WHITAKER'S CONCISE ALMANACK 19⟨

AN

Almanack

For the Year of Our Lord

1999

ESTABLISHED 1868

BY

JOSEPH WHITAKER, FSA

CONTAINING AN ACCOUNT OF THE

ASTRONOMICAL AND OTHER PHENOMENA

AND

A vast Amount of INFORMATION respecting the

GOVERNMENT, FINANCES, POPULATION,

COMMERCE, and GENERAL STATISTICS of

the various Nations of the WORLD

with an INDEX containing

over 7,000

References

LONDON

OFFICE: 51 NINE ELMS LANE

LONDON SW8 5DR

The traditional design of the title page for Whitaker's Almanack which has appeared in each edition since 1868

Whitaker's Concise Almanack

1999

LONDON:
THE STATIONERY OFFICE

The Stationery Office Ltd
51 Nine Elms Lane, London sw8 5DR

Whitaker's Almanack published annually since 1868
© 131st edition The Stationery Office Ltd 1998
Concise Almanack (672 pages)
0 11 702242 X

Designed by Douglas Martin
Jacket designed by Bob Eames
Typeset by Page Bros (Norwich) Ltd
Printed and bound in Great Britain by
Clays Ltd, part of St Ives PLC, Bungay, Suffolk

Editorial Consultants
Sally Whitaker
Gyles Brandreth
Rupert Pennant-Rea

Editorial Staff
Hilary Marsden (Editor)
Bridie Macmahon; Neil Mackay (Assistant Editors, UK)
Daniel Carroll (Assistant Editor, International)
Surekha Davies (Database Co-ordinator)

Published by The Stationery Office and available from:

The Publications Centre
(mail, telephone and fax orders only)
PO Box 276, London sw8 5DT
General enquiries 0171-873 0011
Telephone orders 0171-873 9090
Fax orders 0171-873 8200

The Stationery Office Bookshops
123 Kingsway, London wc2b 6pq
0171-242 6393   Fax 0171-242 6394
16 Arthur Street, Belfast bt1 4gd
01232-238451   Fax 01232-235401
68–69 Bull Street, Birmingham b4 6ad
0121-236 9696   Fax 0121-236 9699
33 Wine Street, Bristol bs1 2bq
0117-926 4306   Fax 0117-929 4515
The Stationery Office Oriel Bookshop
The Friary, Cardiff cf1 4aa
01222-395548   Fax 01222-384347
71 Lothian Road, Edinburgh eh3 9az
0131-228 4181   Fax 0131-622 7017
9–21 Princess Street, Manchester m6o 8as
0161-834 7201   Fax 0161-833 0634

The Stationery Office's Accredited Agents
(see Yellow Pages)

and through good booksellers

Contents

CONTENTS CONTINUED

AVAILABLE IN WHITAKER'S ALMANACK
(1,280 pages, hardback, £35)

FINANCE
British currency, banking, mutual societies, national savings, insurance, financial regulation, Stock Exchange, stamp duties, taxation

LEGAL NOTES
Consumer law, wills, divorce

MEDIA
Broadcasting, the press, book publishers, annual reference books

ORGANIZATIONS
Trade and employers' associations, trade unions, national academies of scholarship, research councils and associations, sports bodies, clubs, societies and institutions

INTERNATIONAL ORGANIZATIONS
European Union, the Commonwealth, CIS, United Nations

COUNTRIES OF THE WORLD
Countries A–Z, UK Overseas Territories

THE YEAR 1997–8
Archaeology, architecture, broadcasting, conservation and heritage, dance, film, literature, opera, Parliament, acts of parliament, white papers, science, sports results and records, theatre, weather

Preface

TO THE 131ST ANNUAL VOLUME

The past year has seen dramatic progress towards a settlement in Northern Ireland, culminating in the historic peace agreement on Good Friday. The consequent moves towards self-government in Northern Ireland with the establishment of the new Northern Ireland assembly herald the similar developments which will take place in Scotland and Wales in the next few years as the Scottish parliament and Welsh assembly are set up. The progress of the legislation and the issues debated in the Westminster Parliament are recorded in the article on the year in Parliament, and developments to date are summarized in the Northern Ireland, Scotland and Wales parts of the Local Government section.

The environment has been of serious concern at both government and grass-roots level for some years. The international, European Union and UK initiatives to implement the Rio declaration are summarized in a new Environment section. The section on wildlife conservation has been expanded to add details of international and EU protection for endangered species and habitats to the existing information.

The nation's health is the subject of a new section of statistical data covering, for instance, the prevalence of drug-taking and the incidence of infectious diseases, as well as the Government's health strategy and targets.

The article about the National Health Service has been revised and expanded to include more information about NHS services, more statistical data and directories of the health authorities in the UK. In addition, new information and statistics about personal social services are included.

New information is included about religious observance in the UK and the existing information about faiths and the churches has been reorganized. The information on the royal households has also been reorganized, clarifying which positions are full-time permanent posts and which are purely honorary.

My thanks are due this year not only to the editorial team and our contributors but also to our new colleagues for ensuring that all ran as smoothly this year as in the past. I also wish to thank the many individuals and organizations who provide us with information or suggestions for further refinements to the contents of the Almanack.

51 NINE ELMS LANE
LONDON SW8 5DR
TEL: 0171-873 8442 (editorial office)
        0171-873 0011 (customer services)
E-MAIL: whitakers.almanack@theso.co.uk
WEB: http://www.whitakers-almanack.co.uk

HILARY MARSDEN
Editor
OCTOBER 1998

The Year 1999

CHRONOLOGICAL CYCLES AND ERAS

Dominical Letter	C
Epact	13
Golden Number (Lunar Cycle)	V
Julian Period	6712
Roman Indiction	7
Solar Cycle	20

	Beginning
Japanese year Heisei 11	1 January
Regnal year 48	6 February
Chinese year of the Rabbit	16 February
Hindu new year	18 March
Indian (Saka) year 1921	22 March
Sikh new year	14 April
Muslim year AH 1420	17 April
Jewish year AM 5760	11 September
Roman year 2752 AUC	

RELIGIOUS CALENDARS

Epiphany	6 January
Makara Sankranti	14 January
Vasant Panchami (Sarasvati-puja)	22 January
Presentation of Christ in the Temple	2 February
Mahashivaratri	14 February
Ash Wednesday	17 February
Holi	1 March
Chaitra (Hindu new year)	18 March
The Annunciation	25 March
Ramanavami	25 March
Maundy Thursday	1 April
Passover, first day	1 April
Good Friday	2 April
Easter Day (western churches)	4 April
Easter Day (Greek Orthodox)	11 April
Baisakhi Mela (Sikh new year)	14 April
Muslim new year	17 April
Rogation Sunday	9 May
Ascension Day	13 May
Feast of Weeks, first day	21 May
Pentecost (Whit Sunday)	23 May
Trinity Sunday	30 May
Corpus Christi	3 June
Martyrdom of Guru Arjan Dev Ji	17 June
Raksha-bandhan	26 August
Janmashtami	2 September
Jewish new year	11 September
Ganesh Chaturthi, first day	13 September
Yom Kippur (Day of Atonement)	20 September
Ganesh festival, last day	24 September
Feast of Tabernacles, first day	25 September
Durga-puja	10 October
Navaratri festival, first day	10 October
Sarasvati-puja	16 October
Dasara	19 October
All Saints' Day	1 November
Diwali (Hindu), first day	5 November
Diwali (Hindu), last day	10 November
Birthday of Guru Nanak Dev Ji	23 November
Advent Sunday	28 November
Chanucah, first day	4 December
Ramadan, first day	9 December
Martyrdom of Guru Tegh Bahadur Ji	13 December
Christmas Day	25 December

CIVIL CALENDAR

Accession of Queen Elizabeth II	6 February
Duke of York's birthday	19 February
St David's Day	1 March
Commonwealth Day	8 March
Prince Edward's birthday	10 March
St Patrick's Day	17 March
Birthday of Queen Elizabeth II	21 April
St George's Day	23 April
Coronation of Queen Elizabeth II	2 June
Duke of Edinburgh's birthday	10 June
The Queen's Official Birthday	12 June
Queen Elizabeth the Queen Mother's birthday	4 August
Princess Royal's birthday	15 August
Princess Margaret's birthday	21 August
Lord Mayor's Day	13 November
Prince of Wales's birthday	14 November
Remembrance Sunday	14 November
Wedding Day of Queen Elizabeth II	20 November
St Andrew's Day	30 November

LEGAL CALENDAR

LAW TERMS

Hilary Term	11 January to 31 March
Easter Term	13 April to 28 May
Trinity Term	8 June to 30 July
Michaelmas Term	1 October to 21 December

QUARTER DAYS

England, Wales and Northern Ireland

Lady	25 March
Midsummer	24 June
Michaelmas	29 September
Christmas	25 December

TERM DAYS

Scotland

Candlemas	28 February
Whitsunday	28 May
Lammas	28 August
Martinmas	28 November
Removal Terms	28 May, 28 November

1999

JANUARY

Sunday		3	10	17	24	31
Monday		4	11	18	25	
Tuesday		5	12	19	26	
Wednesday		6	13	20	27	
Thursday		7	14	21	28	
Friday	1	8	15	22	29	
Saturday	2	9	16	23	30	

FEBRUARY

Sunday		7	14	21	28
Monday	1	8	15	22	
Tuesday	2	9	16	23	
Wednesday	3	10	17	24	
Thursday	4	11	18	25	
Friday	5	12	19	26	
Saturday	6	13	20	27	

MARCH

Sunday		7	14	21	28
Monday	1	8	15	22	29
Tuesday	2	9	16	23	30
Wednesday	3	10	17	24	31
Thursday	4	11	18	25	
Friday	5	12	19	26	
Saturday	6	13	20	27	

APRIL

Sunday		4	11	18	25
Monday		5	12	19	26
Tuesday		6	13	20	27
Wednesday		7	14	21	28
Thursday	1	8	15	22	29
Friday	2	9	16	23	30
Saturday	3	10	17	24	

MAY

Sunday		2	9	16	23	30
Monday		3	10	17	24	31
Tuesday		4	11	18	25	
Wednesday		5	12	19	26	
Thursday		6	13	20	27	
Friday		7	14	21	28	
Saturday	1	8	15	22	29	

JUNE

Sunday		6	13	20	27
Monday		7	14	21	28
Tuesday	1	8	15	22	29
Wednesday	2	9	16	23	30
Thursday	3	10	17	24	
Friday	4	11	18	25	
Saturday	5	12	19	26	

JULY

Sunday		4	11	18	25
Monday		5	12	19	26
Tuesday		6	13	20	27
Wednesday		7	14	21	28
Thursday	1	8	15	22	29
Friday	2	9	16	23	30
Saturday	3	10	17	24	31

AUGUST

Sunday	1	8	15	22	29
Monday	2	9	16	23	30
Tuesday	3	10	17	24	31
Wednesday	4	11	18	25	
Thursday	5	12	19	26	
Friday	6	13	20	27	
Saturday	7	14	21	28	

SEPTEMBER

Sunday		5	12	19	26
Monday		6	13	20	27
Tuesday		7	14	21	28
Wednesday	1	8	15	22	29
Thursday	2	9	16	23	30
Friday	3	10	17	24	
Saturday	4	11	18	25	

OCTOBER

Sunday		3	10	17	24	31
Monday		4	11	18	25	
Tuesday		5	12	19	26	
Wednesday		6	13	20	27	
Thursday		7	14	21	28	
Friday	1	8	15	22	29	
Saturday	2	9	16	23	30	

NOVEMBER

Sunday		7	14	21	28
Monday	1	8	15	22	29
Tuesday	2	9	16	23	30
Wednesday	3	10	17	24	
Thursday	4	11	18	25	
Friday	5	12	19	26	
Saturday	6	13	20	27	

DECEMBER

Sunday		5	12	19	26
Monday		6	13	20	27
Tuesday		7	14	21	28
Wednesday	1	8	15	22	29
Thursday	2	9	16	23	30
Friday	3	10	17	24	31
Saturday	4	11	18	25	

PUBLIC HOLIDAYS

	England and Wales	Scotland	Northern Ireland
New Year	†1 January	1, †4 January	†1 January
St Patrick's Day	—	—	17 March
*Good Friday	2 April	2 April	2 April
Easter Monday	5 April	—	5 April
Early May	†3 May	3 May	†3 May
Spring	31 May	†31 May	31 May
Battle of the Boyne	—	—	‡12 July
Summer	30 August	2 August	30 August
*Christmas	25, 26, 27, †28 December	25, 26, †27, †28 December	25, 26, 27, †28 December
New Year's Eve	†31 December	†31 December	†31 December

*In England, Wales and Northern Ireland, Christmas Day and Good Friday are common law holidays
In the Channel Islands, Liberation Day (9 May) is a bank and public holiday
†Subject to royal proclamation
‡Subject to proclamation by the Secretary of State for Northern Ireland

2000

JANUARY

Sunday		2	9	16	23	30
Monday		3	10	17	24	31
Tuesday		4	11	18	25
Wednesday		5	12	19	26
Thursday		6	13	20	27
Friday		7	14	21	28
Saturday	1	8	15	22	29

FEBRUARY

Sunday		6	13	20	27
Monday		7	14	21	28
Tuesday	1	8	15	22	29
Wednesday	2	9	16	23
Thursday	3	10	17	24
Friday	4	11	18	25
Saturday	5	12	19	26

MARCH

Sunday		5	12	19	26
Monday		6	13	20	27
Tuesday		7	14	21	28
Wednesday	1	8	15	22	29
Thursday	2	9	16	23	30
Friday	3	10	17	24	31
Saturday	4	11	18	25

APRIL

Sunday		2	9	16	23	30
Monday		3	10	17	24
Tuesday		4	11	18	25
Wednesday		5	12	19	26
Thursday		6	13	20	27
Friday		7	14	21	28
Saturday	1	8	15	22	29

MAY

Sunday		7	14	21	28
Monday	1	8	15	22	29
Tuesday	2	9	16	23	30
Wednesday	3	10	17	24	31
Thursday	4	11	18	25
Friday	5	12	19	26
Saturday	6	13	20	27

JUNE

Sunday		4	11	18	25
Monday		5	12	19	26
Tuesday		6	13	20	27
Wednesday		7	14	21	28
Thursday	1	8	15	22	29
Friday	2	9	16	23	30
Saturday	3	10	17	24

JULY

Sunday		2	9	16	23	30
Monday		3	10	17	24	31
Tuesday		4	11	18	25
Wednesday		5	12	19	26
Thursday		6	13	20	27
Friday		7	14	21	28
Saturday	1	8	15	22	29

AUGUST

Sunday		6	13	20	27
Monday		7	14	21	28
Tuesday	1	8	15	22	29
Wednesday	2	9	16	23	30
Thursday	3	10	17	24	31
Friday	4	11	18	25
Saturday	5	12	19	26

SEPTEMBER

Sunday		3	10	17	24
Monday		4	11	18	25
Tuesday		5	12	19	26
Wednesday		6	13	20	27
Thursday		7	14	21	28
Friday	1	8	15	22	29
Saturday	2	9	16	23	30

OCTOBER

Sunday	1	8	15	22	29
Monday	2	9	16	23	30
Tuesday	3	10	17	24	31
Wednesday	4	11	18	25
Thursday	5	12	19	26
Friday	6	13	20	27
Saturday	7	14	21	28

NOVEMBER

Sunday		5	12	19	26
Monday		6	13	20	27
Tuesday		7	14	21	28
Wednesday	1	8	15	22	29
Thursday	2	9	16	23	30
Friday	3	10	17	24
Saturday	4	11	18	25

DECEMBER

Sunday		3	10	17	24	31
Monday		4	11	18	25
Tuesday		5	12	19	26
Wednesday		6	13	20	27
Thursday		7	14	21	28
Friday	1	8	15	22	29
Saturday	2	9	16	23	30

PUBLIC HOLIDAYS

	England and Wales	Scotland	Northern Ireland
New Year	†3 January	3, †4 January	†3 January
St Patrick's Day	—	—	17 March
*Good Friday	21 April	21 April	21 April
Easter Monday	24 April	—	24 April
Early May	†1 May	1 May	†1 May
Spring	29 May	†29 May	29 May
Battle of the Boyne	—	—	‡12 July
Summer	28 August	7 August	28 August
*Christmas	25, 26 December	25, †26 December	25, 26 December

FORTHCOMING EVENTS 1999

This is the UN International Year for the Older Persons
and the Arts Council Year for Architecture and Design
The European City of Culture is Weimar, Germany
* Provisional dates

8 January –	London International Boat Show
17 January	Earls Court, London
23 January –	Monet in the 20th Century
18 April	Exhibition
	Royal Academy of Arts, London
19 February –	J. E. Millais Exhibition
6 June	National Portrait Gallery, London
7 March –	Liberal Democrat Party Spring
9 March	Conference
	Harrogate International Centre
11 March –	Cruft's Dog Show
14 March	National Exhibition Centre, Birmingham
18 March –	Ideal Home Exhibition
11 April	Earls Court, London
25 March –	Arts of the Sikh Kingdoms
25 July	Exhibition
	Victoria and Albert Museum, London
28 March –	London International Book Fair
30 March	Olympia, London
23 April	World Book Day
*May – October	Chichester Festival Theatre season
15 May –	Pitlochry Festival Theatre season
9 October	Tayside
19 May –	Glyndebourne Festival Opera season
28 August	Lewes, E. Sussex
21 May – 6 June	Bath International Music Festival
27 May – 28 May	Chelsea Flower Show
	Royal Hospital, Chelsea, London
28 May – 6 June	Hay Festival of Literature
	Hay-on-Wye, Hereford
*June	York Mystery Plays
	York Minster
*7 June –	Royal Academy Summer Exhibition
22 August	Piccadilly, London
11 June – 27 June	Aldeburgh Festival of Music and Arts
	Suffolk
12 June	Trooping the Colour
	Horse Guards Parade, London
2 July – 11 July	York Early Music Festival
3 July – 18 July	Cheltenham International Festival of Music
5 July – 8 July	The Royal Show
	Stoneleigh Park, Kenilworth, Warks
6 July – 11 July	Hampton Court Palace Flower Show
	East Molesey, Surrey
16 July –	Promenade Concerts season
11 September	Royal Albert Hall, London
*16 July – 24 July	Welsh Proms 1999
	St David's Hall, Cardiff
*16 July – 31 July	Buxton Festival
	Derbyshire
20 July –	Royal Tournament
1 August	Earls Court, London
*27 July – 29 July	Wisley Flower Show
	RHS Garden, Wisley, Surrey
31 July –	Royal National Eisteddfod of Wales
7 August	Anglesey

6 August –	Edinburgh Military Tattoo
28 August	Edinburgh Castle
12 August –	Battle of the Flowers
13 August	Jersey
15 August –	Edinburgh International Festival
4 September	
21 August –	Three Choirs Festival
27 August	Worcester
29 August –	Notting Hill Carnival
30 August	Notting Hill, London
3 September –	Blackpool Illuminations
7 November	
4 September	Braemar Royal Highland Gathering
	Aberdeenshire
11 September –	Southampton International Boat
19 September	Show
	Western Esplanade, Southampton
13 September –	TUC Annual Congress
16 September	Brighton
19 September –	Liberal Democrat Party Autumn
23 September	Conference
	Edinburgh
27 September –	Labour Party Conference
2 October	Bournemouth International Centre
5 October –	Conservative Party Conference
8 October	Blackpool
*5 November –	London International Film Festival
22 November	
7 November	London to Brighton Veteran Car Run
*7 November –	CBI Annual Conference
9 November	Birmingham
11 November	Two-minute silence at 11 a.m.
13 November	Lord Mayor's Procession and Show
	City of London
17 November –	Huddersfield Contemporary Music
28 November	Festival

SPORTS EVENTS

18 January –	Tennis: Australian Open
31 January	Championships
	Melbourne, Australia
*6 February	Rugby Union: Scotland v. Wales
	Murrayfield, Edinburgh
	Rugby Union: Ireland v. France
	Lansdowne Road, Dublin
*20 February	Rugby Union: Wales v. Ireland
	Wembley Stadium, London
	Rugby Union: England v. Scotland
	Twickenham, London
5 March –	Athletics: World Indoor
7 March	Championships
	Maebashi, Japan
*6 March	Rugby Union: Ireland v. England
	Lansdowne Road, Dublin
	Rugby Union: France v. Wales
	Parc des Princes, Paris
*20 March	Rugby Union: Scotland v. Ireland
	Murrayfield, Edinburgh
	Rugby Union: England v. France
	Twickenham, London
27 March –	World Cross-Country
28 March	Championships
	Belfast
*3 April	Oxford and Cambridge Boat Race
	Putney to Mortlake, London

3 April – 11 April	World Curling Championships
	St John, New Brunswick, Canada
*10 April	Rugby Union: France v. Scotland
	Parc des Princes, Paris
	Rugby Union: Wales v. England
	Wembley Stadium, London
*17 April – 3 May	Snooker: World Professional
	Championships
	Crucible Theatre, Sheffield
18 April	Athletics: London Marathon
1 May	Rugby League: Challenge Cup final
6 May – 9 May	Badminton Horse Trial
	Badminton, Wilts
9 May	Football: Welsh FA Cup final
13 May – 16 May	Royal Windsor Horse Show
	Home Park, Windsor
15 May	Rugby Union: Tetley's Bitter Cup
	final
	Twickenham, London
17 May – 23 May	Badminton: World Championships
	Copenhagen, Denmark
22 May	Football: FA Cup final
	Wembley Stadium, London
*22 May	Rugby Union: County
	Championship finals
	Twickenham, London
24 May – 6 June	Tennis: French Open
	Championships
	Paris
29 May	Football: Scottish FA Cup final
	Hampden Park, Glasgow
31 May – 5 June	Golf: British Amateur
	Championship
	Royal County Down Golf Club and
	Kilkeel Golf Club
5 June – 11 June	TT Motorcycle Races
	Isle of Man
20 June	Cricket: World Cup final
	Lord's, London
21 June – 4 July	Lawn Tennis: All-England
	Championships
	Wimbledon, London
30 June – 4 July	Rowing: Henley Royal Regatta
	Henley-on-Thames, Oxon
1 July – 5 July	Cricket: 1st Test Match, England v.
	New Zealand
	Edgbaston, Birmingham
10 July – 24 July	Shooting: NRA Imperial Meeting
	Bisley Camp, Woking, Surrey
*11 July	British Formula 1 Grand Prix
	Silverstone, Northants
*12 July – 25 July	Yachting: Admiral's Cup
	Isle of Wight
15 July – 18 July	Golf: The Open
	Carnoustie
22 July – 26 July	Cricket: 2nd Test Match, England v.
	New Zealand
	Lord's, London
31 July –	Yachting: Cowes Week
7 August	Isle of Wight
1 August –	World Orienteering Championships
8 August	Inverness
5 August –	Cricket: 3rd Test Match, England v.
9 August	New Zealand
	Old Trafford, Manchester
*7 August	Yachting: Fastnet Race
	Isle of Wight

19 August –	Cricket: 4th Test Match, England v.
23 August	New Zealand
	The Oval, London
20 August –	Athletics: World Championships
29 August	Seville, Spain
22 August –	World Rowing Championships
29 August	St Catharine's, Canada
*24 August –	European Show Jumping
30 August	Championships
	Hickstead, Sussex
30 August –	Tennis: US Open Championships
12 September	New York, USA
*2 September –	Burghley Horse Trials
5 September	Burghley, Lincs
*5 September	Cricket: Natwest Trophy final
	Lord's, London
11 September –	Golf: Walker Cup
12 September	Nairn Golf Club
24 September –	Golf: Ryder Cup
26 September	Boston, USA
27 September –	Tennis: Grand Slam Cup
3 October	Munich, Germany
*29 September –	Horse of the Year Show
3 October	Wembley Arena, London
*6 November	Rugby Union: World Cup final
	Cardiff
29 November	Tennis: Davis Cup final

HORSE-RACING*

18 March	Cheltenham Gold Cup
27 March	Lincoln Handicap
10 April	Grand National
	Aintree, Liverpool
1 May	Two Thousand Guineas
	Newmarket
2 May	One Thousand Guineas
	Newmarket
4 June	The Oaks
	Epsom
4 June	Coronation Cup
	Epsom
5 June	The Derby
	Epsom
15 June – 18 June	Royal Ascot
24 July	King George VI and Queen
	Elizabeth Diamond Stakes
	Ascot
8 September	St Leger
	Doncaster
2 October	Cambridgeshire Handicap
	Newmarket
16 October	Cesarewitch
	Newmarket

CENTENARIES OF 1999

1499	
23 November	Perkin Warbeck, pretender to the throne of Henry VII, died
1599	
22 March	Sir Anthony van Dyck, painter, born
25 April	Oliver Cromwell, Lord Protector 1653–8, born
1699	
21 April	Jean Racine, French playwright, died
1799	
19 March	Earl of Derby, Prime Minister 1852, 1858–9, 1866-8
18 May	Pierre de Beaumarchais, French author, died
14 December	George Washington, first President of the United States of America, died
1899	
7 January	Francis Poulenc, composer, born
17 January	Nevil Shute, novelist, born
29 January	Alfred Sisley, painter, died
27 February	Prof. Charles Best, Canadian physiologist who discovered insulin, born
22 April	Vladimir Nabokov, Russian-born novelist, born
23 April	Dame Ngaio Marsh, New Zealand crime novelist, born
29 April	'Duke' Ellington, American jazz pianist and composer, born
8 May	Friedrich von Hayek, Austrian-born political economist, born
10 May	Fred Astaire, American actor, singer and dancer, born
24 May	Suzanne Lenglen, French tennis player, born
3 June	Johann Strauss (the younger), Austrian composer, died
1 July	Charles Laughton, actor, born
13 August	Sir Alfred Hitchcock, film director and producer, born
16 August	Robert Bunsen, German chemist, died
24 August	Jorge Luis Borges, Argentinian novelist and poet, born
27 August	C. S. Forester, novelist and biographer, born
15 December	Harold Abrahams, athlete, born
16 December	Sir Noel Coward, actor and playwright, born
25 December	Humphrey Bogart, American actor, born

CENTENARIES OF 2000

1400	
14 February	Richard II, King 1377–99, killed
25 October	Geoffrey Chaucer, poet, died
1500	
29 May	Bartolomeu Diaz, Portuguese navigator who sailed around the Cape of Good Hope, died
1 November	Benvenuto Cellini, Italian sculptor and engraver, born
1600	
17 January	Pedro Calderón de la Barca, Spanish playwright, born
19 November	Charles I, King 1625–49, born
1700	
1 May	John Dryden, poet, died
1800	
24 January	Sir Edwin Chadwick, social reformer, born
11 February	William Fox Talbot, photography pioneer, born
25 April	William Cowper, poet, died
9 May	John Brown, American slavery abolitionist, born
14 June	Battle of Marengo
25 October	Thomas, Lord Macaulay, historian, born
1900	
20 January	John Ruskin, author and art critic, died
24 January	Battle of Spion Kop, Boer War
22 February	Luis Buñuel, Spanish film director, born
27 February	Labour Party founded
28 February	Relief of Ladysmith, Boer War
2 March	Kurt Weill, German-born composer, born
2 March	Lord Cottesloe, soldier and philanthropist, born
5 April	Spencer Tracy, American actor, born
19 April	Richard Hughes, novelist, born
25 April	Gladwyn Jebb, diplomat, born
17 May	Relief of Mafeking, Boer War
28 May	Sir George Grove, musicologist, died
6 June	Arthur Askey, comedian, born
13 June	Boxer Rebellion broke out in China
25 June	Louis, Earl Mountbatten of Burma, born
2 July	Sir Tyrone Guthrie, theatre producer, born
4 July	Louis Armstrong, American trumpeter, born
10 July	Evelyn Laye, actress, born
4 August	Queen Elizabeth the Queen Mother born
25 August	Friedrich Nietzsche, philosopher, died
7 September	Joan Cross, opera singer, born
8 October	Sir Geoffrey Jellicoe, architect, born
16 October	Edward Ardizzone, illustrator, born
23 October	Douglas Jardine, cricketer, born
14 November	Aaron Copland, American composer, born
22 November	Sir Arthur Sullivan, composer, died
30 November	Oscar Wilde, novelist and playwright, died
16 December	Sir Victor Pritchett, author, born

Astronomy

The following pages give astronomical data for each month of the year 1999. There are four pages of data for each month. All data are given for 0h Greenwich Mean Time (GMT), i.e. at the midnight at the beginning of the day named. This applies also to data for the months when British Summer Time is in operation (for dates, *see* below).

The astronomical data are given in a form suitable for observation with the naked eye or with a small telescope. These data do not attempt to replace the *Astronomical Almanac* for professional astronomers.

A fuller explanation of how to use the astronomical data is given on pages 71–3.

CALENDAR FOR EACH MONTH

The calendar for each month shows dates of religious, civil and legal significance for the year 1999.

The days in bold type are the principal holy days and the festivals and greater holy days of the Church of England as set out in the calendar authorized for use from 1997. Observance of certain festivals and greater holy days is transferred if the day falls on a principal holy day. The calendar shows the date on which holy days and festivals are to be observed in 1999.

The days in small capitals are dates of significance in the calendars of non-Anglican denominations and non-Christian religions.

The days in italic type are dates of civil and legal significance. The royal anniversaries shown in italic type are the days on which the Union flag is to be flown.

The rest of the calendar comprises days of general interest and the dates of birth or death of well-known people.

Fuller explanations of the various calendars can be found under Time Measurement and Calendars (pages 81–9).

The zodiacal signs through which the Sun is passing during each month are illustrated. The date of transition from one sign to the next, to the nearest hour, is given under Astronomical Phenomena.

JULIAN DATE

The Julian date on 1999 January 0.0 is 2451178.5. To find the Julian date for any other date in 1999 (at 0h GMT), add the day-of-the-year number on the extreme right of the calendar for each month to the Julian date for January 0.0.

SEASONS

The seasons are defined astronomically as follows:

Spring from the vernal equinox to the summer solstice
Summer from the summer solstice to the autumnal
          equinox
Autumn from the autumnal equinox to the winter solstice
Winter from the winter solstice to the vernal equinox

The seasons in 1999 are:

Northern hemisphere

Vernal equinox	March 21d 02h GMT
Summer solstice	June 21d 20h GMT
Autumnal equinox	September 23d 12h GMT
Winter solstice	December 22d 08h GMT

Southern hemisphere

Autumnal equinox	March 20d 02h GMT
Winter solstice	June 21d 20h GMT
Vernal equinox	September 23d 12h GMT
Summer solstice	December 22d 08h GMT

The longest day of the year, measured from sunrise to sunset, is at the summer solstice. For the remainder of this century the longest day in the United Kingdom will fall each year on 21 June. *See also* page 81.

The shortest day of the year is at the winter solstice. For the remainder of this century the shortest day in the United Kingdom will fall on 22 December in 1999, and on 21 December in 2000. *See also* page 81.

The equinox is the point at which day and night are of equal length all over the world. *See also* page 81.

In popular parlance, the seasons in the northern hemisphere comprise the following months:

Spring   March, April, May
Summer   June, July, August
Autumn   September, October, November
Winter   December, January, February

BRITISH SUMMER TIME

British Summer Time is the legal time for general purposes during the period in which it is in operation (*see also* page 75). During this period, clocks are kept one hour ahead of Greenwich Mean Time. The hour of changeover is 01h Greenwich Mean Time. The duration of Summer Time in 1999 is from March 28 01h GMT to October 31 01h GMT.

TOTAL ECLIPSE OF THE SUN 1999

On 11 August 1999 the whole of the UK will, weather permitting, be able to see a partial eclipse of the Sun, with a total eclipse being visible in Southern Cornwall and Devon, and Alderney; for full details, *see* page 66. This is the first total eclipse to cross the UK since 1927 (apart from one grazing northern Shetland in 1954); the next will not be until 2090 for the mainland, 2081 for the Channel Islands.

Safety in viewing an eclipse is paramount, as the retina can be damaged if suitable eye protection or instruments are not used. A mylar viewer is recommended.

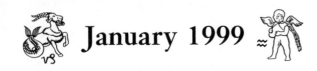

January 1999

FIRST MONTH, 31 DAYS. *Janus*, god of the portal, facing two ways, past and future

1	Friday	**Naming and Circumcision of Jesus.** *Bank Holiday in UK*	*week* 52 *day* 1
2	Saturday	Isaac Asimov b. 1920. David Bailey b. 1938	2
3	Sunday	**2nd S. of Christmas.** Clement Attlee b. 1883	*week* 1 *day* 3
4	Monday	*Bank Holiday in Scotland.* Albert Camus d. 1960	4
5	Tuesday	Twelfth Night. Frederic, Lord Leighton d. 1896	5
6	Wednesday	**The Epiphany.** Gustave Doré b. 1833	6
7	Thursday	Francis Poulenc b. 1899. Gerald Durrell b. 1925	7
8	Friday	Giotto d. 1337. Elvis Presley b. 1935	8
9	Saturday	Simone de Beauvoir b. 1908. Ruskin Spear d. 1990	9
10	Sunday	**Baptism of Christ. 1st S. of Epiphany.**	*week* 2 *day* 10
11	Monday	*Hilary Law Sittings begin.* Richmal Crompton d. 1969	11
12	Tuesday	Edmund Burke b. 1729. Nevil Shute d. 1960	12
13	Wednesday	Jan van Goyen b. 1596. James Joyce d. 1941	13
14	Thursday	Sir Cecil Beaton b. 1904. Humphrey Bogart d. 1957	14
15	Friday	British Museum opened 1759. Martin Luther King b. 1929	15
16	Saturday	Sir John Moore d. 1809. Laura Riding b. 1901	16
17	Sunday	**2nd S. of Epiphany.** Nevil Shute b. 1899	*week* 3 *day* 17
18	Monday	A. A. Milne b. 1882. Arthur Ransome b. 1884	18
19	Tuesday	Edgar Allen Poe b. 1809. Paul Cézanne b. 1839	19
20	Wednesday	Sir John Soane d. 1837. John Ruskin d. 1900	20
21	Thursday	Louis XVI of France executed 1793. George Orwell d. 1950	21
22	Friday	Francis Bacon b. 1561. Queen Victoria d. 1901	22
23	Saturday	Salvador Dali d. 1989. Brian Redhead d. 1994	23
24	Sunday	**3rd S. of Epiphany.** Charles James Fox b. 1749	*week* 4 *day* 24
25	Monday	**Conversion of Paul.** Robert Burns b. 1759	25
26	Tuesday	Gen. Gordon killed 1885. India declared a republic 1950	26
27	Wednesday	Kaiser Wilhelm II b. 1859. Giuseppe Verdi d. 1901	27
28	Thursday	Gen. Gordon b. 1833. W. B. Yeats d. 1939	28
29	Friday	Alfred Sisley d. 1899. Germaine Greer b. 1929	29
30	Saturday	Charles I executed 1649. Gandhi assassinated 1948	30
31	Sunday	**4th S. of Epiphany.** Samuel Goldwyn d. 1974	*week* 5 *day* 31

ASTRONOMICAL PHENOMENA

d	h	
3	13	Earth at perihelion (147 million km)
9	22	Mars in conjunction with Moon. Mars 3° S.
16	16	Mercury in conjunction with Moon. Mercury 4° S.
19	07	Venus in conjunction with Moon. Venus 2° S.
20	13	Sun's longitude 300° ≈
22	01	Jupiter in conjunction with Moon. Jupiter 2° N.
22	08	Neptune in conjunction
24	07	Saturn in conjunction with Moon. Saturn 2° N.

MINIMA OF ALGOL

d	h	d	h	d	h
2	16.1	14	03.4	25	14.7
5	12.9	17	00.2	28	11.5
8	09.7	19	21.0	31	08.3
11	06.6	22	17.9		

CONSTELLATIONS

The following constellations are near the meridian at

	d	h		d	h
December	1	24	January	16	21
December	16	23	February	1	20
January	1	22	February	15	19

Draco (below the Pole), Ursa Minor (below the Pole), Camelopardus, Perseus, Auriga, Taurus, Orion, Eridanus and Lepus

THE MOON

Phases, Apsides and Node	d	h	m
○ Full Moon	2	02	50
☾ Last Quarter	9	14	22
● New Moon	17	15	46
☽ First Quarter	24	19	15
○ Full Moon	31	16	07
Apogee (404,792 km)	11	11	44
Perigee (369,290 km)	26	21	34

Mean longitude of ascending node on January 1, 144°

THE SUN   s.d. 16'.3

Day	Right Ascension	Dec. —	Equation of time	Rise 52°	Rise 56°	Transit	Set 52°	Set 56°	Sidereal time	Transit of First Point of Aries
	h m s	° '	m s	h m	h m	h m	h m	h m	h m s	h m s
1	18 43 58	23 03	− 3 09	8 08	8 31	12 03	15 59	15 36	6 40 49	17 16 21
2	18 48 23	22 58	− 3 38	8 08	8 31	12 04	16 00	15 37	6 44 45	17 12 25
3	18 52 47	22 53	− 4 05	8 08	8 31	12 04	16 01	15 38	6 48 42	17 08 29
4	18 57 12	22 47	− 4 33	8 08	8 30	12 05	16 02	15 39	6 52 39	17 04 33
5	19 01 35	22 41	− 5 00	8 07	8 30	12 05	16 03	15 41	6 56 35	17 00 37
6	19 05 59	22 34	− 5 27	8 07	8 29	12 06	16 05	15 42	7 00 32	16 56 41
7	19 10 22	22 27	− 5 53	8 07	8 29	12 06	16 06	15 44	7 04 28	16 52 45
8	19 14 44	22 20	− 6 19	8 06	8 28	12 07	16 07	15 45	7 08 25	16 48 49
9	19 19 06	22 12	− 6 45	8 06	8 27	12 07	16 09	15 47	7 12 21	16 44 54
10	19 23 28	22 03	− 7 10	8 05	8 27	12 07	16 10	15 49	7 16 18	16 40 58
11	19 27 49	21 54	− 7 34	8 04	8 26	12 08	16 11	15 50	7 20 14	16 37 02
12	19 32 09	21 45	− 7 58	8 04	8 25	12 08	16 13	15 52	7 24 11	16 33 06
13	19 36 29	21 35	− 8 21	8 03	8 24	12 09	16 14	15 54	7 28 08	16 29 10
14	19 40 48	21 25	− 8 44	8 02	8 23	12 09	16 16	15 55	7 32 04	16 25 14
15	19 45 07	21 14	− 9 06	8 02	8 22	12 09	16 17	15 57	7 36 01	16 21 18
16	19 49 24	21 04	− 9 27	8 01	8 21	12 10	16 19	15 59	7 39 57	16 17 22
17	19 53 42	20 52	− 9 48	8 00	8 19	12 10	16 21	16 01	7 43 54	16 13 26
18	19 57 58	20 40	−10 08	7 59	8 18	12 10	16 22	16 03	7 47 50	16 09 30
19	20 02 14	20 28	−10 27	7 58	8 17	12 11	16 24	16 05	7 51 47	16 05 34
20	20 06 29	20 16	−10 46	7 57	8 16	12 11	16 26	16 07	7 55 44	16 01 39
21	20 10 44	20 03	−11 04	7 56	8 14	12 11	16 27	16 09	7 59 40	15 57 43
22	20 14 57	19 49	−11 21	7 54	8 13	12 11	16 29	16 11	8 03 37	15 53 47
23	20 19 10	19 36	−11 37	7 53	8 11	12 12	16 31	16 13	8 07 33	15 49 51
24	20 23 22	19 22	−11 53	7 52	8 10	12 12	16 33	16 15	8 11 30	15 45 55
25	20 27 33	19 07	−12 07	7 51	8 08	12 12	16 34	16 17	8 15 26	15 41 59
26	20 31 44	18 53	−12 21	7 49	8 06	12 12	16 36	16 19	8 19 23	15 38 03
27	20 35 54	18 38	−12 34	7 48	8 05	12 13	16 38	16 21	8 23 19	15 34 07
28	20 40 02	18 22	−12 46	7 47	8 03	12 13	16 40	16 23	8 27 16	15 30 11
29	20 44 10	18 06	−12 58	7 45	8 01	12 13	16 41	16 26	8 31 13	15 26 15
30	20 48 17	17 50	−13 08	7 44	7 59	12 13	16 43	16 28	8 35 09	15 22 19
31	20 52 24	17 34	−13 18	7 42	7 58	12 13	16 45	16 30	8 39 06	15 18 24

DURATION OF TWILIGHT (in minutes)

Latitude	52°	56°	52°	56°	52°	56°	52°	56°
	1 January		11 January		21 January		31 January	
Civil	41	47	40	45	38	43	37	41
Nautical	84	96	82	93	80	90	78	87
Astronomical	125	141	123	138	120	134	117	130

THE NIGHT SKY

Mercury is unsuitably placed for observation throughout the month.

Venus, magnitude − 3.9, is visible in the evenings but will only be seen for a short time after sunset, low above the south-western horizon. It is slowly moving out from the Sun but even by the end of the month it is not visible for much more than an hour after sunset. Shortly after sunset on the 19th, the thin crescent Moon, just over three days old, will be seen about 5° above and to the left of Venus.

Mars will be visible in the night sky throughout 1999. In January it is a morning object, its magnitude brightening during the month from +1.0 to +0.5. It will be seen crossing the meridian during morning twilight. Mars is moving eastwards in Virgo, passing 4° N. of Spica on the night of the 8th to 9th. The Moon, at Last Quarter, is near Mars on the mornings of the 9th and 10th.

Jupiter, magnitude − 2.2, is an evening object and after the end of twilight will be seen in the south-western quadrant of the sky. On the evening of the 21st, Jupiter will be seen about 4° above the thin crescent Moon, only four days old. Early in the month Jupiter moves from Aquarius into Pisces.

Saturn is visible in the south-western quadrant of the sky in the evenings, magnitude +0.4. On the evening of the 23rd the Moon, one day before First Quarter, is near the planet. Saturn is in the constellation of Pisces.

THE MOON

Day	RA	Dec.	Hor. par.	Semi-diam.	Sun's co-long.	PA of Bright Limb	Phase	Age	Rise 52°	Rise 56°	Transit	Set 52°	Set 56°
	h m	°	′	′	°	°	%	d	h m	h m	h m	h m	h m
1	5 39	+19.0	60.1	16.4	72	252	98	13.1	15 49	15 30	23 56	7 00	7 19
2	6 40	+19.6	59.7	16.3	84	208	100	14.1	16 51	16 32	—	8 01	8 21
3	7 41	+18.9	59.1	16.1	97	112	99	15.1	17 59	17 42	0 54	8 52	9 10
4	8 39	+17.0	58.3	15.9	109	108	95	16.1	19 09	18 55	1 51	9 33	9 48
5	9 35	+14.3	57.5	15.7	121	109	90	17.1	20 20	20 10	2 44	10 06	10 17
6	10 27	+10.9	56.7	15.4	133	111	83	18.1	21 29	21 23	3 33	10 34	10 42
7	11 16	+ 7.1	55.9	15.2	145	112	74	19.1	22 36	22 33	4 20	10 58	11 02
8	12 03	+ 3.1	55.2	15.0	157	112	65	20.1	23 42	23 43	5 04	11 20	11 21
9	12 49	− 1.0	54.7	14.9	169	112	56	21.1	—	—	5 47	11 41	11 39
10	13 34	− 4.9	54.4	14.8	182	112	46	22.1	0 46	0 50	6 29	12 03	11 57
11	14 20	− 8.7	54.2	14.8	194	110	37	23.1	1 50	1 57	7 12	12 26	12 17
12	15 06	−12.0	54.2	14.8	206	109	28	24.1	2 53	3 04	7 56	12 51	12 39
13	15 53	−14.9	54.3	14.8	218	106	20	25.1	3 55	4 10	8 41	13 21	13 06
14	16 42	−17.3	54.6	14.9	230	103	13	26.1	4 56	5 14	9 28	13 56	13 39
15	17 33	−18.8	55.1	15.0	242	100	7	27.1	5 55	6 14	10 18	14 39	14 19
16	18 25	−19.5	55.5	15.1	255	98	3	28.1	6 48	7 08	11 08	15 29	15 09
17	19 19	−19.3	56.1	15.3	267	103	1	29.1	7 36	7 55	12 00	16 27	16 09
18	20 13	−18.0	56.6	15.4	279	233	0	0.3	8 18	8 35	12 52	17 32	17 16
19	21 08	−15.8	57.1	15.6	291	251	2	1.3	8 54	9 07	13 44	18 42	18 30
20	22 01	−12.7	57.6	15.7	303	251	6	2.3	9 25	9 35	14 35	19 56	19 47
21	22 54	− 8.9	58.1	15.8	315	250	12	3.3	9 52	9 59	15 26	21 10	21 06
22	23 47	− 4.6	58.4	15.9	328	249	20	4.3	10 18	10 20	16 16	22 26	22 26
23	0 39	0.0	58.7	16.0	340	249	30	5.3	10 43	10 42	17 06	23 43	23 47
24	1 32	+ 4.7	59.0	16.1	352	249	41	6.3	11 10	11 04	17 58	—	—
25	2 26	+ 9.1	59.2	16.1	4	251	52	7.3	11 38	11 29	18 51	1 00	1 08
26	3 21	+13.0	59.3	16.2	16	254	64	8.3	12 11	11 58	19 46	2 17	2 29
27	4 19	+16.2	59.4	16.2	28	257	74	9.3	12 51	12 34	20 43	3 32	3 48
28	5 18	+18.4	59.3	16.2	41	262	84	10.3	13 38	13 19	21 41	4 43	5 02
29	6 18	+19.5	59.1	16.1	53	266	91	11.3	14 34	14 14	22 39	5 47	6 06
30	7 17	+19.3	58.8	16.0	65	270	97	12.3	15 38	15 19	23 36	6 41	7 00
31	8 16	+17.9	58.3	15.9	77	271	99	13.3	16 46	16 31	—	7 26	7 42

MERCURY

Day	RA	Dec.	Diam.	Phase	Transit	5° high 52°	5° high 56°
	h m	°	″	%	h m	h m	h m
1	17 22	−22.6	5	84	10 42	7 36	8 10
3	17 34	−23.0	5	86	10 47	7 43	8 19
5	17 47	−23.3	5	88	10 51	7 51	8 28
7	17 59	−23.6	5	90	10 56	7 58	8 36
9	18 12	−23.8	5	91	11 01	8 05	8 44
11	18 25	−24.0	5	92	11 06	8 12	8 50
13	18 39	−24.0	5	94	11 12	8 17	8 56
15	18 52	−24.0	5	95	11 17	8 22	9 01
17	19 06	−23.8	5	95	11 23	8 27	9 05
19	19 19	−23.6	5	96	11 29	8 30	9 08
21	19 33	−23.3	5	97	11 35	8 33	9 09
23	19 47	−22.9	5	98	11 41	8 36	9 10
25	20 01	−22.4	5	98	11 47	8 37	9 10
27	20 15	−21.8	5	99	11 53	8 38	9 09
29	20 29	−21.1	5	99	11 59	8 38	9 08
31	20 43	−20.3	5	100	12 05	15 33	15 05

VENUS

Day	RA	Dec.	Diam.	Phase	Transit	5° high 52°	5° high 56°
	h m	°	″	%	h m	h m	h m
1	19 50	−22.3	10	97	13 10	16 21	15 48
6	20 17	−21.2	10	96	13 17	16 37	16 08
11	20 43	−19.7	10	96	13 23	16 55	16 29
16	21 08	−18.1	11	95	13 29	17 13	16 50
21	21 33	−16.2	11	94	13 34	17 31	17 11
26	21 58	−14.1	11	94	13 39	17 50	17 33
31	22 22	−11.9	11	93	13 43	18 07	17 53

MARS

Day	RA	Dec.	Diam.	Phase	Transit	5° high 52°	5° high 56°
1	13 11	− 5.4	6	91	6 29	1 31	1 39
6	13 20	− 6.3	6	90	6 19	1 25	1 34
11	13 29	− 7.2	7	90	6 08	1 19	1 29
16	13 37	− 8.0	7	90	5 57	1 13	1 23
21	13 46	− 8.8	7	90	5 46	1 06	1 17
26	13 54	− 9.5	8	90	5 34	0 58	1 10
31	14 01	−10.1	8	90	5 22	0 50	1 02

SUNRISE AND SUNSET

	London		Bristol		Birmingham		Manchester		Newcastle		Glasgow		Belfast	
	0°05'	51°30'	2°35'	51°28'	1°55'	52°28'	2°15'	53°28'	1°37'	54°59'	4°14'	55°52'	5°56'	54°35'
	h m	h m	h m	h m	h m	h m	h m	h m	h m	h m	h m	h m	h m	h m
1	8 06	16 02	8 16	16 12	8 18	16 04	8 25	16 00	8 31	15 49	8 47	15 53	8 46	16 08
2	8 06	16 03	8 16	16 13	8 18	16 05	8 25	16 01	8 31	15 50	8 47	15 55	8 46	16 09
3	8 06	16 04	8 16	16 14	8 18	16 06	8 25	16 02	8 31	15 51	8 47	15 56	8 46	16 11
4	8 06	16 05	8 15	16 15	8 18	16 07	8 24	16 03	8 30	15 52	8 46	15 57	8 45	16 12
5	8 05	16 06	8 15	16 16	8 17	16 09	8 24	16 05	8 30	15 54	8 46	15 59	8 45	16 13
6	8 05	16 07	8 15	16 18	8 17	16 10	8 24	16 06	8 30	15 55	8 45	16 00	8 44	16 15
7	8 05	16 09	8 14	16 19	8 17	16 11	8 23	16 07	8 29	15 56	8 45	16 02	8 44	16 16
8	8 04	16 10	8 14	16 20	8 16	16 13	8 23	16 09	8 28	15 58	8 44	16 03	8 43	16 17
9	8 04	16 11	8 13	16 21	8 16	16 14	8 22	16 10	8 28	15 59	8 43	16 05	8 43	16 19
10	8 03	16 13	8 13	16 23	8 15	16 15	8 21	16 12	8 27	16 01	8 43	16 06	8 42	16 21
11	8 03	16 14	8 12	16 24	8 14	16 17	8 21	16 13	8 26	16 03	8 42	16 08	8 41	16 22
12	8 02	16 15	8 12	16 26	8 14	16 18	8 20	16 15	8 25	16 04	8 41	16 10	8 40	16 24
13	8 01	16 17	8 11	16 27	8 13	16 20	8 19	16 16	8 25	16 06	8 40	16 11	8 40	16 25
14	8 00	16 18	8 10	16 29	8 12	16 21	8 18	16 18	8 24	16 08	8 39	16 13	8 39	16 27
15	8 00	16 20	8 09	16 30	8 11	16 23	8 17	16 20	8 23	16 09	8 38	16 15	8 38	16 29
16	7 59	16 22	8 09	16 32	8 10	16 25	8 16	16 21	8 22	16 11	8 37	16 17	8 37	16 31
17	7 58	16 23	8 08	16 33	8 09	16 26	8 15	16 23	8 20	16 13	8 36	16 19	8 36	16 32
18	7 57	16 25	8 07	16 35	8 08	16 28	8 14	16 25	8 19	16 15	8 34	16 21	8 34	16 34
19	7 56	16 26	8 06	16 37	8 07	16 30	8 13	16 26	8 18	16 17	8 33	16 23	8 33	16 36
20	7 55	16 28	8 05	16 38	8 06	16 31	8 12	16 28	8 17	16 19	8 32	16 25	8 32	16 38
21	7 54	16 30	8 04	16 40	8 05	16 33	8 11	16 30	8 15	16 20	8 30	16 27	8 31	16 40
22	7 53	16 31	8 03	16 42	8 04	16 35	8 10	16 32	8 14	16 22	8 29	16 29	8 29	16 42
23	7 52	16 33	8 01	16 43	8 03	16 37	8 08	16 34	8 13	16 24	8 27	16 31	8 28	16 44
24	7 50	16 35	8 00	16 45	8 02	16 38	8 07	16 36	8 11	16 26	8 26	16 33	8 27	16 45
25	7 49	16 37	7 59	16 47	8 00	16 40	8 06	16 37	8 10	16 28	8 24	16 35	8 25	16 47
26	7 48	16 38	7 58	16 48	7 59	16 42	8 04	16 39	8 08	16 30	8 23	16 37	8 24	16 49
27	7 47	16 40	7 56	16 50	7 57	16 44	8 03	16 41	8 07	16 32	8 21	16 39	8 22	16 51
28	7 45	16 42	7 55	16 52	7 56	16 46	8 01	16 43	8 05	16 34	8 19	16 41	8 20	16 53
29	7 44	16 44	7 54	16 54	7 55	16 47	8 00	16 45	8 03	16 36	8 18	16 43	8 19	16 55
30	7 42	16 45	7 52	16 56	7 53	16 49	7 58	16 47	8 02	16 38	8 16	16 45	8 17	16 57
31	7 41	16 47	7 51	16 57	7 52	16 51	7 56	16 49	8 00	16 41	8 14	16 47	8 15	16 59

JUPITER

Day	RA	Dec.	Transit	5° high	
				52°	56°
	h m	° '	h m	h m	h m
1	23 32.4	− 4 20	16 49	21 53	21 46
11	23 38.1	− 3 41	16 16	21 23	21 17
21	23 44.6	− 2 57	15 43	20 54	20 49
31	23 51.7	− 2 09	15 11	20 26	20 21

Diameters – equatorial 37″ polar 34″

SATURN

Day	RA	Dec.	Transit	5° high	
				52°	56°
	h m	° '	h m	h m	h m
1	1 43.1	+ 7 57	18 59	1 10	1 13
11	1 43.5	+ 8 02	18 20	0 32	0 35
21	1 44.6	+ 8 12	17 42	23 51	23 54
31	1 46.4	+ 8 25	17 05	23 14	23 18

Diameters – equatorial 18″ polar 16″
Rings – major axis 41″ minor axis 10″

URANUS

Day	RA	Dec.	Transit	10° high	
				52°	56°
	h m	° '	h m	h m	h m
1	20 54.4	−18 05	14 11	17 08	16 34
11	20 56.5	−17 56	13 34	16 33	15 59
21	20 58.8	−17 47	12 57	15 57	15 24
31	21 01.2	−17 37	12 20	15 21	14 49

Diameter 4″

NEPTUNE

Day	RA	Dec.	Transit	10° high	
				52°	56°
	h m	° '	h m	h m	h m
1	20 12.8	−19 38	13 30	16 13	15 33
11	20 14.4	−19 33	12 52	15 36	14 56
21	20 15.9	−19 28	12 14	14 59	14 20
31	20 17.5	−19 23	11 37	14 22	13 43

Diameter 2″

February 1999

SECOND MONTH, 28 or 29 DAYS. *Februa*, Roman festival of Purification

1	*Monday*	Piet Mondrian d. 1944. Jo Richardson d. 1994	*week 5 day* 32
2	*Tuesday*	**Presentation of Christ in the Temple (Candlemas)**	33
3	*Wednesday*	Beau Nash d. 1762. Felix Mendelssohn b. 1809	34
4	*Thursday*	George Lillo b. 1693. Charles Lindbergh b. 1902	35
5	*Friday*	Sir Robert Peel b. 1788. John Boyd Dunlop b. 1840	36
6	*Saturday*	*Queen's Accession 1952.* Queen Anne b. 1665	37
7	*Sunday*	**2nd S. before Lent.** Charles Dickens b. 1812	*week 6 day* 38
8	*Monday*	Mary, Queen of Scots executed 1587. John Ruskin b. 1819	39
9	*Tuesday*	Edward Carson b. 1854. Brendan Behan b. 1923	40
10	*Wednesday*	Henry, Lord Darnley killed 1567. Harold Macmillan b. 1894	41
11	*Thursday*	Thomas Edison b. 1847. Mary Quant b. 1934	42
12	*Friday*	Charles Darwin b. 1809. Abraham Lincoln b. 1809	43
13	*Saturday*	Accession of William III and Mary II 1689	44
14	*Sunday*	**S. next before Lent.** St Valentine's Day	*week 7 day* 45
15	*Monday*	Graham Hill b. 1929. Norman Parkinson d. 1990	46
16	*Tuesday*	Shrove Tuesday. *Chinese Year of the Rabbit*	47
17	*Wednesday*	**Ash Wednesday.** Graham Sutherland d. 1980	48
18	*Thursday*	Mary I b. 1516. Michelangelo d. 1564	49
19	*Friday*	*Duke of York b. 1960.* Deng Xiaoping d. 1997	50
20	*Saturday*	Dame Marie Rambert b. 1888. Kurt Cobain b. 1967	51
21	*Sunday*	**1st S. of Lent.** Malcolm X assassinated 1965	*week 8 day* 52
22	*Monday*	Eric Gill b. 1882. Andy Warhol d. 1987	53
23	*Tuesday*	Samuel Pepys b. 1633. Sir Edward Elgar d. 1934	54
24	*Wednesday*	Wilhelm Grimm b. 1786. Joseph Rowntree d. 1925	55
25	*Thursday*	Sir Christopher Wren d. 1723. Pierre Renoir b. 1841	56
26	*Friday*	Frank Bridge b. 1879. Everton Weekes b. 1925	57
27	*Saturday*	John Evelyn d. 1706. Prof. Charles Best b. 1899	58
28	*Sunday*	**2nd S. of Lent.** Relief of Ladysmith 1900	*week 9 day* 59

ASTRONOMICAL PHENOMENA

d   h
2   02   Uranus in conjunction
4   05   Mercury in superior conjunction
7   06   Mars in conjunction with Moon. Mars 3° S.
16   07   Annular eclipse of Sun (*see* page 66)
17   02   Mercury in conjunction with Moon. Mercury 0°.2 N.
18   08   Venus in conjunction with Moon. Venus 2° N.
18   17   Jupiter in conjunction with Moon. Jupiter 2° N.
19   03   Sun's longitude 330° ♓
20   16   Saturn in conjunction with Moon. Saturn 3° N.
23   20   Jupiter in conjunction with Venus. Jupiter 0°.1 S.

MINIMA OF ALGOL

d	h	d	h	d	h
3	05.1	14	16.4	26	03.7
6	02.0	17	13.2		
8	22.8	20	10.1		
11	19.6	23	06.9		

CONSTELLATIONS

The following constellations are near the meridian at

	d	h		d	h
January	1	24	February	15	21
January	16	23	March	1	20
February	1	22	March	16	19

Draco (below the Pole), Camelopardus, Auriga, Taurus, Gemini, Orion, Canis Minor, Monoceros, Lepus, Canis Major and Puppis

THE MOON

Phases, Apsides and Node	d	h	m
☾ Last Quarter	8	11	58
● New Moon	16	06	39
☽ First Quarter	23	02	43
Apogee (404,346 km)	8	08	51
Perigee (368,685 km)	20	14	25

Mean longitude of ascending node on February 1, 143°

THE SUN   s.d. 16′.2

Day	Right Ascension	Dec.	Equation of time	Rise 52°	Rise 56°	Transit	Set 52°	Set 56°	Sidereal time	Transit of First Point of Aries
	h m s	° ′	m s	h m	h m	h m	h m	h m	h m s	h m s
1	20 56 29	17 17	−13 27	7 41	7 56	12 14	16 47	16 32	8 43 02	15 14 28
2	21 00 34	17 00	−13 35	7 39	7 54	12 14	16 49	16 34	8 46 59	15 10 32
3	21 04 38	16 43	−13 43	7 38	7 52	12 14	16 51	16 36	8 50 55	15 06 36
4	21 08 41	16 25	−13 49	7 36	7 50	12 14	16 53	16 39	8 54 52	15 02 40
5	21 12 43	16 07	−13 55	7 34	7 48	12 14	16 54	16 41	8 58 48	14 58 44
6	21 16 45	15 49	−14 00	7 33	7 46	12 14	16 56	16 43	9 02 45	14 54 48
7	21 20 45	15 31	−14 04	7 31	7 44	12 14	16 58	16 45	9 06 41	14 50 52
8	21 24 45	15 12	−14 07	7 29	7 42	12 14	17 00	16 47	9 10 38	14 46 56
9	21 28 44	14 53	−14 10	7 27	7 40	12 14	17 02	16 50	9 14 35	14 43 00
10	21 32 43	14 34	−14 12	7 25	7 37	12 14	17 04	16 52	9 18 31	14 39 04
11	21 36 40	14 14	−14 13	7 24	7 35	12 14	17 06	16 54	9 22 28	14 35 09
12	21 40 37	13 55	−14 13	7 22	7 33	12 14	17 07	16 56	9 26 24	14 31 13
13	21 44 33	13 35	−14 12	7 20	7 31	12 14	17 09	16 58	9 30 21	14 27 17
14	21 48 29	13 15	−14 11	7 18	7 29	12 14	17 11	17 01	9 34 17	14 23 21
15	21 52 23	12 54	−14 09	7 16	7 26	12 14	17 13	17 03	9 38 14	14 19 25
16	21 56 17	12 34	−14 07	7 14	7 24	12 14	17 15	17 05	9 42 10	14 15 29
17	22 00 10	12 13	−14 03	7 12	7 22	12 14	17 17	17 07	9 46 07	14 11 33
18	22 04 03	11 52	−13 59	7 10	7 19	12 14	17 19	17 09	9 50 04	14 07 37
19	22 07 54	11 31	−13 54	7 08	7 17	12 14	17 20	17 12	9 54 00	14 03 41
20	22 11 45	11 09	−13 49	7 06	7 15	12 14	17 22	17 14	9 57 57	13 59 45
21	22 15 36	10 48	−13 43	7 04	7 12	12 14	17 24	17 16	10 01 53	13 55 49
22	22 19 26	10 26	−13 36	7 02	7 10	12 14	17 26	17 18	10 05 50	13 51 54
23	22 23 15	10 04	−13 28	7 00	7 08	12 13	17 28	17 20	10 09 46	13 47 58
24	22 27 03	9 42	−13 20	6 58	7 05	12 13	17 30	17 22	10 13 43	13 44 02
25	22 30 51	9 20	−13 11	6 56	7 03	12 13	17 32	17 25	10 17 39	13 40 06
26	22 34 38	8 58	−13 02	6 53	7 00	12 13	17 33	17 27	10 21 36	13 36 10
27	22 38 25	8 36	−12 52	6 51	6 58	12 13	17 35	17 29	10 25 33	13 32 14
28	22 42 11	8 13	−12 42	6 49	6 55	12 13	17 37	17 31	10 29 29	13 28 18

DURATION OF TWILIGHT (in minutes)

Latitude	52°	56°	52°	56°	52°	56°	52°	56°
	1 February		11 February		21 February		28 February	
Civil	37	41	35	39	34	38	34	38
Nautical	77	86	75	83	74	81	73	81
Astronomical	117	130	114	126	113	125	112	124

THE NIGHT SKY

Mercury is unsuitably placed for observation for most of the month as it passes through superior conjunction on the 4th. For the last week of the month it may be glimpsed as an evening object, magnitude −1.1 to −0.7, low above the west-south-western horizon around the end of evening civil twilight. For observers in the northern hemisphere this is the most favourable evening apparition of the year.

Venus continues to be visible as a brilliant evening object, magnitude −3.9. Its rapid motion northwards in declination makes it visible for longer each night and by the end of February it is still visible low in the western sky two hours after sunset. Venus is moving out from the Sun while Jupiter is moving in towards the Sun, so that the two bodies are close to each other for several days around the 23rd to 24th. During the evening of the 23rd Jupiter will be seen only about 0°.1 to the left of Venus. The thin crescent

Moon is near the planet on the evenings of the 17th and 18th.

Mars continues to be visible as a morning object, its magnitude brightening during February from +0.5 to −0.1. The Moon will be seen about 2° above the planet on the morning of the 7th. Mars moves from Virgo into Libra during the month.

Jupiter continues to be visible in the south-western sky in the early evening, magnitude −2.1. The thin crescent Moon may be detected about 3° below and to the left of Jupiter on the evening of the 18th.

Saturn, magnitude +0.5, continues to be visible in the south-western sky in the evenings. The crescent Moon, four days old, is near Saturn on the evening of the 20th.

Zodiacal Light. The evening cone may be observed in the western sky after the end of twilight from the 2nd to 17th. This faint phenomenon is only visible under good conditions, in the absence of both moonlight and artificial lighting.

THE MOON

Day	RA h m	Dec. °	Hor. par.	Semi-diam.	Sun's co-long. °	PA of Bright Limb °	Phase %	Age d	Rise 52° h m	Rise 56° h m	Transit h m	Set 52° h m	Set 56° h m
1	9 12	+15.6	57.7	15.7	89	115	100	14.3	17 57	17 45	0 30	8 03	8 16
2	10 06	+12.4	57.1	15.6	101	108	98	15.3	19 08	19 00	1 22	8 33	8 43
3	10 57	+ 8.7	56.4	15.4	113	109	94	16.3	20 17	20 13	2 10	8 59	9 05
4	11 46	+ 4.7	55.8	15.2	126	110	88	17.3	21 25	21 24	2 56	9 23	9 25
5	12 33	+ 0.6	55.2	15.0	138	110	81	18.3	22 30	22 33	3 40	9 45	9 44
6	13 18	− 3.5	54.7	14.9	150	110	73	19.3	23 35	23 41	4 23	10 06	10 02
7	14 04	− 7.3	54.4	14.8	162	109	64	20.3	—	—	5 06	10 29	10 21
8	14 50	−10.9	54.2	14.8	174	107	55	21.3	0 38	0 48	5 50	10 53	10 42
9	15 37	−13.9	54.3	14.8	186	104	45	22.3	1 41	1 54	6 34	11 21	11 07
10	16 25	−16.5	54.5	14.8	198	101	36	23.3	2 42	2 59	7 20	11 53	11 36
11	17 15	−18.3	54.8	14.9	211	97	27	24.3	3 42	4 00	8 08	12 32	12 13
12	18 06	−19.3	55.3	15.1	223	93	19	25.3	4 37	4 57	8 58	13 18	12 58
13	18 59	−19.4	55.9	15.2	235	88	12	26.3	5 28	5 47	9 49	14 13	13 54
14	19 53	−18.6	56.6	15.4	247	83	6	27.3	6 13	6 30	10 42	15 15	14 58
15	20 48	−16.7	57.3	15.6	259	78	2	28.3	6 51	7 06	11 34	16 24	16 10
16	21 43	−13.8	58.0	15.8	272	69	0	29.3	7 25	7 36	12 27	17 38	17 28
17	22 37	−10.2	58.6	16.0	284	256	1	0.7	7 54	8 02	13 19	18 54	18 48
18	23 31	− 5.9	59.0	16.1	296	253	4	1.7	8 22	8 25	14 11	20 12	20 10
19	0 25	− 1.2	59.3	16.2	308	252	9	2.7	8 48	8 47	15 02	21 30	21 33
20	1 19	+ 3.5	59.4	16.2	320	252	17	3.7	9 14	9 10	15 54	22 49	22 56
21	2 13	+ 8.1	59.5	16.2	333	253	27	4.7	9 42	9 34	16 47	—	—
22	3 09	+12.2	59.4	16.2	345	256	37	5.7	10 14	10 01	17 42	0 07	0 18
23	4 06	+15.6	59.2	16.1	357	259	49	6.7	10 50	10 35	18 38	1 22	1 37
24	5 03	+18.0	58.9	16.1	9	263	60	7.7	11 34	11 16	19 34	2 34	2 52
25	6 02	+19.3	58.6	16.0	21	268	71	8.7	12 26	12 06	20 31	3 39	3 58
26	7 01	+19.4	58.2	15.9	33	274	80	9.7	13 25	13 07	21 27	4 35	4 54
27	7 58	+18.5	57.8	15.8	46	279	88	10.7	14 31	14 14	22 21	5 22	5 40
28	8 54	+16.4	57.4	15.6	58	284	94	11.7	15 40	15 26	23 13	6 01	6 15

MERCURY

Day	RA h m	Dec. °	Diam. "	Phase %	Transit h m	5° high 52° h m	5° high 56° h m
1	20 50	−19.9	5	100	12 08	15 39	15 13
3	21 04	−19.0	5	100	12 14	15 53	15 28
5	21 18	−17.9	5	100	12 20	16 06	15 44
7	21 32	−16.8	5	100	12 26	16 21	16 00
9	21 46	−15.6	5	99	12 33	16 35	16 16
11	21 59	−14.2	5	98	12 39	16 50	16 33
13	22 13	−12.8	5	97	12 44	17 05	16 50
15	22 27	−11.3	5	96	12 50	17 20	17 06
17	22 40	− 9.7	5	93	12 56	17 35	17 23
19	22 54	− 8.1	5	90	13 01	17 49	17 39
21	23 06	− 6.4	6	86	13 06	18 03	17 55
23	23 19	− 4.7	6	81	13 10	18 16	18 10
25	23 30	− 3.0	6	74	13 13	18 28	18 23
27	23 41	− 1.4	6	67	13 16	18 39	18 35
29	23 50	+ 0.1	7	58	13 17	18 47	18 45
31	23 58	+ 1.4	7	50	13 16	18 53	18 51

VENUS

Day	RA h m	Dec. °	Diam. "	Phase %	Transit h m	5° high 52° h m	5° high 56° h m
1	22 26	−11.4	11	93	13 44	18 11	17 57
6	22 50	− 9.0	11	92	13 47	18 28	18 17
11	23 13	− 6.6	11	91	13 51	18 45	18 37
16	23 35	− 4.0	11	90	13 53	19 02	18 56
21	23 58	− 1.4	12	89	13 56	19 19	19 14
26	0 20	+ 1.2	12	88	13 59	19 35	19 33
31	0 42	+ 3.8	12	87	14 01	19 51	19 51

MARS

Day	RA h m	Dec. °	Diam. "	Phase %	Transit h m	5° high 52° h m	5° high 56° h m
1	14 03	−10.3	8	91	5 19	0 48	1 01
6	14 10	−10.9	8	91	5 07	0 39	0 52
11	14 17	−11.4	9	91	4 54	0 29	0 43
16	14 23	−11.9	9	91	4 40	0 18	0 33
21	14 28	−12.3	10	92	4 26	0 07	0 22
26	14 33	−12.7	10	92	4 10	23 51	0 09
31	14 36	−13.0	11	93	3 55	23 37	23 53

SUNRISE AND SUNSET

	London		Bristol		Birmingham		Manchester		Newcastle		Glasgow		Belfast	
	0°05′	51°30′	2°35′	51°28′	1°55′	52°28′	2°15′	53°28′	1°37′	54°59′	4°14′	55°52′	5°56′	54°35′
	h m	h m	h m	h m	h m	h m	h m	h m	h m	h m	h m	h m	h m	h m
1	7 39	16 49	7 49	16 59	7 50	16 53	7 55	16 51	7 58	16 43	8 12	16 50	8 14	17 01
2	7 38	16 51	7 48	17 01	7 48	16 55	7 53	16 53	7 56	16 45	8 10	16 52	8 12	17 04
3	7 36	16 53	7 46	17 03	7 47	16 57	7 51	16 55	7 54	16 47	8 08	16 54	8 10	17 06
4	7 35	16 54	7 45	17 05	7 45	16 59	7 50	16 57	7 53	16 49	8 06	16 56	8 08	17 08
5	7 33	16 56	7 43	17 06	7 43	17 01	7 48	16 59	7 51	16 51	8 04	16 58	8 06	17 10
6	7 31	16 58	7 41	17 08	7 42	17 03	7 46	17 01	7 49	16 53	8 02	17 00	8 05	17 12
7	7 30	17 00	7 40	17 10	7 40	17 04	7 44	17 03	7 47	16 55	8 00	17 03	8 03	17 14
8	7 28	17 02	7 38	17 12	7 38	17 06	7 42	17 05	7 45	16 57	7 58	17 05	8 01	17 16
9	7 26	17 04	7 36	17 14	7 36	17 08	7 40	17 07	7 43	16 59	7 56	17 07	7 59	17 18
10	7 24	17 05	7 34	17 15	7 34	17 10	7 39	17 09	7 41	17 02	7 54	17 09	7 57	17 20
11	7 23	17 07	7 32	17 17	7 32	17 12	7 37	17 11	7 39	17 04	7 52	17 11	7 55	17 22
12	7 21	17 09	7 31	17 19	7 31	17 14	7 35	17 13	7 36	17 06	7 50	17 14	7 53	17 24
13	7 19	17 11	7 29	17 21	7 29	17 16	7 33	17 15	7 34	17 08	7 47	17 16	7 50	17 26
14	7 17	17 13	7 27	17 23	7 27	17 18	7 31	17 17	7 32	17 10	7 45	17 18	7 48	17 28
15	7 15	17 15	7 25	17 25	7 25	17 20	7 29	17 19	7 30	17 12	7 43	17 20	7 46	17 30
16	7 13	17 16	7 23	17 26	7 23	17 22	7 26	17 21	7 28	17 14	7 41	17 22	7 44	17 32
17	7 11	17 18	7 21	17 28	7 21	17 23	7 24	17 22	7 26	17 16	7 38	17 24	7 42	17 35
18	7 09	17 20	7 19	17 30	7 19	17 25	7 22	17 24	7 23	17 18	7 36	17 27	7 40	17 37
19	7 07	17 22	7 17	17 32	7 17	17 27	7 20	17 26	7 21	17 20	7 34	17 29	7 37	17 39
20	7 05	17 24	7 15	17 34	7 15	17 29	7 18	17 28	7 19	17 23	7 31	17 31	7 35	17 41
21	7 03	17 25	7 13	17 36	7 13	17 31	7 16	17 30	7 17	17 25	7 29	17 33	7 33	17 43
22	7 01	17 27	7 11	17 37	7 10	17 33	7 14	17 32	7 14	17 27	7 27	17 35	7 31	17 45
23	6 59	17 29	7 09	17 39	7 08	17 35	7 11	17 34	7 12	17 29	7 24	17 37	7 28	17 47
24	6 57	17 31	7 07	17 41	7 06	17 37	7 09	17 36	7 10	17 31	7 22	17 40	7 26	17 49
25	6 55	17 33	7 05	17 43	7 04	17 38	7 07	17 38	7 07	17 33	7 19	17 42	7 24	17 51
26	6 53	17 34	7 03	17 44	7 02	17 40	7 05	17 40	7 05	17 35	7 17	17 44	7 21	17 53
27	6 51	17 36	7 01	17 46	7 00	17 42	7 02	17 42	7 02	17 37	7 14	17 46	7 19	17 55
28	6 49	17 38	6 59	17 48	6 57	17 44	7 00	17 44	7 00	17 39	7 12	17 48	7 17	17 57

JUPITER

Day	RA	Dec.	Transit	5° high	
				52°	56°
	h m	° ′	h m	h m	h m
1	23 52.5	− 2 04	15 07	20 24	20 19
11	0 00.2	− 1 13	14 36	19 57	19 52
21	0 08.3	− 0 19	14 05	19 30	19 27
31	0 16.7	+ 0 36	13 34	19 04	19 01

Diameters – equatorial 34″ polar 32″

SATURN

Day	RA	Dec.	Transit	5° high	
				52°	56°
	h m	° ′	h m	h m	h m
1	1 46.6	+ 8 26	17 01	23 11	23 14
11	1 49.1	+ 8 43	16 24	22 36	22 39
21	1 52.1	+ 9 02	15 48	22 01	22 05
31	1 55.6	+ 9 24	15 12	21 27	21 31

Diameters – equatorial 17″ polar 15″
Rings – major axis 39″ minor axis 10″

URANUS

Day	RA	Dec.	Transit	10° high	
				52°	56°
	h m	° ′	h m	h m	h m
1	21 01.4	−17 36	12 16	9 15	9 48
11	21 03.7	−17 26	11 39	8 37	9 09
21	21 06.0	−17 16	11 02	7 58	8 30
31	21 08.2	−17 07	10 25	7 20	7 51

Diameter 4″

NEPTUNE

Day	RA	Dec.	Transit	10° high	
				52°	56°
	h m	° ′	h m	h m	h m
1	20 17.7	−19 23	11 33	8 47	9 26
11	20 19.2	−19 18	10 55	8 09	8 47
21	20 20.7	−19 13	10 17	7 30	8 08
31	20 22.0	−19 08	9 39	6 51	7 29

Diameter 2″

March 1999

THIRD MONTH, 31 DAYS. *Mars*, Roman god of battle

1	*Monday*	St David's Day. David Niven b. 1910	*week* 9 *day* 60
2	*Tuesday*	Kurt Weill b. 1900. Archbishop Basil Hume b. 1923	61
3	*Wednesday*	Robert Adam d. 1792. Sir Henry Wood b. 1869	62
4	*Thursday*	Forth Railway Bridge opened 1890. Kenny Dalglish b. 1951	63
5	*Friday*	Flora Macdonald d. 1790. William Beveridge b. 1879	64
6	*Saturday*	Michelangelo b. 1474. Cyrano de Bergerac b. 1619	65
7	*Sunday*	**3rd S. of Lent.** Sir Edwin Landseer b. 1802	*week* 10 *day* 66
8	*Monday*	Commonwealth Day. Hector Berlioz d. 1869	67
9	*Tuesday*	Ernest Bevin b. 1881. Yuri Gagarin b. 1934	68
10	*Wednesday*	*Prince Edward b. 1964.* Jan Masaryk d. 1948	69
11	*Thursday*	Sir Alexander Fleming d. 1955. Haydn Wood d. 1959	70
12	*Friday*	Gabriele d'Annunzio b. 1864. Nijinsky b. 1890	71
13	*Saturday*	Joseph Priestley b. 1733. Uranus discovered 1781	72
14	*Sunday*	**4th S. of Lent.** Mothering Sunday	*week* 11 *day* 73
15	*Monday*	Lord Melbourne b. 1779. Sir Henry Bessemer d. 1898	74
16	*Tuesday*	Aubrey Beardsley d. 1898. William Beveridge d. 1963	75
17	*Wednesday*	St Patrick's Day. *Bank Holiday in Northern Ireland*	76
18	*Thursday*	Hindu New Year. Neville Chamberlain b. 1869	77
19	*Friday*	**St Joseph of Nazareth.** Dr Livingstone b. 1813	78
20	*Saturday*	Marshal Foch d. 1929. Brendan Behan d. 1964	79
21	*Sunday*	**5th S. of Lent.** Archbishop Cranmer executed 1556	*week* 12 *day* 80
22	*Monday*	Sir Anthony van Dyck b. 1599. Goethe d. 1832	81
23	*Tuesday*	Princess Eugenie of York b. 1990	82
24	*Wednesday*	Elizabeth I d. 1603. William Morris b. 1834	83
25	*Thursday*	**The Annunciation.** Treaty of Rome 1957	84
26	*Friday*	Sir John Vanbrugh d. 1726. Cecil Rhodes d. 1902	85
27	*Saturday*	James I d. 1625. James Callaghan b. 1912	86
28	*Sunday*	**Palm Sunday.** Eugene Ionesco d. 1994	*week* 13 *day* 87
29	*Monday*	Sir Edwin Lutyens b. 1869. John Major b. 1943	88
30	*Tuesday*	Beau Brummell d. 1840. Vincent van Gogh b. 1853	89
31	*Wednesday*	*Hilary Law Sittings end.* Eiffel Tower completed 1889	90

ASTRONOMICAL PHENOMENA

d	h	
3	13	Mercury at greatest elongation E.18°
7	04	Mars in conjunction with Moon. Mars 3° S.
10	09	Mercury at stationary point
13	22	Pluto at stationary point
18	01	Mercury in conjunction with Moon. Mercury 7° N.
18	13	Jupiter in conjunction with Moon. Jupiter 3° N.
18	14	Mars at stationary point
19	19	Mercury in inferior conjunction
20	02	Saturn in conjunction with Venus. Saturn 2° S.
20	04	Saturn in conjunction with Moon. Saturn 3° N.
20	05	Venus in conjunction with Moon. Venus 5° N.
21	02	Sun's longitude 0° ♈

MINIMA OF ALGOL

d	h	d	h	d	h
1	00.5	12	11.8	23	23.1
3	21.4	15	08.6	26	19.9
6	18.2	18	05.5	29	16.7
9	15.0	21	02.3		

CONSTELLATIONS

The following constellations are near the meridian at

	d	h		d	h
February	1	24	March	16	21
February	15	23	April	1	20
March	1	22	April	15	19

Cepheus (below the Pole), Camelopardus, Lynx, Gemini, Cancer, Leo, Canis Minor, Hydra, Monoceros, Canis Major and Puppis

THE MOON

Phases, Apsides and Node

		d	h	m
○	Full Moon	2	06	58
☾	Last Quarter	10	08	40
●	New Moon	17	18	48
☽	First Quarter	24	10	18
○	Full Moon	31	22	49

	d	h	m
Apogee (404,714 km)	8	05	05
Perigee (363,286 km)	20	00	07

Mean longitude of ascending node on March 1, 141°

THE SUN

s.d. 16'.1

Day	Right Ascension	Dec.	Equation of time	Rise 52°	Rise 56°	Transit	Set 52°	Set 56°	Sidereal time	Transit of First Point of Aries
	h m s	° '	m s	h m	h m	h m	h m	h m	h m s	h m s
1	22 45 56	− 7 50	−12 30	6 47	6 53	12 12	17 39	17 33	10 33 26	13 24 22
2	22 49 41	− 7 28	−12 19	6 45	6 50	12 12	17 41	17 35	10 37 22	13 20 26
3	22 53 26	− 7 05	−12 07	6 43	6 48	12 12	17 42	17 37	10 41 19	13 16 30
4	22 57 09	− 6 42	−11 54	6 40	6 45	12 12	17 44	17 39	10 45 15	13 12 34
5	23 00 53	− 6 19	−11 41	6 38	6 43	12 12	17 46	17 42	10 49 12	13 08 39
6	23 04 36	− 5 55	−11 28	6 36	6 40	12 11	17 48	17 44	10 53 08	13 04 43
7	23 08 19	− 5 32	−11 14	6 34	6 38	12 11	17 50	17 46	10 57 05	13 00 47
8	23 12 01	− 5 09	−10 59	6 31	6 35	12 11	17 51	17 48	11 01 02	12 56 51
9	23 15 43	− 4 46	−10 45	6 29	6 32	12 11	17 53	17 50	11 04 58	12 52 55
10	23 19 24	− 4 22	−10 30	6 27	6 30	12 10	17 55	17 52	11 08 55	12 48 59
11	23 23 06	− 3 59	−10 14	6 25	6 27	12 10	17 57	17 54	11 12 51	12 45 03
12	23 26 47	− 3 35	− 9 59	6 22	6 25	12 10	17 58	17 56	11 16 48	12 41 07
13	23 30 27	− 3 11	− 9 43	6 20	6 22	12 10	18 00	17 58	11 20 44	12 37 11
14	23 34 08	− 2 48	− 9 27	6 18	6 19	12 09	18 02	18 00	11 24 41	12 33 15
15	23 37 48	− 2 24	− 9 10	6 15	6 17	12 09	18 04	18 02	11 28 37	12 29 20
16	23 41 27	− 2 00	− 8 54	6 13	6 14	12 09	18 05	18 04	11 32 34	12 25 24
17	23 45 07	− 1 37	− 8 37	6 11	6 12	12 08	18 07	18 07	11 36 31	12 21 28
18	23 48 47	− 1 13	− 8 19	6 09	6 09	12 08	18 09	18 09	11 40 27	12 17 32
19	23 52 26	− 0 49	− 8 02	6 06	6 06	12 08	18 11	18 11	11 44 24	12 13 36
20	23 56 05	− 0 25	− 7 45	6 04	6 04	12 08	18 12	18 13	11 48 20	12 09 40
21	23 59 44	− 0 02	− 7 27	6 02	6 01	12 07	18 14	18 15	11 52 17	12 05 44
22	0 03 23	+ 0 22	− 7 09	5 59	5 58	12 07	18 16	18 17	11 56 13	12 01 48
23	0 07 01	+ 0 46	− 6 51	5 57	5 56	12 07	18 17	18 19	12 00 10	11 57 52
24	0 10 40	+ 1 09	− 6 33	5 55	5 53	12 06	18 19	18 21	12 04 06	11 53 56
25	0 14 18	+ 1 33	− 6 15	5 52	5 50	12 06	18 21	18 23	12 08 03	11 50 00
26	0 17 57	+ 1 57	− 5 57	5 50	5 48	12 06	18 23	18 25	12 11 59	11 46 05
27	0 21 35	+ 2 20	− 5 39	5 48	5 45	12 05	18 24	18 27	12 15 56	11 42 09
28	0 25 13	+ 2 44	− 5 21	5 45	5 43	12 05	18 26	18 29	12 19 53	11 38 13
29	0 28 52	+ 3 07	− 5 03	5 43	5 40	12 05	18 28	18 31	12 23 49	11 34 17
30	0 32 30	+ 3 30	− 4 44	5 41	5 37	12 05	18 29	18 33	12 27 46	11 30 21
31	0 36 09	+ 3 54	− 4 26	5 38	5 35	12 04	18 31	18 35	12 31 42	11 26 25

DURATION OF TWILIGHT (in minutes)

Latitude	52°	56°	52°	56°	52°	56°	52°	56°
	1 March		11 March		21 March		31 March	
Civil	34	38	34	37	34	37	34	38
Nautical	73	81	73	80	74	82	76	84
Astronomical	112	124	113	125	116	129	120	136

THE NIGHT SKY

Mercury reaches its greatest eastern elongation (18°) on the 3rd and continues to be visible low above the western horizon at the end of civil twilight in the evenings for the first week or ten days of the month. During this period its magnitude fades from −0.6 to +1.4. Thereafter it is too close to the Sun for observation, inferior conjunction occurring on the 19th. Mercury and Jupiter are within 5–6 degrees of each other during the first part of the month, Jupiter being much the brighter object, and also further from the Sun.

Venus, magnitude −4.0, is a magnificent object in the western sky in the evenings. On the evening of the 19th the thin crescent Moon, only two days old, will be seen about 9° below Venus.

Mars is now brightening considerably as it moves towards opposition next month, rising by 0.8 magnitudes and ending March with a magnitude of −1.0. The gibbous Moon will be seen about 2° above the planet on the morning of the 7th. Mars is in Libra and reaches its first stationary point on the 18th.

Jupiter, magnitude −2.1, is still visible for a short time in the south-western sky after sunset but only for the first two weeks of the month. Thereafter it is lost in the gathering twilight.

Saturn is still an evening object in the western sky but moving closer to the Sun and only visible for a short time after sunset. Its magnitude is +0.5. The thin crescent Moon, only two days old, is near the planet on the early evening of the 19th.

Zodiacal Light. The evening cone may be observed, stretching up from the western horizon along the ecliptic, after the end of twilight from the 4th to the 19th.

THE MOON

Day	RA	Dec.	Hor. par.	Semi- diam.	Sun's co- long.	PA of Bright Limb	Phase	Age	Rise 52°	Rise 56°	Transit	Set 52°	Set 56°
	h m	°	′	′	°	°	%	d	h m	h m	h m	h m	h m
1	9 48	+13.6	56.9	15.5	70	290	98	12.7	16 50	16 40	—	6 33	6 44
2	10 39	+10.0	56.4	15.4	82	314	100	13.7	17 59	17 53	0 02	7 01	7 08
3	11 28	+ 6.1	55.9	15.2	94	97	99	14.7	19 08	19 05	0 48	7 25	7 29
4	12 16	+ 2.0	55.4	15.1	106	104	97	15.7	20 15	20 16	1 33	7 47	7 48
5	13 02	− 2.1	54.9	15.0	118	106	93	16.7	21 20	21 25	2 17	8 09	8 06
6	13 48	− 6.1	54.5	14.9	131	106	87	17.7	22 24	22 33	3 00	8 31	8 25
7	14 34	− 9.7	54.3	14.8	143	104	80	18.7	23 28	23 40	3 44	8 55	8 45
8	15 21	−13.0	54.2	14.8	155	102	72	19.7	—	—	4 28	9 21	9 08
9	16 08	−15.7	54.2	14.8	167	99	63	20.7	0 30	0 45	5 13	9 51	9 35
10	16 57	−17.8	54.4	14.8	179	96	54	21.7	1 30	1 47	6 00	10 26	10 08
11	17 47	−19.1	54.8	14.9	191	92	44	22.7	2 26	2 45	6 48	11 08	10 49
12	18 39	−19.6	55.4	15.1	204	87	34	23.7	3 18	3 38	7 38	11 58	11 39
13	19 32	−19.1	56.1	15.3	216	83	25	24.7	4 05	4 23	8 29	12 57	12 38
14	20 26	−17.6	56.9	15.5	228	78	17	25.7	4 46	5 02	9 21	14 02	13 46
15	21 20	−15.1	57.7	15.7	240	73	10	26.7	5 21	5 34	10 13	15 14	15 02
16	22 15	−11.8	58.6	16.0	252	67	4	27.7	5 53	6 02	11 06	16 30	16 21
17	23 10	− 7.7	59.3	16.2	265	56	1	28.7	6 21	6 27	11 59	17 48	17 44
18	0 05	− 3.0	59.9	16.3	277	294	0	0.2	6 48	6 49	12 52	19 09	19 09
19	1 00	+ 1.9	60.2	16.4	289	261	2	1.2	7 15	7 12	13 45	20 30	20 35
20	1 56	+ 6.7	60.4	16.4	301	258	7	2.2	7 43	7 36	14 40	21 51	22 01
21	2 53	+11.2	60.2	16.4	313	258	14	3.2	8 14	8 03	15 35	23 10	23 24
22	3 51	+14.9	59.9	16.3	326	261	24	4.2	8 50	8 35	16 32	—	—
23	4 50	+17.6	59.5	16.2	338	265	34	5.2	9 32	9 14	17 30	0 25	0 43
24	5 49	+19.2	58.9	16.1	350	269	45	6.2	10 21	10 02	18 27	1 34	1 53
25	6 48	+19.6	58.4	15.9	2	274	56	7.2	11 19	10 59	19 23	2 33	2 52
26	7 45	+18.9	57.8	15.7	14	279	67	8.2	12 22	12 04	20 17	3 22	3 40
27	8 41	+17.1	57.2	15.6	27	284	77	9.2	13 29	13 15	21 08	4 03	4 18
28	9 34	+14.4	56.6	15.4	39	289	85	10.2	14 38	14 27	21 57	4 36	4 48
29	10 25	+11.1	56.1	15.3	51	293	92	11.2	15 47	15 39	22 44	5 04	5 13
30	11 14	+ 7.3	55.7	15.2	63	298	96	12.2	16 55	16 51	23 29	5 29	5 34
31	12 02	+ 3.3	55.2	15.1	75	310	99	13.2	18 02	18 02	—	5 51	5 53

MERCURY

Day	RA	Dec.	Diam.	Phase	Transit	5° high 52°	5° high 56°
	h m	°	″	%	h m	h m	h m
1	23 50	+ 0.1	7	58	13 17	18 47	18 45
3	23 58	+ 1.4	7	50	13 16	18 53	18 51
5	0 04	+ 2.6	8	41	13 14	18 56	18 55
7	0 08	+ 3.5	8	32	13 09	18 56	18 55
9	0 10	+ 4.2	9	23	13 03	18 52	18 52
11	0 10	+ 4.5	9	16	12 54	18 44	18 45
13	0 08	+ 4.6	10	10	12 44	18 33	18 33
15	0 04	+ 4.3	10	5	12 32	18 19	18 19
17	23 59	+ 3.7	11	2	12 19	18 02	18 02
19	23 53	+ 3.0	11	1	12 05	17 44	17 43
21	23 46	+ 2.0	11	1	11 50	6 15	6 17
23	23 40	+ 1.0	11	2	11 37	6 07	6 09
25	23 35	− 0.1	11	5	11 24	5 59	6 02
27	23 31	− 1.1	11	8	11 12	5 52	5 56
29	23 28	− 2.0	11	12	11 02	5 46	5 51
31	23 26	− 2.7	10	16	10 52	5 40	5 46

VENUS

Day	RA	Dec.	Diam.	Phase	Transit	5° high 52°	5° high 56°
	h m	°	″	%	h m	h m	h m
1	0 33	+ 2.8	12	88	14 00	19 44	19 44
6	0 56	+ 5.4	12	86	14 03	20 00	20 01
11	1 18	+ 7.9	12	85	14 06	20 16	20 19
16	1 41	+10.4	13	84	14 08	20 31	20 37
21	2 03	+12.7	13	83	14 11	20 47	20 54
26	2 26	+15.0	13	81	14 15	21 02	21 12
31	2 50	+17.1	13	80	14 19	21 17	21 29

MARS

Day	RA	Dec.	Diam.	Phase	Transit	5° high 52°	5° high 56°
1	14 35	−12.9	10	93	4 01	23 43	0 01
6	14 38	−13.1	11	93	3 45	23 27	23 44
11	14 40	−13.3	11	94	3 27	23 11	23 27
16	14 42	−13.4	12	95	3 09	22 53	23 09
21	14 42	−13.5	13	96	2 49	22 33	22 49
26	14 40	−13.4	13	96	2 28	22 11	22 28
31	14 38	−13.3	14	97	2 06	21 48	22 04

SUNRISE AND SUNSET

	London		Bristol		Birmingham		Manchester		Newcastle		Glasgow		Belfast	
	0°05'	51°30'	2°35'	51°28'	1°55'	52°28'	2°15'	53°28'	1°37'	54°59'	4°14'	55°52'	5°56'	54°35'
	h m	h m	h m	h m	h m	h m	h m	h m	h m	h m	h m	h m	h m	h m
1	6 47	17 40	6 57	17 50	6 55	17 46	6 58	17 46	6 58	17 41	7 09	17 50	7 14	17 59
2	6 44	17 42	6 54	17 52	6 53	17 48	6 56	17 48	6 55	17 43	7 07	17 52	7 12	18 01
3	6 42	17 43	6 52	17 53	6 51	17 50	6 53	17 50	6 53	17 45	7 04	17 54	7 09	18 03
4	6 40	17 45	6 50	17 55	6 49	17 51	6 51	17 51	6 50	17 47	7 02	17 57	7 07	18 05
5	6 38	17 47	6 48	17 57	6 46	17 53	6 49	17 53	6 48	17 49	6 59	17 59	7 05	18 07
6	6 36	17 49	6 46	17 59	6 44	17 55	6 46	17 55	6 45	17 51	6 57	18 01	7 02	18 09
7	6 34	17 50	6 43	18 00	6 42	17 57	6 44	17 57	6 43	17 53	6 54	18 03	7 00	18 11
8	6 31	17 52	6 41	18 02	6 39	17 59	6 42	17 59	6 40	17 55	6 52	18 05	6 57	18 13
9	6 29	17 54	6 39	18 04	6 37	18 00	6 39	18 01	6 38	17 57	6 49	18 07	6 55	18 15
10	6 27	17 55	6 37	18 06	6 35	18 02	6 37	18 03	6 35	17 59	6 47	18 09	6 52	18 17
11	6 25	17 57	6 35	18 07	6 33	18 04	6 34	18 05	6 33	18 01	6 44	18 11	6 50	18 19
12	6 22	17 59	6 32	18 09	6 30	18 06	6 32	18 07	6 30	18 03	6 41	18 13	6 47	18 21
13	6 20	18 01	6 30	18 11	6 28	18 08	6 30	18 08	6 28	18 05	6 39	18 15	6 45	18 23
14	6 18	18 02	6 28	18 12	6 26	18 09	6 27	18 10	6 25	18 07	6 36	18 17	6 42	18 25
15	6 16	18 04	6 26	18 14	6 23	18 11	6 25	18 12	6 23	18 09	6 34	18 19	6 40	18 27
16	6 13	18 06	6 23	18 16	6 21	18 13	6 22	18 14	6 20	18 11	6 31	18 21	6 37	18 29
17	6 11	18 07	6 21	18 17	6 19	18 15	6 20	18 16	6 18	18 13	6 28	18 24	6 35	18 31
18	6 09	18 09	6 19	18 19	6 16	18 16	6 18	18 18	6 15	18 15	6 26	18 26	6 32	18 32
19	6 07	18 11	6 17	18 21	6 14	18 18	6 15	18 20	6 13	18 17	6 23	18 28	6 30	18 34
20	6 04	18 13	6 14	18 23	6 12	18 20	6 13	18 21	6 10	18 19	6 21	18 30	6 27	18 36
21	6 02	18 14	6 12	18 24	6 09	18 22	6 10	18 23	6 08	18 21	6 18	18 32	6 25	18 38
22	6 00	18 16	6 10	18 26	6 07	18 24	6 08	18 25	6 05	18 23	6 15	18 34	6 22	18 40
23	5 57	18 18	6 07	18 28	6 04	18 25	6 06	18 27	6 03	18 25	6 13	18 36	6 20	18 42
24	5 55	18 19	6 05	18 29	6 02	18 27	6 03	18 29	6 00	18 27	6 10	18 38	6 17	18 44
25	5 53	18 21	6 03	18 31	6 00	18 29	6 01	18 31	5 57	18 29	6 07	18 40	6 15	18 46
26	5 51	18 23	6 01	18 33	5 57	18 31	5 58	18 32	5 55	18 31	6 05	18 42	6 12	18 48
27	5 48	18 24	5 58	18 34	5 55	18 32	5 56	18 34	5 52	18 33	6 02	18 44	6 10	18 50
28	5 46	18 26	5 56	18 36	5 53	18 34	5 53	18 36	5 50	18 35	6 00	18 46	6 07	18 52
29	5 44	18 28	5 54	18 38	5 50	18 36	5 51	18 38	5 47	18 37	5 57	18 48	6 05	18 54
30	5 41	18 29	5 51	18 39	5 48	18 38	5 49	18 40	5 45	18 39	5 54	18 50	6 02	18 56
31	5 39	18 31	5 49	18 41	5 46	18 39	5 46	18 42	5 42	18 41	5 52	18 52	6 00	18 57

JUPITER

Day	RA	Dec.	Transit	5° high	
				52°	56°
	h m	° '	h m	h m	h m
1	0 15.0	+ 0 25	13 40	19 09	19 06
11	0 23.6	+ 1 22	13 09	18 43	18 41
21	0 32.4	+ 2 19	12 39	18 18	18 16
31	0 41.3	+ 3 16	12 08	17 52	17 51

Diameters – equatorial 33″ polar 31″

SATURN

Day	RA	Dec.	Transit	5° high	
				52°	56°
	h m	° '	h m	h m	h m
1	1 54.9	+ 9 19	15 19	21 34	21 38
11	1 58.7	+ 9 42	14 44	21 00	21 05
21	2 02.9	+10 07	14 09	20 27	20 32
31	2 07.4	+10 32	13 34	19 55	20 00

Diameters – equatorial 16″ polar 15″
Rings – major axis 38″ minor axis 10″

URANUS

Day	RA	Dec.	Transit	10° high	
				52°	56°
	h m	° '	h m	h m	h m
1	21 07.8	−17 09	10 33	7 28	7 59
11	21 09.9	−17 00	9 55	6 49	7 20
21	21 11.8	−16 52	9 18	6 11	6 41
31	21 13.5	−16 44	8 40	5 32	6 02

Diameter 4″

NEPTUNE

Day	RA	Dec.	Transit	10° high	
				52°	56°
	h m	° '	h m	h m	h m
1	20 21.7	−19 09	9 47	6 59	7 37
11	20 23.0	−19 05	9 09	6 20	6 58
21	20 24.1	−19 02	8 30	5 42	6 19
31	20 25.0	−18 58	7 52	5 03	5 40

Diameter 2″

April 1999

FOURTH MONTH, 30 DAYS. *Aperire*, to open; Earth opens to receive seed

1	*Thursday*	**Maundy Thursday.** Passover begins	*week* 13 *day* 91
2	*Friday*	**Good Friday.** *Public Holiday in the UK*	92
3	*Saturday*	Easter Eve. Graham Greene d. 1991	93
4	*Sunday*	**Easter Day** (Western churches)	*week* 14 *day* 94
5	*Monday*	*Bank Holiday in England, Wales and Northern Ireland*	95
6	*Tuesday*	Richard I d. 1199. Peary reached the North Pole 1909	96
7	*Wednesday*	William Wordsworth b. 1770. Henry Ford d. 1947	97
8	*Thursday*	Sir Adrian Boult b. 1889. Kurt Cobain d. 1994	98
9	*Friday*	Duke of Monmouth b. 1649. Frank Lloyd Wright d. 1959	99
10	*Saturday*	Gen. William Booth b. 1829. Chris Hani assassinated 1993	100
11	*Sunday*	**2nd S. of Easter.** Easter Day (Eastern Orthodox)	*week* 15 *day* 101
12	*Monday*	Alan Ayckbourn b. 1939. Bobby Moore b. 1941	102
13	*Tuesday*	*Easter Law Sittings begin.* Edict of Nantes 1598	103
14	*Wednesday*	Sikh New Year. Sir John Gielgud b. 1904	104
15	*Thursday*	Greta Garbo d. 1990. John Curry d. 1994	105
16	*Friday*	Mme Tussaud d. 1850. Sir Charles Chaplin b. 1889	106
17	*Saturday*	Muslim New Year. Benjamin Franklin d. 1790	107
18	*Sunday*	**3rd S. of Easter.** Judge Jeffreys d. 1689	*week* 16 *day* 108
19	*Monday*	Primrose Day. Lord Berners d. 1950	109
20	*Tuesday*	Adolf Hitler b. 1889. Bram Stoker d. 1912	110
21	*Wednesday*	*Queen Elizabeth II b. 1926.* Jean Racine d. 1699	111
22	*Thursday*	Kathleen Ferrier b. 1912. Yehudi Menuhin b. 1916	112
23	*Friday*	**St George.** Shakespeare d. 1616. Cervantes d. 1616	113
24	*Saturday*	Easter Rising, Dublin, began 1916	114
25	*Sunday*	**4th S. of Easter.** Oliver Cromwell b. 1599	*week* 17 *day* 115
26	*Monday*	**St Mark.** Eugène Delacroix b. 1798	116
27	*Tuesday*	Samuel Morse b. 1791. Dashiel Hammett b. 1894	117
28	*Wednesday*	Mutiny on the *Bounty.* Mussolini killed 1945	118
29	*Thursday*	Duke Ellington b. 1899. Easter Rising put down 1916	119
30	*Friday*	Mary II b. 1662. Adolf Hitler d. 1945	120

ASTRONOMICAL PHENOMENA

d	h	
1	06	Jupiter in conjunction
2	09	Mercury at stationary point
3	10	Mars in conjunction with Moon. Mars 3° S.
14	05	Mercury in conjunction with Moon. Mercury 1° N.
15	10	Jupiter in conjunction with Moon. Jupiter 3° N.
16	16	Mercury at greatest elongation W.28°
16	20	Saturn in conjunction with Moon. Saturn 3° N.
18	23	Venus in conjunction with Moon. Venus 7° N.
20	13	Sun's longitude 30° ♉
24	18	Mars at opposition
27	11	Saturn in conjunction
29	23	Mars in conjunction with Moon. Mars 4° S.

MINIMA OF ALGOL

d	h	d	h	d	h
1	13.6	13	00.8	24	12.1
4	10.4	15	21.7	27	08.9
7	07.2	18	18.5	30	05.8
10	04.0	21	15.3		

CONSTELLATIONS

The following constellations are near the meridian at

	d	h		d	h
March	1	24	April	15	21
March	16	23	May	1	20
April	1	22	May	16	19

Cepheus (below the Pole), Cassiopeia (below the Pole), Ursa Major, Leo Minor, Leo, Sextans, Hydra and Crater

THE MOON

Phases, Apsides and Node	d	h	m
☾ Last Quarter	9	02	51
● New Moon	16	04	22
☽ First Quarter	22	19	02
○ Full Moon	30	14	55
Apogee (405,568 km)	4	21	22
Perigee (358,904 km)	17	05	18

Mean longitude of ascending node on April 1, 140°

THE SUN
s.d. 16'.0

Day	Right Ascension	Dec. +	Equation of time	Rise 52°	Rise 56°	Transit	Set 52°	Set 56°	Sidereal time	Transit of First Point of Aries
	h m s	° '	m s	h m	h m	h m	h m	h m	h m s	h m s
1	0 39 47	4 17	− 4 08	5 36	5 32	12 04	18 33	18 37	12 35 39	11 22 29
2	0 43 26	4 40	− 3 50	5 34	5 29	12 04	18 35	18 39	12 39 35	11 18 33
3	0 47 04	5 03	− 3 32	5 32	5 27	12 03	18 36	18 41	12 43 32	11 14 37
4	0 50 43	5 26	− 3 15	5 29	5 24	12 03	18 38	18 43	12 47 28	11 10 41
5	0 54 22	5 49	− 2 57	5 27	5 22	12 03	18 40	18 45	12 51 25	11 06 45
6	0 58 01	6 12	− 2 40	5 25	5 19	12 03	18 41	18 47	12 55 22	11 02 50
7	1 01 41	6 35	− 2 23	5 22	5 16	12 02	18 43	18 49	12 59 18	10 58 54
8	1 05 20	6 57	− 2 06	5 20	5 14	12 02	18 45	18 51	13 03 15	10 54 58
9	1 09 00	7 20	− 1 49	5 18	5 11	12 02	18 47	18 54	13 07 11	10 51 02
10	1 12 40	7 42	− 1 33	5 16	5 09	12 01	18 48	18 56	13 11 08	10 47 06
11	1 16 21	8 04	− 1 17	5 13	5 06	12 01	18 50	18 58	13 15 04	10 43 10
12	1 20 02	8 26	− 1 01	5 11	5 03	12 01	18 52	19 00	13 19 01	10 39 14
13	1 23 43	8 48	− 0 45	5 09	5 01	12 01	18 53	19 02	13 22 57	10 35 18
14	1 27 24	9 10	− 0 30	5 07	4 58	12 00	18 55	19 04	13 26 54	10 31 22
15	1 31 06	9 32	− 0 15	5 05	4 56	12 00	18 57	19 06	13 30 51	10 27 26
16	1 34 48	9 53	− 0 01	5 02	4 53	12 00	18 59	19 08	13 34 47	10 23 30
17	1 38 30	10 14	+ 0 14	5 00	4 51	12 00	19 00	19 10	13 38 44	10 19 35
18	1 42 13	10 35	+ 0 27	4 58	4 48	11 59	19 02	19 12	13 42 40	10 15 39
19	1 45 56	10 56	+ 0 41	4 56	4 46	11 59	19 04	19 14	13 46 37	10 11 43
20	1 49 39	11 17	+ 0 54	4 54	4 43	11 59	19 05	19 16	13 50 33	10 07 47
21	1 53 23	11 38	+ 1 07	4 52	4 41	11 59	19 07	19 18	13 54 30	10 03 51
22	1 57 08	11 58	+ 1 19	4 49	4 38	11 59	19 09	19 20	13 58 26	9 59 55
23	2 00 52	12 18	+ 1 31	4 47	4 36	11 58	19 11	19 22	14 02 23	9 55 59
24	2 04 38	12 39	+ 1 42	4 45	4 34	11 58	19 12	19 24	14 06 19	9 52 03
25	2 08 23	12 58	+ 1 53	4 43	4 31	11 58	19 14	19 26	14 10 16	9 48 07
26	2 12 09	13 18	+ 2 03	4 41	4 29	11 58	19 16	19 28	14 14 13	9 44 11
27	2 15 56	13 37	+ 2 13	4 39	4 27	11 58	19 17	19 30	14 18 09	9 40 16
28	2 19 43	13 56	+ 2 23	4 37	4 24	11 58	19 19	19 32	14 22 06	9 36 20
29	2 23 30	14 15	+ 2 32	4 35	4 22	11 57	19 21	19 34	14 26 02	9 32 24
30	2 27 18	14 34	+ 2 40	4 33	4 20	11 57	19 22	19 36	14 29 59	9 28 28

DURATION OF TWILIGHT (in minutes)

Latitude	52°	56°	52°	56°	52°	56°	52°	56°
	1 April		11 April		21 April		30 April	
Civil	34	38	35	40	37	42	39	44
Nautical	76	85	79	90	84	96	89	105
Astronomical	121	137	128	148	138	167	152	200

THE NIGHT SKY

Mercury is unsuitably placed for observation throughout the month.

Venus continues to be visible as a magnificent object in the western sky in the evenings, magnitude −4.1. On the evening of the 18th the thin crescent Moon, less than three days old, will be seen near the planet. Venus passes 7° N. of Aldebaran on the evening of the 21st.

Mars reaches opposition on the 24th, and is thus visible throughout the hours of darkness, attaining a magnitude of −1.7. Because of the eccentricity of its orbit, closest approach to the Earth (87 million km) does not occur until May 1st. The gibbous Moon is near the planet during the night of the 2nd to 3rd: also the Full Moon is near during the night of the 29th to 30th. During April, Mars moves retrograde from Libra back into Virgo.

Jupiter passes through conjunction on the first day of the month and thus remains too close to the Sun for observation.

Saturn, magnitude +0.4, is disappearing into the lengthening evening twilight in the west, and is unlikely to be seen after the first few days of the month. Saturn passes through conjunction on the 27th.

THE MOON

Day	RA h m	Dec. °	Hor. par. '	Semi- diam. '	Sun's co- long. °	PA of Bright Limb °	Phase %	Age d	Rise 52° h m	Rise 56° h m	Transit h m	Set 52° h m	Set 56° h m
1	12 48	− 0.9	54.9	14.9	87	31	100	14.2	19 08	19 11	0 13	6 13	6 11
2	13 34	− 4.9	54.5	14.9	100	91	99	15.2	20 13	20 20	0 56	6 34	6 29
3	14 20	− 8.7	54.3	14.8	112	98	96	16.2	21 17	21 27	1 39	6 57	6 48
4	15 06	−12.2	54.1	14.7	124	98	91	17.2	22 19	22 33	2 23	7 22	7 10
5	15 53	−15.1	54.1	14.7	136	97	85	18.2	23 20	23 37	3 08	7 50	7 35
6	16 42	−17.4	54.1	14.8	148	94	78	19.2	—	—	3 54	8 23	8 05
7	17 31	−19.0	54.4	14.8	160	91	70	20.2	0 18	0 37	4 41	9 02	8 42
8	18 22	−19.7	54.8	14.9	173	87	61	21.2	1 11	1 31	5 30	9 48	9 28
9	19 14	−19.6	55.3	15.1	185	83	51	22.2	1 59	2 19	6 19	10 42	10 22
10	20 06	−18.4	56.0	15.3	197	78	41	23.2	2 41	2 59	7 10	11 43	11 25
11	20 59	−16.4	56.9	15.5	209	74	31	24.2	3 18	3 33	8 01	12 50	12 36
12	21 53	−13.4	57.8	15.7	221	70	22	25.2	3 50	4 02	8 52	14 03	13 52
13	22 46	− 9.6	58.7	16.0	234	66	14	26.2	4 19	4 27	9 44	15 19	15 13
14	23 41	− 5.1	59.6	16.2	246	62	7	27.2	4 46	4 50	10 36	16 39	16 37
15	0 36	− 0.3	60.4	16.4	258	54	2	28.2	5 13	5 12	11 30	18 01	18 04
16	1 32	+ 4.8	60.9	16.6	270	8	0	29.2	5 40	5 35	12 25	19 24	19 32
17	2 29	+ 9.5	61.1	16.6	283	274	1	0.8	6 10	6 01	13 21	20 47	21 00
18	3 29	+13.7	61.0	16.6	295	266	5	1.8	6 44	6 31	14 20	22 08	22 24
19	4 29	+17.0	60.6	16.5	307	267	12	2.8	7 25	7 08	15 20	23 22	23 41
20	5 31	+19.1	60.0	16.4	319	270	20	3.8	8 13	7 54	16 19	—	—
21	6 32	+19.9	59.3	16.2	331	275	31	4.8	9 10	8 50	17 17	0 27	0 47
22	7 31	+19.4	58.5	15.9	344	279	41	5.8	10 13	9 54	18 13	1 21	1 40
23	8 28	+17.8	57.7	15.7	356	284	52	6.8	11 20	11 04	19 06	2 05	2 22
24	9 22	+15.3	56.9	15.5	8	288	63	7.8	12 29	12 17	19 56	2 41	2 54
25	10 14	+12.1	56.3	15.3	20	291	73	8.8	13 38	13 29	20 43	3 10	3 20
26	11 03	+ 8.4	55.7	15.2	32	294	81	9.8	14 46	14 41	21 28	3 35	3 41
27	11 50	+ 4.4	55.2	15.0	45	297	88	10.8	15 52	15 51	22 11	3 57	4 00
28	12 36	+ 0.2	54.8	14.9	57	300	94	11.8	16 58	17 00	22 54	4 18	4 18
29	13 22	− 3.9	54.4	14.8	69	305	97	12.8	18 03	18 09	23 37	4 39	4 35
30	14 07	− 7.8	54.2	14.8	81	325	99	13.8	19 07	19 17	—	5 01	4 54

MERCURY

Day	RA h m	Dec. °	Diam. "	Phase %	Transit h m	5° high 52° h m	5° high 56° h m
1	23 26	− 3.0	10	18	10 48	5 38	5 44
3	23 26	− 3.5	10	22	10 41	5 33	5 39
5	23 28	− 3.8	10	26	10 36	5 29	5 35
7	23 31	− 4.0	9	30	10 31	5 25	5 31
9	23 35	− 3.9	9	34	10 27	5 21	5 28
11	23 40	− 3.8	9	38	10 25	5 17	5 24
13	23 46	− 3.5	8	41	10 23	5 14	5 20
15	23 53	− 3.0	8	44	10 22	5 10	5 16
17	0 00	− 2.5	8	47	10 21	5 07	5 12
19	0 08	− 1.8	8	50	10 22	5 03	5 08
21	0 17	− 1.0	7	53	10 22	5 00	5 04
23	0 26	− 0.2	7	56	10 24	4 56	5 00
25	0 35	+ 0.8	7	59	10 25	4 53	4 56
27	0 45	+ 1.8	7	62	10 28	4 50	4 52
29	0 56	+ 3.0	6	65	10 30	4 47	4 48
31	1 07	+ 4.2	6	68	10 34	4 44	4 44

VENUS

Day	RA h m	Dec. °	Diam. "	Phase %	Transit h m	5° high 52° h m	5° high 56° h m
1	2 54	+17.5	13	80	14 19	21 20	21 32
6	3 18	+19.4	14	78	14 23	21 35	21 49
11	3 42	+21.0	14	76	14 28	21 50	22 05
16	4 07	+22.5	15	75	14 33	22 03	22 21
21	4 32	+23.7	15	73	14 38	22 16	22 35
26	4 57	+24.7	16	71	14 43	22 27	22 47
31	5 22	+25.4	16	69	14 48	22 37	22 58

MARS

Day	RA h m	Dec. °	Diam. "	Phase %	Transit h m	5° high 52° h m	5° high 56° h m
1	14 37	−13.2	14	98	2 01	21 43	21 59
6	14 33	−13.0	15	98	1 37	21 18	21 34
11	14 28	−12.7	15	99	1 13	20 51	21 06
16	14 22	−12.4	16	100	0 47	20 23	20 38
21	14 15	−11.9	16	100	0 20	19 54	20 08
26	14 07	−11.5	16	100	23 48	19 24	19 38
31	14 00	−11.1	16	100	23 21	18 54	19 08

SUNRISE AND SUNSET

	London 0°05' 51°30'		Bristol 2°35' 51°28'		Birmingham 1°55' 52°28'		Manchester 2°15' 53°28'		Newcastle 1°37' 54°59'		Glasgow 4°14' 55°52'		Belfast 5°56' 54°35'	
	h m	h m	h m	h m	h m	h m	h m	h m	h m	h m	h m	h m	h m	h m
1	5 37	18 33	5 47	18 43	5 43	18 41	5 44	18 43	5 40	18 43	5 49	18 54	5 57	18 59
2	5 35	18 34	5 45	18 44	5 41	18 43	5 41	18 45	5 37	18 44	5 46	18 56	5 55	19 01
3	5 32	18 36	5 42	18 46	5 39	18 45	5 39	18 47	5 35	18 46	5 44	18 58	5 52	19 03
4	5 30	18 38	5 40	18 48	5 36	18 46	5 36	18 49	5 32	18 48	5 41	19 00	5 50	19 05
5	5 28	18 39	5 38	18 49	5 34	18 48	5 34	18 51	5 29	18 50	5 39	19 02	5 47	19 07
6	5 26	18 41	5 36	18 51	5 32	18 50	5 32	18 53	5 27	18 52	5 36	19 04	5 45	19 09
7	5 23	18 43	5 33	18 53	5 29	18 52	5 29	18 54	5 24	18 54	5 33	19 06	5 42	19 11
8	5 21	18 44	5 31	18 54	5 27	18 53	5 27	18 56	5 22	18 56	5 31	19 08	5 40	19 13
9	5 19	18 46	5 29	18 56	5 25	18 55	5 25	18 58	5 19	18 58	5 28	19 10	5 37	19 15
10	5 17	18 48	5 27	18 58	5 23	18 57	5 22	19 00	5 17	19 00	5 26	19 12	5 35	19 17
11	5 15	18 49	5 25	18 59	5 20	18 58	5 20	19 02	5 14	19 02	5 23	19 14	5 33	19 18
12	5 12	18 51	5 22	19 01	5 18	19 00	5 18	19 03	5 12	19 04	5 21	19 16	5 30	19 20
13	5 10	18 53	5 20	19 03	5 16	19 02	5 15	19 05	5 10	19 06	5 18	19 18	5 28	19 22
14	5 08	18 55	5 18	19 04	5 13	19 04	5 13	19 07	5 07	19 08	5 16	19 20	5 25	19 24
15	5 06	18 56	5 16	19 06	5 11	19 05	5 11	19 09	5 05	19 10	5 13	19 22	5 23	19 26
16	5 04	18 58	5 14	19 08	5 09	19 07	5 08	19 11	5 02	19 12	5 11	19 24	5 20	19 28
17	5 02	19 00	5 12	19 09	5 07	19 09	5 06	19 13	5 00	19 14	5 08	19 26	5 18	19 30
18	4 59	19 01	5 09	19 11	5 05	19 11	5 04	19 14	4 57	19 16	5 06	19 28	5 16	19 32
19	4 57	19 03	5 07	19 13	5 02	19 12	5 01	19 16	4 55	19 18	5 03	19 31	5 13	19 34
20	4 55	19 05	5 05	19 14	5 00	19 14	4 59	19 18	4 53	19 20	5 01	19 33	5 11	19 36
21	4 53	19 06	5 03	19 16	4 58	19 16	4 57	19 20	4 50	19 21	4 58	19 35	5 09	19 38
22	4 51	19 08	5 01	19 18	4 56	19 18	4 55	19 22	4 48	19 23	4 56	19 37	5 06	19 40
23	4 49	19 10	4 59	19 19	4 54	19 19	4 53	19 23	4 46	19 25	4 53	19 39	5 04	19 41
24	4 47	19 11	4 57	19 21	4 52	19 21	4 50	19 25	4 43	19 27	4 51	19 41	5 02	19 43
25	4 45	19 13	4 55	19 23	4 50	19 23	4 48	19 27	4 41	19 29	4 49	19 43	5 00	19 45
26	4 43	19 15	4 53	19 24	4 48	19 25	4 46	19 29	4 39	19 31	4 46	19 45	4 57	19 47
27	4 41	19 16	4 51	19 26	4 46	19 26	4 44	19 31	4 36	19 33	4 44	19 47	4 55	19 49
28	4 39	19 18	4 49	19 28	4 43	19 28	4 42	19 33	4 34	19 35	4 42	19 49	4 53	19 51
29	4 37	19 19	4 47	19 29	4 41	19 30	4 40	19 34	4 32	19 37	4 39	19 51	4 51	19 53
30	4 35	19 21	4 45	19 31	4 39	19 31	4 38	19 36	4 30	19 39	4 37	19 53	4 48	19 55

JUPITER

Day	RA	Dec.	Transit	5° high 52°	56°
	h m	° '	h m	h m	h m
1	0 42.2	+ 3 21	12 05	6 21	6 21
11	0 51.1	+ 4 18	11 35	5 46	5 45
21	1 00.0	+ 5 13	11 04	5 11	5 10
31	1 08.7	+ 6 07	10 33	4 35	4 34

Diameters – equatorial 33″ polar 31″

SATURN

Day	RA	Dec.	Transit	5° high 52°	56°
	h m	° '	h m	h m	h m
1	2 07.9	+10 35	13 30	19 51	19 57
11	2 12.6	+11 00	12 56	19 19	19 25
21	2 17.4	+11 26	12 21	18 47	18 53
31	2 22.3	+11 51	11 47	18 14	18 21

Diameters – equatorial 16″ polar 15″
Rings – major axis 37″ minor axis 11″

URANUS

Day	RA	Dec.	Transit	10° high 52°	56°
	h m	° '	h m	h m	h m
1	21 13.7	−16 44	8 37	5 28	5 58
11	21 15.1	−16 38	7 59	4 50	5 19
21	21 16.3	−16 33	7 21	4 11	4 40
31	21 17.1	−16 29	6 42	3 32	4 01

Diameter 4″

NEPTUNE

Day	RA	Dec.	Transit	10° high 52°	56°
	h m	° '	h m	h m	h m
1	20 25.1	−18 58	7 48	4 59	5 36
11	20 25.8	−18 56	7 10	4 20	4 57
21	20 26.2	−18 54	6 31	3 41	4 18
31	20 26.5	−18 53	5 52	3 02	3 39

Diameter 2″

May 1999

FIFTH MONTH, 31 DAYS. *Maia*, goddess of growth and increase

1	*Saturday*	**SS Philip and James.** Great Exhibition opened 1851	*week* 17 *day* 121
2	*Sunday*	**5th S. of Easter.** Leonardo da Vinci d. 1519	*week* 18 *day* 122
3	*Monday*	*Bank Holiday in the UK.* Festival of Britain opened 1951	123
4	*Tuesday*	Joseph Whitaker b. 1820. Sir Osbert Sitwell d. 1969	124
5	*Wednesday*	Napoleon Bonaparte d. 1821. Austin Reed d. 1954	125
6	*Thursday*	Tony Blair b. 1953. First four-minute mile 1954	126
7	*Friday*	Robert Browning b. 1812. Sir Huw Wheldon b. 1916	127
8	*Saturday*	John Stuart Mill d. 1873. Friedrich von Hayek b. 1899	128
9	*Sunday*	**6th S. of Easter.** Europe Day	*week* 19 *day* 129
10	*Monday*	Indian Mutiny began 1857. Fred Astaire b. 1899	130
11	*Tuesday*	Paul Nash b. 1889. Martha Graham b. 1894	131
12	*Wednesday*	John Masefield d. 1967. John Smith d. 1994	132
13	*Thursday*	**Ascension Day.** John Nash d. 1835	133
14	*Friday*	**St Matthias.** Thomas Gainsborough baptized 1727	134
15	*Saturday*	Joseph Whitaker d. 1895. James Mason b. 1909	135
16	*Sunday*	**7th S. of Easter.** 'Oscars' first presented 1929	*week* 20 *day* 136
17	*Monday*	Botticelli d. 1510. Relief of Mafeking 1900	137
18	*Tuesday*	Pierre de Beaumarchais d. 1799. Pope John Paul II b. 1920	138
19	*Wednesday*	Anne Boleyn executed 1536. Sir John Betjeman d. 1984	139
20	*Thursday*	John Stuart Mill b. 1806. First Chelsea Flower Show 1913	140
21	*Friday*	FEAST OF WEEKS begins. Lord Clark d. 1983	141
22	*Saturday*	Maria Edgeworth d. 1849. Blackwall Tunnel opened 1897	142
23	*Sunday*	**Pentecost (Whit Sunday).** Thomas Hood b. 1799	*week* 21 *day* 143
24	*Monday*	Queen Victoria b. 1819. Suzanne Lenglen b. 1899	144
25	*Tuesday*	Lord Beaverbrook b. 1879. Gustav Holst d. 1934	145
26	*Wednesday*	Samuel Pepys d. 1703. Queen Mary b. 1867	146
27	*Thursday*	John Calvin d. 1564. Jawaharlal Nehru d. 1964	147
28	*Friday*	*Easter Law Sittings end.* William Pitt (younger) b. 1759	148
29	*Saturday*	Constantinople captured by Turks 1453. Everest conquered 1953	149
30	*Sunday*	**Trinity Sunday.** Alexander Pope d. 1744	*week* 22 *day* 150
31	*Monday*	**Visit of Virgin Mary to Elizabeth.** *Bank Holiday in the UK*	151

ASTRONOMICAL PHENOMENA

d	h	
1	22	Jupiter in conjunction with Mercury. Jupiter 2° N.
7	01	Neptune at stationary point
13	07	Jupiter in conjunction with Moon. Jupiter 3° N.
13	16	Saturn in conjunction with Mercury. Saturn 0°.6 S.
14	12	Saturn in conjunction with Moon. Saturn 3° N.
14	15	Mercury in conjunction with Moon. Mercury 4° N.
18	14	Venus in conjunction with Moon. Venus 6° N.
21	12	Sun's longitude 60° II
21	22	Uranus at stationary point
25	18	Mercury in superior conjunction
26	15	Mars in conjunction with Moon. Mars 5° S.
31	00	Pluto at opposition

MINIMA OF ALGOL

Algol is inconveniently situated for observation during May.

CONSTELLATIONS

The following constellations are near the meridian at

	d	h		d	h
April	1	24	May	16	21
April	15	23	June	1	20
May	1	22	June	15	19

Cepheus (below the Pole), Cassiopeia (below the Pole), Ursa Minor, Ursa Major, Canes Venatici, Coma Berenices, Bootes, Leo, Virgo, Crater, Corvus and Hydra

THE MOON

Phases, Apsides and Node	d	h	m
☾ Last Quarter	8	17	29
● New Moon	15	12	05
☽ First Quarter	22	05	34
○ Full Moon	30	06	40
Apogee (406,265 km)	2	05	59
Perigee (357,095 km)	15	15	01
Apogee (406,404 km)	29	08	00

Mean longitude of ascending node on May 1, 138°

THE SUN   s.d. 15′.8

Day	Right Ascension	Dec. +	Equation of time	Rise 52°	Rise 56°	Transit	Set 52°	Set 56°	Sidereal time	Transit of First Point of Aries
	h m s	° ′	m s	h m	h m	h m	h m	h m	h m s	h m s
1	2 31 07	14 52	+ 2 48	4 31	4 17	11 57	19 24	19 38	14 33 55	9 24 32
2	2 34 56	15 11	+ 2 56	4 29	4 15	11 57	19 26	19 40	14 37 52	9 20 36
3	2 38 46	15 29	+ 3 03	4 28	4 13	11 57	19 27	19 42	14 41 48	9 16 40
4	2 42 36	15 46	+ 3 09	4 26	4 11	11 57	19 29	19 44	14 45 45	9 12 44
5	2 46 27	16 04	+ 3 15	4 24	4 08	11 57	19 31	19 46	14 49 42	9 08 48
6	2 50 18	16 21	+ 3 20	4 22	4 06	11 57	19 32	19 48	14 53 38	9 04 52
7	2 54 10	16 38	+ 3 25	4 20	4 04	11 57	19 34	19 50	14 57 35	9 00 56
8	2 58 02	16 54	+ 3 29	4 18	4 02	11 56	19 36	19 52	15 01 31	8 57 01
9	3 01 55	17 11	+ 3 32	4 17	4 00	11 56	19 37	19 54	15 05 28	8 53 05
10	3 05 49	17 27	+ 3 35	4 15	3 58	11 56	19 39	19 56	15 09 24	8 49 09
11	3 09 43	17 42	+ 3 38	4 13	3 56	11 56	19 40	19 58	15 13 21	8 45 13
12	3 13 38	17 58	+ 3 39	4 12	3 54	11 56	19 42	20 00	15 17 17	8 41 17
13	3 17 34	18 13	+ 3 40	4 10	3 52	11 56	19 44	20 02	15 21 14	8 37 21
14	3 21 30	18 28	+ 3 41	4 08	3 50	11 56	19 45	20 04	15 25 11	8 33 25
15	3 25 26	18 42	+ 3 41	4 07	3 48	11 56	19 47	20 06	15 29 07	8 29 29
16	3 29 23	18 57	+ 3 40	4 05	3 46	11 56	19 48	20 08	15 33 04	8 25 33
17	3 33 21	19 11	+ 3 39	4 04	3 44	11 56	19 50	20 09	15 37 00	8 21 37
18	3 37 19	19 24	+ 3 37	4 02	3 43	11 56	19 51	20 11	15 40 57	8 17 41
19	3 41 18	19 37	+ 3 35	4 01	3 41	11 56	19 53	20 13	15 44 53	8 13 46
20	3 45 18	19 50	+ 3 32	4 00	3 39	11 56	19 54	20 15	15 48 50	8 09 50
21	3 49 18	20 03	+ 3 29	3 58	3 38	11 57	19 56	20 17	15 52 46	8 05 54
22	3 53 18	20 15	+ 3 25	3 57	3 36	11 57	19 57	20 18	15 56 43	8 01 58
23	3 57 19	20 27	+ 3 21	3 56	3 34	11 57	19 58	20 20	16 00 40	7 58 02
24	4 01 20	20 38	+ 3 16	3 55	3 33	11 57	20 00	20 22	16 04 36	7 54 06
25	4 05 22	20 50	+ 3 11	3 53	3 31	11 57	20 01	20 23	16 08 33	7 50 10
26	4 09 25	21 00	+ 3 05	3 52	3 30	11 57	20 02	20 25	16 12 29	7 46 14
27	4 13 27	21 11	+ 2 58	3 51	3 29	11 57	20 04	20 27	16 16 26	7 42 18
28	4 17 31	21 21	+ 2 52	3 50	3 27	11 57	20 05	20 28	16 20 22	7 38 22
29	4 21 35	21 31	+ 2 44	3 49	3 26	11 57	20 06	20 30	16 24 19	7 34 26
30	4 25 39	21 40	+ 2 37	3 48	3 25	11 57	20 07	20 31	16 28 15	7 30 31
31	4 29 44	21 49	+ 2 29	3 47	3 24	11 58	20 09	20 32	16 32 12	7 26 35

DURATION OF TWILIGHT (in minutes)

Latitude	52°	56°	52°	56°	52°	56°	52°	56°
	1 May		11 May		21 May		31 May	
Civil	39	45	41	49	44	53	46	57
Nautical	90	106	97	121	106	143	116	TAN
Astronomical	154	209	179	TAN	TAN	TAN	TAN	TAN

THE NIGHT SKY

Mercury is unsuitably placed for observation throughout the month, superior conjunction occurring on the 25th.

Venus, magnitude −4.2, is still a magnificent object, dominating the western sky in the evenings before setting to the north of west. At the end of the month Venus will be seen passing south of Castor and Pollux, the two bright stars in the constellation of Gemini.

Mars continues to be visible in the southern sky, though by the end of the month it is lost to view before midnight. It is still a conspicuous object, though during the month its magnitude fades from −1.6 to −1.1. The gibbous Moon is near the planet on the evening of the 26th. Mars is moving slowly retrograde in the constellation of Virgo.

Jupiter is too close to the Sun for observation for most of May. However, during the last few days of the month it may be glimpsed for a short time low above the eastern horizon before the morning twilight inhibits observation. Jupiter, magnitude −2.1, is in the constellation of Pisces.

Saturn is unsuitably placed for observation.

THE MOON

Day	RA h m	Dec. °	Hor. par.	Semi- diam.	Sun's co- long.	PA of Bright Limb	Phase %	Age d	Rise 52° h m	Rise 56° h m	Transit h m	Set 52° h m	Set 56° h m
1	14 54	−11.4	54.0	14.7	93	57	100	14.8	20 11	20 24	0 20	5 25	5 14
2	15 40	−14.5	54.0	14.7	105	85	98	15.8	21 13	21 29	1 05	5 51	5 37
3	16 28	−17.0	54.0	14.7	118	89	95	16.8	22 12	22 31	1 50	6 22	6 05
4	17 18	−18.8	54.1	14.7	130	89	90	17.8	23 07	23 27	2 37	6 59	6 40
5	18 08	−19.8	54.4	14.8	142	86	84	18.8	23 57	—	3 25	7 42	7 22
6	18 59	−19.9	54.8	14.9	154	82	76	19.8	—	0 17	4 14	8 32	8 12
7	19 51	−19.1	55.3	15.1	166	79	67	20.8	0 41	0 59	5 03	9 30	9 11
8	20 43	−17.4	55.9	15.2	179	75	58	21.8	1 18	1 35	5 53	10 33	10 18
9	21 35	−14.8	56.7	15.5	191	71	47	22.8	1 51	2 04	6 43	11 42	11 30
10	22 27	−11.3	57.6	15.7	203	68	37	23.8	2 20	2 30	7 33	12 55	12 47
11	23 19	− 7.2	58.6	16.0	215	66	27	24.8	2 47	2 52	8 23	14 11	14 07
12	0 12	− 2.5	59.5	16.2	228	63	17	25.8	3 12	3 14	9 14	15 30	15 30
13	1 07	+ 2.4	60.3	16.4	240	62	9	26.8	3 38	3 36	10 08	16 52	16 57
14	2 03	+ 7.4	61.0	16.6	252	58	4	27.8	4 06	3 59	11 03	18 16	18 25
15	3 02	+12.0	61.3	16.7	264	39	1	28.8	4 37	4 26	12 01	19 39	19 54
16	4 03	+15.8	61.4	16.7	276	293	1	0.5	5 15	5 00	13 02	21 00	21 18
17	5 06	+18.5	61.1	16.6	289	276	4	1.5	6 00	5 42	14 03	22 12	22 32
18	6 09	+19.9	60.5	16.5	301	276	9	2.5	6 55	6 34	15 05	23 14	23 34
19	7 11	+19.9	59.7	16.3	313	279	17	3.5	7 57	7 38	16 04	—	—
20	8 11	+18.7	58.8	16.0	325	283	27	4.5	9 06	8 48	17 00	0 03	0 21
21	9 08	+16.3	57.9	15.8	338	287	37	5.5	10 17	10 02	17 52	0 43	0 58
22	10 01	+13.2	57.0	15.5	350	290	48	6.5	11 27	11 17	18 41	1 15	1 26
23	10 51	+ 9.5	56.2	15.3	2	293	58	7.5	12 36	12 30	19 27	1 41	1 49
24	11 39	+ 5.5	55.5	15.1	14	295	68	8.5	13 44	13 41	20 10	2 04	2 09
25	12 26	+ 1.4	54.9	15.0	27	296	77	9.5	14 50	14 51	20 53	2 26	2 26
26	13 11	− 2.8	54.5	14.9	39	296	84	10.5	15 55	15 59	21 36	2 46	2 43
27	13 56	− 6.8	54.2	14.8	51	297	90	11.5	16 59	17 07	22 19	3 07	3 01
28	14 42	−10.5	54.0	14.7	63	298	95	12.5	18 03	18 15	23 03	3 30	3 20
29	15 29	−13.8	54.0	14.7	75	303	98	13.5	19 06	19 21	23 48	3 55	3 42
30	16 16	−16.5	54.0	14.7	87	337	100	14.5	20 06	20 24	—	4 24	4 08
31	17 05	−18.5	54.1	14.7	100	67	99	15.5	21 03	21 23	0 34	4 58	4 40

MERCURY

Day	RA h m	Dec. °	Diam. "	Phase %	Transit h m	5° high 52° h m	5° high 56° h m
1	1 07	+ 4.2	6	68	10 34	4 44	4 44
3	1 18	+ 5.4	6	71	10 37	4 41	4 40
5	1 30	+ 6.7	6	74	10 41	4 38	4 36
7	1 43	+ 8.1	6	77	10 46	4 36	4 32
9	1 55	+ 9.5	6	80	10 51	4 33	4 29
11	2 09	+11.0	6	83	10 57	4 32	4 26
13	2 23	+12.5	5	86	11 03	4 30	4 23
15	2 38	+14.0	5	89	11 10	4 29	4 20
17	2 53	+15.4	5	92	11 18	4 28	4 19
19	3 09	+16.9	5	95	11 26	4 29	4 17
21	3 26	+18.3	5	97	11 35	4 29	4 17
23	3 43	+19.7	5	99	11 45	4 31	4 17
25	4 01	+21.0	5	100	11 55	4 34	4 18
27	4 19	+22.1	5	100	12 06	19 36	19 53
29	4 38	+23.1	5	99	12 16	19 53	20 11
31	4 57	+23.9	5	96	12 27	20 08	20 28

VENUS

Day	RA h m	Dec. °	Diam. "	Phase %	Transit h m	5° high 52° h m	5° high 56° h m
1	5 22	+25.4	16	69	14 48	22 37	22 58
6	5 47	+25.8	17	67	14 54	22 44	23 06
11	6 11	+26.0	17	65	14 59	22 50	23 12
16	6 36	+25.8	18	63	15 03	22 53	23 15
21	7 00	+25.4	19	61	15 08	22 55	23 16
26	7 23	+24.8	20	58	15 11	22 53	23 13
31	7 46	+23.9	21	56	15 14	22 50	23 09

MARS

Day	RA h m	Dec. °	Diam. "	Phase %	Transit h m	5° high 52° h m	5° high 56° h m
1	14 00	−11.1	16	100	23 21	3 52	3 39
6	13 53	−10.6	16	99	22 54	3 28	3 15
11	13 46	−10.3	16	99	22 28	3 04	2 51
16	13 41	−10.0	16	98	22 03	2 40	2 28
21	13 36	− 9.8	15	97	21 39	2 17	2 05
26	13 33	− 9.7	15	96	21 16	1 55	1 43
31	13 31	− 9.7	14	94	20 55	1 33	1 21

SUNRISE AND SUNSET

	London		Bristol		Birmingham		Manchester		Newcastle		Glasgow		Belfast	
	0°05′	51°30′	2°35′	51°28′	1°55′	52°28′	2°15′	53°28′	1°37′	54°59′	4°14′	55°52′	5°56′	54°35′
	h m	h m	h m	h m	h m	h m	h m	h m	h m	h m	h m	h m	h m	h m
1	4 33	19 23	4 43	19 33	4 38	19 33	4 36	19 38	4 28	19 41	4 35	19 55	4 46	19 57
2	4 31	19 24	4 41	19 34	4 36	19 35	4 34	19 40	4 25	19 43	4 32	19 57	4 44	19 59
3	4 30	19 26	4 40	19 36	4 34	19 37	4 31	19 41	4 23	19 45	4 30	19 59	4 42	20 00
4	4 28	19 28	4 38	19 38	4 32	19 38	4 30	19 43	4 21	19 47	4 28	20 01	4 40	20 02
5	4 26	19 29	4 36	19 39	4 30	19 40	4 28	19 45	4 19	19 48	4 26	20 03	4 38	20 04
6	4 24	19 31	4 34	19 41	4 28	19 42	4 26	19 47	4 17	19 50	4 24	20 05	4 36	20 06
7	4 22	19 32	4 32	19 42	4 26	19 43	4 24	19 49	4 15	19 52	4 22	20 07	4 34	20 08
8	4 21	19 34	4 31	19 44	4 24	19 45	4 22	19 50	4 13	19 54	4 20	20 09	4 32	20 10
9	4 19	19 36	4 29	19 46	4 23	19 47	4 20	19 52	4 11	19 56	4 17	20 11	4 30	20 12
10	4 17	19 37	4 27	19 47	4 21	19 48	4 18	19 54	4 09	19 58	4 15	20 13	4 28	20 13
11	4 16	19 39	4 26	19 49	4 19	19 50	4 16	19 55	4 07	20 00	4 13	20 14	4 26	20 15
12	4 14	19 40	4 24	19 50	4 17	19 52	4 15	19 57	4 05	20 02	4 11	20 16	4 24	20 17
13	4 12	19 42	4 23	19 52	4 16	19 53	4 13	19 59	4 03	20 03	4 10	20 18	4 23	20 19
14	4 11	19 43	4 21	19 53	4 14	19 55	4 11	20 01	4 02	20 05	4 08	20 20	4 21	20 20
15	4 09	19 45	4 19	19 55	4 13	19 56	4 10	20 02	4 00	20 07	4 06	20 22	4 19	20 22
16	4 08	19 46	4 18	19 56	4 11	19 58	4 08	20 04	3 58	20 09	4 04	20 24	4 17	20 24
17	4 06	19 48	4 17	19 58	4 10	19 59	4 06	20 05	3 56	20 10	4 02	20 26	4 16	20 26
18	4 05	19 49	4 15	19 59	4 08	20 01	4 05	20 07	3 55	20 12	4 00	20 27	4 14	20 27
19	4 04	19 51	4 14	20 01	4 07	20 03	4 03	20 09	3 53	20 14	3 59	20 29	4 12	20 29
20	4 02	19 52	4 12	20 02	4 05	20 04	4 02	20 10	3 51	20 16	3 57	20 31	4 11	20 31
21	4 01	19 54	4 11	20 04	4 04	20 06	4 00	20 12	3 50	20 17	3 55	20 33	4 09	20 32
22	4 00	19 55	4 10	20 05	4 03	20 07	3 59	20 13	3 48	20 19	3 54	20 34	4 08	20 34
23	3 58	19 56	4 09	20 06	4 01	20 08	3 58	20 15	3 47	20 20	3 52	20 36	4 06	20 36
24	3 57	19 58	4 07	20 08	4 00	20 10	3 56	20 16	3 45	20 22	3 51	20 38	4 05	20 37
25	3 56	19 59	4 06	20 09	3 59	20 11	3 55	20 18	3 44	20 24	3 49	20 39	4 04	20 39
26	3 55	20 00	4 05	20 10	3 58	20 12	3 54	20 19	3 43	20 25	3 48	20 41	4 02	20 40
27	3 54	20 02	4 04	20 12	3 56	20 14	3 53	20 20	3 41	20 27	3 46	20 43	4 01	20 42
28	3 53	20 03	4 03	20 13	3 55	20 15	3 51	20 22	3 40	20 28	3 45	20 44	4 00	20 43
29	3 52	20 04	4 02	20 14	3 54	20 16	3 50	20 23	3 39	20 29	3 44	20 46	3 59	20 44
30	3 51	20 05	4 01	20 15	3 53	20 18	3 49	20 24	3 38	20 31	3 43	20 47	3 58	20 46
31	3 50	20 06	4 00	20 16	3 52	20 19	3 48	20 26	3 37	20 32	3 41	20 48	3 56	20 47

JUPITER

Day	RA	Dec.	Transit	5° high	
				52°	56°
	h m	° ′	h m	h m	h m
1	1 08.7	+ 6 07	10 33	4 35	4 34
11	1 17.3	+ 6 58	10 03	4 00	3 58
21	1 25.6	+ 7 47	9 32	3 25	3 22
31	1 33.5	+ 8 32	9 00	2 50	2 46

Diameters – equatorial 34″ polar 32″

SATURN

Day	RA	Dec.	Transit	5° high	
				52°	56°
	h m	° ′	h m	h m	h m
1	2 22.3	+11 51	11 47	5 19	5 13
11	2 27.3	+12 16	11 12	4 43	4 36
21	2 32.1	+12 39	10 38	4 06	3 59
31	2 36.8	+13 01	10 03	3 29	3 22

Diameters – equatorial 16″ polar 15″
Rings – major axis 37″ minor axis 12″

URANUS

Day	RA	Dec.	Transit	10° high	
				52°	56°
	h m	° ′	h m	h m	h m
1	21 17.1	−16 29	6 42	3 32	4 01
11	21 17.6	−16 27	6 03	2 53	3 22
21	21 17.8	−16 27	5 24	2 14	2 43
31	21 17.7	−16 28	4 45	1 34	2 04

Diameter 4″

NEPTUNE

Day	RA	Dec.	Transit	10° high	
				52°	56°
	h m	° ′	h m	h m	h m
1	20 26.5	−18 53	5 52	3 02	3 39
11	20 26.5	−18 53	5 12	2 22	2 59
21	20 26.3	−18 54	4 33	1 43	2 20
31	20 25.9	−18 55	3 53	1 03	1 41

Diameter 2″

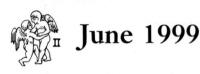

June 1999

SIXTH MONTH, 30 DAYS. *Junius*, Roman *gens* (family)

1	*Tuesday*	John Masefield b. 1878. Marilyn Monroe b. 1926	*week 22 day* 152
2	*Wednesday*	*Coronation Day 1953.* Vita Sackville West d. 1962	153
3	*Thursday*	**Corpus Christi.** Johann Strauss (younger) d. 1899	154
4	*Friday*	Casanova d. 1798. Kaiser Wilhelm II d. 1941	155
5	*Saturday*	World Enviroment Day. Lord Kitchener d. 1916	156
6	*Sunday*	**1st S. after Trinity.** Pushkin b. 1799 (NS)	*week 23 day* 157
7	*Monday*	Beau Brummell b. 1778. Charles Rennie Mackintosh b. 1868	158
8	*Tuesday*	*Trinity Law Sittings begin.* Frank Lloyd Wright b. 1869	159
9	*Wednesday*	Charles Dickens d. 1870. Lord Beaverbrook d. 1964	160
10	*Thursday*	*Duke of Edinburgh b. 1921.* Judy Garland b. 1922	161
11	*Friday*	**St Barnabas.** Jackie Stewart b. 1939	162
12	*Saturday*	*Queen's Official Birthday.* Anne Frank b. 1929	163
13	*Sunday*	**2nd S. after Trinity.** Dorothy L. Sayers b. 1893	*week 24 day* 164
14	*Monday*	Steffi Graf b. 1969. Dame Peggy Ashcroft d. 1991	165
15	*Tuesday*	First non-stop transatlantic flight 1919	166
16	*Wednesday*	Duke of Marlborough d. 1722. Lord Alexander of Tunis d. 1969	167
17	*Thursday*	Edward I b. 1239. Sir Edward Burne-Jones d. 1898	168
18	*Friday*	Ethel Barrymore d. 1959. Jack Harkness d. 1994	169
19	*Saturday*	Lord Haig b. 1861. The Duchess of Windsor b. 1896	170
20	*Sunday*	**3rd S. after Trinity.** Errol Flynn b. 1909	*week 25 day* 171
21	*Monday*	Prince William of Wales b. 1982	172
22	*Tuesday*	Alexandra Rose Day. Fred Astaire d. 1987	173
23	*Wednesday*	The Duke of Windsor b. 1894. Sir Len Hutton b. 1916	174
24	*Thursday*	**John the Baptist.** Book of Common Prayer issued 1559	175
25	*Friday*	Earl Mountbatten of Burma b. 1900. George Orwell b. 1903	176
26	*Saturday*	Laurie Lee b. 1914. Ford Madox Ford d. 1939	177
27	*Sunday*	**4th S. after Trinity.** Charles Parnell b. 1846	*week 26 day* 178
28	*Monday*	Archduke Ferdinand assassinated 1914. Treaty of Versailles 1919	179
29	*Tuesday*	**SS Peter and Paul.** Peter Paul Rubens b. 1577	180
30	*Wednesday*	Tower Bridge opened 1894. Ruskin Spear b. 1911	181

ASTRONOMICAL PHENOMENA

d	h	
4	06	Mars at stationary point
10	02	Jupiter in conjunction with Moon. Jupiter 4° N.
11	03	Saturn in conjunction with Moon. Saturn 3° N.
11	12	Venus at greatest elongation E.45°
15	07	Mercury in conjunction with Moon. Mercury 4° N.
17	02	Venus in conjunction with Moon. Venus 2° N.
21	20	Sun's longitude 90° ♋
23	01	Mars in conjunction with Moon. Mars 6° S.
28	23	Mercury at greatest elongation E.26°

MINIMA OF ALGOL

Algol is inconveniently situated for observation during June.

CONSTELLATIONS

The following constellations are near the meridian at

	d	h		d	h
May	1	24	June	15	21
May	16	23	July	1	20
June	1	22	July	16	19

Cassiopeia (below the Pole), Ursa Minor, Draco, Ursa Major, Canes Venatici, Bootes, Corona, Serpens, Virgo and Libra

THE MOON

Phases, Apsides and Node

	d	h	m
☾ Last Quarter	7	04	20
● New Moon	13	19	03
☽ First Quarter	20	18	13
○ Full Moon	28	21	37
Perigee (358,185 km)	13	00	31
Apogee (405,882 km)	25	15	21

Mean longitude of ascending node on June 1, 136°

THE SUN   s.d. 15'.8

Day	Right Ascension	Dec. +	Equation of time	Rise 52°	Rise 56°	Transit	Set 52°	Set 56°	Sidereal time	Transit of First Point of Aries
	h m s	° ′	m s	h m	h m	h m	h m	h m	h m s	h m s
1	4 33 49	21 58	+ 2 20	3 46	3 23	11 58	20 10	20 34	16 36 09	7 22 39
2	4 37 54	22 06	+ 2 11	3 46	3 21	11 58	20 11	20 35	16 40 05	7 18 43
3	4 42 00	22 14	+ 2 02	3 45	3 20	11 58	20 12	20 36	16 44 02	7 14 47
4	4 46 06	22 21	+ 1 52	3 44	3 20	11 58	20 13	20 38	16 47 58	7 10 51
5	4 50 13	22 28	+ 1 42	3 43	3 19	11 58	20 14	20 39	16 51 55	7 06 55
6	4 54 20	22 35	+ 1 31	3 43	3 18	11 59	20 15	20 40	16 55 51	7 02 59
7	4 58 27	22 41	+ 1 20	3 42	3 17	11 59	20 16	20 41	16 59 48	6 59 03
8	5 02 35	22 47	+ 1 09	3 42	3 16	11 59	20 17	20 42	17 03 44	6 55 07
9	5 06 43	22 52	+ 0 58	3 41	3 16	11 59	20 18	20 43	17 07 41	6 51 11
10	5 10 51	22 57	+ 0 46	3 41	3 15	11 59	20 18	20 44	17 11 38	6 47 15
11	5 15 00	23 02	+ 0 34	3 40	3 15	12 00	20 19	20 45	17 15 34	6 43 20
12	5 19 09	23 06	+ 0 22	3 40	3 14	12 00	20 20	20 45	17 19 31	6 39 24
13	5 23 18	23 10	+ 0 10	3 40	3 14	12 00	20 20	20 47	17 23 27	6 35 28
14	5 27 27	23 14	− 0 03	3 40	3 13	12 00	20 21	20 47	17 27 24	6 31 32
15	5 31 36	23 17	− 0 16	3 39	3 13	12 00	20 21	20 48	17 31 20	6 27 36
16	5 35 46	23 19	− 0 29	3 39	3 13	12 01	20 22	20 48	17 35 17	6 23 40
17	5 39 55	23 21	− 0 42	3 39	3 13	12 01	20 22	20 49	17 39 14	6 19 44
18	5 44 05	23 23	− 0 55	3 39	3 13	12 01	20 23	20 49	17 43 10	6 15 48
19	5 48 14	23 25	− 1 08	3 39	3 13	12 01	20 23	20 50	17 47 07	6 11 52
20	5 52 24	23 26	− 1 21	3 39	3 13	12 01	20 23	20 50	17 51 03	6 07 56
21	5 56 34	23 26	− 1 34	3 40	3 13	12 02	20 24	20 50	17 55 00	6 04 00
22	6 00 43	23 26	− 1 47	3 40	3 13	12 02	20 24	20 51	17 58 56	6 00 05
23	6 04 53	23 26	− 2 00	3 40	3 13	12 02	20 24	20 51	18 02 53	5 56 09
24	6 09 02	23 25	− 2 13	3 40	3 14	12 02	20 24	20 51	18 06 49	5 52 13
25	6 13 12	23 24	− 2 26	3 41	3 14	12 03	20 24	20 51	18 10 46	5 48 17
26	6 17 21	23 23	− 2 38	3 41	3 15	12 03	20 24	20 51	18 14 43	5 44 21
27	6 21 30	23 21	− 2 51	3 42	3 15	12 03	20 24	20 50	18 18 39	5 40 25
28	6 25 39	23 18	− 3 03	3 42	3 16	12 03	20 24	20 50	18 22 36	5 36 29
29	6 29 48	23 16	− 3 16	3 43	3 16	12 03	20 24	20 50	18 26 32	5 32 33
30	6 33 56	23 12	− 3 28	3 43	3 17	12 04	20 24	20 50	18 30 29	5 28 37

DURATION OF TWILIGHT (in minutes)

Latitude	52°	56°	52°	56°	52°	56°	52°	56°
	1 June		11 June		21 June		30 June	
Civil	47	58	48	61	49	63	49	62
Nautical	117	TAN	125	TAN	128	TAN	125	TAN
Astronomical	TAN	TAN	TAN	TAN	TAN	TAN	TAN	TAN

THE NIGHT SKY

Mercury is at greatest eastern elongation (26°) on the 28th and thus theoretically visible as an evening object. The long summer twilight will seriously hinder observation but under good conditions it may be possible to glimpse the planet during the third week of the month, very low above the west-north-western horizon at the end of evening civil twilight. Mercury will be about magnitude 0.

Venus continues to be visible as a magnificent object in the western skies in the evenings, magnitude −4.3. On the evening of the 16th the thin crescent Moon, only three days old, will be seen about 5° from the planet.

Mars is an evening object, visible in the south-western sky, its magnitude fading during the month from −1.0 to −0.4. On the evening of the 22nd the gibbous Moon will be seen approaching the planet. Mars reaches its second stationary point in Virgo on the 5th, resuming its direct motion.

Jupiter, magnitude −2.2, is a morning object, low in the eastern sky before dawn. The old crescent Moon will be seen about 5° below the planet on the morning of the 10th. During the month Jupiter moves eastwards from Pisces into Aries.

Saturn is not visible for the first three weeks of the month, then slowly begins to emerge from the long morning twilight and may be detected low above the east-north-eastern horizon before the sky gets too bright. The fact that in these latitudes even nautical twilight is continuous throughout the night means that it will not be an easy object to locate. Its magnitude is +0.4.

Twilight. Reference to the table above shows that astronomical twilight lasts all night for a period around the summer solstice (i.e. in June and July), even in southern England. Under these conditions the sky never gets completely dark as the Sun is always less than 18° below the horizon.

THE MOON

Day	RA	Dec.	Hor. par.	Semi-diam.	Sun's co-long.	PA of Bright Limb	Phase	Age	Rise 52°	Rise 56°	Transit	Set 52°	Set 56°
	h m	°	'	'	°	°	%	d	h m	h m	h m	h m	h m
1	17 56	−19.8	54.3	14.8	112	80	97	16.5	21 55	22 16	1 22	5 39	5 19
2	18 47	−20.2	54.6	14.9	124	80	93	17.5	22 41	23 01	2 11	6 27	6 06
3	19 38	−19.6	54.9	15.0	136	78	88	18.5	23 21	23 38	3 00	7 22	7 02
4	20 30	−18.1	55.4	15.1	148	75	81	19.5	23 55	—	3 49	8 23	8 06
5	21 21	−15.8	56.0	15.3	161	72	72	20.5	—	0 09	4 39	9 29	9 16
6	22 12	−12.6	56.7	15.4	173	70	63	21.5	0 24	0 35	5 27	10 39	10 29
7	23 03	− 8.7	57.5	15.7	185	67	52	22.5	0 51	0 58	6 16	11 52	11 46
8	23 55	− 4.3	58.3	15.9	197	66	41	23.5	1 15	1 19	7 05	13 07	13 06
9	0 47	+ 0.4	59.1	16.1	210	65	30	24.5	1 40	1 39	7 56	14 25	14 28
10	1 41	+ 5.3	59.9	16.3	222	65	20	25.5	2 05	2 01	8 48	15 46	15 53
11	2 37	+10.0	60.6	16.5	234	66	12	26.5	2 34	2 25	9 43	17 08	17 20
12	3 36	+14.2	61.1	16.6	246	66	5	27.5	3 07	2 54	10 42	18 30	18 46
13	4 37	+17.4	61.2	16.7	259	60	1	28.5	3 47	3 30	11 43	19 48	20 07
14	5 41	+19.5	61.1	16.6	271	321	0	0.2	4 37	4 17	12 45	20 57	21 17
15	6 44	+20.2	60.6	16.5	283	284	2	1.2	5 36	5 16	13 47	21 54	22 13
16	7 47	+19.5	59.9	16.3	295	283	7	2.2	6 44	6 25	14 46	22 40	22 56
17	8 47	+17.5	59.0	16.1	307	286	14	3.2	7 56	7 41	15 42	23 16	23 29
18	9 43	+14.6	58.1	15.8	320	289	23	4.2	9 10	8 58	16 34	23 45	23 55
19	10 36	+11.0	57.1	15.6	332	291	32	5.2	10 22	10 13	17 22	—	—
20	11 26	+ 6.9	56.3	15.3	344	293	42	6.2	11 31	11 27	18 08	0 10	0 16
21	12 13	+ 2.7	55.5	15.1	356	294	53	7.2	12 39	12 38	18 52	0 32	0 34
22	12 59	− 1.5	54.9	15.0	9	294	62	8.2	13 45	13 48	19 34	0 53	0 52
23	13 45	− 5.6	54.5	14.8	21	293	71	9.2	14 50	14 57	20 17	1 14	1 09
24	14 30	− 9.4	54.2	14.8	33	292	80	10.2	15 54	16 04	21 00	1 35	1 27
25	15 17	−12.8	54.0	14.7	45	291	87	11.2	16 57	17 11	21 45	1 59	1 48
26	16 04	−15.8	54.0	14.7	57	289	92	12.2	17 59	18 16	22 31	2 27	2 12
27	16 53	−18.1	54.1	14.7	70	288	97	13.2	18 58	19 17	23 19	2 59	2 41
28	17 43	−19.6	54.3	14.8	82	292	99	14.2	19 52	20 13	—	3 37	3 17
29	18 34	−20.2	54.6	14.9	94	17	100	15.2	20 40	21 01	0 08	4 23	4 02
30	19 26	−19.9	54.9	15.0	106	72	99	16.2	21 23	21 41	0 57	5 16	4 56

MERCURY

Day	RA	Dec.	Diam.	Phase	Transit	5° high 52°	5° high 56°
	h m	°	"	%	h m	h m	h m
1	5 06	+24.3	5	95	12 33	20 16	20 36
3	5 24	+24.8	5	92	12 43	20 29	20 50
5	5 42	+25.2	5	88	12 53	20 41	21 02
7	6 00	+25.4	6	83	13 03	20 51	21 13
9	6 17	+25.4	6	79	13 11	21 00	21 21
11	6 33	+25.3	6	75	13 19	21 07	21 27
13	6 48	+25.0	6	70	13 27	21 12	21 32
15	7 03	+24.7	6	66	13 33	21 15	21 35
17	7 16	+24.2	6	62	13 39	21 17	21 36
19	7 29	+23.6	7	58	13 43	21 18	21 36
21	7 41	+22.9	7	54	13 47	21 17	21 34
23	7 52	+22.2	7	51	13 50	21 15	21 31
25	8 02	+21.5	8	47	13 52	21 12	21 28
27	8 11	+20.7	8	44	13 52	21 08	21 23
29	8 19	+19.9	8	40	13 52	21 03	21 17
31	8 26	+19.1	8	37	13 51	20 57	21 10

VENUS

Day	RA	Dec.	Diam.	Phase	Transit	5° high 52°	5° high 56°
	h m	°	"	%	h m	h m	h m
1	7 50	+23.7	21	55	15 14	22 49	23 08
6	8 11	+22.5	22	53	15 16	22 43	23 00
11	8 32	+21.2	23	50	15 16	22 35	22 51
16	8 51	+19.8	25	47	15 15	22 26	22 39
21	9 09	+18.2	26	44	15 13	22 14	22 26
26	9 25	+16.5	28	41	15 10	22 01	22 12
31	9 40	+14.8	30	37	15 05	21 47	21 55

MARS

Day	RA	Dec.	Diam.	Phase	Transit	5° high 52°	5° high 56°
	h m	°	"	%	h m	h m	h m
1	13 31	− 9.7	14	94	20 51	1 29	1 17
6	13 30	− 9.9	14	93	20 31	1 08	0 56
11	13 31	−10.1	13	92	20 12	0 48	0 35
16	13 33	−10.5	13	91	19 55	0 28	0 15
21	13 36	−10.9	12	90	19 38	0 09	23 52
26	13 40	−11.4	12	89	19 23	23 47	23 32
31	13 45	−12.0	11	89	19 08	23 28	23 14

SUNRISE AND SUNSET

	London		Bristol		Birmingham		Manchester		Newcastle		Glasgow		Belfast	
	0°05'	51°30'	2°35'	51°28'	1°55'	52°28'	2°15'	53°28'	1°37'	54°59'	4°14'	55°52'	5°56'	54°35'
	h m	h m	h m	h m	h m	h m	h m	h m	h m	h m	h m	h m	h m	h m
1	3 49	20 08	3 59	20 17	3 52	20 20	3 47	20 27	3 36	20 34	3 40	20 50	3 55	20 48
2	3 48	20 09	3 59	20 18	3 51	20 21	3 46	20 28	3 35	20 35	3 39	20 51	3 54	20 50
3	3 48	20 10	3 58	20 19	3 50	20 22	3 46	20 29	3 34	20 36	3 38	20 52	3 54	20 51
4	3 47	20 11	3 57	20 20	3 49	20 23	3 45	20 30	3 33	20 37	3 37	20 54	3 53	20 52
5	3 46	20 12	3 57	20 21	3 48	20 24	3 44	20 31	3 32	20 38	3 37	20 55	3 52	20 53
6	3 46	20 13	3 56	20 22	3 48	20 25	3 43	20 32	3 31	20 39	3 36	20 56	3 51	20 54
7	3 45	20 13	3 55	20 23	3 47	20 26	3 43	20 33	3 31	20 40	3 35	20 57	3 50	20 55
8	3 45	20 14	3 55	20 24	3 47	20 27	3 42	20 34	3 30	20 41	3 34	20 58	3 50	20 56
9	3 44	20 15	3 54	20 25	3 46	20 28	3 42	20 35	3 29	20 42	3 34	20 59	3 49	20 57
10	3 44	20 16	3 54	20 26	3 46	20 29	3 41	20 36	3 29	20 43	3 33	21 00	3 49	20 58
11	3 44	20 17	3 54	20 26	3 45	20 29	3 41	20 37	3 28	20 44	3 33	21 01	3 48	20 59
12	3 43	20 17	3 53	20 27	3 45	20 30	3 40	20 37	3 28	20 45	3 32	21 02	3 48	20 59
13	3 43	20 18	3 53	20 28	3 45	20 31	3 40	20 38	3 28	20 46	3 32	21 02	3 48	21 00
14	3 43	20 18	3 53	20 28	3 45	20 31	3 40	20 39	3 27	20 46	3 31	21 03	3 47	21 01
15	3 43	20 19	3 53	20 29	3 44	20 32	3 40	20 39	3 27	20 47	3 31	21 04	3 47	21 01
16	3 43	20 20	3 53	20 29	3 44	20 32	3 40	20 40	3 27	20 47	3 31	21 04	3 47	21 02
17	3 43	20 20	3 53	20 30	3 44	20 33	3 39	20 40	3 27	20 48	3 31	21 05	3 47	21 02
18	3 42	20 20	3 53	20 30	3 44	20 33	3 39	20 41	3 27	20 48	3 31	21 05	3 47	21 03
19	3 43	20 21	3 53	20 30	3 44	20 34	3 39	20 41	3 27	20 49	3 31	21 06	3 47	21 03
20	3 43	20 21	3 53	20 31	3 44	20 34	3 40	20 41	3 27	20 49	3 31	21 06	3 47	21 04
21	3 43	20 21	3 53	20 31	3 45	20 34	3 40	20 42	3 27	20 49	3 31	21 06	3 47	21 04
22	3 43	20 21	3 53	20 31	3 45	20 34	3 40	20 42	3 27	20 49	3 31	21 06	3 47	21 04
23	3 43	20 22	3 53	20 31	3 45	20 34	3 40	20 42	3 27	20 50	3 31	21 07	3 48	21 04
24	3 44	20 22	3 54	20 31	3 45	20 35	3 41	20 42	3 28	20 50	3 32	21 07	3 48	21 04
25	3 44	20 22	3 54	20 31	3 46	20 35	3 41	20 42	3 28	20 50	3 32	21 07	3 48	21 04
26	3 44	20 22	3 55	20 31	3 46	20 35	3 41	20 42	3 29	20 50	3 33	21 06	3 49	21 04
27	3 45	20 22	3 55	20 31	3 47	20 34	3 42	20 42	3 29	20 49	3 33	21 06	3 49	21 04
28	3 45	20 21	3 55	20 31	3 47	20 34	3 42	20 42	3 30	20 49	3 34	21 06	3 50	21 04
29	3 46	20 21	3 56	20 31	3 48	20 34	3 43	20 42	3 30	20 49	3 34	21 06	3 50	21 04
30	3 46	20 21	3 57	20 31	3 48	20 34	3 44	20 41	3 31	20 49	3 35	21 05	3 51	21 03

JUPITER

Day	RA	Dec.	Transit	5° high	
				52°	56°
	h m	° '	h m	h m	h m
1	1 34.3	+ 8 37	8 57	2 46	2 42
11	1 41.8	+ 9 18	8 25	2 11	2 06
21	1 48.7	+ 9 55	7 53	1 35	1 30
31	1 54.9	+10 28	7 19	0 59	0 54

Diameters – equatorial 36″ polar 34″

SATURN

Day	RA	Dec.	Transit	5° high	
				52°	56°
	h m	° '	h m	h m	h m
1	2 37.3	+13 03	10 00	3 26	3 18
11	2 41.8	+13 23	9 25	2 49	2 41
21	2 46.0	+13 41	8 50	2 12	2 04
31	2 49.8	+13 57	8 14	1 36	1 27

Diameters – equatorial 17″ polar 15″
Rings – major axis 38″ minor axis 13″

URANUS

Day	RA	Dec.	Transit	10° high	
				52°	56°
	h m	° '	h m	h m	h m
1	21 17.7	−16 28	4 41	1 30	2 00
11	21 17.2	−16 30	4 01	0 51	1 20
21	21 16.4	−16 34	3 21	0 11	0 41
31	21 15.4	−16 39	2 41	23 28	0 02

Diameter 4″

NEPTUNE

Day	RA	Dec.	Transit	10° high	
				52°	56°
	h m	° '	h m	h m	h m
1	20 25.8	−18 56	3 49	0 59	1 37
11	20 25.2	−18 58	3 09	0 20	0 57
21	20 24.4	−19 01	2 29	23 36	0 18
31	20 23.5	−19 04	1 49	22 56	23 34

Diameter 2″

July 1999

SEVENTH MONTH, 31 DAYS. *Julius* Caesar, formerly *Quintilis*, fifth month of Roman pre-Julian calendar

1	*Thursday*	Diana, Princess of Wales b. 1961	*week* 26 *day* 182
2	*Friday*	Archbishop Cranmer b. 1489. Joseph Chamberlain d. 1914	183
3	*Saturday*	**St Thomas.** Robert Adam b. 1728	184
4	*Sunday*	**5th S. after Trinity.** Independence Day, USA	*week* 27 *day* 185
5	*Monday*	Sir Harold Acton b. 1904. Georgette Heyer d. 1974	186
6	*Tuesday*	Henry II d. 1189. Edward VI d. 1553	187
7	*Wednesday*	Ernest Newman d. 1959. Dame Flora Robson d. 1984	188
8	*Thursday*	Joseph Chamberlain b. 1836. Percy Grainger b. 1882	189
9	*Friday*	Edward Heath b. 1916. David Hockney b. 1937	190
10	*Saturday*	John Calvin b. 1509. Evelyn Laye b. 1900	191
11	*Sunday*	**6th S. after Trinity.** Robert the Bruce b. 1274	*week* 28 *day* 192
12	*Monday*	*Bank Holiday in Northern Ireland.* Thoreau b. 1817	193
13	*Tuesday*	Sidney Webb b. 1859. Lord Clark b. 1903	194
14	*Wednesday*	Storming of the Bastille 1789. Ingmar Bergman b. 1918	195
15	*Thursday*	St Swithin's Day. Inigo Jones b. 1573	196
16	*Friday*	Sir Joshua Reynolds b. 1723. Ginger Rogers b. 1911	197
17	*Saturday*	Isaac Watts b. 1674. Sir Geoffrey Jellicoe d. 1996	198
18	*Sunday*	**7th S. after Trinity.** Jane Austen d. 1817	*week* 29 *day* 199
19	*Monday*	*Mary Rose* sank 1545. Edgar Degas b. 1834	200
20	*Tuesday*	Sir Edmund Hillary b. 1919. Calouste Gulbenkian d. 1955	201
21	*Wednesday*	Ernest Hemingway b. 1898. First men on the Moon 1969	202
22	*Thursday*	**Mary Magdalene.** Tate Gallery opened 1897	203
23	*Friday*	Raymond Chandler b. 1888. Jessica Mitford d. 1996	204
24	*Saturday*	Alexandre Dumas (père) b. 1802. Peter Sellers d. 1980	205
25	*Sunday*	**St James. 8th S. after Trinity**	*week* 30 *day* 206
26	*Monday*	Aldous Huxley b. 1894. Terry Scott d. 1994	207
27	*Tuesday*	Alexandre Dumas (fils) b. 1824. Ivy Compton-Burnett d. 1969	208
28	*Wednesday*	Thomas Cromwell executed 1540. Cyrano de Bergerac d. 1655	209
29	*Thursday*	Marriage of Prince Charles and Lady Diana Spencer 1981	210
30	*Friday*	*Trinity Law Sittings end.* Henry Moore b. 1898	211
31	*Saturday*	Franz Liszt d. 1886. Leonard Cheshire d. 1992	212

ASTRONOMICAL PHENOMENA

d	h	
6	22	Earth at aphelion (152 million km)
7	18	Jupiter in conjunction with Moon. Jupiter 4° N.
8	16	Saturn in conjunction with Moon. Saturn 3° N.
13	00	Mercury at stationary point
14	10	Mercury in conjunction with Moon. Mercury 3° S.
14	19	Venus at greatest brilliancy
16	01	Venus in conjunction with Moon. Venus 3° S.
21	03	Mars in conjunction with Moon. Mars 7° S.
23	07	Sun's longitude 120° ♌
26	10	Neptune at opposition
26	16	Mercury in inferior conjunction
28	11	Partial eclipse of Moon (*see* page 66)
30	02	Venus at stationary point

MINIMA OF ALGOL

d	h	d	h	d	h
2	07.7	13	18.9	25	06.2
5	04.5	16	15.7	28	03.0
8	01.3	19	12.5	30	23.8
10	22.1	22	09.3		

CONSTELLATIONS

The following constellations are near the meridian at

	d	h		d	h
June	1	24	July	16	21
June	15	23	August	1	20
July	1	22	August	16	19

Ursa Minor, Draco, Corona, Hercules, Lyra, Serpens, Ophiuchus, Libra, Scorpius and Sagittarius

THE MOON

Phases, Apsides and Node	d	h	m
☾ Last Quarter	6	11	57
● New Moon	13	02	24
☽ First Quarter	20	09	00
○ Full Moon	28	11	25
Perigee (361,762 km)	11	06	01
Apogee (404,959 km)	23	05	39

Mean longitude of ascending node on July 1, 135°

THE SUN   s.d. 15'.8

Day	Right Ascension	Dec. +	Equation of time	Rise 52°	Rise 56°	Transit	Set 52°	Set 56°	Sidereal time	Transit of First Point of Aries
	h m s	° '	m s	h m	h m	h m	h m	h m	h m s	h m s
1	6 38 05	23 09	− 3 39	3 44	3 18	12 04	20 23	20 49	18 34 25	5 24 41
2	6 42 13	23 05	− 3 51	3 45	3 19	12 04	20 23	20 49	18 38 22	5 20 45
3	6 46 21	23 01	− 4 02	3 45	3 20	12 04	20 22	20 48	18 42 18	5 16 50
4	6 50 28	22 56	− 4 13	3 46	3 21	12 04	20 22	20 47	18 46 15	5 12 54
5	6 54 36	22 51	− 4 24	3 47	3 22	12 04	20 22	20 47	18 50 12	5 08 58
6	6 58 43	22 45	− 4 35	3 48	3 23	12 05	20 21	20 46	18 54 08	5 05 02
7	7 02 49	22 39	− 4 45	3 49	3 24	12 05	20 20	20 45	18 58 05	5 01 06
8	7 06 56	22 33	− 4 54	3 50	3 25	12 05	20 20	20 44	19 02 01	4 57 10
9	7 11 02	22 26	− 5 04	3 51	3 26	12 05	20 19	20 43	19 05 58	4 53 14
10	7 15 07	22 19	− 5 13	3 52	3 27	12 05	20 18	20 43	19 09 54	4 49 18
11	7 19 12	22 11	− 5 22	3 53	3 29	12 05	20 17	20 41	19 13 51	4 45 22
12	7 23 17	22 03	− 5 30	3 54	3 30	12 06	20 17	20 40	19 17 47	4 41 26
13	7 27 22	21 55	− 5 38	3 55	3 31	12 06	20 16	20 39	19 21 44	4 37 30
14	7 31 25	21 47	− 5 45	3 56	3 33	12 06	20 15	20 38	19 25 41	4 33 35
15	7 35 29	21 38	− 5 52	3 57	3 34	12 06	20 14	20 37	19 29 37	4 29 39
16	7 39 32	21 28	− 5 58	3 58	3 36	12 06	20 13	20 35	19 33 34	4 25 43
17	7 43 34	21 18	− 6 04	4 00	3 37	12 06	20 12	20 34	19 37 30	4 21 47
18	7 47 36	21 08	− 6 09	4 01	3 39	12 06	20 11	20 33	19 41 27	4 17 51
19	7 51 37	20 58	− 6 14	4 02	3 40	12 06	20 09	20 31	19 45 23	4 13 55
20	7 55 38	20 47	− 6 18	4 04	3 42	12 06	20 08	20 30	19 49 20	4 09 59
21	7 59 38	20 36	− 6 21	4 05	3 43	12 06	20 07	20 28	19 53 16	4 06 03
22	8 03 37	20 24	− 6 24	4 06	3 45	12 06	20 06	20 27	19 57 13	4 02 07
23	8 07 36	20 12	− 6 27	4 08	3 47	12 06	20 04	20 25	20 01 10	3 58 11
24	8 11 35	20 00	− 6 29	4 09	3 48	12 06	20 03	20 23	20 05 06	3 54 15
25	8 15 32	19 48	− 6 30	4 11	3 50	12 07	20 02	20 22	20 09 03	3 50 20
26	8 19 30	19 35	− 6 30	4 12	3 52	12 07	20 00	20 20	20 12 59	3 46 24
27	8 23 26	19 22	− 6 30	4 13	3 54	12 07	19 59	20 18	20 16 56	3 42 28
28	8 27 22	19 08	− 6 30	4 15	3 56	12 06	19 57	20 16	20 20 52	3 38 32
29	8 31 18	18 54	− 6 29	4 16	3 57	12 06	19 56	20 14	20 24 49	3 34 36
30	8 35 12	18 40	− 6 27	4 18	3 59	12 06	19 54	20 12	20 28 45	3 30 40
31	8 39 06	18 26	− 6 24	4 19	4 01	12 06	19 52	20 10	20 32 42	3 26 44

DURATION OF TWILIGHT (in minutes)

Latitude	52°	56°	52°	56°	52°	56°	52°	56°
	1 July		11 July		21 July		31 July	
Civil	48	61	46	58	44	53	41	49
Nautical	124	TAN	116	TAN	107	144	98	122
Astronomical	TAN	TAN	TAN	TAN	TAN	TAN	180	TAN

THE NIGHT SKY

Mercury is unsuitably placed for observation throughout the month, inferior conjunction occurring on the 26th.

Venus, magnitude −4.5, attains its greatest brilliancy on the 14th. It is visible as a magnificent object in the western sky in the evenings but the period available for observation is shortening noticeably and it will be lost in the glare of sunset a few days before the end of July. On the evenings of the 15th and 16th the thin crescent Moon will be seen within a few degrees of Venus. Through a small telescope Venus exhibits marked changes during the month; its angular diameter increases from 30 to 45 arcseconds while the phase changes from 37 per cent to 16 per cent illuminated.

Mars continues to be visible as an evening object in the south-western sky, magnitude −0.2. The First Quarter Moon is near the planet on the evening of the 20th. Towards the end of the month Mars moves from Virgo into Libra.

Jupiter continues to be visible as a morning object in the south-eastern sky, magnitude −2.4.

Saturn, magnitude +0.4, is a morning object. By the end of the month it may be detected low above the eastern horizon shortly after midnight. On the morning of the 9th the crescent Moon, four days before New, is near Saturn.

Neptune is at opposition on the 26th, in Capricornus. It is not visible to the naked eye as its magnitude is +7.8.

THE MOON

Day	RA	Dec.	Hor. par.	Semi- diam.	Sun's co- long.	PA of Bright Limb	Phase	Age	Rise 52°	56°	Transit	Set 52°	56°
	h m	°	′	′	°	°	%	d	h m	h m	h m	h m	h m
1	20 18	−18.7	55.3	15.1	118	75	96	17.2	21 58	22 14	1 47	6 16	5 58
2	21 10	−16.5	55.8	15.2	131	73	91	18.2	22 29	22 42	2 36	7 21	7 06
3	22 01	−13.5	56.3	15.3	143	71	84	19.2	22 56	23 05	3 25	8 29	8 18
4	22 52	− 9.9	56.9	15.5	155	69	76	20.2	23 21	23 26	4 13	9 41	9 33
5	23 42	− 5.6	57.5	15.7	167	68	66	21.2	23 45	23 46	5 02	10 54	10 51
6	0 33	− 1.0	58.2	15.9	179	67	56	22.2	—	—	5 50	12 09	12 10
7	1 25	+ 3.7	58.9	16.0	192	68	44	23.2	0 09	0 06	6 40	13 26	13 31
8	2 18	+ 8.3	59.5	16.2	204	69	33	24.2	0 35	0 28	7 32	14 45	14 55
9	3 14	+12.6	60.0	16.4	216	71	23	25.2	1 04	0 53	8 27	16 05	16 19
10	4 13	+16.2	60.4	16.5	228	74	14	26.2	1 40	1 24	9 25	17 23	17 41
11	5 14	+18.8	60.6	16.5	241	78	6	27.2	2 23	2 05	10 26	18 35	18 55
12	6 17	+20.1	60.5	16.5	253	80	2	28.2	3 17	2 57	11 28	19 38	19 59
13	7 20	+20.0	60.2	16.4	265	41	0	29.2	4 20	4 00	12 29	20 30	20 49
14	8 22	+18.5	59.7	16.3	277	287	1	0.9	5 32	5 14	13 27	21 12	21 27
15	9 20	+16.0	58.9	16.1	290	287	5	1.9	6 46	6 32	14 22	21 45	21 56
16	10 16	+12.5	58.1	15.8	302	289	11	2.9	8 00	7 50	15 13	22 12	22 20
17	11 08	+ 8.6	57.2	15.6	314	291	18	3.9	9 13	9 07	16 01	22 36	22 40
18	11 57	+ 4.3	56.3	15.4	326	292	27	4.9	10 23	10 21	16 47	22 58	22 58
19	12 45	0.0	55.6	15.1	339	292	37	5.9	11 31	11 33	17 30	23 19	23 15
20	13 31	− 4.2	55.0	15.0	351	291	46	6.9	12 37	12 43	18 14	23 40	23 33
21	14 17	− 8.2	54.5	14.9	3	290	56	7.9	13 42	13 51	18 57	—	23 53
22	15 03	−11.8	54.3	14.8	15	288	65	8.9	14 46	14 59	19 41	0 03	—
23	15 50	−14.9	54.1	14.8	28	285	74	9.9	15 48	16 04	20 27	0 29	0 16
24	16 38	−17.4	54.2	14.8	40	282	82	10.9	16 49	17 07	21 14	0 59	0 43
25	17 28	−19.2	54.4	14.8	52	278	89	11.9	17 45	18 05	22 02	1 35	1 16
26	18 19	−20.1	54.7	14.9	64	274	94	12.9	18 36	18 57	22 52	2 18	1 57
27	19 11	−20.1	55.0	15.0	76	271	98	13.9	19 21	19 40	23 42	3 08	2 48
28	20 03	−19.1	55.5	15.1	89	271	100	14.9	20 00	20 16	—	4 06	3 48
29	20 56	−17.2	56.0	15.2	101	73	100	15.9	20 33	20 46	0 32	5 11	4 55
30	21 48	−14.4	56.5	15.4	113	74	98	16.9	21 01	21 11	1 22	6 19	6 07
31	22 40	−10.8	57.0	15.5	125	72	93	17.9	21 27	21 33	2 11	7 31	7 22

MERCURY

Day	RA	Dec.	Diam.	Phase	Transit	5° high 52°	56°
	h m	°	″	%	h m	h m	h m
1	8 26	+19.1	8	37	13 51	20 57	21 10
3	8 32	+18.3	9	33	13 49	20 50	21 02
5	8 37	+17.6	9	30	13 46	20 43	20 54
7	8 41	+16.8	9	26	13 41	20 34	20 45
9	8 43	+16.2	10	23	13 35	20 25	20 35
11	8 44	+15.6	10	19	13 29	20 15	20 24
13	8 44	+15.0	11	16	13 20	20 04	20 13
15	8 43	+14.6	11	12	13 11	19 52	20 01
17	8 41	+14.3	11	9	13 00	19 40	19 49
19	8 37	+14.1	11	7	12 49	19 28	19 36
21	8 33	+14.1	11	4	12 36	19 15	19 23
23	8 28	+14.2	12	2	12 23	19 02	19 11
25	8 22	+14.4	12	1	12 10	18 50	18 59
27	8 16	+14.7	11	1	11 56	5 14	5 05
29	8 11	+15.0	11	2	11 43	4 59	4 50
31	8 06	+15.5	11	3	11 31	4 44	4 34

VENUS

Day	RA	Dec.	Diam.	Phase	Transit	5° high 52°	56°
	h m	°	″	%	h m	h m	h m
1	9 40	+14.8	30	37	15 05	21 47	21 55
6	9 53	+13.0	33	34	14 58	21 30	21 38
11	10 04	+11.3	35	30	14 49	21 12	21 18
16	10 13	+ 9.6	38	26	14 38	20 52	20 57
21	10 19	+ 8.0	41	21	14 24	20 30	20 33
26	10 22	+ 6.7	45	17	14 07	20 06	20 08
31	10 21	+ 5.5	48	12	13 46	19 40	19 41

MARS

Day	RA	Dec.	Diam.	Phase	Transit	5° high 52°	56°
1	13 45	−12.0	11	89	19 08	23 28	23 14
6	13 51	−12.7	11	88	18 55	23 11	22 55
11	13 58	−13.4	11	88	18 42	22 54	22 37
16	14 05	−14.1	10	87	18 30	22 37	22 19
21	14 13	−14.9	10	87	18 18	22 20	22 02
26	14 22	−15.7	10	86	18 08	22 04	21 44
31	14 32	−16.6	9	86	17 58	21 49	21 28

SUNRISE AND SUNSET

	London		Bristol		Birmingham		Manchester		Newcastle		Glasgow		Belfast	
	0°05'	51°30'	2°35'	51°28'	1°55'	52°28'	2°15'	53°28'	1°37'	54°59'	4°14'	55°52'	5°56'	54°35'
	h m	h m	h m	h m	h m	h m	h m	h m	h m	h m	h m	h m	h m	h m
1	3 47	20 21	3 57	20 31	3 49	20 34	3 44	20 41	3 32	20 48	3 36	21 05	3 52	21 03
2	3 48	20 20	3 58	20 30	3 50	20 33	3 45	20 41	3 33	20 48	3 37	21 05	3 53	21 02
3	3 48	20 20	3 59	20 30	3 50	20 33	3 46	20 40	3 33	20 47	3 38	21 04	3 53	21 02
4	3 49	20 20	3 59	20 29	3 51	20 32	3 47	20 40	3 34	20 47	3 38	21 03	3 54	21 01
5	3 50	20 19	4 00	20 29	3 52	20 32	3 47	20 39	3 35	20 46	3 39	21 03	3 55	21 01
6	3 51	20 19	4 01	20 28	3 53	20 31	3 48	20 38	3 36	20 45	3 40	21 02	3 56	21 00
7	3 52	20 18	4 02	20 28	3 54	20 31	3 49	20 38	3 37	20 45	3 42	21 01	3 57	20 59
8	3 53	20 17	4 03	20 27	3 55	20 30	3 50	20 37	3 38	20 44	3 43	21 00	3 58	20 59
9	3 54	20 17	4 04	20 27	3 56	20 29	3 51	20 36	3 39	20 43	3 44	20 59	3 59	20 58
10	3 55	20 16	4 05	20 26	3 57	20 28	3 52	20 35	3 41	20 42	3 45	20 59	4 00	20 57
11	3 56	20 15	4 06	20 25	3 58	20 28	3 54	20 35	3 42	20 41	3 46	20 57	4 02	20 56
12	3 57	20 14	4 07	20 24	3 59	20 27	3 55	20 34	3 43	20 40	3 48	20 56	4 03	20 55
13	3 58	20 14	4 08	20 23	4 00	20 26	3 56	20 33	3 44	20 39	3 49	20 55	4 04	20 54
14	3 59	20 13	4 09	20 22	4 01	20 25	3 57	20 32	3 46	20 38	3 50	20 54	4 05	20 53
15	4 00	20 12	4 10	20 21	4 03	20 24	3 58	20 31	3 47	20 37	3 52	20 53	4 07	20 52
16	4 01	20 11	4 11	20 20	4 04	20 23	4 00	20 29	3 48	20 36	3 53	20 52	4 08	20 50
17	4 03	20 10	4 13	20 19	4 05	20 22	4 01	20 28	3 50	20 34	3 55	20 50	4 10	20 49
18	4 04	20 09	4 14	20 18	4 06	20 21	4 02	20 27	3 51	20 33	3 56	20 49	4 11	20 48
19	4 05	20 07	4 15	20 17	4 08	20 19	4 04	20 26	3 53	20 32	3 58	20 47	4 12	20 47
20	4 06	20 06	4 16	20 16	4 09	20 18	4 05	20 24	3 54	20 30	4 00	20 46	4 14	20 45
21	4 08	20 05	4 18	20 15	4 10	20 17	4 07	20 23	3 56	20 29	4 01	20 44	4 15	20 44
22	4 09	20 04	4 19	20 14	4 12	20 16	4 08	20 22	3 57	20 27	4 03	20 43	4 17	20 42
23	4 10	20 02	4 20	20 12	4 13	20 14	4 10	20 20	3 59	20 26	4 05	20 41	4 19	20 41
24	4 12	20 01	4 22	20 11	4 15	20 13	4 11	20 19	4 01	20 24	4 06	20 39	4 20	20 39
25	4 13	20 00	4 23	20 10	4 16	20 11	4 13	20 17	4 02	20 22	4 08	20 38	4 22	20 38
26	4 14	19 58	4 25	20 08	4 18	20 10	4 14	20 16	4 04	20 21	4 10	20 36	4 23	20 36
27	4 16	19 57	4 26	20 07	4 19	20 08	4 16	20 14	4 06	20 19	4 11	20 34	4 25	20 34
28	4 17	19 55	4 27	20 05	4 21	20 07	4 17	20 13	4 07	20 17	4 13	20 32	4 27	20 33
29	4 19	19 54	4 29	20 04	4 22	20 05	4 19	20 11	4 09	20 16	4 15	20 31	4 28	20 31
30	4 20	19 52	4 30	20 02	4 24	20 04	4 21	20 09	4 11	20 14	4 17	20 29	4 30	20 29
31	4 22	19 51	4 32	20 01	4 25	20 02	4 22	20 08	4 13	20 12	4 19	20 27	4 32	20 27

JUPITER

Day	RA	Dec.	Transit	5° high	
				52°	56°
	h m	° '	h m	h m	h m
1	1 54.9	+10 28	7 19	0 59	0 54
11	2 00.4	+10 56	6 46	0 23	0 17
21	2 05.1	+11 19	6 11	23 42	23 36
31	2 08.7	+11 36	5 35	23 05	22 59

Diameters – equatorial 39″ polar 37″

SATURN

Day	RA	Dec.	Transit	5° high	
				52°	56°
	h m	° '	h m	h m	h m
1	2 49.8	+13 57	8 14	1 36	1 27
11	2 53.2	+14 10	7 38	0 58	0 50
21	2 56.1	+14 21	7 02	0 21	0 12
31	2 58.5	+14 29	6 25	23 40	23 31

Diameters – equatorial 17″ polar 16″
Rings – major axis 39″ minor axis 14″

URANUS

Day	RA	Dec.	Transit	10° high	
				52°	56°
	h m	° '	h m	h m	h m
1	21 15.4	−16 39	2 41	23 28	0 02
11	21 14.2	−16 45	2 00	22 48	23 18
21	21 12.8	−16 52	1 19	22 08	22 39
31	21 11.2	−16 59	0 38	21 28	21 59

Diameter 4″

NEPTUNE

Day	RA	Dec.	Transit	10° high	
				52°	56°
	h m	° '	h m	h m	h m
1	20 23.5	−19 04	1 49	22 56	23 34
11	20 22.5	−19 07	1 08	22 17	22 55
21	20 21.4	−19 11	0 28	21 37	22 15
31	20 20.3	−19 15	23 44	20 57	21 35

Diameter 2″

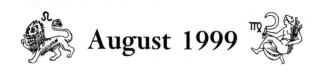

August 1999

EIGHTH MONTH, 31 DAYS. Julius, Caesar *Augustus*, formerly *Sextilis*, sixth month of Roman pre-Julian calendar

1	Sunday	**9th S. after Trinity.** Queen Anne d. 1714	*week* 31 *day* 213
2	Monday	*Bank Holiday in Scotland.* William S. Burroughs d. 1997	214
3	Tuesday	Sir Joseph Paxton b. 1801. P. D. James b. 1920	215
4	Wednesday	*Queen Elizabeth the Queen Mother b. 1900*	216
5	Thursday	Neil Armstrong b. 1930. Marilyn Monroe d. 1962	217
6	Friday	**The Transfiguration.** Alfred, Lord Tennyson b. 1809	218
7	Saturday	Oliver Hardy d. 1957. Ossie Clark d. 1996	219
8	Sunday	**10th S. after Trinity.** Princess Beatrice of York b. 1988	*week* 32 *day* 220
9	Monday	John Dryden b. 1631. Philip Larkin b. 1922	221
10	Tuesday	Sir Charles Napier b. 1782. Charles Keene b. 1823	222
11	Wednesday	Enid Blyton b. 1897. Andrew Carnegie d. 1919	223
12	Thursday	George IV b. 1762. William Blake d. 1827	224
13	Friday	Sir Basil Spence b. 1907. Florence Nightingale d. 1910	225
14	Saturday	John Galsworthy b. 1867. J. B. Priestley d. 1984	226
15	Sunday	**Blessed Virgin Mary. 11th S. after Trinity.** *Princess Royal b. 1950*	*week* 33 *day* 227
16	Monday	Georgette Heyer b. 1902. Ted Hughes b. 1930	228
17	Tuesday	Davy Crockett b. 1786. Rudolf Hess d. 1987	229
18	Wednesday	Willie Rushton b. 1937. Sir Frederick Ashton d. 1988	230
19	Thursday	President Bill Clinton b. 1946. Sir Jacob Epstein d. 1959	231
20	Friday	Soviet invasion of Czechoslovakia 1968	232
21	Saturday	*Princess Margaret b. 1930.* William IV b. 1765	233
22	Sunday	**12th S. after Trinity.** Deng Xiaoping b. 1904	*week* 34 *day* 234
23	Monday	William Wallace executed 1305. Gene Kelly b. 1912	235
24	Tuesday	**St Bartholomew.** Aubrey Beardsley d. 1872	236
25	Wednesday	Ivan the Terrible b. 1530. Friedrich Nietzsche d. 1900	237
26	Thursday	Prince Albert b. 1819. Christopher Isherwood b. 1904	238
27	Friday	C. S. Forester b. 1899. Charles Le Corbusier d. 1965	239
28	Saturday	Goethe b. 1749. Leigh Hunt d. 1859	240
29	Sunday	**13th S. after Trinity.** Ingrid Bergman d. 1982	*week* 35 *day* 241
30	Monday	*Bank Holiday in England, Wales and Northern Ireland*	242
31	Tuesday	Diana, Princess of Wales d. 1997	243

ASTRONOMICAL PHENOMENA

d	h	
4	04	Jupiter in conjunction with Moon. Jupiter 4° N.
5	01	Saturn in conjunction with Moon. Saturn 3° N.
6	03	Mercury at stationary point
7	19	Uranus at opposition
10	03	Mercury in conjunction with Moon. Mercury 1° S.
11	11	Total eclipse of Sun (*see* page 66)
12	10	Venus in conjunction with Moon. Venus 9° S.
14	14	Mercury at greatest elongation W.19°
18	16	Mars in conjunction with Moon. Mars 7° S.
19	02	Pluto at stationary point
20	12	Venus in inferior conjunction
23	14	Sun's longitude 150° ♍
25	03	Jupiter at stationary point
27	21	Venus in conjunction with Mercury. Venus 10° S.
30	01	Saturn at stationary point
31	11	Jupiter in conjunction with Moon. Jupiter 4° N.

MINIMA OF ALGOL

d	h		d	h		d	h
2	20.6		14	07.8		25	19.1
5	17.4		17	04.6		28	15.9
8	14.2		20	01.4		31	12.7
11	11.0		22	22.2			

CONSTELLATIONS

The following constellations are near the meridian at

	d	h			d	h
July	1	24		August	16	21
July	16	23		September	1	20
August	1	22		September	15	19

Draco, Hercules, Lyra, Cygnus, Sagitta, Ophiuchus, Serpens, Aquila and Sagittarius

THE MOON

Phases, Apsides and Node	d	h	m
☾ Last Quarter	4	17	27
● New Moon	11	11	08
☽ First Quarter	19	01	47
○ Full Moon	26	23	48
Perigee (366,679 km)	7	23	26
Apogee (404,301 km)	19	23	25

Mean longitude of ascending node on August 1, 133°

THE SUN

s.d. 15'.8

Day	Right Ascension	Dec. +	Equation of time	Rise 52°	Rise 56°	Transit	Set 52°	Set 56°	Sidereal time	Transit of First Point of Aries
	h m s	° '	m s	h m	h m	h m	h m	h m	h m s	h m s
1	8 43 00	18 11	− 6 21	4 21	4 03	12 06	19 51	20 08	20 36 39	3 22 48
2	8 46 53	17 56	− 6 18	4 22	4 05	12 06	19 49	20 06	20 40 35	3 18 52
3	8 50 45	17 40	− 6 14	4 24	4 07	12 06	19 47	20 04	20 44 32	3 14 56
4	8 54 37	17 25	− 6 09	4 26	4 09	12 06	19 46	20 02	20 48 28	3 11 00
5	8 58 28	17 09	− 6 04	4 27	4 10	12 06	19 44	20 00	20 52 25	3 07 04
6	9 02 19	16 53	− 5 58	4 29	4 12	12 06	19 42	19 58	20 56 21	3 03 09
7	9 06 09	16 36	− 5 51	4 30	4 14	12 06	19 40	19 56	21 00 18	2 59 13
8	9 09 58	16 20	− 5 44	4 32	4 16	12 06	19 38	19 54	21 04 14	2 55 17
9	9 13 47	16 03	− 5 36	4 33	4 18	12 06	19 37	19 52	21 08 11	2 51 21
10	9 17 36	15 45	− 5 28	4 35	4 20	12 05	19 35	19 49	21 12 08	2 47 25
11	9 21 23	15 28	− 5 19	4 37	4 22	12 05	19 33	19 47	21 16 04	2 43 29
12	9 25 11	15 10	− 5 10	4 38	4 24	12 05	19 31	19 45	21 20 01	2 39 33
13	9 28 57	14 52	− 5 00	4 40	4 26	12 05	19 29	19 43	21 23 57	2 35 37
14	9 32 43	14 34	− 4 50	4 41	4 28	12 05	19 27	19 40	21 27 54	2 31 41
15	9 36 29	14 15	− 4 38	4 43	4 30	12 05	19 25	19 38	21 31 50	2 27 45
16	9 40 14	13 57	− 4 27	4 45	4 32	12 04	19 23	19 36	21 35 47	2 23 49
17	9 43 58	13 38	− 4 15	4 46	4 34	12 04	19 21	19 33	21 39 43	2 19 54
18	9 47 42	13 19	− 4 02	4 48	4 36	12 04	19 19	19 31	21 43 40	2 15 58
19	9 51 25	12 59	− 3 49	4 50	4 38	12 04	19 17	19 28	21 47 37	2 12 02
20	9 55 08	12 40	− 3 35	4 51	4 40	12 03	19 15	19 26	21 51 33	2 08 06
21	9 58 50	12 20	− 3 21	4 53	4 42	12 03	19 12	19 24	21 55 30	2 04 10
22	10 02 32	12 00	− 3 06	4 54	4 44	12 03	19 10	19 21	21 59 26	2 00 14
23	10 06 14	11 40	− 2 51	4 56	4 46	12 03	19 08	19 19	22 03 23	1 56 18
24	10 09 55	11 20	− 2 35	4 58	4 47	12 02	19 06	19 16	22 07 19	1 52 22
25	10 13 35	10 59	− 2 19	4 59	4 49	12 02	19 04	19 14	22 11 16	1 48 26
26	10 17 15	10 39	− 2 03	5 01	4 51	12 02	19 02	19 11	22 15 12	1 44 30
27	10 20 55	10 18	− 1 46	5 03	4 53	12 02	18 59	19 09	22 19 09	1 40 35
28	10 24 34	9 57	− 1 28	5 04	4 55	12 01	18 57	19 06	22 23 06	1 36 39
29	10 28 13	9 36	− 1 11	5 06	4 57	12 01	18 55	19 03	22 27 02	1 32 43
30	10 31 51	9 14	− 0 53	5 08	4 59	12 01	18 53	19 01	22 30 59	1 28 47
31	10 35 30	8 53	− 0 34	5 09	5 01	12 00	18 51	18 58	22 34 55	1 24 51

DURATION OF TWILIGHT (in minutes)

Latitude	52°	56°	52°	56°	52°	56°	52°	56°
	1 August		11 August		21 August		31 August	
Civil	41	48	39	45	37	42	35	40
Nautical	97	120	89	106	83	96	79	89
Astronomical	177	TAN	153	205	138	166	127	147

THE NIGHT SKY

Mercury becomes a morning object after the first ten days of the month, low above the east-north-eastern horizon at the beginning of morning civil twilight. It is visible for about a fortnight and during this time its magnitude brightens from +0.5 to −1.2.

Venus passes through inferior conjunction on the 20th and therefore remains too close to the Sun for observation for almost the whole of August. However for the last three or four days of the month it might be glimpsed low in the east for a few minutes before sunrise; its magnitude is −4.2.

Mars, magnitude +0.1, continues to be visible as an evening object in the south-western sky, in Libra. On the evening of the 18th the Moon, at First Quarter, will be seen about 6° above the planet.

Jupiter, magnitude −2.6, is still a splendid morning object in the south-eastern sky. The Moon, at Last Quarter, will be seen about 5° below and to the right of the planet during the early hours of the 4th. By the end of the month Jupiter may be detected low above the eastern horizon by about 21h. Jupiter has been moving eastwards in Aries but reaches its first stationary point on the 25th.

Saturn continues to be visible as a morning object, magnitude +0.3. By the end of the month the planet is visible low in the eastern sky by 22h. On the morning of the 5th, the Moon, at Last Quarter, will be seen about 4° below the planet. Saturn is in Aries and reaches its first stationary point on the last day of August.

Uranus is at opposition on the 7th, in Capricornus. Uranus is barely visible to the naked eye as its magnitude is +5.7, but it is readily located with only small optical aid.

Meteors. The maximum of the famous Perseid meteor shower occurs in the early hours of the 13th. Conditions are particularly favourable as there will be no interference by moonlight.

THE MOON

Day	RA (h m)	Dec. (°)	Hor. par. (')	Semi-diam. (')	Sun's co-long. (°)	PA of Bright Limb (°)	Phase (%)	Age (d)	Rise 52° (h m)	Rise 56° (h m)	Transit (h m)	Set 52° (h m)	Set 56° (h m)
1	23 31	− 6.7	57.5	15.7	137	70	87	18.9	21 51	21 53	3 00	8 44	8 39
2	0 21	− 2.2	57.9	15.8	150	70	79	19.9	22 14	22 13	3 48	9 58	9 58
3	1 13	+ 2.5	58.4	15.9	162	70	69	20.9	22 39	22 33	4 37	11 14	11 18
4	2 05	+ 7.2	58.8	16.0	174	71	58	21.9	23 07	22 57	5 28	12 31	12 39
5	2 59	+11.5	59.2	16.1	186	73	47	22.9	23 39	23 25	6 21	13 49	14 01
6	3 56	+15.2	59.5	16.2	198	77	36	23.9	—	—	7 16	15 05	15 22
7	4 55	+18.0	59.7	16.3	211	81	25	24.9	0 17	0 00	8 13	16 18	16 38
8	5 55	+19.7	59.8	16.3	223	86	16	25.9	1 05	0 45	9 13	17 24	17 44
9	6 57	+20.2	59.7	16.3	235	92	8	26.9	2 03	1 42	10 13	18 19	18 39
10	7 58	+19.3	59.4	16.2	247	97	3	27.9	3 09	2 50	11 12	19 05	19 22
11	8 57	+17.1	59.0	16.1	260	105	0	28.9	4 22	4 06	12 08	19 42	19 55
12	9 54	+14.0	58.4	15.9	272	280	0	0.5	5 37	5 25	13 01	20 12	20 21
13	10 48	+10.2	57.7	15.7	284	286	3	1.5	6 51	6 43	13 51	20 37	20 43
14	11 39	+ 6.0	57.0	15.5	296	288	8	2.5	8 04	8 00	14 38	21 00	21 02
15	12 27	+ 1.6	56.2	15.3	309	289	14	3.5	9 14	9 14	15 24	21 22	21 20
16	13 15	− 2.7	55.5	15.1	321	289	22	4.5	10 22	10 26	16 08	21 43	21 38
17	14 01	− 6.9	55.0	15.0	333	288	31	5.5	11 28	11 36	16 52	22 06	21 57
18	14 48	−10.6	54.6	14.9	345	286	40	6.5	12 33	12 44	17 36	22 31	22 18
19	15 35	−13.9	54.3	14.8	357	284	49	7.5	13 36	13 51	18 21	22 59	22 44
20	16 23	−16.7	54.2	14.8	10	280	59	8.5	14 37	14 55	19 07	23 32	23 14
21	17 12	−18.7	54.3	14.8	22	276	68	9.5	15 35	15 55	19 55	—	23 52
22	18 02	−19.9	54.6	14.9	34	272	77	10.5	16 28	16 49	20 44	0 12	—
23	18 54	−20.2	55.0	15.0	46	267	84	11.5	17 16	17 36	21 34	0 59	0 39
24	19 46	−19.5	55.5	15.1	58	262	91	12.5	17 57	18 15	22 24	1 54	1 35
25	20 39	−17.9	56.0	15.3	71	256	96	13.5	18 32	18 47	23 15	2 57	2 39
26	21 32	−15.4	56.6	15.4	83	248	99	14.5	19 03	19 14	—	4 04	3 50
27	22 24	−12.0	57.2	15.6	95	156	100	15.5	19 30	19 38	0 05	5 16	5 06
28	23 16	− 7.9	57.8	15.7	107	80	99	16.5	19 55	19 58	0 55	6 30	6 24
29	0 08	− 3.4	58.3	15.9	119	75	95	17.5	20 19	20 19	1 44	7 46	7 44
30	1 00	+ 1.4	58.7	16.0	132	73	89	18.5	20 44	20 39	2 34	9 03	9 06
31	1 53	+ 6.2	59.0	16.1	144	73	81	19.5	21 10	21 02	3 25	10 21	10 28

MERCURY

Day	RA (h m)	Dec. (°)	Diam. (")	Phase (%)	Transit (h m)	5° high 52° (h m)	5° high 56° (h m)
1	8 04	+15.8	11	5	11 25	4 37	4 27
3	8 01	+16.3	10	8	11 15	4 23	4 13
5	8 00	+16.8	10	11	11 06	4 11	4 01
7	8 00	+17.3	9	16	10 58	4 01	3 50
9	8 02	+17.7	9	22	10 53	3 53	3 41
11	8 06	+18.1	8	28	10 50	3 48	3 35
13	8 12	+18.3	8	35	10 48	3 44	3 32
15	8 20	+18.5	7	43	10 48	3 44	3 31
17	8 30	+18.5	7	50	10 50	3 45	3 33
19	8 41	+18.3	7	58	10 54	3 50	3 37
21	8 53	+17.9	6	66	10 59	3 56	3 44
23	9 06	+17.4	6	74	11 04	4 05	3 54
25	9 21	+16.7	6	80	11 11	4 16	4 05
27	9 36	+15.8	6	86	11 18	4 28	4 18
29	9 51	+14.7	5	91	11 25	4 41	4 33
31	10 06	+13.5	5	94	11 33	4 55	4 48

VENUS

Day	RA (h m)	Dec. (°)	Diam. (")	Phase (%)	Transit (h m)	5° high 52° (h m)	5° high 56° (h m)
1	10 21	+ 5.4	49	11	13 42	19 35	19 36
6	10 16	+ 4.6	52	7	13 17	19 06	19 07
11	10 08	+ 4.3	55	4	12 48	18 37	18 37
16	9 57	+ 4.4	57	2	12 18	18 07	18 07
21	9 45	+ 4.9	58	1	11 46	17 38	17 39
26	9 33	+ 5.7	57	2	11 15	17 11	17 13
31	9 24	+ 6.7	55	5	10 46	16 48	16 50

MARS

Day	RA (h m)	Dec. (°)	Diam. (")	Phase (%)	Transit (h m)	5° high 52° (h m)	5° high 56° (h m)
1	14 34	−16.7	9	86	17 56	21 46	21 24
6	14 44	−17.6	9	86	17 46	21 30	21 08
11	14 55	−18.4	9	86	17 37	21 16	20 51
16	15 06	−19.2	9	86	17 29	21 01	20 35
21	15 17	−20.0	8	86	17 21	20 47	20 20
26	15 30	−20.8	8	86	17 13	20 34	20 05
31	15 42	−21.5	8	86	17 06	20 21	19 50

SUNRISE AND SUNSET

	London		Bristol		Birmingham		Manchester		Newcastle		Glasgow		Belfast	
	0°05′	51°30′	2°35′	51°28′	1°55′	52°28′	2°15′	53°28′	1°37′	54°59′	4°14′	55°52′	5°56′	54°35′
	h m	h m	h m	h m	h m	h m	h m	h m	h m	h m	h m	h m	h m	h m
1	4 23	19 49	4 33	19 59	4 27	20 00	4 24	20 06	4 14	20 10	4 21	20 25	4 34	20 25
2	4 25	19 47	4 35	19 57	4 28	19 59	4 25	20 04	4 16	20 08	4 22	20 23	4 35	20 24
3	4 26	19 46	4 36	19 56	4 30	19 57	4 27	20 02	4 18	20 06	4 24	20 21	4 37	20 22
4	4 28	19 44	4 38	19 54	4 31	19 55	4 29	20 00	4 20	20 04	4 26	20 19	4 39	20 20
5	4 29	19 42	4 39	19 52	4 33	19 53	4 30	19 58	4 22	20 02	4 28	20 17	4 41	20 18
6	4 31	19 41	4 41	19 51	4 35	19 51	4 32	19 57	4 23	20 00	4 30	20 14	4 42	20 16
7	4 32	19 39	4 42	19 49	4 36	19 50	4 34	19 55	4 25	19 58	4 32	20 12	4 44	20 14
8	4 34	19 37	4 44	19 47	4 38	19 48	4 36	19 53	4 27	19 56	4 34	20 10	4 46	20 12
9	4 35	19 35	4 46	19 45	4 39	19 46	4 37	19 51	4 29	19 54	4 36	20 08	4 48	20 10
10	4 37	19 33	4 47	19 43	4 41	19 44	4 39	19 49	4 31	19 52	4 38	20 06	4 50	20 07
11	4 39	19 31	4 49	19 41	4 43	19 42	4 41	19 47	4 33	19 50	4 40	20 04	4 51	20 05
12	4 40	19 30	4 50	19 39	4 44	19 40	4 42	19 45	4 34	19 47	4 41	20 01	4 53	20 03
13	4 42	19 28	4 52	19 38	4 46	19 38	4 44	19 43	4 36	19 45	4 43	19 59	4 55	20 01
14	4 43	19 26	4 53	19 36	4 48	19 36	4 46	19 40	4 38	19 43	4 45	19 57	4 57	19 59
15	4 45	19 24	4 55	19 34	4 49	19 34	4 48	19 38	4 40	19 41	4 47	19 54	4 59	19 57
16	4 47	19 22	4 57	19 32	4 51	19 32	4 49	19 36	4 42	19 39	4 49	19 52	5 00	19 54
17	4 48	19 20	4 58	19 30	4 53	19 30	4 51	19 34	4 44	19 36	4 51	19 50	5 02	19 52
18	4 50	19 18	5 00	19 28	4 54	19 28	4 53	19 32	4 46	19 34	4 53	19 47	5 04	19 50
19	4 51	19 16	5 01	19 26	4 56	19 26	4 55	19 30	4 47	19 32	4 55	19 45	5 06	19 48
20	4 53	19 14	5 03	19 24	4 58	19 23	4 56	19 27	4 49	19 29	4 57	19 42	5 08	19 45
21	4 54	19 12	5 05	19 21	4 59	19 21	4 58	19 25	4 51	19 27	4 59	19 40	5 10	19 43
22	4 56	19 09	5 06	19 19	5 01	19 19	5 00	19 23	4 53	19 25	5 01	19 38	5 11	19 41
23	4 58	19 07	5 08	19 17	5 03	19 17	5 02	19 21	4 55	19 22	5 03	19 35	5 13	19 38
24	4 59	19 05	5 09	19 15	5 04	19 15	5 03	19 18	4 57	19 20	5 05	19 33	5 15	19 36
25	5 01	19 03	5 11	19 13	5 06	19 13	5 05	19 16	4 59	19 17	5 07	19 30	5 17	19 34
26	5 02	19 01	5 13	19 11	5 08	19 10	5 07	19 14	5 01	19 15	5 09	19 28	5 19	19 31
27	5 04	18 59	5 14	19 09	5 09	19 08	5 08	19 12	5 02	19 13	5 11	19 25	5 21	19 29
28	5 06	18 57	5 16	19 07	5 11	19 06	5 10	19 09	5 04	19 10	5 13	19 23	5 22	19 26
29	5 07	18 54	5 17	19 04	5 13	19 04	5 12	19 07	5 06	19 08	5 15	19 20	5 24	19 24
30	5 09	18 52	5 19	19 02	5 14	19 01	5 14	19 05	5 08	19 05	5 16	19 18	5 26	19 22
31	5 10	18 50	5 20	19 00	5 16	18 59	5 15	19 02	5 10	19 03	5 18	19 15	5 28	19 19

JUPITER

Day	RA	Dec.	Transit	5° high	
				52°	56°
	h m	° ′	h m	h m	h m
1	2 09.0	+11 37	5 32	23 02	22 55
11	2 11.4	+11 47	4 55	22 24	22 17
21	2 12.6	+11 51	4 16	21 45	21 39
31	2 12.6	+11 48	3 37	21 06	21 00

Diameters – equatorial 43″ polar 41″

SATURN

Day	RA	Dec.	Transit	5° high	
				52°	56°
	h m	° ′	h m	h m	h m
1	2 58.7	+14 29	6 21	23 36	23 27
11	3 00.4	+14 34	5 43	22 58	22 49
21	3 01.4	+14 36	5 05	22 19	22 10
31	3 01.8	+14 35	4 26	21 40	21 31

Diameters – equatorial 18″ polar 17″
Rings – major axis 42″ minor axis 15″

URANUS

Day	RA	Dec.	Transit	10° high	
				52°	56°
	h m	° ′	h m	h m	h m
1	21 11.1	−16 59	0 34	3 41	3 10
11	21 09.5	−17 06	23 49	2 59	2 28
21	21 07.9	−17 13	23 08	2 17	1 45
31	21 06.4	−17 20	22 28	1 35	1 03

Diameter 4″

NEPTUNE

Day	RA	Dec.	Transit	10° high	
				52°	56°
	h m	° ′	h m	h m	h m
1	20 20.2	−19 15	23 40	2 30	1 52
11	20 19.1	−19 19	22 59	1 49	1 11
21	20 18.0	−19 23	22 19	1 08	0 29
31	20 17.1	−19 26	21 39	0 28	23 44

Diameter 2″

September 1999

NINTH MONTH, 30 DAYS. *Septem* (seven), seventh month of Roman pre-Julian calendar

1	*Wednesday*	Engelbert Humperdinck b. 1854. Siegfried Sassoon d. 1967	*week 35 day* 244
2	*Thursday*	Thomas Telford d. 1834. J. R. R. Tolkien d. 1973	245
3	*Friday*	Oliver Cromwell d. 1658. Roy Castle d. 1994	246
4	*Saturday*	Anton Bruckner b. 1824. Georges Simenon d. 1989	247
5	*Sunday*	**14th S. after Trinity.** Pieter Brueghel (elder) d. 1569	*week 36 day* 248
6	*Monday*	The *Mayflower* sailed from Plymouth 1620	249
7	*Tuesday*	Elizabeth I b. 1533. Joan Cross b. 1900	250
8	*Wednesday*	Sir Peter Maxwell Davies b. 1934. Richard Strauss d. 1949	251
9	*Thursday*	End of soap rationing 1950. Mao Tse-tung d. 1976	252
10	*Friday*	Mary Wollstonecraft Godwin d. 1797. Arnold Palmer b. 1929	253
11	*Saturday*	JEWISH NEW YEAR. Jessica Mitford b. 1917	254
12	*Sunday*	**15th S. after Trinity.** Marshal von Blücher d. 1819	*week 37 day* 255
13	*Monday*	Gen. Wolfe d. 1759. Arnold Schönberg b. 1874	256
14	*Tuesday*	**Holy Cross Day.** Sir Peter Scott b. 1909	257
15	*Wednesday*	Prince Henry of Wales b. 1984. Battle of Britain Day	258
16	*Thursday*	Peter Darrell b. 1929. Maria Callas d. 1977	259
17	*Friday*	Sir Frederick Ashton b. 1904. Stirling Moss b. 1929	260
18	*Saturday*	Greta Garbo b. 1905. Sean O'Casey d. 1964	261
19	*Sunday*	**16th S. after Trinity.** Emil Zátopek b. 1922	*week 38 day* 262
20	*Monday*	YOM KIPPUR. Stevie Smith b. 1902	263
21	*Tuesday*	**St Matthew.** Gustav Holst b. 1874	264
22	*Wednesday*	Michael Faraday b. 1791. Irving Berlin d. 1989	265
23	*Thursday*	Wilkie Collins d. 1889. Sigmund Freud d. 1939	266
24	*Friday*	Scott Fitzgerald b. 1896. Dr Seuss d. 1991	267
25	*Saturday*	FEAST OF TABERNACLES begins. Johann Strauss (elder) d. 1849	268
26	*Sunday*	**17th S. after Trinity.** *Queen Mary* launched 1934	*week 39 day* 269
27	*Monday*	Adelina Patti d. 1919. Dame Gracie Fields d. 1979	270
28	*Tuesday*	Ellis Peters b. 1913. W. H. Auden d. 1973	271
29	*Wednesday*	**St Michael and All Angels.** Mrs Gaskell b. 1810	272
30	*Thursday*	Pierre Corneille d. 1684. Truman Capote b. 1924	273

ASTRONOMICAL PHENOMENA

d	h	
1	08	Saturn in conjunction with Moon. Saturn 3° N.
7	21	Venus in conjunction with Moon. Venus 8° S.
8	15	Mercury in superior conjunction
10	01	Mercury in conjunction with Moon. Mercury 1° S.
11	00	Venus at stationary point
16	12	Mars in conjunction with Moon. Mars 6° S.
23	12	Sun's longitude 180° ♎
26	14	Venus at greatest brilliancy
27	15	Jupiter in conjunction with Moon. Jupiter 4° N.
28	13	Saturn in conjunction with Moon. Saturn 3° N.

MINIMA OF ALGOL

d	h	d	h	d	h
3	09.5	14	20.7	26	08.0
6	06.3	17	17.5	29	04.8
9	03.1	20	14.3		
11	23.9	23	11.2		

CONSTELLATIONS

The following constellations are near the meridian at

d	h		d	h
August	1	24	September	15	21
August	16	23	October	1	20
September	1	22	October	16	19

Draco, Cepheus, Lyra, Cygnus, Vulpecula, Sagitta, Delphinus, Equuleus, Aquila, Aquarius and Capricornus

THE MOON

Phases, Apsides and Node	d	h	m
☾ Last Quarter	2	22	17
● New Moon	9	22	02
☽ First Quarter	17	20	06
○ Full Moon	25	10	51
Perigee (369,783 km)	2	18	04
Apogee (404,431 km)	16	18	42
Perigee (366,227 km)	28	16	50

Mean longitude of ascending node on September 1, 132°

THE SUN   s.d. 15′.9

Day	Right Ascension	Dec.	Equation of time	Rise 52°	Rise 56°	Transit	Set 52°	Set 56°	Sidereal time	Transit of First Point of Aries
	h m s	° ′	m s	h m	h m	h m	h m	h m	h m s	h m s
1	10 39 07	+ 8 31	− 0 16	5 11	5 03	12 00	18 48	18 56	22 38 52	1 20 55
2	10 42 45	+ 8 10	+ 0 03	5 12	5 05	12 00	18 46	18 53	22 42 48	1 16 59
3	10 46 22	+ 7 48	+ 0 22	5 14	5 07	11 59	18 44	18 51	22 46 45	1 13 03
4	10 49 59	+ 7 26	+ 0 42	5 16	5 09	11 59	18 41	18 48	22 50 41	1 09 07
5	10 53 36	+ 7 04	+ 1 02	5 17	5 11	11 59	18 39	18 45	22 54 38	1 05 11
6	10 57 13	+ 6 41	+ 1 22	5 19	5 13	11 58	18 37	18 43	22 58 34	1 01 15
7	11 00 49	+ 6 19	+ 1 42	5 21	5 15	11 58	18 35	18 40	23 02 31	0 57 20
8	11 04 26	+ 5 57	+ 2 02	5 22	5 17	11 58	18 32	18 38	23 06 28	0 53 24
9	11 08 02	+ 5 34	+ 2 23	5 24	5 19	11 57	18 30	18 35	23 10 24	0 49 28
10	11 11 37	+ 5 11	+ 2 43	5 25	5 21	11 57	18 28	18 32	23 14 21	0 45 32
11	11 15 13	+ 4 49	+ 3 04	5 27	5 23	11 57	18 25	18 30	23 18 17	0 41 36
12	11 18 49	+ 4 26	+ 3 25	5 29	5 25	11 56	18 23	18 27	23 22 14	0 37 40
13	11 22 24	+ 4 03	+ 3 46	5 30	5 27	11 56	18 21	18 24	23 26 10	0 33 44
14	11 26 00	+ 3 40	+ 4 07	5 32	5 28	11 56	18 18	18 22	23 30 07	0 29 48
15	11 29 35	+ 3 17	+ 4 29	5 34	5 30	11 55	18 16	18 19	23 34 03	0 25 52
16	11 33 10	+ 2 54	+ 4 50	5 35	5 32	11 55	18 14	18 16	23 38 00	0 21 56
17	11 36 45	+ 2 31	+ 5 11	5 37	5 34	11 55	18 11	18 14	23 41 57	0 18 00
18	11 40 20	+ 2 08	+ 5 33	5 39	5 36	11 54	18 09	18 11	23 45 53	0 14 05
19	11 43 56	+ 1 44	+ 5 54	5 40	5 38	11 54	18 07	18 08	23 49 50	0 10 09
20	11 47 31	+ 1 21	+ 6 16	5 42	5 40	11 54	18 04	18 06	23 53 46	0 06 13
21	11 51 06	+ 0 58	+ 6 37	5 43	5 42	11 53	18 02	18 03	23 57 43	{ 0 02 17 / 23 58 21
22	11 54 41	+ 0 35	+ 6 58	5 45	5 44	11 53	18 00	18 00	0 01 39	23 54 25
23	11 58 16	+ 0 11	+ 7 19	5 47	5 46	11 52	17 57	17 58	0 05 36	23 50 29
24	12 01 52	− 0 12	+ 7 41	5 48	5 48	11 52	17 55	17 55	0 09 32	23 46 33
25	12 05 27	− 0 35	+ 8 02	5 50	5 50	11 52	17 53	17 52	0 13 29	23 42 37
26	12 09 03	− 0 59	+ 8 22	5 52	5 52	11 51	17 50	17 50	0 17 26	23 38 41
27	12 12 39	− 1 22	+ 8 43	5 53	5 54	11 51	17 48	17 47	0 21 22	23 34 46
28	12 16 15	− 1 46	+ 9 04	5 55	5 56	11 51	17 46	17 44	0 25 19	23 30 50
29	12 19 51	− 2 09	+ 9 24	5 57	5 58	11 50	17 43	17 42	0 29 15	23 26 54
30	12 23 28	− 2 32	+ 9 44	5 58	6 00	11 50	17 41	17 39	0 33 12	23 22 58

DURATION OF TWILIGHT (in minutes)

Latitude	52°	56°	52°	56°	52°	56°	52°	56°
	1 September		11 September		21 September		30 September	
Civil	35	39	34	38	34	37	34	37
Nautical	79	89	76	84	74	82	73	80
Astronomical	127	146	120	135	115	129	113	126

THE NIGHT SKY

Mercury is unsuitably placed for observation throughout the month, superior conjunction occurring on the 8th.

Venus is emerging from the morning twilight and visible in the eastern sky before dawn. Venus attains its greatest brilliancy on the 26th with a magnitude of −4.6.

Mars, magnitude +0.4, is still visible in the south-western sky in the evenings. The Moon is about 6° from Mars on the evening of the 16th. Mars moves from Scorpius into Ophiuchus during September, passing 3° N. of Antares on the 17th.

Jupiter, magnitude −2.8, continues to be visible as a splendid object in the southern half of the sky as it moves towards opposition next month.

Saturn, magnitude +0.1, is still a morning object, in the constellation of Aries. The Moon is near the planet on the mornings of the 1st and the 28th.

Zodiacal Light. The morning cone may be seen reaching up from the eastern horizon along the ecliptic, before the beginning of morning twilight, from the 8th to the 23rd.

THE MOON

Day	RA h m	Dec. °	Hor. par. '	Semi-diam. '	Sun's co-long. °	PA of Bright Limb °	Phase %	Age d	Rise 52° h m	Rise 56° h m	Transit h m	Set 52° h m	Set 56° h m
1	2 47	+10.6	59.2	16.1	156	75	72	20.5	21 41	21 28	4 17	11 38	11 50
2	3 43	+14.5	59.3	16.1	168	78	61	21.5	22 17	22 00	5 11	12 55	13 11
3	4 40	+17.5	59.3	16.2	180	82	49	22.5	23 00	22 41	6 08	14 08	14 27
4	5 40	+19.5	59.2	16.1	193	87	38	23.5	23 53	23 33	7 05	15 15	15 36
5	6 40	+20.2	59.1	16.1	205	92	27	24.5	—	—	8 04	16 13	16 33
6	7 39	+19.7	58.9	16.0	217	98	18	25.5	0 55	0 35	9 02	17 01	17 19
7	8 38	+18.0	58.5	15.9	229	104	10	26.5	2 04	1 47	9 58	17 40	17 54
8	9 34	+15.2	58.1	15.8	241	110	4	27.5	3 17	3 03	10 51	18 12	18 22
9	10 28	+11.7	57.6	15.7	254	121	1	28.5	4 31	4 21	11 41	18 38	18 46
10	11 20	+ 7.6	57.1	15.5	266	221	0	0.1	5 44	5 38	12 30	19 02	19 06
11	12 10	+ 3.2	56.5	15.4	278	277	1	1.1	6 55	6 54	13 16	19 24	19 24
12	12 58	− 1.2	55.9	15.2	290	283	5	2.1	8 05	8 07	14 01	19 46	19 42
13	13 45	− 5.5	55.3	15.1	303	284	10	3.1	9 12	9 19	14 45	20 08	20 00
14	14 32	− 9.5	54.8	14.9	315	284	17	4.1	10 19	10 29	15 29	20 32	20 21
15	15 19	−13.0	54.5	14.8	327	282	24	5.1	11 23	11 37	16 14	20 58	20 44
16	16 06	−15.9	54.3	14.8	339	279	33	6.1	12 25	12 42	17 00	21 29	21 12
17	16 55	−18.2	54.2	14.8	352	276	42	7.1	13 25	13 44	17 47	22 06	21 46
18	17 45	−19.7	54.3	14.8	4	272	52	8.1	14 20	14 40	18 35	22 50	22 29
19	18 36	−20.3	54.6	14.9	16	267	61	9.1	15 09	15 30	19 24	23 41	23 20
20	19 27	−20.0	55.1	15.0	28	262	70	10.1	15 52	16 11	20 14	—	—
21	20 19	−18.7	55.7	15.2	40	257	79	11.1	16 30	16 46	21 04	0 40	0 21
22	21 12	−16.5	56.4	15.4	52	253	87	12.1	17 02	17 15	21 55	1 45	1 29
23	22 04	−13.4	57.2	15.6	65	247	93	13.1	17 31	17 40	22 45	2 55	2 43
24	22 57	− 9.5	57.9	15.8	77	240	97	14.1	17 56	18 02	23 35	4 09	4 01
25	23 49	− 5.0	58.6	16.0	89	216	100	15.1	18 21	18 22	—	5 26	5 22
26	0 42	− 0.1	59.2	16.1	101	98	99	16.1	18 46	18 43	0 26	6 44	6 45
27	1 36	+ 4.8	59.6	16.2	113	81	97	17.1	19 12	19 05	1 18	8 04	8 10
28	2 31	+ 9.5	59.8	16.3	125	79	91	18.1	19 41	19 30	2 11	9 24	9 35
29	3 28	+13.7	59.9	16.3	138	80	84	19.1	20 16	20 01	3 06	10 44	10 58
30	4 26	+17.1	59.7	16.3	150	83	74	20.1	20 58	20 39	4 03	12 00	12 18

MERCURY

Day	RA h m	Dec. °	Diam. "	Phase %	Transit h m	5° high 52° h m	56° h m
1	10 14	+12.8	5	96	11 36	5 03	4 55
3	10 29	+11.5	5	98	11 44	5 17	5 11
5	10 43	+10.0	5	99	11 50	5 32	5 27
7	10 58	+ 8.5	5	100	11 57	5 46	5 42
9	11 12	+ 7.0	5	100	12 03	18 04	18 06
11	11 26	+ 5.4	5	100	12 09	18 01	18 02
13	11 39	+ 3.8	5	99	12 14	17 59	17 58
15	11 52	+ 2.2	5	99	12 19	17 56	17 54
17	12 05	+ 0.6	5	98	12 24	17 52	17 49
19	12 17	− 0.9	5	97	12 28	17 48	17 44
21	12 29	− 2.5	5	96	12 33	17 45	17 39
23	12 41	− 4.0	5	95	12 37	17 41	17 33
25	12 53	− 5.5	5	93	12 40	17 36	17 28
27	13 04	− 6.9	5	92	12 44	17 32	17 22
29	13 16	− 8.3	5	91	12 47	17 28	17 16
31	13 27	− 9.7	5	90	12 51	17 23	17 10

VENUS

Day	RA h m	Dec. °	Diam. "	Phase %	Transit h m	5° high 52° h m	56° h m
1	9 22	+ 6.9	55	5	10 41	4 40	4 37
6	9 17	+ 7.8	52	9	10 17	4 10	4 07
11	9 16	+ 8.6	48	14	9 56	3 46	3 42
16	9 19	+ 9.2	45	18	9 40	3 26	3 21
21	9 25	+ 9.6	41	23	9 27	3 10	3 06
26	9 34	+ 9.8	38	27	9 16	2 59	2 55
31	9 46	+ 9.6	35	31	9 08	2 52	2 47

MARS

Day	RA h m	Dec. °	Diam. "	Phase %	Transit h m	5° high 52° h m	56° h m
1	15 45	−21.7	8	86	17 05	20 19	19 47
6	15 58	−22.3	8	86	16 59	20 07	19 33
11	16 12	−23.0	8	86	16 53	19 55	19 20
16	16 26	−23.5	7	86	16 47	19 45	19 07
21	16 40	−24.0	7	86	16 42	19 35	18 56
26	16 55	−24.4	7	87	16 37	19 26	18 45
31	17 10	−24.8	7	87	16 32	19 19	18 36

SUNRISE AND SUNSET

	London		Bristol		Birmingham		Manchester		Newcastle		Glasgow		Belfast	
	0°05'	51°30'	2°35'	51°28'	1°55'	52°28'	2°15'	53°28'	1°37'	54°59'	4°14'	55°52'	5°56'	54°35'
	h m	h m	h m	h m	h m	h m	h m	h m	h m	h m	h m	h m	h m	h m
1	5 12	18 48	5 22	18 58	5 18	18 57	5 17	19 00	5 12	19 00	5 20	19 12	5 30	19 17
2	5 14	18 46	5 24	18 56	5 19	18 54	5 19	18 57	5 14	18 58	5 22	19 10	5 32	19 14
3	5 15	18 43	5 25	18 53	5 21	18 52	5 21	18 55	5 15	18 55	5 24	19 07	5 33	19 12
4	5 17	18 41	5 27	18 51	5 23	18 50	5 22	18 53	5 17	18 53	5 26	19 05	5 35	19 09
5	5 18	18 39	5 28	18 49	5 24	18 48	5 24	18 50	5 19	18 50	5 28	19 02	5 37	19 07
6	5 20	18 37	5 30	18 47	5 26	18 45	5 26	18 48	5 21	18 48	5 30	18 59	5 39	19 04
7	5 22	18 34	5 32	18 44	5 28	18 43	5 28	18 45	5 23	18 45	5 32	18 57	5 41	19 02
8	5 23	18 32	5 33	18 42	5 29	18 41	5 29	18 43	5 25	18 43	5 34	18 54	5 43	18 59
9	5 25	18 30	5 35	18 40	5 31	18 38	5 31	18 41	5 27	18 40	5 36	18 52	5 44	18 57
10	5 26	18 27	5 36	18 37	5 33	18 36	5 33	18 38	5 28	18 37	5 38	18 49	5 46	18 54
11	5 28	18 25	5 38	18 35	5 34	18 33	5 35	18 36	5 30	18 35	5 40	18 46	5 48	18 52
12	5 29	18 23	5 40	18 33	5 36	18 31	5 36	18 33	5 32	18 32	5 42	18 44	5 50	18 49
13	5 31	18 21	5 41	18 31	5 38	18 29	5 38	18 31	5 34	18 30	5 44	18 41	5 52	18 47
14	5 33	18 18	5 43	18 28	5 39	18 26	5 40	18 28	5 36	18 27	5 46	18 38	5 54	18 44
15	5 34	18 16	5 44	18 26	5 41	18 24	5 42	18 26	5 38	18 25	5 48	18 36	5 55	18 42
16	5 36	18 14	5 46	18 24	5 43	18 22	5 43	18 24	5 40	18 22	5 49	18 33	5 57	18 39
17	5 37	18 11	5 48	18 21	5 44	18 19	5 45	18 21	5 42	18 20	5 51	18 31	5 59	18 37
18	5 39	18 09	5 49	18 19	5 46	18 17	5 47	18 19	5 43	18 17	5 53	18 28	6 01	18 34
19	5 41	18 07	5 51	18 17	5 48	18 15	5 49	18 16	5 45	18 14	5 55	18 25	6 03	18 31
20	5 42	18 05	5 52	18 14	5 49	18 12	5 50	18 14	5 47	18 12	5 57	18 23	6 05	18 29
21	5 44	18 02	5 54	18 12	5 51	18 10	5 52	18 11	5 49	18 09	5 59	18 20	6 06	18 26
22	5 45	18 00	5 55	18 10	5 53	18 07	5 54	18 09	5 51	18 07	6 01	18 17	6 08	18 24
23	5 47	17 58	5 57	18 08	5 54	18 05	5 55	18 06	5 53	18 04	6 03	18 15	6 10	18 21
24	5 49	17 55	5 59	18 05	5 56	18 03	5 57	18 04	5 55	18 01	6 05	18 12	6 12	18 19
25	5 50	17 53	6 00	18 03	5 58	18 00	5 59	18 02	5 56	17 59	6 07	17 59	6 14	18 16
26	5 52	17 51	6 02	18 01	5 59	17 58	6 01	17 59	5 58	17 56	6 09	18 07	6 16	18 14
27	5 54	17 48	6 04	17 58	6 01	17 56	6 03	17 57	6 00	17 54	6 11	18 04	6 17	18 11
28	5 55	17 46	6 05	17 56	6 03	17 53	6 04	17 54	6 02	17 51	6 13	18 01	6 19	18 09
29	5 57	17 44	6 07	17 54	6 04	17 51	6 06	17 52	6 04	17 49	6 15	17 59	6 21	18 06
30	5 58	17 42	6 08	17 52	6 06	17 48	6 08	17 49	6 06	17 46	6 17	17 56	6 23	18 04

JUPITER

Day	RA	Dec.	Transit	5° high	
				52°	56°
	h m	° '	h m	h m	h m
1	2 12.5	+11 48	3 33	21 02	20 56
11	2 11.0	+11 38	2 52	20 22	20 16
21	2 08.3	+11 22	2 10	19 41	19 35
31	2 04.6	+11 01	1 27	19 00	18 54

Diameters – equatorial 47″ polar 45″

SATURN

Day	RA	Dec.	Transit	5° high	
				52°	56°
	h m	° '	h m	h m	h m
1	3 01.7	+14 35	4 22	21 36	21 27
11	3 01.3	+14 31	3 42	20 57	20 48
21	3 00.2	+14 24	3 02	20 17	20 08
31	2 58.4	+14 15	2 21	19 37	19 28

Diameters – equatorial 19″ polar 17″
Rings – major axis 44″ minor axis 16″

URANUS

Day	RA	Dec.	Transit	10° high	
				52°	56°
	h m	° '	h m	h m	h m
1	21 06.3	−17 20	22 24	1 31	0 59
11	21 04.9	−17 26	21 43	0 50	0 18
21	21 03.8	−17 30	21 03	0 09	23 32
31	21 03.0	−17 34	20 22	23 24	22 51

Diameter 4″

NEPTUNE

Day	RA	Dec.	Transit	10° high	
				52°	56°
	h m	° '	h m	h m	h m
1	20 17.0	−19 26	21 35	0 24	23 40
11	20 16.3	−19 29	20 54	23 39	23 00
21	20 15.7	−19 31	20 15	22 59	22 19
31	20 15.3	−19 32	19 35	22 19	21 39

Diameter 2″

October 1999

TENTH MONTH, 31 DAYS. *Octo* (eight), eighth month of Roman pre-Julian calendar

1	*Friday*	*Michaelmas Law Sittings begin.* Stanley Holloway b. 1890	*week* 39 *day* 274
2	*Saturday*	Mahatma Gandhi b. 1869. Graham Greene b. 1904	275
3	*Sunday*	**18th S. after Trinity.** Reunification of Germany 1990	*week* 40 *day* 276
4	*Monday*	Rembrandt d. 1669. *Sputnik I* launched 1957	277
5	*Tuesday*	Louis Lumière b. 1864. *R101* disaster 1930	278
6	*Wednesday*	Thor Heyerdahl b. 1914. Bette Davis d. 1989	279
7	*Thursday*	Edgar Allen Poe d. 1849. Mario Lanza d. 1959	280
8	*Friday*	Sir Geoffrey Jellicoe b. 1900. Kathleen Ferrier d. 1953	281
9	*Saturday*	Alfred Dreyfus b. 1859. John Lennon b. 1940	282
10	*Sunday*	**19th S. after Trinity.** Harold Pinter b. 1930	*week* 41 *day* 283
11	*Monday*	James Joule d. 1889. Boer War began 1899	284
12	*Tuesday*	Elizabeth Fry d. 1845. Edith Cavell executed 1915	285
13	*Wednesday*	Anatole France d. 1924. Margaret Thatcher b. 1925	286
14	*Thursday*	Dwight Eisenhower b. 1890. Cliff Richard b. 1940	287
15	*Friday*	Friedrich Nietzsche b. 1844. Sarah, Duchess of York b. 1959	288
16	*Saturday*	Oscar Wilde b. 1854. Edward Ardizzone b. 1900	289
17	*Sunday*	**20th S. after Trinity.** Frederic Chopin d. 1849	*week* 42 *day* 290
18	*Monday*	**St Luke.** Beau Nash b. 1674	291
19	*Tuesday*	Jonathan Swift d. 1745. Leigh Hunt b. 1784	292
20	*Wednesday*	Lord Palmerston b. 1784. Sir Anthony Quayle d. 1989	293
21	*Thursday*	Battle of Trafalgar 1805. Aberfan disaster 1966	294
22	*Friday*	Thomas Sheraton d. 1806. Pablo Casals d. 1973	295
23	*Saturday*	Dr W. G. Grace d. 1915. Pélé b. 1940	296
24	*Sunday*	**Last S. after Trinity.** Dame Sybil Thorndike b. 1882	*week* 43 *day* 297
25	*Monday*	Chaucer d. 1400. Lord Macauley b. 1800	298
26	*Tuesday*	Georges Danton b. 1759. Leon Trotsky b. 1879 (os)	299
27	*Wednesday*	Theodore Roosevelt b. 1858. Dylan Thomas b. 1914	300
28	*Thursday*	**SS Simon and Jude.** Capt. James Cook b. 1728	301
29	*Friday*	James Boswell b. 1740. Wall Street crash 1929	302
30	*Saturday*	Angelica Kauffmann b. 1741. Sir Barnes Wallis d. 1979	303
31	*Sunday*	**4th S. before Advent.** Hallowmass Eve	*week* 44 *day* 304

ASTRONOMICAL PHENOMENA

d	h	
5	20	Venus in conjunction with Moon. Venus 4° S.
11	08	Mercury in conjunction with Moon. Mercury 7° S.
14	01	Neptune at stationary point
15	13	Mars in conjunction with Moon. Mars 5° S.
23	06	Uranus at stationary point
23	19	Jupiter at opposition
23	21	Sun's longitude 210° ♏
24	19	Jupiter in conjunction with Moon. Jupiter 3° N.
24	22	Mercury at greatest elongation E.24°
25	19	Saturn in conjunction with Moon. Saturn 2° N.
31	00	Venus at greatest elongation W.46°

MINIMA OF ALGOL

d	h	d	h	d	h
2	01.6	13	12.8	25	00.1
4	22.4	16	09.6	27	20.9
7	19.2	19	06.5	30	17.7
10	16.0	22	03.3		

CONSTELLATIONS

The following constellations are near the meridian at

	d	h		d	h
September	1	24	October	16	21
September	15	23	November	1	20
October	1	22	November	15	19

Ursa Major (below the Pole), Cepheus, Cassiopeia, Cygnus, Lacerta, Andromeda, Pegasus, Capricornus, Aquarius and Piscis Austrinus

THE MOON

Phases, Apsides and Node	d	h	m
☾ Last Quarter	2	04	02
● New Moon	9	11	34
☽ First Quarter	17	15	00
○ Full Moon	24	21	02
☾ Last Quarter	31	12	04
Apogee (405,289 km)	14	13	54
Perigee (360,936 km)	26	13	05

Mean longitude of ascending node on October 1, 130°

THE SUN   s.d. 16'.1

Day	Right Ascension	Dec.	Equation of time	Rise 52°	Rise 56°	Transit	Set 52°	Set 56°	Sidereal time	Transit of First Point of Aries
	h m s	° '	m s	h m	h m	h m	h m	h m	h m s	h m s
1	12 27 05	2 56	+10 04	6 00	6 02	11 50	17 39	17 37	0 37 08	23 19 02
2	12 30 42	3 19	+10 23	6 02	6 04	11 49	17 36	17 34	0 41 05	23 15 06
3	12 34 19	3 42	+10 42	6 03	6 06	11 49	17 34	17 31	0 45 01	23 11 10
4	12 37 57	4 05	+11 01	6 05	6 08	11 49	17 32	17 29	0 48 58	23 07 14
5	12 41 35	4 28	+11 19	6 07	6 10	11 49	17 29	17 26	0 52 54	23 03 18
6	12 45 14	4 51	+11 37	6 08	6 12	11 48	17 27	17 24	0 56 51	22 59 22
7	12 48 52	5 15	+11 55	6 10	6 14	11 48	17 25	17 21	1 00 48	22 55 26
8	12 52 32	5 38	+12 12	6 12	6 16	11 48	17 23	17 18	1 04 44	22 51 31
9	12 56 11	6 00	+12 29	6 13	6 18	11 47	17 20	17 16	1 08 41	22 47 35
10	12 59 52	6 23	+12 46	6 15	6 20	11 47	17 18	17 13	1 12 37	22 43 39
11	13 03 32	6 46	+13 02	6 17	6 22	11 47	17 16	17 11	1 16 34	22 39 43
12	13 07 13	7 09	+13 17	6 19	6 24	11 47	17 14	17 08	1 20 30	22 35 47
13	13 10 55	7 31	+13 32	6 20	6 26	11 46	17 11	17 06	1 24 27	22 31 51
14	13 14 37	7 54	+13 47	6 22	6 28	11 46	17 09	17 03	1 28 23	22 27 55
15	13 18 19	8 16	+14 01	6 24	6 30	11 46	17 07	17 01	1 32 20	22 23 59
16	13 22 02	8 38	+14 14	6 26	6 32	11 46	17 05	16 58	1 36 17	22 20 03
17	13 25 46	9 00	+14 27	6 27	6 34	11 45	17 03	16 56	1 40 13	22 16 07
18	13 29 30	9 22	+14 39	6 29	6 36	11 45	17 01	16 53	1 44 10	22 12 11
19	13 33 15	9 44	+14 51	6 31	6 38	11 45	16 59	16 51	1 48 06	22 08 16
20	13 37 00	10 06	+15 02	6 33	6 41	11 45	16 56	16 48	1 52 03	22 04 20
21	13 40 46	10 27	+15 13	6 34	6 43	11 45	16 54	16 46	1 55 59	22 00 24
22	13 44 33	10 49	+15 23	6 36	6 45	11 44	16 52	16 43	1 59 56	21 56 28
23	13 48 20	11 10	+15 32	6 38	6 47	11 44	16 50	16 41	2 03 52	21 52 32
24	13 52 08	11 31	+15 41	6 40	6 49	11 44	16 48	16 39	2 07 49	21 48 36
25	13 55 57	11 52	+15 49	6 41	6 51	11 44	16 46	16 36	2 11 46	21 44 40
26	13 59 46	12 13	+15 56	6 43	6 53	11 44	16 44	16 34	2 15 42	21 40 44
27	14 03 36	12 33	+16 02	6 45	6 55	11 44	16 42	16 32	2 19 39	21 36 48
28	14 07 27	12 53	+16 08	6 47	6 57	11 44	16 40	16 29	2 23 35	21 32 52
29	14 11 19	13 14	+16 13	6 48	6 59	11 44	16 38	16 27	2 27 32	21 28 56
30	14 15 11	13 33	+16 17	6 50	7 02	11 44	16 36	16 25	2 31 28	21 25 01
31	14 19 04	13 53	+16 21	6 52	7 04	11 44	16 34	16 23	2 35 25	21 21 05

DURATION OF TWILIGHT (in minutes)

Latitude	52°	56°	52°	56°	52°	56°	52°	56°
	1 October		11 October		21 October		31 October	
Civil	34	37	34	37	34	38	36	40
Nautical	73	80	73	80	74	81	75	83
Astronomical	113	125	112	124	113	124	114	126

THE NIGHT SKY

Mercury is unsuitably placed for observation throughout October.

Venus, magnitude −4.5, is a magnificent morning object, visible in the eastern sky before 03h; by the end of the month it becomes visible low in the east almost four hours before sunrise. Venus passes 3° S. of Regulus on the 8th. On the mornings of October 5th and 6th the old crescent Moon is in the vicinity of the planet.

Mars, magnitude +0.6, continues to be visible in the south-western sky in the early part of the evening, though since it reaches a southern declination of 25° during the month it will only be seen at a very low altitude. The Moon, two days before First Quarter, will be seen about 5° from the planet on the evening of the 15th. Mars is now moving more rapidly eastwards, passing from Ophiuchus into Sagittarius during the month.

Jupiter, magnitude −2.9, is at opposition on the 23rd, and thus visible throughout the hours of darkness. During the night of the 24th to 25th the Full Moon is near the planet.

Saturn is now visible for the greater part of the night as it approaches opposition early in November. By the end of October it is visible in the eastern sky almost as soon as it gets dark. Its magnitude is −0.1. The Full Moon will be seen about 3° below Saturn on the evening of the 25th, shortly after the two bodies rise above the eastern horizon.

THE MOON

Day	RA	Dec.	Hor. par.	Semi-diam.	Sun's co-long.	PA of Bright Limb	Phase	Age	Rise 52°	Rise 56°	Transit	Set 52°	Set 56°
	h m	°	'	'	°	°	%	d	h m	h m	h m	h m	h m
1	5 26	+19.3	59.5	16.2	162	88	63	21.1	21 48	21 28	5 01	13 10	13 30
2	6 26	+20.4	59.1	16.1	174	93	52	22.1	22 47	22 27	5 59	14 10	14 31
3	7 26	+20.1	58.7	16.0	186	98	41	23.1	23 53	23 35	6 57	15 01	15 20
4	8 24	+18.6	58.2	15.9	199	103	30	24.1	—	—	7 52	15 41	15 57
5	9 20	+16.1	57.8	15.7	211	108	21	25.1	1 04	0 49	8 45	16 14	16 27
6	10 14	+12.8	57.3	15.6	223	113	13	26.1	2 17	2 05	9 36	16 42	16 50
7	11 05	+ 8.9	56.8	15.5	235	118	7	27.1	3 29	3 22	10 24	17 06	17 11
8	11 54	+ 4.6	56.3	15.3	247	125	2	28.1	4 40	4 37	11 10	17 28	17 29
9	12 42	+ 0.2	55.8	15.2	260	150	0	29.1	5 49	5 50	11 55	17 49	17 46
10	13 29	− 4.2	55.3	15.1	272	253	0	0.5	6 58	7 03	12 39	18 10	18 04
11	14 16	− 8.3	54.9	15.0	284	274	2	1.5	8 05	8 13	13 24	18 33	18 23
12	15 03	−12.1	54.5	14.9	296	277	6	2.5	9 11	9 23	14 08	18 58	18 45
13	15 51	−15.2	54.3	14.8	309	277	12	3.5	10 14	10 30	14 54	19 27	19 11
14	16 39	−17.8	54.1	14.7	321	274	18	4.5	11 15	11 34	15 40	20 02	19 42
15	17 29	−19.5	54.1	14.7	333	271	26	5.5	12 12	12 33	16 28	20 42	20 21
16	18 19	−20.4	54.3	14.8	345	267	35	6.5	13 03	13 24	17 16	21 29	21 08
17	19 10	−20.4	54.6	14.9	357	263	44	7.5	13 49	14 09	18 05	22 24	22 04
18	20 01	−19.5	55.1	15.0	9	259	54	8.5	14 28	14 46	18 54	23 26	23 08
19	20 52	−17.6	55.7	15.2	22	254	63	9.5	15 01	15 16	19 43	—	—
20	21 44	−14.9	56.5	15.4	34	250	73	10.5	15 30	15 42	20 33	0 33	0 19
21	22 35	−11.3	57.4	15.6	46	246	82	11.5	15 57	16 04	21 22	1 44	1 34
22	23 27	− 7.0	58.3	15.9	58	243	89	12.5	16 21	16 24	22 13	2 59	2 53
23	0 20	− 2.3	59.1	16.1	70	238	95	13.5	16 45	16 45	23 04	4 17	4 16
24	1 14	+ 2.8	59.9	16.3	82	227	99	14.5	17 11	17 06	23 57	5 37	5 41
25	2 09	+ 7.8	60.4	16.5	95	141	100	15.5	17 39	17 30	—	7 00	7 08
26	3 07	+12.4	60.7	16.5	107	91	98	16.5	18 12	17 58	0 53	8 23	8 35
27	4 07	+16.2	60.7	16.5	119	87	93	17.5	18 52	18 34	1 51	9 44	10 01
28	5 08	+19.0	60.5	16.5	131	89	86	18.5	19 40	19 20	2 51	11 00	11 20
29	6 10	+20.4	60.0	16.4	143	93	77	19.5	20 38	20 17	3 52	12 06	12 27
30	7 11	+20.5	59.4	16.2	155	98	67	20.5	21 44	21 24	4 51	13 00	13 21
31	8 11	+19.3	58.7	16.0	168	103	56	21.5	22 54	22 38	5 49	13 44	14 02

MERCURY

Day	RA	Dec.	Diam.	Phase	Transit	5° high 52°	5° high 56°
	h m	°	"	%	h m	h m	h m
1	13 27	− 9.7	5	90	12 51	17 23	17 10
3	13 38	−11.0	5	88	12 54	17 19	17 04
5	13 49	−12.3	5	87	12 57	17 14	16 58
7	14 00	−13.6	5	85	13 00	17 09	16 52
9	14 10	−14.7	5	84	13 03	17 05	16 46
11	14 21	−15.9	5	82	13 05	17 00	16 39
13	14 32	−16.9	6	80	13 08	16 55	16 33
15	14 42	−18.0	6	78	13 10	16 51	16 27
17	14 52	−18.9	6	75	13 12	16 46	16 20
19	15 02	−19.8	6	73	13 14	16 41	16 14
21	15 11	−20.6	6	70	13 15	16 37	16 08
23	15 20	−21.3	6	66	13 16	16 33	16 02
25	15 29	−21.9	7	62	13 17	16 28	15 56
27	15 36	−22.4	7	58	13 17	16 24	15 50
29	15 43	−22.8	7	53	13 15	16 19	15 44
31	15 49	−23.1	8	48	13 13	16 15	15 39

VENUS

Day	RA	Dec.	Diam.	Phase	Transit	5° high 52°	5° high 56°
	h m	°	"	%	h m	h m	h m
1	9 46	+ 9.6	35	31	9 08	2 52	2 47
6	10 00	+ 9.2	33	35	9 02	2 48	2 44
11	10 15	+ 8.6	31	38	8 58	2 47	2 43
16	10 31	+ 7.8	29	42	8 55	2 48	2 45
21	10 49	+ 6.7	27	45	8 53	2 51	2 49
26	11 07	+ 5.4	26	48	8 51	2 56	2 55
31	11 26	+ 4.0	24	51	8 51	3 03	3 03

MARS

Day	RA	Dec.	Diam.	Phase	Transit	5° high 52°	5° high 56°
1	17 10	−24.8	7	87	16 32	19 19	18 36
6	17 25	−25.0	7	87	16 28	19 12	18 28
11	17 41	−25.2	7	87	16 24	19 07	18 22
16	17 57	−25.2	7	88	16 20	19 02	18 18
21	18 13	−25.2	6	88	16 16	18 59	18 15
26	18 29	−25.0	6	88	16 13	18 57	18 14
31	18 45	−24.7	6	89	16 09	18 57	18 15

SUNRISE AND SUNSET

	London		Bristol		Birmingham		Manchester		Newcastle		Glasgow		Belfast	
	0°05′	51°30′	2°35′	51°28′	1°55′	52°28′	2°15′	53°28′	1°37′	54°59′	4°14′	55°52′	5°56′	54°35′
	h m	h m	h m	h m	h m	h m	h m	h m	h m	h m	h m	h m	h m	h m
1	6 00	17 39	6 10	17 49	6 08	17 46	6 10	17 47	6 08	17 44	6 19	17 54	6 25	18 01
2	6 02	17 37	6 12	17 47	6 10	17 44	6 11	17 45	6 10	17 41	6 21	17 51	6 27	17 59
3	6 03	17 35	6 13	17 45	6 11	17 41	6 13	17 42	6 12	17 39	6 23	17 48	6 29	17 56
4	6 05	17 32	6 15	17 42	6 13	17 39	6 15	17 40	6 14	17 36	6 25	17 46	6 31	17 54
5	6 07	17 30	6 17	17 40	6 15	17 37	6 17	17 37	6 15	17 34	6 27	17 43	6 32	17 51
6	6 08	17 28	6 18	17 38	6 16	17 34	6 19	17 35	6 17	17 31	6 29	17 41	6 34	17 49
7	6 10	17 26	6 20	17 36	6 18	17 32	6 20	17 33	6 19	17 29	6 31	17 38	6 36	17 46
8	6 12	17 23	6 22	17 33	6 20	17 30	6 22	17 30	6 21	17 26	6 33	17 35	6 38	17 44
9	6 13	17 21	6 23	17 31	6 22	17 28	6 24	17 28	6 23	17 24	6 35	17 33	6 40	17 41
10	6 15	17 19	6 25	17 29	6 23	17 25	6 26	17 25	6 25	17 21	6 37	17 30	6 42	17 39
11	6 17	17 17	6 27	17 27	6 25	17 23	6 28	17 23	6 27	17 19	6 39	17 28	6 44	17 36
12	6 18	17 15	6 28	17 25	6 27	17 21	6 29	17 21	6 29	17 16	6 41	17 25	6 46	17 34
13	6 20	17 12	6 30	17 23	6 29	17 19	6 31	17 18	6 31	17 14	6 43	17 23	6 48	17 32
14	6 22	17 10	6 32	17 20	6 30	17 16	6 33	17 16	6 33	17 11	6 45	17 20	6 50	17 29
15	6 23	17 08	6 33	17 18	6 32	17 14	6 35	17 14	6 35	17 09	6 47	17 18	6 52	17 27
16	6 25	17 06	6 35	17 16	6 34	17 12	6 37	17 12	6 37	17 06	6 49	17 15	6 53	17 24
17	6 27	17 04	6 37	17 14	6 36	17 10	6 39	17 09	6 39	17 04	6 51	17 13	6 55	17 22
18	6 28	17 02	6 38	17 12	6 37	17 07	6 41	17 07	6 41	17 02	6 53	17 10	6 57	17 20
19	6 30	17 00	6 40	17 10	6 39	17 05	6 42	17 05	6 43	16 59	6 55	17 08	6 59	17 17
20	6 32	16 58	6 42	17 08	6 41	17 03	6 44	17 03	6 45	16 57	6 57	17 05	7 01	17 15
21	6 34	16 56	6 44	17 06	6 43	17 01	6 46	17 00	6 47	16 55	6 59	17 03	7 03	17 13
22	6 35	16 54	6 45	17 04	6 45	16 59	6 48	16 58	6 49	16 52	7 01	17 01	7 05	17 10
23	6 37	16 52	6 47	17 02	6 46	16 57	6 50	16 56	6 51	16 50	7 03	16 58	7 07	17 08
24	6 39	16 50	6 49	17 00	6 48	16 55	6 52	16 54	6 53	16 48	7 06	16 56	7 09	17 06
25	6 41	16 48	6 51	16 58	6 50	16 53	6 54	16 52	6 55	16 45	7 08	16 54	7 11	17 04
26	6 42	16 46	6 52	16 56	6 52	16 51	6 56	16 50	6 57	16 43	7 10	16 51	7 13	17 02
27	6 44	16 44	6 54	16 54	6 54	16 49	6 57	16 48	6 59	16 41	7 12	16 49	7 15	16 59
28	6 46	16 42	6 56	16 52	6 56	16 47	6 59	16 45	7 01	16 39	7 14	16 47	7 17	16 57
29	6 48	16 40	6 58	16 50	6 57	16 45	7 01	16 43	7 03	16 37	7 16	16 44	7 19	16 55
30	6 49	16 38	6 59	16 48	6 59	16 43	7 03	16 41	7 05	16 35	7 18	16 42	7 21	16 53
31	6 51	16 36	7 01	16 46	7 01	16 41	7 05	16 39	7 07	16 32	7 20	16 40	7 23	16 51

JUPITER

Day	RA	Dec.	Transit	5° high	
				52°	56°
	h m	° ′	h m	h m	h m
1	2 04.6	+11 01	1 27	7 50	7 56
11	2 00.0	+10 36	0 43	7 04	7 09
21	1 55.0	+10 08	23 55	6 17	6 22
31	1 49.9	+ 9 40	23 10	5 30	5 35

Diameters – equatorial 50″ polar 47″

SATURN

Day	RA	Dec.	Transit	5° high	
				52°	56°
	h m	° ′	h m	h m	h m
1	2 58.4	+14 15	2 21	19 37	19 28
11	2 56.1	+14 03	1 39	18 56	18 48
21	2 53.3	+13 50	0 57	18 15	18 07
31	2 50.3	+13 36	0 15	17 34	17 26

Diameters – equatorial 20″ polar 18″
Rings – major axis 46″ minor axis 16″

URANUS

Day	RA	Dec.	Transit	10° high	
				52°	56°
	h m	° ′	h m	h m	h m
1	21 03.0	−17 34	20 22	23 24	22 51
11	21 02.4	−17 36	19 43	22 44	22 11
21	21 02.1	−17 37	19 03	22 04	21 31
31	21 02.2	−17 36	18 24	21 25	20 52

Diameter 4″

NEPTUNE

Day	RA	Dec.	Transit	10° high	
				52°	56°
	h m	° ′	h m	h m	h m
1	20 15.3	−19 32	19 35	22 19	21 39
11	20 15.1	−19 33	18 55	21 39	21 00
21	20 15.1	−19 33	18 16	21 00	20 20
31	20 15.4	−19 32	17 37	20 21	19 41

Diameter 2″

November 1999

ELEVENTH MONTH, 30 DAYS. *Novem* (nine), ninth month of Roman pre-Julian calendar

1	*Monday*	**All Saints' Day.** Benevenuto Cellini b. 1500	*week* 44 *day* 305
2	*Tuesday*	All Souls. George Bernard Shaw d. 1950	306
3	*Wednesday*	Karl Baedeker b. 1801. Henri Matisse d. 1954	307
4	*Thursday*	William III b. 1650. Yitzhak Rabin assassinated 1995	308
5	*Friday*	DIWALI begins. Robert Maxwell d. 1991	309
6	*Saturday*	John Philip Sousa b. 1854. Kate Greenaway d. 1901	310
7	*Sunday*	**3rd S. before Advent.** Steve McQueen d. 1980	*week* 45 *day* 311
8	*Monday*	Munich Putsch 1923. Edward Ardizzone d. 1979	312
9	*Tuesday*	Sir Giles Gilbert Scott b. 1880. Katherine Hepburn b. 1909	313
10	*Wednesday*	Johann von Schiller b. 1759. Sir Jacob Epstein b. 1880	314
11	*Thursday*	Armistice Day 1918. Dame Elizabeth Maconchy d. 1994	315
12	*Friday*	Mrs Elizabeth Gaskell d. 1865. Baroness Orczy d. 1947	316
13	*Saturday*	Archbishop of Canterbury b. 1935	317
14	*Sunday*	**2nd S. before Advent.** *Prince of Wales b. 1948*	*week* 46 *day* 318
15	*Monday*	William Pitt (the elder) b. 1708. Aneurin Bevan b. 1897	319
16	*Tuesday*	Opening of the Suez Canal 1869. Sir Oswald Mosley b. 1896	320
17	*Wednesday*	Eric Gill d. 1940. Martin Scorsese b. 1942	321
18	*Thursday*	Louis Daguerre b. 1789. Cab Calloway d. 1994	322
19	*Friday*	Indira Gandhi b. 1917. Sir Basil Spence d. 1976	323
20	*Saturday*	*Queen's Wedding Day.* Windsor Castle fire 1992	324
21	*Sunday*	**Christ the King. S. next before Advent**	*week* 47 *day* 325
22	*Monday*	George Eliot b. 1819. John Kennedy assassinated 1963	326
23	*Tuesday*	Thomas Tallis d. 1585. Roald Dahl d. 1990	327
24	*Wednesday*	Frances Hodgson Burnett b. 1849. Dodie Smith d. 1990	328
25	*Thursday*	Andrew Carnegie b. 1835. Imran Khan b. 1952	329
26	*Friday*	Eugene Ionesco b. 1912. Michael Bentine d. 1996	330
27	*Saturday*	Fanny Kemble b. 1809. Eugene O'Neill d. 1953	331
28	*Sunday*	**1st S. of Advent.** Ian Serraillier d. 1994	*week* 48 *day* 332
29	*Monday*	Louisa M. Alcott b. 1832. Giacomo Puccini d. 1924	333
30	*Tuesday*	**St Andrew.** Sir Philip Sydney b. 1554	334

ASTRONOMICAL PHENOMENA

d	h	
4	02	Venus in conjunction with Moon. Venus 3° S.
5	03	Mercury at stationary point
6	14	Saturn at opposition
9	10	Mercury in conjunction with Moon. Mercury 6° S.
13	15	Mars in conjunction with Moon. Mars 3° S.
15	22	Mercury in inferior conjunction (transits Sun)
21	01	Jupiter in conjunction with Moon. Jupiter 4° N.
22	03	Saturn in conjunction with Moon. Saturn 2° N.
22	18	Sun's longitude 240° ♐
25	04	Mercury at stationary point

MINIMA OF ALGOL

d	h	d	h	d	h
2	14.5	14	01.8	25	13.0
5	11.3	16	22.6	28	09.9
8	08.1	19	19.4		
11	05.0	22	16.2		

CONSTELLATIONS

The following constellations are near the meridian at

	d	h		d	h
October	1	24	November	15	21
October	16	23	December	1	20
November	1	22	December	16	19

Ursa Major (below the Pole), Cepheus, Cassiopeia, Andromeda, Pegasus, Pisces, Aquarius and Cetus

THE MOON

Phases, Apsides and Node	d	h	m
● New Moon	8	03	53
☽ First Quarter	16	09	03
○ Full Moon	23	07	04
☾ Last Quarter	29	23	19
Apogee (406,238 km)	11	05	41
Perigee (357,272 km)	23	22	01

Mean longitude of ascending node on November 1, 128°

THE SUN   s.d. 16'.2

Day	Right Ascension	Dec. −	Equation of time	Rise 52°	Rise 56°	Transit	Set 52°	Set 56°	Sidereal time	Transit of First Point of Aries
	h m s	° '	m s	h m	h m	h m	h m	h m	h m s	h m s
1	14 22 58	14 13	+16 23	6 54	7 06	11 44	16 33	16 21	2 39 21	21 17 09
2	14 26 53	14 32	+16 25	6 56	7 08	11 44	16 31	16 18	2 43 18	21 13 13
3	14 30 49	14 51	+16 26	6 58	7 10	11 44	16 29	16 16	2 47 15	21 09 17
4	14 34 45	15 10	+16 26	6 59	7 12	11 44	16 27	16 14	2 51 11	21 05 21
5	14 38 42	15 28	+16 26	7 01	7 14	11 44	16 25	16 12	2 55 08	21 01 25
6	14 42 40	15 47	+16 24	7 03	7 16	11 44	16 24	16 10	2 59 04	20 57 29
7	14 46 39	16 05	+16 22	7 05	7 19	11 44	16 22	16 08	3 03 01	20 53 33
8	14 50 39	16 22	+16 18	7 07	7 21	11 44	16 20	16 06	3 06 57	20 49 37
9	14 54 39	16 40	+16 14	7 08	7 23	11 44	16 19	16 04	3 10 54	20 45 41
10	14 58 41	16 57	+16 09	7 10	7 25	11 44	16 17	16 02	3 14 50	20 41 46
11	15 02 43	17 14	+16 04	7 12	7 27	11 44	16 15	16 00	3 18 47	20 37 50
12	15 06 46	17 31	+15 57	7 14	7 29	11 44	16 14	15 58	3 22 44	20 33 54
13	15 10 50	17 47	+15 50	7 15	7 31	11 44	16 12	15 56	3 26 40	20 29 58
14	15 14 55	18 03	+15 42	7 17	7 33	11 44	16 11	15 55	3 30 37	20 26 02
15	15 19 01	18 19	+15 32	7 19	7 35	11 45	16 10	15 53	3 34 33	20 22 06
16	15 23 07	18 34	+15 23	7 21	7 38	11 45	16 08	15 51	3 38 30	20 18 10
17	15 27 14	18 49	+15 12	7 22	7 40	11 45	16 07	15 50	3 42 26	20 14 14
18	15 31 23	19 04	+15 00	7 24	7 42	11 45	16 05	15 48	3 46 23	20 10 18
19	15 35 31	19 18	+14 48	7 26	7 44	11 45	16 04	15 46	3 50 19	20 06 22
20	15 39 41	19 32	+14 35	7 28	7 46	11 46	16 03	15 45	3 54 16	20 02 26
21	15 43 52	19 46	+14 21	7 29	7 48	11 46	16 02	15 43	3 58 13	19 58 31
22	15 48 03	19 59	+14 06	7 31	7 50	11 46	16 01	15 42	4 02 09	19 54 35
23	15 52 15	20 12	+13 51	7 33	7 52	11 46	16 00	15 41	4 06 06	19 50 39
24	15 56 28	20 24	+13 34	7 34	7 53	11 47	15 58	15 39	4 10 02	19 46 43
25	16 00 42	20 37	+13 17	7 36	7 55	11 47	15 58	15 38	4 13 59	19 42 47
26	16 04 56	20 48	+12 59	7 37	7 57	11 47	15 57	15 37	4 17 55	19 38 51
27	16 09 11	21 00	+12 40	7 39	7 59	11 47	15 56	15 36	4 21 52	19 34 55
28	16 13 27	21 11	+12 21	7 40	8 01	11 48	15 55	15 34	4 25 48	19 30 59
29	16 17 44	21 22	+12 01	7 42	8 03	11 48	15 54	15 33	4 29 45	19 27 03
30	16 22 02	21 32	+11 40	7 43	8 04	11 49	15 53	15 32	4 33 42	19 23 07

DURATION OF TWILIGHT (in minutes)

Latitude	52°	56°	52°	56°	52°	56°	52°	56°
	1 November		11 November		21 November		30 November	
Civil	36	40	37	41	38	43	39	45
Nautical	75	84	78	87	80	90	82	93
Astronomical	115	127	117	130	120	134	123	137

THE NIGHT SKY

Mercury is unsuitably placed for observation at first, inferior conjunction (and a transit across the face of the Sun) occurring on the 15th. During the last week of the month the planet is visible as a morning object, magnitude +1.0 to −0.5, low above the south-eastern horizon at the beginning of morning civil twilight. See page 66 for details of the transit.

Venus continues to be visible as a magnificent object, completely dominating the south-eastern sky for several hours before dawn, magnitude −4.3. On the morning of the 4th the old crescent Moon, four days before New, will be seen about 5° to the left of the planet. On the morning of the 29th Venus passes 5° N. of Spica.

Mars is still an evening object, low in the south-western sky in the early part of the evening, magnitude +0.8. The crescent Moon will be seen about 2° above the planet on the evening of the 13th. Towards the end of the month Mars moves from Sagittarius into Capricornus.

Jupiter, just past opposition, continues to be visible for the greater part of the night, magnitude −2.9. On the evening of the 20th the gibbous Moon will be seen passing 5° below the planet.

Saturn, magnitude −0.2, reaches opposition on the 6th and thus is visible throughout the hours of darkness. Saturn is in Aries. On the night of the 21st to 22nd the gibbous Moon will be seen passing 4° below the planet.

Meteors. Although the Leonids do not usually produce a brilliant display, there could be a sharp peak in the number of meteors seen within about an hour of midnight on the 17th to 18th; if so, it will be a noticeable display. The Moon, just past First Quarter, will not provide much interference as it will be low in the south-west, setting at half past midnight.

THE MOON

Day	RA h m	Dec. °	Hor. par. '	Semi-diam. '	Sun's co-long. °	PA of Bright Limb °	Phase %	Age d	Rise 52° h m	Rise 56° h m	Transit h m	Set 52° h m	Set 56° h m
1	9 08	+17.0	58.0	15.8	180	107	45	22.5	—	23 54	6 43	14 19	14 33
2	10 02	+13.8	57.4	15.6	192	111	34	23.5	0 07	—	7 34	14 48	14 58
3	10 53	+10.0	56.7	15.5	204	114	25	24.5	1 18	1 10	8 22	15 12	15 18
4	11 42	+ 5.8	56.2	15.3	216	117	16	25.5	2 29	2 25	9 08	15 34	15 36
5	12 30	+ 1.4	55.6	15.2	228	119	10	26.5	3 38	3 38	9 52	15 55	15 53
6	13 17	− 3.0	55.2	15.0	241	122	5	27.5	4 46	4 50	10 36	16 15	16 10
7	14 03	− 7.2	54.8	14.9	253	131	1	28.5	5 54	6 01	11 20	16 37	16 28
8	14 50	−11.1	54.5	14.8	265	177	0	29.5	7 00	7 11	12 04	17 01	16 49
9	15 37	−14.5	54.2	14.8	277	257	1	0.8	8 04	8 19	12 49	17 28	17 12
10	16 25	−17.3	54.1	14.7	289	268	3	1.8	9 07	9 25	13 36	18 00	17 41
11	17 14	−19.3	54.0	14.7	302	268	7	2.8	10 06	10 26	14 23	18 37	18 17
12	18 04	−20.5	54.0	14.7	314	266	13	3.8	10 59	11 21	15 11	19 22	19 00
13	18 55	−20.8	54.2	14.8	326	263	20	4.8	11 47	12 08	15 59	20 14	19 53
14	19 45	−20.2	54.5	14.8	338	259	28	5.8	12 27	12 47	16 47	21 12	20 53
15	20 36	−18.6	54.9	15.0	350	255	37	6.8	13 02	13 19	17 36	22 15	22 00
16	21 27	−16.2	55.5	15.1	3	252	46	7.8	13 32	13 45	18 24	23 23	23 11
17	22 17	−13.0	56.3	15.3	15	249	56	8.8	13 58	14 08	19 11	—	—
18	23 07	− 9.0	57.2	15.6	27	246	66	9.8	14 22	14 28	20 00	0 35	0 27
19	23 58	− 4.5	58.2	15.8	39	244	76	10.8	14 46	14 47	20 49	1 49	1 45
20	0 50	+ 0.4	59.1	16.1	51	243	85	11.8	15 10	15 07	21 41	3 06	3 07
21	1 44	+ 5.4	60.0	16.4	63	241	92	12.8	15 36	15 28	22 35	4 27	4 32
22	2 40	+10.3	60.8	16.6	75	237	97	13.8	16 06	15 54	23 32	5 50	6 00
23	3 39	+14.6	61.2	16.7	88	208	100	14.8	16 42	16 26	—	7 14	7 29
24	4 41	+18.0	61.4	16.7	100	104	99	15.8	17 27	17 07	0 33	8 36	8 55
25	5 45	+20.2	61.2	16.7	112	96	96	16.8	18 22	18 01	1 35	9 50	10 11
26	6 49	+20.9	60.7	16.5	124	98	89	17.8	19 27	19 07	2 38	10 53	11 14
27	7 52	+20.1	60.0	16.3	136	101	81	18.8	20 39	20 21	3 39	11 43	12 02
28	8 52	+18.0	59.1	16.1	148	106	71	19.8	21 53	21 39	4 37	12 22	12 37
29	9 48	+15.0	58.2	15.9	160	109	61	20.8	23 07	22 57	5 30	12 53	13 05
30	10 41	+11.2	57.4	15.6	173	112	50	21.8	—	—	6 20	13 19	13 27

MERCURY

Day	RA h m	Dec. °	Diam. "	Phase %	Transit h m	5° high 52° h m	5° high 56° h m
1	15 51	−23.1	8	45	13 11	16 12	15 37
3	15 55	−23.2	8	38	13 06	16 08	15 32
5	15 56	−23.0	8	31	12 59	16 02	15 27
7	15 55	−22.7	9	24	12 50	15 56	15 23
9	15 52	−22.1	9	16	12 38	15 50	15 18
11	15 46	−21.2	10	9	12 23	15 43	15 13
13	15 38	−20.2	10	3	12 07	15 35	15 08
15	15 28	−18.9	10	0	11 49	8 12	8 37
17	15 18	−17.6	10	1	11 31	7 45	8 07
19	15 08	−16.3	10	4	11 14	7 20	7 41
21	15 01	−15.3	9	11	11 00	7 00	7 18
23	14 57	−14.6	9	19	10 49	6 44	7 01
25	14 56	−14.2	8	29	10 40	6 33	6 50
27	14 57	−14.2	8	38	10 34	6 26	6 44
29	15 00	−14.4	7	47	10 30	6 24	6 42
31	15 06	−14.9	7	55	10 28	6 25	6 44

VENUS

Day	RA h m	Dec. °	Diam. "	Phase %	Transit h m	5° high 52° h m	5° high 56° h m
1	11 30	+ 3.7	24	51	8 50	3 04	3 05
6	11 49	+ 2.0	23	54	8 50	3 13	3 14
11	12 09	+ 0.3	22	56	8 51	3 22	3 25
16	12 30	− 1.5	21	58	8 51	3 32	3 37
21	12 50	− 3.5	20	61	8 52	3 43	3 50
26	13 12	− 5.4	19	63	8 54	3 55	4 03
31	13 33	− 7.4	18	65	8 56	4 08	4 18

MARS

Day	RA h m	Dec. °	Diam. "	Phase %	Transit h m	5° high 52° h m	5° high 56° h m
1	18 48	−24.7	6	89	16 08	18 57	18 15
6	19 04	−24.3	6	89	16 05	18 57	18 17
11	19 21	−23.8	6	89	16 01	18 58	18 21
16	19 37	−23.2	6	90	15 58	19 01	18 25
21	19 53	−22.5	6	90	15 54	19 03	18 30
26	20 09	−21.6	6	90	15 51	19 07	18 36
31	20 25	−20.7	6	91	15 47	19 10	18 42

SUNRISE AND SUNSET

	London		Bristol		Birmingham		Manchester		Newcastle		Glasgow		Belfast	
	0°05′	51°30′	2°35′	51°28′	1°55′	52°28′	2°15′	53°28′	1°37′	54°59′	4°14′	55°52′	5°56′	54°35′
	h m	h m	h m	h m	h m	h m	h m	h m	h m	h m	h m	h m	h m	h m
1	6 53	16 34	7 03	16 44	7 03	16 39	7 07	16 37	7 09	16 30	7 22	16 38	7 25	16 49
2	6 55	16 32	7 05	16 43	7 05	16 37	7 09	16 35	7 11	16 28	7 24	16 36	7 27	16 47
3	6 56	16 31	7 06	16 41	7 07	16 35	7 11	16 34	7 13	16 26	7 27	16 34	7 29	16 45
4	6 58	16 29	7 08	16 39	7 08	16 33	7 13	16 32	7 15	16 24	7 29	16 31	7 31	16 43
5	7 00	16 27	7 10	16 37	7 10	16 32	7 15	16 30	7 17	16 22	7 31	16 29	7 33	16 41
6	7 02	16 25	7 12	16 36	7 12	16 30	7 17	16 28	7 19	16 20	7 33	16 27	7 35	16 39
7	7 03	16 24	7 13	16 34	7 14	16 28	7 18	16 26	7 21	16 18	7 35	16 25	7 37	16 37
8	7 05	16 22	7 15	16 32	7 16	16 26	7 20	16 24	7 23	16 16	7 37	16 23	7 39	16 35
9	7 07	16 21	7 17	16 31	7 18	16 25	7 22	16 23	7 25	16 14	7 39	16 21	7 41	16 33
10	7 09	16 19	7 19	16 29	7 19	16 23	7 24	16 21	7 27	16 13	7 41	16 19	7 43	16 31
11	7 11	16 17	7 20	16 28	7 21	16 22	7 26	16 19	7 29	16 11	7 44	16 18	7 45	16 30
12	7 12	16 16	7 22	16 26	7 23	16 20	7 28	16 18	7 31	16 09	7 46	16 16	7 47	16 28
13	7 14	16 15	7 24	16 25	7 25	16 18	7 30	16 16	7 33	16 07	7 48	16 14	7 49	16 26
14	7 16	16 13	7 26	16 23	7 27	16 17	7 32	16 14	7 35	16 06	7 50	16 12	7 51	16 25
15	7 17	16 12	7 27	16 22	7 28	16 15	7 34	16 13	7 37	16 04	7 52	16 10	7 53	16 23
16	7 19	16 10	7 29	16 20	7 30	16 14	7 35	16 11	7 39	16 02	7 54	16 09	7 55	16 21
17	7 21	16 09	7 31	16 19	7 32	16 13	7 37	16 10	7 41	16 01	7 56	16 07	7 57	16 20
18	7 23	16 08	7 32	16 18	7 34	16 11	7 39	16 09	7 43	15 59	7 58	16 06	7 59	16 18
19	7 24	16 07	7 34	16 17	7 35	16 10	7 41	16 07	7 45	15 58	8 00	16 04	8 01	16 17
20	7 26	16 05	7 36	16 15	7 37	16 09	7 43	16 06	7 47	15 56	8 02	16 02	8 03	16 15
21	7 28	16 04	7 37	16 14	7 39	16 08	7 44	16 05	7 49	15 55	8 04	16 01	8 04	16 14
22	7 29	16 03	7 39	16 13	7 41	16 06	7 46	16 03	7 51	15 54	8 06	16 00	8 06	16 13
23	7 31	16 02	7 41	16 12	7 42	16 05	7 48	16 02	7 53	15 52	8 08	15 58	8 08	16 12
24	7 32	16 01	7 42	16 11	7 44	16 04	7 50	16 01	7 55	15 51	8 10	15 57	8 10	16 10
25	7 34	16 00	7 44	16 10	7 45	16 03	7 51	16 00	7 56	15 50	8 12	15 56	8 12	16 09
26	7 36	15 59	7 45	16 09	7 47	16 02	7 53	15 59	7 58	15 49	8 13	15 54	8 13	16 08
27	7 37	15 58	7 47	16 08	7 49	16 01	7 55	15 58	8 00	15 48	8 15	15 53	8 15	16 07
28	7 39	15 57	7 48	16 07	7 50	16 00	7 56	15 57	8 02	15 47	8 17	15 52	8 17	16 06
29	7 40	15 57	7 50	16 07	7 52	15 59	7 58	15 56	8 03	15 46	8 19	15 51	8 18	16 05
30	7 42	15 56	7 51	16 06	7 53	15 59	8 00	15 55	8 05	15 45	8 20	15 50	8 20	16 04

JUPITER

Day	RA	Dec.	Transit	5° high	
				52°	56°
	h m	° ′	h m	h m	h m
1	1 49.4	+ 9 38	23 06	5 26	5 30
11	1 44.5	+ 9 12	22 22	4 40	4 44
21	1 40.4	+ 8 51	21 38	3 54	3 58
31	1 37.3	+ 8 36	20 56	3 11	3 14

Diameters – equatorial 49″ polar 46″

SATURN

Day	RA	Dec.	Transit	5° high	
				52°	56°
	h m	° ′	h m	h m	h m
1	2 50.0	+13 35	0 11	6 47	6 55
11	2 46.8	+13 21	23 24	6 03	6 11
21	2 43.7	+13 08	22 41	5 20	5 27
31	2 40.8	+12 56	21 59	4 37	4 44

Diameters – equatorial 20″ polar 18″
Rings – major axis 46″ minor axis 15″

URANUS

Day	RA	Dec.	Transit	10° high	
				52°	56°
	h m	° ′	h m	h m	h m
1	21 02.3	−17 36	18 20	21 21	20 49
11	21 02.7	−17 34	17 41	20 43	20 10
21	21 03.5	−17 30	17 03	20 05	19 32
31	21 04.6	−17 25	16 24	19 27	18 55

Diameter 4″

NEPTUNE

Day	RA	Dec.	Transit	10° high	
				52°	56°
	h m	° ′	h m	h m	h m
1	20 15.5	−19 32	17 33	20 17	19 38
11	20 16.0	−19 31	16 54	19 39	18 59
21	20 16.7	−19 29	16 16	19 01	18 21
31	20 17.7	−19 26	15 38	18 23	17 43

Diameter 2″

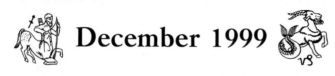

December 1999

TWELFTH MONTH, 31 DAYS. *Decem* (ten), tenth month of Roman pre-Julian calendar

1	*Wednesday*	Henry I d. 1135. Woody Allen b. 1935	*week* 48 *day* 335
2	*Thursday*	John Brown executed 1859. Stephen Potter d. 1969	336
3	*Friday*	Robert Louis Stevenson d. 1894. Pierre Renoir d. 1919	337
4	*Saturday*	CHANUCAH begins. Frank Zappa d. 1993	338
5	*Sunday*	**2nd S. of Advent.** Walt Disney b. 1901	*week* 49 *day* 339
6	*Monday*	Henry VI b. 1421. Anthony Trollope d. 1882	340
7	*Tuesday*	Henry, Lord Darnley b. 1545. Capt Bligh d. 1817	341
8	*Wednesday*	Mary, Queen of Scots b. 1542. John Lennon killed 1980	342
9	*Thursday*	RAMADAN begins. John Milton b. 1608	343
10	*Friday*	Royal Academy founded 1768. Alfred Nobel d. 1896	344
11	*Saturday*	Alexander Solzhenitsyn b. 1918. Willie Rushton d. 1996	345
12	*Sunday*	**3rd S. of Advent.** John Osborne b. 1929	*week* 50 *day* 346
13	*Monday*	Dr Johnson d. 1784. Battle of the River Plate 1939	347
14	*Tuesday*	George Washington d. 1799. Andrei Sakharov d. 1989	348
15	*Wednesday*	Harold Abrahams b. 1899. Walt Disney d. 1966	349
16	*Thursday*	Jane Austen b. 1775. Sir Noel Coward b. 1899	350
17	*Friday*	Sir Humphrey Davy b. 1778. Elizabeth Garrett Anderson d. 1917	351
18	*Saturday*	Sir John Alcock d. 1919. Ben Travers d. 1980	352
19	*Sunday*	**4th S. of Advent.** Stella Gibbons d. 1989	*week* 51 *day* 353
20	*Monday*	Sir Robert Menzies b. 1894. John Steinbeck d. 1968	354
21	*Tuesday*	*Michaelmas Law Sittings end.* Joseph Stalin b. 1879	355
22	*Wednesday*	Dame Peggy Ashcroft b. 1907. Samuel Beckett d. 1989	356
23	*Thursday*	Richard Arkwright b. 1732. Ronnie Scott d. 1996	357
24	*Friday*	King John b. 1167. John Osborne d. 1994	358
25	*Saturday*	**Christmas Day.** Humphrey Bogart b. 1899	359
26	*Sunday*	**St Stephen. 1st S. of Christmas.** Boxing Day	*week* 52 *day* 360
27	*Monday*	**St John.** *Bank Holiday in the UK*	361
28	*Tuesday*	**Holy Innocents.** *Bank Holiday in the UK*	362
29	*Wednesday*	Thomas à Becket killed 1170. Christina Rossetti d. 1894	363
30	*Thursday*	Rudyard Kipling b. 1865. Richard Rodgers d. 1979	364
31	*Friday*	*Bank Holiday in the UK.* Henri Matisse b. 1869	365

ASTRONOMICAL PHENOMENA

d	h	
3	00	Pluto in conjunction
3	01	Mercury at greatest elongation W.20°
3	23	Venus in conjunction with Moon. Venus 3° S.
6	02	Mercury in conjunction with Moon. Mercury 3° S.
12	18	Mars in conjunction with Moon. Mars 0°.6 S.
18	08	Jupiter in conjunction with Moon. Jupiter 4° N.
19	11	Saturn in conjunction with Moon. Saturn 3° N.
20	15	Jupiter at stationary point
22	08	Sun's longitude 270° ♑

MINIMA OF ALGOL

d	h	d	h	d	h
1	06.7	12	17.9	24	05.2
4	03.5	15	14.8	27	02.0
7	00.3	18	11.6	29	22.9
9	21.1	21	08.4		

CONSTELLATIONS

The following constellations are near the meridian at

	d	h		d	h
November	1	24	December	16	21
November	15	23	January	1	20
December	1	22	January	16	19

Ursa Major (below the Pole), Ursa Minor (below the Pole), Cassiopeia, Andromeda, Perseus, Triangulum, Aries, Taurus, Cetus and Eridanus

THE MOON

Phases, Apsides and Node	d	h	m
● New Moon	7	22	32
☽ First Quarter	16	00	50
○ Full Moon	22	17	31
☾ Last Quarter	29	14	04
Apogee (406,628 km)	8	11	20
Perigee (356,656 km)	22	11	01

Mean longitude of ascending node on December 1, 127°

THE SUN

s.d. 16′.3

Day	Right Ascension	Dec. −	Equation of time	Rise 52°	Rise 56°	Transit	Set 52°	Set 56°	Sidereal time	Transit of First Point of Aries
	h m s	° ′	m s	h m	h m	h m	h m	h m	h m s	h m s
1	16 26 20	21 42	+11 18	7 45	8 06	11 49	15 53	15 31	4 37 38	19 19 11
2	16 30 38	21 51	+10 56	7 46	8 08	11 49	15 52	15 30	4 41 35	19 15 16
3	16 34 58	22 00	+10 33	7 48	8 09	11 50	15 51	15 30	4 45 31	19 11 20
4	16 39 18	22 09	+10 10	7 49	8 11	11 50	15 51	15 29	4 49 28	19 07 24
5	16 43 39	22 17	+ 9 46	7 50	8 12	11 50	15 50	15 28	4 53 24	19 03 28
6	16 48 00	22 24	+ 9 21	7 52	8 14	11 51	15 50	15 28	4 57 21	18 59 32
7	16 52 22	22 32	+ 8 56	7 53	8 15	11 51	15 49	15 27	5 01 17	18 55 36
8	16 56 44	22 38	+ 8 30	7 54	8 17	11 52	15 49	15 27	5 05 14	18 51 40
9	17 01 07	22 45	+ 8 03	7 55	8 18	11 52	15 49	15 26	5 09 11	18 47 44
10	17 05 30	22 51	+ 7 37	7 56	8 19	11 53	15 49	15 26	5 13 07	18 43 48
11	17 09 54	22 56	+ 7 10	7 57	8 20	11 53	15 48	15 25	5 17 04	18 39 52
12	17 14 18	23 01	+ 6 42	7 58	8 22	11 54	15 48	15 25	5 21 00	18 35 56
13	17 18 43	23 06	+ 6 14	7 59	8 23	11 54	15 48	15 25	5 24 57	18 32 01
14	17 23 08	23 10	+ 5 46	8 00	8 24	11 54	15 48	15 25	5 28 53	18 28 05
15	17 27 33	23 14	+ 5 17	8 01	8 25	11 55	15 48	15 25	5 32 50	18 24 09
16	17 31 58	23 17	+ 4 48	8 02	8 26	11 55	15 49	15 25	5 36 46	18 20 13
17	17 36 24	23 20	+ 4 19	8 03	8 27	11 56	15 49	15 25	5 40 43	18 16 17
18	17 40 50	23 22	+ 3 50	8 04	8 27	11 56	15 49	15 25	5 44 40	18 12 21
19	17 45 15	23 24	+ 3 21	8 04	8 28	11 57	15 49	15 26	5 48 36	18 08 25
20	17 49 42	23 25	+ 2 51	8 05	8 29	11 57	15 50	15 26	5 52 33	18 04 29
21	17 54 08	23 26	+ 2 21	8 06	8 29	11 58	15 50	15 26	5 56 29	18 00 33
22	17 58 34	23 26	+ 1 52	8 06	8 30	11 58	15 51	15 27	6 00 26	17 56 37
23	18 03 00	23 26	+ 1 22	8 07	8 30	11 59	15 51	15 27	6 04 22	17 52 41
24	18 07 27	23 26	+ 0 52	8 07	8 31	11 59	15 52	15 28	6 08 19	17 48 46
25	18 11 53	23 25	+ 0 23	8 07	8 31	12 00	15 52	15 29	6 12 15	17 44 50
26	18 16 19	23 23	− 0 07	8 08	8 31	12 00	15 53	15 29	6 16 12	17 40 54
27	18 20 45	23 21	− 0 37	8 08	8 32	12 01	15 54	15 30	6 20 09	17 36 58
28	18 25 11	23 19	− 1 06	8 08	8 32	12 01	15 55	15 31	6 24 05	17 33 02
29	18 29 37	23 16	− 1 36	8 08	8 32	12 02	15 56	15 32	6 28 02	17 29 06
30	18 34 03	23 12	− 2 05	8 08	8 32	12 02	15 57	15 33	6 31 58	17 25 10
31	18 38 29	23 09	− 2 34	8 08	8 32	12 03	15 58	15 34	6 35 55	17 21 14

DURATION OF TWILIGHT (in minutes)

Latitude	52°	56°	52°	56°	52°	56°	52°	56°
	1 December		11 December		21 December		31 December	
Civil	40	45	41	47	41	47	41	47
Nautical	82	93	84	96	85	97	84	96
Astronomical	123	138	125	141	126	142	125	141

THE NIGHT SKY

Mercury continues to be visible in the mornings for the first half of the month, magnitude − 0.5. It may be glimpsed low above the south-eastern horizon at the beginning of morning twilight. This is the most suitable morning apparition of the year for observers in the northern hemisphere. On the morning of the 6th, the old crescent Moon, less than two days before New, may be detected about 3° to the left of the planet. For the remainder of the year Mercury is too close to the Sun for observation.

Venus, magnitude − 4.2, is still a brilliant object in the south-eastern sky in the early mornings. On the morning of the 4th the old crescent Moon will be seen about 5° to the left of the planet.

Mars, magnitude +1.0, continues to be visible low in the south-western sky in the early evenings. Although Mars has moved some 7°–8° nearer to the Sun during December, the period of time available for observation increases as the planet moves northward in declination. Shortly before the end of the year it moves from Capricornus into Aquarius. Before the crescent Moon sets on the evening of the 12th it will actually pass in front of the planet, though this will occur at a very low altitude (*see* page 67.)

Jupiter, magnitude − 2.7, continues to be visible as a brilliant object in the night sky, though by the end of the year it has sunk too low in the western sky to be visible after about 01h. On the night of the 17th to 18th the gibbous Moon passes 7° below the planet. Jupiter reaches its second stationary point on the 21st, in Aries, and then resumes its direct motion.

Saturn is an evening object, magnitude 0.0, visible from the end of evening twilight until the early hours of the morning. Jupiter has gradually been catching up with Saturn; the two bodies were 35° apart at the beginning of the year and only 15° at the end. Jupiter will pass Saturn at the end of May 2000; they will then be about 15° from the Sun.

Meteors. The maximum of the well-known Geminid meteor shower occurs on the morning of the 14th. Conditions are favourable as the Moon sets several hours before midnight.

THE MOON

Day	RA	Dec.	Hor. par.	Semi- diam.	Sun's co- long.	PA of Bright Limb	Phase	Age	Rise 52°	Rise 56°	Transit	Set 52°	Set 56°
	h m	°	'	'	°	°	%	d	h m	h m	h m	h m	h m
1	11 32	+ 7.0	56.6	15.4	185	114	39	22.8	0 19	0 13	7 07	13 42	13 45
2	12 19	+ 2.6	55.9	15.2	197	115	30	23.8	1 29	1 27	7 52	14 02	14 02
3	13 06	− 1.8	55.3	15.1	209	116	21	24.8	2 37	2 39	8 35	14 22	14 19
4	13 52	− 6.1	54.8	14.9	221	116	14	25.8	3 44	3 50	9 19	14 43	14 36
5	14 38	−10.1	54.4	14.8	234	116	8	26.8	4 51	5 00	10 02	15 05	14 55
6	15 25	−13.6	54.2	14.8	246	117	4	27.8	5 56	6 09	10 47	15 31	15 16
7	16 12	−16.6	54.0	14.7	258	124	1	28.8	6 59	7 16	11 33	16 01	15 43
8	17 01	−18.9	53.9	14.7	270	196	0	0.1	8 00	8 19	12 19	16 36	16 16
9	17 51	−20.4	53.9	14.7	282	256	1	1.1	8 55	9 17	13 07	17 18	16 56
10	18 42	−20.9	54.0	14.7	294	261	4	2.1	9 45	10 07	13 56	18 07	17 46
11	19 32	−20.6	54.2	14.8	307	259	8	3.1	10 28	10 49	14 44	19 03	18 43
12	20 23	−19.3	54.5	14.9	319	256	14	4.1	11 05	11 23	15 32	20 05	19 47
13	21 13	−17.1	54.9	15.0	331	253	21	5.1	11 36	11 51	16 19	21 10	20 56
14	22 03	−14.2	55.5	15.1	343	251	30	6.1	12 03	12 14	17 06	22 18	22 09
15	22 52	−10.5	56.1	15.3	355	248	40	7.1	12 27	12 34	17 53	23 29	23 24
16	23 41	− 6.3	56.9	15.5	7	247	50	8.1	12 49	12 52	18 40	—	—
17	0 31	− 1.7	57.8	15.8	20	246	60	9.1	13 11	13 11	19 28	0 43	0 41
18	1 22	+ 3.2	58.8	16.0	32	246	71	10.1	13 35	13 30	20 19	1 59	2 02
19	2 15	+ 8.1	59.7	16.3	44	247	81	11.1	14 02	13 52	21 13	3 18	3 26
20	3 12	+12.6	60.5	16.5	56	248	89	12.1	14 33	14 19	22 11	4 40	4 52
21	4 11	+16.5	61.1	16.7	68	250	95	13.1	15 12	14 55	23 12	6 03	6 19
22	5 14	+19.3	61.4	16.7	80	246	99	14.1	16 02	15 41	—	7 22	7 42
23	6 19	+20.8	61.4	16.7	92	126	100	15.1	17 03	16 41	0 16	8 33	8 55
24	7 24	+20.7	61.1	16.6	105	102	98	16.1	18 14	17 54	1 19	9 32	9 52
25	8 28	+19.2	60.4	16.5	117	104	93	17.1	19 30	19 14	2 21	10 18	10 35
26	9 28	+16.4	59.6	16.2	129	107	85	18.1	20 48	20 36	3 19	10 54	11 07
27	10 24	+12.7	58.6	16.0	141	110	76	19.1	22 04	21 56	4 13	11 23	11 32
28	11 17	+ 8.5	57.6	15.7	153	112	66	20.1	23 16	23 13	5 02	11 47	11 52
29	12 06	+ 4.0	56.7	15.5	165	113	56	21.1	—	—	5 49	12 09	12 10
30	12 54	− 0.5	55.9	15.2	177	113	46	22.1	0 26	0 27	6 34	12 29	12 27
31	13 41	− 4.9	55.2	15.0	190	113	36	23.1	1 35	1 39	7 17	12 50	12 44

MERCURY

Day	RA	Dec.	Diam.	Phase	Transit	5° high 52°	5° high 56°
	h m	°	"	%	h m	h m	h m
1	15 06	−14.9	7	55	10 28	6 25	6 44
3	15 13	−15.5	7	62	10 28	6 29	6 48
5	15 22	−16.2	6	68	10 29	6 34	6 55
7	15 31	−17.0	6	73	10 30	6 41	7 03
9	15 41	−17.8	6	77	10 33	6 49	7 13
11	15 52	−18.6	6	81	10 36	6 58	7 23
13	16 03	−19.4	6	84	10 39	7 08	7 34
15	16 15	−20.2	5	86	10 43	7 17	7 45
17	16 27	−20.9	5	88	10 47	7 27	7 57
19	16 40	−21.6	5	90	10 52	7 37	8 09
21	16 52	−22.2	5	92	10 57	7 47	8 21
23	17 05	−22.8	5	93	11 02	7 57	8 32
25	17 18	−23.3	5	94	11 07	8 06	8 43
27	17 31	−23.7	5	95	11 12	8 15	8 54
29	17 45	−24.0	5	96	11 18	8 24	9 03
31	17 58	−24.3	5	97	11 24	8 32	9 12

VENUS

Day	RA	Dec.	Diam.	Phase	Transit	5° high 52°	5° high 56°
	h m	°	"	%	h m	h m	h m
1	13 33	− 7.4	18	65	8 56	4 08	4 18
6	13 55	− 9.4	17	67	8 58	4 21	4 33
11	14 18	−11.3	17	69	9 01	4 35	4 49
16	14 40	−13.2	16	70	9 04	4 50	5 06
21	15 04	−14.9	16	72	9 08	5 05	5 23
26	15 28	−16.6	15	74	9 12	5 20	5 41
31	15 52	−18.0	15	75	9 17	5 35	5 58

MARS

Day	RA	Dec.	Diam.	Phase	Transit	5° high 52°	5° high 56°
	h m	°	"	%	h m	h m	h m
1	20 25	−20.7	6	91	15 47	19 10	18 42
6	20 41	−19.7	5	91	15 43	19 14	18 48
11	20 57	−18.7	5	91	15 39	19 18	18 54
16	21 12	−17.5	5	92	15 35	19 22	19 00
21	21 27	−16.3	5	92	15 30	19 26	19 06
26	21 43	−15.0	5	92	15 26	19 30	19 12
31	21 58	−13.6	5	93	15 21	19 34	19 18

SUNRISE AND SUNSET

	London		Bristol		Birmingham		Manchester		Newcastle		Glasgow		Belfast	
	0°05'	51°30'	2°35'	51°28'	1°55'	52°28'	2°15'	53°28'	1°37'	54°59'	4°14'	55°52'	5°56'	54°35'
	h m	h m	h m	h m	h m	h m	h m	h m	h m	h m	h m	h m	h m	h m
1	7 43	15 55	7 53	16 05	7 55	15 58	8 01	15 54	8 07	15 44	8 22	15 49	8 22	16 03
2	7 44	15 55	7 54	16 05	7 56	15 57	8 02	15 54	8 08	15 43	8 24	15 48	8 23	16 02
3	7 46	15 54	7 56	16 04	7 58	15 57	8 04	15 53	8 10	15 42	8 25	15 47	8 25	16 02
4	7 47	15 53	7 57	16 04	7 59	15 56	8 05	15 52	8 11	15 41	8 27	15 47	8 26	16 01
5	7 48	15 53	7 58	16 03	8 00	15 56	8 07	15 52	8 13	15 41	8 28	15 46	8 28	16 00
6	7 50	15 53	7 59	16 03	8 02	15 55	8 08	15 51	8 14	15 40	8 30	15 45	8 29	16 00
7	7 51	15 52	8 01	16 02	8 03	15 55	8 09	15 51	8 15	15 40	8 31	15 45	8 30	15 59
8	7 52	15 52	8 02	16 02	8 04	15 54	8 11	15 50	8 17	15 39	8 33	15 44	8 32	15 59
9	7 53	15 52	8 03	16 02	8 05	15 54	8 12	15 50	8 18	15 39	8 34	15 44	8 33	15 59
10	7 54	15 51	8 04	16 02	8 06	15 54	8 13	15 50	8 19	15 39	8 35	15 44	8 34	15 58
11	7 55	15 51	8 05	16 01	8 08	15 54	8 14	15 50	8 21	15 38	8 37	15 43	8 35	15 58
12	7 56	15 51	8 06	16 01	8 09	15 54	8 15	15 50	8 22	15 38	8 38	15 43	8 37	15 58
13	7 57	15 51	8 07	16 01	8 10	15 54	8 16	15 49	8 23	15 38	8 39	15 43	8 38	15 58
14	7 58	15 51	8 08	16 01	8 11	15 54	8 17	15 49	8 24	15 38	8 40	15 43	8 39	15 58
15	7 59	15 51	8 09	16 02	8 11	15 54	8 18	15 50	8 25	15 38	8 41	15 43	8 40	15 58
16	8 00	15 52	8 10	16 02	8 12	15 54	8 19	15 50	8 26	15 38	8 42	15 43	8 40	15 58
17	8 01	15 52	8 11	16 02	8 13	15 54	8 20	15 50	8 26	15 38	8 43	15 43	8 41	15 58
18	8 01	15 52	8 11	16 02	8 14	15 54	8 21	15 50	8 27	15 38	8 43	15 43	8 42	15 58
19	8 02	15 52	8 12	16 02	8 14	15 55	8 21	15 50	8 28	15 39	8 44	15 43	8 43	15 58
20	8 03	15 53	8 13	16 03	8 15	15 55	8 22	15 51	8 29	15 39	8 45	15 44	8 43	15 59
21	8 03	15 53	8 13	16 03	8 16	15 55	8 23	15 51	8 29	15 40	8 45	15 44	8 44	15 59
22	8 04	15 54	8 14	16 04	8 16	15 56	8 23	15 52	8 30	15 40	8 46	15 45	8 44	16 00
23	8 04	15 54	8 14	16 04	8 17	15 56	8 24	15 52	8 30	15 41	8 46	15 45	8 45	16 00
24	8 05	15 55	8 15	16 05	8 17	15 57	8 24	15 53	8 31	15 41	8 47	15 46	8 45	16 01
25	8 05	15 55	8 15	16 06	8 17	15 58	8 24	15 53	8 31	15 42	8 47	15 47	8 46	16 02
26	8 05	15 56	8 15	16 06	8 18	15 58	8 25	15 54	8 31	15 43	8 47	15 47	8 46	16 02
27	8 06	15 57	8 15	16 07	8 18	15 59	8 25	15 55	8 31	15 43	8 48	15 48	8 46	16 03
28	8 06	15 58	8 16	16 08	8 18	16 00	8 25	15 56	8 32	15 44	8 48	15 49	8 46	16 04
29	8 06	15 59	8 16	16 09	8 18	16 01	8 25	15 57	8 32	15 45	8 48	15 50	8 46	16 05
30	8 06	15 59	8 16	16 10	8 18	16 02	8 25	15 58	8 32	15 46	8 48	15 51	8 46	16 06
31	8 06	16 00	8 16	16 11	8 18	16 03	8 25	15 59	8 31	15 47	8 48	15 52	8 46	16 07

JUPITER

Day	RA	Dec.	Transit	5° high	
				52°	56°
	h m	° '	h m	h m	h m
1	1 37.3	+ 8 36	20 56	3 11	3 14
11	1 35.3	+ 8 28	20 15	2 29	2 32
21	1 34.6	+ 8 27	19 35	1 49	1 52
31	1 35.3	+ 8 34	18 56	1 11	1 14

Diameters – equatorial 45" polar 42"

SATURN

Day	RA	Dec.	Transit	5° high	
				52°	56°
	h m	° '	h m	h m	h m
1	2 40.8	+12 56	21 59	4 37	4 44
11	2 38.4	+12 47	21 18	3 54	4 01
21	2 36.5	+12 40	20 36	3 12	3 19
31	2 35.2	+12 37	19 56	2 31	2 39

Diameters – equatorial 20" polar 18"
Rings – major axis 45" minor axis 15"

URANUS

Day	RA	Dec.	Transit	10° high	
				52°	56°
	h m	° '	h m	h m	h m
1	21 04.6	−17 25	16 24	19 27	18 55
11	21 06.0	−17 18	15 46	18 50	18 18
21	21 07.7	−17 11	15 09	18 14	17 42
31	21 09.6	−17 03	14 31	17 37	17 06

Diameter 4"

NEPTUNE

Day	RA	Dec.	Transit	10° high	
				52°	56°
	h m	° '	h m	h m	h m
1	20 17.7	−19 26	15 38	18 23	17 43
11	20 18.8	−19 22	14 59	17 45	17 06
21	20 20.1	−19 18	14 21	17 08	16 29
31	20 21.5	−19 14	13 43	16 30	15 52

Diameter 2"

RISING AND SETTING TIMES

TABLE 1. SEMI-DIURNAL ARCS (HOUR ANGLES AT RISING/SETTING)

Dec.	Latitude 0°	10°	20°	30°	40°	45°	50°	52°	54°	56°	58°	60°	Dec.
	h m	h m	h m	h m	h m	h m	h m	h m	h m	h m	h m	h m	
0°	6 00	6 00	6 00	6 00	6 00	6 00	6 00	6 00	6 00	6 00	6 00	6 00	0°
1°	6 00	6 01	6 01	6 02	6 03	6 04	6 05	6 05	6 06	6 06	6 06	6 07	1°
2°	6 00	6 01	6 03	6 05	6 07	6 08	6 10	6 10	6 11	6 12	6 13	6 14	2°
3°	6 00	6 02	6 04	6 07	6 10	6 12	6 14	6 15	6 17	6 18	6 19	6 21	3°
4°	6 00	6 03	6 06	6 09	6 13	6 16	6 19	6 21	6 22	6 24	6 26	6 28	4°
5°	6 00	6 04	6 07	6 12	6 17	6 20	6 24	6 26	6 28	6 30	6 32	6 35	5°
6°	6 00	6 04	6 09	6 14	6 20	6 24	6 29	6 31	6 33	6 36	6 39	6 42	6°
7°	6 00	6 05	6 10	6 16	6 24	6 28	6 34	6 36	6 39	6 42	6 45	6 49	7°
8°	6 00	6 06	6 12	6 19	6 27	6 32	6 39	6 41	6 45	6 48	6 52	6 56	8°
9°	6 00	6 06	6 13	6 21	6 31	6 36	6 44	6 47	6 50	6 54	6 59	7 04	9°
10°	6 00	6 07	6 15	6 23	6 34	6 41	6 49	6 52	6 56	7 01	7 06	7 11	10°
11°	6 00	6 08	6 16	6 26	6 38	6 45	6 54	6 58	7 02	7 07	7 12	7 19	11°
12°	6 00	6 09	6 18	6 28	6 41	6 49	6 59	7 03	7 08	7 13	7 20	7 26	12°
13°	6 00	6 09	6 19	6 31	6 45	6 53	7 04	7 09	7 14	7 20	7 27	7 34	13°
14°	6 00	6 10	6 21	6 33	6 48	6 58	7 09	7 14	7 20	7 27	7 34	7 42	14°
15°	6 00	6 11	6 22	6 36	6 52	7 02	7 14	7 20	7 27	7 34	7 42	7 51	15°
16°	6 00	6 12	6 24	6 38	6 56	7 07	7 20	7 26	7 33	7 41	7 49	7 59	16°
17°	6 00	6 12	6 26	6 41	6 59	7 11	7 25	7 32	7 40	7 48	7 57	8 08	17°
18°	6 00	6 13	6 27	6 43	7 03	7 16	7 31	7 38	7 46	7 55	8 05	8 17	18°
19°	6 00	6 14	6 29	6 46	7 07	7 21	7 37	7 45	7 53	8 03	8 14	8 26	19°
20°	6 00	6 15	6 30	6 49	7 11	7 25	7 43	7 51	8 00	8 11	8 22	8 36	20°
21°	6 00	6 16	6 32	6 51	7 15	7 30	7 49	7 58	8 08	8 19	8 32	8 47	21°
22°	6 00	6 16	6 34	6 54	7 19	7 35	7 55	8 05	8 15	8 27	8 41	8 58	22°
23°	6 00	6 17	6 36	6 57	7 23	7 40	8 02	8 12	8 23	8 36	8 51	9 09	23°
24°	6 00	6 18	6 37	7 00	7 28	7 46	8 08	8 19	8 31	8 45	9 02	9 22	24°
25°	6 00	6 19	6 39	7 02	7 32	7 51	8 15	8 27	8 40	8 55	9 13	9 35	25°
26°	6 00	6 20	6 41	7 05	7 37	7 57	8 22	8 35	8 49	9 05	9 25	9 51	26°
27°	6 00	6 21	6 43	7 08	7 41	8 03	8 30	8 43	8 58	9 16	9 39	10 08	27°
28°	6 00	6 22	6 45	7 12	7 46	8 08	8 37	8 52	9 08	9 28	9 53	10 28	28°
29°	6 00	6 22	6 47	7 15	7 51	8 15	8 45	9 01	9 19	9 41	10 10	10 55	29°
30°	6 00	6 23	6 49	7 18	7 56	8 21	8 54	9 11	9 30	9 55	10 30	12 00	30°
35°	6 00	6 28	6 59	7 35	8 24	8 58	9 46	10 15	10 58	12 00	12 00	12 00	35°
40°	6 00	6 34	7 11	7 56	8 59	9 48	12 00	12 00	12 00	12 00	12 00	12 00	40°
45°	6 00	6 41	7 25	8 21	9 48	12 00	12 00	12 00	12 00	12 00	12 00	12 00	45°
50°	6 00	6 49	7 43	8 54	12 00	12 00	12 00	12 00	12 00	12 00	12 00	12 00	50°
55°	6 00	6 58	8 05	9 42	12 00	12 00	12 00	12 00	12 00	12 00	12 00	12 00	55°
60°	6 00	7 11	8 36	12 00	12 00	12 00	12 00	12 00	12 00	12 00	12 00	12 00	60°
65°	6 00	7 29	9 25	12 00	12 00	12 00	12 00	12 00	12 00	12 00	12 00	12 00	65°
70°	6 00	7 56	12 00	12 00	12 00	12 00	12 00	12 00	12 00	12 00	12 00	12 00	70°
75°	6 00	8 45	12 00	12 00	12 00	12 00	12 00	12 00	12 00	12 00	12 00	12 00	75°
80°	6 00	12 00	12 00	12 00	12 00	12 00	12 00	12 00	12 00	12 00	12 00	12 00	80°

TABLE 2. CORRECTION FOR REFRACTION AND SEMI-DIAMETER

	m	m	m	m	m	m	m	m	m	m	m	m	
0°	3	3	4	4	4	5	5	5	6	6	6	7	0°
10°	3	3	4	4	4	5	5	6	6	6	7	7	10°
20°	4	4	4	4	5	5	6	7	7	8	8	9	20°
25°	4	4	4	4	5	6	7	8	8	9	11	13	25°
30°	4	4	4	5	6	7	8	9	11	14	21	—	30°

NB: Regarding Table 1. If latitude and declination are of the same sign, take out the respondent directly. If they are of opposite signs, subtract the respondent from 12h.
Example:

Lat.	Dec.	Semi-diurnal arc
+52°	+20°	7h 51m
+52°	−20°	4h 09m

SUNRISE AND SUNSET

The local mean time of sunrise or sunset may be found by obtaining the hour angle from Table 1 and applying it to the time of transit. The hour angle is negative for sunrise and positive for sunset. A small correction to the hour angle, which always has the effect of increasing it numerically, is necessary to allow for the Sun's semi-diameter (16′) and for refraction (34′); it is obtained from Table 2. The resulting local mean time may be converted into the standard time of the country by taking the difference between the longitude of the standard meridian of the country and that of the place, adding it to the local mean time if the place is west of the standard meridian, and subtracting it if the place is east.

Example – Required the New Zealand Mean Time (12h fast on GMT) of sunset on May 23 at Auckland, latitude 36° 50′ S. (or minus), longitude 11h 39m E. Taking the declination as +20°.6 (page 33), we find

	h	m
Tabular entry for Lat. 30° and Dec. 20°, opposite signs	+ 5	11
Proportional part for 6° 50′ of Lat.	–	15
Proportional part for 0°.6 of Dec.	–	2
Correction (Table 2)	+	4
Hour angle		4 58
Sun transits (page 33)	11	57
Longitudinal correction	+	21
New Zealand Mean Time	17	16

MOONRISE AND MOONSET

It is possible to calculate the times of moonrise and moonset using Table 1, though the method is more complicated because the apparent motion of the Moon is much more rapid and also more variable than that of the Sun.

The parallax of the Moon, about 57′, is near to the sum of the semi-diameter and refraction but has the opposite effect on these times. It is thus convenient to neglect all three quantities in the method outlined below.

TABLE 3. LONGITUDE CORRECTION

X	40m	45m	50m	55m	60m	65m	70m
A h	m	m	m	m	m	m	m
1	2	2	2	2	3	3	3
2	3	4	4	5	5	5	6
3	5	6	6	7	8	8	9
4	7	8	8	9	10	11	12
5	8	9	10	11	13	14	15
6	10	11	13	14	15	16	18
7	12	13	15	16	18	19	20
8	13	15	17	18	20	22	23
9	15	17	19	21	23	24	26
10	17	19	21	23	25	27	29
11	18	21	23	25	28	30	32
12	20	23	25	28	30	33	35
13	22	24	27	30	33	35	38
14	23	26	29	32	35	38	41
15	25	28	31	34	38	41	44
16	27	30	33	37	40	43	47
17	28	32	35	39	43	46	50
18	30	34	38	41	45	49	53
19	32	36	40	44	48	51	55
20	33	38	42	46	50	54	58
21	35	39	44	48	53	57	61
22	37	41	46	50	55	60	64
23	38	43	48	53	58	62	67
24	40	45	50	55	60	65	70

Notation

φ = latitude of observer
λ = longitude of observer (measured positively towards the west)
T_{-1} = time of transit of Moon on previous day
T_0 = time of transit of Moon on day in question
T_1 = time of transit of Moon on following day
δ_0 = approximate declination of Moon
δ_R = declination of Moon at moonrise
δ_S = declination of Moon at moonset
h_0 = approximate hour angle of Moon
h_R = hour angle of Moon at moonrise
h_S = hour angle of Moon at moonset
t_R = time of moonrise
t_S = time of moonset

Method

1. With arguments φ, δ_0 enter Table 1 on page 64 to determine h_0 where h_0 is negative for moonrise and positive for moonset.

2. Form approximate times from
$t_R = T_0 + \lambda + h_0$
$t_S = T_0 + \lambda + h_0$

3. Determine δ_R, δ_S for times t_R, t_S respectively.

4. Re-enter Table 1 on page 64 with
   (a) arguments φ, δ_R to determine h_R
   (b) arguments φ, δ_S to determine h_S

5. Form $t_R = T_0 + \lambda + h_R + AX$
   $t_S = T_0 + \lambda + h_S + AX$

   where $A = (\lambda + h)$

   and $X = (T_0 - T_{-1})$ if $(\lambda + h)$ is negative
         $X = (T_1 - T_0)$ if $(\lambda + h)$ is positive

   AX is the respondent in Table 3.

Example – To find the times of moonrise and moonset at Vancouver ($\varphi = +49°$, $\lambda = +8h$ 12m) on 1999 March 16. The starting data (page 26) are

$T_{-1} = 10h$ 13m
T_0 = 11h 06m
T_1 = 11h 59m
δ_0 = −10°

1. h_0 = 5h 13m
2. Approximate values
   t_R = 16d 11h 06m + 8h 12m + (−5h 13m)
       = 16d 14h 05m
   t_S = 16d 11h 06m + 8h 12m + (+5h 13m)
       = 17d 00h 31m
3. δ_R = −9°.4
   δ_S = −7°.6
4. h_R = −5h 16m
   h_S = +5h 24m
5. t_R = 16d 11h 06m + 8h 12m + (−5h 16m) + 7m
       = 16d 14h 09m
   t_S = 16d 11h 06m + 8h 12m + (+5h 24m) + 30m
       = 17d 01h 12m

To get the LMT of the phenomenon the longitude is subtracted from the GMT thus:
Moonrise = 16d 14h 09m − 8h 12m = 16d 05h 57m
Moonset = 17d 01h 12m − 8h 12m = 16d 17h 00m

ECLIPSES AND OCCULTATIONS 1999

ECLIPSES

During 1999 there will be two eclipses of the Sun and one of the Moon. (Penumbral eclipses of the Moon are not mentioned in this section as they are too difficult to observe.)

1. An annular eclipse of the Sun on February 16 is visible as a partial eclipse from southern Africa, Madagascar, the Indian Ocean, Malaysia, Indonesia, the Philippines, the Southern Ocean, Australia and Antarctica. It begins at 03h 52m and ends at 09h 15m. The track of the annular phase crosses the Southern Ocean and the Indian Ocean before crossing Australia and ending in the Coral Sea. The annular phase begins at 04h 57m and ends at 08h 11m; the maximum duration is 1m 18s.

2. A partial eclipse of the Moon occurs on July 28 and is visible from the Americas, the Pacific Ocean, Australasia, eastern Asia, the Indian Ocean, and Antarctica. The eclipse begins at 10h 22m and ends at 12h 45m. At maximum, 40 per cent of the Moon is eclipsed.

3. A total eclipse of the Sun on August 11 is visible as a partial eclipse from eastern North America, Greenland, Iceland, the Atlantic Ocean, Europe, northern Africa, Asia and the Indian Ocean. It starts at 08h 26m and ends at 13h 40m. The path of totality starts in the Atlantic Ocean just south of Newfoundland, and crosses extreme south-west England, northern France, Germany, Austria, Hungary, Romania, northern Bulgaria, Turkey, northern Iraq, Iran, Pakistan and India. It ends in the Indian Ocean just east of India.

At Edinburgh the partial phase begins at 09h 06m and ends at 11h 34m, while at Greenwich the times are 09h 04m and 11h 40m respectively. At maximum eclipse, 85 per cent of the Sun is obscured as seen from Edinburgh and 97 per cent from Greenwich.

The path of totality across the British Isles covers the Scilly Isles, southern Cornwall and Devon, and Alderney in the Channel Islands. From Land's End the partial phase begins at 08h 56m and ends at 11h 31m. Totality there lasts for about 2.1 minutes, centred on a mid-time of 10h 11.4m. The spectacle of a total eclipse being visible from mainland Britain is a rarity; the next one does not occur until 2090, and even then is visible only from southern Cornwall and with the Sun only about 6° high in the west.

TRANSIT

A near-grazing transit of Mercury across the northern edge of the Sun occurs on November 15, with a mid-time of about 21h 41m. The transit is visible from the Americas (except the north-east), the Pacific Ocean, extreme eastern Asia, Indonesia and Australasia. At ingress, the exterior contact occurs at about 21h 11m in North America, 21h 15m in Japan (at sunrise), and 21h 18m in New Zealand. At egress, the exterior contact occurs at 22h 10m, 22h 08m and 22h 04m respectively.

LUNAR OCCULTATIONS

Observations of the times of occultations are made by both amateur and professional astronomers. Such observations are later analysed to yield accurate positions of the Moon; this is one method of determining the difference between ephemeris time and universal time.

Many of the observations made by amateurs are obtained with the use of a stop-watch which is compared with a time-signal immediately after the observation. Thus an accuracy of about one-fifth of a second is obtainable,

though the observer's personal equation may amount to one-third or one-half of a second.

The list on page 67 includes most of the occultations visible under favourable conditions in the British Isles. No occultation is included unless the star is at least 10° above the horizon and the Sun sufficiently far below the horizon to permit the star to be seen with the naked eye or with a small telescope. The altitude limit is reduced from 10° to 2° for stars and planets brighter than magnitude 2.0 and such occultations are also predicted in daylight.

The column Phase shows (i) whether a disappearance (D) or reappearance (R) is to be observed; and (ii) whether it is at the dark limb (D) or bright limb (B). The column headed 'El. of Moon' gives the elongation of the Moon from the Sun, in degrees. The elongation increases from 0° at New Moon to 180° at Full Moon and on to 360° (or 0°) at New Moon again. Times and position angles (P), reckoned from the north point in the direction north, east, south, west, are given for Greenwich (lat. 51° 30′, long. 0°) and Edinburgh (lat. 56° 00′, long. 3° 12′ west).

The coefficients a and b are the variations in the GMT for each degree of longitude (positive to the west) and latitude (positive to the north) respectively; they enable approximate times (to within about 1m generally) to be found for any point in the British Isles. If the point of observation is $\Delta\lambda$ degrees west and $\Delta\phi$ degrees north, the approximate time is found by adding $a.\Delta\lambda + b.\Delta\phi$ to the given GMT.

Example: the disappearance of ZC 692 on March 22 at Coventry, found from both Greenwich and Edinburgh.

	Greenwich °	Edinburgh °
Longitude	0.0	+ 3.2
Long. of Coventry	+ 1.5	+ 1.5
$\Delta\lambda$	+ 1.5	− 1.7
Latitude	+ 51.5	+ 56.0
Lat. of Coventry	+ 52.4	+ 52.4
$\Delta\phi$	+ 0.9	− 3.6

	h m	h m
GMT	18 28.3	18 22.3
$a.\Delta\lambda$	− 2.0	+ 2.0
$b.\Delta\phi$	− 0.7	+ 0.7
	18 25.6	18 25.0

If the occultation is given for one station but not the other, the reason for the suppression is given by the following code:

N = star not occulted
A = star's altitude less than 10° (2° for bright stars and planets)
S = Sun not sufficiently below the horizon
G = occultation is of very short duration

In some cases the coefficients a and b are not given; this is because the occultation is so short that prediction for other places by means of these coefficients would not be reliable.

Observers may like to note that ZC 692 = *Aldebaran* (occulted on March 22, May 16 and July 10).

The other first-magnitude star (ZC 1487 = Regulus) is occulted on April 24, July 15 and September 8.

LUNAR OCCULTATIONS 1999

Date		ZC No.	Mag.	Phase	El. of Moon	GREENWICH				EDINBURGH			
						UT	a	b	P	UT	a	b	P
					°	h m	m	m	°	h m	m	m	°
January	7	1644	4.1	R.D.	242	2 26.6	−1.4	0.6	279	2 25.0	−1.1	0.5	290
	23	210	6.6	D.D.	79	22 15.2	−0.3	−2.0	104	22 6.1	−0.4	−1.5	88
	25	462	5.9	D.D.	103	19 9.4	−1.1	1.6	38	19 15.4	−0.7	2.5	19
	26	608	6.0	D.D.	116	18 44.9	−1.1	1.6	54	18 49.8	−0.8	2.0	38
	26	626	6.4	D.D.	118	23 4.8	−0.9	−1.8	105	22 55.1	−0.9	−1.3	92
	27	635	3.9	D.D.	119	0 57.6	−0.3	−1.4	88	0 50.5	−0.4	−1.2	78
	28	814	5.3	D.D.	135	A				4 15.1	0.1	−1.0	69
	28	943	6.2	D.D.	144	22 11.5	−1.5	−2.9	142	21 58.3	−1.3	−1.2	122
	28	947	5.2	D.D.	145	23 3.4	G		21	N			
February	18	20	6.8	D.D.	33	18 28.8	G		149	18 6.6	−0.9	−2.4	114
	19	165	6.7	D.D.	46	19 38.7	−0.5	−1.0	74	19 33.5	−0.5	−0.7	59
	20	306	6.9	D.D.	61	21 19.7	−0.3	−0.4	51	21 17.8	−0.3	0.0	36
	21	444	6.2	D.D.	74	21 0.8	−0.6	−2.9	123	20 48.1	−0.7	−2.0	105
	23	741	5.7	D.D.	100	21 44.2	−0.9	−1.5	98	21 35.4	−1.0	−1.0	86
	28	1337	5.6	D.D.	153	1 58.4	−0.8	−1.5	94	1 49.5	−0.9	−1.3	88
	28	1336	5.2	D.D.	153	2 10.6	0.0	−3.1	161	1 57.2	−0.2	−2.7	152
March	20	405	4.4	D.D.	43	A				21 24.5	−0.1	−0.2	38
	21	526	6.9	D.D.	56	20 5.2	−0.8	1.4	21	N			
	22	692	1.1	D.D.	68	18 28.3	−1.3	−0.8	87	18 22.3	−1.2	−0.2	73
	22	692	1.1	R.B.	69	19 37.9	−1.0	−0.7	254	19 30.6	−0.9	−1.1	267
	23	871	6.9	D.D.	84	23 17.2	−0.6	0.1	37	23 16.9	G		22
	24	1038	6.8	D.D.	97	24 6.3	0.0	−1.9	115	23 57.7	−0.1	−1.8	108
	28	1425	6.9	D.D.	136	3 3.5	−0.1	−1.6	95	2 55.9	−0.2	−1.6	91
	30	1644	4.1	D.D.	160	4 12.7	−0.4	−1.1	61	4 6.2	−0.5	−1.1	55
April	22	1262	6.2	D.D.	92	23 38.9	−0.1	−1.8	115	23 30.2	−0.2	−1.8	110
	23	1375	5.6	D.D.	103	20 51.9	−1.0	−1.8	125	20 41.3	−1.1	−1.4	117
	24	1487	1.3	D.D.	115	21 21.5	−2.0	0.3	64	21 18.0	−2.1	1.1	53
	24	1487	1.3	R.B.	116	22 11.4	−0.4	−3.0	341	21 56.3	−0.1	−3.4	351
	26	1609	4.7	D.D.	129	1 39.4	−0.3	−1.8	105	1 30.1	−0.4	−1.8	102
May	16	692	1.1	D.D.	15	12 11.3	G		147	11 58.1	−1.5	−0.5	120
	16	692	1.1	R.D.	15	12 33.6	G		184	12 46.5	−0.8	−2.2	211
	21	1466	5.2	D.D.	87	23 25.2	0.0	−1.9	125	23 16.3	−0.1	−1.9	121
June	17	1415	6.2	D.D.	56	21 33.3	G		43	S			
	19	1645	6.6	D.D.	80	22 32.5	−0.6	−0.8	53	22 26.5	G		46
	20	1749	6.1	D.D.	92	23 12.8	G		178	22 59.6	−0.1	−2.7	171
	23	2072	6.7	D.D.	126	23 20.5	−1.2	−1.1	72	23 11.6	−1.2	−1.1	68
	25	2291	5.5	D.D.	147	21 50.7	−1.4	−0.8	131	21 44.0	−1.2	−0.4	128
July	10	692	1.1	D.B.	322	8 22.0	−1.8	−0.9	123	8 15.8	−1.3	0.2	105
	10	692	1.1	R.D.	322	9 9.5	−0.9	2.7	206	9 15.5	−1.0	1.6	225
	15	1487	1.3	D.D.	37	A				21 18.0	0.3	−1.9	138
	22	2247	5.6	D.D.	118	N				21 18.8	G		182
	25	2633	4.0	D.D.	150	20 55.9	−1.2	−0.3	140	S			
	25	2638	5.4	D.D.	151	21 49.0	−1.8	0.9	47	21 47.9	−1.6	1.0	41
	26	2797	3.0	D.D.	162	22 59.9	−1.7	−0.2	103	22 54.4	−1.4	0.0	98
September	8	1487	1.3	D.B.	344	15 53.6	0.3	−2.9	169	15 42.0	0.1	−2.6	163
	8	1487	1.3	R.D.	345	16 23.4	−0.5	−0.7	231	16 17.6	−0.5	−1.1	237
	21	3086	6.0	D.D.	136	21 54.7	−1.3	0.1	58	21 51.9	−1.1	0.3	49
	23	3237	4.4	D.D.	150	1 21.0	−0.7	−0.7	63	1 16.7	−0.5	−0.4	49
	27	364	4.3	R.D.	213	22 9.1	−0.7	1.4	269	22 13.4	−0.6	1.4	277
	29	508	4.3	R.D.	228	0 42.4	−0.4	2.7	202	0 51.5	−0.5	2.1	217
November	15	3115	6.3	D.D.	84	20 14.9	−1.3	−1.4	95	20 5.8	−1.1	−1.0	83
	16	3240	6.6	D.D.	95	19 21.3	−1.7	−0.5	91	19 14.9	−1.4	−0.2	81
	20	106	6.8	D.D.	134	0 21.7	−0.8	−0.8	72	0 16.6	−0.7	−0.4	57
	21	364	4.3	D.D.	157	17 33.3	−0.2	1.9	51	17 41.4	−0.1	1.9	44
	22	405	4.4	D.D.	162	2 21.5	−0.8	−1.0	77	2 15.7	−0.7	−0.6	63
December	12	Mars	0.9	D.D.	53	19 14.3	−0.4	−0.5	49	A			
	13	3190	3.0	D.D.	62	15 36.2	−1.7	0.5	87	15 33.9	−1.4	0.7	81
	13	3190	3.0	R.B.	63	16 54.0	−1.3	0.4	232	16 51.3	−1.2	0.2	241
	14	3327	6.8	D.D.	75	18 51.9	−1.7	−1.3	102	18 42.6	−1.4	−0.7	88
	15	3478	6.5	D.D.	88	21 46.9	−0.8	−1.4	85	21 39.5	−0.7	−1.0	70
	19	444	6.2	D.D.	138	18 12.3	−1.1	1.1	96	18 15.0	−0.8	1.4	86
	19	462	5.9	D.D.	141	23 42.7	−1.2	−1.5	100	23 34.1	−1.1	−0.8	84

MEAN PLACES OF STARS 1999.5

Name	Mag.	RA h m	Dec. ° '	Spectrum	Name	Mag.	RA h m	Dec. ° '	Spectrum
α And *Alpheratz*	2.1	0 08.4	+29 05	A0p	γ Corvi	2.6	12 15.8	−17 32	B8
β Cassiopeiae *Caph*	2.3	0 09.2	+59 09	F5	α Crucis	1.0	12 26.6	−63 06	B1
γ Pegasi *Algenib*	2.8	0 13.2	+15 11	B2	γ Crucis	1.6	12 31.1	−57 07	M3
β Mensae	2.9	0 25.7	−77 15	G0	γ Centauri	2.2	12 41.5	−48 57	A0
α Phoenicis	2.4	0 26.3	−42 19	K0	γ Virginis	2.7	12 41.6	− 1 27	F0
α Cassiopeiae *Schedar*	2.2	0 40.5	+56 32	K0	β Crucis	1.3	12 47.7	−59 41	B1
β Ceti *Diphda*	2.0	0 43.6	−17 59	K0	ε Ursae Majoris *Alioth*	1.8	12 54.0	+55 58	A0p
γ Cassiopeiae*	Var.	0 56.7	+60 43	B0p	α Canum Venaticorum	2.9	12 56.0	+38 19	A0p
β Andromedae *Mirach*	2.1	1 09.7	+35 37	M0	ζ Ursae Majoris *Mizar*	2.1	13 23.9	+54 56	A2p
δ Cassiopeiae	2.7	1 25.8	+60 14	A5	α Virginis *Spica*	1.0	13 25.2	−11 10	B2
α Eridani *Achernar*	0.5	1 37.7	−57 14	B5	ε Centauri	2.6	13 39.9	−53 28	B1
β Arietis *Sheratan*	2.6	1 54.6	+20 48	A5	η Ursae Majoris *Alkaid*	1.9	13 47.5	+49 19	B3
γ Andromedae *Almak*	2.3	2 03.9	+42 20	K0	β Centauri *Hadar*	0.6	14 03.8	−60 22	B1
α Arietis *Hamal*	2.0	2 07.1	+23 28	K2	θ Centauri	2.1	14 06.7	−36 22	K0
α Ursae Minoris *Polaris*	2.0	2 31.3	+89 16	F8	α Bootis *Arcturus*	0.0	14 15.6	+19 11	K0
β Persei *Algol**	Var.	3 08.1	+40 57	B8	α Centauri *Rigil Kent*	0.1	14 39.6	−60 50	G0
α Persei *Mirfak*	1.8	3 24.3	+49 52	F5	ε Bootis	2.4	14 45.0	+27 05	K0
η Tauri *Alcyone*	2.9	3 47.5	+24 06	B5p	β UMi *Kochab*	2.1	14 50.7	+74 09	K5
α Tauri *Aldebaran*	0.9	4 35.9	+16 31	K5	γ Ursae Minoris	3.1	15 20.7	+71 50	A2
β Orionis *Rigel*	0.1	5 14.5	− 8 12	B8p	α CrB *Alphecca*	2.2	15 34.7	+26 43	A0
α Aurigae *Capella*	0.1	5 16.7	+46 00	G0	β Trianguli Australis	3.0	15 55.1	−63 26	F0
γ Orionis *Bellatrix*	1.6	5 25.1	+ 6 21	B2	δ Scorpii	2.3	16 00.3	−22 37	B0
β Tauri *Elnath*	1.7	5 26.3	+28 36	B8	β Scorpii	2.6	16 05.4	−19 48	B1
δ Orionis	2.2	5 32.0	− 0 18	B0	α Scorpii *Antares*	1.0	16 29.4	−26 26	M0
α Leporis	2.6	5 32.7	−17 49	F0	α Trianguli Australis	1.9	16 48.6	−69 02	K2
ε Orionis	1.7	5 36.2	− 1 12	B0	ε Scorpii	2.3	16 50.1	−34 18	K0
ζ Orionis	1.8	5 40.7	− 1 57	B0	α Herculis†	Var.	17 14.6	+14 23	M3
κ Orionis	2.1	5 47.7	− 9 40	B0	λ Scorpii	1.6	17 33.6	−37 06	B2
α Orionis *Betelgeuse**	Var.	5 55.1	+ 7 24	M0	α Ophiuchi *Rasalhague*	2.1	17 34.9	+12 34	A5
β Aurigae *Menkalinan*	1.9	5 59.5	+44 57	A0p	θ Scorpii	1.9	17 37.3	−43 00	F0
β CMa *Mirzam*	2.0	6 22.7	−17 57	B1	κ Scorpii	2.4	17 42.5	−39 02	B2
α Carinae *Canopus*	−0.7	6 23.9	−52 42	F0	γ Draconis	2.2	17 56.6	+51 29	K5
γ Geminorum *Alhena*	1.9	6 37.7	+16 24	A0	ε Sgr *Kaus Australis*	1.9	18 24.1	−34 23	A0
α Canis Majoris *Sirius*	−1.5	6 45.1	−16 43	A0	α Lyrae *Vega*	0.0	18 36.9	+38 47	A0
ε Canis Majoris	1.5	6 58.6	−28 58	B1	σ Sagittarii	2.0	18 55.2	−26 18	B3
δ Canis Majoris	1.9	7 08.4	−26 24	F8p	β Cygni *Albireo*	3.1	19 30.7	+27 58	K0
α Geminorum *Castor*	1.6	7 34.6	+31 53	A0	α Aquilae *Altair*	0.8	19 50.8	+ 8 52	A5
α CMi *Procyon*	0.4	7 39.3	+ 5 14	F5	α Capricorni	3.8	20 18.0	−12 33	G5
β Geminorum *Pollux*	1.1	7 45.3	+28 02	K0	γ Cygni	2.2	20 22.2	+40 15	F8p
ζ Puppis	2.3	8 03.6	−40 00	Od	α Pavonis	1.9	20 25.6	−56 44	B3
γ Velorum	1.8	8 09.5	−47 20	Oap	α Cygni *Deneb*	1.3	20 41.4	+45 17	A2p
ε Carinae	1.9	8 22.5	−59 30	K0	α Cephei *Alderamin*	2.4	21 18.6	+62 35	A5
δ Velorum	2.0	8 44.7	−54 42	A0	ε Pegasi	2.4	21 44.2	+ 9 52	K0
λ Velorum *Suhail*	2.2	9 08.0	−43 26	K5	δ Capricorni	2.9	21 47.0	−16 08	A5
β Carinae	1.7	9 13.2	−69 43	A0	α Gruis	1.7	22 08.2	−46 58	B5
ι Carinae	2.2	9 17.1	−59 16	F0	δ Cephei†	3.7	22 29.2	+58 25	†
κ Velorum	2.6	9 22.1	−55 01	B3	β Gruis	2.1	22 42.6	−46 53	M3
α Hydrae *Alphard*	2.0	9 27.6	− 8 39	K2	α PsA *Fomalhaut*	1.2	22 57.6	−29 37	A3
α Leonis *Regulus*	1.3	10 08.3	+11 58	B8	β Pegasi *Scheat*	2.4	23 03.8	+28 05	M0
γ Leonis *Algeiba*	1.9	10 19.9	+19 51	K0	α Pegasi *Markab*	2.5	23 04.7	+15 12	A0
β Ursae Majoris *Merak*	2.4	11 01.8	+56 23	A0					
α Ursae Majoris *Dubhe*	1.8	11 03.7	+61 45	K0					
δ Leonis	2.6	11 14.1	+20 32	A3					
β Leonis *Denebola*	2.1	11 49.0	+14 34	A2					
γ Ursae Majoris *Phecda*	2.4	11 53.8	+53 42	A0					

*γ Cassiopeiae, 1998 mag. 2.5. β Persei, mag. 2.1 to 3.4.
α Orionis, mag. 0.1 to 1.2.

†α Herculis, mag. 3.1 to 3.9. δ Cephei, mag. 3.7 to 4.4,
spectrum F5 to G0.

The positions of heavenly bodies on the celestial sphere are defined by two co-ordinates, right ascension and declination, which are analogous to longitude and latitude on the surface of the Earth. If we imagine the plane of the terrestrial equator extended indefinitely, it will cut the celestial sphere in a great circle known as the celestial equator. Similarly the plane of the Earth's orbit, when extended, cuts in the great circle called the ecliptic. The two intersections of these circles are known as the First Point of Aries and the First Point of Libra. If from any star a perpendicular be drawn to the celestial equator, the length of this perpendicular is the star's declination. The arc, measured eastwards along the equator from the First Point of Aries to the foot of this perpendicular, is the right ascension. An alternative definition of right ascension is that it is the angle at the celestial pole (where the Earth's axis, if prolonged, would meet the sphere) between the great circles to the First Point of Aries and to the star.

The plane of the Earth's equator has a slow movement, so that our reference system for right ascension and declination is not fixed. The consequent alteration in these quantities from year to year is called precession. In right ascension it is an increase of about 3 seconds a year for equatorial stars, and larger or smaller changes in either direction for stars near the poles, depending on the right ascension of the star. In declination it varies between $+20''$ and $-20''$ according to the right ascension of the star.

A star or other body crosses the meridian when the sidereal time is equal to its right ascension. The altitude is then a maximum, and may be deduced by remembering that the altitude of the elevated pole is numerically equal to the latitude, while that of the equator at its intersection with the meridian is equal to the co-latitude, or complement of the latitude.

Thus in London (lat. 51° 30′) the meridian altitude of Sirius is found as follows:

	°	′
Altitude of equator	38	30
Declination south	16	43
Difference	21	47

The altitude of Capella (Dec. $+46°\ 00'$) at lower transit is:

	°	′
Altitude of pole	51	30
Polar distance of star	44	00
Difference	7	30

The brightness of a heavenly body is denoted by its magnitude. Omitting the exceptionally bright stars Sirius and Canopus, the twenty brightest stars are of the first magnitude, while the faintest stars visible to the naked eye are of the sixth magnitude. The magnitude scale is a precise one, as a difference of five magnitudes represents a ratio of 100 to 1 in brightness. Typical second magnitude stars are Polaris and the stars in the belt of Orion. The scale is most easily fixed in memory by comparing the stars with Norton's *Star Atlas* (*see* page 71). The stars Sirius and Canopus and the planets Venus and Jupiter are so bright that their magnitudes are expressed by negative numbers. A small telescope will show stars down to the ninth or tenth magnitude, while stars fainter than the twentieth magnitude may be photographed by long exposures with the largest telescopes.

MEAN AND SIDEREAL TIME

Acceleration					Retardation				
h	m s	m	s	s	h	m s	m	s	s
1	0 10	0	00		1	0 10	0	00	
2	0 20	3	02	0	2	0 20	3	03	0
3	0 30	9	07	1	3	0 29	9	09	1
4	0 39	15	13	2	4	0 39	15	15	2
5	0 49	21	18	3	5	0 49	21	21	3
6	0 59	27	23	4	6	0 59	27	28	4
7	1 09	33	28	5	7	1 09	33	34	5
8	1 19	39	34	6	8	1 19	39	40	6
9	1 29	45	39	7	9	1 28	45	46	7
10	1 39	51	44	8	10	1 38	51	53	8
11	1 48	57	49	9	11	1 48	57	59	9
12	1 58	60	00	10	12	1 58	60	00	10
13	2 08				13	2 08			
14	2 18				14	2 18			
15	2 28				15	2 27			
16	2 38				16	2 37			
17	2 48				17	2 47			
18	2 57				18	2 57			
19	3 07				19	3 07			
20	3 17				20	3 17			
21	3 27				21	3 26			
22	3 37				22	3 36			
23	3 47				23	3 46			
24	3 57				24	3 56			

The length of a sidereal day in mean time is 23h 56m 04s.09. Hence 1h MT = 1h + 9s.86 ST and 1h ST = 1h − 9s.83 MT.

To convert an interval of mean time to the corresponding interval of sidereal time, enter the acceleration table with the given mean time (taking the hours and the minutes and seconds separately) and add the acceleration obtained to the given mean time. To convert an interval of sidereal time to the corresponding interval of mean time, take out the retardation for the given sidereal time and subtract.

The columns for the minutes and seconds of the argument are in the form known as critical tables. To use these tables, find in the appropriate left-hand column the two entries between which the given number of minutes and seconds lies; the quantity in the right-hand column between these two entries is the required acceleration or retardation. Thus the acceleration for 11m 26s (which lies between the entries 9m 07s and 15m 13s) is 2s. If the given number of minutes and seconds is a tabular entry, the required acceleration or retardation is the entry in the right-hand column above the given tabular entry, e.g. the retardation for 45m 46s is 7s.

Example – Convert 14h 27m 35s from ST to MT

	h	m	s
Given ST	14	27	35
Retardation for 14h		2	18
Retardation for 27m 35s			5
Corresponding MT	14	25	12

For further explanation, *see* pages 73–4.

ECLIPSES AND SHADOW TRANSITS OF JUPITER'S SATELLITES 1999

GMT d h m	Sat.	Phen.
JANUARY		
2 20 27	I	Sh.I
3 19 50	I	Ec.R
5 20 34	II	Ec.R
11 19 04	I	Sh.E
18 18 14	III	Ec.D
18 18 48	I	Sh.I
18 21 00	I	Sh.E
19 18 10	I	Ec.R
21 20 02	II	Sh.E
26 20 05	I	Ec.R
28 20 02	II	Sh.I
FEBRUARY		
3 19 21	I	Sh.E
5 19 29	III	Sh.E
10 19 04	I	Sh.I
11 18 24	I	Ec.R
JUNE		
27 01 49	I	Sh.I
29 01 10	III	Sh.I
JULY		
5 00 57	I	Ec.D
12 02 52	I	Ec.D
13 02 15	I	Sh.E
13 02 49	II	Ec.D
15 00 16	II	Sh.E
17 01 32	III	Ec.R
20 01 59	I	Sh.I
22 00 20	II	Sh.I
22 02 53	II	Sh.E
24 03 04	III	Ec.D
28 01 09	I	Ec.D
29 00 30	I	Sh.E
29 02 57	II	Sh.I
30 23 48	II	Ec.R
AUGUST		
3 23 39	III	Sh.E
4 03 03	I	Ec.D
5 00 15	I	Sh.I
5 02 24	I	Sh.E
6 23 50	II	Ec.D
7 02 22	II	Ec.R
11 01 16	III	Sh.I
11 03 38	III	Sh.E
12 02 08	I	Sh.I
12 23 26	I	Ec.D
13 22 46	I	Sh.E
14 02 25	II	Sh.I
16 00 02	II	Sh.E
19 04 02	I	Sh.I
20 01 20	I	Ec.D
20 22 30	I	Sh.I
21 00 40	I	Sh.E
21 21 32	III	Ec.R
23 00 07	II	Sh.I
23 02 38	II	Sh.I
27 03 14	I	Ec.D
28 00 24	I	Sh.I
28 02 34	I	Sh.E
28 21 43	I	Ec.D

GMT d h m	Sat.	Phen.
AUGUST		
28 23 10	III	Ec.D
29 01 33	III	Ec.R
29 21 02	I	Sh.E
30 02 43	II	Sh.I
31 20 52	II	Ec.D
SEPTEMBER		
4 02 18	I	Sh.I
4 04 28	I	Sh.E
4 23 37	I	Ec.D
5 03 11	III	Ec.D
5 20 46	I	Sh.I
5 22 56	I	Sh.E
7 23 28	II	Ec.D
9 21 09	II	Sh.E
11 04 12	I	Sh.I
12 01 32	I	Ec.D
12 22 40	I	Sh.I
13 00 50	I	Sh.E
15 02 03	II	Ec.D
15 21 20	III	Sh.I
15 23 38	III	Sh.E
16 21 14	II	Sh.I
16 23 46	II	Sh.E
19 03 26	I	Ec.D
20 00 34	I	Sh.I
20 02 44	I	Sh.E
20 21 54	I	Ec.D
21 21 13	I	Sh.E
22 04 39	II	Ec.D
23 01 22	III	Sh.I
23 03 38	III	Sh.E
23 23 50	II	Sh.I
24 02 22	II	Sh.E
27 02 28	I	Sh.I
27 23 49	I	Ec.D
28 20 57	I	Sh.I
28 23 07	I	Sh.E
OCTOBER		
1 02 26	II	Sh.I
2 20 34	II	Ec.D
3 19 17	III	Ec.D
3 21 33	III	Ec.R
5 01 43	I	Ec.D
5 22 51	I	Sh.I
6 01 02	I	Sh.E
6 20 12	I	Ec.D
7 19 30	I	Sh.E
9 23 10	II	Ec.D
10 23 18	III	Ec.D
11 20 52	II	Sh.E
12 03 38	I	Ec.D
13 00 46	I	Sh.I
13 02 56	I	Sh.E
13 22 07	I	Ec.D
14 19 15	I	Sh.I
14 21 25	I	Sh.E
17 01 47	II	Ec.D
18 20 57	II	Sh.I
18 23 28	II	Sh.E
20 02 41	I	Sh.I
21 00 01	I	Ec.D
21 19 39	III	Sh.E
21 21 09	I	Sh.I

GMT d h m	Sat.	Phen.
OCTOBER		
21 23 20	I	Sh.E
22 18 30	I	Ec.D
25 23 33	II	Sh.I
26 02 05	II	Sh.E
27 20 15	II	Ec.R
28 21 29	III	Sh.I
28 23 04	I	Sh.I
28 23 41	III	Sh.E
29 01 15	I	Sh.E
29 22 35	I	Ec.R
30 19 44	I	Sh.E
NOVEMBER		
2 02 09	II	Sh.I
3 22 53	II	Ec.R
5 01 00	I	Sh.I
5 01 31	III	Sh.I
5 17 58	II	Sh.E
6 00 30	I	Ec.R
6 19 28	I	Sh.I
6 21 39	I	Sh.E
7 18 58	I	Ec.R
8 17 37	III	Ec.R
11 01 31	II	Ec.R
12 18 04	II	Sh.I
12 20 34	II	Sh.E
13 21 24	I	Sh.I
13 23 34	I	Sh.E
14 20 53	I	Ec.R
15 18 03	I	Sh.E
15 19 27	III	Ec.D
15 21 38	III	Ec.R
19 20 40	II	Sh.I
19 23 10	II	Sh.E
20 23 19	I	Sh.I
21 17 28	II	Ec.R
21 22 48	I	Ec.R
22 17 48	I	Sh.I

GMT d h m	Sat.	Phen.
NOVEMBER		
22 19 58	I	Sh.E
22 23 29	III	Ec.D
26 23 16	II	Sh.I
28 20 07	II	Ec.R
29 19 44	I	Sh.I
29 21 54	I	Sh.E
30 19 12	I	Ec.R
DECEMBER		
3 17 40	III	Sh.I
3 19 47	III	Sh.E
5 22 45	II	Ec.R
6 21 39	I	Sh.I
6 23 49	I	Sh.E
7 17 40	II	Sh.E
7 21 07	I	Ec.R
8 18 18	I	Sh.I
10 21 42	III	Sh.I
14 17 46	II	Sh.I
14 20 16	II	Sh.E
14 23 03	I	Ec.R
15 18 04	I	Sh.I
15 20 14	I	Sh.E
16 17 31	I	Ec.R
21 17 45	III	Ec.R
21 20 22	II	Sh.I
21 22 52	II	Sh.E
22 20 00	I	Sh.I
22 22 10	I	Sh.E
23 17 22	II	Ec.R
23 19 27	I	Ec.R
28 19 41	III	Ec.D
28 21 46	III	Ec.R
29 21 56	I	Sh.I
30 17 28	II	Ec.D
30 20 01	II	Ec.R
30 21 22	I	Ec.R
31 18 34	I	Sh.I

Jupiter's satellites transit across the disk from east to west, and pass behind the disk from west to east. The shadows that they cast also transit across the disk. With the exception at times of Satellite IV, the satellites also pass through the shadow of the planet, i.e. they are eclipsed. Just before opposition the satellite disappears in the shadow to the west of the planet and reappears from occultation on the east limb. Immediately after opposition the satellite is occulted at the west limb and reappears from eclipse to the east of the planet. At times approximately two to four months before and after opposition, both phases of eclipses of Satellite III may be seen. When Satellite IV is eclipsed, both phases may be seen.

The times given refer to the centre of the satellite. As the satellite is of considerable size, the immersion and emersion phases are not instantaneous. Even when the satellite enters or leaves the shadow along a radius of the shadow, the phase can last for several minutes. With Satellite IV, grazing phenomena can occur so that the light from the satellite may fade and brighten again without a complete eclipse taking place.

The list of phenomena gives most of the eclipses and shadow transits visible in the British Isles under favourable conditions.

Ec. = Eclipse   R. = Reappearance
Sh. = Shadow transit   I. = Ingress
D. = Disappearance   E. = Egress

EXPLANATION OF ASTRONOMICAL DATA

Positions of the heavenly bodies are given only to the degree of accuracy required by amateur astronomers for setting telescopes, or for plotting on celestial globes or star atlases. Where intermediate positions are required, linear interpolation may be employed.

Definitions of the terms used cannot be given here. They must be sought in astronomical literature and textbooks. Probably the best source for the amateur is Norton's *Star Atlas and Reference Handbook* (Longman, 18th edition, 1989; £26.99), which contains an introduction to observational astronomy, and a series of star maps for showing stars visible to the naked eye. Certain more extended ephemerides are available in the British Astronomical Association Handbook, an annual popular among amateur astronomers (Secretary: Burlington House, Piccadilly, London W1V 9AG).

A special feature has been made of the times when the various heavenly bodies are visible in the British Isles. Since two columns, calculated for latitudes 52° and 56°, are devoted to risings and settings, the range 50° to 58° can be covered by interpolation and extrapolation. The times given in these columns are Greenwich Mean Times for the meridian of Greenwich. An observer west of this meridian must add his/her longitude (in time) and vice versa.

In accordance with the usual convention in astronomy, + and − indicate respectively north and south latitudes or declinations.

All data are, unless otherwise stated, for 0h Greenwich Mean Time (GMT), i.e. at the midnight at the beginning of the day named. Allowance must be made for British Summer Time during the period that this is in operation (*see* pages 15 and 75).

PAGE ONE OF EACH MONTH

The calendar for each month is explained on page 15.

Under the heading Astronomical Phenomena will be found particulars of the more important conjunctions of the Sun, Moon and planets with each other, and also the dates of other astronomical phenomena of special interest.

Times of Minima of Algol are approximate times of the middle of the period of diminished light.

The Constellations listed each month are those that are near the meridian at the beginning of the month at 22h local mean time. Allowance must be made for British Summer Time if necessary. The fact that any star crosses the meridian 4m earlier each night or 2h earlier each month may be used, in conjunction with the lists given each month, to find what constellations are favourably placed at any moment. The table preceding the list of constellations may be extended indefinitely at the rate just quoted.

The principal phases of the Moon are the GMTs when the difference between the longitude of the Moon and that of the Sun is 0°, 90°, 180° or 270°. The times of perigee and apogee are those when the Moon is nearest to, and farthest from, the Earth, respectively. The nodes or points of intersection of the Moon's orbit and the ecliptic make a complete retrograde circuit of the ecliptic in about 19 years. From a knowledge of the longitude of the ascending node and the inclination, whose value does not vary much from 5°, the path of the Moon among the stars may be plotted on a celestial globe or star atlas.

PAGE TWO OF EACH MONTH

The Sun's semi-diameter, in arc, is given once a month.

The right ascension and declination (Dec.) is that of the true Sun. The right ascension of the mean Sun is obtained by applying the equation of time, with the sign given, to the right ascension of the true Sun, or, more easily, by applying 12h to the Sidereal Time. The direction in which the equation of time has to be applied in different problems is a frequent source of confusion and error. Apparent Solar Time is equal to the Mean Solar Time plus the Equation of Time. For example, at noon on August 8 the Equation of Time is − 5m 40s and thus at 12h Mean Time on that day the Apparent Time is 12h − 5m 40s = 11h 54m 20s.

The Greenwich Sidereal Time at 0h and the Transit of the First Point of Aries (which is really the mean time when the sidereal time is 0h) are used for converting mean time to sidereal time and vice versa.

The GMT of transit of the Sun at Greenwich may also be taken as the local mean time (LMT) of transit in any longitude. It is independent of latitude. The GMT of transit in any longitude is obtained by adding the longitude to the time given if west, and vice versa.

LIGHTING-UP TIME

The legal importance of sunrise and sunset is that the Road Vehicles Lighting Regulations 1989 (SI 1989 No. 1796) make the use of front and rear position lamps on vehicles compulsory during the period between sunset and sunrise. Headlamps on vehicles are required to be used during the hours of darkness on unlit roads or whenever visibility is seriously reduced. The hours of darkness are defined in these regulations as the period between half an hour after sunset and half an hour before sunrise.

In all laws and regulations 'sunset' refers to the local sunset, i.e. the time at which the Sun sets at the place in question. This common-sense interpretation has been upheld by legal tribunals. Thus the necessity for providing for different latitudes and longitudes, as already described, is evident.

SUNRISE AND SUNSET

The times of sunrise and sunset are those when the Sun's upper limb, as affected by refraction, is on the true horizon of an observer at sea-level. Assuming the mean refraction to be 34′, and the Sun's semi-diameter to be 16′, the time given is that when the true zenith distance of the Sun's centre is 90° + 34′ + 16′ or 90° 50′, or, in other words, when the depression of the Sun's centre below the true horizon is 50′. The upper limb is then 34′ below the true horizon, but is brought there by refraction. An observer on a ship might see the Sun for a minute or so longer, because of the dip of the horizon, while another viewing the sunset over hills or mountains would record an earlier time. Nevertheless, the moment when the true zenith distance of the Sun's centre is 90° 50′ is a precise time dependent only on the latitude and longitude of the place, and independent of its altitude above sea-level, the contour of its horizon, the vagaries of refraction or the small seasonal change in the Sun's semi-diameter; this moment is suitable in every way as a definition of sunset (or sunrise) for all statutory purposes. (For further information, *see* footnote on page 72.)

TWILIGHT

Light reaches us before sunrise and continues to reach us for some time after sunset. The interval between darkness and sunrise or sunset and darkness is called twilight. Astronomically speaking, twilight is considered to begin or end when the Sun's centre is 18° below the horizon, as no light from the Sun can then reach the observer. As thus defined twilight may last several hours; in high latitudes at the summer solstice the depression of 18° is not reached, and twilight lasts from sunset to sunrise.

The need for some sub-division of twilight is met by dividing the gathering darkness into four stages.

(1) *Sunrise or Sunset*, defined as above
(2) *Civil twilight*, which begins or ends when the Sun's centre is 6° below the horizon. This marks the time when operations requiring daylight may commence or must cease. In England it varies from about 30 to 60 minutes after sunset and the same interval before sunrise
(3) *Nautical twilight*, which begins or ends when the Sun's centre is 12° below the horizon. This marks the time when it is, to all intents and purposes, completely dark
(4) *Astronomical twilight*, which begins or ends when the Sun's centre is 18° below the horizon. This marks theoretical perfect darkness. It is of little practical importance, especially if nautical twilight is tabulated

To assist observers the durations of civil, nautical and astronomical twilights are given at intervals of ten days. The beginning of a particular twilight is found by subtracting the duration from the time of sunrise, while the end is found by adding the duration to the time of sunset. Thus the beginning of astronomical twilight in latitude 52°, on the Greenwich meridian, on March 11 is found as 06h 25m − 113m = 04h 32m and similarly the end of civil twilight as 17h 57m + 34m = 18h 31m. The letters TAN (twilight all night) are printed when twilight lasts all night.

Under the heading The Night Sky will be found notes describing the position and visibility of the planets and other phenomena.

PAGE THREE OF EACH MONTH

The Moon moves so rapidly among the stars that its position is given only to the degree of accuracy that permits linear interpolation. The right ascension (RA) and declination (Dec.) are geocentric, i.e. for an imaginary observer at the centre of the Earth. To an observer on the surface of the Earth the position is always different, as the altitude is always less on account of parallax, which may reach 1°.

The lunar terminator is the line separating the bright from the dark part of the Moon's disk. Apart from irregularities of the lunar surface, the terminator is elliptical, because it is a circle seen in projection. It becomes the full circle forming the limb, or edge, of the Moon at New and Full Moon. The selenographic longitude of the terminator is measured from the mean centre of the visible disk, which may differ from the visible centre by as much as 8°, because of libration.

Instead of the longitude of the terminator the Sun's selenographic co-longitude (Sun's co-long.) is tabulated. It is numerically equal to the selenographic longitude of the morning terminator, measured eastwards from the mean centre of the disk. Thus its value is approximately 270° at New Moon, 360° at First Quarter, 90° at Full Moon and 180° at Last Quarter.

The Position Angle (PA) of the Bright Limb is the position angle of the midpoint of the illuminated limb, measured eastwards from the north point on the disk. The Phase column shows the percentage of the area of the Moon's disk illuminated; this is also the illuminated percentage of the diameter at right angles to the line of cusps. The terminator is a semi-ellipse whose major axis is the line of cusps, and whose semi-minor axis is determined by the tabulated percentage; from New Moon to Full Moon the east limb is dark, and vice versa.

The times given as moonrise and moonset are those when the upper limb of the Moon is on the horizon of an observer at sea-level. The Sun's horizontal parallax (Hor. par.) is about 9″, and is negligible when considering sunrise and sunset, but that of the Moon averages about 57′. Hence the computed time represents the moment when the true zenith distance of the Moon is 90° 50′ (as for the Sun) minus the horizontal parallax. The time required for the Sun or Moon to rise or set is about four minutes (except in high latitudes). *See also* page 65 and footnote below.

The GMT of transit of the Moon over the meridian of Greenwich is given; these times are independent of latitude but must be corrected for longitude. For places in the British Isles it suffices to add the longitude if west, and vice versa. For other places a further correction is necessary because of the rapid movement of the Moon relative to the stars. The entire correction is conveniently determined by first finding the west longitude λ of the place. If the place is in west longitude, λ is the ordinary west longitude; if the place is in east longitude λ is the complement to 24h (or 360°) of the longitude and will be greater than 12h (or 180°). The correction then consists of two positive portions, namely λ and the fraction $\lambda/24$ (or $\lambda°/360$) multiplied by the difference between consecutive transits. Thus for Sydney, New South Wales, the longitude is 10h 05m east, so λ=13h 55m and the fraction $\lambda/24$ is 0.58. The transit on the local date 1999 January 16 is found as follows:

	d	h	m
GMT of transit at Greenwich Jan.	16	11	08
λ		13	55
0.58×(11h 08m − 10h 18m)			29
GMT of transit at Sydney		17	01	32
Corr. to NSW Standard Time			10	00
Local standard time of transit		17	11	32

As is evident, for any given place the quantities λ and the correction to local standard time may be combined permanently, being here 23h 55m.

Positions of Mercury are given for every second day, and those of Venus and Mars for every fifth day; they may be interpolated linearly. The diameter (Diam.) is given in seconds of arc. The phase is the illuminated percentage of the disk. In the case of the inner planets this approaches 100 at superior conjunction and 0 at inferior conjunction. When the phase is less than 50 the planet is crescent-shaped or horned; for greater phases it is gibbous. In the case of the exterior planet Mars, the phase approaches 100 at conjunction and opposition, and is a minimum at the quadratures.

Since the planets cannot be seen when on the horizon, the actual times of rising and setting are not given; instead, the time when the planet has an apparent altitude of 5° has

---

SUNRISE, SUNSET AND MOONRISE, MOONSET

The tables have been constructed for the meridian of Greenwich, and for latitudes 52° and 56°. They give Greenwich Mean Time (GMT) throughout the year. To obtain the GMT of the phenomenon as seen from any other latitude and longitude in the British Isles, first interpolate or extrapolate for latitude by the usual rules of proportion. To the time thus found, the longitude (expressed in time) is to be added if west (as it usually is in Great Britain) or subtracted if east. If the longitude is expressed in degrees and minutes of arc, it must be converted to time at the rate of 1° = 4m and 15′ = 1m.

A method of calculating rise and set times for other places in the world is given on pages 64 and 65

been tabulated. If the time of transit is between 00h and 12h the time refers to an altitude of 5° above the eastern horizon; if between 12h and 24h, to the western horizon. The phenomenon tabulated is the one that occurs between sunset and sunrise. The times given may be interpolated for latitude and corrected for longitude, as in the case of the Sun and Moon.

The GMT at which the planet transits the Greenwich meridian is also given. The times of transit are to be corrected to local meridians in the usual way, as already described.

PAGE FOUR OF EACH MONTH

The GMTs of sunrise and sunset for seven cities, whose adopted positions in longitude (W.) and latitude (N.) are given immediately below the name, may be used not only for these phenomena, but also for lighting-up times (see page 71 for a fuller explanation).

The particulars for the four outer planets resemble those for the planets on Page Three of each month, except that, under Uranus and Neptune, times when the planet is 10° high instead of 5° high are given; this is because of the inferior brightness of these planets. The diameters given for the rings of Saturn are those of the major axis (in the plane of the planet's equator) and the minor axis respectively. The former has a small seasonal change due to the slightly varying distance of the Earth from Saturn, but the latter varies from zero when the Earth passes through the ring plane every 15 years to its maximum opening half-way between these periods. The rings were last open at their widest extent (and Saturn at its brightest) in 1988; this will occur again in 2002. The Earth passed through the ring plane in 1995–6 and will do so again in 2009.

TIME

From the earliest ages, the natural division of time into recurring periods of day and night has provided the practical time-scale for the everyday activities of the human race. Indeed, if any alternative means of time measurement is adopted, it must be capable of adjustment so as to remain in general agreement with the natural time-scale defined by the diurnal rotation of the Earth on its axis. Ideally, the rotation should be measured against a fixed frame of reference; in practice it must be measured against the background provided by the celestial bodies. If the Sun is chosen as the reference point, we obtain Apparent Solar Time, which is the time indicated by a sundial. It is not a uniform time but is subject to variations which amount to as much as a quarter of an hour in each direction. Such wide variations cannot be tolerated in a practical time-scale, and this has led to the concept of Mean Solar Time in which all the days are exactly the same length and equal to the average length of the Apparent Solar Day.

The positions of the stars in the sky are specified in relation to a fictitious reference point in the sky known as the First Point of Aries (or the Vernal Equinox). It is therefore convenient to adopt this same reference point when considering the rotation of the Earth against the background of the stars. The time-scale so obtained is known as Apparent Sidereal Time.

GREENWICH MEAN TIME

The daily rotation of the Earth on its axis causes the Sun and the other heavenly bodies to appear to cross the sky from east to west. It is convenient to represent this relative motion as if the Sun really performed a daily circuit around

a fixed Earth. Noon in Apparent Solar Time may then be defined as the time at which the Sun transits across the observer's meridian. In Mean Solar Time, noon is similarly defined by the meridian transit of a fictitious Mean Sun moving uniformly in the sky with the same average speed as the true Sun. Mean Solar Time observed on the meridian of the transit circle telescope of the Old Royal Observatory at Greenwich is called Greenwich Mean Time (GMT). The mean solar day is divided into 24 hours and, for astronomical and other scientific purposes, these are numbered 0 to 23, commencing at midnight. Civil time is usually reckoned in two periods of 12 hours, designated a.m. (ante meridiem, i.e. before noon) and p.m. (post meridiem, i.e. after noon).

UNIVERSAL TIME

Before 1925 January 1, GMT was reckoned in 24 hours commencing at noon; since that date it has been reckoned from midnight. To avoid confusion in the use of the designation GMT before and after 1925, since 1928 astronomers have tended to use the term Universal Time (UT) or Weltzeit (WZ) to denote GMT measured from Greenwich Mean Midnight.

In precision work it is necessary to take account of small variations in Universal Time. These arise from small irregularities in the rotation of the Earth. Observed astronomical time is designated UT0. Observed time corrected for the effects of the motion of the poles (giving rise to a 'wandering' in longitude) is designated UT1. There is also a seasonal fluctuation in the rate of rotation of the Earth arising from meteorological causes, often called the annual fluctuation. UT1 corrected for this effect is designated UT2 and provides a time-scale free from short-period fluctuations. It is still subject to small secular and irregular changes.

APPARENT SOLAR TIME

As mentioned above, the time shown by a sundial is called Apparent Solar Time. It differs from Mean Solar Time by an amount known as the Equation of Time, which is the total effect of two causes which make the length of the apparent solar day non-uniform. One cause of variation is that the orbit of the Earth is not a circle but an ellipse, having the Sun at one focus. As a consequence, the angular speed of the Earth in its orbit is not constant; it is greatest at the beginning of January when the Earth is nearest the Sun.

The other cause is due to the obliquity of the ecliptic; the plane of the equator (which is at right angles to the axis of rotation of the Earth) does not coincide with the ecliptic (the plane defined by the apparent annual motion of the Sun around the celestial sphere) but is inclined to it at an angle of 23° 26'. As a result, the apparent solar day is shorter than average at the equinoxes and longer at the solstices. From the combined effects of the components due to obliquity and eccentricity, the equation of time reaches its maximum values in February (−14 minutes) and early November (+16 minutes). It has a zero value on four dates during the year, and it is only on these dates (approximately April 15, June 14, September 1, and December 25) that a sundial shows Mean Solar Time.

SIDEREAL TIME

A sidereal day is the duration of a complete rotation of the Earth with reference to the First Point of Aries. The term sidereal (or 'star') time is a little misleading since the time-scale so defined is not exactly the same as that which would be defined by successive transits of a selected star, as there is a small progressive motion between the stars and the First Point of Aries due to the precession of the Earth's axis. This makes the length of the sidereal day shorter than the true period of rotation by 0.008 seconds. Superimposed on this steady precessional motion are small oscillations (nutation), giving rise to fluctuations in apparent sidereal time amounting to as much as 1.2 seconds. It is therefore customary to employ Mean Sidereal Time, from which these fluctuations have been removed. The conversion of GMT to Greenwich sidereal time (GST) may be performed by adding the value of the GST at 0h on the day in question (Page Two of each month) to the GMT converted to sidereal time using the table on page 69.

Example – To find the GST at August 8d 02h 41m 11s GMT

	h	m	s
GST at 0h	21	05	12
GMT	2	41	11
Acceleration for 2h			20
Acceleration for 41m 11s			7
Sum = GST =	23	46	50

If the observer is not on the Greenwich meridian then his/her longitude, measured positively westwards from Greenwich, must be subtracted from the GST to obtain Local Sidereal Time (LST). Thus, in the above example, an observer 5h east of Greenwich, or 19h west, would find the LST as 4h 46m 50s.

EPHEMERIS TIME

An analysis of observations of the positions of the Sun, Moon and planets taken over an extended period is used in preparing ephemerides. (An ephemeris is a table giving the apparent position of a heavenly body at regular intervals of time, e.g. one day or ten days, and may be used to compare current observations with tabulated positions.) Discrepancies between the positions of heavenly bodies observed over a 300-year period and their predicted positions arose because the time-scale to which the observations were related was based on the assumption that the rate of rotation of the Earth is uniform. It is now known that this rate of rotation is variable. A revised time-scale, Ephemeris Time (ET), was devised to bring the ephemerides into agreement with the observations.

The second of ET is defined in terms of the annual motion of the Earth in its orbit around the Sun (1/31556925.9747 of the tropical year for 1900 January 0d 12h ET). The precise determination of ET from astronomical observations is a lengthy process as the requisite standard of accuracy can only be achieved by averaging over a number of years.

In 1976 the International Astronomical Union adopted a new dynamical time-scale for general use whose scale unit is the SI second (*see* Atomic Time). ET is now of little more than historical interest.

TERRESTRIAL DYNAMICAL TIME

The uniform time system used in computing the ephemerides of the solar system is Terrestrial Dynamical Time (TDT), which has replaced ET for this purpose. Except for the most rigorous astronomical calculations, it may be assumed to be the same as ET. During 1999 the estimated difference TDT – UT is about 64 seconds.

ATOMIC TIME

The fundamental standards of time and frequency must be defined in terms of a periodic motion adequately uniform, enduring and measurable. Progress has made it possible to use natural standards, such as atomic or molecular oscillations. Continuous oscillations are generated in an electrical circuit, the frequency of which is then compared or brought into coincidence with the frequency characteristic

of the absorption or emission by the atoms or molecules when they change between two selected energy levels. The National Physical Laboratory (NPL) routinely uses clocks of high stability produced by locking a quartz oscillator to the frequencies defined by caesium or hydrogen atoms.

International Atomic Time (TAI), established through international collaboration, is formed by combining the readings of many caesium clocks and was set close to the astronomically-based Universal Time (UT) near the beginning of 1958. It was formally recognized in 1971 and since 1988 January 1 has been maintained by the International Bureau of Weights and Measures (BIPM). The second markers are generated according to the International System (SI) definition adopted in 1967 at the 13th General Conference of Weights and Measures: 'The second is the duration of 9 192 631 770 periods of radiation corresponding to the transition between the two hyperfine levels of the ground state of the caesium-133 atom.'

Civil time in almost all countries is now based on Co-ordinated Universal Time (UTC), which was adopted for scientific purposes on 1972 January 1. UTC differs from TAI by an integer number of seconds (determined from studies of the rate of rotation of the Earth) and was designed to make both atomic time and UT accessible with accuracies appropriate for most users. The UTC time-scale is adjusted by the insertion (or, in principle, omission) of leap seconds in order to keep it within ±0.9 s of UT. These leap seconds are introduced, when necessary, at the same instant throughout the world, either at the end of December or at the end of June. So, for example, the 22nd leap second occurs at 0h UTC on 1999 January 1. All leap seconds so far have been positive, with 61 seconds in the final minute of the UTC month. The time 23h 59m 60s UTC is followed one second later by 0h 0m 00s of the first day of the following month. Notices concerning the insertion of leap seconds are issued by the International Earth Rotation Service (IERS) at the Observatoire de Paris.

RADIO TIME-SIGNALS

UTC is made generally available through time-signals and standard frequency broadcasts such as MSF in the UK, CHU in Canada and WWV and WWVH in the USA. These are based on national time-scales that are maintained in close agreement with UTC and provide traceability to the national time-scale and to UTC. The markers of seconds in the UTC scale coincide with those of TAI.

To disseminate the national time-scale in the UK, special signals are broadcast on behalf of the National Physical Laboratory from the BT (British Telecom) radio station at Rugby (call-sign MSF). The signals are controlled from a caesium beam atomic frequency standard and consist of a precise frequency carrier of 60 kHz which is switched off, after being on for at least half a second, to mark every second. In part of the first second of each minute the carrier may be switched on and off to carry data at 100 bits/second. In the other seconds the carrier is always off for at least one tenth of a second at the start and then it carries an on-off code giving the British clock time and date, together with information identifying the start of the next minute. Changes to and from summer time are made following government announcements. Leap seconds are inserted as announced by the IERS and information provided by them on the difference between UTC and UT is also signalled. Other broadcast signals in the UK include the BBC six pips signal, the BT Timeline ('speaking clock'), the NPL Truetime service for computers, and a coded time-signal on the BBC 198 kHz transmitters which is used for timing in the electricity supply industry. From 1972 January 1 the six pips on the BBC have consisted of five short pips from second 55 to second 59 (six pips in the case of a leap second) followed by one lengthened pip, the start of which indicates the exact minute. From 1990 February 5 these signals have been controlled by the BBC with seconds markers referenced to the satellite-based US navigation system GPS (Global Positioning System) and time and day referenced to the MSF transmitter. Formerly they were generated by the Royal Greenwich Observatory. The BT Timeline is compared daily with the National Physical Laboratory caesium beam atomic frequency standard at the Rugby radio station. The NPL Truetime service is directly connected to the national time scale.

Accurate timing may also be obtained from the signals of international navigation systems such as the ground-based Omega, or the satellite-based American GPS or Russian GLONASS systems.

STANDARD TIME

Since 1880 the standard time in Britain has been Greenwich Mean Time (GMT); a statute that year enacted that the word 'time' when used in any legal document relating to Britain meant, unless otherwise specifically stated, the mean time of the Greenwich meridian. Greenwich was adopted as the universal meridian on 13 October 1884. A system of standard time by zones is used world-wide, standard time in each zone differing from that of the Greenwich meridian by an integral number of hours, either fast or slow. The large territories of the USA and Canada are divided into zones approximately 7.5° on either side of central meridians. (For time zones of countries of the world, see Index.)

Variations from the standard time of some countries occur during part of the year; they are decided annually and are usually referred to as Summer Time or Daylight Saving Time.

At the 180th meridian the time can be either 12 hours fast on Greenwich Mean Time or 12 hours slow, and a change of date occurs. The internationally-recognized date or calendar line is a modification of the 180th meridian, drawn so as to include islands of any one group on the same side of the line, or for political reasons. The line is indicated by joining up the following co-ordinates:

Lat.	Long.	Lat.	Long.
60° S.	180°	48° N.	180°
51° S.	180°	53° N.	170° E.
45° S.	172.5° W.	65.5° N. 169° W.	
15° S.	172.5° W.	75° N.	180°
5° S.	180°		

BRITISH SUMMER TIME

In 1916 an Act ordained that during a defined period of that year the legal time for general purposes in Great Britain should be one hour in advance of Greenwich Mean Time. The Summer Time Acts 1922 and 1925 defined the period during which Summer Time was to be in force, stabilizing practice until the Second World War.

During the war the duration of Summer Time was extended and in the years 1941 to 1945 and in 1947 Double Summer Time (two hours in advance of Greenwich Mean Time) was in force. After the war, Summer Time was extended each year in 1948–52 and 1961–4 by Order in Council.

Between 1968 October 27 and 1971 October 31 clocks were kept one hour ahead of Greenwich Mean Time throughout the year. This was known as British Standard Time.

The most recent legislation is the Summer Time Act 1972, which enacted that 'the period of summer time for the purposes of this Act is the period beginning at two o'clock,

Greenwich mean time, in the morning of the day after the third Saturday in March or, if that day is Easter Day, the day after the second Saturday in March, and ending at two o'clock, Greenwich mean time, in the morning of the day after the fourth Saturday in October.'

The duration of Summer Time can be varied by Order in Council and in recent years alterations have been made to bring the operation of Summer Time in Britain closer to similar provisions in other countries of the European Union; for instance, since 1981 the hour of changeover has been 01h Greenwich Mean Time.

The duration of Summer Time in the next few years is:
1999   March 28 01h GMT to October 31 01h GMT
2000   March 26 01h GMT to October 29 01h GMT
2001   March 25 01h GMT to October 28 01h GMT

MEAN REFRACTION

Alt.	Ref.	Alt.	Ref.	Alt.	Ref.
° ′	′	° ′	′	° ′	′
1 20	21	3 12	13	7 54	6
1 30	20	3 34	12	9 27	5
1 41	19	4 00	11	11 39	4
1 52	18	4 30	10	15 00	3
2 05	17	5 06	9	20 42	2
2 19	16	5 50	8	32 20	1
2 35	15	6 44	7	62 17	0
2 52	14	7 54		90 00	
3 12					

The refraction table is in the form of a critical table (see page 69)

ASTRONOMICAL CONSTANTS

Solar parallax	8″.794
Astronomical unit	149597870 km
Precession for the year 1999	50″.291
Precession in right ascension	3s.075
Precession in declination	20″.043
Constant of nutation	9″.202
Constant of aberration	20″.496
Mean obliquity of ecliptic (1999)	23° 26′ 22″
Moon's equatorial hor. parallax	57′ 02″.70
Velocity of light in vacuo per second	299792.5 km
Solar motion per second	20.0 km
Equatorial radius of the Earth	6378.140 km
Polar radius of the Earth	6356.755 km
North galactic pole (IAU standard)	
RA 12h 49m (1950.0). Dec. 27°.4 N.	
Solar apex	RA 18h 06m Dec. + 30°
Length of year (in mean solar days)	
Tropical	365.24219
Sidereal	365.25636
Anomalistic (perihelion to perihelion)	365.25964
Eclipse	346.6200

Length of month (mean values)	d	h	m	s
New Moon to New	29	12	44	02.9
Sidereal	27	07	43	11.5
Anomalistic (perigee to perigee)	27	13	18	33.2

ELEMENTS OF THE SOLAR SYSTEM

Orb	Mean distance from Sun (Earth = 1)	km 10⁶	Sidereal period days	Synodic period days	Incl. of orbit to ecliptic ° '	Diameter km	Mass (Earth = 1)	Period of rotation on axis days
Sun	—	—	—	—	—	1,392,530	332,946	25-35*
Mercury	0.39	58	88.0	116	7 00	4,879	0.0553	58.646
Venus	0.72	108	224.7	584	3 24	12,104	0.8150	243.019r
Earth	1.00	150	365.3	—	—	12,756e	1.0000	0.997
Mars	1.52	228	687.0	780	1 51	6,794e	0.1074	1.026
Jupiter	5.20	778	4,332.6	399	1 18	142,984e / 133,708p	317.89	0.410e
Saturn	9.54	1427	10,759.2	378	2 29	120,536e / 108,728p	95.18	0.426e
Uranus	19.18	2870	30,684.6	370	0 46	51,118e	14.54	0.718r
Neptune	30.06	4497	60,191.0	367	1 46	49,528e	17.15	0.671
Pluto	39.80	5954	91,708.2	367	17 09	2,302	0.002	6.387

e equatorial, p polar, r retrograde, * depending on latitude

THE SATELLITES

Name	Star mag.	Mean distance from primary km	Sidereal period of revolution d
EARTH			
I Moon	—	384,400	27.322
MARS			
I Phobos	12	9,378	0.319
II Deimos	13	23,459	1.262
JUPITER			
XVI Metis	17	127,960	0.295
XV Adrastea	19	128,980	0.298
V Amalthea	14	181,300	0.498
XIV Thebe	16	221,900	0.675
I Io	5	421,600	1.769
II Europa	5	670,900	3.551
III Ganymede	5	1,070,000	7.155
IV Callisto	6	1,883,000	16.689
XIII Leda	20	11,094,000	239
VI Himalia	15	11,480,000	251
X Lysithea	18	11,720,000	259
VII Elara	17	11,737,000	260
XII Ananke	19	21,200,000	631r
XI Carme	18	22,600,000	692r
VIII Pasiphae	17	23,500,000	735r
IX Sinope	18	23,700,000	758r
SATURN			
XVIII Pan	—	133,583	0.575
XV Atlas	18	137,670	0.602
XVI Prometheus	16	139,353	0.613
XVII Pandora	16	141,700	0.629
XI Epimetheus	15	151,422	0.694
X Janus	14	151,472	0.695
I Mimas	13	185,520	0.942
II Enceladus	12	238,020	1.370
III Tethys	10	294,660	1.888
XIII Telesto	19	294,660	1.888
XIV Calypso	19	294,660	1.888
IV Dione	10	377,400	2.737
XII Helene	18	377,400	2.737
V Rhea	10	527,040	4.518
VI Titan	8	1,221,830	15.945

Name	Star mag.	Mean distance from primary km	Sidereal period of revolution d
SATURN			
VII Hyperion	14	1,481,100	21.277
VIII Iapetus	11	3,561,300	79.330
IX Phoebe	16	12,952,000	550.48r
URANUS			
VI Cordelia	—	49,770	0.335
VII Ophelia	—	53,790	0.376
VIII Bianca	—	59,170	0.435
IX Cressida	—	61,780	0.464
X Desdemona	—	62,680	0.474
XI Juliet	—	64,350	0.493
XII Portia	—	66,090	0.513
XIII Rosalind	—	69,940	0.558
XIV Belinda	—	75,260	0.624
XV Puck	—	86,010	0.762
V Miranda	17	129,390	1.413
I Ariel	14	191,020	2.520
II Umbriel	15	266,300	4.144
III Titania	14	435,910	8.706
IV Oberon	14	583,520	13.463
S/1997U1	—	72,000,000	579
S/1997U2	—	122,000,000	1,289
NEPTUNE			
III Naiad	25	48,230	0.294
IV Thalassa	24	50,070	0.311
V Despina	23	52,530	0.335
VI Galatea	22	61,950	0.429
VII Larissa	22	73,550	0.555
VIII Proteus	20	117,650	1.122
I Triton	13	354,760	5.877
II Nereid	19	5,513,400	360.136
PLUTO			
I Charon	17	19,600	6.387

THE EARTH

The shape of the Earth is that of an oblate spheroid or solid of revolution whose meridian sections are ellipses not differing much from circles, whilst the sections at right angles are circles. The length of the equatorial axis is about 12,756 km, and that of the polar axis is 12,714 km. The mean density of the Earth is 5.5 times that of water, although that of the surface layer is less. The Earth and Moon revolve about their common centre of gravity in a lunar month; this centre in turn revolves round the Sun in a plane known as the ecliptic, that passes through the Sun's centre. The Earth's equator is inclined to this plane at an angle of 23.4°. This tilt is the cause of the seasons. In mid-latitudes, and when the Sun is high above the Equator, not only does the high noon altitude make the days longer, but the Sun's rays fall more directly on the Earth's surface; these effects combine to produce summer. In equatorial regions the noon altitude is large throughout the year, and there is little variation in the length of the day. In higher latitudes the noon altitude is lower, and the days in summer are appreciably longer than those in winter.

The average velocity of the Earth in its orbit is 30 km a second. It makes a complete rotation on its axis in about 23h 56m of mean time, which is the sidereal day. Because of its annual revolution round the Sun, the rotation with respect to the Sun, or the solar day, is more than this by about four minutes (see page 73). The extremity of the axis of rotation, or the North Pole of the Earth, is not rigidly fixed, but wanders over an area roughly 20 metres in diameter.

TERRESTRIAL MAGNETISM

A magnetic compass points along the horizontal component of a magnetic line of force. These lines of force converge on the 'magnetic dip-poles', the places where a freely suspended magnetized needle would become vertical. Not only do these poles move with time, but their exact locations are ill-defined, particularly so in the case of the north dip-pole where the lines of force on the north side of it, instead of converging radially, tend to bunch into a channel. Although it is therefore unrealistic to attempt to specify the locations of the dip-poles exactly, the present approximate adopted positions are 79°.8 N., 106°.7 W. and 64°.6 S., 138°.5 E. The two magnetic dip-poles are thus not antipodal, the line joining them passing the centre of the Earth at a distance of about 1,250 km. The distances of the magnetic dip-poles from the north and south geographical poles are about 1,200 km and 2,800 km respectively.

There is also a 'magnetic equator', at all points of which the vertical component of the Earth's magnetic field is zero and a magnetized needle remains horizontal. This line runs between 2° and 10° north of the geographical equator in Asia and Africa, turns sharply south off the west African coast, and crosses South America through Brazil, Bolivia and Peru; it recrosses the geographical equator in mid-Pacific.

Reference has already been made to secular changes in the Earth's field. The following table indicates the changes in magnetic declination (or variation of the compass). Declination is the angle in the horizontal plane between the direction of true north and that in which a magnetic compass points. Similar, though much smaller, changes have occurred in 'dip' or magnetic inclination. Secular changes differ throughout the world. Although the London

observations strongly suggest a cycle with a period of several hundred years, an exact repetition is unlikely.

London		Greenwich	
1580	11° 15′ E.	1850	22° 24′ W.
1622	5° 56′ E.	1900	16° 29′ W.
1665	1° 22′ W.	1925	13° 10′ W.
1730	13° 00′ W.	1950	9° 07′ W.
1773	21° 09′ W.	1975	6° 39′ W.

In order that up-to-date information on declination may be available, many governments publish magnetic charts on which there are lines (isogonic lines) passing through all places at which specified values of declination will be found at the date of the chart.

In the British Isles, isogonic lines now run approximately north-east to south-west. Though there are considerable local deviations due to geological causes, a rough value of magnetic declination may be obtained by assuming that at 50° N. on the meridian of Greenwich, the value in 1999 is 2° 46′ west and allowing an increase of 15′ for each degree of latitude northwards and one of 28′ for each degree of longitude westwards. For example, at 53° N., 5° W., declination will be about 2° 46′ + 45′ + 140′, i.e. 5° 51′ west. The average annual change at the present time is about 11′ decrease.

The number of magnetic observatories is about 200, irregularly distributed over the globe. There are three in Great Britain, run by the British Geological Survey: at Hartland, north Devon; at Eskdalemuir, Dumfriesshire; and at Lerwick, Shetland Islands. The following are some recent annual mean values of the magnetic elements for Hartland.

Year	Declination West ° ′	Dip or inclination ° ′	Horizontal force gauss	Vertical force gauss
1960	9 59	66 44	0.1871	0.4350
1965	9 30	66 34	0.1887	0.4354
1970	9 06	66 26	0.1903	0.4364
1975	8 32	66 17	0.1921	0.4373
1980	7 44	66 10	0.1933	0.4377
1985	6 56	66 08	0.1938	0.4380
1990	6 15	66 10	0.1939	0.4388
1995	5 33	66 07	0.1946	0.4395
1997	5 13	66 06	0.1948	0.4398

The normal world-wide terrestrial magnetic field corresponds approximately to that of a very strong small bar magnet near the centre of the Earth, but with appreciable smooth spatial departures. The origin and the slow secular change of the normal field are not fully understood but are generally ascribed to electric currents associated with fluid motions in the Earth's core. Superimposed on the normal field are local and regional anomalies whose magnitudes may in places approach that of the normal field; these are due to the influence of mineral deposits in the Earth's crust. A small proportion of the field is of external origin, mostly associated with electric currents in the ionosphere. The configuration of the external field and the ionization of the atmosphere depend on the incident particle and radiation flux from the Sun. There are, therefore, short-term and non-periodic as well as diurnal, 27-day, seasonal and 11-year periodic changes in the magnetic field, dependent upon the position of the Sun and the degree of solar activity.

MAGNETIC STORMS

Occasionally, sometimes with great suddenness, the Earth's magnetic field is subject for several hours to marked disturbance. During a severe storm in 1989 the declination at Lerwick changed by almost 8° in less than an hour. In many instances such disturbances are accompanied by widespread displays of aurorae, marked changes in the incidence of cosmic rays, an increase in the reception of 'noise' from the Sun at radio frequencies, and rapid changes in the ionosphere and induced electric currents within the Earth which adversely affect radio and telegraphic communications. The disturbances are caused by changes in the stream of ionized particles which emanates from the Sun and through which the Earth is continuously passing. Some of these changes are associated with visible eruptions on the Sun, usually in the region of sun-spots. There is a marked tendency for disturbances to recur after intervals of about 27 days, the apparent period of rotation of the Sun on its axis, which is consistent with the sources being located on particular areas of the Sun.

ARTIFICIAL SATELLITES

To consider the orbit of an artificial satellite, it is best to imagine that one is looking at the Earth from a distant point in space. The Earth would then be seen to be rotating about its axis inside the orbit described by the rapidly revolving satellite. The inclination of a satellite orbit to the Earth's equator (which generally remains almost constant throughout the satellite's lifetime) gives at once the maximum range of latitudes over which the satellite passes. Thus a satellite whose orbit has an inclination of 53° will pass overhead all latitudes between 53° S. and 53° N., but would never be seen in the zenith of any place nearer the poles than these latitudes. If we consider a particular place on the earth, whose latitude is less than the inclination of the satellite's orbit, then the Earth's rotation carries this place first under the northbound part of the orbit and then under the southbound portion of the orbit, these two occurrences being always less than 12 hours apart for satellites moving in direct orbits (i.e. to the east). (For satellites in retrograde orbits, the words 'northbound' and 'southbound' should be interchanged in the preceding statement.) As the value of the latitude of the observer increases and approaches the value of the inclination of the orbit, so this interval gets shorter until (when the latitude is equal to the inclination) only one overhead passage occurs each day.

Observation of Satellites

The regression of the orbit around the Earth causes alternate periods of visibility and invisibility, though this is of little concern to the radio or radar observer. To the visual observer the following cycle of events normally occurs (though the cycle may start in any position): invisibility, morning observations before dawn, invisibility, evening observations after dusk, invisibility, morning observations before dawn, and so on. With reasonably high satellites and for observers in high latitudes around the summer solstice, the evening observations follow the morning observations without interruption as sunlight passing over the polar regions can still illuminate satellites which are passing over temperate latitudes at local midnight. At the moment all satellites rely on sunlight to make them visible, though a satellite with a flashing light has been suggested for a future launching. The observer must be in darkness or twilight in order to make any useful observations. (For durations of twilight; and sunrise and sunset times, *see* Page Two of each month.)

Some of the satellites are visible to the naked eye and much interest has been aroused by the spectacle of a bright satellite disappearing into the Earth's shadow. The event is even more interesting telescopically as the disappearance occurs gradually as the satellite traverses the Earth's penumbral shadow, and during the last few seconds before the eclipse is complete the satellite may change colour (in suitable atmospheric conditions) from yellow to red. This is because the last rays of sunlight are refracted through the denser layers of our atmosphere before striking the satellite.

Some satellites rotate about one or more axes so that a periodic variation in brightness is observed. This was particularly noticeable in several of the Soviet satellites.

Satellite research has provided some interesting results, including a revised value of the Earth's oblateness (1/298.2), and the discovery of the Van Allen radiation belts.

Launchings

Apart from their names, e.g. Cosmos 6 Rocket, the satellites are also classified according to their date of launch. Thus 1961 α refers to the first satellite launching of 1961. A number following the Greek letter indicated the relative brightness of the satellites put in orbit. From the beginning of 1963 the Greek letters were replaced by numbers and the numbers by roman letters e.g. 1963–01A. For all satellites successfully injected into orbit the following table gives the designation and names of the main objects, the launch date and some initial orbital data. These are the inclination to the equator (i), the nodal period of revolution (P), the eccentricity (e), and the perigee height.

Although most of the satellites launched are injected into orbits less than 1,000 km high, there are an increasing number of satellites in geostationary orbits, i.e. where the orbital inclination is zero, the eccentricity close to zero, and the period of revolution is 1436.1 minutes. Thus the satellite is permanently situated over the equator at one selected longitude at a mean height of 35,786 km. This geostationary band is crowded. In one case there are four television satellites (Astra 1A, Astra 1B, Astra 1C and Astra 1D) orbiting within a few tens of kilometres of each other. In the sky they appear to be separated by only a few arc minutes.

In 1997 a number of *Iridium* satellites have been launched into high inclination orbits (*see* table). These are owned by the mobile telephone company Cellnet. For visual observers, these satellites have an interesting characteristic, namely that the large solar panels they carry can, when in exactly the right orientation with respect to the Sun and the observer, give off a 'flare' in brightness which can on occasion attain a magnitude of −6, much brighter than Venus. The flare can be visible to the naked eye for nearly a minute.

ARTIFICIAL SATELLITE LAUNCHES 1997–8

Desig-nation	Satellite	Launch date	i	P	e	Perigee height
1997–			°	m		km
021	China DHF3-2, rocket	May 11	0.2	1435.3	0.790	25759
022	Cosmos 2342, rocket, platform, rocket	May 14	62.7	717.1	0.733	505
023	Shuttle 84	May 15	51.6	92.3	0.044	384
024	Cosmos 2343, rocket	May 15	64.9	89.4	0.026	206
025	Comsat, rocket, rocket	May 20	19.6	667.5	0.722	1280
026	Telstar 5, rocket, platform, rocket	May 24	7.7	942.3	0.770	15107
027	Inmarsat 3F4, Insat2D, rocket	June 3	7.0	630.0	0.712	218
028	Cosmos 2344, rocket	June 6	63.2	130.1	0.235	1510
029	FY 2, CZ 3A, rocket	June 10	27.8	634.1	0.713	141
030	Iridium 14, 12, 10, 9, 13, 16, 11	June 18	86.4	94.9	0.061	502
031	Intelsat 802, rocket	June 25	0.1	1431.3	0.814	35610
032	Shuttle	June 30	28.5	90.4	0.032	300
033	Progress M35, rocket	July 5	51.6	90.2	0.030	264
034	Iridium 15, 17, 18, 20, 21, rocket	July 9	86.4	97.5	0.077	625
035	GPS Navstar, rocket, rocket	July 23	54.7	712.6	0.732	19875
036	Superbird C, rocket	July 28	25.3	1969.7	0.788	333
037	Orbview 2, rocket	August 1	98.2	99.0	0.000	707
038	Soyuz TM26, rocket	August 5	51.6	91.5	0.042	370
039	Shuttle 85, Christa Spas	August 7	57.0	90.0	0.029	280
040	Panamsat 6, rocket	August 8	0.0	1436.0	0.000	35773
041	Cosmos 2345, rocket, rocket	August 14	50.0	622.0	0.710	233
042	Agila 2, rocket	August 19	24.6	806.4	0.750	171
043	Iridium 26, 25, 24, 23, 22, rocket	August 21	86.7	95.7	0.066	544
044	SSTI Lewis, rocket	August 23	97.5	90.7	0.032	295
045	ACE, rocket	August 25		(unknown)		
046	Panamsat 5, rocket	August 28	14.5	804.4	0.749	8589
047	Forte, rocket	August 29	70.0	101.2	0.099	800
048	Iridium Sim2, Sim1, rocket	September 1	86.2	97.3	0.076	623
049	Hot Bird 3, Meteosat 7, rocket	September 2	7.0	631.2	0.713	213
050	GE 3, rocket	September 4	19.1	796.9	0.748	306
051	Iridium 29, 32, 33, 27, 28, 30, 31, rocket	September 14	86.5	95.0	0.061	506
052	Cosmos 2346, rocket	September 23	82.9	104.5	0.117	939
053	Intelsat 803	September 24	7.0	633.3	0.713	292
054	Molniya 1T, rocket, platform, rocket	September 24	62.7	735.9	0.737	445
055	Shuttle 86	September 26	51.6	91.7	0.044	384
056	Iridium 19, 37, 36, 35, 34, rocket	September 27	86.7	95.7	0.066	545
057	IRS 1D, rocket	September 29	98.5	96.8	0.072	381
058	Progress M36, rocket, Sputnik 40	October 5	51.6	92.2	0.044	383
059	Echostar 3, rocket	October 5	12.0	818.8	0.752	6571
060	Foton 11, rocket	October 9	62.7	90.4	0.031	219
061	Cassini, rocket	October 15		(Heliocentric orbit)		
062	Apstar 2R, rocket	October 16	0.1	1707.3	0.829	34276
063	Step M4, rocket	October 22	45.0	93.8	0.055	434
064	Lacrosse 3, rocket	October 24	57.0	98.0	0.081	665
065	DSCS III B13, rocket	October 25	0.0	1436.0	0.815	35789
066	Maqsat H, Maqsat B, YES, rocket	October 30	7.7	467.3	0.657	535
067	GPS Navstar, rocket, rocket	November 6	35.0	357.4	0.596	185
068	USA 134, rocket	November 8		(unknown)		
069	Iridium 43, 41, 40, 39, 38, rocket	November 9	86.5	97.5	0.077	627
070	Kupon, rocket, platform, rocket	November 12	0.0	1449.9	0.816	36035
071	Sirius 2, Indostar 1, rocket	November 12	0.1	1426.4	0.814	35420
072	Resurs F1M, rocket	November 18	82.2	89.1	0.021	209
073	Shuttle 87, Spartan 201	November 19	28.5	90.0	0.029	281
074	TRMM, Hikoboshi, Orihime, rocket	November 27	35.0	91.9	0.042	369
075	JCSAT 5, Equator S, rocket	December 2	4.0	630.7	0.713	220

Designation	Satellite	Launch date	i	P	e	Perigee height
1997–			°	m		km
076	Astra 1G, Proton, platform, rocket	December 2	12.4	841.5	0.756	10320
077	Iridium 42, 44	December 8	86.2	97.4	0.076	627
078	Galaxy 8I, rocket	December 9	27.0	821.0	0.752	166
079	Cosmos 2347, rocket	December 9	65.0	92.8	0.047	406
080	Cosmos 2348, rocket	December 15	67.0	89.2	0.022	161
081	Progress M37, rocket	December 20	51.6	90.3	0.030	265
082	Iridium 45, 46, 47, 48, 49, rocket	December 20	86.5	97.4	0.076	625
083	Intelsat 804, rocket	December 22	7.0	630.3	0.713	266
084	Orbcomm F 5, 6, 7, 8, 9, 10, 11, 12, rocket, HAPS	December 23	45.0	101.2	0.100	816
085	Earlybird, rocket	December 24	97.2	94.3	0.057	480
086	Asiasat 3, rocket, platform, rocket	December 24	51.5	636.3	0.714	270
1998–						
001	Lunar Prospector, rocket	January 7		(Selenocentric orbit)		
002	Skynet 4D, rocket	January 10	23.6	654.8	0.719	1186
003	Shuttle 89	January 23	51.6	91.1	0.036	299
004	Soyuz TM27, rocket	January 29	51.6	89.9	0.028	256
005	US137 Capric, rocket	January 29		(Heliocentric orbit)		
006	Brasilsat B3, Inmarsat 3F5, platform, Spelda	February 4	7.0	631.2	0.713	212
007	GFO, Orbcomm G-1, Orbcomm G-2, Celestis 02, rocket	February 10	108.0	101.5	0.101	782
008	Globalstar FM1, FM2, FM3, FM4, rocket	February 14	52.0	110.5	0.150	1244
009	Cosmos 2349, rocket	February 17	70.4	89.4	0.023	212
010	Iridium 50, 56, 52, 53, 54, rocket	February 18	86.5	99.3	0.088	722
011	Kakehasha, rocket	February 21	30.1	106.3	0.129	249
012	Snoe, Teledisc-1, rocket	February 26	97.7	95.9	0.067	536
013	Hot Bird 4, rocket	February 27	7.0	627.8	0.712	183
014	Intelsat 806, rocket	February 28	23.8	627.8	0.712	189

Time Measurement and Calendars

MEASUREMENTS OF TIME

Measurements of time are based on the time taken by the earth to rotate on its axis (day); by the moon to revolve round the earth (month); and by the earth to revolve round the sun (year). From these, which are not commensurable, certain average or mean intervals have been adopted for ordinary use.

THE DAY

The day begins at midnight and is divided into 24 hours of 60 minutes, each of 60 seconds. The hours are counted from midnight up to 12 noon (when the sun crosses the meridian), and these hours are designated a.m. (*ante meridiem*); and again from noon up to 12 midnight, which hours are designated p.m. (*post meridiem*), except when the 24-hour reckoning is employed. The 24-hour reckoning ignores a.m. and p.m., numbering the hours 0 to 23 from midnight.

Colloquially the 24 hours are divided into day and night, day being the time while the sun is above the horizon (including the four stages of twilight defined on page 72). Day is subdivided into morning, the early part of daytime, ending at noon; afternoon, from noon to about 6 p.m.; and evening, which may be said to extend from 6 p.m. until midnight. Night, the dark period between day and day, begins at the close of astronomical twilight (*see* page 72) and extends beyond midnight to sunrise the next day.

The names of the days are derived from Old English translations or adaptations of the Roman titles.

Sunday	Sun	Sol
Monday	Moon	Luna
Tuesday	Tiw/Tyr (god of war)	Mars
Wednesday	Woden/Odin	Mercury
Thursday	Thor	Jupiter
Friday	Frigga/Freyja (goddess of love)	
		Venus
Saturday	Saeternes	Saturn

THE MONTH

The month in the ordinary calendar is approximately the twelfth part of a year, but the lengths of the different months vary from 28 (or 29) days to 31.

THE YEAR

The equinoctial or tropical year is the time that the earth takes to revolve round the sun from equinox to equinox, i.e. 365.24219 mean solar days, or 365 days 5 hours 48 minutes and 45 seconds.

The calendar year usually consists of 365 days but a year containing 366 days is called bissextile (*see* Roman calendar, page 89) or leap year, one day being added to the month of February so that a date 'leaps over' a day of the week. In the Roman calendar the day that was repeated was the sixth day before the beginning of March, the equivalent of 24 February.

A year is a leap year if the date of the year is divisible by four without remainder, unless it is the last year of the century. The last year of a century is a leap year only if its number is divisible by 400 without remainder, e.g. the years 1800 and 1900 had only 365 days but the year 2000 will have 366 days.

THE SOLSTICE

A solstice is the point in the tropical year at which the sun attains its greatest distance, north or south, from the Equator. In the northern hemisphere the furthest point north of the Equator marks the summer solstice and the furthest point south the winter solstice.

The date of the solstice varies according to locality. For example, if the summer solstice falls on 21 June late in the day by Greenwich time, that day will be the longest of the year at Greenwich though it may be by only a second, but it will fall on 22 June, local date, in Japan, and so 22 June will be the longest day there. The date of the solstice is also affected by the length of the tropical year, which is 365 days 6 hours less about 11 minutes 15 seconds. If a solstice happens late on 21 June in one year, it will be nearly six hours later in the next (unless the next year is a leap year), i.e. early on 22 June, and that will be the longest day.

This delay of the solstice does not continue because the extra day in leap year brings it back a day in the calendar. However, because of the 11 minutes 15 seconds mentioned above, the additional day in leap year brings the solstice back too far by 45 minutes, and the time of the solstice in the calendar is earlier, in a four-year pattern, as the century progresses. The last year of a century is in most cases not a leap year, and the omission of the extra day puts the date of the solstice later by about six hours too much. Compensation for this is made by the fourth centennial year being a leap year. The solstice has become earlier in date throughout this century and, because the year 2000 is a leap year, the solstice will get earlier still throughout the 21st century.

The date of the winter solstice, the shortest day of the year, is affected by the same factors as the longest day.

At Greenwich the sun sets at its earliest by the clock about ten days before the shortest day. The daily change in the time of sunset is due in the first place to the sun's movement southwards at this time of the year, which diminishes the interval between the sun's transit and its setting. However, the daily decrease of the Equation of Time causes the time of apparent noon to be continuously later day by day, which to some extent counteracts the first effect. The rates of the change of these two quantities are not equal or uniform; their combination causes the date of earliest sunset to be 12 or 13 December at Greenwich. In more southerly latitudes the effect of the movement of the sun is less, and the change in the time of sunset depends on that of the Equation of Time to a greater degree, and the date of earliest sunset is earlier than it is at Greenwich, e.g. on the Equator it is about 1 November.

THE EQUINOX

The equinox is the point at which the sun crosses the Equator and day and night are of equal length all over the world. This occurs in March and September.

DOG DAYS

The days about the heliacal rising of the Dog Star, noted from ancient times as the hottest period of the year in the northern hemisphere, are called the Dog Days. Their incidence has been variously calculated as depending on the Greater or Lesser Dog Star (Sirius or Procyon) and their duration has been reckoned as from 30 to 54 days. A generally accepted period is from 3 July to 15 August.

CHRISTIAN CALENDAR

In the Christian chronological system the years are distinguished by cardinal numbers before or after the birth of Christ, the period being denoted by the letters BC (Before Christ) or, more rarely, AC (*Ante Christum*), and AD (*Anno Domini* – In the Year of Our Lord). The correlative dates of the epoch are the fourth year of the 194th Olympiad, the 753rd year from the foundation of Rome, AM 3761 (Jewish chronology), and the 4714th year of the Julian period. The actual date of the birth of Christ is somewhat uncertain.

The system was introduced into Italy in the sixth century. Though first used in France in the seventh century, it was not universally established there until about the eighth century. It has been said that the system was introduced into England by St Augustine (AD 596), but it was probably not generally used until some centuries later. It was ordered to be used by the Bishops at the Council of Chelsea (AD 816).

THE JULIAN CALENDAR

In the Julian calendar (adopted by the Roman Empire in 45 BC, *see* page 89) all the centennial years were leap years, and for this reason towards the close of the 16th century there was a difference of ten days between the tropical and calendar years; the equinox fell on 11 March of the calendar, whereas at the time of the Council of Nicaea (AD 325), it had fallen on 21 March. In 1582 Pope Gregory ordained that 5 October should be called 15 October and that of the end-century years only the fourth should be a leap year (*see* page 81).

THE GREGORIAN CALENDAR

The Gregorian calendar was adopted by Italy, France, Spain and Portugal in 1582, by Prussia, the Roman Catholic German states, Switzerland, Holland and Flanders on 1 January 1583, by Poland in 1586, Hungary in 1587, the Protestant German and Netherland states and Denmark in 1700, and by Great Britain and Dominions (including the North American colonies) in 1752, by the omission of eleven days (3 September being reckoned as 14 September). Sweden omitted the leap day in 1700 but observed leap days in 1704 and 1708, and reverted to the Julian calendar by having two leap days in 1712; the Gregorian calendar was adopted in 1753 by the omission of eleven days (18 February being reckoned as 1 March). Japan adopted the calendar in 1872, China in 1912, Bulgaria in 1915, Turkey and Soviet Russia in 1918, Yugoslavia and Romania in 1919, and Greece in 1923.

In the same year that the change was made in England from the Julian to the Gregorian calendar, the beginning of the new year was also changed from 25 March to 1 January (*see* page 86).

THE ORTHODOX CHURCHES

Some Orthodox Churches still use the Julian reckoning but the majority of Greek Orthodox Churches and the Romanian Orthodox Church have adopted a modified 'New Calendar', observing the Gregorian calendar for fixed feasts and the Julian for movable feasts.

The Orthodox Church year begins on 1 September. There are four fast periods and, in addition to Pascha (Easter), twelve great feasts, as well as numerous commemorations of the saints of the Old and New Testaments throughout the year.

THE DOMINICAL LETTER

The dominical letter is one of the letters A–G which are used to denote the Sundays in successive years. If the first day of the year is a Sunday the letter is A; if the second, B; the third, C; and so on. A leap year requires two letters, the first for 1 January to 29 February, the second for 1 March to 31 December (*see* page 84).

EPIPHANY

The feast of the Epiphany, commemorating the manifestation of Christ, later became associated with the offering of gifts by the Magi. The day was of great importance from the time of the Council of Nicaea (AD 325), as the primate of Alexandria was charged at every Epiphany feast with the announcement in a letter to the churches of the date of the forthcoming Easter. The day was also of importance in Britain as it influenced dates, ecclesiastical and lay, e.g. Plough Monday, when work was resumed in the fields, fell on the Monday in the first full week after Epiphany.

LENT

The Teutonic word *Lent*, which denotes the fast preceding Easter, originally meant no more than the spring season; but from Anglo-Saxon times at least it has been used as the equivalent of the more significant Latin term Quadragesima, meaning the 'forty days' or, more literally, the fortieth day. Ash Wednesday is the first day of Lent, which ends at midnight before Easter Day.

PALM SUNDAY

Palm Sunday, the Sunday before Easter and the beginning of Holy Week, commemorates the triumphal entry of Christ into Jerusalem and is celebrated in Britain (when palm is not available) by branches of willow gathered for use in the decoration of churches on that day.

MAUNDY THURSDAY

Maundy Thursday is the day before Good Friday, the name itself being a corruption of *dies mandati* (day of the mandate) when Christ washed the feet of the disciples and gave them the mandate to love one another.

EASTER DAY

Easter Day is the first Sunday after the full moon which happens on, or next after, the 21st day of March; if the full moon happens on a Sunday, Easter Day is the Sunday after.

This definition is contained in an Act of Parliament (24 Geo. II c. 23) and explanation is given in the preamble to the Act that the day of full moon depends on certain tables that have been prepared. These tables are summarized in the early pages of the Book of Common Prayer. The moon referred to is not the real moon of the heavens, but a hypothetical moon on whose 'full' the date of Easter depends, and the lunations of this 'calendar' moon consist of twenty-nine and thirty days alternately, with certain necessary modifications to make the date of its full agree as nearly as possible with that of the real moon, which is known as the Paschal Full Moon. At present, Easter falls on one of 35 days (22 March to 25 April).

A FIXED EASTER

In 1928 the House of Commons agreed to a motion for the third reading of a bill proposing that Easter Day shall, in the calendar year next but one after the commencement of the Act and in all subsequent years, be the first Sunday after the second Saturday in April. Easter would thus fall on the second or third Sunday in April, i.e. between 9 and 15 April (inclusive). A clause in the Bill provided that before it shall come into operation, regard shall be had to any opinion expressed officially by the various Christian churches.

Efforts by the World Council of Churches to secure a unanimous choice of date for Easter by its member churches have so far been unsuccessful.

ROGATION DAYS

Rogation Days are the Monday, Tuesday and Wednesday preceding Ascension Day and from the fifth century were observed as public fasts with solemn processions and supplications. The processions were discontinued as religious observances at the Reformation, but survive in the ceremony known as 'beating the parish bounds'. Rogation Sunday is the Sunday before Ascension Day.

EMBER DAYS

The Ember Days at the four seasons are the Wednesday, Friday and Saturday (*a*) before the third Sunday in Advent,

(*b*) before the second Sunday in Lent, and (*c*) before the Sundays nearest to the festivals of St Peter and of St Michael and All Angels.

TRINITY SUNDAY

Trinity Sunday is eight weeks after Easter Day, on the Sunday following Pentecost (Whit Sunday). Subsequent Sundays are reckoned in the Book of Common Prayer calendar of the Church of England as 'after Trinity'.

Thomas Becket (1118–70) was consecrated Archbishop of Canterbury on the Sunday after Whit Sunday and his first act was to ordain that the day of his consecration should be held as a new festival in honour of the Holy Trinity. This observance spread from Canterbury throughout the whole of Christendom.

MOVABLE FEASTS TO THE YEAR 2031

Year	Ash Wednesday	Easter	Ascension	Pentecost (Whit Sunday)	Advent Sunday
1999	17 February	4 April	13 May	23 May	28 November
2000	8 March	23 April	1 June	11 June	3 December
2001	28 February	15 April	24 May	3 June	2 December
2002	13 February	31 March	9 May	19 May	1 December
2003	5 March	20 April	29 May	8 June	30 November
2004	25 February	11 April	20 May	30 May	28 November
2005	9 February	27 March	5 May	15 May	27 November
2006	1 March	16 April	25 May	4 June	3 December
2007	21 February	8 April	17 May	27 May	2 December
2008	6 February	23 March	1 May	11 May	30 November
2009	25 February	12 April	21 May	31 May	29 November
2010	17 February	4 April	13 May	23 May	28 November
2011	9 March	24 April	2 June	12 June	27 November
2012	22 February	8 April	17 May	27 May	2 December
2013	13 February	31 March	9 May	19 May	1 December
2014	5 March	20 April	29 May	8 June	30 November
2015	18 February	5 April	14 May	24 May	29 November
2016	10 February	27 March	5 May	15 May	27 November
2017	1 March	16 April	25 May	4 June	3 December
2018	14 February	1 April	10 May	20 May	2 December
2019	6 March	21 April	30 May	9 June	1 December
2020	26 February	12 April	21 May	31 May	29 November
2021	17 February	4 April	13 May	23 May	28 November
2022	2 March	17 April	26 May	5 June	27 November
2023	22 February	9 April	18 May	28 May	3 December
2024	14 February	31 March	9 May	19 May	1 December
2025	5 March	20 April	29 May	8 June	30 November
2026	18 February	5 April	14 May	24 May	29 November
2027	10 February	28 March	6 May	16 May	28 November
2028	1 March	16 April	25 May	4 June	3 December
2029	14 February	1 April	10 May	20 May	2 December
2030	6 March	21 April	30 May	9 June	1 December
2031	26 February	13 April	22 May	1 June	30 November

NOTES

Ash Wednesday (first day in Lent) can fall at earliest on 4 February and at latest on 10 March

Mothering Sunday (fourth Sunday in Lent) can fall at earliest on 1 March and at latest on 4 April

Easter Day can fall at earliest on 22 March and at latest on 25 April

Ascension Day is forty days after Easter Day and can fall at earliest on 30 April and at latest on 3 June

Pentecost (Whit Sunday) is seven weeks after Easter and can fall at earliest on 10 May and at latest on 13 June

Trinity Sunday is the Sunday after Whit Sunday

Corpus Christi falls on the Thursday after Trinity Sunday

Sundays after Pentecost – there are not less than 18 and not more than 23

Advent Sunday is the Sunday nearest to 30 November

EASTER DAYS AND DOMINICAL LETTERS 1500 TO 2033

Dates up to and including 1752 are according to the Julian calendar

	1500–1599	1600–1699	1700–1799	1800–1899	1900–1999	2000–2033
March						
d 22	1573	1668	1761	1818		
e 23	1505/16	1600	1788	1845/56	1913	2008
f 24		1611/95	1706/99		1940	
g 25	1543/54	1627/38/49	1722/33/44	1883/94	1951	
A 26	1559/70/81/92	1654/65/76	1749/58/69/80	1815/26/37	1967/78/89	
b 27	1502/13/24/97	1608/87/92	1785/96	1842/53/64	1910/21/32	2005/16
c 28	1529/35/40	1619/24/30	1703/14/25	1869/75/80	1937/48	2027/32
d 29	1551/62	1635/46/57	1719/30/41/52	1807/12/91	1959/64/70	
e 30	1567/78/89	1651/62/73/84	1746/55/66/77	1823/34	1902/75/86/97	
f 31	1510/21/32/83/94	1605/16/78/89	1700/71/82/93	1839/50/61/72	1907/18/29/91	2002/13/24
April						
g 1	1526/37/48	1621/32	1711/16	1804/66/77/88	1923/34/45/56	2018/29
A 2	1553/64	1643/48	1727/38	1809/20/93/99	1961/72	
b 3	1575/80/86	1659/70/81	1743/63/68/74	1825/31/36	1904/83/88/94	
c 4	1507/18/91	1602/13/75/86/97	1708/79/90	1847/58	1915/20/26/99	2010/21
d 5	1523/34/45/56	1607/18/29/40	1702/13/24/95	1801/63/74/85/96	1931/42/53	2015/26
e 6	1539/50/61/72	1634/45/56	1729/35/40/60	1806/17/28/90	1947/58/69/80	
f 7	1504/77/88	1667/72	1751/65/76	1822/33/44	1901/12/85/96	
g 8	1509/15/20/99	1604/10/83/94	1705/87/92/98	1849/55/60	1917/28	2007/12
A 9	1531/42	1615/26/37/99	1710/21/32	1871/82	1939/44/50	2023
b 10	1547/58/69	1631/42/53/64	1726/37/48/57	1803/14/87/98	1955/66/77	
c 11	1501/12/63/74/85/96	1658/69/80	1762/73/84	1819/30/41/52	1909/71/82/93	2004
d 12	1506/17/28	1601/12/91/96	1789	1846/57/68	1903/14/25/36/98	2009/20
e 13	1533/44	1623/28	1707/18	1800/73/79/84	1941/52	2031
f 14	1555/60/66	1639/50/61	1723/34/45/54	1805/11/16/95	1963/68/74	
g 15	1571/82/93	1655/66/77/88	1750/59/70/81	1827/38	1900/06/79/90	2001
A 16	1503/14/25/36/87/98	1609/20/82/93	1704/75/86/97	1843/54/65/76	1911/22/33/95	2006/17/28
b 17	1530/41/52	1625/36	1715/20	1808/70/81/92	1927/38/49/60	2022/33
c 18	1557/68	1647/52	1731/42/56	1802/13/24/97	1954/65/76	
d 19	1500/79/84/90	1663/74/85	1747/67/72/78	1829/35/40	1908/81/87/92	
e 20	1511/22/95	1606/17/79/90	1701/12/83/94	1851/62	1919/24/30	2003/14/25
f 21	1527/38/49	1622/33/44	1717/28	1867/78/89	1935/46/57	2019/30
g 22	1565/76	1660	1739/53/64	1810/21/32	1962/73/84	
A 23	1508	1671		1848	1905/16	2000
b 24	1519	1603/14/98	1709/91	1859		2011
c 25	1546	1641	1736	1886	1943	

HINDU CALENDAR

The Hindu calendar is a luni-solar calendar of twelve months, each containing 29 days, 12 hours. Each month is divided into a light fortnight (Shukla or Shuddha) and a dark fortnight (Krishna or Vadya) based on the waxing and waning of the moon. In most parts of India the month starts with the light fortnight, i.e. the day after the new moon, although in some regions it begins with the dark fortnight, i.e. the day after the full moon.

The new year begins in the month of Chaitra (March/April) and ends in the month of Phalgun (March). The twelve months, Chaitra, Vaishakh, Jyeshtha, Ashadh, Shravan, Bhadrapad, Ashvin, Kartik, Margashirsh, Paush, Magh and Phalgun, have Sanskrit names derived from twelve asterisms (constellations). There are regional variations to the names of the months but the Sanskrit names are understood throughout India.

Every lunar month must have a solar transit and is termed pure (shuddha). The lunar month without a solar transit is impure (mala) and called an intercalary month. An intercalary month occurs approximately every 32 lunar months, whenever the difference between the Hindu year of 360 lunar days (354 days 8 hours solar time) and the 365 days 6 hours of the solar year reaches the length of one Hindu lunar month (29 days 12 hours).

The leap month may be added at any point in the Hindu year. The name given to the month varies according to when it occurs but is taken from the month immediately following it. A leap month occurs in 1999–2000 (Jyeshtha).

The days of the week are called Raviwar (Sunday), Somawar (Monday), Mangalwar (Tuesday), Budhawar (Wednesday), Guruwar (Thursday), Shukrawar (Friday) and Shaniwar (Saturday). The names are derived from Sanskrit names of the Sun, the Moon and five planets, Mars, Mercury, Jupiter, Venus and Saturn.

Most fasts and festivals are based on the lunar calendar but a few are determined by the apparent movement of the Sun, e.g. Sankranti and Pongal (in southern India), which are celebrated on 14/15 January to mark the start of the Sun's apparent journey northwards and a change of season.

Festivals celebrated throughout India are Chaitra (the New Year), Raksha-bandhan (the renewal of the kinship bond between brothers and sisters), Navaratri (a nine-night festival dedicated to the goddess Parvati), Dasara (the victory of Rama over the demon army), Diwali (a festival of lights), Makara Sankranti, Shivaratri (dedicated to Shiva), and Holi (a spring festival).

Regional festivals are Durga-puja (dedicated to the goddess Durga (Parvati)), Sarasvati-puja (dedicated to the goddess Sarasvati), Ganesh Chaturthi (worship of Ganesh on the fourth day (Chaturthi) of the light half of Bhadrapad), Ramanavami (the birth festival of the god Rama) and Janmashtami (the birth festival of the god Krishna).

The main festivals celebrated in Britain are Navaratri, Dasara, Durga-puja, Diwali, Holi, Sarasvati-puja, Ganesh Chaturthi, Raksha-bandhan, Ramanavami and Janmashtami.

For dates of the main festivals in 1999, *see* page 9.

JEWISH CALENDAR

The story of the Flood in the Book of Genesis indicates the use of a calendar of some kind and that the writers recognized thirty days as the length of a lunation. However, after the diaspora, Jewish communities were left in considerable doubt as to the times of fasts and festivals. This led to the formation of the Jewish calendar as used today. It is said that this was done in AD 358 by Rabbi Hillel II, though some assert that it did not happen until much later.

The calendar is luni-solar, and is based on the lengths of the lunation and of the tropical year as found by Hipparchus (*c.*120 BC), which differ little from those adopted at the present day. The year AM 5759 (1998–9) is the 2nd year of the 304th Metonic (Minor or Lunar) cycle of 19 years and the 19th year of the 206th Solar (or Major) cycle of 28 years since the Era of the Creation. Jews hold that the Creation occurred at the time of the autumnal equinox in the year known in the Christian calendar as 3760 BC (954 of the Julian period). The epoch or starting point of Jewish chronology corresponds to 7 October 3761 BC. At the beginning of each solar cycle, the Tekufah of Nisan (the vernal equinox) returns to the same day and to the same hour.

The hour is divided into 1080 minims, and the month between one new moon and the next is reckoned as 29 days, 12 hours, 793 minims. The normal calendar year, called a Regular Common year, consists of 12 months of 30 days and 29 days alternately. Since twelve months such as these comprise only 354 days, in order that each of them shall not diverge greatly from an average place in the solar year, a thirteenth month is occasionally added after the fifth month of the civil year (which commences on the first day of the month Tishri), or as the penultimate month of the ecclesiastical year (which commences on the first day of the month Nisan). The years when this happens are called Embolismic or leap years.

Of the 19 years that form a Metonic cycle, seven are leap years; they occur at places in the cycle indicated by the numbers 3, 6, 8, 11, 14, 17 and 19, these places being chosen so that the accumulated excesses of the solar years should be as small as possible.

A Jewish year is of one of the following six types:

Minimal Common	353 days
Regular Common	354 days
Full Common	355 days
Minimal Leap	383 days
Regular Leap	384 days
Full Leap	385 days.

The Regular year has alternate months of 30 and 29 days. In a Full year, whether common or leap, Marcheshvan, the second month of the civil year, has 30 days instead of 29; in Minimal years Kislev, the third month, has 29 instead of 30. The additional month in leap years is called Adar I and precedes the month called Adar in Common years. Adar II is called Adar Sheni in leap years, and the usual Adar festivals are kept in Adar Sheni. Adar I and Adar II always have 30 days, but neither this, nor the other variations mentioned, is allowed to change the number of days in the other months, which still follow the alternation of the normal twelve.

These are the main features of the Jewish calendar, which must be considered permanent because as a Jewish law it cannot be altered except by a great Sanhedrin.

The Jewish day begins between sunset and nightfall. The time used is that of the meridian of Jerusalem, which is 2h 21m in advance of Greenwich Mean Time. Rules for the beginning of sabbaths and festivals were laid down for the latitude of London in the 18th century and hours for nightfall are now fixed annually by the Chief Rabbi.

JEWISH CALENDAR 5759–60

AM 5759 (759) is a Full Common year of 12 months, 50 sabbaths and 355 days; AM 5760 (760) is a Full Leap year of 13 months, 55 sabbaths and 385 days.

Jewish Month	AM 5759	AM 5760
Tishri 1	21 September 1998	11 September 1999
Marcheshvan 1	21 October	11 October
Kislev 1	20 November	10 November
Tebet 1	20 December	10 December
Shebat 1	18 January 1999	8 January 2000
*Adar 1	17 February	7 February
†Adar II		8 March
Nisan 1	18 March	6 April
Iyar 1	17 April	6 May
Sivan 1	16 May	4 June
Tammuz 1	15 June	4 July
Ab 1	14 July	2 August
Elul 1	13 August	1 September

*Known as Adar Rishon in leap years
†Known as Adar Sheni in leap years

JEWISH FASTS AND FESTIVALS

For dates of principal festivals in 1999, *see* page 9

Tishri 1–2	Rosh Hashanah (New Year)
Tishri 3	*Fast of Gedaliah
Tishri 10	Yom Kippur (Day of Atonement)
Tishri 15–21	Succoth (Feast of Tabernacles)
Tishri 21	Hoshana Rabba
Tishri 22	Shemini Atseret (Solemn Assembly)
Tishri 23	Simchat Torah (Rejoicing of the Law)
Kislev 25	Chanucah (Dedication of the Temple) begins
Tebet 10	Fast of Tebet
†*Adar* 13	§Fast of Esther
†*Adar* 14	Purim
†*Adar* 15	Shushan Purim
Nisan 15–22	Pesach (Passover)
Sivan 6–7	Shavuot (Feast of Weeks)
Tammuz 17	*Fast of Tammuz
Ab 9	*Fast of Ab

*If these dates fall on the sabbath the fast is kept on the following day
†Adar Sheni in leap years
§This fast is observed on Adar 11 (or Adar Sheni 11 in leap years) if Adar 13 falls on a sabbath

THE MUSLIM CALENDAR

The Muslim era is dated from the *Hijrah*, or flight of the Prophet Muhammad from Mecca to Medina, the corresponding date of which in the Julian calendar is 16 July AD 622. The lunar *hijri* calendar is used principally in Iran, Egypt, Malaysia, Pakistan, Mauritania, various Arab states and certain parts of India. Iran uses the solar *hijri* calendar as well as the lunar *hijri* calendar. The dating system was adopted about AD 639, commencing with the first day of the month Muharram.

The lunar calendar consists of twelve months containing an alternate sequence of 30 and 29 days, with the intercalation of one day at the end of the twelfth month at stated intervals in each cycle of 30 years. The object of the intercalation is to reconcile the date of the first day of the month with the date of the actual new moon.

Some adherents still take the date of the evening of the first physical sighting of the crescent of the new moon as that of the first of the month. If cloud obscures the moon the present month may be extended to 30 days, after which the new month will begin automatically regardless of whether the moon has been seen. (Under religious law a month must have less than 31 days.) This means that the beginning of a new month and the date of religious festivals can vary from the published calendars.

In each cycle of 30 years, 19 years are common and contain 354 days, and 11 years are intercalary (leap years) of 355 days, the latter being called *kabisah*. The mean length of the Hijrah years is 354 days 8 hours 48 minutes and the period of mean lunation is 29 days 12 hours 44 minutes.

To ascertain if a year is common or kabisah, divide it by 30: the quotient gives the number of completed cycles and the remainder shows the place of the year in the current cycle. If the remainder is 2, 5, 7, 10, 13, 16, 18, 21, 24, 26 or 29, the year is kabisah and consists of 355 days.

MUSLIM CALENDAR 1419–20

Hijrah year 1419 AH (remainder 9) is a common year; 1420 AH (remainder 10) is a kabisah year.

Month (length)	1419 AH	1420 AH
Muharram (30)	28 April 1998	17 April 1999
Safar (29)	28 May	17 May
Rabi' I (30)	26 June	15 June
Rabi' II (29)	26 July	15 July
Jumada I (30)	24 August	13 August
Jumada II (29)	23 September	12 September
Rajab (30)	22 October	11 October
Sha'ban (29)	21 November	10 November
Ramadân (30)	20 December	9 December
Shawwâl (29)	19 January 1999	8 January 2000
Dhû'l-Qa'da (30)	17 February	6 February
Dhû'l-Hijjah (29 or 30)	19 March	7 March

MUSLIM FESTIVALS

Ramadan is a month of fasting for all Muslims because it is the month in which the revelation of the *Qur'an* (Koran) began. During Ramadan Muslims abstain from food, drink and sexual pleasure from dawn until after sunset throughout the month.

The two major festivals are *Id al-Fitr* and *Id al-Adha*. Id al-Fitr marks the end of the Ramadan fast and is celebrated on the day after the sighting of the new moon of the following month. Id al-Adha, the festival of sacrifice (also known as the great festival), celebrates the submission of the Prophet Ibrahim (Abraham) to God. Id al-Adha falls on the tenth day of Dhul-Hijjah, coinciding with the day when those on *hajj* (pilgrimage to Mecca) sacrifice animals.

Other days accorded special recognition are:

Muharram 1	New Year's Day
Muharram 10	Ashura (the day Prophet Noah left the Ark and Prophet Moses was saved from Pharaoh (Sunni), the death of the Prophet's grandson Husain (Shi'ite))
Rabi'u-l-Awwal (Rabi' I) 12	Mawlid al-Nabi (birthday of the Prophet Muhammad)
Rajab 27	Laylat al-Isra' wa'l-Mi'raj (The Night of Journey and Ascension)
Ramadân One of the odd-numbered nights in the last 10 of the month	Laylat al-Qadr (Night of Power)
Dhû'l-Hijjah 10	Id al-Adha (Festival of Sacrifice)

THE SIKH CALENDAR

The Sikh calendar is a lunar calendar of 365 days divided into 12 months. The length of the months varies between 29 and 32 days.

There are no prescribed feast days and no fasting periods. The main celebrations are Baisakhi Mela (the new year and the anniversary of the founding of the Khalsa), Diwali Mela (festival of light), Hola Mohalla Mela (a spring festival held in the Punjab), and the Gurpurbs (anniversaries associated with the ten Gurus).

For dates of the major celebrations in 1999, *see* page 9.

CIVIL AND LEGAL CALENDAR

THE HISTORICAL YEAR

Before 1752, two calendar systems were used in England. The civil or legal year began on 25 March and the historical year on 1 January. Thus the civil or legal date 24 March 1658 was the same day as the historical date 24 March 1659; a date in that portion of the year is written as 24 March 165⅞, the lower figure showing the historical year.

THE NEW YEAR

In England in the seventh century, and as late as the 13th, the year was reckoned from Christmas Day, but in the 12th century the Church in England began the year with the feast of the Annunciation of the Blessed Virgin ('Lady Day') on 25 March and this practice was adopted generally in the 14th century. The civil or legal year in the British Dominions (exclusive of Scotland) began with Lady Day until 1751. But in and since 1752 the civil year has begun with 1 January. New Year's Day in Scotland was changed from 25 March to 1 January in 1600.

Elsewhere in Europe, 1 January was adopted as the first day of the year by Venice in 1522, German states in 1544, Spain, Portugal, and the Roman Catholic Netherlands in 1556, Prussia, Denmark and Sweden in 1559, France in 1564, Lorraine in 1579, the Protestant Netherlands in 1583, Russia in 1725, and Tuscany in 1751.

REGNAL YEARS

Regnal years are the years of a sovereign's reign and each begins on the anniversary of his or her accession, e.g. regnal year 48 of the present Queen begins on 6 February 1999.

The system was used for dating Acts of Parliament until 1962. The Summer Time Act 1925, for example, is quoted as 15 and 16 Geo. V c. 64, because it became law in the parliamentary session which extended over part of both of these regnal years. Acts of a parliamentary session during which a sovereign died were usually given two year numbers, the regnal year of the deceased sovereign and the regnal year of his or her successor, e.g. those passed in 1952 were dated 16 Geo. VI and 1 Elizabeth II. Since 1962 Acts of Parliament have been dated by the calendar year.

QUARTER AND TERM DAYS

Holy days and saints days were the usual means in early times for setting the dates of future and recurrent appointments. The quarter days in England and Wales are the feast of the Nativity (25 December), the feast of the Annunciation (25 March), the feast of St John the Baptist (24 June) and the feast of St Michael and All Angels (29 September).

The term days in Scotland are Candlemas (the feast of the Purification), Whitsunday, Lammas (Loaf Mass), and Martinmas (St Martin's Day). These fell on 2 February, 15 May, 1 August and 11 November respectively. However, by the Term and Quarter Days (Scotland) Act 1990, the dates of the term days were changed to 28 February (Candlemas), 28 May (Whitsunday), 28 August (Lammas) and 28 November (Martinmas).

RED-LETTER DAYS

Red-letter days were originally the holy days and saints days indicated in early ecclesiastical calendars by letters printed in red ink. The days to be distinguished in this way were approved at the Council of Nicaea in AD 325.

These days still have a legal significance, as judges of the Queen's Bench Division wear scarlet robes on red-letter days falling during the law sittings. The days designated as red-letter days for this purpose are:

Holy and saints days (for dates, *see* pages 16, 20, etc.)
The Conversion of St Paul, the Purification, Ash Wednesday, the Annunciation, the Ascension, the feasts of St Mark, SS Philip and James, St Matthias, St Barnabas, St John the Baptist, St Peter, St Thomas, St James, St Luke, SS Simon and Jude, All Saints, St Andrew

Civil calendar (for dates, *see* page 9)
The anniversaries of The Queen's accession, The Queen's birthday and The Queen's coronation, The Queen's official birthday, the birthday of the Duke of Edinburgh, the birthday of Queen Elizabeth the Queen Mother, the birthday of the Prince of Wales, St David's Day and Lord Mayor's Day

PUBLIC HOLIDAYS

Public holidays are divided into two categories, common law and statutory. Common law holidays are holidays 'by habit and custom'; in England, Wales and Northern Ireland these are Good Friday and Christmas Day.

Statutory public holidays, known as bank holidays, were first established by the Bank Holidays Act 1871. They were, literally, days on which the banks (and other public institutions) were closed and financial obligations due on that day were payable the following day. The legislation currently governing public holidays in the UK, which is the Banking and Financial Dealings Act 1971 stipulates the days that are to be public holidays in England, Wales, Scotland and Northern Ireland.

Certain holidays (indicated by * below) are granted annually by royal proclamation, either throughout the UK or in any place in the UK. The public holidays are:

England and Wales

*New Year's Day
Easter Monday
*The first Monday in May
The last Monday in May
The last Monday in August
26 December, if it is not a Sunday
27 December when 25 or 26 December is a Sunday

Scotland

New Year's Day, or if it is a Sunday, 2 January
2 January, or if it is a Sunday, 3 January
Good Friday
The first Monday in May
*The last Monday in May
The first Monday in August
Christmas Day, or if it is a Sunday, 26 December
*Boxing Day – if Christmas Day falls on a Sunday, 26 December is given in lieu and an alternative day is given for Boxing Day

Northern Ireland

*New Year's Day
17 March, or if it is a Sunday, 18 March
Easter Monday
*The first Monday in May
The last Monday in May
*12 July, or if it is a Sunday, 13 July
The last Monday in August
26 December, if it is not a Sunday
27 December if 25 or 26 December is a Sunday

For dates of public holidays in 1999 and 2000, *see* pages 10–11.

CHRONOLOGICAL CYCLES AND ERAS

SOLAR (OR MAJOR) CYCLE

The solar cycle is a period of twenty-eight years in any corresponding year of which the days of the week recur on the same day of the month.

METONIC (LUNAR, OR MINOR) CYCLE

In 432 BC, Meton, an Athenian astronomer, found that 235 lunations are very nearly, though not exactly, equal in duration to 19 solar years and so after 19 years the phases of the Moon recur on the same days of the month (nearly). The dates of full moon in a cycle of 19 years were inscribed in figures of gold on public monuments in Athens, and the number showing the position of a year in the cycle is called the golden number of that year.

JULIAN PERIOD

The Julian period was proposed by Joseph Scaliger in 1582. The period is 7980 Julian years, and its first year coincides with the year 4713 BC. The figure of 7980 is the product of the number of years in the solar cycle, the Metonic cycle and the cycle of the Roman indiction (28 × 19 × 15).

ROMAN INDICTION

The Roman indiction is a period of fifteen years, instituted for fiscal purposes about AD 300.

EPACT

The epact is the age of the calendar Moon, diminished by one day, on 1 January, in the ecclesiastical lunar calendar.

CHINESE CALENDAR

A lunar calendar was the sole calendar in use in China until 1911, when the government adopted the new (Gregorian) calendar for official and most business activities. The Chinese tend to follow both calendars, the lunar calendar playing an important part in personal life, e.g. birth celebrations, festivals, marriages; and in rural villages the lunar calendar dictates the cycle of activities, denoting the change of weather and farming activities.

The lunar calendar is used in Hong Kong, Singapore, Malaysia, Tibet and elsewhere in south-east Asia. The calendar has a cycle of 60 years. The new year begins at the first new moon after the sun enters the sign of Aquarius, i.e. the new year falls between 21 January and 19 February in the Gregorian calendar.

Each year in the Chinese calendar is associated with one of 12 animals: the rat, the ox, the tiger, the rabbit, the dragon, the snake, the horse, the goat or sheep, the monkey, the chicken or rooster, the dog, and the pig.

The date of the Chinese new year and the astrological sign for the years 1999–2003 are:

1999	16 February	Rabbit
2000	5 February	Dragon
2001	—	Snake
2002	—	Horse
2003	—	Goat or Sheep

COPTIC CALENDAR

In the Coptic calendar, which is used in parts of Egypt and Ethiopia, the year is made up of 12 months of 30 days each, followed, in general, by five complementary days. Every fourth year is an intercalary or leap year and in these years there are six complementary days. The intercalary year of the Coptic calendar immediately precedes the leap year of the Julian calendar. The era is that of Diocletian or the Martyrs, the origin of which is fixed at 29 August AD 284 (Julian date).

INDIAN ERAS

In addition to the Muslim reckoning, other eras are used in India. The Saka era of southern India, dating from 3 March AD 78, was declared the national calendar of the Republic of India with effect from 22 March 1957, to be used concurrently with the Gregorian calendar. As revised, the year of the new Saka era begins at the spring equinox, with five successive months of 31 days and seven of 30 days in ordinary years, and six months of each length in leap years. The year AD 1999 is 1921 of the revised Saka era.

The year AD 1999 corresponds to the following years in other eras:

Year 2056 of the Vikram Samvat era
Year 1406 of the Bengali San era
Year 1175 of the Kollam era
Vedanga Jyotisa year 5 of the five-yearly cycle (384th cycle of Paitamah Siddhanta)
Year 6000 of the Kaliyuga era
Year 2543 of the Buddha Nirvana era

JAPANESE CALENDAR

The Japanese calendar is essentially the same as the Gregorian calendar, the years, months and weeks being of the same length and beginning on the same days as those of the Gregorian calendar. The numeration of the years is different, based on a system of epochs or periods each of which begins at the accession of an Emperor or other important occurrence. The method is not unlike the British system of regnal years, except that each year of a period closes on 31 December. The Japanese chronology begins about AD 650 and the three latest epochs are defined by the reigns of Emperors, whose actual names are not necessarily used:

Epoch

Taishō	1 August 1912 to 25 December 1926
Shōwa	26 December 1926 to 7 January 1989
Heisei	8 January 1989

The year Heisei 11 begins on 1 January 1999.

The months are known as First Month, Second Month, etc., First Month being equivalent to January. The days of the week are Nichiyōbi (Sun-day), Getsuyōbi (Moon-day), Kayōbi (Fire-day), Suiyōbi (Water-day), Mokuyōbi (Wood-day), Kinyōbi (Metal-day), Doyōbi (Earth-day).

THE MASONIC YEAR

Two dates are quoted in warrants, dispensations, etc., issued by the United Grand Lodge of England, those for the current year being expressed as *Anno Domini* 1999 – *Anno Lucis* 5999. This *Anno Lucis* (year of light) is based on the Book of Genesis 1:3, the 4000-year difference being derived, in modified form, from *Ussher's Notation*, published in 1654, which places the Creation of the World in 4004 BC.

OLYMPIADS

Ancient Greek chronology was reckoned in Olympiads, cycles of four years corresponding with the periodic Olympic Games held on the plain of Olympia in Elis once every four years. The intervening years were the first, second, etc., of the Olympiad, which received the name of the victor at the Games. The first recorded Olympiad is that of Choroebus, 776 BC.

ZOROASTRIAN CALENDAR

Zoroastrians, followers of the Iranian prophet Zarathushtra (known to the Greeks as Zoroaster) are mostly to be found in Iran and in India, where they are known as Parsees.

The Zoroastrian era dates from the coronation of the last Zoroastrian Sasanian king in AD 631. The Zoroastrian calendar is divided into twelve months, each comprising 30 days, followed by five holy days of the Gathas at the end of each year to make the year consist of 365 days.

In order to synchronize the calendar with the solar year of 365 days, an extra month was intercalated once every 120 years. However, this intercalation ceased in the 12th century and the New Year, which had fallen in the spring, slipped back to August. Because intercalation ceased at different times in Iran and India, there was one month's difference between the calendar followed in Iran (Kadmi calendar) and by the Parsees (Shenshai calendar). In 1906 a group of Zoroastrians decided to bring the calendar back in line with the seasons again and restore the New Year to 21 March each year (Fasli calendar).

The Shenshai calendar (New Year in August) is mainly used by Parsees. The Fasli calendar (New Year, 21 March) is mainly used by Zoroastrians living in Iran, in the Indian subcontinent, or away from Iran.

THE ROMAN CALENDAR

Roman historians adopted as an epoch the foundation of Rome, which is believed to have happened in the year 753 BC. The ordinal number of the years in Roman reckoning followed by the letters AUC (*ab urbe condita*), so that the year 1999 is 2752 AUC (MMDCCLII). The calendar that we know has developed from one said to have been established by Romulus using a year of 304 days divided into ten months, beginning with March. To this Numa added January and February, making the year consist of 12 months of 30 and 29 days alternately, with an additional day so that the total was 355. It is also said that Numa ordered an intercalary month of 22 or 23 days in alternate years, making 90 days in eight years, to be inserted after 23 February.

However, there is some doubt as to the origination and the details of the intercalation in the Roman calendar. It is certain that some scheme of this kind was inaugurated and not fully carried out, for in the year 46 BC Julius Caesar found that the calendar had been allowed to fall into some confusion. He sought the help of the Egyptian astronomer Sosigenes, which led to the construction and adoption (45 BC) of the Julian calendar, and, by a slight alteration, to the Gregorian calendar now in use. The year 46 BC was made to consist of 445 days and is called the Year of Confusion.

In the Roman (Julian) calendar the days of the month were counted backwards from three fixed points, or days, and an intervening day was said to be so many days before the next coming point, the first and last being counted. These three points were the Kalends, the Nones, and the Ides. Their positions in the months and the method of counting from them will be seen in the table below. The year containing 366 days was called *bissextilis annus*, as it had a doubled sixth day (*bissextus dies*) before the March Kalends on 24 February – *ante diem sextum Kalendas Martias*, or a.d. VI Kal. Mart.

Present days of the month	March, May, July, October have thirty-one days	January, August, December have thirty-one days	April, June, September, November have thirty days	February has twenty-eight days, and in leap year twenty-nine
1	Kalendis	Kalendis	Kalendis	Kalendis
2	VI	IV ⎫ ante	IV ⎫ ante	IV ⎫ ante
3	V ⎫ ante	III ⎭ Nonas	III ⎭ Nonas	III ⎭ Nonas
4	IV ⎪ Nonas	pridie Nonas	pridie Nonas	pridie Nonas
5	III ⎭	Nonis	Nonis	Nonis
6	pridie Nonas	VIII ⎫	VIII ⎫	VIII ⎫
7	Nonis	VII ⎪	VII ⎪	VII ⎪
8	VIII ⎫	VI ⎪ ante	VI ⎪ ante	VI ⎪ ante
9	VII ⎪	V ⎭ Idus	V ⎭ Idus	V ⎭ Idus
10	VI ⎪ ante	IV ⎪	IV ⎪	IV ⎪
11	V ⎭ Idus	III ⎭	III ⎭	III ⎭
12	IV	pridie Idus	pridie Idus	pridie Idus
13	III	Idibus	Idibus	Idibus
14	pridie Idus	XIX ⎫	XVIII ⎫	XVI ⎫
15	Idibus	XVIII	XVII	XV
16	XVII ⎫	XVII	XVI	XIV
17	XVI	XVI	XV	XIII
18	XV	XV	XIV	XII
19	XIV	XIV	XIII	XI
20	XIII	XIII	XII ⎫ ante Kalendas	X ⎫ ante Kalendas
21	XII	XII ⎫ ante Kalendas	XI ⎬ (of the month	IX ⎭ Martias
22	XI ⎫ ante Kalendas	XI ⎬ (of the month	X ⎭ following)	VIII
23	X ⎬ (of the month	X ⎭ following)	IX	VII
24	IX ⎭ following)	IX	VIII	*VI
25	VIII	VIII	VII	V
26	VII	VII	VI	IV
27	VI	VI	V	III ⎭
28	V	V	IV	pridie Kalendas Martias
29	IV	IV ⎭	III ⎭	* (repeated in leap year)
30	III ⎭	pridie Kalendas	pridie Kalendas	
31	pridie Kalendas (Aprilis, Iunias, Sextilis, Novembris)	(Februarias, Septembris, Ianuarias)	(Maias, Quinctilis, Octobris, Decembris)	

Calendar for Any Year 1780–2040

To select the correct calendar for any year between 1780 and 2040, consult the index below
* leap year

Year		Year		Year		Year		Year		Year		Year		Year	
1780	N*	1813	K	1846	I	1879	G	1912	D*	1945	C	1978	A	2011	M
1781	C	1814	M	1847	K	1880	J*	1913	G	1946	E	1979	C	2012	B*
1782	E	1815	A	1848	N*	1881	M	1914	I	1947	G	1980	F*	2013	E
1783	G	1816	D*	1849	C	1882	A	1915	K	1948	J*	1981	I	2014	G
1784	J*	1817	G	1850	E	1883	C	1916	N*	1949	M	1982	K	2015	I
1785	M	1818	I	1851	G	1884	F*	1917	C	1950	A	1983	M	2016	L*
1786	A	1819	K	1852	J*	1885	I	1918	E	1951	C	1984	B*	2017	A
1787	C	1820	N*	1853	M	1886	K	1919	G	1952	F*	1985	E	2018	C
1788	F*	1821	C	1854	A	1887	M	1920	J*	1953	I	1986	G	2019	E
1789	I	1822	E	1855	C	1888	B*	1921	M	1954	K	1987	I	2020	H*
1790	K	1823	G	1856	F*	1889	E	1922	A	1955	M	1988	L*	2021	K
1791	M	1824	J*	1857	I	1890	G	1923	C	1956	B*	1989	A	2022	M
1792	B*	1825	M	1858	K	1891	I	1924	F*	1957	E	1990	C	2023	A
1793	E	1826	A	1859	M	1892	L*	1925	I	1958	G	1991	E	2024	D*
1794	G	1827	C	1860	B*	1893	A	1926	K	1959	I	1992	H*	2025	G
1795	I	1828	F*	1861	E	1894	C	1927	M	1960	L*	1993	K	2026	I
1796	L*	1829	I	1862	G	1895	E	1928	B*	1961	A	1994	M	2027	K
1797	A	1830	K	1863	I	1896	H*	1929	E	1962	C	1995	A	2028	N*
1798	C	1831	M	1864	L*	1897	K	1930	G	1963	E	1996	D*	2029	C
1799	E	1832	B*	1865	A	1898	M	1931	I	1964	H*	1997	G	2030	E
1800	G	1833	E	1866	C	1899	A	1932	L*	1965	K	1998	I	2031	G
1801	I	1834	G	1867	E	1900	C	1933	A	1966	M	1999	K	2032	J*
1802	K	1835	I	1868	H*	1901	E	1934	C	1967	A	2000	N*	2033	M
1803	M	1836	L*	1869	K	1902	G	1935	E	1968	D*	2001	C	2034	A
1804	B*	1837	A	1870	M	1903	I	1936	H*	1969	G	2002	E	2035	C
1805	E	1838	C	1871	A	1904	L*	1937	K	1970	I	2003	G	2036	F*
1806	G	1839	E	1872	D*	1905	A	1938	M	1971	K	2004	J*	2037	I
1807	I	1840	H*	1873	G	1906	C	1939	A	1972	N*	2005	M	2038	K
1808	L*	1841	K	1874	I	1907	E	1940	D*	1973	C	2006	A	2039	M
1809	A	1842	M	1875	K	1908	H*	1941	G	1974	E	2007	C	2040	B*
1810	C	1843	A	1876	N*	1909	K	1942	I	1975	G	2008	F*		
1811	E	1844	D*	1877	C	1910	M	1943	K	1976	J*	2009	I		
1812	H*	1845	G	1878	E	1911	A	1944	N*	1977	M	2010	K		

A

January
Sun.	1	8	15	22 29
Mon.	2	9	16	23 30
Tue.	3	10	17	24 31
Wed.	4	11	18	25
Thur.	5	12	19	26
Fri.	6	13	20	27
Sat.	7	14	21	28

February
Day				
Sun.	5	12	19	26
Mon.	6	13	20	27
Tue.	7	14	21	28
Wed.	1	8	15	22
Thur.	2	9	16	23
Fri.	3	10	17	24
Sat.	4	11	18	25

March
Day				
Sun.	5	12	19	26
Mon.	6	13	20	27
Tue.	7	14	21	28
Wed.	1	8	15	22 29
Thur.	2	9	16	23 30
Fri.	3	10	17	24 31
Sat.	4	11	18	25

April
Day				
Sun.	2	9	16	23 30
Mon.	3	10	17	24
Tue.	4	11	18	25
Wed.	5	12	19	26
Thur.	6	13	20	27
Fri.	7	14	21	28
Sat.	1	8	15	22 29

May
Sun.	7	14	21	28
Mon.	1	8	15	22 29
Tue.	2	9	16	23 30
Wed.	3	10	17	24 31
Thur.	4	11	18	25
Fri.	5	12	19	26
Sat.	6	13	20	27

June
Sun.	4	11	18	25
Mon.	5	12	19	26
Tue.	6	13	20	27
Wed.	7	14	21	28
Thur.	1	8	15	22 29
Fri.	2	9	16	23 30
Sat.	3	10	17	24

July
Sun.	2	9	16	23 30
Mon.	3	10	17	24 31
Tue.	4	11	18	25
Wed.	5	12	19	26
Thur.	6	13	20	27
Fri.	7	14	21	28
Sat.	1	8	15	22 29

August
Sun.	6	13	20	27
Mon.	7	14	21	28
Tue.	1	8	15	22 29
Wed.	2	9	16	23 30
Thur.	3	10	17	24 31
Fri.	4	11	18	25
Sat.	5	12	19	26

September
Sun.	3	10	17	24
Mon.	4	11	18	25
Tue.	5	12	19	26
Wed.	6	13	20	27
Thur.	7	14	21	28
Fri.	1	8	15	22 29
Sat.	2	9	16	23 30

October
Sun.	1	8	15	22 29
Mon.	2	9	16	23 30
Tue.	3	10	17	24 31
Wed.	4	11	18	25
Thur.	5	12	19	26
Fri.	6	13	20	27
Sat.	7	14	21	28

November
Sun.	5	12	19	26
Mon.	6	13	20	27
Tue.	7	14	21	28
Wed.	1	8	15	22 29
Thur.	2	9	16	23 30
Fri.	3	10	17	24
Sat.	4	11	18	25

December
Sun.	3	10	17	24 31
Mon.	4	11	18	25
Tue.	5	12	19	26
Wed.	6	13	20	27
Thur.	7	14	21	28
Fri.	1	8	15	22 29
Sat.	2	9	16	23 30

EASTER DAYS

March 26	1815, 1826, 1837, 1967, 1978, 1989
April 2	1809, 1893, 1899, 1961
April 9	1871, 1882, 1939, 1950, 2023, 2034
April 16	1786, 1797, 1843, 1854, 1865, 1911, 1922, 1933, 1995, 2006, 2017
April 23	1905

B (LEAP YEAR)

January
Day				
Sun.	1	8	15	22 29
Mon.	2	9	16	23 30
Tue.	3	10	17	24 31
Wed.	4	11	18	25
Thur.	5	12	19	26
Fri.	6	13	20	27
Sat.	7	14	21	28

February
Day				
Sun.	5	12	19	26
Mon.	6	13	20	27
Tue.	7	14	21	28
Wed.	1	8	15	22 29
Thur.	2	9	16	23
Fri.	3	10	17	24
Sat.	4	11	18	25

March
Day				
Sun.	4	11	18	25
Mon.	5	12	19	26
Tue.	6	13	20	27
Wed.	7	14	21	28
Thur.	1	8	15	22 29
Fri.	2	9	16	23 30
Sat.	3	10	17	24 31

April
Day				
Sun.	1	8	15	22 29
Mon.	2	9	16	23 30
Tue.	3	10	17	24
Wed.	4	11	18	25
Thur.	5	12	19	26
Fri.	6	13	20	27
Sat.	7	14	21	28

May
Day				
Sun.	6	13	20	27
Mon.	7	14	21	28
Tue.	1	8	15	22 29
Wed.	2	9	16	23 30
Thur.	3	10	17	24 31
Fri.	4	11	18	25
Sat.	5	12	19	26

June
Day				
Sun.	3	10	17	24
Mon.	4	11	18	25
Tue.	5	12	19	26
Wed.	6	13	20	27
Thur.	7	14	21	28
Fri.	1	8	15	22 29
Sat.	2	9	16	23 30

July
Day				
Sun.	1	8	15	22 29
Mon.	2	9	16	23 30
Tue.	3	10	17	24 31
Wed.	4	11	18	25
Thur.	5	12	19	26
Fri.	6	13	20	27
Sat.	7	14	21	28

August
Day				
Sun.	5	12	19	26
Mon.	6	13	20	27
Tue.	7	14	21	28
Wed.	1	8	15	22 29
Thur.	2	9	16	23 30
Fri.	3	10	17	24 31
Sat.	4	11	18	25

September
Day				
Sun.	2	9	16	23 30
Mon.	3	10	17	24
Tue.	4	11	18	25
Wed.	5	12	19	26
Thur.	6	13	20	27
Fri.	7	14	21	28
Sat.	1	8	15	22 29

October
Day				
Sun.	7	14	21	28
Mon.	1	8	15	22 29
Tue.	2	9	16	23 30
Wed.	3	10	17	24 31
Thur.	4	11	18	25
Fri.	5	12	19	26
Sat.	6	13	20	27

November
Day				
Sun.	4	11	18	25
Mon.	5	12	19	26
Tue.	6	13	20	27
Wed.	7	14	21	28
Thur.	1	8	15	22 29
Fri.	2	9	16	23 30
Sat.	3	10	17	24

December
Day				
Sun.	2	9	16	23 30
Mon.	3	10	17	24 31
Tue.	4	11	18	25
Wed.	5	12	19	26
Thur.	6	13	20	27
Fri.	7	14	21	28
Sat.	1	8	15	22 29

EASTER DAYS

April 1	1804, 1888, 1956, 2040
April 8	1792, 1860, 1928, 2012
April 22	1832, 1984

C

	January	February	March
Sun.	7 14 21 28	4 11 18 25	4 11 18 25
Mon.	1 8 15 22 29	5 12 19 26	5 12 19 26
Tue.	2 9 16 23 30	6 13 20 27	6 13 20 27
Wed.	3 10 17 24 31	7 14 21 28	7 14 21 28
Thur.	4 11 18 25	1 8 15 22	1 8 15 22 29
Fri.	5 12 19 26	2 9 16 23	2 9 16 23 30
Sat.	6 13 20 27	3 10 17 24	3 10 17 24 31

	April	May	June
Sun.	1 8 15 22 29	6 13 20 27	3 10 17 24
Mon.	2 9 16 23 30	7 14 21 28	4 11 18 25
Tue.	3 10 17 24	1 8 15 22 29	5 12 19 26
Wed.	4 11 18 25	2 9 16 23 30	6 13 20 27
Thur.	5 12 19 26	3 10 17 24 31	7 14 21 28
Fri.	6 13 20 27	4 11 18 25	1 8 15 22 29
Sat.	7 14 21 28	5 12 19 26	2 9 16 23 30

	July	August	September
Sun.	1 8 15 22 29	5 12 19 26	2 9 16 23 30
Mon.	2 9 16 23 30	6 13 20 27	3 10 17 24
Tue.	3 10 17 24 31	7 14 21 28	4 11 18 25
Wed.	4 11 18 25	1 8 15 22 29	5 12 19 26
Thur.	5 12 19 26	2 9 16 23 30	6 13 20 27
Fri.	6 13 20 27	3 10 17 24 31	7 14 21 28
Sat.	7 14 21 28	4 11 18 25	1 8 15 22 29

	October	November	December
Sun.	7 14 21 28	4 11 18 25	2 9 16 23 30
Mon.	1 8 15 22 29	5 12 19 26	3 10 17 24 31
Tue.	2 9 16 23 30	6 13 20 27	4 11 18 25
Wed.	3 10 17 24 31	7 14 21 28	5 12 19 26
Thur.	4 11 18 25	1 8 15 22 29	6 13 20 27
Fri.	5 12 19 26	2 9 16 23 30	7 14 21 28
Sat.	6 13 20 27	3 10 17 24	1 8 15 22 29

EASTER DAYS

March 25	1883, 1894, 1951, 2035
April 1	1866, 1877, 1923, 1934, 1945, 2018, 2029
April 8	1787, 1798, 1849, 1855, 1917, 2007
April 15	1781, 1827, 1838, 1900, 1906, 1979, 1990, 2001
April 22	1810, 1821, 1962, 1973

E

	January	February	March
Sun.	6 13 20 27	3 10 17 24	3 10 17 24 31
Mon.	7 14 21 28	4 11 18 25	4 11 18 25
Tue.	1 8 15 22 29	5 12 19 26	5 12 19 26
Wed.	2 9 16 23 30	6 13 20 27	6 13 20 27
Thur.	3 10 17 24 31	7 14 21 28	7 14 21 28
Fri.	4 11 18 25	1 8 15 22	1 8 15 22 29
Sat.	5 12 19 26	2 9 16 23	2 9 16 23 30

	April	May	June
Sun.	7 14 21 28	5 12 19 26	2 9 16 23 30
Mon.	1 8 15 22 29	6 13 20 27	3 10 17 24
Tue.	2 9 16 23 30	7 14 21 28	4 11 18 25
Wed.	3 10 17 24	1 8 15 22 29	5 12 19 26
Thur.	4 11 18 25	2 9 16 23 30	6 13 20 27
Fri.	5 12 19 26	3 10 17 24 31	7 14 21 28
Sat.	6 13 20 27	4 11 18 25	1 8 15 22 29

	July	August	September
Sun.	7 14 21 28	4 11 18 25	1 8 15 22 29
Mon.	1 8 15 22 29	5 12 19 26	2 9 16 23 30
Tue.	2 9 16 23 30	6 13 20 27	3 10 17 24
Wed.	3 10 17 24 31	7 14 21 28	4 11 18 25
Thur.	4 11 18 25	1 8 15 22 29	5 12 19 26
Fri.	5 12 19 26	2 9 16 23 30	6 13 20 27
Sat.	6 13 20 27	3 10 17 24 31	7 14 21 28

	October	November	December
Sun.	6 13 20 27	3 10 17 24	1 8 15 22 29
Mon.	7 14 21 28	4 11 18 25	2 9 16 23 30
Tue.	1 8 15 22 29	5 12 19 26	3 10 17 24 31
Wed.	2 9 16 23 30	6 13 20 27	4 11 18 25
Thur.	3 10 17 24 31	7 14 21 28	5 12 19 26
Fri.	4 11 18 25	1 8 15 22 29	6 13 20 27
Sat.	5 12 19 26	2 9 16 23 30	7 14 21 28

EASTER DAYS

March 24	1799
March 31	1782, 1793, 1839, 1850, 1861, 1907
	1918, 1929, 1991, 2002, 2013
April 7	1822, 1833, 1901, 1985
April 14	1805, 1811, 1895, 1963, 1974
April 21	1867, 1878, 1889, 1935, 1946, 1957, 2019, 2030

D (LEAP YEAR)

	January	February	March
Sun.	7 14 21 28	4 11 18 25	3 10 17 24 31
Mon.	1 8 15 22 29	5 12 19 26	4 11 18 25
Tue.	2 9 16 23 30	6 13 20 27	5 12 19 26
Wed.	3 10 17 24 31	7 14 21 28	6 13 20 27
Thur.	4 11 18 25	1 8 15 22 29	7 14 21 28
Fri.	5 12 19 26	2 9 16 23	1 8 15 22 29
Sat.	6 13 20 27	3 10 17 24	2 9 16 23 30

	April	May	June
Sun.	7 14 21 28	5 12 19 26	2 9 16 23 30
Mon.	1 8 15 22 29	6 13 20 27	3 10 17 24
Tue.	2 9 16 23 30	7 14 21 28	4 11 18 25
Wed.	3 10 17 24	1 8 15 22 29	5 12 19 26
Thur.	4 11 18 25	2 9 16 23 30	6 13 20 27
Fri.	5 12 19 26	3 10 17 24 31	7 14 21 28
Sat.	6 13 20 27	4 11 18 25	1 8 15 22 29

	July	August	September
Sun.	7 14 21 28	4 11 18 25	1 8 15 22 29
Mon.	1 8 15 22 29	5 12 19 26	2 9 16 23 30
Tue.	2 9 16 23 30	6 13 20 27	3 10 17 24
Wed.	3 10 17 24 31	7 14 21 28	4 11 18 25
Thur.	4 11 18 25	1 8 15 22 29	5 12 19 26
Fri.	5 12 19 26	2 9 16 23 30	6 13 20 27
Sat.	6 13 20 27	3 10 17 24 31	7 14 21 28

	October	November	December
Sun.	6 13 20 27	3 10 17 24	1 8 15 22 29
Mon.	7 14 21 28	4 11 18 25	2 9 16 23 30
Tue.	1 8 15 22 29	5 12 19 26	3 10 17 24 31
Wed.	2 9 16 23 30	6 13 20 27	4 11 18 25
Thur.	3 10 17 24 31	7 14 21 28	5 12 19 26
Fri.	4 11 18 25	1 8 15 22 29	6 13 20 27
Sat.	5 12 19 26	2 9 16 23 30	7 14 21 28

EASTER DAYS

March 24	1940
March 31	1872, 2024
April 7	1844, 1912, 1996
April 14	1816, 1968

F (LEAP YEAR)

	January	February	March
Sun.	6 13 20 27	3 10 17 24	2 9 16 23 30
Mon.	7 14 21 28	4 11 18 25	3 10 17 24 31
Tue.	1 8 15 22 29	5 12 19 26	4 11 18 25
Wed.	2 9 16 23 30	6 13 20 27	5 12 19 26
Thur.	3 10 17 24 31	7 14 21 28	6 13 20 27
Fri.	4 11 18 25	1 8 15 22 29	7 14 21 28
Sat.	5 12 19 26	2 9 16 23	1 8 15 22 29

	April	May	June
Sun.	6 13 20 27	4 11 18 25	1 8 15 22 29
Mon.	7 14 21 28	5 12 19 26	2 9 16 23 30
Tue.	1 8 15 22 29	6 13 20 27	3 10 17 24
Wed.	2 9 16 23 30	7 14 21 28	4 11 18 25
Thur.	3 10 17 24	1 8 15 22 29	5 12 19 26
Fri.	4 11 18 25	2 9 16 23 30	6 13 20 27
Sat.	5 12 19 26	3 10 17 24 31	7 14 21 28

	July	August	September
Sun.	6 13 20 27	3 10 17 24 31	7 14 21 28
Mon.	7 14 21 28	4 11 18 25	1 8 15 22 29
Tue.	1 8 15 22 29	5 12 19 26	2 9 16 23 30
Wed.	2 9 16 23 30	6 13 20 27	3 10 17 24
Thur.	3 10 17 24 31	7 14 21 28	4 11 18 25
Fri.	4 11 18 25	1 8 15 22 29	5 12 19 26
Sat.	5 12 19 26	2 9 16 23 30	6 13 20 27

	October	November	December
Sun.	5 12 19 26	2 9 16 23 30	7 14 21 28
Mon.	6 13 20 27	3 10 17 24	1 8 15 22 29
Tue.	7 14 21 28	4 11 18 25	2 9 16 23 30
Wed.	1 8 15 22 29	5 12 19 26	3 10 17 24 31
Thur.	2 9 16 23 30	6 13 20 27	4 11 18 25
Fri.	3 10 17 24 31	7 14 21 28	5 12 19 26
Sat.	4 11 18 25	1 8 15 22 29	6 13 20 27

EASTER DAYS

March 23	1788, 1856, 2008
April 6	1828, 1980
April 13	1884, 1952, 2036
April 20	1924

G

	January	February	March
Sun.	5 12 19 26	2 9 16 23	2 9 16 23 30
Mon.	6 13 20 27	3 10 17 24	3 10 17 24 31
Tue.	7 14 21 28	4 11 18 25	4 11 18 25
Wed.	1 8 15 22 29	5 12 19 26	5 12 19 26
Thur.	2 9 16 23 30	6 13 20 27	6 13 20 27
Fri.	3 10 17 24 31	7 14 21 28	7 14 21 28
Sat.	4 11 18 25	1 8 15 22	1 8 15 22 29

	April	May	June
Sun.	6 13 20 27	4 11 18 25	1 8 15 22 29
Mon.	7 14 21 28	5 12 19 26	2 9 16 23 30
Tue.	1 8 15 22 29	6 13 20 27	3 10 17 24
Wed.	2 9 16 23 30	7 14 21 28	4 11 18 25
Thur.	3 10 17 24	1 8 15 22 29	5 12 19 26
Fri.	4 11 18 25	2 9 16 23 30	6 13 20 27
Sat.	5 12 19 26	3 10 17 24 31	7 14 21 28

	July	August	September
Sun.	6 13 20 27	3 10 17 24 31	7 14 21 28
Mon.	7 14 21 28	4 11 18 25	1 8 15 22 29
Tue.	1 8 15 22 29	5 12 19 26	2 9 16 23 30
Wed.	2 9 16 23 30	6 13 20 27	3 10 17 24
Thur.	3 10 17 24 31	7 14 21 28	4 11 18 25
Fri.	4 11 18 25	1 8 15 22 29	5 12 19 26
Sat.	5 12 19 26	2 9 16 23 30	6 13 20 27

	October	November	December
Sun.	5 12 19 26	2 9 16 23 30	7 14 21 28
Mon.	6 13 20 27	3 10 17 24	1 8 15 22 29
Tue.	7 14 21 28	4 11 18 25	2 9 16 23 30
Wed.	1 8 15 22 29	5 12 19 26	3 10 17 24 31
Thur.	2 9 16 23 30	6 13 20 27	4 11 18 25
Fri.	3 10 17 24 31	7 14 21 28	5 12 19 26
Sat.	4 11 18 25	1 8 15 22 29	6 13 20 27

EASTER DAYS

March 23	1845, 1913
March 30	1823, 1834, 1902, 1975, 1986, 1997
April 6	1806, 1817, 1890, 1947, 1958, 1969
April 13	1800, 1873, 1879, 1941, 2031
April 20	1783, 1794, 1851, 1862, 1919, 1930, 2003, 2014, 2025

I

	January	February	March
Sun.	4 11 18 25	1 8 15 22	1 8 15 22 29
Mon.	5 12 19 26	2 9 16 23	2 9 16 23 30
Tue.	6 13 20 27	3 10 17 24	3 10 17 24 31
Wed.	7 14 21 28	4 11 18 25	4 11 18 25
Thur.	1 8 15 22 29	5 12 19 26	5 12 19 26
Fri.	2 9 16 23 30	6 13 20 27	6 13 20 27
Sat.	3 10 17 24 31	7 14 21 28	7 14 21 28

	April	May	June
Sun.	5 12 19 26	3 10 17 24 31	7 14 21 28
Mon.	6 13 20 27	4 11 18 25	1 8 15 22 29
Tue.	7 14 21 28	5 12 19 26	2 9 16 23 30
Wed.	1 8 15 22 29	6 13 20 27	3 10 17 24
Thur.	2 9 16 23 30	7 14 21 28	4 11 18 25
Fri.	3 10 17 24	1 8 15 22 29	5 12 19 26
Sat.	4 11 18 25	2 9 16 23 30	6 13 20 27

	July	August	September
Sun.	5 12 19 26	2 9 16 23 30	6 13 20 27
Mon.	6 13 20 27	3 10 17 24 31	7 14 21 28
Tue.	7 14 21 28	4 11 18 25	1 8 15 22 29
Wed.	1 8 15 22 29	5 12 19 26	2 9 16 23 30
Thur.	2 9 16 23 30	6 13 20 27	3 10 17 24
Fri.	3 10 17 24 31	7 14 21 28	4 11 18 25
Sat.	4 11 18 25	1 8 15 22 29	5 12 19 26

	October	November	December
Sun.	4 11 18 25	1 8 15 22 29	6 13 20 27
Mon.	5 12 19 26	2 9 16 23 30	7 14 21 28
Tue.	6 13 20 27	3 10 17 24	1 8 15 22 29
Wed.	7 14 21 28	4 11 18 25	2 9 16 23 30
Thur.	1 8 15 22 29	5 12 19 26	3 10 17 24 31
Fri.	2 9 16 23 30	6 13 20 27	4 11 18 25
Sat.	3 10 17 24 31	7 14 21 28	5 12 19 26

EASTER DAYS

March 22	1818
March 29	1807, 1891, 1959, 1970
April 5	1795, 1801, 1863, 1874, 1885, 1931, 1942, 1953, 2015, 2026, 2037
April 12	1789, 1846, 1857, 1903, 1914, 1925, 1998, 2009
April 19	1829, 1835, 1981, 1987

H (LEAP YEAR)

	January	February	March
Sun.	5 12 19 26	2 9 16 23	1 8 15 22 29
Mon.	6 13 20 27	3 10 17 24	2 9 16 23 30
Tue.	7 14 21 28	4 11 18 25	3 10 17 24 31
Wed.	1 8 15 22 29	5 12 19 26	4 11 18 25
Thur.	2 9 16 23 30	6 13 20 27	5 12 19 26
Fri.	3 10 17 24 31	7 14 21 28	6 13 20 27
Sat.	4 11 18 25	1 8 15 22 29	7 14 21 28

	April	May	June
Sun.	5 12 19 26	3 10 17 24 31	7 14 21 28
Mon.	6 13 20 27	4 11 18 25	1 8 15 22 29
Tue.	7 14 21 28	5 12 19 26	2 9 16 23 30
Wed.	1 8 15 22 29	6 13 20 27	3 10 17 24
Thur.	2 9 16 23 30	7 14 21 28	4 11 18 25
Fri.	3 10 17 24	1 8 15 22 29	5 12 19 26
Sat.	4 11 18 25	2 9 16 23 30	6 13 20 27

	July	August	September
Sun.	5 12 19 26	2 9 16 23 30	6 13 20 27
Mon.	6 13 20 27	3 10 17 24 31	7 14 21 28
Tue.	7 14 21 28	4 11 18 25	1 8 15 22 29
Wed.	1 8 15 22 29	5 12 19 26	2 9 16 23 30
Thur.	2 9 16 23 30	6 13 20 27	3 10 17 24
Fri.	3 10 17 24 31	7 14 21 28	4 11 18 25
Sat.	4 11 18 25	1 8 15 22 29	5 12 19 26

	October	November	December
Sun.	4 11 18 25	1 8 15 22 29	6 13 20 27
Mon.	5 12 19 26	2 9 16 23 30	7 14 21 28
Tue.	6 13 20 27	3 10 17 24	1 8 15 22 29
Wed.	7 14 21 28	4 11 18 25	2 9 16 23 30
Thur.	1 8 15 22 29	5 12 19 26	3 10 17 24 31
Fri.	2 9 16 23 30	6 13 20 27	4 11 18 25
Sat.	3 10 17 24 31	7 14 21 28	5 12 19 26

EASTER DAYS

March 29	1812, 1964
April 5	1896
April 12	1868, 1936, 2020
April 19	1840, 1908, 1992

J (LEAP YEAR)

	January	February	March
Sun.	4 11 18 25	1 8 15 22 29	7 14 21 28
Mon.	5 12 19 26	2 9 16 23	1 8 15 22 29
Tue.	6 13 20 27	3 10 17 24	2 9 16 23 30
Wed.	7 14 21 28	4 11 18 25	3 10 17 24 31
Thur.	1 8 15 22 29	5 12 19 26	4 11 18 25
Fri.	2 9 16 23 30	6 13 20 27	5 12 19 26
Sat.	3 10 17 24 31	7 14 21 28	6 13 20 27

	April	May	June
Sun.	4 11 18 25	2 9 16 23 30	6 13 20 27
Mon.	5 12 19 26	3 10 17 24 31	7 14 21 28
Tue.	6 13 20 27	4 11 18 25	1 8 15 22 29
Wed.	7 14 21 28	5 12 19 26	2 9 16 23 30
Thur.	1 8 15 22 29	6 13 20 27	3 10 17 24
Fri.	2 9 16 23 30	7 14 21 28	4 11 18 25
Sat.	3 10 17 24	1 8 15 22 29	5 12 19 26

	July	August	September
Sun.	4 11 18 25	1 8 15 22 29	5 12 19 26
Mon.	5 12 19 26	2 9 16 23 30	6 13 20 27
Tue.	6 13 20 27	3 10 17 24 31	7 14 21 28
Wed.	7 14 21 28	4 11 18 25	1 8 15 22 29
Thur.	1 8 15 22 29	5 12 19 26	2 9 16 23 30
Fri.	2 9 16 23 30	6 13 20 27	3 10 17 24
Sat.	3 10 17 24 31	7 14 21 28	4 11 18 25

	October	November	December
Sun.	3 10 17 24 31	7 14 21 28	5 12 19 26
Mon.	4 11 18 25	1 8 15 22 29	6 13 20 27
Tue.	5 12 19 26	2 9 16 23 30	7 14 21 28
Wed.	6 13 20 27	3 10 17 24	1 8 15 22 29
Thur.	7 14 21 28	4 11 18 25	2 9 16 23 30
Fri.	1 8 15 22 29	5 12 19 26	3 10 17 24 31
Sat.	2 9 16 23 30	6 13 20 27	4 11 18 25

EASTER DAYS

March 28	1880, 1948, 2032
April 4	1920
April 11	1784, 1852, 2004
April 18	1824, 1976

K

	January	February	March
Sun.	3 10 17 24 31	7 14 21 28	7 14 21 28
Mon.	4 11 18 25	1 8 15 22	1 8 15 22 29
Tue.	5 12 19 26	2 9 16 23	2 9 16 23 30
Wed.	6 13 20 27	3 10 17 24	3 10 17 24 31
Thur.	7 14 21 28	4 11 18 25	4 11 18 25
Fri.	1 8 15 22 29	5 12 19 26	5 12 19 26
Sat.	2 9 16 23 30	6 13 20 27	6 13 20 27

	April	May	June
Sun.	4 11 18 25	2 9 16 23 30	6 13 20 27
Mon.	5 12 19 26	3 10 17 24 31	7 14 21 28
Tue.	6 13 20 27	4 11 18 25	1 8 15 22 29
Wed.	7 14 21 28	5 12 19 26	2 9 16 23 30
Thur.	1 8 15 22 29	6 13 20 27	3 10 17 24
Fri.	2 9 16 23 30	7 14 21 28	4 11 18 25
Sat.	3 10 17 24	1 8 15 22 29	5 12 19 26

	July	August	September
Sun.	4 11 18 25	1 8 15 22 29	5 12 19 26
Mon.	5 12 19 26	2 9 16 23 30	6 13 20 27
Tue.	6 13 20 27	3 10 17 24 31	7 14 21 28
Wed.	7 14 21 28	4 11 18 25	1 8 15 22 29
Thur.	1 8 15 22 29	5 12 19 26	2 9 16 23 30
Fri.	2 9 16 23 30	6 13 20 27	3 10 17 24
Sat.	3 10 17 24 31	7 14 21 28	4 11 18 25

	October	November	December
Sun.	3 10 17 24 31	7 14 21 28	5 12 19 26
Mon.	4 11 18 25	1 8 15 22 29	6 13 20 27
Tue.	5 12 19 26	2 9 16 23 30	7 14 21 28
Wed.	6 13 20 27	3 10 17 24	1 8 15 22 29
Thur.	7 14 21 28	4 11 18 25	2 9 16 23 30
Fri.	1 8 15 22 29	5 12 19 26	3 10 17 24 31
Sat.	2 9 16 23 30	6 13 20 27	4 11 18 25

EASTER DAYS

March 28	1869, 1875, 1937, 2027
April 4	1790, 1847, 1858, 1915, 1926, 1999, 2010, 2021
April 11	1819, 1830, 1841, 1909, 1971, 1982, 1993
April 18	1802, 1813, 1897, 1954, 1965
April 25	1886, 1943, 2038

M

	January	February	March
Sun.	2 9 16 23 30	6 13 20 27	6 13 20 27
Mon.	3 10 17 24 31	7 14 21 28	7 14 21 28
Tue.	4 11 18 25	1 8 15 22	1 8 15 22 29
Wed.	5 12 19 26	2 9 16 23	2 9 16 23 30
Thur.	6 13 20 27	3 10 17 24	3 10 17 24 31
Fri.	7 14 21 28	4 11 18 25	4 11 18 25
Sat.	1 8 15 22 29	5 12 19 26	5 12 19 26

	April	May	June
Sun.	3 10 17 24	1 8 15 22 29	5 12 19 26
Mon.	4 11 18 25	2 9 16 23 30	6 13 20 27
Tue.	5 12 19 26	3 10 17 24 31	7 14 21 28
Wed.	6 13 20 27	4 11 18 25	1 8 15 22 29
Thur.	7 14 21 28	5 12 19 26	2 9 16 23 30
Fri.	1 8 15 22 29	6 13 20 27	3 10 17 24
Sat.	2 9 16 23 30	7 14 21 28	4 11 18 25

	July	August	September
Sun.	3 10 17 24 31	7 14 21 28	4 11 18 25
Mon.	4 11 18 25	1 8 15 22 29	5 12 19 26
Tue.	5 12 19 26	2 9 16 23 30	6 13 20 27
Wed.	6 13 20 27	3 10 17 24 31	7 14 21 28
Thur.	7 14 21 28	4 11 18 25	1 8 15 22 29
Fri.	1 8 15 22 29	5 12 19 26	2 9 16 23 30
Sat.	2 9 16 23 30	6 13 20 27	3 10 17 24

	October	November	December
Sun.	2 9 16 23 30	6 13 20 27	4 11 18 25
Mon.	3 10 17 24 31	7 14 21 28	5 12 19 26
Tue.	4 11 18 25	1 8 15 22 29	6 13 20 27
Wed.	5 12 19 26	2 9 16 23 30	7 14 21 28
Thur.	6 13 20 27	3 10 17 24	1 8 15 22 29
Fri.	7 14 21 28	4 11 18 25	2 9 16 23 30
Sat.	1 8 15 22 29	5 12 19 26	3 10 17 24 31

EASTER DAYS

March 27	1785, 1842, 1853, 1910, 1921, 2005
April 3	1825, 1831, 1983, 1994
April 10	1803, 1814, 1887, 1898, 1955, 1966, 1977, 2039
April 17	1870, 1881, 1927, 1938, 1949, 2022, 2033
April 24	1791, 1859, 2011

L (LEAP YEAR)

	January	February	March
Sun.	3 10 17 24 31	7 14 21 28	6 13 20 27
Mon.	4 11 18 25	1 8 15 22 29	7 14 21 28
Tue.	5 12 19 26	2 9 16 23	1 8 15 22 29
Wed.	6 13 20 27	3 10 17 24	2 9 16 23 30
Thur.	7 14 21 28	4 11 18 25	3 10 17 24 31
Fri.	1 8 15 22 29	5 12 19 26	4 11 18 25
Sat.	2 9 16 23 30	6 13 20 27	5 12 19 26

	April	May	June
Sun.	3 10 17 24	1 8 15 22 29	5 12 19 26
Mon.	4 11 18 25	2 9 16 23 30	6 13 20 27
Tue.	5 12 19 26	3 10 17 24 31	7 14 21 28
Wed.	6 13 20 27	4 11 18 25	1 8 15 22 29
Thur.	7 14 21 28	5 12 19 26	2 9 16 23 30
Fri.	1 8 15 22 29	6 13 20 27	3 10 17 24
Sat.	2 9 16 23 30	7 14 21 28	4 11 18 25

	July	August	September
Sun.	3 10 17 24 31	7 14 21 28	4 11 18 25
Mon.	4 11 18 25	1 8 15 22 29	5 12 19 26
Tue.	5 12 19 26	2 9 16 23 30	6 13 20 27
Wed.	6 13 20 27	3 10 17 24 31	7 14 21 28
Thur.	7 14 21 28	4 11 18 25	1 8 15 22 29
Fri.	1 8 15 22 29	5 12 19 26	2 9 16 23 30
Sat.	2 9 16 23 30	6 13 20 27	3 10 17 24

	October	November	December
Sun.	2 9 16 23 30	6 13 20 27	4 11 18 25
Mon.	3 10 17 24 31	7 14 21 28	5 12 19 26
Tue.	4 11 18 25	1 8 15 22 29	6 13 20 27
Wed.	5 12 19 26	2 9 16 23 30	7 14 21 28
Thur.	6 13 20 27	3 10 17 24	1 8 15 22 29
Fri.	7 14 21 28	4 11 18 25	2 9 16 23 30
Sat.	1 8 15 22 29	5 12 19 26	3 10 17 24 31

EASTER DAYS

March 27	1796, 1864, 1932, 2016
April 3	1836, 1904, 1988
April 17	1808, 1892, 1960

N (LEAP YEAR)

	January	February	March
Sun.	2 9 16 23 30	6 13 20 27	5 12 19 26
Mon.	3 10 17 24 31	7 14 21 28	6 13 20 27
Tue.	4 11 18 25	1 8 15 22 29	7 14 21 28
Wed.	5 12 19 26	2 9 16 23	1 8 15 22 29
Thur.	6 13 20 27	3 10 17 24	2 9 16 23 30
Fri.	7 14 21 28	4 11 18 25	3 10 17 24 31
Sat.	1 8 15 22 29	5 12 19 26	4 11 18 25

	April	May	June
Sun.	2 9 16 23 30	7 14 21 28	4 11 18 25
Mon.	3 10 17 24	1 8 15 22 29	5 12 19 26
Tue.	4 11 18 25	2 9 16 23 30	6 13 20 27
Wed.	5 12 19 26	3 10 17 24 31	7 14 21 28
Thur.	6 13 20 27	4 11 18 25	1 8 15 22 29
Fri.	7 14 21 28	5 12 19 26	2 9 16 23 30
Sat.	1 8 15 22 29	6 13 20 27	3 10 17 24

	July	August	September
Sun.	2 9 16 23 30	6 13 20 27	3 10 17 24
Mon.	3 10 17 24 31	7 14 21 28	4 11 18 25
Tue.	4 11 18 25	1 8 15 22 29	5 12 19 26
Wed.	5 12 19 26	2 9 16 23 30	6 13 20 27
Thur.	6 13 20 27	3 10 17 24	7 14 21 28
Fri.	7 14 21 28	4 11 18 25	1 8 15 22 29
Sat.	1 8 15 22 29	5 12 19 26	2 9 16 23 30

	October	November	December
Sun.	1 8 15 22 29	5 12 19 26	3 10 17 24 31
Mon.	2 9 16 23 30	6 13 20 27	4 11 18 25
Tue.	3 10 17 24 31	7 14 21 28	5 12 19 26
Wed.	4 11 18 25	1 8 15 22 29	6 13 20 27
Thur.	5 12 19 26	2 9 16 23 30	7 14 21 28
Fri.	6 13 20 27	3 10 17 24	1 8 15 22 29
Sat.	7 14 21 28	4 11 18 25	2 9 16 23 30

EASTER DAYS

March 26	1780
April 2	1820, 1972
April 9	1944
April 16	2028
April 23	1848, 1916, 2000

GEOLOGICAL TIME

The earth is thought to have come into existence approximately 4,600 million years ago, but for nearly half this time, the Archean era, it was uninhabited. Life is generally believed to have emerged in the succeeding Proterozoic era. The Archean and the Proterozoic eras are often together referred to as the Precambrian.

Although primitive forms of life, e.g. algae and bacteria, existed during the Proterozoic era, it is not until the strata of Palaeozoic rocks is reached that abundant fossilized remains appear.

Since the Precambrian, there have been three great geological eras:

PALAEOZOIC ('ancient life')
*c.*570–*c.*245 million years ago

Cambrian – Mainly sandstones, slate and shales; limestones in Scotland. Shelled fossils and invertebrates, e.g. trilobites and brachiopods appear
Ordovician – Mainly shales and mudstones, e.g. in north Wales; limestones in Scotland. First fishes
Silurian – Shales, mudstones and some limestones, found mostly in Wales and southern Scotland
Devonian – Old red sandstone, shale, limestone and slate, e.g. in south Wales and the West Country
Carboniferous – Coal-bearing rocks, millstone grit, limestone and shale. First traces of land-living life
Permian – Marls, sandstones and clays. First reptile fossils

There are two great phases of mountain building in the Palaeozoic era: the Caledonian, characterized in Britain by NE–SW lines of hills and valleys; and the later Hercyian, widespread in west Germany and adjacent areas, and in Britain exemplified in E.–W. lines of hills and valleys.

The end of the Palaeozoic era was marked by the extensive glaciations of the Permian period in the southern continents and the decline of amphibians. It was succeeded by an era of warm conditions.

MESOZOIC ('middle forms of life')
*c.*245–*c.*65 million years ago

Triassic – Mostly sandstone, e.g. in the West Midlands
Jurassic – Mainly limestones and clays, typically displayed in the Jura mountains, and in England in a NE–SW belt from Lincolnshire and the Wash to the Severn and the Dorset coast
Cretaceous – Mainly chalk, clay and sands, e.g. in Kent and Sussex

Giant reptiles were dominant during the Mesozoic era, but it was at this time that marsupial mammals first appeared, as well as *Archaeopteryx lithographica*, the earliest known species of bird. Coniferous trees and flowering plants also developed during the era and, with the birds and the mammals, were the main species to survive into the Cenozoic era. The giant reptiles became extinct.

CENOZOIC ('recent life')
from *c.*65 million years ago

Palaeocene ⎱ The emergence of new forms of life, includ-
Eocene   ⎰ ing existing species
Oligocene – Fossils of a few still existing species
Miocene – Fossil remains show a balance of existing and extinct species
Pliocene – Fossil remains show a majority of still existing species
Pleistocene – The majority of remains are those of still existing species

Holocene – The present, post-glacial period. Existing species only, except for a few exterminated by man

In the last 25 million years, from the Miocene through the Pliocene periods, the Alpine-Himalayan and the circum-Pacific phases of mountain building reached their climax. During the Pleistocene period ice-sheets repeatedly locked up masses of water as land ice; its weight depressed the land, but the locking-up of the water lowered the sea-level by 100–200 metres. The glaciations and interglacials of the Ice Age are difficult to date and classify, but recent scientific opinion considers the Pleistocene period to have begun approximately 1.64 million years ago. The last glacial retreat, merging into the Holocene period, was 10,000 years ago.

HUMAN DEVELOPMENT

Any consideration of the history of mankind must start with the fact that all members of the human race belong to one species of animal, i.e. *Homo sapiens*, the definition of a species being in biological terms that all its members can interbreed. As a species of mammal it is possible to group man with other similar types, known as the primates. Amongst these is found a sub-group, the apes, which includes, in addition to man, the chimpanzees, gorillas, orang-utans and gibbons. All lack a tail, have shoulder blades at the back, and a Y-shaped chewing pattern on the surface of their molars, as well as showing the more general primate characteristics of four incisors, a thumb which is able to touch the fingers of the same hand, and finger and toe nails instead of claws. The factors available to scientific study suggest that human beings have chimpanzees and gorillas as their nearest relatives in the animal world. However, there remains the possibility that there once lived creatures, now extinct, which were closer to modern man than the chimpanzees and gorillas, and which shared with modern man the characteristics of having flat faces (i.e. the absence of a pronounced muzzle), being bipedal, and possessing large brains.

There are two broad groups of extinct apes recognized by specialists. The ramapithecines, the remains of which, mainly jaw fragments, have been found in east Africa, Asia, and Turkey. They lived about 14 to 8 million years ago, and from the evidence of their teeth it seems they chewed more in the manner of modern man than the other presently living apes. The second group, the australopithecines, have left more numerous remains amongst which sub-groups may be detected, although the geographic spread is limited to south and east Africa. Living between 5 and 1.5 million years ago, they were closer relatives of modern man to the extent that they walked upright, did not have an extensive muzzle and had similar types of pre-molars. The first australopithecine remains were recognized at Taung in South Africa in 1924 and subsequent discoveries include those at the Olduvai Gorge in Tanzania. The most impressive discovery was made at Hadar, Ethiopia, in 1974 when about half a skeleton, known as 'Lucy', was found.

Also in east Africa, between 2 million and 1.5 million years ago, lived a hominid group which not only walked upright, had a flat face, and a large brain case, but also made simple pebble and flake stone tools. On present evidence these habilines seem to have been the first people to make tools, however crude. This facility is related to the larger brain size and human beings are the only animals to make implements to be used in other processes. These early pebble tool users, because of their distinctive

GEOLOGICAL TIME

Era	Period	Epoch	Date began*	Evolutionary stages
Cenozoic	Quaternary	Holocene	0.01	Man
		Pleistocene	1.64	
	Tertiary	Pliocene	5.2	
		Miocene	23.3	
		Oligocene	35.4	
		Eocene	56.5	
		Palaeocene	65.0	
Mesozoic	Cretaceous		145.6	
	Jurassic		208.0	First birds
	Triassic		245.0	First mammals
Palaeozoic	Permian		290.0	First reptiles
	Carboniferous		362.5	First amphibians and insects
	Devonian		408.5	
	Silurian		439.0	
	Ordovician		510.0	First fishes
	Cambrian		570.0	First invertebrates
	Precambrian		4,600.0	First primitive life forms, e.g. algae and bacteria

*millions of years ago

characteristics, have been grouped as a separate sub-species, now extinct, of the genus *Homo* and are known as *Homo habilis*.

The use of fire, again a human characteristic, is associated with another group of extinct hominids whose remains, about a million years old, are found in south and east Africa, China, Indonesia, north Africa and Europe. Mastery of the techniques of making fire probably helped the colonization of the colder northern areas and in this respect the site of Vertesszollos in Hungary is of particular importance. *Homo erectus* is the name given to this group of fossils and it includes a number of famous individual discoveries, e.g. Solo Man, Heidelberg Man, and especially Peking Man who lived at the cave site at Choukoutien which has yielded evidence of fire and burnt bone.

The well-known group Neanderthal Man, or *Homo sapiens neandertalensis*, is an extinct form of modern man who lived between about 100,000 and 40,000 years ago, thus spanning the last Ice Age. Indeed, its ability to adapt to the cold climate on the edge of the ice-sheets is one of its characteristic features, the remains being found only in Europe, Asia and the Middle East. Complete neanderthal skeletons were found during excavations at Tabun in Israel, together with evidence of tool-making and the use of fire. Distinguished by very large brains, it seems that neanderthal man was the first to develop recognizable social customs, especially deliberate burial rites. Why the neanderthalers became extinct is not clear but it may be connected with the climatic changes at the end of the Ice Ages, which would have seriously affected their food supplies; possibly they became too specialized for their own good.

The Swanscombe skull is the only known human fossil remains found in England. Some specialists see Swanscombe Man (or, more probably, woman) as a neanderthaler. Others group these remains together with the Steinheim skull from Germany, seeing both as a separate sub-species. There is too little evidence as yet on which to form a final judgement.

Modern Man, *Homo sapiens sapiens*, the surviving sub-species of *Homo sapiens*, had evolved to our present physical condition and had colonized much of the world by about 30,000 years ago. There are many previously distinguished individual specimens, e.g. Cromagnon Man, which may now be grouped together as *Homo sapiens sapiens*. It was modern man who spread to the American continent by crossing the landbridge between Siberia and Alaska and thence moved south through North America and into South America. Equally it is modern man who over the last 30,000 years has been responsible for the major developments in technology, art and civilization generally.

One of the problems for those studying fossil man is the lack in many cases of sufficient quantities of fossil bone for analysis. It is important that theories should be tested against evidence, rather than the evidence being made to fit the theory. The Piltdown hoax is a well-known example of 'fossils' being forged to fit what was seen in some quarters as the correct theory of man's evolution.

CULTURAL DEVELOPMENT

The Eurocentric bias of early archaeologists meant that the search for a starting point for the development and transmission of cultural ideas, especially by migration, trade and warfare, concentrated unduly on Europe and the Near East. The Three Age system, whereby pre-history was divided into a Stone Age, a Bronze Age and an Iron Age, was devised by Christian Thomsen, curator of the National Museum of Denmark in the early 19th century, to facilitate the classification of the museum's collections.

The descriptive adjectives referred to the materials from which the implements and weapons were made and came to be regarded as the dominant features of the societies to which they related. The refinement of the Three Age system once dominated archaeological thought and remains a generally accepted concept in the popular mind. However, it is now seen by archaeologists as an inadequate model for human development.

Common sense suggests that there were no complete breaks between one so-called Age and another, any more than contemporaries would have regarded 1485 as a complete break between medieval and modern English history. Nor can the Three Age system be applied universally. In some areas it is necessary to insert a Copper Age, while in Africa south of the Sahara there would seem to be no Bronze Age at all; in Australia, Old Stone Age societies survived, while in South America, New Stone Age communities existed into modern times. The civilizations in other parts of the world clearly invalidate a Eurocentric theory of human development.

The concept of the 'Neolithic revolution', associated with the domestication of plants and animals, was a development of particular importance in the human cultural pattern. It reflected change from the primitive hunter/gatherer economies to a more settled agricultural way of life and therefore, so the argument goes, made possible the development of urban civilization. However, it can no longer be argued that this 'revolution' took place only in one area from which all development stemmed. Though it appears that the cultivation of wheat and barley was first undertaken, together with the domestication of cattle and goats/sheep in the Fertile Crescent (the area bounded by the rivers Tigris and Euphrates), there is evidence that rice was first deliberately planted and pigs domesticated in south-east Asia, maize first cultivated in Central America and llamas first domesticated in South America. It has been recognized in recent years that cultural changes can take place independently of each other in different parts of the world at different rates and different times. There is no need for a general diffusionist theory.

Although scholars will continue to study the particular societies which interest them, it may be possible to obtain a reliable chronological framework, in absolute terms of years, against which the cultural development of any particular area may be set. The development and refinement of radio-carbon dating and other scientific methods of producing absolute chronologies is enabling the cross-referencing of societies to be undertaken. As the techniques of dating become more rigorous in application and the number of scientifically obtained dates increases, the attainment of an absolute chronology for prehistoric societies throughout the world comes closer to being achieved.

Tidal Tables

CONSTANTS

The constant tidal difference may be used in conjunction with the time of high water at a standard port shown in the predictions data (pages 98–103) to find the time of high water at any of the ports or places listed below. These tidal differences are very approximate and should be used only as a guide to the time of high water at the places below. More precise local data should be obtained for navigational and other nautical purposes.

All data allow high water time to be found in Greenwich Mean Time; this applies also to data for the months when British Summer Time is in operation and the hour's time difference should be allowed for. Ports marked * are in a different time zone and the standard time zone difference also needs to be added/subtracted to give local time.

EXAMPLE

Required time of high water at Stranraer at 2 January 1999
Appropriate time of high water at Greenock

Afternoon tide 2 January	1227 hrs
Tidal difference	−0020 hrs
High water at Stranraer	1207 hrs

The columns headed 'Springs' and 'Neaps' show the height, in metres, of the tide above datum for mean high water springs and mean high water neaps respectively.

Port	Diff.		Springs	Neaps
		h m	m	m
Aberdeen	Leith	−1 19	4.3	3.4
*Antwerp (Prosperpolder)	London	+0 50	5.8	4.8
Ardrossan	Greenock	−0 15	3.2	2.6
Avonmouth	London	−6 45	13.2	9.8
Ayr	Greenock	−0 25	3.0	2.5
Barrow (Docks)	Liverpool	0 00	9.3	7.1
Belfast	London	−2 47	3.5	3.0
Blackpool	Liverpool	−0 10	8.9	7.0
*Boulogne	London	−2 44	8.9	7.2
*Calais	London	−2 04	7.2	5.9
*Cherbourg	London	−6 00	6.4	5.0
Cobh	Liverpool	−5 55	4.2	3.2
Cowes	London	−2 38	4.2	3.5
Dartmouth	London	+4 25	4.9	3.8
*Dieppe	London	−3 03	9.3	7.3
Douglas, IOM	Liverpool	−0 04	6.9	5.4
Dover	London	−2 52	6.7	5.3
Dublin	London	−2 05	4.1	3.4
Dun Laoghaire	London	−2 10	4.1	3.4
*Dunkirk	London	−1 54	6.0	4.9
Fishguard	Liverpool	−4 01	4.8	3.4
Fleetwood	Liverpool	0 00	9.2	7.3
*Flushing	London	−0 15	4.7	3.9
Folkestone	London	−3 04	7.1	5.7
Galway	Liverpool	−6 08	5.1	3.9
Glasgow	Greenock	+0 26	4.7	4.0
Harwich	London	−2 06	4.0	3.4
*Le Havre	London	−3 55	7.9	6.6
Heysham	Liverpool	+0 05	9.4	7.4
Holyhead	Liverpool	−0 50	5.6	4.4
*Hook of Holland	London	−0 01	2.1	1.7
Hull (Albert Dock)	London	−7 40	7.5	5.8

Port	Diff.		Springs	Neaps
Immingham	London	−8 00	7.3	5.8
Larne	London	−2 40	2.8	2.5
Lerwick	Leith	−3 48	2.2	1.6
Londonderry	London	−5 37	2.7	2.1
Lowestoft	London	−4 25	2.4	2.1
Margate	London	−1 53	4.8	3.9
Milford Haven	Liverpool	−5 08	7.0	5.2
Morecambe	Liverpool	+0 07	9.5	7.4
Newhaven	London	−2 46	6.7	5.1
Oban	Greenock	+5 43	4.0	2.9
*Ostend	London	−1 32	5.1	4.2
Plymouth (Devonport)	London	+4 05	5.5	4.4
Portland	London	+5 09	2.1	1.4
Portsmouth	London	−2 38	4.7	3.8
Ramsgate	London	−2 32	5.2	4.1
Richmond Lock	London	+1 00	4.9	3.7
Rosslare Harbour	Liverpool	−5 24	1.9	1.4
Rosyth	Leith	+0 09	5.8	4.7
*Rotterdam	London	+1 45	2.0	1.7
St Helier	London	+4 48	11.0	8.1
St Malo	London	+4 27	12.2	9.2
St Peter Port	London	+4 54	9.3	7.0
Scrabster	Leith	−6 06	5.0	4.0
Sheerness	London	−1 19	5.8	4.7
Shoreham	London	−2 44	6.3	4.9
Southampton (1st high water)	London	−2 54	4.5	3.7
Spurn Head	London	−8 25	6.9	5.5
Stornoway	Liverpool	−4 16	4.8	3.7
Stranraer	Greenock	−0 20	3.0	2.4
Stromness	Leith	−5 26	3.6	2.7
Swansea	London	−7 35	9.5	7.2
Tees (River Entrance)	Leith	+1 09	5.5	4.3
Tilbury	London	−0 49	6.4	5.4
Tobermory	Liverpool	−5 11	4.4	3.3
Tyne River (North Shields)	London	−1030	5.0	3.9
Ullapool	Leith	−7 40	5.2	3.9
Walton-on-the-Naze	London	−2 10	4.2	3.4
Wick	Leith	−3 26	3.5	2.8
*Zeebrugge	London	−0 55	4.8	3.9

PREDICTIONS

The data on pages 98–103 are daily predictions of the time and height of high water at London Bridge, Liverpool, Greenock and Leith. The time of the data is Greenwich Mean Time; this applies also to data for the months when British Summer Time is in operation and the hour's time difference should be allowed for. The datum of predictions for each port shows the difference of height, in metres from Ordnance data (Newlyn).

The tidal information for London Bridge, Liverpool, Greenock and Leith is reproduced with the permission of the UK Hydrographic Office and the Controller of HMSO. Crown copyright reserved.

JANUARY 1999   *High water*   GMT

		London Bridge *Datum of predictions 3.20 m below				Liverpool *Datum of predictions 4.93 m below				Greenock *Datum of predictions 1.62 m below				Leith *Datum of predictions 2.90 m below			
		hr	ht m	hr	ht m	hr	ht m	hr	ht m	hr	ht m	hr	ht m	hr	ht m	hr	ht m
1	Friday	00 29	6.9	12 51	7.0	10 17	9.5	22 43	9.6	11 41	3.6	—	—	01 19	5.6	13 47	5.6
2	Saturday	01 21	7.1	13 43	7.3	11 06	9.8	23 31	9.7	00 13	3.5	12 27	3.7	02 11	5.7	14 35	5.7
3	Sunday	02 10	7.2	14 33	7.4	11 52	9.8	—	—	01 04	3.5	13 11	3.8	03 00	5.8	15 22	5.8
4	Monday	02 55	7.2	15 21	7.4	00 17	9.6	12 37	9.8	01 52	3.5	13 53	3.9	03 49	5.7	16 08	5.7
5	Tuesday	03 39	7.1	16 06	7.3	01 02	9.4	13 20	9.6	02 37	3.5	14 34	3.9	04 36	5.6	16 55	5.6
6	Wednesday	04 19	6.9	16 49	7.1	01 45	9.2	14 02	9.3	03 20	3.4	15 15	3.9	05 23	5.4	17 42	5.4
7	Thursday	04 56	6.7	17 30	6.8	02 26	8.8	14 43	8.9	04 01	3.4	15 56	3.8	06 09	5.2	18 29	5.1
8	Friday	05 32	6.5	18 10	6.5	03 08	8.4	15 25	8.5	04 43	3.3	16 38	3.6	06 55	4.9	19 17	4.9
9	Saturday	06 11	6.3	18 52	6.2	03 53	7.9	16 12	8.0	05 28	3.1	17 22	3.4	07 43	4.7	20 09	4.7
10	Sunday	06 57	6.0	19 42	5.9	04 46	7.5	17 10	7.6	06 16	3.0	18 10	3.2	08 35	4.5	21 04	4.6
11	Monday	07 57	5.7	20 42	5.8	05 53	7.3	18 20	7.4	07 09	2.9	19 04	3.1	09 30	4.5	22 04	4.5
12	Tuesday	09 11	5.6	21 49	5.8	07 07	7.4	19 33	7.5	08 18	2.9	20 08	3.0	10 30	4.5	23 09	4.5
13	Wednesday	10 24	5.7	22 51	6.0	08 11	7.7	20 34	7.8	09 43	3.0	21 29	2.9	11 34	4.6	—	—
14	Thursday	11 25	6.0	23 47	6.3	09 02	8.1	21 24	8.1	10 41	3.1	22 36	3.0	00 12	4.6	12 32	4.8
15	Friday	—	—	12 19	6.3	09 47	8.5	22 06	8.5	11 25	3.3	23 23	3.1	01 04	4.8	13 20	5.0
16	Saturday	00 37	6.5	13 06	6.5	10 26	8.9	22 45	8.7	—	—	12 02	3.4	01 47	5.0	14 01	5.2
17	Sunday	01 22	6.7	13 49	6.7	11 04	9.1	23 23	8.9	00 03	3.1	12 36	3.4	02 26	5.2	14 39	5.3
18	Monday	02 03	6.8	14 29	6.8	11 42	9.3	—	—	00 42	3.2	13 08	3.5	03 03	5.3	15 16	5.4
19	Tuesday	02 42	6.9	15 09	6.9	00 01	9.1	12 20	9.4	01 21	3.2	13 43	3.5	03 40	5.4	15 51	5.5
20	Wednesday	03 19	6.9	15 48	7.0	00 41	9.1	13 00	9.5	02 02	3.2	14 20	3.6	04 17	5.4	16 27	5.5
21	Thursday	03 56	6.9	16 29	7.0	01 21	9.2	13 41	9.5	02 43	3.2	14 59	3.6	04 56	5.4	17 05	5.5
22	Friday	04 35	6.9	17 11	6.9	02 03	9.1	14 24	9.4	03 24	3.3	15 38	3.6	05 38	5.3	17 48	5.4
23	Saturday	05 16	6.8	17 56	6.8	02 47	8.9	15 10	9.1	04 05	3.2	16 20	3.5	06 25	5.2	18 35	5.3
24	Sunday	06 01	6.7	18 45	6.5	03 35	8.6	16 02	8.8	04 49	3.2	17 07	3.3	07 16	5.1	19 29	5.1
25	Monday	06 52	6.4	19 41	6.3	04 32	8.2	17 03	8.4	05 38	3.1	18 01	3.2	08 14	4.9	20 33	4.9
26	Tuesday	07 54	6.2	20 49	6.1	05 40	7.9	18 14	8.2	06 35	3.0	19 10	3.0	09 21	4.8	21 48	4.9
27	Wednesday	09 11	6.1	22 03	6.1	06 57	7.9	19 31	8.2	07 48	2.9	20 52	3.0	10 34	4.8	23 04	4.9
28	Thursday	10 29	6.2	23 11	6.3	08 12	8.2	20 43	8.5	09 28	3.0	22 14	3.1	11 44	5.0	—	—
29	Friday	11 38	6.5	—	—	09 15	8.7	21 43	8.9	10 35	3.2	23 15	3.2	00 14	5.1	12 46	5.2
30	Saturday	00 12	6.6	12 39	6.8	10 08	9.2	22 35	9.3	11 28	3.4	—	—	01 14	5.3	13 39	5.4
31	Sunday	01 06	6.9	13 32	7.1	10 56	9.5	23 21	9.5	00 08	3.3	12 15	3.6	02 06	5.5	14 27	5.6

FEBRUARY 1999   *High water*   GMT

		London Bridge				Liverpool				Greenock				Leith			
1	Monday	01 55	7.1	14 21	7.3	11 40	9.7	—	—	00 58	3.4	12 59	3.7	02 52	5.6	15 11	5.7
2	Tuesday	02 40	7.1	15 07	7.3	00 04	9.5	12 22	9.7	01 43	3.4	13 40	3.7	03 35	5.6	15 54	5.7
3	Wednesday	03 22	7.0	15 48	7.2	00 45	9.4	13 01	9.6	02 24	3.4	14 19	3.8	04 17	5.5	16 35	5.6
4	Thursday	03 58	6.9	16 26	7.0	01 22	9.2	13 38	9.4	03 00	3.3	14 56	3.8	04 57	5.4	17 15	5.4
5	Friday	04 31	6.8	16 59	6.8	01 57	9.0	14 13	9.1	03 35	3.3	15 32	3.7	05 36	5.2	17 54	5.2
6	Saturday	05 03	6.7	17 33	6.7	02 33	8.7	14 49	8.7	04 10	3.3	16 09	3.6	06 16	5.0	18 34	5.0
7	Sunday	05 38	6.5	18 09	6.5	03 10	8.3	15 28	8.3	04 47	3.2	16 47	3.4	06 58	4.8	19 18	4.8
8	Monday	06 19	6.3	18 51	6.2	03 52	7.8	16 14	7.8	05 28	3.1	17 29	3.2	07 43	4.6	20 08	4.5
9	Tuesday	07 06	6.0	19 40	6.0	04 46	7.4	17 12	7.3	06 14	2.9	18 17	3.0	08 34	4.4	21 05	4.4
10	Wednesday	08 03	5.7	20 39	5.8	05 56	7.1	18 27	7.1	07 08	2.8	19 13	2.8	09 32	4.3	22 11	4.3
11	Thursday	09 13	5.6	21 51	5.8	07 19	7.3	19 50	7.3	08 21	2.8	20 23	2.8	10 38	4.3	23 25	4.4
12	Friday	10 35	5.7	23 05	6.0	08 28	7.7	20 54	7.7	09 59	2.9	21 50	2.8	11 49	4.5	—	—
13	Saturday	11 44	6.0	—	—	09 20	8.2	21 43	8.2	10 55	3.1	22 57	2.9	00 31	4.6	12 50	4.8
14	Sunday	00 06	6.3	12 40	6.4	10 04	8.7	22 25	8.6	11 36	3.2	23 43	3.0	01 22	4.9	13 37	5.1
15	Monday	00 58	6.6	13 27	6.7	10 44	9.1	23 05	9.0	—	—	12 11	3.3	02 03	5.1	14 17	5.3
16	Tuesday	01 43	6.8	14 10	7.0	11 23	9.4	23 44	9.2	00 24	3.1	12 47	3.4	02 42	5.3	14 54	5.5
17	Wednesday	02 25	6.9	14 52	7.1	—	—	12 02	9.6	01 05	3.2	13 25	3.5	03 19	5.5	15 30	5.7
18	Thursday	03 04	7.0	15 32	7.2	00 23	9.4	12 43	9.8	01 45	3.2	14 03	3.6	03 56	5.6	16 07	5.7
19	Friday	03 42	7.1	16 12	7.2	01 04	9.5	13 24	9.8	02 24	3.3	14 42	3.6	04 35	5.6	16 46	5.7
20	Saturday	04 20	7.1	16 53	7.1	01 45	9.5	14 07	9.7	03 03	3.3	15 22	3.6	05 17	5.5	17 29	5.6
21	Sunday	05 00	7.1	17 36	6.9	02 28	9.3	14 51	9.4	03 41	3.3	16 02	3.5	06 03	5.4	18 16	5.5
22	Monday	05 43	6.9	18 21	6.6	03 13	8.9	15 40	8.9	04 22	3.3	16 46	3.4	06 51	5.1	19 09	5.2
23	Tuesday	06 31	6.6	19 12	6.2	04 05	8.3	16 38	8.3	05 07	3.2	17 36	3.2	07 48	4.9	20 14	4.9
24	Wednesday	07 29	6.2	20 19	5.9	05 12	7.8	17 52	7.8	05 59	3.0	18 39	2.9	08 56	4.7	21 32	4.7
25	Thursday	08 50	5.9	21 42	5.8	06 36	7.6	19 19	7.8	07 06	2.9	20 41	2.8	10 13	4.6	22 54	4.7
26	Friday	10 18	6.0	22 53	6.0	08 00	7.9	20 36	8.1	09 07	2.9	22 11	2.9	11 31	4.8		
27	Saturday	11 28	6.3	23 57	6.4	09 06	8.4	21 35	8.6	10 22	3.1	23 10	3.1	00 10	4.9	12 39	5.0
28	Sunday	—	—	12 27	6.8	09 58	9.0	22 24	9.0	11 15	3.3	—	—	01 11	5.2	13 33	5.3

MARCH 1999   *High water*   GMT

		LONDON BRIDGE *Datum of predictions 3.20 m below				LIVERPOOL *Datum of predictions 4.93 m below				GREENOCK *Datum of predictions 1.62 m below				LEITH *Datum of predictions 2.90 m below			
		hr	ht m	hr	ht m	hr	ht m	hr	ht m	hr	ht m	hr	ht m	hr	ht m	hr	ht m
1	Monday	00 51	6.8	13 20	7.1	10 43	9.4	23 07	9.3	00 00	3.2	12 01	3.5	01 59	5.3	14 18	5.5
2	Tuesday	01 40	7.0	14 07	7.3	11 24	9.6	23 46	9.4	00 46	3.3	12 43	3.5	02 40	5.5	14 58	5.6
3	Wednesday	02 24	7.1	14 49	7.2	—	—	12 02	9.6	01 27	3.3	13 23	3.6	03 18	5.5	15 36	5.6
4	Thursday	03 02	7.0	15 27	7.1	00 22	9.3	12 38	9.5	02 03	3.3	13 59	3.6	03 54	5.5	16 12	5.5
5	Friday	03 36	6.9	15 59	6.9	00 56	9.2	13 11	9.3	02 34	3.3	14 33	3.6	04 29	5.4	16 46	5.4
6	Saturday	04 05	6.8	16 28	6.8	01 28	9.1	13 43	9.1	03 04	3.3	15 06	3.6	05 03	5.2	17 21	5.2
7	Sunday	04 35	6.7	16 59	6.7	02 00	8.8	14 17	8.8	03 35	3.2	15 40	3.5	05 39	5.0	17 57	5.0
8	Monday	05 09	6.6	17 34	6.6	02 34	8.5	14 53	8.4	04 08	3.2	16 15	3.4	06 17	4.8	18 37	4.8
9	Tuesday	05 48	6.5	18 13	6.4	03 12	8.1	15 34	7.9	04 45	3.1	16 55	3.2	06 59	4.6	19 23	4.5
10	Wednesday	06 31	6.2	18 58	6.1	03 58	7.6	16 25	7.3	05 27	2.9	17 40	3.0	07 45	4.4	20 15	4.3
11	Thursday	07 22	5.9	19 52	5.9	04 58	7.2	17 33	7.0	06 19	2.7	18 36	2.8	08 41	4.2	21 19	4.2
12	Friday	08 24	5.6	20 58	5.7	06 18	7.0	18 57	7.0	07 25	2.6	19 43	2.7	09 46	4.2	22 34	4.2
13	Saturday	09 40	5.6	22 19	5.8	07 44	7.3	20 18	7.4	08 51	2.7	21 07	2.7	11 02	4.3	23 51	4.5
14	Sunday	11 06	5.9	23 32	6.1	08 47	7.9	21 14	8.0	10 13	2.9	22 27	2.8	—	—	12 12	4.6
15	Monday	—	—	12 10	6.3	09 35	8.5	21 59	8.6	11 02	3.1	23 19	3.0	00 49	4.8	13 06	5.0
16	Tuesday	00 29	6.5	13 01	6.8	10 18	9.1	22 40	9.1	11 42	3.2	—	—	01 35	5.1	13 49	5.3
17	Wednesday	01 18	6.8	13 47	7.1	10 59	9.5	23 21	9.4	00 02	3.1	12 22	3.4	02 15	5.4	14 27	5.6
18	Thursday	02 01	7.0	14 30	7.3	11 40	9.8	—	—	00 44	3.2	13 03	3.5	02 53	5.6	15 05	5.8
19	Friday	02 42	7.2	15 11	7.4	00 01	9.7	12 22	10.0	01 24	3.3	13 44	3.6	03 32	5.8	15 44	5.9
20	Saturday	03 22	7.3	15 52	7.4	00 43	9.8	13 05	10.0	02 02	3.4	14 25	3.6	04 13	5.8	16 26	5.9
21	Sunday	04 03	7.4	16 34	7.3	01 25	9.7	13 48	9.8	02 40	3.4	15 05	3.6	04 56	5.6	17 11	5.8
22	Monday	04 45	7.3	17 15	7.0	02 08	9.4	14 33	9.4	03 17	3.5	15 46	3.6	05 41	5.4	18 01	5.5
23	Tuesday	05 28	7.1	17 59	6.7	02 54	9.0	15 22	8.8	03 57	3.4	16 30	3.4	06 31	5.2	18 56	5.2
24	Wednesday	06 16	6.7	18 48	6.2	03 45	8.4	16 21	8.1	04 41	3.2	17 20	3.1	07 27	4.8	20 03	4.8
25	Thursday	07 15	6.2	19 55	5.8	04 52	7.8	17 39	7.6	05 34	3.0	18 26	2.8	08 36	4.6	21 21	4.6
26	Friday	08 40	5.9	21 25	5.7	06 20	7.5	19 08	7.5	06 46	2.9	20 41	2.7	09 55	4.5	22 43	4.6
27	Saturday	10 07	6.0	22 37	5.9	07 44	7.7	20 22	7.9	08 45	2.8	22 02	2.9	11 16	4.7	—	—
28	Sunday	11 13	6.4	23 37	6.4	08 48	8.3	21 19	8.4	10 03	3.0	22 57	3.0	00 00	4.8	12 25	4.9
29	Monday	—	—	12 10	6.9	09 40	8.8	22 06	8.8	10 56	3.2	23 44	3.2	00 59	5.1	13 18	5.1
30	Tuesday	00 31	6.7	13 01	7.1	10 24	9.1	22 46	9.1	11 41	3.4	—	—	01 44	5.2	14 01	5.3
31	Wednesday	01 19	7.0	13 47	7.2	11 03	9.3	23 23	9.2	00 26	3.2	12 23	3.4	02 22	5.3	14 39	5.4

APRIL 1999   *High water*   GMT

		LONDON BRIDGE				LIVERPOOL				GREENOCK				LEITH			
1	Thursday	02 02	7.0	14 27	7.2	11 39	9.3	23 56	9.2	01 04	3.2	13 00	3.4	02 56	5.4	15 14	5.4
2	Friday	02 40	7.0	15 01	7.0	—	—	12 12	9.3	01 36	3.2	13 35	3.4	03 28	5.4	15 47	5.4
3	Saturday	03 12	6.8	15 30	6.8	00 27	9.1	12 44	9.1	02 05	3.2	14 07	3.4	04 00	5.3	16 20	5.3
4	Sunday	03 40	6.7	15 57	6.8	00 58	9.0	13 15	8.9	02 33	3.2	14 39	3.4	04 33	5.2	16 53	5.2
5	Monday	04 10	6.7	16 28	6.8	01 30	8.9	13 48	8.7	03 03	3.2	15 12	3.3	05 07	5.1	17 29	5.0
6	Tuesday	04 43	6.6	17 02	6.7	02 03	8.6	14 23	8.4	03 33	3.2	15 48	3.2	05 43	4.9	18 07	4.8
7	Wednesday	05 21	6.5	17 41	6.5	02 39	8.2	15 02	7.9	04 08	3.1	16 27	3.1	06 22	4.7	18 49	4.6
8	Thursday	06 04	6.3	18 25	6.3	03 21	7.8	15 50	7.4	04 47	2.9	17 12	2.9	07 05	4.5	19 39	4.4
9	Friday	06 53	6.0	19 16	6.0	04 16	7.4	16 53	7.0	05 37	2.8	18 07	2.7	07 58	4.3	20 39	4.2
10	Saturday	07 52	5.8	20 18	5.8	05 29	7.1	18 11	7.0	06 42	2.6	19 14	2.6	09 02	4.2	21 49	4.2
11	Sunday	09 02	5.7	21 34	5.8	06 52	7.3	19 32	7.3	08 00	2.6	20 32	2.7	10 16	4.3	23 05	4.4
12	Monday	10 24	6.0	22 51	6.1	08 04	7.8	20 36	8.0	09 23	2.8	21 51	2.8	11 30	4.5	—	—
13	Tuesday	11 34	6.4	23 53	6.4	08 59	8.5	21 26	8.6	10 22	3.0	22 49	3.0	00 10	4.8	12 28	4.8
14	Wednesday	—	—	12 30	6.8	09 46	9.1	22 11	9.2	11 10	3.2	23 35	3.1	01 02	5.2	13 15	5.3
15	Thursday	00 46	6.8	13 19	7.1	10 31	9.6	22 54	9.6	11 54	3.4	—	—	01 45	5.5	13 58	5.6
16	Friday	01 33	7.1	14 05	7.4	11 15	9.9	23 37	9.8	00 18	3.2	12 39	3.5	02 26	5.7	14 39	5.8
17	Saturday	02 18	7.3	14 48	7.5	11 59	10.1	—	—	01 00	3.4	13 24	3.6	03 08	5.8	15 22	6.0
18	Sunday	03 02	7.5	15 31	7.5	00 20	9.9	12 45	10.0	01 40	3.5	14 08	3.6	03 50	5.8	16 08	5.9
19	Monday	03 46	7.5	16 14	7.3	01 05	9.8	13 31	9.8	02 19	3.5	14 51	3.6	04 35	5.7	16 56	5.8
20	Tuesday	04 31	7.4	16 57	7.1	01 50	9.5	14 18	9.3	02 58	3.6	15 34	3.5	05 22	5.5	17 49	5.5
21	Wednesday	05 17	7.2	17 41	6.7	02 38	9.0	15 09	8.7	03 38	3.5	16 21	3.3	06 13	5.2	18 47	5.2
22	Thursday	06 07	6.8	18 30	6.3	03 31	8.4	16 08	8.1	04 23	3.3	17 16	3.0	07 12	4.9	19 53	4.8
23	Friday	07 08	6.3	19 38	5.9	04 37	7.9	17 24	7.6	05 16	3.1	18 30	2.8	08 21	4.6	21 06	4.6
24	Saturday	08 30	6.0	21 03	5.8	06 00	7.6	18 47	7.5	06 23	2.9	20 25	2.7	09 36	4.6	22 22	4.6
25	Sunday	09 47	6.1	22 12	6.0	07 18	7.7	19 56	7.8	08 09	2.9	21 39	2.9	10 52	4.6	23 35	4.8
26	Monday	10 49	6.5	23 11	6.3	08 21	8.1	20 52	8.2	09 35	3.0	22 33	3.0	11 59	4.8	—	—
27	Tuesday	11 45	6.8	—	—	09 13	8.5	21 39	8.6	10 29	3.2	23 18	3.1	00 33	4.9	12 53	5.0
28	Wednesday	00 04	6.7	12 35	7.0	09 58	8.8	22 19	8.8	11 15	3.2	23 58	3.1	01 19	5.1	13 37	5.1
29	Thursday	00 53	6.9	13 20	7.1	10 37	9.0	22 55	9.0	11 56	3.3	—	—	01 57	5.2	14 15	5.2
30	Friday	01 37	6.9	14 00	7.1	11 13	9.0	23 27	9.0	00 34	3.2	12 34	3.2	02 30	5.2	14 50	5.3

MAY 1999   *High water*   GMT

		LONDON BRIDGE *Datum of predictions 3.20 m below*				LIVERPOOL *Datum of predictions 4.93 m below*				GREENOCK *Datum of predictions 1.62 m below*				LEITH *Datum of predictions 2.90 m below*			
		hr	ht m	hr	ht m	hr	ht m	hr	ht m	hr	ht m	hr	ht m	hr	ht m	hr	ht m
1	Saturday	02 15	6.9	14 34	6.9	11 45	9.0	23 59	9.0	01 08	3.2	13 08	3.2	03 02	5.3	15 23	5.3
2	Sunday	02 48	6.7	15 02	6.8	—	—	12 17	8.9	01 37	3.2	13 40	3.2	03 34	5.2	15 56	5.2
3	Monday	03 18	6.6	15 30	6.7	00 30	8.9	12 49	8.8	02 05	3.2	14 12	3.2	04 06	5.2	16 30	5.1
4	Tuesday	03 48	6.6	16 01	6.7	01 03	8.8	13 23	8.6	02 33	3.3	14 46	3.2	04 40	5.1	17 05	5.0
5	Wednesday	04 22	6.6	16 36	6.7	01 37	8.6	13 58	8.4	03 04	3.2	15 24	3.1	05 15	4.9	17 43	4.8
6	Thursday	05 00	6.5	17 15	6.6	02 14	8.4	14 38	8.1	03 38	3.2	16 04	3.0	05 53	4.8	18 24	4.7
7	Friday	05 43	6.4	17 58	6.3	02 55	8.0	15 24	7.7	04 16	3.0	16 51	2.9	06 34	4.6	19 11	4.5
8	Saturday	06 32	6.2	18 49	6.1	03 47	7.7	16 22	7.4	05 03	2.8	17 45	2.8	07 24	4.4	20 07	4.4
9	Sunday	07 28	6.0	19 48	5.9	04 52	7.5	17 32	7.2	06 04	2.7	18 49	2.7	08 25	4.3	21 13	4.4
10	Monday	08 35	6.0	20 58	5.9	06 06	7.5	18 47	7.5	07 19	2.7	19 59	2.7	09 35	4.4	22 24	4.5
11	Tuesday	09 48	6.1	22 11	6.1	07 18	7.9	19 54	8.0	08 37	2.8	21 12	2.8	10 46	4.6	23 30	4.8
12	Wednesday	10 58	6.5	23 16	6.5	08 19	8.5	20 50	8.6	09 44	3.0	22 15	3.0	11 49	4.9	—	—
13	Thursday	11 57	6.8	—	—	09 13	9.1	21 40	9.2	10 38	3.2	23 07	3.1	00 26	5.2	12 42	5.3
14	Friday	00 13	6.9	12 50	7.1	10 03	9.6	22 27	9.6	11 27	3.4	23 53	3.3	01 15	5.5	13 29	5.6
15	Saturday	01 05	7.1	13 39	7.4	10 51	9.9	23 13	9.8	—	—	12 15	3.5	02 00	5.7	14 15	5.8
16	Sunday	01 55	7.4	14 26	7.4	11 38	10.0	23 59	9.9	00 37	3.4	13 04	3.5	02 44	5.8	15 03	5.9
17	Monday	02 43	7.5	15 12	7.4	—	—	12 26	9.9	01 20	3.5	13 52	3.5	03 30	5.8	15 52	5.9
18	Tuesday	03 30	7.6	15 56	7.3	00 46	9.8	13 15	9.7	02 01	3.6	14 39	3.5	04 17	5.7	16 44	5.8
19	Wednesday	04 18	7.5	16 41	7.1	01 35	9.5	14 05	9.3	02 43	3.6	15 27	3.4	05 06	5.5	17 38	5.5
20	Thursday	05 07	7.3	17 27	6.8	02 24	9.1	14 56	8.8	03 25	3.6	16 18	3.2	05 59	5.2	18 35	5.2
21	Friday	05 59	6.9	18 16	6.4	03 17	8.6	15 53	8.2	04 11	3.5	17 14	3.1	06 58	5.0	19 37	4.9
22	Saturday	06 57	6.5	19 18	6.1	04 18	8.1	16 59	7.7	05 03	3.3	18 21	2.9	08 02	4.8	20 41	4.7
23	Sunday	08 08	6.3	20 32	5.9	05 29	7.8	18 12	7.5	06 05	3.1	19 44	2.8	09 10	4.6	21 48	4.6
24	Monday	09 17	6.2	21 38	6.0	06 40	7.7	19 19	7.6	07 23	3.0	21 00	2.8	10 17	4.6	22 55	4.6
25	Tuesday	10 17	6.4	22 37	6.2	07 44	7.9	20 17	7.9	08 51	3.0	21 57	2.9	11 22	4.7	23 55	4.8
26	Wednesday	11 12	6.6	23 31	6.4	08 39	8.2	21 05	8.3	09 54	3.0	22 44	3.0	—	—	12 12	4.8
27	Thursday	—	—	12 03	6.8	09 26	8.4	21 47	8.5	10 43	3.1	23 26	3.1	00 45	4.9	13 07	4.9
28	Friday	00 22	6.6	12 49	6.9	10 08	8.6	22 25	8.7	11 26	3.1	—	—	01 27	5.0	13 48	5.0
29	Saturday	01 08	6.7	13 30	6.9	10 45	8.7	22 59	8.8	00 05	3.1	12 05	3.1	02 03	5.1	14 25	5.1
30	Sunday	01 48	6.7	14 05	6.8	11 20	8.7	23 32	8.9	00 40	3.2	12 40	3.1	02 37	5.2	15 00	5.1
31	Monday	02 24	6.7	14 37	6.8	11 53	8.7	—	—	01 11	3.2	13 12	3.1	03 10	5.2	15 34	5.1

JUNE 1999   *High water*   GMT

		LONDON BRIDGE				LIVERPOOL				GREENOCK				LEITH			
1	Tuesday	02 57	6.6	15 08	6.7	00 06	8.9	12 27	8.6	01 40	3.2	13 46	3.1	03 44	5.2	16 09	5.1
2	Wednesday	03 30	6.6	15 40	6.7	00 40	8.8	13 02	8.6	02 09	3.3	14 23	3.1	04 18	5.1	16 45	5.0
3	Thursday	04 05	6.6	16 16	6.7	01 16	8.7	13 39	8.4	02 41	3.3	15 03	3.0	04 53	5.0	17 22	4.9
4	Friday	04 44	6.5	16 54	6.6	01 54	8.6	14 19	8.3	03 16	3.2	15 46	3.0	05 30	4.9	18 02	4.8
5	Saturday	05 26	6.5	17 37	6.4	02 36	8.4	15 04	8.0	03 55	3.1	16 33	2.9	06 11	4.8	18 48	4.7
6	Sunday	06 14	6.4	18 26	6.3	03 25	8.1	15 56	7.8	04 38	3.0	17 25	2.8	06 58	4.7	19 40	4.6
7	Monday	07 08	6.2	19 22	6.1	04 23	8.0	16 59	7.7	05 33	2.9	18 22	2.8	07 54	4.6	20 41	4.6
8	Tuesday	08 10	6.2	20 27	6.1	05 30	7.9	18 08	7.8	06 41	2.8	19 25	2.8	08 58	4.6	21 47	4.7
9	Wednesday	09 18	6.3	21 36	6.2	06 37	8.2	19 15	8.1	07 56	2.9	20 32	2.8	10 07	4.7	22 53	4.9
10	Thursday	10 25	6.5	22 42	6.5	07 42	8.5	20 17	8.6	09 09	3.0	21 41	2.9	11 12	4.9	23 54	5.1
11	Friday	11 27	6.8	23 43	6.8	08 42	9.0	21 13	9.1	10 11	3.2	22 40	3.1	—	—	12 12	5.2
12	Saturday	—	—	12 24	7.0	09 38	9.4	22 04	9.5	11 05	3.3	23 31	3.3	00 48	5.4	13 06	5.5
13	Sunday	00 41	7.0	13 17	7.2	10 31	9.6	22 53	9.7	11 57	3.4	—	—	01 38	5.6	13 57	5.7
14	Monday	01 35	7.3	14 06	7.3	11 21	9.8	23 42	9.8	00 18	3.4	12 49	3.4	02 25	5.7	14 48	5.8
15	Tuesday	02 26	7.4	14 54	7.4	—	—	12 12	9.7	01 04	3.5	13 41	3.4	03 13	5.7	15 39	5.8
16	Wednesday	03 16	7.5	15 40	7.3	00 31	9.7	13 02	9.6	01 48	3.6	14 31	3.4	04 02	5.7	16 31	5.7
17	Thursday	04 06	7.5	16 26	7.1	01 20	9.5	13 51	9.3	02 31	3.7	15 21	3.3	04 52	5.6	17 24	5.5
18	Friday	04 54	7.3	17 11	6.9	02 08	9.3	14 39	8.9	03 14	3.7	16 10	3.2	05 45	5.4	18 18	5.3
19	Saturday	05 44	7.0	17 57	6.6	02 58	8.9	15 29	8.4	03 58	3.6	17 01	3.1	06 40	5.1	19 13	5.0
20	Sunday	06 35	6.7	18 47	6.3	03 50	8.4	16 23	7.9	04 46	3.4	17 54	3.0	07 37	4.9	20 08	4.8
21	Monday	07 33	6.4	19 48	6.1	04 48	8.0	17 25	7.6	05 39	3.2	18 51	2.9	08 35	4.7	21 05	4.6
22	Tuesday	08 36	6.2	20 54	6.0	05 53	7.7	18 31	7.5	06 37	3.1	19 54	2.8	09 35	4.6	22 04	4.5
23	Wednesday	09 36	6.1	21 56	6.0	06 58	7.6	19 33	7.6	07 45	2.9	21 05	2.8	10 37	4.6	23 06	4.6
24	Thursday	10 32	6.2	22 53	6.1	07 59	7.8	20 27	7.9	09 02	2.9	22 04	2.9	11 38	4.6	—	—
25	Friday	11 24	6.4	23 47	6.3	08 51	8.0	21 14	8.2	10 06	2.9	22 53	3.0	00 03	4.7	12 34	4.7
26	Saturday	—	—	12 13	6.6	09 38	8.2	21 56	8.5	10 55	3.0	23 36	3.1	00 53	4.8	13 20	4.8
27	Sunday	00 36	6.5	12 58	6.7	10 19	8.4	22 34	8.7	11 37	3.0	—	—	01 35	5.0	14 01	5.0
28	Monday	01 21	6.6	13 38	6.8	10 57	8.5	23 10	8.8	00 14	3.2	12 14	3.0	02 12	5.1	14 38	5.1
29	Tuesday	02 02	6.6	14 15	6.8	11 32	8.6	23 45	8.9	00 49	3.2	12 48	3.0	02 48	5.2	15 13	5.1
30	Wednesday	02 39	6.7	14 50	6.8	—	—	12 08	8.6	01 18	3.2	13 24	3.0	03 24	5.2	15 49	5.2

JULY 1999   High water   GMT

		LONDON BRIDGE *Datum of predictions 3.20 m below				LIVERPOOL *Datum of predictions 4.93 m below				GREENOCK *Datum of predictions 1.62 m below				LEITH *Datum of predictions 2.90 m below			
		hr	m (ht)	hr	m (ht)	hr	m (ht)	hr	m (ht)	hr	m (ht)	hr	m (ht)	hr	m (ht)	hr	m (ht)
1	Thursday	03 15	6.6	15 25	6.7	00 21	8.9	12 45	8.6	01 49	3.3	14 04	3.0	03 59	5.2	16 25	5.1
2	Friday	03 51	6.6	16 01	6.6	00 59	8.9	13 23	8.6	02 22	3.3	14 46	3.0	04 34	5.2	17 02	5.1
3	Saturday	04 30	6.7	16 38	6.6	01 38	8.8	14 03	8.6	02 58	3.3	15 28	3.0	05 10	5.1	17 42	5.0
4	Sunday	05 11	6.6	17 19	6.6	02 19	8.8	14 45	8.5	03 37	3.2	16 13	3.0	05 50	5.1	18 26	5.0
5	Monday	05 57	6.6	18 04	6.5	03 05	8.6	15 33	8.3	04 19	3.2	17 00	2.9	06 35	5.0	19 15	4.9
6	Tuesday	06 47	6.4	18 56	6.4	03 57	8.5	16 28	8.1	05 07	3.1	17 51	2.9	07 26	4.9	20 11	4.8
7	Wednesday	07 44	6.3	19 56	6.3	04 57	8.3	17 32	8.0	06 04	3.0	18 46	2.9	08 25	4.8	21 14	4.8
8	Thursday	08 48	6.2	21 04	6.2	06 03	8.3	18 41	8.1	07 14	2.9	19 50	2.8	09 33	4.8	22 21	4.9
9	Friday	09 56	6.3	22 13	6.3	07 12	8.4	19 49	8.4	08 36	2.9	21 07	2.9	10 43	4.9	23 27	5.0
10	Saturday	11 01	6.5	23 20	6.6	08 19	8.7	20 52	8.8	09 49	3.1	22 17	3.0	11 50	5.1	—	—
11	Sunday	—	—	12 02	6.8	09 21	9.0	21 48	9.2	10 51	3.2	23 14	3.2	00 27	5.2	12 51	5.4
12	Monday	00 22	6.9	12 58	7.0	10 17	9.3	22 39	9.5	11 46	3.3	—	—	01 21	5.4	13 46	5.6
13	Tuesday	01 20	7.1	13 50	7.2	11 09	9.5	23 29	9.7	00 04	3.4	12 41	3.3	02 11	5.6	14 38	5.7
14	Wednesday	02 13	7.4	14 38	7.3	11 59	9.6	—	—	00 51	3.5	13 33	3.3	02 59	5.7	15 28	5.8
15	Thursday	03 03	7.4	15 25	7.2	00 16	9.7	12 47	9.5	01 36	3.6	14 23	3.3	03 48	5.7	16 17	5.7
16	Friday	03 51	7.4	16 09	7.2	01 03	9.6	13 33	9.3	02 18	3.7	15 09	3.3	04 36	5.6	17 05	5.5
17	Saturday	04 37	7.3	16 50	7.0	01 48	9.4	14 16	9.0	03 00	3.7	15 52	3.2	05 25	5.5	17 53	5.3
18	Sunday	05 21	7.1	17 30	6.8	02 31	9.1	14 58	8.6	03 41	3.6	16 34	3.2	06 14	5.3	18 41	5.1
19	Monday	06 03	6.7	18 10	6.5	03 14	8.7	15 41	8.2	04 23	3.5	17 17	3.1	07 03	5.0	19 29	4.8
20	Tuesday	06 47	6.4	18 54	6.2	04 00	8.2	16 30	7.7	05 07	3.3	18 02	3.0	07 54	4.8	20 18	4.6
21	Wednesday	07 36	6.1	19 48	6.0	04 53	7.7	17 29	7.4	05 54	3.1	18 50	2.9	08 47	4.6	21 11	4.5
22	Thursday	08 34	5.9	20 55	5.8	05 58	7.4	18 39	7.3	06 46	2.9	19 47	2.8	09 45	4.5	22 09	4.4
23	Friday	09 37	5.8	22 05	5.8	07 10	7.4	19 46	7.5	07 48	2.8	21 07	2.8	10 49	4.4	23 12	4.5
24	Saturday	10 39	6.0	23 09	5.9	08 15	7.5	20 42	7.9	09 08	2.8	22 19	2.9	11 55	4.5	—	—
25	Sunday	11 35	6.2	—	—	09 09	7.9	21 30	8.3	10 23	2.8	23 09	3.0	00 14	4.6	12 51	4.7
26	Monday	00 05	6.2	12 07	6.5	09 55	8.2	22 12	8.6	11 13	2.9	23 51	3.1	01 06	4.8	13 37	4.9
27	Tuesday	00 55	6.5	13 13	6.7	10 36	8.4	22 50	8.9	11 53	2.9	—	—	01 48	5.0	14 15	5.1
28	Wednesday	01 39	6.7	13 55	6.8	11 14	8.6	23 27	9.0	00 26	3.2	12 30	3.0	02 27	5.2	14 52	5.2
29	Thursday	02 20	6.8	14 34	6.8	11 51	8.7	—	—	00 58	3.3	13 07	3.0	03 03	5.3	15 28	5.3
30	Friday	02 59	6.8	15 11	6.8	00 03	9.1	12 28	8.8	01 29	3.3	13 47	3.0	03 39	5.4	16 04	5.3
31	Saturday	03 36	6.8	15 46	6.8	00 41	9.2	13 06	8.9	02 04	3.3	14 27	3.1	04 14	5.4	16 41	5.3

AUGUST 1999   High water   GMT

		LONDON BRIDGE				LIVERPOOL				GREENOCK				LEITH			
		hr	m	hr	m	hr	m	hr	m	hr	m	hr	m	hr	m	hr	m
1	Sunday	04 14	6.8	16 22	6.8	01 20	9.2	13 44	8.9	02 41	3.4	15 08	3.1	04 49	5.4	17 20	5.3
2	Monday	04 54	6.8	17 00	6.8	02 01	9.2	14 25	8.8	03 19	3.4	15 49	3.1	05 28	5.4	18 03	5.2
3	Tuesday	05 36	6.7	17 42	6.7	02 44	9.0	15 09	8.6	03 59	3.3	16 31	3.1	06 12	5.3	18 50	5.1
4	Wednesday	06 22	6.5	18 29	6.5	03 32	8.8	16 00	8.4	04 42	3.2	17 16	3.0	07 01	5.1	19 43	4.9
5	Thursday	07 14	6.3	19 25	6.3	04 28	8.4	17 00	8.0	05 32	3.1	18 07	2.9	07 58	5.0	20 44	4.8
6	Friday	08 17	6.1	20 33	6.1	05 34	8.1	18 13	7.9	06 35	2.9	19 07	2.9	09 08	4.8	21 54	4.8
7	Saturday	09 29	6.0	21 51	6.1	06 49	8.1	19 30	8.1	08 06	2.8	20 34	2.9	10 25	4.9	23 06	4.9
8	Sunday	10 41	6.2	23 05	6.3	08 05	8.3	20 40	8.5	09 40	2.9	22 01	3.0	11 39	5.0	—	—
9	Monday	11 46	6.5	—	—	09 12	8.7	21 39	9.0	10 47	3.1	23 01	3.2	00 13	5.1	12 45	5.2
10	Tuesday	00 11	6.7	12 43	6.8	10 09	9.1	22 30	9.4	11 43	3.2	23 52	3.4	01 11	5.4	13 40	5.5
11	Wednesday	01 09	7.1	13 35	7.1	10 59	9.4	23 17	9.7	—	—	12 35	3.3	02 01	5.6	14 29	5.7
12	Thursday	02 01	7.3	14 23	7.2	11 46	9.5	—	—	00 38	3.5	13 24	3.3	02 47	5.7	15 14	5.7
13	Friday	02 49	7.4	15 07	7.2	00 01	9.7	12 29	9.4	01 22	3.6	14 09	3.3	03 32	5.8	15 58	5.7
14	Saturday	03 33	7.4	15 47	7.1	00 43	9.7	13 09	9.3	02 02	3.7	14 49	3.3	04 16	5.7	16 41	5.5
15	Sunday	04 14	7.2	16 24	7.0	01 22	9.5	13 47	9.0	02 41	3.7	15 25	3.3	04 59	5.6	17 23	5.3
16	Monday	04 52	7.0	16 58	6.8	02 00	9.1	14 23	8.7	03 18	3.6	16 00	3.3	05 41	5.4	18 04	5.1
17	Tuesday	05 26	6.7	17 32	6.6	02 36	8.8	14 59	8.4	03 54	3.6	16 37	3.2	06 24	5.1	18 46	4.9
18	Wednesday	06 00	6.5	18 09	6.4	03 15	8.3	15 40	7.9	04 32	3.4	17 16	3.1	07 08	4.9	19 31	4.7
19	Thursday	06 39	6.2	18 53	6.1	03 59	7.8	16 28	7.5	05 13	3.2	17 59	3.0	07 57	4.6	20 20	4.5
20	Friday	07 25	5.9	19 48	5.7	04 54	7.3	17 33	7.2	06 00	3.0	18 49	2.8	08 52	4.4	21 15	4.4
21	Saturday	08 24	5.7	20 58	5.5	06 08	7.0	18 56	7.2	06 56	2.8	19 52	2.8	09 56	4.3	22 18	4.4
22	Sunday	09 40	5.7	22 23	5.6	07 35	7.1	20 09	7.6	08 07	2.7	21 33	2.8	11 08	4.3	23 28	4.5
23	Monday	10 55	5.9	23 33	6.0	08 41	7.5	21 04	8.1	09 47	2.7	22 40	3.0	—	—	12 18	4.6
24	Tuesday	11 55	6.3	—	—	09 31	8.0	21 49	8.6	10 52	2.9	23 24	3.1	00 32	4.7	13 09	4.8
25	Wednesday	00 28	6.4	12 47	6.6	10 14	8.4	22 28	8.9	11 35	3.0	—	—	01 20	5.0	13 50	5.1
26	Thursday	01 15	6.7	13 32	6.8	10 52	8.7	23 05	9.2	00 00	3.2	12 13	3.1	02 01	5.3	14 27	5.3
27	Friday	01 58	6.9	14 13	6.9	11 29	8.9	23 42	9.4	00 34	3.3	12 49	3.1	02 38	5.5	15 03	5.5
28	Saturday	02 38	7.0	14 51	6.9	—	—	12 06	9.1	01 08	3.4	13 27	3.2	03 14	5.6	15 40	5.6
29	Sunday	03 16	7.1	15 26	7.0	00 19	9.5	12 44	9.2	01 44	3.5	14 06	3.2	03 49	5.7	16 17	5.6
30	Monday	03 54	7.1	16 02	7.0	00 59	9.6	13 23	9.2	02 21	3.5	14 44	3.3	04 26	5.7	16 57	5.6
31	Tuesday	04 32	7.0	16 39	7.0	01 40	9.5	14 03	9.1	03 00	3.5	15 22	3.3	05 06	5.6	17 39	5.4

SEPTEMBER 1999   *High water*   GMT

		LONDON BRIDGE *Datum of predictions 3.20 m below*				LIVERPOOL *Datum of predictions 4.93 m below*				GREENOCK *Datum of predictions 1.62 m below*				LEITH *Datum of predictions 2.90 m below*			
		hr	ht m	hr	ht m	hr	ht m	hr	ht m	hr	ht m	hr	ht m	hr	ht m	hr	ht m
1	Wednesday	05 13	6.9	17 20	6.9	02 23	9.3	14 46	8.9	03 39	3.5	16 01	3.3	05 51	5.5	18 26	5.2
2	Thursday	05 56	6.6	18 06	6.7	03 10	8.9	15 35	8.5	04 20	3.3	16 43	3.2	06 41	5.3	19 18	5.0
3	Friday	06 44	6.3	18 59	6.3	04 05	8.4	16 35	8.0	05 07	3.1	17 33	3.1	07 40	5.0	20 20	4.8
4	Saturday	07 45	5.9	20 09	5.9	05 14	7.9	17 52	7.7	06 07	2.9	18 33	3.0	08 53	4.8	21 34	4.7
5	Sunday	09 07	5.7	21 38	5.9	06 38	7.7	19 19	7.8	07 52	2.8	20 06	2.9	10 15	4.8	22 52	4.8
6	Monday	10 27	5.9	22 57	6.2	08 01	8.0	20 33	8.3	09 43	2.9	21 50	3.1	11 35	4.9	——	—
7	Tuesday	11 32	6.3	——	—	09 07	8.5	21 30	8.9	10 46	3.1	22 49	3.3	00 04	5.1	12 41	5.2
8	Wednesday	00 01	6.7	12 29	6.8	10 00	9.0	22 18	9.4	11 37	3.3	23 38	3.5	01 03	5.3	13 34	5.4
9	Thursday	00 57	7.1	13 19	7.1	10 46	9.3	23 01	9.6	——	—	12 24	3.3	01 50	5.5	14 17	5.6
10	Friday	01 46	7.4	14 04	7.2	11 27	9.4	23 41	9.7	00 22	3.6	13 08	3.4	02 33	5.7	14 57	5.6
11	Saturday	02 31	7.4	14 46	7.2	——	—	12 06	9.4	01 04	3.6	13 47	3.4	03 13	5.7	15 36	5.6
12	Sunday	03 11	7.3	15 23	7.1	00 19	9.6	12 42	9.3	01 42	3.7	14 21	3.4	03 52	5.7	16 13	5.5
13	Monday	03 47	7.1	15 56	6.9	00 54	9.4	13 15	9.1	02 17	3.7	14 52	3.4	04 30	5.5	16 49	5.4
14	Tuesday	04 18	6.9	16 26	6.8	01 27	9.1	13 48	8.8	02 51	3.6	15 24	3.4	05 07	5.4	17 26	5.2
15	Wednesday	04 47	6.7	16 58	6.7	02 01	8.8	14 21	8.5	03 25	3.5	15 57	3.3	05 45	5.1	18 04	5.0
16	Thursday	05 19	6.6	17 34	6.5	02 36	8.3	14 58	8.1	04 00	3.4	16 33	3.2	06 26	4.9	18 46	4.7
17	Friday	05 55	6.4	18 15	6.2	03 17	7.8	15 42	7.7	04 38	3.2	17 14	3.1	07 12	4.6	19 33	4.5
18	Saturday	06 38	6.1	19 03	5.8	04 07	7.3	16 39	7.2	05 23	3.0	18 03	2.9	08 05	4.4	20 27	4.4
19	Sunday	07 29	5.8	20 04	5.5	05 14	6.9	17 57	7.0	06 19	2.8	19 04	2.8	09 06	4.2	21 29	4.3
20	Monday	08 36	5.6	21 23	5.5	06 45	6.9	19 28	7.3	07 29	2.7	20 24	2.8	10 18	4.3	22 41	4.4
21	Tuesday	10 07	5.7	22 54	5.8	08 09	7.3	20 32	7.9	08 58	2.7	21 59	3.0	11 35	4.5	23 52	4.7
22	Wednesday	11 20	6.0	23 56	6.3	09 03	7.9	21 19	8.5	10 24	2.9	22 49	3.2	——	—	12 34	4.8
23	Thursday	——	—	12 15	6.5	09 46	8.4	22 00	9.0	11 10	3.1	23 28	3.3	00 46	5.0	13 19	5.1
24	Friday	00 45	6.7	13 03	6.8	10 24	8.9	22 38	9.4	11 49	3.2	——	—	01 30	5.3	13 58	5.4
25	Saturday	01 30	7.0	13 45	7.0	11 01	9.2	23 16	9.6	00 04	3.4	12 26	3.3	02 08	5.6	14 36	5.6
26	Sunday	02 11	7.2	14 24	7.1	11 39	9.4	23 55	9.8	00 42	3.5	13 04	3.4	02 45	5.8	15 13	5.8
27	Monday	02 51	7.2	15 02	7.2	——	—	12 19	9.6	01 22	3.6	13 41	3.4	03 22	5.9	15 52	5.8
28	Tuesday	03 30	7.2	15 41	7.2	00 36	9.8	13 00	9.5	02 01	3.6	14 18	3.5	04 02	5.9	16 33	5.7
29	Wednesday	04 10	7.2	16 21	7.2	01 19	9.7	13 42	9.4	02 41	3.7	14 56	3.5	04 46	5.8	17 16	5.6
30	Thursday	04 50	7.0	17 03	7.1	02 04	9.4	14 26	9.0	03 20	3.6	15 35	3.5	05 33	5.6	18 04	5.3

OCTOBER 1999   *High water*   GMT

		LONDON BRIDGE				LIVERPOOL				GREENOCK				LEITH			
1	Friday	05 32	6.7	17 49	6.7	02 52	8.9	15 16	8.5	04 02	3.4	16 17	3.4	06 26	5.3	18 57	5.1
2	Saturday	06 18	6.2	18 43	6.3	03 49	8.2	16 17	8.0	04 50	3.2	17 06	3.3	07 29	5.0	20 02	4.8
3	Sunday	07 18	5.8	19 58	5.9	05 02	7.7	17 39	7.6	05 53	2.9	18 08	3.1	08 45	4.8	21 20	4.7
4	Monday	08 51	5.6	21 32	5.9	06 33	7.6	19 09	7.8	08 04	2.8	19 48	3.0	10 07	4.7	22 40	4.8
5	Tuesday	10 11	5.9	22 44	6.3	07 53	7.9	20 19	8.3	09 39	3.0	21 33	3.2	11 26	4.9	23 51	5.1
6	Wednesday	11 13	6.3	23 44	6.8	08 53	8.5	21 14	8.8	10 35	3.2	22 31	3.4	——	—	12 30	5.2
7	Thursday	——	—	12 08	6.8	09 43	8.9	22 00	9.3	11 23	3.4	23 18	3.5	00 48	5.3	13 20	5.4
8	Friday	00 37	7.2	12 58	7.1	10 26	9.2	22 41	9.5	——	—	12 05	3.4	01 35	5.5	14 00	5.5
9	Saturday	01 25	7.4	13 42	7.2	11 04	9.3	23 19	9.5	00 01	3.6	12 45	3.4	02 14	5.6	14 36	5.6
10	Sunday	02 08	7.4	14 22	7.2	11 39	9.3	23 53	9.4	00 41	3.6	13 19	3.4	02 51	5.6	15 10	5.6
11	Monday	02 46	7.2	14 58	7.0	——	—	12 11	9.2	01 17	3.6	13 50	3.4	03 27	5.6	15 44	5.5
12	Tuesday	03 17	7.0	15 28	6.8	00 25	9.2	12 43	9.1	01 51	3.6	14 20	3.5	04 02	5.5	16 17	5.4
13	Wednesday	03 44	6.8	15 57	6.7	00 57	9.0	13 15	8.9	02 23	3.6	14 50	3.5	04 36	5.3	16 52	5.2
14	Thursday	04 11	6.7	16 28	6.6	01 29	8.7	13 48	8.6	02 56	3.5	15 21	3.5	05 13	5.1	17 28	5.0
15	Friday	04 43	6.7	17 04	6.5	02 05	8.4	14 24	8.3	03 31	3.4	15 56	3.4	05 52	4.9	18 07	4.8
16	Saturday	05 19	6.5	17 45	6.3	02 44	7.9	15 06	7.9	04 09	3.3	16 35	3.2	06 36	4.7	18 51	4.6
17	Sunday	06 01	6.2	18 31	6.0	03 31	7.4	15 57	7.4	04 54	3.1	17 23	3.1	07 26	4.5	19 43	4.4
18	Monday	06 49	5.9	19 27	5.7	04 32	7.0	17 06	7.1	05 49	2.9	18 23	2.9	08 24	4.3	20 45	4.4
19	Tuesday	07 49	5.7	20 35	5.6	05 52	6.9	18 31	7.2	06 58	2.8	19 35	2.9	09 32	4.3	21 56	4.4
20	Wednesday	09 08	5.6	22 01	5.8	07 20	7.2	19 46	7.7	08 19	2.8	20 59	3.0	10 46	4.5	23 07	4.7
21	Thursday	10 33	5.9	23 13	6.2	08 23	7.8	20 40	8.4	09 41	3.0	22 04	3.2	11 51	4.8	——	—
22	Friday	11 35	6.3	——	—	09 10	8.5	21 25	9.0	10 36	3.2	22 51	3.3	00 06	5.0	12 42	5.2
23	Saturday	00 09	6.7	12 26	6.7	09 51	9.0	22 07	9.5	11 19	3.3	23 34	3.5	00 55	5.3	13 26	5.5
24	Sunday	00 57	7.0	13 12	7.0	10 32	9.4	22 49	9.8	11 59	3.4	——	—	01 37	5.6	14 06	5.7
25	Monday	01 42	7.2	13 55	7.2	11 12	9.7	23 31	10.0	00 16	3.6	12 38	3.5	02 17	5.9	14 46	5.9
26	Tuesday	02 24	7.3	14 38	7.4	11 54	9.8	——	—	00 59	3.7	13 17	3.6	02 58	6.0	15 27	5.9
27	Wednesday	03 06	7.3	15 21	7.4	00 15	10.0	12 38	9.8	01 42	3.7	13 56	3.7	03 42	6.0	16 10	5.8
28	Thursday	03 48	7.3	16 05	7.4	01 01	9.8	13 23	9.6	02 25	3.7	14 35	3.8	04 29	5.9	16 56	5.7
29	Friday	04 31	7.1	16 51	7.2	01 49	9.4	14 11	9.2	03 07	3.6	15 15	3.7	05 19	5.7	17 45	5.4
30	Saturday	05 14	6.7	17 39	6.9	02 39	8.9	15 02	8.7	03 52	3.5	15 59	3.6	06 16	5.4	18 41	5.1
31	Sunday	06 01	6.3	18 36	6.4	03 38	8.3	16 04	8.1	04 45	3.2	16 49	3.4	07 20	5.0	19 49	4.9

NOVEMBER 1999   *High water*   GMT

	LONDON BRIDGE *Datum of predictions 3.20 m below			LIVERPOOL *Datum of predictions 4.93 m below			GREENOCK *Datum of predictions 1.62 m below			LEITH *Datum of predictions 2.90 m below		
	hr	ht m	hr	ht m	hr	ht m	hr	ht m	hr	ht m	hr	ht m
1 Monday	07 00	5.9	19 51	6.0	04 51	7.7	17 23	7.8	05 56	3.0	17 52	3.2	08 33	4.8	21 04	4.8
2 Tuesday	08 32	5.7	21 14	6.1	06 16	7.6	18 46	7.8	07 54	2.9	19 23	3.1	09 50	4.8	22 20	4.8
3 Wednesday	09 47	5.9	22 21	6.4	07 30	7.9	19 54	8.2	09 17	3.1	21 03	3.2	11 04	4.9	23 28	5.0
4 Thursday	10 47	6.3	23 19	6.7	08 29	8.3	20 49	8.6	10 12	3.3	22 04	3.4	—	—	12 07	5.1
5 Friday	11 41	6.7	—	—	09 18	8.7	21 36	9.0	10 58	3.4	22 53	3.5	00 25	5.2	12 56	5.3
6 Saturday	00 11	7.0	12 32	7.0	10 00	9.0	22 17	9.2	11 39	3.5	23 36	3.5	01 13	5.4	13 37	5.4
7 Sunday	00 59	7.2	13 17	7.1	10 38	9.2	22 54	9.2	—	—	12 16	3.5	01 53	5.4	14 12	5.4
8 Monday	01 41	7.2	13 57	7.0	11 12	9.2	23 27	9.2	00 15	3.5	12 50	3.5	02 30	5.5	14 45	5.5
9 Tuesday	02 18	7.0	14 33	6.9	11 44	9.2	23 58	9.0	00 52	3.5	13 22	3.5	03 04	5.5	15 17	5.4
10 Wednesday	02 48	6.9	15 04	6.7	—	—	12 15	9.1	01 25	3.5	13 51	3.6	03 38	5.4	15 50	5.4
11 Thursday	03 14	6.8	15 33	6.6	00 30	8.9	12 48	8.9	01 57	3.4	14 21	3.6	04 12	5.3	16 23	5.3
12 Friday	03 42	6.7	16 05	6.6	01 04	8.7	13 22	8.8	02 31	3.4	14 52	3.6	04 48	5.1	16 59	5.1
13 Saturday	04 14	6.7	16 41	6.5	01 40	8.4	13 58	8.5	03 07	3.4	15 26	3.5	05 26	5.0	17 36	4.9
14 Sunday	04 50	6.6	17 21	6.4	02 18	8.1	14 38	8.2	03 46	3.3	16 04	3.4	06 08	4.8	18 17	4.8
15 Monday	05 31	6.4	18 07	6.2	03 03	7.7	15 26	7.8	04 31	3.1	16 48	3.2	06 55	4.6	19 06	4.6
16 Tuesday	06 18	6.1	19 00	6.0	03 58	7.3	16 27	7.5	05 24	3.0	17 43	3.0	07 48	4.5	20 04	4.5
17 Wednesday	07 14	5.9	20 02	5.9	05 07	7.2	17 39	7.5	06 28	2.9	18 51	3.0	08 51	4.4	21 12	4.5
18 Thursday	08 22	5.8	21 14	6.0	06 24	7.3	18 51	7.8	07 39	2.9	20 05	3.0	09 59	4.6	22 21	4.7
19 Friday	09 40	5.9	22 26	6.3	07 33	7.8	19 54	8.4	08 52	3.0	21 17	3.2	11 06	4.8	23 24	5.0
20 Saturday	10 48	6.3	23 29	6.6	08 29	8.5	20 48	9.0	09 56	3.2	22 15	3.3	—	—	12 04	5.2
21 Sunday	11 47	6.6	—	—	09 18	9.0	21 36	9.5	10 47	3.3	23 05	3.5	00 18	5.3	12 54	5.5
22 Monday	00 23	7.0	12 40	7.0	10 03	9.5	22 23	9.8	11 32	3.5	23 52	3.6	01 06	5.6	13 39	5.7
23 Tuesday	01 13	7.2	13 29	7.2	10 48	9.8	23 10	10.0	—	—	12 14	3.6	01 52	5.8	14 22	5.9
24 Wednesday	02 00	7.3	14 17	7.4	11 34	10.0	23 58	10.0	00 39	3.7	12 57	3.8	02 37	6.0	15 05	5.9
25 Thursday	02 45	7.4	15 04	7.5	—	—	12 20	9.9	01 26	3.7	13 38	3.8	03 25	6.0	15 51	5.9
26 Friday	03 30	7.3	15 52	7.5	00 46	9.8	13 09	9.7	02 13	3.7	14 20	3.9	04 15	5.9	16 39	5.7
27 Saturday	04 15	7.1	16 41	7.3	01 37	9.5	13 58	9.4	03 00	3.6	15 03	3.9	05 08	5.7	17 30	5.5
28 Sunday	05 00	6.8	17 31	7.0	02 28	9.0	14 51	9.0	03 49	3.5	15 48	3.8	06 05	5.4	18 28	5.2
29 Monday	05 47	6.5	18 27	6.7	03 25	8.5	15 48	8.5	04 44	3.3	16 38	3.6	07 07	5.1	19 32	5.0
30 Tuesday	06 44	6.1	19 32	6.3	04 29	8.0	16 56	8.1	05 51	3.1	17 37	3.4	08 12	4.9	20 41	4.9

DECEMBER 1999   *High water*   GMT

	LONDON BRIDGE			LIVERPOOL			GREENOCK			LEITH		
1 Wednesday	08 01	5.9	20 45	6.2	05 43	7.7	18 10	7.9	07 14	3.0	18 47	3.3	09 20	4.8	21 49	4.9
2 Thursday	09 13	6.0	21 49	6.3	06 54	7.7	19 18	8.0	08 36	3.1	20 14	3.2	10 27	4.8	22 55	4.9
3 Friday	10 14	6.2	22 46	6.5	07 56	8.0	20 17	8.3	09 37	3.2	21 28	3.3	11 31	4.9	23 55	5.0
4 Saturday	11 10	6.4	23 39	6.7	08 47	8.4	21 07	8.5	10 26	3.3	22 23	3.4	—	—	12 24	5.0
5 Sunday	—	—	12 01	6.7	09 32	8.7	21 51	8.8	11 09	3.4	23 09	3.4	00 46	5.1	13 09	5.2
6 Monday	00 28	6.8	12 49	6.8	10 11	8.9	22 29	8.9	11 48	3.5	23 51	3.4	01 30	5.2	13 48	5.3
7 Tuesday	01 11	6.9	13 32	6.8	10 47	9.0	23 04	8.9	—	—	12 24	3.5	02 09	5.3	14 22	5.3
8 Wednesday	01 49	6.9	14 10	6.8	11 20	9.1	23 37	8.9	00 28	3.3	12 58	3.5	02 45	5.3	14 55	5.3
9 Thursday	02 21	6.8	14 43	6.7	11 53	9.1	—	—	01 02	3.3	13 29	3.6	03 19	5.3	15 28	5.3
10 Friday	02 50	6.7	15 15	6.6	00 10	8.8	12 27	9.0	01 35	3.3	13 58	3.6	03 53	5.2	16 02	5.3
11 Saturday	03 20	6.7	15 48	6.6	00 45	8.7	13 02	8.9	02 10	3.3	14 30	3.6	04 28	5.2	16 36	5.2
12 Sunday	03 52	6.6	16 23	6.6	01 21	8.6	13 39	8.7	02 47	3.3	15 04	3.5	05 05	5.1	17 12	5.1
13 Monday	04 29	6.6	17 03	6.5	01 59	8.4	14 18	8.5	03 27	3.2	15 41	3.4	05 44	4.9	17 50	4.9
14 Tuesday	05 09	6.5	17 47	6.4	02 41	8.1	15 02	8.3	04 11	3.1	16 22	3.3	06 28	4.8	18 35	4.8
15 Wednesday	05 54	6.3	18 37	6.3	03 29	7.9	15 54	8.1	04 59	3.0	17 10	3.2	07 17	4.7	19 26	4.7
16 Thursday	06 45	6.1	19 33	6.2	04 28	7.6	16 56	7.9	05 54	3.0	18 07	3.1	08 13	4.6	20 27	4.7
17 Friday	07 46	6.0	20 37	6.2	05 36	7.6	18 04	8.0	06 54	2.9	19 14	3.1	09 16	4.7	21 34	4.8
18 Saturday	08 55	6.1	21 45	6.3	06 45	7.8	19 10	8.3	08 02	3.0	20 30	3.1	10 23	4.8	22 41	4.9
19 Sunday	10 05	6.3	22 52	6.5	07 50	8.3	20 13	8.8	09 12	3.1	21 40	3.2	11 26	5.0	23 44	5.2
20 Monday	11 11	6.5	23 52	6.8	08 48	8.9	21 10	9.2	10 15	3.3	22 39	3.4	—	—	12 23	5.3
21 Tuesday	—	—	12 11	6.8	09 40	9.4	22 03	9.6	11 07	3.4	23 33	3.5	00 40	5.4	13 14	5.6
22 Wednesday	00 47	7.0	13 07	7.1	10 30	9.7	22 55	9.9	11 55	3.6	—	—	01 32	5.7	14 02	5.7
23 Thursday	01 38	7.2	14 00	7.4	11 18	9.9	23 45	9.9	00 24	3.6	12 41	3.7	02 23	5.9	14 48	5.8
24 Friday	02 27	7.3	14 50	7.5	—	—	12 07	10.0	01 16	3.6	13 25	3.9	03 13	6.0	15 35	5.9
25 Saturday	03 14	7.3	15 40	7.5	00 35	9.8	12 57	9.9	02 06	3.6	14 09	3.9	04 04	5.9	16 25	5.8
26 Sunday	04 00	7.2	16 29	7.5	01 25	9.6	13 46	9.7	02 55	3.6	14 53	3.9	04 56	5.7	17 16	5.6
27 Monday	04 45	7.0	17 18	7.2	02 14	9.2	14 34	9.3	03 44	3.5	15 37	3.9	05 50	5.5	18 11	5.4
28 Tuesday	05 31	6.7	18 08	6.9	03 04	8.8	15 25	8.9	04 34	3.4	16 24	3.8	06 45	5.2	19 08	5.2
29 Wednesday	06 18	6.4	19 01	6.5	03 57	8.3	16 19	8.4	05 26	3.2	17 14	3.6	07 42	5.0	20 08	5.0
30 Thursday	07 15	6.1	20 02	6.2	04 56	7.8	17 21	8.0	06 22	3.1	18 09	3.4	08 40	4.8	21 10	4.8
31 Friday	08 24	5.9	21 06	6.1	06 04	7.6	18 30	7.7	07 25	3.0	19 10	3.2	09 40	4.7	22 12	4.7

World Geographical Statistics

THE EARTH

The shape of the Earth is that of an oblate spheroid or solid of revolution whose meridian sections are ellipses, whilst the sections at right angles are circles.

DIMENSIONS

Equatorial diameter = 12,756.27 km (7,926.38 miles)
Polar diameter = 12,713.50 km (7,899.80 miles)
Equatorial circumference = 40,075.01 km (24,901.46 miles)
Polar circumference = 40,007.86 km (24,859.73 miles)

The equatorial circumference is divided into 360 degrees of longitude, which is measured in degrees, minutes and seconds east or west of the Greenwich meridian (0°) to 180°, the meridian 180° E. coinciding with 180° W. This was internationally ratified in 1884.

Distance north and south of the Equator is measured in degrees, minutes and seconds of latitude. The Equator is 0°, the North Pole is 90° N. and the South Pole is 90° S. The Tropics lie at 23° 26′ N. (Tropic of Cancer) and 23° 26′ S. (Tropic of Capricorn). The Arctic Circle lies at 66° 34′ N. and the Antarctic Circle at 66° 34′ S. (NB The Tropics and the Arctic and Antarctic circles are affected by the slow decrease in obliquity of the ecliptic, of about 0.5 arcseconds per century. The effect of this is that the Arctic and Antarctic circles are currently moving towards their respective poles by about 14 metres per century, while the Tropics move towards the Equator by the same amount.

AREA, ETC.

The surface area of the Earth is 510,069,120 km² (196,938,800 miles²), of which the water area is 70.92 per cent and the land area is 29.08 per cent.

The velocity of a given point on the Earth's surface at the Equator is 1,669.79 km per hour (1,037.56 m.p.h.). The Earth's mean velocity in its orbit around the Sun is 107,229 km per hour (66,629 m.p.h.). The Earth's mean distance from the Sun is 149,597,870 km (92,955,807 miles).

Source: Royal Greenwich Observatory

OCEANS

AREA

	km²	miles²
Pacific	166,240,000	64,186,300
Atlantic	86,550,000	33,420,000
Indian	73,427,000	28,350,500
Arctic	13,223,700	5,105,700

The division by the Equator of the Pacific into the North and South Pacific and the Atlantic into the North and South Atlantic makes a total of six oceans.

GREATEST DEPTHS

Greatest depth location	metres	feet
Mariana Trench, Pacific	10,924	35,840
Puerto Rico Trench, Atlantic	9,220	30,249
Java (Sunda) Trench, Indian	7,725	25,344
Eurasian Basin, Arctic	5,450	17,880

SEAS

AREA

	km²	miles²
South China	2,974,600	1,148,500
Caribbean	2,515,900	971,400
Mediterranean	2,509,900	969,100
Bering	2,226,100	873,000
Gulf of Mexico	1,507,600	582,100
Okhotsk	1,392,000	537,500
Japan	1,015,000	391,100
Hudson Bay	730,100	281,900
East China	664,600	256,600
Andaman	564,880	218,100
Black Sea	507,900	196,100
Red Sea	453,000	174,900
North Sea	427,100	164,900
Baltic Sea	382,000	147,500
Yellow Sea	294,000	113,500
Persian/Arabian Gulf	230,000	88,800

GREATEST DEPTHS

| | Maximum depth ||
	metres	feet
Caribbean	9,220	30,250
East China	7,507	24,629
South China	7,258	23,812
Mediterranean	5,150	16,896
Andaman	4,267	14,000
Bering	3,936	12,913
Gulf of Mexico	3,504	11,496
Okhotsk	3,365	11,040
Japan	3,053	10,016
Red Sea	2,266	7,434
Black Sea	2,212	7,257
North Sea	439	1,440
Hudson Bay	111	364
Baltic Sea	90	295
Yellow Sea	73	240
Persian Gulf	73	240

THE CONTINENTS

There are six geographic continents, although America is often divided politically into North and Central America, and South America.

AFRICA is surrounded by sea except for the narrow isthmus of Suez in the north-east, through which is cut the Suez Canal. Its extreme longitudes are 17° 20′ W. at Cape Verde, Senegal, and 51° 24′ E. at Ras Hafun, Somalia. The extreme latitudes are 37° 20′ N. at Cape Blanc, Tunisia, and 34° 50′ S. at Cape Agulhas, South Africa, about 4,400 miles apart. The Equator passes through the middle of the continent.

NORTH AMERICA, including Mexico, is surrounded by ocean except in the south, where the isthmian states of CENTRAL AMERICA link North America with South America. Its extreme longitudes are 168° 5′ W. at Cape Prince of Wales, Alaska, and 55° 40′ W. at Cape Charles,

Newfoundland. The extreme continental latitudes are the tip of the Boothia peninsula, NW Territories, Canada (71° 51′ N.) and 14° 22′ N. at Ocós in the south of Mexico.

SOUTH AMERICA lies mostly in the southern hemisphere; the Equator passes through the north of the continent. It is surrounded by ocean except where it is joined to Central America in the north by the narrow isthmus through which is cut the Panama Canal. Its extreme longitudes are 34° 47′ W. at Cape Branco in Brazil and 81° 20′ W. at Punta Pariña, Peru. The extreme continental latitudes are 12° 25′ N. at Punta Gallinas, Colombia, and 53° 54′ S. at the southernmost tip of the Brunswick peninsula, Chile. Cape Horn, on Cape Island, Chile, lies at 55° 59′ S.

ANTARCTICA lies almost entirely within the Antarctic Circle (66° 34′ S.) and is the largest of the world's glaciated areas. The continent has an area of 5.4 million square miles, 99 per cent of which is permanently ice-covered. The ice amounts to some 7.2 million cubic miles and represents more than 90 per cent of the world's fresh water. The environment is too hostile for unsupported human habitation. *See also* pages 786–7

ASIA is the largest continent and occupies 30 per cent of the world's land surface. The extreme longitudes are 26° 05′ E. at Baba Buran, Turkey and 169° 40′ W. at Mys Dežneva (East Cape), Russia, a distance of about 6,000 miles. Its extreme northern latitude is 77° 45′ N. at Cape Čeljuskin, Russia, and it extends over 5,000 miles south to about 1° 15′ N. of the Equator.

AUSTRALIA is the smallest of the continents and lies in the southern hemisphere. It is entirely surrounded by ocean. Its extreme longitudes are 113° 11′ E. at Steep Point and 153° 11′ E. at Cape Byron. The extreme latitudes are 10° 42′ S. at Cape York and 39° S. at South East Point, Tasmania.

EUROPE, including European Russia, is the smallest continent in the northern hemisphere. Its extreme latitudes are 71° 11′ N. at North Cape in Norway, and 36° 23′ N. at Cape Matapan in southern Greece, a distance of about 2,400 miles. Its breadth from Cabo Carvoeiro in Portugal (9° 34′ W.) in the west to the Kara River, north of the Urals (66° 30′ E.) in the east is about 3,300 miles. The division between Europe and Asia is generally regarded as the watershed of the Ural Mountains; down the Ural river to Gur'yev, Kazakhstan; across the Caspian Sea to Aphsheronskiy Poluostrov, near Baku; along the watershed of the Caucasus Mountains to Anapa and thence across the Black Sea to the Bosporus in Turkey; across the Sea of Marmara to Çanakkale Boğazi (Dardanelles).

	Area km^2	miles^2
Asia	43,998,000	16,988,000
*America	41,918,000	16,185,000
Africa	29,800,000	11,506,000
Antarctica	13,980,000	5,400,000
†Europe	9,699,000	3,745,000
Australia	7,618,493	2,941,526

*North and Central America has an area of 24,255,000 km^2 (9,365,000 miles^2)

†Includes 5,571,000 km^2 (2,151,000 miles^2) of former USSR territory, including the Baltic states, Belarus, Moldova, the Ukraine, that part of Russia west of the Ural Mountains and Kazakhstan west of the Ural river. European Turkey (24,378 km^2/9,412 miles^2) comprises territory to the west and north of the Bosporus and the Dardanelles

GLACIATED AREAS

It is estimated that 15,915,000 km^2 (6,145,000 miles^2) or 10.73 per cent of the world's land surface is permanently covered with ice.

	Area km^2	miles^2
South Polar regions	13,830,000	5,340,000
North Polar regions (incl. Greenland or Kalaallit Nunaat)	1,965,000	758,500
Alaska-Canada	58,800	22,700
Asia	37,800	14,600
South America	11,900	4,600
Europe	10,700	4,128
New Zealand	1,015	391
Africa	238	92

The largest glacier is the 515 km/320 mile-long Lambert-Fisher Ice Passage, Antarctica.

PENINSULAS

	Area km^2	miles^2
Arabian	3,250,000	1,250,000
Southern Indian	2,072,000	800,000
Alaskan	1,500,000	580,000
Labradorian	1,300,000	500,000
Scandinavian	800,300	309,000
Iberian	584,000	225,500

LARGEST ISLANDS

Island, and Ocean	*Area* km^2	miles^2
Greenland (Kalaallit Nunaat), Arctic	2,175,500	840,000
New Guinea, Pacific	821,030	317,000
Borneo, Pacific	725,450	280,100
Madagascar, Indian	587,040	226,658
Baffin Island, Arctic	507,451	195,928
Sumatra, Indian	427,350	165,000
Honshu, Pacific	227,413	87,805
*Great Britain, Atlantic	218,077	84,200
Victoria Island, Arctic	217,292	83,897
Ellesmere Island, Arctic	196,236	75,767
Sulawesi (Celebes), Indian	189,036	72,987
South Island, NZ, Pacific	151,213	58,384
Java, Indian	126,650	48,900
North Island, NZ, (Pacific)	115,777	44,702
Cuba, Atlantic	110,862	42,804
Newfoundland, Atlantic	108,855	42,030
Luzon, Pacific	105,880	40,880
Iceland, Atlantic	102,817	39,698
Mindanao, Pacific	95,247	36,775
Ireland, Atlantic	82,462	31,839

*Mainland only

LARGEST DESERTS

	Area (approx.) km²	miles²
The Sahara, N. Africa	8,400,000	3,250,000
Australian Desert	1,550,000	600,000
Arabian Desert	1,200,000	470,000
The Gobi, Mongolia/China	1,040,000	400,000
Kalahari Desert, Botswana/ Namibia/S. Africa	520,000	200,000
Takla Makan, Mongolia/ China	320,000	125,000
Sonoran Desert, USA/ Mexico	310,000	120,000
*Kara Kum, Turkmenistan	310,000	120,000
Namib Desert, Namibia	285,000	110,000
Thar Desert, India/Pakistan	260,000	100,000
Somali Desert, Somalia	260,000	100,000
Atacama Desert, Chile	180,000	70,000
Dasht-e Lut, Iran	52,000	20,000
Mojave Desert, USA	38,850	15,000

*Together with the Kyzyl Kum known as the Turkestan Desert

DEEPEST DEPRESSIONS

	Maximum depth below sea level metres	feet
Dead Sea, Jordan/Israel	395	1,296
Turfan Depression, Sinkiang, China	153	505
Qattara Depression, Egypt	132	436
Mangyshlak peninsula, Kazakhstan	131	433
Danakil Depression, Ethiopia	116	383
Death Valley, California, USA	86	282
Salton Sink, California, USA	71	235
W. of Ustyurt plateau, Kazakhstan	70	230
Prikaspiyskaya Nizmennost', Russia/Kazakhstan	67	220
Lake Sarykamysh, Uzbekistan/ Turkmenistan	45	148
El Faiyûm, Egypt	44	147
Valdies peninsula, Lago Enriquillo, Dominican Republic	40	131

The world's largest exposed depression is the Prikaspiyskaya Nizmennost' covering the hinterland of the northern third of the Caspian Sea, which is itself 28 m (92 ft) below sea level.

Western Antarctica and Central Greenland largely comprise crypto-depressions under ice burdens. The Antarctic Wilkes subglacial basin has a bedrock 2,341 m (7,680 ft) below sea-level. In Greenland (lat. 73° N., long. 39° W.) the bedrock is 365 m (1,197 ft) below sea-level.

More than a quarter of the area of The Netherlands lies marginally below sea-level, an area of more than 10,000 km²/3,860 miles².

LONGEST MOUNTAIN RANGES

Range, and location	Length km	miles
Cordillera de Los Andes, W. South America	7,200	4,500
Rocky Mountains, W. North America	4,800	3,000
Himalaya-Karakoram-Hindu Kush, S. Central Asia	3,800	2,400
Great Dividing Range, E. Australia	3,600	2,250
Trans-Antarctic Mts, Antarctica	3,500	2,200
Atlantic Coast Range, E. Brazil	3,000	1,900
West Sumatran-Javan Range, Indonesia	2,900	1,800
Aleutian Range, Alaska and NW Pacific	2,650	1,650
Tien Shan, S. Central Asia	2,250	1,400
Central New Guinea Range, Irian Jaya/Papua New Guinea	2,000	1,250

HIGHEST MOUNTAINS

The world's 8,000-metre mountains (with six subsidiary peaks) are all in the Himalaya-Karakoram-Hindu Kush range.

Mountain	Height metres	feet
Mt Everest*	8,848	29,028
K2 (Chogori)†	8,607	28,238
Kangchenjunga	8,597	28,208
Lhotse	8,511	27,923
Makalu I	8,481	27,824
Lhotse Shar (II)	8,383	27,504
Dhaulagiri I	8,171	26,810
Manaslu I (Kutang I)	8,156	26,760
Cho Oyu	8,153	26,750
Nanga Parbat (Diamir)	8,125	26,660
Annapurna I	8,091	26,546
Gasherbrum I (Hidden Peak)	8,068	26,470
Broad Peak I	8,046	26,400
Shisham Pangma (Gosainthan)	8,046	26,400
Gasherbrum II	8,034	26,360
Makalu South-East	8,010	26,280
Broad Peak Central	8,000	26,246

*Named after Sir George Everest (1790–1866), Surveyor-General of India 1830–43, in 1863. He pronounced his name Eve-rest
†Formerly Godwin-Austin

The culminating summits in the other major mountain ranges are:

Mountain, by range or country	Height metres	feet
Pik Pobedy, Tien Shan	7,439	24,406
Cerro Aconcagua, Cordillera de Los Andes	6,960	22,834
Mt McKinley (S. Peak), Alaska Range	6,194	20,320
Kilimanjaro (Kibo), Tanzania	5,894	19,340
Hkakabo Razi, Myanmar	5,881	19,296
El'brus, (W. Peak), Caucasus	5,642	18,510
Citlaltépetl (Orizaba), Sierra Madre Oriental, Mexico	5,610	18,405
Vinson Massif, E. Antarctica	4,900	16,073

Mountain, by range or country	Height metres	feet
Puncak Jaya, Central New Guinea Range	4,884	16,023
Mt Blanc, Alps	4,807	15,771
Klyuchevskaya Sopka, Kamchatka peninsula, Russia	4,750	15,584
Ras Dashan, Ethiopian Highlands	4,620	15,158
Zard Kūh, Zagros Mts, Iran	4,547	14,921
Mt Kirkpatrick, Trans Antarctic	4,529	14,860
Mt Belukha, Altai Mts, Russia/ Kazakhstan	4,505	14,783
Mt Elbert, Rocky Mountains	4,400	14,433
Mt Rainier, Cascade Range, N. America	4,392	14,410
Nevado de Colima, Sierra Madre Occidental, Mexico	4,268	14,003
Jebel Toubkal, Atlas Mts, N. Africa	4,165	13,665
Kinabalu, Crocker Range, Borneo	4,101	13,455
Kerinci, West Sumatran-Javan Range, Indonesia	3,800	12,467
Jabal an Nabī Shu'ayb, N. Tihāmat, Yemen	3,760	12,336
Mt Cook (Aorangi), Southern Alps, New Zealand	3,754	12,315
Teotepec, Sierra Madre del Sur, Mexico	3,703	12,149
Thaban Ntlenyana, Drakensberg, South Africa	3,482	11,425
Pico de Bandeira, Atlantic Coast Range	2,890	9,482
Shishaldin, Aleutian Range	2,861	9,387
Kosciusko, Great Dividing Range	2,228	7,310

HIGHEST VOLCANOES

Volcano (last major eruption), and location	Height metres	feet
Ojos del Salado (1981), Andes, Argentina	6,895	22,588
Llullaillaco (1877), Andes, Argentina/Chile	6,723	22,057
San Pedro (1960), Andes, Chile	6,199	20,325
Guallatiri (1960, 1993), Andes, Chile	6,060	19,882
Láscar (1995), Andes, Chile	5,990	19,652
Cotopaxi (1940, 1975), Andes, Ecuador	5,897	19,347
Tupungatito (1986), Andes, Chile	5,640	18,504
Popocatépetl (1996), Mexico	5,465	17,930
Nevado del Ruiz (1985, 1991), Colombia	5,400	17,716
Sangay (1996), Andes, Ecuador	5,230	17,159
Guagua Pichincha (1993), Andes, Ecuador	4,784	15,696
Purace (1977), Colombia	4,756	15,601
Klyuchevskaya Sopka (1997), Kamchatka peninsula, Russia	4,750	15,584
Galeras (1993), Colombia	4,275	14,028
Nevado de Colima (1991, 1994), Mexico	4,268	14,003
Mauna Loa (1984, 1987), Hawaii Is.	4,170	13,680
Cameroon (1982), Cameroon	4,095	13,435
Acatenango (1972), Guatemala	3,960	12,992
Fuego (1987, 1991), Guatemala	3,835	12,582
Kerinci (1970, 1987), Sumatra, Indonesia	3,800	12,467

Volcano (last major eruption), and location	Height metres	feet
Erebus (1995), Ross Island, Antarctica	3,794	12,450
Tacana (1986, 1988), Guatemala	3,780	12,400
Fuji (1708), Honshu, Japan	3,775	12,388
Santa Maria (1902, 1993), Guatemala	3,768	12,362
Rindjani (1966), Lombok, Indonesia	3,726	12,224
Semeru (1995, 1997), Java, Indonesia	3,675	12,060
Nyiragongo (1994), Dem. Rep. of Congo	3,475	11,400
Koryakskaya (1957), Kamchatka, Russia	3,456	11,339
Irazú (1965, 1992), Costa Rica	3,432	11,260
Slamet (1989), Java, Indonesia	3,428	11,247
Spurr (1953), Alaska, USA	3,374	11,069
Mt Etna (1169, 1669, 1993, 1996, 1997), Sicily, Italy	3,350	10,990
Turrialba (1866, 1992), Costa Rica	3,339	10,956
Raung (1993, 1997), Java, Indonesia	3,322	10,932
Sheveluch (1964, 1997), Kamchatka, Russia	3,283	10,771
Agung (1964), Bali, Indonesia	3,142	10,308
Llaima (1995), Chile	3,128	10,239
Redoubt (1990), Alaska, USA	3,108	10,197
Tjareme (1938), Java, Indonesia	3,078	10,098
On-Take (1980, 1991), Honshu, Japan	3,063	10,049
Nyamuragira (1994), Dem. Rep. of Congo	3,056	10,028
Iliamna (1953, 1978), Alaska, USA	3,052	10,016

OTHER NOTABLE VOLCANOES

	Height metres	feet
Tambora (1815), Sumbawa, Indonesia	2,850	9,353
Mt St Helens (1980, 1986, 1991), Washington State, USA	2,549	8,363
Beerenberg (1985), Jan Mayen Island	2,546	8,347
Pinatubo (1991, 1995), Philippines	1,598	5,249
Hekla (1981, 1991), Iceland	1,501	4,920
Mt Pelée (1902), Martinique	1,397	4,583
Mt Unzen (1792, 1991, 1996), Kyushu, Japan	1,360	4,462
Vesuvius (AD 79, 1631, 1944), Italy	1,280	4,198
Kilauea (1996, 1997), Hawaii, USA	1,249	4,009
Soufrière (1979, 1997), St Vincent	1,234	4,048
Soufrière Hills (1997), Montserrat	942	3,091
Stromboli (1996, 1997), Lipari Is., Italy	926	3,038
Krakatau (1883, 1995), Sunda Strait, Indonesia	813	2,667
Santorini (Thíra) (1628 BC, 1950), Aegean Sea, Greece	566	1,857
Vulcano (Monte Aria) (1988), Lipari Is., Italy	499	1,637
Tristan da Cunha (1961), South Atlantic	243	800
Surtsey (1963–7), off Iceland	173	568

LARGEST LAKES

The areas of some of these lakes are subject to seasonal variation.

	Area km²	miles²	Length km	miles
Caspian Sea, Iran/ Azerbaijan/Russia/ Turkmenistan/ Kazakhstan	371,000	143,000	1,171	728
*Michigan–Huron, USA/Canada	117,610	45,300	1,010	627
Superior, Canada/ USA	82,100	31,700	563	350
Victoria, Uganda/ Tanzania/Kenya	69,500	26,828	362	225
Aral Sea, Kazakhstan/ Uzbekistan	40,000	15,444	134	217
Tanganyika, Dem. Rep. of Congo/ Tanzania/Zambia/ Burundi	32,900	12,665	725	450
Great Bear, Canada	31,328	12,096	309	192
†Baykal (Baikal), Russia	30,500	11,776	620	385
Malawi (Nyasa), Tanzania/Malawi/ Mozambique	29,600	11,430	580	360
Great Slave, Canada	28,570	11,031	480	298
Erie, Canada/USA	25,670	9,910	388	241
Winnipeg, Canada	24,390	9,417	428	266
Ontario, Canada/USA	19,010	7,340	310	193
Ladozhskoye (Ladoga), Russia	17,700	6,835	193	120
Balkhash, Kazakhstan	17,400	6,718	482	299

*Lakes Michigan and Huron are regarded as lobes of the same lake. The Michigan lobe has an area of 57,750 km² (22,300 miles²) and the Huron lobe an area of 59,570 km² (23,000 miles²)
†World's deepest lake (1,940 m/6,365 ft)

UNITED KINGDOM, BY COUNTRY

Lough Neagh, Northern Ireland	381.73	147.39	28.90	18.00
Loch Lomond, Scotland	71.12	27.46	36.44	22.64
Windermere, England	14.74	5.69	16.90	10.50
Lake Vyrnwy, Wales (artificial)	4.53	1.75	7.56	4.70
Llyn Tegid (Bala), Wales (natural)	4.38	1.69	5.80	3.65

LONGEST RIVERS

River, source and outflow	Length km	miles
Nile (Bahr-el-Nil), R. Luvironza, Burundi – E. Mediterranean Sea	6,670	4,145
Amazon (Amazonas), Lago Villafro, Peru – S. Atlantic Ocean	6,448	4,007
Mississippi-Missouri-Red Rock, Montana – Gulf of Mexico	5,970	3,710
Yenisey-Angara, W. Mongolia – Kara Sea	5,540	3,442

River, source and outflow	Length km	miles
Yangtze-Kiang (Chang Jiang), Kunlun Mts, W. China – Yellow Sea	5,530	3,436
Huang He (Yellow River), Bayan Har Shan range, central China – Yellow Sea	5,463	3,395
Ob'-Irtysh, W. Mongolia – Kara Sea	5,410	3,362
Río de la Plata-Paraná, R. Paranáiba, central Brazil – S. Atlantic Ocean	4,880	3,032
Zaïre (Congo), R. Lualaba, Dem. Rep. of Congo-Zambia – S. Atlantic Ocean	4,700	2,920
Lena-Kirenga, R. Kirenga, W. of Lake Baykal – Arctic Ocean	4,400	2,734
Mekong, Lants'ang, Tibet – South China Sea	4,350	2,702
Amur-Argun, R. Argun, Khingan Mts, N. China – Sea of Okhotsk	4,345	2,700
Mackenzie-Peace, Tatlatui Lake, British Columbia – Beaufort Sea	4,240	2,635
Niger, Loma Mts, Guinea – Gulf of Guinea, E. Atlantic Ocean	4,181	2,600
Murray-Darling, SE Queensland – Lake Alexandrina, S. Australia	3,717	2,310
Volga, Valdai plateau – Caspian Sea	3,530	2,193
Zambezi, NW Zambia – S. Indian Ocean	2,736	1,700

OTHER NOTABLE RIVERS

St Lawrence, Minnesota, USA – Gulf of St Lawrence	3,130	1,945
Ganges-Brahmaputra, R. Matsang, SW Tibet – Bay of Bengal	2,900	1,800
Indus, R. Sengge, SW Tibet – N. Arabian Sea	2,880	1,790
Danube (Donau), Black Forest, SW Germany – Black Sea	2,856	1,775
Tigris-Euphrates, R. Murat, E. Turkey – Persian Gulf	2,800	1,740
Irrawaddy, R. Mali Hka, Myanmar – Andaman Sea	2,151	1,337
Don, SE of Novomoskovsk – Sea of Azov	1,969	1,224

BRITISH ISLES

Shannon, Co. Cavan, Rep. of Ireland – Atlantic Ocean	386	240
Severn, Powys, Wales – Bristol Channel	354	220
Thames, Gloucestershire, England – North Sea	346	215
Tay, Perthshire, Scotland – North Sea	188	117
Clyde, Lanarkshire, Scotland – Firth of Clyde	158	98½
Tweed, Peeblesshire, Scotland – North Sea	155	96½
Bann (Upper and Lower), Co. Down, N. Ireland – Atlantic Ocean	122	76

GREATEST WATERFALLS – BY HEIGHT

Waterfall, river and location	Total drop		Greatest single leap	
	metres	feet	metres	feet
Angel, Carrao, Venezuela	979	3,212	807	2,648
Tugela, Tugela, Natal, S. Africa	947	3,110	410	1,350
Utigård, Jostedal Glacier, Norway	800	2,625	600	1,970
Mongefossen, Monge, Norway	774	2,540	—	—
Yosemite, Yosemite Creek, USA	739	2,425	435	1,430
Østre Mardøla Foss, Mardals, Norway	656	2,154	296	974
Tyssestrengane, Tysso, Norway	646	2,120	289	948
Cuquenán, Arabopó, Venezuela	610	2,000	—	—
Sutherland, Arthur, NZ	580	1,904	248	815
*Kjellfossen (Kile), Naeröfjord, Norway	561	1,841	149	490

*Volume often so low the fall atomizes into a 'bridal veil'

BRITISH ISLES, BY COUNTRY

Eas a' Chuàl Aluinn, Glas Bheinn, Sutherland, Scotland	200	658		
Powerscourt Falls, Dargle, Co. Wicklow, Rep. of Ireland	106	350		
Pistyll-y-Llyn, Powys/ Dyfed border, Wales	c.73	230– 240		(cascades)
Pistyll Rhyadr, Clwyd/ Powys border, Wales	71.5	235		(single leap)
Caldron Snout, R. Tees, Cumbria/Durham, England	61	200		(cascades)

GREATEST WATERFALLS – BY VOLUME

Waterfall, river and location	Mean annual flow	
	m³/sec	galls/sec
Boyoma (Stanley), R. Lualaba, Dem. Rep. of Congo	c.17,000	c.3,750,000
Khône, Mekong, Laos	11,500	2,530,000
Niagara (Horseshoe), R. Niagara/Lake Erie–Lake Ontario	5,640	1,260,000
Paulo Afonso, R. São Francisco, Brazil	2,800	625,000
Urubupunga, Alto Paraná, Brazil	2,800	625,000
Cataratas del Iguazú, R. Iguaçu, Brazil/Argentina	1,725	380,000
Patos-Maribando, Rio Grande, Brazil	1,500	330,000
Victoria (Mosi-oa-tunya), R. Zambezi, Zambia/ Zimbabwe	1,100	242,000
Churchill, R. Churchill, Canada	975	215,000
Kaieteur, R. Potaro, Guyana	660	145,000

TALLEST DAMS

	metres	feet
*Rogun, R. Vakhsh, Tajikistan	335	1,098
Nurek, R. Vakhsh, Tajikistan	300	984
Grande Dixence, Switzerland	285	935
*Longtan, R. Hangshui, China	285	935
Inguri, Georgia	272	892
Chicoasén, Mexico	261	856
Tehri, R. Bhagivathi, India	261	856

*Under construction

The world's most massive dam is the Syncrude Tailings dam in Alberta, Canada, which will have a volume of 540 million cubic metres/706 million cubic yards.

The Three Gorges Chang Jiang (Yangtze) Dam, China, with a crest length of 1,983 m/6,505 ft, is due for completion in 2009.

The Yacyretá-Apipe dam across the River Paraná, Argentina-Paraguay, is being completed to a length of 69,600 m/43.24 miles.

TALLEST INHABITED BUILDINGS

Building and city	Height	
	metres	feet
Chongqing Tower, China	457	1,499
Petronas Towers I and II, Kuala Lumpur, Malaysia	451.9	1,482
Sears Tower, Chicago[1]	443	1,454
Jin Mao, Shanghai, China (1998)	420	1,378
One World Trade Center Tower, New York[2]	417	1,368
Plaza Rakyat, Kuala Lumpur, Malaysia	382	1,254
Empire State Building, New York[3]	381	1,250
Central Plaza, Hong Kong	373	1,227
T & C Tower, Kaohsiung, Taiwan	347	1,140
Amoco Building, Chicago	346	1,136
John Hancock Center, Chicago	343	1,127
Shun Hing Square, Shenzhen, China	325	1,066
Sky Central Plaza, Guangzhou, China	321	1,056
Chicago Beach Tower, Dubai	320	1,050
Baiyoke Tower, Bangkok, Thailand	320	1,050
Chrysler Building, New York	319	1,046
Bank of China, Hong Kong[4]	315	1,033
Nation's Bank Tower, Atlanta, USA	312	1,023

1. With TV antennae, 520 m/1,707 ft
2. With TV antennae, 521.2 m/1,710 ft; Two World Trade Center Tower, 415 m/1,362 ft
3. With TV tower (added 1950–1), 430.9 m/1,414 ft
4. With steel mast, 368.5 m/1,209 ft

TALLEST STRUCTURES

Structure and location	Height	
	metres	feet
*Warszawa Radio Mast, Konstantynow, Poland	646	2,120
KTHI-TV Mast, Blanchard, North Dakota (guyed)	629	2,063
CN Tower, Metro Centre, Toronto, Canada	555	1,822
Ostankino Tower, Moscow	537	1,762

*Collapsed during renovation, August 1991

LONGEST BRIDGES – BY SPAN

Bridge and location	Length metres	feet
SUSPENSION SPANS		
*Akashi-Kaikyo, Shikoku, Japan (1998)	1,990	6,529
Store Baelt East Bridge, Denmark	1,624	5,328
Humber Estuary, Humberside, England	1,410	4,626
*Jiangyin (Yangtze), China (1999)	1,385	4,488
Verrazano Narrows, Brooklyn–Staten I, USA	1,298	4,260
Golden Gate, San Francisco Bay, USA	1,280	4,200
Hoga Kustan, Sweden	1,210	3,970
Mackinac Straits, Michigan, USA	1,158	3,800
Minami Bisan-Seto, Japan	1,100	3,609
Bosporus I, Istanbul, Turkey	1,089	3,576
Bosporus II, Istanbul, Turkey	1,074	3,524
George Washington, Hudson River, New York City, USA	1,067	3,500
Kurushima III, Japan	1,030	3,379
Ponte 25 de Abril (Tagus), Lisbon, Portugal	1,013	3,323
Firth of Forth (road), nr Edinburgh, Scotland	1,006	3,300
Kita Bisan-Seto, Japan	990	3,248
Severn River, Severn Estuary, England	988	3,240
*Under construction		

The main span of the 5.15 km/3.2 mile long Second Severn bridging, opened in 1996, is 456 m/1,496 ft.

CANTILEVER SPANS		
Pont de Québec (rail-road), St Lawrence, Canada	548.6	1,800
Ravenswood, W. Virginia, USA	525.1	1,723
Firth of Forth (rail), nr Edinburgh, Scotland	521.2	1,710
Nanko, Osaka, Japan	510.0	1,673
Commodore Barry, Chester, Pennsylvania, USA	494.3	1,622
Greater New Orleans, Louisiana, USA	480.0	1,575
Howrah (rail-road), Calcutta, India	457.2	1,500
STEEL ARCH SPANS		
New River Gorge, Fayetteville, W. Virginia, USA	518.0	1,700
Bayonne (Kill van Kull), Bayonne, NJ – Staten I, USA	503.5	1,652
Sydney Harbour, Sydney, Australia	502.9	1,650

The 'floating' bridging at Evergreen, Seattle, Washington State, USA, is 3,839 m/12,596 ft long.

The longest stretch of bridgings of any kind is that carrying the Interstate 55 and Interstate 10 highways at Manchac, Louisiana, on twin concrete trestles over 55.21 km/34.31 miles.

LONGEST VEHICULAR TUNNELS

Tunnel and location	Length km	miles
*Seikan (rail), Tsugaru Channel, Japan	53.90	33.49
*Channel Tunnel, Cheriton, Kent – Sangatte, Calais	49.94	31.03
Moscow metro, Belyaevo – Bittsevsky, Moscow, Russia	37.90	23.50
Northern line tube, East Finchley – Morden, London	27.84	17.30
Oshimizu (rail), Honshū, Japan	22.17	13.78
Simplon II (rail), Brigue, Switzerland – Iselle, Italy	19.82	12.31
Simplon I (rail), Brigue, Switzerland – Iselle, Italy	19.80	12.30
*Shin-Kanmon (rail), Kanmon Strait, Japan	18.68	11.61
Great Appennine (rail), Vernio, Italy	18.49	11.49
St Gotthard (road), Göschenen – Airolo, Switzerland	16.32	10.14
Rokko (rail), Ōsaka – Kōbe, Japan	16.09	10.00
*Sub-aqueous		

The longest non-vehicular tunnelling in the world is the Delaware Aqueduct in New York State, USA, constructed in 1937–44 to a length of 168.9 km/105 miles.

BRITAIN – RAIL TUNNELS	miles	yards
Severn, Bristol – Newport	4	484
Totley, Manchester – Sheffield	3	950
Standedge, Manchester – Huddersfield	3	66
Sodbury, Swindon – Bristol	2	924
Disley, Stockport – Sheffield	2	346
Ffestiniog, Llandudno – Blaenau Ffestiniog	2	338
Bramhope, Leeds – Harrogate	2	241
Cowburn, Manchester – Sheffield	2	182

The longest road tunnel in Britain is the Mersey Road Tunnel, 2 miles 228 yards long. The longest canal tunnel, at Standedge, W. Yorks, is 3 miles 330 yards long; it was closed in 1944 but is currently being restored.

LONGEST SHIP CANALS

Canal (opening date)	Length km	miles	Min. depth metres	feet
White Sea-Baltic (formerly Stalin) (1933) Canalized river; canal 51.5 km/32 miles	227	141.00	5.0	16.5
*Suez (1869) Links Red and Mediterranean Seas	162	100.60	12.9	42.3
V. I. Lenin Volga-Don (1952) Links Black and Caspian Seas	100	62.20	n/a	n/a

Canal (opening date)	Length		Min. depth	
	km	miles	metres	feet
Kiel (or North Sea) (1895) Links North and Baltic Seas	98	60.90	13.7	45.0
*Houston (1940) Links inland city with sea	91	56.70	10.4	34.0
Alphonse XIII (1926) Gives Seville access to sea	85	53.00	7.6	25.0
Panama (1914) Links Pacific Ocean and Caribbean Sea; lake chain, 78.9 km/49 miles dug	82	50.71	12.5	41.0
Manchester Ship (1894) Links city with Irish Channel	64	39.70	8.5	28.0
Welland (1932) Circumvents Niagara Falls and Rapids	43	26.70	8.8	29.0
Brussels (Rupel Sea) (1922) Renders Brussels an inland port	32	19.80	6.4	21.0

*Has no locks

The first section of China's Grand Canal, running 1,782 km/1,107 miles from Beijing to Hangzhou, was opened AD 610 and completed in 1283. Today it is limited to 2,000 tonne vessels.
The St Lawrence Seaway comprises Beauharnois, Welland and Welland Bypass and Seaway 54–59 canals, and allows access to Duluth, Minnesota, USA via the Great Lakes from the Atlantic end of Canada's Gulf of St Lawrence, a distance of 3,769 km/2,342 miles.

LARGEST CITIES OF THE WORLD

In most cases figures refer to urban agglomerations (Ψ seaport)

	Population
Mexico City, Mexico	15,047,685
Cairo, Egypt	13,000,000
Ψ Bombay/Mumbai, India	12,596,243
Tokyo, Japan	11,927,457
Ψ Calcutta, India	11,021,918
Ψ Buenos Aires, Argentina	10,686,163
Seoul, South Korea	10,412,000
São Paulo, Brazil	9,842,059
Paris, France	9,319,367
Ψ Jakarta, Indonesia	9,160,500
Moscow, Russia	8,600,000
Manila, Philippines	8,594,150
Delhi, India	8,419,084
Ψ Shanghai, China	8,205,598
Bogotá, Colombia	8,000,000
Istanbul, Turkey	7,784,100
Ψ New York, USA	7,380,906
Beijing, China	7,362,426
Ψ Karachi, Pakistan	7,183,000
Washington DC, USA	7,051,495

The United Kingdom

The United Kingdom comprises Great Britain (England, Wales and Scotland) and Northern Ireland. The Isle of Man and the Channel Islands are Crown dependencies with their own legislative systems, and not a part of the United Kingdom.

AREA AS AT 31 MARCH 1981

	Land miles²	km²	*Inland water miles²	km²	Total miles²	km²
United Kingdom	93,006	240,883	1,242	3,218	94,248	244,101
England	50,058	129,652	293	758	50,351	130,410
Wales	7,965	20,628	50	130	8,015	20,758
Scotland	29,767	77,097	653	1,692	30,420	78,789
†Northern Ireland	5,225	13,532	249	628	5,467	14,160
Isle of Man	221	572	—	—	221	572
Channel Islands	75	194	—	—	75	194

*Excluding tidal water
†Excluding certain tidal waters that are parts of statutory areas in Northern Ireland

POPULATION

The first official census of population in England, Wales and Scotland was taken in 1801 and a census has been taken every ten years since, except in 1941 when there was no census because of war. The last official census in the United Kingdom was taken on 21 April 1991 and the next is due in April 2001.

The first official census of population in Ireland was taken in 1841. However, all figures given below refer only to the area which is now Northern Ireland. Figures for Northern Ireland in 1921 and 1931 are estimates based on the censuses taken in 1926 and 1937 respectively.

Estimates of the population of England before 1801, calculated from the number of baptisms, burials and marriages, are:

1570	4,160,221	1670	5,773,646
1600	4,811,718	1700	6,045,008
1630	5,600,517	1750	6,517,035

Thousands	United Kingdom Total	Male	Female	England and Wales Total	Male	Female	Scotland Total	Male	Female	Northern Ireland Total	Male	Female
CENSUS RESULTS 1801–1991												
1801	—	—	—	8,893	4,255	4,638	1,608	739	869	—	—	—
1811	13,368	6,368	7,000	10,165	4,874	5,291	1,806	826	980	—	—	—
1821	15,472	7,498	7,974	12,000	5,850	6,150	2,092	983	1,109	—	—	—
1831	17,835	8,647	9,188	13,897	6,771	7,126	2,364	1,114	1,250	—	—	—
1841	20,183	9,819	10,364	15,914	7,778	8,137	2,620	1,242	1,378	1,649	800	849
1851	22,259	10,855	11,404	17,928	8,781	9,146	2,889	1,376	1,513	1,443	698	745
1861	24,525	11,894	12,631	20,066	9,776	10,290	3,062	1,450	1,612	1,396	668	728
1871	27,431	13,309	14,122	22,712	11,059	11,653	3,360	1,603	1,757	1,359	647	712
1881	31,015	15,060	15,955	25,974	12,640	13,335	3,736	1,799	1,936	1,305	621	684
1891	34,264	16,593	17,671	29,003	14,060	14,942	4,026	1,943	2,083	1,236	590	646
1901	38,237	18,492	19,745	32,528	15,729	16,799	4,472	2,174	2,298	1,237	590	647
1911	42,082	20,357	21,725	36,070	17,446	18,625	4,761	2,309	2,452	1,251	603	648
1921	44,027	21,033	22,994	37,887	18,075	19,811	4,882	2,348	2,535	1,258	610	648
1931	46,038	22,060	23,978	39,952	19,133	20,819	4,843	2,326	2,517	1,243	601	642
1951	50,225	24,118	26,107	43,758	21,016	22,742	5,096	2,434	2,662	1,371	668	703
1961	52,709	25,481	27,228	46,105	22,304	23,801	5,179	2,483	2,697	1,425	694	731
1971	55,515	26,952	28,562	48,750	23,683	25,067	5,229	2,515	2,714	1,536	755	781
1981	55,848	27,104	28,742	49,155	23,873	25,281	5,131	2,466	2,664	*1,533	750	783
1991	56,467	27,344	29,123	49,890	24,182	25,707	4,999	2,392	2,607	1,578	769	809
†RESIDENT POPULATION: PROJECTIONS (MID-YEAR)												
2001	59,618	29,377	30,241	52,818	26,062	26,756	5,106	2,484	2,622	1,694	830	864
2011	60,929	30,206	30,723	54,151	26,881	27,269	5,059	2,476	2,583	1,720	848	872
2021	62,244	30,916	31,328	55,526	27,614	27,913	4,993	2,449	2,544	1,724	853	871

*Figures include 44,500 non-enumerated persons
† Projections are 1996 based

Source: The Stationery Office – *Annual Abstract 1998*; ONS – Census reports (Crown copyright)

ISLANDS: Census Results 1901–91

	Isle of Man			Jersey			*Guernsey		
	Total	Male	Female	Total	Male	Female	Total	Male	Female
1901	54,752	25,496	29,256	52,576	23,940	28,636	40,446	19,652	20,794
1911	52,016	23,937	28,079	51,898	24,014	27,884	41,858	20,661	21,197
1921	60,284	27,329	32,955	49,701	22,438	27,263	38,315	18,246	20,069
1931	49,308	22,443	26,865	50,462	23,424	27,038	40,643	19,659	20,984
1951	55,123	25,749	29,464	57,296	27,282	30,014	43,652	21,221	22,431
1961	48,151	22,060	26,091	57,200	27,200	30,000	45,068	21,671	23,397
1971	56,289	26,461	29,828	72,532	35,423	37,109	51,458	24,792	26,666
1981	64,679	30,901	33,778	77,000	37,000	40,000	53,313	25,701	27,612
1991	69,788	33,693	36,095	84,082	40,862	43,220	58,867	28,297	30,570

* Population of Guernsey, Herm, Jethou and Lithou. Figures for 1901–71 record all persons present on census night; census figures for 1981 and 1991 record all persons resident in the islands on census night

Source: 1991 Census

RESIDENT POPULATION

MID -YEAR ESTIMATE

	1986	1996
United Kingdom	56,852,000	58,801,000
England	47,342,000	49,089,000
Wales	2,820,000	2,921,000
Scotland	5,123,000	5,128,000
Northern Ireland	1,567,000	1,663,000

Source: The Stationery Office – *Annual Abstract of Statistics 1998* (Crown copyright)

BY AGE AND SEX 1996

Males	Under 16	65 and over
United Kingdom	6,205,000	3,768,000
England	5,158,000	3,167,000
Wales	308,000	207,000
Scotland	526,000	309,000
Northern Ireland	212,000	85,000

Females	Under 16	60 and over
United Kingdom	5,893,000	6,900,000
England	4,894,000	5,755,000
Wales	293,000	375,000
Scotland	503,000	606,000
Northern Ireland	203,000	164,000

Source: The Stationery Office – *Annual Abstract of Statistics 1998* (Crown copyright)

BY ETHNIC GROUP (1991 Census (Great Britain))

Ethnic group	Estimated population	Percentage
Caribbean	500,000	16.6
African	212,000	7
Other black	178,000	5.9
Indian	840,000	27.9
Pakistani	477,000	15.8
Bangladeshi	163,000	5.4
Chinese	157,000	5.2
Other Asian	198,000	6.6
Other	290,000	9.6
Total ethnic minority groups	3,015,000	100
White	51,874,000	—
All ethnic groups	54,889,000	—

Source: The Stationery Office – *Population Trends* 72 (Crown copyright)

AVERAGE DENSITY *Persons per hectare*

	1981	1991
England	3.55	3.61
Wales	1.34	1.36
Scotland	0.66	0.65
Northern Ireland	1.12	1.11

Sources: ONS – Census reports (Crown copyright)

IMMIGRATION 1996
Acceptances for settlement in the UK by nationality

Region	Number of persons
Europe: total	7,500
European Economic Area	130
Remainder of Europe	7,370
Americas: total	8,470
USA	4.030
Canada	970
Africa: total	12,970
Asia: total	27,880
Indian sub-continent	13,590
Middle East	4,790
Oceania: total	3,520
British Overseas Citizens	620
Stateless	780
Total	61,730

Source: The Stationery Office – *Annual Abstract of Statistics 1998* (Crown copyright)

LIVE BIRTHS AND BIRTH RATES 1996

	Live births	Birth rate*
United Kingdom	733,000	12.5
England and Wales	649,000	12.5
Scotland	59,000	11.6
Northern Ireland	25,000	14.8

*Live births per 1,000 population
Source: The Stationery Office – *Annual Abstract of Statistics 1998* (Crown copyright)

LEGAL ABORTIONS 1996

Age group	England and Wales	Scotland
Under 16	3,645	323
16–19	28,790	2,355
20–34	113,895	7,966
35–44	21,145	1,290
45 and over	428	27
Age not stated	13	—
Total	179,877	

Source: The Stationery Office – Annual Abstract of Statistics 1998 (Crown copyright)

BIRTHS OUTSIDE MARRIAGE (UK)

Age group	1981	1996
Under 20	30,000	45,000
20–24	33,000	80,000
25–29	16,000	69,000
Over 30	13,000	66,000
Total	91,000	260,000

Source: The Stationery Office – Annual Abstract of Statistics 1998 (Crown copyright)

MARRIAGE AND DIVORCE 1995

	Marriages	Divorces
United Kingdom	322,251p	170,283
England and Wales	283,012p	155,499
Scotland	30,663	12,249
Northern Ireland	8,576	2,535

p provisional
Source: The Stationery Office – Annual Abstract of Statistics 1998 (Crown copyright)

DEATHS AND DEATH RATES 1996

Males	Deaths	Death rate*
United Kingdom	305,323	10.6
England and Wales	268,682	10.6p
Scotland	29,223	11.8
Northern Ireland	7,418	9.1
Females		
United Kingdom	330,701	11.1
England and Wales	291,453	11.1p
Scotland	31,448	11.9
Northern Ireland	7,800	9.2

* Deaths per 1,000 population
p provisional
Sources: The Stationery Office – Annual Abstract of Statistics 1998; ONS; General Register Office for Scotland; Annual Report of the Registrar-General for Northern Ireland 1995 (Crown copyright)

INFANT MORTALITY 1996p
Deaths of infants under 1 year of age per 1,000 live births

	Number
United Kingdom	6.1
England and Wales	6.1
Scotland	6.2
Northern Ireland	5.8

p provisional
Source: The Stationery Office – Annual Abstract of Statistics 1998 (Crown copyright)

EXPECTATION OF LIFE LIFE TABLES 1994–96 (INTERIM FIGURES)

	England and Wales		Scotland		Northern Ireland	
Age	Male	Female	Male	Female	Male	Female
0	74.4	79.6	72.1	77.6	73.3	78.7
5	70.0	75.1	67.7	73.2	68.9	74.2
10	65.0	70.1	62.7	68.2	63.9	69.3
15	60.1	65.2	57.8	63.2	59.0	64.3
20	55.2	60.3	53.1	58.3	54.3	59.4
25	50.5	55.3	48.3	53.4	49.6	54.5
30	45.7	50.4	43.6	48.6	44.8	49.6
35	40.9	45.6	38.9	43.7	40.0	44.7
40	36.2	40.7	34.2	38.9	35.3	39.9
45	31.5	36.0	29.6	34.2	30.6	35.1
50	26.9	31.3	25.2	29.6	26.1	30.5
55	22.6	26.8	21.0	25.2	21.7	26.0
60	18.5	22.5	17.2	21.0	17.7	21.7
65	14.8	18.4	13.7	17.2	14.2	17.8
70	11.6	14.7	10.8	13.7	11.0	14.0
75	8.9	11.4	8.3	10.6	8.3	10.8
80	6.6	8.6	6.2	7.9	6.0	7.9
85	4.9	6.3	4.6	5.7	4.2	5.6

Source: The Stationery Office – Annual Abstract of Statistics 1998 (Crown copyright)

DEATHS ANALYSED BY CAUSE 1996

	England & Wales	Scotland	N. Ireland
TOTAL DEATHS	563,007	60,671	15,218
Infectious and parasitic diseases	3,662	493	54
Neoplasms	140,120	15,419	3,715
Malignant neoplasm of stomach	6,778	699	200
Malignant neoplasm of trachea, bronchus and lung	30,972	4,126	816
Malignant neoplasm of breast	12,298	1,200	309
Malignant neoplasm of uterus	1,309	105	28
Malignant neoplasm of cervix	1,329	138	45
Benign and unspecified neoplasms	1,673	194	60
Leukaemia	3,472	319	92
Endocrine, nutritional and metabolic diseases and immunity disorders	7,551	722	81
Diabetes mellitus	6,027	526	49
Nutritional deficiencies	71	16	—
Other metabolic and immunity disorders	1,060	140	28
Diseases of blood and blood-forming organs	1,992	180	22
Anaemias	725	76	11
Mental disorders	9,354	1,595	100
Diseases of the nervous system and sense organs	9,809	852	236
Meningitis	247	14	7
Diseases of the circulatory system	238,855	26,728	6,633
Rheumatic heart disease	1,694	154	29
Hypertensive disease	3,023	281	75
Ischaemic heart disease	129,680	14,650	3,856
Diseases of pulmonary circulation and other forms of heart disease	26,322	3,063	655
Cerebrovascular disease	60,031	7,130	1,653
Diseases of the respiratory system	89,216	7,863	2,749
Influenza	182	45	6
Pneumonia	54,502	4,158	1,817
Bronchitis, emphysema	4,275	348	137
Asthma	1,356	122	31
Diseases of the digestive system	19,958	2,440	483
Ulcer of stomach and duodenum	4,108	344	102
Appendicitis	103	9	—
Hernia of the abdominal cavity and other intestinal obstruction	1,977	196	52
Chronic liver disease and cirrhosis	3,756	723	88
Diseases of the genitourinary system	6,788	839	254
Nephritis, nephrotic syndrome and nephrosis	3,068	549	168
Hyperplasia of prostate	236	11	3
Complications of pregnancy, childbirth and the puerperium	47	6	1
Abortion	6	—	—
Diseases of the skin and subcutaneous tissue	1,089	75	29
Diseases of the musculo-skeletal system	3,540	252	35
Congenital anomalies	1,238	192	72
Certain conditions originating in the perinatal period	151	181	68
Birth trauma, hypoxia, birth asphyxia and other respiratory conditions	116	94	28
Signs, symptoms and ill-defined conditions	10,842	337	88
Sudden infant death syndrome	337	43	15
Deaths from injury and poisoning	16,120	2,497	598
All accidents	10,438	1,497	402
Motor vehicle accidents	3,217	363	121
Suicide and self-inflicted injury	3,455	596	124
All other external causes	2,227	404	72

Source; The Stationery Office – *Annual Abstract of Statistics 1998* (Crown copyright)

The National Flag

The national flag of the United Kingdom is the Union Flag, generally known as the Union Jack.

The Union Flag is a combination of the cross of St George, patron saint of England, the cross of St Andrew, patron saint of Scotland, and a cross similar to that of St Patrick, patron saint of Ireland.

Cross of St George: cross Gules in a field Argent (red cross on a white ground)

Cross of St Andrew: saltire Argent in a field Azure (white diagonal cross on a blue ground)

Cross of St Patrick: saltire Gules in a field Argent (red diagonal cross on a white ground)

The Union Flag was first introduced in 1606 after the union of the kingdoms of England and Scotland under one sovereign. The cross of St Patrick was added in 1801 after the union of Great Britain and Ireland.

FLYING THE UNION FLAG

The correct orientation of the Union Flag when flying is with the broader diagonal band of white uppermost in the hoist (i.e. near the pole) and the narrower diagonal band of white uppermost in the fly (i.e. furthest from the pole).

It is the practice to fly the Union Flag daily on some customs houses. In all other cases, flags are flown on government buildings by command of The Queen.

Days for hoisting the Union Flag are notified to the Department for Culture, Media and Sport by The Queen's command and communicated by the department to the other government departments. On the days appointed, the Union Flag is flown on government buildings in the United Kingdom from 8 a.m. to sunset.

DAYS FOR FLYING FLAGS

The Queen's Accession	6 February
Birthday of The Duke of York	19 February
*St David's Day (in Wales only)	1 March
Commonwealth Day (1999)	8 March
Birthday of The Prince Edward	10 March
Birthday of The Queen	21 April
*St George's Day (in England only)	23 April
†Europe Day	9 May
Coronation Day	2 June
Birthday of The Duke of Edinburgh	10 June
The Queen's Official Birthday (1999)	12 June
Birthday of Queen Elizabeth the Queen Mother	4 August
Birthday of The Princess Royal	15 August
Birthday of The Princess Margaret	21 August
Remembrance Sunday (1999)	14 November
Birthday of The Prince of Wales	14 November
The Queen's Wedding Day	20 November
*St Andrew's Day (in Scotland only)	30 November

‡The opening of Parliament by The Queen
‡The prorogation of Parliament by The Queen

*Where a building has two or more flagstaffs, the appropriate national flag may be flown in addition to the Union Flag, but not in a superior position
†The Union Flag should fly alongside the European flag. On government buildings that have only one flagpole, the Union Flag should take precedence
‡Flags are flown whether or not The Queen performs the ceremony in person. Flags are flown only in the Greater London area

FLAGS AT HALF-MAST

Flags are flown at half-mast (i.e. two-thirds up between the top and bottom of the flagstaff) on the following occasions:

(a) From the announcement of the death up to the funeral of the Sovereign, except on Proclamation Day, when flags are hoisted right up from 11 a.m. to sunset

(b) The funerals of members of the royal family, subject to special commands from The Queen in each case

(c) The funerals of foreign rulers, subject to special commands from The Queen in each case

(d) The funerals of prime ministers and ex-prime ministers of the UK, subject to special commands from The Queen in each case

(e) Other occasions by special command of The Queen

On occasions when days for flying flags coincide with days for flying flags at half-mast, the following rules are observed. Flags are flown:

(a) although a member of the royal family, or a near relative of the royal family, may be lying dead, unless special commands be received from The Queen to the contrary

(b) although it may be the day of the funeral of a foreign ruler

If the body of a very distinguished subject is lying at a government office, the flag may fly at half-mast on that office until the body has left (provided it is a day on which the flag would fly) and then the flag is to be hoisted right up. On all other government buildings the flag will fly as usual.

THE ROYAL STANDARD

The Royal Standard is hoisted only when The Queen is actually present in the building, and never when Her Majesty is passing in procession.

The Royal Family

THE SOVEREIGN

ELIZABETH II, by the Grace of God, of the United Kingdom of Great Britain and Northern Ireland and of her other Realms and Territories Queen, Head of the Commonwealth, Defender of the Faith

Her Majesty Elizabeth Alexandra Mary of Windsor, elder daughter of King George VI and of HM Queen Elizabeth the Queen Mother
Born 21 April 1926, at 17 Bruton Street, London W1
Ascended the throne 6 February 1952
Crowned 2 June 1953, at Westminster Abbey
Married 20 November 1947, in Westminster Abbey, HRH The Duke of Edinburgh
Official residences: Buckingham Palace, London SW1A 1AA; Windsor Castle, Berks; Palace of Holyroodhouse, Edinburgh
Private residences: Sandringham, Norfolk; Balmoral Castle, Aberdeenshire

HUSBAND OF THE QUEEN

HRH THE PRINCE PHILIP, DUKE OF EDINBURGH, KG, KT, OM, GBE, AC, QSO, PC, Ranger of Windsor Park
Born 10 June 1921, son of Prince and Princess Andrew of Greece and Denmark (*see* page 128), naturalized a British subject 1947, created Duke of Edinburgh, Earl of Merioneth and Baron Greenwich 1947

CHILDREN OF THE QUEEN

HRH THE PRINCE OF WALES (Prince Charles Philip Arthur George), KG, KT, GCB and Great Master of the Order of the Bath, AK, QSO, PC, ADC(P)
Born 14 November 1948, created Prince of Wales and Earl of Chester 1958, succeeded as Duke of Cornwall, Duke of Rothesay, Earl of Carrick and Baron Renfrew, Lord of the Isles and Prince and Great Steward of Scotland 1952
Married 29 July 1981 Lady Diana Frances Spencer (Diana, Princess of Wales (1961–97), youngest daughter of the 8th Earl Spencer and the Hon. Mrs Shand Kydd), marriage dissolved 1996
Issue:
(1) HRH Prince William of Wales (Prince William Arthur Philip Louis), *born* 21 June 1982
(2) HRH Prince Henry of Wales (Prince Henry Charles Albert David), *born* 15 September 1984
Residences of the Prince of Wales: St James's Palace, London SW1A 1BS; Highgrove, Doughton, Tetbury, Glos GL8 8TN

HRH THE PRINCESS ROYAL (Princess Anne Elizabeth Alice Louise), KG, GCVO
Born 15 August 1950, declared The Princess Royal 1987
Married (1) 14 November 1973 Captain Mark Anthony Peter Phillips, CVO (*born* 22 September 1948); marriage dissolved 1992; (2) 12 December 1992 Captain Timothy James Hamilton Laurence, MVO, RN (*born* 1 March 1955)
Issue:

(1) Peter Mark Andrew Phillips, *born* 15 November 1977
(2) Zara Anne Elizabeth Phillips, *born* 15 May 1981
Residence: Gatcombe Park, Minchinhampton, Glos

HRH THE DUKE OF YORK (Prince Andrew Albert Christian Edward), CVO, ADC(P)
Born 19 February 1960, created Duke of York, Earl of Inverness and Baron Killyleagh 1986
Married 23 July 1986 Sarah Margaret Ferguson, now Sarah, Duchess of York (*born* 15 October 1959, younger daughter of Major Ronald Ferguson and Mrs Hector Barrantes), marriage dissolved 1996
Issue:
(1) HRH Princess Beatrice of York (Princess Beatrice Elizabeth Mary), *born* 8 August 1988
(2) HRH Princess Eugenie of York (Princess Eugenie Victoria Helena), *born* 23 March 1990
Residences: Buckingham Palace, London SW1A 1AA; Sunninghill Park, Ascot, Berks

HRH THE PRINCE EDWARD (Prince Edward Antony Richard Louis), CVO
Born 10 March 1964
Residence: Buckingham Palace, London SW1A 1AA

SISTER OF THE QUEEN

HRH THE PRINCESS MARGARET, COUNTESS OF SNOWDON, CI, GCVO, Royal Victorian Chain, Dame Grand Cross of the Order of St John of Jerusalem
Born 21 August 1930, younger daughter of King George VI and HM Queen Elizabeth the Queen Mother
Married 6 May 1960 Antony Charles Robert Armstrong-Jones, GCVO (*born* 7 March 1930, created Earl of Snowdon 1961, Constable of Caernarvon Castle); marriage dissolved 1978
Issue:
(1) David Albert Charles, Viscount Linley, *born* 3 November 1961, *married* 8 October 1993 the Hon. Serena Stanhope
(2) Lady Sarah Chatto (Sarah Frances Elizabeth), *born* 1 May 1964, *married* 14 July 1994 Daniel Chatto, and has issue, Samuel David Benedict Chatto, *born* 28 July 1996
Residence: Kensington Palace, London W8 4PU

MOTHER OF THE QUEEN

HM QUEEN ELIZABETH THE QUEEN MOTHER (Elizabeth Angela Marguerite), Lady of the Garter, Lady of the Thistle, CI, GCVO, GBE, Dame Grand Cross of the Order of St John, Royal Victorian Chain, Lord Warden and Admiral of the Cinque Ports and Constable of Dover Castle
Born 4 August 1900, youngest daughter of the 14th Earl of Strathmore and Kinghorne
Married 26 April 1923 (as Lady Elizabeth Bowes-Lyon) Prince Albert, Duke of York, afterwards King George VI (*see* page 127)
Residences: Clarence House, St James's Palace, London SW1A 1BA; Royal Lodge, Windsor Great Park, Berks; Castle of Mey, Caithness

AUNT OF THE QUEEN

HRH PRINCESS ALICE, DUCHESS OF GLOUCESTER (Alice Christabel), GCB, CI, GCVO, GBE, Grand Cordon of Al Kamal
Born 25 December 1901, third daughter of the 7th Duke of Buccleuch and Queensberry
Married 6 November 1935 (as Lady Alice Montagu-Douglas-Scott) Prince Henry, Duke of Gloucester, third son of King George V (*see* page 127)
Residence: Kensington Palace, London W8 4PU

COUSINS OF THE QUEEN

HRH THE DUKE OF GLOUCESTER (Prince Richard Alexander Walter George), KG, GCVO, Grand Prior of the Order of St John of Jerusalem
Born 26 August 1944
Married 8 July 1972 Birgitte Eva van Deurs, now HRH The Duchess of Gloucester, GCVO (*born* 20 June 1946, daughter of Asger Henriksen and Vivian van Deurs)
Issue:
(1)   Earl of Ulster (Alexander Patrick Gregers Richard), *born* 24 October 1974
(2)   Lady Davina Windsor (Davina Elizabeth Alice Benedikte), *born* 19 November 1977
(3)   Lady Rose Windsor (Rose Victoria Birgitte Louise), *born* 1 March 1980
Residence: Kensington Palace, London W8 4PU

HRH THE DUKE OF KENT (Prince Edward George Nicholas Paul Patrick), KG, GCMG, GCVO, ADC(P)
Born 9 October 1935
Married 8 June 1961 Katharine Lucy Mary Worsley, now HRH The Duchess of Kent, GCVO (*born* 22 February 1933, daughter of Sir William Worsley, Bt.)
Issue:
(1)   Earl of St Andrews (George Philip Nicholas), *born* 26 June 1962, *married* 9 January 1988 Sylvana Tomaselli, and has issue, Edward Edmund Maximilian George, Baron Downpatrick, *born* 2 December 1988; Lady Marina Charlotte Alexandra Katharine Windsor, *born* 30 September 1992; Lady Amelia Sophia Theodora Mary Margaret Windsor, *born* 24 August 1995
(2)   Lady Helen Taylor (Helen Marina Lucy), *born* 28 April 1964, *married* 18 July 1992 Timothy Taylor, and has issue, Columbus George Donald Taylor, *born* 6 August 1994; Cassius Edward Taylor, *born* 26 December 1996
(3)   Lord Nicholas Windsor (Nicholas Charles Edward Jonathan), *born* 25 July 1970

HRH PRINCESS ALEXANDRA, THE HON. LADY OGILVY (Princess Alexandra Helen Elizabeth Olga Christabel), GCVO
Born 25 December 1936
Married 24 April 1963 The Rt. Hon. Sir Angus Ogilvy, KCVO (*born* 14 September 1928, second son of 12th Earl of Airlie)
Issue:
(1)   James Robert Bruce Ogilvy, *born* 29 February 1964, *married* 30 July 1988 Julia Rawlinson, and has issue, Flora Alexandra Ogilvy, *born* 15 December 1994; Alexander Charles Ogilvy, *born* 12 November 1996

(2)   Marina Victoria Alexandra, Mrs Mowatt, *born* 31 July 1966, *married* 2 February 1990 Paul Mowatt (marriage dissolved 1997), and has issue, Zenouska May Mowatt, *born* 26 May 1990; Christian Alexander Mowatt, *born* 4 June 1993
Residence: Thatched House Lodge, Richmond Park, Surrey

HRH PRINCE MICHAEL OF KENT (Prince Michael George Charles Franklin), KCVO
Born 4 July 1942
Married 30 June 1978 Baroness Marie-Christine Agnes Hedwig Ida von Reibnitz, now HRH Princess Michael of Kent (*born* 15 January 1945, daughter of Baron Gunther von Reibnitz)
Issue:
(1)   Lord Frederick Windsor (Frederick Michael George David Louis), *born* 6 April 1979
(2)   Lady Gabriella Windsor (Gabriella Marina Alexandra Ophelia), *born* 23 April 1981
Residences: Kensington Palace, London W8 4PU; Nether Lypiatt Manor, Stroud, Glos.

ORDER OF SUCCESSION

1   HRH The Prince of Wales
2   HRH Prince William of Wales
3   HRH Prince Henry of Wales
4   HRH The Duke of York
5   HRH Princess Beatrice of York
6   HRH Princess Eugenie of York
7   HRH The Prince Edward
8   HRH The Princess Royal
9   Peter Phillips
10   Zara Phillips
11   HRH The Princess Margaret, Countess of Snowdon
12   Viscount Linley
13   Lady Sarah Chatto
14   Samuel Chatto
15   HRH The Duke of Gloucester
16   Earl of Ulster
17   Lady Davina Windsor
18   Lady Rose Windsor
19   HRH The Duke of Kent
20   Baron Downpatrick
21   Lady Marina Charlotte Windsor
22   Lady Amelia Windsor
23   Lord Nicholas Windsor
24   Lady Helen Taylor
25   Columbus Taylor
26   Cassius Taylor
27   Lord Frederick Windsor
28   Lady Gabriella Windsor
29   HRH Princess Alexandra, the Hon. Lady Ogilvy
30   James Ogilvy
31   Alexander Ogilvy
32   Flora Ogilvy
33   Marina, Mrs Paul Mowatt
34   Christian Mowatt
35   Zenouska Mowatt
36   The Earl of Harewood

The Earl of St Andrews and HRH Prince Michael of Kent lost the right of succession to the throne through marriage to a Roman Catholic. Their children remain in succession provided that they are in communion with the Church of England

Royal Households

THE QUEEN'S HOUSEHOLD

Office: Buckingham Palace, London SW1A 1AA
Tel: 0171-930 4832
Web: http://www.royal.gov.uk
The Lord Chamberlain is the most senior member of The Queen's Household and under him come the heads of the six departments: the Private Secretary, the Keeper of the Privy Purse, the Comptroller of the Lord Chamberlain's Office, the Master of the Household, the Crown Equerry, and the Director of the Royal Collection. Positions in these departments are full-time salaried posts.

There are also a number of honorary or now largely ceremonial appointments which carry no remuneration or a small honorarium. In the following list, most honorary appointments have been placed at the end; however, where this is not the case, such appointments are indicated by an asterisk.

GREAT OFFICERS OF STATE

Lord Chamberlain, The Lord Camoys, GCVO, PC
Lord Steward, The Viscount Ridley, KG, GCVO, TD
Master of the Horse, The Lord Somerleyton, KCVO

LADIES-IN-WAITING AND EQUERRIES

Mistress of the Robes, The Duchess of Grafton, GCVO
Ladies of the Bedchamber, The Countess of Airlie, DCVO; The Lady Farnham, CVO
Women of the Bedchamber, Hon. Mary Morrison, DCVO; Lady Susan Hussey, DCVO; Lady Dugdale, DCVO; The Lady Elton, CVO; Mrs Christian Adams (temp.)
Equerries, Lt.-Col. Sir Guy Acland, Bt., MVO; Sqn. Ldr. S. Brailsford

THE PRIVATE SECRETARY'S OFFICE
Buckingham Palace, London SW1A 1AA

Private Secretary to The Queen, The Rt Hon. Sir Robert Fellowes, GCB, GCVO (until Feb. 1999); Sir Robin Janvrin, KCVO, CB (from Feb. 1999)
Deputy Private Secretary, Sir Robin Janvrin, KCVO, CB (until Feb. 1999); Mrs M. Francis (from Feb. 1999)
Communications Secretary, S. Lewis
Assistant Private Secretary, Mrs M. Francis (until Feb. 1999)
Special Assistant to the Private Secretary, A. Dent
Chief Clerk, Mrs G. Middleburgh
Secretary to the Private Secretary, Miss E. Ash

PRESS OFFICE

Press Secretary, G. Crawford, LVO
Deputy Press Secretary, Miss P. Russell-Smith
Assistant Press Secretaries, R. Arbiter, LVO; D. Tuck

THE QUEEN'S ARCHIVES
Round Tower, Windsor Castle, Berks

Keeper of The Queen's Archives, The Rt Hon. Sir Robert Fellowes, GCB, GCVO
Assistant Keeper, O. Everett, CVO
Registrar, Lady de Bellaigue, MVO

THE PRIVY PURSE AND TREASURER'S OFFICE
Buckingham Palace, London SW1A 1AA

Keeper of the Privy Purse and Treasurer to The Queen, Sir Michael Peat, KCVO
Director of Property Services, J. Tiltman, LVO

Director of Royal Travel, Air Cdre the Hon. T. Elworthy
Director of Finance, Property Services and Royal Travel, S. Cawley
Deputy Keeper of the Privy Purse and Deputy Treasurer, J. Parsons, CVO
Chief Accountant and Paymaster, I. McGregor
Personnel Officer, Miss P. Lloyd
Land Agent, Sandringham, M. O'Lone, FRICS
Resident Factor, Balmoral, P. Ord, FRICS

THE LORD CHAMBERLAIN'S OFFICE
Buckingham Palace, London SW1A 1AA

Comptroller, Lt.-Col. W. H. M. Ross, CVO, OBE
Assistant Comptroller, Lt.-Col. A. Mather, CVO, OBE
Secretary, J. Spencer, MVO
Assistant Secretary, Miss A. Krysztofiak
State Invitations Assistant, J. O. Hope
Marshal of the Diplomatic Corps, Vice-Adm. Sir James Weatherall, KBE
Vice-Marshal, P. Astley, LVO

CENTRAL CHANCERY OF THE ORDERS OF KNIGHTHOOD
St James's Palace, London SW1A 1BS

Secretary, Lt.-Col. A. Mather, CVO, OBE
Assistant Secretary, Miss R. Wells, MVO

MASTER OF THE HOUSEHOLD'S DEPARTMENT
Buckingham Palace, London SW1A 1AA

Master of the Household, Maj.-Gen. Sir Simon Cooper, KCVO
Deputy Master of the Household, Lt.-Col. Sir Guy Acland, Bt., MVO
Assistants to the Master of the Household, M. T. Parker, MVO; A. Jarman; A. Smith
Chief Clerk, M. C. W. N. Jephson, LVO
Chief Housekeeper, Miss H. Colebrook, MVO
Palace Steward, P. S. Croasdale, RVM
Royal Chef, L. Mann, RVM
Superintendent, Windsor Castle, Maj. M. Davidson, MBE, BEM
Superintendent, The Palace of Holyroodhouse, Lt.-Col. D. Anderson, OBE

ROYAL MEWS DEPARTMENT
Buckingham Palace, London SW1W 0QH

Crown Equerry, Lt.-Col. S. Gilbart-Denham, CVO
Superintendent, Royal Mews, Buckingham Palace, Maj. I. Kelly

THE ROYAL COLLECTION
St James's Palace, London SW1A 1BS

Director of Royal Collection and Surveyor of The Queen's Works of Art, H. Roberts, CVO, FSA
Surveyor of The Queen's Pictures, C. Lloyd, LVO
Librarian, The Royal Library, Windsor Castle, O. Everett, CVO
Deputy Surveyor of The Queen's Works of Art, J. Marsden
Director of Media Affairs, R. Arbiter, LVO
Curator of the Print Room, The Hon. Mrs Roberts, LVO
Financial Director, M. Stevens
Financial Controller, Mrs G. Johnson
Administrator and Assistant to The Surveyors, D. Rankin-Hunt, MVO, TD
Senior Picture Restorer, Miss V. Pemberton-Pigott, MVO
Chief Restorer, Old Master Drawings, A. Donnithorne
Senior Furniture Restorer, E. Fancourt, MVO, RVM
Armourer, J. Jackson, RVM
Chief Binder, R. Day, MVO, RVM

ROYAL COLLECTION ENTERPRISES LTD
Managing Director, M. E. K. Hewlett, LVO

ECCLESIASTICAL HOUSEHOLD

Clerk of the Closet, The Bishop of Derby
Deputy Clerk of the Closet, Revd W. Booth
Chaplains and Extra Chaplains to The Queen: approx. 30–40
Dean of the Chapels Royal, The Bishop of London
Sub-Dean of the Chapels Royal, Revd W. Booth
Organist, Choirmaster and Composer, R. J. Popplewell, MVO, FRCO, FRCM
Domestic Chaplain, Buckingham Palace, Revd W. Booth
Domestic Chaplain, Windsor Castle, The Dean of Windsor
Domestic Chaplain, Sandringham, Revd Canon G. R. Hall

MEDICAL HOUSEHOLD

Head of the Medical Household and Physician to The Queen, R. Thompson, DM, FRCP
Serjeant Surgeon, B. T. Jackson, FRCS
Apothecary to The Queen and to the Household, N. R. Southward, CVO
Apothecary to the Household at Windsor, J. Holliday
Apothecary to the Household at Sandringham, I. K. Campbell, D.O bst., FRCGP
Coroner of The Queen's Household, J. Burton, CBE

OTHER HONORARY/CEREMONIAL APPOINTMENTS

Lord High Almoner, The Bishop of Wakefield
Master of The Queen's Music, M. Williamson, CBE, AO
Poet Laureate, Ted Hughes, OM, OBE
Keeper of the Royal Philatelic Collection, C. Goodwyn
Bargemaster, R. Crouch
Swan Warden, Prof. C. Perrins, LVO
Swan Marker, D. Barber

POLITICAL (GOVERNMENT WHIPS)
(*see also* page 277)

Captain, Honourable Corps of Gentlemen-at-Arms (Chief Whip in the Lords), The Lord Carter, PC
Captain, Queen's Bodyguard of the Yeomen of the Guard (Deputy Chief Whip in the Lords), The Lord McIntosh of Haringey
Lords-in-Waiting, The Lord Hoyle; The Lord Hunt of King's Heath
Baronesses-in-Waiting, The Baroness Farrington of Ribbleton; The Baroness Ramsay of Cartvale; The Baroness Amos
Treasurer of the Household (Deputy Chief Whip in the Commons), K. Bradley, MP
Comptroller of the Household, T. McAvoy, MP
Vice-Chamberlain, G. Allen, MP

ARMED FORCES

Gold Sticks, Maj.-Gen. Lord Michael Fitzalan-Howard, GCVO, CB, CBE, MC; Gen. Sir Desmond Fitzpatrick, GCB, GCVO, DSO, MBE, MC
Vice-Admiral of the United Kingdom, Adm. Sir Nicholas Hunt, GCB, LVO
Rear-Admiral of the United Kingdom, Adm. Sir John Black
First and Principal Naval Aide-de-Camp, Adm. Sir Michael Boyce, KCB, OBE
Flag Aide-de-Camp, Adm. Sir John Brigstocke, KCB
Aides-de-Camp-General, Gen. Sir Charles Guthrie, GCB, LVO, OBE; Gen. Sir Jeremy Mackenzie, GCB, OBE
Air Aides-de-Camp, Air Chief Marshal Sir Richard Johns, GCB, CBE, LVO; Air Chief Marshal Sir John Allison, KCB, CBE

Gentleman Usher to the Sword of State, Adm. Sir Michael Layard, KCB, CBE
Constable and Governor of Windsor Castle, Gen. Sir Patrick Palmer, KBE
Governor of Edinburgh Castle, Maj.-Gen. M. J. Strudwick, CBE

BODYGUARDS

THE HONOURABLE CORPS OF GENTLEMEN-AT-ARMS
Captain, The Lord Carter, PC
Lieutenant, Lt.-Col. R. Mayfield, DSO
Clerk of the Cheque and Adjutant, Col. D. Fanshawe, OBE;
Gentlemen of the Corps: 27

THE QUEEN'S BODY GUARD OF THE YEOMEN OF THE GUARD
Captain, The Lord McIntosh of Haringey
Lieutenant, Col. G. W. Tufnell
Clerk of the Cheque and Adjutant, Col. S. Longsdon
Yeomen of the Guard: 81

THE QUEEN'S HOUSEHOLD IN SCOTLAND

Hereditary Lord High Constable of Scotland, The Earl of Erroll
Hereditary Master of the Household in Scotland, The Duke of Argyll
Lord Lyon King of Arms, Sir Malcolm Innes of Edingight, KCVO, WS
Hereditary Banner-Bearer for Scotland, The Earl of Dundee
Hereditary Bearer of the National Flag of Scotland, The Earl of Lauderdale
Hereditary Keeper of the Palace of Holyroodhouse, The Duke of Hamilton and Brandon
Historiographer, Prof. T. C. Smout, CBE, FBA, FRSE, FSAScot.
Botanist, Prof. D. Henderson, CBE, FRSE
Painter and Limner, vacant
Sculptor in Ordinary, Prof. Sir Eduardo Paolozzi, CBE, RA
Astronomer, Prof. J. Brown, PH.D., FRSE
Heralds and Pursuivants, see page 282

ECCLESIASTICAL HOUSEHOLD

Dean of the Chapel Royal, Very Revd J. Harkness, CB, OBE
Dean of the Order of the Thistle, Very Revd G. I. Macmillan
Chaplains in Ordinary: 10
Domestic Chaplain, Balmoral, Revd R. P. Sloan

MEDICAL HOUSEHOLD

Physicians in Scotland, P. Brunt, OBE, MD, FRCP; A. Toft, CBE, FRCPE
Surgeons in Scotland, J. Engeset, FRCS; I. Macintyre
Apothecary to the Household at Balmoral, D. J. A. Glass
Apothecary to the Household at the Palace of Holyroodhouse, Dr J. Cormack, MD, FRCPE, FRCGP

ROYAL COMPANY OF ARCHERS (QUEEN'S BODYGUARD FOR SCOTLAND)

Captain-General and Gold Stick for Scotland, Maj. Sir Hew Hamilton-Dalrymple, Bt., KCVO
Adjutant, Maj. the Hon. Sir Lachlan Maclean, Bt.
President of the Council and Silver Stick for Scotland, The Duke of Buccleuch and Queensberry, KT, VRD
Secretary, Capt. J. D. B. Younger
Treasurer, J. M. Haldane of Gleneagles
Members on the active list: c.400

HOUSEHOLD OF THE PRINCE PHILIP, DUKE OF EDINBURGH

Office: Buckingham Palace, London SW1A 1AA
Tel: 0171-930 4832

Treasurer, Sir Brian McGrath, KCVO
Private Secretary, Brig. M. G. Hunt-Davis, CVO, CBE
Equerry, Lt.-Cdr. R. Tarran
Temporary Equerries, Capt. P. Wise; Lt.-Col. P. Denning;
Capt. S. Courtauld
Chief Clerk and Accountant, G. D. Partington

HOUSEHOLD OF QUEEN ELIZABETH THE QUEEN MOTHER

Office: Clarence House, St James's Palace, London SW1A
1BA
Tel: 0171-930 3141

Lord Chamberlain, The Earl of Crawford and Balcarres, KT,
PC
Private Secretary, Comptroller and Equerry, Capt. Sir Alastair
Aird, GCVO
Assistant Private Secretary and Equerry, Maj. R. Seymour, CVO
Treasurer and Extra Equerry, Hon. N. Assheton
Treasurer Emeritus and Equerry, Maj. Sir Ralph Anstruther,
Bt., GCVO, MC
Equerry, Capt. W. de Rouet (temp.)
Apothecary to the Household, Dr N. Southward, CVO
Surgeon-Apothecary to the Household (Royal Lodge, Windsor), J.
Holliday
Ladies of the Bedchamber, The Lady Grimthorpe, DCVO; The
Countess of Scarbrough
Women of the Bedchamber, Dame Frances Campbell-Preston,
DCVO; Lady Angela Oswald, LVO; The Hon. Mrs
Rhodes; Mrs Michael Gordon-Lennox
Clerk Comptroller, A. Kirkpatrick-Smith
Information Officer, Mrs R. Murphy, LVO
Clerks, Miss F. Fletcher, LVO; Mrs W. Stevens

HOUSEHOLD OF THE PRINCE OF WALES

Office: St James's Palace, London SW1A 1BS
Tel: 0171-930 4832

Private Secretary and Treasurer, S. M. J. Lamport
Deputy Private Secretary, M. Bolland
Assistant Private Secretaries, J. Skan; N. S. Archer; Ms E.
Buchanan
Press Secretary, Miss S. Henney
Deputy Press Secretary, Mrs C. Harris
Equerry, Lt. Cdr. J. Lavery, RN
Secretary to the Duchy of Cornwall and Keeper of the Records,
W. R. A. Ross

HOUSEHOLD OF THE DUKE OF YORK

Office: Buckingham Palace, London SW1A 1AA
Tel: 0171-930 4832

Private Secretary, Treasurer and Extra Equerry, Capt. R. N.
Blair, LVO, RN

Comptroller and Assistant Private Secretary, Cdr. C. Manley,
OBE
Equerry, Capt. R. L. Gerrard-Wright

HOUSEHOLD OF THE PRINCE EDWARD

Office: Buckingham Palace, London SW1A 1AA
Tel: 0171-930 4832

Private Secretary, Lt.-Col. S. G. O'Dwyer, LVO
Clerk, Mrs L. Sharp

HOUSEHOLD OF THE PRINCESS ROYAL

Office: Buckingham Palace, London SW1A 1AA
Tel: 0171-930 4832

Private Secretary, R. McGuigan
Assistant Private Secretary, Mrs S. Gee
Ladies-in-Waiting, Lady Carew Pole, LVO; Mrs Andrew
Feilden, LVO; The Hon. Mrs Legge-Bourke, LVO; Mrs
William Nunneley, LVO; Mrs Timothy Holderness-
Roddam; Mrs Charles Ritchie; Mrs David Bowes Lyon

HOUSEHOLD OF THE PRINCESS MARGARET, COUNTESS OF SNOWDON

Office: Kensington Palace, London W8 4PU
Tel: 0171-930 3141

Private Secretary, The Viscount Ullswater, PC
Treasurer, Maj. The Lord Napier and Ettrick, KCVO
Lady-in-Waiting, The Hon. Mrs Whitehead, LVO

HOUSEHOLD OF THE DUKE AND DUCHESS OF GLOUCESTER

Office: Kensington Palace, London W8 4PU
Tel: 0171-937 6374

Private Secretary, Comptroller and Equerry, Maj. N. M. L.
Barne, LVO
Assistant Private Secretary to the Duchess of Gloucester, Miss S.
Marland, LVO
Ladies-in-Waiting, Mrs Michael Wigley, CVO; Mrs Euan
McCorquodale, LVO; Mrs Howard Page, LVO

HOUSEHOLD OF PRINCESS ALICE, DUCHESS OF GLOUCESTER

Office: Kensington Palace, London W8 4PU
Tel: 0171-937 6374

Private Secretary, Comptroller and Equerry, Maj. N. M. L.
Barne, LVO
Ladies-in-Waiting, Dame Jean Maxwell-Scott, DCVO; Mrs
Michael Harvey, LVO

HOUSEHOLD OF THE DUKE AND DUCHESS OF KENT

Office: York House, St James's Palace, London SW1 1BQ
Tel: 0171-930 4872

Private Secretary, N. C. Adamson, OBE
Temporary Equerry, Capt. D. Hampshire
Ladies-in-Waiting, Mrs Fiona Henderson, CVO; Mrs Colin Marsh, LVO; Mrs Julian Tomkins; Mrs Peter Troughton; Mrs Richard Beckett

HOUSEHOLD OF PRINCESS ALEXANDRA, THE HON. LADY OGILVY

Office: Buckingham Palace, London SW1A 1AA
Tel: 0171-930 1860

Comptroller and Private Secretary, Capt. N. Blair, LVO, RN
Lady-in-Waiting, Lady Mary Mumford, DCVO

HOUSEHOLD OF PRINCE AND PRINCESS MICHAEL OF KENT

Office: Kensington Palace, London W8 4PU
Tel: 0171-938 3519

Personal Secretaries, Miss C. Jenkins, Miss K. Garrod
Ladies-in-Waiting, The Hon. Mrs Sanders; Miss A. Frost; Mrs J. Fellowes

Royal Salutes

ENGLAND

A salute of 62 guns is fired on the wharf at the Tower of London on the following occasions:

(a) the anniversaries of the birth, accession and coronation of the Sovereign
(b) the anniversary of the birth of HM Queen Elizabeth the Queen Mother
(c) the anniversary of the birth of HRH Prince Philip, Duke of Edinburgh

A salute of 41 guns only is fired on extraordinary and triumphal occasions, e.g. on the occasion of the Sovereign opening, proroguing or dissolving Parliament in person, or when passing through London in procession, except when otherwise ordered.

A salute of 41 guns is fired from the two saluting stations in London (the Tower of London and Hyde Park) on the occasion of the birth of a royal infant.

Constable of the Royal Palace and Fortress of London, Field Marshal the Lord Inge, GCB
Lieutenant of the Tower of London, Lt.-Gen. Sir Anthony Denison-Smith, KBE
Resident Governor and Keeper of the Jewel House, Maj.-Gen. G. Field, CB, OBE

Master Gunner of St James's Park, Field Marshal the Lord Vincent of Coleshill, GBE, KCB, DSO
Master Gunner within the Tower, Col. S. Lalor

SCOTLAND

Royal salutes are authorized at Edinburgh Castle and Stirling Castle, although in practice Edinburgh Castle is the only operating saluting station in Scotland.

A salute of 21 guns is fired on the following occasions:

(a) the anniversaries of the birth, accession and coronation of the Sovereign
(b) the anniversary of the birth of HM Queen Elizabeth the Queen Mother
(c) the anniversary of the birth of HRH Prince Philip, Duke of Edinburgh

A salute of 21 guns is fired in Edinburgh on the occasion of the opening of the General Assembly of the Church of Scotland.

A salute of 21 guns may also be fired in Edinburgh on the arrival of HM The Queen, HM Queen Elizabeth the Queen Mother, or a member of the royal family who is a Royal Highness on an official visit.

Royal Finances

FUNDING

THE CIVIL LIST

The Civil List dates back to the late 17th century. It was originally used by the sovereign to supplement hereditary revenues for paying the salaries of judges, ambassadors and other government officers as well as the expenses of the royal household. In 1760 on the accession of George III it was decided that the Civil List would be provided by Parliament to cover all relevant expenditure in return for the King surrendering the hereditary revenues of the Crown. At that time Parliament undertook to pay the salaries of judges, ambassadors, etc. In 1831 Parliament agreed also to meet the costs of the royal palaces in return for a reduction in the Civil List. Each sovereign has agreed to continue this arrangement.

The Civil List paid to The Queen is charged on the Consolidated Fund. Until 1972, the amount of money allocated annually under the Civil List was set for the duration of a reign. The system was then altered to a fixed annual payment for ten years but from 1975 high inflation made an annual review necessary. The system of payments reverted to the practice of a fixed annual payment for ten years from 1 January 1991.

The Civil List Acts provide for other members of the royal family to receive parliamentary annuities from government funds to meet the expenses of carrying out their official duties. Since 1975 The Queen has reimbursed the Treasury for the annuities paid to the Duke of Gloucester, the Duke of Kent and Princess Alexandra. Since 1993 The Queen has reimbursed all the annuities except those paid to herself, Queen Elizabeth the Queen Mother and the Duke of Edinburgh.

The Prince of Wales does not receive a parliamentary annuity. He derives his income from the revenues of the Duchy of Cornwall and these monies meet the official and private expenses of the Prince of Wales and his family. The annual payments for the years 1991–2000 are:

The Queen	£7,900,000
Queen Elizabeth the Queen Mother	643,000
The Duke of Edinburgh	359,000
*The Duke of York	249,000
*The Prince Edward	96,000
*The Princess Royal	228,000
*The Princess Margaret, Countess of Snowdon	219,000
*Princess Alice, Duchess of Gloucester	87,000
*The Duke of Gloucester	175,000
*The Duke of Kent	236,000
*Princess Alexandra	225,000
	10,417,000
*Refunded to the Treasury	1,515,000
Total	8,902,000

GRANTS-IN-AID

Several government departments provide grants-in-aid to the royal household to meet various official expenses. Property Services grant-in-aid is provided by the Department for Culture, Media and Sport for the upkeep of English occupied royal palaces which are used as offices, for official or ceremonial purposes and to which there is public access. Royal Travel grant-in-aid is provided by the Department of the Environment, Transport and the Regions to meet the cost of official royal travel by air and rail, using mainly aircraft from 32 (The Royal) Squadron, chartered commercial aircraft for major overseas state visits and the Royal Train. From 1 April 1998 Communications and Information grant-in-aid has been provided by the Central Office of Information to meet the cost of media and information services.

In July 1998 it was announced that control of the budget for overseas royal visits would be transferred from the Foreign and Commonwealth Office to the royal household.

Grant-in-aid for 1998–9 is:

Property Services	£15,800,000
Royal Travel	16,400,000
Communications and Information	471,000

THE PRIVY PURSE

The funds received by the Privy Purse pay for official expenses incurred by The Queen as head of state and for some of The Queen's private expenditure. The revenues of the Duchy of Lancaster are the principal source of income for the Privy Purse. The revenues of the Duchy were retained by George III in 1760 when the hereditary revenues were surrendered in exchange for the Civil List.

PERSONAL INCOME

The Queen's personal income derives mostly from investments, and is used to meet private expenditure.

DEPARTMENTAL VOTES

Items of expenditure connected with the official duties of the royal family which fall directly on votes of government departments include:

Ministry of Defence – equerries
Foreign and Commonwealth Office – Marshal of the Diplomatic Corps; costs (other than travel costs) associated with overseas visits at the request of government departments
HM Treasury – Central Chancery of the Orders of Knighthood
The Post Office – postal services

TAXATION

The sovereign is not legally liable to pay income tax, capital gains tax or inheritance tax. After income tax was reintroduced in 1842, some income tax was paid voluntarily by the sovereign but over a long period these payments were phased out. In 1992 The Queen offered to pay tax on a voluntary basis from 6 April 1993, and the Prince of Wales to pay tax on a voluntary basis on his income from the Duchy of Cornwall. (He was already taxed in all other respects.)

The main provisions for The Queen and the Prince of Wales to pay tax, set out in a Memorandum of Understanding on Royal Taxation presented to Parliament on 11 February 1993, are that The Queen will pay income tax and capital gains tax in respect of her private income and assets, and on the proportion of the income and capital gains of the Privy Purse used for private purposes. Inheritance tax will be paid on The Queen's assets, except for those which pass to the next sovereign, whether automatically or by gift or bequest. The Prince of Wales will pay income tax on income from the Duchy of Cornwall used for private purposes.

The Prince of Wales has confirmed that he intends to pay tax on the same basis following his accession to the throne.

Other members of the royal family are subject to tax as for any taxpayer.

Military Ranks and Titles

THE QUEEN

Lord High Admiral of the United Kingdom

Colonel-in-Chief
The Life Guards; The Blues and Royals (Royal Horse Guards and 1st Dragoons); The Royal Scots Dragoon Guards (Carabiniers and Greys); The Queen's Royal Lancers; Royal Tank Regiment; Corps of Royal Engineers; Grenadier Guards; Coldstream Guards; Scots Guards; Irish Guards; Welsh Guards; The Royal Welch Fusiliers; The Queen's Lancashire Regiment; The Argyll and Sutherland Highlanders (Princess Louise's); The Royal Green Jackets; Adjutant General's Corps; The Royal Mercian and Lancastrian Yeomanry; The Governor General's Horse Guards (of Canada); The King's Own Calgary Regiment; Canadian Forces Military Engineers Branch; Royal 22e Regiment (of Canada); Governor-General's Foot Guards (of Canada); The Canadian Grenadier Guards; Le Regiment de la Chaudiere (of Canada); 2nd Bn Royal New Brunswick Regiment (North Shore); The 48th Highlanders of Canada; The Argyll and Sutherland Highlanders of Canada (Princess Louise's); The Calgary Highlanders; Royal Australian Engineers; Royal Australian Infantry Corps; Royal Australian Army Ordnance Corps; Royal Australian Army Nursing Corps; The Corps of Royal New Zealand Engineers; Royal New Zealand Infantry Regiment; Royal Malta Artillery; The Malawi Rifles

Affiliated Colonel-in-Chief
The Queen's Gurkha Engineers

Captain-General
Royal Regiment of Artillery; The Honourable Artillery Company; Combined Cadet Force Association; Royal Regiment of Canadian Artillery; Royal Regiment of Australian Artillery; Royal Regiment of New Zealand Artillery; Royal New Zealand Armoured Corps

Patron
Royal Army Chaplains' Department

Air Commodore-in-Chief
Royal Auxiliary Air Force; Royal Air Force Regiment; Air Reserve (of Canada); Royal Australian Air Force Reserve; Territorial Air Force (of New Zealand)

Commandant-in-Chief
Royal Air Force College, Cranwell

Hon. Air Commodore
RAF Marham

HRH THE PRINCE PHILIP, DUKE OF EDINBURGH

Admiral of the Fleet
Field Marshal
Marshal of the Royal Air Force
Admiral of the Fleet, Royal Australian Navy
Field Marshal, Australian Military Forces
Marshal of the Royal Australian Air Force
Admiral of the Fleet, Royal New Zealand Navy

Field Marshal, New Zealand Army
Marshal of the Royal New Zealand Air Force
Captain-General, Royal Marines

Admiral
Royal Canadian Sea Cadets

Colonel-in-Chief
The Royal Gloucestershire, Berkshire and Wiltshire Regiment; The Highlanders (Seaforth, Gordons and Camerons); Corps of Royal Electrical and Mechanical Engineers; Intelligence Corps; Army Cadet Force Association; The Royal Canadian Regiment; The Royal Hamilton Light Infantry (Wentworth Regiment) (of Canada); The Cameron Highlanders of Ottawa; The Queen's Own Cameron Highlanders of Canada; The Seaforth Highlanders of Canada; The Royal Canadian Army Cadets; The Royal Corps of Australian Electrical and Mechanical Engineers; The Australian Cadet Corps

Deputy Colonel-in-Chief
The Queen's Royal Hussars (Queen's Own and Royal Irish)

Colonel
Grenadier Guards

Hon. Colonel
City of Edinburgh Universities Officers' Training Corps; The Trinidad and Tobago Regiment

Air Commodore-in-Chief
Air Training Corps; Royal Canadian Air Cadets

Hon. Air Commodore
RAF Kinloss

HM QUEEN ELIZABETH THE QUEEN MOTHER

Colonel-in-Chief
1st The Queen's Dragoon Guards; The Queen's Royal Hussars (Queen's Own and Royal Irish); 9th/12th Royal Lancers (Prince of Wales's); The King's Regiment; The Royal Anglian Regiment; The Light Infantry; The Black Watch (Royal Highland Regiment); Royal Army Medical Corps; The Black Watch (Royal Highland Regiment) of Canada; The Toronto Scottish Regiment; Canadian Forces Medical Services; Royal Australian Army Medical Corps; Royal New Zealand Army Medical Corps

Hon. Colonel
The Royal Yeomanry; The London Scottish; Inns of Court and City Yeomanry; The King's Own Yorkshire Yeomanry (Light Infantry)

Commandant-in-Chief
Women in the Royal Navy; Women, Royal Air Force; Royal Air Force Central Flying School

HRH THE PRINCE OF WALES

Captain, Royal Navy
Group Captain, Royal Air Force

Colonel-in-Chief
The Royal Dragoon Guards; The 22nd (Cheshire) Regiment; The Royal Regiment of Wales (24th/41st Foot); The Parachute Regiment; The Royal Gurkha Rifles; Army Air Corps; The Royal Canadian Dragoons; Lord Strathcona's Horse (Royal Canadians); Royal Regiment of Canada; Royal Winnipeg Rifles; Air Reserve Group of Air Command (of Canada); Royal Australian Armoured Corps; The Royal Pacific Islands Regiment

Deputy Colonel-in-Chief
The Highlanders (Seaforth, Gordons and Camerons)

Colonel
Welsh Guards

Air Commodore-in-Chief
Royal New Zealand Air Force

Hon. Air Commodore
RAF Valley

HRH THE DUKE OF YORK

Lieutenant-Commander, Royal Navy

Admiral
Sea Cadet Corps

Colonel-in-Chief
The Staffordshire Regiment (The Prince of Wales's); The Royal Irish Regiment (27th (Inniskilling), 83rd, 87th and The Ulster Defence Regiment); Royal New Zealand Army Logistic Regiment; The Queen's York Rangers (First Americans)

Hon. Air Commodore
RAF Lossiemouth

HRH THE PRINCESS ROYAL

Rear Admiral
Chief Commandant for Women in the Royal Navy

Colonel-in-Chief
The Household Cavalry; The King's Royal Hussars; Royal Corps of Signals; The Royal Scots (The Royal Regiment); The Worcestershire and Sherwood Foresters Regiment (29th/45th Foot); The Royal Logistic Corps; 8th Canadian Hussars (Princess Louise's); Canadian Forces Communications and Electronics Branch; The Grey and Simcoe Foresters; The Royal Regina Rifle Regiment; Royal Australian Corps of Signals; Royal New Zealand Corps of Signals; Royal New Zealand Nursing Corps

Affiliated Colonel-in-Chief
The Queen's Gurkha Signals; The Queen's Own Gurkha Transport Regiment

Hon. Colonel
University of London Officers' Training Corps

Hon. Air Commodore
RAF Lyneham; University of London Air Squadron

HRH THE PRINCESS MARGARET, COUNTESS OF SNOWDON

Colonel-in-Chief
The Light Dragoons; The Royal Highland Fusiliers (Princess Margaret's Own Glasgow and Ayrshire Regiment); Queen Alexandra's Royal Army Nursing Corps; The Highland Fusiliers of Canada; The Princess Louise Fusiliers (of Canada); The Bermuda Regiment

Deputy Colonel-in-Chief
The Royal Anglian Regiment

Hon. Air Commodore
RAF Coningsby

HRH PRINCESS ALICE, DUCHESS OF GLOUCESTER

Air Chief Marshal

Colonel-in-Chief
The King's Own Scottish Borderers; Royal Australian Corps of Transport

Deputy Colonel-in-Chief
The King's Royal Hussars; The Royal Anglian Regiment

Air Chief Commandant
Women, Royal Air Force

HRH THE DUKE OF GLOUCESTER

Hon. Air Marshal

Deputy Colonel-in-Chief
The Royal Gloucestershire, Berkshire and Wiltshire Regiment; The Royal Logistic Corps

Hon. Colonel
Royal Monmouthshire Royal Engineers (Militia)

Hon. Air Commodore
RAF Odiham

HRH THE DUCHESS OF GLOUCESTER

Colonel-in-Chief
Royal Australian Army Educational Corps; Royal New Zealand Army Educational Corps

Deputy Colonel-in-Chief
Adjutant-General's Corps

HRH THE DUKE OF KENT

Field Marshal
Hon. Air Chief Marshal

Colonel-in-Chief
The Royal Regiment of Fusiliers; The Devonshire and Dorset Regiment; The Lorne Scots (Peel, Dufferin and Hamilton Regiment)

Deputy Colonel-in-Chief
The Royal Scots Dragoon Guards (Carabiniers and
Greys)

Colonel
Scots Guards

Hon. Air Commodore
RAF Leuchars

HRH THE DUCHESS OF KENT

Hon. Major-General

Colonel-in-Chief
The Prince of Wales's Own Regiment of Yorkshire

Deputy Colonel-in-Chief
The Royal Dragoon Guards; Adjutant-General's Corps;
The Royal Logistic Corps

HRH PRINCE MICHAEL OF KENT

Major (retd), The Royal Hussars (Prince of Wales's Own)

Hon. Commodore
Royal Naval Reserve

HRH PRINCESS ALEXANDRA, THE HON. LADY OGILVY

Patron
Queen Alexandra's Royal Naval Nursing Service

Colonel-in-Chief
The King's Own Royal Border Regiment; The Queen's
Own Rifles of Canada; The Canadian Scottish
Regiment (Princess Mary's)

Deputy Colonel-in-Chief
The Queen's Royal Lancers; The Light Infantry

Deputy Hon. Colonel
The Royal Yeomanry; The King's Own Yorkshire
Yeomanry (Light Infantry)

Patron and Air Chief Commandant
Princess Mary's Royal Air Force Nursing Service

The House of Windsor

King George V assumed by royal proclamation (17 July 1917) for his House and family, as well as for all descendants in the male line of Queen Victoria who are subjects of these realms, the name of Windsor.

KING GEORGE V (George Frederick Ernest Albert), second son of King Edward VII, *born* 3 June 1865; *married* 6 July 1893 HSH Princess Victoria Mary Augusta Louise Olga Pauline Claudine Agnes of Teck (Queen Mary, *born* 26 May 1867; *died* 24 March 1953); *succeeded* to the throne 6 May 1910; *died* 20 January 1936. *Issue:*

1. HRH PRINCE EDWARD Albert Christian George Andrew Patrick David, *born* 23 June 1894, *succeeded* to the throne as King Edward VIII, 20 January 1936; *abdicated* 11 December 1936; created *Duke of Windsor* 1937; *married* 3 June 1937, Mrs Wallis Warfield (Her Grace The Duchess of Windsor, *born* 19 June 1896; *died* 24 April 1986), *died* 28 May 1972

2. HRH PRINCE ALBERT Frederick Arthur George, *born* 14 December 1895, *created* Duke of York 1920; *married* 26 April 1923, Lady Elizabeth Bowes-Lyon, youngest daughter of the 14th Earl of Strathmore and Kinghorne (HM Queen Elizabeth the Queen Mother, *see* page 117), *succeeded* to the throne as King George VI, 11 December 1936; *died* 6 February 1952, having had issue (*see* page 117)

3. HRH PRINCESS (Victoria Alexandra Alice) MARY, *born* 25 April 1897, *created* Princess Royal 1932; *married* 28 February 1922, Viscount Lascelles, later the 6th Earl of Harewood (1882–1947), *died* 28 March 1965. *Issue:*
   (1) George Henry Hubert Lascelles, 7th Earl of Harewood, KBE, *born* 7 February 1923; *married* (1) 1949, Maria (Marion) Stein (marriage dissolved 1967); *issue*, (*a*) David Henry George, Viscount Lascelles, *born* 1950; (*b*) James Edward, *born* 1953; (*c*)

(Robert) Jeremy Hugh, *born* 1955; (2) 1967, Mrs Patricia Tuckwell; *issue*, (*d*) Mark Hubert, *born* 1964
   (2) Gerald David Lascelles (1924–98), *married* (1) 1952, Miss Angela Dowding (marriage dissolved 1978); *issue*, (*a*) Henry Ulick, *born* 1953; (2) 1978, Mrs Elizabeth Colvin; *issue*, (*b*) Martin David, *born* 1962

4. HRH PRINCE HENRY William Frederick Albert, *born* 31 March 1900, *created* Duke of Gloucester, Earl of Ulster and Baron Culloden 1928, *married* 6 November 1935, Lady Alice Christabel Montagu-Douglas-Scott, daughter of the 7th Duke of Buccleuch (HRH Princess Alice, Duchess of Gloucester, *see* page 118); *died* 10 June 1974. *Issue:*
   (1) HRH Prince William Henry Andrew Frederick, *born* 18 December 1941; *accidentally killed* 28 August 1972
   (2) HRH Prince Richard Alexander Walter George (HRH The Duke of Gloucester), *see* page 118

5. HRH PRINCE GEORGE Edward Alexander Edmund, *born* 20 December 1902, *created* Duke of Kent, Earl of St Andrews and Baron Downpatrick 1934, *married* 29 November 1934, HRH Princess Marina of Greece and Denmark (*born* 30 November os, 1906; *died* 27 August 1968); *killed on active service*, 25 August 1942. *Issue:*
   (1) HRH Prince Edward George Nicholas Paul Patrick (HRH The Duke of Kent), *see* page 118
   (2) HRH Princess Alexandra Helen Elizabeth Olga Christabel (HRH Princess Alexandra, the Hon. Lady Ogilvy), *see* page 118
   (3) HRH Prince Michael George Charles Franklin (HRH Prince Michael of Kent), *see* page 118

6. HRH PRINCE JOHN Charles Francis, *born* 12 July 1905; *died* 18 January 1919

Descendants of Queen Victoria

QUEEN VICTORIA (Alexandrina Victoria), *born* 24 May 1819; *succeeded* to the throne 20 June 1837; *married* 10 February 1840 (Francis) Albert Augustus Charles Emmanuel, Duke of Saxony, Prince of Saxe-Coburg and Gotha (HRH Albert, Prince Consort, *born* 26 August 1819, *died* 14 December 1861); *died* 22 January 1901. *Issue:*

1. HRH PRINCESS VICTORIA Adelaide Mary Louisa (Princess Royal) (1840–1901), *m.* 1858, Friedrich III (1831–88), German Emperor March–June 1888. *Issue:*
   (1) HIM Wilhelm II (1859–1941), German Emperor 1888–1918, *m.* (1) 1881 Princess Augusta Victoria of Schleswig-Holstein-Sonderburg-Augustenburg (1858–1921); (2) 1922 Princess Hermine of Reuss (1887–1947). *Issue:*
   (*a*) Prince Wilhelm (1882–1951), *Crown Prince* 1888–1918, *m.* 1905 Duchess Cecilie of Mecklenburg-Schwerin; *issue:* Prince Wilhelm (1906–40); Prince Louis Ferdinand (1907–94), *m.* 1938 Grand Duchess Kira (*see* page 128); Prince Hubertus (1909–50); Prince Friedrich Georg (1911–66); Princess Alexandrine Irene (1915–80); Princess Cecilie (1917–75)
   (*b*) Prince Eitel-Friedrich (1883–1942), *m.* 1906 Duchess Sophie of Oldenburg (marriage dissolved 1926)
   (*c*) Prince Adalbert (1884–1948), *m.* 1914 Duchess Adelheid of Saxe-Meiningen; *issue:* Princess Victoria Marina (1917–81); Prince Wilhelm Victor (1919–89)
   (*d*) Prince August Wilhelm (1887–1949), *m.* 1908 Princess Alexandra of Schleswig-Holstein-Sonderburg-Glücksburg (marriage dissolved 1920); *issue:* Prince Alexander (1912–85)
   (*e*) Prince Oskar (1888–1958), *m.* 1914 Countess von Ruppin; *issue:* Prince Oskar (1915–39); Prince Burchard (1917–88); Princess Herzeleide (1918–89); Prince Wilhelm-Karl (*b.* 1922)

(*f*) Prince Joachim (1890–1920), *m.* 1916 Princess Marie of Anhalt; *issue:* Prince (Karl) Franz Joseph (1916–75), and has issue
   (*g*) Princess Viktoria Luise (1892–1980), *m.* 1913 Ernst, Duke of Brunswick 1913–18 (1887–1953); *issue:* Prince Ernst (1914–87); Prince Georg (*b.* 1915), *m.* 1946 Princess Sophie of Greece (*see* page 128) and has issue (two sons, one daughter); Princess Frederika (1917–81), *m.* 1938 Paul I, King of the Hellenes (*see* page 128); Prince Christian (1919–81); Prince Welf Heinrich (*b.* 1923)
   (2) Princess Charlotte (1860–1919), *m.* 1878 Bernhard, Duke of Saxe-Meiningen 1914 (1851–1914). *Issue:* Princess Feodora (1879–1945), *m.* 1898 Prince Heinrich XXX of Reuss
   (3) Prince Heinrich (1862–1929), *m.* 1888 Princess Irene of Hesse (*see* page 128). *Issue:*
   (*a*) Prince Waldemar (1889–1945), *m.* Princess Calixta Agnes of Lippe
   (*b*) Prince Sigismund (1896–1978), *m.* 1919 Princess Charlotte of Saxe-Altenburg; *issue:* Princess Barbara (1920–94); Prince Alfred (*b.* 1924)
   (*c*) Prince Heinrich (1900–4)
   (4) Prince Sigismund (1864–6)
   (5) Princess Victoria (1866–1929), *m.* (1) 1890, Prince Adolf of Schaumburg-Lippe (1859–1916); (2) 1927 Alexander Zubkov
   (6) Prince Waldemar (1868–79)
   (7) Princess Sophie (1870–1932), *m.* 1889 Constantine I (1868–1923), King of the Hellenes 1913–17, 1920–3. *Issue:*
   (*a*) George II (1890–1947), King of the Hellenes 1923–4 and 1935–47, *m.* 1921 Princess Elisabeth of Roumania (marriage dissolved 1935) (*see* page 128)

(*b*) Alexander I (1893–1920), King of the Hellenes 1917–20, *m*. 1919 Aspasia Manos; *issue:* Princess Alexandra (1921–93), *m*. 1944 King Petar II of Yugoslavia (*see* below)
(*c*) Princess Helena (1896–1982), *m*. 1921 King Carol of Roumania (*see* below), (marriage dissolved 1928)
(*d*) Paul I (1901–64), King of the Hellenes 1947–64, *m*. 1938 Princess Frederika of Brunswick (*see* page 127); *issue:* King Constantine II (*b*. 1940), *m*. 1964 Princess Anne-Marie of Denmark (*see* page 129), and has issue (three sons, two daughters); Princess Sophie (*b*. 1938), *m*. 1962 Juan Carlos I of Spain (*see* page 129); Princess Irene (*b*. 1942)
(*e*) Princess Irene (1904–74), *m*. 1939 4th Duke of Aosta; *issue:* Prince Amedeo, 5th Duke of Aosta (*b*. 1943)
(*f*) Princess Katherine (Lady Katherine Brandram) (*b*. 1913), *m*. 1947 Major R. C. A. Brandram, MC, TD; *issue:* R. Paul G. A. Brandram (*b*. 1948)
(8) Princess Margarethe (1872–1954), *m*. 1893 Prince Friedrich Karl of Hesse (1868–1940). *Issue:*
(*a*) Prince Friedrich Wilhelm (1893–1916)
(*b*) Prince Maximilian (1894–1914)
(*c*) Prince Philipp (1896–1980), *m*. 1925 Princess Mafalda of Italy; *issue:* Prince Moritz (*b*. 1926); Prince Heinrich (*b*. 1927); Prince Otto (*b*. 1937); Princess Elisabeth (*b*. 1940)
(*d*) Prince Wolfgang (1896–1989), *m*. (1) 1924 Princess Marie Alexandra of Baden; (2) 1948 Ottilie Möller
(*e*) Prince Richard (1901–69)
(*f*) Prince Christoph (1901–43), *m*. 1930 Princess Sophie of Greece (*see* below) and has issue (two sons, three daughters)

2. HRH PRINCE ALBERT EDWARD (HM KING EDWARD VII), *b*. 9 November 1841, *m*. 1863 HRH Princess Alexandra of Denmark (1844–1925), *succeeded* to the throne 22 January 1901, *d*. 6 May 1910. *Issue:*
(1) Albert Victor, Duke of Clarence and Avondale (1864–92)
(2) George (HM KING GEORGE V) (*see* page 127)
(3) Louise (1867–1931) Princess Royal 1905–31, *m*. 1889 1st Duke of Fife (1849–1912). *Issue:*
(*a*) Princess Alexandra, Duchess of Fife (1891–1959), *m*. 1913 Prince Arthur of Connaught (*see* page 129)
(*b*) Princess Maud (1893–1945), *m*. 1923 11th Earl of Southesk (1893–1992); *issue:* The Duke of Fife (*b*. 1929)
(4) Victoria (1868–1935)
(5) Maud (1869–1938), *m*. 1896 Prince Carl of Denmark (1872–1957), later King Haakon VII of Norway 1905–57. *Issue:*
(*a*) Olav V (1903–91), King of Norway 1957–91, *m*. 1929 Princess Märtha of Sweden (1901–54); *issue:* Princess Ragnhild (*b*. 1930); Princess Astrid (*b*. 1932); Harald V, King of Norway (*b*. 1937)
(6) Alexander (6–7 April 1871)

3. HRH PRINCESS ALICE Maud Mary (1843–78), *m*. 1862 Prince Ludwig (1837–92), Grand Duke of Hesse 1877–92. *Issue:*
(1) Victoria (1863–1950), *m*. 1884 *Admiral of the Fleet* Prince Louis of Battenberg (1854–1921), *cr*. 1st Marquess of Milford Haven 1917. *Issue:*
(*a*) Alice (1885–1969), *m*. 1903 Prince Andrew of Greece (1882–1944); *issue:* Princess Margarita (1905–81), *m*. 1931 Prince Gottfried of Hohenlohe-Langenburg (*see* below); Princess Theodora (1906–69), *m*. Prince Berthold of Baden (1906–63) and has issue (two sons, one daughter); Princess Cecilie (1911–37), *m*. George, Grand Duke of Hesse (*see* below); Princess Sophie (*b*. 1914), *m*. (1) 1930 Prince Christoph of Hesse (*see* above); (2) 1946 Prince Georg of Hanover (*see* page 127); Prince Philip, Duke of Edinburgh (*b*. 1921) (*see* page 117)
(*b*) Louise (1889–1965), *m*. 1923 Gustaf VI Adolf (1882–1973), King of Sweden 1950–73
(*c*) George, 2nd Marquess of Milford Haven (1892–1938), *m*. 1916 Countess Nadejda, daughter of Grand Duke Michael of Russia; *issue:* Lady Tatiana (1917–88); David Michael, 3rd Marquess (1919–70)
(*d*) Louis, 1st Earl Mountbatten of Burma (1900–79), *m*. 1922 Edwina Ashley, daughter of Lord Mount Temple; *issue:* Patricia, Countess Mountbatten of Burma (*b*. 1924), Pamela (*b*. 1929)
(2) Elizabeth (1864–1918), *m*. 1884 Grand Duke Sergius of Russia (1857–1905)
(3) Irene (1866–1953), *m*. 1888 Prince Heinrich of Prussia (*see* page 127)

(4) Ernst Ludwig (1868–1937), Grand Duke of Hesse 1892–1918, *m*. (1) 1894 Princess Victoria Melita of Saxe-Coburg (*see* below) (marriage dissolved 1901); (2) 1905 Princess Eleonore of Solms-Hohensolmslich. *Issue:*
(*a*) Princess Elizabeth (1895–1903)
(*b*) George, Hereditary Grand Duke of Hesse (1906–37), *m*. Princess Cecilie of Greece (*see* above), and had issue, two sons, accidentally killed with parents 1937
(*c*) Ludwig, Prince of Hesse (1908–68), *m*. 1937 Margaret, daughter of 1st Lord Geddes
(5) Frederick William (1870–3)
(6) Alix (Tsaritsa of Russia) (1872–1918), *m*. 1894 Nicholas II (1868–1918) Tsar of All the Russias 1894–1917, assassinated 16 July 1918. *Issue:*
(*a*) Grand Duchess Olga (1895–1918)
(*b*) Grand Duchess Tatiana (1897–1918)
(*c*) Grand Duchess Marie (1899–1918)
(*d*) Grand Duchess Anastasia (1901–18)
(*e*) Alexis, Tsarevich of Russia (1904–18)
(7) Marie (1874–8)

4. HRH PRINCE ALFRED Ernest Albert, Duke of Edinburgh, *Admiral of the Fleet* (1844–1900), *m*. 1874 Grand Duchess Marie Alexandrovna of Russia (1853–1920); succeeded as Duke of Saxe-Coburg and Gotha 22 August 1893. *Issue:*
(1) Alfred, Prince of Saxe-Coburg (1874–99)
(2) Marie (1875–1938), *m*. 1893 Ferdinand (1865–1927), King of Roumania 1914–27. *Issue:*
(*a*) Carol II (1893–1953), King of Roumania 1930–40, *m*. (2) 1921 Princess Helena of Greece (*see* above) (marriage dissolved 1928); *issue:* Michael (*b*. 1921), King of Roumania 1927–30, 1940–7, *m*. 1948 Princess Anne of Bourbon-Parma, and has issue (five daughters)
(*b*) Elisabeth (1894–1956), *m*. 1921 George II, King of the Hellenes (*see* page 127)
(*c*) Marie (1900–61), *m*. 1922 Alexander (1888–1934), King of Yugoslavia 1921–34; *issue:* Petar II (1923–70), King of Yugoslavia 1934–45, *m*. 1944 Princess Alexandra of Greece (*see* above) and has issue (Crown Prince Alexander, *b*. 1945); Prince Tomislav (*b*. 1928), *m*. (1) 1957 Princess Margarita of Baden (daughter of Princess Theodora of Greece and Prince Berthold of Baden, *see* above); (2) 1982 Linda Bonney; and has issue (three sons, one daughter); Prince Andrej (1929–90), *m*. (1) 1956 Princess Christina of Hesse (daughter of Prince Christoph of Hesse and Princess Sophie of Greece, *see* above); (2) 1963 Princess Kira-Melita of Leiningen (*see* below); and has issue (three sons, two daughters)
(*d*) Prince Nicolas (1903–78)
(*e*) Princess Ileana (1909–91), *m*. (1) 1931 Archduke Anton of Austria; (2) 1954 Dr Stefan Issarescu; *issue:* Archduke Stefan (*b*. 1932); Archduchess Maria Ileana (1933–59); Archduchess Alexandra (*b*. 1935); Archduke Dominic (*b*. 1937); Archduchess Maria Magdalena (*b*. 1939); Archduchess Elisabeth (*b*. 1942)
(*f*) Prince Mircea (1913–16)
(3) Victoria Melita (1876–1936), *m*. (1) 1894 Grand Duke Ernst Ludwig of Hesse (*see* above) (marriage dissolved 1901); (2) 1905 the Grand Duke Kirill of Russia (1876–1938). *Issue:*
(*a*) Marie Kirillovna (1907–51), *m*. 1925 Prince Friedrich Karl of Leiningen; *issue:* Prince Emich (1926–91); Prince Karl (1928–90); Princess Kira-Melita (*b*. 1930), *m*. Prince Andrej of Yugoslavia (*see* above); Princess Margarita (*b*. 1932); Prince Mechtilde (*b*. 1936); Prince Friedrich (*b*. 1938)
(*b*) Kira Kirillovna (1909–67), *m*. 1938 Prince Louis Ferdinand of Prussia (*see* page 127); *issue:* Prince Friedrich Wilhelm (*b*. 1939); Prince Michael (*b*. 1940); Princess Marie (*b*. 1942); Princess Kira (*b*. 1943); Prince Louis Ferdinand (1944–77); Prince Christian (*b*. 1946); Princess Xenia (1949–92)
(*c*) Vladimir Kirillovich (1917–92), *m*. 1948 Princess Leonida Bagration-Mukhransky; *issue:* Grand Duchess Maria (*b*. 1953), and has issue
(4) Alexandra (1878–1942), *m*. 1896 Ernst, Prince of Hohenlohe Langenburg. *Issue:*
(*a*) Gottfried (1897–1960), *m*. 1931 Princess Margarita of Greece (*see* above); *issue:* Prince Kraft (*b*. 1935), Princess Beatrice (1936–97); Prince Georg Andreas (*b*. 1938), Prince Ruprecht (1944–76); Prince Albrecht (1944–92)

(*b*) Maria (1899–1967), *m.* 1916 Prince Friedrich of Schleswig-Holstein-Sonderburg-Glücksburg; *issue:* Prince Peter (1922–80); Princess Marie (*b.* 1927)
(*c*) Princess Alexandra (1901–63)
(*d*) Princess Irma (1902–86)
(5) Princess Beatrice (1884–1966), *m.* 1909 Alfonso of Orleans, Infante of Spain. *Issue:*
(*a*) Prince Alvaro (*b.* 1910), *m.* 1937 Carla Parodi-Delfino; *issue:* Doña Gerarda (*b.* 1939); Don Alonso (1941–75); Doña Beatriz (*b.* 1943); Don Alvaro (*b.* 1947)
(*b*) Prince Alonso (1912–36)
(*c*) Prince Ataulfo (1913–74)

5. HRH PRINCESS HELENA Augusta Victoria (1846–1923), *m.* 1866 Prince Christian of Schleswig-Holstein-Sonderburg-Augustenburg (1831–1917). *Issue:*
(1) Prince Christian Victor (1867–1900)
(2) Prince Albert (1869–1931), Duke of Schleswig-Holstein 1921–31
(3) Princess Helena (1870–1948)
(4) Princess Marie Louise (1872–1956), *m.* 1891 Prince Aribert of Anhalt (marriage dissolved 1900)
(5) Prince Harold (12–20 May 1876)

6. HRH PRINCESS LOUISE Caroline Alberta (1848–1939), *m.* 1871 the Marquess of Lorne, afterwards 9th Duke of Argyll (1845–1914); without issue

7. HRH PRINCE ARTHUR William Patrick Albert, Duke of Connaught, *Field Marshal* (1850–1942), *m.* 1879 Princess Louisa of Prussia (1860–1917). *Issue:*
(1) Margaret (1882–1920), *m.* 1905 Crown Prince Gustaf Adolf (1882–1973), afterwards King of Sweden 1950–73. *Issue:*
(*a*) Gustaf Adolf, Duke of Västerbotten (1906–47), *m.* 1932 Princess Sibylla of Saxe-Coburg-Gotha (*see* below); *issue:* Princess Margaretha (*b.* 1934); Princess Birgitta (*b.* 1937); Princess Désirée (*b.* 1938); Princess Christina (*b.* 1943); Carl XVI Gustaf, King of Sweden (*b.* 1946)
(*b*) Count Sigvard Bernadotte (*b.* 1907), *m.*; *issue:* Count Michael (*b.* 1944)
(*c*) Princess Ingrid (Queen Mother of Denmark) (*b.* 1910), *m.* 1935 Frederick IX (1899–1972), King of Denmark 1947–72; *issue:* Margrethe II, Queen of Denmark (*b.* 1940); Princess Benedikte (*b.* 1944); Princess Anne-Marie (*b.* 1946), *m.* 1964 Constantine II of Greece (*see* page 128)
(*d*) Prince Bertil, Duke of Halland (1912–97), *m.* 1976 Mrs Lilian Craig
(*e*) Count Carl Bernadotte (*b.* 1916), *m.* (1) 1946 Mrs Kerstin Johnson; (2) 1988 Countess Gunnila Bussler

(2) Arthur (1883–1938), *m.* 1913 HH the Duchess of Fife (*see* page 128). *Issue:*
Alastair Arthur, 2nd Duke of Connaught (1914–43)
(3) (Victoria) Patricia (1886–1974), *m.* 1919 Adm. Hon. Sir Alexander Ramsay. *Issue:*
Alexander Ramsay of Mar (*b.* 1919), *m.* 1956 Hon. Flora Fraser (Lady Saltoun)

8. HRH PRINCE LEOPOLD George Duncan Albert, Duke of Albany (1853–84), *m.* 1882 Princess Helena of Waldeck (1861–1922). *Issue:*
(1) Alice (1883–1981), *m.* 1904 Prince Alexander of Teck (1874–1957), *cr.* 1st Earl of Athlone 1917. *Issue:*
(*a*) Lady May (1906–94), *m.* 1931 Sir Henry Abel-Smith, KCMG, KCVO, DSO; *issue:* Anne (*b.* 1932); Richard (*b.* 1933); Elizabeth (*b.* 1936)
(*b*) Rupert, Viscount Trematon (1907–28)
(*c*) Prince Maurice (March–September 1910)
(2) Charles Edward (1884–1954), Duke of Albany 1884 until title suspended 1917, Duke of Saxe-Coburg-Gotha 1900–18, *m.* 1905 Princess Victoria Adelheid of Schleswig-Holstein-Sonderburg-Glücksburg. *Issue:*
(*a*) Prince Johann Leopold (1906–72), and has issue
(*b*) Princess Sibylla (1908–72), *m.* 1932 Prince Gustav Adolf of Sweden (*see* above)
(*c*) Prince Dietmar Hubertus (1909–43)
(*d*) Princess Caroline (1912–83), and has issue
(*e*) Prince Friedrich Josias (*b.* 1918), and has issue

9. HRH PRINCESS BEATRICE Mary Victoria Feodore (1857–1944), *m.* 1885 Prince Henry of Battenberg (1858–96). *Issue:*
(1) Alexander, 1st Marquess of Carisbrooke (1886–1960), *m.* 1917 Lady Irene Denison. *Issue:*
Lady Iris Mountbatten (1920–82), *m.*; *issue:* Robin A. Bryan (*b.* 1957)
(2) Victoria Eugénie (1887–1969), *m.* 1906 Alfonso XIII (1886–1941) King of Spain 1886–1931. *Issue:*
(*a*) Prince Alfonso (1907–38)
(*b*) Prince Jaime (1908–75), and has issue
(*c*) Princess Beatrice (*b.* 1909), and has issue
(*d*) Princess Maria (1911–96), and has issue
(*e*) Prince Juan (1913–93), Count of Barcelona; *issue:* Princess Maria (*b.* 1936); Juan Carlos I, King of Spain (*b.* 1938), *m.* 1962 Princess Sophie of Greece (*see* page 128) and has issue (one son, two daughters); Princess Margarita (*b.* 1939)
(*f*) Prince Gonzalo (1914–34)
(3) Major Lord Leopold Mountbatten (1889–1922)
(4) Maurice (1891–1914), died of wounds received in action

Kings and Queens

HOUSES OF CERDIC AND DENMARK

Reign
927–939   ÆTHELSTAN
Son of Edward the Elder, by Ecgwynn, and grandson of Alfred
Acceded to Wessex and Mercia *c.*924, established direct rule over Northumbria 927, effectively creating the Kingdom of England
Reigned 15 years

939–946   EDMUND I
Born 921, son of Edward the Elder, by Eadgifu
Married (1) Ælfgifu (2) Æthelflæd
Killed aged 25, *reigned* 6 years

946–955   EADRED
Son of Edward the Elder, by Eadgifu
Reigned 9 years

955–959   EADWIG
Born before 943, son of Edmund and Ælfgifu

Married Ælfgifu
Reigned 3 years

959–975   EDGAR I
Born 943, son of Edmund and Ælfgifu
Married (1) Æthelflæd (2) Wulfthryth (3) Ælfthryth
Died aged 32, *reigned* 15 years

975–978   EDWARD I (the Martyr)
Born c.962, son of Edgar and Æthelflæd
Assassinated aged c.16, *reigned* 2 years

978–1016   ÆTHELRED (the Unready)
Born c.968/969, son of Edgar and Ælfthryth
Married (1) Ælfgifu (2) Emma, daughter of Richard I, count of Normandy
1013–14 dispossessed of kingdom by Swegn Forkbeard (king of Denmark 987–1014)
Died aged c.47, *reigned* 38 years

1016   EDMUND II (Ironside)
Born before 993, son of Æthelred and Ælfgifu
Married Ealdgyth
Died aged over 23, *reigned* 7 months (April–November)

1016–1035   CNUT (Canute)
Born c.995, son of Swegn Forkbeard, king of Denmark, and Gunhild

Married (1) Ælfgifu (2) Emma, widow of
Æthelred the Unready
Gained submission of West Saxons 1015,
Northumbrians 1016, Mercia 1016, king of all
England after Edmund's death
King of Denmark 1019–35, king of Norway
1028–35
Died aged *c.*40, *reigned* 19 years

1035–1040   HAROLD I (Harefoot)
*Born c.*1016/17, son of Cnut and Ælfgifu
Married Ælfgifu
1035 recognized as regent for himself and his
brother Harthacnut; 1037 recognized as king
Died aged *c.*23, *reigned* 4 years

1040–1042   HARTHACNUT
*Born c.*1018, son of Cnut and Emma
Titular king of Denmark from 1028
Acknowledged king of England 1035–7 with
Harold I as regent; effective king after Harold's
death
Died aged *c.*24, *reigned* 2 years

1042–1066   EDWARD II (the Confessor)
Born between 1002 and 1005, son of Æthelred the
Unready and Emma
Married Eadgyth, daughter of Godwine, earl of
Wessex
Died aged over 60, *reigned* 23 years

1066   HAROLD II (Godwinesson)
*Born c.*1020, son of Godwine, earl of Wessex, and
Gytha
Married (1) Eadgyth (2) Ealdgyth
Killed in battle aged *c.*46, *reigned* 10 months
(January–October)

THE HOUSE OF NORMANDY

1066–1087   WILLIAM I (the Conqueror)
Born 1027/8, son of Robert I, duke of Normandy;
obtained the Crown by conquest
Married Matilda, daughter of Baldwin, count of
Flanders
Died aged *c.*60, *reigned* 20 years

1087–1100   WILLIAM II (Rufus)
Born between 1056 and 1060, third son of
William I; succeeded his father in England only
Killed aged *c.*40, *reigned* 12 years

1100–1135   HENRY I (Beauclerk)
Born 1068, fourth son of William I
Married (1) Edith or Matilda, daughter of
Malcolm III of Scotland (2) Adela, daughter of
Godfrey, count of Louvain
Died aged 67, *reigned* 35 years

1135–1154   STEPHEN
Born not later than 1100, third son of Adela,
daughter of William I, and Stephen, count of Blois
Married Matilda, daughter of Eustace, count of
Boulogne
1141 (February–November) held captive by
adherents of Matilda, daughter of Henry I, who
contested the crown until 1153
Died aged over 53, *reigned* 18 years

THE HOUSE OF ANJOU (PLANTAGENETS)

1154–1189   HENRY II (Curtmantle)
Born 1133, son of Matilda, daughter of Henry I,
and Geoffrey, count of Anjou
Married Eleanor, daughter of William, duke of
Aquitaine, and divorced queen of Louis VII of
France
Died aged 56, *reigned* 34 years

1189–1199   RICHARD I (Coeur de Lion)
Born 1157, third son of Henry II
Married Berengaria, daughter of Sancho VI, king of
Navarre
Died aged 42, *reigned* 9 years

1199–1216   JOHN (Lackland)
Born 1167, fifth son of Henry II

Married (1) Isabella or Avisa, daughter of William,
earl of Gloucester (divorced) (2) Isabella, daughter
of Aymer, count of Angoulême
Died aged 48, *reigned* 17 years

1216–1272   HENRY III
Born 1207, son of John and Isabella of Angoulême
Married Eleanor, daughter of Raymond, count of
Provence
Died aged 65, *reigned* 56 years

1272–1307   EDWARD I (Longshanks)
Born 1239, eldest son of Henry III
Married (1) Eleanor, daughter of Ferdinand III,
king of Castile (2) Margaret, daughter of Philip III
of France
Died aged 68, *reigned* 34 years

1307–1327   EDWARD II
Born 1284, eldest surviving son of Edward I and
Eleanor
Married Isabella, daughter of Philip IV of France
Deposed January 1327, *killed* September 1327 aged
43, *reigned* 19 years

1327–1377   EDWARD III
Born 1312, eldest son of Edward II
Married Philippa, daughter of William, count of
Hainault
Died aged 64, *reigned* 50 years

1377–1399   RICHARD II
Born 1367, son of Edward (the Black Prince), eldest
son of Edward III
Married (1) Anne, daughter of Emperor Charles IV
(2) Isabelle, daughter of Charles VI of France
Deposed September 1399, *killed* February 1400 aged
33, *reigned* 22 years

THE HOUSE OF LANCASTER

1399–1413   HENRY IV
Born 1366, son of John of Gaunt, fourth son of
Edward III, and Blanche, daughter of Henry, duke
of Lancaster
Married (1) Mary, daughter of Humphrey, earl of
Hereford (2) Joan, daughter of Charles, king of
Navarre, and widow of John, duke of Brittany
Died aged *c.* 47, *reigned* 13 years

1413–1422   HENRY V
Born 1387, eldest surviving son of Henry IV and
Mary
Married Catherine, daughter of Charles VI of
France
Died aged 34, *reigned* 9 years

1422–1471   HENRY VI
Born 1421, son of Henry V
Married Margaret, daughter of René, duke of
Anjou and count of Provence
Deposed March 1461, *restored* October 1470
Deposed April 1471, *killed* May 1471 aged 49, *reigned*
39 years

THE HOUSE OF YORK

1461–1483   EDWARD IV
Born 1442, eldest son of Richard of York (grandson
of Edmund, fifth son of Edward III, and son of
Anne, great-granddaughter of Lionel, third son of
Edward III)
Married Elizabeth Woodville, daughter of Richard,
Lord Rivers, and widow of Sir John Grey
Acceded March 1461, *deposed* October 1470, *restored*
April 1471
Died aged 40, *reigned* 21 years

1483   EDWARD V
Born 1470, eldest son of Edward IV
Deposed June 1483, *died* probably July–September
1483, aged 12, *reigned* 2 months (April–June)

1483–1485   RICHARD III
Born 1452, fourth son of Richard of York
Married Anne Neville, daughter of Richard, earl of
Warwick, and widow of Edward, Prince of Wales,
son of Henry VI
Killed in battle aged 32, *reigned* 2 years

THE HOUSE OF TUDOR

1485–1509   HENRY VII
Born 1457, son of Margaret Beaufort (great-granddaughter of John of Gaunt, fourth son of Edward III) and Edmund Tudor, earl of Richmond
Married Elizabeth, daughter of Edward IV
Died aged 52, *reigned* 23 years

1509–1547   HENRY VIII
Born 1491, second son of Henry VII
Married (1) Catherine, daughter of Ferdinand II, king of Aragon, and widow of his elder brother Arthur (divorced) (2) Anne, daughter of Sir Thomas Boleyn (executed) (3) Jane, daughter of Sir John Seymour (died in childbirth) (4) Anne, daughter of John, duke of Cleves (divorced) (5) Catherine Howard, niece of the Duke of Norfolk (executed) (6) Catherine, daughter of Sir Thomas Parr and widow of Lord Latimer
Died aged 55, *reigned* 37 years

1547–1553   EDWARD VI
Born 1537, son of Henry VIII and Jane Seymour
Died aged 15, *reigned* 6 years

1553   JANE
Born 1537, daughter of Frances (daughter of Mary Tudor, the younger daughter of Henry VII) and Henry Grey, duke of Suffolk
Married Lord Guildford Dudley, son of the Duke of Northumberland
Deposed July 1553, *executed* February 1554 aged 16, *reigned* 14 days

1553–1558   MARY I
Born 1516, daughter of Henry VIII and Catherine of Aragon
Married Philip II of Spain
Died aged 42, *reigned* 5 years

1558–1603   ELIZABETH I
Born 1533, daughter of Henry VIII and Anne Boleyn
Died aged 69, *reigned* 44 years

BRITISH KINGS AND QUEENS   SINCE 1603

THE HOUSE OF STUART

Reign
1603–1625   JAMES I (VI OF SCOTLAND)
Born 1566, son of Mary, queen of Scots (granddaughter of Margaret Tudor, elder daughter of Henry VII), and Henry Stewart, Lord Darnley
Married Anne, daughter of Frederick II of Denmark
Died aged 58, *reigned* 22 years
(*see also* page 133)

1625–1649   CHARLES I
Born 1600, second son of James I
Married Henrietta Maria, daughter of Henry IV of France
Executed 1649 aged 48, *reigned* 23 years

COMMONWEALTH DECLARED 19 May 1649
1649–53 Government by a council of state
1653–8 Oliver Cromwell, *Lord Protector*
1658–9 Richard Cromwell, *Lord Protector*

1660–1685   CHARLES II
Born 1630, eldest son of Charles I
Married Catherine, daughter of John IV of Portugal
Died aged 54, *reigned* 24 years

1685–1688   JAMES II (VII of Scotland)
Born 1633, second son of Charles I
Married (1) Lady Anne Hyde, daughter of Edward, earl of Clarendon (2) Mary, daughter of Alphonso, duke of Modena
Reign ended with flight from kingdom December 1688
Died 1701 aged 67, *reigned* 3 years

INTERREGNUM 11 December 1688 to 12 February 1689

1689–1702   WILLIAM III
Born 1650, son of William II, prince of Orange, and Mary Stuart, daughter of Charles I
Married Mary, elder daughter of James II
Died aged 51, *reigned* 13 years
and
1689–1694   MARY II
Born 1662, elder daughter of James II and Anne
Died aged 32, *reigned* 5 years

1702–1714   ANNE
Born 1665, younger daughter of James II and Anne
Married Prince George of Denmark, son of Frederick III of Denmark
Died aged 49, *reigned* 12 years

THE HOUSE OF HANOVER

1714–1727   GEORGE I (Elector of Hanover)
Born 1660, son of Sophia (daughter of Frederick, elector palatine, and Elizabeth Stuart, daughter of James I) and Ernest Augustus, elector of Hanover
Married Sophia Dorothea, daughter of George William, duke of Lüneburg-Celle
Died aged 67, *reigned* 12 years

1727–1760   GEORGE II
Born 1683, son of George I
Married Caroline, daughter of John Frederick, margrave of Brandenburg-Anspach
Died aged 76, *reigned* 33 years

1760–1820   GEORGE III
Born 1738, son of Frederick, eldest son of George II
Married Charlotte, daughter of Charles Louis, duke of Mecklenburg-Strelitz
Died aged 81, *reigned* 59 years

REGENCY 1811–20
Prince of Wales regent owing to the insanity of George III

1820–1830   GEORGE IV
Born 1762, eldest son of George III
Married Caroline, daughter of Charles, duke of Brunswick-Wolfenbüttel
Died aged 67, *reigned* 10 years

1830–1837   WILLIAM IV
Born 1765, third son of George III
Married Adelaide, daughter of George, duke of Saxe-Meiningen
Died aged 71, *reigned* 7 years

1837–1901   VICTORIA
Born 1819, daughter of Edward, fourth son of George III
Married Prince Albert of Saxe-Coburg and Gotha
Died aged 81, *reigned* 63 years

THE HOUSE OF SAXE-COBURG AND GOTHA

1901–1910   EDWARD VII
Born 1841, eldest son of Victoria and Albert
Married Alexandra, daughter of Christian IX of Denmark
Died aged 68, *reigned* 9 years

THE HOUSE OF WINDSOR

1910–1936   GEORGE V
Born 1865, second son of Edward VII
Married Victoria Mary, daughter of Francis, duke of Teck
Died aged 70, *reigned* 25 years

1936   EDWARD VIII
Born 1894, eldest son of George V
Married (1937) Mrs Wallis Warfield
Abdicated 1936, *died* 1972 aged 77, *reigned* 10 months (20 January to 11 December)

1936–1952   GEORGE VI
Born 1895, second son of George V
Married Lady Elizabeth Bowes-Lyon, daughter of 14th Earl of Strathmore and Kinghorne (*see also* page 117)
Died aged 56, *reigned* 15 years

1952–   ELIZABETH II
           Born 1926, elder daughter of George VI
           Married Philip, son of Prince Andrew of Greece
           (see also page 117)
           WHOM GOD PRESERVE

KINGS AND QUEENS OF SCOTS 1016 TO 1603

Reign
1016–1034   MALCOLM II
            Born c.954, son of Kenneth II
            Acceded to Alba 1005, secured Lothian c.1016,
            obtained Strathclyde for his grandson Duncan
            c.1016, thus reigning over an area approximately
            the same as that governed by later rulers of
            Scotland
            Died aged c.80, reigned 18 years

THE HOUSE OF ATHOLL

1034–1040   DUNCAN I
            Son of Bethoc, daughter of Malcolm II, and
            Crinan, mormaer of Atholl
            Married a cousin of Siward, earl of Northumbria
            Reigned 5 years
1040–1057   MACBETH
            Born c.1005, son of a daughter of Malcolm II and
            Finlaec, mormaer of Moray
            Married Gruoch, granddaughter of Kenneth III
            Killed aged c.52, reigned 17 years
1057–1058   LULACH
            Born c.1032, son of Gillacomgan, mormaer of
            Moray, and Gruoch (and stepson of Macbeth)
            Died aged c.26, reigned 7 months (August–March)
1058–1093   MALCOLM III (Canmore)
            Born c.1031, elder son of Duncan I
            Married (1) Ingibiorg (2) Margaret (St Margaret),
            granddaughter of Edmund II of England
            Killed in battle aged c.62, reigned 35 years
1093–1097   DONALD III BÀN
            Born c.1033, second son of Duncan I
            Deposed May 1094, restored November 1094, deposed
            October 1097, reigned 3 years
1094   DUNCAN II
            Born c.1060, elder son of Malcolm III and Ingibiorg
            Married Octreda of Dunbar
            Killed aged c.34, reigned 6 months
            (May–November)
1097–1107   EDGAR
            Born c.1074, second son of Malcolm III and
            Margaret
            Died aged c.32, reigned 9 years
1107–1124   ALEXANDER I (The Fierce)
            Born c.1077, fifth son of Malcolm III and Margaret
            Married Sybilla, illegitimate daughter of Henry I
            of England
            Died aged c.47, reigned 17 years
1124–1153   DAVID I (The Saint)
            Born c.1085, sixth son of Malcolm III and Margaret
            Married Matilda, daughter of Waltheof, earl of
            Huntingdon
            Died aged c.68, reigned 29 years
1153–1165   MALCOLM IV (The Maiden)
            Born c.1141, son of Henry, earl of Huntingdon,
            second son of David I
            Died aged c.24, reigned 12 years
1165–1214   WILLIAM I (The Lion)
            Born c.1142, brother of Malcolm IV
            Married Ermengarde, daughter of Richard,
            viscount of Beaumont
            Died aged c.72, reigned 49 years
1214–1249   ALEXANDER II
            Born 1198, son of William I
            Married (1) Joan, daughter of John, king of
            England (2) Marie, daughter of Ingelram de Coucy
            Died aged 50, reigned 34 years

1249–1286   ALEXANDER III
            Born 1241, son of Alexander II and Marie
            Married (1) Margaret, daughter of Henry III of
            England (2) Yolande, daughter of the Count of
            Dreux
            Killed accidentally aged 44, reigned 36 years
1286–1290   MARGARET (The Maid of Norway)
            Born 1283, daughter of Margaret (daughter of
            Alexander III) and Eric II of Norway
            Died aged 7, reigned 4 years

            FIRST INTERREGNUM 1290–2
            Throne disputed by 13 competitors. Crown
            awarded to John Balliol by adjudication of Edward
            I of England

THE HOUSE OF BALLIOL

1292–1296   JOHN (Balliol)
            Born c.1250, son of Dervorguilla, great-great-
            granddaughter of David I, and John de Balliol
            Married Isabella, daughter of John, earl of Surrey
            Abdicated 1296, died 1313 aged c.63, reigned 3 years

            SECOND INTERREGNUM 1296–1306
            Edward I of England declared John Balliol to have
            forfeited the throne for contumacy in 1296 and
            took the government of Scotland into his own
            hands

THE HOUSE OF BRUCE

1306–1329   ROBERT I (Bruce)
            Born 1274, son of Robert Bruce and Marjorie,
            countess of Carrick, and great-grandson of the
            second daughter of David, earl of Huntingdon,
            brother of William I
            Married (1) Isabella, daughter of Donald, earl of
            Mar (2) Elizabeth, daughter of Richard, earl of
            Ulster
            Died aged 54, reigned 23 years
1329–1371   DAVID II
            Born 1324, son of Robert I and Elizabeth
            Married (1) Joanna, daughter of Edward II of
            England (2) Margaret Drummond, widow of Sir
            John Logie (divorced)
            Died aged 46, reigned 41 years

            1332 Edward Balliol, son of John Balliol, crowned
            King of Scots September, expelled December
            1333–6 Edward Balliol restored as King of Scots

THE HOUSE OF STEWART

1371–1390   ROBERT II (Stewart)
            Born 1316, son of Marjorie (daughter of Robert I)
            and Walter, High Steward of Scotland
            Married (1) Elizabeth, daughter of Sir Robert Mure
            of Rowallan (2) Euphemia, daughter of Hugh, earl
            of Ross
            Died aged 74, reigned 19 years
1390–1406   ROBERT III
            Born c.1337, son of Robert II and Elizabeth
            Married Annabella, daughter of Sir John
            Drummond of Stobhall
            Died aged c.69, reigned 16 years
1406–1437   JAMES I
            Born 1394, son of Robert III
            Married Joan Beaufort, daughter of John, earl of
            Somerset
            Assassinated aged 42, reigned 30 years
1437–1460   JAMES II
            Born 1430, son of James I
            Married Mary, daughter of Arnold, duke of
            Gueldres
            Killed accidentally aged 29, reigned 23 years
1460–1488   JAMES III
            Born 1452, son of James II
            Married Margaret, daughter of Christian I of
            Denmark
            Assassinated aged 36, reigned 27 years

1488–1513	JAMES IV
	Born 1473, son of James III
	Married Margaret Tudor, daughter of Henry VII
	of England
	Killed in battle aged 40, *reigned* 25 years
1513–1542	JAMES V
	Born 1512, son of James IV
	Married (1) Madeleine, daughter of Francis I of
	France (2) Mary of Lorraine, daughter of the Duc
	de Guise
	Died aged 30, *reigned* 29 years
1542–1567	MARY
	Born 1542, daughter of James V and Mary
	Married (1) the Dauphin, afterwards Francis II of
	France (2) Henry Stewart, Lord Darnley (3) James
	Hepburn, earl of Bothwell
	Abdicated 1567, prisoner in England from 1568,
	executed 1587, *reigned* 24 years
1567–1625	JAMES VI (and I of England)
	Born 1566, son of Mary, queen of Scots, and
	Henry, Lord Darnley
	Acceded 1567 to the Scottish throne, *reigned* 58
	years
	Succeeded 1603 to the English throne, so joining
	the English and Scottish crowns in one person.
	The two kingdoms remained distinct until 1707
	when the parliaments of the kingdoms became
	conjoined
	For British Kings and Queens since 1603, *see* pages
	131–2

WELSH SOVEREIGNS AND PRINCES

Wales was ruled by sovereign princes from the earliest times until the death of Llywelyn in 1282. The first English Prince of Wales was the son of Edward I, who was born in Caernarvon town on 25 April 1284. According to a discredited legend, he was presented to the Welsh chieftains as their prince, in fulfilment of a promise that they should have a prince who 'could not speak a word of English' and should be native born. This son, who afterwards became Edward II, was created 'Prince of Wales and Earl of Chester' at the Lincoln Parliament on 7 February 1301.
The title Prince of Wales is borne after individual conferment and is not inherited at birth, though some Princes have been declared and styled Prince of Wales but never formally so created (*s.*). The title was conferred on Prince Charles by The Queen on 26 July 1958. He was invested at Caernarvon on 1 July 1969.

INDEPENDENT PRINCES AD 844 TO 1282

844–878	Rhodri the Great
878–916	Anarawd, son of Rhodri
916–950	Hywel Dda, the Good
950–979	Iago ab Idwal (or Ieuaf)
979–985	Hywel ab Ieuaf, the Bad
985–986	Cadwallon, his brother
986–999	Maredudd ab Owain ap Hywel Dda
999–1008	Cynan ap Hywel ab Ieuaf
1018–1023	Llywelyn ap Seisyll
1023–1039	Iago ab Idwal ap Meurig
1039–1063	Gruffydd Llywelyn ap Seisyll
1063–1075	Bleddyn ap Cynfyn
1075–1081	Trahaern ap Caradog
1081–1137	Gruffydd ap Cynan ab Iago
1137–1170	Owain Gwynedd
1170–1194	Dafydd ab Owain Gwynedd
1194–1240	Llywelyn Fawr, the Great
1240–1246	Dafydd ap Llywelyn
1246–1282	Llywelyn ap Gruffydd ap Llywelyn

ENGLISH PRINCES SINCE 1301

1301	Edward (Edward II)
1343	Edward the Black Prince, s. of Edward III
1376	Richard (Richard II), s. of the Black Prince
1399	Henry of Monmouth (Henry V)
1454	Edward of Westminster, son of Henry VI

1471	Edward of Westminster (Edward V)
1483	Edward, son of Richard III (d. 1484)
1489	Arthur Tudor, son of Henry VII
1504	Henry Tudor (Henry VIII)
1610	Henry Stuart, son of James I (d. 1612)
1616	Charles Stuart (Charles I)
*c.*1638 (*s.*)	Charles Stuart (Charles II)
1688 (*s.*)	James Francis Edward Stuart (The Old Pretender),
	son of James II (d. 1766)
1714	George Augustus (George II)
1729	Frederick Lewis, s. of George II (d. 1751)
1751	George William Frederick (George III)
1762	George Augustus Frederick (George IV)
1841	Albert Edward (Edward VII)
1901	George (George V)
1910	Edward (Edward VIII)
1958	Charles Philip Arthur George

PRINCESSES ROYAL

The style Princess Royal is conferred at the Sovereign's discretion on his or her eldest daughter. It is an honorary title, held for life, and cannot be inherited or passed on. It was first conferred on Princess Mary, daughter of Charles I, in approximately 1642.

*c.*1642	Princess Mary (1631–60), daughter of Charles I
1727	Princess Anne (1709–59), daughter of George II
1766	Princess Charlotte (1766–1828), daughter of
	George III
1840	Princess Victoria (1840–1901), daughter of Victoria
1905	Princess Louise (1867–1931), daughter of
	Edward VII
1932	Princess Mary (1897–1965), daughter of
	George V
1987	Princess Anne (b. 1950), daughter of Elizabeth II

Precedence

ENGLAND AND WALES

The Sovereign
The Prince Philip, Duke of
  Edinburgh
The Prince of Wales
The Sovereign's younger sons
The Sovereign's grandsons
The Sovereign's cousins
Archbishop of Canterbury
Lord High Chancellor
Archbishop of York
The Prime Minister
Lord President of the Council
Speaker of the House of Commons
Lord Privy Seal
Ambassadors and High
  Commissioners
Lord Great Chamberlain
Earl Marshal
Lord Steward of the Household
Lord Chamberlain of the Household
Master of the Horse
Dukes, according to their patent of
  creation:
  (1) of England
  (2) of Scotland
  (3) of Great Britain
  (4) of Ireland
  (5) those created since the Union
Ministers and Envoys
Eldest sons of Dukes of Blood Royal
Marquesses, according to their
  patent of creation:
  (1) of England
  (2) of Scotland
  (3) of Great Britain
  (4) of Ireland
  (5) those created since the Union
Dukes' eldest sons
Earls, according to their patent of
  creation:
  (1) of England
  (2) of Scotland
  (3) of Great Britain
  (4) of Ireland
  (5) those created since the Union
Younger sons of Dukes of Blood
  Royal
Marquesses' eldest sons
Dukes' younger sons
Viscounts, according to their patent
  of creation:
  (1) of England
  (2) of Scotland
  (3) of Great Britain
  (4) of Ireland
  (5) those created since the Union
Earls' eldest sons
Marquesses' younger sons
Bishops of London, Durham and
  Winchester

Other English Diocesan Bishops,
  according to seniority of
  consecration
Suffragan Bishops, according to
  seniority of consecration
Secretaries of State, if of the degree
  of a Baron
Barons, according to their patent of
  creation:
  (1) of England
  (2) of Scotland
  (3) of Great Britain
  (4) of Ireland
  (5) those created since the Union
Treasurer of the Household
Comptroller of the Household
Vice-Chamberlain of the Household
Secretaries of State under the degree
  of Baron
Viscounts' eldest sons
Earls' younger sons
Barons' eldest sons
Knights of the Garter
Privy Counsellors
Chancellor of the Exchequer
Chancellor of the Duchy of
  Lancaster
Lord Chief Justice of England
Master of the Rolls
President of the Family Division
Vice-Chancellor
Lords Justices of Appeal
Judges of the High Court
Viscounts' younger sons
Barons' younger sons
Sons of Life Peers
Baronets, according to date of patent
Knights of the Thistle
Knights Grand Cross of the Bath
Members of the Order of Merit
Knights Grand Commanders of the
  Star of India
Knights Grand Cross of St Michael
  and St George
Knights Grand Commanders of the
  Indian Empire
Knights Grand Cross of the Royal
  Victorian Order
Knights Grand Cross of the British
  Empire
Companions of Honour
Knights Commanders of the Bath
Knights Commanders of the Star of
  India
Knights Commanders of St Michael
  and St George
Knights Commanders of the Indian
  Empire
Knights Commanders of the Royal
  Victorian Order
Knights Commanders of the British
  Empire
Knights Bachelor
Vice-Chancellor of the County
  Palatine of Lancaster

Official Referees of the Supreme
  Court
Circuit judges and judges of the
  Mayor's and City of London
  Court
Companions of the Bath
Companions of the Star of India
Companions of St Michael and St
  George
Companions of the Indian Empire
Commanders of the Royal Victorian
  Order
Commanders of the British Empire
Companions of the Distinguished
  Service Order
Lieutenants of the Royal Victorian
  Order
Officers of the British Empire
Companions of the Imperial Service
  Order
Eldest sons of younger sons of Peers
Baronets' eldest sons
Eldest sons of Knights, in the same
  order as their fathers
Members of the Royal Victorian
  Order
Members of the British Empire
Younger sons of the younger sons of
  Peers
Baronets' younger sons
Younger sons of Knights, in the same
  order as their fathers
Naval, Military, Air, and other
  Esquires by office

WOMEN

Women take the same rank as their
husbands or as their brothers; but the
daughter of a peer marrying a commoner retains her title as Lady or
Honourable. Daughters of peers rank
next immediately after the wives of
their elder brothers, and before their
younger brothers' wives. Daughters
of peers marrying peers of lower
degree take the same order of precedence as that of their husbands; thus
the daughter of a Duke marrying a
Baron becomes of the rank of
Baroness only, while her sisters
married to commoners retain their
rank and take precedence of the
Baroness. Merely official rank on the
husband's part does not give any
similar precedence to the wife.
  Peeresses in their own right take
the same precedence as peers of the
same rank, i.e. from their date of
creation.

Forms of address

It is only possible to cover here the forms of address for peers, baronets and knights, their wife and children, and Privy Counsellors. Greater detail should be sought in one of the publications devoted to the subject.

Both formal and social forms of address are given where usage differs; nowadays, the social form is generally preferred to the formal, which increasingly is used only for official documents and on very formal occasions.

F— represents forename
S— represents surname

BARON – *Envelope (formal)*, The Right Hon. Lord — ; *(social)*, The Lord — . *Letter (formal)*, My Lord; *(social)*, Dear Lord — . *Spoken*, Lord — .
BARON'S WIFE – *Envelope (formal)*, The Right Hon. Lady — ; *(social)*, The Lady — . *Letter (formal)*, My Lady; *(social)*, Dear Lady — . *Spoken*, Lady — .
BARON'S CHILDREN – *Envelope*, The Hon. F— S—. *Letter*, Dear Mr/Miss/Mrs S—. *Spoken*, Mr/Miss/Mrs S—.
BARONESS IN OWN RIGHT – *Envelope*, may be addressed in same way as a Baron's wife or, if she prefers *(formal)*, The Right Hon. the Baroness — ; *(social)*, The Baroness — . Otherwise as for a Baron's wife.
BARONET – *Envelope*, Sir F— S— , Bt. *Letter (formal)*, Dear Sir; *(social)*, Dear Sir F— . *Spoken*, Sir F— .
BARONET'S WIFE – *Envelope*, Lady S— . *Letter (formal)*, Dear Madam; *(social)*, Dear Lady S— . *Spoken*, Lady S— .
COUNTESS IN OWN RIGHT – As for an Earl's wife.
COURTESY TITLES – The heir apparent to a Duke, Marquess or Earl uses the highest of his father's other titles as a courtesy title. (For list, *see* pages 165–6.) The holder of a courtesy title is not styled The Most Hon. or The Right Hon., and in correspondence 'The' is omitted before the title. The heir apparent to a Scottish title may use the title 'Master' (*see* below).
DAME – *Envelope*, Dame F— S—, followed by appropriate post-nominal letters. *Letter (formal)*, Dear Madam; *(social)*, Dear Dame F— . *Spoken*, Dame F— .
DUKE – *Envelope (formal)*, His Grace the Duke of — ; *(social)*, The Duke of — . *Letter (formal)*, My Lord Duke; *(social)*, Dear Duke. *Spoken (formal)*, Your Grace; *(social)*, Duke.
DUKE'S WIFE – *Envelope (formal)*, Her Grace the Duchess of — ; *(social)*, The Duchess of — . *Letter (formal)*, Dear Madam; *(social)*, Dear Duchess. *Spoken*, Duchess.
DUKE'S ELDEST SON – *see* Courtesy titles.
DUKE'S YOUNGER SONS – *Envelope*, Lord F— S—. *Letter (formal)*, My Lord; *(social)*, Dear Lord F— . *Spoken (formal)*, My Lord; *(social)*, Lord F— .
DUKE'S DAUGHTER – *Envelope*, Lady F— S— . *Letter (formal)*, Dear Madam; *(social)*, Dear Lady F— . *Spoken*, Lady F— .
EARL – *Envelope (formal)*, The Right Hon. the Earl (of) — ; *(social)*, The Earl (of) — . *Letter (formal)*, My Lord; *(social)*, Dear Lord — . *Spoken (formal)*, My Lord; *(social)*, Lord — .
EARL'S WIFE – *Envelope (formal)*, The Right Hon. the Countess (of) — ; *(social)*, The Countess (of) — . *Letter (formal)*, Madam; *(social)*, Dear Lady — . *Spoken (formal)*, Madam; *(social)*, Lady — .
EARL'S CHILDREN – *Eldest son*, *see* Courtesy titles. *Younger sons*, The Hon. F— S— (for forms of address, *see* Baron's children). *Daughters*, Lady F— S— (for forms of address, *see* Duke's daughter).

KNIGHT (BACHELOR) – *Envelope*, Sir F— S— . *Letter (formal)*, Dear Sir; *(social)*, Dear Sir F— . *Spoken*, Sir F— .
KNIGHT (ORDERS OF CHIVALRY) – *Envelope*, Sir F— S— , followed by appropriate post-nominal letters. Otherwise as for Knight Bachelor.
KNIGHT'S WIFE – As for Baronet's wife.
LIFE PEER – As for Baron/Baroness in own right.
LIFE PEER'S WIFE – As for Baron's wife.
LIFE PEER'S CHILDREN – As for Baron's children.
MARQUESS – *Envelope (formal)*, The Most Hon. the Marquess of — ; *(social)*, The Marquess of — . *Letter (formal)*, My Lord; *(social)*, Dear Lord — . *Spoken (formal)*, My Lord; *(social)*, Lord — .
MARQUESS'S WIFE – *Envelope (formal)*, The Most Hon. the Marchioness of — ; *(social)*, The Marchioness of — . *Letter (formal)*, Madam; *(social)*, Dear Lady — . *Spoken*, Lady — .
MARQUESS'S CHILDREN – *Eldest son*, *see* Courtesy titles. *Younger sons*, Lord F— S— (for forms of address, *see* Duke's younger sons). *Daughters*, Lady F— S— (for forms of address, *see* Duke's daughter).
MASTER – The title is used by the heir apparent to a Scottish peerage, though usually the heir apparent to a Duke, Marquess or Earl uses his courtesy title rather than 'Master'. *Envelope*, The Master of — . *Letter (formal)*, Dear Sir; *(social)*, Dear Master of — . *Spoken (formal)*, Master, or Sir; *(social)*, Master, or Mr S— .
MASTER'S WIFE – Addressed as for the wife of the appropriate peerage style, otherwise as Mrs S— .
PRIVY COUNSELLOR – *Envelope*, The Right (or Rt.) Hon. F— S— . *Letter*, Dear Mr/Miss/Mrs S— . *Spoken*, Mr/Miss/Mrs S— . It is incorrect to use the letters PC after the name in conjunction with the prefix The Right Hon., unless the Privy Counsellor is a peer below the rank of Marquess and so is styled The Right Hon. because of his rank. In this case only, the post-nominal letters may be used in conjunction with the prefix The Right Hon.
VISCOUNT – *Envelope (formal)*, The Right Hon. the Viscount — ; *(social)*, The Viscount — . *Letter (formal)*, My Lord; *(social)*, Dear Lord — . *Spoken (formal)*, My Lord; *(social)*, Lord — .
VISCOUNT'S WIFE – *Envelope (formal)*, The Right Hon. the Viscountess — ; *(social)*, The Viscountess — . *Letter (formal)*, Madam; *(social)*, Dear Lady — . *Spoken*, Lady — .
VISCOUNT'S CHILDREN – As for Baron's children.

The Peerage

and Members of the House of Lords

The rules which govern the creation and succession of peerages are extremely complicated. There are, technically, five separate peerages, the Peerage of England, of Scotland, of Ireland, of Great Britain, and of the United Kingdom. The Peerage of Great Britain dates from 1707 when an Act of Union combined the two kingdoms of England and Scotland and separate peerages were discontinued. The Peerage of the United Kingdom dates from 1801 when Great Britain and Ireland were combined under an Act of Union. Some Scottish peers have received additional peerages of Great Britain or of the United Kingdom since 1707, and some Irish peers additional peerages of the United Kingdom since 1801.

The Peerage of Ireland was not entirely discontinued from 1801 but holders of Irish peerages, whether predating or created subsequent to the Union of 1801, are not entitled to sit in the House of Lords if they have no additional English, Scottish, Great Britain or United Kingdom peerage. However, they are eligible for election to the House of Commons and to vote in parliamentary elections, which other peers are not. An Irish peer holding a peerage of a lower grade which enables him to sit in the House of Lords is introduced there by the title which enables him to sit, though for all other purposes he is known by his higher title.

In the Peerage of Scotland there is no rank of Baron; the equivalent rank is Lord of Parliament, abbreviated to 'Lord' (the female equivalent is 'Lady'). All peers of England, Scotland, Great Britain or the United Kingdom who are 21 years or over, and of British, Irish or Commonwealth nationality are entitled to sit in the House of Lords.

No fees for dignities have been payable since 1937. The House of Lords surrendered the ancient right of peers to be tried for treason or felony by their peers in 1948.

HEREDITARY WOMEN PEERS

Most hereditary peerages pass on death to the nearest male heir, but there are exceptions, and several are held by women (*see* pages 144 and 156).

A woman peer in her own right retains her title after marriage, and if her husband's rank is the superior she is designated by the two titles jointly, the inferior one second. Her hereditary claim still holds good in spite of any marriage whether higher or lower. No rank held by a woman can confer any title or even precedence upon her husband but the rank of a hereditary woman peer in her own right is inherited by her eldest son (or in some cases daughter).

Since the Peerage Act 1963, hereditary women peers in their own right have been entitled to sit in the House of Lords, subject to the same qualifications as men.

LIFE PEERS

Since 1876 non-hereditary or life peerages have been conferred on certain eminent judges to enable the judicial functions of the House of Lords to be carried out. These Lords are known as Lords of Appeal or law lords and, to date, such appointments have all been male.

Since 1958 life peerages have been conferred upon distinguished men and women from all walks of life, giving them seats in the House of Lords in the degree of Baron or Baroness. They are addressed in the same way as heredi-

tary Lords and Barons, and their children have similar courtesy titles.

PEERAGES EXTINCT SINCE THE LAST EDITION

MARQUESSATES: Ormonde (*cr*.1825)
VISCOUNTCIES: Tonypandy (*cr*.1983)
BARONIES: Morrison (*cr*.1945)
LIFE PEERAGES: Boyd-Carpenter (*cr*.1972);Cudlipp (*cr*.1974); Dainton (*cr*.1986); Denington (*cr*.1978); Donaldson of Kingsbridge (*cr*.1967); Granville of Eye (*cr*. 1967); Howell (*cr*.1992); Kings Norton (*cr*.1965); Kissin (*cr*.1974); Lestor of Eccles (*cr*.1997); Llewelyn-Davies of Hastoe (*cr*.1967); McGregor of Durris (*cr*.1978); Mellish (*cr*.1985); Rayner (*cr*.1983); Smith (*cr*.1978); Wallace of Campsie (*cr*.1974); Wilson of Langside (*cr*.1969); Wyatt of Weeford (*cr*.1987)

DISCLAIMER OF PEERAGES

The Peerage Act 1963 enables peers to disclaim their peerages for life. Peers alive in 1963 could disclaim within twelve months after the passing of the Act (31 July 1963); a person subsequently succeeding to a peerage may disclaim within 12 months (one month if an MP) after the date of succession, or of reaching 21, if later. The disclaimer is irrevocable but does not affect the descent of the peerage after the disclaimant's death, and children of a disclaimed peer may, if they wish, retain their precedence and any courtesy titles and styles borne as children of a peer. The disclaimer permits the disclaimant to sit in the House of Commons if elected as an MP.

The following peerages are currently disclaimed:

EARLDOMS: Durham (1970); Selkirk (1994)
VISCOUNTCIES: Camrose (1995); Hailsham (1963); Stansgate (1963)
BARONIES: Altrincham (1963); Merthyr (1977); Reith (1972); Sanderson of Ayot (1971); Silkin (1972)

PEERS WHO ARE MINORS (i.e. under 21 years of age)
EARLS: Craven (*b*. 1989)
BARONS: Elphinstone (*b*. 1980)

CONTRACTIONS AND SYMBOLS

s.   Scottish title
I.   Irish title
*   The peer holds also an Imperial title, specified after the name by Engl., Brit. or UK
o   there is no 'of' in the title
b. born
s. succeeded
m. married
w. widower or widow
M. minor
†   heir not ascertained at time of going to press

Hereditary Peers

ROYAL DUKES

Style, His Royal Highness The Duke of ___
Style of address (formal) May it please your Royal Highness; *(informal)* Sir

Created	Title, order of succession, name, etc.	Heir
1947	*Edinburgh* (1st), The Prince Philip, Duke of Edinburgh, (*see* page 117)	The Prince of Wales
1337	*Cornwall,* Charles, Prince of Wales, *s.* 1952 (*see* page 117)	‡
1398	*Rothesay,* Charles, Prince of Wales, *s.* 1952 (*see* page 117)	‡
1986	*York* (1st), The Prince Andrew, Duke of York (*see* page 117)	None
1928	*Gloucester* (2nd), Prince Richard, Duke of Gloucester, *s.* 1974 (*see* page 118)	Earl of Ulster (*see* page 118)
1934	*Kent* (2nd), Prince Edward, Duke of Kent, *s.* 1942 (*see* page 118)	Earl of St Andrews (*see* page 118)

‡ The title is not hereditary but is held by the Sovereign's eldest son from the moment of his birth or the Sovereign's accession

---

DUKES

Coronet, Eight strawberry leaves
Style, His Grace the Duke of ___
Wife's style, Her Grace the Duchess of ___
Eldest son's style, Takes his father's second title as a courtesy title
Younger sons' style, 'Lord' before forename and family name
Daughters' style, 'Lady' before forename and family name
For forms of address, *see* page 135

Created	Title, order of succession, name, etc.	Heir
1868 I.*	*Abercorn* (5th), James Hamilton (6th *Brit. Marq., Abercorn,* 1790; 14th *Scott. Earl, Abercorn,* 1606), *b.* 1934, *s.* 1979, *m.*	Marquess of Hamilton, *b.* 1969
1701 S.*	*Argyll* (12th), Ian Campbell (5th *UK Duke, Argyll,* 1892), *b.* 1937, *s.* 1973, *m.*	Marquess of Lorne, *b.* 1968
1703 S.	*Atholl* (11th), John Murray, *b.* 1929, *s.* 1996, *m.*	Marquess of Tullibardine, *b.* 1960
1682	*Beaufort* (11th), David Robert Somerset, *b.* 1928, *s.* 1984, *w.*	Marquess of Worcester, *b.* 1952
1694	*Bedford* (13th), John Robert Russell, *b.* 1917, *s.* 1953, *m.*	Marquess of Tavistock, *b.* 1940
1663 S.*	*Buccleuch* (9th) and *Queensberry* (11th) (S. 1684), Walter Francis John Montagu Douglas Scott, KT, VRD (8th *Engl. Earl, Doncaster,* 1662), *b.* 1923, *s.* 1973, *m.*	Earl of Dalkeith, *b.* 1954
1694	*Devonshire* (11th), Andrew Robert Buxton Cavendish, KG, MC, PC, *b.* 1920, *s.* 1950, *m.*	Marquess of Hartington CBE, *b.* 1944
1900	*Fife* (3rd), James George Alexander Bannerman Carnegie (12th *Scott. Earl, Southesk,* 1633, *s.* 1992), *b.* 1929, *s.* 1959. (*see* page 128)	Earl of Southesk, *b.* 1961
1675	*Grafton* (11th), Hugh Denis Charles FitzRoy, KG, *b.* 1919, *s.* 1970, *m.*	Earl of Euston, *b.* 1947
1643 S.*	*Hamilton* (15th) and *Brandon* (12th) (*Brit.* 1711), Angus Alan Douglas Douglas-Hamilton, *b.* 1938, *s.* 1973. *Premier Peer of Scotland*	Marquess of Douglas and Clydesdale, *b.* 1978
1766 I.*	*Leinster* (8th), Gerald FitzGerald (8th *Brit. Visct., Leinster,* 1747), *b.* 1914, *s.* 1976, *m. Premier Duke and Marquess of Ireland*	Marquess of Kildare, *b.* 1948
1719	*Manchester* (12th), Angus Charles Drogo Montagu, *b.* 1938, *s.* 1985, *m.*	Viscount Mandeville, *b.* 1962
1702	*Marlborough* (11th), John George Vanderbilt Henry Spencer-Churchill, *b.* 1926, *s.* 1972, *m.*	Marquess of Blandford, *b.* 1955
1707 S.*	*Montrose* (8th), James Graham (6th *Brit. Earl, Graham,* 1722), *b.* 1935, *s.* 1992, *m.*	Marquess of Graham, *b.* 1973
1483	*Norfolk* (17th), Miles Francis Stapleton Fitzalan-Howard, KG, GCVO, CB, CBE, MC (12th *Engl. Baron, Beaumont,* 1309, *s.* 1971; 4th *UK Baron Howard of Glossop,* 1869, *s.* 1972), *b.* 1915, *s.* 1975, *m. Premier Duke and Earl Marshal*	Earl of Arundel and Surrey, *b.* 1956
1766	*Northumberland* (12th), Ralph George Algernon Percy, *b.* 1956, *s.* 1995, *m.*	Earl Percy, *b.* 1984
1675	*Richmond* (10th) and *Gordon* (5th) (*UK* 1876), Charles Henry Gordon Lennox (10th *Scott. Duke, Lennox,* 1675), *b.* 1929, *s.* 1989, *m.*	Earl of March and Kinrara, *b.* 1955
1707 S.*	*Roxburghe* (10th), Guy David Innes-Ker (5th *UK Earl, Innes,* 1837), *b.* 1954, *s.* 1974, *m. Premier Baronet of Scotland*	Marquess of Bowmont and Cessford, *b.* 1981

Created	Title, order of succession, name, etc.	Heir
1703	Rutland (10th), Charles John Robert Manners, CBE, b. 1919, s. 1940, m.	Marquess of Granby, b. 1959
1684	St Albans (14th), Murray de Vere Beauclerk, b. 1939, s. 1988, m.	Earl of Burford, b. 1965
1547	Somerset (19th), John Michael Edward Seymour, b. 1952, s. 1984, m.	Lord Seymour, b. 1982
1833	Sutherland (6th), John Sutherland Egerton, TD (5th UK Earl, Ellesmere, 1846, s. 1944), b. 1915, s. 1963, m.	Francis R. E., b. 1940
1814	Wellington (8th), Arthur Valerian Wellesley, KG, LVO, OBE, MC (9th Irish Earl, Mornington, 1760), b. 1915, s. 1972, m.	Marquess of Douro, b. 1945
1874	Westminster (6th), Gerald Cavendish Grosvenor, OBE, b. 1951, s. 1979, m.	Earl Grosvenor, b. 1991

MARQUESSES

Coronet, Four strawberry leaves alternating with four silver balls
Style, The Most Hon. the Marquess (of) ___. In Scotland the spelling 'Marquis' is preferred for pre-Union creations
Wife's style, The Most Hon. the Marchioness (of) ___
Eldest son's style, Takes his father's second title as a courtesy title
Younger sons' style, 'Lord' before forename and family name
Daughters' style, 'Lady' before forename and family name
For forms of address, see page 135

Created	Title, order of succession, name, etc.	Heir
1916	Aberdeen and Temair (6th), Alastair Ninian John Gordon (12th Scott. Earl, Aberdeen, 1682), b. 1920, s. 1984, m.	Earl of Haddo, b. 1955
1876	Abergavenny (5th), John Henry Guy Nevill, KG, OBE, b. 1914, s. 1954, m.	Christopher G. C. N., b. 1955
1821	Ailesbury (8th), Michael Sidney Cedric Brudenell-Bruce, b. 1926, s. 1974.	Earl of Cardigan, b. 1952
1831	Ailsa (8th), Archibald Angus Charles Kennedy (20th Scott. Earl, Cassillis, 1509), b. 1956, s. 1994.	Lord David Kennedy, b. 1958
1815	Anglesey (7th), George Charles Henry Victor Paget, b. 1922, s. 1947, m.	Earl of Uxbridge, b. 1950
1789	Bath (7th), Alexander George Thynn, b. 1932, s. 1992, m.	Viscount Weymouth, b. 1974
1826	Bristol (7th), (Frederick William) John Augustus Hervey, b. 1954, s. 1985.	Lord Frederick W. A. H., b. 1979
1796	Bute (7th), John Colum Crichton-Stuart (12th Scott. Earl, Dumfries, 1633), b. 1958, s. 1993, m.	Earl of Dumfries, b. 1989
1812	°Camden (6th), David George Edward Henry Pratt, b. 1930, s. 1983.	Earl of Brecknock, b. 1965
1815	Cholmondeley (7th), David George Philip Cholmondeley (11th Irish Visct., Cholmondeley, 1661), b. 1960, s. 1990. Lord Great Chamberlain	Charles G. C., b. 1959
1816 I.*	°Conyngham (7th), Frederick William Henry Francis Conyngham (7th UK Baron, Minster, 1821), b. 1924, s. 1974, m.	Earl of Mount Charles, b. 1951
1791 I.*	Donegall (7th), Dermot Richard Claud Chichester, LVO (7th Brit. Baron, Fisherwick, 1790; 6th Brit. Baron, Templemore, 1831, s. 1953), b. 1916, s. 1975, m.	Earl of Belfast, b. 1952
1789 I.*	Downshire (8th), (Arthur) Robin Ian Hill (8th Brit. Earl, Hillsborough, 1772), b. 1929, s. 1989, m.	Earl of Hillsborough, b. 1959
1801 I.*	Ely (8th), Charles John Tottenham (8th UK Baron, Loftus, 1801), b. 1913, s. 1969, m.	Viscount Loftus, b. 1943
1801	Exeter (8th), (William) Michael Anthony Cecil, b. 1935, s. 1988, m.	Lord Burghley, b. 1970
1800 I.*	Headfort (6th), Thomas Geoffrey Charles Michael Taylour (4th UK Baron, Kenlis, 1831), b. 1932, s. 1960, m.	Earl of Bective, b. 1959
1793	Hertford (9th), Henry Jocelyn Seymour (10th Irish Baron, Conway, 1712), b. 1958, s. 1997, m.	Earl of Yarmouth, b. 1993
1599 S.*	Huntly (13th), Granville Charles Gomer Gordon (5th UK Baron, Meldrum, 1815), b. 1944, s. 1987, m. Premier Marquess of Scotland	Earl of Aboyne, b. 1973
1784	Lansdowne (8th), George John Charles Mercer Nairne Petty-Fitzmaurice, PC (8th Irish Earl, Kerry, 1723), b. 1912, s. 1944, m.	Earl of Shelburne, b. 1941
1902	Linlithgow (4th), Adrian John Charles Hope (10th Scott. Earl, Hopetoun, 1703), b. 1946, s. 1987, m.	Earl of Hopetoun, b. 1969
1816 I.*	Londonderry (9th), Alexander Charles Robert Vane-Tempest-Stewart (6th UK Earl, Vane, 1823), b. 1937, s. 1955, m.	Viscount Castlereagh, b. 1972
1701 S.*	Lothian (12th), Peter Francis Walter Kerr, KCVO (6th UK Baron, Kerr, 1821), b. 1922, s. 1940, m.	Earl of Ancram PC, MP, b. 1945
1917	Milford Haven (4th), George Ivar Louis Mountbatten, b. 1961, s. 1970, m.	Earl of Medina, b. 1991
1838	Normanby (5th), Constantine Edmund Walter Phipps (9th Irish Baron, Mulgrave, 1767), b. 1954, s. 1994, m.	Lord Justin C. P., b. 1958

Created	Title, order of succession, name, etc.	Heir
1812	*Northampton* (7th), Spencer Douglas David Compton, *b.* 1946, *s.* 1978, *m.*	Earl Compton, *b.* 1973
1682 s.	*Queensberry* (12th), David Harrington Angus Douglas, *b.* 1929, *s.* 1954.	Viscount Drumlanrig, *b.* 1967
1926	*Reading* (4th), Simon Charles Henry Rufus Isaacs, *b.* 1942, *s.* 1980, *m.*	Viscount Erleigh, *b.* 1986
1789	*Salisbury* (6th), Robert Edward Peter Cecil, *b.* 1916, *s.* 1972, *m.*	Viscount Cranborne PC, *b.* 1946 (see also Baron Cecil, page 148)
1800 I.*	*Sligo* (11th), Jeremy Ulick Browne (11th *UK Baron, Monteagle,* 1806), *b.* 1939, *s.* 1991, *m.*	Sebastian U. B., *b.* 1964
1787	°*Townshend* (7th), George John Patrick Dominic Townshend, *b.* 1916, *s.* 1921, *w.*	Viscount Raynham, *b.* 1945
1694 s.*	°*Tweeddale* (13th), Edward Douglas John Hay (4th *UK Baron Tweeddale,* 1881), *b.* 1947, *s.* 1979.	Lord Charles D. M. H., *b.* 1947
1789 I.*	*Waterford* (8th), John Hubert de la Poer Beresford (8th *Brit. Baron Tyrone,* 1786), *b.* 1933, *s.* 1934, *m.*	Earl of Tyrone, *b.* 1958
1551	*Winchester* (18th), Nigel George Paulet, *b.* 1941, *s.* 1968, *m. Premier Marquess of England*	Earl of Wiltshire, *b.* 1969
1892	*Zetland* (4th), Lawrence Mark Dundas (6th *UK Earl, Zetland,* 1838; 7th *Brit. Baron Dundas,* 1794), *b.* 1937, *s.* 1989, *m.*	Earl of Ronaldshay, *b.* 1965

EARLS

Coronet, Eight silver balls on stalks alternating with eight gold strawberry leaves
Style, The Right Hon. the Earl (of) __
Wife's style, The Right Hon. the Countess (of) __
Eldest son's style, Takes his father's second title as a courtesy title
Younger sons' style, 'The Hon.' before forename and family name
Daughters' style, 'Lady' before forename and family name
For forms of address, *see* page 135

Created	Title, order of succession, name, etc.	Heir
1639 s.	*Airlie* (13th), David George Coke Patrick Ogilvy, KT, GCVO, PC, Royal Victorian Chain, *b.* 1926, *s.* 1968, *m.*	Lord Ogilvy, *b.* 1958
1696	*Albemarle* (10th), Rufus Arnold Alexis Keppel, *b.* 1965, *s.* 1979.	Crispian W. J. K., *b.* 1948
1952	°*Alexander of Tunis* (2nd), Shane William Desmond Alexander, *b.* 1935, *s.* 1969, *m.*	Hon. Brian J. A, *b.* 1939
1662 s.	*Annandale and Hartfell* (11th), Patrick Andrew Wentworth Hope Johnstone, *b.* 1941, claim established 1985, *m.*	Lord Johnstone, *b.* 1971
1789 I.	°*Annesley* (10th), Patrick Annesley, *b.* 1924, *s.* 1979, *m.*	Hon. Philip H. A., *b.* 1927
1785 I.	*Antrim* (9th), Alexander Randal Mark McDonnell, *b.* 1935, *s.* 1977, *m. Viscount Dunluce*	Hon. Randal A. St J. M., *b.* 1967
1762 I.*	*Arran* (9th), Arthur Desmond Colquhoun Gore (5th *UK Baron Sudley,* 1884), *b.* 1938, *s.* 1983, *m.*	Paul A. G. CMG, CVO, *b.* 1921
1955	°*Attlee* (3rd), John Richard Attlee, *b.* 1956, *s.* 1991, *m.*	None
1714	*Aylesford* (11th), Charles Ian Finch-Knightley, *b.* 1918, *s.* 1958, *w.*	Lord Guernsey, *b.* 1947
1937	°*Baldwin of Bewdley* (4th), Edward Alfred Alexander Baldwin, *b.* 1938, *s.* 1976, *m.*	Viscount Corvedale, *b.* 1973
1922	*Balfour* (4th), Gerald Arthur James Balfour, *b.* 1925, *s.* 1968, *m.*	Eustace A. G. B., *b.* 1921
1772	°*Bathurst* (8th), Henry Allen John Bathurst, *b.* 1927, *s.* 1943, *m.*	Lord Apsley, *b.* 1961
1919	°*Beatty* (3rd), David Beatty, *b.* 1946, *s.* 1972, *m.*	Viscount Borodale, *b.* 1973
1797 I.	*Belmore* (8th), John Armar Lowry-Corry, *b.* 1951, *s.* 1960, *m.*	Viscount Corry, *b.* 1985
1739 I.*	*Bessborough* (11th), Arthur Mountifort Longfield Ponsonby (8th *UK Baron Duncannon,* 1834), *b.* 1912, *s.* 1993, *m.*	Hon. Myles F. L. P., *b.* 1941
1815	*Bradford* (7th), Richard Thomas Orlando Bridgeman, *b.* 1947, *s.* 1981, *m.*	Viscount Newport, *b.* 1980
1469 s.*	*Buchan* (17th), Malcolm Harry Erskine (8th *UK Baron Erskine,* 1806), *b.* 1930, *s.* 1984, *m.*	Lord Cardross, *b.* 1960
1746	*Buckinghamshire* (10th), (George) Miles Hobart-Hampden, *b.* 1944, *s.* 1983, *m.*	Sir John Hobart, Bt., *b.* 1945
1800	°*Cadogan* (8th), Charles Gerald John Cadogan, *b.* 1937, *s.* 1997, *m.*	Viscount Chelsea, *b.* 1966
1878	°*Cairns* (6th), Simon Dallas Cairns, CBE, *b.* 1939, *s.* 1989, *m.*	Viscount Garmoyle, *b.* 1965
1455 s.	*Caithness* (20th), Malcolm Ian Sinclair, PC, *b.* 1948, *s.* 1965, *w.*	Lord Berriedale, *b.* 1981
1800 I.	*Caledon* (7th), Nicholas James Alexander, *b.* 1955, *s.* 1980, *m.*	Viscount Alexander, *b.* 1990
1661	*Carlisle* (13th), George William Beaumont Howard (13th *Scott. Baron Ruthven of Freeland,* 1651), *b.* 1949, *s.* 1994.	Hon. Philip C. W. H., *b.* 1963

Created	Title, order of succession, name, etc.	Heir
1793	*Carnarvon* (7th), Henry George Reginald Molyneux Herbert, KCVO, KBE, *b.* 1924, *s.* 1987, *m.*	Lord Porchester, *b.* 1956
1748 I.*	*Carrick* (10th), David James Theobald Somerset Butler (4th *UK Baron Butler*, 1912), *b.* 1953, *s.* 1992, *m.*	Viscount Ikerrin, *b.* 1975
1800 I.	°*Castle Stewart* (8th), Arthur Patrick Avondale Stuart, *b.* 1928, *s.* 1961, *m.*	Viscount Stuart, *b.* 1953
1814	°*Cathcart* (6th), Alan Cathcart, CB, DSO, MC (15th *Scott. Baron Cathcart*, 1447), *b.* 1919, *s.* 1927, *m.*	Lord Greenock, *b.* 1952
1647 I.	*Cavan.* The 12th Earl died in 1988. Heir had not established his claim to the title at the time of going to press	Roger C. *Lambart, b.* 1944
1827	°*Cawdor* (7th), Colin Robert Vaughan Campbell, *b.* 1962, *s.* 1993, *m.*	Hon. Frederick W. *C., b.* 1965
1801	*Chichester* (9th), John Nicholas Pelham, *b.* 1944, *m.*	Richard A. H. *P., b.* 1952
1803 I.*	*Clancarty* (9th), Nicholas Power Richard Le Poer Trench (8th *UK Visct. Clancarty*, 1823), *b.* 1952, *s.* 1995.	None
1776 I.*	*Clanwilliam* (7th), John Herbert Meade (5th *UK Baron Clanwilliam*, 1828), *b.* 1919, *s.* 1989, *m.*	Lord Gillford, *b.* 1960
1776	*Clarendon* (7th), George Frederick Laurence Hyde Villiers, *b.* 1933, *s.* 1955, *m.*	Lord Hyde, *b.* 1976
1620 I.*	*Cork* (14th) and *Orrery* (14th) (I. 1660), John William Boyle, DSC (10th *Brit. Baron Boyle of Marston*, 1711), *b.* 1916, *s.* 1995, *m.*	Hon. John R. *B., b.* 1945
1850	*Cottenham* (8th), Kenelm Charles Everard Digby Pepys, *b.* 1948, *s.* 1968, *m.*	Viscount Crowhurst, *b.* 1983
1762 I.*	*Courtown* (9th), James Patrick Montagu Burgoyne Winthrop Stopford (8th *Brit. Baron Saltersford*, 1796), *b.* 1954, *s.* 1975, *m.*	Viscount Stopford, *b.* 1988
1697	*Coventry* (11th), George William Coventry, *b.* 1934, *s.* 1940, *m.*	Hon. Francis H. *C., b.* 1912
1857	°*Cowley* (7th), Garret Graham Wellesley, *b.* 1934, *s.* 1975, *m.*	Viscount Dangan, *b.* 1965
1892	*Cranbrook* (5th), Gathorne Gathorne-Hardy, *b.* 1933, *s.* 1978, *m.*	Lord Medway, *b.* 1968
1801	*Craven* (9th), Benjamin Robert Joseph Craven, *b.* 1989, *s.* 1990, *M.*	Rupert J. E. *C., b.* 1926
1398 S.*	*Crawford* (29th) and *Balcarres* (12th) (S. 1651), Robert Alexander Lindsay, KT, PC (5th *UK Baron, Wigan*, 1826; *Baron Balniel* (life peerage), 1974), *b.* 1927, *s.* 1975, *m. Premier Earl on Union Roll*	Lord Balniel, *b.* 1958
1861	*Cromartie* (5th), John Ruaridh Blunt Grant Mackenzie, *b.* 1948, *s.* 1989, *m.*	Viscount Tarbat, *b.* 1987
1901	*Cromer* (4th), Evelyn Rowland Esmond Baring, *b.* 1946, *s.* 1991, *m.*	Viscount Errington, *b.* 1994
1633 S.*	*Dalhousie* (16th), Simon Ramsay, KT, GCVO, GBE, MC (4th *UK Baron Ramsay*, 1875), *b.* 1914, *s.* 1950, *w.*	Lord Ramsay, *b.* 1948
1725 I.	*Darnley* (11th), Adam Ivo Stuart Bligh (20th *Engl. Baron Clifton of Leighton Bromswold*, 1608), *b.* 1941, *s.* 1980, *m.*	Lord Clifton, *b.* 1968
1711	*Dartmouth* (10th), William Legge, *b.* 1949, *s.* 1997.	Hon. Rupert *L., b.* 1951
1761	°*De La Warr* (11th), William Herbrand Sackville, *b.* 1948, *s.* 1988, *m.*	Lord Buckhurst, *b.* 1979
1622	*Denbigh* (12th) and *Desmond* (11th) (I. 1622), Alexander Stephen Rudolph Feilding, *b.* 1970, *s.* 1995, *m.*	William D. *F., b.* 1939
1485	*Derby* (19th), Edward Richard William Stanley, *b.* 1962, *s.* 1994, *m.*	Hon. Peter H. C. *S., b.* 1964
1553	*Devon* (17th), Charles Christopher Courtenay, *b.* 1916, *s.* 1935, *m.*	Lord Courtenay, *b.* 1942
1800 I.*	*Donoughmore* (8th), Richard Michael John Hely-Hutchinson (8th *UK Visct. Hutchinson*, 1821), *b.* 1927, *s.* 1981, *m.*	Viscount Suirdale, *b.* 1952
1661 I.*	*Drogheda* (12th), Henry Dermot Ponsonby Moore (3rd *UK Baron Moore*, 1954), *b.* 1937, *s.* 1989, *m.*	Viscount Moore, *b.* 1983
1837	*Ducie* (7th), David Leslie Moreton, *b.* 1951, *s.* 1991, *m.*	Lord Moreton, *b.* 1981
1860	*Dudley* (4th), William Humble David Ward, *b.* 1920, *s.* 1969, *m.*	Viscount Ednam, *b.* 1947
1660 S.*	*Dundee* (12th), Alexander Henry Scrymgeour (2nd *UK Baron Glassary*, 1954), *b.* 1949, *s.* 1983, *m.*	Lord Scrymgeour, *b.* 1982
1669 S.	*Dundonald* (15th), Iain Alexander Douglas Blair Cochrane, *b.* 1961, *s.* 1986, *m.*	Lord Cochrane, *b.* 1991
1686 S.	*Dunmore* (12th), Malcolm Kenneth Murray, *b.* 1946, *s.* 1995, *m.*	Hon. Geoffrey C. *M., b.* 1949
1822 I.	*Dunraven and Mount-Earl* (7th), Thady Windham Thomas Wyndham-Quin, *b.* 1939, *s.* 1965, *m.*	None
1833	*Durham.* Disclaimed for life 1970. (*Antony Claud Frederick Lambton, b.*1922, *s.*1970, *m.*)	Hon. Edward R. *L.* (Baron Durham), *b.* 1961
1837	*Effingham* (7th), David Mowbray Algernon Howard (17th *Engl. Baron Howard of Effingham*, 1554), *b.* 1939, *s.* 1996, *m.*	Lord Howard of Effingham, *b.* 1971
1507 S.*	*Eglinton* (18th) and *Winton* (9th) (S. 1600), Archibald George Montgomerie (6th *UK Earl Winton*, 1859), *b.* 1939, *s.* 1966, *m.*	Lord Montgomerie, *b.* 1966
1733 I.*	*Egmont* (11th), Frederick George Moore Perceval (9th *Brit. Baron Lovel and Holland*, 1762), *b.* 1914, *s.* 1932, *m.*	Viscount Perceval, *b.* 1934
1821	*Eldon* (5th), John Joseph Nicholas Scott, *b.* 1937, *s.* 1976, *m.*	Viscount Encombe, *b.* 1962
1633 S.*	*Elgin* (11th) and *Kincardine* (15th) (S. 1647), Andrew Douglas Alexander Thomas Bruce, KT (4th *UK Baron, Elgin*, 1849), *b.* 1924, *s.* 1968, *m.*	Lord Bruce, *b.* 1961

Created	Title, order of succession, name, etc.	Heir
1789 I.*	*Enniskillen* (7th), Andrew John Galbraith Cole (5th *UK Baron, Grinstead*, 1815), *b.* 1942, *s.* 1989, *m.*	Arthur G. C., *b.* 1920
1789 I.*	*Erne* (6th), Henry George Victor John Crichton (3rd *UK Baron, Fermanagh*, 1876), *b.* 1937, *s.* 1940, *m.*	Viscount Crichton, *b.* 1971
1452 S.	*Erroll* (24th), Merlin Sereld Victor Gilbert Hay, *b.* 1948, *s.* 1978, *m.* Hereditary Lord High Constable and Knight Marischal of Scotland	Lord Hay, *b.* 1984
1661	*Essex* (10th), Robert Edward de Vere Capell, *b.* 1920, *s.* 1981, *m.*	Viscount Malden, *b.* 1944
1711	°*Ferrers* (13th), Robert Washington Shirley, PC, *b.* 1929, *s.* 1954, *m.*	Viscount Tamworth, *b.* 1952
1789	°*Fortescue* (8th), Charles Hugh Richard Fortescue, *b.* 1951, *s.* 1993, *m.*	Hon. Martin D. F., *b.* 1924
1841	*Gainsborough* (5th), Anthony Gerard Edward Noel, *b.* 1923, *s.* 1927, *m.*	Viscount Campden, *b.* 1950
1623 S.*	*Galloway* (13th), Randolph Keith Reginald Stewart (6th *Brit. Baron Stewart of Garlies*, 1796), *b.* 1928, *s.* 1978, *m.*	Andrew C. S., *b.* 1949
1703 S.*	*Glasgow* (10th), Patrick Robin Archibald Boyle (4th *UK Baron, Fairlie*, 1897), *b.* 1939, *s.* 1984, *m.*	Viscount of Kelburn, *b.* 1978
1806 I.*	*Gosford* (7th), Charles David Nicholas Alexander John Sparrow Acheson (5th *UK Baron, Worlingham*, 1835), *b.* 1942, *s.* 1966, *m.*	Hon. Patrick B. V. M. A., *b.* 1915
1945	*Gowrie* (2nd), Alexander Patric Greysteil Hore-Ruthven, PC (3rd *UK Baron Ruthven of Gowrie*, 1919), *b.* 1939, *s.* 1955, *m.*	Viscount Ruthven of Canberra, *b.* 1964
1684 I.*	*Granard* (10th), Peter Arthur Edward Hastings Forbes (5th *UK Baron, Granard*, 1806), *b.* 1957, *s.* 1992, *m.*	Viscount Forbes, *b.* 1981
1833	°*Granville* (6th), Granville George Fergus Leveson-Gower, *b.* 1959, *s.* 1996, *m.*	Hon. Niall J. L.-G., *b.* 1963
1806	°*Grey* (6th), Richard Fleming George Charles Grey, *b.* 1939, *s.* 1963, *m.*	Philip K. G., *b.* 1940
1752	*Guilford* (9th), Edward Francis North, *b.* 1933, *s.* 1949, *w.*	Lord North, *b.* 1971
1619 S.	*Haddington* (13th), John George Baillie-Hamilton, *b.* 1941, *s.* 1986, *m.*	Lord Binning, *b.* 1985
1919	°*Haig* (2nd), George Alexander Eugene Douglas Haig, OBE, *b.* 1918, *s.* 1928, *m.*	Viscount Dawick, *b.* 1961
1944	*Halifax* (3rd), Charles Edward Peter Neil Wood (5th *UK Visct., Halifax*, 1866), *b.* 1944, *s.* 1980, *m.*	Lord Irwin, *b.* 1977
1898	*Halsbury* (3rd), John Anthony Hardinge Giffard, FRS, FEng, *b.* 1908, *s.* 1943, *w.*	Adam E. G., *b.* 1934
1754	*Hardwicke* (10th), Joseph Philip Sebastian Yorke, *b.* 1971, *s.* 1974.	Richard C. J. Y., *b.* 1916
1812	*Harewood* (7th), George Henry Hubert Lascelles, KBE, *b.* 1923, *s.* 1947, *m.* (*see also* page 127)	Viscount Lascelles, *b.* 1950 (*see also* page 127)
1742	*Harrington* (11th), William Henry Leicester Stanhope (8th *Brit. Visct. Stanhope of Mahon*, 1717), *b.* 1922, *s.* 1929, *m.*	Viscount Petersham, *b.* 1945
1809	*Harrowby* (7th), Dudley Danvers Granville Coutts Ryder, TD, *b.* 1922, *s.* 1987, *m.*	Viscount Sandon, *b.* 1951
1605 S.	*Home* (15th), David Alexander Cospatrick Douglas-Home, CVO, *b.* 1943, *s.* 1995, *m.*	Lord Dunglass, *b.* 1987
1821	°*Howe* (7th), Frederick Richard Penn Curzon, *b.* 1951, *s.* 1984, *m.*	Viscount Curzon, *b.* 1994
1529	*Huntingdon* (16th), William Edward Robin Hood Hastings Bass, *b.* 1948, *s.* 1990, *m.*	Hon. Simon A. R. H. H. B., *b.* 1950
1885	*Iddesleigh* (4th), Stafford Henry Northcote, *b.* 1932, *s.* 1970, *m.*	Viscount St Cyres, *b.* 1957
1756	*Ilchester* (9th), Maurice Vivian de Touffreville Fox-Strangways, *b.* 1920, *s.* 1970, *m.*	Hon. Raymond G. F.-S., *b.* 1921
1929	*Inchcape* (4th), (Kenneth) Peter (Lyle) Mackay, *b.* 1943, *s.* 1994, *m.*	Viscount Glenapp, *b.* 1979
1919	*Iveagh* (4th), Arthur Edward Rory Guinness, *b.* 1969, *s.* 1992.	Hon. Rory M. B. G., *b.* 1974
1925	°*Jellicoe* (2nd), George Patrick John Rushworth Jellicoe, KBE, DSO, MC, PC, FRS, *b.* 1918, *s.* 1935, *m.*	Viscount Brocas, *b.* 1950
1697	*Jersey* (10th), (George Francis) William Villiers (13th *Irish Visct., Grandison*, 1620), *b.* 1976, *s.* 1998.	Hon. Jamie C. V., *b.* 1994
1822 I.	*Kilmorey* (6th), Richard Francis Needham, Kt, PC, *b.* 1942, *s.* 1977, *m.*	Viscount Newry and Morne, *b.* 1966
1866	*Kimberley* (4th), John Wodehouse, *b.* 1924, *s.* 1941, *m.*	Lord Wodehouse, *b.* 1951
1768 I.	*Kingston* (11th), Barclay Robert Edwin King-Tenison, *b.* 1943, *s.* 1948, *m.*	Viscount Kingsborough, *b.* 1969
1633 S.*	*Kinnoull* (15th), Arthur William George Patrick Hay (9th *Brit. Baron Hay of Pedwardine*, 1711), *b.* 1935, *s.* 1938, *m.*	Viscount Dupplin, *b.* 1962
1677 S.*	*Kintore* (13th), Michael Canning William John Keith (3rd *UK Visct. Stonehaven*, 1938), *b.* 1939, *s.* 1989, *m.*	Lord Inverurie, *b.* 1976
1914	°*Kitchener of Khartoum* (3rd), Henry Herbert Kitchener, TD, *b.* 1919, *s.* 1937.	None
1756 I.	*Lanesborough* (9th), Denis Anthony Brian Butler, TD, *b.* 1918, *s.* 1950, *m.*	None
1624 S.	*Lauderdale* (17th), Patrick Francis Maitland, *b.* 1911, *s.* 1968, *m.*	Viscount Maitland, *b.* 1937
1837	*Leicester* (7th), Edward Douglas Coke, *b.* 1936, *s.* 1994, *m.*	Viscount Coke, *b.* 1965
1641 S.	*Leven* (14th) and *Melville* (13th) (s. 1690), Alexander Robert Leslie Melville, *b.* 1924, *s.* 1947, *m.*	Lord Balgonie, *b.* 1954
1831	*Lichfield* (5th), Thomas Patrick John Anson, *b.* 1939, *s.* 1960.	Viscount Anson, *b.* 1978

Created	Title, order of succession, name, etc.	Heir
1803 ɪ.*	*Limerick* (6th), Patrick Edmund Pery, KBE (6th *UK Baron Foxford*, 1815), *b.* 1930, *s.* 1967, *m.*	Viscount Glentworth, *b.* 1963
1572	*Lincoln* (18th), Edward Horace Fiennes-Clinton, *b.* 1913, *s.* 1988, *m.*	Hon. Edward G. *F.-C.*, *b.* 1943
1633 s.	*Lindsay* (16th), James Randolph Lindesay-Bethune, *b.* 1955, *s.* 1989, *m.*	Viscount Garnock, *b.* 1990
1626	*Lindsey* (14th) and *Abingdon* (9th) (1682), Richard Henry Rupert Bertie, *b.* 1931, *s.* 1963, *m.*	Lord Norreys, *b.* 1958
1776 ɪ.	*Lisburne* (8th), John David Malet Vaughan, *b.* 1918, *s.* 1965, *m.*	Viscount Vaughan, *b.* 1945
1822 ɪ.*	*Listowel* (6th), Francis Michael Hare (4th *UK Baron Hare*, 1869), *b.* 1964, *s.* 1997, *m.*	Hon. Timothy P. *H.*, *b.* 1966
1905	*Liverpool* (5th), Edward Peter Bertram Savile Foljambe, *b.* 1944, *s.* 1969, *m.*	Viscount Hawkesbury, *b.* 1972
1945	°*Lloyd George of Dwyfor* (3rd), Owen Lloyd George, *b.* 1924, *s.* 1968, *m.*	Viscount Gwynedd, *b.* 1951
1785 ɪ.*	*Longford* (7th), Francis Aungier Pakenham, KG, PC (6th *UK Baron, Silchester*, 1821; 1st *UK Baron Pakenham*, 1945), *b.* 1905, *s.* 1961, *m.*	Thomas F. D. *P.*, *b.* 1933
1807	*Lonsdale* (7th), James Hugh William Lowther, *b.* 1922, *s.* 1953, *m.*	Viscount Lowther, *b.* 1949
1838	*Lovelace* (5th), Peter Axel William Locke King (12th *Brit. Baron King*, 1725), *b.* 1951, *s.* 1964, *m.*	None
1795 ɪ.*	*Lucan* (7th), Richard John Bingham (3rd *UK Baron Bingham*, 1934), *b.* 1934, *s.* 1964, *m.*	Lord Bingham, *b.* 1967
1880	*Lytton* (5th), John Peter Michael Scawen Lytton (18th *Engl. Baron, Wentworth*, 1529), *b.* 1950, *s.* 1985, *m.*	Viscount Knebworth, *b.* 1989
1721	*Macclesfield* (9th), Richard Timothy George Mansfield Parker, *b.* 1943, *s.* 1992, *m.*	Hon. J. David G. *P.*, *b.* 1945
1800	*Malmesbury* (6th), William James Harris, TD, *b.* 1907, *s.* 1950, *w.*	Viscount FitzHarris, *b.* 1946
1776 & 1792	*Mansfield and Mansfield* (8th), William David Mungo James Murray (14th *Scott. Visct. Stormont*, 1621), *b.* 1930, *s.* 1971, *m.*	Viscount Stormont, *b.* 1956
1565 s.	*Mar* (14th) and *Kellie* (16th) (s. 1616), James Thorne Erskine, *b.* 1949, *s.* 1994, *m.*	Hon. Alexander D. *E.*, *b.* 1952
1785 ɪ.	*Mayo* (10th), Terence Patrick Bourke, *b.* 1929, *s.* 1962.	Lord Naas, *b.* 1953
1627 ɪ.*	*Meath* (14th), Anthony Windham Normand Brabazon (5th *UK Baron, Chaworth*, 1831), *b.* 1910, *s.* 1949, *m.*	Lord Ardee, *b.* 1941
1766 ɪ.	*Mexborough* (8th), John Christopher George Savile, *b.* 1931, *s.* 1980, *m.*	Viscount Pollington, *b.* 1959
1813	*Minto* (6th), Gilbert Edward George Lariston Elliot-Murray-Kynynmound, OBE, *b.* 1928, *s.* 1975, *m.*	Viscount Melgund, *b.* 1953
1562 s.*	*Moray* (20th), Douglas John Moray Stuart (12th *Brit. Baron Stuart of Castle Stuart*, 1796), *b.* 1928, *s.* 1974, *m.*	Lord Doune, *b.* 1966
1815	*Morley* (6th), John St Aubyn Parker, KCVO, *b.* 1923, *s.* 1962, *m.*	Viscount Boringdon, *b.* 1956
1458 s.	*Morton* (22nd), John Charles Sholto Douglas, *b.* 1927, *s.* 1976, *m.*	Lord Aberdour, *b.* 1952
1789	*Mount Edgcumbe* (8th), Robert Charles Edgcumbe, *b.* 1939, *s.* 1982.	Piers V. *E.*, *b.* 1946
1831	*Munster* (7th), Anthony Charles FitzClarence, *b.* 1926, *s.* 1983, *m.*	None
1805	°*Nelson* (9th), Peter John Horatio Nelson, *b.* 1941, *s.* 1981, *m.*	Viscount Merton, *b.* 1971
1660 s.	*Newburgh* (12th), Don Filippo Giambattista Camillo Francesco Aldo Maria Rospigliosi, *b.* 1942, *s.* 1986, *m.*	Princess Donna Benedetta F. M. *R.*, *b.* 1974
1827 ɪ.	*Norbury* (6th), Noel Terence Graham-Toler, *b.* 1939, *s.* 1955, *m.*	Viscount Glandine, *b.* 1967
1806 ɪ.*	*Normanton* (6th), Shaun James Christian Welbore Ellis Agar (9th *Brit. Baron, Mendip*, 1794; 4th *UK Baron, Somerton*, 1873), *b.* 1945, *s.* 1967, *m.*	Viscount Somerton, *b.* 1982
1647 s.	*Northesk* (14th), David John MacRae Carnegie, *b.* 1954, *s.* 1994, *m.*	Lord Rosehill, *b.* 1980
1801	*Onslow* (7th), Michael William Coplestone Dillon Onslow, *b.* 1938, *s.* 1971, *m.*	Viscount Cranley, *b.* 1967
1696 s.	*Orkney* (9th), (Oliver) Peter St John, *b.* 1938, *s.* 1998, *m.*	Viscount Kirkwall, *b.* 1969
1328 ɪ.	*Ormonde* and *Ossory*. The 8th Marquess of Ormonde died in 1997, when the marquessate became extinct. The heir to his earldoms had not established his claim at the time of going to press	Viscount Mountgarret, *b.* 1936 (*see* page 146)
1925	*Oxford and Asquith* (2nd), Julian Edward George Asquith, KCMG, *b.* 1916, *s.* 1928, *w.*	Viscount Asquith OBE, *b.* 1952
1929	°*Peel* (3rd), William James Robert Peel (4th *UK Visct. Peel*, 1895), *b.* 1947, *s.* 1969, *m.*	Viscount Clanfield, *b.* 1976
1551	*Pembroke* (17th) and *Montgomery* (14th) (1605), Henry George Charles Alexander Herbert, *b.* 1939, *s.* 1969.	Lord Herbert, *b.* 1978
1605 s.	*Perth* (17th), John David Drummond, PC, *b.* 1907, *s.* 1951, *w.*	Viscount Strathallan, *b.* 1935
1905	*Plymouth* (3rd), Other Robert Ivor Windsor-Clive (15th *Engl. Baron, Windsor*, 1529), *b.* 1923, *s.* 1943, *m.*	Viscount Windsor, *b.* 1951
1785 ɪ.	*Portarlington* (7th), George Lionel Yuill Seymour Dawson-Damer, *b.* 1938, *s.* 1959, *m.*	Viscount Carlow, *b.* 1965
1689	*Portland* (12th), Count Timothy Charles Robert Noel Bentinck, *b.* 1953, *s.* 1997, *m.*	Viscount Woodstock, *b.* 1984
1743	*Portsmouth* (10th), Quentin Gerard Carew Wallop, *b.* 1954, *s.* 1984, *m.*	Viscount Lymington, *b.* 1981
1804	*Powis* (8th), John George Herbert (9th *Irish Baron, Clive*, 1762), *b.* 1952, *s.* 1993, *m.*	Viscount Clive, *b.* 1979

Created	Title, order of succession, name, etc.	Heir
1765	*Radnor* (8th), Jacob Pleydell-Bouverie, *b.* 1927, *s.* 1968, *m.*	Viscount Folkestone, *b.* 1955
1831 I.*	*Ranfurly* (7th), Gerald Françoys Needham Knox (8th *UK Baron, Ranfurly,* 1826), *b.* 1929, *s.* 1988, *m.*	Edward J. K., *b.* 1957
1771 I.	*Roden* (10th), Robert John Jocelyn, *b.* 1938, *s.* 1993, *m.*	Viscount Jocelyn, *b.* 1989
1801	*Romney* (7th), Michael Henry Marsham, *b.* 1910, *s.* 1975, *m.*	Julian C. M., *b.* 1948
1703 S.*	*Rosebery* (7th), Neil Archibald Primrose (3rd *UK Earl Midlothian,* 1911), *b.* 1929, *s.* 1974, *m.*	Lord Dalmeny, *b.* 1967
1806 I.	*Rosse* (7th), William Brendan Parsons, *b.* 1936, *s.* 1979, *m.*	Lord Oxmantown, *b.* 1969
1801	*Rosslyn* (7th), Peter St Clair-Erskine, *b.* 1958, *s.* 1977, *m.*	Lord Loughborough, *b.* 1986
1457 S.	*Rothes* (21st), Ian Lionel Malcolm Leslie, *b.* 1932, *s.* 1975, *m.*	Lord Leslie, *b.* 1958
1861	°*Russell* (5th), Conrad Sebastian Robert Russell, FBA, *b.* 1937, *s.* 1987, *m.*	Viscount Amberley, *b.* 1968
1915	°*St Aldwyn* (3rd), Michael Henry Hicks Beach, *b.* 1950, *s.* 1992, *m.*	Hon. David S. H. B., *b.* 1955
1815	*St Germans* (10th), Peregrine Nicholas Eliot, *b.* 1941, *s.* 1988.	Lord Eliot, *b.* 1966
1660	*Sandwich* (11th), John Edward Hollister Montagu, *b.* 1943, *s.* 1995, *m.*	Viscount Hinchingbrooke, *b.* 1969
1690	*Scarbrough* (12th), Richard Aldred Lumley (13th *Irish Visct. Lumley,* 1628), *b.* 1932, *s.* 1969, *m.*	Viscount Lumley, *b.* 1973
1701 S.	*Seafield* (13th), Ian Derek Francis Ogilvie-Grant, *b.* 1939, *s.* 1969, *m.*	Viscount Reidhaven, *b.* 1963
1882	*Selborne* (4th), John Roundell Palmer, KBE, FRS, *b.* 1940, *s.* 1971, *m.*	Viscount Wolmer, *b.* 1971
1646 S.	*Selkirk.* Disclaimed for life 1994. (*see* Lord Selkirk of Douglas, page 161)	Hon. John A. *Douglas-Hamilton, b.* 1978
1672	*Shaftesbury* (10th), Anthony Ashley-Cooper, *b.* 1938, *s.* 1961, *m.*	Lord Ashley, *b.* 1977
1756 I.*	*Shannon* (9th), Richard Bentinck Boyle (8th *Brit. Baron Carleton,* 1786), *b.* 1924, *s.* 1963.	Viscount Boyle, *b.* 1960
1442	*Shrewsbury and Waterford* (22nd) (I. 1446), Charles Henry John Benedict Crofton Chetwynd Chetwynd-Talbot (7th *Engl. Earl Talbot,* 1784), *b.* 1952, *s.* 1980, *m.* Premier Earl of England and Ireland	Viscount Ingestre, *b.* 1978
1961	*Snowdon* (1st), Antony Charles Robert Armstrong-Jones, GCVO, *b.* 1930, *m.* (*see also* page 117)	Viscount Linley, *b.* 1961 (*see also* page 117)
1765	°*Spencer* (9th), Charles Edward Maurice Spencer, *b.* 1964, *s.* 1992.	Viscount Althorp, *b.* 1994
1703 S.*	*Stair* (14th), John David James Dalrymple (7th *UK Baron, Oxenfoord,* 1841), *b.* 1961, *s.* 1996.	Hon. David H. D., *b.* 1963
1984	*Stockton* (2nd), Alexander Daniel Alan Macmillan, *b.* 1943, *s.* 1986, *m.*	Viscount Macmillan of Ovenden, *b.* 1974
1821	*Stradbroke* (6th), Robert Keith Rous, *b.* 1937, *s.* 1983, *m.*	Viscount Dunwich, *b.* 1961
1847	*Strafford* (8th), Thomas Edmund Byng, *b.* 1936, *s.* 1984, *m.*	Viscount Enfield, *b.* 1964
1606 S.*	*Strathmore and Kinghorne* (18th), Michael Fergus Bowes Lyon (16th *Scott. Earl, Strathmore,* 1677; 18th *Scott. Earl, Kinghorne,* 1606; 5th *UK Earl, Strathmore and Kinghorne,* 1937), *b.* 1957, *s.* 1987, *m.*	Lord Glamis, *b.* 1986
1603	*Suffolk* (21st) and *Berkshire* (14th) (1626), Michael John James George Robert Howard, *b.* 1935, *s.* 1941, *m.*	Viscount Andover, *b.* 1974
1955	*Swinton* (2nd), David Yarburgh Cunliffe-Lister, *b.* 1937, *s.* 1972, *m.*	Hon. Nicholas J. C.-L., *b.* 1939
1714	*Tankerville* (10th), Peter Grey Bennet, *b.* 1956, *s.* 1980.	Revd the Hon. George A. G. B., *b.* 1925
1822	°*Temple of Stowe* (8th), (Walter) Grenville Algernon Temple-Gore-Langton, *b.* 1924, *s.* 1988, *m.*	Lord Langton, *b.* 1955
1815	*Verulam* (7th), John Duncan Grimston (11th *Irish Visct. Grimston,* 1719; 16th *Scott. Baron Forrester of Corstorphine,* 1633), *b.* 1951, *s.* 1973, *m.*	Viscount Grimston, *b.* 1978
1729	°*Waldegrave* (13th), James Sherbrooke Waldegrave, *b.* 1940, *s.* 1995, *m.*	Viscount Chewton, *b.* 1986
1759	*Warwick* (9th) and *Brooke* (9th) (*Brit.* 1746), Guy David Greville, *b.* 1957, *s.* 1996, *m.*	Lord Brooke, *b.* 1982
1633 S.*	*Wemyss* (12th) and *March* (8th) (s. 1697), Francis David Charteris, KT (5th *UK Baron Wemyss,* 1821), *b.* 1912, *s.* 1937, *m.*	Lord Neidpath, *b.* 1948
1621 I.	*Westmeath* (13th), William Anthony Nugent, *b.* 1928, *s.* 1971, *m.*	Hon. Sean C. W. N., *b.* 1965
1624	*Westmorland* (16th), Anthony David Francis Henry Fane, *b.* 1951, *s.* 1993, *m.*	Hon. Harry St C. F., *b.* 1953
1876	*Wharncliffe* (5th), Richard Alan Montagu Stuart Wortley, *b.* 1953, *s.* 1987, *m.*	Viscount Carlton, *b.* 1980
1801	*Wilton* (7th), Seymour William Arthur John Egerton, *b.* 1921, *s.* 1927, *m.*	Baron Ebury, *b.* 1934 (*see* page 149)
1628	*Winchilsea* (16th) and *Nottingham* (11th) (1681), Christopher Denys Stormont Finch Hatton, *b.* 1936, *s.* 1950, *m.*	Viscount Maidstone, *b.* 1967
1766 I.	°*Winterton* (8th), (Donald) David Turnour, *b.* 1943, *s.* 1991, *m.*	Robert C. T., *b.* 1950
1956	*Woolton* (3rd), Simon Frederick Marquis, *b.* 1958, *s.* 1969, *m.*	None
1837	*Yarborough* (8th), Charles John Pelham, *b.* 1963, *s.* 1991, *m.*	Lord Worsley, *b.* 1990

COUNTESSES IN THEIR OWN RIGHT

Style, The Right Hon. the Countess (of) __
Husband, Untitled
Children's style, As for children of an Earl
For forms of address, *see* page 135

Created	Title, order of succession, name, etc.	Heir
1643 s.	*Dysart* (11th in line), Rosamund Agnes Greaves, *b.* 1914, *s.* 1975.	Lady Katherine *Grant of Rothiemurchus*, *b.* 1918
1633 s.	*Loudoun* (13th in line), Barbara Huddleston Abney-Hastings, *b.* 1919, *s.* 1960, *m.*	Lord Mauchline, *b.* 1942
c.1115 s.	*Mar* (31st in line), Margaret of Mar, *b.* 1940, *s.* 1975, *m. Premier Earldom of Scotland*	Mistress of Mar, *b.* 1963
1947	°*Mountbatten of Burma* (2nd in line), Patricia Edwina Victoria Knatchbull, CBE, *b.* 1924, *s.* 1979, *m.*	Lord Romsey, *b.* 1947 (*see also* page 148)
c.1235 s.	*Sutherland* (24th in line), Elizabeth Millicent Sutherland, *b.* 1921, *s.* 1963, *m.*	Lord Strathnaver, *b.* 1947

VISCOUNTS

Coronet, Sixteen silver balls
Style, The Right Hon. the Viscount __
Wife's style, The Right Hon. the Viscountess __
Children's style, 'The Hon.' before forename and family name
In Scotland, the heir apparent to a Viscount may be styled 'The Master of __ (title of peer)'
For forms of address, *see* page 135

Created	Title, order of succession, name, etc.	Heir
1945	*Addison* (4th), William Matthew Wand Addison, *b.* 1945, *s.* 1992, *m.*	Hon. Paul W. *A.*, *b.* 1973
1946	*Alanbrooke* (3rd), Alan Victor Harold Brooke, *b.* 1932, *s.* 1972.	None
1919	*Allenby* (3rd), Lt.-Col. Michael Jaffray Hynman Allenby, *b.* 1931, *s.* 1984, *m.*	Hon. Henry J. H. *A.*, *b.* 1968
1911	*Allendale* (3rd), Wentworth Hubert Charles Beaumont, *b.* 1922, *s.* 1956.	Hon. Wentworth P. I. *B.*, *b.* 1948
1642 s.	*of Arbuthnott* (16th), John Campbell Arbuthnott, KT, CBE, DSC, FRSE, *b.* 1924, *s.* 1966, *m.*	Master of Arbuthnott, *b.* 1950
1751 I.	*Ashbrook* (11th), Michael Llowarch Warburton Flower, *b.* 1935, *s.* 1995, *m.*	Hon. Rowland F. W. *F.*, *b.* 1975
1917	*Astor* (4th), William Waldorf Astor, *b.* 1951, *s.* 1966, *m.*	Hon. William W. *A.*, *b.* 1979
1781 I.	*Bangor* (8th), William Maxwell David Ward, *b.* 1948, *s.* 1993, *m.*	Hon. E. Nicholas *W.*, *b.* 1953
1925	*Bearsted* (5th), Nicholas Alan Samuel, *b.* 1950, *s.* 1996, *m.*	Hon. Harry R. *S.*, *b.* 1988
1963	*Blakenham* (2nd), Michael John Hare, *b.* 1938, *s.* 1982, *m.*	Hon. Caspar J. *H.*, *b.* 1972
1935	*Bledisloe* (3rd), Christopher Hiley Ludlow Bathurst, QC, *b.* 1934, *s.* 1979.	Hon. Rupert E. L. *B.*, *b.* 1964
1712	*Bolingbroke* (7th) and *St John* (8th) (1716), Kenneth Oliver Musgrave St John, *b.* 1927, *s.* 1974.	Hon. Henry F. *St J.*, *b.* 1957
1960	*Boyd of Merton* (2nd), Simon Donald Rupert Neville Lennox-Boyd, *b.* 1939, *s.* 1983, *m.*	Hon. Benjamin A. *L.-B.*, *b.* 1964
1717 I.*	*Boyne* (11th), Gustavus Michael Stucley Hamilton-Russell (5th UK Baron Brancepeth, 1866), *b.* 1965, *s.* 1995, *m.*	Hon. Richard G. *H.-R.* DSO, LVO, *b.* 1909
1929	*Brentford* (4th), Crispin William Joynson-Hicks, *b.* 1933, *s.* 1983, *m.*	Hon. Paul W. *J.-H.*, *b.* 1971
1929	*Bridgeman* (3rd), Robin John Orlando Bridgeman, *b.* 1930, *s.* 1982, *m.*	Hon. William O. C. *B.*, *b.* 1968
1868	*Bridport* (4th), Alexander Nelson Hood (7th *Duke, Brontë in Sicily*, 1799; 6th *Irish Baron Bridport*, 1794), *b.* 1948, *s.* 1969, *m.*	Hon. Peregrine A. N. *H.*, *b.* 1974
1952	*Brookeborough* (3rd), Alan Henry Brooke, *b.* 1952, *s.* 1987, *m.*	Hon. Christopher A. *B.*, *b.* 1954
1933	*Buckmaster* (3rd), Martin Stanley Buckmaster, OBE, *b.* 1921, *s.* 1974.	Hon. Colin J. *B.*, *b.* 1923
1939	*Caldecote* (2nd), Robert Andrew Inskip, KBE, DSC, FEng, *b.* 1917, *s.* 1947, *m.*	Hon. Piers J. H. *I.*, *b.* 1947
1941	*Camrose*. Disclaimed for life 1995. (*see* Baron Hartwell, page 159)	Hon. Adrian M. *Berry*, *b.* 1937

Created	Title, order of succession, name, etc.	Heir
1954	*Chandos* (3rd), Thomas Orlando Lyttelton, *b.* 1953, *s.* 1980, *m.*	Hon. Oliver A. *L.*, *b.* 1986
1665 I.	*Charlemont* (14th), John Day Caulfeild (18th *Irish Baron Caulfeild of Charlemont*, 1620), *b.* 1934, *s.* 1985, *m.*	Hon. John D. *C.*, *b.* 1966
1921	*Chelmsford* (3rd), Frederic Jan Thesiger, *b.* 1931, *s.* 1970, *m.*	Hon. Frederic C. P. *T.*, *b.* 1962
1717 I.	*Chetwynd* (10th), Adam Richard John Casson Chetwynd, *b.* 1935, *s.* 1965, *m.*	Hon. Adam D. *C.*, *b.* 1969
1911	*Chilston* (4th), Alastair George Akers-Douglas, *b.* 1946, *s.* 1982, *m.*	Hon. Oliver I. *A.-D.*, *b.* 1973
1902	*Churchill* (3rd), Victor George Spencer (5th *UK Baron Churchill*, 1815), *b.* 1934, *s.* 1973.	None to Viscountcy. To Barony, Richard H. R. *S.*, *b.* 1926
1718	*Cobham* (11th), John William Leonard Lyttelton (8th *Irish Baron Westcote*, 1776), *b.* 1943, *s.* 1977, *m.*	Hon. Christopher C. *L.*, *b.* 1947
1902	*Colville of Culross* (4th), John Mark Alexander Colville, QC (13th *Scott. Baron Colville of Culross*, 1604), *b.* 1933, *s.* 1945, *m.*	Master of Colville, *b.* 1959
1826	*Combermere* (5th), Michael Wellington Stapleton-Cotton, *b.* 1929, *s.* 1969, *m.*	Hon. Thomas R. W. *S.-C.*, *b.* 1969
1917	*Cowdray* (4th), Michael Orlando Weetman Pearson (4th *UK Baron Cowdray*, 1910), *b.* 1944, *s.* 1995, *m.*	Hon. Charles A. *P.*, *b.* 1956
1927	*Craigavon* (3rd), Janric Fraser Craig, *b.* 1944, *s.* 1974.	None
1886	*Cross* (3rd), Assheton Henry Cross, *b.* 1920, *s.* 1932.	None
1943	*Daventry* (3rd), Francis Humphrey Maurice FitzRoy Newdegate, *b.* 1921, *s.* 1986, *m.*	Hon. James E. *F. N.*, *b.* 1960
1937	*Davidson* (2nd), John Andrew Davidson, *b.* 1928, *s.* 1970, *m.*	Hon. Malcolm W. M. *D.*, *b.* 1934
1956	*De L'Isle* (2nd), Philip John Algernon Sidney, MBE (7th *UK Baron De L'Isle and Dudley*, 1835), *b.* 1945, *s.* 1991, *m.*	Hon. Philip W. E. *S.*, *b.* 1985
1776 I.	*De Vesci* (7th), Thomas Eustace Vesey (8th *Irish Baron Knapton*, 1750), *b.* 1955, *s.* 1983, *m.*	Hon. Oliver I. *V.*, *b.* 1991
1917	*Devonport* (3rd), Terence Kearley, *b.* 1944, *s.* 1973.	Chester D. H. *K.*, *b.* 1932
1964	*Dilhorne* (2nd), John Mervyn Manningham-Buller, *b.* 1932, *s.* 1980, *m.*	Hon. James E. *M.-B.*, *b.* 1956
1622 I.	*Dillon* (22nd), Henry Benedict Charles Dillon, *b.* 1973, *s.* 1982.	Hon. Richard A. L. *D.*, *b.* 1948
1785 I.	*Doneraile* (10th), Richard Allen St Leger, *b.* 1946, *s.* 1983, *m.*	Hon. Nathaniel W. R. St J. *St L.*, *b.* 1971
1680 I.*	*Downe* (11th), John Christian George Dawnay (4th *UK Baron Dawnay*, 1897), *b.* 1935, *s.* 1965, *m.*	Hon. Richard H. *D.*, *b.* 1967
1959	*Dunrossil* (2nd), John William Morrison, CMG, *b.* 1926, *s.* 1961, *m.*	Hon. Andrew W. R. *M.*, *b.* 1953
1964	*Eccles* (1st), David McAdam Eccles, CH, KCVO, PC, *b.* 1904, *m.*	Hon. John D. *E.* CBE, *b.* 1931
1897	*Esher* (4th), Lionel Gordon Baliol Brett, CBE, *b.* 1913, *s.* 1963, *m.*	Hon. Christopher L. B. *B.*, *b.* 1936
1816	*Exmouth* (10th), Paul Edward Pellew, *b.* 1940, *s.* 1970, *m.*	Hon. Edward F. *P.*, *b.* 1978
1620 S.	*Falkland* (15th), Lucius Edward William Plantagenet Cary, *b.* 1935, *s.* 1984, *m. Premier Scottish Viscount on the Roll*	Master of Falkland, *b.* 1963
1720	*Falmouth* (9th), George Hugh Boscawen (26th *Engl. Baron Le Despencer*, 1264), *b.* 1919, *s.* 1962, *m.*	Hon. Evelyn A. H. *B.*, *b.* 1955
1720 I.*	*Gage* (8th), (Henry) Nicolas Gage (7th *Brit. Baron Gage*, 1790), *b.* 1934, *s.* 1993, *m.*	Hon. Henry W. *G.*, *b.* 1975
1727 I.	*Galway* (12th), George Rupert Monckton-Arundell, *b.* 1922, *s.* 1980, *m.*	Hon. J. Philip *M.-A.*, *b.* 1952
1478 I.*	*Gormanston* (17th), Jenico Nicholas Dudley Preston (5th *UK Baron Gormanston*, 1868), *b.* 1939, *s.* 1940, *w. Premier Viscount of Ireland*	Hon. Jenico F. T. *P.*, *b.* 1974
1816 I.	*Gort* (9th), Foley Robert Standish Prendergast Vereker, *b.* 1951, *s.* 1995, *m.*	Hon. Nicholas L. P. *V.*, *b.* 1954
1900	*Goschen* (4th), Giles John Harry Goschen, *b.* 1965, *s.* 1977, *m.*	None
1849	*Gough* (5th), Shane Hugh Maryon Gough, *b.* 1941, *s.* 1951.	None
1937	*Greenwood* (2nd), David Henry Hamar Greenwood, *b.* 1914, *s.* 1948.	Hon. Michael G. H. *G.*, *b.* 1923
1929	*Hailsham.* Disclaimed for life 1963. (*see* Lord Hailsham of St Marylebone, page 159)	Rt. Hon. Douglas M. *Hogg* QC, MP, *b.* 1945
1891	*Hambleden* (4th), William Herbert Smith, *b.* 1930, *s.* 1948, *m.*	Hon. William H. B. *S.*, *b.* 1955
1884	*Hampden* (6th), Anthony David Brand, *b.* 1937, *s.* 1975, *m.*	Hon. Francis A. *B.*, *b.* 1970
1936	*Hanworth* (3rd), David Stephen Geoffrey Pollock, *b.* 1946, *s.* 1996, *m.*	Hon. Richard C. S. *P.*, *b.* 1951
1791 I.	*Harberton* (10th), Thomas de Vautort Pomeroy, *b.* 1910, *s.* 1980, *m.*	Hon. Robert W. *P.*, *b.* 1916
1846	*Hardinge* (6th), Charles Henry Nicholas Hardinge, *b.* 1956, *s.* 1984, *m.*	Hon. Andrew H. *H.*, *b.* 1960
1791 I.	*Hawarden* (9th), (Robert) Connan Wyndham Leslie Maude, *b.* 1961, *s.* 1991, *m.*	Hon. Thomas P. C. *M.*, *b.* 1964
1960	*Head* (2nd), Richard Antony Head, *b.* 1937, *s.* 1983, *m.*	Hon. Henry J. *H.*, *b.* 1980
1550	*Hereford* (18th), Robert Milo Leicester Devereux, *b.* 1932, *s.* 1952. *Premier Viscount of England*	Hon. Charles R. de B. *D.*, *b.* 1975
1842	*Hill* (8th), Antony Rowland Clegg-Hill, *b.* 1931, *s.* 1974, *m.*	Peter D. R. C. *C.-H.*, *b.* 1945
1796	*Hood* (7th), Alexander Lambert Hood (7th *Irish Baron, Hood*, 1782), *b.* 1914, *s.* 1981, *m.*	Hon. Henry L. A. *H.*, *b.* 1958
1956	*Ingleby* (2nd), Martin Raymond Peake, *b.* 1926, *s.* 1966, *w.*	None
1945	*Kemsley* (2nd), (Geoffrey) Lionel Berry, *b.* 1909, *s.* 1968, *m.*	Richard G. *B.*, *b.* 1951

Created	Title, order of succession, name, etc.	Heir
1911	Knollys (3rd), David Francis Dudley Knollys, b. 1931, s. 1966, m.	Hon. Patrick N. M. K., b. 1962
1895	Knutsford (6th), Michael Holland-Hibbert, b. 1926, s. 1986, m.	Hon. Henry T. H.-H., b. 1959
1945	Lambert (3rd), Michael John Lambert, b. 1912, s. 1989, m.	None
1954	Leathers (3rd), Christopher Graeme Leathers, b. 1941, s. 1996, m.	Hon. James F. L., b. 1969
1922	Leverhulme (3rd), Philip William Bryce Lever, KG,TD, b. 1915, s. 1949, w.	None
1781 I.	Lifford (9th), (Edward) James Wingfield Hewitt, b. 1949, s. 1987, m.	Hon. James T. W. H., b. 1979
1921	Long (4th), Richard Gerard Long, CBE, b. 1929, s. 1967, m.	Hon. James R. L., b. 1960
1957	Mackintosh of Halifax (3rd), (John) Clive Mackintosh, b. 1958, s. 1980, m.	Hon. Thomas H. G. M., b. 1985
1955	Malvern (3rd), Ashley Kevin Godfrey Huggins, b. 1949, s. 1978.	Hon. M. James H., b. 1928
1945	Marchwood (3rd), David George Staveley Penny, b. 1936, s. 1979, w.	Hon. Peter G. W. P., b. 1965
1942	Margesson (2nd), Francis Vere Hampden Margesson, b. 1922, s. 1965, m.	Capt. Hon. Richard F. D. M., b. 1960
1660 I.*	Massereene (14th) and Ferrard (7th) (1797), John David Clotworthy Whyte-Melville Foster Skeffington (7th UK Baron, Oriel, 1821), b. 1940, s. 1992, m.	Hon. Charles J. C. W.-M. F. S., b. 1973
1802	Melville (9th), Robert David Ross Dundas, b. 1937, s. 1971, m.	Hon. Robert H. K. D., b. 1984
1916	Mersey (4th), Richard Maurice Clive Bigham (13th Scott. Lord Nairne, 1681, s. 1995), b. 1934, s. 1979, m.	Hon. Edward J. H. B., b. 1966
1717 I.*	Midleton (12th), Alan Henry Brodrick (9th Brit. Baron Brodrick of Peper Harow, 1796), b. 1949, s. 1988, m.	Hon. Ashley R. B., b. 1980
1962	Mills (3rd), Christopher Philip Roger Mills, b. 1956, s. 1988, m.	None
1716 I.	Molesworth (11th), Richard Gosset Molesworth, b. 1907, s. 1961, w.	Hon. Robert B. K. M., b. 1959
1801 I.*	Monck (7th), Charles Stanley Monck (4th UK Baron, Monck, 1866), b. 1953, s. 1982 (does not use title)	Hon. George S. M., b. 1957
1957	Monckton of Brenchley (2nd), Maj.-Gen. Gilbert Walter Riversdale Monckton, CB, OBE, MC, b. 1915, s. 1965, m.	Hon. Christopher W. M., b. 1952
1946	Montgomery of Alamein (2nd), David Bernard Montgomery, CBE, b. 1928, s. 1976, m.	Hon. Henry D. M., b. 1954
1550 I.*	Mountgarret (17th), Richard Henry Piers Butler (4th UK Baron Mountgarret, 1911), b. 1936, s. 1966, m.	Hon. Piers J. R. B., b. 1961
1952	Norwich (2nd), John Julius Cooper, CVO, b. 1929, s. 1954, m.	Hon. Jason C. D. B. C., b. 1959
1651 S.	of Oxfuird (13th), George Hubbard Makgill, CBE, b. 1934, s. 1986, m.	Master of Oxfuird, b. 1969
1873	Portman (9th), Edward Henry Berkeley Portman, b. 1934, s. 1967, m.	Hon. Christopher E. B. P., b. 1958
1743 I.*	Powerscourt (10th), Mervyn Niall Wingfield (4th UK Baron Powerscourt, 1885), b. 1935, s. 1973, m.	Hon. Mervyn A. W., b. 1963
1900	Ridley (4th), Matthew White Ridley, KG, GCVO, TD, b. 1925, s. 1964, m. Lord Steward	Hon. Matthew W. R., b. 1958
1960	Rochdale (2nd), St John Durival Kemp, b. 1938, s. 1993, m.	Hon. Jonathan H. D. K., b. 1961
1919	Rothermere (3rd), Vere Harold Esmond Harmsworth, b. 1925, s. 1978, m.	Hon. H. Jonathan E. V. H., b. 1967
1937	Runciman of Doxford (3rd), Walter Garrison Runciman (Garry), CBE, FBA (4th UK Baron, Runciman, 1933), b. 1934, s. 1989, m.	Hon. David W. R., b. 1967
1918	St Davids (3rd), Colwyn Jestyn John Philipps (20th Engl. Baron Strange of Knokin, 1299; 8th Engl. Baron, Hungerford, 1426; Baron De Moleyns, 1445), b. 1939, s. 1991, m.	Hon. Rhodri C. P., b. 1966
1801	St Vincent (7th), Ronald George James Jervis, b. 1905, s. 1940, m.	Hon. Edward R. J. J., b. 1951
1937	Samuel (3rd), David Herbert Samuel, OBE, PH.D., b. 1922, s. 1978, m.	Hon. Dan J. S., b. 1925
1911	Scarsdale (3rd), Francis John Nathaniel Curzon (7th Brit. Baron Scarsdale, 1761), b. 1924, s. 1977, m.	Hon. Peter G. N. C., b. 1949
1905	Selby (5th), Edward Thomas William Gully, b. 1967, s. 1997, m.	Hon. Christopher R. T. G., b. 1993
1805	Sidmouth (7th), John Tonge Anthony Pellew Addington, b. 1914, s. 1976, m.	Hon. Jeremy F. A., b. 1947
1940	Simon (3rd), Jan David Simon, b. 1940, s. 1993, m.	None
1960	Slim (2nd), John Douglas Slim, OBE, b. 1927, s. 1970, m.	Hon. Mark W. R. S., b. 1960
1954	Soulbury (2nd), James Herwald Ramsbotham, b. 1915, s. 1971, w.	Hon. Sir Peter E. R. GCMG, GCVO, b. 1919
1776 I.	Southwell (7th), Pyers Anthony Joseph Southwell, b. 1930, s. 1960, m.	Hon. Richard A. P. S., b. 1956
1942	Stansgate. Disclaimed for life 1963. (Rt. Hon. Anthony Neil Wedgwood Benn, MP, b.1925, s.1960, m.)	Stephen M. W. B., b. 1951
1959	Stuart of Findhorn (2nd), David Randolph Moray Stuart, b. 1924, s. 1971, m.	Hon. J. Dominic S., b. 1948
1957	Tenby (3rd), William Lloyd George, b. 1927, s. 1983, m.	Hon. Timothy H. G. L. G., b. 1962
1952	Thurso (3rd), John Archibald Sinclair, b. 1953, s. 1995, m.	Hon. James A. R. S., b. 1984
1721	Torrington (11th), Timothy Howard St George Byng, b. 1943, s. 1961, m.	John L. B. MC, b. 1919
1936	Trenchard (3rd), Hugh Trenchard, b. 1951, s. 1987, m.	Hon. Alexander T. T., b. 1978
1921	Ullswater (2nd), Nicholas James Christopher Lowther, PC, b. 1942, s. 1949, m.	Hon. Benjamin J. L., b. 1975

Created	Title, order of succession, name, etc.	Heir
1621 I.	*Valentia* (15th), Richard John Dighton Annesley, *b.* 1929, *s.* 1983, *m.*	Hon. Francis W. D. *A.*, *b.* 1959
1952	*Waverley* (3rd), John Desmond Forbes Anderson, *b.* 1949, *s.* 1990.	None
1938	*Weir* (3rd), William Kenneth James Weir, *b.* 1933, *s.* 1975, *m.*	Hon. James W. H. *W.*, *b.* 1965
1983	*Whitelaw* (1st), William Stephen Ian Whitelaw, KT, CH, MC, PC, *b.* 1918.	None
1918	*Wimborne* (4th), Ivor Mervyn Vigors Guest (5th *UK Baron Wimborne* 1880), *b.* 1968, *s.* 1993.	Hon. Julian J. *G.*, *b.* 1945
1923	*Younger of Leckie* (4th), George Kenneth Hotson Younger, KT, KCVO, TD, PC (*Baron Younger of Prestwick* (life peerage), 1992), *b.* 1931, *s.* 1997, *m.*	Hon. James E. G. *Y.*, *b.* 1955

BARONS/LORDS

Coronet, Six silver balls
Style, The Right Hon. the Lord ___. In the Peerage of Scotland there is no rank of Baron; the equivalent rank is Lord of Parliament (*see* page 136) and Scottish peers should always be styled 'Lord', never 'Baron'
Wife's style, The Right Hon. the Lady ___
Children's style, 'The Hon.' before forename and family name
In Scotland, the heir apparent to a Lord may be styled 'The Master of ___ (title of peer)'
For forms of address, *see* page 135

Created	Title, order of succession, name, etc.	Heir
1911	*Aberconway* (3rd), Charles Melville McLaren, *b.* 1913, *s.* 1953, *m.*	Hon. H. Charles *M.*, *b.* 1948
1873	*Aberdare* (4th), Morys George Lyndhurst Bruce, KBE, PC, *b.* 1919, *s.* 1957, *m.*	Hon. Alastair J. L. *B.*, *b.* 1947
1835	*Abinger* (8th), James Richard Scarlett, *b.* 1914, *s.* 1943, *m.*	Hon. James H. *S.*, *b.* 1959
1869	*Acton* (4th), Richard Gerald Lyon-Dalberg-Acton, *b.* 1941, *s.* 1989, *m.*	Hon. John C. F. H. *L.-D.-A.*, *b.* 1966
1887	*Addington* (6th), Dominic Bryce Hubbard, *b.* 1963, *s.* 1982.	Hon. Michael W. L. *H.*, *b.* 1965
1896	*Aldenham* (6th) and *Hunsdon of Hunsdon* (4th) (1923), Vicary Tyser Gibbs, *b.* 1948, *s.* 1986, *m.*	Hon. Humphrey W. F. *G.*, *b.* 1989
1962	*Aldington* (1st), Toby Austin Richard William Low, KCMG, CBE, DSO, TD, PC, *b.* 1914.	Hon. Charles H. S. *L.*, *b.* 1948
1945	*Altrincham*. Disclaimed for life 1963. (*John Edward Poynder Grigg, b.* 1924, *s.* 1955, *m.*)	Hon. Anthony U. D. D. *G.*, *b.* 1934
1929	*Alvingham* (2nd), Maj.-Gen. Robert Guy Eardley Yerburgh, CBE, *b.* 1926, *s.* 1955, *m.*	Capt. Hon. Robert R. G. *Y.*, *b.* 1956
1892	*Amherst of Hackney* (4th), William Hugh Amherst Cecil, *b.* 1940, *s.* 1980, *m.*	Hon. H. William A. *C.*, *b.* 1968
1881	*Ampthill* (4th), Geoffrey Denis Erskine Russell, CBE, PC, *b.* 1921, *s.* 1973.	Hon. David W. E. *R.*, *b.* 1947
1947	*Amwell* (3rd), Keith Norman Montague, *b.* 1943, *s.* 1990, *m.*	Hon. Ian K. *M.*, *b.* 1973
1863	*Annaly* (6th), Luke Richard White, *b.* 1954, *s.* 1990, *m.*	Hon. Luke H. *W.*, *b.* 1990
1885	*Ashbourne* (4th), Edward Barry Greynville Gibson, *b.* 1933, *s.* 1983, *m.*	Hon. Edward C. d'O. *G.*, *b.* 1967
1835	*Ashburton* (7th), John Francis Harcourt Baring, KG, KCVO, *b.* 1928, *s.* 1991, *m.*	Hon. Mark F. R. *B.*, *b.* 1958
1892	*Ashcombe* (4th), Henry Edward Cubitt, *b.* 1924, *s.* 1962, *m.*	Mark E. *C.*, *b.* 1964
1911	*Ashton of Hyde* (3rd), Thomas John Ashton, TD, *b.* 1926, *s.* 1983, *m.*	Hon. Thomas H. *A.*, *b.* 1958
1800 I.	*Ashtown* (7th), Nigel Clive Crosby Trench, KCMG, *b.* 1916, *s.* 1990, *m.*	Hon. Roderick N. G. *T.*, *b.* 1944
1956	*Astor of Hever* (3rd), John Jacob Astor, *b.* 1946, *s.* 1984, *m.*	Hon. Charles G. J. *A.*, *b.* 1990
1789 I.*	*Auckland* (10th), Robert Ian Burnard Eden (10th *Brit. Baron Auckland*, 1793), *b.* 1962, *s.* 1997, *m.*	Hon. Ronald J. *E.*, *b.* 1931
1313	*Audley*. The 25th Lord Audley died in July 1997, leaving three co-heiresses	
1900	*Avebury* (4th), Eric Reginald Lubbock, *b.* 1928, *s.* 1971, *m.*	Hon. Lyulph A. J. *L.*, *b.* 1954
1718 I.	*Aylmer* (13th), Michael Anthony Aylmer, *b.* 1923, *s.* 1982, *m.*	Hon. A. Julian *A.*, *b.* 1951
1929	*Baden-Powell* (3rd), Robert Crause Baden-Powell, *b.* 1936, *s.* 1962, *m.*	Hon. David M. *B.-P.*, *b.* 1940
1780	*Bagot* (9th), Heneage Charles Bagot, *b.* 1914, *s.* 1979, *m.*	Hon. C. H. Shaun *B.*, *b.* 1944
1953	*Baillieu* (3rd), James William Latham Baillieu, *b.* 1950, *s.* 1973, *m.*	Hon. Robert L. *B.*, *b.* 1979
1607 S.	*Balfour of Burleigh* (8th), Robert Bruce, FRSE, *b.* 1927, *s.* 1967, *m.*	Hon. Victoria B., *b.* 1973
1945	*Balfour of Inchrye* (2nd), Ian Balfour, *b.* 1924, *s.* 1988, *m.*	None
1924	*Banbury of Southam* (3rd), Charles William Banbury, *b.* 1953, *s.* 1981, *m.*	None
1698	*Barnard* (11th), Harry John Neville Vane, TD, *b.* 1923, *s.* 1964.	Hon. Henry F. C. *V.*, *b.* 1959
1887	*Basing* (5th), Neil Lutley Sclater-Booth, *b.* 1939, *s.* 1983, *m.*	Hon. Stuart W. *S.-B.*, *b.* 1969
1917	*Beaverbrook* (3rd), Maxwell William Humphrey Aitken, *b.* 1951, *s.* 1985, *m.*	Hon. Maxwell F. *A.*, *b.* 1977

Created	Title, order of succession, name, etc.	Heir
1647 s.	*Belhaven and Stenton* (13th), Robert Anthony Carmichael Hamilton, *b.* 1927, *s.* 1961, *m.*	Master of Belhaven, *b.* 1953
1848 I.	*Bellew* (7th), James Bryan Bellew, *b.* 1920, *s.* 1981, *m.*	Hon. Bryan E. *B.*, *b.* 1943
1856	*Belper* (4th), (Alexander) Ronald George Strutt, *b.* 1912, *s.* 1956.	Hon. Richard H. *S.*, *b.* 1941
1938	*Belstead* (2nd), John Julian Ganzoni, PC, *b.* 1932, *s.* 1958.	None
1421	*Berkeley* (18th), Anthony Fitzhardinge Gueterbock, OBE, *b.* 1939, *s.* 1992, *m.*	Hon. Thomas F. *G.*, *b.* 1969
1922	*Bethell* (4th), Nicholas William Bethell, *b.* 1938, *s.* 1967, *m.*	Hon. James N. *B.*, *b.* 1967
1938	*Bicester* (3rd), Angus Edward Vivian Smith, *b.* 1932, *s.* 1968.	Hugh C. V. *S.*, *b.* 1934
1903	*Biddulph* (5th), (Anthony) Nicholas Colin Maitland Biddulph, *b.* 1959, *s.* 1988, *m.*	Hon. William I. R. *M. B.*, *b.* 1963
1938	*Birdwood* (3rd), Mark William Ogilvie Birdwood, *b.* 1938, *s.* 1962, *m.*	None
1958	*Birkett* (2nd), Michael Birkett, *b.* 1929, *s.* 1962, *m.*	Hon. Thomas *B.*, *b.* 1982
1907	*Blyth* (4th), Anthony Audley Rupert Blyth, *b.* 1931, *s.* 1977, *m.*	Hon. Riley A. J. *B.*, *b.* 1955
1797	*Bolton* (7th), Richard William Algar Orde-Powlett, *b.* 1929, *s.* 1963, *m.*	Hon. Harry A. N. *O.-P.*, *b.* 1954
1452 s.	*Borthwick* (24th), John Hugh Borthwick, *b.* 1940, *s.* 1997, *m.*	Hon. James H. A. *B. of Glengelt*, *b.* 1940
1922	*Borwick* (4th), James Hugh Myles Borwick, MC, *b.* 1917, *s.* 1961, *m.*	Hon. Robin S. *B.*, *b.* 1927
1761	*Boston* (10th), Timothy George Frank Boteler Irby, *b.* 1939, *s.* 1978, *m.*	Hon. George W. E. B. *I.*, *b.* 1971
1942	*Brabazon of Tara* (3rd), Ivon Anthony Moore-Brabazon, *b.* 1946, *s.* 1974, *m.*	Hon. Benjamin R. *M.-B.*, *b.* 1983
1880	*Brabourne* (7th), John Ulick Knatchbull, CBE, *b.* 1924, *s.* 1943, *m.*	Lord Romsey, *b.* 1947 (*see* page 144)
1925	*Bradbury* (3rd), John Bradbury, *b.* 1940, *s.* 1994, *m.*	Hon. John *B.*, *b.* 1973
1962	*Brain* (2nd), Christopher Langdon Brain, *b.* 1926, *s.* 1966, *m.*	Hon. Michael C. *B.* DM, FRCP, *b.* 1928
1938	*Brassey of Apethorpe* (3rd), David Henry Brassey, OBE, *b.* 1932, *s.* 1967, *m.*	Hon. Edward *B.*, *b.* 1964
1788	*Braybrooke* (10th), Robin Henry Charles Neville, *b.* 1932, *s.* 1990, *m.*	George *N.*, *b.* 1943
1957	*Bridges* (2nd), Thomas Edward Bridges, GCMG, *b.* 1927, *s.* 1969, *m.*	Hon. Mark T. *B.*, *b.* 1954
1945	*Broadbridge* (3rd), Peter Hewett Broadbridge, *b.* 1938, *s.* 1972, *m.*	Martin H. *B.*, *b.* 1929
1933	*Brocket* (3rd), Charles Ronald George Nall-Cain, *b.* 1952, *s.* 1967, *m.*	Hon. Alexander C. C. *N.-C.*, *b.* 1984
1860	*Brougham and Vaux* (5th), Michael John Brougham, CBE, *b.* 1938, *s.* 1967.	Hon. Charles W. *B.*, *b.* 1971
1945	*Broughshane* (3rd), (William) Kensington Davison, DSO, DFC, *b.* 1914, *s.* 1995.	None
1776	*Brownlow* (7th), Edward John Peregrine Cust, *b.* 1936, *s.* 1978, *m.*	Hon. Peregrine E. Q. *C.*, *b.* 1974
1942	*Bruntisfield* (2nd), John Robert Warrender, OBE, MC, TD, *b.* 1921, *s.* 1993, *m.*	Hon. Michael J. V. *W.*, *b.* 1949
1950	*Burden* (3rd), Andrew Philip Burden, *b.* 1959, *s.* 1995.	Hon. Fraser W. E. *B.*, *b.* 1964
1529	*Burgh* (7th), Alexander Peter Willoughby Leith, *b.* 1935, *s.* 1959, *m.*	Hon. A. Gregory D. *L.*, *b.* 1958
1903	*Burnham* (6th), Hugh John Frederick Lawson, *b.* 1931, *s.* 1993, *m.*	Hon. Harry F. A. *L.*, *b.* 1968
1897	*Burton* (3rd), Michael Evan Victor Baillie, *b.* 1924, *s.* 1962, *m.*	Hon. Evan M. R. *B.*, *b.* 1949
1643	*Byron* (13th), Robert James Byron, *b.* 1950, *s.* 1989, *m.*	Hon. Charles R. G. *B.*, *b.* 1990
1937	*Cadman* (3rd), John Anthony Cadman, *b.* 1938, *s.* 1966, *m.*	Hon. Nicholas A. J. *C.*, *b.* 1977
1945	*Calverley* (3rd), Charles Rodney Muff, *b.* 1946, *s.* 1971, *m.*	Hon. Jonathan E. *M.*, *b.* 1975
1383	*Camoys* (7th), (Ralph) Thomas Campion George Sherman Stonor, GCVO, PC, *b.* 1940, *s.* 1976, *m. Lord Chamberlain*	Hon. R. William R. T. *S.*, *b.* 1974
1715 I.	*Carbery* (11th), Peter Ralfe Harrington Evans-Freke, *b.* 1920, *s.* 1970, *m.*	Hon. Michael P. *E.-F.*, *b.* 1942
1834 I.*	*Carew* (7th), Patrick Thomas Conolly-Carew (7th *UK Baron, Carew*, 1838), *b.* 1938, *s.* 1994, *m.*	Hon. William P. *C.-C.*, *b.* 1973
1916	*Carnock* (4th), David Henry Arthur Nicolson, *b.* 1920, *s.* 1982.	Nigel *N.* MBE, *b.* 1917
1796 I.*	*Carrington* (6th), Peter Alexander Rupert Carington, KG, GCMG, CH, MC, PC (6th *Brit. Baron Carrington*, 1797), *b.* 1919, *s.* 1938, *m.*	Hon. Rupert F. J. *C.*, *b.* 1948
1812 I.	*Castlemaine* (8th), Roland Thomas John Handcock, MBE, *b.* 1943, *s.* 1973, *m.*	Hon. Ronan M. E. *H.*, *b.* 1989
1936	*Catto* (2nd), Stephen Gordon Catto, *b.* 1923, *s.* 1959, *m.*	Hon. Innes G. *C.*, *b.* 1950
1918	*Cawley* (3rd), Frederick Lee Cawley, *b.* 1913, *s.* 1954, *m.*	Hon. John F. *C.*, *b.* 1946
1603	*Cecil.* A subsidiary title of the Marquess of Salisbury. His heir Viscount Cranborne, PC, was given a Writ in Acceleration in this title to enable him to sit in the House of Lords whilst his father is still alive (*see also* page 139)	
1937	*Chatfield* (2nd), Ernle David Lewis Chatfield, *b.* 1917, *s.* 1967, *m.*	None
1858	*Chesham* (6th), Nicholas Charles Cavendish, *b.* 1941, *s.* 1989, *m.*	Hon. Charles G. C. *C.*, *b.* 1974
1945	*Chetwode* (2nd), Philip Chetwode, *b.* 1937, *s.* 1950, *m.*	Hon. Roger *C.*, *b.* 1968
1945	*Chorley* (2nd), Roger Richard Edward Chorley, *b.* 1930, *s.* 1978, *m.*	Hon. Nicholas R. D. *C.*, *b.* 1966
1858	*Churston* (5th), John Francis Yarde-Buller, *b.* 1934, *s.* 1991, *m.*	Hon. Benjamin F. A. *Y.-B.*, *b.* 1974
1946	*Citrine* (2nd), Norman Arthur Citrine, *b.* 1914, *s.* 1983, *w.*	Hon. Ronald E. *C.*, *b.* 1919
1800 I.	*Clanmorris* (8th), Simon John Ward Bingham, *b.* 1937, *s.* 1988, *m.*	Robert D. de B. *B.*, *b.* 1942
1672	*Clifford of Chudleigh* (14th), Thomas Hugh Clifford, *b.* 1948, *s.* 1988, *m.*	Hon. Alexander T. H. *C.*, *b.* 1985
1299	*Clinton* (22nd), Gerard Nevile Mark Fane Trefusis, *b.* 1934, *title called out of abeyance* 1965, *m.*	Hon. Charles P. R. F. *T.*, *b.* 1962

Created	Title, order of succession, name, etc.	Heir
1955	*Clitheroe* (2nd), Ralph John Assheton, *b.* 1929, *s.* 1984, *m.*	Hon. Ralph C. *A.*, *b.* 1962
1919	*Clwyd* (3rd), (John) Anthony Roberts, *b.* 1935, *s.* 1987, *m.*	Hon. J. Murray *R.*, *b.* 1971
1948	*Clydesmuir* (3rd), David Ronald Colville, *b.* 1949, *s.* 1996, *m.*	Hon. Richard *C.*, *b.* 1980
1960	*Cobbold* (2nd), David Antony Fromanteel Lytton Cobbold, *b.* 1937, *s.* 1987, *m.*	Hon. Henry F. *L. C.*, *b.* 1962
1919	*Cochrane of Cults* (4th), (Ralph Henry) Vere Cochrane, *b.* 1926, *s.* 1990, *m.*	Hon. Thomas H. V. *C.*, *b.* 1957
1954	*Coleraine* (2nd), (James) Martin (Bonar) Law, *b.* 1931, *s.* 1980, *w.*	Hon. James P. B. *L.*, *b.* 1975
1873	*Coleridge* (5th), William Duke Coleridge, *b.* 1937, *s.* 1984, *m.*	Hon. James D. *C.*, *b.* 1967
1946	*Colgrain* (3rd), David Colin Campbell, *b.* 1920, *s.* 1973, *m.*	Hon. Alastair C. L. *C.*, *b.* 1951
1917	*Colwyn* (3rd), (Ian) Anthony Hamilton-Smith, CBE, *b.* 1942, *s.* 1966, *m.*	Hon. Craig P. *H.-S.*, *b.* 1968
1956	*Colyton* (2nd), Alisdair John Munro Hopkinson, *b.* 1958, *s.* 1996, *m.*	Hon. James P. M. *H.*, *b.* 1983
1841	*Congleton* (8th), Christopher Patrick Parnell, *b.* 1930, *s.* 1967, *m.*	Hon. John P. C. *P.*, *b.* 1959
1927	*Cornwallis* (3rd), Fiennes Neil Wykeham Cornwallis, OBE, *b.* 1921, *s.* 1982, *m.*	Hon. F. W. Jeremy *C.*, *b.* 1946
1874	*Cottesloe* (5th), Cdr. John Tapling Fremantle, *b.* 1927, *s.* 1994, *m.*	Hon. Thomas F. H. *F.*, *b.* 1966
1929	*Craigmyle* (4th), Thomas Columba Shaw, *b.* 1960, *s.* 1998, *m.*	Hon. Alexander F. *S.*, *b.* 1988
1899	*Cranworth* (3rd), Philip Bertram Gurdon, *b.* 1940, *s.* 1964, *m.*	Hon. Sacha W. R. *G.*, *b.* 1970
1959	*Crathorne* (2nd), Charles James Dugdale, *b.* 1939, *s.* 1977, *m.*	Hon. Thomas A. J. *D.*, *b.* 1977
1892	*Crawshaw* (5th), David Gerald Brooks, *b.* 1934, *s.* 1997, *m.*	Hon. John P. *B.*, *b.* 1938
1940	*Croft* (3rd), Bernard William Henry Page Croft, *b.* 1949, *s.* 1997, *w.*	None
1797 I.	*Crofton* (7th), Guy Patrick Gilbert Crofton, *b.* 1951, *s.* 1989, *m.*	Hon. E. Harry P. *C.*, *b.* 1988
1375	*Cromwell* (7th), Godfrey John Bewicke-Copley, *b.* 1960, *s.* 1982, *m.*	Hon. Thomas D. *B.-C.*, *b.* 1964
1947	*Crook* (2nd), Douglas Edwin Crook, *b.* 1926, *s.* 1989, *m.*	Hon. Robert D. E. *C.*, *b.* 1955
1920	*Cullen of Ashbourne* (2nd), Charles Borlase Marsham Cokayne, MBE, *b.* 1912, *s.* 1932, *w.*	Hon. Edmund W. M. *C.*, *b.* 1916
1914	*Cunliffe* (3rd), Roger Cunliffe, *b.* 1932, *s.* 1963, *m.*	Hon. Henry *C.*, *b.* 1962
1927	*Daresbury* (4th), Peter Gilbert Greenall, *b.* 1953, *s.* 1996, *m.*	Hon. Thomas E. *G.*, *b.* 1984
1924	*Darling* (2nd), Robert Charles Henry Darling, *b.* 1919, *s.* 1936, *m.*	Hon. R. Julian H. *D.*, *b.* 1944
1946	*Darwen* (3rd), Roger Michael Davies, *b.* 1938, *s.* 1988, *m.*	Hon. Paul *D.*, *b.* 1962
1932	*Davies* (3rd), David Davies, *b.* 1940, *s.* 1944, *m.*	Hon. David D. *D.*, *b.* 1975
1299	*de Clifford* (27th), John Edward Southwell Russell, *b.* 1928, *s.* 1982, *m.*	Hon. William S. R. *R.*, *b.* 1930
1851	*De Freyne* (7th), Francis Arthur John French, *b.* 1927, *s.* 1935, *m.*	Hon. Fulke C. A. J. *F.*, *b.* 1957
1838	*de Mauley* (6th), Gerald John Ponsonby, *b.* 1921, *s.* 1962, *m.*	Hon. Col. Thomas M. *P.* TD, *b.* 1930
1887	*De Ramsey* (4th), John Ailwyn Fellowes, *b.* 1942, *s.* 1993, *m.*	Hon. Freddie J. *F.*, *b.* 1978
1264	*de Ros* (28th), Peter Trevor Maxwell, *b.* 1958, *s.* 1983, *m. Premier Baron of England*	Hon. Finbar J. *M.*, *b.* 1988
1831	*de Saumarez* (7th), Eric Douglas Saumarez, *b.* 1956, *s.* 1991, *m.*	Hon. Victor T. *S.*, *b.* 1956
1910	*de Villiers* (3rd), Arthur Percy de Villiers, *b.* 1911, *s.* 1934.	Hon. Alexander C. *de V.*, *b.* 1940
1812 I.	*Decies* (7th), Marcus Hugh Tristram de la Poer Beresford, *b.* 1948, *s.* 1992, *m.*	Hon. Robert M. D. *de la P. B.*, *b.* 1988
1821	*Delamere* (5th), Hugh George Cholmondeley, *b.* 1934, *s.* 1979, *m.*	Hon. Thomas P. G. *C.*, *b.* 1968
1937	*Denham* (2nd), Bertram Stanley Mitford Bowyer, KBE, PC, *b.* 1927, *s.* 1948, *m.*	Hon. Richard G. G. *B.*, *b.* 1959
1834	*Denman* (5th), Charles Spencer Denman, CBE, MC, TD, *b.* 1916, *s.* 1971, *w.*	Hon. Richard T. S. *D.*, *b.* 1946
1885	*Deramore* (6th), Richard Arthur de Yarburgh-Bateson, *b.* 1911, *s.* 1964, *m.*	None
1881	*Derwent* (5th), Robin Evelyn Leo Vanden-Bempde-Johnstone, LVO, *b.* 1930, *s.* 1986, *m.*	Hon. Francis P. H. *V.-B.-J.*, *b.* 1965
1930	*Dickinson* (2nd), Richard Clavering Hyett Dickinson, *b.* 1926, *s.* 1943, *m.*	Hon. Martin H. *D.*, *b.* 1961
1620 I.*	*Digby* (12th), Edward Henry Kenelm Digby (6th *Brit. Baron Digby*, 1765), *b.* 1924, *s.* 1964, *m.*	Hon. Henry N. K. *D.*, *b.* 1954
1615	*Dormer* (17th), Geoffrey Henry Dormer, *b.* 1920, *s.* 1995, *m.*	Hon. William R. *D.*, *b.* 1960
1943	*Dowding* (3rd), Piers Hugh Tremenheere Dowding, *b.* 1948, *s.* 1992.	Hon. Mark D. J. *D.*, *b.* 1949
1800 I.	*Dufferin and Clandeboye.* The 10th Baron died in 1991. Heir had not established his claim to the title at the time of going to press	Sir John Blackwood, Bt., *b.* 1944
1929	*Dulverton* (3rd), (Gilbert) Michael Hamilton Wills, *b.* 1944, *s.* 1992, *m.*	Hon. Robert A. H. *W.*, *b.* 1983
1800 I.	*Dunalley* (7th), Henry Francis Cornelius Prittie, *b.* 1948, *s.* 1992, *m.*	Hon. Joel H. *P.*, *b.* 1981
1324 I.	*Dunboyne* (28th), Patrick Theobald Tower Butler, VRD, *b.* 1917, *s.* 1945, *m.*	Hon. John F. *B.*, *b.* 1951
1892	*Dunleath* (6th), Brian Henry Mulholland, *b.* 1950, *s.* 1997, *m.*	Hon. Andrew H. *M.*, *b.* 1981
1439 I.	*Dunsany* (19th), Randal Arthur Henry Plunkett, *b.* 1906, *s.* 1957, *m.*	Hon. Edward J. C. *P.*, *b.* 1939
1780	*Dynevor* (9th), Richard Charles Uryan Rhys, *b.* 1935, *s.* 1962.	Hon. Hugo G. U. *R.*, *b.* 1966
1857	*Ebury* (6th), Francis Egerton Grosvenor, *b.* 1934, *s.* 1957, *m.*	Hon. Julian F. M. *G.*, *b.* 1959
1963	*Egremont* (2nd) and *Leconfield* (7th) (1859), John Max Henry Scawen Wyndham, *b.* 1948, *s.* 1972, *m.*	Hon. George R. V. *W.*, *b.* 1983
1643	*Elibank* (14th), Alan D'Ardis Erskine-Murray, *b.* 1923, *s.* 1973, *w.*	Master of Elibank, *b.* 1964

Created	Title, order of succession, name, etc.	Heir
1802	*Ellenborough* (8th), Richard Edward Cecil Law, *b.* 1926, *s.* 1945, *m.*	Maj. Hon. Rupert E. H. *L.*, *b.* 1955
1509 s.*	*Elphinstone* (19th), Alexander Mountstuart Elphinstone (5th *UK Baron, Elphinstone,* 1885), *b.* 1980, *s.* 1994, *M.*	Hon. Angus J. *E.*, *b.* 1982
1934	*Elton* (2nd), Rodney Elton, TD, *b.* 1930, *s.* 1973, *m.*	Hon. Edward P. *E.*, *b.* 1966
1964	*Erroll of Hale* (1st), Frederick James Erroll, TD, PC, *b.* 1914, *m.*	None
1627 s.	*Fairfax of Cameron* (14th), Nicholas John Albert Fairfax, *b.* 1956, *s.* 1964, *m.*	Hon. Edward N. T. *F.*, *b.* 1984
1961	*Fairhaven* (3rd), Ailwyn Henry George Broughton, *b.* 1936, *s.* 1973, *m.*	Maj. Hon. James H. A. *B.*, *b.* 1963
1916	*Faringdon* (3rd), Charles Michael Henderson, *b.* 1937, *s.* 1977, *m.*	Hon. James H. *H.*, *b.* 1961
1756 I.	*Farnham* (12th), Barry Owen Somerset Maxwell, *b.* 1931, *s.* 1957, *m.*	Hon. Simon K. *M.*, *b.* 1933
1856 I.	*Fermoy* (6th), Patrick Maurice Burke Roche, *b.* 1967, *s.* 1984, *m.*	Hon. E. Hugh B. *R.*, *b.* 1972
1826	*Feversham* (6th), Charles Antony Peter Duncombe, *b.* 1945, *s.* 1963, *m.*	Hon. Jasper O. S. *D.*, *b.* 1968
1798 I.	*ffrench* (8th), Robuck John Peter Charles Mario ffrench, *b.* 1956, *s.* 1986, *m.*	Hon. John C. M. J. F. *ff.*, *b.* 1928
1909	*Fisher* (3rd), John Vavasseur Fisher, DSC, *b.* 1921, *s.* 1955, *m.*	Hon. Patrick V. *F.*, *b.* 1953
1295	*Fitzwalter* (21st), (Fitzwalter) Brook Plumptre, *b.* 1914, *title called out of abeyance* 1953, *m.*	Hon. Julian B. *P.*, *b.* 1952
1776	*Foley* (8th), Adrian Gerald Foley, *b.* 1923, *s.* 1927, *m.*	Hon. Thomas H. *F.*, *b.* 1961
1445 s.	*Forbes* (22nd), Nigel Ivan Forbes, KBE, *b.* 1918, *s.* 1953, *m. Premier Lord of Scotland*	Master of Forbes, *b.* 1946
1821	*Forester* (8th), (George Cecil) Brooke Weld-Forester, *b.* 1938, *s.* 1977, *m.*	Hon. C. R. George *W.-F.*, *b.* 1975
1922	*Forres* (4th), Alastair Stephen Grant Williamson, *b.* 1946, *s.* 1978, *m.*	Hon. George A. M. *W.*, *b.* 1972
1917	*Forteviot* (4th), John James Evelyn Dewar, *b.* 1938, *s.* 1993, *m.*	Hon. Alexander J. E. *D.*, *b.* 1971
1951	*Freyberg* (3rd), Valerian Bernard Freyberg, *b.* 1970, *s.* 1993.	None
1917	*Gainford* (3rd), Joseph Edward Pease, *b.* 1921, *s.* 1971, *m.*	Hon. George *P.*, *b.* 1926
1818 I.	*Garvagh* (5th), (Alexander Leopold Ivor) George Canning, *b.* 1920, *s.* 1956, *m.*	Hon. Spencer G. S. de R. *C.*, *b.* 1953
1942	*Geddes* (3rd), Euan Michael Ross Geddes, *b.* 1937, *s.* 1975, *m.*	Hon. James G. N. *G.*, *b.* 1969
1876	*Gerard* (5th), Anthony Robert Hugo Gerard, *b.* 1949, *s.* 1992, *m.*	Hon. Rupert B. C. *G.*, *b.* 1981
1824	*Gifford* (6th), Anthony Maurice Gifford, QC, *b.* 1940, *s.* 1961, *m.*	Hon. Thomas A. *G.*, *b.* 1967
1917	*Gisborough* (3rd), Thomas Richard John Long Chaloner, *b.* 1927, *s.* 1951, *m.*	Hon. T. Peregrine L. *C.*, *b.* 1961
1960	*Gladwyn* (2nd), Miles Alvery Gladwyn Jebb, *b.* 1930, *s.* 1996.	None
1899	*Glanusk* (5th), Christopher Russell Bailey, *b.* 1942, *s.* 1997, *m.*	Hon. Charles H. *B.*, *b.* 1976
1918	*Glenarthur* (4th), Simon Mark Arthur, *b.* 1944, *s.* 1976, *m.*	Hon. Edward A. *A.*, *b.* 1973
1911	*Glenconner* (3rd), Colin Christopher Paget Tennant, *b.* 1926, *s.* 1983, *m.*	Hon. Cody *T.*, *b.* 1994
1964	*Glendevon* (2nd), Julian John Somerset Hope, *b.* 1950, *s.* 1996.	Hon. Jonathan C. *H.*, *b.* 1952
1922	*Glendyne* (3rd), Robert Nivison, *b.* 1926, *s.* 1967, *m.*	Hon. John *N.*, *b.* 1960
1939	*Glentoran* (3rd), (Thomas) Robin (Valerian) Dixon, CBE, *b.* 1935, *s.* 1995, *m.*	Hon. Daniel G. *D.*, *b.* 1959
1909	*Gorell* (4th), Timothy John Radcliffe Barnes, *b.* 1927, *s.* 1963, *m.*	Hon. Ronald A. H. *B.*, *b.* 1931
1953	*Grantchester* (3rd), Christopher John Suenson-Taylor, *b.* 1951, *s.* 1995, *m.*	Hon. Jesse D. *S.-T.*, *b.* 1977
1782	*Grantley* (8th), Richard William Brinsley Norton, *b.* 1956, *s.* 1995.	Hon. Francis J. H. *N.*, *b.* 1960
1794 I.	*Graves* (9th), Evelyn Paget Graves, *b.* 1926, *s.* 1994, *m.*	Hon. Timothy E. *G.*, *b.* 1960
1445 s.	*Gray* (22nd), Angus Diarmid Ian Campbell-Gray, *b.* 1931, *s.* 1946, *m.*	Master of Gray, *b.* 1964
1950	*Greenhill* (3rd), Malcolm Greenhill, *b.* 1924, *s.* 1989.	None
1927	*Greenway* (4th), Ambrose Charles Drexel Greenway, *b.* 1941, *s.* 1975, *m.*	Hon. Mervyn S. K. *G.*, *b.* 1942
1902	*Grenfell* (3rd), Julian Pascoe Francis St Leger Grenfell, *b.* 1935, *s.* 1976, *m.*	Francis P. J. *G.*, *b.* 1938
1944	*Gretton* (4th), John Lysander Gretton, *b.* 1975, *s.* 1989.	None
1397	*Grey of Codnor* (6th), Richard Henry Cornwall-Legh, *b.* 1936, *s.* 1996, *m.*	Hon. Richard S. C. *C.-L.*, *b.* 1976
1955	*Gridley* (3rd), Richard David Arnold Gridley, *b.* 1956, *s.* 1996, *m.*	Hon. Carl R. *G.*, *b.* 1981
1964	*Grimston of Westbury* (2nd), Robert Walter Sigismund Grimston, *b.* 1925, *s.* 1979, *m.*	Hon. Robert J. S. *G.*, *b.* 1951
1886	*Grimthorpe* (4th), Christopher John Beckett, OBE, *b.* 1915, *s.* 1963, *m.*	Hon. Edward J. *B.*, *b.* 1954
1945	*Hacking* (3rd), Douglas David Hacking, *b.* 1938, *s.* 1971, *m.*	Hon. Douglas F. *H.*, *b.* 1968
1950	*Haden-Guest* (5th), Christopher Haden-Guest, *b.* 1948, *s.* 1996, *m.*	Hon. Nicholas *H.-G.*, *b.* 1951
1886	*Hamilton of Dalzell* (4th), James Leslie Hamilton, *b.* 1938, *s.* 1990, *m.*	Hon. Gavin G. *H.*, *b.* 1968
1874	*Hampton* (6th), Richard Humphrey Russell Pakington, *b.* 1925, *s.* 1974, *m.*	Hon. John H. A. *P.*, *b.* 1964
1939	*Hankey* (3rd), Donald Robin Alers Hankey, *b.* 1938, *s.* 1996, *m.*	Hon. Alexander M. A. *H.*, *b.* 1947
1958	*Harding of Petherton* (2nd), John Charles Harding, *b.* 1928, *s.* 1989, *m.*	Hon. William A. J. *H.*, *b.* 1969
1910	*Hardinge of Penshurst* (4th), Julian Alexander Hardinge, *b.* 1945, *s.* 1997.	Hon. Hugh F. *H.*, *b.* 1948
1876	*Harlech* (6th), Francis David Ormsby-Gore, *b.* 1954, *s.* 1985, *m.*	Hon. Jasset D. C. *O.-G.*, *b.* 1986
1939	*Harmsworth* (3rd), Thomas Harold Raymond Harmsworth, *b.* 1939, *s.* 1990, *m.*	Hon. Dominic M. E. *H.*, *b.* 1973

Created	Title, order of succession, name, etc.	Heir
1815	*Harris* (8th), Anthony Harris, *b.* 1942, *s.* 1996, *m.*	Ronald G. T. *H.*, *b.* 1911
1954	*Harvey of Tasburgh* (2nd), Peter Charles Oliver Harvey, *b.* 1921, *s.* 1968, *w.*	Charles J. G. *H.*, *b.* 1951
1295	*Hastings* (22nd), Edward Delaval Henry Astley, *b.* 1912, *s.* 1956, *m.*	Hon. Delaval T. H. *A.*, *b.* 1960
1835	*Hatherton* (8th), Edward Charles Littleton, *b.* 1950, *s.* 1985, *m.*	Hon. Thomas E. *L.*, *b.* 1977
1776	*Hawke* (11th), Edward George Hawke, TD, *b.* 1950, *s.* 1992, *m.*	None
1927	*Hayter* (3rd), George Charles Hayter Chubb, KCVO, CBE, *b.* 1911, *s.* 1967, *m.*	Hon. G. William M. *C.*, *b.* 1943
1945	*Hazlerigg* (2nd), Arthur Grey Hazlerigg, MC, TD, *b.* 1910, *s.* 1949, *w.*	Hon. Arthur G. *H.*, *b.* 1951
1943	*Hemingford* (3rd), (Dennis) Nicholas Herbert, *b.* 1934, *s.* 1982, *m.*	Hon. Christopher D. C. *H.*, *b.* 1973
1906	*Hemphill* (5th), Peter Patrick Fitzroy Martyn Martyn-Hemphill, *b.* 1928, *s.* 1957, *m.*	Hon. Charles A. M. *M.-H.*, *b.* 1954
1799 I.*	*Henley* (8th), Oliver Michael Robert Eden (6th *UK Baron Northington*, 1885), *b.* 1953, *s.* 1977, *m.*	Hon. John W. O. *E.*, *b.* 1988
1800 I.*	*Henniker* (8th), John Patrick Edward Chandos Henniker-Major, KCMG, CVO, MC (4th *UK Baron Hartismere*, 1866), *b.* 1916, *s.* 1980, *m.*	Hon. Mark I. P. C. *H.-M.*, *b.* 1947
1886	*Herschell* (3rd), Rognvald Richard Farrer Herschell, *b.* 1923, *s.* 1929, *m.*	None
1935	*Hesketh* (3rd), Thomas Alexander Fermor-Hesketh, KBE, PC, *b.* 1950, *s.* 1955, *m.*	Hon. Frederick H. *F.-H.*, *b.* 1988
1828	*Heytesbury* (6th), Francis William Holmes à Court, *b.* 1931, *s.* 1971, *m.*	Hon. James W. H. *à. C.*, *b.* 1967
1886	*Hindlip* (6th), Charles Henry Allsopp, *b.* 1940, *s.* 1993, *m.*	Hon. Henry W. *A.*, *b.* 1973
1950	*Hives* (3rd), Matthew Peter Hives, *b.* 1971, *s.* 1997.	Hon. Michael B. *H.*, *b.* 1926
1912	*Hollenden* (3rd), Gordon Hope Hope-Morley, *b.* 1914, *s.* 1977, *m.*	Hon. Ian H. *H.-M.*, *b.* 1946
1897	*HolmPatrick* (4th), Hans James David Hamilton, *b.* 1955, *s.* 1991, *m.*	Hon. Ion H. J. *H.*, *b.* 1956
1797 I.	*Hotham* (8th), Henry Durand Hotham, *b.* 1940, *s.* 1967, *m.*	Hon. William B. *H.*, *b.* 1972
1881	*Hothfield* (6th), Anthony Charles Sackville Tufton, *b.* 1939, *s.* 1991, *m.*	Hon. William S. *T.*, *b.* 1977
1597	*Howard de Walden* (9th), John Osmael Scott-Ellis, TD (5th *UK Baron Seaford*, 1826), *b.* 1912, *s.* 1946, *m.*	To Barony of Howard de Walden, four co-heiresses. To Barony of Seaford, Colin H. F. *Ellis*, *b.* 1946
1930	*Howard of Penrith* (2nd), Francis Philip Howard, *b.* 1905, *s.* 1939, *m.*	Hon. Philip E. *H.*, *b.* 1945
1960	*Howick of Glendale* (2nd), Charles Evelyn Baring, *b.* 1937, *s.* 1973, *m.*	Hon. David E. C. *B.*, *b.* 1975
1796 I.	*Huntingfield* (7th), Joshua Charles Vanneck, *b.* 1954, *s.* 1994, *m.*	Hon. Gerard C. A. *V.*, *b.* 1985
1866	*Hylton* (5th), Raymond Hervey Jolliffe, *b.* 1932, *s.* 1967, *m.*	Hon. William H. M. *J.*, *b.* 1967
1933	*Iliffe* (3rd), Robert Peter Richard Iliffe, *b.* 1944, *s.* 1996, *m.*	Hon. Edward R. *I.*, *b.* 1968
1543 I.	*Inchiquin* (18th), Conor Myles John O'Brien, *b.* 1943, *s.* 1982, *m.*	Murrough R. *O.*, *b.* 1910
1962	*Inchyra* (2nd), Robert Charles Reneke Hoyer Millar, *b.* 1935, *s.* 1989, *m.*	Hon. C. James C. H. *M.*, *b.* 1962
1964	*Inglewood* (2nd), (William) Richard Fletcher-Vane, *b.* 1951, *s.* 1989, *m.*	Hon. Henry W. F. *F.-V.*, *b.* 1990
1919	*Inverforth* (4th), Andrew Peter Weir, *b.* 1966, *s.* 1982.	Hon. John V. *W.*, *b.* 1935
1941	*Ironside* (2nd), Edmund Oslac Ironside, *b.* 1924, *s.* 1959, *m.*	Hon. Charles E. G. *I.*, *b.* 1956
1952	*Jeffreys* (3rd), Christopher Henry Mark Jeffreys, *b.* 1957, *s.* 1986, *m.*	Hon. Arthur M. H. *J.*, *b.* 1989
1906	*Joicey* (5th), James Michael Joicey, *b.* 1953, *s.* 1993, *m.*	Hon. William J. *J.*, *b.* 1990
1937	*Kenilworth* (4th), (John) Randle Siddeley, *b.* 1954, *s.* 1981, *m.*	Hon. William R. J. *S.*, *b.* 1992
1935	*Kennet* (2nd), Wayland Hilton Young, *b.* 1923, *s.* 1960, *m.*	Hon. W. A. Thoby *Y.*, *b.* 1957
1776 I.*	*Kensington* (8th), Hugh Ivor Edwardes (5th *UK Baron Kensington*, 1886), *b.* 1933, *s.* 1981, *m.*	Hon. W. Owen A. *E.*, *b.* 1964
1951	*Kenswood* (2nd), John Michael Howard Whitfield, *b.* 1930, *s.* 1963, *m.*	Hon. Michael C. *W.*, *b.* 1955
1788	*Kenyon* (6th), Lloyd Tyrrell-Kenyon, *b.* 1947, *s.* 1993, *m.*	Hon. Lloyd N. *T.-K.*, *b.* 1972
1947	*Kershaw* (4th), Edward John Kershaw, *b.* 1936, *s.* 1962, *m.*	Hon. John C. E. *K.*, *b.* 1971
1943	*Keyes* (2nd), Roger George Bowlby Keyes, *b.* 1919, *s.* 1945, *m.*	Hon. Charles W. P. *K.*, *b.* 1951
1909	*Kilbracken* (3rd), John Raymond Godley, DSC, *b.* 1920, *s.* 1950.	Hon. Christopher J. *G.*, *b.* 1945
1900	*Killanin* (3rd), Michael Morris, MBE, TD, *b.* 1914, *s.* 1927, *m.*	Hon. G. Redmond F. *M.*, *b.* 1947
1943	*Killearn* (3rd), Victor Miles George Aldous Lampson, *b.* 1941, *s.* 1996, *m.*	Hon. Miles H. M. *L.*, *b.* 1977
1789 I.	*Kilmaine* (7th), John David Henry Browne, *b.* 1948, *s.* 1978, *m.*	Hon. John F. S. *B.*, *b.* 1983
1831	*Kilmarnock* (7th), Alastair Ivor Gilbert Boyd, *b.* 1927, *s.* 1975, *m.*	Hon. Robin J. *B.*, *b.* 1941
1941	*Kindersley* (3rd), Robert Hugh Molesworth Kindersley, *b.* 1929, *s.* 1976, *m.*	Hon. Rupert J. M. *K.*, *b.* 1955
1223 I.	*Kingsale* (35th), John de Courcy, *b.* 1941, *s.* 1969. *Premier Baron of Ireland*	Nevinson R. *de C.*, *b.* 1920
1902	*Kinross* (5th), Christopher Patrick Balfour, *b.* 1949, *s.* 1985, *m.*	Hon. Alan I. *B.*, *b.* 1978
1951	*Kirkwood* (3rd), David Harvie Kirkwood, PH.D., *b.* 1931, *s.* 1970, *m.*	Hon. James S. *K.*, *b.* 1937
1800 I.	*Langford* (9th), Col. Geoffrey Alexander Rowley-Conwy, OBE, *b.* 1912, *s.* 1953, *m.*	Hon. Owain G. *R.-C.*, *b.* 1958
1942	*Latham* (2nd), Dominic Charles Latham, *b.* 1954, *s.* 1970.	Anthony M. *L.*, *b.* 1954
1431	*Latymer* (8th), Hugo Nevill Money-Coutts, *b.* 1926, *s.* 1987, *m.*	Hon. Crispin J. A. N. *M.-C.*, *b.* 1955
1869	*Lawrence* (5th), David John Downer Lawrence, *b.* 1937, *s.* 1968.	None
1947	*Layton* (3rd), Geoffrey Michael Layton, *b.* 1947, *s.* 1989, *m.*	Hon. David *L.* MBE, *b.* 1914
1839	*Leigh* (5th), John Piers Leigh, *b.* 1935, *s.* 1979, *m.*	Hon. Christopher D. P. *L.*, *b.* 1960

Created	Title, order of succession, name, etc.	Heir
1962	*Leighton of St Mellons* (2nd), (John) Leighton Seager, *b.* 1922, *s.* 1963, *m.*	Hon. Robert W. H. L. *S.*, *b.* 1955
1797	*Lilford* (7th), George Vernon Powys, *b.* 1931, *s.* 1949, *m.*	Hon. Mark V. *P.*, *b.* 1975
1945	*Lindsay of Birker* (3rd), James Francis Lindsay, *b.* 1945, *s.* 1994, *m.*	Alexander S. *L.*, *b.* 1940
1758 I.	*Lisle* (8th), Patrick James Lysaght, *b.* 1931, *s.* 1998.	Hon. John N. G. *L.*, *b.* 1960
1850	*Londesborough* (9th), Richard John Denison, *b.* 1959, *s.* 1968, *m.*	Hon. James F. *D.*, *b.* 1990
1541 I.	*Louth* (16th), Otway Michael James Oliver Plunkett, *b.* 1929, *s.* 1950, *m.*	Hon. Jonathan O. *P.*, *b.* 1952
1458 s.*	*Lovat* (16th), Simon Fraser (5th *UK Baron, Lovat*, 1837), *b.* 1977, *s.* 1995	Hon. Jack *F.*, *b.* 1984
1663	*Lucas* (11th) and *Dingwall* (8th) (s. 1609), Ralph Matthew Palmer, *b.* 1951, *s.* 1991, *m.*	Hon. Lewis E. *P.*, *b.* 1987
1946	*Lucas of Chilworth* (2nd), Michael William George Lucas, *b.* 1926, *s.* 1967, *m.*	Hon. Simon W. *L.*, *b.* 1957
1929	*Luke* (3rd), Arthur Charles St John Lawson-Johnston, *b.* 1933, *s.* 1996, *m.*	Hon. Ian J. St J. *L.-J.*, *b.* 1963
1914	*Lyell* (3rd), Charles Lyell, *b.* 1939, *s.* 1943.	None
1859	*Lyveden* (6th), Ronald Cecil Vernon, *b.* 1915, *s.* 1973, *m.*	Hon. Jack L. *V.*, *b.* 1938
1959	*MacAndrew* (3rd), Christopher Anthony Colin MacAndrew, *b.* 1945, *s.* 1989, *m.*	Hon. Oliver C. J. *M.*, *b.* 1983
1776 I.	*Macdonald* (8th), Godfrey James Macdonald of Macdonald, *b.* 1947, *s.* 1970, *m.*	Hon. Godfrey E. H. T. *M.*, *b.* 1982
1949	*Macdonald of Gwaenysgor* (2nd), Gordon Ramsay Macdonald, *b.* 1915, *s.* 1966, *m.*	None
1937	*McGowan* (3rd), Harry Duncan Cory McGowan, *b.* 1938, *s.* 1966, *m.*	Hon. Harry J. C. *M.*, *b.* 1971
1922	*Maclay* (3rd), Joseph Paton Maclay, *b.* 1942, *s.* 1969, *m.*	Hon. Joseph P. *M.*, *b.* 1977
1955	*McNair* (3rd), Duncan James McNair, *b.* 1947, *s.* 1989, *m.*	Hon. Thomas J. *M.*, *b.* 1990
1951	*Macpherson of Drumochter* (2nd), (James) Gordon Macpherson, *b.* 1924, *s.* 1965, *m.*	Hon. James A. *M.*, *b.* 1979
1937	*Mancroft* (3rd), Benjamin Lloyd Stormont Mancroft, *b.* 1957, *s.* 1987, *m.*	None
1807	*Manners* (5th), John Robert Cecil Manners, *b.* 1923, *s.* 1972, *m.*	Hon. John H. R. *M.*, *b.* 1956
1922	*Manton* (3rd), Joseph Rupert Eric Robert Watson, *b.* 1924, *s.* 1968, *m.*	Maj. Hon. Miles R. M. *W.*, *b.* 1958
1908	*Marchamley* (4th), William Francis Whiteley, *b.* 1968, *s.* 1994.	None
1964	*Margadale* (2nd), James Ian Morrison, TD, *b.* 1930, *s.* 1996, *m.*	Hon. Alastair J. *M.*, *b.* 1958
1961	*Marks of Broughton* (2nd), Michael Marks, *b.* 1920, *s.* 1964, *m.*	Hon. Simon R. *M.*, *b.* 1950
1964	*Martonmere* (2nd), John Stephen Robinson, *b.* 1963, *s.* 1989.	David A. *R.*, *b.* 1965
1776 I.	*Massy* (9th), Hugh Hamon John Somerset Massy, *b.* 1921, *s.* 1958, *m.*	Hon. David H. S. *M.*, *b.* 1947
1935	*May* (3rd), Michael St John May, *b.* 1931, *s.* 1950, *m.*	Hon. Jasper B. St J. *M.*, *b.* 1965
1928	*Melchett* (4th), Peter Robert Henry Mond, *b.* 1948, *s.* 1973.	None
1925	*Merrivale* (3rd), Jack Henry Edmond Duke, *b.* 1917, *s.* 1951, *m.*	Hon. Derek J. P. *D.*, *b.* 1948
1911	*Merthyr.* Disclaimed for life 1977. (*Trevor Oswin Lewis, Bt*, CBE, *b.*1935, *s.*1977, *m.*)	David T. *L.*, *b.* 1977
1919	*Meston* (3rd), James Meston, *b.* 1950, *s.* 1984, *m.*	Hon. Thomas J. D. *M.*, *b.* 1977
1838	*Methuen* (7th), Robert Alexander Holt Methuen, *b.* 1931, *s.* 1994, *m.*	Christopher P. M. C. *Methuen-Campbell*, *b.* 1928
1711	*Middleton* (12th), (Digby) Michael Godfrey John Willoughby, MC, *b.* 1921, *s.* 1970, *m.*	Hon. Michael C. J. *W.*, *b.* 1948
1939	*Milford* (3rd), Hugo John Laurence Philipps, *b.* 1929, *s.* 1993, *m.*	Hon. Guy W. *P.*, *b.* 1961
1933	*Milne* (2nd), George Douglass Milne, TD, *b.* 1909, *s.* 1948, *m.*	Hon. George A. *M.*, *b.* 1941
1951	*Milner of Leeds* (2nd), Arthur James Michael Milner, AE, *b.* 1923, *s.* 1967, *m.*	Hon. Richard J. *M.*, *b.* 1959
1947	*Milverton* (2nd), Revd Fraser Arthur Richard Richards, *b.* 1930, *s.* 1978, *m.*	Hon. Michael H. *R.*, *b.* 1936
1873	*Moncreiff* (5th), Harry Robert Wellwood Moncreiff, *b.* 1915, *s.* 1942, *w.*	Hon. Rhoderick H. W. *M.*, *b.* 1954
1884	*Monk Bretton* (3rd), John Charles Dodson, *b.* 1924, *s.* 1933, *m.*	Hon. Christopher M. *D.*, *b.* 1958
1885	*Monkswell* (5th), Gerard Collier, *b.* 1947, *s.* 1984, *m.*	Hon. James A. *C.*, *b.* 1977
1728	*Monson* (11th), John Monson, *b.* 1932, *s.* 1958, *m.*	Hon. Nicholas J. *M.*, *b.* 1955
1885	*Montagu of Beaulieu* (3rd), Edward John Barrington Douglas-Scott-Montagu, *b.* 1926, *s.* 1929, *m.*	Hon. Ralph *D.-S.-M.*, *b.* 1961
1839	*Monteagle of Brandon* (6th), Gerald Spring Rice, *b.* 1926, *s.* 1946, *m.*	Hon. Charles J. S. *R.*, *b.* 1953
1943	*Moran* (2nd), (Richard) John (McMoran) Wilson, KCMG, *b.* 1924, *s.* 1977, *m.*	Hon. James M. *W.*, *b.* 1952
1918	*Morris* (3rd), Michael David Morris, *b.* 1937, *s.* 1975, *m.*	Hon. Thomas A. S. *M.*, *b.* 1982
1950	*Morris of Kenwood* (2nd), Philip Geoffrey Morris, *b.* 1928, *s.* 1954, *m.*	Hon. Jonathan D. *M.*, *b.* 1968
1831	*Mostyn* (5th), Roger Edward Lloyd Lloyd-Mostyn, MC, *b.* 1920, *s.* 1965, *m.*	Hon. Llewellyn R. L. *L.-M.*, *b.* 1948
1933	*Mottistone* (4th), David Peter Seely, CBE, *b.* 1920, *s.* 1966, *m.*	Hon. Peter J. P. *S.*, *b.* 1949
1945	*Mountevans* (3rd), Edward Patrick Broke Evans, *b.* 1943, *s.* 1974, *m.*	Hon. Jeffrey de C. R. *E.*, *b.* 1948
1283	*Mowbray* (26th), *Segrave* (27th) (1283) and *Stourton* (23rd) (1448), Charles Edward Stourton, CBE, *b.* 1923, *s.* 1965, *w.*	Hon. Edward W. S. *S.*, *b.* 1953

Created	Title, order of succession, name, etc.	Heir
1932	*Moyne* (3rd), Jonathan Bryan Guinness, *b.* 1930, *s.* 1992, *m.*	Hon. Jasper J. R. G., *b.* 1954
1929	*Moynihan* (4th), Colin Berkeley Moynihan, *b.* 1955, *s.* 1997, *m.*	Hon. Nicholas E. B. M., *b.* 1994
1781 I.	*Muskerry* (9th), Robert Fitzmaurice Deane, *b.* 1948, *s.* 1988, *m.*	Hon. Jonathan F. D., *b.* 1986
1627 S.	*Napier* (14th) and *Ettrick* (5th) (*UK* 1872), Francis Nigel Napier, KCVO, *b.* 1930, *s.* 1954, *m.*	Master of Napier, *b.* 1962
1868	*Napier of Magdala* (6th), Robert Alan Napier, *b.* 1940, *s.* 1987, *m.*	Hon. James R. N., *b.* 1966
1940	*Nathan* (2nd), Roger Carol Michael Nathan, *b.* 1922, *s.* 1963, *m.*	Hon. Rupert H. B. N., *b.* 1957
1960	*Nelson of Stafford* (3rd), Henry Roy George Nelson, *b.* 1943, *s.* 1995, *m.*	Hon. Alistair W. H. N., *b.* 1973
1959	*Netherthorpe* (3rd), James Frederick Turner, *b.* 1964, *s.* 1982, *m.*	Hon. Andrew J. E. T., *b.* 1993
1946	*Newall* (2nd), Francis Storer Eaton Newall, *b.* 1930, *s.* 1963, *m.*	Hon. Richard H. E. N., *b.* 1961
1776 I.	*Newborough* (7th), Robert Charles Michael Vaughan Wynn, DSC, *b.* 1917, *s.* 1965, *m.*	Hon. Robert V. W., *b.* 1949
1892	*Newton* (5th), Richard Thomas Legh, *b.* 1950, *s.* 1992, *m.*	Hon. Piers R. L., *b.* 1979
1930	*Noel-Buxton* (3rd), Martin Connal Noel-Buxton, *b.* 1940, *s.* 1980, *m.*	Hon. Charles C. N.-B., *b.* 1975
1957	*Norrie* (2nd), (George) Willoughby Moke Norrie, *b.* 1936, *s.* 1977, *m.*	Hon. Mark W. J. N., *b.* 1972
1884	*Northbourne* (5th), Christopher George Walter James, *b.* 1926, *s.* 1982, *m.*	Hon. Charles W. H. J., *b.* 1960
1866	*Northbrook* (6th), Francis Thomas Baring, *b.* 1954, *s.* 1990, *m.*	None
1878	*Norton* (8th), James Nigel Arden Adderley, *b.* 1947, *s.* 1993, *m.*	Hon. Edward J. A. A., *b.* 1982
1906	*Nunburnholme* (5th), Charles Thomas Wilson, *b.* 1935, *s.* 1998.	Hon. Stephen C. W., *b.* 1973
	Oaksey. See Trevethin and Oaksey	
1950	*Ogmore* (2nd), Gwilym Rees Rees-Williams, *b.* 1931, *s.* 1976, *m.*	Hon. Morgan R.-W., *b.* 1937
1870	*O'Hagan* (4th), Charles Towneley Strachey, *b.* 1945, *s.* 1961.	Hon. Richard T. S., *b.* 1950
1868	*O'Neill* (4th), Raymond Arthur Clanaboy O'Neill, TD, *b.* 1933, *s.* 1944, *m.*	Hon. Shane S. C. O'N., *b.* 1965
1836 I.*	*Oranmore and Browne* (4th), Dominick Geoffrey Edward Browne (2nd *UK Baron, Mereworth*, 1926), *b.* 1901, *s.* 1927, *m.*	Hon. Dominick G. T. B., *b.* 1929
1933	*Palmer* (4th), Adrian Bailie Nottage Palmer, *b.* 1951, *s.* 1990, *m.*	Hon. Hugo B. R. P., *b.* 1980
1914	*Parmoor* (4th), (Frederick Alfred) Milo Cripps, *b.* 1929, *s.* 1977.	Michael L. S. C., *b.* 1942
1937	*Pender* (3rd), John Willoughby Denison-Pender, *b.* 1933, *s.* 1965, *m.*	Hon. Henry J. R. D.-P., *b.* 1968
1866	*Penrhyn* (6th), Malcolm Frank Douglas-Pennant, DSO, MBE, *b.* 1908, *s.* 1967, *m.*	Hon. Nigel D.-P., *b.* 1909
1603	*Petre* (18th), John Patrick Lionel Petre, *b.* 1942, *s.* 1989, *m.*	Hon. Dominic W. P., *b.* 1966
1918	*Phillimore* (5th), Francis Stephen Phillimore, *b.* 1944, *s.* 1994, *m.*	Hon. Tristan A. S. P., *b.* 1977
1945	*Piercy* (3rd), James William Piercy, *b.* 1946, *s.* 1981.	Hon. Mark E. P. P., *b.* 1953
1827	*Plunket* (8th), Robin Rathmore Plunket, *b.* 1925, *s.* 1975, *m.*	Hon. Shaun A. F. S. P., *b.* 1931
1831	*Poltimore* (7th), Mark Coplestone Bampfylde, *b.* 1957, *s.* 1978, *m.*	Hon. Henry A. W. B., *b.* 1985
1690 S.	*Polwarth* (10th), Henry Alexander Hepburne-Scott, TD, *b.* 1916, *s.* 1944, *m.*	Master of Polwarth, *b.* 1947
1930	*Ponsonby of Shulbrede* (4th), Frederick Matthew Thomas Ponsonby, *b.* 1958, *s.* 1990.	None
1958	*Poole* (2nd), David Charles Poole, *b.* 1945, *s.* 1993, *m.*	Hon. Oliver J. P., *b.* 1972
1852	*Raglan* (5th), FitzRoy John Somerset, *b.* 1927, *s.* 1964.	Hon. Geoffrey S., *b.* 1932
1932	*Rankeillour* (4th), Peter St Thomas More Henry Hope, *b.* 1935, *s.* 1967.	Michael R. H., *b.* 1940
1953	*Rathcavan* (3rd), Hugh Detmar Torrens O'Neill, *b.* 1939, *s.* 1994, *m.*	Hon. François H. N. O'N., *b.* 1984
1916	*Rathcreedan* (3rd), Christopher John Norton, *b.* 1949, *s.* 1990, *m.*	Hon. Adam G. N., *b.* 1952
1868 I.	*Rathdonnell* (5th), Thomas Benjamin McClintock-Bunbury, *b.* 1938, *s.* 1959, *m.*	Hon. William L. M.-B., *b.* 1966
1911	*Ravensdale* (3rd), Nicholas Mosley, MC, *b.* 1923, *s.* 1966, *m.*	Hon. Shaun N. M., *b.* 1949
1821	*Ravensworth* (8th), Arthur Waller Liddell, *b.* 1924, *s.* 1950, *m.*	Hon. Thomas A. H. L., *b.* 1954
1821	*Rayleigh* (6th), John Gerald Strutt, *b.* 1960, *s.* 1988, *m.*	Hon. John F. S., *b.* 1993
1937	*Rea* (3rd), John Nicolas Rea, MD, *b.* 1928, *s.* 1981, *m.*	Hon. Matthew J. R., *b.* 1956
1628 S.	*Reay* (14th), Hugh William Mackay, *b.* 1937, *s.* 1963, *m.*	Master of Reay, *b.* 1965
1902	*Redesdale* (6th), Rupert Bertram Mitford, *b.* 1967, *s.* 1991.	None
1940	*Reith.* Disclaimed for life 1972. (*Christopher John Reith, b.1928, s.1971, m.*)	Hon. James H. J. R., *b.* 1971
1928	*Remnant* (3rd), James Wogan Remnant, CVO, *b.* 1930, *s.* 1967, *m.*	Hon. Philip J. R., *b.* 1954
1806 I.	*Rendlesham* (8th), Charles Anthony Hugh Thellusson, *b.* 1915, *s.* 1943, *w.*	Hon. Charles W. B. T., *b.* 1954
1933	*Rennell* (3rd), (John Adrian) Tremayne Rodd, *b.* 1935, *s.* 1978, *m.*	Hon. James R. D. T. R., *b.* 1978
1964	*Renwick* (2nd), Harry Andrew Renwick, *b.* 1935, *s.* 1973, *m.*	Hon. Robert J. R., *b.* 1966
1885	*Revelstoke* (5th), John Baring, *b.* 1934, *s.* 1994.	Hon. James C. B., *b.* 1938
1905	*Ritchie of Dundee* (5th), (Harold) Malcolm Ritchie, *b.* 1919, *s.* 1978, *m.*	Hon. C. Rupert R. R., *b.* 1958
1935	*Riverdale* (3rd), Anthony Robert Balfour, *b.* 1960, *s.* 1998.	Hon. David R. B., *b.* 1938
1961	*Robertson of Oakridge* (2nd), William Ronald Robertson, *b.* 1930, *s.* 1974, *m.*	Hon. William B. E. R., *b.* 1975
1938	*Roborough* (3rd), Henry Massey Lopes, *b.* 1940, *s.* 1992, *m.*	Hon. Massey J. H. L., *b.* 1969
1931	*Rochester* (2nd), Foster Charles Lowry Lamb, *b.* 1916, *s.* 1955, *m.*	Hon. David C. L., *b.* 1944
1934	*Rockley* (3rd), James Hugh Cecil, *b.* 1934, *s.* 1976, *m.*	Hon. Anthony R. C., *b.* 1961
1782	*Rodney* (10th), George Brydges Rodney, *b.* 1953, *s.* 1992, *m.*	Nicholas S. H. R., *b.* 1947

Created	Title, order of succession, name, etc.	Heir
1651 s.*	*Rollo* (14th), David Eric Howard Rollo (5th *UK Baron Dunning*, 1869), *b.* 1943, *s.* 1997, *m.*	Master of Rollo, *b.* 1972
1959	*Rootes* (3rd), Nicholas Geoffrey Rootes, *b.* 1951, *s.* 1992, *m.*	William B. *R.*, *b.* 1944
1796 I.*	*Rossmore* (7th), William Warner Westenra (6th *UK Baron, Rossmore,* 1838), *b.* 1931, *s.* 1958, *m.*	Hon. Benedict W. *W.*, *b.* 1983
1939	*Rotherwick* (3rd), (Herbert) Robin Cayzer, *b.* 1954, *s.* 1996, *m.*	Hon. H. Robin *C.*, *b.* 1989
1885	*Rothschild* (4th), (Nathaniel Charles) Jacob Rothschild, GBE, *b.* 1936, *s.* 1990, *m.*	Hon. Nathaniel P. V. J. *R.*, *b.* 1971
1911	*Rowallan* (4th), John Polson Cameron Corbett, *b.* 1947, *s.* 1993	Hon. Jason W. P. C. *C.*, *b.* 1972
1947	*Rugby* (3rd), Robert Charles Maffey, *b.* 1951, *s.* 1990, *m.*	Hon. Timothy J. H. *M.*, *b.* 1975
1919	*Russell of Liverpool* (3rd), Simon Gordon Jared Russell, *b.* 1952, *s.* 1981, *m.*	Hon. Edward C. S. *R.*, *b.* 1985
1876	*Sackville* (6th), Lionel Bertrand Sackville-West, *b.* 1913, *s.* 1965, *m.*	Hugh R. I. *S.-W.*, MC, *b.* 1919
1964	*St Helens* (2nd), Richard Francis Hughes-Young, *b.* 1945, *s.* 1980, *m.*	Hon. Henry T. *H.-Y.*, *b.* 1986
1559	*St John of Bletso* (21st), Anthony Tudor St John, *b.* 1957, *s.* 1978, *m.*	Hon. Oliver B. *St J.*, *b.* 1995
1887	*St Levan* (4th), John Francis Arthur St Aubyn, DSC, *b.* 1919, *s.* 1978, *m.*	Hon. O. Piers *St A.* MC, *b.* 1920
1885	*St Oswald* (5th), Derek Edward Anthony Winn, *b.* 1919, *s.* 1984, *m.*	Hon. Charles R. A. *W.*, *b.* 1959
1960	*Sanderson of Ayot.* Disclaimed for life 1971. (*Alan Lindsay Sanderson, b.* 1931, *s.* 1971, *m.*)	Hon. Michael *S.*, *b.* 1959
1945	*Sandford* (2nd), Revd John Cyril Edmondson, DSC, *b.* 1920, *s.* 1959, *m.*	Hon. James J. M. *E.*, *b.* 1949
1871	*Sandhurst* (5th), (John Edward) Terence Mansfield, DFC, *b.* 1920, *s.* 1964, *m.*	Hon. Guy R. J. *M.*, *b.* 1949
1802	*Sandys* (7th), Richard Michael Oliver Hill, *b.* 1931, *s.* 1961, *m.*	The Marquess of Downshire (*see* page 138)
1888	*Savile* (3rd), George Halifax Lumley-Savile, *b.* 1919, *s.* 1931.	Hon. Henry L. T. *L.-S.*, *b.* 1923
1447	*Saye and Sele* (21st), Nathaniel Thomas Allen Fiennes, *b.* 1920, *s.* 1968, *m.*	Hon. Richard I. *F.*, *b.* 1959
1932	*Selsdon* (3rd), Malcolm McEacharn Mitchell-Thomson, *b.* 1937, *s.* 1963, *m.*	Hon. Callum M. M. *M.-T.*, *b.* 1969
1489 s.	*Sempill* (21st), James William Stuart Whitemore Sempill, *b.* 1949, *s.* 1995, *m.*	Master of Sempill, *b.* 1979
1916	*Shaughnessy* (3rd), William Graham Shaughnessy, *b.* 1922, *s.* 1938, *m.*	Hon. Michael J. *S.*, *b.* 1946
1946	*Shepherd* (2nd), Malcolm Newton Shepherd, PC, *b.* 1918, *s.* 1954, *w.*	Hon. Graeme G. *S.*, *b.* 1949
1964	*Sherfield* (2nd), Christopher James Makins, *b.* 1942, *s.* 1996, *m.*	Hon. Dwight W. *M.*, *b.* 1951
1902	*Shuttleworth* (5th), Charles Geoffrey Nicholas Kay-Shuttleworth, *b.* 1948, *s.* 1975, *m.*	Hon. Thomas E. *K.-S.*, *b.* 1976
1950	*Silkin.* Disclaimed for life 1972. (*Arthur Silkin, b.* 1916, *s.* 1972, *m.*)	Hon. Christopher L. *S.*, *b.* 1947
1963	*Silsoe* (2nd), David Malcolm Trustram Eve, QC, *b.* 1930, *s.* 1976, *m.*	Hon. Simon R. T. *E.*, *b.* 1966
1947	*Simon of Wythenshawe* (2nd), Roger Simon, *b.* 1913, *s.* 1960, *m.*	Hon. Matthew *S.*, *b.* 1955
1449 s.	*Sinclair* (17th), Charles Murray Kennedy St Clair, CVO, *b.* 1914, *s.* 1957, *m.*	Master of Sinclair, *b.* 1968
1957	*Sinclair of Cleeve* (3rd), John Lawrence Robert Sinclair, *b.* 1953, *s.* 1985.	None
1919	*Sinha* (5th), Anindo Kumar Sinha, *b.* 1930, *s.* 1992.	Hon. Arup K. *S.*, *b.* 1966
1828	*Skelmersdale* (7th), Roger Bootle-Wilbraham, *b.* 1945, *s.* 1973, *m.*	Hon. Andrew *B.-W.*, *b.* 1977
1916	*Somerleyton* (3rd), Savile William Francis Crossley, KCVO, *b.* 1928, *s.* 1959, *m.* Master of the Horse	Hon. Hugh F. S. *C.*, *b.* 1971
1784	*Somers* (9th), Philip Sebastian Somers Cocks, *b.* 1948, *s.* 1995.	Alan B. *C.*, *b.* 1930
1780	*Southampton* (6th), Charles James FitzRoy, *b.* 1928, *s.* 1989, *m.*	Hon. Edward C. *F.*, *b.* 1955
1959	*Spens* (3rd), Patrick Michael Rex Spens, *b.* 1942, *s.* 1984, *m.*	Hon. Patrick N. G. *S.*, *b.* 1968
1640	*Stafford* (15th), Francis Melfort William Fitzherbert, *b.* 1954, *s.* 1986, *m.*	Hon. Benjamin J. B. *F.*, *b.* 1983
1938	*Stamp* (4th), Trevor Charles Bosworth Stamp, MD, FRCP, *b.* 1935, *s.* 1987, *m.*	Hon. Nicholas C. T. *S.*, *b.* 1978
1839	*Stanley of Alderley* (8th) and *Sheffield* (8th) (I. 1738), Thomas Henry Oliver Stanley (7th *UK Baron, Eddisbury,* 1848), *b.* 1927, *s.* 1971, *m.*	Hon. Richard O. *S.*, *b.* 1956
1318	*Strabolgi* (11th), David Montague de Burgh Kenworthy, *b.* 1914, *s.* 1953, *m.*	Andrew D. W. *K.*, *b.* 1967
1954	*Strang* (2nd), Colin Strang, *b.* 1922, *s.* 1978, *m.*	None
1955	*Strathalmond* (3rd), William Roberton Fraser, *b.* 1947, *s.* 1976, *m.*	Hon. William G. *F.*, *b.* 1976
1936	*Strathcarron* (2nd), David William Anthony Blyth Macpherson, *b.* 1924, *s.* 1937, *m.*	Hon. Ian D. P. *M.*, *b.* 1949
1955	*Strathclyde* (2nd), Thomas Galloway Dunlop du Roy de Blicquy Galbraith, PC, *b.* 1960, *s.* 1985, *m.*	Hon. Charles W. du R. de B. *G.*, *b.* 1962
1900	*Strathcona and Mount Royal* (4th), Donald Euan Palmer Howard, *b.* 1923, *s.* 1959, *m.*	Hon. D. Alexander S. *H.*, *b.* 1961
1836	*Stratheden* (6th) and *Campbell* (6th) (1841), Donald Campbell, *b.* 1934, *s.* 1987, *m.*	Hon. David A. *C.*, *b.* 1963
1884	*Strathspey* (6th), James Patrick Trevor Grant of Grant, *b.* 1943, *s.* 1992, *m.*	Hon. Michael P. F. *G.*, *b.* 1953

Created	Title, order of succession, name, etc.	Heir
1838	*Sudeley* (7th), Merlin Charles Sainthill Hanbury-Tracy, *b.* 1939, *s.* 1941.	D. Andrew J. *H.-T.*, *b.* 1928
1786	*Suffield* (11th), Anthony Philip Harbord-Hamond, MC, *b.* 1922, *s.* 1951, *m.*	Hon. Charles A. A. *H.-H.*, *b.* 1953
1893	*Swansea* (4th), John Hussey Hamilton Vivian, *b.* 1925, *s.* 1934, *m.*	Hon. Richard A. H. *V.*, *b.* 1957
1907	*Swaythling* (5th), Charles Edgar Samuel Montagu, *b.* 1954, *s.* 1998, *m.*	Hon. Anthony T. S. *M.*, *b.* 1931
1919	*Swinfen* (3rd), Roger Mynors Swinfen Eady, *b.* 1938, *s.* 1977, *m.*	Hon. Charles R. P. S. *E.*, *b.* 1971
1935	*Sysonby* (3rd), John Frederick Ponsonby, *b.* 1945, *s.* 1956.	None
1831 I.	*Talbot of Malahide* (10th), Reginald John Richard Arundell, *b.* 1931, *s.* 1987, *m.*	Hon. Richard J. T. *A.*, *b.* 1957
1946	*Tedder* (3rd), Robin John Tedder, *b.* 1955, *s.* 1994, *m.*	Hon. Benjamin J. *T.*, *b.* 1985
1884	*Tennyson* (5th), Cdr. Mark Aubrey Tennyson, DSC, *b.* 1920, *s.* 1991, *m.*	Lt.-Cdr. James A. *T.* DSC, *b.* 1913
1918	*Terrington* (5th), (Christopher) Montague Woodhouse, DSO, OBE, *b.* 1917, *s.* 1998, *w.*	Hon. Christopher R. J. *W.*, *b.* 1946
1940	*Teviot* (2nd), Charles John Kerr, *b.* 1934, *s.* 1968, *m.*	Hon. Charles R. *K.*, *b.* 1971
1616	*Teynham* (20th), John Christopher Ingham Roper-Curzon, *b.* 1928, *s.* 1972, *m.*	Hon. David J. H. I. *R.-C.*, *b.* 1965
1964	*Thomson of Fleet* (2nd), Kenneth Roy Thomson, *b.* 1923, *s.* 1976, *m.*	Hon. David K. R. *T.*, *b.* 1957
1792	*Thurlow* (8th), Francis Edward Hovell-Thurlow-Cumming-Bruce, KCMG, *b.* 1912, *s.* 1971, *w.*	Hon. Roualeyn R. *H.-T.-C.-B.*, *b.* 1952
1876	*Tollemache* (5th), Timothy John Edward Tollemache, *b.* 1939, *s.* 1975, *m.*	Hon. Edward J. H. *T.*, *b.* 1976
1564 S.	*Torphichen* (15th), James Andrew Douglas Sandilands, *b.* 1946, *s.* 1975, *m.*	Douglas R. A. *S.*, *b.* 1926
1947	*Trefgarne* (2nd), David Garro Trefgarne, PC, *b.* 1941, *s.* 1960, *m.*	Hon. George G. *T.*, *b.* 1970
1921	*Trevethin* (4th) and *Oaksey* (2nd) (1947), John Geoffrey Tristram Lawrence, OBE, *b.* 1929, *s.* 1971, *m.*	Hon. Patrick J. T. *L.*, *b.* 1960
1880	*Trevor* (5th), Marke Charles Hill-Trevor, *b.* 1970, *s.* 1997, *m.*	Hon. Iain R. *H.-T.*, *b.* 1971
1461 I.	*Trimlestown* (21st), Raymond Charles Barnewall, *b.* 1930, *s.* 1997.	None
1940	*Tryon* (3rd), Anthony George Merrik Tryon, *b.* 1940, *s.* 1976.	Hon. Charles G. B. *T.*, *b.* 1976
1935	*Tweedsmuir* (3rd), William de l'Aigle Buchan, *b.* 1916, *s.* 1996, *m.*	Hon. John W. H. de l'A. *B.*, *b.* 1950
1523	*Vaux of Harrowden* (10th), John Hugh Philip Gilbey, *b.* 1915, *s.* 1977, *m.*	Hon. Anthony W. *G.*, *b.* 1940
1800 I.	*Ventry* (8th), Andrew Wesley Daubeny de Moleyns, *b.* 1943, *s.* 1987, *m.*	Hon. Francis W. *D. de M.*, *b.* 1965
1762	*Vernon* (10th), John Lawrance Vernon, *b.* 1923, *s.* 1963, *m.*	Col. William R. D. *Vernon-Harcourt* OBE, *b.* 1909
1922	*Vestey* (3rd), Samuel George Armstrong Vestey, *b.* 1941, *s.* 1954, *m.*	Hon. William G. *V.*, *b.* 1983
1841	*Vivian* (6th), Nicholas Crespigny Laurence Vivian, *b.* 1935, *s.* 1991, *m.*	Hon. Charles H. C. *V.*, *b.* 1966
1934	*Wakehurst* (3rd), (John) Christopher Loder, *b.* 1925, *s.* 1970, *m.*	Hon. Timothy W. *L.*, *b.* 1958
1723	*Walpole* (10th), Robert Horatio Walpole (8th *Brit. Baron Walpole of Wolterton*, 1756), *b.* 1938, *s.* 1989, *m.*	Hon. Jonathan R. H. *W.*, *b.* 1967
1780	*Walsingham* (9th), John de Grey, MC, *b.* 1925, *s.* 1965, *m.*	Hon. Robert *de G.*, *b.* 1969
1936	*Wardington* (2nd), Christopher Henry Beaumont Pease, *b.* 1924, *s.* 1950, *m.*	Hon. William S. *P.*, *b.* 1925
1792 I.	*Waterpark* (7th), Frederick Caryll Philip Cavendish, *b.* 1926, *s.* 1948, *m.*	Hon. Roderick A. *C.*, *b.* 1959
1942	*Wedgwood* (4th), Piers Anthony Weymouth Wedgwood, *b.* 1954, *s.* 1970, *m.*	John *W.* CBE, MD, FRCP, *b.* 1919
1861	*Westbury* (5th), David Alan Bethell, CBE, MC, *b.* 1922, *s.* 1961, *m.*	Hon. Richard N. *B.* MBE, *b.* 1950
1944	*Westwood* (3rd), (William) Gavin Westwood, *b.* 1944, *s.* 1991, *m.*	Hon. W. Fergus *W.*, *b.* 1972
1935	*Wigram* (2nd), (George) Neville (Clive) Wigram, MC, *b.* 1915, *s.* 1960, *w.*	Maj. Hon. Andrew F. C. *W.* MVO, *b.* 1949
1491	*Willoughby de Broke* (21st), Leopold David Verney, *b.* 1938, *s.* 1986, *m.*	Hon. Rupert G. *V.*, *b.* 1966
1946	*Wilson* (2nd), Patrick Maitland Wilson, *b.* 1915, *s.* 1964, *w.*	None
1937	*Windlesham* (3rd), David James George Hennessy, CVO, PC, *b.* 1932, *s.* 1962, *w.*	Hon. James R. *H.*, *b.* 1968
1951	*Wise* (2nd), John Clayton Wise, *b.* 1923, *s.* 1968, *m.*	Hon. Christopher J. C. *W.* PH.D., *b.* 1949
1869	*Wolverton* (7th), Christopher Richard Glyn, *b.* 1938, *s.* 1988.	Hon. Andrew J. *G.*, *b.* 1943
1928	*Wraxall* (2nd), George Richard Lawley Gibbs, *b.* 1928, *s.* 1931.	Hon. Sir Eustace H. B. *G.* KCVO, CMG, *b.* 1929
1915	*Wrenbury* (3rd), Revd John Burton Buckley, *b.* 1927, *s.* 1940, *m.*	Hon. William E. *B.*, *b.* 1966
1838	*Wrottesley* (6th), Clifton Hugh Lancelot de Verdon Wrottesley, *b.* 1968, *s.* 1977.	Hon. Stephen J. *W.*, *b.* 1955
1919	*Wyfold* (3rd), Hermon Robert Fleming Hermon-Hodge, ERD, *b.* 1915, *s.* 1942.	None
1829	*Wynford* (8th), Robert Samuel Best, MBE, *b.* 1917, *s.* 1943, *m.*	Hon. John P. R. *B.*, *b.* 1950
1308	*Zouche* (18th), James Assheton Frankland, *b.* 1943, *s.* 1965, *m.*	Hon. William T. A. *F.*, *b.* 1984

BARONESSES/LADIES IN THEIR OWN RIGHT

Style, The Right Hon. the Lady __, *or* The Right Hon. the Baroness __, according to her preference. Either style may be used, except in the case of Scottish titles (indicated by s.), which are not baronies (*see* page 136) and whose holders are always addressed as Lady
Husband, Untitled
Children's style, As for children of a Baron
For forms of address, *see* page 135

Created	Title, order of succession, name, etc.	Heir
1455	*Berners* (16th in line), Pamela Vivien Kirkham, *b.* 1929, *title called out of abeyance* 1995, *m.*	Hon. Rupert W. T. K., *b.* 1953
1529	*Braye* (8th in line), Mary Penelope Aubrey-Fletcher, *b.* 1941, *s.* 1985, *m.*	Two co-heiresses
1321	*Dacre* (27th in line), Rachel Leila Douglas-Home, *b.* 1929, *title called out of abeyance* 1970, *w.*	Hon. James T. A. *D.-H.*, *b.* 1952
1332	*Darcy de Knayth* (18th in line), Davina Marcia Ingrams, DBE, *b.* 1938, *s.* 1943, *w.*	Hon. Caspar D. *I.*, *b.* 1962
1439	*Dudley* (14th in line), Barbara Amy Felicity Hamilton, *b.* 1907, *s.* 1972, *m.*	Hon. Jim A. H. *Wallace*, *b.* 1930
1490 s.	*Herries of Terregles* (14th in line), Anne Elizabeth Fitzalan-Howard, *b.* 1938, *s.* 1975, *m.*	Lady Mary *Mumford* CVO, *b.* 1940
1602 s.	*Kinloss* (12th in line), Beatrice Mary Grenville Freeman-Grenville, *b.* 1922, *s.* 1944, *m.*	Master of Kinloss, *b.* 1953
1445 s.	*Saltoun* (20th in line), Flora Marjory Fraser, *b.* 1930, *s.* 1979, *m.*	Hon. Katharine I. M. I. F., *b.* 1957
1628	*Strange* (16th in line), (Jean) Cherry Drummond of Megginch, *b.* 1928, *title called out of abeyance* 1986, *m.*	Hon. Adam H. *D. of M.*, *b.* 1953
1544/5	*Wharton* (11th in line), Myrtle Olive Felix Robertson, *b.* 1934, *title called out of abeyance* 1990, *m.*	Hon. Myles C. D. *R.*, *b.* 1964
1313	*Willoughby de Eresby* (27th in line), (Nancy) Jane Marie Heathcote-Drummond-Willoughby, *b.* 1934, *s.* 1983.	Two co-heiresses

Life Peers

NEW LIFE PEERAGES *1 September 1997 to 31 August 1998*
NEW YEAR'S HONOURS (30 December 1997): Sir Robin Butler, GCB, CVO; Sir Ronald Dearing, CB; Paul Hamlyn, CBE; Rt. Revd David Sheppard
QUEEN'S BIRTHDAY HONOURS (13 June 1998): Sir Terence Burns, GCB; Sir David English (died 11 June 1998); Sir Herbert Laming, CBE; Sir Colin Marshall; Revd Kathleen Richardson, OBE
WORKING PEERS (20 June 1998): Nazir Ahmed; Waheed Alli; William Bach; Sir Tim Bell; Melvyn Bragg; David Brookman; Peta Buscombe; Anthony Christopher, CBE; Anthony Clarke, CBE; Tim Clements-Jones, CBE; Christine Crawley, MEP; David Evans; Mary Goudie; Toby Harris; Christopher Haskins; Rt. Hon. Norman Lamont; Brian Mackenzie, OBE; Sue Miller; Philip Norton; Andrew Phillips, OBE; Tom Sawyer; Margaret Sharp; Glenys Thornton; John Tomlinson, MEP; Manzila Uddin; Norman Warner; Paul White
NEW MINISTER (August 1998): Angus Macdonald*
*Title not gazetted at time of going to press

CREATED UNDER THE APPELLATE JURISDICTION ACT 1876 (AS AMENDED)

BARONS

Created
1986   *Ackner,* Desmond James Conrad Ackner, PC, *b.* 1920, *m.*
1981   *Brandon of Oakbrook,* Henry Vivian Brandon, MC, PC, *b.* 1920, *m.*
1980   *Bridge of Harwich,* Nigel Cyprian Bridge, PC, *b.* 1917, *m.*
1982   *Brightman,* John Anson Brightman, PC, *b.* 1911, *m.*
1991   *Browne-Wilkinson,* Nicolas Christopher Henry Browne-Wilkinson, PC, *b.* 1930, *m.* Lord of Appeal in Ordinary
1996   *Clyde,* James John Clyde, *b.* 1932, *m.* Lord of Appeal in Ordinary
1957   *Denning,* Alfred Thompson Denning, OM, PC, *b.* 1899, *w.*
1986   *Goff of Chieveley,* Robert Lionel Archibald Goff, PC, *b.* 1926, *m.*
1985   *Griffiths,* (William) Hugh Griffiths, MC, PC, *b.* 1923, *m.*
1995   *Hoffmann,* Leonard Hubert Hoffmann, PC, *b.* 1934, *m.* Lord of Appeal in Ordinary
1997   *Hutton,* (James) Brian (Edward) Hutton, PC, *b.* 1931, *m.* Lord of Appeal in Ordinary
1988   *Jauncey of Tullichettle,* Charles Eliot Jauncey, PC, *b.* 1925, *m.*
1977   *Keith of Kinkel,* Henry Shanks Keith, GBE, PC, *b.* 1922, *m.*
1979   *Lane,* Geoffrey Dawson Lane, AFC, PC, *b.* 1918, *m.*
1993   *Lloyd of Berwick,* Anthony John Leslie Lloyd, PC, *b.* 1929, *m.* Lord of Appeal in Ordinary
1992   *Mustill,* Michael John Mustill, PC, *b.* 1931, *m.*
1994   *Nicholls of Birkenhead,* Donald James Nicholls, PC, *b.* 1933, *m.* Lord of Appeal in Ordinary
1994   *Nolan,* Michael Patrick Nolan, PC, *b.* 1928, *m.*
1986   *Oliver of Aylmerton,* Peter Raymond Oliver, PC, *b.* 1921, *m.*
1997   *Saville of Newdigate,* Mark Oliver Saville, PC, *b.* 1936, *m.* Lord of Appeal in Ordinary

1977   *Scarman,* Leslie George Scarman, OBE, PC, *b.* 1911, *m.*
1992   *Slynn of Hadley,* Gordon Slynn, PC, *b.* 1930, *m.* Lord of Appeal in Ordinary
1995   *Steyn,* Johan van Zyl Steyn, PC, *b.* 1932, *m.* Lord of Appeal in Ordinary
1982   *Templeman,* Sydney William Templeman, MBE, PC, *b.* 1920, *m.*
1964   *Wilberforce,* Richard Orme Wilberforce, CMG, OBE, PC, *b.* 1907, *m.*
1992   *Woolf,* Harry Kenneth Woolf, PC, *b.* 1933, *m.* Master of the Rolls

CREATED UNDER THE LIFE PEERAGES ACT 1958

BARONS

Created
1998   *Ahmed,* Nazir Ahmed.
1996   *Alderdice,* John Thomas Alderdice, *b.* 1955, *m.*
1988   *Alexander of Weedon,* Robert Scott Alexander, QC, *b.* 1936, *m.*
1976   *Allen of Abbeydale,* Philip Allen, GCB, *b.* 1912, *m.*
1998   *Alli,* Waheed Alli.
1961   *Alport,* Cuthbert James McCall Alport, TD, PC, *b.* 1912, *w.*
1997   *Alton of Liverpool,* David Patrick Paul Alton, *b.* 1951, *m.*
1965   *Annan,* Noël Gilroy Annan, OBE, *b.* 1916, *m.*
1992   *Archer of Sandwell,* Peter Kingsley Archer, PC, QC, *b.* 1926, *m.*
1992   *Archer of Weston-super-Mare,* Jeffrey Howard Archer, *b.* 1940, *m.*
1988   *Armstrong of Ilminster,* Robert Temple Armstrong, GCB, CVO, *b.* 1927, *m.*
1992   *Ashley of Stoke,* Jack Ashley, CH, PC, *b.* 1922, *m.*
1993   *Attenborough,* Richard Samuel Attenborough, CBE, *b.* 1923, *m.*
1998   *Bach,* William Stephen Goulden Bach.
1997   *Bagri,* Raj Kumar Bagri, CBE, *b.* 1930, *m.*
1997   *Baker of Dorking,* Kenneth Wilfred Baker, CH, PC, *b.* 1934, *m.*
1974   *Balniel,* The Earl of Crawford and Balcarres (*see* page 140)
1974   *Barber,* Anthony Perrinott Lysberg Barber, TD, PC, *b.* 1920, *m.*
1992   *Barber of Tewkesbury,* Derek Coates Barber, *b.* 1918, *m.*
1983   *Barnett,* Joel Barnett, PC, *b.* 1923, *m.*
1997   *Bassam of Brighton,* (John) Steven Bassam, *b.* 1953.
1982   *Bauer,* Prof. Peter Thomas Bauer, D.SC., FBA, *b.* 1915.
1967   *Beaumont of Whitley,* Revd Timothy Wentworth Beaumont, *b.* 1928, *m.*
1998   *Bell,* Timothy John Leigh Bell, *b.* 1941, *m.*
1979   *Bellwin,* Irwin Norman Bellow, *b.* 1923, *m.*
1981   *Beloff,* Max Beloff, FBA, *b.* 1913, *m.*
1997   *Biffen,* (William) John Biffen, PC, *b.* 1930, *m.*
1996   *Bingham of Cornhill,* Thomas Henry Bingham, PC, *b.* 1933, *m. Lord Chief Justice of England*
1997   *Blackwell,* Norman Roy Blackwell, *b.* 1952, *m.*
1971   *Blake,* Robert Norman William Blake, FBA, *b.* 1916, *w.*

1994   *Blaker,* Peter Allan Renshaw Blaker, KCMG, PC, *b.* 1922, *m.*

1978   *Blease,* William John Blease, *b.* 1914, *m.*

1995   *Blyth of Rowington,* James Blyth, *b.* 1940, *m.*

1980   *Boardman,* Thomas Gray Boardman, MC, TD, *b.* 1919, *m.*

1996   *Borrie,* Gordon Johnson Borrie, QC, *b.* 1931, *m.*

1976   *Boston of Faversham,* Terence George Boston, QC, *b.* 1930, *m.*

1996   *Bowness,* Peter Spencer Bowness, CBE, *b.* 1943, *m.*

1998   *Bragg,* Melvyn Bragg, *b.* 1939, *m.*

1992   *Braine of Wheatley,* Bernard Richard Braine, PC, *b.* 1914, *w.*

1987   *Bramall,* Edwin Noel Westby Bramall, KG, GCB, OBE, MC, *b.* 1923, *m. Field Marshal*

1976   *Briggs,* Asa Briggs, FBA, *b.* 1921, *m.*

1997   *Brooke of Alverthorpe,* Clive Brooke, *b.* 1942, *m.*

1975   *Brookes,* Raymond Percival Brookes, *b.* 1909, *m.*

1998   *Brookman,* David Keith Brookman, *b.* 1937, *m.*

1979   *Brooks of Tremorfa,* John Edward Brooks, *b.* 1927, *m.*

1974   *Bruce of Donington,* Donald William Trevor Bruce, *b.* 1912, *m.*

1976   *Bullock,* Alan Louis Charles Bullock, FBA, *b.* 1914, *m.*

1997   *Burlison,* Thomas Henry Burlison, *b.* 1936, *m.*

1998   *Burns,* Terence Burns, GCB, *b.* 1944, *m.*

1998   *Butler of Brockwell,* (Frederick Edward) Robin Butler, GCB, CVO, *b.* 1938, *m.*

1988   *Butterfield,* (William) John (Hughes) Butterfield, OBE, DM, FRCP, *b.* 1920, *m.*

1985   *Butterworth,* John Blackstock Butterworth, CBE, *b.* 1918, *m.*

1978   *Buxton of Alsa,* Aubrey Leland Oakes Buxton, KCVO, MC, *b.* 1918, *m.*

1987   *Callaghan of Cardiff,* (Leonard) James Callaghan, KG, PC, *b.* 1912, *m.*

1984   *Cameron of Lochbroom,* Kenneth John Cameron, PC, *b.* 1931, *m.*

1981   *Campbell of Alloway,* Alan Robertson Campbell, QC, *b.* 1917, *m.*

1974   *Campbell of Croy,* Gordon Thomas Calthrop Campbell, MC, PC, *b.* 1921, *m.*

1987   *Carlisle of Bucklow,* Mark Carlisle, QC, PC, *b.* 1929, *m.*

1983   *Carmichael of Kelvingrove,* Neil George Carmichael, *b.* 1921.

1975   *Carr of Hadley,* (Leonard) Robert Carr, PC, *b.* 1916, *m.*

1987   *Carter,* Denis Victor Carter, PC, *b.* 1932, *m.*

1977   *Carver,* (Richard) Michael (Power) Carver, GCB, CBE, DSO, MC, *b.* 1915, *m. Field Marshal*

1990   *Cavendish of Furness,* (Richard) Hugh Cavendish, *b.* 1941, *m.*

1982   *Cayzer,* (William) Nicholas Cayzer, *b.* 1910, *w.*

1996   *Chadlington,* Peter Selwyn Gummer, *b.* 1942, *m.*

1964   *Chalfont,* (Alun) Arthur Gwynne Jones, OBE, MC, PC, *b.* 1919, *m.*

1985   *Chapple,* Francis (Frank) Joseph Chapple, *b.* 1921, *w.*

1978   *Charteris of Amisfield,* Martin Michael Charles Charteris, GCB, GCVO, OBE, PC, Royal Victorian Chain , *b.* 1913, *m.*

1987   *Chilver,* (Amos) Henry Chilver, FRS, FENG., *b.* 1926, *m.*

1977   *Chitnis,* Pratap Chidamber Chitnis, *b.* 1936, *m.*

1998   *Christopher,* Anthony Martin Grosvenor Christopher, CBE, *b.* 1925, *m.*

1992   *Clark of Kempston,* William Gibson Haig Clark, PC, *b.* 1917, *m.*

1998   *Clarke of Hampstead,* Anthony James Clarke, CBE.

1979   *Cledwyn of Penrhos,* Cledwyn Hughes, CH, PC, *b.* 1916, *m.*

1998   *Clement-Jones,* Timothy Francis Clement-Jones, CBE.

1990   *Clinton-Davis,* Stanley Clinton Clinton-Davis, PC, *b.* 1928, *m.*

1978   *Cockfield,* (Francis) Arthur Cockfield, PC, *b.* 1916, *w.*

1987   *Cocks of Hartcliffe,* Michael Francis Lovell Cocks, PC, *b.* 1929, *m.*

1980   *Coggan,* Rt. Revd (Frederick) Donald Coggan, PC, Royal Victorian Chain, *b.* 1909, *m.*

1981   *Constantine of Stanmore,* Theodore Constantine, CBE, AE, *b.* 1910, *w.*

1992   *Cooke of Islandreagh,* Victor Alexander Cooke, OBE, *b.* 1920, *m.*

1996   *Cooke of Thorndon,* Robin Brunskill Cooke, KBE, PC, PH.D., *b.* 1926, *m.*

1997   *Cope of Berkeley,* John Ambrose Cope, PC, *b.* 1937, *m.*

1997   *Cowdrey of Tonbridge,* (Michael) Colin Cowdrey, CBE, *b.* 1932, *m.*

1991   *Craig of Radley,* David Brownrigg Craig, GCB, OBE, *b.* 1929, *m. Marshal of the Royal Air Force*

1987   *Crickhowell,* (Roger) Nicholas Edwards, PC, *b.* 1934, *m.*

1978   *Croham,* Douglas Albert Vivian Allen, GCB, *b.* 1917, *w.*

1995   *Cuckney,* John Graham Cuckney, *b.* 1925, *m.*

1996   *Currie of Marylebone,* David Anthony Currie, *b.* 1946, *m.*

1979   *Dacre of Glanton,* Hugh Redwald Trevor-Roper, *b.* 1914, *w.*

1993   *Dahrendorf,* Ralf Dahrendorf, KBE, PH.D., D.phil., FBA, *b.* 1929, *m.*

1997   *Davies of Coity,* (David) Garfield Davies, CBE, *b.* 1935, *m.*

1997   *Davies of Oldham,* Bryan Davies, *b.* 1939, *m.*

1983   *Dean of Beswick,* Joseph Jabez Dean, *b.* 1922.

1993   *Dean of Harptree,* (Arthur) Paul Dean, PC, *b.* 1924, *m.*

1998   *Dearing,* Ronald Ernest Dearing, CB, *b.* 1930, *m.*

1986   *Deedes,* William Francis Deedes, MC, PC, *b.* 1913, *m.*

1991   *Desai,* Prof. Meghnad Jagdishchandra Desai, PH.D., *b.* 1940, *m.*

1997   *Dholakia,* Navnit Dholakia, OBE, *b.* 1937, *m.*

1970   *Diamond,* John Diamond, PC, *b.* 1907, *m.*

1997   *Dixon,* Donald Dixon, PC, *b.* 1929, *m.*

1993   *Dixon-Smith,* Robert William Dixon-Smith, *b.* 1934, *m.*

1988   *Donaldson of Lymington,* John Francis Donaldson, PC, *b.* 1920, *m.*

1985   *Donoughue,* Bernard Donoughue, D.phil., *b.* 1934.

1987   *Dormand of Easington,* John Donkin Dormand, *b.* 1919, *m.*

1994   *Dubs,* Alfred Dubs, *b.* 1932, *m.*

1995   *Eames,* Robert Henry Alexander Eames, PH.D., *b.* 1937, *m.*

1992   *Eatwell,* John Leonard Eatwell, *b.* 1945, *m.*

1983   *Eden of Winton,* John Benedict Eden, PC, *b.* 1925, *m.*

1992   *Elis-Thomas,* Dafydd Elis Elis-Thomas, *b.* 1946, *m.*

1985   *Elliott of Morpeth,* Robert William Elliott, *b.* 1920, *m.*

1981   *Elystan-Morgan,* Dafydd Elystan Elystan-Morgan, *b.* 1932, *m.*

1980   *Emslie,* George Carlyle Emslie, MBE, PC, FRSE, *b.* 1919, *m.*

1997	*Evans of Parkside,* John Evans, *b.* 1930, *m.*
1998	*Evans of Watford,* David Charles Evans.
1992	*Ewing of Kirkford,* Harry Ewing, *b.* 1931, *m.*
1983	*Ezra,* Derek Ezra, MBE, *b.* 1919, *m.*
1997	*Falconer of Thoroton,* Charles Leslie Falconer, QC, *b.* 1951, *m.*
1983	*Fanshawe of Richmond,* Anthony Henry Fanshawe Royle, KCMG, *b.* 1927, *m.*
1996	*Feldman,* Basil Feldman, *b.* 1926, *m.*
1983	*Fitt,* Gerard Fitt, *b.* 1926, *w.*
1979	*Flowers,* Brian Hilton Flowers, FRS, *b.* 1924, *m.*
1967	*Foot,* John Mackintosh Foot, *b.* 1909, *m.*
1982	*Forte,* Charles Forte, *b.* 1908, *m.*
1989	*Fraser of Carmyllie,* Peter Lovat Fraser, PC, QC, *b.* 1945, *m.*
1997	*Freeman,* Roger Norman Freeman, PC, *b.* 1942, *m.*
1982	*Gallacher,* John Gallacher, *b.* 1920, *m.*
1997	*Garel-Jones,* (William Armand Thomas) Tristan Garel-Jones, PC, *b.* 1941, *m.*
1992	*Geraint,* Geraint Wyn Howells, *b.* 1925, *m.*
1975	*Gibson,* (Richard) Patrick (Tallentyre) Gibson, *b.* 1916, *m.*
1979	*Gibson-Watt,* (James) David Gibson-Watt, MC, PC, *b.* 1918, *m.*
1997	*Gilbert,* John William Gilbert, PC, PH.D., *b.* 1927, *m.*
1996	*Gillmore of Thamesfield,* David Howe Gillmore, GCMG, *b.* 1934, *m.*
1992	*Gilmour of Craigmillar,* Ian Hedworth John Little Gilmour, PC, *b.* 1926, *m.*
1994	*Gladwin of Clee,* Derek Oliver Gladwin, CBE, *b.* 1930, *m.*
1977	*Glenamara,* Edward Watson Short, CH, PC, *b.* 1912, *m.*
1997	*Goodhart,* William Howard Goodhart, QC, *b.* 1933, *m.*
1997	*Gordon of Strathblane,* James Stuart Gordon, CBE, *b.* 1936, *m.*
1976	*Grade,* Lew Grade, *b.* 1906, *m.*
1983	*Graham of Edmonton,* (Thomas) Edward Graham, *b.* 1925, *m.*
1983	*Gray of Contin,* James (Hamish) Hector Northey Gray, PC, *b.* 1927, *m.*
1974	*Greene of Harrow Weald,* Sidney Francis Greene, CBE, *b.* 1910, *m.*
1974	*Greenhill of Harrow,* Denis Arthur Greenhill, GCMG, OBE, *b.* 1913, *m.*
1975	*Gregson,* John Gregson, *b.* 1924.
1968	*Grey of Naunton,* Ralph Francis Alnwick Grey, GCMG, GCVO, OBE, *b.* 1910, *w.*
1991	*Griffiths of Fforestfach,* Brian Griffiths, *b.* 1941, *m.*
1995	*Habgood,* Rt. Revd John Stapylton Habgood, PC, PH.D., *b.* 1927, *m.*
1970	*Hailsham of St Marylebone,* Quintin McGarel Hogg, KG, CH, PC, FRS, *b.* 1907, *m.*
1994	*Hambro,* Charles Eric Alexander Hambro, *b.* 1930, *m.*
1998	*Hamlyn,* Paul Bertrand Hamlyn, CBE, *b.* 1926, *m.*
1998	*Hanningfield,* Paul Edward Winston White
1983	*Hanson,* James Edward Hanson, *b.* 1922, *m.*
1997	*Hardie,* Andrew Rutherford Hardie, QC, PC, *b.* 1946, *m. Lord Advocate*
1997	*Hardy of Wath,* Peter Hardy, *b.* 1931, *m.*
1974	*Harmar-Nicholls,* Harmar Harmar-Nicholls, *b.* 1912, *m.*
1974	*Harris of Greenwich,* John Henry Harris, PC, *b.* 1930, *m.*
1998	*Harris of Haringey,* (Jonathan) Toby Harris, *b.* 1953, *m.*
1979	*Harris of High Cross,* Ralph Harris, *b.* 1924, *m.*
1996	*Harris of Peckham,* Philip Charles Harris, *b.* 1942, *m.*

1968	*Hartwell,* (William) Michael Berry, MBE, TD, *b.* 1911, *w.*
1993	*Haskel,* Simon Haskel, *b.* 1934, *m.*
1998	*Haskins,* Christopher Robin Haskins, *b.* 1937, *m.*
1990	*Haslam,* Robert Haslam, *b.* 1923, *m.*
1997	*Hattersley,* Roy Sidney George Hattersley, PC, *b.* 1932, *m.*
1992	*Hayhoe,* Bernard John (Barney) Hayhoe, PC, *b.* 1925, *m.*
1992	*Healey,* Denis Winston Healey, CH, MBE, PC, *b.* 1917, *m.*
1984	*Henderson of Brompton,* Peter Gordon Henderson, KCB, *b.* 1922, *m.*
1997	*Higgins,* Terence Langley Higgins, KBE, PC, *b.* 1928, *m.*
1979	*Hill-Norton,* Peter John Hill-Norton, GCB, *b.* 1915, *m. Admiral of the Fleet*
1997	*Hogg of Cumbernauld,* Norman Hogg, *b.* 1938, *m.*
1979	*Holderness,* Richard Frederick Wood, PC, *b.* 1920, *m.*
1991	*Hollick,* Clive Richard Hollick, *b.* 1945, *m.*
1990	*Holme of Cheltenham,* Richard Gordon Holme, CBE, *b.* 1936, *m.*
1979	*Hooson,* (Hugh) Emlyn Hooson, QC, *b.* 1925, *m.*
1995	*Hope of Craighead,* (James Arthur) David Hope, PC, *b.* 1938, *m. Lord of Appeal in Ordinary*
1992	*Howe of Aberavon,* (Richard Edward) Geoffrey Howe, CH, PC, QC, *b.* 1926, *m.*
1997	*Howell of Guildford,* David Arthur Russell Howell, PC, *b.* 1936, *m.*
1978	*Howie of Troon,* William Howie, *b.* 1924, *m.*
1997	*Hoyle,* (Eric) Douglas Harvey Hoyle, *b.* 1930, *w.*
1961	*Hughes,* William Hughes, CBE, PC, *b.* 1911, *w.*
1997	*Hughes of Woodside,* Robert Hughes, *b.* 1932, *m.*
1966	*Hunt,* (Henry Cecil) John Hunt, KG, CBE, DSO, *b.* 1910, *m.*
1997	*Hunt of Kings Heath,* Philip Alexander Hunt, OBE, *b.* 1949, *m.*
1980	*Hunt of Tanworth,* John Joseph Benedict Hunt, GCB, *b.* 1919, *m.*
1997	*Hunt of Wirral,* David James Fletcher Hunt, MBE, PC, *b.* 1942, *m.*
1997	*Hurd of Westwell,* Douglas Richard Hurd, CH, CBE, PC, *b.* 1930, *m.*
1996	*Hussey of North Bradley,* Marmaduke James Hussey, *b.* 1923, *m.*
1978	*Hutchinson of Lullington,* Jeremy Nicolas Hutchinson, QC, *b.* 1915, *m.*
1997	*Inge,* Peter Anthony Inge, GCB, *b.* 1935, *m. Field Marshal*
1982	*Ingrow,* John Aked Taylor, OBE, TD, *b.* 1917, *m.*
1987	*Irvine of Lairg,* Alexander Andrew Mackay Irvine, PC, QC, *b.* 1940, *m. Lord High Chancellor*
1997	*Islwyn,* Royston John (Roy) Hughes, *b.* 1925, *m.*
1997	*Jacobs,* (David) Anthony Jacobs, *b.* 1931, *m.*
1988	*Jakobovits,* Immanuel Jakobovits, *b.* 1921, *m.*
1997	*Janner of Braunstone,* Greville Ewan Janner, QC, *b.* 1928, *w.*
1987	*Jenkin of Roding,* (Charles) Patrick (Fleeming) Jenkin, PC, *b.* 1926, *m.*
1987	*Jenkins of Hillhead,* Roy Harris Jenkins, OM, PC, *b.* 1920, *m.*
1981	*Jenkins of Putney,* Hugh Gater Jenkins, *b.* 1908, *w.*
1987	*Johnston of Rockport,* Charles Collier Johnston, TD, *b.* 1915, *m.*
1997	*Jopling,* (Thomas) Michael Jopling, PC, *b.* 1930, *m.*
1991	*Judd,* Frank Ashcroft Judd, *b.* 1935, *m.*
1980	*Keith of Castleacre,* Kenneth Alexander Keith, *b.* 1916, *m.*
1997	*Kelvedon,* (Henry) Paul Guinness Channon, PC, *b.* 1935, *m.*

1996 *Kilpatrick of Kincraig,* Robert Kilpatrick, CBE, *b.* 1926, *m.*
1985 *Kimball,* Marcus Richard Kimball, *b.* 1928, *m.*
1983 *King of Wartnaby,* John Leonard King, *b.* 1918, *m.*
1993 *Kingsdown,* Robert (Robin) Leigh-Pemberton, KG, PC, *b.* 1927, *m.*
1994 *Kingsland,* Christopher James Prout, TD, PC, QC, *b.* 1942.
1975 *Kirkhill,* John Farquharson Smith, *b.* 1930, *m.*
1987 *Knights,* Philip Douglas Knights, CBE, QPM, *b.* 1920, *m.*
1991 *Laing of Dunphail,* Hector Laing, *b.* 1923, *m.*
1998 *Laming,* (William) Herbert Laming, CBE, *b.* 1936, *m.*
1998 *Lamont of Lerwick,* Norman Stewart Hughson Lamont, PC, *b.* 1942, *m.*
1990 *Lane of Horsell,* Peter Stewart Lane, *b.* 1925, *w.*
1997 *Lang of Monkton,* Ian Bruce Lang, PC, *b.* 1940, *m.*
1992 *Lawson of Blaby,* Nigel Lawson, PC, *b.* 1932, *m.*
1993 *Lester of Herne Hill,* Anthony Paul Lester, QC, *b.* 1936, *m.*
1997 *Levene of Portsoken,* Peter Keith Levene, KBE, *b.* 1941, *m.*
1997 *Levy,* Michael Abraham Levy, *b.* 1944, *m.*
1982 *Lewin,* Terence Thornton Lewin, KG, GCB, LVO, DSC, *b.* 1920, *m. Admiral of the Fleet*
1989 *Lewis of Newnham,* Jack Lewis, FRS, *b.* 1928, *m.*
1997 *Lloyd-Webber,* Andrew Lloyd Webber, *b.* 1948, *m.*
1997 *Lofthouse of Pontefract,* Geoffrey Lofthouse, *b.* 1925, *w.*
1974 *Lovell-Davis,* Peter Lovell Lovell-Davis, *b.* 1924, *m.*
1979 *Lowry,* Robert Lynd Erskine Lowry, PC, PC (NI), *b.* 1919, *m.*
1984 *McAlpine of West Green,* (Robert) Alistair McAlpine, *b.* 1942, *m.*
1988 *Macaulay of Bragar,* Donald Macaulay, QC, *b.* 1933, *m.*
1975 *McCarthy,* William Edward John McCarthy, D.Phil., *b.* 1925, *m.*
1976 *McCluskey,* John Herbert McCluskey, *b.* 1929, *m.*
1989 *McColl of Dulwich,* Ian McColl, CBE, FRCS, FRCSE, *b.* 1933, *m.*
1995 *McConnell,* Robert William Brian McConnell, PC (NI), *b.* 1922, *m.*
1991 *Macfarlane of Bearsden,* Norman Somerville Macfarlane, KT, FRSE, *b.* 1926, *m.*
1982 *McIntosh of Haringey,* Andrew Robert McIntosh, *b.* 1933, *m.*
1991 *Mackay of Ardbrecknish,* John Jackson Mackay, PC, *b.* 1938, *m.*
1979 *Mackay of Clashfern,* James Peter Hymers Mackay, KT, PC, FRSE, *b.* 1927, *m.*
1995 *Mackay of Drumadoon,* Donald Sage Mackay, *b.* 1946, *m.*
1998 *Mackenzie of Framwellgate,* Brian Mackenzie, OBE.
1988 *Mackenzie-Stuart,* Alexander John Mackenzie Stuart, *b.* 1924, *m.*
1974 *Mackie of Benshie,* George Yull Mackie, CBE, DSO, DFC, *b.* 1919, *m.*
1996 *MacLaurin,* Ian Charter MacLaurin, *b.* 1937, *m.*
1982 *MacLehose of Beoch,* (Crawford) Murray MacLehose, KT, GBE, KCMG, KCVO, *b.* 1917, *m.*
1995 *McNally,* Tom McNally, *b.* 1943, *m.*
1991 *Marlesford,* Mark Shuldham Schreiber, *b.* 1931, *m.*
1981 *Marsh,* Richard William Marsh, PC, *b.* 1928, *m.*
1998 *Marshall of Knightsbridge,* Colin Marsh Marshall, *b.* 1933, *m.*
1987 *Mason of Barnsley,* Roy Mason, PC, *b.* 1924, *m.*
1997 *Mayhew of Twysden,* Patrick Barnabas Burke Mayhew, QC, PC, *b.* 1929, *m.*

1993 *Menuhin,* Yehudi Menuhin, OM, KBE, *b.* 1916, *m.*
1992 *Merlyn-Rees,* Merlyn Merlyn-Rees, PC, *b.* 1920, *m.*
1978 *Mishcon,* Victor Mishcon, *b.* 1915, *m.*
1981 *Molloy,* William John Molloy, *b.* 1918
1997 *Molyneaux of Killead,* James Henry Molyneaux, KBE, PC, *b.* 1920
1997 *Monro of Langholm,* Hector Seymour Peter Monro, AE, PC, *b.* 1922, *m.*
1997 *Montague of Oxford,* Michael Jacob Montague, CBE, *b.* 1932.
1992 *Moore of Lower Marsh,* John Edward Michael Moore, PC, *b.* 1937, *m.*
1986 *Moore of Wolvercote,* Philip Brian Cecil Moore, GCB, GCVO, CMG, PC, *b.* 1921, *m.*
1990 *Morris of Castle Morris,* Brian Robert Morris, D.Phil., *b.* 1930, *m.*
1997 *Morris of Manchester,* Alfred Morris, PC, *b.* 1928, *m.*
1971 *Moyola,* James Dawson Chichester-Clark, PC (NI), *b.* 1923, *m.*
1985 *Murray of Epping Forest,* Lionel Murray, OBE, PC, *b.* 1922, *m.*
1979 *Murton of Lindisfarne,* (Henry) Oscar Murton, OBE, TD, PC, *b.* 1914, *m.*
1997 *Naseby,* Michael Wolfgang Laurence Morris, PC, *b.* 1936, *m.*
1997 *Neill of Bladen,* (Francis) Patrick Neill, QC, *b.* 1926, *m.*
1997 *Newby,* Richard Mark Newby, OBE, *b.* 1953, *m.*
1997 *Newton of Braintree,* Antony Harold Newton, OBE, PC, *b.* 1937, *m.*
1994 *Nickson,* David Wigley Nickson, KBE, FRSE, *b.* 1929, *m.*
1975 *Northfield,* (William) Donald Chapman, *b.* 1923.
1998 *Norton of Louth,* Philip Norton.
1997 *Onslow of Woking,* Cranley Gordon Douglas Onslow, KCMG, PC, *b.* 1926, *m.*
1976 *Oram,* Albert Edward Oram, *b.* 1913, *m.*
1997 *Orme,* Stanley Orme, PC, *b.* 1923, *m.*
1971 *Orr-Ewing,* (Charles) Ian Orr-Ewing, OBE, *b.* 1912, *m.*
1992 *Owen,* David Anthony Llewellyn Owen, CH, PC, *b.* 1938, *m.*
1991 *Palumbo,* Peter Garth Palumbo, *b.* 1935, *m.*
1992 *Parkinson,* Cecil Edward Parkinson, PC, *b.* 1931, *m.*
1975 *Parry,* Gordon Samuel David Parry, *b.* 1925, *m.*
1997 *Patten,* John Haggitt Charles Patten, PC, *b.* 1945, *m.*
1996 *Paul,* Swraj Paul, *b.* 1931, *m.*
1990 *Pearson of Rannoch,* Malcolm Everard MacLaren Pearson, *b.* 1942, *m.*
1979 *Perry of Walton,* Walter Laing Macdonald Perry, OBE, FRS, FRSE, *b.* 1921, *m.*
1987 *Peston,* Maurice Harry Peston, *b.* 1931, *m.*
1983 *Peyton of Yeovil,* John Wynne William Peyton, PC, *b.* 1919, *m.*
1994 *Phillips of Ellesmere,* Prof. David Chilton Phillips, KBE, FRS, *b.* 1924, *m.*
1998 *Phillips of Sudbury,* Andrew Wyndham Phillips, OBE.
1996 *Pilkington of Oxenford,* Revd Canon Peter Pilkington, *b.* 1933, *w.*
1992 *Plant of Highfield,* Prof. Raymond Plant, PH.D., *b.* 1945, *m.*
1959 *Plowden,* Edwin Noel Plowden, GBE, KCB, *b.* 1907, *m.*
1987 *Plumb,* (Charles) Henry Plumb, MEP, *b.* 1925, *m.*
1981 *Plummer of St Marylebone,* (Arthur) Desmond (Herne) Plummer, PC, *b.* 1914, *m.*
1990 *Porter of Luddenham,* George Porter, OM, FRS, *b.* 1920, *m.*
1992 *Prentice,* Reginald Ernest Prentice, PC, *b.* 1923, *m.*
1987 *Prior,* James Michael Leathes Prior, PC, *b.* 1927, *m.*

1982 *Prys-Davies*, Gwilym Prys Prys-Davies, *b.* 1923, *m.*
1997 *Puttnam*, David Terence Puttnam, CBE, *b.* 1941, *m.*
1987 *Pym*, Francis Leslie Pym, MC, PC, *b.* 1922, *m.*
1982 *Quinton*, Anthony Meredith Quinton, FBA, *b.* 1925, *m.*
1994 *Quirk*, Prof. (Charles) Randolph Quirk, CBE, FBA, *b.* 1920, *m.*
1997 *Randall of St Budeaux*, Stuart Jeffrey Randall, *b.* 1938, *m.*
1978 *Rawlinson of Ewell*, Peter Anthony Grayson Rawlinson, PC, QC, *b.* 1919, *m.*
1976 *Rayne*, Max Rayne, *b.* 1918, *m.*
1997 *Razzall*, (Edward) Timothy Razzall, CBE, *b.* 1943, *m.*
1987 *Rees*, Peter Wynford Innes Rees, PC, QC, *b.* 1926, *m.*
1988 *Rees-Mogg*, William Rees-Mogg, *b.* 1928, *m.*
1991 *Renfrew of Kaimsthorn*, (Andrew) Colin Renfrew, FBA, *b.* 1937, *m.*
1979 *Renton*, David Lockhart-Mure Renton, KBE, TD, PC, QC, *b.* 1908, *w.*
1997 *Renton of Mount Harry*, (Ronald) Timothy Renton, PC, *b.* 1932, *m.*
1997 *Renwick of Clifton*, Robin William Renwick, KCMG, *b.* 1937, *m.*
1990 *Richard*, Ivor Seward Richard, PC, QC, *b.* 1932, *m.*
1979 *Richardson*, John Samuel Richardson, LVO, MD, FRCP, *b.* 1910, *w.*
1983 *Richardson of Duntisbourne*, Gordon William Humphreys Richardson, KG, MBE, TD, PC, *b.* 1915, *m.*
1992 *Rix*, Brian Norman Roger Rix, CBE, *b.* 1924, *m.*
1961 *Robens of Woldingham*, Alfred Robens, PC, *b.* 1910, *m.*
1997 *Roberts of Conwy*, (Ieuan) Wyn (Pritchard) Roberts, PC, *b.* 1930, *m.*
1992 *Rodger of Earlsferry*, Alan Ferguson Rodger, PC, QC, FBA, *b.* 1944.
1992 *Rodgers of Quarry Bank*, William Thomas Rodgers, PC, *b.* 1928, *m.*
1996 *Rogers of Riverside*, Richard George Rogers, RA, RIBA, *b.* 1933, *m.*
1977 *Roll of Ipsden*, Eric Roll, KCMG, CB, *b.* 1907, *w.*
1991 *Runcie*, Rt Revd Robert Alexander Kennedy Runcie, MC, PC, Royal Victorian Chain, *b.* 1921, *m.*
1997 *Russell-Johnston*, (David) Russell Russell-Johnston, *b.* 1932, *m.*
1975 *Ryder of Eaton Hastings*, Sydney Thomas Franklin (Don) Ryder, *b.* 1916, *m.*
1997 *Ryder of Wensum*, Richard Andrew Ryder, OBE, PC, *b.* 1949, *m.*
1996 *Saatchi*, Maurice Saatchi, *b.* 1946, *m.*
1962 *Sainsbury*, Alan John Sainsbury, *b.* 1902, *w.*
1989 *Sainsbury of Preston Candover*, John Davan Sainsbury, KG, *b.* 1927, *m.*
1997 *Sainsbury of Turville*, David John Sainsbury, *b.* 1940, *m.*
1987 *St John of Fawsley*, Norman Antony Francis St John-Stevas, PC, *b.* 1929.
1997 *Sandberg*, Michael Graham Ruddock Sandberg, CBE, *b.* 1927, *m.*
1985 *Sanderson of Bowden*, Charles Russell Sanderson, *b.* 1933, *m.*
1998 *Sawyer*, Lawrence (Tom) Sawyer.
1979 *Scanlon*, Hugh Parr Scanlon, *b.* 1913, *m.*
1978 *Sefton of Garston*, William Henry Sefton, *b.* 1915, *m.*
1997 *Selkirk of Douglas*, James Alexander Douglas-Hamilton, PC, QC, *b.* 1942, *m.*

1996 *Sewel*, John Buttifant Sewel, CBE.
1994 *Shaw of Northstead*, Michael Norman Shaw, *b.* 1920, *m.*
1959 *Shawcross*, Hartley William Shawcross, GBE, PC, QC, *b.* 1902, *m.*
1994 *Sheppard of Didgemere*, Allan John George Sheppard, KCVO, *b.* 1932, *m.*
1998 *Sheppard of Liverpool*, David Stuart Sheppard, *b.* 1929, *m.*
1997 *Shore of Stepney*, Peter David Shore, PC, *b.* 1924, *m.*
1980 *Sieff of Brimpton*, Marcus Joseph Sieff, OBE, *b.* 1913, *w.*
1971 *Simon of Glaisdale*, Jocelyn Edward Salis Simon, PC, *b.* 1911, *m.*
1997 *Simon of Highbury*, David Alec Gwyn Simon, CBE, *b.* 1939, *m.*
1997 *Simpson of Dunkeld*, George Simpson, *b.* 1942, *m.*
1991 *Skidelsky*, Robert Jacob Alexander Skidelsky, D.phil., *b.* 1939, *m.*
1997 *Smith of Clifton*, Trevor Arthur Smith, *b.* 1937, *m.*
1965 *Soper*, Revd Donald Oliver Soper, ph.D., *b.* 1903, *m.*
1990 *Soulsby of Swaffham Prior*, Ernest Jackson Lawson Soulsby, ph.D., *b.* 1926, *m.*
1983 *Stallard*, Albert William Stallard, *b.* 1921, *m.*
1997 *Steel of Aikwood*, David Martin Scott Steel, KBE, PC, *b.* 1938, *m.*
1991 *Sterling of Plaistow*, Jeffrey Maurice Sterling, CBE, *b.* 1934, *m.*
1987 *Stevens of Ludgate*, David Robert Stevens, *b.* 1936, *m.*
1992 *Stewartby*, (Bernard Harold) Ian (Halley) Stewart, RD, PC, FBA, FRSE, *b.* 1935, *m.*
1981 *Stodart of Leaston*, James Anthony Stodart, PC, *b.* 1916, *w.*
1983 *Stoddart of Swindon*, David Leonard Stoddart, *b.* 1926, *m.*
1969 *Stokes*, Donald Gresham Stokes, TD, FEng., *b.* 1914, *w.*
1997 *Stone of Blackheath*, Andrew Zelig Stone, *b.* 1942, *m.*
1971 *Tanlaw*, Simon Brooke Mackay, *b.* 1934, *m.*
1996 *Taverne*, Dick Taverne, QC, *b.* 1928, *m.*
1978 *Taylor of Blackburn*, Thomas Taylor, CBE, *b.* 1929, *m.*
1968 *Taylor of Gryfe*, Thomas Johnston Taylor, FRSE, *b.* 1912, *m.*
1996 *Taylor of Warwick*, John David Beckett Taylor, *b.* 1952, *m.*
1992 *Tebbit*, Norman Beresford Tebbit, CH, PC, *b.* 1931, *m.*
1996 *Thomas of Gresford*, Donald Martin Thomas, OBE, QC, *b.* 1937, *m.*
1987 *Thomas of Gwydir*, Peter John Mitchell Thomas, PC, QC, *b.* 1920, *w.*
1997 *Thomas of Macclesfield*, Terence James Thomas, CBE, *b.* 1937, *m.*
1981 *Thomas of Swynnerton*, Hugh Swynnerton Thomas, *b.* 1931, *m.*
1977 *Thomson of Monifieth*, George Morgan Thomson, KT, PC, *b.* 1921, *m.*
1990 *Tombs*, Francis Leonard Tombs, FEng., *b.* 1924, *m.*
1998 *Tomlinson*, John Edward Tomlinson, MEP, *b.* 1939.
1994 *Tope*, Graham Norman Tope, CBE, *b.* 1943, *m.*
1981 *Tordoff*, Geoffrey Johnson Tordoff, *b.* 1928, *m.*
1993 *Tugendhat*, Christopher Samuel Tugendhat, *b.* 1937, *m.*
1990 *Varley*, Eric Graham Varley, PC, *b.* 1932, *m.*
1996 *Vincent of Coleshill*, Richard Frederick Vincent, GBE, KCB, DSO, *b.* 1931, *m.* (Field Marshal)
1985 *Vinson*, Nigel Vinson, LVO, *b.* 1931, *m.*

1990 *Waddington*, David Charles Waddington, GCVO, PC, QC, *b.* 1929, *m.*
1990 *Wade of Chorlton*, (William) Oulton Wade, *b.* 1932, *m.*
1992 *Wakeham*, John Wakeham, PC, *b.* 1932, *m.*
1997 *Walker of Doncaster*, Harold Walker, PC, *b.* 1927, *m.*
1992 *Walker of Worcester*, Peter Edward Walker, MBE, PC, *b.* 1932, *m.*
1974 *Wallace of Coslany*, George Douglas Wallace, *b.* 1906, *m.*
1995 *Wallace of Saltaire*, William John Lawrence Wallace, PH.D., *b.* 1941, *m.*
1989 *Walton of Detchant*, John Nicholas Walton, TD, FRCP, *b.* 1922, *m.*
1998 *Warner*, Norman Reginald Warner, *b.* 1940, *m.*
1997 *Watson of Invergowrie*, Michael Goodall Watson, *b.* 1949, *m.*
1992 *Weatherill*, (Bruce) Bernard Weatherill, PC, *b.* 1920, *m.*
1977 *Wedderburn of Charlton*, (Kenneth) William Wedderburn, FBA, QC, *b.* 1927, *m.*
1976 *Weidenfeld*, (Arthur) George Weidenfeld, *b.* 1919, *m.*
1980 *Weinstock*, Arnold Weinstock, *b.* 1924, *m.*
1978 *Whaddon*, (John) Derek Page, *b.* 1927, *m.*
1996 *Whitty*, John Lawrence (Larry) Whitty, *b.* 1943, *m.*
1974 *Wigoder*, Basil Thomas Wigoder, QC, *b.* 1921, *m.*
1985 *Williams of Elvel*, Charles Cuthbert Powell Williams, CBE, *b.* 1933, *m.*
1992 *Williams of Mostyn*, Gareth Wyn Williams, QC, *b.* 1941, *m.*
1992 *Wilson of Tillyorn*, David Clive Wilson, GCMG, PH.D., *b.* 1935, *m.*
1995 *Winston*, Robert Maurice Lipson Winston, FRCOG, *b.* 1940, *m.*
1985 *Wolfson*, Leonard Gordon Wolfson, *b.* 1927, *m.*
1991 *Wolfson of Sunningdale*, David Wolfson, *b.* 1935, *m.*
1994 *Wright of Richmond*, Patrick Richard Henry Wright, GCMG, *b.* 1931, *m.*
1978 *Young of Dartington*, Michael Young, PH.D., *b.* 1915, *m.*
1984 *Young of Graffham*, David Ivor Young, PC, *b.* 1932, *m.*
1992 *Younger of Prestwick*, The Viscount Younger of Leckie. (*see* page 147)

BARONESSES

Created
1997 *Amos*, Valerie Ann Amos, *b.* 1954.
1996 *Anelay of St Johns*, Joyce Anne Anelay, DBE, *b.* 1947, *m.*
1987 *Blackstone*, Tessa Ann Vosper Blackstone, PH.D., *b.* 1942.
1987 *Blatch*, Emily May Blatch, CBE, PC, *b.* 1937, *m.*
1990 *Brigstocke*, Heather Renwick Brigstocke, *b.* 1929, *w.*
1964 *Brooke of Ystradfellte*, Barbara Muriel Brooke, DBE, *b.* 1908, *w.*
1998 *Buscombe*, Peta Jane Buscombe.
1996 *Byford*, Hazel Byford, DBE, *b.* 1941, *m.*
1982 *Carnegy of Lour*, Elizabeth Patricia Carnegy of Lour, *b.* 1925.
1990 *Castle of Blackburn*, Barbara Anne Castle, PC, *b.* 1910, *w.*
1992 *Chalker of Wallasey*, Lynda Chalker, PC, *b.* 1942, *m.*
1982 *Cox*, Caroline Anne Cox, *b.* 1937, *m.*
1998 *Crawley*, Christine Mary Crawley, MEP, *b.* 1950, *m.*
1990 *Cumberlege*, Julia Frances Cumberlege, CBE, *b.* 1943, *m.*

1978 *David*, Nora Ratcliff David, *b.* 1913, *w.*
1993 *Dean of Thornton-le-Fylde*, Brenda Dean, PC, *b.* 1943, *m.*
1974 *Delacourt-Smith of Alteryn*, Margaret Rosalind Delacourt-Smith, *b.* 1916, *m.*
1991 *Denton of Wakefield*, Jean Denton, CBE, *b.* 1935.
1990 *Dunn*, Lydia Selina Dunn, DBE, *b.* 1940, *m.*
1990 *Eccles of Moulton*, Diana Catherine Eccles, *b.* 1933, *m.*
1972 *Elles*, Diana Louie Elles, *b.* 1921, *m.*
1997 *Emerton*, Audrey Caroline Emerton, DBE, *b.* 1935.
1974 *Falkender*, Marcia Matilda Falkender, CBE, *b.* 1932.
1994 *Farrington of Ribbleton*, Josephine Farrington, *b.* 1940, *m.*
1974 *Fisher of Rednal*, Doris Mary Gertrude Fisher, *b.* 1919, *w.*
1990 *Flather*, Shreela Flather, *m.*
1997 *Fookes*, Janet Evelyn Fookes, DBE, *b.* 1936.
1981 *Gardner of Parkes*, (Rachel) Trixie (Anne) Gardner, *b.* 1927, *m.*
1998 *Goudie*, Mary Teresa Goudie, *m.*
1993 *Gould of Potternewton*, Joyce Brenda Gould, *b.* 1932, *m.*
1991 *Hamwee*, Sally Rachel Hamwee, *b.* 1947.
1996 *Hayman*, Helene Valerie Hayman, *b.* 1949, *m.*
1991 *Hilton of Eggardon*, Jennifer Hilton, QPM, *b.* 1936.
1995 *Hogg*, Sarah Elizabeth Mary Hogg, *b.* 1946, *m.*
1990 *Hollis of Heigham*, Patricia Lesley Hollis, D.PHIL., *b.* 1941, *m.*
1985 *Hooper*, Gloria Dorothy Hooper, *b.* 1939.
1965 *Hylton-Foster*, Audrey Pellew Hylton-Foster, DBE, *b.* 1908, *w.*
1991 *James of Holland Park*, Phyllis Dorothy White (P. D. James), OBE, *b.* 1920, *w.*
1992 *Jay of Paddington*, Margaret Ann Jay, PC, *b.* 1939. *Lord Privy Seal*
1979 *Jeger*, Lena May Jeger, *b.* 1915, *w.*
1997 *Kennedy of the Shaws*, Helena Ann Kennedy, QC, *b.* 1950, *m.*
1997 *Knight of Collingtree*, (Joan Christabel) Jill Knight, DBE, *b.* 1923, *w.*
1997 *Linklater of Butterstone*, Veronica Linklater, *b.* 1943, *m.*
1996 *Lloyd of Highbury*, Prof. June Kathleen Lloyd, DBE, FRCP, FRCPE, FRCGP, *b.* 1928.
1978 *Lockwood*, Betty Lockwood, *b.* 1924, *w.*
1997 *Ludford*, Sarah Ann Ludford, *b.* 1951.
1979 *McFarlane of Llandaff*, Jean Kennedy McFarlane, *b.* 1926.
1971 *Macleod of Borve*, Evelyn Hester Macleod, *b.* 1915, *w.*
1997 *Maddock*, Diana Margaret Maddock, *b.* 1945, *m.*
1991 *Mallalieu*, Ann Mallalieu, QC, *b.* 1945, *m.*
1970 *Masham of Ilton*, Susan Lilian Primrose Cunliffe-Lister, *b.* 1935, *m.* (*Countess of Swinton*)
1998 *Miller of Chilthorne Domer*, Susan Elizabeth Miller.
1993 *Miller of Hendon*, Doreen Miller, MBE, *b.* 1933, *m.*
1997 *Nicholson of Winterbourne*, Emma Harriet Nicholson, *b.* 1941, *m.*
1982 *Nicol*, Olive Mary Wendy Nicol, *b.* 1923, *m.*
1991 *O'Cathain*, Detta O'Cathain, OBE, *b.* 1938, *m.*
1989 *Oppenheim-Barnes*, Sally Oppenheim-Barnes, PC, *b.* 1930, *m.*
1990 *Park of Monmouth*, Daphne Margaret Sybil Désirée Park, CMG, OBE, *b.* 1921.
1991 *Perry of Southwark*, Pauline Perry, *b.* 1931, *m.*
1974 *Pike*, (Irene) Mervyn (Parnicott) Pike, DBE, *b.* 1918.
1997 *Pitkeathley*, Jill Elizabeth Pitkeathley, OBE, *b.* 1940.

1981   *Platt of Writtle*, Beryl Catherine Platt, CBE, FEng.,
        b. 1923, *m.*
1996   *Ramsay of Cartvale*, Margaret Mildred (Meta)
        Ramsay, *b.* 1936.
1994   *Rawlings*, Patricia Elizabeth Rawlings, *b.* 1939.
1997   *Rendell of Babergh*, Ruth Barbara Rendell, CBE, *b.*
        1930, *m.*
1998   *Richardson of Calow*, Kathleen Margaret
        Richardson, OBE, *b.* 1938, *m.*
1974   *Robson of Kiddington*, Inga-Stina Robson, *b.* 1919,
        w.
1979   *Ryder of Warsaw*, Margaret Susan Cheshire (Sue
        Ryder), CMG, OBE, *b.* 1923, *w.*
1997   *Scotland of Asthal*, Patricia Janet Scotland, QC, *m.*
1991   *Seccombe*, Joan Anna Dalziel Seccombe, DBE, *b.*
        1930, *m.*
1967   *Serota*, Beatrice Serota, DBE, *b.* 1919, *m.*
1998   *Sharp of Guildford*, Margaret Lucy Sharp, *m.*
1973   *Sharples*, Pamela Sharples, *b.* 1923, *m.*
1995   *Smith of Gilmorehill*, Elizabeth Margaret Smith, *b.*
        1940, *w.*
1996   *Symons of Vernham Dean*, Elizabeth Conway
        Symons, *b.* 1951.
1992   *Thatcher*, Margaret Hilda Thatcher, KG, OM, PC,
        FRS, *b.* 1925, *m.*
1994   *Thomas of Walliswood*, Susan Petronella Thomas,
        OBE, *b.* 1935, *m.*
1998   *Thornton*, (Dorothea) Glenys Thornton.
1980   *Trumpington*, Jean Alys Barker, PC, *b.* 1922, *w.*
1985   *Turner of Camden*, Muriel Winifred Turner, *b.*
        1927, *m.*
1998   *Uddin*, Manzila Pola Uddin.
1985   *Warnock*, Helen Mary Warnock, DBE, *b.* 1924, *w.*
1970   *White*, Eirene Lloyd White, *b.* 1909, *w.*
1996   *Wilcox*, Judith Ann Wilcox, *w.*
1993   *Williams of Crosby*, Shirley Vivien Teresa Brittain
        Williams, PC, *b.* 1930, *m.*
1971   *Young*, Janet Mary Young, PC, *b.* 1926, *m.*
1997   *Young of Old Scone*, Barbara Scott Young, *b.* 1948.

Lords Spiritual

The Lords Spiritual are the Archbishops of Canterbury and York and 24 diocesan bishops of the Church of England. The Bishops of London, Durham and Winchester always have seats in the House of Lords; the other 21 seats are filled by the remaining diocesan bishops in order of seniority. The Bishop of Sodor and Man and the Bishop of Gibraltar are not eligible to sit in the House of Lords.

ARCHBISHOPS

Style, The Most Revd and Right Hon. the Lord Archbishop of __
Addressed as Archbishop, *or* Your Grace

Introduced to House of Lords
1991   *Canterbury* (103rd), George Leonard Carey, PC, PH.D., *b.* 1935, *m., cons.* 1987, *trans.* 1991
1990   *York* (96th), David Michael Hope, KCVO, PC, D.Phil., *b.* 1940, *cons.* 1985, *elected* 1985, *trans.* 1991, 1995

BISHOPS

Style, The Right Revd the Lord Bishop of __
Addressed as My Lord
elected date of election as diocesan bishop

Introduced to House of Lords
1996   *London* (132nd), Richard John Carew Chartres, *b.* 1947, *m., cons.* 1992
1994   *Durham* (93rd), (Anthony) Michael (Arnold) Turnbull, *b.* 1935, *m., cons.* 1988, *elected* 1988, *trans.* 1994
1996   *Winchester* (96th), Michael Charles Scott-Joynt, *b.* 1943, *m., cons.* 1987
1979   *Chichester* (102nd), Eric Waldram Kemp, DD, *b.* 1915, *m., cons.* 1974, *elected* 1974
1984   *Ripon* (11th), David Nigel de Lorentz Young, *b.* 1931, *m., cons.* 1977, *elected* 1977
1989   *Lichfield* (97th), Keith Norman Sutton, *b.* 1934, *m., cons.* 1978, *elected* 1984
1990   *Exeter* (69th), (Geoffrey) Hewlett Thompson, *b.* 1929, *m., cons.* 1974, *elected* 1985
1990   *Bristol* (54th), Barry Rogerson, *b.* 1936, *m., cons.* 1979, *elected* 1985
1991   *Norwich* (70th), Peter John Nott, *b.* 1933, *m., cons.* 1977, *elected* 1985
1993   *Lincoln* (70th), Robert Maynard Hardy, *b.* 1936, *m., cons.* 1980, *elected* 1986
1993   *Oxford* (41st), Richard Douglas Harries, *b.* 1936, *m., cons.* 1987, *elected* 1987
1994   *Birmingham* (7th), Mark Santer, *b.* 1936, *w., cons.* 1981, *elected* 1987
1995   *Southwell* (9th), Patrick Burnet Harris, *b.* 1934, *m., cons.* 1973, *elected* 1988
1995   *Blackburn* (7th), Alan David Chesters, *b.* 1937, *m., cons.* 1989, *elected* 1989
1996   *Carlisle* (65th), Ian Harland, *b.* 1932, *m., cons.* 1985, *elected* 1989
1996   *Ely* (67th), Stephen Whitefield Sykes, *b.* 1939, *m., cons.* 1990, *elected* 1990

1996   *Hereford* (103rd), John Keith Oliver, *b.* 1935, *m., cons.* 1990, *elected* 1990
1996   **Leicester* (5th), Thomas Frederick Butler, *b.* 1940, *m., cons.* 1985, *elected* 1991

Bishops awaiting seats, in order of seniority
Bath and Wells (77th), James Lawton Thompson, *b.* 1936, *m., cons.* 1978, *elected* 1991
Wakefield (11th), Nigel Simeon McCulloch, *b.* 1942, *m., cons.* 1986, *elected* 1992
Bradford (8th), David James Smith, *b.* 1935, *m., cons.* 1987, *elected* 1992
Manchester (10th), Christopher John Mayfield, *b.* 1935, *m., cons.* 1985, *elected* 1993
Salisbury (77th), David Staffurth Stancliffe, *b.* 1942, *m., cons.* 1993, *elected* 1993
Gloucester (39th), David Edward Bentley, *b.* 1935, *m., cons.* 1986, *elected* 1993
Rochester (106th), Michael James Nazir-Ali, PH.D., *b.* 1949, *m., cons.* 1984, *elected* 1995
Guildford (8th), John Warren Gladwin, *b.* 1942, *m., cons.* 1994, *elected* 1994
Portsmouth (8th), Kenneth William Stevenson, *b.* 1949, *m., cons.* 1995, *elected* 1995
Derby (6th), Jonathan Sansbury Bailey, *b.* 1940, *m., cons.* 1992, *elected* 1995
St Albans (9th), Christopher William Herbert, *b.* 1944, *m., cons.* 1995, *elected* 1995
Chelmsford (8th), John Freeman Perry, *b.* 1935, *m., cons.* 1989, *elected* 1996
Peterborough (37th), Ian Cundy, *b.* 1945, *m., cons.* 1992, *elected* 1996
Chester (40th), Peter Robert Forster, PH.D., *b.* 1950, *cons.* 1996, *elected* 1996
St Edmundsbury and Ipswich (9th), (John Hubert) Richard Lewis, *b.* 1943, *m., cons.* 1992, *elected* 1997
Worcester (112th), Peter Stephen Maurice Selby, *b.* 1941, *cons.* 1984, *elected* 1997
Newcastle (11th), (John) Martin Wharton, *b.* 1944, *m., cons.* 1992, *elected* 1997
Sheffield (6th), John Nicholls, *b.* 1943, *m., cons.* 1990, *elected* 1997
Truro (14th), William Ind, *b.* 1942, *m., cons.* 1987, *elected* 1997
Coventry (8th), Colin J. Bennetts, *b.* 1940, *m., cons.* 1994, *elected* 1997
Liverpool (7th), James Jones, *b.* 1948, *m., cons.* 1994, *elected* 1998

*In September 1998 the Bishop of Leicester will become the Bishop of Southwark; he will retain his seat in the House of Lords

COURTESY TITLES

From this list it will be seen that, for example, the Marquess of Blandford is heir to the Dukedom of Marlborough, and Viscount Amberley to the Earldom of Russell. Titles of second heirs are also given, and the courtesy title of the father of a second heir is indicated by *; e.g. Earl of Burlington, eldest son of *Marquess of Hartington
For forms of address, see page 135

MARQUESSES

*Blandford – *Marlborough, D.*
Bowmont and Cessford – *Roxburghe, D.*
Douglas and Clydesdale – *Hamilton, D.*
*Douro – *Wellington, D.*
Graham – *Montrose, D.*
Granby – *Rutland, D.*
Hamilton – *Abercorn, D.*
*Hartington – *Devonshire, D.*
*Kildare – *Leinster, D.*
Lorne – *Argyll, D.*
*Tavistock – *Bedford, D.*
Tullibardine – *Atholl, D.*
*Worcester – *Beaufort, D.*

EARLS

Aboyne – *Huntly, M.*
Altamont – *Sligo, M.*
Ancram – *Lothian, M.*
Arundel and Surrey – *Norfolk, D.*
*Bective – *Headfort, M.*
*Belfast – *Donegall, M.*
Brecknock – *Camden, M.*
Burford – *St Albans, D.*
Burlington – *Hartington, M.*
*Cardigan – *Ailesbury, M.*
Compton – *Northampton, M.*
*Dalkeith – *Buccleuch, D.*
Dumfries – *Bute, M.*
*Euston – *Grafton, D.*
Glamorgan – *Worcester, M.*
Grosvenor – *Westminster, D.*
*Haddo – *Aberdeen and Temair, M.*
Hillsborough – *Downshire, M.*
Hopetoun – *Linlithgow, M.*
March and Kinrara – *Richmond, D.*
*Mount Charles – *Conyngham, M.*
Mornington – *Douro, M.*
Percy – *Northumberland, D.*
Ronaldshay – *Zetland, M.*
*St Andrews – *Kent, D.*
*Shelburne – *Lansdowne, M.*
*Southesk – *Fife, D.*
Sunderland – *Blandford, M.*
*Tyrone – *Waterford, M.*

Ulster – *Gloucester, D.*
*Uxbridge – *Anglesey, M.*
Wiltshire – *Winchester, M.*
Yarmouth – *Hertford, M.*

VISCOUNTS

Althorp – *Spencer, E.*
Amberley – *Russell, E.*
Andover – *Suffolk and Berkshire, E.*
Anson – *Lichfield, E.*
Asquith – *Oxford and Asquith, E.*
Boringdon – *Morley, E.*
Borodale – *Beatty, E.*
Boyle – *Shannon, E.*
Brocas – *Jellicoe, E.*
Calne and Calstone – *Shelburne, E.*
Campden – *Gainsborough, E.*
Carlow – *Portarlington, E.*
Carlton – *Wharncliffe, E.*
Castlereagh – *Londonderry, M.*
Chelsea – *Cadogan, E.*
Chewton – *Waldegrave, E.*
Chichester – *Belfast, E.*
Clanfield – *Peel, E.*
Clive – *Powis, E.*
Coke – *Leicester, E.*
Corry – *Belmore, E.*
Corvedale – *Baldwin of Bewdley, E.*
Cranborne – *Salisbury, M.*
Cranley – *Onslow, E.*
Crichton – *Erne, E.*
Crowhurst – *Cottenham, E.*
Curzon – *Howe, E.*
Dangan – *Cowley, E.*
Dawick – *Haig, E.*
Drumlanrig – *Queensberry, M.*
Dunwich – *Stradbroke, E.*
Dupplin – *Kinnoull, E.*
Ebrington – *Fortescue, E.*
Ednam – *Dudley, E.*
Emlyn – *Cawdor, E.*
Encombe – *Eldon, E.*
Enfield – *Strafford, E.*
Erleigh – *Reading, M.*
Errington – *Cromer, E.*
FitzHarris – *Malmesbury, E.*
Folkestone – *Radnor, E.*
Forbes – *Granard, E.*
Garmoyle – *Cairns, E.*
Garnock – *Lindsay, E.*
Glandine – *Norbury, E.*

Glenapp – *Inchcape, E.*
Glentworth – *Limerick, E.*
Grimstone – *Verulam, E.*
Gwynedd – *Lloyd George of Dwyfor, E.*
Hawkesbury – *Liverpool, E.*
Hinchingbrooke – *Sandwich, E.*
Ikerrin – *Carrick, E.*
Ingestre – *Shrewsbury, E.*
Ipswich – *Euston, E.*
Jocelyn – *Roden, E.*
Kelburn – *Glasgow, E.*
Kilwarlin – *Hillsborough, E.*
Kingsborough – *Kingston, E.*
Kirkwall – *Orkney, E.*
Knebworth – *Lytton, E.*
Lascelles – *Harewood, E.*
Linley – *Snowdon, E.*
Loftus – *Ely, M.*
Lowther – *Lonsdale, E.*
Lumley – *Scarbrough, E.*
Lymington – *Portsmouth, E.*
Macmillan of Ovenden – *Stockton, E.*
Maidstone – *Winchilsea and Nottingham, E.*
Maitland – *Lauderdale, E.*
Malden – *Essex, E.*
Mandeville – *Manchester, D.*
Medina – *Milford Haven, M.*
Melgund – *Minto, E.*
Merton – *Nelson, E.*
Moore – *Drogheda, E.*
Newport – *Bradford, E.*
Newry and Mourne – *Kilmorey, E.*
Parker – *Macclesfield, E.*
Perceval – *Egmont, E.*
Petersham – *Harrington, E.*
Pollington – *Mexborough, E.*
Raynham – *Townshend, M.*
Reidhaven – *Seafield, E.*
Ruthven of Canberra – *Gowrie, E.*
St Cyres – *Iddesleigh, E.*
Sandon – *Harrowby, E.*
Savernake – *Cardigan, E.*
Slane – *Mount Charles, E.*
Somerton – *Normanton, E.*
Stopford – *Courtown, E.*
Stormont – *Mansfield, E.*
Strathallan – *Perth, E.*
Stuart – *Castle Stewart, E.*
Suirdale – *Donoughmore, E.*
Tamworth – *Ferrers, E.*
Tarbat – *Cromartie, E.*

Vaughan – *Lisburne, E.*
Weymouth – *Bath, M.*
Windsor – *Plymouth, E.*
Wolmer – *Selborne, E.*
Woodstock – *Portland, E.*

BARONS (LORD __)

Aberdour – *Morton, E.*
Apsley – *Bathurst, E.*
Ardee – *Meath, E.*
Ashley – *Shaftesbury, E.*
Balgonie – *Leven and Melville, E.*
Balniel – *Crawford and Balcarres, E.*
Berriedale – *Caithness, E.*
Bingham – *Lucan, E.*
Binning – *Haddington, E.*
Brooke – *Warwick, E.*
Bruce – *Elgin, E.*
Buckhurst – *De La Warr, E.*
Burghley – *Exeter, M.*
Cardross – *Buchan, E.*
Carnegie – *Southesk, E.*
Clifton – *Darnley, E.*
Cochrane – *Dundonald, E.*
Courtenay – *Devon, E.*
Dalmeny – *Rosebery, E.*
Doune – *Moray, E.*
Downpatrick – *St Andrews, E.*
Dunglass – *Home, E.*
Eliot – *St Germans, E.*
Eskdail – *Dalkeith, E.*
Formartine – *Haddo, E.*
Gillford – *Clanwilliam, E.*
Glamis – *Strathmore, E.*
Greenock – *Cathcart, E.*
Guernsey – *Aylesford, E.*
Hay – *Erroll, E.*
Herbert – *Pembroke, E.*
Howard of Effingham – *Effingham, E.*
Howland – *Tavistock, M.*
Hyde – *Clarendon, E.*
Inverurie – *Kintore, E.*
Irwin – *Halifax, E.*
Johnstone – *Annandale and Hartfell, E.*
Kenlis – *Bective, E.*
Langton – *Temple of Stowe, E.*
La Poer – *Tyrone, E.*
Leslie – *Rothes, E.*
Loughborough – *Rosslyn, E.*
Maltravers – *Arundel and Surrey, E.*
Mauchline – *Loudoun, C.*
Medway – *Cranbrook, E.*
Montgomerie – *Eglinton and Winton, E.*
Moreton – *Ducie, E.*
Naas – *Mayo, E.*

Neidpath – *Wemyss and March, E.*
Norreys – *Lindsey and Abingdon, E.*
North – *Guilford, E.*

Ogilvy – *Airlie, E.*
Oxmantown – *Rosse, E.*
Paget de Beaudesert – *Uxbridge, E.*
Porchester – *Carnarvon, E.*

Ramsay – *Dalhousie, E.*
Romsey – *Mountbatten of Burma, C.*
Rosehill – *Northesk, E.*
Scrymgeour – *Dundee, E.*

Seymour – *Somerset, D.*
Strathnaver – *Sutherland, C.*
Wodehouse – *Kimberley, E.*
Worsley – *Yarborough, E.*

PEERS' SURNAMES WHICH DIFFER FROM THEIR TITLES

The following symbols indicate the rank of the peer holding each title:

B. Baron/Lord or Baroness/Lady
C. Countess
D. Duke
E. Earl
M. Marquess
V. Viscount
* Life Peer

Abney-Hastings – *Loudoun, C.*
Acheson – *Gosford, E.*
Adderley – *Norton, B.*
Addington – *Sidmouth, V.*
Agar – *Normanton, E.*
Aitken – *Beaverbrook, B.*
Akers-Douglas – *Chilston, V.*
Alexander – *A. of Tunis, E.*
Alexander – *A. of Weedon, B.*
Alexander – *Caledon, E.*
Allen – *A. of Abbeydale, B.*
Allen – *Croham, B.*
Allsopp – *Hindlip, B.*
Alton – *A. of Liverpool, B.*
Anderson – *Waverley, V.*
Anelay – *A. of St Johns, B.*
Annesley – *Valentia, V.*
Anson – *Lichfield, E.*
Arbuthnott – *of Arbuthnott, V.*
Archer – *A. of Sandwell, B.*
Archer – *A. of Weston-super-Mare, B.*
Armstrong – *A. of Ilminster, B.*
Armstrong-Jones – *Snowdon, E.*
Arthur – *Glenarthur, B.*
Arundell – *Talbot of Malahide, B.*
Ashley – *A. of Stoke, B.*
Ashley-Cooper – *Shaftesbury, E.*
Ashton – *A. of Hyde, B.*
Asquith – *Oxford and Asquith, E.*
Assheton – *Clitheroe, B.*
Astley – *Hastings, B.*
Astor – *B. of Hever, B.*
Aubrey-Fletcher – *Braye, B.*
Bailey – *Glanusk, B.*
Baillie – *Burton, B.*
Baillie-Hamilton – *Haddington, E.*
Baker – *B. of Dorking, B.*
Balcarres – *Balniel, B.*
Baldwin – *B. of Bewdley, E.*
Balfour – *B. of Inchrye, B.*
Balfour – *Kinross, B.*
Balfour – *Riverdale, B.*

Bampfylde – *Poltimore, B.*
Banbury – *B. of Southam, B.*
Barber – *B. of Tewkesbury, B.*
Baring – *Ashburton, B.*
Baring – *Cromer, E.*
Baring – *Howick of Glendale, B.*
Baring – *Northbrook, B.*
Baring – *Revelstoke, B.*
Barker – *Trumpington, B.*
Barnes – *Gorell, B.*
Barnewall – *Trimlestown, B.*
Bassam – *B. of Brighton, B.*
Bathurst – *Bledisloe, V.*
Beauclerk – *St Albans, D.*
Beaumont – *Allendale, V.*
Beaumont – *B. of Whitley, B.*
Beckett – *Grimthorpe, B.*
Bellow – *Bellwin, B.*
Benn – *Stansgate, V.*
Bennet – *Tankerville, E.*
Bentinck – *Portland, E.*
Beresford – *Waterford, M.*
Berry – *Hartwell, B.*
Berry – *Kemsley, V.*
Bertie – *Lindsey, E.*
Best – *Wynford, B.*
Bethell – *Westbury, B.*
Bewicke-Copley – *Cromwell, B.*
Bigham – *Mersey, V.*
Bingham – *B. of Cornhill, B.*
Bingham – *Clanmorris, B.*
Bingham – *Lucan, E.*
Bligh – *Darnley, E.*
Blyth – *B. of Rowington, B.*
Bootle-Wilbraham – *Skelmersdale, B.*
Boscawen – *Falmouth, V.*
Boston – *B. of Faversham, B.*
Bourke – *Mayo, E.*
Bowes Lyon – *Strathmore and Kinghorne, E.*
Bowyer – *Denham, B.*
Boyd – *Kilmarnock, B.*
Boyle – *Cork and Orrery, E.*
Boyle – *Glasgow, E.*
Boyle – *Shannon, E.*
Brabazon – *Meath, E.*
Braine – *B. of Wheatley, B.*
Brand – *Hampden, V.*
Brandon – *B. of Oakbrook, B.*
Brassey – *B. of Apethorpe, B.*
Brett – *Esher, V.*
Bridge – *B. of Harwich, B.*
Bridgeman – *Bradford, E.*
Brodrick – *Midleton, V.*
Brooke – *Alanbrooke, V.*
Brooke – *B. of Alverthorpe, B.*
Brooke – *B. of Ystradfellte, B.*
Brooke – *Brookeborough, V.*
Brooks – *B. of Tremorfa, B.*

Brooks – *Crawshaw, B.*
Brougham – *B. and Vaux, B.*
Broughton – *Fairhaven, B.*
Browne – *Kilmaine, B.*
Browne – *Oranmore and Browne, B.*
Browne – *Sligo, M.*
Bruce – *Aberdare, B.*
Bruce – *Balfour of Burleigh, B.*
Bruce – *B. of Donington, B.*
Bruce – *Elgin and Kincardine, E.*
Brudenell-Bruce – *Ailesbury, M.*
Buchan – *Tweedsmuir, B.*
Buckley – *Wrenbury, B.*
Butler – *B. of Brockwell, B.*
Butler – *Carrick, E.*
Butler – *Dunboyne, B.*
Butler – *Lanesborough, E.*
Butler – *Mountgarret, V.*
Buxton – *B. of Alsa, B.*
Byng – *Strafford, E.*
Byng – *Torrington, V.*
Callaghan – *C. of Cardiff, B.*
Cameron – *C. of Lochbroom, B.*
Campbell – *Argyll, D.*
Campbell – *C. of Alloway, B.*
Campbell – *C. of Croy, B.*
Campbell – *Cawdor, E.*
Campbell – *Colgrain, B.*
Campbell – *Stratheden and Campbell, B.*
Campbell-Gray – *Gray, B.*
Canning – *Garvagh, B.*
Capell – *Essex, E.*
Carington – *Carrington, B.*
Carlisle – *C. of Bucklow, B.*
Carmichael – *C. of Kelvingrove, B.*
Carnegie – *Fife, D.*
Carnegie – *Northesk, E.*
Carr – *C. of Hadley, B.*
Cary – *Falkland, V.*
Castle – *C. of Blackburn, B.*
Caulfeild – *Charlemont, V.*
Cavendish – *C. of Furness, B.*
Cavendish – *Chesham, B.*
Cavendish – *Devonshire, D.*
Cavendish – *Waterpark, B.*
Cayzer – *Rotherwick, B.*
Cecil – *Amherst of Hackney, B.*
Cecil – *Exeter, M.*
Cecil – *Rockley, B.*
Cecil – *Salisbury, M.*
Chalker – *C. of Wallasey, B.*
Chaloner – *Gisborough, B.*
Channon – *Kelvedon, B.*
Chapman – *Northfield, B.*
Charteris – *C. of Amisfield, B.*

Charteris – *Wemyss and March, E.*
Cheshire – *Ryder of Warsaw, B.*
Chetwynd-Talbot – *Shrewsbury and Waterford, E.*
Chichester – *Donegall, M.*
Chichester-Clark – *Moyola, B.*
Child Villiers – *Jersey, E.*
Cholmondeley – *Delamere, B.*
Chubb – *Hayter, B.*
Clark – *C. of Kempston, B.*
Clarke – *C. of Hampstead, B.*
Clegg-Hill – *Hill, V.*
Clifford – *C. of Chudleigh, B.*
Cochrane – *C. of Cults, B.*
Cochrane – *Dundonald, E.*
Cocks – *C. of Hartcliffe, B.*
Cocks – *Somers, B.*
Cokayne – *Cullen of Ashbourne, B.*
Coke – *Leicester, E.*
Cole – *Enniskillen, E.*
Collier – *Monkswell, B.*
Colville – *Clydesmuir, B.*
Colville – *C. of Culross, V.*
Compton – *Northampton, M.*
Conolly-Carew – *Carew, B.*
Constantine – *C. of Stanmore, B.*
Cooke – *C. of Islandreagh, B.*
Cooke – *C. of Thorndon, B.*
Cooper – *Norwich, V.*
Cope – *C. of Berkeley, B.*
Corbett – *Rowallan, B.*
Cornwall-Legh – *Grey of Codnor, B.*
Courtenay – *Devon, E.*
Cowdrey – *C. of Tonbridge, B.*
Craig – *C. of Radley, B.*
Craig – *Craigavon, V.*
Crichton – *Erne, E.*
Crichton-Stuart – *Bute, M.*
Cripps – *Parmoor, B.*
Crossley – *Somerleyton, B.*
Cubitt – *Ashcombe, B.*
Cunliffe-Lister – *Masham of Ilton, B.*
Cunliffe-Lister – *Swinton, E.*
Currie – *C. of Marylebone, B.*
Curzon – *Howe, E.*
Curzon – *Scarsdale, V.*
Cust – *Brownlow, B.*
Dalrymple – *Stair, E.*
Daubeny de Moleyns – *Ventry, B.*
Davies – *D. of Coity, B.*
Davies – *D. of Oldham, B.*

Davies – *Darwen, B.*
Davison – *Broughshane, B.*
Dawnay – *Downe, V.*
Dawson-Damer –
  Portarlington, E.
Dean – *D. of Beswick, B.**
Dean – *D. of Harptree, B.**
Dean – *D. of Thornton-le-*
  *Fylde, B.**
Deane – *Muskerry, B.*
de Courcy – *Kingsale, B.*
de Grey – *Walsingham, B.*
Delacourt-Smith – *D. of*
  *Alteryn, B.**
de la Poer Beresford –
  Decies, B.
Denison – *Londesborough, B.*
Denison-Pender – *Pender, B.*
Denton – *D. of Wakefield, B.**
Devereux – *Hereford, V.*
Dewar – *Forteviot, B.*
De Yarburgh-Bateson –
  Deramore, B.
Dixon – *Glentoran, B.*
Dodson – *Monk Bretton, B.*
Donaldson – *D. of Lymington,*
  *B.**
Dormand – *D. of Easington,*
  *B.**
Douglas – *Morton, E.*
Douglas – *Queensberry, M.*
Douglas-Hamilton –
  Hamilton, D.
Douglas-Hamilton – *Selkirk*
  *of Douglas, B.**
Douglas-Home – *Dacre, B.*
Douglas-Home – *Home, E.*
Douglas-Pennant – *Penrhyn,*
  B.
Douglas-Scott-Montagu –
  Montagu of Beaulieu, B.
Drummond – *Perth, E.*
Drummond of Megginch –
  Strange, B.
Dugdale – *Crathorne, B.*
Duke – *Merrivale, B.*
Duncombe – *Feversham, B.*
Dundas – *Melville, V.*
Dundas – *Zetland, M.*
Eady – *Swinfen, B.*
Eccles – *E. of Moulton, B.**
Eden – *Auckland, B.*
Eden – *E. of Winton, B.**
Eden – *Henley, B.*
Edgcumbe – *Mount*
  Edgcumbe, E.
Edmondson – *Sandford, B.*
Edwardes – *Kensington, B.*
Edwards – *Crickhowell, B.**
Egerton – *Sutherland, D.*
Egerton – *Wilton, E.*
Eliot – *St Germans, E.*
Elliot-Murray-
  Kynynmound – *Minto, E.*
Elliott – *E. of Morpeth, B.**
Erroll – *E. of Hale, B.*
Erskine – *Buchan, E.*
Erskine – *Mar and Kellie, E.*
Erskine-Murray – *Elibank,*
  B.
Evans – *E. of Parkside, B.**
Evans – *E. of Watford, B.**

Evans – *Mountevans, B.*
Evans-Freke – *Carbery, B.*
Eve – *Silsoe, B.*
Ewing – *E. of Kirkford, B.**
Fairfax – *F. of Cameron, B.*
Falconer – *F. of Thoroton, B.**
Fane – *Westmorland, E.*
Farrington – *F. of Ribbleton,*
  *B.**
Feilding – *Denbigh, E.*
Fellowes – *De Ramsey, B.*
Fermor-Hesketh – *Hesketh,*
  B.
Fiennes – *Saye and Sele, B.*
Fiennes-Clinton – *Lincoln,*
  E.
Finch Hatton – *Winchilsea,*
  E.
Finch-Knightley – *Aylesford,*
  E.
Fisher – *F. of Rednal, B.**
Fitzalan-Howard – *Herries*
  of Terregles, B.
Fitzalan-Howard – *Norfolk,*
  D.
FitzClarence – *Munster, E.*
FitzGerald – *Leinster, D.*
Fitzherbert – *Stafford, B.*
FitzRoy – *Grafton, D.*
FitzRoy – *Southampton, B.*
FitzRoy Newdegate –
  Daventry, V.
Fletcher-Vane – *Inglewood,*
  B.
Flower – *Ashbrook, V.*
Foljambe – *Liverpool, E.*
Forbes – *Granard, E.*
Fox-Strangways – *Ilchester,*
  E.
Frankland – *Zouche, B.*
Fraser – *F. of Carmyllie, B.**
Fraser – *Lovat, B.*
Fraser – *Saltoun, B.*
Fraser – *Strathalmond, B.*
Freeman-Grenville –
  Kinloss, B.
Fremantle – *Cottesloe, B.*
French – *De Freyne, B.*
Galbraith – *Strathclyde, B.*
Ganzoni – *Belstead, B.*
Gardner – *G. of Parkes, B.**
Gathorne-Hardy –
  Cranbrook, E.
Gibbs – *Aldenham, B.*
Gibbs – *Wraxall, B.*
Gibson – *Ashbourne, B.*
Giffard – *Halsbury, E.*
Gilbey – *Vaux of Harrowden,*
  B.
Gillmore – *G. of Thamesfield,*
  *B.**
Gilmour – *G. of Craigmillar,*
  *B.**
Gladwin – *G. of Clee, B.**
Glyn – *Wolverton, B.*
Godley – *Kilbracken, B.*
Goff – *G. of Chieveley, W.**
Gordon – *Aberdeen and*
  Temair, M.
Gordon – *G. of Strathblane,*
  *B.**
Gordon – *Huntly, M.*

Gordon Lennox – *Richmond,*
  D.
Gore – *Arran, E.*
Gould – *G. of Potternewton,*
  *B.**
Graham – *G. of Edmonton, B.**
Graham – *Montrose, D.*
Graham-Toler – *Norbury, E.*
Grant of Grant – *Strathspey,*
  B.
Gray – *G. of Contin, B.**
Greaves – *Dysart, C.*
Greenall – *Daresbury, B.*
Greene – *G. of Harrow Weald,*
  *B.**
Greenhill – *G. of Harrow, B.**
Greville – *Warwick, E.*
Grey – *G. of Naunton, B.**
Griffiths – *G. of Fforestfach,*
  *B.**
Grigg – *Altrincham, B.*
Grimston – *G. of Westbury, B.*
Grimston – *Verulam, E.*
Grosvenor – *Ebury, B.*
Grosvenor – *Westminster, D.*
Guest – *Wimborne, V.*
Gueterbock – *Berkeley, B.*
Guinness – *Iveagh, E.*
Guinness – *Moyne, B.*
Gully – *Selby, V.*
Gummer – *Chadlington, B.**
Gurdon – *Cranworth, B.*
Gwynne Jones – *Chalfont, B.**
Hamilton – *Abercorn, D.*
Hamilton – *Belhaven and*
  Stenton, B.
Hamilton – *Dudley, B.*
Hamilton – *H. of Dalzell, B.*
Hamilton – *HolmPatrick, B.*
Hamilton-Russell – *Boyne,*
  V.
Hamilton-Smith – *Colwyn,*
  B.
Hanbury-Tracy – *Sudeley, B.*
Handcock – *Castlemaine, B.*
Harbord-Hamond –
  Suffield, B.
Harding – *H. of Petherton, B.*
Hardinge – *H. of Penshurst, B.*
Hardy – *H. of Wath, B.*
Hare – *Blakenham, V.*
Hare – *Listowel, E.*
Harmsworth – *Rothermere, V.*
Harris – *H. of Greenwich, B.**
Harris – *H. of Haringey, B.**
Harris – *H. of High Cross, B.**
Harris – *H. of Peckham, B.**
Harris – *Malmesbury, E.*
Harvey – *H. of Tasburgh, B.*
Hastings Bass – *Huntingdon,*
  E.
Hay – *Erroll, E.*
Hay – *Kinnoull, E.*
Hay – *Tweeddale, M.*
Heathcote-Drummond-
  Willoughby – *Willoughby*
  de Eresby, B.
Hely-Hutchinson –
  Donoughmore, E.
Henderson – *Faringdon, B.*
Henderson – *H. of Brompton,*
  *B.**

Hennessy – *Windlesham, B.*
Henniker-Major – *Henniker,*
  B.
Hepburne-Scott – *Polwarth,*
  B.
Herbert – *Carnarvon, E.*
Herbert – *Hemingford, B.*
Herbert – *Pembroke, E.*
Herbert – *Powis, E.*
Hermon-Hodge – *Wyfold, B.*
Hervey – *Bristol, M.*
Hewitt – *Lifford, V.*
Hicks Beach – *St Aldwyn, E.*
Hill – *Downshire, M.*
Hill – *Sandys, B.*
Hill-Trevor – *Trevor, B.*
Hilton – *H. of Eggardon, B.**
Hobart-Hampden –
  Buckinghamshire, E.
Hogg – *H. of Cumbernauld, B.**
Hogg – *Hailsham of St*
  *Marylebone, B.**
Holland-Hibbert –
  Knutsford, V.
Hollis – *H. of Heigham, B.**
Holme – *H. of Cheltenham, B.**
Holmes à Court –
  Heytesbury, B.
Hood – *Bridport, V.*
Hope – *Glendevon, B.*
Hope – *H. of Craighead, B.**
Hope – *Linlithgow, M.*
Hope – *Rankeillour, B.*
Hope Johnstone – *Annandale*
  and Hartfell, E.
Hope-Morley – *Hollenden, B.*
Hopkinson – *Colyton, B.*
Hore-Ruthven – *Gowrie, E.*
Hovell-Thurlow-
  Cumming-Bruce –
  Thurlow, B.
Howard – *Carlisle, E.*
Howard – *Effingham, E.*
Howard – *H. of Penrith, B.*
Howard – *Strathcona and*
  Mount Royal, B.
Howard – *Suffolk and*
  Berkshire, E.
Howe – *H. of Aberavon, B.**
Howell – *H. of Guildford, B.**
Howells – *Geraint, B.**
Howie – *H. of Troon, B.**
Hubbard – *Addington, B.*
Huggins – *Malvern, V.*
Hughes – *Cledwyn of Penrhos,*
  *B.**
Hughes – *H. of Woodside, B.**
Hughes – *Islwyn, B.**
Hughes-Young – *St Helens,*
  B.
Hunt – *H. of Kings Heath, B.**
Hunt – *H. of Tanworth, B.**
Hunt – *H. of Wirral, B.**
Hurd – *H. of Westwell, B.**
Hussey – *H. of North Bradley,*
  *B.**
Hutchinson – *H. of*
  *Lullington, B.**
Ingrams – *Darcy de Knayth, B.*
Innes-Ker – *Roxburghe, D.*
Inskip – *Caldecote, V.*
Irby – *Boston, B.*

Philipps – *St Davids, V.*
Phillips – *P. of Ellesmere, B.*
Phillips – *P. of Sudbury, B.*
Phipps – *Normanby, M.*
Pilkington – *P. of Oxenford, B.*
Plant – *P. of Highfield, B.*
Platt – *P. of Writtle, B.*
Pleydell-Bouverie – *Radnor, E.*
Plummer – *P. of St Marylebone, B.*
Plumptre – *Fitzwalter, B.*
Plunkett – *Dunsany, B.*
Plunkett – *Louth, B.*
Pollock – *Hanworth, V.*
Pomeroy – *Harberton, V.*
Ponsonby – *Bessborough, E.*
Ponsonby – *de Mauley, B.*
Ponsonby – *P. of Shulbrede, B.*
Ponsonby – *Sysonby, B.*
Porter – *P. of Luddenham, B.*
Powys – *Lilford, B.*
Pratt – *Camden, M.*
Preston – *Gormanston, V.*
Primrose – *Rosebery, E.*
Prittie – *Dunalley, B.*
Prout – *Kingsland, B.*
Ramsay – *Dalhousie, E.*
Ramsay – *R. of Cartvale, B.*
Ramsbotham – *Soulbury, V.*
Randall – *R. of St Budeaux, B.*
Rawlinson – *R. of Ewell, B.*
Rees-Williams – *Ogmore, B.*
Rendell – *R. of Babergh, B.*
Renfrew – *R. of Kaimsthorn, B.*
Renton – *R. of Mount Harry, B.*
Renwick – *R. of Clifton, B.*
Rhys – *Dynevor, B.*
Richards – *Milverton, B.*
Richardson – *R. of Calow, B.*
Richardson – *R. of Duntisbourne, B.*
Ritchie – *R. of Dundee, B.*
Robens – *R. of Woldingham, B.*
Roberts – *Clwyd, B.*
Roberts – *R. of Conwy, B.*
Robertson – *R. of Oakridge, B.*
Robertson – *Wharton, B.*
Robinson – *Martonmere, B.*
Robson – *R. of Kiddington, B.*
Roche – *Fermoy, B.*
Rodd – *Rennell, B.*
Rodger – *R. of Earlsferry, B.*
Rodgers – *R. of Quarry Bank, B.*
Rogers – *R. of Riverside, B.*
Roll – *R. of Ipsden, B.*
Roper-Curzon – *Teynham, B.*
Rospigliosi – *Newburgh, E.*
Rous – *Stradbroke, E.*
Rowley-Conwy – *Langford, B.*
Royle – *Fanshawe of Richmond, B.*
Runciman (Garry) – *Runciman of Doxford, V.*
Russell – *Ampthill, B.*
Russell – *Bedford, D.*

Russell – *de Clifford, B.*
Russell – *R. of Liverpool, B.*
Ryder – *Harrowby, E.*
Ryder – *R. of Eaton Hastings, B.*
Ryder – *R. of Warsaw, B.*
Ryder – *R. of Wensum, B.*
Sackville – *De La Warr, E.*
Sackville-West – *Sackville, B.*
Sainsbury – *S. of Preston Candover, B.*
Sainsbury – *S. of Turville, B.*
St Aubyn – *St Levan, B.*
St Clair – *Sinclair, B.*
St Clair-Erskine – *Rosslyn, E.*
St John – *Bolingbroke, V.*
St John – *Orkney, E.*
St John – *St. J. of Bletso, B.*
St John-Stevas – *St J. of Fawsley, B.*
St Leger – *Doneraile, V.*
Samuel – *Bearsted, V.*
Sanderson – *S. of Ayot, B.*
Sanderson – *S. of Bowden, B.*
Sandilands – *Torphichen, B.*
Saumarez – *de Saumarez, B.*
Savile – *Mexborough, E.*
Saville – *S. of Newdigate, W.*
Scarlett – *Abinger, B.*
Schreiber – *Marlesford, B.*
Sclater-Booth – *Basing, B.*
Scotland – *S. of Asthal, B.*
Scott – *Eldon, E.*
Scott-Ellis – *Howard de Walden, B.*
Scrymgeour – *Dundee, E.*
Seager – *Leighton of St Mellons, B.*
Seely – *Mottistone, B.*
Sefton – *S. of Garston, B.*
Seymour – *Hertford, M.*
Seymour – *Somerset, D.*
Sharp – *S. of Guildford, B.*
Shaw – *Craigmyle, B.*
Shaw – *S. of Northstead, B.*
Sheppard – *S. of Didgemere, B.*
Sheppard – *S. of Liverpool, B.*
Shirley – *Ferrers, E.*
Shore – *S. of Stepney, B.*
Short – *Glenamara, B.*
Siddeley – *Kenilworth, B.*
Sidney – *De L'Isle, V.*
Sieff – *S. of Brimpton, B.*
Simon – *S. of Glaisdale, B.*
Simon – *S. of Highbury, B.*
Simon – *S. of Wythenshawe, B.*
Simpson – *S. of Dunkeld, B.*
Sinclair – *Caithness, E.*
Sinclair – *S. of Cleeve, B.*
Sinclair – *Thurso, V.*
Skeffington – *Massereene, V.*
Slynn – *S. of Hadley, B.*
Smith – *Bicester, B.*
Smith – *Hambleden, V.*
Smith – *Kirkhill, B.*
Smith – *S. of Clifton, B.*
Smith – *S. of Gilmorehill, B.*
Somerset – *Beaufort, D.*
Somerset – *Raglan, B.*
Soulsby – *S. of Swaffham Prior, B.*
Spencer – *Churchill, V.*

Spencer-Churchill – *Marlborough, D.*
Spring Rice – *Monteagle of Brandon, B.*
Stanhope – *Harrington, E.*
Stanley – *Derby, E.*
Stanley – *S. of Alderley and Sheffield, B.*
Stapleton-Cotton – *Combermere, V.*
Steel – *S. of Aikwood, B.*
Sterling – *S. of Plaistow, B.*
Stevens – *S. of Ludgate, B.*
Stewart – *Galloway, E.*
Stewart – *Stewartby, B.*
Stodart – *S. of Leaston, B.*
Stoddart – *S. of Swindon, B.*
Stone – *S. of Blackheath, B.*
Stonor – *Camoys, B.*
Stopford – *Courtown, E.*
Stourton – *Mowbray, B.*
Strachey – *O'Hagan, B.*
Strutt – *Belper, B.*
Strutt – *Rayleigh, B.*
Stuart – *Castle Stewart, E.*
Stuart – *Mackenzie-Stuart, B.*
Stuart – *Moray, E.*
Stuart – *S. of Findhorn, V.*
Suenson-Taylor – *Grantchester, B.*
Symons – *S. of Vernham Dean, B.*
Taylor – *Ingrow, B.*
Taylor – *T. of Blackburn, B.*
Taylor – *T. of Gryfe, B.*
Taylor – *T. of Warwick, B.*
Taylour – *Headfort, M.*
Temple-Gore-Langton – *Temple of Stowe, E.*
Tennant – *Glenconner, B.*
Thellusson – *Rendlesham, B.*
Thesiger – *Chelmsford, V.*
Thomas – *T. of Gresford, B.*
Thomas – *T. of Gwydir, B.*
Thomas – *T. of Macclesfield, B.*
Thomas – *T. of Swynnerton, B.*
Thomas – *T. of Walliswood, B.*
Thomson – *T. of Fleet, B.*
Thomson – *T. of Monifieth, B.*
Thynn – *Bath, M.*
Tottenham – *Ely, M.*
Trefusis – *Clinton, B.*
Trench – *Ashtown, B.*
Trevor-Roper – *Dacre of Glanton, B.*
Tufton – *Hothfield, B.*
Turner – *Netherthorpe, B.*
Turner – *T. of Camden, B.*
Turnour – *Winterton, E.*
Tyrell-Kenyon – *Kenyon, B.*
Vanden-Bempde-Johnstone – *Derwent, B.*
Vane – *Barnard, B.*
Vane-Tempest-Stewart – *Londonderry, M.*
Vanneck – *Huntingfield, B.*
Vaughan – *Lisburne, E.*
Vereker – *Gort, V.*

Verney – *Willoughby de Broke, B.*
Vernon – *Lyveden, B.*
Vesey – *De Vesci, V.*
Villiers – *Clarendon, E.*
Vincent – *V. of Coleshill, B.*
Vivian – *Swansea, B.*
Wade – *W. of Chorlton, B.*
Walker – *W. of Doncaster, B.*
Walker – *W. of Worcester, B.*
Wallace – *W. of Coslany, B.*
Wallace – *W. of Saltaire, B.*
Wallop – *Portsmouth, E.*
Walton – *W. of Detchant, B.*
Ward – *Bangor, V.*
Ward – *Dudley, E.*
Warrender – *Bruntisfield, B.*
Watson – *Manton, B.*
Watson – *W. of Invergowrie, B.*
Webber – *Lloyd-Webber, B.*
Wedderburn – *W. of Charlton, B.*
Weir – *Inverforth, B.*
Weld-Forester – *Forester, B.*
Wellesley – *Cowley, E.*
Wellesley – *Wellington, D.*
Westenra – *Rossmore, B.*
White – *Annaly, B.*
White – *Hanningfield, B.*
White – *James of Holland Park, B.*
Whiteley – *Marchamley, B.*
Whitfield – *Kenswood, B.*
Williams – *W. of Crosby, B.*
Williams – *W. of Elvel, B.*
Williams – *W. of Mostyn, B.*
Williamson – *Forres, B.*
Willoughby – *Middleton, B.*
Wills – *Dulverton, B.*
Wilson – *Moran, B.*
Wilson – *Nunburnholme, B.*
Wilson – *W. of Tillyorn, B.*
Windsor – *Gloucester, D.*
Windsor – *Kent, D.*
Windsor-Clive – *Plymouth, E.*
Wingfield – *Powerscourt, V.*
Winn – *St Oswald, B.*
Wodehouse – *Kimberley, E.*
Wolfson – *W. of Sunningdale, B.*
Wood – *Halifax, E.*
Wood – *Holderness, B.*
Woodhouse – *Terrington, B.*
Wright – *W. of Richmond, B.*
Wyndham – *Egremont and Leconfield, B.*
Wyndham-Quin – *Dunraven and Mount-Earl, E.*
Wynn – *Newborough, B.*
Yarde-Buller – *Churston, B.*
Yerburgh – *Alvingham, B.*
Yorke – *Hardwicke, E.*
Young – *Kennet, B.*
Young – *Y. of Dartington, B.*
Young – *Y. of Graffham, B.*
Young – *Y. of Old Scone, B.*
Younger – *Y. of Leckie, V.*

Orders of Chivalry

THE MOST NOBLE ORDER
OF THE GARTER (1348)

KG

Ribbon, Blue
Motto, Honi soit qui mal y pense
(*Shame on him who thinks evil of it*)
The number of Knights Companions
is limited to 24

SOVEREIGN OF THE ORDER
The Queen

LADIES OF THE ORDER
HM Queen Elizabeth the Queen
Mother, 1936
HRH The Princess Royal, 1994

ROYAL KNIGHTS
HRH The Prince Philip, Duke of
Edinburgh, 1947
HRH The Prince of Wales, 1958
HRH The Duke of Kent, 1985
HRH The Duke of Gloucester, 1997

EXTRA KNIGHTS COMPANIONS AND
LADIES
HRH Princess Juliana of the
Netherlands, 1958
HRH The Grand Duke of
Luxembourg, 1972
HM The Queen of Denmark, 1979
HM The King of Sweden, 1983
HM The King of Spain, 1988
HM The Queen of the Netherlands,
1989
HIM The Emperor of Japan, 1998

KNIGHTS AND LADY COMPANIONS
The Earl of Longford, 1971
The Marquess of Abergavenny, 1974
The Duke of Grafton, 1976
The Lord Hunt, 1979
The Duke of Norfolk, 1983
The Lord Lewin, 1983
The Lord Richardson of
Duntisbourne, 1983
The Lord Carrington, 1985
The Lord Callaghan of Cardiff, 1987
The Viscount Leverhulme, 1988
The Lord Hailsham of St
Marylebone, 1988
The Duke of Wellington, 1990
Field Marshal the Lord Bramall, 1990
Sir Edward Heath, 1992
The Viscount Ridley, 1992
The Lord Sainsbury of Preston
Candover, 1992
The Lord Ashburton, 1994

The Lord Kingsdown, 1994
Sir Ninian Stephen, 1994
The Baroness Thatcher, 1995
Sir Edmund Hillary, 1995
The Duke of Devonshire, 1996
Sir Timothy Colman, 1996

Prelate, The Bishop of Winchester
Chancellor, The Lord Carrington, KG,
GCMG, CH, MC
Register, The Dean of Windsor
Garter King of Arms, P. Gwynn-Jones,
CVO
Gentleman Usher of the Black Rod, Gen.
Sir Edward Jones, KCB, CBE
Secretary, D. H. B. Chesshyre, LVO

THE MOST ANCIENT AND
MOST NOBLE ORDER OF
THE THISTLE (REVIVED 1687)

KT

Ribbon, Green
Motto, Nemo me impune lacessit (*No
one provokes me with impunity*)
The number of Knights is limited to 16

SOVEREIGN OF THE ORDER
The Queen

LADY OF THE THISTLE
HM Queen Elizabeth the Queen
Mother, 1937

ROYAL KNIGHTS
HRH The Prince Philip, Duke of
Edinburgh, 1952
HRH The Prince of Wales, Duke of
Rothesay, 1977

KNIGHTS
The Earl of Wemyss and March, 1966
The Earl of Dalhousie, 1971
Sir Donald Cameron of Lochiel, 1973
The Duke of Buccleuch and
Queensberry, 1978
The Earl of Elgin and Kincardine,
1981
The Lord Thomson of Monifieth,
1981
The Lord MacLehose of Beoch, 1983
The Earl of Airlie, 1985
Capt. Sir Iain Tennant, 1986
The Viscount Whitelaw, 1990
The Viscount Younger of Leckie,
1995
The Viscount of Arbuthnott, 1996
The Earl of Crawford and Balcarres,
1996
Lady Fraser, 1996

The Lord Macfarlane of Bearsden,
1996
The Lord Mackay of Clashfern, 1997
Chancellor, The Duke of Buccleuch
and Queensberry, KT, VRD
Dean, The Very Revd G. I. Macmillan
Secretary and Lord Lyon King of Arms, Sir
Malcolm Innes of Edingight, KCVO,
WS
Usher of the Green Rod, Rear-Adm. C. H.
Layman, CB, DSO, LVO

THE MOST HONOURABLE
ORDER OF THE BATH
(1725)

GCB *Military*   GCB *Civil*

GCB Knight (or Dame) Grand
Cross
KCB Knight Commander
DCB Dame Commander
CB Companion
Ribbon, Crimson
Motto, Tria juncta in uno (*Three joined
in one*)
Remodelled 1815, and enlarged many
times since. The Order is divided into
civil and military divisions. Women
became eligible for the Order from 1
January 1971

THE SOVEREIGN

GREAT MASTER AND FIRST OR
PRINCIPAL KNIGHT GRAND
CROSS
HRH The Prince of Wales, KG, KT,
GCB
Dean of the Order, The Dean of
Westminster
Bath King of Arms, Air Chief Marshal
Sir David Evans, GCB, CBE
Registrar and Secretary, Rear-Adm.
D. E. Macey, CB
Genealogist, P. Gwynn-Jones, CVO
Gentleman Usher of the Scarlet Rod, Air
Vice-Marshal Sir Richard Peirse,
KCVO, CB
Deputy Secretary, The Secretary of the
Central Chancery of the Orders of
Knighthood
Chancery, Central Chancery of the
Orders of Knighthood, St James's
Palace, London SW1A 1BH

THE ORDER OF MERIT
(1902)

OM *Military* OM *Civil*

OM

Ribbon, Blue and crimson

This Order is designed as a special distinction for eminent men and women without conferring a knighthood upon them. The Order is limited in numbers to 24, with the addition of foreign honorary members. Membership is of two kinds, military and civil, the badge of the former having crossed swords, and the latter oak leaves

THE SOVEREIGN

HRH The Prince Philip, Duke of Edinburgh, 1968
Sir George Edwards, 1971
Sir Alan Hodgkin, 1973
Revd Prof. Owen Chadwick, KBE, 1983
Sir Andrew Huxley, 1983
Frederick Sanger, 1986
The Lord Menuhin, 1987
Prof. Sir Ernst Gombrich, 1988
Dr Max Perutz, 1988
Dame Cicely Saunders, 1989
The Lord Porter of Luddenham, 1989
The Baroness Thatcher, 1990
Dame Joan Sutherland, 1991
Prof. Francis Crick, 1991
Dame Ninette de Valois, 1992
Sir Michael Atiyah, 1992
Lucian Freud, 1993
The Lord Jenkins of Hillhead, 1993
Sir Aaron Klug, 1995
Sir John Gielgud, 1996
The Lord Denning, 1997
Sir Norman Foster, 1997
Sir Denis Rooke, 1997
Ted Hughes, 1998
Honorary Member, Nelson Mandela, 1995

Secretary and Registrar, Sir Edward Ford, GCVO, KCB, ERD
Chancery, Central Chancery of the Orders of Knighthood, St James's Palace, London SW1A 1BH

THE MOST EXALTED ORDER OF THE STAR OF INDIA (1861)

GCSI Knight Grand Commander
KCSI Knight Commander
CSI Companion

Ribbon, Light blue, with white edges
Motto, Heaven's Light our Guide

THE SOVEREIGN

Registrar, The Secretary of the Central Chancery of the Orders of Knighthood
No conferments have been made since 1947

THE MOST DISTINGUISHED ORDER OF ST MICHAEL AND ST GEORGE (1818)

GCMG KCMG

GCMG Knight (or Dame) Grand Cross
KCMG Knight Commander
DCMG Dame Commander
CMG Companion

Ribbon, Saxon blue, with scarlet centre
Motto, Auspicium melioris aevi
(*Token of a better age*)

THE SOVEREIGN

GRAND MASTER
HRH The Duke of Kent, KG, GCMG, GCVO, ADC

Prelate, The Rt. Revd Simon Barrington-Ward
Chancellor, Sir Antony Acland, GCMG, GCVO
Secretary, The Permanent Under-Secretary of State at the Foreign and Commonwealth Office and Head of the Diplomatic Service
Registrar, Sir John Graham, Bt., GCMG
King of Arms, Sir Ewen Fergusson, GCMG, GCVO
Gentleman Usher of the Blue Rod, Sir John Margetson, KCMG
Dean, The Dean of St Paul's
Deputy Secretary, The Secretary of the Central Chancery of the Orders of Knighthood
Chancery, Central Chancery of the Orders of Knighthood, St James's Palace, London SW1A 1BH

THE MOST EMINENT ORDER OF THE INDIAN EMPIRE (1868)

GCIE Knight Grand Commander
KCIE Knight Commander
CIE Companion

Ribbon, Imperial purple
Motto, Imperatricis auspiciis (*Under the auspices of the Empress*)

THE SOVEREIGN

Registrar, The Secretary of the Central Chancery of the Orders of Knighthood
No conferments have been made since 1947

THE IMPERIAL ORDER OF THE CROWN OF INDIA (1877) FOR LADIES

CI

Badge, the royal cipher in jewels within an oval, surmounted by an heraldic crown and attached to a bow of light blue watered ribbon, edged white
The honour does not confer any rank or title upon the recipient
No conferments have been made since 1947

HM The Queen, 1947
HM Queen Elizabeth the Queen Mother, 1931
HRH The Princess Margaret, Countess of Snowdon, 1947
HRH Princess Alice, Duchess of Gloucester, 1937

THE ROYAL VICTORIAN ORDER (1896)

GCVO KCVO

GCVO Knight or Dame Grand Cross
KCVO Knight Commander
DCVO Dame Commander
CVO Commander
LVO Lieutenant
MVO Member

Ribbon, Blue, with red and white edges
Motto, Victoria

THE SOVEREIGN
GRAND MASTER
HM Queen Elizabeth the Queen Mother

Chancellor, The Lord Chamberlain
Secretary, The Keeper of the Privy Purse
Registrar, The Secretary of the Central Chancery of the Orders of Knighthood
Chaplain, The Chaplain of the Queen's Chapel of the Savoy
Hon. Genealogist, D. H. B. Chesshyre, LVO

THE MOST EXCELLENT ORDER OF THE BRITISH EMPIRE (1917)

GBE   KBE

The Order was divided into military and civil divisions in December 1918

GBE Knight or Dame Grand Cross
KBE Knight Commander
DBE Dame Commander
CBE Commander
OBE Officer
MBE Member

Ribbon, Rose pink edged with pearl grey with vertical pearl stripe in centre (military division); without vertical pearl stripe (civil division)
Motto, For God and the Empire

THE SOVEREIGN

GRAND MASTER
HRH The Prince Philip, Duke of Edinburgh, KG, KT, OM, GBE, PC

Prelate, The Bishop of London
King of Arms, Air Chief Marshal Sir Patrick Hine, GCB, GBE
Registrar, The Secretary of the Central Chancery of the Orders of Knighthood
Secretary, The Secretary of the Cabinet and Head of the Home Civil Service
Dean, The Dean of St Paul's
Gentleman Usher of the Purple Rod, Sir Robin Gillett, Bt., GBE, RD
Chancery, Central Chancery of the Orders of Knighthood, St James's Palace, London SW1A 1BH

ORDER OF THE COMPANIONS OF HONOUR (1917)

CH

Ribbon, Carmine, with gold edges
This Order consists of one class only and carries with it no title. The number of awards is limited to 65 (excluding honorary members)

Anthony, Rt. Hon. John, 1981
Ashley of Stoke, The Lord, 1975
Astor, Hon. David, 1993
Attenborough, Sir David, 1995
Baker, Dame Janet, 1993

Baker of Dorking, The Lord, 1992
Brenner, Sydney, 1986
Brook, Peter, 1998
Brooke, Rt. Hon. Peter, 1992
Carrington, The Lord, 1983
Casson, Sir Hugh, 1984
Cledwyn of Penrhos, The Lord, 1976
de Valois, Dame Ninette, 1981
Doll, Prof. Sir Richard, 1995
Eccles, The Viscount, 1984
Fraser, Rt. Hon. Malcolm, 1977
Freud, Lucian, 1983
Gielgud, Sir John, 1977
Glenamara, The Lord, 1976
Gorton, Rt. Hon. Sir John, 1971
Guinness, Sir Alec, 1994
Hailsham of St Marylebone, The Lord, 1974
Hawking, Prof. Stephen, 1989
Healey, The Lord, 1979
Heseltine, Rt. Hon. Michael, 1997
Hobsbawm, Prof. Eric, 1998
Hockney, David, 1997
Howe of Aberavon, The Lord, 1996
Hurd of Westwell, The Lord, 1995
Jones, James, 1977
King, Rt. Hon. Tom, 1992
Lange, Rt. Hon. David, 1989
Lasdun, Sir Denys, 1995
Milstein, César, 1994
Owen, The Lord, 1994
Patten, Rt. Hon. Christopher, 1998
Perutz, Dr Max, 1975
Powell, Anthony, 1987
Powell, Sir Philip, 1984
Runciman, Hon. Sir Steven, 1984
Rylands, George, 1987
Sanger, Frederick, 1981
Sisson, Charles, 1993
Smith, Sir John, 1993
Somare, Rt. Hon. Sir Michael, 1978
Talboys, Rt. Hon. Sir Brian, 1981
Tebbit, The Lord, 1987
Trudeau, Rt. Hon. Pierre, 1984
Whitelaw, The Viscount, 1974
Widdowson, Dr Elsie, 1993
Honorary Members, Lee Kuan Yew, 1970; Dr Joseph Luns, 1971

Secretary and Registrar, The Secretary of the Central Chancery of the Orders of Knighthood

THE DISTINGUISHED SERVICE ORDER (1886)

DSO

Ribbon, Red, with blue edges
Bestowed in recognition of especial services in action of commissioned officers in the Navy, Army and Royal Air Force and (since 1942) Mercantile Marine. The members are

Companions only. A Bar may be awarded for any additional act of service

THE IMPERIAL SERVICE ORDER (1902)

ISO

Ribbon, Crimson, with blue centre

Appointment as Companion of this Order is open to members of the Civil Services whose eligibility is determined by the grade they hold. The Order consists of The Sovereign and Companions to a number not exceeding 1,900, of whom 1,300 may belong to the Home Civil Services and 600 to Overseas Civil Services. The Prime Minister announced in March 1993 that he would make no further recommendations for appointments to the Order.

Secretary, The Secretary of the Cabinet and Head of the Home Civil Service
Registrar, The Secretary of the Central Chancery of the Orders of Knighthood, St James's Palace, London SW1A 1BH

THE ROYAL VICTORIAN CHAIN (1902)

It confers no precedence on its holders

HM THE QUEEN
HM Queen Elizabeth the Queen Mother, 1937

HRH Princess Juliana of the Netherlands, 1950
HM The King of Thailand, 1960
HM The King of Jordan, 1966
HM King Zahir Shah of Afghanistan, 1971
HM The Queen of Denmark, 1974
HM The King of Nepal, 1975
HM The King of Sweden, 1975
The Lord Coggan, 1980
HM The Queen of the Netherlands, 1982
Gen. Antonio Eanes, 1985
HM The King of Spain, 1986
HM The King of Saudi Arabia, 1987
HRH The Princess Margaret, Countess of Snowdon, 1990
The Lord Runcie, 1991
The Lord Charteris of Amisfield, 1992
HE Richard von Weizsäcker, 1992
HM The King of Norway, 1994
The Earl of Airlie, 1997

Baronetage and Knightage

BARONETS

Style, 'Sir' before forename and surname, followed by 'Bt.'
Wife's style, 'Lady' followed by surname
For forms of address, *see* page 135

There are five different creations of baronetcies: Baronets of England (creations dating from 1611); Baronets of Ireland (creations dating from 1619); Baronets of Scotland or Nova Scotia (creations dating from 1625); Baronets of Great Britain (creations after the Act of Union 1707 which combined the kingdoms of England and Scotland); and Baronets of the United Kingdom (creations after the union of Great Britain and Ireland in 1801).

Badge of Baronets of the United Kingdom

Badge of Baronets of Nova Scotia

Badge of Ulster

The patent of creation limits the destination of a baronetcy, usually to male descendants of the first baronet, although special remainders allow the baronetcy to pass, if the male issue of sons fail, to the male issue of daughters of the first baronet. In the case of baronetcies of Scotland or Nova Scotia, a special remainder of 'heirs male and of tailzie' allows the baronetcy to descend to heirs general, including women. There are four existing Scottish baronets with such a remainder.

The Official Roll of Baronets is kept at the Home Office by the Registrar of the Baronetage. Anyone who considers that he is entitled to be entered on the Roll may petition the Crown through the Home Secretary. Every person succeeding to a baronetcy must exhibit proofs of succession to the Home Secretary. A person whose name is not entered on the Official Roll will not be addressed or mentioned by the title of baronet in any official document, nor will he be accorded precedence as a baronet.

BARONETCIES EXTINCT SINCE THE LAST EDITION
Bethune (*cr.* 1683); Holland (*cr.* 1917); Platt (*cr.* 1958); Roll (*cr.* 1921)

Registrar of the Baronetage, Miss C. E. C. Sinclair
Assistant Registrar, Mrs F. G. Bright
Office, Home Office, 50 Queen Anne's Gate, London SW1H 9AT. Tel: 0171-273 3498

KNIGHTS

Style, 'Sir' before forename and surname, followed by appropriate post-nominal initials if a Knight Grand Cross, Knight Grand Commander or Knight Commander
Wife's style, 'Lady' followed by surname

For forms of address, *see* page 135
The prefix 'Sir' is not used by knights who are clerics of the Church of England, who do not receive the accolade. Their wives are entitled to precedence as the wife of a knight but not to the style of 'Lady'.

ORDERS OF KNIGHTHOOD

Knight Grand Cross, Knight Grand Commander, and Knight Commander are the higher classes of the Orders of Chivalry (*see* pages 170–2). Honorary knighthoods of these Orders may be conferred on men who are citizens of countries of which The Queen is not head of state. As a rule, the prefix 'Sir' is not used by honorary knights.

KNIGHTS BACHELOR

The Knights Bachelor do not constitute a Royal Order, but comprise the surviving representation of the ancient State Orders of Knighthood. The Register of Knights Bachelor, instituted by James I in the 17th century, lapsed, and in 1908 a voluntary association under the title of The Society of Knights (now The Imperial Society of Knights Bachelor by Royal Command) was formed with the primary objects of continuing the various registers dating from 1257 and obtaining the uniform registration of every created Knight Bachelor. In 1926 a design for a badge to be worn by Knights Bachelor was approved and adopted; in 1974 a neck badge and miniature were added.

Knight Principal, Sir Conrad Swan, KCVO
Chairman of Council, The Lord Lane of Horsell
Prelate, Rt. Revd and Rt. Hon. The Bishop of London
Hon. Registrar, Sir Robert Balchin
Hon. Treasurer, Sir Douglas Morpeth, TD
Clerk to the Council, R. M. Esden
Office, 21 Old Buildings, Lincoln's Inn, London WC2A 3UJ

LIST OF BARONETS AND KNIGHTS
Revised to 31 August 1998

Peers are not included in this list

† Not registered on the Official Roll of the Baronetage at the time of going to press
() The date of creation of the baronetcy is given in parenthesis
I Baronet of Ireland
NS Baronet of Nova Scotia
S Baronet of Scotland

If a baronet or knight has a double barrelled or hyphenated surname, he is listed under the final element of the name
A full entry in italic type indicates that the recipient of a knighthood died during the year in which the honour was conferred. The name is included for purposes of record

Abal, Sir Tei, Kt., CBE
Abbott, Sir Albert Francis, Kt., CBE
Abbott, *Adm.* Sir Peter Charles, KCB
Abdy, Sir Valentine Robert Duff, Bt.
 (1850)
Abel, Sir Seselo (Cecil) Charles
 Geoffrey, Kt., OBE
Abeles, Sir (Emil Herbert) Peter, Kt.
Abercromby, Sir Ian George, Bt.
 (s. 1636)
Abraham, Sir Edward Penley, Kt.,
 CBE, FRS
Acheson, *Prof.* Sir (Ernest) Donald,
 KBE
Ackers, Sir James George, Kt.
Ackroyd, Sir Timothy Robert
 Whyte, Bt. (1956)
Acland, Sir Antony Arthur, GCMG,
 GCVO
Acland, *Lt.-Col.* Sir (Christopher)
 Guy (Dyke), Bt., MVO (1890)
Acland, Sir John Dyke, Bt. (1644)
Acland, *Maj.-Gen.* Sir John Hugh
 Bevil, KCB, CBE
Adam, Sir Christopher Eric Forbes,
 Bt. (1917)
Adams, Sir Philip George Doyne,
 KCMG
Adams, Sir William James, KCMG
Adamson, Sir (William Owen)
 Campbell, Kt.
Adrien, *Hon.* Sir Maurice Latour-, Kt.
Adye, Sir John Anthony, KCMG
Agnew, Sir Crispin Hamlyn, Bt.
 (s. 1629)
Agnew, Sir John Keith, Bt. (1895)
Aiken, *Air Chief Marshal* Sir John
 Alexander Carlisle, KCB
Ainsworth, Sir (Thomas) David, Bt.
 (1916)
Aird, *Capt.* Sir Alastair Sturgis, GCVO
Aird, Sir (George) John, Bt. (1901)
Airey, Sir Lawrence, KCB
Airy, *Maj.-Gen.* Sir Christopher John,
 KCVO, CBE
Aitchison, Sir Charles Walter de
 Lancey, Bt. (1938)
Akehurst, *Gen.* Sir John Bryan, KCB,
 CBE
Albu, Sir George, Bt. (1912)
Alcock, *Air Chief Marshal* Sir (Robert
 James) Michael, GCB, KBE
Aldous, *Rt. Hon.* Sir William, Kt.
Alexander, Sir Charles Gundry, Bt.
 (1945)
Alexander, Sir Claud Hagart-, Bt.
 (1886)
Alexander, Sir Douglas, Bt. (1921)
Alexander, Sir (John) Lindsay, Kt.
Alexander, *Prof.* Sir Kenneth John
 Wilson, Kt.
Alexander, Sir Michael O'Donal
 Bjarne, GCMG
†Alexander, Sir Patrick Desmond
 William Cable-, Bt. (1809)
Allan, Sir Anthony James Allan
 Havelock-, Bt. (1858)
Allen, *Prof.* Sir Geoffrey, Kt., PH.D.,
 FRS
Allen, Sir John Derek, Kt., CBE

Allen, *Hon.* Sir Peter Austin Philip
 Jermyn, Kt.
Allen, Sir William Guilford, Kt.
Allen, Sir (William) Kenneth
 (Gwynne), Kt.
Alleyne, Sir George Allanmoore
 Ogarren, Kt.
Alleyne, *Revd* Sir John Olpherts
 Campbell, Bt. (1769)
Alliance, Sir David, Kt., CBE
Allinson, Sir (Walter) Leonard, KCVO,
 CMG
Alliott, *Hon.* Sir John Downes, Kt.
Allison, *Air Chief Marshal* Sir John
 Shakespeare, KCB, CBE
Alment, Sir (Edward) Anthony John,
 Kt.
Althaus, Sir Nigel Frederick, Kt.
Ambo, *Revd* George, KBE
Amet, *Hon.* Sir Arnold Karibone, Kt.
Amies, Sir (Edwin) Hardy, KCVO
Amory, Sir Ian Heathcoat, Bt. (1874)
Anderson, Sir John Anthony, KBE
Anderson, *Maj.-Gen.* Sir John
 Evelyn, KBE
Anderson, Sir John Muir, Kt., CMG
Anderson, *Hon.* Sir Kevin Victor, Kt.
Anderson, Sir Leith Reinsford
 Steven, Kt., CBE
Anderson, *Vice-Adm.* Sir Neil
 Dudley, KBE, CB
Anderson, *Prof.* Sir (William)
 Ferguson, Kt., OBE
Anderton, Sir (Cyril) James, Kt., CBE,
 QPM
Andrew, Sir Robert John, KCB
Andrews, Sir Derek Henry, KCB, CBE
Andrews, *Hon.* Sir Dormer George,
 Kt.
Angus, Sir Michael Richardson, Kt.
Annesley, Sir Hugh Norman, Kt.,
 QPM
Anson, *Vice-Adm.* Sir Edward
 Rosebery, KCB
Anson, Sir John, KCB
Anson, *Rear-Adm.* Sir Peter, Bt., CB
 (1831)
Anstey, *Brig.* Sir John, Kt., CBE, TD
Anstruther, *Maj.* Sir Ralph Hugo, Bt.,
 GCVO, MC (s. 1694)
Antico, Sir Tristan Venus, Kt.
Antrobus, Sir Charles James, GCMG,
 OBE
Antrobus, Sir Edward Philip, Bt.
 (1815)
Appleyard, Sir Leonard Vincent,
 KCMG
Appleyard, Sir Raymond Kenelm,
 KBE
Arbuthnot, Sir Keith Robert Charles,
 Bt. (1823)
Arbuthnot, Sir William Reierson, Bt.
 (1964)
Arbuthnott, *Prof.* Sir John Peebles,
 Kt., PH.D., FRSE
Archdale, *Capt.* Sir Edward Folmer,
 Bt., DSC, RN (1928)
Archer, *Gen.* Sir (Arthur) John, KCB,
 OBE
Arculus, Sir Ronald, KCMG, KCVO

Armitage, *Air Chief Marshal* Sir
 Michael John, KCB, CBE
Armour, *Prof.* Sir James, Kt., CBE
†Armstrong, Sir Christopher John
 Edmund Stuart, Bt., MBE (1841)
Armytage, Sir John Martin, Bt.
 (1738)
Arnold, *Rt. Hon.* Sir John Lewis, Kt.
Arnold, Sir Malcolm Henry, Kt., CBE
Arnold, Sir Thomas Richard, Kt.
Arnott, Sir Alexander John Maxwell,
 Bt. (1896)
Arnott, *Prof.* Sir (William) Melville,
 Kt., TD, MD
Arrindell, Sir Clement Athelston,
 GCMG, GCVO, QC
Arthur, *Lt.-Gen.* Sir (John) Norman
 Stewart, KCB
Arthur, Sir Stephen John, Bt. (1841)
Ash, *Prof.* Sir Eric Albert, Kt., CBE, FRS,
 FEng.
Ashburnham, Sir Denny Reginald,
 Bt. (1661)
Ashe, Sir Derick Rosslyn, KCMG
Ashley, Sir Bernard Albert, Kt.
Ashmore, *Admiral of the Fleet* Sir
 Edward Beckwith, GCB, DSC
Ashmore, *Vice-Adm.* Sir Peter
 William Beckwith, KCB, KCVO, DSC
Ashworth, Sir Herbert, Kt.
Aske, *Revd* Sir Conan, Bt. (1922)
Askew, Sir Bryan, Kt.
Asscher, *Prof.* (Adolf) William, Kt.,
 MD, FRCP
Astill, *Hon.* Sir Michael John, Kt.
Aston, Sir Harold George, Kt., CBE
Aston, *Hon.* Sir William John, KCMG
Astor, *Hon.* Sir John Jacob, Kt., MBE
Astwood, *Hon.* Sir James Rufus, KBE
Atcherley, Sir Harold Winter, Kt.
Atiyah, Sir Michael Francis, Kt., OM,
 PH.D., FRS
Atkins, *Rt. Hon.* Sir Robert James, Kt.
Atkinson, *Air Marshal* Sir David
 William, KBE
Atkinson, Sir Frederick John, KCB
Atkinson, Sir John Alexander, KCB,
 DFC
Atkinson, Sir Robert, Kt., DSC, FEng.
Atopare, Sir Sailas, GCMG
Attenborough, Sir David Frederick,
 Kt., CH, CVO, CBE, FRS
Atwell, Sir John William, Kt., CBE,
 FRSE, FEng.
Atwill, Sir (Milton) John (Napier),
 Kt.
Audland, Sir Christopher John,
 KCMG
Audley, Sir George Bernard, Kt.
Augier, *Prof.* Sir Fitz-Roy Richard,
 Kt.
Auld, *Rt. Hon.* Sir Robin Ernest, Kt.
†Austin, Sir Anthony Leonard, Bt.
 (1894)
Austin, *Vice-Adm.* Sir Peter Murray,
 KCB
Austin, *Air Marshal* Sir Roger Mark,
 KCB, AFC
Axford, Sir William Ian, Kt.
Ayckbourn, Sir Alan, Kt., CBE

Aykroyd, Sir James Alexander Frederic, Bt. (1929)
Aykroyd, Sir William Miles, Bt., MC (1920)
Aylmer, Sir Richard John, Bt. (I. 1622)
Bacha, Sir Bhinod, Kt., CMG
Backhouse, Sir Jonathan Roger, Bt. (1901)
Bacon, Sir Nicholas Hickman Ponsonby, Bt. *Premier Baronet of England* (1611 and 1627)
Bacon, Sir Sidney Charles, Kt., CB, FEng.
Baddeley, Sir John Wolsey Beresford, Bt. (1922)
Baddiley, *Prof.* Sir James, Kt., PH.D., D.SC., FRS, FRSE
Badge, Sir Peter Gilmour Noto, Kt.
Badger, Sir Geoffrey Malcolm, Kt.
Baer, Sir Jack Mervyn Frank, Kt.
Bagge, Sir (John) Jeremy Picton, Bt. (1867)
Bagnall, *Air Marshal* Sir Anthony John Crowther, KCB, OBE
Bagnall, *Field Marshal* Sir Nigel Thomas, GCB, CVO, MC
Bailey, Sir Alan Marshall, KCB
Bailey, Sir Brian Harry, Kt., OBE
Bailey, Sir Derrick Thomas Louis, Bt., DFC (1919)
Bailey, Sir John Bilsland, KCB
Bailey, Sir Richard John, Kt., CBE
Bailey, Sir Stanley Ernest, Kt., CBE, QPM
Bailhache, Sir Philip Martin, Kt.
Baillie, Sir Gawaine George Hope, Bt. (1823)
Baines, *Prof.* Sir George Grenfell-, Kt., OBE
Baird, Sir David Charles, Bt. (1809)
†Baird, Sir James Andrew Gardiner, Bt. (S. 1695)
Baird, *Lt.-Gen.* Sir James Parlane, KBE, MD
Baird, *Vice-Adm.* Sir Thomas Henry Eustace, KCB
Bairsto, *Air Marshal* Sir Peter Edward, KBE, CB
Baker, Sir Bryan William, Kt.
Baker, Sir Robert George Humphrey Sherston-, Bt. (1796)
Baker, *Hon.* Sir (Thomas) Scott (Gillespie), Kt.
Balchin, Sir Robert George Alexander, Kt.
Balcombe, *Rt. Hon.* Sir (Alfred) John, Kt.
Balderstone, Sir James Schofield, Kt.
Baldwin, *Prof.* Sir Jack Edward, Kt., FRS
Baldwin, Sir Peter Robert, KCB
Ball, *Air Marshal* Sir Alfred Henry Wynne, KCB, DSO, DFC
Ball, Sir Charles Irwin, Bt. (1911)
Ball, Sir Christopher John Elinger, Kt.
Ball, *Prof.* Sir Robert James, Kt., PH.D.
Bamford, Sir Anthony Paul, Kt.

Banham, Sir John Michael Middlecott, Kt.
Bannerman, Sir David Gordon, Bt., OBE (S. 1682)
Bannister, Sir Roger Gilbert, Kt., CBE, DM, FRCP
Barber, Sir (Thomas) David, Bt. (1960)
Barbour, *Very Revd* Sir Robert Alexander Stewart, KCVO, MC
Barclay, Sir Colville Herbert Sanford, Bt. (S. 1668)
Barclay, Sir Peter Maurice, Kt., CBE
Barder, Sir Brian Leon, KCMG
Barker, Sir Alwyn Bowman, Kt., CMG
Barker, Sir Colin, Kt.
Barker, *Hon.* Sir (Richard) Ian, Kt.
Barlow, Sir Christopher Hilaro, Bt. (1803)
Barlow, Sir Frank, Kt., CBE
Barlow, Sir (George) William, Kt., FEng.
Barlow, Sir John Kemp, Bt. (1907)
Barlow, Sir Thomas Erasmus, Bt., DSC (1902)
Barnard, Sir Joseph Brian, Kt.
Barnes, Sir (James) David (Francis), Kt., CBE
Barnes, Sir Kenneth, KCB
Barnewall, Sir Reginald Robert, Bt. (I. 1623)
Baron, Sir Thomas, Kt., CBE
Barraclough, *Air Chief Marshal* Sir John, KCB, CBE, DFC, AFC
Barraclough, Sir Kenneth James Priestley, Kt., CBE, TD
Barran, Sir David Haven, Kt.
Barran, Sir John Napoleon Ruthven, Bt. (1895)
Barratt, Sir Lawrence Arthur, Kt.
Barratt, Sir Richard Stanley, Kt., CBE, QPM
Barrett, *Lt.-Gen.* Sir David William Scott-, KBE, MC
Barrett, Sir Stephen Jeremy, KCMG
Barrington, Sir Alexander (Fitzwilliam Croker), Bt. (1831)
Barrington, Sir Nicholas John, KCMG, CVO
Barron, Sir Donald James, Kt.
Barrow, *Capt.* Sir Richard John Uniacke, Bt. (1835)
Barrowclough, Sir Anthony Richard, Kt., QC
Barry, Sir (Lawrence) Edward (Anthony Tress), Bt. (1899)
†Bartlett, Sir Andrew Alan, Bt. (1913)
Barttelot, *Col.* Sir Brian Walter de Stopham, Bt., OBE (1875)
Batchelor, Sir Ivor Ralph Campbell, Kt., CBE
Bate, Sir David Lindsay, KBE
Bate, Sir (Walter) Edwin, Kt., OBE
Bateman, Sir Cecil Joseph, KBE
Bateman, Sir Geoffrey Hirst, Kt., FRCS
Bates, Sir Geoffrey Voltelin, Bt., MC (1880)
Bates, Sir Malcolm Rowland, Kt.
Batho, Sir Peter Ghislain, Bt. (1928)

Bathurst, *Admiral of the Fleet* Sir (David) Benjamin, GCB
Bathurst, Sir Frederick John Charles Gordon Hervey-, Bt. (1818)
Bathurst, Sir Maurice Edward, Kt., CMG, CBE, QC
Batten, Sir John Charles, KCVO
Battersby, *Prof.* Sir Alan Rushton, Kt., FRS
Battishill, Sir Anthony Michael William, GCB
Batty, Sir William Bradshaw, Kt., TD
Baxendell, Sir Peter Brian, Kt., CBE, FEng.
Bayliss, Sir Richard Ian Samuel, KCVO, MD, FRCP
Bayne, Sir Nicholas Peter, KCMG
Baynes, Sir John Christopher Malcolm, Bt. (1801)
†Bazley, Sir Thomas John Sebastian, Bt. (1869)
Beach, *Gen.* Sir (William Gerald) Hugh, GBE, KCB, MC
Beale, *Lt.-Gen.* Sir Peter John, KBE, FRCP
Beament, Sir James William Longman, Kt., SC.D., FRS
Beattie, *Hon.* Sir Alexander Craig, Kt.
Beattie, *Hon.* Sir David Stuart, GCMG, GCVO
Beauchamp, Sir Christopher Radstock Proctor-, Bt. (1745)
Beaumont, *Capt.* the Hon. Sir (Edward) Nicholas (Canning), KCVO
Beaumont, Sir George (Howland Francis), Bt. (1661)
Beaumont, Sir Richard Ashton, KCMG, OBE
Beavis, *Air Chief Marshal* Sir Michael Gordon, KCB, CBE, AFC
Becher, Sir William Fane Wrixon, Bt., MC (1831)
Beck, Sir Edgar Charles, Kt., CBE, FEng.
Beck, Sir Edgar Philip, Kt.
Beckett, *Capt.* Sir (Martyn) Gervase, Bt., MC (1921)
Beckett, Sir Terence Norman, KBE, FEng.
Bedingfeld, *Capt.* Sir Edmund George Felix Paston-, Bt. (1661)
Bedser, Sir Alec Victor, Kt., CBE
Beecham, Sir Jeremy Hugh, Kt.
Beecham, Sir John Stratford Roland, Bt. (1914)
Beeley, Sir Harold, KCMG, CBE
Beetham, *Marshal of the Royal Air Force* Sir Michael James, GCB, CBE, DFC, AFC
Beevor, Sir Thomas Agnew, Bt. (1784)
Beith, Sir John Greville Stanley, KCMG
Belch, Sir Alexander Ross, Kt., CBE, FRSE
Beldam, *Rt. Hon.* Sir (Alexander) Roy (Asplan), Kt.
Belich, Sir James, Kt.
Bell, Sir Brian Ernest, KBE

Bell, Sir (George) Raymond, KCMG, CB

Bell, Sir John Lowthian, Bt. (1885)

Bell, *Hon.* Sir Rodger, Kt.

Bell, Sir (William) Ewart, KCB

Bell, Sir William Hollin Dayrell Morrison-, Bt. (1905)

Bellew, Sir Henry Charles Gratton-, Bt. (1838)

Bellinger, Sir Robert Ian, GBE

Bellingham, Sir Noel Peter Roger, Bt. (1796)

Bengough, *Col.* Sir Piers, KCVO, OBE

Benn, Sir (James) Jonathan, Bt. (1914)

Bennett, Sir Charles Moihi Te Arawaka, Kt., DSO

Bennett, *Air Vice-Marshal* Sir Erik Peter, KBE, CB

Bennett, *Rt. Hon.* Sir Frederic Mackarness, Kt.

Bennett, Sir Hubert, Kt.

Bennett, *Hon.* Sir Hugh Peter Derwyn, Kt.

Bennett, Sir John Mokonuiarangi, Kt.

Bennett, *Gen.* Sir Phillip Harvey, KBE, DSO

Bennett, Sir Reginald Frederick Brittain, Kt., VRD

Bennett, Sir Richard Rodney, Kt., CBE

Bennett, Sir Ronald Wilfrid Murdoch, Bt. (1929)

Benson, Sir Christopher John, Kt.

Benyon, Sir William Richard, Kt.

Beresford, Sir (Alexander) Paul, Kt., MP

Berger, *Vice-Adm.* Sir Peter Egerton Capel, KCB, LVO, DSC

Berghuser, *Hon.* Sir Eric, Kt., MBE

Berman, Sir Franklin Delow, KCMG

Bernard, Sir Dallas Edmund, Bt. (1954)

Berney, Sir Julian Reedham Stuart, Bt. (1620)

Berridge, *Prof.* Sir Michael John, Kt., FRS

Berrill, Sir Kenneth Ernest, GBE, KCB

Berriman, Sir David, Kt.

Berry, *Prof.* Sir Colin Leonard, Kt., FRCPath.

Berry, *Prof.* Sir Michael Victor, Kt., FRS

Berthon, *Vice-Adm.* Sir Stephen Ferrier, KCB

Berthoud, Sir Martin Seymour, KCVO, CMG

Best, Sir Richard Radford, KCVO, CBE

Bethune, *Hon.* Sir (Walter) Angus, Kt.

Bett, Sir Michael, Kt., CBE

Bevan, Sir Martyn Evan Evans, Bt. (1958)

Bevan, Sir Timothy Hugh, Kt.

Beveridge, Sir Gordon Smith Grieve, Kt., FRSE, FEng., FRSA

Beverley, *Lt.-Gen.* Sir Henry York La Roche, KCB, OBE, RM

Bibby, Sir Derek James, Bt., MC (1959)

Bick, *Hon.* Sir Martin James Moore-, Kt.

Bickersteth, *Rt. Revd* John Monier, KCVO

Biddulph, Sir Ian D'Olier, Bt. (1664)

Bide, Sir Austin Ernest, Kt.

Bidwell, Sir Hugh Charles Philip, GBE

Biggam, Sir Robin Adair, Kt.

Biggs, *Vice-Adm.* Sir Geoffrey William Roger, KCB

Biggs, Sir Norman Paris, Kt.

Bilas, Sir Angmai Simon, Kt., OBE

Billière, *Gen.* Sir Peter Edgar de la Cour de la, KCB, KBE, DSO, MC

Bingham, *Hon.* Sir Eardley Max, Kt., QC

Birch, Sir John Allan, KCVO, CMG

Birch, Sir Roger, Kt., CBE, QPM

Bird, Sir Richard Geoffrey Chapman, Bt. (1922)

Birkin, Sir John Christian William, Bt. (1905)

Birkin, Sir (John) Derek, Kt., TD

Birkmyre, Sir Archibald, Bt. (1921)

Birley, Sir Derek Sydney, Kt.

Birrell, Sir James Drake, Kt.

Birt, Sir John, Kt.

Birtwistle, Sir Harrison, Kt.

Bishop, Sir Frederick Arthur, Kt., CB, CVO

Bishop, Sir George Sidney, Kt., CB, OBE

Bishop, Sir Michael David, Kt., CBE

Bisson, *Rt. Hon.* Sir Gordon Ellis, Kt.

Black, *Prof.* Sir Douglas Andrew Kilgour, Kt., MD, FRCP

Black, Sir James Whyte, Kt., FRCP, FRS

Black, *Adm.* Sir (John) Jeremy, GBE, KCB, DSO

Black, Sir Robert Brown, GCMG, OBE

Black, Sir Robert David, Bt. (1922)

Blackburne, *Hon.* Sir William Anthony, Kt.

Blacker, *Gen.* Sir (Anthony Stephen) Jeremy, KCB, CBE

Blacker, *Gen.* Sir Cecil Hugh, GCB, OBE, MC

Blackett, Sir Hugh Francis, Bt. (1673)

Blacklock, *Surgeon Capt. Prof.* Sir Norman James, KCVO, OBE

Blackman, Sir Frank Milton, KCVO, OBE

Blackwell, Sir Basil Davenport, Kt., FEng.

Blackwood, Sir John Francis, Bt. (1814)

Blair, Sir Alastair Campbell, KCVO, TD, WS

Blair, *Lt.-Gen.* Sir Chandos, KCVO, OBE, MC

Blair, Sir Edward Thomas Hunter, Bt. (1786)

Blake, Sir Alfred Lapthorn, KCVO, MC

Blake, Sir Francis Michael, Bt. (1907)

Blake, Sir Peter James, KBE

Blake, Sir (Thomas) Richard (Valentine), Bt. (I. 1622)

Blaker, Sir John, Bt. (1919)

Blakiston, Sir Ferguson Arthur James, Bt. (1763)

Blanch, Sir Malcolm, KCVO

Bland, Sir (Francis) Christopher (Buchan), Kt.

Bland, Sir Henry Armand, Kt., CBE

Bland, *Lt.-Col.* Sir Simon Claud Michael, KCVO

Blatherwick, Sir David Elliott Spiby, KCMG, OBE

Blelloch, Sir John Nial Henderson, KCB

Blennerhassett, Sir (Marmaduke) Adrian Francis William, Bt. (1809)

Blewitt, *Maj.* Sir Shane Gabriel Basil, GCVO

Blofeld, *Hon.* Sir John Christopher Calthorpe, Kt.

Blois, Sir Charles Nicholas Gervase, Bt. (1686)

Blomefield, Sir Thomas Charles Peregrine, Bt. (1807)

Bloomfield, Sir Kenneth Percy, KCB

Blosse, *Capt.* Sir Richard Hely Lynch-, Bt. (1622)

Blount, Sir Walter Edward Alpin, Bt., DSC (1642)

Blundell, Sir Thomas Leon, Kt., FRS

Blunden, Sir George, Kt.

†Blunden, Sir Philip Overington, Bt. (I. 1766)

Blunt, Sir David Richard Reginald Harvey, Bt. (1720)

Blyth, Sir Charles (Chay), Kt., CBE, BEM

Boardman, *Prof.* Sir John, Kt., FSA, FBA

Bodmer, Sir Walter Fred, Kt., PH.D., FRS

Body, Sir Richard Bernard Frank Stewart, Kt., MP

Boevey, Sir Thomas Michael Blake Crawley-, Bt. (1784)

Bogan, Sir Nagora, KBE

Bogarde, Sir Dirk (Derek Niven van den Bogaerde), Kt.

Boileau, Sir Guy (Francis), Bt. (1838)

Boles, Sir Jeremy John Fortescue, Bt. (1922)

Boles, Sir John Dennis, Kt., MBE

Bolland, Sir Edwin, KCMG

Bollers, *Hon.* Sir Harold Brodie Smith, Kt.

Bolton, Sir Frederic Bernard, Kt., MC

Bona, Sir Kina, KBE

Bonallack, Sir Michael Francis, Kt., OBE

Bond, Sir Kenneth Raymond Boyden, Kt.

Bond, *Prof.* Sir Michael Richard, Kt., FRCP sych., FRCPGlas., FRCSE

Bondi, *Prof.* Sir Hermann, KCB, FRS

Bonfield, Sir Peter Leahy, Kt., CBE, FEng.

Bonham, *Maj.* Sir Antony Lionel Thomas, Bt. (1852)

Bonington, Sir Christian John Storey, Kt., CBE

Bonsall, Sir Arthur Wilfred, KCMG, CBE

Bonsor, Sir Nicholas Cosmo, Bt. (1925)
Boolell, Sir Satcam, Kt.
Boord, Sir Nicolas John Charles, Bt. (1896)
Boorman, *Lt.-Gen.* Sir Derek, KCB
Booth, Sir Christopher Charles, Kt., MD, FRCP
Booth, Hon. Sir David Alwyn Gore-, KCMG, KCVO
Booth, Sir Douglas Allen, Bt. (1916)
Booth, Sir Gordon, KCMG, CVO
Booth, Sir Josslyn Henry Robert Gore-, Bt. (I. 1760)
Booth, Sir Michael Addison John Wheeler-, KCB
Boothby, Sir Brooke Charles, Bt. (1660)
Boreel, Sir Francis David, Bt. (1645)
Boreham, *Hon.* Sir Leslie Kenneth Edward, Kt.
Bornu, The Waziri of, KCMG, CBE
Borthwick, Sir John Thomas, Bt., MBE (1908)
Bossom, *Hon.* Sir Clive, Bt. (1953)
Boswall, Sir (Thomas) Alford Houstoun-, Bt. (1836)
Boswell, *Lt.-Gen.* Sir Alexander Crawford Simpson, KCB, CBE
Bosworth, Sir Neville Bruce Alfred, Kt., CBE
Bottomley, Sir James Reginald Alfred, KCMG
Boughey, Sir John George Fletcher, Bt. (1798)
Boulton, Sir Clifford John, GCB
Boulton, Sir (Harold Hugh) Christian, Bt. (1905)
Boulton, Sir William Whytehead, Bt., CBE, TD (1944)
Bourn, Sir John Bryant, KCB
Bourne, Sir (John) Wilfrid, KCB
Bovell, *Hon.* Sir (William) Stewart, Kt.
Bowater, Sir Euan David Vansittart, Bt. (1939)
Bowater, Sir (John) Vansittart, Bt. (1914)
Bowden, Sir Andrew, Kt., MBE
Bowden, Sir Frank, Bt. (1915)
Bowen, Sir Geoffrey Fraser, Kt.
Bowen, Sir Mark Edward Mortimer, Bt. (1921)
Bowett, *Prof.* Sir Derek William, Kt., CBE, QC, FBA
†Bowlby, Sir Richard Peregrine Longstaff, Bt. (1923)
Bowman, Sir Jeffery Haverstock, Kt.
Bowman, Sir Paul Humphrey Armytage, Bt. (1884)
Bowmar, Sir Charles Erskine, Kt.
Bowness, Sir Alan, Kt., CBE
Boyce, *Adm.* Sir Michael Cecil, KCB, OBE
Boyce, Sir Robert Charles Leslie, Bt. (1952)
Boyd, Sir Alexander Walter, Bt. (1916)
Boyd, Sir John Dixon Iklé, KCMG

Boyd, The Hon. Sir Mark Alexander Lennox-, Kt.
Boyd, *Prof.* Sir Robert Lewis Fullarton, Kt., CBE, D.SC., FRS
Boyes, Sir Brian Gerald Barratt-, KBE
Boyle, Sir Stephen Gurney, Bt. (1904)
Boynton, Sir John Keyworth, Kt., MC
Boys, *Rt. Hon.* Sir Michael Hardie, GCMG
Boyson, *Rt. Hon.* Sir Rhodes, Kt.
Brabham, Sir John Arthur, Kt., OBE
Bradbeer, Sir John Derek Richardson, Kt., OBE, TD
Bradbury, *Surgeon Vice-Adm.* Sir Eric Blackburn, KBE, CB
Bradford, Sir Edward Alexander Slade, Bt. (1902)
Bradman, Sir Donald George, Kt.
Bradshaw, Sir Kenneth Anthony, KCB
Bradshaw, *Lt.-Gen.* Sir Richard Phillip, KBE
Brain, Sir (Henry) Norman, KBE, CMG
Braithwaite, Sir (Joseph) Franklin Madders, Kt.
Braithwaite, *Rt. Hon.* Sir Nicholas Alexander, Kt., OBE
Braithwaite, Sir Rodric Quentin, GCMG
Bramall, Sir (Ernest) Ashley, Kt.
Bramley, *Prof.* Sir Paul Anthony, Kt.
Branigan, Sir Patrick Francis, Kt., QC
Bray, Sir Theodor Charles, Kt., CBE
Brennan, *Hon.* Sir (Francis) Gerard, KBE
Brett, Sir Charles Edward Bainbridge, Kt., CBE
Brickwood, Sir Basil Greame, Bt. (1927)
Bridges, *Hon.* Sir Phillip Rodney, Kt., CMG
Brierley, Sir Ronald Alfred, Kt.
Bright, Sir Graham Frank James, Kt.
Bright, Sir Keith, Kt.
Brigstocke, *Adm.* Sir John Richard, KCB
Brinckman, Sir Theodore George Roderick, Bt. (1831)
†Brisco, Sir Campbell Howard, Bt. (1782)
Briscoe, Sir John Geoffrey James, Bt. (1910)
Brise, Sir John Archibald Ruggles-, Bt., CB, OBE, TD (1935)
Bristow, *Hon.* Sir Peter Henry Rowley, Kt.
Brittan, *Rt. Hon.* Sir Leon, Kt., QC
Brittan, Sir Samuel, Kt.
Britton, Sir Edward Louis, Kt., CBE
Broackes, Sir Nigel, Kt.
†Broadbent, Sir Andrew George, Bt. (1893)
Brocklebank, Sir Aubrey Thomas, Bt. (1885)
Brockman, *Vice-Adm.* Sir Ronald Vernon, KCB, CSI, CIE, CVO, CBE
Brodie, Sir Benjamin David Ross, Bt. (1834)
Broers, *Prof.* Sir Alec Nigel, Kt., PH.D., FRS

Bromhead, Sir John Desmond Gonville, Bt. (1806)
Bromley, Sir Michael Roger, KBE
Bromley, Sir Rupert Charles, Bt. (1757)
Bromley, Sir Thomas Eardley, KCMG
Brook, Sir Robin, Kt., CMG, OBE
†Brooke, Sir Alistair Weston, Bt. (1919)
Brooke, Sir Francis George Windham, Bt. (1903)
Brooke, *Rt. Hon.* Sir Henry, Kt.
Brooke, Sir (Richard) David Christopher, Bt. (1662)
Brookes, Sir Wilfred Deakin, Kt., CBE, DSO
Brooksbank, Sir (Edward) Nicholas, Bt. (1919)
Broom, *Air Marshal* Sir Ivor Gordon, KCB, CBE, DSO, DFC, AFC
Broomfield, Sir Nigel Hugh Robert Allen, KCMG
†Broughton, Sir David Delves, Bt. (1661)
Broun, Sir William Windsor, Bt. (s. 1686)
Brown, Sir Allen Stanley, Kt., CBE
Brown, Sir (Austen) Patrick, KCB
Brown, *Adm.* Sir Brian Thomas, KCB, CBE
Brown, Sir (Cyril) Maxwell Palmer, KCB, CMG
Brown, *Vice-Adm.* Sir David Worthington, KCB
Brown, Sir Derrick Holden-, Kt.
Brown, Sir Douglas Denison, Kt.
Brown, *Hon.* Sir Douglas Dunlop, Kt.
Brown, Sir George Francis Richmond, Bt. (1863)
Brown, Sir George Noel, Kt.
Brown, Sir John Douglas Keith, Kt.
Brown, Sir John Gilbert Newton, Kt., CBE
Brown, Sir Mervyn, KCMG, OBE
Brown, Sir Peter Randolph, Kt.
Brown, *Hon.* Sir Ralph Kilner, Kt., OBE, TD
Brown, Sir Robert Crichton-, KCMG, CBE, TD
Brown, *Rt. Hon.* Sir Simon Denis, Kt.
Brown, *Rt. Hon.* Sir Stephen, Kt.
Brown, Sir Thomas, Kt.
Brown, Sir William Brian Piggott-, Bt. (1903)
Browne, Sir (Edmund) John (Phillip), Kt., FEng.
Brownrigg, Sir Nicholas (Gawen), Bt. (1816)
Browse, *Prof.* Sir Norman Leslie, Kt., MD, FRCS
Bruce, Sir (Francis) Michael Ian, Bt. (s. 1628)
Bruce, Sir Hervey James Hugh, Bt. (1804)
Bruce, *Rt. Hon.* Sir (James) Roualeyn Hovell-Thurlow-Cumming-, Kt.
Brunner, Sir John Henry Kilian, Bt. (1895)
Brunton, Sir (Edward Francis) Lauder, Bt. (1908)

Brunton, Sir Gordon Charles, Kt.

Bryan, Sir Arthur, Kt.

Bryan, Sir Paul Elmore Oliver, Kt., DSO, MC

Bryce, *Hon.* Sir (William) Gordon, Kt., CBE

Bryson, *Adm.* Sir Lindsay Sutherland, KCB, FEng.

Buchan, Sir John, Kt., CMG

Buchanan, Sir Andrew George, Bt. (1878)

Buchanan, Sir Charles Alexander James Leith-, Bt. (1775)

Buchanan, *Prof.* Sir Colin Douglas, Kt., CBE

Buchanan, *Vice-Adm.* Sir Peter William, KBE

Buchanan, Sir (Ranald) Dennis, Kt., MBE

Buchanan, Sir Robert Wilson (Robin), Kt.

Buck, Sir (Philip) Antony (Fyson), Kt., QC

Buckland, Sir Ross, Kt.

Buckley, *Rt. Hon.* Sir Denys Burton, Kt., MBE

Buckley, Sir John William, Kt.

Buckley, *Lt.-Cdr.* Sir (Peter) Richard, KCVO

Buckley, *Hon.* Sir Roger John, Kt.

Budd, Sir Alan Peter, Kt.

Bulkeley, Sir Richard Thomas Williams-, Bt. (1661)

Bull, Sir George Jeffrey, Kt.

Bull, Sir Simeon George, Bt. (1922)

Bullard, Sir Julian Leonard, GCMG

Bullus, Sir Eric Edward, Kt.

Bulmer, Sir William Peter, Kt.

Bultin, Sir Bato, Kt., MBE

Bunbury, Sir Michael William, Bt. (1681)

Bunbury, Sir (Richard David) Michael Richardson-, Bt. (I. 1787)

Bunch, Sir Austin Wyeth, Kt., CBE

Bunyard, Sir Robert Sidney, Kt., CBE, QPM

Burbidge, Sir Herbert Dudley, Bt. (1916)

Burdett, Sir Savile Aylmer, Bt. (1665)

Burgen, Sir Arnold Stanley Vincent, Kt., FRS

Burgess, *Gen.* Sir Edward Arthur, KCB, OBE

Burgess, Sir (Joseph) Stuart, Kt., CBE, Ph.D., FRSC

Burgh, Sir John Charles, KCMG, CB

Burke, Sir James Stanley Gilbert, Bt. (I. 1797)

Burke, Sir (Thomas) Kerry, Kt.

Burley, Sir Victor George, Kt., CBE

Burman, Sir (John) Charles, Kt.

Burnet, Sir James William Alexander (Sir Alastair Burnet), Kt.

Burnett, *Air Chief Marshal* Sir Brian Kenyon, GCB, DFC, AFC

Burnett, Sir David Humphery, Bt., MBE, TD (1913)

Burnett, Sir John Harrison, Kt.

Burnett, Sir Walter John, Kt.

Burney, Sir Cecil Denniston, Bt. (1921)

Burns, Sir (Robert) Andrew, KCMG

Burrell, Sir John Raymond, Bt. (1774)

Burrenchobay, Sir Dayendranath, KBE, CMG, CVO

Burrows, Sir Bernard Alexander Brocas, GCMG

Burston, Sir Samuel Gerald Wood, Kt., OBE

Burt, *Hon.* Sir Francis Theodore Page, KCMG

Burton, Sir Carlisle Archibald, Kt., OBE

Burton, Sir George Vernon Kennedy, Kt., CBE

Burton, Sir Michael St Edmund, KCVO, CMG

Bush, *Adm.* Sir John Fitzroy Duyland, GCB, DSC

Butler, *Rt. Hon.* Sir Adam Courtauld, Kt.

Butler, *Hon.* Sir Arlington Griffith, KCMG

Butler, Sir Clifford Charles, Kt., Ph.D., FRS

Butler, Sir Michael Dacres, GCMG

Butler, Sir (Reginald) Michael (Thomas), Bt. (1922)

Butler, *Hon.* Sir Richard Clive, Kt.

†Butler, Sir Richard Pierce, Bt. (1628)

Butt, Sir (Alfred) Kenneth Dudley, Bt. (1929)

Butter, *Maj.* Sir David Henry, KCVO, MC

Butterfield, *Hon.* Sir Alexander Neil Logie, Kt.

Buxton, Sir Jocelyn Charles Roden, Bt. (1840)

Buxton, *Rt. Hon.* Sir Richard Joseph, Kt.

Buzzard, Sir Anthony Farquhar, Bt. (1929)

Byatt, Sir Hugh Campbell, KCVO, CMG

Byers, Sir Maurice Hearne, Kt., CBE, QC

Byford, Sir Lawrence, Kt., CBE, QPM

Cable, Sir James Eric, KCVO, CMG

Cadbury, Sir (George) Adrian (Hayhurst), Kt.

Cadbury, Sir (Nicholas) Dominic, Kt.

Cadogan, *Prof.* Sir John Ivan George, Kt., CBE, FRS, FRSE

Cahn, Sir Albert Jonas, Bt. (1934)

Cain, Sir Henry Edney Conrad, Kt.

Caine, Sir Michael Harris, Kt.

Caines, Sir John, KCB

Cairncross, Sir Alexander Kirkland, KCMG

Calcutt, Sir David Charles, Kt., QC

Calderwood, Sir Robert, Kt.

Caldwell, *Surgeon Vice-Adm.* Sir (Eric) Dick, KBE, CB

Callard, Sir Eric John, Kt., FEng.

Callaway, *Prof.* Sir Frank Adams, Kt., CMG, OBE

Calman, *Prof.* Sir Kenneth Charles, KCB, MD, FRCP, FRCS, FRSE

Calne, *Prof.* Sir Roy Yorke, Kt., FRS

Calthorpe, Sir Euan Hamilton Anstruther-Gough-, Bt. (1929)

Cameron of Lochiel, Sir Donald Hamish, KT, CVO, TD

Cameron, Sir (Eustace) John, Kt., CBE

Campbell, Sir Alan Hugh, GCMG

Campbell, *Prof.* Sir Colin Murray, Kt.

Campbell, *Prof.* Sir Donald, Kt., CBE, FRCS, FRCPGlas.

Campbell, Sir Ian Tofts, Kt., CBE, VRD

Campbell, Sir Ilay Mark, Bt. (1808)

Campbell, Sir James Alexander Moffat Bain, Bt. (s. 1668)

Campbell, Sir Lachlan Philip Kemeys, Bt. (1815)

Campbell, Sir Matthew, KBE, CB, FRSE

Campbell, Sir Niall Alexander Hamilton, Bt. (1831)

Campbell, Sir Robin Auchinbreck, Bt. (s. 1628)

Campbell, Sir Thomas Cockburn-, Bt. (1821)

Campbell, *Hon.* Sir Walter Benjamin, Kt.

Campbell, *Hon.* Sir William Anthony, Kt.

†Carden, Sir Christopher Robert, Bt. (1887)

Carden, Sir John Craven, Bt. (I. 1787)

Carew, Sir Rivers Verain, Bt. (1661)

Carey, Sir Peter Willoughby, GCB

Carlisle, Sir James Beethoven, GCMG

Carlisle, Sir John Michael, Kt.

Carlisle, Sir Kenneth Melville, Kt.

Carmichael, Sir David Peter William Gibson-Craig-, Bt. (s. 1702 and 1831)

Carnac, *Revd Canon* Sir (Thomas) Nicholas Rivett-, Bt. (1836)

Carnegie, *Lt.-Gen.* Sir Robin Macdonald, KCB, OBE

Carnegie, Sir Roderick Howard, Kt.

Carnwath, Sir Robert John Anderson, Kt., CVO

Caro, Sir Anthony Alfred, Kt., CBE

Carpenter, *Lt.-Gen.* the Hon. Sir Thomas Patrick John Boyd-, KBE

Carr, Sir (Albert) Raymond (Maillard), Kt.

Carrick, *Hon.* Sir John Leslie, KCMG

Carrick, Sir Roger John, KCMG, LVO

Carsberg, *Prof.* Sir Bryan Victor, Kt.

Carswell, *Rt. Hon.* Sir Robert Douglas, Kt.

Carter, Sir Charles Frederick, Kt., FBA

Carter, *Prof.* Sir David Craig, Kt., FRCSE, FRCSG Ias., FRCPE

Carter, Sir John, Kt., QC

Carter, Sir John Alexander, Kt.

Carter, Sir John Gordon Thomas, Kt.

Carter, Sir Philip David, Kt., CBE

Carter, Sir Richard Henry Alwyn, Kt.

Carter, Sir William Oscar, Kt.

Collins, Sir Bryan Thomas Alfred,
Kt., OBE, QFSM
Collins, Sir John Alexander, Kt.
Collyear, Sir John Gowen, Kt., FEng.
Colman, *Hon.* Sir Anthony David, Kt.
Colman, Sir Michael Jeremiah, Bt.
(1907)
Colquhoun of Luss, Sir Ivar Iain, Bt.
(1786)
Colt, Sir Edward William Dutton, Bt.
(1694)
Colthurst, Sir Richard La Touche,
Bt. (1744)
Coltman, Sir (Arthur) Leycester
Scott, KBE, CMG
Colvin, Sir Howard Montagu, Kt.,
CVO, CBE, FBA
Compston, *Vice-Adm.* Sir Peter
Maxwell, KCB
Compton, *Rt. Hon.* Sir John George
Melvin, KCMG
Conant, Sir John Ernest Michael, Bt.
(1954)
Condon, Sir Paul Leslie, Kt., QPM
Connell, *Hon.* Sir Michael Bryan, Kt.
Conran, Sir Terence Orby, Kt.
Cons, *Hon.* Sir Derek, Kt.
Constable, Sir Frederic Strickland-,
Bt. (1641)
Constantinou, Sir Georkios, Kt., OBE
Cook, *Prof.* Sir Alan Hugh, Kt.
Cook, Sir Christopher Wymondham
Rayner Herbert, Bt. (1886)
Cooke, Sir Charles Fletcher-, Kt., QC
Cooke, *Lt.-Col.* Sir David William
Perceval, Bt. (1661)
Cooke, Sir Howard Felix Hanlan,
GCMG, GCVO
Cooksey, Sir David James Scott, Kt.
Cooley, Sir Alan Sydenham, Kt., CBE
Cooper, *Rt. Hon.* Sir Frank, GCB, CMG
Cooper, Sir (Frederick Howard)
Michael Craig-, Kt., CBE, TD
Cooper, *Gen.* Sir George Leslie
Conroy, GCB, MC
Cooper, Sir Louis Jacques Blom-,
Kt., QC
Cooper, Sir Patrick Graham Astley,
Bt. (1821)
Cooper, Sir Richard Powell, Bt.
(1905)
Cooper, Sir Robert George, Kt., CBE
Cooper, *Maj.-Gen.* Sir Simon
Christie, KCVO
Cooper, Sir William Daniel Charles,
Bt. (1863)
Coote, Sir Christopher John, Bt.,
Premier Baronet of Ireland (I. 1621)
Copas, *Most Revd* Virgil, KBE, DD
Copisarow, Sir Alcon Charles, Kt.
Corbett, *Maj.-Gen.* Sir Robert John
Swan, KCVO, CB
Corby, Sir (Frederick) Brian, Kt.
Corfield, *Rt. Hon.* Sir Frederick
Vernon, Kt., QC
Corfield, Sir Kenneth George, Kt.,
FEng.
Cork, Sir Roger William, Kt.
Corley, Sir Kenneth Sholl Ferrand,
Kt.

Cormack, Sir Magnus Cameron, KBE
Cormack, Sir Patrick Thomas, Kt.,
MP
Corness, Sir Colin Ross, Kt.
Cornford, Sir (Edward) Clifford, KCB,
FEng.
Cornforth, Sir John Warcup, Kt., CBE,
D.Phil., FRS
Corry, Sir William James, Bt. (1885)
Cortazzi, Sir (Henry Arthur) Hugh,
GCMG
Cory, Sir (Clinton Charles) Donald,
Bt. (1919)
Cossons, Sir Neil, Kt., OBE
Cotter, *Lt.-Col.* Sir Delaval James
Alfred, Bt., DSO (I. 1763)
Cotterell, Sir John Henry Geers, Bt.
(1805)
Cotton, Sir John Richard, KCMG, OBE
Cotton, *Hon.* Sir Robert Carrington,
KCMG
Cottrell, Sir Alan Howard, Kt., Ph.D.,
FRS, FEng.
†Cotts, Sir Richard Crichton
Mitchell, Bt. (1921)
Couper, Sir (Robert) Nicholas
(Oliver), Bt. (1841)
Court, *Hon.* Sir Charles Walter
Michael, KCMG, OBE
Cousins, *Air Marshal* Sir David, KCB,
AFC
Coutts, Sir David Burdett Money-,
KCVO
Couzens, Sir Kenneth Edward, KCB
Covacevich, Sir (Anthony) Thomas,
Kt., DFC
Cowan, *Lt.-Gen.* Sir Samuel, KCB, CBE
Coward, *Vice-Adm.* Sir John Francis,
KCB, DSO
Cowen, *Rt. Hon. Prof.* Sir Zelman,
GCMG, GCVO, QC
Cowie, Sir Thomas (Tom), Kt., OBE
Cowperthwaite, Sir John James, KBE,
CMG
Cox, Sir Alan George, Kt., CBE
Cox, *Prof.* Sir David Roxbee, Kt., FRS
Cox, Sir Geoffrey Sandford, Kt., CBE
Cox, *Vice-Adm.* Sir John Michael
Holland, KCB
Cradock, *Rt. Hon.* Sir Percy, GCMG
Craig, Sir (Albert) James
(Macqueen), GCMG
Craufurd, Sir Robert James, Bt.
(1781)
Craven, Sir John Anthony, Kt.
Craven, *Air Marshal* Sir Robert
Edward, KBE, CB, DFC
Crawford, *Prof.* Sir Frederick
William, Kt., FEng.
Crawford, Sir (Robert) Stewart,
GCMG, CVO
Crawford, *Vice-Adm.* Sir William
Godfrey, KBE, CB, DSC
Creagh, *Maj.-Gen.* Sir (Kilner)
Rupert Brazier-, KBE, CB, DSO
Cresswell, *Hon.* Sir Peter John, Kt.
Crill, Sir Peter Leslie, KBE
Cripps, Sir Cyril Humphrey, Kt.
Crisp, Sir (John) Peter, Bt. (1913)

Critchett, Sir Ian (George Lorraine),
Bt. (1908)
Critchley, Sir Julian Michael
Gordon, Kt.
Croft, Sir Owen Glendower, Bt.
(1671)
Croft, Sir Thomas Stephen Hutton,
Bt. (1818)
†Crofton, Sir Hugh Denis, Bt. (1801)
Crofton, *Prof.* Sir John Wenman, Kt.
Crofton, Sir Malby Sturges, Bt.
(1838)
Croker, Sir Walter Russell, KBE
Crookenden, *Lt.-Gen.* Sir Napier,
KCB, DSO, OBE
Cross, *Air Chief Marshal* Sir Kenneth
Brian Boyd, KCB, CBE, DSO, DFC
Crossland, *Prof.* Sir Bernard, Kt., CBE,
FEng.
Crossland, Sir Leonard, Kt.
Crossley, Sir Nicholas John, Bt.
(1909)
Cruthers, Sir James Winter, Kt.
Cubbon, Sir Brian Crossland, GCB
Cubitt, Sir Hugh Guy, Kt., CBE
Cullen, Sir (Edward) John, Kt., FEng.
Cumming, Sir William Gordon
Gordon-, Bt. (1804)
Cuninghame, Sir John Christopher
Foggo Montgomery-, Bt. (NS
1672)
†Cuninghame, Sir William Henry
Fairlie-, Bt. (S. 1630)
Cunliffe, Sir David Ellis, Bt. (1759)
Cunningham, *Lt.-Gen.* Sir Hugh
Patrick, KBE
Cunynghame, Sir Andrew David
Francis, Bt. (S. 1702)
†Currie, Sir Donald Scott, Bt. (1847)
Currie, Sir Neil Smith, Kt., CBE
Curtis, Sir Barry John, Kt.
Curtis, Sir (Edward) Leo, Kt.
Curtis, *Hon.* Sir Richard Herbert, Kt.
Curtis, Sir William Peter, Bt. (1802)
Curtiss, *Air Marshal* Sir John Bagot,
KCB, KBE
Curwen, Sir Christopher Keith,
KCMG
Cuschieri, *Prof.* Sir Alfred, Kt.
Cutler, Sir (Arthur) Roden, VC,
KCMG, KCVO, CBE
Cutler, Sir Charles Benjamin, KBE, ED
Dacie, *Prof.* Sir John Vivian, Kt., MD,
FRS
Dain, Sir David John Michael, KCVO
Dale, Sir William Leonard, KCMG
Dalrymple, *Maj.* Sir Hew Fleetwood
Hamilton-, Bt., KCVO (S. 1697)
Dalton, Sir Alan Nugent Goring, Kt.,
CBE
Dalton, *Vice-Adm.* Sir Geoffrey
Thomas James Oliver, KCB
Daly, *Lt.-Gen.* Sir Thomas Joseph,
KBE, CB, DSO
Dalyell, Sir Tam (Thomas), Bt., MP
(NS 1685)
Daniel, Sir Goronwy Hopkin, KCVO,
CB, D.Phil.
Daniel, Sir John Sagar, Kt., D.SC.
Daniell, Sir Peter Averell, Kt., TD

Darby, Sir Peter Howard, Kt., CBE, QFSM

Darell, Sir Jeffrey Lionel, Bt., MC (1795)

Dargie, Sir William Alexander, Kt., CBE

Dark, Sir Anthony Michael Beaumont-, Kt.

Darling, Sir Clifford, GCVO

Darling, Gen. Sir Kenneth Thomas, GBE, KCB, DSO

Darvall, Sir (Charles) Roger, Kt., CBE

Dashwood, Sir Francis John Vernon Hereward, Bt., Premier Baronet of Great Britain (1707)

Dashwood, Sir Richard James, Bt. (1684)

Daunt, Sir Timothy Lewis Achilles, KCMG

Davey, Hon. Sir David Herbert Penry-, Kt.

David, Sir Jean Marc, Kt., CBE, QC

David, His Hon. Sir Robin (Robert) Daniel George, Kt., QC

Davidson, Sir Robert James, Kt., FEng.

Davie, Sir John Ferguson-, Bt. (1847)

Davies, Hon. Sir (Alfred William) Michael, Kt.

Davies, Sir Alun Talfan, Kt., QC

Davies, Sir (Charles) Noel, Kt.

Davies, Prof. Sir David Evan Naughton, Kt., CBE, FRS, FEng.

Davies, Sir David Henry, Kt.

Davies, Hon. Sir (David Herbert) Mervyn, Kt., MC, TD

Davies, Prof. Sir Graeme John, Kt., FEng.

Davies, Vice-Adm. Sir Lancelot Richard Bell, KBE

Davies, Sir Peter Maxwell, Kt., CBE

Davies, Sir Victor Caddy, Kt., OBE

Davis, Sir Charles Sigmund, Kt., CB

Davis, Sir Colin Rex, Kt., CBE

Davis, Sir (Ernest) Howard, Kt., CMG, OBE

Davis, Sir John Gilbert, Bt. (1946)

Davis, Sir Peter John, Kt.

Davis, Sir Rupert Charles Hart-, Kt.

Davis, Hon. Sir Thomas Robert Alexander Harries, KBE

Davison, Rt. Hon. Sir Ronald Keith, GBE, CMG

Davson, Sir Christopher Michael Edward, Bt. (1927)

Dawbarn, Sir Simon Yelverton, KCVO, CMG

Dawson, Hon. Sir Daryl Michael, KBE, CB

Dawson, Sir Hugh Michael Trevor, Bt. (1920)

Dawtry, Sir Alan (Graham), Kt., CBE, TD

Day, Sir Derek Malcolm, KCMG

Day, Sir (Judson) Graham, Kt.

Day, Sir Michael John, Kt., OBE

Day, Sir Robin, Kt.

Day, Sir Simon James, Kt.

Deakin, Sir (Frederick) William (Dampier), Kt., DSO

Deane, Hon. Sir William Patrick, KBE

Dear, Sir Geoffrey James, Kt., QPM

de Bellaigue, Sir Geoffrey, GCVO

Debenham, Sir Gilbert Ridley, Bt. (1931)

de Deney, Sir Geoffrey Ivor, KCVO

de Hoghton, Sir (Richard) Bernard (Cuthbert), Bt. (1611)

De la Bère, Sir Cameron, Bt. (1953)

de la Rue, Sir Andrew George Ilay, Bt. (1898)

Dellow, Sir John Albert, Kt., CBE

de Montmorency, Sir Arnold Geoffroy, Bt. (I. 1631)

Denholm, Sir John Ferguson (Ian), Kt., CBE

Denman, Sir (George) Roy, KCB, CMG

Denny, Sir Anthony Coningham de Waltham, Bt. (I. 1782)

Denny, Sir Charles Alistair Maurice, Bt. (1913)

Dent, Sir John, Kt., CBE, FEng.

Dent, Sir Robin John, KCVO

Denton, Prof. Sir Eric James, Kt., CBE, FRS

Derbyshire, Sir Andrew George, Kt.

Derham, Sir Peter John, Kt.

de Trafford, Sir Dermot Humphrey, Bt. (1841)

Devesi, Sir Baddeley, GCMG, GCVO

De Ville, Sir Harold Godfrey Oscar, Kt., CBE

Devitt, Sir James Hugh Thomas, Bt. (1916)

de Waal, Sir (Constant Henrik) Henry, KCB, QC

Dewey, Sir Anthony Hugh, Bt. (1917)

Dewhurst, Prof. Sir (Christopher) John, Kt.

d'Eyncourt, Sir Mark Gervais Tennyson-, Bt. (1930)

Dhenin, Air Marshal Sir Geoffrey Howard, KBE, AFC, GM, MD

Dhrangadhra, HH the Maharaja Raj Saheb of, KCIE

Dibela, Hon. Sir Kingsford, GCMG

Dick, Maj.-Gen. Sir Iain Charles Mackay-, KCVO, MBE

Dickenson, Sir Aubrey Fiennes Trotman-, Kt.

Dickinson, Sir Harold Herbert, Kt.

Dickinson, Sir Samuel Benson, Kt.

Dilbertson, Sir Geoffrey, Kt., CBE

Dilke, Sir Charles John Wentworth, Bt. (1862)

Dillon, Rt. Hon. Sir (George) Brian (Hugh), Kt.

Dixon, Sir Ian Leonard, Kt., CBE

Dixon, Sir Jonathan Mark, Bt. (1919)

Djanogly, Sir Harry Ari Simon, Kt., CBE

Dobbs, Capt. Sir Richard Arthur Frederick, KCVO

Dobson, Vice-Adm. Sir David Stuart, KBE

Dobson, Gen. Sir Patrick John Howard-, GCB

Dodds, Sir Ralph Jordan, Bt. (1964)

Dodson, Sir Derek Sherborne Lindsell, KCMG, MC

Dodsworth, Sir John Christopher Smith-, Bt. (1784)

Doll, Prof. Sir (William) Richard (Shaboe), Kt., CH, OBE, FRS, DM, MD, D.SC.

Dollery, Sir Colin Terence, Kt.

Donald, Sir Alan Ewen, KCMG

Donald, Air Marshal Sir John George, KBE

Donne, Hon. Sir Gaven John, KBE

Donne, Sir John Christopher, Kt.

Dookun, Sir Dewoonarain, Kt.

Dorey, Sir Graham Martyn, Kt.

Dorman, Sir Philip Henry Keppel, Bt. (1923)

Dougherty, Maj.-Gen. Sir Ivan Noel, Kt., CBE, DSO, ED

Doughty, Sir William Roland, Kt.

Douglas, Sir (Edward) Sholto, Kt.

Douglas, Hon. Sir Roger Owen, Kt.

Douglas, Rt. Hon. Sir William Randolph, KCMG

Dover, Prof. Sir Kenneth James, Kt., D.Litt., FBA, FRSE

Dowell, Sir Anthony James, Kt., CBE

Down, Sir Alastair Frederick, Kt., OBE, MC, TD

Downes, Sir Edward Thomas, Kt., CBE

Downey, Sir Gordon Stanley, KCB

Downs, Sir Diarmuid, Kt., CBE, FEng.

Downward, Sir William Atkinson, Kt.

Dowson, Sir Philip Manning, Kt., CBE, PRA

Doyle, Sir Reginald Derek Henry, Kt., CBE

D'Oyly, Sir Nigel Hadley Miller, Bt. (1663)

Drake, Hon. Sir (Frederick) Maurice, Kt., DFC

Dreyer, Adm. Sir Desmond Parry, GCB, CBE, DSC

Drinkwater, Sir John Muir, Kt., QC

Driver, Sir Antony Victor, Kt.

Driver, Sir Eric William, Kt.

Drummond, Sir John Richard Gray, Kt., CBE

Drury, Sir (Victor William) Michael, Kt., OBE

Dryden, Sir John Stephen Gyles, Bt. (1733 and 1795)

du Cann, Rt. Hon. Sir Edward Dillon Lott, KBE

†Duckworth, Sir Edward Richard Dyce, Bt. (1909)

du Cros, Sir Claude Philip Arthur Mallet, Bt. (1916)

Duff, Rt. Hon. Sir (Arthur) Antony, GCMG, CVO, DSO, DSC

Duffell, Lt.-Gen. Sir Peter Royson, KCB, CBE, MC

Duffus, Hon. Sir William Algernon Holwell, Kt.

Duffy, Sir (Albert) (Edward) Patrick, Kt., Ph.D.

Dugdale, Sir William Stratford, Bt., MC (1936)

Dunbar, Sir Archibald Ranulph, Bt. (s. 1700)

Dunbar, Sir David Hope-, Bt. (s. 1664)

Dunbar, Sir Drummond Cospatrick Ninian, Bt., MC (s. 1698)

Dunbar, Sir James Michael, Bt. (s. 1694)

†Dunbar of Hempriggs, Sir Richard Francis, Bt. (s. 1706)

Duncan, Sir James Blair, Kt.

Duncombe, Sir Philip Digby Pauncefort-, Bt. (1859)

Dunham, Sir Kingsley Charles, Kt., Ph.D., FRS, FRSE, FEng.

Dunlop, Sir Thomas, Bt. (1916)

Dunlop, Sir William Norman Gough, Kt.

Dunn, Air Marshal Sir Eric Clive, KBE, CB, BEM

Dunn, Air Marshal Sir Patrick Hunter, KBE, CB, DFC

Dunn, Rt. Hon. Sir Robin Horace Walford, Kt., MC

Dunne, Sir Thomas Raymond, KCVO

Dunnett, Sir Alastair MacTavish, Kt.

Dunning, Sir Simon William Patrick, Bt. (1930)

Dunphie, Maj.-Gen. Sir Charles Anderson Lane, Kt., CB, CBE, DSO

Dunstan, Lt.-Gen. Sir Donald Beaumont, KBE, CB

Dunt, Vice-Adm. Sir John Hugh, KCB

†Duntze, Sir Daniel Evans, Bt. (1774)

Dupre, Sir Tumun, Kt., MBE

Dupree, Sir Peter, Bt. (1921)

Durand, Sir Edward Alan Christopher David Percy, Bt. (1892)

Durant, Sir (Robert) Anthony (Bevis), Kt.

Durham, Sir Kenneth, Kt.

Durie, Sir Alexander Charles, Kt., CBE

Durkin, Air Marshal Sir Herbert, KBE, CB

Durrant, Sir William Alexander Estridge, Bt. (1784)

Duthie, Prof. Sir Herbert Livingston, Kt.

Duthie, Sir Robert Grieve (Robin), Kt., CBE

Dyer, Prof. Sir (Henry) Peter (Francis) Swinnerton-, Bt., KBE, FRS (1678)

Dyke, Sir David William Hart, Bt. (1677)

Dyson, Hon. Sir John Anthony, Kt.

Eady, Hon. Sir David, Kt.

Earle, Sir (Hardman) George (Algernon), Bt. (1869)

East, Sir (Lewis) Ronald, Kt., CBE

Easton, Sir Robert William Simpson, Kt., CBE

Eaton, Adm. Sir Kenneth John, GBE, KCB

Eberle, Adm. Sir James Henry Fuller, GCB

Ebrahim, Sir (Mahomed) Currimbhoy, Bt. (1910)

Echlin, Sir Norman David Fenton, Bt. (I. 1721)

Eckersley, Sir Donald Payze, Kt., OBE

Edge, Capt. Sir (Philip) Malcolm, KCVO

†Edge, Sir William, Bt. (1937)

Edmonstone, Sir Archibald Bruce Charles, Bt. (1774)

Edwardes, Sir Michael Owen, Kt.

Edwards, Sir Christopher John Churchill, Bt. (1866)

Edwards, Sir George Robert, Kt., OM, CBE, FRS, FEng.

Edwards, Sir (John) Clive (Leighton), Bt. (1921)

Edwards, Sir Llewellyn Roy, Kt.

Edwards, Prof. Sir Samuel Frederick, Kt., FRS

Egan, Sir John Leopold, Kt.

Egerton, Sir John Alfred Roy, Kt.

Egerton, Sir (Philip) John (Caledon) Grey-, Bt. (1617)

Egerton, Sir Stephen Loftus, KCMG

Eggleston, Hon. Sir Richard Moulton, Kt.

Eichelbaum, Rt. Hon. Sir Thomas, GBE

Eliott of Stobs, Sir Charles Joseph Alexander, Bt. (s. 1666)

Ellerton, Sir Geoffrey James, Kt., CMG, MBE

Elliot, Sir Gerald Henry, Kt.

Elliott, Sir Clive Christopher Hugh, Bt. (1917)

Elliott, Sir David Murray, KCMG, CB

Elliott, Prof. Sir John Huxtable, Kt., FBA

Elliott, Sir Randal Forbes, KBE

Elliott, Prof. Sir Roger James, Kt., FRS

Elliott, Sir Ronald Stuart, Kt.

Ellis, Sir Ronald, Kt., FEng.

Ellison, Col. Sir Ralph Harry Carr-, Kt., TD

Elphinstone, Sir John, Bt. (s. 1701)

Elphinstone, Sir John Howard Main, Bt. (1816)

Elton, Sir Arnold, Kt., CBE

Elton, Sir Charles Abraham Grierson, Bt. (1717)

Elwes, Sir Jeremy Vernon, Kt., CBE

Elwood, Sir Brian George Conway, Kt., CBE

Elworthy, Sir Peter Herbert, Kt.

Elyan, Sir (Isadore) Victor, Kt.

Emery, Rt. Hon. Sir Peter Frank Hannibal, Kt., MP

Engineer, Sir Noshirwan Phirozshah, Kt.

Engle, Sir George Lawrence Jose, KCB, QC

English, Sir Terence Alexander Hawthorne, KBE, FRCS

Epstein, Prof. Sir (Michael) Anthony, Kt., CBE, FRS

Ereaut, Sir (Herbert) Frank Cobbold, Kt.

Errington, Col. Sir Geoffrey Frederick, Bt., OBE (1963)

Errington, Sir Lancelot, KCB

Erskine, Sir (Thomas) David, Bt. (1821)

Esmonde, Sir Thomas Francis Grattan, Bt. (I. 1629)

Espie, Sir Frank Fletcher, Kt., OBE

Esplen, Sir John Graham, Bt. (1921)

Eustace, Sir Joseph Lambert, GCMG, GCVO

Evans, Sir Anthony Adney, Bt. (1920)

Evans, Rt. Hon. Sir Anthony Howell Meurig, Kt., RD

Evans, Air Chief Marshal Sir David George, GCB, CBE

Evans, Air Chief Marshal Sir David Parry-, GCB, CBE

Evans, Hon. Sir Haydn Tudor, Kt.

Evans, Prof. Sir John Grimley, Kt., FRCP

Evans, Sir Richard Harry, Kt., CBE

Evans, Sir Richard Mark, KCMG, KCVO

Evans, Sir Robert, Kt., CBE, FEng.

Evans, Sir (William) Vincent (John), GCMG, MBE, QC

Eveleigh, Rt. Hon. Sir Edward Walter, Kt., ERD

Everard, Sir Robin Charles, Bt. (1911)

Everson, Sir Frederick Charles, KCMG

Every, Sir Henry John Michael, Bt. (1641)

Ewans, Sir Martin Kenneth, KCMG

†Ewart, Sir William Michael, Bt. (1887)

Ewbank, Hon. Sir Anthony Bruce, Kt.

Ewin, Sir (David) Ernest Thomas Floyd, Kt., OBE, LVO

Ewing, Sir Ronald Archibald Orr-, Bt. (1886)

Eyre, Sir Graham Newman, Kt., QC

Eyre, Maj.-Gen. Sir James Ainsworth Campden Gabriel, KCVO, CBE

Eyre, Sir Reginald Edwin, Kt.

Eyre, Sir Richard Charles Hastings, Kt., CBE

Faber, Sir Richard Stanley, KCVO, CMG

Fadahunsi, Sir Joseph Odeleye, KCMG

Fagge, Sir John William Frederick, Bt. (1660)

Fairbairn, Sir (James) Brooke, Bt. (1869)

Fairclough, Sir John Whitaker, Kt., FEng.

Fairgrieve, Sir (Thomas) Russell, Kt., CBE, TD

Fairhall, Hon. Sir Allen, KBE

Fairweather, Sir Patrick Stanislaus, KCMG

Falconer, Hon. Sir Douglas William, Kt., MBE

†Falkiner, Sir Benjamin Simon Patrick, Bt. (I. 1778)

Fall, Sir Brian James Proetel, GCVO, KCMG

Falle, Sir Samuel, KCMG, KCVO, DSC

Fang, Prof. Sir Harry, Kt., CBE

Fareed, Sir Djamil Sheik, Kt.

Frost, Sir Terence Ernest Manitou, Kt., RA
Frost, Hon. Sir (Thomas) Sydney, Kt.
Fry, Sir Peter Derek, Kt.
Fry, Hon. Sir William Gordon, Kt.
Fuchs, Sir Vivian Ernest, Kt., ph.d.
†Fuller, Sir James Henry Fleetwood, Bt. (1910)
Fuller, Hon. Sir John Bryan Munro, Kt.
Fung, Hon. Sir Kenneth Ping-Fan, Kt., CBE
Furness, Sir Stephen Roberts, Bt. (1913)
Gadsden, Sir Peter Drury Haggerston, GBE, FEng.
Gage, Hon. Sir William Marcus, Kt.
Gainsford, Sir Ian Derek, Kt., DDS
Gaius, Rt. Revd Sir Getake, KBE
Gallwey, Sir Philip Frankland Payne-, Bt. (1812)
Gam, Rt. Revd Sir Getake, KBE
Gamble, Sir David Hugh Norman, Bt. (1897)
Gambon, Sir Michael John, Kt., CBE
Garden, Air Marshal Sir Timothy, KCB
Gardiner, Sir George Arthur, Kt.
Gardiner, Sir John Eliot, Kt., CBE
Gardner, Sir Edward Lucas, Kt., QC
†Gardner, Sir Robert Henry Bruce-, Bt. (1945)
Garland, Hon. Sir Patrick Neville, Kt.
Garland, Hon. Sir Ransley Victor, KBE
Garlick, Sir John, KCB
Garner, Sir Anthony Stuart, Kt.
Garnett, Vice-Adm. Sir Ian David Graham, KCB
Garnier, Rear-Adm. Sir John, KCVO, CBE
Garrett, Sir Anthony Peter, Kt., CBE
Garrick, Sir Ronald, Kt., CBE, FEng.
Garrioch, Sir (William) Henry, Kt.
Garrod, Lt.-Gen. Sir (John) Martin Carruthers, KCB, OBE
Garthwaite, Sir (William) Mark (Charles), Bt. (1919)
Gaskell, Sir Richard Kennedy Harvey, Kt.
Gatehouse, Hon. Sir Robert Alexander, Kt.
Geno, Sir Makena Viora, KBE
George, Sir Arthur Thomas, Kt.
George, Prof. Sir Charles Frederick, MD, FRCP
George, Sir Richard William, Kt., CVO
Gerken, Vice-Adm. Sir Robert William Frank, KCB, CBE
Gery, Sir Robert Lucian Wade-, KCMG, KCVO
Gethin, Sir Richard Joseph St Lawrence, Bt. (I. 1665)
Getty, Sir (John) Paul, KBE
Ghurburrun, Sir Rabindrah, Kt.
Gibb, Sir Francis Ross (Frank), Kt., CBE, FEng.
Gibbings, Sir Peter Walter, Kt.
Gibbons, Sir (John) David, KBE

Gibbons, Sir William Edward Doran, Bt. (1752)
Gibbs, Hon. Sir Eustace Hubert Beilby, KCVO, CMG
Gibbs, Rt. Hon. Sir Harry Talbot, GCMG, KBE
Gibbs, Lt.-Col. Sir Peter Evan Wyldbore, KCVO
Gibbs, Sir Roger Geoffrey, Kt.
Gibbs, Field Marshal Sir Roland Christopher, GCB, CBE, DSO, MC
†Gibson, Revd Sir Christopher Herbert, Bt. (1931)
Gibson, Revd Sir David, Bt. (1926)
Gibson, Vice-Adm. Sir Donald Cameron Ernest Forbes, KCB, DSC
Gibson, Rt. Hon. Sir Peter Leslie, Kt.
Gibson, Rt. Hon. Sir Ralph Brian, Kt.
Giddings, Air Marshal Sir (Kenneth Charles) Michael, KCB, OBE, DFC, AFC
Gielgud, Sir (Arthur) John, Kt., OM, CH
Giffard, Sir (Charles) Sydney (Rycroft), KCMG
Gilbert, Air Chief Marshal Sir Joseph Alfred, KCB, CBE
Gilbert, Sir Martin John, Kt., CBE
†Gilbey, Sir Walter Gavin, Bt. (1893)
Giles, Rear-Adm. Sir Morgan Charles Morgan-, Kt., DSO, OBE, GM
Gill, Sir Anthony Keith, Kt., FEng.
Gillam, Sir Patrick John, Kt.
Gillett, Sir Robin Danvers Penrose, Bt., GBE, RD (1959)
Gilmour, Col. Sir Allan Macdonald, KCVO, OBE, MC
Gilmour, Sir John Edward, Bt., DSO, TD (1897)
Gina, Sir Lloyd Maepeza, KBE
Gingell, Air Chief Marshal Sir John, GBE, KCB, KCVO
Girolami, Sir Paul, Kt.
Girvan, Hon. Sir (Frederick) Paul, Kt.
Gladstone, Sir (Erskine) William, Bt. (1846)
Glasspole, Sir Florizel Augustus, GCMG, GCVO
Glen, Sir Alexander Richard, KBE, DSC
Glenn, Sir (Joseph Robert) Archibald, Kt., OBE
Glidewell, Rt. Hon. Sir Iain Derek Laing, Kt.
Glock, Sir William Frederick, Kt., CBE
Glover, Gen. Sir James Malcolm, KCB, MBE
Glover, Sir Victor Joseph Patrick, Kt.
Glyn, Sir Richard Lindsay, Bt. (1759 and 1800)
Goavea, Sir Sinaka Vakai, KBE
Godber, Sir George Edward, GCB, DM
Goff, Sir Robert (William) Davis-, Bt. (1905)
Gold, Sir Arthur Abraham, Kt., CBE
Gold, Sir Joseph, Kt.
Goldberg, Prof. Sir Abraham, Kt., MD, D.SC., FRCP

Goldberg, Prof. Sir David Paul Brandes, Kt.
Goldman, Sir Samuel, KCB
Gombrich, Prof. Sir Ernst Hans Josef, Kt., OM, CBE, ph.D., FBA, FSA
Gooch, Sir (Richard) John Sherlock, Bt. (1746)
Gooch, Sir Trevor Sherlock (Sir Peter), Bt. (1866)
Good, Sir John Kennedy-, KBE
Goodall, Sir (Arthur) David Saunders, GCMG
Goodenough, Sir Anthony Michael, KCMG
Goodenough, Sir William McLernon, Bt. (1943)
Goodhart, Sir Philip Carter, Kt.
Goodhart, Sir Robert Anthony Gordon, Bt. (1911)
Goodhew, Sir Victor Henry, Kt.
Goodison, Sir Alan Clowes, KCMG
Goodison, Sir Nicholas Proctor, Kt.
Goodlad, Rt. Hon. Sir Alastair Robertson, KCMG, MP
Goodman, Sir Patrick Ledger, Kt., CBE
Goodson, Sir Mark Weston Lassam, Bt. (1922)
Goodwin, Sir Matthew Dean, Kt., CBE
Goold, Sir George Leonard, Bt. (1801)
Gordon, Sir Alexander John, Kt., CBE
Gordon, Sir Andrew Cosmo Lewis Duff-, Bt. (1813)
Gordon, Sir Charles Addison Somerville Snowden, KCB
Gordon, Sir Keith Lyndell, Kt., CMG
Gordon, Sir (Lionel) Eldred (Peter) Smith-, Bt. (1838)
Gordon, Sir Robert James, Bt. (s. 1706)
Gordon, Sir Sidney Samuel, Kt., CBE
Gordon Lennox, Lord Nicholas Charles, KCMG, KCVO
†Gore, Sir Nigel Hugh St George, Bt. (I. 1622)
Gorham, Sir Richard Masters, Kt., CBE, DFC
Goring, Sir William Burton Nigel, Bt. (1627)
Gorman, Sir John Reginald, Kt., CVO, CBE, MC
Gorst, Sir John Michael, Kt.
Gorton, Rt. Hon. Sir John Grey, GCMG, CH
Goschen, Sir Edward Christian, Bt., DSO (1916)
Gosling, Sir (Frederick) Donald, Kt.
Goswell, Sir Brian Lawrence, Kt.
Goulden, Sir (Peter) John, KCMG
Goulding, Sir (Ernest) Irvine, Kt.
Goulding, Sir Marrack Irvine, KCMG
Goulding, Sir (William) Lingard Walter, Bt. (1904)
Gourlay, Gen. Sir (Basil) Ian (Spencer), KCB, OBE, MC, RM
Gourlay, Sir Simon Alexander, Kt.
Govan, Sir Lawrence Herbert, Kt.
Gow, Gen. Sir (James) Michael, GCB

Gowans, Sir James Learmonth, Kt.,
CBE, FRCP, FRS
Graaff, Sir de Villiers, Bt., MBE (1911)
Grabham, Sir Anthony Henry, Kt.
Graham, Sir Alexander Michael, GBE
Graham, Sir James Bellingham, Bt.
(1662)
Graham, Sir James Fergus Surtees,
Bt. (1783)
Graham, Sir James Thompson, Kt.,
CMG
Graham, Sir John Alexander Noble,
Bt., GCMG (1906)
Graham, Sir John Moodie, Bt. (1964)
Graham, Sir Norman William, Kt.,
CB
Graham, Sir Peter, KCB, QC
Graham, Sir Peter Alfred, Kt., OBE
Graham, *Lt.-Gen.* Sir Peter Walter,
KCB, CBE
†Graham, Sir Ralph Stuart, Bt. (1629)
Graham, *Hon.* Sir Samuel Horatio,
Kt., CMG, OBE
Grandy, *Marshal of the Royal Air Force*
Sir John, GCB, GCVO, KBE, DSO
Grant, Sir Archibald, Bt. (s. 1705)
Grant, Sir Clifford, Kt.
Grant, Sir (John) Anthony, Kt.
Grant, Sir (Matthew) Alistair, Kt.
Grant, Sir Patrick Alexander
Benedict, Bt. (s. 1688)
Gray, Sir John Archibald Browne,
Kt., SC.D., FRS
Gray, Sir John Walton David, KBE,
CMG
Gray, *Lt.-Gen.* Sir Michael Stuart,
KCB, OBE
Gray, Sir Robert McDowall (Robin),
Kt.
Gray, Sir William Hume, Bt. (1917)
Gray, Sir William Stevenson, Kt.
Graydon, *Air Chief Marshal* Sir
Michael James, GCB, CBE
Grayson, Sir Jeremy Brian Vincent
Harrington, Bt. (1922)
Green, Sir Allan David, KCB, QC
Green, Sir Andrew Fleming, KCMG
Green, *Hon.* Sir Guy Stephen
Montague, KBE
Green, Sir Kenneth, Kt.
Green, Sir Owen Whitley, Kt.
†Green, Sir Stephen Lycett, Bt., TD
(1886)
Greenaway, Sir John Michael
Burdick, Bt. (1933)
Greenbury, Sir Richard, Kt.
Greene, Sir (John) Brian Massy-, Kt.
Greengross, Sir Alan David, Kt.
Greening, *Rear-Adm.* Sir Paul
Woollven, GCVO
Greenstock, Sir Jeremy Quentin,
KCMG
Greenwell, Sir Edward Bernard, Bt.
(1906)
Gregson, Sir Peter Lewis, GCB
Greig, Sir (Henry Louis) Carron,
KCVO, OBE
Grenside, Sir John Peter, Kt., CBE
Grey, Sir Anthony Dysart, Bt. (1814)

Grierson, Sir Michael John Bewes,
Bt. (s. 1685)
Grierson, Sir Ronald Hugh, Kt.
Griffin, *Maj.* Sir (Arthur) John
(Stewart), KCVO
Griffin, Sir (Charles) David, Kt., CBE
Griffiths, Sir Eldon Wylie, Kt.
Griffiths, Sir John Norton-, Bt.
(1922)
Grimwade, Sir Andrew Sheppard,
Kt., CBE
Grindrod, *Most Revd* John Basil
Rowland, KBE
Grinstead, Sir Stanley Gordon, Kt.
Grose, *Vice-Adm.* Sir Alan, KBE
Grossart, Sir Angus McFarlane
McLeod, Kt., CBE
Grotrian, Sir Philip Christian Brent,
Bt. (1934)
Grove, Sir Charles Gerald, Bt. (1874)
Grove, Sir Edmund Frank, KCVO
Grugeon, Sir John Drury, Kt.
Grylls, Sir (William) Michael (John),
Kt.
Guinness, Sir Alec, Kt., CH, CBE
Guinness, Sir Howard Christian
Sheldon, Kt., VRD
Guinness, Sir Kenelm Ernest Lee, Bt.
(1867)
Guise, Sir John Grant, Bt. (1783)
Gull, Sir Rupert William Cameron,
Bt. (1872)
Gumbs, Sir Emile Rudolph, Kt.
Gunn, *Prof.* Sir John Currie, Kt., CBE
Gunn, Sir Robert Norman, Kt.
Gunn, Sir William Archer, KBE, CMG
†Gunning, Sir Charles Theodore, Bt.
(1778)
Gunston, Sir John Wellesley, Bt.
(1938)
Gurdon, *Prof.* Sir John Bertrand, Kt.,
D.phil., FRS
Guthrie, *Gen.* Sir Charles Ronald
Llewelyn, GCB, LVO, OBE
Guthrie, Sir Malcolm Connop, Bt.
(1936)
Guy, *Gen.* Sir Roland Kelvin, GCB,
CBE, DSO
Habakkuk, Sir John Hrothgar, Kt.,
FBA
Hadfield, Sir Ronald, Kt., QPM
Hadlee, Sir Richard John, Kt., MBE
Hadley, Sir Leonard Albert, Kt.
Hague, *Prof.* Sir Douglas Chalmers,
Kt., CBE
Halberg, Sir Murray Gordon, Kt.,
MBE
Hale, *Prof.* Sir John Rigby, Kt.
Hall, Sir Arnold Alexander, Kt., FRS,
FEng.
Hall, Sir Basil Brodribb, KCB, MC, TD
Hall, *Air Marshal* Sir Donald Percy,
KCB, CBE, AFC
Hall, Sir Douglas Basil, Bt., KCMG
(s. 1687)
Hall, Sir Ernest, Kt., OBE
Hall, Sir (Frederick) John (Frank),
Bt. (1923)
Hall, Sir John, Kt.
Hall, Sir John Bernard, Bt. (1919)

Hall, Sir Peter Edward, KBE, CMG
Hall, *Prof.* Sir Peter Geoffrey, Kt., FBA
Hall, Sir Peter Reginald Frederick,
Kt., CBE
Hall, Sir Robert de Zouche, KCMG
Hall, *Brig.* Sir William Henry, KBE,
DSO, ED
Halliday, *Vice-Adm.* Sir Roy William,
KBE, DSC
Halpern, Sir Ralph Mark, Kt.
Halsey, *Revd* Sir John Walter Brooke,
Bt. (1920)
Halstead, Sir Ronald, Kt., CBE
Ham, Sir David Kenneth Rowe-, GBE
Hambling, Sir (Herbert) Hugh, Bt.
(1924)
Hamburger, Sir Sidney Cyril, Kt.,
CBE
Hamer, *Hon.* Sir Rupert James,
KCMG, ED
Hamill, Sir Patrick, Kt., QPM
Hamilton, *Rt. Hon.* Sir Archibald
Gavin, Kt., MP
Hamilton, Sir Edward Sydney, Bt.
(1776 and 1819)
Hamilton, Sir James Arnot, KCB, MBE,
FEng.
Hamilton, Sir Malcolm William
Bruce Stirling-, Bt. (s. 1673)
Hamilton, Sir Michael Aubrey, Kt.
Hamilton, Sir (Robert Charles)
Richard Caradoc, Bt. (s. 1646)
Hammett, *Hon.* Sir Clifford James,
Kt.
Hammick, Sir Stephen George, Bt.
(1834)
Hampel, Sir Ronald Claus, Kt.
Hampshire, Sir Stuart Newton, Kt.,
FBA
Hampson, Sir Stuart, Kt.
Hampton, Sir (Leslie) Geoffrey, Kt.
Hancock, Sir David John Stowell,
KCB
Hancock, *Air Marshal* Sir Valston
Eldridge, KCB, CB, DFC
Hand, *Most Revd* Geoffrey David,
KBE
Handley, Sir David John
Davenport-, Kt., OBE
Hanham, Sir Michael William, Bt.,
DFC (1667)
Hanley, *Rt. Hon.* Sir Jeremy James,
KCMG
Hanley, Sir Michael Bowen, KCB
Hanmer, Sir John Wyndham
Edward, Bt. (1774)
Hann, Sir James, Kt., CBE
Hannam, Sir John Gordon, Kt.
Hannay, Sir David Hugh Alexander,
GCMG
Hanson, Sir (Charles) Rupert
(Patrick), Bt. (1918)
Hanson, Sir John Gilbert, KCMG, CBE
Hardcastle, Sir Alan John, Kt.
Hardie, Sir Douglas Fleming, Kt.,
CBE
Harding, Sir Christopher George
Francis, Kt.
Harding, Sir George William, KCMG,
CVO

Harding, *Marshal of the Royal Air Force* Sir Peter Robin, GCB

Harding, Sir Roy Pollard, Kt., CBE

Hardman, Sir Henry, KCB

Hardy, Sir David William, Kt.

Hardy, Sir James Gilbert, Kt., OBE

Hardy, Sir Richard Charles Chandos, Bt. (1876)

Hare, Sir David, Kt., FRSL

Hare, Sir Philip Leigh, Bt. (1818)

Harford, Sir (John) Timothy, Bt. (1934)

Hargroves, *Brig.* Sir Robert Louis, Kt., CBE

Harington, *Gen.* Sir Charles Henry Pepys, GCB, CBE, DSO, MC

Harington, Sir Nicholas John, Bt. (1611)

Harland, *Air Marshal* Sir Reginald Edward Wynyard, KBE, CB

Harley, *Gen.* Sir Alexander George Hamilton, KBE, CB

Harman, *Gen.* Sir Jack Wentworth, GCB, OBE, MC

Harman, *Hon.* Sir Jeremiah LeRoy, Kt.

Harman, Sir John Andrew, Kt.

Harmsworth, Sir Hildebrand Harold, Bt. (1922)

Harpham, Sir William, KBE, CMG

Harris, *Prof.* Sir Alan James, Kt., CBE, FEng.

Harris, *Prof.* Sir Henry, Kt., FRCP, FRCPath., FRS

Harris, *Lt.-Gen.* Sir Ian Cecil, KBE, CB, DSO

Harris, Sir Jack Wolfred Ashford, Bt. (1932)

Harris, *Air Marshal* Sir John Hulme, KCB, CBE

Harris, Sir William Gordon, KBE, CB, FEng.

Harrison, Sir David, Kt., CBE, FEng.

Harrison, *Prof.* Sir Donald Frederick Norris, Kt., FRCS

Harrison, Sir Ernest Thomas, Kt., OBE

Harrison, Sir Francis Alexander Lyle, Kt., MBE, QC

Harrison, *Surgeon Vice-Adm.* Sir John Albert Bews, KBE

Harrison, *Hon.* Sir (John) Richard, Kt., ED

Harrison, *Hon.* Sir Michael Guy Vicat, Kt.

Harrison, Sir Michael James Harwood, Bt. (1961)

Harrison, *Prof.* Sir Richard John, Kt., FRS

Harrison, Sir (Robert) Colin, Bt. (1922)

Harrison, Sir Terence, Kt., FEng

Harrop, Sir Peter John, KCB

Hart, Sir Graham Allan, KCB

Hart, *Hon.* Sir Michael Christopher Campbell, Kt.

Hartopp, *Lt. Cdr* Sir Kenneth Alston Cradock-, Bt., MBE, DSC (1796)

Hartwell, Sir (Francis) Anthony Charles Peter, Bt. (1805)

Harvey, Sir Charles Richard Musgrave, Bt. (1933)

Harvie, Sir John Smith, Kt., CBE

Haselhurst, Sir Alan Gordon Barraclough, Kt., MP

Haskard, Sir Cosmo Dugal Patrick Thomas, KCMG, MBE

Haslam, *Hon.* Sir Alec Leslie, Kt.

Haslam, *Rear-Adm.* Sir David William, KBE, CB

Hassett, *Gen.* Sir Francis George, KBE, CB, DSO, LVO

Hastings, Sir Stephen Lewis Edmonstone, Kt., MC

Hatty, *Hon.* Sir Cyril James, Kt.

Haughton, Sir James, Kt., CBE, QPM

Havelock, Sir Wilfrid Bowen, Kt.

Hawkins, Sir Arthur Ernest, Kt.

†Hawkins, Sir Howard Caesar, Bt. (1778)

Hawkins, Sir Paul Lancelot, Kt., TD

Hawley, Sir Donald Frederick, KCMG, MBE

†Hawley, Sir Henry Nicholas, Bt. (1795)

Haworth, Sir Philip, Bt. (1911)

Hawthorne, *Prof.* Sir William Rede, Kt., CBE, SC.D., FRS, FEng.

Hay, Sir David Osborne, Kt., CBE, DSO

Hay, Sir David Russell, Kt., CBE, FRCP, MD

Hay, Sir Hamish Grenfell, Kt.

Hay, Sir James Brian Dalrymple-, Bt. (1798)

Hay, Sir John Erroll Audley, Bt. (s. 1663)

†Hay, Sir Ronald Frederick Hamilton, Bt. (s. 1703)

Haydon, Sir Walter Robert, KCMG

Hayes, Sir Brian, Kt., CBE, QPM

Hayes, Sir Brian David, GCB

Hayes, *Vice-Adm.* Sir John Osier Chattock, KCB, OBE

Hayr, *Air Marshal* Sir Kenneth William, KCB, KBE, AFC

Hayward, Sir Anthony William Byrd, Kt.

Hayward, Sir Jack Arnold, Kt., OBE

Haywood, Sir Harold, KCVO, OBE

Head, Sir Francis David Somerville, Bt. (1838)

Healey, Sir Charles Edward Chadwyck-, Bt. (1919)

Heap, Sir Peter William, KCMG

Hearne, Sir Graham James, Kt., CBE

Heath, *Rt. Hon.* Sir Edward Richard George, KG, MBE, MP

Heath, Sir Mark Evelyn, KCVO, CMG

Heathcote, *Brig.* Sir Gilbert Simon, Bt., CBE (1733)

Heathcote, Sir Michael Perryman, Bt. (1733)

Heatley, Sir Peter, Kt., CBE

Heaton, Sir Yvo Robert Henniker-, Bt. (1912)

Heiser, Sir Terence Michael, GCB

Hellaby, Sir (Frederick Reed) Alan, Kt.

Henderson, Sir Denys Hartley, Kt.

Henderson, Sir (John) Nicholas, GCMG, KCVO

Henderson, Sir William MacGregor, Kt., D.SC., FRS

Henley, Sir Douglas Owen, KCB

Henley, *Rear-Adm.* Sir Joseph Charles Cameron, KCVO, CB

Hennessy, Sir James Patrick Ivan, KBE, CMG

†Henniker, Sir Adrian Chandos, Bt. (1813)

Henry, Sir Denis Aynsley, Kt., OBE, QC

Henry, *Rt. Hon.* Sir Denis Robert Maurice, Kt.

Henry, *Hon.* Sir Geoffrey Arama, KBE

Henry, Sir Patrick Denis, Bt. (1923)

Henry, *Hon.* Sir Trevor Ernest, Kt.

Hepburn, Sir John Alastair Trant Kidd Buchan-, Bt. (1815)

Herbecq, Sir John Edward, KCB

Herbert, *Adm.* Sir Peter Geoffrey Marshall, KCB, OBE

Hermon, Sir John Charles, Kt., OBE, QPM

Heron, Sir Conrad Frederick, KCB, OBE

Heron, Sir Michael Gilbert, Kt.

Hervey, Sir Roger Blaise Ramsay, KCVO, CMG

Heseltine, *Rt. Hon.* Sir William Frederick Payne, GCB, GCVO

Hetherington, Sir Arthur Ford, Kt., DSC, FEng.

Hetherington, Sir Thomas Chalmers, KCB, CBE, TD, QC

Hewetson, Sir Christopher Raynor, Kt., TD

Hewett, Sir Peter John Smithson, Bt., MM (1813)

Hewitt, Sir (Cyrus) Lenox (Simson), Kt., OBE

Hewitt, Sir Nicholas Charles Joseph, Bt. (1921)

Heygate, Sir Richard John Gage, Bt. (1831)

Heyman, Sir Horace William, Kt.

Heywood, Sir Peter, Bt. (1838)

Hezlet, *Vice-Adm.* Sir Arthur Richard, KBE, CB, DSO, DSC

Hibbert, Sir Jack, KCB

Hibbert, Sir Reginald Alfred, GCMG

Hickey, Sir Justin, Kt.

Hickman, Sir (Richard) Glenn, Bt. (1903)

Hicks, Sir Robert, Kt.

Hidden, *Hon.* Sir Anthony Brian, Kt.

Hielscher, Sir Leo Arthur, Kt.

Higgins, *Hon.* Sir Malachy Joseph, Kt.

Higginson, Sir Gordon Robert, Kt., PH.D., FEng.

Hill, Sir Alexander Rodger Erskine-, Bt. (1945)

Hill, Sir Arthur Alfred, Kt., CBE

Hill, Sir Brian John, Kt.

Hill, Sir James Frederick, Bt. (1917)

Hill, Sir John McGregor, Kt., PH.D., FEng.

Hill, Sir John Maxwell, Kt., CBE, DFC

†Hill, Sir John Rowley, Bt. (I. 1779)
Hill, *Vice-Adm.* Sir Robert Charles Finch, KBE, FEng.
Hill, Sir (Stanley) James (Allen), Kt.
Hillary, Sir Edmund, KG, KBE
Hillhouse, Sir (Robert) Russell, KCB
Hills, Sir Graham John, Kt.
Hine, *Air Chief Marshal* Sir Patrick Bardon, GCB, GBE
Hines, Sir Colin Joseph, Kt., OBE
Hirsch, *Prof.* Sir Peter Bernhard, Kt., PH.D., FRS
Hirst, *Rt. Hon.* Sir David Cozens-Hardy, Kt.
Hirst, Sir Michael William, Kt.
Hoare, Sir Peter Richard David, Bt. (1786)
Hoare, Sir Timothy Edward Charles, Bt., OBE (I. 1784)
Hobart, Sir John Vere, Bt. (1914)
Hobbs, *Maj.-Gen.* Sir Michael Frederick, KCVO, CBE
Hobday, Sir Gordon Ivan, Kt.
Hobhouse, Sir Charles John Spinney, Bt. (1812)
Hobhouse, *Rt. Hon.* Sir John Stewart, Kt.
Hockaday, Sir Arthur Patrick, KCB, CMG
Hockley, *Gen.* Sir Anthony Heritage Farrar-, GBE, KCB, DSO, MC
Hoddinott, Sir John Charles, Kt., CBE, QPM
†Hodge, Sir Andrew Rowland, Bt. (1921)
Hodge, Sir James William, KCVO, CMG
Hodge, Sir Julian Stephen Alfred, Kt.
Hodges, *Air Chief Marshal* Sir Lewis MacDonald, KCB, CBE, DSO, DFC
Hodgkin, *Prof.* Sir Alan Lloyd, OM, KBE, FRS, SC.D.
Hodgkin, Sir Gordon Howard Eliot, Kt., CBE
Hodgkinson, *Air Chief Marshal* Sir (William) Derek, KCB, CBE, DFC, AFC
Hodgson, Sir Maurice Arthur Eric, Kt., FEng.
Hodgson, *Hon.* Sir (Walter) Derek (Thornley), Kt.
Hodson, Sir Michael Robin Adderley, Bt. (I. 1789)
Hoffenberg, *Prof.* Sir Raymond, KBE
Hogg, Sir Christopher Anthony, Kt.
Hogg, Sir Edward William Lindsay-, Bt. (1905)
Hogg, *Vice-Adm.* Sir Ian Leslie Trower, KCB, DSC
Hogg, Sir John Nicholson, Kt., TD
Hogg, Sir Michael David, Bt. (1846)
Holcroft, Sir Peter George Culcheth, Bt. (1921)
Holden, Sir Edward, Bt. (1893)
Holden, Sir John David, Bt. (1919)
Holder, Sir John Henry, Bt. (1898)
Holder, *Air Marshal* Sir Paul Davie, KBE, CB, DSO, DFC, PH.D.

Holdgate, Sir Martin Wyatt, Kt., CB, PH.D.
Holland, *Hon.* Sir Alan Douglas, Kt.
Holland, *Hon.* Sir Christopher John, Kt.
Holland, Sir Clifton Vaughan, Kt.
Holland, Sir Geoffrey, KCB
Holland, Sir Kenneth Lawrence, Kt., CBE, QFSM
Holland, Sir Philip Welsby, Kt.
Holliday, *Prof.* Sir Frederick George Thomas, Kt., CBE, FRSE
Hollings, *Hon.* Sir (Alfred) Kenneth, Kt., MC
Hollis, *Hon.* Sir Anthony Barnard, Kt.
Hollom, Sir Jasper Quintus, KBE
Holloway, *Hon.* Sir Barry Blyth, KBE
Holm, Sir Carl Henry, Kt., OBE
Holm, Sir Ian (Ian Holm Cuthbert), Kt., CBE
Holman, *Hon.* Sir (Edward) James, Kt.
Holmes, *Prof.* Sir Frank Wakefield, Kt.
Holmes, Sir Peter Fenwick, Kt., MC
Holroyd, *Air Marshal* Sir Frank Martyn, KBE, CB, FEng.
Holt, *Prof.* Sir James Clarke, Kt.
Holt, Sir Michael, Kt., CBE
Home, Sir William Dundas, Bt. (S. 1671)
Honeycombe, *Prof.* Sir Robert William Kerr, Kt., FRS, FEng.
Honywood, Sir Filmer Courtenay William, Bt. (1660)
Hood, Sir Harold Joseph, Bt., TD (1922)
Hookway, Sir Harry Thurston, Kt.
Hooper, *Hon.* Sir Anthony, Kt.
Hope, Sir (Charles) Peter, KCMG, TD
Hope, Sir Colin Frederick Newton, Kt.
Hope, *Rt. Revd and Rt. Hon.* David Michael, KCVO
Hope, Sir John Carl Alexander, Bt. (S. 1628)
Hopkin, Sir (William Aylsham) Bryan, Kt., CBE
Hopkins, Sir Anthony Philip, Kt., CBE
Hopkins, Sir Michael John, Kt., CBE, RA, RIBA
Hopwood, *Prof.* Sir David Alan, Kt., FRS
Hordern, *Rt. Hon.* Sir Peter Maudslay, Kt.
Horlick, *Vice-Adm.* Sir Edwin John, KBE, FEng.
Horlick, Sir James Cunliffe William, Bt. (1914)
Horlock, *Prof.* Sir John Harold, Kt., FRS, FEng.
Hornby, Sir Derek Peter, Kt.
Hornby, Sir Simon Michael, Kt.
Horne, Sir Alan Gray Antony, Bt. (1929)
Horsfall, Sir John Musgrave, Bt., MC, TD (1909)
Horsley, *Air Marshal* Sir (Beresford) Peter (Torrington), KCB, CBE, LVO, AFC

†Hort, Sir Andrew Edwin Fenton, Bt. (1767)
Horton, Sir Robert Baynes, Kt.
Hosker, Sir Gerald Albery, KCB, QC
Hoskyns, Sir Benedict Leigh, Bt. (1676)
Hoskyns, Sir John Austin Hungerford Leigh, Kt.
Hotung, Sir Joseph Edward, Kt.
Houghton, Sir John Theodore, Kt., CBE, FRS
†Houldsworth, Sir Richard Thomas Reginald, Bt. (1887)
Hounsfield, Sir Godfrey Newbold, Kt., CBE
Hourston, Sir Gordon Minto, Kt.
House, *Lt.-Gen.* Sir David George, GCB, KCVO, CBE, MC
Houssemayne du Boulay, Sir Roger William, KCVO, CMG
Howard, Sir (Hamilton) Edward de Coucey, Bt., GBE (1955)
Howard, *Prof.* Sir Michael Eliot, Kt., CBE, MC
Howard, *Maj.-Gen.* Lord Michael Fitzalan-, GCVO, CB, CBE, MC
Howard, Sir Walter Stewart, Kt., MBE
Howell, Sir Ralph Frederic, Kt.
Howells, Sir Eric Waldo Benjamin, Kt., CBE
Howlett, *Gen.* Sir Geoffrey Hugh Whitby, KBE, MC
Hoyle, *Prof.* Sir Fred, Kt., FRS
Hoyos, *Hon.* Sir Fabriciano Alexander, Kt.
Huddleston, Most Revd (Ernest Urban) Trevor, KCMG
Hudson, *Lt.-Gen.* Sir Peter, KCB, CBE
Huggins, *Hon.* Sir Alan Armstrong, Kt.
Hughes, *Hon.* Sir Anthony Philip Gilson, Kt.
Hughes, Sir David Collingwood, Bt. (1773)
Hughes, *Prof.* Sir Edward Stuart Reginald, Kt., CBE
Hughes, Sir Jack William, Kt.
Hughes, Sir Trevor Denby Lloyd-, Kt.
Hughes, Sir Trevor Poulton, KCB
Hugo, *Lt.-Col.* Sir John Mandeville, KCVO, OBE
Hull, *Prof.* Sir David, Kt.
Hulse, Sir Edward Jeremy Westrow, Bt. (1739)
Hume, Sir Alan Blyth, Kt., CB
Humphreys, Sir (Raymond Evelyn) Myles, Kt.
Hunn, Sir Jack Kent, Kt., CMG
Hunt, Sir John Leonard, Kt.
Hunt, *Adm.* Sir Nicholas John Streynsham, GCB, LVO
Hunt, Sir Rex Masterman, Kt., CMG
Hunt, Sir Robert Frederick, Kt., CBE, FEng.
Hunter, *Hon.* Sir Alexander Albert, KBE
Hunter, Sir Alistair John, KCMG
Hunter, Sir Ian Bruce Hope, Kt., MBE

Hunter, *Prof.* Sir Laurence Colvin, Kt., CBE, FRSE
Hurn, Sir (Francis) Roger, Kt.
Hurrell, Sir Anthony Gerald, KCVO, CMG
Hurst, Sir Geoffrey Charles, Kt., MBE
Husbands, Sir Clifford Straugh, GCMG
Hutchinson, *Hon.* Sir Ross, Kt., DFC
Hutchinson, *Lt.-Cdr.* Sir (George) Ian Clark, Kt., RN
Hutchison, *Rt. Hon.* Sir Michael, Kt.
Hutchison, Sir Peter Craft, Bt. (1956)
Hutchison, Sir Robert, Bt. (1939)
Huxley, *Prof.* Sir Andrew Fielding, Kt., OM, FRS
Huxtable, *Gen.* Sir Charles Richard, KCB, CBE
Hyatali, *Hon.* Sir Isaac Emanuel, Kt.
Hyslop, Sir Robert John (Robin) Maxwell-, Kt.
Ibbs, Sir (John) Robin, KBE
Imbert, Sir Peter Michael, Kt., QPM
Imray, Sir Colin Henry, KBE, CMG
Ingham, Sir Bernard, Kt.
Ingilby, Sir Thomas Colvin William, Bt. (1866)
Inglis, Sir Brian Scott, Kt.
Inglis of Glencorse, Sir Roderick John, Bt. (s. 1703)
Ingram, Sir James Herbert Charles, Bt. (1893)
Ingram, Sir John Henderson, Kt., CBE
Inkin, Sir Geoffrey David, Kt., OBE
†Innes, Sir David Charles Kenneth Gordon, Bt. (NS 1686)
Innes of Edingight, Sir Malcolm Rognvald, KCVO
Innes, Sir Peter Alexander Berowald, Bt. (s. 1628)
Inniss, *Hon.* Sir Clifford de Lisle, Kt.
Irvine, Sir Donald Hamilton, Kt., CBE, MD, FRCGP
Irving, *Prof.* Sir Miles Horsfall, Kt., MD, FRCS, FRCSE
Isaacs, Sir Jeremy Israel, Kt.
Isham, Sir Ian Vere Gyles, Bt. (1627)
Jack, *Hon.* Sir Alieu Sulayman, Kt.
Jack, Sir David, Kt., CBE, FRS, FRSE
Jack, Sir David Emmanuel, GCMG, MBE
Jackson, *Air Chief Marshal* Sir Brendan James, GCB
Jackson, Sir (John) Edward, KCMG
Jackson, *Lt.-Gen.* Sir Michael David, KCB, CBE
Jackson, Sir Michael Roland, Bt. (1902)
Jackson, Sir Nicholas Fane St George, Bt. (1913)
Jackson, Sir Robert, Bt. (1815)
Jackson, *Gen.* Sir William Godfrey Fothergill, GBE, KCB, MC
Jackson, Sir William Thomas, Bt. (1869)
Jacob, Sir Isaac Hai, Kt., QC
Jacob, *Hon.* Sir Robert Raphael Hayim (Robin), Kt.
Jacobi, Sir Derek George, Kt., CBE
Jacobi, *Dr* Sir James Edward, Kt., OBE

Jacobs, *Hon.* Sir Kenneth Sydney, KBE
Jacobs, Sir Piers, KBE
Jacobs, Sir Wilfred Ebenezer, GCMG, GCVO, OBE, QC
Jacomb, Sir Martin Wakefield, Kt.
Jaffray, Sir William Otho, Bt. (1892)
James, Sir Cynlais Morgan, KCMG
James, Sir Gerard Bowes Kingston, Bt. (1823)
James, Sir John Nigel Courtenay, KCVO, CBE
James, Sir Robert Vidal Rhodes, Kt.
James, Sir Stanislaus Anthony, GCMG, OBE
Jamieson, *Air Marshal* Sir David Ewan, KBE, CB
Jansen, Sir Ross Malcolm, KBE
Janvrin, Sir Robin Berry, KCVO, CB
Jardine of Applegirth, Sir Alexander Maule, Bt. (s. 1672)
Jardine, Sir Andrew Colin Douglas, Bt. (1916)
Jardine, *Maj.* Sir (Andrew) Rupert (John) Buchanan-, Bt., MC (1885)
Jarman, *Prof.* Sir Brian, Kt., OBE
Jarratt, Sir Alexander Anthony, Kt., CB
Jawara, *Hon.* Sir Dawda Kairaba, Kt.
Jay, Sir Antony Rupert, Kt., CVO
Jeewoolall, Sir Ramesh, Kt.
Jefferson, Sir George Rowland, Kt., CBE, FEng.
Jefferson, Sir Mervyn Stewart Dunnington-, Bt. (1958)
Jeffreys, *Prof.* Sir Alec John, Kt., FRS
Jeffries, *Hon.* Sir John Francis, Kt.
Jehangir, Sir Hirji, Bt. (1908)
Jejeebhoy, Sir Rustom, Bt. (1857)
Jenkins, Sir Brian Garton, GBE
Jenkins, Sir Elgar Spencer, Kt., OBE
Jenkins, Sir Michael Nicholas Howard, Kt., OBE
Jenkins, Sir Michael Romilly Heald, KCMG
Jenkinson, Sir John Banks, Bt. (1661)
†Jenks, Sir Maurice Arthur Brian, Bt. (1932)
Jennings, Sir John Southwood, Kt., CBE, FRSE
Jennings, *Prof.* Sir Robert Yewdall, Kt., QC
Jephcott, Sir (John) Anthony, Bt. (1962)
Jessel, Sir Charles John, Bt. (1883)
Jewkes, Sir Gordon Wesley, KCMG
Joel, *Hon.* Sir Asher Alexander, KBE
John, Sir Elton Hercules (Reginald Kenneth Dwight), Kt., CBE
Johns, *Air Chief Marshal* Sir Richard Edward, GCB, CBE, LVO
Johnson, *Rt. Hon.* Sir David Powell Croom-, Kt., DSC, VRD
Johnson, *Gen.* Sir Garry Dene, KCB, OBE, MC
Johnson, Sir John Rodney, KCMG
†Johnson, Sir Patrick Eliot, Bt. (1818)
Johnson, Sir Peter Colpoys Paley, Bt. (1755)
Johnson, *Hon.* Sir Robert Lionel, Kt.
Johnson, Sir Vassel Godfrey, Kt., CBE

Johnston, Sir John Baines, GCMG, KCVO
Johnston, *Lt.-Col.* Sir John Frederick Dame, GCVO, MC
Johnston, *Lt.-Gen.* Sir Maurice Robert, KCB, OBE
Johnston, Sir Thomas Alexander, Bt. (s. 1626)
Johnston, Sir William Robert Patrick Knox- (Sir Robin), Kt., CBE, RD
Johnstone, Sir (George) Richard Douglas, Bt. (s. 1700)
Johnstone, Sir (John) Raymond, Kt., CBE
Jolliffe, Sir Anthony Stuart, GBE
Jones, *Gen.* Sir (Charles) Edward Webb, KCB, CBE
Jones, Sir Christopher Lawrence-, Bt. (1831)
Jones, Sir David Akers-, KBE, CMG
Jones, *Air Marshal* Sir Edward Gordon, KCB, CBE, DSO, DFC
Jones, Sir Ewart Ray Herbert, Kt., D.SC., Ph.D., FRS
Jones, Sir Gordon Pearce, Kt.
Jones, Sir Harry Ernest, Kt., CBE
Jones, Sir (John) Derek Alun-, Kt.
Jones, Sir John Henry Harvey-, Kt., MBE
Jones, Sir John Prichard-, Bt. (1910)
Jones, Sir Keith Stephen, Kt.
Jones, *Hon.* Sir Kenneth George Illtyd, Kt.
Jones, Sir (Owen) Trevor, Kt.
Jones, Sir (Peter) Hugh (Jefferd) Lloyd-, Kt.
Jones, Sir Richard Anthony Lloyd, KCB
Jones, Sir Robert Edward, Kt.
Jones, Sir Simon Warley Frederick Benton, Bt. (1919)
Jones, Sir (Thomas) Philip, Kt., CB
Jones, Sir (William) Emrys, Kt.
Jones, *Hon.* Sir William Lloyd Mars-, Kt., MBE
Jones, Sir Wynn Normington Hugh-, Kt., LVO
†Joseph, *Hon.* Sir James Samuel, Bt. (1943)
Jowitt, *Hon.* Sir Edwin Frank, Kt.
Joyce, *Lt.-Gen.* Sir Robert John Hayman-, KCB, CBE
Judge, *Rt. Hon.* Sir Igor, Kt.
Judge, Sir Paul Rupert, Kt.
Jugnauth, *Rt. Hon.* Sir Anerood, KCMG, QC
Jungius, *Vice-Adm.* Sir James George, KBE
Jupp, *Hon.* Sir Kenneth Graham, Kt., MC
Kaberry, *Hon.* Sir Christopher Donald, Bt. (1960)
Kalms, Sir (Harold) Stanley, Kt.
Kalo, Sir Kwamala, Kt., MBE
Kan Yuet-Keung, Sir, GBE
Kapi, *Hon.* Sir Mari, Kt., CBE
Kaputin, Sir John Rumet, KBE, CMG
Katsina, The Emir of, KBE, CMG
Katz, Sir Bernard, Kt., FRS
Kausimae, Sir David Nanau, KBE

Kavali, Sir Thomas, Kt., OBE
Kawharu, *Prof.* Sir Ian Hugh, Kt.
Kay, *Prof.* Sir Andrew Watt, Kt.
Kay, *Hon.* Sir John William, Kt.
Kay, *Hon.* Sir Maurice Ralph, Kt.
Kaye, Sir Emmanuel, Kt., CBE
Kaye, Sir John Phillip Lister Lister-, Bt. (1812)
Kaye, Sir Paul Henry Gordon, Bt. (1923)
Keane, Sir Richard Michael, Bt. (1801)
Keeble, Sir (Herbert Ben) Curtis, GCMG
Keene, *Hon.* Sir David Wolfe, Kt.
Keith, *Prof.* Sir James, KBE
Kellett, Sir Stanley Charles, Bt. (1801)
Kelly, Sir David Robert Corbett, Kt., CBE
Kelly, *Rt. Hon.* Sir (John William) Basil, Kt.
Kelly, Sir William Theodore, Kt., OBE
Kemball, *Air Marshal* Sir (Richard) John, KCB, CBE
Kemp, Sir (Edward) Peter, KCB
Kenilorea, *Rt. Hon.* Sir Peter, KBE
Kennard, *Lt.-Col.* Sir George Arnold Ford, Bt. (1891)
Kennaway, Sir John Lawrence, Bt. (1791)
Kennedy, Sir Clyde David Allen, Kt.
Kennedy, Sir Francis, KCMG, CBE
Kennedy, *Hon.* Sir Ian Alexander, Kt.
Kennedy, Sir Ludovic Henry Coverley, Kt.
†Kennedy, Sir Michael Edward, Bt., (1836)
Kennedy, *Rt. Hon.* Sir Paul Joseph Morrow, Kt.
Kennedy, *Air Chief Marshal* Sir Thomas Lawrie, GCB, AFC
Kenny, Sir Anthony John Patrick, Kt., D.Phil., D.Litt., FBA
Kenny, *Gen.* Sir Brian Leslie Graham, GCB, CBE
Kent, Sir Harold Simcox, GCB, QC
Kenyon, Sir George Henry, Kt.
Kermode, Sir (John) Frank, Kt., FBA
Kermode, Sir Ronald Graham Quale, KBE
Kerr, *Hon.* Sir Brian Francis, Kt.
Kerr, *Adm.* Sir John Beverley, GCB
Kerr, Sir John Olav, KCMG
Kerr, *Rt. Hon.* Sir Michael Robert Emanuel, Kt.
Kerruish, Sir (Henry) Charles, Kt., OBE
Kerry, Sir Michael James, KCB, QC
Kershaw, Sir (John) Anthony, Kt., MC
Keswick, Sir John Chippendale Lindley, Kt.
Kidd, Sir Robert Hill, KBE, CB
Kikau, *Ratu* Sir Jone Latianara, KBE
Killen, *Hon.* Denis James, KCMG
Killick, Sir John Edward, GCMG
Kimber, Sir Charles Dixon, Bt. (1904)

King, Sir John Christopher, Bt. (1888)
King, *Vice-Adm.* Sir Norman Ross Dutton, KBE
King, Sir Richard Brian Meredith, KCB, MC
King, Sir Wayne Alexander, Bt. (1815)
Kingman, *Prof.* Sir John Frank Charles, Kt., FRS
Kingsland, Sir Richard, Kt., CBE, DFC
Kingsley, Sir Patrick Graham Toler, KCVO
Kinloch, Sir David, Bt. (s. 1686)
Kinloch, Sir David Oliphant, Bt. (1873)
Kipalan, Sir Albert, Kt.
Kirby, *Hon.* Sir Richard Clarence, Kt.
Kirkham, Sir Graham, Kt.
Kirkpatrick, Sir Ivone Elliott, Bt. (s. 1685)
Kirkwood, *Hon.* Sir Andrew Tristram Hammett, Kt.
Kirwan, Sir (Archibald) Laurence Patrick, KCMG, TD
Kitcatt, Sir Peter Julian, Kt., CB
Kitson, *Gen.* Sir Frank Edward, GBE, KCB, MC
Kitson, Sir Timothy Peter Geoffrey, Kt.
Kleinwort, Sir Richard Drake, Bt. (1909)
Klug, Sir Aaron, Kt., OM
Kneller, Sir Alister Arthur, Kt.
Knight, Sir Arthur William, Kt.
Knight, Sir Harold Murray, KBE, DSC
Knight, *Air Chief Marshal* Sir Michael William Patrick, KCB, AFC
Knill, *Prof.* Sir John Lawrence, Kt., FEng.
†Knill, Sir Thomas John Pugin Bartholomew, Bt. (1893)
Knott, Sir John Laurence, Kt., CBE
Knowles, Sir Charles Francis, Bt. (1765)
Knowles, Sir Durward Randolph, Kt., OBE
Knowles, Sir Leonard Joseph, Kt., CBE
Knowles, Sir Richard Marchant, Kt.
Knox, Sir Bryce Muir, KCVO, MC, TD
Knox, Sir David Laidlaw, Kt.
Knox, *Hon.* Sir John Leonard, Kt.
Knox, *Hon.* Sir William Edward, Kt.
Koraea, Sir Thomas, Kt.
Kornberg, *Prof.* Sir Hans Leo, Kt., D.SC., SC.D., ph.D., FRS
Korowi, Sir Wiwa, GCMG
Kroto, *Prof.* Sir Harold Walter, Kt., FRS
Kulukundis, Sir Elias George (Eddie), Kt., OBE
Kurongku, *Most Revd* Peter, KBE
Labouchere, Sir George Peter, GBE, KCMG
Lacon, Sir Edmund Vere, Bt. (1818)
Lacy, Sir Hugh Maurice Pierce, Bt. (1921)
Lacy, Sir John Trend, Kt., CBE
Laddie, *Hon.* Sir Hugh Ian Lang, Kt.

Laidlaw, Sir Christophor Charles Fraser, Kt.
Laing, Sir (John) Martin (Kirby), Kt., CBE
Laing, Sir (John) Maurice, Kt.
Laing, Sir (William) Kirby, Kt., FEng.
Laird, Sir Gavin Harry, Kt., CBE
Lake, Sir (Atwell) Graham, Bt. (1711)
Laker, Sir Frederick Alfred, Kt.
Lakin, Sir Michael, Bt. (1909)
Laking, Sir George Robert, KCMG
Lamb, Sir Albert (Larry), Kt.
Lamb, Sir Albert Thomas, KBE, CMG, DFC
Lambert, Sir Anthony Edward, KCMG
Lambert, Sir John Henry, KCVO, CMG
†Lambert, Sir Peter John Biddulph, Bt. (1711)
Lampl, Sir Frank William, Kt.
Landale, Sir David William Neil, KCVO
Landau, Sir Dennis Marcus, Kt.
Lane, Sir David William Stennis Stuart, Kt.
Lang, *Lt.-Gen.* Sir Derek Boileau, KCB, DSO, MC
Langham, Sir James Michael, Bt. (1660)
Langlands, Sir Robert Alan, Kt.
Langley, *Hon.* Sir Gordon Julian Hugh, Kt.
Langley, *Maj.-Gen.* Sir Henry Desmond Allen, KCVO, MBE
†Langrishe, Sir James Hercules, Bt. (I. 1777)
Lankester, Sir Timothy Patrick, KCB
Lapun, *Hon.* Sir Paul, Kt.
Larcom, Sir (Charles) Christopher Royde, Bt. (1868)
Large, Sir Andrew McLeod Brooks, Kt.
Large, Sir Peter, Kt., CBE
Larmour, Sir Edward Noel, KCMG
Lasdun, Sir Denys Louis, Kt., CH, CBE, FRIBA
Latey, *Rt. Hon.* Sir John Brinsmead, Kt., MBE
Latham, *Hon.* Sir David Nicholas Ramsey, Kt.
Latham, Sir Michael Anthony, Kt.
Latham, Sir Richard Thomas Paul, Bt. (1919)
Latimer, Sir (Courtenay) Robert, Kt., CBE
Latimer, Sir Graham Stanley, KBE
Lauder, Sir Piers Robert Dick-, Bt. (s. 1690)
Laughton, Sir Anthony Seymour, Kt.
Laurantus, Sir Nicholas, Kt., MBE
Laurence, Sir Peter Harold, KCMG, MC
Laurie, Sir Robert Bayley Emilius, Bt. (1834)
Lauterpacht, Sir Elihu, Kt., CBE, QC
Lauti, *Rt. Hon.* Sir Toaripi, GCMG
Lavan, *Hon.* Sir John Martin, Kt.
Law, *Adm.* Sir Horace Rochfort, GCB, OBE, DSC
Lawes, Sir (John) Michael Bennet, Bt. (1882)

Lawler, Sir Peter James, Kt., OBE
Lawrence, Sir David Roland Walter, Bt. (1906)
Lawrence, Sir Guy Kempton, Kt., DSO, OBE, DFC
Lawrence, Sir Ivan John, Kt., QC
Lawrence, Sir John Patrick Grosvenor, Kt., CBE
Lawrence, Sir John Waldemar, Bt., OBE (1858)
Lawrence, Sir William Fettiplace, Bt. (1867)
Laws, *Hon.* Sir John Grant McKenzie, Kt.
Lawson, Sir Christopher Donald, Kt.
Lawson, *Col.* Sir John Charles Arthur Digby, Bt., DSO, MC (1900)
Lawson, Sir John Philip Howard-, Bt. (1841)
Lawson, *Gen.* Sir Richard George, KCB, DSO, OBE
Lawton, *Prof.* Sir Frank Ewart, Kt.
Lawton, *Rt. Hon.* Sir Frederick Horace, Kt.
Layard, *Adm.* Sir Michael Henry Gordon, KCB, CBE
Layfield, Sir Frank Henry Burland Willoughby, Kt., QC
Lea, *Vice-Adm.* Sir John Stuart Crosbie, KBE
Lea, Sir Thomas William, Bt. (1892)
Leach, *Admiral of the Fleet* Sir Henry Conyers, GCB
Leahy, Sir Daniel Joseph, Kt.
Leahy, Sir John Henry Gladstone, KCMG
Learmont, *Gen.* Sir John Hartley, KCB, CBE
Leask, *Lt.-Gen.* Sir Henry Lowther Ewart Clark, KCB, DSO, OBE
Leather, Sir Edwin Hartley Cameron, KCMG, KCVO
Leaver, Sir Christopher, GBE
Le Bailly, *Vice-Adm.* Sir Louis Edward Stewart Holland, KBE, CB
Le Cheminant, *Air Chief Marshal* Sir Peter de Lacey, GBE, KCB, DFC
Lechmere, Sir Berwick Hungerford, Bt. (1818)
Lee, Sir Arthur James, KBE, MC
Lee, *Air Chief Marshal* Sir David John Pryer, GBE, CB
Lee, *Brig.* Sir Leonard Henry, Kt., CBE
Lee, Sir Quo-wei, Kt., CBE
Leeds, Sir Christopher Anthony, Bt. (1812)
Lees, Sir David Bryan, Kt.
Lees, Sir Thomas Edward, Bt. (1897)
Lees, Sir Thomas Harcourt Ivor, Bt. (1804)
Lees, Sir (William) Antony Clare, Bt. (1937)
Leese, Sir John Henry Vernon, Bt. (1908)
Le Fanu, *Maj.* Sir (George) Victor (Sheridan), KCVO
le Fleming, Sir David Kelland, Bt. (1705)
Legard, Sir Charles Thomas, Bt. (1660)

Legg, Sir Thomas Stuart, KCB, QC
Leggatt, *Rt. Hon.* Sir Andrew Peter, Kt.
Leggatt, Sir Hugh Frank John, Kt.
Leggett, Sir Clarence Arthur Campbell, Kt., MBE
Leigh, Sir Geoffrey Norman, Kt.
Leigh, Sir Richard Henry, Bt. (1918)
Leighton, Sir Michael John Bryan, Bt. (1693)
Leitch, Sir George, KCB, OBE
Leith, Sir Andrew George Forbes-, Bt. (1923)
Le Marchant, Sir Francis Arthur, Bt. (1841)
Lemon, Sir (Richard) Dawnay, Kt., CBE
Leng, *Gen.* Sir Peter John Hall, KCB, MBE, MC
Lennard, *Revd* Sir Hugh Dacre Barrett-, Bt. (1801)
Leon, Sir John Ronald, Bt. (1911)
Leonard, *Rt. Revd and Rt. Hon.* Graham Douglas, KCVO
Leonard, *Hon.* Sir (Hamilton) John, Kt.
Lepping, Sir George Geria Dennis, GCMG, MBE
Le Quesne, Sir (Charles) Martin, KCMG
Le Quesne, Sir (John) Godfray, Kt., QC
Leslie, Sir Colin Alan Bettridge, Kt.
Leslie, Sir John Norman Ide, Bt. (1876)
†Leslie, Sir (Percy) Theodore, Bt. (s. 1625)
Leslie, Sir Peter Evelyn, Kt.
Lester, Sir James Theodore, Kt.
Lethbridge, Sir Thomas Periam Hector Noel, Bt. (1804)
Lever, Sir Paul, KCMG
Lever, Sir (Tresham) Christopher Arthur Lindsay, Bt. (1911)
Levey, Sir Michael Vincent, Kt., LVO
Levine, Sir Montague Bernard, Kt.
Levinge, Sir Richard George Robin, Bt. (I. 1704)
Lewando, Sir Jan Alfred, Kt., CBE
Lewinton, Sir Christopher, Kt.
Lewis, Sir David Courtenay Mansel, KCVO
Lewthwaite, *Brig.* Sir Rainald Gilfrid, Bt., CVO, OBE, MC (1927)
Ley, Sir Ian Francis, Bt. (1905)
Leyland, Sir Philip Vyvyan Naylor-, Bt. (1895)
Lickiss, Sir Michael Gillam, Kt.
Lidderdale, Sir David William Shuckburgh, KCB
Liggins, *Prof.* Sir Graham Collingwood, Kt., CBE, FRS
Lightman, *Hon.* Sir Gavin Anthony, Kt.
Lighton, Sir Thomas Hamilton, Bt. (I. 1791)
Lim, Sir Han-Hoe, Kt., CBE
Limon, Sir Donald William, KCB
Linacre, Sir (John) Gordon (Seymour), Kt., CBE, AFC, DFM

Lindop, Sir Norman, Kt.
Lindsay, Sir James Harvey Kincaid Stewart, Kt.
Lindsay, *Hon.* Sir John Edmund Frederic, Kt.
Lindsay, Sir Ronald Alexander, Bt. (1962)
Lipworth, Sir (Maurice) Sydney, Kt.
Lithgow, Sir William James, Bt. (1925)
Little, *Most Revd* Thomas Francis, KBE
Littler, Sir (James) Geoffrey, KCB
Livesay, *Adm.* Sir Michael Howard, KCB
Llewellyn, Sir Henry Morton, Bt., CBE (1922)
Llewelyn, Sir John Michael Dillwyn-Venables-, Bt. (1890)
Lloyd, *Prof.* Sir Geoffrey Ernest Richard, Kt., FBA
Lloyd, Sir Ian Stewart, Kt.
Lloyd, Sir Nicholas Markley, Kt.
Lloyd, *Rt. Hon.* Sir Peter Robert Cable, Kt., MP
Lloyd, Sir Richard Ernest Butler, Bt. (1960)
Lloyd, *Hon.* Sir Timothy Andrew Wigram, Kt.
Loader, Sir Leslie Thomas, Kt., CBE
Loane, *Most Revd* Marcus Lawrence, KBE
Lobo, Sir Rogerio Hyndman, Kt., CBE
Lock, *Cdr.* Sir (John) Duncan, Kt.
Lockhart, Sir Simon John Edward Francis Sinclair-, Bt. (s. 1636)
Loder, Sir Giles Rolls, Bt. (1887)
Logan, Sir Donald Arthur, KCMG
Logan, Sir Raymond Douglas, Kt.
Lokoloko, Sir Tore, GCMG, GCVO, OBE
Lombe, *Hon.* Sir Edward Christopher Evans-, Kt.
Longmore, *Hon.* Sir Andrew Centlivres, Kt.
Loram, *Vice-Adm.* Sir David Anning, KCB, CVO
Lorimer, Sir (Thomas) Desmond, Kt.
Los, *Hon.* Sir Kubulan, Kt., CBE
Lovell, Sir (Alfred Charles) Bernard, Kt., OBE, FRS
Lovelock, Sir Douglas Arthur, KCB
Loveridge, Sir John Warren, Kt.
Lovill, Sir John Roger, Kt., CBE
Low, Sir Alan Roberts, Kt.
Low, Sir James Richard Morrison-, Bt. (1908)
Lowe, *Air Chief Marshal* Sir Douglas Charles, GCB, DFC, AFC
Lowe, Sir Thomas William Gordon, Bt. (1918)
Lowry, Sir John Patrick, Kt., CBE
Lowson, Sir Ian Patrick, Bt. (1951)
Lowther, *Maj.* Sir Charles Douglas, Bt. (1824)
Lowther, Sir John Luke, KCVO, CBE
Loyd, Sir Francis Alfred, KCMG, OBE
Loyd, Sir Julian St John, KCVO
Lu, Sir Tseng Chi, Kt.
Lucas, Sir Cyril Edward, Kt., CMG, FRS

Lucas, Sir Thomas Edward, Bt. (1887)
Luce, *Rt. Hon.* Sir Richard Napier, Kt.
Lucy, Sir Edmund John William Hugh Cameron-Ramsay-Fairfax, Bt. (1836)
Luddington, Sir Donald Collin Cumyn, KBE, CMG, CVO
Lumsden, Sir David James, Kt.
Lus, *Hon.* Sir Pita, Kt., OBE
Lush, *Hon.* Sir George Hermann, Kt.
Lushington, Sir John Richard Castleman, Bt. (1791)
Luttrell, *Col.* Sir Geoffrey Walter Fownes, KCVO, MC
Lyell, *Rt. Hon.* Sir Nicholas Walter, Kt., QC, MP
Lygo, *Adm.* Sir Raymond Derek, KCB
Lyle, Sir Gavin Archibald, Bt. (1929)
Lyons, Sir Edward Houghton, Kt.
Lyons, Sir James Reginald, Kt.
Lyons, Sir John, Kt.
McAdam, Sir Ian William James, Kt., OBE
McAlpine, Sir William Hepburn, Bt. (1918)
Macara, Sir Alexander Wiseman, Kt., FRCP, FRCGP
†Macara, Sir Hugh Kenneth, Bt. (1911)
Macartney, Sir John Barrington, Bt. (I. 1799)
McAvoy, Sir (Francis) Joseph, Kt., CBE
McCaffrey, Sir Thomas Daniel, Kt.
McCall, Sir (Charles) Patrick Home, Kt., MBE, TD
McCallum, Sir Donald Murdo, Kt., CBE, FEng.
McCamley, Sir Graham Edward, Kt., MBE
McCarthy, *Rt. Hon.* Sir Thaddeus Pearcey, KBE
McCartney, Sir (James) Paul, Kt., MBE
McClellan, *Col.* Sir Herbert Gerard Thomas, Kt., CBE, TD
McClintock, Sir Eric Paul, Kt.
McColl, Sir Colin Hugh Verel, KCMG
McCollum, *Rt. Hon.* Sir William, Kt.
McConnell, Sir Robert Shean, Bt. (1900)
McCorkell, *Col.* Sir Michael William, KCVO, OBE, TD
McCowan, *Rt. Hon.* Sir Anthony James Denys, Kt.
McCowan, Sir Hew Cargill, Bt. (1934)
McCrea, *Prof.* Sir William Hunter, Kt., FRS
McCrindle, Sir Robert Arthur, Kt.
McCullough, *Hon.* Sir (Iain) Charles (Robert), Kt.
MacDermott, *Rt. Hon.* Sir John Clarke, Kt.
McDermott, Sir (Lawrence) Emmet, KBE
MacDonald, *Gen.* Sir Arthur Leslie, KBE, CB

Macdonald of Sleat, Sir Ian Godfrey Bosville, Bt. (s. 1625)
Macdonald, Sir Kenneth Carmichael, KCB
Macdonald, *Vice-Adm.* Sir Roderick Douglas, KBE
McDonald, Sir Tom, Kt., OBE
MacDougall, Sir (George) Donald (Alastair), Kt., CBE, FBA
McDowell, Sir Eric Wallace, Kt., CBE
McDowell, Sir Henry McLorinan, KBE
Mace, *Lt.-Gen.* Sir John Airth, KBE, CB
McEwen, Sir John Roderick Hugh, Bt. (1953)
McFarland, Sir John Talbot, Bt. (1914)
Macfarlane, Sir (David) Neil, Kt.
Macfarlane, Sir George Gray, Kt., CB, FEng.
McFarlane, Sir Ian, Kt.
McGeoch, *Vice-Adm.* Sir Ian Lachlan Mackay, KCB, DSO, DSC
McGrath, Sir Brian Henry, KCVO
Macgregor, Sir Edwin Robert, Bt. (1828)
MacGregor of MacGregor, Sir Gregor, Bt. (1795)
McGregor, Sir Ian Alexander, Kt., CBE, FRS
McGrigor, *Capt.* Sir Charles Edward, Bt. (1831)
McIntosh, *Vice-Adm.* Sir Ian Stewart, KBE, CB, DSO, DSC
McIntosh, Sir Malcolm Kenneth, Kt., ph.D.
McIntosh, Sir Ronald Robert Duncan, KCB
McIntyre, Sir Donald Conroy, Kt., CBE
McIntyre, Sir Meredith Alister, Kt.
MacKay, *Prof.* Sir Donald Iain, Kt., FRSE
McKay, Sir John Andrew, Kt., CBE
Mackechnie, Sir Alistair John, Kt.
McKee, *Maj.* Sir (William) Cecil, Kt., ERD
McKellen, Sir Ian Murray, Kt., CBE
McKenzie, Sir Alexander, KBE
Mackenzie, Sir Alexander Alwyne Henry Charles Brinton Muir-, Bt. (1805)
†Mackenzie, Sir (James William) Guy, Bt. (1890)
Mackenzie, *Gen.* Sir Jeremy John George, GCB, OBE
†Mackenzie, Sir Peter Douglas, Bt. (s. 1673)
†Mackenzie, Sir Roderick McQuhae, Bt. (s. 1703)
McKenzie, Sir Roy Allan, KBE
Mackeson, Sir Rupert Henry, Bt. (1954)
MacKinlay, Sir Bruce, Kt., CBE
McKinnon, Sir James, Kt.
McKinnon, *Hon.* Sir Stuart Neil, Kt.
Mackintosh, Sir Cameron Anthony, Kt.
Macklin, Sir Bruce Roy, Kt., OBE

†Mackworth, Sir Digby John, Bt. (1776)
McLaren, Sir Robin John Taylor, KCMG
†Maclean of Dunconnell, Sir Charles Edward, Bt. (1957)
Maclean, Sir Donald Og Grant, Kt.
McLean, Sir Francis Charles, Kt., CBE
MacLean, *Vice-Adm.* Sir Hector Charles Donald, KBE, CB, DSC
Maclean, Sir Lachlan Hector Charles, Bt. (NS 1631)
Maclean, Sir Robert Alexander, KBE
McLennan, Sir Ian Munro, KCMG, KBE
McLeod, Sir Charles Henry, Bt. (1925)
McLeod, Sir Ian George, Kt.
MacLeod, Sir (John) Maxwell Norman, Bt. (1924)
Macleod, Sir (Nathaniel William) Hamish, KBE
McLintock, Sir Michael William, Bt. (1934)
Maclure, Sir John Robert Spencer, Bt. (1898)
McMahon, Sir Brian Patrick, Bt. (1817)
McMahon, Sir Christopher William, Kt.
Macmillan, Sir (Alexander McGregor) Graham, Kt.
MacMillan, *Lt.-Gen.* Sir John Richard Alexander, KCB, CBE
McMullin, *Rt. Hon.* Sir Duncan Wallace, Kt.
Macnaghten, Sir Patrick Alexander, Bt. (1836)
McNamara, *Air Chief Marshal* Sir Neville Patrick, KBE
Macnaughton, *Prof.* Sir Malcolm Campbell, Kt.
McNee, Sir David Blackstock, Kt., QPM
McNulty, Sir (Robert William) Roy, Kt., CBE
MacPhail, Sir Bruce Dugald, Kt.
Macpherson, Sir Ronald Thomas Steward (Tommy), CBE, MC, TD
Macpherson of Cluny, *Hon.* Sir William Alan, Kt., TD
McQuarrie, Sir Albert, Kt.
MacRae, Sir (Alastair) Christopher (Donald Summerhayes), KCMG
Macrae, *Col.* Sir Robert Andrew Scarth, KCVO, MBE
Macready, Sir Nevil John Wilfrid, Bt. (1923)
Mactaggart, Sir John Auld, Bt. (1938)
Macwhinnie, Sir Gordon Menzies, Kt., CBE
McWilliam, Sir Michael Douglas, KCMG
McWilliams, Sir Francis, GBE, FEng.
Madden, *Adm.* Sir Charles Edward, Bt., GCB (1919)
Maddocks, Sir Kenneth Phipson, KCMG, KCVO
Maddox, Sir John Royden, Kt.
Madel, Sir (William) David, Kt., MP

Madigan, Sir Russel Tullie, Kt., OBE

Magnus, Sir Laurence Henry Philip, Bt. (1917)

Maguire, *Air Marshal* Sir Harold John, KCB, DSO, OBE

Mahon, Sir (John) Denis, Kt., CBE

Mahon, Sir William Walter, Bt. (1819)

Maiden, Sir Colin James, Kt., D.Phil.

Main, Sir Peter Tester, Kt., ERD

Maini, Sir Amar Nath, Kt., CBE

Maino, Sir Charles, KBE

†Maitland, Sir Charles Alexander, Bt. (1818)

Maitland, Sir Donald James Dundas, GCMG, OBE

Makins, Sir Paul Vivian, Bt. (1903)

Malcolm, Sir James William Thomas Alexander, Bt. (s. 1665)

Malet, Sir Harry Douglas St Lo, Bt. (1791)

Mallaby, Sir Christopher Leslie George, GCMG, GCVO

Mallick, *Prof.* Sir Netar Prakash, Kt., FRCP, FRCPed

†Mallinson, Sir William James, Bt. (1935)

Malone, *Hon.* Sir Denis Eustace Gilbert, Kt.

Malpas, Sir Robert, Kt., CBE, FEng

Mamo, Sir Anthony Joseph, Kt., OBE

Mance, *Hon.* Sir Jonathan Hugh, Kt.

Manchester, Sir William Maxwell, KBE

Mander, Sir Charles Marcus, Bt. (1911)

Manduell, Sir John, Kt., CBE

Mann, *Rt. Revd* Michael Ashley, KCVO

Mann, Sir Rupert Edward, Bt. (1905)

Mansel, Sir Philip, Bt. (1622)

Mansfield, *Vice-Adm.* Sir (Edward) Gerard (Napier), KBE, CVO

Mansfield, *Prof.* Sir Peter, Kt., FRS

Mansfield, Sir Philip (Robert Aked), KCMG

Mantell, *Rt. Hon.* Sir Charles Barrie Knight, Kt.

Manton, Sir Edwin Alfred Grenville, Kt.

Manuella, Sir Tulaga, GCMG, MBE

Manzie, Sir (Andrew) Gordon, KCB

Mara, *Rt. Hon. Ratu* Sir Kamisese Kapaiwai Tuimacilai, GCMG, KBE

Margetson, Sir John William Denys, KCMG

Marjoribanks, Sir James Alexander Milne, KCMG

Mark, Sir Robert, GBE

Markham, Sir Charles John, Bt. (1911)

Marking, Sir Henry Ernest, KCVO, CBE, MC

Marling, Sir Charles William Somerset, Bt. (1882)

Marr, Sir Leslie Lynn, Bt. (1919)

Marriner, Sir Neville, Kt., CBE

Marriott, Sir Hugh Cavendish Smith-, Bt. (1774)

Marriott, Sir John Brook, KCVO

†Marsden, Sir Simon Neville Llewelyn, Bt. (1924)

Marshall, Sir Arthur Gregory George, Kt., OBE

Marshall, Sir Denis Alfred, Kt.

Marshall, *Prof.* Sir (Oshley) Roy, Kt., CBE

Marshall, Sir Peter Harold Reginald, KCMG

Marshall, Sir Robert Braithwaite, KCB, MBE

Marshall, Sir (Robert) Michael, Kt.

Martell, *Vice-Adm.* Sir Hugh Colenso, KBE, CB

Martin, Sir George Henry, Kt., CBE

Martin, *Vice-Adm.* Sir John Edward Ludgate, KCB, DSC

Martin, *Prof.* Sir (John) Leslie, Kt., Ph.D.

Martin, *Prof.* Sir Laurence Woodward, Kt.

Martin, Sir (Robert) Bruce, Kt., QC

Marychurch, Sir Peter Harvey, KCMG

Masefield, Sir Charles Beech Gordon, Kt.

Masefield, Sir Peter Gordon, Kt.

Masire, Sir Ketumile, GCMG

Mason, *Hon.* Sir Anthony Frank, KBE

Mason, Sir (Basil) John, Kt., CB, D.SC., FRS

Mason, *Prof.* Sir David Kean, Kt., CBE

Mason, Sir Frederick Cecil, KCVO, CMG

Mason, Sir Gordon Charles, Kt., OBE

Mason, Sir John Charles Moir, KCMG

Mason, Sir John Peter, Kt., CBE

Mason, *Prof.* Sir Ronald, KCB, FRS

Matane, Sir Paulias Nguna, Kt., CMG, OBE

Mather, Sir (David) Carol (Macdonell), Kt., MC

Mather, Sir William Loris, Kt., CVO, OBE, MC, TD

Mathers, Sir Robert William, Kt.

Matheson of Matheson, Sir Fergus John, Bt. (1882)

Matheson, Sir (James Adam) Louis, KBE, CMG, FEng.

Matthews, Sir Peter Alec, Kt.

Matthews, Sir Peter Jack, Kt., CVO, OBE, QPM

Matthews, Sir Stanley, Kt., CBE

Maud, The Hon. Sir Humphrey John Hamilton, KCMG

Mawhinney, *Rt. Hon.* Sir Brian Stanley, Kt., MP

Maxwell, Sir Michael Eustace George, Bt. (s. 1681)

Maxwell, Sir Nigel Mellor Heron-, Bt. (s. 1683)

May, *Rt. Hon.* Sir Anthony Tristram Kenneth, Kt.

May, Sir Kenneth Spencer, Kt., CBE

May, *Prof.* Sir Robert McCredie, Kt., FRS

Maynard, *Hon.* Sir Clement Travelyan, Kt.

Mayne, *Very Revd* Michael Clement Otway, KCVO

Meadow, *Prof.* Sir (Samuel) Roy, Kt., FRCP, FRCPE

Medlycott, Sir Mervyn Tregonwell, Bt. (1808)

Megarry, *Rt. Hon.* Sir Robert Edgar, Kt., FBA

Meinertzhagen, Sir Peter, Kt., CMG

Melhuish, Sir Michael Ramsay, KBE, CMG

Mellon, Sir James, KCMG

Melville, Sir Harry Work, KCB, Ph.D., D.SC., FRS

Melville, Sir Leslie Galfreid, KBE

Melville, Sir Ronald Henry, KCB

Mensforth, Sir Eric, Kt., CBE, F.Eng.

Menter, Sir James Woodham, Kt., Ph.D., SC.D., FRS

Menteth, Sir James Wallace Stuart-, Bt. (1838)

Menzies, Sir Peter Thomson, Kt.

Meyer, Sir Anthony John Charles, Bt. (1910)

Meyer, Sir Christopher John Rome, KCMG

Meyjes, Sir Richard Anthony, Kt.

Meyrick, Sir David John Charlton, Bt. (1880)

Meyrick, Sir George Christopher Cadafael Tapps-Gervis-, Bt. (1791)

Miakwe, *Hon.* Sir Akepa, KBE

Michael, Sir Peter Colin, Kt., CBE

Middleton, Sir Lawrence Monck, Bt. (1662)

Middleton, Sir Peter Edward, GCB

Miers, Sir (Henry) David Alastair Capel, KBE, CMG

Milbank, Sir Anthony Frederick, Bt. (1882)

Milburn, Sir Anthony Rupert, Bt. (1905)

Mildmay, Sir Walter John Hugh St John-, Bt. (1772)

Miles, Sir Peter Tremayne, KCVO

Miles, Sir William Napier Maurice, Bt. (1859)

Millais, Sir Geoffrey Richard Everett, Bt. (1885)

Millar, Sir Oliver Nicholas, GCVO, FBA

Millard, Sir Guy Elwin, KCMG, CVO

Miller, Sir Donald John, Kt., FRSE, FEng.

Miller, Sir Harry Holmes, Bt. (1705)

Miller, Sir Hilary Duppa (Hal), Kt.

Miller, *Lt.-Col.* Sir John Mansel, GCVO, DSO, MC

Miller, Sir (Oswald) Bernard, Kt.

Miller, Sir Peter North, Kt.

Miller, Sir Ronald Andrew Baird, Kt., CBE

Miller of Glenlee, Sir Stephen William Macdonald, Bt. (1788)

Millett, *Rt. Hon.* Sir Peter Julian, Kt.

Millichip, Sir Frederick Albert (Bert), Kt.

Mills, *Vice-Adm.* Sir Charles Piercy, KCB, CBE, DSC

Mills, Sir Frank, KCVO, CMG

Mills, Sir John Lewis Ernest Watts, Kt., CBE

Mills, Sir Peter Frederick Leighton, Bt. (1921)

Milman, *Lt.-Col.* Sir Derek, Bt. (1800)

Milne, Sir John Drummond, Kt.

†Milner, Sir Timothy William Lycett, Bt. (1717)

Mirrlees, *Prof.* Sir James Alexander, Kt., FBA

Mitchell, *Air Cdre* Sir (Arthur) Dennis, KBE, CVO, DFC, AFC

Mitchell, Sir David Bower, Kt.

Mitchell, Sir Derek Jack, KCB, CVO

Mitchell, *Prof.* Sir (Edgar) William John, Kt., CBE, FRS

Mitchell, *Rt. Hon.* Sir James FitzAllen, KCMG

Mitchell, *Very Revd* Patrick Reynolds, KCVO

Mitchell, *Hon.* Sir Stephen George, Kt.

Moate, Sir Roger Denis, Kt.

Mobbs, Sir (Gerald) Nigel, Kt.

Moberly, Sir John Campbell, KBE, CMG

Moberly, Sir Patrick Hamilton, KCMG

Moffat, Sir Brian Scott, Kt., OBE

Moffat, *Lt.-Gen.* Sir (William) Cameron, KBE

Mogg, *Gen.* Sir (Herbert) John, GCB, CBE, DSO

†Moir, Sir Christopher Ernest, Bt. (1916)

Moller, *Hon.* Sir Lester Francis, Kt.

†Molony, Sir Thomas Desmond, Bt. (1925)

Monck, Sir Nicholas Jeremy, KCB

Montgomery, Sir (Basil Henry) David, Bt. (1801)

Montgomery, Sir (William) Fergus, Kt.

Mookerjee, Sir Birendra Nath, Kt.

Moollan, Sir Abdool Hamid Adam, Kt.

Moollan, *Hon.* Sir Cassam (Ismael), Kt.

Moon, Sir Peter Wilfred Giles Graham-, Bt. (1855)

†Moon, Sir Roger, Bt. (1887)

Moore, *Most Revd* Desmond Charles, KBE

Moore, Sir Francis Thomas, Kt.

Moore, Sir Henry Roderick, Kt., CBE

Moore, *Hon.* Sir John Cochrane, Kt.

Moore, *Maj.-Gen.* Sir (John) Jeremy, KCB, OBE, MC

Moore, Sir John Michael, KCVO, CB, DSC

Moore, *Vice Adm.* Sir Michael Antony Claës, KBE, LVO

Moore, *Prof.* Sir Norman Winfrid, Bt. (1919)

Moore, Sir Patrick William Eisdell, Kt., OBE

Moore, Sir William Roger Clotworthy, Bt., TD (1932)

Morauta, Sir Mekere, Kt.

Mordaunt, Sir Richard Nigel Charles, Bt. (1611)

Moreton, Sir John Oscar, KCMG, KCVO, MC

Morgan, *Vice-Adm.* Sir Charles Christopher, KBE

Morgan, *Maj.-Gen.* Sir David John Hughes-, Bt., CB, CBE (1925)

Morgan, Sir John Albert Leigh, KCMG

Morison, *Hon.* Sir Thomas Richard Atkin, Kt.

Morland, *Hon.* Sir Michael, Kt.

Morland, Sir Robert Kenelm, Kt.

Morpeth, Sir Douglas Spottiswoode, Kt., TD

Morris, *Air Marshal* Sir Arnold Alec, KBE, CB, FEng.

Morris, Sir (James) Richard (Samuel), Kt., CBE, FEng.

Morris, Sir Keith Elliot Hedley, KBE, CMG

Morris, *Prof.* Sir Peter John, Kt., FRS

Morris, Sir Robert Byng, Bt. (1806)

Morris, Sir Trefor Alfred, Kt., CBE, QPM

Morris, *Very Revd* Sir William James, KCVO, Ph.D.

Morrison, Sir (Alexander) Fraser, Kt., CBE

Morrison, *Hon.* Sir Charles Andrew, Kt.

Morrison, Sir Howard Leslie, Kt., OBE

Morritt, *Hon.* Sir (Robert) Andrew, Kt., CVO

Morrow, Sir Ian Thomas, Kt.

Morse, Sir Christopher Jeremy, KCMG

Mortimer, Sir John Clifford, Kt., CBE, QC

Morton, *Adm.* Sir Anthony Storrs, GBE, KCB

Morton, Sir (Robert) Alastair (Newton), Kt.

Moseley, Sir George Walker, KCB

Moser, *Prof.* Sir Claus Adolf, KCB, CBE, FBA

Moses, *Hon.* Sir Alan George, Kt.

†Moss, Sir David John Edwards-, Bt. (1868)

Mostyn, *Gen.* Sir (Joseph) David Frederick, KCB, CBE

†Mostyn, Sir William Basil John, Bt. (1670)

Mott, Sir John Harmer, Bt. (1930)

Mottram, Sir Richard Clive, KCB

†Mount, Sir (William Robert) Ferdinand, Bt. (1921)

Mountain, Sir Denis Mortimer, Bt. (1922)

Mowbray, Sir John, Kt.

Mowbray, Sir John Robert, Bt. (1880)

Muir, Sir Laurence Macdonald, Kt.

†Muir, Sir Richard James Kay, Bt. (1892)

Muirhead, Sir David Francis, KCMG, CVO

Mulcahy, Sir Geoffrey John, Kt.

Mullens, *Lt.-Gen.* Sir Anthony Richard Guy, KCB, OBE

Mummery, *Hon.* Sir John Frank, Kt.

Munn, Sir James, Kt., OBE

Munro, Sir Alan Gordon, KCMG

†Munro, Sir Kenneth Arnold William, Bt. (s. 1634)

†Munro, Sir Keith Gordon, Bt. (1825)

Munro, Sir Sydney Douglas Gun-, GCMG, MBE

Muria, *Hon.* Sir Gilbert John Baptist, Kt.

Murphy, Sir Leslie Frederick, Kt.

Murray, *Rt. Hon.* Sir Donald Bruce, Kt.

Murray, Sir James, KCMG

Murray, Sir John Antony Jerningham, Kt., CBE

Murray, *Prof.* Sir Kenneth, Kt., FRCPath., FRS, FRSE

Murray, Sir Nigel Andrew Digby, Bt. (s. 1628)

Murray, Sir Patrick Ian Keith, Bt. (s. 1673)

†Murray, Sir Rowland William, Bt. (s. 1630)

Mursell, Sir Peter, Kt., MBE

Musgrave, Sir Christopher Patrick Charles, Bt. (1611)

Musgrave, Sir Richard James, Bt. (I. 1782)

Musson, *Gen.* Sir Geoffrey Randolph Dixon, GCB, CBE, DSO

Myers, Sir Philip Alan, Kt., OBE, QPM

Myers, *Prof.* Sir Rupert Horace, KBE

Mynors, Sir Richard Baskerville, Bt. (1964)

Naipaul, Sir Vidiadhar Surajprasad, Kt.

Nairn, Sir Michael, Bt. (1904)

Nairn, Sir Robert Arnold Spencer-, Bt. (1933)

Nairne, *Rt. Hon.* Sir Patrick Dalmahoy, GCB, MC

Naish, Sir (Charles) David, Kt.

Nall, Sir Michael Joseph, Bt., RN (1954)

Namaliu, *Rt. Hon.* Sir Rabbie Langanai, Kt., CMG

†Napier, Sir Charles Joseph, Bt. (1867)

Napier, Sir John Archibald Lennox, Bt. (s. 1627)

Napier, Sir Oliver John, Kt.

Nasmith, *Prof.* Sir James Duncan Dunbar-, Kt., CBE, RIBA, FRSE

Neal, Sir Eric James, Kt., CVO

Neal, Sir Leonard Francis, Kt., CBE

Neale, Sir Gerrard Anthony, Kt.

Neave, Sir Paul Arundell, Bt. (1795)

Nedd, *Hon.* Sir Robert Archibald, Kt.

Needham, *Rt. Hon.* Sir Richard (The Earl of Kilmorey, *see* page 141)

Neill, Sir Brian Thomas, Kt.

Neill, *Rt. Hon.* Sir Ivan, Kt., PC (NI)

Neill, Sir (James) Hugh, KCVO, CBE, TD

†Nelson, Sir Jamie Charles Vernon Hope, Bt. (1912)

Nelson, *Hon.* Sir Robert Franklyn, Kt.
Nelson, *Air Marshal* Sir (Sidney) Richard (Carlyle), KCB, OBE, MD
Nepean, *Lt.-Col.* Sir Evan Yorke, Bt. (1802)
Neuberger, *Hon.* Sir David Edmond, Kt.
Neubert, Sir Michael John, Kt.
Neville, Sir Roger Albert Gartside, Kt., VRD
New, *Maj.-Gen.* Sir Laurence Anthony Wallis, Kt., CB, CBE
Newall, Sir Paul Henry, Kt., TD
Newington, Sir Michael John, KCMG
Newman, Sir Francis Hugh Cecil, Bt. (1912)
Newman, Sir Geoffrey Robert, Bt. (1836)
Newman, *Hon.* Sir George Michael, Kt.
Newman, Sir Kenneth Leslie, GBE, QPM
Newman, *Vice-Adm.* Sir Roy Thomas, KCB
Newman, *Col.* Sir Stuart Richard, Kt., CBE, TD
Newsam, Sir Peter Anthony, Kt.
Newton, Sir (Charles) Wilfred, Kt., CBE
Newton, Sir (Harry) Michael (Rex), Bt. (1900)
Newton, Sir Kenneth Garnar, Bt., OBE, TD (1924)
Ngata, Sir Henare Kohere, KBE
Nichol, Sir Duncan Kirkbride, Kt., CBE
Nicholas, Sir David, Kt., CBE
Nicholas, Sir John William, KCVO, CMG
Nicholls, *Air Marshal* Sir John Moreton, KCB, CBE, DFC, AFC
Nichols, Sir Richard Everard, Kt.
Nicholson, Sir Bryan Hubert, Kt.
†Nicholson, Sir Charles Christian, Bt. (1912)
Nicholson, *Hon.* Sir David Eric, Kt.
Nicholson, *Rt. Hon.* Sir Michael, Kt.
Nicholson, Sir Paul Douglas, Kt.
Nicholson, Sir Robin Buchanan, Kt., PH.D., FRS, FEng.
Nicoll, Sir William, KCMG
Nightingale, Sir Charles Manners Gamaliel, Bt. (1628)
Nightingale, Sir John Cyprian, Kt., CBE, BEM, QPM
Nimmo, *Hon.* Sir John Angus, Kt., CBE
Nixon, *Maj.* Sir Cecil Dominic Henry Joseph, Bt., MC (1906)
Nixon, Sir Edwin Ronald, Kt., CBE
Noble, Sir David Brunel, Bt. (1902)
Noble, Sir Iain Andrew, Bt., OBE (1923)
Noble, Sir (Thomas Alexander) Fraser, Kt., MBE
Nombri, Sir Joseph Karl, Kt., ISO, BEM
Norman, Sir Arthur Gordon, KBE, DFC
Norman, Sir Mark Annesley, Bt. (1915)

Norman, Sir Robert Henry, Kt., OBE
Norman, Sir Ronald, Kt., OBE
Norrington, Sir Roger Arthur Carver, Kt., CBE
Norris, *Air Chief Marshal* Sir Christopher Neil Foxley-, GCB, DSO, OBE
Norris, Sir Eric George, KCMG
North, Sir Peter Machin, Kt., CBE, QC, DCL, FBA
North, Sir Thomas Lindsay, Kt.
North, Sir (William) Jonathan (Frederick), Bt. (1920)
Norton, *Vice-Adm. Hon.* Sir Nicholas John Hill-, KCB
Norwood, Sir Walter Neville, Kt.
Nossal, Sir Gustav Joseph Victor, Kt., CBE
Nott, *Rt. Hon.* Sir John William Frederic, KCB
Nourse, *Rt. Hon.* Sir Martin Charles, Kt.
Nugent, Sir John Edwin Lavallin, Bt. (1795)
Nugent, *Maj.* Sir Peter Walter James, Bt. (1831)
Nugent, Sir Robin George Colborne, Bt. (1806)
Nursaw, Sir James, KCB, QC
Nuttall, Sir Nicholas Keith Lillington, Bt. (1922)
Nutting, *Rt. Hon.* Sir (Harold) Anthony, Bt. (1903)
Oakeley, Sir John Digby Atholl, Bt. (1790)
Oakes, Sir Christopher, Bt. (1939)
Oakshott, Hon. Sir Anthony Hendrie, Bt. (1959)
Oates, Sir Thomas, Kt., CMG, OBE
Obolensky, *Prof.* Sir Dimitri, Kt.
O'Brien, Sir Frederick William Fitzgerald, Kt.
O'Brien, Sir Richard, Kt., DSO, MC
O'Brien, Sir Timothy John, Bt. (1849)
O'Brien, *Adm.* Sir William Donough, KCB, DSC
O'Connell, Sir Maurice James Donagh MacCarthy, Bt. (1869)
O'Connor, *Rt. Hon.* Sir Patrick McCarthy, Kt.
O'Dea, Sir Patrick Jerad, KCVO
Odell, Sir Stanley John, Kt.
Odgers, Sir Graeme David William, Kt.
Ogden, Sir (Edward) Michael, Kt., QC
Ogilvy, *Rt. Hon.* Sir Angus James Bruce, KCVO
Ogilvy, Sir Francis Gilbert Arthur, Bt. (s. 1626)
Ognall, *Hon.* Sir Harry Henry, Kt.
Ohlson, Sir Brian Eric Christopher, Bt. (1920)
Okeover, *Capt.* Sir Peter Ralph Leopold Walker-, Bt. (1886)
Olewale, *Hon.* Sir Niwia Ebia, Kt.
Oliphant, Sir Mark (Marcus Laurence Elwin), KBE, FRS
O'Loghlen, Sir Colman Michael, Bt. (1838)

Olver, Sir Stephen John Linley, KBE, CMG
O'Neil, *Hon.* Sir Desmond Henry, Kt.
Ongley, *Hon.* Sir Joseph Augustine, Kt.
Onslow, Sir John Roger Wilmot, Bt. (1797)
Oppenheim, Sir Duncan Morris, Kt.
Oppenheimer, Sir Michael Bernard Grenville, Bt. (1921)
Orde, Sir John Alexander Campbell-, Bt. (1790)
O'Regan, *Dr* Sir Stephen Gerard (Tipene), Kt.
Orlebar, Sir Michael Keith Orlebar Simpson-, Kt.
Orr, Sir David Alexander, Kt., MC
Osborn, Sir John Holbrook, Kt.
Osborn, Sir Richard Henry Danvers, Bt. (1662)
Osborne, Sir Peter George, Bt. (I. 1629)
Osifelo, Sir Frederick Aubarua, Kt., MBE
Osmond, Sir Douglas, Kt., CBE
Osmond, Sir (Stanley) Paul, Kt., CB
O'Sullevan, Sir Peter John, Kt., CBE
Oswald, *Admiral of the Fleet* Sir (John) Julian Robertson, GCB
Oswald, Sir (William Richard) Michael, KCVO
Otton, Sir Geoffrey John, KCB
Otton, *Rt. Hon.* Sir Philip Howard, Kt.
Oulton, Sir Antony Derek Maxwell, GCB, QC
Ouseley, Sir Herman George, Kt.
Outram, Sir Alan James, Bt. (1858)
Overall, Sir John Wallace, Kt., CBE, MC
Owen, Sir Geoffrey, Kt.
Owen, Sir Hugh Bernard Pilkington, Bt. (1813)
Owen, Sir Hugo Dudley Cunliffe-, Bt. (1920)
Owen, *Hon.* Sir John Arthur Dalziel, Kt.
Owo, The Olowo of, Kt.
Oxburgh, *Prof.* Sir Ernest Ronald, KBE, PH.D., FRS
Oxford, Sir Kenneth Gordon, Kt., CBE, QPM
Packard, *Lt.-Gen.* Sir (Charles) Douglas, KBE, CB, DSO
Page, Sir (Arthur) John, Kt.
Page, Sir Frederick William, Kt., CBE, FEng.
Page, Sir John Joseph Joffre, Kt., OBE
Paget, Sir Julian Tolver, Bt., CVO (1871)
Paget, Sir Richard Herbert, Bt. (1886)
Pain, *Lt.-Gen.* Sir (Horace) Rollo (Squarey), KCB, MC
Pain, *Hon.* Sir Peter Richard, Kt.
Paine, Sir Christopher Hammon, Kt., FRCP, FRCR
Palin, *Air Chief Marshal* Sir Roger Hewlett, KCB, OBE
Palliser, *Rt. Hon.* Sir (Arthur) Michael, GCMG

Palmar, Sir Derek James, Kt.
Palmer, Sir (Charles) Mark, Bt. (1886)
Palmer, *Gen.* Sir (Charles) Patrick (Ralph), KBE
Palmer, Sir Geoffrey Christopher John, Bt. (1660)
Palmer, *Rt. Hon.* Sir Geoffrey Winston Russell, KCMG
Palmer, Sir John Chance, Kt.
Palmer, Sir John Edward Somerset, Bt. (1791)
Palmer, *Maj.-Gen.* Sir (Joseph) Michael, KCVO
Palmer, Sir Reginald Oswald, GCMG, MBE
Pantlin, Sir Dick Hurst, Kt., CBE
Paolozzi, Sir Eduardo Luigi, Kt., CBE, RA
Parbo, Sir Arvi Hillar, Kt.
Parish, Sir David Elmer Woodbine, Kt., CBE
Park, *Hon.* Sir Andrew Edward Wilson, Kt.
Park, *Hon.* Sir Hugh Eames, Kt.
Parker, Sir (Arthur) Douglas Dodds-, Kt.
Parker, Sir Eric Wilson, Kt.
Parker, *Hon.* Sir Jonathan Frederic, Kt.
Parker, Sir Peter, KBE, LVO
Parker, Sir Richard (William) Hyde, Bt. (1681)
Parker, *Rt. Hon.* Sir Roger Jocelyn, Kt.
Parker, *Vice-Adm.* Sir (Wilfred) John, KBE, CB, DSC
Parker, Sir William Peter Brian, Bt. (1844)
Parkes, Sir Edward Walter, Kt., FEng
Parkinson, Sir Nicholas Fancourt, Kt.
Parsons, Sir (John) Michael, Kt.
Parsons, Sir Richard Edmund (Clement Fownes), KCMG
Partridge, Sir Michael John Anthony, KCB
Pascoe, *Gen.* Sir Robert Alan, KCB, MBE
Pasley, Sir John Malcolm Sabine, Bt. (1794)
Patel, *Prof.* Sir Narendra Babubhai, Kt.
Paterson, Sir Dennis Craig, Kt.
Paterson, Sir John Valentine Jardine, Kt.
Patnick, Sir (Cyril) Irvine, Kt., OBE
Paton, Sir (Thomas) Angus (Lyall), Kt., CMG, FRS, FEng.
Pattie, *Rt. Hon.* Sir Geoffrey Edwin, Kt.
Pattinson, Sir (William) Derek, Kt.
Pattison, *Prof.* Sir John Ridley, Kt., DM, FRCPath.
Pattullo, Sir (David) Bruce, Kt., CBE
Paul, Sir John Warburton, GCMG, OBE, MC
Paul, *Air Marshal* Sir Ronald Ian Stuart-, KBE
Payne, Sir Norman John, Kt., CBE, FEng.

Peach, Sir Leonard Harry, Kt.
Peacock, *Prof.* Sir Alan Turner, Kt., DSC
Pearce, Sir Austin William, Kt., CBE, Ph.D., FEng.
Pearce, Sir (Daniel Norton) Idris, Kt., CBE, TD
Pearce, Sir Eric Herbert, Kt., OBE
Pearse, Sir Brian Gerald, Kt.
Pearson, Sir Francis Nicholas Fraser, Bt. (1964)
Pearson, *Gen.* Sir Thomas Cecil Hook, KCB, CBE, DSO
Peart, *Prof.* Sir William Stanley, Kt., MD, FRS
Pease, Sir (Alfred) Vincent, Bt. (1882)
Pease, Sir Richard Thorn, Bt. (1920)
Peat, Sir Gerrard Charles, KCVO
Peat, Sir Michael Charles Gerrard, KCVO
Peck, Sir Edward Heywood, GCMG
Peckham, *Prof.* Sir Michael John, Kt., FRCP, FRCPGlas., FRCR, FRCPath.
Pedder, *Air Marshal* Sir Ian Maurice, KCB, OBE, DFC
Peek, *Vice-Adm.* Sir Richard Innes, KBE, CB, DSC
Peek, Sir William Grenville, Bt. (1874)
Peel, Sir John Harold, KCVO
Peel, Sir (William) John, Kt.
Peirse, Sir Henry Grant de la Poer Beresford-, Bt. (1814)
Peirse, *Air Vice-Marshal* Sir Richard Charles Fairfax, KCVO, CB
Pelgen, Sir Harry Friedrich, Kt., MBE
Peliza, Sir Robert John, KBE, ED
Pelly, Sir Richard John, Bt. (1840)
Pemberton, Sir Francis Wingate William, Kt., CBE
Penrose, *Prof.* Sir Roger, Kt., FRS
Pereira, Sir (Herbert) Charles, Kt., D.SC., FRS
Perring, Sir John Raymond, Bt. (1963)
Perris, Sir David (Arthur), Kt., MBE
Perry, Sir David Howard, KCB
Perry, Sir (David) Norman, Kt., MBE
Perry, Sir Michael Sydney, Kt., CBE
Pestell, Sir John Richard, KCVO
Peterkin, Sir Neville, Kt.
Peters, *Prof.* Sir David Keith, Kt., FRCP
Petersen, Sir Jeffrey Charles, KCMG
Petersen, Sir Johannes Bjelke-, KCMG
Peterson, Sir Christopher Matthew, Kt., CBE, TD
†Petit, Sir Jehangir, Bt. (1890)
Peto, Sir Henry George Morton, Bt. (1855)
Peto, Sir Michael Henry Basil, Bt. (1927)
Petrie, Sir Peter Charles, Bt., CMG (1918)
Pettigrew, Sir Russell Hilton, Kt.
Pettit, Sir Daniel Eric Arthur, Kt.
Pettitt, Sir Dennis, Kt.
Philips, *Prof.* Sir Cyril Henry, Kt.
Phillips, Sir Fred Albert, Kt., CVO

Phillips, Sir (Gerald) Hayden, KCB
Phillips, Sir Henry Ellis Isidore, Kt., CMG, MBE
Phillips, Sir Horace, KCMG
Phillips, *Hon.* Sir Nicholas Addison, Kt.
Phillips, Sir Peter John, Kt., OBE
Phillips, Sir Robin Francis, Bt. (1912)
Pickard, Sir (John) Michael, Kt.
Pickering, Sir Edward Davies, Kt.
Pickthorn, Sir James Francis Mann, Bt. (1959)
Pidgeon, Sir John Allan Stewart, Kt.
†Piers, Sir James Desmond, Bt. (I. 1661)
Pigot, Sir George Hugh, Bt. (1764)
Pigott, Sir Berkeley Henry Sebastian, Bt. (1808)
Pike, *Lt.-Gen.* Sir Hew William Royston, KCB, DSO, MBE
Pike, Sir Michael Edmund, KCVO, CMG
Pike, Sir Philip Ernest Housden, Kt., QC
Pilditch, Sir Richard Edward, Bt. (1929)
Pile, Sir Frederick Devereux, Bt., MC (1900)
Pilkington, Sir Antony Richard, Kt.
Pilkington, Sir Thomas Henry Milborne-Swinnerton-, Bt. (S. 1635)
Pill, *Rt. Hon.* Sir Malcolm Thomas, Kt.
Pillar, *Adm.* Sir William Thomas, GBE, KCB
Pindling, *Rt. Hon.* Sir Lynden Oscar, KCMG
Pinker, Sir George Douglas, KCVO
Pinsent, Sir Christopher Roy, Bt. (1938)
Pippard, *Prof.* Sir (Alfred) Brian, Kt., FRS
Pirie, *Gp Capt* Sir Gordon Hamish, Kt., CVO, OBE
Pitakaka, Sir Moses Puibangara, GCMG
Pitcher, Sir Desmond Henry, Kt.
Pitman, Sir Brian Ivor, Kt.
Pitoi, Sir Sere, Kt., CBE
Pitt, Sir Harry Raymond, Kt., Ph.D., FRS
Pitts, Sir Cyril Alfred, Kt.
Plastow, Sir David Arnold Stuart, Kt.
Platt, Sir Harold Grant, Kt.
Platt, *Prof.* Hon. Sir Peter, Bt. (1959)
Playfair, Sir Edward Wilder, KCB
Pliatzky, Sir Leo, KCB
Plowman, *Hon.* Sir John Robin, Kt., CBE
Plumb, *Prof.* Sir John Harold, Kt.
Pohai, Sir Timothy, Kt., MBE
Pole, Sir (John) Richard (Walter Reginald) Carew, Bt. (1628)
Pole, Sir Peter Van Notten, Bt. (1791)
Polkinghorne, *Revd Canon* John Charlton, KBE, FRS
Pollen, Sir John Michael Hungerford, Bt. (1795)

Pollock, Sir George Frederick, Bt. (1866)

Pollock, Sir Giles Hampden Montagu-, Bt. (1872)

Pollock, *Admiral of the Fleet* Sir Michael Patrick, GCB, LVO, DSC

Ponsonby, Sir Ashley Charles Gibbs, Bt., KCVO, MC (1956)

Pontin, Sir Frederick William, Kt.

Poole, *Hon.* Sir David Anthony, Kt.

Poore, Sir Herbert Edward, Bt. (1795)

Pope, Sir Joseph Albert, Kt., D.SC., Ph.D.

Popplewell, *Hon.* Sir Oliver Bury, Kt.

†Porritt, Sir Jonathon Espie, Bt. (1963)

Portal, Sir Jonathan Francis, Bt. (1901)

Porter, Sir John Simon Horsbrugh-, Bt. (1902)

Porter, Sir Leslie, Kt.

Porter, *Air Marshal* Sir (Melvin) Kenneth (Drowley), KCB, CBE

Porter, *Rt. Hon.* Sir Robert Wilson, Kt., PC (NI), QC

Posnett, Sir Richard Neil, KBE, CMG

Potter, *Rt. Hon.* Sir Mark Howard, Kt.

Potter, *Maj.-Gen.* Sir (Wilfrid) John, KBE, CB

Potts, *Hon.* Sir Francis Humphrey, Kt.

Pound, Sir John David, Bt. (1905)

Pountain, Sir Eric John, Kt.

Powell, Sir (Arnold Joseph) Philip, Kt., CH, OBE, RA, FRIBA

Powell, Sir Charles David, KCMG

Powell, Sir Nicholas Folliott Douglas, Bt. (1897)

Powell, Sir Raymond, Kt., MP

Powell, Sir Richard Royle, GCB, KBE, CMG

Power, Sir Alastair John Cecil, Bt. (1924)

Prance, *Prof.* Sir Ghillean Tolmie, Kt., FRS

Prendergast, Sir (Walter) Kieran, KCVO, CMG

Prentice, *Hon.* Sir William Thomas, Kt., MBE

Prescott, Sir Mark, Bt. (1938)

Preston, Sir Ronald Douglas Hildebrand, Bt. (1815)

Prevost, Sir Christopher Gerald, Bt. (1805)

Price, Sir Charles Keith Napier Rugge-, Bt. (1804)

Price, Sir David Ernest Campbell, Kt.

Price, Sir Francis Caradoc Rose, Bt. (1815)

Price, Sir Frank Leslie, Kt.

Price, Sir (James) Robert, KBE

Price, Sir Norman Charles, KCB

Price, Sir Robert John Green-, Bt. (1874)

Prickett, *Air Chief Marshal* Sir Thomas Other, KCB, DSO, DFC

Prideaux, Sir Humphrey Povah Treverbian, Kt., OBE

†Primrose, Sir John Ure, Bt. (1903)

Pringle, *Air Marshal* Sir Charles Norman Seton, KBE, FENG.

Pringle, *Hon.* Sir John Kenneth, Kt.

Pringle, *Lt.-Gen.* Sir Steuart (Robert), Bt., KCB, RM (S. 1683)

Pritchard, Sir Neil, KCMG

Proby, Sir Peter, Bt. (1952)

Prosser, Sir Ian Maurice Gray, Kt.

Proud, Sir John Seymour, Kt.

Pryke, Sir David Dudley, Bt. (1926)

Puapua, *Rt. Hon.* Sir Tomasi, KBE

Pugh, Sir Idwal Vaughan, KCB

Pullinger, Sir (Francis) Alan, Kt., CBE

Pumfrey, *Hon.* Sir Nicholas Richard, Kt.

Pumphrey, Sir (John) Laurence, KCMG

Purchas, *Rt. Hon.* Sir Francis Brooks, Kt.

Purves, Sir William, Kt., CBE, DSO

Purvis, *Vice-Adm.* Sir Neville, KCB

Quicke, Sir John Godolphin, Kt., CBE

Quigley, Sir (William) George (Henry), Kt., CB, Ph.D.

Quilliam, *Hon.* Sir (James) Peter, Kt.

Quilter, Sir Anthony Raymond Leopold Cuthbert, Bt. (1897)

Quinlan, Sir Michael Edward, GCB

Quinton, Sir James Grand, Kt.

Radcliffe, Sir Sebastian Everard, Bt. (1813)

Radzinowicz, *Prof.* Sir Leon, Kt., LLD

Rae, *Hon.* Sir Wallace Alexander Ramsay, Kt.

Raeburn, Sir Michael Edward Norman, Bt. (1923)

Raeburn, *Maj.-Gen.* Sir (William) Digby (Manifold), KCVO, CB, DSO, MBE

Raikes, *Vice-Adm.* Sir Iwan Geoffrey, KCB, CBE, DSC

Raison, *Rt. Hon.* Sir Timothy Hugh Francis, Kt.

Ralli, Sir Godfrey Victor, Bt., TD (1912)

Ramdanee, Sir Mookteswar Baboolall Kailash, Kt.

Ramphal, Sir Shridath Surendranath, GCMG

Ramphul, Sir Baalkhristna, Kt.

Ramphul, Sir Indurduth, Kt.

Ramsay, Sir Alexander William Burnett, Bt. (1806)

Ramsay, Sir Allan John (Hepple), KBE, CMG

Ramsbotham, *Gen.* Sir David John, GCB, CBE

Ramsbotham, *Hon.* Sir Peter Edward, GCMG, GCVO

Ramsden, Sir John Charles Josslyn, Bt. (1689)

Ramsey, Sir Alfred Ernest, Kt.

Randle, *Prof.* Sir Philip John, Kt.

Rank, Sir Benjamin Keith, Kt., CMG

Rankin, Sir Alick Michael, Kt., CBE

Rankin, Sir Ian Niall, Bt. (1898)

Rasch, Sir Simon Anthony Carne, Bt. (1903)

Rashleigh, Sir Richard Harry, Bt. (1831)

Ratford, Sir David John Edward, KCMG, CVO

Rattee, *Hon.* Sir Donald Keith, Kt.

Rattle, Sir Simon Dennis, Kt., CBE

Rault, Sir Louis Joseph Maurice, Kt.

Rawlins, *Surgeon Vice-Adm.* Sir John Stuart Pepys, KBE

Rawlinson, Sir Anthony Henry John, Bt. (1891)

Read, *Air Marshal* Sir Charles Frederick, KBE, CB, DFC, AFC

Read, *Gen.* Sir (John) Antony (Jervis), GCB, CBE, DSO, MC

Read, Sir John Emms, Kt.

†Reade, Sir Kenneth Ray, Bt. (1661)

Reay, *Lt.-Gen.* Sir (Hubert) Alan John, KBE

Redgrave, *Maj.-Gen.* Sir Roy Michael Frederick, KBE, MC

Redmayne, Sir Nicholas, Bt. (1964)

Redmond, Sir James, Kt., FENG.

Redwood, Sir Peter Boverton, Bt. (1911)

Reece, Sir Charles Hugh, Kt.

Reece, Sir James Gordon, Kt.

Rees, Sir (Charles William) Stanley, Kt., TD

Rees, Sir David Allan, Kt., Ph.D., D.SC., FRS

Rees, *Prof.* Sir Martin John, Kt., FRS

Reeve, Sir Anthony, KCMG, KCVO

Reeves, *Most Revd* Paul Alfred, GCMG, GCVO

Reffell, *Adm.* Sir Derek Roy, KCB

Refshauge, *Maj.-Gen.* Sir William Dudley, Kt., CBE

Reid, Sir Alexander James, Bt. (1897)

Reid, Sir (Harold) Martin (Smith), KBE, CMG

Reid, Sir Hugh, Bt. (1922)

Reid, Sir Norman Robert, Kt.

Reid, Sir Robert Paul, Kt.

Reid, Sir William Kennedy, KCB

Reiher, Sir Frederick Bernard Carl, KBE, CMG

Reilly, Sir (D'Arcy) Patrick, GCMG, OBE

Reilly, *Lt.-Gen.* Sir Jeremy Calcott, KCB, DSO

Renals, Sir Stanley, Bt. (1895)

Rennie, Sir John Shaw, GCMG, OBE

Renouf, Sir Clement William Bailey, Kt.

Renouf, Sir Francis Henry, Kt.

Renshaw, Sir (Charles) Maurice Bine, Bt. (1903)

Renwick, Sir Richard Eustace, Bt. (1921)

Reporter, Sir Shapoor Ardeshirji, KBE

Reynolds, Sir David James, Bt. (1923)

Reynolds, Sir Peter William John, Kt., CBE

Rhodes, Sir Basil Edward, Kt., CBE, TD

Rhodes, Sir John Christopher Douglas, Bt. (1919)

Rhodes, Sir Peregrine Alexander, KCMG
Rice, *Maj.-Gen.* Sir Desmond Hind Garrett, KCVO, CBE
Rice, Sir Timothy Miles Bindon, Kt.
Richard, Sir Cliff, Kt., OBE
Richards, Sir Brian Mansel, Kt., CBE, Ph.D.
Richards, Sir (Francis) Brooks, KCMG, DSC
Richards, *Lt.-Gen.* Sir John Charles Chisholm, KCB, KCVO, RM
Richards, Sir Rex Edward, Kt., D.SC., FRS
Richards, *Hon.* Sir Stephen Price, Kt.
Richardson, Sir Anthony Lewis, Bt. (1924)
Richardson, *Rt. Hon.* Sir Ivor Lloyd Morgan, Kt.
Richardson, Sir (John) Eric, Kt., CBE
Richardson, Sir Michael John de Rougemont, Kt.
Richardson, *Lt.-Gen.* Sir Robert Francis, KCB, CVO, CBE
Richardson, Sir Simon Alaisdair Stewart-, Bt. (s. 1630)
Richmond, Sir John Frederick, Bt. (1929)
Richmond, *Prof.* Sir Mark Henry, Kt., FRS
Ricketts, Sir Robert Cornwallis Gerald St Leger, Bt. (1828)
Riddell, Sir John Charles Buchanan, Bt., CVO (s. 1628)
Ridley, Sir Adam (Nicholas), Kt.
Ridsdale, Sir Julian Errington, Kt., CBE
Rifkind, *Rt. Hon.* Sir Malcolm Leslie, KCMG, QC
Rigby, *Lt.-Col.* Sir (Hugh) John (Macbeth), Bt. (1929)
Riley, Sir Ralph, Kt., FRS
Rimer, *Hon.* Sir Colin Percy Farquharson, Kt.
Ringadoo, *Hon.* Sir Veerasamy, GCMG
Ripley, Sir Hugh, Bt. (1880)
Risk, Sir Thomas Neilson, Kt.
Ritako, Sir Thomas Baha, Kt., MBE
Rix, *Hon.* Sir Bernard Anthony, Kt.
Rix, Sir John, Kt., MBE, FEng.
Roberts, *Hon.* Sir Denys Tudor Emil, KBE, QC
Roberts, Sir Derek Harry, Kt., CBE, FRS, FEng.
Roberts, Sir (Edward Fergus) Sidney, Kt., CBE
Roberts, *Prof.* Sir Gareth Gwyn, Kt., FRS
Roberts, Sir Gilbert Howland Rookehurst, Bt. (1809)
Roberts, Sir Gordon James, Kt., CBE
Roberts, Sir Samuel, Bt. (1919)
Roberts, Sir Stephen James Leake, Kt.
Roberts, Sir William James Denby, Bt. (1909)
Robertson, Sir John Fraser, KCMG, CBE
Robertson, Sir Lewis, Kt., CBE, FRSE

Robertson, *Prof.* Sir Rutherford Ness, Kt., CMG
Robins, Sir Ralph Harry, Kt., FEng.
Robinson, Sir Albert Edward Phineas, Kt.
†Robinson, Sir Christopher Philipse, Bt. (1854)
Robinson, Sir Dominick Christopher Lynch-, Bt. (1920)
Robinson, Sir John James Michael Laud, Bt. (1660)
Robinson, Sir Wilfred Henry Frederick, Bt. (1908)
Robotham, *Hon.* Sir Lascelles Lister, Kt.
Robson, *Prof.* Sir James Gordon, Kt., CBE
Robson, Sir John Adam, KCMG
Roch, *Rt. Hon.* Sir John Ormond, Kt.
Roche, Sir David O'Grady, Bt. (1838)
Rodgers, Sir (Andrew) Piers (Wingate Aikin-Sneath), Bt. (1964)
Rodrigues, Sir Alberto Maria, Kt., CBE, ED
Roe, *Air Chief Marshal* Sir Rex David, GCB, AFC
Rogers, Sir Frank Jarvis, Kt.
Rogers, *Air Chief Marshal* Sir John Robson, KCB, CBE
Rooke, Sir Denis Eric, Kt., OM, CBE, FRS, FEng.
Ropner, Sir John Bruce Woollacott, Bt. (1952)
Ropner, Sir Robert Douglas, Bt. (1904)
Roscoe, Sir Robert Bell, KBE
Rose, *Rt. Hon.* Sir Christopher Dudley Roger, Kt.
Rose, Sir Clive Martin, GCMG
Rose, Sir David Lancaster, Bt. (1874)
Rose, *Gen.* Sir (Hugh) Michael, KCB, CBE, DSO, QGM
Rose, Sir Julian Day, Bt. (1872 and 1909)
Rosier, *Air Chief Marshal* Sir Frederick Ernest, GCB, CBE, DSO
Ross, Sir (James) Keith, Bt., RD, FRCS (1960)
Ross, *Lt.-Gen.* Sir Robert Jeremy, KCB, OBE
Rosser, Sir Melvyn Wynne, Kt.
Rossi, Sir Hugh Alexis Louis, Kt.
Rotblat, *Prof.* Joseph, KCMG, CBE, FRS
Roth, *Prof.* Sir Martin, Kt., MD, FRCP
Rothschild, Sir Evelyn Robert Adrian de, Kt.
Rougier, *Hon.* Sir Richard George, Kt.
Rous, *Lt.-Gen.* Hon. Sir William Edward, KCB, OBE
Rowell, Sir John Joseph, Kt., CBE
Rowland, *Air Marshal* Sir James Anthony, KBE, DFC, AFC
Rowland, Sir (John) David, Kt.
Rowlands, *Air Marshal* Sir John Samuel, GC, KBE
Rowley, Sir Charles Robert, Bt. (1836) †(1786)

Roxburgh, *Vice-Adm.* Sir John Charles Young, KCB, CBE, DSO, DSC
Royden, Sir Christopher John, Bt. (1905)
Rudd, Sir (Anthony) Nigel (Russell), Kt.
Rumbold, Sir Henry John Sebastian, Bt. (1779)
Rumbold, Sir Jack Seddon, Kt.
Runchorelal, Sir (Udayan) Chinubhai Madhowlal, Bt. (1913)
Runciman, *Hon.* Sir James Cochran Stevenson (Sir Steven), Kt., CH
Rusby, *Vice-Adm.* Sir Cameron, KCB, LVO
†Russell, Sir (Arthur) Mervyn, Bt. (1812)
Russell, Sir Charles Dominic, Bt. (1916)
Russell, *Hon.* Sir David Sturrock West-, Kt.
Russell, Sir George, Kt., CBE
Russell, *Prof.* Sir Peter Edward Lionel, Kt., D.litt., FBA
Russell, Sir (Robert) Mark, KCMG
Russell, *Rt. Hon.* Sir (Thomas) Patrick, Kt.
Rutter, Sir Frank William Eden, KBE
Rutter, *Prof.* Sir Michael Llewellyn, Kt., CBE, MD, FRS
Ryan, Sir Derek Gerald, Bt. (1919)
Rycroft, Sir Richard Newton, Bt. (1784)
Ryrie, Sir William Sinclair, KCB
Sabola, *Hon.* Sir Joaquim Claudino Gonsalves-, Kt.
Sachs, *Hon.* Sir Michael Alexander Geddes, Kt.
Sainsbury, Sir Robert James, Kt.
Sainsbury, *Rt. Hon.* Sir Timothy Alan Davan, Kt.
†St Aubyn, Sir William Molesworth-, Bt. (1689)
†St George, Sir John Avenel Bligh, Bt. (I. 1766)
St Johnston, Sir Kerry, Kt.
Sainty, Sir John Christopher, KCB
Sakzewski, Sir Albert, Kt.
Salisbury, Sir Robert William, Kt.
Salt, Sir Patrick MacDonnell, Bt. (1869)
Salt, Sir (Thomas) Michael John, Bt. (1899)
Sampson, Sir Colin, Kt., CBE, QPM
Samuel, Sir John Michael Glen, Bt. (1898)
Samuelson, Sir (Bernard) Michael (Francis), Bt. (1884)
Samuelson, Sir Sydney Wylie, Kt., CBE
Sanders, Sir John Reynolds Mayhew-, Kt.
Sanders, Sir Robert Tait, KBE, CMG
Sanderson, Sir Frank Linton, Bt. (1920)
Sarei, Sir Alexis Holyweek, Kt., CBE
Sarell, Sir Roderick Francis Gisbert, KCMG, KCVO
Saunders, *Hon.* Sir John Anthony Holt, Kt., CBE, DSO, MC

Saunders, Sir Peter, Kt.
Sauzier, Sir (André) Guy, Kt., CBE, ED
Savage, Sir Ernest Walter, Kt.
Savile, Sir James Wilson Vincent, Kt., OBE
Say, *Rt. Revd* Richard David, KCVO
Schiemann, *Rt. Hon.* Sir Konrad Hermann Theodor, Kt.
Scholey, Sir David Gerald, Kt., CBE
Scholey, Sir Robert, Kt., CBE, FEng.
Scholtens, Sir James Henry, KCVO
Schubert, Sir Sydney, Kt.
Scipio, Sir Hudson Rupert, Kt.
Scoon, Sir Paul, GCMG, GCVO, OBE
Scott, Sir Anthony Percy, Bt. (1913)
Scott, Sir (Charles) Peter, KBE, CMG
Scott, Sir David Aubrey, GCMG
Scott, Sir Dominic James Maxwell-, Bt. (1642)
Scott, Sir Ian Dixon, KCMG, KCVO, CIE
Scott, Sir James Jervoise, Bt. (1962)
Scott, Sir Kenneth Bertram Adam, KCVO, CMG
Scott, Sir Michael, KCVO, CMG
Scott, *Rt. Hon.* Sir Nicholas Paul, KBE
Scott, Sir Oliver Christopher Anderson, Bt. (1909)
Scott, *Prof.* Sir Philip John, KBE
Scott, *Rt. Hon.* Sir Richard Rashleigh Folliott, Kt.
Scott, Sir Robert David Hillyer, Kt.
Scott, Sir Walter John, Bt. (1907)
Scott, *Rear-Adm.* Sir (William) David (Stewart), KBE, CB
Scowen, Sir Eric Frank, Kt., MD, D.SC., LLD, FRCP, FRCS
Scrivenor, Sir Thomas Vaisey, Kt., CMG
Seale, Sir John Henry, Bt. (1838)
Seaman, Sir Keith Douglas, KCVO, OBE
Sebastian, Sir Cuthbert Montraville, GCMG, OBE
†Sebright, Sir Peter Giles Vivian, Bt. (1626)
Seccombe, Sir (William) Vernon Stephen, Kt.
Secombe, Sir Harry Donald, Kt., CBE
Seconde, Sir Reginald Louis, KCMG, CVO
Sedley, *Hon.* Sir Stephen John, Kt.
Seely, Sir Nigel Edward, Bt. (1896)
Seeto, Sir Ling James, Kt., MBE
Seeyave, Sir Rene Sow Choung, Kt., CBE
Seligman, Sir Peter Wendel, Kt., CBE
Sergeant, Sir Patrick, Kt.
Series, Sir (Joseph Michel) Emile, Kt., CBE
Serpell, Sir David Radford, KCB, CMG, OBE
Seton, Sir Iain Bruce, Bt. (s. 1663)
†Seton, Sir James Christall, Bt. (s. 1683)
Severne, *Air Vice-Marshal* Sir John de Milt, KCVO, OBE, AFC
Seymour, *Cdr.* Sir Michael Culme-, Bt., RN (1809)

Shackleton, *Prof.* Sir Nicholas John, Kt., Ph.D., FRS
Shakerley, Sir Geoffrey Adam, Bt. (1838)
Shakespeare, Sir Thomas William, Bt. (1942)
Sharp, Sir Adrian, Bt. (1922)
Sharp, Sir George, Kt., OBE
Sharp, Sir Kenneth Johnston, Kt., TD
Sharp, Sir Leslie, Kt., QPM
Sharp, Sir Richard Lyall, KCVO, CB
†Sharp, Sir Samuel Christopher Reginald, Bt. (1920)
Sharpe, *Hon.* Sir John Henry, Kt., CBE
Sharples, Sir James, Kt., QPM
Shattock, Sir Gordon, Kt.
Shaw, Sir Brian Piers, Kt.
Shaw, Sir (Charles) Barry, Kt., CB, QC
Shaw, Sir (George) Neville Bowan-, Kt.
Shaw, *Prof.* Sir John Calman, Kt., CBE, FRSE
Shaw, Sir (John) Giles (Dunkerley), Kt.
Shaw, Sir John Michael Robert Best-, Bt. (1665)
Shaw, Sir Neil McGowan, Kt.
Shaw, Sir Robert, Bt. (1821)
Shaw, Sir Roy, Kt.
Shaw, Sir Run Run, Kt., CBE
Sheehy, Sir Patrick, Kt.
Sheen, *Hon.* Sir Barry Cross, Kt.
Sheffield, Sir Reginald Adrian Berkeley, Bt. (1755)
Shehadie, Sir Nicholas Michael, Kt., OBE
Sheil, *Hon.* Sir John, Kt.
Sheldon, *Hon.* Sir (John) Gervase (Kensington), Kt.
Shelley, Sir John Richard, Bt. (1611)
Shelton, Sir William Jeremy Masefield, Kt.
Shepheard, Sir Peter Faulkner, Kt., CBE
Shepherd, Sir Colin Ryley, Kt.
Shepperd, Sir Alfred Joseph, Kt.
Sherlock, Sir Philip Manderson, KBE
Sherman, Sir Alfred, Kt.
Sherman, Sir Louis, Kt., OBE
Shields, Sir Neil Stanley, Kt., MC
Shields, *Prof.* Sir Robert, Kt., MD
Shiffner, Sir Henry David, Bt. (1818)
Shillington, Sir (Robert Edward) Graham, Kt., CBE
Shinwell, Sir (Maurice) Adrian, Kt.
Shock, Sir Maurice, Kt.
Short, Sir Apenera Pera, KBE
Short, *Brig.* Sir Noel Edward Vivian, Kt., MBE, MC
Shuckburgh, Sir Rupert Charles Gerald, Bt. (1660)
Siaguru, Sir Anthony Michael, KBE
Siddall, Sir Norman, Kt., CBE, FEng.
Sidey, *Air Marshal* Sir Ernest Shaw, KBE, CB, MD
Sie, Sir Banja Tejan-, GCMG
Simeon, Sir John Edmund Barrington, Bt. (1815)
Simmons, *Air Marshal* Sir Michael George, KCB, AFC

Simmons, Sir Stanley Clifford, Kt., FRCS, FRCOG
Simms, Sir Neville Ian, Kt., FEng.
Simon, Sir David Alec Gwyn, Kt., CBE
Simonet, Sir Louis Marcel Pierre, Kt., CBE
Simpson, *Hon.* Sir Alfred Henry, Kt.
Simpson, *Lt.-Gen.* Sir Roderick Alexander Cordy-, KBE, CB
Simpson, Sir William James, Kt.
Sims, Sir Roger Edward, Kt.
Sinclair, Sir Clive Marles, Kt.
Sinclair, Sir George Evelyn, Kt., CMG, OBE
Sinclair, Sir Ian McTaggart, KCMG, QC
Sinclair, *Air Vice-Marshal* Sir Laurence Frank, GC, KCB, CBE, DSO
Sinclair, Sir Patrick Robert Richard, Bt. (s. 1704)
Sinden, Sir Donald Alfred, Kt., CBE
Singer, *Prof.* Sir Hans Wolfgang, Kt.
Singer, *Hon.* Sir Jan Peter, Kt.
Singh, *Hon.* Sir Vijay Raghubir, Kt.
Sitwell, Sir (Sacheverell) Reresby, Bt. (1808)
Skeet, Sir Trevor Herbert Harry, Kt.
Skeggs, Sir Clifford George, Kt.
Skehel, Sir John James, Kt., FRS
Skingsley, *Air Chief Marshal* Sir Anthony Gerald, GBE, KCB
Skinner, Sir (Thomas) Keith (Hewitt), Bt. (1912)
Skipwith, Sir Patrick Alexander d'Estoteville, Bt. (1622)
Skyrme, Sir (William) Thomas (Charles), KCVO, CB, CBE, TD
Slack, Sir William Willatt, KCVO, FRCS
Slade, Sir Benjamin Julian Alfred, Bt. (1831)
Slade, *Rt. Hon.* Sir Christopher John, Kt.
Slaney, *Prof.* Sir Geoffrey, KBE
Slater, *Adm.* Sir John (Jock) Cunningham Kirkwood, GCB, LVO
Sleight, Sir Richard, Bt. (1920)
Sloan, Sir Andrew Kirkpatrick, Kt., QPM
Sloman, Sir Albert Edward, Kt., CBE
Smart, *Prof.* Sir George Algernon, Kt., MD, FRCP
Smart, Sir Jack, Kt., CBE
Smedley, *Hon.* Sir (Frank) Brian, Kt.
Smedley, Sir Harold, KCMG, MBE
Smiley, *Lt.-Col.* Sir John Philip, Bt. (1903)
Smith, Sir Alan, Kt., CBE, DFC
Smith, Sir Alexander Mair, Kt., Ph.D.
Smith, Sir Andrew Colin Hugh-, Kt.
Smith, *Lt.-Gen.* Sir Anthony Arthur Denison-, KBE
Smith, Sir Charles Bracewell-, Bt. (1947)
Smith, Sir Christopher Sydney Winwood, Bt. (1809)
Smith, *Prof.* Sir Colin Stansfield, Kt., CBE
Smith, Sir Cyril, Kt., MBE

Smith, *Prof.* Sir David Cecil, Kt., FRS
Smith, *Air Chief Marshal* Sir David
 Harcourt-, GBE, KCB, DFC
Smith, Sir David Iser, KCVO
Smith, Sir Douglas Boucher, KCB
Smith, Sir Dudley (Gordon), Kt.
Smith, *Maj.-Gen.* Sir (Francis) Brian
 Wyldbore-, Kt., CB, DSO, OBE
Smith, *Prof.* Sir Francis Graham-, Kt.,
 FRS
Smith, Sir Geoffrey Johnson, Kt., MP
Smith, Sir John Alfred, Kt., QPM
Smith, *Prof.* Sir John Cyril, Kt., CBE,
 QC, FBA
Smith, Sir John Hamilton-Spencer-,
 Bt. (1804)
Smith, Sir John Jonah Walker-, Bt.
 (1960)
Smith, Sir John Lindsay Eric, Kt., CH,
 CBE
Smith, Sir John Rathbone Vassar-,
 Bt. (1917)
Smith, Sir Joseph William Grenville,
 Kt., MD, FRCP
Smith, Sir Leslie Edward George, Kt.
Smith, *Maj.-Gen.* Sir Michael Edward
 Carleton-, Kt., CBE
Smith, Sir Michael John Llewellyn,
 KCVO, CMG
Smith, *Rt. Hon.* Sir Murray Stuart-,
 Kt.
Smith, Sir (Norman) Brian, Kt., CBE,
 ph.D.
†Smith, Sir Peter Frank Graham
 Newson-, Bt. (1944)
Smith, Sir Raymond Horace, KBE
Smith, Sir Robert Courtney, Kt., CBE
Smith, Sir Robert Hill, Bt. (1945)
Smith, *Prof.* Sir Roland, Kt.
Smith, *Air Marshal* Sir Roy David
 Austen-, KBE, CB, CVO, DFC
Smith, *Gen.* Sir Rupert Anthony, KCB,
 DSO, OBE, QGM
Smith, Sir (Thomas) Gilbert, Bt.
 (1897)
Smith, Sir (William) Antony (John)
 Reardon-, Bt. (1920)
Smith, Sir (William) Richard
 Prince-, Bt. (1911)
Smithers, Sir Peter Henry Berry
 Otway, Kt., VRD, D.phil.
Smyth, Sir Thomas Weyland
 Bowyer-, Bt. (1661)
Smyth, Sir Timothy John, Bt. (1955)
Soakimori, Sir Frederick
 Pa-Nukuanca, KBE, CPM
Soame, Sir Charles John Buckworth-
 Herne-, Bt. (1697)
Sobers, Sir Garfield St Auburn, Kt.
Solomon, Sir Harry, Kt.
Somare, *Rt. Hon.* Sir Michael
 Thomas, GCMG, CH
Somers, *Rt. Hon.* Sir Edward
 Jonathan, Kt.
Somerville, *Brig.* Sir John Nicholas,
 Kt., CBE
Somerville, Sir Quentin Charles
 Somerville Agnew-, Bt. (1957)
Soutar, *Air Marshal* Sir Charles John
 Williamson, KBE

South, Sir Arthur, Kt.
Southby, Sir John Richard Bilbe, Bt.
 (1937)
Southern, Sir Richard William, Kt.,
 FBA
Southern, Sir Robert, Kt., CBE
Southey, Sir Robert John, Kt., CMG
Southgate, Sir Colin Grieve, Kt.
Southgate, Sir William David, Kt.
Southward, Sir Leonard Bingley, Kt.,
 OBE
Southwood, *Prof.* Sir (Thomas)
 Richard (Edmund), Kt., FRS
Southworth, Sir Frederick, Kt., QC
Souyave, *Hon.* Sir (Louis) Georges,
 Kt.
Sowrey, *Air Marshal* Sir Frederick
 Beresford, KCB, CBE, AFC
Sparkes, Sir Robert Lyndley, Kt.
Sparrow, Sir John, Kt.
Spearman, Sir Alexander Young
 Richard Mainwaring, Bt. (1840)
Spedding, *Prof.* Sir Colin Raymond
 William, Kt., CBE
Spedding, Sir David Rolland, KCMG,
 CVO, OBE
Speed, Sir (Herbert) Keith, Kt., RD
Speed, Sir Robert William Arney,
 Kt., CB, QC
Speelman, Sir Cornelis Jacob, Bt.
 (1686)
Speight, *Hon.* Sir Graham Davies, Kt.
Speir, Sir Rupert Malise, Kt.
Spencer, Sir Derek Harold, Kt., QC
Spicer, Sir James Wilton, Kt.
Spicer, Sir Nicholas Adrian Albert,
 Bt., MB (1906)
Spicer, Sir (William) Michael Hardy,
 Kt., MP
Spiers, Sir Donald Maurice, Kt., CB,
 TD
Spooner, Sir James Douglas, Kt.
Spotswood, *Marshal of the Royal Air
 Force* Sir Denis Frank, GCB, CBE,
 DSO, DFC
Spratt, *Col.* Sir Greville Douglas, GBE,
 TD
Spring, Sir Dryden Thomas, Kt.
Spry, *Hon.* Sir John Farley, Kt.
Squire, *Air Marshal* Sir Peter Ted,
 KCB, DFC, AFC
Stabb, *Hon.* Sir William Walter, Kt.,
 QC
Stainton, Sir (John) Ross, Kt., CBE
Stakis, Sir Reo Argiros, Kt.
Stamer, Sir (Lovelace) Anthony, Bt.
 (1809)
Stanbridge, *Air Vice-Marshal* Sir
 Brian Gerald Tivy, KCVO, CBE, AFC
Stanier, Sir Beville Douglas, Bt.
 (1917)
Stanier, *Field Marshal* Sir John
 Wilfred, GCB, MBE
Stanley, *Rt. Hon.* Sir John Paul, Kt.,
 MP
†Staples, Sir Thomas, Bt. (I. 1628)
Stark, Sir Andrew Alexander Steel,
 KCMG, CVO
Starkey, Sir John Philip, Bt. (1935)
Starrit, Sir James, KCVO

Statham, Sir Norman, KCMG, CVO
Staughton, *Rt. Hon.* Sir Christopher
 Stephen Thomas Jonathan
 Thayer, Kt.
Staveley, Sir John Malfroy, KBE, MC
Stear, *Air Chief Marshal* Sir Michael
 James Douglas, KCB, CBE
Steel, Sir David Edward Charles, Kt.,
 DSO, MC, TD
Steel, *Hon.* Sir David William, Kt.
Steel, *Maj.* Sir (Fiennes) Michael
 Strang, Bt. (1938)
Steele, Sir (Philip John) Rupert, Kt.
Steere, Sir Ernest Henry Lee-, KBE
Stephen, *Rt. Hon.* Sir Ninian Martin,
 KG, GCMG, GCVO, KBE
Stephens, Sir (Edwin) Barrie, Kt.
Stephenson, Sir Henry Upton, Bt.
 (1936)
Stephenson, *Rt. Hon.* Sir John
 Frederick Eustace, Kt.
Sternberg, Sir Sigmund, Kt.
Stevens, Sir Jocelyn Edward
 Greville, Kt., CVO
Stevens, Sir Laurence Houghton, Kt.,
 CBE
Stevenson, Sir Henry Dennistoun
 (Sir Dennis), Kt., CBE
Stevenson, *Vice-Adm.* Sir (Hugh)
 David, KBE
Stevenson, Sir Simpson, Kt.
Stewart, Sir Alan, KBE
Stewart, Sir Alan d'Arcy, Bt. (I. 1623)
Stewart, Sir David James
 Henderson-, Bt. (1957)
Stewart, Sir David John Christopher,
 Bt. (1803)
Stewart, Sir Edward Jackson, Kt.
Stewart, *Prof.* Sir Frederick Henry,
 Kt., ph.D., FRS, FRSE
Stewart, Sir Houston Mark Shaw-,
 Bt., MC, TD (S. 1667)
Stewart, Sir James Douglas, Kt.
Stewart, Sir James Moray, KCB
Stewart, Sir (John) Simon (Watson),
 Bt. (1920)
Stewart, Sir Robertson Huntly, Kt.,
 CBE
Stewart, Sir Robin Alastair, Bt. (1960)
Stewart, Sir Ronald Compton, Bt.
 (1937)
Stewart, *Prof.* Sir William Duncan
 Paterson, Kt., FRS, FRSE
Stibbon, *Gen.* Sir John James, KCB,
 OBE
Stirling, Sir Alexander John
 Dickson, KBE, CMG
Stirling, Sir Angus Duncan Aeneas,
 Kt.
Stockdale, Sir Arthur Noel, Kt.
Stockdale, Sir Thomas Minshull, Bt.
 (1960)
Stoddart, *Wg Cdr.* Sir Kenneth
 Maxwell, KCVO, AE
Stoker, *Prof.* Sir Michael George
 Parke, Kt., CBE, FRCP, FRS, FRSE
Stokes, Sir John Heydon Romaine,
 Kt.
Stones, Sir William Frederick, Kt.,
 OBE

Stonhouse, *Revd* Sir Michael Philip, Bt. (1628)

Stonor, *Air Marshal* Sir Thomas Henry, KCB

Stoppard, Sir Thomas, Kt., CBE

Storey, *Hon.* Sir Richard, Bt., CBE (1960)

Stormonth Darling, Sir James Carlisle, Kt., CBE, MC, TD

Stott, Sir Adrian George Ellingham, Bt. (1920)

Stoute, Sir Michael Ronald, Kt.

Stow, Sir Christopher Philipson-, Bt., DFC (1907)

Stowe, Sir Kenneth Ronald, GCB, CVO

Stracey, Sir John Simon, Bt. (1818)

Strachan, Sir Curtis Victor, Kt., CVO

Strachey, Sir Charles, Bt. (1801)

Straker, Sir Michael Ian Bowstead, Kt., CBE

Strawson, *Prof.* Sir Peter Frederick, Kt., FBA

Street, *Hon.* Sir Laurence Whistler, KCMG

Streeton, Sir Terence George, KBE, CMG

Stringer, Sir Donald Edgar, Kt., CBE

Strong, Sir Roy Colin, Kt., Ph.D., FSA

Stronge, Sir James Anselan Maxwell, Bt. (1803)

Stroud, *Prof.* Sir (Charles) Eric, Kt., FRCP

Strutt, Sir Nigel Edward, Kt., TD

Stuart, Sir James Keith, Kt.

Stuart, Sir Kenneth Lamonte, Kt.

†Stuart, Sir Phillip Luttrell, Bt. (1660)

Stubblefield, Sir (Cyril) James, Kt., D.SC., FRS

Stubbs, Sir James Wilfrid, KCVO, TD

Stubbs, Sir William Hamilton, Kt., Ph.D.

Stucley, *Lt.* Sir Hugh George Coplestone Bampfylde, Bt. (1859)

Studd, Sir Edward Fairfax, Bt. (1929)

Studd, Sir Peter Malden, GBE, KCVO

Studholme, Sir Henry William, Bt. (1956)

Stuttaford, Sir William Royden, Kt., CBE

Style, *Lt.-Cdr.* Sir Godfrey William, Kt., CBE, DSC, RN

†Style, Sir William Frederick, Bt. (1627)

Suffield, Sir (Henry John) Lester, Kt.

Sugden, Sir Arthur, Kt.

Sullivan, *Hon.* Sir Jeremy Mirth, Kt.

Sullivan, Sir Richard Arthur, Bt. (1804)

Sumner, *Hon.* Sir Christopher John, Kt.

Sutherland, Sir John Brewer, Bt. (1921)

Sutherland, Sir Maurice, Kt.

Sutherland, *Prof.* Sir Stewart Ross, Kt., FBA

Sutherland, Sir William George MacKenzie, Kt.

Suttie, Sir James Edward Grant-, Bt. (s. 1702)

Sutton, Sir Frederick Walter, Kt., OBE

Sutton, *Air Marshal* Sir John Matthias Dobson, KCB

Sutton, Sir Richard Lexington, Bt. (1772)

Swaffield, Sir James Chesebrough, Kt., CBE, RD

Swaine, Sir John Joseph, Kt., CBE

Swan, Sir Conrad Marshall John Fisher, KCVO, Ph.D.

Swan, Sir John William David, KBE

Swann, Sir Michael Christopher, Bt., TD (1906)

Swanwick, Sir Graham Russell, Kt., MBE

Swartz, *Hon.* Sir Reginald William Colin, KBE, ED

Sweetnam, Sir (David) Rodney, KCVO, CBE, FRCS

Swinburn, *Lt.-Gen.* Sir Richard Hull, KCB

Swinson, Sir John Henry Alan, Kt., OBE

Swinton, *Maj.-Gen.* Sir John, KCVO, OBE

Swire, Sir Adrian Christopher, Kt.

Swire, Sir John Anthony, Kt., CBE

Swynnerton, Sir Roger John Massy, Kt., CMG, OBE, MC

Sykes, Sir Francis John Badcock, Bt. (1781)

Sykes, Sir Hugh Ridley, Kt.

Sykes, Sir John Charles Anthony le Gallais, Bt. (1921)

Sykes, *Prof.* Sir (Malcolm) Keith, Kt.

Sykes, Sir Richard, Kt.

Sykes, Sir Tatton Christopher Mark, Bt. (1783)

Symington, *Prof.* Sir Thomas, Kt., MD, FRSE

Symons, *Vice-Adm.* Sir Patrick Jeremy, KBE

Synge, Sir Robert Carson, Bt. (1801)

Tait, *Adm.* Sir (Allan) Gordon, KCB, DSC

Tait, Sir Peter, KBE

Talbot, *Hon.* Sir Hilary Gwynne, Kt.

Talboys, *Rt. Hon.* Sir Brian Edward, CH, KCB

Tancred, Sir Henry Lawson-, Bt. (1662)

Tangaroa, *Hon.* Sir Tangoroa, Kt., MBE

Tange, Sir Arthur Harold, Kt., CBE

Tapsell, Sir Peter Hannay Bailey, Kt., MP

Tate, Sir (Henry) Saxon, Bt. (1898)

Tavaiqia, *Ratu* Sir Josaia, KBE

Tavare, Sir John, Kt., CBE

Taylor, *Lt.-Gen.* Sir Allan Macnab, KBE, MC

Taylor, Sir (Arthur) Godfrey, Kt.

Taylor, Sir Cyril Julian Hebden, Kt.

Taylor, Sir Edward Macmillan (Teddy), Kt., MP

Taylor, *Rt. Revd* John Bernard, KCVO

Taylor, Sir John Lang, KCMG

Taylor, Sir Nicholas Richard Stuart, Bt. (1917)

Taylor, *Prof.* Sir William, Kt., CBE

Teagle, *Vice-Adm.* Sir Somerford Francis, KBE

Tebbit, Sir Donald Claude, GCMG

Telford, Sir Robert, Kt., CBE, FEng.

Temple, Sir Ernest Sanderson, Kt., MBE, QC

Temple, Sir Rawden John Afamado, Kt., CBE, QC

Temple, *Maj.* Sir Richard Anthony Purbeck, Bt., MC (1876)

Templeton, Sir John Marks, Kt.

Tenison, Sir Richard Hanbury-, KCVO

Tennant, Sir Anthony John, Kt.

Tennant, *Capt.* Sir Iain Mark, KT

Teo, Sir Fiatau Penitala, GCMG, GCVO, ISO, MBE

Terry, *Air Marshal* Sir Colin George, KBE, CB

Terry, Sir Michael Edward Stanley Imbert-, Bt. (1917)

Terry, *Air Chief Marshal* Sir Peter David George, GCB, AFC

Tetley, Sir Herbert, KBE, CB

Tett, Sir Hugh Charles, Kt.

Thatcher, Sir Denis, Bt., MBE, TD (1990)

Thesiger, Sir Wilfred Patrick, KBE, DSO

Thomas, Sir Derek Morison David, KCMG

Thomas, Sir Frederick William, Kt.

Thomas, Sir (Godfrey) Michael (David), Bt. (1694)

Thomas, Sir Jeremy Cashel, KCMG

Thomas, Sir (John) Alan, Kt.

Thomas, Sir John Maldwyn, Kt.

Thomas, *Prof.* Sir John Meurig, Kt., FRS

Thomas, Sir Keith Vivian, Kt.

Thomas, Sir Robert Evan, Kt.

Thomas, *Hon.* Sir Roger John Laugharne, Kt.

Thomas, *Hon.* Sir Swinton Barclay, Kt.

Thomas, Sir William James Cooper, Bt., TD (1919)

Thomas, Sir (William) Michael (Marsh), Bt. (1918)

Thomas, *Adm.* Sir (William) Richard Scott, KCB, KCVO, OBE

Thompson, Sir Christopher Peile, Bt. (1890)

Thompson, Sir Clive Malcolm, Kt.

Thompson, Sir Donald, Kt.

Thompson, Sir Gilbert Williamson, Kt., OBE

Thompson, *Surgeon Vice-Adm.* Sir Godfrey James Milton-, KBE

Thompson, Sir (Humphrey) Simon Meysey-, Bt. (1874)

Thompson, *Prof.* Sir Michael Warwick, Kt., D.SC

Thompson, Sir Paul Anthony, Bt. (1963)

Thompson, Sir Peter Anthony, Kt.

Thompson, Sir Richard Hilton Marler, Bt. (1963)

Thompson, Sir (Thomas) Lionel Tennyson, Bt. (1806)

Thomson, Sir Adam, Kt., CBE

Thomson, Sir (Frederick Douglas) David, Bt. (1929)

Thomson, Sir John Adam, GCMG

Thomson, Sir John (Ian) Sutherland, KBE, CMG

Thomson, Sir Mark Wilfrid Home, Bt. (1925)

Thomson, Sir Thomas James, Kt., CBE, FRCP

Thorn, Sir John Samuel, Kt., OBE

Thorne, *Maj.-Gen.* Sir David Calthrop, KBE, CVO

Thorne, Sir Neil Gordon, Kt., OBE, TD

Thorne, Sir Peter Francis, KCVO, CBE

Thornton, Sir (George) Malcolm, Kt.

Thornton, *Lt.-Gen.* Sir Leonard Whitmore, KCB, CBE

Thornton, Sir Peter Eustace, KCB

Thornton, Sir Richard Eustace, KCVO, OBE

Thorold, Sir Anthony Henry, Bt., OBE, DSC (1642)

Thorpe, *Hon.* Sir Mathew Alexander, Kt.

Thouron, Sir John Rupert Hunt, KBE

Thwaites, Sir Bryan, Kt., Ph.D.

Thwin, Sir U, Kt.

Tibbits, *Capt.* Sir David Stanley, Kt., DSC

Tickell, Sir Crispin Charles Cervantes, GCMG, KCVO

Tidbury, Sir Charles Henderson, Kt.

Tikaram, Sir Moti, KBE

Tims, Sir Michael David, KCVO

Tindle, Sir Ray Stanley, Kt., CBE

Tippet, *Vice-Adm.* Sir Anthony Sanders, KCB

†Tipping, Sir David Gwynne Evans-, Bt. (1913)

Tirvengadum, Sir Harry Krishnan, Kt.

Titman, Sir John Edward Powis, KCVO

Tod, *Air Marshal* Sir John Hunter Hunter-, KBE, CB

Tod, *Vice-Adm.* Sir Jonathan James Richard, KCB, CBE

Todd, *Prof.* Sir David, Kt., CBE

Todd, Sir Ian Pelham, KBE, FRCS

Todd, *Hon.* Sir (Reginald Stephen) Garfield, Kt.

Tollemache, Sir Lyonel Humphry John, Bt. (1793)

Tololo, Sir Alkan, KBE

Tomkins, Sir Alfred George, Kt., CBE

Tomkins, Sir Edward Emile, GCMG, CVO

Tomkys, Sir (William) Roger, KCMG

Tomlinson, *Prof.* Sir Bernard Evans, Kt., CBE

Tooley, Sir John, Kt.

Tooth, Sir (Hugh) John Lucas-, Bt. (1920)

ToRobert, Sir Henry Thomas, KBE

Tory, Sir Geofroy William, KCMG

Touche, Sir Anthony George, Bt. (1920)

Touche, Sir Rodney Gordon, Bt. (1962)

Toulson, *Hon.* Sir Roger Grenfell, Kt.

Tovey, Sir Brian John Maynard, KCMG

ToVue, Sir Ronald, Kt., OBE

Towneley, Sir Simon Peter Edmund Cosmo William, KCVO

Townsend, Sir Cyril David, Kt.

Townsend, *Rear-Adm.* Sir Leslie William, KCVO, CBE

Townsing, Sir Kenneth Joseph, Kt., CMG

Traill, Sir Alan Towers, GBE

Trant, *Gen.* Sir Richard Brooking, KCB

Travers, Sir Thomas à'Beckett, Kt.

Treacher, *Adm.* Sir John Devereux, KCB

Trehane, Sir (Walter) Richard, Kt.

Treitel, *Prof.* Sir Guenter Heinz, Kt., FBA, QC

Trelawny, Sir John Barry Salusbury-, Bt. (1628)

Trench, Sir Peter Edward, Kt., CBE, TD

Trescowthick, Sir Donald Henry, KBE

†Trevelyan, Sir Edward (Norman), Bt. (1662)

Trevelyan, Sir Geoffrey Washington, Bt. (1874)

Trewby, *Vice-Adm.* Sir (George Francis) Allan, KCB, FEng.

Trezise, Sir Kenneth Bruce, Kt., OBE

Trippier, Sir David Austin, Kt., RD

Tritton, Sir Anthony John Ernest, Bt. (1905)

Trollope, Sir Anthony Simon, Bt. (1642)

Trotman, Sir Alexander, Kt.

Trotter, Sir Neville Guthrie, Kt.

Trotter, Sir Ronald Ramsay, Kt.

Troubridge, Sir Thomas Richard, Bt. (1799)

Troup, *Vice-Adm.* Sir (John) Anthony (Rose), KCB, DSC

Trowbridge, *Rear-Adm.* Sir Richard John, KCVO

Truscott, Sir George James Irving, Bt. (1909)

Tuck, Sir Bruce Adolph Reginald, Bt. (1910)

Tucker, *Hon.* Sir Richard Howard, Kt.

Tuckey, *Hon.* Sir Simon Lane, Kt.

Tuita, Sir Mariano Kelesimalefo, Kt., OBE

Tuite, Sir Christopher Hugh, Bt., Ph.D. (1622)

Tuivaga, Sir Timoci Uluiburotu, Kt.

Tuke, Sir Anthony Favill, Kt.

Tumim, *His Hon.* Sir Stephen, Kt.

Tupper, Sir Charles Hibbert, Bt. (1888)

Turbott, Sir Ian Graham, Kt., CMG, CVO

Turing, Sir John Dermot, Bt. (s. 1638)

Turnberg, *Prof.* Sir Leslie Arnold, Kt., MD, FRCP

Turnbull, Sir Andrew, KCB, CVO

Turnbull, Sir Richard Gordon, GCMG

Turner, Sir Colin William Carstairs, Kt., CBE, DFC

Turner, *Hon.* Sir Michael John, Kt.

Turnquest, Sir Orville Alton, GCMG, QC

Tuti, *Revd* Dudley, KBE

Tweedie, *Prof.* Sir David Philip, Kt.

Tyree, Sir (Alfred) William, Kt., OBE

Tyrwhitt, Sir Reginald Thomas Newman, Bt. (1919)

Udoma, *Hon.* Sir (Egbert) Udo, Kt.

Unsworth, *Hon.* Sir Edgar Ignatius Godfrey, Kt., CMG

Unwin, Sir (James) Brian, KCB

Ure, Sir John Burns, KCMG, LVO

Urquhart, Sir Brian Edward, KCMG, MBE

Urwick, Sir Alan Bedford, KCVO, CMG

Usher, Sir Leonard Gray, KBE

Usher, Sir (William) John Tevenar, Bt. (1899)

Ustinov, Sir Peter Alexander, Kt., CBE

Utting, Sir William Benjamin, Kt., CB

Vai, Sir Mea, Kt., CBE, ISO

Vallance, Sir Iain David Thomas, Kt.

Vallat, Sir Francis Aimé, GBE, KCMG, QC

Vallings, *Vice-Adm.* Sir George Montague Francis, KCB

Vanderfelt, Sir Robin Victor, KBE

Vane, Sir John Robert, Kt., D.Phil., D.SC., FRS

Vanneck, *Air Cdre* Hon. Sir Peter Beckford Rutgers, GBE, CB, AFC

van Straubenzee, Sir William Radcliffe, Kt., MBE

Vasquez, Sir Alfred Joseph, Kt., CBE, QC

Vaughan, Sir Gerard Folliott, Kt., FRCP

†Vavasour, Sir Eric Michael Joseph Marmaduke, Bt. (1828)

Veale, Sir Alan John Ralph, Kt., FEng.

Verco, Sir Walter John George, KCVO

†Verney, Sir John Sebastian, Bt. (1946)

Verney, *Hon.* Sir Lawrence John, Kt., TD

Verney, Sir Ralph Bruce, Bt., KBE (1818)

Vernon, Sir James, Kt., CBE

Vernon, Sir Nigel John Douglas, Bt. (1914)

Vernon, Sir (William) Michael, Kt.

Vesey, Sir (Nathaniel) Henry (Peniston), Kt.

Vestey, Sir (John) Derek, Bt. (1921)

Vial, Sir Kenneth Harold, Kt., CBE

Vick, Sir (Francis) Arthur, Kt., OBE, Ph.D.

Vickers, *Lt.-Gen.* Sir Richard Maurice Hilton, KCB, LVO, OBE

Victoria, Sir (Joseph Aloysius)
Donatus, Kt., CBE
Vincent, Sir William Percy Maxwell,
Bt. (1936)
Vinelott, Hon. Sir John Evelyn, Kt.
Vines, Sir William Joshua, Kt., CMG
†Vyvyan, Sir Ralph Ferrers
Alexander, Bt. (1645)
Waddell, Sir Alexander Nicol Anton,
KCMG, DSC
Waddell, Sir James Henderson, Kt.,
CB
Wade, Prof. Sir Henry William
Rawson, Kt., QC, FBA
Wade, Air Chief Marshal Sir Ruthven
Lowry, KCB, DFC
Waine, Rt. Revd John, KCVO
Waite, Rt. Hon. Sir John Douglas, Kt.
Wake, Sir Hereward, Bt., MC (1621)
Wakefield, Sir (Edward) Humphry
(Tyrell), Bt. (1962)
Wakefield, Sir Norman Edward, Kt.
Wakefield, Sir Peter George Arthur,
KBE, CMG
Wakeford, Air Marshal Sir Richard
Gordon, KCB, OBE, LVO, AFC
Wakeley, Sir John Cecil Nicholson,
Bt., FRCS (1952)
†Wakeman, Sir Edward Offley
Bertram, Bt. (1828)
Walford, Sir Christopher Rupert, Kt.
Walker, Revd Alan Edgar, Kt., OBE
Walker, Gen. Sir Antony Kenneth
Frederick, KCB
Walker, Sir Baldwin Patrick, Bt.
(1856)
Walker, Sir (Charles) Michael, GCMG
Walker, Sir Colin John Shedlock,
Kt., OBE
Walker, Sir David Alan, Kt.
Walker, Sir Gervas George, Kt.
Walker, Sir Harold Berners, KCMG
Walker, Maj. Sir Hugh Ronald, Bt.
(1906)
Walker, Sir James Graham, Kt., MBE
Walker, Sir James Heron, Bt. (1868)
Walker, Air Marshal Sir John Robert,
KCB, CBE, AFC
Walker, Gen. Sir Michael John
Dawson, KCB, CMG, CBE
Walker, Sir Michael Leolin
Forestier-, Bt. (1835)
Walker, Sir Miles Rawstron, Kt., CBE
Walker, Sir Patrick Jeremy, KCB
Walker, Rt. Hon. Sir Robert, Kt.
Walker, Sir Rodney Myerscough, Kt.
Walker, Hon. Sir Timothy Edward,
Kt.
Walker, Gen. Sir Walter Colyear,
KCB, CBE, DSO
Wall, Sir (John) Stephen, KCMG, LVO
Wall, Hon. Sir Nicholas Peter
Rathbone, Kt.
Wall, Sir Robert William, Kt., OBE
Wallace, Lt.-Gen. Sir Christopher
Brooke Quentin, KBE
Wallace, Sir Ian James, Kt., CBE
Waller, Hon. Sir (George) Mark, Kt.
Waller, Rt. Hon. Sir George Stanley,
Kt., OBE

Waller, Sir Robert William, Bt.
(I. 1780)
Walley, Sir John, KBE, CB
Wallis, Sir Peter Gordon, KCVO
Wallis, Sir Timothy William, Kt.
Walmsley, Vice-Adm. Sir Robert, KCB
Walsh, Sir Alan, Kt., D.SC., FRS
Walsh, Prof. Sir John Patrick, KBE
†Walsham, Sir Timothy John, Bt.
(1831)
Walters, Prof. Sir Alan Arthur, Kt.
Walters, Sir Dennis Murray, Kt., MBE
Walters, Sir Frederick Donald, Kt.
Walters, Sir Peter Ingram, Kt.
Walters, Sir Roger Talbot, KBE, FRIBA
Walton, Sir John Robert, Kt.
Wan, Sir Wamp, Kt., MBE
Wanstall, Hon. Sir Charles Gray, Kt.
Ward, Rt. Hon. Sir Alan Hylton, Kt.
Ward, Sir John Devereux, Kt., CBE
Ward, Sir Joseph James Laffey, Bt.
(1911)
Ward, Maj.-Gen. Sir Philip John
Newling, KCVO, CBE
Ward, Sir Timothy James, Kt.
Wardale, Sir Geoffrey Charles, KCB
Wardlaw, Sir Henry (John), Bt.
(s. 1631)
Waring, Sir (Alfred) Holburt, Bt.
(1935)
Warmington, Sir David Marshall, Bt.
(1908)
Warner, Sir (Edward Courtenay)
Henry, Bt. (1910)
Warner, Sir Edward Redston, KCMG,
OBE
Warner, Prof. Sir Frederick Edward,
Kt., FRS, FEng.
Warner, Sir Gerald Chierici, KCMG
Warner, Hon. Sir Jean-Pierre Frank
Eugene, Kt.
Warren, Sir (Frederick) Miles, KBE
Warren, Sir Kenneth Robin, Kt.
†Warren, Sir Michael Blackley, Bt.
(1784)
Wass, Sir Douglas William Gretton,
GCB
Waterhouse, Hon. Sir Ronald Gough,
Kt.
Waterlow, Sir Christopher Rupert,
Bt. (1873)
Waterlow, Sir (James) Gerard, Bt.
(1930)
Waters, Gen. Sir (Charles) John, GCB,
CBE
Waters, Sir (Thomas) Neil (Morris),
Kt.
Wates, Sir Christopher Stephen, Kt.
Watkins, Rt. Hon. Sir Tasker, VC, GBE
Watson, Sir Bruce Dunstan, Kt.
Watson, Prof. Sir David John, Kt.,
PH.D.
Watson, Sir Duncan Amos, Kt., CBE
Watson, Sir (James) Andrew, Bt.
(1866)
Watson, Sir John Forbes Inglefield-,
Bt. (1895)
Watson, Sir Michael Milne-, Bt., CBE
(1937)
Watson, Sir (Noel) Duncan, KCMG

Watson, Vice-Adm. Sir Philip
Alexander, KBE, LVO
Watson, Sir Ronald Matthew, Kt.,
CBE
Watt, Surgeon Vice-Adm. Sir James,
KBE, FRCS
Watt, Sir James Harvie-, Bt. (1945)
Watts, Sir Arthur Desmond, KCMG
Watts, Lt.-Gen. Sir John Peter Barry
Condliffe, KBE, CB, MC
Wauchope, Sir Roger (Hamilton)
Don-, Bt. (s. 1667)
Way, Sir Richard George Kitchener,
KCB, CBE
Weatherall, Prof. Sir David John, Kt.,
FRS
Weatherall, Vice-Adm. Sir James
Lamb, KBE
Weatherstone, Sir Dennis, KBE
Weaver, Sir Tobias Rushton, Kt., CB
Webb, Sir Thomas Langley, Kt.
Webster, Very Revd Alan Brunskill,
KCVO
Webster, Vice-Adm. Sir John
Morrison, KCB
Webster, Hon. Sir Peter Edlin, Kt.
Wedderburn, Sir Andrew John
Alexander Ogilvy-, Bt. (1803)
Wedgwood, Sir (Hugo) Martin, Bt.
(1942)
Weekes, Sir Everton DeCourcey,
KCMG, OBE
Weinberg, Sir Mark Aubrey, Kt.
Weir, Sir Michael Scott, KCMG
Weir, Sir Roderick Bignell, Kt.
Welby, Sir (Richard) Bruno Gregory,
Bt. (1801)
Welch, Sir John Reader, Bt. (1957)
Weldon, Sir Anthony William, Bt.
(I. 1723)
Weller, Sir Arthur Burton, Kt., CBE
Wellings, Sir Jack Alfred, Kt., CBE
†Wells, Sir Christopher Charles, Bt.
(1944)
Wells, Sir John Julius, Kt.
Wells, Sir William Henry Weston,
Kt., FRICS
Westbrook, Sir Neil Gowanloch, Kt.,
CBE
Westerman, Sir (Wilfred) Alan, Kt.,
CBE
Weston, Sir Michael Charles Swift,
KCMG, CVO
Weston, Sir (Philip) John, KCMG
Whalen, Sir Geoffrey Henry, Kt., CBE
Wheeler, Sir Harry Anthony, Kt.,
OBE
Wheeler, Air Chief Marshal Sir
(Henry) Neil (George), GCB, CBE,
DSO, DFC, AFC
Wheeler, Rt. Hon. Sir John Daniel,
Kt.
Wheeler, Sir John Hieron, Bt. (1920)
Wheeler, Gen. Sir Roger Neil, GCB,
CBE
Wheler, Sir Edward Woodford, Bt.
(1660)
Whent, Sir Gerald Arthur, Kt., CBE
Whishaw, Sir Charles Percival Law,
Kt.

Whitaker, *Maj.* Sir James Herbert Ingham, Bt., OBE (1936)
White, Sir Christopher Robert Meadows, Bt. (1937)
White, *Hon.* Sir Christopher Stuart Stuart-, Kt.
White, Sir David Harry, Kt.
White, Sir Frank John, Kt.
White, Sir George Stanley James, Bt. (1904)
White, *Wg Cdr.* Sir Henry Arthur Dalrymple-, Bt., DFC (1926)
White, *Adm.* Sir Hugo Moresby, GCB, CBE
White, *Hon.* Sir John Charles, Kt., MBE
White, Sir John Woolmer, Bt. (1922)
White, Sir Lynton Stuart, Kt., MBE, TD
White, Sir Nicholas Peter Archibald, Bt. (1802)
White, *Adm.* Sir Peter, GBE
Whitehead, Sir John Stainton, GCMG, CVO
Whitehead, Sir Rowland John Rathbone, Bt. (1889)
Whiteley, Sir Hugo Baldwin Huntington-, Bt. (1918)
Whiteley, *Gen.* Sir Peter John Frederick, GCB, OBE, RM
Whitfield, Sir William, Kt., CBE
Whitford, *Hon.* Sir John Norman Keates, Kt.
Whitmore, Sir Clive Anthony, GCB, CVO
Whitmore, Sir John Henry Douglas, Bt. (1954)
Whitney, Sir Raymond William, Kt., OBE, MP
Whittome, Sir (Leslie) Alan, Kt.
Wickerson, Sir John Michael, Kt.
Wicks, Sir James Albert, Kt.
Wicks, Sir Nigel Leonard, KCB, CVO, CBE
†Wigan, Sir Michael Iain, Bt. (1898)
Wiggin, Sir Alfred William (Jerry), Kt., TD
†Wiggin, Sir Charles Rupert John, Bt. (1892)
Wigram, *Revd Canon* Sir Clifford Woolmore, Bt. (1805)
Wilbraham, Sir Richard Baker, Bt. (1776)
Wilford, Sir (Kenneth) Michael, GCMG
Wilkes, *Gen.* Sir Michael John, KCB, CBE
Wilkins, Sir Graham John, Kt.
Wilkinson, Sir (David) Graham (Brook) Bt. (1941)
Wilkinson, *Prof.* Sir Denys Haigh, Kt., FRS
Wilkinson, Sir Peter Allix, KCMG, DSO, OBE
Wilkinson, Sir Philip William, Kt.
Willcocks, Sir David Valentine, Kt., CBE, MC
Williams, Sir Alastair Edgcumbe James Dudley-, Bt. (1964)

Williams, Sir Alwyn, Kt., PH.D., FRS, FRSE
Williams, Sir Arthur Dennis Pitt, Kt.
Williams, Sir (Arthur) Gareth Ludovic Emrys Rhys, Bt. (1918)
Williams, *Prof.* Sir Bruce Rodda, KBE
Williams, Sir Daniel Charles, GCMG, QC
Williams, *Adm.* Sir David, GCB
Williams, *Prof.* Sir David Glyndwr Tudor, Kt.
Williams, Sir David Innes, Kt.
Williams, *Hon.* Sir Denys Ambrose, KCMG
Williams, Sir Donald Mark, Bt. (1866)
Williams, *Prof.* Sir (Edward) Dillwyn, Kt., FRCP
Williams, *Hon.* Sir Edward Stratten, KCMG, KBE
Williams, *Prof.* Sir Glanmor, Kt., CBE, FBA
Williams, Sir Henry Sydney, Kt., OBE
Williams, Sir John Robert, KCMG
Williams, Sir (Lawrence) Hugh, Bt. (1798)
Williams, Sir Leonard, KBE, CB
Williams, Sir Osmond, Bt., MC (1909)
Williams, Sir Peter Michael, Kt.
Williams, *Prof.* Sir Robert Evan Owen, Kt., MD, FRCP
Williams, Sir (Robert) Philip Nathaniel, Bt. (1915)
Williams, Sir Robin Philip, Bt. (1953)
Williams, Sir (William) Maxwell (Harries), Kt.
Williamson, Sir David Francis, GCMG, CB
Williamson, *Marshal of the Royal Air Force* Sir Keith Alec, GCB, AFC
Williamson, Sir (Nicholas Frederick) Hedworth, Bt. (1642)
Willink, Sir Charles William, Bt. (1957)
Willis, *Hon.* Sir Eric Archibald, KBE, CMG
Willis, *Vice-Adm.* Sir (Guido) James, KBE
Willis, *Air Chief Marshal* Sir John Frederick, GBE, KCB
Willison, *Lt.-Gen.* Sir David John, KCB, OBE, MC
Willison, Sir John Alexander, Kt., OBE
†Wills, Sir David James Vernon, Bt. (1923)
Wills, Sir David Seton, Bt. (1904)
Wills, Sir (Hugh) David Hamilton, Kt., CBE, TD
Wills, Sir John Vernon, Bt., KCVO, TD (1923)
Wilmot, Sir Henry Robert, Bt. (1759)
Wilmot, Sir Michael John Assheton Eardley-, Bt. (1821)
Wilsey, *Gen.* Sir John Finlay Willasey, GCB, CBE
Wilson, *Lt.-Gen.* Sir (Alexander) James, KBE, MC
Wilson, Sir Anthony, Kt.

Wilson, *Vice-Adm.* Sir Barry Nigel, KCB
Wilson, *Lt.-Col.* Sir Blair Aubyn Stewart-, KCVO
Wilson, Sir Charles Haynes, Kt.
Wilson, *Prof.* Sir Colin Alexander St John, Kt., RA, FRIBA
Wilson, Sir David, Bt. (1920)
Wilson, Sir David Mackenzie, Kt.
Wilson, Sir Geoffrey Masterman, KCB, CMG
Wilson, Sir James William Douglas, Bt. (1906)
Wilson, Sir John Foster, Kt., CBE
Wilson, *Brig.* Sir Mathew John Anthony, Bt., OBE, MC (1874)
Wilson, *Hon.* Sir Nicholas Allan Roy, Kt.
Wilson, Sir Patrick Michael Ernest David McNair-, Kt.
Wilson, Sir Reginald Holmes, Kt.
Wilson, Sir Richard Thomas James, KCB
Wilson, Sir Robert, Kt., CBE
Wilson, Sir Robert Donald, KBE
Wilson, *Rt. Revd* Roger Plumpton, KCVO, DD
Wilson, Sir Roland, KBE
Wilson, *Air Chief Marshal* Sir (Ronald) Andrew (Fellowes), KCB, AFC
Wilson, *Hon.* Sir Ronald Darling, KBE, CMG
Wilton, Sir (Arthur) John, KCMG, KCVO, MC
Wingate, *Capt.* Sir Miles Buckley, KCVO
Winnington, Sir Francis Salwey William, Bt. (1755)
Winskill, *Air Cdre* Sir Archibald Little, KCVO, CBE, DFC
Winterbottom, Sir Walter, Kt., CBE
Wiseman, Sir John William, Bt. (1628)
Wolfendale, *Prof.* Sir Arnold Whittaker, Kt., FRS
Wolfson, Sir Brian Gordon, Kt.
Wolseley, Sir Charles Garnet Richard Mark, Bt. (1628)
†Wolseley, Sir James Douglas, Bt. (I. 1745)
Wolstenholme, Sir Gordon Ethelbert Ward, Kt., OBE
Wombwell, Sir George Philip Frederick, Bt. (1778)
Womersley, Sir Peter John Walter, Bt. (1945)
Woo, Sir Leo Joseph, Kt.
Wood, Sir Alan Marshall Muir, Kt., FRS, FEng.
Wood, Sir Andrew Marley, KCMG
Wood, Sir Anthony John Page, Bt. (1837)
Wood, Sir David Basil Hill-, Bt. (1921)
Wood, Sir Frederick Ambrose Stuart, Kt.
Wood, Sir Ian Clark, Kt., CBE
Wood, *Prof.* Sir John Crossley, Kt., CBE

Wood, *Hon.* Sir John Kember, Kt., MC
Wood, Sir Martin Francis, Kt., OBE
Wood, Sir Russell Dillon, KCVO, VRD
Wood, Sir William Alan, KCVO, CB
Woodard, *Rear Adm.* Sir Robert
  Nathaniel, KCVO
Woodcock, Sir John, Kt., CBE, QPM
Woodfield, Sir Philip John, KCB, CBE
Woodhead, *Vice-Adm.* Sir (Anthony)
  Peter, KCB
Woodhouse, *Rt. Hon.* Sir (Arthur)
  Owen, KBE, DSC
Wooding, Sir Norman Samuel, Kt.,
  CBE
Woodroffe, *Most Revd* George
  Cuthbert Manning, KBE
Woodroofe, Sir Ernest George, Kt.,
  ph.D.
Woodruff, *Prof.* Sir Michael Francis
  Addison, Kt., D.SC., FRS, FRCS
Woods, Sir Colin Philip Joseph,
  KCVO, CBE
Woodward, *Hon.* Sir (Albert) Edward,
  Kt., OBE
Woodward, *Adm.* Sir John Forster,
  GBE, KCB
Woolf, Sir John, Kt.
Woollaston, Sir (Mountford)
  Tosswill, Kt.
Worsley, *Gen.* Sir Richard Edward,
  GCB, OBE
Worsley, Sir (William) Marcus
  (John), Bt. (1838)
Worsthorne, Sir Peregrine Gerard,
  Kt.
Wratten, *Air Chief Marshal* Sir
  William John, GBE, CB, AFC
Wraxall, Sir Charles Frederick
  Lascelles, Bt. (1813)
Wrey, Sir George Richard
  Bourchier, Bt. (1628)
Wrigglesworth, Sir Ian William, Kt.
Wright, Sir Allan Frederick, KBE
Wright, Sir David John, KCMG, LVO
Wright, Sir Denis Arthur Hepworth,
  GCMG
Wright, Sir Edward Maitland, Kt.,
  D.Phil., LLD, D.SC., FRSE
Wright, *Hon.* Sir (John) Michael, Kt.
Wright, Sir (John) Oliver, GCMG,
  GCVO, DSC
Wright, Sir Paul Hervé Giraud,
  KCMG, OBE
Wright, Sir Peter Robert, Kt., CBE
Wright, Sir Richard Michael Cory-,
  Bt. (1903)
Wrightson, Sir Charles Mark
  Garmondsway, Bt. (1900)
Wrigley, *Prof.* Sir Edward Anthony
  (Sir Tony), Kt., ph.D., PBA
Wu, Sir Gordon Ying Sheung, KCMG
Wynn, Sir David Watkin Williams-,
  Bt. (1688)
Yacoub, *Prof.* Sir Magdi Habib, Kt.,
  FRCS
Yang, *Hon.* Sir Ti Liang, Kt.
Yapp, Sir Stanley Graham, Kt.
Yardley, Sir David Charles Miller,
  Kt., LLD
Yarranton, Sir Peter George, Kt.

Yarrow, Sir Eric Grant, Bt., MBE
  (1916)
Yellowlees, Sir Henry, KCB
Yocklunn, Sir John (Soong Chung),
  KCVO
Yoo Foo, Sir (François) Henri, Kt.
Youens, Sir Peter William, Kt., CMG,
  OBE
Young, Sir Brian Walter Mark, Kt.
Young, Sir Colville Norbert, GCMG,
  MBE
Young, *Lt.-Gen.* Sir David Tod, KBE,
  CB, DFC
Young, *Rt. Hon.* Sir George Samuel
  Knatchbull, Bt., MP (1813)
Young, *Hon.* Sir Harold William,
  KCMG
Young, Sir John Kenyon Roe, Bt.
  (1821)
Young, *Hon.* Sir John McIntosh,
  KCMG
Young, Sir Leslie Clarence, Kt., CBE
Young, Sir Norman Smith, Kt.
Young, Sir Richard Dilworth, Kt.
Young, Sir Robert Christopher
  Mackworth-, GCVO
Young, Sir Roger William, Kt.
Young, Sir Stephen Stewart
  Templeton, Bt. (1945)
Young, Sir William Neil, Bt. (1769)
Younger, *Maj.-Gen.* Sir John
  William, Bt., CBE (1911)
Yuwi, Sir Matiabe, KBE
Zeeman, *Prof.* Sir (Erik) Christopher,
  Kt., FRS
Zeidler, Sir David Ronald, Kt., CBE
Zissman, Sir Bernard Philip, Kt.
Zochonis, Sir John Basil, Kt.
Zoleveke, Sir Gideon Pitabose, KBE
Zunz, Sir Gerhard Jacob (Jack), Kt.,
  FENG.
Zurenuoc, Sir Zibang, KBE

The Military Knights of Windsor

The Military Knights of Windsor take part in all ceremonies of the Noble Order of the Garter and attend Sunday morning service in St George's Chapel, Windsor Castle, as representatives of the Knights of the Garter. The Knights receive a small stipend in addition to their army pensions and quarters in Windsor Castle.

The Knights of Windsor were originally founded in 1348 after the wars in France to assist English knights, who, having been prisoners in the hands of the French, had become impoverished by the payment of heavy ransoms. When Edward III founded the Order of the Garter later the same year, he incorporated the Knights of Windsor and the College of St George into its foundation and raised the number of Knights to 26 to correspond with the number of the Knights of the Garter. Known later as the Alms Knights or Poor Knights of Windsor, their establishment was

reduced under the will of Henry VIII to 13 and statutes were drawn up by Elizabeth I.

In 1833, William IV changed their designation to The Military Knights and granted them their present uniform which consists of a scarlet tail-coat with white cross sword-belt, crimson sash and cocked hat with plume. The badges are the Shield of St George and the Star of the Order of the Garter.

Governor, Maj.-Gen. Peter Downward, CB, DSO, DFC
Military Knights, Brig. A. L. Atkinson, OBE; Brig. J. F. Lindner, OBE, MC; Maj. W. L. Thompson, MVO, MBE, DCM; Maj. J. C. Cowley, OBE, DCM; Maj. G. R. Mitchell, MBE, BEM; Lt.-Col. R. L. C. Tamplin; Maj. P. H. Bolton, MBE; Brig. T. W. Hackworth, OBE; Maj. R. J. Moore; Lt.-Col. R. R. Giles; Maj. R. J. de M. Gainher; Maj. A. H. Clarkson
Supernumerary, Brig. A. C. Tyler, CBE, MC

The Order of St John

THE MOST VENERABLE ORDER OF THE HOSPITAL OF ST JOHN OF JERUSALEM (1888)

GCStJ Bailiff/Dame Grand Cross
KStJ Knight of Justice/Grace
DStJ Dame of Justice/Grace
ChStJ Chaplain
CStJ Commander
OStJ Officer
SBStJ Serving Brother
SSStJ Serving Sister
EsqStJ Esquire

Mottoes, Pro Fide *and* Pro Utilitate Hominum

The Order of St John, founded in the early 12th century in Jerusalem, was a religious order with a particular duty to care for the sick. In Britain the Order was dissolved by Henry VIII in 1540 but the British branch was revived in the early 19th century. The branch was not accepted by the Grand Magistracy of the Order in Rome but its search for a role in the tradition of the Hospitallers led to the founding of the St John Ambulance Association in 1877 and later the St John Ambulance Brigade; in 1882 the St

John Ophthalmic Hospital was founded in Jerusalem. A royal charter was granted in 1888 establishing the British Order of St John as a British Order of Chivalry with the Sovereign as its head.

Admission to the Order is conferred in recognition of service, usually in St John Ambulance. Membership does not confer any rank, style, title or precedence on a recipient.

SOVEREIGN HEAD OF THE ORDER
HM The Queen

GRAND PRIOR
HRH The Duke of Gloucester, KG, GCVO

Lord Prior, The Lord Vestey
Prelate, The Rt. Revd M. A. Mann, KCVO
Chancellor, Prof. A. R. Mellows, TD
Bailiff of Egle, The Lord Remnant
Headquarters, St John's Gate, Clerkenwell, London EC1M 4DA. Tel: 0171-253 6644

Dames Grand Cross and Dames Commanders

Style, 'Dame' before forename and surname, followed by appropriate post-nominal initials. Where such an award is made to a lady already in enjoyment of a higher title, the appropriate initials follow her name
Husband, Untitled
For forms of address, *see* page 135

Dame Grand Cross and Dame Commander are the higher classes for women of the Order of the Bath, the Order of St Michael and St George, the Royal Victorian Order, and the Order of the British Empire. Dames Grand Cross rank after the wives of Baronets and before the wives of Knights Grand Cross. Dames Commanders rank after the wives of Knights Grand Cross and before the wives of Knights Commanders.

Honorary Dames Commanders may be conferred on women who are citizens of countries of which The Queen is not head of state.

LIST OF DAMES   *Revised to 31 August 1998*

Women peers in their own right and life peers are not included in this list. Female members of the royal family are not included in this list; details of the orders they hold are given on pages 117–8

If a dame has a double barrelled or hyphenated surname, she is listed under the final element of the name
A full entry in italic type indicates that the recipient of an honour died during the year in which the honour was conferred. The name is included for the purposes of record

Abaijah, Dame Josephine, DBE
Abel Smith, Lady, DCVO
Abergavenny, The Marchioness of, DCVO
Airlie, The Countess of, DCVO
Albemarle, The Countess of, DBE
Anderson, *Brig.* Hon. Dame Mary Mackenzie (Mrs Pihl), DBE
Anglesey, The Marchioness of, DBE
Anson, Lady (Elizabeth Audrey), DBE
Anstee, Dame Margaret Joan, DCMG
Arden, *Hon.* Dame Mary Howarth (Mrs Mance), DBE
Baker, Dame Janet Abbott (Mrs Shelley), CH, DBE
Ballin, Dame Reubina Ann, DBE
Barnes, Dame (Alice) Josephine (Mary Taylor), DBE, FRCP, FRCS
Barrow, Dame Jocelyn Anita (Mrs Downer), DBE
Barstow, Dame Josephine Clare (Mrs Anderson), DBE
Basset, Lady Elizabeth, DCVO
Bean, Dame Majorie Louise, DBE
Beaurepaire, Dame Beryl Edith, DBE
Beer, *Prof.* Dame Gillian Patricia Kempster, DBE, FBA
Bergquist, *Prof.* Dame Patricia Rose, DBE
Berry, Dame Alice Miriam, DBE
Blaize, Dame Venetia Ursula, DBE
Blaxland, Dame Helen Frances, DBE
Booth, *Hon.* Dame Margaret Myfanwy Wood, DBE
Bottomley, Dame Bessie Ellen, DBE
Bowman, Dame (Mary) Elaine Kellett-, DBE
Bowtell, Dame Ann Elizabeth, DCB

Boyd, Dame Vivienne Myra, DBE
Bracewell, *Hon.* Dame Joyanne Winifred (Mrs Copeland), DBE
Brain, Dame Margaret Anne (Mrs Wheeler), DBE
Brazill, Dame Josephine (Sister Mary Philippa), DBE
Bridges, Dame Mary Patricia, DBE
Brown, Dame Gillian Gerda, DCVO, CMG
Browne, Lady Moyra Blanche Madeleine, DBE
Bryans, Dame Anne Margaret, DBE
Buttfield, Dame Nancy Eileen, DBE
Bynoe, Dame Hilda Louisa, DBE
Caldicott, Dame Fiona, DBE, FRCP, FRCPsych.
Cartland, Dame Barbara Hamilton, DBE
Cartwright, Dame Silvia Rose, DBE
Casey, Dame Stella Katherine, DBE
Charles, Dame (Mary) Eugenia, DBE
Chesterton, Dame Elizabeth Ursula, DBE
Clark, *Prof.* Dame (Margaret) June, DBE, Ph.D.
Clay, Dame Marie Mildred, DBE
Clayton, Dame Barbara Evelyn (Mrs Klyne), DBE
Cleland, Dame Rachel, DBE
Coll, Dame Elizabeth Anne Loosemore Esteve-, DBE
Collarbone, Dame Patricia, DBE
Corsar, The Hon. Dame Mary Drummond, DBE
Coulshed, Dame (Mary) Frances, DBE, TD
Daws, Dame Joyce Margaretta, DBE
Dell, Dame Miriam Patricia, DBE
Dench, Dame Judith Olivia (Mrs Williams), DBE
de Valois, Dame Ninette, OM, CH, DBE
Digby, Lady, DBE
Donaldson, Dame (Dorothy) Mary (Lady Donaldson of Lymington), GBE
Drake, *Brig.* Dame Jean Elizabeth Rivett-, DBE
Dugdale, Kathryn, Lady, DCVO
Dumont, Dame Ivy Leona, DCMG
Dyche, Dame Rachael Mary, DBE
Ebsworth, *Hon.* Dame Ann Marian, DBE

Engel, Dame Pauline Frances (Sister Pauline Engel), DBE
Evison, Dame Helen June Patricia, DBE
Fenner, Dame Peggy Edith, DBE
Fitton, Dame Doris Alice (Mrs Mason), DBE
Fort, Dame Maeve Geraldine, DCMG
Fraser, Dame Dorothy Rita, DBE
Friend, Dame Phyllis Muriel, DBE
Fritchie, Dame Irene Tordoff (Dame Rennie Fritchie), DBE
Frost, Dame Phyllis Irene, DBE
Fry, Dame Margaret Louise, DBE
Gallagher, Dame Monica Josephine, DBE
Gardiner, Dame Helen Louisa, DBE, MVO
Giles, *Air Comdt.* Dame Pauline (Mrs Parsons), DBE, RRC
Goodman, Dame Barbara, DBE
Gordon, Dame Minita Elmira, GCMG, GCVO
Gow, Dame Jane Elizabeth (Mrs Whiteley), DBE
Grafton, The Duchess of, GCVO
Green, Dame Mary Georgina, DBE
Grey, Dame Beryl Elizabeth (Mrs Svenson), DBE
Grimthorpe, The Lady, DCVO
Guilfoyle, Dame Margaret Georgina Constance, DBE
Guthardt, *Revd Dr* Dame Phyllis Myra, DBE
Haig, Dame Mary Alison Glen-, DBE
Hale, *Hon.* Dame Brenda Marjorie (Mrs Farrand), DBE
Harper, Dame Elizabeth Margaret Way, DBE
Heilbron, *Hon.* Dame Rose, DBE
Henderson, Dame Louise Etiennette Sidonie, DBE
Henrison, Dame Anne Elizabeth Rosina, DBE
Herbison, Dame Jean Marjory, DBE, CMG
Hercus, *Hon.* Dame (Margaret) Ann, DCMG
Hetet, Dame Rangimarie, DBE
Higgins, *Prof.* Dame Rosalyn, DBE, QC
Hill, *Air Cdre* Dame Felicity Barbara, DBE
Hiller, Dame Wendy (Mrs Gow), DBE

Decorations and Medals

PRINCIPAL DECORATIONS AND MEDALS
In order of precedence

VICTORIA CROSS (VC), 1856 (*see* page 209)
GEORGE CROSS (GC), 1940 (*see* pages 209–210)

BRITISH ORDERS OF KNIGHTHOOD, ETC.
Baronet's Badge
Knight Bachelor's Badge

DECORATIONS
Conspicuous Gallantry Cross (CGC), 1995
Royal Red Cross Class I (RRC), 1883
Distinguished Service Cross (DSC), 1914. For all ranks for actions at sea
Military Cross (MC), December 1914. For all ranks for actions on land
Distinguished Flying Cross (DFC), 1918. For all ranks for acts of gallantry when flying in active operations against the enemy
Air Force Cross (AFC), 1918. For all ranks for acts of courage when flying, although not in active operations against the enemy
Royal Red Cross Class II (ARRC)
Order of British India
Kaisar-i-Hind Medal
Order of St John

MEDALS FOR GALLANTRY AND DISTINGUISHED CONDUCT
Union of South Africa Queen's Medal for Bravery, in Gold
Distinguished Conduct Medal (DCM), 1854
Conspicuous Gallantry Medal (CGM), 1874
Conspicuous Gallantry Medal (Flying)
George Medal (GM), 1940
Queen's Police Medal for Gallantry
Queen's Fire Service Medal for Gallantry
Royal West African Frontier Force Distinguished Conduct Medal
King's African Rifles Distinguished Conduct Medal
Indian Distinguished Service Medal
Union of South Africa Queen's Medal for Bravery, in Silver
Distinguished Service Medal (DSM), 1914
Military Medal (MM), 1916
Distinguished Flying Medal (DFM), 1918
Air Force Medal (AFM)
Constabulary Medal (Ireland)
Medal for Saving Life at Sea
Sea Gallantry Medal
Indian Order of Merit (Civil)
Indian Police Medal for Gallantry
Ceylon Police Medal for Gallantry
Sierra Leone Police Medal for Gallantry
Sierra Leone Fire Brigades Medal for Gallantry
Colonial Police Medal for Gallantry (CPM)
Queen's Gallantry Medal, 1974
Royal Victorian Medal (RVM), Gold, Silver and Bronze
British Empire Medal (BEM), (formerly the Medal of the Order of the British Empire, for Meritorious Service; also includes the Medal of the Order awarded before 29 December 1922)
Canada Medal
Queen's Police (QPM) *and Queen's Fire Service Medals* (QFSM) *for Distinguished Service*
Queen's Medal for Chiefs

WAR MEDALS AND STARS (in order of date)
POLAR MEDALS (in order of date)
POLICE MEDALS FOR VALUABLE SERVICE
JUBILEE, CORONATION AND DURBAR MEDALS
King George V, King George VI and Queen Elizabeth II Long and Faithful Service Medals

EFFICIENCY AND LONG SERVICE DECORATIONS AND MEDALS
Medal for Meritorious Service
Accumulated Campaign Service Medal
The Medal for Long Service and Good Conduct (Military)
Naval Long Service and Good Conduct Medal
Royal Marines Meritorious Service Medal
Royal Air Force Meritorious Service Medal
Royal Air Force Long Service and Good Conduct Medal
Medal for Long Service and Good Conduct (Ulster Defence Regiment)
Police Long Service and Good Conduct Medal
Fire Brigade Long Service and Good Conduct Medal
Colonial Police and Fire Brigades Long Service Medals
Colonial Prison Service Medal
Hong Kong Disciplined Services Medal
Army Emergency Reserve Decoration (ERD), 1952
Volunteer Officers' Decoration (VD)
Volunteer Long Service Medal
Volunteer Officers' Decoration for India and the Colonies
Volunteer Long Service Medal for India and the Colonies
Colonial Auxiliary Forces Officers' Decoration
Colonial Auxiliary Forces Long Service Medal
Medal for Good Shooting (Naval)
Militia Long Service Medal
Imperial Yeomanry Long Service Medal
Territorial Decoration (TD), 1908
Efficiency Decoration (ED)
Territorial Efficiency Medal
Efficiency Medal
Special Reserve Long Service and Good Conduct Medal
Decoration for Officers, Royal Navy Reserve (RD), 1910
Decoration for Officers, RNVR (VRD)
Royal Naval Reserve Long Service and Good Conduct Medal
RNVR Long Service and Good Conduct Medal
Royal Naval Auxiliary Sick Berth Reserve Long Service and Good Conduct Medal
Royal Fleet Reserve Long Service and Good Conduct Medal
Royal Naval Wireless Auxiliary Reserve Long Service and Good Conduct Medal
Air Efficiency Award (AE), 1942
Ulster Defence Regiment Medal
Northern Ireland Home Service Medal
The Queen's Medal. For champion shots in the RN, RM, RNZN, Army, RAF
Cadet Forces Medal, 1950
Coastguard Auxiliary Service Long Service Medal (formerly Coast Life Saving Corps Long Service Medal)
Special Constabulary Long Service Medal
Royal Observer Corps Medal
Civil Defence Long Service Medal
Ambulance Service (Emergency Duties) Long Service and Good Conduct Medal
Rhodesia Medal
Royal Ulster Constabulary Service Medal
Service Medal of the Order of St John
Badge of the Order of the League of Mercy
Voluntary Medical Service Medal, 1932

Women's Voluntary Service Medal
Colonial Special Constabulary Medal

FOREIGN ORDERS, DECORATIONS AND MEDALS (in order of date)

THE VICTORIA CROSS (1856)
FOR CONSPICUOUS BRAVERY

VC

Ribbon, Crimson, for all Services (until 1918 it was blue for the Royal Navy)

Instituted on 29 January 1856, the Victoria Cross was awarded retrospectively to 1854, the first being held by Lt. C. D. Lucas, RN, for bravery in the Baltic Sea on 21 June 1854 (gazetted 24 February 1857). The first 62 Crosses were presented by Queen Victoria in Hyde Park, London, on 26 June 1857.

The Victoria Cross is worn before all other decorations, on the left breast, and consists of a cross-pattée of bronze, one and a half inches in diameter, with the Royal Crown surmounted by a lion in the centre, and beneath there is the inscription *For Valour*. Holders of the VC receive a tax-free annuity of £1,300, irrespective of need or other conditions. In 1911, the right to receive the Cross was extended to Indian soldiers, and in 1920 to matrons, sisters and nurses, and the staff of the Nursing Services and other services pertaining to hospitals and nursing, and to civilians of either sex regularly or temporarily under the orders, direction or supervision of the naval, military, or air forces of the Crown.

SURVIVING RECIPIENTS OF THE VICTORIA CROSS *as at 31 August 1998*

Agansing Rai, *Capt.,* MM (5th Royal Gurkha Rifles)
1944 *World War*
Ali Haidar, *Jemadar* (13th Frontier Force Rifles)
1945 *World War*
Annand, *Capt.* R. W. (Durham Light Infantry)
1940 *World War*
Bhan Bhagta Gurung, *Havildar* (2nd Gurkha Rifles)
1945 *World War*
Bhandari Ram, *Capt.* (10th Baluch Regiment)
1944 *World War*
Chapman, *Sgt.* E. T., BEM (Monmouthshire Regiment)
1945 *World War*
Cruickshank, *Flt. Lt.* J. A. (RAFVR)
1944 *World War*
Cutler, *Capt.* Sir Roden, AK, KCMG, KCVO, CBE (Australian Military Forces, 2/5th Field Artillery)
1941 *World War*
Fraser, *Lt.-Cdr.* I. E., DSC (RNR)
1945 *World War*
Gaje Ghale, *Capt.* (5th Royal Gurkha Rifles)
1943 *World War*
Ganju Lama, *Capt.,* MM (7th Gurkha Rifles)
1944 *World War*
Gardner, *Capt.* P. J., MC (Royal Tank Regiment)
1941 *World War*
Gould, *Lt.* T. W. (RN)
1942 *World War*

Jamieson, *Maj.* D. A., CVO (Royal Norfolk Regiment)
1944 *World War*
Kenna, *Pte.* E. (Australian Military Forces, 2/4th (NSW))
1945 *World War*
Kenneally, *Guardsman* J. P. (Irish Guards)
1943 *World War*
Lachhiman Gurung, *Havildar* (8th Gurkha Rifles)
1945 *World War*
Merritt, *Lt.-Col.* C. C. I., CD (South Saskatchewan Regiment)
1942 *World War*
Norton, *Capt.* G. R., MM (South African Forces, Kaffrarian Rifles)
1944 *World War*
Payne, *WO* K., DSC (USA) (Australian Army Training Team)
1969 *Vietnam*
Porteous, *Col.* P. A. (Royal Regiment of Artillery)
1942 *World War*
Rambahadur Limbu, *Capt.,* MVO (10th Princess Mary's Gurkha Rifles)
1965 *Sarawak*
Reid, *Flt. Lt.* W. (RAFVR)
1943 *World War*
Smith, *Sgt.* E. A., CD (Seaforth Highlanders of Canada)
1944 *World War*
Speakman-Pitts, *Sgt.* W. (Black Watch)
1951 *Korea*
Tulbahadur Pun, *Lt.* (6th Gurkha Rifles)
1944 *World War*
Umrao Singh, *Sub Major* (Royal Indian Artillery)
1944 *World War*
Watkins, *Maj. Rt. Hon.* Sir Tasker, GBE (Welch Regiment)
1944 *World War*
Wilson, *Lt.-Col.* E. C. T. (East Surrey Regiment)
1940 *World War*

THE GEORGE CROSS (1940)
FOR GALLANTRY

GC

Ribbon, Dark blue, threaded through a bar adorned with laurel leaves
Instituted 24 September 1940 (with amendments, 3 November 1942)

The George Cross is worn before all other decorations (except the VC) on the left breast (when worn by a woman it may be worn on the left shoulder from a ribbon of the same width and colour fashioned into a bow). It consists of a plain silver cross with four equal limbs, the cross having in the centre a circular medallion bearing a design showing St George and the Dragon. The inscription *For Gallantry* appears round the medallion and in the angle of each limb of the cross is the Royal cypher 'G VI' forming a circle concentric with the medallion. The reverse is plain and bears the name of the recipient and the date of the award. The cross is suspended by a ring from a bar adorned with laurel leaves on dark blue ribbon one and a half inches wide.

The cross is intended primarily for civilians; awards to the fighting services are confined to actions for which purely military honours are not normally granted. It is awarded only for acts of the greatest heroism or of the most conspicuous courage in circumstances of extreme danger. From 1 April 1965, holders of the Cross have received a tax-free annuity, which is now £1,300.

The royal warrant which ordained that the grant of the Empire Gallantry Medal should cease authorized holders of that medal to return it to the Central Chancery of the Orders of Knighthood and to receive in exchange the George Cross. A similar provision applied to posthumous awards of the Empire Gallantry Medal made after the outbreak of war in 1939. In October 1971 all surviving holders of the Albert Medal and the Edward Medal exchanged those decorations for the George Cross.

SURVIVING RECIPIENTS OF THE GEORGE CROSS
as at 31 August 1998

If the recipient originally received the Empire Gallantry Medal (EGM), the Albert Medal (AM) or the Edward Medal (EM), this is indicated by the initials in parenthesis.

Archer, *Col.* B. S. T., GC, OBE, ERD, 1941
Baker, J. T., GC (EM), 1929
Bamford, J., GC, 1952
Beaton, J., GC, CVO, 1974
Bridge, *Lt.-Cdr.* J., GC, GM and BAR, 1944
Butson, *Lt.-Col.* A. R. C., GC, CD, MD (AM), 1948
Bywater, R. A. S., GC, GM, 1944
Errington, H., GC, 1941
Farrow, K., GC (AM), 1948
Flintoff, H. H., GC (EM), 1944
Gledhill, A. J., GC, 1967
Gregson, J. S., GC (AM), 1943
Hawkins, E., GC (AM), 1943
Johnson, *WO1 (SSM)* B., GC, 1990
Kinne, D. G., GC, 1954
Lowe, A. R., GC (AM), 1949
Lynch, J., GC, BEM (AM), 1948
Malta, GC, 1942
Manwaring, T. G., GC (EM), 1949
Moore, R. V., GC, CBE, 1940
Moss, B., GC, 1940
Naughton, F., GC (EGM), 1937
Pearson, Miss J. D. M., GC (EGM), 1940
Pratt, M. K., GC, 1978
Purves, Mrs M., GC (AM), 1949
Raweng, Awang anak, GC, 1951
Riley, G., GC (AM), 1944
Rowlands, *Air Marshal* Sir John, GC, KBE, 1943
Sinclair, *Air Vice-Marshal* Sir Laurence, GC, KCB, CBE, DSO, 1941
Stevens, H. W., GC, 1958
Stronach, *Capt.* G. P., GC, 1943
Styles, *Lt.-Col.* S. G., GC, 1972
Taylor, *Lt.-Cdr.* W. H., GC, MBE, 1941
Walker, C., GC, 1972
Walker, C. H., GC (AM), 1942
Walton, E. W. K., GC (AM), DSO, 1948
Wilcox, C., GC (EM), 1949
• Wiltshire, S. N., GC (EGM), 1930
Wooding, E. A., GC (AM), 1945

Chiefs of Clans and Names in Scotland

Only chiefs of whole Names or Clans are included, except certain special instances (marked *) who, though not chiefs of a whole name, were or are for some reason (e.g. the Macdonald forfeiture) independent. Under decision (*Campbell-Gray*, 1950) that a bearer of a 'double or triple-barrelled' surname cannot be held chief of a part of such, several others cannot be included in the list at present.

THE ROYAL HOUSE: HM The Queen

AGNEW: Sir Crispin Agnew of Lochnaw, Bt., QC, 6 Palmerston Road, Edinburgh EH9 ITN

ANSTRUTHER: Sir Ralph Anstruther of that Ilk, Bt., GCVO, MC, Balcaskie, Pittenweem, Fife KY10 2RD

ARBUTHNOTT: The Viscount of Arbuthnott, KT, CBE, DSC, Arbuthnott House, Laurencekirk, Kincardineshire AB30 IPA

BARCLAY: Peter C. Barclay of Towie Barclay and of that Ilk, 28A Gordon Place, London W8 4JE

BORTHWICK: The Lord Borthwick, Crookston, Heriot, Midlothian EH38 5YS

BOYD: The Lord Kilmarnock, 194 Regent's Park Road, London NW1 8XP

BOYLE: The Earl of Glasgow, Kelburn, Fairlie, Ayrshire KA29 OBE

BRODIE: Ninian Brodie of Brodie, Brodie Castle, Forres, Morayshire IV36 OTE

BRUCE: The Earl of Elgin and Kincardine, KT, Broomhall, Dunfermline, Fife KY11 3DU

BUCHAN: David S. Buchan of Auchmacoy, Auchmacoy House, Ellon, Aberdeenshire

BURNETT: J. C. A. Burnett of Leys, Crathes Castle, Banchory, Kincardineshire

CAMERON: Sir Donald Cameron of Lochiel, KT, CVO, TD, Achnacarry, Spean Bridge, Inverness-shire

CAMPBELL: The Duke of Argyll, Inveraray, Argyll PA32 8XF

CARMICHAEL: Richard J. Carmichael of Carmichael, Carmichael, Thankerton, Biggar, Lanarkshire

CARNEGIE: The Duke of Fife, Elsick House, Stonehaven, Kincardineshire AB3 2NT

CATHCART: Maj.-Gen. The Earl Cathcart, CB, DSO, MC, Moor Hatches, West Amesbury, Salisbury SP4 7BH

CHARTERIS: The Earl of Wemyss and March, KT, Gosford House, Longniddry, East Lothian EH32 OPX

CLAN CHATTAN: M. K. Mackintosh of Clan Chattan, Maxwell Park, Gwelo, Zimbabwe

CHISHOLM: Hamish Chisholm of Chisholm (*The Chisholm*), Elmpine, Beck Row, Bury St Edmunds, Suffolk

COCHRANE: The Earl of Dundonald, Lochnell Castle, Ledaig, Argyllshire

COLQUHOUN: Sir Ivar Colquhoun of Luss, Bt., Camstraddan, Luss, Dunbartonshire G83 8NX

CRANSTOUN: David A. S. Cranstoun of that Ilk, Corehouse, Lanark

CRICHTON: vacant

CUMMING: Sir William Cumming of Altyre, Bt., Altyre, Forres, Moray

DARROCH: Capt. Duncan Darroch of Gourock, The Red House, Branksome Park Road, Camberley, Surrey

DAVIDSON: Alister G. Davidson of Davidston, 21 Winscombe Street, Takapuna, Auckland, New Zealand

DEWAR: Kenneth Dewar of that Ilk and Vogrie, The Dower House, Grayshott, nr Hindhead, Surrey

DRUMMOND: The Earl of Perth, PC, Stobhall, Perth PH2 6DR

DUNBAR: Sir James Dunbar of Mochrum, Bt., Bld 848 C.2, 66877 Flugplatz, Ramstein, Germany

DUNDAS: David D. Dundas of Dundas, 8 Derna Road, Kenwyn 7700, South Africa

DURIE: Raymond V. D. Durie of Durie, Court House, Pewsey, Wilts

ELIOTT: Mrs Margaret Eliott of Redheugh, Redheugh, Newcastleton, Roxburghshire

ERSKINE: The Earl of Mar and Kellie, Erskine House, Kirk Wynd, Alloa, Clackmannan FK10 4JF

FARQUHARSON: Capt. A. Farquharson of Invercauld, MC, Invercauld, Braemar, Aberdeenshire AB35 5TT

FERGUSSON: Sir Charles Fergusson of Kilkerran, Bt., Kilkerran, Maybole, Ayrshire

FORBES: The Lord Forbes, KBE, Balforbes, Alford, Aberdeenshire AB33 8DR

FORSYTH: Alistair Forsyth of that Ilk, Ethie Castle, by Arbroath, Angus DD11 5SP

FRASER: The Lady Saltoun, Inverey House, Aberdeenshire AB35 5YB

*FRASER (OF LOVAT): The Lord Lovat, Beaufort Lodge, Beauly, Inverness-shire IV4 7AZ

GAYRE: R. Gayre of Gayre and Nigg, Minard Castle, Minard, Inverary, Argyll PA32 8YB

GORDON: The Marquess of Huntly, Aboyne Castle, Aberdeenshire AB34 5JP

GRAHAM: The Duke of Montrose, Buchanan Auld House, Drymen, Stirlingshire

GRANT: The Lord Strathspey, The House of Lords, London SW1A OPW

GRIERSON: Sir Michael Grierson of Lag, Bt., 40C Palace Road, London SW2 3NJ

HAIG: The Earl Haig, OBE, Bemersyde, Melrose, Roxburghshire TD6 9DP

HALDANE: Martin Haldane of Gleneagles, Gleneagles, Auchterarder, Perthshire

HANNAY: Ramsey Hannay of Kirkdale and of that Ilk, Cardoness House, Gatehouse-of-Fleet, Kirkcudbrightshire

HAY: The Earl of Erroll, Woodbury Hall, Sandy, Beds

HENDERSON: John Henderson of Fordell, 7 Owen Street, Toowoomba, Queensland, Australia

HUNTER: Pauline Hunter of Hunterston, Plovers Ridge, Lon Cecrist, Treaddur Bay, Holyhead, Gwynedd

IRVINE OF DRUM: David C. Irvine of Drum, 20 Enville Road, Bowden, Altrincham, Cheshire WA14 2PQ

JARDINE: Sir Alexander Jardine of Applegirth, Bt., Ash House, Thwaites, Millom, Cumbria LA18 5HY

JOHNSTONE: The Earl of Annandale and Hartfell, Raehills, Lockerbie, Dumfriesshire

KEITH: The Earl of Kintore, The Stables, Keith Hall, Inverurie, Aberdeenshire AB51 OLD

KENNEDY: The Marquess of Ailsa, Cassillis House, Maybole, Ayrshire

KERR: The Marquess of Lothian, KCVO, Ferniehurst Castle, Jedburgh, Roxburghshire TN8 6NX

KINCAID: Mrs Heather V. Kincaid of Kincaid, 4 Watling Street, Leintwardine, Craven Arms, Shropshire

LAMONT: Peter N. Lamont of that Ilk, St Patrick's College, Manly, NSW 2095, Australia

LEASK: Madam Leask of Leask, 1 Vincent Road, Sheringham, Norfolk

LENNOX: Edward J. H. Lennox of that Ilk, Pools Farm, Downton on the Rock, Ludlow, Shropshire

LESLIE: The Earl of Rothes, Tanglewood, West Tytherley, Salisbury, Wilts SP5 1LX

LINDSAY: The Earl of Crawford and Balcarres, KT, PC, Balcarres, Colinsburgh, Fife

LOCKHART: Angus H. Lockhart of the Lee, Newholme, Dunsyre, Lanark

LUMSDEN: Gillem Lumsden of that Ilk and Blanerne, Stapely Howe, Hoe Benham, Newbury, Berks

MACALESTER: William St J. S. McAlester of Loup and Kennox, 2 Avon Road East, Christchurch, Dorset

MCBAIN: J. H. McBain of McBain, 7025 North Finger Rock Place, Tucson, Arizona, USA

MACDONALD: The Lord Macdonald (*The Macdonald of Macdonald*), Kinloch Lodge, Sleat, Isle of Skye

*MACDONALD OF CLANRANALD: Ranald A. Macdonald of Clanranald, Mornish House, Killin, Perthshire FK21 8TX

*MACDONALD OF SLEAT (CLAN HUSTEAIN): Sir Ian Macdonald of Sleat, Bt., Thorpe Hall, Rudston, Driffield, N. Humberside YO25 0JE

*MACDONELL OF GLENGARRY: Air Cdre Aeneas R. MacDonell of Glengarry, CB, DFC, Elonbank, Castle Street, Fortrose, Ross-shire IV10 8TH

MACDOUGALL: vacant

MACDOWALL: Fergus D. H. Macdowall of Garthland, 9170 Ardmore Drive, North Saanich, British Columbia, Canada

MACGREGOR: Brig. Sir Gregor MacGregor of MacGregor, Bt., Bannatyne, Newtyle, Blairgowrie, Perthshire PH12 8TR

MACINTYRE: James W. MacIntyre of Glenoe, 15301 Pine Orchard Drive, Apartment 3H, Silver Spring, Maryland, USA

MACKAY: The Lord Reay, House of Lords, London SW1

MACKENZIE: The Earl of Cromartie, Castle Leod, Strathpeffer, Ross-shire IV14 9AA

MACKINNON: Madam Anne Mackinnon of Mackinnon, 16 Purleigh Road, Bridgwater, Somerset

MACKINTOSH: *The Mackintosh of Mackintosh*, Moy Hall, Inverness IV13 7YQ

MACLACHLAN: vacant

MACLAREN: Donald MacLaren of MacLaren and Achleskine, Achleskine, Kirkton, Balquidder, Lochearnhead

MACLEAN: The Hon. Sir Lachlan Maclean of Duart, Bt., Arngask House, Glenfarg, Perthshire PH2 9QA

MACLENNAN: vacant

MACLEOD: John MacLeod of MacLeod, Dunvegan Castle, Isle of Skye

MACMILLAN: George MacMillan of MacMillan, Finlaystone, Langbank, Renfrewshire

MACNAB: J. C. Macnab of Macnab (*The Macnab*), Leuchars Castle Farmhouse, Leuchars, Fife KY16 0EY

MACNAGHTEN: Sir Patrick Macnaghten of Macnaghten and Dundarave, Bt., Dundarave, Bushmills, Co. Antrim

MACNEACAIL: Iain Macneacail of Macneacail and Scorrybreac, 12 Fox Street, Ballina, NSW, Australia

MACNEIL OF BARRA: Ian R. Macneil of Barra (*The Macneil of Barra*), 95/6 Grange Loan, Edinburgh

MACPHERSON: The Hon. Sir William Macpherson of Cluny, TD, Newtown Castle, Blairgowrie, Perthshire

MCTAVISH: E. S. Dugald McTavish of Dunardry

MACTHOMAS: Andrew P. C. MacThomas of Finegand, c/o Roslin Cottage, Pitmedden, Aberdeenshire AB41 7NY

MAITLAND: The Earl of Lauderdale, 12 St Vincent Street, Edinburgh

MAKGILL: The Viscount of Oxfuird, Hill House, St Mary Bourne, Andover, Hants SP11 6BG

MALCOLM (MACCALLUM): Robin N. L. Malcolm of Poltalloch, Duntrune Castle, Lochgilphead, Argyll

MAR: The Countess of Mar, St Michael's Farm, Great Witley, Worcs WR6 6JB

MARJORIBANKS: Andrew Marjoribanks of that Ilk, 10 Newark Street, Greenock

MATHESON: Maj. Sir Fergus Matheson of Matheson, Bt., Old Rectory, Hedenham, Bungay, Suffolk NR35 2LD

MENZIES: David R. Menzies of Menzies, Wester Auchnagallin Farmhouse, Braes of Castle Grant, Grantown on Spey PH26 3PL

MOFFAT: Madam Moffat of that Ilk, St Jasual, Bullocks Farm Lane, Wheeler End Common, High Wycombe

MONCREIFFE: vacant

MONTGOMERIE: The Earl of Eglinton and Winton, Balhomie, Cargill, Perth PH2 6DS

MORRISON: Dr Iain M. Morrison of Ruchdi, Magnolia Cottage, The Street, Walberton, Sussex

MUNRO: Hector W. Munro of Foulis, Foulis Castle, Evanton, Ross-shire IV16 9UX

MURRAY: The Duke of Atholl, Blair Castle, Blair Atholl, Perthshire

NESBITT (or NISBET): Robert Nesbitt of that Ilk, Upper Roundhurst Farm, Roundhurst, Haslemere, Surrey

NICOLSON: The Lord Carnock, 90 Whitehall Court, London SW1A 2EL

OGILVY: The Earl of Airlie, KT, GCVO, PC, Cortachy Castle, Kirriemuir, Angus

RAMSAY: The Earl of Dalhousie, KT, GCVO, GBE, MC, Brechin Castle, Brechin, Angus DD7 6SH

RATTRAY: James S. Rattray of Rattray, Craighall, Rattray, Perthshire

ROBERTSON: Alexander G. H. Robertson of Struan (*Struan-Robertson*), The Breach Farm, Goudhurst Road, Cranbrook, Kent

ROLLO: The Lord Rollo, Pitcairns, Dunning, Perthshire

ROSE: Miss Elizabeth Rose of Kilravock, Kilravock Castle, Croy, Inverness

ROSS: David C. Ross of that Ilk, Shandwick, Perth Road, Stanley, Perthshire

RUTHVEN: The Earl of Gowrie, PC, Castlemartin, Kilcullen, Co. Kildare, Republic of Ireland

SCOTT: The Duke of Buccleuch and Queensberry, KT, VRD, Bowhill, Selkirk

SCRYMGEOUR: The Earl of Dundee, Birkhill, Cupar, Fife

SEMPILL: The Lord Sempill, 3 Vanburgh Street, Edinburgh

SHAW: John Shaw of Tordarroch, Newhall, Balblair, by Conon Bridge, Ross-shire

SINCLAIR: The Earl of Caithness, Churchill, Chipping Norton, Oxford OX7 5UX

SKENE: Danus Skene of Skene, Nether Pitlour, Strathmiglo, Fife

STIRLING: Fraser J. Stirling of Cader, 44A Oakley Street, London SW3 5HA

STRANGE: Maj. Timothy Strange of Balcaskie, Little Holme, Porton Road, Amesbury, Wilts

SUTHERLAND: The Countess of Sutherland, House of Tongue, Brora, Sutherland

SWINTON: John Swinton of that Ilk, 123 Superior Avenue SW, Calgary, Alberta, Canada

TROTTER: Alexander Trotter of Mortonhall, Charterhall, Duns, Berwickshire

URQUHART: Kenneth T. Urquhart of Urquhart, 507 Jefferson Park Avenue, Jefferson, New Orleans, Louisiana 70121, USA

WALLACE: Ian F. Wallace of that Ilk, 5 Lennox Street, Edinburgh EH4 1QB

WEDDERBURN OF THAT ILK: The Master of Dundee, Birkhill, Cupar, Fife

WEMYSS: David Wemyss of that Ilk, Invermay, Forteviot, Perthshire

The Privy Council

The Sovereign in Council, or Privy Council, was the chief source of executive power until the system of Cabinet government developed in the 18th century. Now the Privy Council's main functions are to advise the Sovereign and to exercise its own statutory responsibilities independent of the Sovereign in Council (see also page 216).

Membership of the Privy Council is automatic upon appointment to certain government and judicial positions in the United Kingdom, e.g. Cabinet ministers must be Privy Counsellors and are sworn in on first assuming office. Membership is also accorded by The Queen to eminent people in the UK and independent countries of the Commonwealth of which Her Majesty is Queen, on the recommendation of the British Prime Minister. Membership of the Council is retained for life, except for very occasional removals.

The administrative functions of the Privy Council are carried out by the Privy Council Office (see page 334) under the direction of the President of the Council, who is always a member of the Cabinet.

President of the Council, The Rt. Hon.
  Margaret Beckett, MP
Clerk of the Council, N. H. Nicholls, CBE

MEMBERS *as at 31 August 1998*

HRH The Duke of Edinburgh, 1951
HRH The Prince of Wales, 1977

Aberdare, Lord, 1974
Ackner, Lord, 1980
Airlie, Earl of, 1984
Aldington, Lord, 1954
Aldous, Sir William, 1995
Alebua, Ezekiel, 1988
Alison, Michael, 1981
Alport, Lord, 1960
Ampthill, Lord, 1995
Ancram, Michael, 1996
Anthony, Douglas, 1971
Arbuthnot, James, 1998
Archer of Sandwell, Lord, 1977
Arnold, Sir John, 1979
Arthur, Hon. Owen, 1995
Ashdown, Paddy, 1989
Ashley of Stoke, Lord, 1979
Atkins, Sir Robert, 1995
Auld, Sir Robin, 1995
Baker of Dorking, Lord, 1984
Balcombe, Sir John, 1985
Barber, Lord, 1963

Barnett, Lord, 1975
Beckett, Margaret, 1993
Beith, Alan, 1992
Beldam, Sir Roy, 1989
Belstead, Lord, 1983
Benn, Anthony, 1964
Bennett, Sir Frederic, 1985
Biffen, Lord, 1979
Bingham of Cornhill, Lord, 1986
Birch, William, 1992
Bird, Vere, 1982
Bisson, Sir Gordon, 1987
Blair, Anthony, 1994
Blaker, Lord, 1983
Blanchard, Peter, 1998
Blatch, Baroness, 1993
Blunkett, David, 1997
Bolger, James, 1991
Booth, Albert, 1976
Boothroyd, Betty, 1992
Boscawen, Hon. Robert, 1992
Bottomley, Virginia, 1992
Boyson, Sir Rhodes, 1987
Braine of Wheatley, Lord, 1985
Brandon of Oakbrook, Lord, 1978
Brathwaite, Sir Nicholas, 1991
Bridge of Harwich, Lord, 1975
Brightman, Lord, 1979
Brittan, Sir Leon, 1981
Brooke, Sir Henry, 1996
Brooke, Peter, 1988
Brown, Gordon, 1996
Brown, Nicholas, 1997
Brown, Sir Simon, 1992
Brown, Sir Stephen, 1983
Browne-Wilkinson, Lord, 1983
Buckley, Sir Denys, 1970
Butler, Sir Adam, 1984
Butler-Sloss, Dame Elizabeth, 1988
Buxton, Sir Richard, 1997
Byers, Stephen, 1998
Caithness, Earl of, 1990
Callaghan of Cardiff, Lord, 1964
Cameron of Lochbroom, Lord, 1984
Camoys, Lord, 1997
Campbell of Croy, Lord, 1970
Canterbury, The Archbishop of,
  1991
Carlisle of Bucklow, Lord, 1979
Carr of Hadley, Lord, 1963
Carrington, Lord, 1959
Carswell, Sir Robert, 1993
Carter, Lord, 1997
Casey, Sir Maurice, 1986
Castle of Blackburn, Baroness, 1964
Chadwick, Sir John, 1997
Chalfont, Lord, 1964
Chalker of Wallasey, Baroness, 1987
Chan, Sir Julius, 1981
Charteris of Amisfield, Lord, 1972
Chataway, Sir Christopher, 1970
Clark, Alan, 1991
Clark, David, 1997
Clark, Helen, 1990

Clark of Kempston, Lord, 1990
Clarke, Kenneth, 1984
Clarke, Thomas, 1997
Cledwyn of Penrhos, Lord, 1966
Clinton-Davis, Lord, 1998
Clyde, Lord, 1996
Cockfield, Lord, 1982
Cocks of Hartcliffe, Lord, 1976
Coggan, Lord, 1961
Colman, Fraser, 1986
Compton, Sir John, 1983
Concannon, John, 1978
Cook, Robin, 1996
Cooke of Thorndon, Lord, 1977
Cooper, Sir Frank, 1983
Cope of Berkeley, Lord, 1988
Corfield, Sir Frederick, 1970
Cowen, Sir Zelman, 1981
Cradock, Sir Percy, 1993
Cranborne, Viscount, 1994
Crawford and Balcarres, Earl of, 1972
Crickhowell, Lord, 1979
Croom-Johnson, Sir David, 1984
Cullen, *Hon.* Lord, 1997
Cumming-Bruce, Sir Roualeyn,
  1977
Cunningham, Jack, 1993
Curry, David, 1996
Darling, Alistair, 1997
Davies, Denzil, 1978
Davies, Ronald, 1997
Davis, David, 1997
Davison, Sir Ronald, 1978
Dean of Harptree, Lord, 1991
Dean of Thornton-le-Fylde,
  Baroness, 1998
Deedes, Lord, 1962
Dell, Edmund, 1970
Denham, Lord, 1981
Denning, Lord, 1948
Devonshire, Duke of, 1964
Dewar, Donald, 1996
Diamond, Lord, 1965
Dillon, Sir Brian, 1982
Dixon, Lord, 1996
Dobson, Frank, 1997
Donaldson of Lymington, Lord, 1979
Dorrell, Stephen, 1994
Douglas, Sir William, 1977
du Cann, Sir Edward, 1964
Duff, Sir Antony, 1980
Dunn, Sir Robin, 1980
East, Paul, 1998
Eccles, Viscount, 1951
Eden of Winton, Lord, 1972
Eggar, Timothy, 1995
Eichelbaum, Sir Thomas, 1989
Emery, Sir Peter, 1993
Emslie, Lord, 1972
Erroll of Hale, Lord, 1960
Esquivel, Manuel, 1986
Evans, Sir Anthony, 1992
Eveleigh, Sir Edward, 1977
Farquharson, Sir Donald, 1989

Fellowes, Sir Robert, 1990
Ferrers, Earl, 1982
Field, Frank, 1997
Floissac, Sir Vincent, 1992
Foot, Michael, 1974
Forsyth, Sir Michael, 1995
Forth, Eric, 1997
Foster, Derek, 1993
Fowler, Sir Norman, 1979
Fox, Sir Marcus, 1995
Fox, Sir Michael, 1981
Fraser, Malcolm, 1976
Fraser of Carmyllie, Lord, 1989
Freeman, John, 1966
Freeman, Lord, 1993
Freeson, Reginald, 1976
Garel-Jones, Lord, 1992
Gault, Thomas, 1992
Georges, Telford, 1986
Gibbs, Sir Harry, 1972
Gibson, Sir Peter, 1993
Gibson, Sir Ralph, 1985
Gibson-Watt, Lord, 1974
Gilbert, Lord, 1978
Gilmour of Craigmillar, Lord, 1973
Glenamara, Lord, 1964
Glidewell, Sir Iain, 1985
Goff of Chieveley, Lord, 1982
Goodlad, Sir Alastair, 1992
Gorton, Sir John, 1968
Gowrie, Earl of, 1984
Graham, Douglas, 1998
Graham of Edmonton, Lord, 1998
Gray of Contin, Lord, 1982
Griffiths, Lord, 1980
Gummer, John, 1985
Habgood, Rt. Revd Lord, 1983
Hague, William, 1995
Hailsham of St Marylebone, Lord, 1956
Hamilton, Sir Archie, 1991
Hanley, Sir Jeremy, 1994
Hardie, Lord, 1997
Hardie Boys, Sir Michael, 1989
Harman, Harriet, 1997
Harris of Greenwich, Lord, 1998
Harrison, Walter, 1977
Hattersley, Lord, 1975
Hayhoe, Lord, 1985
Healey, Lord, 1964
Heath, Sir Edward, 1955
Heathcoat-Amory, David, 1996
Henry, Sir Denis, 1993
Henry, John, 1996
Heseltine, Michael, 1979
Heseltine, Sir William, 1986
Hesketh, Lord, 1991
Higgins, Lord, 1979
Hirst, Sir David, 1992
Hobhouse, Sir John, 1993
Hoffmann, Lord, 1992
Hogg, Hon. Douglas, 1992
Holderness, Lord, 1959
Hope of Craighead, Lord, 1989
Hordern, Sir Peter, 1993
Howard, Michael, 1990
Howe of Aberavon, Lord, 1972
Howell of Guildford, Lord, 1979
Hughes, Lord, 1970
Hunt, Jonathan, 1989

Hunt of Wirral, Lord, 1990
Hurd of Westwell, Lord, 1982
Hutchison, Sir Michael, 1995
Hutton, Lord, 1988
Ingraham, Hubert, 1993
Irvine of Lairg, Lord, 1997
Jack, Michael, 1997
Jauncey of Tullichettle, Lord, 1988
Jay of Paddington, Baroness, 1998
Jellicoe, Earl, 1963
Jenkin of Roding, Lord, 1973
Jenkins of Hillhead, Lord, 1964
Jones, Aubrey, 1955
Jopling, Lord, 1979
Judge, Sir Igor, 1996
Jugnauth, Sir Anerood, 1987
Kaufman, Gerald, 1978
Keith, Sir Kenneth, 1998
Keith of Kinkel, Lord, 1976
Kelly, Sir Basil, 1984
Kelvedon, Lord, 1980
Kenilorea, Sir Peter, 1979
Kennedy, Sir Paul, 1992
Kerr, Sir Michael, 1981
King, Thomas, 1979
Kingsdown, Lord, 1987
Kingsland, Lord, 1994
Kinnock, Neil, 1983
Knight, Gregory, 1995
Lamont, Norman, 1986
Lane, Lord, 1975
Lang of Monkton, Lord, 1990
Lange, David, 1984
Lansdowne, Marquess of, 1964
Latasi, Kamuta, 1996
Latey, Sir John, 1986
Lauti, Sir Toaripi, 1979
Lawson of Blaby, Lord, 1981
Lawton, Sir Frederick, 1972
Leggatt, Sir Andrew, 1990
Leonard, Rt. Revd Graham, 1981
Lilley, Peter, 1990
Lloyd of Berwick, Lord, 1984
Lloyd, Sir Peter, 1994
London, The Bishop of, 1995
Longford, Earl of, 1948
Louisy, Allan, 1981
Lowry, Lord, 1974
Luce, Sir Richard, 1986
Lyell, Sir Nicholas, 1990
Mabon, Dickson, 1977
McCarthy, Sir Thaddeus, 1968
McCollum, Sir Liam, 1997
McCowan, Sir Anthony, 1989
MacDermott, Sir John, 1987
MacGregor, John, 1985
MacIntyre, Duncan, 1980
Mackay, Andrew, 1998
McKay, Ian, 1992
Mackay of Ardbrecknish, Lord, 1996
Mackay of Clashfern, Lord, 1979
Mackay of Drumadoon, Lord, 1996
McKinnon, Donald, 1992
Maclean, David, 1995
Maclennan, Robert, 1997
McMullin, Sir Duncan, 1980
Major, John, 1987
Mandelson, Peter, 1998
Mantell, Sir Charles, 1997
Mara, Ratu Sir Kamisese, 1973

Marsh, Lord, 1966
Mason of Barnsley, Lord, 1968
Maude, Hon. Francis, 1992
Mawhinney, Sir Brian, 1994
May, Sir Anthony, 1998
Mayhew of Twysden, Lord, 1986
Meacher, Michael, 1997
Megarry, Sir Robert, 1978
Mellor, David, 1990
Merlyn-Rees, Lord, 1974
Millan, Bruce, 1975
Millett, Sir Peter, 1994
Mitchell, Sir James, 1985
Molyneaux of Killead, Lord, 1983
Monro of Langholm, Lord, 1995
Moore, Michael, 1990
Moore of Lower Marsh, Lord, 1986
Moore of Wolvercote, Lord, 1977
Morris, Charles, 1978
Morris, John, 1970
Morris of Manchester, Lord, 1979
Morritt, Sir Robert, 1994
Mowlam, Marjorie, 1997
Moyle, Roland, 1978
Mummery, Sir John, 1996
Murray, Hon. Lord, 1974
Murray, Sir Donald, 1989
Murray of Epping Forest, Lord, 1976
Murton of Lindisfarne, Lord, 1976
Mustill, Lord, 1985
Nairne, Sir Patrick, 1982
Namaliu, Sir Rabbie, 1989
Naseby, Lord, 1994
Needham, Sir Richard, 1994
Neill, Sir Brian, 1985
Newton of Braintree, Lord, 1988
Nicholls of Birkenhead, Lord, 1995
Nicholson, Sir Michael, 1995
Nolan, Lord, 1991
Nott, Sir John, 1979
Nourse, Sir Martin, 1985
Nutting, Sir Anthony, 1954
Oakes, Gordon, 1979
O'Connor, Sir Patrick, 1980
O'Donnell, Turlough, 1979
O'Flynn, Francis, 1987
Ogilvy, Sir Angus, 1997
Oliver of Aylmerton, Lord, 1980
Onslow of Woking, Lord, 1988
Oppenheim-Barnes, Baroness, 1979
Orme, Lord, 1974
Otton, Sir Philip, 1995
Owen, Lord, 1976
Paeniu, Bikenibeu, 1991
Palliser, Sir Michael, 1983
Palmer, Sir Geoffrey, 1986
Parker, Sir Roger, 1983
Parkinson, Lord, 1981
Patten, Christopher, 1989
Patten, Lord, 1990
Patterson, Percival, 1993
Pattie, Sir Geoffrey, 1987
Perth, Earl of, 1957
Peters, Winston, 1998
Peyton of Yeovil, Lord, 1970
Phillips, Sir Nicholas, 1995
Pill, Sir Malcolm, 1995
Pindling, Sir Lynden, 1976
Portillo, Michael, 1992
Potter, Sir Mark, 1996

Prentice, Lord, 1966
Prescott, John, 1994
Price, George, 1982
Prior, Lord, 1970
Puapua, Sir Tomasi, 1982
Purchas, Sir Francis, 1982
Pym, Lord, 1970
Raison, Sir Timothy, 1982
Ramsden, James, 1963
Rawlinson of Ewell, Lord, 1964
Redwood, John, 1993
Rees, Lord, 1983
Reid, John, 1998
Renton, Lord, 1962
Renton of Mount Harry, Lord, 1989
Richard, Lord, 1993
Richardson, Sir Ivor, 1978
Richardson of Duntisbourne, Lord, 1976
Rifkind, Sir Malcolm, 1986
Robens of Woldingham, Lord, 1951
Roberts of Conwy, Lord, 1991
Robertson, George, 1997
Roch, Sir John, 1993
Rodger of Earlsferry, Lord, 1992
Rodgers of Quarry Bank, Lord, 1975
Rose, Sir Christopher, 1992
Ross, *Hon.* Lord, 1985
Rumbold, Dame Angela, 1991
Runcie, Lord, 1980
Russell, Sir Patrick, 1987
Ryder of Wensum, Lord, 1990
Sainsbury, Sir Timothy, 1992
St John of Fawsley, Lord, 1979
Sandiford, Erskine, 1989
Saville of Newdigate, Lord, 1994
Scarman, Lord, 1973
Schiemann, Sir Konrad, 1995
Scott, Sir Nicholas, 1989
Scott, Sir Richard, 1991
Seaga, Edward, 1981

Selkirk of Douglas, Lord, 1996
Shawcross, Lord, 1946
Shearer, Hugh, 1969
Sheldon, Robert, 1977
Shephard, Gillian, 1992
Shepherd, Lord, 1965
Shipley, Jennifer, 1998
Shore of Stepney, Lord, 1967
Short, Clare, 1997
Simmonds, Kennedy, 1984
Simon of Glaisdale, Lord, 1961
Sinclair, Ian, 1977
Slade, Sir Christopher, 1982
Slynn of Hadley, Lord, 1992
Smith, Andrew, 1997
Smith, Christopher, 1997
Smith, Sir Geoffrey Johnson, 1996
Somare, Sir Michael, 1977
Somers, Sir Edward, 1981
Stanley, Sir John, 1984
Staughton, Sir Christopher, 1988
Steel of Aikwood, Lord, 1977
Stephen, Sir Ninian, 1979
Stephenson, Sir John, 1971
Stewartby, Lord, 1989
Steyn, Lord, 1992
Stodart of Leaston, Lord, 1974
Stott, Lord, 1964
Strang, Gavin, 1997
Strathclyde, Lord, 1995
Straw, Jack, 1997
Stuart-Smith, Sir Murray, 1988
Talboys, Sir Brian, 1977
Taylor, Ann, 1997
Tebbit, Lord, 1981
Templeman, Lord, 1978
Thatcher, Baroness, 1970
Thomas, Edmund, 1996
Thomas, Sir Swinton, 1994
Thomas of Gwydir, Lord, 1964
Thomson, David, 1981

Thomson of Monifieth, Lord, 1966
Thorpe, Jeremy, 1967
Thorpe, Sir Matthew, 1995
Tipping, Andrew, 1998
Tizard, Robert, 1986
Trefgarne, Lord, 1989
Trimble, David, 1997
Trumpington, Baroness, 1992
Ullswater, Viscount, 1994
Varley, Lord, 1974
Waddington, Lord, 1987
Waite, Sir John, 1993
Wakeham, Lord, 1983
Waldegrave, William, 1990
Walker of Doncaster, Lord, 1979
Walker of Worcester, Lord, 1970
Walker, Sir Robert, 1997
Waller, Sir George, 1976
Waller, Sir Mark, 1996
Ward, Sir Alan, 1995
Watkins, Sir Tasker, 1980
Weatherill, Lord, 1980
Wheeler, Sir John, 1993
Whitelaw, Viscount, 1967
Widdecombe, Ann, 1997
Wigley, Dafydd, 1997
Wilberforce, Lord, 1964
Williams, Alan, 1977
Williams of Crosby, Baroness, 1974
Windlesham, Lord, 1973
Wingti, Paias, 1987
Withers, Reginald, 1977
Woodhouse, Sir Owen, 1974
Woolf, Lord, 1986
Wylie, *Hon.* Lord, 1970
York, The Archbishop of, 1991
Young, Baroness, 1981
Young, Sir George, 1993
Young of Graffham, Lord, 1984
Younger of Leckie, Viscount, 1979
Zacca, Edward, 1992

The Privy Council of Northern Ireland

The Privy Council of Northern Ireland had responsibilities in Northern Ireland similar to those of the Privy Council in Great Britain until the Northern Ireland Act 1974 instituted direct rule and a UK Cabinet minister became responsible for the functions previously exercised by the Northern Ireland government.

Membership of the Privy Council of Northern Ireland is retained for life. The postnominal initials PC (NI)

are used to differentiate its members from those of the Privy Council.

MEMBERS *as at 31 August 1998*

Bailie, Robin, 1971
Bleakley, David, 1971
Bradford, Roy, 1969
Craig, William, 1963
Dobson, John, 1969
Kelly, Sir Basil, 1969

Kirk, Herbert, 1962
Long, William, 1966
Lowry, The Lord, 1971
McConnell, The Lord, 1964
McIvor, Basil, 1971
Morgan, William, 1961
Moyola, The Lord, 1966
Neill, Sir Ivan, 1950
Porter, Sir Robert, 1969
Taylor, John, MP, 1970
West, Henry, 1960

Parliament

The United Kingdom constitution is not contained in any single document but has evolved in the course of time, formed partly by statute, partly by common law and partly by convention. A constitutional monarchy, the United Kingdom is governed by Ministers of the Crown in the name of the Sovereign, who is head both of the state and of the government.

The organs of government are the legislature (Parliament), the executive and the judiciary. The executive consists of HM Government (Cabinet and other Ministers) (*see* pages 276–7), government departments (*see* pages 278–353), local authorities (*see* Local Government), and public corporations operating nationalized industries or social or cultural services (*see* pages 278–353). The judiciary (*see* Law Courts and Offices) pronounces on the law, both written and unwritten, interprets statutes and is responsible for the enforcement of the law; the judiciary is independent of both the legislature and the executive.

THE MONARCHY

The Sovereign personifies the state and is, in law, an integral part of the legislature, head of the executive, head of the judiciary, commander-in-chief of all armed forces of the Crown and 'Supreme Governor' of the Church of England. The seat of the monarchy is in the United Kingdom. In the Channel Islands and the Isle of Man, which are Crown dependencies, the Sovereign is represented by a Lieutenant-Governor. In the member states of the Commonwealth of which the Sovereign is head of state, her representative is a Governor-General; in UK dependencies the Sovereign is usually represented by a Governor, who is responsible to the British Government.

Although in practice the powers of the monarchy are now very limited, restricted mainly to the advisory and ceremonial, there are important acts of government which require the participation of the Sovereign. These include summoning, proroguing and dissolving Parliament, giving royal assent to bills passed by Parliament, appointing important office-holders, e.g. government ministers, judges, bishops and governors, conferring peerages, knighthoods and other honours, and granting pardon to a person wrongly convicted of a crime. The Sovereign appoints the Prime Minister; by convention this office is held by the leader of the political party which enjoys, or can secure, a majority of votes in the House of Commons. In international affairs the Sovereign as head of state has the power to declare war and make peace, to recognize foreign states and governments, to conclude treaties and to annex or cede territory. However, as the Sovereign entrusts executive power to Ministers of the Crown and acts on the advice of her Ministers, which she cannot ignore, royal prerogative powers are in practice exercised by Ministers, who are responsible to Parliament.

Ministerial responsibility does not diminish the Sovereign's importance to the smooth working of government. She holds meetings of the Privy Council (*see* below), gives audiences to her Ministers and other officials at home and overseas, receives accounts of Cabinet decisions, reads dispatches and signs state papers; she must be informed and

consulted on every aspect of national life; and she must show complete impartiality.

COUNSELLORS OF STATE

In the event of the Sovereign's absence abroad, it is necessary to appoint Counsellors of State under letters patent to carry out the chief functions of the Monarch, including the holding of Privy Councils and giving royal assent to acts passed by Parliament. The normal procedure is to appoint as Counsellors three or four members of the royal family among those remaining in the UK.

In the event of the Sovereign on accession being under the age of 18 years, or at any time unavailable or incapacitated by infirmity of mind or body for the performance of the royal functions, provision is made for a regency.

THE PRIVY COUNCIL

The Sovereign in Council, or Privy Council, was the chief source of executive power until the system of Cabinet government developed. Nowadays its main function is to advise the Sovereign to approve Orders in Council and to advise on the issue of royal proclamations. The Council's own statutory responsibilities (independent of the powers of the Sovereign in Council) include powers of supervision over the registering bodies for the medical and allied professions. A full Council is summoned only on the death of the Sovereign or when the Sovereign announces his or her intention to marry. (For full list of Counsellors, *see* pages 213–5.)

There are a number of advisory Privy Council committees, whose meetings the Sovereign does not attend. Some are prerogative committees, such as those dealing with legislative matters submitted by the legislatures of the Channel Islands and the Isle of Man or with applications for charters of incorporation; and some are provided for by statute, e.g. those for the universities of Oxford and Cambridge and the Scottish universities.

The Judicial Committee of the Privy Council is the final court of appeal from courts of the UK dependencies, courts of independent Commonwealth countries which have retained the right of appeal, courts of the Channel Islands and the Isle of Man, some professional and disciplinary committees, and church sources. The Committee is composed of Privy Counsellors who hold, or have held, high judicial office, although usually only three or five hear each case.

Administrative work is carried out by the Privy Council Office under the direction of the President of the Council, a Cabinet Minister.

PARLIAMENT

Parliament is the supreme law-making authority and can legislate for the UK as a whole or for any parts of it separately (the Channel Islands and the Isle of Man are Crown dependencies and not part of the UK). The main functions of Parliament are to pass laws, to provide (by voting taxation) the means of carrying on the work of government and to scrutinize government policy and administration, particularly proposals for expenditure. International treaties and agreements are by custom presented to Parliament before ratification.

Parliament emerged during the late 13th and early 14th centuries. The officers of the King's household and the King's judges were the nucleus of early Parliaments, joined by such ecclesiastical and lay magnates as the King might summon to form a prototype 'House of Lords', and occasionally by the knights of the shires, burgesses and proctors of the lower clergy. By the end of Edward III's reign a 'House of Commons' was beginning to appear; the first known Speaker was elected in 1377.

Parliamentary procedure is based on custom and precedent, partly formulated in the Standing Orders of both Houses of Parliament, and each House has the right to control its own internal proceedings and to commit for contempt. The system of debate in the two Houses is similar; when a motion has been moved, the Speaker proposes the question as the subject of a debate. Members speak from wherever they have been sitting. Questions are decided by a vote on a simple majority. Draft legislation is introduced, in either House, as a bill. Bills can be introduced by a Government Minister or a private Member, but in practice the majority of bills which become law are introduced by the Government. To become law, a bill must be passed by each House (for parliamentary stages, see Bill, page 221) and then sent to the Sovereign for the royal assent, after which it becomes an Act of Parliament.

Proceedings of both Houses are public, except on extremely rare occasions. The minutes (called Votes and Proceedings in the Commons, and Minutes of Proceedings in the Lords) and the speeches (The Official Report of Parliamentary Debates, *Hansard*) are published daily. Proceedings are also recorded for transmission on radio and television and stored in the Parliamentary Recording Unit before transfer to the National Sound Archive. Television cameras have been allowed into the House of Lords since 1985 and into the House of Commons since 1989; committee meetings may also be televised.

By the Parliament Act of 1911, the maximum duration of a Parliament is five years (if not previously dissolved), the term being reckoned from the date given on the writs for the new Parliament. The maximum life has been prolonged by legislation in such rare circumstances as the two world wars (31 January 1911 to 25 November 1918; 26 November 1935 to 15 June 1945). Dissolution and writs for a general election are ordered by the Sovereign on the advice of the Prime Minister. The life of a Parliament is divided into sessions, usually of one year in length, beginning and ending most often in October or November.

DEVOLUTION

The Northern Ireland Assembly elected in June 1998 is due to be formally established by legislation in early 1999; it will have legislative authority in the fields currently administered by the Northern Ireland departments. The Welsh Assembly due to be elected in May 1999 will have power to make secondary legislation in the areas where executive functions have been transferred to it. The Scottish Parliament due to be elected in 1999 will have legislative power over all devolved matters, i.e. matters not reserved to Westminster or otherwise outside its powers. For further details, *see* Local Government section.

THE HOUSE OF LORDS
London SWIA OPW
Tel 0171-219 3000
Information Office: 0171–219 3107
E-mail: HLINFO@parliament.uk
Web site: http://www.parliament.uk

The House of Lords consists of the Lords Spiritual and Temporal. The Lords Spiritual are the Archbishops of Canterbury and York, the Bishops of London, Durham and Winchester, and the 21 senior diocesan bishops of the Church of England. The Lords Temporal currently consist of all hereditary peers of England, Scotland, Great Britain and the UK who have not disclaimed their peerages, life peers created under the Life Peerages Act 1958, and those Lords of Appeal in Ordinary created life peers under the Appellate Jurisdiction Act 1876, as amended (law lords). The Government is planning to introduce legislation removing the right of hereditary peers to sit in the House of Lords.

Disclaimants of a hereditary peerage lose their right to sit in the House of Lords but gain the right to vote at parliamentary elections and to offer themselves for election to the House of Commons (*see also* page 136). Those peers disqualified from sitting in the House include:

– aliens, i.e. any peer who is not a British citizen, a Commonwealth citizen (under the British Nationality Act 1981) or a citizen of the Republic of Ireland
– peers under the age of 21
– undischarged bankrupts or, in Scotland, those whose estate is sequestered
– peers convicted of treason

Peers who do not wish to attend sittings of the House of Lords may apply for leave of absence for the duration of a Parliament.

Until the beginning of this century the House of Lords had considerable power, being able to veto any bill submitted to it by the House of Commons, but those powers were greatly reduced by the Parliament Acts of 1911 and 1949 (*see* page 221).

Combined with its legislative role, the House of Lords has judicial powers as the ultimate Court of Appeal for courts in Great Britain and Northern Ireland, except for criminal cases in Scotland. These powers are exercised by the Lord Chancellor and the law lords.

Members of the House of Lords are unpaid. However, they are entitled to reimbursement of travelling expenses on parliamentary business within the UK and certain other expenses incurred for the purpose of attendance at sittings of the House, within a maximum for each day of £78 for overnight subsistence, £34.50 for day subsistence and incidental travel, and £33.50 for secretarial costs, postage and certain additional expenses.

COMPOSITION *as at 1 July 1998*

Archbishops and Bishops, 26
Peers by succession, 750 (16 women)
Hereditary peers of first creation (including the Prince of Wales), 9
Life peers under the Appellate Jurisdiction Act 1876, 26
Life peers under the Life Peerages Act 1958, 458 (80 women)
Total 1,269
Of whom:
   Peers without writs of summons, 69 (3 minors)
   Peers on leave of absence from the House, 66

STATE OF PARTIES *as at 1 July 1998* *

More than half of the members of the House of Lords take the whip of one of the three main political parties. The other members sit on the cross-benches as independents, support other parties or have declared no political affiliation.

Conservative, 471
Labour, 158
Liberal Democrats, 66
Cross-bench, 323
Other (including Lords Spiritual), 117
* Excluding peers without writs of summons and peers on leave of absence from the House

OFFICERS

The House is presided over by the Lord Chancellor, who is *ex officio* Speaker of the House. A panel of deputy Speakers is appointed by Royal Commission. The first deputy Speaker is the Chairman of Committees, appointed at the beginning of each session, a salaried officer of the House who takes the chair in committee of the whole House and in some select committees. He is assisted by a panel of deputy chairmen, headed by the salaried Principal Deputy Chairman of Committees, who is also chairman of the European Communities Committee of the House.

The permanent officers include the Clerk of the Parliaments, who is in charge of the administrative and procedural staff collectively known as the Parliament Office; the Gentleman Usher of the Black Rod, who is also Serjeant-at-Arms in attendance upon the Lord Chancellor and is responsible for security and for accommodation and services in the House of Lords; and the Yeoman Usher who is Deputy Serjeant-at-Arms and assists Black Rod in his duties.

Speaker (£148,850), The Lord Irvine of Lairg, PC, QC
    Private Secretary, Ms E. Hutchinson
Chairman of Committees (£53,264), The Lord Boston of Faversham, QC
Principal Deputy Chairman of Committees (£49,052), The Lord Tordoff

DEPARTMENT OF THE CLERK OF THE PARLIAMENTS
Clerk of the Parliaments (£116,045), J. M. Davies
Clerk Assistant and Clerk of Legislation (£70,220–£105,740), P. D. G. Hayter, LVO
Reading Clerk and Principal Finance Officer (£58,590–£94,330), M. G. Pownall
Counsel to Chairman of Committees (£58,590–£94,330), D. Rippengal, CB, QC; Sir James Nursaw, KCB, QC: Dr C. S. Kerse
Principal Clerks (£53,450–£89,090), J. A. Vallance White, CB (*Judicial Office and Fourth Clerk at the Table*); B. P. Keith (*Clerk of the Journals*); (£48,420–£79,230) D. R. Beamish (*Committees and Overseas Office*); R. H. Walters, D.Phil. (*Establishment Officer*); Dr F. P. Tudor (*Private Bills*); E. C. Ollard (*Public Bills*); A. Makower; T. V. Mohan (*Select Committees*)
Senior Clerks (£30,431–£46,108), Mrs M. E. Ollard; E. J. J. Wells; S. P. Burton (*seconded as Secretary to the Leader of the House and Chief Whip*); Mrs M. B. Bloor; T. E. Radice; Dr D. Rolt; D. J. Batt; I. Smyth
Clerks (£15,862–£27,564), Dr C. A. Mylne; Miss L. J. Mouland; J. A. Vaughan
Clerk of the Records (£43,910–£70,430), D. J. Johnson, FSA
Deputy Clerk of the Records (£34,462–£55,915), S. K. Ellison
Librarian (£48,420–£79,230), D. L. Jones
Deputy Librarian (£34,462–£55,915), P. G. Davis, PH.D.
Senior Library Clerk (£30,431–£46,108), Miss J. L. Victory, PH.D.
Examiners of Petitions for Private Bills, Dr F. P. Tudor; W. A. Proctor

Editor, Official Report (*Hansard*), (£43,910–£70,430), Mrs M. E. Villiers
Deputy Editor, Official Report (£34,462–£55,915), G. R. Goodbarne

DEPARTMENT OF THE GENTLEMAN USHER OF THE BLACK ROD
Gentleman Usher of the Black Rod and Serjeant-at-Arms (£58,590–£94,330), Gen. Sir Edward Jones, KCB, CBE
Yeoman Usher of the Black Rod and Deputy Serjeant-at-Arms (£30,431–£46,108), Air Vice-Marshal D. R. Hawkins, CB, MBE

SELECT COMMITTEES

The main House of Lords select committees, as at 8 June 1998, are as follows:

European Communities – Sub-committees:
    A (Economic and Financial Affairs, Trade and External Relations) – Chair, The Lord Barnett, PC; *Clerk,* Dr F. P. Tudor
    B (Energy, Industry and Transport) – Chair, The Lord Geddes; *Clerk,* Ms K. Ball
    C (Environment, Transport and Consumer Protection) – Chair, The Baroness Hilton of Eggardon, QPM; *Clerk,* T. Radice
    D (Agriculture, Fisheries and Food) – Chair, The Lord Reay; *Clerk,* A. Mackersie
    E (Law and Institutions) – Chair, The Lord Hoffmann, PC; *Clerk,* T. Radice
    F (Social Affairs, Education and Home Affairs) – Chair, The Lord Wallace of Saltaire, PH.D.; *Clerk,* Ms M. Bloor
Science and Technology – Chair, The Lord Phillips of Ellesmere, KBE, FRS; *Clerk,* A. Makower
Delegated Powers and Deregulation – Chair, The Lord Alexander of Weedon, QC; *Clerk,* Dr F. P. Tudor

THE HOUSE OF COMMONS
London SW1A 0AA
Tel 0171-219 3000
Information Office: 0171-219 4272
Forthcoming business: 0171-219 5532
E-mail: hcinfo@parliament.uk
Web site: http://www.parliament.uk

The members of the House of Commons are elected by universal adult suffrage. For electoral purposes, the United Kingdom is divided into constituencies, each of which returns one member to the House of Commons, the member being the candidate who obtains the largest number of votes cast in the constituency. To ensure equitable representation, the four Boundary Commissions (*see* page 285) keep constituency boundaries under review and recommend any redistribution of seats which may seem necessary because of population movements, etc. The number of seats was raised to 640 in 1945, reduced to 625 in 1948, and subsequently rose to 630 in 1955, 635 in 1970, 650 in 1983, 651 in 1992 and 659 in 1997. Of the present 659 seats, there are 529 for England, 40 for Wales, 72 for Scotland and 18 for Northern Ireland. The number of Scottish MPs at Westminster is to be cut by about 12 by 2007.

ELECTIONS

Elections are by secret ballot, each elector casting one vote; voting is not compulsory. For entitlement to vote in parliamentary elections, *see* Legal Notes section. When a seat becomes vacant between general elections, a by-election is held.

British subjects and citizens of the Irish Republic can stand for election as Members of Parliament (MPs) provided they are 21 or over and not subject to disqualification. Those disqualified from sitting in the House include:

- undischarged bankrupts
- people sentenced to more than one year's imprisonment
- clergy of the Church of England, Church of Scotland, Church of Ireland and Roman Catholic Church
- members of the House of Lords
- holders of certain offices listed in the House of Commons Disqualification Act 1975, e.g. members of the judiciary, Civil Service, regular armed forces, police forces, some local government officers and some members of public corporations and government commissions

A candidate does not require any party backing but his or her nomination for election must be supported by the signatures of ten people registered in the constituency. A candidate must also deposit with the returning officer £500, which is forfeit if the candidate does not receive more than 5 per cent of the votes cast. All election expenses at a general election, except the candidate's personal expenses, are subject to a statutory limit of £4,965, plus 4.2 pence for each elector in a borough constituency or 5.6 pence for each elector in a county constituency.

See pages 226–33 for an alphabetical list of MPs, pages 236–68 for the results of the last general election, and page 233 for the results of by-elections since the general election.

STATE OF PARTIES *as at 31 July 1998*

Conservative, 162 (14 women)
Labour, 418 (101 women)
Liberal Democrats, 46 (3 women)
Plaid Cymru, 4
Scottish Nationalist, 6 (2 women)
Sinn Fein, 2
Social Democratic and Labour, 3
Ulster Democratic Unionist, 2
Ulster Unionist, 10
United Kingdom Unionist, 1
Independent, 1
The Speaker and three Deputy Speakers, 4 (1 woman)
Total, 659 (121 women)
Government majority, 181

BUSINESS

The week's business of the House is outlined each Thursday by the Leader of the House, after consultation between the Chief Government Whip and the Chief Opposition Whip. A quarter to a third of the time will be taken up by the Government's legislative programme and the rest by other business. As a rule, bills likely to raise political controversy are introduced in the Commons before going on to the Lords, and the Commons claims exclusive control in respect of national taxation and expenditure. Bills such as the Finance Bill, which imposes taxation, and the Consolidated Fund Bills, which authorize expenditure, must begin in the Commons. A bill of which the financial provisions are subsidiary may begin in the Lords; and the Commons may waive its rights in regard to Lords' amendments affecting finance.

The Commons has a public register of MPs' financial and certain other interests; this is published annually as a House of Commons paper. Members must also disclose any relevant financial interest or benefit in a matter before the House when taking part in a debate, in certain other proceedings of the House, or in consultations with other MPs, with Ministers or with civil servants.

MEMBERS' PAY AND ALLOWANCES

Since 1911 members of the House of Commons have received salary payments; facilities for free travel were introduced in 1924. Salary rates since 1911 are as follows:

1911	£400 p.a.	1982 June	£14,510 p.a.
1931	360	1983 June	15,308
1934	380	1984 Jan	16,106
1935	400	1985 Jan	16,904
1937	600	1986 Jan	17,702
1946	1,000	1987 Jan	18,500
1954	1,250	1988 Jan	22,548
1957	1,750	1989 Jan	24,107
1964	3,250	1990 Jan	26,701
1972 Jan	4,500	1991 Jan	28,970
1975 June	5,750	1992 Jan	30,854
1976 June	6,062	1994 Jan	31,687
1977 July	6,270	1995 Jan	33,189
1978 June	6,897	1996 Jan	34,085
1979 June	9,450	1996 July	43,000
1980 June	11,750	1997 April	43,860
1981 June	13,950	1998 April	45,066

In 1969 MPs were granted an allowance for secretarial and research expenses, now known as the Office Costs Allowance. From April 1998 the allowance is £49,232 a year.

Since 1972 MPs have been able to claim reimbursement for the additional cost of staying overnight away from their main residence while on parliamentary business; this is known as the Additional Costs Allowance and from April 1998 is £12,717 a year.

Since 1980 each MP in receipt of the Office Costs Allowance has been able to contribute sums to an approved pension scheme for the provision of a pension, or other benefits, for or in respect of persons whose salary is met by him/her from the Office Costs Allowance.

MEMBERS' PENSIONS

Pension arrangements for MPs were first introduced in 1964. The arrangements currently provide a pension of one-fiftieth of salary for each year of pensionable service with a maximum of two-thirds of salary at age 65. Pension is payable normally at age 65, for men and women, or on later retirement. Pensions may be paid earlier, e.g. on retirement due to ill health. The widow/widower of a former MP receives a pension of five-eighths of the late MP's pension. Pensions are index-linked. Members currently contribute 6 per cent of salary to the pension fund; there is an Exchequer contribution, currently slightly more than the amount contributed by MPs.

The House of Commons Members' Fund provides for annual or lump sum grants to ex-MPs, their widows or widowers, and children whose incomes are below certain limits. Alternatively, payments of £2,325.72 a year to ex-MPs with at least ten years' service and who left the House of Commons before October 1964, and £1,454.16 a year to their widows or widowers are made as of right. Members contribute £24 a year and the Exchequer £215,000 a year to the fund.

OFFICERS AND OFFICIALS

The House of Commons is presided over by the Speaker, who has considerable powers to maintain order in the House. A deputy Speaker, called the Chairman of Ways and Means, and two Deputy Chairmen may preside over sittings of the House of Commons; they are elected by the House, and, like the Speaker, neither speak nor vote other than in their official capacity.

The staff of the House are employed by a Commission chaired by the Speaker. The heads of the six House of Commons departments are permanent officers of the House, not MPs. The Clerk of the House is the principal adviser to the Speaker on the privileges and procedures of the House, the conduct of the business of the House, and committees. The Serjeant-at-Arms is responsible for security, ceremonial, and for accommodation in the Commons part of the Palace of Westminster.

Speaker (£106,716), The Rt. Hon. Betty Boothroyd, MP (West Bromwich West)
Chairman of Ways and Means (£77,047), Sir Alan Haselhurst, MP (Saffron Walden)
First Deputy Chairman of Ways and Means (£73,173), Michael Martin, MP (Glasgow Springburn)
Second Deputy Chairman of Ways and Means (£73,173), Michael Lord, MP (Suffolk Central and Ipswich North)

OFFICES OF THE SPEAKER AND CHAIRMAN OF WAYS AND MEANS
Speaker's Secretary (£43,910–£70,430), N. Bevan, CB
Chaplain to the Speaker, Revd Canon R. Wright
Secretary to the Chairman of Ways and Means,   (£29,533 –£44,678), Ms L. M. Gardner

DEPARTMENT OF THE CLERK OF THE HOUSE
Clerk of the House of Commons (£116,045), W. R. McKay, CB
Clerk Assistant (£64,140–£99,880), G. Cubie
Clerk of Committees (£64,140–£99,880), C. B. Winnifrith, CB
Clerk of Legislation (£64,140–£99,880), R. B. Sands
Principal Clerks (£58,590–£94,330)
   Journals, A. J. Hastings
   Table Office, D. G. Millar
   Domestic Committees, M. R. Jack, PH.D.
Principal Clerks (£48,420–£79,230)
   Overseas Office, R. W. G. Wilson
   Bills, W. A. Proctor
   Select Committees, Ms H. E. Irwin; Mrs J. Sharpe; F. A. Cranmer
   Delegated Legislation, R. J. Rogers
Deputy Principal Clerks (£43,910–£70,430), Ms A. Barry; C. R. M. Ward, PH.D.; D. W. N. Doig; A. Sandall; D. L. Natzler; E. P. Silk; L. C. Laurence Smyth; S. J. Patrick; D. J. Gerhold; C. J. Poyser; D. F. Harrison; S. J. Priestley; A. H. Doherty; P. A. Evans; R. I. S. Phillips; R. G. James, PH.D.; Ms P. A. Helme; D. R. Lloyd; B. M. Hutton; J. S. Benger, D.Phil.; Ms E. C. Samson; N. P. Walker; M. D. Hamlyn; Mrs E. J. Flood; P. C. Seaward, D.Phil.
Senior Clerks (£29,533–£44,678), C. G. Lee; C. D. Stanton; A. Y. A. Azad; C. A. Shaw; Ms L. M. Gardner; K. J. Brown; F. J. Reid; M. Hennessy; G. R. Devine; P. G. Moon; M. Clark; Mrs J. N. St J. Mulley; T. W. P. Healey; Mrs S. A. R. Davies; J. D. Whatley; K. C. Fox; J. D. W. Rhys; Ms J. A. Long; Ms J. Eldred (*acting*); S. T. Fiander (*acting*); D. H. Griffiths (*acting*)
Examiners of Petitions for Private Bills, W. A. Proctor; Dr F. P. Tudor
Registrar of Members' Interests (£58,590–£94,330), R. J. Willoughby (*seconded to Speaker's Office*)
Taxing Officer, W. A. Proctor

Vote Office
Deliverer of the Vote (£43,910–£70,430), H. C. Foster
Deputy Deliverers of the Vote (£29,533–£44,678), J. F. Collins (*Distribution*); O. B. T. Sweeney (*Parliamentary*); F. W. Hallett (*Production*)

Speaker's Counsel
Speaker's Counsel (£58,590–£94,330), J. Mason, CB

Speaker's Counsel (European legislation) (£58,590–£94,330), J. E. G. Vaux
Speaker's Assistant Counsel (£43,910–£70,430), A. Akbar; J. R. Mallinson

DEPARTMENT OF THE SERJEANT-AT-ARMS
Serjeant-at-Arms (£58,590–£94,330), P. N. W. Jennings
Deputy Serjeant-at-Arms (£43,910–£70,430), M. J. A. Cummins
Assistant Serjeant-at-Arms (£33,447–£54,170), P. A. J. Wright
Deputy Assistant Serjeants-at-Arms (£29,533–£44,678), J. M. Robertson; M. Harvey

DEPARTMENT OF THE LIBRARY
Librarian (£58,590–£94,330), Miss J. B. Tanfield
Directors (£43,910–£79,230), Miss P. Baines; K. G. Cuninghame; Mrs J. Wainwright; R. Clements; R. Ware, D.phil.
Heads of Sections (£33,447–£54,170), C. Pond, PH.D.; Mrs C. Andrews; Mrs J. Lourie; C. Barclay; Mrs J. Fiddick; Mrs C. Gillie; R. Twigger; Mrs G. Allen; R. Cracknell
Senior Library Clerks (£29,533–£44,678), Ms F. Poole; T. Edmonds; Ms O. Gay; Miss E. McInnes; Dr D. Gore; B. Winetrobe; Miss M. Baber; Ms A. Walker; Mrs H. Holden; Mrs P. Carling; Miss J. Seaton; Mrs K. Greener; Ms P. Strickland; Miss V. Miller; M. P. Hillyard; Ms J. Roll; Ms W. Wilson; S. Wise; E. Wood; P. Bowers, PH.D.; T. Dodd; A. Seely; Mrs J. Hough; G. Danby, PH.D.; Miss P. Hughes, PH.D.; B. Morgan; Ms K. Wright; Miss L. Conway; C. Blair, PH.D.

DEPARTMENT OF FINANCE AND ADMINISTRATION
Director of Finance and Administration (£58,590–£94,330), A. Walker
Accountant (£48,420–£79,230), A. Marskell
Head of Establishments Office (£48,420–£79,230), B. Wilson

DEPARTMENT OF THE OFFICIAL REPORT
Editor (£48,420–£79,230), I. Church
Deputy Editors (£39,830–£62,570), P. Walker; W. G. Garland; Miss L. Sutherland

SELECT COMMITTEES
The more important committees, as at August 1998, are:

DEPARTMENTAL COMMITTEES
Agriculture – Chair, Peter Luff, MP; *Clerk,* Ms L. M. Gardner
Culture, Media and Sport– Chair, Rt. Hon. Gerald Kaufman, MP; *Clerk,* C. G. Lee
Defence – Chair, Bruce George, MP; *Clerks,* P. A. Evans; Ms S. McGlashan
Education and Employment – Clerks, M. D. Hamlyn; K. C. Fox
   Sub-committees: Education – Chair, vacant; *Clerk,* M. D. Hamlyn; *Employment – Chair,* Derek Foster, MP; *Clerk,* T. W. P. Healey
Environment, Transport and the Regions – Chairs, Andrew Bennett, MP; Gwyneth Dunwoody, MP; *Clerk,* D. F. Harrison
   Sub-committees: Environment – Chair, Andrew Bennett, MP; *Clerk,* H. A. Yardley; *Transport – Chair,* Gwyneth Dunwoody, MP; *Clerk,* G. R. Devine
Foreign Affairs – Chair, Donald Anderson, MP; *Clerks,* E. P. Silk; M. P. Atkins
Health – Chair, David Hinchliffe, MP; *Clerks,* J. S. Benger, D.phil.; J. D. Whatley
Home Affairs – Chair, Chris Mullin, MP; *Clerks,* C. J. Poyser; T. Goldsmith

International Development – Chair, Bowen Wells, MP; *Clerk*, A. Y. A. Azad

Northern Ireland – Chair, Rt. Hon. Peter Brooke, CH, MP; *Clerk*, C. R. M. Ward

Science and Technology – Chair, Dr Michael Clark, MP; *Clerk*, Mrs J. N. St J. Mulley

Scottish Affairs – Chair, David Marshall, MP; *Clerk*, F. A. Cranmer

Social Security – Chair, Archy Kirkwood, MP; *Clerk*, L. C. Laurence Smyth

Trade and Industry – Chair, Martin O'Neill, MP; *Clerk*, Ms A. Barry

Treasury – Chair, Giles Radice, MP; *Clerks*, Mrs J. Sharpe; Ms J. A. Long

  Treasury departments and agencies sub-committee: Chair, rotating chairmanship; *Clerk*, Ms J. A. Long

Welsh Affairs – Chair, Martyn Jones, MP; *Clerk*, Ms P. A. Helme

NON-DEPARTMENTAL COMMITTEES

Deregulation – Chair, Peter Pike, MP; *Clerk*, J. D. W. Rhys

Environmental Audit – Chair, John Horam, MP; *Clerk*, F. J. Reid

European Legislation – Chair, James Hood, MP; *Clerk*, Mrs E. J. Flood

Modernization – Chair, Rt. Hon. Margaret Beckett, MP; *Clerks*, C. B. Winnifrith, CB; A. Sandall

Procedure – Chair, Nicholas Winterton, MP; *Clerks*, Ms E. C. Samson; H. A. Yardley

Public Accounts – Chair, Rt. Hon. David Davis, MP; *Clerk*, K. J. Brown

Public Administration – Chair, Rhodri Morgan, MP; *Clerk*, Dr P. C. Seaward

Standards and Privileges – Chair, Rt. Hon. Robert Sheldon, MP; *Clerks*, A. Sandall; Mrs S. A. R. Davies

---

PARLIAMENTARY INFORMATION

The following is a short glossary of aspects of the work of Parliament. Unless otherwise stated, references are to House of Commons procedures.

BILL – Proposed legislation is termed a bill. The stages of a public bill (for private bills, *see* page 222) in the House of Commons are as follows:

First Reading: There is no debate at this stage, which nowadays merely constitutes an order to have the bill printed

Second Reading: The debate on the principles of the bill

Committee Stage: The detailed examination of a bill, clause by clause. In most cases this takes place in a standing committee, or the whole House may act as a committee. A special standing committee may take evidence before embarking on detailed scrutiny of the bill. Very rarely, a bill may be examined by a select committee (*see* page 222)

Report Stage: Detailed review of a bill as amended in committee

Third Reading: Final debate on a bill

Public bills go through the same stages in the House of Lords, except that in almost all cases the committee stage is taken in committee of the whole House.

A bill may start in either House, and has to pass through both Houses to become law. Both Houses have to agree the same text of a bill, so that the amendments made by the second House are then considered in the originating House, and if not agreed, sent back or themselves amended, until agreement is reached.

CHILTERN HUNDREDS – A legal fiction, a nominal office of profit under the Crown, the acceptance of which requires an MP to vacate his seat. The Manor of Northstead is similar. These are the only means by which an MP may resign.

CONSOLIDATED FUND BILL – A bill to authorize issue of money to maintain Government services. The bill is dealt with without debate.

EARLY DAY MOTION – A motion put on the notice paper by an MP without in general the real prospect of its being debated. Such motions are expressions of back-bench opinion.

FATHER OF THE HOUSE – The Member whose continuous service in the House of Commons is the longest. The present Father of the House is the Rt. Hon. Sir Edward Heath, KG, MBE, MP, elected first in 1950.

HOURS OF MEETING – The House of Commons meets Monday, Tuesday and Thursday at 2.30 p.m., and on Wednesday and Friday at 9.30 a.m.; there are ten Fridays without sittings in each session. The House of Lords normally meets at 2.30 p.m. Monday to Wednesday and at 3 p.m. on Thursday. In the latter part of the session, the House of Lords sometimes sits on Fridays at 11 a.m.

LEADER OF THE OPPOSITION – In 1937 the office of Leader of the Opposition was recognized and a salary was assigned to the post. Since April 1998 the salary has been £101,579 (including parliamentary salary of £45,066). The present Leader of the Opposition is the Rt. Hon. William Hague, MP.

THE LORD CHANCELLOR – The Lord High Chancellor of Great Britain is (*ex officio*) the Speaker of the House of Lords. Unlike the Speaker of the House of Commons, he is a member of the Government, takes part in debates and votes in divisions. He has none of the powers to maintain order that the Speaker in the Commons has, these powers being exercised in the Lords by the House as a whole. The Lord Chancellor sits in the Lords on one of the Woolsacks, couches covered with red cloth and stuffed with wool. If he wishes to address the House in any way except formally as Speaker, he leaves the Woolsack.

NORTHERN IRELAND GRAND COMMITTEE – The Northern Ireland Grand Committee consists of all MPs representing constituencies in Northern Ireland, together with not more than 25 other MPs nominated by the Committee of Selection. The business of the committee includes questions, short debates, ministerial statements, bills, legislative proposals and other matters relating exclusively to Northern Ireland, and delegated legislation.

 The Northern Ireland Affairs Committee is one of the departmental select committees, empowered to examine the expenditure, administration and policy of the Northern Ireland Office and the administration and expenditure of the Crown Solicitor's Office.

OPPOSITION DAY – A day on which the topic for debate is chosen by the Opposition. There are 20 such days in a normal session. On 17 days, subjects are chosen by the Leader of the Opposition; on the remaining three days by the leader of the next largest opposition party.

PARLIAMENT ACTS 1911 AND 1949 – Under these Acts, bills may become law without the consent of the Lords, though the House of Lords has the power to delay a public bill for 13 months from its first second reading in the House of Commons.

PRIME MINISTER'S QUESTIONS – The Prime Minister answers questions from 3.00 to 3.30 p.m. on Wednesdays.

PRIVATE BILL – A bill promoted by a body or an individual to give powers additional to, or in conflict with, the general law, and to which a special procedure applies to enable people affected to object.

PRIVATE MEMBER'S BILL – A public bill promoted by a Member who is not a member of the Government.

PRIVATE NOTICE QUESTION – A question adjudged of urgent importance on submission to the Speaker (in the Lords, the Leader of the House), answered at the end of oral questions, usually at 3.30 p.m.

PRIVILEGE – The following are covered by the privilege of Parliament:
(i) freedom from interference in going to, attending at, and going from, Parliament
(ii) freedom of speech in parliamentary proceedings
(iii) the printing and publishing of anything relating to the proceedings of the two Houses is subject to privilege
(iv) each House is the guardian of its dignity and may punish any insult to the House as a whole

QUESTION TIME – Oral questions are answered by Ministers in the Commons from 2.30 to 3.30 p.m. every day except Friday. They are also taken at the start of the Lords sittings, with a daily limit of four oral questions.

ROYAL ASSENT – The royal assent is signified by letters patent to such bills and measures as have passed both Houses of Parliament (or bills which have been passed under the Parliament Acts 1911 and 1949). The Sovereign has not given royal assent in person since 1854. On occasion, for instance in the prorogation of Parliament, royal assent may be pronounced to the two Houses by Lords Commissioners. More usually royal assent is notified to each House sitting separately in accordance with the Royal Assent Act 1967. The old French formulae for royal assent are then endorsed on the acts by the Clerk of the Parliaments.

The power to withhold assent resides with the Sovereign but has not been exercised in the UK since 1707, in the reign of Queen Anne.

SCOTTISH GRAND COMMITTEE – Established in its present form in 1957, the committee consists of all 72 MPs representing Scottish constituencies, with a quorum of ten. The functions of the committee are to consider the principle of all public bills relating exclusively to Scotland (constituting in effect the bill's second reading); to consider the Scottish estimates on not less than six days a session; and to consider matters relating exclusively to Scotland on not more than six days a session. From the beginning of the 1994–5 session, the committee's powers were enhanced to allow oral questions, short debates, ministerial statements, and consideration of appropriate statutory instruments. The committee can meet on appointed days at specified places in Scotland.

The Scottish Affairs Committee, one of the departmental select committees, is empowered to examine the expenditure, administration and policy of the Scottish Office, and the expenditure and administration of the Lord Advocate's Office.

SELECT COMMITTEES – Consisting usually of ten to 15 members of all parties, select committees are a means used by both Houses in order to investigate certain matters. Most select committees in the House of Commons are now tied to departments: each committee investigates subjects within a government department's remit. There are other House of Commons select committees dealing with public accounts (i.e. the spending by the Government of money voted by Parliament) and European legislation, and also domestic committees dealing, for example, with privilege and procedure. Major select committees usually take evidence in public; their evidence and reports are published by The Stationery Office. House of Commons select committees are reconstituted after a general election. For main committees, *see* pages 220–1.

The principal select committee in the House of Lords is that on the European Communities, which has, at present, six sub-committees dealing with all areas of Community policy. The House of Lords also has a select committee on science and technology, which appoints sub-committees to deal with specific subjects, and a select committee on delegated powers and deregulation. For committees, *see* page 218. In addition, *ad hoc* select committees have been set up from time to time to investigate specific subjects, e.g. overseas trade, murder and life imprisonment. There are also some joint committees of the two Houses, e.g. the committees on statutory instruments and on parliamentary privilege.

THE SPEAKER – The Speaker of the House of Commons is the spokesman and president of the Chamber. He or she is elected by the House at the beginning of each Parliament or when the previous Speaker retires or dies. The Speaker neither speaks in debates nor votes in divisions except when the voting is equal.

VACANT SEATS – When a vacancy occurs in the House of Commons during a session of Parliament, the writ for the by-election is moved by a Whip of the party to which the member whose seat has been vacated belonged. If the House is in recess, the Speaker can issue a warrant for a writ, should two members certify to him that a seat is vacant.

WELSH GRAND COMMITTEE – First appointed in the 1959–60 session, the committee consists of all 40 MPs representing Welsh constituencies plus not more than five other members nominated by the Committee of Selection. The functions of the committee are to consider the principle of all public bills referred to it (constituting in effect the second reading of such a bill); and to consider matters relating exclusively to Wales. Since 1996 the business of the committee may also include questions, ministerial statements and short debates. Since June 1996 members of the committee have been permitted to speak in Welsh.

The Welsh Affairs Committee, one of the departmental select committees, is empowered to examine the expenditure, administration and policy of the Welsh Office.

WHIPS – In order to secure the attendance of Members of a particular party in Parliament on all occasions, and particularly on the occasion of an important vote, Whips (originally known as 'Whippers-in') are appointed. The written appeal or circular letter issued by them is also known as a 'whip', its urgency being denoted by the number of times it is underlined. Failure to respond to a three-line whip, headed 'Most important', is tantamount in the Commons to secession (at any rate temporarily) from the party. Whips are officially recognized by Parliament and are provided with office accommodation in both Houses. In both Houses, Government and some Opposition Whips receive salaries from public funds.

PARLIAMENTARY EDUCATION UNIT – Norman Shaw Building (North), London SW1A 2TT. Tel: 0171-219 2105
E-mail: edunit@parliament.uk

GOVERNMENT OFFICE

The Government is the body of Ministers responsible for the administration of national affairs, determining policy and introducing into Parliament any legislation necessary to give effect to government policy. The majority of Ministers are members of the House of Commons but members of the House of Lords or of neither House may also hold ministerial responsibility. The Lord Chancellor is always a member of the House of Lords. The Prime Minister is, by current convention, always a member of the House of Commons.

THE PRIME MINISTER

The office of Prime Minister, which had been in existence for nearly 200 years, was officially recognized in 1905 and its holder was granted a place in the table of precedence. The Prime Minister, by tradition also First Lord of the Treasury and Minister for the Civil Service, is appointed by the Sovereign and is usually the leader of the party which enjoys, or can secure, a majority in the House of Commons. Other Ministers are appointed by the Sovereign on the recommendation of the Prime Minister, who also allocates functions amongst Ministers and has the power to obtain their resignation or dismissal individually.

The Prime Minister informs the Sovereign of state and political matters, advises on the dissolution of Parliament, and makes recommendations for important Crown appointments, the award of honours, etc.

As the chairman of Cabinet meetings and leader of a political party, the Prime Minister is responsible for translating party policy into government activity. As leader of the Government, the Prime Minister is responsible to Parliament and to the electorate for the policies and their implementation.

The Prime Minister also represents the nation in international affairs, e.g. summit conferences.

THE CABINET

The Cabinet developed during the 18th century as an inner committee of the Privy Council, which was the chief source of executive power until that time. The Cabinet is composed of about 20 Ministers chosen by the Prime Minister, usually the heads of government departments (generally known as Secretaries of State unless they have a special title, e.g. Chancellor of the Exchequer), the leaders of the two Houses of Parliament, and the holders of various traditional offices.

The Cabinet's functions are the final determination of policy, control of government and co-ordination of government departments. The exercise of its functions is dependent upon enjoying majority support in the House of Commons. Cabinet meetings are held in private, taking place once or twice a week during parliamentary sittings and less often during a recess. Proceedings are confidential, the members being bound by their oath as Privy Counsellors not to disclose information about the proceedings.

The convention of collective responsibility means that the Cabinet acts unanimously even when Cabinet Ministers do not all agree on a subject. The policies of departmental Ministers must be consistent with the policies of the Government as a whole, and once the Government's policy has been decided, each Minister is expected to support it or resign.

The convention of ministerial responsibility holds a Minister, as the political head of his or her department, accountable to Parliament for the department's work. Departmental Ministers usually decide all matters within their responsibility, although on matters of political importance they normally consult their colleagues collectively. A decision by a departmental Minister is binding on the Government as a whole.

POLITICAL PARTIES

Before the reign of William and Mary the principal officers of state were chosen by and were responsible to the Sovereign and not to Parliament or the nation at large. Such officers acted sometimes in concert with one another but more often independently, and the fall of one did not, of necessity, involve that of others, although all were liable to be dismissed at any moment.

In 1693 the Earl of Sunderland recommended to William III the advisability of selecting a ministry from the political party which enjoyed a majority in the House of Commons and the first united ministry was drawn in 1696 from the Whigs, to which party the King owed his throne. This group became known as the Junto and was regarded with suspicion as a novelty in the political life of the nation, being a small section meeting in secret apart from the main body of Ministers. It may be regarded as the forerunner of the Cabinet and in course of time it led to the establishment of the principle of joint responsibility of Ministers, so that internal disagreement caused a change of personnel or resignation of the whole body of Ministers.

The accession of George I, who was unfamiliar with the English language, led to a disinclination on the part of the Sovereign to preside at meetings of his Ministers and caused the appearance of a Prime Minister, a position first acquired by Robert Walpole in 1721 and retained by him without interruption for 20 years and 326 days.

DEVELOPMENT OF PARTIES

In 1828 the Whigs became known as Liberals, a name originally given to it by its opponents to imply laxity of principles, but gradually accepted by the party to indicate its claim to be pioneers and champions of political reform and progressive legislation. In 1861 a Liberal Registration Association was founded and Liberal Associations became widespread. In 1877 a National Liberal Federation was formed, with headquarters in London. The Liberal Party was in power for long periods during the second half of the 19th century and for several years during the first quarter of the 20th century, but after a split in the party the numbers elected were small from 1931. In 1988, a majority of the Liberals agreed on a merger with the Social Democratic Party under the title Social and Liberal Democrats; since 1989 they have been known as the Liberal Democrats. A minority continue separately as the Liberal Party.

Soon after the change from Whig to Liberal the Tory Party became known as Conservative, a name believed to have been invented by John Wilson Croker in 1830 and to have been generally adopted about the time of the passing of the Reform Act of 1832 to indicate that the preservation of national institutions was the leading principle of the party. After the Home Rule crisis of 1886 the dissentient Liberals entered into a compact with the Conservatives, under which the latter undertook not to contest their seats, but a separate Liberal Unionist organization was maintained until 1912, when it was united with the Conservatives.

Labour candidates for Parliament made their first appearance at the general election of 1892, when there were 27 standing as Labour or Liberal-Labour. In 1900 the

Labour Representation Committee was set up in order to establish a distinct Labour group in Parliament, with its own whips, its own policy, and a readiness to co-operate with any party which might be engaged in promoting legislation in the direct interest of labour. In 1906 the LRC became known as the Labour Party.

The Council for Social Democracy was announced by four former Labour Cabinet Ministers in January 1981 and on 26 March 1981 the Social Democratic Party was launched. Later that year the SDP and the Liberal Party formed an electoral alliance. In 1988 a majority of the SDP agreed on a merger with the Liberal Party (*see* above) but a minority continued as a separate party under the SDP title. In 1990 it was decided to wind up the party organization and its three sitting MPs were known as independent social democrats. None were returned at the 1992 general election.

Plaid Cymru was founded in 1926 to provide an independent political voice for Wales and to campaign for self-government in Wales.

The Scottish National Party was founded in 1934 to campaign for independence for Scotland.

The Social Democratic and Labour Party was founded in 1970, emerging from the civil rights movement of the 1960s, with the aim of promoting reform, reconciliation and partnership across the sectarian divide in Northern Ireland and of opposing violence from any quarter.

The Ulster Democratic Unionist Party was founded in 1971 to resist moves by the Ulster Unionist Party which were considered a threat to the Union. Its aim is to maintain Northern Ireland as an integral part of the UK.

The Ulster Unionist Council first met formally in 1905. Its objectives are to maintain Northern Ireland as an integral part of the UK and to promote the aims of the Ulster Unionist Party.

GOVERNMENT AND OPPOSITION

The government of the day is formed by the party which wins the largest number of seats in the House of Commons at a general election, or which has the support of a majority of members in the House of Commons. By tradition, the leader of the majority party is asked by the Sovereign to form a government, while the largest minority party becomes the official Opposition with its own leader and a 'Shadow Cabinet'. Leaders of the Government and Opposition sit on the front benches of the Commons with their supporters (the back-benchers) sitting behind them.

FINANCIAL SUPPORT

Financial support to Opposition parties was introduced in 1975 and is commonly known as Short Money, after Edward Short, the Leader of the House at that time, who introduced the scheme. For 1998–9 financial support is:

Conservative	£1,112,885.74
Liberal Democrats	419,559.87
Plaid Cymru	23,921.74
SNP	52,070.47
SDLP	20,925.09
Democratic Unionists	13,103.96
Ulster Unionsts	53,660.30

The parties included here are those with MPs sitting in the House of Commons in the present Parliament. Addresses of other political parties may be found in the Societies and Institutions section.

CONSERVATIVE AND UNIONIST PARTY
Central Office, 32 Smith Square, London SW1P 3HH
Tel 0171-222 9000; fax 0171-233 0701
E-mail: ccoffice@conservative-party.org.uk
Web: http://www.tory.org.uk

Chairman, Rt. Hon. Michael Ancram, QC, MP
Deputy Chairman and Chief Executive, Archie Norman, MP
Vice-Chairmen, The Baroness Buscombe; Andrew Lansley, CBE, MP; Hon. David Prior, MP; Tim Yeo, MP
Treasurer, M. Ashcroft

SHADOW CABINET *as at 3 August 1998*
Leader of the Opposition, Rt. Hon. William Hague, MP
Deputy Leader, Rt. Hon. Peter Lilley, MP
Agriculture, Fisheries and Food, Tim Yeo, MP
Constitutional Affairs, Dr Liam Fox, MP
Culture, Media and Sport, Peter Ainsworth, MP
Defence, John Maples, MP
Education and Employment, David Willetts, MP
Environment, Transport and the Regions, Rt. Hon. Gillian Shephard, MP
Foreign and Commonwealth Affairs, Rt. Hon. Michael Howard, QC, MP
Health, Rt. Hon. Ann Widdecombe, MP
Home Affairs, Rt. Hon. Sir Norman Fowler, MP
International Development, Gary Streeter, MP
Leader of the House of Commons and Chancellor of the Duchy of Lancaster, Rt. Hon. Sir George Young, Bt., MP
Leader of the House of Lords, Viscount Cranborne, PC
Northern Ireland, Rt. Hon. Andrew Mackay, MP
Social Security, Iain Duncan-Smith, MP
Trade and Industry, Rt. Hon. John Redwood, MP
Treasury, Rt. Hon. Francis Maude, MP
Chief Secretary to the Treasury, Rt. Hon. David Heathcoat-Amory, MP

CHIEF WHIPS
House of Lords, The Lord Strathclyde, PC
House of Commons, James Arbuthnot, MP (*Chief Whip*);
Patrick McLoughlin, MP (*Deputy Chief Whip*)

SCOTTISH CONSERVATIVE AND UNIONIST CENTRAL OFFICE
Suite 1/1, 14 Links Place, Leith, Edinburgh EH6 7EZ
Tel 0131-555 2900
E-mail: SCUCO@Scottish.tory.org.uk

Chairman, R. Robertson
Deputy Chairman, Mrs K. Donald
Hon. Treasurer, W. Y. Hughes, CBE
Head of Campaigns and Operations, D. Canzini

LABOUR PARTY
Millbank Tower, Millbank, London SW1P 4GT
Tel 0171-802 1000; fax 0171-802 1234
E-mail: labour-party@geo2.poptel.org.uk
Web: http://www.labour.org.uk

Parliamentary Party Leader, Rt. Hon. Anthony Blair, MP
Deputy Party Leader, Rt. Hon. John Prescott, MP
Leader in the Lords, The Lord Richard, PC, QC
Chair, R. Rosser
Vice-Chair, Rt. Hon. Clare Short, MP
Treasurer, Ms M. Prosser
General Secretary, Ms M. McDonagh
General Secretary, Scottish Labour Party, A. Rowley

LIBERAL DEMOCRATS
4 Cowley Street, London SW1P 3NB
Tel 0171-222 7999; fax 0171-799 2170
E-mail: libdems@cix.co.uk
Web: http://www.libdems.org.uk

President, Rt. Hon. Robert Maclennan, MP
Hon. Treasurer, The Lord Razzall, CBE
Chief Executive, Ms E. Pamplin
Parliamentary Party Leader, Rt. Hon. Paddy Ashdown, MP
Leader in the Lords, The Lord Rodgers of Quarry Bank, PC

LIBERAL DEMOCRAT SPOKESMEN *as at June 1998*
Deputy Leader, Home and Legal Affairs, Alan Beith, MP
Agriculture and Rural Affairs, Charles Kennedy, MP
Culture, Media and Sport, Constitution, Rt. Hon. Robert
  Maclennan, MP
Education and Employment, Don Foster, MP
Environment and Transport, Matthew Taylor, MP
Foreign Affairs, Defence and Europe, Menzies Campbell, MP
Health, Simon Hughes, MP
Local Government and Housing, Paul Burstow, MP
Social Security and Welfare, David Rendel, MP
Trade and Industry, David Chidgey, MP
Treasury, Malcolm Bruce, MP
Women, Jackie Ballard, MP
Young People, Lembit Opik, MP
Northern Ireland, The Lord Holme of Cheltenham
Scotland, Jim Wallace, MP
Wales, Richard Livsey, MP

LIBERAL DEMOCRAT WHIPS
House of Lords, The Lord Harris of Greenwich, PC
House of Commons, Paul Tyler, MP (*Chief Whip*); Andrew
  Stunell, MP (*Deputy Whip*)

LIBERAL DEMOCRATS WALES
Bay View House, 102 Bute Street, Cardiff CF1 6AD
Tel 01222-313400; fax 01222-313401
E-mail: ldwales@cix.co.uk

Party President, A. Carlile, QC
Party Leader, Richard Livsey, CBE, MP
Chairman, C. Davies
Treasurer, N. Howells
Secretary, Ms K. Lloyd
Administrative Officer, Ms H. Northmore

SCOTTISH LIBERAL DEMOCRATS
4 Clifton Terrace, Edinburgh EH12 5DR
Tel 0131-337 2314; fax 0131-337 3566
E-mail: scotlibdem@cix.co.uk
Web: http://www.scotlibdems.org.uk

Party President, R. Thomson
Party Leader, Jim Wallace, MP
Convener, S. Gallagher
Treasurer, D. R. Sullivan
Chief Executive, W. Rennie

PLAID CYMRU
18 Park Grove, Cardiff CF1 3BN
Tel 01222-646000; fax 01222-646001
E-mail: post@plaidcymru.org
Web: http://www/plaidcymru.org

Party President, Dafydd Wigley, MP
Chairman, M. Phillips
Hon. Treasurer, O. Williams
Chief Executive/General Secretary, K. Davies

SCOTTISH NATIONAL PARTY
6 North Charlotte Street, Edinburgh EH2 4JH
Tel 0131-226 3661; fax 0131-225 9597
Web: http://www.snp.org.uk

Parliamentary Party Leader, Margaret Ewing, MP
Chief Whip, Andrew Welsh, MP
National Convener, Alex Salmond, MP
Senior Vice-Convener, Dr A. Macartney, MEP
National Treasurer, K. MacAskill
National Secretary, C. Campbell

NORTHERN IRELAND

SOCIAL DEMOCRATIC AND LABOUR PARTY
121 Ormeau Road, Belfast BT7 1SH
Tel 01232-247700; fax 01232-236699
E-mail: sdlp@indigo.ie
Web: http://www.indigo.ie/sdlp

Parliamentary Party Leader, John Hume, MP, MEP
Deputy Leader, Seamus Mallon, MP
Chief Whip, Eddie McGrady, MP
Chairman, J. Stephenson
Hon. Treasurer, J. Lennon
General Secretary, Mrs G. Cosgrove

ULSTER DEMOCRATIC UNIONIST PARTY
91 Dundela Avenue, Belfast BT4 3BU
Tel 01232-471155; fax 01232-471797
E-mail: info@dup.org.uk
Web: http://www.dup.org.uk

Parliamentary Party Leader, I. Paisley, MP, MEP
Deputy Leader, Peter Robinson, MP
Chairman, W. J. McClure
Hon. Treasurer, G. Campbell
Party Secretary, N. Dodds

ULSTER UNIONIST PARTY
3 Glengall Street, Belfast BT12 5AE
Tel 01232-324601; fax 01232-246738
E-mail: uup@uup.org
Web: http://www.uup.org

Party Leader, Rt. Hon. David Trimble, MP
Chief Whip, Revd Martin Smyth, MP

ULSTER UNIONIST COUNCIL
President, J. Cunningham
Chairman, D. Rogan
Hon. Treasurer, J. Allen, OBE
Party Secretary, J. Wilson

MEMBERS OF PARLIAMENT as at 1 August 1998

For abbreviations, *see* page 235
* Member of last Parliament
† Former Member of Parliament
An entire entry in italic indicates that the MP was elected at the general election but has died since; the name is included for the purposes of record

*Abbott, Ms Diane J. (*b.* 1953) *Lab., Hackney North and Stoke Newington,* maj. 15,627

Adams, Gerard (Gerry) (*b.* 1948) *SF, Belfast West,* maj. 7,909

*Adams, Mrs K. Irene (*b.* 1948) *Lab., Paisley North,* maj. 12,814

*Ainger, Nicholas R. (*b.* 1949) *Lab., Carmarthen West and Pembrokeshire South,* maj. 9,621

*Ainsworth, Peter M. (*b.* 1956) *C., Surrey East,* maj. 15,093

*Ainsworth, Robert W. (*b.* 1952) *Lab., Coventry North East,* maj. 22,569

Alexander, Douglas G. (*b.* 1967) *Lab., Paisley South,* maj. 2,731

Allan, Richard B. (*b.* 1966) *LD, Sheffield Hallam,* maj. 8,271

*Allen, Graham W. (*b.* 1953) *Lab., Nottingham North,* maj. 18,801

*Amess, David A. A. (*b.* 1952) *C., Southend West,* maj. 2,615

*Ancram, Rt. Hon. Michael A. F. J. K. (Earl of Ancram) (*b.* 1945) *C., Devizes,* maj. 9,782

*Anderson, Donald (*b.* 1939) *Lab., Swansea East,* maj. 25,569

*Anderson, Mrs Janet (*b.* 1949) *Lab., Rossendale and Darwen,* maj. 10,949

*Arbuthnot, Rt. Hon. James N. (*b.* 1952) *C., Hampshire North East,* maj. 14,398

*Armstrong, Miss Hilary J. (*b.* 1945) *Lab., Durham North West,* maj. 24,754

*Ashdown, Rt. Hon. J. J. D. (Paddy) (*b.* 1941) *LD, Yeovil,* maj. 11,403

*Ashton, Joseph W. (*b.* 1933) *Lab., Bassetlaw,* maj. 17,460

Atherton, Ms Candice K. (*b.* 1955) *Lab., Falmouth and Camborne,* maj. 2,688

Atkins, Ms Charlotte (*b.* 1950) *Lab., Staffordshire Moorlands,* maj. 10,049

*Atkinson, David A. (*b.* 1940) *C., Bournemouth East,* maj. 4,346

*Atkinson, Peter L. (*b.* 1943) *C., Hexham,* maj. 222

*Austin-Walker, John E. (*b.* 1944) *Lab., Erith and Thamesmead,* maj. 17,424

Baker, Norman J. (*b.* 1957) *LD, Lewes,* maj. 1,300

*Baldry, Antony B. (*b.* 1950) *C., Banbury,* maj. 4,737

Ballard, Mrs Jacqueline M. (*b.* 1953) *LD, Taunton,* maj. 2,443

*Banks, Anthony L. (*b.* 1943) *Lab., West Ham,* maj. 19,494

*Barnes, Harold (*b.* 1936) *Lab., Derbyshire North East,* maj. 18,321

*Barron, Kevin J. (*b.* 1946) *Lab., Rother Valley,* maj. 23,485

*Battle, John D. (*b.* 1951) *Lab., Leeds West,* maj. 19,771

*Bayley, Hugh (*b.* 1952) *Lab., City of York,* maj. 20,523

Beard, C. Nigel (*b.* 1936) *Lab., Bexleyheath and Crayford,* maj. 3,415

*Beckett, Rt. Hon. Margaret M. (*b.* 1943) *Lab., Derby South,* maj. 16,106

*Begg, Ms Anne (*b.* 1955) *Lab., Aberdeen South,* maj. 3,365

*Beggs, Roy (*b.* 1936) *UUP, Antrim East,* maj. 6,389

*Beith, Rt. Hon. Alan J. (*b.* 1943) *LD, Berwick upon Tweed,* maj. 8,042

Bell, Martin, OBE (*b.* 1938) *Ind., Tatton,* maj. 11,077

*Bell, Stuart (*b.* 1938) *Lab., Middlesbrough,* maj. 25,018

*Benn, Rt. Hon. Anthony N. W. (*b.* 1925) *Lab., Chesterfield,* maj. 5,775

*Bennett, Andrew F. (*b.* 1939) *Lab., Denton and Reddish,* maj. 20,311

*Benton, Joseph E. (*b.* 1933) *Lab., Bootle,* maj. 28,421

Bercow, John S. (*b.* 1963) *C., Buckingham,* maj. 12,386

*Beresford, Sir Paul (*b.* 1946) *C., Mole Valley,* maj. 10,221

*Bermingham, Gerald E. (*b.* 1940) *Lab., St Helens South,* maj. 23,739

*Berry, Roger L., D.Phil. (*b.* 1948) *Lab., Kingswood,* maj. 14,253

Best, Harold (*b.* 1939) *Lab., Leeds North West,* maj. 3,844

*Betts, Clive J. C. (*b.* 1950) *Lab., Sheffield Attercliffe,* maj. 21,818

Blackman, Ms Elizabeth M. (*b.* 1949) *Lab., Erewash,* maj. 9,135

*Blair, Rt. Hon. Anthony C. L. (*b.* 1953) *Lab., Sedgefield,* maj. 25,143

Blears, Hazel A. (*b.* 1956) *Lab., Salford,* maj. 17,069

Blizzard, Robert J. (*b.* 1950) *Lab., Waveney,* maj. 12,453

*Blunkett, Rt. Hon. David (*b.* 1947) *Lab., Sheffield Brightside,* maj. 19,954

Blunt, Crispin J. R. (*b.* 1960) *C., Reigate,* maj. 7,741

*Boateng, Paul Y. (*b.* 1951) *Lab., Brent South,* maj. 19,691

*Body, Sir Richard (*b.* 1927) *C., Boston and Skegness,* maj. 647

*Boothroyd, Rt. Hon. Betty (*b.* 1929) *The Speaker, West Bromwich West,* maj. 15,423

Borrow, David S. (*b.* 1952) *Lab., Ribble South,* maj. 5,084

*Boswell, Timothy E. (*b.* 1942) *C., Daventry,* maj. 7,378

*Bottomley, Peter J. (*b.* 1944) *C., Worthing West,* maj. 7,713

*Bottomley, Rt. Hon. Virginia H. B. M. (*b.* 1948) *C., Surrey South West,* maj. 2,694

*Bradley, Keith J. C. (*b.* 1950) *Lab., Manchester Withington,* maj. 18,581

Bradley, Peter C. S. (*b.* 1953) *Lab., Wrekin, The,* maj. 3,025

Bradshaw, Benjamin P. J. (*b.* 1960) *Lab., Exeter,* maj. 11,705

Brady, Graham (*b.* 1967) *C., Altrincham and Sale West,* maj. 1,505

Brake, Thomas A. (*b.* 1962) *LD, Carshalton and Wallington,* maj. 2,267

Brand, Dr Peter (*b.* 1947) *LD, Isle of Wight,* maj. 6,406

*Brazier, Julian W. H., TD (*b.* 1953) *C., Canterbury,* maj. 3,964

Breed, Colin E. (*b.* 1947) *LD, Cornwall South East,* maj. 6,480

Brinton, Ms Helen R. (*b.* 1954) *Lab., Peterborough,* maj. 7,323

*Brooke, Rt. Hon. Peter L., CH (*b.* 1934) *C., Cities of London and Westminster,* maj. 4,881

*Brown, Rt. Hon. J. Gordon, Ph.D. (*b.* 1951) *Lab., Dunfermline East,* maj. 18,751

*Brown, Nicholas H. (*b.* 1950) *Lab., Newcastle upon Tyne East and Wallsend,* maj. 23,811

Brown, Russell L. (*b.* 1951) *Lab., Dumfries,* maj. 9,643

Browne, Desmond (*b.* 1952) *Lab., Kilmarnock and Loudoun,* maj. 7,256

*Browning, Mrs Angela F. (*b.* 1946) *C., Tiverton and Honiton,* maj. 1,653

*Bruce, Ian C. (*b.* 1947) *C., Dorset South,* maj. 77

*Bruce, Malcolm G. (*b.* 1944) *LD, Gordon,* maj. 6,997

Buck, Ms Karen P. (*b.* 1958) *Lab., Regent's Park and Kensington North,* maj. 14,657

*Burden, Richard H. (*b.* 1954) *Lab., Birmingham Northfield,* maj. 11,443

Burgon, Colin (*b.* 1948) *Lab., Elmet,* maj. 8,779

Burnett, John P. A. (*b.* 1945) *LD, Devon West and Torridge,* maj. 1,957

*Burns, Simon H. M. (*b.* 1952) *C., Chelmsford West,* maj. 6,691

Burstow, Paul K. (*b.* 1962) *LD, Sutton and Cheam,* maj. 2,097

Butler, Ms Christine M. (*b.* 1943) *Lab., Castle Point,* maj. 1,116

*Butterfill, John V. (*b*. 1941) *C., Bournemouth West*, maj. 5,710
*Byers, Rt. Hon. Stephen J. (*b*. 1953) *Lab., Tyneside North*, maj. 26,643
Cable, Dr J. Vincent (*b*. 1943) *LD, Twickenham*, maj. 4,281
*Caborn, Richard G. (*b*. 1943) *Lab., Sheffield Central*, maj. 16,906
Campbell, Alan (*b*. 1957) *Lab., Tynemouth*, maj. 11,273
*Campbell, Mrs Anne (*b*. 1940) *Lab., Cambridge*, maj. 14,137
*Campbell, Ronald (*b*. 1943) *Lab., Blyth Valley*, maj. 17,736
*Campbell, W. Menzies, CBE, QC (*b*. 1941) *LD, Fife North East*, maj. 10,356
*Campbell-Savours, Dale N. (*b*. 1943) *Lab., Workington*, maj. 19,656
*Canavan, Dennis A. (*b*. 1942) *Lab., Falkirk West*, maj. 13,783
*Cann, James C. (*b*. 1946) *Lab., Ipswich*, maj. 10,439
Caplin, Ivor K. (*b*. 1958) *Lab., Hove*, maj. 3,959
Casale, Roger M. (*b*. 1960) *Lab., Wimbledon*, maj. 2,980
*Cash, William N. P. (*b*. 1940) *C., Stone*, maj. 3,818
Caton, Martin P. (*b*. 1951) *Lab., Gower*, maj. 13,007
Cawsey, Ian A. (*b*. 1960) *Lab., Brigg and Goole*, maj. 6,389
*Chapman, J. K. (Ben) (*b*. 1940) *Lab., Wirral South*, maj. 7,004
*Chapman, Sir Sydney (*b*. 1935) *C., Chipping Barnet*, maj. 1,035
Chaytor, David M. (*b*. 1949) *Lab., Bury North*, maj. 7,866
*Chidgey, David W. G. (*b*. 1942) *LD, Eastleigh*, maj. 754
*Chisholm, Malcolm G. R. (*b*. 1949) *Lab., Edinburgh North and Leith*, maj. 10,978
Chope, Christopher R., OBE (*b*. 1947) *C., Christchurch*, maj. 2,165
*Church, Mrs Judith A. (*b*. 1953) *Lab., Dagenham*, maj. 17,054
*Clapham, Michael (*b*. 1943) *Lab., Barnsley West and Penistone*, maj. 17,267
*Clappison, W. James (*b*. 1956) *C., Hertsmere*, maj. 3,075
Clark, Rt. Hon. Alan K. M. (*b*. 1928) *C., Kensington and Chelsea*, maj. 9,519
*Clark, Rt. Hon. David G., PH.D. (*b*. 1939) *Lab., South Shields*, maj. 22,153
Clark, Ms Lynda M. (*b*. 1949) *Lab., Edinburgh Pentlands*, maj. 4,862
*Clark, Dr Michael, PH.D. (*b*. 1935) *C., Rayleigh*, maj. 10,684
Clark, Paul G. (*b*. 1957) *Lab., Gillingham*, maj. 1,980
Clarke, Anthony R. (*b*. 1963) *Lab., Northampton South*, maj. 744
Clarke, Charles R. (*b*. 1950) *Lab., Norwich South*, maj. 14,239
*Clarke, Eric L. (*b*. 1933) *Lab., Midlothian*, maj. 9,870
*Clarke, Rt. Hon. Kenneth H., QC (*b*. 1940) *C., Rushcliffe*, maj. 5,055
*Clarke, Rt. Hon. Thomas, CBE (*b*. 1941) *Lab., Coatbridge and Chryston*, maj. 19,295
*Clelland, David G. (*b*. 1943) *Lab., Tyne Bridge*, maj. 22,906
*Clifton-Brown, Geoffrey R. (*b*. 1953) *C., Cotswold*, maj. 11,965
*Clwyd, Mrs Ann (*b*. 1937) *Lab., Cynon Valley*, maj. 19,755
Coaker, Vernon R. (*b*. 1953) *Lab., Gedling*, maj. 3,802
*Coffey, Ms M. Ann (*b*. 1946) *Lab., Stockport*, maj. 18,912
*Cohen, Harry M. (*b*. 1949) *Lab., Leyton and Wanstead*, maj. 15,186
Coleman, Iain (*b*. 1958) *Lab., Hammersmith and Fulham*, maj. 3,842
Collins, Timothy W. G. (*b*. 1964) *C., Westmorland and Lonsdale*, maj. 4,521
Colman, Anthony (*b*. 1943) *Lab., Putney*, maj. 2,976
*Colvin, Michael K. B. (*b*. 1932) *C., Romsey*, maj. 8,585
*Connarty, Michael (*b*. 1947) *Lab., Falkirk East*, maj. 13,385
*Cook, Francis (*b*. 1935) *Lab., Stockton North*, maj. 21,357
*Cook, Rt. Hon. R. F. (Robin) (*b*. 1946) *Lab., Livingston*, maj. 11,747

Cooper, Ms Yvette (*b*. 1969) *Lab., Pontefract and Castleford*, maj. 25,725
*Corbett, Robin (*b*. 1933) *Lab., Birmingham Erdington*, maj. 12,657
*Corbyn, Jeremy B. (*b*. 1949) *Lab., Islington North*, maj. 19,955
*Cormack, Sir Patrick (*b*. 1939) *C., Staffordshire South*, maj. 7,821
*Corston, Ms Jean A. (*b*. 1942) *Lab., Bristol East*, maj. 16,159
Cotter, Brian J. (*b*. 1938) *LD, Weston-Super-Mare*, maj. 1,274
*Cousins, James M. (*b*. 1944) *Lab., Newcastle upon Tyne Central*, maj. 16,480
*Cox, Thomas M. (*b*. 1930) *Lab., Tooting*, maj. 15,011
*Cran, James D. (*b*. 1944) *C., Beverley and Holderness*, maj. 811
Cranston, Ross F. (*b*. 1948) *Lab., Dudley North*, maj. 9,457
Crausby, David A. (*b*. 1946) *Lab., Bolton North East*, maj. 12,669
Cryer, Mrs C. Ann (*b*. 1939) *Lab., Keighley*, maj. 7,132
Cryer, John R. (*b*. 1964) *Lab., Hornchurch*, maj. 5,680
*Cummings, John S. (*b*. 1943) *Lab., Easington*, maj. 30,012
*Cunliffe, Lawrence F. (*b*. 1929) *Lab., Leigh*, maj. 24,496
*Cunningham, Rt. Hon. Dr. J. A. (Jack), PH.D. (*b*. 1939) *Lab., Copeland*, maj. 11,944
*Cunningham, James D. (*b*. 1941) *Lab., Coventry South*, maj. 10,953
*Cunningham, Ms Roseanna (*b*. 1951) *SNP, Perth*, maj. 3,141
*Curry, Rt. Hon. David M. (*b*. 1944) *C., Skipton and Ripon*, maj. 11,620
Curtis-Tansley, Ms Claire (*b*. 1958) *Lab., Crosby*, maj. 7,182
*Dafis, Cynog G. (*b*. 1938) *PC, Ceredigion*, maj. 6,961
*Dalyell, Tam (Sir Thomas Dalyell of the Binns, Bt.) (*b*. 1932) *Lab., Linlithgow*, maj. 10,838
*Darling, Rt. Hon. Alistair M. (*b*. 1953) *Lab., Edinburgh Central*, maj. 11,070
Darvill, Keith E. (*b*. 1948) *Lab., Upminster*, maj. 2,770
Davey, Edward J. (*b*. 1965) *LD, Kingston and Surbiton*, maj. 56
Davey, Ms Valerie (*b*. 1940) *Lab., Bristol West*, maj. 1,493
*Davidson, Ian G. (*b*. 1950) *Lab. Co-op., Glasgow Pollok*, maj. 13,791
*Davies, Rt. Hon. D. J. Denzil (*b*. 1938) *Lab., Llanelli*, maj. 16,039
Davies, Geraint R. (*b*. 1960) *Lab., Croydon Central*, maj. 3,897
*Davies, J. Quentin (*b*. 1944) *C., Grantham and Stamford*, maj. 2,692
*Davies, Rt. Hon. Ronald (*b*. 1946) *Lab., Caerphilly*, maj. 25,839
*Davis, Rt. Hon. David M. (*b*. 1948) *C., Haltemprice and Howden*, maj. 7,514
*Davis, Terence A. G. (*b*. 1938) *Lab., Birmingham Hodge Hill*, maj. 14,200
Dawson, T. Hilton (*b*. 1953) *Lab., Lancaster and Wyre*, maj. 1,295
*Day, Stephen R. (*b*. 1948) *C., Cheadle*, maj. 3,189
Dean, Ms Janet E. A. (*b*. 1949) *Lab., Burton*, maj. 6,330
*Denham, John Y. (*b*. 1953) *Lab., Southampton Itchen*, maj. 14,209
*Dewar, Rt. Hon. Donald C. (*b*. 1937) *Lab., Glasgow Anniesland*, maj. 15,154
Dismore, Andrew H. (*b*. 1954) *Lab., Hendon*, maj. 6,155
Dobbin, James (*b*. 1941) *Lab. Co-op., Heywood and Middleton*, maj. 17,542
*Dobson, Rt. Hon. Frank G. (*b*. 1940) *Lab., Holborn and St Pancras*, maj. 17,903
Donaldson, Jeffrey M. (*b*. 1962) *UUP, Lagan Valley*, maj. 16,925

Heal, Mrs Sylvia L. (*b.* 1942) *Lab. Co-op., Halesowen and Rowley Regis*, maj. 10,337

*Heald, Oliver (*b.* 1954) *C., Hertfordshire North East*, maj. 3,088

Healey, John (*b.* 1960) *Lab., Wentworth*, maj. 23,959

Heath, David W. St J. (*b.* 1954) *LD, Somerton and Frome*, maj. 130

*Heath, Rt. Hon. Sir Edward, KG, MBE (*b.* 1916) *C., Old Bexley and Sidcup*, maj. 3,569

*Heathcoat-Amory, Rt. Hon. David P. (*b.* 1949) *C., Wells*, maj. 528

*Henderson, Douglas J. (*b.* 1949) *Lab., Newcastle upon Tyne North*, maj. 19,332

Henderson, Ivan J. (*b.* 1958) *Lab., Harwich*, maj. 1,216

Hepburn, Stephen (*b.* 1959) *Lab., Jarrow*, maj. 21,933

*Heppell, John B. (*b.* 1948) *Lab., Nottingham East*, maj. 15,419

*Heseltine, Rt. Hon. Michael R. D., CH (*b.* 1933) *C., Henley*, maj. 11,167

Hesford, Stephen (*b.* 1957) *Lab., Wirral West*, maj. 2,738

Hewitt, Ms Patricia H. (*b.* 1948) *Lab., Leicester West*, maj. 12,864

*Hill, T. Keith (*b.* 1943) *Lab., Streatham*, maj. 18,423

*Hinchliffe, David M. (*b.* 1948) *Lab., Wakefield*, maj. 14,604

*Hodge, Mrs Margaret E., MBE (*b.* 1944) *Lab., Barking*, maj. 15,896

*Hoey, Ms Catharine (Kate) L. (*b.* 1946) *Lab., Vauxhall*, maj. 18,660

*Hogg, Rt. Hon. Douglas M., QC (*b.* 1945) *C., Sleaford and North Hykeham*, maj. 5,123

*Home Robertson, John D. (*b.* 1948) *Lab., East Lothian*, maj. 14,221

*Hood, James (*b.* 1948) *Lab., Clydesdale*, maj. 13,809

*Hoon, Geoffrey W. (*b.* 1953) *Lab., Ashfield*, maj. 22,728

Hope, Philip I. (*b.* 1955) *Lab. Co-op., Corby*, maj. 11,860

Hopkins, Kelvin P. (*b.* 1941) *Lab., Luton North*, maj. 9,626

*Horam, John R. (*b.* 1939) *C., Orpington*, maj. 2,952

*Howard, Rt. Hon. Michael, QC (*b.* 1941) *C., Folkestone and Hythe*, maj. 6,332

*Howarth, Alan T., CBE (*b.* 1944) *Lab., Newport East*, maj. 13,523

*Howarth, George E. (*b.* 1949) *Lab., Knowsley North and Sefton East*, maj. 26,147

Howarth, J. Gerald D. (*b.* 1947) *C., Aldershot*, maj. 6,621

*Howells, Kim S., PH.D. (*b.* 1946) *Lab., Pontypridd*, maj. 23,129

Hoyle, Lindsay H. (*b.* 1957) *Lab., Chorley*, maj. 9,870

*Hughes, Ms Beverley J. (*b.* 1950) *Lab., Stretford and Urmston*, maj. 13,640

*Hughes, Kevin M. (*b.* 1952) *Lab., Doncaster North*, maj. 21,937

*Hughes, Simon H. W. (*b.* 1951) *LD, Southwark North and Bermondsey*, maj. 3,387

Humble, Mrs Jovanka (Joan) (*b.* 1951) *Lab., Blackpool North and Fleetwood*, maj. 8,946

*Hume, John, MEP (*b.* 1937) *SDLP, Foyle*, maj. 13,664

*Hunter, Andrew R. F. (*b.* 1943) *C., Basingstoke*, maj. 2,397

Hurst, Alan A. (*b.* 1945) *Lab., Braintree*, maj. 1,451

*Hutton, John M. P. (*b.* 1955) *Lab., Barrow and Furness*, maj. 14,497

Iddon, Brian (*b.* 1940) *Lab., Bolton South East*, maj. 21,311

*Illsley, Eric E. (*b.* 1955) *Lab., Barnsley Central*, maj. 24,501

*Ingram, Adam P. (*b.* 1947) *Lab., East Kilbride*, maj. 17,384

*Jack, Rt. Hon. J. Michael (*b.* 1946) *C., Fylde*, maj. 8,963

*Jackson, Ms Glenda M., CBE (*b.* 1936) *Lab., Hampstead and Highgate*, maj. 13,284

*Jackson, Mrs Helen M. (*b.* 1939) *Lab., Sheffield Hillsborough*, maj. 16,451

*Jackson, Robert V. (*b.* 1946) *C., Wantage*, maj. 6,039

*Jamieson, David C. (*b.* 1947) *Lab., Plymouth Devonport*, maj. 19,067

*Jenkin, Hon. Bernard C. (*b.* 1959) *C., Essex North*, maj. 5,476

*Jenkins, Brian D. (*b.* 1942) *Lab., Tamworth*, maj. 7,496

Johnson, Alan A. (*b.* 1950) *Lab., Hull West and Hessle*, maj. 15,525

Johnson, Ms Melanie J. (*b.* 1955) *Lab., Welwyn Hatfield*, maj. 5,595

*Johnson Smith, Rt. Hon. Sir Geoffrey (*b.* 1924) *C., Wealden*, maj. 14,204

Jones, Ms Fiona E. A. (*b.* 1957) *Lab., Newark*, maj. 3,016

Jones, Ms Helen M. (*b.* 1954) *Lab., Warrington North*, maj. 19,527

*Jones, Ieuan W. (*b.* 1949) *PC, Ynys Môn*, maj. 2,481

Jones, Ms Jennifer G. (*b.* 1948) *Lab., Wolverhampton South West*, maj. 5,118

*Jones, Jonathan O. (*b.* 1954) *Lab. Co-op., Cardiff Central*, maj. 7,923

*Jones, Ms Lynne M., PH.D. (*b.* 1951) *Lab., Birmingham Selly Oak*, maj. 14,088

*Jones, Martyn D. (*b.* 1947) *Lab., Clwyd South*, maj. 13,810

*Jones, Nigel D. (*b.* 1948) *LD, Cheltenham*, maj. 6,645

*Jones, S. Barry (*b.* 1938) *Lab., Alyn and Deeside*, maj. 16,403

*Jowell, Ms Tessa J. H. D. (*b.* 1947) *Lab., Dulwich and West Norwood*, maj. 16,769

*Kaufman, Rt. Hon. Gerald B. (*b.* 1930) *Lab., Manchester Gorton*, maj. 17,342

Keeble, Ms Sally C. (*b.* 1951) *Lab., Northampton North*, maj. 10,000

*Keen, D. Alan (*b.* 1937) *Lab. Co-op., Feltham and Heston*, maj. 15,273

Keen, Mrs Ann L. (*b.* 1948) *Lab., Brentford and Isleworth*, maj. 14,424

Keetch, Paul S. (*b.* 1961) *LD, Hereford*, maj. 6,648

Kelly, Ms Ruth M. (*b.* 1968) *Lab., Bolton West*, maj. 7,072

Kemp, Fraser (*b.* 1958) *Lab., Houghton and Washington East*, maj. 26,555

*Kennedy, Charles P. (*b.* 1959) *LD, Ross, Skye and Inverness West*, maj. 4,019

*Kennedy, Mrs Jane E. (*b.* 1958) *Lab., Liverpool Wavertree*, maj. 19,701

*Key, S. Robert (*b.* 1945) *C., Salisbury*, maj. 6,276

*Khabra, Piara S. (*b.* 1924) *Lab., Ealing Southall*, maj. 21,423

Kidney, David N. (*b.* 1955) *Lab., Stafford*, maj. 4,314

*Kilfoyle, Peter (*b.* 1946) *Lab., Liverpool Walton*, maj. 27,038

King, Andrew (*b.* 1948) *Lab., Rugby and Kenilworth*, maj. 495

King, Ms Oona T. (*b.* 1967) *Lab., Bethnal Green and Bow*, maj. 11,285

*King, Rt. Hon. Thomas J., CH (*b.* 1933) *C., Bridgwater*, maj. 1,796

Kingham, Ms Teresa J. (*b.* 1963) *Lab., Gloucester*, maj. 8,259

Kirkbride, Miss Julie (*b.* 1960) *C., Bromsgrove*, maj. 4,895

*Kirkwood, Archibald J. (*b.* 1946) *LD, Roxburgh and Berwickshire*, maj. 7,906

Kumar, Dr Ashok (*b.* 1956) *Lab., Middlesbrough South and Cleveland East*, maj. 10,607

Ladyman, Dr Stephen J. (*b.* 1952) *Lab., Thanet South*, maj. 2,878

Laing, Mrs Eleanor F. (*b.* 1958) *C., Epping Forest*, maj. 5,252

Lait, Ms Jacqueline A. H. (*b.* 1947) *C., Beckenham*, maj. 1,227

Lansley, Andrew D. (*b.* 1956) *C., Cambridgeshire South*, maj. 8,712

Lawrence, Mrs Jacqueline R. (*b.* 1948) *Lab., Preseli Pembrokeshire*, maj. 8,736

Laxton, Robert (*b.* 1944) *Lab., Derby North*, maj. 10,615

*Leigh, Edward J. E. (*b.* 1950) *C., Gainsborough*, maj. 6,826

Lepper, David (*b.* 1945) *Lab. Co-op., Brighton Pavilion*, maj. 13,181

Leslie, Christopher M. (*b.* 1972) *Lab., Shipley*, maj. 2,996

Letwin, Oliver (*b.* 1956) *C., Dorset West*, maj. 1,840

Levitt, Tom (*b.* 1954) *Lab., High Peak*, maj. 8,791

Mountford, Ms Kali C. J. (*b.* 1954) *Lab., Colne Valley*, maj. 4,840

*Mowlam, Rt. Hon. Marjorie, PH.D. (*b.* 1949) *Lab., Redcar*, maj. 21,664

*Mudie, George E. (*b.* 1945) *Lab., Leeds East*, maj. 17,466

*Mullin, Christopher J. (*b.* 1947) *Lab., Sunderland South*, maj. 19,638

Murphy, Denis (*b.* 1948) *Lab., Wansbeck*, maj. 22,367

Murphy, James (*b.* 1967) *Lab., Eastwood*, maj. 3,236

*Murphy, Paul P. (*b.* 1948) *Lab., Torfaen*, maj. 24,536

Naysmith, J. Douglas (*b.* 1941) *Lab. Co-op., Bristol North West*, maj. 11,382

*Nicholls, Patrick C. M. (*b.* 1948) *C., Teignbridge*, maj. 281

Norman, Archibald J. (*b.* 1954) *C., Tunbridge Wells*, maj. 7,506

Norris, Dan (*b.* 1960) *Lab., Wansdyke*, maj. 4,799

Oaten, Mark (*b.* 1964) *LD, Winchester*, maj. 21,556

*O'Brien, Michael (*b.* 1954) *Lab., Warwickshire North*, maj. 14,767

*O'Brien, William (*b.* 1929) *Lab., Normanton*, maj. 15,893

*O'Hara, Edward (*b.* 1937) *Lab., Knowsley South*, maj. 30,708

*Olner, William J. (*b.* 1942) *Lab., Nuneaton*, maj. 13,540

*O'Neill, Martin J. (*b.* 1945) *Lab., Ochil*, maj. 4,652

Opik, Lembit (*b.* 1965) *LD, Montgomeryshire*, maj. 6,303

Organ, Ms Diana M. (*b.* 1952) *Lab., Forest of Dean*, maj. 6,343

Osborne, Mrs Sandra C. (*b.* 1956) *Lab., Ayr*, maj. 6,543

*Ottaway, Richard G. J. (*b.* 1945) *C., Croydon South*, maj. 11,930

*Page, Richard L. (*b.* 1941) *C., Hertfordshire South West*, maj. 10,021

*Paice, James E. T. (*b.* 1949) *C., Cambridgeshire South East*, maj. 9,349

*Paisley, Revd Ian R. K., MEP (*b.* 1926) *DUP, Antrim North*, maj. 10,574

Palmer, Nicholas D. (*b.* 1950) *Lab., Broxtowe*, maj. 5,575

Paterson, Owen W. (*b.* 1956) *C., Shropshire North*, maj. 2,195

*Pearson, Ian P., PH.D. (*b.* 1959) *Lab., Dudley South*, maj. 13,027

*Pendry, Thomas (*b.* 1934) *Lab., Stalybridge and Hyde*, maj. 14,806

Perham, Ms Linda (*b.* 1947) *Lab., Ilford North*, maj. 3,224

*Pickles, Eric J. (*b.* 1952) *C., Brentwood and Ongar*, maj. 9,690

*Pickthall, Colin (*b.* 1944) *Lab., Lancashire West*, maj. 17,119

*Pike, Peter L. (*b.* 1937) *Lab., Burnley*, maj. 17,062

Plaskitt, James A. (*b.* 1954) *Lab., Warwick and Leamington*, maj. 3,398

Pollard, Kerry P. (*b.* 1944) *Lab., St Albans*, maj. 4,459

Pond, Christopher R. (*b.* 1952) *Lab., Gravesham*, maj. 5,779

*Pope, Gregory J. (*b.* 1960) *Lab., Hyndburn*, maj. 11,448

Pound, Stephen P. (*b.* 1948) *Lab., Ealing North*, maj. 9,160

*Powell, Sir Raymond (*b.* 1928) *Lab., Ogmore*, maj. 24,447

*Prentice, Ms Bridget T. (*b.* 1952) *Lab., Lewisham East*, maj. 12,127

*Prentice, Gordon (*b.* 1951) *Lab., Pendle*, maj. 10,824

*Prescott, Rt. Hon. John L. (*b.* 1938) *Lab., Hull East*, maj. 23,318

*Primarolo, Ms Dawn (*b.* 1954) *Lab., Bristol South*, maj. 19,328

Prior, Hon. David G. L. (*b.* 1954) *C., Norfolk North*, maj. 1,293

Prosser, Gwynfor M. (*b.* 1943) *Lab., Dover*, maj. 11,739

*Purchase, Kenneth (*b.* 1939) *Lab. Co-op., Wolverhampton North East*, maj. 12,987

*Quin, Miss Joyce G. (*b.* 1944) *Lab., Gateshead East and Washington West*, maj. 24,950

Quinn, Lawrence W. (*b.* 1956) *Lab., Scarborough and Whitby*, maj. 5,124

*Radice, Giles H. (*b.* 1936) *Lab., Durham North*, maj. 26,299

Rammell, William E. (*b.* 1959) *Lab., Harlow*, maj. 10,514

Randall, A. John (*b.* 1955) *C., Uxbridge*, maj. 3,766

Rapson, Sydney N. J. (*b.* 1942) *Lab., Portsmouth North*, maj. 4,323

*Raynsford, W. R. N. (Nick) (*b.* 1945) *Lab., Greenwich and Woolwich*, maj. 18,128

*Redwood, Rt. Hon. John A., D.Phil. (*b.* 1951) *C., Wokingham*, maj. 9,365

Reed, Andrew J. (*b.* 1964) *Lab., Loughborough*, maj. 5,712

*Reid, Rt. Hon. John, PH.D. (*b.* 1947) *Lab., Hamilton North and Bellshill*, maj. 17,067

*Rendel, David D. (*b.* 1949) *LD, Newbury*, maj. 8,517

*Robathan, Andrew R. G. (*b.* 1951) *C., Blaby*, maj. 6,474

*Robertson, Rt. Hon. George I. M. (*b.* 1946) *Lab., Hamilton South*, maj. 15,878

Robertson, Laurence A. (*b.* 1958) *C., Tewkesbury*, maj. 9,234

*Robinson, Geoffrey (*b.* 1938) *Lab., Coventry North West*, maj. 16,601

*Robinson, Peter D. (*b.* 1948) *DUP, Belfast East*, maj. 6,754

*Roche, Mrs Barbara M. R. (*b.* 1954) *Lab., Hornsey and Wood Green*, maj. 20,499

*Roe, Mrs Marion A. (*b.* 1936) *C., Broxbourne*, maj. 6,653

*Rogers, Allan R. (*b.* 1932) *Lab., Rhondda*, maj. 24,931

*Rooker, Jeffrey W. (*b.* 1941) *Lab., Birmingham Perry Barr*, maj. 18,957

*Rooney, Terence H. (*b.* 1950) *Lab., Bradford North*, maj. 12,770

*Ross, Ernest (*b.* 1942) *Lab., Dundee West*, maj. 11,859

*Ross, William (*b.* 1936) *UUP, Londonderry East*, maj. 3,794

*Rowe, Andrew J. B. (*b.* 1935) *C., Faversham and Kent Mid*, maj. 4,173

*Rowlands, Edward (*b.* 1940) *Lab., Merthyr Tydfil and Rhymney*, maj. 27,086

Roy, Frank (*b.* 1958) *Lab., Motherwell and Wishaw*, maj. 12,791

Ruane, Christopher S. (*b.* 1958) *Lab., Vale of Clwyd*, maj. 8,955

*Ruddock, Mrs Joan M. (*b.* 1943) *Lab., Lewisham Deptford*, maj. 18,878

Ruffley, David L. (*b.* 1962) *C., Bury St Edmunds*, maj. 368

Russell, Ms Christine M. (*b.* 1945) *Lab., City of Chester*, maj. 10,553

Russell, Robert E. (*b.* 1946) *LD, Colchester*, maj. 1,581

Ryan, Ms Joan M. (*b.* 1955) *Lab., Enfield North*, maj. 6,822

*Salmond, Alexander E. A. (*b.* 1954) *SNP, Banff and Buchan*, maj. 12,845

Salter, Martin J. (*b.* 1954) *Lab., Reading West*, maj. 2,997

Sanders, Adrian M. (*b.* 1959) *LD, Torbay*, maj. 12

Sarwar, Mohammad (*b.* 1952) *Lab., Glasgow Govan*, maj. 2,914

Savidge, Malcolm K. (*b.* 1946) *Lab., Aberdeen North*, maj. 10,010

Sawford, Philip A. (*b.* 1950) *Lab., Kettering*, maj. 189

Sayeed, Jonathan (*b.* 1948) *C., Bedfordshire Mid*, maj. 7,090

*Sedgemore, Brian C. J. (*b.* 1937) *Lab., Hackney South and Shoreditch*, maj. 14,980

Shaw, Jonathan R. (*b.* 1966) *Lab., Chatham and Aylesford*, maj. 2,790

*Sheerman, Barry J. (*b.* 1940) *Lab. Co-op., Huddersfield*, maj. 15,848

*Sheldon, Rt. Hon. Robert E. (*b.* 1923) *Lab., Ashton under Lyne*, maj. 22,965

*Shephard, Rt. Hon. Gillian P. (*b.* 1940) *C., Norfolk South West*, maj. 2,464

*Shepherd, Richard C. S. (*b.* 1942) *C., Aldridge-Brownhills*, maj. 2,526

Shipley, Ms Debra A. (*b.* 1957) *Lab., Stourbridge*, maj. 5,645

*Short, Rt. Hon. Clare (*b.* 1946) *Lab., Birmingham Ladywood*, maj. 23,082

*Simpson, Alan J. (*b.* 1948) *Lab., Nottingham South*, maj. 13,364

Simpson, Keith (*b.* 1949) *C., Norfolk Mid*, maj. 1,336

*Wicks, Malcolm H. (*b*. 1947) *Lab., Croydon North*, maj. 18,398
*Widdecombe, Rt. Hon. Ann N. (*b*. 1947) *C., Maidstone and the Weald*, maj. 9,603
*Wigley, Rt. Hon. Dafydd (*b*. 1943) *PC, Caernarfon*, maj. 7,949
*Wilkinson, John A. D. (*b*. 1940) *C., Ruislip-Northwood*, maj. 7,794
*Willetts, David L. (*b*. 1956) *C., Havant*, maj. 3,729
*Williams, Rt. Hon. Alan J. (*b*. 1930) *Lab., Swansea West*, maj. 14,459
*Williams, Dr Alan W. (*b*. 1945) *Lab., Carmarthen East and Dinefwr*, maj. 3,450
Williams, Mrs Betty H. (*b*. 1944) *Lab., Conwy*, maj. 1,596
Willis, G. Philip (*b*. 1941) *LD, Harrogate and Knaresborough*, maj. 6,236
Wills, Michael D. (*b*. 1952) *Lab., Swindon North*, maj. 7,688
*Wilshire, David (*b*. 1943) *C., Spelthorne*, maj. 3,473
*Wilson, Brian D. H. (*b*. 1948) *Lab., Cunninghame North*, maj. 11,039
*Winnick, David J. (*b*. 1933) *Lab., Walsall North*, maj. 12,588
*Winterton, Mrs J. Ann (*b*. 1941) *C., Congleton*, maj. 6,130

*Winterton, Nicholas R. (*b*. 1938) *C., Macclesfield*, maj. 8,654
Winterton, Ms Rosalie (*b*. 1958) *Lab., Doncaster Central*, maj. 17,856
*Wise, Mrs Audrey (*b*. 1935) *Lab., Preston*, maj. 18,680
Wood, Michael R. (*b*. 1946) *Lab., Batley and Spen*, maj. 6,141
Woodward, Shaun A. (*b*. 1958) *C., Witney*, maj. 7,028
Woolas, Philip J. (*b*. 1959) *Lab., Oldham East and Saddleworth*, maj. 3,389
*Worthington, Anthony (*b*. 1941) *Lab., Clydebank and Milngavie*, maj. 13,320
*Wray, James (*b*. 1938) *Lab., Glasgow Bailieston*, maj. 14,840
Wright, Anthony D. (*b*. 1954) *Lab., Great Yarmouth*, maj. 8,668
*Wright, Anthony W., D.Phil. (*b*. 1948) *Lab., Cannock Chase*, maj. 14,478
Wyatt, Derek M. (*b*. 1949) *Lab., Sittingbourne and Sheppey*, maj. 1,929
*Yeo, Timothy S. K. (*b*. 1945) *C., Suffolk South*, maj. 4,175
*Young, Rt. Hon. Sir George, Bt. (*b*. 1941) *C., Hampshire North West*, maj. 11551

BY-ELECTIONS SINCE THE GENERAL ELECTION

UXBRIDGE
(31 July 1997)
*E.*57,733 *T.*55.2%

J. Randall, *C.*	16,288
A. Slaughter, *Lab.*	12,522
K. Kerr, *LD*	1,792
'Lord Sutch', *Loony*	396
Ms J. Leonard, *Soc.*	259
Ms F. Taylor, *BNP*	205
I. Anderson, *Nat. Dem.*	157
J. McCauley, *NF*	110
H. Middleton, *Original Lib. Party*	69
J. Feisenberger, *UK Ind.*	39
R. Carroll, *Emerald Rainbow Islands Dream Ticket*	30
C. majority	3,766

PAISLEY SOUTH
(6 November 1997)
E. 54,040 *T.*42%

D. Alexander, *Lab.*	10,346
I. Blackford, *SNP*	7,615
Ms E. McCartin, *LD*	2,582
Ms S. Laidlaw, *C.*	1,643
J. Deighan, *ProLife*	578
F. Curran, *Soc. All. Fighting Corruption*	306
C. McLauchlan, *Scottish Ind. Lab.*	155
C. Herriot, *Soc. Lab.*	153
K. Blair, *NLP*	57
Lab. majority	2,731

BECKENHAM
(20 November 1997)
*E.*72,807 *T.*43.7%

Ms J. Lait, *C.*	13,162
R. Hughes, *Lab.*	11,935
Ms R. Vetterlein, *LD*	5,864
P. Rimmer, *Lib.*	330
J. McAuley, *NF*	267
L. Mead, *New Britain Ref.*	237
T. Campion, *Social Foundation*	69
J. Small, *NLP*	44
C. majority	1,227

WINCHESTER
(20 November 1997)
*E.*78,884 *T.*68.7%

M. Oaten, *LD*	37,006
G. Malone, *C.*	15,450
P. Davies, *Lab.*	944
R. Page, *Ref./UK Ind. Alliance*	521
'Lord' Sutch, *Loony*	316
R. Huggett, *Literal Dem.*	59
Ms R. Barry, *NLP*	48
R. Everest, *European C.*	40
LD majority	21,556

General Election statistics

PRINCIPAL PARTIES IN PARLIAMENT since 1970

	1970	1974 Feb.	1974 Oct.	1979	1983	1987	1992	1997
Conservative	330*	296	276	339	397	375	336	165
Labour	287	301	319	268	209	229	270	418
Liberal/LD	6	14	13	11	17	17	20	46
Social Democrat	—	1	—	—	6	5	—	—
Independent	5†	1	1	2	—	—	—	1
Plaid Cymru	—	2	3	2	2	3	4	4
Scottish Nationalist	1	7	11	2	2	3	3	6
Democratic Unionist	—	—	—	3	3	3	3	2
SDLP	—	1	1	1	1	3	4	3
Sinn Fein	—	—	—	—	1	1	—	2
Ulster Popular Unionist	—	—	—	—	1	1	1	—
Ulster Unionist‡	*	11	10	6	10	9	9	10
UK Unionist	—	—	—	—	—	—	—	1
The Speaker	1	1	1	1	1	1	1	1
Total	630	635	635	635	650	650	651	659

* Including 8 Ulster Unionists
† Comprising: Independent Labour 1, Independent Unity 1, Protestant Unity 1, Republican Labour 1, Unity 1
‡ Comprises:
   1974 (February) United Ulster Unionist Council 11
   1974 (October) United Ulster Unionist 10
   1979 Ulster Unionist 5, United Ulster Unionist 1
   1983 Official Unionist 10

PARLIAMENTS since 1970

Assembled	Dissolved	Duration yr	m.	d.
29 June 1970	8 February 1974	3	7	10
6 March 1974	20 September 1974	0	6	14
22 October 1974	7 April 1979	4	5	16
9 May 1979	13 May 1983	4	0	4
15 June 1983	18 May 1987	3	11	3
17 June 1987	16 March 1992	4	8	28
27 April 1992	8 April 1997	4	11	12
7 May 1997				

MAJORITIES IN THE COMMONS since 1970

Year	Party	Maj.
1970	Conservative	31
1974 Feb.	No majority	
1974 Oct.	Labour	5
1979	Conservative	43
1983	Conservative	144
1987	Conservative	102
1992	Conservative	21
1997	Labour	178

VOTES CAST 1992 and 1997

	1992	1997
Conservative	14,089,722	9,600,940
Labour	11,567,764	13,517,911
Liberal Democrats	6,027,552	5,243,440
Scottish Nationalist	629,564	622,260
Plaid Cymru	154,390	161,030
N. Ireland parties	740,859	780,920
Others	401,239	1,361,701
Total	33,619,090	31,287,702

DISTRIBUTION OF SEATS BY COUNTRY 1997

	England	Wales	Scotland	N. Ireland
Conservative	165	—	—	—
Labour	328	34	56	—
Lib. Dem.	34	2	10	—
SNP	—	—	6	—
Plaid Cymru	—	4	—	—
Other	2*	—	—	18

* Includes the Speaker

SIZE OF ELECTORATE 1997

England	36,806,557
Wales	2,222,533
Scotland	3,984,406
Northern Ireland	1,190,198
Total	44,203,694

PARLIAMENTARY CONSTITUENCIES AS AT 1 MAY 1997

The results of voting in each parliamentary division at the general election of 1 May 1997 are given below. The majority in the 1992 general election, and any by-election between 1987 and 1992, is given below the 1992 result where the constituency covers the same area as in 1992. Where the boundaries of a constituency have changed since 1992, a notional result for 1992 is given.

Symbols
E. Total number of electors in the constituency at the 1997 general election
T. Turnout of electors at the 1997 general election
* Member of the last Parliament in unchanged constituency
† Member of the last Parliament in different constituency or one affected by boundary changes

Abbreviations
All.	Alliance Party (NI)
C.	Conservative
DUP	Democratic Unionist Party
Green	Green Party
Ind.	Independent
Lab.	Labour
Lab. Co-op.	Labour Co-operative
LD	Liberal Democrat
PC	Plaid Cymru
SDLP	Social Democratic and Labour Party
SF	Sinn Fein
SNP	Scottish National Party
UKU	United Kingdom Unionist
UUP	Ulster Unionist Party
ACA	Anti-Child Abuse
ACC	Anti-Corruption Candidate
Albion	Albion Party
Alt.	Alternative
ANP	All Night Party
Anti-maj.	Independent Anti-majority Democracy
AS	Anti-sleaze
Barts	Independent Save Barts Candidate
BDP	British Democratic Party
Beanus	Space Age Superhero from Planet Beanus
Beaut.	Independently Beautiful Party
Bert.	Berties Party
BFAIR	British Freedom and Individual Rights
BHMBCM	Black Haired Medium Build Caucasian Male
BHR	British Home Rule
B. Ind.	Beaconsfield Independent: Unity Through Electoral Reform
BIPF	British Isles People First Party
BNP	British National Party
Bypass	Newbury Bypass Stop Construction Now
Byro	Lord Byro versus the Scallywag Tories
Care	Care in the Community
CASC	Conservatives Against the Single Currency
CFSS	Country Field and Shooting Sports
Ch. D.	Christian Democrat

Ch. Nat.	Christian Nationalist
Choice	People's Choice
Ch. P.	Christian Party
Ch. U.	Christian Unity
Comm. L.	Communist League
Comm. P.	Communist Party of Britain
Constit.	Constitutionalist
Consult.	Independent Democracy Means Consulting the People
CRP	Community Representative Party
CSSPP	Common Sense Sick of Politicians Party
Cvty	Conservatory
D. Nat.	Democratic Nationalist
Dream	Rainbow Dream Ticket Party
Dynamic	First Dynamic Party
EDP	English Democratic Party
Embryo	Anti-Abortion Euthanasia Embryo Experiments
EUP	European Unity Party
Fair	Building a Fair Society
FDP	Fancy Dress Party
Fellowship	Fellowship Party for Peace and Justice
FEP	Full Employment Party
FP	Freedom Party
Glow	Glow Bowling Party
GRLNSP	Green Referendum Lawless Naturally Street Party
Heart	Heart 106.2 Alien Party
Hemp	Hemp Coalition
HR	Human Rights '97
Hum.	Humanist Party
IAC	Independent Anti-Corruption in Government/TGWU
Ind. AFE	Independent Against a Federal Europe
Ind. BB	Independent Back to Basics
Ind. CRP	Independent Conservative Referendum Party
Ind. Dean	Independent Royal Forest of Dean
Ind. Dem.	Independent Democrat
Ind. ECR	Independent English Conservative and Referendum
Ind. F.	Independent Forester
Ind. Green	Independent Green: Your Children's Future
Ind. Hum.	English Independent Humanist Party
Ind. Is.	Island Independent
Ind. JRP	Justice and Renewal Independent Party
Ind. No	Independent No to Europe
IZB	Islam Zinda Baad Platform
JP	Justice Party
Juice	Juice Party
KBF	Keep Britain Free and Independent Party
Lab. Change	Labour Time for Change Candidate
LC	Loyal Conservative
LCP	Legalize Cannabis Party
LGR	Local Government Reform
Lib.	Liberal
Loc.	Local
Logic	Logic Party Truth Only Allowed
Loony	Monster Raving Loony Party
Mal	Mal Voice of the People Party
Miss M.	Miss Moneypenny's Glamorous One Party
MK	Mebyon Kernow

Mongolian	Mongolian Barbeque Great Place to Party
MRAC	Multi-racial Anti-Corruption Alliance
Nat. Dem.	National Democrat
New Way	New Millennium New Way Hemp Candidate
NF	National Front
NIFT	Former Captain NI Football Team
NIP	Northern Ireland Party
NI Women	Northern Ireland Women's Coalition
NLP	Natural Law Party
NLPC	New Labour Party Candidate
None	None of the Above Parties
NPC	Non-party Conservative
Pacifist	Pacifist for Peace, Justice, Co-operation, Environment
PAYR	Protecting All Your Rights Locally Effectively
PF	Pathfinders
PLP	People's Labour Party
Plymouth	Plymouth First Group
PP	People's Party
PPP	People's Party Party
ProLife	ProLife Alliance
PUP	Progressive Unionist Party
RA	Residents Association
Rain. Is.	Rainbow Connection Your Island Candidate
Rain. Ref.	Rainbow Referendum
R. Alt.	Radical Alternative
Ref.	Referendum Party
Ren. Dem.	Renaissance Democrat
Rep. GB	Republican Party of Great Britain
Rights	Charter for Basic Rights
Ronnie	Ronnie the Rhino Party
Route 66	Route 66 Party Posse Party
Scrapit	Scrapit Stop Avon Ring Road Now
SCU	Scottish Conservative Unofficial
SEP	Socialist Equality Party
SFDC	Stratford First Democratic Conservative
SG	Sub-genus Party
Shields	Pro Interests of South Shields People
SIP	Sheffield Independent Party
SLI	Scottish Labour Independent
Slough	People in Slough Shunning Useless Politicians
SLU	Scottish Labour Unofficial
Soc.	Socialist Party
Soc. Dem.	Social Democrat
Soc. Lab.	Socialist Labour Party
SPGB	Socialist Party of Great Britain
Spts All.	Sportsman's Alliance: Anything but Mellor
SSA	Scottish Socialist Alliance
Stan	Happiness Stan's Freedom to Party Party
Teddy	Teddy Bear Alliance Party
Top	Top Choice Liberal Democrat
21st Cent.	21st Century Independent Foresters
UA	Universal Alliance
UK Ind.	UK Independence Party
UKPP	UK Pensioners Party
WCCC	West Cheshire College in Crisis Party
Wessex	Wessex Regionalist
WP	Workers' Party
WRP	Workers' Revolutionary Party

ENGLAND

ALDERSHOT
E.76,189   T. 71.07%
G. Howarth, C.   23,119
A. Collett, LD   16,498
T. Bridgeman, Lab.   13,057
J. Howe, UK Ind.   794
A. Pendragon, Ind.   361
Dr D. Stevens, BNP   322
C. majority 6,621
(Boundary change: notional C.)

ALDRIDGE-BROWNHILLS
E.62,441   T. 74.26%
*R. Shepherd, C.   21,856
J. Toth, Lab.   19,330
Ms C. Downie, LD   5,184
C. majority 2,526
(April 1992, C. maj. 11,024)

ALTRINCHAM AND SALE WEST
E.70,625   T. 73.32%
G. Brady, C.   22,348
Ms J. Baugh, Lab.   20,843
M. Ramsbottom, LD   6,535
A. Landes, Ref.   1,348
J. Stephens, ProLife   313
Dr R. Mrozinski, UK Ind.   270
J. Renwick, NLP   125
C. majority 1,505
(Boundary change: notional C.)

AMBER VALLEY
E.72,005   T. 76.07%
Ms J. Mallaber, Lab.   29,943
†P. Oppenheim, C.   18,330
R. Shelley, LD   4,219
Mrs I. McGibbon, Ref.   2,283
Lab. majority 11,613
(Boundary change: notional C.)

ARUNDEL AND SOUTH DOWNS
E.67,641   T. 75.90%
H. Flight, C.   27,251
J. Goss, LD   13,216
R. Black, Lab.   9,376
J. Herbert, UK Ind.   1,494
C. majority 14,035
(Boundary change: notional C.)

ASHFIELD
E.72,269   T. 70.02%
†G. Hoon, Lab.   32,979
M. Simmonds, C.   10,251
W. Smith, LD   4,882
M. Betts, Ref.   1,896
S. Belshaw, BNP   595
Lab. majority 22,728
(Boundary change: notional Lab.)

ASHFORD
E.74,149   T. 74.57%
D. Green, C.   22,899
J. Ennals, Lab.   17,544
J. Williams, LD   10,901
C. Cruden, Ref.   3,201
R. Boden, Green   660
S. Tyrell, NLP   89
C. majority 5,355
(April 1992, C. maj. 17,359)

ASHTON UNDER LYNE
E.72,206   T. 65.48%
†Rt. Hon. R. Sheldon, Lab.   31,919
R. Mayson, C.   8,954
T. Pickstone, LD   4,603
Mrs L. Clapham, Ref.   1,346
Prince Cymbal, Loony   458
Lab. majority 22,965
(Boundary change: notional Lab.)

AYLESBURY
E.79,047   T. 72.81%
†D. Lidington, C.   25,426
Ms S. Bowles, LD   17,007
R. Langridge, Lab.   12,759
M. John, Ref.   2,196
L. Sheaff, NLP   166
C. majority 8,419
(Boundary change: notional C.)

BANBURY
E.77,456   T. 75.46%
†A. Baldry, C.   25,076
Ms H. Peperell, Lab.   20,339
Mrs C. Bearder, LD   9,761
J. Ager, Ref.   2,245
Ms B. Cotton, Green   530
Mrs L. King, UK Ind.   364
I. Pearson, NLP   131
C. majority 4,737
(Boundary change: notional C.)

BARKING
E.53,682   T. 61.41%
†Mrs M. Hodge, Lab.   21,698
K. Langford, C.   5,802
M. Marsh, LD   3,128
C. Taylor, Ref.   1,283
M. Tolman, BNP   894
D. Mearns, ProLife   159
Lab. majority 15,896
(Boundary change: notional Lab.)

BARNSLEY CENTRAL
E.61,133   T. 59.68%
†E. Illsley, Lab.   28,090
S. Gutteridge, C.   3,589
D. Finlay, LD   3,481
J. Walsh, Ref.   1,325
Lab. majority 24,501
(Boundary change: notional Lab.)

BARNSLEY EAST AND MEXBOROUGH
E.67,840   T. 63.88%
†J. Ennis, Lab.   31,699
Miss J. Ellison, C.   4,936
D. Willis, LD   4,489
K. Capstick, Soc. Lab.   1,213
A. Miles, Ref.   797
Ms J. Hyland, SEP   201
Lab. majority 26,763
(Boundary change: notional Lab.)

BARNSLEY WEST AND PENISTONE
E.64,894   T. 65.04%
*M. Clapham, Lab.   25,017
P. Watkins, C.   7,750
Mrs W. Knight, LD   7,613
Mrs J. Miles, Ref.   1,828
Lab. majority 17,267
(April 1992, Lab. maj. 14,504)

BARROW AND FURNESS
E.66,960   T. 72.03%
*J. Hutton, Lab.   27,630
R. Hunt, C.   13,133
Mrs A. Metcalfe, LD   4,264
J. Hamzeian, PLP   1,995
D. Mitchell, Ref.   1,208
Lab. majority 14,497
(April 1992, Lab. maj. 3,578)

BASILDON
E.73,989   T. 71.74%
Ms A. Smith, Lab. Co-op.   29,646
J. Baron, C.   16,366
Ms L. Granshaw, LD   4,608
C. Robinson, Ref.   2,462
Lab. Co-op. majority 13,280
(Boundary change: notional C.)

BASINGSTOKE
E.77,035   T. 74.16%
†A. Hunter, C.   24,751
N. Lickley, Lab.   22,354
M. Rimmer, LD   9,714
E. Selim, Ind.   310
C. majority 2,397
(Boundary change: notional C.)

BASSETLAW
E.68,101   T. 70.37%
†J. Ashton, Lab.   29,298
M. Cleasby, C.   11,838
M. Kerrigan, LD   4,950
R. Graham, Ref.   1,838
Lab. majority 17,460
(Boundary change: notional Lab.)

BATH
E.70,815   T. 76.24%
†D. Foster, LD   26,169
Ms A. McNair, C.   16,850
T. Bush, Lab.   8,828
A. Cook, Ref.   1,192
R. Scrase, Green   580
P. Sandell, UK Ind.   315
N. Pullen, NLP   55
LD majority 9,319
(Boundary change: notional LD)

BATLEY AND SPEN
E.64,209   T. 73.14%
M. Wood, Lab.   23,213
†Mrs E. Peacock, C.   17,072
Mrs K. Pinnock, LD   4,133
E. Wood, Ref.   1,691
R. Smith, BNP   472
C. Lord, Green   384
Lab. majority 6,141
(Boundary change: notional C.)

BATTERSEA
E.66,928   T. 70.82%
M. Linton, Lab.   24,047
†J. Bowis, C.   18,687
Ms P. Keaveney, LD   3,482
M. Slater, Ref.   804
R. Banks, UK Ind.   250
J. Marshall, Dream   127
Lab. majority 5,360
(Boundary change: notional C.)

BEACONSFIELD
E.68,959   T. 72.80%
D. Grieve, C.   24,709
P. Mapp, LD   10,722
A. Hudson, Lab.   10,063
H. Lloyd, Ref.   2,197
C. Story, CASC   1,434
C. Cooke, UK Ind.   451
Ms G. Duval, ProLife   286
T. Dyball, NLP   193
R. Matthews, B. Ind.   146
C. majority 13,987
(Boundary change: notional C.)

BECKENHAM
E.72,807   T. 74.65%
†P. Merchant, C.   23,084
R. Hughes, Lab.   18,131
Ms R. Vetterlein, LD   9,858
L. Mead, Ref.   1,663
P. Rimmer, Lib.   720
C. Pratt, UK Ind.   506
J. Mcauley, NF   388
C. majority 4,953
(Boundary change: notional C.)
See also page 233

BEDFORD
E.66,560   T. 73.53%
P. Hall, Lab.   24,774
R. Blackman, C.   16,474
C. Noyce, LD   6,044
P. Conquest, Ref.   1,503
Ms P. Saunders, NLP   149
Lab. majority 8,300
(Boundary change: notional C.)

BEDFORDSHIRE MID
E.66,979   T. 78.41%
J. Sayeed, C.   24,176
N. Mallett, Lab.   17,086
T. Hill, LD   8,823
Mrs S. Marler, Ref.   2,257
M. Lorys, NLP   174
C. majority 7,090
(Boundary change: notional C.)

BEDFORDSHIRE NORTH EAST
E.64,743   T. 77.83%
†Rt. Hon. Sir N. Lyell, C.   22,311
J. Lehal, Lab.   16,428
P. Bristow, LD   7,179
J. Taylor, Ref.   2,490
L. Foley, Ind. C.   1,842
B. Bence, NLP   138
C. majority 5,883
(Boundary change: notional C.)

BEDFORDSHIRE SOUTH WEST
E.69,781   T. 75.76%
†Sir D. Madel, C.   21,534
A. Date, Lab.   21,402
S. Owen, LD   7,559
Ms R. Hill, Ref.   1,761
T. Wise, UK Ind.   446
A. Le Carpentier, NLP   162
C. majority 132
(Boundary change: notional C.)

BERWICK-UPON-TWEED
E.56,428   T. 74.08%
*A. Beith, LD   19,007
P. Brannen, Lab.   10,965

N. Herbert, C.   10,056
N. Lambton, Ref.   1,423
I. Dodds, UK Ind.   352
LD majority 8,042
(April 1992, LD maj. 5,043)

BETHNAL GREEN AND BOW
E.73,008   T. 61.20%
Ms O. King, Lab.   20,697
K. Choudhury, C.   9,412
S. N. Islam, LD   5,361
D. King, BNP   3,350
T. Milson, Lib.   2,963
S. Osman, Real Lab.   1,117
S. Petter, Green   812
M. Abdullah, Ref.   557
A. Hamid, Soc. Lab.   413
Lab. majority 11,285
(Boundary change: notional Lab.)

BEVERLEY AND HOLDERNESS
E.71,916   T. 73.62%
†J. Cran, C.   21,629
N. O'Neill, Lab.   20,818
J. Melling, LD   9,689
D. Barley, UK Ind.   695
S. Withers, NLP   111
C. majority 811
(Boundary change: notional C.)

BEXHILL AND BATTLE
E.65,584   T. 74.70%
†C. Wardle, C.   23,570
Mrs K. Field, LD   12,470
R. Beckwith, Lab.   8,866
Mrs V. Thompson, Ref.   3,302
J. Pankhurst, UK Ind.   786
C. majority 11,100
(Boundary change: notional C.)

BEXLEYHEATH AND CRAYFORD
E.63,334   T. 76.14%
N. Beard, Lab.   21,942
†D. Evennett, C.   18,527
Mrs F. Montford, LD   5,391
B. Thomas, Ref.   1,551
Ms P. Smith, BNP   429
W. Jenner, UK Ind.   383
Lab. majority 3,415
(Boundary change: notional C.)

BILLERICAY
E.76,550   T. 72.40%
†Mrs T. Gorman, C.   22,033
P. Richards, Lab.   20,677
G. Williams, LD   8,763
B. Hughes, LC   3,377
J. Buchanan, ProLife   570
C. majority 1,356
(Boundary change: notional C.)

BIRKENHEAD
E.59,782   T. 65.78%
*F. Field, Lab.   27,825
J. Crosby, C.   5,982
R. Wood, LD   3,548
M. Cullen, Soc. Lab.   1,168
R. Evans, Ref.   800
Lab. majority 21,843
(April 1992, Lab. maj. 17,613)

BIRMINGHAM EDGBASTON
E.70,204   T. 69.03%
Mrs G. Stuart, Lab.   23,554

A. Marshall, C.   18,712
J. Gallagher, LD   4,691
J. Oakton, Ref.   1,065
D. Campbell, BDP   443
Lab. majority 4,842
(Boundary change: notional C.)

BIRMINGHAM ERDINGTON
E.66,380   T. 60.87%
†R. Corbett, Lab.   23,764
A. Tompkins, C.   11,107
I. Garrett, LD   4,112
G. Cable, Ref.   1,424
Lab. majority 12,657
(Boundary change: notional Lab.)

BIRMINGHAM HALL GREEN
E.58,767   T. 71.16%
S. McCabe, Lab.   22,372
*A. Hargreaves, C.   13,952
A. Dow, LD   4,034
P. Bennett, Ref.   1,461
Lab. majority 8,420
(April 1992, C. maj. 3,665)

BIRMINGHAM HODGE HILL
E.56,066   T. 60.91%
*T. Davis, Lab.   22,398
E. Grant, C.   8,198
H. Thomas, LD   2,891
P. Johnson, UK Ind.   660
Lab. majority 14,200
(April 1992, Lab. maj. 7,068)

BIRMINGHAM LADYWOOD
E.70,013   T. 54.24%
†Ms C. Short, Lab.   28,134
S. Vara, C.   5,052
S. S. Marwa, LD   3,020
Mrs R. Gurney, Ref.   1,086
A. Carmichael, Nat. Dem.   685
Lab. majority 23,082
(Boundary change: notional Lab.)

BIRMINGHAM NORTHFIELD
E.56,842   T. 68.34%
†R. Burden, Lab.   22,316
A. Blumenthal, C.   10,873
M. Ashall, LD   4,078
D. Gent, Ref.   1,243
K. Axon, BNP   337
Lab. majority 11,443
(Boundary change: notional Lab.)

BIRMINGHAM PERRY BARR
E.71,031   T. 64.60%
†J. Rooker, Lab.   28,921
A. Dunnett, C.   9,964
R. Hassall, LD   4,523
S. Mahmood, Ref.   843
A. Baxter, Lib.   718
L. Windridge, BNP   544
A. S. Panesar, Fourth Party   374
Lab. majority 18,957
(Boundary change: notional Lab.)

BIRMINGHAM SELLY OAK
E.72,049   T. 70.16%
*Dr L. Jones, Lab.   28,121
G. Greene, C.   14,033
D. Osborne, LD   6,121
L. Marshall, Ref.   1,520
Dr G. Gardner, ProLife   417

P. Sherriff-Knowles, *Loony* 253
H. Meads, *NLP* 85
Lab. majority 14,088
(April 1992, Lab. maj. 2,060)

BIRMINGHAM SPARKBROOK AND
SMALL HEATH
*E.*73,130　*T.* 57.11%
†R. Godsiff, *Lab.* 26,841
K. Hardeman, *C.* 7,315
R. Harmer, *LD* 3,889
A. Clawley, *Green* 959
R. Dooley, *Ref.* 737
P. Patel, *Fourth Party* 538
R. M. Syed, *PAYR* 513
Ms S. Bi, *Ind.* 490
C. Wren, *Soc. Lab.* 483
Lab. majority 19,526
(Boundary change: notional Lab.)

BIRMINGHAM YARDLEY
*E.*53,058　*T.* 71.22%
*Ms E. Morris, *Lab.* 17,778
J. Hemming, *LD* 12,463
Mrs A. Jobson, *C.* 6,736
D. Livingston, *Ref.* 646
A. Ware, *UK Ind.* 164
Lab. majority 5,315
(April 1992, Lab. maj. 162)

BISHOP AUCKLAND
*E.*66,754　*T.* 68.88%
†Rt. Hon. D. Foster, *Lab.* 30,359
Mrs J. Fergus, *C.* 9,295
L. Ashworth, *LD* 4,223
D. Blacker, *Ref.* 2,104
Lab. majority 21,064
(Boundary change: notional Lab.)

BLABY
*E.*70,471　*T.* 76.05%
†A. Robathan, *C.* 24,564
R. Willmott, *Lab.* 18,090
G. Welsh, *LD* 8,001
R. Harrison, *Ref.* 2,018
J. Peacock, *BNP* 523
T. Stokes, *Ind.* 397
C. majority 6,474
(Boundary change: notional C.)

BLACKBURN
*E.*73,058　*T.* 65.01%
*J. Straw, *Lab.* 26,141
Ms S. Sidhu, *C.* 11,690
S. Fenn, *LD* 4,990
D. Bradshaw, *Ref.* 1,892
Mrs T. Wingfield, *Nat. Dem.* 671
Mrs H. Drummond, *Soc. Lab.* 637
R. Field, *Green* 608
Mrs M. Carmichael-Grimshaw,
　KBF 506
W. Batchelor, *CSSPP* 362
Lab. majority 14,451
(April 1992, Lab. maj. 6,027)

BLACKPOOL NORTH AND
FLEETWOOD
*E.*74,989　*T.* 71.67%
Mrs J. Humble, *Lab.* 28,051
†H. Elletson, *C.* 19,105
Mrs B. Hill, *LD* 4,600
Ms K. Stacey, *Ref.* 1,704
J. Ellis, *BNP* 288

Lab. majority 8,946
(Boundary change: notional C.)

BLACKPOOL SOUTH
*E.*75,720　*T.* 67.80%
G. Marsden, *Lab.* 29,282
R. Booth, *C.* 17,666
Mrs D. Holt, *LD* 4,392
Lab. majority 11,616
(Boundary change: notional C.)

BLAYDON
*E.*64,699　*T.* 70.98%
*J. McWilliam, *Lab.* 27,535
P. Maughan, *LD* 10,930
M. Watson, *C.* 6,048
R. Rook, *Ind. Lab.* 1,412
Lab. majority 16,605
(April 1992, Lab. maj. 13,343)

BLYTH VALLEY
*E.*61,761　*T.* 68.78%
*R. Campbell, *Lab.* 27,276
A. Lamb, *LD* 9,540
Mrs B. Musgrave, *C.* 5,666
Lab. majority 17,736
(April 1992, Lab. maj. 8,044)

BOGNOR REGIS AND
LITTLEHAMPTON
*E.*66,480　*T.* 69.86%
N. Gibb, *C.* 20,537
R. Nash, *Lab.* 13,216
Dr J. Walsh, *LD* 11,153
G. Stride, *UK Ind.* 1,537
C. majority 7,321
(Boundary change: notional C.)

BOLSOVER
*E.*66,476　*T.* 71.32%
†D. Skinner, *Lab.* 35,073
R. Harwood, *C.* 7,924
I. Cox, *LD* 4,417
Lab. majority 27,149
(Boundary change: notional Lab.)

BOLTON NORTH EAST
*E.*67,930　*T.* 72.44%
D. Crausby, *Lab.* 27,621
R. Wilson, *C.* 14,952
Dr E. Critchley, *LD* 4,862
D. Staniforth, *Ref.* 1,096
W. Kelly, *Soc. Lab.* 676
Lab. majority 12,669
(Boundary change: notional Lab.)

BOLTON SOUTH EAST
*E.*66,459　*T.* 65.23%
B. Iddon, *Lab.* 29,856
P. Carter, *C.* 8,545
F. Harasiwka, *LD* 3,805
W. Pickering, *Ref.* 973
L. Walch, *NLP* 170
Lab. majority 21,311
(Boundary change: notional Lab.)

BOLTON WEST
*E.*63,535　*T.* 77.37%
Ms R. Kelly, *Lab.* 24,342
†T. Sackville, *C.* 17,270
Mrs B. Ronson, *LD* 5,309
Mrs D. Kelly, *Soc. Lab.* 1,374
Mrs G. Frankl-Slater, *Ref.* 865

Lab. majority 7,072
(Boundary change: notional C.)

BOOTLE
*E.*57,284　*T.* 66.73%
†J. Benton, *Lab.* 31,668
R. Mathews, *C.* 3,247
K. Reid, *LD* 2,191
J. Elliott, *Ref.* 571
P. Glover, *Soc.* 420
S. Cohen, *NLP* 126
Lab. majority 28,421
(Boundary change: notional Lab.)

BOSTON AND SKEGNESS
*E.*67,623　*T.* 68.87%
†Sir R. Body, *C.* 19,750
P. McCauley, *Lab.* 19,103
J. Dodsworth, *LD* 7,721
C. majority 647
(Boundary change: notional C.)

BOSWORTH
*E.*68,113　*T.* 76.57%
†D. Tredinnick, *C.* 21,189
A. Furlong, *Lab.* 20,162
J. Ellis, *LD* 9,281
S. Halborg, *Ref.* 1,521
C. majority 1,027
(Boundary change: notional C.)

BOURNEMOUTH EAST
*E.*61,862　*T.* 70.20%
†D. Atkinson, *C.* 17,997
D. Eyre, *LD* 13,651
Mrs J. Stevens, *Lab.* 9,181
A. Musgrave-Scott, *Ref.* 1,808
K. Benney, *UK Ind.* 791
C. majority 4,346
(Boundary change: notional C.)

BOURNEMOUTH WEST
*E.*62,028　*T.* 66.22%
†J. Butterfill, *C.* 17,115
Ms J. Dover, *LD* 11,405
D. Gritt, *Lab.* 10,093
R. Mills, *Ref.* 1,910
Mrs L. Tooley, *UK Ind.* 281
J. Morse, *BNP* 165
A. Springham, *NLP* 103
C. majority 5,710
(Boundary change: notional C.)

BRACKNELL
*E.*79,292　*T.* 74.52%
†A. Mackay, *C.* 27,983
Ms A. Snelgrove, *Lab.* 17,596
A. Hilliar, *LD* 9,122
J. Tompkins, *New Lab.* 1,909
W. Cairns, *Ref.* 1,636
L. Boxall, *UK Ind.* 569
Ms D. Roberts, *ProLife* 276
C. majority 10,387
(Boundary change: notional C.)

BRADFORD NORTH
*E.*66,228　*T.* 63.26%
*T. Rooney, *Lab.* 23,493
R. Skinner, *C.* 10,723
T. Browne, *LD* 6,083
H. Wheatley, *Ref.* 1,227
W. Beckett, *Loony* 369

Lab. majority 12,770
(April 1992, Lab. maj. 7,664)

BRADFORD SOUTH
*E.*68,391   *T.* 65.88%
*G. Sutcliffe, *Lab.*   25,558
Mrs A. Hawkesworth, *C.*   12,622
A. Wilson-Fletcher, *LD*   5,093
Mrs M. Kershaw, *Ref.*   1,785
Lab. majority 12,936
(April 1992, Lab. maj. 4,902)
(June 1994, Lab. maj. 9,664)

BRADFORD WEST
*E.*71,961   *T.* 63.32%
M. Singh, *Lab.*   18,932
M. Riaz, *C.*   15,055
Mrs H. Wright, *LD*   6,737
A. Khan, *Soc. Lab.*   1,551
C. Royston, *Ref.*   1,348
J. Robinson, *Green*   861
G. Osborn, *BNP*   839
S. Shah, *Soc.*   245
Lab. majority 3,877
(April 1992, Lab. maj. 9,502)

BRAINTREE
*E.*72,772   *T.* 76.37%
A. Hurst, *Lab.*   23,729
†Rt. Hon. A. Newton, *C.*   22,278
T. Ellis, *LD*   6,418
N. Westcott, *Ref.*   2,165
J. Abbott, *Green*   712
M. Nolan, *New Way*   274
Lab. majority 1,451
(Boundary change: notional C.)

BRENT EAST
*E.*53,548   *T.* 65.87%
†K. Livingstone, *Lab.*   23,748
M. Francois, *C.*   7,866
I. Hunter, *LD*   2,751
S. Keable, *Soc. Lab.*   466
A. Shanks, *ProLife*   218
Ms C. Warrilo, *Dream*   120
D. Jenkins, *NLP*   103
Lab. majority 15,882
(Boundary change: notional Lab.)

BRENT NORTH
*E.*54,149   *T.* 70.50%
B. Gardiner, *Lab.*   19,343
†Rt. Hon. Sir R. Boyson, *C.*   15,324
P. Lorber, *LD*   3,104
A. Davids, *NLP*   204
G. Clark, *Dream*   199
Lab. majority 4,019
(Boundary change: notional C.)

BRENT SOUTH
*E.*53,505   *T.* 64.48%
†P. Boateng, *Lab.*   25,180
S. Jackson, *C.*   5,489
J. Brazil, *LD*   2,670
Ms J. Phythian, *Ref.*   497
D. Edler, *Green*   389
C. Howard, *Dream*   175
Ms A. Mahaldar, *NLP*   98
Lab. majority 19,691
(Boundary change: notional Lab.)

BRENTFORD AND ISLEWORTH
*E.*79,058   *T.* 71.00%
Mrs A. Keen, *Lab.*   32,249
†N. Deva, *C.*   17,825
Dr G. Hartwell, *LD*   4,613
J. Bradley, *Green*   687
Mrs B. Simmerson, *UK Ind.*   614
M. Ahmed, *NLP*   147
Lab. majority 14,424
(Boundary change: notional C.)

BRENTWOOD AND ONGAR
*E.*66,005   *T.* 76.85%
†E. Pickles, *C.*   23,031
Mrs E. Bottomley, *LD*   13,341
M. Young, *Lab.*   11,231
Mrs A. Kilmartin, *Ref.*   2,658
Capt. D. Mills, *UK Ind.*   465
C. majority 9,690
(Boundary change: notional C.)

BRIDGWATER
*E.*73,038   *T.* 74.79%
*Rt. Hon. T. King, *C.*   20,174
M. Hoban, *LD*   18,378
R. Lavers, *Lab.*   13,519
Ms F. Evens, *Ref.*   2,551
C. majority 1,796
(April 1992, C. maj. 9,716)

BRIGG AND GOOLE
*E.*63,648   *T.* 73.53%
I. Cawsey, *Lab.*   23,493
D. Stewart, *C.*   17,104
Mrs M.-R. Hardy, *LD*   4,692
D. Rigby, *Ref.*   1,513
Lab. majority 6,389
(Boundary change: notional C.)

BRIGHTON KEMPTOWN
*E.*65,147   *T.* 70.81%
D. Turner, *Lab.*   21,479
†Sir A. Bowden, *C.*   17,945
C. Gray, *LD*   4,478
D. Inman, *Ref.*   1,526
Ms H. Williams, *Soc. Lab.*   316
J. Bowler, *NLP*   172
Ms L. Newman, *Loony*   123
R. Darlow, *Dream*   93
Lab. majority 3,534
(Boundary change: notional C.)

BRIGHTON PAVILION
*E.*66,431   *T.* 73.69%
D. Lepper, *Lab. Co-op.*   26,737
†Sir D. Spencer, *C.*   13,556
K. Blanshard, *LD*   4,644
P. Stocken, *Ref.*   1,304
P. West, *Green*   1,249
R. Huggett, *Ind. C.*   1,098
F. Stevens, *UK Ind.*   179
R. Dobbs, *SG*   125
A. Card, *Dream*   59
Lab. Co-op. majority 13,181
(Boundary change: notional C.)

BRISTOL EAST
*E.*68,990   *T.* 69.87%
†Ms J. Corston, *Lab.*   27,418
E. Vaizey, *C.*   11,259
P. Tyzack, *LD*   7,121
G. Philp, *Ref.*   1,479
P. Williams, *Soc. Lab.*   766

J. McLaggan, *NLP*   158
Lab. majority 16,159
(Boundary change: notional Lab.)

BRISTOL NORTH WEST
*E.*75,009   *T.* 73.65%
D. Naysmith, *Lab. Co-op.*   27,575
†M. Stern, *C.*   16,193
I. Parry, *LD*   7,263
C. Horton, *Ind. Lab.*   1,718
J. Quintanilla, *Ref.*   1,609
G. Shorter, *Soc. Lab.*   482
S. Parnell, *BNP*   265
T. Leighton, *NLP*   140
Lab. Co-op. majority 11,382
(Boundary change: notional Lab.
Co-op.)

BRISTOL SOUTH
*E.*72,393   *T.* 68.87%
†Ms D. Primarolo, *Lab.*   29,890
M. Roe, *C.*   10,562
S. Williams, *LD*   6,691
D. Guy, *Ref.*   1,486
J. Boxall, *Green*   722
I. Marshall, *Soc.*   355
Louis Taylor, *Glow*   153
Lab. majority 19,328
(Boundary change: notional Lab.)

BRISTOL WEST
*E.*84,870   *T.* 73.81%
Ms V. Davey, *Lab.*   22,068
†Rt. Hon. W. Waldegrave, *C.*   20,575
C. Boney, *LD*   17,551
Lady M. Beauchamp, *Ref.*   1,304
J. Quinnell, *Green*   852
R. Nurse, *Soc. Lab.*   244
J. Brierley, *NLP*   47
Lab. majority 1,493
(Boundary change: notional C.)

BROMLEY AND CHISLEHURST
*E.*71,104   *T.* 74.17%
†Rt. Hon. E. Forth, *C.*   24,428
R. Yeldham, *Lab.*   13,310
Dr P. Booth, *LD*   12,530
R. Bryant, *UK Ind.*   1,176
Ms F. Speed, *Green*   640
M. Stoneman, *NF*   369
G. Aitman, *Lib.*   285
C. majority 11,118
(Boundary change: notional C.)

BROMSGROVE
*E.*67,744   *T.* 77.07%
Miss J. Kirkbride, *C.*   24,620
P. McDonald, *Lab.*   19,725
Mrs J. Davy, *LD*   6,200
Mrs D. Winsor, *Ref.*   1,411
Mrs G. Wetton, *UK Ind.*   251
C. majority 4,895
(Boundary change: notional C.)

BROXBOURNE
*E.*66,720   *T.* 70.41%
†Mrs M. Roe, *C.*   22,952
B. Coleman, *Lab.*   16,299
Mrs J. Davies, *LD*   5,310
D. Millward, *Ref.*   1,633
D. Bruce, *BNP*   610
B. Cheetham, *Third Way*   172

C. majority 6,653
(Boundary change: notional C.)

BROXTOWE
*E.*74,144   *T.* 78.41%
N. Palmer, *Lab.* 27,343
†Sir J. Lester, *C.* 21,768
T. Miller, *LD* 6,934
R. Tucker, *Ref.* 2,092
Lab. majority 5,575
(Boundary change: notional C.)

BUCKINGHAM
*E.*62,945   *T.* 78.48%
J. Bercow, *C.* 24,594
R. Lehmann, *Lab.* 12,208
N. Stuart, *LD* 12,175
Dr G. Clements, *NLP* 421
C. majority 12,386
(Boundary change: notional C.)

BURNLEY
*E.*67,582   *T.* 66.95%
*P. Pike, *Lab.* 26,210
W. Wiggin, *C.* 9,148
G. Birtwistle, *LD* 7,877
R. Oakley, *Ref.* 2,010
Lab. majority 17,062
(April 1992, Lab. maj. 11,491)

BURTON
*E.*72,601   *T.* 75.08%
Ms J. Dean, *Lab.* 27,810
†Sir I. Lawrence, *C.* 21,480
D. Fletcher, *LD* 4,617
K. Sharp, *Nat. Dem.* 604
Lab. majority 6,330
(Boundary change: notional C.)

BURY NORTH
*E.*70,515   *T.* 78.07%
D. Chaytor, *Lab.* 28,523
*A. Burt, *C.* 20,657
N. Kenyon, *LD* 4,536
R. Hallewell, *Ref.* 1,337
Lab. majority 7,866
(April 1992, C. maj. 4,764)

BURY SOUTH
*E.*66,568   *T.* 75.60%
I. Lewis, *Lab.* 28,658
†D. Sumberg, *C.* 16,225
V. D'Albert, *LD* 4,227
B. Slater, *Ref.* 1,216
Lab. majority 12,433
(Boundary change: notional C.)

BURY ST EDMUNDS
*E.*74,017   *T.* 75.02%
D. Ruffley, *C.* 21,290
M. Ereira-Guyer, *Lab.* 20,922
D. Cooper, *LD* 10,102
I. McWhirter, *Ref.* 2,939
Mrs J. Lillis, *NLP* 272
C. majority 368
(Boundary change: notional C.)

CALDER VALLEY
*E.*74,901   *T.* 75.39%
Ms C. McCafferty, *Lab.* 26,050
*Sir D. Thompson, *C.* 19,795
S. Pearson, *LD* 8,322
A. Mellor, *Ref.* 1,380
Ms V. Smith, *Green* 488

C. Jackson, *BNP* 431
Lab. majority 6,255
(April 1992, C. maj. 4,878)

CAMBERWELL AND PECKHAM
*E.*50,214   *T.* 56.71%
†Ms H. Harman, *Lab.* 19,734
K. Humphreys, *C.* 3,383
N. Williams, *LD* 3,198
N. China, *Ref.* 692
Ms A. Ruddock, *Soc. Lab.* 685
G. Williams, *Lib.* 443
Ms J. Barker, *Soc.* 233
C. Eames, *WRP* 106
Lab. majority 16,351
(Boundary change: notional Lab.)

CAMBRIDGE
*E.*71,669   *T.* 71.63%
*Mrs A. Campbell, *Lab.* 27,436
D. Platt, *C.* 13,299
G. Heathcock, *LD* 8,287
W. Burrows, *Ref.* 1,262
Ms M. Wright, *Green* 654
Ms A. Johnstone, *ProLife* 191
R. Athow, *WRP* 107
Ms P. Gladwin, *NLP* 103
Lab. majority 14,137
(April 1992, Lab. maj. 580)

CAMBRIDGESHIRE NORTH EAST
*E.*76,056   *T.* 72.87%
†M. Moss, *C.* 23,855
Mrs V. Bucknor, *Lab.* 18,754
A. Nash, *LD* 9,070
M. Bacon, *Ref.* 2,636
C. Bennett, *Soc. Lab.* 851
L. Leighton, *NLP* 259
C. majority 5,101
(Boundary change: notional C.)

CAMBRIDGESHIRE NORTH WEST
*E.*65,791   *T.* 74.20%
†Rt. Hon. Dr B. Mawhinney, *C.*
23,488
L. Steptoe, *Lab.* 15,734
Mrs B. McCoy, *LD* 7,388
A.Watt, *Ref.* 1,939
W. Wyatt, *UK Ind.* 269
C. majority 7,754
(Boundary change: notional C.)

CAMBRIDGESHIRE SOUTH
*E.*69,850   *T.* 76.85%
A. Lansley, *C.* 22,572
J. Quinlan, *LD* 13,860
A. Gray, *Lab.* 13,485
R. Page, *Ref.* 3,300
D. Norman, *UK Ind.* 298
F. Chalmers, *NLP* 168
C. majority 8,712
(Boundary change: notional C.)

CAMBRIDGESHIRE SOUTH EAST
*E.*75,666   *T.* 75.08%
†J. Paice, *C.* 24,397
R. Collinson, *Lab.* 15,048
Ms S. Brinton, *LD* 14,246
J. Howlett, *Ref.* 2,838
K. Lam, *Fair* 167
P. While, *NLP* 111
C. majority 9,349
(Boundary change: notional C.)

CANNOCK CHASE
*E.*72,362   *T.* 72.37%
†Dr A. Wright, *Lab.* 28,705
J. Backhouse, *C.* 14,227
R. Kirby, *LD* 4,537
P. Froggatt, *Ref.* 1,663
W. Hurley, *New Lab.* 1,615
M. Conroy, *Soc. Lab.* 1,120
M. Hartshorn, *Loony* 499
Lab. majority 14,478
(Boundary change: notional Lab.)

CANTERBURY
*E.*74,548   *T.* 72.58%
†J. Brazier, *C.* 20,913
Ms C. Hall, *Lab.* 16,949
M. Vye, *LD* 12,854
J. Osborne, *Ref.* 2,460
G. Meaden, *Green* 588
J. Moore, *UK Ind.* 281
A. Pringle, *NLP* 64
C. majority 3,964
(Boundary change: notional C.)

CARLISLE
*E.*59,917   *T.* 72.78%
†E. Martlew, *Lab.* 25,031
R. Lawrence, *C.* 12,641
C. Mayho, *LD* 4,576
A. Fraser, *Ref.* 1,233
W. Stevens, *NLP* 126
Lab. majority 12,390
(Boundary change: notional Lab.)

CARSHALTON AND WALLINGTON
*E.*66,038   *T.* 73.33%
T. Brake, *LD* 18,490
*N. Forman, *C.* 16,223
A. Theobald, *Lab.* 11,565
J. Storey, *Ref.* 1,289
P. Hickson, *Green* 377
G. Ritchie, *BNP* 261
L. Povey, *UK Ind.* 218
LD majority 2,267
(April 1992, C. maj. 9,943)

CASTLE POINT
*E.*67,146   *T.* 72.34%
Ms C. Butler, *Lab.* 20,605
*Dr R. Spink, *C.* 19,489
D. Baker, *LD* 4,477
H. Maulkin, *Ref.* 2,700
Miss L. Kendall, *Consult.* 1,301
Lab. majority 1,116
(April 1992, C. maj. 16,830)

CHARNWOOD
*E.*72,692   *T.* 77.28%
†Rt. Hon. S. Dorrell, *C.* 26,110
D. Knaggs, *Lab.* 20,210
R. Wilson, *LD* 7,224
H. Meechan, *Ref.* 2,104
M. Palmer, *BNP* 525
C. majority 5,900
(Boundary change: notional C.)

CHATHAM AND AYLESFORD
*E.*69,172   *T.* 71.07%
J. Shaw, *Lab.* 21,191
R. Knox-Johnston, *C.* 18,401
R. Murray, *LD* 7,389
K. Riddle, *Ref.* 1,538
A. Harding, *UK Ind.* 493

T. Martel, *NLP* 149
Lab. majority 2,790
(Boundary change: notional C.)

CHEADLE
E.67,627 T. 77.58%
†S. Day, *C.* 22,944
Mrs P. Calton, *LD* 19,755
P. Diggett, *Lab.* 8,253
P. Brook, *Ref.* 1,511
C. majority 3,189
(Boundary change: notional C.)

CHELMSFORD WEST
E.76,086 T. 76.99%
†S. Burns, *C.* 23,781
M. Bracken, *LD* 17,090
Dr R. Chad, *Lab.* 15,436
T. Smith, *Ref.* 1,536
G. Rumens, *Green* 411
M. Levin, *UK Ind.* 323
C. majority 6,691
(Boundary change: notional C.)

CHELTENHAM
E.67,950 T. 74.03%
†N. Jones, *LD* 24,877
J. Todman, *C.* 18,232
B. Leach, *Lab.* 5,100
Mrs A. Powell, *Ref.* 1,065
K. Hanks, *Loony* 375
G. Cook, *UK Ind.* 302
Ms A. Harriss, *ProLife* 245
Ms S. Brighouse, *NLP* 107
LD majority 6,645
(Boundary change: notional LD)

CHESHAM AND AMERSHAM
E.69,244 T. 75.38%
†Mrs C. Gillan, *C.* 26,298
M. Brand, *LD* 12,439
P. Farrelly, *Lab.* 10,240
P. Andrews, *Ref.* 2,528
C. Shilson, *UK Ind.* 618
H. Godfrey, *NLP* 74
C. majority 13,859
(Boundary change: notional C.)

CHESTER, CITY OF
E.71,730 T. 78.43%
Ms C. Russell, *Lab.* 29,806
†G. Brandreth, *C.* 19,253
D. Simpson, *LD* 5,353
R. Mullen, *Ref.* 1,487
I. Sanderson, *Loony* 204
J. Gerrard, *WCCC* 154
Lab. majority 10,553
(Boundary change: notional C.)

CHESTERFIELD
E.72,472 T. 70.91%
*Rt. Hon. A. Benn, *Lab.* 26,105
A. Rogers, *LD* 20,330
M. Potter, *C.* 4,752
N. Scarth, *Ind. OAP* 202
Lab. majority 5,775
(April 1992, Lab. maj. 6,414)

CHICHESTER
E.74,489 T. 74.88%
A. Tyrie, *C.* 25,895
Prof. P. Gardiner, *LD* 16,161
C. Smith, *Lab.* 9,605

D. Denny, *Ref.* 3,318
J. Rix, *UK Ind.* 800
C. majority 9,734
(Boundary change: notional C.)

CHINGFORD AND WOODFORD
GREEN
E.62,904 T. 70.66%
†I. Duncan Smith, *C.* 21,109
T. Hutchinson, *Lab.* 15,395
G. Seeff, *LD* 6,885
A. Gould, *BNP* 1,059
C. majority 5,714
(Boundary change: notional C.)

CHIPPING BARNET
E.69,049 T. 71.78%
†Sir S. Chapman, *C.* 21,317
G. Cooke, *Lab.* 20,282
S. Hooker, *LD* 6,121
V. Ribekow, *Ref.* 1,190
B. Miskin, *Loony* 253
B. Scallan, *ProLife* 243
Ms D. Dirksen, *NLP* 159
C. majority 1,035
(Boundary change: notional C.)

CHORLEY
E.74,387 T. 77.58%
L. Hoyle, *Lab.* 30,607
†D. Dover, *C.* 20,737
S. Jones, *LD* 4,900
A. Heaton, *Ref.* 1,319
P. Leadbetter, *NLP* 143
Lab. majority 9,870
(Boundary change: notional C.)

CHRISTCHURCH
E.71,488 T. 78.61%
C. Chope, *C.* 26,095
†Mrs D. Maddock, *LD* 23,930
C. Mannan, *Lab.* 3,884
R. Spencer, *Ref.* 1,684
R. Dickinson, *UK Ind.* 606
C. majority 2,165
(Boundary change: notional C.)

CITIES OF LONDON AND
WESTMINSTER
E.69,047 T. 58.16%
†Rt. Hon. P. Brooke, *C.* 18,981
Ms K. Green, *Lab.* 14,100
M. Dumigan, *LD* 4,933
Sir A. Walters, *Ref.* 1,161
Ms P. Wharton, *Barts* 266
C. Merton, *UK Ind.* 215
R. Johnson, *NLP* 176
N. Walsh, *Loony* 138
G. Webster, *Hemp* 112
J. Sadowitz, *Dream* 73
C. majority 4,881
(Boundary change: notional C.)

CLEETHORPES
E.68,763 T. 73.40%
Ms S. McIsaac, *Lab.* 26,058
†M. Brown, *C.* 16,882
K. Melton, *LD* 5,746
J. Berry, *Ref.* 1,787
Lab. majority 9,176
(Boundary change: notional C.)

COLCHESTER
E.74,743 T.69.58%
R. Russell, *LD* 17,886
S. Shakespeare, *C.* 16,305
R. Green, *Lab.* 15,891
J. Hazell, *Ref.* 1,776
Ms L. Basker, *NLP* 148
LD majority 1,581
(Boundary change: notional C.)

COLNE VALLEY
E.73,338 T.76.92%
Ms K. Mountford, *Lab.* 23,285
*G. Riddick, *C.* 18,445
N. Priestley, *LD* 12,755
A. Brooke, *Soc. Lab.* 759
A. Cooper, *Green* 493
J. Nunn, *UK Ind.* 478
Ms M. Staniforth, *Loony* 196
Lab. majority 4,840
(April 1992, C. maj. 7,225)

CONGLETON
E.68,873 T.77.56%
†Mrs A. Winterton, *C.* 22,012
Mrs J. Walmsley, *LD* 15,882
Ms H. Scholey, *Lab.* 14,714
J. Lockett, *UK Ind.* 811
C. majority 6,130
(Boundary change: notional C.)

COPELAND
E.54,263 T.76.19%
*Rt. Hon. Dr J. Cunningham,
Lab. 24,025
A. Cumpsty, *C.* 12,081
R. Putnam, *LD* 3,814
C. Johnston, *Ref.* 1,036
G. Hanratty, *ProLife* 389
Lab. majority 11,944
(April 1992, Lab. maj. 2,439)

CORBY
E.69,252 T.77.91%
P. Hope, *Lab. Co-op.* 29,888
*W. Powell, *C.* 18,028
I. Hankinson, *LD* 4,045
S. Riley-Smith, *Ref.* 1,356
I. Gillman, *UK Ind.* 507
Ms J. Bence, *NLP* 133
Lab. Co-op. majority 11,860
(April 1992, C. maj. 342)

CORNWALL NORTH
E.80,076 T.73.16%
*P. Tyler, *LD* 31,186
N. Linacre, *C.* 17,253
Ms A. Lindo, *Lab.* 5,523
Ms F. Odam, *Ref.* 3,636
J. Bolitho, *MK* 645
R. Winfield, *Lib.* 186
N. Cresswell, *NLP* 152
LD majority 13,933
(April 1992, LD maj. 1,921)

CORNWALL SOUTH EAST
E.75,825 T.75.74%
C. Breed, *LD* 27,044
W. Lightfoot, *C.* 20,564
Mrs D. Kirk, *Lab.* 7,358
J. Wonnacott, *UK Ind.* 1,428
P. Dunbar, *MK* 573
W. Weights, *Lib* 268

Ms M. Hartley, *NLP* 197
LD majority 6,480
(April 1992, C. maj. 7,704)

COTSWOLD
*E.*67,333   *T.*75.92%
†G. Clifton-Brown, *C.* 23,698
D. Gayler, *LD* 11,733
D. Elwell, *Lab.* 11,608
R. Lowe, *Ref.* 3,393
Ms V. Michael, *Green* 560
H. Brighouse, *NLP* 129
C. majority 11,965
(Boundary change: notional C.)

COVENTRY NORTH EAST
*E.*74,274   *T.*64.74%
†R. Ainsworth, *Lab.* 31,856
M. Burnett, *C.* 9,287
G. Sewards, *LD* 3,866
N. Brown, *Lib.* 1,181
R. Hurrell, *Ref.* 1,125
H. Khamis, *Soc. Lab.* 597
C. Sidwell, *Dream* 173
Lab. majority 22,569
(Boundary change: notional Lab.)

COVENTRY NORTH WEST
*E.*76,439   *T.*71.07%
†G. Robinson, *Lab.* 30,901
P. Bartlett, *C.* 14,300
Dr N. Penlington, *LD* 5,690
D. Butler, *Ref.* 1,269
D. Spencer, *Soc. Lab.* 940
R. Wheway, *Lib.* 687
P. Mills, *ProLife* 359
L. Francis, *Dream* 176
Lab. majority 16,601
(Boundary change: notional Lab.)

COVENTRY SOUTH
*E.*71,826   *T.*69.79%
†J. Cunningham, *Lab.* 25,511
P. Ivey, *C.* 14,558
G. MacDonald, *LD* 4,617
D. Nellist, *Soc.* 3,262
P. Garratt, *Ref.* 943
R. Jenking, *Lib.* 725
J. Astbury, *BNP* 328
Ms A.-M. Bradshaw, *Dream* 180
Lab. majority 10,953
(Boundary change: notional C.)

CRAWLEY
*E.*69,040   *T.*73.03%
Mrs L. Moffatt, *Lab.* 27,750
Miss J. Crabb, *C.* 16,043
H. de Souza, *LD* 4,141
R. Walters, *Ref.* 1,931
E. Saunders, *UK Ind.* 322
A. Kahn, *JP* 230
Lab. majority 11,707
(Boundary change: notional C.)

CREWE AND NANTWICH
*E.*68,694   *T.*73.67%
†Mrs G. Dunwoody, *Lab.* 29,460
M. Loveridge, *C.* 13,662
D. Cannon, *LD* 5,940
P. Astbury, *Ref.* 1,543
Lab. majority 15,798
(Boundary change: notional Lab.)

CROSBY
*E.*57,190   *T.*77.18%
Ms C. Curtis-Tansley, *Lab.* 22,549
†Sir M. Thornton, *C.* 15,367
P. McVey, *LD* 5,080
J. Gauld, *Ref.* 813
J. Marks, *Lib.* 233
W. Hite, *NLP* 99
Lab. majority 7,182
(Boundary change: notional C.)

CROYDON CENTRAL
*E.*80,152   *T.*69.62%
G. Davies, *Lab.* 25,432
†D. Congdon, *C.* 21,535
G. Schlich, *LD* 6,061
C. Cook, *Ref.* 1,886
M.-S. Barnsley, *Green* 595
J. Woollcott, *UK Ind.* 290
Lab. majority 3,897
(Boundary change: notional C.)

CROYDON NORTH
*E.*77,063   *T.*68.21%
†M. Wicks, *Lab.* 32,672
I. Martin, *C.* 14,274
M. Morris, *LD* 4,066
R. Billis, *Ref.* 1,155
J. Feisenberger, *UK Ind.* 396
Lab. majority 18,398
(Boundary change: notional C.)

CROYDON SOUTH
*E.*73,787   *T.*73.45%
†R. Ottaway, *C.* 25,649
C. Burling, *Lab.* 13,719
S. Gauge, *LD* 11,441
A. Barber, *Ref.* 2,631
P. Ferguson, *BNP* 354
A. Harker, *UK Ind.* 309
M. Samuel, *Choice* 96
C. majority 11,930
(Boundary change: notional C.)

DAGENHAM
*E.*58,573   *T.*61.74%
†Mrs J. Church, *Lab.* 23,759
J. Fairrie, *C.* 6,705
T. Dobrashian, *LD* 2,704
S. Kraft, *Ref.* 1,411
W. Binding, *BNP* 900
R. Dawson, *Ind.* 349
M. Hipperson, *Nat. Dem.* 183
Ms K. Goble, *ProLife* 152
Lab. majority 17,054
(Boundary change: notional Lab.)

DARLINGTON
*E.*65,140   *T.*73.95%
*A. Milburn, *Lab.* 29,658
P. Scrope, *C.* 13,633
L. Boxell, *LD* 3,483
M. Blakey, *Ref.* 1,399
Lab. majority 16,025
(April 1992, Lab. maj. 2,798)

DARTFORD
*E.*69,726   *T.*74.57%
H. Stoate, *Lab.* 25,278
†R. Dunn, *C.* 20,950
Mrs D. Webb, *LD* 4,827
P. McHale, *BNP* 428
P. Homden, *FDP* 287

J. Pollitt, *Ch. D.* 228
Lab. majority 4,328
(Boundary change: notional C.)

DAVENTRY
*E.*80,151   *T.*77.04%
†T. Boswell, *C.* 28,615
K. Ritchie, *Lab.* 21,237
J. Gordon, *LD* 9,233
Mrs B. Russocki, *Ref.* 2,018
B. Mahoney, *UK Ind.* 443
R. France, *NLP* 204
C. majority 7,378
(Boundary change: notional C.)

DENTON AND REDDISH
*E.*68,866   *T.*66.92%
†A. Bennett, *Lab.* 30,137
Ms B. Nutt, *C.* 9,826
I. Donaldson, *LD* 6,121
Lab. majority 20,311
(Boundary change: notional Lab.)

DERBY NORTH
*E.*76,116   *T.*73.76%
R. Laxton, *Lab.* 29,844
*Rt. Hon. G. Knight, *C.* 19,229
R. Charlesworth, *LD* 5,059
P. Reynolds, *Ref.* 1,816
J. Waters, *ProLife* 195
Lab. majority 10,615
(April 1992, C. maj. 4,453)

DERBY SOUTH
*E.*76,386   *T.*67.84%
†Rt. Hon. Mrs M. Beckett, *Lab.* 29,154
J. Arain, *C.* 13,048
J. Beckett, *LD* 7,438
J. Browne, *Ref.* 1,862
R. Evans, *Nat. Dem.* 317
Lab. majority 16,106
(Boundary change: notional Lab.)

DERBYSHIRE NORTH EAST
*E.*71,653   *T.*72.54%
*H. Barnes, *Lab.* 31,425
S. Elliott, *C.* 13,104
S. Hardy, *LD* 7,450
Lab. majority 18,321
(April 1992, Lab. maj. 6,270)

DERBYSHIRE SOUTH
*E.*76,672   *T.*78.21%
M. Todd, *Lab.* 32,709
†Mrs E. Currie, *C.* 18,742
R. Renold, *LD* 5,408
R. North, *Ref.* 2,491
Dr I. Crompton, *UK Ind.* 617
Lab. majority 13,967
(Boundary change: notional C.)

DERBYSHIRE WEST
*E.*72,716   *T.*78.23%
†P. McLoughlin, *C.* 23,945
S. Clamp, *Lab.* 19,060
C. Seeley, *LD* 9,940
J. Gouriet, *Ref.* 2,499
G. Meynell, *Ind. Green* 593
H. Price, *UK Ind.* 484
N. Delves, *Loony* 281
M. Kyslun, *Ind. BB* 81

C. *majority* 4,885
(Boundary change: notional C.)

DEVIZES
*E.*80,383   *T.*74.69%
†Rt. Hon. M. Ancram, *C.* 25,710
A. Vickers, *LD* 15,928
F. Jeffrey, *Lab.* 14,551
J. Goldsmith, *Ref.* 3,021
S. Oram, *UK Ind.* 622
S. Haysom, *NLP* 204
C. *majority* 9,782
(Boundary change: notional C.)

DEVON EAST
*E.*69,094   *T.*76.06%
†Rt. Hon. Sir P. Emery, *C.* 22,797
Miss R. Trethewey, *LD* 15,308
A. Siantonas, *Lab.* 9,292
W. Dixon, *Ref.* 3,200
G. Halliwell, *Lib.* 1,363
C. Giffard, *UK Ind.* 459
G. Needs, *Nat. Dem.* 131
C. *majority* 7,489
(Boundary change: notional C.)

DEVON NORTH
*E.*70,350   *T.*77.94%
†N. Harvey, *LD* 27,824
R. Ashworth, *C.* 21,643
Mrs E. Brenton, *Lab.* 5,367
LD *majority* 6,181
(Boundary change: notional LD)

DEVON SOUTH WEST
*E.*69,293   *T.*76.22%
†G. Streeter, *C.* 22,695
C. Mavin, *Lab.* 15,262
K. Baldry, *LD* 12,542
R. Sadler, *Ref.* 1,668
Mrs H. King, *UK Ind.* 491
J. Hyde, *NLP* 159
C. *majority* 7,433
(Boundary change: notional C.)

DEVON WEST AND TORRIDGE
*E.*75,919   *T.*77.91%
J. Burnett, *LD* 24,744
I. Liddell-Grainger, *C.* 22,787
D. Brenton, *Lab.* 7,319
R. Lea, *Ref.* 1,946
M. Jackson, *UK Ind.* 1,841
M. Pithouse, *Ind. Lab.* 508
LD *majority* 1,957
(Boundary change: notional C.)

DEWSBURY
*E.*61,523   *T.*70.01%
†Mrs A. Taylor, *Lab.* 21,286
Dr P. McCormick, *C.* 12,963
K. Hill, *LD* 4,422
Ms F. Taylor, *BNP* 2,232
Ms W. Goff, *Ref.* 1,019
D. Daniel, *Ind. Lab.* 770
I. McCourtie, *Green* 383
Lab. majority 8,323
(Boundary change: notional Lab.)

DONCASTER CENTRAL
*E.*67,965   *T.*63.92%
Ms R. Winterton, *Lab.* 26,961
D. Turtle, *C.* 9,105
S. Tarry, *LD* 4,091

M. Cliff, *Ref.* 1,273
M. Kenny, *Soc. Lab.* 854
J. Redden, *ProLife* 697
P. Davies, *UK Ind.* 462
Lab. majority 17,856
(April 1992, Lab. maj. 10,682)

DONCASTER NORTH
*E.*63,019   *T.*63.30%
†K. Hughes, *Lab.* 27,843
P. Kennerley, *C.* 5,906
M. Cook, *LD* 3,369
R. Thornton, *Ref.* 1,589
M. Swan, *AS Lab.* 1,181
Lab. majority 21,937
(Boundary change: notional Lab.)

DON VALLEY
*E.*65,643   *T.*66.35%
Ms C. Flint, *Lab.* 25,376
Mrs C. Gledhill, *C.* 10,717
P. Johnston, *LD* 4,238
P. Davis, *Ref.* 1,379
N. Ball, *Soc. Lab.* 1,024
S. Platt, *Green* 493
Ms C. Johnson, *ProLife* 330
Lab. majority 14,659
(Boundary change: notional Lab.)

DORSET MID AND POOLE NORTH
*E.*67,049   *T.*75.67%
C. Fraser, *C.* 20,632
A. Leaman, *LD* 19,951
D. Collis, *Lab.* 8,014
D. Nabarro, *Ref.* 2,136
C. *majority* 681
(Boundary change: notional C.)

DORSET NORTH
*E.*68,923   *T.*76.30%
R. Walter, *C.* 23,294
Mrs P. Yates, *LD* 20,548
J. Fitzmaurice, *Lab.* 5,380
Mrs M. Evans, *Ref.* 2,564
Revd D. Wheeler, *UK Ind.* 801
C. *majority* 2,746
(Boundary change: notional C.)

DORSET SOUTH
*E.*66,318   *T.*74.16%
†I. Bruce, *C.* 17,755
J. Knight, *Lab.* 17,678
M. Plummer, *LD* 9,936
P. McAndrew, *Ref.* 2,791
Capt. M. Shakesby, *UK Ind.* 861
G. Napper, *NLP* 161
C. *majority* 77
(Boundary change: notional C.)

DORSET WEST
*E.*70,369   *T.*76.10%
O. Letwin, *C.* 22,036
R. Legg, *LD* 20,196
R. Bygraves, *Lab.* 9,491
P. Jenkins, *UK Ind.* 1,590
M. Griffiths, *NLP* 239
C. *majority* 1,840
(Boundary change: notional C.)

DOVER
*E.*68,669   *T.*78.93%
G. Prosser, *Lab.* 29,535
†D. Shaw, *C.* 17,796

M. Corney, *LD* 4,302
Mrs S. Anderson, *Ref.* 2,124
C. Hyde, *UK Ind.* 443
Lab. majority 11,739
(Boundary change: notional C.)

DUDLEY NORTH
*E.*68,835   *T.*69.45%
R. Cranston, *Lab.* 24,471
C. MacNamara, *C.* 15,014
G. Lewis, *LD* 3,939
M. Atherton, *Soc. Lab.* 2,155
S. Bavester, *Ref.* 1,201
G. Cartwright, *NF* 559
S. Darby, *Nat. Dem.* 469
Lab. majority 9,457
(Boundary change: notional Lab.)

DUDLEY SOUTH
*E.*66,731   *T.*71.78%
†I. Pearson, *Lab.* 27,124
M. Simpson, *C.* 14,097
R. Burt, *LD* 5,214
C. Birch, *Ref.* 1,467
Lab. majority 13,027
(Boundary change: notional Lab.)

DULWICH AND WEST NORWOOD
*E.*69,655   *T.*65.49%
†Ms T. Jowell, *Lab.* 27,807
R. Gough, *C.* 11,038
Mrs S. Kramer, *LD* 4,916
B. Coles, *Ref.* 897
Dr A. Goldie, *Lib.* 587
D. Goodman, *Dream* 173
E. Pike, *UK Ind.* 159
Capt. Rizz, *Rizz Party* 38
Lab. majority 16,769
(Boundary change: notional Lab.)

DURHAM NORTH
*E.*67,891   *T.*69.48%
†G. Radice, *Lab.* 33,142
M. Hardy, *C.* 6,843
B. Moore, *LD* 5,225
I. Parkin, *Ref.* 1,958
Lab. majority 26,299
(Boundary change: notional Lab.)

DURHAM NORTH WEST
*E.*67,156   *T.*68.97%
†Miss H. Armstrong, *Lab.* 31,855
Mrs L. St J. Howe, *C.* 7,101
A. Gillings, *LD* 4,991
R. Atkinson, *Ref.* 2,372
Lab. majority 24,754
(Boundary change: notional Lab.)

DURHAM, CITY OF
*E.*69,340   *T.*70.86%
*G. Steinberg, *Lab.* 31,102
R. Chalk, *C.* 8,598
Dr N. Martin, *LD* 7,499
Ms M. Robson, *Ref.* 1,723
P. Kember, *NLP* 213
Lab. majority 22,504
(April 1992, Lab. maj. 15,058)

EALING ACTON AND SHEPHERD'S BUSH
*E.*72,078   *T.*66.68%
†C. Soley, *Lab.* 28,052
Mrs B. Yerolemou, *C.* 12,405

A. Mitchell, *LD* 5,163
C. Winn, *Ref.* 637
J. Gilbert, *Soc. Lab.* 635
J. Gomm, *UK Ind.* 385
P. Danon, *ProLife* 265
C. Beasley, *Glow* 209
W. Edwards, *Ch. P.* 163
K. Turner, *NLP* 150
Lab. majority 15,647
(Boundary change: notional Lab.)

EALING NORTH
*E.*78,144   *T.*71.31%
S. Pound, *Lab.* 29,904
†H. Greenway, *C.* 20,744
A. Gupta, *LD* 3,887
G. Slysz, *UK Ind.* 689
Ms A. Siebe, *Green* 502
Lab. majority 9,160
(Boundary change: notional C.)

EALING SOUTHALL
*E.*81,704   *T.*66.88%
†P. Khabra, *Lab.* 32,791
J. Penrose, *C.* 11,368
Ms N. Thomson, *LD* 5,687
H. Brar, *Soc. Lab.* 2,107
N. Goodwin, *Green* 934
B. Cherry, *Ref.* 854
Ms K. Klepacka, *ProLife* 473
Dr R. Mead, *UK Ind.* 428
Lab. majority 21,423
(Boundary change: notional Lab.)

EASINGTON
*E.*62,518   *T.*67.01%
*J. Cummings, *Lab.* 33,600
J. Hollands, *C.* 3,588
J. Heppell, *LD* 3,025
R. Pulfrey, *Ref.* 1,179
S. Colborn, *SPGB* 503
Lab. majority 30,012
(April 1992, Lab. maj. 26,390)

EASTBOURNE
*E.*72,347   *T.*72.80%
†N. Waterson, *C.* 22,183
C. Berry, *LD* 20,189
D. Lines, *Lab.* 6,576
T. Lowe, *Ref.* 2,724
Mrs T. Williamson, *Lib.* 741
J. Dawkins, *UK Ind.* 254
C. majority 1,994
(Boundary change: notional C.)

EAST HAM
*E.*65,591   *T.*60.81%
†S. Timms, *Lab.* 25,779
Miss A. Bray, *C.* 6,421
I. Khan, *Soc. Lab.* 2,697
M. Sole, *LD* 2,599
C. Smith, *BNP* 1,258
Mrs J. McCann, *Ref.* 845
G. Hardy, *Nat. Dem.* 290
Lab. majority 19,358
(Boundary change: notional Lab.)

EASTLEIGH
*E.*72,155   *T.*76.91%
†D. Chidgey, *LD* 19,453
S. Reid, *C.* 18,699
A. Lloyd, *Lab.* 14,883
V. Eldridge, *Ref.* 2,013

P. Robinson, *UK Ind.* 446
LD majority 754
(Boundary change: notional C.)

ECCLES
*E.*69,645   *T.*65.60%
I. Stewart, *Lab.* 30,468
G. Barker, *C.* 8,552
R. Boyd, *LD* 4,905
J. De Roeck, *Ref.* 1,765
Lab. majority 21,916
(Boundary change: notional Lab.)

EDDISBURY
*E.*65,256   *T.*75.78%
†Rt.. Hon. A. Goodlad, *C.* 21,027
Ms M. Hanson, *Lab.* 19,842
D. Reaper, *LD* 6,540
Ms N. Napier, *Ref.* 2,041
C. majority 1,185
(Boundary change: notional C.)

EDMONTON
*E.*63,718   *T.*70.37%
A. Love, *Lab. Co-op.* 27,029
*Dr I. Twinn, *C.* 13,557
A. Wiseman, *LD* 2,847
J. Wright, *Ref.* 708
B. Cowd, *BNP* 437
Mrs P. Weald, *UK Ind.* 260
Lab. Co-op. majority 13,472
(April 1992, C. maj. 593)

ELLESMERE PORT AND NESTON
*E.*67,573   *T.*77.79%
†A. Miller, *Lab.* 31,310
Mrs L. Turnbull, *C.* 15,274
Ms J. Pemberton, *LD* 4,673
C. Rodden, *Ref.* 1,305
Lab. majority 16,036
(Boundary change: notional Lab.)

ELMET
*E.*70,423   *T.*76.81%
C. Burgon, *Lab.* 28,348
*S. Batiste, *C.* 19,569
B. Jennings, *LD* 4,691
C. Zawadski, *Ref.* 1,487
Lab. majority 8,779
(April 1992, C. maj. 3,261)

ELTHAM
*E.*57,358   *T.*75.71%
C. Efford, *Lab.* 23,710
C. Blackwood, *C.* 13,528
Ms A. Taylor, *LD* 3,701
M. Clark, *Ref.* 1,414
H. Middleton, *Lib.* 584
W. Hitches, *BNP* 491
Lab. majority 10,182
(Boundary change: notional C.)

ENFIELD NORTH
*E.*67,680   *T.*70.43%
Ms J. Ryan, *Lab.* 24,148
M. Field, *C.* 17,326
M. Hopkins, *LD* 4,264
R. Ellingham, *Ref.* 857
Ms J. Griffin, *BNP* 590
Mrs J. O'Ware, *UK Ind.* 484
Lab. majority 6,822
(April 1992, C. maj. 9,430)

ENFIELD SOUTHGATE
*E.*65,796   *T.*70.72%
S. Twigg, *Lab.* 20,570
†Rt. Hon. M. Portillo, *C.* 19,137
J. Browne, *LD* 4,966
N. Luard, *Ref.* 1,342
A. Storkey, *Ch. D.* 289
A. Malakouna, *Mal* 229
Lab. majority 1,433
(Boundary change: notional C.)

EPPING FOREST
*E.*72,795   *T.*72.82%
Mrs E. Laing, *C.* 24,117
S. Murray, *Lab.* 18,865
S. Robinson, *LD* 7,074
J. Berry, *Ref.* 2,208
P. Henderson, *BNP* 743
C. majority 5,252
(Boundary change: notional C.)

EPSOM AND EWELL
*E.*73,222   *T.*74.00%
†Rt. Hon. Sir A. Hamilton, *C.* 24,717
P. Woodford, *Lab.* 13,192
J. Vincent, *LD* 12,380
C. Macdonald, *Ref.* 2,355
H. Green, *UK Ind.* 544
H. Charlton, *Green* 527
Ms K. Weeks, *ProLife* 466
C. majority 11,525
(Boundary change: notional C.)

EREWASH
*E.*77,402   *T.*77.95%
Ms E. Blackman, *Lab.* 31,196
†Mrs A. Knight, *C.* 22,061
Dr M. Garnett, *LD* 5,181
S. Stagg, *Ref.* 1,404
M. Simmons, *Soc. Lab.* 496
Lab. majority 9,135
(Boundary change: notional C.)

ERITH AND THAMESMEAD
*E.*62,887   *T.*66.13%
†J. Austin-Walker, *Lab.* 25,812
N. Zahawi, *C.* 8,388
A. Grigg, *LD* 5,001
J. Flunder, *Ref.* 1,394
V. Dooley, *BNP* 718
M. Jackson, *UK Ind.* 274
Lab. majority 17,424
(Boundary change: notional Lab.)

ESHER AND WALTON
*E.*72,382   *T.*74.14%
†I. Taylor, *C.* 26,747
Ms J. Reay, *Lab.* 12,219
G. Miles, *LD* 10,937
A. Cruickshank, *Ref.* 2,904
B. Collignon, *UK Ind.* 558
Ms S. Kay, *Dream* 302
C. majority 14,528
(Boundary change: notional C.)

ESSEX NORTH
*E.*68,008   *T.*75.30%
†B. Jenkin, *C.* 22,480
T. Young, *Lab.* 17,000
A. Phillips, *LD* 10,028
R. Lord, *UK Ind.* 1,202
Ms S. Ransome, *Green* 495

C. majority 5,476
(Boundary change: notional C.)

EXETER
*E.*79,154   *T.*78.16%
B. Bradshaw, *Lab.*   29,398
Dr A. Rogers, *C.*   17,693
D. Brewer, *LD*   11,148
D. Morrish, *Lib.*   2,062
P. Edwards, *Green*   643
Mrs C. Haynes, *UK Ind.*   638
J. Meakin, *UKPP*   282
Lab. majority 11,705
(Boundary change: notional C.)

FALMOUTH AND CAMBORNE
*E.*71,383   *T.*75.13%
Ms C. Atherton, *Lab.*   18,151
*S. Coe, *C.*   15,463
Mrs T. Jones, *LD*   13,512
P. de Savary, *Ref.*   3,534
J. Geach, *Ind. Lab.*   1,691
P. Holmes, *Lib.*   527
R. Smith, *UK Ind.*   355
Ms R. Lewarne, *MK*   238
G. Glitter, *Loony*   161
Lab. majority 2,688
(April 1992, C. maj. 3,267)

FAREHAM
*E.*68,787   *T.*75.85%
†Rt. Hon. Sir P. Lloyd, *C.*   24,436
M. Pryor, *Lab.*   14,078
Mrs G. Hill, *LD*   10,234
D. Markham, *Ref.*   2,914
W. O'Brien, *Ind. No*   515
C. majority 10,358
(Boundary change: notional C.)

FAVERSHAM AND KENT MID
*E.*67,490   *T.*73.50%
†A. Rowe, *C.*   22,016
A. Stewart, *Lab.*   17,843
B. Parmenter, *LD*   6,138
R. Birley, *Ref.*   2,073
N. Davidson, *Loony*   511
M. Cunningham, *UK Ind.*   431
D. Currer, *Green*   380
Ms C. Morgan, *GRLNSP*   115
N. Pollard, *NLP*   99
C. majority 4,173
(Boundary change: notional C.)

FELTHAM AND HESTON
*E.*71,093   *T.*65.58%
†A. Keen, *Lab. Co-op.*   27,836
P. Ground, *C.*   12,563
C. Penning, *LD*   4,264
R. Stubbs, *Ref.*   1,099
R. Church, *BNP*   682
D. Fawcett, *NLP*   177
Lab. Co-op. majority 15,273
(Boundary change: notional Lab. Co-op.)

FINCHLEY AND GOLDERS GREEN
*E.*72,225   *T.*69.65%
R. Vis, *Lab.*   23,180
†J. Marshall, *C.*   19,991
J. Davies, *LD*   5,670
G. Shaw, *Ref.*   684
A. Gunstock, *Green*   576
D. Barraclough, *UK Ind.*   205

Lab. majority 3,189
(Boundary change: notional C.)

FOLKESTONE AND HYTHE
*E.*71,153   *T.*73.15%
†Rt. Hon. M. Howard, *C.*   20,313
D. Laws, *LD*   13,981
P. Doherty, *Lab.*   12,939
J. Aspinall, *Ref.*   4,188
J. Baker, *UK Ind.*   378
E. Segal, *Soc.*   182
R. Saint, *CFSS*   69
C. majority 6,332
(Boundary change: notional C.)

FOREST OF DEAN
*E.*63,465   *T.*79.07%
Ms D. Organ, *Lab.*   24,203
†P. Marland, *C.*   17,860
Dr A. Lynch, *LD*   6,165
J. Hopkins, *Ref.*   1,624
G. Morgan, *Ind. Dean*   218
C. Palmer, *21st Cent.*   80
S. Porter, *Ind. F.*   34
Lab. majority 6,343
(Boundary change: notional Lab.)

FYLDE
*E.*71,385   *T.*72.94%
†Rt. Hon. M. Jack, *C.*   25,443
J. Garrett, *Lab.*   16,480
W. Greene, *LD*   7,609
D. Britton, *Ref.*   2,372
T. Kerwin, *NLP*   163
C. majority 8,963
(Boundary change: notional C.)

GAINSBOROUGH
*E.*64,106   *T.*74.56%
†E. Leigh, *C.*   20,593
P. Taylor, *Lab.*   13,767
N. Taylor, *LD*   13,436
C. majority 6,826
(Boundary change: notional C.)

GATESHEAD EAST AND
WASHINGTON WEST
*E.*64,114   *T.*67.19%
†Miss J. Quin, *Lab.*   31,047
Miss J. Burns, *C.*   6,097
A. Ord, *LD*   4,622
M. Daley, *Ref.*   1,315
Lab. majority 24,950
(Boundary change: notional Lab.)

GEDLING
*E.*68,820   *T.*75.80%
V. Coaker, *Lab.*   24,390
*A. Mitchell, *C.*   20,588
R. Poynter, *LD*   5,180
J. Connor, *Ref.*   2,006
Lab. majority 3,802
(April 1992, C. maj. 10,637)

GILLINGHAM
*E.*70,389   *T.*72.00%
P. Clark, *Lab.*   20,187
†J. Couchman, *C.*   18,207
R. Sayer, *LD*   9,649
G. Cann, *Ref.*   1,492
C. MacKinlay, *UK Ind.*   590
D. Robinson, *Loony*   305
C. Jury, *BNP*   195

Ms G. Duguay, *NLP*   58
Lab. majority 1,980
(Boundary change: notional C.)

GLOUCESTER
*E.*78,682   *T.*73.61%
Ms T. Kingham, *Lab.*   28,943
†D. French, *C.*   20,684
P. Munisamy, *LD*   6,069
A. Reid, *Ref.*   1,482
A. Harris, *UK Ind.*   455
Ms M. Hamilton, *NLP*   281
Lab. majority 8,259
(Boundary change: notional C.)

GOSPORT
*E.*68,830   *T.*70.25%
*P. Viggers, *C.*   21,085
I. Gray, *Lab.*   14,827
S. Hogg, *LD*   9,479
A. Blowers, *Ref.*   2,538
P. Ettie, *Ind.*   426
C. majority 6,258
(April 1992, C. maj. 16,318)

GRANTHAM AND STAMFORD
*E.*72,310   *T.*73.25%
†Q. Davies, *C.*   22,672
P. Denning, *Lab.*   19,980
J. Sellick, *LD*   6,612
Ms M. Swain, *Ref.*   2,721
M. Charlesworth, *UK Ind.*   556
Ms R. Clark, *ProLife*   314
I. Harper, *NLP*   115
C. majority 2,692
(Boundary change: notional C.)

GRAVESHAM
*E.*69,234   *T.*76.92%
C. Pond, *Lab.*   26,460
†J. Arnold, *C.*   20,681
Dr M. Canet, *LD*   4,128
Mrs P. Curtis, *Ref.*   1,441
A. Leyshon, *Ind.*   414
D. Palmer, *NLP*   129
Lab. majority 5,779
(Boundary change: notional C.)

GREAT GRIMSBY
*E.*65,043   *T.*66.26%
*A. Mitchell, *Lab.*   25,765
D. Godson, *C.*   9,521
A. De Freitas, *LD*   7,810
Lab. majority 16,244
(April 1992, Lab. maj. 7,504)

GREAT YARMOUTH
*E.*68,625   *T.*71.23%
A. Wright, *Lab.*   26,084
*M. Carttiss, *C.*   17,416
D. Wood, *LD*   5,381
Lab. majority 8,668
(April 1992, C. maj. 5,309)

GREENWICH AND WOOLWICH
*E.*61,352   *T.*65.85%
†N. Raynsford, *Lab.*   25,630
M. Mitchell, *C.*   7,502
Mrs C. Luxton, *LD*   5,049
D. Ellison, *Ref.*   1,670
R. Mallone, *Fellowship*   428
D. Martin-Eagle, *Constit.*   124

Lab. majority 18,128
(Boundary change: notional Lab.)

GUILDFORD
*E.*75,541   *T.*75.40%
N. St Aubyn, *C.* | 24,230
Mrs M. Sharp, *LD* | 19,439
J. Burns, *Lab.* | 9,945
J. Gore, *Ref.* | 2,650
R. McWhirter, *UK Ind.* | 400
J. Morris, *Pacifist* | 294
C. majority 4,791
(Boundary change: notional C.)

HACKNEY NORTH AND STOKE NEWINGTON
*E.*62,045   *T.*52.95%
*Ms D. Abbott, *Lab.* | 21,110
M. Lavender, *C.* | 5,483
D. Taylor, *LD* | 3,806
Yen Chit Chong, *Green* | 1,395
B. Maxwell, *Ref.* | 544
D. Tolson, *None* | 368
Miss L. Lovebucket, *Rain. Ref.* | 146
Lab. majority 15,627
(April 1992, Lab. maj. 10,727)

HACKNEY SOUTH AND SHOREDITCH
*E.*61,728   *T.*54.67%
†B. Sedgemore, *Lab.* | 20,048
M. Pantling, *LD* | 5,068
C. O'Leary, *C.* | 4,494
T. Betts, *New Lab.* | 2,436
R. Franklin, *Ref.* | 613
G. Callow, *BNP* | 531
M. Goldman, *Comm. P.* | 298
Ms M. Goldberg, *NLP* | 145
W. Rogers, *WRP* | 113
Lab. majority 14,980
(Boundary change: notional Lab.)

HALESOWEN AND ROWLEY REGIS
*E.*66,245   *T.*73.61%
Mrs S. Heal, *Lab.* | 26,366
J. Kennedy, *C.* | 16,029
Ms E. Todd, *LD* | 4,169
P. White, *Ref.* | 1,244
Ms K. Meeds, *Nat. Dem.* | 592
T. Weller, *Green* | 361
Lab. majority 10,337
(Boundary change: notional C.)

HALIFAX
*E.*71,701   *T.*70.51%
*Mrs A. Mahon, *Lab.* | 27,465
R. Light, *C.* | 16,253
E. Waller, *LD* | 6,059
Mrs C. Whitaker, *UK Ind.* | 779
Lab. majority 11,212
(April 1992, Lab. maj. 478)

HALTEMPRICE AND HOWDEN
*E.*65,602   *T.*75.53%
†Rt. Hon. D. Davis, *C.* | 21,809
Ms D. Wallis, *LD* | 14,295
G. McManus, *Lab.* | 11,701
T. Pearson, *Ref.* | 1,370
G. Bloom, *UK Ind.* | 301
B. Stevens, *NLP* | 74
C. majority 7,514
(Boundary change: notional C.)

HALTON
*E.*64,987   *T.*68.38%
D. Twigg, *Lab.* | 31,497
P. Balmer, *C.* | 7,847
Ms J. Jones, *LD* | 3,263
R. Atkins, *Ref.* | 1,036
D. Proffitt, *Lib.* | 600
J. Alley, *Rep. GB* | 196
Lab. majority 23,650
(Boundary change: notional Lab.)

HAMMERSMITH AND FULHAM
*E.*78,637   *T.*68.70%
I. Coleman, *Lab.* | 25,262
†M. Carrington, *C.* | 21,420
Ms A. Sugden, *LD* | 4,728
Mrs M. Bremner, *Ref.* | 1,023
W. Johnson-Smith, *New Lab.* | 695
Ms E. Streeter, *Green* | 562
G. Roberts, *UK Ind.* | 183
A. Phillips, *NLP* | 79
A. Elston, *Care* | 74
Lab. majority 3,842
(Boundary change: notional C.)

HAMPSHIRE EAST
*E.*76,604   *T.*75.88%
†M. Mates, *C.* | 27,927
R. Booker, *LD* | 16,337
R. Hoyle, *Lab.* | 9,945
J. Hayter, *Ref.* | 2,757
I. Foster, *Green* | 649
S. Coles, *UK Ind.* | 513
C. majority 11,590
(Boundary change: notional C.)

HAMPSHIRE NORTH EAST
*E.*69,111   *T.*73.95%
†J. Arbuthnot, *C.* | 26,017
I. Mann, *LD* | 11,619
P. Dare, *Lab.* | 8,203
D. Rees, *Ref.* | 2,420
K. Jessavala, *Ind.* | 2,400
C. Berry, *UK Ind.* | 452
C. majority 14,398
(Boundary change: notional C.)

HAMPSHIRE NORTH WEST
*E.*73,222   *T.*74.66%
†Rt. Hon. Sir G. Young, Bt., *C.* | 24,730
C. Fleming, *LD* | 13,179
M. Mumford, *Lab.* | 12,900
Mrs P. Callaghan, *Ref.* | 1,533
T. Rolt, *UK Ind.* | 1,383
W. Baxter, *Green* | 486
H. Anscomb, *Bypass* | 231
R. Dodd, *Ind.* | 225
C. majority 11,551
(Boundary change: notional C.)

HAMPSTEAD AND HIGHGATE
*E.*64,889   *T.*67.86%
†Ms G. Jackson, *Lab.* | 25,275
Miss E. Gibson, *C.* | 11,991
Mrs B. Fox, *LD* | 5,481
Ms M. Siddique, *Ref.* | 667
J. Leslie, *NLP* | 147
R. Carroll, *Dream* | 141
Miss P. Prince, *UK Ind.* | 123
R. J. Harris, *Hum.* | 105
Capt. Rizz, *Rizz Party* | 101

Lab. majority 13,284
(Boundary change: notional Lab.)

HARBOROUGH
*E.*70,424   *T.*75.27%
†E. Garnier, *C.* | 22,170
M. Cox, *LD* | 15,646
N. Holden, *Lab.* | 13,332
N. Wright, *Ref.* | 1,859
C. majority 6,524
(Boundary change: notional C.)

HARLOW
*E.*64,072   *T.*74.62%
W. Rammell, *Lab.* | 25,861
†J. Hayes, *C.* | 15,347
Ms L. Spenceley, *LD* | 4,523
M. Wells, *Ref.* | 1,422
G. Batten, *UK Ind.* | 340
J. Bowles, *BNP* | 319
Lab. majority 10,514
(Boundary change: notional C.)

HARROGATE AND KNARESBOROUGH
*E.*65,155   *T.*73.14%
P. Willis, *LD* | 24,558
†Rt. Hon. N. Lamont, *C.* | 18,322
Ms B. Boyce, *Lab.* | 4,159
J. Blackburn, *LC* | 614
LD majority 6,236
(Boundary change: notional C.)

HARROW EAST
*E.*79,846   *T.*71.37%
A. McNulty, *Lab.* | 29,927
†H. Dykes, *C.* | 20,189
B. Sharma, *LD* | 4,697
B. Casey, *Ref.* | 1,537
A. Scholefield, *UK Ind.* | 464
A. Planton, *NLP* | 171
Lab. majority 9,738
(Boundary change: notional C.)

HARROW WEST
*E.*72,005   *T.*72.92%
G. Thomas, *Lab.* | 21,811
*R. Hughes, *C.* | 20,571
Mrs P. Nandhra, *LD* | 8,127
H. Crossman, *Ref.* | 1,997
Lab. majority 1,240
(Boundary change: notional C.)

HARTLEPOOL
*E.*67,712   *T.*65.65%
*P. Mandelson, *Lab.* | 26,997
M. Horsley, *C.* | 9,489
R. Clark, *LD* | 6,248
Miss M. Henderson, *Ref.* | 1,718
Lab. majority 17,508
(April 1992, Lab. maj. 8,782)

HARWICH
*E.*75,775   *T.*70.62%
I. Henderson, *Lab.* | 20,740
†I. Sproat, *C.* | 19,524
Mrs A. Elvin, *LD* | 7,037
J. Titford, *Ref.* | 4,923
R. Knight, *CRP* | 1,290
Lab. majority 1,216
(Boundary change: notional C.)

HASTINGS AND RYE
*E.*70,388   *T.*69.71%
M. Foster, *Lab.* | 16,867

*Mrs J. Lait, *C.* 14,307
M. Palmer, *LD* 13,717
C. McGovern, *Ref.* 2,511
Ms J. Amstad, *Lib.* 1,046
W. Andrews, *UK Ind.* 472
D. Howell, *Loony* 149
Lab. majority 2,560
(April 1992, C. maj. 6,634)

HAVANT
*E.*68,420   *T.*70.63%
†D. Willetts, *C.* 19,204
Ms L. Armstrong, *Lab.* 15,475
M. Kooner, *LD* 10,806
A. Green, *Ref.* 2,395
M. Atwal, *BIPF* 442
C. majority 3,729
(Boundary change: notional C.)

HAYES AND HARLINGTON
*E.*56,829   *T.*72.31%
J. McDonnell, *Lab.* 25,458
A. Retter, *C.* 11,167
A. Little, *LD* 3,049
F. Page, *Ref.* 778
J. Hutchins, *NF* 504
D. Farrow, *ANP* 135
Lab. majority 14,291
(Boundary change: notional C.)

HAZEL GROVE
*E.*63,694   *T.*77.46%
A. Stunell, *LD* 26,883
B. Murphy, *C.* 15,069
J. Lewis, *Lab.* 5,882
J. Stanyer, *Ref.* 1,055
G. Black, *UK Ind.* 268
D. Firkin-Flood, *Ind. Hum.* 183
LD majority 11,814
(April 1992, C. maj. 929)

HEMEL HEMPSTEAD
*E.*71,468   *T.*77.09%
A. McWalter, *Lab. Co-op.* 25,175
†R. Jones, *C.* 21,539
Mrs P. Lindsley, *LD* 6,789
P. Such, *Ref.* 1,327
Ms D. Harding, *NLP* 262
Lab. Co-op. majority 3,636
(Boundary change: notional C.)

HEMSWORTH
*E.*66,964   *T.*67.91%
†J. Trickett, *Lab.* 32,088
N. Hazell, *C.* 8,096
Ms J. Kirby, *LD* 4,033
D. Irvine, *Ref.* 1,260
Lab. majority 23,992
(Boundary change: notional Lab.)

HENDON
*E.*76,195   *T.*65.67%
A. Dismore, *Lab.* 24,683
†Sir J. Gorst, *C.* 18,528
W. Casey, *LD* 5,427
S. Rabbow, *Ref.* 978
B. Wright, *UK Ind.* 267
Ms S. Taylor, *WRP* 153
Lab. majority 6,155
(Boundary change: notional C.)

HENLEY
*E.*66,424   *T.*77.60%
†Rt. Hon. M. Heseltine, *C.* 23,908
T. Horton, *LD* 12,741
D. Enright, *Lab.* 11,700
S. Sainsbury, *Ref.* 2,299
Mrs S. Miles, *Green* 514
N. Barlow, *NLP* 221
T. Hibbert, *Whig Party* 160
C. majority 11,167
(Boundary change: notional C.)

HEREFORD
*E.*69,864   *T.*75.22%
P. Keetch, *LD* 25,198
†Sir C. Shepherd, *C.* 18,550
C. Chappell, *Lab.* 6,596
C. Easton, *Ref.* 2,209
LD majority 6,648
(Boundary change: notional C.)

HERTFORD AND STORTFORD
*E.*71,759   *T.*76.03%
†B. Wells, *C.* 24,027
S. Speller, *Lab.* 17,142
M. Wood, *LD* 9,679
H. Page Croft, *Ref.* 2,105
B. Smalley, *UK Ind.* 1,223
M. Franey, *ProLife* 259
D. Molloy, *Logic* 126
C. majority 6,885
(Boundary change: notional C.)

HERTFORDSHIRE NORTH EAST
*E.*67,161   *T.*77.42%
†O. Heald, *C.* 21,712
I. Gibbons, *Lab.* 18,624
S. Jarvis, *LD* 9,493
J. Grose, *Ref.* 2,166
C. majority 3,088
(Boundary change: notional C.)

HERTFORDSHIRE SOUTH WEST
*E.*71,671   *T.*77.31%
†R. Page, *C.* 25,462
M. Wilson, *Lab.* 15,441
Mrs A. Shaw, *LD* 12,381
T. Millward, *Ref.* 1,853
C. Adamson, *NLP* 274
C. majority 10,021
(Boundary change: notional C.)

HERTSMERE
*E.*68,011   *T.*74.03%
†J. Clappison, *C.* 22,305
Ms E. Kelly, *Lab.* 19,230
Mrs A. Gray, *LD* 6,466
J. Marlow, *Ref.* 1,703
R. Saunders, *UK Ind.* 453
N. Kahn, *NLP* 191
C. majority 3,075
(Boundary change: notional C.)

HEXHAM
*E.*58,914   *T.*77.52%
*P. Atkinson, *C.* 17,701
I. McMinn, *Lab.* 17,479
Dr P. Carr, *LD* 7,959
R. Waddell, *Ref.* 1,362
D. Lott, *UK Ind.* 1,170
C. majority 222
(April 1992, C. maj. 13,438)

HEYWOOD AND MIDDLETON
*E.*73,898   *T.*68.41%
J. Dobbin, *Lab. Co-op.* 29,179
S. Grigg, *C.* 11,637
D. Clayton, *LD* 7,908
Mrs C. West, *Ref.* 1,076
P. Burke, *Lib.* 750
Lab. Co-op. majority 17,542
(Boundary change: notional Lab. Co-op.)

HIGH PEAK
*E.*72,315   *T.*79.03%
T. Levitt, *Lab.* 29,052
†C. Hendry, *C.* 20,261
Mrs S. Barber, *LD* 6,420
C. Hanson-Orr, *Ref.* 1,420
Lab. majority 8,791
(Boundary change: notional C.)

HITCHIN AND HARPENDEN
*E.*67,219   *T.*77.99%
†Rt. Hon. P. Lilley, *C.* 24,038
Ms R. Sanderson, *Lab.* 17,367
C. White, *LD* 10,515
D. Cooke, *NLP* 290
J. Horton, *Soc.* 217
C. majority 6,671
(Boundary change: notional C.)

HOLBORN AND ST PANCRAS
*E.*63,037   *T.*60.28%
†F. Dobson, *Lab.* 24,707
J. Smith, *C.* 6,804
Ms J. McGuinness, *LD* 4,750
Mrs J. Carr, *Ref.* 790
T. Bedding, *NLP* 191
S. Smith, *JP* 173
Ms B. Conway, *WRP* 171
M. Rosenthal, *Dream* 157
P. Rice-Evans, *EUP* 140
B. Quintavalle, *ProLife* 114
Lab. majority 17,903
(Boundary change: notional Lab.)

HORNCHURCH
*E.*60,775   *T.*72.30%
J. Cryer, *Lab.* 22,066
*R. Squire, *C.* 16,386
R. Martins, *LD* 3,446
R. Khilkoff-Boulding, *Ref.* 1,595
Miss J. Trueman, *Third Way* 259
J. Sowerby, *ProLife* 189
Lab. majority 5,680
(April 1992, C. maj. 9,165)

HORNSEY AND WOOD GREEN
*E.*74,537   *T.*69.08%
*Mrs B. Roche, *Lab.* 31,792
Mrs H. Hart, *C.* 11,293
Ms L. Featherstone, *LD* 5,794
Ms H. Jago, *Green* 1,214
Ms R. Miller, *Ref.* 808
P. Sikorski, *Soc. Lab.* 586
Lab. majority 20,499
(April 1992, Lab. maj. 5,177)

HORSHAM
*E.*75,432   *T.*75.78%
Rt. Hon. F. Maude, *C.* 29,015
Mrs M. Millson, *LD* 14,153
Ms M. Walsh, *Lab.* 10,691
R. Grant, *Ref.* 2,281

H. Miller, *UK Ind.* 819
M. Corbould, *FEP* 206
C. majority 14,862
(Boundary change: notional C.)

**HOUGHTON AND WASHINGTON
EAST**
*E.*67,343   *T.*62.10%
F. Kemp, *Lab.* 31,946
P. Booth, *C.* 5,391
K. Miller, *LD* 3,209
J. Joseph, *Ref.* 1,277
Lab. majority 26,555
(Boundary change: notional Lab.)

HOVE
*E.*69,016   *T.*69.72%
I. Caplin, *Lab.* 21,458
R. Guy, *C.* 17,499
T. Pearce, *LD* 4,645
S. Field, *Ref.* 1,931
J. Furness, *Ind. C.* 1,735
P. Mulligan, *Green* 644
J. Vause, *UK Ind.* 209
Lab. majority 3,959
(April 1992, C. maj. 12,268)

HUDDERSFIELD
*E.*65,824   *T.*67.69%
*B. Sheerman, *Lab. Co-op.* 25,171
W. Forrow, *C.* 9,323
G. Beever, *LD* 7,642
P. McNulty, *Ref.* 1,480
J. Phillips, *Green* 938
Lab. Co-op. majority 15,848
(April 1992, *Lab. majority* 7,258)

HULL EAST
*E.*68,733   *T.*58.90%
*Rt. Hon. J. Prescott, *Lab.* 28,870
A. West, *C.* 5,552
J. Wastling, *LD* 3,965
G. Rogers, *Ref.* 1,788
Ms M. Nolan, *ProLife* 190
D. Whitley, *NLP* 121
Lab. majority 23,318
(April 1992, Lab. maj. 18,719)

HULL NORTH
*E.*68,106   *T.*56.96%
*K. McNamara, *Lab.* 25,542
D. Lee, *C.* 5,837
D. Nolan, *LD* 5,667
A. Scott, *Ref.* 1,533
T. Brotheridge, *NLP* 215
Lab. majority 19,705
(April 1992, Lab. maj. 15,384)

HULL WEST AND HESSLE
*E.*65,840   *T.*58.25%
A. Johnson, *Lab.* 22,520
R. Tress, *LD* 6,995
C. Moore, *C.* 6,933
R. Bate, *Ref.* 1,596
B. Franklin, *NLP* 310
Lab. majority 15,525
(Boundary change: notional Lab.)

HUNTINGDON
*E.*76,094   *T.*74.86%
†Rt. Hon. J. Major, *C.* 31,501
J. Reece, *Lab.* 13,361
M. Owen, *LD* 8,390

D. Bellamy, *Ref.* 3,114
C. Coyne, *UK Ind.* 331
Ms V. Hufford, *Ch. D.* 177
D. Robertson, *Ind.* 89
C. majority 18,140
(Boundary change: notional C.)

HYNDBURN
*E.*66,806   *T.*72.26%
†G. Pope, *Lab.* 26,831
P. Britcliffe, *C.* 15,383
L. Jones, *LD* 4,141
P. Congdon, *Ref.* 1,627
J. Brown, *IAC* 290
Lab. majority 11,448
(Boundary change: notional Lab.)

ILFORD NORTH
*E.*68,218   *T.*71.60%
Ms L. Perham, *Lab.* 23,135
†V. Bendall, *C.* 19,911
A. Dean, *LD* 5,049
P. Wilson, *BNP* 750
Lab. majority 3,224
(Boundary change: notional C.)

ILFORD SOUTH
*E.*72,104   *T.*69.37%
†M. Gapes, *Lab. Co-op.* 29,273
Sir N. Thorne, *C.* 15,073
Ms A. Khan, *LD* 3,152
D. Hodges, *Ref.* 1,073
B. Ramsey, *Soc. Lab.* 868
A. Owens, *BNP* 580
Lab. Co-op. majority 14,200
(Boundary change: notional C.)

IPSWICH
*E.*66,947   *T.*72.24%
†J. Cann, *Lab.* 25,484
S. Castle, *C.* 15,045
N. Roberts, *LD* 5,881
T. Agnew, *Ref.* 1,637
W. Vinyard, *UK Ind.* 208
E. Kaplan, *NLP* 107
Lab. majority 10,439
(Boundary change: notional Lab.)

ISLE OF WIGHT
*E.*101,680   *T.*71.95%
Dr P. Brand, *LD* 31,274
A. Turner, *C.* 24,868
Ms D. Gardiner, *Lab.* 9,646
T. Bristow, *Ref.* 4,734
M. Turner, *UK Ind.* 1,072
H. Rees, *Ind. Is.* 848
P. Scivier, *Green* 544
C. Daly, *NLP* 87
J. Eveleigh, *Rain. Is.* 86
LD majority 6,406
(April 1992, C. maj. 1,827)

ISLINGTON NORTH
*E.*57,385   *T.*62.49%
*J. Corbyn, *Lab.* 24,834
J. Kempton, *LD* 4,879
S. Fawthrop, *C.* 4,631
C. Ashby, *Green* 1,516
Lab. majority 19,955
(April 1992, Lab. maj. 12,784)

ISLINGTON SOUTH AND FINSBURY
*E.*55,468   *T.*63.67%
†C. Smith, *Lab.* 22,079
Ms S. Ludford, *LD* 7,516
D. Berens, *C.* 4,587
Miss J. Bryett, *Ref.* 741
A. Laws, *ACA* 171
M. Creese, *NLP* 121
E. Basarik, *Ind.* 101
Lab. majority 14,563
(Boundary change: notional Lab.)

JARROW
*E.*63,828   *T.*68.84%
S. Hepburn, *Lab.* 28,497
M. Allatt, *C.* 6,564
T. Stone, *LD* 4,865
A. LeBlond, *Ind. Lab.* 2,538
P. Mailer, *Ref.* 1,034
J. Bissett, *SPGB* 444
Lab. majority 21,933
(Boundary change: notional Lab.)

KEIGHLEY
*E.*67,231   *T.*76.57%
Mrs A. Cryer, *Lab.* 26,039
*G. Waller, *C.* 18,907
M. Doyle, *LD* 5,064
C. Carpenter, *Ref.* 1,470
Lab. majority 7,132
(April 1992, C. maj. 3,596)

KENSINGTON AND CHELSEA
*E.*67,786   *T.*54.71%
Rt. Hon. A. Clark, *C.* 19,887
R. Atkinson, *Lab.* 10,368
R. Woodthorpe Browne, *LD* 5,668
Ms A. Ellis-Jones, *UK Ind.* 540
E. Bear, *Teddy* 218
G. Oliver, *UKPP* 176
Ms S. Hamza, *NLP* 122
P. Sullivan, *Dream* 65
P. Parliament, *Heart* 44
C. majority 9,519
(Boundary change: notional C.)

KETTERING
*E.*75,153   *T.*75.79%
P. Sawford, *Lab.* 24,650
†Rt. Hon. R. Freeman, *C.* 24,461
R. Aron, *LD* 6,098
A. Smith, *Ref.* 1,551
Mrs R. le Carpentier, *NLP* 197
Lab. majority 189
(Boundary change: notional C.)

KINGSTON AND SURBITON
*E.*73,879   *T.*75.35%
E. Davey, *LD* 20,411
†R. Tracey, *C.* 20,355
Ms S. Griffin, *Lab.* 12,811
Mrs G. Tchiprout, *Ref.* 1,470
Ms P. Burns, *UK Ind.* 418
C. Port, *Dream* 100
M. Leighton, *NLP* 100
LD majority 56
(Boundary change: notional C.)

KINGSWOOD
*E.*77,026   *T.*77.75%
†Dr R. Berry, *Lab.* 32,181
J. Howard, *C.* 17,928
Mrs J. Pinkerton, *LD* 7,672

Ms A. Reather, *Ref.* 1,463
P. Hart, *BNP* 290
A. Harding, *NLP* 238
A. Nicolson, *Scrapit* 115
Lab. majority 14,253
(Boundary change: notional C.)

KNOWSLEY NORTH AND SEFTON
EAST
*E.*70,918 *T.*70.09%
†G. Howarth, *Lab.* 34,747
C. Doran, *C.* 8,600
D. Bamber, *LD* 5,499
C. Jones, *Soc. Lab.* 857
Lab. majority 26,147
(Boundary change: notional Lab.)

KNOWSLEY SOUTH
*E.*70,532 *T.*67.47%
†E. O'Hara, *Lab.* 36,695
G. Robertson, *C.* 5,987
C. Mainey, *LD* 3,954
A. Wright, *Ref.* 954
Lab. majority 30,708
(Boundary change: notional Lab.)

LANCASHIRE WEST
*E.*73,175 *T.*74.79%
†C. Pickthall, *Lab.* 33,022
C. Varley, *C.* 15,903
A. Wood, *LD* 3,938
M. Carter, *Ref.* 1,025
J. Collins, *NLP* 449
D. Hill, *Home Rule* 392
Lab. majority 17,119
(Boundary change: notional Lab.)

LANCASTER AND WYRE
*E.*78,168 *T.*75.30%
H. Dawson, *Lab.* 25,173
†K. Mans, *C.* 23,878
J. Humberstone, *LD* 6,802
Mrs V. Ivell, *Ref.* 1,516
J. Barry, *Green* 795
Dr J. Whittaker, *UK Ind.* 698
Lab. majority 1,295
(Boundary change: notional C.)

LEEDS CENTRAL
*E.*67,664 *T.*54.70%
†D. Fatchett, *Lab.* 25,766
E. Wild, *C.* 5,077
D. Freeman, *LD* 4,164
P. Myers, *Ref.* 1,042
D. Rix, *Soc. Lab.* 656
C. Hill, *Soc.* 304
Lab. majority 20,689
(Boundary change: notional Lab.)

LEEDS EAST
*E.*56,963 *T.*62.83%
*G. Mudie, *Lab.* 24,151
J. Emsley, *C.* 6,685
Mrs M. Kirk, *LD* 3,689
L. Parish, *Ref.* 1,267
Lab. majority 17,466
(April 1992, Lab. maj. 12,697)

LEEDS NORTH EAST
*E.*63,185 *T.*72.03%
F. Hamilton, *Lab.* 22,368
*T. Kirkhope, *C.* 15,409
Dr W. Winlow, *LD* 6,318

I. Rose, *Ref.* 946
Ms J. Egan, *Soc. Lab.* 468
Lab. majority 6,959
(April 1992, C. maj. 4,244)

LEEDS NORTH WEST
*E.*69,972 *T.*70.57%
H. Best, *Lab.* 19,694
*Dr K. Hampson, *C.* 15,850
Mrs B. Pearce, *LD* 11,689
S. Emmett, *Ref.* 1,325
R. Lamb, *Soc. Lab.* 335
R. Toone, *ProLife* 251
D. Duffy, *Ronnie* 232
Lab. majority 3,844
(April 1992, C. maj. 7,671)

LEEDS WEST
*E.*63,965 *T.*62.88%
*J. Battle, *Lab.* 26,819
J. Whelan, *C.* 7,048
N. Amor, *LD* 3,622
W. Finley, *Ref.* 1,210
D. Blackburn, *Green* 896
N. Nowosielski, *Lib.* 625
Lab. majority 19,771
(April 1992, Lab. maj. 13,828)

LEICESTER EAST
*E.*64,012 *T.*69.37%
*K. Vaz, *Lab.* 29,083
S. Milton, *C.* 10,661
J. Matabudul, *LD* 3,105
P. Iwaniw, *Ref.* 1,015
S. Sidhu, *Soc. Lab.* 436
N. Slack, *Glow* 102
Lab. majority 18,422
(April 1992, Lab. maj. 11,316)

LEICESTER SOUTH
*E.*71,750 *T.*67.06%
*J. Marshall, *Lab.* 27,914
C. Heaton-Harris, *C.* 11,421
B. Coles, *LD* 6,654
J. Hancock, *Ref.* 1,184
J. Dooher, *Soc. Lab.* 634
K. Sills, *Nat. Dem.* 307
Lab. majority 16,493
(April 1992, Lab. maj. 9,440)

LEICESTER WEST
*E.*64,570 *T.*63.36%
Ms P. Hewitt, *Lab.* 22,580
R. Thomas, *C.* 9,716
M. Jones, *LD* 5,795
W. Shooter, *Ref.* 970
G. Forse, *Green* 586
D. Roberts, *Soc. Lab.* 452
Ms J. Nicholls, *Soc.* 327
A. Belshaw, *BNP* 302
C. Potter, *Nat. Dem.* 186
Lab. majority 12,864
(April 1992, Lab. maj. 3,978)

LEICESTERSHIRE NORTH WEST
*E.*65,069 *T.*79.95%
D. Taylor, *Lab.* 29,332
R. Goodwill, *C.* 16,113
S. Heptinstall, *LD* 4,492
M. Abney-Hastings, *Ref.* 2,088
Lab. majority 13,219
(Boundary change: notional C.)

LEIGH
*E.*69,908 *T.*65.69%
†L. Cunliffe, *Lab.* 31,652
E. Young, *C.* 7,156
P. Hough, *LD* 5,163
R. Constable, *Ref.* 1,949
Lab. majority 24,496
(Boundary change: notional Lab.)

LEOMINSTER
*E.*65,993 *T.*76.60%
†P. Temple-Morris, *C.* 22,888
T. James, *LD* 14,053
R. Westwood, *Lab.* 8,831
A. Parkin, *Ref.* 2,815
Ms F. Norman, *Green* 1,086
R. Chamings, *UK Ind.* 588
J. Haycock, *UK Ind.* 292
C. majority 8,835
(Boundary change: notional C.)

LEWES
*E.*64,340 *T.*76.42%
N. Baker, *LD* 21,250
†T. Rathbone, *C.* 19,950
Dr M. Patton, *Lab.* 5,232
Mrs L. Butler, *Ref.* 2,481
J. Harvey, *UK Ind.* 256
LD majority 1,300
(Boundary change: notional C.)

LEWISHAM DEPTFORD
*E.*58,141 *T.*57.87%
†Mrs J. Ruddock, *Lab.* 23,827
Mrs I. Kimm, *C.* 4,949
K. Appiah, *LD* 3,004
J. Mulrenan, *Soc. Lab.* 996
Ms S. Shepherd, *Ref.* 868
Lab. majority 18,878
(Boundary change: notional Lab.)

LEWISHAM EAST
*E.*56,333 *T.*66.41%
†Ms B. Prentice, *Lab.* 21,821
P. Hollobone, *C.* 9,694
D. Buxton, *LD* 4,178
S. Drury, *Ref.* 910
R. Croucher, *NF* 431
P. White, *Lib.* 277
Capt. Rizz, *Dream* 97
Lab. majority 12,127
(Boundary change: notional Lab.)

LEWISHAM WEST
*E.*58,659 *T.*64.00%
*J. Dowd, *Lab.* 23,273
Mrs C. Whelan, *C.* 8,936
Miss K. McGrath, *LD* 3,672
A. Leese, *Ref.* 1,098
N. Long, *Soc. Lab.* 398
Ms E. Oram, *Lib.* 167
Lab. majority 14,337
(April 1992, Lab. maj. 1,809)

LEYTON AND WANSTEAD
*E.*62,176 *T.*63.24%
†H. Cohen, *Lab.* 23,922
R. Vaudry, *C.* 8,736
C. Anglin, *LD* 5,920
S. Duffy, *ProLife* 488
A. Mian, *Ind.* 256
Lab. majority 15,186
(Boundary change: notional Lab.)

LICHFIELD
E.62,720   T.77.48%
†M. Fabricant, C.   20,853
Ms S. Woodward, Lab.   20,615
Dr P. Bennion, LD   5,473
G. Seward, Ref.   1,652
C. majority 238
(Boundary change: notional C.)

LINCOLN
E.65,485   T.71.08%
Ms G. Merron, Lab.   25,563
A. Brown, C.   14,433
Ms L. Gabriel, LD   5,048
J. Ivory, Ref.   1,329
A. Myers, NLP   175
Lab. majority 11,130
(Boundary change: notional Lab.)

LIVERPOOL GARSTON
E.66,755   T.65.14%
Ms M. Eagle, Lab.   26,667
Ms F. Clucas, LD   8,250
N. Gordon-Johnson, C.   6,819
F. Dunne, Ref.   833
G. Copeland, Lib.   666
J. Parsons, NLP   127
S. Nolan, SEP   120
Lab. majority 18,417
(Boundary change: notional Lab.)

LIVERPOOL RIVERSIDE
E.73,429   T.51.93%
Ms L. Ellman, Lab. Co-op.   26,858
Ms B. Fraenkel, LD   5,059
D. Sparrow, C.   3,635
Ms C. Wilson, Soc.   776
D. Green, Lib.   594
G. Skelly, Ref.   586
Ms H. Neilson, ProLife   277
D. Braid, MRAC   179
G. Gay, NLP   171
Lab. Co-op. majority 21,799
(Boundary change: notional Lab.
Co-op.)

LIVERPOOL WALTON
E.67,527   T.59.54%
*P. Kilfoyle, Lab.   31,516
R. Roberts, LD   4,478
M. Kotecha, C.   2,551
C. Grundy, Ref.   620
Ms L. Mahmood, Soc.   444
Ms H. Williams, Lib.   352
Ms V. Mearns, ProLife   246
Lab. majority 27,038
(April 1992, Lab. maj. 28,299)

LIVERPOOL WAVERTREE
E.73,063   T.62.85%
†Ms J. Kennedy, Lab.   29,592
R. Kemp, LD   9,891
C. Malthouse, C.   4,944
P. Worthington, Ref.   576
K. McCullough, Lib.   391
Ms R. Kingsley, ProLife   346
Ms C. Corkhill, WRP   178
Lab. majority 19,701
(Boundary change: notional Lab.)

LIVERPOOL WEST DERBY
E.68,682   T.61.38%
†R. Wareing, Lab.   30,002

S. Radford, Lib.   4,037
Ms A. Hines, LD   3,805
N. Morgan, C.   3,656
P. Forrest, Ref.   657
Lab. majority 25,965
(Boundary change: notional Lab.)

LOUGHBOROUGH
E.68,945   T.75.95%
A. Reed, Lab.   25,448
K. Andrew, C.   19,736
Ms D. Brass, LD   6,190
R. Gupta, Ref.   991
Lab. majority 5,712
(Boundary change: notional C.)

LOUTH AND HORNCASTLE
E.68,824   T.72.58%
†Sir P. Tapsell, C.   21,699
J. Hough, Lab.   14,799
Mrs F. Martin, LD   12,207
Ms R. Robinson, Green   1,248
C. majority 6,900
(Boundary change: notional C.)

LUDLOW
E.61,267   T.75.55%
†C. Gill, C.   19,633
I. Huffer, LD   13,724
Ms N. O'Kane, Lab.   11,745
T. Andrewes, Green   798
E. Freeman-Keel, UK Ind.   385
C. majority 5,909
(Boundary change: notional C.)

LUTON NORTH
E.64,618   T.73.25%
K. Hopkins, Lab.   25,860
D. Senior, C.   16,234
Mrs K. Newbound, LD   4,299
C. Brown, UK Ind.   689
A. Custance, NLP   250
Lab. majority 9,626
(Boundary change: notional C.)

LUTON SOUTH
E.68,395   T.70.45%
Ms M. Moran, Lab.   26,428
†Sir G. Bright, C.   _   15,109
K. Fitchett, LD   4,610
C. Jacobs, Ref.   1,205
C. Lawman, UK Ind.   390
M. Scheimann, Green   356
Ms C. Perrin, NLP   86
Lab. majority 11,319
(Boundary change: notional C.)

MACCLESFIELD
E.72,094   T.75.22%
†N. Winterton, C.   26,888
Ms J. Jackson, Lab.   18,234
M. Flynn, LD   9,075
C. majority 8,654
(Boundary change: notional C.)

MAIDENHEAD
E.67,302   T.75.61%
Mrs T. May, C.   25,344
A. Ketteringham, LD   13,363
Ms D. Robson, Lab.   9,205
C. Taverner, Ref.   1,638
D. Munkley, Lib.   896
N. Spiers, UK Ind.   277

K. Ardley, Glow   166
C. majority 11,981
(Boundary change: notional C.)

MAIDSTONE AND THE WEALD
E.72,466   T.73.98%
†Rt. Hon. Miss A. Widdecombe,
  C.   23,657
J. Morgan, Lab.   14,054
Mrs J. Nelson, LD   11,986
Ms S. Hopkins, Ref.   1,998
Ms M. Cleator, Soc. Lab.   979
Ms P. Kemp, Green   480
Mrs R. Owen, UK Ind.   339
J. Oldbury, NLP   115
C. majority 9,603
(Boundary change: notional C.)

MAKERFIELD
E.67,358   T.66.83%
†I. McCartney, Lab.   33,119
M. Winstanley, C.   6,942
B. Hubbard, LD   3,743
A. Seed, Ref.   1,210
Lab. majority 26,177
(Boundary change: notional Lab.)

MALDON AND CHELMSFORD EAST
E.66,184   T.76.13%
†J. Whittingdale, C.   24,524
K. Freeman, Lab.   14,485
G. Pooley, LD   9,758
L. Overy-Owen, UK Ind.   935
Ms E. Burgess, Green   685
C. majority 10,039
(Boundary change: notional C.)

MANCHESTER BLACKLEY
E.62,227   T.57.46%
G. Stringer, Lab.   25,042
S. Barclay, C.   5,454
S. Wheale, LD   3,937
P. Stanyer, Ref.   1,323
Lab. majority 19,588
(Boundary change: notional Lab.)

MANCHESTER CENTRAL
E.63,815   T.52.55%
†A. Lloyd, Lab.   23,803
Ms A. Firth, LD   4,121
S. McIlwaine, C.   3,964
F. Rafferty, Soc. Lab.   810
J. Maxwell, Ref.   742
T. Rigby, Comm L.   97
Lab. majority 19,682
(Boundary change: notional Lab.)

MANCHESTER GORTON
E.64,349   T.56.43%
†Rt. Hon. G. Kaufman, Lab.   23,704
Dr J. Pearcey, LD   6,362
G. Senior, C.   4,249
K. Hartley, Ref.   812
Dr S. Fitz-Gibbon, Green   683
T. Wongsam, Soc. Lab.   501
Lab. majority 17,342
(Boundary change: notional Lab.)

MANCHESTER WITHINGTON
E.66,116   T.66.59%
†K. Bradley, Lab.   27,103
J. Smith, C.   8,522
Dr Y. Zalzala, LD   6,000

M. Sheppard, *Ref.* 1,079
S. Caldwell, *ProLife* 614
Ms J. White, *Soc.* 376
S. Kingston, *Dream* 181
M. Gaskell, *NLP* 152
Lab. majority 18,581
(Boundary change: notional Lab.)

MANSFIELD
*E.*67,057   *T.*70.72%
*A. Meale, *Lab.* 30,556
T. Frost, *C.* 10,038
P. Smith, *LD* 5,244
W. Bogusz, *Ref.* 1,588
Lab. majority 20,518
(April 1992, Lab. maj. 11,724)

MEDWAY
*E.*61,736   *T.*72.47%
R. Marshall-Andrews, *Lab.* 21,858
*Dame P. Fenner, *C.* 16,504
R. Roberts, *LD* 4,555
J. Main, *Ref.* 1,420
Mrs S. Radlett, *UK Ind.* 405
Lab. majority 5,354
(April 1992, C. maj. 8,786)

MERIDEN
*E.*76,287   *T.*71.73%
Mrs C. Spelman, *C.* 22,997
B. Seymour-Smith, *Lab.* 22,415
A. Dupont, *LD* 7,098
P. Gilbert, *Ref.* 2,208
C. majority 582
(April 1992, C. maj. 14,699)

MIDDLESBROUGH
*E.*70,931   *T.*64.99%
†S. Bell, *Lab.* 32,925
L. Benham, *C.* 7,907
Miss A. Charlesworth, *LD* 3,934
R. Edwards, *Ref.* 1,331
Lab. majority 25,018
(Boundary change: notional Lab.)

MIDDLESBROUGH SOUTH AND
CLEVELAND EAST
*E.*70,481   *T.*76.03%
Dr A. Kumar, *Lab.* 29,319
†M. Bates, *C.* 18,712
H. Garrett, *LD* 4,004
R. Batchelor, *Ref.* 1,552
Lab. majority 10,607
(Boundary change: notional C.)

MILTON KEYNES NORTH EAST
*E.*70,395   *T.*72.78%
B. White, *Lab.* 20,201
†P. Butler, *C.* 19,961
G. Mabbutt, *LD* 8,907
M. Phillips, *Ref.* 1,492
A. Francis, *Green* 576
M. Simson, *NLP* 99
Lab. majority 240
(Boundary change: notional C.)

MILTON KEYNES SOUTH WEST
*E.*71,070 · *T.*71.42%
Mrs P. Starkey, *Lab.* 27,298
*B. Legg, *C.* 17,006
P. Jones, *LD* 6,065
H. Kelly, *NLP* 389

Lab. majority 10,292
(April 1992, C. maj. 4,687)

MITCHAM AND MORDEN
*E.*65,385   *T.*73.33%
Ms S. McDonagh, *Lab.* 27,984
*Rt. Hon. Dame A. Rumbold, *C.*
14,243
N. Harris, *LD* 3,632
P. Isaacs, *Ref.* 810
Ms L. Miller, *BNP* 521
T. Walsh, *Green* 415
K. Vasan, *Ind.* 144
J. Barrett, *UK Ind.* 117
N. Dixon, *ACC* 80
Lab. majority 13,741
(April 1992, C. maj. 1,734)

MOLE VALLEY
*E.*69,140   *T.*78.86%
†P. Beresford, *C.* 26,178
S. Cooksey, *LD* 15,957
C. Payne, *Lab.* 8,057
N. Taber, *Ref.* 2,424
R. Burley, *Ind. CRP* 1,276
Capt. I. Cameron, *UK Ind.* 435
Ms J. Thomas, *NLP* 197
C. majority 10,221
(Boundary change: notional C.)

MORECAMBE AND LUNESDALE
*E.*68,013   *T.*72.41%
Ms G. Smith, *Lab.* 24,061
†Sir M. Lennox-Boyd, *C.* 18,096
Mrs J. Greenwell, *LD* 5,614
I. Ogilvie, *Ref.* 1,313
D. Walne, *NLP* 165
Lab. majority 5,965
(Boundary change: notional C.)

MORLEY AND ROTHWELL
*E.*68,385   *T.*67.12%
†J. Gunnell, *Lab.* 26,836
A. Barraclough, *C.* 12,086
M. Galdas, *LD* 5,087
D. Mitchell-Innes, *Ref.* 1,359
R. Wood, *BNP* 381
Ms P. Sammon, *ProLife* 148
Lab. majority 14,750
(Boundary change: notional Lab.)

NEW FOREST EAST
*E.*65,717   *T.*74.64%
Dr J. Lewis, *C.* 21,053
G. Dawson, *LD* 15,838
A. Goodfellow, *Lab.* 12,161
C. majority 5,215
(Boundary change: notional C.)

NEW FOREST WEST
*E.*66,522   *T.*74.79%
D. Swayne, *C.* 25,149
R. Hale, *LD* 13,817
D. Griffiths, *Lab.* 7,092
Mrs M. Elliott, *Ref.* 2,150
M. Holmes, *UK Ind.* 1,542
C. majority 11,332
(Boundary change: notional C.)

NEWARK
*E.*69,763   *T.*74.50%
Ms F. Jones, *Lab.* 23,496
*R. Alexander, *C.* 20,480

P. Harris, *LD* 5,960
G. Creedy, *Ref.* 2,035
Lab. majority 3,016
(April 1992, C. maj. 8,229)

NEWBURY
*E.*73,680   *T.*76.65%
†D. Rendel, *LD* 29,887
R. Benyon, *C.* 21,370
P. Hannon, *Lab.* 3,107
E. Snook, *Ref.* 992
Ms R. Stark, *Green* 644
R. Tubb, *UK Ind.* 302
Ms K. Howse, *Soc. Lab.* 174
LD majority 8,517
(Boundary change: notional C.)

NEWCASTLE-UNDER-LYME
*E.*66,686   *T.*73.67%
*Mrs L. Golding, *Lab.* 27,743
M. Hayes, *C.* 10,537
Dr R. Studd, *LD* 6,858
Ms K. Suttle, *Ref.* 1,510
S. Mountford, *Lib.* 1,399
Ms B. Bell, *Soc. Lab.* 1,082
Lab. majority 17,206
(April 1992, Lab. maj. 9,839)

NEWCASTLE UPON TYNE CENTRAL
*E.*69,781   *T.*66.05%
†J. Cousins, *Lab.* 27,272
B. Newmark, *C.* 10,792
Ms R. Berry, *LD* 6,911
C. Coxon, *Ref.* 1,113
Lab. majority 16,480
(Boundary change: notional Lab.)

NEWCASTLE UPON TYNE EAST AND
WALLSEND
*E.*63,272   *T.*65.73%
†N. Brown, *Lab.* 29,607
J. Middleton, *C.* 5,796
G. Morgan, *LD* 4,415
P. Cossins, *Ref.* 966
Ms B. Carpenter, *Soc. Lab.* 642
M. Levy, *Comm. P.* 163
Lab. majority 23,811
(Boundary change: notional Lab.)

NEWCASTLE UPON TYNE NORTH
*E.*65,357   *T.*69.20%
*D. Henderson, *Lab.* 28,125
G. White, *C.* 8,793
P. Allen, *LD* 6,578
Mrs D. Chipchase, *Ref.* 1,733
Lab. majority 19,332
(April 1992, Lab. maj. 8,946)

NORFOLK MID
*E.*75,311   *T.*76.29%
K. Simpson, *C.* 22,739
D. Zeichner, *Lab.* 21,403
Mrs S. Frary, *LD* 8,617
N. Holder, *Ref.* 3,229
A. Park, *Green* 1,254
B. Parker, *NLP* 215
C. majority 1,336
(Boundary change: notional C.)

NORFOLK NORTH
*E.*77,113   *T.*76.27%
D. Prior, *C.* 21,456
N. Lamb, *LD* 20,163

M. Cullingham, *Lab.*   14,736
J. Allen, *Ref.*   2,458
C. majority 1,293
(April 1992, C. maj. 12,545)

NORFOLK NORTH WEST
*E.*77,083   *T.*74.72%
Dr G. Turner, *Lab.*   25,250
*H. Bellingham, *C.*   23,911
Ms E. Knowles, *LD*   5,513
R. Percival, *Ref.*   2,923
Lab. majority 1,339
(April 1992, C. maj. 11,564)

NORFOLK SOUTH
*E.*79,239   *T.*78.37%
†Rt. Hon. J. MacGregor, *C.*   24,935
Mrs B. Hacker, *LD*   17,557
Ms J. Ross, *Lab.*   16,188
Mrs P. Bateson, *Ref.*   2,533
Mrs S. Ross-Wagenknecht, *Green* 484
A. Boddy, *UK Ind.*   400
C. majority 7,378
(Boundary change: notional C.)

NORFOLK SOUTH WEST
*E.*80,236   *T.*73.28%
†Rt. Hon. Mrs G. Shephard, *C.*   24,694
A. Heffernan, *Lab.*   22,230
D. Buckton, *LD*   8,178
R. Hoare, *Ref.*   3,694
C. majority 2,464
(Boundary change: notional C.)

NORMANTON
*E.*62,980   *T.*68.28%
†W. O'Brien, *Lab.*   26,046
Miss F. Bulmer, *C.*   10,153
D. Ridgway, *LD*   5,347
K. Shuttleworth, *Ref.*   1,458
Lab. majority 15,893
(Boundary change: notional Lab.)

NORTHAMPTON NORTH
*E.*73,664   *T.*70.18%
Ms S. Keeble, *Lab.*   27,247
†A. Marlow, *C.*   17,247
Ms L. Dunbar, *LD*   6,579
D. Torbica, *UK Ind.*   464
B. Spivack, *NLP*   161
Lab. majority 10,000
(Boundary change: notional C.)

NORTHAMPTON SOUTH
*E.*79,384   *T.*71.94%
A. Clarke, *Lab.*   24,214
†Rt. Hon. M. Morris, *C.*   23,470
A. Worgan, *LD*   6,316
C. Petrie, *Ref.*   1,405
D. Clark, *UK Ind.*   1,159
G. Woollcombe, *NLP*   541
Lab. majority 744
(Boundary change: notional C.)

NORTHAVON
*E.*78,943   *T.*79.21%
Prof. S. Webb, *LD*   26,500
†Rt. Hon. Sir J. Cope, *C.*   24,363
R. Stone, *Lab.*   9,767
J. Parfitt, *Ref.*   1,900
LD majority 2,137
(Boundary change: notional C.)

NORWICH NORTH
*E.*72,521   *T.*75.92%
Dr I. Gibson, *Lab.*   27,346
Dr R. Kinghorn, *C.*   17,876
P. Young, *LD*   6,951
A. Bailey-Smith, *Ref.*   1,777
H. Marks, *LCP*   512
J. Hood, *Soc. Lab.*   495
Mrs D. Mills, *NLP*   100
Lab. majority 9,470
(Boundary change: notional C.)

NORWICH SOUTH
*E.*70,009   *T.*72.56%
C. Clarke, *Lab.*   26,267
B. Khanbhai, *C.*   12,028
A. Aalders-Dunthorne, *LD*   9,457
Dr D. Holdsworth, *Ref.*   1,464
H. Marks, *LCP*   765
A. Holmes, *Green*   736
B. Parsons, *NLP*   84
Lab. majority 14,239
(Boundary change: notional Lab.)

NOTTINGHAM EAST
*E.*65,581   *T.*60.60%
*J. Heppell, *Lab.*   24,755
A. Raca, *C.*   9,336
K. Mulloy, *LD*   4,008
B. Brown, *Ref.*   1,645
Lab. majority 15,419
(April 1992, Lab. maj. 7,680)

NOTTINGHAM NORTH
*E.*65,698   *T.*63.02%
*G. Allen, *Lab.*   27,203
Ms G. Shaw, *C.*   8,402
Ms R. Oliver, *LD*   3,301
J. Neal, *Ref.*   1,858
A. Belfield, *Soc.*   637
Lab. majority 18,801
(April 1992, Lab. maj. 10,743)

NOTTINGHAM SOUTH
*E.*72,418   *T.*67.00%
*A. Simpson, *Lab.*   26,825
B. Kirsch, *C.*   13,461
G. Long, *LD*   6,265
K. Thompson, *Ref.*   1,523
Ms S. Edwards, *Nat. Dem.*   446
Lab. majority 13,364
(April 1992, Lab. maj. 3,181)

NUNEATON
*E.*72,032   *T.*74.29%
*W. Olner, *Lab.*   30,080
R. Blunt, *C.*   16,540
R. Cockings, *LD*   4,732
R. English, *Ref.*   1,533
D. Bray, *Loc. Ind.*   390
P. Everitt, *UK Ind.*   238
Lab. majority 13,540
(April 1992, Lab. maj. 1,631)

OLD BEXLEY AND SIDCUP
*E.*68,044   *T.*75.53%
†Rt. Hon. Sir E. Heath, *C.*   21,608
R. Justham, *Lab.*   18,039
I. King, *LD*   8,284
B. Reading, *Ref.*   2,457
C. Bullen, *UK Ind.*   489

Ms V. Tyndall, *BNP*   415
R. Stephens, *NLP*   99
C. majority 3,569
(Boundary change: notional C.)

OLDHAM EAST AND SADDLEWORTH
*E.*73,189   *T.*73.92%
P. Woolas, *Lab.*   22,546
†C. Davies, *LD*   19,157
J. Hudson, *C.*   10,666
D. Findlay, *Ref.*   1,116
J. Smith, *Soc. Lab.*   470
I. Dalling, *NLP*   146
Lab. majority 3,389
(Boundary change: notional C.)

OLDHAM WEST AND ROYTON
*E.*69,203   *T.*66.09%
†M. Meacher, *Lab.*   26,894
J. Lord, *C.*   10,693
H. Cohen, *LD*   5,434
G. Choudhury, *Soc. Lab.*   1,311
P. Etherden, *Ref.*   1,157
Mrs S. Dalling, *NLP*   249
Lab. majority 16,201
(Boundary change: notional Lab.)

ORPINGTON
*E.*78,749   *T.*76.40%
†J. Horam, *C.*   24,417
C. Maines, *LD*   21,465
Ms S. Polydorou, *Lab.*   10,753
D. Clark, *Ref.*   2,316
J. Carver, *UK Ind.*   526
R. Almond, *Lib.*   494
N. Wilton, *ProLife*   191
C. majority 2,952
(Boundary change: notional C.)

OXFORD EAST
*E.*69,339   *T.*69.05%
†A. Smith, *Lab.*   27,205
J. Djanogly, *C.*   10,540
G. Kershaw, *LD*   7,038
M. Young, *Ref.*   1,391
C. Simmons, *Green*   975
W. Harper-Jones, *Embryo*   318
Dr P. Gardner, *UK Ind.*   234
J. Thompson, *NLP*   108
P. Mylvaganam, *Anti-maj.*   68
Lab. majority 16,665
(Boundary change: notional Lab.)

OXFORD WEST AND ABINGDON
*E.*79,329   *T.*77.14%
Dr E. Harris, *LD*   26,268
L. Harris, *C.*   19,983
Ms S. Brown, *Lab.*   12,361
Mrs G. Eustace, *Ref.*   1,258
Dr M. Woodin, *Green*   691
R. Buckton, *UK Ind.*   258
Mrs L. Hodge, *ProLife*   238
Ms A.-M. Wilson, *NLP*   91
J. Rose, *LGR*   48
LD majority 6,285
(Boundary change: notional C.)

PENDLE
*E.*63,049   *T.*74.60%
*G. Prentice, *Lab.*   25,059
J. Midgeley, *C.*   14,235
A. Greaves, *LD*   5,460

D. Hockney, *Ref.* 2,281
Lab. majority 10,824
(April 1992, Lab. maj. 2,113)

PENRITH AND THE BORDER
*E.*66,496   *T.*73.63%
†Rt. Hon. D. Maclean, *C.* 23,300
G. Walker, *LD* 13,067
Mrs M. Meling, *Lab.* 10,576
C. Pope, *Ref.* 2,018
C. majority 10,233
(Boundary change: notional C.)

PETERBOROUGH
*E.*65,926   *T.*73.46%
Ms H. Brinton, *Lab.* 24,365
Mrs J. Foster, *C.* 17,042
D. Howarth, *LD* 5,170
P. Slater, *Ref.* 924
C. Brettell, *NLP* 334
J. Linskey, *UK Ind.* 317
S. Goldspink, *ProLife* 275
Lab. majority 7,323
(Boundary change: notional C.)

PLYMOUTH DEVONPORT
*E.*74,483   *T.*69.76%
†D. Jamieson, *Lab.* 31,629
A. Johnson, *C.* 12,562
R. Copus, *LD* 5,570
C. Norsworthy, *Ref.* 1,486
Mrs C. Farrand, *UK Ind.* 478
S. Ebbs, *Nat. Dem.* 238
Lab. majority 19,067
(Boundary change: notional Lab.)

PLYMOUTH SUTTON
*E.*70,666   *T.*67.43%
Mrs L. Gilroy, *Lab. Co-op.* 23,881
A. Crisp, *C.* 14,441
S. Melia, *LD* 6,613
T. Hanbury, *Ref.* 1,654
R. Bullock, *UK Ind.* 499
K. Kelway, *Plymouth* 396
F. Lyons, *NLP* 168
Lab. Co-op. majority 9,440
(Boundary change: notional C.)

PONTEFRACT AND CASTLEFORD
*E.*62,350   *T.*66.39%
Ms Y. Cooper, *Lab.* 31,339
A. Flook, *C.* 5,614
W. Paxton, *LD* 3,042
R. Wood, *Ref.* 1,401
Lab. majority 25,725
(April 1992, Lab. maj. 23,495)

POOLE
*E.*66,078   *T.*70.84%
R. Syms, *C.* 19,726
A. Tetlow, *LD* 14,428
H. White, *Lab.* 10,100
J. Riddington, *Ref.* 1,932
P. Tyler, *UK Ind.* 487
Mrs J. Rosta, *NLP* 137
C. majority 5,298
(Boundary change: notional C.)

POPLAR AND CANNING TOWN
*E.*67,172   *T.*58.46%
J. Fitzpatrick, *Lab.* 24,807
B. Steinberg, *C.* 5,892
Ms J. Ludlow, *LD* 4,072

J. Tyndall, *BNP* 2,849
I. Hare, *Ref.* 1,091
Ms J. Joseph, *Soc. Lab.* 557
Lab. majority 18,915
(Boundary change: notional Lab.)

PORTSMOUTH NORTH
*E.*64,539   *T.*70.14%
S. Rapson, *Lab.* 21,339
†P. Griffiths, *C.* 17,016
S. Sollitt, *LD* 4,788
S. Evelegh, *Ref.* 1,757
P. Coe, *UK Ind.* 298
C. Bex, *Wessex* 72
Lab. majority 4,323
(Boundary change: notional C.)

PORTSMOUTH SOUTH
*E.*80,514   *T.*64.21%
M. Hancock, *LD* 20,421
*D. Martin, *C.* 16,094
A. Burnett, *Lab.* 13,086
C. Trim, *Ref.* 1,629
J. Thompson, *Lib.* 184
Mrs J. Evans, *UK Ind.* 141
W. Treend, *NLP* 140
LD majority 4,327
(April 1992, C. maj. 242)

PRESTON
*E.*72,933   *T.*65.92%
†Mrs A. Wise, *Lab.* 29,220
P. Gray, *C.* 10,540
W. Chadwick, *LD* 7,045
J. C. Porter, *Ref.* 924
J. Ashforth, *NLP* 345
Lab. majority 18,680
(Boundary change: notional Lab.)

PUDSEY
*E.*70,922   *T.*74.35%
P. Truswell, *Lab.* 25,370
P. Bone, *C.* 19,163
Dr J. Brown, *LD* 7,375
D. Crabtree, *Ref.* 823
Lab. majority 6,207
(April 1992, C. maj. 8,972)

PUTNEY
*E.*60,176   *T.*73.11%
A. Colman, *Lab.* 20,084
*Rt. Hon. D. Mellor, *C.* 17,108
R. Pyne, *LD* 4,739
Sir J. Goldsmith, *Ref.* 1,518
W. Jamieson, *UK Ind.* 233
L. Beige, *Stan* 101
M. Yardley, *Spts All.* 90
J. Small, *NLP* 66
Ms A. Poole, *Beaut.* 49
D. Vanbraam, *Ren. Dem.* 7
Lab. majority 2,976
(April 1992, C. maj. 7,526)

RAYLEIGH
*E.*68,737   *T.*74.65%
†Dr M. Clark, *C.* 25,516
R. Ellis, *Lab.* 14,832
S. Cumberland, *LD* 10,137
A. Farmer, *Lib.* 829
C. majority 10,684
(Boundary change: notional C.)

READING EAST
*E.*71,586   *T.*70.15%
Ms J. Griffiths, *Lab.* 21,461
†J. Watts, *C.* 17,666
R. Samuel, *LD* 9,307
D. Harmer, *Ref.* 1,042
J. Buckley, *NLP* 254
Miss A. Thornton, *UK Ind.* 252
Ms B. Packer, *BNP* 238
Lab. majority 3,795
(Boundary change: notional C.)

READING WEST
*E.*69,073   *T.*70.05%
M. Salter, *Lab.* 21,841
N. Bennett, *C.* 18,844
Mrs D. Tomlin, *LD* 6,153
S. Brown, *Ref.* 976
I. Dell, *BNP* 320
D. Black, *UK Ind.* 255
Lab. majority 2,997
(Boundary change: notional C.)

REDCAR
*E.*68,965   *T.*70.99%
†Dr M. Mowlam, *Lab.* 32,972
A. Isaacs, *C.* 11,308
Ms J. Benbow, *LD* 4,679
Lab. majority 21,664
(Boundary change: notional Lab.)

REDDITCH
*E.*60,841   *T.*73.55%
Ms J. Smith, *Lab.* 22,280
Miss A. McIntyre, *C.* 16,155
M. Hall, *LD* 4,935
R. Cox, *Ref.* 1,151
P. Davis, *NLP* 227
Lab. majority 6,125
(Boundary change: notional C.)

REGENT'S PARK AND KENSINGTON
NORTH
*E.*73,752   *T.*64.19%
Ms K. Buck, *Lab.* 28,367
P. McGuinness, *C.* 13,710
Miss E. Gasson, *LD* 4,041
Ms S. Dangoor, *Ref.* 867
J. Hinde, *NLP* 192
Ms D. Sadowitz, *Dream* 167
Lab. majority 14,657
(Boundary change: notional Lab.)

REIGATE
*E.*64,750   *T.*74.40%
C. Blunt, *C.* 21,123
A. Howard, *Lab.* 13,382
P. Samuel, *LD* 9,615
†Sir G. Gardiner, *Ref.* 3,352
R. Higgs, *Ind.* 412
S. Smith, *UK Ind.* 290
C. majority 7,741
(Boundary change: notional C.)

RIBBLE SOUTH
*E.*71,670   *T.*77.06%
D. Borrow, *Lab.* 25,856
†Rt. Hon. R. Atkins, *C.* 20,772
T. Farron, *LD* 5,879
G. Adams, *Ref.* 1,475
N. Ashton, *Lib.* 1,127
Ms B. Leadbetter, *NLP* 122

Lab. majority 5,084
(Boundary change: notional C.)

RIBBLE VALLEY
E.72,664   *T*.78.75%
†N. Evans, *C.*   26,702
M. Carr, *LD*   20,062
M. Johnstone, *Lab.*   9,013
J. Parkinson, *Ref.*   1,297
Miss N. Holmes, *NLP*   147
C. majority 6,640
(Boundary change: notional C.)

RICHMOND (Yorks)
E.65,058   *T*.73.38%
†Rt. Hon. W. Hague, *C.*   23,326
S. Merritt, *Lab.*   13,275
Mrs J. Harvey, *LD*   8,773
A. Bentley, *Ref.*   2,367
C. majority 10,051
(Boundary change: notional C.)

RICHMOND PARK
E.71,572   *T*.79.43%
Dr J. Tonge, *LD*   25,393
†Rt. Hon. J. Hanley, *C.*   22,442
Ms S. Jenkins, *Lab.*   7,172
J. Pugh, *Ref.*   1,467
D. Beaupre, *Loony*   204
B. D'Arcy, *NLP*   102
P. Davies, *Dream*   73
LD majority 2,951
(Boundary change: notional C.)

ROCHDALE
E.68,529   *T*.70.16%
Ms L. Fitzsimons, *Lab.*   23,758
†Miss E. Lynne, *LD*   19,213
M. Turnberg, *C.*   4,237
G. Bergin, *BNP*   653
S. Mohammed, *IZB*   221
Lab. majority 4,545
(Boundary change: notional LD)

ROCHFORD AND SOUTHEND EAST
E.72,848   *T*.63.97%
†Sir E. Taylor, *C.*   22,683
N. Smith, *Lab.*   18,458
Ms P. Smith, *LD*   4,387
B. Lynch, *Lib.*   1,070
C. majority 4,225
(Boundary change: notional C.)

ROMFORD
E.59,611   *T*.70.66%
Mrs E. Gordon, *Lab.*   18,187
†Sir M. Neubert, *C.*   17,538
N. Meyer, *LD*   3,341
S. Ward, *Ref.*   1,431
T. Hurlstone, *Lib.*   1,100
M. Carey, *BNP*   522
Lab. majority 649
(Boundary change: notional C.)

ROMSEY
E.67,306   *T*.76.99%
†M. Colvin, *C.*   23,834
M. Cooper, *LD*   15,249
Ms J. Ford, *Lab.*   9,623
Dr A. Sked, *UK Ind.*   1,824
M. Wigley, *Ref.*   1,291
C. majority 8,585
(Boundary change: notional C.)

ROSSENDALE AND DARWEN
E.69,749   *T*.73.42%
†Mrs J. Anderson, *Lab.*   27,470
Mrs P. Buzzard, *C.*   16,521
B. Dunning, *LD*   5,435
R. Newstead, *Ref.*   1,108
A. Wearden, *BNP*   674
Lab. majority 10,949
(Boundary change: notional Lab.)

ROTHER VALLEY
E.68,622   *T*.67.26%
*K. Barron, *Lab.*   31,184
S. Stanbury, *C.*   7,699
S. Burgess, *LD*   5,342
S. Cook, *Ref.*   1,932
Lab. majority 23,485
(April 1992, Lab. maj. 17,222)

ROTHERHAM
E.59,895   *T*.62.86%
*D. MacShane, *Lab.*   26,852
S. Gordon, *C.*   5,383
D. Wildgoose, *LD*   3,919
R. Hollibone, *Ref.*   1,132
A. Neal, *ProLife*   364
Lab. majority 21,469
(April 1992, Lab. maj. 17,561)

RUGBY AND KENILWORTH
E.79,384   *T*.77.10%
A. King, *Lab.*   26,356
†J. Pawsey, *C.*   25,861
J. Roodhouse, *LD*   8,737
M. Twite, *NLP*   251
Lab. majority 495
(Boundary change: notional C.)

RUISLIP-NORTHWOOD
E.60,393   *T*.74.24%
†J. Wilkinson, *C.*   22,526
P. Barker, *Lab.*   14,732
C. Edwards, *LD*   7,279
Ms C. Griffin, *NLP*   296
C. majority 7,794
(Boundary change: notional C.)

RUNNYMEDE AND WEYBRIDGE
E.72,177   *T*.71.44%
P. Hammond, *C.*   25,051
I. Peacock, *Lab.*   15,176
G. Taylor, *LD*   8,397
P. Rolt, *Ref.*   2,150
S. Slater, *UK Ind.*   625
J. Sleeman, *NLP*   162
C. majority 9,875
(Boundary change: notional C.)

RUSHCLIFFE
E.78,735   *T*.78.89%
*Rt. Hon. K. Clarke, *C.*   27,558
Ms J. Pettit, *Lab.*   22,503
S. Boote, *LD*   8,851
Miss S. Chadd, *Ref.*   2,682
J. Moore, *UK Ind.*   403
Ms A. Maszwska, *NLP*   115
C. majority 5,055
(April 1992, C. maj. 19,766)

RUTLAND AND MELTON
E.70,150   *T*.75.02%
†A. Duncan, *C.*   24,107
J. Meads, *Lab.*   15,271

K. Lee, *LD*   10,112
R. King, *Ref.*   2,317
J. Abbott, *UK Ind.*   823
C. majority 8,836
(Boundary change: notional C.)

RYEDALE
E.65,215   *T*.74.80%
†J. Greenway, *C.*   21,351
J. Orrell, *LD*   16,293
Ms A. Hiles, *Lab.*   8,762
J. Mackfall, *Ref.*   1,460
S. Feaster, *UK Ind.*   917
C. majority 5,058
(Boundary change: notional C.)

SAFFRON WALDEN
E.74,097   *T*.76.99%
†Sir A. Haselhurst, *C.*   25,871
M. Caton, *LD*   15,298
M. Fincken, *Lab.*   12,275
R. Glover, *Ref.*   2,308
I. Evans, *UK Ind.*   658
B. Tyler, *Ind.*   486
C. Edwards, *NLP*   154
C. majority 10,573
(Boundary change: notional C.)

ST ALBANS
E.65,560   *T*.77.49%
K. Pollard, *Lab.*   21,338
D. Rutley, *C.*   16,879
A. Rowlands, *LD*   10,692
J. Warrilow, *Ref.*   1,619
Ms S. Craigen, *Dream*   166
I. Docker, *NLP*   111
Lab. majority 4,459
(Boundary change: notional C.)

ST HELENS NORTH
E.71,380   *T*.68.97%
D. Watts, *Lab.*   31,953
P. Walker, *C.*   8,536
J. Beirne, *LD*   6,270
D. Johnson, *Ref.*   1,276
R. Waugh, *Soc. Lab.*   832
R. Rudin, *UK Ind.*   363
Lab. majority 23,417
(April 1992, Lab. maj. 16,244)

ST HELENS SOUTH
E.66,526   *T*.66.53%
†G. Bermingham, *Lab.*   30,367
Ms M. Russell, *C.*   6,628
B. Spencer, *LD*   5,919
W. Holdaway, *Ref.*   1,165
Ms H. Jump, *NLP*   179
Lab. majority 23,739
(Boundary change: notional Lab.)

ST IVES
E.71,680   *T*.75.20%
A. George, *LD*   23,966
W. Rogers, *C.*   16,796
C. Fegan, *Lab.*   8,184
M. Faulkner, *Ref.*   3,714
Mrs P. Garnier, *UK Ind.*   567
G. Stephens, *Lib.*   425
K. Lippiatt, *R. Alt.*   178
W. Hitchins, *BHMBCM*   71
LD majority 7,170
(April 1992, C. maj. 1,645)

SALFORD
E.58,610   T.56.51%
Ms H. Blears, *Lab.*   22,848
E. Bishop, *C.*   5,779
N. Owen, *LD*   3,407
R. Cumpsty, *Ref.*   926
Ms S. Herman, *NLP*   162
Lab. majority 17,069
(Boundary change: notional Lab.)

SALISBURY
E.78,973   T.73.75%
*R. Key, *C.*   25,012
Ms Y. Emmerson-Peirce, *LD* 18,736
R. Rogers, *Lab.*   10,242
N. Farage, *UK Ind.*   3,332
H. Soutar, *Green*   623
W. Holmes, *Ind.*   184
Mrs S. Haysom, *NLP*   110
C. majority 6,276
(April 1992, C. maj. 8,973)

SCARBOROUGH AND WHITBY
E.75,862   T.71.61%
L. Quinn, *Lab.*   24,791
*J. Sykes, *C.*   19,667
M. Allinson, *LD*   7,672
Ms S. Murray, *Ref.*   2,191
Lab. majority 5,124
(April 1992, C. maj. 11,734)

SCUNTHORPE
E.60,393   T.68.84%
†E. Morley, *Lab.*   25,107
M. Fisher, *C.*   10,934
G. Smith, *LD*   3,497
P. Smith, *Ref.*   1,637
B. Hopper, *Soc. Lab.*   399
Lab. majority 14,173
(Boundary change: notional Lab.)

SEDGEFIELD
E.64,923   T.72.57%
†Rt. Hon. A. Blair, *Lab.*   33,526
Mrs E. Pitman, *C.*   8,383
R. Beadle, *LD*   3,050
Miss M. Hall, *Ref.*   1,683
B. Gibson, *Soc. Lab.*   474
Lab. majority 25,143
(Boundary change: notional Lab.)

SELBY
E.75,141   T.74.95%
J. Grogan, *Lab.*   25,838
K. Hind, *C.*   22,002
E. Batty, *LD*   6,778
D. Walker, *Ref.*   1,162
P. Spence, *UK Ind.*   536
Lab. majority 3,836
(Boundary change: notional C.)

SEVENOAKS
E.66,474   T.75.44%
M. Fallon, *C.*   22,776
J. Hayes, *Lab.*   12,315
R. Walshe, *LD*   12,086
N. Large, *Ref.*   2,138
Ms M. Lawrence, *Green*   443
M. Ellis, *PF*   244
A. Hankey, *NLP*   147
C. majority 10,461
(Boundary change: notional C.)

SHEFFIELD ATTERCLIFFE
E.68,548   T.64.65%
*C. Betts, *Lab.*   28,937
B. Doyle, *C.*   7,119
Mrs G. Smith, *LD*   6,973
J. Brown, *Ref.*   1,289
Lab. majority 21,818
(April 1992, Lab. maj. 15,480)

SHEFFIELD BRIGHTSIDE
E.58,930   T.57.47%
*D. Blunkett, *Lab.*   24,901
F. Butler, *LD*   4,947
C. Buckwell, *C.*   2,850
B. Farnsworth, *Ref.*   624
P. Davidson, *Soc. Lab.*   482
R. Scott, *NLP*   61
Lab. majority 19,954
(April 1992, Lab. maj. 22,681)

SHEFFIELD CENTRAL
E.68,667   T.53.04%
†R. Caborn, *Lab.*   23,179
A. Qadar, *LD*   6,273
M. Hess, *C.*   4,341
A. D'Agorne, *Green*   954
A. Brownlow, *Ref.*   863
K. Douglas, *Soc.*   466
Ms M. Aitken, *ProLife*   280
M. Driver, *WRP*   63
Lab. majority 16,906
(Boundary change: notional Lab.)

SHEFFIELD HALLAM
E.62,834   T.72.38%
R. Allan, *LD*   23,345
†Sir I. Patnick, *C.*   15,074
S. Conquest, *Lab.*   6,147
I. Davidson, *Ref.*   788
P. Booler, *SIP*   125
LD majority 8,271
(Boundary change: notional C.)

SHEFFIELD HEELEY
E.66,599   T.64.96%
*W. Michie, *Lab.*   26,274
R. Davison, *LD*   9,196
J. Harthman, *C.*   6,767
D. Mawson, *Ref.*   1,029
Lab. majority 17,078
(April 1992, Lab. maj. 14,954)

SHEFFIELD HILLSBOROUGH
E.74,642   T.71.04%
*Mrs H. Jackson, *Lab.*   30,150
A. Dunworth, *LD*   13,699
D. Nuttall, *C.*   7,707
J. Rusling, *Ref.*   1,468
Lab. majority 16,451
(April 1992, Lab. maj. 7,068)

SHERWOOD
E.74,788   T.75.59%
*P. Tipping, *Lab.*   33,071
R. Spencer, *C.*   16,259
B. Moult, *LD*   4,889
L. Slack, *Ref.*   1,882
P. Ballard, *BNP*   432
Lab. majority 16,812
(April 1992, Lab. maj. 2,910)

SHIPLEY
E.69,281   T.76.32%
C. Leslie, *Lab.*   22,962
*Rt. Hon. Sir M. Fox, *C.*   19,966
J. Cole, *LD*   7,984
Dr S. Ellams, *Ref.*   1,960
Lab. majority 2,996
(April 1992, C. maj. 12,382)

SHREWSBURY AND ATCHAM
E.73,542   T.75.25%
P. Marsden, *Lab.*   20,484
*D. Conway, *C.*   18,814
Mrs A. Woolland, *LD*   13,838
D. Barker, *Ref.*   1,346
D. Rowlands, *UK Ind.*   477
A. Dignan, *CFSS*   257
A. Williams, *PPP*   128
Lab. majority 1,670
(April 1992, C. maj. 10,965)

SHROPSHIRE NORTH
E.70,852   T.72.71%
O. Paterson, *C.*   20,730
I. Lucas, *Lab.*   18,535
J. Stevens, *LD*   10,489
D. Allen, *Ref.*   1,764
C. majority 2,195
(Boundary change: notional C.)

SITTINGBOURNE AND SHEPPEY
E.63,850   T.72.30%
D. Wyatt, *Lab.*   18,723
†Sir R. Moate, *C.*   16,794
R. Truelove, *LD*   8,447
P. Moull, *Ref.*   1,082
C. Driver, *Loony*   644
N. Risi, *UK Ind.*   472
Lab. majority 1,929
(Boundary change: notional C.)

SKIPTON AND RIPON
E.72,042   T.75.44%
†Rt. Hon. D. Curry, *C.*   25,294
T. Mould, *LD*   13,674
R. Marchant, *Lab.*   12,171
Mrs N. Holdsworth, *Ref.*   3,212
C. majority 11,620
(Boundary change: notional C.)

SLEAFORD AND NORTH HYKEHAM
E.71,486   T.74.39%
†Rt. Hon. D. Hogg, *C.*   23,358
S. Harriss, *Lab.*   18,235
J. Marriott, *LD*   8,063
P. Clery, *Ref.*   2,942
R. Overton, *Ind.*   578
C. majority 5,123
(Boundary change: notional C.)

SLOUGH
E.70,283   T.67.91%
Ms F. MacTaggart, *Lab.*   27,029
Mrs P. Buscombe, *C.*   13,958
C. Bushill, *LD*   3,509
Ms A. Bradshaw, *Lib.*   1,835
T. Sharkey, *Ref.*   1,124
P. Whitmore, *Slough*   277
Lab. majority 13,071
(Boundary change: notional Lab.)

SOLIHULL
E.78,898   T.74.66%
†J. Taylor, *C.*   26,299
M. Southcombe, *LD*   14,902
Ms R. Harris, *Lab.*   14,334
M. Nattrass, *Ref.*   2,748
J. Caffery, *ProLife*   623
C. majority 11,397
(Boundary change: notional C.)

SOMERTON AND FROME
E.73,988   T.77.58%
D. Heath, *LD*   22,684
†M. Robinson, *C.*   22,554
R. Ashford, *Lab.*   9,385
R. Rodwell, *Ref.*   2,449
R. Gadd, *UK Ind.*   331
LD majority 130
(Boundary change: notional C.)

SOUTHAMPTON ITCHEN
E.76,869   T.70.06%
†J. Denham, *Lab.*   29,498
P. Fleet, *C.*   15,289
D. Harrison, *LD*   6,289
J. Clegg, *Ref.*   1,660
K. Rose, *Soc. Lab.*   628
C. Hoar, *UK Ind.*   172
G. Marsh, *Soc.*   113
Ms R. Barry, *NLP*   110
F. McDermott, *ProLife*   99
Lab. majority 14,209
(Boundary change: notional Lab.)

SOUTHAMPTON TEST
E.72,983   T.71.85%
A. Whitehead, *Lab.*   28,396
†Sir J. Hill, *C.*   14,712
A. Dowden, *LD*   7,171
P. Day, *Ref.*   1,397
H. Marks, *LCP*   388
A. McCabe, *UK Ind.*   219
P. Taylor, *Glow*   81
J. Sinel, *NLP*   77
Lab. majority 13,684
(Boundary change: notional Lab.)

SOUTHEND WEST
E.66,493   T.69.95%
†D. Amess, *C.*   18,029
Mrs N. Stimson, *LD*   15,414
A. Harley, *Lab.*   10,600
C. Webster, *Ref.*   1,734
B. Lee, *UK Ind.*   636
P. Warburton, *NLP*   101
C. majority 2,615
(April 1992, C. maj. 11,902)

SOUTH HOLLAND AND THE
DEEPINGS
E.69,642   T.71.98%
J. Hayes, *C.*   24,691
J. Lewis, *Lab.*   16,700
P. Millen, *LD*   7,836
G. Erwood, *NPC*   902
C. majority 7,991
(Boundary change: notional C.)

SOUTHPORT
E.70,194   T.72.08%
R. Fearn, *LD*   24,346
*M. Banks, *C.*   18,186
Ms S. Norman, *Lab.*   6,125

F. Buckle, *Ref.*   1,368
Ms S. Ashton, *Lib.*   386
E. Lines, *NLP*   93
M. Middleton, *Nat. Dem.*   92
LD majority 6,160
(April 1992, C. maj. 3,063)

SOUTH SHIELDS
E.62,261   T.62.60%
†Dr D. Clark, *Lab.*   27,834
M. Hoban, *C.*   5,681
D. Ord, *LD*   3,429
A. Loraine, *Ref.*   1,660
I. Wilburn, *Shields*   374
Lab. majority 22,153
(Boundary change: notional Lab.)

SOUTHWARK NORTH AND
BERMONDSEY
E.65,598   T.62.19%
†S. Hughes, *LD*   19,831
J. Fraser, *Lab.*   16,444
G. Shapps, *C.*   2,835
M. Davidson, *BNP*   713
W. Newton, *Ref.*   545
I. Grant, *Comm L.*   175
J. Munday, *Lib.*   157
Ms I. Yngvison, *Nat. Dem.*   95
LD majority 3,387
(Boundary change: notional LD)

SPELTHORNE
E.70,562   T.73.58%
*D. Wilshire, *C.*   23,306
K. Dibble, *Lab.*   19,833
E. Glynn, *LD*   6,821
B. Coleman, *Ref.*   1,495
J. Fowler, *UK Ind.*   462
C. majority 3,473
(April 1992, C. maj. 19,843)

STAFFORD
E.67,555   T.76.64%
D. Kidney, *Lab.*   24,606
D. Cameron, *C.*   20,292
Mrs P. Hornby, *LD*   5,480
S. Culley, *Ref.*   1,146
A. May, *Loony*   248
Lab. majority 4,314
(Boundary change: notional C.)

STAFFORDSHIRE MOORLANDS
E.66,095   T.77.34%
Ms C. Atkins, *Lab.*   26,686
Dr A. Ashworth, *C.*   16,637
Mrs C. Jebb, *LD*   6,191
D. Stanworth, *Ref.*   1,603
Lab. majority 10,049
(Boundary change: notional Lab.)

STAFFORDSHIRE SOUTH
E.68,896   T.74.19%
†Sir P. Cormack, *C.*   25,568
Ms J. LeMaistre, *Lab.*   17,747
Mrs J. Calder, *LD*   5,797
P. Carnell, *Ref.*   2,002
C. majority 7,821
(Boundary change: notional C.)

STALYBRIDGE AND HYDE
E.65,468   T.65.80%
†T. Pendry, *Lab.*   25,363
N. de Bois, *C.*   10,557

M. Cross, *LD*   5,169
R. Clapham, *Ref.*   1,992
Lab. majority 14,806
(Boundary change: notional Lab.)

STEVENAGE
E.66,889   T.76.82%
Ms B. Follett, *Lab.*   28,440
†T. Wood, *C.*   16,858
A. Wilcock, *LD*   4,588
J. Coburn, *Ref.*   1,194
D. Bundy, *ProLife*   196
A. Calcraft, *NLP*   110
Lab. majority 11,582
(Boundary change: notional C.)

STOCKPORT
E.65,232   T.71.54%
†Ms A. Coffey, *Lab.*   29,338
S. Fitzsimmons, *C.*   10,426
Mrs S. Roberts, *LD*   4,951
W. Morley-Scott, *Ref.*   1,280
G. Southern, *Soc. Lab.*   255
C. Newitt, *Loony*   213
C. Dronfield, *Ind.*   206
Lab. majority 18,912
(Boundary change: notional Lab.)

STOCKTON NORTH
E.64,380   T.69.08%
†F. Cook, *Lab.*   29,726
B. Johnston, *C.*   8,369
Mrs S. Fletcher, *LD*   4,816
K. McConnell, *Ref.*   1,563
Lab. majority 21,357
(Boundary change: notional Lab.)

STOCKTON SOUTH
E.68,470   T.76.12%
Ms D. Taylor, *Lab.*   28,790
†T. Devlin, *C.*   17,205
P. Monck, *LD*   4,721
J. Horner, *Ref.*   1,400
Lab. majority 11,585
(Boundary change: notional C.)

STOKE-ON-TRENT CENTRAL
E.64,113   T.62.77%
*M. Fisher, *Lab.*   26,662
N. Jones, *C.*   6,738
E. Fordham, *LD*   4,809
P. Stanyer, *Ref.*   1,071
M. Coleman, *BNP*   606
Ms F. Oborski, *Lib.*   359
Lab. majority 19,924
(April 1992, Lab. maj. 13,420)

STOKE-ON-TRENT NORTH
E.59,030   T.65.50%
†Ms J. Walley, *Lab.*   25,190
C. Day, *C.*   7,798
H. Jebb, *LD*   4,141
Ms J. Tobin, *Ref.*   1,537
Lab. majority 17,392
(Boundary change: notional Lab.)

STOKE-ON-TRENT SOUTH
E.69,968   T.66.08%
*G. Stevenson, *Lab.*   28,645
Mrs S. Scott, *C.*   10,342
P. Barnett, *LD*   4,710
R. Adams, *Ref.*   1,103
Mrs A. Micklem, *Lib.*   580

S. Batkin, *BNP* 568
B. Lawrence, *Nat. Dem.* 288
Lab. majority 18,303
(April 1992, Lab. maj. 6,909)

STONE
*E.*68,242   *T.*77.77%
†W. Cash, *C.* 24,859
J. Wakefield, *Lab.* 21,041
B. Stamp, *LD* 6,392
Ms A. Winfield, *Lib.* 545
Ms D. Grice, *NLP* 237
C. majority 3,818
(Boundary change: notional C.)

STOURBRIDGE
*E.*64,966   *T.*76.50%
Ms D. Shipley, *Lab.* 23,452
†W. Hawksley, *C.* 17,807
C. Bramall, *LD* 7,123
P. Quick, *Ref.* 1,319
Lab. majority 5,645
(Boundary change: notional C.)

STRATFORD-ON-AVON
*E.*81,434   *T.*76.26%
J. Maples, *C.* 29,967
Dr S. Juned, *LD* 15,861
S. Stacey, *Lab.* 12,754
A. Hilton, *Ref.* 2,064
J. Spilsbury, *UK Ind.* 556
J. Brewster, *NLP* 307
S. Marcus, *SFDC* 306
Ms S. Miller, *ProLife* 284
C. majority 14,106
(Boundary change: notional C.)

STREATHAM
*E.*74,509   *T.*60.24%
†K. Hill, *Lab.* 28,181
E. Noad, *C.* 9,758
R. O'Brien, *LD* 6,082
J. Wall, *Ref.* 864
Lab. majority 18,423
(Boundary change: notional Lab.)

STRETFORD AND URMSTON
*E.*69,913   *T.*69.65%
Ms B. Hughes, *Lab.* 28,480
J. Gregory, *C.* 14,840
J. Bridges, *LD* 3,978
Ms C. Dore, *Ref.* 1,397
Lab. majority 13,640
(Boundary change: notional Lab.)

STROUD
*E.*77,494   *T.*80.45%
D. Drew, *Lab. Co-op.* 26,170
†R. Knapman, *C.* 23,260
P. Hodgkinson, *LD* 9,502
J. Marjoram, *Green* 3,415
Lab. Co-op. majority 2,910
(Boundary change: notional C.)

SUFFOLK CENTRAL AND IPSWICH
NORTH
*E.*70,222   *T.*75.22%
†M. Lord, *C.* 22,493
Ms C. Jones, *Lab.* 18,955
Dr M. Goldspink, *LD* 10,886
Ms S. Bennell, *Ind.* 489
C. majority 3,538
(Boundary change: notional C.)

SUFFOLK COASTAL
*E.*74,219   *T.*75.80%
†Rt. Hon. J. Gummer, *C.* 21,696
M. Campbell, *Lab.* 18,442
Ms A. Jones, *LD* 12,036
S. Caulfield, *Ref.* 3,416
A. Slade, *Green* 514
Ms F. Kaplan, *NLP* 152
C. majority 3,254
(Boundary change: notional C.)

SUFFOLK SOUTH
*E.*67,323   *T.*77.20%
†T. Yeo, *C.* 19,402
P. Bishop, *Lab.* 15,227
Mrs K. Pollard, *LD* 14,395
C. de Chair, *Ref.* 2,740
Mrs A. Holland, *NLP* 211
C. majority 4,175
(Boundary change: notional C.)

SUFFOLK WEST
*E.*68,638   *T.*71.51%
†R. Spring, *C.* 20,081
M. Jefferys, *Lab.* 18,214
A. Graves, *LD* 6,892
J. Carver, *Ref.* 3,724
A. Shearer, *NLP* 171
C. majority 1,867
(Boundary change: notional C.)

SUNDERLAND NORTH
*E.*64,711   *T.*59.05%
†W. Etherington, *Lab.* 26,067
A. Selous, *C.* 6,370
G. Pryke, *LD* 3,973
M. Nicholson, *Ref.* 1,394
K. Newby, *Loony* 409
Lab. majority 19,697
(Boundary change: notional Lab.)

SUNDERLAND SOUTH
*E.*67,937   *T.*58.77%
†C. Mullin, *Lab.* 27,174
T. Schofield, *C.* 7,536
J. Lennox, *LD* 4,606
M. Wilkinson, *UK Ind.* 609
Lab. majority 19,638
(Boundary change: notional Lab.)

SURREY EAST
*E.*72,852   *T.*75.02%
†P. Ainsworth, *C.* 27,389
Ms B. Ford, *LD* 12,296
D. Ross, *Lab.* 11,573
M. Sydney, *Ref.* 2,656
A. Stone, *UK Ind.* 569
Ms S. Bartrum, *NLP* 173
C. majority 15,093
(Boundary change: notional C.)

SURREY HEATH
*E.*73,813   *T.*74.14%
†N. Hawkins, *C.* 28,231
D. Newman, *LD* 11,944
Ms S. Jones, *Lab.* 11,511
J. Gale, *Ref.* 2,385
R. Squire, *UK Ind.* 653
C. majority 16,287
(Boundary change: notional C.)

SURREY SOUTH WEST
*E.*72,350   *T.*78.03%
*Rt. Hon. Mrs V. Bottomley, *C.*
25,165
N. Sherlock, *LD* 22,471
Ms M. Leicester, *Lab.* 5,333
Mrs J. Clementson, *Ref.* 2,830
J. Kirby, *UK Ind.* 401
Ms J. Quintavalle, *ProLife* 258
C. majority 2,694
(April 1992, C. maj. 14,975)

SUSSEX MID
*E.*68,784   *T.*77.73%
†N. Soames, *C.* 23,231
Mrs M. Collins, *LD* 16,377
M. Hamilton, *Lab.* 9,969
T. Large, *Ref.* 3,146
J. Barnett, *UK Ind.* 606
E. Tudway, *Ind. JRP* 134
C. majority 6,854
(Boundary change: notional C.)

SUTTON AND CHEAM
*E.*62,785   *T.*75.01%
P. Burstow, *LD* 19,919
*Lady O. Maitland, *C.* 17,822
M. Allison, *Lab.* 7,280
P. Atkinson, *Ref.* 1,784
S. McKie, *UK Ind.* 191
Ms D. Wright, *NLP* 96
LD majority 2,097
(April 1992, C. maj. 10,756)

SUTTON COLDFIELD
*E.*71,864   *T.*72.92%
*Rt. Hon. Sir N. Fowler, *C.* 27,373
A. York, *Lab.* 12,488
J. Whorwood, *LD* 10,139
D. Hope, *Ref.* 2,401
C. majority 14,885
(April 1992, C. maj. 26,036)

SWINDON NORTH
*E.*65,535   *T.*73.66%
M. Wills, *Lab.* 24,029
G. Opperman, *C.* 16,341
M. Evemy, *LD* 6,237
Ms G. Goldsmith, *Ref.* 1,533
A. Fiskin, *NLP* 130
Lab. majority 7,688
(Boundary change: notional Lab.)

SWINDON SOUTH
*E.*70,207   *T.*72.87%
Ms J. Drown, *Lab.* 23,943
†S. Coombs, *C.* 18,298
S. Pajak, *LD* 7,371
D. Mackintosh, *Ref.* 1,273
R. Charman, *Route 66* 181
K. Buscombe, *NLP* 96
Lab. majority 5,645
(Boundary change: notional C.)

TAMWORTH
*E.*67,205   *T.*74.18%
†B. Jenkins, *Lab.* 25,808
Lady A. Lightbown, *C.* 18,312
Mrs J. Pinkett, *LD* 4,025
Mrs D. Livesey, *Ref.* 1,163
C. Lamb, *UK Ind.* 369
Ms C. Twelvetrees, *Lib.* 177

Lab. majority 7,496
(Boundary change: notional C.)

TATTON
E.63,822   T.76.45%

M. Bell, *Ind.*	29,354
†N. Hamilton, *C.*	18,277
S. Hill, *Ind.*	295
S. Kinsey, *Ind.*	187
B. Penhaul, *Miss M.*	128
J. Muir, *Albion*	126
M. Kennedy, *NLP*	123
D. Bishop, *Byro*	116
R. Nicholas, *Ind.*	113
J. Price, *Juice*	73

Ind. majority 11,077
(Boundary change: notional C.)

TAUNTON
E.79,783   T.76.47%

Mrs J. Ballard, *LD*	26,064
*D. Nicholson, *C.*	23,621
Ms E. Lisgo, *Lab.*	8,248
B. Ahern, *Ref.*	2,760
L. Andrews, *BNP*	318

LD majority 2,443
(April 1992, C. maj. 3,336)

TEIGNBRIDGE
E.81,667   T.77.08%

†P. Nicholls, *C.*	24,679
R. Younger-Ross, *LD*	24,398
Ms S. Dann, *Lab.*	11,311
S. Stokes, *UK Ind.*	1,601
N. Banwell, *Green*	817
Mrs L. Golding, *Dream*	139

C. majority 281
(Boundary change: notional C.)

TELFORD
E.56,558   T.65.62%

†B. Grocott, *Lab.*	21,456
B. Gentry, *C.*	10,166
N. Green, *LD*	4,371
C. Morris, *Ref.*	1,119

Lab. majority 11,290
(Boundary change: notional Lab.)

TEWKESBURY
E.68,208   T.76.46%

L. Robertson, *C.*	23,859
J. Sewell, *LD*	14,625
K. Tustin, *Lab.*	13,665

C. majority 9,234
(Boundary change: notional C.)

THANET NORTH
E.71,112   T.68.84%

*R. Gale, *C.*	21,586
Ms I. Johnston, *Lab.*	18,820
P. Kendrick, *LD*	5,576
M. Chambers, *Ref.*	2,535
Ms J. Haines, *UK Ind.*	438

C. majority 2,766
(April 1992, C. maj. 18,210)

THANET SOUTH
E.62,792   T.71.65%

Dr S. Ladyman, *Lab.*	20,777
†Rt. Hon. J. Aitken, *C.*	17,899
Ms B. Hewett-Silk, *LD*	5,263
C. Crook, *UK Ind.*	631
D. Wheatley, *Green*	418

Lab. majority 2,878
(Boundary change: notional C.)

THURROCK
E.71,600   T.65.94%

*A. MacKinlay, *Lab.*	29,896
A. Rosindell, *C.*	12,640
J. White, *LD*	3,843
P. Compobassi, *UK Ind.*	833

Lab. majority 17,256
(April 1992, Lab. maj. 1,172)

TIVERTON AND HONITON
E.75,744   T.78.06%

†Mrs A. Browning, *C.*	24,438
Dr J. Barnard, *LD*	22,785
J. King, *Lab.*	7,598
S. Lowings, *Ref.*	2,952
Mrs J. Roach, *Lib.*	635
Ms E. McIvor, *Green*	485
D. Charles, *Nat. Dem.*	236

C. majority 1,653
(Boundary change: notional C.)

TONBRIDGE AND MALLING
E.64,798   T.75.97%

†Rt. Hon. Sir J. Stanley, *C.*	23,640
Mrs B. Withstandley, *Lab.*	13,410
K. Brown, *LD*	9,467
J. Scrivenor, *Ref.*	2,005
Mrs B. Bullen, *UK Ind.*	502
G. Valente, *NLP*	205

C. majority 10,230
(Boundary change: notional C.)

TOOTING
E.66,653   T.69.17%

*T. Cox, *Lab.*	27,516
J. Hutchings, *C.*	12,505
S. James, *LD*	4,320
Mrs A. Husband, *Ref.*	829
J. Rattray, *Green*	527
P. Boddington, *BFAIR*	161
J. Koene, *Rights*	94
D. Bailey-Bond, *Dream*	83
P. Miller, *NLP*	70

Lab. majority 15,011
(April 1992, Lab. maj. 4,107)

TORBAY
E.72,258   T.73.79%

A. Sanders, *LD*	21,094
*R. Allason, *C.*	21,082
M. Morey, *Lab.*	7,923
G. Booth, *UK Ind.*	1,962
B. Cowling, *Lib.*	1,161
P. Wild, *Dream*	100

LD majority 12
(April 1992, C. maj. 5,787)

TOTNES
E.70,473   T.76.30%

†Sir A. Steen, *C.*	19,637
R. Chave, *LD*	18,760
V. Ellery, *Lab.*	8,796
Ms P. Cook, *Ref.*	2,552
C. Venmore, *Loc. C.*	2,369
H. Thomas, *UK Ind.*	999
A. Pratt, *Green*	548
J. Golding, *Dream*	108

C. majority 877
(Boundary change: notional C.)

TOTTENHAM
E.66,173   T.56.98%

*B. Grant, *Lab.*	26,121
A. Scantlebury, *C.*	5,921
N. Hughes, *LD*	4,064
P. Budge, *Green*	1,059
Ms E. Tay, *ProLife*	210
C. Anglin, *WRP*	181
Ms T. Kent, *SEP*	148

Lab. majority 20,200
(April 1992, Lab. maj. 11,968)

TRURO AND ST AUSTELL
E.76,824   T.73.87%

*M. Taylor, *LD*	27,502
N. Badcock, *C.*	15,001
M. Dooley, *Lab.*	8,697
C. Hearn, *Ref.*	3,682
A. Haithwaite, *UK Ind.*	576
Mrs D. Robinson, *Green*	482
D. Hicks, *MK*	450
Mrs L. Yelland, *PP*	240
P. Boland, *NLP*	117

LD majority 12,501
(April 1992, LD maj. 7,570)

TUNBRIDGE WELLS
E.65,259   T.74.10%

A. Norman, *C.*	21,853
A. Clayton, *LD*	14,347
P. Warner, *Lab.*	9,879
T. Macpherson, *Ref.*	1,858
M. Anderson Smart, *UK Ind.*	264
P. Levy, *NLP*	153

C. majority 7,506
(Boundary change: notional C.)

TWICKENHAM
E.73,281   T.79.34%

Dr V. Cable, *LD*	26,237
†T. Jessel, *C.*	21,956
Ms E. Tutchell, *Lab.*	9,065
Miss J. Harrison, *Ind. ECR*	589
T. Haggar, *Dream*	155
A. Hardy, *NLP*	142

LD majority 4,281
(Boundary change: notional C.)

TYNE BRIDGE
E.61,058   T.57.08%

†D. Clelland, *Lab.*	26,767
A. Lee, *C.*	3,861
Mrs M. Wallace, *LD*	2,785
G. Oswald, *Ref.*	919
Ms E. Brunskill, *Soc.*	518

Lab. majority 22,906
(Boundary change: notional Lab.)

TYNEMOUTH
E.66,341   T.77.11%

A. Campbell, *Lab.*	28,318
M. Callanan, *C.*	17,045
A. Duffield, *LD*	4,509
C. Rook, *Ref.*	819
Dr F. Rogers, *UK Ind.*	462

Lab. majority 11,273
(Boundary change: notional C.)

TYNESIDE NORTH
E.66,449   T.67.90%

†S. Byers, *Lab.*	32,810
M. McIntyre, *C.*	6,167
T. Mulvenna, *LD*	4,762

M. Rollings, *Ref.*   1,382
Lab. majority 26,643
(Boundary change: notional Lab.)

UPMINSTER
*E.*57,149   *T.*72.30%
K. Darvill, *Lab.*   19,085
†Sir N. Bonsor, *C.*   16,315
Mrs P. Peskett, *LD*   3,919
T. Murray, *Ref.*   2,000
Lab. majority 2,770
(Boundary change: notional C.)

UXBRIDGE
*E.*57,497   *T.*72.26%
†Sir M. Shersby, *C.*   18,095
D. Williams, *Lab.*   17,371
Dr A. Malyan, *LD*   4,528
G. Aird, *Ref.*   1,153
Ms J. Leonard, *Soc.*   398
C. majority 724
(Boundary change: notional C.)
See also page 233

VALE OF YORK
*E.*70,077   *T.*76.01%
Miss A. McIntosh, *C.*   23,815
M. Carter, *Lab.*   14,094
C. Hall, *LD*   12,656
C. Fairclough, *Ref.*   2,503
A. Pelton, *Soc. Dem.*   197
C. majority 9,721
(Boundary change: notional C.)

VAUXHALL
*E.*70,402   *T.*55.49%
†Ms K. Hoey, *Lab.*   24,920
K. Kerr, *LD*   6,260
R. Bacon, *C.*   5,942
I. Driver, *Soc. Lab.*   983
S. Collins, *Green*   864
R. Headicar, *SPGB*   97
Lab. majority 18,660
(Boundary change: notional Lab.)

WAKEFIELD
*E.*73,210   *T.*68.96%
†D. Hinchliffe, *Lab.*   28,977
J. Peacock, *C.*   14,373
D. Dale, *LD*   5,656
S. Shires, *Ref.*   1,480
Lab. majority 14,604
(Boundary change: notional Lab.)

WALLASEY
*E.*63,714   *T.*73.52%
*Ms A. Eagle, *Lab.*   30,264
Mrs P. Wilcock, *C.*   11,190
P. Reisdorf, *LD*   3,899
R. Hayes, *Ref.*   1,490
Lab. majority 19,074
(April 1992, Lab. maj. 3,809)

WALSALL NORTH
*E.*67,587   *T.*64.07%
*D. Winnick, *Lab.*   24,517
M. Bird, *C.*   11,929
Ms T. O'Brien, *LD*   4,050
D. Bennett, *Ref.*   1,430
M. Pitt, *Ind.*   911
A. Humphries, *NF*   465
Lab. majority 12,588
(April 1992, Lab. maj. 3,824)

WALSALL SOUTH
*E.*64,221   *T.*67.33%
*B. George, *Lab.*   25,024
L. Leek, *C.*   13,712
H. Harris, *LD*   2,698
Dr T. Dent, *Ref.*   1,662
Mrs L. Meads, *NLP*   144
Lab. majority 11,312
(April 1992, Lab. maj. 3,178)

WALTHAMSTOW
*E.*63,818   *T.*62.76%
†N. Gerrard, *Lab.*   25,287
Mrs J. Andrew, *C.*   8,138
Dr J. Jackson, *LD*   5,491
Revd G. Hargreaves, *Ref.*   1,139
Lab. majority 17,149
(Boundary change: notional Lab.)

WANSBECK
*E.*62,998   *T.*71.70%
D. Murphy, *Lab.*   29,569
A. Thompson, *LD*   7,202
P. Green, *C.*   6,299
P. Gompertz, *Ref.*   1,146
Dr N. Best, *Green*   956
Lab. majority 22,367
(April 1992, Lab. maj. 18,174)

WANSDYKE
*E.*69,032   *T.*79.27%
D. Norris, *Lab.*   24,117
M. Prisk, *C.*   19,318
J. Manning, *LD*   9,205
K. Clinton, *Ref.*   1,327
T. Hunt, *UK Ind.*   438
P. House, *Loony*   225
Ms S. Lincoln, *NLP*   92
Lab. majority 4,799
(Boundary change: notional C.)

WANTAGE
*E.*71,657   *T.*78.23%
*R. Jackson, *C.*   22,311
Ms C. Wilson, *Lab.*   16,272
Ms J. Riley, *LD*   14,822
S. Rising, *Ref.*   1,549
Ms M. Kennet, *Green*   640
Count N. Tolstoy-Miloslausky,
    UK Ind.   465
C. majority 6,039
(April 1992, C. maj. 16,473)

WARLEY
*E.*59,758   *T.*65.08%
†J. Spellar, *Lab.*   24,813
C. Pincher, *C.*   9,362
J. Pursehouse, *LD*   3,777
K. Gamre, *Ref.*   941
Lab. majority 15,451
(Boundary change: notional Lab.)

WARRINGTON NORTH
*E.*72,694   *T.*70.50%
Ms H. Jones, *Lab.*   31,827
Ms R. Lacey, *C.*   12,300
I. Greenhalgh, *LD*   5,308
Dr A. Smith, *Ref.*   1,816
Lab. majority 19,527
(Boundary change: notional Lab.)

WARRINGTON SOUTH
*E.*72,262   *T.*76.23%
Ms H. Southworth, *Lab.*   28,721
C. Grayling, *C.*   17,914
P. Walker, *LD*   7,199
G. Kelly, *Ref.*   1,082
S. Ross, *NLP*   166
Lab. majority 10,807
(Boundary change: notional C.)

WARWICK AND LEAMINGTON
*E.*79,374   *T.*75.71%
J. Plaskitt, *Lab.*   26,747
†Sir D. Smith, *C.*   23,349
N. Hicks, *LD*   7,133
Mrs V. Davis, *Ref.*   1,484
P. Baptie, *Green*   764
G. Warwick, *UK Ind.*   306
M. Gibbs, *EDP*   183
R. McCarthy, *NLP*   125
Lab. majority 3,398
(Boundary change: notional C.)

WARWICKSHIRE NORTH
*E.*72,602   *T.*74.71%
†M. O'Brien, *Lab.*   31,669
S. Hammond, *C.*   16,902
W. Powell, *LD*   4,040
R. Mole, *Ref.*   917
C. Cooke, *UK Ind.*   533
I. Moorecroft, *Bert.*   178
Lab. majority 14,767
(Boundary change: notional Lab.)

WATFORD
*E.*74,015   *T.*74.63%
Ms C. Ward, *Lab.*   25,019
R. Gordon, *C.*   19,227
A. Canning, *LD*   9,272
Dr P. Roe, *Ref.*   1,484
L. Davis, *NLP*   234
Lab. majority 5,792
(Boundary change: notional C.)

WAVENEY
*E.*75,266   *T.*75.21%
R. Blizzard, *Lab.*   31,846
†D. Porter, *C.*   19,393
C. Thomas, *LD*   5,054
N. Clark, *Ind.*   318
Lab. majority 12,453
(Boundary change: notional C.)

WEALDEN
*E.*79,519   *T.*74.32%
†Rt. Hon. Sir G. Johnson Smith,
    C.   29,417
M. Skinner, *LD*   15,213
N. Levine, *Lab.*   10,185
B. Taplin, *Ref.*   3,527
Mrs M. English, *UK Ind.*   569
P. Cragg, *NLP*   188
C. majority 14,204
(Boundary change: notional C.)

WEAVER VALE
*E.*66,011   *T.*73.17%
†M. Hall, *Lab.*   27,244
J. Byrne, *C.*   13,796
T. Griffiths, *LD*   5,949
R. Cockfield, *Ref.*   1,312
Lab. majority 13,448
(Boundary change: notional Lab.)

WELLINGBOROUGH
*E.*74,955 *T.*75.10%
P. Stinchcombe, *Lab.* 24,854
*Sir P. Fry, *C.* 24,667
P. Smith, *LD* 5,279
A. Ellwood, *UK Ind.* 1,192
Ms A. Lowrys, *NLP* 297
Lab. majority 187
(April 1992, C. maj. 11,816)

WELLS
*E.*72,178 *T.*78.11%
*Rt. Hon. D. Heathcoat-Amory,
  C. 22,208
Dr P. Gold, *LD* 21,680
M. Eavis, *Lab.* 10,204
Mrs P. Phelps, *Ref.* 2,196
Ms L. Royse, *NLP* 92
C. majority 528
(April 1992, C. maj. 6,649)

WELWYN HATFIELD
*E.*67,395 *T.*78.59%
Ms M. Johnson, *Lab.* 24,936
†D. Evans, *C.* 19,341
R. Schwartz, *LD* 7,161
E. Cox, *RA* 1,263
Ms H. Harold, *ProLife* 267
Lab. majority 5,595
(Boundary change: notional C.)

WENTWORTH
*E.*63,951 *T.*65.33%
J. Healey, *Lab.* 30,225
K. Hamer, *C.* 6,266
J. Charters, *LD* 3,867
A. Battley, *Ref.* 1,423
Lab. majority 23,959
(April 1992, Lab. maj. 22,449)

WEST BROMWICH EAST
*E.*63,401 *T.*65.44%
†P. Snape, *Lab.* 23,710
B. Matsell, *C.* 10,126
M. Smith, *LD* 6,179
G. Mulley, *Ref.* 1,472
Lab. majority 13,584
(Boundary change: notional Lab.)

WEST BROMWICH WEST
*E.*67,496 *T.*54.37%
†Rt. Hon. Miss B. Boothroyd,
  Speaker 23,969
R. Silvester, *Lab. Change* 8,546
S. Edwards, *Nat. Dem.* 4,181
Speaker majority 15,423
(Boundary change: notional Lab.)

WESTBURY
*E.*74,301 *T.*76.38%
†D. Faber, *C.* 23,037
J. Miller, *LD* 16,969
K. Small, *Lab.* 11,969
G. Hawkins, *Lib.* 1,956
N. Hawkings-Byass, *Ref.* 1,909
R. Westbury, *UK Ind.* 771
C. Haysom, *NLP* 140
C. majority 6,068
(Boundary change: notional C.)

WEST HAM
*E.*57,058 *T.*58.99%
†A. Banks, *Lab.* 24,531

M. MacGregor, *C.* 5,037
Ms S. McDonough, *LD* 2,479
K. Francis, *BNP* 1,198
T. Jug, *Loony* 300
J. Rainbow, *Dream* 116
Lab. majority 19,494
(Boundary change: notional Lab.)

WESTMORLAND AND LONSDALE
*E.*68,389 *T.*74.29%
T. Collins, *C.* 21,470
S. Collins, *LD* 16,949
J. Harding, *Lab.* 10,459
M. Smith, *Ref.* 1,931
C. majority 4,521
(Boundary change: notional C.)

WESTON-SUPER-MARE
*E.*72,445 *T.*73.68%
B. Cotter, *LD* 21,407
Mrs M. Daly, *C.* 20,133
D. Kraft, *Lab.* 9,557
T. Sewell, *Ref.* 2,280
LD majority 1,274
(Boundary change: notional C.)

WIGAN
*E.*64,689 *T.*67.74%
†R. Stott, *Lab.* 30,043
M. Loveday, *C.* 7,400
T. Beswick, *LD* 4,390
A. Bradborne, *Ref.* 1,450
C. Maile, *Green* 442
W. Ayliffe, *NLP* 94
Lab. majority 22,643
(Boundary change: notional Lab.)

WILTSHIRE NORTH
*E.*77,237 *T.*75.11%
J. Gray, *C.* 25,390
S. Cordon, *LD* 21,915
N. Knowles, *Lab.* 8,261
Ms M. Purves, *Ref.* 1,774
A. Wood, *UK Ind.* 410
Ms J. Forsyth, *NLP* 263
C. majority 3,475
(Boundary change: notional C.)

WIMBLEDON
*E.*64,070 *T.*75.47%
R. Casale, *Lab.* 20,674
*Dr C. Goodson-Wickes, *C.* 17,694
Ms A. Willott, *LD* 8,014
H. Abid, *Ref.* 993
R. Thacker, *Green* 474
Ms S. Davies, *ProLife* 346
M. Kirby, *Mongolian* 112
G. Stacey, *Dream* 47
Lab. majority 2,980
(April 1992, C. maj. 14,761)

WINCHESTER
*E.*78,884 *T.*78.66%
M. Oaten, *LD* 26,100
†G. Malone, *C.* 26,098
P. Davies, *Lab.* 6,528
P. Strand, *Ref.* 1,598
R. Huggett, *Top* 640
D. Rumsey, *UK Ind.* 476
J. Browne, *Ind. AFE* 307
P. Stockton, *Loony* 307
LD majority 2
(Boundary change: notional C.)
See also page 233

WINDSOR
*E.*69,132 *T.*73.46%
†M. Trend, *C.* 24,476
C. Fox, *LD* 14,559
Mrs A. Williams, *Lab.* 9,287
J. McDermott, *Ref.* 1,676
P. Bradshaw, *Lib.* 388
Mrs E. Bigg, *UK Ind.* 302
Mr R. Parr, *Dynamic* 93
C. majority 9,917
(Boundary change: notional C.)

WIRRAL SOUTH
*E.*59,372 *T.*81.01%
†B. Chapman, *Lab.* 24,499
L. Byrom, *C.* 17,495
P. Gilchrist, *LD* 5,018
D. Wilcox, *Ref.* 768
Ms J. Nielsen, *ProLife* 264
G. Mead, *NLP* 51
Lab. majority 7,004
(Boundary change: notional C.)

WIRRAL WEST
*E.*60,908 *T.*76.98%
S. Hesford, *Lab.* 21,035
*Rt. Hon. D. Hunt, *C.* 18,297
J. Thornton, *LD* 5,945
D. Wharton, *Ref.* 1,613
Lab. majority 2,738
(April 1992, C. maj. 11,064)

WITNEY
*E.*73,520 *T.*76.72%
S. Woodward, *C.* 24,282
A. Hollingsworth, *Lab.* 17,254
Mrs A. Lawrence, *LD* 11,202
G. Brown, *Ref.* 2,262
M. Montgomery, *UK Ind.* 765
Ms S. Chapple-Perrie, *Green* 636
C. majority 7,028
(Boundary change: notional C.)

WOKING
*E.*70,053 *T.*72.68%
H. Malins, *C.* 19,553
P. Goldenberg, *LD* 13,875
Ms K. Hanson, *Lab.* 10,695
H. Bell, *Ind. C.* 3,933
C. Skeate, *Ref.* 2,209
M. Harvey, *UK Ind.* 512
Miss D. Sleeman, *NLP* 137
C. majority 5,678
(Boundary change: notional C.)

WOKINGHAM
*E.*66,161 *T.*75.74%
†Rt. Hon. J. Redwood, *C.* 25,086
Dr R. Longton, *LD* 15,721
Ms P. Colling, *Lab.* 8,424
P. Owen, *Loony* 877
C. majority 9,365
(Boundary change: notional C.)

WOLVERHAMPTON NORTH EAST
*E.*61,642 *T.*67.17%
K. Purchase, *Lab. Co-op.* 24,534
D. Harvey, *C.* 11,547
B. Niblett, *LD* 2,214
C. Hallmark, *Lib.* 1,560
A. Muchall, *Ref.* 1,192
M. Wingfield, *Nat. Dem.* 356
Lab. Co-op. majority 12,987

(Boundary change: notional Lab. Co-op.)

WOLVERHAMPTON SOUTH EAST
E.54,291   T.64.15%
*D. Turner, Lab. Co-op.	22,202
W. Hanbury, C.	7,020
R. Whitehouse, LD	3,292
T. Stevenson-Platt, Ref.	980
N. Worth, Soc. Lab.	689
K. Bullman, Lib.	647

Lab. Co-op. majority 15,182
(April 1992, Lab. maj. 10,240)

WOLVERHAMPTON SOUTH WEST
E.67,482   T.72.49%
Ms J. Jones, Lab.	24,657
*N. Budgen, C.	19,539
M. Green, LD	4,012
M. Hyde, Lib.	713

Lab. majority 5,118
(April 1992, C. maj. 4,966)

WOODSPRING
E.69,964   T.78.51%
†Dr L. Fox, C.	24,425
Mrs N. Kirsen, LD	16,691
Ms D. Sander, Lab.	11,377
R. Hughes, Ref.	1,614
Dr R. Lawson, Green	667
A. Glover, Ind.	101
M. Mears, NLP	52

C. majority 7,734
(Boundary change: notional C.)

WORCESTER
E.69,234   T.74.56%
M. Foster, Lab.	25,848
N. Bourne, C.	18,423
P. Chandler, LD	6,462
Mrs P. Wood, UK Ind.	886

Lab. majority 7,425
(Boundary change: notional C.)

WORCESTERSHIRE MID
E.68,381   T.74.32%
†P. Luff, C.	24,092
Mrs D. Smith, Lab.	14,680
D. Barwick, LD	9,458
T. Watson, Ref.	1,780
D. Ingles, UK Ind.	646
A. Dyer, NLP	163

C. majority 9,412
(Boundary change: notional C.)

WORCESTERSHIRE WEST
E.64,712   T.76.25%
†Sir M. Spicer, C.	22,223
M. Hadley, LD	18,377

N. Stone, Lab.	7,738
Ms S. Cameron, Green	1,006

C. majority 3,846
(Boundary change: notional C.)

WORKINGTON
E.65,766   T.75.08%
†D. Campbell-Savours, Lab.	31,717
R. Blunden, C.	12,061
P. Roberts, LD	3,967
G. Donnan, Ref.	1,412
C. Austin, UA	217

Lab. majority 19,656
(Boundary change: notional Lab.)

WORSLEY
E.68,978   T.67.82%
†T. Lewis, Lab.	29,083
D. Garrido, C.	11,342
R. Bleakley, LD	6,356

Lab. majority 17,741
(Boundary change: notional Lab.)

WORTHING EAST AND SHOREHAM
E.70,771   T.72.87%
T. Loughton, C.	20,864
M. King, LD	15,766
M. Williams, Lab.	12,335
J. McCulloch, Ref.	1,683
Mrs R. Jarvis, UK Ind.	921

C. majority 5,098
(Boundary change: notional C.)

WORTHING WEST
E.71,329   T.72.12%
†P. Bottomley, C.	23,733
C. Hare, LD	16,020
J. Adams, Lab.	8,347
N. John, Ref.	2,313
T. Cross, UK Ind.	1,029

C. majority 7,713
(Boundary change: notional C.)

WREKIN, THE
E.59,126   T.76.56%
P. Bradley, Lab.	21,243
P. Bruinvels, C.	18,218
I. Jenkins, LD	5,807

Lab. majority 3,025
(Boundary change: notional C.)

WYCOMBE
E.73,589   T.71.10%
†Sir R. Whitney, C.	20,890
C. Bryant, Lab.	18,520
P. Bensilum, LD	9,678
A. Fulford, Ref.	2,394
J. Laker, Green	716
M. Heath, NLP	121

C. majority 2,370
(Boundary change: notional C.)

WYRE FOREST
E.73,063   T.75.35%
D. Lock, Lab.	26,843
†A. Coombs, C.	19,897
D. Cropp, LD	4,377
W. Till, Ref.	1,956
C. Harvey, Lib.	1,670
J. Millington, UK Ind.	312

Lab. majority 6,946
(Boundary change: notional C.)

WYTHENSHAWE AND SALE EAST
E.71,986   T.63.25%
P. Goggins, Lab.	26,448
P. Fleming, C.	11,429
Ms V. Tucker, LD	5,639
B. Stanyer, Ref.	1,060
J. Flannery, Soc. Lab.	957

Lab. majority 15,019
(Boundary change: notional Lab.)

YEOVIL
E.74,165   T.72.88%
†Rt. Hon. J. D. D. Ashdown, LD	26,349
N. Cambrook, C.	14,946
P. Conway, Lab.	8,053
J. Beveridge, Ref.	3,574
D. Taylor, Green	728
J. Archer, Musician	306
C. Hudson, Dream	97

LD majority 11,403
(Boundary change: notional LD)

YORK, CITY OF
E.79,383   T.73.50%
*H. Bayley, Lab.	34,956
S. Mallett, C.	14,433
A. Waller, LD	6,537
J. Sheppard, Ref.	1,083
M. Hill, Green	880
E. Wegener, UK Ind.	319
A. Lightfoot, Ch. Nat.	137

Lab. majority 20,523
(April 1992, Lab. maj. 6,342)

YORKSHIRE EAST
E.69,409   T.70.55%
†J. Townend, C.	20,904
I. Male, Lab.	17,567
D. Leadley, LD	9,070
R. Allerston, Soc. Dem.	1,049
M. Cooper, Nat. Dem.	381

C. majority 3,337
(Boundary change: notional C.)

WALES

ABERAVON
E.50,025   T.71.89%
*Rt. Hon. J. Morris, Lab.	25,650
R. McConville, LD	4,079
P. Harper, C.	2,835
P. Cockwell, PC	2,088
P. David, Ref.	970
Capt. Beany, Beanus	341

Lab. majority 21,571
(April 1992, Lab. maj. 21,310)

ALYN AND DEESIDE
E.58,091   T.72.21%
†B. Jones, Lab.	25,955
T. Roberts, C.	9,552
Mrs E. Burnham, LD	4,076
M. Jones, Ref.	1,627

Mrs S. Hills, PC	738

Lab. majority 16,403
(Boundary change: notional Lab.)

BLAENAU GWENT
E.54,800   T.72.32%
*L. Smith, Lab.	31,493
Mrs G. Layton, LD	3,458
Mrs M. Williams, C.	2,607

J. Criddle, *PC* 2,072
Lab. majority 28,035
(April 1992, Lab. maj. 30,067)

BRECON AND RADNORSHIRE
*E.*52,142   *T.*82.24%
R. Livsey, *LD* 17,516
*J. Evans, *C.* 12,419
C. Mann, *Lab.* 11,424
Ms E. Phillips, *Ref.* 900
S. Cornelius, *PC* 622
LD majority 5,097
(April 1992, C. maj. 130)

BRIDGEND
*E.*59,721   *T.*72.44%
*W. Griffiths, *Lab.* 25,115
D. Davies, *C.* 9,867
A. McKinlay, *LD* 4,968
T. Greaves, *Ref.* 1,662
D. Watkins, *PC* 1,649
Lab. majority 15,248
(April 1992, Lab. maj. 7,326)

CAERNARFON
*E.*46,815   *T.*72.65%
*D. Wigley, *PC* 17,616
E. Williams, *Lab.* 9,667
E. Williams, *C.* 4,230
Ms M. McQueen, *LD* 1,686
C. Collins, *Ref.* 811
PC majority 7,949
(April 1992, PC maj. 14,476)

CAERPHILLY
*E.*64,621   *T.*70.05%
*R. Davies, *Lab.* 30,697
R. Harris, *C.* 4,858
L. Whittle, *PC* 4,383
A. Ferguson, *LD* 3,724
M. Morgan, *Ref.* 1,337
Mrs C. Williams, *ProLife* 270
Lab. majority 25,839
(April 1992, Lab. maj. 22,672)

CARDIFF CENTRAL
*E.*60,354   *T.*70.01%
*J. Owen Jones, *Lab. Co-op.* 18,464
Mrs J. Randerson, *LD* 10,541
D. Melding, *C.* 8,470
T. Burns, *Soc. Lab.* 2,230
W. Vernon, *PC* 1,504
N. Lloyd, *Ref.* 760
C. James, *Loony* 204
A. Hobbs, *NLP* 80
Lab. Co-op. majority 7,923
(April 1992, Lab. maj. 3,465)

CARDIFF NORTH
*E.*60,430   *T.*80.24%
Ms J. Morgan, *Lab.* 24,460
*G. Jones, *C.* 16,334
R. Rowland, *LD* 5,294
Dr C. Palfrey, *PC* 1,201
E. Litchfield, *Ref.* 1,199
Lab. majority 8,126
(April 1992, C. maj. 2,969)

CARDIFF SOUTH AND PENARTH
*E.*61,838   *T.*68.57%
*A. Michael, *Lab. Co-op.* 22,647
Mrs C. Roberts, *C.* 8,766
Dr S. Wakefield, *LD* 3,964

J. Foreman, *New Lab.* 3,942
D. Haswell, *PC* 1,356
P. Morgan, *Ref.* 1,211
M. Shepherd, *Soc.* 344
Ms B. Caves, *NLP* 170
Lab. Co-op. majority 13,881
(April 1992, Lab. maj. 10,425)

CARDIFF WEST
*E.*58,198   *T.*69.21%
†R. Morgan, *Lab.* 24,297
S. Hoare, *C.* 8,669
Ms J. Gasson, *LD* 4,366
Ms G. Carr, *PC* 1,949
T. Johns, *Ref.* 996
Lab. majority 15,628
(Boundary change: notional Lab.)

CARMARTHEN EAST AND DINEFWR
*E.*53,079   *T.*78.62%
†Dr A. Wynne Williams, *Lab.* 17,907
R. Thomas, *PC* 14,457
E. Hayward, *C.* 5,022
Mrs J. Hughes, *LD* 3,150
I. Humphreys-Evans, *Ref.* 1,196
Lab. majority 3,450
(Boundary change: notional Lab.)

CARMARTHEN WEST AND
PEMBROKESHIRE SOUTH
*E.*55,724   *T.*76.52%
†N. Ainger, *Lab.* 20,956
O. J. Williams, *C.* 11,335
R. Llewellyn, *PC* 5,402
K. Evans, *LD* 3,516
Mrs J. Poirrier, *Ref.* 1,432
Lab. majority 9,621
(Boundary change: notional Lab.)

CEREDIGION
*E.*54,378   *T.*73.90%
†C. Dafis, *PC* 16,728
R. Harris, *Lab.* 9,767
D. Davies, *LD* 6,616
Dr F. Aubel, *C.* 5,983
J. Leaney, *Ref.* 1,092
PC majority 6,961
(Boundary change: notional PC)

CLWYD SOUTH
*E.*53,495   *T.*73.62%
†M. Jones, *Lab.* 22,901
B. Johnson, *C.* 9,091
A. Chadwick, *LD* 3,684
G. Williams, *PC* 2,500
A. Lewis, *Ref.* 1,207
Lab. majority 13,810
(Boundary change: notional Lab.)

CLWYD WEST
*E.*53,467   *T.*75.29%
G. Thomas, *Lab.* 14,918
†R. Richards, *C.* 13,070
E. Williams, *PC* 5,421
G. Williams, *LD* 5,151
Ms H. Collins, *Ref.* 1,114
D. Neal, *Cvty* 583
Lab. majority 1,848
(Boundary change: notional C.)

CONWY
*E.*55,092   *T.*75.44%
Mrs B. Williams, *Lab.* 14,561

R. Roberts, *LD* 12,965
D. Jones, *C.* 10,085
R. Davies, *PC* 2,844
A. Barham, *Ref.* 760
R. Bradley, *Alt. LD* 250
D. Hughes, *NLP* 95
Lab. majority 1,596
(April 1992, C. maj. 995)

CYNON VALLEY
*E.*48,286   *T.*69.22%
*Mrs A. Clwyd, *Lab.* 23,307
A. Davies, *PC* 3,552
H. Price, *LD* 3,459
A. Smith, *C.* 2,262
G. John, *Ref.* 844
Lab. majority 19,755
(April 1992, Lab. maj. 21,364)

DELYN
*E.*53,693   *T.*74.02%
†D. Hanson, *Lab.* 22,300
Mrs K. Lumley, *C.* 10,607
P. Lloyd, *LD* 4,160
A. Drake, *PC* 1,558
Ms E. Soutter, *Ref.* 1,117
Lab. majority 11,693
(Boundary change: notional Lab.)

GOWER
*E.*57,691   *T.*75.12%
M. Caton, *Lab.* 23,313
A. Cairns, *C.* 10,306
H. Evans, *LD* 5,624
E. Williams, *PC* 2,226
R. Lewis, *Ref.* 1,745
A. Popham, *FP* 122
Lab. majority 13,007
(April 1992, Lab. maj. 7,018)

ISLWYN
*E.*50,540   *T.*72.03%
*D. Touhig, *Lab. Co-op.* 26,995
C. Worker, *LD* 3,064
R. Walters, *C.* 2,864
D. Jones, *PC* 2,272
Mrs S. Monaghan, *Ref.* 1,209
Lab. Co-op. majority 23,931
(April 1992, Lab. maj. 24,728)
(Feb. 1995, Lab. maj. 13,097)

LLANELLI
*E.*58,323   *T.*70.66%
†Rt. Hon. D. Davies, *Lab.* 23,851
M. Phillips, *PC* 7,812
A. Hayes, *C.* 5,003
N. Burree, *LD* 3,788
J. Willock, *Soc. Lab.* 757
Lab. majority 16,039
(Boundary change: notional Lab.)

MEIRIONNYDD NANT CONWY
*E.*32,345   *T.*75.98%
*E. Llwyd, *PC* 12,465
H. Rees, *Lab.* 5,660
J. Quin, *C.* 3,922
Mrs B. Feeley, *LD* 1,719
P. Hodge, *Ref.* 809
PC majority 6,805
(April 1992, PC maj. 4,613)

MERTHYR TYDFIL AND RHYMNEY
*E.*56,507   *T.*69.27%

*T. Rowlands, *Lab.* 30,012
D. Anstey, *LD* 2,926
J. Morgan, *C.* 2,508
A. Cox, *PC* 2,344
A. Cowdell, *Old Lab.* 691
R. Hutchings, *Ref.* 660
Lab. majority 27,086
(April 1992, Lab. maj. 26,713)

MONMOUTH
*£.*60,703 *T.*80.76%
H. Edwards, *Lab.* 23,404
*R. Evans, *C.* 19,226
M. Williams, *LD* 4,689
N. Warry, *Ref.* 1,190
A. Cotton, *PC* 516
Lab. majority 4,178
(April 1992, C. maj. 3,204)

MONTGOMERYSHIRE
*£.*42,618 *T.*74.91%
L. Opik, *LD* 14,647
G. Davies, *C.* 8,344
Ms A. Davies, *Lab.* 6,109
Ms H. M. Jones, *PC* 1,608
J. Bufton, *Ref.* 879
Ms S. Walker, *Green* 338
LD majority 6,303
(April 1992, LD maj. 5,209)

NEATH
*£.*55,525 *T.*74.28%
*P. Hain, *Lab.* 30,324
D. Evans, *C.* 3,583
T. Jones, *PC* 3,344
F. Little, *LD* 2,597
P. Morris, *Ref.* 975
H. Marks, *LCP* 420
Lab. majority 26,741
(April 1992, Lab. maj. 23,975)

NEWPORT EAST
*£.*50,997 *T.*73.06%
†A. Howarth, *Lab.* 21,481
D. Evans, *C.* 7,958
A. Cameron, *LD* 3,880
A. Scargill, *Soc. Lab.* 1,951
G. Davis, *Ref.* 1,267
C. Holland, *PC* 721
Lab. majority 13,523
(April 1992, Lab. maj. 9,899)

NEWPORT WEST
*£.*53,914 *T.*74.57%
*P. Flynn, *Lab.* 24,331
P. Clarke, *C.* 9,794
S. Wilson, *LD* 3,907
C. Thompsett, *Ref.* 1,199
H. Jackson, *PC* 648
H. Moelwyn Hughes, *UK Ind.* 323

Lab. majority 14,537
(April 1992, Lab. maj. 7,779)

OGMORE
*£.*52,078 *T.*73.10%
*Sir R. Powell, *Lab.* 28,163
D. Unwin, *C.* 3,716
Ms K. Williams, *LD* 3,510
J. Rogers, *PC* 2,679
Lab. majority 24,447
(April 1992, Lab. maj. 23,827)

PONTYPRIDD
*£.*64,185 *T.*71.44%
*Dr K. Howells, *Lab.* 29,290
N. Howells, *LD* 6,161
J. Cowen, *C.* 5,910
O. Llewelyn, *PC* 2,977
J. Wood, *Ref.* 874
P. Skelly, *Soc. Lab.* 380
R. Griffiths, *Comm. P.* 178
A. Moore, *NLP* 85
Lab. majority 23,129
(April 1992, Lab. maj. 19,797)

PRESELI PEMBROKESHIRE
*£.*54,088 *T.*78.40%
Mrs J. Lawrence, *Lab.* 20,477
R. Buckland, *C.* 11,741
J. Clarke, *LD* 5,527
A. Lloyd Jones, *PC* 2,683
D. Berry, *Ref.* 1,574
Ms M. Scott Cato, *Green* 401
Lab. majority 8,736
(Boundary change: notional C.)

RHONDDA
*£.*57,105 *T.*71.46%
*A. Rogers, *Lab.* 30,381
Ms L. Wood, *PC* 5,450
Dr R. Berman, *LD* 2,307
S. Whiting, *C.* 1,551
S. Gardiner, *Ref.* 658
K. Jakeway, *Green* 460
Lab. majority 24,931
(April 1992, Lab. maj. 28,816)

SWANSEA EAST
*£.*57,373 *T.*67.41%
*D. Anderson, *Lab.* 29,151
Ms C. Dibble, *C.* 3,582
E. Jones, *LD* 3,440
Ms M. Pooley, *PC* 1,308
Ms C. Maggs, *Ref.* 904
R. Job, *Soc.* 289
Lab. majority 25,569
(April 1992, Lab. maj. 23,482)

SWANSEA WEST
*£.*58,703 *T.*68.94%

*Rt. Hon. A. Williams, *Lab.* 22,748
A. Baker, *C.* 8,289
J. Newbury, *LD* 5,872
D. Lloyd, *PC* 2,675
D. Proctor, *Soc. Lab.* 885
Lab. majority 14,459
(April 1992, Lab. maj. 9,478)

TORFAEN
*£.*60,343 *T.*71.67%
*P. Murphy, *Lab.* 29,863
N. Parish, *C.* 5,327
Ms J. Gray, *LD* 5,249
Ms D. Holler, *Ref.* 1,245
R. Gough, *PC* 1,042
R. Coghill, *Green* 519
Lab. majority 24,536
(April 1992, Lab. maj. 20,754)

VALE OF CLWYD
*£.*52,418 *T.*74.65%
C. Ruane, *Lab.* 20,617
D. Edwards, *C.* 11,662
D. Munford, *LD* 3,425
Ms G. Kensler, *PC* 2,301
S. Vickers, *Ref.* 834
S. Cooke, *UK Ind.* 293
Lab. majority 8,955
(Boundary change: notional C.)

VALE OF GLAMORGAN
*£.*67,213 *T.*80.21%
J. Smith, *Lab.* 29,054
†W. Sweeney, *C.* 18,522
Mrs S. Campbell, *LD* 4,945
Ms M. Corp, *PC* 1,393
Lab. majority 10,532
(Boundary change: notional C.)

WREXHAM
*£.*50,741 *T.*71.78%
Dr J. Marek, *Lab.* 20,450
S. Andrew, *C.* 8,688
A. Thomas, *LD* 4,833
J. Cronk, *Ref.* 1,195
K. Plant, *PC* 1,170
N. Low, *NLP* 86
Lab. majority 11,762
(Boundary change: notional Lab.)

YNYS MÔN
*£.*52,952 *T.*75.41%
*I. Wyn Jones, *PC* 15,756
O. Edwards, *Lab.* 13,275
G. Owen, *C.* 8,569
D. Burnham, *LD* 1,537
H. Gray Morris, *Ref.* 793
PC majority 2,481
(April 1992, PC maj. 1,106)

SCOTLAND

ABERDEEN CENTRAL
*£.*54,257 *T.*65.64%
F. Doran, *Lab.* 17,745
Mrs J. Wisely, *C.* 6,944
B. Topping, *SNP* 5,767
J. Brown, *LD* 4,714
J. Farquharson, *Ref.* 446

Lab. majority 10,801
(Boundary change: notional Lab.)

ABERDEEN NORTH
*£.*54,302 *T.*70.74%
M. Savidge, *Lab.* 18,389
B. Adam, *SNP* 8,379
J. Gifford, *C.* 5,763

M. Rumbles, *LD* 5,421
A. Mackenzie, *Ref.* 463
Lab. majority 10,010
(Boundary change: notional Lab.)

ABERDEEN SOUTH
*£.*60,490 *T.*72.84%
Ms A. Begg, *Lab.* 15,541

N. Stephen, *LD*	12,176
†R. Robertson, *C.*	11,621
J. Towers, *SNP*	4,299
R. Wharton, *Ref.*	425
Lab. majority 3,365	
(Boundary change: notional C.)	

ABERDEENSHIRE WEST AND KINCARDINE
*E.*59,123   *T.*73.05%

Sir R. Smith, *LD*	17,742
†G. Kynoch, *C.*	15,080
Ms J. Mowatt, *SNP*	5,639
Ms Q. Khan, *Lab.*	3,923
S. Ball, *Ref.*	805
LD majority 2,662	
(Boundary change: notional C.)	

AIRDRIE AND SHOTTS
*E.*57,673   *T.*71.40%

†Mrs H. Liddell, *Lab.*	25,460
K. Robertson, *SNP*	10,048
Dr N. Brook, *C.*	3,660
R. Wolseley, *LD*	1,719
C. Semple, *Ref.*	294
Lab. majority 15,412	
(Boundary change: notional Lab.)	

ANGUS
*E.*59,708   *T.*72.14%

†A. Welsh, *SNP*	20,792
S. Leslie, *C.*	10,603
Ms C. Taylor, *Lab.*	6,733
Dr R. Speirs, *LD*	4,065
B. Taylor, *Ref.*	883
SNP majority 10,189	
(Boundary change: notional SNP)	

ARGYLL AND BUTE
*E.*49,451   *T.*72.23%

*Mrs R. Michie, *LD*	14,359
Prof. N. MacCormick, *SNP*	8,278
R. Leishman, *C.*	6,774
A. Syed, *Lab.*	5,596
M. Stewart, *Ref.*	713
LD majority 6,081	
(April 1992, LD maj. 2,622)	

AYR
*E.*55,829   *T.*80.17%

Mrs S. Osborne, *Lab.*	21,679
†P. Gallie, *C.*	15,136
I. Blackford, *SNP*	5,625
Miss C. Hamblen, *LD*	2,116
J. Enos, *Ref.*	200
Lab. majority 6,543	
(Boundary change: notional Lab.)	

BANFF AND BUCHAN
*E.*58,493   *T.*68.69%

†A. Salmond, *SNP*	22,409
W. Frain-Bell, *C.*	9,564
Ms M. Harris, *Lab.*	4,747
N. Fletcher, *LD*	2,398
A. Buchan, *Ref.*	1,060
SNP majority 12,845	
(Boundary change: notional SNP)	

CAITHNESS, SUTHERLAND AND EASTER ROSS
*E.*41,566   *T.*70.18%

†R. Maclennan, *LD*	10,381
J. Hendry, *Lab.*	8,122

E. Harper, *SNP*	6,710
T. Miers, *C.*	3,148
Ms C. Ryder, *Ref.*	369
J. Martin, *Green*	230
M. Carr, *UK Ind.*	212
LD majority 2,259	
(Boundary change: notional LD)	

CARRICK, CUMNOCK AND DOON VALLEY
*E.*65,593   *T.*74.96%

†G. Foulkes, *Lab. Co-op.*	29,398
A. Marshall, *C.*	8,336
Mrs C. Hutchison, *SNP*	8,190
D. Young, *LD*	2,613
J. Higgins, *Ref.*	634
Lab. Co-op. majority 21,062	
(Boundary change: notional Lab. Co-op.)	

CLYDEBANK AND MILNGAVIE
*E.*52,092   *T.*75.03%

†A. Worthington, *Lab.*	21,583
J. Yuill, *SNP*	8,263
Ms N. Morgan, *C.*	4,885
K. Moody, *LD*	4,086
I. Sanderson, *Ref.*	269
Lab. majority 13,320	
(Boundary change: notional Lab.)	

CLYDESDALE
*E.*63,428   *T.*71.60%

*J. Hood, *Lab.*	23,859
A. Doig, *SNP*	10,050
M. Izatt, *C.*	7,396
Mrs S. Grieve, *LD*	3,796
K. Smith, *BNP*	311
Lab. majority 13,809	
(April 1992, Lab. maj. 10,187)	

COATBRIDGE AND CHRYSTON
*E.*52,024   *T.*72.30%

†T. Clarke, *Lab.*	25,697
B. Nugent, *SNP*	6,402
A. Wauchope, *C.*	3,216
Mrs M. Daly, *LD*	2,048
B. Bowsley, *Ref.*	249
Lab. majority 19,295	
(Boundary change: notional Lab.)	

CUMBERNAULD AND KILSYTH
*E.*48,032   *T.*75.00%

Ms R. McKenna, *Lab.*	21,141
C. Barrie, *SNP*	10,013
I. Sewell, *C.*	2,441
J. Biggam, *LD*	1,368
Ms J Kara, *ProLife*	609
K. McEwan, *SSA*	345
Ms P. Cook, *Ref.*	107
Lab. majority 11,128	
(April 1992, Lab. maj. 9,215)	

CUNNINGHAME NORTH
*E.*55,526   *T.*74.07%

*B. Wilson, *Lab.*	20,686
Mrs M. Mitchell, *C.*	9,647
Ms K. Nicoll, *SNP*	7,584
Ms K. Freel, *LD*	2,271
Ms L. McDaid, *Soc. Lab.*	501
I. Winton, *Ref.*	440
Lab. majority 11,039	
(April 1992, Lab. maj. 2,939)	

CUNNINGHAME SOUTH
*E.*49,543   *T.*71.54%

*B. Donohoe, *Lab.*	22,233
Mrs M. Burgess, *SNP*	7,364
Mrs P. Paterson, *C.*	3,571
E. Watson, *LD*	1,604
K. Edwin, *Soc. Lab.*	494
A. Martlew, *Ref.*	178
Lab. majority 14,869	
(April 1992, Lab. maj. 10,680)	

DUMBARTON
*E.*56,229   *T.*73.39%

*J. McFall, *Lab. Co-op.*	20,470
W. Mackechnie, *SNP*	9,587
P. Ramsay, *C.*	7,283
A. Reid, *LD*	3,144
L. Robertson, *SSA*	283
G. Dempster, *Ref.*	255
D. Lancaster, *UK Ind.*	242
Lab. Co-op. majority 10,883	
(April 1992, Lab. maj. 6,129)	

DUMFRIES
*E.*62,759   *T.*78.92%

R. Brown, *Lab.*	23,528
S. Stevenson, *C.*	13,885
R. Higgins, *SNP*	5,977
N. Wallace, *LD*	5,487
D. Parker, *Ref.*	533
Ms E. Hunter, *NLP*	117
Lab. majority 9,643	
(Boundary change: notional C.)	

DUNDEE EAST
*E.*58,388   *T.*69.41%

†J. McAllion, *Lab.*	20,718
Ms S. Robison, *SNP*	10,757
B. Mackie, *C.*	6,397
Dr G. Saluja, *LD*	1,677
E. Galloway, *Ref.*	601
H. Duke, *SSA*	232
Ms E. MacKenzie, *NLP*	146
Lab. majority 9,961	
(Boundary change: notional Lab.)	

DUNDEE WEST
*E.*57,346   *T.*67.67%

†E. Ross, *Lab.*	20,875
J. Dorward, *SNP*	9,016
N. Powrie, *C.*	5,105
Dr E. Dick, *LD*	2,972
Ms M. Ward, *SSA*	428
J. MacMillan, *Ref.*	411
Lab. majority 11,859	
(Boundary change: notional Lab.)	

DUNFERMLINE EAST
*E.*52,072   *T.*70.25%

†Rt. Hon. G. Brown, *Lab.*	24,441
J. Ramage, *SNP*	5,690
I. Mitchell, *C.*	3,656
J. Tolson, *LD*	2,164
T. Dunsmore, *Ref.*	632
Lab. majority 18,751	
(Boundary change: notional Lab.)	

DUNFERMLINE WEST
*E.*52,467   *T.*69.44%

†Ms R. Squire, *Lab.*	19,338
J. Lloyd, *SNP*	6,984
Mrs E. Harris, *LD*	4,963
K. Newton, *C.*	4,606

J. Bain, *Ref.* 543
Lab. majority 12,354
(Boundary change: notional Lab.)

EAST KILBRIDE
*E.*65,229 *T.*74.81%
†A. Ingram, *Lab.* 27,584
G. Gebbie, *SNP* 10,200
C. Herbertson, *C.* 5,863
Mrs K. Philbrick, *LD* 3,527
J. Deighan, *ProLife* 1,170
Ms J. Gray, *Ref.* 306
E. Gilmour, *NLP* 146
Lab. majority 17,384
(Boundary change: notional Lab.)

EAST LOTHIAN
*E.*57,441 *T.*75.61%
†J. Home Robertson, *Lab.* 22,881
M. Fraser, *C.* 8,660
D. McCarthy, *SNP* 6,825
Ms A. MacAskill, *LD* 4,575
N. Nash, *Ref.* 491
Lab. majority 14,221
(Boundary change: notional Lab.)

EASTWOOD
*E.*66,697 *T.*78.32%
J. Murphy, *Lab.* 20,766
P. Cullen, *C.* 17,530
D. Yates, *SNP* 6,826
Dr C. Mason, *LD* 6,110
D. Miller, *Ref.* 497
Dr M. Tayan, *ProLife* 393
D. McPherson, *UK Ind.* 113
Lab. majority 3,236
(Boundary change: notional C.)

EDINBURGH CENTRAL
*E.*63,695 *T.*67.09%
†A. Darling, *Lab.* 20,125
M. Scott-Hayward, *C.* 9,055
Ms F. Hyslop, *SNP* 6,750
Ms K. Utting, *LD* 5,605
Ms L. Hendry, *Green* 607
A. Skinner, *Ref.* 495
M. Benson, *Ind. Dem.* 98
Lab. majority 11,070
(Boundary change: notional Lab.)

EDINBURGH EAST AND
MUSSELBURGH
*E.*59,648 *T.*70.61%
†Dr G. Strang, *Lab.* 22,564
D. White, *SNP* 8,034
K. Ward, *C.* 6,483
Dr C. MacKellar, *LD* 4,511
J. Sibbet, *Ref.* 526
Lab. majority 14,530
(Boundary change: notional Lab.)

EDINBURGH NORTH AND LEITH
*E.*61,617 *T.*66.45%
†M. Chisholm, *Lab.* 19,209
Ms A. Dana, *SNP* 8,231
E. Stewart, *C.* 7,312
Ms H. Campbell, *LD* 5,335
A. Graham, *Ref.* 441
G. Brown, *SSA* 320
P. Douglas-Reid, *NLP* 97
Lab. majority 10,978
(Boundary change: notional Lab.)

EDINBURGH PENTLANDS
*E.*59,635 *T.*76.70%
Ms L. Clark, *Lab.* 19,675
†Rt. Hon. M. Rifkind, *C.* 14,813
S. Gibb, *SNP* 5,952
Dr J. Dawe, *LD* 4,575
M. McDonald, *Ref.* 422
R. Harper, *Green* 224
A. McConnachie, *UK Ind.* 81
Lab. majority 4,862
(Boundary change: notional C.)

EDINBURGH SOUTH
*E.*62,467 *T.*71.78%
†N. Griffiths, *Lab.* 20,993
Miss E. Smith, *C.* 9,541
M. Pringle, *LD* 7,911
Dr J. Hargreaves, *SNP* 5,791
I. McLean, *Ref.* 504
B. Dunn, *NLP* 98
Lab. majority 11,452
(Boundary change: notional Lab.)

EDINBURGH WEST
*E.*61,133 *T.*77.91%
D. Gorrie, *LD* 20,578
†Rt. Hon. Lord J. Douglas-
Hamilton, *C.* 13,325
Ms L. Hinds, *Lab.* 8,948
G. Sutherland, *SNP* 4,210
Dr S. Elphick, *Ref.* 277
P. Coombes, *Lib.* 263
A. Jack, *AS* 30
LD majority 7,253
(Boundary change: notional C.)

FALKIRK EAST
*E.*56,792 *T.*73.24%
†M. Connarty, *Lab.* 23,344
K. Brown, *SNP* 9,959
M. Nicol, *C.* 5,813
R. Spillane, *LD* 2,153
S. Mowbray, *Ref.* 326
Lab. majority 13,385
(Boundary change: notional Lab.)

FALKIRK WEST
*E.*52,850 *T.*72.60%
†D. Canavan, *Lab.* 22,772
D. Alexander, *SNP* 8,989
Mrs C. Buchanan, *C.* 4,639
D. Houston, *LD* 1,970
Lab. majority 13,783
(Boundary change: notional Lab.)

FIFE CENTRAL
*E.*58,315 *T.*69.90%
†H. McLeish, *Lab.* 23,912
Mrs P. Marwick, *SNP* 10,199
J. Rees-Mogg, *C.* 3,669
R. Laird, *LD* 2,610
J. Scrymgeour-Wedderburn, *Ref.* 375
Lab. majority 13,713
(Boundary change: notional Lab.)

FIFE NORTH EAST
*E.*58,794 *T.*71.16%
*M. Campbell, *LD* 21,432
A. Bruce, *C.* 11,076
C. Welsh, *SNP* 4,545
C. Milne, *Lab.* 4,301
W. Stewart, *Ref.* 485

LD majority 10,356
(Boundary change: notional LD)

GALLOWAY AND UPPER NITHSDALE
*E.*52,751 *T.*79.65%
A. Morgan, *SNP* 18,449
†Rt. Hon. I. Lang, *C.* 12,825
Ms K. Clark, *Lab.* 6,861
J. McKerchar, *LD* 2,700
R. Wood, *Ind.* 566
A. Kennedy, *Ref.* 428
J. Smith, *UK Ind.* 189
SNP majority 5,624
(Boundary change: notional C.)

GLASGOW ANNIESLAND
*E.*52,955 *T.*63.98%
†Rt. Hon. D. Dewar, *Lab.* 20,951
Dr W. Wilson, *SNP* 5,797
A. Brocklehurst, *C.* 3,881
C. McGinty, *LD* 2,453
A. Majid, *ProLife* 374
W. Bonnar, *SSA* 229
A. Milligan, *UK Ind.* 86
Ms G. McKay, *Ref.* 84
T. Pringle, *NLP* 24
Lab. majority 15,154
(Boundary change: notional Lab.)

GLASGOW BAILLIESTON
*E.*51,152 *T.*62.27%
†J. Wray, *Lab.* 20,925
Mrs P. Thomson, *SNP* 6,085
M. Kelly, *C.* 2,468
Ms S. Rainger, *LD* 1,217
J. McVicar, *SSA* 970
J. McClafferty, *Ref.* 188
Lab. majority 14,840
(Boundary change: notional Lab.)

GLASGOW CATHCART
*E.*49,312 *T.*69.17%
†J. Maxton, *Lab.* 19,158
Ms M. Whitehead, *SNP* 6,913
A. Muir, *C.* 4,248
C. Dick, *LD* 2,302
Ms Z. Indyk, *ProLife* 687
R. Stevenson, *SSA* 458
S. Haldane, *Ref.* 344
Lab. majority 12,245
(Boundary change: notional Lab.)

GLASGOW GOVAN
*E.*49,836 *T.*64.70%
M. Sarwar, *Lab.* 14,216
Ms N. Sturgeon, *SNP* 11,302
W. Thomas, *C.* 2,839
R. Stewart, *LD* 1,915
A. McCombes, *SSA* 755
P. Paton, *SLU* 325
I. Badar, *SLI* 319
Z. J. Abbasi, *SCU* 221
K. MacDonald, *Ref.* 201
J. White, *BNP* 149
Lab. majority 2,914
(Boundary change: notional Lab.)

GLASGOW KELVIN
*E.*57,438 *T.*56.85%
†G. Galloway, *Lab.* 16,643
Ms S. White, *SNP* 6,978
Ms E. Buchanan, *LD* 4,629
D. McPhie, *C.* 3,539

A. Green, *SSA* — 386
R. Grigor, *Ref.* — 282
V. Vanni, *SPGB* — 102
G. Stidolph, *NLP* — 95
Lab. majority 9,665
(Boundary change: notional Lab.)

GLASGOW MARYHILL
*E.*52,523   *T.*56.59%
†Ms M. Fyfe, *Lab.* — 19,301
J. Wailes, *SNP* — 5,037
Ms E. Attwooll, *LD* — 2,119
S. Baldwin, *C.* — 1,747
Ms L. Blair, *NLP* — 651
Ms A. Baker, *SSA* — 409
J. Hanif, *ProLife* — 344
R. Paterson, *Ref.* — 77
S. Johnstone, *SEP* — 36
Lab. majority 14,264
(Boundary change: notional Lab.)

GLASGOW POLLOK
*E.*49,284   *T.*66.56%
†I. Davidson, *Lab. Co-op.* — 19,653
D. Logan, *SNP* — 5,862
T. Sheridan, *SSA* — 3,639
E. Hamilton, *C.* — 1,979
D. Jago, *LD* — 1,137
Ms M. Gott, *ProLife* — 380
D. Haldane, *Ref.* — 152
Lab. Co-op. majority 13,791
(Boundary change: notional Lab. Co-op.)

GLASGOW RUTHERGLEN
*E.*50,646   *T.*70.14%
†T. McAvoy, *Lab. Co-op.* — 20,430
I. Gray, *SNP* — 5,423
R. Brown, *LD* — 5,167
D. Campbell Bannerman, *C.* — 3,288
G. Easton, *Ind. Lab.* — 812
Ms R. Kane, *SSA* — 251
Ms J. Kerr, *Ref.* — 150
Lab. Co-op. majority 15,007
(Boundary change: notional Lab. Co-op.)

GLASGOW SHETTLESTON
*E.*47,990   *T.*55.87%
†D. Marshall, *Lab.* — 19,616
H. Hanif, *SNP* — 3,748
C. Simpson, *C.* — 1,484
Ms K. Hiles, *LD* — 1,061
Ms C. McVicar, *SSA* — 482
R. Currie, *BNP* — 191
T. Montguire, *Ref.* — 151
J. Graham, *WRP* — 80
Lab. majority 15,868
(Boundary change: notional Lab.)

GLASGOW SPRINGBURN
*E.*53,473   *T.*59.05%
†M. Martin, *Lab.* — 22,534
J. Brady, *SNP* — 5,208
M.Holdsworth, *C.* — 1,893
J. Alexander, *LD* — 1,349
J. Lawson, *SSA* — 407
A. Keating, *Ref.* — 186
Lab. majority 17,326
(Boundary change: notional Lab.)

GORDON
*E.*58,767   *T.*71.89%
†M. Bruce, *LD* — 17,999
J. Porter, *C.* — 11,002
R. Lochhead, *SNP* — 8,435
Ms L. Kirkhill, *Lab.* — 4,350
F. Pidcock, *Ref.* — 459
LD majority 6,997
(Boundary change: notional C.)

GREENOCK AND INVERCLYDE
*E.*48,818   *T.*71.05%
†Dr N. Godman, *Lab.* — 19,480
B. Goodall, *SNP* — 6,440
R. Ackland, *LD* — 4,791
H. Swire, *C.* — 3,976
Lab. majority 13,040
(Boundary change: notional Lab.)

HAMILTON NORTH AND BELLSHILL
*E.*53,607   *T.*70.88%
†Dr J. Reid, *Lab.* — 24,322
M. Matheson, *SNP* — 7,255
G. McIntosh, *C.* — 3,944
K. Legg, *LD* — 1,924
R. Conn, *Ref.* — 554
Lab. majority 17,067
(Boundary change: notional Lab.)

HAMILTON SOUTH
*E.*46,562   *T.*71.07%
†G. Robertson, *Lab.* — 21,709
I. Black, *SNP* — 5,831
R. Kilgour, *C.* — 2,858
R. Pitts, *LD* — 1,693
C. Gunn, *ProLife* — 684
S. Brown, *Ref.* — 316
Lab. majority 15,878
(Boundary change: notional Lab.)

INVERNESS EAST, NAIRN AND LOCHABER
*E.*65,701   *T.*72.71%
D. Stewart, *Lab.* — 16,187
F. Ewing, *SNP* — 13,848
S. Gallagher, *LD* — 8,364
Mrs M. Scanlon, *C.* — 8,355
Ms W. Wall, *Ref.* — 436
M. Falconer, *Green* — 354
D. Hart, *Ch. U.* — 224
Lab. majority 2,339
(Boundary change: notional LD)

KILMARNOCK AND LOUDOUN
*E.*61,376   *T.*77.24%
D. Browne, *Lab.* — 23,621
A. Neil, *SNP* — 16,365
D. Taylor, *C.* — 5,125
J. Stewart, *LD* — 1,891
W. Sneddon, *Ref.* — 284
W. Gilmour, *NLP* — 123
Lab. majority 7,256
(April 1992, Lab. maj. 6,979)

KIRKCALDY
*E.*52,186   *T.*67.02%
†L. Moonie, *Lab. Co-op.* — 18,730
S. Hosie, *SNP* — 8,020
Miss C. Black, *C.* — 4,779
J. Mainland, *LD* — 3,031
V. Baxter, *Ref.* — 413

Lab. Co-op. majority 10,710
(Boundary change: notional Lab. Co-op.)

LINLITHGOW
*E.*53,706   *T.*73.84%
†T. Dalyell, *Lab.* — 21,469
K. MacAskill, *SNP* — 10,631
T. Kerr, *C.* — 4,964
A. Duncan, *LD* — 2,331
K. Plomer, *Ref.* — 259
Lab. majority 10,838
(Boundary change: notional Lab.)

LIVINGSTON
*E.*60,296   *T.*71.04%
†Rt. Hon. R. Cook, *Lab.* — 23,510
P. Johnston, *SNP* — 11,763
H. Craigie Halkett, *C.* — 4,028
E. Hawthorn, *LD* — 2,876
Ms H. Campbell, *Ref.* — 444
M. Culbert, *SPGB* — 213
Lab. majority 11,747
(Boundary change: notional Lab.)

MIDLOTHIAN
*E.*47,552   *T.*74.13%
†E. Clarke, *Lab.* — 18,861
L. Millar, *SNP* — 8,991
Miss A. Harper, *C.* — 3,842
R. Pinnock, *LD* — 3,235
K. Docking, *Ref.* — 320
Lab. majority 9,870
(Boundary change: notional Lab.)

MORAY
*E.*58,302   *T.*68.21%
†Mrs M. Ewing, *SNP* — 16,529
A. Findlay, *C.* — 10,963
L. Macdonald, *Lab.* — 7,886
Ms D. Storr, *LD* — 3,548
P. Mieklejohn, *Ref.* — 840
SNP majority 5,566
(Boundary change: notional SNP)

MOTHERWELL AND WISHAW
*E.*52,252   *T.*70.08%
F. Roy, *Lab.* — 21,020
J. McGuigan, *SNP* — 8,229
S. Dickson, *C.* — 4,024
A. Mackie, *LD* — 2,331
C. Herriot, *Soc. Lab.* — 797
T. Russell, *Ref.* — 218
Lab. majority 12,791
(Boundary change: notional Lab.)

OCHIL
*E.*56,572   *T.*77.40%
†M. O'Neill, *Lab.* — 19,707
G. Reid, *SNP* — 15,055
A. Hogarth, *C.* — 6,383
Mrs A. Watters, *LD* — 2,262
D. White, *Ref.* — 210
I. McDonald, *D. Nat.* — 104
M. Sullivan, *NLP* — 65
Lab. majority 4,652
(Boundary change: notional Lab.)

ORKNEY AND SHETLAND
*E.*32,291   *T.*64.00%
*J. Wallace, *LD* — 10,743
J. Paton, *Lab.* — 3,775
W. Ross, *SNP* — 2,624

H. Vere Anderson, *C.* 2,527
F. Adamson, *Ref.* 820
Ms C. Wharton, *NLP* 116
A. Robertson, *Ind.* 60
LD majority 6,968
(April 1992, LD maj. 5,033)

PAISLEY NORTH
*E.*49,725   *T.*68.65%
†Mrs I. Adams, *Lab.* 20,295
I. Mackay, *SNP* 7,481
K. Brookes, *C.* 3,267
A. Jelfs, *LD* 2,365
R. Graham, *ProLife* 531
E. Mathew, *Ref.* 196
Lab. majority 12,814
(Boundary change: notional Lab.)

PAISLEY SOUTH
*E.*54,040   *T.*69.12%
†G. McMaster, *Lab. Co-op.* 21,482
W. Martin, *SNP* 8,732
Ms E. McCartin, *LD* 3,500
R. Reid, *C.* 3,237
J. Lardner, *Ref.* 254
S. Clerkin, *SSA* 146
Lab. Co-op. majority 12,750
(Boundary change: notional Lab. Co-op.)
See also page 233

PERTH
*E.*60,313   *T.*73.87%
†Ms R. Cunningham, *SNP* 16,209
J. Godfrey, *C.* 13,068
D. Alexander, *Lab.* 11,036
C. Brodie, *LD* 3,583
R. MacAuley, *Ref.* 366
M. Henderson, *UK Ind.* 289
SNP majority 3,141
(Boundary change: notional C.)

RENFREWSHIRE WEST
*E.*52,348   *T.*76.00%
†T. Graham, *Lab.* 18,525
C. Campbell, *SNP* 10,546
C. Cormack, *C.* 7,387
B. MacPherson, *LD* 3,045
S. Lindsay, *Ref.* 283
Lab. majority 7,979
(Boundary change: notional Lab.)

ROSS, SKYE AND INVERNESS WEST
*E.*55,639   *T.*71.81%
†C. Kennedy, *LD* 15,472
D. Munro, *Lab.* 11,453
Mrs M. Paterson, *SNP* 7,821
Miss M. Macleod, *C.* 4,368
L. Durance, *Ref.* 535
A. Hopkins, *Green* 306
LD majority 4,019
(Boundary change: notional LD)

ROXBURGH AND BERWICKSHIRE
*E.*47,259   *T.*73.91%
†A. Kirkwood, *LD* 16,243
D. Younger, *C.* 8,337
Ms H. Eadie, *Lab.* 5,226
M. Balfour, *SNP* 3,959
J. Curtis, *Ref.* 922
P. Neilson, *UK Ind.* 202
D. Lucas, *NLP* 42
LD majority 7,906
(Boundary change: notional LD)

STIRLING
*E.*52,491   *T.*81.84%
Mrs A. McGuire, *Lab.* 20,382
†Rt. Hon. M. Forsyth, *C.* 13,971
E. Dow, *SNP* 5,752
A. Tough, *LD* 2,675
W. McMurdo, *UK Ind.* 154
Ms E. Olsen, *Value Party* 24
Lab. majority 6,411
(Boundary change: notional C.)

STRATHKELVIN AND BEARSDEN
*E.*62,974   *T.*78.94%
†S. Galbraith, *Lab.* 26,278
D. Sharpe, *C.* 9,986
G. McCormick, *SNP* 8,111
J. Morrison, *LD* 4,843
D. Wilson, *Ref.* 339
Ms J. Fisher, *NLP* 155
Lab. majority 16,292
(Boundary change: notional Lab.)

TAYSIDE NORTH
*E.*61,398   *T.*74.25%
J. Swinney, *SNP* 20,447
†W. Walker, *C.* 16,287
I. McFatridge, *Lab.* 5,141
P. Regent, *LD* 3,716
SNP majority 4,160
(Boundary change: notional C.)

TWEEDDALE, ETTRICK AND LAUDERDALE
*E.*50,891   *T.*76.64%
M. Moore, *LD* 12,178
K. Geddes, *Lab.* 10,689
A. Jack, *C.* 8,623
I. Goldie, *SNP* 6,671
C. Mowbray, *Ref.* 406
J. Hein, *Lib.* 387
D. Paterson, *NLP* 47
LD majority 1,489
(Boundary change: notional LD)

WESTERN ISLES
*E.*22,983   *T.*70.08%
*C. Macdonald, *Lab.* 8,955
Dr A. Lorne Gillies, *SNP* 5,379
J. McGrigor, *C.* 1,071
N. Mitchison, *LD* 495
R. Lionel, *Ref.* 206
Lab. majority 3,576
(April 1992, Lab. maj. 1,703)

NORTHERN IRELAND

ANTRIM EAST
*E.*58,963   *T.*58.26%
†R. Beggs, *UUP* 13,318
S. Neeson, *All.* 6,929
J. McKee, *DUP* 6,682
T. Dick, *C.* 2,334
W. Donaldson, *PUP* 1,757
D. O'Connor, *SDLP* 1,576
R. Mason, *Ind.* 1,145
Ms C. McAuley, *SF* 543
Ms M. McCann, *NLP* 69
UUP majority 6,389
(Boundary change: notional UUP)

ANTRIM NORTH
*E.*72,411   *T.*63.78%
*Revd I. Paisley, *DUP* 21,495
J. Leslie, *UUP* 10,921
S. Farren, *SDLP* 7,333
J. McCarry, *SF* 2,896
Dr D. Alderdice, *All.* 2,845
Ms B. Hinds, *NI Women* 580
J. Wright, *NLP* 116

DUP majority 10,574
(April 1992, DUP maj. 14,936)

ANTRIM SOUTH
*E.*69,414   *T.*57.91%
†C. Forsythe, *UUP* 23,108
D. McClelland, *SDLP* 6,497
D. Ford, *All.* 4,668
H. Smyth, *PUP* 3,490
H. Cushinan, *SF* 2,229
Ms B. Briggs, *NLP* 203
UUP majority 16,611
(Boundary change: notional UUP)

BELFAST EAST
*E.*61,744   *T.*63.21%
†P. Robinson, *DUP* 16,640
R. Empey, *UUP* 9,886
J. Hendron, *All.* 9,288
Miss S. Dines, *C.* 928
D. Corr, *SF* 810
Mrs P. Lewsley, *SDLP* 629
D. Dougan, *NIFT* 541
J. Bell, *WP* 237
D. Collins, *NLP* 70

DUP majority 6,754
(Boundary change: notional DUP)

BELFAST NORTH
*E.*64,577   *T.*64.19%
†C. Walker, *UUP* 21,478
A. Maginness, *SDLP* 8,454
G. Kelly, *SF* 8,375
T. Campbell, *All.* 2,221
P. Emerson, *Green* 539
P. Treanor, *WP* 297
Ms A. Gribben, *NLP* 88
UUP majority 13,024
(Boundary change: notional UUP)

BELFAST SOUTH
*E.*63,439   *T.*62.24%
†Revd M. Smyth, *UUP* 14,201
Dr A. McDonnell, *SDLP* 9,601
D. Ervine, *PUP* 5,687
S. McBride, *All.* 5,112
S. Hayes, *SF* 2,019
Ms A. Campbell, *NI Women* 1,204
Miss M. Boal, *C.* 962
N. Cusack, *Ind. Lab.* 292

P. Lynn, *WP*   286
J. Anderson, *NLP*   120
UUP majority 4,600
(Boundary change: notional UUP)

BELFAST WEST
*E.*61,785   *T.*74.27%
G. Adams, *SF*   25,662
†Dr J. Hendron, *SDLP*   17,753
F. Parkinson, *UUP*   1,556
J. Lowry, *WP*   721
L. Kennedy, *HR*   102
Ms M. Daly, *NLP*   91
SF majority 7,909
(Boundary change: notional SDLP)

DOWN NORTH
*E.*63,010   *T.*58.03%
†R. McCartney, *UKU*   12,817
A. McFarland, *UUP*   11,368
Sir O. Napier, *All.*   7,554
L. Fee, *C.*   1,810
Miss M. Farrell, *SDLP*   1,602
Ms J. Morrice, *NI Women*   1,240
T. Mullins, *NLP*   108
R. Mooney, *NIP*   67
UKU majority 1,449
(Boundary change: notional Popular Unionist)

DOWN SOUTH
*E.*69,855   *T.*70.84%
†E. McGrady, *SDLP*   26,181
D. Nesbitt, *UUP*   16,248
M. Murphy, *SF*   5,127
J. Crozier, *All.*   1,711
Ms R. McKeon, *NLP*   219
SDLP majority 9,933
(Boundary change: notional SDLP)

FERMANAGH AND SOUTH TYRONE
*E.*64,600   *T.*74.75%
†K. Maginnis, *UUP*   24,862
G. McHugh, *SF*   11,174
T. Gallagher, *SDLP*   11,060
S. Farry, *All.*   977
S. Gillan, *NLP*   217
UUP majority 13,688
(Boundary change: notional UUP)

FOYLE
*E.*67,620   *T.*70.71%
†J. Hume, *SDLP*   25,109
M. McLaughlin, *SF*   11,445
W. Hay, *DUP*   10,290
Mrs H.-M. Bell, *All.*   817
D. Brennan, *NLP*   154
SDLP majority 13,664
(Boundary change: notional SDLP)

LAGAN VALLEY
*E.*71,225   *T.*62.21%
J. Donaldson, *UUP*   24,560
S. Close, *All.*   7,635
E. Poots, *DUP*   6,005
Ms D. Kelly, *SDLP*   3,436
S. Sexton, *C.*   1,212
Ms S. Ramsey, *SF*   1,110
Ms F. McCarthy, *WP*   203
H. Finlay, *NLP*   149
UUP majority 16,925
(Boundary change: notional UUP)

LONDONDERRY EAST
*E.*58,831   *T.*64.77%
†W. Ross, *UUP*   13,558
G. Campbell, *DUP*   9,764
A. Doherty, *SDLP*   8,273
M. O'Kane, *SF*   3,463
Ms Y. Boyle, *All.*   2,427
J. Holmes, *C.*   436
Ms C. Gallen, *NLP*   100
I. Anderson, *Nat. Dem.*   81
UUP majority 3,794
(Boundary change: notional UUP)

NEWRY AND ARMAGH
*E.*70,652   *T.*75.40%
†S. Mallon, *SDLP*   22,904
D. Kennedy, *UUP*   18,015
P. McNamee, *SF*   11,218
P. Whitcroft, *All.*   1,015
D. Evans, *NLP*   123
SDLP majority 4,889
(Boundary change: notional SDLP)

STRANGFORD
*E.*69,980   *T.*59.47%
†Rt. Hon. J. Taylor, *UUP*   18,431
Mrs I. Robinson, *DUP*   12,579
K. McCarthy, *All.*   5,467
P. O'Reilly, *SDLP*   2,775
G. Chalk, *C.*   1,743
G. O Fachtna, *SF*   503
Mrs S. Mullins, *NLP*   121
UUP majority 5,852
(Boundary change: notional UUP)

TYRONE WEST
*E.*58,168   *T.*79.55%
W. Thompson, *UUP*   16,003
J. Byrne, *SDLP*   14,842
P. Doherty, *SF*   14,280
Ms A. Gormley, *All.*   829
T. Owens, *WP*   230
R. Johnstone, *NLP*   91
UUP majority 1,161
(Boundary change: notional DUP)

ULSTER MID
*E.*58,836   *T.*86.12%
M. McGuinness, *SF*   20,294
†Revd W. McCrea, *DUP*   18,411
D. Haughey, *SDLP*   11,205
E. Bogues, *All.*   460
Mrs M. Donnelly, *WP*   238
Ms M. Murray, *NLP*   61
SF majority 1,883
(Boundary change: notional DUP)

UPPER BANN
*E.*70,398   *T.*67.88%
*D. Trimble, *UUP*   20,836
Ms B. Rodgers, *SDLP*   11,584
Ms B. O'Hagan, *SF*   5,773
M. Carrick, *DUP*   5,482
Dr W. Ramsay, *All.*   3,017
T. French, *WP*   554
B. Price, *C.*   433
J. Lyons, *NLP*   108
UUP majority 9,252
(Boundary change: notional UUP)

European Parliament

European Parliament elections take place at five-yearly intervals. In mainland Britain MEPs have so far been elected in all constituencies on a first-past-the-post basis; in Northern Ireland three MEPs are elected by the single transferable vote system of proportional representation. From 1979 to 1994 the number of seats held by the UK in the European Parliament was 81. At the June 1994 election the number of seats increased to 87 (England 71, Wales 5, Scotland 8, Northern Ireland 3).

At the European Parliament elections to be held on 10 June 1999, all British MEPs will be elected under a 'closed-list' regional system of proportional representation, with England being divided into nine regions and Scotland and Wales each constituting a region. Parties will submit a list of candidates for each region in their own order of preference. Voters will vote for a party rather than a candidate, and seats will then be allocated in proportion to each party's vote. Candidates further up the party's list will therefore have a better chance of being elected. Each region will return the following number of members: East Midlands, 6; Eastern, 8; London, 10; North-East, 4; North-West, 10; South-East, 11; South-West, 7; West Midlands, 8; Yorkshire and the Humber, 7; Wales, 5; Scotland 8.

British subjects and citizens of the Irish Republic are eligible for election to the European Parliament provided they are 21 or over and not subject to disqualification. Since 1994, nationals of member states of the European Union have had the right to vote in elections to the European Parliament in the UK.

MEPs receive a salary from the parliaments or governments of their respective member states, set at the level of the national parliamentary salary and subject to national taxation rules (for salary of British MPs, *see* page 219).

UK MEMBERS AS AT END JULY 1998

*Denotes membership of the last European Parliament

*Adam, Gordon J., ph.d. (*b.* 1934), *Lab.*, *Northumbria*, maj. 66,158

*Balfe, Richard A. (*b.* 1944), *Lab.*, *London South Inner*, maj. 59,220

*Barton, Roger (*b.* 1945), *Lab.*, *Sheffield*, maj. 50,288

Billingham, Mrs Angela T. (*b.* 1939), *Lab.*, *Northamptonshire and Blaby*, maj. 26,085

*Bowe, David R. (*b.* 1955), *Lab.*, *Cleveland and Richmond*, maj. 57,568

*Cassidy, Bryan M. D. (*b.* 1934), *C.*, *Dorset and Devon East*, maj. 2,264

Chichester, Giles B. (*b.* 1946), *C.*, *Devon and Plymouth East*, maj. 700

*Coates, Kenneth S. (*b.* 1930), *European United Left/Nordic Green Left Group*, *Nottinghamshire North and Chesterfield*, maj. 76,260

*Collins, Kenneth D. (*b.* 1939), *Lab.*, *Strathclyde East*, maj. 52,340

Corbett, Richard (*b.* 1955), *Lab.*, *Merseyside West*, maj. 18,704

Corrie, John A. (*b.* 1935), *C.*, *Worcestershire and Warwickshire South*, maj. 1,204

*Crampton, Peter D. (*b.* 1932), *Lab.*, *Humberside*, maj. 40,618

*Crawley, The Baroness (Christine) (*b.* 1950), *Lab.*, *Birmingham East*, maj. 55,120

Cunningham, Thomas A. (Tony) (*b.* 1952), *Lab.*, *Cumbria and Lancashire North*, maj. 22,988

*David, Wayne (*b.* 1957), *Lab.*, *South Wales Central*, maj. 86,082

*Donnelly, Alan J. (*b.* 1957), *Lab.*, *Tyne and Wear*, maj. 88,380

Donnelly, Brendan P. (*b.* 1950), *C.*, *Sussex South and Crawley*, maj. 1,746

*Elles, James E. M. (*b.* 1949), *C.*, *Buckinghamshire and Oxfordshire East*, maj. 30,665

*Elliott, Michael N. (*b.* 1932), *Lab.*, *London West*, maj. 42,275

Evans, Robert J. E. (*b.* 1956), *Lab.*, *London North West*, maj. 17,442

*Ewing, Mrs Winifred M. (*b.* 1929), *SNP*, *Highlands and Islands*, maj. 54,916

*Falconer, Alexander (*b.* 1940), *Lab.*, *Scotland Mid and Fife*, maj. 31,413

*Ford, J. Glyn (*b.* 1950), *Lab.*, *Greater Manchester East*, maj. 55,986

*Green, Mrs Pauline (*b.* 1948), *Lab.*, *London North*, maj. 48,348

Hallam, David J. A. (*b.* 1948), *Lab.*, *Herefordshire and Shropshire*, maj. 1,850

Hardstaff, Mrs Veronica M. (*b.* 1941), *Lab.*, *Lincolnshire and Humberside South*, maj. 13,745

*Harrison, Lyndon H. A. (*b.* 1947), *Lab.*, *Cheshire West and Wirral*, maj. 47,176

Hendrick, Mark P. (*b.* 1958), *Lab.*, *Lancashire Central*, maj. 12,191

*Hindley, Michael J. (*b.* 1947), *Lab.*, *Lancashire South*, maj. 41,404

Howitt, Richard (*b.* 1961), *Lab.*, *Essex South*, maj. 21,367

*Hughes, Stephen S. (*b.* 1952), *Lab.*, *Durham*, maj. 111,638

*Hume, John, MP (*b.* 1937), *SDLP*, *Northern Ireland*, polled 161,992 votes

*Jackson, Mrs Caroline F., D.phil. (*b.* 1946), *C.*, *Wiltshire North and Bath*, maj. 8,787

*Kellett-Bowman, Edward T. (*b.* 1931), *C.*, *Itchen*, *Test and Avon*, maj. 6,903

Kerr, Hugh (*b.* 1944), *Green*, *Essex West and Hertfordshire East*, maj. 3,067

Kinnock, Mrs Glenys E. (*b.* 1944), *Lab.*, *South Wales East*, maj. 120,247

*Lomas, Alfred (*b.* 1928), *Lab.*, *London North East*, maj. 57,085

Macartney, W. J. Allan, ph.d. (*b.* 1941), *SNP*, *Scotland North East*, maj. 31,227

McAvan, Ms Linda (*b.* 1962), *Lab.*, *Yorkshire South*, maj. 40,224

McCarthy, Ms Arlene (*b.* 1960), *Lab.*, *Peak District*, maj. 49,307

*McGowan, Michael (*b.* 1940), *Lab.*, *Leeds*, maj. 53,082

*McIntosh, Miss Anne C. B., MP (*b.* 1954), *C.*, *Essex North and Suffolk South*, maj. 3,633

*McMahon, Hugh R. (*b.* 1938), *Lab.*, *Strathclyde West*, maj. 25,023

*McMillan-Scott, Edward H. C. (*b.* 1949), *C.*, *Yorkshire North*, maj. 7,072

McNally, Mrs Eryl M. (*b.* 1942), *Lab.*, *Bedfordshire and Milton Keynes*, maj. 33,209

*Martin, David W. (*b.* 1954), *Lab.*, *Lothians*, maj. 37,207

Mather, Graham C. S. (*b.* 1954), *C.*, *Hampshire North and Oxford*, maj. 9,194

*Megahy, Thomas (*b.* 1929), *Lab.*, *Yorkshire South West*, maj. 59,562

Miller, Bill (*b.* 1954), *Lab.*, *Glasgow*, maj. 43,158

*Moorhouse, C. James O. (*b.* 1924), *C.*, *London South and Surrey East*, maj. 8,739

Morgan, Ms Eluned (*b.* 1967), *Lab., Wales Mid and West,* maj. 29,234

*Morris, Revd David R. (*b.* 1930), *Lab., South Wales West,* maj. 84,970

Murphy, Simon F., PH.D . (*b.* 1962), *Lab., Midlands West,* maj. 54,823

Needle, Clive (*b.* 1956), *Lab., Norfolk,* maj. 26,287

*Newens, A. Stanley (*b.* 1930), *Lab., London Central,* maj. 25,059

*Newman, Edward (*b.* 1953), *Lab., Greater Manchester Central,* maj. 42,445

*Nicholson, James F. (*b.* 1945), *UUUP, Northern Ireland,* polled 133,459 votes

*Oddy, Ms Christine M. (*b.* 1955), *Lab., Coventry and Warwickshire North,* maj. 43,901

*Paisley, Revd Ian R. K., MP (*b.* 1926), *DUP, Northern Ireland,* polled 163,246 votes

Perry, Roy J. (*b.* 1943), *C., Wight and Hampshire South,* maj. 5,101

*Plumb, The Lord (*b.* 1925), *C., Cotswolds,* maj. 4,268

*Pollack, Ms Anita J. (*b.* 1946), *Lab., London South West,* maj. 30,975

Provan, James L. C. (*b.* 1936), *C., South Downs West,* maj. 21,067

*Read, Ms I. M. (Mel) (*b.* 1939), *Lab., Nottingham and Leicestershire North West,* maj. 39,668

*Seal, Barry H., PH.D. (*b.* 1937), *Lab., Yorkshire West,* maj. 48,197

*Simpson, Brian (*b.* 1953), *Lab., Cheshire East,* maj. 39,279

Skinner, Peter W. (*b.* 1959), *Lab., Kent West,* maj. 16,777

*Smith, Alexander (*b.* 1943), *Lab., Scotland South,* maj. 45,155

*Spencer, Thomas N. B. (*b.* 1948), *C., Surrey,* maj. 27,018

Spiers, Shaun M. (*b.* 1962), *Lab., London South East,* maj. 8,022

*Stevens, John C. C. (*b.* 1955), *C., Thames Valley,* maj. 758

*Stewart-Clark, Sir John, Bt. (*b.* 1929), *C., Sussex East and Kent South,* maj. 6,212

Sturdy, Robert W. (*b.* 1944), *C., Cambridgeshire,* maj. 3,942

Tappin, Michael (*b.* 1946), *Lab., Staffordshire West and Congleton,* maj. 40,277

Teverson, Robin (*b.* 1952), *LD, Cornwall and Plymouth West,* maj. 29,498

Thomas, David E. (*b.* 1955), *Lab., Suffolk and Norfolk South West,* maj. 12,535

*Titley, Gary (*b.* 1950), *Lab., Greater Manchester West,* maj. 58,635

* Tomlinson, The Lord (John) (*b.* 1939), *Lab., Birmingham West,* maj. 39,350

*Tongue, Ms Carole (*b.* 1955), *Lab., London East,* maj. 57,389

Truscott, Peter, PH.D. (*b.* 1959), *Lab., Hertfordshire,* maj. 10,304

Waddington, Mrs Susan A. (*b.* 1944), *Lab., Leicester,* maj. 20,284

Watson, Graham R. (*b.* 1956), *LD, Somerset and Devon North,* maj. 22,509

Watts, Mark F. (*b.* 1964), *Lab., Kent East,* maj. 635

*White, Ian (*b.* 1947), *Lab., Bristol,* maj. 29,955

Whitehead, Phillip (*b.* 1937), *Lab., Staffordshire East and Derby,* maj. 72,196

*Wilson, A. Joseph (*b.* 1937), *Lab., Wales North,* maj. 15,242

*Wynn, Terence (*b.* 1946), *Lab., Merseyside East and Wigan,* maj. 74,087

UK CONSTITUENCIES AS AT 9 JUNE 1994

Abbreviations

Anti Fed.	UK Independence Anti-Federal
Anti Fed. C.	Official Anti-Federalist Conservative
Beanus	Eurobean from Planet Beanus
C. Non Fed.	Conservative Non-Federal Party
Capital P.	Restoration of Capital Punishment
Comm.	Communist
Comm. YBG	Communist Y Blaid Gomiwyddol
Const. NI	Constitutional Independence for N. Ireland
Corr.	Corrective Party
CPP	Christian People's Party
ICP	International Communist Party
ICP4	International Communist Party (4th International)
Ind. AES	Independent Anti-European Superstate
Ind. Out	Independent Out of Europe
Judo	European People's Party Judo Christian Alliance
Loony C	Raving Loony Commonsense
Loony CP	Monster Raving Loony Christian Party
Loony X	Monster Raving Loony Project X Party
MCCARTHY	Make Criminals Concerned About Our Response To Hostility and Yobbishness
MK	Mebyon Kernow
NCSA	Network Against Child Support Agency

Neeps	North East Ethnic Party, The Neeps
Rainbow	Rainbow Connection – Oui-Say-Non-Party
Sportsman	Sportsman Anti-Common Market Bureaucracy
UUUP	United Ulster Unionist Party

For other abbreviations, *see* page 235

ENGLAND

BEDFORDSHIRE AND MILTON KEYNES
E. 525,524   *T.* 38.74%

E. McNally, *Lab.*	94,837
Mrs E. Currie, *C.*	61,628
Ms M. Howes, *LD*	27,994
A. Sked, *UK Independence*	7,485
A. Francis, *Green*	6,804
A. Howes, *New Britain*	3,878
L. Sheaff, *NLP*	939
Lab. majority	33,209
(Boundary change since June 1989)

BIRMINGHAM EAST
E. 520,782   *T.* 29.77%

*Mrs C. Crawley, *Lab.*	90,291
A. Turner, *C.*	35,171
Ms C. Cane, *LD*	19,455
P. Simpson, *Green*	6,268
R. Cook, *Soc.*	1,969
M. Brierley, *NLP*	1,885
Lab. majority	55,120
(June 1989, Lab. maj. 46,948)

BIRMINGHAM WEST
E. 509,948   *T.* 28.49%

*J. Tomlinson, *Lab.*	77,957
D. Harman, *C.*	38,607
N. McGeorge, *LD*	14,603
Dr B. Juby, *Anti Fed.*	5,237
M. Abbott, *Green*	4,367
A. Carmichael, *NF*	3,727
H. Meads, *NLP*	789
Lab. majority	39,350
(June 1989, Lab. maj. 30,860)

BRISTOL
E. 503,218   *T.* 40.91%

*I. White, *Lab.*	90,790
The Earl of Stockton, *C.*	60,835
J. Barnard, *LD*	40,394
J. Boxall, *Green*	7,163
T. Whittingham, *UK Independence*	5,798
T. Dyball, *NLP*	876
Lab. majority	29,955
(Boundary change since June 1989)

BUCKINGHAMSHIRE AND OXFORDSHIRE EAST
E. 487,692   *T.* 37.31%

*J. Elles, *C.*	77,037
D. Enright, *Lab.*	46,372
Ms S. Bowles, *LD*	42,836
L. Roach, *Green*	8,433
Ms A. Micklem, *Lib.*	5,111
Dr G. Clements, *NLP*	2,156
C. majority	30,665
(Boundary change since June 1989)

CAMBRIDGESHIRE
E. 495,383 *T.* 35.91%
R. Sturdy, *C.* 66,921
Ms M. Johnson, *Lab.* 62,979
A. Duff, *LD* 36,114
Ms M. Wright, *Green* 5,756
P. Wiggin, *Lib.* 4,051
F. Chalmers, *NLP* 2,077
C. majority 3,942
(Boundary change since June 1989)

CHESHIRE EAST
E. 502,726 *T.* 32.46%
*B. Simpson, *Lab.* 87,586
P. Slater, *C.* 48,307
P. Harris, *LD* 20,552
D. Wild, *Green* 3,671
P. Dixon, *Loony CP* 1,600
P. Leadbetter, *NLP* 1,488
Lab. majority 39,279
(Boundary change since June 1989)

CHESHIRE WEST AND WIRRAL
E. 538,571 *T.* 36.78%
*L. Harrison, *Lab.* 106,160
D. Senior, *C.* 58,984
I. Mottershaw, *LD* 20,746
D. Carson, *British Home Rule* 6,167
M. Money, *Green* 5,096
A. Wilmot, *NLP* 929
Lab. majority 47,176
(Boundary change since June 1989)

CLEVELAND AND RICHMOND
E. 499,580 *T.* 35.26%
*D. Bowe, *Lab.* 103,355
R. Goodwill, *C.* 45,787
B. Moore, *LD* 21,574
G. Parr, *Green* 4,375
R. Scott, *NLP* 1,068
Lab. majority 57,568
(Boundary change since June 1989)

CORNWALL AND PLYMOUTH WEST
E. 484,697 *T.* 44.92%
R. Teverson, *LD* 91,113
*C. Beazley, *C.* 61,615
Mrs D. Kirk, *Lab.* 42,907
Mrs P. Garnier, *UK Independence*
6,466
P. Holmes, *Lib.* 6,414
Ms K. Westbrook, *Green* 4,372
Dr L. Jenkin, *MK* 3,315
F. Lyons, *NLP* 921
M. Fitzgerald, *Subsidiarity* 606
LD majority 29,498
(Boundary change since June 1989)

COTSWOLDS
E. 497,588 *T.* 39.27%
*The Lord Plumb, *C.* 67,484
Ms T. Kingham, *Lab.* 63,216
J. Thomson, *LD* 44,269
M. Rendell, *New Britain* 11,044
D. McCanlis, *Green* 8,254
H. Brighouse, *NLP* 1,151
C. majority 4,268
(Boundary change since June 1989)

COVENTRY AND WARWICKSHIRE
NORTH
E. 523,448 *T.* 32.54%
*Ms C. Oddy, *Lab.* 89,500

Ms J. Crabb, *C.* 45,599
G. Sewards, *LD* 17,453
R. Meacham, *Free Trade* 9,432
P. Baptie, *Green* 4,360
R. Wheway, *Lib.* 2,885
R. France, *NLP* 1,098
Lab. majority 43,901
(Boundary change since June 1989)

CUMBRIA AND LANCASHIRE NORTH
E. 498,557 *T.* 40.78%
A. Cunningham, *Lab.* 97,599
*The Lord Inglewood, *C.* 74,611
R. Putnam, *LD* 24,233
R. Frost, *Green* 5,344
I. Docker, *NLP* 1,500
Lab. majority 22,988
(Boundary change since June 1989)

DEVON AND PLYMOUTH EAST
E. 524,320 *T.* 45.07%
G. Chichester, *C.* 74,953
A. Sanders, *LD* 74,253
Ms L. Gilroy, *Lab.* 47,596
D. Morrish, *Lib.* 14,621
P. Edwards, *Green* 11,172
R. Huggett, *Literal Democrat* 10,203
J. Everard, *Ind.* 2,629
A. Pringle, *NLP* 908
C. majority 700
(Boundary change since June 1989)

DORSET AND DEVON EAST
E. 531,842 *T.* 41.21%
*B. Cassidy, *C.* 81,551
P. Goldenberg, *LD* 79,287
A. Gardner, *Lab.* 34,856
M. Floyd, *UK Independence* 10,548
Mrs K. Bradbury, *Green* 8,642
I. Mortimer, *C. Non Fed.* 3,229
M. Griffiths, *NLP* 1,048
C. majority 2,264
(Boundary change since June 1989)

DURHAM
E. 532,051 *T.* 35.62%
*S. Hughes, *Lab.* 136,671
P. Bradbourn, *C.* 25,033
Dr N. Martin, *LD* 20,935
S. Hope, *Green* 5,670
C. Adamson, *NLP* 1,198
Lab. majority 111,638
(June 1989, Lab. maj. 86,848)

ESSEX NORTH AND SUFFOLK
SOUTH
E. 497,098 *T.* 41.33%
*Ms A. McIntosh, *C.* 68,311
C. Pearson, *Lab.* 64,678
S. Mole, *LD* 52,536
S. de Chair, *Ind. AES* 12,409
J. Abbott, *Green* 6,641
N. Pullen, *NLP* 884
C. majority 3,633
(Boundary change since June 1989)

ESSEX SOUTH
E. 487,221 *T.* 33.08%
R. Howitt, *Lab.* 71,883
L. Stanbrook, *C.* 50,516
G. Williams, *LD* 26,132
B. Lynch, *Lib.* 6,780
G. Rumens, *Green* 4,691

M. Heath, *NLP* 1,177
Lab. majority 21,367
(Boundary change since June 1989)

ESSEX WEST AND HERTFORDSHIRE
EAST
E. 504,095 *T.* 36.39%
H. Kerr, *Lab.* 66,379
*Ms P. Rawlings, *C.* 63,312
Ms G. James, *LD* 35,695
B. Smalley, *Britain* 10,277
Ms F. Mawson, *Green* 5,632
P. Carter, *Sportsman* 1,127
L. Davis, *NLP* 1,026
Lab. majority 3,067
(Boundary change since June 1989)

GREATER MANCHESTER CENTRAL
E. 481,779 *T.* 29.11%
*E. Newman, *Lab.* 74,935
Mrs S. Mason, *C.* 32,490
J. Begg, *LD* 22,988
B. Candeland, *Green* 4,952
P. Burke, *Lab.* 3,862
P. Stanley, *NLP* 1,017
Lab. majority 42,445
(Boundary change since June 1989)

GREATER MANCHESTER EAST
E. 501,125 *T.* 27.17%
*G. Ford, *Lab.* 82,289
J. Pinniger, *C.* 26,303
A. Riley, *LD* 20,545
T. Clarke, *Green* 5,823
W. Stevens, *NLP* 1,183
Lab. majority 55,986
(Boundary change since June 1989)

GREATER MANCHESTER WEST
E. 512,618 *T.* 29.70%
*G. Titley, *Lab.* 94,129
D. Newns, *C.* 35,494
F. Harasiwka, *LD* 13,650
R. Jackson, *Green* 3,950
G. Harrison, *MCCARTHY* 3,693
T. Brotheridge, *NLP* 1,316
Lab. majority 58,635
(Boundary change since June 1989)

HAMPSHIRE NORTH AND OXFORD
E. 525,982 *T.* 38.31%
G. Mather, *C.* 72,209
Ms J. Hawkins, *LD* 63,015
J. Tanner, *Lab.* 48,525
D. Wilkinson, *UK Independence* 8,377
Dr M. Woodin, *Green* 7,310
H. Godfrey, *NLP* 1,027
R. Boston, *Boston Tea Party* 1,018
C. majority 9,194
(Boundary change since June 1989)

HEREFORDSHIRE AND SHROPSHIRE
E. 536,470 *T.* 38.69%
D. Hallam, *Lab.* 76,120
*Sir C. Prout, *C.* 74,270
J. Gallagher, *LD* 44,130
Ms F. Norman, *Green* 11,578
T. Mercer, *NLP* 1,480
Lab. majority 1,850
(Boundary change since June 1989)

HERTFORDSHIRE
E. 522,338   T. 40.11%
Dr P. Truscott, *Lab.*	81,821
P. Jenkinson, *C.*	71,517
D. Griffiths, *LD*	38,995
Ms L. Howitt, *Green*	7,741
M. Biggs, *New Britain*	6,555
J. McAuley, *NF*	1,755
D. Lucas, *NLP*	734
J. Laine, *Century*	369
Lab. majority	10,304

(Boundary change since June 1989)

HUMBERSIDE
E. 519,013   T. 32.38%
*P. Crampton, *Lab.*	87,296
D. Stewart, *C.*	46,678
Ms D. Wallis, *LD*	28,818
Ms S. Mummery, *Green*	4,170
Ms A. Miszewska, *NLP*	1,100
Lab. majority	40,618

(Boundary change since June 1989)

ITCHEN, TEST AND AVON
E. 550,406   T. 41.83%
*E. Kellett-Bowman, *C.*	81,456
A. Barron, *LD*	74,553
E. Read, *Lab.*	52,416
N. Farage, *UK Independence*	12,423
Ms F. Hulbert, *Green*	7,998
A. Miller-Smith, *NLP*	1,368
C. majority	6,903

(Boundary change since June 1989)

KENT EAST
E. 499,662   T. 40.34%
M. Watts, *Lab.*	69,641
*C. Jackson, *C.*	69,006
J. Macdonald, *LD*	44,549
C. Bullen, *UK Independence*	9,414
S. Dawe, *Green*	7,196
C. Beckley, *NLP*	1,746
Lab. majority	635

(Boundary change since June 1989)

KENT WEST
E. 505,658   T. 37.33%
P. Skinner, *Lab.*	77,346
*B. Patterson, *C.*	60,569
J. Daly, *LD*	33,869
C. Mackinlay, *UK Independence*	9,750
Ms P. Kemp, *Green*	5,651
J. Bowler, *NLP*	1,598
Lab. majority	16,777

(Boundary change since June 1989)

LANCASHIRE CENTRAL
E. 505,224   T. 33.23%
M. Hendrick, *Lab.*	73,420
*M. Welsh, *C.*	61,229
Ms J. Ross-Mills, *LD*	20,578
D. Hill, *Home Rule*	6,751
C. Maile, *Green*	4,169
Ms J. Ayliffe, *NLP*	1,727
Lab. majority	12,191

(Boundary change since June 1989)

LANCASHIRE SOUTH
E. 514,840   T. 33.14%
*M. Hindley, *Lab.*	92,598
R. Topham, *C.*	51,194
J. Ault, *LD*	17,008
J. Gaffney, *Green*	4,774

Mrs E. Rokas, *Ind.*	3,439
J. Renwick, *NLP*	1,605
Lab. majority	41,404

(Boundary change since June 1989)

LEEDS
E. 521,989   T. 30.03%
*M. McGowan, *Lab.*	89,160
N. Carmichael, *C.*	36,078
Ms J. Harvey, *LD*	17,575
M. Meadowcroft, *Lib.*	6,617
Ms C. Nash, *Green*	6,283
Ms S. Hayward, *NLP*	1,018
Lab. majority	53,082

(June 1989, Lab. maj. 42,518)

LEICESTER
E. 515,343   T. 37.63%
Ms S. Waddington, *Lab.*	87,048
A. Marshall, *C.*	66,764
M. Jones, *LD*	28,890
G. Forse, *Green*	8,941
Ms P. Saunders, *NLP*	2,283
Lab. majority	20,284

(Boundary change since June 1989)

LINCOLNSHIRE AND HUMBERSIDE SOUTH
E. 539,981   T. 36.34%
Mrs V. Hardstaff, *Lab.*	83,172
*W. Newton Dunn, *C.*	69,427
K. Melton, *LD*	27,241
Ms R. Robinson, *Green*	8,563
E. Wheeler, *Lib.*	3,434
I. Selby, *NCSA*	2,973
H. Kelly, *NLP*	1,429
Lab. majority	13,745

(Boundary change since June 1989)

LONDON CENTRAL
E. 494,610   T. 32.57%
*S. Newens, *Lab.*	75,711
A. Elliott, *C.*	50,652
Ms S. Ludford, *LD*	20,176
Ms N. Kortvelyessy, *Green*	7,043
H. Le Fanu, *UK Independence*	4,157
C. Slapper, *Soc.*	1,593
Ms S. Hamza, *NLP*	1,215
G. Weiss, *Rainbow*	547
Lab. majority	25,059

(June 1989, Lab. maj. 11,542)

LONDON EAST
E. 511,523   T. 33.38%
*Ms C. Tongue, *Lab.*	98,759
Ms V. Taylor, *C.*	41,370
K. Montgomery, *LD*	15,566
G. Batten, *UK Independence*	5,974
J. Baguley, *Green*	4,337
O. Tillett, *Third Way Independence*	3,484
N. Kahn, *NLP*	1,272
Lab. majority	57,389

(June 1989, Lab. maj. 27,385)

LONDON NORTH
E. 541,269   T. 34.00%
*Mrs P. Green, *Lab.*	102,059
M. Keegan, *C.*	53,711
I. Mann, *LD*	15,739
Ms H. Jago, *Green*	5,666
I. Booth, *UK Independence*	5,099
G. Sabrizi, *Judo*	880

J. Hinde, *NLP*	856
Lab. majority	48,348

(June 1989, Lab. maj. 5,837)

LONDON NORTH EAST
E. 486,016   T. 26.60%
*A. Lomas, *Lab.*	80,256
S. Gordon, *C.*	23,171
K. Appiah, *LD*	10,242
Ms J. Lambert, *Green*	8,386
E. Murat, *Lib.*	2,573
P. Compobassi, *UK Independence*	2,015
R. Archer, *NLP*	1,111
M. Fischer, *Comm. GB*	869
A. Hyland, *ICP4*	679
Lab. majority	57,085

(June 1989, Lab. maj. 47,767)

LONDON NORTH WEST
E. 481,272   T. 35.13%
R. Evans, *Lab.*	80,192
*The Lord Bethell, *C.*	62,750
Ms H. Leighter, *LD*	18,998
D. Johnson, *Green*	4,743
Ms A. Murphy, *Comm. GB*	858
Ms T. Sullivan, *NLP*	807
C. Palmer, *Century*	740
Lab. majority	17,442

(June 1989, C. maj. 7,400)

LONDON SOUTH AND SURREY EAST
E. 486,358   T. 34.38%
*J. Moorhouse, *C.*	64,813
Ms G. Rolles, *Lab.*	56,074
M. Reinisch, *LD*	32,059
J. Cornford, *Green*	7,046
J. Major, *Loony X*	3,339
A. Reeve, *Capital P.*	2,983
P. Levy, *NLP*	887
C. majority	8,739

(Boundary change since June 1989)

LONDON SOUTH EAST
E. 493,178   T. 35.38%
S. Spiers, *Lab.*	71,505
*P. Price, *C.*	63,483
J. Fryer, *LD*	25,271
I. Mouland, *Green*	6,399
R. Almond, *Lib.*	3,881
K. Lowne, *NF*	2,926
J. Small, *NLP*	1,025
Lab. majority	8,022

(Boundary change since June 1989)

LONDON SOUTH INNER
E. 510,609   T. 27.30%
*R. Balfe, *Lab.*	85,079
A. Boff, *C.*	25,859
A. Graves, *LD*	20,708
S. Collins, *Green*	6,570
M. Leighton, *NLP*	1,179
Lab. majority	59,220

(Boundary change since June 1989)

LONDON SOUTH WEST
E. 479,246   T. 34.35%
*Ms A. Pollack, *Lab.*	81,850
Prof. P. Treleaven, *C.*	50,875
G. Blanchard, *LD*	18,697
T. Walsh, *Green*	5,460
A. Scholefield, *UK Independence*	4,912
C. Hopewell, *Capital P.*	1,840
M. Simson, *NLP*	625

J. Quanjer, *Spirit of Europe*   377
Lab. majority   30,975
(Boundary change since June 1989)

LONDON WEST
E. 505,791   *T.* 36.02%
*M. Elliott, *Lab.*   94,562
R. Guy, *C.*   52,287
W. Mallinson, *LD*   21,561
J. Bradley, *Green*   6,134
G. Roberts, *UK Independence*   4,583
W. Binding, *NF*   1,963
R. Johnson, *NLP*   1,105
Lab. majority   42,275
(June 1989, Lab. maj. 14,808)

MERSEYSIDE EAST AND WIGAN
E. 518,196   *T.* 24.66%
*T. Wynn, *Lab.*   91,986
C. Manson, *C.*   17,899
Ms F. Clucas, *LD*   8,874
J. Melia, *Lib.*   4,765
L. Brown, *Green*   3,280
G. Hutchard, *NLP*   1,009
Lab. majority   74,087
(June 1989, Lab. maj. 76,867)

MERSEYSIDE WEST
E. 515,909   *T.* 26.18%
*K. Stewart, *Lab.*   78,819
C. Varley, *C.*   27,008
D. Bamber, *LD*   19,097
S. Radford, *Lib.*   4,714
Ms L. Lever, *Green*   4,573
J. Collins, *NLP*   852
Lab. majority   51,811
(June 1989, Lab. maj. 49,817)
See also page 275

MIDLANDS WEST
E. 533,742   *T.* 31.28%
S. Murphy, *Lab.*   99,242
M. Simpson, *C.*   44,419
G. Baldauf-Good, *LD*   12,195
M. Hyde, *Lib.*   5,050
C. Mattingly, *Green*   4,390
J. Oldbury, *NLP*   1,641
Lab. majority   54,823
(June 1989, Lab. maj. 42,364)

NORFOLK
E. 513,553   *T.* 44.25%
C. Needle, *Lab.*   102,711
*P. Howell, *C.*   76,424
P. Burall, *LD*   39,107
A. Holmes, *Green*   7,938
B. Parsons, *NLP*   1,075
Lab. majority   26,287
(Boundary change since June 1989)

NORTHAMPTONSHIRE AND BLABY
E. 524,916   *T.* 39.37%
Mrs A. Billingham, *Lab.*   95,317
*A. Simpson, *C.*   69,232
K. Scudder, *LD*   27,616
Ms A. Bryant, *Green*   9,121
I. Whitaker, *Ind.*   4,397
B. Spivack, *NLP*   972
Lab. majority   26,085
(Boundary change since June 1989)

NORTHUMBRIA
E. 516,680   *T.* 33.65%
*G. Adam, *Lab.*   103,087
J. Flack, *C.*   36,929
L. Opik, *LD*   20,195
D. Lott, *UK Independence*   7,210
J. Hartshorne, *Green*   5,714
L. Walch, *NLP*   740
Lab. majority   66,158
(June 1989, Lab. maj. 60,040)

NOTTINGHAM AND
LEICESTERSHIRE NORTH WEST
E. 507,915   *T.* 37.68%
*Ms M. Read, *Lab.*   95,344
M. Brandon-Bravo, *C.*   55,676
A. Wood, *LD*   23,836
Ms S. Blount, *Green*   7,035
J. Downes, *UK Independence*   5,849
P. Walton, *Ind. Out*   2,710
Mrs J. Christou, *NLP*   927
Lab. majority   39,668
(Boundary change since June 1989)

NOTTINGHAMSHIRE NORTH AND
CHESTERFIELD
E. 490,330   *T.* 36.95%
*K. Coates, *Lab.*   114,353
D. Hazell, *C.*   38,093
Ms S. Pearce, *LD*   21,936
G. Jones, *Green*   5,159
Ms S. Lincoln, *NLP*   1,632
Lab. majority   76,260
(Boundary change since June 1989)

PEAK DISTRICT
E. 511,357   *T.* 39.02%
Ms A. McCarthy, *Lab.*   105,853
R. Fletcher, *C.*   56,546
Ms S. Barber, *LD*   29,979
M. Shipley, *Green*   5,598
D. Collins, *NLP*   1,533
Lab. majority   49,307
(Boundary change since June 1989)

SHEFFIELD
E. 476,530   *T.* 27.50%
*R. Barton, *Lab.*   76,397
Ms S. Anginotti, *LD*   26,109
Ms K. Twitchen, *C.*   22,374
B. New, *Green*   4,742
M. England, *Comm.*   834
R. Hurford, *NLP*   577
Lab. majority   50,288
(Boundary change since June 1989)

SOMERSET AND DEVON NORTH
E. 517,349   *T.* 47.09%
G. Watson, *LD*   106,187
*Mrs M. Daly, *C.*   83,678
J. Pilgrim, *Lab.*   34,540
D. Taylor, *Green*   10,870
G. Livings, *New Britain*   7,165
M. Lucas, *NLP*   1,200
LD majority   22,509
(Boundary change since June 1989)

SOUTH DOWNS WEST
E. 486,793   *T.* 39.45%
J. Provan, *C.*   83,813
Dr J. Walsh, *LD*   62,746
Ms L. Armstrong, *Lab.*   32,344
E. Paine, *Green*   7,703

W. Weights, *Lib.*   3,630
P. Kember, *NLP*   1,794
C. majority   21,067
(Boundary change since June 1989)

STAFFORDSHIRE EAST AND DERBY
E. 519,553   *T.* 35.46%
P. Whitehead, *Lab.*   102,393
Ms J. Evans, *C.*   50,197
Ms D. Brass, *LD*   17,469
I. Crompton, *UK Independence*   6,993
R. Clarke, *Green*   4,272
R. Jones, *NF*   2,098
Ms D. Grice, *NLP*   793
Lab. majority   72,196
(Boundary change since June 1989)

STAFFORDSHIRE WEST AND
CONGLETON
E. 502,395   *T.* 31.60%
M. Tappin, *Lab.*   84,337
A. Brown, *C.*   44,060
J. Stevens, *LD*   24,430
D. Hoppe, *Green*   4,533
D. Lines, *NLP*   1,403
Lab. majority   40,277
(Boundary change since June 1989)

SUFFOLK AND NORFOLK SOUTH
WEST
E. 477,668   *T.* 38.38%
D. Thomas, *Lab.*   74,304
*A. Turner, *C.*   61,769
R. Atkins, *LD*   37,975
A. Slade, *Green*   7,760
E. Kaplan, *NLP*   1,530
Lab. majority   12,535
(Boundary change since June 1989)

SURREY
E. 514,130   *T.* 37.51%
*T. Spencer, *C.*   83,405
Mrs S. Thomas, *LD*   56,387
Ms F. Wolf, *Lab.*   30,894
Mrs S. Porter, *UK Independence*   7,717
H. Charlton, *Green*   7,198
J. Walker, *Ind. Britain in Europe*   4,627
Mrs J. Thomas, *NLP*   2,638
C. majority   27,018
(Boundary change since June 1989)

SUSSEX EAST AND KENT SOUTH
E. 513,550   *T.* 41.90%
*Sir J. Stewart-Clark, *C.*   83,141
D. Bellotti, *LD*   76,929
N. Palmer, *Lab.*   35,273
A. Burgess, *UK Independence*   9,058
Ms R. Addison, *Green*   7,439
Ms T. Williamson, *Lib.*   2,558
P. Cragg, *NLP*   765
C. majority   6,212
(Boundary change since June 1989)

SUSSEX SOUTH AND CRAWLEY
E. 492,413   *T.* 37.64%
B. Donnelly, *C.*   62,860
Ms J. Edmond Smith, *Lab.*   61,114
J. Williams, *LD*   41,410
Ms P. Beever, *Green*   9,348
D. Horner, *Ind. Euro-Sceptic*   7,106
N. Furness, *Anti Fed. C.*   2,618
A. Hankey, *NLP*   901

C. majority 1,746
(Boundary change since June 1989)

THAMES VALLEY
E. 543,685   *T.* 34.80%
*J. Stevens, *C.* 70,485
J. Howarth, *Lab.* 69,727
N. Bathurst, *LD* 33,187
P. Unsworth, *Green* 6,120
J. Clark, *Lib.* 5,381
P. Owen, *Loony C* 2,859
M. Grenville, *NLP* 1,453
C. majority 758
(June 1989, C. maj. 26,491)

TYNE AND WEAR
E. 516,436   *T.* 28.02%
*A. Donnelly, *Lab.* 107,604
I. Liddell-Grainger, *C.* 19,224
P. Maughan, *LD* 8,706
G. Edwards, *Green* 4,375
Ms W. Lundgren, *Lib.* 4,164
A. Fisken, *NLP* 650
Lab. majority 88,380
(June 1989, Lab. maj. 95,780)

WIGHT AND HAMPSHIRE SOUTH
E. 488,398   *T.* 37.16%
R. Perry, *C.* 63,306
M. Hancock, *LD* 58,205
Ms S. Fry, *Lab.* 40,442
J. Browne, *Ind.* 12,140
P. Fuller, *Green* 6,697
W. Treend, *NLP* 722
C. majority 5,101
(Boundary change since June 1989)

WILTSHIRE NORTH AND BATH
E. 496,591   *T.* 41.46%
*Mrs C. Jackson, *C.* 71,872
Ms J. Matthew, *LD* 63,085
Ms J. Norris, *Lab.* 50,489
P. Cullen, *Lib.* 6,760
M. Davidson, *Green* 5,974
T. Hedges, *UK Independence* 5,842
D. Cooke, *NLP* 1,148
Dr J. Day, *CPP* 725
C. majority 8,787
(Boundary change since June 1989)

WORCESTERSHIRE AND
WARWICKSHIRE SOUTH
E. 551,162   *T.* 37.98%
J. Corrie, *C.* 73,573
Ms G. Gschaider, *Lab.* 72,369
P. Larner, *LD* 44,168
Ms J. Alty, *Green* 9,273
C. Hards, *National Independence* 8,447
J. Brewster, *NLP* 1,510
C. majority 1,204
(Boundary change since June 1989)

YORKSHIRE NORTH
E. 475,686   *T.* 38.70%
*E. McMillan-Scott, *C.* 70,036
B. Regan, *Lab.* 62,964
M. Pitts, *LD* 43,171
Dr R. Richardson, *Green* 7,036
S. Withers, *NLP* 891
C. majority 7,072
(Boundary change since June 1989)

YORKSHIRE SOUTH
E. 523,401   *T.* 28.64%
*N. West, *Lab.* 109,004
J. Howard, *C.* 20,695
Ms C. Roderick, *LD* 11,798
P. Davies, *UK Independence* 3,948
J. Waters, *Green* 3,775
N. Broome, *NLP* 681
Lab. majority 88,309
(June 1989, Lab. maj. 91,784)
See also page 275

YORKSHIRE SOUTH WEST
E. 547,469   *T.* 29.03%
*T. Megahy, *Lab.* 94,025
Mrs C. Adamson, *C.* 34,463
D. Ridgway, *LD* 21,595
A. Cooper, *Green* 7,163
G. Mead, *NLP* 1,674
Lab. majority 59,562
(Boundary change since June 1989)

YORKSHIRE WEST
E. 490,078   *T.* 34.61%
*B. Seal, *Lab.* 90,652
R. Booth, *C.* 42,455
C. Bidwell, *LD* 20,452
R. Pearson, *New Britain* 8,027
C. Harris, *Green* 7,154
D. Whitley, *NLP* 894
Lab. majority 48,197
(Boundary change since June 1989)

WALES

SOUTH WALES CENTRAL
E. 477,182   *T.* 39.40%
*W. David, *Lab.* 115,396
Ms L. Verity, *C.* 29,314
G. Llywelyn, *PC* 18,857
J. Dixon, *LD* 18,471
C. von Ruhland, *Green* 4,002
R. Griffiths, *Comm. YBG* 1,073
G. Duguay, *NLP* 889
Lab. majority 86,082
(Boundary change since June 1989)

SOUTH WALES EAST
E. 454,794   *T.* 43.07%
Mrs G. Kinnock, *Lab.* 144,907
Mrs R. Blomfield-Smith, *C.* 24,660
C. Woolgrove, *LD* 9,963
C. Mann, *PC* 9,550
R. Coghill, *Green* 4,509
Ms S. Williams, *Welsh Soc.* 1,270
Dr R. Brussatis, *NLP* 1,027
Lab. majority 120,247
(Boundary change since June 1989)

SOUTH WALES WEST
E. 395,131   *T.* 39.92%
*Revd D. Morris, *Lab.* 104,263
R. Buckland, *C.* 19,293
J. Bushell, *LD* 15,499
Ms C. Adams, *PC* 12,364
Ms J. Evans, *Green* 4,114
Ms H. Evans, *NLP* 1,112
Capt. Beany, *Beanus* 1,106
Lab. majority 84,970
(Boundary change since June 1989)

WALES MID AND WEST
E. 401,529   *T.* 48.00%
Ms E. Morgan, *Lab.* 78,092
M. Phillips, *PC* 48,858
P. Bone, *C.* 31,606
Ms J. Hughes, *LD* 23,719
D. Rowlands, *UK Independence* 5,536
Dr C. Busby, *Green* 3,938
T. Griffith-Jones, *NLP* 988
Lab. majority 29,234
(Boundary change since June 1989)

WALES NORTH
E. 475,829   *T.* 45.34%
*J. Wilson, *Lab.* 88,091
D. Wigley, *PC* 72,849
G. Mon Hughes, *C.* 33,450
Ms R. Parry, *LD* 14,828
P. Adams, *Green* 2,850
D. Hughes, *NLP* 2,065
M. Cooksey, *Ind.* 1,623
Lab. majority 15,242
(Boundary change since June 1989)

SCOTLAND

GLASGOW
E. 463,364   *T.* 34.46%
W. Miller, *Lab.* 83,953
T. Chalmers, *SNP* 40,795
T. Sheridan, *SML* 12,113
R. Wilkinson, *C.* 10,888
J. Money, *LD* 7,291
P. O'Brien, *Green* 2,252
J. Fleming, *Soc.* 1,125
M. Wilkinson, *NLP* 868
C. Marsden, *ICP* 381
Lab. majority 43,158
(June 1989, Lab. maj. 59,232)

HIGHLANDS AND ISLANDS
E. 328,104   *T.* 39.09%
*Mrs W. Ewing, *SNP* 74,872
M. Macmillan, *Lab.* 19,956
M. Tennant, *C.* 15,767
H. Morrison, *LD* 12,919
Dr E. Scott, *Green* 3,140
M. Carr, *UK Independence* 1,096
Ms M. Gilmour, *NLP* 522
SNP majority 54,916
(June 1989, SNP maj. 44,695)

LOTHIANS
E. 520,943   *T.* 38.69%
*D. Martin, *Lab.* 90,531
K. Brown, *SNP* 53,324
Dr P. McNally, *C.* 33,526
Ms H. Campbell, *LD* 17,883
R. Harper, *Green* 5,149
J. McGregor, *Soc.* 637
M. Siebert, *NLP* 500
Lab. majority 37,207
(June 1989, Lab. maj. 38,826)

SCOTLAND MID AND FIFE
E. 546,060   *T.* 38.25%
*A. Falconer, *Lab.* 95,667
R. Douglas, *SNP* 64,254
P. Page, *C.* 28,192

Ms H. Lyall, *LD*	17,192
M. Johnston, *Green*	3,015
T. Pringle, *NLP*	532
Lab. majority	31,413
(June 1989, Lab. maj. 52,157)	

SCOTLAND NORTH EAST
E. 575,748   *T.* 37.72%

A. Macartney, *SNP*	92,892
*H. McCubbin, *Lab.*	61,665
Dr R. Harris, *C.*	40,372
S. Horner, *LD*	18,008
K. Farnsworth, *Green*	2,569
Ms M. Ward, *Comm. GB*	689
L. Mair, *Neeps*	584
D. Paterson, *NLP*	371
SNP majority	31,227
(June 1989, Lab. maj. 2,613)	

SCOTLAND SOUTH
E. 500,643   *T.* 40.14%

*A. Smith, *Lab.*	90,750
A. Hutton, *C.*	45,595
Mrs C. Creech, *SNP*	45,032
D. Millar, *LD*	13,363
J. Hein, *Lib.*	3,249
Ms L. Hendry, *Green*	2,429
G. Gay, *NLP*	539
Lab. majority	45,155
(June 1989, Lab. maj. 15,693)	

STRATHCLYDE EAST
E. 492,618   *T.* 37.26%

*K. Collins, *Lab.*	106,476
I. Hamilton, *SNP*	54,136

B. Cooklin, *C.*	13,915
R. Stewart, *LD*	6,383
A. Whitelaw, *Green*	1,874
D. Gilmour, *NLP*	787
Lab. majority	52,340
(June 1989, Lab. maj. 60,317)	

STRATHCLYDE WEST
E. 489,129   *T.* 40.05%

*H. McMahon, *Lab.*	86,957
C. Campbell, *SNP*	61,934
J. Godfrey, *C.*	28,414
D. Herbison, *LD*	14,772
Ms K. Allan, *Green*	2,886
Ms S. Gilmour, *NLP*	918
Lab. majority	25,023
(June 1989, Lab. maj. 39,591)	

NORTHERN IRELAND

Northern Ireland forms a three-member seat with a single transferable vote system
E. 1,150,304 *T.* 48.67%

*Revd I. Paisley, *DUP*	163,246
*J. Hume, *SDLP*	161,992
*J. Nicholson, *UUUP*	133,459
Mrs M. Clark-Glass, *All.*	23,157
T. Hartley, *SF*	21,273
Ms D. McGuinness, *SF*	17,195
F. Molloy, *SF*	16,747
Revd H. Ross, *Ulster Independence*	7,858

Miss M. Boal, *C.*	5,583
J. Lowry, *WP*	2,543
N. Cusack, *Ind. Lab.*	2,464
J. Anderson, *NLP*	1,418
Mrs J. Campion, *Peace Coalition*	1,088
D. Kerr, *Independence for Ulster*	571
Ms S. Thompson, *NLP*	454
M. Kennedy, *NLP*	419
R. Mooney, *Const. NI*	400

BY-ELECTIONS SINCE 9 JUNE 1994

MERSEYSIDE WEST
(12 December 1996)
E. 515,549   *T.* 11.4%

R. Corbett, *Lab.*	31,484
J. Myers, *C.*	12,780
K. J. C. Reid, *LD*	8,829
S. R. Radford, *Lib.*	4,050
S. Darby, *Nat. Dem.*	718
J. D. Collins, *NLP*	680
Lab. majority	18,704

YORKSHIRE SOUTH
(7 May 1998)
E. 221,741   *T.* 28.29%

Ms L. McAvan, *Lab.*	62,275
Ms D. P. Wallis, *LD*	22,051
R. Goodwill, *C.*	21,085
P. Davis, *UK Ind.*	13,830
Lab. majority	40,224

COMMONWEALTH PARLIAMENTARY ASSOCIATION (1911)

The Commonwealth Parliamentary Association consists of 141 branches in the national, state, provincial or territorial parliaments in the countries of the Commonwealth. Conferences and general assemblies are held every year in different countries of the Commonwealth.
President (1998–9), Hon. Hector McClean, MP, Speaker of the House of Representatives, Trinidad and Tobago
Chairman of the Executive Committee (1996–), Hon. Billie Miller, MP (Barbados)
Secretary-General, A. R. Donahoe, QC, Suite 700, Westminster House, 7 Millbank, London SW1P 3JA

UNITED KINGDOM BRANCH
Hon. Presidents, The Lord Chancellor; Madam Speaker
Chairman of Branch, Rt. Hon. Tony Blair, MP
Chairman of Executive Committee, Donald Anderson, MP

Secretary, A. Pearson, Westminster Hall, Houses of Parliament, London, SW1A 0AA

THE INTER-PARLIAMENTARY UNION (1889)

The Union exists to facilitate personal contact between members of all parliaments in the promotion of representative institutions, peace and international co-operation.
Secretary-General, A. Johnsson, Place du Petit-Saconnex, BP 99, 1211 Geneva 19, Switzerland

BRITISH GROUP
Palace of Westminster, London SW1A 0AA
Hon. Presidents, The Lord Chancellor; Madam Speaker
President, Rt. Hon. Tony Blair, MP
Chairman, David Marshall, MP
Secretary, D. Ramsay

The Government

as at 4 August 1998

Prime Minister, First Lord of the Treasury and Minister for the Civil Service
The Rt. Hon. Anthony (Tony) Blair, MP, since May 1997
Deputy Prime Minister and Secretary of State for the Environment, Transport and the Regions
The Rt. Hon. John Prescott, MP, since May 1997
Chancellor of the Exchequer
The Rt. Hon. Gordon Brown, MP, since May 1997
Secretary of State for Foreign and Commonwealth Affairs
The Rt. Hon. Robin Cook, MP, since May 1997
Lord Chancellor
The Lord Irvine of Lairg, PC, QC, since May 1997
Secretary of State for the Home Department
The Rt. Hon. Jack Straw, MP, since May 1997
Secretary of State for Education and Employment
The Rt. Hon. David Blunkett, MP, since May 1997
President of the Council and Leader of the House of Commons
The Rt. Hon. Margaret Beckett, MP, since July 1998
Minister for the Cabinet Office and Chancellor of the Duchy of Lancaster
The Rt. Hon. Dr Jack Cunningham, MP, since July 1998
Secretary of State for Scotland
The Rt. Hon. Donald Dewar, MP, since May 1997
Secretary of State for Defence
The Rt. Hon. George Robertson, MP, since May 1997
Secretary of State for Health
The Rt. Hon. Frank Dobson, MP, since May 1997
Parliamentary Secretary to the Treasury (Chief Whip)
The Rt. Hon. Ann Taylor, MP
Secretary of State for Culture, Media and Sport
The Rt. Hon. Chris Smith, MP, since May 1997
Secretary of State for Northern Ireland
The Rt. Hon. Dr Marjorie (Mo) Mowlam, MP, since May 1997
Secretary of State for Wales
The Rt. Hon. Ron Davies, MP, since May 1997
Secretary of State for International Development
The Rt. Hon. Clare Short, MP, since May 1997
Secretary of State for Social Security
The Rt. Hon. Alistair Darling, MP, since July 1998
Minister of Agriculture, Fisheries and Food
The Rt. Hon. Nick Brown, MP, since July 1998
Leader of the House of Lords and Minister for Women
The Baroness Jay of Paddington*, since July 1998
Secretary of State for Trade and Industry
The Rt. Hon. Peter Mandelson, MP, since July 1998
Chief Secretary to the Treasury
The Rt. Hon. Stephen Byers, MP, since July 1998

The Minister of State at the Department of the Environment, Transport and the Regions with responsibility for Transport, and the Government Chief Whip in the House of Lords will attend Cabinet meetings although they are not members of the Cabinet.
* Appointed as Lord Privy Seal

LAW OFFICERS

Attorney-General
The Rt. Hon. John Morris, QC, MP, since May 1997
Lord Advocate
The Lord Hardie, PC, QC, since May 1997
Solicitor-General
Ross Cranston, MP, since July 1998
Solicitor-General for Scotland
Colin Boyd, QC

MINISTERS OF STATE

Agriculture, Fisheries and Food
Jeff Rooker, MP (*Food Safety*)
Cabinet Office
The Lord Falconer of Thoroton, QC
Defence
Doug Henderson, MP (*Armed Forces*)
The Lord Gilbert, PC, Ph.D. (*Defence Procurement*)
Education and Employment
The Rt. Hon. Andrew Smith, MP (*Welfare to Work, Equal Opportunities*)
Estelle Morris, MP (*School Standards*)
The Baroness Blackstone, Ph.D.
Environment, Transport and the Regions
The Rt. Hon. Dr John Reid, MP (*Transport*)
The Rt. Hon. Michael Meacher, MP (*Environment*)
Hilary Armstrong, MP (*Local Government, Housing*)
Richard Caborn, MP (*Regions, Regeneration, Planning*)
Foreign and Commonwealth Office
Joyce Quin, MP (*Minister for Europe*)
Derek Fatchett, MP
Tony Lloyd, MP
Health
Alan Milburn, MP (*NHS Structure and Resources*)
Tessa Jowell, MP (*Public Health, Women's Issues*)
Home Office
Alun Michael, MP (*Criminal and Police Policy*)
The Lord Williams of Mostyn, QC (*Constitution, Prisons, Probation*)
Lord Chancellor's Department
Geoff Hoon, MP
Northern Ireland Office
Paul Murphy, MP (*Political Development, Finance, Personnel, Information*)
Adam Ingram, MP (*Security, Criminal Justice, Economic Development*)
Scottish Office
Helen Liddell, MP (*Education, Women's Issues, Co-ordination and Presentation of Policy*)
Henry McLeish, MP (*Home Affairs, Devolution, Local Government*)
Social Security
John Denham, MP
Trade and Industry
John Battle, MP (*Energy, Industry, Environment*)
Ian McCartney, MP (*Employment Relations*)
Brian Wilson, MP (*Trade*)
The Lord Simon of Highbury, CBE (*Trade and Competitiveness in Europe*)†

Treasury
Geoffrey Robinson, MP (*Paymaster-General*)
Dawn Primarolo, MP (*Financial Secretary*)
Patricia Hewitt, MP (*Economic Secretary*)
The Lord Simon of Highbury, CBE (*Trade and Competitiveness in Europe*)†
† Joint DTI/Treasury minister

UNDER-SECRETARIES OF STATE

Agriculture, Fisheries and Food
Elliot Morley, MP (*Fisheries, Countryside*)
The Lord Donoughue, D.phil. (*Farming, Food Industry*)
Cabinet Office
Peter Kilfoyle, MP
Culture, Media and Sport
Alan Howarth, MP (*Arts*)
Tony Banks, MP (*Sport*)
Janet Anderson, MP (*Tourism, Film, Broadcasting*)
Defence
John Spellar, MP
Education and Employment
Margaret Hodge, MP (*Employment, Equal Opportunities*)
Charles Clarke, MP (*Schools*)
George Mudie, MP (*Lifelong Learning*)
Environment, Transport and the Regions
Nick Raynsford, MP (*London, Construction*)
Glenda Jackson, MP (*Transport in London*)
The Lord Whitty (*Roads*)
Alan Meale, MP (*Environment, Wildlife, Health and Safety Executive, Regeneration, the Regions*)
Foreign and Commonwealth Office
The Baroness Symons of Vernham Dean
Health
Paul Boateng, MP (*Social Care, Mental Health*)
The Baroness Hayman (*NHS Development, Cancer, Emergency Services*)
Home Office
George Howarth, MP (*Prisons, Probation, Fire and Emergency Planning, Drugs, Elections, Gambling, Data Protection*)
Michael O'Brien, MP (*Immigration, Nationality*)
Kate Hoey, MP (*Metropolitan Police, Women's Issues, International Co-operation*)
International Development
George Foulkes, MP
Northern Ireland Office
John McFall, MP (*Education, Training and Employment, Health, Community Relations*)
The Lord Dubs (*Environment, Agriculture*)
Scottish Office
Dr Calum MacDonald, MP (*Housing, Transport, European Affairs*)
Sam Galbraith, MP (*Health, Arts*)
The Lord Sewel, CBE (*Agriculture, Environment, Fisheries*)
Gus Macdonald‡ (*Business and Industry*)

Social Security
The Baroness Hollis of Heigham, D.phil. (*Child Benefit, Child Support, War Pensions*)
Angela Eagle, MP (*Income-related Benefits, International and Green Issues*)
Stephen Timms, MP (*Disability and Sickness Benefits, National Insurance Contributions, Devolution, Independent Living Fund*)
Trade and Industry
Dr Kim Howells, MP (*Competition, Consumer Affairs*)
Barbara Roche, MP (*Small Firms, Regional Policy*)
The Lord Sainsbury of Turville (*Science*)
Welsh Office
Peter Hain, MP
Jon Owen Jones, MP
‡ Not an MP; will receive a life peerage to enable him to sit in the House of Lords

GOVERNMENT WHIPS

HOUSE OF LORDS

Captain of the Honourable Corps of Gentlemen-at-Arms (Chief Whip)
The Lord Carter, PC
Captain of The Queen's Bodyguard of the Yeoman of the Guard (Deputy Chief Whip)
The Lord McIntosh of Haringey
Lords-in-Waiting
The Lord Hoyle; The Lord Hunt of King's Heath
Baronesses-in-Waiting
The Baroness Farrington of Ribbleton; The Baroness Ramsay of Cartvale; The Baroness Amos

HOUSE OF COMMONS

Parliamentary Secretary to the Treasury (Chief Whip)
The Rt. Hon. Ann Taylor, MP
Treasurer of HM Household (Deputy Chief Whip)
Keith Bradley, MP
Comptroller of HM Household
Thomas McAvoy, MP
Vice-Chamberlain of HM Household
Graham Allen, MP
Lords Commissioners
Robert Ainsworth, MP; James Dowd, MP; Clive Betts, MP; David Jamieson, MP; Jane Kennedy, MP
Assistant Whips
David Clelland, MP; Kevin Hughes, MP; Anne McGuire, MP; David Hanson, MP; Michael Hall, MP; Keith Hill, MP; G regory Pope, MP

Government Departments and Public Offices

For changes notified after 31 August, *see* Stop-press

This section covers central government departments, executive agencies, regulatory bodies, other statutory independent organizations, and bodies which are government-financed or whose head is appointed by a government minister.

THE CIVIL SERVICE

Under the Next Steps programme, launched in 1988, many semi-autonomous executive agencies have been established with the aim of improving the performance of the Civil Service. Executive agencies operate within a framework set by the responsible minister which specifies policies, objectives and available resources. All executive agencies are set annual performance targets by their minister. Each agency has a chief executive, who is responsible for the day-to-day operations of the agency and who is accountable to the minister for the use of resources and for meeting the agency's targets. The minister accounts to Parliament for the work of the agency. Nearly 60 per cent of civil servants now work in executive agencies. Customs and Excise, the Inland Revenue, the Crown Prosecution Service and the Serious Fraud Office, which employ a further 17 per cent of civil servants, also operate on 'Next Steps' lines. In January 1998 there were about 468,180 permanent civil servants.

The Senior Civil Service was created in April 1996 and comprises about 3,000 staff from Permanent Secretary to the former Grade 5 level, including all agency chief executives. All government departments and executive agencies are now responsible for their own pay and grading systems for civil servants outside the Senior Civil Service. In practice the grades of the former Open structure are still in use in some organizations. The Open structure represented the following:

Grade   *Title*
1   Permanent Secretary
1A   Second Permanent Secretary
2   Deputy Secretary
3   Under-Secretary
4   Chief Scientific Officer B, Professional and Technology Directing A
5   Assistant Secretary, Deputy Chief Scientific Officer, Professional and Technology Directing B
6   Senior Principal, Senior Principal Scientific Officer, Professional and Technology Superintending Grade
7   Principal, Principal Scientific Officer, Principal Professional and Technology Officer

SALARIES 1998–9

MINISTERIAL SALARIES *from 1 April 1998*

Ministers who are Members of the House of Commons receive a parliamentary salary (£45,066) in addition to their ministerial salary.

*Prime Minister	£102,750
*Cabinet minister (Commons)	£61,650
*†Cabinet minister (Lords)	£80,107
Minister of State (Commons)	£31,981
Minister of State (Lords)	£53,264
Parliamentary Under-Secretary (Commons)	£24,273
Parliamentary Under-Secretary (Lords)	£44,832

* These ministers have decided not to take the full salaries provided for them for the financial year 1998–9. They will instead draw the following ministerial salaries: Prime Minister, £60,167; Cabinet minister (Commons), £45,201; Cabinet minister (Lords), £60,495
† Except the Lord Chancellor, who receives a salary of £148,850

SPECIAL ADVISERS' SALARIES *from 1 April 1998*

Special advisers are paid out of public funds; their salaries are negotiated individually, but are usually in the range £24,836 to £74,954.

CIVIL SERVICE SALARIES *from 1 December 1998*

Senior Civil Service (SCS)

Secretary of the Cabinet and Head of the Home Civil Service	£95,720–£164,310
Permanent Secretary	£95,720–£164,310
Band 9	£85,080–£120,490
Band 8	£77,840–£113,680
Band 7	£71,250–£107,300
Band 6	£65,080–£101,350
Band 5	£59,450–£95,720
Band 4	£54,230–£90,400
Band 3	£49,130–£80,400
Band 2	£44,560–£71,470
Band 1	£40,420–£63,490

Staff are placed in pay bands according to their level of responsibility and taking account of other factors such as experience and marketability. Movement within and between bands is based on performance. A recruitment and retention allowance of up to £3,000 may be paid in certain circumstances in addition to the salary ranges shown for bands 1 to 9.

Other Civil Servants

Following the delegation of responsibility for pay and grading to government departments and agencies from 1 April 1996, it is no longer possible to show the pay rates for staff outside the Senior Civil Service. Individual departments and agencies now have their own pay systems in operation.

ADJUDICATOR'S OFFICE
Haymarket House, 28 Haymarket, London SW1Y 4SP
Tel 0171-930 2292; fax 0171-930 2298

The Adjudicator's Office opened in 1993 and investigates complaints about the way the Inland Revenue (including the Valuation Office Agency), Customs and Excise, the Contributions Agency and the Contributions Unit of the Social Security Agency in Northern Ireland have handled an individual's affairs.

The Adjudicator, Ms E. Filkin
Head of Office, M. Savage

ADVISORY, CONCILIATION AND ARBITRATION SERVICE

Brandon House, 180 Borough High Street, London
SE1 1LW
Tel 0171-210 3613; fax 0171-210 3708

The Advisory, Conciliation and Arbitration Service (ACAS) was set up under the Employment Protection Act 1975 (the provisions now being found in the Trade Union and Labour Relations (Consolidation) Act 1992). ACAS is directed by a Council consisting of a full-time chairman and part-time employer, trade union and independent members, all appointed by the Secretary of State for Trade and Industry. The functions of the Service are to promote the improvement of industrial relations in general, to provide facilities for conciliation, mediation and arbitration as means of avoiding and resolving industrial disputes, and to provide advisory and information services on industrial relations matters to employers, employees and their representatives.

ACAS has regional offices in Birmingham, Bristol, Cardiff, Fleet, Glasgow, Leeds, Liverpool, London, Manchester, Newcastle upon Tyne and Nottingham.

Chairman, J. Hougham, CBE
Chief Conciliator (G4), D. Evans

MINISTRY OF AGRICULTURE, FISHERIES AND FOOD

Nobel House, 17 Smith Square, London SW1P 3JR
Tel 0171-238 6000; fax 0171-238 6591
E-mail: helpline@inf.maff.gov.uk
Web: http://www.maff.gov.uk/maffhome.htm

The Ministry of Agriculture, Fisheries and Food is responsible for government policies on agriculture, horticulture and fisheries in England and for policies relating to the safety and quality of food in the UK as a whole, including composition, labelling, additives, contaminants and new production processes. In association with the agriculture departments of the Scottish, Welsh and Northern Ireland Offices and with the Intervention Board (*see* page 315–16), the Ministry is responsible for negotiations in the EU on the common agricultural and fisheries policies, and for single European market questions relating to its responsibilities. Its remit also includes international agricultural and food trade policy.

The Ministry exercises responsibilities for the protection and enhancement of the countryside and the marine environment, for flood defence and for other rural issues. It is the licensing authority for veterinary medicines and the registration authority for pesticides. It administers policies relating to the control of animal, plant and fish diseases. It provides scientific, technical and professional services and advice to farmers, growers and ancillary industries, and it commissions research to assist in the formulation and assessment of policy and to underpin applied research and development work done by industry. Responsibility for food safety and standards will be transferred to the new Food Standards Agency, expected to be in operation by mid 1999.

Minister of Agriculture, Fisheries and Food, The Rt. Hon. Nick Brown, MP
Principal Private Secretary (SCS), D. North
Private Secretary, A. K. R. Slade

Minister of State, Jeff Rooker, MP (*Food Safety*)
Private Secretary, Mrs K. Lepper
Parliamentary Private Secretary, R. Burden, MP
Parliamentary Secretaries, Elliot Morley, MP (*Fisheries, the Countryside*); The Lord Donoughue, D.phil. (*Farming, the Food Industry*)
Private Secretary to Mr Morley, C. Porro
Private Secretary to Lord Donoughue, Dr P. Grimley
Parliamentary Clerk, M. Stickings
Permanent Secretary (SCS), R. J. Packer
Private Secretary, Mrs J. Milne

ESTABLISHMENT DEPARTMENT
Director of Establishments (SCS), R. A. Saunderson

ESTABLISHMENTS (GENERAL) AND OFFICE SERVICES DIVISION
Head of Division (G6), Dr J. A. Bailey

WELFARE BRANCH
Whitehall Place (West Block), London SW1A 2HH
Tel 0171-238 6000
Chief Welfare Officer (SEO), D. J. Jones

PERSONNEL MANAGEMENT AND DEVELOPMENT DIVISION
Head of Division (SCS), T. J. Osmond

DEPARTMENTAL HEALTH AND SAFETY UNIT
Spur 6, C Block, Government Buildings, Epsom Road, Guildford GU1 2LD
Tel 01483-403120/403753
Head of Unit (G7), C. R. Bradburn

TRAINING AND DEVELOPMENT BRANCH
Principal (G7), J. M. Cowley

BUILDING AND ESTATE MANAGEMENT
Eastbury House, 30–34 Albert Embankment, London SE1 7TL
Tel 0171-238 6000
Head of Division (SCS), J. A. S. Nickson

INFORMATION TECHNOLOGY DIRECTORATE
Room 755, St Christopher House, Southwark Street, London SE1 0UD
Tel 0171-921 1886
Director (SCS), A. G. Matthews
Head of Strategies (G6), P. Barber
Head of Applications (G6), D. D. Brown
Head of Infrastructure (G6), S. Soper

INFORMATION DIVISION
Tel 0171-238 6000; helpline 0645-335577
Chief Information Officer (SCS), G. Blakeway
Chief Press Officer (G7), M. Smith
Chief Publicity Officer (G7), N. Wagstaffe
Principal Librarian (G7), P. McShane

FINANCE DEPARTMENT
3–8 Whitehall Place (West Block), London SW1A 2HH
Tel 0171-238 6000
Principal Finance Officer (SCS), P. Elliott

FINANCIAL POLICY DIVISION
Head of Division (SCS), B. J. Harding

FINANCIAL MANAGEMENT DIVISION
Head of Division (SCS), J. M. Lowi

PROCUREMENT AND CONTRACTS DIVISION
Director of Audit (SCS), D. V. Fisher

CAP Schemes Management
Head of Division (SCS), L. G. Mitchell

Market Testing and Procurement Advice
Director (SCS), D. B. Rabey

Resource Management Strategy Unit
Head of Division (SCS), Mrs J. Flint

LEGAL DEPARTMENT
55 Whitehall, London swia 2ey
Tel 0171-238 6000
Legal Adviser and Solicitor (SCS), Miss K. M. S. Morton
Principal Assistant Solicitors (SCS), D. J. Pearson; Ms C. A. Crisham

Legal Divisions
Assistant Solicitor, Division A1 (SCS), P. Davis
Assistant Solicitor, Division A2 (SCS), P. Kent
Assistant Solicitor, Division A3 (SCS), C. Gregory
Assistant Solicitor, Division A4 (SCS), C. Allen
Assistant Solicitor, Division A5 (SCS), Mrs C. A. Davis
Assistant Solicitor, Division B1 (SCS), Dr G. Davis
Assistant Solicitor, Division B2 (SCS), Ms S. B. Spence
Assistant Solicitor, Division B3 (SCS), A. I. Corbett
Assistant Solicitor, Division B4 (SCS), Mrs F. C. Nash

Investigation Unit
Chief Investigation Officer, Miss J. Panting

ECONOMICS AND STATISTICS
Under-Secretary (SCS), D. Thompson

Divisions
Senior Economic Adviser, Economics and Statistics (Farm Business) (SCS), H. Fearn
Senior Economic Adviser, Economics (International and Food) (SCS), N. Atkinson
Senior Economic Adviser, Economics (Resource Use) (SCS), J. P. Muriel

Statistics Division
Foss House, Kingspool, 1–2 Peasholme Green, York
yo1 2px
Tel 01904-455328
Chief Statistician (Commodities and Food) (SCS), S. Platt
Chief Statistician (Census and Surveys) (SCS), P. F. Helm

CHIEF SCIENTIST'S GROUP
St Christopher House, 80–112 Southwark Street,
London sei oud
Tel 0171-928 3666
Chief Scientist (SCS), Dr D. W. F. Shannon

Divisions
Head, Agriculture and Food Technology (SCS), Dr J. C. Sherlock
Head, Food and Veterinary Science Division (SCS), Dr K. J. MacOwan
Head, Environment, Fisheries and International Science (SCS), Dr M. Parker
Head, Research Policy Co-ordination (SCS), A. R. Burne

FISHERIES DEPARTMENT
Fisheries Secretary (SCS), S. Wentworth

Divisions
Head, Fisheries I (SCS), A. Kuyk
Head, Fisheries II (SCS), C. I. Llewellyn
Head, Fisheries III (SCS), J. E. Robbs
Head, Fisheries IV (G6), B. S. Edwards
Chief Inspector, Sea Fisheries Inspectorate (G6), S. G. Ellson

AGRICULTURAL COMMODITIES, TRADE AND FOOD PRODUCTION
Deputy Secretary (SCS), Ms V. K. Timms

EUROPEAN UNION AND LIVESTOCK GROUP
Under-Secretary (SCS), D. P. Hunter

Divisions
Head, European Union (SCS), A. J. Lebrecht
Head, Beef and Sheep (SCS), J. R. Cowan
Head, Milk, Pigs, Eggs and Poultry (SCS), P. P. Nash
Head, Livestock Schemes (G6), Ms L. Cornish

ARABLE CROPS AND HORTICULTURE
Under-Secretary (SCS), vacant

Divisions
Head, Cereals and Set-Aside (SCS), R. A. Hathaway
Head, Sugar, Tobacco, Oilseeds and Protein (SCS), H. B. Brown
Head, Horticulture and Potatoes (SCS), G. W. Noble

Plant Variety Rights Office and Seeds Division
White House Lane, Huntingdon Road, Cambridge
cb3 olf
Tel 01223-277151
Head of Office (SCS), D. A. Boreham

FOOD, DRINK AND MARKETING POLICY
Under-Secretary (SCS), N. Thornton

Divisions
Head, Food and Drinks Industry (SCS), Miss C. J. Rabagliati
Head, International Relations and Export Promotion (SCS), D. V. Orchard
Head, Trade Policy and Tropical Foods (SCS), Miss S. E. Brown
Head, Market Task Force (SCS), vacant
Head, Devolution Unit (SCS), Miss V. A. Smith

REGIONAL SERVICES AND DEFENCE GROUP
Under-Secretary (SCS), Mrs K. J. A. Brown
Head, Agricultural Resources and Better Regulation (SCS), Mrs A. M. Blackburn
Head, Plant Health, and Plant Health and Seeds Inspectorate (SCS), A. J. Perrins
Head, Flood and Coastal Protection (SCS), Dr J. Park

Regional Organization
Head, Regional Support Unit (G7), D. Putley

Regional Service Centres
Anglia Region, Block B, Government Buildings, Brooklands Avenue, Cambridge cb2 2dr. Tel: 01223-462727. *Regional Director (G6)*, M. Edwards
East Midlands Region, Block 7, Government Buildings, Chalfont Drive, Nottingham ng8 3sn. Tel: 0115-929 1191. *Regional Director (G6)*, G. Norbury
North-East Region, Government Buildings, Crosby Road, Northallerton, N. Yorks dl6 1ad. Tel: 01609-773751. *Regional Director (G6)*, P. Watson
Northern Region, Eden Bridge House, Lowther Street, Carlisle, Cumbria ca3 8dx. Tel: 01228-23400. *Regional Director (SCS)*, I. G. Pearson
North Mercia Region, Electra Way, Crewe Business Park, Crewe, Cheshire cw1 6gl. Tel: 01270-754000. *Regional Director (G6)*, F. Whitehouse
South-East Region, Block A, Government Buildings, Coley Park, Reading, Berks rg1 6dt. Tel: 01734-581222. *Regional Director (G6)*, Mrs V. Silvester

SOUTH MERCIA REGION, Block C, Government Buildings, Whittington Road, Worcester WR5 2LQ. Tel: 01905-763355. *Regional Director (G6)*, B. Davies
SOUTH-WEST REGION, Clyst House, Winslade Park, Clyst St Mary, Exeter EX5 1DY. Tel: 01392-447400. *Regional Director (G6)*, M. R. W. Highman
WESSEX REGION, Block 3, Government Buildings, Burghill Road, Westbury-on-Trym, Bristol BS10 6NJ. Tel: 01272-591000. *Regional Director (G6)*, Mrs A. J. L. Ould

FOOD SAFETY AND ENVIRONMENT GROUP
Deputy Secretary (SCS), R. J. D. Carden, CB

ENVIRONMENT GROUP
Under-Secretary (SCS), D. J. Coates
Head, Conservation and Rural Development (SCS), Ms J. Allfrey
Head, Conservation Management Division (SCS), P. M. Boyling
Head, Environmental Protection (SCS), D. E. Jones

FOOD SAFETY AND STANDARDS GROUP
Under-Secretary (SCS), G. Podger

DIVISIONS
Head, Additives and Novel Foods (SCS), Dr J. R. Bell
Head, Food Contaminants (SCS), Dr R. Burt
Head, Food Labelling and Standards (SCS), G. F. Meekings
Head, Radiological Safety and Nutrition (SCS), Dr M. G. Segal
Head, Food Hygiene (SCS), R. J. Harding
Head, Meat Hygiene I (SCS), R. C. McIvor
Head, Meat Hygiene II (SCS), C. J. Lawson
Head, Food Standards Agency Division (SCS), Miss E. J. Wordley

ANIMAL HEALTH GROUP
Government Buildings, Hook Rise South, Tolworth, Surbiton, Surrey KT6 7NF
Tel 0181-330 4411
Under-Secretary (SCS), B. H. B. Dickinson

DIVISIONS
Head, Animal Health (BSE and International Trade) (SCS), T. E. D. Eddy
Head, Animal Health (Disease Control) (SCS), T. D. Rossington
Head, Services (G6), R. Gurd
Head, Animal Welfare (SCS), C. J. Ryder

CHIEF VETERINARY OFFICER'S GROUP
Government Buildings, Hook Rise South, Tolworth, Surbiton, Surrey KT6 7NF
Tel 0181-330 8057
Chief Veterinary Officer (SCS), J. M. Scudamore
Assistant Chief Veterinary Officer (SCS), R. J. G. Cawthorne

DIVISIONS
Head, Veterinary International Trade Team (SCS), R. A. Bell
Head, Veterinary Notifiable Disease Team (Exotic Diseases and BSE) (SCS), Dr D. Matthews
Head, Veterinary Notifiable Disease Team (Endemic Animal Diseases and Zoonoses) (SCS), Dr D. Reynolds
Head, Welfare Team (SCS), A. T. Turnbull

VETERINARY FIELD SERVICE
Government Buildings, Hook Rise South, Tolworth, Surbiton, Surrey KT15 3NB
Tel 0181-330 4411
Director of Veterinary Field Services (SCS), M. J. Atkinson

EXECUTIVE AGENCIES
CENTRAL SCIENCE LABORATORY
Sand Hutton, York YO4 1LZ
Tel 01904-462000; fax 01904-462111
The agency provides MAFF with technical support and policy advice on the protection and quality of the food supply and on related environmental issues.
Chief Executive (G3), Prof. P. I. Stanley
Research Directors (G5), Prof. A. R. Hardy (*Agriculture and Environment*); Dr M. Parker (*Food*)

CENTRE FOR ENVIRONMENT, FISHERIES AND AQUACULTURE SCIENCE
Pakefield Road, Lowestoft, Suffolk NR33 0HT
Tel 01502-562244; fax 01502-513865
The Agency, established in April 1997, provides research and consultancy services in fisheries science and management, aquaculture, fish health and hygiene, environmental impact assessment, and environmental quality assessment.
Chief Executive, Dr P. Greig-Smith

FARMING AND RURAL CONSERVATION AGENCY
Nobel House, 17 Smith Square, London SW1P 3JR
Tel 0171-238 5432; fax 0171-238 5588
The Agency, established in April 1997, is responsible jointly to MAFF and the Welsh Office. It assists the Government in the design, development and implementation of policies on the integration of farming and conservation, environmental protection and the rural economy. This includes agri-environment schemes such as Environmentally Sensitive Areas, Countryside Stewardship and access schemes, land use and tenure, milk hygiene inspections and wildlife management.
Chief Executive (SCS), Miss S. Nason

INTERVENTION BOARD
— *see* page 315–16

MEAT HYGIENE SERVICE
Foss House, Kingspool, 1–2 Peasholme Green, York YO1 7PX
Tel 01904-455655; fax 01904-455502
The Agency was launched in April 1995. It protects public health and animal welfare through veterinary supervision and meat inspection in licensed fresh meat establishments.
Chief Executive (G4), J. McNeill

PESTICIDES SAFETY DIRECTORATE
Mallard House, Kingspool, 3 Peasholme Green, York YO1 7PX
Tel 01904-640500; fax 01904-455733
The Pesticides Safety Directorate is responsible for the evaluation and approval of pesticides and the development of policies relating to them, in order to protect consumers, users and the environment.
Chief Executive (G4), G. K. Bruce
Director (Policy) (G5), J. A. Bainton
Director (Approvals) (G5), Dr A. D. Martin

VETERINARY LABORATORIES AGENCY
Woodham Lane, New Haw, Addlestone, Surrey KT15 3NB
Tel 01932-341111; fax 01932-347046
The Veterinary Laboratories Agency provides scientific and technical expertise in animal and public health.
Chief Executive (G3), Dr T. W. A. Little
Director of Research (G4), Dr J. A. Morris
Director of Laboratory Services (G5), Dr S. Edwards
Director of Surveillance (G5), J. W. Harkness
Director of Finance (G6), I. Grattidge
Laboratory Secretary (G6), C. Edwards

VETERINARY MEDICINES DIRECTORATE
Woodham Lane, New Haw, Addlestone, Surrey KT15 3NB
Tel 01932-336911; fax 01932-336618

The Veterinary Medicines Directorate is responsible for all aspects of the authorization and control of veterinary medicines, including post-authorization surveillance of residues in meat and animal products, and the provision of policy advice to ministers.

Chief Executive and Director of Veterinary Medicines (G4), Dr J. M. Rutter
Director (Policy) (G5), R. Anderson
Director (Licensing) (G5), S. Dean
Secretary and Head of Business Unit (G6), J. FitzGerald
Licensing Manager, Pharmaceuticals and Feed Additives (G6), J. P. O'Brien
Licensing Manager, Immunologicals (G6) (acting), Dr D. Fawthrop

COLLEGE OF ARMS OR HERALDS COLLEGE
Queen Victoria Street, London EC4V 4BT
Tel 0171-248 2762

The Sovereign's Officers of Arms (Kings, Heralds and Pursuivants of Arms) were first incorporated by Richard III. The powers vested by the Crown in the Earl Marshal (the Duke of Norfolk) with regard to state ceremonial are largely exercised through the College. The College is also the official repository of the arms and pedigrees of English, Welsh, Northern Irish and Commonwealth (except Canadian) families and their descendants, and its records include official copies of the records of Ulster King of Arms, the originals of which remain in Dublin. The 13 officers of the College specialize in genealogical and heraldic work for their respective clients.

Arms have been and still are granted by letters patent from the Kings of Arms. A right to arms can only be established by the registration in the official records of the College of Arms of a pedigree showing direct male line descent from an ancestor already appearing therein as being entitled to arms, or by making application through the College of Arms for a grant of arms. Grants are made to corporations as well as to individuals.

The College of Arms is open Monday–Friday 10–4.

Earl Marshal, The Duke of Norfolk, KG, GCVO, CB, CBE, MC

KINGS OF ARMS
Garter, P. L. Gwynn-Jones, CVO, FSA
Clarenceux (and Registrar), D. H. B. Chesshyre, LVO, FSA
Norroy and Ulster, T. Woodcock, LVO, FSA

HERALDS
Richmond (and Earl Marshal's Secretary), P. L. Dickinson
York, H. E. Paston-Bedingfeld
Chester, T. H. S. Duke

PURSUIVANTS
Bluemantle, R. J. B. Noel
Portcullis, W. G. Hunt, TD
Rouge Croix, D. V. White

COURT OF THE LORD LYON
HM New Register House, Edinburgh EH1 3YT
Tel 0131-556 7255; fax 0131-557 2148

The Court of the Lord Lyon is the Scottish Court of Chivalry (including the genealogical jurisdiction of the *Ri-Sennachie* of Scotland's Celtic Kings). The Lord Lyon King of Arms has jurisdiction, subject to appeal to the Court of Session and the House of Lords, in questions of heraldry and the right to bear arms. The Court also administers the Scottish Public Register of All Arms and Bearings and the Public Register of All Genealogies. Pedigrees are established by decrees of Lyon Court and by letters patent. As Royal Commissioner in Armory, the Lord Lyon grants patents of arms (which constitute the grantee and heirs noble in the Noblesse of Scotland) to 'virtuous and well-deserving' Scotsmen and to petitioners (personal or corporate) in The Queen's overseas realms of Scottish connection, and issues birthbrieves.

Lord Lyon King of Arms, Sir Malcolm Innes of Edingight, KCVO, WS

HERALDS
Albany, J. A. Spens, RD, WS
Rothesay, Sir Crispin Agnew of Lochnaw, Bt., QC
Ross, C. J. Burnett, FSA Scot

PURSUIVANTS
Kintyre, J. C. G. George, FSA Scot
Unicorn, Alastair Campbell of Airds, FSA Scot
Carrick, Mrs C. G. W. Roads, MVO, FSA Scot

Lyon Clerk and Keeper of Records, Mrs C. G. W. Roads, MVO, FSA Scot
Procurator-Fiscal, D. F. Murby, WS
Herald Painter, Mrs J. Phillips
Macer, A. M. Clark

ARTS COUNCILS

The Arts Council of Great Britain was established as an independent body in 1946 to be the principal channel for the Government's support of the arts. In 1994 the Scottish and Welsh Arts Councils became autonomous and the Arts Council of Great Britain became the Arts Council of England.

The Arts Councils are responsible for the distribution of the proceeds of the National Lottery allocated to the arts (*see* page 610).

ARTS COUNCIL OF ENGLAND
14 Great Peter Street, London SW1P 3NQ
Tel 0171-333 0100; fax 0171-973 6590

The Arts Council of England's objectives are to develop and improve the understanding and practice of the arts and to increase their accessibility to the public. The Council funds the major arts organizations in England and the ten Regional Arts Boards. It is funded by the Department for Culture, Media and Sport but operates at 'arm's length' from Government as regards artistic decision-making, although it is expected to account for such decisions to the Government and the public. The Council also provides advice, information and help to artists and arts organizations. Its members are unpaid.

The Council distributes an annual grant from the Department for Culture, Media and Sport; the grant for 1998–9 is £184.6 million.

In July 1998 the Government published a discussion document including a proposal to merge the Arts Council of England and the Crafts Council.

Chairman, G. Robinson
Members, D. Anderson; D. Brierley, CBE; Ms D. Bull; Prof. C. Frayling; A. Gormley; A. Kapoor; Prof. J. MacGregor; Prof. A. Motion; Ms P. Skene; Ms H. Strong
Chief Executive, P. Hewitt

REGIONAL ARTS BOARDS
EASTERN ARTS BOARD, Cherry Hinton Hall, Cherry Hinton Road, Cambridge CB1 4DW. Tel: 01223-215355. *Chair*, S. Timperley
EAST MIDLANDS ARTS BOARD, Mountfields House, Epinal Way, Loughborough, Leics LE11 0QE. Tel: 01509-218292. *Chair*, Prof. R. Cowell
LONDON ARTS BOARD, Elme House, 133 Long Acre, London WC2E 9AF. Tel: 0171-240 1313. *Chair*, T. Phillips
NORTHERN ARTS BOARD, 9–10 Osborne Terrace, Newcastle upon Tyne NE2 1NZ. Tel: 0191-281 6334. *Chair*, G. Loggie
NORTH-WEST ARTS BOARD, Manchester House, 22 Bridge Street, Manchester M3 3AB. Tel: 0161-834 6644. *Chair*, Prof. B. Cox, CBE
SOUTH-EAST ARTS BOARD, Union House, Eridge Road, Tunbridge Wells, Kent TN4 8HF. Tel: 01892-507200. *Chair*, R. Reed
SOUTHERN ARTS BOARD, 13 St Clement Street, Winchester SO23 9DQ. Tel: 01962-855099. *Chair*, D. Astor
SOUTH-WEST ARTS BOARD, Bradninch Place, Gandy Street, Exeter EX4 3LS. Tel: 01392-218188. *Chair*, D. Brierley, CBE
WEST MIDLANDS ARTS BOARD, 82 Granville Street, Birmingham B1 2LH. Tel: 0121-631 3121. *Chair*, R. Natkiel
YORKSHIRE AND HUMBERSIDE ARTS BOARD, 21 Bond Street, Dewsbury, W. Yorks WF13 1AX. Tel: 01924-455555. *Chair*, C. Price

SCOTTISH ARTS COUNCIL
12 Manor Place, Edinburgh EH3 7DD
Tel 0131-226 6051; fax 0131-225 9833
The Scottish Arts Council funds arts organizations in Scotland and is funded directly by the Scottish Office. The grant for 1998–9 is £26.9 million.
Chairman, M. Linklater
Members, Ms S. Ainsley; H. Buchanan; R. Chester; W. English; J. Faulds; K. Geddes; P. Iles; R. Love; Ms M. Marshall; Dr Ann Matheson; Ms J. Richardson; W. Speirs; Prof. E. Spiller; Ms J. Urquart
Director, Ms S. Reid
Lottery Director, D. Bonnar

ARTS COUNCIL OF WALES
9 Museum Place, Cardiff CF1 3NX
Tel 01222-376500; fax 01222-221447
The Arts Council of Wales funds arts organizations in Wales and is funded directly by the Welsh Office. The grant for 1998–9 is £14.189 million.
Chairman, Sir Richard Lloyd Jones, KCB
Members, Ms E. Bennet; Ms J. Davidson; R. Davies; Ms A. Davis; K. Evans; Ms K. Gass; G. Jenkins; D. Johnston; G. S. Jones; L. Jones; G. Lewis; A. Lloyd; C. Lyddon; D. Richards; A. Roberts; Ms C. Thomas; Ms M. Vincentelli
Chief Executive, Ms J. Weston

ARTS COUNCIL OF NORTHERN IRELAND
MacNeice House, 77 Malone Road, Belfast BT9 6AQ
Tel 01232-385200; fax 01232-661715
The Arts Council of Northern Ireland disburses government funds in support of the arts in Northern Ireland. It is funded by the Department of Education for Northern Ireland, and the grant for 1998–9 is £6.67 million.
Chairman, Prof. B. Walker
Vice-Chairman, vacant

Members, M. Bradley; W. Burns; S. Burnside; F. Cobain; P. Donnelly; Dr Tess Hurson; Mrs R. McMullan; Ms M. O'Neill; G. Patterson; Ms C. Poulter; Ms I. Sandford; A. Shortt; Dr B. Walker
Chief Executive, B. Ferran

ART GALLERIES, ETC

ROYAL FINE ART COMMISSION
7 St James's Square, London SW1Y 4JU
Tel 0171-839 6537; fax 0171-839 8475
Established in 1924, the Commission is an autonomous authority on the aesthetic implications of any project or development, primarily but not exclusively architectural, which affects the visual environment.
In July 1998 the Government published a discussion document including a proposal to reform or abolish the Commission.
Chairman, The Lord St John of Fawsley, PC, FRSL
Commissioners, Miss S. Andreae; Prof. R. D. Carter, CBE; E. Cullinan, CBE, RA; D. H. Fraser, RA; E. Hollinghurst; Sir Michael Hopkins, CBE, RA; S. A. Lipton; Prof. Margaret MacKeith, PH.D.; H. T. Moggridge, OBE; G. Morrison; Mrs J. Nutting; T. Osborne, FRICS; I. Ritchie; Sir Colin Stansfield Smith, CBE; Prof. J. R. Steer, FSA; Miss W. Taylor, CBE; Dr G. Worsley
Secretary, F. Golding

ROYAL FINE ART COMMISSION FOR SCOTLAND
Bakehouse Close, 146 Canongate, Edinburgh EH8 8DD
Tel 0131-556 6699; fax 0131-556 6633
The Commission was established in 1927 and advises ministers and local authorities on the visual impact and quality of design of construction projects. It is an independent body and gives its opinions impartially.
Chairman, The Lord Cameron of Lochbroom, PC, FRSE
Commissioners, Prof. G. Benson; W. A. Cadell; Mrs K. Dalyell; Ms J. Malvenan; R. G. Maund; M. Murray; D. Page; B. Rae; R. Russell; M. Turnbull; A. Wright
Secretary, C. Prosser

NATIONAL GALLERY
Trafalgar Square, London WC2N 5DN
Tel 0171-839 3321; fax 0171-747 2403
The National Gallery, which houses a permanent collection of western painting from the 13th to the 20th century, was founded in 1824, following a parliamentary grant of £60,000 for the purchase and exhibition of the Angerstein collection of pictures. The present site was first occupied in 1838; an extension to the north of the building with a public entrance in Orange Street was opened in 1975, and the Sainsbury wing was opened in 1991. Total government grant-in-aid for 1998–9 is £18.6 million.

BOARD OF TRUSTEES
Chairman, P. Hughes, CBE
Trustees, Lady Bingham; Sir Mark Richmond, SC.D., FRS; A. Bennett; Lady Monck; Mrs P. Ridley; Sir Ewen Fergusson, GCMG, GCVO; R. Gavron, CBE; C. Le Brun; The Hon. R. G. H. Seitz; Dr D. Landau; Sir Colin Southgate

OFFICERS
Director, R. N. MacGregor
Keeper, Dr N. Penny
Senior Curator, vacant
Chief Restorer, M. H. Wyld, CBE

Head of Exhibitions, M. J. Wilson
Scientific Adviser, Dr A. Roy
Director of Administration, J. MacAuslan
Head of Press and Public Relations, Miss J. Liddiard

NATIONAL PORTRAIT GALLERY
St Martin's Place, London WC2H 0HE
Tel 0171-306 0055; fax 0171-306 0058

A grant was made in 1856 to form a gallery of the portraits of the most eminent persons in British history. The present building was opened in 1896 and an extension in 1933. There are four outstations displaying portraits in appropriate settings: Montacute House, Gawthorpe Hall, Beningbrough Hall and Bodelwyddan Castle. Total government grant-in-aid for 1998–9 is £4.697 million.

BOARD OF TRUSTEES
Chairman, H. Keswick
Trustees, The Lord President of the Council (*ex officio*); The President of the Royal Academy of Arts (*ex officio*); J. Roberts, CBE, D.Phil.; The Lord Morris of Castle Morris, D.Phil.; Prof. N. Lynton; J. Tusa; Sir Antony Acland, GCMG, GCVO; Mrs J. E. Benson, LVO, OBE; Lady Tumim, OBE; Sir David Scholey, CBE; Mrs C. Tomalin; Baroness Willoughby de Eresby; M. Hastings; Prof. The Earl Russell, FBA; T. Phillips, RA
Director (*G3*), C. Saumarez Smith, PH.D.

TATE GALLERY
Millbank, London SW1P 4RG
Tel 0171-887 8000; fax 0171-887 8007

The Tate Gallery comprises the national collections of British painting and 20th-century painting and sculpture. The Gallery was opened in 1897, the cost of erection (£80,000) being defrayed by Sir Henry Tate, who also contributed the nucleus of the present collection. The Turner wing was opened in 1910, galleries to contain the collection of modern foreign painting in 1926, and a new sculpture hall in 1937. In 1979 a further extension was built, and the Clore Gallery, for the Turner collection, was opened in 1987. The Tate Gallery Liverpool opened in 1988 and the Tate Gallery St Ives in 1993. The new Tate Gallery of Modern Art at Bankside is due to open in 2000, with the Millbank gallery then being devoted to British art. Total government grant-in-aid for 1998–9 is £18.218 million.

BOARD OF TRUSTEES
Chairman, D. Verey
Trustees, Prof. Dawn Ades; The Hon. Mrs J. de Botton; Sir Richard Carew Pole; Prof. M. Craig-Martin; P. Doig; Sir Christopher Mallaby, GCMG, GCVO; Sir Mark Richmond; Mrs P. Ridley, OBE; W. Woodrow

OFFICERS
Director, N. Serota
Director of Public and Regional Services, S. Nairne
Director of Collections, J. Lewison
Director, Tate Gallery of Modern Art, L. Nittve
Director, Tate Gallery of British Art, S. Deuchar
Curator, Tate Gallery Liverpool, L. Biggs
Curator, Tate Gallery St Ives, M. Tooby

WALLACE COLLECTION
Hertford House, Manchester Square, London W1M 6BN
Tel 0171-935 0687; fax 0171-224 2155

The Wallace Collection was bequeathed to the nation by the widow of Sir Richard Wallace, Bt. in 1897, and Hertford House was subsequently acquired by the Government.

Total government grant-in-aid for 1998–9 is £1.816 million.
Director, Miss R. J. Savill
Head of Administration, A. W. Houldershaw

NATIONAL GALLERIES OF SCOTLAND
The Mound, Edinburgh EH2 2EL
Tel 0131-624 6200; fax 0131-343 3250

The National Galleries of Scotland comprise the National Gallery of Scotland, the Scottish National Portrait Gallery and the Scottish National Gallery of Modern Art. There are also outstations at Paxton House, Berwickshire, and Duff House, Banffshire. Total government grant-in-aid for 1998–9 is £7.460 million.

TRUSTEES
Chairman of the Trustees, The Countess of Airlie, CVO
Trustees, E. Hagman; Dr M. Shea; Mrs A. McCurley; Prof. J. R. Harper, CBE; Prof. Christina Lodder; J. H. Blair; Ms V. Atkinson; Lord Gordon of Strathblane, CBE; G. Weaver; Prof. I. Whyte

OFFICERS
Director (*G4*), T. Clifford
Keeper of Conservation (*G6*), J. P. Dick, OBE
Head of Press and Information (*G7*), Mrs A. M. Wagener
Keeper of Education (*G7*), M. Cassin
Registrar (*G7*), Miss A. Buddle
Secretary (*G6*), Ms S. Edwards
Buildings (*G7*), R. Galbraith
Keeper, National Gallery of Scotland (*G6*), M. Clarke
Keeper, Scottish National Portrait Gallery (*G6*), J. Holloway
Curator of Photography, Miss S. F. Stevenson
Keeper, Scottish National Gallery of Modern Art (*G6*), R. Calvocoressi

UK ATOMIC ENERGY AUTHORITY
Harwell, Didcot, Oxon OX11 0RA
Tel 01235-820220; fax 01235-436401

The UKAEA was established by the Atomic Energy Authority Act 1954 and took over responsibility for the research and development of the civil nuclear power programme. The Authority's commercial arm, AEA Technology PLC, was privatized in 1996. UKAEA is responsible for the safe management and decommissioning of its radioactive plant and for maximizing the income from its still-operating active facilities, buildings and land on its six sites. UKAEA also undertakes special nuclear tasks for the Government, including the UK's contribution to the international fusion programme.
Chairman, Adm. Sir Kenneth Eaton
Chief Executive, Dr J. McKeown

AUDIT COMMISSIONS

AUDIT COMMISSION FOR LOCAL AUTHORITIES AND THE NATIONAL HEALTH SERVICE IN ENGLAND AND WALES
1 Vincent Square, London SW1P 2PN
Tel 0171-828 1212; fax 0171-976 6187

The Audit Commission was set up in 1983 with responsibility for the external audit of local authorities. This remit was extended from 1990 to include the audit of the National Health Service bodies in England and Wales.

The Commission appoints the auditors, who may be from the District Audit Service or from a private firm of accountants. The Commission is also responsible for promoting value for money in the services provided by local authorities and health bodies.

The Commission has 15–17 members who, though appointed by the Secretary of State for the Environment, Transport and the Regions in consultation with the Secretaries of State for Wales and for Health, are responsible to Parliament.

Chairman, R. Brooke
Deputy Chairman, J. Orme
Controller of Audit, A. Foster
Chief Executive of District Audit Service, D. Prince

ACCOUNTS COMMISSION FOR SCOTLAND
18 George Street, Edinburgh EH2 2QU
Tel 0131-477 1234; fax 0131-477 4567

The Commission was set up in 1975. It is responsible for securing the audit of the accounts of Scottish local authorities and certain joint boards and joint committees, and for value-for-money audits of authorities. In 1995 it assumed responsibility for securing the audit of National Health Service bodies in Scotland. The Commission is required to deal with reports made by the Controller of Audit on items of account contrary to law; on incorrect accounting; and on losses due to misconduct, negligence and failure to carry out statutory duties.

Members are appointed by the Secretary of State for Scotland.

Chairman, Prof. J. P. Percy, CBE
Controller of Audit, R. W. Black
Secretary, W. F. Magee

ASSEMBLY OMBUDSMAN FOR NORTHERN IRELAND
— *see* Parliamentary Ombudsman for Northern Ireland

THE BANK OF ENGLAND
Threadneedle Street, London EC2R 8AH
Tel 0171-601 4444; fax 0171-601 4771

The Bank of England was incorporated in 1694 under royal charter. It is the banker of the Government and manages the note issue. Since May 1997 it has been operationally independent and its new Monetary Policy Committee has had responsibility for setting short-term interest rates to meet the Government's inflation target. As the central reserve bank of the country, the Bank keeps the accounts of British banks, who maintain with it a proportion of their cash resources, and of most overseas central banks. The Bank is divided into two divisions, Monetary Stability and Financial Stability. Its responsibility for banking supervision has been transferred to the Financial Services Authority. (*See also* pages 634–5).

Governor, E. A. J. George
Deputy Governors, D. Clementi; M. A. King
Directors, C. J. Allsopp; R. Bailie, OBE; A. R. F. Buxton; Sir David Cooksey; H. J. Davies; G. Hawker; Mrs F. A. Heaton; Sir John Keswick; Sir David Lees; Dame Sheila Masters, DBE; Ms S. McKechnie, OBE; W. Morris; J. Neill, CBE, PH.D.; N. I. Simms; Sir Colin Southgate; J. Stretton
Monetary Policy Committee, The Governor; the Deputy Governors; I. Plenderleith; Prof. C. Goodhart; Dr D. Julius; Sir Alan Budd; Prof. W. Buiter; J. Vickers

Advisers to the Governor, Sir Peter Petrie; L. Berkowitz; M. Foster; D. Brearley
Chief Cashier and Deputy Director, Banking and Market Services, G. E. A. Kentfield
Chief Registrar, G. P. Sparkes
General Manager, Printing Works, A. W. Jarvis
Secretary, P. D. Rodgers
The Auditor, K. Butler

BOUNDARY COMMISSIONS

The Commissions are constituted under the Parliamentary Constituencies Act 1986. The Speaker of the House of Commons is *ex officio* chairman of all four commissions in the UK. Each of the four commissions is required by law to keep the parliamentary constituencies in their part of the UK under review. The latest review was completed in 1995 and its proposals took effect at the 1997 general election. The next review is due to be completed between 2002 and 2006.

ENGLAND
1 Drummond Gate, London SW1V 2QQ
Tel 0171-533 5177; fax 0171-533 5176
Deputy Chairman, The Hon. Mr Justice Harrison
Joint Secretaries, R. Farrance; S. Limpkin

WALES
1 Drummond Gate, London SW1V 2QQ
Tel 0171-533 5172; fax 0171-533 5176
Deputy Chairman, The Hon. Mr Justice Kay
Joint Secretaries, R. Farrance; S. Limpkin

SCOTLAND
Saughton House, Edinburgh EH1 3XD
Tel 0131-244 2196/2188; fax 0131-244 2195
Deputy Chairman, The Hon. Lady Cosgrove
Secretary, vacant

NORTHERN IRELAND
REL Division, 11 Millbank, London SW1P 4QE
Tel 0171-210 6569
Deputy Chairman, The Hon. Mr Justice Pringle
Secretary, Ms C. Marson

BRITISH BROADCASTING CORPORATION
Broadcasting House, Portland Place, London W1A 1AA
Tel 0171-580 4468; fax 0171-637 1630
Television Centre, Wood Lane, London W12 7RJ
Tel 0181-743 8000; fax 0181-749 7520

The BBC was incorporated under royal charter as successor to the British Broadcasting Company Ltd, whose licence expired in 1926. The current charter came into force on 1 May 1996 and extends to 31 December 2006. The chairman, vice-chairman and other governors are appointed by The Queen-in-Council. The BBC is financed by revenue from receiving licences for the home services and by grant-in-aid from Parliament for the World Service (radio). In 1996 the BBC was restructured into six divisions: Production, Broadcast, News, Worldwide, Resources, and Corporate Centre.

For services, *see* Broadcasting section.

286   Government Departments and Public Offices

BOARD OF GOVERNORS

Chairman (£66,000), Sir Christopher Bland
Vice-Chairman (£17,000), The Baroness Young of Old Scone
National Governors (*each* £17,000), Sir Kenneth Bloomfield, KCB (*N. Ireland*); R. S. Jones, OBE (*Wales*); N. Drummond (*Scotland*)
Chairman, English National Forum (£13,000), R. Sondhi
Governors (*each* £8,000), W. B. Jordan, CBE; Mrs J. Cohen; Sir David Scholey, CBE; Sir Richard Eyre, CBE; A. White, CBE; Dame Pauline Neville-Jones, DCMG; A. Young

BOARD OF MANAGEMENT

EXECUTIVE COMMITTEE
Director-General (£354,000), Sir John Birt
Chief Executives, R. Neil (*BBC Production*); W. Wyatt (*BBC Broadcast*); T. Hall (*BBC News*); R. Lynch (*BBC Resources Ltd*); R. Gavin (*BBC Worldwide*)
Managing Director, S. Younger (*World Service*)
Directors, Ms M. Salmon (*Personnel*); Ms P. Hodgson (*Policy and Planning*); J. Smith (*Finance*); C. Browne (*Corporate Affairs*)

OTHER BOARD OF MANAGEMENT MEMBERS
Directors, A. Yentob (*Television*); M. Bannister (*Radio*); Ms J. Drabble (*Education*); M. Byford (*Regional Broadcasting*)

OTHER SENIOR STAFF

The Secretary, C. Graham
Director, Continuous News, Ms J. Abramsky
Controller, BBC1, P. Salmon
Controller, BBC2, M. Thompson
Controller, Radio 1, A. Parfitt
Controller, Radio 2, J. Moir
Controller, Radio 3, R. Wright
Controller, Radio 4, J. Boyle
Controller, Radio 5 Live, R. Mosey
Controller, BBC Proms and Millennium Programmes, N. Kenyon
Controller, BBC Scotland, J. McCormick
Controller, BBC Wales, G. Talfan Davies
Controller, BBC N. Ireland, P. Loughrey
Controller, English Regions, N. Chapman

THE BRITISH COUNCIL
10 Spring Gardens, London SW1A 2BN
Tel 0171-930 8466; fax 0171-839 6347
Bridgewater House, 58 Whitworth Street, Manchester M15 4AA
Tel 0161-957 7755; fax 0161-957 7762
Arts Division: 11 Portland Place, London WIN 4EJ
Tel 0171-389 3001; fax 0171-389 3199

The British Council was established in 1934, incorporated by royal charter in 1940 and granted a supplemental charter in 1993. It is an independent, non-political organization which promotes Britain abroad. It is the UK's international network for education, culture and development services. The Council is represented in 230 towns and cities in 109 countries and runs 209 libraries, 95 teaching centres and 29 resource centres around the world.

Total income in 1997–8, including Foreign and Commonwealth Office grants and contracted money, was £412.662 million.
Chairman, The Baroness Kennedy of The Shaws, QC
Deputy Chairman, The Lord Chorley
Director-General, Dr D. Drewery

BRITISH FILM COMMISSION
70 Baker Street, London WIM 1DJ
Tel 0171-224 5000; fax 0171-224 1013

The British Film Commission was set up in 1991 and is funded by the Department for Culture, Media and Sport. The Commission promotes the UK as an international production centre, encourages the use of locations, facilities, services and personnel, and provides, at no charge to the enquirer, comprehensive advice and information relating to the practical aspects of filming in the UK.

In July 1998 the Government published a discussion document including a proposal to establish a new film body which would incorporate the work currently undertaken by the Commision.
Commissioner and Chief Executive, S. Norris

BRITISH FILM INSTITUTE
21 Stephen Street, London WIP 2LN
Tel 0171-255 1444; fax 0171-436 7950

The British Film Institute was first set up in 1933 and is now established by royal charter. It is the UK national agency with responsibility for encouraging the arts of film and television and conserving them in the national interest. BFI divisions include the National Film and Television Archive, the National Cinema Centre (comprising the National Film Theatre and the London Film Festival) and BFI Films, which deals with distribution and film sales. The BFI also supports a network of regional film theatres and the BFI National Library contains the world's largest collection of material relating to film and television. Total government funding for 1998–9 is £15.1 million.

In July 1998 the Government published a discussion document including a proposal to establish a new film body which would incorporate the work currently undertaken by the Institute.
Chairman, A. Parker
Deputy Chairman, Ms J. Bakewell
Director, J. Woodward

BRITISH PHARMACOPOEIA COMMISSION
Market Towers, 1 Nine Elms Lane, London SW8 5NQ
Tel 0171-273 0561; fax 0171-273 0566

The British Pharmacopoeia Commission sets standards for medicinal products used in human and veterinary medicines and is responsible for publication of the British Pharmacopoeia (a publicly available statement of the standard that a product must meet throughout its shelf-life), the British Pharmacopoeia (Veterinary) and the selection of British Approved Names. It has 13 members who are appointed by the Secretary of State for Health, the Minister for Agriculture, Fisheries and Food, the Secretaries of State for Scotland and Wales, and the relevant Northern Ireland departments.
Chairman, Prof. D. Calam, OBE, D.Phil.
Vice-Chairman, Prof. J. A. Goldsmith
Secretary and Scientific Director, Dr R. C. Hutton

BRITISH RAILWAYS BOARD
Whittles House, 14 Pentonville Road, London NI 9HF
Tel 0171-904 5000; fax 0171-904 5040

The British Railways Board came into being in 1963 under the terms of the Transport Act 1962. Under the Railways Act 1993, the activities of the Board have been restructured and largely transferred to the private sector. Its residual responsibilities include disposing of surplus land and advising the Government on rail policy issues.

The Government announced in July 1998 that British Rail's residual functions would be taken over by a new strategic rail authority.

Chairman and Chief Executive (part-time) (£76,000), J. K. Welsby, CBE
Vice-Chairman, J. J. Jerram, CBE
Executive Member, A. P. Watkinson
Non-executive Members (part-time), A. D. Begg; J. D. Hughes; Miss K. T. Kantor; R. J. Kennedy; N. J. Wakefield
Secretary, P. Trewin

BRITISH STANDARDS INSTITUTION (BSI)
389 Chiswick High Road, London W4 4AL
Tel 0181-996 9000; fax 0181-996 7344

The British Standards Institution is the recognized authority in the UK for the preparation and publication of national standards for industrial and consumer products. About 90 per cent of its standards work is now internationally linked. British Standards are issued for voluntary adoption, though in a number of cases compliance with a British Standard is required by legislation. Industrial and consumer products certified as complying with the relevant British Standard may carry the Institution's certification trade mark, known as the 'Kitemark'.
Chairman, V. E. Thomas, CBE
Chief Executive, K. Tozzi

BRITISH TOURIST AUTHORITY
Thames Tower, Black's Road, London W6 9EL
Tel 0181-846 9000; fax 0181-563 0302

Established under the Development of Tourism Act 1969, the British Tourist Authority has specific responsibility for promoting tourism to Great Britain from overseas. It also has a general responsibility for the promotion and development of tourism and tourist facilities within Great Britain as a whole, and for advising the Secretary of State for Culture, Media and Sport on tourism matters.
Chairman (part-time), D. Quarmby
Chief Executive, A. Sell

BRITISH WATERWAYS
Willow Grange, Church Road, Watford, Herts WD1 3QA
Tel 01923-226422; fax 01923-201400

British Waterways is the navigation authority for over 2,000 miles of canals and rivers in England, Scotland and Wales. It is responsible to the Secretary of State for the Environment, Transport and the Regions. Its responsibilities include maintaining the waterways and structures on and around them; looking after wildlife and the waterway environment; and ensuring that canals and rivers are safe and enjoyable places to visit.
Chairman (part-time), B. Henderson, CBE
Members (part-time), D. H. R. Yorke; Sir Neil Cossons; Ms J. Elvey; Ms J. Lewis-Jones; Ms C. Dobson; P. King; P. Soulsby; C. Christie
Chief Executive, D. Fletcher
Director of Corporate Services, R. J. Duffy

BROADCASTING STANDARDS COMMISSION
7 The Sanctuary, London SW1P 3JS
Tel 0171-233 0544; fax 0171-233 0397

The Commission was established in April 1997 under the Broadcasting Act 1996. It is an independent organization representing the interests of the consumer, and its remit covers all television and radio broadcasting. The Commission considers the portrayal of violence and sexual conduct and matters of taste and decency. It also provides redress for people who believe they have been unfairly treated or subjected to unwarranted infringement of privacy. The Commission conducts research into standards and fairness in broadcasting and produces codes of practice, and it considers and adjudicates on complaints. Members of the Commission are appointed by the Secretary of State for Culture, Media and Sport. The appointments are part-time.
Chair (£45,210), The Lady Howe of Aberavon
Deputy Chairmen (£34,000–£36,000), Ms J. Leighton; Mrs S. Warner
Commissioners (each £14,450), Ms D. Barr; Ms R. Bevan; D. Boulton; Dame Fiona Caldicott, DBE; S. Heppel, CB; R. Kernohan, OBE; the Very Revd J. Lang; Ms S. Lloyd; Ms S. O'Sullivan; M. Parris; Ms S. Wyn Thomas
Director, S. Whittle

THE BROADS AUTHORITY
Thomas Harvey House, 18 Colegate, Norwich NR3 1BQ
Tel 01603-610734; fax 01603-765710

The Broads Authority is a special statutory authority set up under the Norfolk and Suffolk Broads Act 1988. The functions of the Authority are to conserve and enhance the natural beauty of the Broads; to promote the enjoyment of the Broads by the public; and to protect the interests of navigation. The Authority comprises 35 members, appointed by the local authorities in the area covered, environmental conservation bodies, the Environment Agency, and the Great Yarmouth Port Authority.
Chairman, The Viscountess Knollys
Chief Executive, Prof. M. A. Clark, OBE

288   Government Departments and Public Offices

THE CABINET OFFICE
70 Whitehall, London SW1A 2AS
Tel 0171-270 3000
*Horse Guards Road, London SW1P 3AL
Tel 0171-270 1234
Web: http://www.open.gov.uk.cabinetoffice

The Cabinet Office comprises the Secretariat, who support Ministers collectively in the conduct of Cabinet business; and units responsible for the progress and development of the Better Government, Better Regulation, Citizen's Charter and Next Steps programmes, policy on open government, Senior Civil Service and public appointments, market testing and efficiency in the Civil Service, and Civil Service recruitment. The Cabinet Office supports the Prime Minister in his capacity as Minister for the Civil Service, with responsibility for day-to-day supervision delegated to the Chancellor of the Duchy of Lancaster. The former Office of Public Service was merged with the Cabinet Office in July 1998 in order to integrate more closely the formulation and the implementation of policies.

In July 1998 the Prime Minister announced plans to set up a Performance and Innovation Unit, a Centre for Management and Policy Studies (incorporating a reshaped Civil Service College), and a Management Board for the Civil Service within the Cabinet Office.

Prime Minister and Minister for the Civil Service,
The Rt. Hon. Tony Blair, MP
Minister for the Cabinet Office and Chancellor of the Duchy of Lancaster, The Rt. Hon. Dr Jack Cunningham, MP
Principal Private Secretary, Dr M. Taylor
Private Secretary, Ms B. Feeny
Minister of State, The Lord Falconer of Thoroton, QC
Parliamentary Under-Secretary, Peter Kilfoyle, MP
Private Secretary, Dr C. Brake
Secretary of the Cabinet and Head of the Home Civil Service, Sir Richard Wilson, KCB
Private Secretary, Ms J. A. Polley
Second Permanent Secretary, R. Mountfield, CB
Private Secretary, Ms D. Crewe
Parliamentary Clerk, S. Brown
Press Secretary, B. Sutlieff
Head of the Government Information and Communication Service, M. Granatt
Chief Scientific Adviser, Sir Robert May, FRS

PRIME MINISTER'S OFFICE
10 Downing Street, London SW1A 2AA
Tel 0171-270 3000; fax 0171-925 0918
Web: http://www.number-10.gov.uk
Principal Private Secretary, J. E. Holmes, CMG
Chief of Staff, J. Powell
Private Secretaries, J. J. Heywood (*Economic Affairs*); R. Read (*Parliamentary Affairs*); A. Lapsley (*Home Affairs*); P. Barton (*Assistant on Overseas Affairs*); Ms C. Hawley (*Assistant on Home Affairs*)
Diary Secretary, Ms K. Garvey
Special Assistant for Presentation and Planning, Ms A. Hunter
Assistant to Mrs Blair, Ms F. Millar
Political Secretary, Ms S. Morgan
Head of Policy Unit, D. Miliband
Policy Unit, G. Mulgan; R. Liddle; D. Scott; Ms E. Lloyd; P. Hyman; J. Purnell; P. McFadden; R. Hill; G. Norris; Ms S. White; A. Adonis
Parliamentary Private Secretaries, B. Grocott, MP; Ms A. Coffey, MP

Chief Press Secretary, A. Campbell
Deputy Press Secretary, G. Smith
Special Advisers, Press Office, Ms H. Coffman; L. Price
Strategic Communications Unit, A. Evans; P. Bassett; D. Bradshaw; J. Humphreys; Ms S. Kenny; A. Silverman
Secretary for Appointments, and Ecclesiastical Secretary to the Lord Chancellor, J. Holroyd, CB
Parliamentary Clerk, Mrs H. Murray

SECRETARIAT
Economic and Domestic Secretariat, W. Rickett; J. Elvidge
Defence and Overseas Affairs Secretariat, M. Pakenham, CMG; D. Fisher
Joint Intelligence Organization, J. Alpass; R. Gozny
European Secretariat, B. Bender, CB; M. Donnelly
Constitution Secretariat, Q. Thomas

*CITIZEN'S CHARTER UNIT
Tel 0171-270 1826
Director, J. Rees
Deputy Director, Mrs G. Craig

CENTRAL IT UNIT
53 Parliament Street, London SW1A 2NG
Tel 0171-238 2015
Director, D. Cooke

*EFFICIENCY AND EFFECTIVENESS GROUP
Tel 0171-270 0257
Director, J. R. C. Oughton
Head of Next Steps Project Team, Dr J. G. Fuller

*CIVIL SERVICE EMPLOYER GROUP
Director, J. Barker
Development and Equal Opportunities Division, Ms A. Schofield
Fast Stream and European Staffing Division, Ms J. Lemprière
International Public Service Unit, C. J. Parry
Personnel Management and Conditions of Service Division, Ms E. Goodison
Top Management Programme, Ms H. Dudley (*Course Director*)
Civil Service Pensions Division, D. G. Pain

*OFFICE OF THE COMMISSIONER FOR PUBLIC APPOINTMENTS (OCPA)
Tel 0171-270 5792
The role of the Commissioner for Public Appointments (CPA) is to monitor, regulate and approve departmental appointment procedures for ministerial appointments to advisory and executive non-departmental public bodies, public corporations, nationalized industries, regulators and NHS bodies. The Commissioner is appointed by Order-in-Council.
Commissioner, Sir Leonard Peach
Head of Office, J. Barron

*OFFICE OF THE CIVIL SERVICE COMMISSIONERS (OCSC)
Tel 0171-270 5081; fax 0171-270 5967
First Commissioner, Sir Michael Bett, CBE
Commissioners (part-time), D. J. Burr; Ms M. S. Forbes; Ms J. A. Hunt; H. J. F. McLean, CBE; Sir Leonard Peach; J. Shrigley; K. Singh; C. Stevens, CB
Secretary to the Commissioners and Head of the Office, J. Barron

GOVERNMENT INFORMATION AND COMMUNICATION SERVICE DEVELOPMENT CENTRE
Ashley House, 2 Monck Street, London SW1P 2BQ
Tel 0171-270 1234
Director, C. Skinner

*BETTER REGULATION UNIT
Director, M. Stanley

*SENIOR CIVIL SERVICE GROUP
Director, B. M. Fox, CB
Deputy Director, S. Mitha

*MACHINERY OF GOVERNMENT AND STANDARDS GROUP
Director, D. A. Wilkinson
Queen's Printer, Mrs C. Tullo

CEREMONIAL BRANCH
Ashley House, 2 Monck Street, London SW1P 2BQ
Tel 0171-270 1234
Honours Nomination Unit: Tel 0171-276 2775
Ceremonial Officer, A. J. Merifield, CB

ESTABLISHMENT OFFICER'S GROUP
Queen Anne's Chambers, 28 Broadway, London SW1H 9JS
Tel 0171-270 3000
Principal Establishment and Finance Officer, Mrs N. A. Oppenheimer
Deputy Establishment Officer, Miss E. Chennells
Senior Finance Officer, K. Tolladay

EXECUTIVE AGENCIES

THE BUYING AGENCY
Royal Liver Building, Pier Head, Liverpool L3 1PE
Tel 0151-227 4262; fax 0151-227 3315
The Agency provides a professional purchasing service to government departments and other public bodies.
Chief Executive (G5), S. P. Sage

CCTA (CENTRAL COMPUTER AND TELECOMMUNICATIONS AGENCY)
Rosebery Court, St Andrew's Business Park, Norwich NR7 0HS
Tel 01603-704567; fax 01603-704817
Steel House, 11 Tothill Street, London SW1H 9NF
Tel 0171-273 6565; fax 0171-273 6555
CCTA's objective is to develop, maintain and make available expertise about information technology which public sector organizations can draw on in order to operate more effectively and efficiently.
Chief Executive, R. Assirati

CENTRAL OFFICE OF INFORMATION
— *see* below

CIVIL SERVICE COLLEGE
Sunningdale Park, Ascot, Berks SL5 0QE
Tel 01344-634000; fax 01344-634781
11 Belgrave Road, London SW1V 1RB
Tel 0171-834 6644; fax 01344-634451
199 Cathedral Street, Glasgow G4 0QU
Tel 0141-553 6021; fax 0141-553 6171
The College provides training in management and professional skills for the public and private sectors.
Chief Executive (G3), R. Bayley
Business Executives (G5/G6), M. N. Barnes; R. Behrens; G. W. Llewellyn; Ms L. Oliver (*Non-Executive Director*); P. Tebby; M. Timmis; Dr A. Wyatt

GOVERNMENT CAR AND DESPATCH AGENCY
46 Ponton Road, London SW8 5AX
Tel 0171-217 3839; fax 0171-217 3840

*Unless otherwise stated, this is the address and telephone number for divisions of the Cabinet Office

The Agency provides secure transport and document transfers between government departments.
Chief Executive, N. Matheson

PROPERTY ADVISERS TO THE CIVIL ESTATE
6th Floor, Trevelyan House, Great Peter Street, London SW1P 2BY
Tel 0171-271 2626; fax 0171-271 2622
The Agency co-ordinates government activity on the civil estate, and provides general property guidance and support to government departments.
Chief Executive, J. C. Locke, FRICS

CENTRAL ADJUDICATION SERVICES
Quarry House, Quarry Hill, Leeds LS2 7UB
Tel 0113-232 4000; fax 0113-232 4841
New Court, 48 Carey Street, London WC2A 2LS
Tel 0171-412 1504; fax 0171-412 1220

The Chief Adjudication Officer and Chief Child Support Officer are independent statutory authorities under the Social Security Act 1975 (as amended) and the Child Support Act 1991. They are appointed by the Secretary of State for Social Security to give advice to adjudication officers dealing with claims for social security cash benefits and to child support officers, and to keep under review the operation of the systems of adjudication. They report annually to the Secretary of State on adjudication standards.
Chief Adjudication Officer, and Chief Child Support Officer, E. W. Hazlewood

CENTRAL OFFICE OF INFORMATION
Hercules Road, London SE1 7DU
Tel 0171-928 2345; fax 0171-928 5037

The Central Office of Information (COI) is an executive agency which offers consultancy, procurement and project management services to central government for publicity. Though the majority of COI's work is for government departments in the UK, it also procures a range of publicity materials for overseas consumption. Administrative responsibility for the COI rests with the Chancellor of the Duchy of Lancaster within the Cabinet Office.
Chief Executive (G3), A. Douglas
Senior Personal Secretary, Ms L. Sheasgreen

MANAGEMENT BOARD
Members, K. Williamson; R. Smith; P. Buchanan; I. Hamilton; R. Haslam; Ms S. Whetton; M. Reid
Secretary, Ms L. Sheasgreen

DIRECTORS
Director, New Business (G6), Ms S. Whetton
Director, Marketing Communications (G6), P. Buchanan
Director, Films, Radio and Events (G6), I. Hamilton
Director, Publications (G6), M. Reid
Director, Central Services (G5), K. Williamson
Director, Regional Network (G6), R. Haslam

NETWORK OFFICES
EASTERN, Three Crowns House, 72–80 Hills Road, Cambridge CB2 1LL. *Network Director (G7),* P. Powell
MIDLANDS EAST, 1st Floor, Severns House, 20 Middle Pavement, Nottingham NG1 7DW. *Network Director (G7),* P. Smith

MIDLANDS WEST, Five Ways House, Islington Row Middleway, Edgbaston, Birmingham BI5 ISH. *Network Director (G6)*, B. Garner
NORTH-EAST, Wellbar House, Gallowgate, Newcastle upon Tyne NEI 4TB. *Network Director (G7)*, Ms L. Taylor
NORTH-WEST, Sunley Tower, Piccadilly Plaza, Manchester MI 4BD. *Network Director (G7)*, Mrs E. Jones
SOUTH-EAST, Hercules Road, London SEI 7DU. *Network Director (G6)*, Ms V. Burdon
SOUTH-WEST, The Pithay, Bristol BSI 2NF. *Network Director (G7)*, P. Whitbread
YORKSHIRE AND HUMBERSIDE, City House, New Station Street, Leeds LSI 4JG. *Network Director (G7)*, Ms W. Miller

CERTIFICATION OFFICE FOR TRADE UNIONS AND EMPLOYERS' ASSOCIATIONS
180 Borough High Street, London SEI ILW
Tel 0171-210 3734/5; fax 0171-210 3612

The Certification Office is an independent statutory authority. The Certification Officer is appointed by the Secretary of State for Trade and Industry and is responsible for receiving and scrutinizing annual returns from trade unions and employers' associations; for investigating allegations of financial irregularities in the affairs of a trade union or employers' association; for dealing with complaints concerning trade union elections; for ensuring observance of statutory requirements governing political funds and trade union mergers; and for certifying the independence of trade unions.
Certification Officer, E. G. Whybrew
Assistant Certification Officer, G. S. Osborne

SCOTLAND
58 Frederick Street, Edinburgh EH2 ILN
Tel 0131-226 3224; fax 0131-200 1300
Assistant Certification Officer for Scotland, J. L. J. Craig

CHARITY COMMISSION
St Alban's House, 57–60 Haymarket, London SWIY 4QX
Tel 0171-210 4556; fax 0171-210 4545
2nd Floor, 20 King's Parade, Queen's Dock, Liverpool L3 4DQ
Tel 0151-703 1500; fax 0151-703 1557
Woodfield House, Tangier, Taunton, Somerset TAI 4BL
Tel 01823-345000; fax 01823-345008

The Charity Commission is established under the Charities Act 1993 with the general function of promoting the effective use of charitable resources in England and Wales. The Commission gives information and advice to charity trustees to make the administration of their charity more effective; investigates misconduct and the abuse of charitable assets, and takes or recommends remedial action; and maintains a public register of charities. The Commission does not have at its disposal any funds with which to make grants to organizations or individuals.
At the end of 1997 there were 184,000 registered charities.
Chief Commissioner (G3), R. Fries
Legal Commissioner (G3), M. Carpenter
Commissioners (part-time) (G4), J. Bonds; Ms J. Warburton; Ms J. Unwin
Heads of Legal Sections (G5), J. A. Dutton; G. S. Goodchild; K. M. Dibble; S. Slack

Executive Director (G4), Ms L. Berry
Head of Policy Division (G5), R. Carter
Establishment Officer (G5), Ms C. Stewart
Information Systems Controller (G5), Ms G. Cruickshank

The offices responsible for charities in Scotland and Northern Ireland are:
SCOTLAND – Scottish Charities Office, Crown Office, 25 Chambers Street, Edinburgh EHI ILA. Tel: 0131-226 2626
NORTHERN IRELAND – Department of Health and Social Services, Charities Branch, Annexe 3, Castle Buildings, Stormont Estate, Belfast BT4 3RA. Tel: 01232-522780

CHIEF ADJUDICATION OFFICER AND CHIEF CHILD SUPPORT OFFICER
— *see* Central Adjudication Services

CHILD SUPPORT AGENCY
— *see* page 345

CHURCH COMMISSIONERS
1 Millbank, London SWIP 3JZ
Tel 0171-222 7010; fax 0171-233 0171

The Church Commissioners were established in 1948 by the amalgamation of Queen Anne's Bounty (established 1704) and the Ecclesiastical Commissioners (established 1836). They are responsible for the management of most of the Church of England's assets, the income from which is predominantly used to pay, house and pension the clergy. The Commissioners own 131,970 acres of agricultural land, a number of residential estates in central London, and commercial property in Great Britain. They also carry out administrative duties in connection with pastoral reorganization and redundant churches.
The Commissioners are: the Archbishops of Canterbury and of York; four bishops, three clergy and four lay persons elected by the respective houses of the General Synod; two deans or provosts elected by all the deans and provosts; three persons nominated by The Queen; three persons nominated by the Archbishops of Canterbury and York; three persons nominated by the Archbishops after consultation with others including the lord mayors of London and York and the vice-chancellors of the universities of Oxford and Cambridge; the First Lord of the Treasury; the Lord President of the Council; the Home Secretary; the Lord Chancellor; the Secretary of State for Culture, Media and Sport; and the Speaker of the House of Commons.

INCOME AND EXPENDITURE
for year ended 31 December 1997

	£ million
Total income	143.7
Net income	135.3
Investments	80.0
Property	43.2
Interest from loans, etc.	20.5
Total expenditure	131.5
Clergy stipends	24.8
Clergy and widows' pensions	82.1
Episcopal and cathedral housing	2.6
Financial provision for resigning clergy	2.4
Commissioners' administration of central church functions	4.7
Episcopal administration and payments to Chapters	10.6

Church buildings	0.8
Administration costs of other bodies	2.6
Surplus for year	3.8

CHURCH ESTATES COMMISSIONERS
First, Sir Michael Colman, Bt.
Second, S. Bell, MP
Third, Mrs M. H. Laird

OFFICERS
Secretary, H. H. Hughes
Deputy Secretary (Finance and Investment), C. W. Daws
Official Solicitor, N. I. Johnson
Assistant Secretaries:
  The Accountant, G. C. Baines
  Management Accountant, B. J. Hardy
  Chief Surveyor, A. C. Brown
  Computer Manager, J. W. Ferguson
  Bishoprics Secretary, E. G. Peacock
  Investments Manager, A. S. Hardy
  Pastoral, Houses and Redundant Churches, M. D. Elengorn
  Senior Architect, J. A. Taylor

CIVIL AVIATION AUTHORITY
CAA House, 45–59 Kingsway, London WC2B 6TE
Tel 0171-379 7311; fax: 0171-240 1153

The CAA is responsible for the economic regulation of UK airlines and for the safety regulation of UK civil aviation by the certification of airlines and aircraft and by licensing aerodromes, flight crew and aircraft engineers. Through its subsidiary company, National Air Traffic Services Ltd (NATS), it is also responsible for the provision of air traffic control and telecommunications services. The Government announced in June 1998 that it planned to sell 51 per cent of NATS to the private sector.

The CAA advises the Government on aviation issues, represents consumer interests, conducts economic and scientific research, produces statistical data, and provides specialist services and other training and consultancy services to clients world-wide.
Chairman (part-time), Sir Malcolm Field
Secretary, R. J. Britton

THE COAL AUTHORITY
200 Lichfield Lane, Mansfield, Notts NG18 4RG
Tel 01623-427162; fax: 01623-622072

The Coal Authority was established under the Coal Industry Act 1994 to manage certain functions previously undertaken by British Coal, including ownership of unworked coal. It is responsible for licensing coal mining operations and for providing information on coal reserves and past and future coal mining. It settles subsidence claims not falling on coal mining operators. It deals with the management and disposal of property, and with surface hazards such as abandoned coal mine shafts.
Chairman, Sir David White
Chief Executive, K. J. Fergusson

COMMONWEALTH DEVELOPMENT CORPORATION
1 Bessborough Gardens, London SW1V 2JQ
Tel 0171-828 4488; fax 0171-828 6505

The Commonwealth Development Corporation (CDC) assists overseas countries in the development of their economies. Its sponsoring department is the Department for International Development. Its main activity is providing long-term finance, as loans and risk capital, for financially viable and developmentally sound business enterprises. CDC's area of operations includes UK overseas territories and, with ministerial approval, Commonwealth or other developing countries. At present, CDC is authorized to operate in more than 60 countries and territories. Its investments at the end of 1997 were £1,560 million.

The Government announced in June 1998 that it planned to sell its majority stake in CDC.
Chairman (part-time), The Earl Cairns, CBE
Deputy Chairman (part-time), Sir William Ryrie, KCB
Chief Executive, Dr R. Reynolds

COMMONWEALTH SECRETARIAT
— *see* Index

COMMONWEALTH WAR GRAVES COMMISSION
2 Marlow Road, Maidenhead, Berks SL6 7DX
Tel 01628-634221; fax 01628-771208

The Commonwealth War Graves Commission (formerly Imperial War Graves Commission) was founded by royal charter in 1917. It is responsible for the commemoration of 1,695,098 members of the forces of the Commonwealth who fell in the two world wars. More than one million graves are maintained in 23,216 burial grounds throughout the world. Over three-quarters of a million men and women who have no known grave or who were cremated are commemorated by name on memorials built by the Commission.

The funds of the Commission are derived from the six participating governments, i.e. the UK, Canada, Australia, India, New Zealand and South Africa.
President, HRH The Duke of Kent, KG, GCMG, GCVO, ADC
Chairman, The Secretary of State for Defence in the UK
Vice-Chairman, Adm. Sir John Kerr, GCB
Members, The High Commissioners in London for Canada, New Zealand, India, South Africa and Australia; The Viscount Ridley, KG, GCVO, TD; Prof. R. J. O'Neill, AO; Mrs L. Golding, MP; J. Wilkinson, MP; Sir John Gray, KBE, CMG; P. D. Orchard-Lisle, CBE, TD; Air Chief Marshal Sir Michael Stear, KCB, CBE; Gen. Sir John Wilsey, GCB, CBE
Director-General and Secretary to the Commission, D. Kennedy, CMG
Deputy Director-General, R. J. Dalley
Legal Adviser and Solicitor, G. C. Reddie
Directors, D. R. Parker (*Personnel*); A. Coombe (*Works*); R. D. Wilson (*Finance*); D. C. Parker (*Horticulture*); L. J. Hanna (*Information and Secretariat*)

IMPERIAL WAR GRAVES ENDOWMENT FUND
Trustees, The Lord Remnant, CVO (*Chairman*); A. C. Barker; Adm. Sir John Kerr, GCB
Secretary to the Trustees, R. D. Wilson

COUNTRYSIDE COMMISSION

John Dower House, Crescent Place, Cheltenham, Glos
GL50 3RA
Tel 01242-521381; fax 01242-584270

The Countryside Commission was set up in 1968 and is an independent agency which promotes the conservation and enhancement of landscape beauty in England. It encourages the provision and improvement of facilities in the countryside, and works to secure access for open air recreation. The Commission is funded by an annual grant from the Department of the Environment, Transport and the Regions, and members of the Commission are appointed by the Secretary of State. The Government announced in March 1998 that the Countryside Commission would merge with the Rural Development Commission in April 1999.

Chairman, R. Simmonds, CBE
Commissioners, D. Barker, MBE; the Rt. Revd Bishop of Blackburn; The Lord Denham, KBE; Dr Victoria Edwards, FRICS; Dr Susan Owens; W. Rogers-Coltman, OBE; R. Swarbrick, CBE; D. Woodhall, CBE
Chief Executive (G3), R. G. Wakeford
Directors (G5), R. Clarke (*Programmes*); M. Taylor (*Resources*)
Head of Strategic Affairs (G7), D. E. Coleman
Head, Farms and Woodlands Branch (G7), R. Lloyd
Head, National Heritage Unit (G7), P. Walshe
Head, Sustainable Leisure Branch (G7), R. Roberts
Head, Planning for Sustainable Development Branch (G7), J. Worth
Head, Local Identity Branch (G7), T. Robinson
Head, Countryside Around Towns Branch (G7), Dr M. Rawson
Head, Information Services (G7), J. Huntley
Head, Resources Management (G7), V. Ellis
Regional Officers (G7), Dr M. Carroll (*Eastern*); T. Allen (*Midlands*); K. Buchanan (*North-East*); Dr Liz Newton (*North-West*); Ms M. Spain (*South-East*); N. Holliday (*South-West*); Dr S. A. Bucknall (*Yorkshire and Humber*)

COUNTRYSIDE COUNCIL FOR WALES/ CYNGOR CEFN GWLAD CYMRU

Plas Penrhos, Ffordd Penrhos, Bangor LL57 2LQ
Tel 01248-385500; fax 01248-385505

The Countryside Council for Wales is the Government's statutory adviser on wildlife, countryside and maritime conservation matters in Wales, and it is the executive authority for the conservation of habitats and wildlife. It promotes the protection of the Welsh landscape and encourages opportunities for public access and enjoyment of the countryside. It provides grant aid to local authorities, voluntary organizations and individuals to pursue countryside management. It is funded by the Welsh Office and accountable to the Secretary of State for Wales, who appoints its members.

Chairman, E. M. W. Griffith, CBE
Chief Executive, P. E. Loveluck, CBE
Senior Director and Chief Scientist, Dr M. E. Smith
Director, Countryside Policy, Dr J. Taylor
Director, Conservation, Dr D. Parker

COVENT GARDEN MARKET AUTHORITY

Covent House, New Covent Garden Market, London
SW8 5NX
Tel 0171-720 2211; fax 0171-622 5307

The Covent Garden Market Authority is constituted under the Covent Garden Market Acts 1961 to 1977, the members being appointed by the Minister of Agriculture, Fisheries and Food. The Authority owns and operates the 56-acre New Covent Garden Markets (fruit, vegetables, flowers) which have been trading since 1974.

Chairman (part-time), L. Mills, CBE
General Manager, Dr P. M. Liggins
Secretary, C. Farey

CRIMINAL CASES REVIEW COMMISSION

Alpha Tower, Suffolk Street Queensway, Birmingham B1
1TT
Tel 0121-633 1800; fax 0121-633 1823

The Criminal Cases Review Commission is an independent body set up under the Criminal Appeal Act 1995. It is a non-departmental public body reporting to Parliament via the Home Secretary. It is responsible for investigating suspected miscarriages of justice in England, Wales and Northern Ireland, and deciding whether or not to refer cases back to an appeal court. Membership of the Commission is by royal appointment; the senior executive staff are appointed by the Commission.

A commission to investigate alleged miscarriages of justice in Scotland is to be established by 1 April 1999.

Chairman, Sir Frederick Crawford, FENG.
Members, B. Capon; L. Elks; A. Foster; Ms J. Gort; Ms F. King; J. Knox; D. Kyle; J. Leckey; Prof. L. Leigh; J. MacKeith; K. Singh; B. Skitt; E. Weiss
Chief Executive, Ms G. Stacey
Director of Finance and Personnel, D. Robson
Legal Advisers, J. Wagstaff; M. Aspinall
Police Adviser, R. Barrington

CRIMINAL INJURIES COMPENSATION AUTHORITY AND BOARD

Morley House, 26–30 Holborn Viaduct, London EC1A 2JQ
Tel 0171-842 6800; fax 0171-436 0804
Tay House, 300 Bath Street, Glasgow G2 4JR
Tel 0141-331 2726; 0141-331 2287

All applications for compensation for personal injury arising from crimes of violence in England, Scotland and Wales are dealt with at the above locations. (Separate arrangements apply in Northern Ireland.) Applications received up to 31 March 1996 were assessed on the basis of common law damages under the 1990 compensation scheme by the Criminal Injuries Compensation Board (CICB), which also hears appeals. Applications received on or after 1 April 1996 are assessed under a tariff-based scheme by the Criminal Injuries Compensation Authority (CICA); there is a separate avenue of appeal to the Criminal Injuries Compensation Appeals Panel (CICAP). In 1996–7 total compensation paid was £209,208,500.

Chairman of the Criminal Injuries Compensation Board (part-time) (£35,306), The Lord Carlisle of Bucklow, PC, QC
Chief Executive of the Board and of the Criminal Injuries Compensation Authority, P. G. Spurgeon

Head of Legal Services, Mrs A. M. Johnstone
Operations Manager, E. McKeown
Chairman of the Criminal Injuries Compensation Appeals Panel,
M. Lewer, QC
Secretary to the Panel, Miss V. Jenson

CROFTERS COMMISSION
4–6 Castle Wynd, Inverness IV2 3EQ
Tel 01463-663450; fax 01463-711820

The Crofters Commission was established in 1955. It advises the Secretary of State for Scotland on all matters relating to crofting. It controls the letting, subletting and, in certain circumstances, the assignation or enlargement of crofts; the removal of land from crofting tenure; and the regulation of common grazings. It delivers schemes to develop crofts and crofting townships and for the improvement of crofters' livestock.
Chairman, I. MacAskill
Secretary (G6), M. Grantham

CROWN ESTATE
16 Carlton House Terrace, London SW1Y 5AH
Tel 0171-210 4377; fax 0171-930 8202

The land revenues of the Crown in England and Wales have been collected on the public account since 1760, when George III surrendered them to Parliament and received a fixed annual payment or Civil List. At the time of the surrender the gross revenues amounted to about £89,000 and the net return to about £11,000. The land revenues in Ireland have been carried to the Consolidated Fund since 1820; from 1923, as regards the Republic of Ireland, they have been collected and administered by the Irish Government. The land revenues in Scotland were transferred to the predecessors of the Crown Estate Commissioners in 1833.

In the year ended 31 March 1998, the gross revenue from the Crown Estate totalled £160.1 million and £113.2 million was paid to the Exchequer as surplus revenue.
First Commissioner and Chairman (part-time), Sir Denys Henderson
Second Commissioner and Chief Executive, C. K. Howes, CB, CVO
Commissioners (part-time), Sir John James, KCVO, CBE; I. Grant; J. H. M. Norris, CBE; The Lord De Ramsey; Mrs H. Chapman, CBE, FRICS
Commissioner and Deputy Chief Executive, D. E. G. Griffiths
Legal Adviser, D. Harris
Director of Urban Estates, N. Borrett
Urban Estates Managers, M. W. Dillon; A. Bickmore; R. Wyatt
Development and Investment Manager, L. Colgan
Agricultural Estates Manager, C. Bourchier
Marine Estates Manager, F. G. Parrish
Information Systems Manager, D. Kingston-Smith
Valuation and Investment Analysis Manager, P. Shearmur
Internal Audit Manager, J. E. Ford
Finance Manager, J. G. Lelliott
Personnel and Office Services Manager, R. H. Blake
Public Relations and Press Officer, Mrs G. Coates

SCOTLAND
10 Charlotte Square, Edinburgh EH2 4BR
Tel 0131-226 7241; fax 0131-220 1366

Crown Estate Receiver for Scotland, M. J. Gravestock

WINDSOR ESTATE
The Great Park, Windsor, Berks SL4 2HT
Tel 01753-860222; fax 01753-859617
Deputy Ranger and Surveyor, P. Everett

CROWN PROSECUTION SERVICE
— *see* pages 363–4

DEPARTMENT FOR CULTURE, MEDIA AND SPORT
2–4 Cockspur Street, London SW1Y 5DH
Tel 0171-211 6200; fax 0171-211 6032
E-mail: enquiries@culture.gov.uk
Web: http://www.culture.gov.uk

The Department for Culture, Media and Sport was established in July 1997 and is responsible for government policy relating to the arts, broadcasting, the press, museums and galleries, libraries, sport and recreation, historic buildings and ancient monuments, tourism, and the music industry. It funds the Arts Councils and other arts bodies, is responsible for policy on the National Lottery and the Millennium, and sponsors the Millennium Commission.
Secretary of State for Culture, Media and Sport, The Rt. Hon. Chris Smith, MP
Private Secretary, T. Dyer
Special Advisers, J. Eccles; J. Newbigin
Parliamentary Private Secretary, Ms F. Mactaggart, MP
Parliamentary Under-Secretaries, Alan Howarth, MP (*Arts*); Tony Banks, MP (*Sport*); Janet Anderson, MP (*Tourism, Film and Broadcasting*)
Private Secretaries, M. McGann; S. Green; D. Tambling
Parliamentary Clerk, T. English
Permanent Secretary (SCS), R. Young
Private Secretary, J. Priestland

LIBRARIES, GALLERIES AND MUSEUMS GROUP
Head of Group (SCS), Miss S. Booth, CBE
Head of Libraries and Information Division (SCS), N. Mackay
Head of British Library Project and IT Strategy Unit (A(U)), E. D'Silva
Head of Museums and Galleries Division (SCS), H. Corner
Director, Government Art Collection (SCS), Ms P. Johnson
Head of Cultural Property Unit (A(L)), M. Helston

SPORT, TOURISM, NATIONAL LOTTERY CHARITIES BOARD AND MILLENNIUM GROUP
Head of Group (SCS), D. Chesterton
Head of Sport and Recreation Division (SCS), S. Broadley
Head of Tourism Division (SCS), Ms B. Phillips
Head of National Lottery Charities Board Division (A(L)), Mrs V. Molloy
Head of Millennium Unit (A(L)), Miss C. Pillman

ARTS, BUILDING AND CREATIVE INDUSTRIES GROUP
Head of Group (SCS), L. P. Wright
Head of Arts Division (SCS), Ms M. Leech
Head of Buildings, Monuments and Sites Division (SCS), N. Pittman
Head of Creative Industries Unit (A(L)), D. Fawcett

BROADCASTING AND MEDIA GROUP
Head of Group (SCS), N. J. Kroll
Head of Broadcasting Policy Division (SCS), vacant
Head of Media Division (SCS), Ms J. Evans

FINANCE, LOTTERY AND PERSONNEL GROUP
Director (SCS), A. Ramsay
Head of Finance Division (SCS), Ms A. Stewart
Head of National Lottery Division (SCS), A. McLellan

Head of Personnel and Central Services Division (SCS), Ms R. Siemaszko

STRATEGY AND COMMUNICATIONS
Head of Strategy and Communications (SCS), P. Bolt

EXECUTIVE AGENCY

ROYAL PARKS AGENCY
The Old Police House, Hyde Park, London W2 2UH
Tel 0171-298 2000; fax 0171-298 2005

The Agency is responsible for maintaining and developing the royal parks.
Chief Executive (G5), D. Welch

BOARD OF CUSTOMS AND EXCISE
*New King's Beam House, 22 Upper Ground, London
SE1 9PJ
Tel 0171-620 1313
Web: http://www.open.gov.uk/customs/c&ehome/htm

Commissioners of Customs were first appointed in 1671 and housed by the King in London. The Excise Department was formerly under the Inland Revenue Department and was amalgamated with the Customs Department in 1909.

HM Customs and Excise is responsible for collecting and administering customs and excise duties and VAT, and advises the Chancellor of the Exchequer on any matters connected with them. The Department is also responsible for preventing and detecting the evasion of revenue laws and for enforcing a range of prohibitions and restrictions on the importation of certain classes of goods. In addition, the Department undertakes certain agency work on behalf of other departments, including the compilation of UK overseas trade statistics from customs import and export documents.

THE BOARD
Chairman (G1), Dame Valerie Strachan, DCB
    Private Secretaries, Ms J. Mellon; L. Allen
Deputy Chairman, A. W. Russell, CB
Commissioners (G3), A. C. Sawyer; P. R. H. Allen; A. R. Rawsthorne; D. J. Howard; A. Paynter; M. R. Brown; R. N. McAfee; M. W. Norgrove
Head of Board's Secretariat, J. Bone

PUBLIC RELATIONS OFFICE
Tel 0171-865 5665
Head of Public Relations, Ms L. J. Sinclair

INFORMATION SYSTEMS DIRECTORATE
Alexander House, 21 Victoria Avenue, Southend-on-Sea
SS99 1AA
Tel 01702-348944
Director, A. Paynter

CUSTOMS POLICY DIRECTORATE
Director, A. R. Rawsthorne

EXCISE AND CENTRAL POLICY DIRECTORATE
Director, D. J. Howard

VAT POLICY DIRECTORATE
Director, M. R. Brown

PERSONNEL AND FINANCE DIRECTORATE
Director, P. R. H. Allen

---

*Unless otherwise stated, this is the address and telephone number of directorates of the Board

CENTRAL OPERATIONS DIRECTORATE
Director, R. N. McAfee

Tariff and Statistical Office
Portcullis House, 27 Victoria Avenue, Southend-on-Sea
SS2 6AL
Tel 01702-348944
Controller, M. McDowall

Accounting Services Division
Alexander House, 21 Victoria Avenue, Southend-on-Sea
SS99 1AA
Tel 01702-348944
Accountant and Comptroller-General, D. Robinson

OPERATIONS (COMPLIANCE) DIRECTORATE
Director, M. W. Norgrove

OPERATIONS (PREVENTION) DIRECTORATE
Director, A. C. Sawyer

National Investigation Service
Custom House, Lower Thames Street, London EC3R 6EE
Tel 0171-283 5353
Chief Investigation Officer, R. Kellaway

SOLICITOR'S OFFICE
Solicitor, D. Pickup
Deputy Solicitor, G. Fotherby

COLLECTORS OF HM CUSTOMS AND EXCISE (G5)
Anglia, M. Hill
Central England, D. Garlick
Eastern England, A. Durrant
London Airports, M. Peach
London Central, J. Maclean
Northern England, H. Peden
Northern Ireland, T. W. Logan
North-west England, A. Allen
Scotland, C. Arnott
South-east England, W. I. Stuttle
South London and Thames, J. Hendry
Southern England, H. Burnard
Thames Valley, J. Barnard
Wales, the West and Borders, B. Flavill

OFFICE OF THE DATA PROTECTION COMMISSIONER
Wycliffe House, Water Lane, Wilmslow, Cheshire
SK9 5AF
Tel 01625-545745; fax 01625-524510

The Office of the Data Protection Registrar was created by the Data Protection Act 1984; the Registrar was renamed the Data Protection Commissioner under the Data Protection Act 1998, which implemented the EU Data Protection Directive (95/46/EC) in the UK. It is the Commissioner's duty to compile and maintain the register of data users and computer bureaux and to provide facilities for members of the public to examine the register; to promote observance of data protection principles; to consider complaints made by data subjects; to disseminate information about the Data Protection Act; to encourage the production of codes of practice by trade associations and other bodies; to guide data users in complying with data protection principles; and to co-operate with other parties to the Council of Europe Convention and act as UK authority for the purposes of Article 13 of the Convention.
Commissioner, Mrs E. France

DEER COMMISSION FOR SCOTLAND
Knowsley, 82 Fairfield Road, Inverness IV3 5LH
Tel 01463-231751; fax 01463-712931

The Deer Commission for Scotland has the general functions of furthering the conservation and control of deer in Scotland. It has the statutory duty, with powers, to prevent damage to agriculture, forestry and the habitat by deer. It is funded by the Scottish Office.
Chairman (part-time), P. Gordon-Duff-Pennington, OBE
Director, A. Rinning
Technical Director, R. W. Youngson

MINISTRY OF DEFENCE
— *see* pages 384–7

DESIGN COUNCIL
34 Bow Street, London WC2E 7DL
Tel 0171-420 5200; fax 0171-420 5300

The Design Council is incorporated by royal charter and is a registered charity. It works with government, industry and academia to generate information and practical tools for uptake in industry and education which demonstrate the contribution, value and effectiveness of design. Its sponsoring department is the Department of Trade and Industry.
Chairman, J. Sorrell, CBE
Chief Executive, A. Summers

THE DUCHY OF CORNWALL
10 Buckingham Gate, London SW1E 6LA
Tel 0171-834 7346; fax 0171-931 9541

The Duchy of Cornwall was created by Edward III in 1337 for the support of his eldest son Edward, later known as the Black Prince. It is the oldest of the English duchies. The duchy is acquired by inheritance by the sovereign's eldest son either at birth or on the accession of his parent to the throne, whichever is the later. The primary purpose of the estate remains to provide an income for the Prince of Wales. The estate is mainly agricultural, consisting of 129,000 acres in 24 counties mainly in the south-west of England. The duchy also has some residential property, a number of shops and offices, and a Stock Exchange portfolio. Prince Charles is the 24th Duke of Cornwall.

THE PRINCE'S COUNCIL
Chairman, HRH The Prince of Wales, KG, KT, GCB
Lord Warden of the Stannaries, The Earl Peel
Receiver-General, The Earl Cairns, CBE
Attorney-General to the Prince of Wales, N. Underhill, QC
Secretary and Keeper of the Records, W. R. A. Ross
Other members, Earl of Shelburne; J. E. Pugsley; A. M. J. Galsworthy; C. Howes, CB; W. N. Hood, CBE; S. Lamport

OTHER OFFICERS
Auditors, I. Brindle; R. Hughes
Sheriff (1998–9), P. R. Thompson

THE DUCHY OF LANCASTER
Lancaster Place, Strand, London WC2E 7ED
Tel 0171-836 8277; fax 0171-836 3098

The estates and jurisdiction known as the Duchy of Lancaster have belonged to the reigning monarch since 1399 when John of Gaunt's son came to the throne as Henry IV. As the Lancaster Inheritance it goes back as far as 1265 when Henry III granted his youngest son Edmund lands and possessions following the Baron's war. In 1267 Henry gave Edmund the County, Honor and Castle of Lancaster and created him the first Earl of Lancaster. In 1351 Edward III created Lancaster a County Palatine.
The Chancellor of the Duchy of Lancaster is responsible for the administration of the Duchy, the appointment of justices of the peace in Lancashire, Greater Manchester and Merseyside and ecclesiastical patronage in the Duchy gift.
Chancellor of the Duchy of Lancaster (and Minister for the Cabinet Office), The Rt. Hon. Dr Jack Cunningham, MP (*see also* page 288)
Attorney-General, R. G. B. McCombe, QC
Receiver-General, Sir Michael Peat, KCVO
Clerk of the Council, M. K. Ridley, CVO
Chief Clerk, Col. F. N. J. Davies

ECGD (EXPORT CREDITS GUARANTEE DEPARTMENT)
PO Box 2200, 2 Exchange Tower, Harbour Exchange Square, London E14 9GS
Tel 0171-512 7000; fax 0171-512 7649

ECGD (Export Credits Guarantee Department), the UK's official export credit insurer, is a government department responsible to the Secretary of State for Trade and Industry and functions under the Export and Investment Guarantees Act 1991. This enables ECGD to facilitate UK exports by making available export credit insurance to firms engaged in selling overseas and to guarantee repayment to banks providing finance for capital goods. The Act also empowers ECGD to insure UK companies investing overseas against political risks such as war, expropriation and restrictions on remittances.
Chief Executive, H. V. B. Brown
Group Directors (G3), V. P. Lunn-Rockliffe (*Asset Management*); J. R. Weiss (*Underwriting*); T. M. Jaffray (*Resource Management*)

DIVISIONS
Director, Finance (G5), R. J. Healey
Director, Central Services (G5), P. J. Callaghan
Directors, Underwriting Divisions (G5), G. G. W. Welsh (*Division 1*); J. C. W. Croall (*Division 2*); M. D. Pentecost (*Division 3*); Mrs M. E. Maddox (*Division 4*); S. R. Dodgson (*Division 5*); C. J. Leeds (*Division 6*)
Director, Office of the General Counsel (G5), R. G. Elden
Director, International Debt (G5), A. J. T. Steele
Director, Claims (G5), R. F. Lethbridge
Director, Treasury and Export Finance (G5), J. S. Snowdon
Director, Risk Management (G5), P. J. Radford
Director, External Relations (G5), R. Gotts
Director, IT Services (G6), E. J. Walsby
Director, Internal Audit (G6), G. Cassell
Director, Operational Research (G6), Ms R. Kaufman

EXPORT GUARANTEES ADVISORY COUNCIL
Chairman, D. H. A. Harrison
Other Members, Ms E. Airey; Dr A. K. Banerji; R. F. T.
Binyon; S. J. Doughty; M. S. Jaskel; Ms L. Knox;
G. W. Lynch, OBE; P. J. Mason; R. H. Maudslay

DEPARTMENT FOR EDUCATION AND
EMPLOYMENT
Sanctuary Buildings, Great Smith Street, London
SWIP 3BT
Tel 0171-925 5000; fax 0171-925 6000
E-mail: info@dfee.gov.uk
Web: http://www.dfee.gov.uk
Caxton House, Tothill Street, London SWIH 9NF
Tel 0171-273 3000; fax 0171-273 5124
Moorfoot, Sheffield SI 4PQ
Tel 0114-275 3275; fax 0114-259 4724
Mowden Hall, Staindrop Road, Darlington DL3 9BG
Tel 01325-460155

The Department for Education and Employment was
formed in July 1995, bringing together the functions of the
former Department for Education with the training and
labour market functions of the former Employment
Department Group. It includes an executive agency, the
Employment Service. The Department aims to support
economic growth and improve the nation's competitive-
ness and quality of life by raising standards of educational
achievement and skill and by promoting an efficient and
flexible labour market. In April 1998 it took over from the
Department of Health responsibility for day care, includ-
ing the regulation of nurseries and childminders.
Secretary of State for Education and Employment, The Rt. Hon.
David Blunkett, MP
Principal Private Secretary, M. Wardle
Special Advisers, C. Ryan; T. Bently; H. Benn; Ms L.
Barclay
Parliamentary Private Secretary, Ms J. Corston, MP
Minister of State, The Rt. Hon. Andrew Smith, MP (*Welfare
to Work, Equal Opportunities*)
Private Secretary, Ms K. Driver
Parliamentary Private Secretary, Ms J. Ryan, MP
Minister of State, Estelle Morris, MP (*School Standards*)
Private Secretary, Ms C. Maye
Minister in the Lords, The Baroness Blackstone, PH.D.
Private Secretary, M. Boo
Parliamentary Private Secretary, T. McNulty, MP
Parliamentary Under-Secretaries of State, Margaret Hodge,
MP (*Employment and Equal Opportunities*); Charles Clarke,
MP (*Schools*) George Mudie, MP (*Lifelong Learning*)
Private Secretaries, Ms G. Magliocco; D. McGrath; Ms L.
Welsh
Permanent Secretary, M. Bichard
Private Secretary, H. Nicholson-Lailey

EMPLOYMENT, LIFELONG LEARNING
AND INTERNATIONAL DIRECTORATE
Director-General, N. Stuart

INTERNATIONAL
Director, C. Tucker, CB
Heads of Divisions, Miss E. Hodkinson (*EC Education and
Training*); Ms W. Harris (*European Union*); Ms E.
Trewartha (*European Social Fund*); B. Shaw (*International
Relations*)

SKILLS AND LIFELONG LEARNING
Director, D. Grover

Heads of Divisions, J. Temple (*Skills Unit*); Mrs F. Everiss
(*Individual Learning*); vacant (*Learning at Work*); Dr J.
Pugh (*University for Industry*)
EMPLOYMENT POLICY
Director, M. J. Richardson
Heads of Divisions, M. Neale (*New Deal Policy*); C. Barnham
(*Employment and Benefits Policy*); E. Galvin (*Employment
and Training Programmes*); B. Wells (*Economy and Labour
Market*)

EQUAL OPPORTUNITIES, TECHNOLOGY AND OVERSEAS
LABOUR
Director, B. Niven
Heads of Divisions, Ms S. Trundle (*Childcare Unit*); Ms J.
Eastabrook (*Sex and Race Equality*); Miss D. Fordham
(*Disability Policy*); R. Ritzema (*Education and Training
Technology*); N. Atkinson (*Overseas Labour Service*)

FINANCE AND ANALYTICAL SERVICES
DIRECTORATE
Director-General, P. Shaw

FINANCE
Heads of Divisions, D. Sandeman (*Expenditure*); S. Burt
(*Private Finance*); Mrs C. Hunter (*Programmes*); R. Wye
(*Efficiency*); P. Connor (*Financial Accounting*); N. Thirtle
(*Internal Audit*)

ANALYTICAL SERVICES
Director, D. Allnutt
Heads of Divisions, M. Britton (*Qualifications, Pupil
Assessment and International*); J. Elliott (*Youth and Further
Education*); D. Thompson (*Higher Education*); B. Butcher
(*Employability and Adult Learning*); R. Bartholomew
(*Equal Opportunities and Research Programmes*); Ms A.
Brown (*Schools, Teachers and Resources*)

FURTHER AND HIGHER EDUCATION AND
YOUTH TRAINING DIRECTORATE
Director-General, R. Dawe

QUALIFICATIONS AND OCCUPATIONAL STANDARDS
Director, R. Hull
Heads of Divisions, M. Waring (*School and College
Qualifications*); J. West (*Qualifications for Work*)

FURTHER EDUCATION AND YOUTH TRAINING
Director, D. Forrester
Heads of Divisions, Ms C. Tyler (*16–19 Policy*); Mrs L.
Ammon, CBE (*Choice and Careers*); J. Stanyer (*Further
Education Support Unit*); A. Shaw (*Further Education*); A.
Davies (*Training for Young People*); Ms B. Evans (*16–19
Student Support*)

HIGHER EDUCATION
Director, A. C. Clark
Heads of Divisions, Mrs I. Wilde (*Higher Education Funding*);
N. Flint (*Student Support 1*); A. Clarke (*Student Support 2*);
T. Fellowes (*Higher Education and Employment*)

LEGAL ADVISER'S OFFICE
Legal Adviser, F. Croft
Heads of Divisions, F. Clarke; S. Harker; C. House; N.
Lambert

OPERATIONS DIRECTORATE
Director, J. Hedger, CB
Heads of Divisions, R. Houten (*TECs and Careers Service
Operational Policy*); P. Lauener (*Resources and Budget
Management*); Mrs P. Jones (*Financial Control, Operations*);
Ms S. Orr (*Quality and Performance Improvement*); H.
Sharp (*Regional Development and Government Offices*); J.
Fuller (*National Training Organizations*)

PERSONNEL AND SUPPORT SERVICES DIRECTORATE
Director, Mrs H. Douglas
Heads of Divisions, R. Hinchcliffe (*Information Systems*); Ms C. Johnson (*Personnel*); S. Green (*Procurement and Contracting*); J. Gordon (*Training and Development*); L. Webb (*Facilities Management*); T. Jeffery (*Corporate Change and Senior Staff*); B. Hillon (*Senior Equal Opportunities Adviser*)

SCHOOLS DIRECTORATE
Director-General, D. Normington
Heads of Division, S. Kershaw (*Education Bill*); S. Edwards (*Schools Communication*)

SCHOOLS ORGANIZATION AND BUILDINGS
Director, P. Makeham
Heads of Divisions, S. Marston (*Schools Framework*); A. Cranston (*Organization of School Places*); R. Jacobs (*Specialist Schools and School Governance*); K. Beeton (*Schools Capital and Buildings*); M. Hipkins (*Under-Fives Policy*); M. Patel (*Architects and Buildings*)

SCHOOL CURRICULUM, FUNDING, AND TEACHERS
Director, N. J. Sanders, CB
Heads of Divisions, A. Wye (*School Recurrent Funding and LEA Finance*); Ms A. Jackson (*School Teachers' Pay and Pensions*); Ms C. Bienkowska (*Teacher Supply, Training and Qualifications*); I. Berry (*Curriculum and Assessment*)

PUPILS, PARENTS AND YOUTH
Director, R. Smith
Heads of Divisions, Miss C. Macready (*Admissions and Information for Parents*); R. Green (*Special Educational Needs*); P. Cohen (*Discipline and Attendance*); G. Holley (*Youth Service and Preparation for Adulthood*); M. Phipps (*Pupil Welfare and Opportunities*); Ms S. Johnson (*Pupil Motivation and Community Links*)

SCHOOL STANDARDS AND EFFECTIVENESS UNIT
Head of Unit, Prof. M. Barber
Heads of Divisions, S. Adamson (*Standards*); Ms S. Scales (*School Effectiveness*)

STRATEGY AND COMMUNICATIONS DIRECTORATE
Director, P. Wanless
Heads of Divisions, Ms J. Simpson (*Head of News*); T. Cook (*Media Relations*); J. Ross (*Publicity*); R. Harrison (*Strategy and Board Secretariat*); J. Dewsbury (*Briefing*); C. Wells (*Millennium Project*)

EXECUTIVE AGENCY
THE EMPLOYMENT SERVICE
Caxton House, Tothill Street, London SWIH 9NA
Tel 0171-273 6060; fax 0171-273 6099
The aims of the Employment Service are to contribute to high levels of employment and growth by helping all people without a job to find work and by helping employers to fill their vacancies, and to help individuals lead rewarding working lives.
Chief Executive, L. Lewis
Director of Jobcentre Services, J. Turner
Director of Human Resources, K. White
Director of Policy and Process Design, R. Foster
Director of Finance, Planning and Research, P. Collis
Non-executive Directors, R. Dykes; Ms L. de Groot
Regional Directors, M. Groves (*East Midlands and Eastern*); S. Holt (*London and South-East*); P. Robson (*Northern*); J. Roberts (*North-West*); K. Pascoe (*South-West*); S. McIntyre (*West Midlands*); R. Lasko (*Yorkshire and Humberside*)
Director for Scotland, A. R. Brown
Director for Wales, Mrs S. Keyse

OFFICE OF ELECTRICITY REGULATION
Hagley House, Hagley Road, Birmingham B16 8QG
Tel 0121-456 2100; fax 0121-456 4664
SCOTLAND: Regent Court, 70 West Regent Street, Glasgow G2 2QZ
Tel 0141-331 2678; fax 0141-331 2777

The Office of Electricity Regulation (OFFER) was set up under the Electricity Act 1989 and is headed by the Director-General of Electricity Supply. It is the independent regulatory body for the electricity supply industry in England, Scotland and Wales. Its functions are to promote competition in the generation and supply of electricity; to ensure that all reasonable demands for electricity are satisfied; to protect customers' interests in relation to prices, security of supply and quality of services; and to promote the efficient use of electricity.
The Government has announced its intention of establishing an Energy Regulator, with responsibility for both electricity and gas, by 1999.
Director-General of Electricity Supply, Prof. S. C. Littlechild (*until the appointment of the new regulator*)
Deputy Director-General, C. P. Carter
Deputy Director-General for Scotland, D. Wilson
Director of Regulation and Business Affairs, J. Saunders
Director of Supply Competition, A. J. Boorman
Director of Consumer Affairs, Dr D. P. Hauser
Technical Director, Dr B. Wharmby
Director of Public Affairs, Miss J. D. Luke
Director of Administration, H. P. Jones
Legal Adviser, D. R. B. Bevan
Chief Examiner, J. D. Cooper

OFFICE FOR THE REGULATION OF ELECTRICITY AND GAS
Brookmount Buildings, 42 Fountain Street, Belfast BTI 5EE
Tel 01232-311575 (*Electricity*); 01232-314212 (*Gas*); fax 01232-311740

The Office for the Regulation of Electricity and Gas (OFREG) is the combined regulatory body for electricity and gas supply industries in Northern Ireland.
Director-General of Electricity Supply and Director-General of Gas for Northern Ireland, D. B. McIldoon
Deputy Director-General of Electricity and Gas, C. H. Coulthard

ENGLISH HERITAGE
— *see* Historic Buildings and Monuments Commission for England

ENGLISH NATURE
Northminster House, Peterborough PEI IUA
Tel 01733-455000; fax 01733-568834

English Nature (the Nature Conservancy Council for England) was established in 1991 and is responsible for advising the Secretary of State for the Environment, Transport and the Regions on nature conservation in England. It promotes, directly and through others, the conservation of England's wildlife and natural features. It selects, establishes and manages National Nature Reserves and identifies and notifies Sites of Special Scientific Interest. It provides advice and information about nature conservation, and supports and conducts research relevant to these functions. Through the Joint Nature Conservation Committee (*see* page 329), it works with its sister organizations in Scotland and Wales on UK and international nature conservation issues.

Chairman, The Baroness Young of Old Scone
Chief Executive, Dr D. R. Langslow
Directors, Dr K. L. Duff; Miss C. E. M. Wood; Ms S. Collins

ENGLISH PARTNERSHIPS
16–18 Old Queen Street, London SW1H 9HP
Tel 0171-976 7070; fax 0171-976 7740

English Partnerships, in statute the Urban Regeneration Agency, came into operation in 1994. Its task is to regenerate derelict, vacant and under-used land and buildings throughout England. Its aim is to deliver regeneration, economic development, job creation and environmental improvement. It works in partnership with the public, private and voluntary sectors. Its sponsoring department is the Department of the Environment, Transport and the Regions.

English Partnerships' regional responsibilities will transfer to the new regional development agencies in April 1999, and the Government has announced plans for English Partnerships to merge with the Commission for the New Towns (*see* page 496) by 1 April 2000.

Chairman, Sir Alan Cockshaw, FENG.
Deputy Chairman, Sir Idris Pearce, CBE, TD
Chief Executive, A. Dunnett

DEPARTMENT OF THE ENVIRONMENT, TRANSPORT AND THE REGIONS
Eland House, Bressenden Place, London SW1E 5DU
Great Minster House, 76 Marsham Street, London SW1P 4DR
Ashdown House, 123 Victoria Street, London SW1E 6DE
Tel 0171-890 3000
Web: http://www.detr.gov.uk

The Department of the Environment, Transport and the Regions (DETR) was formed in June 1997 by the merger of the Department of the Environment and the Department of Transport. It is responsible for policies relating to the environment, housing, transport services, rural affairs, planning, local government, regional development, regeneration, the construction industry and health and safety.

The Department's ministers are based at Eland House.

Deputy Prime Minister and Secretary of State for the Environment, Transport and the Regions, The Rt. Hon. John Prescott, MP
Private Secretary, P. Unwin
Special Advisers, J. Irvin; Ms J. Hammell
Parliamentary Private Secretary, A. Meale, MP
Minister for Transport, The Rt. Hon. Dr John Reid, MP
Private Secretary, P. Kirk
Minister for the Environment, The Rt. Hon. Michael Meacher, MP
Private Secretary, Mrs T. Vokes
Parliamentary Private Secretary, T. Rooney, MP
Minister of State, Hilary Armstrong, MP (*Local Government, Housing*)
Private Secretary, A. J. Redpath
Special Adviser, D. Murphy
Parliamentary Private Secretary, K. Hill, MP

Minister of State, Richard Caborn, MP (*Regions, Regeneration, Planning*)
Private Secretary, C. T. Wood
Special Adviser, P. Hackett
Parliamentary Private Secretary, B. Chapman, MP
Parliamentary Under-Secretaries of State, Nick Raynsford, MP (*London, Construction*); Glenda Jackson, CBE, MP (*Transport in London*); The Lord Whitty (*Roads*); Alan Meale, MP (*Environment, Wildlife, Health and Safety*)
Executive, Regeneration and the Regions)
Private Secretaries, Ms K. Willison; Ms S. Bolt; L. Sambrook; R. O'Donnell
Parliamentary Clerk, Ms P. Gaunt
Permanent Secretary (*SCS*), Sir Richard Mottram, KCB
Private Secretary, Mrs S. Bishop

DIRECTORATE OF COMMUNICATION*
Director (*SCS*), S. Dugdale
Deputy Directors (*SCS*), K. Kerslake (*Publicity*); D. Plews (*Press*)

ENVIRONMENT PROTECTION GROUP†
Director-General (*SCS*), Miss D. A. Nichols

ENERGY, ENVIRONMENT AND WASTE DIRECTORATE
Director (*SCS*), P. Ward
Heads of Divisions (*SCS*), L. Packer (*Energy Efficiency Policy and Sponsorship*); D. Vincent (*Energy Environment Market Innovation*); H. Cleary (*Environment and Business 1–3*); B. Ryder (*Environment and Business 4–5*); Ms L. Simcock (*Waste Policy*); D. Prior (*Joint Environmental Markets Unit*)

ENVIRONMENT AND INTERNATIONAL DIRECTORATE
Director (*SCS*), Dr D. J. Fisk
Heads of Divisions (*SCS*), Dr P. Hinchcliffe (*Chemicals and Biotechnology*); Dr S. Brown (*Radioactive Substances*); P. F. Unwin (*Global Atmosphere*); Dr B. Hackland (*Air and Environment Quality 1–5*); M. Williams (*Air and Environment Quality 6–8*); Ms S. McCabe (*Environment Protection International*)

ENVIRONMENT PROTECTION STRATEGY DIRECTORATE
Director (*SCS*), B. H. Leonard
Heads of Divisions (*SCS*), Mrs H. C. Hillier (*EP Statistics and Information Management*); B. Glicksman (*Environment Agency Sponsorship and Navigation*); J. Stevens (*European Environment*); R. Wilson (*Environment Protection Economics*); J. Adams (*Sustainable Development Unit*); A. Ring (*EPSDU Special Projects*)

WATER AND LAND DIRECTORATE
Director (*SCS*), A. H. Davis
Heads of Divisions (*SCS*), M. Rouse (*Drinking Water Inspectorate*); A. Simcock (*Land and Liabilities*); S. Hoggan (*Water Quality*); A. Wells (*Water Supply and Regulation*)

FINANCE GROUP†
Director and Principal Finance Officer (*SCS*), J. Ballard
Heads of Divisions (*SCS*), R. Bennett (*Finance Programmes*); I. McBrayne (*Finance Sponsorship and Programme*); R. Anderson (*Finance Departmental Administration*); A. Beard (*Finance Accounting Services, Resource Accounting and Budgeting*); M. Haselip (*Internal Audit*)

HOUSING, CONSTRUCTION, REGENERATION AND COUNTRYSIDE GROUP*
Director-General (*SCS*), Mrs M. McDonald, CB

HOUSING, PRIVATE POLICY AND ANALYSIS
Director (*SCS*), M. Gahagan

Heads of Divisons (SCS), Mrs J. Littlewood (Housing and Urban Monitoring and Analysis); M. Hughes (Housing Data and Statistics); S. Aldridge (Housing and Urban Economics); Ms B. Campbell (Housing Policy and Home Ownership); M. Faulkner (Housing Private Rented Sector); C. Braun (Housing Renewal Policy)

HOUSING, SOCIAL POLICY AND RESOURCES
Director (SCS), Mrs D. S. Phillips
Heads of Divisions (SCS), Mrs H. Chipping (Local Authority Housing Finance); R. J. Dinwiddy (Housing Associations and Private Finance); A. Allberry (Homelessness and Housing Management)

CONSTRUCTION DIRECTORATE
Director (SCS), J. Hobson
Heads of Divisions (SCS), J. P. Channing (Construction Industry Sponsorship); J. Stambollouian (Construction Innovation and Research Management); R. Wood (Construction Export Promotion and Materials Sponsorship); P. Everall (Building Regulations); H. Neuberger (Construction Market Intelligence)

WILDLIFE AND COUNTRYSIDE DIRECTORATE
Director (SCS), Ms S. Lambert
Heads of Divisions (SCS), R. M. Pritchard (European Wildlife); R. Hepworth (Global Wildlife); Ms D. Kahn (Rural Development); Ms S. Carter (Countryside)

REGENERATION DIRECTORATE
Director (SCS), P. Evans
Heads of Divisions (SCS), J. Roberts; W. Chapman; Ms L. Derrick

LEGAL GROUP*
Director-General (SCS), D. Hogg

COUNTRYSIDE, PLANNING AND TRANSPORT
Director (SCS), Ms S. Unerman
Heads of Divisions (SCS), N. Lefton (Countryside and Wildlife); Ms G. Hedley-Dent (Planning); R. Lines (Highways); N. Thomas (Road Traffic); A. Jones (Aviation); C. Ingram (Marine); D. Aries (Railways)

ENVIRONMENT, HOUSING AND LOCAL GOVERNMENT
Director (SCS), A. Roberts
Heads of Divisions (SCS), J. Comber (Environment (National)); Ms C. Cooper (Local Government (Finance)); Ms P. Conlon (Local Government (General)); Ms D. Phillips (Housing Private Sector); K. Baublys (Housing Public Sector); Ms S. Headley (Special Projects); I. Day (Commercial and Establishments); M. Devine (Health and Safety Sponsorship)

ENVIRONMENT (INTERNATIONAL AND EC)
Director (SCS), P. Szell
Head of Division (SCS), A. McGlone

LOCAL AND REGIONAL GOVERNMENT GROUP*
Director-General (SCS), P. Wood

LOCAL GOVERNMENT DIRECTORATE
Director (SCS), A. Whetnall
Heads of Divisions (SCS), P. Rowsell (Local Government Sponsorship); J. R. Footitt (Local Government Competition and Quality)

LOCAL GOVERNMENT FINANCE POLICY DIRECTORATE
Director (SCS), M. Lambirth

Heads of Divisions (SCS), R. J. Gibson (Local Government Grant Distribution); Mrs P. Penneck (Local Government Finance Statistics); Dr C. Myerscough (Local Government Capital Finance); N. Dorling (Local Government Taxation); I. Scotter (Local Government Revenue Expenditure)

GOVERNMENT OFFICES AND REGIONAL POLICY DIRECTORATE
Director (SCS), Miss L. Bell
Heads of Divisions (SCS), M. Coulshed; M. Ross; Mrs J. Scoones (Government Offices Central Unit)

REGIONAL OFFICES
— see pages 304–5

PLANNING, ROADS AND LOCAL TRANSPORT‡
Director-General (SCS), C. J. S. Brearley, CB

MOBILITY UNIT
Head of Unit (SCS), Miss E. A. Frye, OBE

FREIGHT DISTRIBUTION AND LOGISTICS
Director (SCS), B. Wadsworth
Heads of Divisions (SCS), Ms A. Moss (Road Haulage); R. Butchart (Transport Statistics Freight); Ms M. Carleton (Traffic Area Network Unit)

PLANNING DIRECTORATE
Director (SCS), J. Jacobs
Heads of Divisions (SCS), vacant (Plans and Policies); R. Jones (Development Control Policy); M. R. Ash (Planning and Compensation); J. Zetter (Environmental Assessment, Internet and Research); A. M. Oliver (Planning and Land Use Statistics); L. Hicks (Minerals and Waste); J. M. Leigh-Pollitt (Land and Property)

NATIONAL ROADS POLICY DIRECTORATE
Director (SCS), H. Wenban-Smith
Heads of Divisions (SCS), T. Worsley (Highways, Economics and Traffic Appraisal); N. McDonald (Highways Policy and Programmes); Mrs C. M. Dixon (Tolling and Private Finance); R. Donachie (Transport Statistics)

URBAN AND LOCAL TRANSPORT
Director (SCS), R. Bird
Heads of Divisions (SCS), E. C. Neve (Buses and Taxis); P. McCarthy (Local Transport Policy); A. S. D. Whybrow (Traffic Policy); M. F. Talbot (Driver Information and Traffic Management); M. Walsh (Local Transport and General); P. Capell (Transport Statistics: Personal Travel)

ROAD AND VEHICLE SAFETY
Director (SCS), J. Plowman
Heads of Divisions (SCS), M. Fendick (Vehicle Standards and Engineering); R. Peal (Road Safety); I. Todd (Licensing and Roadworthiness Policy); Dr Patricia Diamond, OBE (Chief Medical Adviser)

RAILWAYS, AVIATION AND SHIPPING GROUP‡
Director-General (SCS), D. Rowlands

RAILWAYS
Director (SCS), R. J. Griffins
Heads of Divisions (SCS), M. Fuhr (Channel Tunnel and Rail Link); P. Cox (Railways Economics and Finance); P. Thomas (Railways International and General); B. Linnard (Railways Sponsorship); S. Connolly (Railways National Audit Office)

---

* Based at Eland House
† Based at Ashdown House
‡ Based at Great Minster House

300   Government Departments and Public Offices

AVIATION
Director (*SCS*), A. J. Goldman, CB
Heads of Divisions (*SCS*), M. Fawcett (*Airports Policy*); Ms
M. J. Clare (*CAA*); M. C. Mann (*Economics, Aviation, Maritime and International*); Ms E. Duthie (*Aviation Environmental*); M. Smethers (*Multilateral*); A. T. Baker (*International Aviation*); N. Starling (*International Aviation Negotiations*)

AIR ACCIDENTS INVESTIGATION BRANCH
Defence Evaluation and Research Agency, Farnborough, Hants GU14 6TD
Tel 01252-510300

Chief Inspector of Air Accidents, K. P. R. Smart, CBE
Deputy Chief Inspector, R. McKinlay

SHIPPING AND PORTS
Director (*SCS*), R. E. Clarke
Heads of Divisions (*SCS*), D. Cooke (*Shipping Policy 1*);
G. D. Rowe (*Shipping Policy 2*); J. F. Wall (*Shipping Policy 3*); C. Young (*Radioactive Materials Transport*); S. Reeves (*Ports*); D. Lord (*Director, Transport Security*); W. Gillan (*Deputy Director, Transport Security*)

MARINE ACCIDENTS INVESTIGATION BRANCH
5–7 Brunswick Place, Southampton SO1 2AN
Tel 01703-395500

Chief Inspector of Marine Accidents, Rear-Adm. J. Lang
Deputy Chief Inspector, S. Harwood

STRATEGY AND CORPORATE SERVICES GROUP*
Director-General (*SCS*), R. S. Dudding
Heads of Divisions (*SCS*), I. Heawood (*Information Management*); I. Harris (*Working Environment*); P. Walton (*Corporate, Business and Agencies*); A. Murray (*Driver, Vehicle and Operator Project*); G. Jones (*Procurement, Policy and Advice*); J. O'Callaghan (*IT Services*); A. Apling (*Science and Technology Policy*)

PERSONNEL AND CHANGE MANAGEMENT
Director (*SCS*), Ms J. Cotton
Heads of Divisions (*SCS*), M. Bailey (*Personnel Support*); G. Kemp (*Personnel Advice and Support*); E. Gibbons (*Group Facing Teams*); K. Arnold (*Pay and Industrial Relations*); B. Meakins (*Change Management, Development and Training*)

TRANSPORT STRATEGY DIRECTORATE
Director (*SCS*), A. Burchell
Heads of Divisions (*SCS*), D. McMillan (*Integrated Transport 1*); Ms B. Hill (*Integrated Transport 2*); D. Instone (*Transport and Environment*); I. Jordan (*Europe, Transport and General*)

STRATEGY AND ECONOMIC DIRECTORATE
Director (*SCS*), C. Riley
Head of Division (*SCS*), M. Hurst (*Central Economics and Policy*)

EXECUTIVE AGENCIES

DRIVER AND VEHICLE LICENSING AGENCY
Longview Road, Morriston, Swansea SA6 7JL
Tel 01792-772151 (*drivers*); 01792-772134 (*vehicles*)

The Agency issues driving licences, registers and licenses vehicles, and collects excise duty.
Chief Executive, Dr S. J. Ford

DRIVING STANDARDS AGENCY
Stanley House, Talbot Street, Nottingham NG1 5GU
Tel 0115-947 4222; fax 0115-955 7334

The Agency's role is to carry out driving tests and approve driving instructors.
Chief Executive, B. L. Herdan

HIGHWAYS AGENCY
St Christopher House, Southwark Street, London SE1 0TE
Tel 0645-556575

The Agency is responsible for the operation, management and maintenance of the motorway and trunk road network and for road construction and improvement.
Chief Executive, L. J. Haynes

MARITIME AND COASTGUARD AGENCY
Spring Place, 105 Commercial Road, Southampton SO15 1EG
Tel 01703-329100

The Agency was formed in April 1998 by the merger of the Coastguard Agency and the Marine Safety Agency. Its role is to develop, promote and enforce high standards of marine safety; to minimize loss of life amongst seafarers and coastal users; and to minimize pollution from ships of the sea and coastline.
Chief Executive, M. Storey
Chief Coastguard, J. Astbury

PLANNING INSPECTORATE
Tollgate House, Houlton Street, Bristol BS2 9DJ
Tel 0117-987 8000

The Inspectorate is responsible for casework involving planning, housing, roads, environmental and related legislation. It is a joint executive agency of the Department of the Environment, Transport and the Regions and the Welsh Office.
Chief Executive and Chief Planning Inspector, C. Shepley

QUEEN ELIZABETH II CONFERENCE CENTRE
Broad Sanctuary, London SW1P 3EE
Tel 0171-222 5000; fax 0171-798 4200

The Centre provides conference and banqueting facilities for both private sector and government use.
Chief Executive, M. C. Buck

VEHICLE CERTIFICATION AGENCY
1 Eastgate Office Centre, Eastgate Road, Bristol BS5 6XX
Tel 0117-951 5151; fax 0117-952 4103

The Agency tests and certificates vehicles to UK and international standards.
Chief Executive, D. W. Harvey

VEHICLE INSPECTORATE
Berkeley House, Croydon Street, Bristol BS5 0DA
Tel 0117-954 3200; fax 0117-954 3212

The Agency carries out annual testing and inspection of heavy goods and other vehicles and administers the MOT testing scheme.
Chief Executive, R. J. Oliver

TRAFFIC AREA OFFICES AND COMMISSIONERS
Senior Traffic Commissioner, Brig. M. W. Betts
Eastern, G. Simms
North-Eastern and North-Western, K. R. Waterworth
Scottish, Brig. M. W. Betts
South-Eastern and Metropolitan, Brig. M. H. Turner
Western, C. Heaps
West Midlands and S. Wales, J. M. C. Pugh

TRAFFIC DIRECTOR FOR LONDON
College House, Great Peter Street, London SW1P 3LN
Tel 0171-222 4545; fax 0171-976 8640

The Traffic Director for London is a non-departmental public body which is independent from the Department of

* Based at Eland House
† Based at Ashdown House
‡ Based at Great Minster House

the Environment, Transport and the Regions but is responsible to the Secretary of State and to Parliament. Its role is to co-ordinate the Priority (Red) Route Network in London and monitor its operation.
Traffic Director for London, D. Turner

THE ENVIRONMENT AGENCY
25th Floor, Millbank Tower, 21–24 Millbank, London SW1P 4XL
Tel 0171-863 8600; fax 0171-863 8650
Rio House, Waterside Drive, Aztec West, Almondsbury, Bristol BS12 4UD
Tel 01454-624400; fax 01454-624409

The Environment Agency was established in April 1996 under the Environment Act 1995 and is a non-departmental public body sponsored by the Department of the Environment, Transport and the Regions, MAFF and the Welsh Office. The Agency is responsible for pollution prevention and control in England and Wales, and for the management and use of water resources, including flood defences, fisheries and navigation. It has head offices in London and Bristol and eight regional offices.

THE BOARD
Chairman, The Lord De Ramsey
Members, C. Beardwood; E. Gallagher; Sir Richard George; N. Haigh, OBE; C. Hampson, CBE; Sir John Harman; Prof. Jacqueline McGlade; G. Manning, OBE; Mrs K. Morgan; Dr A. Powell; Prof. D. Ritchie; T. Rodgers; G. Wardell; Mrs J. Wykes

THE EXECUTIVE
Chief Executive, E. Gallagher
Director of Finance, N. Reader
Director of Personnel, G. Duncan
Director of Environmental Protection, Dr P. Leinster
Director of Water Management, G. Mance
Director of Operations, A. Robertson
Director of Corporate Affairs, M. Wilson
Director of Legal Services, R. Navarro
Chief Scientist, J. Pentreath

ROYAL COMMISSION ON ENVIRONMENTAL POLLUTION
Steel House, 11 Tothill Street, London SW1H 9NF
Tel 0171-273 6635

The Commission was set up in 1970 to advise on national and international matters concerning the pollution of the environment.
Chairman, Prof. Sir Thomas Blundell
Members, Sir Geoffrey Allen, FRS; Revd Prof. M. C. Banner; Prof. G. S. Boulton, FRS, FRSE; Prof. C. E. D. Chilvers; Prof. R. Clift, OBE, FEng.; Dr P. Doyle, CBE, FRSE; J. Flemming; Sir Martin Holdgate, CB; Prof. R. Macrory; Prof. M. G. Marmot, PH.D.; Prof. J. G. Morris, CBE, FRS; Dr Penelope A. Rowlatt; The Earl of Selborne, KBE, FRS
Secretary, D. R. Lewis

EQUAL OPPORTUNITIES COMMISSION
Overseas House, Quay Street, Manchester M3 3HN
Tel 0161-833 9244; fax 0161-835 1657

Press Office, 36 Broadway, London SW1H 0XH. Tel: 0171-222 1110
Other Offices, Stock Exchange House, 7 Nelson Mandela

Place, Glasgow G2 1QW. Tel: 0141-248 5833; Windsor House, Windsor Place, Cardiff. Tel: 01222-343552

The Commission was set up in 1975 as a result of the passing of the Sex Discrimination Act. It works towards the elimination of discrimination on the grounds of sex or marital status and to promote equality of opportunity between men and women generally. It is responsible to the Department for Education and Employment.
Chairwoman, Ms K. Bahl, CBE
Deputy Chairwomen, Mrs E. Hodder; Ms G. James
Members, P. Smith; Ms M. Berg; R. Grayson; Dr J. Stringer; Prof. T. Rees; R. Penn; Ms J. Rubin; Dr A. Wright; Prof. M. Schofield
Chief Executive (acting), F. Spencer

EQUAL OPPORTUNITIES COMMISSION FOR NORTHERN IRELAND
Chamber of Commerce House, 22 Great Victoria Street, Belfast BT2 7BA
Tel 01232-242752; fax 01232-331047
Chair and Chief Executive, Mrs J. Smyth, CBE

OFFICE OF FAIR TRADING
Field House, Bream's Buildings, London EC4A 1PR
Tel 0171-211 8000; fax 0171-211 8800

The Office of Fair Trading is a non-ministerial government department headed by the Director-General of Fair Trading. It keeps commercial activities in the UK under review and seeks to protect consumers against unfair trading practices. The Director-General's consumer protection duties under the Fair Trading Act 1973, together with his responsibilities under the Consumer Credit Act 1974, the Estate Agents Act 1979, the Control of Misleading Advertisements Regulations 1988, and the Unfair Terms in Consumer Contracts Regulations 1994, are administered by the Office's Consumer Affairs Division. The Competition Policy Division is concerned with monopolies and mergers (under the Fair Trading Act 1973), and the Director-General's other responsibilities for competition matters, including those under the Restrictive Trade Practices Act 1976, the Resale Prices Act 1976, the Competition Act 1980, the Financial Services Act 1986 and the Broadcasting Act 1990. The Office is the UK competent authority on the application of the European Commission's competition rules, and also liaises with the Commission on consumer protection initiatives.
Director-General, J. Bridgeman

CONSUMER AFFAIRS DIVISION
Director (G3), Miss C. Banks
Assistant Directors (G5), R. Watson; M. Graham

COMPETITION POLICY DIVISION
Director (G3), Mrs M. J. Bloom
Assistant Directors (G5), A. J. White; H. L. Emden; E. L. Whitehorn; S. Wood; P. Bamford

LEGAL DIVISION
Director (G3), Miss P. Edwards
Assistant Directors (G5), M. A. Khan; S. Brindley
Establishment and Finance Officer (G5), Mrs R. Heyhoe
Chief Information Officer (G6), D. Hill

FOREIGN AND COMMONWEALTH OFFICE

Downing Street, London SWIA 2AL
Tel 0171-270 3000
Web: http://www.fco.gov.uk

The Foreign and Commonwealth Office provides, mainly through diplomatic missions, the means of communication between the British Government and other governments and international governmental organizations for the discussion and negotiation of all matters falling within the field of international relations. It is responsible for alerting the British Government to the implications of developments overseas; for protecting British interests overseas; for protecting British citizens abroad; for explaining British policies to, and cultivating friendly relations with, governments overseas; and for the discharge of British responsibilities to the UK overseas territories.

Secretary of State for Foreign and Commonwealth Affairs, The Rt. Hon. Robin Cook, MP
  Principal Private Secretary, J. Grant
  Private Secretaries, T. Barrow; A. Patrick
  Special Advisers, A. Hood; D. Clark
  Parliamentary Private Secretary, K. Purchase, MP
Minister for Europe, Joyce Quin, MP
  Private Secretary, N. Hopton
Minister of State, Derek Fatchett, MP
  Private Secretary, F. Baker
Minister of State, Tony Lloyd, MP
  Private Secretary, Ms P. Phillips
  Parliamentary Private Secretary to the Ministers of State, D. MacShane, MP
Parliamentary Under-Secretary of State, The Baroness Symons of Vernham Dean
Parliamentary Relations Department, E. Jenkinson (*Head*); P. Bromley (*Deputy Head and Parliamentary Clerk*)
Permanent Under-Secretary of State and Head of the Diplomatic Service, Sir John Kerr, KCMG
  Private Secretary, D. Frost
Deputy Under-Secretaries, J. R. Young, CMG (*Chief Clerk*); C. Budd (*Economic Director*); E. Jones Parry (*Political Director*); J. Shepherd (*Trade and Investment*); vacant (*Security/Intelligence*); Sir Franklin Berman, KCMG, QC (*Legal Adviser*)
Directors, J. R. de Fonblanque (*Europe*); J. Rollo, CMG (*Chief Economic Adviser*); R. H. Smith (*International Security*); R. Dales (*Africa and Commonwealth*); P. J. Westmacott (*Americas*); H. N. H. Synnott (*Southern Asia*); D. Hall (*Overseas Trade*); D. Plumbly, CMG (*Middle East and North Africa*); P. Ricketts (*Deputy Political Director*); R. Dibble (*General Services*); P. Nixon (*International Crime and Terrorism*); R. Dalton (*Personnel and Security*); M. Arthur (*Resources and Chief Inspector*); E. Clay (*Public Services*); T. Brenton (*Global Issues*); N. Sheinwald (*European Union*)
Director of Protocol and HM Vice-Marshal of the Diplomatic Corps, P. S. Astley, LVO

HEADS OF DEPARTMENTS

Allowances Review Team, M. Legg
Aviation and Maritime Department, N. Ling
British Diplomatic Spouses Association, Mrs E. Nixon
Central European Department, H. Pearce
Change Management Unit, Dr J. Hughes
China/Hong Kong Department, D. Warren
Commonwealth Co-ordination Department, C. Bright
Commonwealth Foreign and Security Policy Unit, Ms A. Pringle
Conference Unit, M. Dalton
Consular Division, D. Taylor

Counter Terrorism Policy Department, V. Fean
Cultural Relations Department, Ms A. Lewis
Diplomatic Service Language Centre, Dr Vanessa Davies
Drugs and International Crime, M. Raven
Eastern Department, P. Thomas
Eastern Adriatic Department, T. Phillips
Economic Advisers Department, J. Rollo, CMG
Economic Relations Department, N. Westcott
Engineering Services, N. Stickells
Environment, Science and Energy Department, J. Ashton
Equatorial Africa Department, Ms A. Grant
European Union Department (External), R. Stagg
European Union Department (Internal), S. Gass
Far Eastern and Pacific Department, vacant
Financial Compliance Unit, M. Purvis
Financial Policy, M. Brown
General Services Management Department, Ms J. Link
Government Hospitality Fund, Col. T. Earl
Home Estates Department, S. Attwood
Honours Unit, R. M. Sands
Human Rights Policy Unit, R. P. Nash
Information Department, P. J. Dun
Information Systems Department, P. McDermott, MVO
Internal Audit, R. Elias
Investment in Britain Bureau, A. Fraser
†*Joint Export Promotion Directorate*, D. Hall
Latin America and Caribbean Department, H. Hogger
Library and Records Department, J. Thompson
Management Consultancy and Inspection Department, M. Aron
Medical and Welfare, Ms E. Kennedy
Middle East Department, E. Chaplin
Migration and Visa Department, R. White
National Audit Office, J. Pearce
Near East and North Africa Department, P. W. Ford
News Department, K. Darroch
Non-Proliferation Department, P. Hare
North America Department, P. J. Priestley
North-East Asia and Pacific Department, D. Coates
OSCE and Council of Europe Department, S. N. Evans, OBE
Overseas Estates Department, M. H. R. Bertram, CBE
Overseas Territories Department, J. White
Permanent Under-Secretary's Department, D. Martin
Personnel Policy Unit, Ms P. Major
Personnel – Senior Management, Ms D. Holt
Personnel Services Department, R. Fell
Policy Planning, Miss A. M. Leslie
PROSPER, C. J. Edgerton, OBE
Protocol Department, R. S. Gorham (*First Assistant Marshal of the Diplomatic Corps*)
Purchasing Directorate, M. Gower
Republic of Ireland Department, G. Ferguson
Research Analysts, S. Jack
Resource and Planning Department, R. Kinchen
Royal Matters Unit, B. England
Security, T. Duggin
Security Policy, vacant
South Asian Department, C. Elmes
South-East Asian Department, N. J. Cox
Southern Africa Department, C. Wilton
Southern European Department, D. Reddaway
Support Services Department, M. Carr
Training, Ms C. Dharawarkar

---

* Joint Foreign and Commonwealth Office/Department for International Development department
† Joint Foreign and Commonwealth Office/Department of Trade and Industry directorate

United Nations Department, Ms R. M. Marsden
Western European Department, A. Layden
Whitley Council, P. May

EXECUTIVE AGENCY

WILTON PARK CONFERENCE CENTRE
Wiston House, Steyning, W. Sussex BN44 3DZ
Tel 01903-815020; fax 01903-816373

The Centre organizes international affairs conferences and is hired out to government departments and commercial users.
Chief Executive and Director, C. B. Jennings

CORPS OF QUEEN'S MESSENGERS
Support Services Department, Foreign and Commonwealth Office, London SW1A 2AH
Tel 0171-270 2779

Superintendent of the Corps of Queen's Messengers, B. Garside
Queen's Messengers, P. Allen; Maj. J. E. A. Andre; Maj. A. N. D. Bols; Lt.-Cdr. K. E. Brown; Lt.-Col. W. P. A. Bush; Lt.-Col. M. B. de S. Clayton; Maj. P. C. H. Dening-Smitherman; Sqn. Ldr. J. S. Frizzell; Capt. N. C. E. Gardner; Maj. D. A. Griffiths; Maj. K. J. Rowbottom; Maj. M. R. Senior; Cdr. K. M. C. Simmons, AFC; Maj. P. M. O. Springfield; Maj. J. S. Steele

FOREIGN COMPENSATION COMMISSION
Room 03, 4 Central Buildings, Matthew Parker Street, London SW1H 9NL
Tel 0171-210 0400; fax 0171-210 0401

The Commission was set up by the Foreign Compensation Act 1950 primarily to distribute, under Orders in Council, funds received from other governments in accordance with agreements to pay compensation for expropriated British property and other losses sustained by British nationals.
Chairman (£83,586), A. W. E. Wheeler, CBE
Secretary, A. N. Grant

FORESTRY COMMISSION
231 Corstorphine Road, Edinburgh EH12 7AT
Tel 0131-334 0303; fax 0131-334 3047

The Forestry Commission is the government department responsible for forestry policy in Great Britain. It reports directly to forestry ministers (i.e. the Secretary of State for Scotland, who takes the lead role, the Minister of Agriculture, Fisheries and Food and the Secretary of State for Wales), to whom it is responsible for advice on forestry policy and for the implementation of that policy.

The Commission's principal objectives are to protect Britain's forests and woodlands; expand Britain's forest area; enhance the economic value of the forest resources; conserve and improve the biodiversity, landscape and cultural heritage of forests and woodlands; develop opportunities for woodland recreation; and increase public understanding of and community participation in forestry. Forest Enterprise, a trading body operating as an executive agency of the Commission, manages its forestry estate on a multi-use basis.

Chairman (part-time) (£36,965), Sir Peter Hutchison, Bt., CBE
Director-General and Deputy Chairman (G2), D. J. Bills
Head of the Forestry Authority (G3), D. L. Foot, CB
Secretary to the Commissioners (G5), F. Strong

FOREST ENTERPRISE, 231 Corstorphine Road, Edinburgh EH12 7AT. Tel: 0131-334 0303. *Chief Executive,* Dr B. McIntosh

REGISTRY OF FRIENDLY SOCIETIES
Victory House, 30–34 Kingsway, London WC2B 6ES
Tel 0171-663 5000

The Registry of Friendly Societies is a government department serving three statutory bodies, the Building Societies Commission, the Friendly Societies Commission, and the Central Office of the Registry of Friendly Societies (together with the Assistant Registrar of Friendly Societies for Scotland).

The Building Societies Commission was established by the Building Societies Act 1986. The Commission is responsible for the supervision of building societies and administers the system of regulation. It also advises the Treasury and other government departments on matters relating to building societies.

The Friendly Societies Commission was established by the Friendly Societies Act 1992. Its responsibilities for the supervision of friendly societies parallel those of the Building Societies Commission for building societies.

The Central Office of the Registry of Friendly Societies provides a public registry for mutual organizations registered under the Building Societies Act 1986, Friendly Societies Acts 1974 and 1992, and the Industrial and Provident Societies Act 1965. It is responsible for the supervision of credit unions, and advises the Government on issues affecting them.

The Registry of Friendly Societies will be subsumed into the Financial Services Authority (*see* page 634) in January 1999.

BUILDING SOCIETIES COMMISSION
Chairman, G. E. Fitchew
Deputy Chairman, M. Owen
Commissioners, J. M. Palmer; *F. E. Worsley; *F. G. Sunderland; *N. Fox Bassett; *Sir James Birrell; *Ms C. Sergeant
* part-time

FRIENDLY SOCIETIES COMMISSION
Chairman, *M. Roberts
Commissioners, F. da Rocha; *B. Richardson; *J. A. Geddes; *Ms S. Brown; *Ms P. Triggs
* part-time

CENTRAL OFFICE OF THE REGISTRY
Chief Registrar, G. E. Fitchew
Assistant Registrars, A. J. Perrett; Ms S. Eden; E. Engstrom; N. Fawcett

BUILDING SOCIETIES COMMISSION STAFF
Grade 3, M. Owen
Grade 4, J. M. Palmer
Grade 5, W. Champion; E. Engstrom
Grade 6, N. F. Digance; A. G. Tebbutt

FRIENDLY SOCIETIES COMMISSION STAFF
Grade 6, F. da Rocha

CENTRAL SERVICES STAFF
Legal Adviser (G4), A. J. Perrett
Establishment and Finance Officer (G5), J. Stevens
Legal Staff (G5), A. D. Preston; Ms P. Henderson; *(G6)*, Ms S. Bagga

REGISTRY OF FRIENDLY SOCIETIES, SCOTLAND
58 Frederick Street, Edinburgh EH2 1NB
Tel 0131-226 3224
Assistant Registrar (G5), J. L. J. Craig, WS

GAMING BOARD FOR GREAT BRITAIN
Berkshire House, 168–173 High Holborn, London WCIV 7AA
Tel 0171-306 6200; fax 0171-306 6266

The Board was established in 1968 and is responsible to the Home Secretary. It is the regulatory body for casinos, bingo clubs, gaming machines and the larger society and all local authority lotteries in Great Britain. Its functions are to ensure that those involved in organizing gaming and lotteries are fit and proper to do so and to keep gaming free from criminal infiltration; to ensure that gaming and lotteries are run fairly and in accordance with the law; and to advise the Home Secretary on developments in gaming and lotteries.
Chairman (part-time) (£37,105), P. Dean, CBE
Secretary, T. Kavanagh

OFFICE OF GAS SUPPLY
Stockley House, 130 Wilton Road, London SWIV 1LQ
Tel 0171-828 0898; fax 0171-932 1600

The Office of Gas Supply (Ofgas) was set up under the Gas Act 1986 and is headed by the Director-General of Gas Supply. It is the independent regulatory body for the gas industry in England, Scotland and Wales. Its functions are to promote competition in the gas industry and to protect customers' interests in relation to prices, security of supply and quality of services.
The Government has announced its intention of establishing an Energy Regulator, with responsibility for both gas and electricity, by 1999.
Director-General, vacant
Chief Economic Adviser, Dr Eileen Marshall, CBE
Legal Adviser, W. Sprigge
Director, Public Affairs, C. Webb
Director, Administration, R. Field

GOVERNMENT ACTUARY'S DEPARTMENT
22 Kingsway, London WC2B 6LE
Tel 0171-211 2600; fax 0171-211 2640

The Government Actuary provides a consulting service to government departments, the public sector, and overseas governments. The actuaries advise on social security schemes and superannuation arrangements in the public sector at home and abroad, on population and other statistical studies, and on government supervision of insurance companies, friendly societies and pension funds.
Government Actuary, C. D. Daykin, CB
Directing Actuaries, D. G. Ballantine; T. W. Hewitson; A. G. Young

Chief Actuaries, E. I. Battersby; Ms W. M. Beaver; A. J. Chamberlain; Ms C. Cresswell; A. I. Johnston; D. Lewis; J. C. A. Rathbone

GOVERNMENT HOSPITALITY FUND
8 Cleveland Row, London SWIA 1DH
Tel 0171-210 4282; fax 0171-930 1148

The Government Hospitality Fund was instituted in 1908 for the purpose of organizing official hospitality on a regular basis with a view to the promotion of international goodwill. It is responsible to the Foreign and Commonwealth Office.
Minister in Charge, The Baroness Symons of Vernham Dean
Secretary, Col. T. Earl

GOVERNMENT OFFICES FOR THE REGIONS

The Government Offices for the Regions were established in April 1994. The regional directors are accountable to the Secretary of State for the Environment, Transport and the Regions, the Secretary of State for Trade and Industry, and the Secretary of State for Education and Employment. The offices' role is to promote a coherent approach to competitiveness, sustainable economic development and regeneration using public and private resources.
Central Unit, 1st Floor, Eland House, Bressenden Place, London SWIE 5DU
Tel 0171-890 5157; fax 0171-890 5019
Director (G3), Miss L. Bell
Head of Unit (G5), Mrs J. Scoones

EASTERN
Secretariat: Building A, Westbrook Centre, Milton Road, Cambridge CB4 1YG
Tel 01223-346700; fax 01223-461941
Regional Director (G3), A. Riddell
Directors (G5), C. Dunabin (*Housing, Environment and Regeneration*); Ms C. Bowdler (*Planning and Transport*); M. Oldham (*Economic Development*); J. Street (*Skills and Enterprise*)

EAST MIDLANDS
Secretariat: The Belgrave Centre, Stanley Place, Talbot Street, Nottingham NG1 5GG
Tel 0115-971 2755; fax 0115-971 2404
Regional Director (G3), D. Morrison
Directors (G5), Dr S. Kennett (*Environment and Transport*); M. Briggs (*Competitiveness, Trade and Industry*); P. Mucklow (*Skills and Enterprise*)

LONDON
Secretariat: 10th Floor, Riverwalk House, 157–161 Millbank, London SWIP 4RR
Tel 0171-217 3456; fax 0171-217 3450
Director of Office (G2), Miss E. C. Turton, CB

Directors (*G3*), J. A. Owen (*Skills, Education and Regeneration*); S. Lord (*Planning, Transport and Corporate Strategy*); R. Allan (*New London Governance*); (*G5*), B. Glickman (*Skills and Education*); Mrs J. Bridges (*Planning*); Ms A. Munro (*Transport*); K. Timmins (*London North-West/Industry*); Ms H. Ghosh (*London East*); S. Gooding (*London Underground*); P. Sanders (*Transport for London*); A. Melville (*London Transport*); Ms E. Meek (*GLA*); (*G6*), A. Weeden (*Transport Task Force*); Ms C. Lyons (*Corporate Strategy*); J. Sienkiewicz (*London Development Unit*); R. Wragg (*Operations and Business Management*); N. Robinson (*Trade and Business Development*); P. Fiddeman (*London South*); B. Mann (*Home Office/GOL Liaison*)

MERSEYSIDE
Secretariat: Cunard Building, Pier Head, Liverpool L3 9TN
Tel 0151-224 6300; fax 0151-224 6470
Regional Director (*SCS*), Ms M. Neville-Rolfe
Directors (*SCS*), P. Holme (*Skills and Enterprise, Education, Competitiveness and Innovation*); P. Styche (*Regeneration, Transport, Planning and Investment*); Ms K. Himsworth (*European Policy and Implementation*)

NORTH-EAST
Secretariat: Wellbar House, Gallowgate, Newcastle upon Tyne NE1 4TD
Tel 0191-201 3300; fax 0191-202 3744
Regional Director (*G3*), Dr R. Dobbie
Directors (*G5*), J. Darlington (*Planning, Environment and Transport*); Miss D. Caudle (*Regeneration and Housing*); A. Dell (*Competitiveness, Industry and Europe*); S. Geary (*Education Skills and Business Development*); (*G6*), Mrs D. Pearce (*Strategy and Resources*)

NORTH-WEST
Secretariat: 20th Floor, Sunley Tower, Piccadilly Plaza, Manchester M1 4BE
Tel 0161-952 4000; fax 0161-952 4099
Regional Director (*G3*), Ms M. Neville-Rolfe
Directors (*G4*), Dr B. Isherwood (*Regeneration*); D. Higham (*Competitiveness*); Ms I. Hughes (*Infrastructure and Planning*); D. Duff (*Skills and Enterprise*); (*G6*), D. Stewart (*Europe* (*Regeneration*))

SOUTH-EAST
Secretariat: 2nd Floor, Bridge House, 1 Walnut Tree Close, Guildford, Surrey GU1 4GA
Tel 01483-882481; fax 01483-882259
Regional Director (*G3*), D. Saunders
Directors (*G5*), Ms L. Robinson (*Hants/IOW*); N. Wilson (*Berks/Oxon/Bucks*); J. Vaughan (*Kent*); D. Andrews (*Surrey/E. and W. Sussex*); Mrs A. Baker (*Regional Strategy Team*)

SOUTH-WEST
Secretariat: 4th Floor, The Pithay, Bristol BS1 2PB
Tel 0117-900 1708; fax 0117-900 1900
Regional Director (*G3*), Ms J. Henderson
Directors (*G5*), S. McQuillin (*Devon and Cornwall*); M. Quinn (*Environment and Transport*); T. Shearer (*Education, Trade and Industry*); G. Nevitte (*Strategy and Resources*)

WEST MIDLANDS
Secretariat: 6th Floor, 77 Paradise Circus, Queensway, Birmingham B1 2DT
Tel 0121-212 5000; fax 0121-212 5456
Regional Director (*G3*), D. Ritchie

Directors (*G4*), Dr H. M. Sutton (*Trade, Industrial Development and Europe*); (*G5*), Mrs P. Holland (*Housing and Regeneration*); P. Langley (*Planning, Transport and Environment*); D. Way (*Education, Skills and Enterprise*); (*G6*), D. Mahoney (*Strategy and Resource Management*)

YORKSHIRE AND HUMBERSIDE
Secretariat: PO Box 213, City House, New Station Street, Leeds LS1 4US
Tel 0113-280 0600; fax 0113-244 4898
Regional Director (*G3*), J. Walker
Directors (*G4*), G. Dyche (*Strategy and Europe*); (*G5*), J. Jarvis (*Planning and Transport*); D. Stewart (*Regeneration*); S. Perryman (*Business, Enterprise and Skills*); (*G6*), M. Doxey (*Personnel and Resources*)

DEPARTMENT OF HEALTH
Richmond House, 79 Whitehall, London SW1A 2NS
Tel 0171-972 2000
Web: http://www.open.gov.uk/doh/dhhome.htm

The Department of Health is responsible for the provision of the National Health Service in England and for social care, including oversight of personal social services run by local authorities in England for children (except day care, which is now the responsibility of the DfEE), the elderly, the infirm, the handicapped and other persons in need. It is responsible for health promotion and has functions relating to public and environmental health, food safety and nutrition. The Department is also responsible for the ambulance and emergency first aid services, under the Civil Defence Act 1948. The Department represents the UK at the European Union and other international organizations including the World Health Organization. It also supports UK-based healthcare and pharmaceutical industries.

Responsibility for food safety will be transferred to the new Food Standards Agency, expected to be in operation by mid 1999.

Secretary of State for Health, The Rt. Hon. Frank Dobson, MP
  Principal Private Secretary, C. Kenny
  Private Secretaries, H. Rogers; F. Anderson
  Special Advisers, J. McCrea; S. Stevens
  Parliamentary Private Secretary, H. Bayley, MP
Minister of State, Alan Milburn, MP (*NHS Structure and Resources*)
  Private Secretary, S. Roughton
  Parliamentary Private Secretary, Ms H. Blears, MP
Minister of State, Tessa Jowell, MP (*Public Health, Women's Issues*)
  Private Secretary, Ms K. Jarvie
  Parliamentary Private Secretary, J. Ennis, MP
Parliamentary Under-Secretaries of State, Paul Boateng, MP (*Social Care, Mental Health*); The Baroness Hayman (*NHS Development, Cancer, Emergency Services*)
  Private Secretaries, J. Marron; W. Connon
  Parliamentary Clerk, J. Fowles
Permanent Secretary (*SCS*), C. Kelly
  Private Secretary, Mrs H. Steele
Chief Medical Officer (*SCS*), Prof. L. Donaldson, FRCSEd., FRCP
Chief Executive, NHS Executive (*SCS*), Sir Alan Langlands
Deputy Chief Medical Officer (*SCS*), Dr J. S. Metters, CB

REGIONAL CHAIRMEN'S MEETING
Chairman, The Secretary of State for Health

Members, Alan Milburn, MP (*Minister of State*); Tessa Jowell, MP (*Minister of State*); Paul Boateng, MP (*Parliamentary Under-Secretary*); The Baroness Hayman (*Parliamentary Under-Secretary*); Prof. L. Donaldson, FRCSEd., FRCP (*Chief Medical Officer*); Sir Alan Langlands (*Chief Executive, NHS Executive*); C. Kelly (*Permanent Secretary*); Mrs Y. Moores; C. Wilkinson; Mrs Z. Manzoor, CBE; P. Hammersley; Mrs R. Varley; Miss J. Trotter, OBE; I. Mills; W. Wells; Prof. A. Breckenridge, CBE; A. D. M. Liddell, CBE

DEPARTMENTAL RESOURCES AND SERVICES GROUP
Head of Group (*SCS*), Ms A. Perkins

STATISTICS DIVISION
Director of Statistics (*SCS*), Mrs R. J. Butler
Chief Statisticians (*SCS*), R. K. Willmer; G. J. O. Phillpotts

PERSONNEL SERVICES
Director of Personnel (*SCS*), D. J. Clark
Heads of Branches (*SCS*), C. Muir; I. Forsyth; S. Redmond

INFORMATION SERVICES DIVISION
Head of Division (*SCS*), Dr A. A. Holt
Heads of Branches, Mrs L. Wishart; C. Horsey; M. Rainsford; Mrs J. Dainty; M. Smith; R. Long; P. G. Cobb

RESOURCE MANAGEMENT AND FINANCE
Head of Division (*SCS*), A. B. Barton
Heads of Branches, P. Kendall; B. Burleigh; J. Stopes-Roe; A. McNeil

ECONOMICS AND OPERATIONAL RESEARCH DIVISION (HEALTH)
Chief Economic Adviser (*SCS*), C. H. Smee, CB
Heads of Branches, Dr S. Harding; J. W. Hurst; Dr G. Royston; A. Hare; D. Franklin

PRESS AND PUBLICITY DIVISION
Director of Press and Publiciy, Miss R. Christopherson, CB (*until the end of 1998*)
Deputy Directors, P. Aylett (*News*); W. Roberts (*Publicity*)

POLICY MANAGEMENT UNIT
Head of Branch, Mrs F. Goldhill

SOLICITOR'S OFFICE
Solicitor (*SCS*), M. Morgan
Director of Legal Services (*SCS*), Mrs G. S. Kerrigan

PUBLIC HEALTH POLICY GROUP

PROTECTION OF HEALTH DIVISION
Head of Division (*SCS*), Dr Eileen Rubery, CB
Head of Branches, Dr E. Smales; A. Smith; J. Walden

JOINT FOOD SAFETY AND STANDARDS DIVISION
Head of Division (*SCS*), G. Podger
Heads of Branches, Dr R. Skinner; Ms P. Stewart

HEALTH PROMOTION DIVISION
Head of Division (*SCS*), D. P. Walden
Principal Medical Officer (*SCS*), Dr D. McInnes
Heads of Branches (*SCS*), Miss A. Mithani; Dr D. McInnes; R. Kornicki; M. Fry

SOCIAL CARE GROUP
Chief Social Services Inspector, Ms D. Platt
Head of Social Care Policy, T. R. H. Luce, CB
Deputy Chief Inspectors, D. Gilroy; Ms A. Nottage
Heads of Branches (*SCS*), N. F. Duncan; S. Mitchell; N. Boyd; J. Kennedy; Mrs E. Johnson; S. Hiller
Assistant Chief Inspector (*HQ*), J. Cleary

Assistant Chief Inspectors (*Regions*), S. Allard; J. Cypher; B. Riddell; A. Jones; D. G. Lambert, CBE; Mrs P. K. Hall; C. P. Brearley; J. Fraser; Mrs L. Hoare; Ms J. Owen

NURSING GROUP
Chief Nursing Officer/Director of Nursing (*SCS*), Mrs Y. Moores
Assistant Chief Nursing Officers (*SCS*), Mrs P. Cantrill; Mrs G. Stephens; D. Moore

RESEARCH AND DEVELOPMENT DIVISION
Director of Research and Development, Prof. J. D. Swales
Deputy Director of Research and Development (*SCS*), Dr C. Henshall
Heads of Branches (*SCS*), Dr P. Greenaway; J. Ennis; Mrs J. Griffin; Ms A. Kauder

NHS EXECUTIVE
Quarry House, Quarry Hill, Leeds LS2 7UE
Tel 0113-254 5000

Chief Executive, Sir Alan Langlands
Director of Human Resources, H. Taylor
Director of Finance and Performance, C. Reeves
Medical Director, Dr G. Winyard
Chief Nursing Officer, Mrs Y. Moores
Director of Research and Development, Prof. J. D. Swales
Director of Planning and Performance Management, A. D. M. Liddell, CBE

CORPORATE AFFAIRS
Head of Corporate Affairs (*SCS*), M. Staniforth

HUMAN RESOURCES
Deputy Director of Human Resources (*SCS*), M. Deegan

INFORMATION MANAGEMENT
Head of Information Management (*SCS*), F. Burns

PLANNING DIRECTORATE
Director (*SCS*), A. D. M. Liddell, CBE
Chief Economic Adviser, C. Smee, CB
Head of Planning, L. Bradley
Head of Communications, Mrs H. McCallum
Director of Statistics, Mrs R. Butler

HEALTH SERVICES DIRECTORATE
Director (*SCS*), Dr G. Winyard
Deputy Director (*SCS*), Dr S. Adam
Heads of Branches, M. Brown; Mrs L. Wolstenholme; Ms J. McKessack; Ms G. Fletcher-Cooke; L. Percival; Dr G. Radford; Mrs Z. Muth

PRIMARY CARE DIVISION
Head of Division, A. McKeon
Fraud Supremo, J. Gee
Chief Dental Officer, J. R. Wild
Chief Pharmaceutical Officer, B. H. Hartley
Heads of Branches, G. Denham (*Dental and Optical Services*); J. Thompson (*Pharmacy and Prescribing*); Miss H. Gwynn (*White Paper Implementation Team*); M. Farrar (*General Medical Services*)

FINANCE AND PERFORMANCE DIRECTORATE
Director (*SCS*), C. L. Reeves
Deputy Directors, P. Garland; R. Douglas
Heads of Branches, B. McCarthy; J. Lawler; Dr S. Peck; M. Sturges; A. Angilley; M. A. Harris, CBE; J. Thomlinson; P. Coates; J. Havelock; J. Copeland

REGIONAL OFFICES
– *see* page 479

ADVISORY COMMITTEES

ADVISORY COMMITTEE ON THE MICROBIOLOGICAL SAFETY OF FOOD, Room 502A, Skipton House, 80 London Road, London SE1 6LH. Tel: 0171-972 5045. *Chairman*, Prof. D. Georgala, CBE, PH.D.
CLINICAL STANDARDS ADVISORY GROUP, Wellington House, 133–155 Waterloo Road, London SE1 8UG. Tel: 0171-972 4926. *Chairman*, Prof. M. Harris
COMMITTEE ON THE SAFETY OF MEDICINES, Market Towers, 1 Nine Elms Lane, London SW8 5NQ. Tel: 0171-273 0451. *Chairman*, Prof. A. M. Breckenridge, CBE, FRCP, FRCPED., FRSE (from Jan. 1999)
MEDICINES COMMISSION, Market Towers, 1 Nine Elms Lane, London SW8 5NQ. Tel: 0171-273 0652. *Chairman*, Prof. D. H. Lawson, CBE, FRCPED., FRCP(Glas.)

EXECUTIVE AGENCIES

MEDICINES CONTROL AGENCY
Market Towers, 1 Nine Elms Lane, London SW8 5NQ
Tel 0171-273 0000; fax 0171-273 0353
The Agency controls medicines through licensing, monitoring and inspection, and enforces safety standards.
Chief Executive, Dr K. H. Jones, CB

MEDICAL DEVICES AGENCY
Hannibal House, Elephant and Castle, London SE1 6TQ
Tel 0171-972 8000; fax 0171-972 8108
The Agency safeguards the performance, quality and safety of medical devices.
Chief Executive, A. Kent

NHS ESTATES
1 Trevelyan Square, Boar Lane, Leeds LS1 6AE
Tel 0113-254 7000; fax 0113-254 7299
NHS Estates provides advice and support in the area of healthcare estate functions to the NHS and the healthcare industry.
Chief Executive, Mrs K. Priestley

NHS PENSIONS
Hesketh House, 200–220 Broadway, Fleetwood, Lancs FY7 8LG
Tel 01253-774774; fax 01253-774860
NHS Pensions administers the NHS occupational pension scheme.
Chief Executive, A. F. Cowan

NHS SUPPLIES
Premier House, 60 Caversham Road, Reading, Berks RG1 7EB
Tel 0118-980 8600; fax 0118-980 8650
NHS Supplies procures goods and services for the NHS.
Chief Executive, T. Hunt, CBE

SPECIAL HOSPITALS

ASHWORTH HOSPITAL, Parkbourn, Maghull, Merseyside L31 1HW. Tel: 0151-473 0303. *Director of Care Services and Nursing*, K. M. Barron
BROADMOOR HOSPITAL, Crowthorne, Berks RG45 7EG. Tel: 01344-773111. *Chief Executive*, Dr J. Hollyman
RAMPTON HOSPITAL, Retford, Notts DN22 0PD. Tel: 01777-248321. *Chief Executive*, Mrs S. Foley

HEALTH AND SAFETY COMMISSION

Rose Court, 2 Southwark Bridge, London SE1 9HS
Tel 0171-717 6000; fax 0171-717 6717

The Health and Safety Commission was created under the Health and Safety at Work etc. Act 1974, with duties to reform health and safety law, to propose new regulations, and generally to promote the protection of people at work and of the public from hazards arising from industrial and commercial activity, including major industrial accidents and the transportation of hazardous materials. The members of the Commission are appointed by the Secretary of State for the Environment, Transport and the Regions. The Commission is made up of representatives of employers, trades unions and local authorities, and has a full-time chairman.
Chairman, F. J. Davies, CBE
Members, R. Symons, CBE; A. Grant; Ms A. Gibson; Dr M. McKiernan; Ms J. Edmond-Smith; D. Coulston; R. Turney; G. Brumwell; Ms M. Burns
Secretary, T. A. Gates

HEALTH AND SAFETY EXECUTIVE

Rose Court, 2 Southwark Bridge, London SE1 9HS
Tel 0171-717 6000; fax 0171-717 6717

The Health and Safety Executive is the Health and Safety Commission's major instrument. Through its inspectorates it enforces health and safety law in the majority of industrial premises. The Executive advises the Commission in its major task of laying down safety standards through regulations and practical guidance for many industrial processes. The Executive is also the licensing authority for nuclear installations and the reporting officer on the severity of nuclear incidents in Britain. In November 1997 the Executive took over responsibility for the Channel Tunnel Safety Authority.
Director-General, Miss J. H. Bacon, CB
Deputy Director-General, D. C. T. Eves, CB (*HM Chief Inspector of Factories*)
Director, Field Operations Directorate, Dr A. Ellis
Director, Nuclear Safety, Dr L. G. Williams (*HM Chief Inspector of Nuclear Installations*)
Director, Science and Technology, Dr J. McQuaid, CB
Director, Safety Policy, C. Norris
Director, Health Directorate, Dr P. J. Graham
Director, Resources and Planning, R. Hillier
Director, Offshore Safety, A. Sefton

HIGHLANDS AND ISLANDS ENTERPRISE

Bridge House, 20 Bridge Street, Inverness IV1 1QR
Tel 01463-234171; fax 01463-244241

Highlands and Islands Enterprise (HIE) was set up under the Enterprise and New Towns (Scotland) Act 1991. Its role is to design, direct and deliver enterprise development, training, environmental and social projects and services. HIE is made up of a strategic core body and ten Local Enterprise Companies (LECs) to which many of its individual functions are delegated.
Chairman, vacant
Chief Executive, I. A. Robertson, CBE

HISTORIC BUILDINGS AND MONUMENTS COMMISSION FOR ENGLAND (ENGLISH HERITAGE)
23 Savile Row, London WIX IAB
Tel 0171-973 3000; fax 0171-973 3001

Under the National Heritage Act 1983, the duties of the Commission are to secure the preservation of ancient monuments and historic buildings; to promote the preservation and enhancement of conservation areas; and to promote the public's enjoyment of, and advance their knowledge of, ancient monuments and historic buildings and their preservation. The Commission is funded by the Department for Culture, Media and Sport.

In July 1998 the Government published a discussion document including a proposal to merge English Heritage and the Royal Commission on the Historical Monuments of England.

Chairman, Sir Jocelyn Stevens, CVO
Commissioners, HRH The Duke of Gloucester, KG, GCVO; The Lord Cavendish of Furness; Ms B. Cherry; Mrs C. Lycett-Green; J. Seymour; A. Fane; Lady Gass; Prof. E. Fernie, CBE; Ms K. McLeod; Prof. R. Morris, FSA; Miss S. Underwood
Chief Executive, Ms P. Alexander

HISTORIC BUILDINGS COUNCIL FOR SCOTLAND
Longmore House, Salisbury Place, Edinburgh EH9 ISH
Tel 0131-668 8600; fax 0131-668 8749

The Historic Buildings Council for Scotland is the advisory body to the Secretary of State for Scotland on matters related to buildings of special architectural or historical interest and in particular to proposals for awards by him of grants for the repair of buildings of outstanding architectural or historical interest or lying within outstanding conservation areas.
Chairman, Sir Raymond Johnstone, CBE
Members, R. Cairns; Sir Ilay Campbell, Bt.; Mrs A. Dundas-Bekker; M. Ellington; Dr J. Frew; J. Hunter Blair; I. Hutchison, OBE; K. Martin; Revd C. Robertson; Mrs P. Robertson; Ms F. Sinclair
Secretary, Ms S. Adams

HISTORIC BUILDINGS COUNCIL FOR WALES
Crown Building, Cathays Park, Cardiff CFI 3NQ
Tel 01222-500200; fax 01222-826375

The Council's function is to advise the Secretary of State for Wales on the built heritage through Cadw: Welsh Historic Monuments (*see* page 353), which is an executive agency within the Welsh Office.
Chairman, T. Lloyd, FSA
Members, R. Haslam; Dr P. Morgan; Mrs S. Furse; Dr S. Unwin; Dr E. Wiliam; Miss E. Evans
Secretary, R. W. Hughes

HISTORIC ROYAL PALACES
Hampton Court Palace, East Molesey, Surrey KT8 9AU
Tel 0181-781 9752; fax 0181-781 9754

Historic Royal Palaces was formerly an executive agency of the Department for Culture, Media and Sport; it became a non-departmental public body on 1 April 1998 and now has charitable trust status. The Secretary of State for Culture, Media and Sport is still accountable to Parliament for the care and presentation of the palaces, which are owned by the Sovereign in right of the Crown. The chairman of the trustees is appointed by The Queen on the advice of the Secretary of State.

Historic Royal Palaces is responsible for the Tower of London, Hampton Court Palace, Kensington Palace State Apartments and the Royal Ceremonial Dress Collection, Kew Palace with Queen Charlotte's Cottage, and the Banqueting House, Whitehall. Government grant-in-aid for 1998–9 is £3.5 million.

TRUSTEES
Chairman, The Earl of Airlie, KT, GCVO, PC
Appointed by The Queen, The Lord Camoys, GCVO, PC; Sir Michael Peat, KCVO; H. Roberts, CVO, FSA
Appointed by the Secretary of State, M. Herbert; Ms A. Heylin; S. Jones; Ms J. Sharman
Ex officio, Field Marshal the Lord Inge, GCB (*Constable of the Tower of London*)

OFFICERS
Chief Executive, D. C. Beeton, CBE
Director of Finance, Ms A. McLeish
Director of Human Resources, M. Bridger
Surveyor of the Fabric, R. Davidson
Curator, Historic Royal Palaces, Dr E. Impey
Director, Palaces Group, R. Evans, FRICS
Resident Governor, HM Tower of London, Maj.-Gen. G. Field, CB, OBE

ROYAL COMMISSION ON THE HISTORICAL MONUMENTS OF ENGLAND
National Monuments Record Centre, Kemble Drive, Swindon SN2 2GZ
Tel 01793-414700; fax 01793-414707
London Search Room: 55 Blandford Street, London WIH 3AF
Tel 0171-208 8200; fax 0171-224 5333

The Royal Commission on the Historical Monuments of England was established in 1908. It is the national body of architectural and archaeological survey and record and manages England's public archive of heritage information, the National Monuments Record. It is funded by the Department for Culture, Media and Sport.

In July 1998 the Government published a discussion document including a proposal to merge the Commission and English Heritage.
Chairman, The Lord Faringdon
Commissioners, Prof. R. Bradley, FSA; D. J. Keene, PH.D.; R. D. H. Gem, PH.D., FSA; T. R. M. Longman; R. A. Yorke; Miss A. Riches, FSA; Dr M. Airs, FSA; Prof. M. Fulford, PH.D., FSA; Dr M. Palmer, FSA; Miss A. Arrowsmith; P. Addyman, FSA; Prof. E. Fernie, CBE, FSA, FRSE; Ms H. Maclagan; Dr W. Sudbury
Secretary, T. G. Hassall, FSA

ROYAL COMMISSION ON THE ANCIENT AND HISTORICAL MONUMENTS OF SCOTLAND

John Sinclair House, 16 Bernard Terrace, Edinburgh
EH8 9NX
Tel 0131-662 1456; fax 0131-662 1477

The Royal Commission was established in 1908 and is appointed to provide for the survey and recording of ancient and historical monuments connected with the culture, civilization and conditions of life of the people in Scotland from the earliest times. It is funded by the Scottish Office. The Commission compiles and maintains the National Monuments Record of Scotland as the national record of the archaeological and historical environment. The National Monuments Record is open for reference Monday–Thursday 9.30–4.30, Friday 9.30–4.

Chairman, Sir William Fraser, GCB, FRSE
Commissioners, Prof. J. M. Coles, ph.D., FBA; Prof. Rosemary Cramp, CBE, FSA; Prof. T. C. Smout, CBE, FRSE, FBA; Dr Deborah Howard, FSA; Prof. R. A. Paxton, FRSE; Dr Barbara Crawford, FSA, FSA scot.; Miss A. Riches; J. Simpson, FSA scot.; Ms M. Mackay, ph.D.
Secretary, R. J. Mercer, FSA, FRSE

ROYAL COMMISSION ON THE ANCIENT AND HISTORICAL MONUMENTS OF WALES

Crown Building, Plas Crug, Aberystwyth SY23 1NJ
Tel 01970-621200; fax 01970-627701

The Royal Commission was established in 1908 and is currently empowered by a royal warrant of 1992 to survey, record, publish and maintain a database of ancient and historical and maritime sites and structures, and landscapes in Wales. The Commission is funded by the Welsh Office and is also responsible for the National Monuments Record of Wales, which is open daily for public reference, for the supply of archaeological information to the Ordnance Survey, for the co-ordination of archaeological aerial photography in Wales, and for sponsorship of the regional Sites and Monuments Records.

Chairman, Prof. J. B. Smith
Commissioners, Prof. R. A. Griffiths, ph.D., D.Litt.; D. Gruffyd Jones; Prof. G. B. D. Jones, D.phil., FSA; Mrs A. Nicol; Prof. P. Sims-Williams, FBA; Prof. G. J. Wainwright, MBE, ph.D., FSA; E. Wiliam, ph.D., FSA
Secretary, P. R. White, FSA

ANCIENT MONUMENTS BOARD FOR SCOTLAND

Longmore House, Salisbury Place, Edinburgh EH9 1SH
Tel 0131-668 8764; fax 0131-668 8765

The Ancient Monuments Board for Scotland advises the Secretary of State for Scotland on the exercise of his functions, under the Ancient Monuments and Archaeological Areas Act 1979, of providing protection for monuments of national importance.

Chairman, Prof. M. Lynch, ph.D., FRSE, PSA scot.

Members, A. Wright, FRSA; Mrs K. Dalyell, FSA scot.; P. Clarke, FSA; Ms A. Ritchie, OBE, ph.D., FSA, FSA scot.; Prof. C. D. Morris, FRSE, FSA, FSA scot.; R. J. Mercer, FRSE, FSA, FSA scot.; W. D. H. Sellar, FSA scot.; B. Mackie; Miss L. M. Thoms, FSA scot.; J. Higgitt, FSA; Ms C. Swanson, ph.D., FSA scot.; M. Baughan; Ms J. Cannizzo, ph.D.; S. Peake , ph.D.; M. Taylor
Secretary, R. A. J. Dalziel
Assessor, D. J. Breeze, ph. D., FRSE, FSA, FSA scot.

ANCIENT MONUMENTS BOARD FOR WALES

Crown Building, Cathays Park, Cardiff CF1 3NQ
Tel 01222-500200; fax 01222-826375

The Ancient Monuments Board for Wales advises the Secretary of State for Wales on his statutory functions in respect of ancient monuments.

Chairman, Prof. R. R. Davies, CBE, D.phil., FBA
Members, R. G. Keen; Mrs F. M. Lynch Llewellyn, FSA; Prof. W. H. Manning, ph.D., FSA; Prof. J. B. Smith; Prof. W. E. Davies, ph.D., FBA; M. J. Garner
Secretary, Mrs J. Booker

HOME-GROWN CEREALS AUTHORITY

Caledonia House, 223 Pentonville Road, London N1 9NG
Tel 0171-520 3914; fax 0171-520 3918

Set up under the Cereals Marketing Act 1965, the Authority consists of seven members representing UK cereal growers, seven representing dealers in, or processors of, grain and two independent members. The Authority's functions are to improve the production and marketing of UK-grown cereals and oilseeds through a research and development programme, to provide a market information service, and to promote UK cereals in export markets.

Chairman (part-time) (£19,750), A. Pike
Chief Executive, A. J. Williams

HOME OFFICE

50 Queen Anne's Gate, London SW1H 9AT
Tel 0171-273 4000; fax 0171-273 2190
E-mail: gen.ho@gtnet.gov.uk
Web: http://www.homeoffice.gov.uk

The Home Office deals with those internal affairs in England and Wales which have not been assigned to other government departments. The Home Secretary is particularly concerned with the administration of justice; criminal law; the treatment of offenders, including probation and the prison service; the police; immigration and nationality; passport policy matters; community relations; certain public safety matters; and fire and civil emergencies services. The Home Secretary personally is the link between The Queen and the public, and exercises certain powers on her behalf, including that of the royal pardon.

Other subjects dealt with include electoral arrangements; ceremonial and formal business connected with honours; scrutiny of local authority by-laws; granting of licences for scientific procedures involving animals; cremations, burials and exhumations; firearms; dangerous drugs and poisons; general policy on laws relating to shops, liquor licensing, gaming and marriage; theatre and cinema licensing; and race relations policy.

The Home Secretary is also the link between the UK government and the governments of the Channel Islands and the Isle of Man.

Secretary of State for the Home Department, The Rt. Hon. Jack Straw, MP
Principal Private Secretary (SCS), K. D. Sutton
Private Secretaries, Ms C. Sumner; Ms I. Hopton; D. Redhouse
Special Advisers, Lord Warner; E. Owen
Parliamentary Private Secretary, P. Tipping, MP
Minister of State, Alun Michael, MP (*Criminal and Police Policy*)
Parliamentary Private Secretary, C. Pickthall, MP
Minister of State, The Lord Williams of Mostyn, QC (*Constitution, Prisons, Probation*)
Parliamentary Private Secretary, B. Jenkins, MP
Private Secretary to the Ministers of State, A. Smith
Parliamentary Under-Secretaries of State, George Howarth, MP (*Prisons, Probation, Fire and Emergency Planning, Drugs, Elections, Gambling, Data Protection*); Michael O'Brien, MP (*Immigration and Nationality*); Kate Hoey, MP (*Metropolitan Police, Women's Issues, International Co-operation*)
Private Secretaries, Miss C. McCombie; J. Payne
Parliamentary Clerk, Ms A. Scott
Permanent Under-Secretary of State (SCS), D. B. Omand
Private Secretary, Miss A. Rutherford
Chief Medical Officer (at Department of Health), Prof. L. Donaldson, FRCSED., FRCP

COMMUNICATION DIRECTORATE
Director (SCS), B. Butler
Deputy Head of Communication (Head of News) (SCS), vacant
Head of Publicity and Corporate Services (SCS), Miss A. Nash
Assistant Director, News (G6), B. McBride
Assistant Director and Head of Information Services Group (G7), P. Griffiths

CONSTITUTIONAL AND COMMUNITY POLICY DIRECTORATE
Director (SCS), Miss C. Sinclair
Heads of Units (SCS), Mrs G. Catto; R. Evans; M. Gillespie; S. B. Hickson

ANIMALS (SCIENTIFIC PROCEDURES) INSPECTORATE
Chief Inspector (SCS), Dr J. Richmond
Superintendent Inspector (SCS), Dr J. Anderson
Inspectors (G6), Dr R. Curtis; Dr V. Navaratnam; Dr C. Wilkins

GAMING BOARD FOR GREAT BRITAIN
— *see* page 304

CORPORATE DEVELOPMENT DIRECTORATE
Director (SCS), Dr D. Pepper
Heads of Units (SCS), Mrs S. Atkins; T. Edwards; Ms E. Sparrow; S. Wharton
Senior Prinicpals (G6), Mrs C. Burrows; T. Lewis; D. Rigby; S. Thornton

CORPORATE RESOURCES DIRECTORATE
Grenadier House, 99–105 Horseferry Road, London SW1P 2DD
Tel 0171-273 4000
Clive House, Petty France, London SW1H 9HD
Tel 0171-273 4000
Director (SCS), Miss P. Drew
Head of Unit (SCS), Dr M. Allnutt

Senior Principals (G6), T. Cobley; R. Creedon; A. Ford; J. G. Jones; Ms E. Moody

CRIMINAL POLICY DIRECTORATE
Directors (SCS), J. Halliday, CB; W. Fittall; J. Lyon
Heads of Units (SCS), M. Boyle; R. Childs; I. Chisholm; J. Duke-Evans; E. Grant; A. Harding; P. Honour; Ms H. Jackson; H. Marriage; Miss C. Stewart
Senior Principals (G6), Mrs A. Johnstone; A. Macfarlane; Ms L. Rogerson

CENTRAL DRUGS PREVENTION UNIT
Horseferry House, Dean Ryle Street, London SW1P 2AW
Tel 0171-273 4000
Head of Unit (G6), Ms L. Rogerson

HOME OFFICE CRIME PREVENTION COLLEGE
The Hawkhills, Easingwold, York YO6 3EG
Tel 01347-825060
Director, J. Acton

HM INSPECTORATE OF PROBATION
Chief Inspector (SCS), G. W. Smith, CBE
Assistant Chief Inspector (G6), G. Childs

FIRE AND EMERGENCY PLANNING DIRECTORATE
Horseferry House, Dean Ryle Street, London SW1P 2AW
Tel 0171-273 4000
50 Queen Anne's Gate, London SW1H 9AT
Tel 0171-273 4000
Director (SCS), Mrs S. Street
Heads of Units (SCS), E. Guy; Mrs V. Harris; Miss S. Paul; Dr D. Peace

HM FIRE SERVICE INSPECTORATE
HM Chief Inspector, G. Meldrum, CBE, QFSM
HM Territorial Inspectors, A. R. Currie, OBE, QFSM; P. Morphew, QFSM; A. Rule, QFSM
Lay Inspector, vacant
HM Inspectors, W. Ambalino; R. A. M. Baillie, QFSM; D. Berry; G. P. Bowles; S. D. Christian; D. Kent; C. Moseley; R. Pearce; E. G. Pearn, QFSM; K. Phillips; M. Robinson; R. M. Simpson, OBE; A. C. Wells, QFSM; D. Wright
Principal (G7), Miss G. Kirton

EMERGENCY PLANNING COLLEGE
The Hawkhills, Easingwold, Yorks YO6 3EG
Tel 01347-821406

IMMIGRATION AND NATIONALITY DIRECTORATE, AND EU AND INTERNATIONAL UNIT
Lunar House, 40 Wellesley Road, Croydon, Surrey CR9 2BY
Tel 0181-686 0333
Apollo House, 36 Wellesley Road, Croydon, Surrey CR9 3RR
Tel 0181-686 0333
50 Queen Anne's Gate, London SW1H 9AT
Tel 0171-273 4000
India Buildings, 3rd Floor, Water Street, Liverpool L2 0QN
Tel 0151-237 5200
Director-General (SCS), T. E. H. Walker, CB
Deputy Directors-General (SCS), M. J. Eland (*Policy*); Miss K. Collins (*Operations*)
Heads of Directorates (SCS), J. Acton; Miss V. M. Dews; Mrs E. C. L. Pallett; J. Potts; A. Walmsley; R. M. Whalley; R. G. Yates

Senior Principals (G6), Ms C. Checksfield; P. Dawson; B. Downie; M. Rumble

IMMIGRATION SERVICE
Director (Ports) (SCS), T. Farrage
Deputy Director (G6), V. Hogg
Director (Enforcement) (SCS), I. Boon
Deputy Director (G6), C. Harbin

EU AND INTERNATIONAL UNIT
Head of Unit (SCS), P. Edwards

LEGAL ADVISERS'S BRANCH
Legal Adviser (SCS), Miss J. Wheldon, CB
Deputy Legal Advisers (SCS), Mrs S. A. Evans; T. Middleton
Assistant Legal Advisers (SCS), R. J. Clayton; J. R. O'Meara; R. Green; S. A. Parker

ORGANIZED AND INTERNATIONAL CRIME DIRECTORATE
Director (SCS), J. Warne

PLANNING AND FINANCE DIRECTORATE
50 Queen Anne's Gate, London SW1H 9AT
Tel 0171-273 4000
Horseferry House, Dean Ryle Street, London SW1P 2AW
Tel 0171-273 4000
Director (SCS), R. Fulton
Heads of Units (SCS), C. Harnett; A. Mortimer
Senior Principals (G6), P. Dare; P. Davies; T. Williams

POLICE POLICY DIRECTORATE
Director (SCS), S. Boys Smith
Heads of Units (SCS), N. Benger; Ms L. Lockyer; Miss D. Loudon
Senior Principals (G6), R. Ginman; Dr G. Laycock

NATIONAL DIRECTORATE OF POLICE TRAINING
National Director of Police Training, P. Hermitage, QPM

Corporate Services
Senior Principal (G6), P. Curwen

POLICE STAFF COLLEGE
Bramshill House, Bramshill, Hook, Hants RG27 0JW
Tel 0125-126 2931
Head of Higher Training, I. McDonald

HENDON DATA CENTRE
Aerodrome Road, Colindale, London NW9 5LN
Tel 0181-200 2424
Head of Unit (G6), J. Ladley

POLICE SCIENTIFIC DEVELOPMENT BRANCH
Sandridge, St Albans, Herts AL4 9HQ
Tel 01727-865051
Director (SCS), B. R. Coleman, OBE
Chief Scientist/Deputy Director (G6), Dr P. Young

Langhurst House, Langhurstwood Road, Nr Horsham, W. Sussex RH12 4WX
Tel 01403-255451
Head of Unit Langhurst (G6), Dr G. Thomas

HM INSPECTORATE OF CONSTABULARY
HM Chief Inspector of Constabulary (SCS), D. J. O'Dowd, CBE, QPM
HM Inspectors (SCS), D. Crompton, CBE, QPM; K. Povey, QPM; C. Smith, CBE, CVO, QPM; P. J. Winship, CBE, QPM; J. A. Stevens, QPM
Lay Inspector, P. T. G. Hobbs
Senior Principal (G6), L. Davidoff

METROPOLITAN POLICE COMMITTEE AND SECRETARIAT
Clive House, Petty France, London SW1H 9HD
Tel 0171-273 4000
Head of Secretariat (SCS), R. Halward

RESEARCH AND STATISTICS DIRECTORATE
Director (SCS), C. Nuttall
Heads of Units (SCS), C. Lewis; D. Moxon; A. Norbury; P. Ward
Senior Principals (G6), G. Barclay; Ms M. Colledge; Mrs P. Dowdeswell; Dr S. Field; Ms M. FitzGerald; P. Goldblatt; J. Graham; Mrs C. Lehman; Mrs P. Mayhew, OBE; Ms J. Vennard; R. Walmsley

STRATEGY UNIT
Head of Unit (SCS), R. Weatherill

HM INSPECTORATE OF PRISONS
HM Chief Inspector, Gen. Sir David Ramsbotham, GCB, CBE
HM Deputy Chief Inspector, C. Allen
HM Inspectors (Governor 1), R. Jacques; G. Hughes

PRISONS OMBUDSMAN
— see page 334

PAROLE BOARD FOR ENGLAND AND WALES
— see pages 332

HM PRISON SERVICE
— see pages 379 – 81

FIRE SERVICE COLLEGE
Moreton-in-Marsh, Glos GL56 0RH
Tel 01608-650831
An executive agency of the Home Office.
Chief Executive and Commandant, T. Glossop, QFSM
College Secretary, Miss R. Jones

UK PASSPORT AGENCY
Clive House, Petty France, London SW1H 9HD
Tel 0171-799 2728
An executive agency of the Home Office.
Chief Executive (SCS), D. Gatenby
Deputy Chief Executive and Director of Operations (G6), K. J. Sheehan
Director of Systems (G6), J. Davies

HORSERACE TOTALISATOR BOARD
74 Upper Richmond Road, London SW15 2SU
Tel 0181-874 6411; fax 0181-874 6107

The Horserace Totalisator Board was established by the Betting, Gaming and Lotteries Act 1963. Its function is to operate totalisators on approved racecourses in Great Britain, and it also provides on- and off-course cash and credit offices. Under the Horserace Totalisator and Betting Levy Board Act 1972, it is further empowered to offer bets at starting price (or other bets at fixed odds) on any sporting event. The chairman and members of the Board are appointed by the Home Secretary.

The Government announced in June 1998 that it would require the Board to enter into partnerships with the private sector.
Chairman (£75,000), P. I. Jones
Chief Executive, W. J. Heaton

HOUSING CORPORATION
149 Tottenham Court Road, London wip obn
Tel 0171-393 2000; fax 0171-393 2111

Established by Parliament in 1964, the Housing Corporation regulates, funds and promotes the proper performance of registered social landlords, which are non-profit making bodies run by voluntary committees. There are over 2,200 registered social landlords, most of which are housing associations, and they now provide homes for more than 1.5 million people. Under the Housing Act 1996, the Corporation's regulatory role was widened to embrace new types of landlords, in particular local housing companies. The Corporation is funded by the Department of the Environment, Transport and the Regions.
Chairman, The Baroness Dean of Thornton-le-Fylde, pc
Deputy Chairman, E. Armitage
Chief Executive, A. Mayer

HUMAN FERTILIZATION AND EMBRYOLOGY AUTHORITY
Paxton House, 30 Artillery Lane, London ei 7ls
Tel 0171-377 5077; fax 0171-377 1871

The Human Fertilization and Embryology Authority (HFEA) was established under the Human Fertilization and Embryology Act 1990. Its function is to license persons carrying out any of the following activities: the creation or use of embryos outside the body in the provision of infertility treatment services; the use of donated gametes in infertility treatment; the storage of gametes or embryos; and research on human embryos. It maintains a confidential database of all such treatments and of egg and sperm donors, and provides information to patients, clinics and the public. The HFEA also keeps under review information about embryos and, when requested to do so, gives advice to the Secretary of State for Health.
Chairman, Mrs R. Deech
Deputy Chairman, Mrs J. Denton
Members, Dr G. Bahadur; Prof. D. Barlow; Prof. Ruth Chambers; Mrs M. E. Coath; Ms E. Forgan; Prof. Christine Gosden; D. Greggains; Prof. A. Grubb; Prof. M. Johnson; R. Jones; Prof. S. Lewis; Dr B. Lieberman; Dr Anne McLaren; The Rt. Revd Bishop of Rochester; Dr Joan Stringer; Prof. A. Templeton; Prof. the Revd A. Thiselton; Julia, Lady Tugendhat; J. Williams
Chief Executive, Mrs S. McCarthy

HUMAN GENETICS ADVISORY COMMISSION
Room 12, Albany House, 94–98 Petty France, London swih 9st
Tel 0171-271 2131; fax 0171-271 2028

The Human Genetics Advisory Commission was established in December 1996. It is an advisory body with the remit of taking a broad view of developments in human genetics and advising ministers on ways to build public confidence in the application of the new science. Members of the Commission are appointed by the Secretary of State for Trade and Industry and the Secretary of State for Health.
Chairman, Prof. Sir Colin Campbell

Members, Prof. C. Aitken, cbe; Dr Michaela Aldred; Prof. M. Bobrow; Mrs D. Littlejohn, cbe; Prof. N. Nevin; Dr Onora O'Neill; Dr G. Poste, frs; Revd Dr J. Polkinghorne, kbe, frs; Ms M. Stuart
Head of Secretariat, Dr Amanda Goldin

INDEPENDENT COMMISSION FOR POLICE COMPLAINTS FOR NORTHERN IRELAND
Chamber of Commerce House, 22 Great Victoria Street, Belfast bt2 7lp
Tel 01232-244821; fax 01232-248563

The Independent Commission for Police Complaints was established under the Police (Northern Ireland) Order 1987. It has powers to supervise the investigation of certain categories of serious complaints, can direct that disciplinary charges be brought, and has oversight of the informal resolution procedure for less serious complaints.
Subject to legislation currently before Parliament, the Commission will be replaced in March 1999 by a Police Ombudsman.
Chairman, P. A. Donnelly
Chief Executive, B. McClelland

INDEPENDENT COMMISSION ON POLICING FOR NORTHERN IRELAND
67 Tufton Street, London swip 3qs
Tel 0171-210 2625; fax 0171-210 2628
3/F Interpoint, 20–24 York Street, Belfast bt15 1aq
Tel 01232-258848; fax 01232-258843

The Commission was set up following the Belfast Agreement of April 1998. Its remit is to inquire into policing in Northern Ireland and put forward proposals for future policing structures and arrangements, including means of encouraging widespread community support for those arrangements. The Commission will report to the Secretary of State for Northern Ireland by summer 1999.
Chairman, The Rt. Hon. C. F. Patten, ch
Members, Dr M. Hayes; Dr G. Lynch; The Hon. Ms K. O'Toole; Prof. C. Shearing; Sir John Smith, qpm; P. Smith, qc; Mrs L. Woods
Secretary, R. N. Peirce

INDEPENDENT HOUSING OMBUDSMAN
Norman House, 105–109 Strand, London wc2r oaa
Tel 0171-836 3630; fax 0171-836 3900

The Independent Housing Ombudsman was established in April 1997 under the Housing Act 1996. The Ombudsman deals with complaints against registered social landlords (not including local authorities).
Ombudsman, R. Jefferies
Chair of Board, Ms P. Brown
General Manager, L. Greenberg

INDEPENDENT INTERNATIONAL COMMISSION ON DECOMMISSIONING
Dublin Castle, Block M, Ship Street, Dublin 2
Tel 00 353 1-478 0111; fax 00 353 1-478 0600
Rosepark House, Upper Newtownards Road, Belfast
BT4 3NR
Tel 01232-488600; fax 01232-488601

The Commission was established by agreement between the British and Irish governments in August 1997. Its objective is to facilitate the decommissioning of illegally-held firearms and explosives in accordance with the relevant legislation in both jurisdictions. Its members are appointed jointly by the two governments; staff are appointed by the Commission. All are drawn from countries other than the UK and the Republic of Ireland.
Chairman, Gen. J. de Chastelain (Canada)
Members, Brig. T. Nieminen (Finland); Ambassador D. C. Johnson (USA)
Chief of Staff, C. E. Garrard (Canada)

INDEPENDENT REVIEW SERVICE FOR THE SOCIAL FUND
4th Floor, Centre City Podium, 5 Hill Street, Birmingham B5 4UB
Tel 0121-606 2100; fax 0121-606 2180

The Social Fund Commissioner is appointed by the Secretary of State for Social Security. The Commissioner appoints Social Fund Inspectors, who provide an independent review of decisions made by Social Fund Officers in the Benefits Agency of the Department of Social Security.
Social Fund Commissioner, J. Scampion

INDEPENDENT TELEVISION COMMISSION
33 Foley Street, London W1P 7LB
Tel 0171-255 3000; fax 0171-306 7800

The Independent Television Commission replaced the Independent Broadcasting Authority in 1991. The Commission is responsible for licensing and regulating all commercially funded television services broadcast from the UK. Members are appointed by the Secretary of State for Culture, Media and Sport.
Chairman (£65,580), Sir Robin Biggam
Deputy Chairman (£16,830), Earl of Dalkeith
Members (*part-time*) (£12,630), Dr J. Beynon, FEng.; Ms J. Goffe; Dr M. Moloney; J. Ranelagh; Dr M. Shea, CVO; Sir Michael Checkland; A. Balls, CB; W. Roddick
Chief Executive (£140,000), P. Rogers
Secretary, M. Redley

INDUSTRIAL INJURIES ADVISORY COUNCIL
6th Floor, The Adelphi, 1–11 John Adam Street, London WC2N 6HT
Tel 0171-962 8066; fax 0171-712 2255

The Industrial Injuries Advisory Council is a statutory body under the Social Security Administration Act 1992 which considers and advises the Secretary of State for Social Security on regulations and other questions relating to industrial injuries benefits or their administration.
Chairman, Prof. A. J. Newman Taylor, OBE, FRCP
Secretary, A. Packer

BOARD OF INLAND REVENUE
Somerset House, Strand, London WC2R 1LB
Tel 0171-438 6622

The Board of Inland Revenue was constituted under the Inland Revenue Board Act 1849. The Board administers and collects direct taxes – income tax, corporation tax, capital gains tax, inheritance tax, stamp duty, and petroleum revenue tax – and advises the Chancellor of the Exchequer on policy questions involving them. The Department's Valuation Office is an executive agency responsible for valuing property for tax purposes.

The Inland Revenue and the Contributions Agency of the Department of Social Security are to merge in April 1999.

THE BOARD
Chairman (G1), N. Montagu, CB
  Private Secretary, Ms C. Lunney
Deputy Chairmen (G2), S. C. T. Matheson, CB; G. H. Bush, CB
Director-General (G2), T. J. Flesher

DIVISIONS
Director, Human Resources Division (G3), J. Gant
Director, Business and Management Services Division (G3), J. Yard
Head, Strategy and Planning Division, P. Wardle
Principal Finance Officer (G3), R. R. Martin
Director, Business Operations Division (G3), D. A. Smith
Director, Statistics and Economics Division (G3), R. G. Ward
Director, Company Tax Division, Financial Institutions Division and Business Management Unit (G3), M. F. Cayley
Director, Customer Service Division (G3), T. Evans
Director, International Division (G3), I. Spence
Director, Business Profits Division and Compliance Division (G3), E. J. Gribbon
Director, Personal Tax Division (G3), E. McGivern, CB
Director, Capital and Valuation Division, and Savings and Investment Division (G3), B. A. Mace

EXECUTIVE OFFICES

ACCOUNTS OFFICE (CUMBERNAULD), St Mungo's Road, Cumbernauld, Glasgow G70 5TR. *Director,* A. Geddes, OBE
ACCOUNTS OFFICE (SHIPLEY), Shipley, Bradford, W. Yorks BD98 8AA. *Director,* R. J. Warner
CAPITAL TAXES OFFICE, Ferrers House, PO Box 38, Castle Meadow Road, Nottingham NG2 1BB. *Director,* E. McKeegan
CAPITAL TAXES OFFICE (SCOTLAND), Mulberry House, 16 Picardy Place, Edinburgh EH1 3NB. *Registrar,* Mrs J. Templeton
COMMUNICATIONS UNITS, North-West Wing, Bush House, London WC2B 4PP. *Head of External Communications Unit,* P. Whyatt; *Head of Internal Communications Unit,* Mrs S. M. Walton
ENFORCEMENT OFFICE, Durrington Bridge House, Barrington Road, Worthing, W. Sussex BN12 4SE. *Director,* Mrs S. F. Walsh

FINANCIAL ACCOUNTING OFFICE, South Block,
Barrington Road, Worthing, W. Sussex BN12 4XH.
Director, J. D. Easey
FINANCIAL INTERMEDIARIES AND CLAIMS OFFICE, St
John's House, Merton Road, Bootle L26 9BB; Fitz Roy
House, PO Box 46, Castle Meadow, Nottingham NG2
1BD. *Director,* S. W. Jones
INTERNAL AUDIT OFFICE, North-West Wing, Bush
House, London WC2B 4PP. *Director,* N. R. Buckley
OIL TAXATION OFFICE, Melbourne House, Aldwych,
London WC2B 4LL. *Director,* R. C. Mountain
PENSION SCHEME OFFICE, Yorke House, PO Box 62,
Castle Meadow Road, Nottingham NG2 1BG. *Director,*
S. J. McManus
SOLICITOR'S OFFICE, East Wing, Somerset House,
London WC2R 1LB. *Solicitor (G2),* B. E. Cleave, CB
SOLICITOR'S OFFICE (SCOTLAND), Clarendon House,
114–116 George Street, Edinburgh EH2 4LH. *Solicitor,*
I. K. Laing
SPECIAL COMPLIANCE OFFICE, Angel Court, 199
Borough High Street, London SE1 1HZ. *Director,*
F. J. Brannigan
STAMP OFFICE, South-West Wing, Bush House, Strand,
London WC2B 4QN. *Director,* K. S. Hodgson, OBE
TRAINING OFFICE, Lawress Hall, Riseholme Park,
Lincoln LN2 2BJ. *Director,* T. Kuczys

REGIONAL EXECUTIVE OFFICES

INLAND REVENUE EAST, Churchgate, New Road,
Peterborough PE1 1TD. *Director,* M. J. Hodgson
INLAND REVENUE LARGE BUSINESS OFFICE, New Court,
Carey Street, London WC2A 2JE. *Director,* Mrs M. E.
Williams
INLAND REVENUE LONDON, New Court, Carey Street,
London WC2A 2JE. *Director,* J. F. Carling
INLAND REVENUE NORTH, 100 Russell Street,
Middlesbrough TS1 2RZ. *Director,* R. I. Ford
INLAND REVENUE NORTH-WEST, The Triad, Stanley
Road, Bootle, Merseyside L75 2DD. *Director,* G. W. Lunn
INLAND REVENUE SOUTH-EAST, Dukes Court, Dukes
Street, Woking GU21 5XR. *Director,* D. L. S. Bean
INLAND REVENUE SOUTH-WEST, 3rd Floor, Longbrook
House, New North Road, Exeter EX4 4UA. *Director,* R. S.
Hurcombe
INLAND REVENUE SOUTH YORKSHIRE, Concept House, 5
Young Street, Sheffield S1 4LF. *Director,* A. C. Sleeman
INLAND REVENUE WALES AND MIDLANDS, 1st Floor,
Phase II Building, Tŷ Glas Avenue, Llanishen, Cardiff
CF4 5TS; 550 Streetsbrook Road, Solihull, West
Midlands B91 1QU. *Director,* M. W. Kirk
INLAND REVENUE SCOTLAND, Clarendon House,
114–116 George Street, Edinburgh EH2 4LH. *Director,*
I. S. Gerrie
INLAND REVENUE NORTHERN IRELAND, Dorchester
House, 52–58 Great Victoria Street, Belfast BT2 7QE.
Director, R. S. T. Ewing

VALUATION OFFICE AGENCY
New Court, 48 Carey Street, London WC2A 2JE
Tel 0171-324 1183/1057; fax 0171-324 1073
Meldrum House, 15 Drumsheugh Gardens, Edinburgh
EH3 7UN
Tel 0131-225 4938; fax 0131-220 4384
Chief Executive, M. A. Johns
Chief Valuer, Scotland, A. Ainslie

ADJUDICATOR'S OFFICE
— *see* page 278

INTELLIGENCE SERVICES TRIBUNAL
PO Box 4823, London SW1A 9XD
Tel 0171-273 4383

The Intelligence Services Act 1994 established a tribunal
of three senior members of the legal profession, independent of the Government and appointed by The Queen, to
investigate complaints from any person about anything
which they believe the Secret Intelligence Service or the
Government Communications Headquarters has done to
them or to their property.
President, The Rt. Hon. Lord Justice Simon Brown
Vice-President, Sheriff J. McInnes, QC
Member, Sir Richard Gaskell
Secretary, E. R. Wilson

INTERCEPTION COMMISSIONER
c/o PO Box 12376, London SW1P 1XU
Tel 0171-273 4096

The Commissioner is appointed by the Prime Minister.
He keeps under review the issue by the Home Secretary,
the Foreign Secretary, and the Secretaries of State for
Scotland and for Northern Ireland, of warrants under the
Interception of Communications Act 1985 and safeguards
made in respect of intercepted material obtained through
the use of such warrants. He is also required to give all such
assistance as the Interception of Communications Tribunal may require to enable it to carry out its functions, and to
submit an annual report to the Prime Minister with respect
to the carrying out of his functions.
Commissioner, The Lord Nolan, PC
   Private Secretary, E. R. Wilson

INTERCEPTION OF COMMUNICATIONS
TRIBUNAL
PO Box 12376, London SW1P 1XU
Tel 0171-273 4096

Under the Interception of Communications Act 1985, the
Tribunal is required to investigate complaints from any
person who believes that communications sent to or by
them have been intercepted in the course of their
transmission by post or by means of a public telecommunications system. The Tribunal comprises senior members
of the legal profession, who are appointed by The Queen.
President, The Hon. Mr Justice Macpherson of Cluny
Vice-President, Sir David Calcutt, QC
Members, P. Scott, QC; R. Seabrook, QC; W. Carmichael
Secretary, E. R. Wilson

DEPARTMENT FOR INTERNATIONAL
DEVELOPMENT
94 Victoria Street, London SW1E 5JL
Tel 0171-917 7000; fax 0171-917 0016
Web: http://www.dfid.gov.uk
Abercrombie House, Eaglesham Road, East Kilbride,
Glasgow G75 8EA
Tel 01355-844000; fax 01355-844099

The Department for International Development (DFID)
was established in May 1997 from the former Overseas

Development Administration of the Foreign and Commonwealth Office. It takes the lead on British policy towards developing countries. It also manages the development assistance budget, including financial aid and technical assistance (specialist staff abroad and training facilities in the UK), whether provided directly to developing countries or through the various multilateral aid organizations, including the EU, the World Bank and the UN agencies.
Secretary of State for International Development, The Rt. Hon. Clare Short, MP
Private Secretary, A. Smith
Special Advisers, D. Harris; D. Mepham
Parliamentary Private Secretary, D. Turner, MP
Parliamentary Under-Secretary, George Foulkes, MP
Permanent Secretary (SCS), J. M. M. Vereker
Private Secretary, J. Gordon

PROGRAMMES

Director-General (SCS), B. R. Ireton
Head of Conflict and Humanitarian Affairs Department (SCS) (acting), Dr M. Kapila

AFRICA
Director (SCS), P. D. M. Freeman
Heads of Departments (SCS), Mrs B. M. Kelly, CBE (*Africa, Greater Horn and Co-ordination*); S. Ray (*West and North Africa*); D. Fish (*Nairobi*); J. R. Drummond (*Harare*); J. H. S. Chard (*Pretoria*)

ASIA
Director (SCS), S. Unsworth
Heads of Departments (SCS), C. Myhill (*East Asia and Pacific*); R. Graham-Harrison (*India*); Ms M. H. Vowles (*Western Asia*); A. K. C. Wood (*South-East Asia*); K. L. Sparkhall (*Bangladesh*)

EASTERN EUROPE AND WESTERN HEMISPHERE
Director (SCS), J. Kerby
Heads of Departments (SCS), A. Coverdale (*Eastern Europe and Central Asia*); J. S. Laing (*Central and South-Eastern Europe*); B. P. Thomson (*Caribbean*)
Heads of Departments, D. R. Curran (*Latin America, Caribbean and Atlantic*); J. D. Moye (*EBRD Unit*)

ECONOMICS AND GOVERNANCE
Director, and Chief Economic Adviser (SCS), J. Goudie
Chief Statistician (SCS), A. B. Williams
Head of Asia, Latin America and Oceans Economics, P. J. Ackroyd
Head of African Economics Department (SCS), M. G. Foster
Head of International Economics Department (SCS), P. D. Grant
Senior Small Enterprise Development Adviser, D. L. Wright
Senior Economic Advisers, Ms R. L. Turner; P. L. Owen; P. J. Dearden; P. J. Landymore; E. Hawthorn; F. C. Clift; J. L. Hoy
Head of Government Institutions Advisory Department (SCS), R. J. Wilson
Senior Government and Institutions Advisers, Dr G. W. Glentworth; D. W. Baker; Mrs A. Newsum; S. Sharples; J. G. Clarke
Criminal Justice Adviser, vacant

HUMAN RESOURCE DEVELOPMENT
Director, and Chief Health and Population Adviser (SCS), Dr D. N. Nabarro
Senior Health and Population Advisers, J. N. Lambert; T. Martineau; S. Tyson; R. N. Grose; Ms C. M. Sergeant
Chief Social Development Adviser, Dr R. Eyben
Senior Social Development Adviser, Ms P. M. Holden
Chief Education Adviser (SCS), Ms M. A. Harrison

Senior Education Advisers, Dr C. Treffgarne; M. E. Seath; M. D. Francis; R. T. Allsop; Dr D. B. Pennycuick; S. E. Packer; Dr K. M. Lillis; Dr G. R. H. Jones
Senior Technical Education Adviser, C. Lewis

PRODUCTIVE CAPACITY AND ENVIRONMENT
Director, and Chief Natural Resources Adviser (SCS), A. J. Bennett, CMG
Head of Environment Policy Department (SCS), D. P. Turner
Head of Natural Resources Policy and Advisory Department, and Deputy Chief Natural Resources Adviser (SCS), J. M. Scott
Head of Natural Resources Research Department (SCS), Dr J. Tarbit, OBE
Senior Natural Resources Advisers, Ms F. Proctor; R. C. Fox; M. J. Wilson; A. J. Tainsh; J. R. F. Hansell; Dr B. E. Grimwood; J. A. Harvey; A. Hall
Natural Resources Systems Programme Manager, J. C. Barrett
Senior Environment and Research Adviser, Ms L. C. Brown
Senior Fisheries Adviser, R. W. Beales
Senior Forestry Advisers, J. M. Hudson; I. A. Napier
Senior Animal Health Advisers, G. G. Freeland; Ms L. M. Bell
Chief Engineering Adviser (SCS), J. W. Hodges
Senior Engineering Advisers, B. Dolton; C. I. Ellis; P. J. Davies; D. F. Gillett; P. W. D. H. Roberts; M. F. Sergeant; R. J. Cadwallader; C. J. Hunt
Senior Water Resources Adviser, A. Wray
Senior Architectural and Physical Planning Adviser, M. W. Parkes
Senior Electrical and Mechanical Adviser, R. P. Jones
Senior Renewable Energy and Research Adviser, A. Gilchrist
Industrial Training Adviser, D. G. Marr

RESOURCES

Director-General (SCS), R. G. Manning
Heads of Departments (SCS), M. J. Dinham (*Personnel*); D. Sands-Smith (*Procurement, Appointments and NGO*); R. Calvert (*Information*); G. M. Stegmann (*Aid Policy and Resources*); A. D. Davis (*Information Systems*); R. A. Elias (*Internal Audit Unit*); C. P. Raleigh (*Evaluation*)
Head of Department, R. Plumb (*Overseas Pensions*)

INTERNATIONAL DEVELOPMENT AFFAIRS
Director (SCS), J. A. L. Faint
Heads of Departments (SCS), M. Lowcock (*European Union*); D. J. Batt (*International Economic Policy*); G. Toulmin (*United Nations and Commonwealth*); M. E. Cund (*International Financial Institutions*)

INTERVENTION BOARD
PO Box 69, Reading RG1 3YD
Tel 0118-958 3626; fax 0118-953 1370

The Intervention Board was established as a government department in 1972 and became an executive agency in 1990. The Board is responsible for the implementation of European Union regulations covering the market support arrangements of the Common Agricultural Policy. Members are appointed by and are responsible to the Minister of Agriculture, Fisheries and Food and the Secretaries of State for Scotland, Wales and Northern Ireland.
Chairman, I. Kent
Chief Executive (G3), G. Trevelyan

HEADS OF DIVISIONS
External Trade Division (G5), J. P. Bradbury
Internal Market Division (G5), H. MacKinnon
Corporate Services Division (G5), Mrs A. Parker
Finance Division (G5), G. R. R. Jenkins
Legal Division (G5), J. F. McCleary

Chief Accountant (G6), R. Bryant
Procurement and Supply (G6), P. J. Offer
Information Systems (G7), T. G. Lamberstock
Internal Market Operations (G6), J. A. Sutton

LAND AUTHORITY FOR WALES
— *see* Welsh Development Agency

LAND REGISTRIES

HM LAND REGISTRY
Lincoln's Inn Fields, London WC2A 3PH
Tel 0171-917 8888; fax 0171-955 0110

The registration of title to land was first introduced in England and Wales by the Land Registry Act 1862; HM Land Registry operates today under the Land Registration Acts 1925 to 1988. The object of registering title to land is to create and maintain a register of landowners whose title is guaranteed by the state and so to simplify the transfer, mortgage and other dealings with real property. Registration on sale is now compulsory throughout England and Wales. The register has been open to inspection by the public since 1990.

HM Land Registry is an executive agency administered under the Lord Chancellor by the Chief Land Registrar.

HEADQUARTERS OFFICE
Chief Land Registrar and Chief Executive, Dr S. J. Hill
Solicitor to Land Registry, C. J. West
Director of Corporate Services, E. G. Beardsall
Senior Land Registrar, J. V. Timothy
Director of Operations, G. N. French
Director of Information Technology, P. J. Smith
Director of Management Services, P. R. Laker
Land Registrar, M. L. Wood
Deputy Establishment Officer, J. Hodder
Controller of Operations Development, P. Norman
Head of Legal Practice, P. Morris
Head of Survey and Plans Practice, M. K. Brown

COMPUTER SERVICES DIVISION
Burrington Way, Plymouth PL5 3LP
Tel 01752-635600
Head of IT Services Division, P. A. Maycock
Head of IT Development Division, R. T. Davis
Head of National Land Information Service (NLIS), R. J. Smith
Head of IT Management Services, K. Deards

LAND CHARGES AND AGRICULTURAL CREDITS DEPARTMENT
Burrington Way, Plymouth PL5 3LP
Tel 01752-635600
Superintendent of Land Charges, J. Hughes

DISTRICT LAND REGISTRIES
BIRKENHEAD – Old Market House, Hamilton Street, Birkenhead L41 5FL. Tel: 0151-473 1110. *District Land Registrar*, M. G. Garwood
COVENTRY – Leigh Court, Torrington Avenue, Coventry CV4 9XZ. Tel: 01203-860860. *District Land Registrar*, S. P. Kelway
CROYDON – Sunley House, Bedford Park, Croydon CR9 3LE. Tel: 0181-781 9100. *District Land Registrar*, D. M. J. Moss
DURHAM (BOLDON HOUSE) – Boldon House, Wheatlands Way, Pity Me, Durham DH1 5GJ. Tel: 0191-301 2345. *District Land Registrar*, R. B. Fearnley

DURHAM (SOUTHFIELD HOUSE) – Southfield House, Southfield Way, Durham DH1 5TR. Tel: 0191-301 3500. *District Land Registrar*, P. J. Timothy
GLOUCESTER – Twyver House, Bruton Way, Gloucester GL1 1DQ. Tel: 01452-511111. *District Land Registrar*, W. W. Budden
HARROW – Lyon House, Lyon Road, Harrow, Middx HA1 2EU. Tel: 0181-235 1181. *District Land Registrar*, C. Tate
KINGSTON UPON HULL – Earle House, Portland Street, Hull HU2 8JN. Tel: 01482-223244. *District Land Registrar*, S. R. Coveney
LEICESTER – Westbridge Place, Leicester LE3 5DR. Tel: 0116-265 4000. *District Land Registrar*, Mrs J. A. Goodfellow
LYTHAM – Birkenhead House, East Beach, Lytham, Lancs FY8 5AB. Tel: 01253-849849. *District Land Registrar*, J. G. Cooper
NOTTINGHAM (EAST) – Robins Wood Road, Nottingham NG8 3RQ. Tel: 0115-906 5353. *District Land Registrar*, vacant
NOTTINGHAM (WEST) – Chalfont Drive, Nottingham NG8 3RN. Tel: 0115-935 1166. *District Land Registrar*, Ms A. M. Goss
PETERBOROUGH – Touthill Close, City Road, Peterborough PE1 1XN. Tel: 01733-288288. *District Land Registrar*, C. W. Martin
PLYMOUTH – Plumer House, Tailyour Road, Crownhill, Plymouth PL6 5HY. Tel: 01752-636000. *District Land Registrar*, A. J. Pain
PORTSMOUTH – St Andrews Court, St Michael's Road, Portsmouth PO1 2JH. Tel: 01705-768888. *District Land Registrar*, S. R. Schrawat
STEVENAGE – Brickdale House, Swingate, Stevenage, Herts SG1 1XG. Tel: 01438-788888. *District Land Registrar*, vacant
SWANSEA – Tŷ Bryn Glas, High Street, Swansea SA1 1PW. Tel: 01792-458877. *District Land Registrar*, T. M. Lewis
TELFORD – Parkside Court, Hall Park Way, Telford TF3 4LR. Tel: 01952-290355. *District Land Registrar*, A. M. Lewis
TUNBRIDGE WELLS – Curtis House, Hawkenbury, Tunbridge Wells, Kent TN2 5AQ. Tel: 01892-510015. *District Land Registrar*, G. R. Tooke
WALES – Tŷ Cwm Tave, Phoenix Way, Llansamlet, Swansea SA7 9FQ. Tel: 01792-355000. *District Land Registrar*, G. A. Hughes
WEYMOUTH – Melcombe Court, 1 Cumberland Drive, Weymouth, Dorset DT4 9TT. Tel: 01305-363636. *District Land Registrar*, Mrs P. M. Reeson
YORK – James House, James Street, York YO1 1YZ. Tel: 01904-450000. *District Land Registrar*, Mrs R. F. Lovel

REGISTERS OF SCOTLAND (EXECUTIVE AGENCY)
Meadowbank House, 153 London Road, Edinburgh EH8 7AU
Tel 0131-659 6111; fax 0131-479 3688

The Registers of Scotland is an executive agency of the Scottish Office. The Registers consist of: General Register of Sasines and Land Register of Scotland; Register of Deeds in the Books of Council and Session; Register of Protests; Register of Judgments; Register of Service of Heirs; Register of the Great Seal; Register of the Quarter Seal; Register of the Prince's Seal; Register of Crown Grants; Register of Sheriffs' Commissions; Register of the Cachet Seal; Register of Inhibitions and Adjudications; Register of Entails; Register of Hornings.

The General Register of Sasines and the Land Register of Scotland form the chief security in Scotland of the rights of land and other heritable (or real) property.
Chief Executive and Keeper of the Registers of Scotland, A. W. Ramage
Deputy Keeper, A. G. Rennie
Managing Director, F. Manson
Directors, Ms M. Cameron (*Non-Executive Director*); Miss J. Kyle (*Human Resources*); Ms A. Rooney (*Finance and Planning*); M. Traynor (*Business Development and Marketing*); B. J. Corr (*IT*); I. A. Davis (*Legal Services*); D. McCallum (*Production*)

LAW COMMISSION
Conquest House, 37–38 John Street, London WC1N 2BQ
Tel 0171-453 1220; fax 0171-453 1297

The Law Commission was set up in 1965, under the Law Commissions Act 1965, to make proposals to the Government for the examination of the law in England and Wales and for its revision where it is unsuited for modern requirements, obscure, or otherwise unsatisfactory. It recommends to the Lord Chancellor programmes for the examination of different branches of the law and suggests whether the examination should be carried out by the Commission itself or by some other body. The Commission is also responsible for the preparation of Consolidation and Statute Law (Repeals) Bills.
Chairman, The Hon. Mrs Justice Arden, DBE
Commissioners, C. Harpum; A. S. Burrows; Miss D. Faber; S. Silber, QC
Secretary, M. W. Sayers

SCOTTISH LAW COMMISSION
140 Causewayside, Edinburgh EH9 1PR
Tel 0131-668 2131; fax 0131-662 4900

The Commission keeps the law in Scotland under review and makes proposals for its development and reform. It is responsible to the Scottish Courts Administration (*see* page 365).
Chairman (*part-time*), The Hon. Lord Gill
Commissioners (*full-time*), Dr E. M. Clive; N. R. Whitty; (*part-time*) Prof. K. G. C. Reid; P. S. Hodge, QC
Secretary, J. G. S. MacLean

LAW OFFICERS' DEPARTMENTS
Legal Secretariat to the Law Officers, Attorney-General's Chambers, 9 Buckingham Gate, London SW1E 6JP
Tel 0171-828 7155; fax 0171-233 7194
Attorney-General's Chambers, Royal Courts of Justice, Belfast BT1 3JY
Tel 01232-235111; fax 01232-546049

The Law Officers of the Crown for England and Wales are the Attorney-General and the Solicitor-General. The Attorney-General, assisted by the Solicitor-General, is the chief legal adviser to the Government and is also ultimately responsible for all Crown litigation. He has overall responsibility for the work of the Law Officers' Departments (the Treasury Solicitor's Department, the Crown Prosecution Service, the Serious Fraud Office and the Legal Secretariat to the Law Officers). He has a specific statutory duty to superintend the discharge of their duties by the Director of Public Prosecutions (who heads the Crown Prosecution Service) and the Director of the Serious Fraud Office. The Director of Public Prosecutions for Northern Ireland is also responsible to the Attorney-General for the performance of his functions. The Attorney-General has additional responsibilities in relation to aspects of the civil and criminal law.
Attorney-General (**£65,509*), The Rt. Hon. John Morris, QC, MP
  Private Secretary, Ms D. Hermer
  Parliamentary Private Secretary, K. Vaz, MP
Solicitor-General (**£53,716*), Ross Cranston, MP
  Private Secretary, Ms D. Hermer
Legal Secretary (*G2*), D. Seymour
Deputy Legal Secretary (*G3*), S. J. Wooler
* In addition to a parliamentary salary of £45,066

LEGAL AID BOARD
85 Gray's Inn Road, London WC1X 8AA
Tel 0171-813 1000

The Legal Aid Board has the general function of ensuring that advice, assistance, mediation and representation are available to those who need them within the framework of the Legal Aid Act 1988. In 1989 the Board took over from the Law Society responsibility for administering legal aid. The Board is a non-departmental government body whose members are appointed by the Lord Chancellor.
Chairman, Sir Tim Chessells
Deputy Chairman, H. Hodge
Members, S. Orchard (*Chief Executive*); Ms D. Charnock; Ms J. Dunkley; P. Ely; B. Harvey; P. Hollingworth; Ms D. Payne; J. Shearer; D. Sinker

SCOTTISH LEGAL AID BOARD
44 Drumsheugh Gardens, Edinburgh EH3 7SW
Tel 0131-226 7061; fax 0131-220 4878

The Scottish Legal Aid Board was set up under the Legal Aid (Scotland) Act 1986. It is responsible for ensuring that advice, assistance and representation are available in accordance with the Act. The Board is a non-departmental government body whose members are appointed by the Secretary of State for Scotland.
Chairman, Mrs J. Couper
Members, B. C. Adair; Mrs K. Blair; Prof. P. H. Grinyer; Sheriff A. Jessop; N. Kuenssberg; D. O'Carroll; Mrs Y. Osman; Ms M. Scanlan; R. Scott; M. C. Thomson, QC; A. F. Wylie, QC
Chief Executive, R. Scott

OFFICE OF THE LEGAL SERVICES OMBUDSMAN
22 Oxford Court, Oxford Street, Manchester M2 3WQ
Tel 0161-236 9532; fax 0161-236 2651

The Legal Services Ombudsman is appointed by the Lord Chancellor under the Courts and Legal Services Act 1990 to oversee the handling of complaints against solicitors, barristers, licensed conveyancers and legal executives by their professional bodies. A complainant must first complain to the relevant professional body before raising the matter with the Ombudsman. The Ombudsman is independent of the legal profession and his services are free of charge.

Legal Services Ombudsman, Ms A. Abraham
Secretary, S. Murray

OFFICE OF THE SCOTTISH LEGAL SERVICES
OMBUDSMAN
2 Greenside Lane, Edinburgh EH1 3AH
Tel 0131-556 5574; fax 0131-556 1519
Scottish Legal Services Ombudsman, G. S. Watson

LIBRARIES

LIBRARY AND INFORMATION COMMISSION
2 Sheraton Street, London W1V 4BH
Tel 0171-411 0059; fax 0171-411 0057

The Commission is an independent body set up by the
then Secretary of State for National Heritage in 1995 to
advise the Government and others on library and information matters, notably in the areas of research strategy and
international links. It also aims to promote co-operation
and co-ordination between different types of information
services.

In July 1998 the Government published a discussion
document including a proposal to merge the Library and
Information Commission and the Museums and Galleries
Commission.
Chairman, M. Evans, CBE
Commissioners, E. Arram; Sir Charles Chadwyck-Healey;
Prof. M. Collier; Prof. Judith Elkin; Ms G. Kempster;
Dr B. Lang; D. Law; Dr R. McKee; Dr Sandra Ward; M.
Wood
Chief Executive, Ms M. Haines

THE BRITISH LIBRARY
96 Euston Road, London NW1 2DB
Tel 0171-412 7000

The British Library was established in 1973. It is the UK's
national library and occupies a key position in the library
and information network. The Library aims to serve
scholarship, research, industry, commerce and all other
major users of information. Its services are based on
collections which include over 18 million volumes, 1
million discs, and 55,000 hours of tape recordings. By 1999
the Library will be based at two sites: London (St Pancras
and Colindale) and Boston Spa, W. Yorks. The British
Library's new purpose-built accommodation at St Pancras
was opened by The Queen in June 1998 and will be fully
operational by the middle of 1999. Government grant-in-
aid to the British Library in 1998–9 is £80.450 million; the
British Library St Pancras Project receives £349,000. The
Library's sponsoring department is the Department for
Culture, Media and Sport.

Access to the reading rooms at St Pancras is limited to
holders of a British Library Reader's Pass; information
about eligibility is available from the Reader Admissions
Office. The exhibition galleries and public areas are open
to all, free of charge.

Opening hours of services vary; some services may close
for one week each year. Specific information should be
checked by telephone.

In July 1998 the Government published a discussion
document including a proposal to transfer the British
Library's research function to the Library and Information
Commission.

BRITISH LIBRARY BOARD
96 Euston Road, London NW1 2DB
Tel 0171-412 7262

Chairman, Dr J. M. Ashworth
Chief Executive and Deputy Chairman, Dr B. Lang
Deputy Chief Executive, D. Russon
Director-General, Collections and Services, D. Bradbury
Part-time Members, The Hon. E. Adeane, CVO; Sir Matthew
Farrer, GCVO; Mrs P. M. Lively, OBE; Prof. M. Anderson,
FBA, FRSE; A. Bloom; Sir Peter Hordern; C. G. R. Leach;
B. Naylor; J. Ritblat; P. Scherer

BRITISH LIBRARY, BOSTON SPA
Boston Spa, Wetherby, W. Yorks LS23 7BQ
Tel 01937-546000

BIBLIOGRAPHIC SERVICES AND DOCUMENT SUPPLY,
Director (G5), M. Smith
NATIONAL BIBLIOGRAPHIC SERVICE. Tel: 01937-546585.
Director (G6), R. Smith
London Unit, 96 Euston Road, London NW1 2DB. Tel: 0171-
412 7077
ACQUISITIONS PROCESSING AND CATALOGUING,
Director (G5), S. Ede
INFORMATION SYSTEMS. Tel: 01937-546879. *Director*
(G5), J. R. Mahoney

BRITISH LIBRARY, ST PANCRAS
96 Euston Road, London NW1 2DB
Tel 0171-412 7000

PLANNING AND RESOURCES. Tel: 0171-412 7132. *Director*
(G5), D. Gesua

PUBLIC AFFAIRS. *Director* (G5), Ms J. Carr
Press and Public Relations. Tel: 0171-412 7111. *Head* (G7),
M. Jackson
Exhibitions Service, Education Service and Visitor Services. Tel:
0171-412 7332

READER SERVICES AND COLLECTION DEVELOPMENT.
Director (G5), M. J. Crump
Reader Admissions. Tel: 0171-412 7677
Reader Services. Tel: 0171-412 7676
*West European Collections, Slavonic and East European
Collections, English Language Collections*. Tel: 0171-412
7676
Newspaper Library, Colindale Avenue, London NW9 5HE.
Tel: 0171-412 7353

COLLECTIONS AND PRESERVATION. *Director* (G5), Dr
M. Foot
Preservation Service (National Preservation Office). Tel: 0171-
412 7612

SPECIAL COLLECTIONS. Tel: 0171-412 7513. *Director*
(G5), Dr A. Prochaska
Oriental and India Office Collections. Tel: 0171-412 7873
Western Manuscripts. Tel: 0171-412 7513 (opens Jan. 1999)
Map Library. Tel: 0171-412 7700
Music Library. Tel: 0171-412 7635
Philatelic Collections. Tel: 0171-412 7729
National Sound Archive. Tel: 0171-412 7440

SCIENCE REFERENCE AND INFORMATION SERVICE,
25 Southampton Buildings, London WC2A 1AW. Tel:
0171-412 7494; 9 Kean Street, London WC2B 4AT. Tel:
0171-412 7288. Moves to St Pancras early summer
1999. *Director*, A. Gomersall
Social Policy Information Service. Tel: 0171-412 7536
RESEARCH AND INNOVATION CENTRE. Tel: 0171-412
7055. *Director*, N. Macartney

NATIONAL LIBRARY OF SCOTLAND
George IV Bridge, Edinburgh EH1 1EW
Tel 0131-226 4531; fax 0131-622 4803

The Library, which was founded as the Advocates' Library in 1682, became the National Library of Scotland in 1925. It is funded by the Scottish Office. It contains about six million books and pamphlets, 18,000 current periodicals, 230 newspaper titles and 100,000 manuscripts. It has an unrivalled Scottish collection.

The Reading Room is for reference and research which cannot conveniently be pursued elsewhere. Admission is by ticket issued to an approved applicant. Opening hours: Reading Room, weekdays, 9.30–8.30 (Wednesday, 10–8.30); Saturday 9.30–1. Map Library, weekdays, 9.30–5 (Wednesday, 10–5); Saturday 9.30–1. Exhibition, weekdays, 10–5; Saturday 10–5; Sunday 2–5. Scottish Science Library, weekdays, 9.30–5 (Wednesday, 10–8.30).

Chairman of the Trustees, The Earl of Crawford and Balcarres, PC
Librarian and Secretary to the Trustees (G4), I. D. McGowan
Secretary of the Library (G6), M. C. Graham
Keeper of Printed Books (G6), Ms A. Matheson, OBE, PH.D.
Keeper of Manuscripts (G6), I. C. Cunningham
Director of Public Services (G6), A. M. Marchbank, PH.D.

NATIONAL LIBRARY OF WALES / LLYFRGELL GENEDLAETHOL CYMRU

Aberystwyth SY23 3BU
Tel 01970-632800; fax 01970-615709

The National Library of Wales was founded by royal charter in 1907, and is funded by the Welsh Office. It contains about four million printed books, 40,000 manuscripts, four million deeds and documents, numerous maps, prints and drawings, and a sound and moving image collection. It specializes in manuscripts and books relating to Wales and the Celtic peoples. It is the repository for pre-1858 Welsh probate records, manorial records and tithe documents, and certain legal records. Readers' room open weekdays, 9.30–6 (Saturday 9.30–5); closed first week of October. Admission by reader's ticket.

President, Dr R. Brinley Jones
Librarian (G4), A. M. W. Green
Heads of Departments (G6), M. W. Mainwaring (*Administration and Technical Services*); G. Jenkins (*Manuscripts and Records*); Dr W. R. M. Griffiths (*Printed Books*); Dr D. H. Owen (*Pictures and Maps*)

LIGHTHOUSE AUTHORITIES

CORPORATION OF TRINITY HOUSE

Trinity House, Tower Hill, London EC3N 4DH
Tel 0171-480 6601; fax 0171-480 7662

Trinity House, the first general lighthouse and pilotage authority in the kingdom, was granted its first charter by Henry VIII in 1514. The Corporation is the general lighthouse authority for England, Wales and the Channel Islands and maintains 72 lighthouses, 13 major floating aids to navigation (e.g. light vessels) and more than 420 buoys. The last four manned lighthouses will be automated by November 1998. The Corporation also has certain statutory jurisdiction over aids to navigation maintained by local harbour authorities and is responsible for dealing with wrecks dangerous to navigation, except those occurring within port limits or wrecks of HM ships.

The Trinity House Lighthouse Service is maintained out of the General Lighthouse Fund which is provided from light dues levied on ships calling at ports of the UK and the Republic of Ireland. The Corporation is also a deep-sea pilotage authority and a charitable organization.

The affairs of the Corporation are controlled by a board of Elder Brethren and the Secretary. A separate board, which comprises Elder Brethren, senior staff and outside representatives, currently controls the Lighthouse Service. The Elder Brethren also act as nautical assessors in marine cases in the Admiralty Division of the High Court of Justice.

ELDER BRETHREN
Master, HRH The Prince Philip, Duke of Edinburgh, KG, KT
Deputy Master, Rear-Adm. P. B. Rowe, CBE, LVO
Elder Brethren, Capt. D. J. Orr; Capt. N. M. Turner, RD; HRH The Prince of Wales, KG, KT; HRH The Duke of York, CVO, ADC; Capt. Sir David Tibbits, DSC, RN; Capt. D. A. G. Dickens; Capt. J. E. Bury; Capt. J. A. N. Bezant, DSC, RD, RNR (retd.); Capt. D. J. Cloke; Capt. Sir Miles Wingate, KCVO; The Rt. Hon. Sir Edward Heath, KG, MBE, MP; Capt. I. R. C. Saunders; Capt. P. F. Mason, CBE; Capt. T. Woodfield, OBE; The Lord Simon of Glaisdale, PC; Admiral of the Fleet the Lord Lewin, KG, GCB, LVO, DSC; Capt. D. T. Smith, RN; Cdr. Sir Robin Gillett, Bt., GBE, RD, RNR; Capt. Sir Malcolm Edge, KCVO; The Lord Cuckney; The Lord Carrington, KG, GCMG, CH, MC, PC; Sir Brian Shaw; The Lord Mackay of Clashfern, KT, PC; Sir Adrian Swire; Capt. P. H. King; The Lord Sterling of Plaistow, CBE, RNR; Cdr. M. J. Rivett-Carnac, RN; Capt. C. M. C. Stewart; Adm. Sir Jock Slater, GCB, LVO, ADC; Capt. J. R. Burton-Hall, RD; Capt. I. Gibb; Cdre P. J. Melson, CBE, RN

OFFICERS
Secretary, R. F. Dobb
Director of Finance, K. W. Clark
Director of Engineering, M. G. B. Wannell
Director of Administration, D. I. Brewer
Human Resources and Communication Manager, N. J. Cutmore
Navigation Manager, Mrs K. Hossain
Legal and Insurance Manager, J. D. Price
Head of Management Services, S. J. W. Dunning
Deputy Director of Engineering, P. N. Hyde
Senior Inspector of Shipping, J. R. Dunnett
Media and Communication Officer, H. L. Cooper

NORTHERN LIGHTHOUSE BOARD

84 George Street, Edinburgh EH2 3DA
Tel 0131-473 3100; fax 0131-220 2093

The Lighthouse Board is the general lighthouse authority for Scotland and the Isle of Man. The present board owes its origin to an Act of Parliament passed in 1786. At present the Commissioners operate under the Merchant Shipping Act 1894 and are 19 in number.

The Commissioners control 84 major automatic lighthouses, 116 minor lights and many lighted and unlighted buoys. They have a fleet of two motor vessels.

COMMISSIONERS
The Lord Advocate; the Solicitor-General for Scotland; the Lord Provosts of Edinburgh, Glasgow and Aberdeen; the Provost of Inverness; the Convener of Argyll and Bute Council; the Sheriffs-Principal of North Strathclyde, Tayside, Central and Fife, Grampian, Highlands and Islands, South Strathclyde, Dumfries and Galloway, Lothians and Borders, and Glasgow and Strathkelvin; A. J. Struthers; W. F. Hay, CBE; Capt. D. M. Cowell; Adm. Sir Michael Livesay, KCB; The Lord Maclay

OFFICERS
Chief Executive, Capt. J. B. Taylor, RN
Director of Finance, D. Gorman
Director of Engineering, W. Paterson
Director of Operations and Navigational Requirements,
   P. J. Christmas

LOCAL COMMISSIONERS

COMMISSION FOR LOCAL ADMINISTRATION IN ENGLAND
21 Queen Anne's Gate, London SW1H 9BU
Tel 0171-915 3210; fax 0171-233 0396

Local Commissioners (local government ombudsmen) are responsible for investigating complaints from members of the public against local authorities (but not town and parish councils); police authorities; the Commission for New Towns (housing functions); education appeal committees and certain other authorities. The Commissioners are appointed by the Crown on the recommendation of the Secretary of State for the Environment, Transport and the Regions.

Certain types of action are excluded from investigation, including personnel matters and commercial transactions unless they relate to the purchase or sale of land. Complaints can be sent direct to the Local Government Ombudsman or through a councillor, although the Local Government Ombudsman will not consider a complaint unless the council has had an opportunity to investigate and reply to a complainant.

A free leaflet *Complaint about the council? How to complain to the Local Government Ombudsman* is available from the Commission's office.

Chairman and Chief Executive of the Commission and Local Commissioner (£112,011), E. B. C. Osmotherly, CB
Vice-Chairman and Local Commissioner (£84,586), Mrs P. A. Thomas
Local Commissioner (£83,586), J. R. White
Member (ex officio), The Parliamentary Commissioner for Administration
Deputy Chief Executive and Secretary (£57,340), N. J. Karney

COMMISSION FOR LOCAL ADMINISTRATION IN WALES
Derwen House, Court Road, Bridgend CF31 1BN
Tel 01656-661325; fax 01656-658317

The Local Commissioner for Wales has similar powers to the Local Commissioners in England. The Commissioner is appointed by the Crown on the recommendation of the Secretary of State for Wales. A free leaflet *Your Local Ombudsman in Wales* is available from the Commission's office.

Local Commissioner, E. R. Moseley
Secretary, D. Bowen
Member (ex officio), The Parliamentary Commissioner for Administration

COMMISSIONER FOR LOCAL ADMINISTRATION IN SCOTLAND
23 Walker Street, Edinburgh EH3 7HX
Tel 0131-225 5300; fax 0131-225 9495

The Local Commissioner for Scotland has similar powers to the Local Commissioners in England, and is appointed by the Crown on the recommendation of the Secretary of State for Scotland.

Local Commissioner, F. C. Marks, OBE
Deputy Commissioner and Secretary, Ms J. H. Renton

LONDON REGIONAL TRANSPORT
55 Broadway, London SW1H 0BD
Tel 0171-222 5600

Subject to the financial objectives and principles approved by the Secretary of State for the Environment, Transport and the Regions, London Regional Transport has a general duty to provide or secure the provision of public transport services for Greater London.

Chairman (part-time non-executive) (acting), B. Appleton
Chief Executive, D. Tunnicliffe, CBE
Member, and Managing Director of London Transport Buses, C. Hodson, CBE
Member, and Managing Director of London Underground Ltd, vacant

LORD ADVOCATE'S DEPARTMENT
2 Carlton Gardens, London SW1Y 5AA
Tel 0171-210 1050; fax 0171-210 1025

The Law Officers for Scotland are the Lord Advocate and the Solicitor-General for Scotland. The Lord Advocate's Department is responsible for drafting Scottish legislation, for providing legal advice to other departments on Scottish questions and for assistance to the Law Officers for Scotland in certain of their legal duties.

Lord Advocate (£80,219), The Lord Hardie, PC, QC
Private Secretary, J. A. Gibbons
Solicitor-General for Scotland (£68,648), Colin Boyd, QC
Private Secretary, J. A. Gibbons
Legal Secretary and First Scottish Parliamentary Counsel (SCS), J. C. McCluskie, QC
Assistant Legal Secretaries and Scottish Parliamentary Counsel (SCS), G. M. Clark; G. Kowalski; P. J. Layden, TD; C. A. M. Wilson
Assistant Legal Secretary and Depute Scottish Parliamentary Counsel (SCS), J. D. Harkness

LORD CHANCELLOR'S DEPARTMENT
Selborne House, 54–60 Victoria Street, London SW1E 6QW
Tel 0171-210 8500
E-mail: enquiries.lcdhq@gtnet.gov.uk
Web: http://www.open.gov.uk/lcd

The Lord Chancellor appoints Justices of the Peace (except in the Duchy of Lancaster) and advises the Crown on the appointment of most members of the higher judiciary. He is responsible for promoting general reforms in the civil law, for the procedure of the civil courts and for legal aid. He is a member of the Cabinet. He also has ministerial responsibility for magistrates' courts, which are administered locally. Administration of the Supreme Court and county courts in England and Wales was taken over by the Court Service, an executive agency of the department, in April 1995.

The Lord Chancellor is also responsible for ensuring that letters patent and other formal documents are passed in the proper form under the Great Seal of the Realm, of which he is the custodian. The work in connection with this is carried out under his direction in the Office of the Clerk of the Crown in Chancery.

The Lord Chancellor is also the senior Lord of Appeal in Ordinary and speaker of the House of Lords.
Lord Chancellor (£148,850), The Lord Irvine of Lairg, PC, QC
Principal Private Secretary, Ms J. Rowe
Special Adviser, G. Hart
Parliamentary Private Secretaries, A. Wright, MP; D. Lock, MP
Minister of State, Geoff Hoon, MP
Private Secretary, J. Freeman
Permanent Secretary (SCS), Sir Hayden Phillips, KCB
Private Secretary, Ms L. Sullivan

CROWN OFFICE
House of Lords, London SW1A 0PW
Tel 0171-219 4713

Clerk of the Crown in Chancery (SCS), Sir Hayden Phillips, KCB
Deputy Clerk of the Crown in Chancery (SCS), vacant
Clerk of the Chamber, C. I. P. Denyer

JUDICIAL APPOINTMENTS GROUP
Tel 0171-210 8926

Head of Group (SCS), M. Huebner, CB
Heads of Divisions (SCS), D. E. Staff (*Policy and Conditions of Service*); Mrs M. Pigott (*Circuit Bench*); Miss J. Killick (*Circuit Bench*); E. Adams (*District Bench and Tribunals*); R. Venne (*Magistrates' Appointments*)

Judicial Studies Board
9th Floor, Millbank Tower, London SW1P 4QW
Tel 0171-925 4762

Secretary (SCS), D. Hill

POLICY GROUP
Tel 0171-210 8719

Director-General (SCS), I. M. Burns, CB
Heads of Divisions (SCS), P. G. Harris (*Legal Aid*); M. Ormerod (*Criminal Policy*); D. Gladwell (*Civil Justice*); R. Sams (*Law Reform and Tribunals*); W. Arnold (*Family Policy*); A. Cogbill (*Civil Justice and Legal Aid Reform*); vacant (*Special Projects*); Ms M. Morse (*Community Legal Services*); Ms A. Finlay (*ECHR Incorporation Team*); D. A. Hill (*Modernization of Justice and Legal Services Development*)
Head of Secretariat and Agency Monitoring Unit (SCS), Ms A. Jones

LEGAL ADVISER'S GROUP
Tel 0171-210 0711

Legal Adviser (SCS), P. Jenkins
Heads of Divisions (SCS), M. H. Collon (*Legal Advice and Litigation*); A. Wallace (*International and Common Law Services*); M. Kron (*Drafting Services*)

COMMUNICATIONS GROUP
Tel 0171-210 8672

Director of Communications (SCS), A. Percival, LVO

CORPORATE SERVICES GROUP
Tel 0171-210 8503

Director of Corporate Services and Principal Establishment and Finance Officer (SCS), Mrs E. Grimsey
Heads of Divisions (SCS), Mrs S. Anderson (*Personnel Management*); Mrs S. Webber (*Personnel Management*); S. Smith (*Finance*); K. Cregeen (*Facilities and Support Services*); A. Rummins (*Internal Assurance*); K. Garrett (*Statutory Publications Office*)

MAGISTRATES' COURTS GROUP
Tel 0171-210 8809

Director (SCS), L. C. Oates
Heads of Divisions (SCS), Mrs S. Field (*Magistrates' Courts*); P. White (*LIBRA Project and Magistrates' Courts IT*)

ECCLESIASTICAL PATRONAGE
10 Downing Street, London SW1A 2AA
Tel 0171-930 4433

Secretary for Ecclesiastical Patronage, J. H. Holroyd, CB
Assistant Secretary for Ecclesiastical Patronage, N. C. Wheeler

MAGISTRATES' COURTS' SERVICE INSPECTORATE
Southside, 105 Victoria Street, London SW1E 6QJ
Tel 0171-210 1655

Chief Inspector (SCS), C. Chivers
Senior Inspectors (SCS), Ms J. Eeles; D. Gear; C. Monson; Ms S. Steel

LORD CHANCELLOR'S ADVISORY COMMITTEE ON STATUTE LAW
67 Tufton Street, London SW1P 3QS
Tel 0171-210 2600

The Advisory Committee advises the Lord Chancellor on all matters relating to the revision, modernization and publication of the statute book.
Chairman, The Lord Chancellor
Deputy Chairman, Sir Thomas Legg, KCB, QC
Members, C. Jenkins, CB, QC; J. C. McCluskie, QC; R. Brodie, CB; R. H. H White; G. Gray; J. M. Davies; Sir Donald Limon, KCB; The Hon. Mrs Justice Arden, DBE; The Hon. Lord Gill; A. H. Hammond, CB; Mrs E. Grimsey; P. Macdonald, CBE; C. Carey; K. Garrett
Secretary, vacant

EXECUTIVE AGENCIES

THE COURT SERVICE
Southside, 105 Victoria Street, London SW1E 6QT
Tel 0171-210 1775

The Court Service provides administrative support to the Supreme Court of England and Wales, county courts and a number of tribunals.
Chief Executive (SCS), I. Magee
Director of Civil and Family Operations (SCS), P. L. Jacob
Director of Criminal Operations (SCS), N. J. Smedley
Director of Tribunals (SCS), P. Stockton

Resources and Support Services Directorate
Director (SCS), C. W. V. Everett
SCS, K. Pogson (*Resources and Planning*); Miss B. Kenny (*Personnel and Training*); A. Shaw (*Accommodation and Procurement*); I. Hyams (*Information Services*)

Royal Courts of Justice
Strand, London WC2A 2LL
Tel 0171-936 6000
Administrator, G. E. Calvett
For Supreme Court departments and offices and circuit administrators, *see* Law Courts and Offices section

HM LAND REGISTRY
— *see* page 316

PUBLIC RECORD OFFICE
— *see* page 336

PUBLIC TRUST OFFICE
— *see* page 335

LORD GREAT CHAMBERLAIN'S OFFICE
House of Lords, London SW1A 0PW
Tel 0171-219 3100; fax 0171-219 2500

The Lord Great Chamberlain is a Great Officer of State, the office being hereditary since the grant of Henry I to the family of De Vere, Earls of Oxford. It is now a joint hereditary office between the Cholmondeley and Carington families. The Lord Great Chamberlain is responsible for the royal apartments of the Palace of Westminster, i.e. The Queen's Robing Room, the Royal Gallery and, in conjunction with the Lord Chancellor and the Speaker, Westminster Hall. The Lord Great Chamberlain has particular responsibility for the internal administrative arrangements within the House of Lords for State Openings of Parliament.

Lord Great Chamberlain, The Marquess of Cholmondeley
Secretary to the Lord Great Chamberlain, Gen. Sir Edward Jones, KCB, CBE
Clerks to the Lord Great Chamberlain, Miss C. J. Bostock; Miss R. M. Wilkinson

LORD PRIVY SEAL'S OFFICE
Privy Council Office, 68 Whitehall, London SW1A 2AT
Tel 0171-270 3000

The Lord Privy Seal is a member of the Cabinet and Leader of the House of Lords. She has no departmental portfolio, but is a member of a number of domestic and economic Cabinet committees. She is responsible to the Prime Minister for the organization of government business in the House and has a responsibility to the House itself to advise it on procedural matters and other difficulties which arise.

Lord Privy Seal, Leader of the House of Lords and Minister for Women, The Baroness Jay of Paddington, PC
Principal Private Secretary, Ms L. Bainsfair
Private Secretary (House of Lords), S. Burton

LOTTERY, OFFICE OF THE NATIONAL
— *see* page 328

OFFICE OF MANPOWER ECONOMICS
Oxford House, 76 Oxford Street, London W1N 9FD
Tel 0171-467 7244; fax 0171-467 7248

The Office of Manpower Economics was set up in 1971. It is an independent non-statutory organization which is responsible for servicing independent review bodies which advise on the pay of various public service groups (*see* Review Bodies, pages 337–8), the Pharmacists Review Panel and the Police Negotiating Board. The Office is also responsible for servicing *ad hoc* bodies of inquiry and for undertaking research into pay and associated matters as requested by the Government.

OME Director, M. J. Horsman
Director, Statistics, Office Services and Police Secretariat, G. S. Charles
Director, Armed Forces and Teachers' Secretariats, G. McGregor
Director, Health Secretariat, and OME Deputy Director, Miss S. M. Haird
Director, Senior Salaries Secretariat, Mrs C. Haworth
Press Liaison Officer, M. C. Cahill

MENTAL HEALTH ACT COMMISSION
Maid Marian House, 56 Hounds Gate, Nottingham NG1 6BG
Tel 0115-943 7100; fax 0115-943 7101

The Mental Health Act Commission was established in 1983. Its functions are to keep under review the operation of the Mental Health Act 1983; to visit and meet patients detained under the Act; to investigate complaints falling within the Commission's remit; to operate the consent to treatment safeguards in the Mental Health Act; to publish a biennial report on its activities; to monitor the implementation of the Code of Practice; and to advise ministers. Commissioners are appointed by the Secretary of State for Health.

Chairman, The Viscountess Runciman of Doxford, OBE
Vice-Chairman, Prof. R. Williams
Chief Executive (G6), W. Bingley

MILLENNIUM COMMISSION
Portland House, Stag Place, London SW1E 5EZ
Tel 0171-880 2001; fax 0171-880 2000

The Millennium Commission was established in February 1994 and is funded by the Department for Culture, Media and Sport. It is an independent body which distributes money from National Lottery proceeds to projects to mark the millennium.

Chairman, The Rt. Hon. Chris Smith, MP
Members, Dr D. Clarke; Prof. Heather Couper, FRAS; Earl of Dalkeith; The Lord Glentoran, CBE; Sir John Hall; The Rt. Hon. M. Heseltine, MP; S. Jenkins; The Baroness Scotland of Asthal, QC
Director, M. O'Connor

MONOPOLIES AND MERGERS COMMISSION
New Court, 48 Carey Street, London WC2A 2JT
Tel 0171-324 1467; fax 0171-324 1400

The Commission was established in 1948 as the Monopolies and Restrictive Practices Commission and became the Monopolies and Mergers Commission under the Fair Trading Act 1973. Its role is to investigate and report on matters which are referred to it by the Secretary of State for Trade and Industry or the Director-General of Fair Trading or, in the case of privatized industries, by the appropriate regulator. Its decisions are determined by the criteria set out in the legislation covering the different types of reference. The main types of reference which can be made are: monopolies; mergers; newspaper mergers; general, involving general practices in an industry; restrictive labour practices; competition, involving anti-competitive practices of individual firms; public sector audits; privatized industries; and Channel 3 (ITV) networking arrangements between holders of regional Channel 3 licences. References may be made under the Fair Trading Act 1973, the Competition Act 1980, the Broadcasting Act or other relevant statutes.

The Commission consists of about 35 members, including a full-time chairman and three part-time deputy chairmen, all appointed by the Secretary of State for Trade and Industry. Each inquiry is conducted on behalf of the

Commission by a group of four to six members who are appointed by the chairman.

The Government has announced plans to reform competition law and replace the Commission with a Competition Commission, subject to parliamentary approval.

Chairman (£120,000), D. Morris, ph.D.

Deputy Chairmen (£51,000 – £68,000), P. G. Corbett, CBE; Ms D. Kingsmill

Members (£14,731/*£9,821 each), H. Aldous; Prof. J. Beatson; R. Bertram; Mrs S. Brown; Prof. M. Cave; *A. T. Clothier; R. H. F. Croft, CB; C. Darke; *R. O. Davies; *N. H. Finney, OBE; *Sir Archibald Forster; Prof. P. Geroski; *Sir Ronald Halstead, CBE; D. B. Hammond; *Ms J. C. Hanratty; C. Henderson, CB; *Ms P. A. Hodgson, CBE; D. J. Jenkins, MBE; R. Lyons; P. MacKay, CB; *Ms K. M. H. Mortimer; *R. J. Munson; *Prof. D. M. G. Newberry, FBA; Dr Gill Owen; Prof. J. F. Pickering; M. R. Prosser; A. Pryor, CB; R. Rawlinson; Prof. Judith Rees; *T. S. Richmond, MBE; J. Rickford; Dr Ann Robinson; *J. K. Roe; Ms H. Shovelton; *G. H. Stacy, CBE; D. Start; Prof. A. Steele

Secretary, Miss P. Boys

* Reserve members

MUSEUMS

MUSEUMS AND GALLERIES COMMISSION
16 Queen Anne's Gate, London SW1H 9AA
Tel 0171-233 4200; fax 0171-233 3686

Established in 1931 as the Standing Commission on Museums and Galleries, the Commission was renamed in 1981. Its sponsor department is the Department for Culture, Media and Sport. The Commission advises the Government, including the Department of Education for Northern Ireland, the Scottish Education Department and the Welsh Office, on museum affairs. Commissioners are appointed by the Prime Minister.

The Commission's executive functions include providing the services of the Museums Security Adviser; allocating grants to the seven Area Museum Councils in England; funding and monitoring the work of the Museum Documentation Association; and administering grant schemes for non-national museums. The Commission administers the arrangements for government indemnities and the acceptance of works of art in lieu of inheritance tax, and its Conservation Unit advises on conservation and environmental standards. A registration scheme for museums in the UK is operated by the Commission.

In July 1998 the Government published a discussion document including a proposal to merge the Museums and Galleries Commission and the Library and Information Commission.

Chairman, J. Joll

Members, Prof. P. Bateson, FRS (*Vice-Chairman*); The Baroness Brigstocke; Prof. R. Buchanan; Ms R. Butler; Penelope, Viscountess Cobham; R. Foster; L. Grossman; R. Hiscox; Adm. Sir John Kerr, GCB; Dr I. McKenzie Smith, RSA; A. Warhurst, CBE; Mrs C. Wilson

Director and Secretary, T. Mason

THE BRITISH MUSEUM
Great Russell Street, London WC1B 3DG
Tel 0171-636 1555; fax 0171-323 8614

The British Museum houses the national collection of antiquities, ethnography, coins and paper money, medals, and prints and drawings. The British Museum may be said to date from 1753, when Parliament approved the holding of a public lottery to raise funds for the purchase of the collections of Sir Hans Sloane and the Harleian manuscripts, and for their proper housing and maintenance. The building (Montagu House) was opened in 1759. The present buildings were erected between 1823 and the present day, and the original collection has increased to its present dimensions by gifts and purchases. Total government grant-in-aid for 1998 – 9 is £32.921 million.

BOARD OF TRUSTEES
Appointed by the Sovereign, HRH The Duke of Gloucester, KG, GCVO
Appointed by the Prime Minister, N. Barber; Prof. Gillian Beer, FBA; Sir John Boyd; E. J. P. Browne, FE ng.; Sir Matthew Farrer, GCVO; Sir Michael Hopkins, CBE, RA, RIBA; Sir Joseph Hotung; Prof. M. Kemp, FBA; S. Keswick; Hon. Mrs M. Marten, OBE; Sir John Morgan, KCMG; The Rt. Hon. Sir Timothy Raison; Sir Martin Rees, FRS; Prof. Sir Gunter Treitel, DCL, FBA, QC
Nominated by the Learned Societies, Prof. Jean Thomas, CBE (*Royal Society*); A. Jones, RA (*Royal Academy*); Sir Claus Moser, KCB, CBE, FBA (*British Academy*); The Lord Renfrew of Kaimsthorn, FBA, FSA (*Society of Antiquaries*)
Appointed by the Trustees of the British Museum, G. C. Greene, CBE (*Chairman*); Sir David Attenborough, CH, CVO, CBE, FRS; Prof. Rosemary Cramp, CBE, FSA; The Lord Egremont; Dr Jennifer Montagu, FBA

OFFICERS
Director, Dr R. G. W. Anderson, FRSC, FSA
Director of Finance and Resources, A. B. Blackstock
Secretary, Mrs C. Nihoul Parker
Head of Public Services, G. A. L. House
Head of Press and Public Relations, A. E. Hamilton
Head of Design, Miss M. Hall, OBE
Head of Education, J. F. Reeve
Head of Administration, C. E. I. Jones
Head of Building Development and Planning, K. T. Stannard
Head of Building Management, T. R. A. Giles
Head of Finance, Miss S. E. Davies
Head of Personnel and Office Services, Miss B. A. Hughes

KEEPERS
Keeper of Prints and Drawings, A. V. Griffiths
Keeper of Coins and Medals, Dr A. M. Burnett
Keeper of Egyptian Antiquities, W. V. Davies
Keeper of Western Asiatic Antiquities, Dr J. E. Curtis
Keeper of Greek and Roman Antiquities, Dr D. J. R. Williams
Keeper of Medieval and Later Antiquities, J. Cherry
Keeper of Prehistoric and Romano-British Antiquities, Dr T. M. Potter
Keeper of Japanese Antiquities, V. T. Harris
Keeper of Oriental Antiquities, R. J. Knox
Keeper of Ethnography, B. J. Mack
Keeper of Scientific Research, Dr S. G. E. Bowman
Keeper of Conservation, W. A. Oddy

NATURAL HISTORY MUSEUM
Cromwell Road, London SW7 5BD
Tel 0171-938 9123

The Natural History Museum originates from the natural history departments of the British Museum, which grew extensively during the 19th century; in 1860 the natural history collection was moved from Bloomsbury to a new location. Part of the site of the 1862 International Exhibition in South Kensington was acquired for the new museum, and the Museum opened to the public in 1881. In 1963 the Natural History Museum became completely independent with its own board of trustees. The Walter

Rothschild Zoological Museum, Tring, bequeathed by the second Lord Rothschild, has formed part of the Museum since 1938. The Geological Museum merged with the Natural History Museum in 1985. Total government grant-in-aid for 1998–9 is £26.96 million.

BOARD OF TRUSTEES
Appointed by the Prime Minister: Sir Robert May, FRS (*Chairman*); Mrs J. M. d'Abo; Sir Denys Henderson; Sir Crispin Tickell, GCMG, KCVO; Prof. Sir Ronald Oxburgh, FRS; Dame Anne McLaren, DBE, FRS; Sir Richard Sykes; Miss J. Mayhew
Appointed by the Secretary of State for Culture, Media and Sport, Prof. C. Leaver, FRS
Appointed by the Trustees of the Natural History Museum, Prof. Sir Brian Follett, FRS; The Lord Palumbo; Prof. K. O'Nions, FRS

SENIOR STAFF
Director, N. R. Chalmers, PH.D.
Director of Science, Prof. P. Henderson, D.Phil.
Policy and Planning Co-ordinator, Ms N. Donlon
Science Policy Co-ordinator, J. Jackson
Head of Development and Marketing, Ms T. Burman
Keeper of Zoology, P. Rainbow
Director, Tring Zoological Museum, Mrs T. Wild
Keeper of Entomology, R. Vane-Wright
Keeper of Botany, S. Blackmore, PH.D.
Keeper of Palaeontology, Prof. S. K. Donaldson
Keeper of Mineralogy, Dr A. Fleet
Head of Finance, N. Greenwood
Head of Human Resources, Mrs J. Rowe
Head of Library and Information Services, R. Lester
Head of Education and Exhibitions (G5), Dr G. Clarke
Head of Visitor Services, Mrs W. B. Gullick
Head of Estates, G. Pellow

THE SCIENCE MUSEUM
Exhibition Road, London SW7 2DD
Tel 0171-938 8000; fax 0171-938 8112

The Science Museum, part of the National Museum of Science and Industry, houses the national collections of science, technology, industry and medicine. The Museum began as the science collection of the South Kensington Museum and first opened in 1857. In 1883 it acquired the collections of the Patent Museum and in 1909 the science collections were transferred to the new Science Museum, leaving the art collections with the Victoria and Albert Museum.

Some of the Museum's commercial aircraft, agricultural machinery, and road and rail transport collections are at Wroughton, Wilts. The National Museum of Science and Industry also incorporates the National Railway Museum, York and the National Museum of Photography, Film and Television, Bradford.

Total government grant-in-aid for 1998–9 is £21.281 million.

BOARD OF TRUSTEES
Chairman, Sir Peter Williams, CBE, PH.D., FEng.
Members, HRH The Duke of Kent, KG, GCMG, GCVO, ADC; Dr M. Archer; G. Dyke; Dr A. Grocock; Mrs A. Higham, OBE; Mrs J. Kennedy, OBE; Dame Bridget Ogilvie, DBE; The Lord Puttnam, CBE; Sir Michael Quinlan, GCB; D. E. Rayner, CBE; Sir Christopher Wates

OFFICERS
Director, Sir Neil Cossons, OBE, FSA
Assistant Director and Head of Resource Management Division, J. J. Defries
Head of Personnel and Legal Services, C. Gosling

Head of Finance, Ms A. Caine
Head of Information Systems, S. Gordon
Head of Estates, J. Bevin
Assistant Director and Head of Collections Division (*acting*), Dr D. A. Robinson
Head of Physical Sciences and Engineering Group (*acting*), Dr A. Q. Morton
Head of Life and Communications Technologies Group, Dr R. F. Bud
Head of Collections Management Group, Dr S. Keene
Assistant Director and Head of Public Affairs Division, C. M. Pemberton
Head of Corporate Relations, F. Kirk
Head of Commercial Development, M. Sullivan
Head of Marketing and Communications, H. Roderick
Head of Wellcome Wing Commercial and Access, B. Jones
Assistant Director, Wellcome Wing Project Director and Head of Science Communication Division, Prof. J. R. Durant
Head of Education and Programmes, Dr R. Jackson
Head of Exhibition and Wellcome Wing Content, Dr G. Farmelo
Head of Design, T. Molloy
Head of National Railway Museum, A. Scott
Head of National Museum of Photography, Film and Television, Ms A. Nevill

VICTORIA AND ALBERT MUSEUM
Cromwell Road, London SW7 2RL
Tel 0171-938 8500

The Victoria and Albert Museum is the national museum of fine and applied art and design. It descends directly from the Museum of Manufactures, which opened in Marlborough House in 1852 after the Great Exhibition of 1851. The Museum was moved in 1857 to become part of the South Kensington Museum. It was renamed the Victoria and Albert Museum in 1899. It also houses the National Art Library and Print Room.

The Museum administers three branch museums: the National Museum of Childhood in Bethnal Green, the Theatre Museum in Covent Garden, and the Wellington Museum at Apsley House. The museum in Bethnal Green was opened in 1872 and the building is the most important surviving example of the type of glass and iron construction used by Paxton for the Great Exhibition. Total government grant-in-aid for 1998–9 is £29.127 million.

BOARD OF TRUSTEES
Chairman, vacant
Deputy Chairman, J. Scott, CBE, FSA
Members, Miss N. Campbell; Penelope, Viscountess Cobham; Lady Copisarow; R. Fitch, CBE; Prof. C. Frayling, PH.D.; Sir Terence Heiser, GCB; Mrs A. Heseltine; A. Irby III; A. Snow; Prof. J. Steer, FSA, DLitt.; A. Wheatley; Prof. C. White, CVO, FBA
Secretary to the Board of Trustees, P. A. Wilson

OFFICERS
Director, Dr A. C. N. Borg, CBE, FSA
Assistant Directors, T. J. Stevens (*Collections*); J. W. Close (*Administration*)
Head of Buildings and Estate, R. P. Whitehouse
Chief Curator, Ceramics and Glass, Dr O. Watson
Head of Conservation, Dr J. Ashley-Smith
Head of Education, D. Anderson
Chief Curator, Far Eastern, Miss R. Kerr
Head of Finance and Central Services, Miss R. M. Sykes
Chief Curator, Furniture and Woodwork, C. Wilk
Chief Curator, Indian and South-East Asian, Dr D. Swallow
Head of Information Systems Services, A. Cooper
Head of Major Projects, Mrs G. F. Miles

Chief Curator, Metalwork, Silver and Jewellery,
Mrs P. Glanville
Chief Librarian, National Art Library, J. F. van den Wateren
Head of Personnel, Mrs G. Henchley
Chief Curator, Prints, Drawings and Paintings,
Miss S. B. Lambert
Head of Public Services, R. Cole-Hamilton
Head of Records and Collections Services, A. Seal
Head of Research, P. Greenhalgh
Head of Safety and Security, R. Bland
Chief Curator, Sculpture, Dr P. E. D. Williamson
Chief Curator, Textiles and Dress, Mrs V. D. Mendes
Managing Director, V. and A. Enterprises Ltd, M. Cass
Director of Development, Ms C. Morley
Head of National Museum of Childhood (acting), Dr S.
Laurence
Head of Theatre Museum, Miss M. Benton
Head of Wellington Museum, Miss A. Robinson

MUSEUM OF LONDON
London Wall, London EC2Y 5HN
Tel 0171-600 3699; fax 0171-600 1058

The Museum of London illustrates the history of London
from prehistoric times to the present day. It opened in 1976
and is based on the amalgamation of the former Guildhall
Museum and London Museum. The Museum is controlled by a Board of Governors, appointed (nine each) by
the Government and the Corporation of London. The
Museum is currently funded jointly by the Department for
Culture, Media and Sport and the Corporation of London,
each contributing £4.210 million in 1998–9.
Chairman of Board of Governors, P. Revell-Smith, CBE
Director, Dr S. Thurley

COMMONWEALTH INSTITUTE
Kensington High Street, London W8 6NQ
Tel 0171-603 4535; fax 0171-602 7374

The Commonwealth Institute is the UK centre responsible for promoting the Commonwealth in Britain through
exhibitions, educational programmes, publications, resources and information. The Institute houses an Education Centre, a Commonwealth Resource Centre (CRC)
and Literature Library, and a Conference and Events
Centre.
  The Institute is an independent statutory body funded
by the British government with contributions from other
Commonwealth governments. It is controlled by a board of
governors which includes the high commissioners of all
Commonwealth countries represented in London. Total
government grant-in-aid for 1998–9 is £600,000.
Director-General, D. French
Administrative and Commercial Director, P. Kennedy
Head of CRC, Ms K. Peters

IMPERIAL WAR MUSEUM
Lambeth Road, London SE1 6HZ
Tel 0171-416 5000; fax 0171-416 5374

The Museum, founded in 1917, illustrates and records all
aspects of the two world wars and other military operations
involving Britain and the Commonwealth since 1914. It
was opened in its present home, formerly Bethlem
Hospital or Bedlam, in 1936. The Museum also administers HMS *Belfast* in the Pool of London, Duxford Airfield
near Cambridge and the Cabinet War Rooms in Westminster.
  Total government grant-in-aid for 1998–9 is £10.573
million.

OFFICERS
Director-General, R. W. K. Crawford
Secretary, J. J. Chadwick, OBE
Assistant Directors, D. A. Needham (*Administration*); Miss
K. J. Carmichael (*Collections*); G. Marsh (*Planning and
Development*)
Director of Duxford Airfield, E. O. Inman, OBE
Director of HMS Belfast, E. J. Wenzel

KEEPERS
Department of Museum Services, C. Dowling, D.Phil.
Department of Documents, R. W. A. Suddaby
Department of Exhibits and Firearms, D. J. Penn
Department of Printed Books, R. Golland
Department of Art, Miss A. H. Weight
Department of Film, R. B. N. Smither
Department of Photographs, Ms B. Kinally
Department of Sound Records, Mrs M. A. Brooks
Department of Marketing and Trading, Miss A. Godwin
Curator of the Cabinet War Rooms, P. Reed

NATIONAL MARITIME MUSEUM
Greenwich, London SE10 9NF
Tel 0181-858 4422; fax 0181-312 6632

Established by Act of Parliament in 1934, the National
Maritime Museum illustrates the maritime history of
Great Britain in the widest sense, underlining the importance of the sea and its influence on the nation's power,
wealth, culture, technology and institutions. The Museum
is in three groups of buildings in Greenwich Park – the
main building, the Queen's House (built by Inigo Jones,
1616–35) and the Old Royal Observatory (including
Wren's Flamsteed House). Total government grant-in-
aid for 1998–9 is £10.184 million.
Director, R. L. Ormond

NATIONAL ARMY MUSEUM
Royal Hospital Road, London SW3 4HT
Tel 0171-730 0717; fax 0171-823 6573

The National Army Museum covers the history of five
centuries of the British Army. It was established by royal
charter in 1960. Total government grant-in-aid for
1998–9 is £3.2 million.
Director, I. G. Robertson
Assistant Directors, D. K. Smurthwaite; A. J. Guy;
Maj. P. R. Bateman

ROYAL AIR FORCE MUSEUM
Grahame Park Way, London NW9 5LL
Tel 0181-205 2266; fax 0181-200 1751

Situated on the former airfield at RAF Hendon, the
Museum illustrates the development of aviation from
before the Wright brothers to the present-day RAF. Total
government grant-in-aid for 1998–9, including funding
for the aerospace museum at Cosford, is £4.86 million.
Director, Dr M. A. Fopp
Assistant Directors, H. Hall; J. Hutchinson; A. Wright
Senior Keeper, P. Elliott

NATIONAL MUSEUMS AND GALLERIES
ON MERSEYSIDE
PO Box 33, 127 Dale Street, Liverpool L69 3LA
Tel 0151-207 0001; fax 0151-478 4190

The Board of Trustees of the National Museums and
Galleries on Merseyside is responsible for the Liverpool
Museum, the Merseyside Maritime Museum (incorporat-
ing HM Customs and Excise National Museum), the
Museum of Liverpool Life, the Lady Lever Art Gallery,

the Walker Art Gallery and Sudley House, and the Conservation Centre. Total government grant-in-aid for 1998–9 is £12.696 million.

Chairman of the Board of Trustees, D. McDonnell
Director, R. Foster
Keeper of Art Galleries, J. Treuherz
Keeper of Conservation, A. Durham
Keeper, Liverpool Museum, Ms L. Knowles
Keeper, Merseyside Maritime Museum and Museum of Liverpool Life, M. Stammers

NATIONAL MUSEUMS AND GALLERIES OF WALES/AMGUEDDFEYDD AC ORIELAU CENEDLAETHOL CYMRU
Cathays Park, Cardiff CF1 3NP
Tel 01222-573500; fax 01222-577010

The National Museums and Galleries of Wales comprise the National Museum and Gallery, the Museum of Welsh Life, the Roman Legionary Museum, Turner House Art Gallery, the Welsh Slate Museum, the Segontium Roman Museum and the Museum of the Welsh Woollen Industry. Total funding from the Welsh Office for 1998–9 is £12.427 million.

President, M. C. T. Prichard, CBE
Vice-President, A. Thomas

OFFICERS
Director, C. Ford, CBE
Assistant Directors, T. Arnold (*Resource Management*); C. Thomas (*Public Services*); A. Southall (*Museums Development*); I. Fell (*Education and Interpretation*); Dr E. Williams (*Collections and Research*)
Keeper of Geology, M. G. Bassett, ph. D.
Keeper of Bio-diversity and Systematic Diversity, Dr P. G. Oliver
Keeper of Art, D. Alston
Keeper of Archaeology, R. Brewer
Keeper, Museum of Welsh Life, J. Williams-Davies
Officer in Charge, Roman Legionary Museum (*acting*), D. Dollery
Keeper in Charge, Turner House Art Gallery, D. Alston
Keeper in Charge, Welsh Slate Museum, D. Roberts, ph.D.
Officer in Charge, Segontium Roman Museum, R. J. Brewer
Officer in Charge, Museum of the Welsh Woollen Industry, J. Williams-Davies

NATIONAL MUSEUMS OF SCOTLAND
Chambers Street, Edinburgh EH1 1JF
Tel 0131-225 7534; fax 0131-220 4819

The National Museums of Scotland comprise the Royal Museum of Scotland, the Scottish United Services Museum, the Scottish Agricultural Museum, the Museum of Flight, Shambellie House Museum of Costume and (from 1 December 1998) the Museum of Scotland. Total funding from the Scottish Office for 1998–9 is £16.9 million.

BOARD OF TRUSTEES
Chairman, R. Smith, FSA SCOT.
Members, Countess of Dalkeith; Prof. T. Devine; Dr L. Glasser, MBE, FRSE; S. G. Gordon, CBE; Sir Alistair Grant, FRSE; Dr V. van Heyingen, FRSE; G. Johnston, OBE, TD; Prof. P. H. Jones; Prof. A. Manning, OBE; Prof. J. Murray; Sir William Purves, CBE, DSO; Dr A. Ritchie, OBE; The Countess of Rosebery; Sir John Thomson

OFFICERS
Director, M. Jones, FSA, FSA SCOT., FRSA
Depute Director (Resources) and Project Director, Museum of Scotland, I. Hooper, FSA SCOT.

Depute Director (Collections) and Keeper of History and Applied Art, Miss D. Idiens, FRSA, FSA SCOT.
Development Director, C. McCallum
Keeper of Archaeology, D. V. Clarke, ph. D., FSA, FSA SCOT.
Keeper of Geology and Zoology, M. Shaw, D.Phil.
Keeper of Social and Technological History, G. Sprott
Head of Public Affairs, Ms M. Bryden
Head of Museum Services, S. R. Elson, FSA SCOT.
Head of Administration, A. G. Young
Campaign Director, Museum of Scotland, S. Brock, ph.D., FRSA
Keeper, Scottish United Services Museum, S. C. Wood
Curator, Scottish Agricultural Museum, G. Sprott
Curator, Museum of Flight, A. Smith
Keeper, Shambellie House Museum of Costume, Miss N. Tarrant

NATIONAL AUDIT OFFICE
157–197 Buckingham Palace Road, London SW1W 9SP
Tel 0171-798 7000; fax 0171-828 3774
22 Melville Street, Edinburgh EH3 7NS
Tel 0131-244 2736; fax 0131-244 2721
Audit House, 23–24 Park Place, Cardiff CF1 3BA
Tel 01222-378661; fax 01222-388415

The National Audit Office came into existence under the National Audit Act 1983 to replace and continue the work of the former Exchequer and Audit Department. The Act reinforced the Office's total financial and operational independence from the Government and brought its head, the Comptroller and Auditor-General, into a closer relationship with Parliament as an officer of the House of Commons.

The National Audit Office provides independent information, advice and assurance to Parliament and the public about all aspects of the financial operations of government departments and many other bodies receiving public funds. It does this by examining and certifying the accounts of these organizations and by regularly publishing reports to Parliament on the results of its value for money investigations of the economy, efficiency and effectiveness with which public resources have been used. The National Audit Office is also the auditor by agreement of the accounts of certain international and other organizations. In addition, the Office authorizes the issue of public funds to government departments.

Comptroller and Auditor-General, Sir John Bourn, KCB
Private Secretary, F. Grogan
Deputy Comptroller and Auditor-General, R. N. Le Marechal, CB
Assistant Auditors-General, T. Burr; J. A. Higgins; L. H. Hughes, CB; J. Marshall; Miss C. Mawhood; M. C. Pfleger
Directors, Mrs C. Allen; Miss J. Angus; J. Ashcroft; Ms G. Body; A. Burchell; P. Cannon; J. Cavanagh; D. Clarke; J. Colman; M. Daynes; S. Doughty; R. Eales; A. Fiander; R. Frith; N. Gale; Mrs A. Hands; K. Hawkeswell; J. Jones; J. Jones; Ms W. Kenway-Smith; Mrs P. Leahy; J. McEwen; R. Maggs; G. Miller; R. Parker; B. Payne; J. Pearce; Ms M. Radford; J. Rickleton; M. Reeves; A. Roberts; J. Robertson; M. Sinclair; B. Skeen; N. Sloan; Mrs P. Smith; I. Summers; R. Swan; Miss J. Wheeler; M. Whitehouse; D. Woodward; P. Woodward

NATIONAL CONSUMER COUNCIL
20 Grosvenor Gardens, London SW1W 0DH
Tel 0171-730 3469; fax 0171-730 0191

The National Consumer Council was set up by the Government in 1975 to give an independent voice to consumers in the UK. Its job is to advocate the consumer interest to decision-makers in national and local government, industry and regulatory bodies, business and the professions. It does this through a combination of research and campaigning. It is largely funded by grant-in-aid from the Department of Trade and Industry.
Chairman, D. Hatch, CBE
Vice-Chairman, Mrs D. Hutton, CBE
Director, Ms R. Evans

NATIONAL CRIMINAL INTELLIGENCE SERVICE
— *see* Police section

NATIONAL DEBT OFFICE
— *see* National Investment and Loans Office

NATIONAL ENDOWMENT FOR SCIENCE, TECHNOLOGY AND THE ARTS
Department of Culture, Media and Sport, 2–4 Cockspur Street, London SW1Y 5DH
Tel 0171-211 2850; fax 0171-211 2875

The National Endowment for Science, Technology and the Arts (NESTA) was established under the National Lottery Act 1998 with a £200 million endowment from the proceeds of the National Lottery. Its aims are to help talented individuals; to enable innovative ideas to be successfully commercially exploited; and to promote public knowledge of science, technology and the arts.
Chairman, The Lord Puttnam, CBE
Trustees, Dame Bridget Ogilvie, DBE; Prof. Sir Martin Rees, FRS; Dr C. Evans, OBE; Ms C. Vorderman; D. Wardell; F. Matarasso; C. Gillinson; Ms G. McIntosh; Ms C. McKeever; Ms J. Kirkpatrick
Chief Executive (acting), J. Newton

NATIONAL HERITAGE MEMORIAL FUND
7 Holbein Place, London SW1W 0NR
Tel 0171-591 6000; fax 0171-591 6001

The National Heritage Memorial Fund is an independent body established in 1980 as a memorial to those who have died for the UK. The Fund is empowered by the National Heritage Act 1980 to give financial assistance towards the cost of acquiring, maintaining or preserving land, buildings, works of art and other objects of outstanding interest which are also of importance to the national heritage. The Fund is administered by 13 trustees who are appointed by the Prime Minister.
The National Lottery Act 1993 designated the Fund as distributor of the heritage share of proceeds from the National Lottery. As a result, the Fund now operates two funds: the Heritage Memorial Fund and the Heritage Lottery Fund. The Heritage Memorial Fund receives an annual grant from the Department for Culture, Media and Sport (£2 million in 1998–9).

Chairman, Dr E. Anderson
Trustees, R. Boas; Sir Richard Carew Pole, Bt.; W. L. Evans; Sir Alistair Grant; Mrs C. Hubbard; J. Keegan; Ms P. Lankester; Prof. P. J. Newbould; Ms S. Palmer; Mrs C. Porteous; Ms M. A. Sieghart; Dame Sue Tinson, DBE
Director, Ms A. Case

NATIONAL INSURANCE JOINT AUTHORITY
The Adelphi, 1–11 John Adam Street, London WC2N 6HT
Tel 0171-962 8523; fax 0171-962 8647

The Authority's function is to co-ordinate the operation of social security legislation in Great Britain and Northern Ireland, including the necessary financial adjustments between the two National Insurance Funds.
Members, The Secretary of State for Social Security; the Head of the Department of Health and Social Services for Northern Ireland
Secretary, M. Driver

NATIONAL INVESTMENT AND LOANS OFFICE
1 King Charles Street, London SW1A 2AP
Tel 0171-270 3861; fax 0171-270 3860

The National Investment and Loans Office is a non-ministerial government department which was set up in 1980 by the merger of the National Debt Office and the Public Works Loan Board. The Office provides the staff and administrative support for the National Debt Commissioners, the Public Works Loan Commissioners and the Office of HM Paymaster-General. The National Debt Office is responsible for managing the investment portfolios of certain public funds and the management of some residual operations relating to the national debt. The function of the Public Works Loan Board is to make loans from the National Loans Fund to local authorities and certain other statutory bodies, primarily for capital purposes.
The Office of HM Paymaster-General has continuously existed in its present form since 1836; the Paymaster-General has responsibilities assigned from time to time by the Prime Minister and is currently a Treasury minister. The Assistant Paymaster-General is responsible for the banking and financial information services provided to the Government and public sector bodies by the Office of HM Paymaster-General.
Director, I. H. Peattie
Establishment Officer, A. G. Ladd

NATIONAL DEBT OFFICE
Comptroller-General, I. H. Peattie

PUBLIC WORKS LOAN BOARD
Chairman, A. D. Loehnis, CMG
Deputy Chairman, Miss V. J. Di Palma, OBE
Other Commissioners, L. B. Woodhall; Dame Sheila Masters, DBE; Mrs R. V. Hale; R. Burton; J. A. Parkes, CBE; J. Andrews; B. Tanner, CBE; T. Fellowes; Mrs R. Terry
Secretary, I. H. Peattie
Assistant Secretary, Miss L. M. Ashcroft

OFFICE OF HM PAYMASTER-GENERAL
Paymaster-General, Geoffrey Robinson, MP
Assistant Paymaster-General, I. H. Peattie

Deputy Paymaster-General, L. Palmer

BANKING OPERATIONS, National Investment and Loans Office, Sutherland House, Russell Way, Crawley, W. Sussex RH10 1UH. *Banking Manager,* P. Harris

OFFICE OF THE NATIONAL LOTTERY
2 Monck Street, London SW1P 2BQ
Tel 0171-227 2000; fax 0171-227 2005

The Office of the National Lottery (OFLOT) was established as a non-ministerial government department under the National Lottery Act 1993 and is headed by the Director-General of the National Lottery. The Director-General regulates the National Lottery operations and licenses games promoted as part of the Lottery. The Director-General will be replaced by a five-member National Lottery Commission in spring 1999.
Director-General, J. Stoker
Deputy Director-General, K. Jones

For details of National Lottery operations, *see* National Lottery section

NATIONAL LOTTERY CHARITIES BOARD
St Vincent House, 16 Suffolk Street, London SW1Y 4NL
Tel 0171-747 5299; fax 0171-747 5347

The Board is the independent body set up under the National Lottery Act 1993 to distribute funds from the Lottery to support charitable, benevolent and philanthropic organizations. The chairman and members are appointed by the Secretary of State for Culture, Media and Sport. The Board's main aim is to help meet the needs of those at greatest disadvantage in society and to improve the quality of life in the community through grants programmes in the UK and an international grants programme for UK-based agencies working abroad.
Chairman, The Hon. D. Sieff
Deputy Chairman, Sir Adam Ridley
Members, Mrs T. Baring; A. Bhatia, OBE; S. Burkeman; Mrs J. Churchman, OBE; Mrs A. Clark; I. Clarke; Ms S. Clarke, CBE; Ms P. de Lima; Ms K. Hampton; A. Higgins, OBE; T. Jones, OBE; Ms A. Jordan; Ms J. Kaufmann, OBE; W. B. Kirkpatrick, OBE; Mrs B. Lowndes; Ms M. McWilliams; W. G. Morrison, CBE; W. Osborne; R. Partington; J. Simpson, OBE; N. Stewart, OBE; Prof. Sir Eric Stroud, FRCP; Mrs E. Watkins
Chief Executive, T. Hornsby

NATIONAL PHYSICAL LABORATORY
Queens Road, Teddington, Middx TW11 0LW
Tel 0181-977 3222; fax 0181-943 6458

The Laboratory is the UK's national standards laboratory. It develops, maintains and disseminates national measurement standards for physical quantities such as mass, length, time, temperature, voltage, force and pressure. It also conducts underpinning research on engineering materials and information technology and disseminates good measurement practice. It is government-owned but contractor-operated.
Managing Director, Dr J. Rae
Director of Marketing and Communications, D. C. Richardson

NATIONAL RADIOLOGICAL
PROTECTION BOARD
Chilton, Didcot, Oxon OX11 0RQ
Tel 01235-831600; fax 01235-833891

The National Radiological Protection Board is an independent statutory body created by the Radiological Protection Act 1970. It is the national point of authoritative reference on radiological protection for both ionizing and non-ionizing radiations, and has issued recommendations on limiting human exposure to electromagnetic fields and radiation from a range of sources, including X-rays, the Sun and power generators. Its sponsoring department is the Department of Health.
Chairman, vacant
Director, Prof. R. H. Clarke

NATIONAL SAVINGS
Charles House, 375 Kensington High Street, London W14 8SD
Tel 0171-605 9300; fax 0171-605 9438

National Savings was established as a government department in 1969. It became an executive agency of the Treasury in July 1996 and is responsible for the administration of a wide range of schemes for personal savers. The Government is currently considering bids for outsourcing to a private company most of the work undertaken by National Savings.
Chief Executive, P. Bareau
Deputy Chief Executive and Contracting Director, K. Chivers
Operational Services Director, D. H. Monaghan
Personnel Director, D. S. Speedie
Finance Director, V. Raimondo
Commercial Director, C. Moxey
Funding Director, M. Corcoran

For details of schemes, *see* National Savings section

OFFICE FOR NATIONAL STATISTICS
1 Drummond Gate, London SW1V 2QQ
Tel 0171-533 6363; fax 0171-533 5719

The Office for National Statistics was created in April 1996 by the merger of the Central Statistical Office and the Office of Population, Censuses and Surveys. It is an executive agency of the Treasury and is responsible for preparing and interpreting key economic statistics for government policy; collecting and publishing business statistics; publishing annual and monthly statistical digests; providing researchers, analysts and other customers with a statistical service; administration of the marriage laws and local registration of births, marriages and deaths in England and Wales; provision of population estimates and projections and statistics on health and other demographic matters in England and Wales; population censuses in England and Wales; surveys for government departments and public bodies; and promoting these functions within the UK, the European Union and internationally to provide a statistical service to meet European Union and international requirements.

The Office for National Statistics is also responsible for establishing and maintaining a central database of key

economic and social statistics produced to common classifications, definitions and standards.
Chief Executive, Prof. T. Holt
Directors (G3), J. Calder (*Survey and Statistical Services*); J. Fox (*Census, Population and Health*); J. Kidgell (*Macro-Economic Statistics*); D. Roberts (*Administration and Registration*); M. Pepper (*Business Statistics*); (*acting*) J. Pullinger (*Socio-Economic Statistics*)
Principal Establishment Officer (G5), E. Williams
Principal Finance Officer (G5), P. Murphy
Head of Information (G6), I. Scott
Parliamentary Clerk, L. Land

FAMILY RECORDS CENTRE, 1 Myddelton Street, London EC1R 1UW. Tel: 0181-392 5300. Open Mon., Wed., Fri. 9 a.m.-5 p.m.; Tues. 10 a.m.-7 p.m.; Thurs. 9 a.m.-7 p.m.; Sat. 9.30 a.m.-5 p.m.

JOINT NATURE CONSERVATION COMMITTEE
Monkstone House, City Road, Peterborough PE1 1JY
Tel 01733-562626; fax 01733-555948

The Committee was established under the Environmental Protection Act 1990. It advises the Government and others on UK and international nature conservation issues and disseminates knowledge on these subjects. It establishes common standards for the monitoring of nature conservation and research, and provides guidance to English Nature, Scottish Natural Heritage, the Countryside Council for Wales and the Department of the Environment for Northern Ireland.
Chairman, Sir Angus Stirling
Chief Officer, vacant
Director, Dr M. A. Vincent

NEW OPPORTUNITIES FUND
Dacre House, Dacre Street, London SW1H 0DH
Tel 0171-222 3084; fax 0171-222 3085

The New Opportunities Fund was established under the National Lottery Act 1998 and is responsible for distributing funds allocated from the proceeds of the National Lottery to health, education and environment projects within initiatives determined by the Government.
Chair of the Board, The Baroness Pitkeathley
Members of the Board, Ms J. Barrow; Prof. E. Bolton; Ms N. Clarke; Ms M. Letts; Prof. A. Patmore, CBE; D. Mackie; D. Campbell; Ms J. Hutt
Chief Executive (acting), S. Dunmore

NOLAN COMMITTEE (FORMER)
— *see* Committee on Standards in Public Life, page 345

NORTHERN IRELAND AUDIT OFFICE
106 University Street, Belfast BT7 1EU
Tel 01232-251000; fax 01232-251106

The primary aim of the Northern Ireland Audit Office is to provide independent assurance, information and advice to Parliament on the proper accounting for Northern Ireland departmental and certain other public expenditure, revenue, assets and liabilities; on regularity and propriety; and

on the economy, efficiency and effectiveness of the use of resources.
Comptroller and Auditor-General for Northern Ireland, J. M. Dowdall

NORTHERN IRELAND OFFICE
11 Millbank, London SW1P 4QE
Tel 0171-210 3000
Parliament Buildings, Stormont, Belfast BT4 3SS
Tel 01232-520700; fax 01232-528478
Web: http://www.nics.gov.uk/centgov/nio/nio.htm

The Northern Ireland Office was established in 1972, when the Northern Ireland (Temporary Provisions) Act transferred the legislative and executive powers of the Northern Ireland Parliament and Government to the UK Parliament and a Secretary of State.
The Northern Ireland Office is responsible primarily for security issues, law and order and prisons, and for matters relating to the political and constitutional future of the province. It also deals with international issues as they affect Northern Ireland, including the Anglo-Irish Agreement. The Northern Ireland departments are responsible for the administration of social, industrial and economic policies.
The names of most civil servants are not listed for security reasons.
Secretary of State for Northern Ireland, The Rt. Hon. Dr Marjorie (Mo) Mowlam, MP
Special Advisers, N. Warner; Ms A. Healy
Parliamentary Private Secretaries, H. Jackson, MP; S. Timms, MP
Minister of State, Paul Murphy, MP (*Political Development, Finance, Personnel, Information*)
Parliamentary Private Secretary, M. Gapes, MP
Minister of State, Adam Ingram, MP (*Security, Criminal Justice, Economic Development*)
Parliamentary Private Secretary, T. Colman, MP
Parliamentary Under-Secretaries of State, The Lord Dubs (*Environment, Agriculture*); John McFall, MP (*Education, Training and Employment, Health, Community Relations*)
Permanent Under-Secretary of State (SCS), J. Pilling, CB
Second Permanent Under-Secretary of State, Head of the Northern Ireland Civil Service, J. Semple, CB

LONDON
SCS, (Political Director)
SCS, (Associate Political Director); (International and Planning); (Constitutional and Political); (Rights and European); (Personnel and Office Services)
SCS, (Director of Information Services)

BELFAST
SCS, (Political Director)
SCS, (Associate Political Director); (Security); (Criminal Justice); (Political); (Personnel and Finance)

NORTHERN IRELAND INFORMATION SERVICE
Parliament Buildings, Stormont, Belfast BT4 3ST
Tel 01232-520700
Director of Communications

EXECUTIVE AGENCIES
COMPENSATION AGENCY, Royston House, Upper Queen Street, Belfast BT1 6FD. Tel: 01232-2499444
FORENSIC SCIENCE AGENCY, Seapark, 151 Belfast Road, Carrickfergus, Co. Antrim BT38 8PL. Tel: 01232-365744
NORTHERN IRELAND PRISON SERVICE, *see* page 382

330   Government Departments and Public Offices

DEPARTMENT OF AGRICULTURE FOR NORTHERN IRELAND
Dundonald House, Upper Newtownards Road, Belfast BT4 3SB
Tel 01232-520100; fax 01232-525015

Parliamentary Under-Secretary of State, The Lord Dubs
Permanent Secretary (SCS)
Under-Secretaries (SCS), (Central Services and Rural Development); (Food, Farm and Environmental Policy); (Veterinary); (Science); (Agri-Food Development)

EXECUTIVE AGENCIES
INTERVENTION BOARD
— *see* pages 315–16
RIVERS AGENCY, 4 Hospital Road, Belfast BT8 8JP. Tel: 01232-253355

DEPARTMENT OF ECONOMIC DEVELOPMENT NORTHERN IRELAND
Netherleigh, Massey Avenue, Belfast BT4 2JP
Tel 01232-529900; fax 01232-529550

Minister of State, Adam Ingram, MP
Permanent Secretary (SCS)
Under-Secretaries (SCS), (Resources Group); (Regulatory Services Group)

INDUSTRIAL DEVELOPMENT BOARD, IDB House, 64 Chichester Street, Belfast BT1 4JX. Tel: 01232-233233

EXECUTIVE AGENCIES
INDUSTRIAL RESEARCH AND TECHNOLOGY UNIT, 17 Antrim Road, Lisburn BT28 3AL. Tel: 01846-623000
TRAINING AND EMPLOYMENT AGENCY (NORTHERN IRELAND), Adelaide Street, Belfast BT2 8FD. Tel: 01232-257777

DEPARTMENT OF EDUCATION FOR NORTHERN IRELAND
Rathgael House, Balloo Road, Bangor, Co. Down BT19 7PR
Tel 01247-279279; fax 01247-279100

Parliamentary Under-Secretary of State, John McFall, MP
Permanent Secretary (SCS)
Deputy Secretaries (SCS), (Schools); (Finance and Corporate Services)
Chief Inspector (SCS), (Education and Training Inspectorate)

DEPARTMENT OF THE ENVIRONMENT FOR NORTHERN IRELAND
Clarence Court, 10–18 Adelaide Street, Belfast BT2 8GB
Tel 01232-540540

Parliamentary Under-Secretary of State, The Lord Dubs
Permanent Secretary (SCS)
Under-Secretaries (SCS), (Personnel, Finance, Housing and Local Government); (Rural and Urban Affairs); (Roads, Water and Transport); (Planning, Works and Environment)

EXECUTIVE AGENCIES
CONSTRUCTION SERVICE, Churchill House, Victoria Square, Belfast BT1 4QW. Tel: 01232-250284
DRIVER AND VEHICLE LICENSING AGENCY (NORTHERN IRELAND), County Hall, Castlerock Road, Coleraine, Co. Londonderry BT51 3HS. Tel: 01265-41200
DRIVER AND VEHICLE TESTING AGENCY (NORTHERN IRELAND), Balmoral Road, Belfast BT12 6QL. Tel: 01232-681831

ENVIRONMENT AND HERITAGE SERVICE, Commonwealth House, Castle Street, Belfast BT1 1GU. Tel: 01232-251477
LAND REGISTERS OF NORTHERN IRELAND, Lincoln Building, 27–45 Great Victoria Street, Belfast BT2 7SL. Tel: 01232-251515
ORDNANCE SURVEY OF NORTHERN IRELAND, Colby House, Stranmillis Court, Belfast BT9 5BJ. Tel: 01232-255755
PLANNING SERVICE, Clarence Court, 10–18 Adelaide Street, Belfast BT2 8GB. Tel: 01232-540540
PUBLIC RECORD OFFICE (NORTHERN IRELAND) – *see* page 337
RATE COLLECTION AGENCY (NORTHERN IRELAND), Oxford House, 49–55 Chichester Street, Belfast BT1 4HH. Tel: 01232-252252
ROADS SERVICE, Clarence Court, 10–18 Adelaide Street, Belfast BT2 8GB. Tel: 01232-540540
WATER SERVICE, Northland House, 3 Frederick Street, Belfast BT1 2NR. Tel: 01232-244711

ADVISORY BODIES
HISTORIC BUILDINGS COUNCIL FOR NORTHERN IRELAND, c/o Environment and Heritage Service, Historic Monuments and Buildings, Commonwealth House, Castle Street, Belfast BT1 1GU. Tel: 01232-251477
COUNCIL FOR NATURE CONSERVATION AND THE COUNTRYSIDE, c/o Environment and Heritage Service, Commonwealth House, Castle Street, Belfast BT1 1GU. Tel: 01232-251477

DEPARTMENT OF FINANCE AND PERSONNEL
Parliament Buildings, Stormont, Belfast BT4 3SG
Tel 01232-520400

Minister of State, Paul Murphy, MP
Permanent Secretary (SCS)
Under-Secretaries (SCS), (Supply Group); (Resources Control and Professional Services Group); (Central Personnel Group); (Government Purchasing Service)

NORTHERN IRELAND CIVIL SERVICE (NICS)
Parliament Buildings, Stormont, Belfast BT4 3TT
Tel 01232-520700

Head of Civil Service (SCS), J. Semple, CB
Under-Secretaries (SCS), (Central Secretariat); (Legal Services); (Office of the Legislative Council)

GENERAL REGISTER OFFICE (NORTHERN IRELAND), Oxford House, 49–65 Chichester Street, Belfast BT1 4HL. Tel: 01232-252000. *Registrar-General (G6)*

EXECUTIVE AGENCIES
BUSINESS DEVELOPMENT SERVICE, Craigantlet Buildings, Stoney Road, Belfast BT4 3SX. Tel: 01232-520400
GOVERNMENT PURCHASING AGENCY, Rosepark House, Upper Newtownards Road, Belfast BT4 3NR. Tel: 01232-520400
NORTHERN IRELAND STATISTICS AND RESEARCH AGENCY, The Arches Centre, 11–13 Bloomfield Avenue, Belfast BT5 5HD. Tel: 01232-526093
VALUATION AND LANDS AGENCY, Queen's Court, 56–66 Upper Queen Street, Belfast BT4 6FD. Tel: 01232-250700

DEPARTMENT OF HEALTH AND SOCIAL
SERVICES NORTHERN IRELAND
Castle Buildings, Stormont, Belfast BT4 3PP
Tel 01232-520000; fax 01232-520572

Parliamentary Under-Secretary of State, John McFall, MP
Permanent Secretary (SCS)
Chief Medical Officer (SCS)
Under-Secretaries (SCS), (Health and Social Services
  Executive); (Health and Social Policy); (Medical and
  Allied Services); (Central Management and Social
  Security Policy Group)

HEALTH AND SOCIAL SERVICES BOARDS
— *see* page 480

EXECUTIVE AGENCIES
NORTHERN IRELAND CHILD SUPPORT AGENCY, Great
Northern Tower, 17 Great Victoria Street, Belfast
BT2 7AD. Tel: 01232-339000
NORTHERN IRELAND HEALTH AND SOCIAL SERVICES
ESTATES AGENCY, Stoney Road, Dundonald, Belfast
BT16 1US. Tel: 01232-520025
NORTHERN IRELAND SOCIAL SECURITY AGENCY, Castle
Buildings, Stormont, Belfast BT4 3SJ. Tel: 01232-520520

OCCUPATIONAL PENSIONS REGULATORY
AUTHORITY
Invicta House, Trafalgar Place, Brighton BN1 4DW
Tel 01273-627600; fax 01273-627688

The Occupational Pensions Regulatory Authority
(OPRA) was set up under the Pensions Act 1995 and
became fully operational on 6 April 1997. It is the
independent, statutory regulator of occupational pension
schemes in the UK.
Chairman, J. Hayes, CBE
Chief Executive, Ms C. Johnston

OMBUDSMEN
— *see* Local Commissioners *and* Parliamentary
Commissioner. For non-statutory Ombudsmen, *see* Index

ORDNANCE SURVEY
Romsey Road, Maybush, Southampton SO16 4GU
Tel 01703-792000; fax 01703-792452

Ordnance Survey is the national mapping agency for
Britain. It is a government department funded by parlia-
mentary vote, and reports to the Secretary of State for the
Environment, Transport and the Regions.
Director-General and Chief Executive, Prof. D. Rhind

PARADES COMMISSION
12th Floor, Windsor House, 6–12 Bedford Street,
Belfast BT2 7EL
Tel 01232-895900; fax 01232-322988

The Parades Commission was set up under the Public
Processions (Northern Ireland) Act 1998. Its function is to
encourage and facilitate local accommodation on contentious parades; where this is not possible, the Commission is
empowered to make legal determinations about such
parades, which may include imposing conditions on
aspects of the notified parade.

The chairman and members are appointed by the
Secretary of State for Northern Ireland; the membership
must, as far as is practicable, be representative of the
community in Northern Ireland.
Chairman, A. Graham
Members, D. Hewitt, CBE; Mrs R. A. McCormick; A.
  Canavan; F. Guckian, CBE; W. Martin; Dr Barbara Erwin
Secretary (G5), R. Buchanan

OFFICE OF THE PARLIAMENTARY
COMMISSIONER FOR ADMINISTRATION
AND HEALTH SERVICE COMMISSIONER
Millbank Tower, Millbank, London SW1P 4QP
Parliamentary Commissioner: Tel 0171-217 4163; fax 0171-
276 4160; *Health Service Commissioner:* Tel 0171-217 4051;
fax 0171-217 4000

The Parliamentary Commissioner for Administration (the
Parliamentary Ombudsman) is independent of Government and is an officer of Parliament. He is responsible for
investigating complaints referred to him by MPs from
members of the public who claim to have sustained
injustice in consequence of maladministration by or on
behalf of government departments and certain non-
departmental public bodies. Certain types of action by
government departments or bodies are excluded from
investigation. The Parliamentary Commissioner is also
responsible for investigating complaints, referred by MPs,
alleging that access to official information has been
wrongly refused under the Code of Practice on Access to
Government Information 1994.
  The Health Service Commissioners (the Health Service
Ombudsmen) for England, for Scotland and for Wales are
responsible for investigating complaints against National
Health Service authorities and trusts that are not dealt with
by those authorities to the satisfaction of the complainant.
Complaints can be referred direct by the member of the
public who claims to have sustained injustice or hardship in
consequence of the failure in a service provided by a
relevant body, failure of that body to provide a service or in
consequence of any other action by that body. The
Ombudsmens' jurisdiction now covers complaints about
family doctors, dentists, pharmacists and opticians, and
complaints about actions resulting from clinical judgment.
The Health Service Ombudsmen are also responsible for
investigating complaints that information has been wrong-
ly refused under the Code of Practice on Openness in the
National Health Service 1995. The three offices are
presently held by the Parliamentary Commissioner.
Parliamentary Commissioner and Health Service Commissioner
  (G1), M. S. Buckley
Deputy Parliamentary Commissioners (G3), J. E. Avery, CB;
  J. Tate
Deputy Health Service Commissioner (G3), Miss M. I. Nisbet
Directors, Parliamentary Commissioner (G5), N. Cleary;
  D. J. Coffey; Mrs S. P. Maunsell; G. Monk; A. Watson
Directors, Health Service Commissioners (G5), Miss
  H. Bainbridge; N. J. Jordan; D. R. G. Pinchin; R. Tyrrell
Finance and Establishment Officer (G5), T. G. Hull

PARLIAMENTARY COMMISSIONER FOR STANDARDS
House of Commons, London SW1A 0AA
Tel 0171-219 0320

Following recommendations of the Committee on Standards in Public Life (the Nolan Committee) the House of Commons agreed to the appointment of an independent Parliamentary Commissioner for Standards with effect from November 1995. The Commissioner has responsibility for maintaining and monitoring the operation of the Register of Members' Interests; advising Members of Parliament and the select committee on standards and privileges, on the interpretation of the rules on disclosure and advocacy, and on other questions of propriety; and receiving and, if he thinks fit, investigating complaints about the conduct of MPs.
Parliamentary Commissioner for Standards, Sir Gordon Downey, KCB (*until November 1998*)

PARLIAMENTARY COUNSEL
36 Whitehall, London SW1A 2AY
Tel 0171-210 6637; fax 0171-210 6632

Parliamentary Counsel draft all government bills (i.e. primary legislation) except those relating exclusively to Scotland, the latter being drafted by the Lord Advocate's Department. They also advise on all aspects of parliamentary procedure in connection with such bills and draft government amendments to them as well as any motions (including financial resolutions) necessary to secure their introduction into, and passage through, Parliament.
First Counsel (SCS), J. C. Jenkins, CB, QC
Counsel (SCS), D. W. Saunders, CB; E. G. Caldwell, CB;
E. G. Bowman, CB; G. B. Sellers, CB; E. R. Sutherland, CB;
P. F. A. Knowles, CB; S. C. Laws, CB; R. S. Parker, CB;
Miss C. E. Johnston; P. J. Davies

PARLIAMENTARY OMBUDSMAN FOR NORTHERN IRELAND AND NORTHERN IRELAND COMMISSIONER FOR COMPLAINTS
Progressive House, 33 Wellington Place, Belfast BT1 6HN
Tel 01232-233821; fax 01232-234912

The Ombudsman is appointed under legislation with powers to investigate complaints by people claiming to have sustained injustice in consequence of maladministration arising from action taken by a Northern Ireland government department, or any other public body within his remit. Staff are presently seconded from the Northern Ireland Civil Service.
Ombudsman, G. Burns, MBE
Deputy Ombudsman, J. MacQuarrie
Directors, C. O'Hare; R. Doherty; H. Mallon

PAROLE BOARD FOR ENGLAND AND WALES
Abell House, John Islip Street, London SW1P 4LH
Tel 0171-217 5314; 0171-217 5793

The Board was constituted under the Criminal Justice Act 1967 and continued under the Criminal Justice Act 1991. It is an executive non-departmental public body and its duty is to advise the Home Secretary with respect to matters referred to it by him which are connected with the early release or recall of prisoners. Its functions include giving directions concerning the release on licence of prisoners serving discretionary life sentences and of certain prisoners serving long-term determinate sentences.
Chairman, Ms U. Prashar, CBE
Vice-Chairman, The Hon. Mr Justice Tucker
Chief Executive, M. S. Todd

PAROLE BOARD FOR SCOTLAND
Saughton House, Broomhouse Drive, Edinburgh EH11 3XD
Tel 0131-244 8755; fax 0131-244 6974

The Board directs and advises the Secretary of State for Scotland on the release of prisoners on licence, and related matters.
Chairman, I. McNee
Vice-Chairmen, Sheriff G. Shiach; Ms J. Freeman
Secretary, H. P. Boyle

PASSENGER RAIL FRANCHISING, OFFICE OF
— *see* Transport section

PATENT OFFICE
Cardiff Road, Newport NP9 1RH
Tel 0645-500505; fax 01633-814444

The Patent Office is an executive agency of the Department of Trade and Industry. The duties of the Patent Office are to administer the Patent Acts, the Registered Designs Act and the Trade Marks Act, and to deal with questions relating to the Copyright, Designs and Patents Act 1988. The Search and Advisory Service carries out commercial searches through patent information. In 1996 the Office granted 7,132 patents and registered 9,293 designs and 29,196 trade marks.
Comptroller-General, P. R. S. Hartnack
Director, Intellectual Property Policy Directorate, G. Jenkins
Director, Patents and Designs, R. J. Marchant
Director and Assistant Registrar of Trade Marks, P. Lawrence
Director, Administration and Resources and Secretary to the Patent Office, C. Octon
Director, Copyright, J. Startup
Director, Finance, J. Thompson

HM PAYMASTER-GENERAL
— *see* National Investment and Loans Office

PENSIONS COMPENSATION BOARD
5th Floor, 11 Belgrave Road, London SW1V 1RB
Tel 0171-828 9794; fax 0171-931 7239

The Pensions Compensation Board was established under the Pensions Act 1995 and is funded by a levy paid by all eligible occupational pension schemes. Its function is to compensate occupational pension schemes for losses due to dishonesty where the employer is solvent.
Chairman, Dr J. T. Farrand, QC
Secretary, M. Lydon

OFFICE OF THE PENSIONS OMBUDSMAN
6th Floor, 11 Belgrave Road, London SW1V 1RB
Tel 0171-834 9144; fax 0171-821 0065

The Pensions Ombudsman is appointed under the Pension Schemes Act 1993 as amended by the Pensions Act 1995. He investigates and decides complaints and disputes concerning occupational pension schemes. Complaints concerning personal pensions would normally be dealt with only if outside the jurisdiction of the Personal Investment Authority. The Ombudsman is completely independent and there is no charge for bringing a complaint or dispute to him.
Pensions Ombudsman, Dr J. T. Farrand, QC

POLICE COMPLAINTS AUTHORITY
10 Great George Street, London SW1P 3AE
Tel 0171-273 6450; fax 0171-273 6401

The Police Complaints Authority was established under the Police and Criminal Evidence Act 1984 to provide an independent system for dealing with serious complaints by members of the public against police officers in England and Wales. It is funded by the Home Office. The authority has powers to supervise the investigation of certain categories of serious complaints and certain statutory functions in relation to the disciplinary aspects of complaints. It does not deal with police operational matters; these are usually dealt with by the Chief Constable of the relevant force.
Chairman, P. Moorhouse
Deputy Chairman, J. Cartwright
Members, Mrs L. Allan; I. Bynoe; Ms J. Dobry; J. Elliott; M. Meacher; Miss M. Mian; Mrs C. Mitchell; A. Potts; Mrs M. Scorer; Ms L. Whyte; A. Williams

INDEPENDENT COMMISSION FOR POLICE COMPLAINTS FOR NORTHERN IRELAND
— *see* page 312

POLITICAL HONOURS SCRUTINY COMMITTEE
Cabinet Office, Ashley House, 2 Monck Street, London SW1P 2BQ
Tel 0171-276 2770; fax 0171-276 2766

The function of the Political Honours Scrutiny Committee (a committee of Privy Councillors) was set out in an Order in Council in 1991 and amended by Orders in Council in 1994, 1997 and 1998. The Prime Minister submits certain particulars to the Committee about persons proposed to be recommended for honour for their political services. The Committee, after such enquiry as they think fit, report to the Prime Minister whether, so far as they believe, the persons whose names are submitted to them are fit and proper persons to be recommended.
Chairman, The Lord Pym, MC, PC
Members, The Lord Thomson of Monifieth, KT, PC; The Baroness Dean of Thornton-le-Fylde, PC
Secretary, A. J. Merifield, CB

PORT OF LONDON AUTHORITY
Devon House, 58 – 60 St Katharine's Way, London E1 9LB
Tel 0171-265 2656; fax 0171-265 2699

The Port of London Authority is a public trust constituted under the Port of London Act 1908 and subsequent legislation. It is the governing body for the Port of London, covering the tidal portion of the River Thames from Teddington to the seaward limit. The Board comprises a chairman and up to seven but not less than four non-executive members appointed by the Secretary of State for the Environment, Transport and the Regions, and up to four but not less than one executive members appointed by the Board.
Chairman, Sir Brian Shaw
Vice-Chairman, J. H. Kelly, CBE
Chief Executive, D. Jeffery
Secretary, G. E. Ennals

THE POST OFFICE
148 Old Street, London EC1V 9HQ
Tel 0171-490 2888

Crown services for the carriage of government dispatches were set up in about 1516. The conveyance of public correspondence began in 1635 and the mail service was made a parliamentary responsibility with the setting up of a Post Office in 1657. Telegraphs came under Post Office control in 1870 and the Post Office Telephone Service began in 1880. The National Girobank service of the Post Office began in 1968. The Post Office ceased to be a government department in 1969 when responsibility for the running of the postal, telecommunications, giro and remittance services was transferred to a public authority called The Post Office. The 1981 British Telecommunications Act separated the functions of the Post Office, making it solely responsible for postal services and Girobank. Girobank was privatized in 1990. The Government is conducting a review of the Post Office with a view to greater involvement of the private sector in its operations; the results of the review are expected in autumn 1998.

The chairman, chief executive and members of the Post Office Board are appointed by the Secretary of State for Trade and Industry but responsibility for the running of the Post Office as a whole rests with the Board in its corporate capacity.

334   Government Departments and Public Offices

FINANCIAL RESULTS £m	1996–7	1997–8
Post Office Group		
Turnover	6,370	6,759
Profit before tax	577	651
Royal Mail		
Turnover	5,019	5,411
Profit before tax	463	496
Parcelforce		
Turnover	457	465
Profit (loss) before tax	(21)	(14)
Post Office Counters		
Turnover	1,161	1,130
Profit before tax	34	33

POST OFFICE BOARD
Chairman, Dr N. Bain
Chief Executive, J. Roberts, CBE
Members, R. Close (*Managing Director, Finance*); J. Cope (*Managing Director, Strategy and Personnel*)
Secretary, R. Adams
For postal services, *see* pages 515–17

PRIME MINISTER'S OFFICE
— *see* page 288

PRISONS OMBUDSMAN FOR ENGLAND AND WALES
Ashley House, 2 Monck Street, London SW1P 2BQ
Tel 0171-276 2876; fax 0171-276 2860

The post of Prisons Ombudsman was instituted in 1994. The Ombudsman is appointed by the Home Secretary and is an independent point of appeal for prisoners' grievances about their lives in prison, including disciplinary issues. The Ombudsman cannot investigate grievances relating to issues which are the subject of litigation or criminal proceedings, decisions taken by ministers, or actions of bodies outside the prison service.
Prisons Ombudsman, Sir Peter Woodhead, KCB

For Scotland, *see* Scottish Prisons Complaints Commission

PRIVY COUNCIL OFFICE
Whitehall, London SW1A 2AT
Tel 0171-270 0472; fax 0171-270 0109

The Office is responsible for the arrangements leading to the making of all royal proclamations and Orders in Council; for certain formalities connected with ministerial changes; for considering applications for the granting (or amendment) of royal charters; for the scrutiny and approval of by-laws and statutes of chartered bodies; and for the appointment of high sheriffs and many Crown and Privy Council appointments to governing bodies.
President of the Council (and Leader of the House of Commons), The Rt. Hon. Margaret Beckett, MP
Private Secretary, Ms V. A. Scarborough
Clerk of the Council (G3), N. H. Nicholls, CBE
Deputy Clerk of the Council (G5), R. P. Bulling
Senior Clerks, Miss M. A. McCullagh; Mrs P. J. Birleson
Registrar, J. A. C. Watherston

CENTRAL DRUGS CO-ORDINATION UNIT
Government Offices, Great George Street, London SW1P 3AL
Tel 0171-270 5776; fax 0171-270 5857
UK Anti-Drugs Co-ordinator, K. Hellawell
Deputy Anti-Drugs Co-ordinator, M. Trace
Director of Unit, Ms L. Rogerson

PROCURATOR FISCAL SERVICE
— *see* pages 366–7

PUBLIC HEALTH LABORATORY SERVICE
61 Colindale Avenue, London NW9 5DF
Tel 0181-200 1295; fax 0181-200 8130

The Public Health Laboratory Service comprises nine groups of laboratories, the Central Public Health Laboratory and the Communicable Disease Surveillance Centre. The PHLS provides diagnostic microbiological services to hospitals, and has reference facilities that are available nationally. It collates information on the incidence of infection, and when necessary it institutes special inquiries into outbreaks and the epidemiology of infectious disease. It also undertakes bacteriological surveillance of the quality of food and water for local authorities and others.
Chairman (£15,125), Prof. Sir Leslie Turnberg, MD
Deputy Chairman, R. Tabor
Director, Dr Diana Walford, FRCP, FRCpath.
Deputy Directors, Prof. B. I. Duerden, MD, FRCpath. (*Programmes*); K. M. Saunders (*Corporate Planning and Resources*)
Board Secretary, K. M. Saunders

CENTRAL PUBLIC HEALTH LABORATORY
Colindale Avenue, London NW9 5HT
Director, Prof. S. P. Borriello

COMMUNICABLE DISEASES SURVEILLANCE CENTRE
Colindale Avenue, NW9 5EQ
Director, Dr C. L. R. Bartlett

PHLS GROUPS OF LABORATORIES AND GROUP DIRECTORS
East, Dr P. M. B. White
Midlands, Dr R. E. Warren
North, Dr N. F. Lightfoot
North-West, Dr P. Morgan-Capner
South-West, Dr K. A. V. Cartwright
Thames, Dr R. Gross
Trent, Dr P. J. Wilkinson
Wessex, Dr S. A. Rousseau
Wales, Dr A. J. Howard

OTHER SPECIAL LABORATORIES AND UNITS
ANAEROBE REFERENCE UNIT, Public Health Laboratory, Cardiff. *Head*, Prof. B. I. Duerden, MD, FRCpath.
ANTIVIRAL SUSCEPTIBILITY REFERENCE UNIT, Public Health Laboratory, Birmingham. *Head*, Dr D. P. Pillay
CRYPTOSPORIDIUM REFERENCE UNIT, Public Health Laboratory, Rhyl. *Head*, Dr D. Casemore
FOOD MICROBIOLOGY RESEARCH UNIT, Public Health Laboratory, Exeter. *Head*, Prof. T. J. Humphrey
GENITO-URINARY INFECTIONS REFERENCE LABORATORY, Public Health Laboratory, Bristol. *Head*, Dr A. J. Herring
LEPTOSPIRA REFERENCE LABORATORY, Public Health Laboratory, Hereford. *Director*, Dr T. J. Coleman
LYME DISEASE REFERENCE UNIT, Public Health Laboratory, Southampton. *Head*, Dr S. O'Connell

MALARIA REFERENCE LABORATORY, London School of
Hygiene and Tropical Medicine, London WC1E
7HT. *Directors*, Prof. D. J. Bradley, DM; Dr
D. C. Warhurst, FRCpath.
MENINGOCOCCAL REFERENCE LABORATORY, Public
Health Laboratory, Manchester. *Director*, Dr
B. A. Oppenheim
MYCOBACTERIUM REFERENCE UNIT, Public Health
Laboratory, Dulwich, London. *Director*,
Dr F. Drobniewski
MYCOLOGY REFERENCE LABORATORY, Public Health
Laboratory, Bristol. *Head*, Dr D. Warnock; University of
Leeds. *Head*, Prof. E. G. V. Evans
PARASITOLOGY REFERENCE LABORATORY, Hospital for
Tropical Diseases, London. *Director*, Dr P. L. Chiodini
TOXOPLASMA REFERENCE LABORATORY, Public Health
Laboratory, Swansea. *Head*, D. H. M. Joynson
WATER AND ENVIRONMENTAL MICROBIOLOGY
RESEARCH UNIT, Public Health Laboratory,
Nottingham. *Head*, Dr J. V. Lee

REGISTRAR OF PUBLIC LENDING RIGHT
Bayheath House, Prince Regent Street,
Stockton-on-Tees TS18 1DF
Tel 01642-604699; fax 01642-615641

Under the Public Lending Right system, in operation since
1983, payment is made from public funds to authors whose
books are lent out from public libraries. Payment is made
once a year and the amount each author receives is
proportionate to the number of times (established from a
sample) that each registered book has been lent out during
the previous year. The Registrar of PLR, who is appointed
by the Secretary of State for Culture, Media and Sport,
compiles the register of authors and books. Only living
authors resident in the UK or Germany are eligible to
apply. (The term 'author' covers writers, illustrators,
translators, and some editors/compilers.)
  A payment of 2.07 pence was made in 1997–8 for each
estimated loan of a registered book, up to a top limit of
£6,000 for the books of any one registered author; the
money for loans above this level is used to augment the
remaining PLR payments. In February 1998, the sum of
£4.251 million was made available for distribution to
17,512 registered authors and assignees as the annual
payment of PLR.
Registrar, Dr J. G. Parker
Chairman of Advisory Committee, M. Holroyd

PUBLIC RECORD OFFICE
— *see* page 336

PUBLIC TRUST OFFICE
Stewart House, 24 Kingsway, London WC2B 6JX
Tel 0171-664 7000; fax 0171-664 7705
COURT FUNDS OFFICE, 22 Kingsway, London WC2B 6LE
Tel 0171-936 6000

The Public Trust Office became an executive agency of
the Lord Chancellor's Department in 1994. The chief
executive of the agency holds the statutory titles of Public
Trustee and Accountant-General of the Supreme Court.
  The Public Trustee is a trust corporation created to
undertake the business of executorship and trusteeship;
she can act as executor or administrator of the estate of a
deceased person, or as trustee of a will or settlement. The

Public Trustee is also responsible for the performance of
all the administrative, but not the judicial, tasks required of
the Court of Protection under Part VII of the Mental
Health Act 1983, relating to the management and administration of the property and affairs of persons suffering
from mental disorder. The Public Trustee also acts as
Receiver when so directed by the Court, usually where
there is no other person willing or able to act.
  The Accountant-General of the Supreme Court,
through the Court Funds Office, is responsible for the
investment and accounting of funds in court for persons
under a disability, monies in court subject to litigation and
statutory deposits.
Chief Executive (Public Trustee and Accountant-General), Ms
J. C. Lomas
Assistant Public Trustee, Mrs S. Hutcheson
Investment Manager, H. Stevenson
Chief Property Adviser, A. Nightingale

MENTAL HEALTH SECTOR
Director of Mental Health, Mrs H. M. Bratton
Principal of Receivership Division, D. Adams
Principal of Protection Division, P. L. Hales

TRUSTS AND FUNDS SECTOR
Director of Trusts and Funds, F. J. Eddy
Divisional Manager, Court Funds Office, P. MacDermott
Divisional Manager, Trust Division, M. Munt
Finance Officer, M. Guntrip

PLANNING AND PAY POLICY
Head of Human Resources and Planning, Mrs N. M. Hunt

PUBLIC WORKS LOAN BOARD
— *see* National Investment and Loans Office

COMMISSION FOR RACIAL EQUALITY
Elliot House, 10–12 Allington Street, London SW1E 5EH
Tel 0171-828 7022; fax 0171-630 7605

The Commission was established in 1977, under the Race
Relations Act 1976, to work towards the elimination of
discrimination and promote equality of opportunity and
good relations between different racial groups. It is funded
by the Home Office.
Chairman, Sir Herman Ouseley
Deputy Chairman, H. Harris
Commissioners, R. Purkiss; Dr R. Chandran; M. Hastings;
Dr M. Jogee; Ms J. Mellor; Mrs B. Cluff; Dame Simone
Prendergast, DBE; M. Amran; S. Malik; C. Moraes; Ms C.
Short; Dr J. Singh; R. Singh
Executive Director, D. Sharma

THE RADIO AUTHORITY
Holbrook House, 14 Great Queen Street, London
WC2B 5DG
Tel 0171-430 2724; fax 0171-405 7062

The Radio Authority was established in 1991 under the
Broadcasting Act 1990. It is the regulator and licensing
authority for all independent radio services. Members of
the Authority are appointed by the Secretary of State for
Culture, Media and Sport; senior executive staff are
appointed by the Authority.
Chairman, Sir Peter Gibbings
Deputy Chairman, M. Moriarty, CB
Members, M. Reupke; Lady Sheil; A. Reid; Mrs H. Tennant

Chief Executive, A. Stoller
Deputy Chief Executive, D. Vick
Secretary to the Authority and Head of Legal Affairs, Ms E. Salomon

OFFICE OF THE RAIL REGULATOR
1 Waterhouse Square, 138–142 Holborn, London
ECIN 2ST
Tel 0171-282 2000; fax 0171-282 2040

The Office of the Rail Regulator was set up under the Railways Act 1993. It is headed by the Rail Regulator, who is independent of ministerial control. The Regulator's main functions are the licensing of operators of railway assets; the approval of agreements for access by those operators to track, stations and light maintenance depots; the enforcement of domestic competition law; and consumer protection. The Regulator also sponsors a network of Rail Users' Consultative Committees, which represent the interests of passengers.

The Government announced in July 1998 that the consumer protection function of the Rail Regulator would be taken over by a new Strategic Rail Authority.
Rail Regulator, J. A. Swift, QC
Director, Economic Regulation Group, C. W. Bolt
Director, Railway Network Group, C. J. F. Brown
Director, Passenger Services Group, J. A. Rhodes
Chief Legal Adviser, M. R. Brocklehurst
Director, Resources and RUCC Sponsorship, P. D. Murphy
Director, Communications, K. R. Webb

RECORD OFFICES

ADVISORY COUNCIL ON PUBLIC RECORDS
Secretariat: Public Record Office, Kew, Richmond, Surrey
TW9 4DU
Tel 0181-876 3444 ext. 2351; fax 0181-392 5295

Council members are appointed by the Lord Chancellor, under the Public Records Act 1958, to advise him on matters concerning public records in general and, in particular, on those aspects of the work of the Public Record Office which affect members of the public who make use of it.
Chairman, The Master of the Rolls
Secretary, T. R. Padfield

THE PUBLIC RECORD OFFICE
Kew, Richmond, Surrey TW9 4DU
Tel 0181-876 3444; fax 0181-878 8905

The Public Record Office, originally established in 1838 under the Master of the Rolls, was placed under the direction of the Lord Chancellor in 1958; it became an executive agency in 1992. The Lord Chancellor appoints a Keeper of Public Records, whose duties are to co-ordinate and supervise the selection of records of government departments and the law courts for permanent preservation, to safeguard the records and to make them available to the public. There is a separate record office for Scotland, now called the National Archives of Scotland (*see* page 337).

The Office holds records of central government dating from the Domesday Book (1086) to the present. Under the Public Records Act 1967 they are normally open to inspection when 30 years old, and are then available,

without charge, in the reading rooms (Monday, Wednesday, Friday, Saturday, 9.30–5; Tuesday 10–7; Thursday 9.30–7).
Keeper of Public Records (G3), Mrs S. Tyacke, CB
Director, Public Services Division (G5), Dr E. Hallam Smith
Director, Government, Corporate and Information Services Division (G5), Dr D. Simpson

HOUSE OF LORDS RECORD OFFICE
House of Lords, London SW1A 0PW
Tel 0171-219 3074; fax 0171-219 2570

Since 1497, the records of Parliament have been kept within the Palace of Westminster. They are in the custody of the Clerk of the Parliaments. In 1946 a record department was established to supervise their preservation and their availability to the public. The search room of the office is open to the public Monday–Friday, 9.30–5 (Tuesday to 8, by appointment).

Some three million documents are preserved, including Acts of Parliament from 1497, journals of the House of Lords from 1510, minutes and committee proceedings from 1610, and papers laid before Parliament from 1531. Amongst the records are the Petition of Right, the Death Warrant of Charles I, the Declaration of Breda, and the Bill of Rights. The House of Lords Record Office also has charge of the journals of the House of Commons (from 1547), and other surviving records of the Commons (from 1572), including documents relating to private bill legislation from 1818. Among other documents are the records of the Lord Great Chamberlain, the political papers of certain members of the two Houses, and documents relating to Parliament acquired on behalf of the nation. A permanent exhibition was established in the Royal Gallery in 1979.
Clerk of the Records (£43,910–£70,430), D. J. Johnson, FSA
Deputy Clerk of the Records (£34,462–£55,915), S. K. Ellison
Assistant Clerk of the Records (£30,431–£46,108), D. L. Prior

ROYAL COMMISSION ON HISTORICAL MANUSCRIPTS
Quality House, Quality Court, Chancery Lane, London
WC2A 1HP
Tel 0171-242 1198; fax 0171-831 3550

The Commission was set up by royal warrant in 1869 to enquire and report on collections of papers of value for the study of history which were in private hands. In 1959 a new warrant enlarged these terms of reference to include all historical records, wherever situated, outside the Public Records and gave it added responsibilities as a central co-ordinating body to promote, assist and advise on their proper preservation and storage. The Commission is sponsored by the Department for Culture, Media and Sport.

The Commission also maintains the National Register of Archives (NRA), which contains over 41,000 unpublished lists and catalogues of manuscript collections describing the holdings of local record offices, national and university libraries, specialist repositories and others in the UK and overseas. The NRA can be searched using computerized indices which are available in the Commission's search room.

The Commission also administers the Manorial and Tithe Documents Rules on behalf of the Master of the Rolls.
Chairman, The Lord Bingham of Cornhill, PC

Commissioners, Sir Patrick Cormack, FSA, MP; D. G. Vaisey, CBE, FSA; The Lord Egremont and Leconfield; Sir Matthew Farrer, GCVO; Sir John Sainty, KCB, FSA; Prof. R. H. Campbell, OBE, PH.D.; Very Revd H. E. C. Stapleton, FSA; Sir Keith Thomas, PBA; Mrs C. M. Short; The Earl of Scarbrough; Mrs A. Dundas-Bekker; G. E. Aylmer, D.PHIL, FBA; Mrs S. J. Davies, PH.D.; Mrs A. Prochaska, PH.D.; Prof. H. C. G. Matthew, D.PHIL, FBA

Secretary, C. J. Kitching, PH.D., FSA

SCOTTISH RECORDS ADVISORY COUNCIL
HM General Register House, Edinburgh EH1 3YY
Tel 0131-535 1314; fax 0131-535 1360

The Council was established under the Public Records (Scotland) Act 1937. Its members are appointed by the Secretary of State for Scotland and it may submit proposals or make representations to the Secretary of State, the Lord Justice General or the Lord President of the Court of Session on questions relating to the public records of Scotland.

Chairman, Prof. Anne Crowther
Secretary, D. M. Abbott

NATIONAL ARCHIVES OF SCOTLAND
HM General Register House, Edinburgh EH1 3YY
Tel 0131-535 1314; fax 0131-535 1360

The history of the national archives of Scotland can be traced back to the 13th century. The National Archives of Scotland (formerly the Scottish Record Office) is an executive agency of the Scottish Office and keeps the administrative records of pre-Union Scotland, the registers of central and local courts of law, the public registers of property rights and legal documents, and many collections of local and church records and private archives. Certain groups of records, mainly the modern records of government departments in Scotland, the Scottish railway records, the plans collection, and private archives of an industrial or commercial nature, are preserved in the branch repository at the West Register House in Charlotte Square. The search rooms in both buildings are open Monday–Friday, 9–4.45. A permanent exhibition at the West Register House and changing exhibitions at the General Register House are open to the public on weekdays, 10–4. The National Register of Archives (Scotland) is based in the West Register House.

Keeper of the Records of Scotland, P. M. Cadell
Deputy Keeper, Dr P. D. Anderson

PUBLIC RECORD OFFICE (NORTHERN IRELAND)
66 Balmoral Avenue, Belfast BT9 6NY
Tel 01232-251318; fax 01232-255999

The Public Record Office (Northern Ireland) is responsible for identifying and preserving Northern Ireland's archival heritage and making it available to the public. It is an executive agency of the Department of the Environment for Northern Ireland. The search room is open on weekdays, 9.15–4.15 (Thursday, 9.15–8.45).

Chief Executive, Dr A. P. W. Malcomson

CORPORATION OF LONDON RECORDS OFFICE
Guildhall, London EC2P 2EJ
Tel 0171-332 1251; fax 0171-710 8682

The Corporation of London Records Office contains the municipal archives of the City of London which are regarded as the most complete collection of ancient municipal records in existence. The collection includes charters of William the Conqueror, Henry II, and later kings and queens to 1957; ancient custumals: Liber Horn, Dunthorne, Custumarum, Ordinacionum, Memorandorum and Albus, Liber de Antiquis Legibus, and collections of statutes; continuous series of judicial rolls and books from 1252 and Council minutes from 1275; records of the Old Bailey and Guildhall sessions from 1603; financial records from the 16th century; the records of London Bridge from the 12th century; and numerous subsidiary series and miscellanea of historical interest. The Readers' Room is open Monday–Friday, 9.30–4.45.

Keeper of the City Records, The City Secretary
City Archivist, J. R. Sewell
Deputy City Archivist, Mrs J. M. Bankes

RESEARCH COUNCILS
— see pages 704–10

REVIEW BODIES

The secretariat for these bodies is provided by the Office of Manpower Economics (*see* page 322)

ARMED FORCES PAY
The Review Body on Armed Forces Pay was appointed in 1971 to advise the Prime Minister on the pay and allowances of members of naval, military and air forces of the Crown and of any women's service administered by the Defence Council.

Chairman, Sir Gordon Hourston
Members, Mrs K. Coleman, OBE; J. C. L. Cox, CBE; J. Crosby; Vice-Adm. Sir Toby Frere, KCB; The Lord Gladwin of Clee, CBE; Prof. D. Greenaway; Ms G. Haskins

DOCTORS' AND DENTISTS' REMUNERATION
The Review Body on Doctors' and Dentists' Remuneration was set up in 1971 to advise the Prime Minister on the remuneration of doctors and dentists taking any part in the National Health Service.

Chairman, C. B. Gough
Members, Mrs M. Alderson; Prof. N. Bourne; Miss C. Hui; R. Jackson; C. King, CBE; Prof. Sheila McLean; D. Penton

NURSING STAFF, MIDWIVES, HEALTH VISITORS AND PROFESSIONS ALLIED TO MEDICINE
The Review Body for nursing staff, midwives, health visitors and professions allied to medicine was set up in 1983 to advise the Prime Minister on the remuneration of nursing staff, midwives and health visitors employed in the National Health Service; and also of physiotherapists, radiographers, remedial gymnasts, occupational therapists, orthoptists, chiropodists, dietitians and related grades employed in the National Health Service.

Chairman, Prof. C. Booth
Members, J. Bartlett; Mrs S. Gleig; Miss A. Mackie, OBE; M. Malone-Lee, CB; K. Miles; C. Monks, OBE; Prof. G. Raab

SCHOOL TEACHERS
The School Teachers' Review Body (STRB) was set up under the School Teachers' Pay and Conditions Act 1991. It is required to examine and report on such matters relating to the statutory conditions of employment of

school teachers in England and Wales as may be referred to it by the Secretary of State for Education and Employment.
Chairman, A. R. Vineall
Members, Mrs B. Amey; P. Gedling; M. Harding; V. Harris; Miss J. Langdon; C. Lyddon; Mrs P. Sloane

SENIOR SALARIES

The Senior Salaries Review Body (formerly the Top Salaries Review Body) was set up in 1971 to advise the Prime Minister on the remuneration of the judiciary, senior civil servants and senior officers of the armed forces. In 1993 its remit was extended to cover the pay, pensions and allowances of MPs, ministers and others whose pay is determined by a Ministerial and Other Salaries Order, and the allowances of peers.
Chairman, Sir Michael Perry, CBE
Members, The Hon. M. Beloff, QC; D. Clayman; Prof. S. Dawson; Mrs R. Day; Sir Terry Heiser, GCB; Sir Gordon Hourston; Sir Sydney Lipworth, QC; Miss P. Mann, OBE; M. Sheldon, CBE; Prof. Sir David Williams, QC

ROYAL BOTANIC GARDEN EDINBURGH

20A Inverleith Row, Edinburgh EH3 5LR
Tel 0131-552 7171; fax 0131-248 2901

The Royal Botanic Garden Edinburgh (RBGE) originated as the Physic Garden, established in 1670 beside the Palace of Holyroodhouse. The Garden moved to its present 28-hectare site at Inverleith, Edinburgh, in 1821. There are also three specialist gardens: Younger Botanic Garden Benmore, near Dunoon, Argyllshire; Logan Botanic Garden, near Stranraer, Wigtownshire; and Dawyck Botanic Garden, near Stobo, Peeblesshire. Since 1986, RBGE has been administered by a board of trustees established under the National Heritage (Scotland) Act 1985. It receives an annual grant from the Scottish Office.

RBGE is an international centre for scientific research on plant diversity and for education and conservation. It has an extensive library and a herbarium with over two million dried plant specimens. Public opening hours: Edinburgh site, daily (except Christmas Day and New Year's Day) November–January 9.30–4; February and October 9.30–5; March and September 9.30–6; April–August 9.30–7; specialist gardens, 1 March–31 October 9.30–6. Admission free to Edinburgh site; admission charge to specialist gardens.
Chairman of the Board of Trustees, Prof. M. Wilkins, FRSE
Regius Keeper, vacant

ROYAL BOTANIC GARDENS KEW

Richmond, Surrey TW9 3AB
Tel 0181-332 5000; fax 0181-332 5197
Wakehurst Place, Ardingly, nr Haywards Heath,
W. Sussex RH17 6TN
Tel 01444-894066; fax 01444-894069

The Royal Botanic Gardens (RBG) Kew were originally laid out as a private garden for Kew House for George III's mother, Princess Augusta, in 1759. They were much enlarged in the 19th century, notably by the inclusion of the grounds of the former Richmond Lodge. In 1965 the garden at Wakehurst Place was acquired; it is owned by the National Trust and managed by RBG Kew. Under the National Heritage Act 1983 a board of trustees was set up to administer the gardens, which in 1984 became an

independent body supported by grant-in-aid from the Ministry of Agriculture, Fisheries and Food.

The functions of RBG Kew are to carry out research into plant sciences, to disseminate knowledge about plants and to provide the public with the opportunity to gain knowledge and enjoyment from the gardens' collections. There are extensive national reference collections of living and preserved plants and a comprehensive library and archive. The main emphasis is on plant conservation and bio-diversity.

The gardens are open daily (except Christmas Day and New Year's Day) from 9.30 a.m. (Wakehurst, 10 a.m.). The closing hour varies from 4 p.m. in mid-winter to 6 p.m. on weekdays and 7.30 p.m. on Sundays and Bank Holidays in mid-summer. Admission, 1997, £5.00; concessionary schemes available. Glasshouses (Kew only), 9.30–4.30 (winter); 9.30–5.30 (summer). No dogs except guide-dogs for the blind.

BOARD OF TRUSTEES
Chairman, The Viscount Blakenham
Members, The Earl of Selborne, KBE, FRS (*Queen's Trustee*); R. P. Bauman; Sir Jeffery Bowman; Prof. H. Dickinson; Miss A. Ford; S. de Grey; Lady Lennox-Boyd; Prof. M. Crawley; Prof. J. S. Parker; Prof. C. Payne, OBE; Miss M. Black
Director, Prof. Sir Ghillean Prance, FRS

ROYAL COMMISSION FOR THE EXHIBITION OF 1851

Sherfield Building, Imperial College of Science, Technology and Medicine, London SW7 2AZ
Tel 0171-594 8790; fax 0171-594 8794

The Royal Commission was incorporated by supplemental charter as a permanent commission after winding up the affairs of the Great Exhibition of 1851. Its object is to promote scientific and artistic education by means of funds derived from its Kensington estate, purchased with the surplus left over from the Great Exhibition.
President, HRH The Prince Philip, Duke of Edinburgh, KG, KT, PC
Chairman, Board of Management, Sir Denis Rooke, OM, CBE, FRS, FEng.
Secretary to Commissioners, J. P. W. Middleton, CB

THE ROYAL MINT

Llantrisant, Pontyclun CF72 8YT
Tel 01443-623000

The prime responsibility of the Royal Mint is the provision of United Kingdom coinage, but it actively competes in world markets for a share of the available circulating coin business and, based on the last ten years, two-thirds of the 18,000 tonnes of coins produced annually is exported. The Mint also manufactures special proof and uncirculated quality coins in gold, silver and other metals; military and civil decorations and medals; commemorative and prize medals; and royal and official seals.

The Royal Mint became an executive agency of the Treasury in 1990. The Government announced in June 1998 that it would require the Royal Mint to enter into partnerships with the private sector.
Master of the Mint, The Chancellor of the Exchequer (*ex officio*)
Deputy Master and Comptroller, R. de L. Holmes

ROYAL NATIONAL THEATRE BOARD
South Bank, London, SE1 9PX
Tel 0171-452 3333; fax 0171-452 3344

The chairman and members of the Board of the Royal National Theatre are appointed by the Secretary of State for Culture, Media and Sport.
Chairman, Sir Christopher Hogg
Members, Ms J. Bakewell; The Hon. P. Benson; Gabrielle Lady Greenbury; Sir David Hancock, KCB; G. Hutchings; Ms K. Jones; Ms S. MacGregor, OBE; Sir Ian McKellen; M. Oliver; Sir Tom Stoppard, CBE; P. Wiegand
Company Secretary, Mrs M. McGregor
Director, T. Nunn, CBE

RURAL DEVELOPMENT COMMISSION
141 Castle Street, Salisbury, Wilts. SP1 3TP
Tel 01722-336255; fax 01722-332769

The Rural Development Commission is the government agency for economic and social development in rural England. The Commission advises the Government and undertakes activities aimed at stimulating job creation and the provision of essential services in the countryside. Its sponsoring department is the Department of the Environment, Transport and the Regions. The Government announced in March 1998 that the Rural Development Commission would merge with the Countryside Commission in April 1999 and its rural regeneration work would be transferred to the new regional development agencies.
Chairman, M. Middleton, CBE
Chief Executive, J. Edwards

SCOTTISH COURTS ADMINISTRATION
— *see* page 365

SCOTTISH ENTERPRISE
120 Bothwell Street, Glasgow G2 7JP
Tel 0141-248 2700; fax 0141-221 3217

Scottish Enterprise was established in 1991 and its purpose is to create jobs and prosperity for the people of Scotland. It is funded largely by the Scottish Office and is responsible to the Secretary of State for Scotland. Working in partnership with the private and public sectors, Scottish Enterprise aims to further the development of Scotland's economy, to enhance the skills of the Scottish workforce and to promote Scotland's international competitiveness. Through Locate in Scotland (*see* page 341), Scottish Enterprise is also concerned with attracting firms to Scotland.
Chairman (£30,948), Sir Ian Wood, CBE
Chief Executive, C. Beveridge, CBE

SCOTTISH ENVIRONMENT PROTECTION AGENCY
Erskine Court, The Castle Business Park, Stirling FK9 4TR
Tel 01786-457700; fax 01786-446885

The Scottish Environment Protection Agency came into being on 1 April 1996 under the Environment Act 1995. It is responsible for pollution prevention and control in

Scotland, and for the management and use of water resources. It has regional offices in East Kilbride, Riccarton and Dingwall, and 18 local offices throughout Scotland. It receives funding from the Scottish Office.

THE BOARD
Chairman, Prof. W. Turmeau, CBE
Members, A. Buchan; G. Gordon, OBE; D. Hughes Hallett, FRICS; A. Hewat, OBE; Prof. C. Johnston; C. McChord; Ms A. Magee; A. Paton; Ms J. Shaw

THE EXECUTIVE
Chief Executive, A. Paton
Director of Corporate Services, W. Halcrow
Director of Environmental Strategy, Ms P. Henton
Director, North Region, Prof. D. Mackay
Director, East Region (acting), Dr T. Leatherland
Director, West Region, J. Beveridge

SCOTTISH HOMES
Thistle House, 91 Haymarket Terrace, Edinburgh
EH12 5HE
Tel 0131-313 0044; fax 0131-313 2680

Scottish Homes, the national housing agency for Scotland, aims to improve the quality and variety of housing available in Scotland by working in partnership with the public and private sectors. The agency is a major funder of new and improved housing provided by housing associations and private developers. It is currently transferring its own rented houses to alternative landlords. It is also involved in housing research. Board members are appointed by the Secretary of State for Scotland.
Chairman, J. Ward, CBE
Chief Executive, P. McKinlay, CBE

SCOTTISH NATURAL HERITAGE
12 Hope Terrace, Edinburgh EH9 2AS
Tel 0131-447 4784; fax 0131-446 2277

Scottish Natural Heritage was established in 1992 under the Natural Heritage (Scotland) Act 1991. It provides advice on nature conservation to all those whose activities affect wildlife, landforms and features of geological interest in Scotland, and seeks to develop and improve facilities for the enjoyment and understanding of the Scottish countryside. It is funded by the Scottish Office.
Chairman, M. Magnusson, KBE
Chief Executive, R. Crofts
Chief Scientific Adviser, M. B. Usher
Directors of Operations, J. Thomson (*West*); I. Jardine (*East*); J. Watson (*North*)
Director of Corporate Services, L. Montgomery

SCOTTISH OFFICE
*Dover House, Whitehall, London, SW1A 2AU
Tel 0171-270 3000; fax 0171-270 6730
St Andrew's House, Edinburgh EH1 3DG
Tel 0131-556 8400; fax 0131-244 8240
E-mail: ceu@isdoi.scotoff.gov.uk
Web: http://www.scotland.gov.uk

The Secretary of State for Scotland is responsible in Scotland for a wide range of statutory functions which in England and Wales are the responsibility of a number of departmental ministers. He also works closely with minis-

340   Government Departments and Public Offices

ters in charge of Great Britain departments on topics of special significance to Scotland within their fields of responsibility. His statutory functions are administered by five main departments collectively known as the Scottish Office. The departments are: the Scottish Office Agriculture, Environment and Fisheries Department; the Scottish Office Development Department; the Scottish Office Education and Industry Department; the Scottish Office Department of Health; and the Scottish Office Home Department.

In addition there are a number of other Scottish departments for which the Secretary of State has some degree of responsibility; these include the Scottish Courts Administration, the General Register Office, the National Archives of Scotland (formerly the Scottish Record Office) and the Department of the Registers of Scotland. The Secretary of State also bears ministerial responsibility for the activities in Scotland of several statutory bodies, such as the Forestry Commission, whose functions extend throughout Great Britain.

The directly-elected Scottish Parliament which is to be established in 1999 will assume legislative powers in many of the areas of responsibility of the Scottish Office.
Secretary of State for Scotland, The Rt. Hon. Donald Dewar, MP
  Private Secretary (SCS), K. A. L. Thomson
  Special Advisers, M. Elder; Ms W. Alexander; D. Whitton
  Parliamentary Private Secretary, Ms A. McGuire, MP
Minister of State, Helen Liddell, MP (*Education, Women's Issues, the Co-ordination and Presentation of Policy*)
  Private Secretary, Miss S. Davidson
Minister of State, Henry McLeish, MP (*Home Affairs, Devolution, Local Government*)
  Private Secretary, M. Kellet
Parliamentary Under-Secretaries of State, Dr Calum MacDonald, MP (*Housing, Transport, European Affairs*); Sam Galbraith, MP (*Health, the Arts*); The Lord Sewel, CBE (*Agriculture, the Environment, Fisheries*); Gus Macdonald† (*Business and Industry*)
  Private Secretaries, G. Owenson; Ms R. Sunderland; Miss J. Campbell
Parliamentary Clerk, I. Campbell
Permanent Under-Secretary of State, A. M. Russell
  Private Secretary, Miss S. Morrell
† Not an MP; will receive a life peerage to enable him to sit in the House of Lords

*LIAISON DIVISION
Head of Division (SCS), E. W. Ferguson

*MANAGEMENT GROUP SUPPORT STAFF
Head of Group, M. Grant

PERSONNEL GROUP
16 Waterloo Place, Edinburgh EHI 3DN
Tel 0131-556 8400
Principal Establishment Officer (SCS), C. C. MacDonald
Head of Personnel (SCS), D. F. Middleton

FINANCE DIVISION
Victoria Quay, Edinburgh EH6 6QQ
Tel 0131-556 8400
Principal Finance Officer (SCS), Dr P. S. Collings
Assistant Secretaries (SCS), M. T. S. Batho; J. G. Henderson; D. G. N. Reid; W. T. Tait
Head of Accountancy Services Unit, I. M. Smith
Assistant Director of Finance Strategy, I. A. McLeod

SOLICITOR'S OFFICE
For the Scottish departments and certain UK services, including HM Treasury, in Scotland
Solicitor (SCS), R. Brodie, CB
Deputy Solicitor (SCS), R. M. Henderson

Divisional Solicitors (SCS), J. L. Jamieson, CBE; R. Bland (seconded to Scottish Law Commission); G. C. Duke; I. H. Harvie; H. F. Macdiarmid; J. G. S. Maclean; N. Raven; Mrs L. A. Towers

DIRECTORATE OF ADMINISTRATIVE SERVICES
Victoria Quay, Edinburgh EH6 6QQ
Tel 0131-556 8400
Director of Administrative Services (SCS), A. M. Brown
Chief Estates Officer, J. A. Andrew

Saughton House, Broomhouse Drive, Edinburgh EHII 3DX
Head of Information Technology (SCS), Ms M. McGinn
Director of Telecommunications, K. Henderson, OBE

James Craig Walk, Edinburgh EHI 3BA
Head of Purchasing and Supplies (SCS), N. Bowd

CONSTITUTION GROUP
Pentland House, 47 Robb's Loan, Edinburgh EHI4 ITY
Tel 0131-556 8400
Head of Constitution Group (SCS), R. S. B. Gordon
Constitutional Policy (SCS), J. A. Ewing
Referendum and Implementation (SCS), P. E. Grice
Functions and Whitehall Negotiations (SCS), I. N. Walford
Legal Support to Constitution Group, J. L. Jamieson, CBE

SCOTTISH OFFICE INFORMATION DIRECTORATE
For the Scottish departments and certain UK services in Scotland
Director (SCS), R. Williams
Deputy Director, W. A. McNeill

SCOTTISH OFFICE AGRICULTURE, ENVIRONMENT AND FISHERIES DEPARTMENT
Pentland House, 47 Robb's Loan, Edinburgh EHI4 ITY
Tel 0131-556 8400
Secretary (SCS), J. S. Graham
Under-Secretaries (SCS), T. A. Cameron (*Agriculture*); S. F. Hampson (*Environment*)
Fisheries Secretary (SCS), I. W. Gordon
Assistant Secretaries (SCS), I. R. Anderson; D. A. Brew; D. R. Dickson; Ms I. M. Low; A. J. Rushworth; Dr P. Rycroft; G. M. D. Thomson; I. M. Whitelaw; J. R. Wildgoose
Chief Agricultural Officer (SCS), W. A. Macgregor
Deputy Chief Agricultural Officer (SCS), J. I. Woodrow
Assistant Chief Agricultural Officers, J. Henderson; A. Robb; A. J. Robertson
Chief Agricultural Economist, D. J. Greig
Chief Food and Dairy Officer, S. D. Rooke
Principal Surveyor, vacant
Senior Principal Scientific Officers, Mrs L. A. D. Turl; Dr R. Waterhouse

FISHERIES RESEARCH SERVICES
Marine Laboratory, PO Box 101, Victoria Road, Torry, Aberdeen AB9 8DB
Tel 01224-876544
Director of Fisheries Research for Scotland (SCS), Prof. A. D. Hawkins, PH.D., FRSE
Deputy Director (SCS), J. Davies

Freshwater Fisheries Laboratory
Faskally, Pitlochry, Perthshire PH6 5LB
Tel 01796-472060
Senior Principal Scientific Officers, Dr R. M. Cook; Dr J. M. Davies; Dr A. E. Ellis; Dr A. L. S. Munro; R. G. J. Shelton; Dr P. A. Stewart; Dr C. S. Wardle
Inspector of Salmon and Freshwater Fisheries for Scotland, D. A. Dunkley

ENVIRONMENTAL AFFAIRS GROUP
Under-Secretary (SCS), S. F. Hampson
Assistant Secretaries (SCS), J. D. Calder; J. N. Randall; J. A. Rennie
Chief Water Engineer, P. Wright
Ecological Adviser, Dr J. Miles

EXECUTIVE AGENCIES

INTERVENTION BOARD
— *see* pages 315–16

SCOTTISH AGRICULTURAL SCIENCE AGENCY
East Craig, Edinburgh EH12 8NJ
Tel 0131-244 8890; fax 0131-244 8988
The Agency provides scientific information and advice on agricultural and horticultural crops and the environment, and has various statutory and regulatory functions.
Director, Dr R. K. M. Hay
Deputy Director, S. R. Cooper
Senior Principal Scientific Officer, W. J. Rennie

SCOTTISH FISHERIES PROTECTION AGENCY
Pentland House, 47 Robb's Loan, Edinburgh EH14 ITY
Tel 0131-556 8400; fax 0131-244 6086
The Agency enforces fisheries law and regulations in Scottish waters and ports.
Chief Executive, Capt. P. Du Vivier, RN
Director of Corporate Strategy and Resources, J. B. Roddin
Director of Operational Enforcement, R. J. Walker
Marine Superintendent, Capt. W. A. Brown

SCOTTISH OFFICE DEVELOPMENT DEPARTMENT
Victoria Quay, Edinburgh EH6 6QQ
Tel 0131-556 8400
Secretary (SCS), K. MacKenzie
Under-Secretaries (SCS), D. J. Belfall; J. S. B. Martin
Assistant Secretaries (SCS), M. T. Affolter; A. M. Burnside; E. C. Davidson; J. D. Gallacher; R. A. Grant; D. S. Smith; R. Tait
Senior Economic Adviser (SCS), C. L. Wood

PROFESSIONAL STAFF
Director of Construction and Building Control Group and Chief Architect (SCS), J. E. Gibbons, PH.D., FSA SCOT.
Deputy Director of Construction and Building Control Group and Deputy Chief Architect (SCS), Dr J. P. Cornish
Deputy Director of Construction and Building Control Group and Chief Quantity Surveyor (SCS), A. J. Wyllie
Chief Planner (SCS), A. Mackenzie, CBE
Chief Statistician (SCS), C. R. MacLean

INQUIRY REPORTERS
Robert Stevenson House, 2 Greenside Lane, Edinburgh EH1 3AG
Tel 0131-244 5680
Chief Reporter (SCS), R. M. Hickman
Deputy Chief Reporter (SCS), J. M. McCulloch

NATIONAL ROADS DIRECTORATE
Victoria Quay, Edinburgh EH6 6QQ
Tel 0131-556 8400
Director of Roads (SCS), J. Innes
Deputy Chief Engineers (SCS), J. A. Howison (*Roads*); N. B. MacKenzie (*Bridges*)

EXECUTIVE AGENCY

HISTORIC SCOTLAND
Longmore House, Salisbury Place, Edinburgh EH9 ISH
Tel 0131-668 8600; fax 0131-668 8699

The agency's role is to protect Scotland's historic monuments, buildings and lands, and to promote public understanding and enjoyment of them.
Chief Executive (G3), G. N. Munro
Directors (G5), F. J. Lawrie; I. Maxwell; B. Naylor; B. O'Neil; L. Wilson
Chief Inspector of Ancient Monuments, Dr D. J. Breeze
Chief Inspector, Historic Buildings, J. R. Hume, OBE

SCOTTISH OFFICE EDUCATION AND INDUSTRY DEPARTMENT
Victoria Quay, Edinburgh EH6 6QQ
Tel 0131-556 8400
Secretary (SCS), G. R. Wilson, CB
Under-Secretaries (SCS), D. J. Crawley; E. J. Weeple
Assistant Secretaries (SCS), G. F. Dickson; A. W. Fraser; R. N. Irvine; J. W. L. Lonie; S. Y. MacDonald; A. K. MacLeod; Mrs R. Menlowe; Ms J. Morgan; C. M. Reeves; D. A. Stewart
Chief Statistician (SCS), C. R. MacLean

HM INSPECTORS OF SCHOOLS
Senior Chief Inspector (SCS), D. A. Osler
Depute Senior Chief Inspectors (SCS), F. Crawford; G. H. C. Donaldson
Chief Inspectors (SCS), P. Banks; J. Boyes; Miss K. M. Fairweather; D. E. Kelso; J. J. McDonald; A. S. McGlynn; H. M. Stalker
There are 79 Grade 6 Inspectors

INDUSTRIAL EXPANSION
Meridian Court, 5 Cadogan Street, Glasgow G2 6AT
Tel 0141-248 2855
Under-Secretary (SCS), G. Robson
Industrial Adviser, D. Blair
Scientific Adviser, Prof. D. J. Tedford
Assistant Secretaries (SCS), W. Malone; J. K. Mason; Dr J. Rigg

LOCATE IN SCOTLAND
120 Bothwell Street, Glasgow G2 7JP
Tel 0141-248 2700
Director (SCS), M. Togneri

SCOTTISH TRADE INTERNATIONAL
120 Bothwell Street, Glasgow G2 7JP
Tel 0141-248 2700
Director, D. Taylor

EXECUTIVE AGENCIES

STUDENT AWARDS AGENCY FOR SCOTLAND
Gyleview House, 3 Redheughs Rigg, Edinburgh EH12 9HH
Tel 0131-476 8212; fax 0131-244 5887
Chief Executive, K. MacRae

SCOTTISH OFFICE PENSIONS AGENCY
St Margaret's House, 151 London Road, Edinburgh EH8 7TG
Tel 0131-556 8400; fax 0131-244 3334
The Agency is responsible for the pension arrangements of some 300,000 people, mainly NHS and teaching services employees and pensioners.
Chief Executive, R. Garden
Directors, G. Mowat (*Policy*); A. M. Small (*Operations*); M. J. McDermott (*Resources and Customer Services*)

SCOTTISH OFFICE DEPARTMENT OF HEALTH
St Andrew's House, Edinburgh EH1 3DG
Tel 0131-556 8400

NATIONAL HEALTH SERVICE IN SCOTLAND
MANAGEMENT EXECUTIVE
Chief Executive (SCS), G. R. Scaife
Director of Purchasing (SCS), Dr K. J. Woods
Director of Primary Care (SCS), Mrs A. Robson
Director of Finance (SCS), P. Brady
Director of Human Resources (SCS), G. Marr
Director of Nursing, Miss A. Jarvie
Medical Director (SCS), Dr A. B. Young, FRCPE
Director of Trusts (SCS), P. Wilson
Director of Information Services, NHS, C. B. Knox
Director of Estates, H. R. McCallum
Chief Pharmacist (SCS), W. Scott
Chief Scientist, Prof. G. R. D. Catto
Chief Dental Officer, T. R. Watkins

PUBLIC HEALTH POLICY UNIT
Head of Unit and Chief Medical Officer (SCS), Prof. Sir David Carter, FRCSE, FRCSGlas., FRCPE
Deputy Chief Medical Officer (SCS), Dr A. B. Young, FRCPE
Head of Group (SCS), Mrs N. Munro
Assistant Secretary (SCS), J. T. Brown
Principal Medical Officers, Dr J. B. Louden (*part-time*); Dr A. MacDonald (*part-time*); Dr R. Skinner; Dr E. Sowler
Senior Medical Officers, Dr Angela Anderson; Dr P. W. Brooks; Dr K. G. Brotherston; Dr D. Campbell; Dr D. Colin-Thome (*part-time*); Dr J. Cumming; Dr B. Davis; Dr D. J. Ewing; Dr G. R. Foster; Dr A. Keel; Dr Patricia Madden; Dr H. Whyte

STATE HOSPITAL
Carstairs Junction, Lanark ML11 8RP
Tel 01555-840293
Chairman, D. N. James
General Manager, R. Manson

COMMON SERVICES AGENCY
Trinity Park House, South Trinity Road, Edinburgh EH5 3SE
Tel 0131-552 6255
Chairman, G. Scaife
General Manager, Dr F. Gibb

HEALTH BOARDS
— *see* pages 479–80

SCOTTISH OFFICE HOME DEPARTMENT
Saughton House, Broomhouse Drive, Edinburgh EH11 3XD
Tel 0131-556 8400

Secretary (SCS), J. Hamill, CB
Under-Secretaries (SCS), N. G. Campbell; D. Macniven, TD; Mrs G. M. Stewart
Assistant Secretaries (SCS), C. Baxter; Mrs M. H. Brannan; Mrs M. B. Gunn; R. S. T. MacEwen
Chief Research Officer, Dr C. P. A. Levein
Senior Principal Research Officer, Mrs A. Millar

SOCIAL WORK SERVICES GROUP
James Craig Walk, Edinburgh EH1 3BA
Tel 0131-556 8400

Under-Secretary (SCS), N. G. Campbell
Assistant Secretaries (SCS), G. A. Anderson; Dr J. M. Francis; G. A. McHugh; Mrs V. M. Macniven
Chief Inspector of Social Work Services, A. Skinner
Assistant Chief Inspectors, Mrs G. Ottley; D. Pia; I. C. Robertson

OTHER APPOINTMENTS
HM Chief Inspector of Constabulary, W. Taylor, QPM
HM Chief Inspector of Prisons, C. Fairweather, OBE
Commandant, Scottish Police College, H. I. Watson, OBE, QPM
HM Chief Inspector of Fire Services, N. Morrison, CBE, QFSM
Commandant, Scottish Fire Service Training School, D. Grant, QFSM

MENTAL WELFARE COMMISSION FOR SCOTLAND
K Floor, Argyle House, 3 Lady Lawson Street, Edinburgh EH3 9SH
Tel 0131-222 6111

Chairman, Sir William Reid, KCB
Vice-Chairman, Mrs N. Bennie
Commissioners (part-time), C. Campbell, QC; Mrs F. Cotter; W. Gent; Dr P. Jauhar; Dr Shainool Jiwa; Dr Elizabeth McCall-Smith; D. J. Macdonald; C. McKay; Dr Linda Pollock; A. Robb; Dr Margaret Thomas; Ms M. Whoriskey
Director, Dr J. A. T. Dyer

COUNSEL TO THE SECRETARY OF STATE FOR SCOTLAND UNDER THE PRIVATE LEGISLATION PROCEDURE (SCOTLAND) ACT 1936
50 Frederick Street, Edinburgh EH2 1EN
Tel 0131-226 6499

Senior Counsel, G. S. Douglas, QC
Junior Counsel, N. M. P. Morrison

EXECUTIVE AGENCIES

NATIONAL ARCHIVES OF SCOTLAND
— *see* page 337

REGISTERS OF SCOTLAND
— *see* pages 316–17

SCOTTISH COURT SERVICE
— *see* page 365

SCOTTISH PRISON SERVICE
— *see* pages 381–2

GENERAL REGISTER OFFICE
New Register House, Edinburgh EH1 3YT
Tel 0131-334 0380; fax 0131-314 4400

The General Register Office for Scotland is an associated department of the Scottish Office. It is the office of the Registrar-General for Scotland, who has responsibility for civil registration and the taking of censuses in Scotland and has in his custody the following records: the statutory registers of births, deaths, still births, adoptions, marriages and divorces; the old parish registers (recording births, deaths and marriages, etc., before civil registration began in 1855); and records of censuses of the population in Scotland. Hours of public access: Monday–Friday 9–4.30.
Registrar-General, J. Meldrum
Deputy Registrar-General, B. V. Philp
Senior Principal (G6), D. A. Orr
Principals (G7), D. B. L. Brownlee; R. C. Lawson; F. D. Garvie
Statisticians (G7), G. Compton; G. W. L. Jackson; F. G. Thomas

SCOTTISH PRISONS COMPLAINTS COMMISSION
Government Buildings, Broomhouse Drive, Edinburgh EH11 3XD
Tel 0131-244 8423; fax 0131-244 8430

The Commission was established in 1994. It is an independent body to which prisoners in Scottish prisons can make application in relation to any matter where they have failed to obtain satisfaction from the Prison Service's internal grievance procedures. Clinical judgments made by medical officers, matters which are the subject of legal proceedings and matters relating to sentence, conviction and parole decision-making are excluded from the Commission's jurisdiction. The Commissioner is appointed by the Secretary of State for Scotland.
Commissioner, Dr J. McManus

SEA FISH INDUSTRY AUTHORITY
18 Logie Mill, Logie Green Road, Edinburgh EH7 4HG
Tel 0131-558 3331; fax 0131-558 1442

Established under the Fisheries Act 1981, the Authority is required to promote the efficiency of the sea fish industry. It carries out research relating to the industry and gives advice on related matters. It provides training, promotes the marketing, consumption and export of sea fish and sea fish products, and may provide financial assistance for the improvement of fishing vessels in respect of essential safety equipment. It is responsible to the Ministry of Agriculture, Fisheries and Food.
Chairman, E. Davey
Chief Executive, A. C. Fairbairn

THE SECURITY AND INTELLIGENCE SERVICES

Under the Intelligence Services Act 1994, the Intelligence and Security Committee of Parliamentarians was established to oversee the work of GCHQ, MI5 and MI6. The Act also established the Intelligence Services Tribunal (see page 314), which hears complaints made against GCHQ and MI6. The Security Service Tribunal and Commissioner (see below) investigate complaints about MI5.

DEFENCE INTELLIGENCE STAFF
— see Defence section

GOVERNMENT COMMUNICATIONS HEADQUARTERS (GCHQ)
Priors Road, Cheltenham, Glos GL52 5AJ
Tel 01242-221491; fax 01242-226816

GCHQ produces signals intelligence in support of the Government's security, defence and economic policies. It also provides advice and assistance to government departments and the armed forces on the security of their communications and information technology systems. It was placed on a statutory footing by the Intelligence Services Act 1994 and is headed by a director who is directly accountable to the Foreign Secretary.
Director, F. N. Richards, CVO, CMG

THE SECRET INTELLIGENCE SERVICE (MI6)
Vauxhall Cross, PO Box 1300, London SE1 1BD

The Secret Intelligence Service produces secret intelligence in support of the Government's security, defence, foreign and economic policies. It was placed on a statutory footing by the Intelligence Services Act 1994 and is headed by a director-general who is directly accountable to the Foreign Secretary.
Director-General, Sir David Spedding, KCMG, CVO, OBE

THE SECURITY SERVICE (MI5)
Thames House, PO Box 3255, London SW1P 1AE
Tel 0171-930 9000

The function of the Security Service is the protection of national security, in particular against threats from espionage, terrorism, sabotage and the proliferation of weapons of mass destruction, from the activities of agents of foreign powers, and from actions intended to overthrow or undermine parliamentary democracy by political, industrial or violent means. It is also the Service's function to safeguard the economic well-being of the UK against threats posed by the actions or intentions of persons outside the British Islands. Under the Security Service Act 1996, the Service's role was extended to support the police and customs in the prevention and detection of serious crime.

The Security Service was placed on a statutory footing by the Security Service Act 1989 and is headed by a director-general who is directly accountable to the Home Secretary.
Director-General, S. Lander

SECURITY SERVICE COMMISSIONER
c/o PO Box 18, London SE1 0TZ
Tel 0171-273 4095

The Commissioner is appointed by the Prime Minister. He keeps under review the issue of warrants by the Home Secretary under the Intelligence Services Act 1994, and is required to help the Security Service Tribunal by investigating complaints which allege interference with property and by offering all such assistance in discharging its functions as it may require. He is also required to submit an annual report on the discharge of his functions to the Prime Minister.
Commissioner, The Rt. Hon. Lord Justice Stuart-Smith
  Private Secretary, E. R. Wilson

SECURITY SERVICE TRIBUNAL
PO Box 18, London SE1 0TZ
Tel 0171-273 4095

The Security Service Act 1989 established a tribunal of three to five senior members of the legal profession, independent of the Government and appointed by The Queen, to investigate complaints from any person about anything which they believe the Security Service has done to them or to their property.
President, The Rt. Hon. Lord Justice Simon Brown
Vice-President, Sheriff J. McInnes, QC
Member, Sir Richard Gaskell
Secretary, E. R. Wilson

SERIOUS FRAUD OFFICE
Elm House, 10–16 Elm Street, London WCIX OBJ
Tel 0171-239 7272; fax 0171-837 1689

The Serious Fraud Office works under the superintendence of the Attorney-General. Its remit is to investigate and prosecute serious and complex fraud. (Other fraud cases are currently handled by the fraud divisions of the Crown Prosecution Service.) The scope of its powers covers England, Wales and Northern Ireland. The staff includes lawyers, accountants and other support staff; investigating teams work closely with the police.
Director, Mrs R. Wright

DEPARTMENT OF SOCIAL SECURITY
Richmond House, 79 Whitehall, London SW1A 2NS
Tel 0171-238 0800

The Department of Social Security is responsible for the payment of benefits and the collection of contributions under the National Insurance and Industrial Injuries schemes, and for the payment of child benefit, one-parent benefit, income support and family credit. It administers the Social Fund, and is responsible for assessing the means of applicants for legal aid. It is also responsible for the payment of war pensions and the operation of the child maintenance system.
Secretary of State for Social Security, The Rt. Hon. Alistair Darling, MP
  Principal Private Secretary, R. Clark
  Special Advisers, J. McTernan; A. Maugham
  Parliamentary Private Secretary, Ms A. Coffey, MP
Minister of State, John Denham, MP
  Private Secretary, D. Higlett
Parliamentary Under-Secretaries of State, The Baroness Hollis of Heigham, D.Phil. (*Family Policy, Child Benefit, Child Support, War Pensions*); Angela Eagle, MP (*Income-related Benefits, International and Green Issues*); Stephen Timms, MP (*Disability and Sickness Benefits, National Insurance Contributions, Devolution, Independent Living Fund*)
  Private Secretaries, B. Stayte; D. Topping; Ms V. Hutchinson; Ms H. McCarthy; R. Sanguinaza; Ms L. Wright
Permanent Secretary (*G1*), Dame Ann Bowtell, DCB (*until April 1999*)
  Private Secretary, C. Jackson

CORPORATE MANAGEMENT GROUP
Director (*G2*), J. Tross

PERSONNEL AND HQ SUPPORT SERVICES DIRECTORATE
Director, S. Hewitt
Section Heads (*G5*), T. Perl; (*G7*), R. Yeats; B. Glew; J. Elliott

ANALYTICAL SERVICES DIVISION
The Adelphi, 1–11 John Adam Street, London WC2N 6HT
Tel 0171-962 8000

Director (*G3*), D. Stanton
Chief Statistician (*G5*), N. Dyson
Senior Economic Advisers (*G5*), J. Ball; G. Harris; R. D'Souza
Deputy Chief Scientific Officer (*G5*), D. Barnbrook
Chief Research Officers (*G5*), Ms S. Duncan; S. Rice

FINANCE DIVISION
Grade 3, S. Lord

INFORMATION DIRECTORATE
Director of Information (*G4*), M. Sixsmith
Deputy Head of Information (*G6*), J. Bretherton
Chief Press Officer (*G7*), Ms S. Lewis
Chief Publicity Officer (*G7*), Ms A. Martin

SOCIAL SECURITY POLICY GROUP
Head of Policy Group (*G2*), P. R. C. Gray
Policy Directors (*G3*), M. L. Whippman, CB; Miss M. Peirson, CB; D. Brereton; U. Brennan
Head of Women's Unit (*G3*), Ms F. Reynolds, CBE
Policy Managers (*G5*), Mrs A. Lingwood; D. Jackson; B. O'Gorman; M. Street; J. Groombridge; Mrs C. Rookes; B. Calderwood; D. Allsop, CBE; C. Evans; J. Hughes; P. Cleasby; P. Morgan; Mrs L. Richards; Ms J. Shersby; (*G6*), B. Layton; I. Williams; P. Barrett; J. Griffiths-Chayes; K. Sadler; N. Ward

SOLICITOR'S OFFICE
Solicitor (*G2*), Mrs M. A. Morgan, CB

SOLICITOR'S DIVISION A
New Court, 48 Carey Street, London WC2A 2LS
Tel 0171-412 1466

Principal Assistant Solicitor (*G3*), J. A. Catlin
Assistant Solicitors (*G5*), J. M. Swainson; Mrs G. Massiah; Mrs F. A. Logan; C. Cooper; H. Connell; P. Milledge

SOLICITOR'S DIVISION B
New Court, 48 Carey Street, London WC2A 2LS
Tel 0171-412 1528

Solicitor (*G2*), Mrs M. A. Morgan, CB
Assistant Solicitors (*G5*), R. G. S. Aitken; Ms S. Edwards; S. Cooper

SOLICITOR'S DIVISION C
New Court, 48 Carey Street, London WC2A 2LS
Tel 0171-412 1342

Principal Assistant Solicitor (*G3*), Mrs G. S. Kerrigan
Assistant Solicitors (*G5*), R. J. Dormer; Miss M. E. Trefgarne; Mrs S. Walker; G. Aitkin

BENEFITS FRAUD INSPECTORATE
Berkeley House, 12A North Park Road, Harrogate HG1 5QA
Tel 01423-832922
Director-General (*G3*), I. Stewart

EXECUTIVE AGENCIES
BENEFITS AGENCY
Quarry House, Quarry Hill, Leeds LS2 7UA
Tel 0113-232 4000

The Agency administers claims for and payments of social security benefits.
Chief Executive, P. Mathison
  Private Secretary, R. Baldwin
Directors, J. Codling (*Finance*); M. Fisher (*Personnel and Communications*); S. Heminsley (*Strategic and Planning*); A. Cleveland (*Operations Support*); N. Haighton, G. McCorkell (*Projects*)

Medical Policy
Principal Medical Officers, Dr M. Aylward; Dr P. Dewis; Dr P. Sawney; Dr A. Braidwood; Dr P. Stidolph

CHILD SUPPORT AGENCY
DSS Long Benton, Benton Park Road, Newcastle upon Tyne NE98 1YX
Tel 0191-213 5000

The Agency was set up in April 1993. It is responsible for the administration of the Child Support Act and for the assessment, collection and enforcement of maintenance payments for all new cases.
Chief Executive, Ms F. Boardman
Directors, M. Davison; C. Peters; M. Isaacs; T. Read

CONTRIBUTIONS AGENCY
DSS Longbenton, Benton Park Road, Newcastle upon Tyne NE98 1YX
Tel 0191-213 5000

The Agency collects and records National Insurance contributions, maintains individual records, and provides an advisory service on National Insurance matters. The Contributions Agency and the Board of Inland Revenue are to merge in April 1999.
Chief Executive (G3), G. Bertram
Management Board, T. Lord; D. Slater; B. Woodley; A. Fisher
Non-Executive Members, S. Banyard; C. Dodgson

INFORMATION TECHNOLOGY SERVICES AGENCY
4th Floor, Verulam Point, Station Way, St Albans, Herts AL1 5HE
Tel 01727-815835; fax 01727-833740

The Agency maintains and oversees policies on information technology strategy, procurement, technical standards and security.
Chief Executive (acting), P. Sharkey
Directors, J. Thomas; J. Brewood; G. Brown; B. Barnes; B. Gormley; J. Delamere; C. Nicholls
Non-Executive Directors, K. Pfotzer; K. Bogg

WAR PENSIONS AGENCY
Norcross, Blackpool, Lancs FY5 3WP
Tel 01253-856123

The Agency administers the payment of war disablement and war widows' pensions and provides welfare services and support to war disablement pensioners, war widows and their dependants and carers.
Chief Executive, G. Hextall

Central Advisory Committee on War Pensions
6th Floor, The Adelphi, 1–11 John Adam Street, London WC2N 6HT
Tel 0171-962 8062
Secretary, C. Pike

ADVISORY BODIES

NATIONAL DISABILITY COUNCIL, Level 4, Caxton House, Tothill Street, London SW1H 9NA. Tel: 0171-273 5636. *Chairman*, D. Grayson, OBE; *Secretary*, R. Timm
SOCIAL SECURITY ADVISORY COMMITTEE, New Court, Carey Street, London WC2A 2LS. Tel 0171-412 1508. *Chairman*, Lt.-Gen. Sir Thomas Boyd-Carpenter, KBE; *Secretary*, Ms G. Saunders

SPORTS COUNCIL
— *see* United Kingdom Sports Council

OFFICE FOR STANDARDS IN EDUCATION (OFSTED)
Alexandra House, 33 Kingsway, London WC2B 6SE
Tel 0171-421 6574; fax 0171-421 6522

A non-ministerial government department established in 1992 to keep the Secretary of State and the public informed about the standards and management of schools in England, and to establish and monitor an independent inspection system for maintained schools in England. *See also* page 425.
HM Chief Inspector, C. Woodhead
Directors of Inspection, A. J. Rose, CBE; M. J. Tomlinson, CBE

TEAM MANAGERS
Planning and Resources, Miss J. M. Phillips, CBE
Personnel Management, C. Payne
Contracts, C. Bramley
Communications, Media and Public Relations, J. Lawson
Information Systems, vacant
Administrative Support and Estates Management, K. Francis
Training and Assessment of Independent Inspectors, B. McCafferty
Inspection Quality, Monitoring and Development, P. Matthews
LEA Reviews, Reorganization Proposals, D. Singleton
School Improvement, Ms E. Passmore
Nursery and Primary, K. Lloyd
Secondary and Independent, C. Gould
Post-Compulsory, D. West
Special Educational Needs, C. Marshall
Research, Analysis and International, Ms C. Agambar
Teacher Education and Training, D. Taylor
Nursery Education Scheme, D. Bradley
Specialist Advisers, N. Bufton; B. Ponchaud; A. Dobson; M. Ive; P. Smith; Ms J. Mills; G. Clay; P. Jones; J. Hertrich; Ms B. Wintersgill; S. Harrison

There are about 200 HM Inspectors

COMMITTEE ON STANDARDS IN PUBLIC LIFE
Horse Guards Road, London SW1P 3AL
Tel 0171-270 5875; fax 0171-270 5874

The Committee on Standards in Public Life (formerly known as the Nolan Committee, now known as the Neill Committee) was set up in October 1994. It is a standing body whose chairman and members are appointed by the Prime Minister; three members are nominated by the leaders of the three main political parties. The committee's remit is to examine current concerns about standards of conduct of all holders of public office, including arrangements relating to financial and commercial activities, and to make recommendations as to any changes in present arrangements which might be required to ensure the highest standards of propriety in public life. In November 1997 the committee's remit was widened to review issues in relation to the funding of political parties, and to make recommendations as to any changes in present arrangements. The committee does not investigate individual allegations of misconduct.
Chairman, The Lord Neill of Bladen, QC
Members, Sir Clifford Boulton, GCB; Sir Anthony Cleaver; The Lord Goodhart, QC; Ms F. Heaton; Prof. A. King; The Rt. Hon. J. MacGregor, OBE, MP; The Lord Shore of Stepney, PC; Sir William Utting, CB; Ms D. Warwick
Secretary (SCS), R. Horsman

OFFICE OF TELECOMMUNICATIONS
50 Ludgate Hill, London EC4M 7JJ
Tel 0171-634 8700; fax 0171- 634 8943

The Office of Telecommunications (Oftel) is a non-ministerial government department responsible for supervising telecommunications activities and broadcast transmission in the UK. Its principal functions are to ensure that holders of telecommunications licences comply with their licence conditions; to maintain and promote effective competition in telecommunications; and to promote the interests of purchasers and other users of telecommunication services and apparatus in respect of prices, quality and variety.

The Director-General has powers to deal with anti-competitive practices and monopolies. He also has a duty to consider all reasonable complaints and representations about telecommunication apparatus and services.

Director-General, D. Edmonds
Deputy Director-General, Miss A. Lambert
Director of Network Competition, Mrs A. Taylor
Director of Consumer Affairs, Mrs V. Peters
Director of Licensing Policy, Ms S. Chambers
Director of Competition and Fair Trading, Mrs J. Whittles
Technical Director, P. Walker
Economic Director, A. Bell
Legal Director, D. H. M. Ingham
Administration Director, D. Smith
Director of Communications, N. Gammage
Director of Convergence and International Affairs, J. Niblett

TOURIST BOARDS
(For British Tourist Authority, *see* page 287)

The English Tourist Board, the Scottish Tourist Board, the Wales Tourist Board and the Northern Ireland Tourist Board are responsible for developing and marketing the tourist industry in their respective countries. The Boards' main objectives are to promote holidays and to encourage the provision and improvement of tourist amenities.

In July 1998 the Government published a discussion document including a proposal to reform the structure and workings of the English Tourist Board.

ENGLISH TOURIST BOARD, Thames Tower, Black's Road, London W6 9EL. Tel: 0181-846 9000. *Chief Executive,* T. Bartlett
SCOTTISH TOURIST BOARD, 23 Ravelston Terrace, Edinburgh EH4 3EU. Tel: 0131-332 2433; Thistle House, Beechwood Park North, Inverness IV2 3ED. Tel: 01463-716996. *Chief Executive,* T. Buncle
WALES TOURIST BOARD, Brunel House, 2 Fitzalan Road, Cardiff CF2 1UY. Tel: 01222-499909. *Chief Executive,* J. French
NORTHERN IRELAND TOURIST BOARD, St Anne's Court, 59 North Street, Belfast BT1 1NB. Tel: 01232-231221. *Chief Executive,* I. Henderson

DEPARTMENT OF TRADE AND INDUSTRY
1 Victoria Street, London SW1H 0ET
Tel 0171-215 5000; fax 0171-222 2629
Web: http://www.dti.gov.uk

The Department is responsible for international trade policy, including the promotion of UK trade interests in the European Union, GATT, OECD, UNCTAD and other international organizations; the promotion of UK exports and assistance to exporters; policy in relation to industry and commerce, including industrial relations policy; policy towards small firms; regional industrial assistance; legislation and policy in relation to the Post Office; competition policy and consumer protection; the development of national policies in relation to all forms of energy and the development of new sources of energy, including international aspects of energy policy; policy on science and technology research and development; space policy; standards, quality and design; and company legislation.

Secretary of State for Trade and Industry, The Rt. Hon. Peter Mandelson, MP
Principal Private Secretary, A. Phillipson
Private Secretaries, B. Coates; J. Fiennes
Minister of State, John Battle, MP (*Energy, Industry, Environment*)
Senior Private Secretary, R. Riley
Parliamentary Private Secretary, Ms A. Campbell, MP
Minister of State, Ian McCartney, MP (*Employment Relations*)
Private Secretary, Ms R. Hill
Parliamentary Private Secretary, F. Doran, MP
Minister of State, Brian Wilson, MP (*Trade*)
Private Secretary, U. Marthaler
Minister of State, The Lord Simon of Highbury, CBE (*Trade and Competitiveness in Europe*) (*joint DTI/Treasury minister*)
Private Secretary, J. Mitchell
Parliamentary Under-Secretaries of State, Dr Kim Howells, MP (*Competition and Consumer Affairs*); Barbara Roche, MP (*Small Firms and Regional Policy*); The Lord Sainsbury of Turville (*Science*)
Private Secretaries, Ms D. Parr; Ms P. Ciniewicz
British Overseas Trade Board Chairman, M. Laing, CBE
Private Secretary, M. Shute
Parliamentary Clerk, T. Williams
Permanent Secretary, M. Scholar, CB
Private Secretary, R. Collins
Chief Scientific Adviser and Head of Office of Science and Technology, Sir Robert May, FRS
Private Secretary, R. Clay
Directors-General, Sir John Cadogan, CBE, FRS (*Director-General of the Research Councils*); A. Hutton, CB (*Trade Policy*); T. Harris, CMG (*Export Promotion*); D. Durie, CMG (*Regional and Small and Medium Enterprises*); B. Hilton, CB (*Corporate and Consumer Affairs*); D. Nissen (*The Solicitor*); Ms A. Walker (*Energy*); J. Spencer (*Resources and Services*); A. Macdonald, CB (*Industry*)

DIVISIONAL ORGANIZATION

‡BRITISH NATIONAL SPACE CENTRE
Director-General (SCS), D. R. Davis
Deputy Director-General (SCS), D. Leadbeater
Directors (SCS), A. Cooper; Dr P. Murdin; Dr D. Lumley

BUSINESS LINK DIRECTORATE
Director of Business Link (SCS), P. Waller
Directors (SCS), J. Reid; P. Bentley; Mrs P. Jackson; T. Evans

COMPETITIVENESS UNIT
Director of Competitiveness Unit (SCS), D. Evans
Directors (SCS), S. Haddrill; T. Soane; J. Reynolds

‡CHEMICALS AND BIOTECHNOLOGY DIRECTORATE
Director of Chemicals and Biotechnology (SCS), M. Baker
Directors (SCS), Ms G. Alliston; Dr E. A. M. Baker

COAL DIRECTORATE
Director (SCS), M. Atkinson

COMMUNICATIONS DIRECTORATE
Director of Information (SCS), Dr S. Sklaroff
Director of News (SCS), M. Ricketts
Director of Publicity (SCS), Miss P. R. A. Freedman

‡COMMUNICATIONS AND INFORMATION INDUSTRIES DIRECTORATE
Director of Communications and Information Industries (SCS), W. MacIntyre
Directors (SCS), R. King; N. McMillan, CMG; N. Worman; S. Pride

COMPANY LAW AND INVESTIGATIONS DIRECTORATE
Director of Company Law and Investigations (SCS), R. Rogers
Directors (SCS), N. D. Peace; D. E. Love

CONSUMER AFFAIRS AND COMPETITION POLICY DIRECTORATE
Director of Consumer Affairs and Competition Policy (SCS), P. Salvidge
Directors (SCS), P. Mason; Miss D. Gane; Dr A. Eggington; G. Boon; A. Brimelow; M. Higson

CONSUMER GOODS, BUSINESS AND POSTAL SERVICES DIRECTORATE
Director of Consumer Goods, Business and Postal Services (SCS), M. Baker
Directors (SCS), B. Hopson; Ms J. Britton

ECONOMICS AND STATISTICS DIRECTORATE
Chief Economic Adviser (SCS), D. R. Coates
Directors (SCS), K. Warwick; Ms J. Dougharty; M. Bradbury

ELECTRICITY DIRECTORATE
Director of Electricity (SCS), J. Green

EMPLOYMENT RELATIONS DIRECTORATE
Director of Industrial Relations (SCS), Ms H. Leiser
Directors (SCS), Dr E. Baker; R. Niblett; A. Wright; Mrs Z. Hornstein; Ms N. Carter; K. Masson

ENERGY POLICY AND ANALYSIS UNIT
Director of Energy Policy and Analysis (SCS), M. Keay
Directors (SCS), E. Evans; G. C. White

ENERGY TECHNOLOGIES DIRECTORATE
Director (SCS), G. Bevan

‡ENGINEERING INDUSTRIES DIRECTORATE
Director of Engineering Industries (SCS), M. O'Shea
Directors (SCS), J. Neilson; M. Ralph; R. Kingcombe; H. Brown; J. Grewe; R. Poole; A. Vinall; Ms A. Wilks

ENGINEERING INSPECTORATE
Director of Engineering Inspectorate (SCS), Dr P. Fenwick

‡ENVIRONMENT DIRECTORATE
Director of Environment (SCS), Dr C. Hicks
Director (SCS), D. Prior

‡ESTATES AND FACILITIES MANAGEMENT DIRECTORATE
Director (SCS), M. Coolican

EUROPE DIRECTORATE
Kingsgate House, 66–74 Victoria Street, London SW1E 6SW
Director (SCS), B. Stow

EXPORT CONTROL AND NON-PROLIFERATION DIRECTORATE
Kingsgate House, 66–74 Victoria Street, London SW1E 6SW

Director of Export Control and Non-Proliferation (SCS), Dr R. Heathcote
Directors (SCS), A. J. Mantle, J. Neve

EXPORT PROMOTION DIRECTORATES
Kingsgate House, 66–74 Victoria Street, London SW1E 6SW
Director, Markets and Sectors (SCS), M. Gibson
Directors (SCS), M. Mowlam (*The Americas*); M. Cohen (*Asia Pacific*); K. Levinson (*Central and Eastern Europe*); S. Lyle Smythe (*Business in Europe*); S. Khanna (*Middle East, Near East and North Africa*); N. McInnes (*Sub-Saharan Africa and South Asia*); A. Sparkes (*Sectors, Services and Outward Investment*)

EXPORT SERVICES DIRECTORATE
Kingsgate House, 66–74 Victoria Street, London SW1E 6SW
Director (SCS), A. Reynolds

FINANCE AND RESOURCE MANAGEMENT DIRECTORATE
Director of Finance and Resource Management (SCS), J. Phillips
Directors (SCS), E. Hosker; K. Hills; N. Nandra

IMPORT POLICY DIRECTORATE
Kingsgate House, 66–74 Victoria Street, London SW1E 6SW
Director (SCS), A. Berry

‡INDUSTRY ECONOMICS AND STATISTICS DIRECTORATE
Director (SCS), Dr N. Owen

‡INFORMATION MANAGEMENT AND TECHNOLOGY DIRECTORATE
Director (SCS), R. Wheeler

INFRASTRUCTURE AND ENERGY PROJECTS DIRECTORATE
Director of Infrastructure and Energy Projects (SCS), M. Stanley
Directors (SCS), G. Atkinson; Dr K. Forrest; B. Gallagher; J. Campbell

‡INNOVATION UNIT
Director (SCS), Dr A. Keddie

INSURANCE DIRECTORATE
Director of Insurance (SCS), G. Dart
Directors (SCS), R. Allen; K. Long; J. Whitlock; P. Casey

‡INTERNAL AUDIT
Director of Internal Audit (SCS), A. C. Elkington

INTERNATIONAL ECONOMICS DIRECTORATE
Kingsgate House, 66–74 Victoria Street, London SW1E 6SW
Director (SCS), C. Moir

INVEST IN BRITAIN BUREAU
Chief Executive (SCS), A. Fraser

JOINT EXPORT PROMOTION DIRECTORATE (FCO/DTI)
Kingsgate House, 66–74 Victoria Street, London SW1E 6SW
Director-General of Export Promotion (SCS), T. Harris, CMG
Director, JEPD (SCS), D. Hall

LEGAL RESOURCE MANAGEMENT AND BUSINESS LAW UNIT
10 Victoria Street, London SW1H 0NN

‡ At 151 Buckingham Palace Road, London SW1W 9SS

The Solicitor and Director-General (SCS), D. Nissen
Director (SCS), P. Burke

LEGAL SERVICES DIRECTORATE A
10 Victoria Street, London SWIH ONN
Director of Legal A (SCS), J. Stanley
Legal Directors (SCS), J. Roberts; Miss N. O'Flynn;
S. Hyett; Miss G. Richmond

LEGAL SERVICES DIRECTORATE B
10 Victoria Street, London SWIH ONN
Director of Legal B (SCS), P. Bovey
Legal Directors (SCS), R. Baker; T. Susman; B. Welch; R.
Perkins; Ms C. Croft; Ms S. Hardy

LEGAL SERVICES DIRECTORATE C
10 Victoria Street, London SWIH ONN
Director of Legal C (SCS), Ms A. Brett-Holt
Legal Directors (SCS), R. Perkins; R. Green; M. Bucknill; C.
Raikes; A. Woods; C. Osborne

LEGAL SERVICES DIRECTORATE D
10 Victoria Street, London SWIH ONN
Director of Legal D (SCS), Mrs T. Dunstan
Directors (SCS), S. Milligan; S. Clements

MANAGEMENT BEST PRACTICE
Director of Management Best Practice, Dr K. Poulter
Deputy Director (SCS), Dr I. Harrison

NEW ISSUES AND DEVELOPING COUNTRIES
Kingsgate House, 66–74 Victoria Street, London
SWIE 6SW
Director (SCS), C. Bridge

NUCLEAR INDUSTRIES DIRECTORATE
Director of Nuclear Industries (SCS), N. Hirst
Directors (SCS), Dr M. Draper; Dr E. Drage; I. Downing; S.
Bowen

OFFICE OF SCIENCE AND TECHNOLOGY: SCIENCE AND
ENGINEERING BASE DIRECTORATE
Albany House, 84–86 Petty France, London SWIH 9ST
Director, Science and Engineering Base (SCS), A. Quigley
Directors (SCS), Ms F. Price; Dr K. Root

OFFICE OF SCIENCE AND TECHNOLOGY:
TRANSDEPARTMENTAL SCIENCE AND TECHNOLOGY
DIRECTORATE
Albany House, 84–86 Petty France, London SWIH 9ST
Director, Transdepartmental Science and Technology (SCS), Ms
H. Williams
Directors (SCS), R. Wright; S. Spivey; Mrs P. Sellers; Ms J.
Donaldson

OIL AND GAS DIRECTORATE
1 Victoria Street, London SWIH OET
Director of Oil and Gas (SCS), G. Dart
Directors (SCS), J. R. V. Brooks, CBE; D. Saunders

Atholl House, 86–88 Guild Street, Aberdeen AB9 IDR
Tel 01224-254059
Director of Oil and Gas (SCS), S. Toole

REGIONAL ASSISTANCE DIRECTORATE
Director of Regional Assistance (SCS), D. Miner
Director (SCS), S. Robins

REGIONAL EUROPEAN FUNDS DIRECTORATE
Director (SCS), Ms R. Anderson

REGIONAL POLICY DIRECTORATE
Director (SCS), D. Smith

SENIOR STAFF MANAGEMENT
Director (SCS), Ms K. Elliott

SMALL AND MEDIUM-SIZED ENTERPRISES (SME)
POLICY DIRECTORATE
St Mary's House, Level 2, c/o Moorfoot, Sheffield SI 4PQ
Director (SCS), J. Thompson

SMALL AND MEDIUM-SIZED ENTERPRISES (SME)
TECHNOLOGY DIRECTORATE
Director (SCS), R. Allpress

STAFF PAY AND CONDITIONS
Director (SCS), C. Johnston

STAFF PERSONNEL OPERATIONS
Director (SCS), I. Cameron

STAFF POLICY AND DEVELOPMENT UNIT
Director (SCS), Ms B. Habberjam

‡TECHNOLOGY AND STANDARDS DIRECTORATE
Director of Technology and Standards (SCS), R. Foster
Directors (SCS), J. M. Barber; G. C. Riggs; J. Hobday; G.
McGregor; D. Reed

TRADE POLICY DIRECTORATE
Kingsgate House, 66–74 Victoria Street, London
SWIE 6SW
Director (SCS), J. Hunt

UTILITIES REVIEW TEAM
Director of Utilities Review Team (SCS), Dr C. Bell
Director (SCS), R. Bent

BRITISH OVERSEAS TRADE BOARD
Kingsgate House, 66–74 Victoria Street, London SWIE
6SW
Tel 0171-215 5000

President, The Secretary of State for Trade and Industry
Chairman, M. Laing, CBE
Vice-Chairman, HRH The Duke of Kent, KG, GCMG, GCVO
Members, A. Buxton; A. Turner; P. Godwin, CBE; R.
Burman, CBE; T. Harris, CMG; Sir Gilbert Thompson,
OBE; Sir Clive Thompson; R. Turner, OBE; V. Wark; V.
Brown; J. Shepherd, CMG; D. Hall; C. Robinson; A.
Summers
Secretary, Dr D. Walker

REGIONAL OFFICES
— see pages 304–5

EXECUTIVE AGENCIES

COMPANIES HOUSE
Companies House, Crown Way, Cardiff CF4 3UZ
Tel 01222-380801; fax 01222-380900
London Search Room, 55–71 City Road, London ECIY IBB
Tel 0171-253 9393; fax 0171-490 1147
37 Castle Terrace, Edinburgh EHI 2EB
Tel 0131-535 5800; fax 0131-535 5820

Companies House incorporates companies, registers company documents and provides company information.
Registrar of Companies for England and Wales, J. Holden
Registrar for Scotland, J. Henderson

EMPLOYMENT TRIBUNALS SERVICE
19–29 Woburn Place, London WCIH OLU
Tel 0171-273 8666; fax 0171-273 8670

The Service became an executive agency in April 1997 and brought together the administrative support for the industrial tribunals and the Employment Appeal Tribunal.
Chief Executive, I. Jones

---

‡ At 151 Buckingham Palace Road, London SWIW 9SS

THE INSOLVENCY SERVICE
PO Box 203, 21 Bloomsbury Street, London WC1B 3QW
Tel 0171-637 1110; fax 0171-636 4709

The Service administers and investigates the affairs of bankrupts and companies in compulsory liquidation; deals with the disqualification of directors in all corporate failures; regulates insolvency practitioners and their professional bodies; provides banking and investment services for bankruptcy and liquidation estates; and advises ministers on insolvency policy issues.

Inspector-General and Chief Executive, P. R. Joyce
Deputy Inspectors-General, D. J. Flynn; L. T. Cramp

NATIONAL WEIGHTS AND MEASURES LABORATORY
Stanton Avenue, Teddington, Middx TW11 0JZ
Tel 0181-943 7272; fax 0181-943 7270

The Laboratory administers weights and measures legislation, carries out type examination, calibration and testing, and runs courses on metrological topics.

Chief Executive, Dr S. Bennett

PATENT OFFICE
— *see* page 332

RADIOCOMMUNICATIONS AGENCY
New King's Beam House, 22 Upper Ground, London
SE1 9SA
Tel 0171-211 0211; fax 0171-211 0507

The Agency is responsible for the management of the radio spectrum used for civilian purposes within the UK. It also represents UK radio interests internationally.

Chief Executive, D. Hendon

THE TREASURY
Parliament Street, London SW1P 3AG
Tel 0171-270 3000
Web: http://www.hm-treasury.gov.uk

The Office of the Lord High Treasurer has been continuously in commission for well over 200 years. The Lord High Commissioners of HM Treasury are the First Lord of the Treasury (who is also the Prime Minister), the Chancellor of the Exchequer and five junior Lords (who are government whips in the House of Commons). This Board of Commissioners is assisted at present by the Chief Secretary, a Parliamentary Secretary who is also the government Chief Whip, a Financial Secretary, an Economic Secretary, the Paymaster-General, and the Permanent Secretary.

The Prime Minister is not primarily concerned in the day-to-day aspects of Treasury business; the management of the Treasury devolves upon the Chancellor of the Exchequer and the other Treasury ministers.

The Chief Secretary is responsible for the planning and control of public expenditure; value for money in the public services; comprehensive spending reviews; public sector pay; strategic oversight of the financial system and financial services; devolution; and export credit.

The Paymaster-General's responsibilities include enterprise and growth; welfare-to-work issues; competition and deregulation policy; review of corporation tax; Treasury interest in small firms; and government procurement policy and practice. The Paymaster-General's Office is part of the National Investment and Loans Office (*see* pages 327–8).

The Financial Secretary has responsibility for parliamentary financial business; oversight of the Inland Revenue, Customs and Excise and the Valuation Office Agency; Inland Revenue taxes (excluding the windfall levy); Customs and Excise duties and taxes; charities; and the environment, including energy efficiency.

The Economic Secretary has responsibility for the financial system and financial services; Economic and Monetary Union; foreign exchange reserves management; debt management policy; international issues; parliamentary questions; low pay and the minimum wage; women's issues; economic briefing; the Royal Mint; National Savings; the Office for National Statistics; the National Investment and Loans Office; and the Government Actuary's Department.

The Minister for Trade and Competitiveness in Europe deals with *ad hoc* projects and is chairman of an interdepartmental task force and a member of the Economic and European Cabinet committees.

All Treasury ministers are concerned in tax matters.

Prime Minister and First Lord of the Treasury, The Rt. Hon. Tony Blair, MP
Chancellor of the Exchequer, The Rt. Hon. Gordon Brown, MP
Principal Private Secretary, T. Scholar
Private Secretary, vacant
Special Advisers, E. Balls; C. Whelan; E. Miliband; A. Maugham
Parliamentary Private Secretary, D. Touhig, MP
Chief Secretary to the Treasury, The Rt. Hon. Stephen Byers, MP
Private Secretary, P. Schofield
Paymaster-General, Geoffrey Robinson, MP
Private Secretary, S. Field
Parliamentary Private Secretary, I. Pearson, MP
Financial Secretary to the Treasury, Dawn Primarolo, MP
Private Secretary, Ms P. Murray
Parliamentary Private Secretary, A. Johnson, MP
Economic Secretary, Patricia Hewitt, MP
Private Secretary, Ms A. King
Minister of State, The Lord Simon of Highbury, CBE (*Trade and Competitiveness in Europe*) (*joint Treasury/DTI minister*)
Parliamentary Secretary to the Treasury and Government Chief Whip (*£45,201), The Rt. Hon. Ann Taylor, MP
Private Secretary, M. Maclean
Treasurer of HM Household and Deputy Chief Whip (*£31,981), Keith Bradley, MP
Comptroller of HM Household (*£20,580), Thomas McAvoy, MP
Vice-Chamberlain of HM Household (*20,580), Graham Allen, MP
Lord Commissioners of the Treasury (*£20,580), Robert Ainsworth, MP; James Dowd, MP; Clive Betts, MP; David Jamieson, MP; Jane Kennedy, MP
Assistant Whips (*£20,580), David Clelland, MP; Kevin Hughes, MP; Greg Pope, MP; Anne McGuire, MP; David Hanson, MP; Michael Hall, MP; Keith Hill, MP
Parliamentary Clerk, D. S. Martin
Permanent Secretary to the Treasury, Sir Andrew Turnbull, KCB, CVO
Private Secretary, Ms S. Riach
Head of Government Accountancy Service and Chief Accountancy Adviser to the Treasury, A. Likierman

---

* In addition to a parliamentary salary of £45,066

DIRECTORATES
Leader, Ministerial Support Team (SCS), T. Scholar
Leader, Communications Team (SCS), P. Curwen
Leader, Strategy Team (SCS), Dr R. Kosmin

MACROECONOMIC POLICY AND PROSPECTS
Director, and Head of the Government Economic Service (SCS),
A. O'Donnell
Deputy Directors (SCS), J. Grice; J. S. Cunliffe
Team Leaders (SCS), M. Bradbury; Ms M. Dawes; D.
Deaton; C. M. Kelly; Ms S. Killen; A. Kilpatrick

INTERNATIONAL FINANCE
Director (SCS), Sir Nigel Wicks, KCB, CVO, CBE
Deputy Directors (SCS), P. McIntyre; D. L. C. Peretz, CB
Team Leaders (SCS), S. Brooks; A. Gibbs; N. J. Ilett;
Ms S. Owen; M. Richardson

BUDGET AND PUBLIC FINANCES
Director (SCS), E. J. W. Gieve
Deputy Directors (SCS), Ms S. Chakrabarti; C. J. Mowl
Team Leaders (SCS), N. M. Hansford; P. Kane; S. N.
Matthews; A. W. Ritchie; D. Savage; Ms C. Slocock;
P. Wynn Owen

SPENDING
Director (SCS), R. P. Culpin, CB, CVO
Deputy Directors (SCS), †N. Glass; N. Macpherson; Miss
G. M. Noble; P. N. Sedgwick
Team Leaders (SCS), P. Brook; J. Halligan; N. Holgate; A.
Hudson; S. Judge; Ms G. Maklouf; J. Moore; M.
Parkinson; I. V. W. Taylor; Ms R. Thompson; Ms S.
Thomson; Ms S. Walker

FINANCIAL MANAGEMENT, REPORTING AND AUDIT
Director (Chief Accountancy Adviser) (SCS), A. Likierman
Deputy Director (SCS), †J. E. Mortimer
Team Leaders (SCS), J. Breckenbridge; C. Butler; Mrs
R. M. Dunn; Dr R. Kosmin; Ms A. M. Jones; D. Loweth;
D. Slaughter

FINANCE, REGULATION AND INDUSTRY
Director (SCS), S. Robson, CB
Deputy Directors (SCS), H. J. Bush; R. Fellgett; B. Rigby; M.
Roberts
Team Leaders (SCS), R. Allen; M. Burt; P. Casey; J. Colling;
Mrs P. C. Diggle; C. Farthing; D. Griffiths; J. May;
C. R. Pickering; D. Roe; A. Sharples; Ms C. Speck; J.
Whitlock; T. Wilson

PERSONNEL AND SUPPORT
Director (SCS), Ms M. O'Mara
Team Leaders (SCS), I. Cooper; J. Dodds; D. Rayson
† Combined deputy director and head of team

EXECUTIVE AGENCIES

NATIONAL SAVINGS
— *see* page 328

OFFICE FOR NATIONAL STATISTICS
— *see* pages 328–9

ROYAL MINT
— *see* page 338

UNITED KINGDOM DEBT MANAGEMENT OFFICE
1st Floor, Cheapside House, 138 Cheapside, London EC2V
6BB
Tel 0171-862 6500; fax 0171 862 6509

The UK Debt Management Office was launched as an
executive agency of the Treasury in April 1998 after the
transfer from the Bank of England to the Treasury of
responsibility for debt management, the sale of gilts and
oversight of the gilts market. It will in due course take over

responsibility for the management of the Exchequer's daily
cash flow.
Chief Executive, M. L. Williams

THE TREASURY SOLICITOR
DEPARTMENT OF HM PROCURATOR-GENERAL AND
TREASURY SOLICITOR
Queen Anne's Chambers, 28 Broadway, London SW1H 9JS
Tel 0171-210 3000; fax 0171-210 3004

The Treasury Solicitor's Department provides legal
services for many government departments. Those without their own lawyers are provided with legal advice, and
both they and other departments are provided with
litigation services. The Treasury Solicitor is also the
Queen's Proctor, and is responsible for collecting Bona
Vacantia on behalf of the Crown. The Department became
an executive agency in April 1996.
HM Procurator-General and Treasury Solicitor (SCS), A. H.
Hammond, CB
Deputy Treasury Solicitor (SCS), A. M. Inglese

CENTRAL ADVISORY DIVISION
SCS, Mrs I. G. Letwin

LITIGATION DIVISION
SCS, D. Brummell; Mrs D. Babar; A. D. Lawton;
A. Leithead; B. McKay; P. R. Messer; Ms L. Nicoll; Mrs
J. B. C. Oliver; D. Palmer; S. Parkinson; R. J. Phillips;
A. J. Sandal

QUEEN'S PROCTOR DIVISION
Queen's Proctor (SCS), A. H. Hammond, CB
Assistant Queen's Proctor (SCS), Mrs D. Babar

RESOURCES AND SERVICES DIVISION
*Principal Establishment and Finance Officer and Security Officer
(SCS)*, J. P. Burnett
Deputy Establishment Officer (G7), Ms H. Donnelly
Finance Officer (G7), C. A. Woolley
Information Systems Manager (G7), M. Gabbidon
Business Support Manager (SEO), E. Blishen

BONA VACANTIA DIVISION
SCS, R. A. D. Jackson

EUROPEAN DIVISION
SCS, J. E. Collins; A. Ridout; M. C. P. Thomas

CULTURE, MEDIA AND SPORT DIVISION
SCS, C. P. J. Muttukumaru

CABINET OFFICE DIVISION
SCS, M. C. L. Carpenter

MINISTRY OF DEFENCE ADVISORY DIVISION
Metropole Building, Northumberland Avenue, London
WC2N 5BL
Tel 0171-218 4691
SCS, Mrs V. Collett; M. Hemming; D. Macrae

DEPARTMENT FOR EDUCATION AND EMPLOYMENT
ADVISORY DIVISION
Caxton House, Tothill Street, London SW1H 9NF
Tel 0171-273 3000
SCS, F. D. W. Clarke; F. L. Croft; S. T. Harker; C. House;
N. A. D. Lambert

HM TREASURY ADVISORY DIVISION
Treasury Chambers, Parliament Street, London SW1P 3AG
Tel 0171-270 3000
SCS, M. A. Blythe; J. R. J. Braggins; Ms R. Ford; J. Jones;
R. Ricks; Miss J. V. Stokes

CONSTITUTIONAL REFORM DIVISION
70 Whitehall, London SW1A 2AS
Tel 0171-270 6093
SCS, Miss R. A. Jeffreys

GOVERNMENT PROPERTY LAWYERS
Riverside Chambers, Castle Street, Taunton, Somerset
TA1 4AP
Tel 01823-345200; fax 01823-345202

An executive agency of the Treasury Solicitor's Department.
Chief Executive (G3), P. Horner
Group Directors (G5), D. Ager; M. Benmayor; A. M. Scarfe
Director of Lands Advisory (G5), R. C. Paddock

COUNCIL ON TRIBUNALS
7th Floor, 22 Kingsway, London WC2B 6LE
Tel 0171-936 7045; fax 0171-936 7044

The Council on Tribunals is an independent body that operates under the Tribunals and Inquiries Act 1992. It consists of 16 members appointed by the Lord Chancellor and the Lord Advocate; one member is appointed to represent the interests of people in Wales. The Scottish Committee of the Council generally considers Scottish tribunals and matters relating only to Scotland.

The Council advises on and keeps under review the constitution and working of administrative tribunals, and considers and reports on administrative procedures relating to statutory inquiries. Some 70 tribunals are currently under the Council's supervision. It is consulted by and advises government departments on a wide range of subjects relating to adjudicative procedures.
Chairman, The Lord Archer of Sandwell, PC, QC
Members, The Parliamentary Commissioner for
Administration (*ex officio*); R. J. Elliot, WS (*Chairman of the Scottish Committee*); S. M. D. Brown; S. R. Davie, CB; J. H. Eames; Mrs A. Galbraith; ; Mrs S. R. Howdle; I. J. Irvine; R. H. Jones, CVO; S. Jones, CBE; Dr C. A. Kaplan; Prof. T. M. Partington; I. D. Penman, CB; D. G. Readings; P. A. A. Waring
Secretary, A. Twort

SCOTTISH COMMITTEE OF THE COUNCIL ON TRIBUNALS
44 Palmerston Place, Edinburgh EH12 5BJ
Tel 0131-220 1236; fax 0131-225 4271
Chairman, R. J. Elliot, WS
Members, The Parliamentary Commissioner for
Administration; Mrs H. Sheerin, OBE; Ms M. Burns; Mrs A. Middleton; I. D. Penman, CB; Mrs P. Y. Berry, MBE; I. J. Irvine
Secretary, Mrs E. M. MacRae

TRIBUNALS
— see pages 369–72

UNITED KINGDOM SPORTS COUNCIL
Walkden House, 10 Melton Street, London NW1 2EB
Tel 0171-380 8000; fax 0171-380 8010

The UK Sports Council replaced the former Great Britain Sports Council on 1 January 1997. It promotes the development of sport and fosters the provision of facilities for sport and recreation at a UK level. It co-ordinates support to sports which compete internationally as the UK,

works to combat drug misuse, deals with international relations and major events, and undertakes development work on the planned UK Sports Institute. Funding for 1998–9 from the Department for Culture, Media and Sport is £11.6 million.

The Government announced in July 1998 that responsibility for distributing the funds allocated to sport from the proceeds of the National Lottery would be transferred from the English, Welsh, Scottish and Northern Ireland Sports Councils to the UK Sports Council.
Chairman, Sir Rodney Walker
Chief Executive, D. Chesterton

UNRELATED LIVE TRANSPLANT
REGULATORY AUTHORITY
Department of Health, c/o Room 311, Wellington House, 133–155 Waterloo Road, London SE1 8UG
Tel 0171-972 4812; fax 0171-972 4852

The Unrelated Live Transplant Regulatory Authority (ULTRA) is a statutory body established in 1990. In every case where the transplant of an organ within the definition of the Human Organ Transplants Act 1989 is proposed between a living donor and a recipient who are not genetically related, the proposal must be referred to ULTRA. Applications must be made by registered medical practitioners.

The Authority comprises a chairman and ten members appointed by the Secretary of State for Health. The secretariat is provided by Department of Health officials.
Chairman, Prof. M. Bobrow, CBE
Members, Mrs J. H. Callman; Dr J. F. Douglas; Dr H. Draper; Dr P. A. Dyer; Lady Eccles; Miss P. M. Franklin; A. Hooker; S. G. Macpherson; Prof. N. P. Mallick; Prof. J. R. Salaman
Administrative Secretary, W. Kent
Medical Secretary, Dr P. Doyle

WALES YOUTH AGENCY
Leslie Court, Lon-y-Llyn, Caerphilly CF83 1BQ
Tel 01222-880088; fax 01222-880824

The Wales Youth Agency is an independent organization funded by the Welsh Office. Its functions include the encouragement and development of the partnership between statutory and voluntary agencies relating to young people; the promotion of staff development and training; and the extension of marketing and information services in the relevant fields. The board of directors is appointed by the Secretary of State for Wales; directors do not receive a salary.
Chairman of the Board of Directors, R. Noble
Vice-Chairman of the Board of Directors, Dr H. Williamson
Executive Director, B. Williams

OFFICE OF WATER SERVICES
Centre City Tower, 7 Hill Street, Birmingham B5 4UA
Tel 0121-625 1300; fax 0121-625 1400

The Office of Water Services (Ofwat) was set up under the Water Act 1989 and is a non-ministerial government department headed by the Director-General of Water Services. It is the independent economic regulator of the water and sewerage companies in England and Wales.

Ofwat's main duties are to ensure that the companies can finance and carry out the functions specified in the Water Industry Act 1991 and to protect the interests of water customers. There are ten regional customer service committees which are concerned solely with the interests of water customers. Representation of customer interests at national level is the responsibility of the Ofwat National Customer Council (ONCC).

Director-General of Water Services, I. C. R. Byatt
Chairman, Ofwat National Customer Council, Ms S. Reiter

WELSH DEVELOPMENT AGENCY

Principality House, The Friary, Cardiff CF1 4AE
Tel 0345-775577/66; fax 01443-845589

The Agency was established under the Welsh Development Agency Act 1975. Its remit is to help further the regeneration of the economy and improve the environment in Wales. The Agency's main activities include site assembly, provision of premises, encouraging investment by the private sector in property development, grant-aiding land reclamation, stimulating quality urban and rural development, promoting Wales as a location for inward investment, helping to boost the growth, profitability and competitiveness of indigenous Welsh companies, and providing investment capital for industry. Its sponsoring department is the Welsh Office.

Under the Government of Wales Act 1998, the Land Authority for Wales and the Development Board for Rural Wales have merged with the Welsh Development Agency.
Chairman, D. Rowe-Beddoe
Deputy Chairman, R. Lewis, OBE
Chief Executive, W. B. Willott, CB

WELSH OFFICE

*Gwydyr House, Whitehall, London SW1A 2ER
Tel 0171-270 3000
Cathays Park, Cardiff CF1 3NQ
Tel 01222-825111
E-mail: webmaster@wales.gov.uk
Web: http://www.wales.gov.uk

The Welsh Office has responsibility in Wales for ministerial functions relating to health and personal social services; education, except for terms and conditions of service and student awards; training; the Welsh language, arts and culture; the implementation of the Citizen's Charter in Wales; local government; housing; water and sewerage; environmental protection; sport; agriculture and fisheries; forestry; land use, including town and country planning and countryside and nature conservation; new towns; non-departmental public bodies and appointments in Wales; ancient monuments and historic buildings and the Welsh Arts Council; roads; tourism; financial assistance to industry; the Strategic Development Scheme in Wales and the Programme for the Valleys; the operation of the European Regional Development Fund in Wales and other European Union matters; civil emergencies; and all financial aspects of these matters, including Welsh rate support grant.

The directly-elected Welsh Assembly which is to be established in 1999 will take over the budget of the Welsh Office and will be serviced by Welsh Office civil servants.
Secretary of State for Wales, The Rt. Hon. Ron Davies, MP*
Private Secretary, Dr J. E. Milligan*
Special Advisers, J. Adams; H. Roberts

Parliamentary Private Secretary, N. Ainger, MP
Parliamentary Under-Secretaries, Peter Hain, MP; Jon Owen Jones, MP
Private Secretaries, S. George; Ms J. Cole
Parliamentary Clerk, A. Green*
Permanent Secretary (G1), Mrs R. Lomax
Private Secretary, G. Haggaty

LEGAL GROUP
Legal Adviser (G3), D. G. Lambert
Deputy Legal Adviser (G5), J. H. Turnbull

INFORMATION DIVISION
Director of Information (G5), C. P. Wilson
Head of Publicity (G7), W. J. Edwards
Chief Press Officer (G7), D. Clifford

ESTABLISHMENT GROUP
Principal Establishment Officer (G3), S. H. Martin
Heads of Divisions (G5), Mrs B. Wilson; Dr A. G. Thornton; Ms K. Cassidy
Chief Statistician (G5), W. R. L. Alldritt
Head of Health Statistics and Analysis Unit (G6), P. Demery

FINANCE GROUP
Principal Finance Officer (G3), D. T. Richards
Head of Division (G5), L. A. Pavelin
Senior Economic Adviser (G5), M. G. Phelps
Head of Internal Audit (G6), D. A. McNeill

ECONOMIC AFFAIRS
Deputy Secretary (G2), J. D. Shortridge

AGRICULTURE DEPARTMENT
Head of Department (G3), L. K. Walford
Heads of Divisions (G5), Mrs A. M. Jackson; H. D. Brodie

ECONOMIC DEVELOPMENT GROUP
Head of Group (G3), M. J. Cochlin
Heads of Divisions (G5), A. D. Lansdown; L. Conway; P. Fullerton

INDUSTRY AND TRAINING DEPARTMENT
Director (G3), D. W. Jones
Industrial Director (G4), vacant
Heads of Divisions (G5), R. Keveren; N. E. Thomas; W. G. Davies; (G6), Dr R. J. Loveland

SOCIAL POLICY
Deputy Secretary (G2), J. W. Lloyd, CB

EDUCATION DEPARTMENT
Head of Department (G3), R. J. Davies
Heads of Divisions (G5)†, R. Thomas; D. R. Adams; J. Howells; Mrs E. A. Taylor

OFFICE OF HM CHIEF INSPECTOR FOR SCHOOLS IN WALES
Chief Inspector (G4)†, Miss S. Lewis
Staff Inspectors (G5)†, M. G. Haines; C. Abbott
There are 45 Grade 6 Inspectors.
Head of Administration (G7), Mrs S. Howells

LOCAL GOVERNMENT GROUP
Head of Group (G3), B. J. Mitchell
Heads of Divisions (G5), D. A. Pritchard; Ms H. F. O. Thomas; M. J. Shanahan
Chief Inspector, Social Services Inspectorate (Wales) (G5), D. G. Evans
Deputy Chief Inspectors, R. Tebboth; R. C. Woodward; Mrs P. E. White

HEALTH DEPARTMENT
Director (G3), P. R. Gregory

Heads of Divisions (*G5*), D. H. Jones; A. C. Wood; B. Wilcox; R. C. Williams; Dr J. Blamire

HEALTH PROFESSIONAL GROUP
Chief Medical Officer (*G3*), Dr R. Hall
Principal Medical Officers (*G4*), Dr B. Fuge; Dr J. K. Richmond
Senior Medical Officers (*G5*), Dr J. Ludlow; Dr H. N. Williams; Dr D. Salter
Medical Adviser (*part-time*), vacant
Chief Dental Officer (*G5*), P. Langmaid
Chief Scientific Adviser (*G5*), Dr J. A. V. Pritchard
Deputy Scientific Adviser (*G6*), Dr E. O. Crawley
Chief Pharmaceutical Adviser (*G5*), Miss C. W. Howells
Chief Environmental Health Adviser (*G5*), R. Alexander
Deputy Environmental Health Adviser (*G6*), D. Worthington

NURSING DIVISION
Chief Nursing Officer, Miss M. P. Bull, CBE
Nursing Officers, P. Johnson; M. F. Tonkin; Mrs H. Wood; Mrs R. Johnson

TRANSPORT, PLANNING AND ENVIRONMENT GROUP
Head of Group (*G3*), G. C. G. Craig
Director of Highways (*G4*), K. J. Thomas
Heads of Divisions (*G5*), J. R. Rees (*Roads Construction*); G. A. Thomas (*Transport Policy*); (*G6*), R. J. Shaw (*Network Management*); B. H. Hawker, OBE (*Roads Major Projects*)
Grade 7, R. H. Powell; I. P. Davies; R. K. Cones; K. J. A. Tengy; T. J. Collins; S. C. Shouler; M. J. Gilbert; T. C. Dorken; M. J. A. Parker; I. A. Grindulis; A. D. Perry; Dr M. C. Dunn

HEALTH AUTHORITIES
– see page 480

EXECUTIVE AGENCIES

CADW: WELSH HISTORIC MONUMENTS
Crown Building, Cathays Park, Cardiff CF1 3NQ
Tel 01222-500200; fax 01222-826375
Cadw supports the preservation, conservation, appreciation and enjoyment of the built heritage in Wales.
Chief Executive, T. Cassidy
Director of Policy and Administration, R. W. Hughes
Conservation Architect, J. D. Hogg
Principal Inspector of Ancient Monuments and Historic Buildings, J. R. Avent
Inspectors of Ancient Monuments and Historic Buildings, A. D. McLees; Dr S. E. Rees; R. C. Turner; M. J. Yates

FARMING AND RURAL CONSERVATION AGENCY
— see page 281

INTERVENTION BOARD
— see pages 315–16

PLANNING INSPECTORATE
Cathays Park, Cardiff CF1 3NQ
Tel 01222-825670; fax 01222-825150
A joint executive agency of the Department of the Environment, Transport and the Regions and the Welsh Office (*see* page 300).
Chief Executive and Chief Planning Inspector (*G3*), C. Shepley
Director (*G5*), R. Davies

WOMEN'S NATIONAL COMMISSION
5th Floor, The Adelphi, 1–11 John Adam Street, London WC2N 6HT
Tel 0171-712 2443; fax 0171-962 8171

The Women's National Commission is an independent advisory committee to the Government. Its remit is to ensure that the informed opinions of women are given their due weight in the deliberations of the Government and in public debate on matters of public interest including those of special interest to women. The Commission's sponsoring department is the Department for Social Security.
Government Co-Chairman, The Baroness Symons of Vernham Dean
Elected Co-Chairman, Miss V. Evans, CBE
Secretary, Ms J. Bailey

CIVIL SERVICE STAFF

BY MAIN DEPARTMENTS *as at 1 April 1997*

	Total	Of whom in agencies
Agriculture, Fisheries and Food	9,092	3,443
Cabinet Office	2,569	1,542
Customs and Excise	23,071	—
Defence	100,206	62,415
Education and Employment	33,662	29,181
Environment	3,687	681
Foreign Office	5,574	35
Health	4,695	1,013
HM Prison Service	37,704	37,704
Home Office	12,165	2,807
Inland Revenue	54,029	4,301
Lord Chancellor's Department	10,625	9,749
National Heritage	1,004	666
Northern Ireland Office	204	—
Scottish Departments	12,910	7,955
Social Security	93,055	90,372
Trade and Industry	8,398	3,897
Transport	11,154	9,494
Treasury	888	—
Welsh Office	2,180	179
Other departments	48,467	20,100
TOTAL	475,339	285,534

Source: The Stationery Office – *Civil Service Yearbook 1998*

† Based at Tŷ Glas Road, Llanishen, Cardiff CF4 5LE. Tel: 01222-761456

Law Courts and Offices

THE JUDICIAL COMMITTEE OF THE PRIVY COUNCIL

The Judicial Committee of the Privy Council is primarily the final court of appeal for the United Kingdom dependent territories and those independent Commonwealth countries which have retained the avenue of appeal upon achieving independence (Antigua and Barbuda, The Bahamas, Barbados, Belize, Brunei, Dominica, The Gambia, Jamaica, Kiribati, Mauritius, New Zealand, St Christopher and Nevis, St Lucia, St Vincent and the Grenadines, Trinidad and Tobago, and Tuvalu). The Committee also hears appeals from the Channel Islands and the Isle of Man and the disciplinary and health committees of the medical and allied professions. It has a limited jurisdiction to hear appeals under the Pastoral Measure 1983. In 1997 the Judicial Committee heard 69 appeals and 82 petitions for special leave to appeal.

The members of the Judicial Committee include the Lord Chancellor, the Lords of Appeal in Ordinary (*see* page 355), other Privy Counsellors who hold or have held high judicial office and certain judges from the Commonwealth.

PRIVY COUNCIL OFFICE (JUDICIAL COMMITTEE), Downing Street, London SWIA 2AJ. Tel: 0171-270 0483. *Registrar of the Privy Council*, J. A. C. Watherston; *Chief Clerk*, F. G. Hart

The Judicature of England and Wales

The legal system of England and Wales is separate from those of Scotland and Northern Ireland and differs from them in law, judicial procedure and court structure, although there is a common distinction between civil law (disputes between individuals) and criminal law (acts harmful to the community).

The supreme judicial authority for England and Wales is the House of Lords, which is the ultimate Court of Appeal from all courts in Great Britain and Northern Ireland (except criminal courts in Scotland) for all cases except those concerning the interpretation and application of European Community law, including preliminary rulings requested by British courts and tribunals, which are decided by the European Court of Justice (*see* page 778). (At the time of going to press, legislation was before Parliament under which the European Convention on Human Rights would be incorporated into British law; until the legislation comes into force, an applicant must, when all remedies available at national level have been exhausted, petition the European Commission of Human Rights to investigate an alleged violation of the Convention.) As a Court of Appeal the House of Lords consists of the Lord Chancellor and the Lords of Appeal in Ordinary (law lords).

SUPREME COURT OF JUDICATURE

The Supreme Court of Judicature comprises the Court of Appeal, the High Court of Justice and the Crown Court. The High Court of Justice is the superior civil court and is divided into three divisions. The Chancery Division is concerned mainly with equity, bankruptcy and contentious probate business. The Queen's Bench Division deals with commercial and maritime law, serious personal injury and medical negligence cases, cases involving a breach of contract and professional negligence actions. The Family Division deals with matters relating to family law. Sittings are held at the Royal Courts of Justice in London or at 126 district registries outside the capital. High Court judges also sit to hear cases at first instance. Appeals from lower courts are heard by two or three judges, or by single judges of the appropriate division. The Restrictive Practices Court, set up under the Restrictive Trade Practices Act 1956, and the Technology and Construction Court, which deals with cases which require expert evidence on technical and other issues concerning mainly the construction industry, defective products, property valuations, and landlord and tenant disputes, are also part of the High Court. Appeals from the High Court are heard in the Court of Appeal (Civil Division), presided over by the Master of the Rolls, and may go on to the House of Lords.

CRIMINAL CASES

In criminal matters the decision to prosecute in the majority of cases rests with the Crown Prosecution Service, the independent prosecuting body in England and Wales (*see* pages 363–4). The Service is headed by the Director of Public Prosecutions, who works under the superintendence of the Attorney-General. Certain categories of offence continue to require the Attorney-General's consent for prosecution.

The Crown Court sits in about 90 centres, divided into six circuits, and is presided over by High Court judges, full-time circuit judges, and part-time recorders and assistant recorders, sitting with a jury in all trials which are contested. There were 395 assistant recorders at 30 June 1998. The Crown Court deals with trials of the more serious criminal offences, the sentencing of offenders committed for sentence by magistrates' courts (when the magistrates consider their own power of sentence inadequate), and appeals from magistrates' courts. Magistrates usually sit with a circuit judge or recorder to deal with appeals and committals for sentence. Appeals from the Crown Court, either against sentence or conviction, are made to the Court of Appeal (Criminal Division), presided over by the Lord Chief Justice. A further appeal from the Court of Appeal to the House of Lords can be brought if a point of law of general public importance is considered to be involved.

Minor criminal offences (summary offences) are dealt with in magistrates' courts, which usually consist of three unpaid lay magistrates (justices of the peace) sitting without a jury, who are advised on points of law and procedure by a legally-qualified clerk to the justices. There were 30,361 justices of the peace at 1 January 1998. In busier courts a full-time, salaried and legally-qualified stipendiary magistrate presides alone. Cases involving people under 18 are heard in youth courts, specially constituted magistrates' courts which sit apart from other courts. Preliminary proceedings in a serious case to decide whether there is evidence to justify committal for trial in the Crown Court are also dealt with in the magistrates' courts. Appeals from magistrates' courts against sentence or conviction are made to the Crown Court. Appeals upon a point of law are made to the High Court, and may go on to the House of Lords.

CIVIL CASES

Most minor civil cases are dealt with by the county courts, of which there are about 270 (details may be found in the local telephone directory). Cases are heard by circuit judges or district judges. There were 342 district judges at 31 May 1998. For cases involving small claims there are special simplified procedures. Where there are financial limits on county court jurisdiction, claims which exceed those limits may be tried in the county courts with the consent of the parties, or in certain circumstances on transfer from the High Court. Outside London, bankruptcy proceedings can be heard in designated county courts. Magistrates' courts can deal with certain classes of civil case and committees of magistrates license public houses, clubs and betting shops. For the implementation of the Children Act 1989, a new structure of hearing centres was set up in 1991 for family proceedings cases, involving magistrates' courts (family proceedings courts), divorce county courts, family hearing centres and care centres. Appeals in family matters heard in the family proceedings courts go to the Family Division of the High Court; affiliation appeals and appeals from decisions of the licensing committees of magistrates go to the Crown Court. Appeals from county courts are heard in the Court of Appeal (Civil Division), and may go on to the House of Lords.

CORONERS' COURTS

Coroners' courts investigate violent and unnatural deaths or sudden deaths where the cause is unknown. Cases may be brought before a local coroner (a senior lawyer or doctor) by doctors, the police, various public authorities or members of the public. Where a death is sudden and the cause is unknown, the coroner may order a post-mortem examination to determine the cause of death rather than hold an inquest in court.

Judicial appointments are made by The Queen; the most senior appointments are made on the advice of the Prime Minister and other appointments on the advice of the Lord Chancellor.

Under the provisions of the Criminal Appeal Act 1995, a Commission was set up to direct and supervise investigations into possible miscarriages of justice and to refer cases to the courts on the grounds of conviction and sentence (*see* page 292); these functions were formerly the responsibility of the Home Secretary.

For late changes to this section, *see* Stop-Press

THE HOUSE OF LORDS
AS FINAL COURT OF APPEAL

The Lord High Chancellor (£148,850)
The Rt. Hon. the Lord Irvine of Lairg, *born* 1940, *apptd* 1997

LORDS OF APPEAL IN ORDINARY (each £138,889)
Style, The Rt. Hon. Lord —

Rt. Hon. Lord Browne-Wilkinson, *born* 1930, *apptd* 1991
Rt. Hon. Lord Slynn of Hadley, *born* 1930, *apptd* 1992

Rt. Hon. Lord Lloyd of Berwick, *born* 1929, *apptd* 1993
Rt. Hon. Lord Nicholls of Birkenhead, *born* 1933, *apptd* 1994
Rt. Hon. Lord Steyn, *born* 1932, *apptd* 1995
Rt. Hon. Lord Hoffman, *born* 1934, *apptd* 1995
Rt. Hon. Lord Hope of Craighead, *born* 1938, *apptd* 1996
Rt. Hon. Lord Clyde, *born* 1932, *apptd* 1996
Rt. Hon. Lord Hutton, *born* 1931, *apptd* 1997
Rt. Hon. Lord Saville of Newdigate, *born* 1936, *apptd* 1997
*Rt. Hon. Sir John Hobhouse, *born* 1932, *apptd* 1998
*Rt. Hon. Sir Peter Millett, *born* 1932, *apptd* 1998

Registrar, The Clerk of the Parliaments (*see* page 218)
* To receive a life peerage

SUPREME COURT OF JUDICATURE

COURT OF APPEAL

The Master of the Rolls (£138,889), The Rt. Hon. Lord Woolf, *born* 1933, *apptd* 1996
Secretary, Mrs L. Grace
Clerk, Ms J. Jones

LORDS JUSTICES OF APPEAL (each £132,017)
Style, The Rt. Hon. Lord/Lady Justice [surname]

Rt. Hon. Sir Martin Nourse, *born* 1932, *apptd* 1985
Rt. Hon. Dame Elizabeth Butler-Sloss, DBE, *born* 1933, *apptd* 1988
Rt. Hon. Sir Murray Stuart-Smith, *born* 1927, *apptd* 1988
Rt. Hon. Sir Roy Beldam, *born* 1925, *apptd* 1989
Rt. Hon. Sir Paul Kennedy, *born* 1935, *apptd* 1992
Rt. Hon. Sir David Hirst, *born* 1925, *apptd* 1992
Rt. Hon. Sir Simon Brown, *born* 1937, *apptd* 1992
Rt. Hon. Sir Anthony Evans, *born* 1934, *apptd* 1992
Rt. Hon. Sir Christopher Rose, *born* 1937, *apptd* 1992
Rt. Hon. Sir John Roch, *born* 1934, *apptd* 1993
Rt. Hon. Sir Peter Gibson, *born* 1934, *apptd* 1993
Rt. Hon. Sir Denis Henry, *born* 1931, *apptd* 1993
Rt. Hon. Sir Swinton Thomas, *born* 1931, *apptd* 1994
Rt. Hon. Sir Andrew Morritt, CVO, *born* 1938, *apptd* 1994
Rt. Hon. Sir Philip Otton, *born* 1933, *apptd* 1995
Rt. Hon. Sir Robin Auld, *born* 1937, *apptd* 1995
Rt. Hon. Sir Malcolm Pill, *born* 1938, *apptd* 1995
Rt. Hon. Sir William Aldous, *born* 1936, *apptd* 1995
Rt. Hon. Sir Alan Ward, *born* 1938, *apptd* 1995
Rt. Hon. Sir Michael Hutchison, *born* 1933, *apptd* 1995
Rt. Hon. Sir Konrad Schiemann, *born* 1937, *apptd* 1995
Rt. Hon. Sir Nicholas Phillips, *born* 1938, *apptd* 1995
Rt. Hon. Sir Mathew Thorpe, *born* 1938, *apptd* 1995
Rt. Hon. Sir Mark Potter, *born* 1937, *apptd* 1996
Rt. Hon. Sir Henry Brooke, *born* 1936, *apptd* 1996
Rt. Hon. Sir Igor Judge, *born* 1941, *apptd* 1996
Rt. Hon. Sir Mark Waller, *born* 1940, *apptd* 1996
Rt. Hon. Sir John Mummery, *born* 1938, *apptd* 1996
Rt. Hon. Sir Charles Mantell, *born* 1937, *apptd* 1997
Rt. Hon. Sir John Chadwick, ED, *born* 1941, *apptd* 1997
Rt. Hon. Sir Robert Walker, *born* 1938, *apptd* 1997
Rt. Hon. Sir Richard Buxton, *born* 1938, *apptd* 1997
Rt. Hon. Sir Anthony May, *born* 1940, *apptd* 1997

Ex officio Judges, The Lord High Chancellor; the Lord Chief Justice of England; the Master of the Rolls; the President of the Family Division; and the Vice-Chancellor

COURT OF APPEAL (CRIMINAL DIVISION)
Vice-President, The Rt. Hon. Lord Justice Rose
Judges, The Lord Chief Justice of England; the Master of the Rolls; Lords Justices of Appeal; and Judges of the High Court of Justice

COURTS-MARTIAL APPEAL COURT

Judges, The Lord Chief Justice of England; the Master of the Rolls; Lords Justices of Appeal; and Judges of the High Court of Justice

HIGH COURT OF JUSTICE

CHANCERY DIVISION

President, The Lord High Chancellor
The Vice-Chancellor (£132,017), The Rt. Hon. Sir Richard Scott, *born* 1934, *apptd* 1994
　Clerk, W. Northfield, BEM

JUDGES (each £117,752)
Style, The Hon. Mr/Mrs Justice [surname]

Hon. Sir Donald Rattee, *born* 1937, *apptd* 1989
Hon. Sir Francis Ferris, TD, *born* 1932, *apptd* 1990
Hon. Sir Jonathan Parker, *born* 1937, *apptd* 1991
Hon. Sir John Lindsay, *born* 1935, *apptd* 1992
Hon. Dame Mary Arden, DBE, *born* 1947, *apptd* 1993
Hon. Sir Edward Evans-Lombe, *born* 1943, *apptd* 1993
Hon. Sir Robin Jacob, *born* 1941, *apptd* 1993
Hon. Sir William Blackburne, *born* 1944, *apptd* 1993
Hon. Sir Gavin Lightman, *born* 1939, *apptd* 1994
Hon. Sir Robert Carnwath, *born* 1945, *apptd* 1994
Hon. Sir Colin Rimer, *born* 1944, *apptd* 1994
Hon. Sir Hugh Laddie, *born* 1946, *apptd* 1995
Hon. Sir Timothy Lloyd, *born* 1946, *apptd* 1996
Hon. Sir David Neuberger, *born* 1948, *apptd* 1996
Hon. Sir Andrew Park, *born* 1939, *apptd* 1997
Hon. Sir Nicholas Pumfrey, *born* 1951, *apptd* 1997
Hon. Sir Michael Hart, *born* 1948, *apptd* 1998

HIGH COURT OF JUSTICE IN BANKRUPTCY

Judges, The Vice-Chancellor and judges of the Chancery Division of the High Court

COMPANIES COURT

Judges, The Vice Chancellor and judges of the Chancery Division of the High Court

PATENT COURT (APPELLATE SECTION)

Judge, The Hon. Mr Justice Jacob

QUEEN'S BENCH DIVISION

The Lord Chief Justice of England (£148,502) The Rt. Hon. the Lord Bingham of Cornhill, *born* 1933, *apptd* 1996
　Private Secretary, E. Adams
　Clerk, J. Bond
Vice-President, The Rt. Hon. Lord Justice Kennedy

JUDGES (EACH £117,752)
Style, The Hon. Mr/Mrs Justice [surname]

Hon. Sir Oliver Popplewell, *born* 1927, *apptd* 1983
Hon. Sir Richard Tucker, *born* 1930, *apptd* 1985
Hon. Sir Patrick Garland, *born* 1929, *apptd* 1985
Hon. Sir Michael Turner, *born* 1931, *apptd* 1985
Hon. Sir John Alliott, *born* 1932, *apptd* 1986
Hon. Sir Harry Ognall, *born* 1934, *apptd* 1986
Hon. Sir John Owen, *born* 1925, *apptd* 1986
Hon. Sir Humphrey Potts, *born* 1931, *apptd* 1986
Hon. Sir Richard Rougier, *born* 1932, *apptd* 1986
Hon. Sir Ian Kennedy, *born* 1930, *apptd* 1986
Hon. Sir Stuart McKinnon, *born* 1938, *apptd* 1988
Hon. Sir Scott Baker, *born* 1937, *apptd* 1988
Hon. Sir Edwin Jowitt, *born* 1929, *apptd* 1988
Hon. Sir Douglas Brown, *born* 1931, *apptd* 1996
Hon. Sir Michael Morland, *born* 1929, *apptd* 1989
Hon. Sir Roger Buckley, *born* 1939, *apptd* 1989

Hon. Sir Anthony Hidden, *born* 1936, *apptd* 1989
Hon. Sir Michael Wright, *born* 1932, *apptd* 1990
Hon. Sir John Blofeld, *born* 1932, *apptd* 1990
Hon. Sir Peter Cresswell, *born* 1944, *apptd* 1991
Hon. Sir John Laws, *born* 1945, *apptd* 1992
Hon. Dame Ann Ebsworth, DBE, *born* 1937, *apptd* 1992
Hon. Sir Simon Tuckey, *born* 1941, *apptd* 1992
Hon. Sir David Latham, *born* 1942, *apptd* 1992
Hon. Sir Christopher Holland, *born* 1937, *apptd* 1992
Hon. Sir John Kay, *born* 1943, *apptd* 1992
Hon. Sir Richard Curtis, *born* 1933, *apptd* 1992
Hon. Sir Stephen Sedley, *born* 1939, *apptd* 1992
Hon. Dame Janet Smith, DBE, *born* 1940, *apptd* 1992
Hon. Sir Anthony Colman, *born* 1938, *apptd* 1992
Hon. Sir Anthony Clarke, *born* 1943, *apptd* 1993
Hon. Sir John Dyson, *born* 1943, *apptd* 1993
Hon. Sir Thayne Forbes, *born* 1938, *apptd* 1993
Hon. Sir Michael Sachs, *born* 1932, *apptd* 1993
Hon. Sir Stephen Mitchell, *born* 1941, *apptd* 1993
Hon. Sir Rodger Bell, *born* 1939, *apptd* 1993
Hon. Sir Michael Harrison, *born* 1939, *apptd* 1993
Hon. Sir Bernard Rix, *born* 1944, *apptd* 1993
Hon. Dame Heather Steel, DBE, *born* 1940, *apptd* 1993
Hon. Sir William Gage, *born* 1938, *apptd* 1993
Hon. Sir Jonathan Mance, *born* 1943, *apptd* 1993
Hon. Sir Andrew Longmore, *born* 1944, *apptd* 1993
Hon. Sir Thomas Morison, *born* 1939, *apptd* 1993
Hon. Sir David Keene, *born* 1941, *apptd* 1994
Hon. Sir Andrew Collins, *born* 1942, *apptd* 1994
Hon. Sir Maurice Kay, *born* 1942, *apptd* 1995
Hon. Sir Brian Smedley, *born* 1934, *apptd* 1995
Hon. Sir Anthony Hooper, *born* 1937, *apptd* 1995
Hon. Sir Alexander Butterfield, *born* 1942, *apptd* 1995
Hon. Sir George Newman, *born* 1941, *apptd* 1995
Hon. Sir David Poole, *born* 1938, *apptd* 1995
Hon. Sir Martin Moore-Bick, *born* 1946, *apptd* 1995
Hon. Sir Gordon Langley, *born* 1943, *apptd* 1995
Hon. Sir Roger Thomas, *born* 1947, *apptd* 1996
Hon. Sir Robert Nelson, *born* 1942, *apptd* 1996
Hon. Sir Roger Toulson, *born* 1946, *apptd* 1996
Hon. Sir Michael Astill, *born* 1938, *apptd* 1996
Hon. Sir Alan Moses, *born* 1945, *apptd* 1996
Hon. Sir Timothy Walker, *born* 1946, *apptd* 1996
Hon. Sir David Eady, *born* 1943, *apptd* 1997
Hon. Sir Jeremy Sullivan, *born* 1945, *apptd* 1997
Hon. Sir David Penry-Davey, *born* 1942, *apptd* 1997
Hon. Sir Stephen Richards, *born* 1950, *apptd* 1997
Hon. Sir David Steel, *born* 1943, *apptd* 1998

FAMILY DIVISION

President (£132,017) The Rt. Hon. Sir Stephen Brown, *born* 1924, *apptd* 1988
　Secretary, Mrs S. Leung
　Clerk, Mrs S. Bell

JUDGES (each £117,752)
Style, The Hon. Mr/Mrs Justice [surname]

Hon. Sir Edward Cazalet, *born* 1936, *apptd* 1988
Hon. Sir Robert Johnson, *born* 1933, *apptd* 1989
Hon. Dame Joyanne Bracewell, DBE, *born* 1934, *apptd* 1990
Hon. Sir Michael Connell, *born* 1939, *apptd* 1991
Hon. Sir Peter Singer, *born* 1944, *apptd* 1993
Hon. Sir Nicholas Wilson, *born* 1945, *apptd* 1993
Hon. Sir Nicholas Wall, *born* 1945, *apptd* 1993
Hon. Sir Andrew Kirkwood, *born* 1944, *apptd* 1993
Hon. Sir Christopher Stuart-White, *born* 1933, *apptd* 1993
Hon. Dame Brenda Hale, DBE, *born* 1945, *apptd* 1994
Hon. Sir Hugh Bennett, *born* 1943, *apptd* 1995
Hon. Sir Edward Holman, *born* 1947, *apptd* 1995

Hon. Dame Mary Hogg, DBE, born 1947, *apptd* 1995
Hon. Sir Christopher Sumner, *born* 1939, *apptd* 1996
Hon. Sir Anthony Hughes, *born* 1948, *apptd* 1997
Hon. Sir Arthur Charles, *born* 1948, *apptd* 1998

RESTRICTIVE PRACTICES COURT
Room 410, Thomas More Building, Royal Courts of
Justice, Strand, London WC2A 2LL
Tel 0171-936 6727

President, The Hon. Mr Justice Buckley
Judges, The Hon. Mr Justice Ferris; The Hon. Mr Justice
  Lightman
Lay Members, B. M. Currie; Sir Lewis Robertson, CBE;
  R. Garrick, CBE; S. J. Ahearne; J. A. Graham; Mrs D. H.
  Hatfield; J. A. Scott; B. D. Colgate; J. A. C. King
Clerk of the Court, M. Buckley

TECHNOLOGY AND CONSTRUCTION COURT
St Dunstan's House, 133–137 Fetter Lane, London
EC4A 1HD
Tel 0171-936 7427

JUDGES (each £96,214)
The Hon. Mr Justice Dyson (*Presiding Judge*)
His Hon. Judge Bowsher, QC
His Hon. Judge Hicks, QC
His Hon. Judge Havery, QC
His Hon. Judge Lloyd, QC
His Hon. Judge Newman, QC
His Hon. Judge Thornton, QC
His Hon. Judge Wilcox
His Hon. Judge Toulmin, CMG, QC

Court Manager, Miss B. Joy

LORD CHANCELLOR'S DEPARTMENT
— *see* Government Departments and Public Offices

SUPREME COURT DEPARTMENTS AND OFFICES
Royal Courts of Justice, London WC2A 2LL
Tel 0171-936 6000

DIRECTOR'S OFFICE
Director, G. E. Calvett
Group Manager and Deputy Director, J. Selch
Group Manager, Family Proceedings and Probate Service, R. P.
  Knight
Finance and Performance Officer, K. T. Fairweather

ADMIRALTY AND COMMERCIAL REGISTRY AND MARSHAL'S OFFICE
Registrar (£70,820), P. Miller
Admiralty Marshal and Court Manager, A. Ferrigno

BANKRUPTCY DEPARTMENT
Chief Registrar (£84,752), M. C. B. Buckley
Bankruptcy Registrars (£70,820), W. S. James;
  J. A. Simmonds; P. J. S. Rawson; S. Baister; G. W. Jaques
Court Manager, M. A. Brown

CENTRAL OFFICE OF THE SUPREME COURT
*Senior Master of the Supreme Court (QBD), and Queen's
  Remembrancer* (£84,752), R. L. Turner

Masters of the Supreme Court (QBD) (£70,820), D. L.
  Prebble; G. H. Hodgson; J. Trench; M. Tennant; P.
  Miller; N. O. G. Murray; I. H. Foster; G. H. Rose; P. G.
  A. Eyre; H. J. Leslie; J. G. G. Ungley
Senior Court Manager, P. Emery

CHANCERY DIVISION
Senior Court Manager, P. Emery

CHANCERY CHAMBERS
Chief Master of the Supreme Court (£84,752), vacant
Masters of the Supreme Court (£70,820), G. A. Barratt; J. I.
  Winegarten; J. A. Moncaster, R. A. Bowman; N. W.
  Bragge
Court Manager, G. Robinson
Conveyancing Counsel of the Supreme Court, W. D. Ainger;
  H. M. Harrod; A. C. Taussig

COMPANIES COURT
Registrar (£70,820), M. Buckley
Court Manager, M. A. Brown

COURT OF APPEAL CIVIL DIVISION
Registrar (£84,752), vacant
Deputy Registrar, I. M. Joseph
Court Manager, Miss H. M. Goddard

COURT OF APPEAL CRIMINAL DIVISION
Registrar (£84,752), M. McKenzie, QC
Deputy Registrar, Mrs L. G. Knapman
Chief Clerk, M. Bishop

COURTS-MARTIAL APPEALS OFFICE
Registrar (£84,752), M. McKenzie, QC
Chief Clerk, M. Bishop

CROWN OFFICE OF THE SUPREME COURT
Master of the Crown Office, and Queen's Coroner and Attorney
  (£84,752), M. McKenzie, QC
Head of Crown Office, Mrs L. G. Knapman
Chief Clerk, M. Bishop

EXAMINERS OF THE COURT
Empowered to take examination of witnesses in all
Divisions of the High Court
R. G. Wood; Mrs G. M. Kenne; R. M. Planterose; Miss
V. E. I. Selvaratnam

RESTRICTIVE PRACTICES COURT
Clerk of the Court, M. Buckley
Court Manager, M. A. Brown

SUPREME COURT TAXING OFFICE
Chief Master (£84,752), P. T. Hurst
Masters of the Supreme Court (£70,820), M. Ellis; T. H.
  Seager Berry; C. C. Wright; P. A. Rogers; G. N. Pollard;
  J. E. O'Hare; C. D. N. Campbell
Court Manager, Mrs H. Oakey

COURT OF PROTECTION
Stewart House, 24 Kingsway, London WC2B 6HD
Tel 0171-664 7000
Master (£84,752), D. A. Lush

ELECTION PETITIONS OFFICE
Room E218, Royal Courts of Justice, Strand, London
WC2A 2LL
Tel 0171-936 6131

The office accepts petitions and deals with all matters
relating to the questioning of parliamentary, European

Parliament and local government elections, and with applications for relief under the Representation of the People legislation.
Prescribed Officer, R. L. Turner
Chief Clerk, Miss J. L. Waine

OFFICE OF THE LORD CHANCELLOR'S VISITORS
Stewart House, 24 Kingsway, London WC2B 6HD
Tel 0171-664 7317

Legal Visitor, A. R. Tyrrell
Medical Visitors, K. Khan; W. B. Sprey; E. Mateu; S. E. Mahapatra; A. Bailey; A. Kaeser

OFFICIAL RECEIVERS' DEPARTMENT
21 Bloomsbury Street, London WC1B 3SS
Tel 0171-323 3090

Senior Official Receiver, M. C. A. Osborne
Official Receivers, M. J. Pugh; L. T. Cramp; J. Norris

OFFICIAL SOLICITOR'S DEPARTMENT
81 Chancery Lane, London WC2A 6HD
Tel 0171-911 7105

Official Solicitor to the Supreme Court, P. M. Harris
Deputy Official Solicitor, H. J. Baker
Chief Clerk, R. Lancaster

PRINCIPAL REGISTRY (FAMILY DIVISION)
First Avenue House, 42–49 High Holborn, London WC1V 6HA
Tel 0171-936 6000

Senior District Judge (£84,752), G. B. N. A. Angel
District Judges (£70,820), B. P. F. Kenworthy-Browne; Mrs K. T. Moorhouse; M. J. Segal; R. Conn; Miss I. M. Plumstead; G. J. Maple; Miss H. C. Bradley; K. J. White; A. R. S. Bassett-Cross; N. A. Grove; M. C. Berry; Miss S. M. Bowman; C. Million; P. Waller; Miss P. Cushing; R. Harper; G. C. Brasse; Miss D. C. Redgrave
Group Manager, Family Proceedings and Probate Service, R. P. Knight

District Probate Registrars
Birmingham and Stoke-on-Trent, C. Marsh
Brighton and Maidstone, P. Ellwood
Bristol, Exeter and Bodmin, R. H. P. Joyce
Ipswich, Norwich and Peterborough, D. N. Mee
Leeds, Lincoln and Sheffield, A. P. Dawson
Liverpool, Lancaster and Chester, C. Fox
Llandaff, Bangor, Carmarthen and Gloucester, R. F. Yeldam
Manchester and Nottingham, M. A. Moran
Newcastle, Carlisle, York and Middlesbrough, P. Sanderson
Oxford, R. R. Da Costa
Winchester, A. K. Biggs

OFFICE OF THE JUDGE ADVOCATE OF THE FLEET
c/o Group Manager's Office, The Court Service, Concorde House, 10–12 London Road, Maidstone ME16 8QA
Tel 01622-200120

Judge Advocate of the Fleet (£88,077), His Hon. Judge Sessions

OFFICE OF THE JUDGE ADVOCATE-GENERAL OF THE FORCES
(*Joint Service for the Army and the Royal Air Force*)
22 Kingsway, London WC2B 6LE
Tel 0171-218 8079

Judge Advocate-General (£96,214), His Hon. Judge J. W. Rant, CB, QC
Vice-Judge Advocate-General (£84,752), E. G. Moelwyn-Hughes
Judge Advocates (£70,820), D. M. Berkson; M. A. Hunter; J. P. Camp; Miss S. E. Woollam; R. C. C. Seymour; I. H. Pearson; R. G. Chapple; J. F. T. Bayliss

HIGH COURT AND CROWN COURT CENTRES

First-tier centres deal with both civil and criminal cases and are served by High Court and circuit judges. Second-tier centres deal with criminal cases only and are served by High Court and circuit judges. Third-tier centres deal with criminal cases only and are served only by circuit judges.

MIDLAND AND OXFORD CIRCUIT
First-tier – Birmingham, Lincoln, Nottingham, Oxford, Stafford, Warwick
Second-tier – Leicester, Northampton, Shrewsbury, Worcester
Third-tier – Coventry, Derby, Grimsby, Hereford, Peterborough, Stoke-on-Trent, Wolverhampton
Circuit Administrator, P. Handcock, The Priory Courts, 6th Floor, 33 Bull Street, Birmingham B4 6DS. Tel: 0121-681 3000
Group Managers: Birmingham Group, K. Dickerson; *Coventry Group*, Mrs D. Ponsonby; *Lincoln Group*, A. Phillips; *Northampton Group*, S. Smith; *Nottingham Group*, Mrs E. A. Folman; *Stafford Group*, D. Bennett

NORTH-EASTERN CIRCUIT
First-tier – Leeds, Newcastle upon Tyne, Sheffield, Teesside
Second-tier – Bradford, York
Third-tier – Doncaster, Durham, Kingston-upon-Hull
Circuit Administrator, P. J. Farmer, 17th Floor, West Riding House, Albion Street, Leeds LS1 5AA. Tel: 0113-251 1200
Group Managers: Bradford Group, F. Taylor; *Leeds Group*, P. M. Norris; *Newcastle upon Tyne Group*, K. Budgen; *Sheffield Group*, G. Bingham, OBE; *Teesside Group*, Miss E. Yates

NORTHERN CIRCUIT
First-tier – Carlisle, Liverpool, Manchester (Crown Square), Preston
Third-tier – Barrow-in-Furness, Bolton, Burnley, Lancaster; Manchester (Minshull Street)
Circuit Administrator, R. A. Vincent, 15 Quay Street, Manchester M60 9FD. Tel: 0161-833 1005
Group Managers: Liverpool Group, Mrs J. Roche; *Manchester Central Group*, Mrs C. A. Mayer; *Outer Manchester Group*, Mrs B. Handcock; *Preston Group*, B. Wilson

SOUTH-EASTERN CIRCUIT

First-tier – Chelmsford, Croydon, Lewes, Norwich
Second-tier – Ipswich, London (Central Criminal Court), Luton, Maidstone, Reading, St Albans
Third-tier – Aylesbury, Basildon, Bury St Edmunds, Cambridge, Canterbury, Chichester, Guildford, Hove, King's Lynn, London (Croydon, Harrow, Inner London Sessions House, Isleworth, Knightsbridge, Middlesex Guildhall, Snaresbrook, Southwark, Wood Green, Woolwich)
Circuit Administrator, R. J. Clark, New Cavendish House, 18 Maltravers Street, London WC2R 3EU. Tel: 0171-936 7234
Provincial Administrator, J. Powell, Steeple House, Church Lane, Chelmsford CMI INH. Tel: 01245-257425
Group Managers: Chelmsford Group, M. Littlewood; *Maidstone Group*, Mrs H. Hartwell; *Kingston Group*, Miss S. Proudlock; *Lewes Group*, B. Macbeth; *London Group (Civil)*, D. Marsh; *London Group (Crime)*, G. F. Addicott; *Luton Group*, M. McIver

The High Court in Greater London sits at the Royal Courts of Justice.

WALES AND CHESTER CIRCUIT

First-tier – Caernarfon, Cardiff, Chester, Mold, Swansea
Second-tier – Carmarthen, Merthyr Tydfil, Newport, Welshpool
Third-tier – Dolgellau, Haverfordwest, Knutsford, Warrington
Circuit Administrator, P. Risk, Churchill House, Churchill Way, Cardiff CFI 4HH. Tel: 01222-396925
Group Managers: Cardiff Group, G. Pickett; *Chester Group*, G. Kenney; *Swansea Group*, Mrs D. Thomas

WESTERN CIRCUIT

First-tier – Bristol, Exeter, Truro, Winchester
Second-tier – Dorchester, Gloucester, Plymouth, Weymouth
Third-tier – Barnstaple, Bournemouth, Newport (IOW), Portsmouth, Salisbury, Southampton, Swindon, Taunton
Circuit Administrator, D. Ryan, Bridge House, Clifton, Bristol BS8 4BN. Tel: 0117-974 3763
Group Managers: Bristol Group, N. Jeffery; *Exeter Group*, D. Gentry; *Winchester Group*, A. Davison

CIRCUIT JUDGES

Senior Circuit Judges, each £96,214
Circuit Judges at the Central Criminal Court, London (Old Bailey Judges), each £96,214
Circuit Judges, each £88,077
Style, His/Her Hon. Judge [surname]
Senior Presiding Judge, The Rt. Hon. Lord Justice Judge

MIDLAND AND OXFORD CIRCUIT

Presiding Judges, The Hon. Mr Justice Jowitt; The Hon. Mr Justice Astill *(from Jan. 1999)*

F. A. Allan; Miss C. Alton; B. J. Appleby, QC; D. P. Bennett; R. S. A. Benson; J. G. Boggis, QC; R. W. A. Bray; D. W. Brunning; N. B. Cameron Coles, QC; J. J. Cavell; F. A. Chapman; P. N. R. Clark; M. F. Coates; R. R. B. Cole; T. G. E. Corrie; P. F. Crane; *P. J. Crawford, QC (*Recorder of Birmingham*); Mrs P. A. Deeley; P. N. de Mille; T. M. Dillon, QC; C. H. Durman; B. A. Farrer, QC; Miss E. N. Fisher; J. E. Fletcher; A. C. Geddes; R. J. H. Gibbs, QC; J. Hall; V. E. Hall; D. R. D. Hamilton; S. T. Hammond; G. C. W. Harris, QC; M. J. Heath; Miss E. J. Hindley, QC; C. R. Hodson; J. R. Hopkin;

Mrs H. M. Hughes; R. H. Hutchinson; R. A. G. Inglis; R. P. V. Jenkins; A. W. P. King; M. K. Lee, QC; D. L. McCarthy; A. W. McCreath; A. G. MacDuff, QC; D. D. McEvoy, QC; J. V. Machin; M. H. Mander; L. Marshall; K. Matthewman, QC; W. D. Matthews; H. R. Mayor, QC; N. J. Mitchell; P. R. Morrell; J. I. Morris; M. D. Mott; A. J. D. Nicholl; R. T. N. Orme; R. C. C. O'Rorke; J. F. F. Orrell; D. S. Perrett, QC; C. J. Pitchers; R. F. D. Pollard; D. P. Pugsley; J. R. Pyke; R. J. Rubery; J. A. O. Shand; D. P. Stanley; P. J. Stretton; G. C. Styler; H. C. Tayler, QC; A. B. Taylor; J. J. Teare; R. S. W. F. Tonking; J. J. Wait; J. C. Warner; H. Wilson; J. W. Wilson

NORTH-EASTERN CIRCUIT

Presiding Judges, The Hon. Mr Justice Hooper; The Hon. Mr Justice Bennett *(from Jan. 1999)*

J. R. S. Adams; J. Altman; P. M. Baker, QC; T. W. Barber; J. E. Barry; G. N. Barr Young; R. Bartfield; C. O. J. Behrens; D. R. Bentley, QC; P. H. Bowers; A. N. J. Briggs; D. M. A. Bryant; J. W. M. Bullimore; B. Bush; M. C. Carr; M. L. Cartlidge; P. J. Charlesworth; P. J. Cockroft; G. J. K. Coles, QC; J. Crabtree; M. T. Cracknell; W. H. R. Crawford, QC; Mrs J. Davies; I. J. Dobkin; E. J. Faulks; P. J. Fox, QC; A. N. Fricker, QC; M. S. Garner; A. R. Goldsack, QC; R. A. Grant; S. P. Grenfell; S. J. Gullick; G. F. R. Harkins; P. J. M. Heppel, QC; *T. D. T. Hodson (*Recorder of Newcastle upon Tyne*); P. M. L. Hoffman; D. P. Hunt; R. Hunt; A. E. Hutchinson, QC; N. H. Jones, QC; G. H. Kamil; T. D. Kent-Jones, TD; G. M. Lightfoot; R. P. Lowden; A. G. McCallum; C. I. McGonigal; M. K. Mettyear; R. J. Moore; A. L. Myerson, QC; D. A. Orde; Miss H. E. Paling; J. Prophet; P. E. Robertshaw; R. M. Scott; A. Simpson; L. Spittle; Mrs L. Sutcliffe; J. A. Swanson; M. J. Taylor; R. C. Taylor; J. D. G. Walford; M. Walker; P. H. C. Walker; *B. Walsh, QC; C. T. Walton; G. Whitburn, QC; J. S. Wolstenholme; D. R. Wood

NORTHERN CIRCUIT

Presiding Judge, The Hon. Mr Justice Forbes; The Hon. Mr Justice Douglas Brown

M. P. Allweis; H. H. Andrew, QC; J. F. Appleton; S. W. Baker; A. W. Bell; R. C. W. Bennett; Miss I. Bernstein; M. S. Blackburn; C. Bloom, QC; R. Brown; J. K. Burke, QC; I. B. Campbell; F. B. Carter, QC; B. I. Caulfield; D. Clark; *D. C. Clarke, QC (*Recorder of Liverpool*); G. M. Clifton; I. W. Crompton; *R. E. Davies, QC (*Recorder of Manchester*); Miss A. E. Downey; B. R. Duckworth; S. B. Duncan; Miss D. B. Eaglestone; T. K. Earnshaw; G. A. Ensor; D. M. Evans, QC; S. J. D. Fawcus; P. S. Fish; J. R. B. Geake; D. S. Gee; W. George; J. A. D. Gilliland, QC; J. A. Hammond; M. Hedley; T. B. Hegarty, QC; M. J. Henshell; F. R. B. Holloway; R. C. Holman; N. J. G. Howarth; G. W. Humphries; C. E. F. James; P. M. Kershaw, QC (*Commercial Circuit Judge*); H. L. Lachs; P. M. Lakin; B. W. Lewis; R. J. D. Livesey, QC; *R. Lockett; D. Lynch; D. I. Mackay; J. B. Macmillan; D. G. Maddison; B. C. Maddocks; C. J. Mahon; J. A. Morgan; W. P. Morris; T. J. Mort; F. D. Owen, TD; J. A. Phillips; J. C. Phipps; D. A. Pirie; A. J. Proctor; J. H. Roberts; Miss G. D. Ruaux; H. S. Singer; E. Slinger; A. C. Smith; W. P. Smith; Miss E. M. Steel; D. R. Swift; C. B. Tetlow; J. P. Townend; I. J. C. Trigger; P. W. G. Urquhart; K. H. P. Wilkinson; B. Woodward

SOUTH-EASTERN CIRCUIT

Presiding Judges, The Hon. Mr Justice Gage; The Hon. Mr Justice Moses *(from Jan. 1999)*

J. R. D. Adams; M. F. Addison; A. R. L. Ansell;
M. G. Anthony; S. A. Anwyl, QC; M. F. Baker, QC;
M. J. D. Baker; A. F. Balston; G. S. Barham;
C. J. A. Barnett, QC; W. E. Barnett, QC; R. A. Barratt, QC;
K. Bassingthwaighte; *G. A. Bathurst Norman;
P. J. L. Beaumont, QC; N. E. Beddard; Mrs C. V. Bevington;
M. G. Binning; J. E. Bishop; B. M. B. Black; H. O. Blacksell,
QC; J. G. Boal, QC; A. V. Bradbury; P. N. Brandt;
L. J. Bromley, QC; R. G. Brown; J. M. Bull, QC;
*N. M. Butter, QC; H. J. Byrt, QC; C. V. Callman;
J. Q. Campbell; B. E. Capstick, QC; M. J. Carroll;
B. E. F. Catlin; *B. L. Charles, QC; P. C. L. Clark;
P. C. Clegg; Miss S. Coates; S. H. Colgan; P. H. Collins;
C. C. Colston, QC; S. S. Coltart; Viscount Colville of
Culross, QC; J. S. Colyer, QC; C. D. Compston;
T. A. C. Coningsby, QC; J. G. Connor; R. D. Connor;
M. J. Cook; R. A. Cooke; M. R. Coombe; P. E. Copley;
Dr E. Cotran; P. R. Cowell; R. C. Cox; M. L. S. Cripps;
J. F. Crocker; D. L. Croft, QC; H. M. Crush; D. M. Cryan;
P. Curl; G. L. Davies; I. H. Davies, TD; W. L. M. Davies, QC;
M. Dean, QC; W. N. Denison, QC (*Common Serjeant*);
J. E. Devaux; M. N. Devonshire, TD; P. H. Downes;
W. H. Dunn, QC; A. H. Durrant; C. M. Edwards; D. F. Elfer;
QC; D. R. Ellis; R. C. Elly; C. Elwen; F. P. L. Evans;
S. J. Evans; J. D. Farnworth; P. Fingret; J. J. Finney;
P. E. J. Focke, QC; P. Ford; J. J. Fordham; G. C. F. Forrester;
Ms D. A. Freedman; R. Gee; L. Gerber; C. A. H. Gibson;
Miss A. F. Goddard, QC; S. A. Goldstein; M. B. Goodman;
C. G. M. Gordon; J. B. Gosschalk; M. Graham, QC;
B. S. Green, QC; P. B. Greenwood; D. J. Griffiths;
G. D. Grigson; R. B. Groves, TD, VRD; N. T. Hague, QC;
A. B. R. Hallgarten, QC; Miss G. Hallon; J. Hamilton;
Miss S. Hamilton, QC; C. R. H. Hardy;
B. Hargrove, OBE, QC; M. F. Harris; R. G. Hawkins, QC;
J. M. Haworth; R. J. Haworth; R. M. Hayward;
A. N. Hitching; D. Holden; J. F. Holt;
A. C. C. W. Hordern, QC; K. A. D. Hornby; M. Hucker;
Sir David Hughes-Morgan, Bt., CB, CBE; J. G. Hull, QC;
M. J. Hyam (*Recorder of London*); D. A. Inman; A. B. Issard-
Davies; Dr P. J. E. Jackson; T. J. C. Joseph; S. S. Katkhuda;
M. Kennedy, QC; A. M. Kenny; T. R. King; B. J. Knight, QC;
L. G. Krikler; L. H. C. Lait; P. St J. H. Langan, QC;
Capt. J. B. R. Langdon, RN; P. H. Latham; R. Laurie;
T. Lawrence; D. M. Levy, QC; C. C. D. Lindsay, QC;
S. H. Lloyd; F. R. Lockhart; D. B. D. Lowe;
Mrs C. M. Ludlow; Capt. S. Lyons; R. J. McGregor-
Johnson; K. M. McHale; K. A. Machin, QC;
R. G. McKinnon; W. N. McKinnon; K. C. Macrae;
T. Maher; F. J. M. Marr-Johnson; D. N. N. Martineau;
N. A. Medawar, QC; D. B. Meier; D. J. Mellor;
G. D. Mercer; D. Q. Miller; Miss A. E. Mitchell;
F. I. Mitchell; H. M. Morgan; D. Morton Jack; R. T. Moss;
Miss M. J. S. Mowat; J. I. Murchie; T. M. E. Nash;
M. H. D. Neligan; Mrs M. F. Norrie; Brig. A. P. Norris,
OBE; P. W. O'Brien; M. A. Oppenheimer; D. C. J. Paget, QC;
D. A. Paiba; D. J. Parry; Mrs N. Pearce; Prof. D. S. Pearl;
Miss V. A. Pearlman; B. P. Pearson; J. R. Peppitt, QC;
N. A. J. Philpot; T. D. Pillay; D. C. Pitman; J. R. Platt;
P. B. Pollock; T. G. Pontius; W. D. C. Poulton;
H. C. Pownall, QC; S. Pratt; R. J. C. V. Prendergast;
J. E. Previté, QC; B. H. Pryor, QC; J. E. Pullinger;
D. W. Radford; J. W. Rant, CB, QC; E. V. P. Reece;
M. P. Reynolds; G. K. Rice; M. S. Rich, QC; N. P. Riddell;
G. Rivlin, QC; S. D. Robbins; D. A. H. Rodwell, QC;
J. W. Rogers, QC; G. H. Rooke, TD, QC; W. M. Rose;
P. C. R. Rountree; J. H. Rucker; T. R. G. Ryland;
J. E. A. Samuels, QC; R. B. Sanders; A. R. G. Scott-Gall;
J. S. Sennitt; J. L. Sessions; J. D. Sheerin; D. R. A. Sich;
A. G. Simmons; K. T. Simpson; P. R. Simpson;
M. Singh, QC; J. K. E. Slack, TD; S. P. Sleeman;

C. M. Smith, QC; S. A. R. Smith; R. J. Southan; S. B. Spence;
W. F. C. Thomas; P. J. Thompson; A. G. Y. Thorpe;
A. H. Tibber; C. H. Tilling; J. K. Toulmin, CMG, QC;
C. J. M. Tyrer; Mrs A. P. Uziell-Hamilton; J. E. van der
Werff; A. O. R. Vick, QC; T. L. Viljoen;
Miss M. S. Viner, CBE, QC; R. Wakefield; R. Walker;
S. P. Waller; D. B. Watling, QC; V. B. Watts;
C. S. Welchman; A. F. Wilkie, QC; S. R. Wilkinson;
R. J. Winstanley; E. G. Wrintmore; K. H. Zucker, QC

WALES AND CHESTER CIRCUIT

Presiding Judges, The Hon. Mr Justice Maurice Kay; The
Hon. Mr Justice Connell; The Hon. Mr Justice
Thomas

K. E. Barnett; M. R. Burr; S. P. Clarke; T. R. Crowther, QC;
J. T. Curran; Miss J. M. P. Daley; G. H. M. Daniel;
D. T. A. Davies; J. B. S. Diehl, QC; R. T. Dutton;
D. E. H. Edwards; G. O. Edwards, QC; The Lord Elystan-
Morgan; D. R. Evans, QC; M. R. Furness; J. W. Gaskell;
*M. Gibbon, QC; D. R. Halbert; D. J. Hale;
Miss J. E. Hayward; P. J. Jacobs; G. J. Jones; H. D. H. Jones;
G. E. Kilfoil; C. G. Masterman; D. G. Morgan;
D. G. Morris; D. C. Morton; T. H. Moseley, QC;
P. J. Price, QC; E. J. Prosser, QC; J. M. T. Rogers, QC;
S. M. Stephens, QC; H. V. Williams, QC

WESTERN CIRCUIT

Presiding Judges, The Hon. Mr Justice Butterfield; The
Hon. Mr Justice Toulson

P. R. Barclay; P. T. S. Batterbury; J. F. Beashel; R. H. Bond;
Miss J. A. M. Bonvin; C. L. Boothman; M. J. L. Brodrick;
J. M. J. Burford, QC; R. D. H. Bursell, QC; M. G. Cotterill;
G. W. A. Cottle; K. C. Cutler; P. M. Darlow;
S. C. Darwall Smith; Mrs S. P. Darwall Smith;
Mrs L. H. Davies; *M. Dyer; J. D. Foley; D. L. Griffiths;
J. D. Griggs; Mrs C. M. A. Hagen; P. J. C. R. Hooton;
G. B. Hutton; R. E. Jack, QC; A. G. H. Jones;
T. N. Mackean; Miss S. M. D. McKinney; I. S. McKintosh;
J. G. McNaught; T. J. Milligan; J. Neligan; E. G. Neville;
S. K. O'Malley; S. K. Overend; R. Price; R. C. Pryor, QC;
J. N. P. Rudd; A. Rutherford; Miss A. O. H. Sander;
D. H. D. Selwood; R. M. Shawcross; D. A. Smith, QC;
W. E. M. Taylor; P. M. Thomas; A. A. R. Thompson, QC;
D. K. Ticehurst, QC; H. J. M. Tucker, QC;
D. M. Webster, QC; J. H. Weeks, QC; J. S. Wiggs;
J. A. J. Wigmore; J. C. Willis

RECORDERS (each £420 per day)

F. A. Abbott; R. D. I. Adam; P. C. Ader; R. J. P. Aikens, QC;
J. F. Akast; D. J. Ake; R. Akenhead, QC;
I. D. G. Alexander, QC; C. D. Allan, QC; C. J. Alldis;
J. H. Allen, QC; D. M. Altaras; A. J. Anderson, QC;
W. P. Andreae-Jones, QC; Mrs E. H. Andrew;
P. J. Andrews, QC; R. A. Anelay, QC;
Miss L. E. Appleby, QC; J. F. A. Archer, QC; The Lord
Archer of Sandwell, PC, QC; E. K. Armitage, QC;
P. J. B. Armstrong; G. K. Arran; E. G. Aspley;
N. J. Atkinson, QC; D. J. M. Aubrey, QC; D. S. Aubrey;
M. G. Austin-Smith, QC; M. J. S. Axtell; W. S. Aylen, QC;
P. D. Babb; J. F. Badenoch, QC; Miss P. H. Badley;
E. H. Bailey; A. B. Baillie; N. R. J. Baker, QC; Miss A. Ball,
QC; C. G. Ball, QC; A. Barker, QC; B. J. Barker, QC;
D. Barker, QC; G. E. Barling, QC; D. N. Barnard;
H. J. Barnes; T. P. Barnes, QC; A. J. Barnett; D. A. Bartlett;
G. R. Bartlett, QC; J. C. T. Barton, QC; D. C. Bate, QC;
S. D. Batten, QC; P. D. Batty, QC; J. J. Baughan, QC;
R. A. Bayliss; D. M. Bean; J. Beatson; C. H. Beaumont;
R. V. M. E. Behar; R. W. Belben; J. K. Benson; P. C. Benson;
R. A. Benson, QC; H. L. Bentham, QC; D. M. Berkson;

C. R. Berry; M. Bethel, QC; J. P. V. Bevan;
Mrs M. O. Bickford-Smith; N. Bidder; I. G. Bing;
P. V. Birkett, QC; M. I. Birnbaum; W. J. Birtles;
P. W. Birts, QC; B. G. D. Blair, QC; W. J. L. Blair, QC;
J. A. Blair-Gould; A. N. H. Blake; P. E. Bleasdale; R. H. L.
Blomfield, TD; D. J. Blunt, QC; O. S. P. Blunt, QC;
D. R. L. Bodey, QC; G. T. K. Boney, QC; J. J. Boothby;
D. J. Boulton; S. N. Bourne-Arton, QC; Ms M. R. Bowron;
W. Boyce; S. C. Boyd, QC; J. J. Boyle; D. L. Bradshaw;
W. T. S. Braithwaite, QC; N. D. Bratza, QC; G. B. Breen;
D. J. Brennan, QC; M. L. Brent, QC; G. J. B. G. Brice, QC;
A. J. Brigden; D. R. Bright; R. P. Brittain; R. A. Britton;
J. Bromley-Davenport; L. F. M. Brown; S. C. Brown, QC;
D. J. M. Browne, QC; J. N. Browne; A. J. N. Brunner, QC;
W. V. Bryan; Miss B. M. Bucknall, QC; A. Bueno, QC;
J. E. Bullen; P. E. Bullock; J. P. Burke, QC;
H. W. Burnett, QC; R. H. Burns; S. J. Burnton, QC;
G. Burrell, QC; M. J. Burton, QC; K. Bush; A. J. Butcher, QC;
Miss J. Butler; C. W. Byers; D. W. Caddick; D. Calvert-
Smith; R. Camden Pratt, QC; Miss S. M. C. Cameron, QC;
A. N. Campbell, QC; J. M. Caplan, QC; G. M. C. Carey, QC;
A. C. Carlile, QC, MP; H. B. H. Carlisle, QC; The Lord
Carlisle of Bucklow, PC, QC; J. J. Carter-Manning, QC;
R. Carus, QC; Mrs J. R. Case; P. D. Cattan;
Miss M. T. Catterson; R. M. Challinor;
N. M. Chambers, QC; Miss D. C. Champion;
V. R. Chapman; J. M. Cherry, QC; C. F. Chruszcz, QC;
A. V. Chubb; C. H. Clark, QC; C. S. C. S. Clarke, QC;
P. W. Clarke; P. R. J. Clarkson, QC; T. Clayson;
A. S. L. Cleary; W. Clegg, QC; P. Clements; T. A. Clover;
W. P. Coates; D. J. Cocks, QC; J. J. Coffey, QC;
T. A. Coghlan, QC; J. L. Cohen; L. F. R. Cohen, QC;
W. J. Coker, QC; J. R. Cole; A. J. S. Coleman; N. J. Coleman;
P. J. D. Coleridge, QC; A. R. Collender, QC;
P. N. Collier, QC; J. M. Collins; M. G. Collins, QC; I. Collis;
Ms M. Colton; Mrs J. R. Comyns; A. D. Conrad;
C. S. Cook; J. L. Cooke, QC; N. O. Cooke;
K. B. Coonan, QC; A. E. M. Cooper; Miss B. P. Cooper, QC;
P. J. Cooper, QC; C. J. Cornwall; P. J. Cosgrove, QC;
R. M. R. Cotton, QC; J. S. Coward, QC; T. G. Cowling;
Mrs L. M. Cox, QC; P. Crampin, QC; R. F. Cranston, QC;
L. S. Crawford; N. Crichton; D. I. Crigman, QC;
C. A. Critchlow; D. R. Crome; S. R. Crookenden, QC;
Mrs J. Crowley; J. D. Crowley, QC; T. S. Culver;
Miss E. A. M. Curnow, QC; P. D. Curran;
J. W. O. Curtis, QC; M. J. Curwen; A. J. G. Dalziel;
Mrs P. M. T. Dangor; A. M. Darroch; C. P. M. Davidson;
A. M. Davies; A. R. M. Davies; H. Davies; J. T. L. Davies;
Miss N. V. Davies, QC; R. L. Davies, QC; N. A. L. Davis, QC;
W. E. Davis; A. W. Dawson; D. H. Day, QC; P. G. Dedman;
C. F. Dehn, QC; P. A. de la Piquerie; M. A. de Navarro, QC;
R. L. Denyer, QC; H. A. D. de Silva; P. N. Digney;
C. E. Dines; A. D. Dinkin, QC; D. R. Dobbin; P. Dodgson;
R. A. M. Doggett; Ms B. Dohmann, QC;
D. T. Donaldson, QC; A. M. Donne, QC; A. F. S. Donovan;
A. K. Dooley; J. Dowse; J. R. Duggan; P. R. Dunkels, QC;
J. D. Durham Hall, QC; H. W. P. Eccles, QC;
C. N. Edelman, QC; A. H. Edwards;
Miss S. M. Edwards, QC; A. J. C. Edwards-Stuart, QC;
G. Elias, QC; E. A. Elliott; J. A. Elvidge;
R. M. Englehart, QC; D. A. Evans, QC; D. H. Evans, QC;
F. W. H. Evans, QC; G. J. Evans; G. W. R. Evans, QC;
M. Evans, QC; M. J. Evans; M. A. Everall, QC; Miss D.
Faber; T. M. Faber; R. B. Farley, QC; P. M. Farmer, QC;
D. J. Farrer, QC; P. E. Feinberg, QC; R. Fernyhough, QC;
M. C. Field; J. E. Finestein; J. E. P. Finnigan; D. T. Fish;
D. P. Fisher; G. D. Flather, CBE, QC; N. M. Ford, QC;
R. A. Fordham, QC; B. C. Forster; M. D. P. Fortune;
D. R. Foskett, QC; I. H. Foster; J. R. Foster, QC;
Miss R. M. Foster; D. P. Friedman, QC;

C. J. E. Gardner, QC; P. R. Garlick, QC; C. R. Garside, QC;
R. C. Gaskell; S. A. G. L. Gault; A. H. Gee, QC;
I. W. Geering, QC; D. S. Geey; C. R. George, QC; S. M.
Gerlis; D. C. Gerrey; J. S. Gibbons, QC; A. J. Gilbart, QC;
F. H. S. Gilbert, QC; N. J. Gilchrist; K. Gillance;
N. B. D. Gilmour, QC; L. Giovene; A. T. Glass, QC; M. G. J.
Gledhill; H. B. Globe, QC; Miss E. Gloster, QC;
H. K. Goddard, QC; H. A. Godfrey, QC;
Ms L. S. Godfrey, QC; J. J. Goldberg, QC; J. B. Goldring, QC;
P. H. Goldsmith, QC; L. C. Goldstone, QC;
A. J. J. Gompertz, QC; Miss R. M. Goode; J. R. W. Goss;
T. J. C. Goudie, QC; A. A. Goymer; G. Gozem;
A. S. Grabiner, QC; C. A. St J. Gray, QC; H. Green, QC; Miss
J. E. G. Greenberg, QC; A. E. Greenwood;
J. C. Greenwood; J. G. Grenfell, QC; R. D. Grey, QC;
D. E. Griffith-Jones; R. H. Griffith-Jones;
J. P. G. Griffiths, QC; M. G. Grills; M. S. E. Grime, QC;
P. Grobel; P. H. Gross, QC; M. A. W. Grundy; B. P.
Gulbenkian; A. S. Hacking, QC; J. W. Haines; N. J. Hall;
S. J. Hall; J. P. N. Hallam; Miss H. C. Hallett, QC;
G. M. Hamilton, TD, QC; I. M. Hamilton; P. L. Hamlin;
J. L. Hand, QC; Miss R. S. A. Hare, QC; G. T. Harrap; M. K.
Harington; P. J. Harrington, QC; D. M. Harris, QC;
R. D. Harrison; R. M. Harrison, QC; H. M. Harrod;
J. M. Harrow; C. P. Hart-Leverton, QC; B. Harvey;
J. G. Harvey; M. L. T. Harvey, QC; D. W. Hatton, QC;
A. M. D. Havelock-Allan, QC; The Hon. P. N. Havers, QC;
T. S. A. Hawkesworth, QC; W. G. Hawkesworth;
R. W. P. Hay; Prof. D. J. Hayton; R. Hayward-Smith, QC;
A. T. Hedworth, QC; R. A. Henderson, QC;
R. H. Q. Henriques, QC; R. C. Herman; M. S. Heslop, QC;
T. Hewitt; G. R. Hickinbottom; B. J. Higgs, QC;
J. W. Hillyer; A. J. H. Hilton, QC; J. W. Hirst, QC;
W. T. J. Hirst; J. D. Hitchen; S. A. Hockman, QC;
H. E. G. Hodge, OBE; A. J. C. Hoggett, QC; T. V. Holroyde,
QC; R. M. Hone; A. D. Hope; S. Hopkins;
M. A. P. Hopmeier; M. Horowitz, QC; Miss R. Horwood-
Smart; C. P. Hotten, QC; B. F. Houlder, QC;
M. N. Howard, QC; C. I. Howells; M. J. Hubbard, QC; D. L.
Hughes; Miss J. C. A. Hughes, QC; T. P. Hughes, QC;
R. P. Hughes; T. M. Hughes, QC; L. D. Hull;
Capt. D. R. Humphrey, RN; W. G. B. Hungerford;
D. R. N. Hunt, QC; P. J. Hunt, QC; I. G. A. Hunter, QC;
M. A. Hunter; M. Hussain, QC; A. G. K. Hyland;
P. R. Isaacs; S. L. Isaacs, QC; S. Jack; D. G. A. Jackson;
M. R. Jackson; R. M. Jackson, QC; I. E. Jacob;
N. F. B. Jarman, QC; J. M. Jarvis, QC; J. R. Jarvis;
A. H. Jeffreys; D. A. Jeffreys, QC; J. D. Jenkins, QC;
D. B. Johnson, QC; Miss A. M. Jolles; D. A. F. Jones;
D. L. Jones; N. G. Jones; P. H. F. Jones; S. E. Jones, QC;
T. G. Jones; W. J. Jones; W. H. Joss; H. M. Joy;
P. S. L. Joyce, QC; R. W. S. Juckes; M. L. Kallipetis, QC;
Miss L. N. R. Kamill; I. G. F. Karsten, QC; R. G. Kaye, QC;
C. B. Kealy; K. R. Keen, QC; Mrs S. M. Keen;
B. R. Keith, QC; C. J. B. Kemp; D. Kennett Brown;
D. M. Kerr; L. D. Kershen, QC; M. I. Khan;
G. M. Khayat, QC; C. A. Kinch; T. R. A. King, QC;
W. M. Kingston, QC; R. C. Klevan, QC; M. S. Knott;
Miss P. E. Knowles; C. Knox; Miss J. C. M. Korner, QC;
S. E. Kramer, QC; Miss L. J. Kushner, QC; P. E. Kyte, QC;
N. R. W. Lambert; D. A. Landau; D. G. Lane, QC;
T. J. Langdale, QC; B. F. J. Langstaff, QC; D. H. Latham;
R. B. Latham, QC; S. W. Lawler, QC; Sir Ivan Lawrence, QC;
Miss E. A. Lawson, QC; M. H. Lawson, QC; G. S. Lawson-
Rogers, QC; P. L. O. Leaver, QC; D. Lederman, QC;
B. W. T. Leech; I. Leeming, QC; C. H. de V. Leigh, QC;
H. B. G. Lett; B. L. Lever; B. H. Leveson, QC;
A. E. Levy, QC; M. E. Lewer, QC; J. A. Lewis;
K. M. J. Lewison, QC; S. J. Linehan, QC; G. W. Little;
B. J. E. Livesey, QC; C. G. Llewellyn-Jones, QC;

C. J. Lockhart-Mummery, QC; A. J. C. Lodge, QC;
T. Longbotham; D. C. Lovell-Pank, QC; A. C. Lowcock;
G. W. Lowe; J. A. M. Lowen; Rt. Hon. Sir Nicholas Lyell,
QC, MP; A. P. Lyon; E. Lyons, QC; P. G. McCahill, QC;
R. G. B. McCombe, QC; A. G. McDowall; K. M. P. Macgill;
R. D. Machell, QC; B. M. McIntyre; C. C. Mackay, QC;
D. L. Mackie; N. A. McKittrick; I. A. B. McLaren, QC;
I. McLeod; N. R. B. Macleod, QC; A. G. Mainds;
A. H. R. Maitland; A. R. Malcolm; H. J. Malins;
M. E. Mann, QC; The Hon. G. R. J. Mansfield;
A. C. B. Markham-David; R. L. Marks; J. W. Marrin, QC; A.
L. Marriott, QC; G. M. Marriott; A. S. Marron, QC;
P. Marsh; R. G. Marshall-Andrews, QC; G. C. Marson;
H. R. A. Martineau; S. A. Maskrey, QC; C. P. Mather;
D. Matheson, QC; P. R. Matthews; Mrs S. P. Matthews, QC;
P. B. Mauleverer, QC; R. B. Mawrey, QC; J. F. M. Maxwell;
R. Maxwell, QC; Mrs P. R. May; G. M. Mercer;
N. F. Merriman, QC; The Lord Meston, QC;
C. S. J. Metcalf; J. T. Milford, QC; K. S. H. Miller;
R. A. Miller; S. M. Miller, QC; C. J. Millington;
J. B. M. Milmo, QC; D. C. Milne, QC; C. J. M. Miskin, QC;
Miss C. M. Miskin; A. P. Mitchell; C. R. Mitchell;
D. C. Mitchell; J. R. Mitchell; J. E. Mitting, QC; F. R. Moat;
E. G. Moelwyn-Hughes; C. R. D. Moger, QC;
Mrs J. P. Moir; D. R. P. Mole, QC; M. G. C. Moorhouse;
A. G. Moran, QC; D. W. Morgan; P. B. Morgan;
A. P. Morris, QC; C. Morris-Coole; H. A. C. Morrison, OBE;
G. E. Morrow, QC; C. J. Moss, QC; P. C. Mott, QC;
R. W. Moxon-Browne, QC; J. H. Muir; F. J. Muller, QC; A.
H. Munday, QC; G. S. Murdoch, QC; I. P. Murphy, QC;
M. J. A. Murphy, QC; N. O. G. Murray; N. J. Mylne, QC;
H. G. Narayan; A. R. H. Newman, QC; A. I. Niblett;
G. Nice, QC; C. A. A. Nicholls, QC; C. V. Nicholls, QC;
A. S. T. E. Nicol; A. E. R. Noble; B. Nolan, QC;
M. C. Norman; J. M. Norris; P. H. Norris; G. Nuttall;
J. G. Nutting, QC; D. P. O'Brien, QC; Mrs
F. M. Oldham, QC; S. Oliver-Jones, QC; R. W. Onions;
C. P. L. Openshaw, QC; M. N. O'Sullivan;
D. B. W. Ouseley, QC; R. M. Owen, QC; T. W. Owen;
N. D. Padfield, QC; S. R. Page; A. O. Palmer, QC;
A. W. Palmer, QC; D. P. Pannick, QC; A. D. W. Pardoe, QC;
S. A. B. Parish; G. C. Parkins, QC; G. E. Parkinson;
M. P. Parroy, QC; E. O. Parry; N. S. K. Pascoe, QC;
A. Patience, QC; Miss A. E. H. Pauffley, QC; J. G. Paulusz;
W. E. Pawlak; R. J. Pearse Wheatley;
The Hon. I. J. C. Peddie, QC; J. V. Pegden; J. Perry, QC;
M. Pert, QC; N. M. Peters, QC; D. J. Phillips, QC;
W. B. Phillips; M. A. Pickering, QC; J. K. Pickup;
C. J. Pitchford, QC; The Hon. B. M. D. Pitt;
Miss E. F. Platt, QC; R. Platts; J. R. Playford, QC; R. O.
Plender, QC; Miss J. C. Plumptre; Miss I. M. Plumstead; S.
D. Popat; A. R. Porten, QC; L. R. Portnoy; J. R. L.
Posnansky, QC; Mrs R. M. Poulet, QC; S. R. Powles, QC;
T. W. Preston, QC; D. Price; G. A. L. Price, QC;
J. A. Price, QC; J. C. Price; N. P. L. Price, QC; F. S. K.
Privett; H. W. Prosser; A. C. Pugh, QC; G. V. Pugh, QC;
G. F. Pulman, QC; C. P. B. Purchas, QC; R. M. Purchas, QC;
N. R. Purnell, QC; P. O. Purnell, QC; Q. C. W. Querelle;
D. A. Radcliffe; Mrs N. P. Radford, QC;
Ms A. J. Rafferty, QC; T. W. H. Raggatt, QC; Miss E. A.
Ralphs; A. D. Rawley, QC; J. E. Rayner James, QC;
P. R. Raynor, QC; L. F. Read, QC; J. H. Reddihough;
A. R. F. Redgrave, QC; D. W. Rees; G. W. Rees; P. Rees;
C. E. Reese, QC; J. R. Reid, QC; P. C. Reid; D. J. Rennie;
R. E. Rhodes, QC; D. W. Richards; D. J. Richardson;
T. Rigby; S. V. Riordan, QC; G. Risius;
Miss J. H. Ritchie, QC; M. W. Roach; J. M. Roberts;
J. M. G. Roberts, QC; T. D. Roberts; A. J. Robertson;
V. Robinson, QC; D. E. H. Robson, QC; G. W. Roddick, QC;
Miss M. B. Roddy; Miss D. J. Rodgers; P. F. G. Rook, QC;

J. G. Ross; J. G. Ross Martyn; P. C. Rouch; J. J. Rowe, QC;
R. J. Royce, QC; M. W. Rudland; P. E. B. M. Rueff;
A. A. Rumbelow, QC; N. J. Rumfitt, QC; R. J. Rundell;
J. R. T. Rylance; C. R. A. Sallon, QC; C. N. Salmon;
D. A. Salter; A. T. Sander; G. R. Sankey, QC; N. L. Sarony;
J. H. B. Saunders, QC; M. P. Sayers, QC; R. J. Scholes, QC;
Miss P. Scriven, QC; R. J. Seabrook, QC; C. Seagroatt, QC;
M. R. Selfe; W. P. L. Sellick; O. M. Sells, QC; D. Serota, QC;
R. W. Seymour, QC; A. J. Seys-Llewellyn; A. R. F. Sharp;
P. P. Shears; S. J. Sher, QC; Miss J. Shipley;
J. M. Shorrock, QC; S. R. Silber, QC; Miss M. A. Simmons,
QC; P. F. Singer, QC; Miss E. A. Slade, QC; J. C. N. Slater, QC;
A. C. Smith, QC; A. T. Smith, QC; P. W. Smith, QC;
R. D. H. Smith, QC; R. S. Smith, QC; Ms Z. P. Smith;
C. J. Smyth; S. M. Solley, QC; E. Somerset Jones, QC;
R. C. Southwell, QC; R. C. E. Southwell; M. H. Spence, QC;
Sir Derek Spencer, QC; J. Spencer, QC; M. G. Spencer, QC;
R. G. Spencer; S. M. Spencer, QC; R. V. Spencer Bernard;
D. P. Spens, QC; R. W. Spon-Smith; D. Steer, QC;
M. T. Steiger, QC; Mrs L. J. Stern, QC; A. W. Stevenson, TD;
J. S. H. Stewart, QC; N. A. Stewart; R. M. Stewart, QC;
W. R. Stewart Smith; A. C. Steynor; G. J. C. Still;
D. A. Stockdale, QC; Mrs D. M. Stocken;
D. M. A. Stokes, QC; M. G. T. Stokes, QC; J. B. Storey, QC;
P. L. Storr; T. M. F. Stow, QC; D. M. A. Strachan, QC;
M. Stuart-Moore, QC; F. R. C. Such; A. B. Suckling, QC;
Ms L. E. Sullivan, QC; D. M. Sumner;
J. P. C. Sumption, QC; M. A. Supperstone, QC; P. J. Susman;
R. P. Sutton, QC; N. H. Sweeney; Miss C. J. Swift, QC;
M. R. Swift, QC; Miss H. H. Swindells, QC;
C. J. M. Symons, QC; J. P. Tabor, QC; J. A. Tackaberry, QC;
P. J. Talbot, QC; R. K. K. Talbot; R. B. Tansey, QC; J. B. C.
Tanzer; G. F. Tattersall, QC; E. T. H. Teague;
N. J. M. Teare, QC; R. H. Tedd, QC; A. D. Temple, QC;
V. B. A. Temple, QC; M. H. Tennant; D. O. Thomas, QC;
P. A. Thomas; R. L. Thomas, QC; R. M. Thomas;
R. U. Thomas, QC; Miss S. M. Thomas; C. F. J. Thompson;
A. R. Thornhill, QC; P. R. Thornton, QC; A. C. Tickle;
J. Tiley; M. B. Tillett, QC; J. W. Tinnion;
R. N. Titheridge, QC; S. M. Tomlinson, QC;
P. J. H. Towler; J. B. S. Townend, QC; C. M. Treacy, QC;
H. B. Trethowan; A. D. H. Trollope, QC;
M. G. Tugendhat, QC; H. W. Turcan; D. A. Turner, QC;
P. A. Twigg, QC; A. R. Tyrrell, QC; J. F. Uff, QC;
N. E. Underhill, QC; J. G. G. Ungley; N. P. Valios, QC;
N. C. van der Bijl; D. A. J. Vaughan, QC; M. J. D. Vere-
Hodge, QC; C. J. Vosper; J. P. Wadsworth, QC; S. P. Waine;
Miss A. P. Wakefield; R. M. Wakerley, QC; Mrs
E. A. Walker; R. A. Walker, QC; R. J. Walker, QC;
Sir Jonah Walker-Smith, Bt.; T. M. Walsh; J. J. Wardlow;
J. Warren, QC; N. J. Warren; D. E. B. Waters; Miss
B. J. Watson; Sir James Watson, Bt.; B. J. Waylen;
A. R. Webb; R. S. Webb, QC; A. S. Webster, QC;
P. Weitzman; C. H. Whitby; G. B. N. White;
W. J. M. White; D. R. B. Whitehouse, QC; R. P. Whitehurst;
P. G. Whiteman, QC; P. J. M. Whiteman, TD;
A. Whitfield, QC; C. T. Wide, QC; R. Wigglesworth;
A. D. F. Wilcken; N. V. M. Wilkinson; Miss E. Willers;
G. H. G. Williams, QC; Miss J. A. Williams;
J. G. Williams, QC; J. L. Williams, QC; M. J. Williams;
W. L. Williams, QC; The Lord Williams of Mostyn, QC;
Miss H. E. Williamson; S. W. Williamson, QC;
A. J. D. Wilson, QC; A. M. Wilson, QC; I. K. R. Wilson;
C. Wilson-Smith, QC; G. W. Wingate-Saul, QC; Miss S. E.
Wollam; H. Wolton, QC; N. A. Wood; R. L. J. Wood, QC;
W. R. Wood; L. G. Woodley, QC; Miss S. Woodley;
J. T. Woods; W. C. Woodward, QC; A. P. L. Woolman;
T. H. Workman; Miss A. M. Worrall, QC; D. Worsley;
P. F. Worsley, QC; J. J. Wright; M. P. Yelton;
D. E. M. Young, QC

STIPENDIARY MAGISTRATES

PROVINCIAL (each £70,820)

Cheshire, P. K. Dodd, OBE, *apptd* 1991
Derbyshire, M. J. Friel, *apptd* 1997; Mrs J. H. Alderson, *apptd* 1997
Devon, P. H. Wassall, *apptd* 1994
East and West Sussex, P. C. Tain, *apptd* 1992
Essex, K. A. Gray, *apptd* 1995
Greater Manchester, A. Berg, *apptd* 1994; C. R. Darnton, *apptd* 1994
Hampshire, T. G. Cowling, *apptd* 1989
Humberside, N. H. White, *apptd* 1985
Lancashire/Merseyside, J. Finestein, *apptd* 1992
Leicestershire, D. M. Meredith, *apptd* 1995
Merseyside, D. R. G. Tapp, *apptd* 1992; P. S. Ward, *apptd* 1994; P. J. Firth, *apptd* 1994
Middlesex, N. A. McKittrick, *apptd* 1989; S. N. Day, *apptd* 1991; C. S. Wiles, *apptd* 1996
Mid Glamorgan, Miss P. J. Watkins, *apptd* 1995
Norfolk, N. P. Heley, *apptd* 1994
North-East London, G. E. Cawdron, *apptd* 1993
Nottinghamshire, P. F. Nuttall, *apptd* 1991; M. L. R. Harris, *apptd* 1991
Shropshire, P. H. R. Browning, *apptd* 1994
South Glamorgan, C. B. Watkins, *apptd* 1993
South Wales and Gwent, D. V. Manning-Davies, *apptd* 1996
South Yorkshire, J. A. Browne, *apptd* 1992; W. D. Thomas, *apptd* 1989; M. A. Rosenberg, *apptd* 1993; P. H. F. Jones, *apptd* 1995; Mrs S. E. Driver, *apptd* 1995
Staffordshire, P. G. G. Richards, *apptd* 1991
West Midlands, W. M. Probert, *apptd* 1983; B. Morgan, *apptd* 1989; I. Gillespie, *apptd* 1991; M. F. James, *apptd* 1991; C. M. McColl, *apptd* 1994
West Yorkshire, Mrs P. A. Hewitt, *apptd* 1990; G. A. K. Hodgson, *apptd* 1993; N. R. Cadbury, *apptd* 1997

METROPOLITAN

Chief Metropolitan Stipendiary Magistrate and Chairman of Magistrates' Courts Committee for Inner London Area (£88,077), G. E. Parkinson, *apptd* 1997 (*Bow Street*)

Magistrates (each £70,820)
Bow Street, The Chief Magistrate; R. D. Bartle, *apptd* 1972; C. L. Pratt, *apptd* 1990; H. N. Evans, *apptd* 1994
Camberwell Green, C. P. M. Davidson, *apptd* 1984; B. Loosley, *apptd* 1989; H. Gott, *apptd* 1992; Miss E. Roscoe, *apptd* 1994; R. House, *apptd* 1995; Miss C. S. R. Tubbs, *apptd* 1996
Clerkenwell, M. A. Johnstone, *apptd* 1980; I. M. Baker, *apptd* 1990
Greenwich, D. A. Cooper, *apptd* 1991; M. Kelly, *apptd* 1992; P. S. Wallis, *apptd* 1993; H. C. F. Riddle, *apptd* 1995
Highbury Corner, Miss D. Quick, *apptd* 1986; A. T. Evans, *apptd* 1990; Mrs L. Morgan, *apptd* 1995; P. A. M. Clark, *apptd* 1996; Miss D. Lachhar, *apptd* 1996
Horseferry Road, A. R. Davies, *apptd* 1985; G. Breen, *apptd* 1986; T. Workman, *apptd* 1986; Mrs K. R. Keating, *apptd* 1987; G. Wicks, *apptd* 1987; Mrs E. Rees, *apptd* 1994
Inner London and City Family Proceedings Court, N. Crichton, *apptd* 1987
Marylebone, D. Kennett Brown, *apptd* 1982; K. Maitland-Davies, *apptd* 1984; A. C. Baldwin, *apptd* 1990; Ms G. Babington-Browne, *apptd* 1991
South-Western, C. D. Voelcker, *apptd* 1982; A. W. Ormerod, *apptd* 1988; Miss D. Wickham, *apptd* 1989

Thames, Mrs J. Comyns, *apptd* 1982; I. G. Bing, *apptd* 1989; W. A. Kennedy, *apptd* 1991; S. E. Dawson, *apptd* 1984
Tower Bridge, C. S. F. Black, *apptd* 1993; M. Read, *apptd* 1993; S. Somjee, *apptd* 1995
West London Magistrates' Court, Miss A. Jennings, *apptd* 1972; T. English, *apptd* 1986; J. Philips, *apptd* 1989; D. L. Thomas, *apptd* 1990; D. Simpson, *apptd* 1993; J. Coleman, *apptd* 1995

MAGISTRATES' COURTS COMMITTEE FOR THE INNER LONDON AREA
65 Romney Street, London SW1P 3RD
Tel 0171-799 3332
Justices' Chief Executive and Clerk to the Committee (£82,116), Miss C. Glenn
Justices' Clerk (Training) (£46,722), Miss C. Lewis

CROWN PROSECUTION SERVICE
50 Ludgate Hill, London EC4M 7EX
Tel 0171-273 8000

The Crown Prosecution Service (CPS) is responsible for the independent review and conduct of criminal proceedings instituted by police forces in England and Wales, with the exception of cases conducted by the Serious Fraud Office (*see* page 344) and certain minor offences.

The Service is headed by the Director of Public Prosecutions (DPP), who works under the superintendence of the Attorney-General, and a chief executive. The Service currently comprises a headquarters office and 14 areas covering England and Wales, with each area supervised by a Chief Crown Prosecutor. It is in the process of being decentralized, with 42 areas being created to correspond to the police areas in England and Wales.

For salary information, *see* page 278

Director of Public Prosecutions (SCS), Dame Barbara Mills, DBE, QC (*successor to be appointed in autumn 1998*)
Chief Executive (SCS), M. E. Addison
Director of Casework Evaluation (SCS), C. Newell
Director of Casework Services (SCS), G. Duff

CPS AREAS

CPS ANGLIA, Queen's House, 58 Victoria Street, St Albans AL1 3HZ. Tel: 01727-818100. *Chief Crown Prosecutor* (SCS), R. J. Chronnell
CPS CENTRAL CASEWORK, 50 Ludgate Hill, London EC4M 7EX. Tel: 0171-273 8000. *Chief Crown Prosecutor* (SCS), Miss D. Sharpling
CPS EAST MIDLANDS, 2 King Edward Court, King Edward Street, Nottingham NG1 IEL. Tel: 0115-948 0480. *Chief Crown Prosecutor* (SCS), B. T. McArdle
CPS HUMBER, Greenfield House, Scotland Street, Sheffield S3 7DQ. Tel: 0114-291 2164. *Chief Crown Prosecutor* (SCS), D. Adams, CBE
CPS LONDON, Portland House, Stag Place, London SW1E 5BH. Tel: 0171-915 5700. *Chief Crown Prosecutor* (SCS), G. D. Etherington
CPS MERSEY/LANCASHIRE, 7th Floor (South), Royal Liver Building, Pier Head, Liverpool L3 1HN. Tel: 0151-236 7575. *Chief Crown Prosecutor* (SCS), G. Brown
CPS MIDLANDS, 14th Floor, Colmore Gate, 2 Colmore Row, Birmingham B3 2QA. Tel: 0121-629 7202. *Chief Crown Prosecutor* (SCS), D. Blundell

CPS NORTH, 1st Floor, Benton House, 136 Sandyford Road, Newcastle upon Tyne NE2 1QE. Tel: 0191-201 2390. *Chief Crown Prosecutor (SCS)*, M. Graham
CPS NORTH-WEST, PO Box 237, 8th Floor, Sunlight House, Quay Street, Manchester M60 3PS. Tel: 0161-908 2771. *Chief Crown Prosecutor (SCS)*, A. R. Taylor
CPS SEVERN /THAMES, Artillery House, Heritage Way, Droitwich, Worcester WR9 8YB. Tel: 01905-795477. *Chief Crown Prosecutor (SCS)*, N. Franklin
CPS SOUTH-EAST, 1 Onslow Street, Guildford, Surrey GU1 4YA. Tel: 01483-882600. *Chief Crown Prosecutor (SCS)*, C. Nicholls
CPS SOUTH-WEST, 8 Kew Court, Pynes Hill, Rydon Lane, Exeter EX2 5SS. Tel: 01392-422555. *Chief Crown Prosecutor (SCS)*, P. Boeuf
CPS WALES, Tudor House, 16 Cathedral Road, Cardiff CF1 9LJ. Tel: 01222-783000. *Chief Crown Prosecutor (SCS)*, R. A. Prickett
CPS YORKSHIRE, 6th Floor, Ryedale Building, 60 Piccadilly, York YO1 1NS. Tel: 01904-610726. *Chief Crown Prosecutor (SCS)*, D. V. Dickenson

The Scottish Judicature

Scotland has a legal system separate from and differing greatly from the English legal system in enacted law, judicial procedure and the structure of courts.

In Scotland the system of public prosecution is headed by the Lord Advocate and is independent of the police, who have no say in the decision to prosecute. The Lord Advocate, discharging his functions through the Crown Office in Edinburgh, is responsible for prosecutions in the High Court, sheriff courts and district courts. Prosecutions in the High Court are prepared by the Crown Office and conducted in court by one of the law officers, by an advocate-depute, or by a solicitor advocate. In the inferior courts the decision to prosecute is made and prosecution is preferred by procurators fiscal, who are lawyers and full-time civil servants subject to the directions of the Crown Office. A permanent legally-qualified civil servant known as the Crown Agent is responsible for the running of the Crown Office and the organization of the Procurator Fiscal Service, of which he is the head.

Scotland is divided into six sheriffdoms, each with a full-time sheriff principal. The sheriffdoms are further divided into sheriff court districts, each of which has a legally-qualified resident sheriff or sheriffs, who are the judges of the court.

In criminal cases sheriffs principal and sheriffs have the same powers; sitting with a jury of 15 members, they may try more serious cases on indictment, or, sitting alone, may try lesser cases under summary procedure. Minor summary offences are dealt with in district courts which are administered by the district and the islands local government authorities and presided over by lay justices of the peace (of whom there are about 4,000) and, in Glasgow only, by stipendiary magistrates. Juvenile offenders (children under 16) may be brought before an informal children's hearing comprising three local lay people. The superior criminal court is the High Court of Justiciary which is both a trial and an appeal court. Cases on indictment are tried by a High Court judge, sitting with a jury of 15, in Edinburgh and on circuit in other towns. Appeals from the lower courts against conviction or sentence are heard also by the High Court, which sits as

an appeal court only in Edinburgh. There is no further appeal to the House of Lords in criminal cases.

In civil cases the jurisdiction of the sheriff court extends to most kinds of action. Appeal against decisions of the sheriff may be made to the sheriff principal and thence to the Court of Session, or direct to the Court of Session, which sits only in Edinburgh. The Court of Session is divided into the Inner and the Outer House. The Outer House is a court of first instance in which cases are heard by judges sitting singly, sometimes with a jury of 12. The Inner House, itself subdivided into two divisions of equal status, is mainly an appeal court. Appeals may be made to the Inner House from the Outer House as well as from the sheriff court. An appeal may be made from the Inner House to the House of Lords.

The judges of the Court of Session are the same as those of the High Court of Justiciary, the Lord President of the Court of Session also holding the office of Lord Justice General in the High Court. Senators of the College of Justice are Lords Commissioners of Justiciary as well as judges of the Court of Session. On appointment, a Senator takes a judicial title, which is retained for life. Although styled 'The Hon./Rt. Hon. Lord —', the Senator is not a peer.

The office of coroner does not exist in Scotland. The local procurator fiscal inquires privately into sudden or suspicious deaths and may report findings to the Crown Agent. In some cases a fatal accident inquiry may be held before the sheriff.

COURT OF SESSION AND HIGH COURT OF JUSTICIARY

The Lord President and Lord Justice General (£138,889)
   The Rt. Hon. the Lord Rodger of Earlsferry, *born* 1944, *apptd* 1996
   Secretary, A. Maxwell

INNER HOUSE

Lords of Session (each £132,017)

FIRST DIVISION
The Lord President
Hon. Lord Sutherland (Ranald Sutherland), *born* 1932, *apptd* 1985
Hon. Lord Prosser (William Prosser), *born* 1934, *apptd* 1986
Hon. Lord Caplan (Philip Caplan), *born* 1929, *apptd* 1989

SECOND DIVISION
Lord Justice Clerk (£132,017), The Rt. Hon. Lord Cullen (William Cullen), *born* 1935, *apptd* 1997
Rt. Hon. The Lord McCluskey, *born* 1929, *apptd* 1984
Hon. Lord Kirkwood (Ian Kirkwood), *born* 1932, *apptd* 1987
Hon. Lord Coulsfield (John Cameron), *born* 1934, *apptd* 1987

OUTER HOUSE

Lords of Session (each £117,752)

Hon. Lord Milligan (James Milligan), *born* 1934, *apptd* 1988
Rt. Hon. The Lord Cameron of Lochbroom, *born* 1931, *apptd* 1989
Hon. Lord Marnoch (Michael Bruce), *born* 1938, *apptd* 1990
Hon. Lord MacLean (Ranald MacLean), *born* 1938, *apptd* 1990
Hon. Lord Penrose (George Penrose), *born* 1938, *apptd* 1990

Hon. Lord Osborne (Kenneth Osborne), *born* 1937, *apptd* 1990
Hon. Lord Abernethy (Alistair Cameron), *born* 1938, *apptd* 1992
Hon. Lord Johnston (Alan Johnston), *born* 1942, *apptd* 1994
Hon. Lord Gill (Brian Gill), *born* 1942, *apptd* 1994
Hon. Lord Hamilton (Arthur Hamilton), *born* 1942, *apptd* 1995
Hon. Lord Dawson (Thomas Dawson), *born* 1948, *apptd* 1995
Hon. Lord Macfadyen (Donald Macfadyen), *born* 1945, *apptd* 1995
Hon. Lady Cosgrove (Hazel Aronson), *born* 1946, *apptd* 1996
Hon. Lord Nimmo Smith (William Nimmo Smith), *born* 1942, *apptd* 1996
Hon. Lord Philip (Alexander Philip), *born* 1942, *apptd* 1996
Hon. Lord Kingarth (Derek Emslie), *born* 1949, *apptd* 1997
Hon. Lord Bonomy (Iain Bonomy), *born* 1946, *apptd* 1997
Hon. Lord Eassie (Ronald Mackay), *born* 1945, *apptd* 1997

COURT OF SESSION AND HIGH COURT OF JUSTICIARY
Parliament House, Parliament Square, Edinburgh EHI IRQ
Tel 0131-225 2595

Principal Clerk of Session and Justiciary (£30,991–£51,608), J. L. Anderson
Deputy Principal Clerk of Justiciary and Administration (£27,172–£42,023), T. Fyffe
Deputy Principal Clerk of Session and Principal Extractor (£27,172–£42,023), G. McKeand
Deputy Principal Clerk (Keeper of the Rolls) (£27,172–£42,023), R. Cockburn
Depute Clerks of Session and Justiciary (£20,741–£27,216), N. J. Dowie; I. F. Smith; T. Higgins; T. B. Cruickshank; Q. A. Oliver; F. Shannly; A. S. Moffat; D. J. Shand; G. G. Ellis; W. Dunn; A. M. Finlayson; C. C. Armstrong; G. M. Prentice; R. Jenkins; J. O. McLean; M. Weir; R. M. Sinclair; E. G. Appelbe; B. Watson; D. W. Cullen; D. J. Cullum; I. D. Martin; N. McGinley; J. Lynn; E. Dickson

SCOTTISH COURTS ADMINISTRATION
Hayweight House, 23 Lauriston Street, Edinburgh EH3 9DQ
Tel 0131-229 9200

The Scottish Courts Administration is responsible to the Secretary of State for Scotland for the performance of the Scottish Court Service and central administration pertaining to the judiciary in the Supreme and Sheriff Courts; and to the Lord Advocate for certain aspects of court procedures, jurisdiction and legislation, law reform and other matters.
Director (G2), J. Hamill, CB
Deputy Director (Legal Policy) (Assistant Solicitor) (G5), P. M. Beaton
Deputy Director (Resources and Liaison) (G5), D. Stewart

SCOTTISH COURT SERVICE
Hayweight House, 23 Lauriston Street, Edinburgh EH3 9DQ
Tel 0131-229 9200

The Scottish Court Service became an executive agency within the Scottish Courts Administration in 1995. It is responsible to the Secretary of State for Scotland for the provision of staff, court houses and associated services for the Supreme and Sheriff Courts.
Chief Executive, M. Ewart

SHERIFF COURT OF CHANCERY
27 Chambers Street, Edinburgh EHI ILB
Tel 0131-225 2525
The Court deals with service of heirs and completion of title in relation to heritable property.
Sheriff of Chancery, C. G. B. Nicholson, QC

HM COMMISSARY OFFICE
27 Chambers Street, Edinburgh EHI ILB
Tel 0131-225 2525
The Office is responsible for issuing confirmation, a legal document entitling a person to execute a deceased person's will, and other related matters.
Commissary Clerk, J. M. Ross

SCOTTISH LAND COURT
1 Grosvenor Crescent, Edinburgh EHI2 5ER
Tel 0131-225 3595
The court deals with disputes relating to agricultural and crofting land in Scotland.
Chairman (£96,214), The Hon. Lord McGhie (James McGhie), QC
Members, D. J. Houston; D. M. Macdonald; J. Kinloch (*part-time*)
Principal Clerk, K. H. R. Graham, WS

SHERIFFDOMS

SALARIES

Sheriff Principal	£96,214
Sheriff	£88,077
Regional Sheriff Clerk/Area Director	£30,991–£59,000
Sheriff Clerk	£12,206–£42,023

*Floating Sheriff

GRAMPIAN, HIGHLANDS AND ISLANDS
Sheriff Principal, D. J. Risk
Area Director North, J. Robertson

SHERIFFS AND SHERIFF CLERKS
Aberdeen and Stonehaven, D. Kelbie; L. A. S. Jessop; A. Pollock; Mrs A. M. Cowan; C. J. Harris, QC *Sheriff Clerks*, Mrs E. Laing (*Aberdeen*); B. McBride (*Stonehaven*)
Peterhead and Banff, K. A. McLernan; *Sheriff Clerk*, A. Hempseed (*Peterhead*); *Sheriff Clerk Depute*, Mrs F. L. MacPherson (*Banff*)
Elgin, N. McPartlin; *Sheriff Clerk*, M. McBey
Inverness, Lochmaddy, Portree, Stornoway, Dingwall, Tain, Wick and Dornoch, W. J. Fulton; D. Booker-Milburn; J. O. A. Fraser; I. A. Cameron; *G. K. Buchanan; *Sheriff Clerks*, J. Robertson (*Inverness*); W. Cochrane (*Dingwall*); *Sheriff Clerks Depute*, Miss M. Campbell (*Lochmaddy and Portree*); Mrs M. Macdonald (*Stornoway*); L. MacLachlan (*Tain*); Mrs J. McEwan (*Wick*); K. Kerr (*Dornoch*)
Kirkwall and Lerwick, C. S. Mackenzie; *Sheriff Clerks Depute*, P. Cushen (*Kirkwall*); M. Flanagan (*Lerwick*)
Fort William, C. G. McKay (also *Oban*); *Sheriff Clerk Depute*, D. Hood

TAYSIDE, CENTRAL AND FIFE
Sheriff Principal, J. J. Maguire, QC
Area Director East, M. Bonar (*from Dec. 1998*)

SHERIFFS AND SHERIFF CLERKS

Arbroath and Forfar, K. A. Veal; *C. N. R. Stein; *Sheriff Clerks*, M. Herbertson (*Arbroath*); S. Munro (*Forfar*)
Dundee, R. A. Davidson; A. L. Stewart, QC; *J. P. Scott; G. J. Evans (also *Cupar*); *Sheriff Clerk*, J. S. Doig (*until late 1998*)
Perth, J. F. Wheatley, QC; J. C. McInnes, QC; *Mrs P. M. M. Bowman; *Sheriff Clerk*, J. Murphy
Falkirk, A. V. Sheehan; A. J. Murphy; *Sheriff Clerk*, D. Forrester
Stirling, The Hon. R. E. G. Younger; *Sheriff Clerk*, J. Clark
Alloa, W. M. Reid; *Sheriff Clerk*, R. G. McKeand
Cupar, G. J. Evans (also *Dundee*); *Sheriff Clerk*, R. Hughes
Dunfermline, J. S. Forbes; C. W. Palmer; *Sheriff Clerk*, W. McCulloch
Kirkcaldy, F. J. Keane; Mrs L. G. Patrick; *I. D. Dunbar; *Sheriff Clerk*, W. Jones

LOTHIAN AND BORDERS

Sheriff Principal, C. G. B. Nicholson, QC
Area Director East, M. Bonar (*from Dec. 1998*)

SHERIFFS AND SHERIFF CLERKS

Edinburgh, R. G. Craik, QC (also *Peebles*); R. J. D. Scott (also *Peebles*); Miss I. A. Poole; A. M. Bell; J. M. S. Horsburgh, QC; G. W. S. Presslie (also *Haddington*); J. A. Farrell; *A. Lothian; I. D. Macphail, QC; C. N. Stoddart; A. B. Wilkinson, QC; Mrs D. J. B. Robertson; N. M. P. Morrison, QC; *Miss M. M. Stephen; Mrs M. L. E. Jarvie, QC; *Sheriff Clerk*, M. Bonar
Peebles, R. G. Craik, QC (also *Edinburgh*); R. J. D. Scott (also *Edinburgh*); *Sheriff Clerk Depute*, R. McArthur
Linlithgow, H. R. MacLean; G. R. Fleming; *K. A. Ross; *Sheriff Clerk*, R. D. Sinclair
Haddington, G. W. S. Presslie (also *Edinburgh*); *Sheriff Clerk*, J. O'Donnell
Jedburgh and Duns, J. V. Paterson; *Sheriff Clerk*, I. W. Williamson
Selkirk, J. V. Paterson; *Sheriff Clerk Depute*, L. McFarlane

NORTH STRATHCLYDE

Sheriff Principal, R. C. Hay, CBE
Area Director West, I. Scott

SHERIFFS AND SHERIFF CLERKS

Oban, C. G. McKay (also *Fort William*); *Sheriff Clerk Depute*, G. Whitelaw
Dumbarton, J. T. Fitzsimons; T. Scott; S. W. H. Fraser; *Sheriff Clerk*, P. Corcoran
Paisley, R. G. Smith; J. Spy; C. K. Higgins; N. Douglas; *D. J. Pender; *W. Dunlop (also *Campbeltown*); *Sheriff Clerk (acting)*, R. McMillan
Greenock, J. Herald (also *Rothesay*); Sir Stephen Young; *Sheriff Clerk*, J. Tannahill
Kilmarnock, T. M. Croan; D. B. Smith; T. F. Russell; *Sheriff Clerk*, G. Waddell
Dunoon, A. W. Noble; *Sheriff Clerk Depute*, Mrs C. Carson
Campbeltown, *W. Dunlop (also *Paisley*); *Sheriff Clerk Depute*, P. G. Hay
Rothesay, J. Herald (also *Greenock*); *Sheriff Clerk Depute*, Mrs C. K. McCormick

GLASGOW AND STRATHKELVIN

Sheriff Principal, E. F. Bowen, QC
Area Director West, I. Scott

SHERIFFS AND SHERIFF CLERKS

Glasgow, B. Kearney; G. H. Gordon, CBE, PH.D., QC; B. A. Lockhart; I. G. Pirie; Mrs A. L. A. Duncan;

A. C. Henry; J. K. Mitchell; A. G. Johnston; J. P. Murphy; Miss S. A. O. Raeburn, QC; D. Convery; J. McGowan; B. A. Kerr, QC; Mrs C. M. A. F. Gimblett; I. A. S. Peebles, QC; C. W. McFarlane, QC; K. M. Maciver; H. Matthews, QC; J. D. Lowe, CB; J. A. Baird; Miss R. E. A. Rae, QC; T. A. K. Drummond, QC; *Sheriff Clerk*, D. Nicoll

SOUTH STRATHCLYDE, DUMFRIES AND GALLOWAY

Sheriff Principal, G. L. Cox, QC
Area Director West, I. Scott

SHERIFFS AND SHERIFF CLERKS

Hamilton, L. Cameron; A. C. MacPherson; W. F. Lunny; D. C. Russell; V. J. Canavan (also *Airdrie*); W. E. Gibson; H. Stirling; J. H. Stewart; *H. S. Neilson; *Sheriff Clerk*, P. Feeney
Lanark, J. D. Allan; *Sheriff Clerk*, A. Whyte
Ayr, N. Gow, QC; R. G. McEwan, QC; *C. B. Miller; *Sheriff Clerk*, Miss C. D. Cockburn
Stranraer and Kirkcudbright, J. R. Smith (also *Dumfries*); *Sheriff Clerks*, W. McIntosh (*Stranraer*); B. Lindsay (*Kirkcudbright*)
Dumfries, K. G. Barr; M. J. Fletcher; J. R. Smith (also *Stranraer and Kirkcudbright*); *Sheriff Clerk*, P. McGonigle
Airdrie, V. J. Canavan (also *Hamilton*); R. H. Dickson; I. C. Simpson; *J. C. Morris, QC; Sheriff Clerk, K. Carter

STIPENDIARY MAGISTRATES

GLASGOW

R. Hamilton, *apptd* 1984; J. B. C. Nisbet, *apptd* 1984; R. B. Christie, *apptd* 1985; Mrs J. A. M. MacLean, *apptd* 1990

PROCURATOR FISCAL SERVICE

CROWN OFFICE

25 Chambers Street, Edinburgh EH1 1LA
Tel 0131-226 2626
Crown Agent (£76,710–£112,040), A. C. Normand
Deputy Crown Agent (£53,450–£89,090), F. R. Crowe (*from Jan. 1999*)

PROCURATORS FISCAL

SALARIES

Regional Procurator Fiscal – grade 3	£58,590–£94,330
Regional Procurator Fiscal – grade 4	£53,450–£89,090
Procurator Fiscal – upper level	£39,830–£62,570
Procurator Fiscal – lower level	£36,000–£42,000

GRAMPIAN, HIGHLANDS AND ISLANDS REGION

Regional Procurator Fiscal, L. A. Higson (*Aberdeen*)
Procurators Fiscal, E. K. Barbour (*Stonehaven*); A. J. M. Colley (*Banff*); Miss A. Thom (*Peterhead*) (*interim*); J. F. MacKay (*Elgin*); A. N. Perry (*Wick*); J. Bamber (*Portree, Lochmaddy*); F. Redman (*Stornoway*); G. Napier (*Inverness*); R. W. Urquhart (*Kirkwall, Lerwick*); Mrs A. Neizer (*Fort William*); A. N. MacDonald (*Dingwall, Tain*)

TAYSIDE, CENTRAL AND FIFE REGION

Regional Procurator Fiscal, B. K. Heywood (*Dundee*)

Procurators Fiscal, I. C. Walker (*Forfar*); I. A. McLeod (*Perth*); J. J. Miller (*Falkirk*); C. Ritchie (*Stirling and Alloa*); E. B. Russell (*Cupar*); R. G. Stott (*Dunfermline*); Miss E. C. Munro (*Kirkcaldy*)

LOTHIAN AND BORDERS REGION
Regional Procurator Fiscal, N. McFadyen (*from Jan. 1999*) (*Edinburgh*)
Procurators Fiscal, Miss L. M. Ruxton (*Linlithgow*); A. J. P. Reith (*Haddington*); A. R. G. Fraser (*Duns, Jedburgh*); D. MacNeill (*Selkirk*)

NORTH STRATHCLYDE REGION
Regional Procurator Fiscal, J. D. Friel (*Paisley*)
Procurators Fiscal, I. Henderson (*Campbeltown*); C. C. Donnelly (*Dumbarton*); W. S. Carnegie (*Greenock*); D. L. Webster (*Dunoon*); J. G. MacGlennan (*Kilmarnock*); B. R. Maguire (*Oban*)

GLASGOW AND STRATHKELVIN REGION
Regional Procurator Fiscal, A. D. Vannet (*Glasgow*)

SOUTH STRATHCLYDE, DUMFRIES AND GALLOWAY REGION
Regional Procurator Fiscal, vacant (*Hamilton*)
Procurators Fiscal, S. R. Houston (*Lanark*); J. T. O'Donnell (*Ayr*); F. R. Crowe (*Stranraer*) (*interim*); D. J. Howdle (*Dumfries, Stranraer, Kirkcudbright*); D. Spiers (*Airdrie*)

Northern Ireland Judicature

In Northern Ireland the legal system and the structure of courts closely resemble those of England and Wales; there are, however, often differences in enacted law.

The Supreme Court of Judicature of Northern Ireland comprises the Court of Appeal, the High Court of Justice and the Crown Court. The practice and procedure of these courts is similar to that in England. The superior civil court is the High Court of Justice, from which an appeal lies to the Northern Ireland Court of Appeal; the House of Lords is the final civil appeal court.

The Crown Court, served by High Court and county court judges, deals with criminal trials on indictment. Cases are heard before a judge and, except those involving offences specified under emergency legislation, a jury. Appeals from the Crown Court against conviction or sentence are heard by the Northern Ireland Court of Appeal; the House of Lords is the final court of appeal.

The decision to prosecute in cases tried on indictment and in summary cases of a serious nature rests in Northern Ireland with the Director of Public Prosecutions, who is responsible to the Attorney-General. Minor summary offences are prosecuted by the police.

Minor criminal offences are dealt with in magistrates' courts by a legally qualified resident magistrate and, where an offender is under 17, by juvenile courts each consisting of a resident magistrate and two lay members specially qualified to deal with juveniles (at least one of whom must be a woman). In July 1998 there were 919 justices of the peace in Northern Ireland. Appeals from magistrates' courts are heard by the county court, or by the Court of Appeal on a point of law or an issue as to jurisdiction.

Magistrates' courts in Northern Ireland can deal with certain classes of civil case but most minor civil cases are dealt with in county courts. Judgments of all civil courts

are enforceable through a centralized procedure administered by the Enforcement of Judgments Office.

SUPREME COURT OF JUDICATURE
The Royal Courts of Justice, Belfast BT1 3JF
Tel 01232-235111

Lord Chief Justice of Northern Ireland (£138,889)
The Rt. Hon. Sir Robert Carswell, *born* 1934, *apptd* 1997
Principal Secretary, G. W. Johnston

LORDS JUSTICES OF APPEAL (each £132,017)
Style, The Rt. Hon. Lord Justice [surname]
Rt. Hon. Sir John MacDermott, *born* 1927, *apptd* 1987
Rt. Hon. Sir Michael Nicholson, *born* 1933, *apptd* 1995
Rt. Hon. Sir William McCollum, *born* 1933, *apptd* 1997

PUISNE JUDGES (each £117,752)
Style, The Hon. Mr Justice [surname]
Hon. Sir Anthony Campbell, *born* 1936, *apptd* 1988
Hon. Sir John Sheil, *born* 1938, *apptd* 1989
Hon. Sir Brian Kerr, *born* 1948, *apptd* 1993
Hon. Sir John Pringle, *born* 1929, *apptd* 1993
Hon. Sir Malachy Higgins, *born* 1944, *apptd* 1993
Hon. Sir Paul Girvan, *born* 1948, *apptd* 1995
Hon. Sir Patrick Coghlin, *born* 1945, *apptd* 1997

MASTERS OF THE SUPREME COURT (each £70,820)
Master, Queen's Bench and Appeals and Clerk of the Crown, J. W. Wilson, QC
Master, High Court, Mrs D. M. Kennedy
Master, Office of Care and Protection, F. B. Hall
Master, Chancery Office, R. A. Ellison
Master, Bankruptcy and Companies Office, C. W. G. Redpath
Master, Probate and Matrimonial Office, N. Lockie
Master, Taxing Office, J. C. Napier

OFFICIAL SOLICITOR
Official Solicitor to the Supreme Court of Northern Ireland, vacant

COUNTY COURTS

Judges (each £88,077–£96,214)
Style, His Hon. Judge [surname]
Judge Curran, QC; Judge McKee, QC; Judge Gibson, QC; Judge Petrie, QC; Judge Smyth, QC; Judge Markey, QC; Judge McKay, QC; Judge Martin, QC (*Chief Social Security and Child Support Commissioner*); Judge Brady, QC; Judge Rodgers; Judge Foote, QC

RECORDERS (each £96,214)
Belfast, Judge Hart, QC
Londonderry, Judge Burgess

MAGISTRATES' COURTS

RESIDENT MAGISTRATES (each £70,820)
There are 17 resident magistrates in Northern Ireland.

CROWN SOLICITOR'S OFFICE
PO Box 410, Royal Courts of Justice, Belfast BT1 3JY
Tel 01232-542555

Crown Solicitor, N. P. Roberts

DEPARTMENT OF THE DIRECTOR OF
PUBLIC PROSECUTIONS
Royal Courts of Justice, Belfast BTI 3NX
Tel 01232-542444

Director of Public Prosecutions, A. Fraser, CB, QC
Deputy Director of Public Prosecutions, vacant

NORTHERN IRELAND COURT SERVICE
Windsor House, Bedford Street, Belfast BT2 7LT
Tel 01232-328594

Director (G3)

Crime Statistics

ENGLAND AND WALES

NOTIFIABLE OFFENCES RECORDED 1996

Violence against the person	239,300
Sexual offences	31,400
Burglary	1,164,600
Robbery	74,000
Theft and handling stolen goods	2,383,900
Fraud and forgery	136,200
Criminal damage	951,300
Other offences	55,800
Total offences	5,036,600

Source: The Stationery Office – Annual Abstract of Statistics 1998

CRIMINAL JUSTICE STATISTICS 1996

Number of arrests	1,750,000
Notifiable offences cleared up	1,288,000
Clear-up rate	26%
*Number of offenders cautioned	286,200
Defendants proceeded against at magistrates' courts	1,919,500
Defendants found guilty at magistrates' courts	1,368,900
Defendants tried at Crown Courts	85,900
Defendants found guilty at Crown Courts	72,100
Defendants sentenced at Crown Courts after summary conviction	4,600
Total offenders found guilty at both courts	1,441,000
*Total offenders found guilty or cautioned	1,727,200

*Excludes motoring offences

OFFENDERS SENTENCED BY TYPE OF SENTENCE OR
ORDER 1996

Absolute discharge	20,100
Conditional discharge	104,800
Fine	1,075,500
Probation order	50,900
Supervision order	10,900
Community service order	45,900
Attendance sentence order	7,500
Combination order	17,300
Curfew order	200
Young offender institution	20,600
Imprisonment:	
Suspended	3,400
Unsuspended	64,000
Otherwise dealt with	19,400
All sentences or orders: total	1,440,600

AVERAGE LENGTH OF SENTENCE 1996 in months

	Males aged 21 and over	Females aged 21 and over
Magistrates' courts	2.7	2.3
Crown court	24.0	20.0

Source: The Stationery Office – Criminal Statistics England and Wales 1996

SCOTLAND

CRIMES AND OFFENCES RECORDED 1996

Non-sexual crimes of violence against the person	21,500
Crimes involving indecency	5,700
Crimes involving dishonesty	295,400
Fire-raising, vandalism, etc.	89,000
Other crimes	40,300
Miscellaneous offences	146,100
Motor vehicle offences	305,900
Total crimes and offences	903,900*

Source: The Stationery Office – Annual Abstract of Statistics 1998

CRIMINAL JUSTICE STATISTICS 1996

Number of persons proceeded against	177,168
Persons with charge proved	156,707

PERSONS WITH CHARGE PROVED BY MAIN PENALTY
1996

Absolute discharge	1,008
Remit to children's hearing	193
Admonition or caution	15,859
Compensation order	1,415
Fine	105,384
Probation	6,435
Community service order	5,711
Insanity or hospital order	159
Detention of child	45
Young offender institution	4,744
Prison	12,134
All penalties: total	153,087

Source: The Scottish Office

Tribunals

AGRICULTURAL LAND TRIBUNALS
c/o Rural and Marine Environment Division, Ministry of Agriculture, Fisheries and Food, Nobel House, 17 Smith Square, London SW1P 3JR
Tel 0171-238 6991

Agricultural Land Tribunals settle disputes and other issues between agricultural landlords and tenants, and drainage disputes between neighbours.

There are seven tribunals covering England and one covering Wales. For each tribunal the Lord Chancellor appoints a chairman and one or more deputies (barristers or solicitors of at least seven years standing). The Lord Chancellor also appoints lay members to three statutory panels: the 'landowners' panel, the 'farmers' panel and the 'drainage' panel.

Each tribunal is an independent statutory body with jurisdiction only within its own area. A separate tribunal is constituted for each case, and consists of a chairman (who may be the chairman or one of the deputy chairmen) and two lay members nominated by the chairman.
Chairmen (England) (£253 a day), W. D. Greenwood;
K. J. Fisher; P. A. de la Piquerie; C. H. Beaumont; His Hon. Judge Lee; G. L. Newsom; His Hon. Judge Robert Taylor
Chairman (Wales) (£253 a day), W. J. Owen

COMMONS COMMISSIONERS
Room 818, Tollgate House, Houlton Street, Bristol BS2 9DJ
Tel 0117-987 8928

The Commons Commissioners are responsible for deciding disputes arising under the Commons Registration Act 1965 and the Common Land (Rectification of Registers) Act 1989. They also enquire into the ownership of unclaimed common land. Commissioners are appointed by the Lord Chancellor.
Chief Commons Commissioner (part-time) (£34,720), D. M. Burton
Commissioner, I. L. R. Romer
Clerk, Miss S. Hargreaves

COPYRIGHT TRIBUNAL
25 Southampton Buildings, London WC2A 1AY
Tel 0171-438 4776

The Copyright Tribunal, which replaced the Performing Right Tribunal, resolves disputes over copyright licences, principally where there is collective licensing.

The chairman and two deputy chairmen are appointed by the Lord Chancellor. Up to eight ordinary members are appointed by the Secretary of State for Trade and Industry.
Chairman (£316 a day), C. P. Tootal
Secretary, Miss J. E. M. Durdin

DATA PROTECTION TRIBUNAL
c/o The Home Office, Queen Anne's Gate, London SW1H 9AT
Tel 0171-273 3492

The Data Protection Tribunal determines appeals against decisions of the Data Protection Registrar (now Commissioner) (*see* page 294). The chairman and two deputy chairmen are appointed by the Lord Chancellor and must be legally qualified. Lay members are appointed by the Home Secretary to represent the interests of data users or data subjects.

A tribunal consists of a legally-qualified chairman sitting with equal numbers of the lay members appointed to represent the interests of data users and data subjects.
Chairman (£370 a day), J. A. C. Spokes, QC
Secretary, D. Anderson

EMPLOYMENT TRIBUNALS

CENTRAL OFFICE (ENGLAND AND WALES)
19–29 Woburn Place, London WC1H 0LU
Tel 0171-273 8666

Employment Tribunals for England and Wales sit in 11 regions. The tribunals deal with matters of employment law, redundancy, dismissal, contract disputes, sexual, racial and disability discrimination, and related areas of dispute which may arise in the workplace. A central registration unit records all applications and maintains a public register at Southgate Street, Bury St Edmunds, Suffolk IP33 2AQ. The tribunals are funded by the Department of Trade and Industry; administrative support is provided by the Employment Tribunal Service (*see* pages 348–9).

Chairmen, who may be full-time or part-time, are legally qualified. They are appointed by the Lord Chancellor. Tribunal members are nominated by specified employer and employee groups and appointed by the Secretary of State for Trade and Industry.
President, His Hon. Judge Prophet

CENTRAL OFFICE (SCOTLAND)
Eagle Building, 215 Bothwell Street, Glasgow G2 7TS
Tel 0141-204 0730

Tribunals in Scotland have the same remit as those in England and Wales. Chairmen are appointed by the Lord President of the Court of Session and lay members by the Secretary of State for Trade and Industry.
President (£96,214), Mrs D. Littlejohn, CBE

EMPLOYMENT APPEAL TRIBUNAL
Central Office, Audit House, 58 Victoria Embankment, London EC4Y 0DS
Tel 0171-273 1041
Divisional Office, 52 Melville Street, Edinburgh EH3 7HF
Tel 0131-225 3963

The Employment Appeal Tribunal hears appeals on a question of law arising from any decision of an employment tribunal. A tribunal consists of a high court judge and

two lay members, one from each side of industry. They are appointed by The Queen on the recommendation of the Lord Chancellor and the Secretary of State for Trade and Industry. Administrative support is provided by the Employment Tribunal Service (*see* pages 348–9).
President, The Hon. Mr Justice Morison
Scottish Chairman, The Hon. Lord Johnston
Registrar, Miss V. J. Selio

IMMIGRATION APPELLATE AUTHORITIES
Taylor House, 88 Rosebery Avenue, London EC1R 4QU
Tel 0171-862 4200

The Immigration Appeal Adjudicators hear appeals from immigration decisions concerning the need for, and refusal of, leave to enter or remain in the UK, refusals to grant asylum, decisions to make deportation orders and directions to remove persons subject to immigration control from the UK. The Immigration Appeal Tribunal hears appeals direct from decisions to make deportation orders in matters concerning conduct contrary to the public good and refusals to grant asylum. Its principal jurisdiction is, however, the hearing of appeals from adjudicators by the party (Home Office or individual) who is aggrieved by the decision. Appeals are subject to leave being granted by the tribunal.

An adjudicator sits alone. The tribunal sits in divisions of three, normally a legally qualified member and two lay members. Members of the tribunal and adjudicators are appointed by the Lord Chancellor.

IMMIGRATION APPEAL TRIBUNAL
President, His Hon. Judge Pearl
Vice-Presidents, Mrs J. Chatwani; A. F. Hatt; M. Rapinet; A. O'Brien-Quinn

IMMIGRATION APPEAL ADJUDICATORS
Chief Adjudicator, His Hon. Judge Dunn, QC
Deputy Chief Adjudicator, J. Latter

INDEPENDENT TRIBUNAL SERVICE
Whittington House, 19–30 Alfred Place, London
WC1E 7LW
Tel 0171-814 6500

The service is the judicial authority which exercises judicial and administrative control over the independent social security and child support appeal tribunals, medical and disability appeal tribunals, and vaccine damage tribunals.
President, His Hon. Judge Michael Harris
Chief Executive, vacant

INDUSTRIAL TRIBUNALS AND THE FAIR EMPLOYMENT TRIBUNAL (NORTHERN IRELAND)
Long Bridge House, 20–24 Waring Street, Belfast BT1 2EB
Tel 01232-327666

The industrial tribunal system in Northern Ireland was set up in 1965 and has a similar remit to the employment tribunals in the rest of the UK. There is also in Northern Ireland a Fair Employment Tribunal, which hears and determines individual cases of alleged religious or political discrimination in employment. Employers can appeal to the Fair Employment Tribunal if they consider the directions of the Fair Employment Commission to be

unreasonable, inappropriate or unnecessary, and the Fair Employment Commission can make application to the Tribunal for the enforcement of undertakings or directions with which an employer has not complied.

The president, vice-president and part-time chairmen of the Fair Employment Tribunal are appointed by the Lord Chancellor. The full-time chairman and the part-time chairmen of the industrial tribunals and the panel members to both the industrial tribunals and the Fair Employment Tribunal are appointed by the Department of Economic Development Northern Ireland.
President of the Industrial Tribunals and the Fair Employment Tribunal (£88,077), J. Maguire, CBE
Vice-President of the Industrial Tribunals and the Fair Employment Tribunal, Mrs M. P. Price
Secretary, Mrs P. McVeigh

LANDS TRIBUNAL
48–49 Chancery Lane, London WC2A 1JR
Tel 0171-936 7200

The Lands Tribunal is an independent judicial body which determines questions relating to the valuation of land, rating appeals from valuation tribunals, the discharge or modification of restrictive covenants, and compulsory purchase compensation. The tribunal may also arbitrate under references by consent. The president and members are appointed by the Lord Chancellor.
President, vacant
Members (£84,752), M. St J. Hopper, FRICS; P. H. Clarke, FRICS; N. J. Rose, FRICS; P. R. Francis
Member (part-time), His Hon. Judge Rich, QC
Members (part-time) (£400 a day), J. C. Hill, TD; A. P. Musto, FRICS
Registrar, C. A. McMullan

LANDS TRIBUNAL FOR SCOTLAND
1 Grosvenor Crescent, Edinburgh EH12 5ER
Tel 0131-225 7996

The Lands Tribunal for Scotland has the same remit as the tribunal for England and Wales but also covers questions relating to tenants' rights. The president is appointed by the Lord President of the Court of Session.
President, The Hon. Lord McGhie, QC
Members (£84,752), A. R. MacLeary, FRICS; J. Devine, FRICS
Members (part-time), Sheriff A. C. Henry; R. A. Edwards, CBE, WS
Clerk, N. M. Tainsh

MENTAL HEALTH REVIEW TRIBUNALS

The Mental Health Review Tribunals are independent judicial bodies which review the cases of patients compulsorily detained under the provisions of the Mental Health Act 1983. They have the power to discharge the patient, to recommend leave of absence, delayed discharge, transfer to another hospital or that a guardianship order be made, to reclassify both restricted and unrestricted patients, and to recommend consideration of a supervision application. There are eight tribunals in England, each headed by a regional chairman who is appointed by the Lord Chancellor on a part-time basis. Each tribunal is made up of at least three members, and must include a lawyer, who acts as president (£239 a day), a medical member (£226 a day) and a lay member (£97 a day).

The Mental Health Review Tribunals' secretariat is based in five regional offices:

LIVERPOOL, 3rd Floor, Cressington House, 249 St Mary's Road, Garston, Liverpool L19 ONF. Tel: 0151-494 0095. *Clerk*, Mrs B. Foot

LONDON (NORTH), Spur 3, Block 1, Government Buildings, Honeypot Lane, Stanmore, Middx HA7 IAY. Tel: 0171-972 3734. *Clerk*, Ms K. Vale

LONDON (SOUTH), Block 3, Crown Offices, Kingston Bypass Road, Surbiton, Surrey KT6 5QN. Tel: 0181-268 4520. *Clerk*, C. Lilly

NOTTINGHAM, Spur A, Block 5, Government Buildings, Chalfont Drive, Western Boulevard, Nottingham NG8 3RZ. Tel: 0115-929 4222. *Clerk*, M. Chapman

WALES, 4th Floor, Crown Buildings, Cathays Park, Cardiff CFI 3NQ. Tel: 01222-825328. *Clerk*, Mrs C. Thomas

---

NATIONAL HEALTH SERVICE TRIBUNAL

The NHS Tribunal considers representations that the continued inclusion of a doctor, dentist, pharmacist or optician on a health authority's list would be prejudicial to the efficiency of the service concerned. The tribunal sits when required, about eight times a year, and usually in London. The chairman is appointed by the Lord Chancellor and members by the Secretary of State for Health.
Chairman, A. Whitfield, QC
Deputy Chairmen, Miss E. Platt, QC; Dr R. N. Ough
Clerk, I. D. Keith, East Hookers, Twineham, nr Haywards Heath, W. Sussex RH17 5NN. Tel: 01444-881345

NATIONAL HEALTH SERVICE TRIBUNAL (SCOTLAND)
Clerk: 66 Queen Street, Edinburgh EH2 4NE
Tel 0131-226 4771

The tribunal considers representations that the continued inclusion of a registered doctor, dentist, optometrist or pharmacist on a health board's list would be prejudicial to the continuing efficiency of the service concerned.

The tribunal meets when required and is composed of a chairman, one lay member, and one practitioner member drawn from a representative professional panel. The chairman is appointed by the Lord President of the Court of Session, and the lay member and the members of the professional panel are appointed by the Secretary of State for Scotland.
Chairman, M. G. Thomson, QC
Lay member, J. D. M. Robertson
Clerk to the Tribunal, D. G. Brash, WS

PENSIONS APPEAL TRIBUNALS

CENTRAL OFFICE (ENGLAND AND WALES)
48–49 Chancery Lane, London WC2A IJR
Tel 0171-936 7032/3/4

The Pensions Appeal Tribunals are responsible for hearing appeals from ex-servicemen or women and widows who have had their claims for a war pension rejected by the Secretary of State for Social Security. The Entitlement Appeal Tribunals hear appeals in cases where the Secretary of State has refused to grant a war pension. The Assessment Appeal Tribunals hear appeals against the

Secretary of State's assessment of the degree of disablement caused by an accepted condition. The tribunal members are appointed by the Lord Chancellor.
President (£70,820), Dr H. M. G. Concannon
Secretary, Miss N. Collins

PENSIONS APPEAL TRIBUNALS FOR SCOTLAND
20 Walker Street, Edinburgh EH3 7HS
Tel 0131-220 1404
President (£285 a day), C. N. McEachran, QC

OFFICE OF THE SOCIAL SECURITY AND CHILD SUPPORT COMMISSIONERS
5th Floor, Newspaper House, 8–16 Great New Street, London EC4A 3BN
Tel 0171-353 5145
23 Melville Street, Edinburgh EH3 7PW
Tel 0131-225 2201

The Social Security Commissioners are the final statutory authority to decide appeals relating to entitlement to social security benefits. The Child Support Commissioners are the final statutory authority to decide appeals relating to child support. Appeals may be made in relation to both matters only on a point of law. The Commissioners' jurisdiction covers England, Wales and Scotland. There are 17 commissioners; they are all qualified lawyers.
Chief Social Security Commissioner and Chief Child Support Commissioner, His Hon. Judge Machin, QC
Secretary, S. Hill (*London*); E. Barschtschyk (*Edinburgh*)

OFFICE OF THE SOCIAL SECURITY AND CHILD SUPPORT COMMISSIONERS FOR NORTHERN IRELAND
Lancashire House, 5 Linenhall Street, Belfast BT2 8AA
Tel 01232-332344

The role of Northern Ireland Social Security and Child Support Commissioners is similar to that of the Commissioners in Great Britain. There are two commissioners for Northern Ireland.
Chief Commissioner, His Hon. Judge Martin, QC
Registrar of Appeals, W. D. Pollock

THE SOLICITORS' DISCIPLINARY TRIBUNAL
50–52 Chancery Lane, London WC2A ISX
Tel 0171-242 0219

The Solicitors' Disciplinary Tribunal is an independent statutory body whose members are appointed by the Master of the Rolls. The tribunal considers applications made to it alleging either professional misconduct and/or a breach of the statutory rules by which solicitors are bound against an individually named solicitor, former solicitor, registered foreign lawyer, or solicitor's clerk. The president and solicitor members do not receive remuneration.
President, G. B. Marsh
Clerk, Mrs S. C. Elson

THE SCOTTISH SOLICITORS' DISCIPLINE TRIBUNAL
22 Rutland Square, Edinburgh EH1 2BB
Tel 0131-229 5860

The Scottish Solicitors' Discipline Tribunal is an independent statutory body with a panel of 18 members, ten of whom are solicitors; members are appointed by the Lord President of the Court of Session. Its principal function is to consider complaints of misconduct against solicitors in Scotland.
Chairman, J. W. Laughland
Clerk, J. M. Barton, WS

SPECIAL COMMISSIONERS OF INCOME TAX
15–19 Bedford Avenue, London WC1B 3AS
Tel 0171-631 4242

The Special Commissioners are an independent body appointed by the Lord Chancellor to hear complex appeals against decisions of the Board of Inland Revenue and its officials. In addition to the Presiding Special Commissioner there are two full-time and 13 deputy special commissioners; all are legally qualified.
Presiding Special Commissioner, His Hon. Stephen Oliver, QC
Special Commissioners (£84,752), T. H. K. Everett; D. A. Shirley
Clerk, R. P. Lester

SPECIAL IMMIGRATION APPEALS COMMISSION
Taylor House, 88 Rosebery Avenue, London EC1R 4QU
Tel 0171-862 4200

The Commission was set up under the Special Immigration Appeals Commission Act 1998. Its main function is to consider appeals against orders for deportations in cases which involve, in the main, considerations of national security. Members are appointed by the Lord Chancellor.
Chairman, The Hon. Mr Justice Potts
Secretary, Ms P. Dews

TRAFFIC COMMISSIONERS
c/o Scottish Traffic Area, Argyle House, 3 Lady Lawson Street, Edinburgh EH3 9SE
Tel 0131-529 8500

The Traffic Commissioners are responsible for licensing operators of heavy goods and public service vehicles. They also have responsibility for appeals relating to the licensing of operators and for disciplinary cases involving the conduct of drivers of these vehicles. There are six Commissioners in the eight traffic areas covering Britain. Each Traffic Commissioner constitutes a tribunal for the purposes of the Tribunals and Inquiries Act 1971. For Traffic Area Offices and Commissioners, *see* page 300.
Senior Traffic Commissioner (£56,520), M. Betts

TRANSPORT TRIBUNAL
48–49 Chancery Lane, London WC2A 1JR
Tel 0171-936 7493

The Transport Tribunal hears appeals against decisions made by Traffic Commissioners at public inquiries. The tribunal consists of a legally-qualified president, two legal members who may sit as chairmen, and five lay members. The president and legal members are appointed by the Lord Chancellor and the lay members by the Secretary of State for the Environment, Transport and the Regions.
President (part-time), H. B. H. Carlisle, QC
Legal member (*part-time*) (£290 a day), His Hon. Judge Brodrick
Lay members (£232 a day), T. W. Hall; J. W. Whitworth; Miss E. B. Haran; P. Rogers
Secretary, P. J. Fisher

VALUATION TRIBUNALS
c/o Warwickshire Valuation Tribunal, 2nd Floor, Walton House, 11 Parade, Leamington Spa, Warks CV32 4DG
Tel 01926-421875

The Valuation Tribunals hear appeals concerning the council tax, non-domestic rating and land drainage rates in England and Wales, and have residual jurisdiction to hear appeals concerning the community charge, the pre-1990 rating list, disabled rating and mixed hereditaments. There are 56 tribunals in England and eight in Wales; those in England are funded by the Department of the Environment, Transport and the Regions and those in Wales by the Welsh Office. A separate tribunal is constituted for each hearing, and normally consists of a chairman and two other members. Members are appointed by the local authorities and serve on a voluntary basis. A National Association of Valuation Tribunals considers all matters affecting valuations tribunals in England, and the Council of Wales Valuation Tribunals performs the same function in Wales.
President, National Association of Valuation Tribunals, P. Wood
Secretary, National Committee of Valuation Tribunals, B. P. Massen
President, Council of Wales Valuation Tribunals, P. J. Law

VAT AND DUTIES TRIBUNALS
15–19 Bedford Avenue, London WC1B 3AS
Tel 0171-631 4242

VAT and Duties Tribunals are administered by the Lord Chancellor in England and Wales, and by the Secretary of State in Scotland. They are independent, and decide disputes between taxpayers and Customs and Excise. In England and Wales, the president and chairmen are appointed by the Lord Chancellor and members by the Treasury. Chairmen in Scotland are appointed by the Lord President of the Court of Session.
President, His Hon. Stephen Oliver, QC
Vice-President, England and Wales (£84,752), A. W. Simpson
Vice-President, Scotland (£84,752), T. G. Coutts, QC
Vice-President, Northern Ireland (£84,752), His Hon. Judge McKee, QC
Registrar, R. P. Lester

TRIBUNAL CENTRES
EDINBURGH, 44 Palmerston Place, Edinburgh EH12 5BJ. Tel: 0131-226 3551
LONDON (including Belfast), 15–19 Bedford Avenue, London WC1B 3AS. Tel: 0171-631 4242
MANCHESTER, Warwickgate House, Warwick Road, Old Trafford, Manchester M16 0GP. Tel: 0161-872 6471

The Police Service

There are 52 police forces in the United Kingdom, each responsible for policing in its area. Most forces' area is conterminous with one or more local authority areas. Policing in London is carried out by the Metropolitan Police and the City of London Police; in Northern Ireland by the Royal Ulster Constabulary; and by the Isle of Man, States of Jersey, and Guernsey forces in their respective islands and bailiwicks. National services include the National Criminal Intelligence Service and the National Missing Persons Bureau and the National Crime Squad.

Police authorities are responsible for maintaining an effective and efficient police force in their areas. The authorities of English and Welsh forces comprise local councillors, magistrates and independent members. In Scotland, there are six joint police boards made up of local councillors; the other two police authorities are councils. In London the authority for the Metropolitan Police is the Home Secretary, advised by the Metropolitan Police Committee; for the City of London Police the authority is a committee of the Corporation of London and includes councillors and magistrates. In Northern Ireland the Secretary of State appoints the police authority.

Police authorities are financed by central and local government grants and a precept on the council tax. Subject to the approval of the Home Secretary and to regulations, they appoint the chief constable. In England and Wales they are responsible for publishing annual policing plans and annual reports, setting local objectives and a budget, and levying the precept. The police authorities in Scotland are responsible for setting a budget, providing the resources necessary to police the area adequately, appointing officers of the rank of Assistant Chief Constable and above, and determining the number of officers and civilian staff in the force. The structure and responsibilities of the police authority in Northern Ireland are under review.

The Home Secretary and the Secretaries of State for Scotland and Northern Ireland are responsible for the organization, administration and operation of the police service. They make regulations covering matters such as police ranks, discipline, hours of duty, and pay and allowances. All police forces are subject to inspection by HM Inspectors of Constabulary, who report to the respective Secretary of State. In Scotland, a review of the structure of police forces began in April 1998. In Northern Ireland a commission on policing was established by the Belfast Agreement in April 1998. It will make recommendations to the Secretary of State by summer 1999.

COMPLAINTS

The investigation and resolution of a serious complaint against a police officer in England and Wales is subject to the scrutiny of the Police Complaints Authority. An officer who is disciplined by his chief constable, whether as a result of a complaint or not, may appeal to the Home Secretary. In Scotland, chief constables are obliged to investigate a complaint against one of their officers; if there is a suggestion of criminal activity, the complaint is investigated by an independent public prosecutor. In Northern Ireland complaints are investigated by the Independent Commission for Police Complaints, which will be replaced by the Police Ombudsman in spring 1999.

BASIC RATES OF PAY *since 1 September 1997*

Chief Constable	
No fixed term	£68,325–£101,241
Fixed term appointment	£71,745–£106,182
Assistant Chief Constable-designate	80% of their Chief Constable's pay
Assistant Chief Constable	
No fixed term	£57,012–£65,445
Fixed term appointment	£59,865–£68,718
Superintendent	£41,484–£51,495
Chief Inspector	£33,189–£35,499
Inspector	£30,498–£32,295
Sergeant	£23,583–£27,504
Constable	£15,438–£24,432

Metropolitan Police

Metropolitan Commissioner	£133,212
Deputy Commissioner	£95,739–£108,183
Assistant Commissioner	£86,574–£95,316
Commander	£57,012–£68,718

The rank of Chief Superintendent was abolished in April 1995. Existing appointments continue and receive the higher ranges of the pay scale for Superintendents
1998 pay negotiations still in progress at time of going to press

THE SPECIAL CONSTABULARY

Each police force has its own special constabulary, made up of volunteers who work in their spare time. Special Constables have full police powers within their force and adjoining force areas, and assist regular officers with routine policing duties.

NATIONAL CRIME SQUAD

The National Crime Squad (NCS) was established on 1 April 1998, replacing the six regional crime squads in England and Wales. It investigates organized and serious crime occurring across police force boundaries and abroad. It also supports police forces investigating serious crime. The squad is accountable to the National Crime Squad Service Authority.
Headquarters: PO Box 2500, London
SW1V 2WF. Tel: 0171-238 2500
Director General, Roy Penrose, OBE, QPM

NATIONAL CRIMINAL INTELLIGENCE SERVICE

The National Criminal Intelligence Service (NCIS) provides intelligence about serious and organized crime to law enforcement, government and other relevant agencies nationally and internationally. Previously run by the Home Office, on 1 April 1998 NCIS was placed on a statutory footing. It is accountable to the NCIS Service Authority.
Headquarters: PO Box 8000, London
SE11 5EN. Tel: 0171-238 8000
Strength, 564
Director-General, J. Abbott, QPM
Deputy Director-General (Director (Intelligence)), R. Gaspar
Director, International Division, N. Bailly
Director, UK Division, V. Harvey
Director, Resources Division, J. Bamfield

NCS and NCIS Service Authorities
The Service Authorities are responsible for ensuring the effective operation of the National Crime Squad and NCIS, and direct policy; they fulfill a similar role to a police authority. The chairman and nine other core members serve on both authorities.
Headquarters: PO Box 2600, London SW1V 2WG. Tel: 0171-238 2600
Chairman, Rt. Hon. Sir John Wheeler
Clerk, T. Simmons
Treasurer, B. Harty

National Missing Persons Bureau
The Police National Missing Persons Bureau (PNMPB) acts as a central clearing house of information, receiving reports about vulnerable missing persons that are still outstanding after 28 days and details of unidentified persons or remains within 48 hours of being found from all forces in England and Wales. Reports are also received from Scottish police forces, the RUC, and foreign police forces via Interpol.
Headquarters: New Scotland Yard, Broadway, London SW1H 0BG. Tel: 0171-230 1212
Director, C. J. Coombes

Police Information Technology Organization
The Police Information Technology Organization (PITO) became a non-departmental public body on 1 April 1998. It develops and manages the delivery of national police information technology services, such as the Police National Computer, co-ordinates the development of local information technology systems where common standards and systems are needed, and provides a procurement service.
Headquarters: Horseferry House, Dean Ryle Street, London SW1P 2AW. Tel: 0181-358 5367
Chairman, Sir Trefor Morris
Chief Executive, Miss J. MacNaughton

Forensic Science Service
The Forensic Science Service (FSS) provides forensic science support to the police forces in England and Wales for the investigation of scenes of crime, scientific analysis of material, and interpretation of scientific results. The FSS is organized into serious crime, volume crime, drugs and specialist services, supported by intelligence and consultancy services. Laboratories are located at Birmingham, Chepstow, Chorley, Huntingdon, London and Wetherby.
Headquarters: Priory House, Gooch Street North, Birmingham B5 6QQ. Tel: 0121-607 6800
Chief Executive, Dr J. Thompson

POLICE FORCES AND AUTHORITIES

Strength: actual strength of force as at mid 1998
Chair: chairman/convener of the police authority/police committee/joint police board

ENGLAND

Avon and Somerset Constabulary, *HQ,* PO Box 37, Valley Road, Portishead, Bristol BS20 8QJ. Tel: 01275-818181. *Strength,* 2,980; *Chief Constable,* S. Pilkington, QPM; *Chair,* I. Hoddell
Bedfordshire Police, *HQ,* Woburn Road, Kempston, Bedford MK43 9AX. Tel: 01234-841212. *Strength,* 1,095; *Chief Constable,* M. O'Byrne, QPM; *Chair,* A. P. Hendry, CBE

Cambridgeshire Constabulary, *HQ,* Hinchingbrooke Park, Huntingdon, Cambs PE18 8NP. Tel: 01480-456111. *Strength,* 1,296; *Chief Constable,* D. G. Gunn, QPM; *Chair,* J. Reynolds
Cheshire Constabulary, *HQ,* Nuns Road, Chester CH1 2PP. Tel: 01244-350000. *Strength,* 2,070; *Chief Constable,* N. Burgess, QPM; *Chair,* R. Nichols
Cleveland Police, *HQ,* PO Box 70, Ladgate Lane, Middlesbrough TS8 9EH. Tel: 01642-326326. *Strength,* 1,509; *Chief Constable,* B. D. D. Shaw, QPM; *Chair,* K. Walker
Cumbria Constabulary, *HQ,* Carleton Hall, Penrith, Cumbria CA10 2AU. Tel: 01768-891999. *Strength,* 1,154; *Chief Constable,* C. Phillips, QPM; *Chair,* R. Watson
Derbyshire Constabulary, *HQ,* Butterley Hall, Ripley, Derbyshire DE5 3RS. Tel: 01773-570100. *Strength,* 1,767; *Chief Constable,* J. F. Newing, QPM; *Chair,* K. Wilkinson
Devon and Cornwall Constabulary, *HQ,* Middlemoor, Exeter EX2 7HQ. Tel: 0990-777444. *Strength,* 2,997; *Chief Constable,* J. S. Evans, QPM; *Chair,* O. May
Dorset Police Force, *HQ,* Winfrith, Dorchester, Dorset DT2 8DZ. Tel: 01929-462727. *Strength,* 1,305; *Chief Constable,* D. W. Aldous, QPM; *Chair,* P. I. Jones
Durham Constabulary, *HQ,* Aykley Heads, Durham DH1 5TT. Tel: 0191-386 4929. *Strength,* 1,533; *Chief Constable,* G. Hedges; *Chair,* A. Barker
Essex Police, *HQ,* PO Box 2, Springfield, Chelmsford CM2 6DA. Tel: 01245-491491. *Strength,* 2,990; *Chief Constable,* D. F. Stevens; *Chair,* E. A. Peel
Gloucestershire Constabulary, *HQ,* Holland House, Lansdown Road, Cheltenham, Glos GL51 6QH. Tel: 01242-521321. *Strength,* 1,121; *Chief Constable,* A. J. P. Butler, QPM; *Chair,* Brig. M. A. Browne, CBE
Greater Manchester Police, *HQ,* PO Box 22 (S. West PDO), Chester House, Boyer Street, Manchester M16 0RE. Tel: 0161-872 5050. *Strength,* 6,958; *Chief Constable,* D. Wilmot, QPM; *Chair,* S. Murphy
Hampshire Constabulary, *HQ,* West Hill, Winchester, Hants SO22 5DB. Tel: 01962-841500. *Strength,* 3,490; *Chief Constable,* Sir John. Hoddinott, Kt., CBE, QPM; *Chair,* M. J. Clark
Hertfordshire Constabulary, *HQ,* Stanborough Road, Welwyn Garden City, Herts AL8 6XF. Tel: 01707-354200. *Strength,* 1,741; *Chief Constable,* P. Sharpe, QPM; *Chair,* P. Holland
Humberside Police, *HQ,* Queens Gardens, Kingston upon Hull HU1 3DJ. Tel: 01482-326111. *Strength,* 2,024; *Chief Constable,* D. A. Leonard, QPM; *Chair,* F. Bovill
Kent Constabulary, *HQ,* Sutton Road, Maidstone, Kent ME15 9BZ. Tel: 01622-690690. *Strength,* 3,235; *Chief Constable,* J. D.Phillips, QPM; *Chair,* Mrs P. F. Stubbs
Lancashire Constabulary, *HQ,* PO Box 77, Hutton, Preston, Lancs PR4 5SB. Tel: 01772-614444. *Strength,* 3,347; *Chief Constable,* Mrs P. A. Clare, QPM; *Chair,* Dr R. B. Henig
Leicestershire Constabulary, *HQ,* St Johns, Narborough, Leicester LE9 5BX. Tel: 0116-222 2222. *Strength,* 1,993; *Chief Constable,* D. J. Wyrko, QPM; *Chair,* vacant
Lincolnshire Police, *HQ,* PO Box 999, Lincoln LN5 7PH. Tel: 01522-532222. *Strength,* 1,190; *Chief Constable,* R. Childs, QPM; *Chair,* M. D. Kennedy
Merseyside Police, *HQ,* PO Box 59, Canning Place, Liverpool L69 1JD. Tel: 0151-709 6010. *Strength,* 4,360; *Chief Constable,* Sir James Sharples, QPM; *Chair,* Ms C. Gustafson
Norfolk Constabulary, *HQ,* Martineau Lane, Norwich NR1 2DJ. Tel: 01603-768769. *Strength,* 1,425; *Chief Constable,* K. R. Williams, QPM; *Chair,* B. J. Landale

NORTHAMPTONSHIRE POLICE, *HQ,* Wootton Hall, Northampton NN4 0JQ. Tel: 01604-700700. *Strength,* 1,170; *Chief Constable,* C. Fox, QPM; *Chair,* Dr M. Dickie
NORTHUMBRIA POLICE, *HQ,* Ponteland, Newcastle upon Tyne NE20 0BL. Tel: 01661-872555. *Strength,* 3,846; *Chief Constable,* C. STRACHAN, QPM; *Chair,* G. Gill
NORTH YORKSHIRE POLICE, *HQ,* Newby Wiske Hall, Newby Wiske, Northallerton, N. Yorks DL7 9HA. Tel: 01609-783131. *Strength,* 1,369; *Chief Constable,* D. R. Kenworthy, QPM; *Chair,* Mrs A. F. Harris
NOTTINGHAMSHIRE POLICE, *HQ,* Sherwood Lodge, Arnold, Nottingham NG5 8PP. Tel: 0115-967 0999. *Strength,* 2,352; *Chief Constable,* C. F. Bailey, QPM; *Chair,* R. A. Hassett
SOUTH YORKSHIRE POLICE, *HQ,* Snig Hill, Sheffield s3 8LY. Tel: 0114-220 2020. *Strength,* 3,180; *Chief Constable,* M. Hedges; *Chair,* C. Swindells
STAFFORDSHIRE POLICE, *HQ,* Cannock Road, Stafford ST17 0QG. Tel: 01785-257717. *Strength,* 2,292; *Chief Constable,* J. W. Giffard, QPM; *Chair,* J. T. Meir
SUFFOLK CONSTABULARY, *HQ,* Martlesham Heath, Ipswich IP5 3QS. Tel: 01473-613500. *Strength,* 1,177; *Chief Constable,* P. J. Scott-Lee, QPM; *Chair,* M. N. Smith
SURREY POLICE, *HQ,* Mount Browne, Sandy Lane, Guildford, Surrey GU3 1HG. Tel: 01483-571212. *Strength,* 2,451; *Chief Constable,* I. Blair; *Chair,* A. Peirce
SUSSEX POLICE, *HQ,* Malling House, Church Lane, Lewes, E. Sussex BN7 2DZ. Tel: 01273-475432. *Strength,* 3,089; *Chief Constable,* P. Whitehouse, QPM; *Chair,* K. Bodfish
THAMES VALLEY POLICE, *HQ,* Oxford Road, Kidlington, Oxon OX5 2NX. Tel: 01865-846000. *Strength,* 3,864; *Chief Constable,* C. Pollard, QPM; *Chair,* Mrs D. J. Priestley, OBE
WARWICKSHIRE CONSTABULARY, *HQ,* PO Box 4, Leek Wootton, Warwick CV35 7QB. Tel: 01926-415000. *Strength,* 940; *Chief Constable,* A. Timpson; *Chair,* C. Cleaver
WEST MERCIA CONSTABULARY, *HQ,* Hindlip Hall, PO Box 55, Hindlip, Worcester WR3 8SP. Tel: 01905-723000. *Strength,* 2,016; *Chief Constable,* D. C. Blakey, CBE, QPM; *Chair,* D. B. Watkins
WEST MIDLANDS POLICE, *HQ,* PO Box 52, Lloyd House, Colmore Circus, Queensway, Birmingham B4 6NQ. Tel: 0121-626 5000. *Strength,* 7,205; *Chief Constable,* E. Crew, QPM; *Chair,* R. Jones
WEST YORKSHIRE POLICE, *HQ,* PO Box 9, Laburnum Road, Wakefield, W. Yorks WF1 3QP. Tel: 01924-375222. *Strength,* 5,167; *Chief Constable,* G. Moore, QPM; *Chair,* N. Taggart
WILTSHIRE CONSTABULARY, *HQ,* London Road, Devizes, Wilts SN10 2DN. Tel: 01380-722341. *Strength,* 1,196; *Chief Constable,* Miss E. Neville, QPM, PH.D.; *Chair,* H. A. Woolnough

WALES

DYFED-POWYS POLICE, *HQ,* PO Box 99, Llangunnor, Carmarthen SA31 2PF. Tel: 01267-222020. *Strength,* 1,002; *Chief Constable,* R. White, CBE, QPM; *Chair,* Ms M. Roberts
GWENT CONSTABULARY, *HQ,* Croesyceiliog, Cwmbran NP44 2XJ. Tel: 01633-838111. *Strength,* 1,241; *Chief Constable,* F. J. Wilkinson; *Chair,* D. Turnbull
NORTH WALES POLICE, *HQ,* Glan-y-don, Colwyn Bay, Conwy LL29 8AW. Tel: 01492-517171. *Strength,* 1,401; *Chief Constable,* M. J. Argent, QPM; *Chair,* C. M. Ley
SOUTH WALES POLICE, *HQ,* Cowbridge Road, Bridgend CF31 3SU. Tel: 01656-655555. *Strength,* 3,055; *Chief Constable,* A. T. Burden, QPM; *Chair,* B. P. Murray

SCOTLAND

CENTRAL SCOTLAND POLICE, *HQ,* Randolphfield, Stirling FK8 2HD. Tel: 01786-456000. *Strength,* 702; *Chief Constable,* W. J. M. Wilson, QPM; *Convener,* Mrs J. Burness
DUMFRIES AND GALLOWAY CONSTABULARY, *HQ,* Cornwall Mount, Dumfries DG1 1PZ. Tel: 01387-252112. *Strength,* 436; *Chief Constable,* W. Rae, QPM; *Chair,* K. Cameron
FIFE CONSTABULARY, *HQ,* Detroit Road, Glenrothes, Fife KY6 2RJ. Tel: 01592-418888. *Strength,* 840; *Chief Constable,* J. P. Hamilton, QPM; *Chair,* A. Keddie
GRAMPIAN POLICE, *HQ,* Queen Street, Aberdeen AB10 1ZA. Tel: 01224-386000. *Strength,* 1,176; *Chief Constable,* A. G. Brown, QPM; *Chair,* P. Chalmers
LOTHIAN AND BORDERS POLICE, *HQ,* Fettes Avenue, Edinburgh EH4 1RB. Tel: 0131-311 3131. *Strength,* 2,590; *Chief Constable,* R. Cameron, QPM; *Convenor,* E. Drummond
NORTHERN CONSTABULARY, *HQ,* Old Perth Road, Inverness IV2 3SY. Tel: 01463-715555. *Strength,* 654; *Chief Constable,* W. A. Robertson, QPM; *Chair,* Maj. N. Graham
STRATHCLYDE POLICE, *HQ,* 173 Pitt Street, Glasgow G2 4JS. Tel: 0141-532 2000. *Strength,* 7,178; *Chief Constable,* J. Orr, OBE, QPM; *Chair,* W. Timoney
TAYSIDE POLICE, *HQ,* PO Box 59, West Bell Street, Dundee DD1 9JU. Tel: 01382-223200. *Strength,* 1,143; *Chief Constable,* W. A. Spence, QPM; *Chair,* A. Shand

NORTHERN IRELAND

ROYAL ULSTER CONSTABULARY, *HQ,* Brooklyn, Knock Road, Belfast BT5 6LD. Tel: 01232-650222. *Strength,* 8,450; *Chief Constable,* R. Flanagan, OBE; *Chair,* P. Armstrong

ISLANDS

ISLAND POLICE FORCE, *HQ,* Hospital Lane, St Peter Port, Guernsey GY1 2QN. Tel: 01481-725111. *Strength,* 146; *Chief Officer,* M. H. Wyeth; *President, States Committee for Home Affairs,* M. W. Torode
STATES OF JERSEY POLICE, *HQ,* Rouge Bouillon, PO Box 789, St Helier, Jersey JE4 8ZD. Tel: 01534-612612. *Strength,* 240; *Chief Officer,* R. H. Le Breton; *President, Defence Committee,* M. Wavell
ISLE OF MAN CONSTABULARY, *HQ,* Glencrutchery Road, Douglas, Isle of Man IM2 4RG. Tel: 01624-631212. *Strength,* 213; *Chief Constable,* R. E. N. Oake, QPM; *Chairman, Police Committee,* Hon. A. R. Bell

METROPOLITAN POLICE SERVICE
New Scotland Yard, Broadway, London SW1H 0BG
Tel 0171-230 1212

Establishment, 26,902
Commissioner, Sir Paul Condon, QPM
Deputy Commissioner, J. Stevens, QPM
Receiver, P. Fletcher
Chair, Sir John Quinton

OPERATIONAL AREAS
Assistant Commissioners, A. J. Speed, QPM (*Central*); A. Dunn, QPM (*North-East*); P. A. Manning, QPM (*North-West*); W. I. R. Johnston, QPM (*South-East*); D. F. O'Connor, QPM (*South-West*)
Deputy Assistant Commissioner, D. Flanders, QPM; J. Townsend, QPM; J. Stichbury; A. S. Trotter; B. Wilding; M. Todd

Commanders, D. M. T. Kendrick, QPM; T. D. Laidlaw, LVO, QPM; A. L. Rowe, QPM; M. Briggs, QPM; M. R. Campbell; W. I. Griffiths, BEM, QPM; S. C. Pilkington; D. A. Ray, QPM; R. Gaspar; D. Gilbertson; P. Tomkins; R. Currie, QPM ; C. A. Howlett; Mrs S. E. Becks

SPECIALIST OPERATIONS DEPARTMENT
Assistant Commissioner, D. C. Veness, QPM
Deputy Assistant Commissioner, A. G. Fry, QPM
Commanders, R. C. Marsh, CVO, QPM; B. G. Moss, QPM; J. G. D. Grieve, QPM; N. G. Mulvihill, QPM

COMPLAINTS INVESTIGATION BUREAU
Commander, I. G. Quinn, QPM

INSPECTORATE
Commander, B. J. Luckhurst, QPM

OTHER DEPARTMENTS
Director, Strategic Co-ordination, Commander T. C. Lloyd
Director, Personnel, Mrs P. Woods
Director, Consultancy and Information Services, Mrs S. Merchant
Director, Public Affairs, R. Fedorcio
Solicitor, D. Hamilton
Director, Technology, N. Boothman
Director, Property Services, T. G. Lawrence

CITY OF LONDON POLICE
26 Old Jewry, London EC2R 8DJ
Tel 0171-601 2222

Strength, 824
The City of London Police is responsible for policing the City of London. Though small, the area includes one of the most important financial centres in the world and the force has particular expertise in areas such as fraud investigation as well as the areas required of any police force.
The force has a wholly elected police authority, the police committee of the Corporation of London, which appoints the Commissioner.
Commissioner (£95,316), P. Nove, QPM
Assistant Commissioner (acting) (£76,254), J. Davison
Commander (acting) (£66,393), J. Kitchen
Chairman of Police Committee, L. St J. T. Jackson

BRITISH TRANSPORT POLICE
15 Tavistock Place, London WC1H 9SJ
Tel 0171-388 7541

Strength (March 1998), 2,095
British Transport Police is the national police force for the railways in England, Wales and Scotland, including the London Underground system and the Docklands Light Railway. The Chief Constable reports to the British Transport Police Committee. The members of the Committee are appointed by the British Railways Board and include representatives of Railtrack and London Underground Ltd as well as independent members.
Chief Constable, D. J. Williams, QPM
Deputy Chief Constable, A. Parker, QPM

MINISTRY OF DEFENCE POLICE
MDP Wethersfield, Braintree, Essex CM7 4AZ
Tel 01371-854000

Strength (March 1998), 3,856
The Ministry of Defence Police is an agency of the Ministry of Defence. It is a national civilian police force whose officers are appointed by the Secretary of State for Defence. It is responsible for the policing of all military land, stations and establishments in the United Kingdom. The agency also has certain responsibilities for the civilian Ministry of Defence Guard Service.
Chief Constable, W. E. E. Boreham, OBE
Deputy Chief Constable, A. V. Comben
Head of Secretariat, P. A. Crowther

ROYAL PARKS CONSTABULARY
The Old Police House, Hyde Park, London W2 2UH
Tel 0171-298 2000

Strength (June 1998), 166
The Royal Parks Constabulary is maintained by the Royal Parks Agency, an executive agency of the Department of National Heritage, and is responsible for the policing of eight royal parks in and around London. These comprise an area in excess of 6,300 acres. Officers of the force are appointed under the Parks Regulations Act 1872 as amended.
Chief Officer, W. Ross, OBE
Deputy Chief Officer, A. McLean

UK ATOMIC ENERGY AUTHORITY CONSTABULARY
Building E6, Culham Science Centre, Abingdon, Oxon OX14 3DB
Tel 01235-463760

Strength (June 1998), 490
The Constabulary is responsible for policing UK Atomic Energy Authority and British Nuclear Fuels PLC establishments and for escorting nuclear material between establishments. The Chief Constable is responsible, through the Atomic Energy Authority Police Authority, to the President of the Board of Trade.
Chief Constable, W. F. Pryke
Assistant Chief Constable (acting), J. S. Thomas

STAFF ASSOCIATIONS

Police officers are not permitted to join a trade union or to take strike action. All ranks have their own staff associations.
ASSOCIATION OF CHIEF POLICE OFFICERS OF ENGLAND, WALES AND NORTHERN IRELAND, 7th Floor, 25 Victoria Street, London SW1H 0EX. Tel: 0171-227 3434. Represents Chief Constables, Deputy and Assistant Chief Constables in England, Wales and Northern Ireland; officers of the rank of Commander and above in the Metropolitan and City of London Police and senior civilian members of these forces. *General Secretary*, Miss M. C. E. Barton

THE POLICE SUPERINTENDENTS' ASSOCIATION OF
ENGLAND AND WALES, 67A Reading Road, Pangbourne,
Reading RG8 7JD. Tel: 0118-984 4005. Represents
officers of the rank of Superintendent. *Secretary,* Chief
Supt. D. C. Parkinson
THE POLICE FEDERATION OF ENGLAND AND WALES,
15–17 Langley Road, Surbiton, Surrey KT6 6LP. Tel:
0181-399 2224. Represents officers up to and including
the rank of Chief Inspector. *General Secretary,* J. Moseley
ASSOCIATION OF CHIEF POLICE OFFICERS IN SCOTLAND,
Police Headquarters, Fettes Avenue, Edinburgh EH4 1RB.
Tel: 0131-311 3051. Represents the Chief Constables,
Deputy and Assistant Chief Constables of the Scottish
police forces. *Hon. Secretary,* H. R. Cameron, QPM
THE ASSOCIATION OF SCOTTISH POLICE
SUPERINTENDENTS, Secretariat, 173 Pitt Street,
Glasgow G2 4JS. Tel: 0141-221 5796. Represents officers
of the rank of Superintendent. *President,* Chief Supt. S.
Davidson
THE SCOTTISH POLICE FEDERATION, 5 Woodside Place,
Glasgow G3 7QF. Tel: 0141-332 5234. Represents officers
up to and including the rank of Chief Inspector. *General
Secretary,* D. J. Keil, QPM
THE SUPERINTENDENTS' ASSOCIATION OF NORTHERN
IRELAND, RUC Training Centre, Garnerville Road,
Belfast BT4 2NX. Tel: 01232-700660. Represents
Superintendents and Chief Superintendents in the
RUC. *Hon. Secretary,* Supt. W. T. Brown
THE POLICE FEDERATION FOR NORTHERN IRELAND,
Royal Ulster Constabulary, Garnerville, Garnerville
Road, Belfast BT4 2NX. Tel: 01232-760831. Represents
officers up to and including the rank of Chief Inspector.
Secretary, D. A. McClurg

POLICE STRENGTHS 1998

	Male	Female	Total
ENGLAND AND WALES p			
Total officers	107,028	19,828	126,856
Ethnic minority officers	1,957	526	2,483
Special constables	12,483	6,680	19,163
Civilians	22,502	34,260	56,762
SCOTLAND*			
Officers	12,752	2,036	14,788
Special constables	1,336	450	1,786
Civilians	1,861	3,316	5,177
NORTHERN IRELAND			
Officers	7,529	921	8,450
Special constables	829	451	1,280
Civilians	1,212	2,328	3,540

p provisonal
* Figures for Scotland as at 31 March 1997
Sources: Home Office; Scottish Office; RUC

The Prison Service

The prison services in the United Kingdom are the responsibility of the Home Secretary, the Secretary of State for Scotland and the Secretary of State for Northern Ireland. The chief executives of the Prison Service, the Scottish Prison Service and the Northern Ireland Prison Service are responsible for the day-to-day running of the system.

There are 135 prison establishments in England and Wales, 20 in Scotland and four in Northern Ireland. Convicted prisoners are classified according to their perceived security risk and are housed in establishments appropriate to that level of security. There are no open prisons in Northern Ireland. Female prisoners are housed in women's establishments or in separate wings of mixed prisons. Remand prisoners are, where possible, housed separately from convicted prisoners. Offenders under the age of 21 are usually detained in a young offenders' institution, which may be a separate establishment or part of a prison.

Seven prisons are now run by the private sector, and in England and Wales all escort services have been contracted out to private companies. Four prisons are being built and financed under the Private Finance Initiative and will also be run by private contractors.

There are independent prison inspectorates in England and Wales (*see* page 311) and Scotland (*see* page 342) which report annually to the Secretary of State on prison conditions and the treatment of prisoners. HM Chief Inspector of Prisons for England and Wales also performs an inspectorate role for prisons in Northern Ireland. Every prison establishment also has an independent board of visitors or visiting committee made up of local volunteers appointed by the Secretary of State. Any prisoner whose complaint is not satisfied by the internal complaints procedures may complain to the Prisons Ombudsman for England and Wales (*see* page 334) or the Scottish Prisons Complaints Commission (*see* page 343). There is no Prisons Ombudsman for Northern Ireland, but complaints by prisoners regarding maladministration may be made to the Parliamentary Commissioner for Administration (*see* page 331).

The Home Secretary is currently conducting a review into the organization of and links between the prison and probation services in England and Wales.

AVERAGE PRISON POPULATION 1997–8 (UK)

	Remand	Sentenced	Other
ENGLAND AND WALES*			
Male	11,532	46,360	547
Female	599	2,052	25
Total	12,131	48,412	572
SCOTLAND			
Male	n/a	n/a	—
Female	n/a	n/a	—
Total	927	5,133	—
N. IRELAND			
Male	359	1,190	10
Female	9	21	—
Total	368	1,211	10
UK TOTAL	13,426	54,756	582

* 1997 figures

The prison population for 2005 in England and Wales is projected to reach 82,800 if current trends continue

Sources: Home Office – *Statistical Bulletin 5/98*; Scottish Prison Service – *Annual Report and Accounts 1997–8*; Northern Ireland Prison Service – *Annual Report 1997–8*

SENTENCED PRISON POPULATION BY SEX AND OFFENCE (ENGLAND AND WALES) AS AT JUNE 1997

	Male	Female
Violence against the person	9,836	387
Sexual offences	3,973	9
Burglary	7,642	96
Robbery	6,069	154
Theft, handling, fraud and forgery	5,068	453
Drugs offences	6,309	675
Other offences	5,242	193
Offence not known	2,599	100
Total	46,739	2,066

Source: Home Office – *Statistical Bulletin 5/98*

AVERAGE SENTENCED POPULATION BY LENGTH OF SENTENCE 1996 (ENGLAND AND WALES)

	Adults	Young Offenders
Up to 18 months	8,199	2,930
18 months–4 years	10,320	2,606
Over 4 years	17,644	1,164
Total	36,162	6,700

Source: HMSO – *Annual Abstract of Statistics 1998*

AVERAGE DAILY SENTENCED POPULATION BY LENGTH OF SENTENCE 1997–8 (SCOTLAND)

	Adults	Young Offenders
Less than 4 years	2,141	574
4 years or over (including life)	2,218	200
Total	4,359	774

Source: Scottish Prison Service – *Annual Report and Accounts 1997–8*

PRISON SUICIDES 1997–8 (ENGLAND AND WALES)

Adults	66
Young offenders	9
Total	75

Source: HM Prison Service – *Annual Report and Accounts 1997–8*

AVERAGE NUMBER OF PRISON SERVICE STAFF 1997–8 (GREAT BRITAIN)

	England and Wales	Scotland
No. of prison service staff	39,553	4,791

Sources: HM Prison Service – *Annual Report and Accounts 1997–8*; Scottish Prison Service – *Annual Report and Accounts 1997–8*

OPERATING COSTS OF PRISON SERVICE IN ENGLAND AND WALES 1997–8

	£ million
Staff costs	935.9
Other operating costs	752.8
Operating income	(16.4)
Net operating costs before notional charge on capital employed	1,672.3
Charge on capital employed	231.3
Net operating costs	1,903.6
Average net operating costs per prisoner per annum	18,700

Source: HM Prison Service – *Annual Report and Accounts 1997–8*

OPERATING COSTS OF SCOTTISH PRISON SERVICE
1997–8

	£
Total income	1,598,000
Total expenditure	172,071,000
Staff costs	110,874,000
Running costs	47,675,000
Other current expenditure	13,522,000
Operating deficit	(170,473,000)
Interest on capital	(23,199,000)
Interest payable and similar charges	(15,000)
Interest receivable	145,000
Deficit for financial year	(193,542,000)
Average annual cost per prisoner per place	26,170

Source: Scottish Prison Service – Annual Report and Accounts 1997–8

OPERATING COSTS OF NORTHERN IRELAND PRISON
SERVICE 1997–8

	£
Custodial	120,159,080
Non-custodial	5,967,549
Headquarters	7,600,935
Total	133,727,565
Average annual cost per prisoner place	75,297

Source: Northern Ireland Prison Service

THE PRISON SERVICES

HM PRISON SERVICE

Cleland House, Page Street, London SW1P 4LN
Tel 0171-217 6000

SALARIES 1997–8

Governor 1	£49,058–£50,703
Governor 2	£44,298–£45,615
Governor 3	£38,256–£39,300
Governor 4	£31,479–£33,756
Governor 5	£27,761–£30,236

For civil service salaries, see page 278

THE PRISONS BOARD

Director-General (SCS), R. R. Tilt
  Private Secretary, R. Hughes
  Staff Officer, J. Heavens
Director of Security and Deputy Director-General (SCS),
  A. J. Pearson
Director of Personnel (SCS), B. Clark
Director of Finance (SCS), J. Le Vay
Directors of Operations (SCS), A. Papps (North); A. Walker
  (South)
Director of Dispersals (SCS), P. Wheatley
Director of Regimes (SCS), M. Narey
Director of Health Care (SCS), Dr M. Longfield
Director of Service Delivery (Quantum), J. Powls
Non-Executive Members, Sir Duncan Nichol, CBE; Mrs R.
  Thomson, CBE; Mrs P. A. Clare, QPM
Board Secretary, N. Newcomen

Chaplain-General and Archdeacon of the Prison Service,
  Ven. D. Fleming
Senior Roman Catholic Chaplain, Mgr J. Branson

AREA MANAGERS (SCS)

Directorate of Operations (North)
East Midlands, M. Egan; Mercia, D. Curtis; Mersey and
  Manchester, A. Fitzpatrick; North-East, R. Mitchell; North-
  West, D. I. Lockwood; Yorkshire, J. Staples

Directorate of Operations (South)
Central, J. Dring; Kent, T. Murtagh, OBE; London North and
  East Anglia, I. Ward; London South, P. J. Kitteridge, CBE;
  South Coast, J. Perriss; Wales and the West, J. May

PRISON ESTABLISHMENTS

CNA Average number of in use certified normal
  accommodation places 1997–8
Prisoners/Young Offenders Average number of prisoners/
  young offenders 1997–8

ACKLINGTON, Morpeth, Northumberland NE65 9XF. CNA,
  662. Prisoners, 654. Governor, L. Woods
ALBANY, Newport, Isle of Wight PO30 5RS. CNA, 436.
  Prisoners, 429. Governor, I. Murray
ALDINGTON, Ashford, Kent TN25 7BQ. CNA, 145. Prisoners,
  137. Governor, L. Cruttenden
ALTCOURSE (private prison), Higher Lane, Fazakerley,
  Liverpool L9 7LH. CNA, 450. Prisoners, 478. Director, W.
  MacGowan
ASHWELL, Oakham, Leics LE15 7LF. CNA, 444. Prisoners, 453.
  Governor, C. Bushell
*‡ASKHAM GRANGE, Askham Richard, York YO2 3PT. CNA,
  130. Prisoners and Young Offenders, 127. Governor,
  H. E. Crew
‡AYLESBURY, Bierton Road, Aylesbury, Bucks HP20 1EH.
  CNA, 318. Young Offenders, 311. Governor, N. Pascoe
BEDFORD, St Loyes Street, Bedford MK40 1HG. CNA, 343.
  Prisoners, 381. Governor, vacant
BELMARSH, Western Way, Thamesmead, London SE28 0EB.
  CNA, 823. Prisoners, 865. Governor, W. S. Duff
BIRMINGHAM, Winson Green Road, Birmingham B18 4AS.
  CNA, 719. Prisoners, 1,040. Governor, G. Gregory-Smith
BLAKENHURST (private prison), Hewell Lane, Redditch,
  Worcs B97 6QS. CNA, 647. Prisoners, 803. Director,
  P. Siddons
BLANTYRE HOUSE, Goudhurst, Cranbrook, Kent TN17 2NH.
  CNA, 120. Prisoners, 120. Governor, E. McLennan-Murray
BLUNDESTON, Lowestoft, Suffolk NR32 5BG. CNA, 417.
  Prisoners, 402. Governor, S. Robinson
†‡BRINSFORD, New Road, Featherstone, Wolverhampton
  WV10 7PY. CNA, 477. Young Offenders, 521. Governor, C.
  Davidson
BRISTOL, Cambridge Road, Bristol BS7 8PS. CNA, 487.
  Prisoners, 583. Governor, N. Wall
BRIXTON, PO Box 369, Jebb Avenue, London SW2 5XF.
  CNA, 492. Prisoners, 598. Governor, M. O'Sullivan
*†‡BROCKHILL, Redditch, Worcs B97 6RD. CNA, 159.
  Prisoners and Young Offenders, 129. Governor, N. Croft
BUCKLEY HALL (private prison), Buckley Farm Lane,
  Rochdale, Lancs OL12 9DP. CNA, 350. Prisoners, 374.
  Director, S. Mitson
BULLINGDON, PO Box 50, Bicester, Oxon OX6 0PR. CNA,
  655. Prisoners, 687. Governor, J. Cann
*‡BULLWOOD HALL, High Road, Hockley, Essex SS5 4TE.
  CNA, 131. Prisoners and Young Offenders, 131. Governor,
  Mrs C. H. Cawley
CAMP HILL, Newport, Isle of Wight PO30 5PB. CNA, 467.
  Prisoners, 502. Governor, W. Preston
CANTERBURY, 46 Longport, Canterbury CT1 1PJ. CNA, 165.
  Prisoners, 268. Governor, Ms J. Galbally
†‡CARDIFF, Knox Road, Cardiff CF2 1UG. CNA, 527.
  Prisoners and Young Offenders, 710. Governor, J. Thomas-
  Ferrand
‡CASTINGTON, Morpeth, Northumberland NE65 9XG.
  CNA, 320. Young Offenders, 316. Governor, M. Lees
CHANNINGS WOOD, Denbury, Newton Abbot, Devon
  TQ12 6DW. CNA, 482. Prisoners, 605. Governor, R. Mullen

††CHELMSFORD, 200 Springfield Road, Chelmsford, Essex CM2 6LQ. *CNA*, 448. *Prisoners and Young Offenders*, 469. *Governor*, Ms A. Gomme

COLDINGLEY, Bisley, Woking, Surrey GU24 9EX. *CNA*, 298. *Prisoners*, 296. *Governor*, E. R. Butt

*COOKHAM WOOD, Rochester, Kent ME1 3LU. *CNA*, 120. *Prisoners*, 147. *Governor*, Miss C. Kershaw

DARTMOOR, Princetown, Yelverton, Devon PL20 6RR. *CNA*, 620. *Prisoners*, 627. *Governor*, J. Lawrence

‡DEERBOLT, Bowes Road, Barnard Castle, Co. Durham DL12 9BG. *CNA*, 435. *Young Offenders*, 418. *Governor*, P. Atkinson

††DONCASTER (private prison), Off North Bridge, Marshgate, Doncaster DN5 8UX. *CNA*, 771. *Prisoners and Young Offenders*, 1,066. *Director*, H. Jones

††DORCHESTER, North Square, Dorchester DT1 1JD. *CNA*, 147. *Prisoners and Young Offenders*, 230. *Governor*, Mrs D. Calvert

‡DOVER, The Citadel, Western Heights, Dover CT17 9DR. *CNA*, 316. *Young Offenders*, 304. *Governor*, B. Pollett

DOWNVIEW, Sutton Lane, Sutton, Surrey SM2 5PD. *CNA*, 327. *Prisoners*, 337. *Governor*, C. Lambert

*‡DRAKE HALL, Eccleshall, Staffs ST21 6LQ. *CNA*, 281. *Prisoners and Young Offenders*, 267. *Governor*, P. Tidball

*DURHAM, Old Elvet, Durham DH1 3HU. *CNA*, 663. *Prisoners*, 932. *Governor*, N. Clifford

*‡EAST SUTTON PARK, Sutton Valence, Maidstone, Kent ME17 3DF. *CNA*, 94. *Prisoners and Young Offenders*, 96. *Governor (acting)*, Miss P. Nearney

*††EASTWOOD PARK, Falfield, Wotton-under-Edge, Glos GL12 8DB. *CNA*, 175. *Prisoners and Young Offenders*, 157. *Governor*, P. Winkley.

ELMLEY, Church Road, Eastchurch, Sheerness, Kent ME12 4AY. *CNA*, 740. *Prisoners*, 843. *Governor*, A. Smith

ERLESTOKE HOUSE, Devizes, Wilts SN10 5TU. *CNA*, 310. *Prisoners*, 307. *Governor*, M. Cook

EVERTHORPE, Brough, E. Yorks HU15 1RB. *CNA*, 433. *Prisoners*, 460. *Governor*, P. Midgley

††EXETER, New North Road, Exeter EX4 4EX. *CNA*, 266. *Prisoners and Young Offenders*, 458. *Governor*, N. Evans

FEATHERSTONE, New Road, Wolverhampton WV10 7PU. *CNA*, 599. *Prisoners*, 596. *Governor*, C. Scott

††FELTHAM, Bedfont Road, Feltham, Middx TW13 4ND. *CNA*, 849. *Prisoners and Young Offenders*, 894. *Governor*, C. Welsh

FORD, Arundel, W. Sussex BN18 0BX. *CNA*, 481. *Prisoners*, 448. *Governor*, R. S. Brandon

*‡FOSTON HALL, Foston, Derbys DE65 5DN. *CNA*, 142. *Prisoners and Young Offenders*, 123. *Governor*, Ms P. Scriven

FRANKLAND, Brasside, Durham DH1 5YD. *CNA*, 447. *Prisoners*, 448. *Governor*, I. Woods

FULL SUTTON, Full Sutton, York YO41 1PS. *CNA*, 481. *Prisoners*, 500. *Governor*, R. Tasker

GARTH, Ulnes Walton Lane, Leyland, Preston PR5 3NE. *CNA*, 603. *Prisoners*, 617. *Governor*, W. Rose-Quirie

GARTREE, Gallow Field Road, Market Harborough, Leics LE16 7RP. *CNA*, 364. *Prisoners*, 363. *Governor*, R. J. Perry

††GLEN PARVA, Tigers Road, Wigston, Leicester LE8 4TN. *CNA*, 720. *Young Offenders*, 872. *Governor*, B. Payling

††GLOUCESTER, Barrack Square, Gloucester GL1 2JN. *CNA*, 220. *Prisoners and Young Offenders*, 282. *Governor*, R. Dempsey

GRENDON/SPRING HILL, HMP Grendon, Grendon Underwood, Aylesbury, Bucks HP18 0TL. *CNA*, 454. *Prisoners*, 430. *Governor*, T. C. Newell

‡GUYS MARSH, Shaftesbury, Dorset SP7 0AH. *CNA*, 360. *Prisoners and Young Offenders*, 370. *Governor*, D. Godfrey

HASLAR, 2 Dolphin Way, Gosport, Hants PO12 2AW. *CNA*, 158. *Prisoners*, 141. *Governor*, I. Truffet

‡HATFIELD, Thorne Road, Hatfield, Doncaster DN7 6EL. *CNA*, 180. *Young Offenders*, 151. *Governor*, Ms C. Davies

HAVERIGG, Millom, Cumbria LA18 4NA. *CNA*, 530. *Prisoners*, 550. *Governor*, G. Brunskill

HEWELL GRANGE, Redditch, Worcs B97 6QQ. *CNA*, 203. *Prisoners*, 193. *Governor*, D. W. Bamber

HIGH DOWN, Sutton Lane, Sutton, Surrey SM2 5PJ. *CNA*, 649. *Prisoners*, 696. *Governor*, D. Wilson

*HIGHPOINT, Stradishall, Newmarket, Suffolk CB8 9YG. *CNA*, 679. *Prisoners*, 695. *Governor*, R. Woolford

††HINDLEY, Gibson Street, Bickershaw, Wigan, Lancs WN2 5TH. *CNA*, 528. *Prisoners and Young Offenders*, 522. *Governor*, C. Sheffield

‡HOLLESLEY BAY COLONY, Woodbridge, Suffolk IP12 3JW. *CNA*, 458. *Prisoners and Young Offenders*, 424. *Governor*, J. Forster

*††HOLLOWAY, Parkhurst Road, London N7 0NU. *CNA*, 517. *Prisoners and Young Offenders*, 521. *Governor*, M. Sheldrick

HOLME HOUSE, Holme House Road, Stockton-on-Tees TS18 2QU. *CNA*, 918. *Prisoners*, 894. *Governor*, D. Roberts

††HULL, Hedon Road, Hull HU9 5LS. *CNA*, 522. *Prisoners and Young Offenders*, 508. *Governor*, M. Newell

‡HUNTERCOMBE, Huntercombe Place, Nuffield, Henley-on-Thames RG9 5SB. *CNA*, 256. *Young Offenders*, 260. *Governor*, P. Manwaring

KINGSTON, 122 Milton Road, Portsmouth PO3 6AS. *CNA*, 129. *Prisoners*, 116. *Governor*, S. McLean

KIRKHAM, Freckleton Road, Preston PR4 2RN. *CNA*, 702. *Prisoners*, 658. *Governor*, A. F. Jennings, OBE

KIRKLEVINGTON GRANGE, Yarm, Cleveland TS15 9PA. *CNA*, 177. *Prisoners*, 174. *Governor*, Ms S. Anthony

LANCASTER, The Castle, Lancaster LA1 1YL. *CNA*, 218. *Prisoners*, 216. *Governor*, D. G. McNaughton

††LANCASTER FARMS, Far Moor Lane, Stone Row Head, off Quernmore Road, Lancaster LA1 3QZ. *CNA*, 496. *Prisoners and Young Offenders*, 502. *Governor*, D. Thomas

LATCHMERE HOUSE, Church Road, Ham Common, Richmond, Surrey TW10 5HH. *CNA*, 192. *Prisoners*, 179. *Governor*, T. Hinchliffe

LEEDS, Armley, Leeds LS12 2TJ. *CNA*, 907. *Prisoners*, 1,008. *Governor*, R. Daly

LEICESTER, Welford Road, Leicester LE2 7AJ. *CNA*, 215. *Prisoners*, 346. *Governor*, Ms M. Bartlett

††LEWES, Brighton Road, Lewes, E. Sussex BN7 1EA. *CNA*, 485. *Prisoners and Young Offenders*, 482. *Governor*, J. F. Dixon

LEYHILL, Wotton-under-Edge, Glos GL12 8BT. *CNA*, 410. *Prisoners*, 390. *Governor*, D. T. Williams

LINCOLN, Greetwell Road, Lincoln LN2 4BD. *CNA*, 434. *Prisoners*, 625. *Governor*, B. McCourt

LINDHOLME, Bawtry Road, Hatfield Woodhouse, Doncaster DN7 6EE. *CNA*, 682. *Prisoners*, 679. *Governor*, A. Holman

LITTLEHEY, Perry, Huntingdon PE18 0SR. *CNA*, 624. *Prisoners*, 640. *Governor*, C. Morris

LIVERPOOL, 68 Hornby Road, Liverpool L9 3DF. *CNA*, 1,216. *Prisoners*, 1,460. *Governor*, W. Abbott

LONG LARTIN, South Littleton, Evesham, Worcs WR11 5TZ. *CNA*, 379. *Prisoners*, 381. *Governor*, J. Mullen

LOWDHAM GRANGE (private prison), Lowdham, Notts NG14 7TA. *CNA*, 175. *Prisoners*, 175. *Director*, A. Reid

---

* Women's establishment or establishment with units for women
† Remand Centre or establishment with units for remand prisoners
‡ Young Offender Institution or establishment with units for young offenders

*†‡LOW NEWTON, Brasside, Durham DH1 5SD. *CNA*, 199. *Prisoners and Young Offenders*, 298. *Governor*, M. Kirby
MAIDSTONE, 36 County Road, Maidstone ME14 1UZ. *CNA*, 541. *Prisoners*, 558. *Governor*, M. Conway
MANCHESTER, Southall Street, Manchester M60 9AH. *CNA*, 883. *Prisoners*, 1,056. *Governor*, J. Smith
‡MOORLAND, Bawtry Road, Hatfield Woodhouse, Doncaster DN7 6BW. *CNA*, 650. *Prisoners and Young Offenders*, 674. *Governor*, D. J. Waplington, OBE
MORTON HALL, Swinderby, Lincoln LN6 9PS. *CNA*, 203. *Prisoners*, 200. *Governor*, M. Murphy
THE MOUNT, Molyneaux Avenue, Bovingdon, Hemel Hempstead HP3 0NZ. *CNA*, 588. *Prisoners*, 620. *Governor*, P. Wailen
*†‡NEW HALL, Dial Wood, Flockton, Wakefield WF4 4AX. *CNA*, 313. *Prisoners and Young Offenders*, 331. *Governor*, M. Goodwin
†‡NORTHALLERTON, 15a East Road, Northallerton, N. Yorks DL6 1NW. *CNA*, 152. *Prisoners and Young Offenders*, 271. *Governor*, D. P. G. Appleton
NORTH SEA CAMP, Freiston, Boston, Lincs PE22 0QX. *CNA*, 213. *Prisoners*, 199. *Governor*, M. A. Lewis
†‡NORWICH, Mousehold, Norwich NR1 4LU. *CNA*, 570. *Prisoners and Young Offenders*, 722. *Governor*, M. Spurr
NOTTINGHAM, Perry Road, Sherwood, Nottingham NG5 3AG. *CNA*, 388. *Prisoners*, 389. *Governor*, P. J. Bennett
‡ONLEY, Willoughby, Rugby CV23 8AP. *CNA*, 583. *Young Offenders*, 578. *Governor*, J. N. Brooke
†‡PARC (private prison), Heol Hopcyn John, Bridgend CF35 6AR. *CNA*, 470. *Prisoners and Young Offenders*, 411. *Director*, R. Dixon
PARKHURST, Newport, Isle of Wight PO30 5NX. *CNA*, 365. *Prisoners*, 353. *Governor*, D. M. Morrison
PENTONVILLE, Caledonian Road, London N7 8TT. *CNA*, 740. *Prisoners*, 934. *Governor*, R. Duncan
‡PORTLAND, Easton, Portland, Dorset DT5 1DL. *CNA*, 526. *Young Offenders*, 549. *Governor*, Miss S. F. McCormick
‡PRESCOED, 47 Maryport Street, Usk, Gwent NP5 1XP. *CNA*, see Usk. *Prisoners and Young Offenders*, see Usk. *Governor*, R. J. Comber
PRESTON, 2 Ribbleton Lane, Preston PR1 5AB. *CNA*, 398. *Prisoners*, 354. *Governor*, R. J. Crouch
RANBY, Ranby, Retford, Notts DN22 8EU. *CNA*, 519. *Prisoners*, 561. *Governor*, J. Slater
†‡READING, Forbury Road, Reading RG1 3HY. *CNA*, 203. *Prisoners and Young Offenders*, 228. *Governor*, R. Fielder
*RISLEY, Risley, Warrington WA3 6BP. *CNA*, 851. *Prisoners*, 872. *Governor*, J. Harrison
†‡ROCHESTER, 1 Fort Road, Rochester, Kent ME1 3QS. *CNA*, 432. *Prisoners and Young Offenders*, 401. *Governor*, R. A. Chapman
*SEND, Ripley Road, Send, Woking, Surrey GU23 7LJ. *CNA*, 224. *Prisoners*, 219. *Governor*, S. Guy-Gibbons
SHEPTON MALLET, Cornhill, Shepton Mallet, Somerset BA4 5LU. *CNA*, 159. *Prisoners*, 213. *Governor*, R. Bennett
SHREWSBURY, The Dana, Shrewsbury SY1 2HR. *CNA*, 180. *Prisoners*, 324. *Governor*, K. Beaumont
SPRING HILL, see GRENDON
STAFFORD, 54 Gaol Road, Stafford ST16 3AW. *CNA*, 568. *Prisoners*, 622. *Governor*, P. Wright
STANDFORD HILL, Church Road, Eastchurch, Isle of Sheppey, Kent ME12 4AA. *CNA*, 384. *Prisoners*, 336. *Governor*, K. Naisbitt
STOCKEN, Stocken Hall Road, Stretton, nr Oakham, Leics LE15 7RD. *CNA*, 436. *Prisoners*, 458. *Governor*, R. Curtis
‡STOKE HEATH, Stoke Heath, Market Drayton, Shropshire TF9 2JL. *CNA*, 455. *Young Offenders*, 448. *Governor*, J. Alldridge
*‡STYAL, Wilmslow, Cheshire SK9 4HR. *CNA*, 271. *Prisoners and Young Offenders*, 272. *Governor*, Ms M. Moulden

SUDBURY, Ashbourne, Derbys DE6 5HW. *CNA*, 511. *Prisoners*, 492. *Governor*, P. E. Salter
SWALESIDE, Brabazon Road, Eastchurch, Isle of Sheppey, Kent ME12 4AX. *CNA*, 572. *Prisoners*, 593. *Governor*, J. Podmore
†SWANSEA, 200 Oystermouth Road, Swansea SA1 3SR. *CNA*, 260. *Prisoners*, 334. *Governor*, G. Deighton
‡SWINFEN HALL, Lichfield, Staffs WS14 9QS. *CNA*, 203. *Young Offenders*, 201. *Governor*, Ms J. P. Francis
‡THORN CROSS, Arley Road, Appleton Thorn, Warrington WA4 4RL. *CNA*, 316. *Young Offenders*, 221. *Governor*, I. Windebank
USK, 47 Maryport Street, Usk, Gwent NP5 1XP. *CNA* (*Usk and Prescoed*), 243. *Prisoners* (*Usk and Prescoed*), 281. *Governor*, R. J. Comber
THE VERNE, Portland, Dorset DT5 1EQ. *CNA*, 552. *Prisoners*, 571. *Governor*, T. M. Turner
WAKEFIELD, 5 Love Lane, Wakefield WF2 9AG. *CNA*, 531. *Prisoners*, 608. *Governor*, D. Shaw
WANDSWORTH, Heathfield Road, London SW18 3HS. *CNA*, 810. *Prisoners*, 881. *Governor*, M. Knight
WAYLAND, Griston, Thetford, Norfolk IP25 6RL. *CNA*, 620. *Prisoners*, 644. *Governor* (*acting*), R. Orton
WEALSTUN, Wetherby, W. Yorks LS23 7AZ. *CNA*, 599. *Prisoners*, 591. *Governor*, S. Tasker
WEARE, Portland Dock, Castletown, Portland, Dorset DT5 1PZ. *CNA*, 365. *Prisoners*, 284. *Governor*, P. O'Sullivan
WELLINGBOROUGH, Millers Park, Doddington Road, Wellingborough, Northants NN8 2NH. *CNA*, 354. *Prisoners*, 321. *Governor*, E. Willetts
‡WERRINGTON, Werrington, Stoke-on-Trent ST9 0DX. *CNA*, 153. *Young Offenders*, 155. *Governor*, S. Habgood
‡WETHERBY, York Road, Wetherby, W. Yorks LS22 5ED. *CNA*, 320. *Young Offenders*, 285. *Governor*, D. Hall
WHATTON, 14 Cromwell Road, Nottingham NG13 9FQ. *CNA*, 231. *Prisoners*, 228. *Governor*, D. Walmesley
WHITEMOOR, Longhill Road, March, Cambs PE15 0PR. *CNA*, 521. *Prisoners*, 522. *Governor*, T. Williams
*WINCHESTER, Romsey Road, Winchester SO22 5DF. *CNA*, 463. *Prisoners*, 606. *Governor*, R. J. Gaines
THE WOLDS (private prison), Everthorpe, Brough, E. Yorks HU15 2JZ. *CNA*, 360. *Prisoners*, 400. *Director*, Ms A. Rose-Quirie
†‡WOODHILL, Tattenhoe Street, Milton Keynes MK4 4DA. *CNA*, 616. *Prisoners and Young Offenders*, 688. *Governor*, Mrs M. Boon
WORMWOOD SCRUBS, PO Box 757, Du Cane Road, London W12 0AE. *CNA*, 1,171. *Prisoners*, 1,333. *Governor*, S. Moore
WYMOTT, Ulnes Walton Lane, Leyland, Preston PR5 3LW. *CNA*, 809. *Prisoners*, 797. *Governor*, R. Doughty

SCOTTISH PRISON SERVICE

Calton House, 5 Redheughs Rigg, Edinburgh EH12 9HW
Tel 0131-556 8400

SALARIES 1997–8

Senior managers in the Scottish Prison Service, including governors and deputy governors of prisons, are paid across three pay bands in the range £24,200–£53,625.

Chief Executive of Scottish Prison Service (*SCS*), E. W. Frizzell
Director of Custody, J. Durno
Director, Human Resources, Ms A. Mitchell
Director, Finance and Information Systems, W. Pretswell
Director, Strategy and Corporate Affairs, Ms J. Hutchison
Deputy Director, Regime Services and Supplies, J. McNeill
Deputy Director, Estates and Buildings, B. Paterson
Area Director, South and West, P. Withers
Area Director, North and East, P. Russell
Head of Training, Scottish Prison Service College, J. Matthews

PRISON ESTABLISHMENTS
Prisoners/Young Offenders Average number of prisoners/
young offenders 1997–8

*ABERDEEN, Craiginches, Aberdeen AB9 2HN. *Prisoners,* 201.
Governor, I. Gunn
BARLINNIE, Barlinnie, Glasgow G33 2QX. *Prisoners,* 1,208.
Governor, R. L. Houchin
CASTLE HUNTLY, Castle Huntly, Longforgan, nr Dundee
DD2 5HL. *Prisoners,* 107. *Governor,* K. Rennie
*‡CORNTON VALE, Cornton Road, Stirling FK9 5NY.
Prisoners and Young Offenders, 166. *Governor,* Mrs K.
Donegan
*‡DUMFRIES, Terregles Street, Dumfries DG2 9AX. *Young
Offenders,* 147. *Governor,* G. Taylor
DUNGAVEL, Dungavel House, Strathaven, Lanarkshire
ML10 6RF. *Prisoners,* 100. *Governor,* T. Pitt
EDINBURGH, 33 Stenhouse Road, Edinburgh EH1 3LN.
Prisoners, 728. *Governor,* A. Spencer
FRIARTON, Friarton, Perth PH2 8DW. *Prisoners,* 60. *Governor,*
E. A. Gordon
‡GLENOCHIL, King O'Muir Road, Tullibody,
Clackmannanshire FK10 3AD. *Prisoners and Young
Offenders,* 584. *Governor,* L. McBain
GREENOCK, Gateside, Greenock PA16 9AH. *Prisoners,* 242.
Governor, R. MacCowan
*INVERNESS, Porterfield, Inverness IV2 3HH. *Prisoners,* 140.
Governor, H. Ross
LONGRIGGEND, Longriggend, nr Airdrie, Lanarkshire ML6
7TL. *Prisoners,* 151. *Governor,* Ms R. Kite
LOW MOSS, Low Moss, Bishopbriggs, Glasgow G64 2QB.
Prisoners, 362. *Governor,* W. Middleton
NATIONAL INDUCTION UNIT, Shotts ML7 4LE. *Prisoners,*
46. *Governor,* J. Gerrie
NORANSIDE, Noranside, Fern, by Forfar, Angus DD8 3QY.
Prisoners, 118. *Governor,* A. MacDonald
PENNINGHAME, Penninghame, Newton Stewart DG8 6RG.
Prisoners, 60. *Governor,* S. Swan
PERTH, 3 Edinburgh Road, Perth PH2 8AT. *Prisoners,* 472.
Governor, M. Duffy
PETERHEAD, Salthouse Head, Peterhead, Aberdeenshire
AB4 6YY. *Prisoners,* 221. *Governor,* W. Rattray; *Governor,
Peterhead Unit,* B. McConnell
‡POLMONT, Brightons, Falkirk, Stirlingshire FK2 0AB.
Young Offenders, 473. *Governor,* D. Gunn
SHOTTS, Shotts ML7 4LF. *Prisoners,* 471. *Governor,* W.
McKinlay; *Governor, Shotts Unit,* A. MacVicar

NORTHERN IRELAND PRISON SERVICE

Dundonald House, Upper Newtownards Road, Belfast BT4
3SU
Tel 01232-520700

§SALARIES 1997–8

Governor 1	£50,530
Governor 2	£45,627
Governor 3	£39,404
Governor 4	£32,423–£33,887
Governor 5	£28,568–£30,419

§A Northern Ireland allowance is also payable

PRISON ESTABLISHMENTS
Prisoners/Young Offenders Average number of prisoners/
young offenders 1997–8
‡HYDEBANK WOOD, Hospital Road, Belfast BT8 8NA.
Young Offenders, 159
*‡MAGHABERRY, Old Road, Ballinderry Upper, Lisburn,
Co. Antrim BT28 2PT. *Prisoners and Young Offenders,* 512
MAGILLIGAN, Point Road, Magilligan, Co. Londonderry
BT49 0LR. *Prisoners,* 371

MAZE, Halftown Road, Maze, Lisburn, Co. Antrim BT27
5RF. *Prisoners,* 547

---

*   Women's establishment or establishment with units for women
†   Remand Centre or establishment with units for remand prisoners
‡   Young Offender Institution or establishment with units for young
offenders

Defence

The armed forces of the United Kingdom comprise the Royal Navy, the Army and the Royal Air Force. The Queen is commander-in-chief of all the armed forces. The Ministry of Defence, headed by a Secretary of State, provides the support structure for the armed forces. Within the Ministry of Defence, the Defence Council has overall responsibility for running the armed forces. The Chief of Staff of each service reports through the Chief of the Defence Staff to the Secretary of State on matters relating to the running of his service. The Chief of Staff also chairs the executive committee of the appropriate service board, which manages the service in accordance with centrally determined objectives and budgets. The military-civilian Central Staffs, headed by the Vice-Chief of the Defence Staff and the Second Permanent Under-Secretary of State, are responsible for policy, operational requirements, commitments, financial management, resource planning and civilian personnel management. The Procurement Executive is responsible for purchasing equipment. The Defence Scientific Staff and the Defence Intelligence Staff also form part of the Ministry of Defence; names of the latter are not listed for security reasons.

A permanent Joint Headquarters for the conduct of joint operations was set up at Northwood in 1996. The Joint Headquarters connects the policy and strategic functions of the MoD Head Office with the conduct of operations and is intended to strengthen the policy/executive division. A Joint Rapid Deployment Force was established in August 1996.

Britain pursues its defence and security policies through its membership of NATO (to which most of its armed forces are committed), the Western European Union, the European Union, the Organization for Security and Co-operation in Europe and the UN (*see* International Organizations section).

In July 1998 the Government published the results of a review of Britain's defence needs and the role of the armed forces, including plans to enhance joint capabilities, create a new post of Chief of Defence Logistics (*see* below) and turn the Procurement Executive into a defence agency by April 1999 (for details, *see* White Papers section).

ARMED FORCES STRENGTHS *as at 1 January 1998*

All Services	210,587
Men	195,091
Women	15,496
Royal Naval Services	44,468
Men	41,236
Women	3,232
Army	110,055
Men	102,808
Women	7,247
Royal Air Force	56,064
Men	51,047
Women	5,017

Source: Ministry of Defence

DEPLOYMENT OF UK PERSONNEL

Service personnel in UK *as at 1 July 1997*	171,600
England	142,600
Wales	3,300
Scotland	13,900
N. Ireland	11,500

Service personnel overseas *as at 1 April 1998*	43,444
Royal Naval Services	5,221
Army	29,810
Royal Air Force	8,413

Forces overseas were deployed in Continental Europe, Gibraltar, Cyprus and elsewhere in the Mediterranean, the Near East, the Gulf, the Far East and other locations.

There were also 4,007 locally entered army personnel as at 1 April 1998, of whom 1,983 were deployed in the UK, 367 in Gibraltar, 1,556 in the Far East and 101 in other areas.

At 1 August 1997 there were 11,646 US forces based in the UK (9,570 Air Force, 1,700 Navy and 376 Army).

Sources: The Stationery Office: *UK Defence Statistics 1998*; *The Military Balance 1997–8* (OUP)

NUCLEAR FORCES

Britain's nuclear forces comprise three ballistic missile submarines carrying Trident missiles and equipped with nuclear warheads. The fourth and final Trident submarine is due to be launched in late 1998. All nuclear free-fall bombs have now been taken out of service.

ARMS CONTROL

The 1990 Conventional Armed Forces in Europe Treaty (the CFE Treaty), which is currently being revised, commits all NATO and former Warsaw Pact members to limiting five major classes of conventional weapons. In 1968 Britain signed the Nuclear Non-Proliferation Treaty, which was indefinitely and unconditionally extended in 1995. In September 1996 it signed a Comprehensive Nuclear Test Ban Treaty. Britain was a party to the 1972 Biological and Toxin Weapons Convention, which provides for a world-wide ban on biological weapons, and the 1993 Chemical Weapons Convention, which came into force in April 1997 and provides for a world-wide ban on chemical weapons. In December 1997 Britain signed the Ottawa Convention, which provides for an immediate ban on the use, production and transfer of anti-personnel land-mines; the convention enters into force on 1 March 1999. Britain ratified the convention on 31 July 1998 and announced a complete ban on the use of anti-personnel land-mines by British forces.

DEFENCE CUTS

DEFENCE BUDGET

	£ million
1996–7 outturn	22,345
1997–8 estimated outturn	21,840
1998–9 plans	22,240
1999–2000 plans	22,295
2000–1 plans	22,830
2001–2 plans	22,987

The Government estimated in July 1998 that defence expenditure as a percentage of GDP would fall from 2.7 per cent to 2.4 per cent by 2001–2.

Sources: The Stationery Office: *Financial Statement and Budget Report March 1998*; Ministry of Defence: *The Strategic Defence Review*

SERVICE PERSONNEL
1 April

	Royal Navy	Army	RAF	All Services
1975 strength	76,200	167,100	95,000	338,400
1990 strength	63,200	152,800	89,700	305,700
1998 strength	44,500	109,800	55,800	210,100

Source: The Stationery Office: UK Defence Statistics 1998

CIVILIAN PERSONNEL
1 April
1975 level	316,700
1990 level	172,300
1998 level	119,100

Source: The Stationery Office: UK Defence Statistics 1998

MINISTRY OF DEFENCE
Main Building, Whitehall, London SW1A 2HB
Tel 0171-218 9000
Public Enquiry Office: Tel 0171-218 6645
Web http://www.mod.uk.

For ministerial and civil service salaries, *see* page 278
For Services salaries, *see* pages 391–2
Officers promoted in an acting capacity to a more senior rank are listed under the more senior rank. Promotion to five-star rank is no longer usual in peacetime.
For changes after 31 August 1998, *see* Stop-press

Secretary of State for Defence, The Rt. Hon. George Robertson, MP
  Private Secretary (SCS), T. C. McKane
  Special Advisers, A. McGowan; B. Gray
  Parliamentary Private Secretary, Ms S. Heal, MP
Minister of State for the Armed Forces, The Rt. Hon. Doug Henderson, MP
  Private Secretary (SCS), D. King
Minister of State for Defence Procurement, The Lord Gilbert, PC, Ph.D.
  Private Secretary (SCS), R. D. Keen
Parliamentary Under-Secretary of State, John Spellar, MP
  Private Secretary (SCS), Dr S. Cholerton
Permanent Under-Secretary of State (SCS), K. R. Tebbit
Chief of the Defence Staff, Gen. Sir Charles Guthrie, GCB, LVO, OBE, ADC (*Gen.*)

THE DEFENCE COUNCIL
The Defence Council is responsible for running the Armed Forces. It is chaired by the Secretary of State for Defence and consists of: the Ministers of State; the Parliamentary Under-Secretary of State; the Chief of the Defence Staff; the Permanent Under-Secretary of State; the Chief of the Naval Staff; the Chief of the General Staff; the Chief of the Air Staff; the Vice-Chief of the Defence Staff; the Chief Scientific Adviser; the Chief of Defence Procurement; and the Second Permanent Under-Secretary of State.

CHIEFS OF STAFF

CHIEF OF THE NAVAL STAFF
Chief of the Naval Staff and First Sea Lord, Adm. Sir Michael Boyce, KCB, OBE, ADC
Asst Chief of the Naval Staff, Rear-Adm. J. Band
Secretariat (Naval Staff) (SCS), C. Verey

CHIEF OF THE GENERAL STAFF
Chief of the General Staff, Gen. Sir Roger Wheeler, GCB, CBE, ADC (*Gen.*)
Asst Chief of the General Staff, Maj.-Gen. M. A. Willcocks, CB

Director-General, Development and Doctrine, Maj.-Gen. A. D. Pigott, CBE

CHIEF OF THE AIR STAFF
Chief of the Air Staff, Air Chief Marshal Sir Richard Johns, GCB, CBE, LVO, ADC
Asst Chief of the Air Staff, Air Vice-Marshal G. E. Stirrup, AFC
Secretariat (Air Staff) (SCS), M. J. D. Fuller
British-American Community Relations Co-ordinator, Air Marshal Sir John Kemball, KCB, CBE, RAF (retd)
Chief Executive, National Air Traffic Services (SCS), D. J. McLauchlan
Director, Airspace Policy, Air Vice-Marshal R. D. Elder, CBE

CENTRAL STAFFS
Vice-Chief of the Defence Staff, Adm. Sir Peter Abbott, KCB
Second Permanent Under-Secretary of State (SCS), R. T. Jackling, CB, CBE
Deputy CDS (Systems), Lt.-Gen. E. F. G. Burton, OBE
Asst CDS, Operational Requirements (Sea Systems), Rear-Adm. R. T. R. Phillips, CB
Asst CDS, Operational Requirements (Land Systems), Maj.-Gen. P. J. Russell-Jones, OBE
Asst CDS, Operational Requirements (Air Systems), Air Vice-Marshal S. M. Nicholl, CBE, AFC
Deputy CDS (Programmes and Personnel), Air Marshal Sir Peter Squire, KCB, DFC, AFC
Asst CDS (Programmes), Maj.-Gen. J. P. Kiszely, MC
Asst Under-Secretary of State (Service Personnel Policy) (SCS), Miss P. M. Aldred
Defence Housing Executive (SCS), C. J. I. James
Surgeon-General, Air Marshal J. A. Baird, QHP
Chief Executive, Defence Medical Training Organization, and Chief Executive, Defence Secondary Care Agency, Maj.-Gen. C. G. Callow, OBE, QHP
Deputy Under-Secretary of State (Resources, Programmes and Finance) (SCS), C. V. Balmer
Asst Under-Secretary of State (Programmes) (SCS), D. J. Seammen
Asst Under-Secretary of State (Systems) (SCS), T. A. Woolley
Asst Under-Secretary of State (Financial Management) (SCS), D. G. Jones
Asst Under-Secretary of State (General Finance) (SCS), D. C. R. Heyhoe
Defence Services Secretary, Rear-Adm. R. B. Lees
Deputy CDS (Commitments), Air Marshal J. R. Day, OBE
Asst CDS (Operations), Rear-Adm. S. Moore
Asst Under-Secretary of State (Home and Overseas) (SCS), E. V. Buckley
Chief of Defence Logistics, Gen. Sir Samuel Cowan, KCB, CBE
Chief of Staff to the Chief of Defence Logistics, Air Vice-Marshal I. Brackenbury, OBE
Asst CDS (Logistics), Maj.-Gen. G. A. Ewer, CBE
Director of Policy (SCS), R. P. Hatfield, CBE
Asst CDS (Policy), Maj.-Gen. C. F. Drewry, CBE
Deputy Under-Secretary of State (Civilian Management (SCS), J. Howe
Director-General, Management and Organization (SCS), N. K. J. Witney
Asst Under-Secretary of State, Civilian Management (Personnel) (SCS), B. A. E. Taylor
Chief Constable, MOD Police, W. E. E. Boreham, OBE
Asst Under-Secretary of State (Security and Support) (SCS), A. G. Rucker
Legal Adviser (SCS), M. J. Hemming
Director-General, Information and Communications Services (SCS), A. C. Sleigh

Defence Estate Organization (SCS), B. L. Hirst
Commandant, Joint Services Command and Staff College, Maj.-
  Gen. T. J. Granville-Chapman, CBE

DEFENCE INFORMATION STAFF

Director, Information Strategy and News (SCS), Ms O.
  Muirhead
Director, Internal Communications and Media Training (SCS),
  A. Boardman
Director, Public Relations (Navy), Cdre B. Leighton
Director, Public Relations (Army), Brig. R. D. S. Gordon, CBE
Director, Public Relations (RAF), Air Cdre G. L. McRobbie

DEFENCE INTELLIGENCE STAFF

Old War Office Building, Whitehall, London SW1A 2EU
Tel 0171-218 6645; fax 0171-218 1562

Chief of Defence Intelligence
Deputy Chief of Defence Intelligence
Director-General, Intelligence and Geographic Resources

DEFENCE SCIENTIFIC STAFF

Chief Scientific Adviser (SCS), Prof. Sir David Davies, KBE
Chief Scientist (SCS), G. H. B. Jordan
Deputy Chief Scientists (Scrutiny and Analysis) (SCS), M. J.
  Earwicker; P. M. Sutcliffe
Asst Chief Scientific Adviser (Nuclear) (SCS), P. W. Roper
Nuclear Weapon Safety Adviser (SCS), Dr A. Ferguson

SECOND SEA LORD/COMMANDER-IN-
CHIEF NAVAL HOME COMMAND

Second Sea Lord and C.-in-C. Naval Home Command, Adm. Sir
  John Brigstocke, KCB
*Director-General, Naval Personnel (Strategy and Plans) and
  Chief of Staff to Second Sea Lord and C.-in-C. Naval Home
  Command*, Rear-Adm. P. A. Dunt
Asst Under-Secretary of State (Naval Personnel) (SCS), B.
  Miller
*Flag Officer Training and Recruiting and Chief Executive,
  Naval Recruiting and Training Agency*, Rear-Adm. J.
  Chadwick
Naval Secretary and Chief Executive, Naval Manning Agency,
  Rear-Adm. F. M. Malbon (until Jan. 1999)
Director-General, Naval Medical Services, Surgeon Rear-
  Adm. M. P. W. H. Paine, QHS, FRCS
Director-General, Naval Chaplaincy Services, Revd Dr C.
  Stewart

NAVAL SUPPORT COMMAND

Chief of Fleet Support, Vice-Adm. Sir John Dunt, KCB
Director-General, Fleet Support (Operations and Plans), Rear-
  Adm. B. B. Perowne
Asst Under-Secretary of State (Fleet Support) (SCS), D. J.
  Gould
Chief Executive, Ships Support Agency (SCS), J. Coles
*Chief Executive, Naval Bases and Supply Agency, and Chief
  Naval Engineering Officer*, Rear-Adm. J. A. Trewby
Director-General, Aircraft (Navy), Rear-Adm. J. A. Burch
Flag Officer Scotland, N. England and N. Ireland, Rear-Adm.
  A. M. Gregory, OBE

COMMANDER-IN-CHIEF FLEET

C.-in-C. Fleet, Adm. N. R. Essenhigh
Deputy Commander Fleet, Vice-Adm. J. J. Blackham (until
  Jan. 1999); Vice-Adm. F. M. Malbon (from Jan. 1999)
Chief of Staff (Operations) and Flag Officer Submarines, Rear-
  Adm. R. P. Stevens, OBE
Flag Officer Surface Flotilla, Rear-Adm. P. M. Franklyn, MVO
Flag Officer Sea Training, Rear-Adm. R. J. Lippiett, MBE

*Commander, UK Task Group/Commander, Anti-Submarine
  Warfare Strike Force*, Rear-Adm. I. A. Forbes
Flag Officer Naval Aviation, Rear-Adm. I. R. Henderson
Commandant-General, Royal Marines, Maj.-Gen. R. H. G.
  Fulton

QUARTERMASTER-GENERAL'S
DEPARTMENT

Quartermaster-General, Lt.-Gen. S. C. Grant, CB
Chief of Staff, Maj.-Gen. K. O'Donoghue, CBE
Asst Under-Secretary (Quartermaster) (SCS), N. H. R. Evans
Director of Contracts (Army) (SCS), P. D. Batt
Director-General, Logistic Support (Army), Maj.-Gen. A. W.
  Lyons, CBE
Director-General, Equipment Support (Army), Maj.-Gen. P. V.
  R. Besgrove, CBE

ADJUTANT-GENERAL'S DEPARTMENT

Adjutant-General, Gen. Sir Alexander Harley, KBE, CB
Chief of Staff, Maj.-Gen. R. A. Oliver, OBE
Head, Command Secretariat (SCS), M. E. McLoughlin
*Director-General, Army Training and Recruiting and Chief
  Executive, Army Training and Recruiting Agency*, Maj.-Gen.
  C. L. Elliott, MBE
Chaplain-General, Revd Dr V. Dobbin, MBE, QHC
Director-General, Army Medical Services, Maj.-Gen. W. R.
  Short, QHP
Director, Army Legal Services, Maj.-Gen. G. Risius
Military Secretary and Chief Executive, Army Personnel Centre,
  Maj.-Gen. D. L. Burden, CB, CBE
Commandant, Royal Military Academy, Sandhurst, Maj.-Gen.
  A. G. Denaro, CBE
Commandant, Royal Military College of Science, Maj.-Gen. A. S.
  H. Irwin, CBE

COMMANDER-IN-CHIEF LAND COMMAND

C.-in-C., Land Command, Gen. Sir Michael Walker, KCB,
  CMG, CBE, ADC (Gen.)
*Deputy C.-in-C., Land Command, and Inspector-General,
  Territorial Army*, Maj.-Gen. J. D. Stokoe (until March
  1999)
Chief of Staff, HQ Land Command, Maj.-Gen. P. C. C.
  Trousdell
Deputy Chief of Staff, HQ Land Command, Maj.-Gen. P. A.
  Chambers, MBE

HQ STRIKE COMMAND

Air Officer Commanding-in-Chief, Air Chief Marshal Sir
  John Allison, KCB, CBE, ADC
Chief of Staff and Deputy C.-in-C., Air Marshal T. I. Jenner,
  CB
*Senior Air Staff Officer and Air Officer Commanding, No. 38
  Group*, Air Vice-Marshal P. O. Sturley, MBE
Air Officer Logistics and Communications Information Systems,
  Air Vice-Marshal P. J. Scott
Air Officer Administration, Air Vice-Marshal A. J. Burton
Head, Command Secretariat (SCS), C. J. Wright
Air Officer Commanding, No. 1 Group, Air Vice-Marshal J. H.
  Thompson
Air Officer Commanding, No. 11/18 Group, Air Vice-Marshal
  B. K. Burridge, CBE

HQ LOGISTICS COMMAND

*Air Officer Commanding-in-Chief, Air Member for Logistics and
  Chief Engineer (RAF)*, Air Marshal Sir Colin Terry, KBE,
  CB
*Chief of Staff (Air Officer Commanding Directly Administered
  Units)*, Air Vice-Marshal M. D. Pledger, OBE, AFC

Command Secretary (SCS), H. Griffiths
Air Officer Communications Information Systems and Support
Services, Air Vice-Marshal B. C. McCandless, CBE
Director-General, Support Management (RAF), Air Vice-
Marshal P. W. Henderson, MBE
Chief Executive, RAF Maintenance Group Agency, Cdre K. J.
M. Proctor

HQ PERSONNEL AND TRAINING COMMAND

Air Member for Personnel and Air Officer Commanding-in-
Chief, Air Marshal Sir Anthony Bagnall, KCB, OBE
Chief of Staff, Air Vice-Marshal R. A. Wright, AFC
Chief Executive, Training Group Defence Agency, Air Vice-
Marshal A. J. Stables, CBE
Commandant, RAF College, Cranwell, Air Vice-Marshal T. W.
Rimmer, OBE
Air Secretary and Chief Executive, RAF Personnel Management
Agency, Air Vice-Marshal I. M. Stewart, AFC
Director-General, Medical Services (RAF), Air Vice-Marshal
C. J. Sharples, QHP
Director, Legal Services (RAF), Air Vice-Marshal J. Weeden
Chaplain-in-Chief (RAF), Revd A. P. Bishop, QHC
Command Secretary (SCS), L. D. Kyle

PROCUREMENT EXECUTIVE

EXECUTIVE

Chief of Defence Procurement, Vice-Adm. Sir Robert
Walmsley, KCB
Deputy Chief of Defence Procurement (Operations), and Master-
General of the Ordnance, Lt.-Gen. Sir Robert Hayman-
Joyce, KCB, CBE
Deputy Chief of Defence Procurement (Support) (SCS), J. F.
Howe, CB, OBE

BUSINESS UNITS

Principal Directors of Contracts (SCS), P. A. Gerard (Navy); A.
V. Carey (Ordnance); J. A. Harford (Air)
Director-General, Commercial (SCS), A. T. Phipps
Director-General (Resources) (SCS), S. Webb
Director-General, Technical Services, and President of the
Ordnance Board, Air Vice-Marshal P. J. O'Reilly
Chief, Strategic Systems Executive, and Director-General,
Submarines (SCS), G. N. Beaven
Director-General, Surface Ships, and Controller of the Navy,
Rear-Adm. P. Spencer
Director-General, Land Systems, Maj.-Gen. D. J. M. Jenkins,
CBE
Director-General, Command Information Systems (SCS), A. W.
McClelland
Director-General, Air Systems 1, and Controller, Aircraft, Air
Vice-Marshal P. C. Norriss, CB, AFC
Director-General, Air Systems 2 (SCS), I. Fauset
Director-General, Weapons and Electronic Systems (SCS), J.
Allen
Head of Defence Export Services (SCS), C. B. G. Masefield
Asst Under-Secretary (Export Policy and Finance) (SCS), Dr A.
M. Fox
Military Deputy to Head of DES, Rear-Adm. J. F. T. G. Salt,
CB (retd)
Director-General, Saudi Armed Forces Projects, Air Vice-
Marshal C. R. Spink, CBE
Director-General, Marketing (SCS), D. J. Bowen

DEFENCE AGENCIES

ARMED FORCES PERSONNEL ADMINSTRATION AGENCY,
Building 182, RAF Innsworth, Gloucester GL3 1HW. Tel:
01452-712612 ext. 7347. Chief Executive, Air Cdre C. G.
Winsland, OBE

ARMY BASE REPAIR ORGANIZATION, Monxton Road,
Andover, Hants SP11 8HT. Tel: 01264-383295. Chief
Executive, J. R. Drew, CBE
ARMY BASE STORAGE AND DISTRIBUTION AGENCY,
Monxton Road, Andover, Hants SP11 8HT. Tel: 01264-
383332. Chief Executive, Brig. P. D. Foxton
ARMY PERSONNEL CENTRE, Kentigern House, 65 Brown
Street, Glasgow G2 8EX. Tel: 0141-248 7890. Chief
Executive, Maj.-Gen. D. L. Burden, CB, CBE
ARMY TECHNICAL SUPPORT AGENCY, Room 60/1, HQ
QMG, Monxton Road, Andover, Hants SP11 8HT. Tel:
01264-383161. Chief Executive, Brig. A. D. Ball, CBE
ARMY TRAINING AND RECRUITING AGENCY, Trenchard
Lines, Upavon, Pewsey, Wilts SN9 6BE. Tel: 01980-
615024. Chief Executive, Maj.-Gen. C. L. Elliott, MBE
DEFENCE ANALYTICAL SERVICES AGENCY,
Northumberland House, Northumberland Avenue,
London WC2N 5BP. Tel: 0171-218 0729. Chief Executive,
P. Altobell
DEFENCE ANIMAL CENTRE, Welby Lane, Melton
Mowbray, Leics LE13 0SL. Tel: 01664-411811, ext. 8628.
Chief Executive, Col. Julia Kneale, MBE
DEFENCE BILLS AGENCY, Room 410, Mersey House,
Drury Lane, Liverpool L2 7PX. Tel: 0151-242 2234.
Chief Executive, I. S. Elrick
DEFENCE CLOTHING AND TEXTILES AGENCY,
Skimmingdish Lane, Caversfield, Oxon OX6 9TS. Tel:
01869-875501. Chief Executive, Brig. M. J. Roycroft
DEFENCE CODIFICATION AGENCY, Kentigern House, 65
Brown Street, Glasgow G2 8EX. Tel: 0141-224 2066.
Chief Executive, K. A. Bradshaw
DEFENCE COMMUNICATION SERVICES AGENCY,
Building 111, Basil Hill Barracks, Park Lane, Corsham,
Wilts SN13 9NR. Tel: 01225-814886. Chief Executive, Maj-
Gen. A. J. Raper, CBE
DEFENCE DENTAL AGENCY, RAF Halton, Aylesbury,
Bucks HP22 5PG. Tel: 01296-623535, ext. 6851. Chief
Executive, Air Vice-Marshal I. G. McIntyre, QHDS
DEFENCE ESTATE ORGANIZATION, St George's House,
Blakemore Drive, Sutton Coldfield, W. Midlands B95
7RL. Tel: 0121-311 2140. Chief Executive, I. Andrews, CBE
DEFENCE EVALUATION AND RESEARCH AGENCY, Ively
Road, Farnborough, Hants GU14 0LX. Tel: 01252-
392000. Chief Executive, J. A. R. Chisholm
DEFENCE INTELLIGENCE AND SECURITY CENTRE,
Chicksands, Shefford, Beds SG17 5PR. Tel: 01462-
752125. Chief Executive, Brig. C. G. Holtom
DEFENCE MEDICAL TRAINING ORGANIZATION, Brunel
House, 42 The Hard, Portsmouth PO1 3DS. Tel: 01705-
822341. Chief Executive, Maj.-Gen. C. G. Callow, OBE,
QHP
DEFENCE POSTAL AND COURIER SERVICE AGENCY,
Inglis Barracks, Mill Hill, London NW7 1PX. Tel: 0181-
818 6417. Director and Chief Executive, Brig. T. M. Brown,
OBE
DEFENCE SECONDARY CARE AGENCY, Room 564, St
Giles Court, 1–13 St Giles High Street, London WC2H
8LD. Tel: 0171-305 6190. Chief Executive, Maj.-Gen. C.
G. Callow, OBE, QHP
DEFENCE TRANSPORT AND MOVEMENTS EXECUTIVE,
Monxton Road, Andover, Hants SP11 8HT. Tel: 01264-
382537. Chief Executive, Brig. R. E. Ratazzi, CBE
DEFENCE VETTING AGENCY, Room 4/54, Metropole
Building, Northumberland Avenue, London WC2N 5BL.
Tel: 0171-807 0435. Chief Executive, M. P. B. G. Wilson
DISPOSAL SALES AGENCY, 7th Floor, 6 Hercules Road,
London SE1 7DJ. Tel: 0171-261 8853. Chief Executive, M.
Westgate
JOINT AIR RECONNAISSANCE INTELLIGENCE CENTRE,
RAF Brampton, Huntingdon, Cambs PE18 8QL. Tel:
01480-52151. Chief Executive, Gp Capt S. J. Lloyd

LOGISTICS INFORMATION SYSTEMS AGENCY, Monxton Road, Andover, Hants SP11 8HT. Tel: 01264-382025. *Chief Executive*, Brig. P. A. Flanagan
MEDICAL SUPPLIES AGENCY, Drummond Barracks, Ludgershall, Andover, Hants SP11 9RU. Tel: 01980-608606. *Chief Executive*, B. Nimick
METEOROLOGICAL OFFICE, London Road, Bracknell, Berks RG12 2SZ. Tel: 01344-420242. *Chief Executive*, P. D. Ewins, CB, FEng.
MILITARY SURVEY, Elmwood Avenue, Feltham, Middx TW13 7AH. Tel: 0181-818 2181. *Chief Executive*, Brig. P. R. Wildman, OBE
MINSTRY OF DEFENCE POLICE, Wethersfield, Braintree, Essex CM7 4AZ. Tel: 01371-854000. *Chief Executive*, Chief Constable W. E. E. Boreham, OBE
NAVAL AIRCRAFT REPAIR ORGANIZATION, Fareham Road, Gosport, Hants PO13 0AA. Tel: 01705-544910. *Chief Executive*, S. R. Hill
NAVAL BASES AND SUPPLY AGENCY, Room 8, C Block, Ensleigh, Bath BA1 5AB. Tel: 01225-467707. *Chief Executive*, Rear-Adm. J. A. Trewby
NAVAL MANNING AGENCY, Victory Building, HM Naval Base, Portsmouth PO1 3LS. Tel: 01705-727340. *Chief Executive*, Rear-Adm. F. M. Malbon (until Jan. 1999)
NAVAL RECRUITING AND TRAINING AGENCY, Victory Building, HM Naval Base, Portsmouth PO1 3LS. Tel: 01705-727602. *Chief Executive*, Rear-Adm. J. Chadwick
PAY AND PERSONNEL AGENCY, Warminster Road, Bath BA1 5AA. Tel: 01225-828105. *Chief Executive*, M. A. Rowe
RAF LOGISTICS SUPPORT SERVICES, H105, RAF Wyton, PO Box 70, Huntingdon, Cambs PE17 2PY. Tel: 01480-52451, ext. 6604. *Chief Executive*, Air Cdre I. Sloss
RAF MAINTENANCE GROUP AGENCY, RAF Brampton, Huntingdon, Cambs PE18 8QL. Tel: 01480-52151, ext. 6302. *Chief Executive*, Air Cdre K. J. M. Proctor
RAF PERSONNEL MANAGEMENT AGENCY, RAF Innsworth, Gloucester GL3 1EZ. Tel: 01452-712612, ext. 7810. *Chief Executive*, Air Vice-Marshal I. M. Stewart, AFC
RAF SIGNALS ENGINEERING ESTABLISHMENT, RAF Henlow, Beds SG16 6DN. Tel: 01462-851515, ext. 7625. *Chief Executive*, Air Cdre G. Jones, MBE
SERVICE CHILDREN'S EDUCATION, HQ SCE, Building 5, Wegberg Military Complex, BFPO 40. Tel: 00-49 2161-908 2295. *Chief Executive*, D. G. Wadsworth
SHIPS SUPPORT AGENCY, B Block, Foxhill, Bath BA1 5AB. Tel: 01225-883935. *Chief Executive*, J. Coles
SPECIALIST PROCUREMENT SERVICES, MOD Abbey Wood #185, Bristol BS34 8JH. Tel: 0117-913 2721. *Chief Executive*, N. J. Bennett
TRAINING GROUP DEFENCE AGENCY, RAF Innsworth, Gloucester GL3 1EZ. Tel: 01452-712612, ext. 5344. *Chief Executive*, Air Vice-Marshal A. J. Stables, CBE
UNITED KINGDOM HYDROGRAPHIC OFFICE, Admiralty Way, Taunton, Somerset TA1 2DN. Tel: 01823-337900. *Chief Executive, and Hydrographer of the Royal Navy*, Rear-Adm. J. P. Clarke, CB, LVO, MBE

The Royal Navy
LORD HIGH ADMIRAL OF THE UNITED KINGDOM
HM THE QUEEN

ADMIRALS OF THE FLEET
HRH The Prince Philip, Duke of Edinburgh, KG, KT, OM, GBE, AC, QSO, PC, *apptd* 1953
The Lord Hill-Norton, GCB, *apptd* 1971
Sir Michael Pollock, GCB, LVO, DSC, *apptd* 1974
Sir Edward Ashmore, GCB, DSC, *apptd* 1977
The Lord Lewin, KG, GCB, LVO, DSC, apptd 1979

Sir Henry Leach, GCB, *apptd* 1982
Sir Julian Oswald, GCB, *apptd* 1993
Sir Benjamin Bathurst, GCB, *apptd* 1995

ADMIRALS
Boyce, Sir Michael, KCB, OBE, ADC (*Chief of the Naval Staff and First Sea Lord*)
Abbott, Sir Peter, KCB (*Vice-Chief of the Defence Staff*)
Brigstocke, Sir John, KCB, ADC (*C.-in-C. Naval Home Command and Second Sea Lord*)
Essenhigh, N. R. (*C.-in-C. Fleet, C.-in-C. Eastern Atlantic Area and Commander Allied Forces North-Western Europe*)

VICE-ADMIRALS
Dunt, Sir John, KCB (*Chief of Fleet Support*)
Garnett, Sir Ian, KCB (*Chief of Joint Operations*)
Haddacks, P. K. (*UK Military Rep. at NATO HQ*)
Blackham, J. J. (*Deputy Commander Fleet* until Jan. 1999)
Blackburn, D. A. J., LVO (*Chief of Staff to Commander, Allied Naval Forces Southern Europe*)
West, A. W. J., DSC
McAnally, J. H. S., LVO (*Commandant, Royal College of Defence Studies*)
Malbon, F. M. (*Deputy Commander Fleet*) (from Jan. 1999)

REAR-ADMIRALS
Trewby, J. A. (*Chief Executive, Naval Bases and Supply Agency, and Chief Naval Engineering Officer*)
Clarke, J. P., CB, LVO, MBE (*Hydrographer of the Navy and Chief Executive, UK Hydrographic Office*)
Franklin, P. M., MVO (*Flag Officer Surface Flotilla*)
Perowne, J. F., OBE (*Dep. SACLANT*)
Lees, R. B. (*Defence Services Secretary*)
Spencer, P. (*Director-General, Surface Ships, and Controller of the Navy*)
Malbon, F. M. (*Naval Secretary and Chief Executive, Naval Manning Agency*) (until Jan. 1999)
Phillips, R. T. R., CB (*Asst CDS Operational Requirements (Sea Systems)*)
Ross, A. B., CBE (*Asst Director Operations Divn International Military Staff*)
Perowne, B. B. (*Director-General, Fleet Support (Operations and Plans)*)
Forbes, I. A. (*Commander, UK Task Group/Commander, Anti-Submarine Warfare Strike Force*)
Gough, A. B. (*Asst CDS (Policy and Requirements) to Supreme Allied Commander Europe*)
Paine, M. P. W. H., QHS, FRCS (*Director-General, Naval Medical Services*)
Band, J. (*Asst Chief of Naval Staff*)
Lippiett, R. J., MBE (*Flag Officer Sea Training*)
Gregory, A. M., OBE (*Flag Officer Scotland, N. England and N. Ireland*)
Moore, S. (*Asst CDS (Operations)*)
Dunt, P. A. (*Director-General, Naval Personnel (Strategy and Plans) and Chief of Staff to Second Sea Lord and C.-in-C. Naval Home Command*)
Burch, J. A. (*Director-General, Aircraft (Navy)*)
Rickard, H. W. (*Senior Directing Staff (Naval), Royal College of Defence Studies*)
Stevens, R. P., OBE (*Chief of Staff (Operations), Flag Officer Submarines, COMSUBEASTLANT and COMSUBNORTHWEST*)
Henderson, I. R. (*Flag Officer Naval Aviation*)
Chadwick, J. (*Flag Officer Training and Recruiting and Chief Executive, Naval Recruiting and Training Agency*)

Enquiries regarding records of serving officers should be directed to The Naval Secretary, Room 161, Victory Building, HM Naval Base, Portsmouth, Hants PO1 3LS.

HM FLEET *as at 1 April 1998*

SUBMARINES

Trident	Vanguard, Victorious, Vigilant
Fleet	Sceptre, Sovereign, Spartan, Splendid, Superb, Talent, Tireless, Torbay, Trafalgar, Trenchant, Triumph, Turbulent

ANTI-SUBMARINE

WARFARE CARRIERS	Ark Royal, Illustrious, Invincible
ASSAULT SHIPS	Fearless, Intrepid

LANDING PLATFORM

HELICOPTER	Ocean

DESTROYERS

Type 42	Birmingham, Cardiff, Edinburgh, Exeter, Glasgow, Gloucester, Liverpool, Manchester, Newcastle, Nottingham, Southampton, York

FRIGATES

Type 23	Argyll, Grafton, Iron Duke, Lancaster, Marlborough, Monmouth, Montrose, Norfolk, Northumberland, Richmond, Somerset, Sutherland, Westminster
Type 22	Beaver, Boxer, Brave, Campbeltown, Chatham, Cornwall, Coventry, Cumberland, London, Sheffield

OFFSHORE PATROL

Castle Class	Dumbarton Castle, Leeds Castle
Island Class	Alderney, Anglesey, Guernsey, Lindisfarne, Orkney, Shetland

MINEHUNTERS

Hunt Class	Atherstone, Berkeley, Bicester, Brecon, Brocklesby, Cattistock, Chiddingfold, Cottesmore, Dulverton, Hurworth, Ledbury, Middleton, Quorn
Sandown Class	Bridport, Cromer, Inverness, Penzance, Sandown, Walney

PATROL CRAFT

River Class	Arun, Blackwater, Orwell, Spey
Coastal Training Craft*	Archer, Biter, Blazer, Charger, Dasher, Example, Exploit, Explorer, Express, Puncher, Pursuer, Raider, Smiter, Tracker

Gibralter Search and Rescue Craft	Ranger, Trumpeter
ICE PATROL SHIP	Endurance
SURVEY SHIPS	Beagle, Bulldog, Gleaner, Herald, Roebuck, Scott

SOLD/DECOMMISSIONED

1997–8	Britannia, Hecla, Itchen, Loyal Chancellor, Loyal Watcher, Peacock, Plover, Starling

* Operated by the University Royal Naval Units

OTHER PARTS OF THE NAVAL SERVICE

ROYAL MARINES

The Royal Marines were formed in 1664 and are part of the Naval Service. Their primary purpose is to conduct amphibious and land warfare. The principal operational units are 3 Commando Brigade Royal Marines, an amphibious all-arms brigade trained to operate in arduous environments, which is a core element of the UK's Joint Rapid Reaction Force; Comacchio Group Royal Marines, which is responsible for the security of nuclear weapon facilities; and Special Boat Service Royal Marines, the maritime special forces. The Royal Marines also provide detachments for warships and land-based naval parties as required. The Royal Marines Band Service provides military musical support for the Naval Service. The headquarters of the Royal Marines is at Portsmouth, along with the Royal Marines School of Music, and principal bases are at Plymouth, Arbroath, Poole, Taunton and Chivenor. The Corps of Royal Marines is about 6,500 strong.

Commandant-General, Royal Marines, Maj.-Gen. R. H. G. Fulton

ROYAL MARINES RESERVE (RMR)

The Royal Marines Reserve is a commando-trained volunteer force with the principal role, when mobilized, of supporting the Royal Marines. There are RMR centres in London, Glasgow, Bristol, Liverpool and Newcastle. The current strength of the RMR is about 1,000.

Director, RMR, Lt.-Col. A. W. MacCormick

ROYAL FLEET AUXILIARY (RFA)

The Royal Fleet Auxiliary supplies ships of the fleet with fuel, food, water, spares and ammunition while at sea. Its ships are manned by merchant seamen. In April 1997 there were 22 ships in the RFA.

FLEET AIR ARM

The Fleet Air Arm was established in 1937 and operates aircraft (including helicopters) for the Royal Navy. In April 1997 there were 203 aircraft in the Fleet Air Arm.

ROYAL NAVAL RESERVE (RNR)

The Royal Naval Reserve is an integral part of the Naval Service. It comprises up to 3,500 men and women nation-wide who volunteer to train in their spare time to enable the Royal Navy to meet its operational commitments, at sea and ashore, in crisis or war. Under the Strategic Defence Review, the strength of the RNR will be increased by 350.

Director, Naval Reserves, Capt N. R. Hodgson, RN

QUEEN ALEXANDRA'S ROYAL NAVAL NURSING SERVICE

The first nursing sisters were appointed to naval hospitals in 1884 and the Queen Alexandra's Royal Naval Nursing Service (QARNNS) gained its current title in 1902. Nursing ratings were introduced in 1960 and men were integrated into the Service in 1982; both men and women serve as officers and ratings. Female medical assistants were introduced in 1987.

Patron, HRH Princess Alexandra, the Hon. Lady Ogilvy, GCVO

Matron-in-Chief, Capt. P. M. Hambling, QHNS

The Army

THE QUEEN

FIELD MARSHALS

HRH The Prince Philip, Duke of Edinburgh, KG, KT, OM, GBE, AC, QSO, PC, *apptd* 1953
The Lord Carver, GCB, CBE, DSO, MC, *apptd* 1973
Sir Roland Gibbs, GCB, CBE, DSO, MC, *apptd* 1979
The Lord Bramall, KG, GCB, OBE, MC, *apptd* 1982
Sir John Stanier, GCB, MBE, *apptd* 1985
Sir Nigel Bagnall, GCB, CVO, MC, *apptd* 1988
The Lord Vincent of Coleshill, GBE, KCB, DSO (Col. Cmdt. RA), *apptd* 1991
Sir John Chapple, GCB, CBE, *apptd* 1992
HRH The Duke of Kent, KG, GCMG, GCVO, ADC, *apptd* 1993
The Lord Inge, GCB (Col. Green Howards, Col. Cmdt. APTC), *apptd* 1994

GENERALS

Guthrie, Sir Charles, GCB, LVO, OBE, ADC (*Gen.*) (*Chief of the Defence Staff*)
Mackenzie, Sir Jeremy, GCB, OBE, ADC (*Gen.*), Col. Cmdt. AG Corps, Col. The Highlanders
Wheeler, Sir Roger, GCB, CBE, ADC (*Gen.*), Col. Cmdt. Int. Corps, Col. R. Irish (*Chief of the General Staff*)
Walker, Sir Michael, KCB, CMG, CBE, ADC (*Gen.*), Col. Cmdt. The Queen's Division, Col. Cmdt. AAC (*C.-in-C., Land*)
Harley, Sir Alexander, KBE (*Adjutant-General*)
Smith, Sir Rupert, KCB, DSO, OBE, QGM, Col. Cmdt. Parachute Regiment, Col. Cmdt. REME (*D. SACEUR*)
Cowan, Sir Samuel, KCB, CBE, Col. Cmdt. Bde of Gurkhas (*Chief of Defence Logistics*)

LIEUTENANT-GENERALS

Hayman-Joyce, Sir Robert, KCB, CBE, Col. Cmdt. RAC (*Deputy Chief of Defence Procurement (Operations), and Master-General of the Ordnance*)
Pike, Sir Hew, KCB, DSO, MBE (*GOC Northern Ireland*)
Grant, S. C., CB, Col. QLR, Col. Cmdt. King's Division, Col. Cmdt. RE (*Quartermaster-General*)
Wallace, Sir Christopher, KBE, Col. Cmdt. RGJ, Col Cmdt. LI (*Commander Permanent Joint HQ*)
Jackson, Sir Michael, KCB, CBE (*Commander ACE Rapid Reaction Corps*)
Burton, E. F. G., OBE, Col. Cmdt. RA (*Deputy CDS (Systems)*)
Deverell, J. F., OBE, Col. LI, Col. Cmdt. SASC (*Deputy Commander (Operations) SFOR*)

MAJOR-GENERALS

Burden, D. L., CB, CBE (*Military Secretary and Chief Executive, Army Personnel Centre*)
Cordingley, P. A. J., DSO (*Senior British Loan Service Officer, Oman*)
Willcocks, M. A., CB (*Asst Chief of the General Staff*)
Pigott, A. D., CBE, Col. The Queen's Gurkha Engineers, Col. Cmdt. RE (*Director-General, Development and Doctrine*)
McAfee, R. W. M., Col. Cmdt. RTR (*Commander Multinational Divn Central (Airmobile)*)
Vyvyan, C. G. C., CB, CBE, Col. Cmdt. RGJ (*Head of British Defence Staff, Washington*)
White, M. S., CB, CBE, Col. Cmdt. RLC
Jenkins, D. J. M., CBE, Col. Cmdt. REME (*Director-General, Land Systems*)
Granville-Chapman, T. J., CBE (*Commandant, Joint Services Command and Staff College*)

Drewienkiewicz, K. J., CB, Col. Cmdt. RE (*Senior Army Member, Royal College of Defence Studies*)
Oliver, R. A., OBE (*Chief of Staff to Adjutant-General*)
Sulivan, T. J., CBE (*GOC HQ 4 Divn*)
Drewry, C. F., CBE (*Asst CDS (Policy)*)
Elliott, C. L., MBE (*Director-General, Army Training and Recruiting and Chief Executive, Army Training and Recruiting Agency*)
Kiszely, J. P., MC (*Asst CDS (Programmes)*)
O'Donoghue, K., CBE (*Chief of Staff, HQ Quartermaster-General*)
Ewer, G. A., CBE (*Asst CDS (Logistics)*)
Short, W. R., QHP (*Director-General, Army Medical Services*)
Callow, C. G., OBE, QHP (*Chief Executive, Defence Medical Training Organization, and Chief Executive, Defence Secondary Care Agency*)
Denaro, A. G., CBE (*Commandant, RMAS*)
Irwin, A. S. H., CBE (*Commandant, RMCS*)
Trousdell, P. C. C., Col. The Queen's Own Gurkha Transport Regiment (*Chief of Staff, HQ Land Command*)
Besgrove, P. V. R., CBE (*Director-General, Equipment Support (Army)*)
Farrar-Hockley, C. D., MC (*GOC HQ 2 Divn*)
Searby, R. V. (*GOC HQ 5 Divn*)
Russell-Jones, P. J., OBE (*Asst CDS, Operational Requirements (Land Systems)*)
Risius, G. (*Director, Army Legal Services*)
Chambers, P. A., MBE (*Deputy Chief of Staff, HQ Land Command*)
Stokoe, J. D., Col. Cmdt R SIGNALS (*Deputy C.-in-C., Land Command, and Inspector-General, Territorial Army until March 1999*)
Reith, J. G., CBE (*Commander Allied Command Europe Mobile Force*)
Ramsay, A. I., CBE, DSO, Col. Cmdt. RHF (*Commander British Forces Cyprus*)
Webb-Carter, E. J., OBE
Pringle, A. R. D., CBE (*Chief of Staff to Chief of Joint Operations*)
Strudwick, M. J., CBE, Col. Cmdt. The Scottish Division (*GOC Scotland*)
Milne, J. (*Director Support, HQ Allied Land Forces Central Europe*)
Raper, A. J., CBE (*Chief Executive, Defence Communications Services Agency*)
Ridgway, A. P., CBE (*Chief of Staff HQ ACE Rapid Reaction Corps*)
Truluck, A. E. G., CBE (*Executive Assistant to the Chief of Staff Supreme HQ Allied Powers Europe*)
Currie, A. P. N. (*Military Assistant to the High Representative in Sarajevo*)
Lyons, A. W., CBE (*Director-General, Logistic Support (Army)*)
Watt, C. R., CBE (*GOC 1 (UK) Armd Divn*)

CONSTITUTION OF THE ARMY

The regular forces include the following arms, branches and corps. They are listed in accordance with the order of precedence within the British Army. All enquiries with regard to records of officers and soldiers should be directed to Relations with the Public, Army Personnel Office, Kentigern House, 65 Brown Street, Glasgow G2 8EX. Tel: 0141-224 3508/3509/3510.

THE ARMS

HOUSEHOLD CAVALRY – The Household Cavalry Regiment (The Life Guards and The Blues and Royals)

ROYAL ARMOURED CORPS – Cavalry Regiments: 1st The Queen's Dragoon Guards; The Royal Scots Dragoon Guards (Carabiniers and Greys); The Royal Dragoon Guards; The Queen's Royal Hussars (The Queen's Own and Royal Irish); 9th/12th Royal Lancers (Prince of Wales's); The King's Royal Hussars; The Light Dragoons; The Queen's Royal Lancers; Royal Tank Regiment, comprising two regular regiments

ARTILLERY – Royal Regiment of Artillery
ENGINEERS – Corps of Royal Engineers
SIGNALS – Royal Corps of Signals

THE INFANTRY

The Foot Guards and regiments of Infantry of the Line are grouped in divisions as follows:

GUARDS DIVISION – Grenadier, Coldstream, Scots, Irish and Welsh Guards. *Divisional Office*, HQ Infantry, Imber Road, Warminster, Wilts. *Training Centre*, Infantry Training Centre, Vimy Barracks, Catterick, N. Yorks

SCOTTISH DIVISION – The Royal Scots (The Royal Regiment); The Royal Highland Fusiliers (Princess Margaret's Own Glasgow and Ayrshire Regiment); The King's Own Scottish Borderers; The Black Watch (Royal Highland Regiment); The Highlanders (Seaforth, Gordons and Camerons); The Argyll and Sutherland Highlanders (Princess Louise's). *Divisional Office*, HQ Infantry, Imber Road, Warminster, Wilts. *Training Centre*, Infantry Training Centre, Vimy Barracks, Catterick, N. Yorks

QUEEN'S DIVISION – The Princess of Wales's Royal Regiment (Queen's and Royal Hampshire's); The Royal Regiment of Fusiliers; The Royal Anglian Regiment. *Divisional Office*, HQ Infantry, Imber Road, Warminster, Wilts. *Training Centre*, Infantry Training Centre, Vimy Barracks, Catterick, N. Yorks

KING'S DIVISION – The King's Own Royal Border Regiment; The King's Regiment; The Prince of Wales's Own Regiment of Yorkshire; The Green Howards (Alexandra, Princess of Wales's Own Yorkshire Regiment); The Queen's Lancashire Regiment; The Duke of Wellington's Regiment (West Riding). *Divisional Office*, HQ Infantry, Imber Road, Warminster, Wilts. *Training Centre*, Infantry Training Centre, Vimy Barracks, Catterick, N. Yorks

THE ROYAL IRISH REGIMENT (one general service and six home service battalions) – 27th (Inniskilling), 83rd, 87th and the Ulster Defence Regiment. *Regimental HQ and Training Centre*, St Patrick's Barracks, BFPO 808

PRINCE OF WALES'S DIVISION – The Devonshire and Dorset Regiment; The Cheshire Regiment; The Royal Welch Fusiliers; The Royal Regiment of Wales (24th/41st Foot); The Royal Gloucestershire, Berkshire and Wiltshire Regiment; The Worcestershire and Sherwood Foresters Regiment (29th/45th Foot); The Staffordshire Regiment (The Prince of Wales's). *Divisional Office*, HQ Infantry, Imber Road, Warminster, Wilts. *Training Centre*, Infantry Training Centre, Vimy Barracks, Catterick, N. Yorks

LIGHT DIVISION – The Light Infantry; The Royal Green Jackets. *Divisional Office*, HQ Infantry, Imber Road, Warminster, Wilts. *Training Centre*, Infantry Training Centre, Vimy Barracks, Catterick, N. Yorks

BRIGADE OF GURKHAS – The Royal Gurkha Rifles; The Queen's Gurkha Engineers; Queen's Gurkha Signals; The Queen's Own Gurkha Transport Regiment. *Regimental HQ and Training Centre*, Queen Elizabeth Barracks, Church Crookham, Fleet, Aldershot, Hants

THE PARACHUTE REGIMENT (three regular battalions) – *Regimental HQ*, Browning Barracks, Aldershot, Hants.

Training Centre, Infantry Training Centre, Vimy Barracks, Catterick, N. Yorks

SPECIAL AIR SERVICE REGIMENT – *Regimental HQ and Training Centre*, Stirling Lines, Hereford

ARMY AIR CORPS – *Regimental HQ and Training Centre*, Middle Wallop, Stockbridge, Hants

SERVICES/ARMS*

Royal Army Chaplains' Department – *Regimental HQ.* HQ AG, Upavon, Pewsey, Wilts. *Training Centre*, Netheravon House, Netheravon, Wilts SP 4 9NF (until end 1998); Amport House, Amport, Andover, Hants (from end 1998)

The Royal Logistic Corps – *Regimental HQ*, Blackdown Barracks, Deepcut, Camberley, Surrey. *Training Centre*, Princess Royal Barracks, Deepcut, Camberley, Surrey

Royal Army Medical Corps – *Regimental HQ*, Keogh Barracks, Ash Vale, Aldershot, Hants. *Training Centre*, Defence Medical Services Training Centre, Keogh Barracks, Ash Vale, Aldershot, Hants

Corps of Royal Electrical and Mechanical Engineers – *Regimental HQ and Training Centre*, Hazebrouck Barracks, Isaac Newton Road, Arborfield, Reading, Berks

Adjutant-General's Corps – *Corps HQ and Training Centre*, Worthy Down, Winchester, Hants

Royal Army Veterinary Corps – *Regimental HQ*, Keogh Barracks, Ash Vale, Aldershot, Hants. *Training Centre*, Defence Animal Centre, Welby Lane Camp, Melton Mowbray, Leics

Small Arms School Corps – *Corps HQ and Training Centre*, School of Infantry, Imber Road, Warminster, Wilts

Royal Army Dental Corps – *Regimental HQ*, Keogh Barracks, Ash Vale, Aldershot, Hants. *Training Centre*, Defence Dental Agency Training Establishment, Evelyn Wood Road, Aldershot, Hants

*Intelligence Corps – *Corps HQ and Training Centre*, Chicksands, Shefford, Beds

Army Physical Training Corps – *Regimental HQ and Depot*, Queen's Avenue, Aldershot, Hants

General Service Corps

Queen Alexandra's Royal Army Nursing Corps – *Regimental HQ*, Keogh Barracks, Ash Vale, Aldershot, Hants. *Training Centre*, Health Studies Division, Royal Defence Medical College, Vulcan Block, HMS Dolphin, Gosport, Hants

Corps of Army Music – *Corps HQ and Training Centre*, Army School of Music, Kneller Hall, Kneller Road, Twickenham, Middx

ARMY EQUIPMENT HOLDINGS *as at July 1998*

Tanks	483
Armoured combat vehicles or ACV lookalikes	6,000
Artillery pieces	371
Landing craft	
Large	2
Medium	6
Assorted personnel landing craft	many
Helicopters	222

THE TERRITORIAL ARMY (TA)

The Territorial Army is designed to be a General Reserve to the Army. It exists to reinforce the regular Army as and when required, with individuals, sub-units or units either in the UK or overseas, and to provide the framework and basis for regeneration and reconstitution in times of national emergency. The TA also provides an essential link between the military and civilian communities. Its

peacetime establishment is currently 59,000, but is to be cut to 40,000 under the Strategic Defence Review.
Inspector-General, Maj.-Gen. J. D. Stokoe (until March 1998)

QUEEN ALEXANDRA'S ROYAL ARMY NURSING CORPS

The Queen Alexandra's Royal Army Nursing Corps (QARANC) was founded in 1902 as Queen Alexandra's Imperial Military Nursing Service (QAIMNS) and gained its present title in 1949. The QARANC has trained nurses for the register since 1950 and also trains and employs health care assistants. Qualified Registered General Nurses are also recruited. Since 1992 men have been eligible to join the QARANC. Members of the Corps serve in military hospitals in the UK and abroad and in MOD hospital units in the UK.
Colonel-in-Chief, HRH The Princess Margaret, Countess of Snowdon, GCVO, CI
Matron-in-Chief (Army) and Director, Army Nursing Services, Brig. J. Arigho, QHNS

The Royal Air Force

THE QUEEN

MARSHALS OF THE ROYAL AIR FORCE
HRH The Prince Philip, Duke of Edinburgh, KG, KT, OM, GBE, AC, QSO, PC, *apptd* 1953
Sir John Grandy, GCB, GCVO, KBE, DSO, *apptd* 1971
Sir Denis Spotswood, GCB, CBE, DSO, DFC, *apptd* 1974
Sir Michael Beetham, GCB, CBE, DFC, AFC, *apptd* 1982
Sir Keith Williamson, GCB, AFC, *apptd* 1985
The Lord Craig of Radley, GCB, OBE, *apptd* 1988

AIR CHIEF MARSHALS
Johns, Sir Richard, GCB, CBE, LVO, ADC (*Chief of the Air Staff*)
Allison, Sir John, KCB, CBE, ADC (*Air Officer Commanding-in-Chief, HQ Strike Command, and Commander Allied Air Forces NW Europe*)
Cheshire, Sir John, KBE, CB (*C.-in-C. Allied Forces NW Europe*)

AIR MARSHALS
Squire, Sir Peter, KCB, DFC, AFC (*Deputy CDS (Programmes and Personnel)*)
Bagnall, Sir Anthony, KCB, OBE (*Air Member for Personnel and Air Officer C.-in-C., HQ Personnel and Training Command*)
Baird, J. A., QHP (*Surgeon-General*)
Day, J. R., OBE (*Deputy CDS (Commitments)*)
Terry, Sir Colin, KBE, CB (*Air Officer C.-in-C., HQ Logistics Command, Air Member for Logistics and Chief Engineer (RAF)*)
Coville, C. C. C., CB (*Deputy C.-in-C. Allied Forces Central Europe*)
Jenner, T. I., CB (*Chief of Staff and Deputy C.-in-C., HQ Strike Command*)

AIR VICE-MARSHALS
Norriss, P. C., CB, AFC (*Director-General, Air Systems 1, and Controller, Aircraft*)
Feesey, J. D. L., AFC (*Deputy Commander ICAOC 4, Messtetten*)
Goodall, R. H., CBE, AFC
Stables, A. J., CBE (*Chief Executive, Training Group Defence Agency*)

French, J. C., CBE (*Director-General, Intelligence and Geographical Resources*)
McCandless, B. C., CBE (*Air Officer Communications Information Systems and Support Services*)
Elder, R. D., CBE (*Director, Airspace Policy, Joint Air Navigation Services Council*)
Spink, C. R., CBE (*Director-General, Saudi Armed Forces Projects*)
Thompson, J. H. (*AOC No. 1 Group*)
O'Reilly, P. J. (*Director-General, Technical Services (Procurement Executive), and President of the Ordnance Board*)
Stewart, I. M., AFC (*Air Secretary and Chief Executive, RAF Personnel Management Agency*)
Weeden, J. (*Director, Legal Services (RAF)*)
Pledger, M. D., OBE, AFC (*Chief of Staff, HQ Logistics Command (Air Officer Commanding Directly Administered Units)*)
Stirrup, G. E., AFC (*Asst Chief of Air Staff*)
Wright, R. A., AFC (*Chief of Staff, HQ Personnel and Training Command*)
McIntyre, I. G., QHDS (*Chief Executive, Defence Dental Agency*)
Sharples, C. J., QHP (*Director-General, Medical Services (RAF)*)
Filbey, K. D., CBE (*Senior Directing Staff (Air), Royal College of Defence Studies*)
Sturley, P. O., MBE (*Senior Air Staff Officer, HQ Strike Command, and AOC No. 38 Group*)
Brackenbury, I., OBE (*Chief of Staff to Chief of Defence Logistics*)
Henderson, P. W., MBE (*Director-General, Support Management, HQ Logistics Command*)
Burridge, B. K., CBE (*AOC No. 11/18 Group*)
Nicholl, S. M., CBE, AFC (*Asst CDS Operational Requirements (Air Systems)*)
Niven, D. M., CBE (*Leader, Joint Helicopter Command Study Team*)
Scott, P. J. (*Air Officer Logistics and Communications Information Systems, HQ Strike Command*)
Burton, A. J. (*Air Officer Administration, HQ Strike Command*)
Rimmer, T. W., OBE (*Commandant, RAF College, Cranwell*)

CONSTITUTION OF THE ROYAL AIR FORCE

The RAF consists of three commands: Strike Command, Personnel and Training Command and Logistics Command. Strike Command is responsible for all the RAF's front-line forces. Its roles include strike/attack, air defence, reconnaissance, maritime patrol, strategic air transport, air-to-air refuelling, search and rescue, and aeromedical facilities. Personnel and Training Command is responsible for personnel administration and training in the RAF. Logistics Command is responsible for all logistics, engineering and materiel support.
Enquiries regarding records of serving officers should be directed to the RAF Personnel Management Agency (*see* Defence Agencies, above).

RAF EQUIPMENT *as at 1 July 1998*

AIRCRAFT

Tornado ADV	107
Tornado	IDS 142
Harrier	70
Jaguar	54
Canberra	7
Nimrod	28
VC10	24
Tristar	9
Hercules	55
BAe 125	6
BAe 146	3
Sentry	7
Hawk	98
Bulldog	115
Domenie	10
Islander	2
Jetstream	11
Tucano	73

HELICOPTERS

Chinook	34
Puma	41
Sea King	25
Wessex	15
Gazelle	1

ROYAL AUXILIARY AIR FORCE (RAUXAF)

Formed in 1924, the Auxiliary Air Force received the prefix 'Royal' in 1947 in recognition of its war record. The RAuxAF amalgamated with the Royal Air Force Volunteer Reserve in April 1997. The RAuxAF supports the RAF in many roles, including maritime air operations, air and ground defence of airfields, air movements, aeromedical evacuation, intelligence and public relations. In August 1998 there were 1,732 reservists; under the Strategic Defence Review, an additional 270 reserve posts will be created.

Air Commodore-in-Chief, HM The Queen
Controller of Reserve Forces (RAF), Air Cdre C. Davison, MBE

PRINCESS MARY'S ROYAL AIR FORCE NURSING SERVICE

The Princess Mary's Royal Air Force Nursing Service (PMRAFNS) offers commissions to Registered General Nurses (RGN) with a minimum of two years experience after obtaining RGN and normally with a second qualification. RGNs with no additional experience or qualification are recruited as non-commissioned officers in the grade of Staff Nurse.

Air Chief Commandant, HRH Princess Alexandra, the Hon. Lady Ogilvy, GCVO
Matron-in-Chief, Gp Capt R. H. Williams, QHNS

SERVICE SALARIES

The following rates of pay apply from 1 December 1998. Annual salaries are derived from daily rates in whole pence and rounded to the nearest £.

The pay rates shown are for Army personnel. The rates apply also to personnel of equivalent rank and pay band in the other services (*see* page 394 for table of relative ranks).

OFFICERS' SALARIES

MAIN SCALE

Rank	Daily	Annual
Second Lieutenant	£41.58	£15,177
Lieutenant		
On appointment	54.98	20,068
After 1 year in the rank	56.42	20,593
After 2 years in the rank	57.86	21,119
After 3 years in the rank	59.30	21,645
After 4 years in the rank	60.74	22,170
Captain		
On appointment	70.09	25,583
After 1 year in the rank	71.99	26,276
After 2 years in the rank	73.89	26,970
After 3 years in the rank	75.79	27,663
After 4 years in the rank	77.69	28,357
After 5 years in the rank	79.59	29,050
After 6 years in the rank	81.49	29,744
Major		
On appointment	88.88	32,441
After 1 year in the rank	91.08	33,244
After 2 years in the rank	93.28	34,047
After 3 years in the rank	95.48	34,850
After 4 years in the rank	97.68	35,653
After 5 years in the rank	99.88	36,456
After 6 years in the rank	102.08	37,259
After 7 years in the rank	104.28	38,062
After 8 years in the rank	106.48	38,865
Special List Lieutenant-Colonel	122.93	44,869
Lieutenant-Colonel		
On appointment with less than 19 years' service	125.39	45,767
After 2 years in the rank or with 19 years' service	128.69	46,972

Rank	Daily	Annual
Lieutenant-Colonel *contd*		
After 4 years in the rank or with 21 years' service	£131.99	£48,176
After 6 years in the rank or with 23 years' service	135.29	49,381
After 8 years in the rank or with 25 years' service	138.59	50,585
Colonel		
On appointment	145.74	53,195
After 2 years in the rank	149.58	54,597
After 4 years in the rank	153.42	55,998
After 6 years in the rank	157.26	57,400
After 8 years in the rank	161.10	58,802
Brigadier	178.88	65,291
Major-General		
Range 1	190.35	69,478
Range 2	194.56	71,014
Range 3	200.24	73,088
Lieutenant-General		
Range 4	216.93	79,179
Range 5	230.88	84,271
General		
Range 6	290.68	106,098
Range 7	304.28	111,062
Range 8	368.64	134,554

Field Marshal – appointments to this rank will not usually be made in peacetime. The salary for existing holders of the rank is equivalent to the salary of a range 8 General

---

SALARIES OF OFFICERS COMMISSIONED FROM THE RANKS (LIEUTENANTS AND CAPTAINS ONLY)

YEARS OF COMMISSIONED SERVICE	YEARS OF NON-COMMISSIONED SERVICE FROM AGE 18					
	Less than 12 years		12 years but less than 15 years		15 years or more	
	Daily	Annual	Daily	Annual	Daily	Annual
On commissioning	£77.32	£28,222	£81.32	£29,682	£85.30	£31,135
After 1 year's service	79.32	28,952	83.31	30,408	86.62	31,616
After 2 years' service	81.32	29,682	85.30	31,135	87.91	32,087
After 3 years' service	83.31	30,408	86.62	31,616	89.19	32,554
After 4 years' service	85.30	31,135	87.91	32,087	90.48	33,025
After 5 years' service	86.62	31,616	89.19	32,554	91.77	33,496
After 6 years' service	87.91	32,087	90.48	33,025	93.05	33,963
After 8 years' service	89.19	32,554	91.77	33,496	94.34	34,434
After 10 years' service	90.48	33,025	93.05	33,963	94.34	34,434
After 12 years' service	91.77	33,496	94.34	34,434	94.34	34,434
After 14 years' service	93.05	33,963	94.34	34,434	94.34	34,434
After 16 years' service	94.34	34,434	94.34	34,434	94.34	34,434

SOLDIERS' SALARIES

The pay structure below officer level is divided into pay bands. Jobs at each rank are allocated to bands according to their score in the job evaluation system. Length of service is from age 18.

Scale A: committed to serve for less than 6 years, or those with less than 9 years' service who are serving on Open Engagement

Scale B: committed to serve for 6 years but less than 9 years

Scale C: committed to serve for 9 years or more, or those with more than 9 years' service who are serving on Open Engagement

Daily rates of pay effective from 1 December 1998 are:

RANK	SCALE A		
	Band 1	Band 2	Band 3
Private			
Class 4	£26.10	£ —	£ —
Class 3	29.37	34.09	39.33
Class 2	32.83	37.59	42.83
Class 1	35.70	40.45	45.68
Lance Corporal			
Class 3	35.70	40.45	45.68
Class 2	38.00	42.75	48.40
Class 1	40.88	45.63	51.27
Corporal			
Class 2	43.72	48.45	54.10
Class 1	46.94	51.65	57.29

	Band 4	Band 5	Band 6	Band 7
Sergeant	£51.62	£56.75	£62.35	£ —
Staff Sergeant	54.58	59.70	65.33	72.10
Warrant Officer				
Class 2	58.36	63.50	70.41	77.33
Class 1	62.23	67.36	74.37	81.27

	SCALE B		
	Band 1	Band 2	Band 3
Private			
Class 4	£26.40	£ —	£ —
Class 3	29.67	34.39	39.63
Class 2	33.13	37.89	43.13
Class 1	36.00	40.75	45.98

SCALE B			
	Band 1	Band 2	Band 3
Lance Corporal			
Class 3	£36.00	£40.75	£45.98
Class 2	38.30	43.05	48.70
Class 1	41.18	45.93	51.57
Corporal			
Class 2	44.02	48.75	54.40
Class 1	47.24	51.95	57.59

	Band 4	Band 5	Band 6	Band 7
Sergeant	£51.92	£57.05	£62.65	£ —
Staff Sergeant	54.88	60.00	65.63	72.40
Warrant Officer				
Class 2	58.66	63.80	70.71	77.63
Class 1	62.53	67.66	74.67	81.57

SCALE C			
	Band 1	Band 2	Band 3
Private			
Class 4	£26.85	£ —	£ —
Class 3	30.12	34.84	40.08
Class 2	33.58	38.34	43.58
Class 1	36.45	41.20	46.43
Lance Corporal			
Class 3	36.45	41.20	46.43
Class 2	38.75	43.50	49.15
Class 1	41.63	46.38	52.02
Corporal			
Class 2	44.47	49.20	54.85
Class 1	47.69	52.40	58.04

	Band 4	Band 5	Band 6	Band 7
Sergeant	£52.37	£57.50	£63.10	£ —
Staff Sergeant	55.33	60.45	66.08	72.85
Warrant Officer				
Class 2	59.11	64.25	71.16	78.08
Class 1	62.98	68.11	75.12	82.02

RELATIVE RANK – ARMED FORCES

	Royal Navy		Army		Royal Air Force
1	Admiral of the Fleet	1	Field Marshal	1	Marshal of the RAF
2	Admiral (Adm.)	2	General (Gen.)	2	Air Chief Marshal
3	Vice-Admiral (Vice-Adm.)	3	Lieutenant-General (Lt.-Gen.)	3	Air Marshal
4	Rear-Admiral (Rear-Adm.)	4	Major-General (Maj.-Gen.)	4	Air Vice-Marshal
5	Commodore (Cdre)	5	Brigadier (Brig.)	5	Air Commodore (Air Cdre)
6	Captain (Capt.)	6	Colonel (Col.)	6	Group Captain (Gp Capt)
7	Commander (Cdr.)	7	Lieutenant-Colonel (Lt.-Col.)	7	Wing Commander (Wg Cdr.)
8	Lieutenant-Commander (Lt.-Cdr.)	8	Major (Maj.)	8	Squadron Leader (Sqn. Ldr.)
9	Lieutenant (Lt.)	9	Captain (Capt.)	9	Flight Lieutenant (Flt. Lt.)
10	Sub-Lieutenant (Sub-Lt.)	10	Lieutenant (Lt.)	10	Flying Officer (FO)
11	Acting Sub-Lieutenant (Acting Sub-Lt.)	11	Second Lieutenant (2nd Lt.)	11	Pilot Officer (PO)

SERVICE RETIRED PAY ON COMPULSORY RETIREMENT

Those who leave the services having served at least five years, but not long enough to qualify for the appropriate immediate pension, now qualify for a preserved pension and terminal grant, both of which are payable at age 60. The tax-free resettlement grants shown below are payable on release to those who qualify for a preserved pension and who have completed nine years service from age 21 (officers) or 12 years from age 18 (other ranks).

The annual rates for army personnel are given. The rates apply also to personnel of equivalent rank in the other services, including the nursing services.

OFFICERS

Applicable to officers who give full pay service on the active list on or after 30 November 1998. Senior officers (*) can elect to receive a pension calculated as a percentage of their pensionable earnings.

Capt. and below	Major	Lt.-Col.	Colonel	Brigadier	Major-General*	Lieutenant-General*	General*
16 £ 8,477	£10,161	£13,387	£ —	£ —	£ —	£ —	£ —
17 8,871	10,644	14,006	—	—	—	—	—
18 9,264	11,126	14,626	17,000	—	—	—	—
19 9,658	11,609	15,245	17,720	—	—	—	—
20 10,051	12,092	15,864	18,440	—	—	—	—
21 10,445	12,575	16,483	19,160	—	—	—	—
22 10,839	13,057	17,103	19,880	22,961	—	—	—
23 11,232	13,540	17,722	20,600	23,686	—	—	—
24 11,626	14,023	18,341	21,320	24,412	26,652	—	—
25 12,019	14,505	18,961	22,039	25,137	27,445	—	—
26 12,413	14,988	19,580	22,759	25,862	28,238	—	—
27 12,807	15,471	20,199	23,479	26,588	29,031	33,280	—
28 13,200	15,954	20,818	24,199	27,313	29,824	34,189	—
29 13,594	16,436	21,438	24,919	28,039	30,617	35,098	—
30 13,988	16,919	22,057	25,639	28,764	31,410	36,007	47,836
31 14,381	17,402	22,676	26,359	29,490	32,203	36,916	49,043
32 14,775	17,885	23,295	27,079	30,215	32,996	37,825	50,250
33 15,168	18,367	23,915	27,799	30,941	33,789	38,734	51,457
34 15,562	18,850	24,534	28,519	31,666	34,572	39,637	52,661

Field Marshal – active list half pay at the rate of £67,277 a year

WARRANT OFFICERS, NCOs AND PRIVATES

Applicable to soldiers who give full pay service on or after 30 November 1998

No. of years reckonable service	Below Corporal	Corporal	Sergeant	Staff Sergeant	Warrant Officer Class II	Warrant Officer Class I
22	£4,931	£6,264	£ 6,938	£ 7,897	£ 8,164	£ 9,025
23	5,103	6,483	7,180	8,173	8,453	9,349
24	5,275	6,701	7,422	8,448	8,743	9,674
25	5,447	6,920	7,664	8,724	9,032	9,998
26	5,620	7,138	7,907	9,000	9,321	10,323
27	5,792	7,357	8,149	9,275	9,610	10,647
28	5,964	7,576	8,391	9,551	9,900	10,971
29	6,136	7,794	8,633	9,827	10,189	11,296
30	6,308	8,013	8,875	10,102	10,478	11,620
31	6,480	8,231	9,117	10,378	10,767	11,945
32	6,652	8,450	9,359	10,654	11,057	12,269
33	6,824	8,669	9,601	10,929	11,346	12,593
34	6,997	8,887	9,844	11,205	11,635	12,918
35	7,169	9,106	10,086	11,481	11,924	13,242
36	7,341	9,324	10,328	11,756	12,214	13,567
37	7,513	9,543	10,570	12,032	12,503	13,891

RESETTLEMENT GRANTS

Terminal grants are in each case three times the rate of retired pay or pension. There are special rates of retired pay for certain other ranks not shown above. Lower rates are payable in cases of voluntary retirement.

A gratuity of £2,880 is payable for officers with short service commissions for each year completed. Resettlement grants are: officers £9,915; non-commissioned ranks £6,526.

Religion in the UK

There are two established, i.e. state, churches in the United Kingdom: the Church of England and the Church of Scotland. There are no established churches in Wales or Northern Ireland, though the Church in Wales, the Scottish Episcopal Church and the Church of Ireland are members of the Anglican Communion.

About 65 per cent of the population of the UK (38.1 million people) would call itself broadly Christian (in the Trinitarian sense), with 45 per cent (26.1 million) identifying with Anglican churches, 10 per cent (5.7 million) with the Roman Catholic Church, 4 per cent (2.6 million) with Presbyterian Churches, 2 per cent (1.3 million) with Methodist Churches and 4 per cent (2.6 million) with other Christian churches; but only about 8.7 per cent of the population of Great Britain (3.98 million people) regularly attends a Christian church. Church attendance in Northern Ireland is estimated at 30–35 per cent of the population.

About 2 per cent of the population (1.3 million people) is affiliated to non-Trinitarian churches, e.g. Jehovah's Witnesses, the Church of Jesus Christ of Latter-Day Saints (Mormons), the Church of Christ, Scientist and the Unitarian churches.

A further 5 per cent of the population (3.25 million people) are adherents of other faiths, including Hinduism, Islam, Judaism and Sikhism.

About 28 per cent of the population is non-religious.

ADHERENTS TO RELIGIONS IN UK *(millions)*

	1975	1985	1995
Christian (Trinitarian)	40.2	39.1	38.1
Non-Trinitarian	0.7	1.0	1.3
Hindu	0.3	0.4	0.4
Jew	0.4	0.3	0.3
Muslim	0.4	0.9	1.2
Sikh	0.2	0.3	0.6
Other	0.1	0.3	0.3
Total	42.3	42.3	42.2

PERCENTAGE OF UK POPULATION ADHERING TO RELIGIONS

	1975	1985	1995
Christian (Trinitarian)	72	69	65
Non-Trinitarian	1	2	2
Non-Christian religions	3	3	5
All religions	76	74	72

Source: Christian Research/Paternoster Publishing – *UK Christian Handbook Religious Trends No. 1 1998–9*; figures in text are for 1995

INTER-CHURCH AND INTER-FAITH CO-OPERATION

The main umbrella body for the Christian churches in the UK is the Council of Churches for Britain and Ireland (formerly the British Council of Churches). There are also ecumenical bodies in each of the constituent countries of the UK: Churches Together in England, Action of Churches Together in Scotland, CYTUN (Churches Together in Wales), and the Irish Council of Churches. The Free Churches' Council comprises most of the Free Churches in England and Wales, and the Evangelical Alliance represents evangelical Christians.

The Inter Faith Network for the United Kingdom promotes co-operation between faiths, and the Council of Christians and Jews works to improve relations between the two religions. The Council of Churches for Britain and Ireland also has a Commission on Inter Faith Relations.

ACTION OF CHURCHES TOGETHER IN SCOTLAND, Scottish Churches House, Kirk Street, Dunblane,

Perthshire FK15 0AJ. Tel: 01786-825844. *General Secretary,* Revd M. Craig

CHURCHES TOGETHER IN ENGLAND, Inter-Church House, 35–41 Lower Marsh, London SE1 7RL. Tel: 0171-620 4444. *Administration Officer,* Ms J. Lampard

COUNCIL OF CHRISTIANS AND JEWS, Drayton House, 30 Gordon Street, London WC1H 0AN. Tel: 0171-388 3322. *Executive Director,* P. Mendel

COUNCIL OF CHURCHES FOR BRITAIN AND IRELAND, Inter-Church House, 35–41 Lower Marsh, London SE1 7RL. Tel: 0171-620 4444. *General Secretary,* Revd J. Reardon

CYTUN (CHURCHES TOGETHER IN WALES) - Tŷ John Penri, 11 St Helen's Road, Swansea SA1 4AL. Tel: 01792-460876. *General Secretary,* Revd N. A. Davies

EVANGELICAL ALLIANCE, Whitefield House, 186 Kennington Park Road, London SE11 4BT. Tel: 0171-207 2100. *General Director,* Revd J. Edwards

FREE CHURCHES' COUNCIL, 27 Tavistock Square, London WC1H 9HH. Tel: 0171-387 8413. *General Secretary,* Revd G. H. Roper

INTER FAITH NETWORK FOR THE UNITED KINGDOM, 5–7 Tavistock Place, London WC1H 9SN. Tel: 0171-388 0008. *Director,* B. Pearce

IRISH COUNCIL OF CHURCHES, Inter-Church Centre, 48 Elmwood Avenue, Belfast BT9 6AZ. Tel: 01232-663145. *General Secretary,* Dr R. D. Stevens

Christianity

In the first millennium of the Christian era the faith was slowly formulated. Between AD 325 and 787 there were seven Oecumenical Councils at which bishops from the entire Christian world assembled to resolve various doctrinal disputes which had arisen. The estrangement between East and West began after Constantine moved the centre of the Roman Empire from Rome to Constantinople, and it gained momentum after the temporal administration was divided. Linguistic and cultural differences between Greek East and Latin West served to encourage separate ecclesiastical developments which became pronounced in the tenth and early 11th centuries.

The administration of the church was divided between five ancient patriarchates: Rome and all the West, Constantinople (the imperial city – the 'New Rome'), Jerusalem and all Palestine, Antioch and all the East, and Alexandria and all Africa. Of these, only Rome was in the Latin West and after the Great Schism in 1054, Rome developed a structure of authority centralized on one source, the Papacy, while the Orthodox East maintained the style of localized administration.

Papal authority over the doctrine and jurisdiction of the Church in western Europe was unrivalled after the split with the Eastern Orthodox Church until the Protestant Reformation in the 16th century.

CHRISTIANITY IN BRITAIN

A Church of England already existed when Pope Gregory sent Augustine to evangelize the English in AD 596. Conflicts between Church and State during the Middle Ages culminated in the Act of Supremacy in 1534. This repudiated papal supremacy and declared Henry VIII to be the supreme head of the Church in England. Since 1559 the English monarch has been termed the Supreme Governor of the Church of England.

In 1560 the jurisdiction of the Roman Catholic Church in Scotland was abolished and the first assembly of the

Church of Scotland ratified the Confession of Faith, drawn up by a committee including John Knox. In 1592 Parliament passed an Act guaranteeing the liberties of the Church and its presbyterian government. James VI (James I of England) and later Stuart monarchs attempted to restore episcopacy, but a presbyterian church was finally restored in 1690 and secured by the Act of Settlement (1690) and the Act of Union (1707).

PORVOO DECLARATION

The Porvoo Declaration was drawn up by representatives of the British and Irish Anglican churches and the Nordic and Baltic Lutheran churches and was approved by the General Synod of the Church of England in July 1995. Churches that approve the Declaration regard baptized members of each other's churches as members of their own, and allow free interchange of episcopally ordained ministers within the rules of each church.

For Christian churches in the UK, *see* pages 400–22

Non-Christian Religions

BUDDHISM

Buddhism originated in northern India, in the teachings of Siddharta Gautama, who was born near Kapilavastu about 560 BC. After a long spiritual quest he experienced enlightenment beneath a tree at the place now known as Bodhgaya, and began missionary work.

Fundamental to Buddhism is the concept that there is no such thing as a permanent soul or self; when someone dies, consciousness is the only one of the elements of which they were composed which is lost. All the other elements regroup in a new body and carry with them the consequences of the conduct of the earlier life (known as the law of *karma*). This cycle of death and rebirth is broken only when the state of *nirvana* has been reached. Buddhism steers a middle path between belief in personal immortality and belief in death as the final end.

The Four Noble Truths of Buddhism (*dukkha*, suffering; *tanha*, a thirst or desire for continued existence which causes dukkha; *nirvana*, the final liberation from desire and ignorance; and *ariya*, the path to nirvana) are all held to be universal and to sum up the *dhamma* or true nature of life. Necessary qualities to promote spiritual development are *sila* (morality), *samadhi* (meditation) and *panna* (wisdom).

There are two main schools of Buddhism: *Theravada* Buddhism, the earliest extant school, which is more traditional, and *Mahayana* Buddhism, which began to develop about 100 years after the Buddha's death and is more liberal; it teaches that all people may attain Buddhahood. Important schools which have developed within Mahayana Buddhism are *Zen* Buddhism, *Nichiren* Buddhism and Pure Land Buddhism or *Amidism*. There are also distinctive Tibetan forms of Buddhism. Buddhism began to establish itself in the West in the early 20th century.

The scripture of Theravada Buddhism is the *Pali Canon*, which dates from the first century BC. Mahayana Buddhism uses a Sanskrit version of the Pali Canon but also has many other works of scripture.

There is no set time for Buddhist worship, which may take place in a temple or in the home. Worship centres around *paritta* (chanting), acts of devotion centering on the image of the Buddha, and, where possible, offerings to a relic of the Buddha. Buddhist festivals vary according to local traditions and within Theravada and Mahayana Buddhism. For religious purposes Buddhists use solar and lunar calendars, the New Year being celebrated in April. Other festivals mark events in the life of the Buddha.

There is no supreme governing authority in Buddhism. In the United Kingdom communities representing all schools of Buddhism have developed and operate independently. The Buddhist Society was established in 1924; it runs courses and lectures, and publishes books about Buddhism. It represents no one school of Buddhism.

There are estimated to be at least 300 million Buddhists world-wide, and more than 500 groups and centres, an estimated 25,000 adherents and up to 20 temples or monasteries in the UK.

THE BUDDHIST SOCIETY, 58 Eccleston Square, London SW1V 1PH. Tel: 0171-834 5858. *General Secretary*, R. C. Maddox

HINDUISM

Hinduism has no historical founder but had become highly developed in India by about 1200 BC. Its adherents originally called themselves Aryans; Muslim invaders first called the Aryans 'Hindus' (derived from 'Sindhu', the name of the river Indus) in the eighth century.

Hinduism's evolution has been complex and it embraces many different religious beliefs, mythologies and practices. Most Hindus hold that *satya* (truthfulness), *ahimsa* (non-violence), honesty, physical labour and tolerance of other faiths are essential for good living. They believe in one supreme spirit (*Brahman*), and in the transmigration of *atman* (the soul). Most Hindus accept the doctrine of *karma* (consequences of actions), the concept of *samsara* (successive lives) and the possibility of all atmans achieving *moksha* (liberation from samsara) through *jnana* (knowledge), *yoga* (meditation), *karma* (work or action) and *bhakti* (devotion).

Most Hindus offer worship to *murtis* (images or statues) representing different aspects of Brahman, and follow their *dharma* (religious and social duty) according to the traditions of their *varna* (social class), *ashrama* (stage in life), *jati* (caste) and *kula* (family).

Hinduism's sacred texts are divided into *shruti* ('heard' or divinely inspired), including the *Vedas*; or *smriti* ('remembered' tradition), including the *Ramayana*, the *Mahabharata*, the *Puranas* (ancient myths), and the sacred law books. Most Hindus recognize the authority of the *Vedas*, the oldest holy books, and accept the philosophical teachings of the *Upanishads*, the *Vedanta Sutras* and the *Bhagavad-Gita*.

Brahman is formless, limitless and all-pervading, and is represented in worship by murtis which may be male or female and in the form of a human, animal or bird. Brahma, Vishnu and Shiva are the most important gods worshipped by Hindus; their respective consorts are Saraswati, Lakshmi and Durga or Parvati, also known as Shakti. There are held to have been ten *avatars* (incarnations) of Vishnu, of whom the most important are Rama and Krishna. Other popular gods are Ganesha, Hanuman and Subrahmanyam. All gods are seen as aspects of the supreme God, not as competing deities.

Orthodox Hindus revere all gods and goddesses equally, but there are many sects, including the Hare-Krishna movement (ISKCon), the Arya Samaj, the Swami Narayan Hindu mission and the Satya Sai-Baba movement, in which worship is concentrated on one deity to the exclusion of others. In some sects a human *guru* (spiritual teacher) is revered more than the deity, while in other sects the guru is seen as the source of spiritual guidance.

Hinduism does not have a centrally-trained and ordained priesthood. The pronouncements of the *shankaracharyas* (heads of monasteries) of Shringeri, Puri,

Dwarka and Badrinath are heeded by the orthodox but may be ignored by the various sects.

The commonest form of worship is a *puja*, in which offerings of red and yellow powders, rice grains, water, flowers, food, fruit, incense and light are made to the *murti* (image) of a deity. Puja may be done either in a home shrine or a *mandir* (temple). Many British Hindus celebrate life-cycle rituals with Sanskrit mantras for naming a baby, the sacred thread (an initiation ceremony), marriage and cremation. For details of the Hindu calendar, main festivals etc, *see* pages 84–5.

The largest communities of Hindus in Britain are in Leicester, London, Birmingham and Bradford, and developed as a result of immigration from India, eastern Africa and Sri Lanka.

There are an estimated 800 million Hindus world-wide; there are about 360,000 adherents and over 150 temples in the UK.

ARYA PRATINIDHI SABHA (UK) AND ARYA SAMAJ LONDON, 69A Argyle Road, London WI3 OLY. Tel: 0181-991 1732. *President*, Prof. S. N. Bharadwaj

BHARATIYA VIDYA BHAVAN, Institute of Indian Art and Culture, 4A Castletown Road, London WI4 9HQ. Tel: 0171-381 4608. *Executive Director*, Dr M. N. Nandakumara

INTERNATIONAL SOCIETY FOR KRISHNA CONSCIOUSNESS (ISKCon), Bhaktivedanta Manor, Dharam Marg, Hilfield Lane, Aldenham, Watford, Herts WD2 8EZ. Tel: 01923-857244. *Governing Body Commissioner*, P. Latai

NATIONAL COUNCIL OF HINDU TEMPLES (UK), Bhaktivedanta Manor, Dharam Marg, Hilfield Lane, Aldenham, Watford WD2 8EZ. Tel: 01923-856269. *Secretary*, V. Aery

SWAMINARAYAN HINDU MISSION, 105–119 Brentfield Road, London NWI0 8JB. Tel: 0181-965 2651. *Head of Mission*, Pujya Atmaswarup Swami

VISHWA HINDU PARISHAD (UK), 48 Wharfedale Gardens, Thornton Heath, Surrey CR7 6LB. Tel: 0181-684 9716. *General Secretary*, K. Ruparelia

ISLAM

Islam (which means 'peace arising from submission to the will of Allah' in Arabic) is a monotheistic religion which was taught in Arabia by the Prophet Muhammad, who was born in Mecca (Makkah) in AD 570. Islam spread to Egypt, North Africa, Spain and the borders of China in the century following the prophet's death, and is now the predominant religion in Indonesia, the Near and Middle East, northern and parts of western Africa, Pakistan, Bangladesh, Malaysia and some of the former Soviet republics. There are also large Muslim communities in other countries.

For Muslims (adherents of Islam), God (*Allah*) is one and holds absolute power. His commands were revealed to mankind through the prophets, who include Abraham, Moses and Jesus, but his message was gradually corrupted until revealed finally and in perfect form to Muhammad through the angel *Jibril* (Gabriel) over a period of 23 years. This last, incorruptible message has been recorded in the *Qur'an* (Koran), which contains 114 divisions called *surahs*, each made up of *ayahs*, and is held to be the essence of all previous scriptures. The *Ahadith* are the records of the Prophet Muhammad's deeds and sayings (the *Sunnah*) as recounted by his immediate followers. A culture and a system of law and theology gradually developed to form a distinctive Islamic civilization. Islam makes no distinction between sacred and worldly affairs and provides rules for

every aspect of human life. The *Shari'ah* is the sacred law of Islam based upon prescriptions derived from the Qur'an and the Sunnah of the Prophet.

The 'five pillars of Islam' are *shahadah* (a declaration of faith in the oneness and supremacy of Allah and the messengership of Muhammad); *salat* (formal prayer, to be performed five times a day facing the *Ka'bah* (sacred house) in the holy city of Mecca); *zakat* (welfare due); *sawm* (fasting during the month of Ramadan); and *hajj* (pilgrimage to Mecca); some Muslims would add *jihad* (striving for the cause of good and resistance to evil).

Two main groups developed among Muslims. *Sunni* Muslims accept the legitimacy of Muhammad's first four *caliphs* (successors as head of the Muslim community) and of the authority of the Muslim community as a whole. About 90 per cent of Muslims are Sunni Muslims. *Shi'ites* recognize only Muhammad's son-in-law Ali as his rightful successor and the *Imams* (descendants of Ali, not to be confused with *imams* (prayer leaders or religious teachers)) as the principal legitimate religious authority. The largest group within Shi'ism is *Twelver Shi'ism*, which has been the official school of law and theology in Iran since the 16th century; other subsects include the *Ismailis* and the *Druze*, the latter being an offshoot of the Ismailis and differing considerably from the main body of Muslims.

There is no organized priesthood, but learned men such as *ulama*, *imams* and *ayatollahs* are accorded great respect. The *Sufis* are the mystics of Islam. Mosques are centres for worship and teaching and also for social and welfare activities. For details of the Muslim calendar and festivals, *see* page 86.

Islam was first known in western Europe in the eighth century AD when 800 years of Muslim rule began in Spain. Later, Islam spread to eastern Europe. More recently, Muslims came to Europe from Africa, the Middle East and Asia in the late 19th century. Both the Sunni and Shi'ah traditions are represented in Britain, but the majority of Muslims in Britain adhere to Sunni Islam.

The largest communities are in London, Liverpool, Manchester, Birmingham, Bradford, Cardiff, Edinburgh and Glasgow. There is no central organization, but the Islamic Cultural Centre, which is the London Central Mosque, and the Imams and Mosques Council are influential bodies; there are many other Muslim organizations in Britain.

There are about 1,000 million Muslims world-wide, with more than one million adherents and about 900 mosques in Britain.

IMAMS AND MOSQUES COUNCIL, 20–22 Creffield Road, London W5 3RP. Tel: 0181-992 6636. *Director of the Council and Principal of the Muslim College*, Dr M. A. Z. Badawi

ISLAMIC CULTURAL CENTRE, 146 Park Road, London NW8 7RG. Tel: 0171-724 3363. *Director*, H. Al-Majed

MUSLIM WORLD LEAGUE, 46 Goodge Street, London WIP IFJ. Tel: 0171-636 7568. *Director*, U. A. Baidulmaal

UNION OF MUSLIM ORGANIZATIONS OF THE UK AND EIRE, 109 Campden Hill Road, London W8 7TL. Tel: 0171-229 0538. *Geneal Secretary*, Dr S. A. Pasha

JUDAISM

Judaism is the oldest monotheistic faith. The primary authority of Judaism is the Hebrew Bible or *Tanakh*, which records how the descendants of Abraham were led by Moses out of their slavery in Egypt to Mount Sinai where God's law (*Torah*) was revealed to them as the chosen people. The *Talmud*, which consists of commentaries on the *Mishnah* (the first text of rabbinical Judaism), is also held to be authoritative, and may be divided into two main categories: the *halakah* (dealing with legal and ritual matters) and the *Aggadah* (dealing with theological and ethical matters not directly concerned with the regulation of conduct). The *Midrash* comprises rabbinic writings containing biblical interpretations in the spirit of the Aggadah. The *halakah* has become a source of division; Orthodox Jews regard Jewish law as derived from God and therefore unalterable; Reform and Liberal Jews seek to interpret it in the light of contemporary considerations; and Conservative Jews aim to maintain most of the traditional rituals but to allow changes in accordance with tradition. Reconstructionist Judaism, a 20th-century movement, regards Judaism as a culture rather than a theological system and accepts all forms of Jewish practice.

The family is the basic unit of Jewish ritual, with the synagogue playing an important role as the centre for public worship and religious study. A synagogue is led by a group of laymen who are elected to office. The Rabbi is primarily a teacher and spiritual guide. The Sabbath is the central religious observance. For details of the Jewish calendar, fasts and festivals, *see* page 85. Most British Jews are descendants of either the *Ashkenazim* of central and eastern Europe or the *Sephardim* of Spain and Portugal.

The Chief Rabbi of the United Hebrew Congregations of the Commonwealth is appointed by a Chief Rabbinate Conference, and is the rabbinical authority of the Orthodox sector of the Ashkenazi Jewish community. His authority is not recognized by the Reform Synagogues of Great Britain (the largest progressive group), the Union of Liberal and Progressive Synagogues, the Union of Orthodox Hebrew Congregations, the Federation of Synagogues, the Sephardi community, or the Assembly of Masorti Synagogues. He is, however, generally recognized both outside the Jewish community and within it as the public religious representative of the totality of British Jewry.

The *Beth Din* (Court of Judgment) is the rabbinic court. The *Dayanim* (Assessors) adjudicate in disputes or on matters of Jewish law and tradition; they also oversee dietary law administration. The Chief Rabbi is President of the *Beth Din* of the United Synagogue.

The Board of Deputies of British Jews, established in 1760, is the representative body of British Jewry. The basis of representation is mainly synagogal, but communal organizations are also represented. It watches over the interests of British Jewry, acts as a voice of the community and seeks to counter anti-Jewish discrimination and anti-Semitic activities.

There are over 12.5 million Jews world-wide; in Great Britain and Ireland there are an estimated 285,000 adherents and about 365 synagogues. Of these, 191 congregations and about 150 rabbis and ministers are under the jurisdiction of the Chief Rabbi; 99 orthodox congregations have a more independent status; and 75 congregations do not recognize the authority of the Chief Rabbi.

CHIEF RABBINATE, 735 High Road, London NI2 OUS. Tel: 0181-343 6301. *Chief Rabbi*, Dr Jonathan Sacks; *Executive Director*, Mrs S. Weinberg
BETH DIN (COURT OF THE CHIEF RABBI), 735 High Road, London NI2 OUS. Tel: 0181-343 6280. *Registrar*, vacant; *Dayanim*, Rabbi C. Ehrentreu; Rabbi I. Binstock; Rabbi C. D. Kaplin; Rabbi M. Gelley
BOARD OF DEPUTIES OF BRITISH JEWS, Commonwealth House, 1–11 New Oxford Street, London WCIA INF. Tel: 0171-543 5400. *President*, E. Tabachnik, QC; *Director-General*, N. A. Nagler
ASSEMBLY OF MASORTI SYNAGOGUES, 1097 Finchley Road, London NWII OPU. Tel: 0181-201 8772. *Director*, H. Freedman
FEDERATION OF SYNAGOGUES, 65 Watford Way, London NW4 3AQ. Tel: 0181-202 2263. *Administrator*, G. Coleman
REFORM SYNAGOGUES OF GREAT BRITAIN, The Sternberg Centre for Judaism, 80 East End Road,

London N3 2SY. Tel: 0181-349 4731. *Chief Executive*, Rabbi T. Bayfield
SPANISH AND PORTUGUESE JEWS' CONGREGATION, 2 Ashworth Road, London W9 IJY. Tel: 0171-289 2573. *Chief Administrator and Secretary*, H. Miller
UNION OF LIBERAL AND PROGRESSIVE SYNAGOGUES, The Montagu Centre, 21 Maple Street, London WIP 6DS. Tel: 0171-580 1663. *Director*, Rabbi Dr C. H. Middleburgh
UNION OF ORTHODOX HEBREW CONGREGATIONS, 140 Stamford Hill, London NI6 6QT. Tel: 0181-802 6226.
UNITED SYNAGOGUE HEAD OFFICE, 735 High Road, London NI2 OUS. Tel: 0181-343 8989. *Chief Executive*, vacant

SIKHISM

The Sikh religion dates from the birth of Guru Nanak in the Punjab in 1469. 'Guru' means teacher but in Sikh tradition has come to represent the divine presence of God giving inner spiritual guidance. Nanak's role as the human vessel of the divine guru was passed on to nine successors, the last of whom (Guru Gobind Singh) died in 1708. The immortal guru is now held to reside in the sacred scripture, *Guru Granth Sahib*, and so to be present in all Sikh gatherings.

Guru Nanak taught that there is one God and that different religions are like different roads leading to the same destination. He condemned religious conflict, ritualism and caste prejudices. The fifth Guru, Guru Arjan Dev, largely compiled the Sikh Holy Book, a collection of hymns (*gurbani*) known as the *Adi Granth*. It includes the writings of the first five Gurus and the ninth Guru, and selected writings of Hindu and Muslim saints whose views are in accord with the Gurus' teachings. Guru Arjan Dev also built the Golden Temple at Amritsar, the centre of Sikhism. The tenth Guru, Guru Gobind Singh, passed on the guruship to the sacred scripture, Guru Granth Sahib. He also founded the *Khalsa*, an order intended to fight against tyranny and injustice. Male initiates to the order added 'Singh' to their given names and women added 'Kaur'. Guru Gobind Singh also made five symbols obligatory: *kaccha* (a special undergarment), *kara* (a steel bangle), *kirpan* (a small sword), *kesh* (long unshorn hair, and consequently the wearing of a turban), and *kangha* (a comb). These practices are still compulsory for those Sikhs who are initiated into the Khalsa (the *Amritdharis*). Those who do not seek initiation are known as *Sehajdharis*.

There are no professional priests in Sikhism; anyone with a reasonable proficiency in the Punjabi language can conduct a service. Worship can be offered individually or communally, and in a private house or a *gurdwara* (temple). Sikhs are forbidden to eat meat prepared by ritual slaughter; they are also asked to abstain from smoking, alcohol and other intoxicants. Such abstention is compulsory for the *Amritdharis*. For details of the Sikh calendar and main celebrations, *see* page 86.

There are about 20 million Sikhs world-wide and about 400,000 adherents and 250 gurdwaras in Great Britain. The largest communities are in London, Bradford, Leeds, Huddersfield, Birmingham, Coventry and Wolverhampton. Every gurdwara manages its own affairs and there is no central body in the UK. The Sikh Missionary Society provides an information service.

SIKH MISSIONARY SOCIETY UK, 10 Featherstone Road, Southall, Middx UB2 5AA. Tel: 0181-574 1902. *Hon. General Secretary*, M. Singh
WORLD SIKH FOUNDATION, 33 Wargrave Road, South Harrow, Middx HA2 8LL. Tel: 0181-864 9228. *Secretary*, Mrs H. Bharara

The Churches

For changes notified after 31 August, *see* Stop-press

The Church of England

The Church of England is the established (i.e. state) church in England and the mother church of the Anglican Communion. The Thirty-Nine Articles, a set of doctrinal statements which, together with the Book of Common Prayer of 1662 and the Ordinal, define the position of the Church of England, were adopted in their final form in 1571 and include the emphasis on personal faith and the authority of the scriptures common to the Protestant Reformation throughout Europe.

THE ANGLICAN COMMUNION

The Anglican Communion consists of 38 independent provincial or national Christian churches throughout the world, many of which are in Commonwealth countries and originated from missionary activity by the Church of England. There is no single world authority linking the Communion, but all recognize the leadership of the Archbishop of Canterbury and have strong ecclesiastical and historical links with the Church of England. Every ten years all the bishops in the Communion meet at the Lambeth Conference, convened by the Archbishop of Canterbury. The Conference has no policy-making authority but is an important forum for the discussion of issues of common concern. The Anglican Consultative Council was set up in 1968 to function between conferences and the meeting of the Primates every two years.

There are about 70 million Anglicans and 800 archbishops and bishops world-wide.

STRUCTURE

The Church of England is divided into the two provinces of Canterbury and York, each under an archbishop. The two provinces are subdivided into 44 dioceses. Decisions on matters concerning the Church of England are made by the General Synod, established in 1970. It also discusses and expresses opinion on any other matter of religious or public interest. The General Synod has 574 members in total, divided between three houses: the House of Bishops, the House of Clergy and the House of Laity. It is presided over jointly by the Archbishops of Canterbury and York and normally meets twice a year. The Synod has the power, delegated by Parliament, to frame statute law (known as a Measure) on any matter concerning the Church of England. A Measure must be laid before both Houses of Parliament, who may accept or reject it but cannot amend it. Once accepted the Measure is submitted for royal assent and then has the full force of law. There are a number of committees, boards and councils answerable to the Synod, which deal with, or advise on, a wide range of matters. In addition to the General Synod, there are synods of clergy and laity at diocesan level.

Changes to the national structures of the Church of England were recommended in a report accepted by the General Synod in November 1995. The National Institutions Measure was subsequently approved by the Synod and Parliament. An Archbishops' Council has been created and will begin work in January 1999. The Council will oversee the work of all the central institutions of the Church and will report frequently to the General Synod. The Archbishops' Council comprises six appointed members – the Archbishops of Canterbury and York, the

prolocutors of the Convocations of Canterbury and York, the chairman and vice-chairman of the House of Laity – and two bishops, two clergy and two lay members each elected by their respective Houses of the General Synod.

GENERAL SYNOD OF THE CHURCH OF ENGLAND, Church House, Great Smith Street, London SW1P 3NZ. Tel: 0171-222 9011. *Secretary-General,* P. Mawer
HOUSE OF BISHOPS: *Chairman,* The Archbishop of Canterbury; *Vice-Chairman,* The Archbishop of York
HOUSE OF CLERGY: *Chairmen (alternating),* Canon J. Stanley; Canon H. Wilcox
HOUSE OF LAITY: *Chairman,* Dr Christina Baxter; *Vice-Chairman,* Dr P. Giddings

THE ORDINATION OF WOMEN

The canon making it possible for women to be ordained to the priesthood was promulged in the General Synod in February 1994 and the first 32 women priests were ordained on 12 March 1994. The Priests (Ordination of Women) Measure 1993 contains provisions safeguarding the position of bishops and parishes who are opposed to the priestly ministry of women. The General Synod agreed to the appointment of up to three 'provincial episcopal visitors' to work with those who are unable to accept the ministry of bishops ordaining women priests. The provincial episcopal visitors, who are suffragan bishops in the newly created sees of Ebbsfleet and Richborough (Province of Canterbury) and Beverley (Province of York) are allowed to carry out confirmations and ordinations in parishes opposed to women priests, as long as they have the permission of the diocesan bishop.

MEMBERSHIP

In 1996 the Church of England had an electoral roll membership of 1.3 million, of whom up to 1 million regularly attended Sunday services. There are (1997 figures) two archbishops, 107 diocesan, suffragan and (stipendiary) assistant bishops, 8,984 other male and 919 female full-time stipendiary clergy, and over 16,000 churches and places of worship. (The Diocese in Europe is not included in these figures.)

STIPENDIARY CLERGY 1997 AND ELECTORAL ROLL MEMBERSHIP 1996

	Clergy		Membership
	Male	Female	
Bath and Wells	228	23	42,700
Birmingham	177	28	19,300
Blackburn	239	10	37,400
Bradford	113	9	12,700
Bristol	135	19	19,000
Canterbury	162	12	21,000
Carlisle	153	12	24,900
Chelmsford	387	36	50,800
Chester	275	17	48,600
Chichester	341	7	58,200
Coventry	133	16	17,700
Derby	185	15	20,100
Durham	215	26	27,400
Ely	139	22	20,900
Exeter	259	9	33,900

	Clergy		Membership
	Male	Female	
Gloucester	153	15	26,300
Guildford	182	25	30,600
Hereford	103	14	18,900
Leicester	152	18	16,100
Lichfield	335	38	52,200
Lincoln	194	33	31,300
Liverpool	221	35	32,500
London	509	44	52,500
Manchester	293	31	38,000
Newcastle	149	10	17,500
Norwich	186	14	25,900
Oxford	391	56	60,600
Peterborough	145	16	19,500
Portsmouth	106	10	18,000
Ripon	140	22	19,300
Rochester	212	22	31,300
St Albans	258	40	43,100
St Edmundsbury			
and Ipswich	161	14	25,300
Salisbury	223	16	45,900
Sheffield	181	20	20,700
Sodor and Man	22	0	2,800
Southwark	333	59	45,400
Southwell	170	28	18,700
Truro	119	4	17,600
Wakefield	156	16	23,200
Winchester	234	13	42,100
Worcester	144	17	22,400
York	262	28	38,200
TOTAL	8,875	919	1,290,500

STIPENDS 1998–9

Archbishop of Canterbury	£51,020
Archbishop of York	£44,700
Bishop of London	£41,660
Other diocesan bishops	£27,660
Suffragan bishops	£22,740
Deans and provosts	£22,740
Residentiary canons	£18,600
Incumbents and clergy of similar	
status	£15,220*

*national average, provisional estimate

CANTERBURY

103RD ARCHBISHOP AND PRIMATE OF ALL ENGLAND
Most Revd and Rt. Hon. George L. Carey, PH.D., *cons.* 1987, *trans.* 1991, *apptd* 1991; Lambeth Palace, London SE1 7JU. *Signs* George Cantuar:

BISHOPS SUFFRAGAN
Dover, Rt. Revd J. Richard A. Llewellin, *cons.* 1985, *apptd* 1992; Upway, St Martin's Hill, Canterbury, Kent CT1 1PR
Maidstone, Rt. Revd Gavin H. Reid, *cons.* 1992, *apptd* 1992; Bishop's House, Pett Lane, Charing, Ashford, Kent TN27 0DL
Ebbsfleet, Rt. Revd Michael A. Houghton, *apptd* 1998 (provincial episcopal visitor); c/o Bishop of Richborough (*see* address below)
Richborough, Rt. Revd Edwin Barnes, *cons.* 1995, *apptd* 1995 (provincial episcopal visitor); 14 Hall Place Gardens, St Albans, Herts AL1 3SP

DEAN
Very Revd John Arthur Simpson, *apptd* 1986

CANONS RESIDENTIARY
P. Brett, *apptd* 1983; R. H. C. Symon, *apptd* 1994; Dr M. Chandler, *apptd* 1995; Ven. J. Pritchard, *apptd* 1996

Organist, D. Flood, FRCO, *apptd* 1988

ARCHDEACONS
Canterbury, Ven. J. Pritchard, *apptd* 1996
Maidstone, Ven. P. Evans, *apptd* 1989

Vicar-General of Province and Diocese, Chancellor S. Cameron, QC
Commissary-General, His Hon. Judge Richard Walker
Joint Registrars of the Province, F. E. Robson, OBE; B. J. T. Hanson, CBE
Diocesan Registrar and Legal Adviser, R. H. B. Sturt
Diocesan Secretary, D. Kemp, Diocesan House, Lady Wootton's Green, Canterbury CT1 1NQ. Tel: 01227-459401

YORK

96TH ARCHBISHOP AND PRIMATE OF ENGLAND
Most Revd and Rt. Hon. David M. Hope, KCVO, D.Phil., LLD, *cons.* 1985, *trans.* 1995, *apptd* 1995; Bishopthorpe, York YO23 2GE. *Signs* David Ebor:

BISHOPS SUFFRAGAN
Hull, Rt. Revd Richard M. C. Frith, *cons.* 1998, *apptd* 1998; Hullen House, Woodfield Lane, Hessle, Hull HU13 0ES
Selby, Rt. Revd Humphrey V. Taylor, *cons.* 1991, *apptd* 1991; 10 Precentor's Court, York YO1 2ES
Whitby, Rt. Revd Gordon Bates, *cons.* 1983, *apptd* 1983; 60 West Green, Stokesley, Middlesbrough TS9 5BD
Beverley, Rt. Revd John Gaisford, *cons.* 1994, *apptd* 1994 (provincial episcopal visitor); 3 North Lane, Roundhay, Leeds LS8 2QJ

DEAN
Very Revd Raymond Furnell, *apptd* 1994

CANONS RESIDENTIARY
J. Toy, PH.D., *apptd* 1983; R. Metcalfe, *apptd* 1988; P. J. Ferguson, *apptd* 1995; E. R. Norman, PH.D., DD, *apptd* 1995
Organist, P. Moore, FRCO, *apptd* 1983

ARCHDEACONS
Cleveland, Ven. C. J. Hawthorn, *apptd* 1991
East Riding, Ven. P. R. W. Harrison, *apptd* 1998
York, Ven. G. B. Austin, *apptd* 1988

Official Principal and Auditor of the Chancery Court, Sir John Owen, QC
Chancellor of the Diocese, His Hon. Judge Coningsby, QC, *apptd* 1977
Vicar-General of the Province and Official Principal of the Consistory Court, His Hon. Judge Coningsby, QC
Registrar and Legal Secretary, L. P. M. Lennox
Diocesan Secretary, C. Sheppard, Church House, Ogleforth, York YO1 7JE. Tel: 01904-611696

LONDON (Province of Canterbury)

132ND BISHOP
Rt. Revd and Rt. Hon Richard J. C. Chartres; The Old Deanery, Dean's Court, London EC4V 5AA. *Signs* Richard Londin:

AREA BISHOPS
Edmonton, Rt. Revd Brian J. Masters, *cons.* 1982, *apptd* 1984; 1 Regent's Park Terrace, London NW1 7EE
Kensington, Rt. Revd Michael Colclough, *cons.* 1996, *apptd* 1996; 19 Campden Hill Square, London W8 7JY
Stepney, Rt. Revd Dr John M. Sentamu, *cons.* 1996, *apptd* 1996; 63 Coborn Road, London E3 2DB

Willesden, Rt. Revd Graham G. Dow, *cons.* 1992, *apptd* 1992; 173 Willesden Lane, London NW6 7YN

BISHOP SUFFRAGAN
Fulham, Rt. Revd John Broadhurst, *cons.* 1996, *apptd* 1996; 26 Canonbury Park South, London N1 2FN

DEAN OF ST PAUL'S
Very Revd John H. Moses, PH.D., *apptd* 1996

CANONS RESIDENTIARY
Ven. G. Cassidy, *apptd* 1987; R. J. Halliburton, *apptd* 1990; M. J. Saward, *apptd* 1991; S. J. Oliver, *apptd* 1997
Registrar and Receiver of St Paul's, Brig. R. W. Acworth, CBE
Organist, J. Scott, FRCO, *apptd* 1990

ARCHDEACONS
Charing Cross, Ven. Dr W. Jacob, *apptd* 1996
Hackney, Ven. C. Young, *apptd* 1992
Hampstead, Ven. P. Wheatley, *apptd* 1995
London, Ven. G. Cassidy, *apptd* 1987
Middlesex, Ven. M. Colmer, *apptd* 1996
Northolt, Ven. P. Broadbent, *apptd* 1995

Chancellor, Miss S. Cameron, QC, *apptd* 1992
Registrar and Legal Secretary, P. C. E. Morris
Diocesan Secretary, C. J. A. Smith, 36 Causton Street, London SW1P 4AU. Tel: 0171-932 1100

DURHAM (Province of York)

92ND BISHOP
Rt. Revd A. Michael A. Turnbull, *cons.* 1988, *apptd* 1994; Auckland Castle, Bishop Auckland DL14 7NR. *Signs* Michael Dunelm:

BISHOP SUFFRAGAN
Jarrow, Rt. Revd Alan Smithson, *cons.* 1990, *apptd* 1990; The Old Vicarage, Hallgarth, Pittington, Durham DH6 1AB

DEAN
Very Revd John R. Arnold, *apptd* 1989

CANONS RESIDENTIARY
D. W. Brown, *apptd* 1990; T. Willmott, *apptd* 1997; M. Kitchen, *apptd* 1997; D. J. Whittington, *apptd* 1998; N. Stock, *apptd* 1998
Organist, J. B. Lancelot, FRCO, *apptd* 1985

ARCHDEACONS
Auckland, Ven. G. G. Gibson, *apptd* 1993
Durham, Ven. T. Willmott, *apptd* 1997
Sunderland, Ven. F. White, *apptd* 1997

Chancellor, His Hon. Judge Bursell, QC, *apptd* 1989
Registrar and Legal Secretary, A. N. Fairclough
Diocesan Secretary, W. Hurworth, Auckland Castle, Bishop Auckland, Co. Durham DL14 7QJ. Tel: 01388-604515

WINCHESTER (Canterbury)

96TH BISHOP
Rt. Revd Michael C. Scott-Joynt, *cons.* 1987, *trans.* 1995, *apptd* 1995; Wolvesey, Winchester SO23 9ND. *Signs* Michael Winton:

BISHOPS SUFFRAGAN
Basingstoke, Rt. Revd D. Geoffrey Rowell, *cons.* 1994, *apptd* 1994; Bishopswood End, Kingswood Rise, Four Marks, Alton, Hants GU34 5BD

Southampton, Rt. Revd Jonathan M. Gledhill, *cons.* 1996, *apptd* 1996; Ham House, The Crescent, Romsey SO51 7NG

DEAN
Very Revd Michael Till, *apptd* 1996

Dean of Jersey (A Peculiar), Very Revd John Seaford, *apptd* 1993
Dean of Guernsey (A Peculiar), Very Revd Marc Trickey, *apptd* 1995

CANONS RESIDENTIARY
A. K. Walker, *apptd* 1987; P. B. Morgan, *apptd* 1994; C. Stewart, *apptd* 1997; Ven. J. A. Guille, *apptd* 1998 (from Jan. 1999)
Organist, D. Hill, FRCO, *apptd* 1988

ARCHDEACONS
Basingstoke, Ven. J. A. Guille, *apptd* 1998 (from Jan. 1999)
Winchester, Ven. A. G. Clarkson, *apptd* 1984

Chancellor, C. Clark, *apptd* 1993
Registrar and Legal Secretary, P. M. White
Diocesan Secretary, R. Anderton, Church House, 9 The Close, Winchester, Hants SO23 9LS. Tel: 01962-844644

BATH AND WELLS (Canterbury)

76TH BISHOP
Rt. Revd James L. Thompson, *cons.* 1978, *apptd* 1991; The Palace, Wells BA5 2PD. *Signs* James Bath Wells

BISHOP SUFFRAGAN
Taunton, Rt. Revd Andrew John Radford, *cons.* Dec. 1998, *apptd* 1998; Sherford Farm House, Sherford, Taunton TA1 3RF

DEAN
Very Revd Richard Lewis, *apptd* 1990

CANONS RESIDENTIARY
P. de N. Lucas, *apptd* 1988; R. Acworth, *apptd* 1993; P. G. Walker, *apptd* 1994; M. W. Matthews, *apptd* 1997
Organist, M. Archer, *apptd* 1996

ARCHDEACONS
Bath, Ven. R. J. S. Evens, *apptd* 1996
Taunton, Ven. R. M. C. Frith, *apptd* 1992
Wells, Ven. R. Acworth, *apptd* 1993

Chancellor, T. Briden, *apptd* 1993
Registrar and Legal Secretary, T. Berry
Diocesan Secretary, N. Denison, The Old Deanery, Wells, Somerset BA5 2UG. Tel: 01749-670777

BIRMINGHAM (Canterbury)

7TH BISHOP
Rt. Revd Mark Santer, *cons.* 1981, *apptd* 1987; Bishop's Croft, Harborne, Birmingham B17 0BG. *Signs* Mark Birmingham

BISHOP SUFFRAGAN
Aston, Rt. Revd John Austin, *cons.* 1992, *apptd* 1992; Strensham House, 8 Strensham Hill, Moseley, Birmingham B13 8AG

PROVOST
Very Revd Peter A. Berry, *apptd* 1986

CANONS RESIDENTIARY
Ven. C. J. G. Barton, *apptd* 1990; Revd D. Lee, *apptd* 1996;
Revd G. O'Neill, *apptd* 1997
Organist, M. Huxley, FRCO, *apptd* 1986

ARCHDEACONS
Aston, Ven. C. J. G. Barton, *apptd* 1990
Birmingham, Ven. J. F. Duncan, *apptd* 1985
Chancellor, His Hon. Judge Aglionby, *apptd* 1970
Registrar and Legal Secretary, H. Carslake
Diocesan Secretary, J. Drennan, 175 Harborne Park Road,
Harborne, Birmingham B17 0BH. Tel: 0121-427 5141

BLACKBURN (York)

7TH BISHOP
Rt. Revd Alan D. Chesters, *cons.* 1989, *apptd* 1989; Bishop's
House, Ribchester Road, Blackburn BB1 9EF. *Signs* Alan
Blackburn

BISHOPS SUFFRAGAN
Burnley, Rt. Revd Martyn W. Jarrett, *cons.* 1994, *apptd* 1994;
Dean House, 449 Padiham Road, Burnley BB12 6TE
Lancaster, Rt. Revd Stephen Pedley, *cons.* 1998, *apptd* 1997;
The Vicarage, Shireshead, Forton, Preston PR3 0AE

PROVOST
Very Revd David Frayne, *apptd* 1992

CANONS RESIDENTIARY
D. M. Galilee, *apptd* 1995; A. D. Hindley, *apptd* 1996; P. J.
Ballard, *apptd* 1998
Organist, R. Tanner, *apptd* 1998

ARCHDEACONS
Blackburn, Ven. F. J. Marsh, *apptd* 1996
Lancaster, Ven. R. S. Ladds, *apptd* 1997

Chancellor, J. W. M. Bullimore, *apptd* 1990
Registrar and Legal Secretary, T. A. Hoyle
Diocesan Secretary, Revd M. J. Wedgeworth, Diocesan
Office, Cathedral Close, Blackburn BB1 5AA. Tel: 01254-
54421

BRADFORD (York)

8TH BISHOP
Rt. Revd David J. Smith, *cons.* 1987, *apptd* 1992; Bishopscroft,
Ashwell Road, Heaton, Bradford BD9 4AU. *Signs* David
Bradford

PROVOST
Very Revd John S. Richardson, *apptd* 1990

CANONS RESIDENTIARY
C. G. Lewis, *apptd* 1993; G. Smith, *apptd* 1996
Organist, A. Horsey, FRCO, *apptd* 1986

ARCHDEACONS
Bradford, Ven. D. H. Shreeve, *apptd* 1984
Craven, Ven. M. L. Grundy, *apptd* 1994

Chancellor, D. M. Savill, QC, *apptd* 1976
Registrar and Legal Secretary, J. G. H. Mackrell
Diocesan Secretary, M. Halliday, Cathedral Hall, Stott Hill,
Bradford BD1 4ET. Tel: 01274-725958

BRISTOL (Canterbury)

54TH BISHOP
Rt. Revd Barry Rogerson, *cons.* 1979, *apptd* 1985; Bishop's
House, Clifton Hill, Bristol BS8 1BW. *Signs* Barry Bristol

BISHOP SUFFRAGAN
Swindon, Rt. Revd Michael Doe, *cons.* 1994, *apptd* 1994;
Mark House, Field Rise, Old Town, Swindon SN1 4HP

DEAN
Very Revd Robert W. Grimley, *apptd* 1997

CANONS RESIDENTIARY
J. L. Simpson, *apptd* 1989; P. F. Johnson, *apptd* 1990; D. R.
Holt, *apptd* 1998
Organist, vacant

ARCHDEACONS
Bristol, Ven. D. J. Banfield, *apptd* 1990
Swindon, Ven. A. F. Hawker, *apptd* 1998

Chancellor, Sir David Calcutt, QC, *apptd* 1971
Registrar and Legal Secretary, T. Berry
Diocesan Secretary, Mrs L. Farrall, Diocesan Church House,
23 Great George Street, Bristol, Avon BS1 5QZ. Tel:
0117-921 4411

CARLISLE (York)

65TH BISHOP
Rt. Revd Ian Harland, *cons.* 1985, *apptd* 1989; Rose Castle,
Dalston, Carlisle CA5 7BZ. *Signs* Ian Carliol:

BISHOP SUFFRAGAN
Penrith, Rt. Revd Richard Garrard, *cons.* 1994, *apptd* 1994;
Holm Croft, Castle Road, Kendal, Cumbria LA9 7AU

DEAN
Very Revd Graeme P. Knowles, apptd 1998

CANONS RESIDENTIARY
R. A. Chapman, *apptd* 1978; Ven. D. C. Turnbull, *apptd* 1993;
D. W. V. Weston, *apptd* 1994; C. Hill, *apptd* 1996
Organist, J. Suter, FRCO, *apptd* 1991

ARCHDEACONS
Carlisle, Ven. D. C. Turnbull, *apptd* 1993
West Cumberland, Ven. A. N. Davis, *apptd* 1996
Westmorland and Furness, Ven. D. T. I. Jenkins, *apptd* 1995

Chancellor, His Hon. Judge Aglionby, *apptd* 1991
Registrar and Legal Secretary, Mrs S. Holmes
Diocesan Secretary, Canon C. Hill, Church House, West
Walls, Carlisle CA3 8UE. Tel: 01228-522573

CHELMSFORD (Canterbury)

8TH BISHOP
Rt. Revd John F. Perry, *cons.* 1989, *apptd* 1996;
Bishopscourt, Margaretting, Ingatestone CM4 0HD. *Signs*
John Chelmsford

BISHOPS SUFFRAGAN
Barking, Rt. Revd Roger F. Sainsbury, *cons.* 1991, *apptd*
1991; 110 Capel Road, Forest Gate, London E7 0JS
Bradwell, Rt. Revd Laurence Green, *cons.* 1993, *apptd* 1993;
The Vicarage, Orsett Road, Horndon-on-the-Hill,
Stanford-le-Hope, Essex SS17 8NS

Colchester, Rt. Revd Edward Holland, *cons.* 1986, *apptd* 1995; 1 Fitzwalter Road, Lexden, Colchester CO3 3SS

PROVOST
Very Revd Peter S. M. Judd, *apptd* 1997

CANONS RESIDENTIARY
T. Thompson, *apptd* 1988; B. P. Thompson, *apptd* 1988; D. Knight, *apptd* 1991

Organist, Dr G. Elliott, PH.D., FRCO, *apptd* 1981

ARCHDEACONS
Colchester, Ven. M. W. Wallace, *apptd* 1997
Harlow, Ven. P. F. Taylor, *apptd* 1996
Southend, Ven. D. Jennings, *apptd* 1992
West Ham, Ven. M. J. Fox, *apptd* 1996

Chancellor, Miss S. M. Cameron, QC, *apptd* 1970
Registrar and Legal Secretary, B. Hood
Diocesan Secretary, D.Phillips, 53 New Street, Chelmsford, Essex CM1 1AT. Tel: 01245-266731

CHESTER (York)

40TH BISHOP
Rt. Revd Peter R. Forster, PH.D., *cons.* 1996, *apptd* 1996; Bishop's House, Chester CH1 2JD. *Signs* Peter Cestr:

BISHOPS SUFFRAGAN
Birkenhead, Rt. Revd Michael L. Langrish, *cons.* 1993, *apptd* 1993; Bishop's Lodge, 67 Bidston Road, Oxton, Birkenhead L43 6TR
Stockport, Rt. Revd Geoffrey M. Turner, *cons.* 1994, *apptd* 1994; Bishop's Lodge, Back Lane, Dunham Town, Altrincham, Cheshire WA14 4SG

DEAN
Very Revd Dr Stephen S. Smalley, *apptd* 1986

CANONS RESIDENTIARY
R. M. Rees, *apptd* 1990; O. A. Conway, *apptd* 1991; Dr T. J. Dennis, *apptd* 1994; J. W. S. Newcome, *apptd* 1994

Organist and Director of Music, D. G. Poulter, FRCO, *apptd* 1997

ARCHDEACONS
Chester, Ven. C. Hewetson, *apptd* 1994
Macclesfield, Ven. R. J. Gillings, *apptd* 1994

Chancellor, D. G. P. Turner, *apptd* 1998
Registrar and Legal Secretary, A. K. McAllester
Diocesan Secretary, S. P. A. Marriott, Diocesan House, Raymond Street, Chester CH1 4PN. Tel: 01244-379222

CHICHESTER (Canterbury)

102ND BISHOP
Rt. Revd Eric W. Kemp, DD, *cons.* 1974, *apptd* 1974; The Palace, Chichester PO19 1PY. *Signs* Eric Cicestr:

BISHOPS SUFFRAGAN
Horsham, Rt. Revd Lindsay G. Urwin, *cons.* 1993, *apptd* 1993; Bishop's House, 21 Guildford Road, Horsham, W. Sussex RH12 1LU
Lewes, Rt. Revd Wallace P. Benn, *cons.* 1997, *apptd* 1997; 16A Prideaux Road, Eastbourne, E. Sussex BN21 2NB

DEAN
Very Revd John D. Treadgold, LVO, *apptd* 1989

CANONS RESIDENTIARY
R. T. Greenacre, *apptd* 1975; F. J. Hawkins, *apptd* 1981; P. G. Atkinson, *apptd* 1997

Organist, A. J. Thurlow, FRCO, *apptd* 1980

ARCHDEACONS
Chichester, Ven. M. Brotherton, *apptd* 1991
Horsham, Ven. W. C. L. Filby, *apptd* 1983
Lewes and Hastings, Ven. N. S. Reade, *apptd* 1997

Chancellor, His Hon. Judge Q. T. Edwards, QC, *apptd* 1978
Registrar and Legal Secretary, C. L. Hodgetts
Diocesan Secretary, J. Prichard, Diocesan Church House, 211 New Church Road, Hove, E. Sussex BN3 4ED. Tel: 01273-421021

COVENTRY (Canterbury)

8TH BISHOP
Rt. Revd Colin J. Bennetts; *cons.* 1994, *apptd* 1997; The Bishop's House, 23 Davenport Road, Coventry CV5 6PW. *Signs* Colin Coventry

BISHOP SUFFRAGAN
Warwick, Rt. Revd Anthony M. Priddis, *cons.* 1996, *apptd* 1996; 139 Kenilworth Road, Coventry CV4 7AF

PROVOST
Very Revd John F. Petty, *apptd* 1987

CANONS RESIDENTIARY
V. Faull, *apptd* 1994; J. C. Burch, *apptd* 1995; A. White, *apptd* 1998

Director of Music, R. Jeffcoat, *apptd* 1997

ARCHDEACONS
Coventry, Ven. H. I. L. Russell, *apptd* 1989
Warwick, Ven. M. J. J. Paget-Wilkes, *apptd* 1990

Chancellor, Sir William Gage, *apptd* 1980
Registrar and Legal Secretary, D. J. Dumbleton
Diocesan Secretary, Mrs I. Chapman, Church House, Palmerston Road, Coventry CV5 6FJ. Tel: 01203-674328

DERBY (Canterbury)

6TH BISHOP
Rt. Revd Jonathan S. Bailey, *cons.* 1992, *apptd* 1995; Derby Church House, Full Street, Derby DE1 3DR. *Signs* Jonathan Derby

BISHOP SUFFRAGAN
Repton, vacant

PROVOST
Very Revd Michael F. Perham, *apptd* 1998

CANONS RESIDENTIARY
G. A. Chesterman, *apptd* 1989; Ven. I. Gatford, *apptd* 1992; G. O. Marshall, *apptd* 1992; D. C. Truby, *apptd* 1998

Organist, P. Gould, *apptd* 1982

ARCHDEACONS
Chesterfield, Ven. D. C. Garnett, *apptd* 1996
Derby, Ven. I. Gatford, *apptd* 1992

Chancellor, J. W. M. Bullimore, *apptd* 1981
Registrar and Legal Secretary, J. S. Battie
Diocesan Secretary, R. J. Carey, Derby Church House, Full Street, Derby DE1 3DR. Tel: 01332-382233

ELY (Canterbury)

67TH BISHOP
Rt. Revd Stephen W. Sykes, *cons.* 1990, *apptd* 1990; The Bishop's House, Ely, Cambs CB7 4DW. *Signs* Stephen Ely

BISHOP SUFFRAGAN
Huntingdon, Rt. Revd John R. Flack, *cons.* 1997, *apptd* 1996; 14 Lynn Road, Ely, Cambs CB6 IDA

DEAN
Very Revd Michael Higgins, apptd 1991

CANONS RESIDENTIARY
D. J. Green, *apptd* 1980; J. Inge, *apptd* 1996
Organist, P. Trepte, FRCO, *apptd* 1991

ARCHDEACONS
Ely, Ven. J. Watson, *apptd* 1993
Huntingdon, Ven. J. Beer, *apptd* 1997
Wisbech, Ven. J. Rone, *apptd* 1995

Chancellor, W. Gage, QC
Joint Registrars, W. H. Godfrey; P. F. B. Beesley (*Legal Secretary*)
Diocesan Secretary, Dr M. Lavis, Bishop Woodford House, Barton Road, Ely, Cambs CB7 4DX. Tel: 01353-663579

EXETER (Canterbury)

69TH BISHOP
Rt. Revd G. Hewlett Thompson, *cons.* 1974, *apptd* 1985; The Palace, Exeter EXI IHY. *Signs* Hewlett Exon:

BISHOPS SUFFRAGAN
Crediton, Rt. Revd Richard S. Hawkins, *cons.* 1988, *apptd* 1996; 10 The Close, Exeter EXI IEZ
Plymouth, Rt. Revd John H. Garton, *cons.* 1996, *apptd* 1996; 31 Riverside Walk, Tamerton Foliot, Plymouth PL5 4AQ

DEAN
Very Revd Keith B. Jones, *apptd* 1996

CANONS RESIDENTIARY
A. C. Mawson, *apptd* 1979; K. C. Parry, *apptd* 1991
Organist, L. A. Nethsingha, FRCO, *apptd* 1973

ARCHDEACONS
Barnstaple, Ven. T. Lloyd, *apptd* 1989
Exeter, Ven. A. F. Tremlett, *apptd* 1994
Plymouth, Ven. R. G. Ellis, *apptd* 1982
Totnes, Preb. R. T. Gilpin, *apptd* 1996

Chancellor, Sir David Calcutt, QC, *apptd* 1971
Registrar and Legal Secretary, R. K. Wheeler
Diocesan Secretary, M. Beedell, Diocesan House, Palace Gate, Exeter, Devon EXI IHX. Tel: 01392-72686

GIBRALTAR IN EUROPE (Canterbury)

BISHOP
Rt. Revd John Hind, *cons.* 1991, *apptd* 1993; 14 Tufton Street, London SW1P 3QZ

BISHOP SUFFRAGAN
In Europe Rt. Revd Henry Scriven, *cons.* 1995, *apptd* 1994; 14 Tufton Street, London SW1P 3QZ

Dean, Cathedral Church of the Holy Trinity, Gibraltar, Very Revd W. G. Reid

Chancellor, Pro-Cathedral of St Paul, Valletta, Malta, Canon A. Woods
Chancellor, Pro-Cathedral of the Holy Trinity, Brussels, Belgium, Canon N. Walker

ARCHDEACONS
Eastern, Ven. S. J. B. Peake
North-West Europe, Ven. G. G. Allen
France, Ven. M. Draper, OBE
Gibraltar, Ven. K. Robinson
Italy, Ven. W. E. Edebohls
Scandinavia and Germany, Ven. D. Ratcliff
Switzerland, Ven. P. J. Hawker, OBE

Chancellor, Sir David Calcutt, QC
Registrar and Legal Secretary, J. G. Underwood
Diocesan Secretary, A. C. Mumford, 14 Tufton Street, London SW1P 3QZ. Tel: 0171-976 8001

GLOUCESTER (Canterbury)

39TH BISHOP
Rt. Revd David Bentley, *cons.* 1986, *apptd* 1993; Bishopscourt, Gloucester GL1 2BQ. *Signs* David Gloucestr

BISHOP SUFFRAGAN
Tewkesbury, Rt. Revd John S. Went, *cons.* 1995, *apptd* 1995; Green Acre, Hempsted, Gloucester GL2 6LG

DEAN
Very Revd Nicholas A. S. Bury, *apptd* 1997

CANONS RESIDENTIARY
R. D. M. Grey, *apptd* 1982; N. Chatfield, *apptd* 1992; N. Heavisides, *apptd* 1993; C. H. Morgan, *apptd* 1996
Organist, D. Briggs, FRCO, *apptd* 1994

ARCHDEACONS
Cheltenham, Ven. H. S. Ringrose, *apptd* 1998
Gloucester, Ven. C. J. H. Wagstaff, *apptd* 1982

Chancellor and Vicar-General, Ms D. J. Rodgers, *apptd* 1990
Registrar and Legal Secretary, C. G. Peak
Diocesan Secretary, M. Williams, Church House, College Green, Gloucester GL1 2LY. Tel: 01452-410022

GUILDFORD (Canterbury)

8TH BISHOP
Rt. Revd John W. Gladwin, *cons.* 1994, *apptd* 1994; Willow Grange, Woking Road, Guildford GU4 7QS. *Signs* John Guildford

BISHOP SUFFRAGAN
Dorking, Rt. Revd Ian Brackley, *cons.* 1996, *apptd* 1995; Dayspring, 13 Pilgrims Way, Guildford GU4 8AD

DEAN
Very Revd Alexander G. Wedderspoon, *apptd* 1987

CANONS RESIDENTIARY
J. Schofield, *apptd* 1995; Dr Maureen Palmer, *apptd* 1996
Organist, A. Millington, FRCO, *apptd* 1982

ARCHDEACONS
Dorking, Ven. M. Wilson, *apptd* 1995
Surrey, Ven. R. Reiss, *apptd* 1995

Chancellor, His Hon. Judge Goodman
Registrar and Legal Secretary, P. F. B. Beesley

Diocesan Secretary, Mrs K. Ingate, Diocesan House, Quarry Street, Guildford GU1 3XG. Tel: 01483-571826

HEREFORD (Canterbury)

103RD BISHOP
Rt. Revd John Oliver, *cons.* 1990, *apptd* 1990; The Palace, Hereford HR4 9BN. *Signs* John Hereford

BISHOP SUFFRAGAN
Ludlow, Rt. Revd Dr John Saxbee, *cons.* 1994, *apptd* 1994; Bishop's House, Halford, Craven Arms, Shropshire SY7 9BT

DEAN
Very Revd Robert A. Willis, *apptd* 1992

CANONS RESIDENTIARY
P. Iles, *apptd* 1983; J. Tiller, *apptd* 1984; J. Butterworth, *apptd* 1994

Organist, Dr R. Massey, FRCO, *apptd* 1974

ARCHDEACONS
Hereford, Ven. M. W. Hooper, *apptd* 1997
Ludlow, Rt. Revd J. C. Saxbee, *apptd* 1992

Chancellor, J. M. Henty
Joint Registrars and Legal Secretaries, V. T. Jordan; P. F. B. Beesley
Diocesan Secretary, Miss S. Green, The Palace, Hereford HR4 9BL. Tel: 01432-353863

LEICESTER (Canterbury)

BISHOP
vacant; Bishop's Lodge, 10 Springfield Road, Leicester LE2 3BD. *Signs:* — Leicester

STIPENDIARY ASSISTANT BISHOP
Rt. Revd William Down, *cons.* 1990, *apptd* 1995

PROVOST
Very Revd Derek Hole, *apptd* 1992

CANONS RESIDENTIARY
M. T. H. Banks, *apptd* 1988; M. Wilson, *apptd* 1988
Organist, J. T. Gregory, *apptd* 1994

ARCHDEACONS
Leicester, Ven. M. Edson, *apptd* 1994
Loughborough, Ven. I. Stanes, *apptd* 1992

Chancellor, N. Seed, *apptd* 1989
Registrars and Legal Secretaries, P. C. E. Morris; R. H. Bloor
Diocesan Secretary, vacant; Church House, 3–5 St Martin's East, Leicester LE1 5FX. Tel: 0116-262 7445

LICHFIELD (Canterbury)

97TH BISHOP
Rt. Revd Keith N. Sutton, *cons.* 1978, *apptd* 1984; Bishop's House, The Close, Lichfield WS13 7LG. *Signs* Keith Lichfield

BISHOP SUFFRAGAN
Shrewsbury, Rt. Revd David M. Hallatt, *cons.* 1994, *apptd* 1994; 68 London Road, Shrewsbury SY2 6PG

Stafford, Rt. Revd Christopher J. Hill, *cons.* 1996, *apptd* 1996; Ash Garth, Broughton Crescent, Barlaston, Staffs ST12 9DD
Wolverhampton, Rt. Revd Michael G. Bourke, *cons.* 1993, *apptd* 1993; 61 Richmond Road, Wolverhampton WV3 9JH

DEAN
Very Revd Tom Wright, *apptd* 1993

CANONS RESIDENTIARY
A. N. Barnard, *apptd* 1977; C. W. Taylor, *apptd* 1995; Ven. G. Frost, *apptd* 1998
Organist, A. Lumsden, *apptd* 1992

ARCHDEACONS
Lichfield, Ven. G. Frost, *apptd* 1998
Salop, Ven . J. B. Hall, *apptd* 1998
Stoke-on-Trent, Ven. A. G. C. Smith, *apptd* 1997
Walsall, Ven. A. G. Sadler, *apptd* 1997

Chancellor, His Hon. Judge Shand
Registrar and Legal Secretary, J. P. Thorneycroft
Diocesan Secretary, D. R. Taylor, St Mary's House, The Close, Lichfield, Staffs WS13 7LD. Tel: 01543-306030

LINCOLN (Canterbury)

70TH BISHOP
Rt. Revd Robert M. Hardy, *cons.* 1980, *apptd* 1987; Bishop's House, Eastgate, Lincoln LN2 1QQ. *Signs* Robert Lincoln

BISHOPS SUFFRAGAN
Grantham, Rt. Revd Alastair L. J. Redfern, *cons.* 1997, *apptd* 1997; Fairacre, 234 Barronby Road, Grantham, Lincs NG31 8NP
Grimsby, Rt. Revd David Tustin, *cons.* 1979, *apptd* 1979; Bishop's House, Church Lane, Irby-upon-Humber, Grimsby DN37 7JR

DEAN
Very Revd Alexander F. Knight, *apptd* 1998

CANONS RESIDENTIARY
B. R. Davis, *apptd* 1977; A. J. Stokes, *apptd* 1992; V. White, *apptd* 1994
Organist, C. S. Walsh, FRCO, *apptd* 1988

ARCHDEACONS
Lincoln, Ven. A. Hawes, *apptd* 1995
Lindsey, vacant
Stow, Ven. R. J. Wells, *apptd* 1989

Chancellor, His Hon. Judge Goodman, *apptd* 1971
Registrar and Legal Secretary, D. M. Wellman
Diocesan Secretary, P. Hamlyn Williams, The Old Palace, Lincoln LN2 1PU. Tel: 01522-529241

LIVERPOOL (York)

7TH BISHOP
Rt. Revd James Jones, *cons.* 1994, *apptd* 1998; Bishop's Lodge, Woolton Park, Liverpool L25 6DT. *Signs* James Liverpool

BISHOP SUFFRAGAN
Warrington, Rt. Revd John Packer, *cons.* 1996, *apptd* 1996; 34 Central Avenue, Eccleston Park, Prescot, Merseyside L34 2QP

DEAN
Very Revd Rhys D. C. Walters, OBE, *apptd* 1983

CANONS RESIDENTIARY
D. J. Hutton, *apptd* 1983; M. C. Boyling, *apptd* 1994; N. T. Vincent, *apptd* 1995
Organist, Prof. I. Tracey, *apptd* 1980

ARCHDEACONS
Liverpool, Ven. R. L. Metcalf, *apptd* 1994
Warrington, Ven. C. D. S. Woodhouse, *apptd* 1981

Chancellor, R. G. Hamilton
Registrar and Legal Secretary, R. H. Arden
Diocesan Secretary, K. Cawdron, Church House, 1 Hanover Street, Liverpool LI 3DW. Tel: 0151-709 9722

MANCHESTER (York)

10TH BISHOP
Rt. Revd Christopher J. Mayfield, *cons.* 1985, *apptd* 1993; Bishopscourt, Bury New Road, Manchester M7 4LE. *Signs* Christopher Manchester

BISHOPS SUFFRAGAN
Bolton, Rt. Revd David Bonser, *cons.* 1991, *apptd* 1991; 4 Sandfield Drive, Lostock, Bolton BL6 4DU
Hulme, Rt. Revd Colin J. F. Scott, *cons.* 1984, *apptd* 1984 (retires 31 Dec. 1998); 1 Raynham Avenue, Didsbury, Manchester M20 0BW
Middleton, Rt. Revd Stephen Venner, *cons.* 1994, *apptd* 1994; The Hollies, Manchester Road, Rochdale OL11 3QY

DEAN
Very Revd Kenneth Riley, *apptd* 1993

CANONS RESIDENTIARY
J. R. Atherton, PH.D., *apptd* 1984; A. E. Radcliffe, *apptd* 1991; P. Denby, *apptd* 1995
Organist, C. Stokes, *apptd* 1992

ARCHDEACONS
Bolton, Ven. L. M. Davies, *apptd* 1992
Manchester, vacant
Rochdale, Ven. J. M. M. Dalby, *apptd* 1991

Chancellor, J. Holden, *apptd* 1997
Registrar and Legal Secretary, M. Darlington
Diocesan Secretary, Mrs J. Park, Diocesan Church House, 90 Deansgate, Manchester M3 2GH. Tel: 0161-833 9521

NEWCASTLE (York)

11TH BISHOP
Rt. Revd J. Martin Wharton, *cons.* 1992, *apptd* 1997; Bishop's House, 29 Moor Road, Gosforth, Newcastle upon Tyne NE3 IPA. *Signs* Martin Newcastle

STIPENDIARY ASSISTANT BISHOP
Rt. Revd Kenneth Gill, *cons.* 1972, *apptd* 1980

PROVOST
Very Revd Nicholas G. Coulton, *apptd* 1990

CANONS RESIDENTIARY
R. Langley, *apptd* 1985; P. R. Strange, *apptd* 1986; Ven. P. Elliott, *apptd* 1993
Organist, T. G. Hone, FRCO, *apptd* 1987

ARCHDEACONS
Lindisfarne, Ven. M. E. Bowering, *apptd* 1987
Northumberland, Ven. P. Elliott, *apptd* 1993

Chancellor, Prof. D. McClean, *apptd* 1998

Registrar and Legal Secretary, Mrs B. J. Lowdon
Diocesan Secretary, P. Davies, Church House, Grainger Park Road, Newcastle upon Tyne NE4 8SX. Tel: 0191-273 0120

NORWICH (Canterbury)

70TH BISHOP
Rt. Revd Peter J. Nott, *cons.* 1977, *apptd* 1985; Bishop's House, Norwich NR3 ISB. *Signs* Peter Norvic:

BISHOPS SUFFRAGAN
Lynn, vacant
Thetford, Rt. Revd Hugo F. de Waal, *cons.* 1992, *apptd* 1992; Rectory Meadow, Bramerton, Norwich NR14 7DW

DEAN
Very Revd Stephen Platten, *apptd* 1995

CANONS RESIDENTIARY
J. M. Haselock, *apptd* 1998; Ven. C. J. Offer, *apptd* 1994; R. J. Hanmer, *apptd* 1994
Organist, D. Dunnett, *apptd* 1996

ARCHDEACONS
Lynn, Ven. A. C. Foottit, *apptd* 1987
Norfolk, Ven. A. M. Handley, *apptd* 1993
Norwich, Ven. C. J. Offer, *apptd* 1994

Chancellor, The Hon. Mr Justice Blofeld, *apptd* 1998
Registrar and Legal Secretary, J. W. F. Herring
Diocesan Secretary, D. Adeney, Diocesan House, 109 Dereham Road, Easton, Norwich, Norfolk NR9 5ES. Tel: 01603-880853

OXFORD (Canterbury)

41ST BISHOP
Rt. Revd Richard D. Harries, *cons.* 1987, *apptd* 1987; Diocesan Church House, North Hinksey, Oxford OX2 0NB. *Signs* Richard Oxon:

AREA BISHOPS
Buckingham, Rt. Revd Michael A. Hill *cons.* 1998, *apptd* 1998; 28 Church Street, Great Missenden, Bucks HP16 OAZ
Dorchester, Rt. Revd Anthony J. Russell, *cons.* 1988, *apptd* 1988; Holmby House, Sibford Ferris, Banbury, Oxon OX15 5RG
Reading, Rt. Revd Edward W. M. (Dominic) Walker, *cons.* 1997, *apptd* 1997; Bishop's House, Tidmarsh Lane, Tidmarsh, Reading RG8 8HA

DEAN OF CHRIST CHURCH
Very Revd John H. Drury, *apptd* 1991

CANONS RESIDENTIARY
O. M. T. O'Donovan, D.Phil., *apptd* 1982; J. M. Pierce, *apptd* 1987; J. S. K. Ward, *apptd* 1991; R. Jeffery, *apptd* 1996; Prof. J. Webster, *apptd* 1996; Prof. H. M. R. E. Mayr-Harting, *apptd* 1997; Ven. J. A. Morrison, *apptd* 1998
Organist, S. Darlington, FRCO, *apptd* 1985

ARCHDEACONS
Berkshire, Ven. N. A. Russell, *apptd* 1998
Buckingham, Ven. D. Goldie, *apptd* 1998
Oxford, Ven. J. A. Morrison, *apptd* 1998

Chancellor, P. T. S. Boydell, QC, *apptd* 1958
Registrar and Legal Secretary, Dr F. E. Robson
Diocesan Secretary, R. Pearce, Diocesan Church House, North Hinksey, Oxford OX2 0NB. Tel: 01865-244566

PETERBOROUGH (Canterbury)

37TH BISHOP
Rt. Revd Ian P. M. Cundy, *cons.* 1992, *apptd* 1996; The
    Palace, Peterborough PE1 1YA. *Signs* Ian Petriburg:

BISHOP SUFFRAGAN
Brixworth, Rt. Revd Paul E. Barber, *cons.* 1989, *apptd* 1989; 4
    The Avenue, Dallington, Northampton NN1 4RZ

DEAN
Very Revd Michael Bunker, *apptd* 1992

CANONS RESIDENTIARY
T. R. Christie, *apptd* 1980; J. Higham, *apptd* 1983; P. A.
    Spence, *apptd* 1998

Organist, C. S. Gower, FRCO, *apptd* 1977

ARCHDEACONS
Northampton, Ven. M. R. Chapman, *apptd* 1991
Oakham, Ven. B. Fernyhough, *apptd* 1977

Chancellor, T. A. C. Coningsby, QC, *apptd* 1989
Registrar and Legal Secretary, R. Hemingray
Diocesan Secretary, Revd Canon R. J. Cattle, The Palace,
    Peterborough, Cambs PE1 1YB. Tel: 01733-64448

PORTSMOUTH (Canterbury)

8TH BISHOP
Rt. Revd Dr Kenneth W. Stevenson, *cons.* 1995, *apptd* 1995;
    Bishopsgrove, 26 Osborn Road, Fareham, Hants PO16
    7DQ. *Signs* Kenneth Portsmouth

PROVOST
Very Revd Michael L. Yorke, *apptd* 1994

CANONS RESIDENTIARY
D. T. Isaac, *apptd* 1990; Jane B. Hedges, *apptd* 1993; G. Kirk,
    apptd 1998

Organist, D. J. C. Price, *apptd* 1996

ARCHDEACONS
Isle of Wight, Ven. K. M. L. H. Banting, *apptd* 1996
Portsmouth, vacant

Chancellor, His Hon. Judge Aglionby, *apptd* 1978
Registrar and Legal Secretary, Miss H. A. G. Tyler
Diocesan Secretary, M. F. Jordan, Cathedral House, St
    Thomas's Street, Portsmouth, Hants PO1 2HA. Tel:
    01705-825731

RIPON (York)

11TH BISHOP
Rt. Revd David N. de L. Young, *cons.* 1977, *apptd* 1977;
    Bishop Mount, Ripon HG4 5DP. *Signs* David Ripon

BISHOP SUFFRAGAN
Knaresborough, Rt. Revd Frank V. Weston, *cons.* 1997, *apptd*
    1997; 16 Shaftesbury Avenue, Roundhay, Leeds LS8 1DT

DEAN
Very Revd John Methuen, *apptd* 1995

CANONS RESIDENTIARY
M. R. Glanville-Smith, *apptd* 1990; K. Punshon, *apptd* 1996;
    J. Bell, *apptd* 1997

Organist, K. Beaumont, FRCO, *apptd* 1994

ARCHDEACONS
Leeds, Ven. J. M. Oliver, *apptd* 1992
Richmond, Ven. K. Good, *apptd* 1993

Chancellor, His Hon. Judge Grenfell, *apptd* 1992
Registrar and Legal Secretary, J. R. Balmforth
Diocesan Secretary, P. M. Arundel, Diocesan Office, St
    Mary's Street, Leeds LS9 7DP. Tel: 0113-248 7487

ROCHESTER (Canterbury)

106TH BISHOP
Rt. Revd Dr Michael Nazir-Ali, *cons.* 1984, *apptd* 1994;
    Bishopscourt, Rochester ME1 1TS. *Signs* Michael Roffen:

BISHOP SUFFRAGAN
Tonbridge, Rt. Revd Brian A. Smith, *cons.* 1993, *apptd* 1993;
    Bishop's Lodge, 48 St Botolph's Road, Sevenoaks TN13
    3AG

DEAN
Very Revd Edward F. Shotter, *apptd* 1990

CANONS RESIDENTIARY
E. R. Turner, *apptd* 1981; J. M. Armson, *apptd* 1989; N. L.
    Warren, *apptd* 1989; C. J. Meyrick, *apptd* 1998

Organist, R. Sayer, FRCO, *apptd* 1995

ARCHDEACONS
Bromley, Ven. G. Norman, *apptd* 1994
Rochester, Ven. N. L. Warren, *apptd* 1989
Tonbridge, Ven. Judith Rose, *apptd* 1996

Chancellor, His Hon. Judge Goodman, *apptd* 1971
Registrar and Legal Secretary, M. Thatcher
Diocesan Secretary, P. Law, St Nicholas Church, Boley Hill,
    Rochester ME1 1SL. Tel: 01634-830333

ST ALBANS (Canterbury)

9TH BISHOP
Rt. Revd Christopher W. Herbert, *cons.* 1995, *apptd* 1995;
    Abbey Gate House, St Albans AL3 4HD. *Signs* Christopher
    St Albans

BISHOPS SUFFRAGAN
Bedford, Rt. Revd John H. Richardson, *cons.* 1994, *apptd*
    1994; 168 Kimbolton Road, Bedford MK41 8DN
Hertford, Rt. Revd Robin J. N. Smith, *cons.* 1990, *apptd* 1990;
    Hertford House, Abbey Mill Lane, St Albans AL3 4HE

DEAN
Very Revd Christopher Lewis, *apptd* 1993

CANONS RESIDENTIARY
C. Garner, *apptd* 1984; G. R. S. Ritson, *apptd* 1987;
    M. Sansom, *apptd* 1988; C. R. J. Foster, *apptd* 1994

Organist, A. Lucas, *apptd* 1998

ARCHDEACONS
Bedford, Ven. M. L. Lesiter, *apptd* 1993
Hertford, Ven. T. P. Jones, *apptd* 1997
St Albans, Ven. R. I. Cheetham, *apptd* 1998 (from March
    1999)

Chancellor, His Hon. Judge Bursell, QC, *apptd* 1992
Registrar and Legal Secretary, D. N. Cheetham
Diocesan Secretary, L. Nicholls, Holywell Lodge, 41
    Holywell Hill, St Albans AL1 1HE. Tel: 01727-854532

ST EDMUNDSBURY AND IPSWICH
(Canterbury)

9TH BISHOP
Rt. Revd J. H. Richard Lewis, *cons.* 1992, *apptd* 1997;
Bishop's House, 4 Park Road, Ipswich IP1 3ST. *Signs*
Richard St Edmundsbury and Ipswich

BISHOP SUFFRAGAN
Dunwich, Rt. Revd Timothy J. Stevens, *cons.* 1995, *apptd*
1995; The Old Vicarage, Stowupland, Stowmarket
IP14 4BQ

PROVOST
Very Revd J. Atwell, *apptd* 1995

CANONS RESIDENTIARY
A. M. Shaw, *apptd* 1989; M. E. Mingins, *apptd* 1993

Organist, J. Thomas, *apptd* 1997

ARCHDEACONS
Ipswich, Ven. T. A. Gibson, *apptd* 1987
Sudbury, Ven. J. Cox, *apptd* 1995
Suffolk, Ven. G. Arrand, *apptd* 1994

Chancellor, The Hon. Mr Justice Blofeld, *apptd* 1974
Registrar and Legal Secretary, J. Hall
Diocesan Secretary, N. Edgell, 13–15 Tower Street, Ipswich
IP1 3BG. Tel: 01473-211028

SALISBURY (Canterbury)

77TH BISHOP
Rt. Revd David S. Stancliffe, *cons.* 1993, *apptd* 1993; South
Canonry, The Close, Salisbury SP1 2ER. *Signs* David
Sarum

BISHOPS SUFFRAGAN
Ramsbury, vacant
Sherborne, Rt. Revd John D. G. Kirkham, *cons.* 1976, *apptd*
1976; Little Bailie, Sturminster Marshall, Wimborne
BH21 4AD

DEAN
Very Revd Derek Watson, *apptd* 1996

CANONS RESIDENTIARY
D. J. C. Davies, *apptd* 1985; D. M. K. Durston, *apptd* 1992;
June Osborne, *apptd* 1995

Organist, S. R. A. Lole, *apptd* 1997

ARCHDEACONS
Dorset, Ven. G. E. Walton, *apptd* 1982
Sherborne, Ven. P. C. Wheatley, *apptd* 1991
Wilts, Ven. B. J. Hopkinson, *apptd* 1986 (Sarum), 1998
(Wilts)

Chancellor, His Hon. Judge Wiggs, *apptd* 1997
Registrar and Legal Secretary, A. Johnson
Diocesan Secretary, Revd Karen Curnock, Church House,
Crane Street, Salisbury SP1 2QB. Tel: 01722-411922

SHEFFIELD (York)

6TH BISHOP
Rt. Revd John (Jack) Nicholls, *cons.* 1990, *apptd* 1997;
Bishopscroft, Snaithing Lane, Sheffield S10 3LG. *Signs*
Jack Sheffield

BISHOP SUFFRAGAN
Doncaster, Rt. Revd Michael F. Gear, *cons.* 1993, *apptd* 1993;
Bishops Lodge, Hooton Roberts, Rotherham S65 4PF

PROVOST
Very Revd Michael Sadgrove, *apptd* 1995

CANONS RESIDENTIARY
T. M. Page, *apptd* 1982; Ven. S. R. Lowe, *apptd* 1988;
C. M. Smith, *apptd* 1991; Jane E. M. Sinclair, *apptd* 1993

Organist, N. Taylor, *apptd* 1997

ARCHDEACONS
Doncaster, Ven. B. L. Holdridge, *apptd* 1994
Sheffield, Ven. S. R. Lowe, *apptd* 1988

Chancellor, Prof. J. D. McClean, *apptd* 1992
Registrar and Legal Secretary, Mrs M. Myers
Diocesan Secretary, C. A. Beck, FCIS, Diocesan Church
House, 95–99 Effingham Street, Rotherham S65 1BL.
Tel: 01709-511116

SODOR AND MAN (York)

79TH BISHOP
Rt. Revd Noel D. Jones, CB, *cons.* 1989, *apptd* 1989; The
Bishop's House, Quarterbridge Road, Douglas, Isle of
Man IM2 3RF. *Signs* Noel Sodor and Man

CANONS
B. H. Kelly, *apptd* 1980; F. H. Bird, *apptd* 1993; D. Whitworth,
apptd 1996; P. Robinson *apptd* 1998

ARCHDEACON
Isle of Man, Ven. B. H. Partington, *apptd* 1996

Vicar-General and Chancellor, Ms C. Faulds
Registrar and Legal Secretary, C. J. Callow
Diocesan Secretary, The Hon. C. Murphy, c/o 26 The
Fountains, Ramsey, Isle of Man IM8 2AR. Tel: 01624-
816545

SOUTHWARK (Canterbury)

9TH BISHOP
Rt. Revd Thomas F. Butler, PH.D, LLD, *cons.* 1985, *apptd*
1998; Bishop's House, 38 Tooting Bec Gardens, London
SW16 1QZ. *Signs* Thomas Southwark

AREA BISHOPS
Croydon, Rt. Revd Dr Wilfred D. Wood, DD, *cons.* 1985, *apptd*
1985; St Matthew's House, George Street, Croydon CR0
1PE
Kingston upon Thames, Rt Revd Peter B. Price, *cons.* 1997,
apptd 1998; *Kingston Episcopal Area Office,* Whitelands
College, West Hill, London SW15 3SN
Woolwich, Rt. Revd Colin O. Buchanan, *cons.* 1985, *apptd*
1996; 37 South Road, Forest Hill, London SE23 2UJ

PROVOST
Very Revd Colin B. Slee, *apptd* 1994

CANONS RESIDENTIARY
D. Painter, *apptd* 1991; R. White, *apptd* 1991; Helen Cunliffe,
apptd 1995; J. John, *apptd* 1997; B. Saunders, *apptd* 1997

Organist, P. Wright, FRCO, *apptd* 1989

ARCHDEACONS
Croydon, Ven. V. A. Davies, *apptd* 1994
Lambeth, Ven. C. R. B. Bird, *apptd* 1988
Lewisham, Ven. D. J. Atkinson, *apptd* 1996
Reigate, Ven. M. Baddeley, *apptd* 1996

Southwark, Ven. D. L. Bartles-Smith, *apptd* 1985
Wandsworth, Ven. D. Gerrard, *apptd* 1989

Chancellor, C. George, QC
Registrar and Legal Secretary, P. Morris
Diocesan Secretary, S. Parton, Trinity House, 4 Chapel Court, Borough High Street, London SE1 1HW. Tel: 0171-403 8686

SOUTHWELL (York)

9TH BISHOP
Rt. Revd Patrick B. Harris, *cons.* 1973, *apptd* 1988; Bishop's Manor, Southwell NG25 0JR. *Signs* Patrick Southwell

BISHOP SUFFRAGAN
Sherwood, Rt. Revd Alan W. Morgan, *cons.* 1989, *apptd* 1989; Sherwood House, High Oakham Road, Mansfield NG18 5AJ

PROVOST
Very Revd David Leaning, *apptd* 1991

CANONS RESIDENTIARY
I. G. Collins, *apptd* 1985; G. A. Hendy *apptd* 1997
Organist, P. Hale, *apptd* 1989

ARCHDEACONS
Newark, Ven. D. C. Hawtin, *apptd* 1992
Nottingham, Ven. G. Ogilvie, *apptd* 1996

Chancellor, J. Shand, *apptd* 1981
Registrar and Legal Secretary, C. C. Hodson
Diocesan Secretary, B. Noake, Dunham House, Westgate, Southwell, Notts NG25 0JL. Tel: 01636-814331

TRURO (Canterbury)

14TH BISHOP
Rt. Revd William Ind, *cons.* 1987, *apptd* 1997; Lis Escop, Truro TR3 6QQ. *Signs* William Truro

BISHOP SUFFRAGAN
St Germans, Rt. Revd Graham R. James, *cons.* 1993, *apptd* 1993; 32 Falmouth Road, Truro TR1 2HX

DEAN
Very Revd Michael A. Moxon, LVO, *apptd* 1998

CANONS RESIDENTIARY
P. R. Gay, *apptd* 1994; K. P. Mellor, *apptd* 1994; P. D. Goodridge, *apptd* 1996

Organist, A. Nethsingha, FRCO, *apptd* 1994

ARCHDEACONS
Cornwall, Ven. J. T. McCabe, *apptd* 1996
Bodmin, Ven. R. D. C. Whiteman, *apptd* 1989

Chancellor, T. Briden, *apptd* 1998
Registrar and Legal Secretary, M. J. Follett
Diocesan Secretary, B. C. Laite, Diocesan House, Kenwyn, Truro TR1 3DU. Tel: 01872-274351

WAKEFIELD (York)

11TH BISHOP
Rt. Revd Nigel S. McCulloch, *cons.* 1986, *apptd* 1992; Bishop's Lodge, Woodthorpe Lane, Wakefield WF2 6JL. *Signs* Nigel Wakefield

BISHOP SUFFRAGAN
Pontefract, Rt. Revd David James, *cons.* 1998, *apptd* 1998; Pontefract House, 181A Manygates Lane, Wakefield WF2 7DR

PROVOST
Very Revd George P. Nairn-Briggs, *apptd* 1997

CANONS RESIDENTIARY
R. Capper, *apptd* 1997; R. Gage, *apptd* 1997; I. Gaskell, *apptd* 1998; J. Holmes, *apptd* 1998
Organist, J. Bielby, FRCO, *apptd* 1972

ARCHDEACONS
Halifax, Ven. R. Inwood, *apptd* 1995
Pontefract, Ven. A. Robinson, *apptd* 1997

Chancellor, P. Collier, QC, *apptd* 1992
Registrar and Legal Secretary, L. Box
Diocesan Secretary, W. J. B. Smith, Church House, 1 South Parade, Wakefield WF1 1LP. Tel: 01924-371802

WORCESTER (Canterbury)

112TH BISHOP
Rt. Revd Dr Peter S. M. Selby, *cons.* 1984, *apptd* 1997; The Bishop's House, Hartlebury Castle, Kidderminster DY11 7XX. *Signs* Peter Wigorn:

BISHOP SUFFRAGAN
Dudley, Rt. Revd Dr Rupert Hoare, *cons.* 1993, *apptd* 1993; The Bishop's House, Brooklands, Halesowen Road, Cradley Heath B64 7JF

DEAN
Very Revd Peter J. Marshall, *apptd* 1997

CANONS RESIDENTIARY
Ven. F. Bentley, *apptd* 1984; D. G. Thomas, *apptd* 1987; I. M. MacKenzie, *apptd* 1989
Organist, A. Lucas, *apptd* 1996

ARCHDEACONS
Dudley, Ven. J. Gathercole, *apptd* 1987
Worcester, Ven. F. Bentley, *apptd* 1984

Deputy Chancellor, C. Nynors, *apptd* 1998
Registrar and Legal Secretary, M. Huskinson
Diocesan Secretary, J. Stanbury (until 31 Dec. 1998), The Old Palace, Deansway, Worcester WR1 2JE. Tel: 01905-20537

ROYAL PECULIARS

WESTMINSTER
The Collegiate Church of St Peter

Dean, Very Revd Dr A. W. Carr, *apptd* 1997
Sub Dean and Archdeacon, A. E. Harvey, *apptd* 1987
Canons of Westminster, A. E. Harvey, *apptd* 1982; D. H. Hutt, *apptd* 1995; M. J. Middleton, *apptd* 1997; R. Wright, *apptd* 1998
Chapter Clerk and Receiver-General, vacant
Organist, vacant
Registrar, S. J. Holmes, MVO, 20 Dean's Yard, London SW1P 3PA
Legal Secretary, C. L. Hodgetts

WINDSOR
The Queen's Free Chapel of St George within Her Castle of Windsor

Dean, Very Revd D. J. Conner, *apptd* 1998
Canons Residentiary, J. A. White, *apptd* 1982; L. F. P. Gunner, *apptd* 1996; B. P. Thompson, PH.D., *apptd* 1998; J. A. Ovenden, *apptd* 1998
Chapter Clerk, Lt.-Col. N. J. Newman, *apptd* 1990, Chapter Office, The Cloisters, Windsor Castle, Windsor, Berks SL4 1NJ
Organist, J. Rees-Williams, FRCO, *apptd* 1991

Other Anglican Churches

THE CHURCH IN WALES

The Anglican Church was the established church in Wales from the 16th century until 1920, when the estrangement of the majority of Welsh people from Anglicanism resulted in disestablishment. Since then the Church in Wales has been an autonomous province consisting of six sees. The bishops are elected by an electoral college comprising elected lay and clerical members, who also elect one of the diocesan bishops as Archbishop of Wales.

The legislative body of the Church in Wales is the Governing Body, which has 365 members divided between the three orders of bishops, clergy and laity. Its President is the Archbishop of Wales and it meets twice annually. Its decisions are binding upon all members of the Church. The Church's property and finances are the responsibility of the Representative Body. There are about 96,000 members of the Church in Wales, with about 700 stipendiary clergy and 1,142 parishes.

THE GOVERNING BODY OF THE CHURCH IN WALES, 39 Cathedral Road, Cardiff CF1 9XF. Tel: 01222-231638. *Secretary-General,* J. W. D. McIntyre

10TH ARCHBISHOP OF WALES, Most Revd Alwyn R. Jones (Bishop of St Asaph), *elected* 1991

BISHOPS
Bangor (79th), Rt. Revd Dr Barry C. Morgan, *b.* 1947, *cons.* 1993, *elected* 1992; Tŷ'r Esgob, Bangor LL57 2SS. *Signs* Barry Bangor. *Stipendiary clergy,* 65
Llandaff (101st), Rt. Revd Roy T. Davies, *b.* 1934, *cons.* 1985, *elected* 1985; Llys Esgob, The Cathedral Green, Llandaff, Cardiff CF5 2YE. *Signs* Roy Landav. *Stipendiary clergy*, 167
Monmouth (8th), Rt. Revd Rowan D. Williams, *b* 1950, *cons.* 1992, *elected* 1992; Bishopstow, Stow Hill, Newport NP9 4EA. *Signs* Rowan Monmouth. *Stipendiary clergy,* 120
St Asaph (74th), Most Revd Alwyn R. Jones, *b.* 1934, *cons.* 1982, *elected* 1982; Esgobty, St Asaph, Clwyd LL17 0TW. *Signs* Alwyn Cambrensis. *Stipendiary clergy,* 112
St David's (126th), Rt. Revd D. Huw Jones, *b.* 1934, *cons.* 1993, *elected* 1995; Llys Esgob, Abergwili, Carmarthen SA31 2JG. *Signs* Huw St Davids. *Stipendiary clergy,* 138
Swansea and Brecon (7th), Rt. Revd Dewi M. Bridges, *b.* 1933, *cons.* 1988, *elected* 1988 (retires 30 Nov. 1998); Ely Tower, Brecon, Powys LD3 9DE. *Signs* Dewi Swansea Brecon. *Stipendiary clergy,* 100

The stipend of a diocesan bishop of the Church in Wales is £26,674 a year from 1998

THE SCOTTISH EPISCOPAL CHURCH

The Scottish Episcopal Church was founded after the Act of Settlement (1690) established the presbyterian nature of the Church of Scotland. The Scottish Episcopal Church is in full communion with the Church of England but is autonomous. The governing authority is the General Synod, an elected body of 180 members which meets once a year. The diocesan bishop who convenes and presides at meetings of the General Synod is called the Primus and is elected by his fellow bishops.

There are 54,382 members of the Scottish Episcopal Church, of whom 33,795 are communicants. There are seven bishops, 210 stipendiary clergy, and 320 churches and places of worship.

THE GENERAL SYNOD OF THE SCOTTISH EPISCOPAL CHURCH, 21 Grosvenor Crescent, Edinburgh EH12 5EE. Tel: 0131-225 6357. *Secretary-General,* J. F. Stuart
PRIMUS OF THE SCOTTISH EPISCOPAL CHURCH, Most Revd Richard F. Holloway (Bishop of Edinburgh), *elected* 1992

BISHOPS
Aberdeen and Orkney, A. Bruce Cameron, *b.* 1941, *cons.* 1992, *elected* 1992. *Clergy,* 19
Argyll and the Isles, Douglas M. Cameron, *b.* 1935, *cons.* 1993, *elected* 1992. *Clergy,* 9
Brechin, Neville Chamberlain, *b.* 1939, *cons.* 1997, *elected* 1997. *Clergy,* 19
Edinburgh, Richard F. Holloway, *b.* 1933, *cons.* 1986, *elected* 1986. *Clergy,* 53
Glasgow and Galloway, vacant. *Clergy,* 48
Moray, Ross and Caithness, Gregor Macgregor, *b.* 1933, *cons.* 1994, *elected* 1994. *Clergy,* 13
St Andrews, Dunkeld and Dunblane, Michael H. G. Henley, *b.* 1938, *cons.* 1995, *elected* 1995. *Clergy,* 30

The minimum stipend of a diocesan bishop of the Scottish Episcopal Church was £21,510 in 1998 (i.e. 1.5 × the minimum clergy stipend of £14,340)

THE CHURCH OF IRELAND

The Anglican Church was the established church in Ireland from the 16th century but never secured the allegiance of a majority of the Irish and was disestablished in 1871. The Church in Ireland is divided into the provinces of Armagh and Dublin, each under an archbishop. The provinces are subdivided into 12 dioceses.

The legislative body is the General Synod, which has 660 members in total, divided between the House of Bishops and the House of Representatives. The Archbishop of Armagh is elected by the House of Bishops; other episcopal elections are made by an electoral college.

There are about 375,000 members of the Church of Ireland, with two archbishops, ten bishops, about 600 clergy and about 1,000 churches and places of worship.

CENTRAL OFFICE, Church of Ireland House, Church Avenue, Rathmines, Dublin 6. Tel: 00-353-1-4978422. *Chief Officer and Secretary of the Representative Church Body,* R. H. Sherwood; *Assistant Secretary of the General Synod,* V. F. Beatty

PROVINCE OF ARMAGH

ARCHBISHOP OF ARMAGH AND PRIMATE OF ALL IRELAND, Most Revd Robert H. A. Eames, PH.D., *b.* 1937, *cons.* 1975, *trans.* 1986. *Clergy,* 51

BISHOPS
Clogher, Brian D. A. Hannon, *b.* 1936, *cons.* 1986, *apptd* 1986. *Clergy,* 32
Connor, James E. Moore, *b.* 1933, *cons.* 1995, *apptd.* 1995. *Clergy,* 106
Derry and Raphoe, James Mehaffey, PH.D., *b.* 1931, *cons.* 1980, *apptd* 1980. *Clergy,* 50
Down and Dromore, Harold C. Miller, *b.* 1950, *cons.* 1997, *apptd* 1997. *Clergy,* 109
Kilmore, Elphin and Ardagh, Michael H. G. Mayes, *b.* 1941, *cons.* 1993, *apptd* 1993. *Clergy,* 24
Tuam, Killala and Achonry, Richard C. A. Henderson, *b.* 1957, *cons.* 1998, *apptd* 1998. *Clergy,* 12

PROVINCE OF DUBLIN

ARCHBISHOP OF DUBLIN, BISHOP OF GLENDALOUGH, AND PRIMATE OF IRELAND, Most Revd Walton N. F. Empey, *b.* 1934, *cons.* 1981, *trans.* 1985, 1996. *Clergy,* 90

BISHOPS
Cashel and Ossory, John R. W. Neill, *b.* 1945, *cons.* 1986, *trans.* 1997. *Clergy,* 37
Cork, Cloyne and Ross, Robert A. Warke, *b.* 1930, *cons.* 1988, *apptd* 1988. *Clergy,* 28
Limerick and Killaloe, Edward F. Darling, *b.* 1933, *cons.* 1985, *apptd* 1985. *Clergy,* 23
Meath and Kildare, (Most Revd) Robert L. Clarke, PH.D., *b.* 1949, *cons.* 1996, *apptd* 1996. *Clergy,* 23

OVERSEAS

PRIMATES

PRIMATE AND PRESIDING BISHOP OF AOTEAROA, NEW ZEALAND AND POLYNESIA, Rt. Revd John Paterson (Bishop of Auckland), *cons.* 1995, *apptd* 1998
PRIMATE OF AUSTRALIA, Most Revd Keith Rayner (Archbishop of Melbourne), *cons.* 1969, *apptd* 1991
PRIMATE OF BRAZIL, Most Revd Glauco Soares de Lima (Bishop of São Paulo), *cons.* 1989, *apptd* 1994
ARCHBISHOP OF THE PROVINCE OF BURUNDI, Most Revd Samuel Ndayisenga (Bishop of Buye), *apptd* 1998
ARCHBISHOP AND PRIMATE OF CANADA, Most Revd Michael G. Peers, *cons.* 1977, *elected* 1986
ARCHBISHOP OF THE PROVINCE OF CENTRAL AFRICA, Most Revd Walter P. K. Makhulu (Bishop of Botswana), *cons.* 1979, *apptd* 1980
PRIMATE OF THE CENTRAL REGION OF AMERICA, Most Revd Cornelius J. Wilson (Bishop of Costa Rica)
ARCHBISHOP OF THE PROVINCE OF CONGO, Most Revd Byankya Njojo (Bishop of Boga), *cons.* 1980, *apptd* 1992
ARCHBISHOP OF THE PROVINCE OF THE INDIAN OCEAN, Most Revd Remi Rabenirina (Bishop of Antananarivo), *cons.* 1984, *apptd* 1995
PRIMATE OF JAPAN, Rt. Revd John M. Takeda (Bishop of Tokyo), *cons.* 1988, *apptd* 1998
PRESIDENT -BISHOP OF JERUSALEM AND THE MIDDLE EAST, Rt. Revd Ghais A. Malik (Bishop of Egypt), *cons.* 1984, *apptd* 1996
ARCHBISHOP OF THE PROVINCE OF KENYA, Most Revd Dr David Gitari (Bishop of Nairobi), *cons.* 1975, *apptd* 1996
ARCHBISHOP OF THE PROVINCE OF KOREA, Most Revd Bundo C. H. Kim (Bishop of Pusan), *cons.* 1988, *apptd* 1995

ARCHBISHOP OF THE PROVINCE OF MELANESIA, Most Revd Ellison L. Pogo (Bishop of Central Melanesia), *cons.* 1981, *apptd* 1994
ARCHBISHOP OF MEXICO, Most Revd José G. Saucedo (Bishop of Cuernavaca), *cons.* 1958, *elected* 1995
ARCHBISHOP OF THE PROVINCE OF MYANMAR, Most Revd Andrew Mya Han (Bishop of Yangon), *cons.* 1988, *apptd* 1988
ARCHBISHOP OF THE PROVINCE OF NIGERIA, Most Revd Joseph Adetiloye (Bishop of Lagos), *apptd* 1991
ARCHBISHOP OF PAPUA NEW GUINEA, Most Revd James Ayong (Bishop of Aipo Rongo), *cons.* 1995, *elected* 1996
PRIME BISHOP OF THE PHILIPPINES, Most Revd Ignacio C. Soliba, *cons.* 1990, *apptd* 1997
ARCHBISHOP OF THE PROVINCE OF RWANDA, Most Revd Kolini Mboni (Bishop of Kigali)
METROPOLITAN OF THE PROVINCE OF SOUTHERN AFRICA, Most Revd Winston H. N. Ndungane (Archbishop of Cape Town), *cons.* 1991, *trans.* 1996
PRESIDING BISHOP OF THE SOUTHERN CONE OF AMERICA, Rt. Revd Maurice Sinclair (Bishop of Northern Argentina), *cons.* 1990
ARCHBISHOP OF THE PROVINCE OF THE SUDAN, Most Revd Benjamin W. Yugusuk (Bishop of Juba)
ARCHBISHOP OF THE PROVINCE OF TANZANIA, Most Revd Donald Mtetemela (Bishop of Ruaha), *cons.* 1982, *apptd* 1998
ARCHBISHOP OF THE PROVINCE OF UGANDA, Most Revd Livingstone Mpalanyi-Nkoyoyo (Bishop of Kampala)
PRESIDING BISHOP AND PRIMATE OF THE USA, Most Revd Frank T. Griswold III, *cons.* 1985, *apptd* 1997
ARCHBISHOP OF THE PROVINCE OF WEST AFRICA, Most Revd Robert Okine (Bishop of Koforidua), *cons.* 1981, *apptd* 1993
ARCHBISHOP OF THE PROVINCE OF THE WEST INDIES, Most Revd Orland Lindsay (Bishop of North-Eastern Caribbean and Aruba), *cons.* 1970, *apptd* 1986

OTHER CHURCHES AND EXTRA-PROVINCIAL DIOCESES

ANGLICAN CHURCH OF BERMUDA, Rt. Revd Ewen Ratteray, *apptd* 1996
EPISCOPAL CHURCH OF CUBA, Rt. Revd Jorge Perera Hurtado, *apptd* 1995
HONG KONG AND MACAO, Rt. Revd Peter Kwong Kuching, Rt. Revd Made Katib, *apptd* 1995
LUSITANIAN CHURCH (*Portuguese Episcopal Church***),** Rt. Revd Fernando da Luz Soares, *apptd* 1971
SPANISH REFORMED EPISCOPAL CHURCH, Rt. Revd Carlos Lozano Lopez, *apptd* 1995

The Church of Scotland

The Church of Scotland is the established (i.e. state) church of Scotland. The Church is Reformed and evangelical in doctrine, and presbyterian in constitution, i.e. based on a hierarchy of councils of ministers and elders and, since 1990, of members of a diaconate. At local level the kirk session consists of the parish minister and ruling elders. At district level the presbyteries, of which there are 47, consist of all the ministers in the district, one ruling elder from each congregation, and those members of the diaconate who qualify for membership. The General Assembly is the supreme authority, and is presided over by a Moderator chosen annually by the Assembly. The Sovereign, if not present in person, is represented by a Lord High Commissioner who is appointed each year by the Crown.

The Church of Scotland has about 700,000 members, 1,200 ministers and 1,600 churches. There are about 100 ministers and other personnel working overseas.

Lord High Commissioner (1998), The Lord Hogg of Cumbernauld
Moderator of the General Assembly (1998), The Rt. Revd Prof. A. Main, TD, ph.D.
Principal Clerk, Revd F. A. J. Macdonald
Depute Clerk, Revd M. A. MacLean
Procurator, A. Dunlop, QC
Law Agent and Solicitor of the Church, Mrs J. S. Wilson
Parliamentary Agent, I. McCulloch (*London*)
General Treasurer, D. F. Ross
CHURCH OFFICE, 121 George Street, Edinburgh EH2 4YN. Tel: 0131-225 5722

PRESBYTERIES AND CLERKS

Edinburgh, Revd W. P. Graham
West Lothian, Revd D. Shaw
Lothian, J. D. McCulloch

Melrose and Peebles, Revd J. H. Brown
Duns, Revd A. C. D. Cartwright
Jedburgh, Revd A. D. Reid

Annandale and Eskdale, Revd C. B. Haston
Dumfries and Kirkcudbright, Revd G. M. A. Savage
Wigtown and Stranraer, Revd D. Dutton

Ayr, Revd J. Crichton
Irvine and Kilmarnock, Revd C. G. F. Brockie
Ardrossan, Revd D. Broster

Lanark, Revd I. D. Cunningham
Paisley, Revd D. Kay
Greenock, Revd D. Mill
Glasgow, Revd A. Cunningham
Hamilton, Revd J. H. Wilson
Dumbarton, Revd D. P. Munro

South Argyll, M. A. J. Gossip
Dunoon, Revd R. Samuel
Lorn and Mull, Revd W. Hogg

Falkirk, Revd D. E. McClements
Stirling, Revd B. W. Dunsmore

Dunfermline, Revd W. E. Farquhar
Kirkcaldy, Revd B. L. Tomlinson
St Andrews, Revd J. W. Patterson

Dunkeld and Meigle, Revd A. B. Reid
Perth, Revd M. Ward
Dundee, Revd J. A. Roy
Angus, Revd M. I. G. Rooney

Aberdeen, Revd A. Douglas
Kincardine and Deeside, Revd J. W. S. Brown
Gordon, Revd I. U. Thomson
Buchan, Revd R. Neilson
Moray, Revd D. J. Ferguson

Abernethy, Revd J. A. I. MacEwan
Inverness, Revd A. S. Younger
Lochaber, Revd A. Ramsay

Ross, Revd R. M. MacKinnon
Sutherland, Revd J. L. Goskirk
Caithness, Revd M. G. Mappin
Lochcarron/Skye, Revd A. I. Macarthur
Uist, Revd A. P. J. Varwell
Lewis, Revd T. S. Sinclair

Orkney (*Finstown*), Revd T. Hunt
Shetland (*Lerwick*), Revd N. R. Whyte
England (*London*), Revd W. A. Cairns

Europe (*Portugal*), Revd J. W. McLeod

The minimum stipend of a minister in the Church of Scotland in 1998 was £16,093

The Roman Catholic Church

The Roman Catholic Church is one world-wide Christian Church acknowledging as its head the Bishop of Rome, known as the Pope (Father). The Pope is held to be the successor of St Peter and thus invested with the power which was entrusted to St Peter by Jesus Christ. A direct line of succession is therefore claimed from the earliest Christian communities. With the fall of the Roman Empire the Pope also became an important political leader. His temporal power is now limited to the 107 acres of the Vatican City State.

The Pope exercises spiritual authority over the Church with the advice and assistance of the Sacred College of Cardinals, the supreme council of the Church. He is also advised about the concerns of the Church locally by his ambassadors, who liaise with the Bishops' Conference in each country.

In addition to advising the Pope, those members of the Sacred College of Cardinals who are under the age of 80 also elect a successor following the death of a Pope. The assembly of the Cardinals at the Vatican for the election of a new Pope is known as the Conclave in which, in complete seclusion, the Cardinals elect by a secret ballot; a two-thirds majority is necessary before the vote can be accepted as final. When a Cardinal receives the necessary votes, the Dean of the Sacred College formally asks him if he will accept election and the name by which he wishes to be known. On his acceptance of the office the Conclave is dissolved and the First Cardinal Deacon announces the election to the assembled crowd in St Peter's Square. On the first Sunday or Holyday following the election, the new Pope assumes the pontificate at High Mass in St Peter's Square. A new pontificate is dated from the assumption of the pontificate.

The number of cardinals was fixed at 70 by Pope Sixtus V in 1586, but has been steadily increased since the pontificate of John XXIII and at the end of June 1998 stood at 166, plus two cardinals created 'in pectore' (their names being kept secret by the Pope for fear of persecution; they are thought to be Chinese).

The Roman Catholic Church universally and the Vatican City State are run by the Curia, which is made up of the Secretariat of State, the Sacred Council for the Public Affairs of the Church, and various congregations, secretariats and tribunals assisted by commissions and offices. The congregations are permanent commissions for conducting the affairs of the Church and are made up of cardinals, one of whom occupies the office of prefect. Below the Secretariat of State and the congregations are the secretariats and tribunals, all of which are headed by cardinals. (The Curial cardinals are analogous to ministers in charge of government departments.)

The Vatican State has its own diplomatic service, with representatives known as nuncios. Papal nuncios with full diplomatic recognition are given precedence over all other ambassadors to the country to which they are appointed; where precedence is not recognized the Papal representative is known as a pro-nuncio. Where the representation is only to the local churches and not to the government of a country, the Papal representative is known as an apostolic delegate. The Roman Catholic Church has an estimated 890.9 million adherents world-wide.

SOVEREIGN PONTIFF

His Holiness Pope John Paul II (Karol Wojtyla), *born* Wadowice, Poland, 18 May 1920; *ordained priest* 1946; *appointed Archbishop* of Krakow 1964; *created Cardinal* 1967; *assumed pontificate* 16 October 1978

SECRETARIAT OF STATE

Secretary of State, HE Cardinal Angelo Sodano
First Section (General Affairs), Mgr G. Re (Archbishop of Vescovio)
Second Section (Relations with other states), Mgr J. L. Tauran (Archbishop of Telepte)

BISHOPS' CONFERENCE

The Roman Catholic Church in England and Wales is governed by the Bishops' Conference, membership of which includes the Diocesan Bishops, the Apostolic Exarch of the Ukrainians, the Bishop of the Forces and the Auxiliary Bishops. The Conference is headed by the President (Cardinal Basil Hume, Archbishop of Westminster) and Vice-President. There are five departments, each with an episcopal chairman: the Department for Christian Life and Worship (the Archbishop of Southwark), the Department for Mission and Unity (the Bishop of Arundel and Brighton), the Department for Catholic Education and Formation (the Bishop of Leeds), the Department for Christian Responsibility and Citizenship (the Bishop of Plymouth), and the Department for International Affairs.

The Bishops' Standing Committee, made up of all the Archbishops and the chairman of each of the above departments, has general responsibility for continuity and policy between the plenary sessions of the Conference. It prepares the Conference agenda and implements its decisions. It is serviced by a General Secretariat. There are also agencies and consultative bodies affiliated to the Conference.

The Bishops' Conference of Scotland has as its president Archbishop Winning of Glasgow and is the permanently constituted assembly of the Bishops of Scotland. To promote its work, the Conference establishes various agencies which have an advisory function in relation to the Conference. The more important of these agencies are called Commissions and each one has a Bishop President who, with the other members of the Commissions, are appointed by the Conference.

The Irish Episcopal Conference has as its acting president Archbishop Connell of Dublin. Its membership comprises all the Archbishops and Bishops of Ireland and it appoints various Commissions to assist it in its work. There are three types of Commissions: (a) those made up of lay and clerical members chosen for their skills and experience, and staffed by full-time expert secretariats; (b) Commissions whose members are selected from existing institutions and whose services are supplied on a part-time basis; and (c) Commissions of Bishops only.

The Roman Catholic Church in Britain and Ireland has an estimated 8,992,000 members, 11 archbishops, 67 bishops, 11,260 priests, and 8,588 churches and chapels open to the public.

Bishops' Conferences secretariats:

ENGLAND AND WALES, 39 Eccleston Square, London SW1V 1PD. Tel: 0171-630 8220. *General Secretary*, The Rt. Revd Arthur Roche

SCOTLAND, Candida Casa, 8 Corsehill Road, Ayr, Scotland KA7 2ST. Tel: 01292-256750. *General Secretary*, The Rt. Revd Maurice Taylor (Bishop of Galloway)

IRELAND, Iona, 65 Newry Road, Dundalk, Co. Louth. *Executive Secretary*, Revd Hugh G. Connelly

---

GREAT BRITAIN

APOSTOLIC NUNCIO TO GREAT BRITAIN

The Most Revd Pablo Puente, 54 Parkside, London SW19 5NE. Tel: 0181-946 1410

ENGLAND AND WALES

THE MOST REVD ARCHBISHOPS
Westminster, HE Cardinal Basil Hume, *cons.* 1976
Auxiliaries, Vincent Nichols, *cons.* 1992; James J. O'Brien, *cons.* 1977; Patrick O'Donoghue, *cons.* 1993
Clergy, 789
Archbishop's Residence, Archbishop's House, Ambrosden Avenue, London SW1P 1QJ. Tel: 0171-834 4717
Birmingham, Maurice Couve de Murville, *cons.* 1982, *apptd* 1982
Auxiliaries, Philip Pargeter, *cons.* 1989
Clergy, 490
Diocesan Curia, Cathedral House, St Chad's Queensway, Birmingham B4 6EX. Tel: 0121-236 5535
Cardiff, John A. Ward, *cons.* 1981, *apptd* 1983
Clergy, 137
Diocesan Curia, Archbishop's House, 41–43 Cathedral Road, Cardiff CF1 9HD. Tel: 01222-220411
Liverpool, Patrick Kelly, *cons.* 1984, *apptd* 1996
Auxiliary, Vincent Malone, *cons.* 1989
Clergy, 533
Diocesan Curia, 152 Brownlow Hill, Liverpool L3 5RQ. Tel: 0151-709 4801
Southwark, Michael Bowen, *cons.* 1970, *apptd* 1977
Auxiliaries, Charles Henderson, *cons.* 1972; Howard Tripp, *cons.* 1980; John Jukes, *cons.* 1980
Clergy, 516
Diocesan Curia, Archbishop's House, 150 St George's Road, London SE1 6HX. Tel: 0171-928 5592

THE RT. REVD BISHOPS
Arundel and Brighton, Cormac Murphy-O'Connor, *cons.* 1977. *Clergy*, 313. *Diocesan Curia*, Bishop's House, The Upper Drive, Hove, E. Sussex BN3 6NE. Tel: 01273-506387
Brentwood, Thomas McMahon, *cons.* 1980, *apptd* 1980. *Clergy*, 174. *Bishop's Office*, Cathedral House, Ingrave Road, Brentwood, Essex CM15 8AT. Tel: 01277-232266
Clifton, Mervyn Alexander, *cons.* 1972, *apptd* 1975. *Clergy*, 251. *Diocesan Curia*, Egerton Road, Bishopston, Bristol BS7 8HU. Tel: 0117-924 1378
East Anglia, Peter Smith, *cons.* 1995, *apptd* 1995. *Clergy*, 173. *Diocesan Curia*, The White House, 21 Upgate, Poringland, Norwich NR14 7SH. Tel: 01508-492202
Hallam, John Rawsthorne, *cons.* 1981, *apptd* 1997. *Clergy*, 89. *Bishop's Residence*, 'Quarters', Carsick Hill Way, Sheffield S10 3LT. Tel: 0114-230 9101
Hexham and Newcastle, Michael Ambrose Griffiths, *cons.* 1992. *Clergy*, 259. *Diocesan Curia*, Bishop's House, East Denton Hall, 800 West Road, Newcastle upon Tyne NE5 2BJ. Tel: 0191-228 0003
Lancaster, John Brewer, *cons.* 1971, *apptd* 1985. *Clergy*, 256. *Bishop's Residence*, Bishop's House, Cannon Hill, Lancaster LA1 5NG. Tel: 01524-32231
Leeds, David Konstant, *cons.* 1977, *apptd* 1985. *Clergy*, 253. *Diocesan Curia*, 7 St Marks Avenue, Leeds LS2 9BN. Tel: 0113-244 4788

Menevia (*Wales*), Daniel Mullins, *cons.* 1970, *apptd* 1987. *Clergy*, 61. *Diocesan Curia*, 115 Walter Road, Swansea SAI 5RE. Tel: 01792-644017

Middlesbrough, John Crowley, *cons.* 1986, *apptd* 1992. *Clergy*, 187. *Diocesan Curia*, 50A The Avenue, Linthorpe, Middlesbrough, Cleveland TS5 6QT. Tel: 01642-850505

Northampton, Patrick Leo McCartie, *cons.* 1977, *apptd* 1990. *Clergy*, 154. *Diocesan Curia*, Bishop's House, Marriott Street, Northampton NN2 6AW. Tel: 01604-715635

Nottingham, James McGuinness, *cons.* 1972, *apptd* 1975. *Clergy*, 217. *Diocesan Curia*, Willson House, Derby Road, Nottingham NGI 5AW. Tel: 0115-953 9800

Plymouth, Christopher Budd, *cons.* 1986. *Clergy*, 143. *Diocesan Curia*, Vescourt, Hartley Road, Plymouth PL3 5LR. Tel: 01752-772950

Portsmouth, F. Crispian Hollis, *cons.* 1987, *apptd* 1989. *Clergy*, 268. *Bishop's Residence*, Bishop's House, Edinburgh Road, Portsmouth, Hants POI 3HG. Tel: 01705-820894

Salford, Terence J. Brain, *cons.* 1994, *apptd* 1997. *Clergy*, 394. *Diocesan Curia*, Cathedral House, 250 Chapel Street, Salford M3 5LL. Tel: 0161-834 9052

Shrewsbury, Brian Noble, *cons.* 1995, *apptd* 1995. *Clergy* 196. *Diocesan Curia*, 2 Park Road South, Birkenhead, Merseyside L43 4UX. Tel: 0151-652 9855

Wrexham (*Wales*), Edwin Regan, *apptd* 1994. *Clergy*, 86. *Diocesan Curia*, Bishop's House, Sontley Road, Wrexham, Clwyd LL13 7EW. Tel: 01978-262726

SCOTLAND

THE MOST REVD ARCHBISHOPS
St Andrews and Edinburgh, Keith Patrick O'Brien, *cons.* 1985 *Clergy*, 201 *Diocesan Curia*, 106 Whitehouse Loan, Edinburgh EH9 1BD. Tel: 0131-452 8244

Glasgow, HE Cardinal Thomas Winning, *cons.* 1971, *apptd* 1974 *Clergy*, 303 *Diocesan Curia*, 196 Clyde Street, Glasgow GI 4JY. Tel: 0141-226 5898

THE RT. REVD BISHOPS
Aberdeen, Mario Conti, *cons.* 1977. *Clergy*, 58. *Bishop's Residence*, 156 King's Gate, Aberdeen AB2 6BR. Tel: 01224-319154

Argyll and the Isles, vacant. *Clergy*, 32. *Diocesan Curia*, St Mary's, Belford Road, Fort William, Inverness-shire PH33 6BT. Tel: 01397-706046

Dunkeld, Vincent Logan, *cons.* 1981. *Clergy*, 55. *Diocesan Curia*, 26 Roseangle, Dundee DDI 4LR. Tel: 01382-25453

Galloway, Maurice Taylor, *cons.* 1981. *Clergy*, 66. *Diocesan Curia*, 8 Corsehill Road, Ayr KA7 2ST. Tel: 01292-266750

Motherwell, Joseph Devine, *cons.* 1977, *apptd* 1983. *Clergy*, 180. *Diocesan Curia*, Coursington Road, Motherwell MLI 1PW. Tel: 01698-269114

Paisley, John A. Mone, *cons.* 1984, *apptd* 1988. *Clergy*, 95. *Diocesan Curia*, Cathedral House, 8 East Buchanan Street, Paisley, Renfrewshire PAI IHS. Tel: 0141-889 3601

IRELAND

There is one hierarchy for the whole of Ireland. Several of the dioceses have territory partly in the Republic of Ireland and partly in Northern Ireland.

APOSTOLIC NUNCIO TO IRELAND
Most Revd Giovanni Ceirano (titular Archbishop of Tigimma), 183 Navan Road, Dublin 7. Tel: 00 353 1-380577

THE MOST REVD ARCHBISHOPS
Armagh, HE Cardinal Sean Brady, *cons.* 1993, *apptd* 1996 *Auxiliary*, Gerard Clifford, *cons.* 1991 *Clergy*, 183 *Diocesan Curia*, Ara Coeli, Armagh BT61 7QY. Tel: 01861-522045

Cashel, Dermot Clifford, *cons.* 1986 *Clergy*, 136 *Archbishop's Residence*, Archbishop's House, Thurles, Co. Tipperary. Tel: 00 353 504-21512

Dublin, Desmond Connell, *cons.* 1988, *apptd* 1988 *Auxiliaries*, James Moriarty, *cons.* 1992; Eamonn Walsh, *cons.* 1990; Fiachra O'Ceallaigh, *cons* 1994; James Kavanagh, *cons.* 1996 *Clergy*, 994 *Archbishop's Residence*, Archbishop's House, Drumcondra, Dublin 9. Tel: 00 353 1-8373732

Tuam, Michael Neary, *cons.* 1992 *Clergy*, 180 *Archbishop's Residence*, Archbishop's House, Tuam, Co. Galway. Tel: 00 353 93-24166

THE MOST REVD BISHOPS
Achonry, Thomas Flynn, *cons.* 1975. *Clergy*, 62. *Bishop's Residence*, Bishop's House, Ballaghaderreen, Co. Roscommon. Tel: 00 353 907-60021

Ardagh and Clonmacnois, Colm O'Reilly, *cons.* 1983. *Clergy*, 100. *Diocesan Office*, Bishop's House, St Michael's, Longford, Co. Longford. Tel: 00 353 43-46432

Clogher, Joseph Duffy, *cons.* 1979. *Clergy*, 108. *Bishop's Residence*, Bishop's House, Monaghan. Tel: 00 353 47-81019

Clonfert, Joseph Kirby, *cons.* 1988. *Clergy*, 71. *Bishop's Residence*, St Brendan's, Coorheen, Loughrea, Co. Galway. Tel: 00 353 91-41560

Cloyne, John Magee, *cons.* 1987. *Clergy*, 158. *Diocesan Centre*, Cobh, Co. Cork. Tel: 00 353 21-811430

Cork and Ross, John Buckley, *cons.* 1984, *apptd* 1998. *Clergy*, 338. *Diocesan Office*, Bishop's House, Redemption Road, Cork. Tel: 00 353 21-301717

Derry, Seamus Hegarty, *cons.* 1984, *apptd* 1994. *Clergy*, 157. *Bishop's Residence*, Bishop's House, St Eugene's Cathedral, Derry BT48 9AP. Tel: 01504-262302 *Auxiliary*, Francis Lagan, *cons.* 1988

Down and Connor, Patrick J. Walsh, *cons.* 1991. *Clergy*, 248. *Bishop's Residence*, Lisbreen, 73 Somerton Road, Belfast, Co. Antrim DT15 4DE. Tel: 01232-776185 *Auxiliaries*, Anthony Farquhar, *cons.* 1983; Michael Dallat, *cons.* 1994

Dromore, Francis Brooks, *cons.* 1976. *Clergy*, 78. *Bishop's Residence*, Bishop's House, Violet Hill, Newry, Co. Down BT35 6PN. Tel: 01693-62444

Elphin, Christopher Jones, *cons.* 1994. *Clergy*, 101. *Bishop's Residence*, St Mary's, Sligo. Tel: 00 353 71-62670

Ferns, Brendon Comiskey, *cons.* 1980. *Clergy*, 161. *Bishop's Office*, Bishop's House, Summerhill, Wexford. Tel: 00 353 53-22177

Galway and Kilmacduagh, James McLoughlin, *cons.* 1993. *Clergy*, 90. *Diocesan Office*, The Cathedral, Galway. Tel: 00 353 91-63566

Kerry, William Murphy, *cons.* 1995. *Clergy*, 149. *Bishop's Residence*, Bishop's House, Killarney, Co. Kerry. Tel: 00 353 64-31168

Kildare and Leighlin, Laurence Ryan, *cons.* 1984. *Clergy*, 136. *Bishop's Residence*, Bishop's House, Carlow. Tel: 00 353 503-31102

Killala, Thomas Finnegan, *cons.* 1970. *Clergy*, 62. *Bishop's Residence*, Bishop's House, Ballina, Co. Mayo. Tel: 00 353 96-21518

Killaloe, William Walsh, *cons.* 1994. *Clergy*, 149. *Bishop's Residence*, Westbourne, Ennis, Co. Clare. Tel: 00 353 65-28638
Kilmore, Francis McKiernan, *cons.* 1972. *Coadjutor*, Leo O'Reilly. *Clergy*, 115. *Bishop's Residence*, Bishop's House, Cullies, Co. Cavan. Tel: 00 353 49-31496
Limerick, Donal Murray, *cons.* 1996. *Clergy*, 152. *Diocesan Offices*, 66 O'Connell Street, Limerick. Tel: 00 353 61-315856
Meath, Michael Smith, *cons.* 1984, *apptd* 1990. *Clergy*, 141. *Bishop's Residence*, Bishop's House, Dublin Road, Mullingar, Co. Westmeath. Tel: 00 353 44-48841
Ossory, Laurence Forristal, *cons.* 1980. *Clergy*, 111. *Bishop's Residence*, Sion House, Kilkenny. Tel: 00 353 56-62448
Raphoe, Philip Boyce, *cons.* 1994. *Clergy*, 96. *Bishop's Residence*, Ard Adhamhnáin, Letterkenny, Co. Donegal. Tel: 00 353 74-21208
Waterford and Lismore, William Lee, *cons.* 1993. *Clergy*, 130. *Bishop's Residence*, Woodleigh, Summerville Avenue, Waterford. Tel: 00 353 51-71432

PATRIARCHS IN COMMUNION WITH THE ROMAN CATHOLIC CHURCH

Alexandria, HB Stephanos II Ghattas (Patriarch for Catholic Copts)
Antioch, HB Ignace Antoine II Hayek (Patriarch for Syrian rite Catholics); HB Maximos V. Hakim (Patriarch for Greek Melekite rite Catholics); HE Cardinal Nasrallah Pierre Sfeir (Patriarch for Maronite rite Catholics)
Jerusalem, HB Michel Sabbah (Patriarch for Latin rite Catholics); HB Maximos V. Hakim (Patriarch for Greek Melekite rite Catholics)
Babilonia of the Chaldeans, HB Raphael I Bidawid
Cilicia of the Armenians, HB Jean Pierre XVIII Kasparian (Patriarch for Armenian rite Catholics)
Oriental India, Archbishop Raul Nicolau Gonsalves
Lisbon, vacant
Venice, HE Cardinal Marco Ce

Other Churches in the UK

AFRICAN AND AFRO-CARIBBEAN CHURCHES

There are more than 160 Christian churches or groups of African or Afro-Caribbean origin in the UK. These include the Apostolic Faith Church, the Cherubim and Seraphim Church, the New Testament Church Assembly, the New Testament Church of God, the Wesleyan Holiness Church and the Aladura Churches.

The Afro-West Indian United Council of Churches and the Council of African and Afro-Caribbean Churches UK (which was initiated as the Council of African and Allied Churches in 1979 to give one voice to the various Christian churches of African origin in the UK) are the media through which the member churches can work jointly to provide services they cannot easily provide individually.

There are about 70,000 adherents of African and Afro-Caribbean churches in the UK, and about 1,000 congregations. The Afro-West Indian United Council of Churches has about 30,000 individual members, 135 ministers and 65 places of worship. The Council of African and Afro-

Caribbean Churches UK has about 17,000 members, 250 ministers and 75 congregations.
AFRO-WEST INDIAN UNITED COUNCIL OF CHURCHES, c/o New Testament Church of God, Arcadian Gardens, High Road, London N22 5AA. Tel: 0181-888 9427. *Secretary*, Revd E. Brown
COUNCIL OF AFRICAN AND AFRO-CARIBBEAN CHURCHES UK, 31 Norton House, Sidney Road, London SW9 0UJ. Tel: 0171-274 5589. *Chairman*, His Grace The Most Revd Father Olu A. Abiola

ASSOCIATED PRESBYTERIAN CHURCHES OF SCOTLAND

The Associated Presbyterian Churches came into being in 1989 as a result of a division within the Free Presbyterian Church of Scotland. Following two controversial disciplinary cases, the culmination of deepening differences within the Church, a presbytery was formed calling itself the Associated Presbyterian Churches (APC). The Associated Presbyterian Churches has about 1,000 members, 15 ministers and 20 churches.
Clerk of the Scottish Presbytery, Revd Dr M. MacInnes, Drumalin, 16 Drummond Road, Inverness IV2 4NB. Tel: 01463-223983

THE BAPTIST CHURCH

Baptists trace their origins to John Smyth, who in 1609 in Amsterdam reinstituted the baptism of conscious believers as the basis of the fellowship of a gathered church. Members of Smyth's church established the first Baptist church in England in 1612. They came to be known as 'General' Baptists and their theology was Arminian, whereas a later group of Calvinists who adopted the baptism of believers came to be known as 'Particular' Baptists. The two sections of the Baptists were united into one body, the Baptist Union of Great Britain and Ireland, in 1891. In 1988 the title was changed to the Baptist Union of Great Britain.

Baptists emphasize the complete autonomy of the local church, although individual churches are linked in various kinds of associations. There are international bodies (such as the Baptist World Alliance) and national bodies, but some Baptist churches belong to neither. However, in Great Britain the majority of churches and associations belong to the Baptist Union of Great Britain. There are also Baptist Unions in Wales, Scotland and Ireland which are much smaller than the Baptist Union of Great Britain, and there is some overlap of membership.

There are over 40 million Baptist church members world-wide; in the Baptist Union of Great Britain there are 157,000 members, 1,864 pastors and 2,130 churches. In the Baptist Union of Scotland there are 13,882 members, 160 pastors and 172 churches. In the Baptist Union of Wales there are 22,500 members, 112 pastors and 530 churches. In the Baptist Union of Ireland there are 8,393 members, 90 pastors and 110 churches.
President of the Baptist Union of Great Britain (1998−9), Revd D. G. T. McBain
General Secretary, Revd D. R. Coffey, Baptist House, PO Box 44, 129 Broadway, Didcot, Oxon OX11 8RT. Tel: 01235-512077

THE CONGREGATIONAL FEDERATION

The Congregational Federation was founded by members of Congregational churches in England and Wales who did not join the United Reformed Church (q.v.) in 1972. There are also churches in Scotland and Australia affiliated to the Federation. The Federation exists to encourage congregations of believers to worship in free assembly, but it has no authority over them and emphasizes their right to independence and self-government.

The Federation has 11,923 members, 71 recognized ministers and 313 churches in England, Wales and Scotland.

President of the Federation (1998–9), Revd. I. Gregory
General Secretary, G. M. Adams, The Congregational Centre, 4 Castle Gate, Nottingham NG1 7AS. Tel: 0115-911 1460

THE FREE CHURCH OF ENGLAND

The Free Church of England is a union of two bodies in the Anglican tradition, the Free Church of England, founded in 1844 as a protest against the Oxford Movement in the established Church, and the Reformed Episcopal Church, founded in America in 1873 but which also had congregations in England. As both Churches sought to maintain the historic faith, tradition and practice of the Anglican Church since the Reformation, they decided to unite as one body in England in 1927. The historic episcopate was conferred on the English Church in 1876 through the line of the American bishops, who had pioneered an open table Communion policy towards members of other denominations.

The Free Church of England has 1,500 members, 42 ministers and 25 churches in England. It also has three house churches and three ministers in New Zealand, two churches and two ministers in Queensland, Australia, and one church and one minister in St Petersburg, Russia.

General Secretary, Revd W. J. Lawler, 45 Broughton Road, Wallasey, Merseyside L44 4DT. Tel: 0151-638 2564

THE FREE CHURCH OF SCOTLAND

The Free Church of Scotland was formed in 1843 when over 400 ministers withdrew from the Church of Scotland as a result of interference in the internal affairs of the church by the civil authorities. In 1900, all but 26 ministers joined with others to form the United Free Church (most of which rejoined the Church of Scotland in 1929). In 1904 the remaining 26 ministers were recognized by the House of Lords as continuing the Free Church of Scotland.

The Church maintains strict adherence to the Westminster Confession of Faith (1648) and accepts the Bible as the sole rule of faith and conduct. Its General Assembly meets annually. It also has links with Reformed Churches overseas. The Free Church of Scotland has 6,000 members, 110 ministers and 140 churches.

General Treasurer, I. D. Gill, The Mound, Edinburgh EH1 2LS. Tel: 0131-226 5286

THE FREE PRESBYTERIAN CHURCH OF SCOTLAND

The Free Presbyterian Church of Scotland was formed in 1893 by two ministers of the Free Church of Scotland who refused to accept a Declaratory Act passed by the Free Church General Assembly in 1892. The Free Presbyterian Church of Scotland is Calvinistic in doctrine and emphasizes observance of the Sabbath. It adheres strictly to the Westminster Confession of Faith of 1648.

The Church has about 3,000 members in Scotland and about 7,000 in overseas congregations. It has 26 ministers and 50 churches.

Moderator, Revd D. A. Ross, Free Presbyterian Manse, Laide, Ross-shire IV22 2NB
Clerk of Synod, Revd J. MacLeod, 16 Matheson Road, Stornoway, Isle of Lewis HS1 2LA. Tel: 01851-702755

THE INDEPENDENT METHODIST CHURCHES

The Independent Methodist Churches seceded from the Wesleyan Methodist Church in 1805 and remained independent when the Methodist Church in Great Britain was formed in 1932. They are mainly concentrated in industrial areas of the north of England.

The churches are Methodist in doctrine but their organization is congregational. All the churches are members of the Independent Methodist Connexion of Churches. The controlling body of the Connexion is the Annual Meeting, to which churches send delegates. The Connexional President is elected annually. Between annual meetings the affairs of the Connexion are handled by departmental committees. Ministers are appointed by the churches and trained through the Connexion. The ministry is open to both men and women and is unpaid. There are 3,050 members, 106 ministers and 100 churches in Great Britain.

Connexional President (1998–9), M. Bolt
General Secretary, J. M. Day, The Old Police House, Croxton, Stafford ST21 6PE. Tel: 0163-062 0671

THE LUTHERAN CHURCH

Lutheranism is based on the teachings of Martin Luther, the German leader of the Protestant Reformation. The authority of the scriptures is held to be supreme over Church tradition and creeds, and the key doctrine is that of justification by faith alone.

Lutheranism is one of the largest Protestant denominations and it is particularly strong in northern Europe and the USA. Some Lutheran churches are episcopal, while others have a synodal form of organization; unity is based on doctrine rather than structure. Most Lutheran churches are members of the Lutheran World Federation, based in Geneva.

Lutheran services in Great Britain are held in many languages to serve members of different nationalities. English-language congregations are members either of the Lutheran Church in Great Britain-United Synod, or of the Evangelical Lutheran Church of England. The United Synod and most of the various national congregations are members of the Lutheran Council of Great Britain.

There are over 70 million Lutherans world-wide; in Great Britain there are 27,000 members, 45 ministers and 100 churches.
Chairman of the Lutheran Council of Great Britain, Very Revd R. J. Patkai, 30 Thanet Street, London wc1h 9qh. Tel: 0171-383 3081

THE METHODIST CHURCH

The Methodist movement started in England in 1729 when the Revd John Wesley, an Anglican priest, and his brother Charles met with others in Oxford and resolved to conduct their lives and study by 'rule and method'. In 1739 the Wesleys began evangelistic preaching and the first Methodist chapel was founded in Bristol in the same year. In 1744 the first annual conference was held, at which the Articles of Religion were drawn up. Doctrinal emphases included repentance, faith, the assurance of salvation, social concern and the priesthood of all believers. After John Wesley's death in 1791 the Methodists withdrew from the established Church to form the Methodist Church. Methodists gradually drifted into many groups, but in 1932 the Wesleyan Methodist Church, the United Methodist Church and the Primitive Methodist Church united to form the Methodist Church in Great Britain as it now exists.

The governing body and supreme authority of the Methodist Church is the Conference, but there are also 33 district synods, consisting of all the ministers and selected lay people in each district, and circuit meetings of the ministers and lay people of each circuit.

There are over 60 million Methodists world-wide; in Great Britain (1995 figures) there are 380,269 members, 3,660 ministers, 12,611 lay preachers and 6,678 churches.
President of the Conference in Great Britain (1998–9), Revd Prof. W. P. Stephens
Vice-President of the Conference (1998–9), Mrs M. Parker
Secretary of the Conference, Revd Dr N. T. Collinson,
Methodist Church, Conference Office, 25 Marylebone Road, London nw1 5jr. Tel: 0171-486 5502

THE METHODIST CHURCH IN IRELAND

The Methodist Church in Ireland is closely linked to British Methodism but is autonomous. It has 17,349 members, 196 ministers, 307 lay preachers and 229 churches.
President of the Methodist Church in Ireland (1998–9), Revd D. J. Kerr, Grosvenor House, 5 Glengall Street, Belfast bt12 5ad. Tel: 01232-241917
Secretary of the Methodist Church in Ireland, Revd E. T. I. Mawhinney, 1 Fountainville Avenue, Belfast bt9 6an. Tel: 01232-324554

THE (EASTERN) ORTHODOX CHURCH

The Eastern (or Byzantine) Orthodox Church is a communion of self-governing Christian churches recognizing the honorary primacy of the Oecumenical Patriarch of Constantinople.

The position of Orthodox Christians is that the faith was fully defined during the period of the Oecumenical Councils. In doctrine it is strongly trinitarian, and stresses the mystery and importance of the sacraments. It is episcopal in government. The structure of the Orthodox Christian year differs from that of western Churches (*see* page 82).

Orthodox Christians throughout the world are estimated to number about 300 million.

PATRIARCHS OF THE EASTERN ORTHODOX CHURCH
Archbishop of Constantinople, New Rome and Oecumenical Patriarch, Bartholomew, *elected* 1991
Pope and Patriarch of Alexandria and All Africa, Petros VII, *elected* 1997
Patriarch of Antioch and All the East, Ignatios IV, *elected* 1979
Patriarch of Jerusalem and All Palestine, Diodoros, *elected* 1981
Patriarch of Moscow and All Russia, Alexei II, *elected* 1990
Archbishop of Pec, Metropolitan of Belgrade and Karlovci, Patriarch of Serbia, Paul, *elected* 1990
Archbishop of Bucharest and Patriarch of Romania, Teoctist, *elected* 1986
Metropolitan of Sofia and Patriarch of Bulgaria, Maxim, *elected* 1971
Archbishop of Tbilisi and Mtskheta, Catholicos-Patriarch of All Georgia, Ilia II, *elected* 1977

EASTERN ORTHODOX CHURCHES IN THE UK

THE PATRIARCHATE OF ANTIOCH
There are ten parishes served by 12 clergy. In Great Britain the Patriarchate is represented by the Revd Fr Samir Gholam, 1a Redhill Street, London nw1 4bg. Tel: 0171-383 0403.

THE GREEK ORTHODOX CHURCH (PATRIARCHATE OF CONSTANTINOPLE)
The presence of Greek Orthodox Christians in Britain dates back at least to 1677 when Archbishop Joseph Geogirenes of Samos fled from Turkish persecution and came to London. The present Greek cathedral in Moscow Road, Bayswater, was opened for public worship in 1879 and the Diocese of Thyateira and Great Britain was established in 1922. There are now 113 parishes and other communities (including monasteries) in Great Britain, served by six bishops, 97 clergy and 101 churches.

In Great Britain the Patriarchate of Constantinople is represented by Archbishop Gregorios of Thyateira and Great Britain, 5 Craven Hill, London w2 3en. Tel: 0171-723 4787.

THE RUSSIAN ORTHODOX CHURCH (PATRIARCHATE OF MOSCOW) AND THE RUSSIAN ORTHODOX CHURCH OUTSIDE RUSSIA
The records of Russian Orthodox Church activities in Britain date from the visit to England of Tsar Peter I in the early 18th century. Clergy were sent from Russia to serve the chapel established to minister to the staff of the Imperial Russian Embassy in London.

In Great Britain the Patriarchate of Moscow is represented by Metropolitan Anthony of Sourozh, 67 Ennismore Gardens, London sw7 1nh. Fax only: 0171-584 9864. He is assisted by one archbishop, one vicar bishop and 28 clergy. There are 27 parishes and smaller communities.

The Russian Orthodox Church Outside Russia is represented by Archbishop Mark of Berlin, Germany and Great Britain, c/o 57 Harvard Road, London w4 4ed. Tel: 0181-742 3493. There are eight communities, including two monasteries, served by six priests.

THE SERBIAN ORTHODOX CHURCH (PATRIARCHATE OF SERBIA)
There are 33 parishes and smaller communities in Great Britain served by 12 clergy. The Patriarchate of Serbia is represented by the Episcopal Vicar, the Very Revd Milenko Zebic, 131 Cob Lane, Bournville, Birmingham b30 1qe. Tel: 0121-458 5273.

OTHER NATIONALITIES

Most of the Ukrainian parishes in Britain have joined the Patriarchate of Constantinople, leaving five Ukrainian parishes in Britain under the care of the Patriarch of Kiev (who is not recognized by the other Orthodox churches). The Latvian, Polish and some Belorussian parishes are also under the care of the Patriarchate of Constantinople. The Patriarchate of Romania has one parish served by two clergy. The Patriarchate of Bulgaria has one parish served by one priest. The Belorussian Autocephalous Orthodox Church has five parishes served by two priests.

THE ORIENTAL ORTHODOX CHURCHES

The term 'Oriental Orthodox Churches' is now generally used to describe a group of six ancient eastern churches which reject the Christological definition of the Council of Chalcedon (AD 451) and use Christological terms in different ways from the Eastern Orthodox Church. There are about 34 million members of the Oriental Orthodox Churches.

PATRIARCHS OF THE ORIENTAL ORTHODOX CHURCHES

ARMENIAN ORTHODOX CHURCH – *Supreme Patriarch Catholicos of All Armenians (Etchmiadzin)*, Karekin I, *elected* 1995; *Catholicos of Cilicia*, Aram I, *elected* 1995; *Patriarch of Jerusalem*, Torkom, *elected* 1994; *Patriarch of Constantinople*, vacant

COPTIC ORTHODOX CHURCH – *Pope of Alexandria and Patriarch of the See of St Mark*, Shenouda III, *elected* 1971

ERITREAN ORTHODOX CHURCH – *Patriarch of Eritrea*, Philipos I, *elected* 1998

ETHIOPIAN ORTHODOX CHURCH – *Patriarch of Ethopia*, Paulos, *elected* 1992

MALANKARA ORTHODOX SYRIAN CHURCH – *Catholicos of the East*, Basilios Mar Thoma Mathews II, *elected* 1991

SYRIAN ORTHODOX CHURCH – *Patriarch of Antioch and All the East*, Ignatius Zakka I, *elected* 1980

ORIENTAL ORTHODOX CHURCHES IN THE UK

THE ARMENIAN ORTHODOX CHURCH (PATRIARCHATE OF ETCHMIADZIN)

The Armenian Orthodox Church is the longest-established Oriental Orthodox community in Great Britain. It is represented by Archbishop Yeghishe Gizirian, Armenian Primate of Great Britain, Armenian Vicarage, Iverna Gardens, London W8 6TP. Tel: 0171-937 0152.

THE COPTIC ORTHODOX CHURCH

The Coptic Orthodox Church is the largest Oriental Orthodox community in Great Britain. It has four dioceses (Birmingham; Scotland, Ireland and North-East England; the British Orthodox Church; and churches directly under Pope Shenouda III). The representative in Great Britain of Pope Shenouda III is Fr Antonious Thabit Shenouda, 14 Newton Mansions, Queen's Club Gardens, London W14 9RR. Tel: 0171-385 1991.

THE ERITREAN ORTHODOX CHURCH

In Great Britain the Eritrean Orthodox Church is represented by Bishop Markos, 11 Anfield Close, Weir Road, London SW12 0NT. Tel: 0181-675 5115.

THE ETHIOPIAN ORTHODOX CHURCH

The acting head of the Ethiopian Orthodox Church in Europe is Revd Berhanu Beserat, 33 Jupiter Crescent, London NW1 8HA. Tel: 0956-513700.

THE MALANKARA ORTHODOX SYRIAN CHURCH

The Malankara Orthodox Syrian Church is part of the Diocese of Europe under Metropolitan Thomas Mar Makarios. His representative in Great Britain is Fr M. S. Skariah, Paramula House, 44 Newbury Road, Newbury Park, Ilford, Essex IG2 7HD. Tel: 0181-599 3836.

THE SYRIAN ORTHODOX CHURCH

The Syrian Orthodox Church in Great Britain comes under the Patriarchal Vicar, whose representative is Fr Thomas H. Dawood, Antiochian, 5 Canning Road, Croydon CR0 6QA. Tel: 0181-654 7531. The Indian congregation under the Syrian Patriarch of Antioch is represented by Fr Eldhose Koungampillil, 1 Roslyn Court, Roslyn Avenue, East Barnet, Herts EN4 8DJ. Tel: 0181-368 2794.

THE COUNCIL OF ORIENTAL ORTHODOX CHURCHES, 34 Chertsey Road, Church Square, Shepperton, Middx TW17 9LF. Tel: 0181-368 8447. *Secretary*, Deacon Aziz M. A. Nour

---

PENTECOSTAL CHURCHES

Pentecostalism is inspired by the descent of the Holy Spirit upon the apostles at Pentecost. The movement began in Los Angeles, USA, in 1906 and is characterized by baptism with the Holy Spirit, divine healing, speaking in tongues (glossolalia), and a literal interpretation of the scriptures. The Pentecostal movement in Britain dates from 1907. Initially, groups of Pentecostalists were led by laymen and did not organize formally. However, in 1915 the Elim Foursquare Gospel Alliance (more usually called the Elim Pentecostal Church) was founded in Ireland by George Jeffreys and in 1924 about 70 independent assemblies formed a fellowship, the Assemblies of God in Great Britain and Ireland. The Apostolic Church grew out of the 1904–5 revivals in South Wales and was established in 1916, and the New Testament Church of God was established in England in 1953. In recent years many aspects of Pentecostalism have been adopted by the growing charismatic movement within the Roman Catholic, Protestant and Eastern Orthodox churches.

There are about 105 million Pentecostalists worldwide, with about 200,000 adult adherents in Great Britain and Ireland.

THE APOSTOLIC CHURCH, International Administration Offices, PO Box 389, 24–27 St Helens Road, Swansea SA1 1ZH. Tel: 01792-473992. *President*, Pastor R. W. Jones; *Administrator*, Pastor A. Saunders. The Apostolic Church has about 130 churches, 5,500 adherents and 83 ministers

THE ASSEMBLIES OF GOD IN GREAT BRITAIN AND IRELAND, General Offices, 16 Bridgford Road, West Bridgford, Nottingham NG2 6AF. Tel: 0115-981 1188. *General Superintendent*, P. Weaver; *General Administrator*, D. H. Gill. The Assemblies of God has 652 churches, about 75,000 adherents (including children) and 1,100 accredited ministers

THE ELIM PENTECOSTAL CHURCH, PO Box 38, Cheltenham, Glos GL50 3HN. Tel: 01242-519904. *General Superintendent*, Pastor I. W. Lewis; *Administrator*, Pastor B. Hunter. The Elim Pentecostal Church has 600 churches, 68,500 adherents and 650 accredited ministers

THE NEW TESTAMENT CHURCH OF GOD, Main House, Overstone Park, Overstone, Northampton NN6 OAD. Tel: 01604-643311. *National Overseer*, Revd Dr R. O. Brown.
The New Testament Church of God has 110 organized congregations, 7,500 baptized members, about 20,000 adherents and 242 accredited ministers

THE PRESBYTERIAN CHURCH IN IRELAND

The Presbyterian Church in Ireland is Calvinistic in doctrine and presbyterian in constitution. Presbyterianism was established in Ireland as a result of the Ulster plantation in the early 17th century, when English and Scottish Protestants settled in the north of Ireland.
There are 21 presbyteries and five regional synods under the chief court known as the General Assembly. The General Assembly meets annually and is presided over by a Moderator who is elected for one year. The ongoing work of the Church is undertaken by 18 boards under which there are a number of specialist committees.
There are about 295,000 Presbyterians in Ireland, mainly in the north, in 562 congregations and with 400 ministers.
Moderator (1998–9), Rt. Revd S. J. Dixon
Clerk of Assembly and General Secretary (acting), Very Revd Dr S. Hutchinson, Church House, Belfast BT1 6DW. Tel: 01232-322284

THE PRESBYTERIAN CHURCH OF WALES

The Presbyterian Church of Wales or Calvinistic Methodist Church of Wales is Calvinistic in doctrine and presbyterian in constitution. It was formed in 1811 when Welsh Calvinists severed the relationship with the established church by ordaining their own ministers. It secured its own confession of faith in 1823 and a Constitutional Deed in 1826, and since 1864 the General Assembly has met annually, presided over by a Moderator elected for a year. The doctrine and constitutional structure of the Presbyterian Church of Wales was confirmed by Act of Parliament in 1931–2.
The Church has 49,765 members, 130 ministers and 921 churches.
Moderator (1998–9), Revd W. I. Cynwill Williams
General Secretary, Revd D. H. Owen, 53 Richmond Road, Cardiff CF2 3UP. Tel: 01222-494913

THE RELIGIOUS SOCIETY OF FRIENDS (QUAKERS)

Quakerism is a movement, not a church, which was founded in the 17th century by George Fox and others in an attempt to revive what they saw as 'primitive Christianity'. The movement was based originally in the Midlands, Yorkshire and north-west England, but there are now Quakers in 36 countries around the world. The colony of Pennsylvania, founded by William Penn, was originally Quaker.
Emphasis is placed on the experience of God in daily life rather than on sacraments or religious occasions. There is no church calendar. Worship is largely silent and there are no appointed ministers; the responsibility for conducting a meeting is shared equally among those present. Social reform and religious tolerance have always been important

to Quakers, together with a commitment to non-violence in resolving disputes.
There are 213,800 Quakers world-wide, with over 19,000 in Great Britain and Ireland. There are about 490 meeting houses in Great Britain.
CENTRAL OFFICES: (GREAT BRITAIN) Friends House, Euston Road, London NW1 2BJ. Tel: 0171-387 3601; (IRELAND) Swanbrook House, Morehampton Road, Dublin 4. Tel: 00 353 1-683684

THE SALVATION ARMY

The Salvation Army was founded by a Methodist minister, William Booth, in the east end of London in 1865, and has since become established in 103 countries world-wide. It was first known as the Christian Mission, and took its present name in 1878 when it adopted a quasi-military command structure intended to inspire and regulate its endeavours and to reflect its view that the Church was engaged in spiritual warfare. Salvationists emphasize evangelism, social work and the relief of poverty.
The world leader, known as the General, is elected by a High Council composed of the Chief of the Staff and senior ranking officers known as commissioners.
There are about 1.5 million members, 17,389 active officers (full-time ordained ministers) and 16,080 worship centres and outposts world-wide. In Great Britain and Ireland there are 65,168 members, 1,732 active officers and 986 worship centres.
General, P. A. Rader
UK Territorial Commander, Commissioner J. Gowans
TERRITORIAL HEADQUARTERS, 101 Queen Victoria Street, London EC4P 4EP. Tel: 0171-332 0022

THE SEVENTH-DAY ADVENTIST CHURCH

The Seventh-day Adventist Church was founded in 1863 in the USA. Its members look forward to the second coming of Christ and observe the Sabbath (the seventh day) as a day of rest, worship and ministry. The Church bases its faith and practice wholly on the Bible and has developed 27 fundamental beliefs.
The World Church is divided into 14 divisions, each made up of unions of churches. The Seventh-day Adventist Church in the British Isles is known as the British Union of Seventh-day Adventists and is a member of the Trans-European Division. In the British Isles the administrative organization of the church is arranged in three tiers: the local churches; the regional conferences for south England, north England, Wales, Scotland and Ireland; and the national 'union' conference.
There are about 9 million Adventists and 40,905 churches in 208 countries world-wide. In the UK and Ireland there are 19,145 members, 145 ministers and 238 churches.
President of the British Union Conference, Pastor C. R. Perry
BRITISH ISLES HEADQUARTERS, Stanborough Park, Watford WD2 6JP. Tel: 01923-672251

UNDEB YR ANNIBYNWYR CYMRAEG
The Union of Welsh Independents

The Union of Welsh Independents was formed in 1872 and is a voluntary association of Welsh Congregational

Churches and personal members. It is entirely Welsh-speaking. Congregationalism in Wales dates back to 1639 when the first Welsh Congregational Church was opened in Gwent. Member churches are Calvinistic in doctrine and congregationalist in organization. Each church has complete independence in the government and administration of its affairs.

The Union has 39,174 members, 231 ministers and 535 member churches.

President of the Union (1998–9), Revd Dr N. A. Davies

General Secretary, Revd D. Morris Jones, Tŷ John Penry, 11 Heol Sant Helen, Swansea SA1 4AL. Tel: 01792-652542

THE UNITED REFORMED CHURCH

The United Reformed Church was formed by the union of most of the Congregational churches in England and Wales with the Presbyterian Church of England in 1972.

Congregationalism dates from the mid 16th century. It is Calvinistic in doctrine, and its followers form independent self-governing congregations bound under God by covenant, a principle laid down in the writings of Robert Browne (1550–1633). From the late 16th century the movement was driven underground by persecution, but the cause was defended at the Westminster Assembly in 1643 and the Savoy Declaration of 1658 laid down its principles. Congregational churches formed county associations for mutual support and in 1832 these associations merged to form the Congregational Union of England and Wales.

The Presbyterian Church in England also dates from the mid 16th century, and was Calvinistic and evangelical in its doctrine. It was governed by a hierarchy of courts.

In the 1960s there was close co-operation locally and nationally between Congregational and Presbyterian Churches. This led to union negotiations and a Scheme of Union, supported by Act of Parliament in 1972. In 1981 a further unification took place, with the United Association of Churches of Christ becoming part of the URC. In its basis the United Reformed Church reflects local church initiative and responsibility with a conciliar pattern of oversight. The General Assembly is the central body, and is made up of equal numbers of ministers and lay members.

The United Reformed Church is divided into 12 Provinces, each with a Provincial Moderator who chairs the Synod, and 75 Districts. There are 96,917 members, 650 full-time stipendiary ministers, 190 non-stipendiary ministers and 1,739 local churches.

General Secretary, Revd A. G. Burnham, 86 Tavistock Place, London WC1H 9RT. Tel: 0171-916 2020

THE WESLEYAN REFORM UNION

The Wesleyan Reform Union was founded by Methodists who left or were expelled from Wesleyan Methodism in 1849 following a period of internal conflict. Its doctrine is conservative evangelical and its organization is congregational, each church having complete independence in the government and administration of its affairs. The main concentration of churches is in Yorkshire.

The Union has 2,250 members, 20 ministers, 137 lay preachers and 114 churches.

President (1998–9), P. H. Norton

General Secretary, Revd E. W. Downing, Wesleyan Reform Church House, 123 Queen Street, Sheffield S1 2DU. Tel: 0114-272 1938

Non-Trinitarian Churches

THE CHURCH OF CHRIST, SCIENTIST

The Church of Christ, Scientist was founded by Mary Baker Eddy in the USA in 1879 to 'reinstate primitive Christianity and its lost element of healing'. Christian Science teaches the need for spiritual regeneration and salvation from sin, but is best known for its reliance on prayer alone in the healing of sickness. Adherents believe that such healing is a law, or Science, and is in direct line with that practised by Jesus Christ (revered, not as God, but as the Son of God) and by the early Christian Church.

The denomination consists of The First Church of Christ, Scientist, in Boston, Massachusetts, USA (the Mother Church) and its branch churches in over 60 countries world-wide. Branch churches are democratically governed by their members, while a five-member Board of Directors, based in Boston, is authorized to transact the business of the Mother Church. The Bible and Mary Baker Eddy's book, *Science and Health with Key to the Scriptures*, are used at services; there are no clergy. Those engaged in full-time healing are called practitioners, of whom there are 3,500 world-wide.

No membership figures are available, since Mary Baker Eddy felt that numbers are no measure of spiritual vitality and ruled that such statistics should not be published. There are over 2,400 branch churches world-wide, including nearly 200 in the UK.

CHRISTIAN SCIENCE COMMITTEE ON PUBLICATION, 2 Elysium Gate, 126 New Kings Road, London SW6 4LZ. Tel: 0171-371 0600. *District Manager for Great Britain and Ireland*, A. Grayson

THE CHURCH OF JESUS CHRIST OF LATTER-DAY SAINTS

The Church (often referred to as 'the Mormons') was founded in New York State, USA, in 1830, and came to Britain in 1837. The oldest continuous branch in the world is to be found in Preston, Lancs. Mormons are Christians who claim to belong to the 'Restored Church' of Jesus Christ. They believe that true Christianity died when the last original apostle died, but that it was given back to the world by God and Christ through Joseph Smith, the Church's founder and first president. They accept and use the Bible, but believe in continuing revelation from God and use additional scriptures, including *The Book of Mormon: Another Testament of Jesus Christ*. The importance of the family is central to the Church's beliefs and practices. Church members set aside Monday evenings as Family Home Evenings when Christian family values are taught. Polygamy was formally discontinued in 1890.

The Church has no paid ministry; local congregations are headed by a leader chosen from amongst their number. The world governing body, based in Utah, USA, is the three-man First Presidency, assisted by the Quorum of the Twelve Apostles.

There are more than 10 million members world-wide, with about 180,000 adherents in Britain in over 350 congregations.

President of the Europe North Area (including Britain), Elder S. J. Condie

BRITISH HEADQUARTERS, Church Offices, 751 Warwick
Road, Solihull, W. Midlands B91 3DQ. Tel: 0121-712 1202

JEHOVAH'S WITNESSES

The movement now known as Jehovah's Witnesses grew
from a Bible study group formed by Charles Taze Russell
in 1872 in Pennsylvania, USA. In 1896 it adopted the name
of the Watch Tower Bible and Tract Society, and in 1931
its members became known as Jehovah's Witnesses.
Jehovah's (God's) Witnesses believe in the Bible as the
word of God, and consider it to be inspired and historically
accurate. They take the scriptures literally, except where
there are obvious indications that they are figurative or
symbolic, and reject the doctrine of the Trinity. Witnesses
also believe that the earth will remain for ever and that all
those approved of by Jehovah will have eternal life on a
cleansed and beautified earth; only 144,000 will go to
heaven to rule with Christ. They believe that the second
coming of Christ and his thousand-year reign on earth
have been imminent since 1914, and that Armageddon (a
final battle in which evil will be defeated) will precede
Christ's rule of peace. They refuse to take part in military
service, and do not accept blood transfusions. They publish
two magazines, *The Watchtower* and *Awake!*
   The 12-member world governing body is based in New
York, USA. Witnesses world-wide are divided into branches, countries or areas, districts, circuits and congregations. There are overseers at each level, and two assemblies
are held annually for each circuit. There is no paid
ministry, but each congregation has elders assigned to
look after various duties and every Witness is assigned
homes to visit in their congregation.
   There are over 5 million Jehovah's Witnesses world-
wide, with 130,000 Witnesses in the UK organized into
over 1,400 congregations.
BRITISH ISLES HEADQUARTERS, Watch Tower House,
   The Ridgeway, London NW7 1RN. Tel: 0181-906 2211

UNITARIAN AND FREE CHRISTIAN CHURCHES

Unitarianism has its historical roots in the Judaeo-
Christian tradition but rejects the deity of Christ and the
doctrine of the trinity. It allows the individual to embrace
insights from all the world's faiths and philosophies, as
there is no fixed creed. It is accepted that beliefs may evolve
in the light of personal experience.
   Unitarian communities first became established in Poland and Transylvania in the 16th century. The first
avowedly Unitarian place of worship in the British Isles
opened in London in 1774. The General Assembly of
Unitarian and Free Christian Churches came into existence in 1928 as the result of the amalgamation of two
earlier organizations.   There are about 7,000 Unitarians
in Great Britain and Ireland, and 150 Unitarian ministers.
About 200 self-governing congregations and fellowship
groups, including a small number overseas, are members of
the General Assembly.
GENERAL ASSEMBLY OF UNITARIAN AND FREE
   CHRISTIAN CHURCHES, Essex Hall, 1–6 Essex Street,
   Strand, London WC2R 3HY. Tel: 0171-240 2384. *General
   Secretary*, J. J. Teagle

Nobel Prizes

For prize winners for the years 1901–94, *see* earlier editions of *Whitaker's Almanack*.

The Nobel Prizes are awarded each year from the income of a trust fund established by the Swedish scientist Alfred Nobel, the inventor of dynamite, who died on 10 December 1896 leaving a fortune of £1,750,000. The prizes are awarded to those who have contributed most to the common good in the domain of:

Physics – awarded by the Royal Swedish Academy of Sciences
Chemistry – awarded by the Royal Swedish Academy of Sciences
Physiology or Medicine – awarded by the Karolinska Institute
Literature – awarded by the Swedish Academy of Arts
Peace – awarded by a five-person committee elected by the Norwegian Storting
Economic Sciences (instituted 1969) – awarded by the Royal Swedish Academy of Sciences

The prizes are awarded every year on 10 December, the anniversary of Nobel's death. The first awards were made on 10 December 1901.

The Trust is administered by the board of directors of the Nobel Foundation, Stockholm, consisting of five members and three deputy members. The Swedish Government appoints a chairman and a deputy chairman, the remaining members being appointed by the awarding authorities.

The awards have been distributed as follows:

PHYSICS
American 65, British 20, German 19 (1948–90, West German 8), French 12, Soviet 7, Dutch 6, Swedish 4, Austrian 3, Danish 3, Italian 3, Japanese 3, Canadian 2, Chinese 2, Swiss 2, Indian 1, Irish 1, Pakistani 1

CHEMISTRY
American 42, German 27 (1948–90, West German 10), British 25, French 7, Swiss 5, Swedish 4, Canadian 3, Dutch 3, Argentinian 1, Austrian 1, Belgian 1, Czech 1, Finnish 1, Hungarian 1, Italian 1, Japanese 1, Mexican 1, Norwegian 1, Soviet 1

PHYSIOLOGY OR MEDICINE
American 75, British 23, German 15 (1948–90, West German 4), French 7, Swedish 7, Swiss 6, Danish 5, Austrian 4, Belgian 4, Australian 3, Italian 3, Canadian 2, Dutch 2, Hungarian 2, Russian 2, Argentinian 1, Japanese 1, Portuguese 1, South African 1, Spanish 1

LITERATURE
French 12, American 10, British 8, Swedish 7, German 6 (1948–90, West German 1), Italian 6, Spanish 5, Danish 3, Irish 3, Norwegian 3, Polish 3, Soviet 3, Chilean 2, Greek 2, Japanese 2, Swiss 2, Australian 1, Belgian 1, Colombian 1, Czech 1, Egyptian 1, Finnish 1, Guatemalan 1, Icelandic 1, Indian 1, Israeli 1, Mexican 1, Nigerian 1, South African 1, Trinidadian 1, Yugoslav 1, Stateless 1

PEACE
American 18, Institutions 18, British 10, French 9, Swedish 5, German 4 (1948–90, West German 1), South African 4, Belgian 3, Israeli 3, Swiss 3, Argentinian 2, Austrian 2, East Timorese 2, Norwegian 2, Soviet 2, Burmese 1, Canadian 1, Costa Rican 1, Danish 1, Dutch 1, Egyptian 1, Guatemalan 1, Irish 1, Italian 1, Japanese 1, Mexican 1, Palestinian 1, Polish 1, Tibetan 1, Vietnamese 1, Yugoslav 1

ECONOMICS
American 26, British 7, Norwegian 2, Swedish 2, Canadian 1, Dutch 1, French 1, German 1, Soviet 1

The Swedish Embassy (*see* page 1026) can provide a full list of winners.

Prize	1995	1996	1997
Physics	Dr M. Perl (American) Dr F. Reines (American)	Prof. D. Lee (American) Prof. D. Osheroff (American) Prof. R. Richardson (American)	Prof. S. Chu (American) Prof. C. Cohen-Tannoudji (French) Dr W. Phillips (American)
Chemistry	P. Crutzen (Dutch) Dr M. Molina (Mexican) Dr S. Rowland (American)	Prof. R. Curl (American) Sir Harold Kroto, Kt., FRS (British) Prof. R. Smalley (American)	Dr J. Walker (British)
Physiology or Medicine	Dr E. Lewis (American) Dr C. Nuesslein-Volhard (German) Dr E. Wieschaus (American)	Prof. P. Doherty (Australian) Prof. R. Zinkernagel (Swiss)	Prof. S. Prusiner (American)
Literature	S. Heaney (Irish)	W. Szymborska (Polish)	Dario Fo (Italian)
Peace	Prof. J. Rotblat (British) The Pugwash Conference on Science and World Affairs	Bishop Carlos Belo (East Timorese) J. Ramos-Horta (East Timorese)	The International Campaign to Ban Land-mines and the campaign co-ordinator, Jody Williams (American)
Economics	R. Lucas (American)	Prof. J. Mirrlees (British) Prof. W. Vickrey (Canadian)	Prof. M. Scholes (American) Prof. R. Merton (American)

Education

For addresses of national education departments, *see* Government Departments and Public Offices. For other addresses, *see* Education Directory

Responsibility for education in the United Kingdom is largely decentralized. Overall responsibility for all aspects of education lies in England with the Secretary of State for Education and Employment; in Wales with the Secretary of State for Wales; in Scotland with the Secretary of State for Scotland acting through the Scottish Office Education and Industry Department; and in Northern Ireland with the Secretary of State for Northern Ireland.

The main concerns of the education departments (the Department for Education and Employment (DfEE), the Welsh Office, the Scottish Office Education and Industry Department (SOEID), and the Department of Education for Northern Ireland (DENI)) are the formulation of national policies for education and the maintenance of consistency in educational standards. They are responsible for the broad allocation of resources for education, for the rate and distribution of educational building and for the supply, training and superannuation of teachers.

EXPENDITURE

In the UK in 1995–6, expenditure on education was (£ million):

Schools	20,977.9
Further and higher education	9,770.4
Other education and related expenditure	4,680.7

Most of this expenditure is incurred by local authorities, which make their own expenditure decisions according to their local situations and needs. Expenditure on education by central government departments, in real terms, was (£ million):

	1997–8 estimated outturn	1998–9 planned
DfEE	11,692	11,498
Welsh Office	569	527.3
SOEID	1,276	1,182
DENI	1,259	1,284

The bulk of direct expenditure by the DfEE, the Welsh Office and SOEID is directed towards supporting higher education in universities and colleges through the Higher Education Funding Councils (HEFCs) and further education and sixth form colleges through the Further Education Funding Councils (FEFCs) in England and Wales and directly from central government in Scotland. In addition, the DfEE funds student support in England and Wales, the City Technology Colleges (CTCs), the City College for the Technology of the Arts, and pays grants under the specialist schools programme.

The Welsh Office also funds grant-maintained schools, educational services and research, and supports bilingual education and the Welsh language.

In Scotland the main elements of central government expenditure, in addition to those outlined above, are grant-aided special schools, student awards and bursaries (through the Student Award Agency for Scotland), curriculum development, special educational needs and community education.

The Department of Education for Northern Ireland directly funds higher education, teacher education,

teacher salaries and superannuation, student awards, further education, grant-maintained integrated schools, and voluntary grammar schools.

Current net expenditure on education by local education authorities in England, Wales, and Scotland, and education and library boards in Northern Ireland is (£ million):

	1997–8 estimated outturn	1998–9 planned
England	18.50	18.40
Wales	1.20	1.30
Scotland	2.40	2.40
Northern Ireland	0.99	0.88

LOCAL EDUCATION ADMINISTRATION

The education service at present is a national service in which the provision of most school education is locally administered.

In England and Wales the education service is administered by local education authorities (LEAs), which carry the day-to-day responsibility for providing most state primary and secondary education in their areas. They share with the FEFCs the duty to provide adult education to meet local needs.

The LEAs own and maintain most schools and some colleges, build new ones and provide equipment. LEAs are financed largely from the council tax and aggregate external finance (AEF) from the Department for the Environment, Transport and the Regions in England and the Welsh Office in Wales.

All LEA-maintained schools manage their own budgets. The LEA allocates funds to the school, largely on the basis of pupil numbers, and the school governing body is responsible for overseeing spending and for most aspects of staffing, including appointments and dismissals. The School Standards and Framework Act has given LEAs greater powers to monitor, maintain and improve standards. An Education Association can be set up to take over the management of failing schools where both the LEA and the governing body have not brought about improvements identified as necessary by inspection.

The duty of providing education locally in Scotland rests with the education authorities. They are responsible for the construction of buildings, the employment of teachers and other staff, and the provision of equipment and materials. Devolved School Management (DSM) is in place for all primary, secondary and special schools.

Education authorities are required to establish school boards consisting of parents and teachers as well as co-opted members, responsible among other things for the appointment of staff.

Education is administered locally in Northern Ireland by five education and library boards, whose costs are met in full by DENI. All grant-aided schools include elected parents and teachers on their boards of governors. Provision has been made for schools wishing to provide integrated education to have grant-maintained integrated status from the outset. All schools and colleges of further education have full responsibility for their own budgets, including staffing costs. The Council for Catholic Maintained Schools forms an upper tier of management for

Catholic schools and provides advice on matters relating to management and administration.

THE INSPECTORATE

The Office for Standards in Education (OFSTED) is a non-ministerial government department in England headed by HM Chief Inspector of Schools (HMCI). OFSTED's remit is regularly to inspect all maintained schools and report on and thereby improve standards of achievement. All state schools are inspected by teams of OFSTED-trained, self-employed inspectors, including educationalists and lay people and headed by registered inspectors. Registered inspectors are required to follow procedures set out in two key documents, the *Framework for Inspection of Schools* and the *Framework for Nursery Settings* to ensure consistency in the process of inspection and the criteria used. HM Inspectors (HMI) within OFSTED report on good practice in schools and other educational issues based on inspection evidence. From 1997 for secondary and from 1998 for primary, schools will be inspected once every six years or more frequently if there is cause. A summary of the inspection report must be sent to the parents of each pupil by the school, followed by a copy of the governors' action plan thereon. OFSTED's counterpart in Wales is the Office of HM Chief Inspector of Schools in Wales (OHMCI Wales), where inspection of maintained schools is carried out on a five-year cycle. The inspection of further and higher education in England and Wales is the responsibility of inspectors appointed to the respective funding councils. From 2000, each LEA will be inspected on a five-year cycle by OFSTED supported by the Audit Commission.

HM Inspectors of Schools in Scotland inspect schools and publish reports on further education institutions and community education, and are involved in assessing the quality of teacher education. HMIs work in teams alongside lay people and associate assessors, who are practising teachers seconded for the inspection. The inspection of higher education is the responsibility of inspectors appointed to the Higher Education Funding Council for Scotland.

Inspection is carried out in Northern Ireland by the Department of Education's Education and Training Inspectorate, using teams which on occasion include lay people. The Inspectorate also performs an advisory function to the Secretary of State for Northern Ireland. From September 1992 a five-year cycle of inspection was introduced.

There are, in 1998–9, 200 HMIs on OFSTED's permanent staff, 2,000 trained registered inspectors, 9,500 team inspectors in England, 38 HMIs, about 350 registered inspectors and 820 team members in Wales, 78 HMIs and eight Chief Inspectors in Scotland and 58 members of the Inspectorate in Northern Ireland.

SCHOOLS AND PUPILS

Schooling is compulsory in Great Britain for all children between five and 16 years and between four and 16 years in Northern Ireland. Provision is being increased for children under five and many pupils remain at school after the minimum leaving age. No fees are charged in any publicly maintained school in England, Wales and Scotland. In Northern Ireland, fees are paid by pupils in preparatory departments of grammar schools, but pupils admitted to the secondary departments of grammar schools do not pay fees.

In the UK, parents have a right to express a preference for a particular school and have a right to appeal if dissatisfied. The policy, known as more open enrolment, requires schools to admit children up to the limit of their capacity if there is a demand for places, and to publish their criteria for selection if they are over-subscribed, in which case parents have a right of appeal.

The 'Parents' Charter', available free from education departments, is a booklet which tells parents about the education system. Schools are now required to make available information about themselves, their public examination and national test results, truancy rates, and destination of leavers. Corporal punishment is no longer legal in publicly maintained schools in the UK.

FALL AND RISE IN NUMBERS

In primary education, and increasingly in secondary education, pupil numbers in the UK declined through the 1980s. In maintained nursery and primary schools pupil numbers reached their lowest figure of 4.6 million in 1986. They stood at 5.3 million in 1997 and are expected to decline to 5.1 million by 2002. In secondary schools pupil numbers peaked at 4.6 million in 1981. They stood at 3.7 million in 1997 and are projected to rise to about 4 million in 2007.

ENGLAND AND WALES

There are two main types of school in England and Wales: publicly maintained schools, which charge no fees; and independent schools, which charge fees (*see* pages 428–9). Publicly maintained schools are maintained by local education authorities except for grant-maintained schools and City Technology Colleges.

The number of schools by category in 1996 was:

Maintained schools	29,872
County	15,638
Voluntary	7,079
controlled	2,982
aided	4,116
special agreement*	39
Grant-maintained	1,135
Wales	16
CTCs and CCTAs	15
Independent schools	2,318
TOTAL	33,340

* In England only

County schools are owned by LEAs and wholly funded by them. They are non-denominational and provide primary and secondary education. Voluntary schools also provide primary and secondary education. Although the buildings are in many cases provided by the voluntary bodies (mainly religious denominations), they are financially maintained by an LEA. In controlled schools the LEA bears all costs. In aided schools the building is usually provided by the voluntary body. The managers or governors are responsible for repairs to the school building and for improvements and alterations to it, though the DfEE may reimburse up to 85 per cent of approved capital expenditure, while the LEA pays for internal maintenance and other running costs. Special agreement schools are those where the LEA may, by special agreement, pay between one-half and three-quarters of the cost of building a new, or extending an existing, voluntary school, almost always a secondary school.

From September 1999, all existing publicly funded schools will be incorporated into a new school framework. County schools will become community schools. A new voluntary category will be subdivided into two categories, voluntary controlled and voluntary aided schools, which latter will comprise aided and special agreement schools. Most grant-maintained schools will be categorized as foundation schools (*see* below). From 1 September 2000, provision is proposed for schools to opt to transfer between categories.

Under the Local Management of Schools (LMS) initiative, LEAs are required to delegate at least 85 per cent of school budgets, including staffing costs, directly to schools. LEAs continue to retain responsibility for various common services, including transport and school meals.

Governing bodies – All publicly maintained schools have a governing body, usually made up of a number of parent and local community representatives, governors appointed by the LEA if the school is LEA maintained, the headteacher (unless he or she chooses otherwise), and serving teachers. Schools can appoint up to four sponsor governors from business who will be expected to provide financial and managerial assistance. Governors are responsible for the overall policies of schools and their academic aims and objectives; they also control matters of school discipline and the appointment and dismissal of staff. Governing bodies select inspectors for their schools, are responsible for action as a result of inspection reports and are required to make those reports and their action plans thereon available to parents.

The Specialist Schools Programme – The programme is open to all state secondary schools in England which teach the national curriculum and wish to specialize in the teaching of technology, mathematics and science (technology colleges), modern foreign languages (language colleges), sports colleges and arts colleges. In addition to the normal funding arrangements, the schools receive business sponsorship (up to four sponsor governors may sit on governing bodies) and complementary capital grants up to £100,000 from central government, together with extra annual funding of £100 a pupil to assist the delivery of an enhanced curriculum. By September 1998, there were 227 technology colleges, 58 language colleges, 26 sports colleges and 19 arts colleges.

Grant-maintained (GM) schools – Under the Conservative government, all secondary and primary schools, whether maintained or independent, were eligible to apply for grant-maintained status, subject to a ballot of parents. GM schools were maintained directly by the Secretary of State (through the Funding Agency for Schools) and the Welsh Office, not the LEA, and were wholly run by their own governing body. From 1 September 1999, the name and status of GM schools will change. Former county and voluntary controlled schools and those established by the Funding Agency for Schools will become foundation schools, while former voluntary aided and special agreement schools and those founded by promoters will join the voluntary aided subdivision of the voluntary category. They will have the option to express a preference as to category. GM schools will no longer be directly funded and will be included in LEA funding arrangements. About 60 per cent of grant-maintained schools are secondary schools.

City Technology Colleges (CTCs) and *City Colleges for the Technology of the Arts (CCTAs)* are state-aided but independent of LEAs. Their aim is to widen the choice of secondary education in disadvantaged urban areas and to teach a broad curriculum with an emphasis on science, technology, business understanding and arts technologies. Capital costs are shared by government and business sponsors, and running costs are covered by a per capita grant from the DfEE in line with comparable costs in an LEA maintained school. The first city technology college opened in 1988 in Solihull. The first CCTA, known as Britschool, opened in Croydon in 1991.

SCOTLAND

The number of schools by category in 1997 was:
Publicly maintained schools:

Education authority	3,565
Self-governing	2
Independent schools	114
TOTAL	3,681

Education authority schools (known as public schools) are financed by local government, partly through revenue support grants from central government, and partly from local taxation. A small number of grant-aided schools, mainly in the special sector, are conducted by boards of managers and receive grants direct from the SOEID. Independent schools receive no direct grant and charge fees, but are subject to inspection and registration. An additional category exists of self-governing schools opting to be managed entirely by a board of management. These schools remain in the public sector and are funded by direct government grant set to match the resources the school would receive under education authority management. Two were established, but it is planned to return them to the education authority framework.

Education authorities are required to establish school boards to participate in the administration and management of schools. These boards consist of elected parents and staff members as well as co-opted members.

NORTHERN IRELAND

The number of schools by category in 1997 was:
Grant-aided schools:

Controlled	662
Voluntary maintained	549
Voluntary grammar	53
Integrated schools	32
Independent schools	19
TOTAL	1,296

Controlled schools are maintained by the education and library boards with all costs paid from public funds. Voluntary maintained schools, mainly under Roman Catholic management, receive grants towards capital costs and running costs in whole or in part. Voluntary grammar schools may be under Roman Catholic or non-denominational management and receive grants from DENI. All grant-aided schools include elected parents and teachers on their boards of governors, whose responsibilities also include financial management under the Local Management of Schools (LMS) initiative. All secondary schools now have fully delegated budgets and as of 1996–7 84 per cent of primary schools. Voluntary maintained and voluntary grammar schools can apply for designation as a new category of voluntary school, which is eligible for a 100 per cent as opposed to 85 per cent grant. Such schools are managed by a board of governors on which no single interest group has a majority of nominees.

The majority of children in Northern Ireland are educated in schools which in practice are segregated on religious lines. Integrated schools exist to educate Protestant and Roman Catholic children together. There are two types: grant-maintained integrated schools which are funded by DENI; and controlled integrated schools funded by the education and library boards. Procedures are in place for balloting parents in existing segregated schools to determine whether they want instead to have integrated schools, subject to the satisfaction of certain criteria. By

September 1998, 38 integrated schools had been established, 14 of them secondary.

THE STATE SYSTEM

NURSERY EDUCATION – Nursery education is for children
from two to five years and is not compulsory. It takes place
in nursery schools (1,538 in the public sector in 1997) or
nursery classes in primary schools. The number of children
receiving nursery education in the UK in 1996–7 was:

In maintained nursery schools	82,200
In primary schools	989,700
In non-maintained nursery schools	69,300
In special schools	8,000
TOTAL	1,149,200

Many children also attend pre-school playgroups organized by parents and voluntary bodies such as the Pre-
School Learning Alliance. The nursery voucher scheme,
whereby every parent of a four-year-old received a
voucher worth £1,100 exchangeable for up to three terms
of pre-school education, was introduced in England and
Wales in April 1997. It was discontinued by the present
government in summer 1997, before it had been introduced in Northern Ireland. Education authorities are
responsible for funding nursery education in their areas
using a range of providers on the basis of an Early Years
Development Plan after reviewing and consulting on local
provision for under-fives. In Scotland vouchers remained
in place until June 1998; thereafter local authorities
undertook the funding and management of services as
elsewhere in the UK. All providers of pre-school education
are subject to inspection.

PRIMARY EDUCATION – Primary education begins at five
years in Great Britain and four years in Northern Ireland,
and is almost always co-educational. In England, Wales and
Northern Ireland the transfer to secondary school is
generally made at 11 years. In Scotland, the primary school
course lasts for seven years and pupils transfer to secondary
courses at about the age of 12.

Primary schools consist mainly of infants' schools for
children aged five to seven, junior schools for those aged
seven to 11, and combined junior and infant schools for
both age groups. First schools in some parts of England
cater for ages five to ten as the first stage of a three-tier
system: first, middle and secondary. Many primary schools
provide nursery classes for children under five (see above).

Primary schools (UK) 1996–67

No. of primary schools	23,306
No. of pupils	5,380,200
Pupils under five years	989,700

Pupil-teacher ratios in maintained primary schools
were:

	1995–6	1996–7
England	23.2	23.4
Wales	22.5	n/a
Scotland	19.6	19.6
Northern Ireland	19.5	19.8
UK	21.2	20.9

The average size of classes 'as taught' was 25.5 in 1996 but
rose to 25.6 in 1997.

MIDDLE SCHOOLS – Middle schools (which take children
from first schools), mostly in England, cover varying age
ranges between eight and 14 and usually lead on to
comprehensive upper schools.

SECONDARY EDUCATION – Secondary schools are for
children aged 11 to 16 and for those who choose to stay on
to 18. At 16, many students prefer to move on to tertiary or

sixth form colleges (see pages 432–3). Most secondary
schools in England, Wales and Scotland are co-educational. The largest secondary schools have over 1,500 pupils
but only 30.8 per cent of the schools take over 1,000 pupils.

Secondary schools 1997

	England and Wales	Scotland	N. Ireland
No. of pupils	3,240,100	316,600	152,700
% 16 and 17 years	31.3%	63.1%	41.3%
Average class size	21.2	19.5	n/a
Pupil-teacher ratio	16.3	13.2	14.5

In England and Wales the main types of secondary
schools are: comprehensive schools (87.2 per cent of pupils
in England, 100 in Wales), whose admission arrangements
are without reference to ability or aptitude; middle
deemed secondary schools for children aged variously
between eight and 14 years who then move on to senior
comprehensive schools at 12, 13 or 14 (5.1 per cent of pupils
in England); secondary modern schools (2.1 per cent of
pupils in England) providing a general education with a
practical bias; secondary grammar schools (4.2 per cent of
pupils in England) with selective intake providing an
academic course from 11 to 16–18 years; and technical
schools (0.1 per cent in England), providing an integrated
academic and technical education.

In Scotland all pupils in education authority secondary
schools attend schools with a comprehensive intake. Most
of these schools provide a full range of courses appropriate
to all levels of ability from first to sixth year.

In most areas of Northern Ireland there is a selective
system of secondary education with pupils transferring
either to grammar schools (41 per cent of pupils in 1997) or
secondary schools (59 per cent of pupils in 1997) at 11–12
years of age. Parents can choose the school they would like
their children to attend and all those who apply must be
admitted if they meet the criteria. If a school is over-
subscribed beyond its statutory admissions number, selection is on the basis of published criteria, which, for most
grammar schools, place emphasis on performance in the
transfer procedure tests which are set and administered by
the Northern Ireland Council for the Curriculum, Examinations and Assessment. When parents consider that a
school has not applied its criteria fairly they have access to
independent appeals tribunals. Grammar schools provide
an academic type of secondary education with A-levels at
the end of the seventh year, while secondary non-grammar
schools follow a curriculum suited to a wider range of
aptitudes and abilities.

SPECIAL EDUCATION – Special education is provided for
children with special educational needs, usually because
they have a disability which either prevents or hinders
them from making use of educational facilities of a kind
generally provided for children of their age in schools
within the area of the local authority concerned. Wherever
possible, such children are educated in ordinary schools,
taking the parents' wishes into account, and schools are
required to publish their policy for pupils with special
educational needs. LEAs in England and Wales and
Education and Library Boards in Northern Ireland are
required to identify and secure provision for the needs of
children with learning difficulties, to involve the parents in
any decision and draw up a formal statement of the child's
special educational needs and how they intend to meet
them, all within statutory time limits. Parents have a right
to appeal to a Special Educational Needs (SEN) Tribunal if
they disagree with the statement.

Maintained special schools are run by education authorities which pay all the costs of maintenance, but under the
terms of Local Management of Schools (LMS), those able

and wishing to manage their own budgets may choose to do so. Non-maintained special schools are run by voluntary bodies; they may receive some grant from central government for capital expenditure and for equipment but their current expenditure is met primarily from the fees charged to education authorities for pupils placed in the schools. Some independent schools provide education wholly or mainly for children with special educational needs and are required to meet similar standards to those for maintained and non-maintained special schools. It is intended that pupils with special education needs should have access to as much of the national curriculum as possible, but there is provision for them to be exempt from it or for it to be modified to suit their capabilities.

The number of full-time pupils with statements of special needs in January 1997 was:

In special schools: total	100,600
England	87,300
Wales*	3,400
Scotland	6,300
N. Ireland	3,600
In public sector primary and secondary	
schools: total	157,100
England	133,700
Wales*	11,600
Scotland	8,000
N. Ireland	3,800

*January 1996 figures

In Scotland, school placing is a matter of agreement between education authorities and parents. Parents have the right to say which school they want their child to attend, and a right of appeal where their wishes are not being met. Whenever possible, children with special needs are integrated into ordinary schools. However, for those who require a different environment or specialized facilities, there are special schools, both grant-aided by central government and independent, and special classes within ordinary schools. Education authorities are required to respond to reasonable requests for independent special schools and to send children with special needs to schools outside Scotland if appropriate provision is not available within the country.

ALTERNATIVE PROVISION

There is no legal obligation on parents in the UK to educate their children at school provided that the local education authority is satisfied that the child is receiving full-time education suited to its age, abilities and aptitudes. The education authority need not be informed that a child is being educated at home unless the child is already registered at a state school. In this case the parents must arrange for the child's name to be removed from the school's register (by writing to the headteacher) before education at home can begin. Failure to do so leaves the parents liable to prosecution for condoning non-attendance.

In most cases an initial visit is made by an education adviser or education welfare officer, and sometimes subsequent inspections are made, but practice varies according to the individual education authority. There is no requirement for parents educating their children at home to be in possession of a teaching qualification.

Information and support on all aspects of home education can be obtained from Education Otherwise (see page 443).

INDEPENDENT SCHOOLS

Independent schools receive no grants from public funds. They charge fees, and are owned and managed under special trusts, with profits being used for the benefit of the schools concerned. There is a wide variety of provision, from kindergartens to large day and boarding schools, and from experimental schools to traditional institutions. A number of independent schools have been instituted by religious and ethnic minorities.

All independent schools in the UK are open to inspection by approved inspectors (see page 425) and must register with the appropriate government education department. The education departments lay down certain minimum standards and can make schools remedy any unacceptable features of their building or instruction and exclude any unsuitable teacher or proprietor. Most independent schools offer a similar range of courses to state schools and enter pupils for the same public examinations. Introduction of the national curriculum and the associated education targets and assessment procedures is not obligatory in the independent sector.

The term public schools is often applied to those independent schools in membership of the Headmasters' and Headmistresses' Conference, the Governing Bodies Association or the Governing Bodies of Girls' Schools Association. Most public schools are single-sex but there are some mixed schools and an increasing number of schools have mixed sixth forms.

Preparatory schools are so-called because they prepare pupils for the common entrance examination to senior independent schools. Most cater for pupils from about seven to 13 years. The common entrance examination is set by the Common Entrance Examination Board, but marked by the independent school to which the pupil intends to go. It is taken at 13 by boys, and between 11 and 13 by girls.

The number of schools and pupils in 1996–7 was:

	No. of schools	No. of pupils	Pupil-teacher ratio
England	2,258	567,700	10.3
Wales*	62	10,000	10.1
Scotland	114	32,000	11.5
N. Ireland	19	900	9.7

*1995–6 figures

Most independent schools in Scotland follow the English examination system, i.e. GCSE followed by A-levels, although some take the Scottish Education Certificate at Standard grade followed by Highers or Advanced Highers.

ASSISTED PLACES SCHEME

The Assisted Places Scheme is being phased out after the September 1997 entry. It enables children to attend independent secondary schools which their parents could not otherwise afford. The scheme provides help with tuition fees and other expenses, except boarding costs, on a sliding scale depending on the family's income. The proportion of pupils receiving full fee remission is about 46 per cent. In the 1997–8 academic year, about 38,900 places were offered at the 494 participating schools in England and Wales. In Scotland about 3,800 pupils participated in the scheme in 52 schools in 1997–8. Pupils in secondary education holding their places at the beginning of the 1997–8 school year will keep them until they have completed their education at their current school. Those at the primary stage will hold them until they have completed that phase of their education, although some may exceptionally be allowed to hold their places for a further period to complete their secondary education.

The scheme is administered and funded in England by the DfEE, in Wales by the Welsh Office, and in Scotland by the SOEID. The scheme does not operate in Northern Ireland as the independent sector admits non-fee-paying pupils. There is, however, a similar scheme known as the Talented Children's Scheme to help pupils gifted in music and dance.

Further information can be obtained from the Independent Schools Information Service (*see* page 443).

THE CURRICULUM

ENGLAND AND WALES

The national curriculum was introduced in primary and secondary schools between autumn 1989 and autumn 1996, for the period of compulsory schooling from five to 16. It is mandatory in all maintained schools. As originally proposed, it was widely criticized for being too prescriptive and time-consuming. Following revision in 1994 its requirements were substantially reduced; the revisions were implemented in August 1995 for key stages one to three and from August 1996 for key stage four. Consultation is under way for a revised national curriculum to be introduced in schools from September 2000.

The statutory subjects at key stages one and two (five–11-year olds) are:

Core subjects	Foundation subjects
English	Design and technology
Welsh (Welsh-speaking schools in Wales)	Information technology
	History
Mathematics	Geography
Science	Welsh (non-Welsh-speaking schools in Wales)
	Art
	Music
	PE

At key stage three (11- to 14-year-olds) all pupils must study a modern foreign language. At key stage four (14- to 16-year-olds) pupils are required to continue to study the core subjects, PE and, in England only, a modern foreign language, design and technology and information technology. Other foundation subjects are optional. In Wales the national curriculum has separate and distinctive characteristics which are reflected, where appropriate, in the programmes of study. Religious education must be taught across all key stages, following a locally agreed syllabus; parents have the right to remove their children if they wish.

National tests and tasks in English, Welsh (in Welsh-speaking schools in Wales) and mathematics at key stage one, with the addition of science at key stages two and three, are in place. Teachers make their own assessments of their pupils' progress to set alongside the test results. At key stage four the GCSE and vocational equivalents are the main form of assessment.

The DfEE and the Welsh Office publish tables showing pupils' performance in A-level, AS-level, GCSE and GNVQ examinations school by school. In England only, local education authorities are required to publish similar information in November each year showing the results of national curriculum tests and teacher assessments for seven-, 11- and 14-year-olds. Approximately 600,000 pupils in each of the age groups take the tests each year in England and Wales (38,000).

Percentage of pupils reaching the expected level of performance at that age:

	Key stage 1 7-year olds (level 2)	Key stage 2 11-year olds (level 4)	Key stage 3 14-year olds (level 5)
ENGLAND			
English	80.0	63.0	57.5
Mathematics	84.0	63.0	61.5
Science	85.0	69.0	60.5
WALES			
English	80.0	64.5	59.5
Welsh (first language)	85.0	57.0	68.0
Mathematics	83.5	65.0	60.5
Science	84.0	72.0	61.0

National targets have been set for 11-year-olds in England: 80 per cent to reach level four in the English test and 75 per cent to reach level four in the mathematics test by 2002. In Wales the targets are: 70–80 per cent to reach the expected level of performance for that age at key stages two and three by 2002.

In Wales, Welsh is a compulsory subject for all pupils at key stages one, two and three where it is taught either as a first or second language. At key stage four it is compulsory in schools which are Welsh-speaking (as defined by the Education Act 1996). It will also become compulsory at key stage four from September 1999 in schools which are not Welsh-speaking. Schools also use Welsh as the medium of teaching; some 27 per cent of primary schools use Welsh as the sole or main medium of instruction and a further 6 per cent use it for part of the curriculum; nearly 21 per cent of secondary schools use Welsh as the medium of instruction for at least half of their foundation subjects.

In October 1997 in England the Qualifications and Curriculum Authority (QCA) was formed by the amalgamation of the School Curriculum and Assessment Authority (SCAA) and the National Council for Vocational Qualifications. An independent government agency funded by the DfEE, its remit ranges from the under-fives to higher level vocational qualifications. It is responsible for ensuring that the curriculum and qualifications available to young people and adults are of high quality, coherent and flexible. In Wales, the Qualifications, Curriculum and Assessment Authority for Wales/Awdurdod Cymwyster-au, Cwricwlwm ac Asesu Cymru (ACCAC) exercises similar functions. ACCAC is funded by the Welsh Office.

SCOTLAND

The content and management of the curriculum in Scotland are not prescribed by statute but are the responsibility of education authorities and individual headteachers. Advice and guidance is provided by the SOEID and the Scottish Consultative Council on the Curriculum, which also has a developmental role. SOEID has produced guidelines on the structure and balance of the curriculum for the five–14 age group as well as for each of the curriculum areas for this age group and a major programme to extend modern language teaching to primary schools is in progress. There are also guidelines on assessment across the whole curriculum, on reporting to parents, and on standardized national tests for English language and mathematics at five levels. The curriculum for 14- to 16-year-olds includes study within each of eight modes: language and communication, mathematical studies, science, technology, social studies, creative activities, physical education, and religious and moral education. There is a recommended percentage of class time to be devoted to each area over the two years. Provision is made for teaching in Gaelic in Gaelic-speaking areas. Testing is carried out on a voluntary basis when the teacher deems it appropriate; most pupils are expected to move from one level to the next at roughly two-year intervals. National testing is largely in place in most primary schools but secondary school participation rates are lower.

For 16- to 18-year-olds, there is available a modular system of vocational courses, certificated by the Scottish Qualifications Authority (SQA), in addition to academic courses. A new unified framework of courses and awards, known as 'Higher Still', which will bring together both academic and vocational courses will be introduced in 1999 (see page 431). The SQA will award the new certificates.

NORTHERN IRELAND

A curriculum common to all grant-aided schools exists. Pupils are required to study religious education and, depending on which key stage they have reached, certain subjects from six broad areas of study: English, mathematics, science and technology; the environment and society; creative and expressive studies and, in key stages three and four, language studies. The statutory curriculum requirements at key stages one to three have been revised and new programmes of study were introduced in September 1996. Six cross-curricular educational themes, which include information technology and education for mutual understanding, are woven through the main subjects of the curriculum. Irish is a foundation subject in schools that use it as a medium of instruction.

The assessment of pupils is broadly in line with practice in England and Wales and takes place at the ages of eight, 11 and 14. The GCSE is used to assess 16-year-olds.

NATIONAL TESTING AND TEACHERS' ASSESSMENT RESULTS IN CORE SUBJECTS 1997
Percentage of pupils reaching the expected level of performance at that age:

	Key stage 1 8-year olds (level 2)	Key stage 2 11-year olds (level 4)	Key stage 3 14-year olds (level 5)
English	92.2	63.0	66.5
Mathematics	92.0	69.0	73.0
Science	—	—	63.0

National targets have been set for 11-year-olds: 80 per cent to reach level four in English and mathematics by 2002.

The Northern Ireland Council for the Curriculum, Examinations and Assessment (NICCEA) monitors and advises the department and teachers on all matters relating to the curriculum, assessment arrangements and examinations in grant-aided schools. It conducts GCSE, A- and AS-level examinations, pupil assessment at key stages one, two and three and administers the transfer procedure tests.

RECORDS OF ACHIEVEMENT

The National Record of Achievement (NRA) has been reviewed and will be relaunched in February 1999 as 'Progress File'. It sets down the range of a school-leaver's achievements and activities both inside and outside the classroom, including those not tested by examination, and covers achievement in further and higher education, training and employment. It will be implemented in schools from September 1999. It is not compulsory in Scotland but is available to all education authorities for issue to school leavers. Parents in England and Wales must receive a written yearly progress report on all aspects of their child's achievements. There is a similar commitment

for Northern Ireland. In Scotland the school report card gives parents information on their child's progress.

THE PUBLIC EXAMINATION SYSTEM

ENGLAND, WALES AND NORTHERN IRELAND

Until the end of 1987, secondary school pupils at the end of compulsory schooling around the age of 16, and others, took the General Certificate of Education (GCE) Ordinary-level or the Certificate of Secondary Education (CSE). From 1988 these were replaced by a single system of examinations, the General Certificate of Secondary Education (GCSE), which is usually taken after five years of secondary education. The GCSE is the main method of assessing the performance of pupils at age 16 in all national curriculum subjects required to be assessed at the end of compulsory schooling. The structure of the examination is being adapted in accordance with national curriculum requirements; new subject criteria were published in 1995 to govern GCSE syllabuses introduced in 1996 for first examination in 1998. GCSE short-course qualifications are available in some subjects. As a rule the syllabus takes half the time of a full GCSE course.

The GCSE differs from its predecessors in that there are syllabuses based on national criteria covering course objectives, content and assessment methods; differentiated assessment (i.e. different papers or questions for different ranges of ability); and grade-related criteria (i.e. grades awarded on absolute rather than relative performance). The GCSE certificates are awarded on a seven-point scale, A to G. From 1994 there has been an additional 'starred' A grade (A*), to recognize the achievement of the highest attainers at GCSE. Grades A to C are the equivalent of the corresponding O-level grades A to C or CSE grade 1. Grades D, E, F and G record achievement at least as high as that represented by CSE grades 2 to 5. All GCSE syllabuses, assessments and grading procedures are monitored by the Qualifications and Curriculum Authority (see page 429) to ensure that they conform to the national criteria.

In the UK in 1996–7, 94.5 per cent of all 16-year-olds achieved one or more graded GCSE, SCE Standard grade, or equivalent results.

In Wales the Certificate of Education is intended for 16-year-olds for whom no suitable examination exists. In 1996, 24,524 candidates took the examination, of whom 93.4 per cent obtained pass or better.

Many maintained schools offer BTEC Firsts (see page 433) and an increasing number offer BTEC Nationals. National Vocational Qualifications in the form of General NVQs are also available to students in schools (see page 434). The Part 1 GNVQ is a shortened version of the full GNVQ. Designed for 14- to 16-year-olds, it is a two-year course at foundation and intermediate levels broadly equivalent to two GCSEs at grades A* to C. It has been piloted from 1995 and is planned to be available in schools from September 1998.

Advanced (A-level) examinations are taken by those who choose to continue their education after GCSE. A-level courses last two years and have traditionally provided the foundation for entry to higher education. A-levels are marked on a seven-point scale, from A to E, N (narrow failure) and U (unclassified), which latter grade will not be certificated.

Advanced Supplementary level (AS-level) examinations were introduced in 1987 as an alternative to, and to complement, A-level examinations. AS-levels are for full-time A-level students but are also open to other students. An AS-level syllabus covers not less than half the amount of ground covered by the corresponding A-level syllabus and, where possible, is related to it. An AS-level course lasts two years and requires not less than half the teaching time of the corresponding A-level course, and two AS-levels are equivalent to one A-level. AS-level passes are graded A to E, with grade standards related to the A-level grades.

In the UK in 1996–7, 283,000 students (45.6 per cent boys, 54.4 per cent girls) achieved one or more passes at A-level or SCE H-grade. Of those in Great Britain who entered for at least one A-level, or at least two SCE H-grades, 32 per cent studied sciences (60 per cent boys, 40 per cent girls) and 68 per cent studied arts/social studies (41 per cent of boys, 59 per cent of girls).

Most examining boards allow the option of an additional paper of greater difficulty to be taken by A-level candidates to obtain what is known as a Special-level or Scholarship-level qualification. S-level papers are available in most of the traditional academic subjects and are marked on a three-point scale.

The City & Guilds Diploma of Vocational Education is intended for a wide ability range. The Diploma provides recognition of achievement at two levels: foundation at pre-16 and intermediate at post-16. The intermediate level is being phased out in favour of the corresponding GNVQs. Within guidelines and to meet specified criteria, schools and colleges design their own courses, which stress activity-based learning, core skills which include application of number, communication and information technology, and work experience. The Diploma is of value to those who want to find out what aptitudes they may have and to prepare themselves for work, but who may not yet be committed to a particular occupation. At foundation level, it can be taken alongside GCSEs and can provide a context for the introduction of GNVQ units into the key stage four curriculum.

The various examining boards in England have combined into three unitary awarding bodies, which offer both academic and vocational qualifications: GNVQs, GCSEs and A-levels. The new bodies are Edexcel, the Assessment and Qualifications Alliance (AQA), and Oxford, Cambridge and RSA Examinations (OCR) (see page 444). At present the existing examination boards are still separate bodies, working in alliance to develop single courses.

SCOTLAND

Scotland has its own system of public examinations. At the end of the fourth year of secondary education, at about the age of 16, pupils take the Standard grade (which has replaced the Ordinary grade) of the Scottish Certificate of Education. Standard grade courses and examinations have been designed to suit every level of ability, with assessment against nationally determined standards of performance.

For most courses there are three separate examination papers at the end of the two-year Standard grade course. They are set at Credit (leading to awards at grade 1 or 2), General (leading to awards at grade 3 or 4) and Foundation (leading to awards at grade 5 or 6) levels. Grade 7 is available to those who, although they have completed the course, have not attained any of these levels. Normally pupils will take examinations covering two pairs of grades, either grades 1–4 or grades 3–6. Most candidates take seven or eight Standard grade examinations.

The Higher grade of the Scottish Certificate of Education is normally taken one year after Standard grade, at the age of 17 or thereabouts. It is common for pupils to be presented for four or more Higher grades at a single diet of the examination.

The Certificate of Sixth Year Studies (CSYS) is designed to give direction and purpose to sixth-year work by encouraging pupils who have completed their main subjects at Higher grade to study a maximum of three of

these subjects in depth. Pupils may also use the sixth year to gain improved or additional Higher grades or Standard grades. National Certificates may also be taken in the fifth and six years of secondary school as an alternative to or in addition to Highers.

In 1999–2000 the 'Higher Still' reforms will introduce a new system of courses and qualifications, replacing SCE Highers, CSYS and many national certificate modules, for everyone studying beyond Standard grade in Scottish schools, and for non-advanced students in further education colleges. Qualifications will be available at five levels: Access, Intermediate 1, Intermediate 2, Higher, and Advanced Higher. Courses will be made up of internally assessed units and students possessing a number of units and courses may be able to build them into a Scottish Group Award. Achievement of that award will also indicate that the holder has attained a defined level of competence in the core skills of communication, problem-solving, information technology and working with others.

All of these qualifications are awarded by the Scottish Qualifications Authority (SQA), which on 1 April 1997 assumed the functions of the Scottish Examinations Board and the Scottish Vocational Education Council.

THE INTERNATIONAL BACCALAUREATE

The International Baccalaureate is an internationally recognized two-year pre-university course and examination designed to facilitate the mobility of students and to promote international understanding. Candidates must offer one subject from each of six subject groups, at least three at higher level and the remainder at subsidiary level. Single subjects can be offered, for which a certificate is received. There are 33 schools and colleges in the UK which offer the International Baccalaureate diploma.

TEACHERS

ENGLAND AND WALES

Teachers are appointed by local education authorities, school governing bodies, or school managers. Those in publicly maintained schools must be approved as qualified by the Secretary of State. With certain exceptions the profession at present has an all-graduate entry. To obtain Qualified Teacher Status (QTS) it is necessary to have successfully completed a course of initial teacher training, traditionally either a Bachelor of Education (B.Ed.) degree or the Postgraduate Certificate of Education (PGCE) at an accredited institution. New entrants to the profession are statutorily required to serve a one-year induction period during which they will have a structured programme of support. In recent years various employment-based routes to teaching have been developed. The Graduate Teacher Programme allows graduates with teaching experience to undergo between one term's and one year's school-based training. The Registered Teacher Scheme is designed to attract into the teaching profession entrants over 24 years of age without formal teaching qualifications but with relevant training and experience; entrants are paid a salary and undertake one to two years higher education depending on whether they possess relevant teaching experience. Teachers in further education are not required to have Qualified Teacher Status, though roughly half have a teaching qualification and most have industrial, commercial or professional experience. A mandatory qualification for aspiring head-teachers, the National Professional Qualification for Headship (NPQH), was introduced in September 1997.

From September 1998 the national curriculum for initial teacher training was introduced for primary English and mathematics, and information and communications technology; that for primary science and secondary English, mathematics and science will become mandatory from September 1999.

Teacher training is now largely school-based, with student teachers on secondary PGCE courses spending two-thirds of their training in the classroom. Changes have also been made to primary phase teacher training to make it more school-based and to give schools a role in course design and delivery. Individual schools or consortia of schools and CTCs can bid for funds from the DfEE to carry out their own teacher training, including recruitment of students, subject to approval of their proposed training programme by the Teacher Training Agency (TTA) and monitoring and evaluation by the Office for Standards in Education (OFSTED). Funds are given to schools to meet the costs of designing and delivering the courses.

The TTA accredits institutions in England providing initial teacher training for school teachers which meet certain criteria published by the Secretary of State and quality standards. The TTA funds all types of teacher training in England, whether run by universities, colleges or schools, and some educational research. An independent professional council, the General Teaching Council, is to be established by 2000 to advise the Secretary of State and the TTA, with a separate council for Wales.

The TTA Unit in Wales has a similar remit in respect of Wales. The TTA also acts as a central source of information and advice for both England and Wales about entry to teaching, and has responsibilities relating to the continuing professional development of teachers.

The Specialist Teacher Assistant (STA) scheme was introduced in September 1994 to provide trained support to qualified teachers in the teaching of reading, writing and arithmetic to young pupils.

SCOTLAND

All teachers in maintained schools must be registered with the General Teaching Council for Scotland. They are registered provisionally for a two-year probationary period which can be extended if necessary. Only graduates are accepted as entrants to the profession; primary school teachers undertake either a four-year vocational degree course or a one-year postgraduate course, while teachers of academic subjects in secondary schools undertake the latter. Most initial teacher training is classroom-based. The colleges of education provide both in-service and pre-service training for teachers which is subject to inspection by HM Inspectors. The colleges are funded by the Scottish Higher Education Funding Council.

NORTHERN IRELAND

All new entrants to teaching in grant-aided schools are graduates and hold an approved teaching qualification. Teacher training is provided by the two universities and two colleges of education. The colleges are concerned with teacher education mainly for the primary school sector. They also provide B.Ed. courses for intending secondary school teachers of religious education, commercial studies, and craft, design and technology. With these exceptions, the professional training of teachers for secondary schools is provided in the education departments of the universities. A review of primary and secondary teacher training has taken place as a result of which all student teachers spend more time in the classroom. All newly qualified teachers undertake a two-year induction period.

ACCREDITATION OF TRAINING INSTITUTIONS

Advice to central government on the accreditation, content and quality of initial teacher training courses is given in England by the TTA, in Wales by the HEFCW and in

Northern Ireland by validating bodies. These bodies also monitor and disseminate good practice, assisted in Northern Ireland by the Teacher Education Committee. In Scotland the General Teaching Council advises SOEID on the professional suitability of all training courses in colleges of education.

SHORTAGE SUBJECTS

Because of a shortage of teachers in certain secondary subjects, providers of initial teacher training in England and Wales can receive funds from the TTA to help promote courses in certain subjects and to offer students on courses in those subjects financial support. The subjects are: science; mathematics; modern languages (including Welsh in Wales); design and technology; information technology; religious education; music, and geography.

SERVING TEACHERS 1995–6 *(full-time and part-time)* (thousands)

	All	% graduate
Public sector schools	451	62
Nursery and primary	212	50
Secondary	222	72
Special	17	44
FE and HE establishments	127	82
TOTAL	578	72

SALARIES

Qualified teachers in England, Wales and Northern Ireland, other than heads and deputy heads, are paid on an 18-point scale. Entry points and placement depend on qualifications, experience, responsibilities, excellence, and recruitment and retention factors as calculated by the relevant body, i.e. the governing body or the LEA. There is a statutory superannuation scheme in maintained schools.

Teachers in Scotland are paid on a ten-point scale. The entry point depends on type of qualification, and additional allowances are payable under certain circumstances.

Salaries from 1 December 1998*

	England, Wales and N. Ireland	Scotland
Head	£27,204–£59,580	£27,846–£51,582
Deputy head	£26,337–£43,326	£27,846–£38,589
Teacher	£13,362–£35,787	£13,206–£28,893

*From 1 April 1998 for Scotland

FURTHER EDUCATION

Further education is defined as all provision outside schools to people aged over 16 of education up to and including A-level and its equivalent. The Further Education Funding Councils for England and Wales, the Scottish Office Education and Industry Department and the Department of Education for Northern Ireland have a duty to secure provision of adequate facilities for further education in their areas.

ENGLAND AND WALES

Further education and sixth form colleges are funded directly by central government through the Further Education Funding Council for England (FEFCE) and the Further Education Funding Council for Wales (FEFCW). These councils are also responsible for the assessment of quality, in which the Councils' inspectorates play a key role. The colleges are controlled by autonomous further education corporations, which include substantial representation from industry and commerce, and which own their own assets and employ their own staff. Their funding is determined in part by the number of students enrolled.

In England and Wales further education courses are taught at a variety of institutions. These include universities which were formerly polytechnics, colleges of higher education, colleges of further education (some of which also offer higher education courses), and tertiary colleges and sixth form colleges, which concentrate on the provision of normal sixth form school courses as well as a range of vocational courses. A number of institutions specific to a particular form of training, e.g. the Royal College of Music, are also involved.

Teaching staff in further education establishments are not necessarily required to have teaching qualifications although many do so, but they are subject to regular appraisal of teaching performance.

Further education tends to be broadly vocational in purpose and employers are often involved in designing courses. It ranges from lower-level technical and commercial courses through courses for those aiming at higher-level posts in industry, commerce and administration, to professional courses. Facilities exist for GCE A and AS levels, GCSEs, GNVQs and a full range of vocational qualifications (*see* pages 430–1). These courses can form the foundation for progress to higher education qualifications.

The main courses and examinations in the vocational field, all of which link in with the National Vocational Qualification (NVQ) framework (*see* page 434), are offered by the following bodies, but there are also many others.

The Edexcel Foundation was formed by the merger of the Business and Technology Education Council (BTEC) and London Examinations. They provide programmes of study across a wide range of subject areas. The main qualifications offered are GCSEs, A-levels, GNVQs, NVQs, BTEC First, National and Higher National diplomas and certificates, key skills and entry certificates.

City & Guilds specialize in developing qualifications and assessments for work-related and leisure qualifications. They offer nationally and internationally recognized certificates in over 500 qualifications, many of which are NVQs, SVQs and GNVQs. The progressive structure of awards spans seven levels, from foundation to the highest level of professional competence.

RSA Examinations Board schemes cover a wide range of vocational qualifications, including accounting, business administration, customer service, management, language schemes, information technology and teaching qualifications. A wide range of NVQs and GNVQs are offered and a policy operates of credit accumulation, so that candidates can take a single unit or complete qualifications.

There are 480 further education establishments and sixth form colleges in England and Wales. In 1997–8 there were 720,500 full-time and sandwich-course students and 840,900 part-time day students on further education courses.

SCOTLAND

Further education comprises non-advanced courses up to SCE Higher grade, GCE A-level and work-based awards. Courses are taught mainly at colleges of further education, including technical colleges, and in some schools.

There are 46 further education colleges. The responsibility for 43 of these (incorporated colleges) has been transferred to individual boards of management, funded directly by the Secretary of State, which run the colleges and employ staff. The boards include the principal, staff and student representatives among their ten to 16 members; at least half the members must have experience of commerce, industry or the practice of a profession. Two colleges, on Orkney and Shetland, are under Islands Council control and receive payment from the Secretary of State, as do the trustees of the remaining college, Sabhal Mor Ostaig, the Gaelic college on Skye.

The Scottish Qualifications Authority (SQA) awards qualifications for most occupations. It awards at non-advanced level the National Certificate, which is available in over 4,000 individual modules and covers the whole range of non-advanced further education provision in Scotland. Students may study for the National Certificate on a full-time, part-time, open learning or work-based learning basis. National Certificate modules can be taken in further education colleges, secondary schools and other centres, normally from the age of 16 onwards. In August 1999 the 'Higher Still' reforms will introduce a unified curriculum and assessment system for non-advanced post-16 education. Courses will be available at five levels, replacing SCE Higher grades, CSYS courses and many National Certificate modules. SQA also offers modular advanced-level HNC/HND qualifications, which are available in further education colleges and higher education institutions. SQA accredits and awards Scottish Vocational Qualifications (SVQs) which have mutual recognition with the NVQs available in the rest of the UK. SVQs are work-place assessed, but can also be taken in further education colleges and other centres where work-place conditions can be simulated.

The Record of Education and Training (RET) has been introduced to provide a single certificate recording SQA achievements; an updated version is provided as and when necessary. SQA also administers the National Record of Achievement (now 'Progress File') in Scotland on behalf of the Scottish Office.

In the academic year 1996–7 there were 33,799 full-time and sandwich-course students and 254,065 part-time students on non-advanced vocational courses of further education in the 46 further education colleges.

NORTHERN IRELAND

On 1 April 1998 all further education colleges became free-standing corporate bodies like their counterparts in the rest of the UK. Planning, which was previously undertaken by the Education and Library Boards, is now the responsibility of the Department of Education for Northern Ireland, which also funds the colleges direct. The colleges own their own property, are responsible for their own services and employ their own staff.

The governing bodies of the colleges must include at least 50 per cent membership from the professions, local business or industry, or other fields of employment relevant to the activities of the college.

On reaching school-leaving age, pupils may attend colleges of further education to pursue the same type of vocational courses as are provided in colleges in England and Wales, administered by the same examining bodies.

In 1997–8 Northern Ireland had 17 institutions of further education, and there were 21,642 full-time students and 53,952 part-time students on non-advanced vocational courses of further education.

COURSE INFORMATION

Applications for further education courses are generally made directly to the colleges concerned. Information on further education courses in the UK and addresses of colleges can be found in the *Directory of Further Education* published annually by the Careers Research and Advisory Centre.

NATIONAL VOCATIONAL QUALIFICATIONS

Bodies responsible for the regulation of GNVQs and NVQs in the UK are: in England, the Qualifications and Curriculum Authority (QCA); in Wales, the Curriculum and Assessment Authority/Awdurdod Cymwysterau, Cwricwlwm ac Asesu Cymru (ACCAC); in Northern Ireland, the Council for the Curriculum, Examinations and Assessment (NICCEA); and in Scotland, the Scottish Qualifications Authority (SQA). Those bodies do not award qualifications (except for the SQA) but accredit National Vocational Qualifications (NVQs), General National Vocational Qualifications (GNVQs) and core skills. Assessment is carried out through awarding bodies who bestow the qualifications where candidates reach the required standards.

National Vocational Qualifications (NVQs) are work-place based occupational qualifications. In September 1992 General National Vocational Qualifications (GNVQs) were introduced into colleges and schools as a vocational alternative to academic qualifications. They cover broad categories in the NVQ framework and are aimed at those wishing to familiarize themselves with a range of opportunities. Advanced GNVQ or the vocational A-level is equivalent to two A-levels; from September 2000 a revised version equivalent to a single A-level is planned. Intermediate GNVQ is equivalent to four GCSEs at A* to C grade. Foundation GNVQ is equivalent to four GCSEs at D to G grade.

HIGHER EDUCATION

The term higher education is used to describe education above A-level, Higher and Advanced Higher grade and their equivalent, which is provided in universities, colleges of higher education and in some further education colleges.

The Further and Higher Education Act 1992 and parallel legislation in Scotland removed the distinction between higher education provided by the universities, and that provided in England and Wales by the former polytechnics and colleges of higher education and in Scotland by the former central institutions and other institutions, allowing all polytechnics, and other higher education institutions which satisfy the necessary criteria, to award their own taught course and research degrees and to adopt the title of university. All the polytechnics, art colleges and some colleges of higher education have since adopted the title of university. The change of name does not affect the legal constitution of the institutions. All are funded by the Higher Education Funding Councils for England, Wales and Scotland.

The number of students in higher education in the UK in 1996–7 was:

Full-time, sandwich	1,194,600
% female	50.9%
Part-time	696,900
% female	53.3%
TOTAL	1,891,500
of which overseas	201,400

The proportion of 18- to 21-year-olds undertaking full-time and part-time courses in higher education in the UK was 26 per cent in 1995. The number of mature entrants (those aged 21 and over when starting an undergraduate course and 25 and over when starting a postgraduate course) to higher education in Great Britain in 1996–7 (excluding those at the Open University) was 1,560,100.

The number of full-time and part-time students on science courses in 1996–7 was 1,052,900, of whom 22.7 per cent were female.

UNIVERSITIES AND COLLEGES

The universities are self-governing institutions established in most cases by royal charter or Act of Parliament. They have academic freedom and are responsible for their own academic appointments, curricula and student admissions and award their own degrees.

Responsibility for universities in England rests with the Secretary of State for Education and Employment, and in their territories with the Secretaries of State for Scotland, Wales and Northern Ireland. Advice to the Government on matters relating to the universities is provided by the Higher Education Funding Councils for England, Wales and Scotland, and by the Northern Ireland Higher Education Council. The HEFCs receive a block grant from central government which they allocate to the universities and colleges. The grant is allocated directly by central government in Northern Ireland on the advice of the Northern Ireland Higher Education Council.

There are now 88 universities in the UK, where only 47 existed prior to the Further and Higher Education Acts 1992. Of the 88, 71 are in England (including one federal university), two (one a federal institution) in Wales, 13 in Scotland and two in Northern Ireland.

The pre-1992 universities each have their own system of internal government but broad similarities exist. Most are run by two main bodies: the senate, which deals primarily with academic issues and consists of members elected from within the university; and the council, which is the supreme body and is responsible for all appointments and promotions, and bidding for and allocation of financial resources. At least half the members of the council are drawn from outside the university. Joint committees of senate and council are becoming increasingly common.

Those universities which were formerly polytechnics (38) or other higher education institutions (three) and the colleges of higher education (47) are run by higher education corporations (HECs), which are controlled by boards of governors whose members were initially appointed by the Secretaries of State but which will subsequently make their own appointments. At least half the members of each board must be drawn from industry, business, commerce and the professions.

In 1996–7 full-time and part-time student enrolments in England and Wales were:

England

Undergraduates	1,159,600
% overseas	8.5%
Postgraduates	299,100
% overseas	21.2%

Wales

Undergraduates	77,200
% overseas	8.4%
Postgraduates	17,500
% overseas	24.0%

Higher education courses funded by the respective HEFCs are also taught in some further education colleges in England and Wales. In England in 1996–7 there were over 36,000 students (2.5 per cent of total higher education student numbers) on such courses and 549 (0.6 per cent of higher education student numbers) in Wales.

The non-residential Open University provides courses nationally leading to degrees. Teaching is through a combination of television and radio programmes, correspondence, tutorials, short residential courses and local audio-visual centres. No qualifications are needed for entry. The Open University offers a modular programme of undergraduate courses by credit accumulation and post-experience and postgraduate courses, including a programme of higher degrees which comprises B.Phil., M.Phil. and Ph.D. through research, and MA, MBA and M.Sc. through taught courses. The Open University throughout the UK is funded by the Higher Education Funding Council for England. Its recurrent grant for 1996–7 was £110.7 million from the Higher Education Funding Council for England and £6.8 million from the Teacher Training Agency. In 1998, about 116,000 undergraduates were registered at the Open University, of whom about 52 per cent were women. Estimated cost (1998) of a six-credit degree was around £3,800 including course fees of about £2,300.

The independent University of Buckingham provides a two-year course leading to a bachelor's degree and its tuition fees were £9,996 for 1998. It receives no capital or recurrent income from the Government but its students are eligible for mandatory awards from local education authorities. Its academic year consists of four terms of ten weeks each.

ACADEMIC STAFF

Each university and college appoints its own academic staff on its own conditions. However, there is a common salary structure and, except for Oxford and Cambridge, a common career structure in those universities formerly funded by the UFC and a common salary structure for the former PCFC sector. The Universities and Colleges Employers Association (UCEA) acts as a pay agency for universities and colleges.

Teaching staff in higher education require no formal teaching qualification, but teacher trainers are required to spend a certain amount of time in schools to ensure that they have sufficient recent practical experience.

In 1996–7, there were 64,257 full-time and part-time teaching and research staff (UK nationals) in institutions of higher education in the UK.

Salary scales for staff in the pre-1992 universities sector differ from those in the former polytechnics and colleges; it is planned eventually to amalgamate them. The 1998–9 salary scales for non-clinical academic staff in universities formerly funded by the UFC are:

Professor from	£35,120
Senior lecturer	£30,498–£34,464
Lecturer grade B	£22,726–£29,048
Lecturer grade A	£15,735 –£21,815

The salaries of clinical academic staff are kept broadly comparable to those of doctors and dentists in the National Health Service.

Salary scales for lecturers in the former polytechnics, now universities, and colleges of higher education in England, Wales and Northern Ireland are:

	September 1998	*March 1999*
Head of Department	from £26,304	from £26,304
Principal lecturer	£27,512–£34,543	£27,746–£35,204
Senior lecturer	£22,012–£29,086	£22,400–£29,600
Lecturer	£14,148–£23,585	£14,398–£24,002

The salary scales for staff in Scotland are determined at individual college level.

FINANCE

Although universities and colleges are expected to look to a wider range of funding sources than before, and to generate additional revenue in collaboration with indus-

try, they are still largely financed, directly or indirectly, from government resources.

In 1996–7 the total income of institutions of higher education in the UK was £11,143.5 million (£10,647.4 million in 1995–6). Grants from the funding councils amounted to £4,400 million (£4,428.2 million in 1995–6), forming 39.5 per cent of total income (41.6 per cent in 1995–6). Income from research grants and contracts was £1,642.3 million, 14.7 per cent of total income (14.5 per cent in 1995–6).

In the academic year 1996–7 the HEFCs' recurrent grant to institutions outside their sector and to LEAs for the provision of higher education courses was £84.5 million.

COURSES

In the UK all universities, including the Open University, and some colleges award their own degrees and other qualifications and can act as awarding and validating bodies for neighbouring colleges which are not yet accredited. The Quality Assurance Agency for Higher Education, funded by institutional contributions, advises the Secretaries of State on applications for degree-awarding powers.

Higher education courses last full-time for at least four weeks or, if part-time, involve more than 60 hours of instruction. Facilities exist for full-time and part-time study, day release, sandwich or block release. Credit accumulation and transfer (CATS) is a system of study which is becoming widely available. It allows a student to achieve a final qualification by accumulating credits for courses of study successfully achieved, or even professional experience, over a period. Credit transfer information and values are carried on an electronic database called ECCTIS 2000, which is available in most careers offices and many schools and colleges.

Higher education courses comprise: first degree and postgraduate (including research); Diploma in Higher Education (Dip.HE); Higher National Diploma (HND) and Higher National Certificate (HNC); and preparation for professional examinations. The in-service training of teachers is also included, but from September 1994 has been funded in England by the TTA (*see* page 432), not the HEFC.

The Diploma of Higher Education (Dip.HE) is a two-year diploma usually intended to serve as a stepping-stone to a degree course or other further study. The Dip.HE is awarded by the institution itself if it is accredited; by an accredited institution of its choice if not. The BTEC Higher National Certificate (HNC) is awarded after two years part-time study. The BTEC Higher National Diploma (HND) is awarded after two years full-time, or three years sandwich-course or part-time study.

With the exception of certain Scottish universities where master is sometimes used for a first degree in arts subjects, undergraduate courses lead to the title of Bachelor, Bachelor of Arts (BA) and Bachelor of Science (B.Sc.) being the most common. For a higher degree the titles are: Master of Arts (MA), Master of Science (M.Sc.) (usually taught courses) and the research degrees of Master of Philosophy (M.Phil.) and Doctor of Philosophy (Ph.D. or, at a few universities, D.Phil.).

Most undergraduate courses at British universities and colleges of higher education run for three years, except modern language courses and those at Scottish universities and at the University of Keele which usually take four years. Professional courses in subjects such as medicine, dentistry and veterinary science take longer. Details of courses on offer and of predicted entry requirements for the following year's intake are provided in *University and*

College Entrance: Official Guide, published annually by the Universities and Colleges Admissions Service (UCAS), which includes degree, Dip.HE and HND courses at all universities (excluding the Open University) and most colleges of HE; it is available from bookshops.

Postgraduate studies vary in length. Taught courses which lead to certificates, diplomas or master's degrees usually take one year full-time or two years part-time. Research degrees take from two to three years full-time and much longer if completed on a part-time basis. Details of taught courses and research degree opportunities can be found in *Graduate Studies*, published annually for the Careers Research and Advisory Centre (CRAC) by Hobsons Publishing plc (for address, *see* page 444).

Post-experience short courses are forming an increasing part of higher education provision, reflecting the need to update professional and technical training. Most of these courses fund themselves.

ADMISSIONS

The target number of students entering full-time higher education has been set at 30 to 31 per cent of the 18- to 19-year-old age group. Institutions suffer financial penalties if the number of students laid down for them by the funding councils is exceeded, but the individual university or college decides which students to accept. The formal entry requirements to most degree courses are two A-levels at grade E or above (or equivalent), and to HND courses one A-level (or equivalent). In practice, most offers of places require qualifications in excess of this, higher requirements usually reflecting the popularity of a course. These requirements do not, however, exclude applications from students with a variety of non-GCSE qualifications or unquantified experience and skills.

For admission to a degree, Dip.HE or HND, potential students apply through a central clearing house. All universities and most colleges providing higher education courses in the UK are members of the Universities and Colleges Admission Service (UCAS). Applicants are supplied with an application form and a *UCAS Handbook*, available from schools, colleges and careers offices or direct from UCAS, and may apply to a maximum of six institutions/courses on the UCAS form. The only exception among universities is the Open University, which conducts its own admissions.

Applications for undergraduate teacher training courses are made through UCAS. Details of initial teacher training courses in Scotland can be obtained from colleges of education and those universities offering such courses, and from the Committee of Scottish Higher Education Principals (COSHEP).

For admission as a postgraduate student, universities and colleges normally require a good first degree in a subject related to the proposed course of study or research, but other experience and qualifications will be considered on merit. Most applications are made to individual institutions but there are two clearing houses of relevance. Postgraduate teacher training courses in England and Wales utilize the Graduate Teacher Training Registry (*see* page 444). Applications to postgraduate teacher training courses in Scotland are made through the Teacher Education Admissions Clearing House (TEACH) (*see* page 444). Applications for PGCE courses at institutions in Northern Ireland are made to the Department of Education for Northern Ireland. For social work the Social Work Admissions System operates (*see* page 444).

SCOTLAND

The Scottish Higher Education Funding Council (SHEFC) funds 21 institutions of higher education, including 13 universities. The universities are broadly managed as described above and each institution of higher education is managed by an independent governing body which includes representatives of industrial, commercial, professional and educational interests. Most of the courses outside the universities have a vocational orientation and a substantial number are sandwich courses.

Student enrolments in 1996–7 in universities and other higher education institutions were:

Undergraduates	125,600
% overseas	8.8%
Postgraduates	37,500
% overseas	29.9%

There were 32,114 students on higher education courses in further education colleges, 19.6 per cent of total higher education students.

NORTHERN IRELAND

In Northern Ireland advanced courses are provided by 17 institutions of further education, the two universities and the two colleges of education. As well as offering first and postgraduate degrees, the University of Ulster offers courses leading to the BTEC Higher National Diploma and professional qualifications. Applications to undertake courses of higher education other than degree courses are made to the institutions direct. Higher education student enrolments in 1996–7 were (thousands):

Undergraduates	30,200
% overseas	16.8%
Postgraduates	9,500
% overseas	18.2%

There were 10,075 students enrolled on advanced courses of higher education in the institutions of further education, 25.4 per cent of higher education student numbers.

FEES

Tuition fees for existing students with mandatory awards (*see* below) are paid by the grant-awarding body. From September 1998, new entrants to undergraduate courses will pay an annual contribution to their fees of up to £1,000, depending on their own level of income and that of their spouse or parents. Students will pay the fee contribution direct to the institution. Among the classes of students exempt from payment are Scottish and EU students in the fourth year of a four-year degree course at a Scottish institution and medical students in the fifth year of their course. Students from EU member countries pay fees at home student rates and will also be liable to make an annual contribution to fees assessed against family income. Since 1980–1 students from outside the EU have paid fees that are meant to cover the cost of their education, but financial help is available under a number of schemes. Information about these schemes is available from British Council offices world-wide.

Universities and colleges are free to set their own charges for students from non-EU countries. Undergraduate fees for the academic year 1998–9 for home and EU students are set at a flat rate of £1,000.

For postgraduate students, the maximum tuition fee that will be reimbursed through the awards system is £2,610 in 1998–9.

GRANTS FOR STUDENTS

Students in the UK who plan to take a full-time or sandwich course of further study after leaving school may currently be eligible for a grant. A parental contribution is deductible on a sliding scale dependent on income. For married students this may be deducted from their spouse's income instead. However, parental contribution is not deducted from the grant to students over 25 years of age who have been self-supporting for at least three years. The main rates of mandatory grant have been frozen since 1991–2 and although existing students will continue to be eligible for grants and loans in similar proportions as now, grants for new entrants to higher education in 1998–9 will be paid at about half the rate for 1997–8, while loans will increase in compensation. From 1999–2000 maintenance grants for the latter category of students and for all new entrants will be replaced entirely by income-related loans.

Grants are paid by local education authorities in England, Wales and Northern Ireland, of which 100 per cent of the cost is reimbursed by central government. Applications are made to the authority in the area in which the student normally lives. In Scotland grants are made by the SOEID through the Student Awards Agency. Applications should not be made earlier than the January preceding the start of the course.

TYPES OF GRANT

Grants are currently of two kinds: mandatory and discretionary. Mandatory grants are those which awarding authorities must pay to students who are attending designated courses and who can satisfy certain other conditions. Such a grant is awarded normally to enable the student to attend only one designated course and there is no general entitlement to an award for any particular number of years. Discretionary grants are those for which each awarding authority has discretion to decide its own policy.

Designated courses are those full-time or sandwich courses leading to: a degree; the Diploma of Higher Education; the Higher National Diploma; initial teacher-training courses, including those for the postgraduate certificate of education and the art teachers' certificate or diploma; a university certificate or diploma course lasting at least three years and other qualifications which are specifically designated as being comparable to first degree courses. The local education authority should be consulted for advice about eligibility for a grant.

A means-tested maintenance grant, usually paid once a term, covers periods of attendance during term as well as the Christmas and Easter vacations, but not the summer vacation. The basic grant rates for 1998–9 (rates for Scottish students in parenthesis) are:

Living in	Existing students	New entrants (1998–9 only)
College/lodgings in London area	£2,225 (£2,145)	£1,225 (£1,145)
College/lodgings outside London area	£1,810 (£1,735)	£810 (£735)
Parental home	1,480 (£1,325)	£480 (£325)

Additional allowances are available if, for example, the course requires a period of study abroad.

LEA and SOEID expenditure on student fees and maintenance in 1996–7 was £2,380.3 million; about 927,900 mandatory awards were made.

STUDENT LOANS

In the academic year 1998–9 students will be eligible to apply for interest-free but indexed loans of up to £2,145 (£3,145 for new entrants).

Students apply direct to the Student Loans Company Ltd (see page 444), which will require a certificate of eligibility from their place of study. Loans are available to students on designated courses within the scope of current mandatory awards and certain residency conditions apply. In 1996–7, 589,600 loans were taken up, to the value of £877.2 million. Repayment arrangements differ for exist-

ing students and new entrants in 1998–9. Existing students still normally repay over five to seven years, although repayment can be deferred if annual income is at or below 85 per cent of national average earnings (£16,488 at 31 August 1998). New entrants will not be required to make repayments if their annual income is below a designated threshold (£10,000 in 1998–9); otherwise a percentage of the income above that amount is taken to repay the loan.

ACCESS FUNDS

Access funds are allocated by education departments to the appropriate funding councils in England, Wales and Scotland and administered by further and higher education institutions. In Northern Ireland they are allocated by central government to the institutions direct. They are available to students whose access to education might otherwise be inhibited by financial considerations or where real financial difficulties are faced. For the academic year 1998–9, provision in the UK will be £49.4 million.

POSTGRADUATE AWARDS

Grants for postgraduate study are of two types, both discretionary: 30-week bursaries, which are means-tested and are available for certain vocational and diploma courses; and studentship awards, which are dependent on the class of first degree, especially for research degrees, are not means-tested, and cover students undertaking research degrees or taught masters degrees. Postgraduate students, with the exception of students on loan-bearing diploma courses such as teacher training, are not eligible to apply for student loans.

An increasing number of scholarships are available from research charities, endowments, and particular industries or companies. For residents in England and Wales, several schemes of postgraduate bursaries (administered by the British Academy) or studentships are funded by the DfEE, the government research councils, the Ministry of Agriculture, Fisheries and Food, and the British Academy, which awards grants for study in the humanities.

In Scotland postgraduate funding is provided by the SOEID through the Student Awards Agency for Scotland, the Scottish Office Agriculture and Fisheries Department, and the research councils as in England and Wales.

Awards in Northern Ireland are made by DENI, the Department of Agriculture for Northern Ireland, and the Medical Research Council.

The rates for 30-week bursaries for professional and vocational training in 1998–9 (Scottish rates in parenthesis) are:

Living in	
College/lodgings in London area	£4,010 (£3,685)
College/lodgings outside London area	£3,010 (£2,806)
Parental home	£2,520 (£2,180)

Studentship awards are payable at between £5,295 and £6,855 a year (1997–8).

ADULT AND CONTINUING EDUCATION

The term adult education covers a broad spectrum of educational activities ranging from non-vocational courses of general interest, through the acquiring of special vocational skills needed in industry or commerce, to study for a degree at the Open University.

The responsibility for securing adult and continuing education in England and Wales is statutory and shared between the Further Education Funding Councils, which are responsible for and fund those courses which take place in their sector and lead to academic and vocational qualifications, prepare students to undertake further or higher education courses, or confer basic skills; the Higher Education Funding Councils, which fund advanced courses of continuing education; and LEAs, which are responsible for those courses which do not fall within the remit of the funding councils. Funding in Northern Ireland is through the education and library boards and in Scotland by the Scottish Office Education and Industry Department.

PROVIDERS

Courses specifically for adults are provided by many bodies. They include, in the statutory sector: local education authorities in England and Wales; in Scotland the education authorities and the SOEID; education and library boards in Northern Ireland; further education colleges; higher education colleges; universities, especially the Open University and Birkbeck College of the University of London; residential colleges; the BBC, independent television and local radio stations. There are also a number of voluntary bodies.

The LEAs in England and Wales operate through 'area' adult education centres, institutes or colleges, and the adult studies departments of colleges of further education. The SOEID funds adult education, including that provided by the universities and the Workers' Educational Association, at vocational further education colleges (46 in 1997) and evening centres (91 in 1997). In addition, SOEID provides grants to a number of voluntary organizations. Provision in the statutory sector in Northern Ireland is the responsibility of the universities, the education and library boards, the 17 further education colleges and a number of community schools.

The involvement of universities in adult education and continuing education has diversified considerably and is supported by a variety of administrative structures ranging from dedicated departments to a university approach. Birkbeck College in the University of London caters solely for part-time students. Those institutions and colleges formerly in the PCFC sector in England and Wales, because of their range of courses and flexible patterns of student attendance, provide opportunities in the field of adult and continuing education. The Forum for the Advancement of Continuing Education (FACE) promotes collaboration between institutions of higher education active in this area. The Open University, in partnership with the BBC, provides distance teaching leading to first degrees, and also offers post-experience and higher degree courses (see page 453).

Of the voluntary bodies, the biggest is the Workers' Educational Association (WEA) which operates throughout the UK, reaching about 150,000 adult students annually. The FEFC for England, the SOEID, and LEAs make grants towards provision.

The National Institute of Adult Continuing Education (England and Wales) (NIACE) provides information and advice to organizations and providers on all aspects of adult continuing education. NIACE conducts research, project and development work, and is funded by the DfEE, the LEAs and other funding bodies. The Welsh committee, NIACE Cymru, receives financial support from the Welsh Office, support in kind from Welsh local authorities, and advises government, voluntary bodies and education providers on adult continuing education and training matters in Wales. In Scotland advice on adult and community education, and promotion thereof, is provided by the Scottish Community Education Council. Following the

demise of the Northern Ireland Council for Adult Education, its functions have been taken over by DENI until a successor body can be set up.

Membership of the Universities Association for Continuing Education is open to any university or university college in the UK. It promotes university continuing education, facilitates the interchange of information, and supports research and development work in continuing education.

COURSES

Although lengths vary, most courses are part-time. Long-term residential colleges in England and Wales are grant-aided by the FEFCs and provide full-time courses lasting one or two years. Some colleges and centres offer short-term residential courses, lasting from a few days to a few weeks, in a wide range of subjects. Local education authorities directly sponsor many of the colleges, while others are sponsored by universities or voluntary organizations. A directory of learning holidays, *Time to Learn*, is published by NIACE.

GRANTS

Although full-time courses at first degree level attract mandatory awards or student loans, for courses below that level all students over the age of 19 must pay a fee. However, discretionary grants may be available. Adult education bursaries for students at the long-term residential colleges of adult education are the responsibility of the colleges themselves. The awards are administered for the colleges by the Awards Officer of the Residential Colleges Committee for students resident in England and are funded by the FEFC for England in English colleges; for colleges in Wales they are funded and administered by the FEFC for Wales; and for colleges in Scotland and Northern Ireland they are funded by central government and administered by the education authorities. A booklet, *Adult Education Bursaries*, can be obtained from the Awards Officer, Adult Education Bursaries, c/o Ruskin College (see page 454).

Education Directory

LOCAL EDUCATION AUTHORITIES

ENGLAND

County Councils

BEDFORDSHIRE, County Hall, Cauldwell Street, Bedford MK42 9AP. Tel: 01234-362222. *Director*, P. Brett

BUCKINGHAMSHIRE, County Hall, Walton Street, Aylesbury HP20 1UA. Tel: 01296-382641. *Director*, D. McGahey

CAMBRIDGESHIRE, Shire Hall, Castle Hill, Cambridge CB3 0AP. Tel: 01223-717990. *Director*, A. Baxter

CHESHIRE, County Hall, Chester CH1 1SQ. Tel: 01244-602424. *Director*, D. Cracknell

CORNWALL, County Hall, Truro TR1 3AY. Tel: 01872-322400. *Secretary*, J. Harris

CUMBRIA, 5 Portland Square, Carlisle CA1 1PU. Tel: 01228-606868. *Director*, J. Nellist

DERBYSHIRE, County Hall, Matlock DE4 3AG. Tel: 01629-580000. *Chief Education Officer*, Ms V. Hannon

DEVON, County Hall, Topsham Road, Exeter EX2 4QD. Tel: 01392-382059. *Director*, A Smith

DORSET, County Hall, Colliton Park, Dorchester DT1 1XJ. Tel: 01305-224171. *Director*, R. Ely

DURHAM, County Hall, Durham DH1 5UL. Tel: 0191-383 3319. *Director*, K. Mitchell

EAST SUSSEX, County Hall, St Anne's Crescent, Lewes BN7 1SG. Tel: 01273-481000. *County Education Officer*, D. Mallen

ESSEX, PO Box 47, Victoria Road South, Chelmsford CM1 1LD. Tel: 01245-492211. *Director of Learning Services*, P. A. Lincoln

GLOUCESTERSHIRE, Shire Hall, Westgate Street, Gloucester GL1 2TG. Tel: 01452-425300. *Director*, R. Crouch

HAMPSHIRE, The Castle, Winchester SO23 8UG. Tel: 01962-841841. *Director*, P. J. Coles

HERTFORDSHIRE, County Hall, Pegs Lane, Hertford SG13 8DE. Tel: 01992-555704. *Director*, R. Shostak

ISLE OF WIGHT, County Hall, High Street, Newport PO30 1UD. Tel: 01983-823455. *Director*, A. Kaye

KENT, Sessions House, County Hall, Maidstone ME14 1XQ. Tel: 01622-671411. *Director*, N. Henwood

LANCASHIRE, PO Box 61, County Hall, Preston PR1 8RJ. Tel: 01772-254868. *Chief Education Officer*, C. J. Trinick

LEICESTERSHIRE, County Hall, Glenfield, Leicester LE3 8RA. Tel: 0116-265 6631. *Director*, Mrs J. A. M. Strong

LINCOLNSHIRE, County Offices, Newland, Lincoln LN1 1YL. Tel: 01522-553201. *Director*, N. J. Riches

NORFOLK, County Hall, Martineau Lane, Norwich NR1 2DH. Tel: 01603-222300. *Director*, Dr B. Slater

NORTHAMPTONSHIRE, PO Box 233, County Hall, Northampton NN1 1AU. Tel: 01604-236252. *Director*, Mrs B. Bignold

NORTHUMBERLAND, County Hall, Morpeth NE61 2EF. Tel: 01670-533000. *Director*, C. C. Tipple

NORTH YORKSHIRE, County Hall, Northallerton, N. Yorks DL7 8AD. Tel: 01609-780780. *Director*, Miss C. Welbourn

NOTTINGHAMSHIRE, County Hall, West Bridgford, Nottingham NG2 7QP. Tel: 0115-982 3823. *Director*, R. Valentine

OXFORDSHIRE, Macclesfield House, New Road, Oxford OX1 1NA. Tel: 01865-815449. *Director*, G. Badman

SHROPSHIRE, The Shirehall, Abbey Foregate, Shrewsbury SY2 6ND. Tel: 01743-254307. *County Education Officer*, Mrs C. Adams

SOMERSET, County Hall, Taunton TA1 4DY. Tel: 01823-355455. *Chief Education Officer*, M. Jennings

STAFFORDSHIRE, Tipping Street, Stafford ST16 2DH. Tel: 01785-223121. *County Education Officer*, Dr P. J. Hunter

SUFFOLK, St Andrew House, County Hall, Ipswich IP4 1LJ. Tel: 01473-584627. *County Education Officer*, D. J. Peachey

SURREY, County Hall, Penrhyn Road, Kingston upon Thames KT1 2DN. Tel: 0181-541 9500. *County Education Officer*, Dr P. Gray

WARWICKSHIRE, PO Box 24, 22 Northgate Street, Warwick CV34 4SR. Tel: 01926-410410. *Director*, E. Wood

WEST SUSSEX, County Hall, Chichester PO19 1RF. Tel: 01243-777100. *Director*, R. D. C. Bunker

WILTSHIRE, County Hall, Bythesea Road, Trowbridge BA14 8JN. Tel: 01225-713750. *Chief Education Officer*, Dr L. Davies

WORCESTERSHIRE, County Hall, Spetchley Road, Worcester WR5 2NP. Tel: 01905-763763. *Director*, J. Kramer

Unitary Councils

BARNSLEY, Berneslai Close, Barnsley S70 2HS. Tel: 01226-773501. *Programme Director (Education and Leisure)*, D. Dalton

BATH AND NORTH-EAST SOMERSET, PO Box 25, Riverside, Temple Street, Keynsham, Bristol BS31 1EA. Tel: 01225-394200. *Director*, R. Jones

BIRMINGHAM, Margaret Street, Birmingham B3 3BU. Tel: 0121-303 2590. *Chief Education Officer*, Prof. T. Brighouse

BLACKBURN WITH DARWEN, Town Hall, Blackburn BB1 7DY. Tel: 01254-585585. *Director*, Dr M. Pattison

BLACKPOOL, Progress House, Clifton Road, Blackpool FY4 4US. Tel: 01253-476501. *Director*, Dr D. Sanders

BOLTON, Paderborn House, Civic Centre, Bolton BL1 1JW. Tel: 01204-522311. *Director*, Mrs M. Blenkinsop

BOURNEMOUTH, Dorset House, 20–22 Christchurch Road, Bournemouth BH1 3NL. Tel: 01202-451451. *Director*, K. Shaikh

BRACKNELL FOREST, Skimped Hill Lane, Bracknell, Berks RG12 1LY. Tel: 01344-424642. *Director*, A. Ecclestone

BRADFORD, Flockton House, Flockton Road, Bradford BD7 7RY. Tel: 01274-751840. *Director*, Mrs D. Cavanagh

BRIGHTON AND HOVE, PO Box 2503, Kings House, Grand Avenue, Hove BN3 2SR. Tel: 01273-290000. *Director*, Ms D. Stokoe

BRISTOL, Avon House, St James Barton, Bristol BS99 1NB. Tel: 0117-922 4402. *Director*, R. Riddell

BURY, Athenaeum House, Market Street, Bury BL9 0BN. Tel: 0161-253 5603. *Chief Education Officer*, H. Williams

CALDERDALE, Northgate House, Halifax HX1 1UN. Tel: 01422-357257. *Director*, I. Jennings

COVENTRY, New Council Offices, Earl Street, Coventry CV1 5RS. Tel: 01203-831511. *Chief Education Officer*, Ms C. Goodwin

DARLINGTON, Town Hall, Darlington DL1 5QT. Tel: 01325-380651. *Director*, G. Pennington

DERBY, Middleton House, 27 St Mary's Gate, Derby DE1 3NN. Tel: 01332-716922. *Director*, D. D'Hooghe

440   Education

DONCASTER, PO Box 266, The Council House, College Road, Doncaster DN1 3AD. Tel: 01302-737222. *Director,* M. Simpson

DUDLEY, Westox House, 1 Trinity Road, Dudley DY1 1JB. Tel: 01384-814200. *Chief Education Officer,* R. P. Colligan

EAST RIDING OF YORKSHIRE, County Hall, Beverley HU17 9BA. Tel: 01482-887700. *Director,* J. Ginnever

GATESHEAD, Civic Centre, Regent Street, Gateshead NE8 1HH. Tel: 0191-477 1011. *Director,* B. H. Edwards

HALTON, Grosvenor House, Halton Lea, Runcorn, Cheshire WA7 2WD. Tel: 0151-424 2061. *Director,* G. Talbot

HARTLEPOOL, Civic Centre, Victoria Road, Hartlepool TS24 8AY. Tel: 01429-266522. *Director,* J. J. Fitt

HEREFORDSHIRE, PO Box 185, Herefordshire Council, Blackfriars Street, Hereford HR4 9ZR. Tel: 01432-260908. *Director,* Dr E. Oram

KINGSTON UPON HULL, Essex House, Manor Street, Hull HU1 1YD. Tel: 01482-613161. *Director,* Miss J. E. Taylor

KIRKLEES, Oldgate House, 2 Oldgate, Huddersfield HD1 6QW. Tel: 01484-225242. *Chief Education Officer,* G. Tomkin

KNOWSLEY, Huyton Hey Road, Huyton, Knowsley, Merseyside L36 5YH. Tel: 0151-443 3232. *Director,* P. Wylie

LEEDS, Merrion House, Merrion Way, Leeds LS2 8DT. Tel: 0113-247 5612. *Director (acting),* M. R. Shaw

LEICESTER, Marlborough House, 38 Welford Road, Leicester LE2 7AA. Tel: 0116-252 7700. *Director,* T. Warren

LIVERPOOL, 14 Sir Thomas Street, Liverpool L1 6BJ. Tel: 0151-227 3911. *Director,* M. F. Cogley

LUTON, Unity House, 111 Stuart Street, Luton LU1 5NP. Tel: 01582-548000. *Director,* T. Dessent

MANCHESTER, Cumberland House, Crown Square, Manchester M60 3BB. Tel: 0161-234 7125. *Chief Education Officer,* R. Jobson

MEDWAY, Compass Centre, Chatham Maritime, Chatham, Kent ME7 4OD. Tel: 01634-881638. *Director,* R Bolsin

MIDDLESBROUGH, PO Box 191, 2nd Floor, Civic Centre, Middlesbrough TS1 2XS. Tel: 01642-262001. *Director,* Ms C. Berry

MILTON KEYNES, Saxon Court, 502 Avebury Boulevard, Central Milton Keynes MK9 3HS. Tel: 01908-691691. *Director,* A. Flack

NEWBURY, Avon Bank House, West Street, Newbury, Berks RG14 1BZ. Tel: 01635-519728. *Director,* J. Mercer

NEWCASTLE UPON TYNE, Civic Centre, Newcastle upon Tyne NE1 8PU. Tel: 0191-232 8520. *Director,* D. Bell

NORTH EAST LINCOLNSHIRE, 7 Eleanor Street, Grimsby DN32 9DU. Tel: 01472-323090. *Head of Education,* G. Hill

NORTH LINCOLNSHIRE, PO Box 35, Hewson House, Station Road, Brigg DN20 8XJ. Tel: 01724-297240. *Director,* T. Thomas

NORTH SOMERSET, Town Hall, Weston-super-Mare BS23 1AE. Tel: 01934-888829. *Director,* Ms J. Wreford

NORTH TYNESIDE, Stevenson House, Stevenson Street, North Shields NE30 1QA. Tel: 0191-200 5022. *Director,* L. Watson

NOTTINGHAM CITY, Sandfield Centre, Sandfield Road, Nottingham NG2 6JE. Tel: 0115-915 5555. *Director,* P. Roberts

OLDHAM, PO Box 40, Civic Centre, Oldham OL1 1XJ. Tel: 0161-911 3000. *Director,* M. Willis

PETERBOROUGH, Bayard Place, Broadway, Peterborough PE1 1FB. Tel: 01733-563141. *Director,* W. Goodwin

PLYMOUTH, Civic Centre, Armada Way, Plymouth PL1 2EW. Tel: 01752-304977. *Director,* S. Faruqi

POOLE, Civic Centre, Poole, Dorset BH15 2RU. Tel: 01202-633202. *Policy Director,* Dr S. Goodwin

PORTSMOUTH, Civic Offices, Guildhall Square, Portsmouth PO1 2AL. Tel: 01705-841200. *City Education Officer (acting),* A. Seber

READING, Civic Centre, Reading RG1 7TD. Tel: 0118-939 0120. *Director,* A. Daykin

REDCAR AND CLEVELAND, Council Offices, Kirkleatham Street, Redcar TS10 1RT. Tel: 01642-444342. *Chief Education Officer,* K. Burton

ROCHDALE, PO Box 70, Municipal Offices, Smith Street, Rochdale OL16 1YD. Tel: 01706-647474. *Director,* B. Atkinson

ROTHERHAM, Norfolk House, Walker Place, Rotherham S60 1QT. Tel: 01709-382121. *Education Officer,* H. C. Bower

RUTLAND, Catmose, Oakham, Rutland LE15 6HP. Tel: 01572-772704. *Director,* K. Bartley

ST HELENS, Rivington Centre, Rivington Road, St Helens WA10 4ND. Tel: 01744-456000. *Director,* C. Hilton

SALFORD, Chapel Street, Salford M3 5TL. Tel: 0161-832 9751. *Chief Education Officer,* D. C. Johnston

SANDWELL, PO Box 41, Shaftesbury House, 402 High Street, West Bromwich B70 9LT. Tel: 0121-569 8205. *Director,* S. Gallacher

SEFTON, Town Hall, Oriel Road, Bootle, Merseyside L20 7AE. Tel: 0151-922 4040. *Education Officer,* B. Marsh

SHEFFIELD, Leopold Street, Sheffield S1 1RJ. Tel: 0114-273 5722. *Director,* J. Crossley-Holland

SLOUGH, Town Hall, Bath Road, Slough SL1 3UQ. Tel: 01753-552288. *Director,* J. Christie

SOLIHULL, PO Box 20, Council House, Solihull B91 3QU. Tel: 0121-704 6656. *Director,* D. Nixon

SOUTHAMPTON, 5th Floor, Frobisher House, Commercial Road, Southampton SO15 1GX. Tel: 01703-223855. *Executive Director,* R. Hogg

SOUTH GLOUCESTERSHIRE, Bowling Hill, Chipping Sodbury, S. Glos BS37 6JX. Tel: 01454-863253. *Director,* Ms T. Gillespie

SOUTHEND, Civic Centre, Victoria Avenue, Southend-on-Sea SS2 6ER. Tel: 01702-215921. *Director,* S. Hay

SOUTH TYNESIDE, Town Hall and Civic Offices, Westoe Road, South Shields NE33 2RL. Tel: 0191-427 1717. *Director,* I. Reid

STOCKPORT, Stopford House, Piccadilly, Stockport SK1 3XE. Tel: 0161-474 3813. *Chief Education Officer,* M. Hunt

STOCKTON-ON-TEES, PO Box 228, Municipal Buildings, Church Road, Stockton-on-Tees TS18 1XE. Tel: 01642-393939. *Director,* S. T. Bradford

STOKE-ON-TRENT, PO Box 758, Swann House, Boothen Road, Stoke-on-Trent ST4 1RU. Tel: 01782-232014. *Director of Education,* N. Rigby

SUNDERLAND, Civic Centre, Burdon Road, Sunderland SR2 7DN. Tel: 0191-553 1355. *Director,* Dr J. W. Williams

SWINDON, Civic Offices, Euclid Street, Swindon SN1 2JH. Tel: 01793-463069. *Director,* M. Lusty

TAMESIDE, Council Offices, Wellington Road, Ashton under Lyne, Lancs OL6 6LD. Tel: 0161-342 3200. *Director,* A. M. Webster

TELFORD AND WREKIN, Civic Offices, Telford, Shropshire TF3 4LD. Tel: 01952-202402. *Corporate Director,* Ms C. Davies

THURROCK, PO Box 118, Grays, Essex RM17 6GF. Tel: 01375-652652. *Director,* R. Wilkins

TORBAY, Oldway Mansion, Paignton, Devon TQ3 2TE. Tel: 01803-208201. *Director,* G. Cave

TRAFFORD, PO Box 40, Trafford Town Hall, Talbot Road, Stretford, Trafford, Greater Manchester M32 0EL. Tel: 0161-912 1212. *Director*, Mrs K. August

WAKEFIELD, County Hall, Wakefield WF1 2QL. Tel: 01924-305501. *Education Officer*, J. McLeod

WALSALL, Civic Centre, Darwall Street, Walsall WS1 1TP. Tel: 01922-652301. *Director*, T. Howard

WARRINGTON, New Town House, Buttermarket Street, Warrington, Cheshire WA1 2NH. Tel: 01925-444400. *Director*, M. Roxborgh

WIGAN, Gateway House, Standishgate, Wigan, Lancs WN1 1AE. Tel: 01942-828891. *Education Officer*, R. Clark

WINDSOR AND MAIDENHEAD, Town Hall, St Ives Road, Maidenhead, Berks SL6 1RF. Tel: 01628-796258. *Director*, M. Peckham

WIRRAL, Hamilton Building, Conway Street, Birkenhead L41 4FD. Tel: 0151-666 4288. *Director*, C. Rice

WOKINGHAM, Shute End, Wokingham, Berks RG40 1WQ. Tel: 0118-974 6106. *Director*, Mrs J. Griffin

WOLVERHAMPTON, Civic Centre, St Peter's Square, Wolverhampton WV1 1RR. Tel: 01902-554100. *Director*, R. Lockwood

YORK, 10–12 George Hudson Street, York YO1 1ZG. Tel: 01904-613161. *Director*, M. Peters

LONDON

*Inner London borough

BARKING AND DAGENHAM, Town Hall, Barking, Essex IG11 7LU. Tel: 0181-592 4500. *Education Officer*, A. Larbalestier

BARNET, Former Friern Barnet Town Hall, Friern Barnet Lane, London N11 3DL. Tel: 0181-359 3001. *Director (acting)*, M. Kempson

BEXLEY, Hill View, Hill View Drive, Welling, Kent DA16 3RY. Tel: 0181-303 7777. *Director*, P. McGee

BRENT, Chesterfield House, 9 Park Lane, Wembley, Middx HA9 7RW. Tel: 0181-937 3190. *Director*, J. Simpson

BROMLEY, Civic Centre, Stockwell Close, Bromley BR1 3UH. Tel: 0181-464 3333. *Director*, K. Davis

*CAMDEN, Crowndale Centre, 218–220 Eversholt Street, London NW1 1BD. Tel: 0171-911 1525. *Director*, R. Litchfield

*CITY OF LONDON, Education Department, Corporation of London, PO Box 270, Guildhall, London EC2P 2EJ. Tel: 0171-332 1750. *City Education Officer*, D. Smith

*CITY OF WESTMINSTER, City Hall, 64 Victoria Street, London SW1E 6QP. Tel: 0171-641 3338. *Director*, Ms D. McGrath

CROYDON, Taberner House, Park Lane, Croydon CR9 1TP. Tel: 0181-686 4433. *Director*, D. Sands

EALING, Perceval House, 14–16 Uxbridge Road, London W5 2HL. Tel: 0181-758 5410. *Director*, A. Parker

ENFIELD, PO Box 56, Civic Centre, Silver Street, Enfield, Middx EN1 3XQ. Tel: 0181-379 3201. *Director*, Ms E. Graham

*GREENWICH, Riverside House, Beresford Street, London SE18 6DN. Tel: 0181-854 8888. *Director*, G. Gyte

*HACKNEY, Edith Cavell Building, Enfield Road, London N1 5BA. Tel: 0181-356 5000. *Director*, Ms E. Reid

*HAMMERSMITH AND FULHAM, Cambridge House, Cambridge Grove, London W6 0LE. Tel: 0181-748 3020. *Director*, Ms C. Whatford

HARINGEY, 48 Station Road, Wood Green, London N22 4TY. Tel: 0181-975 9700. *Director*, Ms F. Magee

HARROW, PO Box 22, Civic Centre, Station Road, Harrow HA1 2UW. Tel: 0181-424 1304. *Director*, P. Osburn

HAVERING, The Broxhill Centre, Broxhill Road, Harold Hill, Romford RM4 1XN. Tel: 01708-773839. *Director*, C. Hardy

HILLINGDON, Civic Centre, High Street, Uxbridge UB8 1UW. Tel: 01895-250111. *Director (acting)*, G. Moss

HOUNSLOW, Civic Centre, Lampton Road, Hounslow TW3 4DN. Tel: 0181-862 5301. *Director*, J. D. Tricket

*ISLINGTON, Laycock Street, London N1 1TH. Tel: 0171-457 5753. *Education Officer*, Dr H. Nicolle

*KENSINGTON AND CHELSEA, Town Hall, Hornton Street, London W8 7NX. Tel: 0171-361 3334. *Director*, R. Wood

KINGSTON UPON THAMES, Guildhall, Kingston upon Thames KT1 1EU. Tel: 0181-547 5220. *Director*, J. Braithwaite

*LAMBETH, Bluestar House, 234–244 Stockwell Road, London SW9 9SP. Tel: 0171-926 1000. *Director*, Ms H. Du Quesnay

*LEWISHAM, Laurence House, Catford, London SE6 4RU. Tel: 0181-314 6200. *Director*, Ms A. Efunshile

MERTON, Civic Centre, London Road, Morden, Surrey SM4 5DX. Tel: 0181-543 2222. *Director*, Ms J. Cairns

NEWHAM, Broadway House, 322 High Street, Stratford, London E15 1AJ. Tel: 0181-555 5552. *Director*, I. Harrison

REDBRIDGE, Lynton House, 255–259 High Road, Ilford IG1 1NN. Tel: 0181-478 3020. *Chief Education Officer*, D. Kapper

RICHMOND UPON THAMES, Regal House, London Road, Twickenham TW1 3QS. Tel: 0181-891 1411. *Director*, R. Hancock

*SOUTHWARK, 1 Bradenham Close, Albany Road, London SE17 2BA. Tel: 0171-525 5000. *Director*, G. Mott

SUTTON, The Grove, Carshalton, Surrey SM5 3AL. Tel: 0181-770 6500. *Director*, Dr I. Birnbaum

*TOWER HAMLETS, Mulberry Place, 5 Clove Crescent, London E14 2BG. Tel: 0171-364 5000. *Director*, Ms C. Gilbert

WALTHAM FOREST, Municipal Offices, High Road, Leyton, London E10 5QJ. Tel: 0181-527 5544. *Chief Education Officer*, A. Lockhart

*WANDSWORTH, Town Hall, Wandsworth High Street, London SW18 2PU. Tel: 0181-871 7890. *Director*, P. Robinson

WALES

ANGLESEY, Swyddfa'r Sir, Llangefni, Anglesey LL77 7EY. Tel: 01248-752900. *Director*, R. L. P. Jones

BLAENAU GWENT, Victoria House, Victoria Business Park, Ebbw Vale NP3 6ER. Tel: 01495-355434. *Director*, B. Mawby

BRIDGEND, Sunnyside, Sunnyside Road, Bridgend CF31 4AR. Tel: 01656-642600. *Director*, D. Matthews

CAERPHILLY, Council Offices, Caerphilly Road, Ystrad Mynach, Hengoed CF82 7EP. Tel: 01443-864956. *Director*, N. Harries

CARDIFF, County Hall, Atlantic Wharf, Cardiff CF1 5UW. Tel: 01222-872700. *Director*, T. Davies

CARMARTHENSHIRE, Pibwrlwyd, Carmarthen SA31 2NH. Tel: 01267-224501. *Director*, K. Davies

CEREDIGION, Swyddfa'r Sir, Marine Terrace, Aberystwyth SY23 2DE. Tel: 01970-633601. *Director*, R Williams

CONWY, Government Buildings, Dinerth Road, Rhos-on-Sea LL28 4UL. Tel: 01492-574000. *Director*, R. E. Williams

DENBIGHSHIRE, County Hall, Mold, Flintshire CH7 6GR. Tel: 01824-706700. *Director*, E. Lewis

FLINTSHIRE, County Hall, Mold, Flintshire CH7 6NW. Tel: 01352-704400. *Director*, K. McDonogh

442   Education

GWYNEDD, Shire Hall Street, Caernarfon LL55 1SH. Tel: 01286-672255. *Director,* D. Whittall

MERTHYR TYDFIL, Ty Keir Hardie, Riverside Court, Avenue De Clichy, Merthyr Tydfil CF47 8XO. Tel: 01685-724600. *Director,* D. Jones

MONMOUTHSHIRE, County Hall, Cwmbran NP44 2XH. Tel: 01633-644644. *Director,* D. Young

NEATH PORT TALBOT, Civic Centre, Port Talbot SA13 1PJ. Tel: 01639-763333. *Corporate Director,* V. Thomas

NEWPORT, Civic Centre, Newport, South Wales NP9 4UR. Tel: 01633-232204. *Director,* G. Bingham

PEMBROKESHIRE, Cambria House, Haverfordwest SA61 1TP. Tel: 01437-764551. *Director,* G. Davies

POWYS, County Hall, Llandrindod Wells LD1 5LG. Tel: 01597-826006. *Director,* M. Barker

RHONDDA, CYNON, TAFF, Education Centre, Grawen Street, Porth CF39 0BU. Tel: 01443-687666. *Director,* K. Ryley

SWANSEA, County Hall, Oystermouth Road, Swansea SA1 3SN. Tel: 01792-636351. *Director,* R. Parry

TORFAEN, County Hall, Croesyceiliog, Cwmbran, Torfaen NP44 2WN. Tel: 01633-648609. *Director,* M. de Val

VALE OF GLAMORGAN, Civic Offices, Holton Road, Barry CF63 4RU. Tel: 01446-709106. *Director,* A. Davies

WREXHAM, Roxburgh House, Hill Street, Wrexham LL11 1SN. Tel: 01978-297421. *Director,* T. Garner

SCOTLAND

ABERDEEN CITY, Summerhill, Stronsay Drive, Aberdeen AB15 6JA. Tel: 01224-522000. *Director,* J. Stodter

ABERDEENSHIRE, Woodhill House, Westburn Road, Aberdeen AB16 5GB. Tel: 01224-665420. *Director,* M. White

ANGUS, County Buildings, Market Street, Forfar DD8 3WE. Tel: 01307-461460. *Director,* J. Anderson

ARGYLL AND BUTE, Argyll House, Alexandra Parade, Dunoon PA23 8AG. Tel: 01369-704000. *Director,* A. C. Morton

CITY OF EDINBURGH, *(from Dec. 1998)* Wellington Court, 10 Waterloo Place, Edinburgh EH1 3EG. Tel: 0131-200 2000. *Director,* R. Jobson

CLACKMANNANSHIRE, Lime Tree House, Alloa FK10 1EX. Tel: 01259-452431. *Director,* K. Bloomer

DUMFRIES AND GALLOWAY, Education Department, 30 Edinburgh Road, Dumfries DG1 1JG. Tel: 01384-260000. *Director (acting),* F. Sanderson

DUNDEE CITY, 8th Floor, Tayside House, 28 Crichton Street, Dundee DD1 3RJ. Tel: 01382-433088. *Director,* Ms A. Wilson

EAST AYRSHIRE, Council Headquarters, London Road, Kilmarnock KA3 7BU. Tel: 01563-576017. *Director,* J. Mulgrew

EAST DUNBARTONSHIRE, Boclair House, 100 Milngavie Road, Bearsden, Glasgow G61 2TQ. Tel: 0141-942 9000. *Director,* I. Mills

EAST LOTHIAN, Council Buildings, 25 Court Street, Haddington EH41 3HA. Tel: 01620-827588. *Director,* A. Blackie

EAST RENFREWSHIRE, Council Offices, Eastwood Park, Rouken Glen Road, Giffnock G46 6UG. Tel: 0141-577 3430. *Director,* Ms E. J. Currie

FALKIRK, McLaren House, Marchmont Avenue, Polmont, Falkirk FK2 0NZ. Tel: 01324-506600. *Director,* Dr G. Young

FIFE, Rothesay House, North Street, Glenrothes KY7 5PN. Tel: 01592-413656. *Director,* A. Mackay

GLASGOW CITY, Charing Cross Complex, House 1, 20 India Street, Glasgow G2 4PF. Tel: 0141-287 2000. *Director,* K. Corsar

HIGHLAND, Council Buildings, Glenurquhart Road, Inverness IV3 5NX. Tel: 01463-702802. *Director,* A. Gilchrist

INVERCLYDE, 105 Dalrymple Street, Greenock PA15 1HT. Tel: 01475-712828. *Director,* B. McLeary

MIDLOTHIAN, Fairfield House, 8 Lothian Road, Dalkeith EH22 3ZJ. Tel: 0131-270 7500. *Director,* D. MacKay

MORAY, Council Offices, High Street, Elgin IV30 1BX. Tel: 01343-563134. *Director,* K. Gavin

NORTH AYRSHIRE, Cunninghame House, Irvine KA12 8EE. Tel: 01294-324412. *Director,* J. Travers

NORTH LANARKSHIRE, Municipal Buildings, Kildonan Street, Coatbridge ML5 3BT. Tel: 01236-812222. *Director,* M. O'Neill

ORKNEY ISLANDS, Council Offices, School Place, Kirkwall, Orkney KW15 1NY. Tel: 01856-873535. *Director,* L. Manson

PERTH AND KINROSS, Blackfriars, Perth PH1 5LU. Tel: 01738-476200. *Director,* R. McKay

RENFREWSHIRE, Council Headquarters, South Building, Cotton Street, Paisley PA1 1LE. Tel: 0141-842 5601. *Director,* Ms S. Rae

SCOTTISH BORDERS, Council Headquarters, Newtown St Boswells, Melrose TD6 0SA. Tel: 01835-824000. *Director,* J. Christie

SHETLAND ISLANDS, Hayfield House, Hayfield Lane, Lerwick, Shetland ZE1 0QD. Tel: 01595-744000. *Director,* J. Halcrow

SOUTH AYRSHIRE, County Buildings, Wellington Square, Ayr KA7 1DR. Tel: 01292-612201. *Director,* M. McCabe

SOUTH LANARKSHIRE, Council Headquarters, Almada Street, Hamilton ML3 0AE. Tel: 01698-454379. *Executive Director,* Ms M. Allan

STIRLING, Viewforth, Stirling FK8 2ET. Tel: 01786-442680. *Director,* G. Jeyes

WEST DUNBARTONSHIRE, Garshake Road, Dumbarton G82 3PU. Tel: 01389-737000. *Director,* I. McMurdo

WESTERN ISLES, Council Offices, Sandwick Road, Stornoway, Isle of Lewis HS1 2BW. Tel: 01851-703773. *Director,* N. R. Galbraith

WEST LOTHIAN, Lindsay House, South Bridge Street, Bathgate EH48 1TS. Tel: 01506-776358. *Corporate Manager,* R. Stewart

NORTHERN IRELAND

EDUCATION AND LIBRARY BOARDS

BELFAST, 40 Academy Street, Belfast BT1 2NQ. Tel: 01232-564122. *Chief Executive,* T. G. J. Moag, OBE

NORTH, County Hall, 182 Galgorm Road, Ballymena, Co. Antrim BT42 1HN. Tel: 01266-653333. *Chief Executive,* G. Topping

SOUTH EASTERN, 18 Windsor Avenue, Belfast BT9 6EF. Tel: 01232-381188. *Chief Executive,* J. B. Fitzsimons

SOUTHERN, 3 Charlemont Place, The Mall, Armagh BT61 9AX. Tel: 01861-512200. *Chief Executive,* J. G. Kelly

WESTERN, 1 Hospital Road, Omagh, Co. Tyrone BT79 0AW. Tel: 01662-411411. *Chief Executive,* P. J. Martin

ISLANDS

GUERNSEY, Grange Road, St Peter Port, Guernsey GY1 1RQ. Tel: 01481-710821. *Director,* D. T. Neale

JERSEY, PO Box 142, Jersey JE4 8QJ. Tel: 01534-509500. *Director,* T. W. McKeon

ISLE OF MAN, Murray House, 5–11 Mount Havelock, Douglas, Isle of Man IM1 2SG. Tel: 01624-685820. *Director,* R. B. Cowin

ISLES OF SCILLY, Town Hall, St Mary's, Isles of Scilly TR21 0LW. Tel: 01720-422537 ext. 145. *Secretary for Education,* P. S. Hygate

ADVISORY BODIES

SCHOOLS

EDUCATION OTHERWISE, PO Box 7420, London N9 9SG. Tel: Helpline: 0891-518303

BRITISH EDUCATIONAL COMMUNICATIONS AND TECHNOLOGY AGENCY (formerly National Council for Educational Technology), Milburn Hill Road, Science Park, Coventry CV4 7JJ. Tel: 01203-416994. *Chief Executive*, O. Lynch

INTERNATIONAL BACCALAUREATE ORGANIZATION, Peterson House, Fortran Road, St Mellons, Cardiff CF3 OLT. Tel: 01222-774000. *Director of Academic Affairs*, Dr H. Drennan

NATIONAL ADVISORY COUNCIL FOR EDUCATION AND TRAINING TARGETS, 7th Floor, 222 Grays Inn Road, London WCIX 8HL. Tel: 0171-211 5012. *Chairman*, D. Wanless; *Director*, P. Chorley

SPECIAL EDUCATIONAL NEEDS TRIBUNAL, 7th Floor, Windsor House, 50 Victoria Street, London SWIH ONW. Tel: 0171-925 6925. *President*, T. Aldridge, QC

INDEPENDENT SCHOOLS

GOVERNING BODIES ASSOCIATION, The Ancient Foresters, Bush End, Takeley, Bishop's Stortford, Herts CM22 6NN. Tel: 01279-871865. *Secretary*, F. V. Morgan

GOVERNING BODIES OF GIRLS' SCHOOLS ASSOCIATION, The Ancient Foresters, Bush End, Takeley, Bishop's Stortford, Herts CM22 6NN. Tel: 01279-871865. *Secretary*, F. V. Morgan

INDEPENDENT SCHOOLS COUNCIL, Grosvenor Gardens House, 35–37 Grosvenor Gardens, London SWIW OBS. Tel: 0171-630 0144. *Administrator*, Ms E. Sutton

INDEPENDENT SCHOOLS EXAMINATIONS BOARD, Jordan House, Christchurch Road, New Milton, Hants BH25 6QJ. Tel: 01425-621111. *Administrator*, Mrs J. Williams

INDEPENDENT SCHOOLS INFORMATION SERVICE, 56 Buckingham Gate, London SWIE 6AG. Tel: 0171-630 8793. *National Director*, D. J. Woodhead

THE ISJC ASSISTED PLACES COMMITTEE, 100 Rochester Row, London SWIP IJP. Tel: 0171-393 6666. *Secretary*, P. F. V. Waters

FURTHER EDUCATION

FURTHER EDUCATION DEVELOPMENT AGENCY, Citadel Place, Tinworth Street, London SEII 5EH. Tel: 0171-962 1280. *Chief Executive*, C. Hughes

Regional Advisory Councils

ASSOCIATION OF COLLEGES IN THE EASTERN REGION, Merlin Place, Milton Road, Cambridge CB4 4DP. Tel: 01223-424022. *Chief Executive*, J. Graystone

CENTRA (EDUCATION AND TRAINING SERVICES) LTD, Duxbury Park, Duxbury Hall Road, Chorley, Lancs PR7 4AT. Tel: 01257-241428. *Chief Executive*, P. Wren

EMFEC (formerly East Midlands Further Education Council), Robins Wood House, Robins Wood Road, Aspley, Nottingham NG8 3NH. Tel: 0115-929 3291. *Chief Executive*, J. Gardiner

NCFE (formerly Northern Council for Further Education), Portland House, 2nd Floor, Block D, New Bridge Street, Newcastle upon Tyne NEI 8AN. Tel: 0191-201 3100. *Chief Executive*, J. F. Pearce

SOUTHERN REGIONAL COUNCIL FOR EDUCATION AND TRAINING, Building 33, The University of Reading, London Road, Reading RGI 5AQ. Tel: 0118-931 6320. *Chief Executive*, B. J. Knowles

SOUTH WEST ASSOCIATION FOR FURTHER EDUCATION AND TRAINING, Bishops Hull House, Bishops Hull, Taunton, Somerset TAI 5RA. Tel: 01823-335491. *Chief Executive*, Ms L. McGrath

WELSH JOINT EDUCATION COMMITTEE, 245 Western Avenue, Cardiff CF5 2YX. Tel: 01222-265000. *Chief Executive*, I. Hume

YORKSHIRE AND HUMBERSIDE ASSOCIATION FOR FURTHER AND HIGHER EDUCATION, 13 Wellington Road East, Dewsbury, W. Yorks WFI3 IXG. Tel: 01924-450900. *Director (acting)*, C. Daniel

HIGHER EDUCATION

ASSOCIATION OF COMMONWEALTH UNIVERSITIES, John Foster House, 36 Gordon Square, London WCIH OPF. Tel: 0171-387 8572. *Secretary-General*, Prof. M. G. Gibbons

COMMITTEE OF SCOTTISH HIGHER EDUCATION PRINCIPALS (COSHEP), St Andrew House, 141 West Nile Street, Glasgow GI 2RN. Tel: 0141-353 1880. *Secretary*, Dr R. L. Crawford

COMMITTEE OF VICE-CHANCELLORS AND PRINCIPALS OF THE UNIVERSITIES OF THE UNITED KINGDOM, Woburn House, 20 Tavistock Square, London WCIH 9HQ. Tel: 0171-419 4111. *Chairman*, Prof. M. Harris; *Chief Executive*, Ms D. Warwick

NORTHERN IRELAND HIGHER EDUCATION COUNCIL, Rathgael House, Balloo Road, Bangor BTI9 7PR. Tel: 01247-279333. *Chairman*, Sir Kenneth Bloomfield, KCB; *Secretary*, J. Coote

QUALITY ASSURANCE AGENCY FOR HIGHER EDUCATION, Southgate House, Southgate Street, Gloucester GLI IUB. Tel: 01452-557000. *Secretary*, S. Bushell

CURRICULUM COUNCILS

AWDURDOD CYMWYSTERAU CWRICWLWM AC ASESU CYMRU/QUALIFICATIONS, CURRICULUM AND ASSESSMENT AUTHORITY FOR WALES, Castle Buildings, Womanby Street, Cardiff CFI 9SX. Tel: 01222-375400. *Chief Executive*, J. V. Williams

NORTHERN IRELAND COUNCIL FOR THE CURRICULUM, EXAMINATIONS AND ASSESSMENT, Clarendon Dock, 29 Clarendon Road, Belfast BTI 3BG. Tel: 01232-261200. *Chief Executive*, Mrs C. Coxhead

QUALIFICATIONS AND CURRICULUM AUTHORITY, 29 Bolton Street, London WIY 7PD. Tel: 0171-509 5555. *Chairman*, Sir William Stubbs, PH.D; *Chief Executive*, N. Tate, PH.D.

SCOTTISH CONSULTATIVE COUNCIL ON THE CURRICULUM, Gardyne Road, Broughty Ferry, Dundee DD5 INY. Tel: 01382-455053. *Chief Executive*, M. Baughan

EXAMINING BODIES

UNITARY AWARDING BODIES

ASSESSMENT AND QUALIFICATIONS ALLIANCE (AQA), Stag Hill House, Guildford GU2 5XJ. Tel: 01483-506506. Devas Street, Manchester MI5 6EX. Tel: 0161-953 1180. *Director-General*, Ms K. Tattersall

THE EDEXCEL FOUNDATION, Stewart House, 32 Russell Square, London WCIB 5DN. Tel: 0171-393 4444. *Chief Executive*, Ms C. Townsend, PH.D

OXFORD, CAMBRIDGE AND RSA EXAMINATIONS, 1 Regent Street, Cambridge CB2 IGG. Tel: 01223-552552. *Chief Executive*, B. Swift

GCSE

THE EDEXCEL FOUNDATION, *see* above
NORTHERN EXAMINATIONS AND ASSESSMENT BOARD,
Devas Street, Manchester M15 6EX. Tel: 0161-953 1180.
Chief Executive, Ms H. M. James
NORTHERN IRELAND COUNCIL FOR THE CURRICULUM,
EXAMINATIONS AND ASSESSMENT, Clarendon Dock,
29 Clarendon Road, Belfast BT1 3BG. Tel: 01232-261200.
Chief Executive, Mrs C. Coxhead
OXFORD, CAMBRIDGE AND RSA EXAMINATIONS, *see*
above
SEG (SOUTHERN EXAMINING GROUP), Stag Hill House,
Guildford, Surrey GU2 5XJ. Tel: 01483-506506.
Secretary-General, Dr C. P. Hughes
WELSH JOINT EDUCATION COMMITTEE, 245 Western
Avenue, Cardiff CF5 2YX. Tel: 01222-265000. *Chief
Executive*, I. Hume

A-LEVEL

THE ASSOCIATED EXAMINING BOARD, Stag Hill House,
Guildford, Surrey GU2 5XJ. Tel: 01483-506506.
Secretary-General, Dr C. P. Hughes
THE EDEXCEL FOUNDATION, *see* above
NORTHERN EXAMINATIONS AND ASSESSMENT BOARD,
Devas Street, Manchester M15 6EX. Tel: 0161-953 1180.
Chief Executive, Ms H. M. James
NORTHERN IRELAND COUNCIL FOR THE CURRICULUM,
EXAMINATIONS AND ASSESSMENT, Clarendon Dock,
29 Clarendon Road, Belfast BT1 3BG. Tel: 01232-261200.
Chief Executive, Mrs C. Coxhead
OXFORD, CAMBRIDGE AND RSA EXAMINATIONS, *see*
above
WELSH JOINT EDUCATION COMMITTEE, 245 Western
Avenue, Cardiff CF5 2YX. Tel: 01222-265000. *Chief
Executive*, I. Hume

SCOTLAND

SCOTTISH QUALIFICATIONS AUTHORITY, Hanover
House, 24 Douglas Street, Glasgow G2 7NQ. Tel: 0141-
248 7900. Ironmills Road, Dalkeith EH12 1LE. Tel: 0131-
663 6601. *Chief Executive*, R. Tuck

FURTHER EDUCATION

CITY & GUILDS, 1 Giltspur Street, London EC1A 9DD. Tel:
0171-294 2468. *Director-General*, N. Carey, PH.D
THE EDEXCEL FOUNDATION, *see* above
OXFORD, CAMBRIDGE AND RSA EXAMINATIONS, *see*
above

FUNDING COUNCILS

SCHOOLS

FUNDING AGENCY FOR SCHOOLS, Albion Wharf, 25
Skeldergate, York YO1 2XL. Tel: 01904-661661.
Chairman, Vice-Adm. Sir Antony Tippett, KCB; *Chief
Executive*, M. Collier

FURTHER EDUCATION

FURTHER EDUCATION FUNDING COUNCIL FOR
ENGLAND, Cheylesmore House, Quinton Road,
Coventry CV1 2WT. Tel: 01203-863000. *Chief Executive*,
Prof. D. Melville
FURTHER EDUCATION FUNDING COUNCIL FOR WALES,
Linden Court, The Orchards, Ty Glas Avenue, Cardiff
CF4 5DZ. Tel: 01222-761861. *Chief Executive*, Prof. J.
Andrews

SCOTTISH FURTHER EDUCATION FUNDING DIVISION,
Scottish Office Education and Industry Department,
1st Floor West, Victoria Quay, Edinburgh EH6 6QQ.
Tel: 0131-244 0286. *Head of Division*, C. M. Reeves

HIGHER EDUCATION

HIGHER EDUCATION FUNDING COUNCIL FOR
ENGLAND, Northavon House, Coldharbour Lane,
Bristol BS16 1QD. Tel: 0117-931 7317. *Chief Executive*,
Prof. B. Fender
HIGHER EDUCATION FUNDING COUNCIL FOR WALES,
Linden Court, The Orchards, Ty Glas Avenue, Cardiff
CF4 5DZ. Tel: 01222-761861. *Chief Executive*, Prof. J. A.
Andrews
SCOTTISH HIGHER EDUCATION FUNDING COUNCIL,
Donaldson House, 97 Haymarket Terrace, Edinburgh
EH12 5HD. Tel: 0131-313 6500. *Chief Executive*, Prof. J.
Sizer, CBE
STUDENT AWARDS AGENCY FOR SCOTLAND, Gyleview
House, 3 Redheughs Rigg, Edinburgh EH12 9HH. Tel:
0131-244 5823. *Chief Executive*, K. MacRae
STUDENT LOANS COMPANY LTD, 100 Bothwell Street,
Glasgow G2 7JD. Tel: 0141-306 2000. *Chief Executive*, C.
Ward
TEACHER TRAINING AGENCY, Portland House, Stag
Place, London SW1E 5TT. Tel: 0171-925 3700. *Chairman*,
Prof. C. Booth; *Chief Executive*, Ms A. Millett

ADMISSIONS AND COURSE
INFORMATION

CAREERS RESEARCH AND ADVISORY CENTRE, Sheraton
House, Castle Park, Cambridge CB3 0AX. Tel: 01223-
460277. *Chief Executive*, D. McGregor. *Publishers*,
Hobsons Publishing PLC, Bateman Street, Cambridge
CB2 1LZ
COMMITTEE OF SCOTTISH HIGHER EDUCATION
PRINCIPALS (COSHEP), St Andrew House, 141 West
Nile Street, Glasgow Tel: 0141-353 1880. *Secretary*,
Dr R. L. Crawford
GRADUATE TEACHER TRAINING REGISTRY, Fulton
House, Jessop Avenue, Cheltenham, Glos GL50 3SH.
Tel: 01242-544788. *Registrar*, Mrs M. Griffiths
SOCIAL WORK ADMISSIONS SYSTEM, Fulton House,
Jessop Avenue, Cheltenham, Glos GL50 3SH. Tel:
01242-544600. *Admissions Officer*, Mrs M. Griffiths
TEACHER EDUCATION ADMISSIONS CLEARING HOUSE
(TEACH), PO Box 165, Edinburgh EH12 6YA. Tel:
0131-314 6070.
UNIVERSITIES AND COLLEGES ADMISSIONS SERVICE,
Fulton House, Jessop Avenue, Cheltenham, Glos
GL50 3SH. Tel: 01242-222444. *Chief Executive*, M. A.
Higgins, PH.D

UNIVERSITIES

THE UNIVERSITY OF ABERDEEN (1495)
Regent Walk, Aberdeen AB24 3FX
Tel 01224-272000
Full-time students (1997–8), 11,061
Chancellor, The Lord Wilson of Tillyorn, GCMG (1997)
Vice-Chancellor, Prof. C. D. Rice
Registrar, Dr P. J. Murray
Secretary, S. Cannon
Rector, vacant

THE UNIVERSITY OF ABERTAY DUNDEE
(1994)
Bell Street, Dundee DD1 1HG
Tel 01382-308080
Full-time students (1997–8), 3,577
Chancellor, The Earl of Airlie, KT, GCVO, PC (1994)
Vice-Chancellor, Prof. B. King
Registrar, Dr. D. Button
Secretary, D. Hogarth

ANGLIA POLYTECHNIC UNIVERSITY (1992)
Bishop Hall Lane, Chelmsford CM1 1SQ
Tel 01245-493131
Full-time students (1997–8), 7,672
Chancellor, The Lord Prior, PC (1992)
Vice-Chancellor, M. Malone-Lee, CB
Secretary, S. G. Bennett

ASTON UNIVERSITY (1966)
Aston Triangle, Birmingham B4 7ET
Tel 0121-359 3611
Full-time students (1997–8), 5,346
Chancellor, Sir Adrian Cadbury (1979)
Vice-Chancellor, Prof. M. Wright
Registrar and Secretary, R. D. A. Packham

THE UNIVERSITY OF BATH (1966)
Claverton Down, Bath BA2 7AY
Tel 01225-826826
Full-time students (1997–8), 6,299
Chancellor, The Lord Tugendhat (1998)
Vice-Chancellor, Prof. V. D. Vandelinde
Registrar, J. A. Bursey

THE UNIVERSITY OF BIRMINGHAM (1900)
Edgbaston, Birmingham B15 2TT
Tel 0121-414 3344
Full-time students (1997–8), 17,993
Chancellor, Sir Alexander Jarratt, CB (1983)
Vice-Chancellor, Prof. M. Irvine, PH.D
Registrar and Secretary, D. Allen

BOURNEMOUTH UNIVERSITY (1992)
Talbot Campus, Fern Barrow, Poole BH12 5BB
Tel 01202-524111
Full-time students (1997–8), 4,486
Chancellor, The Baroness Cox (1992)
Vice-Chancellor, Prof. G. Slater
Registrar, N. O. G. Richardson

THE UNIVERSITY OF BRADFORD (1966)
Bradford BD7 1DP
Tel 01274-232323
Full-time students (1997–8), 7,517
Chancellor, The Baroness Lockwood (1997)
Director, Prof. C. Bell
Registrar and Secretary, N. J. Andrew

THE UNIVERSITY OF BRIGHTON (1992)
Mithras House, Lewes Road, Brighton BN2 4AT
Tel 01273-600900
Full-time students (1997–8), 13,000
Chairman of the Board, M. C. M. Hume
Director, Prof. Sir David Watson
Deputy Director, D. E. House

THE UNIVERSITY OF BRISTOL (1909)
Senate House, Tyndall Avenue, Bristol BS8 1TH
Tel 0117-928 9000
Full-time students (1997–8), 11,611
Chancellor, Sir Jeremy Morse, KCMG (1989)
Vice-Chancellor, Sir John Kingman, FRS

Registrar, J. H. M. Parry
Secretary, Ms K. E. McKenzie, D.Phil.

BRUNEL UNIVERSITY (1966)
Uxbridge, Middx UB8 3PH
Tel 01895-274000
Full-time students (1997–8), 13,070
Chancellor, The Lord Wakeham, PC (1998)
Vice-Chancellor, Prof. M. J. H. Sterling, PH.D, FEng.
Registrar, vacant
Academic Secretary, J. B. Alexander

THE UNIVERSITY OF BUCKINGHAM (1983)
(Founded 1976 as University College at Buckingham)
Buckingham MK18 1EG
Tel 01280-814080
Full-time students (1996–7), 798
Chancellor, Sir Martin Jacomb (1998)
Vice-Chancellor, Prof. R. H. Taylor
Registrar and Secretary, J. P. Elder

THE UNIVERSITY OF CAMBRIDGE
University Offices, The Old Schools, Cambridge CB2 1TN
Tel 01223-337733
Undergraduates (1997–8) 11,160

UNIVERSITY OFFICERS, ETC.
Chancellor, HRH The Prince Philip, Duke of Edinburgh,
    KG, KT, OM, GBE, PC (1977)
Vice-Chancellor, Prof. Sir Alec Broers, FRS (1996)
High Steward, The Lord Runcie, PC, DD (1991)
Deputy High Steward, The Lord Richardson of
    Duntisbourne, MBE, TD, PC (1983)
Commissary, The Lord Oliver of Aylmerton, PC (*Trinity
    Hall*) (1989)
Proctors, B. L. Hebbelthwaite (*Queens'*); A. S. Browne, PH.D.
    (*Trinity*) (1998)
Orator, A. J. Bowen (*Jesus*) (1993)
Registrary, T. J. Mead, PH.D. (*Wolfson*) (1997)
Librarian, P. K. Fox (*Selwyn*) (1994)
Treasurer, Mrs J. Womack (*Trinity Hall*) (1993)
Secretary-General of the Faculties, D. A. Livesey, PH.D.
    (*Emmanuel*) (1992)
Director of the Fitzwilliam Museum, D. D. Robinson (*Clare*)
    (1995)

COLLEGES AND HALLS, ETC.
with dates of foundation

CHRIST'S (1505), *Master*, A. J. Munro, PH.D. (1995)
CHURCHILL (1960), *Master*, Sir John Boyd, KCMG (1996)
CLARE (1326), *Master*, Prof. B. A. Hepple, LLD (1993)
CLARE HALL (1966), *President*, Prof. Dame Gillian Beer,
    DBE, Litt. D., FBA (1994)
CORPUS CHRISTI (1352), *Master*, Prof. Sir Tony Wrigley,
    PH.D. (1994)
DARWIN (1964), *Master*, Prof. Sir Geoffrey Lloyd, PH.D.,
    FBA (1989)
DOWNING (1800), *Master*, Prof. D. A. King, FRS (1995)
EMMANUEL (1584), *Master*, Prof. J. E. Ffowcs-Williams,
    SC.D. (1996)
FITZWILLIAM (1966), *Master*, Prof. A. W. Cuthbert, PH.D.,
    FRS (1991)
GIRTON (1869), *Mistress*, Prof. A. M. Strathern, PH.D.
    (1998)
GONVILLE AND CAIUS (1348), *Master*, N. McKendrick
    (1996)
HOMERTON (1824) (for B.Ed. Students), *Principal*, Mrs K.
    B. Pretty, PH.D. (1991)
HUGHES HALL (1885) (for post-graduate students),
    President, Prof. P. Richards (1998)
JESUS (1496), *Master*, Prof. D. G. Crighton, SC.D., FRS (1997)

KING's (1441), *Provost*, Prof. P. P. G. Bateson, SC.D., FRS (1987)

*LUCY CAVENDISH COLLEGE (1965) (for women research students and mature and affiliated undergraduates), *President*, The Baroness Perry of Southwark (1994)

MAGDALENE (1542), *Master*, Prof. Sir John Gurdon, D.Phil., FRS (1995)

*NEW HALL (1954), *President*, Mrs A. Lonsdale (1996)

*NEWNHAM (1871), *Principal*, Ms O. S. O'Neill, CBE (1992)

PEMBROKE (1347), *Master*, Sir Roger Tomkys, KCMG (1992)

PETERHOUSE (1284), *Master*, Prof. Sir John Meurig Thomas, FRS (1993)

QUEENS' (1448), *President*, The Lord Eatwell

ROBINSON (1977), *Warden*, Prof. the Lord Lewis of Newnham, SC.D., FRS (1977)

ST CATHARINE's (1473), *Master*, Prof. Sir Terence English (1993)

ST EDMUND's (1896), *Master*, Prof. R. B. Heap, SC.D. (1996)

ST JOHN's (1511), *Master*, Prof. P. Goddard, PH.D., FRS (1994)

SELWYN (1882), *Master*, Sir David Harrison, CBE, SC.D., F.Eng (1993)

SIDNEY SUSSEX (1596), *Master*, Prof. G. Horn, SC.D., FRS (1992)

TRINITY (1546), *Master*, Prof. A. K. Sen (1998)

TRINITY HALL (1350), *Master*, Sir John Lyons, PH.D. (1984)

WOLFSON (1965), *President*, G. Johnson PH.D. (1994)

*College for women only

UNIVERSITY OF CENTRAL ENGLAND IN BIRMINGHAM (1992)
Perry Barr, Birmingham B42 2SU
Tel 0121-331 5000
Full-time students (1997–8), 18,500
Chancellor, The Lord Mayor of Birmingham
Vice-Chancellor, Dr P. C. Knight, CBE
Registrar and Secretary, Ms M. Penlington

UNIVERSITY OF CENTRAL LANCASHIRE (1992)
Preston PR1 2HE
Tel 01772-201201
Full-time students (1997–8), 14,600
Chancellor, Sir Francis Kennedy, KCMG, CBE (1995)
Vice-Chancellor, Dr M. McVicar
Secretary, Mrs P. M. Ackroyd

CITY UNIVERSITY (1966)
Northampton Square, London EC1V 0HB
Tel 0171-477 8000
Full-time students (1997–8), 6,961
Chancellor, The Rt. Hon. the Lord Mayor of London
Vice-Chancellor, Prof. D. W. Rhind
Academic Registrar, A. H. Seville, PH.D.
Secretary, M. M. O'Hara

COVENTRY UNIVERSITY (1992)
Priory Street, Coventry CV1 5FB
Tel 01203-631313
Full-time students (1997–8), 12,060
Chancellor, The Lord Plumb, MEP (1995)
Vice-Chancellor, M. Goldstein, CBE, PH.D., D.SC.
Academic Registrar, J. Gledhill, PH.D.
Secretary, Ms L. Arlidge

CRANFIELD UNIVERSITY (1969)
(Founded as Cranfield Institute of Technology)
Cranfield, Beds MK43 0AL
Tel 01234-750111

Full-time students (1997–8), 2,321
Chancellor, The Lord Vincent of Coleshill, GBE, KCB, DSO (1998)
Vice-Chancellor, Prof. F. R. Hartley, D.SC.
Secretary and Registrar, J. K. Pettifer

DE MONTFORT UNIVERSITY (1992)
The Gateway, Leicester LE1 9BH
Tel 0116-255 1551
Full-time students (1997–8), 22,700
Chancellor, Dr J. White (1998)
Vice-Chancellor, Prof. K. Barker, CBE
Academic Registrar, V. E. Critchlow

UNIVERSITY OF DERBY (1993)
(formerly Derbyshire College of Higher Education)
Kedleston Road, Derby DE22 1GB
Tel 01332-622222
Full-time students (1997–8), 14,000
Chancellor, Sir Christopher Ball
Vice-Chancellor, Prof. R. Waterhouse
Registrar, Mrs J. Fry
Secretary, R. Gillis

THE UNIVERSITY OF DUNDEE (1967)
Dundee DD1 4HN
Tel 01382-344000
Full-time students (1997–8), 9,835
Chancellor, Sir James Black, FRCP, FRS (1992)
Vice-Chancellor, Dr I. J. Graham-Bryce
Secretary, R. Seaton
Rector, T. Slattery (1998–2001)

THE UNIVERSITY OF DURHAM
(Founded 1832; re-organized 1908, 1937 and 1963)
Old Shire Hall, Durham DH1 3HP
Tel 0191-374 2000
Full-time students (1997–8), 8,157
Chancellor, Sir Peter Ustinov, CBE, FRSL
Vice-Chancellor, Prof. Sir Kenneth Calman, KCB, MD, FRCP, FRCGP, FRCR, FRSE
Registrar and Secretary, J. C. F. Hayward

COLLEGES
COLLINGWOOD, *Principal*, Prof. G. H. Blake, PH.D.
GRADUATE SOCIETY, *Principal*, M. Richardson, PH.D.
GREY, *Master*, V. E. Watts
HATFIELD, *Master*, Prof. T. P. Burt, PH.D.
ST AIDAN's, *Principal*, J. S. Ashworth
ST CHAD's, *Principal*, J. P. M. Cassidy, PH.D.
ST CUTHBERT'S SOCIETY, *Principal*, S. G. C. Stoker
ST HILD AND ST BEDE, *Principal*, Prof. D. J. Davies, PH.D.
ST JOHN's, *Principal*, D. V. Day
ST MARY's, *Principal*, Miss J. M. Kenworthy
TREVELYAN, *Principal*, Prof. M. Todd, D.Litt
UNIVERSITY (DURHAM), *Master*, Prof. M. E. Tucker, PH.D.
UNIVERSITY (STOCKTON), *Principal*, J. C. F. Hayward
USHAW, *President*, Revd J. O'Keefe
VAN MILDERT, *Principal*, Prof. I. R. Taylor, PH.D.

THE UNIVERSITY OF EAST ANGLIA (1963)
Norwich NR4 7TJ
Tel 01603-456161
Full-time students (1997–8), 9,750
Chancellor, Sir Geoffrey Allen, FEng, FRS (1994)
Vice-Chancellor, V. Watts
Registrar and Secretary, M. G. E. Paulson-Ellis, OBE

UNIVERSITY OF EAST LONDON (1992)
Longbridge Road, Dagenham, Essex RM8 2AS
Tel 0181-590 7000/7722
Full-time students (1997–8), c.12,000

Chancellor, The Lord Rix, CBE (1997)
Vice-Chancellor, Prof. F. W. Gould
Secretary and Registrar, A. Ingle

THE UNIVERSITY OF EDINBURGH (1583)
Old College, South Bridge, Edinburgh EH8 9YL
Tel 0131-650 1000
Full-time students (1997–8), 17,845
Chancellor, HRH The Prince Philip, Duke of Edinburgh,
KG, KT, OM, GBE, PC, FRS (1952)
Vice-Chancellor, Prof. Sir Stewart Sutherland, FBA, FRSE
Secretary, M. J. B. Lowe, PH.D.
Rector, J. Colquhoun (1997–2000)

THE UNIVERSITY OF ESSEX (1964)
Wivenhoe Park, Colchester CO4 3SQ
Tel 01206-873333
Full-time students (1997–8), 5,710
Chancellor, The Lord Nolan, PC (1997)
Vice-Chancellor, Prof. I. Crewe
Registrar and Secretary, A. F. Woodburn

THE UNIVERSITY OF EXETER (1955)
Northcote House, The Queen's Drive, Exeter EX4 4QJ
Tel 01392-263263
Full-time students (1997–8), 8,514
Chancellor, The Lord Alexander of Weedon (1998)
Vice-Chancellor, Sir Geoffrey Holland, KCB
Registrar and Secretary, I. H. C. Powell

UNIVERSITY OF GLAMORGAN (1992)
Treforest, Pontypridd CF37 1DL
Tel 01443-480480
Full-time students (1997–8), 10,931
Chancellor, The Lord Merlyn-Rees, PC, QC (1994)
Vice-Chancellor, Prof. A. L. Webb
Academic Registrar, J. O'Shea
Secretary, J. L. Bracegirdle

THE UNIVERSITY OF GLASGOW (1451)
University Avenue, Glasgow G12 8QQ
Tel 0141-330 5911
Full-time students (1997–8), 23,572
Principal, Prof. Sir Graeme Davies, FEng.
Registrar, Mrs C. R. Lowther
Secretary, Mrs J. Ellis
Rector, R. Wilson (1996–9)

GLASGOW CALEDONIAN UNIVERSITY
(1993)
Cowcaddens Road, Glasgow G4 0BA
Tel 0141-331 3000
Full-time students (1997–8), 13,399
Secretary, B. M. Murphy
Chancellor, The Lord Nickson, KBE (1993)
Principal and Vice-Chancellor, W. Laurie
Registrar, B. Ferguson

UNIVERSITY OF GREENWICH (1992)
Bexley Road, Eltham, London SE9 2PQ
Tel 0181-331 8000
Full-time students (1997–8), 14,138
Chancellor, vacant
Vice-Chancellor, Dr D. E. Fussey
Academic Registrar, Ms C. H. Rose
Secretary, J. M. Charles

HERIOT-WATT UNIVERSITY (1966)
Riccarton, Edinburgh EH14 4AS
Tel 0131-449 5111
Full-time students (1997–8), 4,700

Chancellor, The Lord Mackay of Clashfern, PC, QC, FRSE
(1979)
Vice-Chancellor, Prof. J. S. Archer, FEng.
Secretary, P. L. Wilson

UNIVERSITY OF HERTFORDSHIRE (1992)
College Lane, Hatfield, Herts AL10 9AB
Tel 01707-284000
Full-time students (1997–8), 18,607
Chancellor, The Lord MacLaurin of Knebworth (1996)
Vice-Chancellor, Prof. N. K. Buxton
Registrar and Secretary, P. G. Jeffreys

UNIVERSITY OF HUDDERSFIELD (1992)
Queensgate, Huddersfield HD1 3DH
Tel 01484-422288
Full-time students (1997–8), 10,885
Chancellor, Sir Ernest Hall, OBE (1996)
Vice-Chancellor, Prof. J. R. Tarrant
Registrar and Secretary, Mrs M. H. Andrew

THE UNIVERSITY OF HULL (1954)
Cottingham Road, Hull HU6 7RX
Tel 01482-346311
Full-time students (1997–8), 13,500
Chancellor, The Lord Armstrong of Ilminster, GCB, CVO
(1994)
Vice-Chancellor, Prof. D. N. Dilks, FRSL
Registrar and Secretary, D. J. Lock

KEELE UNIVERSITY (1962)
Newcastle under Lyme, Staffs ST5 5BG
Tel 01782-621111
Full-time students (1997–8), 6,319
Chancellor, Sir Claus Moser, KCB, CBE, FBA (1986)
Vice-Chancellor, Prof. J. V. Finch
Registrar and Secretary, S. J. Morris

THE UNIVERSITY OF KENT AT
CANTERBURY (1965)
Canterbury CT2 7NZ
Tel 01227-764000
Full-time students (1997–8), 9,904
Chancellor, Sir Crispin Tickell, GCMG, KCVO
Vice-Chancellor, Prof. R. Sibson
Secretary and Registrar, N. A. McHard

KINGSTON UNIVERSITY (1992)
Kingston upon Thames, Surrey KT1 1LQ
Tel 0181-547 2000
Full-time students (1997–8), 12,658
Chancellor, Sir Frank Lampl
Vice-Chancellor, Prof. P. Scott
Secretary, R. Abdulla

THE UNIVERSITY OF LANCASTER (1964)
Bailrigg, Lancaster LA1 4YW
Tel 01524-65201
Full-time students (1997–8), 8,535
Chancellor, HRH Princess Alexandra, the Hon. Lady
Ogilvy, GCVO (1964)
Vice-Chancellor, Prof. W. Ritchie, OBE
Secretary, S. A. C. Lamley

THE UNIVERSITY OF LEEDS (1904)
Leeds LS2 9JT
Tel 0113-243 1751
Full-time students (1997–8), 19,727
Chancellor, HRH The Duchess of Kent, GCVO (1966)
Vice-Chancellor, Prof. A. G. Wilson
Registrar and Secretary, D. S. Robinson, PH.D.

LEEDS METROPOLITAN UNIVERSITY
(1992)
Calverley Street, Leeds LS1 3HE
Tel 0113-283 2600
Full-time students (1997–8), 15,074
Chairman of the Board of Governors, L. Silver (1989)
Vice-Chancellor, Prof. L. Wagner
Academic Registrar, Ms C. Orange
Secretary, M. Wilkinson

THE UNIVERSITY OF LEICESTER (1957)
University Road, Leicester LE1 7RH
Tel 0116-252 2522
Full-time students (1997–8), 8,657
Chancellor, Sir Michael Atiyah, OM, FRS, Ph.D., D.SC. (1995)
Vice-Chancellor, K. J. R. Edwards, Ph.D.
Registrar and Secretary, K. J. Julian

UNIVERSITY OF LINCOLNSHIRE AND
HUMBERSIDE
(University of Humberside founded 1992; re-organized
1996)
Humberside campus: Hull HU6 7RT
Tel 01482–440550
Lincoln campus: Lincoln LN2 4VF
Tel 01522–882000
Full-time students (1997–8), 10,562
Chancellor, Dr J. H. Hooper, CBE
Vice-Chancellor, Prof. R. P. King
Registrar and Secretary, Dr K. Pardoe

THE UNIVERSITY OF LIVERPOOL (1903)
Senate House, Abercromby Square, Liverpool L69 3BX
Tel 0151-794 2000
Full-time students (1997–8), 13,184
Chancellor, The Lord Owen, CH, PC (1996)
Vice-Chancellor, Prof. P. N. Love, CBE
Registrar and Secretary, M. D. Carr

LIVERPOOL JOHN MOORES UNIVERSITY
(1992)
Rodney House, 70 Mount Pleasant, Liverpool L3 5UX
Tel 0151-231 2121
Full-time students (1997–8), 20,000
Chancellor, J. Moores, CBE
Vice-Chancellor, Prof. P. Toyne
Registrar, Ms A. Wild

THE UNIVERSITY OF LONDON (1836)
Senate House, Malet Street, London WC1E 7HU
Tel 0171-636 8000
Internal students (1997–8), 101,576; External students,
26,000
Visitor, HM The Queen in Council
Chancellor, HRH The Princess Royal, KG, GCVO, FRS (1981)
Vice-Chancellor, Prof. G. Zellick, Ph.D.
Chairman of the Council, The Lord Woolf, PC
Chairman of Convocation, D. Leslie

COLLEGES

BIRKBECK COLLEGE, Malet Street, London WC1E 7HX.
Master, Prof. T. O'Shea
CHARING CROSS AND WESTMINSTER MEDICAL SCHOOL,
see Imperial College of Science, Technology and
Medicine
GOLDSMITHS COLLEGE, Lewisham Way, New Cross,
London SE14 6NW. *Warden*, Prof. B. Pimlott, FBA
HEYTHROP COLLEGE, Kensington Square, London
W8 5HQ. *Principal*, B. Callaghan

IMPERIAL COLLEGE OF SCIENCE, TECHNOLOGY AND
MEDICINE (includes Imperial College Schools of
Medicine at Charing Cross, Hammersmith and St
Mary's hospitals and at the National Heart and Lung
Institute), South Kensington, London SW7 2AZ. *Rector*,
Prof. Sir Ronald Oxburgh, KBE, FRS
INSTITUTE OF CANCER RESEARCH, Royal Cancer
Hospital, Chester Beatty Laboratories, 17A Onslow
Gardens, London SW7 3AL. *Chief Executive*, Prof.
P. B. Garland, Ph.D., FRSE
INSTITUTE OF EDUCATION, 20 Bedford Way, London
WC1H 0AL. *Director*, Prof. P. Mortimore, OBE
KING'S COLLEGE LONDON (includes King's College
School of Medicine and Dentistry, United Medical and
Dental Schools of Guy's and St Thomas' Hospitals),
Strand, London WC2R 2LS. *Principal*, Prof. A. Lucas, Ph.D.
Associated Institute:
Institute of Psychiatry, De Crespigny Park, Denmark Hill,
London SE5 8AF. *Dean*, Prof. S. Checkley.
LONDON BUSINESS SCHOOL, Sussex Place, Regent's Park,
London NW1 4SA. *Principal*, Prof. J. Quelch
THE LONDON HOSPITAL MEDICAL COLLEGE, *see* Queen
Mary and Westfield College.
LONDON SCHOOL OF ECONOMICS AND POLITICAL
SCIENCE, Houghton Street, London WC2A 2AE. *Director*,
Prof. A. Giddens
LONDON SCHOOL OF HYGIENE AND TROPICAL
MEDICINE, Keppel Street, London WC1E 7HT. *Dean*,
Prof. H. Spencer
QUEEN MARY AND WESTFIELD COLLEGE (incorporating
St Bartholomew's and the Royal London School of
Medicine and Dentistry and the London Hospital
Medical College), Mile End Road, London E1 4NS.
Principal, Prof. A. Smith
ROYAL FREE HOSPITAL SCHOOL OF MEDICINE, *see*
University College London
ROYAL HOLLOWAY, Egham Hill, Egham, Surrey TW20
0EX. *Principal*, Prof. N. Gowar
ROYAL POSTGRADUATE MEDICAL SCHOOL, *see* Imperial
College of Science, Technology and Medicine
ROYAL VETERINARY COLLEGE, Royal College Street,
London NW1 0TU. *Principal and Dean*, Prof. L. E. Lanyon,
Ph.D.
ST BARTHOLOMEW'S AND THE ROYAL LONDON SCHOOL
OF MEDICINE AND DENTISTRY, *see* Queen Mary and
Westfield College
ST GEORGE'S HOSPITAL MEDICAL SCHOOL, Cranmer
Terrace, London SW17 0RE. *Dean*, Prof. R. Boyd, FRCP
SCHOOL OF ORIENTAL AND AFRICAN STUDIES,
Thornhaugh Street, Russell Square, London WC1H 0XG.
Director, Sir Tim Lankester, KCB
SCHOOL OF PHARMACY, 29–39 Brunswick Square,
London WC1N 1AX. *Dean*, Prof. A. T. Florence, CBE, Ph.D.,
FRSE
SCHOOL OF SLAVONIC AND EAST EUROPEAN STUDIES,
Senate House, Malet Street, London WC1E 7HU. *Director*,
Prof. M. A. Branch, Ph.D.
UNITED MEDICAL AND DENTAL SCHOOLS OF GUY'S AND
ST THOMAS' HOSPITALS, *see* King's College London
UNIVERSITY COLLEGE LONDON (including UCL
Medical School), Gower Street, London WC1E 6BT.
Provost, Sir Derek Roberts, CBE, FRS, FEng.
WYE COLLEGE, Wye, near Ashford, Kent TN25 5AH.
Principal, Prof. J. H. D. Prescott, Ph.D.

INSTITUTES

BRITISH INSTITUTE IN PARIS, 9–11 rue de Constantine,
75340 Paris, Cedex 07, France. *Director*, Prof.
C. L. Campos, CBE, Ph.D. *London office*: Senate House,
Malet Street, London WC1E 7HU

CENTRE FOR DEFENCE STUDIES, King's College London, Strand, London WC2R 2LS. *Director,* Prof. L. Freedman, CBE, FBA
COURTAULD INSTITUTE OF ART, North Block, Somerset House, Strand, London WC2R ORN. *Director,* Prof. E. C. Fernie, CBE, FSA, FRSE
UNIVERSITY MARINE BIOLOGICAL STATION MILLPORT, Isle of Cumbrae, Scotland KA28 OEG. *Director,* Prof. J. Davenport, PH.D., D.SC., FRSE
SCHOOL OF ADVANCED STUDY
Senate House, Malet Street, London WC1E 7HU *Dean,* Prof. T. C. Daintith
Comprises:
CENTRE FOR ENGLISH STUDIES, Senate House, Malet Street, London WC1E 7HU *Director,* Dr W. Gould
INSTITUTE OF ADVANCED LEGAL STUDIES, Charles Clore House, 17 Russell Square, London WC1B 5DR. *Director,* Prof. B. A. K. Rider
INSTITUTE OF CLASSICAL STUDIES, Senate House, Malet Street, London WC1E 7HU. *Director,* Prof. G. B. Waywell, FSA
INSTITUTE OF COMMONWEALTH STUDIES, 27–28 Russell Square, London WC1B 5DS. *Director,* Prof. P. Caplan
INSTITUTE OF GERMANIC STUDIES, 29 Russell Square, London WC1B 5DP. *Hon. Director,* E. M. Batley
INSTITUTE OF HISTORICAL RESEARCH, Senate House, Malet Street, London WC1E 7HU. *Director,* Prof. D. Cannadine
INSTITUTE OF LATIN AMERICAN STUDIES, 31 Tavistock Square, London WC1H 9HA. *Director,* Prof. V. G. Bulmer-Thomas, OBE, D.Phil.
INSTITUTE OF ROMANCE STUDIES, Senate House, Malet Street, London WC1E 7HU. *Director,* Prof. J. Labanyi
INSTITUTE OF UNITED STATES STUDIES, Senate House, Malet Street, London WC1E 7HU. *Director,* Prof. G. L. McDowell, PH.D.
WARBURG INSTITUTE, Woburn Square, London WC1H OAB. *Director,* Prof. C. N. J. Mann, PH.D.

ASSOCIATE INSTITUTIONS
INSTITUTE OF JEWISH STUDIES, 44A Albert Road, London NW4 2SJ. *Principal,* Rabbi Dr D. Sinclair
INSTITUTE OF ZOOLOGY, Royal Zoological Society, Regent's Park, London NW1 4RY. *Director,* Prof. M. Gosling
ROYAL ACADEMY OF MUSIC, Marylebone Road, London NW1 5HT. *Principal,* Prof. C. Price
ROYAL COLLEGE OF MUSIC, Prince Consort Road, London SW7 2BS. *Director,* Dr J. Ritterman
TRINITY COLLEGE OF MUSIC 11–13 Mandeville Place, London W1M 6AQ. *Principal,* G. Henderson

LONDON GUILDHALL UNIVERSITY (1993)
31 Jewry Street, London EC3N 2EY
Tel 0171-320 1000
Full-time students (1997–8), 13,726
Patron, HRH The Prince Philip, Duke of Edinburgh, KG, KT, OM, GBE, PC (1952)
Provost, Prof. R. Floud, D.Phil.
Secretary, M. Weaver
Academic Registrar, Ms J. Grinstead

LOUGHBOROUGH UNIVERSITY (1966)
Loughborough, Leics LE11 3TU
Tel 01509-263171
Full-time students (1997–8), 10,500
Chancellor, Sir Denis Rooke, CBE, FRS, FEng (1989)
Vice-Chancellor, Prof. D.Wallace, FRS, FRSE
Registrar, D. E. Fletcher, PH.D.

UNIVERSITY OF LUTON (1993)
Park Square, Luton LU1 3JU
Tel 01582-734111
Full-time students (1997–8), 10,700
Chancellor, Sir David Plastow
Vice-Chancellor, Dr D. John
Registrar, Ms P. Vachon
Secretary, R. Williams

THE UNIVERSITY OF MANCHESTER
(Founded 1851; re-organized 1880 and 1903)
Oxford Road, Manchester M13 9PL
Tel 0161-275 2000
Full-time students (1997–8), 19,508
Chancellor, The Lord Flowers, FRS (1994)
Vice-Chancellor, Prof. M. B. Harris, CBE, PH.D.
Registrar and Secretary, E. Newcomb
Academic Registrar, A. McMenemy

UNIVERSITY OF MANCHESTER INSTITUTE OF SCIENCE AND TECHNOLOGY (1824)
PO Box 88, Manchester M60 1QD
Tel 0161-236 3311
Full-time students (1997–8), 6,000
Chancellor, Prof. Sir Roland Smith (1995)
Vice-Chancellor, Prof. R. F. Boucher, FEng.
Registrar, P. C. C. Stephenson

MANCHESTER METROPOLITAN UNIVERSITY (1992)
All Saints, Manchester M15 6BH
Tel 0161-247 2000
Full-time students (1997–8), 22,000
Chancellor, The Duke of Westminster, OBE, TD (1993)
Vice-Chancellor, Mrs A. V. Burslem, OBE
Academic Registrar, J. D. M. Karczewski-Slowikowski
Secretary, T. A. Hendley

MIDDLESEX UNIVERSITY (1992)
White Hart Lane, London N17 8HR N14 4XS
Tel 0181-362 5000
Full-time students (1997–8), 19,790
Chancellor, The Baroness Platt of Writtle (1993)
Vice-Chancellor, Prof. M. Driscoll
Registrar, G. Jones

NAPIER UNIVERSITY (1992)
219 Colinton Road, Edinburgh EH14 1DJ
Tel 0131-444 2266
Full-time students (1997–8), 11,412
Chancellor, The Viscount Younger of Leckie, KCVO, TD, PC, FRSE (1993)
Principal and Vice-Chancellor, Prof. J. Mavor
Secretary and Registrar, I. J. Miller

THE UNIVERSITY OF NEWCASTLE UPON TYNE
(Founded 1852; re-organized 1908, 1937 and 1963)
6 Kensington Terrace, Newcastle upon Tyne NE1 7RU
Tel 0191-222 6000
Full-time students (1997–8), 11,922
Chancellor, The Viscount Ridley, KG, GCVO, TD (*until 31 Dec. 1998*)
Vice-Chancellor, J. R. G. Wright
Registrar, D. E. T. Nicholson

UNIVERSITY OF NORTH LONDON (1992)
166–220 Holloway Road, London N7 8DB
Tel 0171-607 2789

Full-time students (1997–8), *c.*11,500
Secretary, J. McParland
Vice-Chancellor, B. A. Roper
Academic Director, G. Holmes

UNIVERSITY OF NORTHUMBRIA AT NEWCASTLE (1992)
Ellison Place, Newcastle upon Tyne NEI 8ST
Tel 0191-232 6002
Full-time students (1997–8), 18,533
Chancellor, The Lord Glenamara, CH, PC (1984)
Vice-Chancellor, Prof. G. Smith
Registrar, Ms C. Penna
Secretary, R. A. Bott

THE UNIVERSITY OF NOTTINGHAM (1948)
University Park, Nottingham NG7 2RD
Tel 0115-951 5151
Full-time students (1997–8), 16,000
Chancellor, The Lord Dearing, CB (1993)
Vice-Chancellor, Prof. Sir Colin Campbell
Registrar, K. Jones

NOTTINGHAM TRENT UNIVERSITY (1992)
Burton Street, Nottingham NGI 4BU
Tel 0115-948 8418
Full-time students (1997–8), 23,410
Vice-Chancellor, Prof. R. Cowell, PH.D.
Academic Registrar, D. W. Samson
Corporate Secretary and Solicitor, S. Smith

THE UNIVERSITY OF OXFORD
University Offices, Wellington Square, Oxford OXI 2JD
Tel 01865-270001
Students in residence 1997–8, 15,623
Chancellor, The Lord Jenkins of Hillhead, OM, PC (*Balliol*),
  elected 1987
High Steward, The Lord Goff of Chieveley, PC (*Lincoln* and
  New College), elected 1990
Vice-Chancellor, Dr C. R. Lucas (*Balliol*), elected 1997
Proctors, Dr R. W. Ainsworth (*St Catherine's*); Dr A. M. Hart
  (*Exeter*), elected 1998
Assessor, Dr A. M. Bowie (*Queen's*), elected 1998
Public Orator, Prof. J. Griffin (*Balliol*), elected 1992
Bodley's Librarian, R. P. Carr (*Balliol*), elected 1997
Keeper of Archives, D. G. Vaisey (*Exeter*), elected 1995
Director of the Ashmolean Museum, Dr C. Brown (*St Catherine's*), elected 1998
Registrar of the University, D. R. Holmes (*Merton*), elected 1998
Surveyor to the University, P. M. R. Hill, elected 1993
Secretary of Faculties, A. P. Weale (*Worcester*), elected 1984
Secretary of the Chest, J. R. Clements, elected 1995
Deputy Registrar (Administration), P. W. Jones (*Green*), elected 1991

OXFORD COLLEGES AND HALLS
with dates of foundation

ALL SOULS (1438), *Warden,* Prof. J. Davis, FBA (1995)
BALLIOL (1263), *Master,* A. Graham (1998)
BRASENOSE (1509), *Principal,* The Lord Windlesham, CVO, PC (1989)
CHRIST CHURCH (1546), *Dean,* Very Revd J. H. Drury (1991)
CORPUS CHRISTI (1517), *President,* Prof. Sir Keith Thomas, FBA (1986)
EXETER (1314), *Rector,* Dr M. Butler (1993)
GREEN (1979), *Warden,* Sir John Hanson, KCMG, CBE (1997)

HARRIS MANCHESTER (1786), *Principal,* Revd R. Waller, PH.D. (1990)
HERTFORD (1874), *Principal,* Sir Walter Bodmer, FRS (1996)
JESUS (1571), *Principal,* Sir Peter North, CBE, DCL, QC, FBA (1984)
KEBLE (1868), *Warden,* Dr A. Cameron, FBA, FSA (1994)
KELLOGG (1990), *President,* Dr G. P. Thomas (1990)
LADY MARGARET HALL (1878), *Principal,* Sir Brian Fall, GVCO, KCMG (1995)
LINACRE (1962), *Principal,* Dr P. A. Slack, FBA (1996)
LINCOLN (1427), *Rector,* Dr W. E. K. Anderson, FRSE (1994)
MAGDALEN (1458), *President,* A. D. Smith, CBE (1988)
MANSFIELD (1886), *Principal,* Prof. D. I. Marquand (1996)
MERTON (1264), *Warden,* Dr. J Rawson, CBE, FBA (1994)
NEW COLLEGE (1379), *Warden,* Dr. A. J. Ryan, FBA (1996)
NUFFIELD (1937), *Warden,* A. Atkinson, FBA (1994)
ORIEL (1326), *Provost,* Dr E. W. Nicholson, DD, FBA (1990)
PEMBROKE (1624), *Master,* Dr R. Stevens, DCL (1993)
QUEEN'S (1340), *Provost,* Dr G. Marshall, FBA (1993)
ST ANNE'S (1952 (Society of Oxford Home-Students (1879)), *Principal,* Mrs R. L. Deech (1991)
ST ANTONY'S (1950), *Warden,* Sir Marrack Goulding, KCMG (1997)
ST CATHERINE'S (1962), *Master,* The Lord Plant of Highfield (1994)
ST CROSS (1965), *Master,* Dr R. C. Repp (1987)
ST EDMUND HALL (*c.*1278), *Principal (acting),* J. P. D. Dunbabin (1996)
*ST HILDA'S (1893), *Principal,* Miss E. Llewellyn-Smith, CB (1990)
ST HUGH'S (1886), *Principal,* D. Wood, CBE, QC (1991)
ST JOHN'S (1555), *President,* Dr W. Hayes (1987)
ST PETER'S (1929), *Master,* Dr J. P. Barron, FSA (1991)
SOMERVILLE (1879), *Principal,* Dame Fiona Caldicott, DBE, FRCP (1996)
TEMPLETON (1965), *President,* Sir David Rowland (1998)
TRINITY (1554), *President,* The Hon. Michael J. Beloff, QC (1996)
UNIVERSITY (1249), *Master,* Sir Robin Butler, GCB, CVO (1998)
WADHAM (1612), *Warden,* J. S. Flemming, FBA (1993)
WOLFSON (1966), *President,* Sir David Smith, D.PHIL., FRS, FRSE (1994)
WORCESTER (1714), *Provost,* R. G. Smethurst (1991)

BLACKFRIARS (1921), *Regent,* Very Revd P. M. Parvis, D.Phil (1996)
CAMPION HALL (1896), *Master,* Revd G. J. Hughes, D.phil (1998)
GREYFRIARS (1910), *Warden,* Revd T. G. Weinandy, PH.D (1996)
REGENT'S PARK (1810), *Principal,* Revd P. S. Fiddes, D.phil. (1989)
ST BENET'S HALL (1897), *Master,* Revd H. Wansbrough, OSB (1991)
WYCLIFFE HALL (1877), *Principal,* Revd A. E. McGrath, D.phil (1995)
*College for women only

OXFORD BROOKES UNIVERSITY (1993)
Headington, Oxford OX3 OBP
Tel 01865-741111
Full-time students (1997–8), 12,600
Chancellor, Baroness Kennedy of the Shaws, QC
Vice-Chancellor, Prof. G. Upton
Academic Registrar, Ms E. N. Winders
Academic Secretary, B. Summers

UNIVERSITY OF PAISLEY (1992)
Paisley PA1 2BE
Tel 0141-848 3000
Full-time students (1997–8), 10,793
Chancellor, Sir Robert Easton, CBE (1993)
Vice-Chancellor, Prof. R. W. Shaw, CBE
Registrar, D. Rigg
Secretary, J. Fraser

UNIVERSITY OF PLYMOUTH (1992)
Drake Circus, Plymouth PL4 8AA
Tel 01752-600600
Full-time students (1997–8), 15,660
Vice-Chancellor, Prof. J. Bull
Secretary and Academic Registrar, Miss J. Hopkinson

UNIVERSITY OF PORTSMOUTH (1992)
University House, Winston Churchill Avenue, Portsmouth
PO1 2UP
Tel 01705-876543
Full-time students (1997–8), 14,500
Chancellor, The Lord Palumbo (1992)
Vice-Chancellor, Prof. J. Craven
Academic Registrar, A. Rees

THE QUEEN'S UNIVERSITY OF BELFAST
(1908)
Belfast BT7 1NN
Tel 01232-245133
Full-time students (1995–6), 14,500
Chancellor, Sir David Orr, MC (1992)
Vice-Chancellor, Prof. G. Bain
Registrar, J. Town
Administrative Secretary, D. H. Wilson

THE UNIVERSITY OF READING (1926)
Whiteknights, PO Box 217, Reading RG6 6AH
Tel 0118-987 5123
Full-time students (1997–8), 11,096
Chancellor, The Lord Carrington, KG, GCMG, CH, MC, PC
(1992)
Vice-Chancellor, Prof. R. Williams
Registrar, D. C. R. Frampton

THE ROBERT GORDON UNIVERSITY (1992)
Schoolhill, Aberdeen AB10 1FR
Tel 01224-262000
Full-time students (1997–8), 7,760
Chancellor, Sir Bob Reid (1993)
Vice-Chancellor, Prof. B. Stevely
Secretary, D. Caldwell

THE UNIVERSITY OF ST ANDREWS (1411)
College Gate, St Andrews KY16 9AJ
Tel 01334-476161
Full-time students (1997–8), 5,629
Chancellor, Sir Kenneth Dover, D.Litt., FRSE, FBA (1981)
Vice-Chancellor, Prof. S. Arnott, CBE, FRS, FRSE
Secretary, D. J. Corner
Rector, D. R. Findlay, QC (1997–1999)

THE UNIVERSITY OF SALFORD (1967)
Salford M5 4WT
Tel 0161-295 5000
Full-time students (1997–8), 12,539
Chancellor, Sir Walter Bodmer, PH.D., FRS
Vice-Chancellor, Prof. M. Harloe
Registrar, M. D. Winton, PH.D.

THE UNIVERSITY OF SHEFFIELD (1905)
Western Bank, Sheffield S10 2TN
Tel 0114-222 2000
Full-time students (1997–8), 16,683
Chancellor, vacant
Vice-Chancellor, Prof. Sir Gareth Roberts, FRS
Registrar, vacant
Secretary, J. O'Donovan

SHEFFIELD HALLAM UNIVERSITY (1992)
Howard Street, Sheffield S1 1WB
Tel 0114-225 5555
Full-time students (1997–8), 18,000
Chancellor, Sir Bryan Nicholson (1992)
Vice-Chancellor, Ms D. Green
Registrar, Ms J. Tory
Secretary, Ms S. Neocosmos

THE UNIVERSITY OF SOUTHAMPTON
(1952)
Highfield, Southampton SO17 1BJ
Tel 01703-595000
Full-time students (1997–8), 13,480
Chancellor, The Earl of Selbourne, KBE, FRS (1996)
Vice-Chancellor, Prof. H. Newby, CBE
Secretary and Registrar, J. F. D. Lauwerys

SOUTH BANK UNIVERSITY (1992)
103 Borough Road, London SE1 0AA
Tel 0171-928 8989
Full-time students (1997–8), 15,000
Chancellor, C. McLaren
Vice-Chancellor, Prof. G. Bernbaum
Registrar, R. Phillips
Secretary, Mrs L. Gander

STAFFORDSHIRE UNIVERSITY (1992)
College Road, Stoke-on-Trent ST4 2DE
Tel 01782-294000
Full-time students (1997–8), 14,500
Chancellor, The Lord Ashley of Stoke, CH, PC (1993)
Vice-Chancellor, Prof. C. E. King, PH.D.
Academic Registrar, Ms F. Francis
Secretary, K. Sproston

THE UNIVERSITY OF STIRLING (1967)
Stirling FK9 4LA
Tel 01786-473171
Full-time students (1997–8), 7,500
Chancellor, Dame Diana Rigg, DBE
Vice-Chancellor, Prof. A. Miller, FRSE
Academic Registrar, D. G. Wood
Secretary, K. J. Clarke

THE UNIVERSITY OF STRATHCLYDE (1964)
McCance Building, John Anderson Campus, Glasgow
G1 1XQ
Tel 0141-552 4400
Full-time students (1997–8), 14,300
Chancellor, The Lord Hope of Craighead, PC (1998)
Principal and Vice-Chancellor, Prof. Sir John Arbuthnott,
FRSE
Secretary, P. W. A. West

UNIVERSITY OF SUNDERLAND (1992)
Langham Tower, Ryhope Road, Sunderland SR2 7EE
Tel 0191-515 2000
Full-time students (1997–8), 11,966
Chancellor, The Lord Puttnam, CBE (1998)
Vice-Chancellor, Ms A. Wright, CBE, PH.D.
Academic Registrar, S. Porteous
Secretary, J. D. Pacey

452 Education

THE UNIVERSITY OF SURREY (1966)
Guildford, Surrey GU2 5XH
Tel 01483-300800
Full-time students (1997–8), 8,204
Chancellor, HRH The Duke of Kent, KG, GCMG, GCVO (1977)
Vice-Chancellor, Prof. P. J. Dowling, FRS, FEng.
Secretary and Registrar, H. W. B. Davies

THE UNIVERSITY OF SUSSEX (1961)
Falmer, Brighton BN1 9RH
Tel 01273-606755
Full-time students (1997–8), 9,085
Chancellor, The Lord Attenborough (1998)
Vice-Chancellor (acting), Prof. M. A. M. Smith
Registrar and Secretary, B. K. Gooch

UNIVERSITY OF TEESSIDE (1992)
Middlesbrough TS1 3BA
Tel 01642-218121
Full-time students (1997–8), 8,216
Chancellor, The Rt. Hon.Sir Leon Brittan QC (1993)
Vice-Chancellor, Prof. D. Fraser
Secretary, J. M. McClintock

THAMES VALLEY UNIVERSITY (1992)
St Mary's Road, Ealing, London W5 5RF
Tel 0181-579 5000
Full-time students (1997–8), 5,793
Chancellor, The Lord Hamlyn, CBE
Vice-Chancellor, M. Fitzgerald, Ph.D.
Director of Registry Services, P. Head

THE UNIVERSITY OF ULSTER (1984)
Cromore Road, Coleraine BT52 1SA
Tel 01265-44141
Full-time students (1997–8), 16,543
Chancellor, Rabbi J. Neuberger (1993)
Vice-Chancellor, Prof. Lord Smith of Clifton (1991)
Academic Registrar, Dr K. Miller

THE UNIVERSITY OF WALES (1893)
King Edward VII Avenue, Cathays Park, Cardiff CF1 3NS
Tel 01222-382656
Students (1997–8), 68,000
Chancellor, HRH The Prince of Wales, KG, KT, GCB, PC (1976)
Senior Vice-Chancellor, Prof. K. G. Robbins, FRSE
Secretary-General, J. D. Pritchard

MEMBER INSTITUTIONS

UNIVERSITY OF WALES, ABERYSTWYTH, Old College, King Street, Aberystwyth SY23 2AX. Tel: 01970-623111. Vice-Chancellor, Prof. D. Llwyd Morgan, D.phil. (1995)
UNIVERSITY OF WALES BANGOR, Bangor LL57 2DG. Tel: 01248-351151. Vice-Chancellor, Prof. H. R. Evans, Ph.D., FEng. (1995)
UNIVERSITY OF WALES, CARDIFF, PO Box 920, Cardiff CF1 3XP. Tel: 01222-874000. Vice-Chancellor, Prof. E. B. Smith, Ph.D., D.Sc. (1993)
UNIVERSITY OF WALES COLLEGE, NEWPORT, Caerleon Campus, PO Box 179, Newport NP6 1YG. Tel: 01633-430088. Principal, Prof. K. J. Overshott, Ph.D. (1990)
UNIVERSITY OF WALES COLLEGE OF MEDICINE, Heath Park, Cardiff CF4 4XN. Tel: 01222-747747. Vice-Chancellor, Prof. I. R. Cameron, DM, FRCP (1994)
UNIVERSITY OF WALES INSTITUTE, CARDIFF, Llandaff Centre, Western Avenue, Cardiff CF5 2SG. Tel: 01222-506070. Principal, A. J. Chapman, Ph.D. (1998)
UNIVERSITY OF WALES, LAMPETER, Lampeter SA48 7ED. Tel: 01570-422351. Vice-Chancellor, Prof. K. G. Robbins, D.Litt., D.phil., FRSE (1992)

UNIVERSITY OF WALES SWANSEA, Singleton Park, Swansea SA2 8PP. Tel: 01792-205678. Vice-Chancellor, Prof. R. H. Williams, Ph.D., D.SC, FRS (1994)

THE UNIVERSITY OF WARWICK (1965)
Coventry CV4 7AL
Tel 01203-523523
Full-time students (1997–8), 15,291
Chancellor, Sir Shridath Surendranath Ramphal, GCMG, QC (1989)
Vice-Chancellor, Prof. Sir Brian Follett, FRS
Registrar, M. L. Shattock, OBE
Academic Registrar, Dr J. W. Nicholls

UNIVERSITY OF WESTMINSTER (1992)
309 Regent Street, London W1R 8AL
Tel 0171-911 5000
Full-time students (1997–8), 9,825
Vice-Chancellor and Rector, Dr G. M. Copland (1996)
Academic Registrar, E. Green

UNIVERSITY OF THE WEST OF ENGLAND, BRISTOL (BRISTOL UWE) (1992)
Coldharbour Lane, Bristol BS16 1QY
Tel 0117-965 6261
Full-time students (1997–8), 19,769
Academic Secretary, Ms C. Webb
Chancellor, The Rt. Hon. Dame Elizabeth Butler-Sloss, DBE (1993)
Vice-Chancellor, A. C. Morris
Academic Registrar, Ms M. J. Carter

THE UNIVERSITY OF WOLVERHAMPTON (1992)
Wulfruna Street, Wolverhampton WV1 1SB
Tel 01902-321000
Full-time students (1997–8), 14,147
Chancellor, The Earl of Shrewsbury and Talbot (1993)
Vice-Chancellor, Prof. J. S. Brooks, Ph.D.
Registrar, J. F. Baldwin
Secretary, A. W. Lee

THE UNIVERSITY OF YORK (1963)
Heslington, York YO10 5DD
Tel 01904-430000
Full-time students (1997–8), 7,000
Chancellor, Dame Janet Baker, CH, DBE (1991)
Vice-Chancellor, Prof. R. U. Cooke, Ph.D.
Registrar, D. J. Foster

THE OPEN UNIVERSITY (1969)
Walton Hall, Milton Keynes MK7 6AA
Tel 01908-274066
Students and clients (1998), c.200,000
Tuition by correspondence linked with special radio and television programmes, video and audio cassettes, computing, residential schools and a locally-based tutorial and counselling service. The University awards degrees of BA, B.Sc, B.Phil., MA, MBA, MBA (Technology), M.Eng., M.Maths, M.Sc., M.Phil., Ph.D., D.Ed., D.Sc. and D.Litt. There are faculties and schools of arts; education; health and social welfare; law; management; mathematics and computing; modern languages; science; social sciences; technology; and a wide range of qualification courses and study packs.
Chancellor, The Rt. Hon. Betty Boothroyd, MP
Vice-Chancellor, Sir John Daniel
Secretary, D. J. Clinch, OBE

ROYAL COLLEGE OF ART (1837)
Kensington Gore, London SW7 2EU
Tel 0171-590 4444
Students (1998–9), 800 (all postgraduate)
Provost, The Earl of Snowdon, GCVO (1995)
Rector and Vice-Provost, Prof. C. Frayling
Registrar, A. Selby

COLLEGES

It is not possible to name here all the colleges offering courses of higher or further education. The list does not include colleges forming part of a polytechnic or a university. The English colleges that follow are confined to those in the Higher Education Funding Council for England sector; there are many more colleges in England providing higher education courses, some with HEFCFE funding. The list of colleges in Wales, Scotland and Northern Ireland includes institutions providing at least one full-time course leading to a first degree granted by an accredited validating body.

ENGLAND

BATH SPA UNIVERSITY COLLEGE, Newton Park, Newton St Loe, Bath BA2 9BN. Tel: 01225-875875. *Director*, F. Morgan
BISHOP GROSSETESTE COLLEGE, Lincoln LN1 3DY. Tel: 01522-527347. *Principal*, Ms E. Baker
BOLTON INSTITUTE OF HIGHER EDUCATION, Deane Road, Bolton BL3 5AB. Tel: 01204-528851. *Principal*, Ms M. Temple (*from Jan. 1999*)
BRETTON HALL, West Bretton, Wakefield, W. Yorks WF4 4LG. Tel: 01924-830261. *Principal*, Prof. G. H. Bell
BUCKINGHAMSHIRE CHILTERNS UNIVERSITY COLLEGE, Queen Alexandra Road, High Wycombe, Bucks HP11 2JZ. Tel: 01494-522141. *Director*, Prof. P. B. Mogford
CANTERBURY CHRIST CHURCH UNIVERSITY COLLEGE, North Holmes Road, Canterbury, Kent CT1 1QU. Tel: 01227-767700. *Principal*, Prof. M. Wright
THE CENTRAL SCHOOL OF SPEECH AND DRAMA, Embassy Theatre, 64 Eton Avenue, London NW3 3HY. Tel: 0171-722 8183. *Principal*, Prof. R. S. Fowler
CHELTENHAM AND GLOUCESTER COLLEGE OF HIGHER EDUCATION, PO Box 220, The Park, Cheltenham, Glos GL50 2QF. Tel: 01242-532700. *Director*, Miss J. O. Trotter, OBE
CHICHESTER INSTITUTE OF HIGHER EDUCATION, College Lane, Chichester, W. Sussex PO19 4PE. Tel: 01243-816000. *Director*, P. E. D. Robinson
DARTINGTON COLLEGE OF ARTS, Totnes, Devon TQ9 6EJ. Tel: 01803-862224. *Principal*, Prof. K. Thompson
EDGE HILL UNIVERSITY COLLEGE, St Helens Road, Ormskirk, Lancs L39 4QP. Tel: 01695-575171. *Director*, Dr. J. Cater
FALMOUTH COLLEGE OF ARTS, Woodlane, Falmouth, Cornwall TR11 4RH. Tel: 01326-211077. *Principal*, Prof. A. G. Livingston
HARPER ADAMS AGRICULTURAL COLLEGE, Newport, Shropshire TF10 8NB. Tel: 01952-820280. *Principal*, Prof. E. W. Jones
HOMERTON COLLEGE, Cambridge CB2 2PH. Tel: 01223-507111. *Principal*, Mrs K. Pretty, PH.D.
KENT INSTITUTE OF ART AND DESIGN, Oakwood Park, Maidstone, Kent ME16 8AG (*also* New Dover Road, Canterbury CT1 3AN; and Fort Pitt, Rochester ME1 1DZ). Tel: 01622-757286. *Director*, Prof. V. Grylls

KING ALFRED'S COLLEGE, Sparkford Road, Winchester, Hants SO22 4NR. Tel: 01962-841515. *Principal*, Prof. J. P. Dickinson
LIVERPOOL HOPE UNIVERSITY COLLEGE, Hope Park, Liverpool L16 9JD. Tel: 0151-291 3477. *Rector*, Prof. S. Lee
THE LONDON INSTITUTE, 65 Davies Street, London W1Y 2AA. Tel: 0171-514 6000. *Rector*, Sir William Stubbs Comprising:
Camberwell College of Arts, Peckham Road, London SE5 8UF
Central St Martins College of Art and Design, Southampton Row, London WC1B 4AP
Chelsea College of Art and Design, Manresa Road, London SW3 6LS
London College of Fashion, 20 John Prince's Street, London W1M 0BJ
London College of Printing, Elephant and Castle, London SE1 6SB
LOUGHBOROUGH COLLEGE OF ART AND DESIGN, Epinal Way, Loughborough, Leics LE11 3GE. Tel: 01509-261515. *Principal*, T. Kavanagh
LSU COLLEGE OF HIGHER EDUCATION, The Avenue, Southampton SO17 1BG. Tel: 01703-216200. *Principal (acting)*, J. Layman
NENE COLLEGE OF HIGHER EDUCATION, Park Campus, Boughton Green Road, Northampton NN2 7AL. Tel: 01604-735500. *Director*, Dr S. M. Gaskell
NEWMAN COLLEGE, Genners Lane, Bartley Green, Birmingham B32 3NT. Tel: 0121-476 1181. *Principal*, Prof. B. Ray
RCN INSTITUTE, The Royal College of Nursing, 20 Cavendish Square, London WIM 0AB. Tel: 0171-409 3333. *Director*, Prof. A. Kitson
ROEHAMPTON INSTITUTE LONDON, Whitelands College, West Hill, London SW15 3SN. Comprises Digby Stuart College, Froebel College, Southlands College and Whitelands College. Tel: 0181-392 3000. *Rector*, Prof. S. C. Holt
ROSE BRUFORD COLLEGE, Lamorbey Park, Sidcup, Kent DA15 9DF. Tel: 0181-300 3024. *Principal*, Prof. R. Ely
ROYAL AGRICULTURAL COLLEGE, Cirencester, Glos GL7 6JS. Tel: 01285-652531. *Principal*, Prof. J. B. Dent
ROYAL NORTHERN COLLEGE OF MUSIC, 124 Oxford Road, Manchester M13 9RD. Tel: 0161-907 5200. *Principal*, Prof. E. Gregson
SOUTHAMPTON INSTITUTE, East Park Terrace, Southampton SO14 0YN. Tel: 01703-319000. *Director*, Dr R. Brown
SURREY INSTITUTE OF ART AND DESIGN, Falkner Road, Farnham, Surrey GU9 7DS. Tel: 01252-722441. *Director*, Prof. N. J. Taylor
TRINITY AND ALL SAINTS' COLLEGE, Brownberrie Lane, Horsforth, Leeds LS18 5HD. Tel: 0113-283 7100. *Principal*, Dr M. J. Coughlan
UNIVERSITY COLLEGE CHESTER, Parkgate Road, Chester CH1 4BJ. Tel: 01244-375444. *Principal*, Prof. T. J. Wheeler
UNIVERSITY COLLEGE OF RIPON AND YORK ST JOHN, Lord Mayor's Walk, York YO3 7EX. Tel: 01904-656771. *Principal*, Prof. R. A. Butlin
UNIVERSITY COLLEGE OF ST MARK AND ST JOHN, Derriford Road, Plymouth PL6 8BH. Tel: 01752-636829. *Principal*, Dr W. J. Rea
UNIVERSITY COLLEGE OF ST MARTIN, Lancaster LA1 3JD. Tel: 01524-384384. *Principal*, Prof. C. J. Carr
UNIVERSITY COLLEGE SCARBOROUGH, Filey Road, Scarborough YO11 3AZ. Tel: 01723-362392. *Principal*, Dr. R. A. Withers

WESTHILL COLLEGE OF HIGHER EDUCATION, Weoley Park Road, Selly Oak, Birmingham B29 6LL. Tel: 0121-472 7245. *Principal,* Prof. J. H. Y. Briggs

WESTMINSTER COLLEGE, Oxford OX2 9AT. Tel: 01865-247644. *Principal,* Revd Dr R. Ralph

WINCHESTER SCHOOL OF ART, Park Avenue, Winchester, Hants SO23 8DL. Tel: 01962-842500. *Head of School,* Prof. K. Crouan

WORCESTER COLLEGE OF HIGHER EDUCATION, Henwick Grove, Worcester WR2 6AJ. Tel: 01905-855000. *Principal,* Ms D. Unwin

WALES

CARMARTHENSHIRE COLLEGE, Graig Campus, Sandy Road, Llanelli SA15 4DN. Tel: 01554-748000. *Principal,* B. Robinson

NORTH EAST WALES INSTITUTE OF HIGHER EDUCATION, Plas Coch, Mold Road, Wrexham LL11 2AW. Tel: 01978-290666. *Principal,* Prof. J. O. Williams

SWANSEA INSTITUTE OF HIGHER EDUCATION, Mount Pleasant, Swansea SA1 6ED. Tel: 01792-481000. *Principal,* Prof. D. Warner

TRINITY COLLEGE, Carmarthen SA31 3EP. Tel: 01267-676767. *Principal,* D. C. Jones-Davies, OBE

WELSH COLLEGE OF MUSIC AND DRAMA, Castle Grounds, Cathays Park, Cardiff CF1 3ER. Tel: 01222-342854. *Principal,* E. Fivet

SCOTLAND

BELL COLLEGE OF TECHNOLOGY, Almada Street, Hamilton, Lanarkshire ML3 0JB. Tel: 01698-283100. *Principal,* Dr K. MacCallum

DUMFRIES AND GALLOWAY COLLEGE, Heathhall, Dumfries DG1 3QZ. Tel: 01387-261261. *Principal,* J. W. M. Neil

FIFE COLLEGE OF FURTHER AND HIGHER EDUCATION, St Brycedale Avenue, Kirkcaldy, Fife KY1 1EX. Tel: 01592-268591. *Principal,* Mrs J. S. R. Johnston

GLASGOW SCHOOL OF ART, 167 Renfrew Street, Glasgow G3 6RQ. Tel: 0141-353 4500. *Director,* Prof. D. Cameron

INVERNESS COLLEGE, Longman Road, Inverness IV1 1SA. Tel: 01463-236681. *Principal,* Ms J. Price

NORTHERN COLLEGE OF EDUCATION, Hilton Place, Aberdeen AB24 4FA. Tel: 01224-283500. Gardyne Road, Dundee DD5 1NY. Tel: 01382-464000. *Principal,* D. A. Adams

QUEEN MARGARET COLLEGE, Duke Street, Edinburgh EH6 8HF. Tel: 0131-317 3000. *Principal,* Dr J. Stringer

ROYAL SCOTTISH ACADEMY OF MUSIC AND DRAMA, 100 Renfrew Street, Glasgow G2 3DB. Tel: 0141-332 4101. *Principal,* Dr P. Ledger, CBE, FRSE

SAC (SCOTTISH AGRICULTURAL COLLEGE), Central Office, West Mains Road, Edinburgh EH9 3JG. Tel: 0131-535 4000. Campuses at Aberdeen, Auchincruive, Ayr and Edinburgh. *Principal,* Prof. P. C. Thomas

ST ANDREW'S COLLEGE OF EDUCATION, Duntocher Road, Bearsden, Glasgow G61 4QA. Tel: 0141-943 3400. *Principal,* Prof. B. J. McGettrick, OBE

NORTHERN IRELAND

EAST DOWN INSTITUTE OF FURTHER AND HIGHER EDUCATION, Market Street, Downpatrick, Co. Down BT30 6ND. Tel: 01396-615815. *Principal,* T. L. Place

ST MARY'S COLLEGE, 191 Falls Road, Belfast BT12 6FE. Tel: 01232-327678. *Principal,* Revd M. O'Callaghan

STRANMILLIS COLLEGE, Stranmillis Road, Belfast BT9 5DY. Tel: 01232-381271. *Principal,* Dr J. R. McMinn

ADULT AND CONTINUING EDUCATION

FORUM FOR THE ADVANCEMENT OF CONTINUING EDUCATION (FACE), Continuing Education, Goldsmiths' College, London SE14 6NW. Tel: 0171-919 7221. *Chair,* M. Barry

NATIONAL INSTITUTE OF ADULT CONTINUING EDUCATION, 21 De Montfort Street, Leicester LE1 7GE. Tel: 0116-204 4200. *Director,* A. Tuckett

NIACE CYMRU, 245 Western Avenue, Cardiff CF5 2YX. Tel: 01222-265002. *Director for Wales,* Ms A. Poole

THE RESIDENTIAL COLLEGES COMMITTEE, c/o Ruskin College, Oxford OX1 2HE. Tel: 01865-556360. *Awards Officer,* Mrs F. A. Bagchi

SCOTTISH COMMUNITY EDUCATION COUNCIL, Rosebery House, 9 Haymarket Terrace, Edinburgh EH12 5EZ. Tel: 0131-313 2488. *Chief Executive,* C. McConnell

THE UNIVERSITIES ASSOCIATION FOR CONTINUING EDUCATION, University of Cambridge Board of Continuing Education, Madingley Hall, Madingley, Cambridge CB3 8AQ. Tel: 01954-210636. *Secretary,* Miss S. E. Rawlings

WORKERS' EDUCATIONAL ASSOCIATION, Temple House, 17 Victoria Park Square, London E2 9PB. Tel: 0181-983 1515. *General Secretary,* R. Lochrie

LONG-TERM RESIDENTIAL COLLEGES FOR ADULT EDUCATION

COLEG HARLECH, Harlech, Gwynedd LL46 2PU. Tel: 01766-780363. *Warden,* J. W. England

CO-OPERATIVE COLLEGE, Stanford Hall, Loughborough, Leics LE12 5QP. Tel: 01509-852333. *Chief Executive,* R. Wildgusp

FIRCROFT COLLEGE, 1018 Bristol Road, Selly Oak, Birmingham B29 6LH. Tel: 0121-471 0116. *Principal,* Ms F. Larden

HILLCROFT COLLEGE, South Bank, Surbiton, Surrey KT6 6DF. Tel: 0181-399 2688. For women only. *Principal,* Ms J. Ireton

NEWBATTLE ABBEY COLLEGE, Dalkeith, Midlothian EH22 3LL. Tel: 0131-663 1921. *Principal,* W. M. Conboy

NORTHERN COLLEGE, Wentworth Castle, Stainborough, Barnsley, S. Yorks S75 3ET. Tel: 01226-776000. *Principal,* Prof. R. H. Fryer

PLATER COLLEGE, Pullens Lane, Oxford OX3 0DT. Tel: 01865-740500. *Principal,* M. Blades

RUSKIN COLLEGE, Walton Street, Oxford OX1 2HE. Tel: 01865-554331. *Principal,* J. Durcan

PROFESSIONAL EDUCATION
Excluding postgraduate study

The organizations listed below are those which, by providing specialist training or conducting examinations, control entry into a profession, or are responsible for maintaining a register of those with professional qualifications in their sector.

Many professions now have a largely graduate entry, and possession of a first degree can exempt entrants from certain of the professional examinations. Enquiries about obtaining professional qualifications should be made to the relevant professional organization(s). Details of higher education providers of first degrees may be found in *University and College Entrance: Official Guide* (available from UCAS, *see* page 444).

EC RECOGNITION

It is now possible for those with professional qualifications obtained in the UK to have these recognized in other European Union countries. A booklet, *Europe Open for Professions*, and further information can be obtained from: DEPARTMENT OF TRADE AND INDUSTRY, Bay 212 Kingsgate House, 66–74 Victoria Street, London SW1E 6SW. Tel: 0171-215 4648. *Contact*, Ms A. Wilson

ACCOUNTANCY

The main bodies granting membership on examination after a period of practical work are:
ASSOCIATION OF CHARTERED CERTIFIED ACCOUNTANTS, 29 Lincoln's Inn Fields, London WC2A 3EE. Tel: 0171-242 6855. *Chief Executive*, Mrs A. L. Rose
CHARTERED INSTITUTE OF MANAGEMENT ACCOUNTANTS, 63 Portland Place, London WIN 4AB. Tel: 0171-637 2311. *Secretary*, J. S. Chester, OBE
CHARTERED INSTITUTE OF PUBLIC FINANCE AND ACCOUNTANCY, 3 Robert Street, London WC2N 6BH. Tel: 0171-543 5600. *Chief Executive*, D. Adams
INSTITUTE OF CHARTERED ACCOUNTANTS IN ENGLAND AND WALES, Chartered Accountants' Hall, PO Box 433, Moorgate Place, London EC2P 2BJ. Tel: 0171-920 8100. *Chief Executive*, J. Collier
INSTITUTE OF CHARTERED ACCOUNTANTS OF SCOTLAND, 27 Queen Street, Edinburgh EH2 1LA. Tel: 0131-225 5673. *Chief Executive*, P. W. Johnston

ACTUARIAL SCIENCE

Two professional organizations grant qualifications after examination:
FACULTY OF ACTUARIES, 18 Dublin Street, Edinburgh EH1 3PP. Tel: 0131-240 1300. *Secretary*, W. W. Mair
INSTITUTE OF ACTUARIES, Staple Inn Hall, High Holborn, London WC1V 7QJ. Tel: 0171-632 2100. *Secretary-General*, G. B. L. Campbell. Education enquiries to Napier House, 4 Worcester Street, Oxford OX1 2AW. Tel: 01865-268200

ARCHITECTURE

The Education and Professional Development Board of the Royal Institute of British Architects sets standards and guides the whole system of architectural education throughout the UK. The RIBA recognizes courses at 35 schools of architecture in the UK for exemption from their own examinations and at some 50 courses overseas.
ARCHITECTS REGISTRATION BOARD, 73 Hallam Street, London WIN 6EE. Tel: 0171-580 5861. *Chief Officer and Registrar*, A. Finch
THE ROYAL INSTITUTE OF BRITISH ARCHITECTS, 66 Portland Place, London WIN 4AD. Tel: 0171-580 5533. Information Unit: 0891-234400. *President*, D. Rock; *Director-General*, A. Reid, PH.D.

Schools of architecture outside the universities include:
THE ARCHITECTURAL ASSOCIATION, 34–36 Bedford Square, London WC1B 3ES. Tel: 0171-887 4000. *Secretary*, E. A. Le Maistre
PRINCE OF WALES'S INSTITUTE OF ARCHITECTURE, 14–15 Gloucester Gate, London NW1 4HG. Tel: 0171-916 7380. *Director*, Prof. A. Gale

BANKING

Professional organizations granting qualifications after examination are:
CHARTERED INSTITUTE OF BANKERS, 90 Bishopsgate, London EC2N 4AS. Tel: 0171-444 7111. *Chief Executive*, G. Shreeve
CHARTERED INSTITUTE OF BANKERS IN SCOTLAND, Drumsheugh House, 38B Drumsheugh Gardens, Edinburgh EH3 7SW. Tel: 0131-473 7777. *Chief Executive*, Dr C. W. Munn

BUILDING

Examinations are conducted by:
CHARTERED INSTITUTE OF BUILDING, Englemere, King's Ride, Ascot, Berks SL5 7TB. Tel: 01344-630700. *Chief Executive*, K. Banbury
INSTITUTE OF BUILDING CONTROL, 92–104 East Street, Epsom, Surrey KT17 1EB. Tel: 01372-745577. *Chief Executive*, Ms R. Raywood
INSTITUTE OF CLERKS OF WORKS OF GREAT BRITAIN, 41 The Mall, London W5 3TJ. Tel: 0181-579 2917/8. *Secretary*, A. P. Macnamara

BUSINESS, MANAGEMENT AND ADMINISTRATION

Professional bodies conducting training and/or examinations in business, administration, management or commerce include:
AMETS (ASSOCIATION FOR MANAGEMENT EDUCATION AND TRAINING IN SCOTLAND), c/o Cottrell Building, University of Stirling, Stirling FK9 4LA. Tel: 01786-450906. *Chairman*, Prof. F. Pignatelli
THE ASSOCIATION OF MBAs, 15 Duncan Terrace, London N1 8BZ. Tel: 0171-837 3375. Publishes a directory giving details of MBA courses provided at UK institutions. *Director*, M. Jones
CAM FOUNDATION (COMMUNICATIONS, ADVERTISING AND MARKETING EDUCATION FOUNDATION), Abford House, 15 Wilton Road, London SW1V 1NJ. Tel: 0171-828 7506. *General Secretary*, J. Knight
CHARTERED INSTITUTE OF HOUSING, Octavia House, Westwood Business Park, Westwood Way, Coventry CV4 8JP. Tel: 01203-851700. *Chief Executive*, D. Butler
CHARTERED INSTITUTE OF MARKETING, Moor Hall, Cookham, Maidenhead, Berks SL6 9QH. Tel: 01628-427500. *Director-General*, S. Cuthbert
CHARTERED INSTITUTE OF PURCHASING AND SUPPLY, Easton House, Easton on the Hill, Stamford, Lincs PE9 3NZ. Tel: 01780-756777. *Chief Executive*, C. Holden
CHARTERED INSTITUTE OF TRANSPORT, 80 Portland Place, London WIN 4DP. Tel: 0171-467 9400. *Director*, Mrs D. de Carvalho
HENLEY MANAGEMENT COLLEGE, Greenlands, Henley-on-Thames, Oxon RG9 3AU. Tel: 01491-571454. *Principal*, Prof. R. Wild, PH.D., D.SC.
INSTITUTE OF ADMINISTRATIVE MANAGEMENT, 40 Chatsworth Parade, Petts Wood, Orpington, Kent BR5 1RW. Tel: 01689-875555. *Chief Executive*, Prof. G. Robinson
INSTITUTE OF CHARTERED SECRETARIES AND ADMINISTRATORS, 16 Park Crescent, London WIN 4AH. Tel: 0171-580 4741. *Chief Executive*, M. J. Ainsworth
INSTITUTE OF CHARTERED SHIPBROKERS, 3 St Helen's Place, London EC3A 6EJ. Tel: 0171-628 5559. *Director*, Mrs B. Fletcher

INSTITUTE OF EXPORT, Export House, 64 Clifton Street, London EC2A 4HB. Tel: 0171-247 9812. *Director-General*, I. J. Campbell

INSTITUTE OF HEALTH SERVICES MANAGEMENT, 7–10 Chandos Street, London WIM 9DE. Tel: 0171-460 7654. *Director*, Ms K. Caines

INSTITUTE OF MANAGEMENT, Management House, Cottingham Road, Corby, Northants NN17 ITT. Tel: 01536-204222. *Director-General*, Mrs M. Chapman

INSTITUTE OF PERSONNEL AND DEVELOPMENT, IPD House, Camp Road, London SW19 4UX. Tel: 0181-971 9000. *Director-General*, G. Armstrong

INSTITUTE OF PRACTITIONERS IN ADVERTISING, 44 Belgrave Square, London SWIX 8QS. Tel: 0171-235 7020. *Secretary*, J. Raad

INSTITUTE OF QUALITY ASSURANCE, 12 Grosvenor Crescent, London SWIX 7EE. Tel: 0171-245 6722. *Secretary-General*, D. Campbell

CHIROPRACTIC

Chiropractic is accorded statutory regulation by the Chiropractic Act 1994. There are currently four professional associations operating voluntary registration schemes. These schemes will be replaced by a General Chiropractic Council when it opens a new register, probably in late 1998 or early 1999. Once the register is in place it will be illegal for anyone to call themselves a chiropractor unless they have undertaken a recognized course of training and are registered with the General Chiropractic Council.

There are currently five training centres for chiropractic. Two of these provide four-year part-time training programmes leading to internal academic awards; the other three provide full-time training leading to a B.Sc. and M.Sc. in chiropractic. In future, the General Chiropractic Council will determine the training requirements to qualify for registration and accredit courses.

BRITISH CHIROPRACTIC ASSOCIATION, Blagrave House, 17 Blagrave Street, Reading RGI 1QB. Tel: 0118-950 5950. *Executive Director*, Ms S. A. Wakefield

GENERAL CHIROPRACTIC COUNCIL, c/o Department of Science and Technology Studies, University College London, Gower Street, London WCIE 6BT. *Chairman*, Mrs N. Morris

SCOTTISH CHIROPRACTIC ASSOCIATION, St Boswells Chiropractic Clinic, Main Street, St Boswells, Melrose TD6 OAP. Tel: 01835-823645. *Secretary*, Dr C. How

DANCE

IMPERIAL SOCIETY OF TEACHERS OF DANCING, Imperial House, 22–26 Paul Street, London EC2A 4QE. Tel: 0171-377 1577. *Chief Executive*, M. J. Browne

INTERNATIONAL DANCE TEACHERS' ASSOCIATION, International House, 76 Bennett Road, Brighton BN2 5JL. Tel: 01273-685652. *Company Secretary*, J. Dearling

ROYAL ACADEMY OF DANCING, 36 Battersea Square, London SWII 3RA. Tel: 0171-223 0091. *Chief Executive*, D. Watchman; *Artistic Director*, Miss L. Wallis

ROYAL BALLET SCHOOL, 155 Talgarth Road, London WI4 9DE. Tel: 0181-748 6335. Also at White Lodge, Richmond Park, Surrey TWIO 5HR. Tel: 0181-876 5547. *Director*, Dame Merle Park, DBE

DEFENCE

ROYAL COLLEGE OF DEFENCE STUDIES, Seaford House, 37 Belgrave Square, London SWIX 8NS. Tel: 0171-915 4800. Prepares selected senior officers and officials for responsibilities in the direction and management of defence and security. *Commandant*, Vice-Adm. J. H. S. McNally, LVO

JOINT SERVICES COMMAND AND STAFF COLLEGE, Bracknell, Berks RGI2 9DD. Tel: 01344-54593. *Commandant*, Maj.-Gen. T. Granville-Chapman, CBE; *Dean of Academic Studies*, Prof. G. Till, PH.D.

ROYAL NAVAL COLLEGE

BRITANNIA ROYAL NAVAL COLLEGE, Dartmouth, Devon TQ6 OHJ. Tel: 01803-832141. Provides professional training and education for all new entry RN officers and officers from foreign and Commonwealth navies. *Commodore*, Cdre R. A. G. Clare

MILITARY COLLEGES

DIRECTORATE OF EDUCATIONAL AND TRAINING SERVICES, Trenchard Lines, Upavon, Pewsey, Wilts SN9 6BE. Tel: 01980-618730. *Director*, Brig. C. F. P. Horsfall

ROYAL MILITARY ACADEMY SANDHURST, Camberley, Surrey GUI5 4PQ. Tel: 01276-63344. *Commandant*, Maj.-Gen. A. G. Denaro, CBE

ROYAL MILITARY COLLEGE OF SCIENCE, Shrivenham, Swindon, Wilts SN6 8LA. Tel: 01793-785435. Students from UK and overseas study from degree to postgraduate levels in engineering, management, science and technology. The College is a faculty of Cranfield University. *Commandant*, Maj.-Gen. A. S. H. Irwin, CBE; *Principal*, Prof. P. Hutchinson

ROYAL AIR FORCE COLLEGES

ROYAL AIR FORCE COLLEGE, Cranwell, Sleaford, Lincs. NG34 8HB. Selects all officer and aircrew entrants to the RAF and provides initial training for all officer entrants to the RAF. Also provides initial specialist training for junior officers of some ground branches, elementary flying training for all three services, general service training for University Air Squadrons, and supervision of the Air Cadet Organization. *Air Officer Commanding and Commandant*, Air Vice-Marshal T. W. Rimmer, OBE

ROYAL AIR FORCE TRAINING, DEVELOPMENT AND SUPPORT UNIT, RAF Halton, Aylesbury, Bucks HP22 5PG. Tel: 01296-623535. *Commanding Officer*, Gp Capt. A. Harris

DENTISTRY

In order to practise in the UK, a dentist must be entered in the Dentists Register. To be registered, a person must hold the degree or diploma in dental surgery of a university in the UK or the diploma of any of the licensing authorities (the Royal Colleges of Surgeons of England and of Edinburgh, and the Royal College of Physicians and Surgeons of Glasgow). Nationals of EU or European Economic Area member states holding an appropriate European diploma, and holders of certain overseas diplomas, may also be registered. Temporary registration may be available for those dentists who do not hold a diploma described above. The Dentists Register is maintained by:

THE GENERAL DENTAL COUNCIL, 37 Wimpole Street, London WIM 8DQ. Tel: 0171-887 3800. *Chief Executive and Registrar*, Mrs R. M. J. Hepplewhite

DIETETICS

See also FOOD AND NUTRITION SCIENCE

The professional association is the British Dietetic Association. Full membership is open to dietitians holding a recognized qualification, who may also become State Registered Dietitians through the Council for Professions Supplementary to Medicine (*see* Medicine)

THE BRITISH DIETETIC ASSOCIATION, 7th Floor, Elizabeth House, 22 Suffolk Street, Queensway, Birmingham BI ILS. Tel: 0121-643 5483. *Secretary*, J. Grigg

DRAMA

The national validating body for courses providing training in drama for the professional theatre is the National Council for Drama Training. It currently has accredited courses at the following: Academy of Live and Recorded Arts; Arts Educational Schools; Birmingham School of Speech Training and Dramatic Art; Bristol Old Vic Theatre School; Central School of Speech and Drama; Cygnet Training Theatre, Exeter; Drama Centre, London; Drama Studio, London; Guildford School of Acting; Guildhall School of Music and Drama, London; London Academy of Music and Dramatic Art; Manchester Metropolitan University School of Theatre; Mountview Theatre School; Oxford School of Drama, Woodstock; Queen Margaret College, Edinburgh; Rose Bruford College, Sidcup; Royal Academy of Dramatic Art, London; Royal Scottish Academy of Music and Drama; Webber Douglas Academy of Dramatic Art, London; Welsh College of Music and Drama.

The accreditation of a course in a school does not necessarily imply that other courses of different type or duration in the same school are also accredited.

THE NATIONAL COUNCIL FOR DRAMA TRAINING, 5 Tavistock Place, London WC1H 9SN. *Executive Secretary,* Mrs A. Bailey

ENGINEERING

The Engineering Council supervises the engineering profession through the 39 nominated engineering institutions who are represented on its Board for Engineers' Regulation. Working with and through the institutions, the Council sets the standards for the registration of individuals, and also the accreditation for academic courses in universities and colleges and the practical training in industry.

THE ENGINEERING COUNCIL, 10 Maltravers Street, London WC2R 3ER. Tel: 0171-240 7891. *Director-General,* M. Shirley

The principal qualifying bodies are:

BRITISH COMPUTER SOCIETY, 1 Sanford Street, Swindon SN1 1HJ. Tel: 01793-417417. *Chief Executive,* Mrs J. M. Scott

BRITISH INSTITUTE OF NON-DESTRUCTIVE TESTING, 1 Spencer Parade, Northampton NN1 5AA. Tel: 01604-630124. *Secretary,* M. E. Gallagher

CHARTERED INSTITUTION OF BUILDING SERVICES ENGINEERS, 222 Balham High Road, London SW12 9BS. Tel: 0181-675 5211. *Secretary,* R. John

INSTITUTION OF AGRICULTURAL ENGINEERS, West End Road, Silsoe, Bedford MK45 4DU. Tel: 01525-861096. *Chief Executive,* J. H. Neville

INSTITUTE OF BRITISH FOUNDRYMEN, Bordesley Hall, The Holloway, Alvechurch, Birmingham B48 7QA. Tel: 01527-596100. *Secretary,* G. A. Schofield

INSTITUTION OF CHEMICAL ENGINEERS, Davis Building, 165–189 Railway Terrace, Rugby, Warks CV21 3HQ. Tel: 01788-578214. *Chief Executive,* Dr T. J. Evans

INSTITUTION OF CIVIL ENGINEERS, 1–7 Great George Street, London SW1P 3AA. Tel: 0171-222 7722. *Director-General,* R. S. Dobson, OBE, FEng.

INSTITUTION OF ELECTRICAL ENGINEERS, Savoy Place, London WC2R 0BL. Tel: 0171-240 1871. *Secretary,* Dr J. C. Williams, OBE, FEng.

INSTITUTE OF ENERGY, 18 Devonshire Street, London W1N 2AU. Tel: 0171-580 7124. *Secretary,* Mrs D. Davy

INSTITUTION OF ENGINEERING DESIGNERS, Courtleigh, Westbury Leigh, Westbury, Wilts BA13 3TA. Tel: 01373-822801. Secretary, M. Osborne

INSTITUTION OF FIRE ENGINEERS, 148 New Walk, Leicester LE1 7QB. Tel: 0116-255 3654. *General Secretary,* D. W. Evans

INSTITUTION OF GAS ENGINEERS, 21 Portland Place, London W1N 3AF. Tel: 0171-636 6603. *Secretary,* Mrs S. M. Raine

INSTITUTE OF HEALTHCARE ENGINEERING AND ESTATE MANAGEMENT, 2 Abingdon House, Cumberland Business Centre, Northumberland Road, Portsmouth PO5 1DS. Tel: 01705-823186. *Secretary,* W. R. Pym

INSTITUTION OF INCORPORATED ENGINEERS, Savoy Hill House, Savoy Hill, London WC2R 0BS. Tel: 0171-836 3357. *Chief Executive,* P. F. Wason

INSTITUTION OF INCORPORATED EXECUTIVE ENGINEERS, Wix Hill House, West Horsley, Surrey KT24 6DZ. Tel: 01483-222383. *Secretary,* D. Dacam, OBE

INSTITUTE OF LIGHTING ENGINEERS, Lennox House, 9 Lawford Road, Rugby CV21 2DZ. Tel: 01788-576492. *Chief Executive,* R. G. Frost

INSTITUTE OF MARINE ENGINEERS, The Memorial Building, 76 Mark Lane, London EC3R 7JN. Tel: 0171-481 8493. *Secretary,* J. E. Sloggett, OBE

INSTITUTE OF MATERIALS, 1 Carlton House Terrace, London SW1Y 5DB. Tel: 0171-451 7300. *Secretary,* Dr B. A. Rickinson

INSTITUTE OF MEASUREMENT AND CONTROL, 87 Gower Street, London WC1E 6AA. Tel: 0171-387 4949. *Secretary,* M. J. Yates

INSTITUTION OF MECHANICAL ENGINEERS, 1 Birdcage Walk, London SW1H 9JJ. Tel: 0171-222 7899. *Director-General (acting),* R. Howard-Jones

INSTITUTION OF MINING AND METALLURGY, Danum House, 6A South Parade, Doncaster DN1 2DY. Tel: 01302-320486. *Secretary,* Dr G. J. M. Woodrow

INSTITUTION OF NUCLEAR ENGINEERS, 1 Penerley Road, London SE6 2LQ. Tel: 0181-698 1500. *Secretary,* W. J. Hurst

INSTITUTE OF PHYSICS, 76 Portland Place, London W1N 4AA. Tel: 0171-470 4800. *Chief Executive,* Dr A. D. W. Jones

INSTITUTION OF PLANT ENGINEERS, 77 Great Peter Street, London SW1P 2EZ. Tel: 0171-233 2855. *Secretary,* P. F. Tye

INSTITUTE OF PLUMBING, 64 Station Lane, Hornchurch, Essex RM12 6NB. Tel: 01708-472791. *Chief Executive,* W. A. Watts, MBE

INSTITUTE OF QUALITY ASSURANCE, 12 Grosvenor Crescent, London SW1X 7EE. Tel: 0171-245 6722. *Secretary-General,* D. Campbell

INSTITUTION OF STRUCTURAL ENGINEERS, 11 Upper Belgrave Street, London SW1X 8BH. Tel: 0171-235 4535. *Chief Executive,* Dr J. W. Dougill, FEng.

INSTITUTION OF WATER OFFICERS, Heriot House, 12 Summerhill Terrace, Newcastle upon Tyne NE4 6EB. Tel: 0191-230 5150. *Company Secretary (acting),* Ms L. Harding

ROYAL AERONAUTICAL SOCIETY, 4 Hamilton Place, London W1V 0BQ. Tel: 0171-499 3515. *Director,* K. Mans

ROYAL INSTITUTION OF NAVAL ARCHITECTS, 10 Upper Belgrave Street, London SW1X 8BQ. Tel: 0171-235 4622. *Chief Executive,* T. Blakeley

THE WELDING INSTITUTE, Abington Hall, Abington, Cambridge CB1 6AL. Tel: 01223-891162. *Chief Executive,* B. Braithwaite, OBE

FILM AND TELEVISION

Postgraduate training for those intending to make a career in film and television production is provided by the National Film and Television School, which provides courses in production, direction, animation, screenwriting, editing, cinematography, screen sound, art direction

and screen music. Short post-experience courses to enable professionals to update or expand their skills are also provided.
NATIONAL FILM AND TELEVISION SCHOOL, Station Road, Beaconsfield, Bucks HP9 1LG. Tel: 01494-671234. *Director*, S. Bayly

FOOD AND NUTRITION SCIENCE
See also DIETETICS

Scientific and professional bodies include:
INSTITUTE OF FOOD SCIENCE & TECHNOLOGY, 5 Cambridge Court, 210 Shepherd's Bush Road, London W6 7NJ. Tel: 0171-603 6316. *Chief Executive*, Ms H. G. Wild

FORESTRY AND TIMBER STUDIES

Professional organizations include:
COMMONWEALTH FORESTRY ASSOCIATION, c/o Oxford Forestry Institute, South Parks Road, Oxford OX1 3RB. Tel: 01865-271037. *Chairman*, Dr J. S. Maini
INSTITUTE OF CHARTERED FORESTERS, 7A St Colme Street, Edinburgh EH3 6AA. Tel: 0131-225 2705. *Secretary*, Mrs M. W. Dick
ROYAL FORESTRY SOCIETY OF ENGLAND, WALES AND NORTHERN IRELAND, 102 High Street, Tring, Herts HP23 4AF. Tel: 01442-822028. *Director*, J. E. Jackson, PH.D.
ROYAL SCOTTISH FORESTRY SOCIETY, The Stables, Dalkeith Country Park, Dalkeith, Midlothian EH22 2NA. Tel: 0131-660 9480. *Director*, M. Osborne

FUEL AND ENERGY SCIENCE

The principal professional bodies are:
INSTITUTE OF ENERGY, 18 Devonshire Street, London W1N 2AU. Tel: 0171-580 7124. *Secretary* Mrs D. Davy
INSTITUTION OF GAS ENGINEERS, 21 Portland Place, London W1N 3AF. Tel: 0171-636 6603. *Secretary*, Mrs S. M. Raine
INSTITUTE OF PETROLEUM, 61 New Cavendish Street, London W1M 8AR. Tel: 0171-467 7100. *Director-General*, I. Ward

HOTELKEEPING, CATERING AND INSTITUTIONAL MANAGEMENT
See also DIETETICS, and FOOD AND NUTRITION SCIENCE

The qualifying professional body in these areas is:
HOTEL AND CATERING INTERNATIONAL MANAGEMENT ASSOCIATION, 191 Trinity Road, London SW17 7HN. Tel: 0181-672 4251. *Chief Executive*, D. Wood

INDUSTRIAL AND VOCATIONAL TRAINING

The NTO National Council represents national training organizations (NTOs), a new network of sector training bodies established in 1997. NTOs are independent, employer-owned bodies which represent the education and training interests of their respective sectors to government and ensure the development and adoption of occupational standards, particularly through National and Scottish Vocational Qualifications.
NTO NATIONAL COUNCIL, 10 Meadowcourt, Amos Road, Sheffield S9 1BX. Tel: 0114-261 9926. *Chief Executive*, Dr. A. Powell

INSURANCE

Organizations conducting examinations and awarding diplomas are:

ASSOCIATION OF AVERAGE ADJUSTERS, 200 Aldersgate Street, London ECIA 4JJ. Tel: 0171-956 0099. *Secretary*, D. W. Taylor
CHARTERED INSTITUTE OF LOSS ADJUSTERS, Manfield House, 1 Southampton Street, London WC2R 0LR. Tel: 0171-240 1496. *Director*, A. F. Clack
CHARTERED INSURANCE INSTITUTE, 20 Aldermanbury, London EC2V 7HY. Tel: 0181-989 8464. *Director-General*, Prof. D. E. Bland

JOURNALISM

Courses for trainee newspaper journalists are available at 30 centres. One-year full-time courses are available for selected students and 18-week courses for graduates. Particulars of all these courses are available from the National Council for the Training of Journalists. Short courses for mid-career development can be arranged, as can various distance learning courses. The NCTJ also offers Assessor, Internal Verifier (IV) and Accreditation of Prior Achievement (APA) training, and NVQs.
For periodical journalists, there are ten centres running courses approved by the Periodicals Training Council.
THE NATIONAL COUNCIL FOR TRAINING OF JOURNALISTS, Latton Bush Centre, Southern Way, Harlow, Essex CM18 7BL. Tel: 01279-430009. *Chief Executive*, R. Selwood
THE PERIODICALS TRAINING COUNCIL, Queen's House, 55–56 Lincoln's Inn Fields, London WC2A 3LJ. Tel: 0171-404 4168. *Director*, Ms J. Butcher

LAW

THE BAR

Admission to the Bar of England and Wales is controlled by the Inns of Court, admission to the Bar of Northern Ireland by the Honorable Society of the Inn of Court of Northern Ireland and admission as an Advocate of the Scottish Bar is controlled by the Faculty of Advocates. The governing body of the barristers' branch of the legal profession in England and Wales is the General Council of the Bar. The governing body in Northern Ireland is the Honorable Society of the Inn of Court of Northern Ireland, and the Faculty of Advocates is the governing body of the Scottish Bar. The education and examination of students training for the Bar of England and Wales is regulated by the General Council of the Bar. Those who intend to practise at the Bar of England and Wales must pass the Bar's vocational course. The Inns of Court School of Law is the largest provider of initial training for those wishing to practise at the Bar, but since September 1997 six other institutions have been validated to provide the course.
FACULTY OF ADVOCATES, Advocates Library, Parliament House, Edinburgh EH1 1RF. Tel: 0131-226 5071. *Dean*, G. N. H. Emslie, QC; *Clerk*, I. G. Armstrong
THE GENERAL COUNCIL OF THE BAR, 3 Bedford Row, London WC1R 4DB. Tel: 0171-242 0082. *Chairman*, H. Hallett, QC; *Chief Executive*, N. Morison
THE HONORABLE SOCIETY OF THE INN OF COURT OF NORTHERN IRELAND, Royal Courts of Justice, Belfast BT1 3JF. Tel: 01232-235111. *Treasurer* (1998), E. A. Comerton, QC; *Under-Treasurer*, J. W. Wilson, QC

The Inns of Court

GRAY'S INN, 8 South Square, London WC1R 5EU. Tel: 0171-405 8164. *Treasurer*, M. Collins, QC; *Under-Treasurer*, D. Machin
THE INNER TEMPLE, London EC4Y 7HL. Tel: 0171-797 8250. *Treasurer*, The Rt. Hon. The Lord Lloyd of Berwick; *Sub-Treasurer*, Brig. P. A. Little, CBE

INNS OF COURT SCHOOL OF LAW 4 Gray's Inn Place, Gray's Inn, London WCIR 5DX. Tel: 0171-404 5787. *Chairman*, The Hon. Mr Justice Hooper; *Principal*, R. Stone

LINCOLN'S INN, London WC2A 3TL. Tel: 0171-405 1393. *Treasurer*, The Rt. Hon. Sir John Balcombe; *Under-Treasurer*, Col. D. H. Hills, MBE

THE MIDDLE TEMPLE, London EC4Y 9AT. Tel: 0171-427 4800. *Treasurer*, Sir David Calcutt, QC; *Under-Treasurer*, Brig. C. T. J. Wright

SOLICITORS

Qualifications for solicitors are obtainable only from one of the Law Societies, which control the education and examination of trainee solicitors and the admission of solicitors.

THE COLLEGE OF LAW provides courses for the Common Professional Examination and Legal Practice Course at Braboeuf Manor, St Catherine's, Guildford, Surrey GU3 IHA; 14 Store Street, London WCIE 7DE; Christleton Hall, Chester CH3 7AB; Bishopthorpe Road, York YO23 2GA. The college also provides the Bar Vocational Course in London branch

LAW SOCIETY OF ENGLAND AND WALES, 113 Chancery Lane, London WC2A IPL. Tel: 0171-242 1222. *President* (1998–9), M. Mathews; *Secretary-General*, Mrs J. M. Betts

LAW SOCIETY OF NORTHERN IRELAND, Law Society House, 98 Victoria Street, Belfast BTI 3JZ. Tel: 01232-231614. *Chief Executive*, J. W. Bailie

LAW SOCIETY OF SCOTLAND, Law Society's Hall, 26 Drumsheugh Gardens, Edinburgh EH3 7YR. Tel: 0131-226 7411. *President* (1998–9), P. Dry; *Secretary*, D. R. Mill

OFFICE FOR THE SUPERVISION OF SOLICITORS, Victoria Court, 8 Dormer Place, Leamington Spa, Warks CV32 5AE. Tel: 01926-820082. The Office is an establishment of the Law Society set up to handle complaints about solicitors and regulate solicitors' practices

LIBRARIANSHIP AND INFORMATION SCIENCE/MANAGEMENT

The Library Association accredits degree and post-graduate courses in library and information science which are offered by 17 universities in the UK. A full list of accredited degree and postgraduate courses is available from its Information Services and on its web site (*see* below) The Association also maintains a professional register of Chartered Members open to graduate ordinary members of the Association.

THE LIBRARY ASSOCIATION, 7 Ridgmount Street, London WCIE 7AE. Tel: 0171-636 7543. Web: http://www.la-hq.org.uk. *Chief Executive*, R. Shimmon

MATERIALS STUDIES

The qualifying body is:
INSTITUTE OF MATERIALS, 1 Carlton House Terrace, London SWIY 5DB. Tel: 0171-541 7300. *Chief Executive*, Dr B. A. Rickinson

MEDICINE

All doctors must be registered with the General Medical Council. In order to register, medical students must complete a five-year undergraduate degree at one of the 19 universities with medical schools, followed by a year of general clinical training. Once registered, doctors undertake general professional and basic specialist training as senior house officers. Further specialist training is provided by the royal colleges, faculties and societies listed

below. The General Medical Council keeps a register of those doctors who have been awarded Certificates of Completion of Specialist Training.

The United Examining Board holds qualifying examinations for candidates who have trained overseas. These candidates must also have spent a period at a UK medical school.

GENERAL MEDICAL COUNCIL, 178 Great Portland Street, London WIN 6JE. Tel: 0171-580 7642. *President*, Sir Donald Irvine, CBE, MD, FRGCP; *Chief Executive*, F. Scott

UNITED EXAMINING BOARD, Apothecaries Hall, Black Friars Lane, London EC4V 6EJ. Tel: 0171-236 1180. *Chairman*, H. B. Devlin; *Registrar*, A. M. Wallington-Smith

COLLEGES/SOCIETIES HOLDING POSTGRADUATE MEMBERSHIP AND DIPLOMA EXAMINATIONS

FACULTY OF ACCIDENT AND EMERGENCY MEDICINE, Royal College of Surgeons of England, 35–43 Lincoln's Inn Fields, London WC2A 3PN. Tel: 0171-405 7071. *President*, Dr K. Little

FACULTY OF OCCUPATIONAL MEDICINE, 6 St Andrew's Place, London NWI 4LB. Tel: 0171-487 3414. *Administrator*, Ms F. M. Quinn

FACULTY OF PHARMACEUTICAL MEDICINE, 1 St Andrew's Place, London NWI 4LB. Tel: 0171-224 0343. *President*, Prof. P. Stonier

FACULTY OF PUBLIC HEALTH MEDICINE, 4 St Andrew's Place, London NWI 4LB. Tel: 0171-935 0243. *Chief Executive*, P. Scourfield

ROYAL COLLEGE OF ANAESTHETISTS, 48–49 Russell Square, London WCIB 4JY. Tel: 0171-813 1900. *President*, Prof. L. Strunin; *Chief Executive*, Ms W. Cogger

ROYAL COLLEGE OF GENERAL PRACTITIONERS, 14 Princes Gate, London SW7 IPU. Tel: 0171-581 3232. *President*, Prof. D. P. Gray, OBE, FRCGP; *Hon. Secretary*, Dr W. Reith, FRCPEd, FRCGP

ROYAL COLLEGE OF OBSTETRICIANS AND GYNAECOLOGISTS, 27 Sussex Place, London NWI 4RG. Tel: 0171-772 6200. *President*, Prof. R. Shaw; *Secretary*, P. A. Barnett

ROYAL COLLEGE OF PAEDIATRICS AND CHILD HEALTH, 50 Hallam Street, London WIN 6DE. Tel: 0171-307 5600. *President*, Prof. J. D. Baum; *Secretary*, Ms L. Tyler

ROYAL COLLEGE OF PATHOLOGISTS, 2 Carlton House Terrace, London SWIY 5AF. Tel: 0171-930 5861. *President*, Prof. R. N. M. MacSween; *Secretary*, K. Lockyer

ROYAL COLLEGE OF PHYSICIANS, 11 St Andrew's Place, London NWI 4LE. Tel: 0171-935 1174. *President*, Prof. K. G. M. M. Alberti, FRCP; *Secretary*, P. Masterton-Smith

ROYAL COLLEGE OF PHYSICIANS AND SURGEONS OF GLASGOW, 232–242 St Vincent Street, Glasgow G2 5RJ. Tel: 0141-221 6072. *President*, C. Mackay; *Hon. Secretary*, Dr C. Semple

ROYAL COLLEGE OF PHYSICIANS OF EDINBURGH, 9 Queen Street, Edinburgh EH2 IJQ. Tel: 0131-225 7324. *President*, Prof. J. C. Petrie; *Secretary*, Dr J. St J. Thomas

ROYAL COLLEGE OF PSYCHIATRISTS, 17 Belgrave Square, London SWIX 8PG. Tel: 0171-235 2351. *President*, Dr R. E. Kendell, CBE; *Secretary*, Mrs V. Cameron

ROYAL COLLEGE OF RADIOLOGISTS, 38 Portland Place, London WIN 4QJ. Tel: 0171-636 4432. *President*, Prof. P. Armstrong; *Secretary*, A. J. Cowles

ROYAL COLLEGE OF SURGEONS OF EDINBURGH, Nicolson Street, Edinburgh EH8 9DW. Tel: 0131-527 1600. *President*, Prof. A. G. D. Maran; *Secretary*, Ms A. S. Campbell

ROYAL COLLEGE OF SURGEONS OF ENGLAND, 35–43 Lincoln's Inn Fields, London WC2A 3PN. Tel: 0171-405 3474. *President*, B. T. Jackson; *Secretary*, C. Duncan

SOCIETY OF APOTHECARIES OF LONDON, 14 Black Friars Lane, London EC4V 6EJ. Tel: 0171-236 1189. *Clerk,* R. J. Stringer

PROFESSIONS SUPPLEMENTARY TO MEDICINE

The standard of professional education in art, drama and music therapies, biomedical sciences, chiropody, dietetics, occupational therapy, orthoptics, physiotherapy and radiography is the responsibility of nine professional boards, which also publish an annual register of qualified practitioners. The work of the boards is co-ordinated by the Council for Professions Supplementary to Medicine.

In 1997 permission was given for two new boards to be set up, one for prosthetists and orthotists and one for art therapists. These will set up registers of qualified practitioners over the next two years.

THE COUNCIL FOR PROFESSIONS SUPPLEMENTARY TO MEDICINE, Park House, 184 Kennington Park Road, London SE11 4BU. Tel: 0171-582 0866. *Registrar,* M. D. Hall

BIOMEDICAL SCIENCES

Qualifications from higher education establishments and training in medical laboratories are required for membership of the Institute of Biomedical Science.
INSTITUTE OF BIOMEDICAL SCIENCE, 12 Coldbath Square, London EC1R 5HL. Tel: 0171-636 8192. *Chief Executive,* A. Potter

CHIROPODY

Professional recognition is granted by the Society of Chiropodists and Podiatrists to students who are awarded B.Sc. degrees in Podiatry or Podiatric Medicine after attending a course of full-time training for three or four years at one of the 14 recognized schools in the UK (11 in England and Wales, two in Scotland and one in Northern Ireland). Qualifications granted and degrees recognized by the Society are approved by the Chiropodists Board for the purpose of State Registration, which is a condition of employment within the National Health Service.
THE SOCIETY OF CHIROPODISTS AND PODIATRISTS, 53 Welbeck Street, London W1M 7HE. Tel: 0171-486 3381. *General Secretary,* M. Paulson

See also DIETETICS

OCCUPATIONAL THERAPY

The professional qualification may be obtained upon successful completion of a validated course in any of the 28 institutions approved by the College of Occupational Therapists. The courses are normally degree-level courses based in higher education institutions.
COLLEGE OF OCCUPATIONAL THERAPISTS, 106–114 Borough High Street, London SE1 1LB. Tel: 0171-357 6480. *Secretary,* J. Thompson

ORTHOPTICS

Orthoptists undertake the diagnosis and treatment of all types of squint and other anomalies of binocular vision, working in close collaboration with ophthalmologists. The training and maintenance of professional standards are the responsibility of the Orthoptists Board of the Council for the Professions Supplementary to Medicine. The professional body is the British Orthoptic Society. Training is at degree level.
THE BRITISH ORTHOPTIC SOCIETY, Tavistock House North, Tavistock Square, London WC1H 9HX. Hon. Secretary, Ms R. Auld

PHYSIOTHERAPY

Full-time three- or four-year degree courses are available at 28 recognized schools in the UK. Information about courses leading to eligibility for Membership of the Chartered Society of Physiotherapy and to State Registration is available from the Chartered Society of Physiotherapy.
THE CHARTERED SOCIETY OF PHYSIOTHERAPY, 14 Bedford Row, London WC1R 4ED. Tel: 0171-306 6666. *Chief Executive,* P. Gray

RADIOGRAPHY AND RADIOTHERAPY

In order to practise both diagnostic and therapeutic radiography in the UK, it is necessary to have successfully completed a course of education and training recognized by the Privy Council. Such courses are offered by universities throughout the UK and lead to the award of a degree in radiography. Further information is available from the college.
THE COLLEGE OF RADIOGRAPHERS, 2 Carriage Row, 183 Eversholt Street, London NW1 1BU. Tel: 0171-391 4500. *Chief Executive,* S. Evans

COMPLEMENTARY MEDICINE

Professional courses are validated by:
INSTITUTE FOR COMPLEMENTARY MEDICINE, PO Box 194, London SE16 1QZ. Tel: 0171-237 5165. Director A. Baird

MERCHANT NAVY TRAINING SCHOOLS

OFFICERS

WARSASH MARITIME CENTRE, Southampton Institute, Newtown Road, Warsash, Southampton SO31 9ZL. Tel: 01489-576161. *Dean,* Capt. G. B. Angas

SEAFARERS

NATIONAL SEA TRAINING CENTRE, North West Kent College, Dering Way, Gravesend, Kent DA12 2JJ. Tel: 01474-363656. *Director of Faculty,* R. MacDonald

MUSIC

ASSOCIATED BOARD OF THE ROYAL SCHOOLS OF MUSIC, 14 Bedford Square, London WC1B 3JG. Tel: 0171-636 5400. The Board conducts graded music examinations in over 80 countries and provides other services to music education through its professional development department and publishing company. *Chief Executive,* R. Morris
GUILDHALL SCHOOL OF MUSIC AND DRAMA, Silk Street, London EC2Y 8DT. Tel: 0171-628 2571. *Principal,* I. Horsbrugh
LONDON COLLEGE OF MUSIC, Thames Valley University, St Mary's Road, London W5 5RF. Tel: 0181-231 2304. *Dean,* Ms P. Thompson
ROYAL ACADEMY OF MUSIC, Marylebone Road, London NW1 5HT. Tel: 0171-873 7373. *Principal,* Prof. C. Price
ROYAL COLLEGE OF MUSIC, Prince Consort Road, London SW7 2BS. Tel: 0171-589 3643. *Director,* Dr J. Ritterman.
ROYAL COLLEGE OF ORGANISTS, 7 St Andrew Street, London EC4A 3LQ. Tel: 0171-936 3606. *Senior Executive,* A. Dear
ROYAL NORTHERN COLLEGE OF MUSIC, 124 Oxford Road, Manchester M13 9RD. Tel: 0161-273 6283. *Principal,* Prof. E. Gregson
ROYAL SCOTTISH ACADEMY OF MUSIC AND DRAMA, 100 Renfrew Street, Glasgow G2 3DB. Tel: 0141-332 4101. *Principal,* Dr P. Ledger, CBE, FRSE

TRINITY COLLEGE OF MUSIC, 11–13 Mandeville Place, London WIM 6AQ. Tel: 0171-935 5773. *Principal*, G. Henderson

NURSING

All nurses must be registered with the UK Central Council for Nursing, Midwifery and Health Visiting. Courses leading to registration as a nurse are at least three years in length. There are also some programmes which are combined with degrees. Students study in colleges of nursing or in institutions of higher education. Courses offer a combination of theoretical and practical experience in a variety of settings. Different courses lead to different types of registration, including: Registered Nurse (RN), Registered Mental Nurse (RMN), Registered Mental Handicap Nurse (RMHN), Registered Sick Children's Nurse (RSCN), Registered Midwife (RM) and Registered Health Visitor (RHV). The various national boards, listed below, are responsible for validating courses in nursing.

The Royal College of Nursing is the main professional union representing nurses and provides higher education through its Institute.

ENGLISH NATIONAL BOARD FOR NURSING, MIDWIFERY AND HEALTH VISITING, Victory House, 170 Tottenham Court Road, London WIP 0HA. Tel: 0171-388 3131. *Chief Executive*, A. P. Smith

NATIONAL BOARD FOR NURSING, MIDWIFERY AND HEALTH VISITING FOR NORTHERN IRELAND, Centre House, 79 Chichester Street, Belfast BTI 4JE. Tel: 01232-238152. *Chief Executive*, Prof. O. D'A. Slevin, PH.D.

NATIONAL BOARD FOR NURSING, MIDWIFERY AND HEALTH VISITING FOR SCOTLAND, 22 Queen Street, Edinburgh EH2 1NT. Tel: 0131-226 7371. *Chief Executive*, D. C. Benton

THE ROYAL COLLEGE OF NURSING OF THE UNITED KINGDOM, 20 Cavendish Square, London WIM 0AB. Tel: 0171-409 3333. *General Secretary*, Miss C. Hancock; *Director of the RCN Institute*, Prof. A. Kitson

WELSH NATIONAL BOARD FOR NURSING, MIDWIFERY AND HEALTH VISITING, 2nd Floor, Golate House, 101 St Mary Street, Cardiff CFI 1DX. Tel: 01222-261400. *Chief Executive*, D. A. Ravey

UK CENTRAL COUNCIL FOR NURSING, MIDWIFERY AND HEALTH VISITING, 23 Portland Place, London WIN 4JT. Tel: 0171-637 7181. *Chief Executive and Registrar*, Ms S. Norman

OPHTHALMIC AND DISPENSING OPTICS

Professional bodies are:
THE ASSOCIATION OF BRITISH DISPENSING OPTICIANS, 6 Hurlingham Business Park, Sulivan Road, London SW6 3DU. Tel: 0171-736 0088. Grants qualifications as a dispensing optician. *Registrar*, D. G. Baker

THE COLLEGE OF OPTOMETRISTS, 42 Craven Street, London WC2N 5NG. Tel: 0171-839 6000. Grants qualifications as an optometrist. *General Secretary*, P. D. Leigh

OSTEOPATHY

Osteopathy is accorded statutory regulation by the Osteopaths Act 1993. The existing voluntary registration schemes were taken over by the General Osteopathic Council, which opened a new statutory register on 9 May 1998. From 2000 it will be an offence for anyone who is not on the statutory register to call themselves an osteopath.

The General Osteopathic Council is now responsible for regulating, developing and promoting the profession. Osteopathic education is currently undergoing considerable change. Courses vary in length from four to six years,

granting various qualifications from diploma to honours degree. Shorter courses are available for qualified doctors. Details of accrediting institutions and courses can be obtained from the General Osteopathic Council.

GENERAL OSTEOPATHIC COUNCIL, Premier House, 10 Greycoat Place, London SWIP 1SB. Tel: 0171-799 2442. *Chief Executive and Registrar*, Miss M. Craggs

PHARMACY

Information may be obtained from the Secretary and Registrar of the Royal Pharmaceutical Society of Great Britain.

ROYAL PHARMACEUTICAL SOCIETY OF GREAT BRITAIN, 1 Lambeth High Street, London SE1 7JN. Tel: 0171-735 9141. *Secretary and Registrar*, J. Ferguson, OBE

PHOTOGRAPHY

The professional body is:
BRITISH INSTITUTE OF PROFESSIONAL PHOTOGRAPHY, Fox Talbot House, Amwell End, Ware, Herts SG12 9HN. Tel: 01920-464011. *Chief Executive*, A. Mair

PRINTING

Details of training courses in printing can be obtained from the Institute of Printing and the British Printing Industries Federation. In addition to these examining and organizing bodies, examinations are held by various independent regional examining boards in further education.

BRITISH PRINTING INDUSTRIES FEDERATION, 11 Bedford Row, London WCIR 4DX. Tel: 0171-242 6904. *Chief Executive*, T. P. E. Machin

INSTITUTE OF PRINTING, 8A Lonsdale Gardens, Tunbridge Wells, Kent TNI 1NU. Tel: 01892-538118. *Secretary-General*, D. Freeland

SCIENCE

Professional qualifications are awarded by:
GEOLOGICAL SOCIETY, Burlington House, Piccadilly, London WIV 0JU. Tel: 0171-434 9944. *Chief Executive*, E. Nickless

INSTITUTE OF BIOLOGY, 20–22 Queensberry Place, London SW7 2DZ. Tel: 0171-581 8333. *President*, Dr J. Norris; *Chief Executive*, Prof. A. Malcolm

INSTITUTE OF PHYSICS, 76 Portland Place, London WIN 3DH. Tel: 0171-470 4800. *Chief Executive*, Dr A. D. W. Jones

ROYAL SOCIETY OF CHEMISTRY, Burlington House, Piccadilly, London WIV 0BN. Tel: 0171-437 8656. *President*, E. Abel, CBE; *Secretary-General*, T. D. Inch, PH.D., D.SC.

SOCIAL WORK

The Central Council for Education and Training in Social Work promotes education and training for social work and social care in the UK. It approves education and training programmes, including those leading to its qualifying award, the Diploma in Social Work.

THE CENTRAL COUNCIL FOR EDUCATION AND TRAINING IN SOCIAL WORK, Derbyshire House, St Chad's Street, London WCIH 8AD. Tel: 0171-278 2455. *Chairman*, Ms Z. Alexander; *Chief Executive*, J. Bernard

SPEECH AND LANGUAGE THERAPY

The Royal College of Speech and Language Therapists provides details of courses leading to qualification as a speech and language therapist. Other professionals may become Associates of the College. A directory of registered members is published annually.

THE ROYAL COLLEGE OF SPEECH AND LANGUAGE THERAPISTS, 7 Bath Place, Rivington Street, London EC2A 3DR. Tel: 0171-613 3855. *Director,* Mrs P. Evans

SURVEYING

The qualifying professional bodies include:

ARCHITECTS AND SURVEYORS INSTITUTE, St Mary House, 15 St Mary Street, Chippenham, Wilts SN15 3WD. Tel: 01249-444505. *Chief Executive,* I. N. Norris

ASSOCIATION OF BUILDING ENGINEERS, Jubilee House, Billing Brook Road, Weston Favell, Northampton NN3 8NW. Tel: 01604-404121. *Chief Executive,* D. Gibson

INCORPORATED SOCIETY OF VALUERS AND AUCTIONEERS (1968), 3 Cadogan Gate, London SW1X 0AS. Tel: 0171-235 2282. *Chief Executive,* C. Evans

INSTITUTE OF REVENUES, RATING AND VALUATION, 41 Doughty Street, London WC1N 2LF. Tel: 0171-831 3505. *Director,* C. Farrington

ROYAL INSTITUTION OF CHARTERED SURVEYORS (incorporating The Institute of Quantity Surveyors), 12 Great George Street, London SW1P 3AD. Tel: 0171-222 7000. *Chief Executive,* J. Armstrong

TEACHING

Teachers in maintained schools must have Qualified Teacher Status (QTS). With certain exceptions, teaching is an all-graduate profession, and QTS may be gained by a number of different routes. Those without a first degree may take a Bachelor of Education (B.Ed) or a Bachelor of Arts/Science (BA/B.Sc) with QTS, full-time for three or four years, depending on the programme followed. These degrees combine subject and professional studies with teaching practice. Shortened courses of these degrees are available for those who have successfully completed one or two years of higher education. The Licensed Teacher Scheme, for those with two years higher education who wished to be employed as teachers at the same time as they trained for QTS, was replaced by the Registered Teacher Scheme in 1998; entrants are paid a salary and undertake one to two years higher education.

For those who already have a first degree, the most common route is through a one-year Postgraduate Certificate of Education (PGCE). This may be taken full-time or part-time, or as a distance-learning programme. Postgraduates may also gain QTS through training in a school (School-Centred Initial Teacher Training). Since January 1998, graduates have been able to join the Graduate Teacher Programme which provides teaching and training for one year (*see also* pages 431–2).

Details of courses in England and Wales are contained in the *Handbook of Initial Teacher Training in England and Wales,* published by NATFHE. Further information about teaching in England and Wales is available from the Teaching Information Line, 01245-454454. Details of courses in Scotland can be obtained from colleges of education, universities, COSHEP and TEACH (*see* page 444). Details of courses in Northern Ireland can be obtained from the Department of Education for Northern Ireland. Applications for teacher training courses in Northern Ireland are made to the institutions direct. For applications, *see* page 436.

TEXTILES

THE TEXTILE INSTITUTE, International Headquarters, 10 Blackfriars Street, Manchester M3 5DR. Tel: 0161-834 8457. *Operations Manager,* P. Daniels

THEOLOGICAL COLLEGES

The number of students training for the ministry in the academic year 1997–8 is shown in parenthesis. Those marked * show figures for 1996–7.

ANGLICAN

COLLEGE OF THE RESURRECTION, Mirfield, W. Yorks WF14 0BW. Tel: 01924-481910. (35). *Principal,* Revd C. Irvine

CRANMER HALL, St John's College, Durham DH1 3RJ. Tel: 0191-374 3579. (65). *Principal,* D. V. Day

OAK HILL COLLEGE, Chase Side, London N14 4PS. Tel: 0181-449 0467. (40). *Principal,* Revd Dr D. Peterson

RIDLEY HALL, Cambridge CB3 9HG. Tel: 01223-741080. (50). *Principal,* Revd G. A. Cray

RIPON COLLEGE, Cuddesdon, Oxford OX44 9EX. Tel: 01865-874427. (76). *Principal,* Revd J. Clarke

ST JOHN'S COLLEGE, Chilwell Lane, Bramcote, Nottingham NG9 3DS. Tel: 0115-925 1114. (70). *Principal,* Revd Canon Dr C. Baxter

ST MICHAEL'S THEOLOGICAL COLLEGE, Llandaff, Cardiff CF5 2YJ. Tel: 01222-563379. (32). *Warden,* Revd Dr J. I. Holdsworth

ST STEPHEN'S HOUSE, 16 Marston Street, Oxford OX4 1JX. Tel: 01865-247874. (50). *Principal,* Revd Dr J. P. Sheehy

THEOLOGICAL INSTITUTE OF THE SCOTTISH EPISCOPAL CHURCH, Oldcoates House, 32 Manor Place, Edinburgh EH3 7EB. Tel: 0131-220 2272. (25). *Principal,* Revd Canon R. A. Nixon

TRINITY COLLEGE, Stoke Hill, Bristol BS9 1JP. Tel: 0117-968 2803. (73). *Principal,* Revd Canon D. Gillett

WESTCOTT HOUSE, Jesus Lane, Cambridge CB5 8BP. Tel: 01223-741000. (58). *Principal,* Revd M. G. V. Roberts

WYCLIFFE HALL, 54 Banbury Road, Oxford OX2 6PW. Tel: 01865-274200. (67). *Principal,* Revd Dr A. E. McGrath

BAPTIST

BRISTOL BAPTIST COLLEGE, The Promenade, Clifton, Bristol BS8 3NF. Tel: 0117-946 7050. (23). *Principal,* Revd Dr B. Haymes

NORTHERN BAPTIST COLLEGE, Luther King House, Brighton Grove, Rusholme, Manchester M14 5JP. Tel: 0161-224 2214. (15). *Principal,* Revd Dr R. L. Kidd

NORTH WALES BAPTIST COLLEGE, Ffordd Ffriddoedd, Bangor LL57 2EH. Tel: 01248-362608. (2*). *Warden,* Revd Dr D. D. Morgan

REGENT'S PARK COLLEGE, Oxford OX1 2LB. Tel: 01865-288120. (26). *Principal,* Revd Dr P. S. Fiddes

THE SCOTTISH BAPTIST COLLEGE, 12 Aytoun Road, Glasgow G41 5RN. Tel: 0141-424 0747. (13). *Principal,* Revd Dr K. B. E. Roxburgh

SOUTH WALES BAPTIST COLLEGE, 54 Richmond Road, Cardiff CF2 3UR. Tel: 01222-256066. (23). *Principal,* Revd D. H. Matthews

CHURCH OF SCOTLAND

TRINITY COLLEGE, 4 The Square, University of Glasgow, Glasgow G12 8QQ. Tel: 0141-330 6840. (26). *Principal,* Revd Dr D. M. Murray

CONGREGATIONAL

SCOTTISH CONGREGATIONAL COLLEGE, 18 Inverleith Terrace, Edinburgh EH3 5NS. Tel: 0131-315 3595. (0). *Principal,* Revd Dr J. W. S. Clark

METHODIST

EDGHILL THEOLOGICAL COLLEGE, 9 Lennoxvale, Belfast BT9 5BY. Tel: 01232-665870. (15). *Principal,* Revd Dr W. D. D. Cooke

HARTLEY VICTORIA COLLEGE, Luther King House, Brighton Grove, Manchester M14 5JP. Tel: 0161-224 2215. (25*). *Principal,* Revd Dr J. A. Harrod
WESLEY COLLEGE, College Park Drive, Henbury Road, Bristol BS10 7QD. Tel: 0117-959 1200. (49). *Principal,* Revd Dr N. Richardson
WESLEY HOUSE, Jesus Lane, Cambridge CB5 8BJ. Tel: 01223-741051. (33). *Principal,* Revd Dr I. H. Jones
WESLEY STUDY CENTRE, 55 The Avenue, Durham DH1 4EB. Tel: 0191-386 1833. (24*). *Director,* Revd Dr P. Luscombe

NON-DENOMINATIONAL
CHRIST'S COLLEGE, 25 High Street, Old Aberdeen AB24 3EE. Tel: 01224-272380. (26). *Master,* Revd Prof. D. Fergusson
NEW COLLEGE, Mound Place, Edinburgh EH1 2LX. Tel: 0131-650 8912. (40). *Principal,* Revd Dr R. Page
QUEENS' COLLEGE, Somerset Road, Edgbaston, Birmingham B15 2QH. Tel: 0121-454 1527. (120). *Principal,* Revd P. Fisher
ST MARY'S COLLEGE, The University, St Andrews, Fife KY16 9JU. Tel: 01334-462851. (7*). *Principal,* Dr R. A. Piper
SPURGEON'S COLLEGE, South Norwood Hill, London SE25 6DJ. Tel: 0181-653 0850. (250). *Principal,* Revd M. J. Quicke

PRESBYTERIAN
UNION THEOLOGICAL COLLEGE, 108 Botanic Avenue, Belfast BT7 1JT. Tel: 01232-205080. (40*). *Principal,* Revd Prof. J. C. McCullough

PRESBYTERIAN CHURCH OF WALES
UNITED THEOLOGICAL COLLEGE, Aberystwyth SY23 2LT. Tel: 01970-624574. (9). *Principal,* Revd Dr J. T. Williams

ROMAN CATHOLIC
ALLEN HALL, 28 Beaufort Street, London SW3 5AA. Tel: 0171-351 1296. (30). *Principal,* Revd J. Overton, STL
CAMPION HOUSE COLLEGE, 112 Thornbury Road, Isleworth, Middx TW7 4NN. Tel: 0181-560 1924. (*c*.15). *Principal,* Revd C. C. Dykehoff, SJ
OSCOTT COLLEGE, Chester Road, Sutton Coldfield, W. Midlands B73 5AA. Tel: 0121-354 7117. (46). *Rector,* Very Revd Mgr K. McDonald
ST JOHN'S SEMINARY, Wonersh, Guildford, Surrey GU5 0QX. Tel: 01483-892217. (56). *Rector,* Revd K. Haggerty, STL
SCOTUS COLLEGE, 2 Chesters Road, Bearsden, Glasgow G61 4AG. Tel: 0141-942 8384. (*35). *Rector,* Rt. Revd M. J. Conway
USHAW COLLEGE, Durham DH7 9RH. Tel: 0191-373 1366. (46). *President,* Revd J. P. O'Keefe

UNITARIAN
UNITARIAN COLLEGE, Luther King House, Brighton Grove, Rusholme, Manchester M14 5JP. Tel: 0161-224 2849. (7). *Principal,* Revd Dr L. Smith

UNITED REFORMED
MANSFIELD COLLEGE, Mansfield Road, Oxford OX1 3TF. Tel: 01865-270999. (20). *Principal,* Prof. D. Marquand
NORTHERN COLLEGE, Luther King House, Brighton Grove, Rusholme, Manchester M14 5JP. Tel: 0161-224 4381. (26). *Principal,* Revd Dr D. R. Peel
WESTMINSTER COLLEGE, Madingley Road, Cambridge CB3 0AA. Tel: 01223-741084. (32). *Principal,* Revd Dr D. G. Cornick

JEWISH
JEWS' COLLEGE, Schaller House, Albert Road, London NW4 2SJ. Tel: 0181-203 6427. (6). *Director,* Prof. D. H. Ruben
LEO BAECK COLLEGE, Sternberg Centre for Judaism, 80 East End Road, London N3 2SY. Tel: 0181-349 4525. (19). *Principal,* Rabbi Prof. J. Magonet

TOWN AND COUNTRY PLANNING
Degree and diploma courses in town planning are accredited by the Royal Town Planning Institute.
THE ROYAL TOWN PLANNING INSTITUTE, 26 Portland Place, London W1N 4BE. Tel: 0171-636 9107. *Secretary-General,* R. Upton

TRANSPORT
Qualifying examinations in transport management and logistics leading to chartered professional status are conducted by the Chartered Institute of Transport.
THE CHARTERED INSTITUTE OF TRANSPORT, 80 Portland Place, London W1N 4DP. Tel: 0171-467 9425. *Director,* Mrs D. de Carvalho

VETERINARY MEDICINE
The regulatory body for veterinary medicine is the Royal College of Veterinary Surgeons, which keeps the register of those entitled to practise veterinary medicine. In order to be registered, a person must complete a five-year undergraduate degree (BvetMed, BVSc., BVMS, BVM and S) at one of the six authorized institutions.
The British Veterinary Association is the professional body representing veterinary surgeons. The British Veterinary Nursing Association is the professional body representing veterinary nurses who are also registered with the Royal College of Veterinary Surgeons.
BRITISH VETERINARY ASSOCIATION, 7 Mansfield Street, London W1M 0AT. Tel: 0171-636 6541. *Chief Executive,* J. Baird
BRITISH VETERINARY NURSING ASSOCIATION, Level 15, Terminus House, Terminus Street, Harlow, Essex CM20 1XA. Tel: 01279-450567. *Chairman,* Ms J. Costello
ROYAL COLLEGE OF VETERINARY SURGEONS, Belgravia House, 62–64 Horseferry Road, London SW1P 2AF. Tel: 0171-222 2001. *President,* Dr A. Brown; *Registrar,* Ms J. Hern

Independent Schools

The following pages list those independent schools whose
Head is a member of the Headmasters' and Headmistress'
Conference, the Society of Headmasters and
Headmistresses of Independent Schools or the Girls'
Schools Association

THE HEADMASTERS' AND HEADMISTRESSES' CONFERENCE

Chairman (1999), J. Sabben-Clare (Winchester College)
Secretary, V. S. Anthony, 130 Regent Road, Leicester
LEI 7PG. Tel: 0116-285 4810
Membership Secretary, D. E. Prince. Tel: 0116-285 1567
The annual meeting is held early in October

* Woodard Corporation School, 1 The Sanctuary, London
SWIP 3JT. Tel: 0171-222 5381
† Girls in VI form
‡ Co-educational
° 1997 figures

Name of School	Foun-ded	No. of pupils	Annual fees £ Boarding	Day	Head (with date of appointment)
ENGLAND AND WALES					
Abbotsholme School, Rocester	1889	156‡	13,200	8,820	I. M. Allison (1997)
Abingdon School, Oxon	1256	800	11,511	6,246	M. St J. Parker (1975)
Ackworth School, W. Yorks	1779	370‡	10,761	6,120	M. J. Dickinson (1995)
Aldenham School, Elstree, Herts	1597	385†	13,170	9,075	S. R. Borthwick (1994)
Alleyn's School, London SE22	1619	920‡	—	6,630	Dr C. H. R. Niven (1992)
Ampleforth College (*RC*), N. Yorks	1802	495†	13,305	6,870	Revd G. F. L. Chamberlain, OSB (1993)
*Ardingly College, Haywards Heath	1858	460‡	13,455	10,185	J. Framlin (1998)
Arnold School, Blackpool	1896	800‡	—	4,200	W. T. Gillen (1993)
Ashville College, Harrogate	1877	610‡	10,329	5,550	M. H. Crosby (1987)
Bablake School, Coventry	1560	850‡	—	4,497	Dr S. Nuttall (1991)
Bancroft's School, Woodford Green, Essex	1727	770‡	—	6,681	Dr P. R. Scott (1996)
Barnard Castle School, Co. Durham	1883	500‡	10,047	5,949	M. D. Featherstone (1997)
Batley Grammar School, W. Yorks	1612	510‡	—	4,527	B. Battye (1998)
Bedales School, Petersfield	1893	409‡	15,045	11,502	Mrs A. A. Willcocks (1995)
Bedford Modern School	1566	950	10,575	5,664	S. Smith (1996)
Bedford School	1552	703	12,720	8,010	Dr I. P. Evans (1990)
Berkhamsted Collegiate School, Herts	1541	970†	12,381	7,683	Dr P. Chadwick (*Principal*) (1996)
Birkdale School, Sheffield	1904	530†	—	5,037	R. J. Court (1998)
°Birkenhead School, Merseyside	1860	677	—	4,155	S. J. Haggett (1988)
Bishop's Stortford College, Herts	1868	324‡	11,610	8,370	J. G. Trotman (1997)
*Bloxham School, Banbury	1860	340‡	14,160	11,085	D. K. Exham (1991)
Blundell's School, Tiverton	1604	454‡	13,395	8,175	J. Leigh (1992)
Bolton School	1524	850	—	4,998	A. W. Wright (1983)
Bootham School, York	1823	375‡	11,550	7,515	I. M. Small (1988)
Bradfield College, Reading	1850	580†	14,160	10,620	P. B. Smith (1985)
Bradford Grammar School	1662	850	—	4,900	S. R. Davidson (1996)
Brentwood School, Essex	1557	1,053‡	11,975	6,875	J. A. B. Kelsall (1993)
Brighton College, E. Sussex	1845	480‡	14,055	9,066	Dr A. F. Seldon (1997)
°Bristol Cathedral School	1140	470†	—	4,362	K. J. Riley (1993)
Bristol Grammar School	1532	1,030‡	—	4,545	C. E. Martin (1986)
Bromsgrove School, Worcs	1553	670‡	11,340	7,110	T. M. Taylor (1986)
Bryanston School, Blandford Forum	1928	640‡	14,982	10,338	T. D. Wheare (1983)
Bury Grammar School, Lancs	1634	700	—	4,194	K. Richards (1990)
Canford School, Wimborne	1923	554‡	14,415	10,815	J. D. Lever (1992)
Caterham School, Surrey	1811	700‡	12,507	6,747	R. A. E. Davey (1995)
Charterhouse, Godalming	1611	675†	14,706	12,153	Revd J. S. Witheridge (1996)
Cheadle Hulme School, Cheshire	1855	1,015‡	—	4,797	D. J. Wilkinson (1990)
Cheltenham College, Glos	1841	546‡	13,860	10,425	P. A. Chamberlain (1997)
Chetham's School of Music, Manchester	1653	265‡	16,902	13,083	Revd Canon P. F. Hullah (1992)
Chigwell School, Essex	1629	362‡	11,019	7,248	D. F. Gibbs (1996)

Name of School	Foun-ded	No. of pupils	Annual fees £		Head (with date of appointment)
			Boarding	Day	
Christ College, Brecon	1541	340‡	11,364	8,805	D. P. Jones (1996)
Christ's Hospital, Horsham	1553	794‡	varies	—	Dr P. C. D. Southern (1996)
Churcher's College, Petersfield	1722	550‡	—	5,820	G. W. Buttle (1988)
City of London Freemen's School, Ashtead	1854	420‡	11,187	7,002	D. C. Haywood (1987)
City of London, London EC4	1442	875	—	6,741	W. Duggan (1998)
Clifton College, Bristol	1862	666‡	14,085	9,660	A. H. Monro (1990)
Colfe's School, London SE12	1652	710†	—	5,985	Dr D. J. Richardson (1990)
Colston's Collegiate School, Bristol	1710	501‡	11,460	6,210	D. G. Crawford (1995)
Cranleigh School, Surrey	1863	480†	14,535	10,755	G. de W. Waller (1997)
Culford School, Bury St Edmunds	1881	360‡	12,330	8,022	J. S. Richardson (1992)
Dame Allan's Boys' School, Newcastle upon Tyne	1705	440†	—	4,305	D. W. Welsh (*Principal*) (1995)
Dauntsey's School, Devizes	1543	670‡	12,318	7,512	S. B. Roberts (1997)
Dean Close School, Cheltenham	1884	453‡	14,055	9,810	Rev. T. M. Hastie-Smith (1998)
*Denstone College, Uttoxeter	1873	335‡	10,248	6,798	D. M. Derbyshire (1997)
Douai School (*RC*), Upper Woolhampton, Reading	1903	200‡	12,114	8,034	Dr P. McLaughlin (1997)
Downside School (*RC*), Somerset	1607	265	12,612	6,402	Revd Dom. A. Sutch (1996)
Dulwich College, London SE21	1619	1,209	13,965	7,080	G. G. Able (*Master*) (1997)
Durham School	1414	275‡	12,360	8,091	N. G. Kern (1997)
Eastbourne College	1867	501‡	13,590	9,360	C. M. P. Bush (1993)
*Ellesmere College, Shropshire	1884	308‡	12,294	8,142	B. J. Wignall (1996)
Eltham College, London SE9	1842	580†	13,227	6,402	D. M. Green (1990)
Emanuel School, London SW11	1594	780‡	—	5,700	Mrs A-M. Sutcliffe (1998)
Epsom College, Surrey	1855	657‡	13,590	10,095	A. H. Beadles (1993)
Eton College, Windsor	1440	1,284	14,796	—	J. E. Lewis (1994)
Exeter School	1633	690‡	9,339	4,929	N. W. Gamble (1992)
Felsted School, Dunmow, Essex	1564	380‡	14,310	11,280	S. C. Roberts (1993)
Forest School, London E17	1834	970†	10,284	6,552	A. G. Boggis (*Warden*) (1992)
Framlingham College, Woodbridge, Suffolk	1864	450‡	11,373	7,299	Mrs. G. M. Randall (1994)
Frensham Heights, Farnham	1925	300‡	13,800	9,150	P. M. de Voil (1993)
Giggleswick School, Settle	1512	326‡	13,515	8,970	A. P. Millard (1993)
The Grange School, Northwich, Cheshire	1978	592‡	—	4,020	Mrs J. E. Stephen (1997)
Gresham's School, Holt, Norfolk	1555	518‡	13,965	9,945	J. H. Arkell (1991)
Haberdashers' Aske's School, Elstree, Herts	1690	1,100	—	6,696	J. W. R. Goulding (1996)
Haileybury, Hertford	1862	630‡	14,640	10,590	S. A. Westley (*Master*) (1996)
Hampton School, Middx	1557	950	—	6,150	B. R. Martin (1987)
Harrow School, Middx	1571	775	15,000	—	N. R. Bomford (1991)
Hereford Cathedral School	1384	620‡	9,555	5,340	Dr H. C. Tomlinson (1987)
Highgate School, London N6	1565	580	—	8,265	R. P. Kennedy (1989)
Hulme Grammar School, Oldham	1611	690	—	4,185	T. J. Turvey (1995)
*Hurstpierpoint College, Hassocks, W. Sussex	1849	360‡	13,170	10,200	S. D. A. Meek (1995)
Hymers College, Hull	1889	750‡	—	4,266	J. C. Morris (1990)
Ipswich School	1390	583‡	10,026	5,823	I. G. Galbraith (1993)
John Lyon School, Harrow	1876	525	—	6,450	Revd T. J. Wright (1986)
Kelly College, Tavistock	1877	350‡	13,095	8,220	M. Turner (1995)
Kent College, Canterbury	1885	480‡	12,100	6,795	E. B. Halse (1995)
Kimbolton School, Huntingdon	1600	560‡	10,560	5,163	R. V. Peel (1987)
King Edward VI School, Southampton	1553	950‡	—	5,625	P. B. Hamilton (1996)
King Edward VII School, Lytham St Annes	1908	490	—	4,260	P. J. Wilde (1993)
King Edward's School, Bath	1552	680‡	—	5,286	P. J. Winter (1994)
King Edward's School, Birmingham	1552	886	—	5,235	R. M. Dancey (*Chief Master*) (1998)
King Edward's School, Witley, Surrey	1553	396‡	10,695	7,320	R. J. Fox (1988)
King Henry VIII School, Coventry	1545	808‡	—	4,497	T. J. Vardon (1994)
*King's College, Taunton	1880	450‡	13,215	8,700	R. S. Funnell (1988)
King's College School, London SW19	1829	720	—	7,800	A. C. V. Evans (1997)
King's School, Bruton, Somerset	1519	352‡	12,360	5,850	R. I. Smyth (1993)
King's School, Canterbury	600	754‡	14,955	10,335	Revd Canon K. H. Wilkinson (1996)
King's School, Chester	1541	520†	—	4,788	A. R. D. Wickson (1981)
King's School, Ely	970	386‡	13,263	9,108	R. H. Youdale (1992)
King's School, Gloucester	1541	320‡	12,500	6,000	P. Lacey (1992)
King's School, Macclesfield	1502	1,200‡	—	4,755	A. G. Silcock (1987)

Name of School	Founded	No. of pupils	Annual fees £		Head (with date of appointment)
			Boarding	Day	
King's School, Rochester, Kent	604	326‡	14,025	8,085	Dr I. R. Walker (1987)
*King's School, Tynemouth	1860	638‡	—	4,491	Dr D. Younger (1993)
King's School, Worcester	1541	790‡	11,439	5,919	T. H. Keyes (1998)
Kingston Grammar School, Surrey	1561	600‡	—	6,338	C. D. Baxter (1991)
Kingswood School, Bath	1748	495‡	13,266	7,125	G. M. Best (1987)
*Lancing College, W. Sussex	1848	495‡	14,070	10,575	P. M. Tinniswood (1998)
Latymer Upper School, London w6	1624	950†	—	6,966	C. Diggory (1991)
°Leeds Grammar School	1552	1,104	—	5,316	B. W. Collins (1986)
Leicester Grammar School	1981	646‡	—	4,890	J. B. Sugden (1989)
Leighton Park School, Reading	1890	365‡	12,807	9,612	J. Dunston (1996)
The Leys School, Cambridge	1875	450‡	13,290	8,460	Revd Dr J. C. A. Barrett (1990)
Liverpool College	1840	620‡	—	4,515	J. P. Siviter (Principal) (1997)
Llandovery College, Carmarthenshire	1848	230‡	11,095	7,368	Dr C. E. Evans (Warden) (1988)
Lord Wandsworth College, Long Sutton, Hants	1912	470‡	11,625	9,045	I. G. Power (1997)
Loughborough Grammar School	1495	970	9,999	5,148	P. B. Fisher (1998)
Magdalen College School, Oxford	1480	538	—	5,664	A. D. Halls (Master) (1998)
Malvern College, Worcs	1865	555‡	14,175	8,985	H. C. K. Carson (1997)
Manchester Grammar School	1515	1,450	—	4,800	Dr G. M. Stephen (High Master) (1994)
Marlborough College, Wilts	1843	820‡	14,790	10,830	E. J. H. Gould (Master) (1993)
Merchant Taylors' School, Liverpool	1620	730	—	1,452	S. J. R. Dawkins (1985)
Merchant Taylors' School, Northwood, Middx	1561	774	12,550	7,550	J. R. Gabitass (1991)
Millfield, Street, Somerset	1935	1,248‡	15,105	9,870	P. M. Johnson (1998)
Mill Hill School, London nw7	1807	560‡	13,290	8,700	W. R. Winfield (1995)
Monkton Combe School, Bath	1868	335‡	13,725	9,375	M. J. Cuthbertson (1990)
Monmouth School	1614	568	9,780	5,871	T. H. P. Haynes (1995)
Mount St Mary's College (RC), Sheffield	1842	269‡	10,200	6,150	P. Macdonald (1998)
Newcastle-under-Lyme School	1874	1,120‡	—	4,194	Dr R. M. Reynolds (Principal) (1990)
Norwich School	1250	633†	—	5,343	C. D. Brown (1984)
°Nottingham High School	1513	834	—	4,923	C. S. Parker (1995)
Oakham School, Rutland	1584	788‡	13,530	8,100	A. R. M. Little (1996)
The Oratory School (RC), Woodcote, Berks	1859	356	13,635	9,540	S. W. Barrow (1991)
Oundle School, Northants	1556	845‡	14,616	—	D. B. McMurray (1984)
Pangbourne College, Berks	1917	320‡	13,197	10,485	A. B. E. Hudson (1988)
Perse School, Cambridge	1615	570†	—	5,526	N. P. V. Richardson (1994)
Plymouth College	1877	604‡	10,977	5,721	A. J. Morsley (1992)
Pocklington School, York	1514	600‡	9,900	5,800	J. N. D. Gray (1992)
Portsmouth Grammar School	1732	800‡	—	5,367	Dr T. R. Hands, D.Phil. (1997)
Prior Park College (RC), Bath	1830	510‡	12,054	6,669	R. G. G. Mercer, D.Phil. (1996)
Queen Elizabeth GS, Wakefield	1591	700†	—	5,001	R. P. Mardling (1985)
Queen Elizabeth's GS, Blackburn	1567	840†	—	4,740	Dr D. S. Hempsall (1995)
Queen Elizabeth's Hospital, Bristol	1590	530	8,385	4,560	Dr R. Gliddon (1985)
Queen's College, Taunton	1843	462‡	10,590	6,945	C. T. Bradnock (1991)
Radley College, Abingdon	1847	620	14,550	—	R. M. Morgan (Warden) (1991)
Ratcliffe College (RC), Leicester	1844	508‡	10,329	6,888	T. A. Kilbride (1996)
Reading Blue Coat School	1646	614‡	11,082	6,081	S. J. W. McArthur (1997)
Reed's School, Cobham, Surrey	1813	405†	11,970	9,048	D. W. Jarrett (1997)
Reigate Grammar School, Surrey	1675	810‡	—	5,910	P. V. Dixon (1996)
Rendcomb College, Cirencester	1920	242‡	9,270	7,020	J. Tolputt (1987)
Repton School, Derby	1557	554‡	13,400	10,110	G. E. Jones (1987)
RNIB New College, Worcester	1987	42‡	24,667	22,200	Mrs H. Williams (Principal) (1995)
Rossall School, Fleetwood, Lancs	1844	253‡	12,600	4,725	R. D. W. Rhodes (1987)
Royal Grammar School, Guildford	1552	850	—	6,660	T. M. S. Young (1992)
Royal Grammar School, Newcastle upon Tyne	1545	915	—	4,527	J. F. X. Miller (1994)
Royal Grammar School, Worcester	1291	745	—	5,130	W. A. Jones (1993)
Royal Hospital School, Ipswich	1712	650‡	12,054	6,450	N. K. D. Ward (1995)
Rugby School	1567	730‡	14,610	8,760	M. B. Mavor, cvo (1990)
Rydal Penrhos School, Colwyn Bay	1880	387‡	11,562	8,152	M. S. James (1998)
Ryde School with Upper Chine, Isle of Wight	1921	450‡	9,690	4,740	Dr N. J. England (1997)
St Albans School	1570	680†	—	6,570	A. R. Grant (1993)
°St Bede's College (RC), Manchester	1876	1,002‡	—	4,170	J. Byrne (1983)

Name of School	Foun-ded	No. of pupils	Annual fees £		Head (with date of appointment)
			Boarding	Day	
St Bees School, Cumbria	1583	292‡	12,435	8,556	Mrs J. D. Pickering (1998)
St Benedict's School (RC), London w5	1902	582†	—	5,790	Dr A. J. Dachs (1987)
St Dunstan's College, London se6	1888	670‡	—	6,114	D. I. Davies (1998)
St Edmund's College (RC), Ware, Herts	1568	400‡	11,535	7,185	D. J. J. McEwen (1984)
St Edmund's School, Canterbury	1749	260‡	13,923	8,988	A. N. Ridley (1994)
St Edward's School, Oxford	1863	555‡	14,250	10,140	D. Christie (Warden) (1988)
St George's College (RC), Addlestone, Surrey	1869	600‡	—	7,290	J. A. Peake (1995)
St John's School, Leatherhead, Surrey	1851	425‡	12,300	8,550	C. H. Tongue (1993)
St Lawrence College in Thanet, Ramsgate	1879	340‡	13,635	8,745	M. Slater (1996)
St Mary's College (RC), Liverpool	1919	617‡	—	4,253	W. Hammond (1991)
St Paul's School, London sw13	1509	770	14,235	9,435	R. S. Baldock (High Master) (1992)
St Peter's School, York	627	508‡	11,679	8,061	A. F. Trotman (1995)
Sedbergh School, Cumbria	1525	287	13,920	10,305	C. H. Hirst (1995)
Sevenoaks School, Kent	1418	946‡	14,355	9,108	T. R. Cookson (1996)
Sherborne School, Dorset	1550	555	14,400	10,800	P. H. Lapping (1988)
Shiplake College, Henley-on-Thames	1959	300†	12,945	8,730	N. Bevan (1988)
Shrewsbury School	1552	695	14,325	10,080	F. E. Maidment (1988)
Silcoates School, Wakefield	1820	426‡	—	5,760	A. P. Spillane (1991)
Solihull School	1560	794‡	—	4,740	P. S. J. Derham (1996)
°Stamford School, Lincs	1532	550	9,048	4,524	J. Hale (Principal) (1997)
Stockport Grammar School	1487	1,000‡	—	4,527	I. Mellor (1996)
Stonyhurst College (RC), Clitheroe	1593	395‡	12,540	7,800	A. J. F. Aylward (1996)
Stowe School, Bucks	1923	580†	14,940	10,800	J. G. L. Nichols (1989)
Sutton Valence School, Kent	1576	374‡	13,140	8,400	N. A. Sampson (1994)
Taunton School	1847	450‡	12,585	8,070	J. P. Whiteley (1997)
Tettenhall College, Wolverhampton	1863	284‡	9,798	6,039	Dr P. C. Bodkin (1994)
Tonbridge School, Kent	1553	702	15,075	10,650	J. M. Hammond (1990)
Trent College, Nottingham	1868	640‡	11,850	7,300	J. S. Lee (1989)
Trinity School, Croydon	1596	850	—	5,961	B. J. Lenon (1995)
Truro School	1879	780‡	10,065	5,304	G. A. G. Dodd (1993)
University College School, London nw3	1830	700	—	8,010	K. J. Durham (1996)
°Uppingham School, Oakham, Rutland	1584	642†	13,920	9,000	Dr S. C. Winkley, d.phil. (1991)
Warwick School	914	820	11,667	5,466	Dr P. J. Cheshire (1988)
Wellingborough School, Northants	1595	380‡	10,890	6,195	F. R. Ullmann (1993)
Wellington College, Crowthorne, Berks	1856	808‡	14,370	10,560	C. J. Driver (Master) (1989)
Wellington School, Somerset	1837	516‡	9,300	5,088	A. J. Rogers (1990)
Wells Cathedral School, Somerset	1180	595‡	11,502	6,831	J. S. Baxter (1986)
West Buckland School, Barnstaple, Devon	1858	493‡	10,380	5,880	J. F. Vick (1997)
Westminster School, London sw1	1560	655‡	15,375	11,550	T. Jones-Parry (1998)
Whitgift School, South Croydon	1596	1,100	—	6,699	C. A. Barnett, d.phil. (1991)
William Hulme's GS, Manchester	1887	725‡	—	4,527	B. J. Purvis (1997)
Winchester College	1382	680	15,345	11,709	J. P. Sabben-Clare (1985)
Wisbech Grammar School, Cambs	1379	630‡	—	5,400	R. S. Repper (1988)
Wolverhampton Grammar School	1512	785‡	—	5,700	Dr B. Trafford (1990)
Woodbridge School, Suffolk	1662	550‡	10,656	6,330	S. H. Cole (1994)
Woodhouse Grove School, Bradford	1812	575‡	10,500	6,120	D. C. Humphreys (1996)
*Worksop College, Notts	1895	370‡	12,375	8,490	R. A. Collard (1994)
Worth School (RC), Crawley	1959	320	13,179	9,024	Fr C. Jamison, ocb (1994)
Wrekin College, Telford	1880	320‡	13,080	7,920	S. Drew (1998)
Wycliffe College, Stonehouse, Glos	1882	393‡	14,805	9,660	Dr R. A. Collins (1998)
Yarm School, Stockton-on-Tees	1978	560†	—	5,673	R. N. Tate (1978)

Scotland

Daniel Stewart's and Melville College, Edinburgh	1832	778	9,810	5,091	P. J. F. Tobin (1989)
Dollar Academy, Clackmannanshire	1818	756‡	10,701	4,833	J. S. Robertson (Rector) (1994)
The High School of Dundee	1239	715‡	—	4,398	A. M. Duncan (1997)
The Edinburgh Academy	1824	483†	12,159	5,703	J. V. Light (Rector) (1995)
Fettes College, Edinburgh	1870	392‡	14,205	9,585	M. C. B. Spens (1998)
George Heriot's School, Edinburgh	1659	931‡	—	4,404	A. G. Hector (1998)
George Watson's College, Edinburgh	1741	1,265‡	9,798	4,800	F. E. Gerstenberg (Principal) (1986)
Glasgow Academy	1845	568‡	—	4,875	D. Comins (Rector) (1994)
Glenalmond College, Perth	1841	370‡	13,785	9,195	I. G. Templeton (Warden) (1992)

Name of School	Foun-ded	No. of pupils	Annual fees £		Head (with date of appointment)
			Boarding	Day	
Gordonstoun School, Elgin	1934	430‡	13,563	8,754	M. C. Pyper (1990)
High School of Glasgow	1124	644‡	—	4,995	R. G. Easton (*Rector*) (1983)
Hutcheson's Grammar School, Glasgow	1641	1,252‡	—	4,473	D. R. Ward (*Rector*) (1987)
Kelvinside Academy, Glasgow	1878	400	—	5,200	J. L. Broadfoot (*Rector*) (1998)
°Loretto School, Musselburgh	1827	319‡	12,195	8,130	K. J. Budge (1995)
Merchiston Castle School, Edinburgh	1833	375	13,470	9,045	A. R. Hunter (1998)
Morrison's Academy, Crieff	1860	393‡	12,450	4,440	G. H. Edwards (*Rector*) (1996)
Robert Gordon's College, Aberdeen	1729	940‡	—	4,800	B. R. W. Lockhart (1996)
°St Aloysius' College, Glasgow	1859	811‡	—	3,500	Revd A. Porter, sj (1995)
St Colomba's School, Kilmacolm	1897	360‡	—	4,473	A. H. Livingstone (1987)
Strathallan School, Perth	1913	420‡	13,500	9,300	A. W. McPhail (1993)
NORTHERN IRELAND					
°Bangor Grammar School	1856	913	—	450	T. W. Patton (1979)
Belfast Royal Academy	1785	1,374‡	—	80	W. M. Sillery (1980)
Campbell College, Belfast	1894	725	6,204	1,317	Dr R. J. I. Pollock (1987)
Coleraine Academical Institution	1856	220	—	75	R. S. Forsythe (1984)
°Methodist College, Belfast	1868	1,864‡	3,449	244	T. W. Mulryne (*Principal*) (1988)
Portora Royal School, Enniskillen	1618	460	—	42	R. L. Bennett (1983)
Royal Belfast Academical Institution	1810	1,050	—	495	R. M. Ridley (*Principal*) (1990)
CHANNEL ISLANDS AND ISLE OF MAN					
Elizabeth College, Guernsey	1563	514†	7,410	2,910	D. E. Toze (1998)
King William's College, Isle of Man	1668	300‡	12,630	9,090	P. K. Fulton-Peebles (*Principal*) (1996)
Victoria College, Jersey	1852	619	—	2,064	J. Hydes (1992)
EUROPE					
Aiglon College, Switzerland	1949	224‡	Fr.58,400	Fr.38,410	R. McDonald (1994)
British School in The Netherlands	1935	560‡	—	Gld.21,720	M. J. Cooper (1990)
British School of Brussels	1970	518‡	—	Fr.697,000	Ms J. M. Bray (*Principal*) (1992)
British School of Paris	1954	340‡	Fr.115,000	Fr.85,000	M. Honour (*Principal*) (1992)
The International School of Geneva	1924	1,074‡	—	Fr.19,420	G. Walker, obe (*Director-General*) (1991)
King's College, Madrid	1969	580‡	Pesetas 2.18m	Pesetas 1.29m	C. T. G. Leech (1997)
St Columba's College, Dublin	1843	265‡	Ir6,675	Ir3,855	T. E. Macey (*Warden*) (1988)
°St Edward's College, Malta	1929	400†	—	LM.780	G. Briscoe (1989)
°St George's English School, Rome	1958	320‡	—	L.18m	Mrs B. Gardner (1994)
St Julian's School, Portugal	1932	475‡	—	Esc.1.2m	F. D. Styan, obe (1994)

OTHER OVERSEAS MEMBERS

AFRICA

DIOCESAN COLLEGE, Rondebosch, SA. *Head,* C. N. Watson
FALCON COLLEGE, PO Esigodini, Zimbabwe. *Head,* P. N. Todd
HILTON COLLEGE, Kwazulu-Natal, SA. *Head,* M. J. Nicholson
MICHAELHOUSE, Balgowan, SA. *Head,* R. D. Forde
PETERHOUSE, Marondera, Zimbabwe. *Head,* M. A. Bawden
ST GEORGE'S COLLEGE, Harare, Zimbabwe. *Head,* Fr P. Edwards
ST JOHN'S COLLEGE, Johannesburg, SA. *Head,* R. J. D. Clarence
ST STITHIAN'S COLLEGE, Randburg, SA. *Head,* D. B. Wylde

AUSTRALIA

BRIGHTON GRAMMAR SCHOOL, Brighton, Victoria. *Head,* M. S. Urwin
BRISBANE BOYS' COLLEGE, Toowong, Queensland. *Head,* acting head

CAMBERWELL GRAMMAR SCHOOL, Balwyn, Victoria. *Head,* C. F. Black
CANBERRA GRAMMAR SCHOOL, Red Hill, ACT. *Head,* T. C. Murray
CAULFIELD GRAMMAR SCHOOL, Elsternwick, Victoria. *Head,* S. H. Newton
CHRIST CHURCH GRAMMAR SCHOOL, Claremont, W. Australia. *Head,* J. J. S. Madin
CRANBROOK SCHOOL, Sydney, NSW. *Head,* Dr B. N. Carter
THE GEELONG COLLEGE, Geelong, Victoria. *Head,* Dr P. Turner
GEELONG GRAMMAR SCHOOL, Corio, Victoria. *Head,* L. Hannah
GUILDFORD GRAMMAR SCHOOL, Guildford, W. Australia. *Head,* K. Walton
HAILEYBURY COLLEGE, Keysborough, Victoria. *Head,* A. H. M. Aikman
THE HALE SCHOOL, Wembley Downs, W. Australia. *Head,* R. J. Inverarity
IVANHOE GRAMMAR SCHOOL, Ivanhoe, Victoria. *Head,* R. D. Fraser

KINROSS WOLAROI SCHOOL, Orange, NSW. *Head*,
A. E. S. Anderson
KNOX GRAMMAR SCHOOL, Wahroonga, NSW. *Head*,
Dr I. Paterson
MELBOURNE GRAMMAR SCHOOL, South Yarra, Victoria.
Head, A. P. Sheahan
MENTONE GRAMMAR SCHOOL, Mentone, Victoria. *Head*,
N. Clark
NEWINGTON COLLEGE, Stanmore, NSW. *Head*,
M. E. Smee
ST PETER'S COLLEGE, St Peter's, S. Australia. *Head*,
R. L. Burchnall
SCOTCH COLLEGE, Adelaide, S. Australia. *Head*, K. Webb
SCOTCH COLLEGE, Melbourne, Victoria. *Head*,
Dr F. G. Donaldson
THE SCOTS COLLEGE, Sydney, NSW. *Head*, Dr R. L. Iles
THE SOUTHPORT SCHOOL, Southport, Queensland. *Head*,
B. A. Cook
SYDNEY CHURCH OF ENGLAND GRAMMAR SCHOOL,
Sydney, NSW. *Head*, R. A. I. Grant
SYDNEY GRAMMAR SCHOOL, Darlinghurst, NSW. *Head*,
Dr R. D. Townsend
TRINITY GRAMMAR SCHOOL, Strathfield, NSW. *Head*,
G. M. Cujes
WESLEY COLLEGE, Melbourne, Victoria. *Head*,
D. G. McArthur
WESTBOURNE AND WILLIAMSTOWN GRAMMAR
SCHOOLS, Hoppers Crossing, Victoria. *Head*, G. G. Ryan

BERMUDA

SALTUS GRAMMAR SCHOOL, Hamilton. *Head*,
R. T. Rowell

CANADA

BRENTWOOD COLLEGE SCHOOL, Mill Bay, BC. *Head*,
W. T. Ross
GLENLYON-NORFOLK SCHOOL, Victoria, BC. *Head*,
D. Brooks
HILLFIELD STRATHALLAN COLLEGE, Hamilton, Ontario.
Head, W. S. Boyer
RIDLEY COLLEGE, St Catherine, Ontario. *Head*, R. D. Lane
ST ANDREW'S COLLEGE, Aurora, Ontario. *Head*,
R. P. Bedard
TRINITY COLLEGE SCHOOL, Port Hope, Ontario. *Head*,
R. C. N. Wright
UPPER CANADA COLLEGE, Toronto, Ontario. *Head*,
J. D. Blakey

HONG KONG

ISLAND SCHOOL, Borrett Road. *Head*, D. J. James
KING GEORGE V SCHOOL, Kowloon. *Head*, M. J. Behennah

INDIA

BISHOP COTTON SCHOOL, Shimla. *Head*, K. K. Mustafi
THE CATHEDRAL AND JOHN CONNON SCHOOL, Bombay.
Head, Mrs M. Isaacs
THE LAWRENCE SCHOOL, Sanawar. *Head*, Dr H. S. Dhillon
THE SCINDIA SCHOOL, Gwalior. *Head*, A. N. Dar

KOREA

YANG CHUNG HIGH SCHOOL, Seoul. *Head*, Dr K. B. Uhm

MALAYSIA

KOLEJ TUANKU JA'AFAR, Negeri Sembilan. *Head*,
P. D. Briggs

NEW ZEALAND

BALLARAT AND CLARENDON COLLEGE, Victoria. *Head*,
D. S. Shepherd
CHRIST'S COLLEGE, Christchurch. *Head*, R. A. Zordan
KING'S COLLEGE, Auckland. *Head*, J. S. Taylor

ST ANDREW'S COLLEGE, Christchurch. *Head*, B. J. Maister
WANGANUI COLLEGIATE SCHOOL, Wanganui. *Head*,
J. R. Hensman

PAKISTAN

AITCHISON COLLEGE, Lahore. *Head*, S. Khan
KARACHI GRAMMAR SCHOOL, Karachi. *Head*,
H. H. A. Pullau

SOUTH AND CENTRAL AMERICA

ACADEMIA BRITANICA CUSCATLECA, Santa Tecla, El
Salvador. *Head*, R. Braund
THE BRITISH SCHOOLS, Montevideo, Uruguay. *Head*,
C. D. T. Smith
MARKHAM COLLEGE, Lima, Peru. *Head*, W. J. Baker
ST ANDREW'S SCOTS SCHOOL, Buenos Aires, Argentina.
Head, A. G. F. Fisher
ST GEORGE'S COLLEGE, Buenos Aires, Argentina. *Head*,
N. P. O. Green
ST PAULS' SCHOOL, São Paulo, Brazil. *Head*,
M. T. M. C. McCann

USA

ST MARK'S COLLEGE, Southborough, Massachusetts.
Head, A. J. de V. Hill

ADDITIONAL MEMBERS

The headteachers of some maintained schools are by
invitation Additional Members of the HMC. They
include the following:

BISHOP WORDSWORTH'S SCHOOL, Salisbury. *Head*,
C. D. Barnett
DURHAM JOHNSTON COMPREHENSIVE SCHOOL, Durham.
Head, Dr J. Dunford, OBE
EGGBUCKLAND COLLEGE, Plymouth. *Head*, H. E. Green
GORDANO SCHOOL, Bristol. *Head*, R. Sommers
HABERDASHERS' ASKE'S HATCHAM COLLEGE, London
SE14. *Head*, Dr E. M. Sidwell
HAYWARDS HEATH COLLEGE, W. Sussex. *Head*,
B. W. Derbyshire
THE JUDD SCHOOL, Tonbridge, Kent. *Head*, K. A. Starling
KING EDWARD VI FIVE WAYS SCHOOL, Birmingham.
Head, J. Knowles
LANCASTER ROYAL GRAMMAR SCHOOL, Lancaster. *Head*,
P. J. Mawby
THE LONDON ORATORY SCHOOL, London SW6. *Head*,
J. C. McIntosh, OBE
PRINCE HENRY'S GRAMMAR SCHOOL, Otley, W Yorks.
Head, M. Franklin
PRINCE WILLIAM SCHOOL, Oundle, Cambs. *Head*,
C. J. Lowe
ROYAL GRAMMAR SCHOOL, High Wycombe, Bucks. *Head*,
D. R. Levin
ST AMBROSE COLLEGE, Altrincham, Cheshire. *Head*,
G. E. Hester
ST ANSELM'S COLLEGE, Birkenhead, Merseyside. *Head*,
C. J. Cleugh
ST EDWARD'S COLLEGE, Liverpool. *Head*, John Waszek
ST OLAVE'S GRAMMAR SCHOOL, Orpington, Kent. *Head*,
T. Jarvis

SOCIETY OF HEADMASTERS AND HEADMISTRESSES OF INDEPENDENT SCHOOLS

The Society was founded in 1961 and, in general, represents smaller boarding schools.

General Secretary, I. D. Cleland, Celedston, Rhosesmor Road, Halkyn, Holywell CH8 8DL. Tel: 01352-781102

Headmasters/mistresses of the following schools are members of both HMC and SHMIS; details of these schools appear in the HMC list: Abbotsholme School, Ackworth School, Bedales School, Churcher's College, Colston's Collegiate School, King's School, Gloucester, King's School, Tynemouth, Leighton Park School, Lord Wandsworth College, Pangbourne College, Reading Blue Coat School, Reed's School, Rendcomb College, Royal Hospital School, Rydal Penrhos School, Ryde School, St

George's College, Shiplake College, Silcoates School, Tettenhall College, Wisbech Grammar School, Yarm School

The Headmistress of King Edward VI High School for Girls is a member of both SHMIS and GSA; details of the school are given in the GSA list

CSC Church Schools Company, Church Schools House, Chapel Street, Titchmarsh, Kettering, Northants NN14 3DA. Tel: 01832-735105

* Woodard Corporation School
† Girls in VI form
‡ Co-educational

Name of School	Foun-ded	No. of pupils	Annual fees £		Head (with date of appointment)
			Boarding	Day	
Abbey Gate College, Saighton, Chester	1977	264‡	—	4,755	E. W. Mitchell (1991)
Austin Friars School (*RC*), Carlisle	1951	304‡	9,009	5,215	Revd D. Middleton (1996)
Battle Abbey School, E. Sussex	1912	120‡	10,485	6,510	R. Clark (1998)
Bearwood College, Wokingham	1827	230‡	11,700	6,825	S. G. G. Aiano (1998)
Bedstone College, Bucknell, Shropshire	1948	155‡	11,700	6,450	M. S. Symonds (1990)
Bentham Grammar School, N. Yorks	1726	200‡	10,485	5,640	T. Halliwell (1995)
Bethany School, Cranbrook, Kent	1866	290‡	11,136	7,125	N. Dorey (1998)
Birkdale School, Sheffield	1904	530†	—	5,037	R. Court (1998)
Box Hill School, Dorking	1959	265‡	11,694	6,804	Dr P. A. S. Atwood (1987)
Claremont Fan Court School, Esher	1932	348‡	10,695	6,750	Mrs. P. B. Farrar (*Principal*) (1994)
Clayesmore School, Blandford Forum	1896	307‡	12,726	8,913	D. J. Beeby (1986)
Cokethorpe School, Witney, Oxon	1957	280‡	13,200	7,600	P. J. S. Cantwell (1995)
Duke of York's Royal Military School, Dover	1803	495‡	855	—	G. H. Wilson (1992)
Elmhurst Ballet School, Camberley	1903	200‡	10,965	8,064	J. McNamara (*Principal*) (1995)
Embley Park School, Romsey, Hants	1946	275‡	10,695	6,510	D. F. Chapman (1987)
Ewell Castle School, Epsom	1926	300	—	5205	R. A. Fewtrell (*Principal*) (1983)
Friends' School, Saffron Walden	1702	200‡	11,700	7,020	Ms J. Laing (1996)
Fulneck School (Boys), Pudsey, W. Yorks	1753	260‡	10,095	5,385	Mrs H. Gordon, (*Principal*) (1996)
*Grenville College, Bideford	1954	270‡	11,631	5,760	Dr M. C. V. Cane (1992)
Halliford School, Shepperton, Middx	1956	300†	—	5,220	J. R. Crook (1984)
Hipperholme Grammar School, Halifax	1648	335‡	—	4,320	C. C. Robinson (1988)
Keil School, Dumbarton	1915	200‡	11,034	6,186	J. A. Cummings (1993)
Kingham Hill School, Chipping Norton	1886	220‡	10,170	6,090	M. H. Payne (1991)
Kirkham Grammar School, Preston	1549	600‡	8,463	4,335	B. Stacey (1991)
Langley School, Norwich	1910	260‡	11,850	6,120	J. Malcolm (1997)
Lincoln Minster School (*CSC*)	1905	216‡	9,450	5,295	Mrs M. Bradley (1996)
Lomond School, Helensburgh, Argyll and Bute	1977	300‡	11,190	5,220	A. D. Macdonald (1986)
Milton Abbey School, Blandford Forum	1954	210	13,500	9,450	W. J. Hughes-D'Aeth (1995)
Oswestry School, Shropshire	1407	350‡	11,442	6,816	P. K. Smith (1995)
The Purcell School (music), Harrow	1962	151‡	15,348	9,060	K. J. Bain (1983)
Rannoch School, Rannoch, By Pitlochry	1959	230‡	11,655	6,105	Dr J. D. Halliday (1997)
Rishworth School, W. Yorks	1724	360‡	9,720	5,265	R. A. Baker (1998)
Rougemont School, Newport	1974	300‡	—	4,941	I. Brown (1995)
Royal Russell School, Croydon	1853	450‡	11,955	6,165	Dr J. R. Jennings (1996)
Royal School, Dungannon, N. Ireland	1614	690‡	3,970	110	P. D. Hewitt (1986)
Royal Wolverhampton School	1850	298‡	11,625	5,880	Mrs B. A. Evans (1995)
Ruthin School, Denbighshire	1574	169‡	11,235	7,185	J. S. Rowlands (1993)
St Bede's School, Hailsham	1979	500‡	13,050	7,875	R. A. Perrin (1978)
St Christopher School, Letchworth	1915	345‡	11,910	6,750	C. Reid (1981)
St David's College, Llandudno	1965	200	10,740	6,987	W. Seymour (1991)
St Edward's School, Cheltenham	1987	500‡	—	6,075	A. J. Martin (1991)
Scarborough College, N. Yorks	1898	387‡	10,539	5,715	T. L. Kirkup (1996)
Seaford College, Petworth, W. Sussex	1884	275‡	11,400	7,500	T. J. Mullins (1997)
Shebbear College, North Devon	1841	225‡	10,905	5,850	L. D. Clark (1997)
Sibford School, Banbury	1842	252‡	11,700	5,805	Ms S. Freestone (1997)

Name of School	Foun-ded	No. of pupils	Annual fees £		Head (with date of appointment)
			Boarding	Day	
Sidcot School, North Somerset	1808	410‡	11,625	6,450	A. Slesser (1997)
Stafford Grammar School	1982	303‡	—	4,491	M. Darley (1998)
Stanbridge Earls School, Romsey, Hants	1952	186‡	13,500	10,050	H. Moxon (1984)
Sunderland High School (*CSC*)	1887	310‡	—	4,530	Dr A. Slater (1998)
Thetford Grammar School, Norfolk	1119	220‡	—	4,827	J. R. Weeks (1990)
Warminster School, Wilts	1707	272‡	10,605	5,985	D. Dowdles (1998)
Yehudi Menuhin School (music), Surrey	1963	46‡	varies	—	P. N. Chisholm (1988)

GIRLS' SCHOOLS ASSOCIATION

THE GIRLS' SCHOOLS ASSOCIATION, 130 Regent Road, Leicester LE1 7PG. Tel: 0116-254 1619
President, Mrs J. Anderson
Secretary, Ms S. Cooper

Headmasters/mistresses of the following schools are members of both HMC and GSA; details of these schools appear in the HMC list: Berkhamsted Collegiate School, Rydal Penrhos School, Stamford Endowed Schools

CSC Church Schools Company
§ Girls Day School Trust, 100 Rochester Row, London SW1P 1JP. Tel: 0171-393 6666
* Woodard Corporation School
† Boys in VI form
‡ Co-educational
° 1997 figures

Name of School	Foun-ded	No. of pupils	Annual fees £		Head (with date of appointment)
ENGLAND AND WALES			Boarding	Day	
Abbey School, Reading	1887	692	—	4,820	Miss B. C. L. Sheldon (1991)
°Abbot's Hill, Hemel Hempstead	1912	153	11,250	6,645	Mrs K. Lewis (1997)
Adcote School for Girls, Shrewsbury	1907	76	10,710	6,150	Mrs A. E. Read (1997)
Alice Ottley School, Worcester	1883	510	—	5,760	Miss C. Sibbit (1986)
Amberfield School, Ipswich	1952	151	—	4,410	Mrs L. A. Lewis (1992)
Ashford School, Kent	1910	400	12,897	7,422	Mrs J. Burnett (1997)
Atherley School, Southampton (*CSC*)	1926	220	—	4,941	Miss A. Burrows (1997)
Badminton School, Bristol	1858	306	13,425	7,425	Mrs J. A. Scarrow (1997)
Bedford High School	1882	700	10,890	5,832	Mrs B. E. Stanley (1995)
Bedgebury School, Goudhurst, Kent	1860	209	12,570	7,806	Mrs L. J. Griffin (1995)
Beechwood Sacred Heart (*RC*), Tunbridge Wells	1915	180	11,940	7,365	Dr S. Price-Cabrera (1997)
§Belvedere School, Liverpool	1880	469	—	4,356	Mrs G. Richards (1997)
Benenden School, Cranbrook, Kent	1923	450	14,997	—	Mrs G. du Charme (1985)
§Birkenhead High School	1901	640	—	4,356	Mrs C. H. Evans (1997)
§Blackheath High School, London SE3	1880	354	—	5,268	Miss R. K. Musgrave (1989)
Bolton School	1877	786	—	4,998	Miss E. J. Panton (1994)
Bradford Girls' Grammar School	1875	659	—	4,728	Mrs L. J. Warrington (1987)
§Brighton and Hove High School	1876	507	—	4,356	Miss R. A. Woodbridge (1989)
Brigidine School, Windsor	1948	192	—	5,280	Mrs M. B. Cairns (1986)
§Bromley High School, Kent	1883	551	—	5,268	Mrs E. J. Hancock (1989)
Bruton School, Somerset	1900	480	9,450	5,200	Mrs A. Napier (*acting*) (1998)
Burgess Hill School, W. Sussex	1906	350	10,635	6,285	Mrs R. F. Lewis (1992)
Bury Grammar School, Lancs	1884	793	—	4,194	Miss C. H. Thompson (1998)
Casterton School, Carnforth, Lancs	1823	351	10,755	6,840	A. F. Thomas (1990)
§Central Newcastle High School	1895	597	—	4,356	Mrs A. M. Chapman (1985)
°Channing School, London N6	1885	335	—	6,210	Mrs I. R. Raphael (1984)
Cheltenham Ladies' College, Glos	1853	856	15,720	10,080	Mrs A. V. Tuck (*Principal*) (1996)
City of London School for Girls, London EC2	1894	566	—	6,237	Mrs Y. A. Burne, PH.D. (1995)
Clifton High School, Bristol	1877	387	8,565	4,965	Mrs M. C. Culligan (1998)
Cobham Hall, Kent	1962	200	12,750	8,700	Mrs R. J. McCarthy (1989)
Colston's Girls' School, Bristol	1891	453	—	4,285	Mrs J. P. Franklin (1989)
Combe Bank School, Sevenoaks	1868	200	—	6,780	Miss N. Spurr (1993)
Commonweal Lodge School, Purley, Surrey	1916	100	—	5,100	Mrs S. C. Law (*Principal*) (1995)
Cranford House School, Moulsford, Oxon	1931	85	—	5,850	Mrs A. B. Gray (1992)
Croham Hurst School, South Croydon	1899	327	—	5,490	Miss S. C. Budgen (1994)
§Croydon High School	1874	685	—	5,268	Miss L. M. Ogilvie (1998)
Dame Alice Harpur School, Bedford	1882	725	—	5,340	Mrs R. Randle (1990)

Name of School	Founded	No. of pupils	Annual fees £ Boarding	Day	Head (with date of appointment)
Dame Allan's Girls' School, Newcastle upon Tyne	1705	390†	—	4,305	D. W. Welsh (*Principal*) (1995)
°Derby High School for Girls	1892	313	—	4,680	G. H. Goddard, ph.d. (1983)
Downe House, Newbury	1907	581	14,175	10,275	Mrs E. McKendrick (1997)
Dunottar School, Reigate	1926	280	—	5,655	Ms M. J. Skinner (1997)
Durham High School for Girls	1884	259	—	5,739	Mrs A. J. Temploman (1998)
Edgbaston Church of England College, Birmingham	1886	149	—	5,100	Mrs A. Varley-Tipton (1992)
Edgbaston High School for Girls, Birmingham	1876	510	—	4,860	Miss E. Mullenger (1998)
Elmslie Girls' School, Blackpool	1918	150	—	4,620	Miss S. J. Woodward (1997)
Farlington School, Horsham	1896	270	11,040	6,795	Mrs P. M. Mawer (1992)
Farnborough Hill, Hants	1889	500	—	5,499	Miss J. Thomas (1998)
°Farringtons and Stratford House, Chislehurst	1911	300	10,914	5,595	Mrs B. J. Stock (1987)
Francis Holland School, London nw1	1878	380	—	6,345	Mrs G. Low (1998)
Francis Holland School, London sw1	1881	250	—	7,110	Miss S. Pattenden (1997)
Gateways School, Harewood, W. Yorks	1941	185	—	4,698	Mrs D. Davidson (1997)
Godolphin and Latymer School, London w6	1905	703	—	6,630	Miss M. Rudland (1986)
Godolphin School, Salisbury	1726	400	12,480	7,476	Miss M. J. Horsburgh (1996)
Greenacre School, Banstead	1933	228	—	5,625	Mrs P. M. Wood (1990)
Guildford High School (*CSC*)	1888	539	—	5,967	Mrs S. H. Singer (1991)
Haberdashers' Aske's School for Girls, Elstree, Herts	1873	850	—	4,980	Mrs P. Penney (1991)
Haberdashers' Monmouth School	1891	585	9,837	5,223	Dr B. Despontin (1997)
Harrogate Ladies' College	1893	356	10,935	6,900	Dr M. J. Hustler (1996)
Headington School, Oxford	1915	530	11,385	5,940	Mrs H. A. Fender (1996)
Heathfield School, Ascot, Berks	1900	220	14,625	—	Mrs J. M. Benammar (1992)
§Heathfield School, Pinner, Middx	1900	326	—	5,268	Miss C. M. Juett (1997)
Hethersett Old Hall School, Norwich	1928	188	10,800	5,430	Mrs V. M. Redington (1983)
Highclare School, Birmingham	1932	196†	—	4,905	Mrs C. A. Hanson (1974)
Hollygirt School, Nottingham	1877	224	—	4,116	Mrs M. I. Connolly (1997)
Holy Child School, Birmingham	1933	147	—	5,109	Mrs J. M. C. Hill (1995)
Holy Trinity College, Bromley	1886	258	—	4,930	Mrs D. A. Bradshaw (1994)
Holy Trinity School, Kidderminster	1903	173	—	4,260	Mrs E. L. Thomas (1998)
Howell's School, Denbigh	1859	200	10,785	7,485	Mrs S. Gordon (1998)
§Howell's School, Llandaff, Cardiff	1860	561	—	4,356	Mrs C. J. Fitz (1991)
Hull High School (*CSC*)	1890	153	—	4,572	Mrs M. A. Benson (1994)
Hulme Grammar School, Oldham	1895	522	—	4,185	Miss M. S. Smolenski (1992)
§Ipswich High School	1878	448	—	4,356	Miss V. C. MacCuish (1993)
James Allen's Girls' School, London se22	1741	740	—	6,501	Mrs M. O. Gibbs (1994)
Kent College, Tunbridge Wells	1885	244	13,080	7,710	Miss B. J. Crompton (1990)
King Edward VI High School for Girls, Birmingham	1883	550	—	5,034	Ms S. H. Evans (1996)
King's High School for Girls, Warwick	1879	550	—	4,980	Mrs J. M. Anderson (1987)
°Kingsley School, Leamington Spa	1884	460	—	4,725	Mrs Mannion Watson (1997)
Lady Eleanor Holles School, Hampton, Middx	1711	726	—	6,600	Miss E. M. Candy (1981)
°La Retraite School, Salisbury	1953	120	—	4,845	Mrs R. A. Simmons (1994)
La Sagesse Convent High School, Newcastle upon Tyne	1906	340	—	4,728	Miss L. Clark (1994)
Lavant House and Rosemead, Chichester	1919	100	11,490	6,450	Mrs S. E. Watkins (1996)
Leeds Girls' High School	1876	617	—	5,199	Mrs S. Fishburn (1997)
Leicester High School	1906	306	—	4,950	Mrs P. A. Watson (1992)
Loughborough High School	1850	549	—	4,689	Miss J. E. L. Harvatt (1978)
Luckley-Oakfield School, Wokingham	1895	264	10,092	5,805	R. C. Blake (1984)
Malvern Girls' College, Worcs	1893	250	13,800	9,210	Mrs P. Leggate (1996)
Manchester High School	1874	726‡	—	4,590	Mrs C. Lee-Jones (1998)
Manor House School, Little Bookham, Surrey	1927	145	8,940	6,210	Mrs L. Mendes (1989)
Marymount International School, Kingston upon Thames	1955	237	15,550	9,050	Sr R. Sheridan (1990)
Maynard School, Exeter	1877	440	—	5,055	Miss F. Murdin (1980)
Merchant Taylors' School, Liverpool	1888	660	—	4,356	Mrs J. I. Mills (1994)
Moira House School, Eastbourne	1875	210	12,930	8,190	Mrs A. Harris (*Principal*) (1997)
More House School, London sw1	1953	220	—	6,300	Miss M. Connell (1991)
Moreton Hall, Oswestry	1913	260	13,230	9,135	J. Forster (1992)
Mount School, York	1831	280	11,655	7,176	Miss B. J. Windle (1986)
Newcastle upon Tyne Church High School	1885	385	—	4,494	Mrs L. G. Smith (1996)

Name of School	Foun-ded	No. of pupils	Annual fees £		Head (with date of appointment)
			Boarding	Day	
New Hall School, Chelmsford	1642	420	12,240	7,950	Sr Anne-Marie (1996)
Northampton High School	1878	599	—	4,650	Mrs L. A. Mayne (1988)
°North Foreland Lodge, Hook	1909	150	11,550	7,050	Miss S. Cameron (1996)
North London Collegiate School, Edgware	1850	760	—	5,850	Mrs B. McCabe (1997)
Northwood College, Middx	1878	451	—	5,790	Mrs J. A. Mayou (1992)
§Norwich High School	1875	662	—	4,356	Mrs V. C. Bidwell (1985)
Notre Dame Senior School, Cobham, Surrey	1937	300	—	5,325	Sr F. Ede (1987)
§Nottingham High School for Girls	1875	849	—	4,356	Mrs A. C. Rees (1996)
§Notting Hill and Ealing High School, London W13	1873	567	—	5,268	Mrs S. M. Whitfield (1991)
Ockbrook School, Derby	1799	480	8,085	4,380	Miss D. P. Bolland (1995)
Old Palace School, Croydon	1887	600	—	4,950	Miss K. L. Hilton (1974)
§Oxford High School	1875	548	—	4,356	Miss F. Lusk (1997)
Palmers Green High School, London N21	1905	150	—	5,235	Mrs S. Grant (1989)
Parsons Mead, Ashtead, Surrey	1897	199	11,010	6,210	Miss E. B. Plant (1990)
Perse School for Girls, Cambridge	1881	540	—	5,499	Miss H. S. Smith (1989)
*Peterborough High School	1939	180	9,930	4,944	Mrs A. J. V. Storey (1977)
Pipers Corner School, High Wycombe	1930	300	11,010	6,588	Mrs V. M. Stattersfield (1996)
Polam Hall School, Darlington	1848	300	10,240	5,034	Mrs H. C. Hamilton (1987)
§Portsmouth High School	1882	458	—	4,356	Mrs J. M. Dawtrey (1984)
°Princess Helena College, Hitchin, Herts	1820	145	10,935	7,605	Mrs A. M. Hodgkiss (acting) (1997)
°Prior's Field, Godalming	1902	230	10,905	7,290	Mrs J. M. McCallum (1987)
§Putney High School, London SW15	1893	562	—	5,268	Mrs E. Merchant (1991)
Queen Anne's School, Reading	1698	309	13,215	8,655	Mrs D. Forbes (1993)
Queen Ethelburga's College, York	1912	200	12,675	7,725	Mrs E. I. E. Taylor (1997)
Queen Margaret's School, York	1901	365	11,937	7,653	Dr G. A. H. Chapman (1993)
°Queen Mary School, Lytham St Anne's	1930	470	—	4,062	Miss M. C. Ritchie (1981)
Queen's College, London W1	1848	386	—	6,990	Lady Goodhart (1991)
Queen's Gate School, London SW7	1891	240	—	6,000	Mrs A. M. Holyoak (Principal) (1989)
Queen's School, Chester	1878	467	—	4,950	Miss D. M. Skilbeck (1989)
Queenswood, Hatfield, Herts	1894	400	13,425	8,310	Ms C. Farr (Principal) (1996)
Redland High School for Girls, Bristol	1882	483	—	4,665	Mrs C. Lear (1989)
Red Maids' School, Bristol	1634	508	8,520	4,260	Miss S. Hampton (1987)
Roedean School, Brighton	1885	422	14,925	9,720	Mrs P. Metham (1997)
§The Royal High School, Bath	1864	670	11,550	4,356	Miss M. A. Winfield (1985)
Royal Masonic School, Herts	1788	500	9,273	5,643	Mrs I. M. Andrews (1992)
Rye St Antony School (RC), Oxford	1930	330	9,510	5,565	Miss A. M. Jones (1990)
St Albans High School	1889	560	—	5,640	Mrs C. Y. Daly (1994)
St Andrew's School, Bedford	1897	140	—	4,410	Mrs J. M. Mark (1996)
St Anne's School, Windermere	1863	210	10,590	7,380	R. D. Hunter (1996)
St Antony's-Leweston School (RC), Sherborne	1891	250	12,402	8,172	Miss B. A. King (1996)
St Catherine's School, Guildford	1885	481	10,890	6,630	Mrs C. M. Oulton (1994)
St David's School, Ashford, Middx	1716	237†	10,920	6,060	Mrs J. G. Osborne (1985)
St Dunstan's Abbey School, Plymouth	1850	170	9,960	5,580	Mrs B. K. Brown (1998)
St Elphin's School, Matlock	1844	150	11,115	6,474	Mrs V. E. Fisher (1994)
St Felix School, Southwold, Suffolk	1897	170	11,550	7,650	R. Williams (1998)
St Francis' College (RC), Letchworth	1933	180	11,535	5,925	Miss M. Hegarty (1993)
St Gabriel's School, Newbury	1929	150	—	5,736	D. J. Cobb (1990)
St George's School, Ascot, Berks	1923	280	13,350	8,550	Mrs A. M. Griggs (1989)
School of St Helen and St Katharine, Abingdon	1903	545	—	5,235	Mrs C. L. Hall (1993)
St Helen's School, Northwood, Middx	1899	630	10,656	5,665	Mrs D. M. Jefkins (1995)
*St Hilary's School, Alderley Edge	1880	100	—	4,635	Ms P. Bristow (1997)
St James' and the Abbey, West Malvern	1896	150	12,366	7,722	Mrs S. Kershaw (1998)
°St Joseph's Convent School (RC), Reading	1909	378	—	4,350	Mrs V. Brookes (1990)
St Leonards-Mayfield School, Mayfield	1850	500	12,213	8,142	Sr J. Sinclair (1980)
St Margaret's School, Bushey, Herts	1749	350	10,695	6,405	Miss M. de Villiers (1992)
*St Margaret's School, Exeter	1904	375	—	4,764	Mrs M. D'Albertanson (1993)
St Martin's School, Solihull	1941	245	—	5,025	Mrs S. J. Williams (1988)
*School of S. Mary and S. Anne, Abbots Bromley, Staffs	1874	219	12,180	8,136	Mrs M. Steel (1998)
St Mary's Convent School, Worcester	1934	200	—	4,230	C. Garner (1997)
St Mary's Hall, Brighton	1836	242	10,215	6,675	Mrs S. M. Meek (1997)
St Mary's School (RC), Ascot, Berks	1885	353	13,440	8,730	Mrs M. Breen (1998)

Name of School	Foun-ded	No. of pupils	Annual fees £ Boarding	Day	Head (with date of appointment)
St Mary's School, Calne, Wilts	1872	300	13,620	8,370	Mrs C. Shaw (1996)
St Mary's School, Cambridge	1898	450	8,745	4,890	Mrs G. Piotrowska (1998)
St Mary's School, Colchester	1908	210	—	4,380	Mrs G. M. G. Mouser (1981)
St Mary's School, Gerrards Cross	1872	140	—	5,900	Mrs F. Balcombe (1995)
St Mary's School (RC), Shaftesbury	1945	262	11,340	7,350	Mrs S. Pennington (1998)
St Mary's School, Wantage, Oxon	1873	210	13,035	8,690	Mrs S. Bodinham (1994)
°St Maur's Senior School, Weybridge	1898	372	—	4,800	Mrs M. E. Dodds (1991)
St Nicholas' School, Fleet, Hants	1935	161	—	4,950	Mrs A. V. Whatmough (1995)
St Paul's Girls' School, London w6	1904	658	—	7,377	Miss E. Diggory (High Mistress) (1998)
St Swithun's School, Winchester	1884	465	12,795	7,740	Dr H. Harvey (1995)
St Teresa's School, Dorking	1928	350	11,700	6,450	Mrs M. E. Prescott (1997)
§Sheffield High School	1878	597	—	4,356	Mrs M. A. Houston (1989)
Sherborne School for Girls, Dorset	1899	420	13,950	9,780	Miss J. M. Taylor (1985)
§Shrewsbury High School	1885	353	—	4,356	Miss S. Gardner (1990)
Sir William Perkins's School, Chertsey, Surrey	1725	580	—	4,950	Miss S. Ross (1994)
§South Hampstead High School, London nw3	1876	608	—	5,268	Mrs J. G. Scott (1993)
Stonar School, Melksham, Wilts	1921	340	10,722	5,955	Mrs C. Homan (1997)
Stover School, Newton Abbot	1932	200	9,885	5,085	P. E. Bujak (1994)
§Streatham Hill and Clapham High School, London sw2	1887	419	—	5,268	Miss G. M. Ellis (1979)
°Surbiton High School, Kingston-upon-Thames (CSC)	1884	612	—	5,115	Miss M. G. Perry (1993)
§Sutton High School, Surrey	1884	500	—	5,268	Mrs A. J. Coutts (1995)
§Sydenham High School, London se26	1887	473	—	5,268	Mrs G. Baker (1988)
Talbot Heath, Bournemouth	1886	431	10,050	5,790	Mrs C. Dipple (1991)
Teesside High School, Stockton-on-Tees	1970	360	—	4,620	Miss J. F. Hamilton (1995)
Tormead School, Guildford	1905	427	—	5,985	Mrs H. E. M. Alleyne (1992)
Truro High School	1880	355	9,285	5,025	J. Graham-Brown (1992)
Tudor Hall School, Banbury	1850	262	11,955	7,455	Miss N. Godfrey (1984)
Wakefield Girls' High School	1878	720†	—	5,001	Mrs P. A. Langham (1987)
Walthamstow Hall, Sevenoaks	1838	260	13,500	7,290	Mrs J. S. Lang (1984)
Wentworth College, Bournemouth	1871	250	10,140	6,360	Miss S. D. Coe (1990)
Westfield School, Newcastle upon Tyne	1962	224	—	4,797	Mrs M. Farndale (1990)
Westholme School, Blackburn	1923	705	—	4,080	Mrs L. Croston (Principal) (1988)
Westonbirt School, Tetbury, Glos	1928	200	12,828	8,430	Mrs G. Hylson-Smith (1986)
§Wimbledon High School, London sw19	1880	586	—	5,268	Dr J. L. Clough (1995)
Wispers School, Haslemere, Surrey	1946	107	10,860	6,990	L. H. Beltran (1980)
Withington Girls' School, Manchester	1890	530	—	4,425	Mrs M. Kenyon (1986)
Woldingham School, Surrey	1842	550	13,431	7,124	Mrs M. M. Ribbins (1997)
Wychwood School, Oxford	1897	150	8,040	5,070	Mrs S. Wingfield Digby (1997)
Wycombe Abbey School, High Wycombe	1896	522	14,250	10,689	Mrs P. E. Davies (1998)
Wykeham House School, Fareham, Hants	1913	160	—	4,554	Mrs R. M. Kamaryc (1995)

SCOTLAND

Kilgraston School, Bridge of Earn, Perth	1930	190	10,965	6,750	Mrs J. L. Austin (1993)
Laurel Park School, Glasgow	1996	357	—	4,653	Mrs E. Surber (1995)
Mary Erskine School, Edinburgh	1694	692	9,810	5,091	P. F. J. Tobin (Principal) (1989)
St George's School, Edinburgh	1888	550	10,185	5,220	Dr J. McClure (1994)
St Leonards School, St Andrews	1877	255‡	13,110	6,930	Mrs M. James (1988)
St Margaret's School, Aberdeen	1846	206	—	4,536	Miss A. C. Ritchie (1998)
St Margaret's School and St Denis and Cranley, Edinburgh	1890	385	9,675	4,755	Miss A. Mitchell (1994)

CHANNEL ISLANDS

°The Ladies' College, Guernsey	1872	350	—	2,340	Miss M. E. Macdonald (Principal) (1992)

Health

SELECTED CAUSES OF DEATH, BY GENDER AND AGE 1996 (United Kingdom)
Percentages and number

	Under 1*	1–14	15–24	25–34	35–54	55–64	65–74	75 and over	All ages
Males									
Circulatory diseases	4	5	4	9	33	43	45	45	42
Cancer	1	16	7	10	28	37	33	22	27
Respiratory diseases	10	7	4	5	5	7	12	20	15
Injury and poisoning	4	30	63	51	15	3	1	1	4
Infectious diseases	7	8	2	5	3	1	—	—	1
Other causes	73	34	19	20	16	9	8	11	11
All males (number)	2,600	1,100	2,800	4,700	22,600	35,100	81,700	155,900	306,500
Females									
Circulatory diseases	6	6	7	12	18	29	39	47	43
Cancer	1	18	17	26	52	48	36	15	23
Respiratory diseases	9	7	5	6	5	9	13	19	16
Injury and poisoning	6	23	43	28	8	2	1	1	2
Infectious diseases	6	8	4	5	1	1	1	—	1
Other causes	73	37	24	24	16	12	11	16	15
All females (number)	1,900	800	1,100	2,200	14,500	21,500	58,200	232,300	332,400

* Excluding deaths at ages under 28 days
Source: The Stationery Office – *Social Trends 28*

NOTIFICATIONS OF INFECTIOUS DISEASES (UK) 1996

Measles	6,865
Mumps	2,182
Rubella	11,720
Whooping cough	2,721
Scarlet fever	6,101
Dysentery	2,641
Food poisoning	89,741
Typhoid and paratyphoid fevers	291
Hepatitis	2,876
Tuberculosis	6,238
Malaria	1,739

Source: The Stationery Office – *Annual Abstract of Statistics 1998*

HIV/AIDS AND SEXUALLY TRANSMITTED DISEASES (ENGLAND)

	1985	1995
HIV cases diagnosed	2,528	2,225
Exposure category		
Homosexual intercourse	67%	57%
Heterosexual intercourse	2%	32%
Injecting drug use	4%	6%
Blood products	24%	1%
Aids cases diagnosed	236	1,524
Sexually transmitted diseases (new cases)		
All, except HIV/Aids	—	404,600
Syphilis	2,400	1,400
Gonorrhoea	46,300	12,400
Chlamydia	—	39,300
Herpes	18,900	27,100
Wart virus	52,200	93,300

Source: The Stationery Office – *Health and Personal Social Services Statistics for England 1997*

PREVALENCE OF SMOKING CIGARETTES (ENGLAND)
Percentages among adults aged 16 and over, by sex

	1986	1996
Males		
Current smoker	34	28
Ex-regular smoker	33	32
Never smoked	33	40
Females		
Current smoker	31	27
Ex-regular smoker	18	20
Never smoked	51	53

Source: The Stationery Office – *Health and Personal Social Services Statistics for England 1997*

ALCOHOL CONSUMPTION - UNITS PER WEEK (ENGLAND) 1996
Percentage

Men	
Non-drinker	7
Under one	7
1–10	31
11–21	24
22–35	17
36–50	7
51 and over	7
Women	
Non-drinker	10
Under one	17
1–10	39
11–21	17
22–35	11
36–50	3
51 and over	3

Source: The Stationery Office – *Health in England 1996*

PEOPLE WHO HAVE EVER TAKEN DRUGS (ENGLAND AND WALES) 1996 *by type of drug and age*
Percentage

Age	16–19	20–24	25–34	35–44	45–59	All aged 16–59
Cannabis	35	42	30	23	8	22
Amphetamines	16	21	11	7	3	9
LSD	10	15	6	4	1	5
Magic mushroom	7	12	8	4	1	5
Ecstasy	9	13	4	1	1	3
Cocaine	2	6	4	3	1	3
Solvents	5	7	3	1	—	2
Crack	1	2	1	1	—	1
Heroin	1	1	1	1	—	1
Any drug	45	49	37	29	13	29

Source: The Stationery Office - *Social Trends 28*

HEALTH IN ENGLAND
A report, *Health in England 1996*, was published by the Health Education Authority and the Office for National Statistics in May 1997. It included the following main findings:
- 31 per cent of men and 29 per cent of women were cigarette smokers
- the mean alcohol consumption was 18.0 units a week for men and 7.7 units a week for women
- 25 per cent of respondents were sedentary
- 38 per cent of men and 26 per cent of women had taken drugs not prescribed by their doctor or bought from the chemist
- 16 per cent of men and 10 per cent of women aged 16–54 had had two or more sexual partners in the previous year

- 80 per cent of men and 78 per cent of women said that their general health was 'very good' or 'good'
- 62 per cent of men and 69 per cent of women had experienced a 'moderate' or 'large' amount of stress in the previous year
- 60 per cent of men and 73 per cent of women had visited their GP in the previous year

HEALTH OF THE NATION TARGETS
The Government in 1992 published a White Paper, *The Health of the Nation*, identifying five key health areas in England (coronary heart disease and stroke, cancers, mental illness, HIV/Aids and sexual health, and accidents) where improvements were deemed to be most necessary. It also identified risk factors associated with the five key areas (including smoking, alcohol, diet and nutrition, obesity and blood pressure). The White Paper set 27 targets, including the following:
- a reduction of 40 per cent in the number of deaths from coronary heart disease and strokes among people under 65 by 2000
- a reduction of 30 per cent in the number of deaths from lung cancer among men and of 15 per cent among women by 2010
- a reduction of 25 per cent in the number of deaths from breast cancer by 2000
- a reduction of 20 per cent in the number of deaths from cervical cancer by 2000
- a reduction of 15 per cent in the number of deaths from suicide by 2000
- a reduction of one third in the number of fatal accidents among children and people over 64 by 2005
- a reduction of 50 per cent in conceptions among girls under 16 by 2000

CONSUMPTION OF FOODS CONTAINING FIBRE AND STARCHY CARBOHYDRATES (ENGLAND) 1996 *by age and sex*
Percentage consuming each food

Age	16–24	25–34	35–44	45–54	55–64	65–74	Total
Men							
Eats wholemeal bread	7	14	16	21	23	22	17
Eats bread daily	83	77	87	84	89	92	84
Eats fruit, vegetables and salad daily	43	51	56	69	72	73	59
Eats potatoes, pasta or rice daily	35	51	55	56	63	66	53
Eats bread; fruit, vegetables and salad; and potatoes, pasta or rice daily	19	31	34	41	45	51	36
Women							
Eats wholemeal bread	16	23	24	30	29	34	25
Eats bread daily	76	75	79	83	83	93	81
Eats fruit, vegetables and salad daily	57	60	74	81	86	83	72
Eats potatoes, pasta or rice daily	44	51	55	62	67	64	56
Eats bread; fruit, vegetables and salad; and potatoes, pasta or rice daily	24	32	38	45	53	53	40

Source: The Stationery Office – *Health in England 1996*

FREQUENCY OF AT LEAST MODERATE-INTENSITY EXERCISE FOR 30 MINUTES OR MORE *by age and sex*
Percentages

Age	16–24	25–34	35–44	45–54	55–64	65–74	Total
Men							
Less than one day a week	9	19	20	26	38	42	24
1–2 days a week	21	20	25	25	23	29	23
3–4 days a week	14	12	12	11	7	14	12
5 or more days a week	56	48	43	39	32	14	41
Women							
Less than one day a week	20	18	19	22	37	46	26
1–2 days a week	29	27	33	28	33	28	30
3–4 days a week	18	15	14	14	9	11	14
5 or more days a week	32	39	34	35	21	14	31

Source: The Stationery Office – *Health in England 1996*

- a reduction of one third in the number of smokers and of 40 per cent in the number of cigarettes sold by 2000
- a reduction of 25 per cent in obesity levels among men and of one third among women by 2005
- a reduction of 30 per cent in the number of people drinking to excess by 2005
- a reduction in the incidence of drug misuse

Annual reports have been published to document progress towards these targets. Some of the targets have been met ahead of schedule, others are on course to be achieved, and others (in particular those relating to obesity and teenage smoking) are currently showing increases rather than reductions.

Similar initiatives were undertaken in Scotland, Wales and Northern Ireland. A policy document, *Scotland's Health: A Challenge to Us All,* published in 1992, included the following main targets:
- a reduction of 40 per cent in the number of deaths from coronary heart disease among people under 65 by 2000
- a reduction of 15 per cent in the number of deaths from cancer by 2000

New Health Strategy

In February 1997 the Government published a Green Paper, *Our Healthier Nation,* which identified four main areas of illness in England (heart disease and stroke, accidents, cancer and mental health) to be improved, and replaced the targets in *The Health of the Nation* with four main targets:
- a reduction in the number of deaths from coronary heart disease and strokes by one third by 2010
- a reduction in the number of deaths from cancer by one fifth by 2010
- a reduction in the number of deaths by suicide by one sixth by 2010
- a reduction in the number of deaths from accidents by one fifth by 2010

Similar reviews are being undertaken in Scotland, Wales and Northern Ireland. A Green Paper, *Working Together for a Healthier Scotland,* was published in February 1998; it invited comments on whether current targets should be revised and/or new targets set. A definitive public health strategy was to be published by the Government in summer 1998.

Health Education

Health education in the UK is the responsibility of the Health Education Authority, Health Promotion Wales, the Health Education Board for Scotland and the Health Promotion Agency for Northern Ireland (*see* page 480). The role of the four authorities is to provide health information and advice to the public, health professionals, and other organizations, and to advise the Government on health education.

Social Welfare

National Health Service

The National Health Service (NHS) came into being on 5 July 1948 under the National Health Service Act 1946, covering England and Wales, and under separate legislation for Scotland and Northern Ireland. The NHS is administered in England by the Secretary of State for Health, and in Wales, Scotland and Northern Ireland by the respective Secretaries of State. During 1999, responsibility for administering the NHS will transfer from the Secretaries of State for Scotland, Wales and Northern Ireland to the Scottish parliament, Welsh assembly and New Northern Ireland Assembly.

The function of the NHS is to provide a comprehensive health service designed to secure improvement in the physical and mental health of the people and to prevent, diagnose and treat illness. It was founded on the principle that treatment should be provided according to clinical need rather than ability to pay, and should be free at the point of delivery. However, prescription charges were provided for by legislation in 1949 and implemented in 1952, and charges for some dental and ophthalmic treatment have also been introduced.

The NHS covers a comprehensive range of hospital, specialist, family practitioner (medical, dental, ophthalmic and pharmaceutical), artificial limb and appliance, ambulance, and community health services. Everyone normally resident in the UK is entitled to use any of these services.

STRUCTURE

The structure of the NHS remained relatively stable for the first 30 years of its existence. In 1974, a three-tier management structure comprising Regional Health Authorities, Area Health Authorities and District Management Teams was introduced in England, and the NHS became responsible for community health services. In 1979 Area Health Authorities were abolished and District Management Teams were replaced by District Health Authorities.

THE INTERNAL MARKET

The National Health Service and Community Care Act 1990 provided for more streamlined Regional Health Authorities and District Health Authorities, and for the establishment of Family Health Services Authorities (FHSAs) and NHS Trusts. The concept of the 'internal market' was introduced into health care, whereby care was provided through NHS contracts where health authorities or boards and GP fundholders (the purchasers) were responsible for buying health care from hospitals, nonfundholding GPs, community services and ambulance services (the providers).

The Act provided for the establishment of NHS Trusts. Trusts operate as self-governing health care providers independent of health authority control and responsible to the Secretary of State. They derive their income principally from contracts to provide services to health authorities and fund-holding GPs. In Northern Ireland, 20 health and social services trusts are responsible for providing health and social services in an organizational model unique to Northern Ireland.

The Act also paved the way for the Community Care reforms, which were introduced in April 1993 and changed in the way care is administered for elderly people, the mentally ill, the physically handicapped and people with learning disabilities.

The eight Regional Health Authorities in England were abolished in April 1996 and replaced by eight regional offices which, together with the headquarters in Leeds, form the NHS Executive. The regional offices are part of the Department of Health, and their functions include financial and performance monitoring of local purchasers and providers, public health, regional research and development, and education programmes.

In April 1996 the District Health Authorities and Family Health Service Authorities were merged to form 100 unified Health Authorities (HAs) in England. The HAs are responsible for health and health services in their areas. They are also responsible for assessing the health care needs of the local population and developing integrated strategies for meeting these needs in partnership with GPs and in consultation with the public, hospitals and others. HAs' resources are allocated by the NHS Executive headquarters, to which they are also accountable for their performance. HA chairmen are appointed by the Health Secretary and non-executive members by the regional offices of the NHS Executive.

In Wales the chairman and non-executive members of the five HAs which replaced the former 17 HAs and FHSAs in April 1996 are appointed by the Welsh Secretary. The Welsh Health Common Services Authority provides a range of specialist services to the NHS in Wales. In Scotland there are 15 Health Boards with similar responsibilities to those of HAs, and in Northern Ireland there are four Health and Social Services Boards.

There are also Community Health Councils (called Local Health Councils in Scotland and Health and Social Services Councils in Northern Ireland) throughout the UK; their role is to represent the interests of the public to health authorities and boards. The Government announced in March 1998 that public consultation and patient representation in the NHS would be increased.

PROPOSED REFORMS

In December 1997 the Government published a White Paper, *The New NHS*, outlining plans for replacing the NHS internal market in England and establishing teams of GPs and community nurses to work together in primary care groups, with long-term service agreements replacing annual contracts between health authorities, primary care groups and NHS Trusts. The White Paper also proposed to create a National Institute of Clinical Excellence to produce new national guidelines, National Service Frameworks to guarantee consistency in access and quality of care, and a Commission for Health Improvement to promote best practice. Other White Papers, *Putting Patients First* and *Designed to Care*, covered similar plans for reforming the NHS in Wales and Scotland respectively. The reforms should be in place in late 1999 or 2000, subject to the passage of legislation through Parliament. For details, *see* White Papers section.

FINANCE

The NHS is still funded mainly (81.5 per cent) through general taxation, although in recent years more reliance has been placed on the NHS element of National Insurance contributions, patient charges and other sources of income. Total UK expenditure on the NHS in 1997–8 was £44,719 million, of which £42,787 million was from public monies and £1,932 million from patient charges and other receipts. NHS expenditure represented 5.7 per cent of GDP. The total cost per head was £758. The planned expenditure for 1998–9 is £46,844 million. The Government announced in July 1998 that an additional £21,000 million would be spent on the NHS between 1999 and 2002.

ENGLAND

NATIONAL HEALTH CURRENT EXPENDITURE 1996–7

	£ million
National Health Service:	
Hospitals, Community Health Services and Family Health Services	39,425
Departmental administration	265
Other central services	3,124
Less payments by patients	865
TOTAL	41,949

PERSONAL SOCIAL SERVICES CURRENT EXPENDITURE 1996–7

	£ million
Central government	101
Local authorities running expenses	9,996
Capital expenditure	221
TOTAL	10,318

Source: The Stationery Office – *Annual Abstract of Statistics 1998*

WALES

CENTRAL GOVERNMENT EXPENDITURE 1996–7

	£ thousand
Hospital, community health and family health services	1,769,500
NHS Trusts	46,600
General medical	122,800
Pharmaceutical	206,400
General dental	72,300
General ophthalmic	17,200
Other	100
TOTAL	2,234,900

Source: Welsh Office Departmental Report 1998

SCOTLAND

NET COSTS OF THE NATIONAL HEALTH SERVICE 1995–6

	£ thousand
Central administration	7,651
Total NHS cost	4,384,174
NHS contributions	452,536
Net costs to Exchequer	3,931,638
Health Board administration	95,274
Hospital and community health services	3,160,044
Family practitioner services	914,012
Central health services	145,943
State hospital	21,563
Training	3,243
Research	10,234
Disabled services	2,247
Welfare foods	14,434
Miscellaneous health services	17,180
TOTAL	4,391,825

Source: Scottish Office – *Annual Abstract of Statistics 1996*

ORGANIZATIONS

HEALTH AUTHORITIES (ENGLAND)

There are 100 health authorities in England. For details, contact the relevant NHS Executive regional office (*see* below).

NHS EXECUTIVE REGIONAL OFFICES

ANGLIA AND OXFORD, 6–12 Capital Drive, Linford Wood, Milton Keynes MK14 6QP. Tel: 01908-844400. *Chairman*, Mrs R. Varley; *Regional Director*, Ms B. Stocking

NORTHERN AND YORKSHIRE, John Snow House, Durham University Science Park, Durham DH1 3YG. Tel: 0191-301 1300. *Chairman*, Mrs Z. Manzoor; *Regional Director*, Prof. L. Donaldson

NORTH THAMES, 40 Eastbourne Terrace, London W2 3QR. Tel: 0171-725 5300. *Chairman*, I. Mills; *Regional Director*, R. Kerr

NORTH WEST, 930–932 Birchwood Boulevard, Millennium Park, Birchwood, Warrington WA3 7QN. Tel: 01925-704000. *Chairman*, Prof. A. Breckenridge; *Regional Director*, R. Tinston

SOUTH AND WEST, Westward House, Lime Kiln Close, Stoke Gifford, Bristol BS34 8SR. Tel: 0117-984 1750. *Chairman*, Miss J. Trotter, OBE; *Regional Director*, A. Laurance

SOUTH THAMES, 40 Eastbourne Terrace, London W2 3QR. Tel: 0171-725 2500. *Chairman*, Sir William Wells; *Regional Director*, N. Crisp

TRENT, Fulwood House, Old Fulwood Road, Sheffield S10 3TH. Tel: 0114-263 0300. *Chairman*, P. Hammersley; *Regional Director*, N. McKay

WEST MIDLANDS, Bartholomew House, 142 Hagley Road, Birmingham B16 9PA. Tel: 0121-224 4600. *Chairman*, C. Wilkinson; *Regional Director*, S. Day

In April 1999 four of the regional offices will be replaced. North and South Thames will be replaced by London and South-East Regions; Anglia and Oxford by Eastern Region; and South and West by South-West Region. The new regional offices will operate from the addresses of their predecessors.

HEALTH BOARDS (SCOTLAND)

ARGYLL AND CLYDE, Ross House, Hawkhead Road, Paisley PA2 7BN. Tel: 0141-842 7200. *Chairman*, M. D. Jones; *General Manager*, N. McConachie

AYRSHIRE AND ARRAN, PO Box 13, Boswell House, 10 Arthur Street, Ayr KA7 1QJ. Tel: 01292-611040. *Chairman*, Dr J. Morrow; *General Manager*, Mrs W. Hatton

BORDERS, Newstead, Melrose, Roxburghshire TD9 0SE. Tel: 01896-822727. *Chairman*, D. A. C. Kilshaw; *General Manager*, L. Burley

DUMFRIES AND GALLOWAY, Grierson House, Crichton Royal Hospital, Bankend Road, Dumfries DG1 4ZH. Tel: 01387-272700. *Chairman*, J. Ross; *General Manager*, N. Campbell

FIFE, Springfield House, Cupar KY15 9UP. Tel: 01334-656200. *Chairman*, Mrs C. Stenhouse; *General Manager*, Miss P. Frost

FORTH VALLEY, 33 Spittal Street, Stirling FK8 1DX. Tel: 01786-463031. *Chairman*, E. Bell-Scott; *General Manager*, D. Hird

GRAMPIAN, Summerfield House, 2 Eday Road, Aberdeen AB15 6RE. Tel: 01224-663456. *Chairman*, Dr C. MacLeod, CBE; *General Manager*, F. E. L. Hartnett, OBE

GREATER GLASGOW, Dalian House, PO Box 15329, 350 St Vincent Street, Glasgow G3 8YZ. Tel: 0141-201 4444. *Chairman*, Prof. D. Hamblen; *Chief Executive*, C. J. Spry

480   Social Welfare

HIGHLAND, Beechwood Park, Inverness IV2 3HG. Tel:
01463-704800. *Chairman*, Mrs C. Thomson; *General
Manager*, Dr G. V. Stone
LANARKSHIRE, 14 Beckford Street, Hamilton, Lanarkshire
ML3 0TA. Tel: 01698-281313. *Chairman*,
I. Livingstone, CBE; *General Manager*, Prof. T. A. Divers
LOTHIAN, 148 Pleasance, Edinburgh EH8 9RS. Tel: 0131-
536 9000. *Chairman*, Mrs M. Ford; *General Manager*, T.
Jones
ORKNEY, Garden House, New Scapa Road, Kirkwall,
Orkney KW15 1BQ. Tel: 01856-885400. *Chairman*,
J. Leslie; *General Manager (acting)*, E. Iseec
SHETLAND, Brevik House, South Road, Lerwick ZE1 0RB.
Tel: 01595-696767. *Chairman*, J. Telford; *General
Manager*, B. J. Atherton
TAYSIDE, Gateway House, Luna Place, Dundee
Technology Park, Dundee DD2 1TP. Tel: 01382-561818.
Chairman, Mrs F. Havenga; *General Manager*, T. Rett
WESTERN ISLES, 37 South Beach Street, Stornoway, Isle of
Lewis HS1 2BN. Tel: 01851-702997. *Chairman*,
A. Matheson; *General Manager*, B. Skilbeck

HEALTH AUTHORITIES (WALES)

BRO TAF, Churchill House, Churchill Way, Cardiff CF1
4TW. Tel: 01222-226216. *Chairman*, Mrs K. Thomas;
Chief Executive, Dr G. Todd
DYFED POWYS, St David's Hospital, Carmarthen SA31 3HB.
Tel: 01267-225225. *Chairman*, Ms M. Price; *Chief
Executive*, P. Stansbie
GWENT, Mamhilad House, Mamhilad, Pontypool NP4 0YP.
Tel: 01495-765065. *Chairman*, Mrs F. Peel; *Chief
Executive*, G. Coomber
MORGANNWG, 41 High Street, Swansea SA1 1LT. Tel:
01792-458066. *Chairman*, D. H. Thomas; *Chief Executive*,
Mrs J. Williams
NORTH WALES, Preswylfa, Hendy Road, Mold CH7 1PZ.
Tel: 01352-700227. *Chairman (acting)*, Mrs A. Roberts;
Chief Executive, B. Jones
WELSH HEALTH COMMON SERVICES AUTHORITY,
Crickhowell House, Pierhead Street, Capital Waterside,
Cardiff CF1 5XT. Tel: 01222-500500. Chairman, T. Rees;
Chief Executive, N. Kirk

NORTHERN IRELAND HEALTH AND
SOCIAL SERVICES BOARDS

EASTERN, Champion House, 12-22 Linenhall Street,
Belfast BT2 BS. Tel: 01232-321313
NORTHERN, County Hall, 182 Galgorm Road, Ballymena
BT42 1QB. Tel: 01266-653333
SOUTHERN, Tower Hill, Armagh BT61 9DR. Tel: 01861-
410041
WESTERN, 15 Gransha Park, Clooney Road, Londonderry
BT47 6TG. Tel: 01504-860086

HEALTH PROMOTION AUTHORITIES

HEALTH EDUCATION AUTHORITY, Trevelyan House, 30
Great Peter Street, London SW1P 2HW. Tel: 0171-222
5300. *Chairman*, vacant; *Chief Executive*, S. Fortescue
HEALTH PROMOTION WALES, Ffynnon-las, Ty Glas
Avenue, Llanishen, Cardiff CF4 5DZ. Tel: 01222-752222.
Chairman, J. I. Davies; *Chief Executive*, M. Ponton
HEALTH EDUCATION BOARD FOR SCOTLAND, Woodburn
House, Canaan Lane, Edinburgh EH10 4SG. Tel 0131-536
5500. *Chairman*, D. Campbell; *Chief Executive*,
Prof. A. Tannahill
HEALTH PROMOTION AGENCY FOR NORTHERN IRELAND,
18 Ormeau Avenue, Belfast BT2 8HS. Tel: 01232-311611

EMPLOYEES AND SALARIES

EMPLOYEES

HEALTH AND PERSONAL SOCIAL SERVICES WORKFORCE
(*Great Britain*) *as at 30 September 1996*

General medical practitioners	*34,421
General dental practitioners	19,147
Ophthalmic medical practitioners	†766
Ophthalmic opticians	†7,652
Medical staff	62,176
Dental staff	3,127
Nursing and midwifery staff	356,109
Professional and technical staff	105,496
Administrative and clerical staff	178,461
Health care assistants and support staff	93,901
Ambulance staff	16,330
Other Health Service staff	6,834
‡Personal social services staff	233,655

*1994 figure
†Figures for England and Wales relate to 31 December 1996. Figures for
Scotland relate to 31 March 1997. Those with contracts with more than
one authority/board will be counted more than once.
‡England only
Source: The Stationery Office – *Annual Abstract of Statistics 1998*

SALARIES *as at 1 December 1998*

General Practitioners (GPs), dentists, optometrists and
pharmacists are self-employed, and are employed by the
NHS under contract. GPs are paid for their NHS work in
accordance with a scheme of remuneration which includes
a basic practice allowance, capitation fees, reimbursement
of certain practice expenses and payments for out-of-hours
work. Dentists receive payment for items of treatment for
individual adult patients and, in addition, a continuing care
payment for those registered with them. Optometrists
receive approved fees for each sight test they carry out.
Pharmacists receive professional fees from the NHS and
are refunded the cost of prescriptions supplied.

Consultant	£45,740–£59,040
Specialist Registrar	£22,510–£32,830
Registrar	£22,510–£27,310
Senior House Officer	£20,135–£26,910
House Officer	£16,145–£18,225
GP	*£49,030
Nursing Grades G–I	
(Senior Ward Sister)	£19,240–£26,965
Nursing Grade F (Ward Sister)	£16,310–£19,985
Nursing Grade E (Senior Staff Nurse)	£14,705–£17,030
Nursing Grades C–D	
(Staff/Enrolled Nurse)	£11,210–£14,705
Nursing Grades A–B (Nursing Auxiliary)	£8,315–£11,210

* average intended net remuneration

HEALTH SERVICES

PRIMARY AND COMMUNITY HEALTH
CARE SERVICES
Primary and community health care services comprise the
family health services (i.e. the general medical, personal
medical, pharmaceutical, dental, and ophthalmic services)
and community services (including preventive activities
such as vaccination, immunization and fluoridation)
commissioned by HAs and provided by NHS Trusts,
health centres and clinics.

The primary and community nursing services include practice nurses based in general practice, district nurses and health visitors, community psychiatric nursing for mentally ill people living outside hospital, and school nursing for the health surveillance of schoolchildren of all ages. Ante- and post-natal care are also an integral part of the primary health care service.

FAMILY DOCTOR SERVICE

In England and Wales the Family Doctor Service (or General Medical Service) is now the responsibility of the HAs.

Any doctor may take part in the Family Doctor Service (provided the area in which he/she wishes to practise has not already an adequate number of doctors) and about 29,000 GPs in England and Wales do so. The distribution of GPs is controlled by the Medical Practices Committee, a statutory body. The average number of patients on a doctor's list in 1997 was:

England	1,878
Wales	1,706
Scotland	1,478

GPs may also have private fee-paying patients.

The National Health Service and Community Care Act 1990 allowed GP practices to apply for fundholding status, under which the practice is responsible for its own NHS budget for a specified range of goods and services. Since April 1996 there have been three types of GP fundholding: total purchasing (a pilot scheme), under which GPs purchase all hospital and community health services for their patients; standard fundholders, for practices with at least 5,000 patients, who purchase a wide range of in- and out-patient services; and community fundholders, who purchase only community nursing services, drugs and diagnostic tests. There are currently 3,481 fundholding units, comprising 4,243 practices and representing more than 50 per cent of GPs. The Government plans to replace the fundholding system by allowing the new primary care groups to assume one of four levels of responsibility, including managing a single unified budget for health care in their area. Around 480 primary care groups were established in shadow form in August 1998. In April 1999 they will become fully operational and all practices will be represented within a primary care group. A board consisting of GPs, nurses, a social services officer, a health authority representative and a local member of the public will administer each group.

Everyone aged 16 or over can choose their doctor (parents or guardians choose for children under 16); the doctor is free to accept a person or not. Should a patient have difficulty in registering with a doctor, HAs have powers to assign the patient to a GP. A person may change their doctor if they wish, by going to the surgery of a GP of their choice who is willing to accept them, and either handing in their medical card to register or filling in a form. When people are away from home they can still use the Family Doctor Service if they ask to be treated as temporary residents, and in an emergency, any doctor in the service will give treatment and advice.

PHARMACEUTICAL SERVICE

Patients may obtain medicines, appliances and oral contraceptives prescribed under the NHS from any pharmacy whose owner has entered into arrangements with the HA to provide this service; the number of these pharmacies in England and Wales in March 1998 was about 10,500. There are also some appliance suppliers who only provide special appliances. In rural areas, where access to a pharmacy may be difficult, patients may be able to obtain medicines, etc., from their doctor.

Except for contraceptives (for which there is no charge), a charge of £5.80 is payable for each item supplied unless the patient is exempt and the declaration on the back of the prescription form is completed. Prepayment certificates (£30.10 valid for four months, £82.70 valid for a year) may be purchased by those patients not entitled to exemption who require frequent prescriptions.

The following people are exempt from prescription charges:
– children under 16
– full-time students under 19
– men and women aged 60 and over
– pregnant women who hold an exemption certificate
– women who have had a baby in the last 12 months and who hold an exemption certificate
– people suffering from certain medical conditions who hold an exemption certificate
– people who receive income support, family credit, disability working allowance or income-based jobseeker's allowance, and their partners
– people who are named on an HC2 certificate issued by the Health Benefits Division
– war pensioners (for their accepted disablements)

Booklet HC11, available from main post offices and local social security offices, gives further details.

The number of prescriptions dispensed in the community in 1997 was:

England	500,200,000
Wales	38,500,000
Scotland	57,200,000

DENTAL SERVICE

Dentists, like doctors, may take part in the NHS and also have private patients. About 16,000 dentists in England provide NHS general dental services. They are responsible to the HAs in whose areas they provide services.

Patients may go to any dentist who is taking part in the NHS and is willing to accept them. Patients are required to pay 80 per cent of the cost of NHS dental treatment. Since 1 April 1998 the maximum charge for a course of treatment has been £340. There is no charge for arrest of bleeding or repairs to dentures; home visits by the dentist or re-opening a surgery in an emergency are charged for as treatment given in the normal way. The following people are exempt from dental charges or have charges remitted:
– people under 18
– full-time students under 19
– women who were pregnant when accepted for treatment
– women who have had a child in the previous 12 months
– people who receive income support, family credit, disability working allowance or income-based jobseeker's allowance, and their partners
– people who are named on an HC2 certificate issued by the Health Benefits Division

Booklet HC11, available from main post offices and local social security offices, gives further details.

GENERAL DENTAL SERVICE 1996–7 (ENGLAND)

Number of dentists	16,336
Number of patients registered	
Adults	19,524,000
Children	7,270,000
Number of courses of treatment	
Adults	24,580,000
Expenditure (£ million)	
Gross expenditure	1,323.1
Paid by patients	383.0
Paid out of public funds	940.1

Source: The Stationery Office – *Health and Personal Social Services Statistics for England 1997*

GENERAL OPHTHALMIC SERVICES

General Ophthalmic Services are administered by HAs. Testing of sight may be carried out by any ophthalmic medical practitioner or ophthalmic optician (optometrist). The optician must give the prescription to the patient, who can take this to any supplier of glasses to have them dispensed. Only registered opticians can supply glasses to children and to people registered as blind or partially sighted.

The NHS sight test costs £14.10. Those on a low income may qualify for help with the cost. The test is available free to:
- children under 16*
- full-time students under 19*
- people who receive income support, income-based jobseeker's allowance, disability working allowance or family credit, and their partners*
- people who are named on an HC2 certificate issued by the Health Benefits Division*
- people prescribed complex lenses*
- people registered as blind or partially sighted
- diagnosed diabetic and glaucoma patients
- close relatives aged 40 or over of diagnosed glaucoma patients

The categories indicated by * above are automatically entitled to help with the purchase of glasses under an NHS voucher scheme, as are people whose spectacles are lost or damaged as a result of their disability, injury or illness. Booklet HC11, available from main post offices and local social security offices, gives further details.

Diagnosis and specialist treatment of eye conditions, and the provision of special glasses, are available through the Hospital Eye Service.

COMMUNITY CHILD HEALTH SERVICES

Pre-school services at GP surgeries or child health clinics provide regular monitoring of children's physical, mental and emotional health and development, and advice to parents on their children's health and welfare.

The School Health Service provides for the medical and dental examination of schoolchildren, and advises the local education authority, the school, the parents and the pupil of any health factors which may require special consideration during the pupil's school life. GPs are increasingly undertaking child health monitoring in order to improve the preventive health care of children.

HOSPITALS AND OTHER SERVICES

Hospital, medical, dental, nursing, ophthalmic and ambulance services are provided by the NHS to meet all reasonable requirements. Facilities for the care of expectant and nursing mothers and young children, and other services required for the diagnosis and treatment of illness, are also provided. Rehabilitation services (occupational therapy, physiotherapy and speech therapy) may also be provided, and surgical and medical appliances are supplied where appropriate.

Specialists and consultants who work in NHS hospitals can also engage in private practice, including the treatment of their private patients in NHS hospitals.

PRIVATE FINANCE INITIATIVE

The Private Finance Initiative (PFI) was launched in 1992, and involves the private sector in designing, building, financing and operating new hospitals, which are then leased to the NHS. In July 1997 a new programme of hospital building under the PFI was announced by the Government.

CHARGES

Certain hospitals have accommodation in single rooms or small wards which, if not required for patients who need privacy for medical reasons, may be made available to patients who desire it as an amenity for a small charge. These patients are still NHS patients and are treated as such.

In a number of hospitals, accommodation is available for the treatment of private in-patients who undertake to pay the full costs of hospital accommodation and services and (usually) separate medical fees to a specialist as well. The amount of the medical fees is a matter for agreement between doctor and patient. Hospital charges for private in-patients are set locally at a commercial rate.

There is no charge for drugs supplied to NHS hospital in-patients, but out-patients pay £5.80 an item unless they are exempt. With certain exceptions, hospital out-patients have to pay fixed charges for dentures, contact lenses and certain appliances. Glasses may be obtained either from the hospital or an optician, and the charge will be related to the type of lens prescribed and the choice of frame.

AMBULANCE SERVICE

The NHS provides emergency ambulance services free of charge via the 999 emergency telephone service. There are 44 ambulance services in the UK, all of which are NHS Trusts or form part of larger trusts. Helicopter ambulances are used in some areas where heavy traffic could hinder road progress, and an air ambulance service is available throughout Scotland. Non-emergency ambulance services are provided free of charge to patients who are deemed to require them on medical grounds.

In 1997–8 in England about 3,576,200 emergency calls were made to the ambulance service, an increase of 7 per cent on the previous year. Emergency patient journeys rose from about 2,600,000 to 2,700,000. The Patients' Charter requires emergency ambulances to respond to 95 per cent of calls within 14 minutes in urban areas and 19 minutes in rural areas, and to reach 50 per cent of cases within eight minutes. In 1997 two-thirds of ambulances met the Charter standard.

NHS DIRECT

NHS Direct is a telephone service staffed by nurses which gives patients advice on how to look after themselves as well as directing them to the appropriate part of the NHS for treatment if necessary. The Government intends that the service will cover 40 per cent of England by April 1999 and all parts of England by the end of 2000.

BLOOD SERVICES

There are four national bodies which co-ordinate the blood donor programme in each constituent country of the UK. About two million donations of blood are given each year; donors give blood at local centres on a voluntary basis.

NATIONAL BLOOD AUTHORITY, Oak House, Reeds Crescent, Watford, Herts WD1 1QH. Tel: 01923-486800. *Chairman,* M. Fogden; *Chief Executive,* J. Adey

SCOTTISH NATIONAL BLOOD TRANSFUSION SERVICE, 21 Ellens Glen Road, Edinburgh EH17 7QT. Tel: 0131-536 5700. *National Director,* A. McMillan-Douglas

WELSH BLOOD SERVICE, Ely Valley Road, Talbot Green, Pontyclun CF72 9WB. Tel: 01443-622000. *Director,* Dr F. G. Williams

NORTHERN IRELAND BLOOD TRANSFUSION SERVICE, City Hospital Complex, Lisburn Road, Belfast BT9 7TS. Tel: 01232-321414

HOSPICES

Hospice or palliative care may be available for patients with life-threatening illnesses. It may be provided at the patient's home or in a voluntary or NHS hospice or in hospital, and is intended to ensure the best possible quality of life for the patient during their illness, and to provide help and support to both the patient and the patient's family. The National Council for Hospices and Specialist Palliative Care Services co-ordinates NHS and voluntary services in England, Wales and Northern Ireland; the Scottish Partnership Agency for Palliative and Cancer Care performs the same function in Scotland.

NATIONAL COUNCIL FOR HOSPICE AND SPECIALIST PALLIATIVE CARE SERVICES, 7th Floor, 1 Great Cumberland Place, London WH1 7AL. Tel: 0171-723 1639. *Executive Director,* Mrs J. Gaffin, OBE
SCOTTISH PARTNERSHIP AGENCY FOR PALLIATIVE AND CANCER CARE, 1A Cambridge Street, Edinburgh EH1 2DY. Tel: 0131-229 0538. *Director,* Mrs M. Stevenson

NUMBER OF BEDS AND PATIENT ACTIVITY 1996

	England*	Wales
In-patients:		
Average daily available beds	206,000	15,600
Average daily occupation of beds	n/a	12,200
Persons waiting for admission at 31 March	†1,048,000	65,000
Day-case admissions	2,845,000	286,400
Ordinary admissions	8,379,000	516,400
Out-patient attendances:		
New patients	10,989,000	667,100
Total attendances	40,118,000	2,569,500
Accident and emergency:		
New patients	12,404,000	798,400
Total attendances	14,234,000	975,300

* 1995 figures
† 1996 figure
n/a not available

SCOTLAND

In-patients:	
Average available staffed beds	40,600
Average occupied beds	32,800
Out-patient attendances:	
New patients	2,666,000
Total attendances	6,338,000

Source: The Stationery Office – *Annual Abstract of Statistics 1998*

WAITING LISTS

At the end of March 1998 the total number of patients waiting to be admitted to NHS hospitals in England was 1,297,662, an increase of 12.1 per cent on the previous year. The number of patients who had been waiting more than one year was 68,023, an increase of 118 per cent on the previous year; however, some 70 per cent of elective in-patients are treated within three months of being placed on a waiting list. Under the Patient's Charter, patients are guaranteed admission within 18 months of being placed on a waiting list.

PATIENT'S CHARTERS

The original Patient's Charter was published in 1991 and came into force in 1992; an expanded version was published in 1995. The Charter sets out the rights of patients in relation to the NHS (i.e. the standards of service which all patients will receive at all times); and patients' reasonable expectations (i.e. the standards of service that the NHS aims to provide, even if they cannot in

exceptional circumstances be met). The Charter covers areas such as access to services, personal treatment of patients, the provision of information, registering with a doctor, hospital waiting times, care in hospitals, community services, ambulance waiting times, dental, optical and pharmaceutical services, and maternity services. In England there are separate Patient's Charter leaflets setting out standards in relation to services for children and young people, maternity services, mental health services and blood donation.

The Government is developing a new NHS Charter, expected to be introduced in 1999. Further information is available free of charge from the national Health Information Service (Tel 0800-665544).

Health authorities and boards, NHS Trusts and GP practices may also have their own local charters setting out the standard of service they aim to provide.

COMPLAINTS

The Patient's Charter includes the right to have any complaint about the service provided by the NHS dealt with quickly, with a full written reply being provided by a relevant chief executive. There are two levels to the NHS complaints procedure: the first level involves resolution of a complaint locally, following a direct approach to the relevant service provider; the second level involves an independent review procedure if the complaint is not resolved locally. As a final resort, patients may approach the Health Service Commissioner or Ombudsman (*see* page 311) (in Northern Ireland, the Commissioner for Complaints (*see* page 332)) if they are dissatisfied with the response of the NHS to a complaint.

In 1996–7 there were 92,974 written complaints about hospital and community health services, of which 67 per cent were resolved locally within the target period of four weeks; 1.7 per cent of complainants requested an independent review. There were 36,990 written complaints about family health services and in 1,040 cases the complainant requested an independent review.

NHS TRIBUNALS

The National Health Service Tribunal and the National Health Service Tribunal (Scotland) (*see* page 371) consider representations that the continued inclusion of a doctor, dentist, optician or pharmacist on the list of a health authority or health board would be prejudicial to the efficiency of the service concerned. The Mental Health Review Tribunals (*see* page 371) are responsible for reviewing the cases of patients compulsorily detained under the Mental Health Act 1983.

RECIPROCAL ARRANGEMENTS

Citizens of countries in the European Economic Area (EEA - *see* page 776) are entitled to receive emergency health care either free of charge or for a reduced charge when they are temporarily visiting other member states of the EEA. Form E111, available at post offices, should be obtained before travelling. Non-EEA nationals, or visitors receiving routine, non-emergency care, are normally required to pay for treatment in Britain. There are bilateral agreements with several other countries, including Australia and New Zealand, for the provision of urgent medical treatment either free of charge or for a reduced charge.

Personal Social Services

The Secretary of State for Health is responsible, under the Local Authority Social Services Act 1970, for the provision of social services for elderly people, disabled people, families and children, and those with mental disorders. Personal Social Services are administered by local authorities according to policies and standards set by central government. Each authority has a Director of Social Services and a Social Services Committee responsible for the social services functions placed upon them. Local authorities provide, enable and commission care after assessing the needs of their population. The private and voluntary sectors also play an important role in the delivery of social services, and an estimated six million people in Great Britain provide substantial regular care for a member of their family.

The Community Care reforms introduced in 1993 were intended to enable vulnerable groups to live in the community rather than in residential homes wherever possible, and to offer them as independent a lifestyle as possible.

At 31 March 1997, there were 519,115 places in residential and nursing care homes in England. About 240,000 residents were supported by local authorities (an increase of 12 per cent on the previous year). Of the local authority-supported residents, 24 per cent were in local authority-run homes (down from 29 per cent), 46 per cent were in independent residential care homes (up from 42 per cent) and 27 per cent were in independent nursing homes (the same percentage as in the previous year).

FINANCE

The Personal Social Services programme is financed partly by central government, with decisions on expenditure allocations being made at local authority level.

STAFF

STAFF OF LOCAL AUTHORITY SOCIAL SERVICES DEPARTMENTS 1997 (ENGLAND)
Full- time equivalents

Area office/field work staff	114,900
Residential care staff	65,400
Day care staff	30,800
Central/strategic HQ staff	16,400
Other staff	1,900
Total staff	229,400

Source: Department of Health

ELDERLY PEOPLE

Services for elderly people are designed to enable them to remain living in their own homes for as long as possible. Local authority services include advice, domestic help, meals in the home, alterations to the home to aid mobility, emergency alarm systems, day and/or night attendants, laundry services and the provision of day centres and recreational facilities. Charges may be made for these services. Respite care may also be provided in order to allow carers temporary relief from their responsibilities.

Local authorities and the private sector also provide 'sheltered housing' for elderly people, sometimes with resident wardens.

If an elderly person is admitted to a residential home, charges are made according to a means test; if the person cannot afford to pay, the costs are met by the local authority.

DISABLED PEOPLE

Services for disabled people are designed to enable them to remain living in their own homes wherever possible. Local authority services include advice, adaptations to the home, meals in the home, help with personal care, occupational therapy, educational facilities and recreational facilities. Respite care may also be provided in order to allow carers temporary relief from their responsibilities.

Special housing may be available for disabled people who can live independently, and residential accommodation for those who cannot.

FAMILIES AND CHILDREN

Local authorities are required to provide services aimed at safeguarding the welfare of children in need and, wherever possible, allowing them to be brought up by their families. Services include advice, counselling, help in the home and the provision of family centres. Many authorities also provide short-term refuge accommodation for women and children.

DAY CARE

In allocating day-care places to children, local authorities give priority to children with special needs, whether in terms of their health, learning abilities or social needs. They also provide a registration and inspection service in relation to childminders, play groups and private day nurseries in the local authority area. In England in 1997 there were 6,100 day nurseries providing 194,000 places, 98,500 registered child-minders providing 365,000 places, and 15,800 play groups providing 384,000 places.

A national child care strategy is being developed by the Government, under which day care and out-of-school child care facilities will be extended to match more closely the needs of working parents.

CHILD PROTECTION

Children considered to be at risk of physical injury, neglect or sexual abuse are placed on the local authority's child protection register. Local authority social services staff, school nurses, health visitors and other agencies work together to prevent and detect cases of abuse. In England at 31 March 1997 there were 16,400 boys and 15,700 girls on child protection registers. Of these, 38 per cent were at risk of neglect, 34 per cent of physical abuse, 23 per cent of sexual abuse and 16 per cent of emotional abuse.

LOCAL AUTHORITY CARE

Local authorities are required to provide accommodation for children who have no parent or guardian or whose parents or guardians are unable or unwilling to care for them. A family proceedings court may also issue a care order in cases where a child is being neglected or abused, or is not attending school; the court must be satisfied that this would positively contribute to the well-being of the child.

The welfare of children in local authority care must be properly safeguarded. Children may be placed with foster families, who receive payments to cover the expenses of caring for the child or children, or in residential care. Children's homes may be run by the local authority or by the private or voluntary sectors; all homes are subject to inspection procedures. In England at 31 March 1997, 51,600 children were in the care of local authorities. Of these, 65 per cent were placed with foster parents and 5 per cent were placed for adoption.

ADOPTION

Local authorities are required to provide an adoption service, either directly or via approved voluntary societies.

In England and Wales in 1996, 6,000 children (3,000 boys and 3,000 girls) were adopted.

PEOPLE WITH LEARNING DISABILITIES

Services for people with learning disabilities (i.e. mental handicap) are designed to enable them to remain living in the community wherever possible. Local authority services include short-term care, support in the home, the provision of day care centres, and help with other activities outside the home. Residential care is provided for the severely or profoundly disabled.

MENTALLY ILL PEOPLE

Under the Care Programme Approach, mentally ill people should be assessed by specialist services and receive a care plan, and a key worker should be appointed for each patient. Regular reviews of the patient's progress should be conducted. Local authorities provide help and advice to mentally ill people and their families, and places in day centres and social centres. Social workers can apply for a mentally disturbed person to be compulsorily detained in hospital. Where appropriate, mentally ill people are provided with accommodation in special hospitals, local authority accommodation, or homes run by private or voluntary organizations. Patients who have been discharged from hospitals may be placed on a supervision register. In July 1998 the Government announced that the system of care for mentally ill people would be replaced. A new mental health strategy will be announced in late 1998 and national standards of patient care will be produced by April 1999. The Mental Health Act 1983 will be replaced by new legislation.

TOTAL PLACES IN RESIDENTIAL AND NURSING HOMES (ENGLAND) *as at 31 March 1997*

By client group

Elderly people	374,302
Physically/sensorily disabled adults	11,494
Elderly mentally infirm people	39,373
People with mental illness	22,646
People with learning disabilities	50,872
Other people	20,428
All client groups	519,115

Source: Department of Health

LOCAL AUTHORITY-SUPPORTED RESIDENTS IN STAFFED RESIDENTIAL AND NURSING CARE (ENGLAND) *as at 31 March 1997*

All staffed homes	236,083
Local authority	58,651
Independent residential care	111,444
Independent nursing care	65,988
Elderly people	180,219
Physically/sensorily disabled adults	8,628
People with mental health problems	17,271
People with learning disabilities	26,872
Other people	3,093

Source: The Stationery Office – *Health and Personal Social Services Statistics for England 1997*

LOCAL AUTHORITY PERSONAL SOCIAL SERVICES GROSS EXPENDITURE BY CLIENT GROUP 1995–6 (ENGLAND)
£ million

	Elderly	Children	Learning disability	Adults	Mental health	HQ costs	Total
HQ costs	—	—	—	—	—	122.4	122.4
Area officers/senior managers	99.0	152.1	22.5	29.1	22.7	—	325.5
Care management/care assessment	221.5	289.1	46.9	61.6	69.0	—	688.1
Residential care	2,282.3	631.1	560.7	153.0	147.2	—	3,774.3
Non-residential care	1,405.7	840.9	430.0	333.6	141.2	—	3,151.4
Field social work	61.3	120.1	19.6	18.8	26.1	—	245.8
Other	—	—	—	85.7	—	—	85.7
TOTAL	4,069.8	2,033.2	1,079.7	681.8	406.3	122.4	8,393.0

Source: The Stationery Office – *Health and Personal Social Services Statistics for England 1997*

National Insurance and Related Cash Benefits

NB All leaflets referred to in this section can be obtained from local social security offices unless an alternative source is given

The state insurance and assistance schemes, comprising schemes of national insurance and industrial injuries insurance, national assistance, and non-contributory old age pensions, came into force from 5 July 1948. The Ministry of Social Security Act 1966 replaced national assistance and non-contributory old age pensions with a scheme of non-contributory benefits. These and subsequent measures relating to social security provision in Great Britain were consolidated by the Social Security Act 1975, the Social Security (Consequential Provisions) Act 1975, and the Industrial Injuries and Diseases (Old Cases) Act 1975. Corresponding measures were passed for Northern Ireland. The Social Security Pensions Act 1975 introduced a new state pensions scheme in 1978, and the graduated pension scheme 1961 to 1975 has been wound up, existing rights being preserved. Under the Pensions Act 1995 the age of retirement is to be 65 for both men and women, this being phased in between 2010 and 6 April 2020. The Pensioners' Payments and Social Security Act 1979 provided for a Christmas bonus for pensioners in 1979 and in succeeding years. The Child Benefit Act 1975 replaced family allowances (introduced 1946) with child benefit and one-parent benefit. Some of this legislation has been superseded by the provisions of the Social Security Acts 1969 to 1992. The Government has announced its intention to reform the social security system and a green paper, *New Ambitions for Our Country – A New Contract for Welfare*, was published in March 1998.

NATIONAL INSURANCE SCHEME

The National Insurance (NI) scheme operates under the Social Security Contributions and Benefits Act 1992 and the Social Security Administration Act 1992, and orders and regulations made thereunder. The scheme is financed by contributions payable by earners, employers and others (*see* below) and by a Treasury grant. Money collected under the scheme is used to finance the National Insurance Fund (from which contributory benefits are paid) and to contribute to the cost of the National Health Service.

NATIONAL INSURANCE FUND

Approximate receipts and payments of the National Insurance Fund for the year ended 31 March 1997 were:

Receipts	£'000
Balance, 1 April 1996	7,835,829
Contributions under the Social Security	
Acts (net of SSP and SMP)	41,874,927
Treasury grant	1,901,500
Compensation from	
Consolidated Fund for SSP	
and SMP recoveries	524,000
Income from investments	473,876
Other receipts	107,977
	52,718,109

Payments	£'000	£'000
Unemployment benefit	587,298	
Jobseeker's allowance		
(contributory)	332,708	
Incapacity benefit	7,661,624	
Maternity allowance	32,725	
Widow's benefit	981,241	
Guardian's allowance and		
child's special allowance	1,496	
Retirement pension	31,994,561	
Pensioners' lump sum		
payments	128,614	41,720,267
Personal pensions		1,997,607
Transfers to Northern Ireland		75,000
Administration		1,038,415
Other payments		17,392
Redundancy payments		132,003
Balance, 31 March 1997		7,737,423
		52,718,107

CONTRIBUTIONS

There are five classes of NI contributions:

Class 1   paid by employees and their employers
Class 1A paid by employers who provide employees with cars/fuel for private use
Class 2   paid by self-employed people
Class 3   voluntary contributions paid to protect entitlement to certain benefits
Class 4   paid by the self-employed on their taxable profits over a set limit

The lower and upper earnings limits and the percentage rates referred to below apply from 6 April 1998 to 5 April 1999.

CLASS 1

Class 1 contributions are paid where a person:
– is an employed earner (employee) or office holder (e.g. company director)
– is 16 or over and under state pension age
– earns at or above the lower earning limit of £64.00 per week (including overtime pay, bonus, commission, etc., without deduction of superannuation contributions)
Class 1 contributions are not paid where a person earns less than the lower earnings limit.

Class 1 contributions are made up of primary and secondary contributions. Primary contributions are those paid by the employee and these are deducted from earnings by the employer. The percentage rates paid by the employee are as follows:
– 2 per cent on all earnings up to and including the lower earnings limit of £64.00
– 10 per cent on earnings between the lower earnings limit and the upper earnings limit of £485.00 per week (8.4 per cent for contracted-out employment, *see* page 488)
Some married women or widows pay a reduced rate of 3.85 per cent on all earnings up to and including the upper earnings limit. It is no longer possible to elect to pay the reduced rate but those who had reduced liability before 12 May 1977 may retain it so long as certain conditions are met. *See* leaflet CA09 (widows) or leaflet CA13 (married women).

Secondary contributions are paid by employers of employed earners on all earnings at or above the lower earnings limit. There is no upper earnings limit for employers' contributions, which are as follows:

Weekly earnings	Percentage of reckonable income Not contracted out	Contracted-out schemes COSR*	COMP*
£64.00–109.99	3.0	0	1.5
110.00–154.99	5.0	2.0	3.5
155.00–209.99	7.0	4.0	5.5
210.00–485.00	10.0	7.0	8.5
over 485.00	10.0	10.0	10.0

* For explanation of COSR and COMP schemes, *see* page 488

The contracted-out rate applies only to that portion of earnings between the lower and upper earnings limits. Employers' contributions below and above those respective limits are assessed at the appropriate not contracted-out rate.

Class 2

Class 2 contributions are paid where a person is self-employed and is 16 or over and under state pension age. Contributions are paid at a flat rate of £6.35 per week regardless of the amount earned. However, those with earnings of less than £3,590 a year can apply for Small Earnings Exception, i.e. exemption from liability to pay Class 2 contributions. Those granted exemption from Class 2 contributions may pay Class 2 or Class 3 contributions voluntarily. Self-employed earners (whether or not they pay Class 2 contributions) may also be liable to pay Class 4 contributions based on profits. There are special rules for those who are concurrently employed and self-employed.

Married women and widows can no longer choose not to pay Class 2 contributions but those who elected not to pay Class 2 contributions before 12 May 1977 may retain the right so long as certain conditions are met.

Class 2 contributions are collected by the Contributions Agency, an executive agency of the Department of Social Security, by direct debit or quarterly bills. *See* leaflets CA03 and CA02.

Class 3

Class 3 contributions are voluntary flat-rate contributions of £6.25 per week payable by persons over the age of 16 who would otherwise be unable to qualify for retirement pension and certain other benefits because they have an insufficient record of Class 1 or Class 2 contributions. This may include those who are not working, those not liable for Class 1 or Class 2 contributions or those excepted from Class 2 contributions. Married women and widows who on or before 11 May 1977 elected not to pay Class 1 (full rate) or Class 2 contributions cannot pay Class 3 contributions while they retain this right.

Class 3 contributions are collected by the Contributions Agency by quarterly bills or direct debit. *See* leaflet CA08.

Class 4

Self-employed people whose profits and gains are over £7,310 a year pay Class 4 contributions in addition to Class 2 contributions. This applies to self-employed earners over 16 and under the state pension age. Class 4 contributions are calculated at 6 per cent of annual profits or gains between £7,310 and £25,220. The maximum Class 4 contribution payable on £25,220 or more is £1,074.60.

Class 4 contributions are assessed and collected by the Inland Revenue together with Schedule D tax. It is possible, in some circumstances, to apply for exceptions from liability to pay Class 4 contributions or to have the amount of contribution reduced (where Class 1 contributions are payable on earnings assessed for Class 4 contributions). *See* leaflet CA03.

PENSIONS

The Social Security Pensions Act came into force in 1978. It aimed to:
– reduce reliance on means-tested benefit in old age, widowhood and chronic ill-health
– ensure that occupational pension schemes which are contracted out of the state scheme fulfil the conditions of a good scheme
– ensure that pensions are adequately protected against inflation
– ensure that men and women are treated equally in state and occupational schemes

Legislation and regulations introduced since 1978 go further towards fulfilling these aims and more changes came into effect in April 1997 (*see* below). One of the changes is to equalize the state pension age for men (currently 65 years) and women (currently 60 years) from 6 April 2020. The change will be phased in over the ten years leading up to 6 April 2020. As a result the state pension age is as follows:
– the pension age for men remains at 65
– the pension age for women born on or before 5 April 1950 remains at 60
– the pension age for women born on or after 6 April 1955 is now 65
– for women born after 5 April 1950 and before 6 April 1955, the pension age is 60 plus one month for every month, or part of a month, that their date of birth fell after 5 April 1950

STATE PENSION SCHEME

The state pension scheme consists of the basic flat-rate pension and the state earnings-related pension scheme (SERPS), also known as additional pension.

The amount of basic pension paid is dependent on the number of 'qualifying years' a person is in their 'working life'. A 'qualifying year' is a tax year in which a person pays Class 1 (at the standard rate), 2 or 3 NI contributions for the whole year (*see* above). Those in receipt of invalid care allowance, disability working allowance, jobseeker's allowance, incapacity benefit, severe disablement allowance or approved training have contributions credited to them for each week they receive benefit or fulfil certain other conditions. For those reaching pensionable age on or after 6 April 1999, a Class 3 credit of earnings will be awarded for each week from 6 April 1995 that family credit has been received. 'Working life' is counted from the start of the tax year in which a person reaches 16 to the end of the tax year before the one in which they reach pensionable age: for men this is normally 49 years and for women this varies between 44 and 49 years because the pension ages vary (*see* above). To get the full rate (100 per cent) basic pension a person must have qualifying years for about 90 per cent of their working life. To get the minimum basic pension (25 per cent) a person will need nine or ten qualifying years. Married women who are not entitled to a pension on their own contributions may get a pension on their husband's contributions. It is possible for people who are unable to work because they care for children or a sick or disabled person at home to reduce the number of qualifying years required. This is called home responsibilities protection (HRP) and can be given for any tax year since April 1978; the number of years for which HRP is given is deducted from the number of qualifying years needed.

The amount of SERPS or additional pension paid depends on the amount of earnings a person has between the lower and upper earnings limits (*see* page 486) for each complete tax year between 6 April 1978 (when the scheme started) and the tax year before they reach state pension age. The right to additional pension does not depend on the person's right to basic pension. The amount of additional pension paid also depends on when a person reaches retirement; changes being phased in from 6 April 1999 mean that pensions will be calculated differently from that date. Women widowed before 6 April 2000 will inherit all their late husband's additional pension and women widowed on or after this date will inherit half of the husband's additional pension.

There are four categories of state pension provided under the Social Security Contributions and Benefits Act 1992:

- Category A, a contributory pension made up of basic and additional elements, payable to those of pensionable age who satisfy the entitlement conditions described above (see pages 489–90)
- Category B, a contributory pension made up of basic and additional elements, payable to married women and widows and based on their husband's contributions. This category of pension is to be extended to men from 6 April 2010 (see pages 489–90)
- Category C, a non-contributory pension payable to those who reached pensionable age before 5 July 1948 (see page 491)
- Category D, a non-contributory pension for those over 80 (see page 491)

Graduated retirement benefit is also available to those who paid graduated NI contributions into the scheme when it existed between April 1961 and April 1975 (see page 492).

It is possible to find out how much basic and additional pension a person might receive by filling in form BR19, available from local social security offices or by telephoning 0191-225 5240.

CONTRACTED-OUT AND PERSONAL PENSION SCHEMES

Under the Pensions Schemes Act 1993, an employer can contract out of SERPS those employees who are members of an occupational scheme, so long as the occupational scheme satisfies certain conditions. The occupational pension takes the place of the additional pension from April 1997 (previously it took the place of part of the additional pension); the state remains responsible for the basic pension. Until April 1997 members of contracted-out occupational and personal pension schemes accrued additional pension in the same way as someone who is not contracted-out but the rate payable was reduced by contracted-out deductions. Since 5 April 1997, it has not been possible to accrue any SERPS while being a member of a contracted-out occupational or personal pension scheme. Members of a COSR, COMP or personal pension scheme can no longer earn additional pension but they are still entitled to those rights earned before April 1997. From April 1997 there are age-related NI contribution rebates for people who leave SERPS and become members of a COMP or personal pension scheme; these will be lower for younger people and higher for older people.

There are two types of contracted-out occupational schemes.

Contracted-Out Salary Related Scheme (COSR)

- this scheme must provide a pension related to earnings
- the pension provided must not be less than a person's guaranteed minimum pension (GMP), i.e. worth about the same as the additional pension provided by the state scheme
- any additional pension earned from 6 April 1978 to 5 April 1997 will be reduced by the amount of GMP earned during that period

- from 6 April 1997 these schemes no longer have to provide a GMP but do have to satisfy a new scheme-based test in order to be issued with a contracting-out certificate

Contracted-Out Money Purchase Scheme (COMP)

- this scheme must provide a pension based on the value of the fund built up, i.e. the money paid in, along with returns from investment
- part of the pension, known as protected rights, takes the place of the additional pension. A contracted-out deduction, which may be more or less than the pension provided by the scheme, will be made from any additional pension earned from 6 April 1987 to 5 April 1997

In contracted-out occupational pension schemes, both the employee and employer pay lower NI contribution rates in recognition that SERPS will not be paid.

Personal Pension Schemes

The option of a personal pension scheme is open to all employees, even if their employer has an occupational pension scheme. A personal pension scheme must provide a pension based on the value of the fund built up, i.e. the money paid in, along with returns from investment. Part of the pension, known as protected rights, takes the place of the additional pension. A contracted-out deduction, which may be more or less than the pension provided by the scheme, will be made from any additional pension earned from 6 April 1987 to 5 April 1997.

Employees who are members of a personal pension plan and their employers pay NI contributions at the full rate and the DSS pays the difference between the full rate and the contracted-out rate into the personal pension scheme.

A Pensions Ombudsman deals with complaints about maladministration of pensions schemes. The Occupational Pensions Board, which supervised contracting-out and approved personal pension schemes, was abolished in April 1997 and replaced by the Occupational Pensions Regulatory Authority. See leaflet NP46.

BENEFITS

Leaflets relating to the various benefits and contribution conditions for different benefits are available from local social security offices; leaflets NI196 *Social Security Benefit Rates*, FB2 *Which Benefit?* and MG1 *A Guide to Benefits* are general guides to benefits, benefit rates and contributions.

The benefits payable under the Social Security Acts are:

CONTRIBUTORY BENEFITS
Jobseeker's allowance (contribution-based)
Incapacity benefit
Maternity allowance
Widow's benefit (comprising widow's payment, widowed mother's allowance and widow's pension)
Retirement pensions, categories A and B

NON-CONTRIBUTORY BENEFITS
Child benefit
Guardian's allowance
Jobseeker's allowance (income-based)
Invalid care allowance
Severe disablement allowance
Attendance allowance
Disability living allowance
Disability working allowance
Retirement pensions, categories C and D
Income support
Family credit

Housing benefit
Council tax benefit
Social fund

BENEFITS FOR INDUSTRIAL INJURIES AND
DISABLEMENT

OTHER
Statutory sick pay
Statutory maternity pay

CONTRIBUTORY BENEFITS

Entitlement to contributory benefits depends on contri-bution conditions being satisfied either by the claimant or by some other person (depending on the kind of benefit). The class or classes of contribution which for this purpose are relevant to each benefit are:

Jobseeker's allowance (contribution-based)	Class 1
Incapacity benefit	Class 1 or 2
Maternity allowance	Class 1 or 2
Widow's benefits	Class 1, 2 or 3
Retirement pensions, categories A and B	Class 1, 2 or 3

The system of contribution conditions relates to yearly levels of earnings on which contributions have been paid.

JOBSEEKER'S ALLOWANCE

Jobseeker's allowance (JSA) replaced unemployment benefit and income support for unemployed people under pension age from 7 October 1996. There are two routes of entitlement. Contribution-based JSA is paid as a personal rate (i.e. additional benefit for dependants is not paid) to those who have made sufficient NI contributions. Savings and partner's earnings are not taken into account and payment can be made for up to six months. Those who do not qualify for contribution-based JSA, those who have exhausted their entitlement to contribution-based JSA or those for whom contribution-based JSA provides insuffi-cient income may qualify for income-based JSA. The amount paid depends on age and number of dependants and income and savings are taken into account. Income-based JSA may comprise three parts: a personal allowance for the jobseeker and his/her partner and one for each child or young person for whom they are responsible; premiums for groups of people with special needs; and housing costs. This is payable for the claimant and their dependants for as long as they satisfy the rules. Rates of jobseeker's allowance correspond to income support rates.

Claims for this benefit are made through job centres/employment offices. A person wishing to claim jobseeker's allowance must be unemployed, capable of work and available for any work which they can reasonably be expected to do, usually for at least 40 hours per week. They must agree and sign a 'jobseeker's agreement', which will set out each claimant's plans to find work, and must actively seek work.

A person will be disqualified from jobseeker's allowance if they have left a job voluntarily or through misconduct, if they refuse to take up an offer of employment or if they fail to attend a training scheme or employment programme. In these circumstances, it may be possible to receive hardship payments, particularly where the claimant or their family is vulnerable, e.g. if sick or pregnant, or for those with children or caring responsibilities. *See* leaflet JSAL5.

INCAPACITY BENEFIT

Incapacity benefit is available to those who are incapable of work but cannot get statutory sick pay from their employer. It is not payable to those over state pension age. However, people who are already in receipt of short-term incapacity benefit when they reach state pension age may continue to receive this benefit for up to 52 weeks. There are three rates of incapacity benefit:
– short-term lower rate for the first 28 weeks of sickness
– short-term higher rate from weeks 29 to 52
– long-term rate after week 52
The terminally ill and those entitled to the highest rate care component of disability living allowance are paid the long-term rate after 28 weeks. Incapacity benefit is taxable after 28 weeks.

Two rates of age addition are paid with long-term benefit based on the claimant's age when incapacity started. The higher rate is payable where incapacity for work commenced before the age of 35; and the lower rate where incapacity commenced before the age of 45. Increases for dependents are also payable with short and long-term incapacity benefit.

There are two medical tests of incapacity: the 'own occupation' test and the 'all work' test. Those who worked before becoming incapable of working will be assessed, for the first 28 weeks of incapacity, on their ability to do their own job. After 28 weeks (or from the start of incapacity for those who were not working) claimants are assessed on their ability to carry out a range of work-related activities. The 'all work' test applies to most former sickness and invalidity benefit claimants. *See* leaflets IB202 and FB28.

MATERNITY ALLOWANCE

The maternity allowance (MA) scheme covers women who are self-employed or otherwise do not qualify for statutory maternity pay (*see* page 494). In order to qualify the woman must have been working and paying standard rate NI contributions for at least 26 weeks in the 66-week period which ends with the week before the week in which the baby is due. A woman can choose to start receiving MA between the beginning of the 11th week before the week in which the baby is due and the Sunday after the baby is born, depending on when she stops working. MA is paid for a period of up to 18 weeks. MA is only paid while the woman is not working. *See* leaflet NI17A.

WIDOW'S BENEFITS

Only the late husband's contributions of any class count for widow's benefit in any of its three forms:
Widow's payment – may be received by a woman who at her husband's death is under 60, or whose husband was not entitled to a Category A retirement pension when he died. It is a single tax-free lump sum payable immedi-ately the woman becomes a widow
Widowed mother's allowance – a taxable benefit payable to a widow if she is entitled or treated as entitled to child benefit, or if she is expecting her husband's baby
Widow's pension – a widow may receive this pension if aged 45 or over at the time of her husband's death (40 or over if widowed before 11 April 1988) or when her widowed mother's allowance ends. If aged 55 or over (50 or over if widowed before 11 April 1988) she will receive the full widow's pension rate
It is not possible to receive widowed mother's allowance and widow's pension at the same time, and widow's benefit in any form ceases upon remarriage or during a period in which a widow lives with a man as his wife. Different rules and conditions (other than those mentioned) apply to women widowed before 11 April 1988. See leaflet NP45.

RETIREMENT PENSION: CATEGORIES A AND B

A Category A pension is payable for life to men and women who reach state pension age and who satisfy the contribu-tions conditions (*see* page 487). A Category B pension is payable for life to a woman and is based on her husband's contributions. It becomes payable only when the husband has claimed his pension and the woman has reached state pension age. It is also payable on widowhood after 60 regardless of whether the late husband had qualified for his pension. There are special rules for those who are widowed before reaching pensionable age.

A person may defer claiming their pension for five years after state pension age. In doing so they may earn increments which will increase the weekly amount paid when they claim their pension. If a married man defers his Category A pension, his wife cannot claim a Category B pension on his contributions but she may earn increments on her pension during this time. A woman can defer her Category B pension, and earn increments, even if her husband is claiming his Category A pension.

The basic state pension is £64.70 per week plus any additional (earnings-related) pension the person may be entitled to (*see* page 487). An increase of £38.70 is paid for an adult dependant, providing the dependant's earnings do not exceed the rate of jobseeker's allowance for a single person (*see* below). It is also possible to get an increase of Category A and B pensions for a child or children. An age addition of 25p per week is payable if a retirement pensioner is aged 80 or over.

Since 1989 pensioners have been allowed to have unlimited earnings without affecting their retirement pension. Income support is payable on top of a pension where a pension does not give the person enough to live on and to those who are entitled to retirement pension but who have not claimed it. Pensioners may also be entitled to housing and council tax benefits.

GRADUATED RETIREMENT BENEFIT

Graduated NI contributions were first payable from 1961 and were calculated as a percentage of earnings between certain bands. They were discontinued in 1975. Any graduated pension which an employed person over 18 and under 70 (65 for a woman) had earned by paying graduated contributions will be paid when the contributor claims retirement pension or at 70 (65 for a woman), in addition to any retirement pension for which he or she qualifies. A wife can get a graduated pension in return for her own graduated contributions, but not for her husband's.

Graduated retirement benefit is at a weekly rate for each 'unit' of graduated contributions paid by the employee (half a unit or more counts as a whole unit); the rate varies from person to person. A unit of graduated pension can be calculated by adding together all graduated contributions and dividing by 7.5 (men) or 9.0 (women). If a person defers making a claim beyond 65 (60 for a woman), entitlement may be increased by one seventh of a penny per £1 of its weekly rate for each complete week of deferred retirement, as long as the retirement is deferred for a minimum of seven weeks.

WEEKLY RATES OF BENEFIT
from April 1998

Jobseeker's allowance (contribution-based)

Person under 18	£30.30
Person aged 18–24	39.85
Person over 25	50.35

Short-term incapacity benefit

Person under pension age – lower rate	48.80
*Person under pension age – higher rate	57.70
Increase for adult dependant	30.20
*Person over pension age	62.05
Increase for adult dependant	37.20

Long-term incapacity benefit

Person (under or over pension age)	64.70
Increase for adult dependant	38.70
Age addition – lower rate	6.80
Age addition – higher rate	13.60

Invalidity allowance: maximum amount payable

Higher rate	13.60
Middle rate	8.60
Lower rate	4.30

Maternity allowance

Employed	57.70
Self-employed or unemployed	50.10

Widow's benefits

Widow's payment (lump sum)	1,000.00
*Widowed mother's allowance	64.70
*Widow's pension	64.70

Retirement pension: categories A and B

Single person	64.70
Increase for wife/other adult dependant	38.70

*These benefits attract an increase for each dependent child (in addition to child benefit) of £9.90 for the first or only child and £11.30 for each subsequent child

NON-CONTRIBUTORY BENEFITS

These benefits are paid from general taxation and are not dependent on NI contributions. Unless otherwise stated, a benefit is tax-free and is not means tested.

CHILD BENEFIT

Child benefit is payable for virtually all children aged under 16, and for those aged 16 to 18 who are studying full-time up to and including A-level or equivalent standard. It is also payable for a short period if the child has left school recently and is registered for work or work-based training for young people at a careers office.

A higher rate of benefit (child benefit (lone parent)) may be paid to a person who is responsible for bringing up one or more children on his/her own. It is a flat rate benefit payable for the eldest child only. Since 6 July 1998 child benefit (lone parent) has not been available to new lone parents but it may still be payable in certain circumstances. *See* leaflets CH1 and CH11.

GUARDIAN'S ALLOWANCE

Where the parents of a child are dead, the person who has the child in his/her family may claim a guardian's allowance in addition to child benefit. In exceptional circumstances the allowance is payable on the death of only one parent. *See* leaflet NI14.

INVALID CARE ALLOWANCE

Invalid care allowance (ICA) is a taxable benefit payable to people of working age who give up the opportunity of full-time paid employment because they are regularly and substantially engaged (spending at least 35 hours per week as a carer) in caring for a severely disabled person. To qualify for ICA a person must be caring for someone in receipt of one of the following benefits:
- the middle or highest rate of disability living allowance care component
- either rate of attendance allowance
- constant attendance allowance, paid at not less than the normal maximum rate, under the industrial injuries or war pension schemes

See leaflets FB31 and FB28.

SEVERE DISABLEMENT ALLOWANCE

Persons who have been incapable of work for a continuous period of at least 28 weeks but who do not qualify for contributory incapacity benefit may be entitled to severe disablement allowance (SDA). This benefit is available to people over 16 and under 65. Those who are over 65 can only get SDA if they were entitled to it on the day before their 65th birthday. People who became incapable of work on or before their 20th birthday do not have to have their disability assessed but those who became incapable after their 20th birthday must be assessed as at least 80 per cent disabled. *See* leaflet NI252.

ATTENDANCE ALLOWANCE

This is payable to disabled people over 65 who need a lot of care or supervision because of physical or mental disability for a period of at least six months. People not expected to live for six months because of an illness do not have to wait six months. The allowance has two rates: the lower rate is for day or night care, and the higher rate is for day and night care. *See* leaflets DS702 and FB28.

DISABILITY LIVING ALLOWANCE

This is payable to disabled people under 65 who have personal care and mobility needs because of an illness or disability for a period of at least three months and are likely to have those needs for a further six months or more. People not expected to live for six months because of an illness do not have to wait three months. The allowance has two components: the care component, which has three rates, and the mobility component, which has two rates. The rates depend on the care and mobility needs of the claimant. The mobility component is payable only to those aged five or over. *See* leaflet DS704.

DISABILITY WORKING ALLOWANCE

This is an income-related benefit for people who are working 16 hours per week or more but have an illness or disability which puts them at a disadvantage in getting a job. To qualify a person must be aged 16 or over and must, at the date of the claim, have one of the 'qualifying benefits', such as disability living allowance. The amount payable depends on the size of the family and weekly income. The allowance is not payable if any savings exceed £16,000. *See* leaflet DS703.

RETIREMENT PENSION: CATEGORIES C AND D

A Category C pension is provided, subject to a residence test, for persons who were over pensionable age on 5 July 1948, and for the wives and widows of men who qualified if they are over pension age. A Category D pension is provided for people aged 80 and over if they are not entitled to another category of pension or are entitled to less than the Category D rate.

WEEKLY RATES OF BENEFIT
from April 1998

Child benefit

Eldest child	£11.45
Eldest child of certain lone parents	17.10
Each subsequent child	9.30

Guardian's allowance

Eldest child	9.90
Each subsequent child	11.30

*Invalid care allowance

	38.70
Increase for wife/other adult dependant	23.15

*Severe disablement allowance

†Basic rate	39.10
Under 40	13.60
40–49	8.60
50–59	4.30
Increase for wife/other adult dependant	23.20

Attendance allowance

Higher rate	51.30
Lower rate	34.30

Disability living allowance
Care component

Higher rate	51.30

Middle rate	34.30
Lower rate	13.60

Mobility component

Higher rate	35.85
Lower rate	13.60

Disability working allowance

Single person	50.75
Couple or single parent	79.40
Child aged under 11	12.35
aged 11–15	20.45
aged 16–18	25.40
Disabled child allowance	21.45
Thirty hours allowance	10.80
‡Applicable amount (income threshold)	
Single person	59.25
Couple or single parent	79.00

Retirement pension: categories *C and D

Single person	38.70
Increase for wife/other adult dependant	23.15
(not payable with Category D pension)	

*These benefits attract an increase for each dependent child (in addition to child benefit) of £9.90 for the first or only child and £11.30 for each subsequent child

†The age addition applies to the age when incapacity began

‡70 pence is deducted from the maximum DWA payable (this is obtained by adding up the appropriate allowance for each person in the family) for every £ coming in each week over the appropriate applicable amount. Where weekly income is below the applicable amount, maximum DWA is payable

INCOME SUPPORT

Income support is a benefit for those aged 16 and over whose income is below a certain level. It can be paid to people who are not expected to sign on as unemployed (income support for unemployed people was replaced by jobseeker's allowance in October 1996) and who are:
– incapable of work due to sickness or disability
– bringing up children alone
– 60 or over
– looking after a person who has a disability
– registered blind
Some people who are not in these categories may also be able to claim income support.

Income support is also payable to people who work for less than 16 hours a week on average (or 24 hours for a partner). Some people can claim income support if they work longer hours.

Income support is not payable if the claimant, or claimant and partner, have capital or savings in excess of £8,000. For capital and savings in excess of £3,000, a deduction of £1 is made for every £250 or part of £250 held. The maximum amount of capital is £16,000 for those in residential homes, and £19,000 for those in nursing homes.

Sums payable depend on fixed allowances laid down by law for people in different circumstances. If both partners are entitled to income support, either may claim it for the couple. People receiving income support may be able to receive housing benefit, help with mortgage or home loan interest and help with health care. They may also be eligible for help with exceptional expenses from the Social Fund. Special rates may apply to some people living in residential care or nursing homes. Leaflet IS20 gives a detailed explanation of income support.

In July 1997 the Government initiated a pilot programme for lone parents, and from October 1998 this was extended to the whole of the UK. All lone parents receiving income support are assigned a personal adviser at a jobcentre who will provide guidance and support with a view to enabling the claimant to find work.

INCOME SUPPORT PREMIUMS

Income support premiums are additional weekly payments for those with special needs. People qualifying for more than one premium will normally only receive the highest single premium for which they qualify. However, family premium, disabled child premium, severe disability premium and carer premium are payable in addition to other premiums.

People with children may qualify for:
- the family premium if they have at least one child (a higher rate is paid to lone parents, although from 6 April 1998 it has not generally been available to new claimants)
- the disabled child premium if they have a child who receives disability living allowance or is registered blind
Carers may qualify for:
- the carer premium if they or their partner are in receipt of invalid care allowance
Long-term sick or disabled people may qualify for:
- the disability premium if they or their partner are receiving certain benefits because they are disabled or cannot work; are registered blind; or if the claimant has been incapable of work or receiving statutory sick pay for at least 364 days (196 days if the person is terminally ill), including periods of incapacity separated by eight weeks or less
- the severe disability premium if the person lives alone and receives attendance allowance or the middle or higher rate of disability living allowance care component and no one receives invalid care allowance for caring for that person. This premium is also available to couples where both partners meet the above conditions
People aged 60 and over may qualify for:
- the pensioner premium if they or their partner are aged 60 to 74
- the enhanced pensioner premium if they or their partner are aged 75 to 79
- the higher pensioner premium if they or their partner are aged 80 or over. This is also available to people over 60 who receive attendance allowance, disability living allowance, long-term incapacity benefit or severe disablement allowance, or who are registered blind

WEEKLY RATES OF BENEFIT
from April 1998

Income support

Single person	
under 18	£30.30
under 18 (higher)	39.85
aged 18–24	39.85
aged 25 and over	50.35
aged 18 and over and a single parent	50.35
Couples*	
both under 18	60.10
one or both aged 18 or over	79.00
For each child in a family	
until September following 11th birthday	17.30
from September following 11th birthday to September following 16th birthday	25.35
†from September following 16th birthday to day before 19th birthday	30.30

Premiums

Family premium	11.05
Family (lone parent) premium	15.75
Disabled child premium	21.45
Carer premium	13.65
Disability premium	
Single	21.45
Couple	30.60

Severe disability premium	
Single	38.50
Couple (one person qualified)	38.50
Couple (both qualified)	77.00
Pensioner premium	
Single	20.10
Couple	30.35
Higher pensioner premium	
Single	27.20
Couple	38.90
Enhanced pensioner premium	
Single	22.85
Couple	33.55

*Where one or both partners are aged under 18, their personal allowance will depend on their situation
†If in full-time education up to A-level or equivalent standard

FAMILY CREDIT

Family credit is a tax-free benefit for working families with children. To qualify, a family must include at least one child under 16 (under 19 if in full-time education up to A-level or equivalent standard) and the claimant, or partner if there is one, must be working for at least 16 hours per week. It does not matter which partner is working and they may be employed or self-employed. Family credit is not payable if the claimant, or claimant and partner, have capital or savings in excess of £8,000. The rate of benefit is affected if capital or savings in excess of £3,000 are held.

Family credit is usually paid at the same rate for 26 weeks, after which a new claim can be made. The rate of family credit depends on:
- the family's net income, excluding child benefit, child benefit (lone-parent) and the first £15.00 of any maintenance in payment
- the number of children and the children's ages
- the number of hours the claimant or their partner work
- in certain circumstances, the amount of childcare charges paid for children under 12
Family credit is claimed by post and in two-parent families the woman should claim. A claim pack, FC1, is available from social security offices or the Family Credit Helpline on 01253-500050. *See* leaflet NI261.

WEEKLY RATES OF BENEFIT
from 7 April 1998

The maximum amount of family credit is payable where income is less than £79.00 per week. For every pound earned over £79.00, 70 pence will be deducted from the maximum amount of family credit that can be paid. The maximum rate consists of:

Adult credit (amount is the same for lone parents and couples)	£48.80
30-hour credit (where one parent works at least 30 hours per week)	10.80
Child credit	
each child under 11	12.35
each child aged 11–15	20.45
each child aged 16–18	25.40

HOUSING BENEFIT

Housing benefit is designed to help people with rent (including rent for accommodation in guest houses, lodgings or hostels). It does not cover mortgage payments. The amount of benefit paid depends on:
- the income of the claimant, and partner if there is one, including earned income, unearned income (any other income including some other benefits) and savings
- number of dependents

– certain extra needs of the claimant, partner or any dependants
– number of people sharing the home who are not dependent on the claimant
– how much rent is paid

Housing benefit is not payable if the claimant, or claimant and partner, have savings of over £16,000. The amount of benefit is affected if savings held exceed £3,000. Housing benefit is not paid for meals, fuel or certain service charges that may be included in the rent. Deductions are also made for most non-dependents who live in the same accommodation as the claimant (and their partner).

The maximum amount of benefit (which is not necessarily the same as the amount of rent paid) may be paid where the claimant is in receipt of income support or income-based jobseeker's allowance or where the claimant's income is less than the amount allowed for their needs. Any income over that allowed for their needs will mean that their benefit is reduced.

Claims for housing benefit are made to the local council. Those who are also claiming income support or income-based jobseeker's allowance may claim housing benefit at the local benefits or employment services office. *See* leaflets RR1 and RR2.

COUNCIL TAX BENEFIT

Nearly all the rules which apply to housing benefit apply to council tax benefit, which helps people on low incomes to pay council tax bills. The amount payable depends on how much council tax is paid and who lives with the claimant.

The maximum amount that is payable for those living in properties in council tax bands A to E is 100 per cent of the claimant's council tax liability. This also applies to those living in properties in bands F to H who were in receipt of the benefit at 31 March 1998. From 1 April 1998 council tax benefit for new claimants living in property bands F to H is restricted to the level payable for Band E. This may be available to those receiving income support or income-based jobseeker's allowance or to those whose income is less than that allowed for their needs. Any income over that allowed for their needs will mean that their council tax benefit is reduced. Deductions are made for non-dependents.

If a person shares a home with one or more adults (not their partner) who are on a low income, it may be possible to claim a second adult rebate. Those who are entitled to both council tax benefit and second adult rebate will be awarded whichever is the greater. Second adult rebate may be claimed by those not in receipt of council tax benefit.

THE SOCIAL FUND

The Social Fund helps people with expenses which are difficult to meet from regular income. Regulated maternity and funeral payments are decided by Adjudication Officers and cold weather payments are made automatically. These payments are not limited by the district's Social Fund budget. Discretionary community care grants, and budgeting and crisis loans are decided by Social Fund Officers and come out of a yearly budget which is allocated to each district (1997–8, grants £97 million; loans £370.5 million; £0.5 million set aside as a contingency reserve). *See* leaflet SB16.

REGULATED PAYMENTS

Maternity Payments

A payment of up to £100 for each baby expected, born, adopted, or the subject of a parental order. It is payable to people on income support, income-based jobseeker's allowance, disability working allowance and family credit and does not have to be repaid.

Funeral Payments

Payable for specified funeral director's charges, including the necessary cost of all burial or cremation expenses, plus other funeral expenses reasonably incurred up to £600, by people receiving income support, income-based jobseeker's allowance, disability working allowance, family credit, council tax benefit or housing benefit who have good reason for taking responsibility for the funeral expenses. Savings in excess of £500 (£1,000 for those aged 60 or over) are taken into account. These payments are recoverable from the estate of the deceased.

Cold-Weather Payments

£8.50 for any consecutive seven days when the average temperature is recorded as or forecast to be 0°C or below in their area. Payments are made to people on income support or income-based jobseeker's allowance and who have a child under five or whose benefit includes a pensioner or disability premium. They do not have to be repaid. Winter 1998–9 will be the second of a two-year winter fuel payments scheme helping pensioners with fuel bills. Every eligible pensioner household receives £20 (£50 if they receive income support).

DISCRETIONARY PAYMENTS

Community Care Grants

These are intended to help people on income support or income-based jobseeker's allowance to move into the community or avoid institutional or residential care; ease exceptional pressures on families; care for a prisoner on release on temporary licence; and/or meet certain essential travelling expenses. They do not have to be repaid.

Budgeting Loans

These are interest-free loans to people who have been receiving income support or income-based jobseeker's allowance for at least 26 weeks, for intermittent expenses that may be difficult to budget for.

Crisis Loans

These are interest-free loans to anyone, whether receiving benefit or not, who is without resources in an emergency, where there is no other means of preventing serious damage or serious risk to their health or safety.

SAVINGS

Savings over £500 (£1,000 for people aged 60 or over) are taken into account for maternity and funeral payments, community care grants and budgeting loans. All savings are taken into account for crisis loans. Savings are not taken into account for cold-weather payments.

INDUSTRIAL INJURIES AND DISABLEMENT BENEFITS

The industrial injuries scheme, administered under the Social Security Contributions and Benefits Act 1992, provides a range of benefits designed to compensate for disablement resulting from an industrial accident (i.e. an accident arising out of and in the course of an employed earner's employment) or from a prescribed disease due to the nature of a person's employment. Those who are self-employed are not covered by this scheme.

INDUSTRIAL INJURIES DISABLEMENT BENEFIT

A person must be at least 14 per cent disabled (except for certain respiratory diseases) in order to qualify for this benefit. The amount paid depends on the degree of disablement:

- those assessed as 14–19 per cent disabled are paid at the 20 per cent rate
- those with disablement of over 20 per cent will have the percentage rounded up or down to the nearest 10 per cent, e.g. a disablement of 44 per cent will be paid at the 40 per cent rate while a disablement of 45 per cent will be paid at the 50 per cent rate

Benefit is payable 15 weeks (90 days) after the date of the accident or onset of the disease and may be payable for a limited period or for life. The benefit is payable whether the person works or not and those who are incapable of work are entitled to draw statutory sick pay or incapacity benefit in addition to industrial injuries disablement benefit. It may also be possible to claim the following allowances:

- reduced earnings allowance for those who are unable to return to their regular work or work of the same standard and who had their accident (or whose disease started) before 1 October 1990
- retirement allowance for those who were entitled to reduced earnings allowance who have reached state pension age
- constant attendance allowance for those with a disablement of 95 per cent or more who need constant care. There are four rates of allowance depending on how much care the person needs
- exceptionally severe disablement allowance for those who are entitled to constant care attendance allowance at one of the higher rates and who need constant care permanently

See leaflets NI6 and N12.

OTHER BENEFITS

People who are disabled because of an accident or disease that was the result of work that they did before 5 July 1948 are not entitled to industrial injuries disablement benefit. They may, however, be entitled to payment under the workmen's compensation scheme or the pneumoconiosis, byssinosis and miscellaneous diseases benefit scheme. *See* leaflets WS1 and PN1.

WEEKLY RATES OF BENEFIT
from April 1998

*Disablement benefit/pension	
Degree of disablement	
100 per cent	£104.70
90	94.23
80	83.76
70	73.29
60	62.82
50	52.35
40	41.85
30	31.41
20	20.94
†Unemployability supplement	64.70
Addition for adult dependant (subject to earnings rule)	38.70
Reduced earnings allowance (maximum)	41.88
Retirement allowance (maximum)	10.47
Constant attendance allowance (normal maximum rate)	42.00
Exceptionally severe disablement allowance	42.00

*There is a weekly benefit for those under 18 with no dependants which is set at a lower rate
†This benefit attracts an increase for each dependent child (in addition to child benefit) of £9.90 for the first child and £11.30 for each subsequent child

CLAIMS AND QUESTIONS

With a few exceptions, claims and questions relating to social security benefits are decided by statutory authorities who act independently of the Department of Social Security and Department for Education and Employment. *See* leaflets NI246 and NI260.

Entitlement to benefit and regulated Social Fund payments is determined by the Adjudication Officer. A claimant who is dissatisfied with that decision has the right of appeal to an independent Social Security Appeal Tribunal. There is a further right of appeal to a Social Security Commissioner against the tribunal's decision but leave to appeal must first be obtained. Appeals to the Commissioner must be on a point of law. Provision is also made for the determination of certain questions by the Secretary of State for Social Security.

Disablement questions are decided by adjudicating medical authorities or medical appeal tribunals. Appeal to the Commissioner against a tribunal's decision is with leave and on a point of law only.

Decisions on applications to the discretionary Social Fund are made by Social Fund Officers. Applicants can ask for a review within 28 days of the date on the decision letter. The Social Fund Review Officer will review the case and there is a further right of review to an independent Social Fund Inspector.

Reviews of housing and council tax benefit decisions are dealt with initially by the council. The claimant must ask for a review within six weeks of being told how much benefit they will receive. Further reviews are dealt with by an independent review board.

OTHER BENEFITS

STATUTORY SICK PAY

Employers usually pay statutory sick pay (SSP) to their employees for up to 28 weeks of sickness in any period of incapacity for work that lasts longer than four days. SSP is paid at £57.70 per week and is subject to PAYE tax and NI deductions. Employees who cannot obtain SSP may be able to claim incapacity benefit. Employers may be able to recover some SSP costs. See leaflets NI244 and NI245.

STATUTORY MATERNITY PAY

In general, employers pay statutory maternity pay (SMP) to pregnant women who have been employed by them full or part-time for at least 26 weeks before the end of the 'qualifying week', which is 15 weeks before the week the baby is due, and whose earnings are on average at least at the lower earnings limit for the payment of NI contributions. All women who meet these conditions receive payment of 90 per cent of their average earnings for six weeks, followed by a maximum of 12 weeks at £57.70. SMP can be paid from the beginning of the 11th week before the week in which the baby is due but women can decide to begin maternity leave later than this. SMP is not payable for any week in which the woman works. Employers are reimbursed for 92 per cent of the SMP they pay (107 per cent for those whose annual NI liability (excluding Class 1A) is £20,000 or less). *See* Leaflet NI17A.

War Pensions

The War Pensions Agency, an executive agency of the Department of Social Security (DSS), awards war pensions under The Naval, Military and Air Forces, Etc. (Disablement and Death) Service Pensions Order 1983 to members of the armed forces in respect of the periods 4 August 1914 to 30 September 1921 and subsequent to 3 September 1939 (including present members of the armed forces). War pensions for the period 1 October 1921 to 2 September 1939 were dealt with by the Ministry of Defence until July 1996 when responsibility passed to the DSS. There is also a scheme for civilians and civil defence workers in respect of the 1939–45 war, and other schemes for groups such as merchant seamen and Polish armed forces who served under British command.

Pensions

War disablement pension is awarded for the disabling effects of any injury, wound or disease which is the result of, or has been aggravated by, conditions of service in the armed forces. It can only be paid once the person has left the armed forces. The amount of pension paid depends on the severity of disablement, which is assessed by comparing the health of the claimant with that of a healthy person of the same age and sex. The person's earning capacity or occupation are not taken into account in this assessment. A pension is awarded if the person has a disablement of 20 per cent or more and a lump sum is usually payable to those with a disablement of less than 20 per cent. No award is made for noise-induced sensorineural hearing loss where the assessment of disablement is less than 20 per cent.

War widow's pension is payable where the husband's death was due to, or hastened by, his service in the armed forces or where the husband was in receipt of a war disablement pension constant attendance allowance (or would have been had he not been in hospital). Since April 1997 a war widow's pension is also payable if the husband was getting unemployability supplement at the time of his death and his pensionable disablement was at least 80 per cent. Most war widows receive a standard rank-related rate but a lower weekly rate is payable to war widows of men below the rank of Lieutenant-Colonel who are under the age of 40, without children and capable of maintaining themselves. This is increased to the standard rate at age 40. Allowances are paid for children (in addition to child benefit) and adult dependents. An age allowance may also be given when the woman reaches 65 and increased at age 70 and age 80.

A war widower's pension may be payable to a man whose wife died because of service in the armed forces, if he was dependent on his wife before her death and cannot support himself.

All war pensions and war widow's pensions are tax-free and pensioners living overseas receive the same amount as those resident in the UK.

Supplementary Allowances

A number of supplementary allowances may be awarded to a war pensioner which are intended to meet various needs which may result from disablement or death and take account of its particular effect on the pensioner or spouse. The principal supplementary allowances are unemployability supplement, allowance for lowered standard of occupation and constant attendance allowance. Others include exceptionally severe disablement allowance, severe disablement occupational allowance, treatment allowance, mobility supplement, comforts allowance, clothing allowance, age allowance and widow's age allowance. There is a rent allowance available on a war widow's pension.

Social Security Benefits

Most social security benefits are paid in addition to the basic war disablement pension or war widow's pension. Any retirement pension for which a war widow qualifies on her own NI contribution record can be paid in addition to her war widow's pension.

A war pensioner or war widow who claims income support, family credit or disability working allowance has the first £10 of pension disregarded. A similar provision operates for housing benefit and council tax benefit; but the local authority may, at its discretion, disregard any or all of the balance.

Claims and Questions

To claim a war pension it is necessary to contact the nearest war pensioners' welfare service office, the address of which is available from local social security offices, or to write to the War Pensions Agency, Norcross, Blackpool FY5 3WP. The war pensioners' welfare service advises and assists war pensioners and war widows on any matters affecting their welfare. General advice can also be obtained from the War Pension Helpline on 01253-858858.

Independent pensions appeal tribunals hear appeals against decisions, made by the DSS, on entitlement and on the assessment of disability with respect to the 1939–45 war and subsequent service cases. War widows from the 1914 war may appeal against decisions about entitlement but there are now no rights of appeal in disablement cases from the 1914 war. Decisions on supplementary allowances are made on a discretionary basis and there is no provision for a statutory right of appeal against them. The DSS send information about how to appeal and the time limits that exist for appeals when they notify claimants of their decision. See leaflet WPA2.

Weekly Rates of Pensions and Allowances
from week commencing 6 April 1998

War disablement pension
Degree of disablement

100 per cent	£111.10
90	99.99
80	88.88
70	77.77
60	66.66
50	55.55
40	44.44
30	33.33
20	22.22

Unemployability supplement
Personal allowance	68.65
Increase for wife/other adult dependant	38.70
Increase for first child	9.90
Increase for other children	11.30

Allowance for lowered standard of occupation (maximum) 41.88
Constant attendance allowance
Half day rate	21.00
Full day rate	42.00
Intermediate rate	63.00
Exceptional rate	84.00

Widow's pension
(widow of Private or equivalent rank)
Standard rate	83.90
Increase for first child	14.25
Increase for other children	15.65
Childless widow under 40	19.41

Widow's age allowance
aged 65–69	9.60
aged 70–79	18.40
aged 80 and over	27.40

The rates for officers and widows of officers differ from those given above. See leaflet WPA9.

Development Corporations

NEW TOWNS

COMMISSION FOR THE NEW TOWNS
Central Business Exchange, 414-428 Midsummer Boulevard, Central Milton Keynes MK9 2EA
Tel 01908-692692; fax: 01908-691333

The Commission was established under the New Towns Act 1959. Its remit is to hold, manage and turn to account the property of development corporations transferred to the Commission; and to dispose of property so transferred and any other property held by it, as soon as it considers it expedient to do so. In carrying out its remit the Commission must have due regard to the convenience and welfare of persons residing, working or carrying on business there and, until disposal, the maintenance and enhancement of the value of the land held and return obtained from it.

The Commission has such responsibilities in Basildon, Bracknell, Central Lancashire, Corby, Crawley, Harlow, Hatfield, Hemel Hempstead, Milton Keynes, Northampton, Peterborough, Redditch, Skelmersdale, Stevenage, Telford, Warrington and Runcorn, Washington, and Welwyn Garden City. The Commission has minimal responsibilities (principally financial and litigation) in Aycliffe and Peterlee, and Cwmbran following the winding-up of their development corporations in 1988.

From April 1998 the Commission took over responsibility for any assets and liabilities remaining in the urban development corporations and housing action trusts of Tyne and Wear, Teesside, Trafford Park, Merseyside, Plymouth, Birmingham Heartlands, Black Country and London Docklands when these were wound up.
Chairman, Sir Alan Cockshaw, FEng
Deputy Chairman, M. H. Mallinson, CBE
Members, J. Trustram Eve; D. Hone; Sir Brian Jenkins, GBE; J. Walker
Chief Executive, N. J. Walker

REGIONAL OFFICES
NORTH (Central Lancashire, Skelmersdale, Warrington and Runcorn, Washington, Aycliffe and Peterlee, Merseyside, Teesside, Trafford Park, and Tyne and Wear), New Town House, Buttermarket Street, Warrington WA1 2LF. Tel: 01925-651144. *Director, Commercial Land Sales,* M. Anderson
CENTRAL (Milton Keynes, Corby, Northampton, Plymouth), Central Business Exchange, 414–428 Midsummer Boulevard, Central Milton Keynes MK9 2EA. Tel: 01908-692692. *Director, Commercial Land Sales,* R. Jamieson
WEST MIDLANDS (Redditch, Telford, Birmingham Heartlands, Black Country), Jordan House West, Hall Court, Hall Park Way, Telford TF3 4NN. Tel: 01952-293131. *Director, Land Sales,* E. Jones
SOUTH (Basildon, Bracknell, Crawley, Harlow, Hatfield, Hemel Hempstead, Peterborough, Stevenage, Welwyn Garden City, London Docklands), Central Business Exchange, 414–428 Midsummer Boulevard, Central Milton Keynes MK9 2EA. Tel: 01908-692692 *Director, Land Sales,* G. D. Johnston

DEVELOPMENT CORPORATIONS

WALES
DEVELOPMENT BOARD FOR RURAL WALES (1977), merged with Welsh Development Agency on 1 October 1998 (*see* page 352)

SCOTLAND
CUMBERNAULD (1956), wound up 31 December 1996
EAST KILBRIDE (1947), wound up 31 December 1995
GLENROTHES (1948), wound up 31 December 1995
IRVINE (1966), wound up 31 March 1997
LIVINGSTON (1962), wound up 31 March 1997

URBAN DEVELOPMENT CORPORATIONS

Urban development corporations were established under the Local Government, Planning and Land Act 1980, as short-life public bodies. Their objectives were to bring land and buildings back into effective use; to develop existing and new industry and commerce; to improve the environment; and to ensure that housing and social facilities are available in the area. All the corporations in England have now been wound up; the last eight (Birmingham Heartlands, Black Country, London Docklands, Merseyside, Plymouth, Teesside, Trafford Park and Tyne and Wear) ceased operations on 31 March 1998.

CARDIFF BAY (1987), Baltic House, Mount Stuart Square, Cardiff CF1 6DH. Tel: 01222-585858. *Chairman,* Sir Geoffrey Inkin, OBE; *Chief Executive,* M. Boyce. Area, 1,094 hectares
LAGANSIDE (1989), Clarendon Building, 15 Clarendon Road, Belfast BT1 3BG. Tel: 01232-328507. *Chairman,* A. Hopkins; *Chief Executive,* M. Smith. Area, 200 hectares

REGIONAL DEVELOPMENT AGENCIES

The creation of regional development agencies in England was announced in a White Paper *Building Partnerships for Prosperity* in December 1997. The agencies' responsibilities will include economic development and regeneration, competitiveness, business support and investment, skills, employment, and sustainable development. There will be eight in England outside London, to be set up in April 1999, and one in London, to be set up at a later date. Some of the functions currently undertaken by English Partnerships, the Government Offices for the Regions and the Rural Development Commission (which is to be merged with the Countryside Commission) will transfer to the agencies.

The Water Industry

ENGLAND AND WALES

In England and Wales the Secretary of State for the Environment, Transport and the Regions and the Secretary of State for Wales have overall responsibility for water policy and set the environmental and health and safety standards for the water industry. The Director-General of Water Services, as the independent economic regulator, is responsible for ensuring that the private water companies are able to fulfil their statutory obligation to provide water supply and sewerage services, and for protecting the interests of consumers.

The Minister of Agriculture, Fisheries and Food and the Secretary of State for Wales are responsible for policy relating to land drainage, flood protection, sea defences and the protection and development of fisheries.

The Environment Agency is responsible for water quality and the control of pollution, the management of water resources and nature conservation. The Drinking Water Inspectorate and local authorities are responsible for the quality of drinking water.

THE WATER COMPANIES

Until 1989 nine regional water authorities in England and the Welsh Water Authority in Wales were responsible for water supply and the development of water resources, sewerage and sewage disposal, pollution control, freshwater fisheries, flood protection, water recreation, and environmental conservation. The Water Act 1989 provided for the creation of a privatized water industry under public regulation, and the functions of the regional water authorities were taken over by ten holding companies and the regulatory bodies.

Of the 99 per cent of the population of England and Wales who are connected to a public water supply, 75 per cent are supplied by the water companies (through their principal operating subsidiaries, the water service companies). The remaining 25 per cent are supplied by statutory water companies which were already in the private sector. Most of these have public limited company (PLC) status; many are now French-owned and one is American-owned. They are represented by Water UK, which also represents the ten water service companies responsible for sewerage and sewage disposal in England and Wales, and the state-owned water authorities of Scotland and Northern Ireland. Water UK is the trade association for all the water service companies except Mid Kent Water.

WATER UK, 1 Queen Anne's Gate, London, SW1H 9BT. Tel: 0171-344 1844. *Chief Executive*, Ms P. Taylor

Water Service Companies

ANGLIAN WATER SERVICES LTD, Anglian House, Ambury Road, Huntingdon, Cambs PE18 6NZ
DWR CYMRU (WELSH WATER), Cambrian Way, Brecon, Powys LD3 7HP
NORTHUMBRIAN WATER LTD, Abbey Road, Pity Me, Durham DH1 5FJ
NORTH WEST WATER LTD, Dawson House, Liverpool Road, Great Sankey, Warrington WA5 3LW
SEVERN TRENT WATER LTD, 2297 Coventry Road, Sheldon, Birmingham B26 3PU
SOUTHERN WATER SERVICES LTD, Southern House, Yeoman Road, Worthing, W. Sussex BN13 3NX
SOUTH WEST WATER SERVICES LTD, Peninsula House, Rydon Lane, Exeter EX2 7HR
THAMES WATER UTILITIES LTD, Nugent House, Vastern Road, Reading RG1 8DB
WESSEX WATER SERVICES LTD, Wessex House, Passage Street, Bristol BS2 0JQ
YORKSHIRE WATER SERVICES LTD, West Riding House, 67 Albion Street, Leeds LS1 5AA

WATER SUPPLY AND CONSUMPTION 1996-7

	Supply		Consumption			
	Supply from treatment works (*Ml/day*)	Total leakage (*Ml/day*)	Household (*l/head/day*) Unmetered	Metered	Non-household (*l/prop/day*) Unmetered	Metered
WATER SERVICE COMPANIES						
Anglian	1,179.3	212.6	177.0	139.8	1,488.6	3,672.6
Dwr Cymru (Welsh)	1,031.2	357.2	173.6	181.1	1,030.6	3,502.0
Northumbrian	798.8	192.4	165.7	133.4	927.2	5,002.2
North West	2,176.5	665.9	157.1	114.7	703.5	3,153.6
Severn Trent	2,022.0	478.6	158.2	138.6	740.0	2.970.6
Southern	622.3	112.7	175.9	140.0	995.1	2,966.6
South West	478.1	129.1	175.3	140.7	1,101.1	1,814.9
Thames	2,857.7	1,082.9	199.3	165.5	1,004.6	3,708.5
Wessex	426.5	128.8	168.0	137.7	1,838.2	2,814.7
Yorkshire	1,350.5	419.8	154.0	130.3	718.3	2,985.9
Total	12,942.9	3,779.8	—	—	—	—
Average	—	—	170.4	138.9	962.5	3,236.3
WATER COMPANIES						
Total	3,422.2	724.9	—	—	—	—
Average	—	—	182.2	156.1	942.5	3,403.4

Source: Office of Water Services

The Office of Water Services (Ofwat) (*see* pages 351–2) was set up under the Water Act 1989 and is the independent economic regulator of the water and sewerage companies in England and Wales. Ofwat's main duty is to ensure that the companies can finance and carry out their statutory functions and to protect the interests of water customers. Ofwat is a non-ministerial government department headed by the Director-General of Water Services, who is appointed by the Secretary of State for the Environment, Transport and the Regions and the Secretary of State for Wales.

The Environment Agency (*see* page 301) has statutory duties and powers in relation to water resources, pollution control, flood defence, fisheries, recreation, conservation and navigation in England and Wales.

The Drinking Water Inspectorate is responsible for assessing the quality of the drinking water supplied by the water companies, inspecting the com-panies themselves and investigating any accidents affecting drinking water quality. The Chief Inspector presents an annual report to the Secretary of State for the Environment, Transport and the Regions and the Secretary of State for Wales.

Methods of Charging

In England and Wales, most domestic customers still pay for domestic water supply and sewerage services through charges based on the old rateable value of their property, although about 10 per cent of householders are now charged according to consumption, which is recorded by meter. Industrial and most commercial customers are charged according to consumption.

Under the Water Industry Act 1991, water companies must discontinue basing their charges on the old rateable value of property after 31 March 2000. In May 1997 the Government announced a review of the system of charging for water. Among other issues, the review considered alternative bases of charging, including continuing the use of rateable values after 2000, the use of council tax bands and metering policy. The Government issued a consulta-tion paper, *Water Charging in England and Wales: A New Approach*, on 1 April 1998.

SCOTLAND

Overall responsibility for national water policy in Scotland rests with the Secretary of State for Scotland. Most aspects of water policy are administered through the Scottish Office Agriculture, Environment and Fisheries Depart-ment.

Water supply and sewerage services were formerly local authority responsibilities and the Central Scotland Water Development Board had the function of developing new sources of water supply for the purpose of providing water in bulk to water authorities whose limits of supply were within the board's area. The Local Government etc. (Scotland) Act 1994 provided for three new public water authorities, covering the north, east and west of Scotland respectively, to be established to take over the provision of water and sewerage services from April 1996. From that date the Central Scotland Water Development Board was abolished. The new authorities are accountable to Parlia-ment through the Secretary of State for Scotland; from July 1999 parliamentary responsibility for the water and sew-erage industry in Scotland and for its regulation will be devolved to the Scottish Parliament. The Act also provi-ded for a Scottish Water and Sewerage Customers Council to be established to represent consumer interests. It monitors the performance of the authorities; approves charges schemes; investigates complaints; and keeps the

Secretary of State advised on standards of service and customer relations.

The Scottish Environment Protection Agency (SEPA) (*see* page 339) is responsible for promoting the cleanliness of Scotland's rivers, lochs and coastal waters. SEPA is also responsible for controlling pollution.

Water Resources 1996

	No.	Yield (Ml/day)
Reservoirs and lochs	287	2,943
Feeder intakes	27	—
River intakes	223	422
Bore-holes	35	77
Underground springs	103	46
Total	*692	3,487

* Including compensation reservoirs

Water Consumption 1996

Total (Ml/day)		2,311.6
Potable		2,254.8
Unmetered		1,686.4
Metered		568.4
Non-potable†		56.8*
Total (l/head/day)		462.7
Unmetered		337.6
Metered and non-potable†		116.9

† 'Non-potable' supplied for industrial purposes. Metered supplies in general relate to commercial and industrial use and unmetered to domestic use
* Includes 41.6 Ml/d supplied by East of Scotland Water Authority to West of Scotland Water Authority from Loch Lomond
Source: The Scottish Office

East of Scotland Water Authority, Pentland Gait, 597 Calder Road, Edinburgh EH11 4HJ. Tel: 0131-453 7500. *Chief Executive*, R. Rennet

North of Scotland Water Authority, Cairngorm House, Beechwood Park North, Inverness IV2 3ED. Tel: 01463-245400. *Chief Executive*, A. Findlay

Scottish Water and Sewerage Customers Council, Ochil House, Springkerse Business Park, Stirling FK7 7XE. Tel: 01786-430200. *Director*, Dr V. Nash

West of Scotland Water Authority, 419 Balmore Road, Glasgow G22 6NU. Tel: 0141-355 5333. *Chief Executive*, E. Chambers

Methods of Charging

The water authorities set charges for domestic and non-domestic water and sewerage provision through charges schemes which have to be approved by the Scottish Water and Sewerage Customers Council. The authorities must publish a summary of their charges schemes.

NORTHERN IRELAND

In Northern Ireland ministerial responsibility for water services lies with the Secretary of State for Northern Ireland. The Water Service, which is an executive agency of the Department of the Environment for Northern Ireland, is responsible for policy and co-ordination with regard to supply, distribution and cleanliness of water, and the provision and maintenance of sewerage services.

The Water Service (*see* page 330) is divided into four regions, the Eastern, Northern, Western and Southern Divisions. These are based in Belfast, Ballymena, London-derry and Craigavon respectively.

On major issues the Department of the Environment for Northern Ireland seeks the views of the Northern Ireland Water Council, a body appointed to advise the Department on the exercise of its water and sewerage functions. The Council includes representatives from agriculture, angling, industry, commerce, tourism, trade unions and local government.

METHODS OF CHARGING

Usually householders do not pay separately for water and sewerage services; the costs of these services are allowed for in the Northern Ireland regional rate. Water consumed by industry, commerce and agriculture in excess of 100 cubic metres (22,000 gallons) per half year is charged through meters. Traders operating from industrially derated premises are required to pay for the treatment and disposal of the trade effluent which they discharge into the public sewerage system.

HM Coastguard

Founded in 1822, originally to guard the coasts against smuggling, HM Coastguard's role today is the very different one of guarding and saving life at sea. The Service is responsible for co-ordinating all civil maritime search and rescue operations around the 10,500 mile coastline of Great Britain and Northern Ireland and 1,000 miles into the Atlantic. In addition, it co-operates with search and rescue organizations of neighbouring countries in western Europe and around the Atlantic seaboard. The Service maintains a 24-hour radar watch on the Dover Strait, providing a Channel navigation information service for all shipping in one of the busiest sea lanes in the world. It also liaises very closely with the off-shore oil and gas industry and with merchant shipping companies.

Since 1997 HM Coastguard has been organized into five regions, each with a regional controller. Each region is subdivided into districts under district controllers, operating from maritime rescue co-ordination centres or sub-centres. In all there are 21 of these centres. They are on 24-hour watch and are fitted with a comprehensive range of communications equipment. They are supported by smaller stations staffed by part-time auxiliary coastguards under the direction of regulars, each of which keeps its parent centre fully informed of day-to-day casualty risk, particularly on the more remote danger spots around the coast.

Between 1 January and 31 December 1997, HM Coastguard co-ordinated 11,667 incidents requiring search and rescue facilities; 16,884 people were assisted and 251 lives were lost. All distress telephone and radio calls are centralized on the 21 centres, which are on the alert for people or vessels in distress, shipping hazards and pollution incidents. Using telecommunications equipment, including satellite, they can alert and co-ordinate the most appropriate rescue facilities; RNLI lifeboats, Royal Navy, RAF or Coastguard helicopters, fixed-wing aircraft, vessels in the vicinity, or Coastguard shore and cliff rescue teams.

For those who regularly sail in local waters or make longer passages, the Coastguard Yacht and Boat Safety Scheme provides a valuable free service. Its aim is to give the Coastguard a record of the details of craft, their equipment fit and normal operating areas. Yacht and Boat Safety Scheme cards are available from all Coastguard stations, harbourmasters' offices, and most yacht clubs and marinas as well as Coastguard headquarters.

Members of the public who see an accident or a potentially dangerous incident on or around the coast should dial 999 and ask for the Coastguard.

In April 1998 the Coastguard Agency and the Marine Safety Agency merged, forming the Maritime and Coastguard Agency, an executive agency of the Department of the Environment, Transport and the Regions.

Coastguard Headquarters and Office of the Chief Coastguard,
Spring Place, 105 Commercial Road, Southampton SO15 1EG. Tel: 01703-329100

Energy

The main primary sources of energy in Britain are oil, natural gas, coal, nuclear power and water power. The main secondary sources (i.e. sources derived from the primary sources) are electricity, coke and smokeless fuels, and petroleum products. The Department of the Environment, Transport and the Regions is responsible for promoting energy efficiency.

INDIGENOUS PRODUCTION OF PRIMARY FUELS
Million tonnes of oil equivalent

	1996	1997p
Coal	31.7	30.8
Petroleum	143.1	141.3
Natural gas	84.7	87.0
Primary electricity		
Nuclear	22.12	23.01
Natural flow hydro	0.33	0.38
Total	282.0	282.4

p provisional

INLAND ENERGY CONSUMPTION BY PRIMARY FUEL
Million tonnes of oil equivalent, seasonally adjusted

	1996	1997p
Coal	46.7	41.7
Petroleum	78.6	75.9
Natural gas	82.4	83.4
Primary electricity	23.89	24.85
Nuclear	22.12	23.01
Natural flow hydro	0.33	0.38
Net imports	1.44	1.46
Total	231.6	225.8

p provisional

TRADE IN FUELS AND RELATED MATERIALS 1997p

	Quantity*	Value†
IMPORTS		
Coal and other solid fuel	14.2	714
Crude petroleum	45.3	3,647
Petroleum products	15.3	1,442
Natural gas	1.3	103
Electricity	1.4	406
Total	77.6	6,312
Total (fob)‡	—	5,875
EXPORTS		
Coal and other solid fuel	1.1	82
Crude petroleum	76.7	6,334
Petroleum products	29.2	3,214
Natural gas	1.7	80
Electricity	—	1
Total	108.6	9,712
Total (fob)‡	—	9,712

p provisional
* Million tonnes of oil equivalent
† £ million
‡ Adjusted to exclude estimated costs of insurance, freight, etc.
Source: Department of Trade and Industry

OIL

Until the 1960s Britain imported almost all its oil supplies. In 1969 oil was discovered in the Arbroath field of the UK Continental Shelf (UKCS). The first oilfield to be brought into production was the Argyll field in 1975, and since the mid-1970s Britain has been a major producer of crude oil.

Licences for exploration and production are granted to companies by the Department of Trade and Industry; the leading British oil companies are British Petroleum (BP) and Shell Transport and Trading. At the end of 1997, 938 offshore licences and 129 onshore licences had been awarded, and there were 98 offshore oilfields in production. In 1997 there were 10 oil refineries and four smaller refining units processing crude and process oils. There are estimated to be reserves of 2,015 million tonnes of oil in the UKCS. Royalties are payable on fields approved before April 1982 and petroleum revenue tax is levied on fields approved between 1975 and March 1993.

DRILLING ACTIVITY 1997p

Number of wells started	Offshore	Onshore
Exploration and appraisal	98	13
Exploration	63	—
Appraisal	35	—
Development	256	29

p provisional

VALUE OF UKCS OIL AND GAS PRODUCTION AND INVESTMENT
£ million

	1996	1997p
Total income	21,052	18,955
Operating costs	3,978	4,150
Exploration expenditure	1,097	1,194
Gross trading profits*	14,387	12,638
Percentage contribution to GDP	2.4	2.1
Capital investment	4,440	4,336
Percentage contribution to industrial investment	18	16

* Net of stock appreciation
p provisional

INDIGENOUS PRODUCTION AND REFINERY RECEIPTS

	1996	1997p
Indigenous production (thousand tonnes)	130,007	128,205
Crude oil	121,930	120,116
NGLs*	8,077	8,089
Refinery receipts (thousand tonnes)		
Indigenous	49,449	47,602
Other†	997	794
Net foreign arrivals	48,275	48,636

p provisional
* Natural gas liquids: condensates and petroleum gases derived at onshore treatment plants
† Mainly recycled products

DELIVERIES OF PETROLEUM PRODUCTS FOR INLAND CONSUMPTION BY ENERGY USE
Thousand tonnes

	1996	1997p
Electricity generators	3,316	1,326
Gas works	50	46
Iron and steel industry	737	719
Other industries	6,436	5,813
Transport	46,642	47,322

Domestic	3,167	3,057
Other	3,744	3,264
Total	64,092	61,547

p provisional
Source: Department of Trade and Indusrty

GAS

From the late 18th century gas in Britain was produced from coal. In the 1960s town gas began to be produced from oil-based feedstocks using imported oil. In 1965 gas was discovered in the North Sea in the West Sole field, which became the first gasfield in production in 1967, and from the late 1960s natural gas began to replace town gas. Britain is now the world's fourth largest producer of gas and in 1997 only 1.5 per cent of gas available for consumption in the UK was imported.

By the end of 1997 there were 75 offshore gasfields producing natural gas and associated gas (mainly methane). There are estimated to be between 765,000 million and 1,985,000 million cubic metres of recoverable gas reserves in existing discoveries. There are about 8,704.5 km of major submarine pipelines for transporting hydro-carbons, and onshore pipelines for carrying refined products and chemicals. Natural gas is transported around Britain by about 270,000 km of pipelines supplied by five pipeline terminals. This pipeline system is owned by Transco and transports gas on behalf of suppliers or shippers under a network code.

The Office of Gas Supply (*see* page 304) is the regulatory body for the gas industry. The Government announced in 1998 plans to merge the Office of Gas Supply and the Office of Electricity Regulation to create a single Energy Regulator for Great Britain.

The gas industry in Britain was nationalized in 1949 and operated as the Gas Council. The Gas Council was replaced by the British Gas Corporation in 1972 and the industry became more centralized. The British Gas Corporation was privatized in 1986 as British Gas PLC.

In 1993 the Monopolies and Mergers Commission found that British Gas's integrated business in Great Britain as a gas trader and the owner of the gas transportation system could be expected to operate against the public interest. In February 1997 British Gas demerged its trading arm into two separate companies: BG PLC, which runs the Transco pipeline business in Britain and oil and gas exploration and production in the UK and abroad; and Centrica PLC, which runs the trading, service and retail operations under the British Gas name.

Competition was gradually introduced into the industrial gas market from 1986. Supply of gas to the domestic market was opened to companies other than British Gas, starting in April 1996 with a pilot project in the West Country and Wales. From spring 1997 competition was progressively introduced throughout the rest of Britain in stages which were completed in May 1998. Gas companies can now also sell electricity to their customers. Similarly, electricity companies can also offer gas.

BG PLC, 100 Thames Valley Park Drive, Reading RG6 1PT. Tel: 0118-935 3222. *Chairman,* R. V. Giordano; *Chief Executive,* D. Varney
CENTRICA PLC, Charter Court, 50 Windsor Road, Slough, Berks SL1 2HA. Tel: 01753-758000. *Chief Executive,* R. Gardner

NATURAL GAS PRODUCTION AND SUPPLY
GWh

	1996	1997p
Gross gas production	980,064	1,000,676
Exports	15,203	21,666
Imports	19,804	14,062
Gas available	923,260	929,252
Gas transmitted‡	908,647	912,844

p provisional
‡ Figures differ from gas available mainly because of stock changes

NATURAL GAS CONSUMPTION
GWh

	1996	1997p
Electricity generators	190,691	240,346
Iron and steel industry	21,961	20,525
Other industries	169,293	161,763
Domestic	375,841	342,353
Public administration, commerce and agriculture	119,935	108,766
Total	877,721	873,753

p provisional
Source: Deaprtment of Trade and Industry

COAL

Coal has been mined in Britain for centuries and the availability of coal was crucial to the industrial revolution of the 18th and 19th centuries. Mines were in private ownership until 1947 when they were nationalized and came under the management of the National Coal Board, later the British Coal Corporation. In addition to producing coal at its own deep-mine and opencast sites, of which there were 850 in 1955, British Coal was responsible for licensing private operators.

Under the Coal Industry Act 1994, the Coal Authority (*see* page 291) was established to take over ownership of coal reserves and to issue licences to private mining companies as part of the privatization of British Coal. The Coal Authority also deals with the physical legacy of mining, e.g. subsidence damage claims, and is responsible for holding and making available all existing records. The mines were sold as five separate businesses in 1994 and coal production in the UK is now undertaken entirely in the private sector. At the end of 1997 there were 21 large deep mines in operation.

The main UK customer for coal is the electricity supply industry, but the latter's demand for coal declined and National Power (*see* page 502) announced that it expected to close ten of its 18 coal-fired power stations by 2000. However, following a review of energy policy, the Government announced measures in June 1998 which included a freeze on new applications to build gas-fired power stations in order to increase opportunities for coal-fired power stations; there is a possibility that the EU might challenge the Government's plans.

COAL PRODUCTION AND FOREIGN TRADE
Thousand tonnes

	1996	1997p
Total production	50,197	48,540
Deep-mined	32,223	30,351
Opencast	16,315	16,675
Imports	17,799	20,230
Exports	988	1,147

p provisional

INLAND COAL USE
Thousand tonnes

	1996	1997p
Fuel producers		
Collieries	8	8
Electricity generators	54,893	46,990
Coke ovens	8,635	8,750
Other conversion industries	946	864
Total	71,403	63,667
Final users		
Industry	3,639	3,323
Domestic	2,705	3,364
Public administration, commerce and agriculture	577	368

p provisional
Source: Department of Trade and Industry

ELECTRICITY

The first power station in Britain generating electricity for public supply began operating in 1882. In the 1930s a national transmission grid was developed, and it was reconstructed and extended in the 1950s and 1960s. Power stations were operated by the Central Electricity Generating Board.

Under the Electricity Act 1989, 12 regional electricity companies (RECs), which are responsible for the distribution of electricity from the national grid to consumers, were formed from the former area electricity boards in England and Wales. Four companies were formed from the Central Electricity Generating Board: three generating companies (National Power PLC, Nuclear Electric PLC and PowerGen PLC) and the National Grid Company PLC, which owns and operates the transmission system. National Power and PowerGen were floated on the stock market in 1991. Nuclear Electric was split into two parts in 1995; the part comprising the more modern nuclear stations was incorporated into a new company, British Energy, which was floated on the stock market in 1996. Magnox Electric, which owns the magnox nucleur reactors, remains in the public sector ans was merged with British Nuclear Fuels (BNFL) in early 1998. Ownership of the National Grid Company was transferred to the RECs and subsequently floated in 1995.

There are now 27 electricity generating companies in Britain. The RECs currently have a monopoly on sales of 100 kW or less to consumers in their franchise areas; over this limit competition has been introduced. Competition was due to be introduced into the domestic electricity market in April 1998, but was postponed due to technical difficulties. Competition is now being introduced from September 1998 and will be completed in June 1999. Generators will sell the electricity they produce into an open commodity market (the Pool) from which buyers will purchase electricity.

Electricity companies can now also sell gas to their customers. Similarly, gas companies can also offer electricity.

In Scotland, three new companies were formed under the Electricity Act 1989: Scottish Power PLC and Scottish Hydro-Electric PLC, which are responsible for generation, transmission, distribution and supply; and Scottish Nuclear Ltd. Scottish Power and Scottish Hydro-Electric were floated on the stock market in 1991; Scottish Nuclear was incorporated into British Energy in 1995.

In Northern Ireland, Northern Ireland Electricity PLC was set up in 1993 under a 1991 Order in Council. It is responsible for transmission, distribution and supply and has been floated on the stock market. There is no Pool in Northern Ireland; three private companies are responsible for electricity generation and the electricity is sold to Northern Ireland Electricity under a series of power purchase agreements.

The Office of Electricity Regulation (*see* page 297) is the regulatory body for the electricity industry. The Government has announced plans to merge the Office of Gas Supply and the Office of Electricity Regulation to create a single Energy Regulator for Great Britain.

The Electricity Association is the electricity industry's main trade association, providing representational and professional services for the electricity companies. EA Technology Ltd provides distribution and utilization research, development and technology transfer.

NUCLEAR POWER

Nuclear reactors began to supply electricity to the national grid in 1956. It is generated at six magnox reactors, seven advanced gas-cooled reactors (AGRs) and one pressurized water reactor (PWR), Sizewell 'B' in Suffolk. Nuclear stations now generate about 28 per cent of the UK's electricity.

In preparation for privatization, the nuclear industry was restructured in December 1995. A holding company, British Energy PLC, was formed with two operational subsidiaries, Nuclear Electric Ltd and Scottish Nuclear Ltd. Nuclear Electric operates the five AGRs and the PWR in England and Wales; Scottish Nuclear operates the two AGRs in Scotland. British Energy was floated on the stock market in 1996. The Magnox reactors were transferred to Magnox Electric PLC, which remained in public ownership. In January 1998 the Government's shareholding in Magnox Electric was transferred to British Nuclear Fuels Ltd (BNFL). BNFL is in public ownership, providing reprocessing, waste management and effluent treatment services. The UK Atomic Energy Authority (*see* page 284) is responsible for the decommissioning of nuclear reactors and other nuclear facilities used in research and development. UK Nirex, which is owned by the nuclear generating companies and the Government, is responsible for the disposal of intermediate and some low-level nuclear waste. The Nuclear Installations Inspectorate of the Health and Safety Executive (*see* page 307) is the nuclear industry's regulator.

SUPPLY COMPANIES

BRITISH ENERGY PLC, 10 Lochside Place, Edinburgh EH12 9DF. Tel: 0131-527 2000. *Chief Executive (acting),* J. Robb

MAGNOX ELECTRIC PLC, Berkeley Centre, Berkeley, Glos GL13 9PB. Tel: 01453-810451. *Chief Executive,* R. Hall

THE NATIONAL GRID COMPANY PLC, National Grid House, Kirby Corner Road, Coventry CV4 8JY. Tel: 01203-423000. *Chief Executive,* D. Jones

NATIONAL POWER PLC, Windmill Hill Business Park, Whitehill Way, Swindon, Wilts SN5 6PB. Tel: 01793-877777. *Chief Executive,* K. Henry

POWERGEN PLC, Westwood Way, Westwood Business Park, Coventry CV4 8LG. Tel: 01203-424000. *Chairman,* E. Wallis

REGIONAL ELECTRICITY COMPANIES

EASTERN ELECTRICITY PLC, PO Box 40, Wherstead Park, Wherstead, Ipswich IP9 2AQ. Tel: 01473-688688

EAST MIDLANDS ELECTRICITY PLC, PO Box 444, Wollaton, Nottingham NG8 1EZ. Tel: 0115-901 0101

LONDON ELECTRICITY PLC, Templar House, 81–87 High Holborn, London WC1V 6NU. Tel: 0171-242 9050

MANWEB PLC, Manweb House, Kingsfield Court, Chester Business Park, Chester CH4 9RF. Tel: 0845-272 3636

MIDLANDS ELECTRICITY PLC, Mucklow Hill, Halesowen, W. Midlands B62 8BP Tel: 0121-423 2345
NORTHERN ELECTRIC PLC, Carliol House, Market Street, Newcastle upon Tyne NE1 6NE. Tel: 0191-210 2000
NORWEB PLC, Talbot Road, Manchester M16 0HQ. Tel: 0161-873 8000
SEEBOARD PLC, Forest Gate, Brighton Road, Crawley, W. Sussex RH11 9BH. Tel: 01293-565888
SOUTHERN ELECTRIC PLC, Southern Electric House, Westacott Way, Littlewick Green, Maidenhead, Berks SL6 3QB. Tel: 01628-822166
SWALEC PLC, Newport Road, St Mellons, Cardiff CF3 9XW. Tel: 01222-792111
SWEB PLC, 800 Park Avenue, Aztec West, Almondsbury, Bristol BS32 4SE. Tel: 01454-201101
YORKSHIRE ELECTRICITY GROUP PLC, Wetherby Road, Scarcroft, Leeds LS14 3HS. Tel: 0113-289 2123

SCOTLAND

HYDRO-ELECTRIC PLC, Dunkeld Road, Perth PH1 5WA. Tel: 01738-455040. *Chief Executive*, R. Young
SCOTTISH POWER PLC, 1 Atlantic Quay, Glasgow G2 8SP. Tel: 0141-248 8200. *Chief Executive*, I. Robinson

NORTHERN IRELAND

NORTHERN IRELAND ELECTRICITY PLC, 120 Malone Road, Belfast BT9 5HT. Tel: 01232-661100. *Chief Executive*, Dr P. Haren
ELECTRICITY ASSOCIATION LTD, 30 Millbank, London SW1P 4RD. Tel: 0171-963 5700. *Chief Executive*, P. E. G. Daubeney
EA TECHNOLOGY LTD, Capenhurst, Chester CH1 6ES. Tel: 0151-339 4181. *Managing Director*, Dr S. F. Exell

ELECTRICITY GENERATION, SUPPLY AND CONSUMPTION
GWh

	1995	1996
Electricity generated: total	34,047	347,369
Major power producers: total	310,292	323,155
Conventional steam stations	169,866	160,565
Nuclear stations	85,298	91,040
Gas turbines and oil engines	190	226
Combined cycle gas turbine stations	48,720	65,880
Hydro-electric stations:		
Natural flow	4,096	2,801
Pumped storage	1,552	1,556
Renewables other than hydro	570	1,087
Other generators	23,755	24,214
Electricity used on works: total	17,391	17,728
Major generating companies	15,799	16,064
Other generators	1,592	1,664
Electricity supplied (gross): total	316,655	329,641
Major power producers: total	294,493	307,091
Conventional steam stations	162,084	—
Nuclear stations	77,643	82,871
Gas turbines and oil engines	181	216
Combined cycle gas turbine stations	48,525	65,604
Hydro-electric stations:		
Natural flow	4,051	2,763
Pumped storage	1,502	1,507
Renewables other than hydro	506	960
Other generators	22,163	22,550
Electricity used in pumping		
Major power producers	2,282	2,430
Electricity supplied (net): total	314,374	327,209
Major power producers	292,211	304,659
Other generators	22,163	22,550
Net imports	16,313	16,677
Electricity available	330,687	343,866
Losses in transmission, etc.	28,457	29,601
Electricity consumption: total	302,230	314,285
Fuel industries	8,289	8,629
Final users: total	293,942	305,656
Industrial sector	99,909	103,129
Domestic sector	102,210	107,513
Other sectors	91,823	95,014

Source: The Stationery Office – Annual Abstract of Statistics 1998

RENEWABLE SOURCES

Renewable sources of energy principally include biofuels, hydro, wind, waste and solar. Renewable sources accounted for 2.3 million tonnes of oil equivalent of primary energy use in 1997; of this, about 1.4 million tonnes was used to generate electricity and about 0.9 million tonnes to generate heat.

The Non-Fossil Fuel Obligation (NFFO) Renewables Orders are the Government's principal mechanism for developing renewable energy sources. NFFO Renewables Orders require the regional electricity companies to buy specified amounts of electricity from specified non-fossil fuel sources. The technologies covered by NFFO Orders are landfill gas, municipal and industrial waste, small-scale hydro, onshore wind and energy crops. The fifth NFFO Renewables Order is expected to be made in late 1998.

The Government is reviewing renewable energy policy, including what measures would be necessary and practicable to achieve 10 per cent of the UK's electricity needs from renewables by 2010, and how renewables can contribute to meeting commitments to future reductions in greenhouse gases.

RENEWABLE ENERGY SOURCES 1996

	Percentages
Biofuels	80.3
Landfill gas	14.4
Sewage gas	11.0
Wood combustion	11.8
Straw combustion	4.2
Refuse combustion	25.6
Other biofuels	13.3
Hydro	16.7
Large-scale	16.3
Small-scale	0.4
Wind	2.4
Active solar heating	0.5
Other	0.1
Total	100

Source: Department of Trade and Industry

Transport

CIVIL AVIATION

Since the privatization of British Airways in 1987, UK airlines have been operated entirely by the private sector. In 1997, total capacity on British airlines amounted to 35,539,000 tonne-km, of which 26,504,000 tonne-km was on scheduled services. British airlines carried 84.7 million passengers, 56.2 million on scheduled services and 28.5 million on charter flights.

Leading British airlines include British Airways, Air UK, Britannia Airways, British Midland, Monarch Airlines and Virgin Atlantic.

There are 143 licensed civil aerodromes in Britain, with Heathrow and Gatwick handling the highest volume of passengers. BAA PLC owns and operates the seven major airports: Heathrow, Gatwick, Stansted, Southampton, Glasgow, Edinburgh and Aberdeen, which between them handle about 71 per cent of air passengers and 81 per cent of air cargo traffic in Britain. Many other airports, including Manchester, are controlled by local authorities or private companies.

The Civil Aviation Authority, an independent statutory body, is responsible for the economic regulation of UK airlines and for the safety regulation of the UK civil aviation industry. Through its wholly-owned subsidiary company National Air Traffic Services Ltd the CAA is also responsible for the provision of air traffic control services over Britain and its surrounding seas and at most major British airports. The Government has announced plans to privatize a majority holding in National Air Traffic Services.

The CAA is responsible for ensuring that UK airlines provide services at the lowest charges possible, given the requirement to meet stringent safety standards. It is also responsible for the economic regulation of the larger airports.

All commercial airline companies must be granted an Air Operator's Certificate, which is issued by the CAA to operators meeting the required safety standards. The CAA also issues airport safety licences, which must be obtained by any airport used for public transport and training flights. All British-registered aircraft must be granted an airworthiness certificate, and the CAA also issues professional licences to pilots, flight crew, ground engineers and air traffic controllers.

AIR PASSENGERS 1997*

ALL UK AIRPORTS: TOTAL	148,249,560
LONDON AREA AIRPORTS: TOTAL	94,984,589
Battersea Heliport	5,072
Gatwick (BAA)	26,959,015
Heathrow (BAA)	58,185,398
London City	1,161,121
Luton	3,238,458
Southend	8,666
Stansted (BAA)	5,426,859
OTHER UK AIRPORTS: TOTAL	53,264,971
Aberdeen (BAA)	2,573,376
Barra	8,670
Barrow-in-Furness	206
Belfast City	1,285,712

Belfast International	2,476,834
Benbecula (HIAL)	37,105
Biggin Hill	7,269
Birmingham	6,025,485
Blackpool	84,060
Bournemouth	269,339
Bristol	1,614,837
Cambridge	19,973
Campbeltown (HIAL)	11,361
Cardiff	1,155,186
Carlisle	840
Coventry	1,694
Dundee	18,469
East Midlands	1,885,767
Edinburgh (BAA)	4,214,919
Exeter	228,449
Glasgow (BAA)	6,117,005
Gloucestershire	2,104
Hawarden	4,467
Humberside	334,623
Inverness (HIAL)	401,991
Islay (HIAL)	20,414
Isle of Man	693,012
Kent International	2,936
Kirkwall (HIAL)	97,388
Leeds/Bradford	1,254,853
Lerwick (Tingwall)	4,248
Liverpool	689,468
Londonderry	56,256
Lydd	2,596
Manchester	15,948,373
Newcastle upon Tyne	2,642,615
Norwich	271,848
Penzance Heliport	108,805
Plymouth	130,526
Prestwick (BAA)	581,191
St Mary's, Isles of Scilly	128,265
Scatsta	102,344
Sheffield City	†254
Shoreham	2,685
Southampton	632,472
Stornoway (HIAL)	97,242
Sumburgh (HIAL)	361,505
Teesside	577,532
Tiree (HIAL)	5,201
Tresco, Isles of Scilly (H)	29,694
Unst	2,520
Wick (HIAL)	40,987
CHANNEL Is. AIRPORTS: TOTAL	2,748,432
Alderney	81,048
Guernsey	930,299
Jersey	1,737,085

*Total terminal, transit, scheduled and charter passengers
† Sheffield City began reporting June 1997
Source: Civil Aviation Authority

RAILWAYS

Britain pioneered railways and a railway network was developed across Britain by private companies in the course of the 19th century. In 1948 the main railway companies were nationalized and were run by a public authority, the British Transport Commission. The Commission was replaced by the British Railways Board in 1963, operating as British Rail. On 1 April 1994, responsibility for managing the railway infrastructure passed to a newly-formed company, Railtrack; the British Railways Board continued as operator of all train services until they were sold or franchised to the private sector. All passenger activities have now been franchised and all British Rail's freight, technical support and specialist function businesses have been sold.

PRIVATIZATION

Since 1 April 1994, ownership of operational track and land has been vested in Railtrack, which was floated on the Stock Exchange in 1996. Railtrack manages the track and charges for access to it and is responsible for signalling and timetabling. It does not operate train services. It owns the stations, and leases most of them out to the train operating companies. Infrastructure support functions are now provided by private sector companies. Railtrack invests in infrastructure principally using finance raised by track charges, and takes investment decisions in consultation with rail operators. Railtrack is also responsible for overall safety on the railways.

RAIL REGULATOR

The independent Rail Regulator is responsible for the licensing of new railway operators, approving access agreements, promoting the use and development of the network, preventing anti-competitive practices (in conjunction with the Director General of Fair Trading) and protecting the interests of rail users. The Regulator indicated in July 1998 that he would be looking to tighten the funding regime for Railtrack after 2001 to promote improvements in the infrastructure. The White Paper *New Deal for Transport* contains proposals to strengthen the Regulator's power to impose sanctions and broaden the scope of his duties.

Separate regulations, which took effect on 28 June 1998, established licensing and access arrangements for certain international train services in Great Britain. These will be overseen by the International Rail Regulator, a position at present held by the Rail Regulator.

The White Paper *New Deal for Transport*, published in July 1998, announced plans to establish a Strategic Rail Authority which will manage passenger railway franchising, take responsibility for increasing the use of the railways for freight transport, and lead strategic planning of passenger and freight rail services.

Proposals to privatize part of London Underground were announced in July 1997. The Government intends the infrastructure to be run by between one and three private companies, with the operating company remaining in public ownership.

SERVICES

For privatization, domestic passenger services were divided into 25 train-operating units, which have been franchised to private sector operators via a competitive tendering process overseen by the Director of the Office of Passenger Rail Franchising. The Government continues to subsidize loss-making but socially necessary rail services. The Franchising Director is responsible for monitoring the performance of the franchisees and allocating and administering government subsidy payments.

There are currently 25 train operating companies: Anglia Railways; Cardiff Railway; Central Trains; Chiltern Railways; Connex South Central; Connex South Eastern; Eurostar (which is not subject to a franchise agreement); Gatwick Express; Great Eastern Railway; Great North Eastern Railway; Great Western Trains; Island Line (Isle of Wight); LTS Rail (London to Southend and Shoeburyness); Merseyrail Electrics; Midland Mainline; North Western Trains; Northern Spirit; Scotrail Railways; Silverlink Train Services (North London); South West Trains; Thameslink Rail; Thames Trains; Virgin Trains (which operates two franchises); Wales and West Passenger Trains; and West Anglia Great Northern Railway.

Railtrack publishes a national timetable which contains details of rail services operated over the Railtrack network, coastal shipping information and connections with Ireland, the Isle of Man, the Isle of Wight, the Channel Islands and some European destinations.

The national rail enquiries service offers information about train times and fares for any part of the country:

National Rail Enquiries	0345-484950
London Transport	0171-222 1234
Eurostar	0345-303030

Rail Users' Consultative Committees monitor the policies and performance of train and station operators in their area (there are nine, covering Great Britain). They are statutory bodies and have a legal right to make recommendations for changes. The London Regional Passengers Committee represents users of buses, the Underground and the Docklands Light Railway as well as users of rail services in the London area.

British Rail's passenger rolling stock was divided between three subsidiary companies, which were privatized in 1996. The companies lease rolling stock to passenger service operators. On privatization, British Rail's bulk freight haulage companies and Rail Express Systems, which carries Royal Mail traffic, were sold to English, Welsh and Scottish Railways, which also purchased Railfreight Distribution (international freight) in 1997. In 1997–8 an average 1,159,000 tonnes of freight was transported by an average of 1,900 trains a day.

BRITISH RAILWAYS BOARD, *see* page 287
RAILTRACK, Railtrack House, Euston Square, London NW1 2EE. Tel: 0171-557 8000. *Chairman*, Sir Robert Horton. *Chief Executive*, G. Corbett
ASSOCIATION OF TRAIN OPERATING COMPANIES, 40 Bernard Street, London WC1N 1BY. Tel: 0171-904 3000. *Chairman*, I. W. Warburton
OFFICE OF PASSENGER RAIL FRANCHISING (OPRAF), Golding's House, 2 Hay's Lane, London SE1 2HR. Tel: 0171-940 4200. *Franchising Director*, J. O'Brien
OFFICE OF THE RAIL REGULATOR (ORR) 1 Waterhouse Square, 138–142 Holborn, London EC1N 2ST. Tel: 0171-282 2000. *Rail Regulator*, J. Swift, QC

RAILTRACK

At 31 March 1998, Railtrack had about 20,000 miles of standard gauge lines and sidings in use, representing 10,343 miles of route of which 3,208 miles were electrified. Standard rail on main line has a weight of 110 lb per yard. Railtrack owns 2,495 stations, 90 light maintenance depots, about 40,000 bridges, viaducts and tunnels, and over 9,000 level crossings.

Passenger journeys made in 1997–8 totalled 845.7 million, including 364.8 million made by holders of season tickets. The average distance of each passenger journey on ordinary fare was 27.43 miles; and on season ticket, 15.45 miles. Passenger stations in use numbered 2,500. The number of ticket transactions in the year was 269.5 million, earning a total ticket revenue of £2,957 million.

In 1997–8 Railtrack showed an operating profit of £380 million and a pre-tax profit of £388 million. On 31 March 1997 Railtrack employed 10,937 staff.

	£ million
Income	
Passenger	2,131
Freight	164
Property rental	127
Other	45
Total	2,467
Costs	
Production and management	523
Infrastructure maintenance	702
Asset maintenance plan charge	501
Joint industry costs	213
Depreciation	148
Total	2,087

RAIL SAFETY

The Railways (Safety Case) Regulations 1994 require infrastructure controllers (e.g. Railtrack, London Underground) to have systems in place to manage safety on the railway networks for which they are responsible.

The infrastructure controllers are required to present a safety case to the Railway Inspectorate (part of the Health and Safety Executive). The safety case must be accepted by the Inspectorate, and is subsequently subject to regular compliance audits.

The infrastructure controllers require companies bidding to operate services to present a safety case. The safety case must be accepted by the infrastructure controller before a service operator can receive a licence and begin to provide services. If any variation is required, the safety case must be re-presented. Safety cases must be reviewed at least every three years. The Inspectorate may examine the safety case of service operators as part of its compliance audit of infrastructure operators.

ACCIDENTS ON RAILWAYS

	1995–6	*1996–97
Train accidents: total	989	1,781
Persons killed: total	7	1
Passengers	1	1
Railway staff	1	0
Others	5	0
Persons injured: total	166	257
Passengers	62	182
Railway staff	75	61
Others	29	14
Other accidents through movement of railway vehicles		
Persons killed	17	20
Persons injured	3,078	828
Other accidents on railway premises		
Persons killed	4	4
Passengers	2	3
Railway staff	2	0
Others	0	1
Persons injured	9,046	3,669
Trespassers and suicides		
Persons killed	246	251
Persons injured	82	106

* New accident reporting regulations came into force on 1 April 1996

THE CHANNEL TUNNEL

The earliest recorded scheme for a submarine transport connection between Britain and France was in 1802. Tunnelling has begun simultaneously on both sides of the Channel three times: in 1881, in the early 1970s, and on 1 December 1987, when construction workers began to bore the first of the three tunnels which form the Channel tunnel. They 'holed through' the first tunnel (the service tunnel) on 1 December 1990 and tunnelling was completed in June 1991. The tunnel was officially inaugurated by The Queen and President Mitterrand of France on 6 May 1994.

The submarine link comprises three tunnels. There are two rail tunnels, each carrying trains in one direction, which measure 24.93 ft (7.6 m) in diameter. Between them lies a smaller service tunnel, measuring 15.75 ft (4.8 m) in diameter. The service tunnel is linked to the rail tunnels by 130 cross-passages for maintenance and safety purposes. The tunnels are 31 miles (50 km) long, 24 miles (38 km) of which is under the sea-bed at an average depth of 132 ft (40 m). The rail terminals are situated at Folkestone and Calais, and the tunnels go underground at Shakespeare Cliff, Dover, and Sangatte, west of Calais.

Passenger services (Eurostar) run from Waterloo station in London and Ashford, Kent, to Paris, Brussels and Lille. Connecting services from Edinburgh and Manchester via London began in 1997. The introduction of through services from these cities, not stopping in London, is the subject of a government review, due to report in late 1998. Vehicle shuttle services (Le Shuttle) operate between Folkestone and Calais.

RAIL LINKS

The route for the British Channel Tunnel rail link will run from Folkestone to a new terminal at St Pancras station, London, with new intermediate stations at Ebbsfleet, Kent, and Stratford, east London; at present services run into a terminal at Waterloo station, London.

Construction of the rail link will be financed by the private sector with a substantial government contribution. A private sector consortium, London and Continental Railways Ltd (LCR), is responsible for the design, construction and ownership of the rail link, and has taken over Union Railways and European Passenger Services Ltd, the UK operator of Eurostar (now renamed Eurostar (UK) Ltd). Construction was expected to be completed in 2003, but on 28 January 1998 LCR informed the Government that it was unable to fulfil its obligations. On 3 June 1998 the Government announced a new funding agreement with LCR. The rail link will be constructed in two phases: phase one, from the Channel Tunnel to Fawkham Junction (where an existing connection allows trains to continue to Waterloo), begins in October 1998 and will be completed in 2003; phase two, from Fawkham Junction to St Pancras, will be built between 2001 and 2007. Railtrack will buy phase one when it is completed and has an option to buy phase two by 2003.

Infrastructure developments in France have been completed and high-speed trains run from Calais to Paris, linking the Channel tunnel with the high-speed European network.

ROADS

HIGHWAY AUTHORITIES

The powers and responsibilities of highway authorities in England and Wales are set out in the Highways Acts 1980; for Scotland there is separate legislation.

Responsibility for trunk road motorways and other trunk roads in Great Britain rests in England with the Secretary of State for the Environment, Transport and the Regions, in Scotland with the Secretary of State for Scotland, and in Wales with the Secretary of State for Wales. The costs of construction, improvement and maintenance are paid for by central government. The White Paper *New Deal for Transport*, published in July 1998, proposes that the Highways Agency should take over responsibility for operating, maintaining and improving the trunk road network.

The highway authority for non-trunk roads in England, Wales and Scotland is, in general, the unitary authority, county council or London borough council in whose area the roads lie.

In Northern Ireland the Department of the Environment for Northern Ireland is the statutory road authority responsible for public roads and their maintenance and construction; the Roads Service executive agency (*see* page 330) carries out these functions on behalf of the Department.

FINANCE

The Government contributes towards capital expenditure through Transport Supplementary Grant (TSG) in England and Transport Grant (TG) in Wales. Grant rates are determined by the respective Secretaries of State; at present, grant is paid at 50 per cent of expenditure accepted for grant in England and Wales.

In England TSG is paid towards capital spending on highways and the regulation of traffic; current expenditure is funded by revenue support grant (i.e. central government grants to local authorities for non-specific services). TSG is also paid towards capital spending on bridge assessment and strengthening; towards structural maintenance on the primary route network; and towards all principal 'A' roads. In Wales TG is paid towards capital expenditure only; current expenditure is funded by revenue support grant.

For the financial year 1998–9 local authorities in England will receive £155 million in TSG. Total estimated expenditure on building and maintaining motorways and trunk roads in England in 1996–7 was £1,584 million; estimated outturn for 1997–8 is £1,491 million.

For the financial year 1998–9 local authorities in Wales will receive up to £21.7 million in TG. Total expenditure on motorways and trunk roads in Wales in 1997–8 was £113.5 million and estimated expenditure in 1998–9 is £102.4 million.

The Scottish Office receives a block vote from Parliament and the Secretary of State for Scotland determines how much is allocated towards roads. Total expenditure on building and maintaining trunk roads in Scotland was estimated at £170 million in 1997–8.

In Northern Ireland expenditure on roads in 1997–8 was £154.3 million, and estimated expenditure for 1998–9 is £145.3 million.

The Government is currently considering the possibility of introducing tolls on certain roads. The White Paper *New Deal for Transport* contains proposals to enable local authorities to levy charges for driving cars into town centres and for workplace parking; the income would be used to improve public transport.

PRIVATE FINANCE

Contracts have been let which allow greater involvement by the private sector in the design, finance, construction and operation of roads. Results of research projects carried out into road pricing technology were published in May 1998; further associated research reports were published in July 1998.

ROADS REVIEW

In June 1997 the Government launched a roads review to determine the role which roads should play in an integrated transport policy and to establish a forward investment programme for the road network in England. The review was published in July 1998 and the Government announced a reduction of over two-thirds in the road building programme. Thirty-seven schemes will go ahead and will be built by 2005 at a cost of £1,400 million; 17 schemes were cancelled; 19 will go ahead only if funded by local authorities; 43 schemes are under review, and seven await a decision. In Wales, a review resulted in four schemes going ahead, six being cancelled, eight being referred for further study and three deferred. A separate review of roads policy in Scotland is to be published in November 1998.

ROAD LENGTHS (in miles) *as at April 1997*

	Total roads	Trunk roads (including motorways)	Motorways*
England	175,587	6,522	1,729
Wales	21,270	1,066	83
Scotland	34,348	2,030	214
N. Ireland	15,251	153	70

*There were in addition 43.9 miles of local authority motorway in England

MOTORWAYS

England and Wales:

M1	London to Yorkshire
M2	London to Faversham
M3	London to Southampton
M4	London to South Wales
M5	Birmingham to Exeter
M6	Catthorpe to Carlisle
M10	St Albans spur
M11	London to Cambridge
M18	Rotherham to Goole
M20	London to Folkestone
M23	London to Gatwick
M25	London orbital
M26	M20 to M25 spur
M27	Southampton bypass
M32	M4 to Bristol spur
M40	London to Birmingham
M41	London to West Cross
M42	South-west of Birmingham to Measham
M45	Dunchurch spur
M50	Ross spur
M53	Chester to Birkenhead
M54	M6 to Telford
M55	Preston to Blackpool
M56	Manchester to Chester
M57	Liverpool outer ring
M58	Liverpool to Wigan
M61	Manchester to Preston
M62	Liverpool to Hull
M63	Manchester southern ring road
M65	Calder Valley
M66	Manchester eastern ring road to Rochdale
M67	Manchester Hyde to Denton
M69	Coventry to Leicester
M180	South Humberside

Scotland:

M8	Edinburgh-Newhouse, Baillieston-West Ferry Interchange
M9	Edinburgh to Dunblane
M73	Maryville to Mollinsburn
M74	Glasgow-Paddy's Rickle Bridge, Cleuchbrae-Gretna
M77	Ayr Road Route
M80	Stirling to Haggs/Glasgow (M8) to Stepps
M90	Inverkeithing to Perth
M876	Dennyloanhead (M80) to Kincardine Bridge

Northern Ireland:

M1	Belfast to Dungannon
M2	Belfast to Antrim
M2	Ballymena bypass
M3	Belfast Cross Harbour Bridge
M5	M2 to Greencastle
M12	M1 to Craigavon
M22	Antrim to Randalstown

ROAD USE

ESTIMATED TRAFFIC ON ALL ROADS (GREAT BRITAIN) 1997

Million vehicle kilometres

All motor vehicles	448,900
Cars and taxis	367,800
Two-wheeled motor vehicles	4,000
Buses and coaches	4,900
Light vans	40,500
Other goods vehicles	31,800
Total goods vehicles	72,300
Pedal cycles	4,000

ROAD GOODS TRANSPORT (GREAT BRITAIN) 1997
Analysis by mode of working and by gross weight of vehicle

Estimated tonne kilometres (thousand million)	149.6
Own account	37.4
Public haulage	112.2
By gross weight of vehicle (billion tonne kilometres)	
Not over 25 tonnes	24.3
Over 25 tonnes	125.2
Estimated tonnes carried (millions)	1,643.0
Own account	599.0
Public haulage	1,044.0
By gross weight of vehicle (million tonnes)	
Not over 25 tonnes	419.0
Over 25 tonnes	1,224.0

ROAD PASSENGER SERVICES

Until 1988 most road passenger transport services in Great Britain were provided by the public sector; the National Bus Company was the largest bus and coach operator in England and Wales and the Scottish Bus Group the largest operator in Scotland. The privatization of the National Bus Company was completed in 1988 and that of the Scottish Bus Group in 1991. London Transport's bus operating subsidiaries were privatized by the end of 1994. Almost all bus and coach services in Great Britain are now provided by private sector companies.

Bus services outside London were deregulated in 1986, although local authorities can subsidise the provision of socially necessary services after competitive tendering. In London, London Transport retains overall responsibility for the provision of services.

The largest bus operators in Great Britain are Stagecoach Holdings, FirstGroup (formerly FirstBus) and Arriva (formerly Cowie British Bus), which between them account for over 40 per cent of all passenger journeys. There are also 17 municipal bus companies in England and Wales, and thousands of smaller private sector operators.

National Express runs a national network of coach routes, mainly operating through franchises.

In Northern Ireland, almost all passenger transport services are provided by subsidiaries of Translink (formerly the Northern Ireland Transport Holding Company), which is publicly owned. The two main operators are Citybus Ltd (in Belfast) and Ulsterbus Ltd (outside Belfast). There are also about 75 small private sector operators.

The transport White Paper announced plans to promote bus use, primarily through agreements between local authorities and bus operators to improve the standard and efficiency of services in an area.

There are about 64,000 licensed taxis in Great Britain, of which about 19,000 are in London. There are also about 66,000 licensed private hire vehicles in Great Britain outside London, and an estimated 60,000 in London; an exact figure is not known because there is currently no licensing system in London.

BUSES AND COACHES (GREAT BRITAIN) 1996-7

Number of vehicles (31 March 1997)	75,900
Vehicle kilometres (millions)	4,199
Local bus passenger journeys (millions)	4,355
Passenger receipts (£ million)	3,586

ROAD SAFETY

The Government in 1987 set a target of reducing road traffic casualties by a third by the year 2000 compared to the average for 1981-5. Measures to achieve this were successful in reducing the number of deaths on the road by 36 per cent by 1997, and the number of serious casualties by 42 per cent. Over the same period the number of slight casualties increased by 16 per cent, but as road traffic increased by 52 per cent, the number of casualties per 100 km travelled has increased by only one per cent.

Government consultations with local authorities, the police and road safety organizations in 1996 produced strong support for setting new road safety targets. Proposals for discussion were produced in autumn 1997, and in late 1998 the Government will set new road safety targets for Britain for the period to 2010; similar targets are being set in Northern Ireland.

ROAD ACCIDENTS 1997

Road accidents	240,046
Vehicles involved:	
Pedal cycles	25,144
Motor vehicles	413,333
Total casualties	327,544
Pedestrians	45,531
Vehicle users	282,013
Killed*	3,599
Pedestrians	973
Pedal cycles	183
All two-wheeled motor vehicles	509
Cars and taxis	1,795
Others	139

*Died within 30 days of accident

	Killed	Injured
1965	7,952	389,985
1970	7,499	355,869
1975	6,366	318,584
1980	6,010	322,590
1985	5,165	312,359
1990	5,217	335,924
1995	3,621	306,885
1996	3,598	316,704
1997	3,599	323,945

Source: Department of the Environment, Transport and the Regions

DRIVING LICENCES

It is necessary to hold a valid full licence in order to drive on public roads in the UK. Learner drivers obtain a provisional driving licence before starting to learn to drive and must then pass a test to obtain a full driving licence. Application forms for a driving licence (form D1) are available from post offices. A phased introduction of driving licences including the driver's photograph began in July 1998; all licences for newly qualified drivers will include a photograph, and qualified drivers will be issued with the new licence when their licence details need updating.

There are separate tests for driving motor cycles, cars, passenger-carrying vehicles (PCVs) and large goods vehicles (LGVs). Drivers must hold full car entitlement before they can apply for PCV or LGV entitlements. At 5 April 1998, 37.6 million people in the UK (20.8 male, 16.8 female) held a valid driving licence (full or provisional). The minimum age for driving motor cars, light goods vehicles up to 3.5 tonnes and motor cycles is 17 (moped, 16). Since June 1997, drivers who collect six or more penalty points within two years of qualifying lose their licence and are required to take another test. A leaflet, *What You Need to Know About Driving Licences* (form D100), is available from post offices.

The Driver and Vehicle Licensing Agency is responsible for issuing driving licences, registering and licensing vehicles, and collecting excise duty in Great Britain. In Northern Ireland the Driver and Vehicle Licensing Agency (Northern Ireland) has similar responsibilities.

DRIVING LICENCE FEES *as at 1 July 1998*

First provisional licence	£21.00
Changing a provisional to a full licence after	
passing a driving test	free
First full	£6.00
Renewal of licence	£6.00
Renewal of licence including PCV or LGV	
entitlements	£26.00
Renewal after disqualification	£17.00
Renewal after drinking and driving	
disqualification	£26.00
Medical renewal	free
Medical renewal (over 70)	£6.00
Duplicate licence	£11.00
Exchange licence	£11.00
Removing endorsements	£11.00
Replacement (change of name or address)	Free

DRIVING TESTS

The Driving Standards Agency is responsible for carrying out driving tests and approving driving instructors in Great Britain. In Northern Ireland the Driver and Vehicle Testing Agency (Northern Ireland) is responsible for testing drivers and vehicles.

More than 1.1 million car driving tests were conducted in Great Britain in 1997–8, of which 46.7 per cent resulted in a pass. In addition over 41,000 lorry tests were undertaken, of which 52.8 per cent were successful. There were more than 5,000 bus tests, with a pass rate of 47.7 per cent. Over 68,000 motorcycle tests were undertaken, of which 68.6 per cent were successful.

Since 1 March 1997 driving test candidates have been required to produce photographic confirmation of their identity.

*DRIVING TEST FEES (weekday rate/evening and Saturday rate) *as at 1 April 1998*

For cars	£32.75/£43
†For motor cycles	£39/£52
For lorries, buses	£73.50/£92
For invalid carriages	free

*Since 1 July 1996 most candidates for car and motor cycle tests have also been required to take a written driving theory test, for which there is a separate fee of £15. Theory tests for lorry and bus drivers were introduced on 1 January 1997
†Before riding on public roads, learner motor cyclists and learner moped riders are required to have completed Compulsory Basic Training, provided by DSA-approved training bodies. Prices vary. All exemptions from CBT were removed on 1 January 1997

An extended driving test was introduced in 1992 for those convicted of dangerous driving. The fee is £65.50/£86 (car) or £78/£104 (motorcycle).

MOTOR VEHICLES

Vehicles must be licensed by the DVLA or the DVLA (Northern Ireland) before they can be driven on public roads. They must also be approved as roadworthy by the Vehicle Certification Agency. The Vehicle Inspectorate carries out annual testing and inspection of goods vehicles, buses and coaches.

There were 39.3 million vehicles registered at the DVLA at March 1998, of which 27.3 million were licensed:

Private and light goods	24,267,758
Motor cycles, scooters, mopeds	655,137
Coaches and buses	79,663
Large goods vehicles	417,646
Electric vehicles	11,651
Others	1,897,227
Total	27,329,082

VEHICLE LICENCES

Registration and first licensing of vehicles is through local offices (known as Vehicle Registration Offices) of the Driver and Vehicle Licensing Agency in Swansea (*see* page 300). Local facilities for relicensing are available at any post office which deals with vehicle licensing. Applicants will need to take their vehicle registration document; if this is not available the applicant must complete form V62 which is held at post offices. Postal applications can be made to the post offices shown on form V100, available at any post office. This form also provides guidance on registering and licensing vehicles.

Details of the present duties chargeable on motor vehicles are available at post offices and Vehicle Registration Offices. The Vehicle Excise and Registration Act 1994 provides *inter alia* that any vehicle kept on a public road but not used on roads is chargeable to excise duty as if it were in use. All non-commercial vehicles constructed before 1 January 1973 are exempt from vehicle excise duty.

VEHICLE EXCISE DUTY RATES *from 15 November 1997*

	Twelve months £	Six months £
Motor Cars		
Light vans, cars, taxis, etc.	150.00	82.50
Motor Cycles		
With or without sidecar, not over 150 cc	15.00	—
With or without sidecar, 150–250 cc	40.00	—
Others	60.00	33.00
Electric motorcycles (including tricycles)	15.00	—
Tricycles (not over 450 kg)		
Not over 150 cc	15.00	—
Others	60.00	33.00
Buses		
Seating 9–16 persons	160.00	88.00
Seating 17–35 persons	210.00	115.50
Seating 36–60 persons	320.00	176.00
Seating over 60 persons	480.00	264.00

MoT TESTING

Cars, motor cycles, motor caravans, light goods and dual-purpose vehicles more than three years old must be covered by a current MoT test certificate. The certificate must be renewed annually. The MoT testing scheme is administered by the Vehicle Inspectorate.

A fee is payable to MoT testing stations, which must be authorized to carry out tests. The maximum fees, which are prescribed by regulations, are:

For cars and light vans	£30.87
For solo motor cycles	£12.74
For motor cycle combinations	£21.28
For three-wheeled vehicles	£25.02
For non-public service vehicle buses	£38.08
For light goods vehicles	£32.77
For goods vehicles up to 3,500 kg	£32.77

SHIPPING AND PORTS

Since earliest times sea trade has played a central role in Britain's economy. By the 17th century Britain had built up a substantial merchant fleet and by the early 20th century it dominated the world shipping industry. In recent years the size and tonnage of the UK-registered trading fleet have declined; the UK-flagged merchant fleet now constitutes about 1 per cent of the world fleet.

Freight is carried by liner and bulk services, almost all scheduled liner services being containerized. About 95 per cent by weight of Britain's overseas trade is carried by sea; this amounts to 77 per cent of its total value. Passengers and vehicles are carried by roll-on, roll-off ferries, hovercraft, hydrofoils and high-speed catamarans. There are about 55 million ferry passengers a year, of whom 35 million travel internationally. The leading British operators of passenger services are Stena Line (which has a Swedish parent company), P. & O. European Ferries and Hoverspeed.

Lloyd's of London provides the most comprehensive shipping intelligence service in the world. *Lloyd's Shipping Index*, published daily, lists some 25,000 ocean-going vessels and gives the latest known report of each.

PORTS

There are about 70 commercially significant ports in Great Britain, including such ports as London, Dover, Forth, Tees and Hartlepool, Grimsby and Immingham, Sullom

Voe, Milford Haven, Southampton, Felixstowe and Liverpool. Belfast is the principal freight port in Northern Ireland.

Broadly speaking, ports are owned and operated by private companies, local authorities or trusts. The largest operator is Associated British Ports (formerly the British Transport Docks Board, privatized in 1981), which owns 23 ports. Total traffic through British ports in 1997 amounted to 557 million tonnes, an increase of 1 per cent on the previous year.

MARINE SAFETY

By 1 October 2002 all roll-on, roll-off ferries operating to and from the UK will be required to meet the new international safety standards on stability established by the Stockholm Agreement.

The Maritime and Coastguard Agency (MCA) was established on 1 April 1998 by the merger of the Coastguard Agency and the Marine Safety Agency. It is an executive agency of the Department of the Environment, Transport and the Regions. The Agency's aims are to develop, promote and enforce high standards of marine safety, to minimize loss of life amongst seafarers and coastal users, and to minimize pollution of the sea and coastline from ships. In 1997 HM Coastguard co-ordinated 11,667 incidents requiring search and rescue facilities; 16,884 people were assisted and 251 lives were lost.

Locations hazardous to shipping in coastal waters are marked by lighthouses and other lights and buoys. The lighthouse authorities are the Corporation of Trinity House (for England, Wales and the Channel Islands), the Northern Lighthouse Board (for Scotland and the Isle of Man), and the Commissioners of Irish Lights (for Northern Ireland and the Republic of Ireland). Trinity House maintains 72 lighthouses, 13 major floating aids to navigation and more than 429 buoys; and the Northern Lighthouse Board 84 lighthouses, 116 minor lights and many buoys.

Harbour authorities are responsible for pilotage within their harbour areas; and the Ports Act 1991 provides for the transfer of lights and buoys to harbour authorities where these are used for mainly local navigation.

PRINCIPAL MERCHANT FLEETS 1997

Flag	No.	Gross tonnage
Panama	6,188	91,127,912
Liberia	1,697	60,058,368
Bahamas	1,221	25,523,201
Greece	1,641	25,288,452
Cyprus	1,650	23,652,626
Malta	1,378	22,984,206
Norway (NIS)	715	19,780,346
Singapore	1,656	18,874,767
Japan	9,310	18,516,363
†China	3,175	16,338,610
Russia	4,814	12,282,373
*United States of America	5,260	11,788,820
Philippines	1,699	8,849,248
St Vincent	1,343	8,374,491
Korea (South)	2,441	7,429,510
Germany	1,125	6,949,555
India	941	6,934,329
Turkey	1,146	6,567,295
Marshall Islands	168	6,314,364
Italy	1,324	6,193,692
Taiwan	692	5,931,264
Hong Kong	375	5,770,563
Denmark (DIS)	468	5,075,438
Malaysia	838	4,842,053
Isle of Man	202	4,759,132
Bermuda	110	4,610,468
Brazil	536	4,372,419
Netherlands	1,178	3,879,532
Iran	417	3,552,950
United Kingdom	1,424	3,485,692
Indonesia	2,383	3,195,007
Norway	1,559	3,058,844
Sweden	588	2,754,113
†Ukraine	1,025	2,689,977
Australia	617	2,606,573
Canada	852	2,526,567
French Antarctic Territory	79	2,462,746
Romania	413	2,344,701
Antigua and Barbuda	516	2,214,334
Thailand	576	2,157,803
Other countries	21,754	46,078,489
WORLD TOTAL	85,494	522,197,193

DIS   Danish International Register of Shipping – offshore registry
NIS   Norwegian International Ship Register – offshore registry
*Excluding ships of United States Reserve Fleet
†Information incomplete

Source: Lloyd's Register of Shipping

MERCHANT SHIPS COMPLETED 1997

Country of Build	No.	Gross tonnage
Japan	624	9,864,236
Korea (South)	202	8,124,454
†China	131	1,394,347
Germany	76	1,088,260
Taiwan	35	722,012
Poland	50	643,223
Denmark	16	465,983
Italy	24	413,107
Finland	6	348,273
Netherlands	98	322,470
Spain	72	225,951
France	15	190,996
Norway	58	163,291
Romania	15	155,263
Croatia	7	121,732
Turkey	26	102,456
Russia	15	87,901
Bulgaria	7	84,339
United Kingdom	17	72,642
†Ukraine	6	71,835
*United States of America	39	70,872
Singapore	42	57,488
Brazil	2	51,861
Malaysia	50	43,742
India	25	41,858
Other countries	162	306,255
For Registration in		
Panama	360	8,119,129
Liberia	65	2,254,515
Germany	146	2,226,880
Singapore	141	1,621,303
Marshall Islands	10	922,058
Norway (NIS)	22	899,978
Bahamas	36	856,269
Hong Kong	27	846,015
Greece	14	791,969
Japan	256	674,487
Philippines	37	630,830
Malaysia	34	474,967
Denmark (DIS)	7	457,188
Barbados	5	389,951
Taiwan	9	322,344
Cyprus	25	286,287
Netherlands	50	249,821
Bermuda	4	243,250
Malta	21	242,888
Israel	8	208,653
Norway	35	181,798
Italy	24	181,440
Korea (South)	26	181,049
Canada	4	157,573
France	13	141,823
Other countries	441	1,672,382
WORLD TOTAL	1,820	25,234,847

DIS   Danish International Register of Shipping – offshore registry
NIS   Norwegian International Ship Register – offshore registry
*Excluding ships of United States Reserve Fleet
†Information incomplete

Source: Lloyd's Register of Shipping

UK-REGISTERED TRADING VESSELS of 500 GROSS TONS AND OVER as at end 1996

Type of vessel	No.	Gross tonnage
Tankers[1]	129	2,958,000
Bulk carriers[2]	42	1,775,000
Specialized carriers[3]	19	87,000
Container (fully cellular)	54	1,491,000
Ro-Ro[4]	87	834,000
Other general cargo	168	681,000
Passenger[5]	15	484,000
TOTAL	514	8,309,000

1 Includes oil, gas, chemical and other specialized tankers
2 Includes combination bulk carriers: ore/oil and ore/bulk/oil carriers
3 Includes livestock, car and chemical carriers
4 Roll-on, roll-off passenger and cargo vessels
5 Cruise liner and other passenger vessels

Source: The Stationery Office – Annual Abstract of Statistics 1998

SEABORNE TRADE OF THE UK 1996
EXPORTS (INCLUDING RE-EXPORTS) PLUS IMPORTS BY SEA

	Million tonnes
By weight	
All cargo	354.3
Dry bulk cargo	89.8
Other dry cargo	113.5
Tanker cargo	151.0

	£ million
By value	
All cargo	260,900
Dry bulk cargo	8,500
Other dry cargo	236,200
Tanker cargo	16,200

Source: The Stationery Office – Annual Abstract of Statistics 1998

SEAPORT TRAFFIC OF GREAT BRITAIN 1996
BY MODE OF APPEARANCE*

	Million gross tonnes
FOREIGN TRAFFIC: Imports	177.6
Bulk fuel traffic	69.4
Other bulk traffic	44.4
Container and roll-on traffic	50.5
Semi-bulk traffic	12.0
Conventional traffic	1.4
FOREIGN TRAFFIC: Exports	167.4
Bulk fuel traffic	103.5
Other bulk traffic	15.6
Container and roll-on traffic	42.5
Semi-bulk traffic	4.8
Conventional traffic	1.1
DOMESTIC TRAFFIC†	150.9
Bulk fuel traffic	113.7
Other bulk traffic	29.0
Container and roll-on traffic	5.5
Semi-bulk traffic	0.2
Conventional traffic	0.4
Non-oil traffic with UK offshore installations	2.2
TRAFFIC THROUGH MINOR PORTS‡	35.0
TOTAL FOREIGN AND DOMESTIC TRAFFIC	531.0

* Detailed statistics only available for major ports, i.e. generally those with at least 2 million tonnes of traffic
† Domestic traffic refers to traffic through the ports of Great Britain only, to all parts of the UK, Isle of Man and the Channel Islands. Traffic to and from offshore installations, landing of sea-dredged aggregates and material shipped for dumping at sea included
‡ Ports with less than 2 million tonnes of traffic

Source: The Stationery Office – Annual Abstract of Statistics 1998

PASSENGER MOVEMENT BY SEA 1996

Arrivals plus departures at UK seaports by place of embarkation or landing*

All passenger movements	34,828,000
Irish Republic	3,887,000
Belgium	2,053,000
France†	25,470,000
Netherlands	1,956,000
Other EU countries	1,014,000
Other European and Mediterranean countries‡	191,000
USA	20,400
Rest of the world	3,500
Pleasure cruises beginning and/or ending at UK seaports	233,000

* Passengers are included at both departure and arrival if their journeys begin and end at a UK seaport
† Includes hovercraft passengers
‡ Includes North Africa and Middle East Mediterranean countries

Source: The Stationery Office – Annual Abstract of Statistics 1998

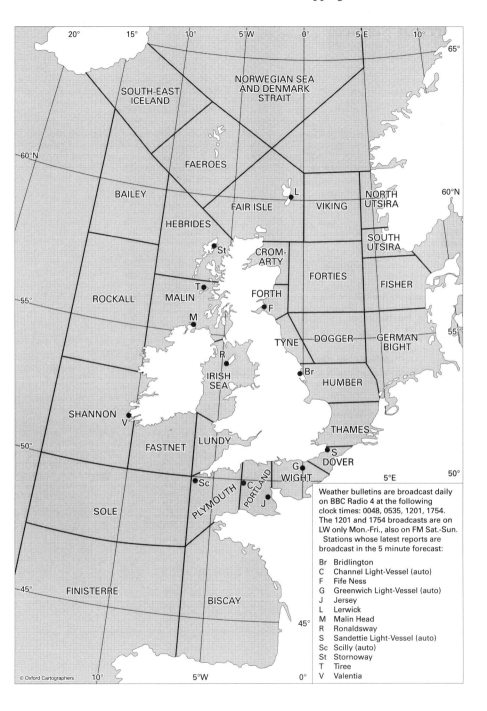

Weather bulletins are broadcast daily on BBC Radio 4 at the following clock times: 0048, 0535, 1201, 1754. The 1201 and 1754 broadcasts are on LW only Mon.-Fri., also on FM Sat.-Sun.
Stations whose latest reports are broadcast in the 5 minute forecast:

Br   Bridlington
C   Channel Light-Vessel (auto)
F   Fife Ness
G   Greenwich Light-Vessel (auto)
J   Jersey
L   Lerwick
M   Malin Head
R   Ronaldsway
S   Sandettie Light-Vessel (auto)
Sc   Scilly (auto)
St   Stornoway
T   Tiree
V   Valentia

© Oxford Cartographers

Forecast Services

WEATHERCALL SERVICE

To obtain local weather forecasts by telephone or fax, dial the prefix code followed by the appropriate area code. The prefix for telephone calls is 0891-500 4; the prefix for faxes is 0897-300 1. A helpdesk can be faxed on 0171-729 8811

National	00
Greater London	01
Kent, Surrey and Sussex	02
Dorset, Hampshire and IOW	03
Devon and Cornwall	04
Wiltshire, Glos, Avon and Somerset	05
Berks, Bucks and Oxfordshire	06
Beds, Herts and Essex	07
Norfolk, Suffolk and Cambridgeshire	08
Glamorgan and Gwent	09
Shropshire, Hereford and Worcester	10
West Midlands, Staffs and Warwickshire	11
Notts, Leics, Northants and Derbyshire	12
Lincolnshire and Humberside	13
Dyfed and Powys	14
Gwynedd and Clwyd	15
North-west England	16
West and South Yorkshire and the Dales	17
North-east England	18
Cumbria and the Lake District	19
Dumfries and Galloway	20
West and Central Scotland	21
Edinburgh, Fife, Lothian and Borders	22
East and Central Scotland	23
Grampian and East Highlands	24
North-west Scotland	25
Highlands, Orkney and Shetland	26
Northern Ireland	27

0891 calls are charged at 50p a minute, 0897 calls at £1.50 per minute (as at September 1998)

MARINECALL SERVICE

To obtain information about weather conditions up to 12 miles off the coast for the following five days, dial the prefix code 0891 500 followed by the appropriate area code

Scotland North	451
Scotland East	452
North-east	453
East	454
Anglia	455
Channel East	456
Mid-Channel	457
South-west	458
Bristol	459
Wales	460
North-west	461
Clyde	462
Caledonia	463
Minch	464
Ulster	465
English Channel	992

0891 calls are charged at 50p a minute, 0897 calls at £1.50 per minute (as at September 1998)

Communications

Postal Services

Responsibility for running postal services rests in the UK with a public authority, the Post Office (*see* pages 333–4). The Secretary of State for Trade and Industry has powers to suspend the letter monopoly of the Post Office in certain areas and to issue licences to other bodies to provide an alternative service. Non-Post Office bodies are permitted to transfer mail between document exchanges and to deliver letters, provided that a minimum fee of £1 per letter is charged. Charitable organizations are allowed to carry and deliver Christmas and New Year cards.

INLAND POSTAL SERVICES AND REGULATIONS

INLAND LETTER POST RATES*

Not over	1st class†	2nd class†
60 g	26p	20p
100 g	39p	31p
150 g	49p	38p
200 g	60p	45p
250 g	70p	55p
300 g	80p	64p
350 g	92p	73p
400 g	£1.04	83p
450 g	£1.17	93p
500 g	£1.30	£1.05
600 g	£1.60	£1.25
700 g	£2.00	£1.45
750 g	£2.15	£1.55 (not
800 g	£2.30	admissible
900 g	£2.55	over 750 g)
1,000 g	£2.50	
Each extra 250 g or part thereof	70p	

UK PARCEL RATES

Not over	
1 kg	£2.70
2 kg	£3.65
4 kg	£5.65
6 kg	£6.15
8 kg	£7.55
10 kg	£7.55
30 kg	£8.85

*Postcards travel at the same rates as letter post
†There is a two-tier postal delivery system in the UK with first class letters normally being delivered the following day and second class post within three days

OVERSEAS POSTAL SERVICES AND REGULATIONS

OVERSEAS SURFACE MAIL RATES

Letters

Not over		Not over	
20 g	31p	450 g	£2.88
60 g	52p	500 g	£3.18
100 g	75p	750 g	£4.70
150 g	£1.06	1,000 g	£6.21
200 g	£1.36	1,250 g	£7.71
250 g	£1.66	1,500 g	£9.21
300 g	£1.97	1,750 g	£10.71
350 g	£2.27	2,000 g	£12.21
400 g	£2.57		

Postcards travel at 20 g letter rate

AIRMAIL LETTER RATES

Europe: Letters

Not over		Not over	
20 g	30p	280 g	£1.95
40 g	44p	300 g	£2.07
60 g	56p	320 g	£2.20
80 g	69p	340 g	£2.32
100 g	82p	360 g	£2.45
120 g	94p	380 g	£2.57
140 g	£1.07	400 g	£2.70
160 g	£1.19	420 g	£2.82
180 g	£1.32	440 g	£2.95
200 g	£1.44	460 g	£3.08
220 g	£1.57	480 g	£3.20
240 g	£1.69	*500 g	£3.33
260 g	£1.82		

* Max. 2 kg
Postcards to Europe travel at 20 g letter rate

Outside Europe: Letters

	Not over 10 g	Not over 20 g	Over 20 g	Post cards
Zone 1	43p	63p	varies	37p
Zone 2	43p	63p	varies	37p

For airmail letter zones outside Europe, *see* pages 520–1

STAMPS

Postage stamps are sold in values of 1p, 2p, 4p, 5p, 6p, 10p, 19p, 20p, 25p, 26p, 29p, 30p, 31p, 35p, 36p, 37p, 38p, 39p, 41p, 43p, 50p, 63p, £1, £1.50, £2.00, £5.00, and £10.00. Books or rolls of first and second class stamps are also available. Stamps are sold at Post Offices and some other outlets, including stationers and newsagents.

PREPAID STATIONERY

Aerogrammes to all destinations are 36p, with a packet of six costing £1.99. Pictorial aerogrammes are 45p; a packet of six, £2.50. Forces aerogrammes are free to certain destinations.

Prepaid envelopes:
Standard services (DL size)

	1st class	2nd class
single	31p	25p
packet of 10	£2.85	£2.25

Guaranteed services	Special Delivery	Registered	Registered Plus
C4, 500g	£3.50	£3.80	£4.85
C5, 250g	3.20	3.60	4.55

Printed postage stamps cut from envelopes, postcards, newspaper wrappers, etc., may be used as stamps in payment of postage, provided that they are not imperfect or defaced.

POSTAL ORDERS

Postal orders (British pattern) are issued and paid at nearly all post offices in the UK and in many other countries.

Postal orders are printed with a counterfoil for denominations of 50p and £1, followed by £1 steps to £10, £15 and £20. Postage stamps may be affixed in the space provided to increase the value of the postal order by up to 49p. Charges (in addition to the value of the postal order): up to £1, 25p; £2–£4, 45p; £5–£7, 65p; £8–£10, 80p; £15, 90p; £20, 95p.

The name of the payee must be inserted on the postal order. If not presented within six months of the last day of the month of issue, orders must be sent to the local customer services manager of Post Office Counters Ltd (listed in the telephone directory) to ascertain whether the order may still be paid. If the counterfoil has been retained postal orders not more than four years out of date may be paid when presented with the counterfoil at a post office.

RESTRICTIONS

Articles which may not be sent in the post include offensive or dangerous articles (such as explosives, articles containing batteries, or aerosol products), packets likely to impede Post Office sorters, and certain kinds of advertisement. Certain other articles (such as biological specimens, liquids, or perishable foodstuffs) may be posted only if packed correctly. Advice is available from Royal Mail (tel: 0345-740740) for letters and small packets; Parcelforce (tel: 0800-224466) for parcels; or local post office counter staff.

The exportation of some goods by post is prohibited except under Department of Trade licence. Enquiries should be addressed to the Export Data Branch, Overseas Trade Divisions, Department of Trade and Industry, 1 Victoria Street, London SW1H 0ET. Tel: 0171-215 5000.

SPECIAL DELIVERY SERVICES

DATAPOST

A guaranteed service for the delivery of documents and packages: (i) Datapost Sameday offers same working day collection and delivery in many areas; (ii) Datapost 10 (for delivery before 10 a.m.) and Datapost 12 (for delivery before noon) offer next working day delivery nationwide and are available only to certain destinations. Items may be collected or handed in at post offices. There are also Datapost links with a number of overseas countries. Parcelforce 24 (next working day delivery) and 48 (delivery in two working days) offer a similar guaranteed service.

ROYAL MAIL SPECIAL DELIVERY

A guaranteed next-day delivery service by 12.30 p.m. to most UK destinations for first class letters and packets. The fee of £3.20 plus first class postage for a 100 g item is refunded if next working day delivery is not achieved, provided that items are posted before latest recommended posting times.

SWIFTAIR

Express delivery of airmail letters and packets up to 2 kg anywhere in the world. Items are normally placed on the first available flight to the destination country. Charge (in addition to postage), £2.70.

OTHER SERVICES

ADVICE OF DELIVERY

Written confirmation of delivery from the post office at the stated destination. Charge: 33p (inland); 40p (international); plus postage.

CERTIFICATE OF POSTING

Issued free on request at time of posting.

COMPENSATION (INLAND AND INTERNATIONAL)

Inland: compensation up to a maximum of £26 may be paid where it can be shown that a letter was damaged or lost in the post due to the fault of the Post Office, its employees or agents. The Post Office does not accept responsibility for loss or damage arising from faulty packing.

International: if a certificate of posting is produced, compensation up to a maximum of £26 may be given for loss or damage in the UK to uninsured parcels to or from most overseas countries. No compensation will be paid for any loss or damage due to the action of the Queen's Enemies.

INTERNATIONAL REPLY COUPONS

Coupons used to prepay replies to letters, exchangeable abroad for stamps representing the lowest airmail letter rate from the country concerned to the UK. Charge: 60p each.

NEWSPAPER POST

Copies of newspapers registered at the Post Office may be posted only by the publisher or their agents in open-ended wrappers or unsealed envelopes approved by the Post Office, or tied with string removable without cutting. Wrappers and envelopes must be prominently marked 'newspaper post' in the top left-hand corner. The only additional writing or printing permitted is 'with compliments', the name and address of sender, request for return if undeliverable, and a page reference. Items receive first class letter service.

POSTE RESTANTE

Poste Restante is solely for travellers and is for three months in any one town. A packet may be addressed to any post office, except town sub-offices, and should state 'Poste Restante' or 'to be called for' in the address. Redirection from a Poste Restante is undertaken for up to three months. Letters for an expected ship at a port are kept for two months, otherwise letters are kept for two weeks, or one month if from abroad. At the end of this period mail is treated as undeliverable or is returned.

PRIVATE BOX

Provides an alternative address (e.g. PO Box 123) and mail is held at the local delivery office for collection. Charge: £42 (six months); £52 (12 months).

RECORDED MAIL

Provides a record of posting and delivery of letters and ensures a signature on delivery. This service is recommended for items of little or no monetary value. All packets must be handed to the post office and a certificate of posting issued. Charges: 60p plus postage (inland); £2.50 plus postage (international).

REDIRECTION

By agent of addressee: mail other than parcels, business reply and freepost items may be reposted free not later than the day after delivery (not counting Sundays and public holidays) if unopened and if original addressee's name is unobscured. Parcels may be redirected free within the same time limits only if the original and substituted address are in the same local parcel delivery area (or the London postal area). Registered packets must be taken to a post office and are re-registered free up to the day after delivery.

By the Post Office: a printed form obtainable from the Post Office must be signed by the person to whom the letters are to be addressed. A fee is payable for each different surname on the application form. Charges: up to 1 calendar month, £6.00 (abroad, £12.00); up to 3 calendar months, £13.00 (£26.00); up to 12 calendar months, £30.00 (£60.00).

REGISTERED MAIL (INLAND AND INTERNATIONAL)

Inland: all packets must be handed to the post office and a certificate of posting obtained. Charges (plus postage): up to £500 compensation, £3.50; Registered Plus for compensation between £500 and £1,500, £4.10; up to £2,200 compensation, £4.55. Consequential Loss Insurance provides cover up to £10,000:

Compensation up to	Registered fee plus postage
£1,000	£1.20
£2,500	£1.50
£5,000	£2.00
£7,500	£2.50
£10,000	£3.00

Compensation in respect of currency or other forms of monetary worth is given only if money is sent by registered letter post. Compensation cannot be paid in the case of any packet containing prohibited articles (*see* Restrictions). Compensation is only paid for well-packed fragile articles and not for exceptionally fragile or perishable articles.

International: ensures a signature in delivery and compensation for valuables sent by letter or small packet post by air or surface mail. Some countries are not covered. Registered fee plus postage: compensation up to £500, £3.00; up to £2,200, £4.00.

SMALL PACKETS POST AND PRINTED PAPERS (INTERNATIONAL)

Permits the transmission of goods up to 2 kg to all countries, in the same mails as printed papers. Packets can be sealed and can contain personal correspondence relating to the contents. Registration is allowed as insurance as long as the item is packed in a way complying with any insurance regulations. A customs declaration is required and the packet must be marked with 'small packet' and a return address. Instructions for the disposal of undelivered packets must be given at the time of posting. An undeliverable packet will be returned to the sender at his/her expense.

Surface mail: world-wide

Not over		Not over	
100 g	50p	450 g	£1.67
150 g	67p	500 g	£1.84
200 g	84p	750 g	£2.68
250 g	£1.00	1,000 g	£3.51
300 g	£1.17	1,500 g	£5.21
350 g	£1.34	2,000 g	£6.91
400 g	£1.51		

Printed papers only, per extra 50 g, 17p

UNDELIVERED AND UNPAID MAIL

Undelivered mail is returned to the sender provided the return address is indicated either on the outside of the envelope or inside. If the sender's address is not available items not containing property are destroyed. If the packet contains something of value it is retained for up to three months. Undeliverable second class mail containing newspapers, magazines or commercial advertising is destroyed.

All unpaid or underpaid letters are treated as second class mail. The recipient is charged the amount of underpayment plus 15p per item. Parcels over 750 g are charged at first class rates plus 15p.

Public Telecommunications Services

Under the British Telecommunications Act 1981 British Telecom (now BT) was created to provide a national public telecommunications service. The Telecommunications Act 1984 removed BT's monopoly on running the public telecommunications system and BT was privatized in 1984.

The Telecommunications Act 1984 also established the Office of Telecommunications (Oftel) as the independent regulatory body for the telecommunications industry (*see also* Government Departments and Public Offices).

PUBLIC TELECOMMUNICATIONS OPERATORS

Until 1991 the three licensed fixed-link public telecommunications operators (PTOs) in the UK were BT, Mercury Communications Ltd, and Kingston Communications (Hull) PLC. In 1991 the Government announced that it was opening up the existing duopoly of the two major fixed-link operators, BT and Mercury, and would be encouraging applications for telecommunications licences. The Department of Trade and Industry has granted over 280 PTO licences.

BT's obligations under its operating licence continue to include the provision of a universal telecommunications

service; a service in rural areas; and essential services, such as public call boxes and emergency services.

Cable and Wireless Communications PLC (which was formed from the merger of Mercury Communications with other communications companies in 1997) is licensed to provide national and international public telecommunications services for residential and business customers. These services utilize the digital network created by Mercury. Cable and Wireless can also provide the following services: public and private telephone services; national and international switched voice and data services; electronic messaging (private circuits and networks (national and international), integrated voice and data); data network services; customer equipment cable television, Internet service provision and mobile communications services.

In December 1996 the Government liberalized international facilities licensing in the UK. The end of the BT/Mercury duopoly means that other operators are now able to apply for licences to own and operate their own international telecommunications networks. By July 1998, 89 operators had been granted international facilities licences. In January 1998 the telecommunications market throughout the European Union was liberalized.

PRIVATE TELEPHONE SERVICES

There are over 260 private telephone companies which offer information on a variety of subjects such as the weather, stock market analysis, horoscopes, etc., on the various networks.

The lines and equipment are provided by BT under condition that services adhere to the codes of practice of the Independent Committee for the Supervision of Standards of Telephone Information Services. Services are charged at different rates from 5p to £1.50 per minute.

MOBILE TELEPHONE SYSTEMS

Cellular telephone network systems allow calls to be made to and from mobile telephones. The four companies licensed by the Department of Trade and Industry to provide competing cellular telephone systems are Cellnet, jointly owned by BT and Securicor; One-2-One, jointly owned by Cable and Wireless and US West; Orange; and Vodafone.

INLAND TELEPHONES

An individual customer can install an extension telephone socket or apparatus in their own home without the need to buy the items from any of the licensed public telecommunications operators. Although an individual need not buy or rent an apparatus from a PTO, a telephone bought from a retail outlet must be of an approved standard compatible with the public network (indicated by a green disc on the label).

BT EXCHANGE LINE RENTALS (*including VAT*)

	Per quarter
Residential, exclusive	£26.62
Light user scheme	from £9.24
Business, exclusive	£43.88

BT TELEPHONE APPARATUS RENTAL *Per quarter*

Residential	from £4.47
Business	from £5.53
Private payphone	from £50.53

EXCHANGE LINE CONNECTION AND TAKE-OVER CHARGES (*including VAT*)

BT

New line	£116.33
Removing customer	£0.00
Take-over of existing lines:	
Simultaneous (same day)	£0.00
Non-simultaneous	£9.99

Cable and Wireless

Monthly line rental	£7.98

RATES

BT and Cable and Wireless local and dialled national calls are charged by the second. Calls made from payphones are charged in 10p units. There is a 5p minimum charge on all BT calls and a 3.5p or 4.2p minimum charge on Cable and Wireless calls depending on the charging package. All charges are subject to VAT, except those from payphones which are VAT inclusive. VAT charges on ordinary lines are calculated as a percentage of the total quarterly (BT)/ monthly (Cable and Wireless) bill.

The charge per second depends on the time of day and the distance of the call:

BT	Cable and Wireless	
Daytime	Daytime	Monday to Friday 8 a.m. to 6 p.m.
Evening and night-time	Evening	Monday to Friday 6 p.m. to 8 a.m.
Weekend	Weekend	Midnight Friday to midnight Sunday

Local rate
Regional rate – up to 35 miles (56 km)
National rate – over 35 miles (56 km) (including Channel Islands and Isle of Man)
Calls to mobile phones

DIALLED CALL TIME pence per minute charges (*including VAT*)*

BT	Local rate
Daytime	4.00
Evening and night-time	1.50
Weekend	1.00
Regional rate	7.91
Daytime	
Evening and night-time	4.00
Weekend	3.00
National rate	
Daytime	7.91
Evening and night-time	4.20
Weekend	3.00
Calls to Cellnet and Vodafone mobile phones	
Daytime	30.00
Evening and night-time	20.00
Weekend	10.00
Calls to Orange and One-2-One mobile phones	
Daytime	30.00
Evening and night-time	20.00
Weekend	10.00

*Cable and Wireless customers choose from a range of packages depending on the time of day they use the telephone most and the distance of their calls. Charges vary with each package.

OPERATOR-CONNECTED CALLS

Operator-connected calls from ordinary lines are generally subject to a one-minute minimum charge (and thereafter by the minute) which varies with distance and time of day. Operator-connected calls from payphones are charged in three-minute periods at the payphone tariff. There is also a £1.80 handling charge for operator-connected calls. For calls that have to be placed through the operator because a dialled call has failed, the charge is equivalent to the dialled rate, subject normally to the one-minute minimum.

Higher charges apply to other operator-connected calls, including special services calls and those to mobile phones, the Irish Republic and the Channel Islands.

PHONECARDS

BT phonecards to the value of £2, £5, £10 and £20 are available from post offices and other outlets for use in specially designated public telephone boxes. Each phonecard unit is equivalent to a 10p coin in a payphone. Special public payphones at major railway stations and airports also accept commercial credit cards.

INTERNATIONAL TELEPHONES

All UK customers have access to International Direct Dialling (IDD) and can dial direct to numbers on most exchanges in over 230 countries world-wide. Details about how to make calls are given in dialling code information and in the International Telephone Guide.

For countries without IDD, calls have to be made through the International Operator. All operator-connected calls are subject to a £1.80 handling charge. Thereafter the call is charged by the minute.

Countries which can be called on IDD fall into one of 18 international charge bands depending on location. Charges in each band also vary according to the time of day; cheap rate dialled calls are available to all countries at certain times, but there is no reduced rate for operator-connected calls. Details of current international telephone charges can be obtained from the International Operator.

For International Dialling Codes, *see* pages 520–1.

OTHER TELECOMMUNICATIONS SERVICES

Telex Service

There are now more than 240 countries that can be reached by the BT telex network from the UK. Calls can be sent to mobile terminals, including ships via the Inmarsat satellite service. Call charges start at 4.8p per minute for inland calls. International calls are charged by the second.

Telemessage

Telemessages can be sent by telephone or telex within the UK for 'hard copy' delivery the next working day, including Saturdays. To achieve this, a telemessage must be telephoned/telexed before 10 p.m. Monday to Saturday (7 p.m. Sundays and Bank Holidays). Dial 0800-190190 and ask for the Telemessage Service.

A telemessage costs £8.99 for the first 50 words and £5.00 for each subsequent group of 50 words – the name and address are free. A sender's copy costs £1.20. A selection of cards is available for special occasions at £1.00 per card. (All prices are include VAT.)

BT SERVICES

Operator Services – 100
For difficulties
For the following call services: alarm calls (booking charge £2.70); advice of duration and charge (charge £1.80); charge card calls (charge £1.50); freephone calls; international personal calls (charge £2.15–£4.30); transferred charge calls (charge £1.80); subscriber controlled transfer (All charges exclude VAT)
International Operator – 155
Directory Enquiries – 192 (35p charge per call)
International Directory Enquiries – 153 (80p charge per call)
Emergency Services – 999
Services include fire service; police service; ambulance service; coastguard; lifeboat; cave rescue; mountain rescue
Faults 151 (residential), 154 (business)
Telemessage 0800-190190
International Telegrams – 100

Maritime Services – 100
Includes Ship's Telegram Service and Ship's Telephone Service
BT Inmarsat Satellite Service – 155
All Other Call Enquiries – 100

Airmail and IDD Codes

AIRMAIL ZONES (AZ)
The table includes airmail letter zones for countries outside Europe, and destinations to which European and European Union airmail letter rates apply (*see also* page 515).
(*Source:* Post Office)
1   airmail zone 1
2   airmail zone 2
e   Europe

INTERNATIONAL DIRECT DIALLING (IDD)
International dialling codes are composed of four elements which are dialled in sequence:

(i)   the international code
(ii)   the country code (*see* below)
(iii) the area code
(iv)   the customer's telephone number

Calls to some countries must be made via the international operator. (*Source:* BT)

†   Calls must be made via the international operator
p   A pause in dialling is necessary whilst waiting for a second tone
*   Varies in some areas
**   Varies depending on carrier

Country	AZ	IDD from UK	IDD to UK
Afghanistan	1	00 93	†
Albania	e	00 355	00 44
Algeria	1	00 213	00p44
Andorra	e	00 376	00 44
Angola	1	00 244	00 44
Anguilla	1	00 1 264	00 11 44
Antigua and Barbuda	1	00 1 268	011 44
Argentina	1	00 54	00 44
Armenia	e	00 374	810 44
Aruba	1	00 297	00 44
Ascension Island	1	00 247	01 44
Australia	2	00 61	00 11 44
Austria	e	00 43	00 44
Azerbaijan	e	00 994	810 44
Azores	e	00 351	00 44
Bahamas	1	00 1 242	011 44
Bahrain	1	00 973	0 44
Bangladesh	1	00 880	00 44
Barbados	1	00 1 246	011 44
Belarus	e	00 375	810 44
Belgium	e	00 32	00 44
Belize	1	00 501	011 44
Benin	1	00 229	00p44
Bermuda	1	00 1 441	011 44
Bhutan	1	00 975	00 44
Bolivia	1	00 591	00 44
Bosnia-Hercegovina	e	00 396	99 44
Botswana	1	00 267	00 44
Brazil	1	00 55	00 44
British Virgin Islands	1	00 1 809	011 44
Brunei	1	00 673	01 44
Bulgaria	e	00 359	00 44
Burkina Faso	1	00 226	00 44
Burundi	1	00 257	90 44
Cambodia	1	00 855	00 44
Cameroon	1	00 237	00 44
Canada	1	00 1	011 44
Canary Islands	e	00 34	07p44
Cape Verde	1	00 238	0 44

Country	AZ	IDD from UK	IDD to UK
Cayman Islands	1	00 1 345	011 44
Central African Republic	1	00 236	00p44
Chad	1	00 235	†
Chile	1	00 56	00 44
China	2	00 86	00 44
Hong Kong	1	00 852	001 44
Colombia	1	00 57	90 44
Comoros	1	00 269	10 44
Congo, Dem. Rep. of	1	00 243	00 44
Congo, Republic of	1	00 242	00 44
Cook Islands	2	00 682	00 44
Costa Rica	1	00 506	00 44
Côte d'Ivoire	1	00 225	00 44
Croatia	e	00 385	00 44
Cuba	1	00 53	119 44
Cyprus	e	00 357	00 44
Czech Republic	e	00 420	00 44
Denmark	e	00 45	00 44
Djibouti	1	00 253	00 44
Dominica	1	00 1 809	011 44
Dominican Republic	1	00 1 809	011 44
Ecuador	1	00 593	01 44
Egypt	1	00 20	00 44
Equatorial Guinea	1	00 240	19 44
Eritrea	1	00 291	†
Estonia	e	00 372	800 44
Ethiopia	1	00 251	00 44
Falkland Islands	1	00 500	01 44
Faroe Islands	e	00 298	009 44
Fiji	2	00 679	05 44
Finland	e	00 358	00 44**
France	e	00 33	00 44
French Guiana	1	00 594	†
French Polynesia	2	00 689	00 44
Gabon	1	00 241	00 44
The Gambia	1	00 220	00 44
Georgia	e	00 995	810 44
Germany	e	00 49	00 44
Ghana	1	00 233	00 44
Gibraltar	e	00 350	00 44
Greece	e	00 30	00 44
Greenland	e	00 299	009 44
Grenada	1	00 1 809	011 44
Guadeloupe	1	00 590	19 44
Guam	2	00 671	001 44
Guatemala	1	00 502	00 44
Guinea	1	00 224	00 44
Guinea-Bissau	1	00 245	†
Guyana	1	00 592	001 44
Haiti	1	00 509	†
Honduras	1	00 504	00 44
Hungary	e	00 36	00 44
Iceland	e	00 354	00 44
India	1	00 91	00 44
Indonesia	1	00 62	001 44**
			00844**
Iran	1	00 98	00 44
Iraq	1	00 964	00 44
Ireland, Republic of	e	00 353	00 44
Israel	1	00 972	00 44
Italy	e	00 39	00 44
Jamaica	1	00 1 809	011 44
Japan	2	00 81	001 44
			004144**
			006144**
Jordan	1	00 962	00 44*
Kazakhstan	e	00 7	810 44
Kenya	1	00 254	00 44

Country	AZ	IDD from UK	IDD to UK		Country	AZ	IDD from UK	IDD to UK
Kiribati	2	00 686	0 44		Russia	e	00 7	810 44
Korea, North	2	00 850	010 44		Rwanda	1	00 250	00 44
Korea, South	2	00 82	001 44**		St Christopher and			
			002 44**		Nevis	1	00 1 869	†
Kuwait	1	00 965	00 44		St Helena	1	00 290	01 44
Kyrgystan	e	00 996	810 44		St Lucia	1	00 1 758	011 44
Laos	1	00 856	†		St Pierre and			
Latvia	e	00 371	810 44		Miquelon	1	00 508	19p44
Lebanon	1	00 961	00 44		St Vincent and the			
Lesotho	1	00 266	00 44		Grenadines	1	00 1 809	00 44
Liberia	1	00 231	00 44		El Salvador	1	00 503	00 44
Libya	1	00 218	00 44		Samoa	2	00 685	0 44
Liechtenstein	e	00 41	00 44		Samoa, American	2	00 684	1 44
Lithuania	e	00 370	810 44		San Marino	e	00 378	00 44
Luxembourg	e	00 352	00 44		São Tomé and			
Macao	1	00 853	00 44		Princípe	1	00 239	00 44
Macedonia	e	00 389	99 44		Saudi Arabia	1	00 966	00 44
Madagascar	1	00 261	16p44		Senegal	1	00 221	00p44
Madeira	e	00 351 91	00 44*		Serbia	e	00 381	99 44
Malawi	1	00 265	101 44		Seychelles	1	00 248	0 44
Malaysia	1	00 60	00 44		Sierra Leone	1	00 232	0 44
Maldives	1	00 960	00 44		Singapore	1	00 65	001 44
Mali	1	00 223	00 44		Slovak Republic	e	00 42	00 44
Malta	e	00 356	00 44		Slovenia	e	00 386	00 44
Mariana Islands,					Solomon Islands	2	00 677	00 44
Northern	2	00 1 670	011 44		Somalia	1	00 252	†
Marshall Islands	2	00 692	012 44		South Africa	1	00 27	09 44
Martinique	1	00 596	19p44		Spain	e	00 34	07p44
Mauritania	1	00 222	00 44		Sri Lanka	1	00 94	00 44
Mauritius	1	00 230	00 44		Sudan	1	00 249	00 44
Mayotte	1	00 269	19p44		Suriname	1	00 597	001 44
Mexico	1	00 52	98 44		Swaziland	1	00 268	00 44
Micronesia, Federated					Sweden	e	00 46	007 44**
States of	2	00 691	011 44					009 44**
Moldova	e	00 373	810 44					008744**
Monaco	e	00 377 93	00 44		Switzerland	e	00 41	00 44
Mongolia	2	00 976	†		Syria	1	00 963	00 44
Montenegro	e	00 381	99 44		Taiwan	2	00 886	002 44
Montserrat	1	00 1 664	†		Tajikistan	e	00 7	810 44
Morocco	1	00 212	00p44		Tanzania	1	00 255	00 44
Mozambique	1	00 258	00 44		Thailand	1	00 66	001 44
Myanmar	1	00 95	0 44		Tibet	1	00 86	00 44
Namibia	1	00 264	09 44		Togo	1	00 228	00 44
Nauru	2	00 674	00 44		Tonga	2	00 676	00 44
Nepal	1	00 977	00 44		Trinidad and Tobago	1	00 1 868	011 44
Netherlands	e	00 31	00 44		Tristan da Cunha	1	00 2 897	†
Netherlands Antilles	1	00 599	00 44		Tunisia	1	00 216	00 44
New Caledonia	2	00 687	00 44		Turkey	e	00 90	00 44
New Zealand	2	00 64	00 44		Turkmenistan	e	00 993	810 44
Nicaragua	1	00 505	00 44		Turks and Caicos			
Niger	1	00 227	00 44		Islands	1	00 1 649	0 44
Nigeria	1	00 234	009 44		Tuvalu	1	00 688	00 44
Niue	2	00 683	†		Uganda	1	00 256	00 44
Norfolk Island	2	00 672	00 44		Ukraine	e	00 380	810 44
Norway	e	00 47	00 44		United Arab Emirates	1	00 971	00 44
Oman	1	00 968	00 44		Uruguay	1	00 598	00 44
Pakistan	1	00 92	00 44		USA	1	00 1	011 44
Palau	2	00 680	†		Alaska		00 1 907	011 44
Panama	1	00 507	00 44		Hawaii		00 1 808	011 44
Papua New Guinea	2	00 675	05 44		Uzbekistan	e	00 7	810 44
Paraguay	1	00 595	002 44		Vanuatu	2	00 678	00 44
			003 44		Vatican City State	e	00 39 66982	00 44
Peru	1	00 51	00 44		Venezuela	1	00 58	00 44
Philippines	2	00 63	00 44		Vietnam	1	00 84	00 44
Poland	e	00 48	0p044		Virgin Islands (US)	1	00 1 340	011 44
Portugal	e	00 351	00 44		Yemen	1	00 967	00 44
Puerto Rico	1	00 1 787	011 44		Yugoslav Fed. Rep.	e	00 381	99 44
Qatar	1	00 974	044		Zambia	1	00 260	00 44
Réunion	1	00 262	19p44		Zimbabwe	1	00 263	110 44
Romania	e	00 40	00 44					

The Internet

The Internet is a rapidly-growing world-wide network of computer networks which use the same protocols (agreed methods of communication). It has its origins in the Advanced Research Projects Agency Network (ARPANET), a government-funded defence network in the USA, and other research and academic networks, such as the UK Joint Academic Network (JANET), a network linking universities and higher education institutions in the UK. JANET has extensive links to international and other national academic networks, and also to commercial and public network services. It is funded by the higher education funding agencies in the UK.

The main protocol used by the networks is Transmission Control Protocol/Internet Protocol (TCP/IP). Other protocols include:
- file transfer protocol (ftp), which allows files to be transferred between computers
- simple mail transfer protocol (smtp), which allows electronic mail (e-mail) to be sent
- hypertext transfer protocol (http), which allows hypertext facilities to be provided
- telnet, a facility which allows users to log on to other computers on the Internet

The most common uses of the Internet include:
- sending and receiving e-mail; text can be sent directly to another computer linked to the Internet
- playing computer games
- commercial transactions
- mailing lists, which enable users to send and receive information on specialist interests
- 'newsgroups' or bulletin boards, where messages on specialist interests can be left for users to read
- the publication of information

The World-Wide Web (WWW or the Web) is a vast collection of computers able to support multi-media formats and accessible via Web 'browsers' (search and navigation tools). Data stored on these computers (servers) is organized into pages with hypertext links; each page has a unique address. It is estimated that the number of pages on the Web trebled between 1995 and 1997 and is now doubling every three months. One estimate put the total number of pages at approximately 320 million in July 1998. For practical purposes the WWW and the Internet are now almost synonymous. The main Web browsers are Netscape Navigator and Internet Explorer. The Internet is increasingly used by commercial organizations for the conduct of electronic business. Policies and standards are being developed to ensure an appropriate level of privacy; tools include access control mechanisms, data labelling and cryptography standards.

The speed of access to Internet sources and of downloading information depends on the number of users on the system (which varies according to the time of day), the location of the information, and the amount of information being downloaded.

CONNECTIONS

Connection to the Internet usually requires access to a computer, a modem and a telephone line, although it is now possible to receive television-based Internet services. Internet service providers (ISPs) supply an Internet address and password, an electronic mailbox and some or all of the necessary software. Most providers provide only a connection to the Internet, but a few also offer more sophisticated on-line services which are usually easier to use but more expensive than direct Internet access. Leading service providers include AOL, CompuServe, Demon, UU net and Microsoft Network. Details of providers are available in computer magazines and specialist Internet publications.

The main methods of connecting to the Internet are by a dial-up connection or a leased-line connection. A dial-up connection may be made over standard telephone lines or over ISDN lines. There are two types of dial-up connection: an online account, which allows the user to log on to an account on a remote computer which is connected to the Internet; and a dial-up IP connection, where a full Internet connection is made from the user's computer. The latter requires more complicated software. A permanent leased-line connection (a data line requiring no modem) is likely to be used where there are a large number of potential users, e.g. where all the users on a local area network (LAN) are to be connected.

In Great Britain, an estimated 6.3 million households own personal computers. Of the 5.5 million people who used the Internet in the first half of 1998, 40 per cent logged on from home compared to 36 per cent from their workplace. The number of Internet users world-wide is estimated to be between 100 million and 130 million.

TERMS

Home page – the introductory section of a site on the Web

Hypertext mark-up language (HTML) – a standard document mark-up language used on the Web

Java – a programming language for writing client/server and networked applications; its uses include creating interactive Web sites

Search engine – a means of finding Web pages or other material on the Internet containing specific words or phrases

Server – a computer storing data and software which can be used by other computers on a network

Uniform/Universal resource locators (URLs) – the address system for the Web

Users' network (USENET) – a large bulletin board system on the Internet

Local Government

Major changes in local government were introduced in England and Wales in 1974 and in Scotland in 1975 by the Local Government Act 1972 and the Local Government (Scotland) Act 1973. Further significant alterations were made in England by the Local Government Acts of 1985 and 1992.

The structure in England was based on two tiers of local authorities (county councils and district councils) in the non-metropolitan areas; and a single tier of metropolitan councils in the six metropolitan areas of England and London borough councils in London.

Following reviews of the structure of local government in England by the Local Government Commission, 46 unitary (all-purpose) authorities were created between April 1995 and April 1998 to cover certain areas in the non-metropolitan counties. The remaining county areas continue to have two tiers of local authorities. The county and district councils in the Isle of Wight were replaced by a single unitary authority on 1 April 1995; the former counties of Avon, Cleveland, Humberside and Berkshire have been replaced by unitary authorities; and Hereford and Worcester was replaced by a new county council for Worcestershire (with district councils) and a unitary authority for Herefordshire.

The Local Government (Wales) Act 1994 and the Local Government etc. (Scotland) Act 1994 abolished the two-tier structure in Wales and Scotland with effect from 1 April 1996, replacing it with a single tier of unitary authorities.

Local authorities are empowered or required by various Acts of Parliament to carry out functions in their areas. The legislation concerned comprises public general Acts and 'local' Acts which local authorities have promoted as private bills.

ELECTIONS

Local elections are normally held on the first Thursday in May. Generally, all British subjects and citizens of the Republic of Ireland who are 18 years or over and resident on the qualifying date in the area for which the election is being held, are entitled to vote at local government elections. A register of electors is prepared and published annually by local electoral registration officers.

A returning officer has the overall responsibility for an election. Voting takes place at polling stations, arranged by the local authority and under the supervision of a presiding officer specially appointed for the purpose. Candidates, who are subject to various statutory qualifications and disqualifications designed to ensure that they are suitable persons to hold office, must be nominated by electors for the electoral area concerned.

In England, the Local Government Commission is responsible for carrying out periodic reviews of electoral arrangements and making proposals to the Secretary of State for changes found necessary. In Wales and Scotland these matters are the responsibility of the Local Government Boundary Commission for Wales and the Local Boundary Commission for Scotland respectively.

LOCAL GOVERNMENT COMMISSION FOR ENGLAND, Dolphyn Court, 10–11 Great Turnstile, Lincoln's Inn Fields, London WCIV 7JU. Tel: 0171-430 8400

LOCAL GOVERNMENT BOUNDARY COMMISSION FOR WALES, 1–6 St Andrew's Place, Cardiff CFI 3BE. Tel: 01222-395031

LOCAL GOVERNMENT BOUNDARY COMMISSION FOR SCOTLAND, 3 Drumsheugh Gardens, Edinburgh EH3 7QJ. Tel: 0131-538 7510.

INTERNAL ORGANIZATION

The council as a whole is the final decision-making body within any authority. Councils are free to a great extent to make their own internal organizational arrangements.

Normally, questions of policy are settled by the full council, while the administration of the various services is the responsibility of committees of councillors. Day-to-day decisions are delegated to the council's officers, who act within the policies laid down by the councillors.

FINANCE

Local government in England, Wales and Scotland is financed from four sources: the council tax, non-domestic rates, government grants, and income from fees and charges for services. (For arrangements in Northern Ireland, *see* page 528.)

COUNCIL TAX

Under the Local Government Finance Act 1992, from 1 April 1993 the council tax replaced the community charge (which had been introduced in April 1989 in Scotland and April 1990 in England and Wales in place of domestic rates).

The council tax is a local tax levied by each local council. Liability for the council tax bill usually falls on the owner-occupier or tenant of a dwelling which is their sole or main residence. Council tax bills may be reduced because of the personal circumstances of people resident in a property, and there are discounts in the case of dwellings occupied by fewer than two adults.

In England, each county council, each district council and each police authority sets its own council tax rate. The district councils collect the combined council tax, and the county councils and police authorities claim their share from the district councils' collection funds. In Wales, each unitary authority and each police authority sets its own council tax rate. The unitary authorities collect the combined council tax and the police authorities claim their share from the funds. In Scotland, each island council and unitary authority sets its own rate of council tax.

The tax relates to the value of the dwelling. Each dwelling is placed in one of eight valuation bands, ranging from A to H, based on the property's estimated market value as at 1 April 1991.

The valuation bands and ranges of values in England, Wales and Scotland are:

England

A	Up to £40,000	E	£88,001–£120,000
B	£40,001–£52,000	F	£120,001–£160,000
C	£52,001–£68,000	G	£160,001–£320,000
D	£68,001–£88,000	H	Over £320,000

Wales

A	Up to £30,000	E	£66,001–£90,000
B	£30,001–£39,000	F	£90,001–£120,000
C	£39,001–£51,000	G	£120,001–£240,000
D	£51,001–£66,000	H	Over £240,000

Scotland

A	Up to £27,000	E	£58,001–£80,000
B	£27,001–£35,000	F	£80,001–£106,000
C	£35,001–£45,000	G	£106,001–£212,000
D	£45,001–£58,000	H	Over £212,000

The council tax within a local area varies between the different bands according to proportions laid down by law. The charge attributable to each band as a proportion of the Band D charge set by the council is approximately:

A	67%	E	122%
B	78%	F	144%
C	89%	G	167%
D	100%	H	200%

The band D rate is given in the tables on pages 545–50 (England), 557 (London), 560 (Wales), and 565 (Scotland). There may be variations from the given figure within each district council area because of different parish or community precepts being levied.

Non-Domestic Rates

Non-domestic (business) rates are collected by billing authorities; these are the district councils in those areas of England with two tiers of local government and unitary authorities in other parts of England, in Wales and in Scotland. In respect of England and Wales, the Local Government Finance Act 1988 provides for liability for rates to be assessed on the basis of a poundage (multiplier) tax on the rateable value of property (hereditaments). Separate multipliers are set by the appropriate Secretaries of State in England, Wales and Scotland, and rates are collected by the billing authority for the area where a property is located. Rate income collected by billing authorities is paid into a national non-domestic rating (NNDR) pool and redistributed to individual authorities on the basis of the adult population figure as prescribed by the appropriate Secretary of State. The rates pools are maintained separately in England, Wales and Scotland. For the years 1995–6 to 2000–1 actual payment of rates in certain cases is subject to transitional arrangements, to phase in the larger increases and reductions in rates resulting from the effects of the 1995 revaluation.

Rates are levied in Scotland in accordance with the Local Government (Scotland) Act 1975. For 1995–6, the Secretary of State for Scotland prescribed a single non-domestic rates poundage to apply throughout the country at the same level as the uniform business rate (UBR) in England. Rate income is pooled and redistributed to local authorities on a per capita basis. For the year 1995–6 payment of rates was subject to transitional arrangements to phase in the effect of the 1995 revaluation.

Rateable values for the rating lists came into force on 1 April 1995. They are derived from the rental value of property as at 1 April 1993 and determined on certain statutory assumptions by the Valuation Office Agency in England and Wales, and by Regional Assessors in Scotland. New property which is added to the list, and significant changes to existing property, necessitate amendments to the rateable value on the same basis. Rating lists (valuation rolls in Scotland) remain in force until the next general revaluation. Such revaluations take place every five years, the next being in 2000.

Certain types of property are exempt from rates, e.g. agricultural land and buildings, and places of public religious worship. Charities and other non-profit-making organizations may receive full or partial relief. Empty property is liable to pay rates at 50 per cent, except for certain specified classes which are exempt entirely.

Government Grants

In addition to specific grants in support of revenue expenditure on particular services, central government pays revenue support grant to local authorities. This grant is paid to each local authority so that if each authority spends at a level sufficient to provide a standard level of service, all authorities in the same class can set broadly the same council tax.

Complaints

Commissioners for Local Administration in England, Wales and Scotland (*see* page 320) are responsible for investigating complaints from members of the public who claim to have suffered injustice as a consequence of maladministration in local government or in certain local bodies.

The Northern Ireland Commissioner for Complaints fulfils a similar function in Northern Ireland, investigating complaints about local authorities and certain public bodies.

Complaints are made to the relevant local authority in the first instance and are referred to the Commissioners if the complainant is not satisfied.

The Queen's Representatives

The Lord-Lieutenant of a county is the permanent local representative of the Crown in that county. The appointment of Lord-Lieutenants is now regulated by the Lieutenancies Act 1997. They are appointed by the Sovereign on the recommendation of the Prime Minister. The retirement age is 75. The office of Lord-Lieutenant dates from 1557, and its holder was originally responsible for the maintenance of order and for local defence in the county. The duties of the post include attending on royalty during official visits to the county, performing certain duties in connection with armed forces of the Crown (and in particular the reserve forces), and making presentations of honours and awards on behalf of the Crown. In England, Wales and Northern Ireland, the Lord-Lieutenant usually also holds the office of *Custos Rotulorum*. As such, he or she acts as head of the county's commission of the peace (which recommends the appointment of magistrates).

The office of Sheriff (from the Old English shire-reeve) of a county was created in the tenth century. The Sheriff was the special nominee of the Sovereign, and the office reached the peak of its influence under the Norman kings. The Provisions of Oxford (1258) laid down a yearly tenure of office. Since the mid-16th century the office has been purely civil, with military duties taken over by the Lord-Lieutenant of the county. The Sheriff (commonly known as 'High Sheriff') attends on royalty during official visits to the county, acts as the returning officer during parliamentary elections in county constituencies, attends the opening ceremony when a High Court judge goes on circuit, executes High Court writs, and appoints under-sheriffs to act as deputies. The appointments and duties of the High Sheriffs in England and Wales are laid down by the Sheriffs Act 1887.

The serving High Sheriff submits a list of names of possible future sheriffs to a tribunal which chooses three names to put to the Sovereign. The tribunal nominates the High Sheriff annually on 12 November and the Sovereign pricks the name of the Sheriff to succeed in the following year. The term of office runs from 25 March to the following 24 March (the civil and legal year before 1752). No person may be chosen twice in three years if there is any other suitable person in the county.

CIVIC DIGNITIES

District councils in England may petition for a royal charter granting borough or 'city' status to the district. Local councils in Wales may petition for a royal charter granting county borough or 'city' status to the council.

In England and Wales the chairman of a borough or county borough council may be called a mayor, and the chairman of a city council a Lord Mayor. Parish councils in England and community councils in Wales may call themselves 'town councils', in which case their chairman is the town mayor.

In Scotland the chairman of a local council may be known as a convenor; a provost is the equivalent of a mayor. The chairmen of the councils for the cities of Aberdeen, Dundee, Edinburgh and Glasgow are Lord Provosts.

ENGLAND
(For London, *see* below)

There are currently 35 non-metropolitan counties; all (apart from the Isle of Wight) are divided into non-metropolitan districts. In addition, there are 45 unitary authorities (13 created in April 1996, 13 in April 1997 and 19 in April 1998). At present there are 237 non-metropolitan districts. The populations of most of the new unitary authorities are in the range of 100,000 to 300,000. The non-metropolitan districts have populations broadly in the range of 60,000 to 100,000; some, however, have larger populations, because of the need to avoid dividing large towns, and some in mainly rural areas have smaller populations.

The main conurbations outside Greater London – Tyne and Wear, West Midlands, Merseyside, Greater Manchester, West Yorkshire and South Yorkshire – are divided into 36 metropolitan districts, most of which have a population of over 200,000.

There are also about 10,000 parishes, in 219 of the non-metropolitan and 18 of the metropolitan districts.

ELECTIONS

For districts, non-metropolitan counties and for about 8,000 parishes, there are elected councils, consisting of directly elected councillors. The councillors elect annually one of their number as chairman.

Generally, councillors serve four years and there are no elections of district and parish councillors in county election years. In metropolitan districts, one-third of the councillors for each ward are elected each year except in the year when county elections take place elsewhere. Non-metropolitan districts can choose whether to have elections by thirds or whole council elections. In the former case, one-third of the council, as nearly as may be, is elected in each year of metropolitan district elections. If whole council elections are chosen, these are held in the year midway between county elections.

FUNCTIONS

In non-metropolitan areas, functions are divided between the districts and counties, those requiring the larger area or population for their efficient performance going to the county. The metropolitan district councils, with the larger population in their areas, already had wider functions than non-metropolitan councils, and following abolition of the metropolitan county councils were given most of their functions also. A few functions continue to be exercised over the larger area by joint bodies, made up of councillors from each district.

The allocation of functions is as follows:

County councils: education; strategic planning; traffic, transport and highways; fire service; consumer protection; refuse disposal; smallholdings; social services; libraries

Non-metropolitan district councils: local planning; housing; highways (maintenance of certain urban roads and off-street car parks); building regulations; environmental health; refuse collection; cemeteries and crematoria

Unitary councils: their functions are all those listed above, except that the fire service is exercised by a joint body

Concurrently by county and district councils: recreation (parks, playing fields, swimming pools); museums; encouragement of the arts, tourism and industry

The Police and Magistrates Court Act 1994 set up police authorities in England and Wales separate from the local authorities.

PARISH COUNCILS

Parishes with 200 or more electors must generally have parish councils, which means that over three-quarters of the parishes have councils. A parish council comprises at least five members, the number being fixed by the district council. Elections are held every four years, at the time of the election of the district councillor for the ward including the parish. All parishes have parish meetings, comprising the electors of the parish. Where there is no council, the meeting must be held at least twice a year.

Parish council functions include: allotments; encouragement of arts and crafts; community halls, recreational facilities (e.g. open spaces, swimming pools), cemeteries and crematoria; and many minor functions. They must also be given an opportunity to comment on planning applications. They may, like county and district councils, spend limited sums for the general benefit of the parish. They levy a precept on the district councils for their funds. The Local Government and Rating Act 1997 gave additional powers to parish councils to spend money on community transport initiatives and crime prevention equipment.

FINANCE

Aggregate external finance for 1998–9 was originally determined at £37,521 million. Of this, specific and special grants were estimated at £5,372 million; £19,506 million was in respect of revenue support grant and £12,524 million was support from the national non-domestic rate pool. Total standard spending by local authorities considered for grant purposes was £48,192 million.

The average council taxes, expressed in terms of Band C, two-adult properties for 1998–9, were: inner London boroughs and the City of London £585; outer London boroughs £625; metropolitan districts £740; shire areas £655. The average for England was £664.

National non-domestic rate (or uniform business rate) for 1998–9 is 47.4p. The provisional amount estimated to be raised from central, local and Crown lists is £12,500 million. Total rateable value held on draft local authority lists at 31 December 1997 was £29,700 million. The amount to be redistributed to authorities from the pool in 1998–9 is £12,500 million.

Under the Local Government and Housing Act 1989, local authorities have four main ways of paying for capital expenditure: borrowing and other forms of extended credit; capital grants from central government towards some types of capital expenditure; 'usable' capital receipts from the sale of land, houses and other assets; and revenue.

The amount of capital expenditure which a local authority can finance by borrowing (or other forms of credit) is effectively limited by the credit approvals issued to it by central government. Most credit approvals can be used for any local authority service; these are known as basic credit approvals. Others (supplementary credit approvals) are for particular projects or services.

Generally, the 'usable' part of a local authority's capital receipts consists of 25 per cent of receipts from the sale of council houses and 50 per cent of most other receipts. The balance has to be set aside as provision for repaying debt and meeting other credit liabilities.

EXPENDITURE

Local authority budgeted net revenue expenditure for 1998–9 was (1998–9 cash prices):

Service	£m
Education	20,163
Personal social services	8,933
Police	6,809
Highway maintenance	1,702
Fire	1,417
Civil defence and other Home Office services	554
Magistrates courts	312
Public transport and parking	671
Housing benefit administration	5,649
Non-housing revenue account housing	386
Libraries, culture and heritage	864
Sport	517
Local environmental services	5,576
Other services	395
Net current expenditure	53,948
Capital charges	2,168
Capital charged to revenue	759
Other non-current expenditure	4,053
Interest receipts	−810
Gross revenue expenditure	60,118
Specific and special grants outside AEF	−9,218
Revenue expenditure	50,900
Specific and special grants inside AEF	−2,065
Net revenue expenditure	48,835

AEF = aggregate external finance

LONDON

Since the abolition of the Greater London Council in 1986, the Greater London area has not had a single local government body. The area is divided into 32 borough councils, which have a status similar to the metropolitan district councils in the rest of England, and the Corporation of the City of London.

In March 1998 the Government announced proposals for a Greater London Authority (GLA) covering the area of the 32 London boroughs and the City of London, which would comprise a directly elected mayor and a 25-member assembly. A referendum was held in London on 7 May 1998; the turnout was approximately 34 per cent, of whom 72 per cent voted in favour of the GLA. The GLA will be responsible for transport, economic development, strategic planning, culture, health, the environment, the police and fire and emergency planning. The separately elected assembly will scrutinize the mayor's activities and approve plans and budgets. Fourteen of the assembly's members will be directly elected to represent specific areas. The remaining 11 members will be elected on the basis of proportional representation from party political lists. The

Government plans to introduce legislation late in 1998 establishing the new authority, and elections will take place in late 1999 or early 2000.

LONDON BOROUGH COUNCILS

The London boroughs have whole council elections every four years, in the year immediately following the county council election year. The next elections will be in 2002.

The borough councils have responsibility for the following functions: building regulations; cemeteries and crematoria; consumer protection; education; youth employment; environmental health; electoral registration; food; drugs; housing; leisure services; libraries; local planning; local roads; museums; parking; recreation (parks, playing fields, swimming pools); refuse collection and street cleansing; social services; town planning; and traffic management.

THE CORPORATION OF LONDON
(*see also* pages 552–4)

The Corporation of London is the local authority for the City of London. Its legal definition is 'The Mayor and Commonalty and Citizens of the City of London'. It is governed by the Court of Common Council, which consists of the Lord Mayor, 24 other aldermen, and 130 common councilmen. The Lord Mayor and two sheriffs are nominated annually by the City guilds (the livery companies) and elected by the Court of Aldermen. Aldermen and councilmen are elected from the 25 wards into which the City is divided; councilmen must stand for re-election annually. The Council is a legislative assembly, and there are no political parties.

The Corporation has the same functions as the London borough councils. In addition, it runs the City of London Police; is the health authority for the Port of London; has health control of animal imports throughout Greater London, including at Heathrow airport; owns and manages public open spaces throughout Greater London; runs the Central Criminal Court; and runs Billingsgate, Smithfield and Spitalfields markets.

THE CITY GUILDS (LIVERY COMPANIES)

The livery companies of the City of London grew out of early medieval religious fraternities and began to emerge as trade and craft guilds, retaining their religious aspect, in the 12th century. From the early 14th century, only members of the trade and craft guilds could call themselves citizens of the City of London. The guilds began to be called livery companies, because of the distinctive livery worn by the most prosperous guild members on ceremonial occasions, in the late 15th century.

By the early 19th century the power of the companies within their trades had begun to wane, but those wearing the livery of a company continued to play an important role in the government of the City of London. Liverymen still have the right to nominate the Lord Mayor and sheriffs, and most members of the Court of Common Council are liverymen (*see also* page 554).

GREATER LONDON SERVICES

After the abolition of the Greater London Council (GLC) in 1986, the London boroughs took over most of its functions. Successor bodies have also been set up for certain functions. The London Residuary Body (LRB) was set up in 1986 to deal with residual matters of the GLC. It completed its work and was wound up in 1995.

WALES

The Local Government (Wales) Act 1994 abolished the two-tier structure of eight county and 37 district councils which had existed since 1974, and replaced it, from 1 April 1996, with 22 unitary authorities. The new authorities were elected in May 1995. Each unitary authority has inherited all the functions of the previous county and district councils, except fire services (which are provided by three combined fire authorities, composed of representatives of the unitary authorities) and National Parks (which are the responsibility of three independent National Park authorities).

The Police and Magistrates Courts Act 1994 set up four police authorities with effect from 1 April 1995: Dyfed-Powys, Gwent, North Wales, and South Wales.

COMMUNITY COUNCILS

In Wales parishes are known as communities. Unlike England, where many areas are not in any parish, communities have been established for the whole of Wales, approximately 865 communities in all. Community meetings may be convened as and when desired.

Community councils exist in 735 communities and further councils may be established at the request of a community meeting. Community councils have broadly the same range of powers as English parish councils. Community councillors are elected at the same time as a unitary authority election and for a term of four years.

FINANCE

Aggregate external finance for 1998–9 is £2,701.9 million. This comprises revenue support grant of £1,799.9 million, specific grants of £258.9 million, support from the national non-domestic rate pool of £612 million, and £31.2 million in council tax reduction grants. Total standard spending by local authorities considered for grant purposes is £3,090.5 million.

The average Band D council tax levied in Wales for 1998–9 is £555, comprising unitary authorities £513, police authorities £57, community councils £16 and an average grant reduction of £31.

National non-domestic rates (or uniform business rate) in Wales for 1998–9 is 42.9p. The amount estimated to be raised is £612 million. Total rateable value held on local authority lists at 31 December 1997 was £1,342 million.

EXPENDITURE

Local authority budgeted net revenue expenditure for 1998–9 was (1998–9 cash prices):

Service	£m
Education	1,355
Personal social services	578
Police	355
Highway maintenance	147
Fire	88
Civil defence and other Home Office services	33
Magistrates courts	19
Public transport and parking	14
Housing benefit administration	265
Non-housing revenue account housing	17
Libraries, museums and art galleries	47
Swimming pools and recreation	53
Local environmental services	268
Other services	120
Net current expenditure	3,359

Capital charges	256
Capital charged to revenue	20
Other non-current expenditure	136
Interest receipts	−21
Gross revenue expenditure	3,750
Specific grants outside AEF	−488
Revenue expenditure	3,262
Specific grants inside AEF	−73
Net revenue expenditure	3,189

AEF = aggregate external finance

SCOTLAND

The Local Government etc. (Scotland) Act 1994 abolished the two-tier structure of nine regional and 53 district councils which had existed since 1975 and replaced it, from 1 April 1996, with 29 unitary authorities on the mainland; the three islands councils remain. The new authorities were elected in April 1995. Each unitary authority has inherited all the functions of the regional and district councils, except water and sewerage (now provided by three public bodies whose members are appointed by the Secretary of State for Scotland) and reporters panels (now a national agency).

When the Scottish Parliament takes office it will assume responsibility for legislation on local government. The Government has established a Commission on Local Government and the Scottish Parliament to make recommendations on the relationship between local authorities and the new Parliament and on increasing local authorities' accountability. The Commission will report to the First Minister of the Scottish Parliament soon after the Parliament is elected.

ELECTIONS

The unitary authorities consist of directly elected councillors. Elections take place every three years; the next elections are in 1999. In 1998 the register showed 4,005,720 electors in Scotland.

FUNCTIONS

The functions of the councils and islands councils are: education; social work; strategic planning; the provision of infrastructure such as roads; consumer protection; flood prevention; coast protection; valuation and rating; the police and fire services; civil defence; electoral registration; public transport; registration of births, deaths and marriages; housing; leisure and recreation; development control and building control; environmental health; licensing; allotments; public conveniences; and the administration of district courts.

COMMUNITY COUNCILS

Unlike the parish councils and community councils in England and Wales, Scottish community councils are not local authorities. Their purpose as defined in statute is to ascertain and express the views of the communities which they represent, and to take in the interests of their communities such action as appears to be expedient or practicable. Over 1,000 community councils have been established under schemes drawn up by district and islands councils in Scotland.

Since April 1996 community councils have had an enhanced role, becoming statutory consultees on local planning issues and on the decentralization schemes which the new councils have to draw up for delivery of services.

528   Local Government

FINANCE

Figures for 1997–8 show total receipts from non-domestic rates of £1,395 million and £991 million from the council tax. The unified business rate for 1997–8 was 44.9p for property with a rateable value of less than £10,000 and 45.8p otherwise. The average Band D council tax payable was £783.

EXPENDITURE

Local authority current expenditure supported by aggregate external finance for 1998–9 was (1998–9 cash prices):

Service	£m
Tourism	8
Roads and transport	340
Housing	3
Other environmental services	701
Law, order and protective services	871
Education	2,703
Arts and libraries	111
Social work services	1,108
Housing benefit administration	32
Sheltered employment	9
Consumer protection	17
Total	5,903
Total excluding housing benefits, sheltered employment and consumer protection	5,845

NORTHERN IRELAND

For the purpose of local government Northern Ireland has a system of 26 single-tier district councils.

ELECTIONS

There are 582 members of the councils, elected for periods of four years at a time on the principle of proportional representation.

FUNCTIONS

The district councils have three main roles. These are:

Executive: responsibility for a wide range of local services including building regulations; community services; consumer protection; cultural facilities; environmental health; miscellaneous licensing and registration provisions, including dog control; litter prevention; recreational and social facilities; refuse collection and disposal; street cleansing; and tourist development

Representative: nominating representatives to sit as members of the various statutory bodies responsible for the administration of regional services such as drainage, education, fire, health and personal social services, housing, and libraries

Consultative: acting as the medium through which the views of local people are expressed on the operation in their area of other regional services, notably conservation (including water supply and sewerage services), planning, and roads, provided by those departments of central government which have an obligation, statutory or otherwise, to consult the district councils about proposals affecting their areas

FINANCE

Local government in Northern Ireland is funded by a system of rates (a local property tax calculated by using the rateable value of a property multiplied by an amount per pound of rateable value). Rates are collected by the Rate Collection Agency, an executive agency within the Department of the Environment for Northern Ireland. A general revaluation of non-domestic properties became effective on 1 April 1997. As a result of this, separate regional rates are now made at standard uniform amounts by the Department of Finance and Personnel for both domestic and non-domestic sectors. District councils now make their individual district rates on the same basis.

In 1997–8 approximately £495 million was raised in rates. The average domestic poundage levied was 189.59p and the average non-domestic rate poundage was 41.37p.

Political Composition of Local Councils

AS AT END MAY 1998

Abbreviations:
C.	Conservative
Com.	Communist
Dem.	Democrat
Green	Green
Ind.	Independent
Lab.	Labour
Lib.	Liberal
LD	Liberal Democrat
MK	Mebyon Kernow
NP	Non-political/Non-party
PC	Plaid Cymru
RA	Ratepayers'/Residents' Associations
SD	Social Democrat
SNP	Scottish National Party

ENGLAND

COUNTY COUNCILS

*Unitary council

Bedfordshire	*C.* 25, *Lab.* 14, *LD* 10
Buckinghamshire	*C.* 37, *LD* 9, *Lab.* 5, *Ind.* 1, *Ind. C.*1, *Lib.* 1
Cambridgeshire	*C.* 33, *Lab.* 10, *LD* 16
Cheshire	*Lab.* 20, *C.* 19, *LD* 9
Cornwall	*LD, Ind. coalition* 39, *Ind.* 23, *C.* 8, *Lab.* 8, *MK* 1
Cumbria	*Lab.* 44, *C.* 23, *LD* 11, *Ind.* 4, *vacant* 1
Derbyshire	*Lab.* 45, *C.* 12, *LD* 6, *Ind.* 1
Devon	*LD* 31, *C.* 14, *Lab.* 4, *Ind.* 3, *Lib.* 2
Dorset	*LD* 21, *C.* 15, *Lab.* 5, *Ind.* 1
Durham	*Lab.* 53, *Ind.* 4, *C.* 2, *LD* 2
East Sussex	*C.* 21, *LD* 16, *Lab.* 7
Essex	*C.* 39, *Lab.* 24, *LD* 15, *Ind.* 1
Gloucestershire	*LD* 22, *C.* 21, *Lab.* 18, *Ind.* 2
Hampshire	*C.* 42, *LD* 22, *Lab.* 8, *Ind.* 2
Hertfordshire	*C.* 38, *Lab.* 30, *LD* 9
*Isle of Wight	*LD* 16, *C.* 16, *Ind.* 9, *Lab.* 4, *Lib.* 2, *others* 2
Kent	*C.* 46, *Lab.* 22, *LD* 15, *vacant* 1
Lancashire	*Lab.* 47, *C.* 23, *LD* 7, *Ind. Lab.* 1
Leicestershire	*C.* 24, *Lab.* 17, *LD* 11, *Ind. C.* 1, *others* 1
Lincolnshire	*C.* 43, *Lab.* 19, *LD* 11, *Ind.* 3
Norfolk	*C.* 36, *Lab.* 34, *LD* 13, *Ind.* 1
Northamptonshire	*Lab.* 38, *C.* 27, *LD* 3
Northumberland	*Lab.* 43, *C.* 14, *LD* 8, *Ind.* 1
North Yorkshire	*C.* 35, *LD* 21, *Lab.* 12, *Ind.* 6
Nottinghamshire	*Lab.* 42, *C.* 17, *LD* 4
Oxfordshire	*C.* 27, *Lab.* 22, *LD* 19, *Green* 2
Shropshire	*C.* 19, *LD* 13, *Lab.* 7, *Ind. Lab.* 2, *Ind.* 1, *others* 2
Somerset	*LD* 37, *C.* 17, *Lab.* 3
Staffordshire	*Lab.* 40, *C.* 20, *LD* 2
Suffolk	*Lab.* 32, *C.* 31, *LD* 15, *Ind.* 2
Surrey	*C.* 47, *LD* 17, *Lab.* 6, *Ind.* 3, *RA* 3

Warwickshire	*Lab.* 31, *C.* 21, *LD* 7, *Ind.* 3
West Sussex	*C.* 37, *LD* 24, *Lab.* 9, *Ind.* 1
Wiltshire	*C.* 23, *LD* 19, *Lab.* 4, *Ind.* 1
Worcestershire	*C.* 25, *Lab* 22, *LD* 8, *Ind.* 1, *Lib.* 1

UNITARY COUNCILS

Barnsley	*Lab.* 63, *Ind.* 2, *C.* 1
Bath and North-East Somerset	*LD*28 , *Lab.* 21, *C.* 16
Birmingham	*Lab.* 83, *C.* 17, *LD* 16, *Ind.* 1
Blackburn with Darwen	*Lab.* 46, *C.* 12, *LD* 4
Blackpool	*Lab.* 33, *C.* 8, *LD* 3
Bolton	*Lab.* 47, *C.* 8, *LD* 5
Bournemouth	*LD* 25, *C.* 20, *Ind.* 6, *Lab.* 6
Bracknell Forest	*C.* 23, *Lab.* 17
Bradford	*Lab.* 65, *C.* 18, *LD* 7
Brighton and Hove	*Lab.* 53, *C.* 23, *Green* 1, *Ind.* 1
Bristol	*Lab.* 45, *LD* 16, *C.* 6
Bury	*Lab.* 39, *C.* 6, *LD* 3
Calderdale	*Lab.* 27, *C.* 13, *LD* 13, *Ind.* 1
Coventry	*Lab.* 47, *C.* 6, *SDP* 1
Darlington	*Lab.* 36, *C.* 13, *LD* 2, *Ind.* 1
Derby	*Lab.* 37, *C.* 4, *LD* 3
Doncaster	*Lab.* 49, *LD* 6, *Ind.* 5, *C.* 3
Dudley	*Lab.* 58, *C.* 7, *LD* 7
East Riding of Yorkshire	*Lab.* 22, *C.* 19, *LD* 19, *Ind.* 5, *SDP* 1, *vacant* 1
Gateshead	*Lab.* 50, *LD* 14, *Lib.* 1, *others* 1
Halton	*Lab.* 47, *LD* 8, *C.* 1
Hartlepool	*Lab.* 33, *LD* 8, *C.* 5, *Ind.* 1
Herefordshire	*LD* 32, *Ind.* 18, *C.* 8, *Lab.* 2
Kingston upon Hull	*Lab.* 50, *Ind. Lab.* 5, *LD* 4, *C.* 1
Kirklees	*Lab.* 43, *LD* 20, *C.* 7, *Green* 2
Knowsley	*Lab.* 65, *LD* 1
Leeds	*Lab.* 80, *C.* 9, *LD* 9, *Green* 1
Leicester	*Lab.* 39, *LD* 10, *C.* 7
Liverpool	*LD* 52, *Lab.* 39, *Lib.* 4, *Ind. Lab.* 1, *others* 3
Luton	*Lab.* 36, *LD* 9, *C.* 3
Manchester	*Lab.* 84, *LD* 15
Medway	*Lab.* 39, *LD* 21, *C.* 20
Middlesbrough	*Lab.* 46, *LD* 4, *C.* 2, *Ind.* 1
Milton Keynes	*Lab.* 27, *LD* 19, *C.* 4, *Ind.* 1
Newcastle upon Tyne	*Lab.* 64, *LD* 13, *vacant* 1
North East Lincolnshire	*Lab.* 33, *LD* 6, *C.* 2, *Ind.* 1
North Lincolnshire	*Lab.* 35, *C.* 7
North Somerset	*LD* 29, *C.* 17, *Ind.* 7, *Lab.* 5, *others* 1
North Tyneside	*Lab.* 44, *C.* 8, *LD* 7, *Ind.* 1
Nottingham City	*Lab.* 50, *C.* 3, *LD* 2
Oldham	*Lab.* 36, *LD* 23, *Ind. Lab.* 1
Peterborough	*Lab.* 25, *C.* 24, *Ind. Lab.* 3, *Lib.* 3, *LD* 2
Plymouth	*Lab.* 47, *C.* 13
Poole	*LD* 23, *C.* 13, *Lab.* 3
Portsmouth	*Lab.* 21, *C.* 10, *LD* 8
Reading	*Lab.* 35, *LD* 6, *C.* 3, *Ind.* 1
Redcar and Cleveland	*Lab.* 48, *LD* 8, *Ind. Lab.* 2, *C.* 1
Rochdale	*Lab.* 36, *LD* 18, *C.* 6
Rotherham	*Lab.* 64, *C.* 1, *vacant* 1
Rutland	*Ind.* 8, *LD* 7, *C.* 2, *Lab.* 2, *Green* 1
St Helens	*Lab.* 42, *LD* 10, *C.* 2
Salford	*Lab.* 57, *LD* 3
Sandwell	*Lab.* 60, *LD* 9, *C.* 2, *Ind. Lab.* 1
Sefton	*Lab.* 31, *LD* 23, *C.* 14, *Ind. Lab.* 1
Sheffield	*Lab.* 50, *LD* 36, *C.* 1

Slough	*Lab.* 34, *C.* 4, *Lib.*3
Solihull	*C.* 20, *Lab.* 17, *LD* 11, *others* 2, *vacant* 1
Southampton	*Lab.* 28, *LD* 14, *C.* 3
Southend	*C.* 19, *LD* 13, *Lab.* 7
South Gloucestershire	*Lab.* 31, *LD* 30, *C.* 8, *others* 1
South Tyneside	*Lab.* 50, *LD* 6, *others* 3, *vacant* 1
Stockport	*LD* 30, *Lab.* 26, *Ind.* 4, *C.* 3
Stockton-on-Tees	*Lab.* 43, *C.* 6, *LD* 4, *Ind. Lab.* 1, *vacant* 1
Stoke-on-Trent	*Lab.* 54, *LD* 3, *C.* 1, *Ind.* 1, *others* 1
Sunderland	*Lab.* 68, *C.* 4, *LD* 2, *Lib.* 1
Swindon	*Lab.* 40, *LD* 9, *C.* 5
Tameside	*Lab.* 49, *C.* 2, *LD* 2, *others* 4
Telford and Wrekin	*Lab.* 38, *C.* 10, *LD* 5
Thurrock	*Lab.* 45, *C.* 4
Torbay	*LD* 21, *C.* 9, *Lab.* 2, *others* 3, *vacant* 1
Trafford	*Lab.* 36, *C.* 23, *LD* 4
Wakefield	*Lab.* 60, *C.* 2, *Ind. Lab.* 1
Walsall	*Lab.* 30, *C.* 16, *LD* 5, *Ind.* 1, *others* 8
Warrington	*Lab.* 43, *LD* 11, *C.* 4, *vacant* 2
West Berkshire	*LD* 37, *C.* 15, *Ind.* 1, *vacant* 1
Wigan	*Lab.* 70, *Ind. Lab.* 1, *LD* 1
Windsor and Maidenhead	*LD* 29, *C.* 22, *Ind.* 7
Wirral	*Lab.* 41, *C.* 16, *LD* 8, *Ind. LD* 1
Wokingham	*C.* 31, *LD* 23
Wolverhampton	*Lab.* 44, *C.* 14, *LD* 2
York	*Lab.* 30, *LD* 18, *C.* 3, *Ind.* 2

DISTRICT COUNCILS

*Denotes councils where one-third of councillors retire each year except in the year of county council elections

*Adur	*LD* 21, *Lab.* 10, *C.* 6, *Ind.* 2
Allerdale	*Lab.* 36, *Ind.* 7, *C.* 6, *LD* 5, *vacant* 1
Alnwick	*LD* 12, *Rural Alliance* 8, *Lab.* 6, *others* 3
Amber Valley	*Lab.* 36, *C.* 6, *vacant* 1
Arun	*C.* 29, *LD* 14, *Lab.* 10, *Ind.* 3
Ashfield	*Lab.* 33
Ashford	*C.* 19, *LD* 14, *Lab.* 11, *Ind. C.* 1, *Ind.* 1, *Lib.* 1, *others* 1
Aylesbury Vale	*LD* 29, *C.* 14, *Ind.* 9, *Lab.* 5, *vacant* 1
Babergh	*Ind.* 11, *C.* 9, *Lab.* 9, *LD* 9, *Ind. Soc.* 2, *others* 2
*Barrow-in-Furness	*Lab.* 23, *C.* 11, *others* 4
*Basildon	*Lab.* 22, *LD* 13, *C.* 6, *vacant* 1
*Basingstoke and Deane	*C.* 25, *Lab.* 15, *LD* 13, *Ind.* 3, *NP* 1
*Bassetlaw	*Lab.* 32, *C.* 9, *LD* 3, *Ind.* 2, *New Ind.* 2, *Ind. Lab.* 1, *vacant* 1
*Bedford	*Lab.* 22, *LD* 15, *C.* 9, *Ind.* 7
Berwick-upon-Tweed	*LD* 13, *Ind.* 10, *C.* 2, *Lab.* 1, *others* 2
Blaby	*Lab.* 17, *C.* 11, *LD* 9, *Ind.* 1, *Ind. C.* 1
Blyth Valley	*Lab.* 39, *LD* 6, *Ind.* 1, *vacant* 1
Bolsover	*Lab.* 35, *Ind.* 1, *RA* 1
Boston	*Lab.* 14, *Ind.* 7, *C.* 6, *LD* 6, *vacant* 1
Braintree	*Lab.* 37, *C.* 10, *Ind.* 7, *LD* 6
Breckland	*C.* 21, *Lab.* 20, *Ind.* 8, *LD* 2, *Green* 1, *vacant* 1

*Brentwood	*LD* 25, *C.* 10, *Lab.* 2, *Lib.* 1, *vacant* 1
Bridgnorth	*Ind.* 9, *Lab.* 6, *LD* 5, *Ind. C.* 4, *C.* 3, *Ind. Lab.* 1, *others* 5
Broadland	*C.* 21, *Lab.* 16, *LD* 8, *Ind.* 4
Bromsgrove	*Lab.* 24, *C.* 12, *RA* 2, *Lib.* 1
*Broxbourne	*C.* 30, *Lab.* 11, *vacant* 1
Broxtowe	*Lab.* 36, *C.* 6, *LD* 6, *Ind.* 1
*Burnley	*Lab.* 31, *LD* 9, *Ind.* 5, *C.* 3
*Cambridge	*Lab.* 21, *LD* 18, *C.* 3
*Cannock Chase	*Lab.* 39, *LD* 3
Canterbury	*LD* 21, *Lab.* 15, *C.* 11, *Ind.* 1, *others* 1
Caradon	*Ind.* 18, *LD* 18, *Lab.* 2, *C.* 1, *others* 2
*Carlisle	*Lab.* 33, *C.* 14, *LD/Ind.* 4
Carrick	*LD* 17, *Ind.* 9, *C.* 8, *Lab.* 8, *MK* 1, *others* 2
Castle Morpeth	*Lab.* 12, *Ind.* 9, *C.* 6, *LD* 4, *Lib.* 2, *others* 1
Castle Point	*Lab.* 33, *C.* 5, *Ind. Lab.* 1
Charnwood	*Lab.* 30, *C.* 15, *LD* 5, *Ind.* 2
Chelmsford	*LD* 32, *C.* 14, *Lab.* 7, *Ind.* 3
*Cheltenham	*LD* 26, *C.* 9, *Lab.* 1, *others* 5
*Cherwell	*Lab.* 23, *C.* 18, *LD* 7, *Ind.* 3, *vacant* 1
*Chester	*Lab.* 26, *LD* 17, *C.* 15, *Ind.* 2
Chesterfield	*Lab.* 37, *LD* 10
Chester-le-Street	*Lab.* 30, *C.* 1, *Ind.* 1, *LD* 1
Chichester	*LD* 23, *C.* 22, *Ind.* 4, *Lab.* 1
Chiltern	*LD* 24, *C.* 21, *Ind.* 2, *RA* 2, *Lab.* 1
*Chorley	*Lab.* 33, *C.* 6, *LD* 6, *Ind.* 2, *Ind. Lab.* 1
Christchurch	*C.* 9, *Ind.* 8, *LD* 8
*Colchester	*LD* 27, *Lab.* 17, *C.* 15, *RA* 1
*Congleton	*LD* 26, *Lab.* 11, *C.* 7, *Ind.* 1
Copeland	*Lab.* 32, *C.* 14, *Ind.* 2, *Ind. Lab.* 2, *vacant* 1
Corby	*Lab.* 23, *C.* 1, *Ind. Lab.* 1, *LD* 1, *vacant* 1
Cotswold	*Ind.* 17, *LD* 8, *Ind. C.* 4, *Lab.* 4, *C.* 3, *others* 9
*Craven	*C.* 13, *LD* 13, *Ind.* 4, *Lab.* 4
*Crawley	*Lab.* 27, *C.* 3, *LD* 2
*Crewe and Nantwich	*Lab.* 37, *C.* 15, *LD* 4, *Ind.* 1
Dacorum	*Lab.* 31, *C.* 20, *LD* 4, *Ind.* 3
Dartford	*Lab.* 34, *C.* 10, *Ind.* 3
*Daventry	*C.* 17, *Lab.* 13, *LD* 3, *Ind.* 2
Derbyshire Dales	*LD* 16, *Ind. C.* 15, *Lab.* 8
Derwentside	*Lab.* 50, *Ind.* 5
Dover	*Lab.* 37, *C.* 15, *LD* 3, *vacant* 1
Durham	*Lab.* 39, *LD* 7, *Ind.* 3
Easington	*Lab.* 44, *Lib.* 3, *Ind.* 2, *Ind. Lab.* 2
*Eastbourne	*LD* 18, *C.* 12
East Cambridgeshire	*Ind.* 14, *LD* 13, *NP* 5, *Lab.* 4, *Ind. C.* 1
East Devon	*C.* 32, *LD* 19, *Ind.* 8, *Lib.* 1
East Dorset	*LD* 23, *C.* 12, *Ind. C.* 1
East Hampshire	*LD* 25, *C.* 13, *Ind.* 3, *vacant* 1
East Hertfordshire	*C.* 23, *LD* 16, *Lab.* 8, *Ind.* 2, *others* 1
*Eastleigh	*LD* 29, *Lab.* 8, *C.* 7
East Lindsey	*NP* 34, *Lab.* 14, *LD* 7, *Green* 3, *others* 2
East Northamptonshire	*Lab.* 24, *C.* 10, *Lib.* 2
East Staffordshire	*Lab.* 34, *C.* 6, *Ind. C.* 3, *LD* 3
Eden	*Ind. Group* 28, *LD* 4, *Ind.* 3, *Lab.* 2

*Ellesmere Port and Neston	Lab. 36, C. 5
*Elmbridge	C. 23, RA 21, LD 8, Lab. 7, Ind. 1
*Epping Forest	Lab. 17, C. 16, LD 15, RA 9, Ind. 2
Epsom and Ewell	RA 32, LD 4, Lab. 3
Erewash	Lab. 39, C. 10, LD 2, Ind. 1
*Exeter	Lab. 22, LD 8, C. 3, Lib. 3
*Fareham	LD 16, C. 14, Lab. 8, Loyal C. 4
Fenland	C. 16, Lab. 15, Ind. 4, Socialist Lab. 3, LD 2
Forest Heath	C. 10, Ind. 6, LD 5, Lab. 4
Forest of Dean	Lab. 29, Ind. 12, LD 5, C. 1, others 2
Fylde	C. 18, Lab. 5, LD 4, others 22
Gedling	Lab. 30, C. 19, LD 7, Ind. 1
*Gloucester	Lab. 25, LD 8, C. 6
*Gosport	Lab. 10, C. 9, Ind. LD 8, LD 3
Gravesham	Lab. 33, C. 10, Ind. 1
*Great Yarmouth	Lab. 36, C. 12
Guildford	LD 19, C. 13, Ind. 7, Lab. 6
Hambleton	C./Ind. 30, Ind. 10, Lab. 4, LD 3
Harborough	LD 15, C. 12, Lab. 8, Ind. 2
*Harlow	Lab. 38, LD 3, C. 1
*Harrogate	LD 40, C. 14, Lab. 4, Ind. 1
*Hart	LD 15, C. 14, Ind. 4, Ind. C. 2
*Hastings	Lab. 18, LD 13, C. 1
*Havant	C. 14, LD 14, Lab. 8, Ind. 3, Ind. Lab. 3
*Hertsmere	Lab. 22, C. 11, LD 6
High Peak	Lab. 30, LD 6, C. 5, Ind. 3
Hinckley and Bosworth	LD 17, Lab. 13, C. 4
Horsham	LD 22, C. 18, Ind. 3
*Huntingdonshire	C. 34, LD 14, Lab. 3, Ind. 2
*Hyndburn	Lab. 35, C. 12
*Ipswich	Lab. 40, C. 8
Kennet	Ind. 14, C. 9, Lab. 9, LD 8
Kerrier	Lab. 15, Ind. 10, LD 8, C. 2, others 9
Kettering	Lab. 32, C. 7, Ind. 3, LD 3
King's Lynn and West Norfolk	Lab. 37, C./Ind. 16, LD 6, Ind. 1
Lancaster	Lab. 35, Ind. 11, C. 8, LD 4, Ind. C. 1, others 1
Lewes	LD 28, C. 16, Lab. 2, Ind. 1, others 1
Lichfield	Lab. 31, C. 19, LD 2, Ind. 1, Ind. Lab. 1, others 2
*Lincoln	Lab. 28, Ind. Lab. 3, C. 1, vacant 1
*Macclesfield	C. 37, Lab. 10, LD 10, others 3
*Maidstone	LD 22, Lab. 15, C. 13, Ind. 5
Maldon	C. 15, Ind. 8, Lab. 7
Malvern Hills	LD 19, C./Ind. 11, Ind. 10, Lab. 1, vacant 1
Mansfield	Lab. 45, C. 1
Melton	C. 8, Lab. 8, LD 6, Ind. 4
Mendip	LD 19, Lab. 9, C. 8, RA 4, Ind. 3
Mid Bedfordshire	C. 23, Lab. 20, Ind. 5, LD 5
Mid Devon	Ind. 19, LD 19, Lab. 1, Lib. 1
Mid Suffolk	Lab. 15, LD 11, C. 7, Ind. 4, Ind. Lab. 2, others 1
*Mid Sussex	LD 27, C. 19, Ind. 4, Lab. 4
*Mole Valley	LD 16, C. 14, Ind. 9, Lab. 2
Newark and Sherwood	Lab. 33, C. 12, LD 5, Ind. 4
*Newcastle under Lyme	Lab. 42, Lib. 9, C. 5
New Forest	LD 31, C. 23, Ind. 4
Northampton	Lab. 34, Lib. 7, C. 1, vacant 1
North Cornwall	Ind. 27, LD 10, C. 1
North Devon	LD 31, Ind. 10, NP 2, C. 1
North Dorset	LD 17, Ind. 11, others 5
North East Derbyshire	Lab. 42, C. 5, LD 3, Ind. Lab. 2, Ind. 1
*North Hertfordshire	Lab. 26, C. 17, LD 6, Ind. 1
North Kesteven	Lab. 16, LD 8, C. 5, Ind. 4, others 6
North Norfolk	Lab. 19, LD 12, NP 8, Ind. C. 7
North Shropshire	Ind. 6, Lab. 6, LD 4, C. 2, others 22
North Warwickshire	Lab. 28, C. 4, Ind. 1, vacant 1
North West Leicestershire	Lab. 35, C. 3, Ind. 2
North Wiltshire	LD 33, C. 11, Lab. 6, Ind. 2
*Norwich	Lab. 35, LD 13
*Nuneaton and Bedworth	Lab. 41, C. 4
*Oadby and Wigston	LD 25, C. 1
Oswestry	Ind. 9, Lab. 8, C. 5, LD 5, others 2
*Oxford	Lab. 33, LD 14, Green 4
*Pendle	LD 29, Lab. 18, C. 3, Ind. 1
*Penwith	LD 12, C. 7, Ind. 7, Lab. 6, MK 2
*Preston	Lab. 30, C. 13, LD 13, Ind. Lab. 1
*Purbeck	LD 8, C. 6, Ind. 5, Lab. 3
*Redditch	Lab. 23, C. 4, LD 2
*Reigate and Banstead	C. 19, Lab. 13, LD 11, RA 5, Ind. 1
Restormel	LD 28, Ind. 7, Lab. 3, C. 2, Ind. LD 1, others 2, vacant 1
Ribble Valley	LD 19, C. 18, Ind. 1, Lab. 1
Richmondshire	NP 20, LD 8, C. 3, Ind. C. 1, SD 1, others 1
*Rochford	LD 18, Lab. 12, C. 6, RA 3, Ind. 1
*Rossendale	Lab. 25, C. 11
Rother	C. 16, LD 16, Ind. 8, Lab. 5
*Rugby	Lab. 22, C. 12, LD 5, others 9
*Runnymede	C. 23, Lab. 12, Ind. 6, LD 1
Rushcliffe	C. 24, Lab. 17, LD 8, Ind. 5
*Rushmoor	C. 17, Lab. 14, LD 14
Ryedale	Ind. 10, LD 8, C. 4, Lab. 1
*St Albans	LD 30, Lab. 16, C. 11
St Edmundsbury	Lab. 22, C. 13, LD 6, Ind. 3
Salisbury	LD 29, Lab. 11, C. 10, Ind. 8
Scarborough	Lab. 24, C. 13, Ind. 8, LD 4
Sedgefield	Lab. 47, Ind. 2
Sedgemoor	C. 22, Lab. 13, LD 12, Ind. 2
Selby	Lab. 27, C. 9, Ind. 4, LD 1
Sevenoaks	LD 19, C. 18, Lab. 12, Ind. 4
Shepway	C. 19, LD 19, Lab. 15, Ind. 3
*Shrewsbury and Atcham	Lab. 21, LD 12, C. 11, Ind. 4
*South Bedfordshire	Lab. 21, LD 16, C. 13, RA 2, Ind. 1
South Bucks	C. 20, Ind. 14, LD 5, NP 1
*South Cambridgeshire	C. 15, LD 13, Lab. 9
South Derbyshire	Lab. 28, C. 6
South Hams	C. 18, Ind. 15, LD 9, Lab. 2
South Holland	Ind. 16, C. 9, Lab. 8, others 5
South Kesteven	Ind. 17, C. 15, Lab. 15, LD 7, Lib. 2, vacant 1
*South Lakeland	LD 20, C. 13, Lab. 10, Ind. 9
South Norfolk	LD 30, C. 12, Lab. 3, Ind. 2
South Northamptonshire	C. 16, Lab. 10, Ind. 7, LD 6, vacant 1
South Oxfordshire	LD 21, Lab. 13, C. 9, Ind. 5, RA 2
South Ribble	Lab. 27, C. 16, LD 9, others 2
South Shropshire	Ind. 8, LD 7, Lab. 1, NP 24

South Somerset	*LD* 44, *C.* 10, *Ind.* 5, *Lab.* 1
South Staffordshire	*C.* 28, *Lab.* 15, *LD* 4, *RA* 2, *Ind.* 1
Spelthorne	*C.* 22, *Lab.* 14, *LD* 3, *vacant* 1
Stafford	*Lab.* 33, *C.* 16, *LD* 10, *Ind. C.* 1
*Staffordshire Moorlands	*Lab.* 26, *Ind. C.* 11, *LD* 7, *Ind.* 3, *NP* 1, *RA* 8
*Stevenage	*Lab.* 37, *LD* 2
*Stratford-on-Avon	*LD* 23, *C.* 18, *Ind.* 7, *Lab.* 5, *others* 2
*Stroud	*Lab.* 26, *C.* 10, *LD* 9, *Ind.* 6, *Green* 4
Suffolk Coastal	*C.* 20, *Lab.* 15, *LD* 15, *Ind.* 5
Surrey Heath	*C.* 24, *LD* 7, *Lab.* 4, *vacant* 1
*Swale	*LD* 22, *Lab.* 19, *C.* 7, *Ind.* 1
*Tamworth	*Lab.* 28, *C.* 1, *Ind.* 1
*Tandridge	*LD* 18, *C.* 17, *Lab.* 7
Taunton Deane	*LD* 29, *C.* 15, *Lab.* 6, *Ind.* 3
Teesdale	*Ind.* 13, *Lab.* 11, *NP* 7
Teignbridge	*LD* 24, *Ind.* 21, *C.* 7, *Lab.* 6
Tendring	*Lab.* 35, *Ind.*12, *C.* 8, *LD* 5
Test Valley	*C.* 20, *LD* 18, *Ind. LD* 3, *Ind.* 2, *vacant* 1
Tewkesbury	*Ind.* 14, *C./Ind.* 8, *LD* 7, *Lab.* 5, *NP* 2
Thanet	*Lab.* 44, *C.* 4, *LD* 4, *Ind.* 2
*Three Rivers	*LD* 23, *C.* 17, *Lab.* 8
*Tonbridge and Malling	*C.* 23, *LD* 21, *Lab.* 11
Torridge	*LD* 13, *Ind.* 10, *Lab.* 5, *C.* 2, *NP* 2, *others* 4
*Tunbridge Wells	*C.* 27, *LD* 12, *Lab.* 7, *Ind.* 2
Tynedale	*Lab.* 19, *LD* 13, *C.* 11, *Ind.* 4
Uttlesford	*LD* 18, *C.* 14, *Ind.* 6, *Lab.* 4
Vale of White Horse	*LD* 34, *C.* 11, *Lab.* 6
Vale Royal	*Lab.* 41, *C.* 15, *LD* 4
Wansbeck	*Lab.* 46
Warwick	*Lab.* 17, *C.* 13, *LD* 11, *Ind.* 4
*Watford	*Lab.* 21, *LD* 8, *C.* 7
*Waveney	*Lab.* 41, *C.* 3, *LD* 2, *Ind.* 1, *others* 1
Waverley	*LD* 33, *C.* 19, *Lab.* 2, *Ind.* 1, *others* 2
Wealden	*C.* 31, *LD* 23, *NP.* 4
Wear Valley	*Lab.* 35, *Ind.* 3, *LD* 2
Wellingborough	*Lab.* 17, *C.* 13, *Ind.* 3, *Ind. C.* 1
*Welwyn Hatfield	*Lab.* 27, *C.* 20
West Devon	*LD* 15, *Ind.* 14, *Lab.* 1
West Dorset	*Ind.* 20, *C.* 18, *LD* 12, *Lab.* 5
*West Lancashire	*Lab.* 33, *C.* 20, *Ind.* 2
*West Lindsey	*LD* 18, *Ind.* 10, *Lab.* 5, *C.* 4
*West Oxfordshire	*C.* 14, *Ind.* 13, *LD* 12, *Lab.* 10
West Somerset	*Ind.* 13, *C.* 9, *Lab.* 8, *LD* 2
West Wiltshire	*LD* 27, *C.* 7, *Lab.* 5, *Ind.* 4
*Weymouth and Portland	*Lab.* 16, *LD* 13, *Ind.* 6
*Winchester	*LD* 37, *C.* 10, *Ind.* 4, *Lab.* 4
*Woking	*LD* 16, *C.* 11, *Lab.* 7, *Ind.* 1
*Worcester	*Lab.* 21, *C.* 10, *Ind.* 3, *LD* 2
*Worthing	*LD* 20, *C.* 16
Wychavon	*C.* 18, *LD* 16, *Lab.* 10, *Ind.* 5
Wycombe	*C.* 24, *LD* 19, *Lab.* 15, *Ind.* 2
Wyre	*Lab.* 32, *C.* 18, *LD* 4, *Ind.* 1, *RA* 1
*Wyre Forest	*Lab.* 28, *LD* 6, *C.* 4, *Lib.* 3, *Ind.* 1

GREATER LONDON BOROUGHS

Barking and Dagenham	*Lab.* 47, *RA* 3, *LD* 1
Barnet	*C.* 28, *Lab.* 26, *LD* 6
Bexley	*C.* 32, *Lab.* 24, *LD* 6

Brent	*Lab.* 43, *C.* 19, *LD* 4
Bromley	*C.* 28, *LD* 25, *Lab.* 7
Camden	*Lab.* 43, *C.* 10, *LD* 6
City of Westminster	*C.* 47, *Lab.* 13
Croydon	*Lab.* 37, *C.* 31, *LD* 1, *vacant* 1
Ealing	*Lab.* 53, *C.* 15, *LD* 3
Enfield	*Lab.* 43, *C.* 23
Greenwich	*Lab.* 51, *C.* 8, *LD* 2
Hackney	*Lab.* 28, *LD* 17, *C.* 12, *Green* 2, *Ind.* 1
Hammersmith and Fulham	*Lab.* 36, *C.* 14
Haringey	*Lab.* 54, *LD* 3, *C.* 2
Harrow	*Lab.* 32, *C.* 20, *Lib.* 9, *Ind.* 2
Havering	*Lab.* 30, *RA* 16, *C.* 14, *LD* 3
Hillingdon	*C.* 33, *Lab.* 32, *LD* 4
Hounslow	*Lab.* 44, *C.* 11, *LD* 4, *RA* 1
Islington	*Lab.* 26, *LD* 26
Kensington and Chelsea	*C.* 39, *Lab.* 15
Kingston upon Thames	*C.* 21, *LD* 19, *Lab.* 10
Lambeth	*Lab.* 47, *LD* 12, *C.* 5
Lewisham	*Lab.* 61, *LD* 4, *C.* 2
Merton	*Lab.* 39, *C.* 12, *Ind.* 3, *LD* 3
Newham	*Lab.* 59, *vacant* 1
Redbridge	*Lab.* 30, *C.* 23, *LD* 9
Richmond upon Thames	*LD* 34, *C.* 14, *Lab.* 4
Southwark	*Lab.* 33, *LD* 27, *C.* 4
Sutton	*LD* 46, *C.* 5, *Lab.* 5
Tower Hamlets	*Lab.* 41, *LD* 9
Waltham Forest	*Lab.* 30, *C.* 14, *LD* 12, *Ind.* 1
Wandsworth	*C.* 50, *Lab.* 11

WALES

Anglesey	*Ind.* 22, *PC* 6, *Lab.* 4, *NP* 4, *others* 3, *vacant* 1
Blaenau Gwent	*Lab.* 34, *Ind.* 5, *C.* 1, *Lib.* 1, *PC* 1
Bridgend	*Lab.* 39, *Ind.* 3, *C.* 2, *LD* 2, *Ind. Lab.* 1, *PC* 1
Caerphilly	*Lab.* 56, *PC* 9, *Ind.* 3
Cardiff	*Lab.* 56, *LD* 9, *C.* 1, *PC* 1
Carmarthenshire	*Lab.* 37, *Ind.* 29, *PC* 8, *Ind. Lab.* 2, *LD* 2, *RA* 2, *others* 1
Ceredigion	*Ind.* 23, *LD* 10, *PC* 8, *Lab.* 1, *others* 1, *vacant* 1
Conwy	*Lab.* 18, *C.* 10, *Ind.* 10, *LD* 6, *PC* 5, *others* 11
Denbighshire	*Ind.* 19, *Lab.* 16, *PC* 7, *Ind. Lab.* 3, *LD* 3
Flintshire	*Lab.* 46, *Ind.* 13, *LD* 7, *C.* 3, *PC* 1, *others* 2
Gwynedd	*PC* 48, *Ind.* 18, *Lab.* 11, *LD* 4, *others* 2
Merthyr Tydfil	*Lab.* 29, *Ind.* 3, *RA* 1
Monmouthshire	*Lab.* 25, *C.* 11, *Ind.* 4, *LD* 1, *vacant* 1
Neath Port Talbot	*Lab.* 50, *PC* 3, *RA* 3, *Ind.* 2, *LD* 2, *SD* 1, *others* 2, *vacant* 1
Newport	*Lab.* 46, *C.* 1
Pembrokeshire	*Ind.* 39, *Lab.* 11, *LD* 4, *PC* 4, *others* 1, *vacant* 1
Powys	*Ind.* 59, *Lab.* 9, *LD* 9, *C.* 3, *PC* 1, *vacant* 2
Rhondda, Cynon, Taff	*Lab.* 57, *PC* 13, *Ind.* 4, *RA* 1
Swansea	*Lab.* 54, *Ind.* 9, *LD* 7, *C.* 1, *vacant* 2

Torfaen	*Lab.* 41, *C.* 1, *Ind.* 1, *LD* 1
Vale of Glamorgan	*Lab.* 35, *C.* 7, *PC* 5
Wrexham	*Lab.* 34, *Ind. C.* 6, *Ind. Lab.* 2, *others* 9

SCOTLAND

Aberdeen City	*Lab.* 29, *LD* 11, *C.* 9, *SNP* 1
Aberdeenshire	*LD* 16, *SNP* 15, *Ind.* 11, *C.* 5
Angus	*SNP* 21, *C.* 2, *LD* 2, *Ind.* 1
Argyll and Bute	*Ind.* 19, *SNP* 5, *LD* 4, *C.* 3, *Lab.* 2
City of Edinburgh	*Lab.* 33, *C.* 14, *LD* 10, *SNP* 1
Clackmannanshire	*Lab.* 8, *SNP* 3, *C.* 1
Dumfries and Galloway	Ind. 25, *Lab.* 18, *LD* 10, *SNP* 9, *C.* 2, *Ind. Lab.* 2, *others* 4
Dundee City	*Lab.* 28, *C.* 4, *SNP* 3, *Ind. Lab.* 1
East Ayrshire	*Lab.* 21, *SNP* 9
East Dunbartonshire	*Lab.* 15, *LD* 9, *C.* 2
East Lothian	*Lab.* 15, *C.* 3
East Renfrewshire	*C.* 9, *Lab.* 8, *LD* 2, *RA* 1
Falkirk	*Lab.* 22, *SNP* 8, *C.* 2, *Ind.* 2, *others* 2
Fife	*Lab.* 54, *LD* 25, *SNP* 9, *Ind.* 4
Glasgow City	*Lab.* 73, *SNP* 4, *C.* 3, *LD* 1, *others* 1, *vacant* 1
Highland	*Ind.* 50, *LD* 8, *SNP* 7, *Lab.* 6, *C.* 1
Inverclyde	*Lab.* 13, *LD* 6, *C.* 1
Midlothian	*Lab.* 14, *SNP* 1
Moray	*SNP* 11, *Lab.* 3, *Ind.* 2, *others* 2
North Ayrshire	*Lab.* 27, *C.* 1, *Ind.* 1, *SNP* 1
North Lanarkshire	*Lab.* 59, *SNP* 7, *Ind.* 2, *vacant* 1
Orkney Islands	*Ind.* 28
Perth and Kinross	*SNP* 18, *Lab.* 6, *LD* 5, *C.* 2, *Ind.* 1
Renfrewshire	*Lab.* 20, *SNP* 13, *LD* 3, *C.* 2, *Ind.* 2
Scottish Borders	*Ind.* 22, *LD* 15, *SNP* 7, *NP* 6, *Lab.* 4, *C.* 3, *vacant* 1
Shetland Islands	*NP* 11, *Ind.* 5, *LD* 4, *Lab.* 2, *Ind. Lab.* 1, *others* 3
South Ayrshire	*Lab.* 20, *C.* 5
South Lanarkshire	*Lab.* 60, *SNP* 7, *C.* 2, *LD* 2, *Ind.* 1, *vacant* 2
Stirling	*Lab.* 12, *C.* 8, *SNP* 2
West Dunbartonshire	*Lab.* 13, *SNP* 9
Western Isles	*NP* 25, *Lab.* 5
West Lothian	*Lab.* 15, *SNP* 11, *C.* 1

England

The Kingdom of England lies between 55° 46′ and 49° 57′ 30″ N. latitude (from a few miles north of the mouth of the Tweed to the Lizard), and between 1° 46′ E. and 5° 43′ W. (from Lowestoft to Land's End). England is bounded on the north by the Cheviot Hills; on the south by the English Channel; on the east by the Straits of Dover (Pas de Calais) and the North Sea; and on the west by the Atlantic Ocean, Wales and the Irish Sea. It has a total area of 50,351 sq. miles (130,410 sq. km): land 50,058 sq. miles (129,652 sq. km); inland water 293 sq. miles (758 sq. km).

POPULATION

The population at the 1991 census was 46,382,050 (males 22,469,707; females 23,912,343). The average density of the population in 1991 was 3.6 persons per hectare.

FLAG

The flag of England is the cross of St George, a red cross on a white field (cross gules in a field argent). The cross of St George, the patron saint of England, has been used since the 13th century.

RELIEF

There is a marked division between the upland and lowland areas of England. In the extreme north the Cheviot Hills (highest point, The Cheviot, 2,674 ft) form a natural boundary with Scotland. Running south from the Cheviots, though divided from them by the Tyne Gap, is the Pennine range (highest point, Cross Fell, 2,930 ft), the main orological feature of the country. The Pennines culminate in the Peak District of Derbyshire (Kinder Scout, 2,088 ft). West of the Pennines are the Cumbrian mountains, which include Scafell Pike (3,210 ft), the highest peak in England, and to the east are the Yorkshire Moors, their highest point being Urra Moor (1,490 ft).

In the west, the foothills of the Welsh mountains extend into the bordering English counties of Shropshire (the Wrekin, 1,334 ft; Long Mynd, 1,694 ft) and Hereford and Worcester (the Malvern Hills – Worcestershire Beacon, 1,394 ft). Extensive areas of high land and moorland are also to be found in the south-western peninsula formed by Somerset, Devon and Cornwall: principally Exmoor (Dunkery Beacon, 1,704 ft), Dartmoor (High Willhays, 2,038 ft) and Bodmin Moor (Brown Willy, 1,377 ft). Ranges of low, undulating hills run across the south of the country, including the Cotswolds in the Midlands and south-west, the Chilterns to the north of London, and the North (Kent) and South (Sussex) Downs of the south-east coastal areas.

The lowlands of England lie in the Vale of York, East Anglia and the area around the Wash. The lowest-lying are the Cambridgeshire Fens in the valleys of the Great Ouse and the River Nene, which are below sea-level in places. Since the 17th century extensive drainage has brought much of the Fens under cultivation. The North Sea coast between the Thames and the Humber, low-lying and formed of sand and shingle for the most part, is subject to erosion and defences against further incursion have been built along many stretches.

HYDROGRAPHY

The Severn is the longest river in Great Britain, rising in the north-eastern slopes of Plynlimon (Wales) and entering England in Shropshire with a total length of 220 miles (354 km) from its source to its outflow into the Bristol Channel, where it receives on the east the Bristol Avon, and on the west the Wye, its other tributaries being the

Vyrnwy, Tern, Stour, Teme and Upper (or Warwickshire) Avon. The Severn is tidal below Gloucester, and a high bore or tidal wave sometimes reverses the flow as high as Tewkesbury (13½ miles above Gloucester). The scenery of the greater part of the river is very picturesque and beautiful, and the Severn is a noted salmon river, some of its tributaries being famous for trout. Navigation is assisted by the Gloucester and Berkeley Ship Canal (16¾ miles), which admits vessels of 350 tons to Gloucester. The Severn Tunnel was begun in 1873 and completed in 1886 at a cost of £2 million and after many difficulties from flooding. It is 4 miles 628 yards in length (of which 2¼ miles are under the river). The Severn road bridge between Haysgate, Gwent, and Almondsbury, Glos, with a centre span of 3,240 ft, was opened in 1966.

The longest river wholly in England is the Thames, with a total length of 215 miles (346 km) from its source in the Cotswold hills to the Nore, and is navigable by ocean-going ships to London Bridge. The Thames is tidal to Teddington (69 miles from its mouth) and forms county boundaries almost throughout its course; on its banks are situated London, Windsor Castle, the oldest royal residence still in regular use, Eton College and Oxford, the oldest university in the kingdom.

Of the remaining English rivers, those flowing into the North Sea are the Tyne, Wear, Tees, Ouse and Trent from the Pennine Range, the Great Ouse (160 miles), which rises in Northamptonshire, and the Orwell and Stour from the hills of East Anglia. Flowing into the English Channel are the Sussex Ouse from the Weald, the Itchen from the Hampshire Hills, and the Axe, Teign, Dart, Tamar and Exe from the Devonian hills. Flowing into the Irish Sea are the Mersey, Ribble and Eden from the western slopes of the Pennines and the Derwent from the Cumbrian mountains.

The English Lakes, noteworthy for their picturesque scenery and poetic associations, lie in Cumbria, the largest being Windermere (10 miles long), Ullswater and Derwent Water.

ISLANDS

The Isle of Wight is separated from Hampshire by the Solent. The capital, Newport, stands at the head of the estuary of the Medina, Cowes (at the mouth) being the chief port. Other centres are Ryde, Sandown, Shanklin, Ventnor, Freshwater, Yarmouth, Totland Bay, Seaview and Bembridge.

Lundy (the name means Puffin Island), 11 miles northwest of Hartland Point, Devon, is about two miles long and about half a mile wide on average, with a total area of about 1,116 acres, and a population of about 20. It became the property of the National Trust in 1969 and is now principally a bird sanctuary.

The Isles of Scilly consist of about 140 islands and skerries (total area, 6 sq. miles/10 sq. km) situated 28 miles south-west of Land's End. Only five are inhabited: St Mary's, St Agnes, Bryher, Tresco and St Martin's. The population is 1,978. The entire group has been designated a Conservation Area, a Heritage Coast, and an Area of Outstanding Natural Beauty, and has been given National Nature Reserve status by the Nature Conservancy Council because of its unique flora and fauna. Tourism and the winter/spring flower trade for the home market form the basis of the economy of the Isles. The island group is a recognized rural development area.

EARLY HISTORY

Archaeological evidence suggests that England has been inhabited since at least the Palaeolithic period, though the extent of the various Palaeolithic cultures was dependent upon the degree of glaciation. The succeeding Neolithic and Bronze Age cultures have left abundant remains throughout the country, the best-known of these being the henges and stone circles of Stonehenge (ten miles north of Salisbury, Wilts) and Avebury (Wilts), both of which are believed to have been of religious significance. In the latter part of the Bronze Age the Goidels, a people of Celtic race, and in the Iron Age other Celtic races of Brythons and Belgae, invaded the country and brought with them Celtic civilization and dialects, place names in England bearing witness to the spread of the invasion over the whole kingdom.

THE ROMAN CONQUEST

The Roman conquest of Gaul (57–50 BC) brought Britain into close contact with Roman civilization, but although Julius Caesar raided the south of Britain in 55 BC and 54 BC, conquest was not undertaken until nearly 100 years later. In AD 43 the Emperor Claudius dispatched Aulus Plautius, with a well-equipped force of 40,000, and himself followed with reinforcements in the same year. Success was delayed by the resistance of Caratacus (Caractacus), the British leader from AD 48–51, who was finally captured and sent to Rome, and by a great revolt in AD 61 led by Boudicca (Boadicea), Queen of the Iceni; but the south of Britain was secured by AD 70, and Wales and the area north to the Tyne by about AD 80.

In AD 122, the Emperor Hadrian visited Britain and built a continuous rampart, since known as Hadrian's Wall, from Wallsend to Bowness (Tyne to Solway). The work was entrusted by the Emperor Hadrian to Aulus Platorius Nepos, legate of Britain from AD 122 to 126, and it was intended to form the northern frontier of the Roman Empire.

The Romans administered Britain as a province under a Governor, with a well-defined system of local government, each Roman municipality ruling itself and its surrounding territory, while London was the centre of the road system and the seat of the financial officials of the Province of Britain. Colchester, Lincoln, York, Gloucester and St Albans stand on the sites of five Roman municipalities, and Wroxeter, Caerleon, Chester, Lincoln and York were at various times the sites of legionary fortresses. Well-preserved Roman towns have been uncovered at or near Silchester (*Calleva Atrebatum*), ten miles south of Reading, Wroxeter (*Viroconium Cornoviorum*), near Shrewsbury, and St Albans (*Verulamium*) in Hertfordshire.

Four main groups of roads radiated from London, and a fifth (the Fosse) ran obliquely from Lincoln through Leicester, Cirencester and Bath to Exeter. Of the four groups radiating from London, one ran south-east to Canterbury and the coast of Kent, a second to Silchester and thence to parts of western Britain and south Wales, a third (later known as Watling Street) ran through Verulamium to Chester, with various branches, and the fourth reached Colchester, Lincoln, York and the eastern counties.

In the fourth century Britain was subject to raids along the east coast by Saxon pirates, which led to the establishment of a system of coast defence from the Wash to Southampton Water, with forts at Brancaster, Burgh Castle (Yarmouth), Walton (Felixstowe), Bradwell, Reculver, Richborough, Dover, Lympne, Pevensey and Porchester (Portsmouth). The Irish (Scoti) and Picts in the north were also becoming more aggressive; from about AD 350 incur-

sions became more frequent and more formidable. As the Roman Empire came under attack increasingly towards the end of the fourth century, many troops were removed from Britain for service in other parts of the empire. The island was eventually cut off from Rome by the Teutonic conquest of Gaul, and with the withdrawal of the last Roman garrison early in the fifth century, the Romano-British were left to themselves.

SAXON SETTLEMENT

According to legend, the British King Vortigern called in the Saxons to defend him against the Picts, the Saxon chieftains being Hengist and Horsa, who landed at Ebbsfleet, Kent, and established themselves in the Isle of Thanet; but the events during the one and a half centuries between the final break with Rome and the re-establishment of Christianity are unclear. However, it would appear that in the course of this period the raids turned into large-scale settlement by invaders traditionally known as Angles (England north of the Wash and East Anglia), Saxons (Essex and southern England) and Jutes (Kent and the Weald), which pushed the Romano-British into the mountainous areas of the north and west, Celtic culture outside Wales and Cornwall surviving only in topographical names. Various kingdoms were established at this time which attempted to claim overlordship of the whole country, hegemony finally being achieved by Wessex (capital, Winchester) in the ninth century. This century also saw the beginning of raids by the Vikings (Danes), which were resisted by Alfred the Great (871–899), who fixed a limit to the advance of Danish settlement by the Treaty of Wedmore (878), giving them the area north and east of Watling Street, on condition that they adopt Christianity.

In the tenth century the kings of Wessex recovered the whole of England from the Danes, but subsequent rulers were unable to resist a second wave of invaders. England paid tribute (*Danegeld*) for many years, and was invaded in 1013 by the Danes and ruled by Danish kings from 1016 until 1042, when Edward the Confessor was recalled from exile in Normandy. On Edward's death in 1066 Harold Godwinson (brother-in-law of Edward and son of Earl Godwin of Wessex) was chosen King of England. After defeating (at Stamford Bridge, Yorkshire, 25 September) an invading army under Harald Hadraada, King of Norway (aided by the outlawed Earl Tostig of Northumbria, Harold's brother), Harold was himself defeated at the Battle of Hastings on 14 October 1066, and the Norman conquest secured the throne of England for Duke William of Normandy, a cousin of Edward the Confessor.

CHRISTIANITY

Christianity reached the Roman province of Britain from Gaul in the third century (or possibly earlier); Alban, traditionally Britain's first martyr, was put to death as a Christian during the persecution of Diocletian (22 June 303), at his native town Verulamium; and the Bishops of Londinium, Eboracum (York), and Lindum (Lincoln) attended the Council of Arles in 314. However, the Anglo-Saxon invasions submerged the Christian religion in England until the sixth century when conversion was undertaken in the north from 563 by Celtic missionaries from Ireland led by St Columba, and in the south by a mission sent from Rome in 597 which was led by St Augustine, who became the first archbishop of Canterbury. England appears to have been converted again by the end of the seventh century and followed, after the Council of Whitby in 663, the practices of the Roman Church, which brought the kingdom into the mainstream of European thought and culture.

PRINCIPAL CITIES

BIRMINGHAM

Birmingham is Britain's second city. It is a focal point in national communications networks with a rapidly expanding international airport. The generally accepted derivation of 'Birmingham' is the *ham* (dwelling-place) of the *ing* (family) of *Beorma*, presumed to have been Saxon. During the Industrial Revolution the town grew into a major manufacturing centre and in 1889 was granted city status.

Despite the decline in manufacturing, Birmingham is still a major hardware trade and motor component industry centre. As well as the National Exhibition Centre and the Aston Science Park, recent developments include the International Convention Centre, the National Indoor Arena and Brindleyplace.

The principal buildings are the Town Hall (1834–50); the Council House (1879); Victoria Law Courts (1891); Birmingham University (1906–9); the 13th-century Church of St Martin-in-the-Bull-Ring (rebuilt 1873); the Cathedral (formerly St Philip's Church) (1711) and the Roman Catholic Cathedral of St Chad (1839–41).

BRADFORD

Bradford lies on the southern edge of the Yorkshire Dales National Park, including within its boundaries the village of Haworth, home of the Brontë sisters, and Ilkley Moor.

Originally a Saxon township, Bradford received a market charter in 1251 but developed only slowly until the industrialization of the textile industry brought rapid growth during the 19th century; it was granted its city charter in 1897. The prosperity of that period is reflected in much of the city's architecture, particularly the public buildings: City Hall (1873), Wool Exchange (1867), St George's Hall (Concert Hall, 1853), Cartwright Hall (Art Gallery, 1904) and the Technical College (1882). Other chief buildings are the Cathedral (15th century) and Bolling Hall (14th century).

Textiles still play an important part in the city's economy but industry is now more broadly based, including engineering, micro-electronics, printing and chemicals. The city has a strong financial services sector, and a growing tourism industry.

BRISTOL

Bristol was a Royal Borough before the Norman Conquest. The earliest form of the name is *Bricgstow*. In 1373 Edward III granted Bristol county status.

The chief buildings include the 12th-century Cathedral (with later additions), with Norman chapter house and gateway, the 14th-century Church of St Mary Redcliffe, Wesley's Chapel, Broadmead, the Merchant Venturers' Almshouses, the Council House (1956), Guildhall, Exchange (erected from the designs of John Wood in 1743), Cabot Tower, the University and Clifton College. The Roman Catholic Cathedral at Clifton was opened in 1973.

The Clifton Suspension Bridge, with a span of 702 feet over the Avon, was projected by Brunel in 1836 but was not completed until 1864. Brunel's SS *Great Britain*, the first ocean-going propeller-driven ship, is now being restored in the City Docks from where she was launched in 1843. The docks themselves have been extensively restored and redeveloped and are becoming a focus for the arts and recreation.

CAMBRIDGE

Cambridge, a settlement far older than its ancient University, lies on the River Cam or Granta. The city is a county town and regional headquarters. Its industries include electronics, high technology research and development, and biotechnology. Among its open spaces are Jesus Green, Sheep's Green, Coe Fen, Parker's Piece, Christ's Pieces, the University Botanic Garden, and the Backs, or lawns and gardens through which the Cam winds behind the principal line of college buildings. East of the Cam, King's Parade, upon which stand Great St Mary's Church, Gibbs' Senate House and King's College Chapel with Wilkins' screen, joins Trumpington Street to form one of the most beautiful throughfares in Europe.

University and college buildings provide the outstanding features of Cambridge architecture but several churches (especially St Benet's, the oldest building in the city, and St Sepulchre's, the Round Church) are also notable. The Guildhall (1939) stands on a site of which at least part has held municipal buildings since 1224.

CANTERBURY

Canterbury, the Metropolitan City of the Anglican Communion, dates back to prehistoric times. It was the Roman *Durovernum Cantiacorum* and the Saxon *Cant-wara-byrig* (stronghold of the men of Kent). Here in 597 St Augustine began the conversion of the English to Christianity, when Ethelbert, King of Kent, was baptized.

Of the Benedictine St Augustine's Abbey, burial place of the Jutish Kings of Kent (whose capital Canterbury was), only ruins remain. St Martin's Church, on the eastern outskirts of the city, is stated by Bede to have been the place of worship of Queen Bertha, the Christian wife of King Ethelbert, before the advent of St Augustine.

In 1170 the rivalry of Church and State culminated in the murder in Canterbury Cathedral, by Henry II's knights, of Archbishop Thomas Becket. His shrine became a great centre of pilgrimage, as described in Chaucer's *Canterbury Tales*. After the Reformation pilgrimages ceased, but the prosperity of the city was strengthened by an influx of Huguenot refugees, who introduced weaving. The poet and playwright Christopher Marlowe was born and reared in Canterbury, and there are also literary associations with Defoe, Dickens, Joseph Conrad and Somerset Maugham.

The Cathedral, with architecture ranging from the 11th to the 15th centuries, is world famous. Modern pilgrims are attracted particularly to the Martyrdom, the Black Prince's Tomb, the Warriors' Chapel and the many examples of medieval stained glass.

The medieval city walls are built on Roman foundations and the 14th-century West Gate is one of the finest buildings of its kind in the country.

The 1,000-seat Marlowe Theatre is a centre for the Canterbury Arts Festival each autumn.

CARLISLE

Carlisle is situated at the confluence of the River Eden and River Caldew, 309 miles north-west of London and about ten miles from the Scottish border. It was granted a charter in 1158.

The city stands at the western end of Hadrian's Wall and dates from the original Roman settlement of *Luguvalium*. Granted to Scotland in the tenth century, Carlisle is not included in the Domesday Book. William Rufus reclaimed the area in 1092 and the castle and city walls were built to guard Carlisle and the western border; the citadel is a Tudor addition to protect the south of the city. Border disputes were common until the problem of the Debatable Lands was settled in 1552. During the Civil War the city remained Royalist; in 1745 Carlisle was besieged for the last time by the Young Pretender.

The Cathedral, originally a 12th-century Augustinian priory, was enlarged in the 13th and 14th centuries after the diocese was created in 1133. To the south is a restored Tithe Barn and nearby the 18th-century church of St Cuthbert, the third to stand on a site dating from the seventh century.

Carlisle is the major shopping, commercial and agricultural centre for the area, and industries include the manufacture of metal goods, biscuits and textiles. However, the largest employer is the services sector, notably in central and local government, retailing and transport. The city has an important communications position at the centre of a network of major roads, as a stage on the main west coast rail services, and with its own airport at Crosby-on-Eden.

CHESTER

Chester is situated on the River Dee, and was granted borough and city status in 1974. Its recorded history dates from the first century when the Romans founded the fortress of *Deva*. The city's name is derived from the Latin *castra* (a camp or encampment). During the Middle Ages, Chester was the principal port of north-west England but declined with the silting of the Dee estuary and competition from Liverpool. The city was also an important military centre, notably during Edward I's Welsh campaigns and the Elizabethan Irish campaigns. During the Civil War, Chester supported the King and was besieged from 1643 to 1646. Chester's first charter was granted *c.* 1175 and the city was incorporated in 1506. The office of Sheriff is the earliest created in the country (*c.* 1120s), and in 1992 the Mayor was granted the title of Lord Mayor. He/she also enjoys the title 'Admiral of the Dee'.

The city's architectural features include the city walls (an almost complete two-mile circuit), the unique 13th-century Rows (covered galleries above the street-level shops), the Victorian Gothic Town Hall (1869), the Castle (rebuilt 1788 and 1822) and numerous half-timbered buildings. The Cathedral was a Benedictine abbey until the Dissolution. Remaining monastic buildings include the chapter house, refectory and cloisters and there is a modern free-standing bell tower. The Norman church of St John the Baptist was a cathedral church in the early Middle Ages. Chester is a thriving retail, business and tourist centre.

COVENTRY

Coventry is an important industrial centre, producing vehicles, machine tools, agricultural machinery, man-made fibres, aerospace components and telecommunications equipment. New investment has come from financial services, power transmission, professional services and education.

The city owes its beginning to Leofric, Earl of Mercia, and his wife Godiva who, in 1043, founded a Benedictine monastery. The guildhall of St Mary dates from the 14th century, three of the city's churches date from the 14th and 15th centuries, and 16th-century almshouses may still be seen. Coventry's first cathedral was destroyed at the Reformation, its second in the 1940 blitz (the walls and spire remain) and the new cathedral designed by Sir Basil Spence, consecrated in 1962, now draws innumerable visitors.

Coventry is the home of the University of Warwick and its Science Park, Coventry University, the Westwood Business Park, the Cable and Wireless College, and the Museum of British Road Transport.

DERBY

Derby stands on the banks of the River Derwent, and its name dates back to 880 when the Danes settled in the locality and changed the original Saxon name of *Northworthy* to *Deoraby*.

Derby has a wide range of industries including aero engines, cars, pipework, specialized mechanical engineering equipment, textiles, chemicals, plastics and the Royal Crown Derby porcelain. The city is an established railway centre with rail research, engineering, safety testing, infrastructure and train-operating companies.

Buildings of interest include St Peter's Church and the Old Abbey Building (14th century), the Cathedral (1525), St Mary's Roman Catholic Church (1839) and the Industrial Museum, formerly the Old Silk Mill (1721). The traditional city centre is complemented by the Eagle Centre and 'out-of-centre' retail developments. In addition to the Derby Playhouse, the Assembly Rooms are a multi-purpose venue.

The first charter granting a Mayor and Aldermen was that of Charles I in 1637. Previous charters date back to 1154. It was granted city status in 1977.

DURHAM

The city of Durham is a district in the county of Durham and a major tourist attraction because of its prominent Norman Cathedral and Castle set high on a wooded peninsula overlooking the River Wear. The Cathedral was founded as a shrine for the body of St Cuthbert in 995. The present building dates from 1093 and among its many treasures is the tomb of the Venerable Bede (673–735). Durham's Prince Bishops had unique powers up to 1836, being lay rulers as well as religious leaders. As a palatinate Durham could have its own army, nobility, coinage and courts. The Castle was the main seat of the Prince Bishops for nearly 800 years; it is now used as a college by the University. The University, founded on the initiative of Bishop William Van Mildert, is England's third oldest.

Among other buildings of interest is the Guildhall in the Market Place which dates originally from the 14th century. Work has been carried out to conserve this area as part of the city's contribution to the Council of Europe's Urban Renaissance Campaign. Annual events include Durham's Regatta in June (claimed to be the oldest rowing event in Britain) and the Annual Gala (formerly Durham Miners' Gala) in July.

The economy has undergone a significant change with the replacement of mining as the dominant industry by 'white collar' employment. Although still a predominantly rural area, the industrial and commercial sector is growing and a wide range of manufacturing and service industries are based on industrial estates in and around the city. A research and development centre, linked to the University, also plays an important role in the local economy.

EXETER

Exeter lies on the River Exe ten miles from the sea. It was granted a charter by Henry II. The Romans founded *Isca Dumnoniorum* in the first century AD, and in the third century a stone wall (much of which remains) was built, providing protection against Saxon, and then Danish invasions. After the Conquest, the city led resistance to William in the west until reduced by siege. The Normans built the ringwork castle of Rougemont, the gatehouse and one tower of which remain, although the rest was pulled down in 1784. The first bridge across the Exe was built in the early 13th century. The city's main port was situated downstream at Topsham until the construction in the 1560s of the first true canal in England, the redevelopment of which in 1700 brought seaborne trade direct to the city. Exeter was the Royalist headquarters in the west during the Civil War.

The diocese of Exeter was established by Edward the Confessor in 1050, although a minster existed near the Cathedral site from the late seventh century. A new cathedral was built in the 12th century but the present building was begun c. 1275, although incorporating the Norman towers, and completed about a century later. The Guildhall dates from the 12th century and there are many other medieval buildings in the city, as well as architecture in the Georgian and Regency styles, and the Custom House (1680). Damage suffered by bombing in 1942 led to the redevelopment of the city centre.

Exeter's prosperity from medieval times was based on trade in wool and woollen cloth (commemorated by Tuckers Hall), which remained at its height until the late 18th century when export trade was hit by the French wars. Subsequently Exeter has developed as an administrative and commercial centre, notably in the distributive trades, light manufacturing industries and tourism.

KINGSTON UPON HULL

Hull (officially Kingston upon Hull) lies at the junction of the River Hull with the Humber, 22 miles from the North Sea. It is one of the major seaports of the United Kingdom, comprising 2,000 acres in four main dock installations. The port provides a wide range of cargo services, including ro-ro and container traffic, and handles a million passengers annually on daily sailings to Rotterdam and Zeebrugge. There is a variety of industry and service industries, as well as increasing tourism and conference business.

The city, restored after heavy air raid damage during the Second World War, has good office and administrative buildings, its municipal centre being the Guildhall, its educational centres the University of Hull and the University of Lincolnshire and Humberside and its religious centre the Parish Church of the Holy Trinity. The old town area has been renovated and includes a marina and shopping complex. Just west of the city is the Humber Bridge, the world's longest single-span suspension bridge.

Kingston upon Hull was so named by Edward I. City status was accorded in 1897 and the office of Mayor raised to the dignity of Lord Mayor in 1914.

LEEDS

Leeds, situated in the lower Aire Valley, is a junction for road, rail, canal and air services and an important manufacturing and commercial centre. Seventy-three per cent of employment is in services, notably the distributive trades, public administration, medical services and business services. The main manufacturing industries are mechanical engineering, printing and publishing, metal goods and furniture.

The principal buildings are the Civic Hall (1933), the Town Hall (1858), the Municipal Buildings and Art Gallery (1884) with the Henry Moore Gallery (1982), the Corn Exchange (1863) and the University. The Parish Church (St Peter's) was rebuilt in 1841; the 17th-century St John's Church has a fine interior with a famous English Renaissance screen; the last remaining 18th-century church in the city is Holy Trinity in Boar Lane (1727). Kirkstall Abbey (about three miles from the centre of the city), founded by Henry de Lacy in 1152, is one of the most complete examples of Cistercian houses now remaining. Temple Newsam, birthplace of Lord Darnley, was acquired by the Council in 1922. The present house was largely rebuilt by Sir Arthur Ingram in about 1620. Adel Church, about five miles from the centre of the city, is a fine Norman structure. The new Royal Armouries Museum houses the collection of antique arms and armour formerly held at the Tower of London.

Leeds was first incorporated by Charles I in 1626. The earliest forms of the name are *Loidis* or *Ledes*, the origins of which are obscure.

LEICESTER

Leicester is situated geographically in the centre of England. It dates back to pre-Roman times and was one of the five Danish *Burghs*. In 1589 Queen Elizabeth I granted a charter to the city and the ancient title was confirmed by letters patent in 1919.

The principal industries are hosiery, knitwear, footwear manufacturing and engineering. The growth of Leicester as a hosiery centre increased rapidly from the introduction there of the first stocking frame in 1670 and today it has some of the largest hosiery factories in the world.

The principal buildings are the Town Hall, the New Walk Centre, the University of Leicester, De Montfort University, De Montfort Hall, one of the finest concert halls in the provinces seating over 2,750 people, and the Granby Halls, an indoor sports facility. The ancient churches of St Martin (now Leicester Cathedral), St Nicholas, St Margaret, All Saints, St Mary de Castro, and buildings such as the Guildhall, the 14th-century Newarke Gate, the Castle and the Jewry Wall Roman site still exist. The Haymarket Theatre was opened in 1973 and The Shires shopping centre in 1992.

LINCOLN

Situated 40 miles inland on the River Witham, Lincoln derives its name from a contraction of *Lindum Colonia*, the settlement founded in AD 48 by the Romans to command the crossing of Ermine Street and Fosse Way. Sections of the third-century Roman city wall can be seen, including an extant gateway (Newport Arch), and excavations have discovered traces of a sewerage system unique in Britain. The Romans also drained the surrounding fenland and created a canal system, laying the foundations of Lincoln's agricultural prosperity and also of the city's importance in the medieval wool trade as a port and Staple town.

As one of the Five Boroughs of the Danelaw, Lincoln was an important trading centre in the ninth and tenth centuries and medieval prosperity from the wool trade lasted until the 14th century, enabling local merchants to build parish churches (of which three survive), and attracting in the 12th century a Jewish community (Jew's House and Court, Aaron's House). However, the removal of the Staple to Boston in 1369 heralded a decline from which the city only recovered fully in the 19th century when improved fen drainage made Lincoln agriculturally important and improved canal and rail links led to industrial development, mainly in the manufacture of machinery, components and engineering products.

The castle was built shortly after the Conquest and is unusual in having two mounds; on one motte stands a Keep (Lucy's Tower) added in the 12th century. It currently houses one of the four surviving copies of the Magna Carta. The Cathedral was begun c. 1073 when the first Norman bishop moved the see of Lindsey to Lincoln, but was mostly destroyed by fire and earthquake in the 12th century. Rebuilding was begun by St Hugh and completed over a century later. Other notable architectural features are the 12th-century High Bridge, the oldest in Britain still to carry buildings, and the Guildhall situated above the 15th–16th-century Stonebow gateway.

LIVERPOOL

Liverpool, on the right bank of the River Mersey, three miles from the Irish Sea, is the United Kingdom's foremost port for the Atlantic trade. Tunnels link Liverpool with Birkenhead and Wallasey.

There are 2,100 acres of dockland on both sides of the river and the Gladstone and Royal Seaforth Docks can accommodate Panamax–sized vessels. Approximately 31 million tonnes of cargo is handled annually. The main cargoes are crude oil, grain, fossil fuels, edible oils, timber, scrap metal, containers and break-bulk cargo. Liverpool Free Port, Britain's largest, was opened in 1984.

Liverpool was created a free borough in 1207 and a city in 1880. From the early 18th century it expanded rapidly with the growth of industrialization and the Atlantic trade. Surviving buildings from this period include the Bluecoat Chambers (1717, formerly the Bluecoat School), the Town Hall (1754, rebuilt to the original design 1795), and buildings in Rodney Street, Canning Street and the suburbs. Notable from the 19th and 20th centuries are the Anglican Cathedral, built from the designs of Sir Giles Gilbert Scott (the foundation stone was laid in 1904, and the building was completed only in 1980), the Catholic Metropolitan Cathedral (designed by Sir Frederick Gibberd, consecrated 1967) and St George's Hall (1838–54), regarded as one of the finest modern examples of classical architecture. The refurbished Albert Dock (designed by Jesse Hartley) contains the Merseyside Maritime Museum and Tate Gallery, Liverpool.

In 1852 an Act was obtained for establishing a public library, museum and art gallery; as a result Liverpool had one of the first public libraries in the country. The Brown, Picton and Hornby libraries now form one of the country's major libraries. The Victoria Building of Liverpool University, the Royal Liver, Cunard and Mersey Docks Harbour Company buildings at the Pier Head, the Municipal Buildings and the Philharmonic Hall are other examples of the city's fine buildings.

MANCHESTER

Manchester (the *Mamucium* of the Romans, who occupied it in AD 79) is a commercial and industrial centre with a population engaged in the engineering, chemical, clothing, food processing and textile industries and in education. Banking, insurance and a growing leisure industry are among the prime commercial activities. The city is connected with the sea by the Manchester Ship Canal, opened in 1894, 35½ miles long, and accommodating ships up to 15,000 tons. Manchester Airport handles 15 million passengers yearly.

The principal buildings are the Town Hall, erected in 1877 from the designs of Alfred Waterhouse, with a large extension of 1938; the Royal Exchange (1869, enlarged 1921); the Central Library (1934); Heaton Hall; the 17th-century Chetham Library; the Rylands Library (1900), which includes the Althorp collection; the University precinct; the 15th-century Cathedral (formerly the parish church); G-MEX exhibition centre and the Free Trade Hall. Recent developments include the Manchester Arena, the largest indoor arena in Europe, and the Bridgewater Hall. Manchester is the home of the Hallé Orchestra, the Royal Northern College of Music, the Royal Exchange Theatre and seven public art galleries. Metrolink, the new light rail system, opened in 1992.

The Commonwealth Games are to be held in Manchester in 2002 and new sports facilities include a stadium, a swimming pool complex and the National Cycling Centre.

The town received its first charter of incorporation in 1838 and was created a city in 1853.

NEWCASTLE UPON TYNE

Newcastle upon Tyne, on the north bank of the River Tyne, is eight miles from the North Sea. A cathedral and university city, it is the administrative, commercial and cultural centre for north-east England and the principal port. It is an important manufacturing centre with a wide variety of industries.

The principal buildings include the Castle Keep (12th century), Black Gate (13th century), Blackfriars (13th century), West Walls (13th century), St Nicholas's Cathedral (15th century, fine lantern tower), St Andrew's Church (12th–14th century), St John's (14th–15th century), All Saints (1786 by Stephenson), St Mary's Roman Catholic Cathedral (1844), Trinity House (17th century), Sandhill (16th-century houses), Guildhall (Georgian), Grey Street (1834–9), Central Station (1846–50), Laing Art Gallery (1904), University of Newcastle Physics Building (1962) and Medical Building (1985), Civic Centre (1963), Central Library (1969) and Eldon Square Shopping Development (1976). Open spaces include the Town Moor (927 acres) and Jesmond Dene. Nine bridges span the Tyne at Newcastle.

The city's name is derived from the 'new castle' (1080) erected as a defence against the Scots. In 1400 it was made a county, and in 1882 a city.

NORWICH

Norwich grew from an early Anglo-Saxon settlement near the confluence of the Rivers Yare and Wensum, and now serves as provincial capital for the predominantly agricultural region of East Anglia. The name is thought to relate to the most northerly of a group of Anglo-Saxon villages or *wics*. The city's first known charter was granted in 1158 by Henry II.

Norwich serves its surrounding area as a market town and commercial centre, banking and insurance being prominent among the city's businesses. From the 14th century until the Industrial Revolution, Norwich was the regional centre of the woollen industry, but now the biggest single industry is financial services and principal trades are engineering, printing, shoemaking, double glazing, the production of chemicals and clothing, food processing and technology. Norwich is accessible to sea-going vessels by means of the River Yare, entered at Great Yarmouth, 20 miles to the east.

Among many historic buildings are the Cathedral (completed in the 12th century and surmounted by a 15th-century spire 315 feet in height), the keep of the Norman castle (now a museum and art gallery), the 15th-century flint-walled Guildhall (now a tourist information centre), some thirty medieval parish churches, St Andrew's and Blackfriars' Halls, the Tudor houses preserved in Elm Hill and the Georgian Assembly House. The University of East Anglia is on the city's western boundary.

NOTTINGHAM

Nottingham stands on the River Trent and is connected by canal with the Atlantic Ocean and the North Sea. *Snotingaham* or *Notingeham*, literally the homestead of the people of Snot, is the Anglo-Saxon name for the Celtic settlement of *Tigguocobauc*, or the house of caves. In 878, Nottingham became one of the Five Boroughs of the Danelaw. William the Conqueror ordered the construction of Nottingham Castle, while the town itself developed rapidly under Norman rule. Its laws and rights were later formally recognized by Henry II's charter in 1155. The Castle became a favoured residence of King John. In 1642 King Charles I raised his personal standard at Nottingham Castle at the start of the Civil War.

Nottingham is a major sporting centre, home to Nottingham Forest FC, Notts County FC (the world's oldest football league side), Nottingham Racecourse and the National Watersports Centre. The principal industries include textiles, pharmaceuticals, food manufacturing, engineering and telecommunications. There are two universities within the city boundaries.

Architecturally, Nottingham has a wealth of notable buildings, particularly those designed in the Victorian era by T. C. Hine and Watson Fothergill. The City Council owns the Castle, of Norman origin but restored in 1878, Wollaton Hall (1580–8), Newstead Abbey (home of Lord Byron), the Guildhall (1888) and Council House (1929). St Mary's, St Peter's and St Nicholas's Churches are of interest, as is the Roman Catholic Cathedral (Pugin, 1842–4).

Nottingham was granted city status in 1897.

OXFORD

Oxford is a university city, an important industrial centre, and a market town. Industry played a minor part in Oxford until the motor industry was established in 1912.

It is for its architecture that Oxford is of most interest to the visitor, its oldest specimens being the reputedly Saxon tower of St Michael's church, the remains of the Norman castle and city walls, and the Norman church at Iffley. It is chiefly famous, however, for its Gothic buildings, such as the Divinity Schools, the Old Library at Merton College, William of Wykeham's New College, Magdalen College and Christ Church and many other college buildings. Later centuries are represented by the Laudian quadrangle at St John's College, the Renaissance Sheldonian Theatre by Wren, Trinity College Chapel, and All Saints Church; Hawksmoor's mock-Gothic at All Souls College, and the 18th-century Queen's College. In addition to individual buildings, High Street and Radcliffe Square, just off it, both form architectural compositions of great beauty. Most of the Colleges have gardens, those of Magdalen, New College, St John's and Worcester being the largest.

PLYMOUTH

Plymouth is situated on the borders of Devon and Cornwall at the confluence of the Rivers Tamar and Plym. The city has a long maritime history; it was the home port of Sir Francis Drake and the starting point for his circumnavigation of the world, as well as the last port of call for the *Mayflower* when the Pilgrim Fathers sailed for the New World in 1620. Today Plymouth is host to many international yacht races. The Barbican harbour area has many Elizabethan buildings and on Plymouth Hoe stands Smeaton's lighthouse, the third to be built on the Eddystone Rocks 13 miles offshore.

The city centre was rebuilt following extensive war damage, and comprises a large shopping centre, municipal offices, law courts and public buildings. The main employment is provided at the naval base, though many industrial firms and service industries have become established in the post-war period and the city is a growing tourism centre. In 1982 the Theatre Royal was opened. In conjunction with the Cornwall County Council, the Tamar Bridge was constructed linking the city by road with Cornwall.

PORTSMOUTH

Portsmouth occupies Portsea Island, Hampshire, with boundaries extending to the mainland. It is a centre of industry and commerce, including many high technology and manufacturing industries. It is the British headquarters of several major international companies. The Royal Navy base still has a substantial work-force, although this has decreased in recent years. The commercial port and continental ferry port is owned and run by the City Council, and carries passengers and vehicles to France and northern Spain.

A major port since the 16th century, Portsmouth is also a thriving seaside resort catering for thousands of visitors annually. Among many historic attractions are Lord Nelson's flagship, HMS *Victory*, the Tudor warship *Mary Rose*, Britain's first 'ironclad' warship, HMS *Warrior*, the D-Day Museum, Charles Dickens' birthplace at 393 Old Commercial Road, the Royal Naval and Royal Marine museums, Southsea Castle (built by Henry VIII), the Round Tower and Point Battery, which for hundreds of years have guarded the entrance to Portsmouth Harbour, Fort Nelson on Portsdown Hill and the Sealife Centre.

ST ALBANS

The origins of St Albans, situated on the River Ver, stem from the Roman town of *Verulamium*. Named after the first Christian martyr in Britain, who was executed here, St Albans has developed around the Norman Abbey and Cathedral Church (consecrated 1115), built partly of materials from the old Roman city. The museums house Iron Age and Roman artefacts and the Roman Theatre, unique in Britain, has a stage as opposed to an amphitheatre. Archaeological excavations in the city centre have revealed evidence of pre-Roman, Saxon and medieval occupation.

The town's significance grew to the extent that it was a signatory and venue for the drafting of the Magna Carta. It was also the scene of riots during the Peasants' Revolt, the French King John was imprisoned there after the Battle of Poitiers, and heavy fighting took place there during the Wars of the Roses.

Previously controlled by the Abbot, the town achieved a charter in 1553 and city status in 1877. The street market, first established in 1553, is still an important feature of the city, as are many hotels and inns which survive from the days when St Albans was an important coach stop. Tourist attractions include historic churches and houses, and a 15th-century clock tower.

The city now contains a wide range of firms, with special emphasis on information and legal services. In addition, it is the home of the Royal National Rose Society, and of Rothamsted Park, the agricultural research centre.

SHEFFIELD

Sheffield, the centre of the special steel and cutlery trades, is situated at the junction of the Sheaf, Porter, Rivelin and Loxley valleys with the River Don. Though its cutlery, silverware and plate have long been famous, Sheffield has other and now more important industries: special and alloy steels, engineering, tool-making, medical equipment and media-related industries (in its new Cultural Industries Quarter). Sheffield has two universities and is an important research centre.

The parish church of St Peter and St Paul, founded in the 12th century, became the Cathedral Church of the Diocese of Sheffield in 1914. The Roman Catholic Cathedral Church of St Marie (founded 1847) was created Cathedral for the new diocese of Hallam in 1980. Parts of the present building date from c.1435. The principal buildings are the Town Hall (1897), the Cutlers' Hall (1832), City Hall (1932), Graves Art Gallery (1934), Mappin Art Gallery, the Crucible Theatre and the restored 19th-century Lyceum theatre, which dates from 1897 and was reopened in 1990. Three major sports venues were opened in 1990 to 1991.

Sheffield was created a city in 1893.

Master Cutler of the Company of Cutlers in Hallamshire 1997–8, P. J. Tear

SOUTHAMPTON

Southampton is the leading British deep-sea port on the Channel and is situated on one of the finest natural harbours in the world. The first charter was granted by Henry II and Southampton was created a county of itself in 1447. In 1964 it was granted city status.

There were Roman and Saxon settlements on the site of the city, which has been an important port since the time of the Conquest due to its natural deep-water harbour. The oldest church is St Michael's (1070) which has an unusually tall spire built in the 18th century as a landmark for navigators of Southampton Water. Other buildings and monuments within the city walls are the Tudor House Museum, God's House Tower, the Bargate museum, the Tudor Merchants Hall, the Weigh-house, West Gate, King John's House, Long House, Wool House, the ruins of Holy Rood Church, St Julien's Church and the Mayflower Memorial. The medieval town walls, built for artillery, are among the most complete in Europe. Public open spaces total over 1,000 acres and comprise 9 per cent of the city's area. The Common covers an area of 328 acres in the central district of the city and is mostly natural parkland. Two recent additions to work in marine technology in Southampton are Europe's leading oceanographic research centre (part of the University) and the marine science and technology business park.

STOKE-ON-TRENT

Stoke-on-Trent, standing on the River Trent and familiarly known as The Potteries, is the main centre of employment for the population of North Staffordshire. The city is the largest clayware producer in the world (china, earthenware, sanitary goods, refractories, bricks and tiles) and also has a wide range of other manufacturing industry, including steel, chemicals, engineering and tyres. Extensive reconstruction has been carried out in recent years.

The city was formed by the federation of the separate municipal authorities of Tunstall, Burslem, Hanley, Stoke, Fenton, and Longton in 1910 and received its city status in 1925.

WINCHESTER

Winchester, the ancient capital of England, is situated on the River Itchen. The city is rich in architecture of all types but the Cathedral takes pride of place. The longest Gothic cathedral in the world, it was built in 1079–93 and exhibits examples of Norman, Early English and Perpendicular styles. Winchester College, founded in 1382, is one of the most famous public schools, the original building (1393) remaining largely unaltered. St Cross Hospital, another great medieval foundation, lies one mile south of the city. The almshouses were founded in 1136 by Bishop Henry de Blois, and Cardinal Henry Beaufort added a new almshouse of 'Noble Poverty' in 1446. The chapel and dwellings are of great architectural interest, and visitors may still receive the 'Wayfarer's Dole' of bread and ale.

Excavations have done much to clarify the origins and development of Winchester. Part of the forum and several of the streets of the Roman town have been discovered; excavations in the Cathedral Close have uncovered the entire site of the Anglo-Saxon cathedral (known as the Old Minster) and parts of the New Minster which was built by Alfred's son Edward the Elder and is the burial place of the Alfredian dynasty. The original burial place of St Swithun, before his remains were translated to a site in the present cathedral, was also uncovered.

Excavations in other parts of the city have thrown much light on Norman Winchester, notably on the site of the Royal Castle (adjacent to which the new Law Courts have been built) and in the grounds of Wolvesey Castle, where the great house built by Bishops Giffard and Henry de Blois in the 12th century has been uncovered. The Great Hall, built by Henry III between 1222 and 1236 survives and houses the Arthurian Round Table.

YORK

The city of York is an archiepiscopal seat. Its recorded history dates from AD 71, when the Roman Ninth Legion established a base under Petilius Cerealis which later became the fortress of *Eburacum*. In Anglo-Saxon times the city was the royal and ecclesiastical centre of Northumbria, and after capture by a Viking army in AD 866 it became the capital of the Viking kingdom of Jorvik. By the 14th century the city had become a great mercantile centre, mainly because of its control of the wool trade, and was used as the chief base against the Scots. Under the Tudors its fortunes declined, though Henry VIII made it the headquarters of the Council of the North. Excavations on many sites, including Coppergate, have greatly expanded knowledge of Roman, Viking and medieval urban life.

With its development as a railway centre in the 19th century the commercial life of York expanded. The principal industries are the manufacture of chocolate, scientific instruments and sugar. It is the location of several government departments.

The city is rich in examples of architecture of all periods. The earliest church was built in AD 627 and, in the 12th to 15th centuries, the present Minster was built in a succession of styles. Other examples within the city are the medieval city walls and gateways, churches and guildhalls. Domestic architecture includes the Georgian mansions of The Mount, Micklegate and Bootham.

English Counties and Shires

LORD-LIEUTENANTS AND HIGH SHERIFFS

County/Shire	Lord-Lieutenant	High Sheriff, 1998–9
Bedfordshire	S. C. Whitbread	G. R. D. Farr
Berkshire	P. L. Wroughton	A. R. Wiseman
Bristol	J. Tidmarsh, MBE	E. H. Webber
Buckinghamshire	Sir Nigel Mobbs	E. R. Verney
Cambridgeshire	J. G. P. Crowden	R. B. Bamford
Cheshire	W. A. Bromley-Davenport	M. A. T. Trevor-Barnston
Cornwall	Lady Holborow	P. R. Thompson
Cumbria	J. A. Cropper	S. P. Pease
Derbyshire	J. K. Bather	G. R. W. Turbutt
Devon	E. Dancer, CBE	The Lady Clinton
Dorset	The Lord Digby	Cdr. P. G. Gregson
Durham	Sir Paul Nicholson	Sir William Gray
East Riding of Yorkshire	R. Marriott, TD	C. A. Maxsted
East Sussex	Admiral Sir Lindsay Bryson, KCB, FRSE, FENG.	Viscountess Brentford, OBE
Essex	The Lord Braybrooke	R. G. Newman
Gloucestershire	H. W. G. Elwes	W. J. Eykyn
Greater London	Field Marshal the Lord Bramall, KG, GCB, OBE, MC	J. P. Gough
Greater Manchester	Col. J. B. Timmins, OBE, TD	J. R. L. Lee
Hampshire	Mrs F. M. Fagan	J. J. L. G. Sheffield
Herefordshire	Sir Thomas Dunne, KCVO	S. W. B. Dereham
Hertfordshire	S. A. Bowes Lyon	The Hon. R. O. Pleydell–Bouverie
Isle of Wight	*C. D. J. Bland	D. C. Biles
Kent	The Lord Kingsdown, KG, PC	J. P. Merricks
Lancashire	The Lord Shuttleworth	C. A. B. Brennan
Leicestershire	T. G. M. Brooks·¹	I. M. McAlpine
Lincolnshire	Mrs B. K. Cracroft-Eley	G. O. Hutchison
Merseyside	A. W. Waterworth	Col. Sir Christopher Hewetson
Norfolk	Sir Timothy Colman, KG	A. E. Buxton
Northamptonshire	Lady Juliet Townsend, LVO	Lady Morton
Northumberland	The Viscount Ridley, KG, GCVO, TD	C. A. F. Baker–Cresswell, OBE, TD
North Yorkshire	Sir Marcus Worsley, Bt.	Lady Clarissa Collin
Nottinghamshire	Sir Andrew Buchanan, Bt.	Mrs J. M. Farr
Oxfordshire	H. L. J. Brunner	R. Ovey
Rutland	Air Chief Marshal Sir Thomas Kennedy, GCB, AFC	Mrs L. L. Taylor
Shropshire	A. E. H. Heber-Percy	L. C. N. Bury
Somerset	Sir John Wills, Bt., KCVO, TD	Mrs M. E. B. Beckett
South Yorkshire	The Earl of Scarbrough	Mrs K. E. Riddle
Staffordshire	J. A. Hawley, TD	A. E. R. Manners
Suffolk	The Lord Belstead, PC	The Hon. P. V. Fisher
Surrey	Mrs S. J. F. Goad	R. H. S. Stilgoe
Tyne and Wear	Sir Ralph Carr-Ellison, TD	J. S. Ward
Warwickshire	M. Dunne	D. J. Barnes
West Midlands	R. R. Taylor, OBE	W. G. K. Carter
West Sussex	Maj.-Gen. Sir Philip Ward, KCVO, CBE	B. S. L. Trafford
West Yorkshire	J. Lyles, CBE	J. J. E. Brennan
Wiltshire	Lt.-Gen. Sir Maurice Johnston, KCB, OBE	Lady Hawley
Worcestershire	Sir Thomas Dunne, KCVO	S. W. B. Dereham

* Lord-Lieutenant and Governor

COUNTY COUNCILS: Area, Population, Finance

Council	Administrative headquarters	Area (hectares)	Population 1996	Total demand upon collection fund 1998–9
Bedfordshire	County Hall, Bedford	123,468	367,300	£83,800,000
Buckinghamshire	County Hall, Aylesbury	188,279	474,600	96,022,000
Cambridgeshire	Shire Hall, Cambridge	306,821	544,600	96,600,000
Cheshire	County Hall, Chester	207,773	668,000	162,108,375
Cornwall	County Hall, Truro	356,442†	483,300†	89,575,000
Cumbria	The Courts, Carlisle	682,451	490,600	102,929,000
Derbyshire	County Hall, Matlock	263,098	728,300	147,817,756
Devon	County Hall, Exeter	656,904	680,100	146,010,000
Dorset	County Hall, Dorchester	265,433	382,090	92,511,952
Durham	County Hall, Durham	243,369	506,900	89,757,000
East Sussex	Pelham House, St Andrew's Lane, Lewes	179,530	485,400	107,110,000
Essex	County Hall, Chelmsford	344,571	1,281,600	277,790,000
Gloucestershire	Shire Hall, Gloucester	264,270	556,300	106,305,850
Hampshire	The Castle, Winchester	378,022	1,222,100	254,437,000
Hertfordshire	County Hall, Hertford	163,601	1,015,800	215,000,000
§Isle of Wight	County Hall, Newport	38,063	125,500	32,345,480
Kent	County Hall, Maidstone	352,556	1,317,800	266,923,000
Lancashire	County Hall, Preston	288,899	1,132,700	237,446,000
Leicestershire	County Hall, Glenfield, Leicester	255,297	597,400	117,462,750
Lincolnshire	County Offices, Newland, Lincoln	591,791	615,900	109,602,000
Norfolk	County Hall, Norwich	537,482	777,000	147,841,234
North Yorkshire	County Hall, Northallerton	803,741	559,600	110,800,000
Northamptonshire	County Hall, Northampton	236,721	604,400	104,406,000
Northumberland	County Hall, Morpeth	503,165	307,400	64,807,000
Nottinghamshire	County Hall, Nottingham	208,620	747,800	158,977,000
Oxfordshire	County Hall, Oxford	260,798	603,200	116,550,537
Shropshire	The Shirehall, Shrewsbury	320,063	277,100	53,720,235
Somerset	County Hall, Taunton	345,233	482,700	95,000,000
Staffordshire	County Buildings, Stafford	271,616	801,300	137,394,388
Suffolk	County Hall, Ipswich	379,664	661,600	120,225,000
Surrey	County Hall, Kingston upon Thames	167,924	1,047,100	248,922,103
Warwickshire	Shire Hall, Warwick	198,052	500,600	105,701,357
West Sussex	County Hall, Chichester	198,935	737,300	161,589,000
Wiltshire	County Hall, Trowbridge	347,883	418,700	87,000,000
Worcestershire	County Hall, Worcester	173,529	505,050	97,586,466

Source for population figures: ONS Monitor PP1 97/1, 28 August 1997
† Including Isles of Scilly
§ Unitary authority since April 1995

544   Local Government

COUNTY COUNCILS: Officers and Chairman

Council	Chief Executive	County Treasurer	Chairman of County Council
Bedfordshire	D. Cleggett	°W. Dodds	J. Hawksby
Buckinghamshire	I. Crookall	§§S. Nolan	K. Ross
Cambridgeshire	A. Barnish	D. T. Earle	J. McKay
Cheshire	C. Cheesman (acting)	A. Cope	D. Newton
Cornwall	J. F. Mills	F. P. Twyning	W. R. Hosking
Cumbria	W. A. Swarbrick	R. F. Mather	R. Calvin
Derbyshire	A. R. N. Hodgson	P. Swaby	L. G. Cannon
Devon	P. Jenkinson	§J. Glasby	Mrs M. Rogers
Dorset	P. K. Harvey	A. P. Peel	Mrs P. Hymers
Durham	K. W. Smith	J. Kirkby	M. Nicholls
East Sussex	Mrs C. Miller	J. Davies	M. Skilton
Essex	K. W. S. Ashurst	K. D. Neale	D. F. Rex
Gloucestershire	R. Cockroft	‖R. Cockroft	J. Rawson
Hampshire	P. C. B. Robertson	J. C. Pittam	Capt. M. P. R. Boyle
Hertfordshire	W. D. Ogley	*C. Sweeney	Sir Norman Lindop
Isle of Wight	††F. Hetherington	J. Pulsford	J. Bowker
Kent	M. Pitt	**D. Lewis	Sir John Grugeon
Lancashire	G. A. Johnson	B. G. Aldred	Mrs I. Short
Leicestershire	J. B. Sinnott	A. Youd	Mrs C. Brock
Lincolnshire	M. Spink (acting)	‡‡M. Spink	J. Libell
Norfolk	T. Byles	R. D. Summers	G. B. Hemming
Northamptonshire	J. V. Picking	†R. Paver	M. Young
Northumberland	°°K. Morris	*K. Morris	P. Hillman
North Yorkshire	J. A. Ransford	†J. S. Moore	W. F. Barton
Nottinghamshire	P. J. Housden	R. Latham	Mrs S. M. Smedley
Oxfordshire	J. Harwood	C. Gray	B. Hook
Shropshire	N. T. Pursey	N. T. Pursey	Mrs J. Marsh
Somerset	Dr D. Radford	C. N. Bilsland	R. B. Clark
Staffordshire	B. A. Price, CBE	R. G. Tettenborn, OBE	T. R. Wright
Suffolk	L. Homer	‡‡P. B. Atkinson	D. F. Smith
Surrey	P. Coen	**P. Derrick	Mrs H. Hawker
Warwickshire	I. G. Caulfield	S. R. Freer	R. Sweet
West Sussex	D. P. Rigg	Mrs H. Kilpatrick	I. R. W. Elliott
Wiltshire	Dr K. Robinson	D. Chalker	Mrs B. M. Jay
Worcestershire	R. Sykes	‡M. Weaver	R. Clayton

* Director of Finance
° Corporate Finance Adviser
°° Managing Director
† Chief Financial Services Officer
‡ Director of Finance Services
†† Head of Paid Service
§ Director of Resources
§§ Head of Finance
** Director of Corporate Services
‡‡ Director of Finance and Resources
‖ County Director

Unitary Councils

Small capitals denote City status
§ Denotes Borough council

Council	Population 1996	Band D charge 1998*	Chief Executive	Mayor (a) Lord Mayor (b) Chairman 1998–9
§Barnsley	227,200	£734.89	J. Edwards, OBE	F. Wright
Bath and North-East Somerset	164,700	762.68	J. Everitt	(b) T. Ball
§Birmingham	1,020,600	846.00	M. Lyons	(a) Ms S. Anderson
Blackburn with Darwen	139,500	870.41	P. S. Watson	Ms F. Oldfield
Blackpool	152,500	632.93	G. E. Essex-Crosby	H. Mitchell
§Bolton	265,400	845.39	B. Knight	P. Finch
Bournemouth	160,700	702.60	D. Newell	K. Rawlings
Bracknell Forest	110,100	670.30	G. Mitchell	J. Finnie
§Bradford	483,400	761.48	R. Penn	(a) T. Miller
Brighton and Hove	249,500	652.00	G. Jones	F. Tonks
§Bristol	399,600	986.00	Ms L. de Groot	(a) G. Robertson
§Bury	181,900	752.71	D. Taylor	Ms C. M. Fitzgerald
§Calderdale	192,800	839.12	P. Sheehan	A. Worth
§Coventry	306,500	897.22	I. Roxburgh	(a) Ms M. Rosher
Darlington	101,300	658.31	B. Keel	Miss P. Buttle
§Derby	233,700	728.67	R. H. Cowlishaw	A. Rehman
§Doncaster	291,800	716.51	A. M. Taylor (acting)	Mrs Y. Woodock
§Dudley	312,200	744.30	A. V. Astling	K. Finch
East Riding of Yorkshire	308,700	808.54	D. Stephenson	(b) D. Ireland
§Gateshead	201,000	927.06	L. N. Elton	B. Richmond
Halton	123,000	643.38	M. Cuff	T. McDermott
Hartlepool	92,100	924.36	B. J. Dinsdale	H. Clouth
Herefordshire	191,550	658.17	N. Pringle	(b) G. Hyde
Kingston upon Hull	266,800	756.79	I. Crookham	(a) B. A. Petch
§Kirklees	388,800	843.00	T. Elson	M. Bower
§Knowsley	154,100	942.83	D. G. Henshaw	S. Byron
§Leeds	726,900	734.71	†J. P. Smith	(a) G. P. Kirkland
Leicester	294,800	764.61	R. Green	(a) J. Mugglestone
§Liverpool	468,000	1,171.54	P. Bounds	(a) H. Herrity
Luton	181,500	653.98	Mrs K. Jones	D. Patten
§Manchester	430,800	949.49	H. Bernstein	(a) G. Conquest
Medway	239,500	634.21	Ms J. Armitt	N. Carter
Middlesbrough	146,800	746.16	¶J. E. Foster	F. Gill
Milton Keynes	197,100	687.00	H. Miller	G. Gillingham
§Newcastle upon Tyne	282,300	905.89	K. G. Lavery	(a) T. D. Marshall
North East Lincolnshire	158,500	827.35	R. Bentham	Ms C. Dixon
North Lincolnshire	152,800	977.81	Dr M. Garnett	A. Smith
North Somerset	185,300	682.66	P. May	J. Hayes
§North Tyneside	193,600	846.30	Executive Directorate	Ms A. Richardson
Nottingham City	284,000	832.19	E. F. Cantle	(a) J. A. Donn
§Oldham	220,200	865.00	C. Smith	(a) Ms M. Riley
Peterborough	158,700	695.48	W. E. Samuel	Ms M. Rainey
Plymouth	255,800	645.49	Mrs A. Stone	(a) Mrs E. Evans
Poole	139,200	673.83	J. Brooks	J. G. S. Curtis
Portsmouth	190,400	634.41	N. Gurney	(a) Ms P. Webb
Reading	142,900	799.83	Ms J. Markham	D. Geary
Redcar and Cleveland	139,800	977.00	A. W. Kilburn	G. Houchen
§Rochdale	207,600	820.72	Mrs F. W. Done	H. Hardiker
§Rotherham	255,300	760.14	A. G. Carruthers	R. Windle
Rutland	35,300	864.04	Dr J. R. Morphet	(b) Col. J. M. K. Weir
§St Helens	179,500	948.65	Mrs C. Hudson	D. Craig
§Salford	229,200	917.79	J. C. Willis	W. Moores
§Sandwell	292,200	800.47	F. N. Summers	B. James
§Sefton	289,700	872.17	G. J. Haywood	P. J. McVey
§Sheffield	530,400	836.74	B. Kerslake	(a) T. Arber
Slough	110,500	648.73	Ms C. Coppell	G. S. Thind
§Solihull	203,900	693.15	Dr N. H. Perry	P. Hogarth

Council	Population 1996	Band D charge 1998*	Chief Executive	Mayor (a) Lord Mayor (b) Chairman 1998–9
SOUTHAMPTON	214,900	663.66	J. Cairns	vacant
South Gloucestershire	235,100	705.20	M. Robinson	(b) R Springer
Southend	172,300	648.06	J. K. M. Krawiec	Mrs N. T. Goodman
§South Tyneside	156,100	837.97	‡P. J. Haigh	B. Scorer
§Stockport	291,100	871.24	J. Schultz	G. Cooper
Stockton-on-Tees	179,000	801.85	G. Garlick	Mrs A. McCoy
STOKE-ON-TRENT	254,400	707.20	B. Smith	(a) Ms K. M. Banks
§SUNDERLAND	294,300	760.30	Dr C. W. Sinclair	W. Scott
Swindon	174,600	638.77	P. Doherty	B. Ford
§Tameside	220,700	862.20	M. J. Greenwood	J. Middleton
Telford and Wrekin	144,200	522.95	D. Hutchison	(b) M. Smith
Thurrock	132,300	630.27	K. Barnes	A. Bennett
Torbay	123,400	645.26	A. Hodgkiss	V. McCann
§Trafford	218,900	657.00	W. Allan Lewis	Mrs C. S. Merry
§WAKEFIELD	317,300	711.78	R. Mather	A. Barlow
§Walsall	262,600	741.18	D. C. Winchurch	E. W. Newman
Warrington	189,000	688.35	S. Broomhead	A. Clemow
West Berkshire	143,700	799.41	Ms S. Manzie	G. Vernon-Jackson
§Wigan	309,800	747.58	S. M. Jones	S. Little
Windsor and Maidenhead	141,500	708.70	D. C. Lunn	Mrs K. Newbound
§Wirral	329,200	913.99	S. Maddox	Ms M. Green
Wokingham	142,400	765.99	Mrs G. Norton	(b) Mrs P. Helliar-Symons
§Wolverhampton	244,500	913.68	D. Anderson	Mrs G. M. Stafford-Good
YORK	175,100	669.37	D. Clark	(a) D. Smallwood

Source of population figures: ONS Monitor PP1 97/1, 28 August 1997
* For explanation of council tax, *see* pages 523–4
† The Chief Officer
‡ Head of Paid Service
¶ Managing Director

District Councils

SMALL CAPITALS denote CITY status
§ Denotes Borough status
Source of population figures: ONS Monitor PP1 97/2, 28 August 1997
For explanation of council tax, *see* pages 523–4
* Executive Director
† General Manager
‡ Head of Paid Service
†† The Chief Officer
¶ Managing Director

Council	Population 1996	Band D charge 1998	Chief Executive	Chairman 1998–9 (a) Mayor (b) Lord Mayor
Adur	58,900	748.19	I. Lowrie	Ms G. Hammond
§Allerdale	95,700	818.61	C. J. Hart	(a) Mrs J. McKeown
Alnwick	31,100	849.31	L. A. B. St Ruth	J. Hobson
§Amber Valley	115,200	764.76	P. M. Carney	(a) Mrs J. M. Sanders
Arun	138,000	724.75	I. Sumnall	A. M. Williamson
Ashfield	108,600	840.84	E. N. Bernasconi	J. M. A. Wilmott
§Ashford	97,900	689.60	A. Baker	(a) D. S. Madgett
Aylesbury Vale	154,900	683.37	B. Hurley	Mrs F. Roberts, MBE
Babergh	79,000	707.78	D. C. Bishop	R. E. Kemp
§Barrow-in-Furness	71,600	833.92	T. O. Campbell	(a) Mrs M. T. Irwin
Basildon	163,300	760.40	J. Robb	R. Sears
§Basingstoke and Deane	147,900	705.00	Mrs K. Sporle	(a) D. Mirfin
Bassetlaw	106,300	829.05	M. S. Havenhand	Mrs J. Pimperton
§Bedford	137,500	791.16	L. W. Gould	(a) A. Ruffin
§Berwick-upon-Tweed	26,600	818.03	E. O. Cawthorn, TD	(a) J. F. Hills
Blaby	85,600	571.34	E. Hemsley	F. G. H. Jackson
§Blyth Valley	80,000	812.49	D. Crawford	(a) Mrs M. E. Gilchrist

Council	Population 1996	Band D charge 1998	Chief Executive	Chairman 1998–9 (a) Mayor (b) Lord Mayor
Bolsover	70,900	838.58	J. R. Fotherby	S. Patrick
§Boston	54,200	740.96	M. James	(a) A. Day
Braintree	126,200	731.26	Ms A. F. Ralph	Mrs R. Mayes
Breckland	113,700	682.23	R. Garnett	J. Boddy
§Brentwood	71,700	714.69	C. P. Sivell	(a) Ms M. Hogan
Bridgnorth	50,800	715.91	Mrs T. M. Elliott	D. Beechey
Broadland	113,900	699.44	J. Bryant	G. E. Debbage
Bromsgrove	85,200	652.39	D. A. H. Bryant	T. M. Crashley
§Broxbourne	81,800	663.61	M. J. Walker	(a) M. Milovanovic
§Broxtowe	111,400	840.68	M. Brown	(a) R. Todd
§Burnley	90,500	879.79	R. Ellis	(a) E. Selby
CAMBRIDGE	116,700	682.32	R. Hammond	(a) P. Cowell
Cannock Chase	90,800	716.79	M. G. Kemp	Mrs P. Z. Stretton
CANTERBURY	136,500	696.31	C. Carmichael	(b) P. Wales
Caradon	79,700	695.43	Dr. J. Neal	B. G. Wilson, TD
CARLISLE	103,100	843.60	R. S. Brackley	(a) Mrs H. Bradley
Carrick	84,900	711.53	J. P. Winskill	Mrs S. C. Shaw
§Castle Morpeth	49,600	833.73	P. Wilson	(a) N. Weatherly
§Castle Point	84,900	747.36	B. Rollinson	(a) Mrs V. Wells
§Charnwood	155,700	773.54	Mr S. M. Peatfield	(a) Mrs I. Thurlby
§Chelmsford	156,600	723.88	M. Easteal	(a) W. R. C. Lane
§Cheltenham	106,700	705.47	L. Davison	(a) Rev. J. Whales
Cherwell	132,700	643.84	G. J. Handley	Mrs W. Humphries
CHESTER	119,200	820.51	P. F. Durham	(b) D. Neild
§Chesterfield	100,700	795.36	D. R. Shaw	(a) M. Fanshawe
Chester-le-Street	56,100	794.97	J. A. Greensmith	J. Lines
Chichester	104,100	696.00	J. S. Marsland	A. J. French, TD
Chiltern	92,500	711.43	A. Goodrum	S. W. James
§Chorley	96,600	822.17	J. W. Davies	(a) A. Whittaker
§Christchurch	43,200	763.56	M. A. Turvey	(a) J. Lofts
§Colchester	154,200	713.53	J. Cobley	(a) D. Cannon
§Congleton	86,600	811.82	¶P. Cooper	(a) R. Fletcher
§Copeland	70,700	821.89	†Dr J. Stanforth	(a) Mrs H. Richardson
§Corby	52,100	707.12	N. Rudd	(a) G. McCart
Cotswold	81,500	703.46	N. C. Abbott	Mrs P. Pretty
Craven	51,300	625.04	Dr G. Taylor	Mrs J. Gott
§Crawley	93,200	709.56	M. D. Sander	(a) A. Kane
§Crewe and Nantwich	113,700	697.19	A. Wenham	(a) R. Stafford
§Dacorum	134,700	676.60	K. Hunt	(a) Ms M. Flint
§Dartford	83,900	705.87	C. R. Shepherd	(a) I. Jones
Daventry	65,300	677.95	P. Cook	A. Goodridge
Derbyshire Dales	69,600	990.00	D. Wheatcroft	A. S. Thomas
Derwentside	87,700	859.54	‡A. Hodgson	R. McArdle
Dover	107,400	708.21	J. P. Moir, TD	W. V. Newman
DURHAM	90,100	815.91	C. Shearsmith	(a) D. Young
Easington	95,200	885.72	†P. Innes	J. Atkinson
§Eastbourne	89,000	734.18	Mrs S. E. Conway	(a) Mrs B. Healy
East Cambridgeshire	67,500	645.82	R. C. Carr	P. I. Warren
East Devon	123,100	705.30	F. J. Vallender	Miss S. M. Randall Johnson
East Dorset	82,000	778.06	A. Breakwell	D. Mills
East Hampshire	110,800	735.36	Miss J. Hunter	J. Palmer
East Hertfordshire	123,600	656.38	R. J. Bailey	R. Parker
§Eastleigh	111,700	737.00	C. Tapp	(a) Mrs M. Kyrle, OBE
East Lindsey	123,100	722.39	P. Haigh	T. Carpenter
East Northamptonshire	70,800	709.07	R. K. Heath	Mrs E. M. Dicks
§East Staffordshire	100,400	720.08	F. W. Saunders	(a) T. M. Dawn
Eden	48,600	822.17	I. W. Bruce	J. B. Thornborrow
§Ellesmere Port and Neston	80,700	828.83	S. Ewbank	(a) R. J. Santo
§Elmbridge	124,500	721.58	D. W. L. Jenkins	(a) D. Denyer
Epping Forest	119,500	733.50	J. Burgess	M. Heavens
§Epsom and Ewell	69,300	692.44	D. J. Smith	(a) P. Ardern-Jones
§Erewash	106,800	795.03	G. A. Pook	(a) Ms B. White
EXETER	107,700	684.78	P. Bostock	(a) B. McNamara
§Fareham	103,700	702.54	A. A. Davies	(a) G. Neill
Fenland	79,200	660.00	N. R. Topliss	A. R. German

Council	Population 1996	Band D charge 1998	Chief Executive	Chairman 1998–9 (a) Mayor (b) Lord Mayor
Forest Heath	68,600	666.58	††D. W. Burnip, R. D. Bolton, P. Nock	Mrs P. J. Barker
Forest of Dean	76,000	721.62	Ms M. Holborow	Mrs S. M. McDonagh
§Fylde	75,000	821.94	J. R. Wilkinson	(a) Mrs E. A. Smith, OBE
§Gedling	112,200	825.07	D. Kennedy	(a) Mrs J. P. Collins
GLOUCESTER	106,800	698.45	G. Garbutt	(a) Ms J. Lugg
§Gosport	76,400	719.20	M. Crocker	(a) Mrs L. G. Barker
§Gravesham	91,700	672.34	E. C. Anderson	(a) E. A. Brook
§Great Yarmouth	89,300	694.57	R. W. Packham	J. Barnes
§Guildford	124,600	701.65	D. T. Watts	(a) K. Childs
Hambleton	84,700	628.89	P. Simpson	Mrs B. Walkington
Harborough	73,700	762.99	M. C. Wilson	Mrs E. D. Derrick
Harlow	73,400	820.57	†D. F. Byrne	P. Bellairs
§Harrogate	147,600	702.31	P. M. Walsh	(a) Mrs R. Timmis
Hart	85,800	700.00	G. R. Jelbart	Ms S. Wallis
§Hastings	82,000	757.37	R. Mawford	(a) G. Daniel
§Havant	117,300	714.23	R. G. Smith	(a) F. W. G. Pearce
§Hertsmere	94,900	706.98	P. H. Copland	(a) D. Banks
§High Peak	88,200	805.79	R. P. H. Brady	(a) Ms J. Brocklehurst
§Hinckley and Bosworth	97,800	729.87	vacant	(a) G. H. Payne
Horsham	118,600	682.12	M. J. Pearson	Mrs C. A. Sully
Huntingdonshire	152,700	656.63	D. Monks	Mrs P. Newbon
§Hyndburn	79,900	868.45	M. J. Chambers	(a) I. J. Ormerod
§Ipswich	113,600	768.96	J. D. Hehir	(a) G. H. Clarke
Kennet	75,500	715.76	P. L. Owens	Mrs S. Findlay
Kerrier	89,100	710.92	G. G. Fox	N. Stevens
§Kettering	80,800	716.04	P. Walker	(a) D. Whyte
§King's Lynn and West Norfolk	131,200	705.86	A. E. Pask	(a) P. Richards
LANCASTER	136,900	822.31	D. Corker	(a) A. C. Bryning
Lewes	86,900	743.25	J. N. Crawford	P. E. C. McCausland
Lichfield	93,200	707.47	J. T. Thompson	J. A. Brookes
LINCOLN	83,500	750.24	A. Sparke	(a) B. Robinson
§Macclesfield	152,600	807.19	B. W. Longden	(a) T. C. Scanlon
§Maidstone	140,700	730.53	J. D. Makepeace	(a) R. T. Judd
Maldon	54,600	717.10	E. A. P. Plumridge	J. Smith
Malvern Hills	91,000	667.14	C. Brook	Mrs E. Williams
Mansfield	101,400	840.01	R. P. Goad	S.Cornish
§Melton	46,500	758.42	P. M. Murphy	(a) R. F. Moore-Coltman
Mendip	98,400	726.35	G. Jeffs	J. Gilham
Mid Bedfordshire	118,900	771.30	C. A. Tucker	N. Cliff
Mid Devon	66,000	720.27	M. I. R. Bull	D. F. Pugsley
Mid Suffolk	80,400	705.66	G. R. Chilton	R. D. Snell
Mid Sussex	125,300	715.39	W. J. H. Hatton	D. Coombes
Mole Valley	79,400	772.95	Mrs H. Kerswell	J. Butcher
Newark and Sherwood	104,500	896.94	R. G. Dix	A. P. Hannaford
§Newcastle under Lyme	122,300	709.76	F. Harley	(a) Mrs B. Blaise
New Forest	169,500	741.50	¶I. B. Mackintosh	Mrs A. M. Howe
§Northampton	192,400	724.72	R. J. B. Morris	(a) U. E. Gravesande
North Cornwall	78,700	717.53	D. Brown	D. Coad
North Devon	86,200	737.48	D. T. Cunliffe	L. H. Ellway
North Dorset	58,200	734.78	Ms E. Peters	M. F. Lane
North East Derbyshire	99,000	843.31	‡Ms C. A. Gilby	Mrs P. Booker
North Hertfordshire	114,900	706.31	S. Philp	Mrs J. Billing
North Kesteven	86,600	712.21	Mrs R. Barlow	J. C. Rose
North Norfolk	96,900	691.02	B. A. Barrell	T. H. Moore
North Shropshire	54,100	746.43	R. J. Hughes	Ms P. Dee
§North Warwickshire	61,400	804.37	J. Hutchinson	(a) Ms B. Stuart
North West Leicestershire	84,300	784.67	M. J. Diaper	H. Sankey
North Wiltshire	121,700	740.44	R. Marshall	B. E. Atfield
NORWICH	126,200	663.75	J. R. Packer	(b) D. Wood
§Nuneaton and Bedworth	118,300	783.82	Ms C. Kerr	(a) R. Chattaway
§Oadby and Wigston	53,500	755.61	Mrs R. E. Hyde	(a) Mrs L. Thornton
§Oswestry	34,600	727.76	D. A. Towers	(a) S. F. Brown
OXFORD	137,300	759.31	R. S. Block	(b) Ms C. Roberts
§Pendle	84,300	875.06	S. Barnes	(a) C. Waite

Council	Population 1996	Band D charge 1998	Chief Executive	Chairman 1998–9 (a) Mayor (b) Lord Mayor
Penwith	59,600	694.50	‡D. H. Hosken	W. T. Trevorrow
§Preston	134,800	890.61	J. E. Carr	(a) Mrs R. Kinsella
Purbeck	45,300	762.68	P. B. Croft	S. C. S. Hinn
§Redditch	77,200	699.22	Ms K. Kerswell	(a) A. Fry
§Reigate and Banstead	119,300	713.00	M. Bacon	(a) J. H. Prevett, OBE
§Restormel	89,500	697.98	Mrs P. Crowson	(a) M. E. R. Burley
§Ribble Valley	52,700	835.29	D. Morris	(a) D. Smith
Richmondshire	47,300	695.53	H. Tabiner	Mrs S. P. Golding
Rochford	76,500	722.07	R. A. Lovell	G. Fox
§Rossendale	64,900	873.74	J. S. Hartley	(a) Ms M. Disley
Rother	89,500	721.63	D. F. Powell	A. Fleming
§Rugby	87,100	778.50	Mrs D. M. Colley	(a) Mrs H. Bell
§Runnymede	76,000	634.59	T. N. Williams	(a) G. B. Woodger
§Rushcliffe	103,500	823.80	K. Beaumont	(a) P. Smith
§Rushmoor	85,800	717.29	J. A. Lloyd	(a) P. J. Moyle
Ryedale	49,100	717.75	H. W. Mosley	G. W. Hobbs
St Albans	130,300	701.77	E. A. Hackford	(a) B. Peyton
§St Edmundsbury	93,600	692.96	G. R. N. Toft	(a) Mrs M. Martin
Salisbury	112,500	724.86	R. Sheard	M. Humphreys
§Scarborough	108,300	698.00	J. M. Trebble	(a) F. Standing
§Sedgefield	90,000	928.45	N. Vaulks	(a) J. Moran
Sedgemoor	101,900	610.75	A. G. Lovell	P. I. Johnstone
Selby	71,300	719.00	M. Connor	Mrs M. Stone
Sevenoaks	110,500	715.12	N. Howells	Mrs N. Munson
Shepway	98,700	726.91	R. J. Thompson	K. D. Hudson
§Shrewsbury and Atcham	97,100	693.76	D. Bradbury	(a) Ms J. A. Williams
South Bedfordshire	110,900	840.92	J. Ruddick	S. H. M. Owen
South Bucks	63,100	693.40	C. R. Furness	R. J. Worrall
South Cambridgeshire	128,400	596.59	J. S. Ballantyne	A. W. Wyatt
South Derbyshire	77,800	795.86	D. J. Dugdale	J. Ford
South Hams	79,300	722.01	M. S. Carpenter	Miss J. A. Westacott
South Holland	71,400	746.80	C. J. Simpkins	R. B. Hartfil
South Kesteven	120,000	722.01	C. Farmer	Mrs J. Gaffigan
South Lakeland	100,900	816.77	A. F. Winstanley	J. Studholme
South Norfolk	105,800	714.45	A. G. T. Kellett	Mrs S. Beare
South Northamptonshire	75,000	738.22	R. Tinlin	B. Stimpson
South Oxfordshire	124,600	704.99	R. Watson	Ms C. Heath-Whyte
§South Ribble	103,000	821.85	P. Halsall	(a) J. Owen
South Shropshire	40,500	732.44	G. C. Biggs, MBE	R. D. Phillips
South Somerset	150,700	730.08	M. Usher, OBE	N. Speakman
South Staffordshire	103,300	632.25	L. T. Barnfield	K. E. Mackie
§Spelthorne	89,200	707.45	M. B. Taylor	(a) Mrs D. L. Grant
§Stafford	124,500	705.12	D. Rawlings	(a) H. Brunt
Staffordshire Moorlands	94,400	743.87	B. J. Preedy	Mrs D. Lythgoe
§Stevenage	76,800	705.25	I. Paske	(a) W. L. Lawrence
Stratford-on-Avon	111,200	733.51	I. B. Prosser	Ms A. Simpson
Stroud	108,000	757.24	R. M. Ollin	Mrs M. E. A. Nolder
Suffolk Coastal	118,700	697.83	T. K. Griffin	Mrs M. J. Dixon
§Surrey Heath	82,400	703.17	B. R. Catchpole	(a) Mrs J. P. White
§Swale	117,600	687.23	J. C. Edwards	(a) G. Lewin
§Tamworth	72,400	676.50	C. Moore	(a) D. N. Thompson
Tandridge	77,600	712.62	P. J. D. Thomas	R. Harling
§Taunton Deane	98,900	695.61	†Mrs S. Douglas	(a) W. E. Softley
Teesdale	24,500	809.00	C. M. Anderson	Mrs K. M. Mitchell
Teignbridge	116,700	725.00	B. T. Jones	M. J. Haines
Tendring	132,300	722.28	J. Hawkins	L. Randall
§Test Valley	107,200	696.74	A. Jones	(a) A. Jackson
§Tewkesbury	77,300	648.26	H. Davis	(a) Mrs P. E. Stokes
Thanet	125,500	722.65	D. Ralls, CBE, DFC	Mrs M. Davies
Three Rivers	84,600	707.45	A. Robertson	Ms B. Lamb
§Tonbridge and Malling	105,000	718.02	T. Thompson	(a) Ms S. Levett
Torridge	54,400	721.74	R. K. Brasington	F. Howard, MBE
§Tunbridge Wells	102,600	870.39	R. J. Stone	(a) A. J. Baker
Tynedale	58,000	833.45	A. Baty	Mrs D. Elwell
Uttlesford	68,500	734.45	K. Ivory	R. B. Tyler

Council	Population 1996	Band D charge 1998	Chief Executive	Chairman 1998–9 (a) Mayor (b) Lord Mayor
Vale of White Horse	112,500	663.47	T. Stock	Mrs J. Hutchinson
§Vale Royal	115,200	833.71	W. R. T. Woods	(a) K. Musgrave
Wansbeck	62,200	832.00	A. G. White	Ms M. Wallace
Warwick	122,500	754.33	Miss J. Barrett	G. Darmody
§Watford	78,900	768.30	Ms C. Hassan	(a) Ms D. Thornhill
Waveney	107,700	675.08	M. Berridge	F. Devereux
§Waverley	114,100	717.60	Miss C. L. Pointer	(a) J. M. Savage
Wealden	138,000	763.05	D. R. Holness	R. I. F. Parsons
Wear Valley	63,300	832.95	*Mrs C. Hughes	H. Douthwaite
§Wellingborough	67,900	628.43	T. McArdle	(a) M. Prescod
Welwyn Hatfield	95,400	702.10	M. Saminaden	Mrs S. Jones
§West Devon	46,400	743.95	D. J. Incoll	(a) D. Bater
West Dorset	90,300	769.98	R. C. Rennison	Mrs N. M. Penfold
West Lancashire	109,800	840.62	W. J. Taylor	D. Thompson
West Lindsey	77,200	757.98	R. W. Nelsey	C. R. Ireland
West Oxfordshire	96,000	656.45	G. Bonner	A. Walker
West Somerset	32,800	727.47	C. W. Rockall	Mrs A. Cave-Browne-Cave
West Wiltshire	108,900	872.75	J. Ligo	P. J. Bryant
§Weymouth and Portland	62,800	770.54	M. N. Ashby	(a) H. R. Legg
WINCHESTER	106,000	716.96	D. H. Cowan	(a) G. Fothergill
§Woking	90,700	710.46	P. Russell	(a) Mrs R. P. Johnson
WORCESTER	92,300	661.09	D. Wareing	(a) D. Prodger
§Worthing	99,200	709.29	M. J. Ball	(a) D. Chapman
Wychavon	108,000	677.45	W. S. Nott	J. Payne
Wycombe	164,000	704.28	R. J. Cummins	E. H. Collins
§Wyre	104,300	829.98	M. Brown	(a) R. Sharrock
Wyre Forest	96,700	691.00	W. S. Baldwin	C. D. Nicholls

The Cinque Ports

As their name implies, the Cinque Ports were originally five in number: Hastings, New Romney, Hythe, Dover and Sandwich. They were formed during the 11th century to defend the Channel coast and, after the Norman Conquest, were recognized as a Confederation by a charter of 1278. The 'antient towns' of Winchelsea and Rye were added at some time after the Conquest. The other members of the Confederation, known as Limbs, are Lydd, Faversham, Folkestone, Deal, Tenterden, Margate and Ramsgate.

Until 1855 the duty of the Cinque Ports was to provide ships and men for the defence of the state in return for considerable privileges, such as tax exemptions and the framing of by-laws. Of these privileges only jurisdiction in Admiralty remains.

The Barons of the Cinque Ports have the ancient privilege of attending the Coronation ceremony and are allotted special places in Westminster Abbey.

Lord Warden of the Cinque Ports, HM Queen Elizabeth the Queen Mother

Judge, Court of Admiralty, Hon. Sir Anthony Clarke

Registrar, I. G. Gill, LVO, 7 Rosetower Court, Broadstairs, Kent CT10 3BG. Tel: 01843-861177

LORD WARDENS OF THE CINQUE PORTS since 1904

The Marquess Curzon	1904
The Prince of Wales	1905
The Earl Brassey	1908
The Earl Beauchamp	1913
The Marquess of Reading	1934
The Marquess of Willingdon	1936
Winston Churchill	1941
Sir Robert Menzies	1965
HM Queen Elizabeth the Queen Mother	1978

1   Stockton-on-Tees
2   Middlesbrough
3   Blackpool
4   Blackburn
    with Darwen
5   Bolton
6   Bury
7   Rochdale
8   Salford
9   Oldham
10 Liverpool
11 Knowsley
12 St Helens
13 Halton
14 Warrington
15 Trafford
16 Manchester
17 Tameside
18 Stockport
19 Nottingham
20 Telford and
    Wrekin
21 Wolverhampton

22 Walsall
23 Sandwell
24 Dudley
25 Birmingham
26 Solihull
27 Coventry
28 Peterborough
29 South Glos
30 Bristol
31 Bath and
    NE Somerset
32 Windsor and
    Maidenhead
33 Slough
34 Reading
35 Wokingham
36 Bracknell Forest
37 Thurrock
38 Southend
39 Medway
40 Plymouth
41 Torbay

LONDON

1   Hillingdon
2   Harrow
3   Barnet
4   Enfield
5   Waltham Forest
6   Redbridge
7   Barking and Dagenham
8   Havering
9   Ealing
10 Brent
11 Camden
12 Haringey
13 Islington
14 Hackney
15 Newham
16 Hounslow
17 Hammersmith and Fulham

18 Kensington and Chelsea
19 City of Westminster
20 City of London
21 Tower Hamlets
22 Richmond upon Thames
23 Wandsworth
24 Lambeth
25 Southwark
26 Lewisham
27 Greenwich
28 Bexley
29 Kingston upon Thames
30 Merton
31 Sutton
32 Croydon
33 Bromley

London

THE CORPORATION OF LONDON
(*see also* page 526)

The City of London is the historic centre at the heart of London known as 'the square mile' around which the vast metropolis has grown over the centuries. The City's residential population is 5,500. The civic government is carried on by the Corporation of London through the Court of Common Council.

The City is an international financial centre, generating over £20 billion a year for the British economy. It includes the head offices of the principal banks, insurance companies and mercantile houses, in addition to buildings ranging from the historic Roman Wall and the 15th-century Guildhall, to the massive splendour of St Paul's Cathedral and the architectural beauty of Wren's spires.

The City of London was described by Tacitus in AD 62 as 'a busy emporium for trade and traders'. Under the Romans it became an important administration centre and hub of the road system. Little is known of London in Saxon times, when it formed part of the kingdom of the East Saxons. In 886 Alfred recovered London from the Danes and reconstituted it a burgh under his son-in-law. In 1066 the citizens submitted to William the Conqueror who in 1067 granted them a charter, which is still preserved, establishing them in the rights and privileges they had hitherto enjoyed.

THE MAYORALTY

The Mayoralty was probably established about 1189, the first Mayor being Henry Fitz Ailwyn who filled the office for 23 years and was succeeded by Fitz Alan (1212–14). A new charter was granted by King John in 1215, directing the Mayor to be chosen annually, which has ever since been done, though in early times the same individual often held the office more than once. A familiar instance is that of 'Whittington, thrice Lord Mayor of London' (in reality four times, 1397, 1398, 1406, 1419); and many modern cases have occurred. The earliest instance of the phrase 'Lord Mayor' in English is in 1414. It was used more generally in the latter part of the 15th century and became invariable from 1535 onwards. At Michaelmas the liverymen in Common Hall choose two Aldermen who have served the office of Sheriff for presentation to the Court of Aldermen, and one is chosen to be Lord Mayor for the following mayoral year.

LORD MAYOR'S DAY

The Lord Mayor of London was previously elected on the feast of St Simon and St Jude (28 October), and from the time of Edward I, at least, was presented to the King or to the Barons of the Exchequer on the following day, unless that day was a Sunday. The day of election was altered to 16 October in 1346, and after some further changes was fixed for Michaelmas Day in 1546, but the ceremonies of admittance and swearing-in of the Lord Mayor continued to take place on 28 and 29 October respectively until 1751. In 1752, at the reform of the calendar, the Lord Mayor continued in office until 8 November, the 'New Style' equivalent of 28 October. The Lord Mayor is now presented to the Lord Chief Justice at the Royal Courts of Justice on the second Saturday in November to make the final declaration of office, having been sworn in at Guildhall on the preceding day. The procession to the

Royal Courts of Justice is popularly known as the Lord Mayor's Show.

REPRESENTATIVES

Aldermen are mentioned in the 11th century and their office is of Saxon origin. They were elected annually between 1377 and 1394, when an Act of Parliament of Richard II directed them to be chosen for life.

The Common Council, elected annually on the first Friday in December, was, at an early date, substituted for a popular assembly called the *Folkmote*. At first only two representatives were sent from each ward, but the number has since been greatly increased.

OFFICERS

Sheriffs were Saxon officers; their predecessors were the *wic-reeves* and *portreeves* of London and Middlesex. At first they were officers of the Crown, and were named by the Barons of the Exchequer; but Henry I (in 1132) gave the citizens permission to choose their own Sheriffs, and the annual election of Sheriffs became fully operative under King John's charter of 1199. The citizens lost this privilege, as far as the election of the Sheriff of Middlesex was concerned, by the Local Government Act 1888; but the liverymen continue to choose two Sheriffs of the City of London, who are appointed on Midsummer Day and take office at Michaelmas.

The office of Chamberlain is an ancient one, the first contemporary record of which is 1237. The Town Clerk (or Common Clerk) is mentioned in 1274.

ACTIVITIES

The work of the Corporation is assigned to a number of committees which present reports to the Court of Common Council. These Committees are: City Lands and Bridge House Grants Estates, Policy and Resources, Finance, Planning and Transportation, Central Markets, Billingsgate and Leadenhall Markets, Spitalfields Market, Police, Port and City of London Health and Social Services, Libraries, Art Galleries and Records, Board of Governors of City of London Freemen's School, Music and Drama (Guildhall School of Music and Drama), Establishment, Housing and Sports Development, Gresham (City side), Hampstead Heath Management, Epping Forest and Open Spaces, West Ham Park, Privileges, Barbican Residential and Barbican Centre (Barbican Arts and Conference Centre).

The City's estate, in the possession of which the Corporation of London differs from other municipalities, is managed by the City Lands and Bridge House Grants Estates Committee, the chairmanship of which carries with it the title of Chief Commoner.

The Honourable the Irish Society, which manages the Corporation's estates in Ulster, consists of a Governor and five other Aldermen, the Recorder, and 19 Common Councilmen, of whom one is elected Deputy Governor.

THE LORD MAYOR 1997–8*

The Rt. Hon. the Lord Mayor, Sir Richard Nichols
  Secretary, Air Vice-Marshal M. Dicken, CB

THE SHERIFFS 1998–9

G. F. Arthur (*Alderman, Cripplegate*) and B. N. Harris (*Councilman, Broad Street*); *elected*, 24 June 1998; *assumed office*, 28 September 1998

---

* The Lord Mayor for 1998–9 was elected on Michaelmas Day. *See* Stop-press

OFFICERS, ETC

Town Clerk and Chamberlain, B. P. Harty
Chief Commoner (1998), R. G. Scriven
Clerk, The Honourable the Irish Society, S. Waley, The Irish
Chamber, 1st Floor, 75 Watling Street, London EC4M 9BJ

THE ALDERMEN

Name and Ward	CC	Ald.	Shff.	Lord Mayor
Sir Peter Gadsden, GBE,				
Farringdon Wt.	1969	1971	1970	1979
Sir Christopher Leaver, GBE,				
Dowgate	1973	1974	1979	1981
Sir Alan Traill, GBE,				
Langbourn	1970	1975	1982	1984
Sir David Rowe-Ham, GBE,				
Bridge and Bridge Wt.	—	1976	1984	1986
Sir Christopher Collett, GBE,				
Broad Street	1973	1979	1985	1988
Sir Alexander Graham, GBE,				
Queenhithe	1978	1979	1986	1990
Sir Brian Jenkins, GBE,				
Cordwainer	—	1980	1987	1991
Sir Paul Newall, TD, Walbrook	1980	1981	1989	1993
Sir Christopher Walford,				
Farringdon Wn.	—	1982	1990	1994
Sir John Chalstrey, Vintry	1981	1984	1993	1995
Sir Roger Cork, Tower	1978	1983	1992	1996
Richard Nichols, Candlewick	1983	1984	1994	1997

All the above have passed the Civic Chair

Lord Levene of Portsoken,			
KBE, Portsoken	1983	1984	1995
Clive Martin, OBE, TD, Aldgate	—	1985	1996
David Howard, Cornhill	1972	1986	1997
James Oliver, Bishopsgate	1980	1987	1997
Peter Bull, Cheap	1968	1984	
Gavyn Arthur, Cripplegate	1988	1991	1998
Robert Finch, Coleman Street	—	1992	
Richard Agutter, Castle			
Baynard	—	1995	
Michael Savory, Bread Street	1980	1996	
David Brewer, Bassishaw	1992	1996	
Nicholas Anstee, Aldersgate	1987	1996	
Michael Everard, CBE, Lime			
Street	—	1996	
John Hughesdon, Billingsgate	1991	1997	

THE COMMON COUNCIL

Deputy: Each Common Councilman so described serves as
deputy to the Alderman of her/his ward

Absalom, J. D. (1994)	*Farringdon Wt.*
Altman, L. P. (1996)	*Cripplegate Wn.*
Angell, E. H. (1991)	*Cripplegate Wt.*
Archibald, *Deputy* W. W. (1986)	*Cornhill*
Ayers, K. E. (1996)	*Bassishaw*
Bailey, J. (1993)	*Cripplegate Wt.*
Balls, H. D. (1970)	*Castle Baynard*
Barker, *Deputy* J. A. (1981)	*Cripplegate Wn.*
Barnes-Yallowley, H. M. F. (1986)	*Coleman Street*
Beale, *Deputy* M. J. (1979)	*Lime Street*
Bird, J. L. (1977)	*Bridge*
Biroum-Smith, P. L. (1988)	*Dowgate*
Block, S. A. A. (1983)	*Cheap*
Bowman, J. C. R. (1995)	*Aldgate*
Bradshaw, D. J. (1991)	*Cripplegate Wn.*
Bramwell, F. M. (1983)	*Langbourn*
Branson, N. A. C. (1996)	*Bassishaw*

Brewster, J. W., OBE (1994)	*Bassishaw*
Brighton, R. L. (1984)	*Portsoken*
Brooks, W. I. B. (1988)	*Billingsgate*
Brown, *Deputy* D. T. (1971)	*Walbrook*
Byllam-Barnes, J. (1997)	*Cheap*
Caspi, D. R. (1994)	*Bridge*
Cassidy, *Deputy* M. J. (1989)	*Coleman Street*
Catt, B. F. (1982)	*Farringdon Wn.*
Chadwick, R. A. H. (1994)	*Tower*
Challis, G. H., CBE (1978)	*Langbourn*
Charkham, J. P. (1996)	*Farringdon Wt.*
Cohen, Mrs C. M. (1986)	*Lime Street*
Cole, Lt.-Col. Sir Colin, KCB, KCVO, TD	
(1964)	*Castle Baynard*
Cotgrove, D. (1991)	*Lime Street*
Coven, *Deputy* Mrs E. O., CBE (1972)	*Dowgate*
Currie, *Deputy* Miss S. E. M. (1985)	*Cripplegate Wt.*
Daily-Hunt, R. B. (1989)	*Cripplegate Wt.*
Darwin, G. E. (1995)	*Farringdon Wt.*
Davis, C. B. (1991)	*Bread Street*
Dove, W. H., MBE (1993)	*Bishopsgate*
Dunitz, A. A. (1984)	*Portsoken*
Eskenzi, A. N. (1970)	*Farringdon Wn.*
Eve, R. A. (1980)	*Cheap*
Everett, K. M. (1984)	*Candlewick*
Falk, F. A., TD (1997)	*Broad Street*
Farrow, M. W. W. (1996)	*Farringdon Wt.*
Farthing, R. B. C. (1981)	*Aldgate*
Fell, J. A. (1982)	*Queenhithe*
FitzGerald, *Deputy* R. C. A. (1981)	*Bread Street*
Forbes, S. J. (1993)	*Bishopsgate*
Fraser, S. J. (1993)	*Coleman Street*
Fraser, W. B. (1981)	*Vintry*
Galloway, A. D. (1981)	*Broad Street*
Gillon, G. M. F. (1995)	*Cordwainer*
Ginsburg, S. (1990)	*Bishopsgate*
Gowman, Miss A. (1991)	*Dowgate*
Graves, A. C. (1985)	*Bishopsgate*
Green, C. (1994)	*Aldersgate*
Griffiths, Mrs R. M. (1996)	*Cripplegate Wt.*
Hall, B. R. H. (1995)	*Farringdon Wn.*
Halliday, Mrs P. (1992)	*Walbrook*
Hardwick, Dr P. B. (1987)	*Aldgate*
Harries, R. E. (1995)	*Cripplegate Wt.*
Harris, B. N. (1996)	*Broad Street*
Hart, *Deputy* M. G. (1970)	*Bridge*
Haynes, J. E. H. (1986)	*Cornhill*
Henderson, *Deputy* J. S., OBE (1975)	*Langbourn*
Henderson-Begg, M. (1977)	*Coleman Street*
Holland, *Deputy* J., CBE (1972)	*Aldgate*
Holliday, Mrs E. H. L. (1987)	*Vintry*
Horlock, *Deputy* H. W. S. (1969)	*Farringdon Wn.*
Jackson, L. St J. T. (1978)	*Bread Street*
Kellett, Mrs M. W. F. (1986)	*Tower*
Kemp, D. L. (1984)	*Coleman Street*
Knowles, S. K. (1984)	*Candlewick*
Lawrence, A. (1994)	*Farringdon Wt.*
Lawson, G. C. H. (1971)	*Portsoken*
Littlestone, N. (1993)	*Aldersgate*
McGuinness, C. (1997)	*Castle Baynard*
MacLellan, A. P. W. (1989)	*Walbrook*
McNeil, I. D. (1977)	*Lime Street*
Malins, *Deputy* J. H., QC (1981)	*Farringdon Wt.*
Martin, R. C. (1986)	*Queenhithe*
Martinelli, *Deputy* P. J. (1994)	*Bassishaw*
Mayhew, Miss J. (1986)	*Queenhithe*
Mayhew, J. P. (1996)	*Aldersgate*
Mitchell, *Deputy* C. R. (1971)	*Castle Baynard*
Mizen, *Deputy* D. H. (1979)	*Broad Street*

Mobsby, *Deputy* D. J. L. (1985)   *Billingsgate*
Morgan, *Deputy* B. L., CBE (1963)   *Bishopsgate*
Moss, A. D. (1989)   *Tower*
Nash, *Deputy* Mrs J. C. (1983)   *Aldersgate*
Newman, Mrs P. B. (1989)   *Aldersgate*
Northall-Laurie, P. D. (1975)   *Walbrook*
O'Ferrall, P. C. K., OBE (1996)   *Aldgate*
Owen, Mrs J. (1975)   *Langbourn*
Owen-Ward, J. R. (1983)   *Bridge*
Parmley, A. C. (1992)   *Vintry*
Pembroke, *Deputy* Mrs A. M. F. (1978)   *Cheap*
Platts-Mills, J. F. F., QC   *Farringdon Wt.*
Ponsonby of Shulbrede, *Deputy* Lady
    (1981)   *Farringdon Wt.*
Price, E. E. (1996)   *Farringdon Wt.*
Pulman, *Deputy* G. A. G. (1983)   *Tower*
Punter, C. (1993)   *Cripplegate Wn.*
Reed, *Deputy* J. L., MBE (1967)   *Farringdon Wn.*
Revell-Smith, *Deputy* P. A., CBE (1959)   *Vintry*
Rigby, P. P., CBE (1972)   *Farringdon Wn.*
Robinson, Mrs D. C. (1989)   *Bishopsgate*
Roney, *Deputy* E. P. T., CBE (1974)   *Bishopsgate*
Samuel, *Deputy* Mrs I., MBE (1971)   *Portsoken*
Sargant, K. A. (1991)   *Cornhill*
Saunders, *Deputy* R. (1975)   *Candlewick*
Scriven, R. G. (1984)   *Candlewick*
Sellon, S. A., OBE, TD (1990)   *Cordwainer*
Shalit, D. M. (1972)   *Farringdon Wn.*
Sharp, *Deputy* Mrs I. M. (1974)   *Queenhithe*
Sherlock, M. R. C. (1992)   *Dowgate*
Simpson, A. S. J. (1987)   *Aldersgate*
Smith, Miss A. M. (1995)   *Farringdon Wt.*
Snyder, *Deputy* M. J. (1986)   *Cordwainer*
Spanner, J. H., TD (1984)   *Broad Street*
Stevenson, F. P. (1994)   *Cripplegate Wn.*
Taylor, J. A. F., TD (1991)   *Bread Street*
Thorp, C. R. (1996)   *Billingsgate*
Trotter, J. (1993)   *Billingsgate*
Walsh, S. (1989)   *Farringdon Wt.*
Warner, D. W. (1994)   *Cripplegate Wn.*
White, Dr J. W. (1986)   *Cornhill*
Willoughby, P. J. (1985)   *Bishopsgate*
Wilmot, R. T. D. (1973)   *Cordwainer*
Wixley, G. R. A., CBE, TD (1964)   *Coleman Street*
Wooldridge, F. D. (1988)   *Farringdon Wn.*

The City Guilds
(Livery Companies)

The constitution of the livery companies has been unchanged for centuries. There are three ranks of membership: freemen, liverymen and assistants. A person can become a freeman by patrimony (through a parent having been a freeman); by servitude (through having served an apprenticeship to a freeman); or by redemption (by purchase).

Election to the livery is the prerogative of the company, who can elect any of its freemen as liverymen. Assistants are usually elected from the livery and form a Court of Assistants which is the governing body of the company. The Master (in some companies called the Prime Warden) is elected annually from the assistants.

As at June 1998, 22,923 liverymen of the guilds were entitled to vote at elections at Common Hall.

The order of precedence, omitting extinct companies, is given in parenthesis after the name of each company in the list below. In certain companies the election of Master or

Prime Warden for the year does not take place till the autumn. In such cases the Master or Prime Warden for 1997–8 is given.

THE TWELVE GREAT COMPANIES
In order of civic precedence

MERCERS (*1*). *Hall*, Ironmonger Lane, London EC2V 8HE. *Livery*, 253. *Clerk*, C. H. Parker. *Master*, R. K. Westmacott

GROCERS (*2*). *Hall*, Princes Street, London EC2R 8AD. *Livery*, 316. *Clerk*, C. G. Mattingley, CBE. *Master*, T. V. Carter

DRAPERS (*3*). *Hall*, Throgmorton Avenue, London EC2N 2DQ. *Livery*, 248. *Clerk*, A. L. Lang, MBE. *Master*, N. G. W. Playne

FISHMONGERS (*4*). *Hall*, London Bridge, London EC4R 9EL. *Livery*, 368. *Clerk*, K. S. Waters. *Prime Warden*, The Hon. Sir Mark Lennox-Boyd

GOLDSMITHS (*5*). *Hall*, Foster Lane, London EC2V 6BN. *Livery*, 280. *Clerk*, R. D. Buchanan-Dunlop, CBE. *Prime Warden*, R. F. H. Vanderpump

MERCHANT TAYLORS (*6/7*). *Hall*, 30 Threadneedle Street, London EC2R 8AY. *Livery*, 323. *Clerk*, D. A. Peck. *Master*, P. M. Franklin-Adams

SKINNERS (*6/7*). *Hall*, 8 Dowgate Hill, London EC4R 2SP. *Livery*, 370. *Clerk*, Capt. D. Hart Dyke, CBE, LVO, RN. *Master*, Prof. C. Seymour-Ure

HABERDASHERS (*8*). *Livery*, 320. *Clerk*, Capt. R. J. Fisher, RN, 39–40 Bartholomew Close, London EC1A 7JN. *Master*, D. G. C. Inglefield

SALTERS (*9*). *Hall*, 4 Fore Street, London EC2Y 5DE. *Livery*, 165. *Clerk*, Col. M. P. Barneby. *Master*, The Lord Rockley

IRONMONGERS (*10*). *Hall*, Shaftesbury Place, Barbican, London EC2Y 8AA. *Livery*, 128. *Clerk*, J. A. Oliver. *Master*, H. S. Johnson

VINTNERS (*11*). *Hall*, Upper Thames Street, London EC4V 3BJ. *Livery*, 309. *Clerk*, Brig. M. Smythe, OBE. *Master*, P. E. Cooper

CLOTHWORKERS (*12*). *Hall*, Dunster Court, Mincing Lane, London EC3R 7AH. *Livery*, 200. *Clerk*, M. G. T. Harris. *Master*, A. P. Leslie, TD

OTHER CITY GUILDS
In alphabetical order

ACTUARIES (*91*). *Livery*, 190. *Clerk*, P. D. Esslemont, 16A Cadogan Square, London SW1X 0JU. *Master*, A. S. Fishman

AIR PILOTS AND AIR NAVIGATORS, GUILD OF (*81*). *Livery*, 500. *Grand Master*, HRH The Prince Philip, Duke of Edinburgh, KG, KT, OM, GBE, PC. *Clerk*, Air Vice-Marshal R. G. Peters, CB, Cobham House, 291 Gray's Inn Road, London WC1X 8QF. *Master*, Capt. T. R. Fulton

APOTHECARIES, SOCIETY OF (*58*). *Hall*, 14 Black Friars Lane, London EC4V 6EJ. *Livery*, 1750. *Clerk*, Lt.-Col. R. J. Stringer. *Master*, Dr I. T. Field

ARBITRATORS (*93*). *Livery*, 224. *Clerk*, Lt.-Col. I. R. P. Green, 2 Bolts Hill, Castle Camps, Cambs CB1 6TL. *Master*, I. W. Menzies

ARMOURERS AND BRASIERS (*22*). *Hall*, 81 Coleman Street, London EC2R 5BJ. *Livery*, 120. *Clerk*, Cdr. T. J. K. Sloane, OBE, RN. *Master*, J. H. Hale

BAKERS (*19*). *Hall*, Harp Lane, London EC3R 6DP. *Livery*, 390. *Clerk*, J. W. Tompkins. *Master*, C. Gilford

BARBERS (*17*). *Hall*, Monkwell Square, Wood Street, London EC2Y 5BL. *Livery*, 200. *Clerk*, Brig. A. F. Eastburn. *Master*, Sir John Chalstrey, MD, FRCS

BASKETMAKERS (*52*). *Livery*, 330. *Clerk*, Maj. G. J. Flint-Shipman, TD, 48 Seymour Walk, London SW10 9NF. *Prime Warden*, P. J. Costain

BLACKSMITHS (*40*). *Livery*, 237. *Clerk*, R. C. Jorden, 27 Cheyne Walk, Grange Park, London N21 1DB. *Prime Warden*, J. M. Latham

BOWYERS (*38*). *Livery*, 110. *Clerk*, J. R. Owen-Ward, 11 Aldermans Hill, London N13 4YD. *Master*, W. P. Forrester

BREWERS (*14*). *Hall*, Aldermanbury Square, London EC2V 7HR. *Livery*, 120. *Clerk*, C. W. Dallmeyer. *Master*, C. J. R. Pope

BRODERERS (*48*). *Livery*, 165. *Clerk*, P. J. C. Crouch, 11 Bridge Road, East Molesey, Surrey KT8 9EU. *Master*, C. A. Hart

BUILDERS MERCHANTS (*88*). *Livery*, 180. *Clerk*, Miss S. M. Robinson, TD, 4 College Hill, London EC4R 2RA. *Master*, J. Hauxwell

BUTCHERS (*24*). *Hall*, 87 Bartholomew Close, London EC1A 7EB. *Livery*, 682. *Clerk*, G. J. Sharp. *Master*, R. Moore

CARMEN (*77*). *Livery*, 430. *Clerk*, Cdr. R. M. H. Bawtree, OBE, 35–37 Ludgate Hill, London EC4M 7JN. *Master*, B. J. Hooper, CBE

CARPENTERS (*26*). *Hall*, 1 Throgmorton Avenue, London EC2N 2JJ. *Livery*, 175. *Clerk*, Maj.-Gen. P. T. Stevenson, OBE. *Master*, V. G. Morton-Smith

CHARTERED ACCOUNTANTS (*86*). *Livery*, 345. *Clerk*, C. Bygrave, The Rustlings, Valley Close, Studham, Dunstable LU6 2QN. *Master*, W. K. Gardener

CHARTERED ARCHITECTS (*98*). *Livery*, 104. *Clerk*, J. Griffiths, 28 Palace Road, East Molesey, Surrey KT8 9DL. *Master*, J. H. Penton, MBE

CHARTERED SECRETARIES AND ADMINISTRATORS (*87*). *Livery*, 210. *Clerk*, Maj. I. Stewart, Saddlers' Hall, 3rd Floor, 40 Gutter Lane, London EC2V 6BR. *Master*, Gp Capt. J. Hurn

CHARTERED SURVEYORS (*85*). *Livery*, 350. *Clerk*, Mrs A. L. Jackson, 16 St Mary-at-Hill, London EC3R 8EE. *Master*, S. Hibberdine

CLOCKMAKERS (*61*). *Livery*, 220. *Clerk*, Gp Capt. P. H. Gibson, MBE, Room 66-67 Albert Buildings, 49 Queen Victoria Street, London EC4N 4SE. *Master*, Dr C. R. Lattimore

COACHMAKERS AND COACH-HARNESS MAKERS (*72*). *Livery*, 421. *Clerk*, Gp Capt. G. Bunn, CBE, 8 Chandler's Court, Burwell, Cambridge CB5 0AZ. *Master*, Adm. Sir Derek Reffell, KCB

CONSTRUCTORS (*99*). *Livery*, 118. *Clerk*, L. L. Brace, 181 Fentiman Road, London SW8 1JY. *Master*, P. Heath

COOKS (*35*). *Livery*, 75. *Clerk*, M. C. Thatcher, 35 Great Peter Street, London SW1P 3LR. *Master*, D. Hodgson

COOPERS (*36*). *Hall*, 13 Devonshire Square, London EC2M 4TH. *Livery*, 260. *Clerk*, J. A. Newton. *Master*, J. R. Lawes

CORDWAINERS (*27*). *Livery*, 153. *Clerk*, Lt.-Col. J. R. Blundell, RM, Eldon Chambers, 30 Fleet Street, London EC4Y 1AA. *Master*, J. G. Church, CBE

CURRIERS (*29*). *Livery*, 96. *Clerk*, Gp Capt. F. J. Hamilton, Kestrel Cottage, East Knoyle, Salisbury SP3 6AD. *Master*, D. H. Pertwee

CUTLERS (*18*). *Hall*, Warwick Lane, London EC4M 7BR. *Livery*, 100. *Clerk*, K. S. G. Hinde, OBE, TD. *Master*, P. Watts

DISTILLERS (*69*). *Livery*, 260. *Clerk*, C. V. Hughes, 71 Lincoln's Inn Fields, London WC2A 3JF. *Master*, I. Coombs

DYERS (*13*). *Hall*, 10 Dowgate Hill, London EC4R 2ST. *Livery*, 120. *Clerk*, J. R. Chambers. *Prime Warden*, H. D. M. Morley-Fletcher, FSA

ENGINEERS (*94*). *Livery*, 282. *Clerk*, Cdr. B. D. Gibson, Kiln Bank, Bodle Street Green, Hailsham, E. Sussex BN27 4UA. *Master*, Dr D. S. Mitchell, CBE

ENVIRONMENTAL CLEANERS (*97*). *Livery*, 245. *Clerk*, J. C. M. Chapman, Woodside Cottage, 41 New Road, Bengeo, Hertford SG14 3JL. *Master*, B. Cole

FAN MAKERS (*76*). *Livery*, 202. *Clerk*, Lt.-Col. I. R. P. Green, 2 Bolts Hill, Castle Camps, Cambs CB1 6TL. *Master*, N. G. Crispin

FARMERS (*80*). *Hall*, 3 Cloth Street, London EC1A 7LD. *Livery*, 300. *Clerk*, Miss M. L. Winter. *Master*, C. Pertwee

FARRIERS (*55*). *Livery*, 358. *Clerk*, Mrs C. C. Clifford, 19 Queen Street, Chipperfield, Kings Langley, Herts WD4 9BT. *Master*, T. F. M. Head

FELTMAKERS (*63*). *Livery*, 170. *Clerk*, Lt.-Col. C. J. Holroyd, Providence Cottage, Chute Cadley, Andover, Hants SP11 9EB. *Master*, P. A. Grant

FLETCHERS (*39*). *Hall*, 3 Cloth Street, Long Lane, London EC1A 7LD. *Livery*, 110. *Clerk*, J. R. Owen-Ward. *Master*, R. H. Upton

FOUNDERS (*33*). *Hall*, 1 Cloth Fair, London EC1A 7HT. *Livery*, 170. *Clerk*, A. J. Gillett. *Master*, R. L. Savory

FRAMEWORK KNITTERS (*64*). *Livery*, 211. *Clerk*, H. W. H. Ellis, Whitegarth Chambers, 37 The Uplands, Loughton, Essex IG10 1NQ. *Master*, D. J. Goodenday

FRUITERERS (*45*). *Livery*, 260. *Clerk*, Lt.-Col. L. G. French, Chapelstones, 84 High Street, Codford St Mary, Warminster, Wilts BA12 0ND. *Master*, A. E. Redsell

FUELLERS (*95*). *Livery*, 110. *Clerk*, S. J. Lee, Fords, 134 Ockford Road, Godalming, Surrey GU7 1RG. *Master*, D. R. T. Waring

FURNITURE MAKERS (*83*). *Livery*, 292. *Clerk*, Mrs J. A. Wright, 9 Little Trinity Lane, London EC4V 2AD. *Master*, C. T. A. Hammond

GARDENERS (*66*). *Livery*, 249. *Clerk*, Col. N. G. S. Gray, 25 Luke Street, London EC2A 4AR. *Master*, R. L. Payton

GIRDLERS (*23*). *Hall*, Basinghall Avenue, London EC2V 5DD. *Livery*, 80. *Clerk*, Lt.-Col. R. Sullivan. *Master*, A. R. Westall

GLASS-SELLERS (*71*). *Livery*, 165. *Hon. Clerk*, B. J. Rawles, 43 Aragon Avenue, Thames Ditton, Surrey KT7 0PY. *Master*, C. N. K. Tizard

GLAZIERS AND PAINTERS OF GLASS (*53*). *Hall*, 9 Montague Close, London SE1 9DD. *Livery*, 265. *Clerk*, P. R. Batchelor. *Master*, G. D. Cracknell

GLOVERS (*62*). *Livery*, 275. *Clerk*, Mrs M. Hood, 71 Ifield Road, London SW10 9AU. *Master*, M. O. Penney

GOLD AND SILVER WYRE DRAWERS (*74*). *Livery*, 307. *Clerk*, J. R. Williams, 50 Cheyne Avenue, London E18 2DR. *Master*, G. X. Constantinidi

GUNMAKERS (*73*). *Livery*, 265. *Clerk*, J. M. Riches, The Proof House, 48–50 Commercial Road, London E1 1LP. *Master*, Col. D. C. Munn

HORNERS (*54*). *Livery*, 243. *Clerk*, A. R. Layard, c/o EMAP Fashion Ltd, Angel House, 338 Goswell Road, London EC1V 7QP. *Master*, J. J. Cartwright

INFORMATION TECHNOLOGISTS (*100*). *Livery*, 256. *Clerk*, Mrs G. Davies, 30 Aylesbury Street, London EC1R 0ER. *Master*, Mrs P. Drakes

INNHOLDERS (*32*). *Hall*, 30 College Street, London EC4R 2RH. *Livery*, 129. *Clerk*, J. R. Edwardes Jones. *Master*, A. C. Lorkin

INSURERS (*92*). *Hall*, 20 Aldermanbury, London EC2V 7HY. *Livery*, 385. *Clerk*, L. J. Walters. *Master*, P. H. Purchon

JOINERS AND CEILERS (*41*). *Livery*, 125. *Clerk*, Mrs A. L. Jackson, 75 Meadway Drive, Horsell, Woking, Surrey GU21 4TF. *Master*, T. F. K. Boucher

LAUNDERERS (*89*). *Hall*, 9 Montague Close, London SE1 9DD. *Livery*, 230. *Clerk*, Mrs J. Polek. *Master*, M. Bennett

LEATHERSELLERS (*15*). *Hall*, 15 St Helen's Place, London EC3A 6DQ. *Livery*, 150. *Clerk*, Capt. J. G. F. Cooke, OBE, RN. *Master*, G. L. Dove

LIGHTMONGERS (*96*). *Livery*, 155. *Clerk*, D. B. Wheatley, Crown Wharf, 11A Coldharbour, Blackwall Reach, London E14 9NS. *Master*, J. S. Webb

LORINERS (*57*). *Livery*, 353. *Clerk*, G. B. Forbes, 8 Portland Square, London W1 9QR. *Master*, E. I. Walker-Arnott

MAKERS OF PLAYING CARDS (*75*). *Livery*, 149. *Clerk*, M. J. Smyth, 6 The Priory, Godstone, Surrey RH9 8NL. *Master*, A. H. Wilcox

MARKETORS (*90*). *Livery*, 231. *Clerk*, Mrs G. Duffy, 13 Hall Gardens, Colney Heath, St Albans, Herts AL4 0QF. *Master*, J. Petersen

MASONS (*30*). *Livery*, 125. *Clerk*, T. F. Ackland, 22 Cannon Hill, London N14 6LS. *Master*, N. R. Barnes

MASTER MARINERS, HONOURABLE COMPANY OF (*78*). *Hall*, HQS [Wellington], Temple Stairs, Victoria Embankment, London WC2R 2PN. *Livery*, 248. *Admiral*, HRH The Prince Philip, Duke of Edinburgh, KG, KT, OM, GBE, PC. *Clerk*, J. A. V. Maddock. *Master*, Capt. A. D. Munro

MUSICIANS (*50*). *Livery*, 357. *Clerk*, S. F. N. Waley, 75 Watling Street, London EC4M 9BJ. *Master*, Prof. M. Troup

NEEDLEMAKERS (*65*). *Livery*, 240. *Clerk*, M. G. Cook, 5 Staple Inn, London WC1V 7QH. *Master*, D. A. Culling

PAINTER-STAINERS (*28*). *Hall*, 9 Little Trinity Lane, London EC4V 2AD. *Livery*, 316. *Clerk*, Col. W. J. Chesshyre. *Master*, R. C. Houghton

PATTENMAKERS (*70*). *Livery*, 180. *Clerk*, C. L. K. Ledger, 17 Orchard Close, The Rutts, Bushey Heath, Herts WD2 1LW. *Master*, R. Paice

PAVIORS (*56*). *Livery*, 235. *Clerk*, J. L. White, 3 Ridgemount Gardens, Enfield, Middx EN2 8QL. *Master*, J. H. Lelliott

PEWTERERS (*16*). *Hall*, Oat Lane, London EC2V 7DE. *Livery*, 118. *Clerk*, Cdr. A. St J. Steiner, OBE. *Master*, M. J. W. Piercy

PLAISTERERS (*46*). *Hall*, 1 London Wall, London EC2Y 5JU. *Livery*, 207. *Clerk*, R. Vickers. *Master*, E. Pilgrim

PLUMBERS (*31*). *Livery*, 350. *Clerk*, Lt.-Col. R. J. A. Paterson-Fox, 49 Queen Victoria Street, London EC4N 4SA. *Master*, P. Brunner

POULTERS (*34*). *Livery*, 180. *Clerk*, A. W. Scott, 23 Orchard Drive, Chorleywood, Herts WD3 5QN. *Master*, R. J. C. Gilpin

SADDLERS (*25*). *Hall*, 40 Gutter Lane, London EC2V 6BR. *Livery*, 72. *Clerk*, Gp Capt. W. S. Brereton Martin, CBE. *Master*, D. S. Snowden

SCIENTIFIC INSTRUMENT MAKERS (*84*). *Hall*, 9 Montague Close, London SE1 9DD. *Livery*, 235. *Clerk*, F. G. Everard. *Master*, B. G. Atherton

SCRIVENERS (*44*). *Livery*, 228. *Clerk*, G. A. Hill, HQS [Wellington], Temple Stairs, Victoria Embankment, London WC2R 2PN. *Master*, O. J. R. Kinsey

SHIPWRIGHTS (*59*). *Livery*, 427. *Permanent Master*, HRH The Prince Philip, Duke of Edinburgh, KG, KT, OM, GBE, PC. *Clerk*, Capt. R. F. Channon, RN, Ironmongers' Hall, Barbican, London EC2Y 8AA. *Prime Warden*, The Earl of Inchcape

SOLICITORS (*79*). *Livery*, 267. *Clerk*, Miss S. M. Robinson, TD, 4 College Hill, London EC2R 2RA. *Master*, R. D. Fox

SPECTACLE MAKERS (*60*). *Livery*, 310. *Clerk*, Lt.-Col. J. A. B. Salmon, OBE, Apothecaries' Hall, Black Friars Lane, London EC4V 6EL. *Master*, F. G. Norville

STATIONERS AND NEWSPAPER MAKERS (*47*). *Hall*, Ave Maria Lane, London EC4M 7DD. *Livery*, 446. *Clerk*, Brig. D. G. Sharp, AFC. *Master*, V. F. Sullivan

TALLOW CHANDLERS (*21*). *Hall*, 4 Dowgate Hill, London EC4R 2SH. *Livery*, 180. *Clerk*, Brig. W. K. L. Prosser, CBE, MC. *Master*, R. A. B. Nicolle

TIN PLATE WORKERS (ALIAS WIRE WORKERS) (*67*). *Livery*, 180. *Clerk*, M. Henderson-Begg, Bartholomew House, 66 Westbury Road, New Malden, Surrey KT3 5AS. *Master*, W. A. Warbey

TOBACCO PIPE MAKERS AND TOBACCO BLENDERS (*82*). *Livery*, 161. *Clerk*, N. J. Hallings-Pott, Hackhurst Farm, Lower Dicker, Hailsham, E. Sussex BN27 4BP. *Master*, S. G. Orlik

TURNERS (*51*). *Livery*, 190. *Clerk*, Lt.-Col. J. A. B. Salmon, OBE, c/o Apothecaries' Hall, Black Friars Lane, London EC4V 6EL. *Master*, C. P. J. Field

TYLERS AND BRICKLAYERS (*37*). *Livery*, 123. *Clerk*, J. A. Norris, 28 Palace Road, East Molesey, Surrey KT8 9DL. *Master*, D. R. Munnery

UPHOLDERS (*49*). *Livery*, 225. *Clerk*, J. P. Cody, c/o KES Ltd, 147 Portland Road, London SE25 4UX. *Master*, R. A. Wood

WAX CHANDLERS (*20*). *Hall*, Gresham Street, London EC2V 7AD. *Livery*, 110. *Clerk*, Cdr J. Stevens. *Master*, Lt.-Cdr N. Bailey

WEAVERS (*42*). *Livery*, 127. *Clerk*, Mrs F. Newcombe, Saddlers' House, Gutter Lane, London EC2V 6BR. *Upper Bailiff*, The Hon. G. W. M. Chubb

WHEELWRIGHTS (*68*). *Livery*, 250. *Clerk*, P. J. C. Crouch, 11 Bridge Road, East Molesey, Surrey KT8 9EU. *Master*, E. C. Wakefield

WOOLMEN (*43*). *Livery*, 130. *Clerk*, F. Allen, Hollands, Hedsor Road, Bourne End, Bucks SL8 5EE. *Master*, P. Rippon

FIREFIGHTERS (*No livery*). *Freemen*, 127. *Clerk*, G. P. Ellis, 20 Aldermanbury, London EC2V 7GF. *Master*, K. Knight

PARISH CLERKS (*No livery*). *Members*, 92. *Clerk*, B. J. N. Coombes, 1 Dean Trench Street, London SW1P 3HB. *Master*, J. D. Hebblethwaite

WATER CONSERVATORS (*No livery*). *Hall*, 16 St Mary-at-Hill, London EC2R 8EE. *Freemen*, 183. *Hon. Clerk*, H. B. Berridge, MBE. *Master*, C. Bland

WATERMEN AND LIGHTERMEN (*No livery*). *Hall*, 16 St Mary-at-Hill, London EC3R 8EE. *Craft Owning Freemen*, 360. *Clerk*, C. Middlemiss. *Master*, C. Livett

WORLD TRADERS (*No livery*). *Freemen*, 130. *Clerk*, N. R. Pullman, 36 Ladbroke Grove, London W11 2PA. *Master*, P. Wildblood, OBE

LONDON BOROUGH COUNCILS

Council	Municipal offices	Population 1996	Band D charge 1998	Chief Executive (*Managing Director)	Mayor (a) Lord Mayor 1998–9
Barking and Dagenham	°Dagenham, RM10 7BN	153,700	697.50	W. C. Smith	I. S. Jamu
Barnet	†The Burroughs, Hendon, NW4 4BG	319,400	728.07	M. Caller	Ms U. Chopra
Bexley	‡Bexleyheath, Kent DA6 7LB	219,300	695.20	C. Duffield	C. Ball
Brent	†Forty Lane, Wembley, HA9 9EZ	247,500	588.93	G. Daniel (*acting*)	Ms B. Joseph
Bromley	°Bromley, BR1 3UH	295,600	609.57	M. Blanch	P. Ayers
§Camden	†Judd Street, WC1H 9JE	189,100	765.38	S. Bundred	R. Hall
§City of Westminster	City Hall, Victoria Street, SW1E 6QP	204,100	325.00	W. Roots	(*a*) D. Harvey
Croydon	Taberner House, Park Lane, Croydon, CR9 3JS	333,800	691.93	D. Wechsler	P. Ryan
Ealing	†Uxbridge Road, W5 2HL	297,000	643.00	Ms G. Guy	U. Chander
Enfield	°Enfield, EN1 3XA	262,600	680.00	D. Plank	S. Carter
§Greenwich	†Wellington Street, SE18 6PW	212,100	883.35	D. Brooks (*acting*)	D. Austen
§Hackney	†Mare Street, E8 1EA	193,800	789.60	A. Elliston	J. Lobenstein, MBE
§Hammersmith and Fulham	†King Street, W6 9JU	156,700	790.00	*N. Newton	A. Slaughter
Haringey	°Wood Green, N22 4LE	216,100	856.00	G. Singh	Ms S. Peacock
Harrow	°Harrow, HA1 2UJ	210,700	723.51	A. Redmond	C. Harrison
Havering	†Romford, RM1 3BD	230,900	724.00	H. W. Tinworth	H. Webb
Hillingdon	°Uxbridge, UB8 1UW	247,700	703.84	D. Leatham	A. Langley
Hounslow	°Lampton Road, Hounslow, TW3 4DN	205,800	730.05	D. Myers	R. Bath
§Islington	†Upper Street, N1 2UD	176,000	912.00	Ms L. Fullick	Ms M. Hillier
§Kensington and Chelsea (RB)	†Hornton Street, W8 7NX	159,000	534.63	A. Taylor	Dr J. Munday
Kingston upon Thames (RB)	Guildhall, Kingston upon Thames, KT1 1EU	141,800	623.65	B. Quoroll	D. Cunningham
§Lambeth	†Brixton Hill, SW2 1RW	264,700	647.00	Ms H. Rabbatts	Ms D. Hayes-Mojon
§Lewisham	†Catford, SE6 4RU	241,500	683.45	Dr B. Quirk	M. Nottingham
Merton	°London Road, Morden, SM4 5DX	182,300	747.41	R. Paine (*acting*)	Ms L. Kirby
§Newham	†East Ham, E6 2RP	228,900	679.50	Dr W. Thomson	A. K. Sheikh
Redbridge	†Ilford, IG1 1DD	230,600	676.00	M. Frater	J. Lovell
Richmond upon Thames	°Richmond Road, Twickenham, TW1 3AA	179,900	745.00	R. L. Harbord	Ms M. Weber
§Southwark	†Peckham Road, SE5 8UB	229,900	786.58	R. Coomber	Ms J. Heatley
Sutton	‡St Nicholas Way, Sutton, SM1 1EA	175,500	701.73	Mrs P. Hughes	Ms J. Lowne
§Tower Hamlets	107A Commercial Street, E1 6BG	176,600	658.78	Ms S. Pierce	A. Asad
Waltham Forest	†Forest Road, Walthamstow, E17 4JF	220,200	813.66	A. Tobias	T. Bhogal
§Wandsworth	†Wandsworth, SW18 2PU	266,200	318.62	G. K. Jones	Mrs E. Howlett

§   Inner London Borough
RB Royal Borough
°   Civic Centre
†   Town Hall
‡   Civic Offices
Source of population statistics: ONS Monitor PP1 97/1, 28 August 1997
For explanation of council tax, *see* pages 523–4

Wales

The Principality of Wales (Cymru) occupies the extreme west of the central southern portion of the island of Great Britain, with a total area of 8,015 sq. miles (20,758 sq. km): land 7,965 sq. miles (20,628 sq. km); inland water 50 sq. miles (130 sq. km). It is bounded on the north by the Irish Sea, on the south by the Bristol Channel, on the east by the English counties of Cheshire, Shropshire, Worcestershire, and Gloucestershire, and on the west by St George's Channel.

Across the Menai Straits is the island of Anglesey (Ynys Môn) (276 sq. miles), communication with which is facilitated by the Menai Suspension Bridge (1,000 ft long) built by Telford in 1826, and by the tubular railway bridge (1,100 ft long) built by Stephenson in 1850. Holyhead harbour, on Holy Isle (north-west of Anglesey), provides accommodation for ferry services to Dublin (70 miles).

POPULATION

The population at the 1991 census was 2,811,865 (males 1,356,886; females 1,454,979). The average density of population in 1991 was 1.36 persons per hectare.

RELIEF

Wales is a country of extensive tracts of high plateau and shorter stretches of mountain ranges deeply dissected by river valleys. Lower-lying ground is largely confined to the coastal belt and the lower parts of the valleys. The highest mountains are those of Snowdonia in the north-west (Snowdon, 3,559 ft), Berwyn (Aran Fawddwy, 2,971 ft), Cader Idris (Pen y Gadair, 2,928 ft), Dyfed (Plynlimon, 2,467 ft), and the Black Mountain, Brecon Beacons and Black Forest ranges in the south-east (Carmarthen Van, 2,630 ft, Pen y Fan, 2,906 ft, Waun Fâch, 2,660 ft).

HYDROGRAPHY

The principal river rising in Wales is the Severn (*see also* page 534), which flows from the slopes of Plynlimon to the English border. The Wye (130 miles) also rises in the slopes of Plynlimon. The Usk (56 miles) flows into the Bristol Channel, through Gwent. The Dee (70 miles) rises in Bala Lake and flows through the Vale of Llangollen, where an aqueduct (built by Telford in 1805) carries the Pontcysyllte branch of the Shropshire Union Canal across the valley. The estuary of the Dee is the navigable portion, 14 miles in length and about five miles in breadth, and the tide rushes in with dangerous speed over the 'Sands of Dee'. The Towy (68 miles), Teifi (50 miles), Taff (40 miles), Dovey (30 miles), Taf (25 miles) and Conway (24 miles), the last named broad and navigable, are wholly Welsh rivers.

The largest natural lake is Bala (Llyn Tegid) in Gwynedd, nearly four miles long and about one mile wide. Lake Vyrnwy is an artificial reservoir, about the size of Bala, and forms the water supply of Liverpool; Birmingham is supplied from reservoirs in the Elan and Claerwen valleys.

WELSH LANGUAGE

According to the 1991 census results, the percentage of persons of three years and over able to speak Welsh was:

Clwyd	18.2	Powys	20.2
Dyfed	43.7	S. Glamorgan	6.5
Gwent	2.4	W. Glamorgan	15.0
Gwynedd	61.0		
Mid Glamorgan	8.5	Wales	18.7

The 1991 figure represents a slight decline from 18.9 per cent in 1981 (1971, 20.8 per cent; 1961, 26 per cent).

FLAG

The flag of Wales, the Red Dragon (Y Ddraig Goch), is a red dragon on a field divided white over green (per fess argent and vert a dragon passant gules). The flag was augmented in 1953 by a royal badge on a shield encircled with a riband bearing the words *Ddraig Goch Ddyry Cychwyn* and imperially crowned, but this augmented flag is rarely used.

EARLY HISTORY

The earliest inhabitants of whom there is any record appear to have been subdued or exterminated by the Goidels (a people of Celtic race) in the Bronze Age. A further invasion of Celtic Brythons and Belgae followed in the ensuing Iron Age. The Roman conquest of southern Britain and Wales was for some time successfully opposed by Caratacus (Caractacus or Caradog), chieftain of the Catuvellauni and son of Cunobelinus (Cymbeline). South-east Wales was subjugated and the legionary fortress at Caerleon-on-Usk established by about AD 75–77; the conquest of Wales was completed by Agricola about AD 78. Communications were opened up by the construction of military roads from Chester to Caerleon-on-Usk and Caerwent, and from Chester to Conwy (and thence to Carmarthen and Neath). Christianity was introduced during the Roman occupation, in the fourth century.

ANGLO-SAXON ATTACKS

The Anglo-Saxon invaders of southern Britain drove the Celts into the mountain stronghold of Wales, and into Strathclyde (Cumberland and south-west Scotland) and Cornwall, giving them the name of *Waelisc* (Welsh), meaning 'foreign'. The West Saxons' victory at Deorham (AD 577) isolated Wales from Cornwall and the battle of Chester (AD 613) cut off communication with Strathclyde and northern Britain. In the eighth century the boundaries of the Welsh were further restricted by the annexations of Offa, King of Mercia, and counter-attacks were largely prevented by the construction of an artificial boundary from the Dee to the Wye (Offa's Dyke).

In the ninth century Rhodri Mawr (844–878) united the country and successfully resisted further incursions of the Saxons by land and raids of Norse and Danish pirates by sea, but at his death his three provinces of Gwynedd (north), Powys (mid) and Deheubarth (south) were divided among his three sons, Anarawd, Mervyn and Cadell. Cadell's son Hywel Dda ruled a large part of Wales and codified its laws but the provinces were not united again until the rule of Llewelyn ap Seisyllt (husband of the heiress of Gwynedd) from 1018 to 1023.

THE NORMAN CONQUEST

After the Norman conquest of England, William I created palatine counties along the Welsh frontier, and the Norman barons began to make encroachments into Welsh territory. The Welsh princes recovered many of their losses during the civil wars of Stephen's reign and in the early 13th century Owen Gruffydd, prince of Gwynedd, was the dominant figure in Wales. Under Llewelyn ap Iorwerth (1194–1240) the Welsh united in powerful resistance to English incursions and Llywelyn's privileges and *de facto* independence were recognized in Magna Carta. His grandson, Llywelyn ap Gruffydd, was the last native prince; he was killed in 1282 during hostilities between the

Welsh and English, allowing Edward I of England to establish his authority over the country. On 7 February 1301, Edward of Caernarvon, son of Edward I, was created Prince of Wales, a title which has subsequently been borne by the eldest son of the sovereign.

Strong Welsh national feeling continued, expressed in the early 15th century in the rising led by Owain Glyndŵr, but the situation was altered by the accession to the English throne in 1485 of Henry VII of the Welsh House of Tudor. Wales was politically assimilated to England under the Act of Union of 1535, which extended English laws to the Principality and gave it parliamentary representation for the first time.

EISTEDDFOD

The Welsh are a distinct nation, with a language and literature of their own, and the national bardic festival (Eisteddfod), instituted by Prince Rhys ap Griffith in 1176, is still held annually (for date, *see* page 12). These *Eisteddfodau* (sessions) form part of the *Gorsedd* (assembly), which is believed to date from the time of Prydian, a ruling prince in an age many centuries before the Christian era.

PRINCIPAL CITIES

CARDIFF

Cardiff, at the mouth of the Rivers Taff, Rhymney and Ely, is the capital city of Wales and a major administrative, commercial and business centre. It has many industries, including steel, and its flourishing port is within the Cardiff Bay area, subject of a major redevelopment until the year 2000.

The many fine buildings include the City Hall, the National Museum of Wales, University Buildings, Law Courts, Welsh Office, County Hall, Police Headquarters, the Temple of Peace and Health, Llandaff Cathedral, the Welsh National Folk Museum at St Fagans, Cardiff Castle, the New Theatre, the Sherman Theatre and the Welsh College of Music and Drama. More recent buildings include St David's Hall, Cardiff International Arena and World Trade Centre, and the Welsh National Ice Rink. The Millennium Stadium is to be completed for the 1999 rugby World Cup.

SWANSEA

Swansea (*Abertawe*) is a city and a seaport. The Gower peninsula was brought within the city boundary under local government reform in 1974. The trade of the port includes coal, steel products, containerized goods, petroleum products and petrochemicals.

The principal buildings are the Norman Castle (rebuilt *c.*1330), the Royal Institution of South Wales, founded in 1835 (including Library), the University College at Singleton, and the Guildhall, containing the Brangwyn panels. More recent buildings include the Industrial and Maritime Museum, the new Maritime Quarter and Marina and the leisure centre.

Swansea was chartered by the Earl of Warwick, *c.* 1158–84, and further charters were granted by King John, Henry III, Edward II, Edward III and James II, Cromwell (two) and the Marcher Lord William de Breos.

CONSTITUTIONAL DEVELOPMENTS

On 22 July 1997, the Government announced plans to establish a Welsh assembly. The assembly will take over the annual budget of the Welsh Office and pass secondary legislation but will have no tax-raising powers of its own. In a referendum on 18 September 1997 about 50 per cent of the electorate voted, of whom 50.3 per cent voted in favour of the assembly. The assembly will have 60 members, of whom 40 will be representatives of a constituency and the remaining 20 elected by proportional representation on the basis of party political lists. A leader will be elected from the majority party to chair an executive committee of ten members. The assembly will be elected for four years, with the first elections taking place in May 1999.

LOCAL COUNCILS

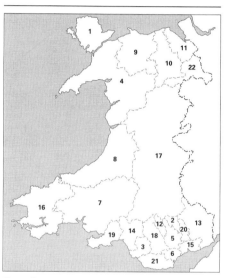

Key	County
1	Anglesey
2	Blaenau Gwent
3	Bridgend
4	Gwynedd
5	Caerphilly
6	Cardiff
7	Carmarthenshire
8	Ceredigion
9	Conwy
10	Denbighshire
11	Flintshire
12	Merthyr Tydfil
13	Monmouthshire
14	Neath and Port Talbot
15	Newport
16	Pembrokeshire
17	Powys
18	Rhondda, Cynon, Taff
19	Swansea
20	Torfaen
21	The Vale of Glamorgan
22	Wrexham

LORD-LIEUTENANTS AND HIGH SHERIFFS

County	Lord-Lieutenant	High Sheriff, 1997–8
Clwyd	Sir William Gladstone, Bt.	Col. H. M. E. Cadogan
Dyfed	Sir David Mansel Lewis, KCVO	J. S. Allen-Mirehouse
Gwent	Sir Richard Hanbury Tenison, KCVO	R. L. Dean
Gwynedd	R. E. Meuric Rees, CBE	Prof. E. Sunderland
Mid Glamorgan	M. A. McLaggan	A. R. Lewis
Powys	The Hon. Mrs S. Legge-Bourke, LVO	J. T. K. Trevor
South Glamorgan	Capt. N. Lloyd-Edwards	D. M. Jones
West Glamorgan	R. C. Hastie, CBE	R. H. Lloyd-Griffiths

LOCAL COUNCILS

SMALL CAPITALS denote CITY status
§ Denotes Borough status

Council	Administrative headquarters	Population 1996	Band D charge 1998	Chief Executive	Chairman 1998–9 (a) Mayor (b) Lord Mayor
Anglesey	Llangefni	67,100	477.32	L. Gibson	H. M. Morgan MBE
§Blaenau Gwent	Ebbw Vale	73,000	567.81	R. Leadbeter, OBE	(a) S. Bartlett
§Bridgend	Bridgend	130,100	601.69	I. K. Lewis	(a) H. C. Davies
§Caerphilly	Hengoed	169,100	601.00	M. Davies	(a) B. Rogers
CARDIFF	Cardiff	315,000	544.58	B. Davies	(b) Ms M. Drake
Carmarthenshire	Carmarthen	169,100	613.33	B. Roynon	J. A. Harries
Ceredigion	Aberaeron	69,500	622.66	O. Watkin	H. Lewis
§Conwy	Conwy	110,600	459.50	C. D. Barker	D. Parry-Jones
Denbighshire	Ruthin	92,200	582.03	H. V. Thomas	P. Williams
Flintshire	Mold	144,900	562.75	P. McGreevy	A. Jones
Gwynedd	Caernarfon	117,800	568.14	G. R. Jones	J. E. James
§Merthyr Tydfil	Merthyr Tydfil	58,100	638.31	G. Meredith	(a) E. C. Galsworthy
Monmouthshire	Cwmbran	86,800	451.88	Ms J. Redfearn	A. R. Carrington
§Neath Port Talbot	Port Talbot	139,500	687.00	K. R. Sawyers	(a) M. Jones
§Newport	Newport	136,800	461.78	R. D. Blair	(a) K. Powell
Pembrokeshire	Haverfordwest	113,600	490.09	B. Parry-Jones	A. Luke
Powys	Llandrindod Wells	124,400	500.89	Ms J. Tonge	M. W. Shaw
§Rhondda, Cynon, Taff	Tonypandy	240,100	600.00	G. R. Thomas	(a) J. David
SWANSEA	Swansea	230,200	542.22	Ms V. Sugar	(b) D. J. E. Jones
§Torfaen	Pontypool	90,500	532.34	Dr C. Grace	(a) B. Smith
§Vale of Glamorgan	Barry	119,400	485.07	D. Foster	J. Batey
§Wrexham	Wrexham	123,300	574.70	D. Griffin	(a) B. Williams

For explanation of council tax, see pages 523–4
Source of population figures: ONS Monitor PP1 97/1, 28 August 1997

Scotland

The Kingdom of Scotland occupies the northern portion of the main island of Great Britain and includes the Inner and Outer Hebrides, and the Orkney, Shetland, and many other islands. It lies between 60° 51′ 30″ and 54° 38′ N. latitude and between 1° 45′ 32″ and 6° 14′ W. longitude, with England to the south, the Atlantic Ocean on the north and west, and the North Sea on the east.

The greatest length of the mainland (Cape Wrath to the Mull of Galloway) is 274 miles, and the greatest breadth (Buchan Ness to Applecross) is 154 miles. The customary measurement of the island of Great Britain is from the site of John o' Groats house, near Duncansby Head, Caithness, to Land's End, Cornwall, a total distance of 603 miles in a straight line and approximately 900 miles by road.

The total area of Scotland is 30,420 sq. miles (78,789 sq. km); land 29,767 sq. miles (77,097 sq. km), inland water 653 sq. miles (1,692 sq. km).

POPULATION

The population at the 1991 census was 4,998,567 (males 2,391,961; females 2,606,606). The average density of the population in 1991 was 0.65 persons per hectare.

RELIEF

There are three natural orographic divisions of Scotland. The southern uplands have their highest points in Merrick (2,766 ft), Rhinns of Kells (2,669 ft), and Cairnsmuir of Carsphairn (2,614 ft), in the west; and the Tweedsmuir Hills in the east (Hartfell 2,651 ft, Dollar Law 2,682 ft, Broad Law 2,756 ft).

The central lowlands, formed by the valleys of the Clyde, Forth and Tay, divide the southern uplands from the northern Highlands, which extend almost from the extreme north of the mainland to the central lowlands, and are divided into a northern and a southern system by the Great Glen.

The Grampian Mountains, which entirely cover the southern Highland area, include in the west Ben Nevis (4,406 ft), the highest point in the British Isles, and in the east the Cairngorm Mountains (Cairn Gorm 4,084 ft, Braeriach 4,248 ft, Ben Macdui 4,296 ft). The north-western Highland area contains the mountains of Wester and Easter Ross (Carn Eige 3,880 ft, Sgurr na Lapaich 3,775 ft).

Created, like the central lowlands, by a major geological fault, the Great Glen (60 miles long) runs between Inverness and Fort William, and contains Loch Ness, Loch Oich and Loch Lochy. These are linked to each other and to the north-east and south-west coasts of Scotland by the Caledonian Canal, providing a navigable passage between the Moray Firth and the Inner Hebrides.

HYDROGRAPHY

The western coast is fragmented by peninsulas and islands, and indented by fjords (sea-lochs), the longest of which is Loch Fyne (42 miles long) in Argyll. Although the east coast tends to be less fractured and lower, there are several great drowned inlets (firths), e.g. Firth of Forth, Firth of Tay, Moray Firth, as well as the Firth of Clyde in the west.

The lochs are the principal hydrographic feature. The largest in Scotland and in Britain is Loch Lomond (27 sq. miles), in the Grampian valleys; the longest and deepest is Loch Ness (24 miles long and 800 feet deep), in the Great Glen; and Loch Shin (20 miles long) and Loch Maree in the Highlands.

The longest river is the Tay (117 miles), noted for its salmon. It flows into the North Sea, with Dundee on the estuary, which is spanned by the Tay Bridge (10,289 ft) opened in 1887 and the Tay Road Bridge (7,365 ft) opened

in 1966. Other noted salmon rivers are the Dee (90 miles) which flows into the North Sea at Aberdeen, and the Spey (110 miles), the swiftest flowing river in the British Isles, which flows into Moray Firth. The Tweed, which gave its name to the woollen cloth produced along its banks, marks in the lower stretches of its 96-mile course the border between Scotland and England.

The most important river commercially is the Clyde (106 miles), formed by the junction of the Daer and Portrail water, which flows through the city of Glasgow to the Firth of Clyde. During its course it passes over the picturesque Falls of Clyde, Bonnington Linn (30 ft), Corra Linn (84 ft), Dundaff Linn (10 ft) and Stonebyres Linn (80 ft), above and below Lanark. The Forth (66 miles), upon which stands Edinburgh, the capital, is spanned by the Forth (Railway) Bridge (1890), which is 5,330 feet long, and the Forth (Road) Bridge (1964), which has a total length of 6,156 feet (over water) and a single span of 3,000 feet.

The highest waterfall in Scotland, and the British Isles, is Eas a'Chùal Aluinn with a total height of 658 feet (200 m), which falls from Glas Bheinn in Sutherland. The Falls of Glomach, on a head-stream of the Elchaig in Wester Ross, have a drop of 370 feet.

GAELIC LANGUAGE

According to the 1991 census, 1.4 per cent of the population of Scotland, mainly in the Highlands and western coastal regions, were able to speak the Scottish form of Gaelic.

FLAG

The flag of Scotland is known as the Saltire. It is a white diagonal cross on a blue field (saltire argent in a field azure) and represents St Andrew, the patron saint of Scotland.

THE SCOTTISH ISLANDS

ORKNEY

The Orkney Islands (total area 375½ sq. miles) lie about six miles north of the mainland, separated from it by the Pentland Firth. Of the 90 islands and islets (holms and skerries) in the group, about one-third are inhabited.

The total population at the 1991 census was 19,612; the 1991 populations of the islands shown here include those of smaller islands forming part of the same civil parish.

Mainland, 15,128	Rousay, 291
Burray, 363	Sanday, 533
Eday, 166	Shapinsay, 322
Flotta and Fara, 126	South Ronaldsay, 943
Graemsay and Hoy, 477	Stronsay, 382
North Ronaldsay, 92	Westray, 704
Papa Westray, 85	

The islands are rich in prehistoric and Scandinavian remains, the most notable being the Stone Age village of Skara Brae, the burial chamber of Maeshowe, the many brochs (towers) and the 12th-century St Magnus Cathedral. Scapa Flow, between the Mainland and Hoy, was the war station of the British Grand Fleet from 1914 to 1919 and the scene of the scuttling of the surrendered German High Seas Fleet (21 June 1919).

Most of the islands are low-lying and fertile, and farming (principally beef cattle) is the main industry. Flotta, to the south of Scapa Flow, is the site of the oil terminal for the Piper, Claymore and Tartan fields in the North Sea.

The capital is Kirkwall (population 6,881) on Mainland.

SHETLAND

The Shetland Islands have a total area of 551 sq. miles and a population at the 1991 census of 22,522. They lie about 50 miles north of the Orkneys, with Fair Isle about half-way between the two groups. Out Stack, off Muckle Flugga, one mile north of Unst, is the most northerly part of the British Isles (60° 51′ 30″ N. lat.).

There are over 100 islands, of which 16 are inhabited. Populations at the 1991 census were:

Mainland, 17,596	Muckle Roe, 115
Bressay, 352	Trondra, 117
East Burra, 72	Unst, 1,055
Fair Isle, 67	West Burra, 857
Fetlar, 90	Whalsay, 1,041
Housay, 85	Yell, 1,075

Shetland's many archaeological sites include Jarlshof, Mousa and Clickhimin, and its long connection with Scandinavia has resulted in a strong Norse influence on its place-names and dialect.

Industries include fishing, knitwear and farming. In addition to the fishing fleet there are fish processing factories, while the traditional handknitting of Fair Isle and Unst is supplemented now with machine-knitted garments. Farming is mainly crofting, with sheep being raised on the moorland and hills of the islands. Latterly the islands have become a centre of the North Sea oil industry, with pipelines from the Brent and Ninian fields running to the terminal at Sullom Voe, the largest of its kind in Europe. Lerwick is the main centre for supply services for offshore oil exploration and development.

The capital is Lerwick (population 7,901) on Mainland.

THE HEBRIDES

Until the late 13th century the Hebrides included other Scottish islands in the Firth of Clyde, the peninsula of Kintyre (Argyll), the Isle of Man, and the (Irish) Isle of Rathlin. The origin of the name is stated to be the Greek *Eboudai*, latinized as *Hebudes* by Pliny, and corrupted to its present form. The Norwegian name *Sudreyjar* (Southern Islands) was latinized as *Sodorenses*, a name that survives in the Anglican bishopric of Sodor and Man.

There are over 500 islands and islets, of which about 100 are inhabited, though mountainous terrain and extensive peat bogs mean that only a fraction of the total area is under cultivation. Stone, Bronze and Iron Age settlement has left many remains, including those at Callanish on Lewis, and Norse colonization influenced language, customs and place-names. Occupations include farming (mostly crofting and stock-raising), fishing and the manufacture of tweeds and other woollens. Tourism is also an important factor in the economy.

The Inner Hebrides lie off the west coast of Scotland and relatively close to the mainland. The largest and best-known is Skye (area 643 sq. miles; pop. 8,868; chief town, Portree), which contains the Cuillin Hills (Sgurr Alasdair 3,257 ft), the Red Hills (Beinn na Caillich 2,403 ft), Bla Bheinn (3,046 ft) and The Storr (2,358 ft). Skye is also famous as the refuge of the Young Pretender in 1746. Other islands in the Highland council area include Raasay (pop. 163), Rum, Eigg and Muck.

Further south the Inner Hebridean islands include Arran (pop. 4,474) containing Goat Fell (2,868 ft); Coll and Tiree (pop. 940); Colonsay and Oronsay (pop. 106); Islay (area 235 sq. miles; pop. 3,538); Jura (area 160 sq. miles; pop. 196) with a range of hills culminating in the Paps of Jura (Beinn-an-Oir, 2,576 ft, and Beinn Chaolais, 2,477 ft); and Mull (area 367 sq. miles; pop. 2,708; chief town Tobermory) containing Ben More (3,171 ft).

The Outer Hebrides, separated from the mainland by the Minch, now form the Western Isles Islands Council

area (area 1,119 sq. miles; population at the 1991 census 29,600). The main islands are Lewis with Harris (area 770 sq. miles, pop. 21,737), whose chief town, Stornoway, is the administrative headquarters; North Uist (pop. 1,404); South Uist (pop. 2,106); Baleshare (55); Benbecula (pop. 1,803) and Barra (pop. 1,244). Other inhabited islands include Bernera (262), Berneray (141), Eriskay (179), Grimsay (215), Scalpay (382) and Vatersay (72).

EARLY HISTORY

There is evidence of human settlement in Scotland dating from the third millennium BC, the earliest settlers being Middle Stone Age hunters and fishermen. Early in the second millennium BC, New Stone Age farmers began to cultivate crops and rear livestock; their settlements were on the west coast and in the north, and included Skara Brae and Maeshowe (Orkney). Settlement by the Early Bronze Age 'Beaker folk', so-called from the shape of their drinking vessels, in eastern Scotland dates from about 1800 BC. Further settlement is believed to have occurred from 700 BC onwards, as tribes were displaced from further south by new incursions from the Continent and the Roman invasions from AD 43.

Julius Agricola, the Roman governor of Britain AD 77–84, extended the Roman conquests in Britain by advancing into Caledonia, culminating with a victory at Mons Graupius, probably in AD 84; he was recalled to Rome shortly afterwards and his forward policy was not pursued. Hadrian's Wall, mostly completed by AD 30, marked the northern frontier of the Roman empire except for the period between about AD 144 and 190 when the frontier moved north to the Forth–Clyde isthmus and a turf wall, the Antonine Wall, was manned.

After the Roman withdrawal from Britain, there were centuries of warfare between the Picts, Scots, Britons, Angles and Vikings. The Picts, believed to be a non-Indo-European race, occupied the area north of the Forth. The Scots, a Gaelic-speaking people of northern Ireland, colonized the area of Argyll and Bute (the kingdom of Dalriada) in the fifth century AD and then expanded eastwards and northwards. The Britons, speaking a Brythonic Celtic language, colonized Scotland from the south from the first century BC; they lost control of south-eastern Scotland (incorporated into the kingdom of Northumbria) to the Angles in the early seventh century but retained Strathclyde (south-western Scotland and Cumbria). Viking raids from the late eighth century were followed by Norse settlement in the western and northern isles, Argyll, Caithness and Sutherland from the mid-ninth century onwards.

UNIFICATION

The union of the areas which now comprise Scotland began in AD 843 when Kenneth mac Alpin, king of the Scots from c.834, became also king of the Picts, joining the two lands to form the kingdom of Alba (comprising Scotland north of a line between the Forth and Clyde rivers). Lothian, the eastern part of the area between the Forth and the Tweed, seems to have been leased to Kenneth II of Alba (reigned 971–995) by Edgar of England c.973/4, and Scottish possession was confirmed by Malcolm II's victory over a Northumbrian army at Carham c.1016. At about this time Malcolm II (reigned 1005–34) placed his grandson Duncan on the throne of the British kingdom of Strathclyde, bringing under Scots rule virtually all of what is now Scotland.

The Norse possessions were incorporated into the kingdom of Scotland from the 12th century onwards. An uprising in the mid-12th century drove the Norse from most of mainland Argyll. The Hebrides were ceded to Scotland by the Treaty of Perth in 1266 after a Norwegian expedition in 1263 failed to maintain Norse authority over the islands. Orkney and Shetland fell to Scotland in 1468–9 as a pledge for the unpaid dowry of Margaret of Denmark, wife of James III, though Danish claims of suzerainty were relinquished only with the marriage of Anne of Denmark to James VI in 1590.

From the 11th century, there were frequent wars between Scotland and England over territory and the extent of England's political influence. The failure of the Scottish royal line with the death of Margaret of Norway in 1290 led to disputes over the throne which were resolved by the adjudication of Edward I of England. He awarded the throne to John Balliol in 1292 but Balliol's refusal to be a puppet king led to war. Balliol surrendered to Edward I in 1296 and Edward attempted to rule Scotland himself. Resistance to Scotland's loss of independence was led by William Wallace, who defeated the English at Stirling Bridge (1297), and Robert Bruce, crowned in 1306, who held most of Scotland by 1311 and routed Edward II's army at Bannockburn (1314). England recognized the independence of Scotland in the Treaty of Northampton in 1328. Subsequent clashes include the disastrous battle of Flodden (1513) in which James IV and many of his nobles fell.

THE UNION

In 1603 James VI of Scotland succeeded Elizabeth I on the throne of England (his mother, Mary Queen of Scots, was the great-granddaughter of Henry VII), his successors reigning as sovereigns of Great Britain. Political union of the two countries did not occur until 1707.

THE JACOBITE REVOLTS

After the abdication (by flight) in 1688 of James VII and II, the crown devolved upon William III (grandson of Charles I) and Mary II (elder daughter of James VII and II). In 1689 Graham of Claverhouse roused the Highlands on behalf of James VII and II, but died after a military success at Killiecrankie.

After the death of Anne (younger daughter of James VII and II), the throne devolved upon George I (great-grandson of James VI and I). In 1715, armed risings on behalf of James Stuart (the Old Pretender) and of James VII and II) led to the indecisive battle of Sheriffmuir, and the Jacobite movement died down until 1745, when Charles Stuart (the Young Pretender) defeated the Royalist troops at Prestonpans and advanced to Derby (1746). From Derby, the adherents of 'James VIII and III' (the title claimed for his father by Charles Stuart) fell back on the defensive and were finally crushed at Culloden (16 April 1746).

PRINCIPAL CITIES

ABERDEEN

Aberdeen, 130 miles north-east of Edinburgh, received its charter as a Royal Burgh in 1179. Scotland's third largest city, Aberdeen is the second largest Scottish fishing port and the main centre for offshore oil exploration and production. It is also an ancient university town and distinguished research centre. Other industries include engineering, food processing, textiles, paper manufacturing and chemicals.

Places of interest include King's College, St Machar's Cathedral, Brig o' Balgownie, Duthie Park and Winter Gardens, Hazlehead Park, the Kirk of St Nicholas, Mercat Cross, Marischal College and Marischal Museum, Provost Skene's House, Art Gallery, Gordon Highlanders Museum, Satrosphere Hands-On Discovery Centre, and Aberdeen Maritime Museum in Provost Ross's House.

DUNDEE

Dundee, a Royal Burgh, is situated on the north bank of the Tay estuary. The city's port and dock installations are important to the offshore oil industry and the airport also provides servicing facilities. Principal industries include textiles, computers and other electronic industries, lasers, printing, tyre manufacture, food processing, carpets, engineering, clothing manufacture and tourism.

The unique City Churches – three churches under one roof, together with the 15th-century St Mary's Tower – are the most prominent architectural feature. Dundee has two historic ships: the Dundee-built RRS *Discovery* which took Capt. Scott to the Antarctic lies alongside Discovery Quay, and the frigate *Unicorn*, the only British-built wooden warship still afloat, is moored in Victoria Dock. Places of interest include Mills Public Observatory, the Tay road and rail bridges, McManus Galleries, Barrack Street Museum, Claypotts Castle, Broughty Castle and Verdant Works (Textile Heritage Centre).

EDINBURGH

Edinburgh is the capital of and seat of government in Scotland. The city is built on a group of hills and contains in Princes Street one of the most beautiful thoroughfares in the world.

The principal buildings are the Castle, which now houses the Stone of Scone and also includes St Margaret's Chapel, the oldest building in Edinburgh, and near it, the Scottish National War Memorial; the Palace of Holyroodhouse; Parliament House, the present seat of the judicature; three universities (Edinburgh, Heriot-Watt, Napier); St Giles' Cathedral; St Mary's (Scottish Episcopal) Cathedral (Sir George Gilbert Scott); the General Register House (Robert Adam); the National and the Signet Libraries; the National Gallery; the Royal Scottish Academy; the National Portrait Gallery; and the Edinburgh International Conference Centre, opened in 1995.

GLASGOW

Glasgow, a Royal Burgh, is the principal commercial and industrial centre in Scotland. The city occupies the north and south banks of the Clyde, formerly one of the chief commercial estuaries in the world. The principal industries include engineering, electronics, finance, chemicals and printing. The city has also developed recently as a tourism and conference centre.

The chief buildings are the 13th-century Gothic Cathedral, the University (Sir George Gilbert Scott), the City Chambers, the Royal Concert Hall, St Mungo Museum of Religious Life and Art, Pollok House, the School of Art (Mackintosh), Kelvingrove Art Galleries, the Gallery of Modern Art, the Burrell Collection museum and the Mitchell Library. The city is home to the Scottish National Orchestra, Scottish Opera and Scottish Ballet.

CONSTITUTIONAL DEVELOPMENTS

On 24 July 1997, the Government announced plans to establish a Scottish parliament. The parliament will have responsibility for areas such as education, health, law, the environment, economic development and local government, with such areas as foreign and economic policy, defence and security being retained by Westminster. The parliament will also be able to raise or reduce the basic rate of income tax by up to three pence. In a referendum in

Scotland on 11 September 1997 about 62 per cent of the electorate turned out, of whom 74.3 per cent voted in favour of the parliament and 63.5 per cent in favour of its having tax-raising powers.

There will be 129 members in the new parliament, of whom 73 will be elected by majority vote in a constituency and the remaining 56 by proportional representation on the basis of party political lists. Elections will be held every four years, with the first elections taking place in May 1999. A First Minister will be appointed by The Queen to head a Scottish executive comprising ministers and law officers. The parliament is due to begin sitting in 2000, although there is a possibility of the timetable being brought forward. The number of Scottish MPs at Westminster is to be cut by about 12 by 2007.

The Secretary of State for Scotland will remain a Cabinet minister, responsible for communication between the Scottish and Westminster parliaments and for representing Scottish interests in those policy areas not devolved. In the event of a dispute between the two parliaments, the judicial committee of the Privy Council will act as arbiter.

LORD-LIEUTENANTS

Title	Name
Aberdeenshire	A. Farquharson
Angus	The Earl of Airlie, KT, GCVO, PC
Argyll and Bute	The Duke of Argyll
Ayrshire and Arran	Maj. R. Y. Henderson, TD
Banffshire	J. A. S. McPherson, CBE
Berwickshire	Maj.-Gen. Sir John Swinton, KCVO, OBE
Caithness	Maj. G. T. Dunnett, TD
Clackmannan	Lt.-Col. R. C. Stewart, CBE, TD
Dumfries	Capt. R. C. Cunningham-Jardine
Dumbartonshire	Brig. D. D. G. Hardie, TD
East Lothian	Sir Hew Hamilton-Dalrymple, Bt., KCVO
Fife	The Earl of Elgin and Kincardine, KT
Inverness	The Lord Gray of Contin, PC
	The Viscount of Arbuthnott, KT,
Kincardineshire	CBE, DSC, FRSE
Lanarkshire	H. B. Sneddon, CBE
Midlothian	Capt. G. W. Burnet, LVO
Moray	Air Vice-Marshal G. A. Chesworth, CB, OBE, DFC
Nairn	The Earl of Leven and Melville
Orkney	G. R. Marwick
Perth and Kinross	Sir David Montgomery, Bt.
Renfrewshire	C. H. Parker, OBE
Ross and Cromarty	Capt. R. W. K. Stirling of Fairburn, TD
Roxburgh, Ettrick and Lauderdale	Dr June Paterson-Brown
Shetland	J. H. Scott
Stirling and Falkirk	Lt.-Col. J. Stirling of Garden, CBE, TD, FRICS
Sutherland	Maj.-Gen. D. Houston, CBE
The Stewartry of Kirkcudbright	Lt.-Gen. Sir Norman Arthur, KCB
Tweeddale	Capt. J. D. B. Younger
West Lothian	The Earl of Morton
Western Isles	The Viscount Dunrossil, CMG
Wigtown	Maj. E. S. Orr-Ewing

The Lord Provosts of the four city districts of Aberdeen, Dundee, Edinburgh and Glasgow are Lord-Lieutenants for those districts *ex officio*

LOCAL COUNCILS

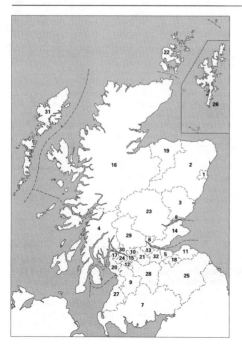

Key	Council
1	Aberdeen City
2	Aberdeenshire
3	Angus
4	Argyll and Bute
5	City of Edinburgh
6	Clackmannanshire
7	Dumfries and Galloway
8	Dundee City
9	East Ayrshire
10	East Dumbartonshire
11	East Lothian
12	East Renfrewshire
13	Falkirk
14	Fife
15	Glasgow City
16	Highland
17	Inverclyde
18	Midlothian
19	Moray
20	North Ayrshire
21	North Lanarkshire
22	Orkney
23	Perth and Kinross
24	Renfrewshire
25	Scottish Borders
26	Shetland
27	South Ayrshire
28	South Lanarkshire
29	Stirling
30	West Dumbartonshire
31	Western Isles
32	West Lothian

LOCAL COUNCILS

Council	Administrative headquarters	Population (latest estimate)	Band D charge 1998	Chief Executive	Chairman (a) Convener (b) Provost (c) Lord Provost
Aberdeen City	Aberdeen	217,260	£794.00	D. Paterson	(c) Ms M. Farquhar
Aberdeenshire	Aberdeen	227,430	695.00	A. G. Campbell	(a) Dr C. S. Millar
Angus	Forfar	111,750	709.00	A. B. Watson	(b) Mrs F. E. Duncan
Argyll and Bute	Lochgilphead	90,550	881.00	J. A. McLellan	(a) J. Wilson
City of Edinburgh	Edinburgh	448,850	867.00	T. N. Aitchison	(c) Rt. Hon. E. Milligan
Clackmannanshire	Alloa	48,810	959.73	R. Allan	(b) R. Elder
Dumfries and Galloway	Dumfries	147,300	886.33	I. F. Smith	(a) A. T. Baldwick
Dundee City	Dundee	149,160	1,148.52	A. Stephen	(c) M. J. Rolfe
East Ayrshire	Kilmarnock	124,000	974.33	D. Montgomery	(b) R. Stirling
East Dunbartonshire	Glasgow	110,679	790.00	C. Mallon	(b) J. Dempsey
East Lothian	Haddington	88,140	760.00	J. Lindsay	(a) P. O'Brien
East Renfrewshire	Glasgow	89,383	682.00	P. Daniels	(b) A. Steele
Falkirk	Falkirk	143,040	699.00	Ms M. Pitcaithly	(b) A. H. Fowler
Fife	Glenrothes	349,300	917.73	J. Markland	(a) J. MacDougall
Glasgow City	Glasgow	611,660	1,229.33	J. Andrews (acting)	(c) P. J. Lally
Highland	Inverness	208,700	776.47	A. D. McCourt	(a) P. J. Peacock, CBE
Inverclyde	Greenock	86,500	1,018.33	R. Cleary	(b) Mrs C. Allan
Midlothian	Dalkeith	80,000	892.00	T. Muir	(b) D. Molloy
Moray	Elgin	86,030	699.00	A. A. Connell	(a) G. McDonald
North Ayrshire	Irvine	139,000	906.33	B. Devine	(a) G. Steven
North Lanarkshire	Motherwell	325,940	967.33	A. Cowe	(b) V. Mathieson
Orkney Islands	Kirkwall	20,000	765.52	A. Buchan	(a) H. Halcro-Johnston
Perth and Kinross	Perth	132,750	884.63	H. Robertson	(b) J. Culliven
Renfrewshire	Paisley	178,260	938.33	T. Scholes	(b) Ms N. Allison
Scottish Borders	Melrose	106,100	639.00	A. M. Croall	(a) A. L Tulley
Shetland Islands	Lerwick	22,522	558.00	N. Reiter	(a) L. S. Smith
South Ayrshire	Ayr	114,247	792.00	G. W. F. Thorley	(b) R. Campbell
South Lanarkshire	Hamilton	307,350	859.00	A. MacNish	(b) S. Casserly
Stirling	Stirling	83,580	910.73	K. Yates	(b) J. Paterson
West Dunbartonshire	Dumbarton	95,760	1,166.00	M. Waters	(b) G. Cairney
Western Isles	Stornoway	28,240	656.00	B. W. Stewart	(a) D. M. Mackay
West Lothian	Livingston	149,540	792.00	A. M. Linkston	(b) J. Thomas

For explanation of council tax, see pages 523–4

Northern Ireland

Northern Ireland has a total area of 5,467 sq. miles (14,144 sq. km): land, 5,225 sq. miles (13,532 sq. km); inland water and tideways, 249 sq. miles (628 sq. km).

The population of Northern Ireland at the 1991 census was 1,577,836 (males, 769,071; females, 808,765). The average density of population in 1991 was 1.11 persons per hectare.

In 1991 the number of persons in the various religious denominations (expressed as percentages of the total population) were: Roman Catholic, 38.4; Presbyterian, 21.4; Church of Ireland, 17.7; Methodist, 3.8; others 7.7; none, 3.7; not stated, 7.3.

FLAG

The official national flag of Northern Ireland is now the Union Flag. The flag formerly in use (a white, six-pointed star in the centre of a red cross on a white field, enclosing a red hand and surmounted by a crown) has not been used since the imposition of direct rule.

PRINCIPAL CITIES

BELFAST

Belfast, the administrative centre of Northern Ireland, is situated at the mouth of the River Lagan at its entrance to Belfast Lough. The city grew, owing to its easy access by sea to Scottish coal and iron, to be a great industrial centre.

The principal buildings are of a relatively recent date and include the Parliament Buildings at Stormont, the City Hall, the Law Courts, the Public Library and the Museum and Art Gallery.

Belfast received its first charter of incorporation in 1613 and was created a city in 1888; the title of Lord Mayor was conferred in 1892.

LONDONDERRY

Londonderry (originally Derry) is situated on the River Foyle, and has important associations with the City of London. The Irish Society was created by the City of London in 1610, and under its royal charter of 1613 it fortified the city and was for long closely associated with its administration. Because of this connection the city was incorporated in 1613 under the new name of Londonderry.

The city is famous for the great siege of 1688–9, when for 105 days the town held out against the forces of James II until relieved by sea. The city walls are still intact and form a circuit of almost a mile around the old city.

Interesting buildings are the Protestant Cathedral of St Columb's (1633) and the Guildhall, reconstructed in 1912 and containing a number of beautiful stained glass windows, many of which were presented by the livery companies of London.

CONSTITUTION AND GOVERNMENT

Northern Ireland is subject to the same fundamental constitutional provisions which apply to the rest of the United Kingdom. It had its own parliament and government from 1921 to 1972, but after increasing civil unrest the Northern Ireland (Temporary Provisions) Act 1972 transferred the legislative and executive powers of the Northern Ireland parliament and government to the UK Parliament and a Secretary of State. The Northern Ireland Constitution Act 1973 provided for devolution in North-

ern Ireland through an assembly and executive, but a power-sharing executive formed by the Northern Ireland political parties in January 1974 collapsed in May 1974; since then Northern Ireland has been governed by direct rule under the provisions of the Northern Ireland Act 1974. This allows Parliament to approve all laws for Northern Ireland and places the Northern Ireland department under the direction and control of the Secretary of State for Northern Ireland.

Attempts were made by successive governments to find a means of restoring a widely acceptable form of devolved government to Northern Ireland. In 1985 the governments of the United Kingdom and the Republic of Ireland signed the Anglo-Irish Agreement, establishing an intergovernmental conference in which the Irish government may put forward views and proposals on certain aspects of Northern Ireland affairs.

Discussions between the British and Irish governments and the main Northern Ireland parties began in 1991. It was agreed that any political settlement would need to address three key relationships: those within Northern Ireland; those within the island of Ireland (north/south); and those between the British and Irish governments (east/west). Although round table talks ended in 1992 the process continued from September 1993 as separate bilateral discussions with three of the Northern Ireland parties (the DUP declined to participate).

In December 1993 the British and Irish governments published the Joint Declaration complementing the political talks, and making clear that any settlement would need to be founded on principles of democracy and consent. The declaration also stated that all democratically mandated parties could be involved in political talks as long as they permanently renounced paramilitary violence.

The provisional IRA and loyalist paramilitary groups announced cease-fires on 31 August and 13 October 1994 respectively. The Government initiated exploratory meetings with Sinn Fein and loyalist representatives in December 1994.

In February 1995 the Prime Minister (John Major) launched *A Framework for Accountable Government in Northern Ireland* and, with the Irish Prime Minister, *A New Framework for Agreement*. These outlined what a comprehensive political settlement might look like. The ideas were intended to facilitate multilateral dialogue involving the Northern Ireland parties and the British government. To this end the Secretary of State for Northern Ireland (Sir Patrick Mayhew) initiated separate bilateral meetings with the leaders of the main parties.

In autumn 1995 the Prime Minister said that Sinn Fein would not be invited to all-party talks until the IRA had decommissioned its arms; the IRA ruled out any decommissioning of weapons in advance of a political settlement. In November 1995 the Prime Minister and the Irish Prime Minister agreed to set up a three-member international body chaired by a former US senator, George Mitchell, to advise both governments on suitable methods of decommissioning arms. The international body reported in January 1996 that no weapons would be decommissioned before the start of all-party talks and that a compromise agreement was necessary under which weapons would be decommissioned during negotiations. The Prime Minister accepted the report and proposed that elections should be held to provide a pool of representatives to conduct all-party talks. On 9 February 1996 the IRA called off its cease-fire.

PEACE TALKS

Following elections on 30 May 1996, all-party talks opened at Stormont Castle on 10 June 1996 which included nine of the ten parties returned at the election; Sinn Fein representatives were turned away because the IRA had failed to reinstate its cease-fire.

The participants of the all-party talks agreed the rules of procedure and set up a business committee. On 29 July 1996 the all-party talks were suspended after disagreements over the issue of decommissioning arms. From September 1996 discussion focused on the issue of decommissioning arms, and an opening agenda for the talks was agreed in October 1996. The talks were suspended from 5 March 1997 until 3 June because of the UK general election and local government elections in Northern Ireland.

On 25 June 1997 the newly-elected Labour Government said that substantive negotiations should begin in September 1997 with a view to reaching conclusions by May 1998. The British and Irish governments issued a joint paper outlining their proposals for resolving the decommissioning issue. The Government also indicated that if the IRA were to call a cease-fire, it would assess whether it was genuine over a period of six weeks, and if satisfied that it was so, would then invite Sinn Fein to the talks. An IRA cease-fire was declared on 20 July 1997.

The Northern Ireland Secretary (Mo Mowlam) met a Sinn Fein delegation on 6 August 1997 and later announced that Sinn Fein would be present when the substantive talks opened on 15 September. The Unionist and loyalist parties, unhappy at the terms on which Sinn Fein had been admitted, boycotted the opening of the talks. The Ulster Unionist Party, the Progressive Unionist Party and the Ulster Democratic Party re-entered the negotiations on 17 September. Full-scale peace talks began on 7 October. The parties had agreed to concentrate on constitutional issues, with the issue of decommissioning terrorist weapons to be handled by a new independent commission.

On 12 January 1998 the British and Irish governments issued a joint document, *Propositions on Heads of Agreement*, proposing the establishment of various new cross-border bodies; further proposals were presented on 27 January. A draft peace settlement was issued by the talks' chairman, Sen. George Mitchell, on 6 April 1998 but was rejected by the Unionists the following day. On 10 April agreement was reached between the British and Irish governments and the eight Northern Ireland political parties still involved in the talks. The agreement provided for an elected New Northern Ireland Assembly; a North/South Ministerial Council, and a British-Irish Council comprising representatives of the British, Irish, Channel Islands and Isle of Man governments and members of the new assemblies for Scotland, Wales and Northern Ireland. Further points included the abandonment of the Republic of Ireland's constitutional claim to Northern Ireland; the decommissioning of weapons; the release of paramilitary prisoners; and changes in policing (*see also* Events of the Year).

Referendums on the agreement were held in Northern Ireland and the Republic of Ireland on 22 May 1998. In Northern Ireland the turnout was 81 per cent, of which 71.12 per cent voted in favour of the agreement. In the Republic of Ireland, the turnout was about 55 per cent, of which 94.4 per cent voted in favour of both the agreement and the necessary constitutional change.

NORTHERN IRELAND ASSEMBLY

Elections to the New Northern Ireland Assembly took place on 25 June 1998 and members met for the first time on 1 July 1998. The Assembly will meet in shadow form until early 1999, when it will become fully operational. It will have executive and legislative authority over those areas formerly the responsibility of the Northern Ireland government departments: agriculture, economic development, education, the environment, finance, health and social security. Its powers might be extended further in future.

The Assembly has 108 members elected by single transferable vote (six from each of the 18 Westminster constituencies). Safeguards ensure that key decisions have cross-community support. The executive powers of the Assembly will be discharged by an executive committee comprising a First Minister and Deputy First Minister (jointly elected by the Assembly on a cross-community basis) and up to ten ministers with departmental responsibilities. Ministerial posts are allocated on the basis of the number of seats each party holds.

Composition

Party	Seats
UUP	28
SDLP	24
DUP	20
Sinn Fein	18
Alliance Party	6
UK Unionist Party	5
Progressive Unionist Party	2
Northern Ireland Women's Coalition	2
Others	3

Presiding Officer, Lord Alderdice
First Minister, David Trimble, MP (UUP)
Deputy First Minister, Seamus Mallon, MP (SDLP)

OTHER BODIES

By 31 October 1998 the Northern Ireland Assembly will identify at least 12 areas in which decisions are to be reached by a North/South Ministerial Council comprising ministers from the Assembly and the Irish government. In at least six of these categories, cross-border agencies will be established.

The intergovernmental conference established by the 1985 Anglo-Irish Agreement (*see* above) was replaced by a new British-Irish Intergovernmental Conference which will discuss all areas of mutual bilateral interest.

The British-Irish Council will operate on the basis of consensus and may reach agreements and pursue common policies in areas of mutual interest.

ECONOMY

FINANCE

Taxation in Northern Ireland is largely imposed and collected by the UK government. After deducting the cost of collection and of Northern Ireland's contributions to the European Union, the balance, known as the Attributed Share of Taxation, is paid over to the Northern Ireland Consolidated Fund. Northern Ireland's revenue is insufficient to meet its expenditure and is supplemented by a grant-in-aid.

	1997–8*	1998–9**
Public income	£6,830,248,928	£7,422,000,000
Public expenditure	6,862,559,199	7,422,000,000

* Outturn
** Estimate

PRODUCTION

The products of the engineering and allied industries, which employed 26,100 persons in 1995, were valued at £2,090 million. The textiles industry (manufacture of textiles and textile products), employing about 24,300 persons, produced goods valued at approximately £999 million. The food products, beverages and tobacco industry, employing about 19,400 persons, produced goods valued at £3,910 million.

In 1997, 1,478 persons were employed in mining and quarrying operations in Northern Ireland and the minerals raised (21,591,000 tonnes) were valued at £55,553,000.

COMMUNICATIONS

The total tonnage handled by Northern Ireland ports in 1997 was 19.5 million. Regular ferry, freight and container services operate to ports in Great Britain and Europe from a number of ports, with most trade passing through Belfast (60 per cent of the total), Larne and Warrenpoint.

The Northern Ireland Transport Holding Company is largely responsible for the supervision of the subsidiary

companies, Ulsterbus and Citybus (which operate the public road passenger services) and Northern Ireland Railways (collectively known as Translink). Road freight services are also provided by a large number of hauliers operating competitively under licence.

Belfast International Airport was privatized in July 1994. It provides scheduled and chartered services on domestic and international routes. In 1997–8 the airport handled approximately 2.5 million passengers and 41,000 tonnes of freight. Scheduled services also operate from Belfast City Airport (BCA) to 20 UK destinations. In 1997–8 the airport handled approximately 1.3 million passengers. City of Derry Airport (Londonderry) provides services to 14 UK and four European destinations and to Belfast, providing links to many of the locations serviced by BCA. In 1997–8 City of Derry Airport handled approximately 68,000 passengers.

NORTHERN IRELAND COUNTIES

County	Area* (sq. miles)	Lord-Lieutenant	High Sheriff, 1998
Antrim	1,093	The Lord O'Neill, TD	R. Conway
Armagh	484	The Earl of Caledon	Dr D. E. Dorman
‡Belfast City	25	Col. J. E. Wilson, OBE	J. Clarke
Down	945	Maj. W. J. Hall	B. L. Henderson
Fermanagh	647	The Earl of Erne	R. A. D. Kells
†Londonderry	798	Sir Michael McCorkell, KCVO, OBE, TD	Maj.-Gen. P. M. Welsh
‡Londonderry City	3.4	J. T. Eaton, CBE, TD	A. D. McClure
Tyrone	1,211	The Duke of Abercorn	Capt. G. H. Caldecott

* Excluding inland waters and tideways
‡ Denotes County Borough
† Excluding the City of Londonderry

DISTRICT COUNCILS

SMALL CAPITALS denotes CITY status
§ Denotes Borough Council

Council	Population (30 June 1996)	Net Annual Value	Council Clerk	Chairman †Mayor 1998
§Antrim, Co. Antrim	47,100	£30,178,161	S. J. Magee	†P. Marks
§Ards, Co. Down	67,500	29,070,618	D. J. Fallows	†G. Ennis
§ARMAGH, Co. Armagh	52,900	19,660,325	D. R. D. Mitchell	†P. Brannigan
§Ballymena, Co. Antrim	58,000	33,959,906	M. G. Rankin	†J. Currie
§Ballymoney, Co. Antrim	24,800	8,699,661	J. Dempsey	†F. Campbell
Banbridge, Co. Down	37,400	14,154,306	R. Gilmore	Mrs J. Baird
BELFAST, Co. Antrim and Co. Down	296,200	287,078,814	B. Hanna	A. Maginnis
§Carrickfergus, Co. Antrim	35,400	15,715,675	R. Boyd	†D. W. Hilditch
§Castlereagh, Co. Down	64,200	30,267,118	A. Donaldson	†J. Norris
§Coleraine, Co. Londonderry	54,500	28,265,513	W. Moore	†J. McClure
Cookstown, Co. Tyrone	31,700	13,755,959	M. J. McGuckin	S. Begley
§Craigavon, Co. Armagh	78,400	43,269,959	T. Reaney	†K. Twyble
DERRY, Co. Londonderry	103,500	60,139,480	T. J. Keaney	†M. Bradley
Down, Co. Down	60,900	22,586,030	O. O'Connor	P. Toman
Dungannon, Co. Tyrone	46,800	22,971,711	W. J. Beattie	P. Daly
Fermanagh, Co. Fermanagh	55,200	27,285,345	Mrs A. McGinley	F. McQuillan
§Larne, Co. Antrim	30,200	17,868,183	C. McGarry	†Mrs J. Drummond
§Limavady, Co. Londonderry	30,500	11,679,636	J. K. Stevenson	†G. Lynch
§Lisburn, Co. Antrim and Co. Down	105,700	56,847,179	N. Davidson	†G. Morrison
Magherafelt, Co. Londonderry	37,500	14,780,022	J. A. McLaughlin	P. Groogan
Moyle, Co. Antrim	14,900	4,703,049	R. G. Lewis	R. Kerr
Newry and Mourne, Co. Down and Co. Armagh	83,900	33,920,343	K. O'Neill	C. Smyth
§Newtownabbey, Co. Antrim	79,200	43,063,458	N. Dunn	†N. Crilly
§North Down, Co. Down	73,400	38,068,752	A. McDowell	†Mrs R. Cooling
Omagh, Co. Tyrone	46,600	21,958,441	J. P. McKinney	J. Byrne
Strabane, Co. Tyrone	36,500	13,004,829	Dr V. R. Eakin	E. Mullen

The Isle of Man

Ellan Vannin

The Isle of Man is an island situated in the Irish Sea, in latitude 54° 3'–54° 25' N. and longitude 4° 18'–4° 47' W., nearly equidistant from England, Scotland and Ireland. Although the early inhabitants were of Celtic origin, the Isle of Man was part of the Norwegian Kingdom of the Hebrides until 1266, when this was ceded to Scotland. Subsequently granted to the Stanleys (Earls of Derby) in the 15th century and later to the Dukes of Atholl, it was brought under the administration of the Crown in 1765. The island forms the bishopric of Sodor and Man.

The total land area is 221 sq. miles (572 sq. km). The report on the 1991 census showed a resident population of 69,788 (males, 33,693; females, 36,095). The main language in use is English. There are no remaining native speakers of Manx Gaelic but 643 people are able to speak the language.
CAPITAL – ΨDouglas; population (1991), 22,214.ΨCastletown (3,152) is the ancient capital; the other towns are ΨPeel (3,829) and ΨRamsey (6,496)
FLAG – A red flag charged with three conjoined armoured legs in white and gold
TYNWALD DAY – 5 July

GOVERNMENT

The Isle of Man is a self-governing Crown dependency, having its own parliamentary, legal and administrative system. The British Government is responsible for international relations and defence. Under the UK Act of Accession, Protocol 3, the island's relationship with the European Union is limited to trade alone and does not extend to financial aid. The Lieutenant-Governor is The Queen's personal representative in the island.

The legislature, Tynwald, is the oldest parliament in the world in continuous existence. It has two branches: the Legislative Council and the House of Keys. The Council consists of the President of Tynwald, the Bishop of Sodor and Man, the Attorney-General (who does not have a vote) and eight members elected by the House of Keys. The House of Keys has 24 members, elected by universal adult suffrage. The branches sit separately to consider legislation and sit together, as Tynwald Court, for most other parliamentary purposes.

The presiding officer in Tynwald Court is the President of Tynwald, elected by the members, who also presides over sittings of the Legislative Council. The presiding officer of the House of Keys is Mr Speaker, who is elected by members of the House.

The principal members of the Manx Government are the Chief Minister and nine departmental ministers, who comprise the Council of Ministers.

Lieutenant-Governor, HE Sir Timothy Daunt, KCMG
  ADC to the Lieutenant-Governor, vacant
President of Tynwald, The Hon. Sir Charles Kerruish, OBE
Speaker, House of Keys, The Hon. N. Q. Cringle
The First Deemster and Clerk of the Rolls, His Honour T. W. Cain
Clerk of Tynwald, Secretary to the House of Keys and Counsel to the Speaker, Prof. T. St J. N. Bates
Clerk of Legislative Council and Clerk Assistant of Tynwald, T. A. Bawden
Attorney-General, W. J. H. Corlett
Chief Minister, The Hon. D. J. Gelling
Chief Secretary, J. F. Kissack
Chief Financial Officer, J. A. Cashen

ECONOMY

Most of the income generated in the island is earned in the services sector with financial and professional services accounting for just over half of the national income. Tourism and manufacturing are also major generators of income whilst the island's other traditional industries of agriculture and fishing now play a smaller role in the economy.

Under the terms of Protocol 3, the island has tariff-free access to EU markets for its goods.

The island's unemployment rate is approximately 1.5 per cent and price inflation is around 3 per cent per annum.

FINANCE

The budget for 1998–9 provided for net revenue expenditure of £264 million. The principal sources of government revenue are taxes on income and expenditure. Income tax is payable at a rate of 15 per cent on the first £9,500 of taxable income for single resident individuals and 20 per cent on the balance, after personal allowances of £7,070. These bands are doubled for married couples. The rate of income tax is 20 per cent on the whole taxable income of non-residents and companies. By agreement with the British Government, the island keeps most of its rates of indirect taxation (VAT and duties) the same as those in the United Kingdom, but this agreement may be terminated by either party. However, VAT on tourist accommodation is charged at 5 per cent. A reciprocal agreement on national insurance benefits and pensions exists between the governments of the Isle of Man and the United Kingdom. Taxes are also charged on property (rates), but these are comparatively low.

The major government expenditure items are health, social security and education, which account for 60 per cent of the government budget. The island makes a voluntary annual contribution to the United Kingdom for defence and other external services.

The island has a special relationship with the European Union and neither contributes money to nor receives funds from the EU budget.

The Channel Islands

The Channel Islands, situated off the north-west coast of France (at distances of from ten to 30 miles), are the only portions of the Dukedom of Normandy still belonging to the Crown, to which they have been attached since the Conquest. They were the only British territory to come under German occupation during the Second World War, following invasion on 30 June to 1 July 1940. The islands were relieved by British forces on 9 May 1945, and 9 May (Liberation Day) is now observed as a bank and public holiday.

The islands consist of Jersey (28,717 acres/11,630 ha), Guernsey (15,654 acres/6,340 ha), and the dependencies of Guernsey: Alderney (1,962 acres/795 ha), Brechou (74/30), Great Sark (1,035/419), Little Sark (239/97), Herm (320/130), Jethou (44/18) and Lihou (38/15) – a total of 48,083 acres/19,474 ha, or 75 sq. miles/194 sq. km. In 1991 the population of Jersey was 84,082; and of Guernsey, 58,867; Alderney, 2,297 and Sark, 575. The official languages are English and French but French is being supplanted by English, which is the language in daily use. In country districts of Jersey and Guernsey and throughout Sark a Norman-French *patois* is also in use, though to a declining extent.

GOVERNMENT

The islands are Crown dependencies with their own legislative assemblies (the States in Jersey, Guernsey and Alderney, and the Court of Chief Pleas in Sark), and systems of local administration and of law, and their own courts. Acts passed by the States require the sanction of The Queen-in-Council. The British Government is responsible for defence and international relations. The Channel Islands have trading rights alone within the European Union; these rights do not include financial aid.

In both Bailiwicks the Lieutenant-Governor and Commander-in-Chief, who is appointed by the Crown, is the personal representative of The Queen and the channel of communication between the Crown (via the Privy Council) and the island's government.

The government of each Bailiwick is conducted by committees appointed by the States. Justice is administered by the Royal Courts of Jersey and Guernsey, each consisting of the Bailiff and 12 elected Jurats. The Bailiffs of Jersey and Guernsey, appointed by the Crown, are President of the States and of the Royal Courts of their respective islands.

Each Bailiwick constitutes a deanery under the jurisdiction of the Bishop of Winchester (*see* Index).

ECONOMY

A mild climate and good soil have led to the development of intensive systems of agriculture and horticulture, which form a significant part of the economy. Equally important are invisible earnings, principally from tourism and banking and finance, the low rate of income tax (20p in the £ in Jersey and Guernsey; no tax of any kind in Sark) and the absence of super-tax and death duties making the islands a popular tax-haven.

Principal exports are agricultural produce and flowers; imports are chiefly machinery, manufactured goods, food, fuel and chemicals. Trade with the UK is regarded as internal.

British currency is legal tender in the Channel Islands but each Bailiwick issues its own coins and notes (*see* page 612). They also issue their own postage stamps; UK stamps are not valid.

JERSEY

Lieutenant-Governor and Commander-in-Chief of Jersey, HE Gen. Sir Michael Wilkes, KCB, CBE, *apptd* 1995
  Secretary and ADC, Lt.-Col. A. J. C. Woodrow, OBE, MC
Bailiff of Jersey, Sir Philip Bailhache, Kt.
Deputy Bailiff, F. C. Hamon
Attorney-General, M. C. St J. Burt, QC
Receiver-General, Gp Capt. R. Green, OBE
Solicitor-General, Miss S. C. Nicolle, QC
Greffier of the States, G. H. C. Coppock
States Treasurer, G. M. Baird

FINANCE

Year to 31 Dec.	1996	1997
Revenue income	£427,619,424	£423,764,968
Revenue expenditure	395,666,525	395,662,095
Capital expenditure	86,728,614*	93,476,388
Public debt	0	0

* restated

CHIEF TOWN – ΨSt Helier, on the south coast of Jersey
FLAG – A white field charged with a red saltire cross, and the arms of Jersey in the upper centre

GUERNSEY AND DEPENDENCIES

Lieutenant-Governor and Commander-in-Chief of the Bailiwick of Guernsey and its Dependencies, HE Vice-Adm. Sir John Coward, KCB, DSO, *apptd* 1994
  Secretary and ADC, Capt. D. P. L. Hodgetts
Bailiff of Guernsey, Sir Graham Dorey
Deputy Bailiff, de V. G. Carey
HM Procureur and Receiver-General, A. C. K. Day, QC
HM Comptroller, G. R. Rowland, QC
States Supervisor, M. J. Brown

FINANCE

Year to 31 Dec.	1996	1997
Revenue	£182,016,695	£183,273,000
Expenditure	166,817,571	168,712,000

CHIEF TOWNS – ΨSt Peter Port, on the east coast of Guernsey; St Anne on Alderney
FLAG – White, bearing a red cross of St George, with a gold cross overall in the centre

ALDERNEY

President of the States, J. Kay-Mouat, OBE
Clerk of the States, D. V. Jenkins
Clerk of the Court, A. Johnson

SARK

Seigneur of Sark, J. M. Beaumont
The Seneschal, L. P. de Carteret
The Greffier, J. P. Hamon

OTHER DEPENDENCIES

Brechou, Lihou and Jethou are leased by the Crown. Herm is leased by the States of Guernsey.

The Environment

THE RIO EARTH SUMMIT

The UN Conference on Environment and Development (UNCED) took place in Rio, Brazil, in 1992. At the conference 103 heads of state or government adopted the Rio Declaration, 27 principles intended to guide governments in pursuing economic development in ways that would benefit all and protect the environment. In particular the declaration stressed that the environment should be protected as part of development and that poorer developing countries should be helped so that they could develop in ways that would minimize damage to the environment. The measures needed to ensure such sustainable development were outlined in the document *Agenda 21*. Neither the Rio Declaration nor Agenda 21 were binding agreements. The UN Commission on Sustainable Development was set up to monitor the progress of Agenda 21.

The second UNCED took place in New York in June 1997. It was found that progress towards the goals set at Rio had been slow. The UK agreed to reverse the decline in the amount of aid it was giving to developing countries and to reduce greenhouse gas emissions to 20 per cent below their 1990 levels by 2010.

CONVENTION ON BIOLOGICAL DIVERSITY

This binding agreement was adopted by 153 states at Rio, came into force in December 1993 and was ratified by the UK in June 1994. Its aim is to lessen the destruction of biological species and habitats, and parties to the convention are required to take inventories of their plants and animals, to protect endangered species and to ensure the diversity of species and habitats in the world. The convention is being implemented through a series of scientific advisory meetings (the third of which took place in September 1997) and meetings of parties (the fourth of which took place in May 1998).

FRAMEWORK CONVENTION ON CLIMATE CHANGE

This convention, also a binding agreement, was adopted by 153 states at Rio, ratified by the UK in December 1993 and came into force in March 1994. It is intended to reduce the risks of global warming by limiting 'greenhouse' gas emissions. It recommended that industrialized countries reduce 'greenhouse' gas emissions to 1990 levels by 2000. Parties are required to reduce emissions but are not bound to the recommended targets.

Progress towards the convention's targets is reviewed at regular conferences. The most recent of these was held in Kyoto, Japan, in December 1997 and the 159 countries represented agreed the Kyoto Protocol, which covers the six main 'greenhouse' gases (carbon dioxide, methane, nitrous oxide, hydrofluorocarbons (HFCs), perfluorocarbons (PFCs), sulphur hexafluoride (SF_6)). Under the protocol:

– 38 industrial countries agreed to legally binding targets for cutting their emissions of greenhouse gases to at least 5.2 per cent below 1990 levels between 2008 and 2012. EU members agreed to an 8 per cent reduction in emissions
– nations are permitted to trade carbon permits, i.e. those close to their ceiling of allowed emissions could buy the right to pollute from those who had not used up their capacity
– nations can also offset emissions by using features such as forests that absorb carbon gases

Sanctions for those not meeting their targets are to be agreed at a later date. A framework convention detailing how these commitments will be met is to be agreed before the protocol comes into force. Follow-up talks are to take place in Buenos Aires, Argentina, in November 1998.

STATEMENT OF PRINCIPLES ON FORESTS

This non-binding agreement was intended to preserve tropical rain forests. It was recognized that forests must meet human needs (as a national resource providing timber and fuel) and that forests are important for absorbing carbon dioxide. The statement recommends the development of sustainable forest management policies and financial aid to developing countries so that they can preserve their forests.

EUROPEAN UNION PROGRAMMES

The EC environmental action programmes are underpinned by the following principles: preventative action; the rectification of environmental damage at source where possible; and the 'polluter pays' principle (i.e. the polluter meets the full cost of the control of pollution). Since the first environmental action plan was adopted in 1972 over 300 EC directives concerning the protection of the environment have been agreed. These must be transposed into national law and policy to be effective.

The EC Fifth Environmental Action Programme, called 'Towards Sustainability', was endorsed in December 1992 and is the EC programme for sustainable development to 2000. It is based on the concept of joint action by national governments, local authorities, private companies and individuals. A review of the programme, setting out priorities for further action, including further integration of environmental considerations into other policy areas, was completed in 1998.

The European Environment Agency was established in 1993 to monitor the state of the environment in Europe and to provide comparable environmental information at pan-European level.

UK MEASURES

The UK's international commitments on the environment have been incorporated into annual white papers called *This Common Inheritance*. These reports summarize the Government's commitments, state what has been achieved in the previous year and outline future action and targets. Among the issues covered by the reports are climate change, wildlife and habitats, rural and urban development, air and water quality, pollution and waste, forestry and soil, and transport.

UK governments have increasingly seen environmental policy as part of a broader concept of sustainable development. This involves achieving environmental, economic and social objectives simultaneously, with environmental impact taken into account in all areas of policy (including transport and agriculture) rather than being considered in isolation. Government policy and operations are subject to scrutiny by the parliamentary environmental audit committee.

The UK produced its first national sustainable development strategy in 1994 and its first set of sustainable development indicators in 1996. Consultation on a new strategy took place in early 1998 and a White Paper is to be published (probably in 1999) which will include revised indicators and targets. (For targets set in 1995 and achievements, see below.)

BIOLOGICAL DIVERSITY

The UK Biodiversity Group was set up after the Rio Earth Summit to identify and draw up costed action plans to protect the most threatened and declining species in the UK. The group's report, published in December 1995, identified 1,250 species and 38 key habitats which require action to protect them. Action plans for 116 species and 14 habitats have been produced so far, and a further 286 species and 24 habitat plans are expected to be completed by the end of 1998.

CLIMATE CHANGE AND POLLUTION

The Climate Change Impact Review Group was set up after Rio to review all previously published work on the effects of climate change. In July 1996 the group published the *Review of the Potential Effects of Climate Change in the UK*, a sector by sector analysis of the impacts of climate change on sea level, the natural environment, energy and transport for the 2020s and 2050s in the UK.

The National Air Quality Strategy was adopted in March 1997. It is a framework for improving air quality. It sets quality standards for the main air pollutants and specific air quality objectives to be met by 2005, and outlines how industry, central and local government, transport and other sectors can contribute to improving air quality.

Progress towards sustainable development is measured by indicators first published in 1996. There are 118 indicators in 21 categories, e.g. economy, leisure and tourism, wildlife and habitats. A revised set of indicators is to be published in 1998 and the Ministry of Agriculture, Fisheries and Food has also begun work on a set of indicators of some of the pressures that agriculture exerts on the environment.

LOCAL AGENDA 21

Local authorities (and local communities) are being encouraged to play their part in meeting the UK's commitments under Agenda 21 and to a lesser degree the Biological Diversity and Climate Change Conventions. Under Local Agenda 21, local authorities draw up a sustainable development strategy for their areas. The main aims of the strategy are to protect and enhance the local environment while meeting social needs and promoting economic success.

Each strategy should identify the local sustainability issues, set explicit objectives and priorities, state which organizations or sectors will take which actions, show how the objectives will be achieved and progress assessed, and outline the procedures for updating the strategy over time. Issues that might be covered by a local sustainability strategy include health, housing, home energy conservation, development plans, transport, air quality, biodiversity and recycling.

Local Agenda 21 is managed by the Local Agenda 21 Steering Group, made up of representatives from the Local Government Association, the Convention of Scottish Local Authorities, the Association of Local Authorities of Northern Ireland, the TUC, the Advisory Committee on Business and the Environment, the World-Wide Fund for Nature, and other organizations. The International Council for Local Environmental Initiatives (ICLEI) is co-ordinating the international Local Agenda 21 initiative and the results of these efforts are reported via local government associations to the United Nations Commission on Sustainable Development.

Local authorities are under no statutory obligation to take part in Local Agenda 21 but a survey in 1996 found that 70 per cent of local authorities are engaged in or committed to Local Agenda 21. The Government would like all local authorities to adopt a Local Agenda 21 strategy by 2000.

BUSINESSES

The Environmental Technology Best Practice Programme was set up in 1994 to help businesses to improve their environmental performance. Businesses are advised on how to minimize waste and to reduce waste at source and in the production process in ways that are low-cost or offer potential savings. The programme publishes free guides to good practice and case studies on low-cost waste minimization measures, cleaner technologies and on specific sectors and pollutants. The specific sectors covered so far are foundries, metal finishing, volatile organic compounds (solvents), textiles, paper and board, glass, printing, food and drink, and chemicals. Work is currently being carried out on guides for engineering and ceramics.

The Environmental Helpline offers advice to business on any environmental issue.

UK TARGETS AND RECENT ACHIEVEMENTS *as at February 1997*

Global Atmosphere
– return carbon dioxide and other greenhouse gas emissions to 1990 levels by 2000
– phase out production and supply of CFCs by end of 1994 (*achieved*)
– return atmospheric chlorine and bromide to 1994 levels by 2012
– phase out HCFCs by 2015 and cut consumption of methyl bromide by 25 per cent by 1998

Air Quality and Noise
– reduce sulphur dioxide emissions by 80 per cent on 1980 levels by 2010
– maintain emissions of oxides of nitrogen at 1987 levels from 1994 (*being achieved*)
– cut emissions from large combustion plants by 60 per cent between 1980 and 2003 (sulphur dioxide) and by 30 per cent between 1980 and 1988 (oxides of nitrogen)

Fresh Water and the Sea
– bring drinking water standards up to EC Directive standards by the mid-1990s (*largely achieved: in 1995, 99.5 per cent of tests in England and Wales met standards*)
– bring bathing waters fully up to EC Directive standards by the mid-1990s (*90 per cent of UK bathing waters met the standards in 1996*)
– phase out dumping of waste from collieries at sea by 1997 (*achieved in 1995*) and dumping of sewage sludge at sea by end of 1998
– halve atmospheric inputs of 17 harmful substances by 1999

Forestry
– double England's forest in the next 50 years (currently 7.5 per cent of total land area), subject to the necessary Common Agricultural Policy reform
– increase woodland cover in Wales by 50 per cent in next 50 years (currently 12 per cent of total land area)

Energy
– achieve energy savings of 250 petajoules per year by 2000

– achieve 15 per cent improvement in energy efficiency of government estate over five years to March 1996 (*achieved 14.5 per cent improvement*). New target set of 20 per cent improvement by 2000
– create 1500 MW of new electricity generating capacity from renewable resources by 2000

Waste
Reduce proportion of controlled waste going to landfill from 70 per cent to 60 per cent by 2005:
– recycle or compost 25 per cent of household waste by 2000
– 1 million tonnes of organic household waste a year to be composted by 2000, and 40 per cent of domestic properties with a garden to carry out composting by 2000
– 40 per cent of soil improvers and growing media in UK to be supplied by non-peat materials by 2005
– maintain at least 90 per cent recycling rate for waste lead-acid batteries
– increase use of waste/recycled materials as aggregates in England from about 30 to 55 million tonnes a year by 2006
– recover 50–65 per cent of packaging waste by 2001 and recycle 25–45 per cent by 2001 (minimum of 15 per cent for each material)
– ensure 40 per cent of UK newspaper feedstock to be waste paper by 2000
– recover 65 per cent of scrap tyres
– achieve easily accessible recycling facilities for 80 per cent of households by 2000

Housing
– reduce the proportion of homes lying empty to 3 per cent by 2005
– ensure that half of all new housing is built on re-used sites by 2005
– reduce number of government-owned empty homes. By April 1997 Home and Scottish Offices to have vacant (for no more than six months) only 1 per cent of their homes which are or could be made habitable, Welsh Office 5 per cent and Department of Transport 7 per cent

ADDRESSES

ADVISORY COMMITTEE ON BUSINESS AND THE ENVIRONMENT, Floor 6/D9, Ashdown House, 123 Victoria Street, London SWIE 6DE. Tel: 0171-890 6624
ENVIRONMENT AGENCY, *see* page 301
ENVIRONMENTAL TECHNOLOGY BEST PRACTICE PROGRAMME, The Environmental Helpline: 0800-585794
EUROPEAN ENVIRONMENT AGENCY, Kongens Nytorv 6, DK-1050 Copenhagen K, Denmark. Tel: Copenhagen 3336 7100. Web: http://www.eea.eu.int
GOVERNMENT PANEL ON SUSTAINABLE DEVELOPMENT, Zone 4/F5 Ashdown House, 123 Victoria Street, London SWIE 6DE. Tel: 0171-890 4962
INTERNATIONAL COUNCIL FOR LOCAL ENVIRONMENTAL INITIATIVES (ICLEI), City Hall, East Tower, 8th Floor, Toronto, Ontario M5H 2N2, Canada. Tel: Toronto 392 1462. Web: http://wwww.iclei.org
LOCAL AGENDA 21, The Local Government Management Board, Layden House, 76-78 Turnmill Street, London ECIM 5QU. Tel: 0171-296 6599. Web: http://www.lgmb.gov.uk
ROYAL COMMISSION ON ENVIRONMENTAL POLLUTION, *see* page 301
SCOTTISH ENVIRONMENT PROTECTION AGENCY, *see* page 339

UK BIODIVERSITY GROUP, c/o Biodiversity Action Plan Secretariat, European Wildlife Division, Department of the Environment, Transport and the Regions, Room 902D Tollgate House, Houlton Street, Bristol BS2 9DJ. Tel: 0117-987 8974
UK ROUND TABLE ON SUSTAINABLE DEVELOPMENT, Zone 4/F4 Ashdown House, 123 Victoria Street, London SWIE 6DE. Tel: 0171-890 4962
UN COMMISSION ON SUSTAINABLE DEVELOPMENT, Division for Sustainable Development, Room DC2, 2220 United Nations, New York, NY 10017, USA. Tel: New York 963 3170

Conservation and Heritage

Conservation of the Countryside

NATIONAL PARKS

ENGLAND AND WALES

The ten National Parks of England and Wales were set up under the provisions of the National Parks and Access to the Countryside Act 1949 to conserve and protect scenic landscapes from inappropriate development and to provide access to the land for public enjoyment.

The Countryside Commission is the statutory body which has the power to designate National Parks in England, and the Countryside Council for Wales is responsible for National Parks in Wales. Designations in England are confirmed by the Secretary of State for the Environment, and those in Wales by the Secretary of State for Wales. The designation of a National Park does not affect the ownership of the land or remove the rights of the local community. The majority of the land in the National Parks is owned by private landowners (74 per cent) or by bodies such as the National Trust (7 per cent) and the Forestry Commission (7 per cent). The National Park Authorities own only 2.3 per cent of the land.

The Environment Act 1995 replaced the existing National Park boards and committees with free-standing National Park Authorities (NPAs). NPAs are the sole local planning authorities for their areas and as such influence land use and development, and deal with planning applications. Their duties include conserving and enhancing the natural beauty, wildlife and cultural heritage of the National Parks; promoting opportunities for public understanding and enjoyment of the National Parks; and fostering the economic and social well-being of the communities within National Parks. The NPAs publish management plans as statements of their policies and appoint their own officers and staff.

Membership of the NPAs differs slightly between England and Wales. In England membership is split between representatives of the constituent local authorities and members appointed by the Secretary of State (of whom one half minus one are nominated by the parish councils in the park), with the local authority representatives in a majority of one. The Countryside Commission advises the Secretary of State on appointments not nominated by the parish councils. In Wales two-thirds of NPA members are appointed by the constituent local authorities and one-third are appointed by the Secretary of State for Wales, advised by the Countryside Council for Wales.

Central government provides 75 per cent of the funding for the parks through the National Park Grant. The remaining 25 per cent is supplied by the local authorities concerned. Approved net expenditure for all National Parks in 1998–9 was £23,285,900 for England and £8,045,333 for Wales.

Two areas considered as having equivalent status are the Broads and the New Forest (see page 575).

The National Parks (with date designation confirmed) are:

BRECON BEACONS (1957), Powys (66 per cent)/Carmarthenshire/Rhondda, Cynon and Taff/Merthyr Tydfil/Blaenau Gwent/Monmouthshire,

1,351 sq. km/522 sq. miles – The park is centred on the Beacons, Pen y Fan, Corn Du and Cribyn, but also includes the valley of the Usk, the Black Mountains to the east and the Black Mountain to the west. There are information centres at Brecon, Craig-y-nos Country Park, Abergavenny and Llandovery, a study centre at Danywenallt and a day visitor centre near Libanus. *Information Office*, 7 Glamorgan Street, Brecon, Powys LD3 7DP. Tel: 01874-624437. *National Park Officer*, M. Fitton

DARTMOOR (1951 and 1994), Devon, 954 sq. km/368 sq. miles – The park consists of moorland and rocky granite tors, and is rich in prehistoric remains. There are information centres at Newbridge, Tavistock, Bovey Tracey, Steps Bridge, Princetown and Postbridge. *Information Office*, Parke, Haytor Road, Bovey Tracey, Devon TQ13 9JQ. Tel: 01626-832093. *National Park Officer*, N. Atkinson

EXMOOR (1954), Somerset (71 per cent)/Devon, 693 sq. km/268 sq. miles – Exmoor is a moorland plateau inhabited by wild ponies and red deer. There are information centres at Lynmouth, County Gate, Dulverton and Combe Martin. *Information Office*, Exmoor House, Dulverton, Somerset TA22 9HL. Tel: 01398-23665. *National Park Officer*, K. Bungay

LAKE DISTRICT (1951), Cumbria, 2,292 sq. km/885 sq. miles – The Lake District includes England's highest mountains (Scafell Pike, Helvellyn and Skiddaw) but it is most famous for its glaciated lakes. There are information centres at Keswick, Waterhead, Hawkshead, Seatoller, Bowness, Grasmere, Coniston, Glenridding and Pooley Bridge, an information van at Gosforth and a park centre at Brockhole, Windermere. *Information Office*, Brockhole, Windermere, Cumbria LA23 1LJ. Tel: 01539-446601. *National Park Officer*, P. Tiplady

NORTHUMBERLAND (1956), Northumberland, 1,049 sq. km/405 sq. miles – The park is an area of hill country stretching from Hadrian's Wall to the Scottish Border. There are information centres at Ingram, Once Brewed, Rothbury, Housesteads, Harbottle and Kielder, and an information caravan at Cawfields. *Information Office*, Eastburn, South Park, Hexham, Northumberland NE46 1BS. Tel: 01434-605555. *National Park Officer*, G. Taylor

NORTH YORK MOORS (1952), North Yorkshire (96 per cent)/Redcar and Cleveland, 1,436 sq. km/554 sq. miles – The park consists of woodland and moorland, and includes the Hambleton Hills and the Cleveland Way. There are information centres at Danby, Pickering, Sutton Bank, Ravenscar, Helmsley and Hutton-le-Hole, and a day study centre at Danby. *Information Office*, The Old Vicarage, Bondgate, Helmsley, York YO6 5BP. Tel: 01439-70657. *National Park Officer*, D. Arnold-Forster

PEAK DISTRICT (1951), Derbyshire (64 per cent)/Staffordshire/South Yorkshire/Cheshire/West Yorkshire/Greater Manchester, 1,438 sq. km/555 sq. miles – The Peak District includes the gritstone moors

of the 'Dark Peak' and the limestone dales of the 'White Peak'. There are information centres at Bakewell, Edale, Fairholmes and Castleton, and information points at Torside (in the Longdendale Valley) and at Hartington (former station).
Information Office, Aldern House, Baslow Road, Bakewell, Derbyshire DE45 1AE. Tel: 01629-814321. *National Park Officer*, C. Harrison
PEMBROKESHIRE COAST (1952 and 1995), Pembrokeshire, 584 sq. km/225 sq. miles – The park includes cliffs, moorland and a number of islands, including Skomer. There are information centres at Tenby, St David's, Pembroke, Newport, Kilgetty, Haverfordwest and Broad Haven.
Information Office, Winch Lane, Haverfordwest, Pembrokeshire SA61 1PY. Tel: 01437-764636. *National Park Officer*, N. Wheeler
SNOWDONIA (1951), Gwynedd/Conwy, 2,142 sq. km/827 sq. miles – Snowdonia is an area of deep valleys and rugged mountains. There are information centres at Aberdyfi, Bala, Betws y Coed, Blaenau Ffestiniog, Conwy, Harlech, Dolgellau and Llanberis.
Information Office, Penrhyndeudraeth, Gwynedd LL48 6LF. Tel: 01766-770274. *National Park Officer*, I. Huws
YORKSHIRE DALES (1954), North Yorkshire (88 per cent)/Cumbria, 1,769 sq. km/683 sq. miles – The Yorkshire Dales are composed primarily of limestone overlaid in places by millstone grit. The three peaks of Ingleborough, Whernside and Pen-y-Ghent are within the park. There are information centres at Clapham, Grassington, Hawes, Aysgarth Falls, Malham and Sedbergh.
Information Office, Yorebridge House, Bainbridge, Leyburn, N. Yorks DL8 3BP. Tel: 01969-50456. *National Park Officer*, H. Hancock

Two other areas considered to have equivalent status to national parks are the Broads and the New Forest. The Broads Authority, a special statutory authority, was established in 1989 to develop, conserve and manage the Norfolk and Suffolk Broads (*see also* page 287). The Government declared in 1992 its intention of giving the New Forest a status equivalent to that of a National Park by declaring it an 'area of national significance'.

THE BROADS (1989), Norfolk, 303 sq. km/117 sq. miles – The Broads are located between Norwich and Great Yarmouth on the flood plains of the five rivers flowing through the area to the sea. The area is one of fens, winding waterways, woodland and marsh. The 40 or so broads are man-made, and are connected to the rivers by dykes, providing over 200 km of navigable waterways. There are information centres at Beccles, Hoveton, North-west Tower (Yarmouth), Ranworth and Toad Hole.
Broads Authority, Thomas Harvey House, 18 Colegate, Norwich NR3 1BQ. Tel: 01603-610734. *Chief Executive*, A. Clark
THE NEW FOREST, Hampshire, 376 sq. km/145 sq. miles – The forest has been protected since 1079 when it was declared a royal hunting forest. The area consists of forest, ancient woodland and heathland. Much of the Forest is managed by the Forestry Commission, which provides several camp-sites. The main villages are Brockenhurst, Burley and Lyndhurst, which has a visitor centre.
The Forestry Commission, Office of the Deputy Surveyor of the New Forest and the New Forest Committee, The Queen's House, Lyndhurst, Hants SO43 7NH. Tel: 01703-284149

SCOTLAND AND NORTHERN IRELAND

The National Parks and Access to the Countryside Act 1949 dealt only with England and Wales and made no provision for Scotland or Northern Ireland. Although there are no national parks in these two countries, there is power to designate them in Northern Ireland under the Amenity Lands Act 1965 and the Nature Conservation and Amenity Lands Order (Northern Ireland) 1985. In 1989 the Scottish Office asked Scottish Natural Heritage to report on whether national parks should be designated in Scotland.

AREAS OF OUTSTANDING NATURAL BEAUTY

ENGLAND AND WALES

Under the National Parks and Access to the Countryside Act 1949, provision was made for the designation of Areas of Outstanding Natural Beauty (AONBs) by the Countryside Commission. The Countryside Commission continues to be responsible for AONBs in England but since April 1991 the Countryside Council for Wales has been responsible for the Welsh AONBs. Designations in England are confirmed by the Secretary of State for the Environment and those in Wales by the Secretary of State for Wales.

Although less emphasis is placed upon the provision of open-air enjoyment for the public than in the national parks, AONBs are areas which are no less beautiful and require the same degree of protection to conserve and enhance the natural beauty of the countryside. This includes protecting flora and fauna, geological and other landscape features. In AONBs planning and management responsibilities are split between county and district councils; where unitary authorities exist they have sole responsibility for planning and management. Several AONBs cross local authority boundaries. Finance for the AONBs is provided by grant-aid.

The 41 Areas of Outstanding Natural Beauty (with date designation confirmed) are:

ANGLESEY (1967), Anglesey, 221 sq. km/85 sq. miles
ARNSIDE AND SILVERDALE (1972), Cumbria/Lancashire, 75 sq. km/29 sq. miles
BLACKDOWN HILLS (1991), Devon/Somerset, 370 sq. km/143 sq. miles
CANNOCK CHASE (1958), Staffordshire, 68 sq. km/26 sq. miles
CHICHESTER HARBOUR (1964), Hampshire/West Sussex, 74 sq. km/29 sq. miles
CHILTERNS (1965; extended 1990), Bedfordshire/Hertfordshire/Buckinghamshire/Oxfordshire, 833 sq. km/322 sq. miles
CLWYDIAN RANGE (1985), Denbighshire/Flintshire, 157 sq. km/60 sq. miles
CORNWALL (1959; Camel estuary 1983), 958 sq. km/370 sq. miles
COTSWOLDS (1966; extended 1990), Gloucestershire/Wiltshire/Warwickshire/Worcestershire/Somerset, 2,038 sq. km/787 sq. miles
CRANBORNE CHASE AND WEST WILTSHIRE DOWNS (1983), Dorset/Hampshire/Somerset/Wiltshire, 983 sq. km/379 sq. miles
DEDHAM VALE (1970; extended 1978, 1991), Essex/Suffolk, 90 sq. km/35 sq. miles
DORSET (1959), 1,129 sq. km/436 sq. miles
EAST DEVON (1963), 268 sq. km/103 sq. miles
EAST HAMPSHIRE (1962), 383 sq. km/148 sq. miles
FOREST OF BOWLAND (1964), Lancashire/North Yorkshire, 802 sq. km/310 sq. miles

576   Conservation and Heritage

GOWER (1956), Swansea/Carmarthenshire, 189 sq. km/73 sq. miles

HIGH WEALD (1983), Kent/Surrey/East Sussex/West Sussex, 1,460 sq. km/564 sq. miles

HOWARDIAN HILLS (1987), North Yorkshire, 204 sq. km/ 79 sq. miles

ISLE OF WIGHT (1963), 189 sq. km/73 sq. miles

ISLES OF SCILLY (1976), 16 sq. km/6 sq. miles

KENT DOWNS (1968), 878 sq. km/339 sq. miles

LINCOLNSHIRE WOLDS (1973), 558 sq. km/215 sq. miles

LLŶN (1957), Gwynedd, 161 sq. km/62 sq. miles

MALVERN HILLS (1959), Herefordshire/Worcestershire/ Gloucestershire, 105 sq. km/40 sq. miles

MENDIP HILLS (1972; extended 1989), Somerset, 198 sq. km/76 sq. miles

NIDDERDALE (1994), North Yorkshire, 603 sq. km/233 sq. miles

NORFOLK COAST (1968), 451 sq. km/174 sq. miles

NORTH DEVON (1960), 171 sq. km/66 sq. miles

NORTH PENNINES (1988), Cumbria/Durham/ Northumberland, 1,983 sq. km/766 sq. miles

NORTHUMBERLAND COAST (1958), 135 sq. km/52 sq. miles

QUANTOCK HILLS (1957), Somerset, 99 sq. km/38 sq. miles

SHROPSHIRE HILLS (1959), 804 sq. km/310 sq. miles

SOLWAY COAST (1964), Cumbria, 115 sq. km/44 sq. miles

SOUTH DEVON (1960), 337 sq. km/130 sq. miles

SOUTH HAMPSHIRE COAST (1967), 77 sq. km/30 sq.miles

SUFFOLK COAST AND HEATHS (1970), 403 sq. km/156 sq. miles

SURREY HILLS (1958), 419 sq. km/162 sq. miles

SUSSEX DOWNS (1966), 983 sq. km/379 sq. miles

TAMAR VALLEY (1995), Cornwall/Devon, 195 sq. km/115 sq. miles

NORTH WESSEX DOWNS (1972), Berkshire/Hampshire/ Oxfordshire/Wiltshire, 1,730 sq. km/668 sq. miles

WYE VALLEY (1971), Monmouthshire/Gloucestershire/ Herefordshire, 326 sq. km/126 sq. miles

NORTHERN IRELAND

The Department of the Environment for Northern Ireland, with advice from the Council for Nature Conservation and the Countryside, designates Areas of Outstanding Natural Beauty in Northern Ireland. At present there are nine and these cover a total area of approximately 284,948 hectares (704,121 acres).

ANTRIM COAST AND GLENS , Co. Antrim, 70,600 ha/ 174,452 acres

CAUSEWAY COAST , Co. Antrim, 4,200 ha/10,378 acres

LAGAN VALLEY , Co. Down, 2,072 ha/5,119 acres

LECALE COAST , Co. Down, 3,108 ha/7,679 acres

MOURNE , Co. Down, 57,012 ha/140,876 acres

NORTH DERRY , Co. Londonderry, 12,950 ha/31,999 acres

RING OF GULLION , Co. Armagh, 15,353 ha/37,938 acres

SPERRIN , Co. Tyrone/Co. Londonderry, 101,006 ha/ 249,585 acres

STRANGFORD LOUGH , Co. Down, 18,647 ha/46,077 acres

NATIONAL SCENIC AREAS

No Areas of Outstanding Natural Beauty are designated in Scotland. However, National Scenic Areas have a broadly equivalent status. Scottish Natural Heritage recognizes areas of national scenic significance. At mid 1998 there

were 40, covering a total area of 1,001,800 hectares (2,475,448 acres).

Development within National Scenic Areas is dealt with by the local planning authority, who are required to consult Scottish Natural Heritage concerning certain categories of development. Land management uses can also be modified in the interest of scenic conservation. The Secretary of State for Scotland has limited powers of intervention should a planning authority and Scottish Natural Heritage disagree.

ASSYNT-COIGACH, Highland, 90,200 ha/222,884 acres

BEN NEVIS AND GLEN COE, Highland/Argyll and Bute/ Perthshire and Kinross, 101,600 ha/251,053 acres

CAIRNGORM MOUNTAINS, Highland/Aberdeenshire/ Moray, 67,200 ha/166,051 acres

CUILLIN HILLS, Highland, 21,900 ha/54,115 acres

DEESIDE AND LOCHNAGAR, Aberdeenshire/Angus, 40,000 ha/98,840 acres

DORNOCH FIRTH, Highland, 7,500 ha/18,532 acres

EAST STEWARTRY COAST, Dumfries and Galloway, 4,500 ha/11,119 acres

EILDON AND LEADERFOOT, Borders, 3,600 ha/8,896 acres

FLEET VALLEY, Dumfries and Galloway, 5,300 ha/13,096 acres

GLEN AFFRIC, Highland, 19,300 ha/47,690 acres

GLEN STRATHFARRAR, Highland, 3,800 ha/9,390 acres

HOY AND WEST MAINLAND, Orkney Islands, 14,800 ha/ 36,571 acres

JURA, Argyll and Bute, 21,800 ha/53,868 acres

KINTAIL, Highland, 15,500 ha/38,300 acres

KNAPDALE, Argyll and Bute, 19,800 ha/48,926 acres

KNOYDART, Highland, 39,500 ha/97,604 acres

KYLE OF TONGUE, Highland, 18,500 ha/45,713 acres

KYLES OF BUTE, Argyll and Bute, 4,400 ha/10,872 acres

LOCH NA KEAL, MULL, Argyll and Bute, 12,700 ha/ 31,382 acres

LOCH LOMOND, Argyll and Bute/Stirling/West Dumbartonshire, 27,400 ha/67,705 acres

LOCH RANNOCH AND GLEN LYON, Perthshire and Kinross/Stirling, 48,400 ha/119,596 acres

LOCH SHIEL, Highland, 13,400 ha/33,111 acres

LOCH TUMMEL, Perthshire and Kinross, 9,200 ha/22,733 acres

LYNN OF LORN, Argyll and Bute, 4,800 ha/11,861 acres

MORAR, MOIDART AND ARDNAMURCHAN, Highland, 13,500 ha/33,358 acres

NORTH-WEST SUTHERLAND, Highland, 20,500 ha/50,655 acres

NITH ESTUARY, Dumfries and Galloway, 9,300 ha/ 22,980 acres

NORTH ARRAN, North Ayrshire, 23,800 ha/58,810 acres

RIVER EARN, Perthshire and Kinross, 3,000 ha/7,413 acres

RIVER TAY, Perthshire and Kinross, 5,600 ha/13,838 acres

ST KILDA, Western Isles, 900 ha/2,224 acres

SCARBA, LUNGA AND THE GARVELLACHS, Argyll and Bute, 1,900 ha/4,695 acres

SHETLAND, Shetland Islands, 11,600 ha/28,664 acres

SMALL ISLES, Highland, 15,500 ha/38,300 acres

SOUTH LEWIS, HARRIS AND NORTH UIST, Western Isles, 109,600 ha/270,822 acres

SOUTH UIST MACHAIR, Western Isles, 6,100 ha/15,073 acres

THE TROSSACHS, Stirling, 4,600 ha/11,367 acres

TROTTERNISH, Highland, 5,000 ha/12,355 acres

UPPER TWEEDDALE, Borders, 10,500 ha/25,945 acres

WESTER ROSS, Highland, 145,300 ha/359,036 acres

THE NATIONAL FOREST

The National Forest is being planted in about 200 square miles of Derbyshire, Leicestershire and Staffordshire. About 30 million trees, of mixed species but mainly broadleaved, will be planted over the next 20 years and beyond, and will eventually cover about one-third of the designated area. The project is funded by the Department of the Environment, Transport and the Regions. It was developed in 1992–5 by the Countryside Commission and is now run by the National Forest Company. Competitive bids for woodland creation projects are submitted to the National Forest Company by anybody who wishes to undertake a project, and are considered under the National Forest tender scheme. Sixteen tenders were approved in the first round of the scheme in 1995. Approval of tenders in the second round of the scheme was given in autumn 1996 and the results of the third round were announced in autumn 1997.

NATIONAL FOREST COMPANY, Enterprise Glade, Bath Lane, Moira, Swadlincote, Derbys DE12 6BD. Tel: 01283-551211. *Chief Executive*, Miss S. Bell

Nature Conservation Areas

SITES OF SPECIAL SCIENTIFIC INTEREST

Site of Special Scientific Interest (SSSI) is a legal notification applied to land in England, Scotland or Wales which English Nature (EN), Scottish Natural Heritage (SNH), or the Countryside Council for Wales (CCW) identifies as being of special interest because of its flora, fauna, geological or physiographical features. In some cases, SSSIs are managed as nature reserves.

EN, SNH and CCW must notify the designation of a SSSI to the local planning authority, every owner/occupier of the land, and the relevant Secretary of State. Forestry and agricultural departments and a number of other bodies are also informed of this notification.

Objections to the notification of a SSSI can be made and ultimately considered at a full meeting of the Council of EN or CCW. In Scotland an objection will be dealt with by the appropriate regional board or the main board of SNH, depending on the nature of the objection. Unresolved objections on scientific grounds must be referred to the Advisory Committee for SSSI.

The protection of these sites depends on the co-operation of individual landowners and occupiers. Owner/occupiers must consult EN, SNH or CCW and gain written consent before they can undertake certain listed activities on the site. Funds are available through management agreements and grants to assist owners and occupiers in conserving sites' interests. As a last resort a site can be purchased.

The number and area of SSSIs in Britain as at 31 March 1998 was:

	no.	hectares	acres
England	4,000	955,000	2,359,805
Scotland	1,442	916,080	2,263,634
Wales	942	217,807	538,202

NORTHERN IRELAND

In Northern Ireland 142 Areas of Special Scientific Interest (ASSIs) have been established by the Department of the Environment for Northern Ireland. These cover a total area of 79,822.206 hectares (197,160.8 acres).

NATIONAL NATURE RESERVES

National Nature Reserves are defined in the National Parks and Access to the Countryside Act 1949 as land designated for the study and preservation of flora and fauna, or of geological or physiographical features.

English Nature (EN), Scottish Natural Heritage (SNH) or the Countryside Council for Wales (CCW) can designate as a National Nature Reserve land which is being managed as a nature reserve under an agreement with one of the statutory nature conservation agencies; land held and managed by EN, SNH or CCW; or land held and managed as a nature reserve by another approved body. EN, SNH or CCW can make by-laws to protect reserves from undesirable activities; these are subject to confirmation by the relevant Secretary of State.

The number and area of National Nature Reserves in Britain as at 31 March 1998 was:

	no.	hectares	acres
England	189	70,623	174,509
Scotland	70	113,238	279,811
Wales	62	18,592	45,922

NORTHERN IRELAND

National Nature Reserves are established and managed by the Department of the Environment for Northern Ireland, with advice from the Council for Nature Conservation and the Countryside. There are 45 National Nature Reserves covering 4,322.1 hectares (10,676 acres).

LOCAL NATURE RESERVES

Local Nature Reserves are defined in the National Parks and Access to the Countryside Act 1949 as land designated for the study and preservation of flora and fauna, or of geological or physiographical features. The Act gives local authorities in England, Scotland and Wales the power to acquire, declare and manage local nature reserves in consultation with English Nature, Scottish Natural Heritage and the Countryside Council for Wales. Conservation trusts can also own and manage non-statutory local nature reserves.

The number and area of designated Local Nature Reserves in Britain as at 31 March 1998 was:

	no.	hectares	acres
England	566	20,428	50,479
Scotland	26	8,031	19,845
Wales	40	4,256	10,517

An additional 38 km of linear trails are designated as Local Nature Reserves.

FOREST NATURE RESERVES

Forest Enterprise (an executive agency of the Forestry Commission) is responsible for the management of the Commission's forests. It has created 46 Forest Nature Reserves with the aim of protecting and conserving special forms of natural habitat, flora and fauna. There are about 300 SSSIs on the estates, some of which are also Nature Reserves.

Forest Nature Reserves extend in size from under 50 hectares (124 acres) to over 500 hectares (1,236 acres). The largest include the Black Wood of Rannoch, by Loch Rannoch; Cannop Valley Oakwoods, Forest of Dean; Culbin Forest, near Forres; Glen Affric, near Fort Augustus; Kylerhea, Skye; Pembrey, Carmarthen Bay; Starr Forest, in Galloway Forest Park; and Wyre Forest, near Kidderminster.

Forest Enterprise also manages 18 Caledonian Forest Reserves in Scotland. These reserves are intended to protect and expand 16,000 hectares of native oak and pine woods in the Scottish highlands.

NORTHERN IRELAND

There are 36 Forest Nature Reserves in Northern Ireland, covering 1,759 hectares (4,346 acres). They are designated and administered by the Forest Service, an agency of the Department of Agriculture for Northern Ireland. There are also 15 National Nature Reserves on Forest Service-owned property.

MARINE NATURE RESERVES

The Wildlife and Countryside Act 1981 gives the Secretary of State for the Environment (and the Secretaries of State for Wales and for Scotland where appropriate) power to designate Marine Nature Reserves, and English Nature, Scottish Natural Heritage and the Countryside Council for Wales powers to select and manage these reserves. Marine Nature Reserves may be established in Northern Ireland under a 1985 Order.

Marine Nature Reserves provide protection for marine flora and fauna, and geological and physiographical features on land covered by tidal waters or parts of the sea in or adjacent to the UK. Reserves also provide opportunities for study and research.

The three statutory Marine Nature Reserves are:

LUNDY (1986), Bristol Channel
SKOMER (1990), Dyfed
STRANGFORD LOUGH (1995), Northern Ireland

Two other areas proposed for designation as reserves are: the Menai Strait, and Bardsey Island and part of the Llŷn peninsula, both in Wales.

A number of non-statutory marine reserves have been set up by conservation groups.

Conservation of Wildlife and Habitats

The United Kingdom is party to a number of international conservation conventions.

RAMSAR CONVENTION

The Convention on Wetlands of International Importance especially as Waterfowl Habitat was adopted at Ramsar, Iran, in 1971 and ratified by the UK in 1976. By June 1998, 110 countries were party to the convention. The aim of the convention is to promote the protection and conservation of wetlands (e.g. areas of marsh, fen) and their flora and fauna, especially waterfowl. Governments who are party to the convention are obliged to designate wetlands in their territory for inclusion in the List of Wetlands of International Importance and to include wetland conservation considerations in their national land-use planning. As at 30 March 1998, there were 124 sites in the UK.

RAMSAR CONVENTION BUREAU, Rue Mauverney 28, CH-1196 Gland, Switzerland. Tel: Gland 999 0170. Web: http://ramsar.org

BONN CONVENTION

The Bonn Convention on the Conservation of Migratory Species of Wild Animals was adopted in 1979 and came into force in the UK on 1 October 1979. The convention requires the protection of listed endangered migratory species and encourages international agreements covering these and other threatened species.

The United Kingdom has signed and ratified two regional agreements under the convention: the Agreement on the Conservation of Small Cetaceans of the Baltic and North Seas (ASCOBANS), protecting dolphins and porpoises, etc; and the Agreement on the Conservation of Bats in Europe. The UK is also a signatory to the African-Eurasian Migratory Waterbird Agreement (AEWA), which is aimed at protecting migrant waterbirds, and is working towards becoming a signatory (on behalf of Gibraltar) to the Agreement on the Conservation of Cetaceans in the Mediterranean and Black Seas (ACCOBAMS).

UNEP/CMS SECRETARIAT, United Nations Premises in Bonn, Martin-Luther-King Strasse 8, D-53175 Bonn, Germany. Tel: Bonn 815 2401. Web: http://www.wcmc.org.uk/cms

BERN CONVENTION

The Convention on the Conservation of European Wildlife and Natural Habitats was adopted in 1979 and ratified by the UK in 1982. The aim of the convention is to conserve flora and fauna and their natural habitats in Europe. Particular emphasis is placed on the protection of endangered and vulnerable species (both endemic and migratory) and on those species and habitats whose conservation requires the co-operation of several states.

Parties to the convention undertake to maintain populations (or take steps to increase populations where necessary) of species covered by the convention while taking account of local cultural, economic and recreational requirements and the requirements of sub-species. They must also ensure that national and local planning and development policies take account of wildlife and fauna.

SECRETARIAT OF THE BERN CONVENTION STANDING COMMITTEE, Council of Europe, F-67075 Strasbourg Cedex, France. Tel: Strasbourg 8841 2253. Web: http://www.coe.com

HABITATS DIRECTIVE

The Council (EC) Directive on the Conservation of Natural Habitats of Wild Fauna and Flora was adopted by the Council in 1992 and became law in the UK in 1994 as the Conservation (Natural Habitats) Regulations. Under this directive EU members are required to maintain or restore natural habitats and wild species (other than birds) and to designate Special Areas of Conservation (SACs). SACs are those areas that are considered to be of European-wide importance because they are rare, threatened or important for the maintenance of biological diversity in Europe. The directive specifies the habitat types and species which require site designation: 75 habitat types and 47 species are proposed for site designation in the UK.

Member states compile a national list from which a final list of European importance will be drawn by 2004. By June 1998 the UK had submitted a total of 315 candidate sites to the Commission.

BIRDS DIRECTIVE

The Council (EC) Directive on the Conservation of Wild Birds was adopted by the Council in 1979 and came into force in April 1981. Under this directive EU members are required to maintain populations of wild birds and to preserve the diversity and area of their habitats. The species that are to be protected are listed in Annex 1 to the directive and are those species that are in danger of extinction, rare, or vulnerable to changes in their habitat.

Members are also obliged, under the directive, to notify the Commission of sites which are of particular importance to the conservation of wild birds. These sites are designated as Special Protection Areas (SPAs). Any site that is to be designated as a SPA in the UK must first have been notified as a Site of Special Scientific Interest or Area of Special Scientific Interest (see page 577). Sites may be designated as SPAs if they are of national or international importance.

By February 1998, a total of 1,740 SPAs had been designated, of which 169 are in the UK. The UK designations cover over 700,000 hectares.

CITES

The Convention on Trade in Endangered Species of Wild Fauna and Flora (CITES) was agreed in 1973 and came into force in 1975. It aims to prevent international trade in wildlife and their products, e.g. skins, from threatening species with extinction. Plant and animal species subject to regulation are listed according to the degree of protection they need:

– appendix I is a list of species threatened with extinction that are, or may be, affected by trade. International trade in these species is prohibited

– appendix II is a list of species which might become threatened if trade in them is not controlled. A permit is required to trade in these species

– appendix III is a list of species, protected within individual countries, where the country has asked other parties to the convention to assist in controlling international trade. A permit is required to trade in these species

Approximately 30,000 species are covered by the regulations.

The Wildlife Licensing and Registration Service (Wildlife and Countryside Directorate) of the Department of Environment, Transport and the Regions (see page 299) is responsible for issuing permits and compiling annual

580   Conservation and Heritage

trade reports. The Joint Nature Conservation Committee (*see* page 329) and the Royal Botanic Gardens (*see* page 338) are the officially designated scientific authorities (on animals and plants respectively) who provide the expertise on which import and export approvals are based. CITES is financed by contributions from the member countries.
CITES Secretariat, 15 Chemin des Anémones, CH-1219 Châtelaine, Geneva, Switzerland. Tel: Geneva 2979 9139

European Wildlife Trade Regulation

The Council (EC) Regulation on the Protection of Species of Wild Fauna and Flora by Regulating Trade Therein came into force in the UK on 1 June 1997. It is intended to standardize wildlife trade regulations across Europe and to improve the application of CITES. Approximately 30,000 plant and animal species are protected under the regulation.

UK Legislation

The Wildlife and Countryside Act 1981 gives legal protection to a wide range of wild animals and plants. Subject to parliamentary approval, the Secretary of State for the Environment may vary the animals and plants given legal protection. The most recent variation of Schedules 5 and 8 came into effect in March and April 1998.

Under Section 9 and Schedule 5 of the Act it is illegal without a licence to kill, injure, take, possess or sell any of the listed animals (whether alive or dead) and to disturb its place of shelter and protection or to destroy that place.

Under Section 13 and Schedule 8 of the Act it is illegal without a licence to pick, uproot, sell or destroy any of the listed plants and, unless authorized, to uproot any wild plant.

The Act lays down a close season for wild birds (other than game birds) from 1 February to 31 August inclusive, each year. Exceptions to these dates are made for:
Capercaillie and (except Scotland) *Woodcock* – 1 February to 30 September
Snipe – 1 February to 11 August
Wild Duck and *Wild Goose* (below high water mark) – 21 February to 31 August

Birds which may be killed or taken outside the close season (except on Sundays and on Christmas Day in Scotland, and on Sundays in prescribed areas of England and Wales) are the above-named, plus coot, certain wild duck (gadwall, goldeneye, mallard, pintail, pochard, shoveler, teal, tufted duck, wigeon), certain wild geese (Canada, greylag, pink-footed, white-fronted (in England and Wales only)), moorhen, golden plover and woodcock.

Certain wild birds may be killed or taken subject to the conditions of a general licence at any time by authorized persons: crow, collared dove, gull (great and lesser black-backed or herring), jackdaw, jay, magpie, pigeon (feral or wood), rook, sparrow (house), and starling. Conditions usually apply where the birds pose a threat to agriculture, public health, air safety, other bird species, and to prevent the spread of disease.

All other British birds are fully protected by law throughout the year.

Animals

‡Adder (*Vipera berus*)
Anemone, Ivell's Sea (*Edwardsia ivelli*)
Anemone, Starlet Sea (*Nematosella vectensis*)
Apus, Tadpole shrimp (*Triops cancriformis*)
Bat, Horseshoe (*Rhinolophidae*, all species)
Bat, Typical (*Vespertilionidae*, all species)
Beetle (*Graphoderus zonatus*)
Beetle (*Hypebaeus flavipes*)

Beetle, Lesser Silver Water (*Hydrochara caraboides*)
§§Beetle, Mire Pill (*Curimopsis nigrita*)
Beetle, Rainbow Leaf (*Chrysolina cerealis*)
*Beetle, Stag (*Lucanus cervus*)
Beetle, Violet Click (*Limoniscus violaceus*)
Beetle, Water (*Graphoderus zonatus*)
Beetle, Water (*Paracymus aeneus*)
Burbot (*Lota lota*)
*Butterfly, Adonis Blue (*Lysandra bellargus*)
*Butterfly, Black Hairstreak (*Strymonidia pruni*)
*Butterfly, Brown Hairstreak (*Thecla betulae*)
*Butterfly, Chalkhill Blue (*Lysandra coridon*)
*Butterfly, Chequered Skipper (*Carterocephalus palaemon*)
*Butterfly, Duke of Burgundy Fritillary (*Hamearis lucina*)
*Butterfly, Glanville Fritillary (*Melitaea cinxia*)
Butterfly, Heath Fritillary (*Mellicta athalia* (or *Melitaea athalia*))
Butterfly, High Brown Fritillary (*Argynnis adippe*)
Butterfly, Large Blue (*Maculinea arion*)
Butterfly, Large Copper (*Lycaena dispar*)
*Butterfly, Large Heath (*Coenonympha tullia*)
*Butterfly, Large Tortoiseshell (*Nymphalis polychloros*)
*Butterfly, Lulworth Skipper (*Thymelicus acteon*)
Butterfly, Marsh Fritillary (*Eurodryas aurinia*)
*Butterfly, Mountain Ringlet (*Erebia epiphron*)
*Butterfly, Northern Brown Argus (*Aricia artaxerxes*)
*Butterfly, Pearl-bordered Fritillary (*Boloria euphrosyne*)
*Butterfly, Purple Emperor (*Apatura iris*)
*Butterfly, Silver Spotted Skipper (*Hesperia comma*)
*Butterfly, Silver-studded Blue (*Plebejus argus*)
*Butterfly, Small Blue (*Cupido minimus*)
Butterfly, Swallowtail (*Papilio machaon*)
*Butterfly, White Letter Hairstreak (*Stymonida w-album*)
*Butterfly, Wood White (*Leptidea sinapis*)
Cat, Wild (*Felis silvestris*)
Cicada, New Forest (*Cicadetta montana*)
**Crayfish, Atlantic stream (*Austropotamobius pallipes*)
Cricket, Field (*Gryllus campestris*)
Cricket, Mole (*Gryllotalpa gryllotalpa*)
Damselfly, Southern (*Coenagrion mercuriale*)
Dolphin (*Cetacea*)
Dormouse (*Muscardinus avellanarius*)
Dragonfly, Norfolk Aeshna (*Aeshna isosceles*)
*Frog, Common (*Rana temporaria*)
Goby, Couch's (*Gobius couchii*)
Goby, Giant (*Gobius cobitis*)
Grasshopper, Wart-biter (*Decticus verrucivorus*)
Hatchet Shell, Northern (*Thyasira gouldi*)
Hydroid, Marine (*Clavopsella navis*)
Lagoon Snail (*Paludinella littorina*)
Lagoon Snail, De Folin's (*Caecum armoricum*)
Lagoon Worm, Tentacled (*Alkmaria romijni*)
Leech, Medicinal (*Hirudo medicinalis*)
Lizard, Sand (*Lacerta agilis*)
‡Lizard, Viviparous (*Lacerta vivipara*)
Marten, Pine (*Martes martes*)
Moth, Barberry Carpet (*Pareulype berberata*)
Moth, Black-veined (*Siona lineata* (or *Idaea lineata*))
Moth, Essex Emerald (*Thetidia smaragdaria*)
Moth, Fiery clearwing (*Bembecia chrysidiformis*)

*   The offence relates to sale only
**   The offence relates to 'taking' and 'sale' only
†   The offence relates to 'killing and injuring' only
‡   The offence relates to 'killing, injuring and sale'
§   The offence relates to 'killing, injuring and taking'
§§ The offence relates only to damaging, destroying or obstructing access to a shelter or protection
†† The offence relates to killing, injuring, taking, possession and sale
‡‡ The offence relates to killing, injuring, taking and damaging, etc., a shelter

Moth, Fisher's estuarine (*Gortyna borelii*)
Moth, New Forest Burnet (*Zygaena viciae*)
Moth, Reddish Buff (*Acosmetia caliginosa*)
Moth, Sussex Emerald (*Thalera fimbrialis*)
††Mussel, Fan (*Atrina fragilis*)
†Mussel, Freshwater Pearl (*Margaritifera margaritifera*)
Newt, Great Crested (or Warty) (*Triturus cristatus*)
*Newt, Palmate (*Triturus helveticus*)
*Newt, Smooth (*Triturus vulgaris*)
Otter, Common (*Lutra lutra*)
Porpoise (*Cetacea*)
Sandworm, Lagoon (*Armandia cirrhosa*)
††Sea Fan, Pink (*Eunicella verrucosa*)
Sea-Mat, Trembling (*Victorella pavida*)
Sea Slug, Lagoon (*Tenellia adspersa*)
‡‡Shad, Allis (*alosa alosa*)
§§Shad, Twaite (*alosa fallax*)
Shark, Basking (*Cetorhinus maximus*)
Shrimp, Fairy (*Chirocephalus diaphanus*)
Shrimp, Lagoon Sand (*Gammarus insensibilis*)
‡Slow-worm (*Anguis fragilis*)
Snail, Glutinous (*Myxas glutinosa*)
Snail, Sandbowl (*Catinella arenaria*)
‡Snake, Grass (*Natrix natrix* (*Natrix helvetica*))
Snake, Smooth (*Coronella austriaca*)
Spider, Fen Raft (*Dolomedes plantarius*)
Spider, Ladybird (*Eresus niger*)
Squirrel, Red (*Sciurus vulgaris*)
Sturgeon (*Actipenser sturio*)
*Toad, Common (*Bufo bufo*)
Toad, Natterjack (*Bufo calamita*)
Turtle, Marine (*Dermochelyidae* and *Cheloniidae*, all species)
Vendace (*Coregonus albula*)
§§Vole, Water (*Arvicola terrestris*)
Walrus (*Odobenus rosmarus*)
Whale (*Cetacea*)
Whitefish (*Coregonus lavaretus*)

Plants

Adder's tongue, Least (*Ophioglossum lusitanicum*)
Alison, Small (*Alyssum alyssoides*)
Blackwort (*Southbya nigrella*)
°Bluebell (*Hyacinthoides non-scripta*)
Broomrape, Bedstraw (*Orobanche caryophyllacea*)
Broomrape, Oxtongue (*Orobanche loricata*)
Broomrape, Thistle (*Orobanche reticulata*)
Cabbage, Lundy (*Rhynchosinapis wrightii*)
Calamint, Wood (*Calamintha sylvatica*)
Caloplaca, Snow (*Caloplaca nivalis*)
Catapyrenium, Tree (*Catapyrenium psoromoides*)
Catchfly, Alpine (*Lychnis alpina*)
Catillaria, Laurer's (*Catellaria laureri*)
Centaury, Slender (*Centaurium tenuiflorum*)
Cinquefoil, Rock (*Potentilla rupestris*)
Clary, Meadow (*Salvia pratensis*)
Club-rush, Triangular (*Scirpus triquetrus*)
Colt's-foot, Purple (*Homogyne alpina*)
Cotoneaster, Wild (*Cotoneaster integerrimus*)
Cottongrass, Slender (*Eriophorum gracile*)
Cow-wheat, Field (*Melampyrum arvense*)
Crocus, Sand (*Romulea columnae*)
Crystalwort, Lizard (*Riccia bifurca*)
Cudweed, Broad-leaved (*Filago pyramidata*)
Cudweed, Jersey (*Gnaphalium luteoalbum*)
Cudweed, Red-tipped (*Filago lutescens*)
Cut-grass (*Leersia oryzoides*)

° The sale of plants taken from the wild is prohibited; the sale of cultivated plants is still permitted

Diapensia (*Diapensia lapponica*)
Dock, Shore (*Rumex rupestris*)
Earwort, Marsh (*Jamesoniella undulifolia*)
Eryngo, Field (*Eryngium campestre*)
Fern, Dickie's bladder (*Cystopteris dickieana*)
Fern, Killarney (*Trichomanes speciosum*)
Flapwort, Norfolk (*Leiocolea rutheana*)
Fleabane, Alpine (*Erigeron borealis*)
Fleabane, Small (*Pulicaria vulgaris*)
Fleawort, South stack (*Tephroseris integrifolia* (*ssp maritima*))
Frostwort, Pointed (*Gymnomitrion apiculatum*)
Fungus, Hedgehog (*Hericium erinaceum*)
Fungus, Oak polypore (*Buglossoporus pulvinus*)
Fungus, Royal bolete (*Boletus regius*)
Fungus, Sandy stilt puffball (*Battarraea phalloides*)
Galingale, Brown (*Cyperus fuscus*)
Gentian, Alpine (*Gentiana nivalis*)
Gentian, Dune (*Gentianella uliginosa*)
Gentian, Early (*Gentianella anglica*)
Gentian, Fringed (*Gentianella ciliata*)
Gentian, Spring (*Gentiana verna*)
Germander, Cut-leaved (*Teucrium botrys*)
Germander, Water (*Teucrium scordium*)
Gladiolus, Wild (*Gladiolus illyricus*)
Goosefoot, Stinking (*Chenopodium vulvaria*)
Grass-poly (*Lythrum hyssopifolia*)
Grimmia, Blunt-leaved (*Grimmia unicolor*)
Gyalecta, Elm (*Gyalecta ulmi*)
Hare's-ear, Sickle-leaved (*Bupleurum falcatum*)
Hare's-ear, Small (*Bupleurum baldense*)
Hawk's-beard, Stinking (*Crepis foetida*)
Hawkweed, Northroe (*Hieracium northroense*)
Hawkweed, Shetland (*Hieracium zetlandicum*)
Hawkweed, Weak-leaved (*Hieracium attenuatifolium*)
Heath, Blue (*Phyllodoce caerulea*)
Helleborine, Red (*Cephalanthera rubra*)
Helleborine, Young's (*Epipactis youngiana*)
Horsetail, Branched (*Equisetum ramosissimum*)
Hound's-tongue, Green (*Cynoglossum germanicum*)
Knawel, Perennial (*Scleranthus perennis*)
Knotgrass, Sea (*Polygonum maritimum*)
Lady's-slipper (*Cypripedium calceolus*)
Lecanactis, Churchyard (*Lecanactis hemisphaerica*)
Lecanora, Tarn (*Lecanora archariana*)
Lecidea, Copper (*Lecidea inops*)
Leek, Round-headed (*Allium sphaerocephalon*)
Lettuce, Least (*Lactuca saligna*)
Lichen, Alpine sulphur-tresses (*Alectoria ochroleuca*)
Lichen, Arctic kidney (*Nephroma arcticum*)
Lichen, Ciliate strap (*Heterodermia leucomelos*)
Lichen, Convoluted cladonia (*Cladonia convoluta*)
Lichen, Coralloid rosette (*Heterodermia propagulifera*)
Lichen, Ear-lobed dog (*Peltigera lepidophora*)
Lichen, Forked hair (*Bryoria furcellata*)
Lichen, Goblin lights (*Catolechia wahlenbergii*)
Lichen, Golden hair (*Teloschistes flavicans*)
Lichen, New Forest beech-lichen (*Enterographa elaborata*)
Lichen, Orange fruited Elm (*Caloplaca luteoalba*)
Lichen, River jelly (*Collema dichotomum*)
Lichen, Scaly breck (*Squamarina lentigera*)
Lichen, Stary breck (*Buellia asterella*)
Lichen, Upright mountain cladonia (*Cladonia stricta*)
Lily, Snowdon (*Lloydia serotina*)
Liverwort, Leafy (*Petallophyllum ralfsi*)
Liverwort, Lindenberg's (*Adelanthus lindenbergianus*)
Marsh-mallow, Rough (*Althaea hirsuta*)
Marshwort, Creeping (*Apium repens*)
Milk-parsley, Cambridge (*Selinum carvifolia*)
Moss (*Drepanocladius vernicosus*)
Moss, Alpine copper (*Mielichoferia mielichoferi*)
Moss, Anomodon, long-leaved (*Anomodon longifolius*)

Moss, Baltic bog (*Sphagnum balticum*)
Moss, Blue dew (*Saelania glaucescens*)
Moss, Blunt-leaved bristle (*Orthotrichum obtusifolium*)
Moss, Bright green cave (*Cyclodictyon laetevirens*)
Moss, Cordate beard (*Barbula cordata*)
Moss, Cornish path (*Ditrichum cornubicum*)
Moss, Derbyshire feather (*Thamnobryum angustifolium*)
Moss, Dune thread (*Bryum mamillatum*)
Moss, Flamingo (*Desmatodon cernuus*)
Moss, Glaucous beard (*Barbula glauca*)
Moss, Green shield (*Buxbaumia viridis*)
Moss, Hair silk (*Plagiothecium piliferum*)
Moss, Knothole (*Zygodon forsteri*)
Moss, Large yellow feather (*Scorpidium turgescens*)
Moss, Millimetre (*Micromitrium tenerum*)
Moss, Multifruited river (*Cryphaea lamyana*)
Moss, Nowell's limestone (*Zygodon gracilis*)
Moss, Polar feather-moss (*Hygrohypnum polare*)
Moss, Rigid apple (*Bartramia stricta*)
Moss, Round-leaved feather (*Rhyncostegium rotundifolium*)
Moss, Schleicher's thread (*Bryum schleicheri*)
Moss, Threadmoss, long-leaved (*Bryum neodamense*)
Moss, Triangular pygmy (*Acaulon triquetrum*)
Moss, Vaucher's feather (*Hypnum vaucheri*)
Mudwort, Welsh (*Limosella australis*)
Naiad, Holly-leaved (*Najas marina*)
Naiad, Slender (*Najas flexilis*)
Orache, Stalked (*Halimione pedunculata*)
Orchid, Early spider (*Ophrys sphegodes*)
Orchid, Fen (*Liparis loeselii*)
Orchid, Ghost (*Epipogium aphyllum*)
Orchid, Lapland marsh (*Dactylorhiza lapponica*)
Orchid, Late spider (*Ophrys fuciflora*)
Orchid, Lizard (*Himantoglossum hircinum*)
Orchid, Military (*Orchis militaris*)
Orchid, Monkey (*Orchis simia*)
Panneria, Caledonia (*Panneria ignobilis*)
Parmelia, New Forest (*Parmelia minarum*)
Parmentaria, Oil stain (*Parmentaria chilensis*)
Pear, Plymouth (*Pyrus cordata*)
Penny-cress, Perfoliate (*Thlaspi perfoliatum*)
Pennyroyal (*Mentha pulegium*)
Pertusaria, Alpine moss (*Pertusaria bryontha*)
Physcia, Southern grey (*Physcia tribacioides*)
Pigmyweed (*Crassula aquatica*)
Pine, Ground (*Ajuga chamaepitys*)
Pink, Cheddar (*Dianthus gratianopolitanus*)
Pink, Childing (*Petroraghia nanteuilii*)
Pink, Deptford (*Dianthus armeria*) (England and Wales only)
Plantain, Floating water (*Luronium natans*)
Pseudocyphellaria, Ragged (*Pseudocyphellaria lacerata*)
Psora, Rusty Alpine (*Psora rubiformis*)
Ragwort, Fen (*Senecio paludosus*)
Ramping-fumitory, Martin's (*Fumaria martinii*)
Rampion, Spiked (*Phyteuma spicatum*)
Restharrow, Small (*Ononis reclinata*)
Rock-cress, Alpine (*Arabis alpina*)
Rock-cress, Bristol (*Arabis stricta*)
Rustwort, Western (*Marsupella profunda*)
Sandwort, Norwegian (*Arenaria norvegica*)
Sandwort, Teesdale (*Minuartia stricta*)
Saxifrage, Drooping (*Saxifraga cernua*)
Saxifrage, Marsh (*Saxifrage hirulus*)
Saxifrage, Tufted (*Saxifraga cespitosa*)
Solenopsora, Serpentine (*Solenopsora liparina*)
Solomon's-seal, Whorled (*Polygonatum verticillatum*)
Sow-thistle, Alpine (*Cicerbita alpina*)
Spearwort, Adder's-tongue (*Ranunculus ophioglossifolius*)
Speedwell, Fingered (*Veronica triphyllos*)

Speedwell, Spiked (*Veronica spicata*)
Spike rush, Dwarf (*Eleocharis parvula*)
Star-of-Bethlehem, Early (*Gagea bohemica*)
Starfruit (*Damasonium alisma*)
Stonewort, Bearded (*Chara canescens*)
Stonewort, Foxtail (*Lamprothamnium papulosum*)
Strapwort (*Corrigiola litoralis*)
Turpswort (*Geocalyx graveolens*)
Violet, Fen (*Viola persicifolia*)
Viper's-grass (*Scorzonera humilis*)
Water-plantain, Ribbon-leaved (*Alisma gramineum*)
Wood-sedge, Starved (*Carex depauperata*)
Woodsia, Alpine (*Woodsia alpina*)
Woodsia, Oblong (*Woodsia ilvenis*)
Wormwood, Field (*Artemisia campestris*)
Woundwort, Downy (*Stachys germanica*)
Woundwort, Limestone (*Stachys alpina*)
Yellow-rattle, Greater (*Rhinanthus serotinus*)

MOST UNDER THREAT

The animals and birds considered to be most under threat in Great Britain by the Joint Nature Conservation Committee are the high brown fritillary butterfly; violet click beetle; new forest burnet moth; corncrake; aquatic warbler; tree sparrow; wryneck; water vole; red squirrel; allis shad; and twaite shad.

Close Seasons and Times

GAME BIRDS

In each case the dates are inclusive:

Black game – 11 December to 19 August (31 August in Somerset, Devon and New Forest)
*Grouse – 11 December to 11 August
*Partridge – 2 February to 31 August
*Pheasant – 2 February to 30 September
*Ptarmigan – (Scotland only) 11 December to 11 August

*It is also unlawful in England and Wales to kill this game on a Sunday or Christmas Day

HUNTING AND GROUND GAME

There is no statutory close time for fox-hunting or rabbit-shooting, nor for hares. However, by an Act passed in 1892 the sale of hares or leverets in Great Britain is prohibited from 1 March to 31 July inclusive. The recognized date for the opening of the fox-hunting season is 1 November, and it continues till the following April.

DEER

The statutory close seasons for deer (all dates inclusive) are:

	England and Wales	Scotland
Fallow deer		
Male	1 May–31 July	1 May–31 July
Female	1 Mar.–31 Oct.	16 Feb.–20 Oct.
Red deer		
Male	1 May–31 July	21 Oct.–30 June
Female	1 Mar.–31 Oct.	16 Feb.–20 Oct.
Roe deer		
Male	1 Nov.–31 Mar.	21 Oct.–31 Mar.
Female	1 Mar.–31 Oct.	1 April–20 Oct.
Sika deer		
Male	1 May–31 July	21 Oct.–30 June
Female	1 Mar.–31 Oct.	16 Feb.–20 Oct.
Red/Sika hybrids		
Male	—	21 Oct.–30 June
Female	—	16 Feb.–20 Oct

ANGLING

GAME FISHING

Where local by-laws neither specify nor dispense with an annual close season, the statutory close times for game fishing are: Trout, 1 October to end February; Salmon, 1 November to 31 January.

COARSE FISHING

Responsibility for the fisheries function of the National Rivers Authority, including licensing and regulation, passed to the Environment Agency on 1 April 1996. The statutory close season for coarse fish in England and Wales runs from 15 March to 15 June on all rivers, streams and drains. Close season arrangements for canals vary from region to region. The close season on all lakes, ponds and reservoirs is at the discretion of the fishery owner, except on the Norfolk Broads and certain Sites of Special Scientific Interest where the statutory close season still applies. It is necessary in all cases to check with the Environment Agency regional office concerning the area (details can be found in the local telephone directory).

LICENCES

Purchase of a national rod fishing licence is legally required of anglers wishing to fish with rod and line in all waters within the area of the Environment Agency.

	Salmon and sea trout	Non-migratory trout and coarse fish
Full	£55.00	£16.00
Concessionary	27.50	8.00
Eight-day	15.00	6.00
One-day	5.00	2.00

Concessionary licences are available for juniors (12–16 years), for senior citizens (65 years and over), and disabled who are in receipt of long-term incapacity benefit, short-term incapacity benefit (at the higher rate) or severe disablement allowance. Those in receipt of a war pension which includes unemployability supplements are also eligible.

Historic Buildings and Monuments

LISTING

Under the Planning (Listed Buildings and Conservation Areas) Act 1990, the Secretary of State for National Heritage has a statutory duty to compile lists of buildings or groups of buildings in England which are of special architectural or historic interest. Under the Ancient Monuments and Archaeological Areas Act 1979 as amended by the National Heritage Act 1983, the Secretary of State is also responsible for compiling a schedule of ancient monuments. Decisions are taken on the advice of English Heritage (*see* page 308).

Listed buildings are classified into Grade I, Grade II* and Grade II. There are currently about 500,000 individual listed buildings in England, of which about 95 per cent are Grade II listed. Almost all pre-1700 buildings are listed, and most buildings of 1700 to 1840. English Heritage is carrying out thematic surveys of particular types of buildings with a view to making recommendations for listing, and members of the public may propose a building for consideration. The main purpose of listing is to ensure that care is taken in deciding the future of a building. No changes which affect the architectural or historic character of a listed building can be made without listed building consent (in addition to planning permission where relevant). Applications for listed building consent are normally dealt with by the local planning authority, although English Heritage is always consulted about proposals affecting Grade I and Grade II* properties. It is a criminal offence to demolish a listed building, or alter it in such a way as to affect its character, without consent.

There are currently about 22,500 scheduled monuments in England. English Heritage is carrying out a Monuments Protection Programme assessing archaeological sites with a view to making recommendations for scheduling, and members of the public may propose a monument for consideration. All monuments proposed for scheduling are considered to be of national importance. Where buildings are both scheduled and listed, ancient monuments legislation takes precedence. The main purpose of scheduling a monument is to preserve it for the future and to protect it from damage, destruction or any unnecessary interference. Once a monument has been scheduled, scheduled monument consent is required before any works are carried out which would damage or alter the monument in any way. The scope of the control is more extensive and more detailed than that applied to listed buildings, but certain minor works, as detailed in the Ancient Monuments Class Consents Order 1994, may be carried out without consent. It is a criminal offence to carry out unauthorized work to scheduled monuments.

Under the Planning (Listed Buildings and Conservation Areas) Act 1990 and the Ancient Monuments and Archaeological Areas Act 1979, the Secretary of State for Wales is responsible for listing buildings and scheduling monuments in Wales on the advice of Cadw (*see* page 353), the Historic Buildings Council for Wales (*see* page 308) and the Ancient Monuments Board for Wales (*see* page 309). The criteria for evaluating buildings are similar to those in England and the same listing system is used. In April 1997 there were 19,161 listed buildings and 2,999 scheduled monuments in Wales.

Under the Town and Country Planning (Scotland) Act 1972 and the Ancient Monuments and Archaeological Areas Act 1979, the Secretary of State for Scotland is responsible for listing buildings and scheduling monu-

ments in Scotland on the advice of Historic Scotland (*see* page 341), the Historic Buildings Council for Scotland (*see* page 308) and the Ancient Monuments Board for Scotland (*see* page 309). The criteria for evaluating buildings are similar to those in England but an A, B, C grading system is used. There are about 43,783 listed buildings and about 6,800 scheduled monuments in Scotland.

Under the Planning (Northern Ireland) Order 1991 and the Historic Monuments and Archaeological Objects (Northern Ireland) Order 1995, the Department of the Environment for Northern Ireland (*see* page 330) is responsible for listing buildings and scheduling monuments in Northern Ireland on the advice of the Historic Buildings Council for Northern Ireland and the Historic Monuments Council for Northern Ireland. The criteria for evaluating buildings are similar to those in England but no statutory grading system is used. In June 1997 there were 8,589 listed buildings and 1,295 scheduled monuments in Northern Ireland.

OPENING TO THE PUBLIC

The following is a selection of the many historic buildings and monuments open to the public. The admission charges given are the standard charges for 1998–9; many properties have concessionary rates for children, etc. Opening hours vary. Many properties are closed in winter and some are also closed in the mornings. Most properties are closed on Christmas Eve, Christmas Day, Boxing Day and New Year's Day, and many are closed on Good Friday. During the winter season, most English Heritage monuments are closed on Mondays and Tuesdays and monuments in the care of Cadw are closed on Sunday mornings. In Northern Ireland most monuments are closed on Mondays except on bank holidays. Information about a specific property should be checked by telephone.

*Closed in winter (usually November-March)
†Closed in winter, and in mornings in summer

ENGLAND

EH English Heritage property
NT National Trust property

*A LA RONDE (NT), Exmouth, Devon. Tel: 01395-265514. Closed Fri. and Sat. Adm. £3.20. Unique 16-sided house completed *c*.1796

†ALNWICK CASTLE, Northumberland. Tel: 01665-510777. Closed Fri. (except Good Friday). Adm. charge. Seat of the Dukes of Northumberland since 1309; Italian Renaissance-style interior

ALTHORP, Northants. Tel: 01604-770107, ticket reservations 01604-592020. Open 1 July to 30 August. Adm £9.50. Spencer family seat. Diana, Princess of Wales memorabilia

†ANGLESEY ABBEY (NT), Cambs. Tel: 01223-811200. Closed Mon. (except Bank Holidays) and Tues. Gardens open daily July to Sept. Adm. £5.80 (£6.80 Sun. and Bank Holidays); gardens only, £3.40. House built *c*.1600. Outstanding grounds with unique statuary

APSLEY HOUSE, London W1. Tel: 0171-499 5676. Closed Mon. Adm. £4.50. Built by Robert Adam 1771-8, home of the Dukes of Wellington since 1817 and known as 'No. 1 London'. Collection of fine and decorative arts

†ARUNDEL CASTLE, W. Sussex. Tel: 01903-883136. Closed Sat. Adm. charge. Castle dating from the Norman Conquest. Seat of the Dukes of Norfolk

AVEBURY (NT), Wilts. Adm. free. Remains of stone circles constructed 4,000 years ago surrounding the later village of Avebury. Also *Alexander Keiller Museum*. Tel: 01672-539250. Adm. £1.60

BANQUETING HOUSE, Whitehall, London SW1. Tel: 0171-930 4179. Closed Sun. and Bank Holidays. Adm. £3.55. Designed by Inigo Jones; ceiling paintings by Rubens. Site of the execution of Charles I

†BASILDON PARK (NT), Berks. Tel: 0118-984 3040. Closed Mon. (except Bank Holidays), Tues. and Good Friday. Adm. £4.00; grounds only, £1.60. Palladian house built in 1776

BATTLE ABBEY (EH), E. Sussex. Tel: 01424-773792. Adm. £4.00. Remains of the abbey founded by William the Conqueror on the site of the Battle of Hastings

BEAULIEU, Hants. Tel: 01590-612345. Adm. charge. House and gardens, Beaulieu Abbey and exhibition of monastic life, National Motor Museum (*see also* page 591)

BEESTON CASTLE (EH), Cheshire. Tel: 01829-260464. Adm. £2.70. Thirteenth-century inner ward with gatehouse and towers, and remains of outer ward

†BELTON HOUSE (NT), Grantham, Lincs. Tel: 01476-566116. Closed Mon. (except Bank Holidays), Tues. and Good Friday. Adm. £5.00. Fine 17th-century house in landscaped park

*BELVOIR CASTLE, nr Grantham, Lincs. Tel: 01476-870262. Closed Mon. (except Bank Holidays) and Fri.; also closed Mon.-Sat. in Oct. Adm. £5.00. Seat of the Dukes of Rutland; 19th-century Gothic-style castle

*BERKELEY CASTLE, Glos. Tel: 01453-810332. Opening times vary. Adm. £4.95. Completed 1153; site of the murder of Edward II (1327)

*BLENHEIM PALACE, Woodstock, Oxon. Tel: 01993-811325. Adm. charge. Seat of the Dukes of Marlborough and Winston Churchill's birthplace; designed by Vanbrugh

†BLICKLING HALL (NT), Norfolk. Tel: 01263-733084. Opening times vary. Adm. £6.00; garden only, £3.30. Jacobean house with state rooms, temple and 18th-century orangery

BODIAM CASTLE (NT), E. Sussex. Tel: 01580-830436. Closed Mon. in winter. Adm. £3.30. Well-preserved medieval moated castle

BOLSOVER CASTLE (EH), Derbys. Tel: 01246-823349. Closed Mon. and Tues. in winter. Adm. £2.95. Notable 17th-century buildings

BOSCOBEL HOUSE (EH), Shropshire. Tel: 01902-850244. Closed Mon. and Tues. in winter; also closed in Jan. Adm. £3.95. Timber-framed 17th-century hunting lodge, refuge of fugitive Charles II

†BOUGHTON HOUSE, Northants. Tel: 01536-515731. House open Aug. only; grounds May to Sept. except Fri.; state rooms by prior booking. Adm. £4.00; grounds, £1.50. A 17th-century house with French-style additions

*BOWOOD HOUSE, Wilts. Tel: 01249-812102. Adm. charge. An 18th-century house in Capability Brown park, with lake, temple and arboretum

†BROADLANDS, Hants. Tel: 01794-517888. Open June-Sept. Adm. £5.00. Palladian mansion in Capability Brown parkland. Mountbatten exhibition

BRONTË PARSONAGE, Haworth, W. Yorks. Tel: 01535-642323. Closed Jan.-Feb. Adm. charge. Home of the Brontë sisters; museum and memorabilia

BUCKFAST ABBEY, Devon. Tel: 01364-642519. Adm. free. Benedictine monastery on medieval foundations

*BUCKINGHAM PALACE, London SW1. Tel: 0171-839 1377. Open daily for eight weeks from early Aug. each year. Adm. £9.50. Purchased by George III in 1762, and the Sovereign's official London residence since 1837. Eighteen state rooms, including the Throne Room, and Picture Gallery

BUCKLAND ABBEY (NT), Devon. Tel: 01822-853607. Closed Thurs.; in winter open only weekend afternoons, closed 4-22 January 1999. Adm. £4.30; grounds only, £2.20. A 13th-century Cistercian monastery. Home of Sir Francis Drake

BURGHLEY HOUSE, Stamford, Lincs. Tel: 01780-752451. Adm. £5.85. Late Elizabethan house; vast state apartments

†CALKE ABBEY (NT), Derbys. Tel: 01332-863822. Closed Thurs. and Fri. Adm. £4.90, by timed ticket; garden only, £2.20. Baroque 18th-century mansion

CARISBROOKE CASTLE (EH), Isle of Wight. Tel: 01983-522107. Adm. £4.00. Norman castle; prison of Charles I 1647-8

CARLISLE CASTLE (EH), Cumbria. Tel: 01228-591922. Adm. £2.90. Medieval castle, prison of Mary Queen of Scots

*CARLYLE'S HOUSE (NT), Cheyne Row, London SW3. Tel: 0171-352 7087. Closed Mon. (except Bank Holidays), Tues. and Good Friday. Adm. £3.20. Home of Thomas Carlyle

CASTLE ACRE PRIORY (EH), Norfolk. Tel: 01760-755394. Closed Mon. and Tues. in winter. Adm. £2.95. Remains include 12th-century church and prior's lodgings

*CASTLE DROGO (NT), Devon. Tel: 01647-433306. Castle closed Fri. (except Good Friday). Adm. £5.20; grounds only, £2.40. Granite castle designed by Lutyens

*CASTLE HOWARD, N. Yorks. Tel: 01653-648444. Adm. £6.50; grounds only, £4.00. Designed by Vanbrugh 1699-1726; mausoleum designed by Hawksmoor

CASTLE RISING CASTLE (EH), Norfolk. Tel: 01553-631330. Closed Mon. and Tues. in winter. Adm. £2.30. A 12th-century keep in a massive earthwork with gatehouse and bridge

†CHARTWELL (NT), Kent. Tel: 01732-866368. Closed Mon. (except Bank Holidays) and Tues. (except July and Aug.). Adm. £5.20 by timed ticket; grounds only, £2.60. Home of Sir Winston Churchill

*CHATSWORTH, Derbys. Tel: 01246-582204. Adm. charge. Tudor mansion in magnificent parkland

CHESTERS ROMAN FORT (EH), Northumberland. Tel: 01434-681379. Adm. £2.70. Roman cavalry fort

*CHYSAUSTER ANCIENT VILLAGE (EH), Cornwall. £1.60. Romano-Cornish village, 2nd and 3rd century AD, on a probably late Iron Age site

CLIFFORD'S TOWER (EH), York. Tel: 01904-646940. Adm. £1.70. A 13th-century tower built on a mound

†CLIVEDEN (NT), Berks. Tel: 01628-605069. House open Thurs. and Sun. only, gardens daily. Adm. £4.80; £1.00 extra for house. Former home of the Astors, now a hotel set in garden and woodland

CORBRIDGE ROMAN SITE (EH), Northumberland. Tel: 01434-632349. Closed Mon. and Tues. in winter. Adm. £2.70. Excavated central area of a Roman town and successive military bases

CORFE CASTLE (NT), Dorset. Tel: 01929-481294. Adm. £3.80. Ruined former royal castle dating from 11th century

†CROFT CASTLE (NT), Herefordshire. Tel: 01568-780246. Closed Mon. (except Bank Holidays), Tues. and Good Friday; April and Oct. open weekends only; grounds open all year. Adm. £3.30; grounds only, £1.50 per car. Pre-Conquest border castle with Georgian-Gothic interior

DEAL CASTLE (EH), Kent. Tel: 01304-372762. Closed Mon. and Tues. in winter. Adm. £3.00. Largest of the coastal defence forts built by Henry VIII

DICKENS HOUSE, Doughty Street, London WC1. Tel: 0171-405 2127. Closed Sun. Adm. £3.50. House occupied by Dickens 1837-9; manuscripts, furniture and portraits

DR JOHNSON'S HOUSE, 17 Gough Square, London EC4. Tel: 0171-353 3745. Closed Sun. and Bank Holidays. Adm. charge. Home of Samuel Johnson

DOVE COTTAGE, Grasmere, Cumbria. Tel: 01539-435544. Closed Jan. and early Feb. Adm. £4.40; museum only, £2.20. Wordsworth's home 1799-1808; museum

DOVER CASTLE (EH), Kent. Tel: 01304-201628. Adm. £6.50. Castle with Roman, Saxon and Norman features; wartime operations rooms

DUNSTANBURGH CASTLE (EH), Northumberland. Tel: 01665-576231. Closed Mon. and Tues. in winter. Adm. £1.70. A 14th-century castle on a cliff, with a substantial gatehouse-keep

FARLEIGH HUNGERFORD CASTLE (EH), Somerset. Tel: 01225-754026. Closed Mon. and Tues. in winter. Adm. £2.10. Late 14th-century castle with two courts; chapel with tomb of Sir Thomas Hungerford

*FARNHAM CASTLE KEEP (EH), Surrey. Tel: 01252-713393. Adm. £2.00. Large 12th-century shell-keep

FOUNTAINS ABBEY (NT), nr Ripon, N. Yorks. Tel: 01765-608888. Closed Fri. Nov.-Jan.; deer park open daily all year. Adm. £4.20; visitor centre, deer park and St Mary's Church free. Ruined Cistercian monastery; 18th-century landscaped gardens of Studley Royal estate

FRAMLINGHAM CASTLE (EH), Suffolk. Tel: 01728-724189. Adm. £2.95. Castle (c.1200) with high curtain walls enclosing an almshouse (1639)

FURNESS ABBEY (EH), Cumbria. Tel: 01229-823420. Closed Mon. and Tues. in winter. Adm. £2.50. Remains of church and conventual buildings founded in 1123

GLASTONBURY ABBEY, Somerset. Tel: 01458-832267. Adm. £2.50. Ruins of a 12th-century abbey rebuilt after fire. Site of an early Christian settlement

GOODRICH CASTLE (EH), Herefordshire. Tel: 01600-890538. Adm. £2.95. Remains of 13th- and 14th-century castle with 12th-century keep

GREENWICH, London SE10. *Royal Observatory.* Tel: 0181-858 4422. Adm. £5.00 (joint ticket for Royal Observatory, The Queen's House and National Maritime Museum). Former Royal Observatory (founded 1675) housing the time ball and zero meridian of longitude. *The Queen's House.* Tel: 0181-858 4422. Closed Sun. mornings. Adm. charge. Designed for Queen Anne, wife of James I, by Inigo Jones. *Painted Hall and Chapel* (Royal Naval College). Closed mornings. Visitors admitted to Sunday service (11 a.m.) in the chapel during college term

GRIME'S GRAVES (EH), Norfolk. Tel: 01842-810656. Closed Mon. and Tues. in winter. Adm. £1.75. Neolithic flint mines. One shaft can be descended

GUILDHALL, London EC2. Tel: 0171-332 1460. Closed Sun. in winter. Adm. free. Centre of civic government of the City. Built c.1440; facade built 1788-9

*HADDON HALL, Derbys. Tel: 01629-812855. Adm. £5.50. Well-preserved 12th-century manor house

HAILES ABBEY (EH), Glos. Tel: 01242-602398. Closed Mon. to Fri. in winter. Adm. £2.50. Ruins of a 13th-century Cistercian monastery

†HAM HOUSE (NT), Richmond, Surrey. Tel: 0181-940 1950. Closed Thurs. and Fri. Adm. £5.00. Garden open all year except Thurs. and Fri. Adm. £1.50. Stuart house with fine interiors

HAMPTON COURT PALACE, East Molesey, Surrey. Tel: 0181-781 9500. Adm. £9.25. A 16th-century palace with additions by Wren. Gardens with maze; Tudor tennis court (summer only)

†HARDWICK HALL (NT), Derbys. Tel: 01246-850430. Closed Mon. (except Bank Holidays), Tues. and Fri.; grounds open daily, all year. Adm. £6.00; grounds only, £2.70. Built 1591-7 for Bess of Hardwick; notable furnishings

*HARDY'S COTTAGE (NT), Higher Bockhampton, Dorset. Tel: 01305-262366. Closed Fri. (except Good Friday) and Sat. Adm. £2.60. Birthplace of Thomas Hardy

*HAREWOOD HOUSE, W. Yorks. Tel: 0113-288 6331. Closed 5 June. Adm. £6.75. An 18th-century house designed by John Carr and Robert Adam; park by Capability Brown

†HATFIELD HOUSE, Herts. Tel: 01707-262823. Closed Mon. (except Bank Holidays). Adm. £5.70; grounds, £3.10. Jacobean house built by Robert Cecil; surviving wing of Royal Palace of Hatfield (1497)

HELMSLEY CASTLE (EH), N. Yorks. Tel: 01439-770442. Closed Mon. and Tues. in winter. Adm. £2.20. A 12th-century keep and curtain wall with 16th-century buildings. Spectacular earthwork defences

†HEVER CASTLE, Kent. Tel: 01732-865224. Adm. charge. A 13th-century double-moated castle, childhood home of Anne Boleyn

*HOLKER HALL, Cumbria. Tel: 015395-58328. Closed Sat. Adm. charge. Former home of the Dukes of Devonshire; award-winning gardens

†HOLKHAM HALL, Norfolk. Tel: 01328-710227. Closed Fri. and Sat. Adm. £4.00. Fine Palladian mansion

HOUSESTEADS ROMAN FORT (EH), Northumberland. Tel: 01434-344363. Adm. £2.70. Excavated infantry fort on Hadrian's Wall with extra-mural civilian settlement

†HUGHENDEN MANOR (NT), High Wycombe. Tel: 01494-532580. Closed Mon. (except Bank Holidays) and Tues.; open weekends only in March. Adm. £4.00. Home of Disraeli; small formal garden

JANE AUSTEN'S HOUSE, Chawton, Hants. Tel: 01420-83262. Closed Mon.-Fri. in Jan. and Feb. Adm. charge. Jane Austen's home 1809-17

*KELMSCOTT MANOR, nr Lechlade, Oxon. Tel: 01367-252486. Open Wed. and afternoon of third Sat. in every month, Thurs. and Fri. by appointment. Adm. £6.00. Summer home of William Morris, with products of Morris and Co.

KENILWORTH CASTLE (EH), Warks. Tel: 01926-852078. Adm. £3.10. Castle with building styles from 1155 to 1649

*KENSINGTON PALACE, London W8. Closed Mon. and Tues. in winter. Adm. £7.50. Built in 1605 and enlarged by Wren; bought by William and Mary in 1689. Birthplace of Queen Victoria. Royal Ceremonial Dress Collection

KENWOOD (EH), Hampstead Lane, London NW3. Tel: 0181-348 1286. Adm. free. Adam villa housing the Iveagh bequest of paintings and furniture. Open-air concerts in summer

*KEW PALACE, Surrey. Tel: 0181-332 5189. Closed for refurbishment until spring 1999. Also *Queen Charlotte's Cottage*, weekends and Bank Holidays in May-Sept. Adm. free (but £4.50 adm. to Kew Gardens)

†KINGSTON LACY HOUSE (NT), Dorset. Tel: 01202-883402. Closed Thurs. and Fri. Adm. £6.00; grounds only, £2.50. A 17th-century house with 19th-century alterations; important art collection

†KNEBWORTH HOUSE, Herts. Tel: 01438-812661. Closed Mon. (except Bank Holidays); grounds open daily except mid-Sept. Mon.-Fri. Adm. charge. Tudor manor house concealed by 19th-century Gothic decoration; Lutyens gardens

*KNOLE (NT), Kent. Tel: 01732-450608. Closed Mon. (except Bank Holidays) and Tues.; park open daily; garden open first Wed. of each month. Adm. £5.00; garden,£1.00; park free to pedestrians. House dating from 1456 set in parkland; fine art treasures

LAMBETH PALACE, London SE1. Tel: 0171-928 8282. Visits by written application. Official residence of the Archbishop of Canterbury. A 19th-century house with parts dating from the 12th century

*LANERCOST PRIORY (EH), Cumbria. Tel: 01697-73030. Adm. £1.90. The nave of the Augustinian priory church, c.1166, is still used; remains of other claustral buildings

*LANHYDROCK (NT), Cornwall. Tel: 01208-73320. Closed Mon. (except Bank Holidays). Garden open all year. Adm. £6.20; garden and grounds only, £3.10. House dating from the 17th century; 45 rooms, including kitchen and nursery

LEEDS CASTLE, Kent. Tel: 01622-765400. Adm. charge. Castle dating from 9th century, on two islands in lake

*LEVENS HALL, Cumbria. Tel: 015395-60321. Closed Fri. and Sat. Adm. £5.20; grounds only, £3.80. Elizabethan house with unique topiary garden (1694). Steam engine collection

LINCOLN CASTLE. Tel: 01522-511068. Adm. charge. Closed Mon.-Fri. in summer. Built by William the Conqueror in 1068

LINDISFARNE PRIORY (EH), Northumberland. Tel: 01289-389200. Open all year, subject to tide times. Adm. £2.70. Bishopric of the Northumbrian kingdom destroyed by the Danes; re-established in the 11th century as a Benedictine priory, now ruined

†LITTLE MORETON HALL (NT), Cheshire. Tel: 01260-272018. Closed Mon. (except Bank Holidays) and Tues.; 7 Nov.-20 Dec. open Sat. and Sun. only. Adm. £4.00; free 7 Nov.-20 Dec. Timber-framed moated manor house with knot garden

LONGLEAT HOUSE, Warminster, Wilts. Tel: 01985-844400. Open daily; safari park closed winter. Adm. charge. Elizabethan house in Italian Renaissance style

LULLINGSTONE ROMAN VILLA (EH), Kent. Tel: 01322-863467. Adm. £2.50. Large villa occupied for much of the Roman period; fine mosaics

†LUTON HOO, Beds. Tel: 01582-722955. Open Fri.-Sun. and Bank Holiday Mon. Adm. charge. Houses the Wernher collection of china, glass, pictures and other objets d'art

MANSION HOUSE, London EC4. Tel: 0171-626 2500. Group visits only, by prior arrangement. Adm. free. The official residence of the Lord Mayor of London

MARBLE HILL HOUSE (EH), Twickenham, Middx. Tel: 0181-892 5115. Closed Mon. and Tues. in winter. Adm. £3.00. English Palladian villa with Georgian paintings and furniture

*MICHELHAM PRIORY, E. Sussex. Closed Mon. and Tues. except in Aug. Tel: 01323-844224. Adm. £4.00. Tudor house built onto an Augustinian priory

MIDDLEHAM CASTLE (EH), N. Yorks. Tel: 01969-623899. Closed Mon. and Tues. in winter. Adm. £2.20. A 12th-century keep within later fortifications. Childhood home of Richard III

†MONTACUTE HOUSE (NT), Somerset. Tel: 01935-823289. Closed Tues; grounds open all year. Adm. £5.20; grounds only, £2.90. Elizabethan house with National Portrait Gallery portraits from period

MOUNT GRACE PRIORY (EH), N. Yorks. Tel: 01609-883494. Closed Mon. and Tues. in winter. Adm. £2.70. Carthusian monastery, with remains of monastic buildings

NETLEY ABBEY (EH), Hants. Tel: 01703-453076. Adm. free. Remains of Cistercian abbey, used as house in Tudor period

OLD SARUM (EH), Wilts. Tel: 01722-335398. Adm. £2.00. Earthworks enclosing remains of the castle and the 11th-century cathedral

ORFORD CASTLE (EH), Suffolk. Tel: 01394-450472. Closed Mon. and Tues. in winter. Adm. £2.30. Circular keep of c.1170 and remains of coastal defence castle built by Henry II

*OSBORNE HOUSE (EH), Isle of Wight. Tel: 01983-200022. Adm. £6.50; grounds only, £3.50. Queen Victoria's seaside residence

†OSTERLEY PARK HOUSE (NT), Isleworth, Middx. Tel: 0181-560 3918. Closed Mon. (except Bank Holidays), Tues. and Good Friday; grounds open all year. Adm. £4.00; grounds free. Elizabethan mansion set in parkland

PENDENNIS CASTLE (EH), Cornwall. Tel: 01326-316594. Adm. £3.00. Well-preserved coastal defence castle built by Henry VIII

†PENSHURST PLACE, Kent. Tel: 01892-870307. Closed Mon.-Fri. in Mar. Adm. £5.70; grounds only, £4.20. House with medieval Baron's Hall and 14th-century gardens

†PETWORTH (NT), W. Sussex. Tel: 01798-342207. Closed Thur. and Fri. (except Good Friday); grounds open all year. Adm. £5.00; grounds free. Late 17th-century house set in deer park

PEVENSEY CASTLE (EH), E. Sussex. Tel: 01323-762604. Closed Mon. and Tues. in winter. Adm. £2.50. Walls of a 4th-century Roman fort; remains of an 11th-century castle

PEVERIL CASTLE (EH), Derbys. Tel: 01433-620613. Closed Mon. and Tues. in winter. Adm. £1.75. A 12th-century castle defended on two sides by precipitous rocks

†POLESDEN LACY (NT), Surrey. Tel: 01372-458203. Closed Mon. (except Bank Holidays) and Tues.; grounds open daily all year. Adm. £6.00; grounds only, £3.00. Regency villa remodelled in the Edwardian era. Fine paintings and furnishings

PORTCHESTER CASTLE (EH), Hants. Tel: 01705-378291. Adm. £2.50. Walls of a late Roman fort enclosing a Norman keep and an Augustinian priory church

*POWDERHAM CASTLE, Devon. Tel: 01626-890243. Closed Sat. Adm. charge. Medieval castle with 18th- and 19th-century alterations

†RABY CASTLE, Co. Durham. Tel: 01833-660202. Closed Sat. (except Bank Holiday weekends); open Wed. and Sun. only in May and June. Adm. charge. A 14th-century castle with walled gardens

*RAGLEY HALL, Warks. Tel: 01789-762090. Closed Mon.-Wed.; grounds open daily in July and Aug. Adm. charge. A 17th-century house with gardens, park and lake

*RICHBOROUGH ROMAN FORT (EH), Kent. Tel: 01304-612013. Closed Mon. and Tues. in Nov. and March, Mon.-Fri. Dec.-Feb. Adm. £2.50. Landing-site of the Claudian invasion in AD 43, with 3rd-century stone walls

RICHMOND CASTLE (EH), N. Yorks. Tel: 01748-822493. Adm. £2.20. A 12th-century keep with 11th-century curtain wall and domestic buildings

RIEVAULX ABBEY (EH), N. Yorks. Tel: 01439-798228. Adm. £2.90. Remains of a Cistercian abbey founded c.1131

ROCHESTER CASTLE (EH), Kent. Tel: 01634-402276. Adm. £2.60. An 11th-century castle partly on the Roman city wall, with a square keep of c.1130

†Rockingham Castle, Northants. Tel: 01536-770240. Open Sun. and Thurs. only (and Bank Holiday Mon. and Tues., and Tues. in Aug.). Adm. £3.90; gardens only, £2.50. Built by William the Conqueror

Royal Pavilion, Brighton. Tel: 01273-290900. Adm. charge. Palace of George IV, in Chinese style with Indian exterior and Regency gardens

†Rufford Old Hall (nt), Lancs. Tel: 01704-821254. Closed Thurs. and Fri. Adm. £3.50; garden only, £1.80. A 16th-century hall with unique screen

St Augustine's Abbey (eh), Canterbury, Kent. Tel: 01227-767345. Adm. £2.50. Remains of Benedictine monastery, with Norman church, on site of abbey founded AD 598 by St Augustine

St Mawes Castle (eh), Cornwall. Tel: 01326-270526. Closed Wed. and Thurs. in winter. Adm. £2.50. Coastal defence castle built by Henry VIII

St Michael's Mount (nt), Cornwall. Tel: 01736-710507. Opening times vary. Adm. £3.90. A 14th-century castle with later additions, off the coast at Marazion

*Sandringham, Norfolk. Tel: 01553-772675. Closed for two weeks in summer and when the Royal Family is in residence. Adm. £4.50; grounds only, £3.50. The Queen's private residence; a neo-Jacobean house built in 1870

Scarborough Castle (eh), N. Yorks. Tel: 01723-372451. Closed Mon. and Tues. in winter. Adm. £2.20. Remains of 12th-century keep and curtain walls

†Sherborne Castle, Dorset. Tel: 01935-813182. Open Tues., Thurs., Sat., Sun. and Bank Holiday Mon. Adm. charge. Sixteenth-century castle built by Sir Walter Raleigh

*Shugborough (nt), Staffs. Tel: 01889-881388. Open Sun. only in October; open for booked parties in winter. Adm. house, county museum and farm, £8.00; each site alone, £3.50. House set in 18th-century park with monuments, temples and pavilions in the Greek Revival style

Skipton Castle, N. Yorks. Tel: 01756-792442. Closed Sun. mornings. Adm. £3.80. D-shaped castle with six round towers and beautiful inner courtyard

†Smallhythe Place (nt), Kent. Tel: 01580-762334. Closed Thurs. and Fri. (except Good Friday). Adm. £3.00. Half-timbered 16th-century house; home of Ellen Terry 1899-1928

†Stanford Hall, Leics. Tel: 01788-860250. Open Sat.-Sun.; also Bank Holiday Mon. and Tues. Adm. £3.80; grounds only, £2.10. William and Mary house with Stuart portraits. Motorcycle museum

Stonehenge (eh), Wilts. Tel: 01980-624715. Adm. £3.90. Prehistoric monument consisting of concentric stone circles surrounded by a ditch and bank

†Stonor Park, Oxon. Tel: 01491-638587. Opening days vary. Adm. £4.50. Medieval house with Georgian facade. Centre of Roman Catholicism after the Reformation

†Stourhead (nt), Wilts. Tel: 01747-841152. Closed Thurs.-Fri. Gardens open daily all year. Adm. £4.40; gardens, £3.40; combined ticket £7.90. English Palladian mansion with famous gardens

*Stratfield Saye House, Hants. Tel: 01256-882882. Closed Fri.; May and Sept. open weekends and Bank Holidays only. Adm. charge. House built 1630-40; home of the Dukes of Wellington since 1817

Stratford-upon-Avon, Warks. *Shakespeare's Birthplace* with Shakespeare Centre; *Anne Hathaway's Cottage*, home of Shakespeare's wife; *Mary Arden's House*, home of Shakespeare's mother; *New Place*, where Shakespeare died; and *Hall's Croft*, home of Shakespeare's daughter.

Tel: 01789-204016. Adm. charges. Also *Grammar School* attended by Shakespeare, *Holy Trinity Church*, where Shakespeare is buried, *Royal Shakespeare Theatre* (burnt down 1926, rebuilt 1932) and *Swan Theatre* (opened 1986)

*Sudeley Castle, Glos. Tel: 01242-602308. Adm. £5.50; grounds only, £4.00. Castle built in 1442; restored in the 19th century

Syon House, Brentford, Middx. Tel: 0181-560 0881. Opening times vary. Adm. charges vary. Built on the site of a former monastery; Adam interior

Tilbury Fort (eh), Essex. Tel: 01375-858489. Closed Mon. and Tues. in winter. Adm. £2.30. A 17th-century coastal fort

Tintagel Castle (eh), Cornwall. Tel: 01840-770328. Adm. £2.80. A 12th-century cliff-top castle and Dark Age settlement site

Tower of London, London EC3. Tel: 0171-709 0765. Adm. £9.00. Royal palace and fortress begun by William the Conqueror in 1078. Houses the Crown Jewels

*Trerice (nt), Cornwall. Tel: 01637-875404. Closed Tues. and Sat. (except in Aug.). Adm. £4.00. Elizabethan manor house

Tynemouth Priory and Castle (eh), Tyne and Wear. Tel: 0191-257 1090. Closed Mon.-Tues. in winter. Adm. £1.70. Remains of a Benedictine priory, founded c.1090, on Saxon monastic site

†Uppark (nt), W. Sussex. Tel: 01730-825415. Closed Fri. and Sat. Adm. £5.50 by timed ticket. Late 17th-century house, completely restored after fire. Fetherstonhaugh art collection

Walmer Castle (eh), Kent. Tel: 01304-364288. Closed Mon. and Tues. in winter; closed Jan.-Feb. and when the Lord Warden is in residence. Adm. £4.00. One of Henry VIII's coastal defence castles, now the residence of the Lord Warden of the Cinque Ports

Waltham Abbey (eh), Essex. Tel: 01992-702200. Adm. free. Ruined abbey including the nave of the abbey church, 'Harold's Bridge' and late 14th-century gatehouse. Traditionally the burial place of Harold II (1066)

Warkworth Castle (eh), Northumberland. Tel: 01665-711423. Adm. £2.70. A 15th-century keep amidst earlier ruins, with 14th-century hermitage (open Wed., Sun. and Bank Holidays in summer) upstream

Warwick Castle. Tel: 01926-406600. Adm. charge. Medieval castle with Madame Tussaud's waxworks, in Capability Brown parkland

Whitby Abbey (eh), N. Yorks. Tel: 01947-603568. Adm. £1.70. Remains of Norman church on the site of a monastery founded in AD 657

*Wilton House, Wilts. Tel: 01722-746729. Adm. £6.50. A 17th-century house on the site of a Tudor house and Saxon abbey

Windsor Castle, Berks. Tel: 01753-831118 for recorded information on opening times. Adm. £9.50, including the Castle precincts. Official residence of The Queen; oldest royal residence still in regular use. Also *St George's Chapel*

Woburn Abbey, Beds. Tel: 01525-290666. Closed Nov. and Dec.; also Mon.-Fri. in Jan. and Feb. Adm. charge. Built on the site of a Cistercian abbey; seat of the Dukes of Bedford. Important art collection; antiques centre

Wroxeter Roman City (eh), Shropshire. Tel: 01743-761330. Closed Mon. and Tues. in winter. Adm. £2.95. Second-century public baths and part of the forum of the Roman town of Viroconium

WALES

c Property of Cadw: Welsh Historic Monuments
nt National Trust property

BEAUMARIS CASTLE (C), Anglesey. Tel: 01222-500200.
Adm. £2.20. Concentrically-planned castle, still almost
intact

CAERLEON ROMAN BATHS AND AMPHITHEATRE (C), nr
Newport. Tel: 01633-422518. Closed Sun. morning in
winter. Adm. £2.00, joint ticket with Roman Legionary
Museum £3.30. Rare example of a legionary bath-
house and late 1st-century arena surrounded by bank
for spectators

CAERNARFON CASTLE (C). Tel: 01222-500200. Adm.
£4.00. Important Edwardian castle built, with the town
wall, between 1283 and 1330

CAERPHILLY CASTLE (C). Tel: 01222-500200. Adm. £2.40.
Concentrically-planned castle (c.1270) notable for its
scale and use of water defences

CARDIFF CASTLE. Tel: 01222-878100. Adm. charge.
Castle built on the site of a Roman fort; spectacular
towers and rich interior

CASTELL COCH (C), nr Cardiff. Tel: 01222-500200. Adm.
£2.50. Rebuilt 1875-90 on medieval foundations

CHEPSTOW CASTLE (C). Tel: 01222-500200. Adm. £3.00.
Rectangular keep amid extensive fortifications

CONWY CASTLE (C). Tel: 01222-500200. Adm. £3.50.
Built by Edward I, 1283-7

*CRICCIETH CASTLE (C). Tel: 01222-500200. Adm. £2.20.
Native Welsh 13th-century castle, altered by Edward I

DENBIGH CASTLE (C). Tel: 01222-500200. Adm. £1.70.
Remains of the castle (begun 1282), including triple-
towered gatehouse

HARLECH CASTLE (C). Tel: 01222-500200. Adm. £3.00.
Well-preserved Edwardian castle, constructed 1283-
90, on an outcrop above the former shore-line

PEMBROKE CASTLE. Tel: 01646-681510. Adm. £3.00.
Castle founded in 1093; Great Tower built 1200;
birthplace of King Henry VII

†PENRHYN CASTLE (NT), Bangor. Tel: 01248-353084.
Closed Tues. Adm. £4.80; grounds only, £3.00. Neo-
Norman castle built in the 19th century. Industrial
railway museum

PORTMEIRION, Penrhyndeudraeth. Tel: 01766-770228.
Adm. £3.75. Village in Italianate style

†POWIS CASTLE (NT), nr Welshpool. Tel: 01938-554338.
Closed Mon. (except Bank Holidays) and Tues. (except
July and Aug.). Adm. £7.50; garden only, £5.00.
Medieval castle with interior in variety of styles; 17th-
century gardens and Clive of India museum

RAGLAN CASTLE (C). Tel: 01222-500200. Adm. £2.40.
Remains of 15th-century castle with moated hexagonal
keep

ST DAVIDS BISHOP'S PALACE (C), St Davids. Tel: 01222-
500200. Closed Sun. mornings in winter. Adm. £1.70.
Remains of residence of Bishops of St Davids built
1328-47

TINTERN ABBEY (C), nr Chepstow. Tel: 01222-500200.
Adm. £2.20. Remains of 13th-century church and
conventual buildings of a Cistercian monastery

*TRETOWER COURT AND CASTLE (C), nr Crickhowell.
Tel: 01222-500200. Adm. £2.20. Medieval house with
remains of 12th-century castle nearby

SCOTLAND

HS Historic Scotland property
NTS National Trust for Scotland property

ANTONINE WALL (HS), between the Clyde and the Forth.
Adm. free. Built about AD 142, consists of ditch, turf
rampart and road, with forts every two miles

BALMORAL CASTLE, nr Braemar. Tel: 013397-42334.
Open mid-April to end July; closed Sun. in April and
May. Adm. £4.00. Baronial-style castle built for
Victoria and Albert. The Queen's private residence

BLACK HOUSE, ARNOL (HS), Lewis, Western Isles. Tel:
01851-710395. Closed Sun.; also Fri. in winter. Adm.
£1.80. Traditional Lewis thatched house

*BLAIR CASTLE, Blair Atholl. Tel: 01796-481207. Adm.
£5.50. Mid 18th-century mansion with 13th-century
tower; seat of the Dukes of Atholl

*BONAWE IRON FURNACE (HS), Argyll and Bute. Tel:
01866-822432. Closed Sun. mornings. Adm. £2.30.
Charcoal-fuelled ironworks founded in 1753

†BOWHILL, Selkirk. Tel: 01750-22204. House open July
only; grounds open April-Aug. except Fri. Adm. £4.00;
grounds only, £1.00. Seat of the Dukes of Buccleuch
and Queensberry; fine collection of paintings,
including portrait miniatures

BROUGH OF BIRSAY (HS), Orkney. Adm. £1.00. Remains of
Norse church and village on the tidal island of Birsay

CAERLAVEROCK CASTLE (HS), nr Dumfries. Tel: 01387-
770244. Closed Sun. mornings. Adm. £2.30. Fine early
classical Renaissance building

CALANAIS STANDING STONES (HS), Lewis, Western Isles.
Tel: 01851-621422. Adm. £1.50. Standing stones in a
cross-shaped setting, dating from 3000 BC

CATHERTUNS (BROWN AND WHITE) (HS), nr Brechin.
Adm. free. Two large Iron Age hill forts

*CAWDOR CASTLE, Inverness. Tel: 01667-404615. Adm.
£5.20; grounds only, £2.80. A 14th-century keep with
15th- and 17th-century additions

CLAVA CAIRNS (HS), Highland. Adm. free. Late Neolithic
or early Bronze Age cairns

*CRATHES CASTLE (NTS), nr Banchory. Tel: 01330-
844525. Garden and grounds open all year. Adm. castle,
garden and grounds, £4.80; each site, £2.00. A 16th-
century baronial castle in woodland, fields and gardens

*CULZEAN CASTLE (NTS), S. Ayrshire. Tel: 01655-760274.
Country park open all year. Adm. £6.50; country park
only, £3.50. An 18th-century Adam castle with oval
staircase and circular saloon

DRYBURGH ABBEY (HS), Scottish Borders. Tel: 01835-
822381. Closed Sun. mornings. Adm. £2.30. A 12th-
century abbey containing tomb of Sir Walter Scott

*DUNVEGAN CASTLE, Skye. Tel: 01470-521206. Adm.
£5.00; gardens only, £3.50. A 13th-century castle with
later additions; home of the chiefs of the Clan
MacLeod; trips to seal colony

EDINBURGH CASTLE (HS). Tel: 0131-225 9846. Adm.
£6.00; war memorial free. Includes the Scottish
National War Memorial, Scottish United Services
Museum and historic apartments

EDZELL CASTLE (HS), nr Brechin. Tel: 01356-648631.
Closed Sun. mornings, Thurs. afternoons and Fri. in
winter. Adm. £2.30. Medieval tower house; unique
walled garden

*EILEAN DONAN CASTLE, Wester Ross. Tel: 01599-
555202. Adm. £3.00. A 13th-century castle with
Jacobite relics

ELGIN CATHEDRAL (HS), Moray. Tel: 01343-547171.
Closed Sun. mornings, Thurs. afternoons and Fri. in
winter. Adm. £1.80. A 13th-century cathedral with fine
chapterhouse

*FLOORS CASTLE, Kelso. Tel: 01573-223333. Adm.
charge. Largest inhabited castle in Scotland; seat of the
Dukes of Roxburghe

FORT GEORGE (HS), Highland. Tel: 01667-462777. Closed Sunday mornings in winter. Adm. £3.00. An 18th-century fort

*GLAMIS CASTLE, Angus. Tel: 01307-840393. Adm. £5.20; grounds only, £2.40. Seat of the Lyon family (later Earls of Strathmore and Kinghorne) since 1372

GLASGOW CATHEDRAL (HS). Tel: 0141-552 6891. Closed Sun. mornings. Adm. free. Medieval cathedral with elaborately vaulted crypt

GLENELG BROCH (HS), Highland. Adm. free. Two broch towers with well-preserved structural features

*HOPETOUN HOUSE, nr Edinburgh. Tel: 0131-331 2451. Adm. £4.70. House designed by Sir William Bruce, enlarged by William Adam

HUNTLY CASTLE (HS). Tel: 01466-793191. Closed Sun. mornings; also Thurs. afternoons and Fri. in winter. Adm. £2.30. Ruin of a 16th- and 17th-century house

*INVERARAY CASTLE, Argyll. Tel: 01499-302203. Adm. charge. Gothic-style 18th-century castle; seat of the Dukes of Argyll

IONA ABBEY, Inner Hebrides. Tel: 01828-640411. Adm. £2.00. Monastery founded by St Columba in AD 563

*JARLSHOF (HS), Shetland. Tel: 01950-460112. Closed Sun. mornings. Adm. £2.30. Remains from Stone Age

JEDBURGH ABBEY (HS), Scottish Borders. Tel: 01835-863925. Closed Sun. mornings in winter. Adm. £2.80. Romanesque and early Gothic church founded c.1138

KELSO ABBEY (HS), Scottish Borders. Adm. free. Remains of great abbey church founded 1128

LINLITHGOW PALACE (HS). Tel: 01506-842896. Closed Sun. mornings in winter. Adm. £2.30. Ruin of royal palace in park setting. Birthplace of Mary, Queen of Scots

MAES HOWE (HS), Orkney. Tel: 01856-761606. Closed Sun. mornings, Thurs. afternoons and Fri. in winter. Adm. £2.30. Neolithic tomb

*MEIGLE SCULPTURED STONE (HS), Angus. Tel: 01828-640612. Adm. £1.50. Celtic Christian stones

MELROSE ABBEY (HS), Scottish Borders. Tel: 01896-822562. Closed Sun. mornings in winter. Adm. £2.80. Ruin of Cistercian abbey founded c.1136

MOUSA BROCH (HS), Shetland. Adm. free. Finest surviving Iron Age broch tower

NETHER LARGIE CAIRNS (HS), Argyll and Bute. Adm. free. Bronze Age and Neolithic cairns

NEW ABBEY CORN MILL (HS), nr Dumfries. Tel: 01387-850260. Closed Sun. mornings, Thurs. afternoons and Fri. in winter. Adm. £2.30. Water-powered mill

PALACE OF HOLYROODHOUSE, Edinburgh. Tel: 0131-556 7371. Closed when The Queen is in residence. Adm. £5.30. The Queen's official Scottish residence. Main part of the palace built 1671-9

RING OF BROGAR (HS), Orkney. Adm. free. Neolithic circle of upright stones with an enclosing ditch

RUTHWELL CROSS (HS), Dumfries and Galloway. Adm. free. Seventh-century Anglian cross

ST ANDREWS CASTLE AND CATHEDRAL (HS), Fife. Tel: 01334-477196 (castle); 01334-472563 (cathedral). Adm. £2.30 (castle); £1.80 (cathedral); £3.50 (combined ticket). Closed Sun. mornings in winter. Ruins of 13th-century castle and remains of the largest cathedral in Scotland

*SCONE PALACE, Perth. Tel: 01738-552300. Adm. £5.20. House built 1802-13 on the site of a medieval palace

SKARA BRAE (HS), Orkney. Tel: 01856-841815. Closed Sun. mornings in winter. Adm. £3.20 (winter); £4.00 (summer, joint ticket with Skaill House). Stone-Age village with adjacent 17th-century house

*SMAILHOLM TOWER (HS), Scottish Borders. Tel: 01573-460365. Closed Sun. mornings. Adm. £1.80. Well-preserved tower-house

STIRLING CASTLE (HS). Tel: 01786-450000. Adm. £4.50. Great Hall and gatehouse of James IV, palace of James V, Chapel Royal remodelled by James VI

TANTALLON CASTLE (HS), E. Lothian. Tel: 01620-892727. Closed Sun. mornings, Thurs. afternoons and Fri. in winter. Adm. £2.30. Fortification with earthwork defences and a 14th-century curtain wall with towers

*THREAVE CASTLE (HS), Dumfries and Galloway. Tel: 0831-168512. Adm. £1.80, including ferry trip. Late 14th-century tower on an island; reached by boat, long walk to castle

URQUHART CASTLE (HS), Loch Ness. Tel: 01456-450551. Adm. £3.50. Castle remains with well-preserved tower

NORTHERN IRELAND

DE Property in the care of the Northern Ireland Department of the Environment
NT National Trust property

CARRICKFERGUS CASTLE (DE), Co. Antrim. Tel: 01960-351273. Closed Sun. mornings. Adm. £2.70. Castle begun in 1180 and garrisoned until 1928

†CASTLE COOLE (NT), Enniskillen. Tel: 01365-322690. Closed Thurs, also Mon.-Fri. in April and Sept. (except Bank Holidays). Adm. house, £2.80; estate, £2.00 per car. An 18th-century mansion by James Wyatt in parkland

†CASTLE WARD (NT), Co. Down. Tel: 01396-881204. Closed Thurs; also closed Mon.-Fri. in April, Sept. and Oct.; grounds open all year. Adm. £2.60. An 18th-century house with Classical and Gothic facades

*DEVENISH ISLAND (DE), Co. Fermanagh. Closed Sun. mornings and Mon. Adm. £2.25. Island monastery founded in the 6th century by St Molaise

DOWNHILL CASTLE (NT), Co. Londonderry. Tel: 01265-848728. Adm. free. Ruins of palatial house in landscaped estate including Mussenden Temple. Opening times of temple vary

DUNLUCE CASTLE (DE), Co. Antrim. Tel: 012657-31938. Closed Sun. morning (except July and Aug.). Adm. £1.50. Ruins of 16th-century stronghold of the MacDonnells

†FLORENCE COURT (NT), Co. Fermanagh. Tel: 01365-348249. Closed Tues.; also closed Mon.-Fri. (except Bank Holidays) in April and Sept.; grounds open all year. Adm. £2.80; estate £2.00 per car. Mid 18th-century house with rococo plasterwork

*GREY ABBEY (DE), Co. Down. Tel: 01247-788585. Closed Sun. morning and Mon. Adm £1.00. Substantial remains of a Cistercian abbey founded in 1193

HILLSBOROUGH FORT (DE), Co. Down. Closed Sun. mornings and Mon. Adm. free. Built in 1650

†MOUNT STEWART (NT), Co. Down. Tel: 012477-88387. Closed Tues.; also closed Mon.-Fri. in April and Oct. Adm. £3.50; garden only, £3.00. An 18th-century house, childhood home of Lord Castlereagh

NENDRUM MONASTERY (DE), Mahee Island, Co. Down. Closed Sun. mornings and Mon.; also Mon.-Fri. in winter. Adm 75p. Founded in the 5th century by St Machaoi

*TULLY CASTLE (DE), Co. Fermanagh. Closed Sun. mornings and Mon. Adm. £1.00. Fortified house and bawn built in 1613

*WHITE ISLAND (DE), Co. Fermanagh. Closed Sun. mornings and Mon. Adm. £2.25. Tenth-century monastery and 12th-century church. Access by ferry

Museums and Galleries

There are more than 2,500 museums and galleries in the United Kingdom. Over 1,700 are registered with the Museums and Galleries Commission (*see* page 323), which indicates that they have an appropriate constitution, are soundly financed, have adequate collection management standards and public services, and have access to professional curatorial advice. Museums must achieve full or provisional registration status in order to be eligible for grants from the Museums and Galleries Commission and from Area Museums Councils. Over 700 of the registered museums are run by a local authority.

The national museums and galleries receive direct government grant-in-aid. These are:
- British Museum
- Imperial War Museum
- National Army Museum
- National Galleries of Scotland
- National Gallery
- National Maritime Museum
- National Museums and Galleries on Merseyside
- National Museum of Wales
- National Museums of Scotland
- National Portrait Gallery
- Natural History Museum
- RAF Museum
- Royal Armouries
- Science Museum
- Tate Gallery
- Ulster Folk and Transport Museum
- Ulster Museum
- Victoria and Albert Museum
- Wallace Collection

Local authority museums are funded by the local authority and may also receive grants from the Museums and Galleries Commission. Independent museums and galleries mainly rely on their own resources but are also eligible for grants from the Museums and Galleries Commission.

The Museums and Galleries Commission has identified 26 non-national museum bodies which have pre-eminent collections of more than local or regional importance. Some of those designated are museum services with a wide variety of collections; others are small and more focused in a particular field. Ten Area Museum Councils in the UK, which are independent charities that receive an annual grant from the Museums and Galleries Commission, give advice and support to the museums in their area and may offer improvement grants. They also circulate exhibitions and assist with training and marketing.

OPENING TO THE PUBLIC

The following is a selection of the museums and art galleries in the United Kingdom. The admission charges given are the standard charges for 1998–9, where a charge is made; many museums have concessionary rates for children, etc. Opening hours vary. Most museums are closed on Christmas Eve, Christmas Day, Boxing Day and New Year's Day; many are closed on Good Friday, and some are closed on May Day Bank Holiday. Some smaller museums close at lunchtimes. Information about a specific museum or gallery should be checked by telephone.

* Local authority museum/gallery
† Museum/gallery contains a collection designated pre-eminent

ENGLAND

BARNARD CASTLE, Co. Durham – *† *The Bowes Museum*, Westwick Road. Tel: 01833-690606. Closed Sun. mornings. Adm. £3.50. European art from the late medieval period to the 19th century; music and costume galleries; English period rooms from Elizabeth I to Victoria; local archaeology

BATH – *American Museum in Britain*, Claverton Manor. Tel: 01225-460503. Closed mornings and Mon. (except Bank Holidays); also closed in winter (except on application). Adm. £5.00 (including house); grounds and galleries only, £2.50. American decorative arts from the 17th to 19th century
**Museum of Costume*, Bennett Street. Tel: 01225-477752. Adm. £3.80. Fashion from the 16th century to the present day
**Roman Baths Museum*, Abbey Church Yard. Tel: 01225-477774. Adm. (excluding 18th-century Pump Room, which is free) £6.30. Museum adjoins the remains of a Roman baths and temple complex
**Victoria Art Gallery*, Bridge Street. Tel: 01225-477772. Closed Bank Holidays. Adm. free. European Old Masters and British art since the 18th century

BEAMISH, Co. Durham – *† *Beamish, The North of England Open Air Museum*. Tel: 01207-231811. Closed Mon. and Fri. in winter. Adm. charge. Recreated northern town *c.*1900, with rebuilt and furnished local buildings, colliery village, farm, railway station, tramway, Pockerley Manor and horse-yard (set *c.*1800)

BEAULIEU, Hants – † *National Motor Museum*. Tel: 01590-612345. Adm. charge. Displays of over 250 vehicles dating from 1895 to the present day

BIRMINGHAM – *† *Aston Hall*, Albert Road. Tel: 0121-327 0062. Closed mornings and in winter. Adm. free. Jacobean house containing paintings, furniture and tapestries from 17th to 19th century
**Birmingham Nature Centre*, Edgbaston. Tel: 0121-472 7775. Closed Mon.-Sat. in winter. Adm. £1.50. Indoor and outdoor enclosures displaying British wildlife
*† *City Museum and Art Gallery*, Chamberlain Square. Tel: 0121-303 2834. Closed Sun. mornings. Adm. free (except Gas Hall). Includes notable collection of Pre-Raphaelites
*† *Museum of the Jewellery Quarter*, Vyse Street, Hockley. Tel: 0121-554 3598. Closed Sun. Adm. £2.00. Built around a real jewellery workshop
*† *Soho House*, Soho Avenue. Tel: 0121-554 9122. Closed Sun. mornings and Mon. (except Bank Holidays). Adm. £2.00. Eighteenth-century home of industrialist Matthew Boulton

BOVINGTON CAMP, Dorset – *Tank Museum*. Tel: 01929-405096. Adm. £6.00. Collection of 300 tanks from the earliest days of tank warfare to the present

BRADFORD – **Cartwright Hall Art Gallery*, Lister Park. Tel: 01274-493313. Closed Sun. mornings and Mon. (except Bank Holidays). Adm. free. British 19th- and 20th-century fine art
**Industrial Museum and Horses at Work*, Moorside Road. Tel: 01274-631756. Closed Sun. mornings and Mon. (except Bank Holidays). Adm. charge. Engineering, textiles, transport and social history exhibits, including recreated back-to-back cottages, shire horses and horse tram-rides

BRIGHTON – *†Booth Museum of Natural History, Dyke Road. Tel: 01273-292777. Closed Thurs. and Sun. mornings. Adm. free. Zoology, botany and geology collections; British birds in recreated habitats

*†Brighton Museum and Art Gallery, Church Street. Tel: 01273-290900. Closed Sun. mornings and Wed. Adm. free. Includes fine art, design, fashion, archaeology, Brighton history

BRISTOL – Arnolfini Gallery, Narrow Quay. Tel: 0117-929 9191. Adm. free; charge for cinema and events. Contemporary visual arts, dance, theatre, film and music

*†Blaise Castle House Museum, Henbury. Tel: 0117-950 6789. Closed Thurs. and Fri.; also closed 1 Nov. to 31 Mar. Adm. free. Agricultural and social history collections in an 18th-century mansion

*†Bristol Industrial Museum, Prince Street. Tel: 0117-925 1470. Closed Thurs. and Fri.; closed Mon.-Fri. in winter. Adm. charge (except on Sun.). Industrial, maritime and transport collections

*†City Museum and Art Gallery, Queen's Road. Tel: 0117-922 3571. Adm. charge (except on Sun.). Includes fine and decorative art, oriental art, Egyptology and Bristol ceramics and paintings

CAMBRIDGE – Duxford Airfield, Duxford. Tel: 01223-835000. Adm. £5.95. Displays of military and civil aircraft, tanks, guns and naval exhibits

†Fitzwilliam Museum, Trumpington Street. Tel: 01223-332900. Closed Mon. (except some Bank Holidays) and Sun. mornings. Adm. free. Antiquities, fine and applied arts, clocks, ceramics, manuscripts, furniture, sculpture, coins and medals, temporary exhibitions

†University Museum of Archaeology and Anthropology, Downing Street. Tel: 01223-333516. Closed Sun., Mon. and mornings. Adm. free. Archaeology and anthropology from all parts of the world

† Whipple Museum of the History of Science, Free School Lane. Tel: 01223-330906. Closed mornings and weekends. Adm. free. Scientific instruments from the 14th century to the present day

CARLISLE – *Tullie House Museum and Art Gallery, Castle Street. Tel: 01228-34781. Closed Sun. mornings. Adm. charge to Border galleries only; ground floor, Old Tullie House and Jacobean galleries, adm. free. Prehistoric archaeology, Hadrian's Wall, Viking and medieval Cumbria, and the social history of Carlisle; also British 19th- and 20th-century art and English porcelain

CHATHAM – The Historic Dockyard. Tel: 01634-823800. Closed Mon., Tues., Thurs. and Fri. in Feb., Mar. and Nov., also closed Dec.-Jan. Adm. charge. Maritime attractions including lifeboat collection

†Royal Engineers Museum, Brompton Barracks. Tel: 01634-406397. Closed Fri. Adm. £3.00. Regimental history, ethnography, decorative art and photography

CHESTER – *Grosvenor Museum, Grosvenor Street. Tel: 01244-321616. Closed Sun. mornings. Adm. free. Roman collections, natural history, art, Chester silver, local history and costume

CHICHESTER – †Weald and Downland Open Air Museum, Singleton. Tel: 01243-811348. Closed Mon.,Tues., Thurs., Fri. in winter. Adm. £5.20. Rebuilt vernacular buildings from south-east England; includes medieval houses, agricultural and rural craft buildings and a working watermill

COLCHESTER – *†Colchester Castle Museum, Castle Park. Tel: 01206-282939. Closed Sun. mornings. Adm. £3.60. Local archaeological antiquities and displays on Roman Colchester; tours of the Roman vaults, castle walls and chapel with medieval and prison displays

COVENTRY – *Herbert Art Gallery and Museum, Jordan Well. Tel: 01203-832381. Closed Sun. mornings. Local

history, archaeology and industry, oriental ceramics, and fine and decorative art

*†Museum of British Road Transport, Hales Street. Tel: 01203-832425. Adm. free. Hundreds of motor vehicles and bicycles

CRICH, nr Matlock, Derbys – †National Tramway Museum. Tel: 01773-852565. Closed in winter and most Fri. in April, Sept. and Oct. Adm. £5.90. Open-air working museum with tram rides

DERBY – *Derby Museum and Art Gallery, The Strand. Tel: 01332-716659. Closed Bank Holiday mornings and Sun. Adm. free. Includes paintings by Joseph Wright of Derby and Derby porcelain

*Industrial Museum, off Full Street. Tel: 01332-255308. Closed Bank Holiday mornings and Sun. Adm. free. Rolls-Royce aero engine collection and a railway engineering gallery

DEVIZES – †Devizes Museum, Long Street. Tel: 01380-727369. Closed Sun. Adm. £2.00. Natural and local history, art gallery, archaeological finds from Bronze Age, Iron Age, Roman and Saxon sites

DORCHESTER – Dorset County Museum, High West Street. Tel: 01305-262735. Closed Sun. (except July and Aug.). Adm. charge. Includes a collection of Thomas Hardy's manuscripts, books, notebooks and drawings

EXETER – *†Royal Albert Memorial Museum, Queen Street. Tel: 01392-265858. Closed Sun. Adm. free. Natural history, archaeology, and fine and decorative art including Exeter silver

GAYDON, Warwick – British Motor Industry Heritage Trust, Heritage Motor Centre, Banbury Road. Tel: 019626-641188. Adm. charge. History of British motor industry from 1895 to present; classic vehicles; engineering gallery; Corgi and Lucas collections

GLOUCESTER, – National Waterways Museum, Llanthony Warehouse, The Docks. Tel: 01452-318054. Adm. £4.50. Two-hundred-year history of Britain's canals and inland waterways

GOSPORT, Hants – Royal Navy Submarine Museum, Haslar Jetty Road. Tel: 01705-529217. Adm. £3.75. Underwater warfare, including the submarine Alliance; historical and nuclear galleries; and first Royal Navy submarine

GRASMERE, Cumbria – †Dove Cottage and the Wordsworth Museum (see page 586)

HALIFAX – Eureka! The Museum for Children, Discovery Road. Tel: 01426-983191. Adm. £4.75 (over age 12), £3.75 (ages 3-12), free (under age 3). Saver ticket £14.75. Hands-on museum designed for children up to age 12

HULL – *Ferens Art Gallery, Queen Victoria Square. Tel: 01482-613902. Closed Sun. mornings. Adm. non-residents £1.00; residents free. European art, especially Dutch 17th-century paintings, British portraits from 17th to 20th centuries and marine paintings

*Town Docks Museum, Queen Victoria Square. Tel: 01482-613902. Closed Sun. mornings. Adm.: non-residents £1.00; residents free. Whaling, fishing and navigation exhibits

HUNTINGDON – *Cromwell Museum, Grammar School Walk. Tel: 01480-375830. Closed Mon., and mornings (except Sat.) in winter. Adm. free. Portraits and memorabilia relating to Oliver Cromwell

IPSWICH – *Christchurch Mansion and Wolsey Art Gallery, Christchurch Park. Tel: 01473-253246. Closed Sun. mornings and Mon. (except Bank Holidays). Adm. free. Tudor house with paintings by Gainsborough, Constable and other Suffolk artists; furniture and 18th-century ceramics. Art gallery for temporary exhibitions

LEEDS – *†City Art Gallery, The Headrow. Tel: 0113-247 8248. Closed Sun. mornings. Adm. free. British and

European paintings including English watercolours, modern sculpture, Henry Moore gallery, print room
*†*City Museum*, Calverley Street. Tel: 0113-247 8275. Closed Sun. and Mon. Adm. free. Natural history, archaeology, ethnography and coin collections
*†*Lotherton Hall*, Aberford. Tel: 0113-281 3259. Closed Sun. mornings and Mon.; also closed Jan.-Feb. Adm. charge. Costume and oriental collections in furnished Edwardian house; deer park and bird garden
Royal Armouries Museum, Armouries Drive. Tel: 0990-106666. Adm. £4.95 low season, £7.95 high season. National collection of arms and armour from BC to present; demonstrations of foot combat in museum's five galleries; falconry and mounted combat in the tiltyard
*† *Temple Newsam House*. Tel: 0113-264 7321. Closed Sun. mornings and Mon.; also closed Jan.-Feb. Adm. charge. Old Masters and 17th- and 18th-century decorative art in furnished Jacobean/Tudor house
LEICESTER – **Jewry Wall Museum*, St Nicholas Circle. Tel: 0116-247 3021. Closed Sun. mornings. Adm. free. Archaeology, Roman Jewry Wall and baths, and mosaics
**New Walk Museum and Art Gallery*, New Walk. Tel: 0116-255 4100. Closed Sun. mornings. Adm. free. Natural history, geology, ancient Egypt gallery, European art and decorative arts
**Snibston Discovery Park*, Coalville. Tel: 01530-510851. Adm. £4.75. Open-air science and industry museum on site of coal mine; country park with nature trail
LINCOLN – **Museum of Lincolnshire Life*, Burton Road. Tel: 01522-528448. Closed Sun. mornings in winter. Adm. charge. Social history and agricultural collection
*Usher Gallery, Lindum Road. Tel: 01522-527980. Closed Sun. mornings. Adm. £2.00. Watches, miniatures, porcelain, silver; collection of Peter de Wint works; Lincolnshire topography; Royal Lincs Regiment and Tennyson memorabilia
LIVERPOOL – *Lady Lever Art Gallery*, Wirral. Tel: 0151-478 4136. Closed Sun. mornings. Adm. £3.00 for an 'Eight Pass' which is valid for 12 months and for all National Museums and Galleries on Merseyside. Paintings, furniture and porcelain
Liverpool Museum, William Brown Street. Tel: 0151-478 4399. Closed Sun. mornings. Adm. 'Eight Pass' as above. Includes Egyptian mummies, weapons and classical sculpture; planetarium, aquarium, vivarium and natural history centre
Merseyside Maritime Museum, Albert Dock. Tel: 0151-478 4499. Adm. 'Eight Pass' as above. Floating exhibits, working displays and craft demonstrations; incorporates HM Customs and Excise National Museum
Museum of Liverpool Life, Mann Island. Tel: 0151-478 4080. Adm. 'Eight Pass' as above. The history of Liverpool
Sudley House, Mossley Hill Road. Tel: 0151-724 3245. Closed Sun. mornings. Adm. 'Eight Pass' as above. Late 18th- and 19th-century British paintings in former shipowner's home
Tate Gallery Liverpool, Albert Dock. Tel: 0151-709 3223. Twentieth-century painting and sculpture
Walker Art Gallery, William Brown Street. Tel: 0151-478 4199. Closed Sun. mornings. Adm. 'Eight Pass' as above. Paintings from the 14th to 20th century
LONDON: GALLERIES – **Barbican Art Gallery*, Barbican Centre, EC2. Tel: 0171-382 7105. Temporary exhibitions
†*Courtauld Gallery*, Somerset House, Strand, WC2. Tel: 0171-873 2526. Closed Sun. mornings. Adm. £4.00. The University of London galleries
†*Dulwich Picture Gallery*, College Road, SE21. Tel: 0181-693 5254. Closed Sun. mornings and Mon. (except Bank

Holidays). Adm. £3.00 (free on Fri.). Built by Sir John Soane to house 17th- and 18th-century paintings
Hayward Gallery, South Bank, SE1. Tel: 0171-928 3144. Adm. £5.00. Temporary exhibitions
National Gallery, Trafalgar Square, WC2. Tel: 0171-839 3321. Closed Sun. mornings. Adm. free. Western painting from the 13th to 20th century; early Renaissance collection in the Sainsbury wing
National Portrait Gallery, St Martin's Place, WC2. Tel: 0171-306 0055. Closed Sun. mornings and some Bank Holidays. Adm. free (except for some special exhibitions). Portraits of eminent people in British history
Percival David Foundation of Chinese Art, Gordon Square, WC1. Tel: 0171-387 3909. Closed weekends and Bank Holidays. Adm. free (charge for use of reference library). Chinese ceramics from tenth to 18th century
Photographers Gallery, Great Newport Street, WC2. Tel: 0171-831 1772. Closed Sun. mornings. Adm. free. Temporary exhibitions
The Queen's Gallery, Buckingham Palace, SW1. Tel: 0171-839 1377. Adm. £3.50. Art from the Royal Collection
Royal Academy of Arts, Piccadilly, W1. Tel: 0171-300 8000. Adm. charge. British art since 1750 and temporary exhibitions; annual Summer Exhibition
Saatchi Gallery, Boundary Road, NW8. Tel: 0171-624 8299. Closed mornings and Mon.-Wed. Adm. £4.00. Contemporary art including paintings, photographs, sculpture and installations
Serpentine Gallery, Kensington Gardens, W2. Tel: 0171-402 6075. Adm. free. Temporary exhibitions of British and international contemporary art
Tate Gallery, Millbank, SW1. Tel: 0171-887 8000. Adm. free (charge for special exhibitions). British painting and 20th-century painting and sculpture
Wallace Collection, Manchester Square, W1. Tel: 0171-935 0687. Closed Sun. mornings. Adm. free. Paintings and drawings, French 18th-century furniture, armour, porcelain and clocks
Whitechapel Art Gallery, Whitechapel High Street, E1. Tel: 0171-522 7878. Closed Mon. Adm. free to most exhibitions. Temporary exhibitions of modern art
LONDON: MUSEUMS – *Bank of England Museum*, Threadneedle Street, EC2 (entrance from Bartholomew Lane). Tel: 0171-601 5545. Closed weekends and Bank Holidays. Adm. free. History of the Bank since 1694
Bethnal Green Museum of Childhood, Cambridge Heath Road, E2. Tel: 0181-983 5200. Closed Sun. mornings and Fri. Adm. free but donations invited. Toys, games and exhibits relating to the social history of childhood
British Museum, Great Russell Street, WC1. Tel: 0171-636 1555. Closed Sun. mornings. Adm. free. Antiquities, coins, medals, prints and drawings
Cabinet War Rooms, King Charles Street, SW1. Tel: 0171-930 6961. Adm. £4.40. Underground rooms used by Churchill and the Government during the Second World War
Commonwealth Experience, Kensington High Street, W8. Tel: 0171-603 4535. Exhibitions on Commonwealth nations, visual arts and crafts; Interactive World
Cutty Sark, Greenwich, SE10. Tel: 0181-858 3445. Adm. £3.50. Restored and rerigged tea clipper with exhibits on board. Sir Francis Chichester's round-the-world yacht, *Gipsy Moth IV*, can also be seen
Design Museum, Shad Thames, SE1. Tel: 0171-378 6055. Adm. £5.25. The development of design and the mass-production of consumer objects
Geffrye Museum, Kingsland Road, E2. Tel: 0171-739 9893. Closed Mon.; also Sun. and Bank Holiday mornings. Adm. free. English urban domestic interiors from 1600

to present day; also paintings, furniture, decorative arts, walled herb garden
HMS Belfast, Morgans Lane, Tooley Street, se1. Tel: 0171-407 6434. Adm £4.40. Life on a warship, illustrated on World War II warship
†*Horniman Museum and Gardens*, London Road, se23. Tel: 0181-699 1872. Adm. free. Museum of ethnography, musical instruments, natural history and aquarium; reference library; sunken, water and flower gardens
Imperial War Museum, Lambeth Road, se1. Tel: 0171-416 5000. Reference departments closed Sat. (except by appointment) and Sun. Adm. £4.70 (free after 4.30 p.m. daily). All aspects of the two world wars and other military operations involving Britain and the Commonwealth since 1914
†*Jewish Museum*, Albert Street, nw1. Tel: 0171-284 1997. Closed Fri., Sat., public and Jewish holidays. Adm. £3.00. Jewish life, history and religion
Jewish Museum, East End Road, n3. Tel: 0181-349 1143. Closed Fri., Sat., public and Jewish holidays. Adm. £2.00. Jewish life in London and Holocaust education
†*London Transport Museum*, Covent Garden, wc2. Tel: 0171-379 6344. Adm. charge. Vehicles, photographs and graphic art relating to the history of transport in London
MCC Museum, Lord's, nw8. Tel: 0171-289 1611. Open match days (closed most Sun. mornings); also conducted tours by appointment with Tours Manager. Adm. charge. Cricket museum
Museum of Garden History, Lambeth Palace Road se1. Tel: 0171-401 8865. Closed Sat. and Dec.-Feb. Adm. free. Exhibition of aspects of garden history and re-created 17th-century garden
†*Museum of London*, London Wall, ec2. Tel: 0171-600 3699. Adm. £5.00 (ticket valid for one year); free after 4.30 p.m. History of London from prehistoric times to present day
Museum of the Moving Image, South Bank, se1. Tel: 0171-401 2636. Adm. £6.25. History of the moving image in cinema and television
National Army Museum, Royal Hospital Road, sw3. Tel: 0171-730 0717. Adm. free. Five-hundred-year history of the British soldier; exhibits include model of the Battle of Waterloo and *Army for Today* gallery
National Maritime Museum, Greenwich, se10. Tel: 0181-858 4422. Reference library closed Sat. (except by appointment) and Sun. Adm. £5.50. Comprises the main building, the Old Royal Observatory and the Queen's House (*see page 586*). Maritime history of Britain; collections include globes, clocks, telescopes and paintings
Natural History Museum, Cromwell Road, sw7. Tel: 0171-938 9123. Adm. £6.00. Natural history collections
Royal Air Force Museum, Colindale, nw9. Tel: 0181-205 2266. Adm. £5.85. National museum of aviation with over 70 full-size aircraft; aviation from before the Wright brothers to the present-day RAF; flight simulator
Royal Mews, Buckingham Palace, sw1. Tel: 0171-839 1377. Open Tues.-Thurs. afternoons. Adm. £4.00. Carriages, coaches, stables and horses
Science Museum, Exhibition Road, sw7. Tel: 0171-938 8000. Adm. charge. Science, technology, industry and medicine collections
Shakespeare Globe Exhibition, Bankside, se1. Tel: 0171-902 1500. Adm. £5.00. Recreation of Elizabethan theatre using 16th-century techniques
Sherlock Holmes Museum, Baker Street, nw1. Tel: 0171-935 8866. Adm. £5.00. Recreated rooms of the fictional detective

Sir John Soane's Museum, Lincoln's Inn Fields, wc2. Tel: 0171-430 0175. Closed Sun. and Mon. Adm. free (groups by appointment only). Art and antiques
Theatre Museum, Russell Street, wc2. Tel: 0171-836 2330. Closed Mon. Adm. £3.50. History of the performing arts
*Tower Bridge Experience, se1. Tel: 0171-378 1928. Adm. £5.95. History of the bridge and display of Victorian steam machinery; panoramic views from walkways
Victoria and Albert Museum, Cromwell Road, sw7. Tel: 0171-938 8500. Closed Mon. mornings. Adm. £5.00. Includes National Art Library and Print Room (closed Sun. and Mon.). Fine and applied art and design, including furniture, glass, textiles, dress collections (British Galleries closed 1998-9)
Wellington Museum, Apsley House, w1 (*see* page 584)
Wimbledon Lawn Tennis Museum, Church Road, sw19. Tel: 0181-946 6131. Closed Sun. mornings and Mon. (except summer Bank Holidays). Adm. £3.00. Tennis trophies, fashion and memorabilia; view of Centre Court

MANCHESTER – **Gallery of Costume*, Rusholme. Tel: 0161-224 5217. Closed Sun., Mon. Adm. free. Exhibits from the 16th to 20th century
†*Manchester Museum*, Oxford Road. Tel: 0161-275 2634. Closed Sun. Adm. free. Archaeology, archery, botany, Egyptology, entomology, ethnography, geology, natural history, numismatics, oriental and zoology collections
†*Museum of Science and Industry*, Castlefield. Tel: 0161-832 1830. Adm. £6.50. On site of world's oldest passenger railway station; galleries relating to space, energy, power, transport, aviation and social history; interactive science centre
†*Whitworth Art Gallery*, Oxford Road. Tel: 0161-275 7450. Closed Sun. mornings. Adm. free. Watercolours, drawings, prints, textiles, wallpapers and 20th-century British art

NEWCASTLE UPON TYNE – **Laing Art Gallery*, New Bridge Street. Tel: 0191-232 7734. Closed Sun. mornings. Adm. free. British and European art, ceramics, glass, silver, textiles and costume; *Art on Tyneside* display
*†Newcastle Discovery Museum, West Blandford Square. Tel: 0191-232 6789. Closed Sun. mornings. Adm. free. Science and industry, local history, fashion and Tyneside's maritime history; Turbinia (first steam-driven engine) gallery

NEWMARKET – *National Horseracing Museum*, High Street. Tel: 01638-667333. Closed Mon. (except July and Aug.) and Nov.-March. Adm. £3.50. Paintings, trophies and exhibits relating to horseracing and tours of local trainers' yards and studs

NORWICH – **†Castle Museum*. Tel: 01603-493624. Closed Sun. mornings. Adm. £3.20 (£2.40 in winter). Art (including Norwich school), archaeology, natural history, teapot collection; guided tours of battlements and dungeons

NOTTINGHAM – **Brewhouse Yard Museum*, Castle Boulevard. Tel: 0115-915 3600. Adm. free (except weekends and Bank Holidays). Daily life from the 17th to 20th century
*Castle Museum. Tel: 0115-915 3700. Adm. free (except weekends and Bank Holidays). Paintings, ceramics, silver and glass; history of Nottingham
*Industrial Museum, Wollaton Park. Tel: 0115-915 3910. Adm. free (except weekends and Bank Holidays). Lacemaking machinery, steam engines and transport exhibits
*Museum of Costume and Textiles, Castle Gate. Tel: 0115-915 3500. Closed Mon. and Tues. Adm. free. Costume

displays from 1790 to the mid-20th century in period rooms

Natural History Museum, Wollaton Park. Tel: 0115-915 3900. Adm. free (except weekends and Bank Holidays). Local natural history and wildlife dioramas

OXFORD – †*Ashmolean Museum*, Beaumont Street. Tel: 01865-278000. Closed Mon. (except Bank Holidays) and Sun. mornings. Adm. free. European and Oriental fine and applied arts, archaeology, Egyptology and numismatics

Museum of Modern Art, Pembroke Street. Tel: 01865-722733. Closed Mon. Adm. £2.50. Temporary exhibitions

†*Museum of the History of Science*, Broad Street. Tel: 01865-277280. Closed mornings and Sun.-Mon. Adm. free. Displays include early scientific instruments, chemical apparatus, clocks and watches

†*Oxford University Museum of Natural History*, Parks Road. Tel: 01865-272950. Closed mornings (except for school parties by appointment) and Sun. Adm. free. Entomology, geology, mineralogy and zoology

†*Pitt Rivers Museum*, South Parks Road. Tel: 01865-270927. Closed mornings (except by appointment) and Sun. Adm. free. Ethnological and archaeological artefacts. Check for periods of closure in 1999

PLYMOUTH – *†*City Museum and Art Gallery*, Drake Circus. Tel: 01752-264878. Closed Mon. (except Bank Holidays) and Sun. Adm. free. Local and natural history, ceramics, silver, Old Masters, temporary exhibitions

The Dome, The Hoe. Tel: 01752-603300. Adm. charge. Maritime history museum

PORTSMOUTH – *Charles Dickens Birthplace Museum*, Old Commercial Road. Tel: 01705-827261. Closed in winter. Adm. charge. Dickens memorabilia

D-Day Museum, Clarence Esplanade. Tel: 01705-827261. Adm. charge. Includes the Overlord Embroidery

Flagship Portsmouth, HM Naval Base. Incorporates the *Royal Naval Museum* (tel: 01705-727562), HMS *Victory* (tel: 01705-822034), HMS *Warrior* (tel: 01705-291379), the †*Mary Rose* (tel: 01705-750521) and the *Dockyard Museum*. Adm. charge to each (combined ticket available). History of the Royal Navy and of the dockyard and the trades in it

PRESTON – *Harris Museum and Art Gallery*, Market Square. Tel: 01772-258248. Closed Sun. and Bank Holidays. Adm. free. British art since the 18th century, ceramics, glass, costume and local history; also contemporary exhibitions

READING – †*Rural History Centre*, University of Reading. Tel: 0118-931 8660. Closed Sun. and Mon. Adm. £1.00. History of farming and the countryside over the last 200 years

ST ALBANS – *Verulamium Museum*, St Michael's. Tel: 01727-819339. Closed Sun. mornings. Adm. £2.80. Iron Age and Roman Verulamium, including wall plasters, jewellery, mosaics and room reconstructions

ST IVES, Cornwall – *Tate Gallery St Ives*, Porthmeor Beach. Tel: 01736-796226. Opening times vary seasonally; closed Mon. Oct.-March. Adm. £3.50. Painting and sculpture by artists associated with St Ives

SHEFFIELD – *City Museum and Mappin Art Gallery*, Weston Park. Tel: 0114-276 8588. Closed Mon. and Tues. Adm. free. Includes applied arts, natural history, Bronze Age archaeology and ethnography, 19th- and 20th-century art

Graves Art Gallery, Surrey Street. Tel: 0114-273 5158. Closed Sun. and Mon. Adm. free. 20th-century British art, Grice Collection of Chinese ivories

Kelham Island Industrial Museum, off Alma Street. Tel: 0114-272 2106. Closed Fri. and Sat. Adm. charge. Local industrial and social history

STOKE-ON-TRENT – *Etruria Industrial Museum*, Etruria. Tel: 01782-287557. Closed Mon. and Tues. Adm. charge. Britain's sole surviving steam-powered potter's mill

Gladstone Pottery Museum, Longton. Tel: 01782-319232. Adm. charge. A working Victorian pottery. Pottery factory tours are available by arrangement Mon.-Fri., except during factory holidays, at the following: *Royal Doulton*, Burslem; *Spode*, Stoke; *Wedgwood*, Barlaston; *W. Moorcroft*, Cobridge; *H R Johnson Tiles*, Tunstall; *Moorland Pottery*, Burslem; *Peggy Davies Ceramics*, Stoke; *Staffordshire Enamels*, Longton; *St George's Fine Bone China*, Hanley

*†*Potteries Museum and Art Gallery*, Hanley. Tel: 01782-232323. Closed Sun. mornings. Adm. free. Pottery, china and porcelain collections

STYAL, Cheshire – *Quarry Bank Mill*. Tel: 01625-527468. Closed Mon. in winter. Adm. charge. Working mill illustrating history of cotton industry; costumed guides at restored Apprentice House

TELFORD – *†*Ironbridge Gorge Museums*. Tel: 01952-433522. Smaller sites closed in winter. Adm. charge for each site; £9.50 for all sites (ticket valid until all sites have been visited). Includes first iron bridge; Blists Hill (late Victorian working town); Museum of Iron; Jackfield Tile Museum; Coalport China Museum; Tar Tunnel; Broseley Pipeworks

TRING, Herts – *Tring Zoological Museum*, Akeman Street. Tel: 01442-824181. Closed Sun. mornings. Adm. £2.50. Display of more than 4,000 animal species

WAKEFIELD – *Yorkshire Sculpture Park*, West Bretton. Tel: 01924-830302. Adm. free. Open-air sculpture gallery including works by Moore, Hepworth, Frink and others

WORCESTER – *City Museum and Art Gallery*, Foregate Street. Tel: 01905-25371. Closed Thurs. and Sun. Adm. free. Includes a military museum, 19th-century chemist's shop and changing art exhibitions

Museum of Worcester Porcelain and Royal Worcester Factory, Severn Street. Tel: 01905-23221. Factory tours on weekdays

WROUGHTON, nr Swindon, Wilts – *Science Museum*, Wroughton Airfield. Tel: 01793-814466. Open selected summer weekends only. Adm. charge. Aircraft displays and some of the Science Museum's transport and agricultural collection

YEOVIL, Somerset – *Fleet Air Arm Museum*, Royal Naval Air Station, Yeovilton. Tel: 01935-840565. Adm. charge. History of naval aviation; historic aircraft, including Concorde 002

Montacute House, Montacute (*see* page 587). Elizabethan and Jacobean portraits from the National Portrait Gallery

YORK – *Beningbrough Hall*, Shipton-by-Beningbrough. Tel: 01904-470666. Closed Thurs. and Fri. (except Good Friday and July-Aug.); also closed in winter. Adm. £4.75. Portraits from the National Portrait Gallery

*†*Castle Museum*. Tel: 01904-653611. Adm. £4.75. Reconstructed streets; costume and military collections

*†*City Art Gallery*, Exhibition Square. Tel: 01904-551861. Closed Sun. mornings. Adm. free. European and British painting spanning seven centuries; modern pottery

Jorvik Viking Centre, Coppergate. Tel: 01904-643211. Adm. £4.99. Reconstruction of Viking York

National Railway Museum, Leeman Road. Tel: 01904-621261. Adm. £4.80. Includes locomotives, rolling stock and carriages

*†*Yorkshire Museum*, Museum Gardens. Tel: 01904-629745. Adm. £3.75. Yorkshire life from Roman to medieval times; geology gallery

WALES

BODELWYDDAN, Denbighshire – *Bodelwyddan Castle.* Tel: 01745-584060. Opening times vary. Adm. charge. Portraits from the National Portrait Gallery, furniture from the Victoria and Albert Museum and sculptures from the Royal Academy

CAERLEON – *Roman Legionary Museum.* Tel: 01633-423134. Adm. charge. Material from the site of the Roman fortress of Isca and its suburbs

CARDIFF – *National Museum and Gallery Cardiff,* Cathays Park. Tel: 01222-397951. Closed Mon. (except Bank Holidays). Adm. charge. Includes natural sciences, archaeology and Impressionist paintings

Museum of Welsh Life, St Fagans. Tel: 01222-573500. Adm. charge. Open-air museum with re-erected buildings, agricultural equipment and costume

DRE-FACH FELINDRE, nr Llandysul – *Museum of the Welsh Woollen Industry.* Tel: 01559-370929. Closed Sun., and Sat. in winter. Adm. charge. Exhibitions, a working woollen mill and craft workshops

LLANBERIS, nr Caernarfon – *Welsh Slate Museum.* Tel: 01286-870630. Closed in winter (except by appointment). Adm. charge. Former slate quarry with original machinery and plant; slate crafts demonstrations

LLANDRINDOD WELLS – *National Cycle Exhibition,* Exhibition Palace, Temple Street. Tel: 01597-825531. Adm £2.50. Over 200 bicycles on display, from 1818 to the present day

SWANSEA – *Glyn Vivian Art Gallery and Museum,* Alexandra Road. Tel: 01792-655006. Closed Mon. (except Bank Holidays). Adm. free. Paintings, ceramics, Swansea pottery and porcelain, clocks, glass and Welsh art

Swansea Maritime and Industrial Museum, Museum Square. Tel: 01792-650351. Closed Mon. (except Bank Holidays). Adm. free. Includes a working woollen mill and historic boats afloat

SCOTLAND

ABERDEEN – *Aberdeen Art Gallery,* Schoolhill. Tel: 01224-646333. Closed Sun. mornings. Adm. free. Art from the 18th to 20th century

Aberdeen Maritime Museum, Shiprow. Tel: 01224-337700. Adm. £3.50. Maritime history, including shipbuilding and North Sea oil

EDINBURGH – *Britannia,* Leith docks. Tel: 0131-555 8800. Former royal yacht; opening Oct. 1998

City Art Centre, Market Street. Tel: 0131-529 3993. Closed Sun. Adm. free. Late 19th- and 20th-century art and temporary exhibitions

Huntly House Museum, Canongate. Tel: 0131-529 4143. Closed Sun. Adm. free. Local history, silver, glass and Scottish pottery

Museum of Childhood, High Street. Tel: 0131-529 4142. Closed Sun. Adm. free. Toys, games, clothes and exhibits relating to the social history of childhood

Museum of Flight, East Fortune Airfield, nr North Berwick. Tel: 01620-880308. Closed in winter. Adm. £3.00. Display of aircraft

National Gallery of Scotland, The Mound. Tel: 0131-624 6200. Closed Sun. mornings. Adm. free. Paintings, drawings and prints from the 16th to 20th century, and the national collection of Scottish art

The People's Story, Canongate. Tel: 0131-529 4057. Closed Sun. Adm. free. Edinburgh life since the 18th century

Royal Museum of Scotland, Chambers Street. Tel: 0131-225 7534. Closed Sun. mornings. Adm. £3.00. Scottish and international collections from prehistoric times to the present

Scottish Agricultural Museum, Ingliston. Tel: 0131-225 7534. Closed Sat. and Sun. Adm. free. History of agriculture in Scotland

Scottish National Portrait Gallery, Queen Street. Tel: 0131-624 6200. Closed Sun. mornings. Adm. free. Portraits of eminent people in Scottish history, and the national collection of photography

Scottish National Gallery of Modern Art, Belford Road. Tel: 0131-624 6200. Closed Sun. mornings. Adm. free. Twentieth-century painting, sculpture and graphic art

The Writer's Museum, Lawnmarket. Tel: 0131-529 4901. Closed Sun. Adm. free. Robert Louis Stevenson, Walter Scott and Robert Burns exhibits

FORT WILLIAM – *West Highland Museum,* Cameron Square. Tel: 01397-702169. Closed Sun. Adm. £2.00. Includes tartan collections and exhibits relating to 1745 uprising

GLASGOW – *Burrell Collection,* Pollokshaws Road. Tel: 0141-649 7151. Adm. free. Paintings, textiles, furniture, ceramics, stained glass and silver from classical times to the 19th century

Gallery of Modern Art, Queen Street. Tel: 0141-229 1996. Adm. free. Collection of contemporary Scottish and world art

Glasgow Art Gallery and Museum, Kelvingrove. Tel: 0141-287 2699. Adm. free. Includes Old Masters, 19th-century French paintings and armour collection

Hunterian Art Gallery, Hillhead Street. Tel: 0141-330 5431. Closed Sun. Adm. free. Rennie Mackintosh and Whistler collections; Old Masters, Scottish paintings and modern paintings, sculpture and prints

McLellan Galleries, Sauchiehall Street. Tel: 0141-331 1854. Adm. charge. Temporary exhibitions

Museum of Transport, Bunhouse Road. Tel: 0141-287 2720. Adm. free. Includes a reproduction of a 1938 Glasgow street, cars since the 1930s, trams and a Glasgow subway station

People's Palace Museum, Glasgow Green. Tel: 0141-554 0223. Adm. free. History of Glasgow since 1175

St Mungo Museum of Religious Life and Art, Castle Street. Tel: 0141-553 2557. Adm. free. Explores universal themes through objects of all the main world religions

NORTHERN IRELAND

BELFAST – *Ulster Museum,* Botanic Gardens. Tel: 01232-383000. Closed weekend mornings. Adm. free. Irish antiquities, natural and local history, fine and applied arts

HOLYWOOD, Co. Down – *Ulster Folk and Transport Museum,* Cultra. Tel: 01232-428428. Closed Sun. mornings. Adm. £4.00. Open-air museum with original buildings from Ulster town and rural life c. 1900; indoor galleries including Irish rail and road transport and Titanic exhibitions

LONDONDERRY – *The Tower Museum,* Union Hall Place. Tel: 01504-372411. Closed Sun. and Mon. Adm. £3.25. Tells the story of Ireland through the history of Londonderry

OMAGH, Co. Tyrone – *Ulster American Folk Park,* Castletown. Tel: 01662-243292. Closed in winter. Adm. £3.50. Open-air museum telling the story of Ulster's emigrants to America; restored or recreated dwellings and workshops; ship and dockside gallery

Countries of the World

The total population of the world in mid-1990 was estimated at 5,292 million, compared with 3,019 million in 1960 and 2,070 million in 1930.

Continent, etc.	Area sq. miles '000	sq. km '000	Estimated population mid-1990
Africa	11,704	30,313	642,000,000
North America[1]	8,311	21,525	276,000,000
Latin America[2]	7,933	20,547	448,000,000
Asia[3]	10,637	27,549	3,113,000,000
Europe[4]	1,915	4,961	498,000,000
Former USSR	8,649	22,402	289,000,000
Oceania[5]	3,286	8,510	26,500,000
TOTAL	52,435	135,807	5,292,000,000

[1] Includes Greenland and Hawaii
[2] Mexico and the remainder of the Americas south of the USA
[3] Includes European Turkey, excludes former USSR
[4] Excludes European Turkey and former USSR
[5] Includes Australia, New Zealand and the islands inhabited by Micronesian, Melanesian and Polynesian peoples
Source: UN Demographic Yearbook 1990 (pub. 1992)

A United Nations report *The Sex and Age Distribution of the World Populations* (revised 1994) puts the world's population in the late 20th and the 21st centuries at the following levels (medium variant data):

1995	5,716.4m	2030	8,670.6m
2000	6,158.0m	2040	9,318.2m
2010	7,032.3m	2050	9,833.2m
2020	7,887.8m		

The population forecast for the years 2000 and 2050 is:

Continent, etc.	Estimated population (million) 2000	2050
Africa	831.596	2,140.844
North America[1]	306.280	388.997
Latin America[2]	523.875	838.527
Asia	3,753.846	5,741.005
Europe	729.803	677.764
Oceania	30.651	46.070
TOTAL	6,158.051	9,833.207

[1] Includes Bermuda, Greenland, and St Pierre and Miquelon
[2] Mexico and the remainder of the Americas south of the USA

AREA AND POPULATION BY CONTINENT

No complete survey of many countries has yet been achieved and consequently accurate area figures are not always available. Similarly, many countries have not recently, or have never, taken a census. The areas of countries given below are derived from estimated figures published by the United Nations. The conversion factors used are:
(i) to convert square miles to square km, multiply by 2.589988
(ii) to convert square km to square miles, multiply by 0.3861022
Population figures for countries are derived from the most recent estimates available. Accurate and up-to-date data for the populations of capital cities are scarce, and definitions of cities' extent differ. The figures given below are the latest estimates available.

Ψ   seaport

AFRICA

COUNTRY/TERRITORY	AREA sq. miles	sq. km	POPULATION	CAPITAL	POPULATION OF CAPITAL
Algeria	919,595	2,381,741	28,548,000	Ψ Algiers	1,740,461
Angola	481,354	1,246,700	11,072,000	Ψ Luanda	475,328
Benin	43,484	112,622	5,561,000	Ψ Porto Novo	179,138
Botswana	224,607	581,730	1,456,000	Gaborone	133,468
Burkina Faso	105,792	274,000	10,200,000	Ouagadougou	634,479
Burundi	10,747	27,834	5,982,000	Bujumbura	235,440
Cameroon	183,569	475,442	13,277,000	Yaoundé	653,670
Cape Verde	1,557	4,033	392,000	Ψ Praia	80,000
Central African Republic	240,535	622,984	3,315,000	Bangui	473,817
Chad	495,755	1,284,000	6,361,000	N'Djaména	179,000
The Comoros	863	2,235	653,000	Moroni	17,267
Congo, Dem. Rep. of	905,355	2,344,858	43,901,000	Kinshasa	2,664,309
Congo, Rep. of	132,047	342,000	2,590,000	Brazzaville	596,200
Côte d'Ivoire	124,504	322,463	14,230,000	Yamoussoukro	126,191
Djibouti	8,958	23,200	577,000	Ψ Djibouti	340,700
Egypt	386,662	1,001,449	59,226,000	Cairo	13,000,000
Equatorial Guinea	10,831	28,051	400,000	Ψ Malabo	30,418
Eritrea	45,406	117,600	3,531,000	Asmara	358,100
Ethiopia	426,373	1,104,300	56,677,000	Addis Ababa	2,316,400
Gabon	103,347	267,668	1,320,000	Ψ Libreville	251,000

Country/Territory	Area sq. miles	sq. km	Population	Capital	Population of Capital
Gambia	4,361	11,295	1,118,000	Ψ Banjul	109,986
Ghana	92,098	238,533	17,453,000	Ψ Accra	738,498
Guinea	94,926	245,857	6,700,000	Ψ Conakry	763,000
Guinea-Bissau	13,948	36,125	1,073,000	Ψ Bissau	109,214
Kenya	224,081	580,367	30,522,000	Nairobi	1,400,000
Lesotho	11,720	30,355	2,050,000	Maseru	288,951
Liberia	43,000	111,369	2,760,000	Ψ Monrovia	421,053
Libya	679,362	1,759,540	5,407,000	Ψ Tripoli	1,000,000
Madagascar	226,658	587,041	14,763,000	Antananarivo	377,600
Malawi	45,747	118,484	9,788,000	Lilongwe	233,973
Mali	478,841	1,240,192	10,795,000	Bamako	658,275
Mauritania	395,956	1,025,520	2,284,000	Nouakchott	850,000
Mauritius	788	2,040	1,122,000	Ψ Port Louis	144,776
Mayotte (Fr.)	144	372	94,410	Mamoudzou	12,000
Morocco	172,414	446,550	27,111,000	Ψ Rabat	1,300,000
Western Sahara	102,703	266,000	283,000	Laayoune	96,784
Mozambique	309,496	801,590	17,423,000	Ψ Maputo	882,601
Namibia	318,261	824,292	1,540,000	Windhoek	169,000
Niger	489,191	1,267,000	9,151,000	Niamey	392,169
Nigeria	356,669	923,768	111,721,000	Abuja	378,671
Réunion (Fr.)	969	2,510	653,000	St Denis	121,999
Rwanda	10,169	26,338	7,952,000	Kigali	156,000
St Helena (UK)	47	122	7,000	Ψ Jamestown	1,332
Ascension Island (UK)	34	88	1,051	Ψ Georgetown	—
Tristan da Cunha (UK)	38	98	288	Ψ Edinburgh of the Seven Seas	—
São Tomé and Príncipe	372	964	127,000	Ψ São Tomé	43,420
Senegal	75,955	196,722	8,312,000	Ψ Dakar	1,641,358
Seychelles	176	455	75,000	Ψ Victoria	24,324
Sierra Leone	27,699	71,740	4,509,000	Ψ Freetown	469,776
Somalia	246,201	637,657	9,250,000	Ψ Mogadishu	1,000,000
South Africa	471,445	1,221,031	41,244,000	{ Pretoria	525,583
				{ Ψ Cape Town	1,911,521
Sudan	967,500	2,505,813	28,098,000	Khartoum	924,505
Swaziland	6,704	17,364	908,000	Mbabane	38,290
Tanzania	362,162	938,000	30,337,000	Dodoma	88,474
Togo	21,925	56,785	4,138,000	Ψ Lomé	366,476
Tunisia	62,592	162,155	8,896,000	Ψ Tunis	1,830,634
Uganda	93,065	241,038	21,297,000	Kampala	750,000
Zambia	290,587	752,618	9,373,000	Lusaka	982,362
Zimbabwe	150,872	390,757	11,526,000	Harare	1,189,103

AMERICA

North America

Country/Territory	Area sq. miles	sq. km	Population	Capital	Population of Capital
Canada	3,849,674	9,970,610	29,606,000	Ottawa	1,010,288
Greenland (Den.)	840,004	2,175,600	58,000	Ψ Godthåb	12,483
Mexico	756,066	1,958,201	90,487,000	Mexico City	15,047,685
St Pierre and Miquelon (Fr.)	93	242	6,000	Ψ St Pierre	5,416
United States	3,540,321	9,169,389	263,034,000	Washington DC	7,051,495

Central America and the West Indies

Country/Territory	Area sq. miles	sq. km	Population	Capital	Population of Capital
Anguilla (UK)	37	96	8,000	The Valley	1,400
Antigua and Barbuda	171	442	66,000	Ψ St John's	22,342
Aruba (Neth.)	75	193	70,000	Ψ Oranjestad	25,000
Bahamas	5,358	13,878	278,000	Ψ Nassau	172,196
Barbados	166	430	264,000	Ψ Bridgetown	108,000
Belize	8,763	22,696	217,000	Belmopan	44,087
Bermuda (UK)	20	53	63,000	Ψ Hamilton	2,277
Cayman Islands (UK)	102	264	35,000	Ψ George Town	20,000
Costa Rica	19,730	51,100	3,333,000	San José	1,186,417
Cuba	42,804	110,861	11,041,000	Ψ Havana	2,175,888
Dominica	290	751	71,000	Ψ Roseau	16,243
Dominican Republic	18,816	48,734	7,915,000	Ψ Santo Domingo	2,134,779

Country/Territory	Area sq. miles	sq. km	Population	Capital	Population of Capital
Grenada	133	344	92,000	Ψ St George's	4,788
Guadeloupe (*Fr.*)	658	1,705	428,000	Ψ Basse Terre	29,522
Guatemala	42,042	108,889	10,621,000	Guatemala City	1,675,589
Haiti	10,714	27,750	7,180,000	Ψ Port-au-Prince	690,168
Honduras	43,277	112,088	5,953,000	Tegucigalpa	670,100
Jamaica	4,243	10,990	2,530,000	Ψ Kingston	103,962
Martinique (*Fr.*)	425	1,102	379,000	Ψ Fort de France	97,814
Montserrat (*UK*)	39	102	3,500	Ψ Plymouth	—
Netherlands Antilles (*Neth.*)	309	800	199,000	Ψ Willemstad	50,000
Nicaragua	50,193	130,000	4,539,000	Managua	608,020
Panama	29,157	75,517	2,631,000	Ψ Panama City	658,000
Puerto Rico (*USA*)	3,427	8,875	3,674,000	Ψ San Juan	1,222,316
Saint Christopher and Nevis	101	261	41,000	Ψ Basseterre	14,161
St Lucia	240	622	145,000	Ψ Castries	56,000
St Vincent and the Grenadines	150	388	111,000	Ψ Kingstown	33,694
El Salvador	8,124	21,041	5,768,000	San Salvador	422,570
Trinidad and Tobago	1,981	5,130	1,306,000	Ψ Port of Spain	46,222
Turks and Caicos Is. (*UK*)	166	430	19,000	Ψ Grand Turk	3,691
Virgin Islands:					
British (*UK*)	58	151	19,107	Ψ Road Town	3,983
US (*USA*)	134	347	105,000	Ψ Charlotte Amalie	11,842
South America					
Argentina	1,073,518	2,780,400	34,587,000	Ψ Buenos Aires	10,686,163
Bolivia	424,165	1,098,581	7,414,000	La Paz	784,976
Brazil	3,300,171	8,547,403	155,822,000	Brasilia	1,601,094
Chile	292,135	756,626	14,210,000	Santiago	5,257,937
Colombia	439,737	1,138,914	35,099,000	Bogotá	8,000,000
Ecuador	109,484	283,561	11,460,000	Quito	1,387,887
Falkland Islands (*UK*)	4,700	12,173	2,000	Ψ Stanley	1,636
French Guiana (*Fr.*)	34,749	90,000	147,000	Ψ Cayenne	41,164
Guyana	83,000	214,969	835,000	Ψ Georgetown	250,000
Paraguay	157,048	406,752	5,085,325	Asunción	718,690
Peru	496,225	1,285,216	23,532,000	Lima	6,483,901
South Georgia (*UK*)	1,580	4,092	—	—	—
Suriname	63,037	163,265	423,000	Ψ Paramaribo	200,970
Uruguay	68,500	177,414	3,186,000	Ψ Montevideo	1,383,660
Venezuela	352,145	912,050	21,644,000	Caracas	2,784,042

ASIA

Country/Territory	Area sq. miles	sq. km	Population	Capital	Population of Capital
Afghanistan	251,773	652,090	20,141,000	Kabul	1,424,400
Bahrain	268	694	586,000	Ψ Manama	140,401
Bangladesh	55,598	143,998	120,433,000	Dhaka	3,397,187
Bhutan	18,147	47,000	1,638,000	Thimphu	15,000
Brunei	2,226	5,765	285,000	Bandar Seri Begawan	49,902
Cambodia	69,898	181,035	9,836,000	Ψ Phnom Penh	832,000
China[1]	3,705,408	9,596,961	1,221,462,000	Beijing (Peking)	7,362,426
Hong Kong (*China*)	415	1,075	6,311,000	—	—
India	1,269,346	3,287,590	935,744,000	New Delhi	301,297
Indonesia	735,358	1,904,569	193,750,000	Ψ Jakarta	9,160,500
Iran	630,577	1,633,188	67,283,000	Tehran	6,750,043
Iraq	169,235	438,317	20,449,000	Baghdad	3,841,268
Israel[2]	8,130	21,056	5,695,000	Tel Aviv	1,880,200
West Bank and Gaza Strip	2,406	6,231	1,635,000	Gaza City	120,000
Japan	145,870	377,801	125,197,000	Tokyo	11,927,457
Jordan	37,738	97,740	5,439,000	Amman	1,270,000
Kazakhstan	1,049,156	2,717,300	15,671,000	Astana	292,000
Korea, (D.P.R.) (North)	46,540	120,538	23,917,000	Pyongyang	2,000,000
Korea, Rep. of (South)	38,330	99,274	46,430,000	Seoul	10,412,000
Kuwait	6,880	17,818	1,691,000	Ψ Kuwait City	400,000
Kyrgyzstan	76,641	198,500	4,500,000	Bishkek	627,800
Laos	91,429	236,800	4,882,000	Vientiane	132,253
Lebanon	4,015	10,400	3,009,000	Ψ Beirut	1,500,000
Macao (*Port.*)	7	18	418,000	Ψ Macao	—
Malaysia	127,320	329,758	20,140,000	Kuala Lumpur	1,145,075

Country/Territory	Area sq. miles	sq. km	Population	Capital	Population of Capital
Maldives	115	298	254,000	Ψ Malé	62,973
Mongolia	604,829	1,566,500	2,410,000	Ulan Bator	515,100
Myanmar (Burma)	261,228	676,578	46,527,000	Ψ Yangon (Rangoon)	2,513,023
Nepal	56,827	147,181	21,918,000	Kathmandu	419,073
Oman	119,498	309,500	2,020,000	Ψ Muscat	400,000
Pakistan	307,374	796,095	129,808,000	Islamabad	350,000
Philippines	115,831	300,000	70,267,000	Ψ Manila	8,594,150
Qatar	4,247	11,000	551,000	Ψ Doha	217,294
Saudi Arabia	830,000	2,149,690	17,880,000	Riyadh	1,800,000
Singapore	239	618	2,987,000	—	—
Sri Lanka	25,332	65,610	18,354,000	Ψ Colombo	615,000
Syria	71,498	185,180	14,315,000	Damascus	1,549,000
Taiwan	13,800	35,742	21,450,183	Taipei	2,607,010
Tajikistan	55,251	143,100	5,513,400	Dushanbe	602,000
Thailand	198,115	513,115	60,206,000	Ψ Bangkok	5,876,000
Turkey[3]	299,158	774,815	61,644,000	Ankara	3,103,000
Turkmenistan	188,456	488,100	3,808,900	Ashkhabad	407,000
United Arab Emirates	32,278	83,600	2,377,453	Abu Dhabi	450,000
Uzbekistan	172,742	447,400	21,206,800	Tashkent	2,094,000
Vietnam	128,066	331,689	74,545,000	Hanoi	3,056,146
Yemen	203,850	527,968	14,501,000	Sana'a	926,595

[1] Including Tibet
[2] Including East Jerusalem, the Golan Heights and Israeli citizens on the West Bank
[3] Including Turkey in Europe

EUROPE

Country/Territory	Area sq. miles	sq. km	Population	Capital	Population of Capital
Albania	11,099	28,748	3,645,000	Tirana	244,153
Andorra	175	453	68,000	Andorra la Vella	16,151
Armenia	11,506	29,800	3,762,000	Yerevan	1,254,400
Austria	32,378	83,859	8,053,000	Vienna	1,806,737
Azerbaijan	33,436	86,600	7,499,000	Ψ Baku	1,149,000
Belarus	80,155	207,600	10,141,000	Minsk	1,687,400
Belgium	11,783	30,519	10,113,000	Brussels	960,324
Bosnia-Hercegovina	19,735	51,129	4,484,000	Sarajevo	415,631
Bulgaria	42,823	110,912	8,402,000	Sofia	1,188,563
Croatia	34,022	88,117	4,495,000	Zagreb	867,717
Cyprus	3,572	9,251	742,000	Nicosia	188,800
Czech Republic	30,450	78,864	10,331,000	Prague	1,216,568
Denmark	16,639	43,094	5,228,000	Ψ Copenhagen	1,353,333
Faroe Islands	540	1,399	47,000	Ψ Tórshavn	16,218
Estonia	17,413	45,100	1,530,000	Tallinn	447,672
Finland	130,559	338,145	5,108,000	Ψ Helsinki	1,016,291
France	212,935	551,500	58,143,000	Paris	9,319,367
Georgia	26,911	69,700	5,401,000	Tbilisi	1,268,000
Germany	137,735	356,733	81,642,000	Berlin	3,472,009
Gibraltar (UK)	2.3	6	28,000	Ψ Gibraltar	
Greece	50,949	131,957	10,458,000	Athens	3,027,922
Hungary	35,920	93,032	10,225,000	Budapest	2,002,121
Iceland	39,769	103,000	272,064	Ψ Reykjavik	106,617
Ireland, Republic of	27,137	70,284	3,626,087	Ψ Dublin	952,700
Italy	116,320	301,268	57,187,000	Rome	2,693,383
Latvia	24,942	64,600	2,479,870	Riga	847,976
Liechtenstein	62	160	31,000	Vaduz	5,072
Lithuania	25,174	65,200	3,715,000	Vilnius	581,500
Luxembourg	998	2,586	418,300	Luxembourg	76,446
Macedonia, Former Yugoslav Republic of	9,928	25,713	2,163,000	Skopje	448,229
Malta	122	316	371,000	Ψ Valletta	9,144
Moldova	13,012	33,700	4,335,000	Kishinev	667,100
Monaco	0.4	1	32,000	Monaco-Ville	27,063
Netherlands	15,770	40,844	15,451,000	Ψ Amsterdam	1,100,764
Norway[1]	125,050	323,877	4,360,000	Ψ Oslo	758,949
Poland	124,808	323,250	38,588,000	Warsaw	1,643,203
Portugal[2]	35,514	91,982	9,920,760	Ψ Lisbon	2,561,225

Country/Territory	Area sq. miles	sq. km	Population	Capital	Population of Capital
Romania	92,043	238,391	22,680,000	Bucharest	2,060,551
Russia[3]	6,592,850	17,075,400	147,500,000	Moscow	8,600,000
San Marino	24	61	25,000	San Marino	4,251
Slovakia	18,924	49,012	5,364,000	Bratislava	451,272
Slovenia	7,821	20,256	1,984,000	Ljubljana	330,000
Spain[4]	195,365	505,992	39,210,000	Madrid	3,084,673
Sweden	173,732	449,964	8,831,000	Ψ Stockholm	1,532,803
Switzerland	15,940	41,284	7,040,000	Berne	321,932
Ukraine	233,090	603,700	50,500,000	Kiev	2,646,100
United Kingdom[5]	94,248	244,101	58,258,000	Ψ London	6,962,319
England	50,351	130,410	48,903,000	—	—
Wales	8,015	20,758	2,917,000	Ψ Cardiff	303,000
Scotland	30,420	78,789	5,137,000	Ψ Edinburgh	448,000
Northern Ireland	5,467	14,160	1,649,000	Ψ Belfast	297,000
Vatican City State	0.2	0.44	1,000	Vatican City	766
Yugoslavia, Fed. Rep. of	39,449	102,173	10,544,000	Belgrade	1,136,786

[1] Excludes Svalbard and Jan Mayen Islands (approx. 24,101 sq. miles (62,422 sq. km) and 3,000 population)
[2] Includes Madeira (314 sq. miles) and the Azores (922 sq. miles)
[3] Includes Russia in Asia
[4] Includes Balearic Islands, Canary Islands, Ceuta and Melilla
[5] Excludes Isle of Man (221 sq. miles (572 sq. km), 69,788 population), and Channel Islands (75 sq. miles (194 sq. km), 142,949 population)

OCEANIA

Country/Territory	Area sq. miles	sq. km	Population	Capital	Population of Capital
American Samoa (USA)	77	199	56,000	Ψ Pago Pago	3,519
Australia	2,988,902	7,741,220	18,054,000	Canberra	307,100
Norfolk Island (Aust.)	14	36	1,772	Ψ Kingston	—
Fiji	7,056	18,274	796,000	Ψ Suva	141,273
French Polynesia (Fr.)	1,544	4,000	220,000	Ψ Papeete	36,784
Guam (USA)	212	549	149,000	Hagatna	1,139
Kiribati	280	726	79,000	Tarawa	17,921
Marshall Islands	70	181	56,000	Dalap-Uliga-Darrit	20,000
Micronesia, Fed. States of	271	702	105,000	Palikir	—
Nauru	8	21	11,000	Ψ Nauru	—
New Caledonia (Fr.)	7,172	18,575	186,000	Ψ Noumea	97,581
New Zealand	104,454	270,534	3,681,546	Ψ Wellington	326,900
Cook Islands	91	236	19,000	Rarotonga	—
Niue	100	260	2,000	Alofi	—
Ross Dependency[1]	175,000	453,248	—	—	—
Tokelau	5	12	2,000	—	—
Northern Mariana Islands (USA)	179	464	47,000	Saipan	52,706
Palau (USA)	177	459	17,000	Koror	10,493
Papua New Guinea	178,704	462,840	4,074,000	Ψ Port Moresby	173,500
Pitcairn Islands (UK)	2	5	42	—	—
Samoa	1,093	2,831	171,000	Ψ Apia	36,000
Solomon Islands	11,157	28,896	378,000	Ψ Honiara	40,000
Tonga	288	747	98,000	Ψ Nuku'alofa	29,018
Tuvalu	10	26	10,000	Ψ Funafuti	2,856
Vanuatu	4,706	12,189	165,000	Ψ Port Vila	26,100
Wallis and Futuna Islands (Fr.)	77	200	14,000	Ψ Mata-Utu	—

[1] Includes permanent shelf ice

Currencies of the World
AND EXCHANGE RATES AGAINST £ STERLING

Franc CFA = Franc de la Communauté financière africaine
Franc CFP = Franc des Comptoirs français du Pacifique
*Rouble rebased 1 January 1998: 1 new rouble=1,000 old roubles

COUNTRY/TERRITORY	MONETARY UNIT	AVERAGE RATE TO £ 5 September 1997	AVERAGE RATE TO £ 4 September 1998
Afghanistan	Afghani (Af) of 100 puls	Af 7531.12	Af 7947.70
Albania	Lek (Lk) of 100 qindarka	Lk 242.978	Lk 251.231
Algeria	Algerian dinar (DA) of 100 centimes	DA 95.1300	DA 98.4813
American Samoa	Currency is that of the USA	US$ 1.5855	US$ 1.6732
Andorra	French and Spanish currencies in use	—	—
Angola	Readjusted kwanza (Kzrl) of 100 lwei	Kzrl 407676.4	Kzrl 430226.7
Anguilla	East Caribbean dollar (EC$) of 100 cents	EC$ 4.2809	EC$ 4.5177
Antigua and Barbuda	East Caribbean dollar (EC$) of 100 cents	EC$ 4.2809	EC$ 4.5177
Argentina	Peso of 10,000 australes	Pesos 1.5847	Pesos 1.6720
Armenia	Dram of 100 louma	Dram 794.494*	Dram 840.583*
Aruba	Aruban florin	Florins 2.8381	Florins 2.9950
Ascension Island	Currency is that of St Helena	*at parity with £ sterling*	
Australia	Australian dollar ($A) of 100 cents	$A 2.1703	$A 2.8507
Norfolk Island	Currency is that of Australia	$A 2.1703	$A 2.8507
Austria	Schilling of 100 Groschen	Schilling 20.1585	Schilling 20.4216
Azerbaijan	Manat of 100 gopik	Manat 6262.72*	Manat 6609.14*
The Bahamas	Bahamian dollar (B$) of 100 cents	B$ 1.5855	B$ 1.6732
Bahrain	Bahraini dinar (BD) of 1,000 fils	BD 0.5977	BD 0.6308
Bangladesh	Taka (Tk) of 100 poisha	Tk 70.6341	Tk 78.8078
Barbados	Barbados dollar (BD$) of 100 cents	BD$ 3.1889	BD$ 3.3653
Belarus	Rouble of 100 kopeks	Roubles 68710.7*	Roubles 402404.7*
Belgium	Belgian franc (or frank) of 100 centimes (centiemen)	Francs 59.1551	Francs 59.8839
Belize	Belize dollar (BZ$) of 100 cents	BZ$ 3.1710	BZ$ 3.3464
Benin	Franc CFA	Francs 964.080	Francs 973.140
Bermuda	Bermuda dollar of 100 cents	$ 1.5855	$ 1.6732
Bhutan	Ngultrum of 100 chetrum (Indian currency is also legal tender)	Ngultrum 58.0294	Ngultrum 71.2156
Bolivia	Boliviano ($b) of 100 centavos	$b 8.3715	$b 9.3365
Bosnia-Hercegovina	Convertible marka		
Botswana	Pula (P) of 100 thebe	P 5.8511	P 7.8389
Brazil	Real of 100 centavos	Real 1.7330	Real 1.9711
Brunei	Brunei dollar (B$) of 100 sen (fully interchangeable with Singapore currency)	$ 2.4021	$ 2.9256
Bulgaria	Lev of 100 stotinki	Leva 2857.07	Leva 2894.22
Burkina Faso	Franc CFA	Francs 964.080	Francs 973.140
Burundi	Burundi franc of 100 centimes	Francs 562.187	Francs 747.541
Cambodia	Riel of 100 sen	Riel 4785.04	Riel 6241.04
Cameroon	Franc CFA	Francs 964.080	Francs 973.140
Canada	Canadian dollar (C$) of 100 cents	C$ 2.1930	C$ 2.5605
Cape Verde	Escudo Caboverdiano of 100 centavos	Esc 154.142	Esc 166.795
Cayman Islands	Cayman Islands dollar (CI$) of 100 cents	CI$ 1.3131	CI$ 1.3858
Central African Republic	Franc CFA	Francs 964.080	Francs 973.140
Chad	Franc CFA	Francs 964.080	Francs 973.140
Chile	Chilean peso of 100 centavos	Pesos 657.824	Pesos 793.515
China	Renminbi Yuan of 10 jiao or 100 fen	Yuan 13.1413	Yuan 13.8534
Hong Kong	Hong Kong dollar (HK$) of 100 cents	HK$ 12.2837	HK$ 12.9481
Colombia	Colombian peso of 100 centavos	Pesos 1880.09	Pesos 2585.26
Comoros	Comorian franc (KMF) of 100 centimes	Francs 726.996	Francs 729.663
Congo, Dem. Rep. of	Congolese franc	Zaïre 218006.2	CFr 230065.1
Congo, Rep. of	Franc CFA	Francs 964.080	Francs 973.140
Costa Rica	Costa Rican colón (₡) of 100 céntimos	₡ 375.779	₡ 437.793
Côte d'Ivoire	Franc CFA	Francs 964.080	Francs 973.140
Croatia	Kuna of 100 lipas	Kuna 10.1121	Kuna 10.5468
Cuba	Cuban peso of 100 centavos	Pesos 33.2955	Pesos 38.4836
Cyprus	Cyprus pound (C£) of 100 cents	C£ 0.8458	C£ 0.8558
Czech Republic	Koruna (Kčs) of 100 haléřu	Kčs 54.3629	Kčs 51.6208

COUNTRY/TERRITORY	MONETARY UNIT	AVERAGE RATE TO £ 5 September 1997	AVERAGE RATE TO £ 4 September 1998
Denmark	Danish krone of 100 øre	Kroner 10.9075	Kroner 11.0523
Faroe Islands	Currency is that of Denmark	Kroner 10.9075	Kroner 11.0523
Djibouti	Djibouti franc of 100 centimes	Francs 281.775	Francs 297.361
Dominica	East Caribbean dollar (EC$) of 100 cents	EC$ 4.2809	EC$ 4.5177
Dominican Republic	Dominican Republic peso (RD$) of 100 centavos	RD$ 22.3476	RD$ 25.7673
Ecuador	Sucre of 100 centavos	Sucres 6536.22*	Sucres 9283.75*
Egypt	Egyptian pound (£E) of 100 piastres or 1,000 millièmes	£E 5.3879	£E 5.7203
Equatorial Guinea	Franc CFA	Francs 964.080	Francs 973.140
Eritrea	Nakfa	—	Nakfa 7.45
Estonia	Kroon of 100 sents	Kroons 22.9141	Kroons 23.4228
Ethiopia	Ethiopian birr (EB) of 100 cents	EB 10.6609	EB 11.6923
Falkland Islands	Falkland pound of 100 pence	*at parity with £ sterling*	
Fiji	Fiji dollar (F$) of 100 cents	F$ 2.3163	F$ 3.4536
Finland	Markka (Mk) of 100 penniä	Mk 8.5887	Mk 8.8297
France	Franc of 100 centimes	Francs 9.6408	Francs 9.7314
French Guiana	Currency is that of France	Francs 9.6408	Francs 9.7314
French Polynesia	Franc CFP	Francs 176.241	Francs 176.887
Gabon	Franc CFA	Francs 964.080	Francs 973.140
The Gambia	Dalasi (D) of 100 butut	D 15.9057	D 17.0918
Georgia	Lari of 100 tetri	—	—
Germany	Deutsche Mark (DM) of 100 Pfennig	DM 2.8647	DM 2.9023
Ghana	Cedi of 100 pesewas	Cedi 3472.25	Cedi 3890.20
Gibraltar	Gibraltar pound of 100 pence	*at parity with £ sterling*	
Greece	Drachma of 100 leptae	Drachmae 451.519	Drachmae 501.358
Greenland	Currency is that of Denmark	Kroner 10.9075	Kroner 11.0523
Grenada	East Caribbean dollar (EC$) of 100 cents	EC$ 4.2809	EC$ 4.5177
Guadeloupe	Currency is that of France	Francs 9.6408	Francs 9.7314
Guam	Currency is that of USA	US$ 1.5855	US$ 1.6732
Guatemala	Quetzal (Q) of 100 centavos	Q 9.6459	Q 10.9173
Guinea	Guinea franc of 100 centimes	Francs 1759.90	Francs 2079.79
Guinea-Bissau	Franc CFA	Francs 964.080	Francs 973.140
Guyana	Guyana dollar (G$) of 100 cents	G$ 225.934	G$ 271.561
Haiti	Gourde of 100 centimes	Gourdes 26.1766	Gourdes 27.5488
Honduras	Lempira of 100 centavos	Lempiras 20.6115	Lempiras 22.7555
Hungary	Forint of 100 fillér	Forints 311.939	Forints 372.505
Iceland	Icelandic króna (Kr) of 100 aurar	Kr 114.568	Kr 118.496
India	Indian rupee (Rs) of 100 paisa	Rs 58.0294	Rs 71.2156
Indonesia	Rupiah (Rp) of 100 sen	Rp 4653.45	Rp 18321.6
Iran	Rial	Rials 4756.50	Rials 5019.60
Iraq	Iraqi dinar (ID) of 1,000 fils	ID 0.4929*	ID 0.5202*
Ireland, Rep. of	Punt (IR£) of 100 pence	IR£ 1.0672	IR£ 1.1582
Israel	Shekel of 100 agora	Shekels 5.5770	Shekels 6.4222
Italy	Lira of 100 centesimi	Lire 2792.53	Lire 2866.48
Jamaica	Jamaican dollar (J$) of 100 cents	J$ 54.6205	J$ 59.9006
Japan	Yen of 100 sen	Yen 192.171	Yen 224.769
Jordan	Jordanian dinar (JD) of 1,000 fils	JD 1.1249	JD 1.1913
Kazakhstan	Tenge	Tenge 120.260	Tenge 132.518
Kenya	Kenya shilling (Ksh) of 100 cents	Ksh 100.481	Ksh 99.8064
Kiribati	Australian dollar ($A) of 100 cents	$A 2.1703	$A 2.8507
Korea, North	Won of 100 chon	Won 3.4881	Won 3.6811
Korea, South	Won of 100 jeon	Won 1437.26	Won 2247.11
Kuwait	Kuwaiti dinar (KD) of 1,000 fils	KD 0.4838	KD 0.5094
Kyrgyzstan	Som	—	—
Laos	Kip (K) of 100 at	K 1523.67	K 4353.67
Latvia	Lats of 100 santimes	Lats 0.9287	Lats 0.9952
Lebanon	Lebanese pound (L£) of 100 piastres	L£ 2439.29	L£ 2539.08
Lesotho	Loti (M) of 100 lisente	M 7.4384	M 10.4153
Liberia	Liberian dollar (L$) of 100 cents	L$ 1.5855	L$ 1.6732
Libya	Libyan dinar (LD) of 1,000 dirhams	LD 0.6081	LD 0.6454
Liechtenstein	Swiss franc of 100 rappen (or centimes)	Francs 2.3467	Francs 2.3816
Lithuania	Litas	Litas 6.3429	Litas 6.6946
Luxembourg	Luxembourg franc (LF) of 100 centimes (Belgian currency is also legal tender)	LF 59.1551	LF 59.8839
Macao	Pataca of 100 avos	Pataca 12.6877	Pataca 13.3943

Country/Territory	Monetary Unit	Average Rate to £ 5 September 1997	Average Rate to £ 4 September 1998
Macedonia (Former Yugoslav Republic of)	Dinar of 100 paras	Dinars 89.2816	Dinars 90.8466
Madagascar	Franc malgache (FMG) of 100 centimes	FMG 7848.22	FMG 9035.28
Malawi	Kwacha (K) of 100 tambala	K 27.3118	K 69.6029
Malaysia	Malaysian dollar (ringgit) (M$) of 100 sen	M$ 4.6713	M$ 6.3582
Maldives	Rufiyaa of 100 laaris	Rufiyaa 18.6613	Rufiyaa 19.6936
Mali	Franc CFA	Francs 964.080	Francs 973.140
Malta	Maltese lira (LM) of 100 cents or 1,000 mils	LM 0.6337	LM 0.6432
Marshall Islands	Currency is that of USA	US$ 1.5855	US$ 1.6732
Martinique	Currency is that of France	Francs 9.6408	Francs 9.7314
Mauritania	Ouguiya (UM) of 5 khoums	UM 246.142	UM 338.932
Mauritius	Mauritius rupee of 100 cents	Rs 34.6749	Rs 40.7843
Mayotte	Currency is that of France	Francs 9.6408	Francs 9.7314
Mexico	Peso of 100 centavos	Pesos 12.3733	Pesos 16.9704
Federated States of Micronesia	Currency is that of USA	US$ 1.5855	US$ 1.6732
Moldova	Leu	Leu 7.2457	Leu 8.0565
Monaco	French franc of 100 centimes	Francs 9.6408	Francs 9.7314
Mongolia	Tugrik of 100 möngö	Tugriks 1244.24	Tugriks 1368.03
Montserrat	East Caribbean dollar (EC$) of 100 cents	EC$ 4.2809	EC$ 4.5177
Morocco	Dirham (DH) of 100 centimes	DH 15.5997	DH 15.8718
Mozambique	Metical (MT) of 100 centavos	MT 18226.1	MT 19233.4
Myanmar	Kyat (K) of 100 pyas	K 9.8541	K 10.4604
Namibia	Namibian dollar of 100 cents	at parity with SA Rand	
Nauru	Australian dollar ($A) of 100 cents	$A 2.1703	$A 2.8507
Nepal	Nepalese rupee of 100 paisa	Rs 90.2942	Rs 114.330
The Netherlands	Gulden (guilder) or florin of 100 cents	Guilders 3.2267	Guilders 3.2753
Netherlands Antilles	Netherlands Antilles guilder of 100 cents	Guilders 2.8381	Guilders 2.9950
New Caledonia	Franc CFP	Francs 176.241	Francs 176.887
New Zealand	New Zealand dollar (NZ$) of 100 cents	NZ$ 2.4912	NZ$ 3.3058
Cook Islands	Currency is that of New Zealand	NZ$ 2.4912	NZ$ 3.3058
Niue	Currency is that of New Zealand	NZ$ 2.4912	NZ$ 3.3058
Tokelau	Currency is that of New Zealand	NZ$ 2.4912	NZ$ 3.3058
Nicaragua	Córdoba (C$) of 100 centavos	C$ 15.2761	C$ 17.9869
Niger	Franc CFA	Francs 964.080	Francs 973.140
Nigeria	Naira (N) of 100 kobo	N 34.7003*	N 36.6197*
Northern Mariana Islands	Currency is that of USA	US$ 1.5855	US$ 1.6732
Norway	Krone of 100 øre	Kroner 11.7812	Kroner 12.8929
Oman	Rial Omani (OR) of 1,000 baiza	OR 0.6105	OR 0.6442
Pakistan	Pakistan rupee of 100 paisa	Rs 64.1803	Rs 83.5680
Palau	Currency is that of the USA	US$ 1.5855	US$ 1.6732
Panama	Balboa of 100 centésimos (US notes are also in circulation)	Balboa 1.5855	Balboa 1.6732
Papua New Guinea	Kina (K) of 100 toea	K 2.2554	K 3.3376
Paraguay	Guaraní (Gs) of 100 céntimos	Gs 3448.46	Gs 4718.43
Peru	New Sol of 100 cénts	New Sol 4.1960	New Sol 5.0966
The Philippines	Philippine peso (P) of 100 centavos	P 50.8946	P 76.1189
Pitcairn Islands	Currency is that of New Zealand	NZ$ 2.4912	NZ$ 3.3058
Poland	Złoty of 100 groszy	Złotys 5.5532	Złotys 6.1658
Portugal	Escudo (Esc) of 100 centavos	Esc 290.543	Esc 297.403
Puerto Rico	Currency is that of USA	US$ 1.5855	US$ 1.6732
Qatar	Qatar riyal of 100 dirhams	Riyals 5.7723	Riyals 6.0913
Réunion	Currency is that of France	Francs 9.6408	Francs 9.7314
Romania	Leu (Lei) of 100 bani	Lei 11851.6	Lei 15038.7
Russia	*New Rouble of 100 kopeks	Roubles 9260.91	Roubles 33.0877
Rwanda	Rwanda franc of 100 centimes	Francs 478.907	Francs 522.708
St Christopher and Nevis	East Caribbean dollar (EC$) of 100 cents	EC$ 4.2809	EC$ 4.5177
St Helena	St Helena pound (£) of 100 pence	at parity with £ sterling	
St Lucia	East Caribbean dollar (EC$) of 100 cents	EC$ 4.2809	EC$ 4.5177
St Pierre and Miquelon	Currency is that of France	Francs 9.6408	Francs 9.7314
St Vincent and the Grenadines	East Caribbean dollar (EC$) of 100 cents	EC$ 4.2809	EC$ 4.5177
El Salvador	El Salvador colón (¢) of 100 centavos	¢ 13.8811	¢ 14.6489
Samoa	Tala (S$) of 100 sene	S$ 4.1515	S$ 5.1546

Country/Territory	Monetary Unit	Average Rate to £ 5 September 1997	Average Rate to £ 4 September 1998
San Marino	San Marino and Italian currencies are in circulation	Lire 2792.53	Lire 2866.48
São Tomé and Príncipe	Dobra of 100 centavos	Dobra 3781.62	Dobra 3998.95
Saudi Arabia	Saudi riyal (SR) of 20 qursh or 100 halala	SR 5.9465	SR 6.2754
Senegal	Franc CFA	Francs 964.080	Francs 973.140
Seychelles	Seychelles rupee of 100 cents	Rs 8.0861	Rs 8.7007
Sierra Leone	Leone (Le) of 100 cents	Le 1236.69	Le 2526.53
Singapore	Singapore dollar (S$) of 100 cents	S$ 2.4021	S$ 2.9253
Slovakia	Koruna (Sk) of 100 haliers	Kčs 55.3197	Kčs 58.8113
Slovenia	Tolar (SIT) of 100 stotin	Tolars 268.058	Tolars 273.541
Solomon Islands	Solomon Islands dollar (SI$) of 100 cents	SI$ 5.8184	SI$ 8.0261
Somalia	Somali shilling of 100 cents	Shillings 4154.01	Shillings 4383.79
South Africa	Rand (R) of 100 cents	R 7.4384	R 10.4153
Spain	Peseta of 100 céntimos	Pesetas 241.694	Pesetas 246.396
Sri Lanka	Sri Lankan rupee of 100 cents	Rs 94.3373	Rs 110.808
Sudan	Sudanese dinar (SD) of 10 pounds	SD 244.167	SD 305.526
Suriname	Suriname guilder of 100 cents	Guilders 635.785	Guilders 670.953
Swaziland	Lilangeni (E) of 100 cents (South African currency is also in circulation)	E 7.4384	E 10.4153
Sweden	Swedish krona of 100 öre	Kronor 12.3493	Kronor 13.2891
Switzerland	Swiss franc of 100 rappen (or centimes)	Francs 2.3467	Francs 2.3816
Syria	Syrian pound (S£) of 100 piastres	S£ 63.4200	S£ 66.9280
Taiwan	New Taiwan dollar (NT$) of 100 cents	NT$ 45.3730	NT$ 58.0508
Tajikistan	Tajik rouble (TJR) of 100 tanga	—	—
Tanzania	Tanzanian shilling of 100 cents	Shillings 976.589	Shillings 1102.97
Thailand	Baht of 100 satang	Baht 58.7825	Baht 68.2415
Togo	Franc CFA	Francs 964.080	Francs 973.140
Tonga	Pa'anga (T$) of 100 seniti	T$ 2.1703	T$ 2.8507
Trinidad and Tobago	Trinidad and Tobago dollar (TT$) of 100 cents	TT$ 9.6795	TT$ 10.4441
Tristan da Cunha	Currency is that of the UK		
Tunisia	Tunisian dinar of 1,000 millimes	Dinars 1.8103	Dinars 1.8806
Turkey	Turkish lira (TL) of 100 kurus	TL 269281.4	TL 464062.1
Turkmenistan	Manat of 100 tenesi	—	—
Turks and Caicos Islands	US dollar (US$)	US$ 1.5855	US$ 1.6732
Tuvalu	Australian dollar ($A) of 100 cents	$A 2.1703	$A 2.8507
Uganda	Uganda shilling of 100 cents	Shillings 1744.05	Shillings 2098.19
Ukraine	Hryvna of 100 kopiykas	Hryvnas 2.9494	Hryvnas 5.1033
United Arab Emirates	UAE dirham of 100 fils	Dirham 5.8234	Dirham 6.1457
United Kingdom	Pound sterling (£) of 100 pence	£ 1.00	£ 1.00
United States of America	US dollar (US$) of 100 cents	US$ 1.5855	US$ 1.6732
Uruguay	Uruguayan peso of 100 centésimos	Pesos 15.4586	Pesos 17.9702
Uzbekistan	Sum	—	Sum 481.045
Vanuatu	Vatu of 100 centimes	Vatu 186.479	Vatu 221.700
Vatican City State	Italian currency is legal tender	Lire 2792.53	Lire 2866.48
Venezuela	Bolívar (Bs) of 100 céntimos	Bs 786.606	Bs 976.530
Vietnam	Dông of 10 hào or 100 xu	Dông 18545.6	Dông 23270.0
Virgin Islands, British	US dollar (US$) (£ sterling and EC$ also circulate)	US$ 1.5855	US$ 1.6732
Virgin Islands, US	Currency is that of the USA	US$ 1.5855	US$ 1.6732
Wallis and Futuna Islands	Franc CFP	Francs 176.241	Francs 176.887
Yemen	Riyal of 100 fils	Riyals 206.115	Riyals 219.173
Yugoslavia	New dinar of 100 paras	New Dinars 9.0507	New Dinars 17.5608
Zambia	Kwacha (K) of 100 ngwee	K 2100.00	K 3363.15
Zimbabwe	Zimbabwe dollar (Z$) of 100 cents	Z$ 18.9626	Z$ 41.4120

Time Zones

Standard time differences from the Greenwich meridian

+   hours ahead of GMT
−   hours behind GMT
*   may vary from standard time at some part of the year (Summer Time or Daylight Saving Time)
h   hours
m   minutes

	h m
Afghanistan	+ 4 30
*Albania	+ 1
Algeria	+ 1
*Andorra	+ 1
Angola	+ 1
Anguilla	− 4
Antigua and Barbuda	− 4
Argentina	− 3
*Armenia	+ 3
Aruba	− 4
Ascension Island	0
*Australia	+10
*Broken Hill area (NSW)	+ 9 30
*Lord Howe Island	+10 30
Northern Territory	+ 9 30
*South Australia	+ 9 30
Western Australia	+ 8
*Austria	+ 1
*Azerbaijan	+ 4
*Azores	− 1
*Bahamas	− 5
Bahrain	+ 3
Bangladesh	+ 6
Barbados	− 4
*Belarus	+ 2
*Belgium	+ 1
Belize	− 6
Benin	+ 1
*Bermuda	− 4
Bhutan	+ 6
Bolivia	− 4
*Bosnia-Hercegovina	+ 1
Botswana	+ 2
Brazil	
Acre	− 5
*eastern, including all coast and Brasilia	− 3
Fernando de Noronha Island	− 2
*southern	− 4
western	− 4
British Antarctic Territory	− 3
British Indian Ocean Territory	+ 5
Diego Garcia	+ 6
British Virgin Islands	− 4
Brunei	+ 8
*Bulgaria	+ 2
Burkina Faso	0
Burundi	+ 2
Cambodia	+ 7
Cameroon	+ 1
Canada	
*Alberta	− 7
*British Columbia	− 8
*Labrador	− 4

	h m
*Manitoba	− 6
*New Brunswick	− 4
*Newfoundland	− 3 30
*Northwest Territories	
east of 85° W.	− 5
85° W.–102° W.	− 6
west of 102° W.	− 7
*Nova Scotia	− 4
*Ontario	
east of 90° W.	− 5
west of 90° W.	− 6
*Prince Edward Island	− 4
Quebec	
east of 63° W.	− 4
*west of 63° W.	− 5
Saskatchewan	− 6
*Yukon	− 8
*Canary Islands	0
Cape Verde	− 1
Cayman Islands	− 5
Central African Republic	+ 1
Chad	+ 1
*Chatham Islands	+12 45
*Chile	− 4
China	+ 8
Christmas Island (Indian Ocean)	+ 7
Cocos Keeling Islands	+ 6 30
Colombia	− 5
Comoros	+ 3
Congo (Dem. Rep.)	
east	+ 2
west	+ 1
Congo (Rep. of)	+ 1
Cook Islands	− 10
Costa Rica	− 6
Côte d'Ivoire	0
*Croatia	+ 1
*Cuba	− 5
*Cyprus	+ 2
*Czech Republic	+ 1
*Denmark	+ 1
Djibouti	+ 3
Dominica	− 4
Dominican Republic	− 4
Ecuador	− 5
Galápagos Islands	− 6
*Egypt	+ 2
Equatorial Guinea	+ 1
Eritrea	+ 3
*Estonia	+ 2
Ethiopia	+ 3
*Falkland Islands	− 4
*Faröe Islands	0
Fiji	+12
*Finland	+ 2
*France	+ 1
French Guiana	− 3
French Polynesia	−10
Marquesas Islands	− 9 30
Gabon	+ 1
The Gambia	0
Georgia	+ 5
*Germany	+ 1
Ghana	0
*Gibraltar	+ 1
*Greece	+ 2

	h m
*Greenland	− 3
Danmarkshavn	0
Mesters Vig	0
*Scoresby Sound	− 1
*Thule area	− 4
Grenada	− 4
Guadeloupe	− 4
Guam	+10
Guatemala	− 6
Guinea	0
Guinea-Bissau	0
Guyana	− 4
*Haiti	− 5
Honduras	− 6
*Hungary	+ 1
Iceland	0
India	+ 5 30
Indonesia	
Bali	+ 8
Flores	+ 8
Irian Jaya	+ 9
Java	+ 7
Kalimantan (south and east)	+ 8
Kalimantan (west and central)	+ 7
Molucca Islands	+ 9
Sulawesi	+ 8
Sumatra	+ 7
Sumbawa	+ 8
Tanimbar	+ 9
Timor	+ 8
*Iran	+ 3 30
*Iraq	+ 3
*Ireland, Republic of	0
*Israel	+ 2
*Italy	+ 1
Jamaica	− 5
Japan	+ 9
*Jordan	+ 2
*Kazakhstan	
western (Aktau)	+ 4
central (Atyrau)	+ 5
eastern	+ 6
Kenya	+ 3
Kiribati	+12
Line Islands	+14
Phoenix Islands	+13
Korea, North	+ 9
Korea, South	+ 9
Kuwait	+ 3
*Kyrgyzstan	+ 5
Laos	+ 7
*Latvia	+ 2
*Lebanon	+ 2
Lesotho	+ 2
Liberia	0
*Libya	+ 1
*Liechtenstein	+ 1
Line Islands not part of Kiribati	−10
*Lithuania	+ 2
*Luxembourg	+ 1
Macao	+ 8
*Macedonia (Former Yug. Rep. of)	+ 1
Madagascar	+ 3

	h m		h m
*Madeira	0	St Lucia	− 4
Malawi	+ 2	*St Pierre and Miquelon	− 3
Malaysia	+ 8	St Vincent and the	
Maldives	+ 5	Grenadines	− 4
Mali	0	El Salvador	− 6
*Malta	+ 1	Samoa	−11
Marshall Islands	+12	Samoa, American	−11
Ebon Atoll	−12	*San Marino	+ 1
Martinique	− 4	São Tomé and Princípe	0
Mauritania	0	Saudi Arabia	+ 3
Mauritius	+ 4	Senegal	0
*Mexico	− 6	Seychelles	+ 4
central	− 7	Sierra Leone	0
*Quintana Roo	− 5	Singapore	+ 8
western	− 8	*Slovakia	+ 1
Micronesia		*Slovenia	+ 1
Caroline Islands	+10	Solomon Islands	+11
Kosrae	+11	Somalia	+ 3
Pingelap	+11	South Africa	+ 2
Pohnpei	+11	South Georgia	− 2
*Moldova	+ 2	*Spain	+ 1
*Monaco	+ 1	Sri Lanka	+ 6
*Mongolia	+ 8	Sudan	+ 2
Montserrat	− 4	Suriname	− 3
Morocco	0	Swaziland	+ 2
Mozambique	+ 2	*Sweden	+ 1
Myanmar	+ 6 30	*Switzerland	+ 1
*Namibia	+ 1	*Syria	+ 2
Nauru	+12	Taiwan	+ 8
Nepal	+ 5 45	Tajikistan	+ 5
*Netherlands	+ 1	Tanzania	+ 3
Netherlands Antilles	− 4	Thailand	+ 7
New Caledonia	+11	Togo	0
*New Zealand	+12	Tonga	+13
Nicaragua	− 6	Trinidad and Tobago	− 4
Niger	+ 1	Tristan da Cunha	0
Nigeria	+ 1	Tunisia	+ 1
Niue	−11	*Turkey	+ 2
Norfolk Island	+11 30	Turkmenistan	+ 5
Northern Mariana Islands	+10	*Turks and Caicos Islands	− 5
*Norway	+ 1	Tuvalu	+12
Oman	+ 4	Uganda	+ 3
Pakistan	+ 5	*Ukraine	+ 2
Palau	+ 9	United Arab Emirates	+ 4
Panama	− 5	*United Kingdom	0
Papua New Guinea	+10	*United States of America	
*Paraguay	− 4	Alaska	− 9
Peru	− 5	Aleutian Islands, east of	
Philippines	+ 8	169° 30′ W.	− 9
*Poland	+ 1	Aleutian Islands, west	
*Portugal	+ 0	of 169° 30′ W.	−10
Puerto Rico	− 4	eastern time	− 5
Qatar	+ 3	central time	− 6
Réunion	+ 4	Hawaii	−10
*Romania	+ 2	mountain time	− 7
*Russia		Pacific time	− 8
Zone 1	+ 2	Uruguay	− 3
Zone 2	+ 3	Uzbekistan	+ 5
Zone 3	+ 4	Vanuatu	+11
Zone 4	+ 5	*Vatican City State	+ 1
Zone 5	+ 6	Venezuela	− 4
Zone 6	+ 7	Vietnam	+ 7
Zone 7	+ 8	Virgin Islands (US)	− 4
Zone 8	+ 9	Yemen	+ 3
Zone 9	+10	*Yugoslavia (Fed. Rep. of)	+ 1
Zone 10	+11	Zambia	+ 2
Zone 11	+12	Zimbabwe	+ 2
Rwanda	+ 2		
St Helena	0		
St Christopher and Nevis	− 4		

Source: reproduced with permission from data produced by HM Nautical Almanac Office

Travel Overseas

PASSPORT REGULATIONS

Applications for United Kingdom passports must be made on the forms obtainable from regional passport offices (see below), main post offices, WorldChoice travel agents and Lloyds Bank.

LONDON – Passport Office, Clive House, 70–78 Petty France, London SW1H 9HD

LIVERPOOL – Passport Office, 5th Floor, India Buildings, Water Street, Liverpool L2 0QZ

NEWPORT – Passport Office, Olympia House, Upper Dock Street, Newport, Gwent NP9 1XA

PETERBOROUGH – Passport Office, Aragon Court, Northminster Road, Peterborough PE1 1QG

GLASGOW – Passport Office, 3 Northgate, 96 Milton Street, Cowcaddens, Glasgow G4 0BT

BELFAST – Passport Office, Hampton House, 47–53 High Street, Belfast BT1 2QS

Central telephone number: 0870-521 0410
Central fax number: 0171-271 8581
Web site: http://www.open.gov.ukpass/ukpass.htm

Telephone calls are normally routed automatically to the nearest office unless all lines are busy, when the call will be rerouted to other offices. Recorded messages to deal with routine enquiries operate 24 hours a day.

The passport offices are open Monday–Friday 9 a.m. to 4.30 p.m. (8.15 a.m. to 4 p.m. in London). The Passport Office in London is also open for cases of emergency (e.g. death or serious illness) arising outside normal office hours between 4 p.m. and 6 p.m. Monday to Friday, between 10 a.m. and 7 p.m. on Saturdays, and between 9.30 a.m. and 2.30 p.m. on Sundays and Bank Holidays.

Straightforward, properly completed applications are processed within 15 working days from April to August, the busiest period, and within ten working days for the rest of the year. Applying in person does not guarantee that an application will be given priority.

The completed application form should be posted, with the appropriate documents and fee, to the regional passport office indicated on the addressed envelope which is provided with each application form (an exception to this is the London office which is a calling-in office only). Accompanying cheques and postal orders should be crossed and made payable to 'The Passport Office'.

A passport cannot be issued or extended on behalf of a person already abroad; such persons should apply to the nearest British High Commission or Consulate.

UK passports are granted to:
(i)   British citizens
(ii) British Dependent Territories citizens
(iii) British Nationals (Overseas)
(iv) British Overseas citizens
(v)   British Subjects
(vi) British Protected Persons

UK passports are generally available for travel to all countries. The possession of a passport does not, however, exempt the holder from compliance with any immigration regulations in force in British or foreign countries, or from the necessity of obtaining a visa where required.

A new, machine-readable application form is being introduced from July 1998. This replaces the five different application forms previously used, and takes into account the fact that all children will require their own passports (see below). The new form also covers amendments and extensions.

ADULTS

A passport granted to a person over 16 will normally be valid for ten years and will not be renewable. Thereafter, or if at any time the passport contains no further space for visas, a new passport must be obtained.

The issue of passports including details of the holder's spouse has been discontinued, but existing family passports may be used until expiry. A spouse who is included in a family passport cannot travel on the passport without the holder.

CHILDREN

From 5 October 1998 all children under the age of 16 will be required to have their own passport, primarily to help prevent child abductions. They will normally be valid for five years, after which point a new passport application must be made. This replaces the system whereby children under the age of 16 could either have their own document or be added to their parents's passports.

A passport granted to a child prior to this date is still valid for five years, although the free, five-year extension option no longer exists. On expiry, a new application must be made. Children included in their parents' passports when the new regulations come into force will not be affected and, assuming that the documents do not expire, can continue to travel on them until they reach the age of 16 or the passport expires or is amended.

COUNTERSIGNATURES

The completed application form should be countersigned by an MP, justice of the peace, minister of religion, a professionally qualified person (e.g. doctor, engineer, lawyer, teacher), bank officer, established Civil Servant, police officer or a person of similar standing who has known the applicant for at least two years, and who is either a British citizen, British Dependent Territories citizen, British National (Overseas), British Overseas citizen, British Subject or a citizen of a Commonwealth country. A relative must not countersign the application.

If the application is for a child under the age of 16, the countersignature should be by someone of relevant standing who has known the parent or person with parental responsibility who signs the declaration of consent, rather than the child.

PHOTOGRAPHS

Two identical unmounted photographs of the applicant must be sent. These photographs should be printed on normal thin photographic paper. They should measure 45 mm × 35 mm (1.77 in × 1.38 in) and should be taken full face against a white background. One photograph should be certified as a true likeness of the applicant by the person who countersigns the application form.

DOCUMENTATION

The applicant's birth certificate or previous British passport, and other documents in support of the statements made in the application must be produced at the time of applying. Details of which documents are required are set out in the notes accompanying the application form.

If the applicant for a passport is a British national by naturalization or registration, the certificate proving this must be produced with the application, unless the applicant holds a previous UK passport issued after registration or naturalization.

48-PAGE PASSPORTS

The 48-page passport is intended to meet the needs of frequent travellers who fill standard passports well before the validity has expired. It is valid for ten years.

PASSPORT FEES* from March 1998

New adult passport	£21
New child passport	£11
Renewal of passport	£21
Amendment of passport	£11
48-page passport	£31

* postal applications only. A £10 charge is added for applications made in person at a passport office in the UK or made abroad

VISAS

British nationals planning to travel overseas should enquire about visa requirements at the Foreign and Commonwealth Office, or the high commission or consulate of their country of destination (*see* the Countries of the World section). Visa requirements may vary depending on the purpose or the length of the visit, and regulations are also liable to change, sometimes at short notice.

Overseas nationals who wish to enter the UK must satisfy the immigration officer at the port of arrival that they meet the requirements of the UK immigration rules. Separate rules apply to nationals of a member state of the European Economic Area (member states of the European Union and Iceland, Liechtenstein and Norway). Details are available from the nearest British mission (*see* the Countries of the World section).

Nationals from the following countries must have a valid visa issued prior to travel to the UK, unless they are settled in the UK or are in the UK for some long-term purpose (more than six months) and returning within the period of a permission to stay granted previously:
Afghanistan; Albania; Algeria; Angola; Armenia; Azerbaijan; Bahrain; Bangladesh; Belarus; Benin; Bhutan; Bosnia-Hercegovina; Bulgaria; Burkina Faso; Burundi; Cambodia; Cameroon; Cape Verde; Central African Republic; Chad; China; Colombia; Comoros; Democratic Republic of Congo; Republic of Congo; Côte d'Ivoire; Cuba; Northern Cyprus ('Turkish Republic of Northern Cyprus'); Djibouti; Dominican Republic; Ecuador; Egypt; Equatorial Guinea; Eritrea; Ethiopia; Fiji; Gabon; Gambia; Georgia; Ghana; Guinea; Guinea-Bissau; Guyana; Haiti; India; Indonesia; Iran; Iraq; Jordan; Kazakhstan; Kenya; Korea (North); Kuwait; Kyrgyzstan; Laos; Lebanon; Liberia; Libya; Macedonia (Former Yugoslav Republic of); Madagascar; Maldives; Mali; Mauritania; Mauritius; Moldova; Mongolia; Morocco; Mozambique; Myanmar (Burma); Nepal; Niger; Nigeria; Oman; Pakistan; Papua New Guinea; Peru; Philippines; Qatar; Romania; Russia; Rwanda; São Tomé and Príncipe; Saudi Arabia; Senegal; Sierra Leone; Somalia; Sri Lanka; Sudan; Suriname; Syria; Taiwan; Tajikistan; Tanzania; Thailand; Togo; Tunisia; Turkey; Turkmenistan; Uganda; Ukraine; United Arab Emirates; Uzbekistan; Vietnam; Yemen; Yugoslavia (Federal Republic of); Zambia.

A valid entry clearance is also required by people who are stateless or who hold a non-national travel document or passport issued by an authority not recognized by the UK.

Nationals of any country not listed above do not need an entry clearance to visit or study in the UK but must obtain entry clearance to settle, work or set up business. Entry clearances take the form of an entry certificate for non-visa nationals.

UK entry clearances can be obtained from British embassies, consulates and high commissions overseas (*see* Countries of the World section).

HEALTH ADVICE

Health Advice for Travellers (booklet T6), published by the Department of Health, contains information on health precautions, reciprocal health agreements with other countries, and immunization. It is available from some travel agents, local post offices or the Department of Health, PO Box 410, Wetherby, W. Yorks LS23 7LN. Tel: 0800-555777 (single copy orders).

IMMUNIZATION

In very general terms immunization against typhoid, polio and hepatitis A should be considered for all countries where standards of hygiene and sanitation may be less than ideal. Protection against malaria, in the form of tablets, as well as measures to avoid mosquito bites, is advised for visits to malarious areas.

Immunization against yellow fever is compulsory for entry into some countries, either for all travellers or for those arriving from a yellow fever-infected area, and is recommended for all travellers to infected areas.

A doctor should be consulted, preferably at least eight weeks before departure, and will advise travellers and arrange vaccinations. If children will be travelling outside Europe, North America, Australia and New Zealand, the doctor should be informed, especially if they have not completed their full course of childhood immunization.

Country-by-country guidance is set out in *Health Advice for Travellers*. Health care professionals can obtain up-to-date information about immunization recommendations from the Department of Health publication *Health Information for Overseas Travel* or from:
ENGLAND – Communicable Disease Surveillance Centre, 61 Colindale Avenue, London NW9 5EQ. Tel: 0181-200 6868
WALES – Welsh Office, Cathays Park, Cardiff CF1 3NQ. Tel: 01222-825111
SCOTLAND – Scottish Office Department of Health, St Andrew's House, Edinburgh EH1 3DG. Tel: 0131-556 8400; or The Scottish Centre for Infection and Environmental Health, Clifton House, Clifton Place, Glasgow G3 7LN. Tel: 0141-300 1130
NORTHERN IRELAND – DHSS, Dundonald House, Upper Newtownards Road, Belfast BT4 3SF. Tel: 01232-520000

MEDICAL TREATMENT ABROAD

Details of free or reduced cost emergency medical treatment when visiting European countries, and countries with which the UK has reciprocal health arrangements, are set out in *Health Advice for Travellers*. It also contains Form E111, the certificate that entitles people to urgent medical treatment in the European Economic Area (EEA), as well as guidance on its completion.

For countries where the UK has no health care agreements, including Canada, the USA, India, the Far East, and the whole of Africa and Latin America, it is advisable to take out medical insurance. A certain amount of insurance is also needed in countries with which the UK has health care agreements.

BUSINESS ABROAD

Working Abroad

A passport issued after 31 December 1982 showing the holder's national status as British citizen will secure for the holder the right to take employment or to establish himself/herself in business or other self-employed activity in another member state of the European Union. A passport bearing the endorsement 'holder has the right of abode in the United Kingdom' where the holder so qualifies will also secure the same right.

In most other countries, employment permits are required, even for casual labour. The nearest representative of the country concerned should be consulted. Local employment offices have a booklet entitled *Working Abroad*.

Export Business

Those planning to travel overseas on export business are advised to contact Overseas Trade Services (OTS), the joint Department of Trade and Industry (DTI) and Foreign and Commonwealth Office export operation. The aim of the OTS is to encourage potential exporters to consider selling overseas and existing exporters to sell more, and its offices can offer advice and information about the markets to be visited. OTS can be contacted through the following:

England – London: Government Office for London, Riverwalk House, 157–161 Millbank, London SW1P 4RR. Tel: 0171-217 3199.

Wales – Welsh Office Industry Department, Cathays Park, Cardiff CF1 3NQ. Tel: 01222-825097

Scotland – Scottish Trade International, 120 Bothwell Street, Glasgow G2 7PJ. Tel: 0141-228 2808

Northern Ireland – Export Development Branch, IDB House, 64 Chichester Street, Belfast BT1 4JX. Tel: 01232-233233

Information about specific overseas markets is available from the country desks at the DTI's headquarters: 1 Victoria Street, London SW1H 0ET. Tel: 0171-215 5000.

For details of the nearest Business Link, contact the Business Links Network. Tel: 0345-567765

Events of the Year

1 September 1997 to 31 August 1998

BRITISH AFFAIRS

SEPTEMBER 1997

2. In Paris, seven *paparazzi* present at the scene of the car crash that killed Diana, Princess of Wales were charged with involuntary manslaughter and failing to assist at the scene of an accident. An official memorial fund was set up for donations to the Princess's favourite charities. 4. The royal family returned to London from Balmoral and The Queen broadcast to the nation from Buckingham Palace. 5. The Princess's coffin was taken from the Chapel Royal at St James's Palace to Kensington Palace. 6. The funeral of Diana, Princess of Wales took place at Westminster Abbey at 11 a.m. After the service a minute's silence was observed throughout the UK. The Princess was buried in a private ceremony on an island in a lake in the grounds of the Spencer family estate at Althorp, Northants. 8. The TUC conference opened in Brighton. 11. A referendum was held in Scotland on whether a Scottish Parliament should be set up and whether it should have the power to adjust tax rates; the turnout was about 62 per cent, of which 74.3 per cent voted in favour of a parliament and 63.5 per cent in favour of it having the power to adjust tax rates. 13. The Duchess of Kent and the Deputy Prime Minister (John Prescott) attended the funeral of Mother Teresa in Calcutta, India. 14. The leader of the Conservative Party (William Hague) was criticized for accusing the Prime Minister (Tony Blair) of making political capital out of the death of the Princess of Wales by leaking reports to the press of his dealings with the royal family in the week before the funeral. 15. Buckingham Palace issued a statement denying that there had been disputes between the royal family and the Spencer family over arrangements for the funeral of the Princess of Wales, and saying that press reports that The Queen had opposed aspects of the arrangements were 'the direct opposite of the truth'. 17. A referendum was held in Wales on whether an assembly should be set up; the turnout was 50 per cent, of which 50.3 per cent voted in favour of an assembly. 22. The Liberal Democrat conference opened in Eastbourne. 24. The Labour Party suspended nine councillors in Glasgow, including the Lord Provost, over allegations that they had accepted overseas trips in return for their support in important votes. 25. The Home Secretary (Jack Straw) announced measures intended to cut youth crime and force parents to take responsi-bility for the behaviour of their children. 29. The Labour Party conference opened in Brighton.

OCTOBER 1997

5. The Prime Minister arrived in Moscow for a two-day visit. 7. The Queen and the Duke of Edinburgh arrived in Islamabad at the beginning of a state visit to Pakistan and India to mark the 50th anniversary of the two countries' independence. The Queen's arrival in India was marred by a diplomatic row over British foreign policy on Kashmir. The Conservative Party conference opened in Blackpool. The results of a ballot of the party's membership were announced: 80.78 per cent of those who voted endorsed William Hague as leader of the party and his principles for reforming the party. 10. The Defence Secretary (George Robertson) announced that the royal yacht *Britannia* would not be replaced after being decommissioned in November 1997. 14. The Conservative MP Piers Merchant resigned, denying newspaper allegations that he had had an affair with an 18-year-old woman; he later admitted that the affair had occurred. 17–20. About two hundred gypsies from the Czech Republic and Slovakia arrived in Dover claiming political asylum; they were granted temporary leave to remain in Britain. 24. The biennial Commonwealth Heads of Government meeting opened in Edinburgh. 26. A silent march led by Cardinal Basil Hume was held in London to mark the 30th anniversary of the passing of the Abortion Act. 29. The Prince of Wales arrived in Swaziland at the start of an eight-day tour of southern Africa. Ian Taylor resigned as a junior Opposition spokesman on Northern Ireland because of the Shadow Cabinet's decision to oppose European monetary union (EMU) at the next general election. The Government published a bill proposing that the next elections for the European Parliament should be held under a system of proportional representation.

NOVEMBER 1997

1. David Curry resigned from the Shadow Cabinet because of its decision to oppose EMU at the next general election. 4. The Government said that Formula One motor racing would be exempt from its proposed ban on sponsorship of sporting events by tobacco companies. On 10 November after taking advice from Sir Patrick Neill, the incoming chairman of the Committee on Standards in Public Life, the Labour Party said that it would return a £1 million donation to party funds which had been made before the general election by Bernie Ecclestone, vice-president of the Formula One Associa-

tion. After conflicting reports as to whether Mr Ecclestone had offered the party a further donation and allegations that the Government's policy had been changed because of his financial support, the Prime Minister gave a television interview on 16 November in which he apologized for the Government's handling of the affair and denied that there had been any impropriety in its dealings with Mr Ecclestone. **5.** The Government published the first White Paper on overseas aid since 1975 (*see* page 1168). **6.** Labour won the Paisley South by-election with a reduced majority (*see* page 233). **7.** The Prime Minister held talks with President Chirac and the French Prime Minister, Lionel Jospin, at the Canary Wharf tower in London's docklands. **13.** The aircraft carrier *Invincible* was ordered to sail to the Mediterranean because of increased tension in the Middle East over Iraq's expulsion of six American weapons inspectors. **17.** Six Britons, including a five-year-old girl, were among 68 people killed when Islamic militants disguised as policemen shot and stabbed tourists at the Pharaonic temples in Luxor, Egypt. **19.** A report by a former Chief Social Services Inspector, Sir William Utting, was published; it disclosed high levels of child abuse in residential and foster homes, and recommended a wider choice of care places, better staff recruitment procedures and a new code of practice for choosing foster carers. **20.** A service of thanksgiving was held at Westminster Abbey to mark the 50th wedding anniversary of The Queen and the Duke of Edinburgh; it was followed by a lunch in their honour at the Banqueting House. In the evening a private ball was held at Windsor Castle following the completion of restoration work after the fire in November 1992. The Conservatives won the Beckenham by-election with a reduced majority (*see* page 233). The Liberal Democrats won the Winchester by-election with a majority of 21,556 (*see* page 233). Sixty-year-old Elizabeth Buttle became the oldest British woman to have a child when she gave birth to a son; it was later alleged that she had received fertility treatment after lying about her age. **21.** The Conservative whip was withdrawn from Peter Temple-Morris, the MP for Leominster, who had threatened to resign the party whip unless Mr Hague changed his stance on EMU; Mr Temple-Morris resigned from the Conservative Party. **22.** The royal yacht *Britannia* entered Portsmouth harbour after her final voyage before being decommissioned. **25.** The Chancellor of the Exchequer (Gordon Brown) delivered a pre-Budget statement in the House of Commons. **28.** MPs voted by a majority of 260 in favour of a private member's bill to ban hunting with dogs.

DECEMBER 1997

1. The Prime Minister appointed Lord Jenkins of Hillhead to lead a commission with the remit of recommending a 'broadly proportional' alternative to the first-past-the-post system for parliamentary elections. **2-10.** Farmers blockaded Holyhead, Stranraer, Dover and other ports in protest against the import of cheap beef from Ireland. **3.** The Government said that the sale of beef on the bone would be banned because of the 'very small risk' that it could cause Creutzfeldt-Jakob disease (CJD). The Prime Minister announced a moratorium on the building of gas-fired power stations in order to protect the deep-mined coal industry. **4.** The Government announced the establishment of a Royal Commission to examine the funding of long-term care of the elderly. **9.** The Government published a White Paper on the NHS (*see* pages 1168-9). The oldest person in Britain, Lucy Askew, died at the age of 114. **10.** A junior Scottish Office minister, Malcolm Chisholm, and three parliamentary private secretaries, Gordon Prentice, Mick Clapham and Neil Gerrard, resigned in order to oppose government plans to cut single-parent benefit. In the House of Commons, 47 Labour back-benchers voted in favour of an amendment opposing the plans. Another parliamentary private secretary, Alice Mahon, was sacked for voting for the amendment. **11.** The royal yacht *Britannia* was decommissioned at a ceremony in Portsmouth. **14.** The Opposition called for the resignation of the Paymaster-General, Geoffrey Robinson, after revelations concerning his involvement with an offshore trust. On 20 January 1998 the Parliamentary Commissioner for Standards (Sir Gordon Downey) said that Mr Robinson had not breached House of Commons rules by not registering his interest in the trust, but that it would have been better if he had done so. **15.** The Agriculture Minister (Jack Cunningham) said that Britain would ban EU meat imports that were not subject to the same hygiene standards as British meat. **19.** William Hague married Ffion Jenkins in a ceremony in the chapel of the crypt of the House of Commons. **22.** The Government announced an £85 million aid package for beef farmers, and said that an independent inquiry would be held into the handling of the bovine spongiform encephalopathy (BSE)/CJD crisis. **24-26.** At least six people were killed when strong winds hit many parts of Britain.

JANUARY 1998

3-5. Violent storms hit many parts of Britain. **8.** At least 1,000 homes were damaged when a tornado hit Selsey, W. Sussex. **9.** The Prime Minister arrived in Japan for a five-day visit. Two independent primary schools became the first Muslim schools in Britain to qualify for state funding when their application for grant-maintained status was approved. Stephen Bayley resigned as creative director of the Millennium Dome in Greenwich, London. **12.** The Japanese government apologized for the suffering of British prisoners during the Second World War. **13.** The Education and Employment Secretary (David Blunkett) announced far-ranging reforms to the national curriculum in primary schools. **14.** The Government published proposals to establish an independent Food Standards Agency (see page 1169). Conservative MPs voted to introduce a one member, one vote system for electing party leaders. **15.** The House of Commons Home Affairs select committee recommended radical changes to the procedures for investigating complaints against police officers. **16.** The aircraft carrier *Invincible* was ordered to sail to the Gulf because of increased tension in the area over Iraq's placing of restrictions on UN weapons inspection. **19.** Twelve-year-old Sean Stewart became the youngest father in Britain when his 16-year-old girlfriend gave birth to a boy in Sharnbrook, Beds. **25.** Queen Elizabeth the Queen Mother broke her left hip in a fall at Sandringham and underwent a hip replacement operation in London the following day. **26.** Liverpool dockers reached a settlement with the Mersey Docks and Harbour Company to bring to an end a dispute which had lasted since September 1995.

FEBRUARY 1998

3. After a meeting with the Culture, Media and Sport Secretary (Chris Smith), Peter Davis resigned as director-general of the Office of the National Lottery in the light of a libel action involving Richard Branson (see page 1088). The Health Secretary (Frank Dobson) said that St Bartholomew's Hospital, London, which the previous Government had earmarked for closure, would remain open. The Prime Minister arrived in Washington DC for a three-day official visit. The Prince of Wales arrived in Sri Lanka for a four-day visit coinciding with celebrations to mark the 50th anniversary of the island's independence; he then visited Nepal and Bhutan. **9.** At the Brit Awards in London a member of the anarchist band Chumbawumba emptied an icebucket over the Deputy Prime Minister (John Prescott). **12.** The Cabinet agreed to the use of force against Iraq if diplomatic efforts failed to secure a resolution in the crisis over UN weapons inspections; on 17 February MPs voted by 493 votes to 25 in favour of the use of force against Iraq if diplomatic efforts failed. **13.** About 1,100 people were evacuated from their homes after a 1,000 lb German Second World War bomb was found in a field outside Chippenham, Wilts; on 15 February army bomb experts carried out a controlled explosion. **16.** The Leader of the Opposition (William Hague) announced a set of proposals, *Fresh Future*, for reforming the internal workings of the Conservative Party; the proposals were approved by party members on 28 March. **17.** The Home Secretary said that future judges, magistrates, police officers, Crown prosecutors, prison staff and probation officers would be required to declare if they were freemasons; a voluntary register would also be set up for current employees to declare membership. **24.** Princess Margaret suffered a mild stroke while on holiday on the Caribbean island of Mustique. **26.** More than 5,000 beacons were lit in the evening throughout Britain in protest at the Government's policies on rural issues.

MARCH 1998

1. At least 250,000 people marched through central London to protest against a bill before Parliament intended to ban hunting with dogs, and to highlight concerns about the Government's policies on the countryside in general. On 13 March the bill was 'talked out' in the House of Commons. **6.** In a change to existing protocol, Buckingham Palace announced that the Union flag would fly over the palace, and other royal palaces, unless The Queen was in residence. **9.** The Prince of Wales underwent surgery on his right knee. **17.** The Israeli prime minister (Binyamin Netanyahu) cancelled a dinner with the Foreign Secretary (Robin Cook) in Jerusalem after Mr Cook visited the controversial Har Homa settlement in east Jerusalem. **31.** All the RAF's nuclear bombs were withdrawn from service, leaving submarine-launched Trident missiles as Britain's only nuclear weapons.

APRIL 1998

2. The Prime Minister held talks with the Chinese prime minister (Zhu Rongji) at Downing Street. **9–12.** At least five people died in severe flooding in central England. **17.** A British teacher, David Mitchell, and his wife and son were kidnapped in Yemen; they were released unharmed on 4 May. **20.** The Scottish Secretary (Donald Dewar) called on the Chief Constable of Grampian (Ian Oliver) to resign after the publication of a report highly critical of the investigation by Grampian police of the abduction and murder of a nine-year-old boy by a known paedophile in July 1997. On 21 April the Grampian Police Board called for Mr Oliver's immediate resignation; on 24 April he resigned. **27.** The Government published a White Paper outlining a ten-year national anti-drugs strategy (see page 1170). **28.** *The Times* began serialization of a controversial book about Mary Bell, who was convicted of the manslaughter of two children in 1968 when she was ten years old and who had been paid for her contribution to the book; on 29 April Mary Bell and her daughter were taken into protective custody after being tracked down by tabloid newspaper reporters. On 30 April the Home Secretary (Jack Straw) launched an inquiry into the affair.

MAY 1998

4. The Prime Minister held talks with the Israeli prime minister and the Palestinian president (Yasser Arafat) in separate sessions at Downing Street. **6.** The Foreign Secretary (Robin Cook) said that an independent inquiry would be held into allegations that Britain had exported arms to Sierra Leone in contravention of the UN ban on the sale of weapons to the state. **7.** A referendum was held in London on whether a strategic authority for London with a directly-elected mayor should be established; the turnout was 34 per cent, of which 72 per cent supported the proposal. Local elections were also held in London, the metropolitan authorities, and some shire districts and unitary authorities in England. 8. Sandline International, the company involved in supplying arms to Sierra Leone as part of a covert operation to restore the country's exiled civilian government, said that it had acted with the full prior knowledge and approval of the British government. 10. The Foreign Secretary said that Sandline International had acted without ministerial approval. 11. The Prime Minister said that although it would be wrong for officials to have deliberately breached the UN arms embargo, both the UN and the UK had been trying to help restore the democratic government of Sierra Leone. 12. The Foreign Secretary said that civil servants at the Foreign Office had not been involved in a 'conspiracy' to supply arms to Sierra Leone. 14. The permanent secretary at the Foreign Office (Sir John Kerr) withdrew an earlier statement that ministers had been told in early March about an imminent Customs and Excise inquiry into Sandline's activities. 18. Customs and Excise said that Sandline may have breached the UN arms embargo, but that it could not press charges because of clear evidence of meetings between the company and Foreign Office officials. 24. It was reported that Christopher Howes, a British mine clearance expert kidnapped by the Khmer Rouge in Cambodia in March 1996, had been murdered three days after the abduction. 25. The Emperor and Empress of Japan arrived in London at the beginning of a six-day state visit. On 26 May hundreds of veterans turned their backs as the royal carriage moved down the Mall, in protest at Japan's refusal to make a formal apology for the treatment of prisoners of war during the Second World War. At a state banquet at Buckingham Palace, Emperor Akihito made a speech in which he expressed the 'deep pain' he felt because of the suffering caused by the war. 29. Two heart surgeons and the chief executive at the Bristol Royal Infirmary, where 29 babies died during heart operations between 1988 and 1995, were found by a General Medical Council committee to have failed to pay sufficient regard to the safety and best interests of patients. On 18 June the three men were found guilty of serious professional misconduct; two of them were struck off and the third was ordered not to operate on children for three years. The Government announced a public inquiry into the case.

JUNE 1998
1. The Leader of the Opposition (William Hague) reshuffled the Shadow Cabinet. 3. The Secretary of State for the Environment, Transport and the Regions (John Prescott) announced a 'public-private partnership' rescue package for the Channel Tunnel rail link. 5. The Government announced that the nuclear reprocessing plant at Dounreay, Caithness, would close. 18. The President of the Board of Trade (Margaret Beckett) announced that a national minimum wage of £3.60 per hour would be introduced in April 1999, with workers aged

18–21 receiving a minimum of £3 per hour. 22. MPs voted to lower the age of consent for homosexuals to 16; on 22 July the House of Lords voted to keep the age of consent at 18, and the relevant clause was subsequently dropped from the legislation.

JULY 1998
5. The *Observer* published allegations that certain lobbyists had privileged access to senior ministers. On 6 July Derek Draper, a director of GPC Market Access, was suspended pending an inquiry into his activities; on 8 July he resigned. 8. In the House of Commons, the Leader of the Opposition attacked the Government for being surrounded by 'money-grabbing cronies'. The Government published the results of its strategic defence review (*see* pages 1070–1). 19. The Lambeth Conference opened in Canterbury. 20. The Government published a White Paper on transport (*see* page 1071). 27. The Prime Minister reshuffled the Cabinet; Harriet Harman, Lord Richard, Gavin Strang and David Clark were sacked, and Peter Mandelson, Alistair Darling, Baroness Jay of Paddington and Stephen Byers entered the Cabinet for the first time. The report of an inquiry conducted by Sir Thomas Legg into the 'arms to Sierra Leone' affair was published; it cleared ministers of having had prior knowledge of Sandline's plans to ship arms to the country, but criticized the judgement of the British High Commissioner, Peter Penfold, and the internal communications systems at the Foreign Office. 28. A range of middle-ranking and junior ministerial appointments was announced. 31. The Government announced a ban on the use of anti-personnel landmines by British troops.

AUGUST 1998
3. Gus Macdonald, the chairman of the Scottish Media Group, was appointed Minister for Business and Industry at the Scottish Office; he will receive a life peerage to enable him to sit in the House of Lords. 24. Sudan recalled its ambassador in London and requested the withdrawal of the British ambassador in Khartoum because of Britain's support for the USA's missile attack on a chemical factory in Khartoum on 20 August. On 27 August Britain temporarily withdrew its diplomats from Khartoum.

NORTHERN IRELAND AFFAIRS

SEPTEMBER 1997
9. Sinn Fein leaders agreed during cross-party talks at Stormont to abide by the Mitchell principles of democracy and non-violence. Five Unionist parties left the talks in protest at the presence of Sinn Fein members. 11. The IRA said that it would have problems with some of the Mitchell principles; it ruled out any disarmament during the talks process and rejected the principle that constitutional

change should have the consent of the majority of the population of Northern Ireland. **15.** Substantive talks opened at Stormont. The Unionist and loyalist parties boycotted the talks; the Ulster Unionist Party (UUP) said that before it would join the negotiations it required assurances that the IRA would hand over weapons during the talks process. **16.** A 400 lb bomb believed to have been planted by a republican splinter group exploded outside an RUC base in Co. Armagh; the UUP later called for Sinn Fein's expulsion from the talks. **17.** The UUP, the Progressive Unionist Party and the Ulster Democratic Party re-entered the negotiations. **23.** In an historic meeting, Unionist, loyalist, nationalist and republican leaders met for face-to-face negotiations at Stormont; the Unionists argued unsuccessfully that Sinn Fein should be expelled from the talks. **24.** It was agreed at the talks that the issue of decommissioning terrorist weapons would be dealt with by a new independent commission and that the substantive talks would concentrate on constitutional issues. **30.** The Northern Ireland Secretary (Mo Mowlam) said that the Government would give up its power to intern suspected terrorists without trial.

OCTOBER 1997

7. Full-scale peace negotiations opened at Stormont. **13.** The Prime Minister met the participants in the peace negotiations; he shook hands with Gerry Adams during the first meeting between a British prime minister and Sinn Fein leaders since 1921. The Prime Minister was later jostled by a hostile loyalist crowd during a walk-about in east Belfast. **25.** A man was killed by a car bomb in Bangor, Co. Down. **30.** The Home Secretary (Jack Straw) announced a comprehensive review of anti-terrorist legislation. A bomb planted by the Continuity IRA, a republican splinter group, exploded in Londonderry.

NOVEMBER 1997

6–7. Several leading IRA members were reported to have resigned in protest at the restoration of the cease-fire and Sinn Fein's adoption of the Mitchell principles of democracy and non-violence. **8.** Gerry Adams said that he was 'deeply sorry' about the IRA bombing at Enniskillen in 1987. **25.** The Chief Constable of the RUC (Ronnie Flanagan) announced the end of army foot patrols in west Belfast.

DECEMBER 1997

10. An IRA prisoner escaped from the Maze prison, Co. Antrim. **11.** Gerry Adams and Martin McGuinness led the first Sinn Fein delegation to be received at Downing Street since 1921. **13–14.** Rioting broke out in Londonderry after an Apprentice Boys' parade. **27.** Billy Wright, the leader of the Loyalist Volunteer Force (LVF) who was serving an eight-year sentence at the Maze prison, Co. Antrim, was shot dead by INLA prisoners. A former IRA prisoner was shot dead and three other people were shot and wounded by the LVF in Dungannon, Co.

Tyrone, and there were disturbances in Portadown, Co. Armagh, and Ballymena, Co. Antrim. **31.** A man was killed and five people were wounded when two loyalist gunmen opened fire in a Roman Catholic bar in Cliftonville, north Belfast.

JANUARY 1998

4. UDA prisoners in the Maze prison voted to withhold their support for the peace process. **9.** The Northern Ireland Secretary met UDA, UVF and IRA prisoners in the Maze prison; the UDA prisoners subsequently restored their support for the peace process. **11.** A Roman Catholic man related by marriage to the Sinn Fein president Gerry Adams was shot dead by the LVF outside a nightclub in Belfast. **12.** The British and Irish governments issued a joint document, *Propositions on Heads of Agreement*, to be debated at the Stormont talks. Its main proposals were an elected Northern Ireland Assembly; a Council of the Isles, to be attended by the British and Irish governments and representatives of the new Scottish, Welsh and Northern Ireland assemblies; a North-South Council to promote co-operation between Northern Ireland and the Irish Republic; and balanced constitutional change. **14.** During an undercover operation in Belfast a policeman was shot and critically injured by a woman soldier who had mistaken him for a terrorist. **18.** A Roman Catholic man was shot dead in Maghera, Co. Londonderry. **19.** A prominent UDA member was shot dead by the INLA in Dunmurry, Co. Antrim. A Roman Catholic man was shot dead in south Belfast. The Prime Minister met a Sinn Fein delegation led by Gerry Adams at Downing Street. **21.** A Roman Catholic man was shot dead in central Belfast and two other men were injured in shootings in the city. **22.** A Roman Catholic man was shot and injured in north Belfast. **23.** A Roman Catholic man was shot dead in north Belfast. **24.** A Roman Catholic man was shot dead in west Belfast. A car bomb believed to have been planted by the Continuity IRA exploded outside an entertainment complex in Enniskillen, Co. Fermanagh. **25.** A Roman Catholic man was shot and injured in Lurgan, Co. Armagh. **26.** The Ulster Democratic Party (UDP) withdrew from the multiparty talks when it became clear that it was about to be excluded because of the sectarian murders perpetrated by its paramilitary associates, the UFF; the Northern Ireland Secretary said that the UDP could be reinstated at the talks if an unconditional cease-fire were restored. **27.** The British and Irish governments presented to the talks further proposals on cross-border bodies. **29.** Tony Blair announced that a judicial tribunal would be set up to establish the truth about 'Bloody Sunday', when 14 people were shot dead by soldiers in Londonderry in 1972.

FEBRUARY 1998

9. A Roman Catholic man was shot dead in Belfast by republican gunmen acting under the name

Direct Action Against Drugs. **10.** A member of the UDA was shot dead in south Belfast. **17.** Sinn Fein sought a temporary injunction at the High Court in Dublin to suspend proceedings to expel it from the multi-party talks as a result of the murders in Belfast in the preceding week; the talks were adjourned until 23 February. **18.** A Roman Catholic man was shot dead in Aghalee, Co. Antrim. **20.** Sinn Fein delegates were suspended from the multi-party talks for two weeks; Mo Mowlam said that any further IRA activity would lead to Sinn Fein's permanent exclusion. About eight people were injured when a 500 lb car bomb exploded outside a police station in Moira, Co. Down. **23.** A 300 lb bomb exploded in Portadown, Co. Armagh. The UDP were re-admitted to the multi-party talks.

MARCH 1998

3. Two men, one a Protestant and one a Roman Catholic, were shot dead in a bar in Poyntzpass, Co. Armagh. **9.** The Government halted the extradition to Germany of Roisin McAliskey on the grounds of her ill health; she was wanted in connection with an IRA bomb attack on a British army base at Osnabrück in June 1996. **10.** A mortar attack was launched on the RUC station in Armagh. **15.** David Keys, one of four men charged in connection with the Poyntzpass murders on 3 March, was found murdered at the Maze prison. **24.** Four mortar bombs were fired at the RUC base in Forkhill, South Armagh. **27.** A former RUC officer was shot dead by the INLA in Armagh.

APRIL 1998

1. The Irish Taoiseach, Bertie Ahern, said before talks with Tony Blair at Downing Street that there were 'large disagreements' between the two governments over the powers of proposed cross-border bodies. **2.** A 980 lb bomb was seized by police at Dun Laoghaire, near Dublin, from a car being driven onto a ferry bound for Anglesey. **6.** The chairman of the Northern Ireland cross-party talks, Sen. George Mitchell, issued a draft document outlining proposals for a peace settlement. **7.** The Ulster Unionists rejected the draft agreement; Tony Blair flew to Belfast to further attempts to reach a settlement. **8.** A man with links to the LVF was shot dead by the INLA in Londonderry. **10.** The British and Irish governments and the Northern Ireland politicians involved in the cross-party talks signed an agreement on achieving a political settlement in Northern Ireland. The main points of the agreement, to be put to the people of the Republic of Ireland and Northern Ireland in a referendum, were:
– a Northern Ireland assembly of 108 members, six elected by proportional representation from each existing parliamentary constituency
– a 12-member executive drawn from the assembly's membership and headed by a First Minister and a Deputy First Minister
– a North-South ministerial council, established by the assembly within a year, to direct co-operation

between Northern Ireland and the Republic of Ireland on a range of issues
– the Republic of Ireland to give up its constitutional claim to Northern Ireland and Britain to repeal the Government of Ireland Act 1920
– a British-Irish Council, with members drawn from the British and Irish governments and the assemblies in Scotland, Wales and Northern Ireland
– a smaller British police and army presence in Northern Ireland, and the removal of security installations as early as possible
– a commitment by all participants to the decommissioning of weapons and to working with an independent international commission on decommissioning, with the aim of achieving decommissioning of all paramilitary weapons within two years
– paramilitary prisoners to be released within two or three years, as long as their organization maintains the cease-fire
– an independent commission on the future of policing in Northern Ireland, to report no later than summer 1999
– human rights commissions in Northern Ireland and the Republic of Ireland
14. The Irish government released nine IRA prisoners from Portlaoise prison, near Dublin, as a 'confidence-building measure'. **17.** A Roman Catholic taxi driver was shot dead in west Belfast in what was believed to be a feud within the INLA. **21.** A Roman Catholic man was shot dead in Portadown, Co. Armagh. **25.** A Roman Catholic man was shot dead in Crumlin, Co. Antrim. **30.** The IRA said that it would not decommission any arms. A 700 lb car bomb was defused in Lisburn, Co. Antrim.

MAY 1998

1. A man believed to be a republican dissident was shot dead and five men were arrested during an attempted raid on a security van near Ashford, Co. Wicklow. **10.** At its conference in Dublin, Sinn Fein delegates voted in favour of the Belfast Agreement and supported changing the party's constitution in order to allow its members take seats in a Northern Ireland assembly; 27 IRA prisoners were allowed to leave prison temporarily in order to attend the conference. **13.** Sir Kenneth Bloomfield, the former head of the Northern Ireland Civil Service, published a report, *We Will Remember Them*, about the treatment of people bereaved or injured during the Troubles. **14.** The Prime Minister visited Northern Ireland and said that four tests would be written into forthcoming legislation to ascertain whether parties with paramilitary links had genuinely renounced violence; any party failing the tests would not be entitled to early release of prisoners or places on the proposed power-sharing executive. The loyalist terrorist Michael Stone was temporarily released from prison and attended a UDP rally in Belfast in support of the peace agreement. **15.** The LVF declared an unequivocal cease-fire. **19.** The pop group U2 gave a concert in Belfast in support of the Belfast Agreement. **20.** On a visit to Belfast, the Prime Minister drew up a handwritten pledge to the people of Northern Ireland, to encourage Unionists to support the Belfast Agreement. **22.** Referendums on the Belfast Agreement were held in Northern Ireland and the Republic of Ireland; voters in the Republic were also asked if they supported a change in the country's constitution to give up its claim to Northern Ireland. In Northern Ireland, the turn-out was about 81 per cent, of which 71.12 per cent voted in favour of the agreement. In the Republic of Ireland, the turn-out was about 55 per cent, of which 94.4 per cent voted in favour of both the agreement and the change to the constitution. **30.** Rioting broke out in Portadown, Co. Armagh, in protest at a junior Orange Order march.

JUNE 1998

24. A 200 lb car bomb believed to have been planted by republicans exploded in the centre of New-townhamilton, Co. Armagh, injuring a 13-year-old boy and causing widespread damage. **25.** Elections were held to the new Northern Ireland Assembly under a system of proportional representation; the SDLP received 22 per cent of first preference votes, the UUP 21.3 per cent, the DUP 18.1 per cent and Sinn Fein 17.6 per cent. The final distribution of seats in the Assembly was: UUP 28, SDLP 24, DUP 20, Sinn Fein 18, Alliance Party 6, UK Unionist Party 5, Progressive Unionist Party 2, Northern Ireland Women's Coalition 2, others 3. **29.** Lord Alderdice resigned as leader of the Alliance Party and was appointed interim Presiding Officer (Speaker) of the Northern Ireland Assembly.

JULY 1998

1. Members of the Northern Ireland Assembly met for the first time at Stormont; David Trimble was elected First Minister and Seamus Mallon was elected Deputy First Minister. **2.** Ten Roman Catholic churches in Northern Ireland were badly damaged in arson attacks believed to have been instigated by the LVF. **5.** Members of the Orange Order were barred by security forces from marching along the Garvaghy Road in Drumcree, Co. Armagh; the marchers had been refused permission to pass down the road by the Parades Commission. A stand-off ensued and violence broke out in loyalist areas of Northern Ireland. **6–9.** Violent protests continued in many areas of Northern Ireland and sectarian attacks were carried out on Roman Catholic properties. On 9 July the Prime Minister met four Orangemen, but the stand-off continued and there were clashes overnight between members of the security forces and loyalists attempting to breach the barricades barring them from the Garvaghy Road. **10.** Three men believed to belong to republican splinter groups were arrested in central London and several explosive devices were made safe after a surveillance operation by MI5 and anti-terrorist police. **12.** Three young brothers whose

mother was a Roman Catholic were burned to death in a sectarian arson attack on their home in Ballymoney, Co. Antrim. The stand-off at Drumcree continued, although some Orangemen called for it to be abandoned. By late July few marchers remained at the site.

AUGUST 1998

1. A car bomb believed to have been planted by republican dissidents exploded in the centre of Banbridge, Co. Down. **6.** Thomas McMahon, who planted the IRA bomb that killed Lord Mountbatten and three other people in 1979, was released from Mountjoy prison under the terms of the Belfast Agreement. **8.** The LVF said that it had given up its campaign of violence for good. **15.** Twenty-eight people were killed and more than 200 injured when a car bomb exploded in the centre of Omagh, Co. Tyrone. On 18 August the dissident republican group the Real IRA claimed responsibility for the bombing but said that it had not intended to kill civilians; it said that its campaign of violence had been suspended. **22.** The INLA announced a cease-fire. **25.** The Prime Minister visited Omagh, and announced that Parliament would be recalled to debate new anti-terrorism measures.

ACCIDENTS AND DISASTERS

SEPTEMBER 1997

3. Sixty-five people were killed when a jet crashed outside Phnom Penh airport. **8.** More than 500 people were reported to have drowned when a ferry sank off the coast of Haiti. **19.** Six people were killed and more than 160 injured when an InterCity 125 Swansea–London train crashed into a freight train in Southall, west London; a seventh person died on 25 September. **26.** All 234 people on board were killed when an airliner crashed in smog near Medan, Sumatra. At least ten people were killed, hundreds were left homeless, and the Basilica of St Francis was badly damaged when an earthquake registering 5.5 on the Richter scale hit Assisi, Italy. **27.** At least 30 people were feared drowned when two cargo vessels collided in smog in the Straits of Malacca.

OCTOBER 1997

1. Four fishermen were missing presumed drowned after their boat sank in rough seas off north-east Scotland. **4.** All passengers and crew were rescued after fire broke out on the Cypriot-owned *Romantica* cruise ship off Cyprus. **9.** At least 400 people died when Hurricane Pauline hit the Pacific coast of Mexico. **October–December.** At least 1,500 people died when torrential rain caused flooding in Somalia.

NOVEMBER 1997

4. At least 265 people were killed and up to 2,800 were missing after Typhoon Linda hit the southern coast of Vietnam. **5.** Eight people were injured when a Virgin Atlantic Airbus was forced to crash-land at Heathrow after its undercarriage jammed. **6.** At least 31 people drowned when violent storms hit western Spain and southern Portugal. **18.** Thirty children were killed and 67 were injured when a school bus crashed off a bridge in Delhi, India. **19.** A helicopter winchman drowned off Shetland after rescuing ten crew from a wrecked cargo ship in 70-m.p.h. gales.

DECEMBER 1997

6. At least 66 people were killed when a military cargo plane crashed into a block of flats in Irkutsk, Siberia. **12.** More than 300 flights were cancelled when fire broke out in Terminal One at Heathrow airport. **15.** Eighty-five people were killed when a plane crashed on its approach to Sharjah airport, UAE. **17.** Up to 70 people were feared dead when a Ukrainian plane crashed as it approached Salonika, Greece. **19.** A Boeing 737 crashed on the island of Sumatra, Indonesia, killing 104 people.

JANUARY 1998

10. At least 50 people were killed and 10,000 injured when an earthquake registering 6.2 on the Richter scale hit northern China.

FEBRUARY 1998

2. All 104 people on board a DC9 plane were feared dead after it crashed into a mountain in the Philippines. **3.** Twenty people were killed when an American military aircraft sliced through the wire supporting a cable car at a ski resort near Cavalese in the Dolomites, Italy. **4.** At least 4,000 people were killed when an earthquake registering 6.1 on the Richter scale hit north-east Afghanistan; a further 250 people died in an aftershock on 8 February. **14.** About 100 people were killed when two trains carrying oil were derailed in Yaoundé, Cameroon. **16.** A Taiwanese airliner crashed at Taipei airport, killing all 197 people on board and seven people on the ground. **23.** At least 38 people were killed and hundreds of homes destroyed when dozens of tornadoes hit central Florida, USA.

MARCH 1998

18. Sixty-two passengers and crew were evacuated safely after the nose wheel of an aircraft collapsed on landing at Manchester airport. **21.** At least 13 people were killed when tornadoes hit the southern USA. **31.** A light aircraft carrying the Leeds United football team crash-landed at Stansted airport after an engine caught fire on take-off; there were no serious injuries.

APRIL 1998

5. Sixty-three people died in a mining accident near Donetsk, Ukraine. **9.** At least 118 Muslims were killed in a stampede near Mena, Saudi Arabia. At least 38 people were killed when a tornado hit central Alabama, USA. **21.** Fifty-three people were

killed when a Boeing 727 crashed after taking off from Bogotá, Colombia.

MAY 1998

6. At least 135 people died and more than 100 were missing after heavy rain caused severe flooding and mud slides in the hills around Naples, southern Italy. **22.** A series of earthquakes registering up to 6.8 on the Richter scale hit central Bolivia, killing at least 60 people. **22–26.** At least 111 people died in a heatwave in India. **31.** At least 4,000 people were killed when an earthquake registering 7.1 on the Richter scale hit north-east Afghanistan.

JUNE 1998

3. At least 96 people were killed when a high-speed train was derailed and crashed into a road bridge in Eschede, Germany. **14.** Five Scottish fishermen were drowned when their trawler, the *Silvery Sea,* was struck by a German coaster in the North Sea. **27.** At least 119 people were killed when an earthquake registering 6.3 on the Richter scale hit southern Turkey.

JULY 1998

16. Floods caused by heavy summer rains were reported to have killed 760 people in southern China. **17.** An earthquake registering 7.1 on the Richter scale hit the northern coast of Papua New Guinea, causing a tidal wave that swept away whole villages and killed at least 1,600 people. **27.** The Mayor of Southampton, Michael Andrews, and another man were killed when a 1940s flying boat crashed into the Solent; 16 people were rescued.

AUGUST 1998

18. At least 178 people were killed when a landslide destroyed the village of Malpa in Uttar Pradesh, northern India. **27.** The government of Bangladesh appealed for international help to cope with flooding that had killed at least 390 people since early July and left 25 million people homeless. **29.** At least 82 people were killed when a Cuban aircraft crashed during take-off at Quito airport, Ecuador.

ARTS, SCIENCE AND THE MEDIA

SEPTEMBER 1997

1. After receiving an ultimatum from the Scottish Arts Council, the board of Scottish Ballet agreed to stand down in order to secure funding for the company for the following season. **16.** The BBC announced plans to merge its television and radio news operations; after strong protests from senior journalists and editors, a compromise plan was agreed. **18.** A portrait of the child murderer Myra Hindley, part of an exhibition of work by young British artists at the Royal Academy, was damaged when protesters threw paint and eggs at it. The Academy's exhibitions secretary had defended the portrait and the exhibition, saying that 'there is no such thing as art that is immoral'. 25. A British team led by Richard Noble set a new world land speed record of 714.144 m.p.h. in a ThrustSSC car driven by Andy Green in the Black Rock Desert, Nevada. The chairman of the Press Complaints Commission (Lord Wakeham) put forward proposals for a revised code of practice for newspapers to protect the privacy of individuals, particularly children, and preventing intrusive photography. The new code was published on 18 December and came into force on 1 January 1998. 29. Gary Hume won the Jerwood prize for painting.

OCTOBER 1997

6. The British-born astronaut Michael Foale returned to earth after 4½ months aboard the space station *Mir*. 8. Astronomers at the University of California, Los Angeles, said that the Hubble telescope had revealed the Pistol Star, a star in the Milky Way ten million times brighter than the Sun. 13. Andy Green became the first person to break the sound barrier on land when he drove at 764.168 m.p.h. in ThrustSSC in the Black Rock Desert; he failed, however, to set a new world land-speed record because he did not complete a second run within an hour of the first. On the 15th Andy Green set a new world land-speed record of 763.035 m.p.h., the first supersonic record, in ThrustSSC. 15. A rocket was launched from Cape Canaveral, Florida, carrying the Cassini-Huygens space probe on a seven-year mission to explore Saturn. 21. Elton John's single *Candle in the Wind 1997* was named the best-selling record ever, having sold 31.8 million copies since the funeral of Diana, Princess of Wales. 22. At the British Fashion Awards, John Galliano and Alexander McQueen shared the award for Designer of the Year. 25. The British Library Reading Room at the British Museum closed. 30. The chief executive of the Royal Opera House (Mary Allen) told a House of Commons select committee that the theatre was facing a financial crisis. A special parliamentary commission ruled that Glasgow City Council could lend some of the Burrell Collection's works to overseas galleries in spite of the fact that this had been expressly forbidden in Sir William Burrell's bequest.

NOVEMBER 1997

3. The Secretary of State for Culture, Media and Sport (Chris Smith) said that London could not afford two opera houses and proposed that English National Opera should move out of the London Coliseum and share the Royal Opera House with the Royal Opera and the Royal Ballet. National Libraries Week began. 4. The Broadcasting Standards Commission warned that children's television was becoming dominated by cartoons. 5. The chairman of the Royal Opera House (Lord Chadlington) announced that a private-sector rescue package had saved the theatre from bankruptcy. 10. Archaeologists announced that they had discovered a huge neolithic temple at Stanton Drew, near Bristol. 17. The Royal Shakespeare Company announced a trading loss of £1.8 million for 1996–7. 19. The first

septuplets to be delivered alive were born in Iowa, USA. 24. The Humanities Reading Room at the new British Library at St Pancras opened. The Broadcasting Standards Commission published a new code of practice, to take effect from 1 January 1998, including the guideline that an individual's privacy should be infringed only when there is an overriding public interest in disclosure of the information.

DECEMBER 1997

2. The video artist Gillian Wearing won the Turner Prize for modern art. 3. A report calling for the resignation of the board and the chief executive of the Royal Opera House was published by a House of Commons select committee; Chris Smith said in response that substantial changes were necessary in the management of the theatre but that precipitate change could worsen the crisis. On 4 December Lord Chadlington resigned as chairman of the board; the other members of the board offered to resign but agreed to stay until a new board could be appointed. The chief executive offered her resignation but it was refused. 8. The DJ Chris Evans bought Virgin Radio.

JANUARY 1998

15. Sir Colin Southgate was appointed chairman of the Royal Opera House. 17. *The Times* began to publish extracts from *Birthday Letters,* a book of poems by the poet laureate Ted Hughes about his relationship with his wife, Sylvia Plath, who committed suicide in 1963. 20. The BBC, the ITC, the Radio Authority and S4C proposed that party political broadcasts be allowed only at election times.

FEBRUARY 1998

1. A £1 million trust fund to encourage new playwrights was launched by a theatre-loving multi-millionaire, Peter Wolff. 2. The director of the Royal Opera, Nicholas Payne, was appointed general director of English National Opera. 4. The Lord Chancellor (Lord Irvine of Lairg) proposed that the Press Complaints Commission should use the principle of 'prior restraint' in regulating press reporting of people's private lives; the idea was widely opposed. 5. At the British Book Awards, *Bridget Jones's Diary* by Helen Fielding was named Book of the Year. The Hallé Orchestra was saved from immediate bankruptcy by reaching a deal with its endowment appeal fund. 9. In a vote on the Competition Bill in the House of Lords, peers supported an amendment to prevent national newspapers from running price-cutting campaigns in order to eliminate rivals. At the Brit Awards in London, All Saints won the award for best single for *Never Ever* and The Verve were named best British group. 15. A third symphony by Elgar, completed from the composer's sketches by Anthony Payne, was premièred at the Royal Festival Hall, London. 15–19. A 65 ft sculpture by Antony Gormley, *The Angel of the North,* was erected at Gateshead. 20–27. An auction of 40,000 items belonging to the late

Duke and Duchess of Windsor raised £14.5 million at Sotheby's in New York. **28.** Senior authors threatened to leave HarperCollins, the publishing company owned by Rupert Murdoch's News Corporation, after it cancelled plans, on the instructions of Mr Murdoch, to publish a book by the former governor of Hong Kong, Chris Patten, which criticised China. On 6 March HarperCollins apologized to Mr Patten for having suggested that the book had been rejected because it was not up to standard.

MARCH 1998

5. Nasa announced that a space probe had found large amounts of frozen water on the moon. **11.** The Irish businessman Tony O'Reilly bought out the Mirror Group in order to take full ownership of the *Independent* and the *Independent on Sunday*. **19.** The 22-member board of the Arts Council resigned at the request of the new secretary-general, Gerry Robinson; it was later replaced by a new ten-member board. **24.** At the Academy Awards ceremony in Los Angeles, *Titanic* won 11 Oscars, including best picture and best director. **25.** The chief executive of the Royal Opera House, Mary Allen, resigned. **29.** The percussionist Adrian Spillett was named BBC Young Musician of the Year.

APRIL 1998

20. Richard Jarman, the former general director of Scottish Opera, was appointed caretaker artistic director of the Royal Opera House. **27.** Scientists in Scotland said that they had isolated a gene believed to play an important role in the susceptibility of smokers to lung cancer. **28.** The British explorer David Hempleman-Adams reached the geographic North Pole, becoming the first person to complete the adventurers' grand slam of 11 mountaineering and polar exploration tasks.

MAY 1998

12. The European Parliament approved the controversial Life Patents Directive, allowing the patenting of biotechnological inventions. **13.** The chairman of the Press Complaints Commission (Lord Wakeham) warned newspapers not to incite violence or xenophobia in their coverage of the football world cup in summer 1998. **19.** English Heritage published the first national register of listed buildings at risk. **20.** All the members of the Arts Council's drama advisory panel resigned in protest at a reorganization of the Council's operations under its new chairman Gerry Robinson. **28.** Nasa announced that the Hubble telescope had photographed TMR-1C, the first planet ever to be seen outside the solar system. **31.** Geri Halliwell, known as 'Ginger Spice', announced that she had left the pop group the Spice Girls.

JUNE 1998

3. English Heritage published the first national survey of monuments at risk. **6.** Dame Ninette de Valois, the founder of the Royal Ballet, celebrated her 100th birthday. **17.** The Culture Secretary announced that ten people, including the sculptor Antony Gormley and the ballerina Deborah Bull, had been appointed to the newly-constituted Arts Council of England. **24.** Thomas Watson won the 1998 National Portrait Gallery BP Portrait Award. **25.** The Queen formally opened the new British Library at St Pancras, London. **30.** A report on the Royal Opera House by Sir Richard Eyre, which had been commissioned by the Culture Secretary, was published; it condemned the House for arrogance and presumption in its handling of public funds, but said that its funding should be increased and its management reformed.

JULY 1998

1. A museum dedicated to the life of Diana, Princess of Wales, opened at Althorp. *Water-lily Pond and Path by the Water* by Claude Monet was sold at Sotheby's in London for £19.8 million, a world record price for a painting by the artist. **2.** The Old Vic theatre was sold to the newly-formed Old Vic Theatre Trust for £3.5 million. **8.** A first edition of Chaucer's *Canterbury Tales* was sold at Christie's in London for £4.6 million, a record price for a printed book. Tina Brown resigned as editor of the *New Yorker*. **9.** Statues of ten Christian martyrs of the 20th century were unveiled at Westminster Abbey. **24.** The Government guaranteed free entry to national museums and galleries by 2001.

AUGUST 1998

12. The New Oxford Dictionary of English was published. **30.** Sir Simon Rattle conducted his last concert as director of the City of Birmingham Symphony Orchestra.

CRIMES AND LEGAL AFFAIRS

SEPTEMBER 1997

6. Eighteen-year-old Rachel Barraclough was found stabbed to death in Wakefield, W. Yorks. **9.** Sixteen-year-old Nathan Brown was ordered to be detained at Her Majesty's pleasure for murdering 14-year-old Carl Rickard with a machete outside a school in London in January 1997. **10.** Dennis Leckey, a senior education welfare officer, was sentenced at Manchester Crown Court to 18 years' imprisonment for sexually abusing boys in his care over a period of more than 20 years. **23.** A British nurse, Lucille McLauchlan, was sentenced in Saudi Arabia to 500 lashes and eight years' imprisonment for being an accessory to the murder of a colleague in December 1996. On 16 November the victim's brother officially accepted a cash settlement to spare the life of a second British nurse, Deborah Parry, if she were convicted of the murder.

OCTOBER 1997

2. A coroner called for an urgent review of the use by police of CS gas after an inquest jury returned a verdict of unlawful killing on a man who died in police custody in May 1996 after being sprayed with the gas. **6.** The High Court ruled that the result of the parliamentary election in Winchester on 1 May 1997, which was won by the Liberal Democrats by two votes, was void because 55 unstamped ballot papers which had been rejected could have changed the result. Two people were killed when their car was rammed from behind and crashed into oncoming traffic in Hanworth, London; Jason Humble was convicted of manslaughter and sentenced to 12 years' imprisonment on 2 April 1998. The Lord Chancellor announced plans to reform the civil justice system and to abolish legal aid in most civil cases (*see* page 1168). **22.** Duncan Bermingham was sentenced in Manchester to life imprisonment for murdering 21-year-old Rachel Thacker in August 1996. **23.** Heather Hallett was elected the first woman chairman of the Bar Council from January 1998. **24.** A woman police officer, Nina Mackay, was stabbed to death in Stratford, London. The Government published a White Paper proposing to incorporate the European Convention on Human Rights into British law (*see* page 1168). The Provincial Court of the Church in Wales found a rector, Clifford Williams, guilty of having had a six-year adulterous affair with a parishioner. **27.** Terence Storey was sentenced in Preston to life imprisonment for the murder of Revd Christopher Gray in Liverpool in August 1996. John Barr, the butcher who supplied meat linked to the outbreak of E. coli-0157 food poisoning in which 20 people died in Scotland in 1996–7, was cleared in Hamilton of recklessly supplying cooked meat for a birthday party in November 1996. **31.** A British au pair, Louise Woodward, was sentenced in Cambridge, Massachusetts, to life imprisonment for the murder of Matthew Eappen, an eight-month-old baby in her care, in February 1996. On 4 November the judge heard applications from her defence lawyers that the verdict be overturned or the conviction be reduced to manslaughter. On 10 November the judge reduced the conviction to manslaughter and sentenced her to 279 days' imprisonment; since she had already served this time on remand she was released immediately.

NOVEMBER 1997

3. Mohan Singh Kular was sentenced in Bristol to life imprisonment for the murder of his wife in the Punjab, India, in 1987. **5.** Six Iraqi men were sentenced at the Central Criminal Court to terms of up to nine years' imprisonment for hijacking a passenger jet to seek asylum in Britain in August 1996. **10.** Stephen Leisk was sentenced in Aberdeen to life imprisonment for the abduction and murder of nine-year-old Scott Simpson. **12.** A court in Brazil ruled that Ronnie Biggs, who escaped from Wandsworth prison in 1965, 15 months into a 30-year sentence for his part in the Great Train Robbery of 1963, would not be extradited to Britain to serve the remainder of his sentence. **14.** Alvin

Black was sentenced at the Central Criminal Court to life imprisonment for the murder of Johanna Czardebon, a German tourist, in Bedford in May 1996. **15.** Fourteen-year-old Kate Bushell was found stabbed to death near her home in Exeter. Small incendiary devices believed to have been planted by the self-styled 'Mardi Gra' blackmailer exploded outside two Sainsbury's stores in west London. **19.** Peter Smith was sentenced in Manchester to life imprisonment for torturing and murdering his girlfriend, Kelly-Anne Bates, in April 1997. **27.** The Government published a White Paper proposing reforms to the youth justice system (*see* page 1168).

DECEMBER 1997

1. Detective Superintendent Raymond Mallon, the head of Middlesbrough CID and the leading exponent in Britain of 'zero tolerance' policing, was suspended over allegations that he had leaked confidential information and may have been involved in criminal activity. **2.** Derek Christian was sentenced in Leeds to life imprisonment for murdering Margaret Wilson in Burton Fleming, E. Yorks, in 1995. **3.** Andrew Evans, who was sentenced in 1972 to life imprisonment for the murder of 14-year-old Judith Roberts, was released from prison after the Court of Appeal quashed the conviction. **5.** John O'Shaughnessy was sentenced in Mold to life imprisonment for the rape and murder of nine-year-old Kayleigh Ward in December 1996. Squadron Leader Nicholas Tucker was sentenced in Norwich to life imprisonment for murdering his wife in 1995 after becoming infatuated with a Serbian interpreter while serving in Bosnia. A three-hour-old baby, Karli Hawthorne, was stolen from the maternity ward at Basildon General Hospital, Essex; she was found at an address in Basildon 14 hours later and a woman was charged with the kidnap. Barry Horne, an animal rights activist, was sentenced in Bristol to 18 years' imprisonment for carrying out arson attacks on shops in the south of England in 1994–6. **15.** Robert and Marius Maczka were sentenced in London to life imprisonment for murdering an elderly Polish couple, Josef and Kornela Ploch, in Fulham in June 1996. **16.** Brian McHugh, Patrick Kelly and James Murphy were sentenced at the Central Criminal Court to 25, 20 and 17 years' imprisonment respectively for plotting IRA bombing campaigns in mainland Britain. **17.** The Labour MP for Glasgow Govan, Mohammed Sarwar, appeared in court charged with fraud relating to his victory in the general election in May 1997. **22.** The 17-year-old son of the Home Secretary (Jack Straw) was arrested and questioned over allegations that he had sold cannabis to an undercover reporter from the *Mirror*; he was later cautioned.

JANUARY 1998

6. A murder charge against the former husband of Carol Park, who went missing in 1976 and whose body was found in Coniston Water in August 1997, was dropped because of lack of evidence. **14.** The former England football coach Terry Venables was banned for seven years by the DTI from holding company directorships after he was found to have acted dishonestly and failed to keep proper accounts. **15.** An unarmed man was shot dead by police at his home in Hastings, E. Sussex, during an investigation into drug trafficking and attempted murder. **16.** The Revd Michael Golightly was sentenced in Newcastle to five years' imprisonment for hitting his wife with a hammer in an apparently motiveless attack. **19.** George Lewis, who spent five years in prison after being framed by members of the former West Midlands serious crime squad for robberies he did not commit, was awarded £200,000 compensation in the High Court. **20.** Michael Steele and Jack Whomes were sentenced at the Central Criminal Court to life imprisonment for murdering three men in Rettendon, Essex, in 1995; all five men had been drug dealers. John M. Barr and Son, the butcher's shop implicated in the outbreak of E. coli-0157 food poisoning which killed 20 people in Scotland in 1996–7, was fined £2,250 for breaching food hygiene and safety laws. **22.** A woman and her four children died in a suspected arson attack at their home in Braunstone, Leicester. **23.** The High Court allowed compensation claims from six miners after ruling that British Coal had failed to take reasonable steps to minimize the harmful effects of coal dust, particularly in 1949–70. **27.** Detectives raided the homes of 19 serving or former CID officers as part of a major anti-corruption operation; 12 officers were suspended from duty. **29.** Victor Farrant was sentenced in Winchester to life imprisonment for the murder of Glenda Hoskins, an accountant, in 1996, and the attempted murder of Ann Fidler, a prostitute, in 1995.

FEBRUARY 1998

2. The American businessman Guy Snowden resigned from the board of the National Lottery operator Camelot after losing a High Court action against Richard Branson, who had alleged that he had been offered a bribe to abandon his bid for the franchise in 1993; Mr Snowden was ordered to pay £100,000 libel damages to Mr Branson. **3.** Carla Faye Tucker, who murdered two people in 1983, became the first woman to be executed in Texas, USA, since the Civil War. **5.** Sheila Bowler, who spent more than four years in prison after being convicted of the murder of her elderly aunt near Rye in 1992, was cleared of murder after a retrial at the Central Criminal Court. Two ten-year-old boys and an 11-year-old were cleared at the Central Criminal Court of raping a nine-year-old girl at their school in west London in 1997. **9.** David Frost was sentenced in Bristol to life imprisonment for the rape and murder of Louise Smith in 1995. **12.** Fr John Lloyd, a Roman Catholic priest, was convicted in Cardiff of indecently assaulting a 13-year-old girl in the mid 1970s; he was later sentenced to 21

months' imprisonment. **13.** A High Court judge, Mr Justice Harman, resigned after the Court of Appeal criticized him for an 'intolerable' delay of 20 months in delivering a judgment. **24.** The conviction of Mahmood Hussein Mattan, who was hanged in 1952 in Cardiff for the murder of Lily Volpert, a shopkeeper, was quashed by the Court of Appeal. Michael Gallagher, an IRA 'sleeper', was sentenced at Woolwich Crown Court to 20 years' imprisonment for conspiring to cause explosions on the mainland. **26.** Paul Longworth was sentenced in Liverpool to life imprisonment for murdering his wife Tina in January 1997 and attempting to make it look like suicide. The racehorse trainer Lynda Ramsden, her husband Jack and the champion jockey Kieren Fallon, were awarded £195,000 damages in the High Court over allegations in the *Sporting Life* that they had conspired to cheat the racing public. **27.** The Northern Ireland Court of Appeal quashed the conviction of Lee Clegg, the paratrooper who served two years of a life sentence for murdering Karen Reilly in Belfast in 1990; a retrial was ordered. Tony Neary, the former England rugby union player, was sentenced in Liverpool to five years' imprisonment for stealing £288,000 in the early 1990s.

MARCH 1998

2. Grant Harris, a consultant gynaecologist, was sentenced at the Central Criminal Court to six years' imprisonment for murdering his wife in June 1997 after she had begun divorce proceedings. **5.** A student was injured when a small incendiary device believed to have been planted by the self-styled 'Mardi Gra' blackmailer exploded near a Sainsbury's store in Forest Hill, London. **9.** Peter Humphrey was sentenced in Exeter to 12 years' imprisonment for arranging an acid attack on his estranged wife in July 1996; a babysitter at his home was badly injured instead of his wife. **19.** The conviction of John Roberts for the murder of a farmer in 1982, based solely on his confession, was quashed by the Court of Appeal on the basis of new psychiatric evidence. **24.** In a landmark civil ruling, a High Court judge ruled that Tony Diedrick, against whom no criminal charges had been brought, had murdered a doctor, Joan Francisco, in London in 1994. Four children and a teacher were shot dead when two boys opened fire at their school in Jonesboro, Arkansas. **28.** A Fulham football fan died from head injuries sustained in fighting after a match at Gillingham, Kent. **30.** The pop star Gary Glitter was charged with holding indecent images of children on his home computer.

APRIL 1998

2. Miles Evans was sentenced in Bristol to life imprisonment for the murder of his stepdaughter Zoe in January 1997. Maurice Papon was sentenced in Bordeaux to ten years' imprisonment for crimes against humanity in relation to his role in deporting Jews from the German-occupied city between 1942 and 1944. **3.** Anthony-Noel Kelly, an artist, was sentenced in London to nine months' imprisonment for stealing body parts from the Royal College of Surgeons to cast sculptures; the sentence was reduced to three months on appeal. **6.** Jong Rhee was sentenced in Chester to life imprisonment for murdering his wife Natalie by burning down the guesthouse in which they were staying in April 1997, in order to claim on insurance policies. **7.** Nicholas Burton was sentenced in Liverpool to life imprisonment for the murder of Rachel McGrath in Manchester in April 1997. **8.** The body of Kirsty Carver, a police computer operator who went missing on 5 March 1998, was found at Spurn Point, E. Yorks; on 9 April a man was charged with her murder. Patricia Bass, who was twice convicted of the murder of her mother in 1992, was released after the Court of Appeal quashed her conviction for a second time. **9.** A taxi driver who was beaten up by policemen in Liverpool in 1989 was awarded record damages of nearly £450,000 against Merseyside Police. **17.** Magdi Elgizouli, a paranoid schizophrenic, was ordered at the Central Criminal Court to be sent to a mental hospital indefinitely after he admitted murdering WPC Nina Mackay in London in October 1997. **30.** Eric Taylor, a Roman Catholic priest, was sentenced in Warwick to seven years' imprisonment for sexually abusing boys in his care in the 1950s and 1960s.

MAY 1998

4. The newly-appointed head of the Swiss Guards, Col. Alois Estermann, and his wife were shot dead in the Vatican City by another member of the Guards, who then shot himself. Theodore Kaczynski, known as the 'Unabomber', was sentenced in Sacramento, USA, to four terms of life imprisonment for an 18-year bombing campaign in which three people were killed and 29 injured. **5.** The pop star Gary Glitter was charged on five counts of indecently assaulting two young girls in the 1970s and 1980s. **7.** A nurse, Vicky Fletcher, was shot dead outside a pub in Castleford, W. Yorks; her lover, Dr Thomas Shanks, was charged with the murder. The Court of Appeal ruled that social workers and doctors had acted unlawfully in sectioning a woman under the Mental Health Act and performing a Caesarean section on her against her will, even though her life and that of the unborn baby were in danger. James Fraser Darling, a British teacher, was sentenced in Phuket, Thailand, to 33 years' imprisonment for indecent assaults on young boys. **14.** A woman, her two children and a 16-year-old babysitter were killed when an arsonist set fire to a house in Newcastle upon Tyne. **15.** Thomas 'Slab' Murphy lost a libel action in the High Court in Dublin against the *Sunday Times*, which had published an article in 1985 naming him as an IRA leader. **18.** The US Attorney-General (Janet Reno) launched an anti-trust lawsuit against Microsoft, alleging that the company's chairman, Bill Gates, had participated in an illegal conspiracy to eliminate competition from the

Internet browser market. **19.** King Fahd of Saudi Arabia commuted the sentences of Lucille McLauchlan and Deborah Parry, two British nurses imprisoned in 1996 over the murder of an Australian nurse, Yvonne Gilford. The nurses arrived in Britain on 21 May and said that they were not guilty of the murder and had been coerced into signing confessions. **20.** Two Van Goghs and a Cézanne were stolen from the Museum of Modern Art in Rome; they were recovered on 6 July and eight people were arrested. **21.** A 15-year-old boy who had been expelled from school in Oregon, USA, shot his parents dead and then fired indiscriminately at people in the school, killing one pupil and seriously injuring eight others.

JUNE 1998

A report critical of the efficiency and effectiveness of the Crown Prosecution Service (CPS) was published; the Government accepted the thrust of its recommendations, including the appointment of 42 Chief Crown Prosecutors and a chief executive to administer the CPS. **9.** PC Andrew Taylor, who sprayed CS gas in the face of an elderly motorist who had parked on double yellow lines, was cleared in Luton of causing actual him bodily harm. **12.** The conviction of Patrick Nicholls, who was sentenced in 1975 to life imprisonment for the murder of 74-year-old Gladys Heath, was quashed by the Court of Appeal. **13.** In Texas, USA, James Byrd, a partially disabled black man, was tied to a van and dragged several miles to his death by three white men allegedly linked to the Ku Klux Klan. **14.** About 50 English football fans were arrested during rioting in Marseilles, France; trouble continued in the city the following day, before and during England's opening world cup match against Tunisia. **16.** The British au pair Louise Woodward, who was sentenced in November 1997 in Cambridge, Massachusetts, to 279 days' imprisonment for the manslaughter of a baby in her care, was given permission to return to Britain after the Massachusetts supreme court upheld both the verdict and the sentence. **17.** An assistant commissioner of the Metropolitan Police, Ian Johnston, publicly apologized to the family of the black teenager Stephen Lawrence, who was murdered in south London in 1993, for the handling of the police investigation into the case. **24.** James McArdle was convicted in London of planting the bomb that exploded in London's Docklands in February 1996; he was sentenced to 25 years' imprisonment. **29.** A public inquiry in London into the handling of the investigation of the murder of Stephen Lawrence was temporarily suspended after 20 members of the militant black group the Nation of Islam stormed the tribunal chamber.

JULY 1998

2. Sion Jenkins was sentenced in Lewes, E. Sussex, to life imprisonment for the murder of his 13-year-old foster daughter Billie-Jo in Hastings in February 1997. **3.** The former champion sprinter Linford Christie won a libel action in the High Court against the journalist John McVicar, who had written an article in a satirical magazine in 1995 in which he said that there was evidence that the athlete may have taken performance-enhancing drugs. **6.** Albert Walker was sentenced in Exeter to life imprisonment for the murder of Roland Platt, whose identity he had stolen in 1991 after leaving Canada to escape charges of theft and money laundering. **20.** Helen Stacey, a registered childminder, was sentenced in Norwich to life imprisonment for shaking to death a five-month-old baby in her care in May 1997. A senior warden at the Masai Mara game reserve in Kenya was charged with the murder of the British tourist Julie Ward in 1988. **24.** Two policemen were killed and a woman tourist was injured when a gunman opened fire in the Congress building in Washington DC, USA. **28.** Ryan James, a veterinary surgeon sentenced to life imprisonment in 1995 for the murder of his wife, was released after the Court of Appeal quashed his conviction because a suicide note written by his wife had been found. **30.** The Court of Appeal quashed the murder conviction of Derek Bentley, a 19-year-old epileptic with a mental age of 11, who was hanged in 1953 for the murder of a policeman in spite of the fact that his accomplice had fired the fatal shot.

August 1998

1. A former MI5 officer, David Shayler, was arrested in Paris; proceedings were instigated to extradite him to face charges under the Official Secrets Act. **29.** Kenneth Noye was arrested in southern Spain and an application was made to extradite him to Britain for questioning about the murder of Stephen Cameron in May 1996.

ECONOMIC AND BUSINESS AFFAIRS

September 1997

5. Transco, the pipeline business of British Gas plc, announced 2,500 redundancies. **18.** Price Waterhouse and Coopers and Lybrand announced plans to merge, creating the largest accountancy practice in the world. **26.** The FT-SE 100 index closed at a record high of 5,226.3 and sterling fell to DM 2.8324 following speculation that the Government was adopting a more positive approach to EMU.

October 1997

1. The American telecommunications group WorldCom made a $30 billion all-stock bid for MCI to rival an earlier bid by BT; on 15 October GTE Corporation offered $28 billion in cash, the largest cash offer ever for a company. On 10 November MCI accepted the bid from WorldCom. The FT-SE 100 index closed at a record high of 5,317.1. **2.** Bill Harrison resigned as chief executive of BZW, the investment arm of Barclays Bank. On 3

October Barclays Bank announced that it would sell the equities and advisory business of BZW; on 12 November it was bought by Crédit Suisse First Boston for £100 million. **10.** Brent Walker agreed to sell the betting chain William Hill to the Japanese investment bank Nomura for £700 million, leaving the company without an on-going business and with a debt of about £500 million; it was reported that the company would be wound up after the sale. **17.** The Chancellor of the Exchequer (Gordon Brown) said that it was extremely unlikely that the UK would join the first wave of EMU in 1999; confusion arose about his stance when an aide, Charlie Whelan, briefed journalists to the effect that the Chancellor would rule out membership of EMU during the lifetime of the current Parliament. On 27 October Gordon Brown said in the House of Commons that the UK would not achieve economic convergence with the rest of Europe, and therefore would not join EMU before the end of the current Parliament, but that there were no constitutional objections to joining and if EMU were successful the Government would want to join early in the next Parliament. Richard Branson launched a new Virgin bank account designed to cover banking, mortgage and loan requirements in one account. **20.** A new automated share dealing system (SETS) was introduced at the London Stock Exchange. **22.** The Hang Seng index in Hong Kong lost 6 per cent of its value. **23.** The Hang Seng index lost a further 10 per cent of its value. The Dow Jones index in New York closed 186.88 points down. The FT-SE 100 index closed 157.3 points down at 4,991.5, the biggest one-day fall for five years. **27.** The Hang Seng index fell a further 5.8 per cent, triggering the biggest-ever one-day fall on Wall Street where the Dow Jones index fell 554.26 points to 7,161.15. Vickers put the Rolls-Royce luxury car business up for sale. **28.** The Hang Seng index fell a further 13.7 per cent. The Dow Jones index closed 337.17 points up at 7,498.32, its largest-ever one-day rise. The FT-SE 100 index closed 85 points down at 4,755.4, having fallen at one stage by 457 points. **29.** The FT-SE 100 index closed 116.4 points up at 4,871.8. **30.** The Hang Seng index fell a further 4 per cent. The Dow Jones index closed 125 points down at 7,381.67. The FT-SE 100 index closed 69.9 points down at 4,801.9.

November 1997

3. The Hang Seng index rose nearly 6 per cent. The Dow Jones index closed 232.31 points up at 7,674.39. The FT-SE 100 index closed 64.1 points up at 4,906.4. **4.** Marks and Spencer announced a £2 billion expansion programme. **5.** Indonesia agreed to implement an IMF rescue package worth up to $43 billion. **6.** The Bank of England raised bank base rates by 0.25 per cent to 7.25 per cent. **7.** The Nikkei-225 index in Tokyo fell more than 4 per cent, causing big falls in the stock markets in Hong Kong, New York and London; the FT-SE 100 index closed 99.5 points down at 4,764.3. **10.** At the CBI conference in London, the Chancellor outlined proposed legislation to pave the way for the introduction of a single European currency. **13.** The Industry Minister (John Battle) said that Rolls-Royce would receive £200 million of state funding in a commercial deal for an aircraft engine development project. **17.** Ann Iverson was ousted as chief executive of Laura Ashley; she was replaced by David Hoare. **18.** The President of the Board of Trade (Margaret Beckett) blocked the planned acquisition by Littlewoods of the home shopping catalogue business Freeman's on the grounds that it would reduce competition in the mail order sector. **19.** Merrill Lynch announced an agreed £3.1 billion cash offer for Mercury Asset Management. **20.** Simon Hughes was ousted as managing director of Mothercare; he was replaced by Greg Tufnell. **23.** Yamaichi Securities, a leading Japanese stockbroking firm, collapsed with debts of $14.6 billion. **25.** The Chancellor delivered a pre-Budget statement in the House of Commons, including the announcement that advance corporation tax would be abolished and corporation tax reduced from April 1999. The Nikkei-225 index in Tokyo closed 854.05 points down at 15,867.53. **30.** South Korea signed an IMF rescue package worth up to $55 billion.

December 1997

2. The Government announced the introduction of individual savings accounts (ISAs) to replace personal equity plans (PEPs) and tax-exempt special savings accounts (TESSAs) from April 1999. **8.** Swiss Bank Corporation and Union Bank of Switzerland announced a merger. **11.** Stock markets in Asia, Europe and the USA fell sharply because of the financial crisis in South Korea. **16.** The Financial Services Authority published a report critical of the management and operations of Prudential Assurance. **22.** The Nikkei-225 index in Tokyo fell 3.4 per cent after the sovereign debts of South Korea, Indonesia and Thailand were downgraded to junk bond status by the international credit rating agency Moody's.

January 1998

1. Ladbroke Group bought the Coral betting shop chain from Bass; on 31 March the sale was referred to the Monopolies and Mergers Commission. **5.** IPC Magazines was sold by Reed Elsevier to a management group backed by the venture capitalist Cinven. **8.** The Indonesian rupiah lost 20 per cent of its value against the dollar. **9.** The Hang Seng index closed 360 points down at 8,894.6; the Nikkei-225, the Dow Jones and the FT-SE 100 indices also suffered heavy falls. **12.** After a meeting with the IMF, President Suharto of Indonesia promised to implement reforms which had been a condition of the rescue package agreed in November 1997. The Hang Seng index closed 773.58 points down at 8,121.06 after Peregrine Investment Holdings, the largest independent stock broker in Hong Kong, went into liquidation. **21.** The Indonesian rupiah lost more than 15 per cent of its value against the

dollar. **22.** The newsagent and newspaper distribution chain John Menzies announced that it would withdraw from retailing and concentrate on distribution. **26.** Compaq Computer Corporation agreed to buy Digital Equipment Corporation for $9.6 billion. **28.** John Prescott said in the House of Commons that a request from London and Continental Railways, the Eurostar operator, for a further £1.2 billion of public money to build the high-speed rail link to the Channel Tunnel had been refused and that the company could not fulfil its obligation to build the link. The FT-SE 100 index closed at a record high of 5,372.6. **30.** The pharmaceutical companies Glaxo-Wellcome and SmithKline Beecham announced plans for a merger; on 23 February the merger talks were broken off.

February 1998

2. The FT-SE 100 index closed at a record high of 5,590.0. **3.** The FT-SE 100 index closed at a record high of 5,612.8; the companies constituting the index were valued at more than £1,000 billion for the first time. Great Universal Stores launched a hostile £1.68 billion bid for the catalogue retailer Argos. **6.** Figures were published showing that the output of the UK's manufacturing industry fell by 0.5 per cent in December 1997, the fifth successive monthly fall. **13.** Lloyds TSB disclosed a 26 per cent rise in pre-tax profits for 1997 to £3.16 billion. **19.** The supermarket groups Kwik Save and Somerfield announced a £1.4 billion merger. **25.** The insurance companies Commercial Union and General Accident announced a £15 billion merger. **27.** The FT-SE 100 index closed at a record high of 5,767.3.

March 1998

4. The National Audit Office published a report stating that Britain's rail leasing companies were sold into the private sector in 1996 for £700 million less than they were worth. **6.** The sale of Great Western Trains to FirstGroup for £140 million was approved by the rail franchise director. The last working tin min in Europe, at South Crofty, Cornwall, closed. **9.** Halifax launched a £780 million take-over bid for the Birmingham Midshires building society. W. H. Smith bought John Menzies for £68 million. Reed Elsevier and Wolters Kluwer abandoned plans to merge. **13.** Sterling closed at $1.6705, its highest level for nine years. **17.** The Chancellor of the Exchequer (Gordon Brown) presented the Budget to the House of Commons. **23.** National Parking Corporation announced an agreed £801 million take-over by Cendant Corporation. The publishing company Random House was bought by the German company Bertelsmann for an estimated £655 million. **30.** Vickers announced that a £340 million bid for Rolls-Royce from BMW had been accepted. The sterling index rose to 108.9, its highest level for ten years.

APRIL 1998

6. The FT-SE 100 index closed at a record high of 6,105.8. Citicorp and Travelers Group announced a $140 billion merger. 7. The Savoy Group agreed to a £520 million take-over by an American consortium led by Blackstone Group. 13. Nationsbank and Bank of America announced a $130 billion merger. 22. Bank of New York launched a hostile $24 billion take-over bid for Mellon Bank. 24. Great Universal Stores won control of the catalogue retailer Argos. 27. The FT-SE 100 index closed 2.4 per cent down at 5,722.4 after heavy falls on Wall Street prompted by rumours of an interest rate rise in the USA. 28. Trade figures for February 1998 showed a deficit of £1.74 billion, the biggest since March 1990.

MAY 1998

2. The European single currency, the Euro, was officially launched at a summit meeting in Brussels. 6. Daimler-Benz and Chrysler announced plans for a $35 billion merger. Lord Sainsbury announced his retirement as chairman of the Sainsbury's supermarket chain. 7. Sterling fell to DM2.9032. Vickers said that Volkswagen had submitted a bid for Rolls-Royce higher than the offer from BMW agreed in March 1998; on 5 June shareholders accepted the Volkswagen offer. On 28 July BMW and Volkswagen reached a deal under which BMW would take over the Rolls-Royce name in 2003, leaving Volkswagen with only the Bentley marque. On 30 July the chief executive of Roll-Royce Motors, Graham Morris, resigned. 11. Shares in Thomson Travel began conditional dealings on the Stock Exchange. 18. The fine art auction house Christie's agreed to a £721 million take-over by the French entrepreneur Francois Pinault. 19. Dr Keith McCullagh said that he would resign as chief executive of the troubled drug development company British Biotech in September 1998. 25. The 18 biggest banks in Japan wrote off about £45 billion in bad loans as the yen fell to its lowest level against the dollar since 1991. 27. Share prices fell in Europe and the USA after the Russian Central Bank tripled its main interest rate to 150 per cent and the financial crisis in Asia deepened.

JUNE 1998

4. The Bank of England raised bank base rates by 0.25 per cent to 7.5 per cent. 9. Members of the London Financial Futures and Options Exchange voted to reform the exchange and end open-outcry trading. 11. The Chancellor of the Exchequer announced that the annual spending round would be abolished and that in future government departments would be set fixed three-year budgets. He also announced the partial privatization of National Air Traffic Services, the Commonwealth Development Corporation, the Horserace Totalisator Board and the Royal Mint. 12. Japan released figures showing that the economy was technically in recession for the first time since 1975. 13. The world's leading investment bank Goldman Sachs

voted to become a public company. 15. The yen fell to 146.55 against the dollar, its lowest level for eight years. 16. Figures were published showing that the headline inflation rate for May 1998 was 4.2 per cent, the highest level for six years. 17. The US Federal Reserve and the Bank of Japan spent an estimated $2 billion buying the yen, which rose to 137.60 against the dollar. 19. Members of the RAC voted in favour of the demutualization of the club's rescue service. 22. Plans were announced for Stagecoach to buy a 49 per cent stake in Virgin Rail for £158 million. 23. Britain's balance of payments figures for January to March 1998 showed a deficit of £3.2 billion. 24. The leading jewellers Asprey and Garrard announced a merger. 29. PowerGen agreed to buy East Midlands Electricity in a deal worth £1.9 billion.

JULY 1998

7. The London Stock Exchange and the Deutsche Börse in Frankfurt announced an alliance designed to allow investors access to leading quoted companies in both markets. 13. The IMF agreed a £13.8 billion aid package for Russia. 14. The Chancellor of the Exchequer announced the Government's spending plans until 2001, and said that an extra £40 billion would be spent on health and education (see page 1171). 15. The FT-SE 100 index closed at a record high of 6,151.5. 24. Wessex Water agreed to a £1.4 billion take-over by the American group Enron. 26. BT announced a £6 billion joint venture with the American company AT and T. 31. Siemens announced the closure of a semi-conductor plant on Tyneside with the loss of at least 1,100 jobs.

AUGUST 1998

11. BP announced a take-over of the American oil group Amoco in a £67.4 billion deal. 13. Trading in Russian shares was temporarily suspended and prices on other stock markets fell sharply after the financier George Soros said that the rouble should be devalued by up to 25 per cent. 17. The Russian Central Bank said that it would allow the rouble to float on the currency markets within a band of between six and 9.5 roubles to the dollar until the end of 1998. 21. The FT-SE 100 index fell 190.4 points to close at 5,477.0. 26. The rouble collapsed and the Russian Central Bank suspended trading in the currency; stock markets across Europe fell sharply. The perfume and cosmetics firm Yardley went into receivership. 27. Trading in the rouble was again suspended and share prices fell on world stock markets. 28. Share prices fell as the economic and political crisis in Russia continued. 31. The Dow Jones industrial average fell 512 points, the second-biggest fall in its history.

ENVIRONMENT

SEPTEMBER 1997

2. The Government ended its opt-out of the international ban on dumping radioactive waste at sea and said that it supported proposals that discharges of hazardous and radioactive substances into the sea should be reduced to as close to zero as possible by 2020. **11.** National Power abandoned plans to burn orimulsion at Pembroke power station.

OCTOBER 1997

2. The National Trust upheld its ban on deer-hunting on its land. **13.** The UK ratified an amendment to the Basle Convention which banned the export of hazardous waste from developed countries. **29.** The Secretary of State for the Environment, Transport and the Regions (John Prescott) said that Britain would cut its carbon dioxide emissions by 20 per cent by 2010.

NOVEMBER 1997

7. As the damming of the Yangtze River in China was completed, environmentalists voiced concerns that the project would further threaten endangered animals, fish, birds and plants. **12.** The Planning Minister (Richard Caborn) said that the Government intended half of the 4.4 million new homes to be built by 2016 to be sited on farmland and in the green belt.

DECEMBER 1997

1. The UN Convention on Climate Change opened in Kyoto, Japan; on 11 December a treaty was agreed reducing emissions of 'greenhouse' gases by an average of 5.2 per cent between 2008 and 2012. **22.** The Energy and Science Minister (John Battle) announced that British Nuclear Fuels Ltd (BNFL) and Magnox Electric would merge.

JANUARY 1998

14. A 50-year ban on mining and mineral extraction in Antarctica, agreed under a protocol to the Antarctica Treaty in April 1991, came into force. **15.** The Government launched a review of planning regulations. **16.** John Prescott approved the building of up to 10,000 houses on green-belt land west of Stevenage, Herts. **25.** John Prescott said that more than half of new houses required should be built on 'brownfield' sites and that the 'predict and provide' policy, according to which councils have to identify land for new houses many years before they are to be built, should be abandoned.

FEBRUARY 1998

13. A temperature of 19.6° C was recorded at Barbourne, Worcs, making it the hottest February day ever recorded in Britain. **23.** John Prescott said that 60 per cent of new houses required should be

built on 'recycled' land and that developers would have to prove that no urban site existed before building in the countryside.

MARCH 1998

3. At least 300 tons of fish died after the waters of the River Dun, Berks, were contaminated by an unknown pollutant. **27.** The Government announced that the Countryside Commission and the Rural Development Commission would be merged.

APRIL 1998

17. Scientists at the University of Colorado, USA, said that a 25-mile long section of an ice shelf had broken away from Antarctica. **29.** John Prescott signed the Kyoto protocol, which set targets for the UK and other industrialized countries to cut their emissions of the gases responsible for global warming. The World Bank, the World Wide Fund for Nature and the government of Brazil announced a deal under which 62 million acres of rainforest would be declared a protected area.

JUNE 1998

17. The Government announced that Britain would reduce its emissions of greenhouse gases by at least 12.5 per cent of the 1990 level by 2010.

JULY 1998

23. Britain and 14 other countries signed an agreement in Sintra, Portugal, under which the remaining Magnox nuclear power stations in Britain would close by 2010 and discharges from Sellafield would be reduced to 'close to zero' by 2020. **31.** The Government cancelled more than 100 road-widening and bypass schemes; 37 schemes, including a cut-and-cover tunnel at Stonehenge, were given the go-ahead.

AUGUST 1998

5. Members of the agriculture select committee of the House of Commons said that parts of the coastline of south-east England and East Anglia should be sacrificed to the sea as part of a 'peaceful accommodation' with nature. Up to 6,000 mink were released from a farm in Ringwood, Hants, by the Animal Liberation Front, threatening 80 square miles of countryside including the New Forest. **10.** Average world-wide temperatures showed that July 1998 was the hottest month ever recorded.

SPORT

SEPTEMBER 1997

2. The West Ham defender Rio Ferdinand was dropped from the England football squad for a world cup qualifier against Moldova on 10 September because he had been convicted on 1 September of drinking and driving. **6.** Greg Rusedski became the first British tennis player to reach the final of the US

Open since 1936 when he beat Jonas Bjorkman; on 7 September he lost in the final to Patrick Rafter. **6–7.** At the world rowing championships in Aïguebelette, France, British rowers won two gold medals, two silvers and four bronzes. **15.** The first-class cricket counties voted 19–12 not to divide the county championship into two divisions. Sir John Hall announced his retirement as chairman of Newcastle United FC. After a bad-tempered match in Brive, France, a brawl broke out in a bar between members of Pontypridd and Brive rugby union clubs; both clubs were fined £30,000 by the European Rugby Cup Ltd for bringing the tournament into disrepute by their conduct during the match. **17.** Clive Woodward was appointed England rugby union coach. **19.** The Football Association (FA) said that it was investigating possible charges following breaches of its rules in the light of a Premier League report into illegal payments surrounding transfer deals.

OCTOBER 1997

8. The British yachtsman and Olympic silver medallist John Merricks was killed in a car crash in Italy. **11.** The England football team qualified for the world cup finals for the first time for eight years after drawing 0–0 with Italy in Rome; violence broke out between England fans and the Italian police during the match. On 24 October the FA published a report that blamed the Italian police for the violence. **14.** The British Athletic Federation called in administrators after declaring itself insolvent. **23.** Bryan Hamilton was sacked as manager of the Northern Ireland football team. **26.** Jacques Villeneuve won the Formula One world motor racing championship for the first time after finishing third in the European grand prix at Jerez, Spain; his main rival, Michael Schumacher, span off the track after hitting the side of Villeneuve's car. On 11 November Schumacher was stripped of his second place in the championship because he was found to have deliberately rammed Villeneuve's car. **29.** Lawrence Dallaglio was appointed England rugby union captain. **30.** An FA inquiry revealed widespread betting on football matches by players and officials in contravention of the FA's rules.

NOVEMBER 1997

7. A charge of manslaughter brought against Frank Williams, the head of the Williams-Renault Formula One motor racing team, over the death of Ayrton Senna in the San Marino grand prix in 1994, was dropped at a court in Italy. On 16 December the remaining members of the team and track officials charged with manslaughter were acquitted. **19.** Gerry Francis resigned as manager of Tottenham Hotspur FC; he was replaced by Christian Gross. **29.** Sir Peter O'Sullevan retired after 50 years of commentating on horse-racing for the BBC.

DECEMBER 1997

11. The Football League put forward five proposals for reforming its operations. The chairman of the management board of the Rugby Football Union (RFU), Cliff Brittle, put forward a blueprint for reforming rugby union in England. **12.** John Searson set a new world record of 59 days for rowing single-handedly across the Atlantic. The footballers Bruce Grobbelaar and Hans Segers were each given a six-month ban and a £10,000 fine, both suspended for two years, by the FA for assisting a Far East syndicate to forecast the results of matches. The Wales rugby union captain, Gwyn Jones, suffered a serious spinal injury while playing for Cardiff against Swansea; he subsequently announced his retirement from the sport. **14.** Greg Rusedski was voted BBC Sports Personality of the Year. **16.** The Government announced that the UK Sports Institute would be based in Sheffield. **22.** The German striker Jurgen Klinsmann, who played for Tottenham Hotspur in 1994–5, rejoined the club on loan from Sampdoria.

JANUARY 1998

7. The 12 rugby union Premiership first division clubs voted to pull out of European competition in 1998. **8.** Phials of synthetic human growth hormone were found in the luggage of a member of the Chinese team arriving for the world swimming championships in Perth, Australia; she was subsequently ordered to return to China. On 14 January four Chinese swimmers at the championships tested positive for drugs. Maurice Lindsay resigned as chief executive of the Rugby Football League to become managing director of Super League Europe. **9.** The former England rugby union captain Will Carling announced his retirement from the first-class game. **11.** The London Scottish rugby union player Simon Fenn lost part of his ear lobe in an alleged biting incident during a match at the Recreation Ground; on 13 January the Bath prop Kevin Yates was suspended pending a disciplinary hearing. On 10 February Yates was banned for six months by the RFU. **13.** Lord Wakeham resigned as chairman of the British Horseracing Board over a financial plan for racing, produced by an industry study group, which called for a 1.75 per cent cut in general betting duty. **25.** Non-league Stevenage Borough held Newcastle United to a 1–1 draw in an FA Cup fourth-round tie at Broadhall Way; Newcastle United later won the replay. **27.** Three jockeys (Jamie Osborne, Dean Gallagher and Leighton Aspell) and another man were arrested and questioned by police over allegations of horse-doping and race-fixing; they were released on bail without charge. On 28 January the three jockeys were suspended for a week by the Jockey Club. **29.** The first Test between the West Indies and England in Kingston, Jamaica, was abandoned after only 62 balls because the pitch was deemed to be dangerously uneven. The vice-chairman of the RFU, Fran Cotton, put forward radical plans for reforming the game in England, including the proposal that top players should be contracted to the RFU.

FEBRUARY 1998

7. The Winter Olympics opened in Nagano, Japan. **9.** Lawrie McMenemy was appointed manager of the Northern Ireland football team. **11.** The 18-year-old Liverpool striker Michael Owen became the youngest footballer to play for England since the 1880s in a match against Chile at Wembley. The first Olympic giant slalom snowboarding champion, Ross Rebagliati, was disqualified by the International Olympic Committee (IOC) after testing positive for marijuana; on 12 February he was reinstated after the Court of Arbitration for Sport ruled that the IOC had acted improperly. Snooker, pool and billiards were granted Olympic status. **12.** Ruud Gullit was sacked as player-manager of Chelsea FC and replaced by Gianluca Vialli. **20.** The RFU announced that Italy would be admitted to the Five Nations' Championship in 2000. Fifteen-year-old Tara Lipinski became the youngest-ever individual Winter Olympic gold medallist when she won the figure skating title at the games in Nagano. **21.** England achieved the highest-ever score in the Five Nations' Championship, beating Wales 60–26 at Twickenham. **24.** Brian Ashton resigned as coach of the Ireland rugby union team. **28.** At the European indoor athletics championships, Ashia Hansen set a new world record of 15.16 metres for the women's triple jump.

MARCH 1998

8. At the Australian grand prix in Melbourne, David Coulthard controversially pulled aside when in the lead in order to allow his McLaren team-mate, Mika Hakkinen, to win the race because of a pre-race pact. **15.** The *News of the World* published allegations that the chairman and vice-chairman of Newcastle United FC had insulted the club's fans and been abusive about local women; the two men resigned on 23 March. **24.** Mike Atherton resigned as captain of the England cricket team after England lost the final Test to the West Indies by an innings and 52 runs; Adam Hollioake took over as captain for the rest of the Caribbean tour. Paul Gascoigne joined Middlesbrough FC from Rangers for £3.45 million. **28.** Cambridge won the University Boat Race in a record time of 16 minutes, 19 seconds. The referee was forced to leave the pitch for several minutes during a match between Barnsley and Liverpool after being threatened by a fan who ran onto the pitch after a Barnsley player had been sent off; two more Barnsley players were sent off during the match. **29.** The Women's Cricket Association voted to merge with the England and Wales Cricket Board. **30.** The Football Task Force published a report on tackling racism in football.

APRIL 1998

3. The popular grey steeplechaser One Man was put down after breaking a leg during a race at Aintree. **4.** The Grand National at Aintree was won by Earth Summit, which became the first horse to win the Scottish, Welsh and English Grand Nationals; only six out of 37 starters finished the race, during which one horse died and two were put down. England won the Five Nations' Championship grand slam for the fourth successive year after beating Ireland at Twickenham. Fran Cotton resigned as vice-chairman of the RFU's management board. **5.** France achieved the highest-ever points total in a Five Nations match when they beat Wales 51–0 at Wembley. **7.** The shot putter Paul Edwards was banned for life by the British Athletic Federation after testing positive for drugs for a second time; he lodged an appeal against the ruling. **22.** Pat Whelan resigned as manager of the Ireland rugby union team. **29.** The Irish Olympic swimming champion Michelle de Bruin denied that she had taken performance-enhancing drugs after the sport's international governing body, FINA, said that a urine sample taken from her in January had shown signs of adulteration. On 6 August de Bruin was banned for four years for manipulating the sample; she accused FINA of conspiring to destroy her career.

MAY 1998

1. Dennis Bergkamp was named Footballer of the Year. **2.** The British boxer Spencer Oliver was taken to hospital in a coma after being knocked out during a European title fight at the Albert Hall, London; on 3 May he underwent an operation to remove a blood clot on his brain. **4.** John Higgins became the world no. 1 snooker player, a position held by Stephen Hendry since 1990, when he won the world championship in Sheffield. **5.** Alec Stewart was named England cricket captain for the summer Test matches. **6.** Alan Shearer, the England football captain, was charged by the FA with misconduct for appearing to kick Neil Lennon in the face during a match against Leicester City on 29 April; on 12 May he was cleared of deliberately kicking the player. **7.** Ray Wilkins was sacked as manager of Fulham FC and replaced by the club's chief operating officer, Kevin Keegan. **8.** The RFU and English rugby union clubs reached agreement over arrangements for the future running of the sport. Kevin Bowring resigned as coach of the Wales rugby union team. **9.** Celtic won the Scottish football championship for the first time in ten years; on 11 May the club's manager, Wim Jansen, resigned. Saracens equalled the highest-ever score in the rugby union Cup final when they beat Wasps 48–18 at Twickenham. **11.** The swimming commentator Hamilton Bland was sacked after a report found that he taken secret payments from manufacturers while acting as a supposedly impartial adviser to local councils on the construction of swimming pools. **13.** Chelsea FC won a European cup for the first time since 1971 when they beat Stuttgart 1–0 to win the European Cup Winners' Cup in Stockholm. **16.** Arsenal became the second team to achieve the

League and FA Cup double twice when they beat Newcastle United 2–0 at Wembley to win the FA Cup. 27. Eighteen-year-old Michael Owen became the youngest player to score for England when he scored the winning goal in a match against Morocco in Casablanca. The Scotland goalkeeper Andy Goram left the world cup squad after newspaper reports about his private life. 31. Paul Gascoigne was controversially left out of the England world cup squad by the coach, Glen Hoddle.

JUNE 1998

8. Sepp Blatter was elected president of FIFA. 10. The football world cup opened in Paris. 13. The French yachtsman Eric Tabarly was drowned after falling from his yacht off the Welsh coast. 20. Danny Grewcock became only the second England player to be sent off during a Test match when he was dismissed during England's defeat by New Zealand at Dunedin. 27. Wales suffered their worst-ever rugby union defeat when they were beaten 96–13 by South Africa in Pretoria. Sam Smith became the first British woman since 1985 to reach the fourth round of the women's singles at Wimbledon when she beat the former champion Conchita Martinez in three sets. 30. England were knocked out of the football world cup by Argentina in St Etienne in a penalty shoot-out after the match had ended in a 2–2 draw; David Beckham was sent off during the match.

JULY 1998

1. Tim Henman became the first Briton for 25 years to reach the semi-finals of the men's singles at Wimbledon when he beat Petr Korda in straight sets. 3. A British boat, *Adventurer*, set a new world record of 74 days, 20 hours and 58 minutes for the circumnavigation of the globe by powered vessel. 4. Jana Novotna won the ladies' singles title at Wimbledon at the third attempt, beating Nathalie Tauziat in straight sets. 5. Pete Sampras became the third player to win five men's singles titles at Wimbledon when he beat Goran Ivanisevic in five sets. 12. France won the football world cup for the first time when they beat Brazil 3–0 in the final in Paris. 17. The Festina cycling team was expelled from the Tour de France after its director admitted that the team's cyclists had been provided with performance-enhancing drugs. On 24 July the 12th stage of the race was delayed by a strike by riders in protest at their treatment by the press and the police. On 29 July three teams withdrew from the race and the riders staged a go-slow, causing the 17th stage to be annulled. On 30 July two more teams withdrew from the race. 19. A 17-year-old British amateur golfer, Justin Rose, finished joint fourth in The Open championship at Royal Birkdale; he immediately turned professional. 21. A Briton, Brian Milton, became the first person to circumnavigate the globe in a microlight aircraft when he landed his plane at Brooklands airfield, Surrey. 27. Two American athletes, the sprinter Dennis Mitchell and the shot-putter Randy Barnes, were suspended after failing drugs tests. 28. The rugby union club Coventry went into receivership.

AUGUST 1998

2. The former Olympic 400 metres silver medallist Roger Black retired from athletics after failing to be selected for the European championships in Budapest. 10. England won a five-Test cricket series for the first time since 1986 when they beat South Africa in the fifth Test at Headingley. 23. Great Britain finished top of the medal table at the European athletics championships in Budapest, with nine gold medals. 27. Kenny Dalglish was sacked as manager of Newcastle United FC; he was replaced by Ruud Gullit. 27–31. The Sri Lankan bowler Muttiah Muralitharan took 16 wickets for 220 runs in a match against England at the Oval.

APPOINTMENTS AND RESIGNATIONS

In addition to those mentioned above, the following appointments and resignations were announced:

1997

1 September: Peter Salmon was appointed controller of BBC1

9 September: Colette Bowe resigned as director of the Personal Investment Authority

12 September: Bob Phillis was appointed chief executive of Guardian Media Group

19 September: Dennis Marks resigned as general director of English National Opera; Richard Handover was appointed chief executive of W. H. Smith

25 September: Kevin Keegan was appointed chief operating officer of Fulham FC; Anthony Whitworth-Jones resigned as general manager of Glyndebourne opera house

1 October: Lord Gowrie resigned as chairman of the Arts Council of England from spring 1998; Sir Alistair Grant was appointed governor of the Bank of Scotland from May 1998

2 October: Sir Patrick Neill was appointed chairman of the Committee on Standards in Public Life

14 October: Keith Hellawell, chief constable of West Yorkshire, was appointed the first co-ordinator of government strategy against drug abuse

23 October: Ian Harley was appointed chief executive of Abbey National from February 1998

28 October: Bob Ingram was appointed chief executive-designate of Glaxo Wellcome

2 December: Richard Gamble resigned as chief executive of Royal and Sun Alliance; he was replaced by Bob Mendelsohn

18 December: Andreas Whittam Smith was appointed president of the British Board of Film Classification

1998

14 January: Gerry Robinson was appointed chairman of the Arts Council of England from April 1998

16 January: Kelvin MacKenzie was appointed deputy chief executive of Mirror Group Newspapers

21 January: Bridget Rowe resigned as editor of the *Sunday Mirror* and was replaced by Brendan Parsons, who was replaced as editor of the *People* by Neil Wallis; Derek Morris was appointed chairman of the Monopolies and Mergers Commission

30 January: Andrew Marr was replaced as editor of the *Independent* by Rosie Boycott, the editor of the *Independent on Sunday*, who took over responsibility for both titles; Mr Marr returned as editor-in-chief after the purchase of the two titles by Tony O'Reilly in March 1998

6 April: Nicholas Snowman, the head of the South Bank Centre in London, was appointed general director of Glyndebourne from September 1998

24 April: Rosie Boycott was appointed editor of the *Express*

1 May: Simon Kelner was appointed editor of the *Independent;* Andrew Marr resigned as editor-in-chief of the newspaper

12 May: Anita Roddick resigned as chief executive of the Body Shop, and became co-chairman; she was replaced as chief executive by Patrick Gournay

4 June: Stuart Higgins resigned as editor of the *Sun;* he was replaced by David Yelland

8 June: Kelvin MacKenzie resigned as deputy chief executive of the Mirror Group

21 July: Brian Williamson was appointed chairman of the London International Financial Futures and Options Exchange; Daniel Hodson resigned as its chief executive

28 July: Roger Alton was appointed editor of the *Observer* in succession to Will Hutton, who was appointed editor-in-chief

---

AFRICA

SEPTEMBER 1997

3. Troops from Great Comoro landed on the island of Anjouan in an unsuccessful attempt to quell a separatist movement. 7. Islamic militants murdered 87 people in a suburb of Algiers. 9. Algerian troops killed at least 127 members of the militant Armed Islamic Group. 16. The Moroccan government and Polisario guerrillas agreed to hold a referendum to determine whether Western Sahara should remain part of Morocco. 22. Islamic militants were suspected of killing at least 85 civilians in Algiers. 24. The Islamic Salvation Army (AIS), the military wing of the Islamic Salvation Front party in Algeria, declared a cease-fire on military activities to begin on 1 October.

OCTOBER 1997

13. Islamic militants killed 43 people in Algeria. 14. Angolan troops from the enclave of Cabinda joined Congolese rebels fighting government troops in the Republic of Congo. On 15 October the rebels took control of Brazzaville, the capital of the Republic of Congo. 26. Angola agreed to withdraw its troops from the Republic of Congo. 28. An attempted coup was put down in Zambia. 31. The UN Security Council imposed sanctions on the Angolan guerrilla movement UNITA for failing to implement the Lusaka Protocol, a 1994 UN-mediated peace agreement.

NOVEMBER 1997

17–19. More than 300 people died in Rwanda when Hutu extremists attacked a prison in an attempt to free prisoners charged with genocide. 28. The Zimbabwean government published a list of 1,503 farms to be confiscated.

DECEMBER 1997

11. At least 1,000 people were killed in north-west Rwanda in an attack by Hutus on a camp for Tutsi refugees from the Democratic Republic of Congo. 16. Nelson Mandela resigned as president of the African National Congress. 21. A group of army officers failed in an attempt to overthrow the Nigerian government. 25. Kenneth Kaunda, the former president of Zambia, was arrested in connection with the coup attempt in October 1997; he was released on 31 December. 29–30. Daniel arap Moi was re-elected president of Kenya. 31. Muslim extremists in Algeria killed 412 people.

JANUARY 1998

1. At least 284 civilians were killed in Burundi by Hutu rebels who were retreating after attacking a government military camp. 14. The government of Equatorial Guinea resigned; a new government was appointed nine days later. 16. The government of Zimbabwe agreed to delay plans to appropriate large, mainly white-owned farms, as a precondition for obtaining EU and World Bank loans. 19–21. Government troops attempted to quell unrest in Harare, Zimbabwe, which had begun in response to rises in basic food prices. 23. The former president of South Africa, P. W. Botha, was charged with contempt of the Truth and Reconciliation Commission, having ignored three subpoenas to appear before it.

FEBRUARY 1998

9. Hutu rebels were reported to have killed 58 people in a village in north-west Rwanda. Nigerian troops launched an air and artillery offensive against Sierra Leone's military junta. 12. Nigerian troops were reported to have taken control of Freetown, the capital of Sierra Leone. Four Sudanese government officials, including the Vice-President, died when the aircraft they were travelling in crashed on landing in southern Sudan. 15. Islamic

militants were suspected of killing 36 people on the outskirts of Algiers. **15–17.** Government troops killed 88 Islamic militants in Algeria. **18.** Islamic militants killed 23 people in western Algeria. **24.** Eighteen people died when a bomb exploded on a train south of Algiers.

MARCH 1998

7. About 100 people were killed in tribal clashes in western Sudan. **10.** Ahmad Tejan Kabbah, the exiled president of Sierra Leone, returned to Freetown after the military junta which had ousted him was ejected by Nigerian peacekeepers. **11.** The rebel group UNITA was declared a legal political party by the Angolan government. **23.** Albert René was elected for a second term as president of the Seychelles.

APRIL 1998

20. In Algeria, 120 policemen were arrested on charges of human rights abuses. Two Roman Catholic priests were convicted in Rwanda of the murders of over 2,000 Tutsis. **21.** At the close of nominations for the Nigerian presidential elections, President Abacha was the only candidate put forward by any of the five government-sanctioned parties. **24.** In Rwanda, thousands of people attended the executions of 22 people found guilty of genocide. **27.** Forty people were killed in a massacre in Chouardia, Algeria.

MAY 1998

1. Jean Kambanda, Rwanda's former prime minister, pleaded guilty to six charges of genocide. **7.** Peace talks in Kenya between the Sudanese government and rebels from the south ended with the announcement of a referendum on self-determination for the south of the country. **13.** Ethiopia called on Eritrea to withdraw immediately from a border area it had occupied.

JUNE 1998

2. The chief of the Armed Islamic Groups (GIA) in Algiers, Mohamed Kebaili, was killed by troops in a suburb of the city. **3.** Fighting flared up on the border between Ethiopia and Eritrea, each side accusing the other of initiating hostilities. **8.** President Abacha of Nigeria died of a heart attack. Ugandan rebels killed more than 60 people in an attack on a school in Fort Portal. **9.** Gen. Abdulsalami Abubakar was sworn in as Nigeria's new president. **15.** Hundreds of people died in Guinea-Bissau in fighting between mutinous troops led by the sacked army chief Ansumane Mane and forces loyal to President Vieira. Nigeria's new military government ordered the release of nine political prisoners. **24.** President Eyadema of Togo was re-elected. **27.** The UN mediator Alioune Blondin Beye, who played a key role in negotiations in Angola, was killed in a plane crash in Côte d'Ivoire. **31.** The UN Secretary-General Kofi Annan held talks with Chief Moshood Abiola, the jailed Niger-

ian pro-democracy leader, in an attempt to secure the chief's release.

JULY 1998

3. Talks aimed at ending the conflict in Guinea-Bissau broke down. **7.** In Nigeria, Chief Abiola died of a heart attack during a meeting with US officials. **8.** There was rioting throughout Nigeria following Chief Abiola's death; 45 people died. **9.** Athmane Khelifi, the leader of the GIA in Algiers, was shot dead outside the city. **15.** The Sudan People's Liberation Army announced a three-month cease-fire in the south of the country to allow aid to reach the 1.2 million people affected by famine. **18.** President Nelson Mandela of South Africa married Gracia Machel, the widow of President Machel of Mozambique. **20.** Fighting resumed in Angola after UNITA seized a number of towns across the country. President Abubakar of Nigeria announced that he would hand over control to a civilian government in early 1999 and announced the release of all political prisoners. **23.** At least 150 people died in Angola following an attack by UNITA troops.

AUGUST 1998

2. In Rwanda, 102 people died in an attack by Hutu rebels. **3.** A rebel movement in the Democratic Republic of Congo announced that it had set up an autonomous zone in the east of the country and intended to oust President Kabila. Sudan announced a unilateral cease-fire in the famine-affected south of the country. **6.** Rebel troops in the Democratic Republic of Congo, allegedly backed by Rwandan troops, reached the west of the country. **7.** Bomb attacks on the US embassies in Nairobi, Kenya, and Dar-es-Salaam, Tanzania, left 240 people dead and 5,000 injured. **9.** Ugandan troops entered the Democratic Republic of Congo to support President Kabila's government. **17.** Two people were killed after police opened fire on pro-democracy demonstrators in Maseru, Lesotho. **20.** The USA carried out a cruise missile attack on a site in Sudan linked to terrorists it believed to be responsible for the bombing of its embassies on 7 August. **21.** Zimbabwe sent troops to the Democratic Republic of Congo to support President Kabila's government. Former South African President P. W. Botha was sentenced to 12 months in jail or a fine of 10,000 rands (£1,000) after being found guilty of contempt by the Truth and Reconciliation Committee. **23.** Rebel troops advancing on Kinshasa were attacked by Angolan forces, who successfully cut off the rebel's supply lines. **25.** It was announced that democratic elections in Nigeria will be held on 20 and 27 February 1999. A bomb exploded in a restaurant in Cape Town, killing two people and injuring 24, in a suspected revenge attack following the US cruise missile strikes in Sudan and Afghanistan on 20 August. **26.** Fighting in the Democratic Republic of Congo reached Kinshasa. **31.** UNITA forces were reported to have joined the anti-government troops in the Democratic Republic of Congo.

THE AMERICAS

SEPTEMBER 1997

2. Costa Rica, Guatemala, Honduras, Nicaragua and El Salvador signed the Managua Declaration, which will create a European Union-style organization. 13–14. The leaders of Canada's provinces and territories agreed to recognize Quebec's 'unique character'; the premier of Quebec boycotted the meeting. 17. President Clinton rescinded a commitment to support an international ban on land-mines.

OCTOBER 1997

14. The Nevis Island Assembly voted to end Nevis's federation with St Christopher. 26. Congressional elections were held in Argentina.

NOVEMBER 1997

5. Rudolph Giuliani was re-elected mayor of New York, USA.

DECEMBER 1997

15. Janet Jagan was elected president of Guyana. 19. The ruling People's National Party won a general election in Jamaica.

JANUARY 1998

17. President Clinton was questioned by lawyers over allegations that he had sexually harassed Paula Jones when he was governor of Arkansas. 19. The People's Progressive Party reached agreement with the opposition People's National Congress in Guyana to initiate a constitutional review, thereby ending protests about the election result in December. 21. An investigation began into an alleged affair between a White House assistant, Monica Lewinsky, and President Clinton, who was accused of persuading her to lie under oath.

FEBRUARY 1998

24. Fidel Castro was reappointed president of Cuba.

MARCH 1998

7. Eighty government soldiers were killed by Marxist guerrillas in Colombia. 10. The former Chilean dictator Gen. Augusto Pinochet retired as commander-in-chief of the armed forces and took a seat in the Senate which he will hold for life. 20. The USA eased sanctions against Cuba.

APRIL 1998

1. The sexual harrassment case bought by Paula Jones against President Clinton was dismissed by the judge, who said that there were no 'genuine issues' worthy of a trial. 20. Colombia's top human rights lawyer was found murdered in Bogotá. 27.

Bishop Conedera, a leading defender of human rights in Guatemala, was found murdered at his home two days after publishing a damning report on human rights violations by the Guatemalan army during the country's 36-year civil war.

MAY 1998

11. The right-wing Colorado Party claimed victory in the Paraguayan general elections, amid widespread allegations of electoral fraud. 20. Congress initiated an investigation of President Clinton's campaign funding in response to allegations that he had received a donation from a Chinese army officer. 21. Marion Barry resigned as mayor of Washington DC. 24. Thirty people were injured when a bomb went off in a church in Danville, Illinois.

JUNE 1998

21. Andres Pastrana, the Conservative candidate, won the Colombian presidential election.

JULY 1998

4. There were mass evacuations in Florida as forest fires burned out of control along the state's Atlantic coast. 20. Jamil Mahaud was elected president of Ecuador. 24. A gunman shot and killed two security staff in the Capitol building, Washington DC. 26. President Clinton was subpoenaed by the grand jury investigating his alleged affair with Monica Lewinsky; on the 28th, Miss Lewinsky was granted immunity from prosecution in return for her testimony concerning her alleged sexual relations with the president.

AUGUST 1998

4. Wall Street suffered the third-biggest fall in its history; it was blamed on the Asian economic crisis. 6. Monica Lewinsky gave evidence to a grand jury about her relationship with President Clinton and contradicted his sworn statement that they did not have sexual relations. 7. The US embassies in Kenya and Tanzania were bombed; 240 people were killed and 5,000 injured. 10. On Nevis, 61 per cent of the islanders voted for independence from St Christopher, but this fell short of the two-thirds majority needed for constitutional change. 17. President Clinton testified before the grand jury regarding his relationship with Monica Lewinsky, and in a televised address admitted to 'an inappropriate physical relationship' with her. 20. The USA launched cruise missile attacks on targets in Afghanistan and Sudan linked to the terrorists believed to be responsible for the bombing of the US embassies in Kenya and Tanzania on 7 August. Canada's Supreme Court ruled that the province of Quebec does not have the right to separate from the rest of the country under either Canadian or international law. 31. The general election in Belize was won by the opposition People's United Party, its leader Said Musa becoming the new Prime Minister. The Dow Jones

index suffered the second largest fall in its history in the aftermath of the Russian economic crisis.

ASIA

SEPTEMBER 1997

12–18. The 15th congress of the Chinese Communist Party (CCP) was held in Beijing; on 19 September a new Politburo standing committee was selected. 25. In Indonesia, forest fires started by landowners attempting to clear land worsened, causing widespread pollution across the region. 31. Indian and Pakistani troops exchanged fire across their disputed border in Kashmir, killing 25 people.

OCTOBER 1997

6–7. More than 400 people died in fighting between Sri Lankan troops and Tamil Tiger rebels. 7. Surya Bahadur Thapa was sworn in as prime minister of Nepal. 8. Kim Jong-il was elected general secretary of North Korea's ruling Worker's Party. 15. A bomb explosion in Colombo, Sri Lanka, killed at least 18 people.

NOVEMBER 1997

7. The Thai government resigned following criticism of its handling of the country's economic crisis; a new coalition government was formed two days later. 10. China and Russia signed an agreement delineating their mutual border. 16. The Chinese pro-democracy activist Wei Jingsheng was released from prison and flown to the USA. 28. The Indian prime minister Inder Kumar Gujral resigned following the withdrawal of the Congress (I) Party from the coalition government.

DECEMBER 1997

2. President Farooq Leghari of Pakistan resigned. 9. Peace talks opened between North and South Korea, the USA and China, seeking a formal ending to the Korean War. 10. The capital of Kazakhstan was moved from Alma-Ata to Akmola. 18. Kim Dae-jung was elected president of South Korea.

JANUARY 1998

11. Gunmen shot dead 24 Shia Muslims in a sectarian attack in Lahore, Pakistan. 15. Indonesia agreed to implement an economic reform package in exchange for a US$43 billion loan from the IMF. 25. Tamil Tiger suicide bombers detonated a bomb in Kandy, Sri Lanka, killing 11 people.

FEBRUARY 1998

4. Sri Lanka celebrated the 50th anniversary of its independence. 6. At least nine people died when a suicide bomber detonated a bomb in Columbo, Sri Lanka. 14. Islamic fundamentalist suicide bombers killed 43 people in Coimbatore, India. 16. Twenty-six people died during violence on the first day of voting in India's general election. 22. At least 66 people died when Tamil Tiger rebels launched an

attack on two navy vessels off northern Sri Lanka. Ten people died during violence in the second round of voting in India's general election. 25. Kim Dae-jung was sworn in as president of South Korea. 27. Both factions in Cambodia's civil war declared a cease-fire.

MARCH 1998

5. Thirty-two people were killed in a Tamil Tiger suicide bomb attack in Colombo, Sri Lanka. 15. The Bharatiya Janata Party (BJP) was invited to form a coalition government following the general election in India, in which no party won an overall majority. 16. At least 100 people died during fighting between the forces of Gen. Rashid Dostum and Hezb-i-Wahdat in Mazar-i-Sharif, northern Afghanistan. Further peace talks between North and South Korea, also attended by representatives from the USA and China, opened in Geneva, Switzerland. 17. Zhu Rongji was elected prime minister of China by the National People's Congress. 19. Atal Behari Vajpayee of the BJP was sworn in as prime minister of India. 26. The Cambodian government claimed that the Khmer Rouge headquarters in Cambodia had been captured by defectors in a mutiny. 30. Prince Norodom Ranariddh returned to Cambodia for the first time since being ousted in a coup in July 1997.

APRIL 1998

6. Pakistan conducted a test flight of a nuclear missile capable of hitting Delhi, India. 15. Pol Pot, the 73-year old former dictator of Cambodia responsible for the deaths of an estimated 1.7 million people, died of a heart attack. 20. In India's Jammu and Kashmir state, 29 people, mostly Hindus, were shot dead by militants. Wang Dan, the Chinese dissident and a student leader during the Tiananmen Square demonstrations, was released from prison and allowed to leave China. Khmer Rouge guerrillas killed 21 people in an attack on a Cambodian fishing village. 22. The French government, separatists and French settlers agreed to hold a referendum in December to determine the constitutional future of New Caledonia. 25. Talks between the Taleban and Afghans from the country's non-Taleban northern enclave took place in Islamabad under US mediation.

MAY 1998

11. India carried out three nuclear tests, raising fears of an arms race with Pakistan; the tests drew widespread international condemnation. 16. Indonesia's President Suharto cancelled the unpopular austerity measures required under the IMF deal in January; 500 people had died in three months of protests. On 21 May President Suharto resigned and was replaced by Vice-President Habibie. 24. Hong Kong's pro-democracy candidates won more than 50 per cent of the vote in legislative elections. 27. Workers in South Korea began a nationwide strike, protesting against a wave of redundancies. 28.

Pakistan carried out five nuclear tests, and announced that because of the severe economic sanctions applied by the international community, it would cut spending in all areas by 50 per cent. **29.** Joseph Estrada won the presidential election in the Philippines.

JUNE 1998

4. In Hong Kong 25,000 people attended a commemoration of the Tiananmen Square massacre, the first such commemoration since Hong Kong reverted to Chinese rule. **25.** President Clinton began an official visit to China. **27.** President Clinton criticized China over human rights issues at a press conference which was televised live across China.

JULY 1998

8. The Taleban banned television sets in Afghanistan. **12.** The Japanese Prime Minister Ryutaro Hashimoto resigned after his Liberal Democratic party lost 17 seats in the elections to the upper house. The Taleban captured Maimana, an opposition stronghold in the north of Afghanistan. **24.** Keizo Obuchi was elected leader of Japan's Liberal Democratic Party. **26.** The Cambodian elections were marred by violence and accusations of voter intimidation by the ruling Cambodian People's Party, although UN observers declared that in general, 'the polling achieved democratic standards'. **27.** The former Pakistani prime minister Benazir Bhutto appeared in court in Lahore to face charges of corruption. **28.** Indonesia began withdrawing its troops from East Timor. **31.** Aung San Suu Kyi, the Burmese opposition leader, was prevented from meeting colleagues and held in her car at a roadblock outside Yangon for six days before being forcibly returned home. The Diet elected Keizo Obuchi prime minister of Japan.

AUGUST 1998

3. More than 100 people were killed in heavy fighting in Kashmir. Flooding along the Yangtze river in China left millions homeless. **5.** The Cambodian People's Party won the largest share of the vote in the recent elections, but was short of the two-thirds majority needed to form a government. **8.** Prince Ranariddh rejected the Cambodian election results and refused to join a coalition government led by Hun Sen. **10.** Prince Billah of Brunei was formally invested as heir to the throne. Taleban forces took control of Mazar-i-Sharif, the last major opposition stronghold in Afghanistan. **12.** Aung San Suu Kyi was once more halted at a police roadblock after attempting to visit her supporters outside the Myanmar capital Yangon. **20.** The USA carried out a cruise missile attack on a site in Afghanistan linked to terrorists it believed to be responsible for the bombing of its embassies in Kenya and Tanzania on 7 August. **24.** Aung San Suu Kyi returned to Yangon after government officials agreed to meet members of her National League for Democracy for talks. **31.** North Korea successfully tested a new ballistic missile capable of hitting Japan.

AUSTRALASIA AND THE PACIFIC

OCTOBER 1997

10. The Papua New Guinea government and rebels from the island of Bougainville signed a truce.

NOVEMBER 1997

3. Jim Bolger announced that he would resign as prime minister of New Zealand from the end of the month; following his resignation, Jenny Shipley became prime minister.

FEBRUARY 1998

2. A ten-day constitutional convention on whether Australia should become a republic opened in Canberra; on 13 February the convention voted in favour of a republic, with a head of state elected by a two-thirds majority of parliament.

MARCH 1998

12. A four-week state of emergency was imposed in Vanuatu after riots broke out in the capital, Port Vila, as investors tried to withdraw their bank savings following rumours of a financial scandal.

APRIL 1998

20. Riot police clashed with dockers on strike in Melbourne, Australia, in protest against mass redundancies. **22.** The Australian Federal Court ordered the reinstatement of all the sacked dock workers, who had been replaced with non-union workers. **31.** In Papua New Guinea rebels gave up their weapons and signed a peace treaty formally ending a decade of civil war on the island of Bougainville.

JULY 1998

8. The New Zealand government was ordered to return land confiscated from the Maoris 30 years ago. The Australian Senate passed a bill declaring farmers' land rights more important than traditional Aborigine claims. **18.** More than 1,600 people were killed when a tidal wave swept away entire villages on the northern coast of Papua New Guinea.

AUGUST 1998

18. New Zealand's ruling coalition was formally dissolved after ministers from the New Zealand First party walked out of a Cabinet meeting. **31.** In Australia, a general election was called for 3 October 1998.

EUROPE

SEPTEMBER 1997

16. The Labour government in Norway promised to resign after receiving less than 37 per cent of the vote in the general election on 15 September. **21.** In Poland, the Solidarity Electoral Alliance defeated the ruling former communists in a legislative election; on 17 October it formed a coalition government with the Freedom Unity party. Presidential and legislative elections in Serbia produced no outright winners.

OCTOBER 1997

1. NATO-led Stabilization Force (SFOR) troops in Bosnia took control of four radio and television transmitters controlled by the Bosnian Serb leader Radovan Karadzic. 5. Less than 50 per cent of the electorate voted in a run-off for the presidential election in Serbia which was therefore ruled invalid. 6. Ten Bosnian Croats charged with war crimes were taken into detention by the International Court in the Hague after giving themselves up for trial. 9. The Italian prime minister Romano Prodi resigned after failing to gain support from within the ruling coalition for his finance bill; he was asked to remain as caretaker prime minister. 19. Milo Djukanovic was elected president of Montenegro. 31. Mary McAleese was elected president of Ireland.

NOVEMBER 1997

2–7. French lorry drivers blockaded roads across France in a strike over pay. 16. In a referendum, Hungarians voted in favour of joining NATO. 22–23. Elections were held to the People's Assembly in Bosnia. 23. Milan Kučan was re-elected president of Slovenia. 29. The Czech government resigned following a scandal over funding of the ruling party.

DECEMBER 1997

2–4. A conference on the disposal of gold confiscated by the Nazis was held in London. 7. A presidential election in Serbia produced no outright winner. 16. Josef Tosovsky, an independent, was appointed as interim prime minister of the Czech Republic. 18. Two Bosnian Croats charged with war crimes were arrested by SFOR troops in Vitez, Bosnia. 19. The International Criminal Tribunal for the Former Yugoslavia released three war crimes suspects after charges were withdrawn because of lack of evidence. 22. Milan Milutinovic, the Socialist Party candidate, was elected president of Serbia.

JANUARY 1998

5. Valdas Adamkus was elected president of Lithuania. 15. The UN Transitional Administration for Eastern Slavonia withdrew, leaving the area under Croatian control. 16. The constitutional court of Turkey banned the pro-Islamic Welfare Party. 18. Milorad Dodik was elected by the legislature as prime minister of Republika Srpska, the Serb part of federal Bosnia. 20. Vaclav Havel was re-elected president of the Czech Republic. 22. NATO troops arrested Goran Jelisic, a Bosnian Serb war crimes suspect, in Bijeljina, Bosnia.

FEBRUARY 1998

3. Levon Ter-Petrosyan resigned as president of Armenia. 9. Troops were ordered on to the streets of Tbilisi, Georgia, following an unsuccessful attempt to assassinate President Shevardnadze. 12. Glafcos Clerides was re-elected president of Cyprus. 14. Two suspected Bosnian Serb war criminals, Milan Simic and Miroslav Tadic, surrendered to SFOR. 23. Government troops quelled riots led by rebel police units in Shkodër, Albania. 24. Simo Zaric, suspected of war crimes in Bosnia, surrendered to SFOR.

MARCH 1998

1–2. At least 20 people died during clashes between Serb police and ethnic Albanians in Pristina, the capital of Kosovo province, Serbia. 4. Dragoljub Kunarac, suspected of war crimes in Bosnia, surrendered to SFOR. 5. Serb forces killed at least 20 ethnic Albanians in Kosovo during attacks on villages suspected of harbouring separatist guerrillas. 7. A military court in Rome, Italy, sentenced Erich Priebke to life imprisonment for his part in the massacre of 335 people in 1944. 11. The Danish general elections were won by the governing centre-left social democratic coalition of prime minister Poul Nyrop Rasmussen. 23. President Yeltsin of Russia sacked his entire Cabinet, including Prime Minister Chernomyrdin. The Communist Party won legislative elections in Moldova. 29. Legislative elections were held in Ukraine. 31. Victor Ciorbea resigned as prime minister of Romania. Robert Kocharyan was elected president of Armenia. 31. The UN Security Council imposed an arms embargo on the Federal Republic of Yugoslavia in an attempt to force the government to negotiate with Kosovo nationalists.

APRIL 1998

2. Radu Vasile was appointed prime minister of Romania. 15. The Czech legislature approved membership of NATO. 20. Thomas Klestil was re-elected president of Austria. 23. Twenty-two people were killed in fighting between Serbian forces and ethnic Albanians. Two Belgian cabinet ministers resigned after Marc Dutroux, the main suspect in the country's child murder scandal, escaped from police custody for three hours; the escape was seen as a further example of incompetence in the police and at all levels of the state. 24. Sergei Kiriyenko's nomination as prime minister of Russia was accepted by the Duma at the third round of voting, after his nomination had twice been vetoed. 25. The Christian Democratic party suffered a heavy defeat in regional elections in Saxony-Anhalt, Germany. 27. Serb tanks entered Kosovo in an attempt to quell ethnic unrest in the area, as fighting continued between Serb forces and ethnic Albanians. Half a million workers in Denmark began a general strike in a dispute over paid leave.

May 1998

4. The newly appointed commander of the Vatican's Swiss Guard and his wife were shot dead by a junior officer. **6.** The Labour Party won 40 per cent of the vote in the Dutch general election, gaining a second term in office as the largest single party in the governing coalition. **7.** The Danish parliament agreed a new pay deal to end the general strike. **10.** A coalition government was formed in the Faröe Islands by parties that seek independence from Denmark over foreign and legal affairs. **24.** Serb forces burned whole villages in Albanian areas of Kosovo, as the conflict between the Serbs and the Kosovo Liberation Army escalated. Hungary's right-wing opposition won the election. Georgia and the breakaway region of Abkhazia agreed on a cease-fire, troop withdrawals and the return of refugees in exchange for the region's autonomy within a federation. **31.** A reformist coalition led by President Djukanovic won the Montenegrin parliamentary elections.

June 1998

1. An international aid package to rescue Russia from its worst financial crisis since economic reforms began was announced, halting the losses on the Moscow stock market. **2.** Violence in Kosovo escalated, with thousands of refugees leaving for Albania after reports of massacres of entire villages by the Serb forces. **8.** The USA banned investment in Yugoslavia and froze all Yugoslav assets within American jurisdiction in response to what it called 'indiscriminate violence' against ethnic Albanians in Kosovo. **20.** All EU ambassadors were withdrawn from Belarus following a dispute in which President Lukashenka of Belarus attempted to evict them from the diplomatic complex adjacent to his residence. **21.** The Social Democrats won the largest share of the vote in the Czech general election, and became the major partners in a centre-left coalition government.

July 1998

6. Russia and Turkmenistan signed an accord dividing up oil resources in the Caspian Sea. **7.** The Italian opposition leader Silvio Berlusconi was sentenced to two years and nine months in prison for bribing tax officials. **8.** Viktor Orban was sworn in as Hungary's prime minister. **9.** Seven people died and 87 were injured in an explosion at the Egyptian bazaar in Istanbul. **13.** The IMF and Russia agreed a US$13.7 billion package to bolster the rouble against speculation. **17.** The remains of Nicholas II, the last Tsar of Russia, were buried in the Peter and Paul Fortress in St Petersburg. **23.** President Maskhadov of Chechenia survived an assassination attempt when his armoured car was destroyed by a bomb. **26.** Serb tanks and heavy artillery attacked rebel Albanian positions in Kosovo in the most widespread and co-ordinated Serb military effort since April. **28.** The Kosovo Libera-

tion Army's stronghold of Malisevo was overrun by Serb forces.

August 1998

13. Trading on the Moscow stock exchange was suspended for the second time in a week after shares fell by 15 per cent. **14.** The Kosovo Liberation Army announced that Adem Demaci would negotiate on its behalf in peace talks over the future of Kosovo. **17.** Russia's central bank loosened its control on the rouble's exchange rate, effectively devaluing the currency by 50 per cent. **23.** President Yeltsin sacked his entire Cabinet for the second time in five months, replacing Prime Minister Kiriyenko with Victor Chernomyrdin. **26.** The rouble lost 40 per cent of its value against the Deutsche Mark after trading in dollars was suspended.

EUROPEAN UNION

October 1997

2. The Treaty of Amsterdam was signed by the member states' foreign ministers. **25.** Italy became part of the Schengen Agreement. **25–26.** The foreign ministers of the EU member states, meeting in Mondorf, Luxembourg, failed to agree on which countries should be invited to attend accession talks in December.

November 1997

20–21. The EU heads of government attended a special summit in Luxembourg at which an agreement to combat unemployment was signed.

December 1997

1. The UK was refused permission to attend meetings of the planned council for co-ordinating monetary union (Euro-X). **12–13.** The European Council, meeting in Luxembourg, agreed to consider two waves of potential new members, comprising ten eastern European countries and Cyprus. **17.** Turkey threatened to withdraw its application to join the EU unless it was included on a list of prospective candidates by June 1998.

January 1998

1. The UK assumed the presidency of the EU Council of Ministers. The constitutional council in France ruled that the constitution would have to be revised before France could ratify the Treaty of Amsterdam. **27.** The EU's statistical arm, Eurostat, said that Italy could not use capital gains tax from a gold transfer to the Bank of Italy to reduce the government's budget deficit.

March 1998

12. The EU heads of state and government and those of 11 aspiring member states attended a conference in London to discuss EU enlargement.

Turkey, which had been refused accession negotiations, turned down an invitation to attend. **15.** The Greek drachma was admitted to the European Exchange Rate Mechanism (ERM). **25.** The EU Commission proclaimed that 11 member states had met the requirements for economic and monetary union. **31.** The Schengen Agreement came into force, ending routine checks at the borders of participating countries.

APRIL 1998

1. Italy became a full member of the Schengen Agreement. **27.** Greece vetoed £240 million of EU aid to Turkey, saying that the EU should not 'reward an uncivilized regime'. **31.** Staff at the European Commission staged a one-day strike in protest at reforms that threaten to end the job security of thousands of civil servants.

MAY 1998

1. EU finance ministers at the Brussels summit announced that 11 countries of the EU would go ahead with the European single currency to be launched on 1 January 1999: Austria, Belgium, Finland, France, Germany, Ireland, Italy, Luxembourg, the Netherlands, Portugal and Spain. Wim Duisenberg was appointed president of the European Central Bank. **12.** The European Parliament approved a biotechnology law that will allow patents to be taken out on the genes of humans, plants and animals, although human cloning and genetic manipulation was outlawed. **13.** The European Parliament approved a Europe-wide ban on tobacco advertising, to be introduced over the next four years. In a speech in Berlin President Clinton announced his support for Turkish membership of the EU. **18.** EU countries won exemption from US trade sanctions against companies that trade with Cuba, Iran and Libya. **25.** A meeting between Turkey and EU officials to improve the strained relations between the two was called off when the Turkish delegation failed to turn up.

JUNE 1998

1. The European Central Bank governing council held its inaugural meeting in Frankfurt. **8.** The EU froze Yugoslavia's assets and banned investment in the country in response to the violence in Kosovo. **9.** The members of the European Central Bank held their first meeting. **10.** The European Commission declared meat from younger animals to be safe from BSE, and called on the EU to allow sales of British beef to resume. **16.** At the EU summit in Cardiff, Chancellor Kohl threatened to withhold Germany's payments to the EU unless the German contribution was reduced. **17.** EU states agreed on an environmental package to cut greenhouse gas emissions by 8 per cent. **29.** The EU announced that it would hold annual summits with China in recognition of the country's growing economic and political importance.

JULY 1998

1. Austria assumed the EU presidency. **13.** President Lukashenka of Belarus and his entire government were banned from setting foot on EU soil following a row over ambassadorial residences in Belarus. **16.** The European Court of Justice ruled that trademark owners can prevent products bearing their mark from being brought into the EU without consent, which prevents supermarkets from selling branded goods at reduced prices. **20.** The EU suspended all humanitarian aid to the Taleban regime in Afghanistan in protest at its denial of equal treatment to women. **31.** The EU approved sanctions against the Angolan opposition group UNITA for failing to implement the 1994 peace accords.

THE MIDDLE EAST

SEPTEMBER 1997

4. Three bombs exploded in Jerusalem, killing at least eight people. **5.** Twelve Israeli commandos died in an ambush in southern Lebanon. **10.** The US Secretary of State Madeleine Albright arrived in Israel for talks with Israeli and Palestinian leaders. **18.** Ten people were killed in a gun and bomb attack on a bus in Cairo, Egypt. **23.** Turkish troops launched an attack on Kurdish positions in northern Iraq. **25.** The Israeli government approved the building of 300 new houses for Jews on the West Bank.

OCTOBER 1997

1. Sheikh Ahmed Yassin, the spiritual founder of the Palestinian fundamentalist movement Hamas, was released from detention in Israel. **7.** Turkey announced that its forces had killed 538 Kurdish separatists in northern Iraq. **8.** Israeli and Palestinian leaders held their first summit for eight months. **13.** Israel released nine Arab prisoners as part of a deal to secure the return of two secret agents arrested in Jordan. **29.** Iraq ordered ten US members of the UN Special Commission on Iraq to leave the country.

NOVEMBER 1997

4. Candidates loyal to King Hussein won the majority of seats in a parliamentary election in Jordan which was boycotted by the Islamist opposition. **12.** The UN Security Council imposed a travel ban on Iraqi officials responsible for blocking UN weapons inspections. **13.** Six American UN weapons inspectors were expelled from Iraq; the UN withdrew all but 19 of its 78-member inspection team. **17.** Islamic militants opened fire on tourists at Luxor, Egypt, killing more than 60 people. **21.** Iraq agreed to allow Americans to return as part of a team of UN weapons inspectors. **31.** The Israeli Cabinet approved a further, conditional withdrawal from the West Bank.

DECEMBER 1997

1. The Israeli government granted permission for the building of 900 more houses for Jews on the West Bank.

JANUARY 1998

12. Iraq banned a team of UN weapons inspectors from a suspected arms site.

FEBRUARY 1998

9. Turkey sent thousands of troops into northern Iraq to prevent Kurdish refugees from fleeing across the border in the event of American and British attacks on Iraq. **11.** Turkish air attacks were reported to have killed at least 20 members of the Kurdistan Workers' Party (PKK) in northern Iraq. The UK and USA rejected an Iraqi offer to open eight sites for inspection for 60 days. **23.** The UN Secretary-General signed an agreement with Iraq allowing UN weapons inspectors unlimited access to sites. **25.** Iraq said it would not allow weapons inspectors unlimited access.

MARCH 1998

1. Israeli troops seized a weapons shipment allegedly destined for the Palestinian National Authority. **4.** Ezer Weisman was re-elected president of Israel. **10.** Three Palestinians were shot dead by Israeli soldiers near Hebron, prompting three days of rioting on the West Bank. **12.** Mordechai Vanunu, who was imprisoned in Israel in 1986 for exposing Israel's nuclear weapons programme, was released from solitary confinement.

APRIL 1998

22. The Israeli prime minister Binyamin Netanyahu made a pact with the extreme right-wing Molodet party to strengthen his government's position in parliament. **27.** Five Israeli soldiers were injured when their vehicle was blown up by Hizbollah guerrillas in southern Lebanon. The UN Security Council extended the oil embargo against Iraq after it failed to comply fully with the UN weapons inspection team. **31.** Israel celebrated the 50th anniversary of the founding of the state of Israel.

MAY 1998

1. The US Secretary of State had separate meetings with Binyamin Netanyahu and Yasser Arafat, the Palestinian president, for discussions on the Middle East peace process. **10.** Binyamin Netanyahu rejected an invitation to further peace talks on the Middle East peace process, citing unreasonable diplomatic pressure from the USA. **14.** Eight Palestinians were killed and 200 wounded by Israeli forces during protests in the Palestinian territories to mark the anniversary of the creation of Israel.

JUNE 1998

17. The US Secretary of State called on Iran to join the USA in drawing a 'road map leading to normal relations', a move seen as a first step towards rapprochement with Iran and its moderate president Mohammed Khatami. **23.** UN weapons inspectors found traces of VX nerve gas in Iraqi missiles, contradicting Iraq's claims that it had never developed chemical warheads. **22.** Abdollah Nouri, the Iranian interior minister and a key ally of President Khatami, was impeached by hardliners in the Iranian parliament.

JULY 1998

8. The Palestinian Authority had its special observer status at the UN upgraded to a higher level. **24.** The reformist mayor of Tehran was found guilty of corruption in a trial seen by many as a political battle between hardline Iranians and moderate supporters of President Khatami.

AUGUST 1998

5. Iraq's Deputy Prime Minister Tariq Aziz announced that Iraq was to end immediately all co-operation with the UN weapons inspection teams. **21.** The Israeli government approved the largest expansion in settlements on the Golan Heights since the territory was occupied in 1967. **25.** The terrorist Abu Nidal was arrested in Egypt. **26.** Scott Ritter, a senior member of the UN weapons inspection team, resigned and accused the UN Security Council of giving in to Saddam Hussein.

INTERNATIONAL RELATIONS

OCTOBER 1997

4. Togo was admitted as the 55th member of the Organization of the Islamic Conference. **20–21.** Members of the South Pacific Commission agreed in Canberra, Australia, to rename the organization the Pacific Community; the UK announced that it would rejoin in 1998. **23.** The heads of state of 11 of the 12 members of the CIS met in Kishinev, Moldova. **24–27.** The Commonwealth heads of government meeting was held in Edinburgh; an economic agreement, the Edinburgh Declaration, was signed.

NOVEMBER 1997

16. The Democratic Republic of Congo withdrew from the Francophone group of countries. **24–25.** The heads of state and government of the member states of the Asia–Pacific Economic Co-operation (APEC) forum met in Vancouver, Canada.

DECEMBER 1997

9–11. Muslim leaders met at an Islamic summit in Tehran, Iran.

FEBRUARY 1998

18. NATO approved the formation of a Dissuasion Force (DFOR) to replace SFOR in Bosnia. 21. The G7 group of industrial nations met in London; an employment summit involving Russia was held the following day. 23. The UN Secretary-General signed an agreement with the Iraqi government allowing UN weapons inspectors unlimited access to sites; the USA agreed to the deal but said that it would maintain its forces in the Gulf on alert for six months. 25. The Iraqi government said that it would not allow weapons inspectors unlimited access to sites.

MARCH 1998

2. Austria rejected an invitation to join NATO. The UN Security Council adopted a resolution which threatened 'the severest consequences' if Iraq were to block access to suspected weapons sites.

APRIL 1998

6. The UK and France ratified the Comprehensive Test Ban Treaty, the first nuclear powers to do so. 22. The UN Human Rights Commission adopted a resolution criticizing Nigeria and urging the junta 'to restore democratic government without delay'. 29. The government of Gibraltar accepted a Spanish proposal for direct talks on the future of the colony, but rejected the idea of Spain 'sharing' sovereignty with Britain.

MAY 1998

1. The US Senate ratified NATO enlargement, opening the possibility of membership to the Czech Republic, Hungary and Poland. 15. The G8 met in Birmingham, with the issues of high-technology crime, debt in developing countries and the nuclear crisis in India and Pakistan on the agenda.

JUNE 1998

17. The USA launched a $2 billion rescue package to help the plummeting Japanese yen, following fears that China would devalue its currency and exacerbate the region's economic crisis.

JULY 1998

10. The US Senate voted to resume agricultural exports to India and Pakistan, reducing the sanctions imposed on the countries following their nuclear tests two months previously. 17. An international conference in Rome attended by delegates from 156 countries agreed to establish a permanent international court for crimes against humanity. 21. The British and American governments discussed holding the trial of two suspects in the Lockerbie bombing in the Netherlands, under Scottish law.

AUGUST 1998

13. Swiss banks agreed to pay US$1.25 billion to survivors of the Holocaust. 20. The UN Security Council announced that Iraq had not met the conditions for sanctions to be lifted.

Obituaries

Abacha, Gen. Sani, president of Nigeria since 1993, aged 54 – 8 June 1998

Abiola, Chief Moshood, Nigerian opposition leader, political prisoner since 1994 after winning annulled presidential election in 1993, aged 60 – 7 July 1998

Albert, Harold, royal biographer under the pseudonym Helen Cathcart, aged 88 – 20 October 1997

Bairstow, David, England and Yorkshire cricketer, aged 46 – found dead 5 January 1998

Banda, Dr Hastings, prime minister of Malawi 1964–6, president 1966–71, life president 1971–94, aged 99 – 25 November 1997

Barton, Sir Derek, FRS, FRSE, chemist, Nobel laureate in 1969, aged 79 – March 1998

Beningfield, Gordon, wildlife and landscape artist, aged 61 – May 1998

Berlin, Sir Isaiah, OM, CBE, FBA, philosopher and first President of Wolfson College, Oxford, aged 88 – 6 November 1997

Bernard, Jeffrey, journalist and bon viveur, aged 65 – 4 September 1997

Berni, Aldo, co-founder of the Berni Inns restaurant chain, aged 88 – 12 October 1997

Biggs, Kenneth, GC, wartime ordnance officer, led containment of Savernake ammunition explosion in January 1946, aged 86 – 11 January 1998

Bing, Sir Rudolf, KBE, general manager of the Metropolitan Opera, New York, 1950–72, aged 95 – 2 September 1997

Bono, Sonny, American pop singer, actor and US Congressman, aged 62 – in an accident, 5 January 1998

Boyd-Carpenter, Lord (John), Conservative MP for Kingston-upon-Thames 1945–72, Chief Secretary to the Treasury 1962–4, aged 90 – 11 July 1998

Bremner, Billy, Leeds United and Scotland footballer, aged 54 – 7 December 1997

Bridges, Lloyd, American actor, aged 85 – 10 March 1998

Brook, Lady (Helen), founder of the Brook Advisory Centres, aged 89 – 3 October 1997

Burgess, Alan, writer and BBC radio producer, aged 83 – 10 April 1998

Cartwright, Dame Mary, DBE, FRS, mathematician, Mistress of Girton College 1949–68, aged 97 – 3 April 1998

Chisholm, George, OBE, jazz trombonist, aged 82 – 6 December 1997

Clark, Roger, MBE, international rally driver, aged 58 – 12 January 1998

Conan Doyle, Air Commandant Dame Jean, DBE, director of the Women's Royal Air Force 1963–6 and administrator of the literary estate of Sir Arthur Conan Doyle since 1971, aged 84 – 18 November 1997

Cookson, Dame Catherine, DBE, writer, aged 91 – 11 June 1998

Cormack, Alan, American physicist and co-winner of the Nobel prize for medicine in 1979 for work leading to the development of the CAT scan, aged 74 – May 1998

Coulson, Francis, MBE, co-proprietor and chef of the Sharrow Bay Hotel, reviver of post-war British gastronomy, aged 78 – 20 February 1998

Crabtree, Shirley (Big Daddy), wrestler, aged 67 – 2 December 1997

Craigmyle, 3rd Baron, aged 74 – 30 April 1998

Crawshaw, 4th Baron, landowner, aged 64 – 7 November 1997

Cross, Beverley, playwright, librettist and screenwriter, aged 66 – 20 March 1998

Crouch, Sir David, Conservative MP for Canterbury 1966–87, aged 78 – 18 February 1998

Cudlipp, Lord, OBE, newspaperman, chairman of the International Publishing Corporation 1963–73, aged 84 – 17 May 1998

Cummings, Michael, OBE, cartoonist, aged 78 – 9 October 1997

Curran, Sir Samuel, FRS, FRSE, FEng, physicist involved in the development of radar and of Britain's hydrogen bomb, first Principal of Strathclyde University and founder of the country's first science park, co-founder of the Enable charity, aged 85 – 25 February 1998

Dainton, Lord, PH.D., SC.D., FRS, chemist, chairman of the University Grants Committee 1973–8, chairman of the British Library board 1978–85, chancellor of Sheffield University since 1979, aged 83 – 5 December 1997

Dartmouth, 9th Earl, aged 73 – 14 December 1997

Davis, Fred, OBE, snooker player, eight times world champion, aged 84 – 15 April 1998

Denington, Baroness, DBE, chairman of the Greater London Council 1975–6, aged 91 – 22 August 1998

Denison, Michael, CBE, actor, aged 82 – 22 July 1998

Denver, John, American folk singer, aged 53 – 12 October 1997

Diamand, Peter, director of the Holland Festival 1948–65 and of the Edinburgh Festival 1965–78, aged 84 – 16 January 1998

Diemer, Walter, American inventor of bubble gum, aged 93 – January 1998

Donaldson of Kingsbridge, Lord, OBE, Labour and subsequently SDP politician, Arts minister 1976–9, aged 90 – 8 March 1998

Dufferin and Ava, Maureen, Marchioness of, socialite, aged 91 – 3 May 1998

Dunnachie, James, Labour MP for Glasgow Pollok 1987–97, aged 66 – 7 September 1997

Durbridge, Francis, crime writer, aged 85 – 11 April 1998

Edwards, Monica, children's author, aged 85 – 18 January 1998

Empson, Adm. Sir Derek, GBE, KCB, aged 78 – 20 September 1997

English, Sir David, editor of the *Daily Mail* 1971–92, aged 67 – 10 June 1998

English, Revd Donald, CBE, chairman of the World Methodist Council 1991–6, aged 68 – 28 August 1998

Eysenck, Prof. Hans, psychologist and writer, aged 81 – 4 September 1997

Fairfax, Frederick, GC, aged 80 – 23 February 1998

Farr, Sir John, Conservative MP for Harborough 1959–92, aged 75 – 26 October 1997

Fashanu, Justin, footballer, aged 37 – committed suicide, 2 May 1998

Fell, Sir Anthony, Conservative MP for Yarmouth 1951–66 and 1970–83, aged 83 – 20 March 1998

Fleming, George, international cyclist, British champion and record holder, aged 80 – 28 December 1997

Francis, Fred, inventor of Scalextric, aged 79 – January 1998

Frank, Sir Charles, OBE, FRS, physicist, aged 87 – 5 April 1998

Frankl, Viktor, psychiatrist and psychotherapist, aged 92 – 3 September 1997

Freeman, Joan, nuclear physicist, aged 80 – 18 March 1998

French, Harold, actor and theatre director, aged 97 – 19 October 1997

Gellhorn, Martha, American journalist and novelist, first female war correspondent, aged 89 – 15 February 1998

George, Frank, cybernetics pioneer, aged 76 – 10 September 1997

Gibbons, Vic, all-round time trial cycling champion 1953 and 1954, 50-miles time trial record-breaker 1955, aged 75 – 21 January 1998

Gibbs, J. C., former England rugby international, aged 95 – 11 January 1998

Gilbey, Monsignor Alfred, Roman Catholic chaplain to Cambridge University 1932–65, aged 96 – 26 March 1998

Glyn, Sir Alan, Conservative MP for Clapham 1959–64 and for Windsor (later Windsor and Maidenhead) 1970–92, aged 79 – 4 May 1998

Goizueta, Roberto, chief executive of Coca-Cola, aged 65 – 18 October 1997

Goldwater, Senator Barry, American politician, Republican presidential candidate 1964, aged 89 – 29 May 1998

Graham, Gordon, CBE, architect, aged 77 – 21 September 1997

Granville of Eye, Lord, Gallipoli veteran, Liberal/Liberal National MP for Eye 1929–51 (Independent 1943–5), aged 100 – 14 February 1998

Grappelli, Stephane, jazz violinist, aged 89 – 1 December 1997

Gray, Milner, CBE, graphic designer, aged 97 – 29 September 1997

Green, Benny, jazz saxophonist, writer and broadcaster, aged 70 – 22 June 1998

Grieve, Mary, OBE, editor of *Woman* 1940–63, aged 91 – 19 February 1998

Grieve, Percy, QC, Conservative MP for Solihull, 1964–83, aged 83 – 22 August 1998

Hackett, Gen. Sir John, GCB, CBE, DSO and BAR, MC, commander-in-chief, British Army of the Rhine 1966–8, principal of King's College London 1968–75, author, aged 86 – 9 September 1997

Hambling, Harry, banker and artist, aged 95 – 22 January 1998

Hertford, 8th Marquess, aged 67 – 22 December 1997

Hicks, David, interior decorator and designer, aged 69 – 29 March 1998

Hinsley, Prof. Sir Harry, OBE, FBA, historian and Master of St John's College 1979–89, aged 79 – 16 February 1998

Hives, 2nd Baron, CBE, aged 83 – November 1997

Hollis, Prof. Martin, FBA, philosopher, aged 59 – 27 February 1998

Howell, Lord (Denis), PC, Labour MP for Birmingham All Saints 1955–9, for Birmingham Small Heath 1961–92, minister for sport in various ministries 1964–70 and 1974–9, and minister responsible for water resources 1974–9, aged 74 – 19 April 1998

Huddleston, Rt. Revd Trevor, KCMG, Anglican monk, anti-apartheid campaigner from the 1950s, Bishop of Masasi 1960–3, suffragan Bishop of Stepney 1968–78, Bishop of Mauritius and first Archbishop of the Church of the Province of the Indian Ocean 1978–83, aged 84 – 20 April 1998

Hughes, Alex (Judge Dread), reggae singer, aged 53 – 13 March 1998

Hunt, Sir David, KCMG, private secretary to Churchill and Attlee, diplomat and *Mastermind* champion, aged 84 – 30 July 1998

Hunt, Sir Peter, FRICS, chairman from 1987 and managing director from 1978 of Land Securities property company, aged 64 – 8 December 1997

Hutchence, Michael, Australian rock star, aged 37 – 22 November 1997

Ibuka, Masaru, co-founder of the Sony Corporation of Japan, aged 89 – 19 December 1997

Ingham, Bryan, painter and sculptor, aged 61 – 22 September 1997

Innes, Hammond, CBE, writer, aged 84 – 10 June 1998

Jersey, 9th Earl, aged 88 – 9 August 1998

Jones, Prof. R. V., CH, CB, CBE, FRS, wartime intelligence scientist, professor of natural philosophy at the University of Aberdeen 1946–81, aged 86 – 17 December 1997

Jones, Sir John, KCB, CMG, director-general of MI5 1981–5, aged 75 – 9 March 1998

Josephs, Wilfred, composer, aged 70 – 18 November 1997

Karamanlis, Constantine, prime minister of Greece 1955–63 and 1974–80, and president 1980–5 and 1990–5, aged 91 – 23 April 1998

Kaye, Stubby, American actor and singer, aged 79 – 15 December 1997

Kendal, Geoffrey, actor-manager, aged 88 – 14 May 1998

Khaldei, Yevgeni, Ukrainian war photographer, aged 80 – 7 October 1997

King, Gen. Sir Frank, GCB, MBE, aged 79 – 30 March 1998

Kings Norton, Lord (Harold Roxbee Cox), PH.D., FENG, aeronautical engineer, industrialist, chancellor of Cranfield University 1969–97, aged 95 – 21 December 1997

Kissin, Lord, financier, aged 85 – 22 November 1997

Lascelles, Hon. Gerald, president of the British Racing Drivers' Club 1964–91, aged 73 – 27 February 1998

Lawrence, Syd, bandleader, aged 74 – 5 May 1998

Laxness, Halldor, Icelandic writer, Nobel laureate 1955, aged 95 – 8 February 1998

Lees-Milne, James, FRSL, FSA, conservationist, architectural historian and diarist, aged 89 – 28 December 1997

Lestor of Eccles, Baroness (Joan), Labour MP for Eton and Slough 1966–83 and for Eccles 1987–97, junior minister 1969–70 and 1974–6, chairman of the Labour Party 1977–8, aged 66 – 27 March 1998

Lewis, Shari, American puppeteer and ventriloquist, aged 65 – 2 August 1998

Lichtenstein, Roy, American artist, aged 73 – 29 September 1997

Lippert, Albert, co-founder of Weight Watchers, aged 72 – 28 February 1998

Lisle, 7th Baron, aged 94 – 29 December 1997

Llewelyn-Davies of Hastoe, Baroness, PC, Labour politician, government chief whip in the House of Lords (first woman to hold the post) 1974–9 and opposition chief whip 1973–4 and 1979–82, aged 82 – 6 November 1997

Lorant, Stefan, Hungarian-born photojournalist, first editor of *Picture Post*, aged 96 – 14 November 1997

Macartney, Allan, PH.D., deputy leader of the Scottish National Party since 1992, MEP for North-East Scotland since 1994, rector of Aberdeen University since 1986, aged 57 – 25 August 1998

McCartney, Lady (Linda), photographer, animal rights campaigner and founder of a vegetarian food business, aged 56 – 17 April 1998

MacGregor, Sir Ian, chairman of British Leyland 1977–80, British Steel 1980–3 and the National Coal Board 1983–6, aged 85 – 13 April 1998

McGregor of Durris, Lord, social historian, chairman of the Press Complaints Commission 1991–4, aged 76 – 10 November 1997

McIntyre, Dr Robert, first SNP MP (for Motherwell April–July 1945), first SNP member of Stirling council and its first SNP provost, party chairman 1948–56 and president 1958–80, aged 84 – 2 February 1998

Mankowitz, Wolf, author, playwright and scriptwriter, aged 73 – 20 May 1998

Mann, Rt. Hon. Sir Michael, a Lord Justice of Appeal 1988–95, aged 67 – 14 June 1998

Marchais, Georges, secretary-general of the French Communist Party 1972–94, aged 77 – 16 November 1997

Marsden, Betty, actress, aged 79 – 18 July 1998

Marx, Enid, artist and designer, aged 95 – 18 May 1998

Massey, Daniel, actor, aged 64 – 25 March 1998

Maynard, Joan, Labour MP for Sheffield Brightside 1974–87, aged 76 – 27 March 1998

Megaw, Rt. Hon. Sir John, CBE, a Lord Justice of Appeal 1969–80, aged 88 – 27 December 1997

Mellish, Lord (Robert), PC, Labour MP for Rotherhithe (later Bermondsey) 1946–82, Chief Whip 1969–70, 1974–6, aged 85 – 9 May 1998

Meredith, Burgess, American actor, aged 89 – 9 September 1997

Merricks, John, yachtsman and Olympic silver medallist, aged 26 – 8 October 1997

Michener, James, American novelist, aged 90 – 16 October 1997

Milburn, Rod, American hurdler, Olympic champion and world record holder in the 110 metres hurdles, aged 47 – 12 November 1997

Millar, Sir Ronald, playwright and political speechwriter, aged 78 – 16 April 1998

Mobutu Sese Seko, president of Zaïre 1965–97, aged 66 – 7 September 1997

Morgan, Dermot, Irish actor, comedian and writer, aged 45 – 1 March 1998

Morrison, 2nd Baron, aged 83 – 29 October 1997

Morroco, Alberto, OBE, RSA, artist, aged 80 – 10 March 1998

Mother Teresa, HON. OM, missionary, founder of the Missionaries of Charity, Nobel peace prize winner 1979, aged 87 – 5 September 1997

Muir, Frank, CBE, writer and broadcaster, aged 77 – 2 January 1998

Newton, Sir Gordon, editor of the *Financial Times* 1950–72, aged 90 – 31 August 1998

Nunburnholme, 4th Lord, aged 70 – August 1998

O'Sullivan, Maureen, Irish-American actress, aged 87 – 21 June 1998

Orkney, 8th Earl, aged 78 – 5 February 1998

Ormonde, 7th Marquess, MBE, aged 98 – 25 October 1997

Passmore, Victor, CH, CBE, RA, artist, aged 89 – 23 January 1998

Percival, Rt. Hon. Sir Ian, QC, Conservative MP for Southport 1959–87 and Solicitor-General 1979–83, aged 76 – 4 April 1998

Philpott, Trevor, journalist, aged 74 – 29 July 1998

Pinkerton, John, computer pioneer who designed the world's first business computer in 1951, aged 78 – 22 December 1997

Pol Pot, leader of the Khmer Rouge and dictator of Cambodia 1975–8, aged in his 70s – 15 April 1998

Porsche, Ferdinand, Austrian car designer, aged 88 – 27 March 1998

Powell, Rt. Hon. Enoch, MBE, Conservative MP for Wolverhampton South West 1950–74, Unionist MP for South Down 1974–87, Cabinet and Shadow Cabinet minister 1960–8, scholar, aged 85–8 February 1998

Ray, James Earl, assassin of Martin Luther King, aged 70–23 April 1998

Rayner, Lord, chairman of Marks and Spencer 1984–91, aged 72–26 June 1998

Riverdale, 2nd Baron, industrialist, aged 96–26 June 1998

Robbins, Harold, American novelist, aged 81–14 October 1997

Robbins, Jerome, American choreographer, aged 79–29 July 1998

Roberts, Sir Frank, GCMG, GCVO, diplomat, aged 90–7 January 1998

Rogers, Roy, American actor, aged 86–6 July 1998

Rollo, 13th Lord, aged 81–25 September 1997

Rowland, R. W. 'Tiny', entrepreneur, aged 80–24 July 1998

Rowse, A. L. (Alfred), CH, historian, aged 93–3 October 1997

Schnittke, Alfred, Russian composer, aged 63–3 August 1998

Schumann, Maurice, French foreign minister 1969–73, playing a leading role in the development of the European Common Market, aged 86–10 February 1998

Scoular, Jimmy, Scottish football player and manager, aged 73–19 March 1998

Shepard, Alan, astronaut, the first American in space and the fifth man to walk on the Moon, aged 74–21 July 1998

Sinatra, Frank, American singer and actor, aged 82–14 May 1998

Skelton, Red, American comic actor, aged 84–17 September 1997

Smith, Lord (Rodney), KBE, president of the Royal College of Surgeons 1973–7, aged 84–1 July 1998

Smythe, Capt. Quentin, VC, aged 81–21 October 1997

Smythe, Reg, cartoonist, creator of Andy Capp, aged 80–13 June 1998

Solti, Sir Georg, KBE, Hungarian-born conductor, aged 84–5 September 1997

Speight, Johnny, television scriptwriter and playwright, aged 78–5 July 1998

Spock, Dr Benjamin, American paediatrician and child psychologist, aged 94–15 March 1998

Squires, Dorothy, popular singer, aged 83–14 April 1998

Staveley, Admiral of the Fleet Sir William, GCB, First Lord of the Admiralty 1985–9, aged 68–13 October 1997

Swaythling, 4th Baron, merchant banker, aged 69–1 July 1998

Tabarly, Eric, yachtsman, aged 66–13 June 1998

Tait, Sir James, electrical engineer, creator and first Vice-Chancellor of the City University, London, aged 85–18 February 1998

Taylor, Lady (Charity), Assistant Director and Inspector of Prisons (Women) 1959–66, aged 83–4 January 1998

Tennstedt, Klaus, German conductor, aged 71–11 January 1998

Terrington, 4th Baron, aged 82–May 1998

Tippett, Sir Michael, OM, CH, CBE, composer, aged 93–8 January 1998

Tonypandy, 1st Viscount, PC, Labour MP for Cardiff Central 1945–50, Cardiff West 1950–83, Speaker of the House of Commons 1976–83, aged 88–22 September 1997

Trease, Geoffrey, FRSL, novelist, playwright, historian and biographer, aged 88–January 1998

Tryon, Lady (Dale), society hostess and dress designer, aged 49–15 November 1997

Tuzo, Gen. Sir Harry, GCB, OBE, MC, Director of Operations Northern Ireland 1971–3, Deputy Supreme Allied Commander Europe 1976–8, aged 80–7 August 1998

Ulanova, Galina, Russian ballerina, aged 88–21 March 1998

Urban, George, director of Radio Free Europe 1983–6 and director of the Centre for Policy Studies, aged 76–3 October 1997

Vernon, Richard, actor, aged 72–4 December 1997

Villiers, James, actor, aged 64–18 January 1998

Wall, Maj. Sir Patrick, MC, Conservative MP for Haltemprice 1954–83, Beverley 1983–7, aged 81–15 May 1998

Wallace of Campsie, Lord, aged 82–23 December 1997

Wells, John, writer, actor and director, aged 61–11 January 1998

Wills Moody, Helen, American tennis player, winner of eight Wimbledon, seven US and four French singles titles, aged 92–1 January 1998

Wilson, Carl, singer with the Beach Boys, aged 51–6 February 1998

Wilson of Langside, Lord (Harry), PC, QC, Solicitor-General for Scotland 1965–7, Lord Advocate 1967–70, aged 81–23 November 1997

Wingfield Digby, Simon, Conservative MP for West Dorset 1941–74, aged 88–22 March 1998

Wood, Kenneth, inventor of the Kenwood Chef electric food mixer, aged 81–19 October 1997

Wootton, Frank, OBE, aviation artist, aged 83–21 April 1998

Wyatt of Weeford, Lord, Labour MP for Birmingham Aston 1945–55 and for Leicester Bosworth 1959–70, junior minister 1951, newspaper columnist, chairman of the Horserace Totalisator Board 1976–97, aged 79–7 December 1997

Wynette, Tammy, American country singer, aged 55–7 April 1998

Yates, Philip, GC, aged 85–14 February 1998

Young, Robert, American actor, aged 91–21 July 1998

Zhivkov, Todor, president of Bulgaria 1971–89, aged 86–5 August 1998

World Heritage Sites

The Convention Concerning the Protection of the World Cultural and Natural Heritage was adopted by UNESCO in 1972 and ratified by the UK in 1984. By December 1997 the convention had been ratified by 152 states. The convention provides for the identification, protection and conservation of cultural and natural sites of outstanding universal value.

Cultural sites may be:
– monuments
– groups of buildings
– sites of historic, aesthetic, archaeological, scientific, ethnologic or anthropologic value
– historic areas of towns
– 'cultural landscapes', i.e. sites whose characteristics are marked by significant interactions between human populations and their natural environment

Natural sites may be:
– those with remarkable physical, biological or geological formations
– those with outstanding universal value from the point of view of science, conservation or natural beauty
– the habitat of threatened species and plants

Governments which are party to the convention nominate sites in their country for inclusion in the World Cultural and Natural Heritage List. Nominations are considered by the World Heritage Committee, an inter-governmental committee composed of 21 representatives of the parties to the convention. The committee is advised by the International Council on Monuments and Sites (ICOMOS) and the International Union for the Conservation of Nature (IUCN). ICOMOS evaluates and reports on proposed cultural sites and IUCN on proposed natural sites. The International Centre for the Study of the Preservation and Restoration of Cultural Property (ICCROM) provides the committee with expert advice on monument restoration. The Department for Culture, Media and Sport represents the UK government in matters relating to the convention.

A prerequisite for inclusion in the World Cultural and Natural Heritage List is the existence of an effective legal protection system in the country in which the site is situated (e.g. listing, conservation areas and planning controls in the United Kingdom) and a detailed management plan to ensure the conservation of the site. Inclusion in the list does not confer any greater degree of protection on the site than that offered by the national protection framework.

If a site is considered to be in serious danger of decay or damage the committee may add it to a complementary list, the World Heritage in Danger List. Sites on this list may benefit from particular attention or emergency measures. There were 25 sites on this list in February 1998.

Financial support for the conservation of sites on the World Cultural and Natural Heritage List is provided by the World Heritage Fund. This is administered by the World Heritage Committee, which determines the financial and technical aid to be allocated. The fund's income is derived from the obligatory contributions of the parties to the convention, amounting to 1 per cent of their contribution to UNESCO. The fund may also receive voluntary contributions from the parties to the convention, donations from institutions or individuals, and income from national and international promotional activities.

DESIGNATED SITES

As at December 1997 there were 552 sites in 112 countries on the World Cultural and Natural Heritage List. Of these, 15 were in the United Kingdom and two in British overseas territories; 13 were listed for their cultural significance (†) and four for their natural significance (*).

United Kingdom

†Bath – the city
†Blenheim Palace and park, Oxfordshire
†Canterbury Cathedral, St Augustine's Abbey, St Martin's Church, Kent
†Castle and town walls of King Edward I, north Wales – Beaumaris, Anglesey, Caernarfon Castle, Conwy Castle, Harlech Castle
†Durham Cathedral and Castle
†Edinburgh Old and New Towns
*Giant's Causeway and Causeway coast, Co. Antrim
†Greenwich, London – maritime Greenwich, including the Royal Naval College, Old Royal Observatory, Queen's House, town centre
†Hadrian's Wall, northern England
†Ironbridge Gorge, Shropshire – the world's first iron bridge and other early industrial sites
*St Kilda, Western Isles
†Stonehenge, Avebury and related megalithic sites, Wiltshire
†Studley Royal Park, Fountains Abbey, St Mary's Church, N. Yorkshire
†Tower of London
†Westminster Abbey, Palace of Westminster, St Margaret's Church, London

British Overseas Territories

*Henderson Island, Pitcairn Islands, South Pacific Ocean
*Gough Island wildlife reserve (part of Tristan da Cunha), South Atlantic Ocean

BUILDINGS, MONUMENTS AND SITES DIVISION, Department for Culture, Media and Sport, 2-4 Cockspur Street, London SW1Y 5DH. Tel: 0171-211 2072
WORLD HERITAGE CENTRE, UNESCO, 7 place de Fontenoy, 75352 Paris 07SP, France. Tel: Paris 4568 1889
INTERNATIONAL CENTRE FOR THE STUDY OF THE PRESERVATION AND RESTORATION OF CULTURAL PROPERTY (ICCROM), Via di San Michele 13, I-00396 Rome, Italy. Tel: Rome 585531
INTERNATIONAL COUNCIL ON MONUMENTS AND SITES (ICOMOS), 10 Barley Mow Passage, London W4 4PH. Tel. 0181-994 6477
INTERNATIONAL UNION FOR THE CONSERVATION OF NATURE (IUCN), UK Committee, c/o 36 Kingfisher Court, Hambridge Road, Newbury, Berks RG14 5SJ. Telephone: 01635-522925

Index

Ascension Day 9, 83
Ashfield 530, 546
  MP 236
Ashford 530, 546
  MP 236
Ashton-under-Lyne, MP 236
Ash Wednesday 9, 83
Asia:
  area 105
  continent 105
  countries of 599–600
  events (1997–8) 632–3
  migration to UK 113
Assemblies of God in Great Britain and
    Ireland 419
Assessment and Qualifications
    Alliance 431
Assisted Places Scheme 428–9
Associated Presbyterian Churches of
    Scotland 416
Aston:
  Archdeacon 403
  Bishop Suffragan 402
  University 445
Astronomical constants 75
Astronomical phenomena (1999) 16, 20,
    24, etc., 71
Astronomical predictions (1999) 16–63
Astronomical unit 75
Atcham, Shrewsbury and 531, 549
  MP 255
Atomic Energy Authority, UK 284
  constabulary 376
Atomic time 74
Attendance allowance 491
Attercliffe (Sheffield), MP 255
Attorney-General 276, 317, 354
  department 317
Auckland, Archdeacon 402
Audit Commission for England and
    Wales 284–5
Audit Office:
  National 326
  Northern Ireland 329
Australasia:
  countries of 601
  events (1997–8) 635
Australia 105
  Anglican Church 412
  continent 105
Autumn:
  defined 15
  equinox 15, 81
Avon and Somerset, Police Authority 374
Avon, Itchen, Test and, MEP 272
Aylesbury, MP 236
Aylesbury Vale 530, 546
Aylesford, Chatham and, MP 240–1
Ayr, MP 264
Ayrshire:
  East 533, 565
  Education Authorities 442
  Lord Lieutenant 564
  North 533, 565
  South 533, 565

Babergh 530, 546
Baillieston (Glasgow), MP 265
Ballymena 568
Ballymoney 568
Banbridge 568
Banbury, MP 236
Banff and Buchan, MP 264
Banffshire, Lord Lieutenant 564
Bangor:
  Bishop 411
  University College of 452
Bank holidays 87
  (1999) 10
  (2000) 11

Banking, professional organizations 455
Bank of England 285
  Museum 593
Bankruptcy, High Court 356
Banqueting House 585
Banstead, Reigate and 531, 549
Baptist Church 416
Barking:
  Bishop (Suffragan) 403
  MP 236
Barking and Dagenham 532, 557
  Education Authority 441
Barnet 532, 557
  Education Authority 441
Barnsley 529, 545
  Education Authority 439
  MPs 236
Barnstaple, Archdeacon 405
Bar of England and Wales 458–9
Bar of Northern Ireland 458
Baronesses:
  form of address 135, 156
  in own right 156
  life 162–3
Baronets 173, 173–204
  form of address 135, 173
  premier 137, 175, 180, 181
Barons:
  courtesy titles 165–6
  form of address 135, 147
  hereditary 147–56
  life 157–63
  premier 137, 150, 151
Barony, premier 150
Barristers' training 458–9
Barrow and Furness, MP 236
Barrow-in-Furness 530, 546
Basildon 496, 530, 546
  MP 236
Basingstoke:
  Archdeacon 402
  Bishop (Suffragan) 402
  MP 236
Basingstoke and Deane 530, 546
Bassetlaw 530, 546
  MP 236
Bath:
  Archdeacon 402
  MP 236
  University 445
  Wiltshire North and, MEP 274
Bath and North East Somerset 529, 545
  Education Authority 439
Bath, Order of 170
  Dames 206–7
  Knights 174–204
Bath and Wells, Bishop 164, 402
Batley and Spen, MP 236
Battersea, MP 236
Battle, Bexhill and, MP 237
BBC 285–6
Beaconsfield, MP 237
Bearsden, Strathkelvin and, MP 267
Beckenham, MP 237
Bedford 530, 546
  Archdeacon 408
  Bishop (Suffragan) 408
  MP 237
Bedfordshire 529, 543, 544
  Education Authority 439
  MEPs 270
  Mid 531, 548
  MPs 237
  Police Authority 374
  South 531, 549
Bedworth, Nuneaton and 531, 548
Belfast 566, 568
  Agreement 567
  airports 504
  Education and Library Board 442

Belfast *continued*
  MPs 267–8
  Queen's University 451
Bellshill, Hamilton North and, MP 266
Benefits:
  Agency 344
  contributory 489–90
  non-contributory 490–1
Berkshire, Archdeacon 407
Berkshire West 530, 546
Bermondsey, Southwark North and,
    MP 256
Bermuda, Bishop (Anglican) 412
Berne Convention 579
Berwickshire:
  Lord Lieutenant 564
  Roxburgh and, MP 267
Berwick-upon-Tweed 530, 546
  MP 237
Beth Din 399
Bethnal Green and Bow, MP 237
Bethnal Green Museum of
    Childhood 324, 593
Beverley and Holderness, MP 237
Beverley, Bishop (Suffragan) 401
Bexhill and Battle, MP 237
Bexley 532, 557
  Education Authority 441
Bexleyheath and Crayford, MP 237
Biggin Hill airport 504
Billericay, MP 237
Bills, Parliamentary 217, 219, 221
Biological Diversity Convention 571
  UK Group 572
Biology, qualifying body 461
Birds Directive 579
Birkenhead:
  Bishop (Suffragan) 404
  MP 237
Birmingham 529, 536, 545
  airport 504
  Archbishop (RC) 414
  Archdeacon 403
  Bishop 164, 402
  Education Authority 439
  MEPs 270
  MPs 237–8
  Universities 445
Births:
  registration 328
  registration, Scotland 342
  statistics 113–14
Bishop Auckland, MP 238
Bishops:
  Anglican, overseas 412
  Church of England 164, 400–10
  Roman Catholic 414–15
  Suffragan 400–10
Blaby 530, 546
  MP 238
  Northamptonshire and, MEP 273
Blackburn:
  Archdeacon 403
  Bishop 164, 403
  MP 238
Blackburn with Darwen 529, 545
  Education Authority 439
Blackley (Manchester), MP 250
Blackpool 529, 545
  airport 504
  Education Authority 439
  MPs 238
Black Rod:
  Gentleman Usher 120, 170, 218
  Yeoman Usher 218
Blaenau Gwent 532, 560
  Education Authority 441
  MP 261–2
Blaydon, MP 238
Blood service 482
Blue Rod 171

Stop-press

CHANGES SINCE PAGES WENT TO PRESS

ROYAL HOUSEHOLDS

Master of the Horse – The Lord Vestey replaces The Lord Somerleyton

PEERAGE

Baron Coleraine married
Died: 3rd Viscount Rothermere; 2nd Baron Marks of Broughton

BARONETAGE AND KNIGHTAGE

Died: Sir Geoffrey Bateman; Rt. Hon. Sir Denys Buckley; Sir Eric Callard; Sir Frank Ereaut; Vice-Adm. Sir John Hayes; Sir Horace Heyman; Sir Francis Renoug; Air Chief Marshal Sir Frederick Rosier; Sir Guy Sauzier; Sir Rupert Speir; Sir Michael Straker; Sir Arthur Vick

PRIVY COUNCIL

Sir Denys Buckley died

PARLIAMENT

Political parties – David McLetchie elected leader of the Scottish Conservatives; Allan Macartney, MEP, senior vice-convenor of the SNP, died
MPs – Tommy Graham, *Lab.* Renfrewshire West, expelled from Labour Party and will sit as an independent
MEPs – Allan Macartney, MEP, died

GOVERNMENT DEPARTMENTS AND PUBLIC OFFICES

Arts Council of Northern Ireland – Miss M. O'Neill appointed vice-chairman
Bank of England – Ms M. Lowther appointed Chief Cashier
BBC – Matthew Banister appointed chief executive, BBC Productions; Sam Younger replaced by Mark Byford as head of the World Service
ECGD – A. Brown appointed to Export Guarantees Advisory Council
Offer – Prof. Littlechild to be replaced as Director-General of Electricity Supply by Callum McCarthy
Equal Opportunities Commission – chairwoman Ms K. Bahl relinquishes post Nov. 1998
Ofgas – C. Spottiswood to be replaced as Director-General of Gas Supply by Callum McCarthy
Victoria and Albert Museum – J. Scott is acting chairman of board of trustees until new chairman appointed
Museum of London – R. Hambro replaces P. Revell-Smith as chairman of board of governors
National Investment and Loans Board – D. W. Midgley to be a commissioner of Public Works Loan Board
Rail Regulator – J. Swift to relinquish post in Nov. 1998
DTI – Dr J. Taylor replaces Sir John Cadogan as director-general of Research Councils from Jan. 1999

LAW COURTS AND OFFICES

Lord Justice of Appeal – Sir Simon Tuckey; Sir Anthony Clarke appointed
High Court appointments – C. A. St J. Gray, QC; R. C. Klevan, QC (Queen's Bench Division)

Circuit judges – D. B. D. Lowe; D. A. Paiba (SE circuit) retired
Sheriffs – Sheriff J. D. Lowe (Glasgow and Strathkelvin) died
Sheriff-clerks – D. Nicoll appointed to Dundee; R. Cockburn appointed to Glasgow

DEFENCE

Navy – J. M. de Halpert promoted Rear Admiral; replaces Rear Adm. Malbon as Naval Secretary/Chief Executive of Naval Manning Agency in Dec. 1998
RAF – Air Vice-Marshal P. Norriss promoted Air Marshal; replaced Lt.-Gen. Sir Robert Hayman-Joyce as Deputy Chief of Defence Procurement (Operations); Norriss replaced as Director-General Air Systems 1 by Air Vice-Marshal A. Nicholson

CHURCH OF ENGLAND

London – Brian Masters, Area Bishop of Edmonton, died

ENERGY

Director-Generals of Electricity Supply and of Gas Supply to be replaced by Callum McCarthy, who will become Energy Regulator

TRANSPORT

Rail Regulator – J. Swift to relinquish post in Nov. 1998

LOCAL GOVERNMENT

Lord Mayor of London 1998–9 – The Lord Levene of Portsoken, elected 29 September

TRADE UNIONS

President of the TUC 1998–9 – Hector MacKenzie (UNISON)
Union for Bradford and Bingley Staff affiliated to TUC

SOCIETIES AND INSTITUTIONS

RNLI – B. Miles replaced as director by A. Freemantle

COUNTRIES OF THE WORLD

Albania – British Ambassador now Stephen Nash
Belize – Said Musa (People's United Party) became prime minister on 1 September
Bosnia-Hercegovina – Elections on 12 September won in Republika Srpska by ultra-nationalist Nikola Poplasen, and in Bosniac-Croat federation by Ante Jelevic and Alija Izetbegovic; overall federation president will be Zivko Radisic
Brunei – British High Commissioner now Stuart Laing
Germany – general election on 27 September lost by ruling Christian Democratic Union party; Kohl resigned as Chancellor and CDU party leader
Malta – Nationalist Party won legislative elections on 5 September; Eddie Fenech-Adami became prime minister
Russian Federation – Alexander Shokhin resigned as Russian deputy prime minister on 25 September
Sweden – Social Democratic Party lost support in the general election on 20 September, but will probably stay in power in a coalition

SPORTS RECORDS
Swimming – men's 4 × 200 freestyle relay: Australia,
7 min. 11.86 sec.

OBITUARIES
August 1998
26 Frederick Reines, American physicist and Nobel
    laureate in 1995, aged 80
September 1998
2 Roy Bradford, MP at Stormont 1965–73, aged 77
   3rd Viscount Rothermere, newspaper proprietor,
   aged 73
6 Akira Kurosawa, Japanese film director, aged 88
11 Frank Haynes, Labour MP for Ashfield 1979–92,
   aged 72
13 George Wallace, former governor of Alabama, aged
   79
14 Yang Shangkun, president of China 1988–92, aged
   91
19 Patricia Hayes, actress, aged 88
21 Florence Griffith-Joyner, athlete, aged 38

EVENTS – SEPTEMBER 1998
2. The British and Irish parliaments were recalled to
debate and pass anti-terrorist legislation drawn up after
the bombing at Omagh on 15 August. Thousands of
students in Myanmar demonstrated against the country's military rulers. **3.**   President Clinton visited
Northern Ireland. The Russian rouble reached a new
low of 17.5 to the US$. **6.** Iran moved troops to its
border with Afghanistan after Iranian diplomats and
journalists in Afghanistan were killed by Taleban
soldiers. **7.** The seven states involved in fighting in the
Democratic Republic of Congo held talks on the
conflict and the future of the country. The satellite
television group BSkyB announced a £625 million
agreement to buy Manchester United FC. **8.** There
were anti-government demonstrations in Jakarta, Indonesia and Phnom Penh, Cambodia. The Commonwealth
Games opened in Malaysia. **9.** The Royal Opera House
announced plans to shut down the Royal Opera
company for 11 months in 1999 in order to save money.
11. The report of independent prosecutor Kenneth
Starr was published on the Internet and alleged 11
offences that might constitute grounds for the impeach-
ment of President Clinton. **13.** The death toll as a result
of the flooding in Bangladesh rose to 950. President
Zeroual of Algeria called early presidential elections for
February 1999 and announced he would not be standing for re-election. **14.** The Northern Ireland Assembly
met for the first time at Stormont. **16.** Turkish forces
killed 53 Kurdish rebels near the border with Iraq. **17.**
The Queen and the Duke of Edinburgh arrived in
Brunei for a three-day state visit; on 20 September they
arrived in Malaysia for a four-day state visit, during
which The Queen closed the Commonwealth Games in
Kuala Lumpur. **20.** Camilla Carr and Jon James, British
aid workers who were kidnapped by rebels in Cheche-
nia in July 1997, were released from captivity. Anwar
Ibrahim, the former deputy prime minister of Malaysia,
was arrested for demonstrating against the government.
21. President Clinton's videotaped testimony to the
grand jury investigating his alleged misconduct was
broadcast unedited on television. **21–25.** Hurricane
Georges hit the Caribbean. **24.** Diplomatic relations
between the UK and Iran were upgraded after the
Iranian government withdrew its support for the *fatwa*
against Salman Rushdie.